# Pocket
# Oxford–Hachette
# French Dictionary

## Second edition, revised

French ---> English
English ---> French

**Edited by**
Marianne Chalmers
Martine Pierquin

D0970881

**OXFORD**
UNIVERSITY PRESS

# OXFORD

UNIVERSITY PRESS

Great Clarendon Street, Oxford OX2 6DP

Oxford University Press is a department of the University of Oxford.
It furthers the University's objective of excellence in research, scholarship,
and education by publishing worldwide in

Oxford New York

Auckland Bangkok Buenos Aires Cape Town Chennai
Dar es Salaam Delhi Hong Kong Istanbul Karachi Kolkata
Kuala Lumpur Madrid Melbourne Mexico City Mumbai Nairobi
São Paulo Shanghai Taipei Tokyo Toronto

Oxford is a registered trade mark of Oxford University Press
in the UK and in certain other countries

Published in the United States
by Oxford University Press Inc., New York

First published 1996
Second edition 2000
Second edition revised 2003

British Library Cataloguing in Publication Data
Data available

Library of Congress Cataloging in Publication Data
Data available


ISBN 0–19–860704–0

10 9 8 7 6 5 4 3 2 1

Designed by Information Design Unit, Newport Pagnell
Typeset in Nimrod, Arial and Meta by Tradespools
Printed in Great Britain by Clays Ltd, Bungay, Suffolk

# Preface to the second edition

This major new edition of the *Pocket Oxford-Hachette French Dictionary* has been expanded and extensively updated to reflect recent additions to both the French and English languages, with the needs of both the general and school user in mind. The dictionary provides comprehensive coverage of core vocabulary across a broad spectrum of contemporary written and spoken language, incorporating many idiomatic phrases and expressions. The wordlist is further enhanced by the addition of new words and phrases generated by recent developments in information technology, science, and popular culture, for effective and up-to-date communication.

Essential information on grammar, style, and pronunciation is provided in a convenient and accessible format, making the dictionary an ideal reference tool and study aid. The user is guided in selecting appropriate translations by clear examples of usage and construction and by information on the register of language, where required.

All grammatical terms used are explained in a glossary at the back of the dictionary, and French verbs are cross-referenced to a set of verb tables.

New features of the dictionary include an A – Z of French life and culture, providing information on contemporary French society, a calendar of traditions, festivals, and holidays in France, and a practical guide to writing letters in French. A series of sample letters illustrates the differences between French and English usage, highlighting important features of style and format in a variety of situations.

Designed to meet the needs of a wide range of users, from the student at intermediate level and above to the enthusiastic traveller or business professional, the *Pocket Oxford-Hachette Dictionary* is an invaluable practical resource for learners of contemporary, idiomatic French at the start of the twenty-first century.

*The Editors*

# Editors and contributors

## First edition

**Chief Editor**
Marie-Hélène Corréard

**Editors**
Frances Illingworth
Natalie Pomier

**Associate Editor**
Mary O'Neill

## Second edition

**Chief Editors**
Marianne Chalmers
Martine Pierquin

**Data Capture**
Anne McConnell
Anna Cotgreave
Marianne Selby-Smith

**A–Z of French Life and Culture**
**Calendar of French traditions, festivals, and holidays**
*Ella Associates*
Valerie Grundy

## Second edition revised

**Summary of French Grammar**
Glynnis Chantrell

# Note on proprietary status

# Contents

# The structure of French-English entries

headword •——— **délice** /delis/ *nm* delight

**délicieusement** /delisjøzmã/ *adv* **(a)** deliciously

**délicieux, -ieuse** /delisjø, øz/ *adj* **(a)** delicious •—— feminine form of the headword

**demandeur¹, -euse** /dəmãdœʀ, øz/ *nm,f* applicant.

compounds in •——— ■ ~ **d'asile** asylum-seeker; ~ **d'emploi** job-seeker
block at end of entry

**épaule** /epol/ *nf* shoulder
IDIOMS **changer son fusil d'**~ to change one's •—— idioms in block at end of entry
tactics; **avoir la tête sur les** ~**s** to have one's head screwed on (colloq)

pronunciation •——— **épicier, -ière** /episje, ɛʀ/ *nm,f* grocer
in IPA

**francophone** /fʀãkɔfɔn/ **1** *adj* French- •—— grammatical categories
speaking; ⟨literature⟩ in the French language
**2** *nmf* French speaker

part of speech •——— **free-lance** /fʀilãs/ *nmf* freelance, freelancer;
plus gender

sense categories •——— **juguler** /ʒygyle/ [1] *vtr* to stamp out ⟨epidemic, ——• number of verb group referring to the French verb tables at the end of the dictionary

**liquider** /likide/ [1] *vtr* **(a)** to settle ⟨accounts⟩;
to liquidate ⟨company, business⟩
**(b)** to clear ⟨goods, stock⟩

**lot** /lo/ *nm* **(a)** (of inheritance) share; (of land) plot •—— sense indicators
**(b)** (in lottery) prize; **gagner le gros** ~ to hit the jackpot

field labels for •——— **luth** /lyt/ *nm* **(a)** (Mus) lute
specialist terms **(b)** (Zool) leatherback

**magner**: **se magner** /maɲe/ [1] *v refl* •—— style labels
(+ *v être*) (slang) to get a move on (colloq)

**pomponner**: **se pomponner** /pɔ̃pɔne/ [1]
grammatical •——— *v refl* (+ *v être*) to get dolled up
information

**précédent, ~e** /pʀesedã, ãt/ **1** *adj* ——— translations
previous
**2** *nm,f* **le** ~, **la** ~**e** the previous one

**profaner** /pʀɔfane/ [1] *vtr* to desecrate
typical collocates •——— ⟨temple⟩; to defile ⟨memory⟩; to debase
– words used with ⟨institution⟩
the headword,
shown to help select **RN** /ɛʀɛn/ *nf* (*abbr* = **route nationale**) ≈ A ——— approximate
the right translation road (GB), highway (US) translation
examples, with •——— **souci** /susi/ *nm* **(a)** **se faire du** ~ to worry
a swung dash **(b)** problem; **j'ai d'autres** ~**s** (**en tête**) I've got
representing the other things to worry about
headword

**transfusé, ~e** /tʀãsfyze/ **1** *pp* ▶ ——— cross-reference
TRANSFUSER

# The structure of English-French entries

headword •————— **battery** *n* pile *f*; (in car) batterie *f*

**battery charger** *n* chargeur *m* de batteries — • separate entries for compounds
**battery farming** *n* élevage *m* en batterie

**beat** ① *n* (a) (of drum, heart) battement *m* ...
phrasal verbs •———— ■ **beat back** repousser ⟨*group, flames*⟩
■ **beat down** ⟨*rain*⟩ tomber à verse (**on** sur)

**cat** *n* (domestic) chat *m*; (female) chatte *f*; **the big ~s** les grands félins *mpl*
**IDIOMS to let the ~ out of the bag** vendre la mèche; **to rain ~s and dogs** pleuvoir des cordes — • idioms in block at end of entry

grammatical • categories and parts of speech —— **clutter** ① *n* désordre *m*
② *vtr* (*also* ~ **up**) encombrer

**edge** ① *n* (a) (outer limit) bord *m*; (of wood, clearing) lisière *f*; **the film had us on the ~ of our seats** le film nous a tenus en haleine (b) (of blade) tranchant *m* — • sense categories

sense indicators •———— **especially** *adv* (a) (above all) surtout, en particulier; **him ~** lui en particulier; **~ as it's so hot** d'autant plus qu'il fait si chaud (b) (on purpose) exprès, spécialement

**fishy** *adj* (a) ⟨*smell, taste*⟩ de poisson (b) (colloq) (suspect) louche (colloq) — • style labels

field labels for • specialist terms —— **message window** *n* (Comput) feuille *f* de message
**mushroom** *n* (a) (Bot, Culin) champignon

**non-smoking** *adj* non fumeur *inv* — • grammatical information

translations •———— **nuisance** *n* (gen) embêtement *m*; (Law) nuisance *f*; **what a ~!** que c'est agaçant!

**official** ① *n* fonctionnaire *mf*; (of party, union) officiel/-ielle *m/f*; (at town hall) employé/-e *m/f* — • feminine ending in translation

typical collocates • – words used with the headword, shown to help select the right translation —— **plump** *adj* ⟨*person, arm, leg*⟩ potelé/-e; ⟨*cheek, face*⟩ rond/-e, plein/-e
**plunge** ① *vtr* plonger (**into** dans) ② *vi* ⟨*road, cliff, waterfall*⟩ plonger; ⟨*bird, plane*⟩ piquer

**secondary school** *n* ≈ école *f* secondaire — • approximate translation equivalent

examples, with • a swung dash representing the headword —— **shut** ① *adj* fermé/-e; **her eyes were ~** elle avait les yeux fermés; **to slam the door ~** claquer la porte (pour bien la fermer); **to keep one's mouth ~** (colloq) se taire

**these** ▶ THIS — • cross-reference

# The pronunciation of French

## Vowels

| | | | |
|---|---|---|---|
| a | *as in* | *patte* | /pat/ |
| ɑ | | *pâte* | /pɑt/ |
| ɑ̃ | | *clan* | /klɑ̃/ |
| e | | *dé* | /de/ |
| ɛ | | *belle* | /bɛl/ |
| ɛ̃ | | *lin* | /lɛ̃/ |
| ə | | *demain* | /dəmɛ̃/ |
| i | | *gris* | /gʀi/ |
| o | | *gros* | /gʀo/ |
| ɔ | | *corps* | /kɔʀ/ |
| ɔ̃ | | *long* | /lɔ̃/ |
| œ | | *leur* | /lœʀ/ |
| œ̃ | | *brun* | /bʀœ̃/ |
| ø | | *deux* | /dø/ |
| u | | *fou* | /fu/ |
| y | | *pur* | /pyʀ/ |

## Semi-vowels

| | | | |
|---|---|---|---|
| j | *as in* | *fille* | /fij/ |
| ɥ | | *huit* | /ɥit/ |
| w | | *oui* | /wi/ |

## Consonants

| | | | |
|---|---|---|---|
| b | *as in* | *bal* | /bal/ |
| d | | *dent* | /dɑ̃/ |
| f | | *foire* | /fwaʀ/ |
| g | | *gomme* | /gɔm/ |
| k | | *clé* | /kle/ |
| l | | *lien* | /ljɛ̃/ |
| m | | *mer* | /mɛʀ/ |
| n | | *nage* | /naʒ/ |
| ɲ | | *gnon* | /ɲɔ̃/ |
| ŋ | | *dancing* | /dɑ̃siŋ/ |
| p | | *porte* | /pɔʀt/ |
| ʀ | | *rire* | /ʀiʀ/ |
| s | | *sang* | /sɑ̃/ |
| ʃ | | *chien* | /ʃjɛ̃/ |
| t | | *train* | /tʀɛ̃/ |
| v | | *voile* | /vwal/ |
| z | | *zèbre* | /zɛbʀ/ |
| ʒ | | *jeune* | /ʒœn/ |

The symbols used in this dictionary for the pronunciation of French are those of the IPA (International Phonetic Alphabet). Certain differences in pronunciation are shown in the phonetic transcription, although many speakers do not observe them—e.g. the long 'a' /ɑ/ in *pâte* and the short 'a' /a/ in *patte*, or the difference between the nasal vowels 'un' /œ̃/ as in *brun* and 'in' /ɛ̃/ as in *brin*.

## Transcription

Each entry is followed by its phonetic transcription between slashes, with a few exceptions.

## Morphological variations

The phonetic transcription of the plural and feminine forms of certain nouns and adjectives does not repeat the root, but shows only the change in ending. Therefore, in

. . . . . . . . . . . . . . . . . . . . . . . . . . . . . . . . . . . . . . . . . . . . .

certain cases, the presentation of the entry does not correspond to that of the phonetic transcripton e.g. *électricien, -ienne* /elɛktʀisjɛ̃, ɛn/.

## Phrases

Full phonetic transcription is given for adverbial or prepositional phrases which are shown in alphabetical order within the main headword e.g. *emblée, d'emblée* /dɑ̃ble/, *plain-pied, de plain-pied* /d(ə)plɛ̃pje/.

## Consonants

*Aspiration of 'h'*

Where it is impossible to make a liaison this is indicated by /'/ immediately after the slash e.g. *haine* /'ɛn/.

*Assimilation*

A voiced consonant can become unvoiced when it is followed by an unvoiced consonant within a word e.g. *absorber* /apsɔʀbe/.

## Vowels

*Open 'e' and closed 'e'*

A clear distinction is made at the end of a word between a closed 'e' and an open 'e' e.g. *pré* /pʀe/ and *près* /pʀɛ/, *complet* /kɔ̃plɛ/ and *combler* /kɔ̃ble/.

Within a word the following rules apply:
- 'e' is always open in a syllable followed by a syllable containing a mute 'e' e.g. *règle* /ʀɛgl/, *réglementaire* /ʀɛgləmɑ̃tɛʀ/

- in careful speech 'e' is pronounced as a closed 'e' when it is followed by a syllable containing a closed vowel (y, i, e) e.g. *pressé* /pʀese/
- 'e' is pronounced as an open 'e' when it is followed by a syllable containing an open vowel e.g. *pressant* /pʀɛsɑ̃/.

*Mute 'e'*

The pronunciation of mute 'e' varies considerably depending on the level of language used and on the region from which the speaker originates. As a general rule it is only pronounced at the end of a word in the South of France or in poetry and it is, therefore, not shown. In an isolated word the mute 'e' preceded by a single consonant is dropped e.g. *parfaitement* /paʀfɛtmɑ̃/, but *probablement* /pʀɔbabləmɑ̃/. In many cases the pronunciation of the mute 'e' depends on the surrounding context. Thus one would say *une reconnaissance de dette* /ynʀəkɔnɛsɑ̃sdədɛt/, but, *ma reconnaissance est éternelle* /maʀkɔnɛsɑ̃sɛtetɛʀnɛl/. The mute 'e' is shown in brackets in order to account for this phenomenon.

*Stress*

There is no real stress as such in French. In normal unemphasized speech a slight stress falls on the final syllable of a word or group of words, providing that it does not contain a mute 'e'. This is not shown in the phonetic transcription of individual entries.

# Abbreviations

| | | | |
|---|---|---|---|
| abbr | abbreviation | Naut | nautical |
| adj | adjective | phr | phrase |
| adv | adverb | pl | plural |
| Anat | anatomy | Pol | politics |
| Aut | automobile | pp | past participle |
| aux | auxiliary | pp adj | past participle adjective |
| Bot | botany | pr n | proper noun |
| colloq | colloquial | pref | prefix |
| Comput | computing | prep | preposition |
| conj | conjunction | pres p adj | present participle adjective |
| Culin | culinary | pron | pronoun |
| dem pron | demonstrative pronoun | qch | quelque chose (something) |
| det | determiner | qn | quelqu'un (somebody) |
| Econ | economy | quantif | quantifier |
| excl | exclamation | ® | registered trademark |
| f | feminine | rel pron | relative pronoun |
| Fr | French | sb | somebody |
| GB | British English | Sch | school |
| gen | generally | sg | singular |
| Hist | history, historical | sth | something |
| indic | indicative | subj | subjunctive |
| inv | invariable | Tech | technology |
| m | masculine | Univ | university |
| Med | medicine | US | American English |
| Mil | military | v | verb |
| Mus | music | v aux | auxiliary verb |
| n | noun | vi | intransitive verb |
| nf | feminine noun | v impers | impersonal verb |
| nm | masculine noun | v refl | reflexive verb |
| nmf | masculine and feminine noun | vtr | transitive verb |
| nm,f | masculine and feminine noun | Zool | zoology |

# Aa

**a¹, A** /a, ɑ/ **1** *nm inv* a, A; **démontrer qch à qn par A plus B** to demonstrate sth conclusively to sb
**2 A** *nf* (*abbr* = **autoroute**) motorway (GB), freeway (US)

**a²** /a/ ▸ AVOIR¹

**à** /a/ *prep*

■ **Note** You will find translations for expressions such as *machine à écrire*, *aller à la pêche* etc, at the entries MACHINE, PÊCHE etc.
– For the uses of *à* with the verbs *aller, être, avoir, penser* etc, see the entries for these verbs.

**(a)** to; **aller ~ Paris** to go to Paris; **se rendre au travail** to go to work
**(b)** at; in; **~ la maison** at home; **être ~ Paris** to be in Paris; **au printemps** in (the) spring; **~ midi** at midday; **~ quatre kilomètres d'ici** four kilometres (GB) from here; **~ 100 kilomètres-heure** at 100 kilometres (GB) per *or* an hour; **un timbre ~ 0,46 euro** a 0.46 euro stamp; **(de) huit ~ dix heures par jour** between eight and ten hours a day
**(c)** with; **le garçon aux cheveux bruns** the boy with dark hair
**(d)** **~ qui est cette montre?** whose is this watch?; **elle est ~ elle** it's hers; **je suis ~ vous tout de suite** I'll be with you in a minute; **c'est ~ qui de jouer?** whose turn is it?
**(e)** **il est ~ plaindre** he's to be pitied
**(f)** **~ nous tous on devrait y arriver** between all of us we should be able to manage; **~ trois on est serrés** with three people it's a squash
**(g)** **~ ce qu'il paraît** apparently; **~ ta santé**, **~ la tienne!** cheers!; **~ tes souhaits!** bless you!

**abaisser** /abese/ [1] **1** *vtr* to pull down ⟨*lever*⟩; to lower ⟨*safety curtain, window*⟩
**2 s'abaisser** *v refl* (+ *v être*) **(a)** ⟨*stage curtain*⟩ to fall
**(b)** **s'~ à faire** to stoop to doing

**abandon** /abɑ̃dɔ̃/ *nm* **(a)** **être à l'~** ⟨*house*⟩ to be abandoned; ⟨*garden*⟩ to be neglected
**(b)** (of project, method) abandonment; (of right) relinquishment
**(c)** (from race, competition) withdrawal

**abandonné**, **~e** /abɑ̃dɔne/ **1** *pp* ▸ ABANDONNER
**2** *pp adj* **(a)** ⟨*spouse, friend, cause*⟩ deserted; ⟨*vehicle, house, nation*⟩ abandoned
**(b)** ⟨*path, factory*⟩ disused

**abandonner** /abɑ̃dɔne/ [1] *vtr* **(a)** (gen) to give up; (in school) to drop ⟨*subject*⟩
**(b)** (from game, tournament) to withdraw; to retire

**(c)** to leave ⟨*person, place*⟩; to abandon ⟨*car, object*⟩
**(d)** to abandon ⟨*child, animal*⟩; to desert ⟨*home, post, cause*⟩
**(e)** ⟨*courage, chance*⟩ to fail ⟨*person*⟩

**abat-jour** /abaʒuʀ/ *nm inv* lampshade

**abats** /aba/ *nm pl* offal; (of poultry) giblets

**abattement** /abatmɑ̃/ *nm*
**(a)** despondency
**(b)** **~ fiscal** tax allowance (GB) *or* deduction (US)

**abattoir** /abatwaʀ/ *nm* abattoir, slaughterhouse

**abattre** /abatʀ/ [61] **1** *vtr* **(a)** to shoot [sb] down ⟨*person*⟩; to shoot ⟨*animal*⟩; to slaughter ⟨*cattle, sheep*⟩
**(b)** to pull down ⟨*building*⟩; to knock down ⟨*wall*⟩; ⟨*person*⟩ to fell ⟨*tree*⟩; ⟨*storm*⟩ to bring down ⟨*tree*⟩
**(c)** to show ⟨*card, hand*⟩
**(d)** to demoralize
**(e)** **~ de la besogne** to get through a lot of work
**2 s'abattre** *v refl* (+ *v être*) **s'~ sur** ⟨*storm*⟩ to break over; ⟨*rain*⟩ to beat down on; ⟨*bird of prey*⟩ to swoop down on

**abbaye** /abei/ *nf* abbey

**abbé** /abe/ *nm* **(a)** priest
**(b)** abbot

**abc** /abese/ *nm* ABC, rudiments

**abcès** /apsɛ/ *nm inv* abscess; **crever l'~** to resolve a crisis

**abdication** /abdikasjɔ̃/ *nf* abdication

**abdiquer** /abdike/ [1] *vi* ⟨*sovereign*⟩ to abdicate

**abdomen** /abdɔmɛn/ *nm* abdomen, stomach

**abdominal**, **~e**, *mpl* **-aux** /abdɔminal, o/ **1** *adj* abdominal
**2 abdominaux** *nm pl* abdominal muscles

**abeille** /abɛj/ *nf* bee

**aberrant**, **~e** /abeʀɑ̃, ɑ̃t/ *adj* **(a)** absurd
**(b)** aberrant

**aberration** /abeʀasjɔ̃/ *nf* aberration

**abêtir** /abetiʀ/ [3]: **s'abêtir** *v refl* (+ *v être*) to become stupid

**abêtissant**, **~e** /abetisɑ̃, ɑ̃t/ *adj* mindless

**abîme** /abim/ *nm* **(a)** abyss
**(b)** (figurative) gulf

**abîmer** /abime/ [1] **1** *vtr* to damage
**2 s'abîmer** *v refl* (+ *v être*) ⟨*object*⟩ to get damaged; ⟨*fruit*⟩ to spoil

**abject**, **~e** /abʒɛkt/ *adj* despicable, abject

**ablation** /ablasjɔ̃/ *nf* excision, removal

**abnégation** /abnegasjɔ̃/ *nf* self-sacrifice

**aboiement** /abwamɑ̃/ *nm* barking

**abolir** /abɔliʀ/ [3] *vtr* to abolish

**abominable** /abɔminabl/ *adj* abominable

**abomination** /abɔminɑsjɔ̃/ *nf* abomination

**abondamment** /abɔ̃damɑ̃/ *adv* ⟨drink⟩ a lot; ⟨illustrate⟩ amply; **rincer** ~ rinse thoroughly

**abondance** /abɔ̃dɑ̃s/ *nf* **(a)** (of information) wealth; (of resources) abundance
**(b)** affluence

**abondant**, ~**e** /abɔ̃dɑ̃, ɑ̃t/ *adj* ⟨food⟩ plentiful; ⟨illustrations⟩ numerous; ⟨vegetation⟩ lush

**abonder** /abɔ̃de/ [1] *vi* to be plentiful; to abound
IDIOMS ~ **dans le sens de qn** to agree wholeheartedly with sb

**abonné**, ~**e** /abɔne/ ⏢1 *pp* ▶ ABONNER
⏢2 *nm,f* **(a)** subscriber
**(b)** season ticket holder

**abonnement** /abɔnmɑ̃/ *nm*
**(a)** subscription
**(b)** (carte d')~ season ticket

**abonner** /abɔne/ [1] ⏢1 *vtr* ~ **qn à qch** (to magazine) to take out a subscription to sth for sb; (for theatre) to buy sb a season ticket for sth
⏢2 **s'abonner** *v refl* (+ *v être*) to subscribe (à to); to buy a season ticket (à for)

**abord** /abɔʀ/ ⏢1 *nm* **(a) elle est d'un** ~ **difficile** she is rather unapproachable
**(b) être d'un** ~ **aisé** ⟨subject, book⟩ to be accessible
**(c) au premier** ~ at first sight
⏢2 **d'abord** *phr* first; **tout d'**~ first of all
⏢3 **abords** *nm pl* surrounding area, area around

**abordable** /abɔʀdabl/ *adj* ⟨product, price⟩ affordable; ⟨text⟩ accessible

**abordage** /abɔʀdaʒ/ *nm* (by pirates) boarding

**aborder** /abɔʀde/ [1] ⏢1 *vtr* **(a)** to tackle ⟨problem⟩
**(b)** to approach ⟨person⟩
**(c)** to reach ⟨place, shore⟩
⏢2 *vi* ⟨traveller, ship⟩ to land

**aboutir** /abutiʀ/ [3] ⏢1 **aboutir à** *v+prep* to lead to
⏢2 *vi* ⟨negotiations, project⟩ to succeed

**aboutissants** /abutisɑ̃/ *nm pl* **les tenants et les** ~ **de qch** the ins and outs of sth

**aboutissement** /abutismɑ̃/ *nm*
**(a)** culmination
**(b)** (successful) outcome

**aboyer** /abwaje/ [23] *vi* ⟨dog⟩ to bark (**après** at)

**abracadabrant**, ~**e** /abʀakadabʀɑ̃, ɑ̃t/ *adj* bizarre

**abrasif**, **-ive** /abʀazif, iv/ *adj* abrasive

**abrégé** /abʀeʒe/ *nm* (book) concise guide

**abréger** /abʀeʒe/ [15] *vtr* **(a)** to shorten ⟨word, expression⟩
**(b)** to cut short ⟨visit, career⟩

**abreuver**: **s'abreuver** /abʀøve/ [1] *v refl* (+ *v être*) ⟨animal⟩ to drink

**abreuvoir** /abʀøvwaʀ/ *nm* drinking trough

**abréviation** /abʀevjasjɔ̃/ *nf* abbreviation

**abri** /abʀi/ *nm* **(a)** shelter; **à l'**~ **de** sheltered from; (figurative) safe from
**(b)** shed

**abricot** /abʀiko/ *nm* apricot

**abricotier** /abʀikɔtje/ *nm* apricot tree

**abriter** /abʀite/ [1] ⏢1 *vtr* **(a)** ⟨building⟩ to shelter ⟨people, animals⟩
**(b)** ⟨country, region⟩ to provide a habitat for ⟨animals, plant life⟩
⏢2 **s'abriter** *v refl* (+ *v être*) to take shelter

**abrogation** /abʀɔgasjɔ̃/ *nf* repeal

**abroger** /abʀɔʒe/ [13] *vtr* to repeal

**abrupt**, ~**e** /abʀypt/ *adj* **(a)** ⟨hill, road⟩ steep; ⟨cliff⟩ sheer
**(b)** ⟨person, tone⟩ abrupt

**abruti**, ~**e** /abʀyti/ *nm,f* (offensive) moron (colloq)

**abrutir** /abʀytiʀ/ [3] ⏢1 *vtr* ⟨noise⟩ to deafen; ⟨alcohol, medication, fatigue⟩ to have a numbing effect on; ⟨blow⟩ to stun
⏢2 **s'abrutir** *v refl* (+ *v être*) **(a)** to become dull-witted
**(b) s'**~ **de travail** to wear oneself out with work

**abrutissant**, ~**e** /abʀytisɑ̃, ɑ̃t/ *adj* ⟨music, noise⟩ deafening; ⟨job⟩ mind-numbing

**absence** /apsɑ̃s/ *nf* **(a)** absence
**(b)** lack; **l'**~ **de pluie** the lack of rain

**absent**, ~**e** /apsɑ̃, ɑ̃t/ ⏢1 *adj* **(a) être** ~ to be away; (for brief spell) to be out
**(b)** ⟨pupil, employee⟩ absent
**(c)** (missing) absent (**de** from)
**(d)** absent-minded
⏢2 *nm,f* absentee

**absentéisme** /apsɑ̃teism/ *nm* absenteeism

**absenter**: **s'absenter** /apsɑ̃te/ [1] *v refl* (+ *v être*) to go away; to go out

**absolu**, ~**e** /apsɔly/ *adj* absolute; ⟨rule⟩ hard and fast

**absolument** /apsɔlymɑ̃/ *adv* absolutely

**absolution** /apsɔlysjɔ̃/ *nf* absolution

**absolutisme** /apsɔlytism/ *nm* absolutism

**absorbant**, ~**e** /apsɔʀbɑ̃, ɑ̃t/ *adj*
**(a)** ⟨substance⟩ absorbent
**(b)** ⟨job, work⟩ absorbing

**absorber** /apsɔʀbe/ [1] *vtr* **(a)** ⟨material, plant⟩ to absorb
**(b)** to take ⟨food, medicine⟩
**(c)** to occupy ⟨mind⟩

**absorption** /apsɔʀpsjɔ̃/ *nf* **(a)** (of liquid) absorption
**(b)** (of food, medicine) taking

**abstenir**: **s'abstenir** /apstəniʀ/ [36] *v refl* (+ *v être*) **(a)** (from voting) to abstain
**(b) s'**~ **de faire** to refrain from doing

**abstention** /apstɑ̃sjɔ̃/ *nf* abstention

**abstinence** /apstinɑ̃s/ *nf* abstinence

**abstraction** /apstʀaksjɔ̃/ *nf* abstraction; faire ~ de to set aside

**abstrait, ~e** /apstʀɛ, ɛt/ **1** *adj* abstract **2** *nm* (gen) abstract; (art) abstract art

**absurde** /apsyʀd/ *adj, nm* absurd

**absurdité** /apsyʀdite/ *nf* absurdity

**abus** /aby/ *nm inv* abuse

**abuser** /abyze/ [1] **1** *vtr* to fool
**2 abuser de** *v+prep* (a) ~ de l'alcool to drink to excess
(b) ~ de to exploit ⟨situation, credibility⟩
(c) ~ de qn to sexually abuse sb
**3** *vi* to go too far; je ne voudrais pas ~ I don't want to impose
**4 s'abuser** *v refl* (+ *v être*) si je ne m'abuse if I'm not mistaken

**abusif, -ive** /abyzif, iv/ *adj* (a) excessive
(b) unfair
(c) improper
(d) over-possessive

**acabit** /akabi/ *nm* du même ~ of that sort

**acacia** /akasja/ *nm* (a) (European) (faux) ~ locust tree
(b) (tropical) acacia

**académicien, -ienne** /akademisjɛ̃, ɛn/ *nm,f* academician

**académie** /akademi/ *nf* (Sch) ≈ local education authority (GB), school district (US)

**académique** /akademik/ *adj* (a) (gen) academic; of the Académie française
(b) (Sch, Univ) ≈ of the local education authority (GB) *or* school district (US)
(c) (in art) academic

**acajou** /akaʒu/ *nm* mahogany

**acariâtre** /akaʀjɑtʀ/ *adj* cantankerous

**accablant, ~e** /akablɑ̃, ɑ̃t/ *adj* (a) ⟨heat, silence⟩ oppressive
(b) ⟨evidence, testimony⟩ damning

**accabler** /akable/ [1] *vtr* (a) ⟨bad news⟩ to devastate; être accablé par to be overcome by ⟨heat, grief⟩
(b) ⟨testimony, person⟩ to condemn

**accalmie** /akalmi/ *nf* (a) lull
(b) slack period

**accaparant, ~e** /akapaʀɑ̃, ɑ̃t/ *adj* very demanding

**accaparer** /akapaʀe/ [1] *vtr* to corner ⟨market⟩; to monopolize ⟨person, power⟩

**accédant, ~e** /aksedɑ̃, ɑ̃t/ *nm,f* ~ à la propriété home-buyer

**accéder** /aksede/ [14] *v+prep* (a) ~ à to reach ⟨place⟩
(b) ~ à to achieve ⟨fame, glory⟩; to obtain ⟨job⟩; to rise to ⟨high office⟩

**accélérateur** /akseleʀatœʀ/ *nm* accelerator

**accélération** /akseleʀasjɔ̃/ *nf* acceleration; (of consumption) sharp increase (de in)

**accélérer** /akseleʀe/ [14] **1** *vtr* to speed up ⟨rhythm, process⟩; ~ le pas to quicken one's step
**2** *vi* ⟨driver⟩ to accelerate

**3 s'accélérer** *v refl* (+ *v être*) ⟨pulse, movement⟩ to become faster; ⟨phenomenon⟩ to accelerate

**accent** /aksɑ̃/ *nm* (a) (of region) accent
(b) (on a letter) accent
(c) (on a syllable) ~ tonique stress; mettre l'~ sur qch to emphasize sth, to put the emphasis on sth
(d) ~ de sincérité hint of sincerity

**accentuer** /aksɑ̃tɥe/ [1] **1** *vtr* (a) (gen) to emphasize, to accentuate
(b) to heighten ⟨tension⟩; to increase ⟨tendency⟩
(c) (in pronouncing) to stress ⟨syllable⟩
**2 s'accentuer** *v refl* (+ *v être*) to become more marked

**acceptable** /aksɛptabl/ *adj* (a) acceptable
(b) passable; satisfactory

**acceptation** /aksɛptasjɔ̃/ *nf* acceptance

**accepter** /aksɛpte/ [1] *vtr* to accept; to agree to

**acception** /aksɛpsjɔ̃/ *nf* sense; dans toute l'~ du terme *or* mot in every sense of the word

**accès** /aksɛ/ *nm inv* (a) access; d'un ~ facile ⟨place⟩ easy to get to; '~ aux quais' 'to the trains'; '~ interdit' 'no entry'; l'~ à access to ⟨profession, course⟩; admission to ⟨club, school⟩
(b) ~ de colère fit of anger; ~ de fièvre bout of fever; par ~ by fits and starts
(c) (Comput) access

**accessible** /aksesibl/ *adj* (a) ⟨place, book, information⟩ accessible
(b) ~ à ⟨job⟩ open to
(c) ⟨price, fare⟩ affordable

**accession** /aksesjɔ̃/ *nf* ~ à accession to ⟨throne, power⟩; attainment of ⟨independence⟩

**accessoire** /akseswaʀ/ **1** *adj* incidental
**2** *nm* (a) accessory; attachment; ~s de toilette toilet requisites
(b) (in the theatre) ~s props

**accessoirement** /akseswaʀmɑ̃/ *adv*
(a) incidentally, as it happens
(b) if desired

**accessoiriste** /akseswaʀist/ *nmf* props man/woman

**accident** /aksidɑ̃/ *nm* (a) accident
(b) hitch; mishap; ~ de parcours (colloq) hitch
■ ~ domestique accident in the home

**accidenté, ~e** /aksidɑ̃te/ **1** *adj*
(a) ⟨person⟩ injured; ⟨car⟩ involved in an accident
(b) ⟨road, ground⟩ uneven
**2** *nm,f* accident victim

**accidentel, -elle** /aksidɑ̃tɛl/ *adj* accidental

**accidentellement** /aksidɑ̃tɛlmɑ̃/ *adv*
(a) in an accident
(b) by accident, accidentally

**acclamation** /aklamasjɔ̃/ *nf* cheering

**acclamer** /aklame/ [1] *vtr* to cheer, to acclaim

**acclimater** /aklimate/ [1] **1** *vtr* to acclimatize
**2 s'acclimater** *v refl* (+ *v être*) to become acclimatized; to adapt

**accointances** /akwɛ̃tɑ̃s/ *nf pl* contacts

**accolade** /akɔlad/ *nf* embrace

**accommoder** /akɔmɔde/ [1] **1** *vtr* to prepare
**2** *vi* ⟨eyes⟩ to focus
**3 s'accommoder** *v refl* (+ *v être*) **s'~ de qch** to make the best of sth; to put up with sth

**accompagnateur, -trice** /akɔ̃paɲatœr, tris/ *nm,f* **(a)** (Mus) accompanist
**(b)** (with children) accompanying adult; (with tourists) courier

**accompagnement** /akɔ̃paɲmɑ̃/ *nm* accompaniment

**accompagner** /akɔ̃paɲe/ [1] *vtr*
**(a)** ⟨person⟩ to accompany, to go with, to come with
**(b)** to accompany ⟨phenomenon, event⟩
**(c)** (Mus) to accompany
**(d)** ⟨wine⟩ to be served with

**accomplir** /akɔ̃plir/ [3] **1** *vtr* to accomplish ⟨task⟩; to fulfil (GB) ⟨obligation⟩
**2 s'accomplir** *v refl* (+ *v être*) to be fulfilled

**accomplissement** /akɔ̃plismɑ̃/ *nm* (of mission) accomplishment, fulfilment (GB); (of ambition, aim) realization, achievement

**accord** /akɔr/ *nm* **(a)** agreement; (tacit) understanding; **d'~** all right, OK (colloq); **je suis d'~** I agree (**avec** with); **se mettre** *or* **tomber d'~** to come to an agreement
**(b)** harmony
**(c)** (in grammar) **~ en genre/en nombre** gender/number agreement
**(d)** (Mus) chord

**accordéon** /akɔrdeɔ̃/ *nm* accordion

**accorder** /akɔrde/ [1] **1** *vtr* **(a)** **~ qch à qn** to grant sb sth ⟨favour, loan, interview, permission, right⟩; to give sb sth ⟨grant, reduction, chance⟩; **il n'a pas entièrement tort, je te l'accorde** he's not entirely wrong, I'll give you that
**(b)** to attach ⟨importance, value⟩ (**à** to); to pay ⟨attention⟩
**(c)** (Mus) to tune ⟨instrument⟩
**(d)** to make [sth] agree ⟨word, adjective⟩
**2 s'accorder** *v refl* (+ *v être*) **(a)** to give oneself ⟨rest, time off⟩
**(b)** to agree (**sur** about, on)
**(c)** ⟨colours, clothes⟩ to go (together) well
**(d)** ⟨adjective, verb⟩ to agree (**avec** with)

**accordeur** /akɔrdœr/ *nm* tuner

**accostage** /akɔstaʒ/ *nm* docking

**accoster** /akɔste/ [1] **1** *vtr* to accost ⟨person⟩
**2** *vi* ⟨ship⟩ to dock

**accotement** /akɔtmɑ̃/ *nm* verge

**accouchement** /akuʃmɑ̃/ *nm* delivery

**accoucher** /akuʃe/ [1] *vi* to give birth (**de** to)

**accoucheur** /akuʃœr/ *nm* obstetrician

**accouder: s'accouder** /akude/ [1] *v refl* (+ *v être*) to lean on one's elbows

**accoudoir** /akudwar/ *nm* arm-rest

**accouplement** /akupləmɑ̃/ *nm* mating

**accourir** /akurir/ [26] *vi* to run up

**accoutrement** /akutrəmɑ̃/ *nm* get-up (colloq)

**accoutrer: s'accoutrer** /akutre/ [1] *v refl* (+ *v être*) to get oneself up (**de** in)

**accoutumance** /akutymɑ̃s/ *nf* addiction

**accoutumer** /akutyme/ [1] **1** *vtr* to accustom (**à** to)
**2 s'accoutumer** *v refl* (+ *v être*) to grow accustomed (**à** to)

**accrédité, ~e** /akredite/ *adj* authorized; accredited

**accréditer** /akredite/ [1] *vtr* **(a)** to give credence to ⟨rumour⟩
**(b)** to accredit ⟨ambassador⟩

**accro** /akro/ *adj* (colloq) hooked (colloq) (**à** on)

**accroc** /akro/ *nm* tear (**à** in)

**accrochage** /akrɔʃaʒ/ *nm* (between people) clash; (between vehicles) collision

**accrocher** /akrɔʃe/ [1] **1** *vtr* **(a)** to hang (**à** from)
**(b)** to hook [sth] on (**à** to)
**(c)** to catch ⟨stocking, sweater⟩ (**à** on)
**(d)** to catch ⟨eye, attention⟩
**2 s'accrocher** *v refl* (+ *v être*) **(a)** (to ledge) to hang on; (to post) to cling (on) (**à** to)
**(b)** ⟨person⟩ **s'~ à qn** to cling to sb
**(c) l'hameçon s'est accroché à ma veste** the hook got caught in my jacket
**(d)** (colloq) **s'~ pour faire** to try hard to do
IDIOMS **avoir le cœur** *or* **l'estomac bien accroché** to have a strong stomach

**accrocheur, -euse** /akrɔʃœr, øz/ *adj* ⟨song, tune⟩ catchy; ⟨picture, title⟩ eye-catching

**accroissement** /akrwasmɑ̃/ *nm* growth

**accroître** /akrwatr/ [72] *vtr*, **s'accroître** *v refl* (+ *v être*) to increase

**accroupir: s'accroupir** /akrupir/ [3] *v refl* (+ *v être*) to squat (down); to crouch (down)

**accru, ~e** /akry/ ▸ ACCROÎTRE

**accueil** /akœj/ *nm* **(a)** welcome
**(b)** reception desk

**accueillant, ~e** /akœjɑ̃, ɑ̃t/ *adj*
**(a)** hospitable, welcoming
**(b)** homely (GB), homey (US)

**accueillir** /akœjir/ [27] *vtr* **(a)** to welcome
**(b)** to receive, to greet
**(c)** ⟨room, hotel⟩ to accommodate
**(d)** ⟨hospital, organization⟩ to cater for

**accumulation** /akymylasjɔ̃/ *nf*
**(a)** accumulation
**(b)** storage

**accumuler** /akymyle/ [1] **1** *vtr* **(a)** to store (up) ⟨things⟩; to accumulate ⟨capital⟩; to make a succession of ⟨mistakes⟩

**(b)** to store (up) ⟨*energy*⟩

**2 s'accumuler** *v refl* (+ *v être*) ⟨*snow, rubbish*⟩ to pile up; ⟨*stocks, debts*⟩ to accrue

**accusateur, -trice** /akyzatœR, tRis/

**1** *adj* ⟨*silence, finger*⟩ accusing; ⟨*presence, speech*⟩ accusatory

**2** *nm,f* accuser; ∼ **public** public prosecutor

**accusation** /akyzasjɔ̃/ *nf* **(a)** accusation; (Law) charge

**(b) l'**∼ the prosecution

**accusé, ∼e** /akyze/ **1** *pp* ▶ ACCUSER

**2** *pp adj* ⟨*wrinkles*⟩ deep; ⟨*relief*⟩ marked

**3** *nm,f* defendant; **les** ∼**s** the accused

■ ∼ **de réception** acknowledgement (of receipt)

**accuser** /akyze/ [1] **1** *vtr* **(a)** to accuse ⟨*person*⟩; to blame ⟨*fate*⟩; ⟨*evidence*⟩ to point to ⟨*person*⟩; ⟨*judge*⟩ to charge ⟨*defendant*⟩ (**de** with)

**(b)** to show, to register ⟨*fall, deficit*⟩

**2 s'accuser** *v refl* (+ *v être*) **(a)** ⟨*person*⟩ to take the blame

**(b)** to become more marked

**IDIOMS** ∼ **le coup** to be visibly shaken

**acerbe** /asɛRb/ *adj* acerbic

**acéré, ∼e** /asere/ *adj* sharp

**acharné, ∼e** /aʃaRne/ *adj* ⟨*supporter*⟩ passionate; ⟨*work*⟩ unremitting; ⟨*struggle*⟩ fierce

**acharnement** /aʃaRnəmã/ *nm* furious energy

**acharner: s'acharner** /aʃaRne/ [1] *v refl* (+ *v être*) **(a)** to persevere; **s'**∼ **contre** to fight against ⟨*project*⟩

**(b) s'**∼ **sur** ⟨*person, animal*⟩ to keep going at ⟨*victim, prey*⟩; (figurative) to hound ⟨*person*⟩; **la malchance s'acharne contre lui** he is dogged by bad luck

**achat** /aʃa/ *nm* purchase

**acheminement** /aʃ(ə)minmã/ *nm* transportation

**acheminer** /aʃ(ə)mine/ [1] **1** *vtr* to transport

**2 s'acheminer** *v refl* (+ *v être*) **s'**∼ **vers** to make one's way toward(s); to move toward(s)

**acheter** /aʃte/ [18] **1** *vtr* to buy; ∼ **qch à qn** to buy sth from sb; to buy sth for sb

**2 s'acheter** *v refl* (+ *v être*) **(a) s'**∼ **qch** to buy oneself sth

**(b) cela s'achète où?** where can you get it?

**acheteur, -euse** /aʃtœR, øz/ *nm,f* buyer

**achever** /aʃve/ [16] **1** *vtr* **(a)** to finish ⟨*work*⟩; to conclude ⟨*discussions*⟩; to complete ⟨*project, inquiry*⟩; to end ⟨*life*⟩

**(b)** to destroy ⟨*animal*⟩; to finish off ⟨*person*⟩

**2 s'achever** *v refl* (+ *v être*) to end

**achoppement** /aʃɔpmã/ *nm* **pierre d'**∼ stumbling block

**acide** /asid/ *adj, nm* acid

**acidité** /asidite/ *nf* acidity, tartness, sharpness

**acidulé, ∼e** /asidyle/ *adj* slightly acid; tangy

**acier** /asje/ **1** *adj inv* steel(y)

**2** *nm* steel; **d'**∼ ⟨*girder, column*⟩ steel; ⟨*nerves*⟩ of steel

**aciérie** /asjeRi/ *nf* steelworks

**acné** /akne/ *nf* acne; ∼ **juvénile** teenage acne

**acolyte** /akɔlit/ *nmf* henchman, acolyte

**acompte** /akɔ̃t/ *nm* **(a)** deposit

**(b)** part payment

**acoquiner: s'acoquiner** /akɔkine/ [1] *v refl* (+ *v être*) **s'**∼ **avec qn** to get thick (colloq) with sb

**à-côté,** *pl* ∼**s** /akote/ *nm* **(a)** perk

**(b)** extra expense

**(c)** extra profit

**à-coup,** *pl* ∼**s** /aku/ *nm* jolt; **par** ∼**s** by fits and starts

**acoustique** /akustik/ **1** *adj* acoustic

**2** *nf* acoustics

**acquéreur** /akeRœR/ *nm* buyer, purchaser

**acquérir** /akeRiR/ [35] *vtr* **(a)** to acquire; (by buying) to purchase

**(b)** to acquire ⟨*reputation*⟩

**acquiescement** /akjɛsmã/ *nm* **donner son** ∼ **à** to acquiesce to

**acquiescer** /akjese/ [12] *vi* to acquiesce

**acquis, ∼e** /aki, iz/ **1** *pp* ▶ ACQUÉRIR

**2** *pp adj* **(a)** ⟨*skills*⟩ acquired

**(b)** ⟨*principle, right*⟩ accepted, established; **les avantages** ∼ the gains made; **tenir qch pour** ∼ to take sth for granted

**3** *nm inv* **(a)** acquired knowledge

**(b)** ∼ **sociaux** social benefits

**IDIOMS bien mal** ∼ **ne profite jamais** (Proverb) ill-gotten gains never prosper

**acquisition** /akizisjɔ̃/ *nf* **(a)** purchase

**(b)** acquisition

**acquit** /aki/ *nm* **je le ferai par** ∼ **de conscience** I'll do it to put my mind at rest

**acquittement** /akitmã/ *nm* (Law) acquittal

**acquitter** /akite/ [1] **1** *vtr* (Law) to acquit

**2 s'acquitter** *v refl* (+ *v être*) **s'**∼ **de son devoir** to do one's duty; **s'**∼ **d'une dette** to pay off a debt

**acre** /akR/ *nf* acre

**âcre** /ɑkR/ *adj* ⟨*taste*⟩ sharp; ⟨*smell*⟩ acrid

**acrobate** /akRɔbat/ *nmf* acrobat

**acrobatie** /akRɔbasi/ *nf* acrobatics

**acronyme** /akRɔnim/ *nm* acronym

**acrylique** /akRilik/ *adj, nm* acrylic

**acte** /akt/ *nm* **(a)** act; ∼ **manqué** Freudian slip; **être libre de ses** ∼**s** to do as one wishes; **faire** ∼ **de candidature** to put oneself forward as a candidate

**(b)** (Law) deed; ∼ **de naissance** birth certificate

**(c)** (in play) act

**acteur, -trice** /aktœR, tRis/ *nm,f*

**(a)** actor/actress

**(b)** protagonist

**actif, -ive** /aktif, iv/ **1** *adj* (gen) active; ⟨market⟩ buoyant; **la vie active** working life **2** *nm* **(a)** l'~ the assets
**(b)** à l'~ **de qn** in sb's favour (GB)

**action** /aksjɔ̃/ *nf* **(a)** action, act; **une bonne** ~ a good deed
**(b)** l'~ action; **moyens d'**~ courses of action; **en** ~ in operation
**(c)** effect; l'~ **de qn sur** sb's influence on
**(d)** ~ **en justice** legal action
**(e)** (in finance) share

**actionnaire** /aksjɔnɛʀ/ *nmf* shareholder

**actionner** /aksjɔne/ [1] *vtr* to activate

**activement** /aktivmɑ̃/ *adv* actively

**activer** /aktive/ [1] **1** *vtr* **(a)** to speed up ⟨work⟩; to stimulate ⟨digestion⟩
**(b)** ⟨wind⟩ to stir up ⟨flames⟩
**(c)** to stoke ⟨fire⟩
**2** **s'activer** *v refl* (+ *v être*) (colloq) to hurry up

**activiste** /aktivist/ *adj, nmf* activist

**activité** /aktivite/ *nf* **(a)** activity; ~ **professionnelle** occupation
**(b)** **être en pleine** ~ ⟨street⟩ to be bustling with activity; ⟨person⟩ to be very busy; **volcan en** ~ active volcano

**actrice** *nf* ▶ ACTEUR

**actualisation** /aktɥalizasjɔ̃/ *nf* ⟨process⟩ updating; ⟨result⟩ update

**actualiser** /aktɥalize/ [1] *vtr* to update

**actualité** /aktɥalite/ **1** *nf* **(a)** current affairs; l'~ **culturelle** cultural events
**(b)** d'~ topical; **toujours d'**~ still relevant today
**2** **actualités** *nf pl* **(a)** news
**(b)** newsreel

**actuel, -elle** /aktɥɛl/ *adj* **(a)** present, current
**(b)** ⟨film, discussion⟩ topical

**actuellement** /aktɥɛlmɑ̃/ *adv* **(a)** at the moment
**(b)** currently

**acuité** /akɥite/ *nf* **(a)** acuity
**(b)** shrillness
**(c)** (of pain) intensity

**acupuncteur, -trice** /akypɔ̃ktœʀ, tʀis/ *nm,f* acupuncturist

**acupuncture** /akypɔ̃ktyʀ/ *nf* acupuncture

**adage** /adaʒ/ *nm* saying, adage

**adaptable** /adaptabl/ *adj* **(a)** (flexible) adaptable (à to)
**(b)** ⟨height, pressure⟩ adjustable; ~ **à toutes les circonstances** *or* **tous les besoins** all-purpose

**adaptateur, -trice** /adaptatœʀ, tʀis/ **1** *nm,f* (for cinema, theatre) (Théát) adapter
**2** *nm* (Tech) adapter

**adaptation** /adaptasjɔ̃/ *nf* adaptation

**adapté, ~e** /adapte/ *adj* **(a)** suitable
**(b)** ~ **à** ⟨solution⟩ suited to
**(c)** (for TV, stage) adapted

**adapter** /adapte/ [1] **1** *vtr* **(a)** to fit (à to)
**(b)** to adapt ⟨equipment⟩
**(c)** to adapt ⟨novel⟩

**2** **s'adapter** *v refl* (+ *v être*) **(a)** ⟨tool, part⟩ to fit
**(b)** to adapt, to adjust (à to)

**addition** /adisjɔ̃/ *nf* **(a)** addition
**(b)** bill, check (US)

**additionner** /adisjɔne/ [1] *vtr* to add up

**adduction** /adyksjɔ̃/ *nf* adduction; ~ **d'eau** water conveyance

**adepte** /adɛpt/ *nmf* **(a)** (of theory) supporter; (of person) disciple
**(b)** enthusiast

**adéquat, ~e** /adekwa, at/ *adj*
**(a)** appropriate, suitable
**(b)** adequate

**adéquation** /adekwasjɔ̃/ *nf*
**(a)** (correspondence) appropriateness (à, avec to)
**(b)** (of model) adequacy (à to)

**adhérence** /adeʀɑ̃s/ *nf* (of tyre, sole) grip

**adhérent, ~e** /adeʀɑ̃, ɑ̃t/ *nm,f* member

**adhérer** /adeʀe/ [14] *v+prep* **(a)** ~ **à** ⟨glue⟩ to stick to; ⟨tyre⟩ to grip
**(b)** ~ **à** to join

**adhésif, -ive** /adezif, iv/ *adj* adhesive

**adhésion** /adezjɔ̃/ *nf* **(a)** membership
**(b)** support

**adieu, *pl* ~x** /adjø/ *nm* goodbye, farewell

**adipeux, -euse** /adipø, øz/ *adj* fatty

**adjectif** /adʒɛktif/ *nm* adjective

**adjoint, ~e** /adʒwɛ̃, ɛ̃t/ *nm,f* assistant; deputy; ~ **au maire** deputy mayor

**adjudant** /adʒydɑ̃/ *nm* ≈ warrant officer

**adjudication** /adʒydikasjɔ̃/ *nf* auction; ~ **judiciaire** sale by order of the court

**adjuger** /adʒyʒe/ [13] *vtr* to auction; **une fois, deux fois, adjugé!** going, going, gone!

**adjuvant** /adʒyvɑ̃/ *nm* additive

**admettre** /admɛtʀ/ [60] *vtr* **(a)** to accept, to admit ⟨fact⟩
**(b)** to admit ⟨person, student⟩; **être admis à un examen** to pass an exam
**(c)** ~ **que** to suppose (that)

**administrateur, -trice** /administʀatœʀ, tʀis/ *nm,f* **(a)** administrator
**(b)** director
**(c)** trustee

**administratif, -ive** /administʀatif, iv/ *adj* **(a)** ⟨staff, building⟩ administrative
**(b)** ⟨report⟩ official

**administration** /administʀasjɔ̃/ *nf*
**(a)** administration
**(b)** civil service
**(c)** **être placé sous** ~ **judiciaire** to go into receivership
**(d)** management
**(e)** (of drugs, sacrament) administration, giving

**administrer** /administʀe/ [1] *vtr* **(a)** to administer ⟨funds⟩; to run ⟨company, country⟩
**(b)** to administer, to give ⟨drug, sacrament⟩

**admirable** /admiʀabl/ *adj* admirable

**admirablement** /admiʀabləmɑ̃/ *adv* ⟨do⟩ admirably; ⟨done⟩ superbly

**admirateur**, **-trice** /admiʀatœʀ, tʀis/ *nm,f* admirer

**admiration** /admiʀasjɔ̃/ *nf* admiration

**admirer** /admiʀe/ [1] *vtr* to admire

**admis**, **~e** /admi, iz/ ① *pp* ▶ ADMETTRE
② *pp adj* accepted; ⟨*candidate*⟩ successful

**admissible** /admisibl/ *adj* (a) acceptable
(b) eligible

**admission** /admisjɔ̃/ *nf* admission;
**service des ~s** reception

**ado** /ado/ *nmf* (colloq) teenager

**adolescence** /adɔlesɑ̃s/ *nf* adolescence

**adolescent**, **~e** /adɔlesɑ̃, ɑ̃t/ ① *adj*
teenage
② *nm,f* teenager, adolescent

**adonner**: **s'adonner** /adɔne/ [1] *v refl*
(+ *v être*) **s'~ à** to devote all one's time to; **il
s'adonne à la boisson** he drinks too much

**adopter** /adɔpte/ [1] *vtr* to adopt ⟨*child,
method*⟩; to pass ⟨*law*⟩

**adoptif**, **-ive** /adɔptif, iv/ *adj* (a) ⟨*child,
country*⟩ adopted
(b) ⟨*parent*⟩ adoptive

**adoption** /adɔpsjɔ̃/ *nf* (a) adoption
(b) passing

**adorable** /adɔʀabl/ *adj* adorable

**adorateur**, **-trice** /adɔʀatœʀ, tʀis/ *nm,f*
worshipper (GB)

**adoration** /adɔʀasjɔ̃/ *nf* worship,
adoration

**adorer** /adɔʀe/ [1] *vtr* to adore, to worship

**adosser**: **s'adosser** /adose/ [1] *v refl*
(+ *v être*) **s'~ à** to lean back on

**adoucir** /adusiʀ/ [3] ① *vtr* to soften ⟨*skin,
water*⟩; to moderate ⟨*tone of voice*⟩; to soothe
⟨*throat*⟩; to ease ⟨*suffering*⟩
② **s'adoucir** *v refl* (+ *v être*) ⟨*temperature*⟩
to become milder; ⟨*slope*⟩ to become more
gentle

**adoucissant**, **~e** /adusisɑ̃, ɑ̃t/ ① *adj*
soothing
② *nm* softener

**adrénaline** /adʀenalin/ *nf* adrenalin

**adresse** /adʀɛs/ *nf* (a) address; **se tromper
d'~** to get the wrong address; (figurative) to
pick the wrong person; **remarque lancée à
l'~ de qn** remark directed at sb
(b) dexterity
(c) skill

**adresser** /adʀese/ [1] ① *vtr* (a) to direct
⟨*criticism*⟩ (à at); to make ⟨*request,
declaration, appeal*⟩; to deliver ⟨*ultimatum*⟩;
to present ⟨*petition*⟩; to aim ⟨*blow*⟩; **~ la
parole à qn** to speak to sb
(b) to send ⟨*letter*⟩
(c) to refer [sb] (à to)
② **s'adresser** *v refl* (+ *v être*) (a) **s'~ à qn**
to speak to sb
(b) **s'~ à** to contact ⟨*embassy*⟩; **s'~ au
guichet 8** to go to window 8
(c) **s'~ à** ⟨*measure*⟩ to be aimed at

**adroit**, **~e** /adʀwa, at/ *adj* skilful (GB);
clever

**adulte** /adylt/ *adj*, *nmf* adult

**adultère** /adyltɛʀ/ ① *adj* adulterous
② *nm* adultery

**advenir** /advəniʀ/ [36] *v impers* **(a)** to
happen; **advienne que pourra** come what
may
**(b)** **~ de** to become of

**adverbe** /advɛʀb/ *nm* adverb

**adversaire** /advɛʀsɛʀ/ *nmf* (gen)
opponent; (Mil) adversary

**adverse** /advɛʀs/ *adj* (a) opposing
(b) opposite

**adversité** /advɛʀsite/ *nf* adversity

**aérer** /aeʀe/ [14] ① *vtr* (a) to air
(b) to space out
② **s'aérer** *v refl* (+ *v être*) to get some
fresh air

**aérien**, **-ienne** /aeʀjɛ̃, ɛn/ *adj* ⟨*transport*⟩
air; ⟨*photography*⟩ aerial; **métro ~** elevated
section of the underground (GB), elevated
railroad (US)

**aéro-club**, *pl* **~s** /aeʀoklœb/ *nm* flying
club

**aérodrome** /aeʀodʀom/ *nm* aerodrome
(GB), (small) airfield

**aérodynamique** /aeʀodinamik/ *adj*
aerodynamic

**aérogare** /aeʀogaʀ/ *nf* air terminal

**aéroglisseur** /aeʀoglisœʀ/ *nm* hovercraft

**aéronautique** /aeʀonotik/ *nf* aeronautics

**aérophagie** /aeʀofaʒi/ *nf* aerophagia

**aéroport** /aeʀopɔʀ/ *nm* airport

**aéroporté** /aeʀopɔʀte/ *adj* ⟨*troops*⟩
airborne; ⟨*equipment*⟩ transported by air

**aérosol** /aeʀosɔl/ *nm* (a) aerosol
(b) spray

**aérospatiale** /aeʀospasjal/ *nf* aerospace
industry

**affabulation** /afabylasjɔ̃/ *nf* fabrication

**affaiblir** /afɛbliʀ/ [3] ① *vtr* to weaken
② **s'affaiblir** *v refl* (+ *v être*) to get weaker

**affaiblissement** /afɛblismɑ̃/ *nm*
(a) weakening
(b) weakened state

**affaire** /afɛʀ/ ① *nf* (a) affair; (political)
crisis, affair; (moral) scandal; (legal) case
(b) affair, matter; **une ~ délicate** a delicate
matter; **c'est l'~ de quelques jours** it'll only
take a few days; **j'en fais mon ~** I'll deal
with it; **c'est une autre ~** that's another
matter; **c'est une ~ d'argent** there's money
involved; **et voilà toute l'~** and that's that;
**c'est toute une ~, ce n'est pas une petite ~**
it's quite a business
(c) (skill, trade) **il connaît bien son ~** he
knows his job; **la mécanique, c'est leur ~**
mechanics is their thing
(d) deal; **faire ~ avec** to do a deal with;
**avoir ~ à** to be dealing with
(e) bargain; **la belle ~!** (colloq) big deal!;
(colloq) **ça fera l'~** that'll do
(f) business, concern
(g) (difficulty) **être tiré d'~** to be out of danger
② **affaires** *nf pl* (a) business ⋯⟶

**(b)** (personal) business affairs; **occupe-toi de tes ~s!** mind your own business!
**(c)** things, belongings
■ **~s courantes** daily business

**affairer: s'affairer** /afeʀe/ [1] *v refl*
(+ *v être*) to bustle about (**à faire** doing)

**affairisme** /afeʀism/ *nm* wheeling and dealing (colloq)

**affaisser: s'affaisser** /afese/ [1] *v refl*
(+ *v être*) **(a)** to subside
**(b)** ⟨shoulders, roof⟩ to sag
**(c)** ⟨person⟩ to collapse

**affaler: s'affaler** /afale/ [1] *v refl* (+ *v être*)
**(a)** to collapse
**(b)** (colloq) to fall

**affamé, ~e** /afame/ **1** *pp* ▶ AFFAMER
**2** *pp adj* **(a)** starving
**(b)** **~ de** hungry for

**affamer** /afame/ [1] *vtr* to starve

**affectation** /afɛktasjɔ̃/ *nf* **(a)** allocation (à to)
**(b)** appointment (à to); posting (à to)
**(c)** affectation

**affecter** /afɛkte/ [1] *vtr* **(a)** to feign, to affect ⟨interest⟩; to affect ⟨behaviour⟩; **~ de faire/d'être** to pretend to do/to be
**(b)** to allocate ⟨funds⟩ (à to)
**(c)** to appoint; to post (à, en to)
**(d)** to affect ⟨market, person⟩

**affectif, -ive** /afɛktif, iv/ *adj* **(a)** emotional
**(b)** affective

**affection** /afɛksjɔ̃/ *nf* **(a)** affection; **prendre qn en ~** to become fond of sb
**(b)** (Med) disease

**affectionner** /afɛksjɔne/ [1] *vtr* to be fond of

**affectivité** /afɛktivite/ *nf* feelings

**affectueusement** /afɛktɥøzmɑ̃/ *adv* affectionately, fondly

**affectueux, -euse** /afɛktɥø, øz/ *adj* affectionate

**affermir** /afɛʀmiʀ/ [3] **1** *vtr* to strengthen ⟨will⟩; to consolidate ⟨power⟩; to firm up ⟨muscles⟩
**2 s'affermir** *v refl* (+ *v être*) ⟨power⟩ to be consolidated; ⟨voice⟩ to become stronger; ⟨muscles⟩ to firm up; ⟨ground⟩ to become firmer

**affermissement** /afɛʀmismɑ̃/ *nm* (of power, recovery) consolidation; (of will, muscles, voice) strengthening; (economic) improvement (de in)

**affichage** /afiʃaʒ/ *nm* **(a)** billsticking; **campagne d'~** poster campaign
**(b)** (Comput) display
■ **~ à cristaux liquides** liquid crystal display, LCD

**affiche** /afiʃ/ *nf* poster; (official) notice; **à l'~** ⟨film⟩ now showing; ⟨play⟩ on; **quitter l'~** to come off
■ **~ de théâtre** playbill

**affiché, ~e** /afiʃe/ **1** *pp* ▶ AFFICHER
**2** *pp adj* **(a)** ⟨ad, picture⟩ (put) up; ⟨information⟩ posted (up)

**(b)** ⟨result⟩ published
**(c)** ⟨optimism, opinion⟩ declared
**(d)** (Comput) ⟨data⟩ displayed

**afficher** /afiʃe/ [1] **1** *vtr* **(a)** to put up ⟨poster, notice⟩
**(b)** to display ⟨prices, result⟩; **~ complet** ⟨film, play⟩ to be sold out; ⟨hotel⟩ to be fully booked
**(c)** ⟨market⟩ to show ⟨rise⟩
**(d)** to declare ⟨ambitions⟩; to display ⟨scorn⟩; to flaunt ⟨opinions, liaison⟩
**2 s'afficher** *v refl* (+ *v être*) **(a)** to flaunt oneself
**(b)** ⟨smile⟩ to appear (**sur** on)

**afficheur** /afiʃœʀ/ *nm* **(a)** poster (GB) *or* billboard (US) sticker
**(b)** (Comput) visual display unit, VDU

**affichiste** /afiʃist/ *nmf* poster artist

**affilé, ~e**[1] /afile/ *adj* ⟨blade⟩ sharpened

**affilée**[2]: **d'affilée** /dafile/ *phr* in a row

**affiler** /afile/ [1] *vtr* to sharpen

**affilier: s'affilier** /afilje/ [2] *v refl* (+ *v être*) to become affiliated

**affiner** /afine/ [1] **1** *vtr* **(a)** to hone ⟨style⟩
**(b)** to slim down ⟨waistline⟩
**2 s'affiner** *v refl* (+ *v être*) **(a)** ⟨style, taste⟩ to become (more) refined
**(b)** ⟨waistline⟩ to slim down

**affinité** /afinite/ *nf* affinity

**affirmatif, -ive**[1] /afiʀmatif, iv/ *adj* affirmative; **faire un signe de tête ~** to nod agreement

**affirmation** /afiʀmasjɔ̃/ *nf* assertion; **l'~ de soi** assertiveness

**affirmative**[2] /afiʀmativ/ **1** *adj f* ▶ AFFIRMATIF
**2** *nf* affirmative

**affirmer** /afiʀme/ [1] **1** *vtr* **(a)** to maintain; **~ faire** to claim to do
**(b)** to assert ⟨talent, authority⟩
**(c)** to declare, to affirm ⟨will⟩
**2 s'affirmer** *v refl* (+ *v être*) ⟨tendency⟩ to become apparent; ⟨personality⟩ to assert itself

**affleurer** /aflœʀe/ [1] *vi* ⟨reef⟩ to show on the surface; ⟨rock⟩ to come through the soil

**affligeant, ~e** /afliʒɑ̃, ɑ̃t/ *adj* pathetic

**affliger** /afliʒe/ [13] *vtr* **(a)** to afflict (**de** with)
**(b)** to distress

**affluence** /aflyɑ̃s/ *nf* crowd(s)

**affluent** /aflyɑ̃/ *nm* tributary

**affluer** /aflye/ [1] *vi* ⟨people⟩ to flock (**à, vers** to); ⟨letters⟩ to pour in

**affolant, ~e** /afɔlɑ̃, ɑ̃t/ *adj* (colloq) frightening

**affolement** /afɔlmɑ̃/ *nm* panic

**affoler** /afɔle/ [1] **1** *vtr* to throw [sb] into a panic
**2 s'affoler** *v refl* (+ *v être*) to panic

**affranchi, ~e** /afʀɑ̃ʃi/ *nm,f* emancipated slave

**affranchir** /afʀɑ̃ʃiʀ/ [3] **1** *vtr* **(a)** to stamp ⟨letter⟩

**(b)** to free ‹slave, country›
**2 s'affranchir** v refl (+ v être) to free oneself

**affranchissement** /afʀɑ̃ʃismɑ̃/ nm
**(a)** stamping; (cost) postage
**(b)** liberation; freeing

**affres** /afʀ/ nf pl (of pain) agony; (of hunger) pangs; (of jealousy) throes; **les ~ de la mort** death throes

**affréter** /afʀete/ [14] vtr to charter

**affréteur** /afʀetœʀ/ nm charter company

**affreusement** /afʀøzmɑ̃/ adv (colloq) terribly

**affreux, -euse** /afʀø, øz/ adj **(a)** hideous
**(b)** awful, dreadful

**affront** /afʀɔ̃/ nm affront

**affrontement** /afʀɔ̃tmɑ̃/ nm confrontation

**affronter** /afʀɔ̃te/ [1] vtr to face ‹situation›; to brave ‹weather›

**affubler** /afyble/ [1] vtr **~ qn de** to deck sb out in ‹clothes›; to saddle sb with ‹nickname›

**affût** /afy/ nm **se tenir** or **être à l'~** to lie in wait; (figurative) to be on the lookout (**de** for)

**affûter** /afyte/ [1] vtr **(a)** to sharpen
**(b)** to grind

**afin** /afɛ̃/ **1 afin de** phr **~ de faire** in order to do
**2 afin que** phr so that

**AFP** /aɛfpe/ nf (abbr = **Agence France-Presse**) AFP (French news agency)

**africain, ~e** /afʀikɛ̃, ɛn/ adj African

**Afrique** /afʀik/ pr nf Africa

**AG** /aʒe/ nf: abbr ▶ ASSEMBLÉE

**agaçant, ~e** /agasɑ̃, ɑ̃t/ adj annoying

**agacement** /agasmɑ̃/ nm irritation

**agacer** /agase/ [12] vtr to annoy, to irritate

**agapes** /agap/ nf pl feast, banquet

**agate** /agat/ nf **(a)** agate
**(b)** marble

**âge** /aʒ/ nm **(a)** age; **faire son ~** to look one's age; **un homme d'un certain ~** a middle-aged man
**(b)** old age; **avec l'~** as one gets older; **prendre de l'~** to grow old
**(c)** age, era
■ **l'~ bête** or **ingrat** the awkward or difficult age; **l'~ mûr** maturity

**âgé, ~e** /aʒe/ adj old

**agence** /aʒɑ̃s/ nf **(a)** agency
**(b)** (of bank) branch
■ **~ immobilière** estate agents (GB), real-estate agency (US; ) **~ de placement** employment agency; **Agence nationale pour l'emploi, ANPE** French national employment agency

**agencer** /aʒɑ̃se/ [12] vtr to lay out ‹room›

**agenda** /aʒɛ̃da/ nm diary

**agenouiller: s'agenouiller** /aʒnuje/ [1] v refl (+ v être) to kneel (down)

**agent** /aʒɑ̃/ nm **(a)** officer, official
**(b)** agent
**(c)** employee

■ **~ de change** stockbroker; **~ de la circulation** traffic policeman; **~ commercial** sales representative; **~ de police** policeman

**agglomération** /aglɔmeʀasjɔ̃/ nf town; village; **l'~ lyonnaise** Lyons and its suburbs

**aggloméré** /aglɔmeʀe/ nm chipboard

**agglomérer** /aglɔmeʀe/ [14] **1** vtr to agglomerate
**2 s'agglomérer** v refl (+ v être) ‹people› to gather together; ‹houses› to be grouped together

**agglutiner: s'agglutiner** /aglytine/ [1] v refl (+ v être) ‹onlookers› to crowd together (**à** at); ‹insects› to cluster together

**aggravation** /agʀavasjɔ̃/ nf (of situation) worsening; (in debt) increase

**aggraver** /agʀave/ [1] **1** vtr to aggravate, to make [sth] worse
**2 s'aggraver** v refl (+ v être) to get worse

**agile** /aʒil/ adj agile, nimble

**agilité** /aʒilite/ nf agility

**agios** /aʒjo/ nm pl bank charges

**agir** /aʒiʀ/ [3] **1** vi **(a)** to act
**(b)** to behave; **~ en lâche** to act like a coward
**(c)** ‹medicine› to take effect, to work
**2 s'agir de** v impers (+ v être) **de quoi s'agit-il?** what is it about?; **il s'agit de votre mari** it's about your husband; **mais il ne s'agit pas de ça!** but that's not the point!; **il s'agit de faire vite** we must act quickly

**âgisme** /aʒism/ nm ageism

**agissements** /aʒismɑ̃/ nm pl activities

**agitateur, -trice** /aʒitatœʀ, tʀis/ nm,f agitator

**agitation** /aʒitasjɔ̃/ nf **(a)** restlessness
**(b)** bustle (**de** in); activity
**(c)** unrest

**agité, ~e** /aʒite/ adj **(a)** ‹sea› rough, choppy; ‹sleep› troubled; ‹period› turbulent; ‹night› restless
**(b)** ‹street› bustling; ‹life› hectic

**agiter** /aʒite/ [1] **1** vtr to wave ‹hand›; to shake ‹can›; to shake up ‹liquid›
**2 s'agiter** v refl (+ v être) **(a)** to fidget; (in bed) to toss and turn
**(b)** to sway (in the wind)
**(c)** to bustle about
**(d)** to become restless

**agneau, pl ~x** /aɲo/ nm **(a)** lamb
**(b)** lambskin

**agonie** /agɔni/ nf death throes

**agonir** /agɔniʀ/ [3] vtr **~ qn d'injures** to hurl insults at sb; **en rentrant, il s'est fait ~** when he got home he was told off soundly

**agoniser** /agɔnize/ [1] vi to be dying

**agrafe** /agʀaf/ nf **(a)** (for paper) staple
**(b)** (on waistband, bra) hook
**(c)** (Med) skin clip

**agrafer** /agʀafe/ [1] vtr **(a)** to staple [sth] (together)
**(b)** to fasten

**agrafeuse** /agʀaføz/ nf stapler

**a**

**agraire** /agRɛR/ *adj* agrarian; **réforme ~** land reform

**agrandir** /agRɑ̃diR/ [3] **1** *vtr* **(a)** to enlarge ⟨*town, photo*⟩; to extend ⟨*house*⟩
**(b)** to expand ⟨*organization*⟩
**2 s'agrandir** *v refl* (+ *v être*) ⟨*hole*⟩ to get bigger; ⟨*town, family*⟩ to expand; ⟨*eyes*⟩ to widen

**agrandissement** /agRɑ̃dismɑ̃/ *nm* enlargement

**agréable** /agReabl/ *adj* nice, pleasant; **~ à vivre** ⟨*person*⟩ pleasant to be with

**agréer** /agRee/ [11] *vtr* **(a)** to agree to ⟨*request*⟩; **veuillez ~ mes salutations distinguées** yours faithfully; yours sincerely
**(b)** to register ⟨*taxi, doctor*⟩; **agent agréé** authorized dealer

**agrégat** /agRega/ *nm* aggregate; (figurative) jumble

**agrégation** /agRegasjɔ̃/ *nf*: *high-level competitive examination for the recruitment of teachers*

**agrément** /agRemɑ̃/ *nm* **(a)** charm; **plein d'~** very pleasant; full of charm; **sans ~** dull; unattractive; cheerless; **voyage d'~** pleasure trip
**(b)** (by official body) approval

**agrémenter** /agRemɑ̃te/ [1] *vtr* to liven up ⟨*story*⟩; to brighten up ⟨*garden*⟩

**agrès** /agRɛ/ *nm pl* (Sport) apparatus

**agresser** /agRese/ [1] *vtr* **(a)** to attack
**(b)** to mug
**(c)** to be aggressive with

**agresseur** /agRescœR/ *nm* **(a)** attacker
**(b)** (in war) aggressor

**agressif, -ive** /agResif, iv/ *adj*
**(a)** aggressive
**(b)** violent; ear-splitting; harsh

**agression** /agResjɔ̃/ *nf* **(a)** attack
**(b)** mugging
**(c)** act of aggression

**agressivité** /agResivite/ *nf* aggressiveness, aggression

**agricole** /agRikɔl/ *adj* **produit ~** farm produce; **coopérative ~** farming cooperative

**agriculteur, -trice** /agRikyltœR, tRis/ *nm,f* farmer

**agriculture** /agRikyltyR/ *nf* farming

**agripper** /agRipe/ [1] **1** *vtr* to grab
**2 s'agripper** *v refl* (+ *v être*) to cling (à to)

**agro-alimentaire**, *pl* **~s**
/agRoalimɑ̃tɛR/ *adj* food-processing

**agrochimie** /agRoʃimi/ *nf* agro-chemistry

**agronomie** /agRɔnɔmi/ *nf* agronomy

**agrume** /agRym/ *nm* citrus fruit

**aguerrir** /ageRiR/ [3] **1** *vtr* to harden ⟨*person*⟩
**2 s'aguerrir** *v refl* (+ *v être*) to become hardened

**aguets**: **aux aguets** /ozagɛ/ *phr* **être aux ~** to be on one's guard

**aguicher** /agiʃe/ [1] *vtr* to lead [sb] on

**aguicheur, -euse** /agiʃœR, øz/ *adj* alluring

**ah** /ɑ/ *excl* oh!; **~ oui?, ~ bon?** really?

**ahuri, ~e** /ayRi/ *adj* **(a)** dazed
**(b)** stunned

**ahurissant, ~e** /ayRisɑ̃, ɑ̃t/ *adj* ⟨*news, strength*⟩ incredible; ⟨*figure*⟩ staggering

**ai** /ɛ/ ▸ AVOIR[1]

**aide**[1] /ɛd/ **1** *nmf* assistant
**2 aide-** (*combining form*) **~-soignant** nursing auxiliary (GB), nurse's aide (US)

**aide**[2] /ɛd/ *nf* **(a)** (from individual, group) help, assistance; (from state) assistance; **apporter son ~ à qn** to help sb
**(b)** (financial) aid; **~ au développement** foreign aid; **~ judiciaire** legal aid

**aider** /ede/ [1] **1** *vtr* **(a)** to help (à faire to do)
**(b)** to aid; to give aid to
**2 aider à** *v+prep* to help toward(s) ⟨*understanding, funding*⟩
**3 s'aider** *v refl* (+ *v être*) **(a) s'~ de** to use ⟨*dictionary, tool*⟩
**(b)** to help each other

**aie** /ɛ/ ▸ AVOIR[1]

**aïe** /aj/ *excl* (in pain) ouch!; (in concern) **~ (~ ~), que se passe-t-il?** oh dear, what's going on?; (in anticipation) **~ ~ ~!... oh NO!...**

**aient** /ɛ/ ▸ AVOIR[1]

**aies** /ɛ/ ▸ AVOIR[1]

**aïeul, ~e** /ajœl/ *nm,f* grandfather/ grandmother

**aïeux** /ajø/ *nm pl* ancestors

**aigle** /ɛgl/ *nm, nf* eagle

**aiglefin** /ɛgləfɛ̃/ *nm* haddock

**aigre** /ɛgR/ *adj* ⟨*smell, taste*⟩ sour

**aigre-doux, -douce**, *pl* **aigres-doux, aigres-douces** /ɛgRədu, dus/ *adj* (Culin) ⟨*fruit,taste*⟩ bitter-sweet; ⟨*sauce*⟩ sweet and sour

**aigrette** /ɛgRɛt/ *nf* (Zool) (bird) egret; (plumes) crest

**aigreur** /ɛgRœR/ *nf* **(a)** sourness; sharpness
**(b) ~s d'estomac** heartburn
**(c)** (figurative) bitterness

**aigrir** /egRiR/ [3] *vtr* to embitter

**aigu, aiguë** /egy/ **1** *adj* **(a)** ⟨*sound, voice*⟩ high-pitched
**(b)** ⟨*pain, symptom*⟩ acute
**(c)** ⟨*sense*⟩ keen
**2** *nm* (Mus) treble; high notes

**aigue-marine**, *pl* **aigues-marines** /ɛgmaRin/ *nf* aquamarine

**aiguillage** /egɥijaʒ/ *nm* (for trains) points (GB), switch (US); **une erreur d'~** a signalling (GB) error

**aiguille** /egɥij/ *nf* **(a)** needle; **~ à coudre** sewing needle
**(b)** (of watch, chronometer) hand; (of gauge) needle; (of weighing scales) pointer; **dans le sens des ~s d'une montre** clockwise

**aiguiller** /egɥije/ [1] *vtr* **(a)** to direct ⟨*person*⟩; to send ⟨*mail*⟩
**(b)** (towards career) to guide ⟨*person*⟩

**aiguilleur** /eguijœr/ *nm* ~ du ciel air traffic controller

**aiguillonner** /eguijɔne/ [1] *vtr* **(a)** to spur ⟨*person*⟩; to stimulate ⟨*ambition*⟩; la faim m'aiguillonnant... driven by hunger...
**(b)** to goad ⟨*ox*⟩

**aiguiser** /egize/ [1] *vtr* **(a)** to sharpen ⟨*knife*⟩
**(b)** to whet ⟨*appetite*⟩; to arouse ⟨*curiosity*⟩

**aiguiseur** /egizœr/ *nm* knife grinder

**ail**, *pl* ~s *or* **aulx** /aj, o/ *nm* garlic

**aile** /ɛl/ *nf* (gen) wing; (of windmill) sail; (of car) wing (GB), fender (US); (of army) flank
IDIOMS **battre de l'~** to be in a bad way; **se sentir pousser des ~s** to feel exhilarated; **prendre un coup dans l'~** to suffer a setback; **voler de ses propres ~s** to stand on one's own two feet

**aileron** /ɛlrɔ̃/ *nm* (of bird) wing tip; (of shark) fin; (of plane) aileron; (of ship) fin

**ailier** /elje/ *nm* (in football) winger; (in rugby) wing three-quarter

**ailleurs** /ajœr/ [1] *adv* elsewhere
[2] **d'ailleurs** *phr* besides, moreover
[3] **par ailleurs** *phr* ils se sont par ~ engagés à faire they have also undertaken to do
IDIOMS **être ~** to be miles away

**aimable** /ɛmabl/ *adj* **(a)** ⟨*word*⟩ kind
**(b)** ⟨*remark*⟩ polite

**aimablement** /ɛmabləmɑ̃/ *adv* politely; kindly

**aimant**, ~e /ɛmɑ̃, ɑ̃t/ [1] *pp* ▶ AIMER
[2] *pp adj* affectionate
[3] *nm* magnet

**aimé**, ~e /eme/ ▶ AIMER

**aimer** /eme/ [1] [1] *vtr* **(a)** to love ⟨*person*⟩; ~ qn à la folie to adore sb
**(b)** to like, to be fond of ⟨*person, activity, thing*⟩; ~ faire to like doing; il aime autant le vin que la bière he likes wine as much as he likes beer; j'aime autant te dire que I may as well tell you that; ~ mieux to prefer; il n'a rien de cassé? j'aime mieux ça! (in relief) nothing's broken? thank goodness!; j'aime mieux ça! (threateningly) that's more like it!
[2] **s'aimer** *v refl* (+ *v être*) **(a)** to love each other
**(b)** to like each other

**aine** /ɛn/ *nf* groin

**aîné**, ~e /ene/ [1] *adj* elder; eldest
[2] *nm,f* **(a)** elder son/daughter, elder child
**(b)** eldest son/daughter, eldest child
**(c)** elder brother/sister
**(d)** elder; oldest

**ainsi** /ɛ̃si/ [1] *adv* **(a)** thus; le mélange ~ obtenu the mixture obtained in this way; Charlotte, c'est ~ qu'on m'appelait Charlotte, that's what they used to call me; s'il en est ~ if that's the way it is; le jury se compose ~ the panel is made up as follows; ~ soit-il amen
**(b)** thus, so
[2] **ainsi que** *phr* **(a)** as well as

**(b)** as; ~ que nous en avions convenu as we had agreed

**air** /ɛr/ *nm* **(a)** air; le bon ~ clean air; concert en plein ~ open-air concert; activités de plein ~ outdoor activities; aller prendre l'~ to go and get some fresh air; on manque d'~ ici it's stuffy in here; être dans l'~ ⟨*reform, idea*⟩ to be in the air; regarder en l'~ to look up; avoir le nez en l'~ to daydream; en l'~ ⟨*threat, words*⟩ empty; ⟨*plan, idea*⟩ vague; tout mettre en l'~ (colloq) to make a dreadful mess; de l'~! (colloq) get lost! (colloq)
**(b)** il y a de l'~ (in room) there's a draught (GB) *or* draft (US); (outside) there's a breeze; il n'y a pas d'~ there's no wind; un courant d'~ a draught (GB) *or* draft (US)
**(c)** manner; expression; avoir un drôle d'~ to look odd; d'un ~ fâché angrily; il y a un ~ de famille entre vous deux you two share a family likeness; cela m'en a tout l'~ it seems like it to me; j'aurais l'~ de quoi? I'd look a right idiot!; cela a l'~ d'être une usine it looks like a factory; il a l'~ de vouloir faire beau it looks as if it's going to be fine
**(d)** tune; un ~ d'opéra an aria
IDIOMS **il ne manque pas d'~!** (colloq) he's got a nerve!; **se donner de grands ~s** to put on airs; **j'ai besoin de changer d'~** I need a change of scene

**aire** /ɛr/ *nf* **(a)** (surface) area
**(b)** eyrie
■ ~ **d'atterrissage** (for plane) landing strip; (for helicopter) landing pad; ~ **de jeu** playground; ~ **de services** motorway (GB) *or* freeway (US) service station; ~ **de stationnement** parking area

**airelle** /ɛrɛl/ *nf* **(a)** bilberry
**(b)** cranberry

**aisance** /ɛzɑ̃s/ *nf* **(a)** ease
**(b)** affluence, comfort

**aise** /ɛz/ [1] **aises** *nf pl* aimer ses ~s to like one's creature comforts; il prenait ses ~s sur le canapé he was stretched out on the sofa
[2] **à l'aise** *phr* être à l'~ *or* à son ~ (physically) to be comfortable; (financially) to be comfortably off; (psychologically) to be at ease; mal à l'~ ill at ease; à votre ~! as you wish *or* like!

**aisé**, ~e /eze/ *adj* **(a)** easy
**(b)** wealthy

**aisément** /ezemɑ̃/ *adv* easily

**aisselle** /ɛsɛl/ *nf* armpit

**ait** /ɛ/ ▶ AVOIR[1]

**Aix-la-Chapelle** /ɛkslaʃapɛl/ *pr n* Aachen

**ajonc** /aʒɔ̃/ *nm* gorse bush

**ajouré**, ~e /aʒure/ *adj* ⟨*tablecloth*⟩ openwork; ⟨*edge, border*⟩ hemstitched

**ajournement** /aʒurnəmɑ̃/ *nm* (of decision) postponement; (of trial) adjournment

**ajourner** /aʒurne/ [1] *vtr* to postpone ⟨*decision, plan*⟩; to adjourn ⟨*debate, trial*⟩

**ajout** /aʒu/ *nm* addition
■ (Comput) ~ **de mémoire** memory upgrade
**ajouter** /aʒute/ [1] **1** *vtr* to add (à to)
　**2 s'ajouter** *v refl* (+ *v être*) **s'~ à** to be
　added to
**ajustement** /aʒystəmã/ *nm* **(a)** (Tech) fit
　**(b)** adjustment; ~ **des prix** price adjustment
**ajuster** /aʒyste/ [1] *vtr* **(a)** to adjust ⟨strap,
　price, timetable⟩; to alter ⟨garment⟩ (à to); to
　calibrate ⟨weighing scales⟩; ~ **qch à** *or* **sur**
　**qch** to make sth fit sth; **corsage ajusté** close-
　fitting bodice
　**(b)** to arrange ⟨hair⟩; to straighten ⟨hat, tie⟩
　**(c)** ~ **son tir** to adjust one's aim
**ajusteur** /aʒystœʀ/ *nm* fitter
**alaise** = ALÈSE
**alambic** /alɑ̃bik/ *nm* still
**alambiqué, ~e** /alɑ̃bike/ *adj* ⟨expression,
　style⟩ convoluted; ⟨explanation⟩ tortuous
**alangui, ~e** /alɑ̃gi/ *adj* **(a)** languid
　**(b)** listless
**alarmant, ~e** /alaʀmɑ̃, ɑ̃t/ *adj* alarming
**alarme** /alaʀm/ *nf* alarm
**alarmer** /alaʀme/ [1] **1** *vtr* to alarm
　**2 s'alarmer** *v refl* (+ *v être*) to become
　alarmed (**de qch** about sth)
**albanais, ~e** /albanɛ, ɛz/ **1** *adj*
　Albanian
　**2** *nm* (language) Albanian
**Albanie** /albani/ *pr nf* Albania
**albâtre** /albɑtʀ/ *nm* alabaster
**albatros** /albatʀos/ *nm inv* albatross
**albinos** /albinos/ *adj inv, nmf inv* albino
**album** /albɔm/ *nm* **(a)** illustrated book;
　~ **de bandes dessinées** comic strip book
　**(b)** album
■ ~ **à colorier** colouring (GB) book
**albumine** /albymin/ *nf* albumin
**alchimie** /alʃimi/ *nf* alchemy
**alcool** /alkɔl/ *nm* **(a)** alcohol; ~ **de poire**
　pear brandy; **teneur en** ~ alcohol content
　**(b)** drink; **l'~ au volant** drink-driving
　**(c) un** ~ a spirit
■ ~ **à brûler** methylated spirits; ~ **à 90°** ≈
　surgical spirit (GB), rubbing alcohol (US)
**alcoolémie** /alkɔlemi/ *nf* presence of
　alcohol in the blood
**alcoolique** /alkɔlik/ *adj, nmf* alcoholic
**alcoolisé, ~e** /alkɔlize/ *adj* alcoholic
**alcoolisme** /alkɔlism/ *nm* alcoholism
**alcootest** /alkɔtɛst/ *nm* **(a)** Breathalyzer®
　**(b)** breath test
**alcôve** /alkov/ *nf* alcove
**aléas** /alea/ *nm pl* vagaries; (financial)
　hazards
**aléatoire** /aleatwaʀ/ *adj* **(a)** ⟨events⟩
　unpredictable; ⟨profession⟩ insecure
　**(b)** ⟨number⟩ random
**alentours** /alɑ̃tuʀ/ *nm pl* surrounding
　area
**alerte** /alɛʀt/ **1** *adj* alert; lively
　**2** *nf* alert; **donner l'~** to raise the alarm;
　~ **générale** full alert

■ ~ **à la bombe** bomb scare
**alerter** /alɛʀte/ [1] *vtr* to alert (**sur** to)
**alèse** /alɛz/ *nf* undersheet, mattress
　protector
**alexandrin** /alɛksɑ̃dʀɛ̃/ *adj m, nm*
　alexandrine
**algèbre** /alʒɛbʀ/ *nf* algebra
**Algérie** /alʒeʀi/ *pr nf* Algeria
**algérien, -ienne** /alʒeʀjɛ̃, ɛn/ *adj*
　Algerian
**algue** /alg/ *nf* **(a) des** ~**s** algae
　**(b)** seaweed
**alias** /aljas/ *adv* alias
**alibi** /alibi/ *nm* **(a)** (Law) alibi
　**(b)** excuse
**aliénation** /aljenasjɔ̃/ *nf* alienation
**aliéné, ~e** /aljene/ *nm,f* insane person
**alignement** /aliɲ(ə)mɑ̃/ *nm* **(a)** row, line
　**(b)** alignment
　**(c)** ~ **de qch sur qch** ⟨currency, salaries⟩
　bringing into line of sth with sth
**aligner** /aliɲe/ [1] **1** *vtr* **(a)** to line [sth] up
　**(b)** ~ **qch sur qch** to bring sth into line with
　sth
　**(c)** to give a list of ⟨figures⟩
　**(d)** to line up ⟨players⟩
　**2 s'aligner** *v refl* (+ *v être*) **(a)** ⟨houses,
　trees⟩ to be in a line
　**(b)** ⟨people⟩ to line up
　**(c) s'~ sur** to align oneself with ⟨country,
　party, ideas⟩
**aliment** /alimã/ *nm* (gen) food; (for farm
　animals) feed; (for plants) nutrient
**alimentaire** /alimɑ̃tɛʀ/ *adj* ⟨needs, habits⟩
　dietary; ⟨industry, shortage⟩ food; **régime** ~
　diet
**alimentation** /alimɑ̃tasjɔ̃/ *nf* **(a)** diet
　**(b)** feeding
　**(c)** food; **magasin d'~** food shop
　**(d)** food industry
　**(e)** supply, feeding; **l'~ en eau** the water
　supply
**alimenter** /alimɑ̃te/ [1] **1** *vtr* **(a)** to feed
　⟨person, animal⟩
　**(b)** to feed, to supply ⟨engine, boiler⟩
　**(c)** to fuel ⟨conversation, hostility⟩
　**2 s'alimenter** *v refl* (+ *v être*) **(a)** ⟨person⟩
　to eat; ⟨animal⟩ to feed
　**(b)** (with water, gas) **s'~ en** to be supplied with
**alinéa** /alinea/ *nm* **(a)** indentation
　**(b)** indented line
　**(c)** paragraph
**alité, ~e** /alite/ *adj* **être** ~ to be confined
　to bed
**alla** /ala/ ▶ ALLER[1]
**allai** /alɛ/ ▶ ALLER[1]
**allaient** /alɛ/ ▶ ALLER[1]
**allais** /alɛ/ ▶ ALLER[1]
**allait** /alɛ/ ▶ ALLER[1]
**allaitement** /alɛtmɑ̃/ *nm* **(a)** breast-
　feeding
　**(b)** suckling
**allaiter** /alete/ [1] *vtr* **(a)** to breast-feed

**(b)** to suckle

**allâmes** /alɑm/ ▶ ALLER[1]

**allant**, **~e** /alɑ̃, ɑ̃t/ [1] pp ▶ ALLER[1]

[2] adj active, lively

[3] nm drive, bounce; **avoir de l'~**, **être plein d'~** to have plenty of drive, to be full of bounce; **perdre son ~** to run out of steam

**allâtes** /alɑt/ ▶ ALLER[1]

**allé**, **~e** /ale/ ▶ ALLER[1]

**allécher** /aleʃe/ [14] vtr to tempt (**avec** with)

**allée** /ale/ [1] nf **(a)** (in garden, wood) path; (leading to house) drive; (in town) avenue

**(b)** aisle

[2] **allées** nf pl **~s et venues** comings and goings

**allégé**, **~e** /aleʒe/ [1] pp ▶ ALLÉGER

[2] pp adj low-fat; ‹chocolate› diet

**allégeance** /aleʒɑ̃s/ nf allegiance

**allégement** /aleʒmɑ̃/ nm (of charges) reduction; (of restrictions, controls) relaxing; **~ fiscal** tax relief

**alléger** /aleʒe/ [15] [1] vtr **(a)** to lighten ‹load, weight›

**(b)** to reduce ‹debt› (**de** by); to cut ‹taxes›; to relax ‹control, restrictions›

[2] **s'alléger** v refl (+ v être) **(a)** ‹load› to get lighter

**(b)** ‹debt, taxation› to be reduced; ‹embargo› to be relaxed

**allégorie** /alegɔʀi/ nf allegory

**allègre** /alɛgʀ/ adj ‹style› light; ‹tone› light-hearted; ‹step, mood› buoyant

**allégrement** /alegʀəmɑ̃/ adv joyfully; (ironic) blithely

**allégresse** /alegʀɛs/ nf joy

**allegro** /alegʀo/ adv allegro

**alléguer** /alege/ [14] vtr **(a)** to invoke

**(b)** to allege

**Allemagne** /almaɲ/ pr nf Germany

**allemand**, **~e** /almɑ̃, ɑ̃d/ [1] adj German

[2] nm (language) German

**aller[1]** /ale/ [9] [1] v aux **je vais apprendre l'italien** I'm going to learn Italian; **j'allais partir quand il est arrivé** I was about to leave when he arrived; **il est allé voir l'exposition** he went to see the exhibition; **va leur parler** go and speak to them

[2] vi (+ v être) **(a) comment vas-tu**, **comment ça va?** how are you?; **ça va (bien)** I'm fine; **~ beaucoup mieux** to be much better; **bois ça**, **ça ira mieux** drink this, you'll feel better; **les affaires vont bien** business is good; **qu'est-ce qui ne va pas?** what's the matter?; **ne pas ~ sans peine** or **mal** not to be easy; **ça devrait ~ de soi** it should be obvious; **ça va pas non?** (colloq), **ça va pas la tête?** (colloq) are you crazy?

**(b)** to go; **où vas-tu?** where are you going?; **~ nager/au travail** to go swimming/to work; **vas-y**, **demande-leur!** go on, ask them!; **allons-y!** let's go!; **allons!**, **allez!** come on!; **~ et venir** to pace up and down; to run in and out; **les nouvelles vont vite** news travels

fast; **j'y vais** (answering phone, door) I'll get it; (when leaving) (colloq) I'm off (colloq); **~ contre la loi** to break the law; to be against the law

**(c) ça va**, **ça ira** (colloq), **ça peut aller** (colloq) that'll do; it'll do; **ça va comme ça** it's all right as it is; **ça ne va pas du tout** that's no good at all; **lundi ça (te) va?** would Monday suit you?

**(d) ~ à qn** to fit sb

**(e) ~ à qn** to suit sb; **ta cravate ne va pas avec ta chemise** your tie doesn't go with your shirt

**(f) ~ jusqu'à tuer** to go as far as to kill; **la voiture peut ~ jusqu'à 200 km/h** the car can do up to 200 km/h; **la période qui va de 1918 à 1939** the period between 1918 and 1939; **~ sur ses 17 ans** to be going on 17

**(g) y ~ de sa petite larme** to shed a little tear

[3] **s'en aller** v refl (+ v être) **(a) s'en aller** to go, to leave, to be off; to go away

**(b) la tache ne s'en va pas** the stain won't come out

**(c)** (formal) to pass away, to die

[4] v impers **(a) il y va de ma réputation** my reputation is at stake

**(b) il en va de même pour toi** that goes for you too

**aller[2]** /ale/ nm **(a) j'ai pris le bus à l'~** I took the bus there; I took the bus here; **il n'arrête pas de faire des ~s et retours entre chez lui et son bureau** he's always going to and fro between the house and the office

**(b) ~ (simple)** single (ticket) (GB), one-way ticket ( **pour** to); **~ retour** return ticket, round trip (US)

**(c)** (Sport) (match) **~** first leg

**allèrent** /alɛʀ/ ▶ ALLER[1]

**allergie** /alɛʀʒi/ nf (Med) allergy

**allergique** /alɛʀʒik/ adj allergic (**à** to)

**allergologue** /alɛʀɡɔlɔg/ nmf allergist

**allez** /ale/ ▶ ALLER[1]

**alliage** /aljaʒ/ nm **(a)** alloy

**(b)** (figurative) combination

**alliance** /aljɑ̃s/ nf **(a)** wedding ring

**(b)** alliance

**allié**, **~e** /alje/ [1] pp ▶ ALLIER

[2] pp adj allied

[3] nm,f **(a)** ally; **les ~s** the Allies

**(b)** relative

**allier** /alje/ [2] [1] vtr **(a)** to combine (**et**, **à** with)

**(b)** (Tech) to alloy ‹metals› (**à**, **avec** with)

[2] **s'allier** v refl (+ v être) to form an alliance

**alliez** /alje/ ▶ ALLER[1]

**alligator** /aligatɔʀ/ nm alligator

**allions** /aljɔ̃/ ▶ ALLER[1]

**allô** /alo/ excl hello!, hallo!

**allocation** /al(l)ɔkasjɔ̃/ nf **(a)** allocation, granting

**(b)** benefit (GB), benefits (US)

■ **~ chômage** unemployment benefit (GB) or benefits (US); **~s familiales** family allowance

**allocution** /al(l)ɔkysjɔ̃/ nf address

**allongé**, **~e** /alɔ̃ʒe/ adj **(a)** être ~ ⟨person⟩ to be lying down; to be reclining; **(b)** elongated

**allonger** /alɔ̃ʒe/ [13] **1** vtr **(a)** to lay [sb] down
**(b)** to extend ⟨list, holiday⟩; cette coiffure t'allonge le visage that hairstyle makes your face look longer
**(c)** to water [sth] down ⟨coffee⟩
**2 s'allonger** v refl (+ v être) **(a)** to lie down
**(b)** to get longer

**allons** /alɔ̃/ ▶ ALLER¹

**allouer** /alwe/ [1] vtr to allocate ⟨sum, allowance, budget⟩; to grant ⟨loan⟩; to allot ⟨time⟩

**allumage** /alymaʒ/ nm (Aut) ignition

**allumé**, **~e** /alyme/ adj (colloq) **(a)** mad (colloq)
**(b)** tipsy (colloq)

**allume-gaz** /alymgaz/ nm inv gas lighter

**allumer** /alyme/ [1] **1** vtr **(a)** to light ⟨candle, gas⟩; to start ⟨fire⟩
**(b)** to switch [sth] on, to turn [sth] on; laisser ses phares allumés to leave one's headlights on
**2 s'allumer** v refl (+ v être) **(a)** ⟨heating, radio, lighting⟩ to come on
**(b)** son regard s'alluma his face lit up

**allumette** /alymɛt/ nf match, matchstick

**allumeur, -euse** /alymœr, øz/ nm,f (colloq) tease

**allure** /alyr/ nf **(a)** (of walker) pace; (of vehicle) speed; ralentir son ~ to slow down; à toute ~ at top speed; à cette ~ at this rate
**(b)** (of animal) gait
**(c)** (of person) appearance
**(d)** style; avoir de l'~ to have style

**allusif, -ive** /alyzif, iv/ adj ⟨remark⟩ allusive; ⟨person⟩ indirect

**allusion** /alyzjɔ̃/ nf allusion (à to); faire ~ à to allude to

**alluvial**, **~e**, mpl **-iaux** /alyvjal, o/ adj alluvial

**alluvion** /alyvjɔ̃/ nf alluvium; des ~s alluvia

**almanach** /almana(k)/ nm almanac

**aloi** /alwa/ nm un succès de bon ~ a well-deserved success; une plaisanterie de mauvais ~ a tasteless joke; une gaieté de bon ~ a simple cheerfulness

**alors** /alɔr/ **1** adv **(a)** then; il avait ~ 18 ans he was 18 at the time; la mode d'~ the fashion in those days; jusqu'~ until then
**(b)** then; (mais) ~ cela change tout! but that changes everything!; et ( puis) ~? so what?
**(c)** so; il y avait une grève des trains, ~ j'ai pris l'autobus there was a train strike, so I took the bus
**(d)** ou ~ or else
**(e)** (colloq) so; ~ il me dit... so he said to me...
**(f)** non mais ~! honestly!
**2 alors que** phr **(a)** while
**(b)** when

**3 alors même que** phr even though

**alouette** /alwɛt/ nf lark

**alourdir** /alurdir/ [3] **1** vtr **(a)** to weigh [sb] down ⟨person⟩; to make [sth] tense ⟨atmosphere⟩
**(b)** to increase ⟨tax, charges⟩
**2 s'alourdir** v refl (+ v être) ⟨eyelids⟩ to begin to droop; ⟨air⟩ to grow heavy

**alourdissement** /alurdismɑ̃/ nm (of tax, deduction) increase (de in)

**alpestre** /alpɛstr/ adj alpine

**alphabet** /alfabɛ/ nm alphabet

**alphabétique** /alfabetik/ adj alphabetical

**alphabétiser** /alfabetize/ [1] vtr to teach [sb] to read and write

**alpin**, **~e** /alpɛ̃, in/ adj alpine

**alpinisme** /alpinism/ nm mountaineering

**alpiniste** /alpinist/ nmf mountaineer, climber

**altération** /alterasjɔ̃/ nf (of faculties) impairment (de of); (of foodstuff) spoiling (de of); (in environment) deterioration (de in)

**altérer** /altere/ [14] vtr **(a)** to affect ⟨taste, health⟩
**(b)** to spoil ⟨foodstuff⟩; to fade ⟨colour⟩
**(c)** to distort ⟨text⟩; to adulterate ⟨substance⟩

**alternance** /altɛrnɑ̃s/ nf alternation; en ~ avec alternately with

**alternateur** /altɛrnatœr/ nm alternator

**alternatif, -ive¹** /altɛrnatif, iv/ adj
**(a)** (gen) alternate
**(b)** ⟨current⟩ alternating
**(c)** ⟨culture, theatre⟩ alternative

**alternative²** /altɛrnativ/ **1** adj f ▶ ALTERNATIF
**2** nf alternative

**alterner** /altɛrne/ [1] **1** vtr to alternate
**2** vi **(a)** to alternate
**(b)** ~ avec qn pour faire to take turns with sb (at) doing

**altesse** /altɛs/ nf **(a)** highness
**(b)** prince/princess

**altier, -ière** /altje, ɛr/ adj haughty

**altitude** /altityd/ nf altitude; en ~ high up (in the mountains)

**alto** /alto/ **1** adj alto
**2** nm **(a)** (instrument) viola
**(b)** viola player (GB), violin (US)
**(c)** (voice) alto

**altruiste** /altrɥist/ adj altruistic

**alu** /aly/ (colloq), **aluminium** /alyminjɔm/ nm aluminium (GB), aluminum (US)

**alvéole** /alveɔl/ nf **(a)** (in honeycomb) cell
**(b)** (in rock) cavity

**alvéolé**, **~e** /alveɔle/ adj honeycombed

**amabilité** /amabilite/ nf **(a)** kindness
**(b)** courtesy

**amadouer** /amadwe/ [1] vtr to coax, to cajole

**amaigrir** /amegrir/ [3] vtr to make [sb] thinner

**amaigrissant**, **~e** /amegrisɑ̃, ɑ̃t/ adj slimming

**amalgame** /amalgam/ *nm* **(a)** (gen) mixture
**(b)** (in dentistry, chemistry) amalgam
**amalgamer** /amalgame/ [1] *vtr* **(a)** to lump together ⟨*problems*⟩; to mix ⟨*feelings, people*⟩
**(b)** to blend, to amalgamate ⟨*ingredients*⟩
**amande** /amɑ̃d/ *nf* **(a)** almond
**(b)** kernel
**amanite** /amanit/ *nf* amanita; ∼ **phalloïde** death cap
**amant** /amɑ̃/ *nm* lover
**amarre** /amaʀ/ *nf* rope; **les** ∼**s** moorings
**amarrer** /amaʀe/ [1] *vtr* **(a)** to moor ⟨*boat*⟩
**(b)** to tie (**à, sur** to)
**amas** /ama/ *nm inv* pile; heap
**amasser** /amase/ [1] **1** *vtr* to amass, to accumulate ⟨*fortune, books*⟩; to collect ⟨*proof*⟩
**2** **s'amasser** *v refl* (+ *v être*) ⟨*snow, objects*⟩ to pile up; ⟨*proof, evidence*⟩ to build up
**amateur** /amatœʀ/ **1** *adj inv* amateur
**2** *nm* **(a)** (non-professional) amateur
**(b)** (of sport, photography) enthusiast; (of wine) connoisseur
**(c) il vend sa voiture, vous êtes** ∼**?** he's selling his car, are you interested?
**amazone** /amazon/ *nf* **en** ∼ sidesaddle
**ambassade** /ɑ̃basad/ *nf* embassy
**ambassadeur** /ɑ̃basadœʀ/ *nm* ambassador
**ambassadrice** /ɑ̃basadʀis/ *nf*
**(a)** ambassador
**(b)** ambassador's wife
**ambiance** /ɑ̃bjɑ̃s/ *nf* atmosphere
**ambiant**, ∼**e** /ɑ̃bjɑ̃, ɑ̃t/ *adj* ⟨*air*⟩ surrounding; **à température** ∼**e** at room temperature
**(b)** prevailing
**ambigu, ambiguë** /ɑ̃bigy/ *adj* ⟨*remark, situation*⟩ ambiguous; ⟨*feeling, attitude*⟩ ambivalent
**ambiguïté** /ɑ̃biguite/ *nf* ambiguity; enigmatic nature; ambivalence
**ambitieux, -ieuse** /ɑ̃bisjø, øz/ *adj* ambitious
**ambition** /ɑ̃bisjɔ̃/ *nf* ambition
**ambitionner** /ɑ̃bisjɔne/ [1] *vtr* to aspire to
**ambivalent**, ∼**e** /ɑ̃bivalɑ̃, ɑ̃t/ *adj* ambivalent
**ambre** /ɑ̃bʀ/ *nm* **(a)** ∼ **(jaune)** amber
**(b)** ∼ **(gris)** ambergris
**ambulance** /ɑ̃bylɑ̃s/ *nf* ambulance
**ambulancier, -ière** /ɑ̃bylɑ̃sje, ɛʀ/ *nm,f* ambulance driver
**ambulant**, ∼**e** /ɑ̃bylɑ̃, ɑ̃t/ *adj* ⟨*circus*⟩ travelling (GB); **vendeur** ∼ (in station) snack trolley man; **un cadavre** ∼ (colloq) a walking skeleton (colloq)
**âme** /ɑm/ *nf* soul; **Dieu ait son** ∼ God rest his/her soul; **socialiste dans l'**∼ a socialist

to the core; **en mon** ∼ **et conscience** in all honesty; **pas** ∼ **qui vive** not a (single) soul; ∼ **sœur** soul mate
**amélioration** /ameljɔʀasjɔ̃/ *nf* improvement
**améliorer** /ameljɔʀe/ [1] *vtr*, **s'améliorer** *v refl* (+ *v être*) to improve
**amen** /amɛn/ *nm inv* amen
**aménagé**, ∼**e** /amenaʒe/ **1** *pp* ▸ AMÉNAGER
**2** *pp adj* **(a)** converted
**(b)** equipped
**aménagement** /amenaʒmɑ̃/ *nm*
**(a)** (of region, town) development
**(b)** (of roads) construction; (of parks, green spaces) creation
**(c)** (of house, boat) fitting
**(d)** (of timetable) adjustment; **l'**∼ **du temps de travail** flexible working hours
**aménager** /amenaʒe/ [13] *vtr* **(a)** to convert; to do up ⟨*house, attic*⟩
**(b)** to equip ⟨*kitchen*⟩; to develop ⟨*region*⟩
**(c)** to create ⟨*parks, green spaces*⟩; to build ⟨*road*⟩; to lay out ⟨*garden*⟩
**(d)** to arrange ⟨*timetable*⟩; to adjust ⟨*regulations*⟩
**amende** /amɑ̃d/ *nf* fine
**amendement** /amɑ̃dmɑ̃/ *nm* **(a)** (in law) amendment (**à** to; **sur** on)
**(b)** (of soil) enrichment
**amener** /amne/ [16] *vtr* **(a)** ∼ **qn quelque part** to take sb somewhere
**(b)** (accompany) ∼ **qn (quelque part)** to bring sb (somewhere)
**(c)** (controversial) ∼ **qch (à qn)** to bring (sb) sth
**(d)** to cause ⟨*problems, illness*⟩; to bring ⟨*rain, fame*⟩
**(e)** to bring up ⟨*issue, subject*⟩; **être bien amené** ⟨*conclusion*⟩ to be well-presented
**(f)** ∼ **qn à qch/faire** to lead sb to sth/to do
**amenuiser: s'amenuiser** /amənɥize/ [1] *v refl* (+ *v être*) ⟨*supplies*⟩ to dwindle; ⟨*risk*⟩ to lessen
**amer, -ère** /amɛʀ/ *adj* bitter
**américain**, ∼**e** /ameʀikɛ̃, ɛn/ **1** *adj* American; **à l'**∼**e** (gen) in the American style; (Culin) à l'américaine
**2** *nm* American English
**Amérindien, -ienne** /ameʀɛ̃djɛ̃, ɛn/ *nm,f* Amerindian, American Indian
**Amérique** /ameʀik/ *pr nf* America
**amerrir** /ameʀiʀ/ [3] *vi* ⟨*hydroplane*⟩ to land (on water); ⟨*spacecraft*⟩ to splash down
**amertume** /amɛʀtym/ *nf* bitterness
**ameublement** /amœbləmɑ̃/ *nm*
**(a)** furniture
**(b)** furniture trade
**(c)** (of room, house) furnishing
**ameuter** /amøte/ [1] *vtr* **(a)** ⟨*person, noise*⟩ to bring [sb] out
**(b)** to stir [sb] up
**ami, ∼e** /ami/ **1** *adj* friendly

**2** *nm,f* friend; **en ~** as a friend; **un ~ des bêtes** an animal lover; ▶ FAUX¹
IDIOMS **les bons comptes font les bons ~s** (Proverb) a debt paid is a friend kept

**amiable**: **à l'amiable** /alamjabl/ *phr* ⟨*separate*⟩ on friendly terms; ⟨*separation*⟩ amicable; ⟨*divorce*⟩ by mutual consent; ▶ CONSTAT

**amiante** /amjãt/ *nm* asbestos

**amical**, **~e¹**, *pl* **-aux** /amikal, o/ *adj* friendly

**amicale²** /amikal/ *nf* association

**amicalement** /amikalmã/ *adv* (a) ⟨*greet, receive*⟩ warmly; ⟨*compete*⟩ in a friendly way (b) (at end of letter) **(bien) ~** best wishes

**amidon** /amidõ/ *nm* starch

**amincir** /amẽsiʀ/ [3] *vtr* to make [sb] look slimmer

**amiral**, *mpl* **-aux** /amiral, o/ *nm* admiral

**amitié** /amitje/ **1** *nf* friendship; **se lier d'~ avec qn** to strike up a friendship with sb **2 amitiés** *nf pl* (at end of letter) kindest regards

**ammoniac** /amɔnjak/ *nm* (gas) ammonia

**ammoniaque** /amɔnjak/ *nf* ammonia

**amnésie** /amnezi/ *nf* amnesia

**amnésique** /amnezik/ *adj* amnesic

**amnistie** /amnisti/ *nf* amnesty

**amocher** /amɔʃe/ (colloq) [1] **1** *vtr* to bash (colloq) [sb/sth] up ⟨*person, car*⟩ **2 s'amocher** *v refl* (+ *v être*) to bash oneself up (colloq); **s'~ le nez** to bash up (colloq) one's nose

**amoindrir** /amwẽdʀiʀ/ [3] *vtr* to reduce ⟨*resistance*⟩; to weaken ⟨*person*⟩

**amonceler** /amõsle/ [19] **1** *vtr* to pile up **2 s'amonceler** *v refl* (+ *v être*) ⟨*clouds, snow*⟩ to build up; ⟨*evidence, problems*⟩ to pile up

**amoncellement** /amõsɛlmã/ *nm* pile; mass

**amont** /amõ/ *nm* (of river) upper reaches; **en ~** upstream (**de** from); **naviguer d'~ en aval** to sail downstream

**amoral**, **~e**, *mpl* **-aux** /amɔral, o/ *adj* amoral

**amorce** /amɔʀs/ *nf* (a) (of discussion) initiation (b) bait (c) (of explosive) cap, primer; (of gun) cap

**amorcer** /amɔʀse/ [12] *vtr* (a) to begin (b) to prime

**amorphe** /amɔʀf/ *adj* apathetic

**amortir** /amɔʀtiʀ/ [3] *vtr* (a) to deaden ⟨*noise*⟩; to absorb ⟨*shock, impact*⟩; to break ⟨*fall*⟩ (b) to pay off ⟨*debt*⟩ (c) **j'ai amorti mon ordinateur en quelques mois** my computer paid for itself in a few months

**amortissement** /amɔʀtismã/ *nm* (a) (of noise) deadening; (of shock) absorption; (of fall) cushioning (b) (of debt) paying off (c) (of equipment) depreciation

**amortisseur** /amɔʀtisœʀ/ *nm* shock absorber

**amour** /amuʀ/ **1** *nm* love; **pour l'~ de** for the sake of; out of love for; **c'était un ~ de jeunesse** it was a youthful romance **2 amours** *nm pl or nf pl* (a) (Zool) mating (b) love affairs; **à tes ~s!** (to somebody sneezing) bless you!

**amouracher**: **s'amouracher** /amuʀaʃe/ [1] *v refl* (+ *v être*) **s'~ de** to become infatuated with

**amourette** /amuʀɛt/ *nf* passing infatuation

**amoureux**, **-euse** /amuʀø, øz/ *adj* in love

**amour-propre** /amuʀpʀɔpʀ/ *nm* self-esteem; pride

**amovible** /amɔvibl/ *adj* detachable; removable

**ampère** /ãpɛʀ/ *nm* amp, ampère

**amphibie** /ãfibi/ *adj* (Zool, Aut) amphibious

**amphithéâtre** /ãfiteatʀ/ *nm* (a) (natural, ancient) amphitheatre (GB) (b) (at university) lecture hall

**amphore** /ãfɔʀ/ *nf* amphora

**ample** /ãpl/ *adj* (a) ⟨*coat, dress*⟩ loose-fitting; ⟨*skirt, sleeve*⟩ full; ⟨*gesture*⟩ sweeping (b) ⟨*quantity*⟩ ample; ⟨*harvest*⟩ abundant; ⟨*details*⟩ full

**amplement** /ãpləmã/ *adv* fully; **c'est ~ suffisant** that's more than enough!

**ampleur** /ãplœʀ/ *nf* (of problem) size; (of project, subject, survey) scope; (of event, disaster, task) scale; (of damage, reaction) extent

**amplificateur** /ãplifikatœʀ/ *nm* amplifier

**amplification** /ãplifikasjõ/ *nf* (a) (in physics) amplification (b) (extension) (of relations) development; (of strike) escalation; (of debate) expansion

**amplifier** /ãplifje/ [2] **1** *vtr* to amplify ⟨*sound, current*⟩; to magnify ⟨*rumour*⟩ **2 s'amplifier** *v refl* (+ *v être*) ⟨*sound*⟩ to grow louder; ⟨*trade*⟩ to increase; ⟨*strike*⟩ to intensify

**ampoule** /ãpul/ *nf* (a) **~ (électrique)** (light) bulb (b) (Med) (drinkable) phial; (injectable) ampoule (c) blister

**ampoulé**, **~e** /ãpule/ *adj* bombastic

**amputation** /ãpytasjõ/ *nf* amputation

**amputer** /ãpyte/ [1] *vtr* (a) (Med) to amputate ⟨*limb*⟩; to perform an amputation on ⟨*person*⟩ (b) to cut [sth] drastically ⟨*budget*⟩

**amusant**, **~e** /amyzã, ãt/ *adj* (a) entertaining (b) funny

**amuse-gueule** /amyzgœl/ *nm inv* cocktail snack (GB), munchies (US)

**amusement** /amyzmã/ *nm* entertainment

**amuser** /amyze/ [1] **1** *vtr* (a) to entertain; to amuse (b) to distract

**2** **s'amuser** *v refl* (+ *v être*) **(a)** to play;
**pour s'~** for fun
**(b) bien s'~** to have a good time
**amuseur, -euse** /amyzœʀ, øz/ *nm,f*
entertainer
**amygdale** /amidal/ *nf* tonsil
**an** /ɑ̃/ *nm* year; **avoir huit ~s** to be eight
(years old); **en l'~ deux mille** in the year
two thousand; **l'~ 55 avant J.-C./après J.-C.**
55 BC/AD
IDIOMS **bon ~, mal ~** year in, year out
**anabolisant** /anabolizɑ̃/ *nm* anabolic
steroid
**anachronique** /anakʀɔnik/ *adj*
anachronistic
**anachronisme** /anakʀɔnism/ *nm*
anachronism
**anal, ~e,** *mpl* **-aux** /anal, o/ *adj* anal
**analogie** /analɔʒi/ *nf* analogy
**analogue** /analɔg/ *adj* similar (à to)
**analphabète** /analfabɛt/ *adj, nmf*
illiterate
**analphabétisme** /analfabetism/ *nm*
illiteracy
**analyse** /analiz/ *nf* **(a)** analysis; **faire l'~**
**de qch** to analyse (GB) sth
**(b)** (Med) test
**(c)** psychoanalysis
**analyser** /analize/ [1] *vtr* **(a)** (gen) to
analyse (GB)
**(b)** (Med) to test ‹*blood, urine*›
**ananas** /anana(s)/ *nm inv* pineapple
**anarchie** /anaʀʃi/ *nf* anarchy
**anarchiste** /anaʀʃist/ **1** *adj* anarchistic
**2** *nmf* anarchist
**anatomie** /anatɔmi/ *nf* anatomy
**ancêtre** /ɑ̃sɛtʀ/ *nmf* ancestor
**anchois** /ɑ̃ʃwa/ *nm inv* anchovy
**ancien, -ienne¹** /ɑ̃sjɛ̃, ɛn/ **1** *adj*
**(a)** ‹*champion, president, capital*› former
**(b)** ‹*history, language*› ancient
**(c)** ‹*style, book, building*› old; ‹*car*› vintage;
‹*piece of furniture*› antique
**(d) c'est lui le plus ~** (in job) he's been here
longest
**2** *nm* **(a)** (in tribe, congregation) elder;
(in company) senior member; **les ~s** the older
people
**(b)** old member; former student
**(c) l'~** older property; (furniture) antiques
■ **~ combattant** veteran
**ancienne²: à l'ancienne** /alɑ̃sjɛn/ *phr*
‹*jam, piece of furniture*› traditional-style
**anciennement** /ɑ̃sjɛnmɑ̃/ *adv* formerly
**ancienneté** /ɑ̃sjɛnte/ *nf* **(a)** (of person)
seniority; **trois ans d'~** three years' service
**(b)** (of tradition, relic) antiquity; (of building) age
**ancre** /ɑ̃kʀ/ *nf* (Naut) anchor
**ancrer** /ɑ̃kʀe/ [1] **1** *vtr* **(a)** to anchor
‹*ship*›
**(b)** to fix ‹*idea*›; to establish ‹*custom*›
**2** **s'ancrer** *v refl* (+ *v être*) **(a)** to anchor
**(b)** ‹*idea*› to become fixed; ‹*custom*› to
become established

**Andorre** /ɑ̃dɔʀ/ *pr nf* Andorra
**andouille** /ɑ̃duj/ *nf* **(a)** (Culin) andouille
**(b)** (colloq) fool
**âne** /ɑn/ *nm* **(a)** (Zool) donkey, ass
**(b)** (colloq) dimwit (colloq)
IDIOMS **faire l'~ pour avoir du son** to act
dumb to find out more
**anéantir** /aneɑ̃tiʀ/ [3] *vtr* **(a)** to ruin
‹*crops, harvest*›; to lay waste to ‹*town*›; to
shatter ‹*hopes*›
**(b)** ‹*news*› to crush; ‹*strain*› to exhaust
**anéantissement** /aneɑ̃tismɑ̃/ *nm*
**(a)** destruction, devastation
**(b)** (of hope) shattering
**(c)** (of person) total collapse
**anecdote** /anɛkdɔt/ *nf* anecdote
**anémie** /anemi/ *nf* **(a)** anaemia
**(b)** weakness
**anémier** /anemje/ [2] **1** *vtr* **(a)** (Med) to
make [sb] anaemic ‹*person*›
**(b)** (figurative) to weaken
**2** **s'anémier** *v refl* (+ *v être*) **(a)** (Med) to
become anaemic
**(b)** (figurative) to grow feeble
**anémique** /anemik/ *adj* **(a)** anaemic
**(b)** weak
**anémone** /anemɔn/ *nf* anemone
**ânerie** /ɑnʀi/ *nf* **(a)** silly remark
**(b)** silly blunder
**ânesse** /anɛs/ *nf* she-ass, female donkey
**anesthésie** /anɛstezi/ *nf* anaesthesia
**aneth** /anɛt/ *nm* dill
**anfractuosité** /ɑ̃fʀaktɥozite/ *nf* crevice
**ange** /ɑ̃ʒ/ *nm* angel
IDIOMS **être aux ~s** to be in (one's) seventh
heaven
**angélique¹** /ɑ̃ʒelik/ *adj* angelic
**angélique²** /ɑ̃ʒelik/ *nf* angelica
**angelot** /ɑ̃ʒlo/ *nm* cherub
**angine** /ɑ̃ʒin/ *nf* throat infection
**anglais, ~e¹** /ɑ̃glɛ, ɛz/ **1** *adj* English
**2** (language) English
**Anglais, ~e** /ɑ̃glɛ, ɛz/ *nm,f* Englishman/
Englishwoman
**anglaise²** /ɑ̃glɛz/ **1** *adj f* ▶ ANGLAIS 1
**2** *nf* ringlet
**angle** /ɑ̃gl/ *nm* **(a)** angle
**(b)** corner
**Angleterre** /ɑ̃glətɛʀ/ *pr nf* England
**anglo-américain, ~e,** *mpl* **~s**
/ɑ̃gloamerikɛ̃, ɛn/ **1** *adj* **(a)** Anglo-
American
**(b)** American English
**2** *nm* (language) American English
**anglo-normand, ~e,** *mpl* **~s**
/ɑ̃glonɔʀmɑ̃, ɑ̃d/ *adj* Anglo-Norman
**Anglo-Normande** /ɑ̃glonɔʀmɑ̃d/ *adj f*
**les îles ~s** the Channel Islands
**anglophone** /ɑ̃glofɔn/ **1** *adj* English-
speaking
**2** *nmf* English speaker; Anglophone
**anglo-saxon, -onne,** *mpl* **~s**
/ɑ̃glosaksɔ̃, ɔn/ *adj* Anglo-Saxon

**angoissant**, **∼e** /ãgwasã, ãt/ *adj*
⟨*prospect*⟩ alarming; ⟨*film, silence*⟩
frightening

**angoisse** /ãgwas/ *nf* anxiety

**angoissé**, **∼e** /ãgwase/ *adj* anxious

**angoisser** /ãgwase/ [1] **1** *vtr* to worry
**2** *vi* (colloq) to be anxious, to be nervous

**anguille** /ãgij/ *nf* eel

**angulaire** /ãgylɛʀ/ *adj* angular

**anicroche** /anikʀɔʃ/ *nf* hitch; **sans ∼(s)**
without a hitch

**animal**, **∼e**, *mpl* **-aux** /animal, o/ **1** *adj*
animal
**2** *nm* animal; **∼ familier** pet; **∼ domestique**
domestic animal; **∼ nuisible** pest

**animalier**, **-ière** /animalje, ɛʀ/ **1** *adj*
wildlife
**2** *nm,f* (in a lab) animal keeper
**3** *nm* wildlife artist

**animateur**, **-trice** /animatœʀ, tʀis/ *nm,f*
**(a)** (of group of holidaymakers, club) coordinator;
(of association) leader; (of festival) organizer
**(b)** presenter

**animation** /animasjɔ̃/ *nf* **(a)** (of group,
exhibition, festival) organization; (of sales)
coordination
**(b)** life, liveliness; **ville qui manque d'∼** dull
town
**(c)** (of street, market) hustle and bustle;
(of people) excitement

**animé**, **∼e** /anime/ *adj* **(a)** animated;
lively; busy
**(b)** **∼ de mauvaises intentions** spurred on by
bad intentions

**animer** /anime/ [1] **1** *vtr* **(a)** to lead
⟨*discussion, group*⟩; to run ⟨*course, show*⟩; to
present ⟨*programme*⟩
**(b)** to liven up ⟨*town, story, meeting*⟩
**2 s'animer** *v refl* (+ *v être*)
**(a)** ⟨*conversation*⟩ to become lively; ⟨*meeting*⟩
to liven up; ⟨*face*⟩ to light up
**(b)** ⟨*statue*⟩ to come to life

**animosité** /animɔzite/ *nf* animosity
(**envers** toward(s); **entre** between)

**anis** /ani/ *nm inv* **(a)** anise
**(b)** aniseed

**ankyloser**: **s'ankyloser** /ãkiloze/ [1]
*v refl* (+ *v être*) to get stiff

**annales** /anal/ *nf pl* **(a)** annals
**(b)** (of exams) (book of ) past papers

**anneau**, *pl* **∼x** /ano/ *nm* ring

**année** /ane/ *nf* year; **l'∼ en cours** this year,
the current year; **avec les ∼s** over the years;
**d'∼ en ∼** year by year; **ces dix dernières ∼s**
over the last ten years; **souhaiter la bonne ∼**
**à qn** to wish sb a happy new year; **(dans) les**
**∼s 80** (in) the eighties; **location à l'∼** annual
rent
∎ **∼ bissextile** leap year; **∼ civile** calendar
year; **∼ universitaire** academic year

**année-lumière**, *pl* **années-lumière**
/anelymjɛʀ/ *nf* light-year

**annexe¹** /anɛks/ *adj* **(a)** ⟨*room*⟩ adjoining

**(b)** ⟨*questions*⟩ additional; ⟨*file, document*⟩
attached

**annexe²** /anɛks/ *nf* **(a)** (building) annexe
(GB), annex (US)
**(b)** (document) appendix

**annexer** /anɛkse/ [1] *vtr* to annex

**annihiler** /aniile/ [1] *vtr* to destroy ⟨*efforts,*
*hopes*⟩; to cancel out ⟨*effect, results*⟩

**anniversaire** /anivɛʀsɛʀ/ **1** *adj* **date** *or*
**jour ∼ de** anniversary of
**2** *nm* **(a)** birthday
**(b)** anniversary

**annonce** /anɔ̃s/ *nf* **(a)** announcement
**(b)** advertisement, ad (colloq); **petite ∼**
classified advertisement
**(c)** declaration; **faire une ∼** (in bridge) to bid
**(d)** sign

**annoncer** /anɔ̃se/ [12] **1** *vtr* **(a)** to
announce
**(b)** to forecast ⟨*rain, event*⟩
**(c)** ⟨*event, signal*⟩ to herald
**2 s'annoncer** *v refl* (+ *v être*) **(a)** ⟨*crisis,*
*storm*⟩ to be brewing
**(b)** **la récolte 92 s'annonce excellente** the '92
harvest promises to be very good

**annonciateur**, **-trice** /anɔ̃sjatœʀ, tʀis/
*adj* ⟨*sign, signal*⟩ warning

**annoter** /anɔte/ [1] *vtr* to annotate ⟨*work*⟩;
to write notes on ⟨*worksheet, homework*⟩

**annuaire** /anɥɛʀ/ *nm* **(a)** directory
**(b)** yearbook

**annuel**, **-elle** /anɥɛl/ *adj* (gen) annual,
yearly; ⟨*contract*⟩ one-year

**annulaire** /anylɛʀ/ *nm* ring finger

**annulation** /anylasjɔ̃/ *nf* **(a)** (gen)
cancellation; (of law) repeal
**(b)** (Law) (of verdict) quashing; (of elections)
cancellation (GB); (of marriage) annulment

**annuler** /anyle/ [1] **1** *vtr* **(a)** to cancel
⟨*appointment, trip*⟩; to write off ⟨*debt*⟩; to
discount ⟨*result of match*⟩
**(b)** (Law) to declare [sth] void ⟨*elections*⟩; to
quash ⟨*verdict*⟩
**2 s'annuler** *v refl* (+ *v être*) to cancel each
other out

**anodin**, **∼e** /anɔdɛ̃, in/ *adj* ⟨*subject*⟩ safe,
neutral; ⟨*question, joke*⟩ innocent

**anomalie** /anɔmali/ *nf* **(a)** anomaly
**(b)** fault

**anonymat** /anɔnima/ *nm* **(a)** anonymity
**(b)** confidentiality

**anonyme** /anɔnim/ *adj* anonymous

**anorexie** /anɔʀɛksi/ *nf* anorexia

**anormal**, **∼e**, *mpl* **-aux** /anɔʀmal, o/ *adj*
abnormal

**ANPE** /aɛnpeœ/ *nf* (*abbr* = **Agence**
**nationale pour l'emploi**) *French*
*national employment agency*

**anse** /ãs/ *nf* (of cup, basket) handle

**antagoniste** /ãtagɔnist/ *adj* ⟨*groups*⟩
opposing; ⟨*interests*⟩ conflicting

**antan**: **d'antan** /dãtã/ *phr* ⟨*wars, festivals*⟩

of old; ⟨*prestige*⟩ former; **les métiers d'~** the old trades; **le Lyon d'~** the Lyons of yesteryear

**antarctique** /ɑ̃taʀktik/ *adj* Antarctic

**Antarctique** /ɑ̃taʀktik/ *pr nm*
(a) Antarctic; **océan ~** Antarctic Ocean
(b) Antarctica

**antécédent, ~e** /ɑ̃tesedɑ̃, ɑ̃t/ ①*adj* previous
②*nm* (a) past history
(b) medical history
(c) (in grammar, mathematics) antecedent

**antenne** /ɑ̃tɛn/*nf* (a) (of radio, television) aerial; (of radar, satellite) antenna; **passer à l'~** ⟨*programme, person*⟩ to go on the air
(b) (of organization, service) branch
(c) (of insect, shrimp) antenna; **avoir des ~s** (figurative) to have a sixth sense

**antérieur, ~e** /ɑ̃teʀjœʀ/ *adj*
(a) ⟨*situation, work*⟩ previous
(b) ⟨*limb, ligament*⟩ anterior

**anthracite** /ɑ̃tʀasit/ *adj inv* charcoal grey (GB), charcoal gray (US)

**anthropologie** /ɑ̃tʀɔpɔlɔʒi/ *nf* anthropology

**anthropophage** /ɑ̃tʀɔpɔfaʒ/ *nmf* cannibal

**antiaérien, -ienne** /ɑ̃tiaeʀjɛ̃, ɛn/ *adj* anti-aircraft

**antiatomique** /ɑ̃tiatɔmik/ *adj* (anti-) radiation; **abri ~** nuclear shelter .

**antibiotique** /ɑ̃tibjɔtik/ *adj, nm* antibiotic

**antibrouillard** /ɑ̃tibʀujaʀ/ *adj inv* **phare ~** fog light

**antibruit** /ɑ̃tibʀɥi/ *adj inv* soundproof

**antichambre** /ɑ̃tiʃɑ̃bʀ/ *nf* anteroom

**antichoc** /ɑ̃tiʃɔk/ *adj inv* (a) **casque ~** crash helmet
(b) ⟨*watch*⟩ shockproof

**anticipation** /ɑ̃tisipasjɔ̃/ *nf* anticipation; **roman d'~** science fiction novel

**anticipé, ~e** /ɑ̃tisipe/ *adj* early

**anticiper** /ɑ̃tisipe/ [1] ①*vtr* to anticipate ⟨*reaction, change, movement*⟩
②*vi* (a) to get ahead of oneself
(b) to think ahead

**anticonformiste** /ɑ̃tikɔ̃fɔʀmist/ *adj, nmf* nonconformist

**anticorps** /ɑ̃tikɔʀ/ *nm inv* antibody

**antidater** /ɑ̃tidate/ [1] *vtr* to backdate

**antidémocratique** /ɑ̃tidemɔkʀatik/ *adj* undemocratic

**antidérapant, ~e** /ɑ̃tideʀapɑ̃, ɑ̃t/ *adj* ⟨*tyre*⟩ nonskid; ⟨*sole*⟩ nonslip

**antidopage** /ɑ̃tidɔpaʒ/ *adj* ⟨*measure*⟩ anti-doping; **contrôle ~** dope test

**antidote** /ɑ̃tidɔt/ *nm* antidote

**antigang** /ɑ̃tigɑ̃g/ *adj inv* **brigade ~** crime squad

**antigel** /ɑ̃tiʒɛl/ *adj inv, nm* antifreeze

**anti-inflammatoire,** *pl* **~s** /ɑ̃tiɛ̃flamatwaʀ/ *adj, nm* anti-inflammatory

**antillais, ~e** /ɑ̃tijɛ, ɛz/ *adj* West Indian

**Antilles** /ɑ̃tij/ *pr nf pl* **les ~** the West Indies; **les Petites/Grandes ~** the Lesser/Greater Antilles

**antilope** /ɑ̃tilɔp/ *nf* antelope

**antimite** /ɑ̃timit/ *adj, nm* moth-repellent

**antipathie** /ɑ̃tipati/ *nf* antipathy

**antipathique** /ɑ̃tipatik/ *adj* unpleasant

**antipelliculaire** /ɑ̃tipɛlikylɛʀ/ *adj* antidandruff

**antipode** /ɑ̃tipɔd/ *nm* antipodes

**antipoison** /ɑ̃tipwazɔ̃/ *adj inv* **centre ~** poisons unit

**antiquaire** /ɑ̃tikɛʀ/ *nmf* antique dealer

**antique** /ɑ̃tik/ *adj* ancient

**antiquité** /ɑ̃tikite/ ①*nf* antique
②**antiquités** *nf pl* antiquities

**Antiquité** /ɑ̃tikite/ *nf* antiquity

**antireflet** /ɑ̃tiʀəflɛ/ *adj inv* nonreflective; (in photography) antiglare

**antirouille** /ɑ̃tiʀuj/ *adj inv* (a) rust-proofing
(b) rust-removing

**antisèche** /ɑ̃tisɛʃ/ *nf* (colloq) (students' slang) crib (colloq)

**antisémite** /ɑ̃tisemit/ ①*adj* anti-Semitic
②*nmf* anti-Semite

**antitabac** /ɑ̃titaba/ *adj inv* antismoking

**antiterroriste** /ɑ̃titɛʀɔʀist/ *adj* **lutte ~** fight against terrorism

**antithèse** /ɑ̃titɛz/ *nf* antithesis

**antituberculeux, -euse** /ɑ̃titybɛʀkylø, øz/ *adj* **vaccin ~** tuberculosis vaccine

**antivol** /ɑ̃tivɔl/ *nm* (of bicycle, motorbike) lock; (of car) anti-theft device

**anus** /anys/ *nm inv* anus

**Anvers** /ɑ̃vɛʀ/ *pr n* Antwerp

**anxiété** /ɑ̃ksjete/ *nf* anxiety

**anxieux, -ieuse** /ɑ̃ksjø, øz/ *adj* ⟨*person*⟩ anxious; ⟨*attitude*⟩ concerned

**aorte** /aɔʀt/ *nf* aorta

**août** /u(t)/ *nm* August

**apaisant, ~e** /apɛzɑ̃, ɑ̃t/ *adj* (a) soothing
(b) calming

**apaiser** /apeze/ [1] ①*vtr* (a) to pacify, to appease
(b) to ease ⟨*conflict*⟩
(c) to calm ⟨*rage*⟩
②**s'apaiser** *v refl* (+ *v être*) (a) to die down
(b) to calm down

**apanage** /apanaʒ/ *nm* **être l'~ de qch/qn** to be the prerogative of sth/sb

**aparté** /apaʀte/ *nm* **en ~** in private; (in a play) in an aside

**apathie** /apati/ *nf* (a) apathy
(b) stagnation

**apatride** /apatʀid/ *adj* stateless

**APEC** /apɛk/ *nf* (abbr = **Agence pour l'emploi des cadres**) executive employment agency

**apercevoir** /apɛʀsəvwaʀ/ [5] **1** *vtr* (a) to make out
(b) to catch sight of
**2 s'apercevoir** *v refl* (+ *v être*) (a) s'~ que to realize that; s'~ de to notice ⟨*mistake*⟩
(b) to catch sight of each other
(c) to meet briefly

**aperçu** /apɛʀsy/ **1** *pp* ▶ APERCEVOIR
**2** *nm* (a) glimpse
(b) outline
(c) insight

**apéritif** /apeʀitif/ *nm* drink

**apesanteur** /apəzɑ̃tœʀ/ *nf* weightlessness

**à-peu-près** /apøpʀɛ/ *nm inv* vague approximation

**apeuré**, ~**e** /apœʀe/ *adj* (scared) frightened; (shy) timid

**aphone** /afɔn/ *adj* être ~ to have lost one's voice

**aphte** /aft/ *nm* mouth ulcer

**apiculture** /apikyltyʀ/ *nf* beekeeping

**apitoiement** /apitwamɑ̃/ *nm* pity (**sur** for)

**apitoyer** /apitwaje/ [23] **1** *vtr* to move [sb] to pity
**2 s'apitoyer** *v refl* (+ *v être*) s'~ sur (le sort de) qn to feel sorry for sb

**aplanir** /aplaniʀ/ [3] *vtr* to level

**aplati**, ~**e** /aplati/ **1** *pp* ▶ APLATIR
**2** *pp adj* (a) flattened
(b) ⟨*nose*⟩ flat

**aplatir** /aplatiʀ/ [3] *vtr* (a) to flatten
(b) to smooth out ⟨*cushion*⟩; to smooth down ⟨*hair*⟩
(c) to press ⟨*seams*⟩

**aplomb** /aplɔ̃/ **1** *nm* (a) confidence; **vous ne manquez pas d'~!** you've got a nerve!
(b) plumb, perpendicularity
**2 d'aplomb** *phr* (a) être d'~ to be straight, to be plumb vertical
(b) (colloq) **ça va te remettre d'~** it will put you back on your feet

**apocalypse** /apɔkalips/ *nf* apocalypse

**apogée** /apɔʒe/ *nm* (a) (of moon, satellite) apogee
(b) (of career, empire) peak

**apologie** /apɔlɔʒi/ *nf* panegyric; apologia; **faire l'~ de** to justify; to praise

**a posteriori** /apɔsteʀjɔʀi/ *phr* after the event

**apostolat** /apɔstɔla/ *nm* (a) apostolate
(b) (figurative) apostolic mission

**apostrophe** /apɔstʀɔf/ *nf* apostrophe

**apostropher** /apɔstʀɔfe/ [1] *vtr* to heckle

**apothéose** /apɔteoz/ *nf* (a) (of show) high point
(b) (of career, work) culmination

**apôtre** /apotʀ/ *nm* apostle

**apparaître** /apaʀɛtʀ/ [73] **1** *vi* (+ *v être*)
(a) ⟨*person, problem*⟩ to appear; ⟨*sun, moon*⟩ to come out
(b) **laisser** *or* **faire** ~ to show
(c) to seem

**2** *v impers* **il apparaît que** it appears that

**apparat** /apaʀa/ *nm* grandeur; **d'~** ceremonial

**appareil** /apaʀɛj/ *nm* (a) device
(b) appliance
(c) telephone; **qui est à l'~?** who's calling please?
(d) aircraft
(e) system; **l'~ digestif** the digestive system
(f) apparatus; **l'~ du parti** the party apparatus
■ ~ **auditif** hearing aid; ~ ⟨**dentaire**⟩ brace (GB), braces (US); ~ **à sous** slot machine; ~ **photo** camera
IDIOMS **être dans son plus simple** ~ to be in one's birthday suit

**appareiller** /apaʀeje/ [1] *vi* to cast off

**apparemment** /apaʀamɑ̃/ *adv*
(a) apparently
(b) seemingly

**apparence** /apaʀɑ̃s/ *nf* appearance

**apparent**, ~**e** /apaʀɑ̃, ɑ̃t/ *adj* (a) visible
(b) ⟨*embarrassment*⟩ apparent
(c) seeming, apparent

**apparenté**, ~**e** /apaʀɑ̃te/ *adj* (a) ⟨*person*⟩ related (**à** to)
(b) ⟨*company*⟩ allied

**apparenter**: **s'apparenter** /apaʀɑ̃te/ [1] *v refl* (+ *v être*) s'~ à to resemble

**apparition** /apaʀisjɔ̃/ *nf* (a) (of product) appearance; (of problem) emergence
(b) apparition

**appartement** /apaʀtəmɑ̃/ *nm* flat (GB), apartment; ~ **témoin** show flat (GB), show apartment (US)

**appartenance** /apaʀtənɑ̃s/ *nf* membership (**à** of)

**appartenir** /apaʀtəniʀ/ [36]
**1 appartenir à** *v+prep* (a) ~ à to belong to
(b) ~ à to be a member of
**2** *v impers* **il appartient à qn de faire** it is up to sb to do

**appât** /apɑ/ *nm* (a) bait
(b) lure

**appâter** /apɑte/ [1] *vtr* (a) to bait
(b) to lure

**appauvrir** /apovʀiʀ/ [3] **1** *vtr* to impoverish
**2 s'appauvrir** *v refl* (+ *v être*) to become impoverished

**appel** /apɛl/ *nm* (a) call; (urgent) appeal; ~ **à** call for ⟨*solidarity*⟩; appeal for ⟨*calm*⟩; ~ **au secours** call for help; cry for help; **faire** ~ **à** to appeal to ⟨*person*⟩; to call ⟨*fire brigade*⟩; ⟨*task*⟩ to call for ⟨*skills*⟩
(b) roll call; (Sch) registration
(c) (Mil) call up (GB), draft (US)
(d) (Law) appeal; **faire** ~ to appeal
(e) (Sport) take off
■ ~ **d'air** draught (GB), draft (US); ~ **de phares** flash of headlights (GB) *or* high beams (US)

**appelé**, ~**e** /aple/ **1** *pp* ▶ APPELER

**2** *pp adj* ~ à qch/à faire destined for sth/to do

**3** *nm* (Mil) conscript, draftee (US)

**appeler** /aple/ [19] **1** *vtr* (a) to call; ~ (qn) à l'aide to call (to sb) for help

(b) to phone (GB), to call

(c) to call ⟨*doctor, taxi*⟩; to send for ⟨*pupil*⟩; ~ qn sous les drapeaux (Mil) to call sb up

(d) ~ qn à faire to call on sb to do; ~ à la grève to call for strike action

(e) mon travail m'appelle à beaucoup voyager my work involves a lot of travel

**2 en appeler à** *v+prep* to appeal to

**3 s'appeler** *v refl* (+ *v être*) to be called; comment t'appelles-tu? what's your name?; je m'appelle Vladimir my name is Vladimir; voilà ce qui s'appelle une belle voiture! now, that's what you call a nice car!

IDIOMS ~ les choses par leur nom, ~ un chat un chat to call a spade a spade

**appellation** /apɛlasjɔ̃/ *nf* name, appellation

**appendice** /apɛ̃dis/ *nm* (Anat) appendix

**appendicite** /apɛ̃disit/ *nf* appendicitis

**appesantir: s'appesantir** /apəzɑ̃tiʀ/ [3] *v refl* (+ *v être*) s'~ sur to dwell on

**appétissant, ~e** /apetisɑ̃, ɑ̃t/ *adj* appetizing

**appétit** /apeti/ *nm* appetite

**applaudir** /aplodiʀ/ [3] **1** *vtr* to applaud

**2** *vi* (a) to applaud, to clap

(b) (figurative) to approve; ~ des deux mains to approve heartily

**applaudissement** /aplodismɑ̃/ *nm*

(a) applause

(b) acclaim

**applicateur** /aplikatœʀ/ *nm* applicator

**application** /aplikasjɔ̃/ *nf* (a) care; il manque d'~ he doesn't apply himself

(b) implementation, enforcement; mettre en ~ to apply ⟨*theory*⟩; to implement ⟨*law*⟩

(c) (of device, program) ~s applications

(d) (of ointment) application

(e) (Comput) application program

**applique** /aplik/ *nf* wall light

**appliqué, ~e** /aplike/ *adj*

(a) hardworking

(b) ⟨*work*⟩ careful

(c) ⟨*science*⟩ applied

**appliquer** /aplike/ [1] **1** *vtr* (a) to apply ⟨*ointment*⟩ (sur to); to put ⟨*stamp*⟩ (sur on)

(b) to implement ⟨*policy, law*⟩

(c) to apply ⟨*technique*⟩ (à to)

**2 s'appliquer** *v refl* (+ *v être*) (a) to take great care (à faire to do)

(b) s'~ à qn/qch ⟨*law, remark*⟩ to apply to sb/sth

**appoint** /apwɛ̃/ *nm* (a) exact change; faire l'~ to give the exact change

(b) d'~ ⟨*salary*⟩ supplementary; ⟨*heating*⟩ additional

**appointements** /apwɛ̃tmɑ̃/ *nm pl* salary

**apport** /apɔʀ/ *nm* (a) provision

(b) contribution

**apporter** /apɔʀte/ [1] *vtr* (a) to bring

⟨*improvement, news*⟩; to bring in ⟨*revenue*⟩; to bring about ⟨*change*⟩; ~ qch à qn to bring sb sth, to take sb sth

(b) to give ⟨*support, explanation*⟩

**apposer** /apoze/ [1] *vtr* to affix (sur on)

**apposition** /apozisjɔ̃/ *nf* apposition

**appréciable** /apʀesjabl/ *adj*

(a) substantial

(b) c'est ~ it's nice

**appréciatif, -ive** /apʀesjatif, iv/ *adj*

(a) appreciative

(b) appraising

**appréciation** /apʀesjasjɔ̃/ *nf* (a) (of quantity) estimate

(b) (financial) evaluation

(c) (of quality) assessment; être laissé à l'~ de qn to be left to sb's discretion

**apprécier** /apʀesje/ [2] *vtr* (a) to appreciate ⟨*art*⟩; to like ⟨*person*⟩

(b) (financially) to value

(c) to estimate ⟨*distance*⟩

(d) to assess ⟨*situation*⟩

**appréhender** /apʀeɑ̃de/ [1] *vtr* (a) to arrest

(b) to dread

(c) to comprehend, to understand

**appréhension** /apʀeɑ̃sjɔ̃/ *nf* apprehension

**apprendre** /apʀɑ̃dʀ/ [52] *vtr* (a) to learn (à faire to do)

(b) to learn ⟨*truth*⟩; to hear (about) ⟨*news*⟩

(c) to teach

(d) ~ qch à qn to tell sb sth

**apprenti, ~e** /apʀɑ̃ti/ *nm,f* (a) apprentice, trainee

(b) novice; ~ poète novice poet

**apprentissage** /apʀɑ̃tisaʒ/ *nm*

(a) training, apprenticeship

(b) learning

**apprêté, ~e** /apʀɛte/ **1** *pp* ▸ APPRÊTER

**2** *pp adj* (a) affected

(b) ⟨*hairstyle*⟩ fussy

**apprêter: s'apprêter** /apʀɛte/ [1] *v refl* (+ *v être*) s'~ à faire to get ready to do

**apprivoiser** /apʀivwaze/ [1] *vtr* to tame

**approbateur, -trice** /apʀɔbatœʀ, tʀis/ *adj* sourire ~ smile of approval

**approbation** /apʀɔbasjɔ̃/ *nf* approval

**approche** /apʀɔʃ/ *nf* approach

**approcher** /apʀɔʃe/ [1] **1** *vtr* (a) ~ qch de la fenêtre to move sth near to the window

(b) to go up to; to come up to

(c) to come into contact with

**2 approcher de** *v+prep* to be (getting) close to

**3** *vi* to approach

**4 s'approcher** *v refl* (+ *v être*) s'~ de to go near; to come near

**approfondi, ~e** /apʀɔfɔ̃di/ **1** *pp* ▸ APPROFONDIR

**2** *pp adj* detailed, in-depth

**approfondir** /apʀɔfɔ̃diʀ/ [3] *vtr* (a) to go into [sth] in depth  ····∴

**(b)** ~ ses connaissances en français to improve one's knowledge of French
**(c)** to make [sth] deeper

**approprié**, ~e /apʀɔpʀije/ adj appropriate

**approprier**: **s'approprier** /apʀɔpʀije/ [2] v refl (+ v être) **(a)** to take, to appropriate ⟨object, idea⟩
**(b)** to seize ⟨power⟩

**approuver** /apʀuve/ [1] vtr **(a)** to approve of; je t'approuve d'avoir accepté I think you were right to accept
**(b)** to approve ⟨budget⟩

**approvisionnement** /apʀɔvizjɔnmɑ̃/ nm supply (en of)

**approvisionner** /apʀɔvizjɔne/ [1] **1** vtr **(a)** to supply (en with); mal approvisionné ⟨shop⟩ badly stocked
**(b)** to pay money into ⟨account⟩
**2 s'approvisionner** v refl (+ v être) **(a)** s'~ en to get one's supplies of (auprès de from)
**(b)** to stock up (en on, with)

**approximatif**, **-ive** /apʀɔksimatif, iv/ adj ⟨estimate, translation⟩ rough

**approximation** /apʀɔksimasjɔ̃/ nf **(a)** rough estimate
**(b)** approximation

**appui** /apɥi/ nm support; à l'~ de in support of ⟨theory⟩; prendre ~ sur to lean on

**appui-tête**, pl **appuis-tête** /apɥitɛt/ nm headrest

**appuyé**, ~e /apɥije/ **1** pp ▶ APPUYER
**2** pp adj ⟨look⟩ intent
**(b)** ⟨joke⟩ laboured (GB)

**appuyer** /apɥije/ [22] **1** vtr **(a)** to rest (sur on); to lean (sur on)
**(b)** to press (contre against)
**(c)** to support, to back (up)
**2** vi **(a)** ~ sur to press ⟨switch⟩; to put one's foot on ⟨brake⟩
**(b)** ~ sur to stress ⟨word⟩
**3 s'appuyer** v refl (+ v être) **(a)** to lean (sur on; contre against)
**(b)** s'~ sur to rely on ⟨theory⟩; to draw on ⟨report⟩

**âpre** /ɑpʀ/ adj **(a)** ⟨taste, cold⟩ bitter
**(b)** ⟨voice⟩ harsh
**(c)** ⟨struggle⟩ fierce; ⟨argument⟩ bitter

**après** /apʀɛ/ **1** adv afterward(s), after; later; peu/bien ~ shortly/long afterward(s); une heure ~ one hour later; peu ~ il y a un lac a bit further on there's a lake; et ~? and then what? so what? (colloq)
**2** prep after; ~ mon départ after I leave; after I left; ~ coup afterward(s); il est toujours ~ son fils (colloq) he's always on at his son (colloq)
**3 d'après** phr **(a)** d'~ moi in my opinion; d'~ lui/la météo according to him/the weather forecast; d'~ ma montre by my watch
**(b)** from; based on; d'~ un dessin de Gauguin from a drawing by Gauguin

**(c)** l'année d'~ the year after; la fois d'~ the next time
**4** après que phr after; ~ qu'il a parlé after he had spoken
**5** après- (combining form) l'~-guerre the postwar years

**après-demain** /apʀɛdmɛ̃/ adv the day after tomorrow

**après-midi** /apʀɛmidi/ nm inv or nf inv afternoon

**après-rasage**, pl ~s /apʀɛʀazaʒ/ adj inv, nm after-shave

**après-ski** /apʀɛski/ nm inv snowboot

**après-vente** /apʀɛvɑ̃t/ adj inv after-sales

**a priori** /apʀijɔʀi/ **1** phr a priori
**2** phr ~, ça ne devrait pas poser de problèmes on the face of it there shouldn't be any problems

**à-propos** /apʀopo/ nm inv intervenir avec ~ to make an apposite remark; agir avec ~ to do the right thing

**apte** /apt/ adj ~ à qch/à faire capable of sth/of doing; fit for sth/to do

**aptitude** /aptityd/ nf aptitude; fitness

**aquarelle** /akwaʀɛl/ nf **(a)** watercolours (GB)
**(b)** watercolour (GB)

**aquarium** /akwaʀjɔm/ nm aquarium, fish tank

**aquatique** /akwatik/ adj **(a)** aquatic
**(b)** sport ~ water sport

**aqueduc** /akdyk/ nm aqueduct

**aquilin** /akilɛ̃/ adj m aquiline

**aquitain**, ~e /akitɛ̃, ɛn/ adj of Aquitaine; le bassin ~ the Aquitaine Basin

**arabe** /aʀab/ **1** adj **(a)** Arab
**(b)** Arabic
**2** nm (language) Arabic

**Arabe** /aʀab/ nmf Arab

**arabesque** /aʀabɛsk/ nf arabesque

**Arabie** /aʀabi/ pr nf Arabia
■ ~ Saoudite Saudi Arabia

**arabique** /aʀabik/ adj Arabian

**arachide** /aʀaʃid/ nf groundnut, peanut

**araignée** /aʀɛɲe/ nf spider
■ ~ de mer spider crab
IDIOMS avoir une ~ au plafond (colloq) to have a screw loose (colloq)

**arbalète** /aʀbalɛt/ nf crossbow

**arbitraire** /aʀbitʀɛʀ/ adj arbitrary

**arbitrairement** /aʀbitʀɛʀmɑ̃/ adv arbitrarily

**arbitre** /aʀbitʀ/ nm **(a)** referee, umpire
**(b)** arbitrator

**arbitrer** /aʀbitʀe/ [1] **1** vtr **(a)** to referee, to umpire
**(b)** to arbitrate in
**2** vi to arbitrate (entre between)

**arborer** /aʀbɔʀe/ [1] vtr **(a)** to wear ⟨smile⟩; to sport ⟨badge⟩
**(b)** to bear ⟨banner⟩; to fly ⟨flag⟩

**arboriculture** /aʀbɔʀikyltyʀ/ nf arboriculture

**arbre** /aʀbʀ/ *nm* **(a)** tree
 **(b)** (Tech) shaft
■ ~ **généalogique** family tree
**arbrisseau**, *pl* ~**x** /aʀbʀiso/ *nm* small
 tree
**arbuste** /aʀbyst/ *nm* shrub
**arc** /aʀk/ *nm* **(a)** (Sport) bow
 **(b)** arc
 **(c)** arch
**arcade** /aʀkad/ *nf* arcade; ~**s** archways.
■ ~ **sourcilière** arch of the eyebrow
**arc-bouter: s'arc-bouter** /aʀkbute/ [1]
 *v refl* (+ *v être*) to brace oneself
**arceau**, *pl* ~**x** /aʀso/ *nm* **(a)** arch
 **(b)** (in croquet) hoop
 **(c)** (in car) roll bar
**arc-en-ciel**, *pl* **arcs-en-ciel**
 /aʀkãsjɛl/ *nm* rainbow
**archaïque** /aʀkaik/ *adj* archaic
**archange** /aʀkãʒ/ *nm* archangel
**arche** /aʀʃ/ *nf* arch; ~ **de Noé** Noah's Ark
**archéologie** /aʀkeɔlɔʒi/ *nf* archaeology
**archéologique** /aʀkeɔlɔʒik/ *adj*
 archaeological
**archet** /aʀʃɛ/ *nm* (Mus) bow
**archétype** /aʀketip/ *nm* archetype
**archevêché** /aʀʃəveʃe/ *nm*
 **(a)** archdiocese
 **(b)** archbishop's palace
**archevêque** /aʀʃəvɛk/ *nm* archbishop
**archi** /aʀʃi/ *pref* (colloq) ~**connu** really well-
 known
**archipel** /aʀʃipɛl/ *nm* archipelago
**architecte** /aʀʃitɛkt/ *nmf* architect
**architecture** /aʀʃitɛktyʀ/ *nf*
 **(a)** architecture
 **(b)** structure
**archives** /aʀʃiv/ *nf pl* archives, records
**arctique** /aʀktik/ *adj* arctic
**Arctique** /aʀktik/ *pr nm* Arctic
**ardemment** /aʀdamã/ *adv* passionately
**ardent**, ~**e** /aʀdã, ãt/ *adj* **(a)** ⟨ember⟩
 glowing; ⟨sun⟩ blazing
 **(b)** ⟨faith⟩ burning; ⟨patriot⟩ fervent;
 ⟨speech⟩ impassioned; ⟨nature⟩ passionate
**ardeur** /aʀdœʀ/ *nf* (of person) ardour (GB);
 (of beliefs) fervour (GB); (of beginner)
 enthusiasm
**ardoise** /aʀdwaz/ *nf* **(a)** slate
 **(b)** (colloq) account
**ardu**, ~**e** /aʀdy/ *adj* **(a)** arduous
 **(b)** taxing
**arène** /aʀɛn/ *nf* **(a)** arena
 **(b)** bullring
 **(c)** ~**s** amphitheatre (GB)
**arête** /aʀɛt/ *nf* **(a)** fishbone
 **(b)** (of roof, mountain) ridge; (of prism) edge;
 (of nose) bridge
**argent** /aʀʒã/ *nm* **(a)** money
 **(b)** silver
■ ~ **liquide** cash
 **IDIOMS prendre qch pour** ~ **comptant** to
 take sth at face value

**argenté**, ~**e** /aʀʒãte/ *adj* **(a)** silver-plated
 **(b)** (in colour) silvery
**argenterie** /aʀʒãtʀi/ *nf* silverware, silver
**Argentine** /aʀʒãtin/ *pr nf* Argentina
**argile** /aʀʒil/ *nf* clay
**argot** /aʀgo/ *nm* slang
**arguer** /aʀge/ [1] **1** *vtr* ~ **que** to claim
 that
 **2 arguer de** *v+prep* to give [sth] as a
 reason
**argument** /aʀgymã/ *nm* argument
**argumentation** /aʀgymãtasjõ/ *nf* line of
 argument
**argumenter** /aʀgymãte/ [1] *vi* to argue
**argus** /aʀgys/ *nm inv:* used car prices guide
**aride** /aʀid/ *adj* arid
**aridité** /aʀidite/ *nf* aridity
**aristocratie** /aʀistɔkʀasi/ *nf* aristocracy
**aristocratique** /aʀistɔkʀatik/ *adj*
 aristocratic
**arithmétique** /aʀitmetik/ **1** *adj*
 arithmetical
 **2** *nf* arithmetic
**arlequin** /aʀləkɛ̃/ *nm* harlequin
**armateur** /aʀmatœʀ/ *nm* shipowner
**armature** /aʀmatyʀ/ *nf* **(a)** (of tent) frame
 **(b)** (in construction) framework
**arme** /aʀm/ **1** *nf* **(a)** weapon; **charger une**
 ~ to load a gun; **rendre les** ~**s** to surrender;
 **en** ~**s** armed; **à** ~**s égales** on equal terms;
 **faire ses premières** ~**s dans l'enseignement**
 to start out as a teacher
 **(b)** branch of the armed services
 **2 armes** *nf pl* coat of arms
■ ~ **blanche** *weapon with a blade*; ~ **à feu**
 firearm
**armé**, ~**e¹** /aʀme/ **1** *pp* ▶ ARMER
 **2** *pp adj* **(a)** armed; **vol à main** ~**e** armed
 robbery
 **(b)** equipped (**de** with; **contre** against)
**armée²** /aʀme/ *nf* army
■ ~ **de l'air** air force; **l'**~ **de réserve** the
 reserves; **l'**~ **de terre** the army
**armement** /aʀməmã/ *nm* **(a)** armament;
 arming
 **(b)** arms, weapons
 **(c)** (of rifle) cocking; (of camera) winding on
 **(d)** (of ship) fitting out
**armer** /aʀme/ [1] **1** *vtr* **(a)** to arm (**de**
 with; **contre** against)
 **(b)** to fit out ⟨ship⟩
 **(c)** to wind on ⟨camera⟩; to cock ⟨rifle⟩
 **2 s'armer** *v refl* (+ *v être*) to arm oneself
**armistice** /aʀmistis/ *nm* armistice
**armoire** /aʀmwaʀ/ *nf* **(a)** cupboard
 **(b)** wardrobe
■ ~ **à glace** wardrobe with a full length
 mirror; **c'est une** ~ **à glace** (colloq) he/she is
 built like a tank (colloq); ~ **métallique** metal
 locker; ~ **à pharmacie** medicine cabinet;
 ~ **de toilette** bathroom cabinet
**armoiries** /aʀmwaʀi/ *nf pl* arms
**armure** /aʀmyʀ/ *nf* armour (GB)

**armurier** /aRmyRje/ nm **(a)** gunsmith
**(b)** armourer (GB)

**aromates** /aROmat/ nm pl herbs and
spices

**aromatique** /aROmatik/ adj aromatic

**aromatiser** /aROmatize/ [1] vtr to flavour
(GB)

**arôme** /aROm/ nm **(a)** aroma
**(b)** flavouring (GB)

**arpège** /aRpɛʒ/ nm arpeggio

**arpenter** /aRpãte/ [1] vtr **(a)** to stride
along
**(b)** to pace up and down
**(c)** to survey ⟨piece of land⟩

**arqué, ~e** /aRke/ adj ⟨brows⟩ arched;
⟨nose⟩ hooked; ⟨legs⟩ bandy

**arquebuse** /aRkəbyz/ nf arquebus

**arquer** /aRke/ [1] **1** vtr to bend ⟨bar⟩
**2** s'arquer v refl (+ v être) to become
bowed

**arrachage** /aRaʃaʒ/ nm (of crop) picking;
(of tooth, post) pulling out; (of scrub, root)
digging out; **~ des mauvaises herbes**
weeding

**arraché** /aRaʃe/ nm snatch; **obtenir à l'~** to
snatch ⟨victory⟩; **vol à l'~** bag snatching

**arrache-pied: d'arrache-pied**
/daRaʃpje/ phr ⟨work⟩ flat out

**arracher** /aRaʃe/ [1] **1** vtr **(a)** to pull up
or dig up ⟨weeds⟩; to pull out ⟨tooth⟩; to tear
down ⟨poster⟩; to rip out ⟨page⟩; to tear off
⟨mask⟩; to uproot ⟨tree⟩; to blow off ⟨tiles⟩
**(b)** **~ à qn** to snatch [sth] from sb ⟨bag,
victory⟩; to extract [sth] from sb ⟨promise⟩; to
get [sth] from sb ⟨smile⟩
**(c)** **~ qn à** to uproot sb from ⟨home⟩; to drag
sb away from ⟨work⟩; to rouse sb from
⟨thoughts⟩; to rescue sb from ⟨poverty⟩
**2** s'arracher v refl (+ v être) **(a)** **~ qch** to
fight over sth
**(b)** **s'~ à** to rouse oneself from ⟨thoughts⟩; to
tear oneself away from ⟨work⟩
**IDIOMS c'est à s'~ les cheveux!** (colloq) it's
enough to make you tear your hair out!; **~
les yeux à** or **de qn** to scratch sb's eyes out

**arracheur** /aRaʃœR/ nm **mentir comme un
~ de dents** to be a born liar

**arraisonner** /aRezɔne/ [1] vtr to board and
inspect

**arrangeant, ~e** /aRãʒã, ãt/ adj obliging

**arrangement** /aRãʒmã/ nm arrangement

**arranger** /aRãʒe/ [13] **1** vtr **(a)** to arrange,
to organize
**(b)** to sort out; **pour ne rien ~, pour tout ~**
to make matters worse
**(c)** to arrange ⟨flowers⟩
**(d)** to tidy ⟨hair⟩; to straighten ⟨skirt⟩
**(e)** (Mus) to arrange
**(f)** ⟨events⟩ to suit ⟨person⟩
**2** s'arranger v refl (+ v être) **(a)** to get
better, to improve
**(b)** **s'~ avec qn** to arrange it with sb
**(c)** to manage
**(d)** **on s'arrangera après** we'll sort it out
later

**(e)** (colloq) **elle ne sait pas s'~** she doesn't
know how to make the most of herself

**arrangeur, -euse** /aRãʒœR, øz/ nm,f
(Mus) arranger

**arrestation** /aRɛstasjõ/ nf arrest

**arrêt** /aRɛ/ nm **(a)** (gen) stopping; (of conflict)
cessation; (of delivery) cancellation;
(in production) halt
**(b)** stop; **sans ~** ⟨travel⟩ nonstop; ⟨interrupt⟩
constantly; **à l'~** ⟨vehicle⟩ stationary;
⟨machine⟩ idle; ⟨electrical appliance⟩ off;
**marquer un temps d'~** to pause; **être aux ~s**
(Mil) to be under arrest
**(c)** stop; **un ~ de bus** a bus stop
**(d)** (Law) ruling
■ **~ du cœur** heart failure; **~ sur image**
freeze-frame, still; **~ de jeu** stoppage time;
**~ de mort** death sentence; **~ de travail**
stoppage of work; sick leave; sick note

**arrêté, ~e** /aRete/ **1** pp ▶ ARRÊTER
**2** pp adj **(a)** ⟨matter⟩ settled
**(b)** ⟨ideas⟩ fixed
**3** nm order, decree

**arrêter** /aRete/ [1] **1** vtr **(a)** to stop ⟨de
faire doing⟩; **être arrêté pour trois semaines**
to be given a sick note for three weeks
**(b)** to switch off ⟨machine⟩; to halt ⟨process⟩
**(c)** to give up ⟨de faire doing⟩
**(d)** to arrest
**(e)** to decide on ⟨plan⟩
**2** vi to stop; **arrête!** stop it!
**3** s'arrêter v refl (+ v être) **(a)** to stop
**(b)** to give up ⟨de faire doing⟩
**(c)** to end
**(d)** **s'~ sur** to dwell on; **s'~ à** to focus on

**arrhes** /aR/ nf pl deposit

**arriéré, ~e** /aRjere/ **1** adj **(a)** outdated
**(b)** backward
**(c)** behind the times
**(d)** retarded
**2** nm arrears

**arrière** /aRjɛR/ **1** adj inv back; rear
**2** nm **(a)** rear; **à l'~** (in car) in the back; (on
plane, train, ship) at the rear; **en ~**
backward(s); (position) behind; **pencher la tête
en ~** to tilt one's head back; **revenir en ~**
⟨person⟩ to turn back; (figurative) to take a
backward step; (on tape) to rewind
**(b)** (Sport) fullback

**arrière-cour,** pl **~s** /aRjɛRkuR/ nf
backyard

**arrière-goût,** pl **~s** /aRjɛRgu/ nm
aftertaste

**arrière-grand-mère,** pl **arrière-
grands-mères** /aRjɛRgRãmɛR/ nf great-
grandmother

**arrière-grand-père,** pl **arrière-
grands-pères** /aRjɛRgRãpɛR/ nm great-
grandfather

**arrière-grands-parents**
/aRjɛRgRãpaRã/ nm pl great-grandparents

**arrière-pays** /aRjɛRpei/ nm inv hinterland

**arrière-pensée,** pl **~s** /aRjɛRpãse/ nf
**(a)** ulterior motive
**(b)** **sans ~** without reservation

**arrière-petits-enfants** /aʀjɛʀpətizɑ̃fɑ̃/
*nm pl* great-grandchildren

**arrière-plan**, *pl* ~**s** /aʀjɛʀplɑ̃/ *nm*
(of picture) background

**arrière-saison**, *pl* ~**s** /aʀjɛʀsezõ/ *nf*
late autumn (GB), late fall (US)

**arrière-train**, *pl* ~**s** /aʀjɛʀtʀɛ̃/ *nm*
hindquarters

**arrimer** /aʀime/ [1] *vtr* **(a)** to fasten
**(b)** (Naut) to stow

**arrivage** /aʀivaʒ/ *nm* delivery,
consignment

**arrivant**, ~**e** /aʀivɑ̃, ɑ̃t/ *nm,f* **un nouvel**
~ a newcomer

**arrivé**, ~**e**¹ /aʀive/ 1 *pp* ▶ ARRIVER
2 *pp adj* **(a)** **le premier** ~ the first person
to arrive
**(b)** **être** ~ to have made it (socially)

**arrivée²** /aʀive/ *nf* **(a)** arrival; **trains à l'**~
arrivals
**(b)** (in race) finish
**(c)** (Tech) inlet

**arriver** /aʀive/ [1] (+ *v être*) 1 *vi* **(a)** (gen)
to arrive; (Sport) to finish; ~ **à/de Paris** to
arrive in/from Paris
**(b)** to come; ~ **en courant** to come running
up
**(c)** ~ **à** to reach ‹*level, agreement*›; to find
‹*solution*›; ~ **(jusqu')à qn** to reach sb
**(d)** ~ **à faire** to manage to do; **je n'y arrive
pas** I can't do it; ~ **à ses fins** to achieve
one's ends
**(e)** **en** ~ **à** to come to
**(f)** to happen
2 *v impers* **qu'est-il arrivé?** what happened?
(à to); **il m'arrive d'y aller, il arrive que j'y
aille** I sometimes go there

**arrivisme** /aʀivism/ *nm* ruthless ambition

**arrogance** /aʀɔgɑ̃s/ *nf* arrogance

**arrogant**, ~**e** /aʀɔgɑ̃, ɑ̃t/ *adj* arrogant

**arroger**: **s'arroger** /aʀɔʒe/ [13] *v refl*
(+ *v être*) to appropriate ‹*title*›; to assume
‹*right, role*›

**arrondi**, ~**e** /aʀõdi/ 1 *adj* rounded;
round
2 *nm* (of face) roundness; (of shoulder) curve

**arrondir** /aʀõdiʀ/ [3] 1 *vtr* **(a)** to round off
‹*edge*›; **coiffure qui arrondit le visage**
hairstyle that makes one's face look round
**(b)** to open wide ‹*eyes*›
**(c)** to round off ‹*figure*› (à to)
2 **s'arrondir** *v refl* (+ *v être*) **(a)** ‹*object*› to
become round(ed); ‹*eyes*› to widen
**(b)** ‹*face*› to fill out
**(c)** ‹*fortune*› to be growing
IDIOMS ~ **les angles** to smooth the rough
edges

**arrondissement** /aʀõdismɑ̃/ *nm*
**(a)** (in city) arrondissement
**(b)** (region) *administrative division in France*

**arrosage** /aʀozaʒ/ *nm* watering

**arroser** /aʀoze/ [1] *vtr* **(a)** to water, to
spray; **on va se faire** ~! (colloq) we're going
to get soaked!
**(b)** to baste ‹*meat*›; to sprinkle ‹*cake*›

**(c)** to drink to
**(d)** **repas arrosé au bourgogne** meal washed
down with Burgundy
2 **s'arroser** *v refl* (+ *v être*) (colloq) **ça
s'arrose** that calls for a drink

**arroseur** /aʀozœʀ/ *nm* sprinkler

**arrosoir** /aʀozwaʀ/ *nm* watering can

**arsenal**, *pl* -**aux** /aʀsənal, o/ *nm* **(a)** naval
shipyard
**(b)** arsenal
**(c)** (colloq) gear

**art** /aʀ/ *nm* **(a)** art
**(b)** art, skill; **avoir l'**~ **de faire** to have a
knack of doing
■ ~ **dramatique** drama; ~ **lyrique** opera; ~ **de
vivre** art of living; ~**s ménagers** home
economics; ~**s plastiques** plastic arts

**Artaban** /aʀtabɑ̃/ *n pr* **fier comme** ~
proud as a peacock

**artère** /aʀtɛʀ/ *nf* **(a)** (Anat) artery
**(b)** arterial road
**(c)** main street

**artériel**, -**ielle** /aʀteʀjɛl/ *adj* arterial

**arthrite** /aʀtʀit/ *nf* arthritis

**arthrose** /aʀtʀoz/ *nf* osteoarthritis

**artichaut** /aʀtiʃo/ *nm* (globe) artichoke.
IDIOMS **avoir un cœur d'**~ to be fickle (*in
love*)

**article** /aʀtikl/ *nm* **(a)** (in paper, law) article;
(in contract) clause
**(b)** (in grammar) article
**(c)** item; ~**s de consommation courante**
basic consumer goods; **faire l'**~ **à qn** to give
sb the sales pitch
IDIOMS **être à l'**~ **de la mort** to be at death's
door

**articulaire** /aʀtikylɛʀ/ *adj* articular

**articulation** /aʀtikylasjõ/ *nf* **(a)** (Anat)
joint
**(b)** (of lamp, sunshade) mobile joint
**(c)** (in phonetics) articulation
**(d)** (in sentence) link
**(e)** (of speech, essay) structure

**articuler** /aʀtikyle/ [1] 1 *vtr* **(a)** to
articulate; **articule!** speak clearly!
**(b)** to utter
**(c)** to structure ‹*ideas*›
2 **s'articuler** *v refl* (+ *v être*) **s'**~ **autour
de** to be based on, to hinge on

**artifice** /aʀtifis/ *nm* **(a)** trick
**(b)** device; **les** ~**s du style** stylistic devices
**(c)** **sans** ~ unpretentious

**artificiel**, -**ielle** /aʀtifisjɛl/ *adj*
**(a)** artificial; man-made
**(b)** superficial; forced

**artificier** /aʀtifisje/ *nm* **(a)** bomb disposal
expert
**(b)** explosives manufacturer
**(c)** fireworks manufacturer

**artillerie** /aʀtijʀi/ *nf* artillery

**artisan** /aʀtizɑ̃/ *nm* **(a)** artisan, craftsman
**(b)** architect, author

**artisanal**, ∼**e**, *mpl* **-aux** /aʀtizanal, o/ *adj* ⟨*method*⟩ traditional; **de fabrication** ∼**e** hand-crafted; home-made

**artisanat** /aʀtizana/ *nm* (a) craft industry, cottage industry
(b) artisans
■ ∼ **d'art** arts and crafts

**artiste** /aʀtist/ ⨯1⨯ *adj* (a) artistic
(b) **il est un peu** ∼ he's a bit of a dreamer
⨯2⨯ *nmf* (a) artist; ∼ **peintre** painter
(b) (on stage) performer; (in music hall) artiste; ∼ **lyrique** opera singer

**artistique** /aʀtistik/ *adj* artistic

**as¹** /a/ ▶ AVOIR¹

**as²** /ɑs/ *nm inv* ace
IDIOMS **être plein aux** ∼ (colloq) to be loaded (colloq); **passer à l'**∼ (colloq) ⟨*money*⟩ to go down the drain; ⟨*holidays*⟩ to go by the board; **être fagoté comme l'**∼ **de pique** (colloq) to look a mess

**ascendance** /asɑ̃dɑ̃s/ *nf* descent, ancestry

**ascendant**, ∼**e** /asɑ̃dɑ̃, ɑ̃t/ ⨯1⨯ *adj* ⟨*curve*⟩ rising; ⟨*movement*⟩ upward; ⟨*star*⟩ ascending
⨯2⨯ *nm* (a) influence (**sur** over)
(b) (Law) ascendant

**ascenseur** /asɑ̃sœʀ/ *nm* lift (GB), elevator (US)
IDIOMS **renvoyer l'**∼ to return the favour (GB)

**ascension** /asɑ̃sjɔ̃/ *nf* (a) ascent; **faire l'**∼ **de** to climb
(b) (figurative) rise

**ascensionnel**, **-elle** /asɑ̃sjɔnɛl/ *adj* ⟨*movement*⟩ upward; **parachute** ∼ parascending

**ascète** /asɛt/ *nmf* ascetic

**ascétisme** /asetism/ *nm* asceticism

**aseptique** /asɛptik/ *adj* aseptic

**aseptisé**, ∼**e** /asɛptize/ *adj* ⟨*art*⟩ sanitized; ⟨*world*⟩ sterile; ⟨*decor*⟩ impersonal

**aseptiser** /asɛptize/ [1] *vtr* to disinfect ⟨*wound*⟩; to sterilize ⟨*instrument*⟩

**asexué**, ∼**e** /asɛksɥe/ *adj* asexual

**asiatique** /azjatik/ *adj* Asian

**Asie** /azi/ *pr nf* Asia; ∼ **Mineure** Asia Minor

**asile** /azil/ *nm* (a) refuge; **chercher** ∼ **à** to seek refuge
(b) (political) asylum
(c) ∼ **de vieillards** old people's home; ∼ **de nuit** night shelter

**asocial**, ∼**e**, *mpl* **-iaux** /asɔsjal, o/ ⨯1⨯ *adj* antisocial
⨯2⨯ *nm,f* social misfit

**aspect** /aspɛ/ *nm* (a) side; **voir qch sous son** ∼ **positif** to see the good side of sth
(b) aspect; **par bien des** ∼**s** in many respects
(c) appearance

**asperge** /aspɛʀʒ/ *nf* (a) asparagus
(b) (colloq) beanpole (colloq), string bean (US)

**asperger** /aspɛʀʒe/ [13] *vtr* to spray; to splash

**aspérité** /aspeʀite/ *nf* (in terrain) bump

**asphalte** /asfalt/ *nm* asphalt

**asphyxiant**, ∼**e** /asfiksjɑ̃, ɑ̃t/ *adj* asphyxiating

**asphyxie** /asfiksi/ *nf* asphyxiation

**asphyxier** /asfiksje/ [2] ⨯1⨯ *vtr* (a) to asphyxiate ⟨*person*⟩
(b) to paralyse ⟨*network, company*⟩
⨯2⨯ **s'asphyxier** *v refl* (+ *v être*) (a) to suffocate to death
(b) to gas oneself
(c) ⟨*network, company*⟩ to become paralysed

**aspirateur** /aspiʀatœʀ/ *nm* vacuum cleaner, hoover® (GB)

**aspiration** /aspiʀasjɔ̃/ *nf* (a) aspiration (**à** for)
(b) sucking up, drawing up
(c) inhalation

**aspirer** /aspiʀe/ [1] ⨯1⨯ *vtr* (a) to breathe in, to inhale
(b) to suck [sth] up
(c) **consonne aspirée** aspirated consonant
⨯2⨯ **aspirer à** *v+prep* to yearn for; to aspire to

**aspirne®** /aspiʀin/ *nf* aspirin
IDIOMS **être blanc comme un cachet d'**∼ to be lily white

**assagir: s'assagir** /asaʒiʀ/ [3] *v refl* (+ *v être*) to quieten down (GB), to quiet down (US)

**assaillant**, ∼**e** /asajɑ̃, ɑ̃t/ *nm,f* (a) attacker
(b) (Mil) **les** ∼**s** the attacking forces

**assaillir** /asajiʀ/ [28] *vtr* (a) to attack
(b) to plague; ∼ **qn de questions** to bombard sb with questions

**assainir** /aseniʀ/ [3] *vtr* (a) to clean up
(b) to stabilize ⟨*economy*⟩; to streamline ⟨*company*⟩

**assainissement** /asenismɑ̃/ *nm*
(a) cleaning up
(b) (of economy) stabilization; (of company) streamlining

**assaisonnement** /asɛzɔnmɑ̃/ *nm* (Culin) seasoning; (on salad) dressing

**assaisonner** /asɛzɔne/ [1] *vtr* to season ⟨*dish*⟩; to dress ⟨*salad*⟩

**assassin**, ∼**e** /asasɛ̃, in/ ⨯1⨯ *adj*
(a) murderous
(b) ⟨*campaign*⟩ vicious
⨯2⨯ *nm* (a) murderer
(b) assassin

**assassinat** /asasina/ *nm* (a) murder
(b) assassination

**assassiner** /asasine/ [1] *vtr* (a) to murder
(b) to assassinate
(c) (colloq) to slate (colloq)

**assaut** /aso/ *nm* attack, assault; **se lancer** *or* **monter à l'**∼ **de** to launch an attack on; **prendre d'**∼ to storm; **les** ∼**s du froid** the onslaught of cold weather

**assécher** /aseʃe/ [14] *vtr* (a) to drain
(b) ⟨*heat*⟩ to dry up

**ASSEDIC** /asedik/ *nf* (*abbr* = **Association pour l'emploi dans**

l'industrie et le commerce)
*organization managing unemployment
contributions and payments*

**assemblage** /asɑ̃blaʒ/ *nm* **(a)** (of motor)
assembly (**de of**)
**(b)** (of ideas) assemblage; (of objects)
collection; (of colours) combination

**assemblée** /asɑ̃ble/ *nf* **(a)** gathering
**(b)** meeting
**(c)** assembly
■ ∼ **générale, AG** general meeting;
**l'Assemblée nationale** the French National
Assembly

**assembler** /asɑ̃ble/ [1] **1** *vtr* to
assemble, to put together
**2 s'assembler** *v refl* (+ *v être*) ⟨*crowd*⟩ to
gather; ⟨*ministers*⟩ to assemble
IDIOMS **qui se ressemble s'assemble** (Proverb)
birds of a feather flock together

**asséner** /asene/ [14] *vtr* ∼ **un coup à qn/
qch** to deal sb/sth a blow

**assentiment** /asɑ̃timɑ̃/ *nm* assent,
consent

**asseoir** /aswaʀ/ [41] **1** *vtr* **(a)** to sit [sb]
down; (in bed) to sit [sb] up; **faire** ∼ **qn** to
make sb sit down; (politely) to offer a seat to
sb
**(b)** to establish ⟨*reputation*⟩
**(c)** (colloq) to stagger, to astound
**2 s'asseoir** *v refl* (+ *v être*) to sit (down);
(in bed) to sit up

**assermenté, ∼e** /asɛʀmɑ̃te/ *adj* sworn,
on oath

**assertion** /asɛʀsjɔ̃/ *nf* assertion

**asservir** /asɛʀviʀ/ [3] *vtr* **(a)** to enslave
⟨*person*⟩
**(b)** to subjugate ⟨*country*⟩

**asservissement** /asɛʀvismɑ̃/ *nm*
**(a)** (of country, people) subjugation
**(b)** subjection
**(c)** subservience

**assesseur** /asesœʀ/ *nm* magistrate's
assistant

**assez** /ase/ *adv* **(a)** enough; ∼ **fort** strong
enough; **j'en ai** ∼ I've got enough; I'm fed up
(colloq)
**(b)** quite; **je suis** ∼ **pressé** I'm in rather a
hurry; **je suis** ∼ **d'accord** I tend to agree

**assidu, ∼e** /asidy/ *adj* **(a)** diligent
**(b)** ⟨*care*⟩ constant
**(c)** ⟨*presence, visits*⟩ regular
**(d)** devoted

**assiduité** /asidyite/ *nf* **(a)** diligence; **avec**
∼ ⟨*work*⟩ diligently; ⟨*train*⟩ assiduously;
⟨*read*⟩ regularly
**(b)** regular attendance
**(c)** ∼**s** assiduities

**assiégeant, ∼e** /asjeʒɑ̃, ɑ̃t/ *nm,f*
besieger

**assiéger** /asjeʒe/ [15] *vtr* to besiege

**assiette** /asjɛt/ *nf* **(a)** (for food) plate
**(b)** ∼ (fiscale) tax base
■ ∼ **anglaise** assorted cold meats; ∼ **en
carton** paper plate; ∼ **creuse** soup plate; ∼ **à
dessert** dessert plate

IDIOMS **ne pas être dans son** ∼ to be out of
sorts

**assignation** /asiɲasjɔ̃/ *nf* **(a)** allocation
**(b)** (Law) summons

**assigner** /asiɲe/ [1] *vtr* **(a)** to assign
⟨*task*⟩
**(b)** to set ⟨*objective*⟩
**(c)** to ascribe ⟨*value, role*⟩ (**à** to)
**(d)** (Law) ∼ **à comparaître** to summons; ∼ **qn
à résidence** to put sb under house arrest

**assimilation** /asimilasjɔ̃/ *nf*
**(a)** comparison
**(b)** assimilation

**assimilé, ∼e** /asimile/ *adj* similar

**assimiler** /asimile/ [1] **1** *vtr* **(a)** to
assimilate; **être assimilé cadre** to have
executive status
**(b)** ∼ **qn/qch à** to liken sb/sth to
**2 s'assimiler** *v refl* (+ *v être*) **(a)** s'∼ **à**
⟨*method*⟩ to be comparable to; ⟨*person*⟩ to
compare oneself to
**(b)** ⟨*minority*⟩ to become assimilated;
⟨*substances*⟩ to be assimilated

**assis, ∼e¹** /asi, iz/ **1** *pp* ▶ ASSEOIR
**2** *pp adj* **(a)** seated; **être** ∼ to be sitting
down; (in bed) to be sitting up; **reste** ∼ don't
get up; (as reprimand) sit still
**(b)** ⟨*reputation*⟩ well-established
**(c)** (colloq) staggered

**assise²** /asiz/ *nf* basis, foundation

**assises** /asiz/ *nf pl* **(a)** meeting
**(b)** (Law) assizes

**assistanat** /asistana/ *nm* **(a)** (Univ)
assistantship
**(b)** (state aid) (pej) charity

**assistance** /asistɑ̃s/ *nf* **(a)** assistance;
aid
**(b)** audience
**(c)** attendance (**à** at)
■ ∼ **respiratoire** artificial respiration;
**l'Assistance publique** ≈ welfare services

**assistant, ∼e** /asistɑ̃, ɑ̃t/ *nm,f* assistant
■ ∼**e sociale** social worker

**assisté, ∼e** /asiste/ **1** *pp* ▶ ASSISTER
**2** *pp adj* **(a)** assisted (**de** by)
**(b)** receiving benefit (GB), on welfare (US)
**(c)** ∼ **par ordinateur** computer-aided
**(d)** **direction** ∼**e** power steering
**3** *nm,f*: *person receiving benefit (GB) or
welfare (US)*

**assister** /asiste/ [1] **1** *vtr* to assist; to aid
**2 assister à** *v+prep* **(a)** ∼ **à** to be at, to
attend
**(b)** ∼ **à** to witness

**associatif, -ive** /asɔsjatif, iv/ *adj*
**(a)** ⟨*memory*⟩ associative
**(b)** **vie associative** community life

**association** /asɔsjasjɔ̃/ *nf* **(a)** association
**(b)** combination

**associé, ∼e** /asɔsje/ **1** *adj* ⟨*member*⟩
associate; ⟨*companies*⟩ associated
**2** *nm,f* associate, partner

**associer** /asɔsje/ [2] **1** *vtr* **(a)** ∼ **qn à** to
include sb in ⟨*success*⟩; to make sb a partner
in ⟨*business*⟩; to give sb a share of ⟨*profits*⟩ ⋯⟶

**(b)** ~ qch à to combine sth with; to associate sth with

**2** **s'associer** v refl (+ v être) **(a)** to go into partnership, to link up; **s'~ pour faire** to join forces to do

**(b)** **s'~ à** to join ⟨movement⟩; to share in ⟨grief⟩

**(c)** to combine

**assoiffé**, **~e** /aswafe/ adj **(a)** thirsty

**(b)** **~ de** thirsting for

**assombrir** /asɔ̃bʀiʀ/ [3] **1** vtr **(a)** to make [sth] dark, to darken

**(b)** to spoil; **la tristesse assombrit son visage** his/her face clouded

**2** **s'assombrir** v refl (+ v être) **(a)** ⟨sky⟩ to darken

**(b)** ⟨face⟩ to become gloomy

**assommant**, **~e** /asɔmɑ̃, ɑ̃t/ adj (colloq)

**(a)** (dull) deadly boring (colloq)

**(b)** (irritating) **tu es ~ avec tes questions** you're a real pain (colloq) with your questions

**assommer** /asɔme/ [1] vtr **(a)** to knock [sb] senseless

**(b)** (colloq) **~ qn** to get on sb's nerves

**(c)** (colloq) ⟨news⟩ to stagger; ⟨heat⟩ to overcome

**assorti**, **~e** /asɔʀti/ adj **(a)** matching

**(b)** assorted

**assortiment** /asɔʀtimɑ̃/ nm **(a)** set

**(b)** assortment, selection

**(c)** (in shop) stock

**assortir** /asɔʀtiʀ/ [3] **1** vtr **(a)** to match (à to; avec with)

**(b)** **~ qch de qch** to add sth to sth

**2** **s'assortir** v refl (+ v être) **(a)** **s'~ à** or **avec** to match

**(b)** **s'~ de** to come with

**assoupir** /asupiʀ/ [3] **1** vtr **(a)** to make [sb] drowsy

**(b)** to dull ⟨senses, passion⟩

**2** **s'assoupir** v refl (+ v être) to doze off

**assoupissement** /asupismɑ̃/ nm drowsiness; (sleep) doze

**assouplir** /asupliʀ/ [3] **1** vtr **(a)** to soften ⟨washing⟩

**(b)** to make [sth] more supple ⟨body, leather⟩

**(c)** to relax ⟨rule⟩

**2** **s'assouplir** v refl (+ v être) **(a)** to get softer

**(b)** to become more supple

**(c)** ⟨person, rule⟩ to become more flexible

**assouplissant** /asuplisɑ̃/ nm fabric softener

**assouplissement** /asuplismɑ̃/ nm

**(a)** (of leather, woollens) softening; (of washing) conditioning

**(b)** (sport) **faire des ~s** or **des exercices d'~** to limber up

**(c)** (of rules, policy, attitude) relaxing

**assouplisseur** /asuplisœʀ/ nm fabric conditioner

**assourdir** /asuʀdiʀ/ [3] vtr **(a)** to deafen

**(b)** to muffle

**assouvir** /asuviʀ/ [3] vtr to satisfy ⟨hunger⟩; to assuage ⟨anger⟩

**assouvissement** /asuvismɑ̃/ nm

**(a)** (of hunger) satisfying; (of anger) assuaging

**(b)** satisfaction

**assujetti**, **~e** /asyʒeti/ adj **~ à** liable for ⟨tax⟩; subject to ⟨rule⟩

**assujettir** /asyʒetiʀ/ [3] **1** vtr **(a)** to subject (à to)

**(b)** to subjugate, to subdue

**(c)** to secure

**2** **s'assujettir** v refl (+ v être) ⟨person⟩ to submit (à to)

**assumer** /asyme/ [1] **1** vtr **(a)** to take ⟨responsibility⟩; to hold ⟨post⟩; to meet ⟨costs⟩

**(b)** to come to terms with ⟨conditions, identity, past⟩; to accept ⟨consequences⟩

**2** **s'assumer** v refl (+ v être) **(a)** to take responsibility for oneself

**(b)** to come to terms with oneself

**assurable** /asyʀabl/ adj insurable

**assurance** /asyʀɑ̃s/ nf **(a)** (self-) confidence, assurance; **avec ~** confidently

**(b)** assurance; **donner à qn l'~ que** to assure sb that

**(c)** insurance (policy)

**(d)** insurance company

**(e)** insurance (premium)

**(f)** insurance (sector)

**(g)** benefit (GB), benefits (US)

■ **~ au tiers** third-party insurance; **~ maladie** health insurance; sickness benefit (GB) or benefits (US); **~ tous risques** comprehensive insurance; **~s sociales** social insurance

**assurance-crédit**, pl **assurances-crédit** /asyʀɑ̃skʀedi/ nf credit insurance

**assurance-vie**, pl **assurances-vie** /asyʀɑ̃svi/ nf life insurance

**assuré**, **~e** /asyʀe/ **1** pp ▶ ASSURER

**2** pp adj **(a)** sure, certain (**de faire** of doing); **soyez ~ de ma reconnaissance** I am very grateful to you

**(b)** insured

**3** adj **(a)** ⟨step, air⟩ confident; ⟨hand⟩ steady; **mal ~** ⟨step, voice⟩ faltering; ⟨gesture⟩ nervous

**(b)** certain, assured

**4** nm,f insured party

■ **~ social** social insurance contributor

**assurément** /asyʀemɑ̃/ adv **(a)** definitely

**(b)** most certainly

**assurer** /asyʀe/ [1] **1** vtr **(a)** **~ à qn que** to assure sb that; **ce n'est pas drôle, je t'assure** believe me, it's no joke

**(b)** **~ qn de** to assure sb of ⟨support⟩

**(c)** to insure ⟨property, goods⟩

**(d)** to carry out ⟨maintenance⟩; to provide ⟨service⟩; **~ la liaison entre** ⟨train, bus, ferry⟩ to operate between; **~ la gestion de** to manage

**(e)** to ensure ⟨victory⟩; to secure ⟨right, post⟩ (**à qn** for sb); to assure ⟨future⟩; **~ un revenu à qn** to give sb an income; **~ ses vieux jours** to provide for one's old age

**(f)** to secure ⟨rope⟩; to belay ⟨climber⟩

**2** **s'assurer** *v refl* (+ *v être*) **(a)** s'~ de qch to make sure of sth
**(b)** to secure ‹*advantage, help*›
**(c)** to take out insurance
**(d)** (figurative) s'~ **contre** to insure against ‹*eventuality, risk*›

**assureur** /asyʀœʀ/ *nm* **(a)** insurance agent
**(b)** insurance company

**astérisque** /asteʀisk/ *nm* asterisk

**asthmatique** /asmatik/ *adj, nmf* asthmatic

**asthme** /asm/ *nm* asthma

**asticot** /astiko/ *nm* maggot

**astigmate** /astigmat/ *adj* astigmatic

**astiquer** /astike/ [1] *vtr* to polish

**astral, ~e,** *mpl* **-aux** /astʀal, o/ *adj* astral

**astre** /astʀ/ *nm* star

**astreindre** /astʀɛ̃dʀ/ [55] **1** *vtr* ~ qn à qch ‹*person*› to force sth upon sb; ‹*rule*› to bind sb to sth; ~ qn à faire to compel sb to do
**2** **s'astreindre** *v refl* (+ *v être*) s'~ à qch to subject oneself to sth

**astringent, ~e** /astʀɛ̃ʒɑ̃, ɑ̃t/ *adj* astringent

**astrologie** /astʀɔlɔʒi/ *nf* astrology

**astrologique** /astʀɔlɔʒik/ *adj* astrological

**astrologue** /astʀɔlɔg/ *nmf* astrologer

**astronaute** /astʀɔnot/ *nmf* astronaut

**astronautique** /astʀɔnotik/ *nf* astronautics

**astronomie** /astʀɔnɔmi/ *nf* astronomy

**astronomique** /astʀɔnɔmik/ *adj* astronomical

**astrophysique** /astʀɔfizik/ *nf* astrophysics

**astuce** /astys/ *nf* **(a)** cleverness
**(b)** shrewdness, astuteness
**(c)** trick
**(d)** pun; joke

**astucieux, -ieuse** /astysjø, øz/ *adj*
**(a)** clever
**(b)** shrewd, sharp

**asymétrique** /asimetʀik/ *adj* asymmetrical

**atchoum** /atʃum/ *nm* atishoo

**atelier** /atəlje/ *nm* **(a)** (place) workshop; (artist's) studio
**(b)** working group
**(c)** (seminar) workshop

**atermoyer** /atɛʀmwaje/ [23] *vi* to procrastinate

**athée** /ate/ **1** *adj* atheistic
**2** *nmf* atheist

**athéisme** /ateism/ *nm* atheism

**athénien, -ienne** /atenjɛ̃, ɛn/ *adj* Athenian

**athlète** /atlɛt/ *nmf* athlete

**athlétique** /atletik/ *adj* athletic

**athlétisme** /atletism/ *nm* athletics (GB), track and field events

**Atlantique** /atlɑ̃tik/ *pr nm* l'~ the Atlantic

**atlas** /atlas/ *nm inv* atlas

**atmosphère** /atmɔsfɛʀ/ *nf* atmosphere

**atoll** /atɔl/ *nm* atoll

**atome** /atom/ *nm* atom
IDIOMS avoir des ~s crochus avec qn (colloq) to get on well with sb

**atomique** /atɔmik/ *adj* atomic

**atomiseur** /atɔmizœʀ/ *nm* spray, atomizer

**atone** /atɔn/ *adj* **(a)** lifeless, apathetic
**(b)** ‹*syllable*› unstressed

**atours** /atuʀ/ *nm pl* finery

**atout** /atu/ *nm* **(a)** trump (card); trumps
**(b)** (figurative) asset; trump card; **mettre tous les ~s dans son jeu** to leave nothing to chance

**âtre** /atʀ/ *nm* hearth

**atroce** /atʀɔs/ *adj* atrocious, dreadful, terrible

**atrocité** /atʀɔsite/ *nf* **(a)** atrocity
**(b)** monstrosity

**atrophie** /atʀɔfi/ *nf* atrophy

**atrophier: s'atrophier** /atʀɔfje/ [2] *v refl* (+ *v être*) to atrophy; **bras atrophié** wasted arm

**attabler: s'attabler** /atable/ [1] *v refl* (+ *v être*) to sit down at (the) table

**attachant, ~e** /ataʃɑ̃, ɑ̃t/ *adj* engaging

**attache** /ataʃ/ *nf* **(a)** tie; string; rope; strap; ~s **familiales** family ties
**(b)** avoir des ~s **fines** to have delicate ankles and wrists

**attaché, ~e** /ataʃe/ *nm,f* attaché
■ ~ de presse press attaché

**attachement** /ataʃmɑ̃/ *nm* **(a)** (to person) attachment
**(b)** (to principle, cause) commitment

**attacher** /ataʃe/ [1] **1** *vtr* **(a)** to tie ‹*person, hands, laces*› (à to); to tether ‹*horse, goat*›; to chain ‹*dog*› (à to); to lock ‹*bicycle*› (à to); to tie up ‹*person, parcel*›
**(b)** to fasten ‹*belt*›
**(c)** to attach ‹*importance*›
**(d)** les privilèges attachés à un poste the privileges attached to a post
**2** **s'attacher** *v refl* (+ *v être*) **(a)** to fasten
**(b)** s'~ à qn/qch to become attached to sb/sth

**attaquable** /atakabl/ *adj* **(a)** ‹*place*› facilement ~ easy to attack
**(b)** ‹*theory, position*› shaky
**(c)** ‹*will*› contestable

**attaquant, ~e** /atakɑ̃, ɑ̃t/ *nm,f* attacker

**attaque** /atak/ **1** *nf* **(a)** attack; (on bank) raid; **passer à l'~** to move into the attack; (figurative) to go on the attack; ~ **à main armée** armed raid
**(b)** (Med) stroke; ~ **cardiaque** heart attack
**2** **d'attaque** *phr* (colloq) on (GB) *or* in (US) form; **être d'~ pour faire** to feel up to doing

a

**attaquer** /atake/ [1] **1** *vtr* **(a)** to attack; to raid ‹*bank*›
**(b)** (Law) to contest ‹*contract, will*›; ~ **qn en justice** to bring a lawsuit against sb
**(c)** to tackle ‹*problem*›
**2** *vi* **(a)** (in tennis, golf) to drive
**(b)** ‹*speaker*› to begin (brusquely)
**3** **s'attaquer** *v refl* (+ *v être*) **s'~ à** to attack ‹*person, policy*›; to tackle ‹*problem*›

**attardé**, **~e** /atarde/ **1** *adj* retarded
**2** *nm,f* mentally retarded person

**attarder: s'attarder** /atarde/ [1] *v refl* (+ *v être*) **(a)** to stay until late; to linger
**(b)** **s'~ sur** to dwell on ‹*point*›

**atteindre** /atɛdR/ [55] **1** *vtr* **(a)** to reach ‹*place, age, level, target*›; to achieve ‹*aim*›
**(b)** ‹*projectile, marksman*› to hit ‹*target*›
**(c)** ‹*illness*› to affect
**2** **atteindre à** *v+prep* to reach; to achieve

**atteint**, **~e¹** /atɛ̃, ɛ̃t/ **1** *pp* ▸ ATTEINDRE
**2** *pp adj* affected (**de, par** by); **être ~ de** to be suffering from ‹*illness*›
**(b)** hit (**de, par** by)

**atteinte²** /atɛ̃t/ **1** *nf* **~ à** attack on; **porter ~ à** to undermine ‹*prestige*›; to damage ‹*reputation*›; to endanger ‹*security*›; to infringe ‹*right*›; **~ à la vie privée** breach of privacy
**2** **hors d'atteinte** *phr* **hors d'~** ‹*person*› beyond reach; ‹*target*› out of range

**attelage** /atlaʒ/ *nm* **(a)** (of horse) harness; (of oxen) yoke; (of wagon) coupling; (of trailer) towing attachment
**(b)** (animals) team; (of oxen) yoke
**(c)** horse-drawn carriage

**atteler** /atle/ [19] **1** *vtr* to harness ‹*horse*›; to yoke ‹*oxen*›; to couple ‹*wagon*›
**2** **s'atteler** *v refl* (+ *v être*) **s'~ à une tâche** to get down to a job

**attelle** /atɛl/ *nf* (Med) splint

**attenant**, **~e** /atnã, ãt/ *adj* adjacent

**attendre** /atɑ̃dR/ [6] **1** *vtr* **(a)** to wait for ‹*person, event*›; **j'attends de voir pour le croire** I'll believe it when I see it; **se faire ~** to keep people waiting; **la réaction ne se fit pas ~** the reaction was instantaneous; **~ son jour** *or* **heure** to bide one's time; **en attendant mieux** until something better turns up; **on ne t'attendait plus!** we'd given up on you!
**(b)** to await, to be in store for ‹*person*›
**(c)** to expect; **~ qch de qn/qch** to expect sth from sb/sth; **elle attend un bébé** she's expecting a baby
**2** *vi* to wait; (on phone) to hold; **faire ~ qn** to keep sb waiting; **en attendant** in the meantime; all the same, nonetheless; **tu ne perds rien pour ~!** (colloq) I'll get you (colloq), just you wait!
**3** **s'attendre** *v refl* (+ *v être*) **s'~ à qch** to expect sth; **s'~ à ce que qn fasse** to expect sb to do

**attendrir** /atɑ̃dRiR/ [3] **1** *vtr* to touch, to move ‹*person*›; **se laisser ~** to soften
**2** **s'attendrir** *v refl* (+ *v être*) to feel moved

**attendrissant**, **~e** /atɑ̃dRisɑ̃, ɑ̃t/ *adj* touching, moving; ‹*innocence*› endearing

**attendrissement** /atɑ̃dRismɑ̃/ *nm* emotion

**attendu¹: attendu que** /atɑ̃dy/ *phr* **(a)** given *or* considering that
**(b)** (Law) whereas

**attendu²**, **~e** /atɑ̃dy/ *adj* **(a)** expected
**(b)** **le jour (tant) ~** the long-awaited day

**attentat** /atɑ̃ta/ *nm* assassination attempt, attack; **~ à la bombe** bomb attack.
■ **~ à la pudeur** (Law) indecent assault

**attente** /atɑ̃t/ *nf* **(a)** waiting; wait; **mon ~ a été vaine** I waited in vain; **dans l'~ de vous lire** looking forward to hearing from you; **en ~** ‹*passenger*› waiting; ‹*file*› pending; ‹*call*› on hold
**(b)** expectation; **répondre à l'~ de qn** to come up to sb's expectations

**attenter** /atɑ̃te/ [1] *v+prep* **~ à ses jours** to attempt suicide; **~ à la vie de qn** to make an attempt on sb's life

**attentif**, **-ive** /atɑ̃tif, iv/ *adj* attentive; **sous l'œil ~ de leur mère** under the watchful eye of their mother

**attention** /atɑ̃sjɔ̃/ **1** *nf* **(a)** attention; **faire ~ à qch** to mind ‹*cars, step*›; to watch out for ‹*black ice*›; to take care of ‹*clothes, belongings*›; to watch ‹*diet, health*›; to pay attention to ‹*fashion, details*›; **faire ~ à qn** to pay attention to sb; to keep an eye on sb; to take notice of sb
**(b)** kind gesture; **être plein d'~s pour qn** to be very attentive to sb
**2** *excl* **(a)** (cry) look out!, watch out!; (written) attention!; (in case of danger) warning!; (on road sign) caution!
**(b)** **~, je ne veux pas dire...** don't get me wrong, I don't mean...

**attentionné**, **~e** /atɑ̃sjɔne/ *adj* attentive, considerate

**attentisme** /atɑ̃tism/ *nm* wait-and-see attitude

**attentivement** /atɑ̃tivmɑ̃/ *adv*
**(a)** attentively
**(b)** carefully

**atténuantes** /atenɥɑ̃t/ *adj f pl* **circonstances ~** (Law) mitigating circumstances

**atténuer** /atenɥe/ [1] **1** *vtr* to ease ‹*pain, distress*›; to lessen ‹*impact*›; to smooth over ‹*differences*›; to weaken ‹*effect*›; to soften ‹*blow*›; to reduce ‹*inequalities*›; to dim ‹*light*›; to make [sth] less strong ‹*smell, taste*›
**2** **s'atténuer** *v refl* (+ *v être*) ‹*pain*› to ease; ‹*anger, grief*› to subside; ‹*corruption, pessimism*› to lessen; ‹*gaps*› to be reduced; ‹*wrinkles, colour*› to fade; ‹*storm, noise*› to die down

**atterrant**, **~e** /ateRɑ̃, ɑ̃t/ *adj* **(a)** appalling
**(b)** shattering

**atterré**, **~e** /ateRe/ *adj* **(a)** appalled
**(b)** shattered

**atterrir** /ateRiR/ [3] *vi* to land

**atterrissage** /ateʀisaʒ/ *nm* landing
**attestation** /atɛstasjɔ̃/ *nf* **(a)** attestation
  **(b)** certificate
**attester** /atɛste/ [1] *vtr* **(a)** to vouch for; to
  testify to
  **(b)** to prove, to attest to
**attirail** /atiʀaj/ *nm* gear, equipment
**attirance** /atiʀɑ̃s/ *nf* attraction
**attirant**, **∼e** /atiʀɑ̃, ɑ̃t/ *adj* attractive
**attirer** /atiʀe/ [1] **1** *vtr* **(a)** to attract
  ⟨person, capital⟩; to draw ⟨crowd, attention⟩;
  **∼ qn dans un coin** to take sb into a corner;
  **∼ qn dans un piège** to lure sb into a trap
  **(b)** ⟨country, profession⟩ to appeal to
  **(c)** to bring ⟨shame, anger⟩; **∼ des ennuis à
  qn** to cause sb problems
  **2 s'attirer** *v refl* (+ *v être*) **s'∼ le soutien
  de qn** to win sb's support; **s'∼ des ennuis** to
  get into trouble
**attiser** /atize/ [1] *vtr* **(a)** to kindle ⟨feeling⟩;
  to fuel ⟨discord⟩; to stir up ⟨hatred⟩
  **(b)** to fan ⟨fire⟩
**attitré**, **∼e** /atitʀe/ *adj* **(a)** ⟨chauffeur⟩
  official
  **(b)** ⟨customer⟩ regular
**attitude** /atityd/ *nf* **(a)** bearing; posture
  **(b)** attitude
**attouchement** /atuʃmɑ̃/ *nm*
  **(a)** molesting
  **(b)** fondling
  **(c)** (by healer) laying on of hands
**attractif, -ive** /atʀaktif, iv/ *adj* attractive
**attraction** /atʀaksjɔ̃/ *nf* attraction
  ■ **∼ terrestre** earth's gravity; **∼ universelle**
  gravitation
**attrait** /atʀɛ/ *nm* **(a)** appeal, attraction;
  lure
  **(b)** **l'∼ de qn pour qn/qch** sb's liking for
  sb/sth
**attraper** /atʀape/ [1] *vtr* **(a)** to catch; **se
  faire ∼** to get caught; **attrapez-le!** stop him!
  **(b)** to catch hold of ⟨rope, hand, leg⟩
  **(c)** (colloq) to catch ⟨cold, illness⟩
  **(d)** (colloq) to tell [sb] off
**attrayant**, **∼e** /atʀɛjɑ̃, ɑ̃t/ *adj*
  **(a)** attractive
  **(b)** pleasant
**attribuer** /atʀibɥe/ [1] **1** *vtr* **(a)** to
  allocate ⟨seat, task⟩; to grant ⟨right⟩; to
  award ⟨prize⟩; to lend ⟨importance⟩; **∼ qch à
  la fatigue** to put sth down to tiredness
  **(b)** **∼ qch à qn** to credit sb with sth
  ⟨quality⟩; to attribute sth to sb ⟨work⟩
  **2 s'attribuer** *v refl* (+ *v être*) **s'∼ la
  meilleure part** to give oneself the largest
  share; **s'∼ tout le mérite** to take all the
  credit
**attribut** /atʀiby/ *nm* **(a)** (quality, symbol)
  attribute
  **(b)** (in grammar) complement; **adjectif ∼**
  predicative adjective; **nom ∼** complement
**attribution** /atʀibysjɔ̃/ **1** *nf* **(a)** allocation
  **(b)** awarding
  **2 attributions** *nf pl* (of individual) remit;
  (of court) competence

**attristant**, **∼e** /atʀistɑ̃, ɑ̃t/ *adj*
  **(a)** distressing, upsetting
  **(b)** depressing; **d'une bêtise ∼e** depressingly
  stupid
**attrister** /atʀiste/ [1] *vtr* to sadden; **j'ai été
  attristé d'apprendre** I was sorry to hear
**attroupement** /atʀupmɑ̃/ *nm* gathering
**attrouper: s'attrouper** /atʀupe/ [1] *v refl*
  (+ *v être*) to gather
**au** /o/ *prep* (= **à le**) ▶ À
**aubade** /obad/ *nf* dawn serenade
**aubaine** /obɛn/ *nf* **(a)** godsend
  **(b)** bargain
**aube** /ob/ *nf* **(a)** dawn
  **(b)** alb; cassock
**aubépine** /obepin/ *nf* hawthorn
**auberge** /obɛʀʒ/ *nf* inn; **∼ de jeunesse**
  youth hostel
  IDIOMS **tu n'es pas sorti de l'∼!** (colloq)
  you're not out of the woods yet!
**aubergine** /obɛʀʒin/ *nf* aubergine,
  eggplant
**aubergiste** /obɛʀʒist/ *nmf* innkeeper
**aucun**, **∼e** /okœ̃, yn/ **1** *adj* no, not any;
  **en ∼ cas** under no circumstances
  **2** *pron* none; **je n'ai lu ∼ de vos livres** I
  haven't read any of your books; **∼ de ses
  arguments n'est convaincant** none of his
  arguments are convincing
**aucunement** /okynmɑ̃/ *adv* in no way
**audace** /odas/ *nf* **(a)** boldness
  **(b)** daring
  **(c)** audacity, nerve (colloq); impudence
**audacieux, -ieuse** /odasjø, øz/ *adj*
  **(a)** bold
  **(b)** audacious, daring
**au-delà** /od(ə)la/ **1** *nm* **l'∼** the hereafter
  **2** *adv* beyond; **jusqu'à 150 euros mais pas
  ∼** up to 150 euros but no more
  **3 au-delà de** *phr* beyond; over
**au-dessous** /odəsu/ **1** *adv* **(a)** below
  **(b)** under; **les enfants de dix ans et ∼**
  children of ten years and under
  **2 au-dessous de** *phr* below; **être ∼ de
  tout** (colloq) to be absolutely useless
**au-dessus** /odəsy/ **1** *adv* above; **les
  enfants de 10 ans et ∼** children of 10 and
  over; **la taille ∼** the next size up
  **2 au-dessus de** *phr* above; **∼ de chez
  moi** in the apartment above mine; **un pont
  ∼ de la rivière** a bridge over the river; **se
  pencher ∼ de la table** to lean across the
  table
**au-devant: au-devant de** /odəvɑ̃də/
  *phr* **aller ∼ de qn** to go to meet sb; **aller ∼
  des ennuis** to let oneself in for trouble
**audible** /odibl/ *adj* audible
**audience** /odjɑ̃s/ *nf* **(a)** (Law) hearing;
  **salle d'∼** courtroom
  **(b)** (interview) audience
  **(c)** (public) audience
**Audimat®** /odimat/ *nm* audience ratings
**audiovisuel, -elle** /odjɔvizɥɛl/ **1** *adj*
  **(a)** broadcasting

(b) audiovisual
**2** *nm* (a) broadcasting
(b) audiovisual equipment
(c) audiovisual methods

**audit** /odit/ *nm* audit

**auditeur**, **-trice** /oditœʀ, tʀis/ *nm,f*
listener

**auditif**, **-ive** /oditif, iv/ *adj* ‹nerve›
auditory; ‹problems› hearing; ‹memory›
aural

**audition** /odisjɔ̃/ *nf* (a) (sense) hearing
(b) audition
(c) (Law) hearing, examination

**auditionner** /odisjɔne/ [1] *vtr*, *vi* to
audition

**auditoire** /oditwaʀ/ *nm* audience

**auge** /oʒ/ *nf* (for animal feed) trough

**augmentation** /ogmɑ̃tasjɔ̃/ *nf* increase;
une ~ (de salaire) a pay rise (GB) *or* raise
(US)

**augmenter** /ogmɑ̃te/ [1] **1** *vtr* to raise, to
increase; to extend; ~ le loyer de qn to put
sb's rent up
**2** *vi* to increase, to go up, to rise

**augure** /ogyʀ/ *nm* (a) omen
(b) augury

**augurer** /ogyʀe/ [1] *vtr* que peut-on ~ de
cette attitude? what should we expect from
this attitude?

**auguste** /ogyst/ *adj* august, noble

**aujourd'hui** /oʒuʀdɥi/ *adv* (a) today
(b) nowadays, today; la France d'~ present-
day France

**aulne** /on/ *nm* alder

**aumône** /omon/ *nf* hand-out, alms;
demander l'~ to ask for charity

**aumônerie** /omonʀi/ *nf* chaplaincy

**aumônier** /omonje/ *nm* chaplain

**aune** /on/ *nm* = AULNE

**auparavant** /opaʀavɑ̃/ *adv* before;
beforehand; previously; formerly

**auprès**: **auprès de** /opʀɛdə/ *phr* (a) next
to, beside; il s'est rendu ~ de sa tante he
went to see his aunt
(b) compared with
(c) s'excuser ~ de qn to apologize to sb;
renseigne-toi ~ de la mairie ask for
information at the town hall; représentant ~
de l'ONU representative to the UN

**auquel** ▶ LEQUEL

**aura** /oʀa/ ▶ AVOIR[1]

**aurai** /oʀe/ ▶ AVOIR[1]

**auras** /oʀa/ ▶ AVOIR[1]

**auréole** /oʀeɔl/ *nf* (a) (stain) ring
(b) halo

**auréolé**, **~e** /oʀeɔle/ *adj* ~ de basking in
the glow of

**aurez** /oʀe/ ▶ AVOIR[1]

**auriculaire** /oʀikylɛʀ/ **1** *adj* auricular
**2** *nm* little finger, pinkie

**aurifère** /oʀifɛʀ/ *adj* (a) ‹mineral›
auriferous
(b) valeurs ~s gold stocks

**aurons** /oʀɔ̃/ ▶ AVOIR[1]

**auront** /oʀɔ̃/ ▶ AVOIR[1]

**aurore** /oʀɔʀ/ *nf* dawn; ~ boréale Northern
Lights, aurora borealis

**auscultation** /oskyltasjɔ̃/ *nf* examination

**ausculter** /oskylte/ [1] *vtr* (Med) to
examine

**auspices** /ospis/ *nm pl* auspices

**aussi** /osi/ **1** *adv* (a) too, as well, also; il
sera absent et moi ~ he'll be away and so
will I
(b) ~ bien que as well as; ~ âgé que as old
as
(c) so; je ne savais pas qu'il était ~ vieux I
didn't know he was so old; dans une ~ belle
maison in such a nice house
**2** *conj* so, consequently

**aussitôt** /osito/ **1** *adv* (a) immediately,
straight away
(b) ~ arrivé as soon as he arrived; ~ dit ~
fait no sooner said than done
**2** **aussitôt que** *phr* as soon as

**austère** /ostɛʀ, osteʀ/ *adj* austere; severe

**austérité** /osteʀite/ *nf* austerity; severity

**austral**, **~e**, *mpl* **~s** /ostʀal/ *adj*
southern, south

**Australie** /ostʀali/ *pr nf* Australia

**australien**, **-ienne** /ostʀaljɛ̃, ɛn/ *adj*
Australian

**autant** /otɑ̃/ **1** *adv* il n'a jamais ~ neigé it
has never snowed so much; je t'aime
toujours ~ I still love you as much; essaie
d'en faire ~ try and do the same; je les hais
tous ~ qu'ils sont I hate every single one of
them; j'aime ~ partir tout de suite I'd rather
leave straight away; ~ dire que la réunion
est annulée in other words the meeting is
cancelled (GB); ~ parler à un mur you might
as well be talking to the wall; ~ que je
sache as far as I know; ~ que tu peux as
much as you can
**2** **autant de** *quantif* (a) ~ de cadeaux so
many presents; il y a ~ de femmes que
d'hommes there are as many women as
(there are) men
(b) ~ de gentillesse such kindness; je n'ai
pas eu ~ de chance que lui I haven't had as
much luck as he has
**3** **d'autant** *phr* cela va permettre de
réduire d'~ les coûts de production this will
allow an equivalent reduction in production
costs; d'~ plus! all the more reason!; d'~
moins even less, all the less; d'~ que all the
more so as
**4** **pour autant** *phr* for all that; sans pour
~ tout modifier without necessarily
changing everything; pour ~ que je sache as
far as I know

**autarcie** /otaʀsi/ *nf* autarky; vivre en ~ to
be self-sufficient

**autel** /otɛl/ *nm* altar

**auteur** /otœʀ/ *nm* (a) author
(b) creator; (of song) composer; (of crime)
perpetrator
■ ~ dramatique playwright

**auteur-compositeur**, *pl* **auteurs-compositeurs** /otœrkɔ̃pozitœr/ *nm* songwriter

**authenticité** /otɑ̃tisite/ *nf* authenticity

**authentifier** /otɑ̃tifje/ [2] *vtr* to authenticate

**authentique** /otɑ̃tik/ *adj* ⟨*story*⟩ true; ⟨*painting, document*⟩ authentic; ⟨*feeling*⟩ genuine

**autiste** /otist/ *nm,f* autistic person

**auto** /oto/ *nf* car, automobile (US)
■ ∼ **tamponneuse** bumper car, dodgem

**autobiographie** /otobjografi/ *nf* autobiography

**autobus** /otɔbys/ *nm inv* bus

**autocar** /otɔkar/ *nm* coach (GB), bus (US)

**autochtone** /otɔkton/ *adj, nmf* native

**autocollant**, ∼**e** /otɔkɔlɑ̃, ɑ̃t/ **1** *adj* self-adhesive
**2** *nm* sticker

**autocuiseur** /otokɥizœr/ *nm* pressure cooker

**autodéfense** /otodefɑ̃s/ *nf* self-defence (GB)

**autodestructeur**, **-trice** /otodɛstryktœr, tris/ *adj* self-destructive

**autodestruction** /otodɛstryksjɔ̃/ *nf* self-destruction

**autodétruire: s'autodétruire** /otodetrɥir/ [69] *v refl* (+ *v être*) ⟨*person*⟩ to destroy oneself; ⟨*tape*⟩ to self-destruct; ⟨*missile*⟩ to autodestruct

**autodidacte** /otodidakt/ *nmf* self-educated person

**auto-école**, *pl* ∼**s** /otoekɔl/ *nf* driving school

**autogérer: s'autogérer** /otoʒere/ [14] *v refl* (+ *v être*) ⟨*company*⟩ to be run on a cooperative basis

**autographe** /otɔgraf/ *adj, nm* autograph

**automate** /otɔmat/ *nm* robot, automaton

**automatique** /otɔmatik/ **1** *adj*
(a) automatic
(b) inevitable
**2** *nm* (a) automatic (revolver)
(b) automatic camera

**automatiquement** /otɔmatikmɑ̃/ *adv*
(a) automatically
(b) (colloq) inevitably

**automatiser** /otɔmatize/ [1] *vtr* to automate

**automatisme** /otɔmatism/ *nm* automatism; automatic functioning; **acquérir des** ∼**s** to acquire automatic reflexes

**automne** /otɔn/ *nm* autumn (GB), fall (US)

**automobile** /otɔmɔbil/ **1** *adj* (a) car
(b) (Sport) ⟨*racing*⟩ motor; ⟨*circuit*⟩ motor racing
**2** *nf* (a) (motor) car, automobile (US)
(b) the motor (GB) *or* automobile (US) industry

**automobiliste** /otɔmɔbilist/ *nmf* motorist

**autonome** /otɔnɔm/ *adj* autonomous; independent; self-sufficient

**autonomie** /otɔnɔmi/ *nf* (a) autonomy
(b) (of car, plane) range; ∼ **de vol** flight range

**autonomiste** /otɔnɔmist/ *adj, nmf* separatist

**autoportrait** /otopɔrtrɛ/ *nm* self-portrait

**autopsie** /otɔpsi/ *nf* postmortem (examination)

**autoradio** /otoradjo/ *nm* car radio

**autorisation** /otɔrizasjɔ̃/ *nf*
(a) permission; authorization
(b) permit

**autorisé**, ∼**e** /otɔrize/ *adj* authorized; legal; accredited; permitted

**autoriser** /otɔrize/ [1] *vtr* (a) to allow, to authorize
(b) ∼ **qn à faire** to entitle sb to do
(c) to make [sth] possible

**autoritaire** /otɔritɛr/ *adj, nmf* authoritarian

**autorité** /otɔrite/ *nf* (a) authority; **faire qch d'**∼ to do sth without consultation; **il n'a aucune** ∼ **sur ses enfants** he has no control over his children; **faire** ∼ ⟨*person*⟩ to be an authority; ⟨*work*⟩ to be authoritative
(b) (person) authority, expert

**autoroute** /otɔrut/ *nf* motorway (GB), freeway (US); ∼ **à péage** toll motorway
■ ∼ **de l'information** information highway

**autoroutier**, **-ière** /otɔrutje, ɛr/ *adj* motorway (GB), freeway (US)

**auto-stop** /otostɔp/ *nm* hitchhiking

**auto-stoppeur**, **-euse**, *mpl* ∼**s** /otostɔpœr, øz/ *nm,f* hitchhiker

**autour** /otur/ **1** *adv* **un parterre de fleurs avec des pierres** ∼ a flower bed with stones around it; **tout** ∼ all around
**2 autour de** *phr* (a) around, round (GB); ∼ **de la table** around the table
(b) around, about; ∼ **de 10 heures** around 10 o'clock
(c) about, on; **un débat** ∼ **du thème du pouvoir** a debate on the theme of power

**autre** /otr/ **1** *det* (a) other; **une** ∼ **histoire** another story; **rien d'**∼ nothing else; **l'effet obtenu est tout** ∼ the effect produced is completely different
(b) (colloq) **nous** ∼**s professeurs/Français** we teachers/French
**2** *pron* (a) **où sont les** ∼**s?** where are the other ones?; where are the others?; **je t'ai pris pour un** ∼ I mistook you for someone else; **ils se respectent les uns les** ∼**s** they respect each other; **chez lui c'est tout l'un ou tout l'**∼ with him it's all or nothing; **à d'**∼**s!** (colloq) pull the other one! (colloq)
(b) **prends-en un** ∼ have another one; **si je peux je t'en apporterai d'**∼**s** if I can I'll bring you some more
**3 autre part** *phr* somewhere else

**autrefois** /otrəfwa/ *adv* in the past; before, formerly; in the old days; ∼, **quand** ⋯∴

Paris s'appelait Lutèce long ago, when Paris was called Lutetia; **les légendes d'~** old legends

**autrement** /otʀəmɑ̃/ *adv* **(a)** differently, in a different way; **c'est comme ça, et pas ~** that's just the way it is; **je n'ai pas pu faire ~ que de les inviter** I had no alternative but to invite them; **on ne peut y accéder ~ que par bateau** you can only get there by boat; **je ne l'ai jamais vue ~ qu'en jean** I've never seen her in anything but jeans; **~ dit** in other words
**(b)** otherwise
**(c)** (colloq) **~ grave** (much) more serious; **il n'était pas ~ impressionné** he wasn't particularly impressed

**Autriche** /otʀiʃ/ *pr nf* Austria

**autrichien, -ienne** /otʀiʃjɛ̃, ɛn/ *adj* Austrian

**autruche** /otʀyʃ/ *nf* ostrich
IDIOMS **pratiquer la politique de l'~** to bury one's head in the sand

**autrui** /otʀɥi/ *pron* others, other people

**auvent** /ovɑ̃/ *nm* **(a)** canopy
**(b)** awning

**aux** /o/ *prep* (= **à les**) ▶ À

**auxiliaire** /oksiljɛʀ/ **1** *adj* **(a)** ⟨*verb*⟩ auxiliary
**(b)** ⟨*equipment, service*⟩ auxiliary; ⟨*motor*⟩ back-up
**(c) maître ~** assistant teacher; **infirmier ~** nursing auxiliary (GB), nurse's aide (US)
**2** *nmf* assistant, helper
**3** *nm* auxiliary (verb)

**auxquels, auxquelles** ▶ LEQUEL

**avachir: s'avachir** /avaʃiʀ/ [3] *v refl* (+ *v être*) **(a)** ⟨*chair*⟩ to sag
**(b)** ⟨*person*⟩ to let oneself go

**avaient** /avɛ/ ▶ AVOIR¹

**avais** /avɛ/ ▶ AVOIR¹

**avait** /avɛ/ ▶ AVOIR¹

**aval** /aval/ *nm* **(a)** (of river) lower reaches; **en ~** downstream
**(b)** approval

**avalanche** /avalɑ̃ʃ/ *nf* avalanche

**avaler** /avale/ [1] *vtr* **(a)** to swallow; **'ne pas ~'** (Med) 'not to be taken internally'
**(b)** to inhale ⟨*smoke, fumes*⟩

**avaleur** /avalœʀ/ *nm* **~ de sabres** sword swallower

**à-valoir** /avalwaʀ/ *nm inv* instalment (GB)

**avance** /avɑ̃s/ **1** *nf* **(a)** advance
**(b)** lead; **avoir/prendre de l'~ sur** to be/pull ahead of
**(c) une ~ (sur salaire)** an advance (on one's salary)
**2 à l'avance** *phr* in advance
**3 d'avance** *phr* in advance; **avoir cinq minutes d'~** to be five minutes early
**4 en avance** *phr* **(a)** early
**(b) être en ~ sur qn** to be ahead of sb
**(c) il est en ~ pour son âge** he's advanced for his age
**5 avances** *nf pl* advances

**avancé, ~e¹** /avɑ̃se/ **1** *pp* ▶ AVANCER
**2** *pp adj* ⟨*ideas*⟩ progressive; **la saison est bien ~e** it's late in the season; **te voilà bien ~!** that's done you a lot of good!

**avancée²** /avɑ̃se/ *nf* (of roof, rock) overhang

**avancement** /avɑ̃smɑ̃/ *nm* **(a)** promotion
**(b)** progress
**(c) ~ de l'âge de la retraite** lowering of the retirement age

**avancer** /avɑ̃se/ [12] **1** *vtr* **(a)** to move [sth] forward ⟨*object*⟩; to push [sth] forward ⟨*plate*⟩
**(b)** to bring forward ⟨*trip, meeting*⟩
**(c) ~ sa montre de cinq minutes** to put one's watch forward (by) five minutes
**(d)** to get ahead with ⟨*work*⟩; **cela ne nous avance à rien** that doesn't get us anywhere
**(e) ~ de l'argent à qn** ⟨*bank*⟩ to advance money to sb
**(f)** to put forward ⟨*argument, theory*⟩; to propose ⟨*figure*⟩
**2** *vi* **(a)** ⟨*person, vehicle*⟩ to move (forward); ⟨*army*⟩ to advance; **elle avança vers le guichet** she went up to the ticket office
**(b)** to make progress, to progress; **faire ~ la science** to further science
**(c) ma montre avance de deux minutes** my watch is two minutes fast
**(d)** ⟨*teeth, chin*⟩ to stick out; ⟨*peninsula*⟩ to jut out
**3 s'avancer** *v refl* (+ *être*) **(a) s'~ vers qch** to move toward(s) sth; **s'~ vers qn** to go toward(s) sb; to come up to sb
**(b)** to get ahead
**(c)** to jut out, to protrude
**(d) je me suis un peu avancé en lui promettant le dossier pour demain** I shouldn't have committed myself by promising him/her I'd have the file ready for tomorrow

**avant¹** /avɑ̃/ **1** *adv* before; first; **bien ~** long before; **il l'a mentionné ~ dans l'introduction** he mentioned it earlier in the introduction
**2** *prep* before; **~ mon retour** before I get back; **before I got back; ~ le 1ᵉʳ juillet** by 1 July; **~ peu** shortly; **~ tout, ~ toute chose** above all; first and foremost
**3 d'avant** *phr* **la séance d'~** the previous performance; **la fois d'~ nous étions déjà perdus** we got lost the last time as well
**4 avant de** *phr* **~ de faire** before doing
**5 avant que** *phr* before
**6 en avant** *phr* forward(s); **en ~ toute!** full steam ahead!; **mettre en ~ le fait que** to point out the fact that; **se mettre en ~** to push oneself forward
**7 en avant de** *phr* ahead of ⟨*group*⟩

**avant²** /avɑ̃/ **1** *adj inv* ⟨*wheel, seat, paw*⟩ front
**2** *nm* **(a) l'~** the front; **aller de l'~** to forge ahead
**(b)** (Sport) forward
**3 avant-** (*combining form*) **l'~-Thatcher** the pre-Thatcher era

**avantage** /avɑ̃taʒ/ *nm* **(a)** advantage; tirer
~ de qch to take advantage of sth; **paraître à
son** ~ to look one's best
**(b)** benefit; ~ **fiscaux** tax benefits

**avantager** /avɑ̃taʒe/ [13] *vtr* **(a)** ‹*person*›
to favour (GB); ‹*situation*› to be to the
advantage of
**(b)** ‹*clothes*› to show [sb/sth] off to
advantage

**avantageusement** /avɑ̃taʒøzmɑ̃/ *adv*
favourably (GB)

**avantageux, -euse** /avɑ̃taʒø, øz/ *adj*
**(a)** ‹*conditions, offer*› favourable (GB),
advantageous; ‹*rate, price*› attractive; **tirer
un parti** ~ **de qch** to use sth to one's
advantage
**(b)** ‹*description, outfit*› flattering

**avant-bras** /avɑ̃bʀa/ *nm inv* forearm

**avant-centre**, *pl* **avants-centres**
/avɑ̃sɑ̃tʀ/ *nm* centre (GB) forward; **jouer** ~
to play centre (GB) forward

**avant-coureur**, *pl* ~**s** /avɑ̃kuʀœʀ/ *adj*
**signes** ~**s** early warning signs

**avant-dernier, -ière**, *pl* ~**s**
/avɑ̃dɛʀnje, ɛʀ/ **1** *adj* penultimate; **l'**~ **jour**
the last day but one
**2** *nm,f* the last but one; **l'**~ **d'une famille de
cinq** the second youngest of five children

**avant-garde**, *pl* ~**s** /avɑ̃gaʀd/ *nf*
**(a)** avant-garde
**(b)** vanguard; **à l'**~ in the vanguard

**avant-goût**, *pl* ~**s** /avɑ̃gu/ *nm* foretaste

**avant-guerre**, *pl* ~**s** /avɑ̃gɛʀ/ *nm or f*
**l'**~ the prewar period; **l'Espagne d'**~
prewar Spain

**avant-hier** /avɑ̃tjɛʀ/ *adv* the day before
yesterday

**avant-poste**, *pl* ~**s** /avɑ̃pɔst/ *nm* (Mil)
outpost; **être aux** ~**s** to be in the vanguard

**avant-première**, *pl* ~**s** /avɑ̃pʀəmjɛʀ/
*nf* preview

**avant-propos** /avɑ̃pʀɔpo/ *nm inv*
foreword

**avant-veille**, *pl* ~**s** /avɑ̃vɛj/ *nf* two days
before

**avare** /avaʀ/ **1** *adj* mean, miserly; ~ **de**
sparing with
**2** *nm,f* miser

**avarice** /avaʀis/ *nf* meanness (GB),
miserliness

**avarier**: **s'avarier** /avaʀje/ [2] *v refl*
(+ *v être*) ‹*meat, fish*› to go rotten

**avatar** /avataʀ/ *nm* **(a)** mishap
**(b)** change

**avec** /avɛk/ **1** *adv* (colloq) **elle est partie** ~
she went off with it
**2** *prep* with; ~ **attention** carefully; **et** ~
**cela, que désirez-vous?** what else would you
like?; **je fais tout son travail et** ~ **ça il n'est
pas content!** I do all his work and he's still
not happy!; **sa séparation d'**~ **sa femme** his
separation from his wife

**avenant, -e** /avnɑ̃, ɑ̃t/ **1** *adj* pleasant
**2** **à l'avenant** *phr* in keeping

**avènement** /avɛnmɑ̃/ *nm* **(a)** (of monarch)
accession; (of politician, era) advent; ~ **au trône**
accession to the throne
**(b)** Advent

**avenir** /avniʀ/ *nm* future; **d'**~ ‹*job*› with a
future; ‹*technique, science*› of the future

**aventure** /avɑ̃tyʀ/ *nf* **(a)** adventure
**(b)** **il m'est arrivé une drôle d'**~ something
strange happened to me
**(c)** venture
**(d)** (love) affair
**IDIOMS dire la bonne** ~ **à qn** to tell sb's
fortune

**aventurer**: **s'aventurer** /avɑ̃tyʀe/ [1]
*v refl* (+ *v être*) to venture

**aventurier, -ière** /avɑ̃tyʀje, ɛʀ/ *nm,f*
adventurer/adventuress

**avenue** /avny/ *nf* avenue

**avérer**: **s'avérer** /avere/ [14] *v refl*
(+ *v être*) **s'**~ **utile** to prove useful; **il s'avère
que** it turns out that

**averse** /avɛʀs/ *nf* shower

**aversion** /avɛʀsjɔ̃/ *nf* aversion; **avoir qn/
qch en** ~ to loathe sb/sth

**averti, -e** /avɛʀti/ **1** *pp* ▶ AVERTIR
**2** *pp adj* **(a)** ‹*reader*› informed
**(b)** experienced

**avertir** /avɛʀtiʀ/ [3] *vtr* **(a)** to inform
**(b)** to warn

**avertissement** /avɛʀtismɑ̃/ *nm*
**(a)** warning
**(b)** (Sport) caution
**(c)** (in book) foreword

**avertisseur** /avɛʀtisœʀ/ *nm* **(a)** alarm
**(b)** (of car) horn

**aveu**, *pl* ~**x** /avø/ *nm* confession;
admission

**aveuglant, -e** /avœglɑ̃, ɑ̃t/ *adj* blinding

**aveugle** /avœgl/ **1** *adj* **(a)** blind
**(b)** ‹*faith, love*› blind; ‹*violence*›
indiscriminate
**2** *nm,f* blind person; **les** ~**s** the blind

**aveuglement** /avœgləmɑ̃/ *nm* blindness

**aveuglément** /avœglemɑ̃/ *adv* blindly

**aveugler** /avœgle/ [1] *vtr* to blind

**aveuglette**: **à l'aveuglette** /alavœglɛt/
*phr* **(a)** blindly
**(b)** at random

**avez** /ave/ ▶ AVOIR¹

**aviateur** /avjatœʀ/ *nm* airman

**aviation** /avjasjɔ̃/ *nf* **(a)** aviation
**(b)** aircraft industry
**(c)** **l'**~ the air force

**aviatrice** /avjatʀis/ *nf* woman pilot

**aviculteur, -trice** /avikyltœʀ, tʀis/ *nm,f*
**(a)** (of fowl) poultry farmer
**(b)** (of birds) aviculturist

**aviculture** /avikyltyʀ/ *nf* **(a)** (of fowl)
poultry farming
**(b)** (of birds) aviculture

**avide** /avid/ *adj* **(a)** greedy
**(b)** ~ **de** avid for, eager for

**avidement** /avidmɑ̃/ adv ‹eat› greedily; ‹read› avidly; ‹look, search› eagerly

**avidité** /avidite/ nf **(a)** greed
**(b)** eagerness

**aviez** /avje/ ▶ AVOIR¹

**avilir** /aviliʀ/ [3] vtr to demean

**avilissant**, **~e** /avilisɑ̃, ɑ̃t/ adj demeaning

**avilissement** /avilismɑ̃/ nm degradation

**aviné**, **~e** /avine/ adj ‹person› inebriated; ‹look, face› drunken

**avion** /avjɔ̃/ nm **(a)** (aero)plane (GB), airplane (US), aircraft; **aller à Rome en ~** to fly to Rome; **'par ~'** 'by air mail'
**(b)** flight
■ **~ de chasse** fighter; **~ à réaction** jet; **~ de tourisme** light passenger aircraft

**avions** /avjɔ̃/ ▶ AVOIR¹

**aviron** /aviʀɔ̃/ nm **(a)** rowing
**(b)** oar

**avis** /avi/ nm inv **(a)** opinion; **je suis de ton ~** I agree with you; **changer d'~** to change one's mind
**(b)** advice; **sauf ~ contraire** unless otherwise informed
**(c)** (of jury, commission) recommendation
**(d)** notice; **lancer un ~ de recherche** to issue a description of a missing person/wanted person
■ **~ au lecteur** foreword; **~ de passage** calling card (left by postman etc)

**avisé**, **~e** /avize/ adj sensible; **être bien/mal ~** to be well-/ill-advised

**aviser** /avize/ [1] **1** vtr to notify
**2** vi to decide
**3** **s'aviser** v refl (+ v être) **ne t'avise pas de recommencer** don't dare do that again

**aviver** /avive/ [1] **1** vtr **(a)** to intensify ‹feelings›; to stir up ‹quarrel›; to make [sth] more acute ‹pain›
**(b)** to liven up ‹colour›
**(c)** to kindle ‹fire›
**2** **s'aviver** v refl (+ v être) ‹desire, anger› to grow; ‹pain, grief› to become more acute

**avocat** /avɔka/ nm **(a)** lawyer, solicitor (GB), attorney (at law) (US)
**(b)** barrister (GB), (trial) lawyer (US); **~ de l'accusation** counsel for the prosecution
**(c)** (of idea) advocate; (of cause, person) champion
**(d)** avocado (pear)

**avocate** /avɔkat/ nf woman lawyer

**avoine** /avwan/ nf oats

**avoir¹** /avwaʀ/ [8]

■ **Note** You will find translations for expressions such as avoir raison, avoir beau, en avoir marre etc, at the entries RAISON, BEAU, MARRE etc.

**1** v aux to have; **j'ai perdu mon briquet** I've lost my lighter; **il aurait aimé te parler** he would have liked to speak to you
**2** vtr **(a)** to have (got) ‹child, book, room, time›; **elle avait les larmes aux yeux** there were tears in her eyes

**(b)** to get ‹object, job›; to catch ‹train, plane›; (on the phone) **j'ai réussi à l'~** I managed to get through to him
**(c)** to wear, to have [sth] on
**(d)** to feel; **~ du chagrin** to feel sad; **qu'est-ce que tu as?** what's wrong with you?
**(e)** **avoir faim/froid/20 ans** to be hungry/cold/20 years old
**(f)** to beat; to have (colloq), to con (colloq); **j'ai été eu** I've been had
**3** **avoir à** v+prep to have to; **tu n'as pas à le critiquer** you shouldn't criticize him; **j'ai beaucoup à faire** I have a lot to do; **tu n'as qu'à leur écrire** all you have to do is write to them
**4** **en avoir pour** v+prep **(a)** **vous en avez pour combien de temps?** how long will it take you?; how long are you going to be?
**(b)** **j'en ai eu pour 75 euros** it cost me 75 euros
**5** **il y a** v impers **(a)** there is/there are; **qu'est-ce qu'il y a?** what's wrong?; what's going on?; **il y a qu'elle m'énerve** she's getting on my nerves, that's what's wrong; **il y a à manger pour quatre** there's enough food for four; **il y en a toujours qui se plaignent** there's always someone who complains; **il n'y en a que pour leur chien** their dog comes first
**(b)** **il y a longtemps** a long time ago; **il n'y a que cinq ans que j'habite ici** I have only been living here for five years
**(c)** **combien y a-t-il jusqu'à la gare?** how far is it to the station?; **il y a au moins 15 kilomètres** it's at least 15 kilometres (GB) away

**avoir²** /avwaʀ/ nm **(a)** credit
**(b)** credit note
**(c)** assets, holdings

**avoisinant**, **~e** /avwazinɑ̃, ɑ̃t/ adj neighbouring (GB)

**avoisiner** /avwazine/ [1] vtr **(a)** ‹costs, sum› to be close to, to be about
**(b)** ‹place› to be near

**avons** /avɔ̃/ ▶ AVOIR¹

**avortement** /avɔʀtəmɑ̃/ nm (Med) abortion

**avorter** /avɔʀte/ [1] vi **(a)** (Med) to have an abortion
**(b)** ‹cow, ewe› to abort, to miscarry
**(c)** ‹plan› to be aborted; ‹uprising› to fail

**avorton** /avɔʀtɔ̃/ nm runt

**avouable** /avwabl/ adj worthy; respectable

**avoué**, **~e** /avwe/ **1** pp ▶ AVOUER
**2** pp adj ‹enemy› declared; ‹intention› avowed
**3** nm ≈ solicitor (GB), attorney(-at-law) (US)

**avouer** /avwe/ [1] **1** vtr to confess, to admit
**2** vi to confess; to own up
**3** **s'avouer** v refl (+ v être) **s'~ rassuré** to say one feels reassured; **s'~ vaincu** to admit defeat

**avril** /avʀil/ nm April

**axe** /aks/ nm **(a)** axis

**(b)** (Tech) axle
**(c)** major road
**(d) dans l'~ du bâtiment** in a line with the building; **la cible est dans l'~ du viseur** the target is lined up in the sights
**axer** /akse/ [1] *vtr* **(a)** to centre (GB) ‹*screw*›; to line up ‹*part*›
**(b)** to base, to centre (GB) (**sur** on)
**axiome** /aksjom/ *nm* axiom
**ayant** /εjɑ̃/ ▶ AVOIR[1]
**ayant droit**, *pl* **ayants droit** /εjɑ̃dRwa/ *nm* **(a)** legal claimant, beneficiary
**(b)** assignee

**ayez** /aje/ ▶ AVOIR[1]
**ayons** /ajɔ̃/ ▶ AVOIR[1]
**azalée** /azale/ *nf* azalea
**Azerbaïdjan** /azεRbajdʒɑ̃/ *pr nm* Azerbaijan
**azimut** /azimyt/ *nm* **(a)** (in astronomy) azimuth
**(b)** (figurative) **une offensive tous ~s** an all-out offensive; **dans tous les ~s** everywhere
**azote** /azɔt/ *nm* nitrogen
**aztèque** /astεk/ *adj* Aztec
**azur** /azyR/ *nm* azure
**azyme** /azim/ *adj* unleavened

# Bb

**b, B** /be/ *nm inv* b, B; **le b a ba** the rudiments
**baba** /baba/ *adj inv* (colloq) **en être** *or* **rester ~** to be flabbergasted (colloq)
**babillage** /babijaʒ/ *nm* babbling
**babiller** /babije/ [1] *vi* to babble, to chatter
**babines** /babin/ *nf pl* lips; **retrousser les ~** ‹*dog*› to bare its teeth; **se lécher les ~** to lick one's chops
**babiole** /babjɔl/ *nf* **(a)** trinket
**(b)** trifle
**bâbord** /babɔR/ *nm* port (side)
**babouche** /babuʃ/ *nf* oriental slipper
**babouin** /babwɛ̃/ *nm* baboon
**baby-foot** /babifut/ *nm inv* table football (GB), table soccer
**bac** /bak/ *nm* **(a)** (colloq) *abbr* = **baccalauréat**
**(b)** ferry
**(c)** tub; **évier à deux ~s** double sink
■ **~ à sable** sandpit (GB), sandbox (US)
**baccalauréat** /bakalɔRea/ *nm* baccalaureate (*school-leaving certificate taken at 17–18*); **~ professionnel** vocational baccalaureate (*vocationally-oriented school-leaving certificate*)
**bâche** /baʃ/ *nf* tarpaulin
**bachelier, -ière** /baʃəlje, εR/ *nm,f*: holder of the baccalaureate
**bâcher** /baʃe/ [1] *vtr* to cover [sth] with tarpaulin ‹*vehicle*›; **un camion bâché** a covered truck
**bachotage** /baʃɔtaʒ/ *nm* (Sch) (colloq) cramming
**bâcler** /bakle/ [1] *vtr* to dash [sth] off ‹*piece of work*›; to rush through ‹*ceremony*›
**bactérie** /bakteRi/ *nf* bacterium
**badaud, ~e** /bado, od/ *nm,f* **(a)** passerby
**(b)** onlooker

**badigeonner** /badiʒɔne/ [1] *vtr* **(a)** to paint
**(b)** to daub (**de** with)
**(c)** (Culin) to brush (**de** with)
**badin, ~e** /badɛ̃, in/ *adj* ‹*tone*› bantering
**baffe** /baf/ *nf* (colloq) clout, slap
**baffle** /bafl/ *nm* **(a)** speaker
**(b)** baffle
**bafouille** /bafuj/ *nf* (colloq) letter
**bafouiller** /bafuje/ [1] *vtr, vi* to mumble
**bagage** /bagaʒ/ *nm* piece of luggage; **faire ses ~s** to pack
IDIOMS **plier ~** (colloq) to pack up and go
**bagagiste** /bagaʒist/ *nm* baggage handler
**bagarre** /bagaR/ *nf* fight, scuffle
**bagarrer: se bagarrer** /bagaRe/ [1] *v refl* (+ *v être*) (colloq) to fight
**bagarreur, -euse** /bagaRœR, øz/ *adj* (colloq) aggressive
**bagatelle** /bagatεl/ *nf* **(a)** trifle, triviality
**(b) pour la ~ de** (ironic) for the trifling sum of
**bagne** /baɲ/ *nm* penal colony
**bagou(t)** /bagu/ *nm* (colloq) **avoir du ~** to have the gift of the gab
**bague** /bag/ *nf* **(a)** ring
**(b)** (around pipe) collar
**baguette** /bagεt/ *nf* **(a)** baguette, French stick
**(b)** stick; **mener qn à la ~** to rule sb with a rod of iron; **~ de chef d'orchestre** conductor's baton
**(c)** drumstick
**(d)** chopstick
■ **~ magique** magic wand
**bahut** /bay/ *nm* **(a)** sideboard
**(b)** (students' slang) school
**(c)** (colloq) truck
**bai, ~e** /bε/ *adj* bay
**baie** /bε/ *nf* **(a)** bay
⸱⸱⸱⸙

**(b)** berry
**(c)** ~ **(vitrée)** picture window

**baignade** /bɛɲad/ *nf* swimming

**baigner** /beɲe/ [1] ☐ *vtr* **(a)** to give [sb] a bath
**(b)** to bathe ⟨*wound*⟩
☐ *vi* ~ **dans l'huile** to be swimming in grease
☐ **se baigner** *v refl* (+ *v être*) to go swimming
**IDIOMS ça baigne** (colloq) things are going fine

**baigneur, -euse** /bɛɲœʀ, øz/ *nm,f* swimmer

**baignoire** /bɛɲwaʀ/ *nf* bathtub; ~ **sabot** hip bath

**bail**, *pl* **baux** /baj, bo/ *nm* lease; **ça fait un** ~ (colloq) it's been ages **(que** since)

**bâiller** /bɑje/ [1] *vi* **(a)** to yawn
**(b)** to gape (open)

**bailleur, bailleresse** /bajœʀ, bajʀɛs/ *nm,f* lessor
■ ~ **de fonds** backer, silent partner

**bâillon** /bɑjɔ̃/ *nm* gag

**bain** /bɛ̃/ *nm* **(a)** bath
**(b)** swim
**(c) grand/petit** ~ deep/shallow pool
■ ~ **de bouche** mouthwash; ~ **de foule** walkabout; **prendre un** ~ **de soleil** to sunbathe
**IDIOMS se remettre dans le** ~ to get back into the swing of things

**baïonnette** /bajɔnɛt/ *nf* bayonet

**baiser** /beze/ *nm* kiss

**baisse** /bɛs/ *nf* **(a)** fall; **en** ~ falling
**(b)** fading
**(c)** decline
**(d)** cut; **la** ~ **du dollar** the fall in the value of the dollar; **une** ~ **des loyers de 2%** a 2% drop in rents; **être en** ~ ⟨*rates, stocks, shares*⟩ to be going down; ⟨*results*⟩ to be decreasing; **le marché est à la** ~ (Econ) the market is bearish; **revoir des prévisions à la** ~ to revise estimates downward(s); **spéculations à la** ~ bear speculations

**baisser** /bese/ [1] ☐ *vtr* **(a)** to lower ⟨*blind*⟩; to wind [sth] down ⟨*window*⟩; to turn down ⟨*collar*⟩; ~ **les bras** (figurative) to give up; ~ **le nez** (figurative) to hang one's head
**(b)** to turn down ⟨*volume*⟩; to dim ⟨*light*⟩; to cut ⟨*prices*⟩
☐ *vi* to go down, to fall, to drop **(à** to; **de** by); (drop in value) ⟨*price, profit, rates, production*⟩ to fall; ⟨*wages, shares*⟩ to go down; ⟨*purchasing power, unemployment*⟩ to decrease; ⟨*productivity, market*⟩ to decline; ⟨*budget*⟩ to be cut; ⟨*currency*⟩ to slide; ⟨*water*⟩ to subside; ⟨*sight*⟩ to fail; ⟨*hearing*⟩ to deteriorate; ~ **d'un ton** (colloq) ⟨*person*⟩ to calm down
☐ **se baisser** *v refl* (+ *v être*) **(a)** to bend down
**(b)** to duck
**(c)** to go down

**baissier, -ière** /besje, ɛʀ/ ☐ *adj* bearish

☐ *nm* (on stock exchange) bear

**bajoue** /baʒu/ *nf* cheek

**bal** /bal/ *nm* **(a)** ball, dance
**(b)** dancehall

**balade** /balad/ *nf* walk; ride

**balader** /balade/ [1] (colloq) ☐ *vtr* **(a)** to take [sb] for a walk/drive
**(b)** to carry [sth] around
☐ **se balader** *v refl* (+ *v être*) to go for a walk/ride/drive
**IDIOMS envoyer qn** ~ (colloq) to send sb packing (colloq)

**baladeur** /baladœʀ/ *nm* walkman®, personal stereo

**balafre** /balafʀ/ *nf* **(a)** scar
**(b)** slash, gash

**balai** /balɛ/ *nm* broom; **passer le** ~ to sweep the floor; **du** ~ (colloq)! go away!

**balance** /balɑ̃s/ *nf* **(a)** (weighing) scales; **faire pencher la** ~ (figurative) to tip the scales
**(b)** (Econ) balance; ~ **commerciale** balance of trade; ~ **des comptes,** ~ **des paiements** balance of payments

**Balance** /balɑ̃s/ *pr nf* Libra

**balancelle** /balɑ̃sɛl/ *nf* swing seat

**balancement** /balɑ̃smɑ̃/ *nm* swaying; swinging

**balancer** /balɑ̃se/ [12] ☐ *vtr* **(a)** to sway; to swing
**(b)** (colloq) to chuck (colloq) **(sur** at); to chuck out (colloq) ⟨*old clothes, junk*⟩
**(c)** (colloq) to squeal on (colloq)
☐ *vi* **(a)** to sway
**(b)** to hesitate
☐ **se balancer** *v refl* (+ *v être*) **(a)** ⟨*person*⟩ to sway; ⟨*boat*⟩ to rock
**(b)** (colloq) **je m'en balance** I couldn't care less

**balancier** /balɑ̃sje/ *nm* pendulum

**balançoire** /balɑ̃swaʀ/ *nf* swing

**balayer** /baleje/ [21] *vtr* **(a)** to sweep (up); ~ **le sol** ⟨*coat*⟩ to brush the ground
**(b)** to brush [sth] aside ⟨*objections*⟩
**(c)** ⟨*radar*⟩ to scan

**balayette** /balɛjɛt/ *nf* (short-handled) brush

**balayeur, -euse** /balɛjœʀ, øz/ *nm,f* roadsweeper

**balbutiement** /balbysimɑ̃/ *nm* **les** ~**s du cinéma** the early days of the cinema

**balbutier** /balbysje/ [2] *vtr, vi* to mumble

**balcon** /balkɔ̃/ *nm* **(a)** balcony
**(b)** (in theatre, cinema) balcony, circle

**Bâle** /bɑl/ *pr n* Basel

**baleine** /balɛn/ *nf* **(a)** whale
**(b)** whalebone; stay; rib

**balisage** /balizaʒ/ *nm* (in port, channel) beaconing; (on airstrip) runway lighting; (on road) signposting; (on path) marking; (of text) tagging

**balise** /baliz/ *nf* **(a)** beacon
**(b)** signpost, waymark
**(c)** (Comput) tag

**b**

**baliser** /balize/ [1] *vtr* **(a)** to mark [sth] out with beacons
**(b)** to signpost, to waymark
**(c)** (Comput) to tag ⟨*text*⟩
**balistique** /balistik/ *nf* ballistics
**baliverne** /balivɛʀn/ *nf* nonsense
**ballade** /balad/ *nf* ballad; ballade
**balle** /bal/ *nf* **(a)** ball; **renvoyer la ∼ (à qn)** (figurative) to retort (to sb); **se renvoyer la ∼** to keep up an animated discussion; to keep passing the buck
**(b)** (in ball games) shot; **faire des ∼s** to knock the ball around; **∼ de jeu** game point
**(c)** bullet
**(d)** (colloq) franc
**ballerine** /balʀin/ *nf* **(a)** ballerina
**(b)** ballet pump
**ballet** /balɛ/ *nm* ballet
**ballon** /balɔ̃/ *nm* **(a)** ball
**(b)** balloon
**(c)** wine glass
**(d)** ∼ (alcootest) Breathalyzer®
■ ∼ dirigeable airship (GB), blimp (US); ∼ d'eau chaude hot water tank; ∼ ovale rugby ball; ∼ rond soccer ball
**ballonnement** /balɔnmɑ̃/ *nm* bloating
**ballot** /balo/ *nm* (colloq) nerd (colloq), fool
**ballottage** /balɔtaʒ/ *nm: absence of an absolute majority in the first round of an election*
**ballotter** /balɔte/ [1] *vtr* **(a)** ⟨*sea*⟩ to toss [sb/sth] around; ⟨*movement*⟩ to jolt
**(b) être ballotté entre sa famille et son travail** to be torn between one's family and one's job
**balluchon** = BALUCHON
**balnéaire** /balneɛʀ/ *adj* ⟨*resort*⟩ seaside
**balte** /balt/ *adj* Baltic; **les pays ∼s** the Baltic States
**baluchon** /balyʃɔ̃/ *nm* bundle
**balustrade** /balystʀad/ *nf* **(a)** parapet
**(b)** railing
**(c)** balustrade
**bambin, ∼e** /bɑ̃bɛ̃, in/ *nm,f* kid (colloq), child
**bambou** /bɑ̃bu/ *nm* bamboo
**ban** /bɑ̃/ ① *nm* round of applause
② **bans** *nm pl* banns
IDIOMS **mettre qn au ∼ de la société** to ostracize sb
**banal, ∼e** /banal/ *adj* **(a)** commonplace, ordinary; **peu ∼** unusual
**(b)** trivial, trite
**banalisation** /banalizasjɔ̃/ *nf* **la ∼ de l'informatique** the way in which computing has become part of everyday life
**banaliser** /banalize/ [1] *vtr* **(a)** to make [sth] commonplace
**(b) voiture banalisée** unmarked car
**banalité** /banalite/ *nf* **(a)** ordinariness
**(b)** triteness
**(c)** trite remark
**banane** /banan/ *nf* **(a)** banana
**(b)** quiff

**(c)** bumbag (GB), fanny pack (US)
**banc** /bɑ̃/ *nm* **(a)** bench
**(b)** (of fish) shoal
■ ∼ des accusés dock; ∼ d'essai test bench; testing ground; ∼ de sable sandbank
**bancaire** /bɑ̃kɛʀ/ *adj* **(a)** ⟨*business*⟩ banking
**(b)** ⟨*card*⟩ bank
**bancal, ∼e** /bɑ̃kal/ *adj* **(a)** ⟨*chair*⟩ rickety
**(b)** ⟨*solution*⟩ unsatisfactory
**bande** /bɑ̃d/ *nf* **(a)** gang; group; ∼ de crétins! you bunch of idiots!; **ils font ∼ à part** they don't join in
**(b)** (of animals) pack
**(c)** (of material, paper) strip; band
**(d)** bandage
**(e)** broad stripe
**(f)** (for recording) tape
■ ∼ d'arrêt d'urgence, BAU hard shoulder; ∼ dessinée, BD (colloq) comic strip; comic book; ∼ de fréquences waveband; ∼ originale (of film) original soundtrack
**bande-annonce**, *pl* **bandes-annonces** /bɑ̃danɔ̃s/ *nf* trailer
**bandeau**, *pl* **∼x** /bɑ̃do/ *nm* **(a)** blindfold
**(b)** eye patch
**(c)** headband
**bandelette** /bɑ̃dlɛt/ *nf* bandage
**bander** /bɑ̃de/ [1] *vtr* **(a)** to bandage
**(b) ∼ les yeux à qn** to blindfold sb
**banderole** /bɑ̃dʀɔl/ *nf* banner
**bande-son**, *pl* **bandes-son** /bɑ̃dsɔ̃/ *nm* soundtrack
**bandit** /bɑ̃di/ *nm* **(a)** bandit; ∼ de grand chemin highwayman
**(b)** crook
**(c)** rascal
**banditisme** /bɑ̃ditism/ *nm* **le (grand) ∼** (organized) crime
**bandoulière** /bɑ̃duljɛʀ/ *nf* shoulder strap
**bang** /bɑ̃g/ *nm* sonic boom
**banlieue** /bɑ̃ljø/ *nf* **(a)** suburbs; **de ∼** suburban
**(b)** suburb
**banlieusard, ∼e** /bɑ̃ljøzaʀ, aʀd/ *nm,f* suburbanite
**bannière** /banjɛʀ/ *nf* banner; **la ∼ étoilée** the star-spangled banner.
IDIOMS **c'est la croix et la ∼** it's hell (**pour faire** doing)
**bannir** /baniʀ/ [3] *vtr* **(a)** to banish (**de** from)
**(b)** to ban
**bannissement** /banismɑ̃/ *nm* banishment (**de** from)
**banque** /bɑ̃k/ *nf* **(a)** bank
**(b)** banking
■ ∼ de données data bank
**banqueroute** /bɑ̃kʀut/ *nf* bankruptcy
**banquet** /bɑ̃kɛ/ *nm* **(a)** banquet
**(b)** feast
**banquette** /bɑ̃kɛt/ *nf* (in café) wall seat; (in car, train) seat
**banquier** /bɑ̃kje/ *nm* banker

**banquise** /bãkiz/ *nf* ice floe
**baptême** /batɛm/ *nm* (a) baptism,
christening
(b) (of ship) christening; (of bell) blessing
■ ∼ de l'air first flight
**baptiser** /batize/ [1] *vtr* (a) to baptize, to
christen
(b) to call, to name; to nickname
(c) to christen ⟨ship⟩; to bless ⟨bell⟩
**bar** /baʀ/ *nm* (a) bar
(b) (Zool) sea bass
**baragouiner** /baʀagwine/ [1] *vtr* (colloq) to
gabble ⟨sentence⟩; to speak [sth] badly
⟨language⟩
**baraka** /baʀaka/ *nf* (colloq) luck
**baraque** /baʀak/ *nf* (a) shack
(b) (colloq) pad (colloq), house
**baraqué**, ∼e /baʀake/ *adj* (colloq) hefty
**baraquement** /baʀakmã/ *nm* (a) group
of huts
(b) hut
(c) army camp
**baratin** /baʀatɛ̃/ *nm* (colloq) (a) sales pitch
(b) sweet-talk; smooth talk (GB) (colloq)
**baratiner** /baʀatine/ [1] *vtr* (colloq) (a) to
give [sb] the spiel (colloq)
(b) to chat [sb] up (colloq)
(c) to try to persuade
**baratineur, -euse** /baʀatinœʀ, øz/ *nm,f*
(colloq) smooth talker (colloq); (dishonest) liar
**barbant**, ∼e /baʀbã, ãt/ *adj* (colloq) boring
**barbare** /baʀbaʀ/ [1] *adj* barbaric;
barbarian
[2] *nmf* barbarian
**barbarie** /baʀbaʀi/ *nf* barbarity, barbarism
**barbe** /baʀb/ [1] *nf* beard; ∼ naissante
stubble
[2] *excl* (colloq) la ∼! I've had enough!; la ∼
avec leurs consignes! to hell with their
orders! (colloq)
■ ∼ à papa candyfloss (GB), cotton candy (US)
IDIOMS à la ∼ de qn under sb's nose
**barbelé** /baʀbəle/ *nm* barbed wire (GB),
barbwire (US)
**barbiche** /baʀbiʃ/ *nf* (a) goatee (beard)
(b) (on goat) (small) beard
**barbier** /baʀbje/ *nm* barber
**barbiturique** /baʀbityʀik/ *nm* barbiturate
**barboteuse** /baʀbɔtøz/ *nf* romper suit
**barbouiller** /baʀbuje/ [1] [1] *vtr* (a) to
smear (de with)
(b) to daub (de with)
(c) ∼ des toiles to do daubs; ∼ du papier to
write drivel
(d) être barbouillé to feel queasy
[2] **se barbouiller** *v refl* (+ *v être*) se ∼ le
visage de qch to get one's face all covered in
sth
**barbu**, ∼e /baʀby/ *adj* bearded; il est ∼ he
has a beard
**barde** /baʀd/ *nf* thin slice of bacon, bard
**bardé**, ∼e /baʀde/ *adj* covered (de in)
**barème** /baʀɛm/ *nm* scale; ∼ des prix price
list; ∼ d'imposition tax schedule *or* scale

**baril** /baʀil/ *nm* barrel, cask; keg; drum
**barillet** /baʀijɛ/ *nm* cylinder
**bariolé**, ∼e /baʀjole/ *adj* multicoloured
(GB)
**baromètre** /baʀɔmɛtʀ/ *nm* barometer
**baron** /baʀɔ̃/ *nm* baron
**baronne** /baʀɔn/ *nf* baroness
**baroque** /baʀɔk/ *adj* (a) baroque
(b) bizarre
**baroudeur** /baʀudœʀ/ *nm* (a) fighter,
warrior
(b) adventurer
**barque** /baʀk/ *nf* (small) boat
**barquette** /baʀkɛt/ *nf* punnet (GB), basket
(US); tub; container
**barrage** /baʀaʒ/ *nm* (a) dam
(b) roadblock; barricade; faire ∼ à to block
**barre** /baʀ/ *nf* (a) bar, rod
(b) (of chocolate) piece
(c) tiller, helm
(d) band, stripe
(e) stroke; la ∼ du t the cross on the t
(f) (of goal) crossbar; (in high jump) bar
(g) (in ballet practice) barre
(h) (Law) bar; ≈ witness box (GB), witness
stand (US)
(i) mark; franchir la ∼ des 13% to go over
the 13% mark
■ ∼ fixe horizontal bar; ∼ oblique slash
IDIOMS avoir un coup de ∼ (colloq) to feel
drained all of a sudden
**barreau**, *pl* ∼x /baʀo/ *nm* (a) (of cage) bar
(b) rung
(c) (Law) le ∼ the Bar
**barrer** /baʀe/ [1] *vtr* (a) to block ⟨way⟩;
'route barrée' 'road closed'
(b) to cross out
**barrette** /baʀɛt/ *nf* (hair) slide (GB),
barrette (US)
**barreur, -euse** /baʀœʀ, øz/ *nm,f* (gen)
helmsman; (in rowing) cox; avec ∼ coxed; sans
∼ coxless
**barricade** /baʀikad/ *nf* barricade
**barrière** /baʀjɛʀ/ *nf* (a) fence
(b) gate
(c) barrier
**barrique** /baʀik/ *nf* barrel
**barrir** /baʀiʀ/ [3] *vi* ⟨elephant⟩ to trumpet
**bar-tabac**, *pl* **bars-tabac** /baʀtaba/
*nm* café ⟨selling stamps and cigarettes⟩
**baryton** /baʀitɔ̃/ *adj, nm* baritone
**bas, basse¹** /ba, bas/ [1] *adj* low; ⟨room⟩
low-ceilinged; ⟨land⟩ low-lying; le ciel est ∼
the sky is overcast; un enfant en ∼ âge a
very young child; être au plus ∼ ⟨prices⟩ to
have reached rock bottom; les cours sont au
plus ∼ (en Bourse) prices have reached rock
bottom
[2] *adv* (a) low; comment peut-on tomber si
∼! how can one sink so low!
(b) voir plus ∼ see below
(c) quietly; tout ∼ ⟨speak⟩ in a whisper;
⟨sing⟩ softly

**(d) être au plus** ∼ to be extremely weak; to be at one's lowest

**3** *nm inv* **(a)** bottom; **le** ∼ **du visage** the lower part of the face; **les pièces du** ∼ the downstairs rooms
**(b)** stocking

**4** **en bas** *phr* downstairs; down below; at the bottom

■ ∼ **de gamme** *adj* low-quality; *nm* lower end of the market; ∼ **morceaux** (Culin) cheap cuts; **basse saison** low season

IDIOMS **avoir des hauts et des** ∼ to have one's ups and downs; **à** ∼ **les tyrans!** down with tyranny!

**basané**, ∼**e** /bazane/ *adj* swarthy

**bas-côté**, *pl* ∼**s** /bɑkote/ *nm* **(a)** verge (GB), shoulder (US)
**(b)** (side) aisle

**basculant**, ∼**e** /baskylɑ̃, ɑ̃t/ *adj* **pont** ∼ bascule bridge; **camion à benne** ∼**e** dump truck

**bascule** /baskyl/ *nf* **fauteuil à** ∼ rocking chair

**basculer** /baskyle/ [1] **1** *vtr* to transfer ⟨*call*⟩
**2** *vi* **(a)** to topple over; **faire** ∼ to tip up ⟨*skip*⟩; to tip out ⟨*load*⟩; to knock [sb] off balance ⟨*person*⟩
**(b)** (figurative) to change radically

**base** /bɑz/ *nf* **(a)** base; **le riz forme la** ∼ **de leur alimentation** rice is their staple diet
**(b)** basis; **reposer sur des** ∼**s solides** to rest on a firm foundation; **à la** ∼ **de qch** at the root *or* heart of sth; **salaire de** ∼ basic salary; **repartir sur de nouvelles** ∼**s** to make a fresh start
**(c)** (in politics) **la** ∼ the rank and file

■ ∼ **de données** database; ∼ **de lancement** launching site

**baser** /bɑze/ [1] **1** *vtr* to base (**sur** on)
**2** **se baser** *v refl* (+ *v être*) **se** ∼ **sur qch** to go by sth

**bas-fond**, *pl* ∼**s** /bɑfɔ̃/ **1** *nm* **(a)** shallows
**(b)** dip
**2** **bas-fonds** *nm pl* seedy areas

**basilic** /bazilik/ *nm* basil

**basilique** /bazilik/ *nf* basilica

**basket** /baskɛt/ *nm* **(a)** basketball
**(b)** trainer (GB), sneaker (US)
IDIOMS **être bien** *or* **à l'aise dans ses** ∼**s** (colloq) to be very together (colloq)

**basque** /bask/ *adj*, *nm* Basque

**basse²** /bɑs/ **1** *adj* ▶ BAS 1
**2** *nf* (Mus) bass

**basse-cour**, *pl* **basses-cours** /bɑskur/ *nf* **(a)** poultry-yard
**(b)** poultry

**bassement** /bɑsmɑ̃/ *adv* basely

**bassesse** /bɑsɛs/ *nf* **(a)** baseness
**(b)** base act

**bassin** /basɛ̃/ *nm* **(a)** pond; fountain; pool
**(b)** (in geography) basin
**(c)** pelvis
**(d)** bedpan

■ ∼ **houiller** coal field

**bassine** /basin/ *nf* bowl; basin

**bassiste** /basist/ *nmf* bass player

**bastingage** /bastɛ̃gaʒ/ *nm* ship's rail

**bas-ventre**, *pl* ∼**s** /bavɑ̃tʀ/ *nm* lower abdomen

**bât** /bɑ/ *nm* pack-saddle
IDIOMS **c'est là que le** ∼ **blesse** that's where the shoe pinches

**bataille** /batɑj/ **1** *nf* **(a)** battle
**(b)** fight
**2** **en bataille** *phr* ⟨*hair*⟩ dishevelled (GB); ⟨*eyebrows*⟩ bushy

**batailler** /batɑje/ [1] *vi* to fight, to battle

**bataillon** /batɑjɔ̃/ *nm* battalion; **Dupont?, inconnu au** ∼ Dupont?, never heard of him

**bâtard**, ∼**e** /bɑtaʀ, aʀd/ **1** *adj* **(a)** ⟨*dog*⟩ mongrel
**(b)** ⟨*work, style*⟩ hybrid
**(c)** (offensive) ⟨*child*⟩ bastard
**2** *nm,f* **(a)** mongrel
**(b)** (offensive) bastard

**bateau**, *pl* ∼**x** /bato/ **1** *adj inv* hackneyed
**2** *nm* **(a)** boat, ship; ∼ **à voile/moteur/vapeur** sailing/motor/steam boat; **faire du** ∼ to go boating; to go sailing
**(b)** dropped kerb (GB) *or* curb (US)

■ ∼ **amiral** flagship; ∼ **pneumatique** rubber dinghy; ∼ **de sauvetage** lifeboat

**bateau-école**, *pl* **bateaux-écoles** /batoekɔl/ *nm* training ship

**bateau-mouche**, *pl* **bateaux-mouches** /batomuʃ/ *nm: large river boat for sightseeing*

**bateleur**, **-euse** /batlœʀ, øz/ *nm, f* tumbler, juggler

**batelier**, **-ière** /batəlje, ɛʀ/ *nm,f* boatman/boatwoman

**bâti**, ∼**e** /bɑti/ **1** *pp* ▶ BÂTIR
**2** *pp adj* **(a)** built; **terrain** ∼ developed site
**(b)** **un homme bien** ∼ a well-built man

**batifoler** /batifɔle/ [1] *vi* **(a)** to romp about
**(b)** to flirt

**bâtiment** /bɑtimɑ̃/ *nm* **(a)** building
**(b)** building trade
**(c)** ship

**bâtir** /bɑtiʀ/ [3] *vtr* **(a)** to build
**(b)** to tack ⟨*hem*⟩

**bâtisse** /bɑtis/ *nf* (dwelling) house; (structure) building

**bâtisseur**, **-euse** /bɑtisœʀ, øz/ *nm, f* master-builder; (figurative) builder

**bâton** /bɑtɔ̃/ *nm* **(a)** stick
**(b)** vertical stroke
**(c)** (colloq) ten thousand francs

■ ∼ **de rouge** (à lèvres) lipstick
IDIOMS **discuter à** ∼**s rompus** to talk about this and that; **mettre des** ∼**s dans les roues de qn** to put a spoke in sb's wheel

**bâtonnet** /bɑtɔnɛ/ *nm* stick

■ ∼ **de poisson** fish finger (GB), fish stick (US)

**batracien** /batʀasjɛ̃/ *nm* batrachian

**battage** /bataʒ/ nm (colloq) publicity, hype (colloq)

**battant**, ∼**e** /batɑ̃, ɑ̃t/ ⓵ adj le cœur ∼ with a beating heart
⓶ nm,f fighter
⓷ nm porte à deux ∼s double door

**batte** /bat/ nf (Sport) bat (GB), paddle (US)

**battement** /batmɑ̃/ nm (a) beating; beat; fluttering; flutter
(b) break, gap; wait

**batterie** /batRi/ nf (a) percussion section
(b) drum kit
(c) battery
■ ∼ **de cuisine** pots and pans

**batteur** /batœR/ nm (a) percussionist
(b) drummer
(c) whisk

**battre** /batR/ [61] ⓵ vtr (a) (defeat) to beat ⟨opponent⟩; to break ⟨record⟩
(b) (hit) to beat ⟨person, animal, carpet⟩; to thresh ⟨corn⟩
(c) ⟨rain, sea⟩ to beat against
(d) to whisk ⟨eggs⟩; to whip ⟨cream⟩
(e) to shuffle ⟨cards⟩
(f) (Mus) ∼ **la mesure** to beat time
(g) to scour ⟨countryside⟩
⓶ **battre de** v+prep ▶ **des ailes** to flap its wings; ∼ **des cils** to flutter one's eyelashes; ∼ **des mains** to clap (one's hands)
⓷ vi (a) ⟨heart, pulse⟩ to beat
(b) ⟨door⟩ to bang
⓸ **se battre** v refl (+ v être) to fight
IDIOMS ∼ **en retraite devant qch** to retreat before sth; ∼ **son plein** to be in full swing

**battu**, ∼**e** /baty/ ⓵ pp ▶ **BATTRE**
⓶ pp adj ⟨child, wife⟩ battered

**BAU** /beay/ nf: abbr ▶ **BANDE**

**baudet** /bodɛ/ nm (colloq) donkey, ass

**baume** /bom/ nm balm, balsam

**baux** /bo/ nm pl ▶ **BAIL**

**bavard**, ∼**e** /bavaR, aRd/ ⓵ adj
(a) talkative
(b) indiscreet
(c) long-winded
⓶ nm,f (a) chatterbox
(b) blabbermouth (colloq)

**bavardage** /bavaRdaʒ/ nm (a) gossip
(b) idle chatter

**bavarder** /bavaRde/ [1] vi (a) to talk, to chatter
(b) to chat
(c) to gossip (sur about)

**bavarois**, ∼**e** /bavaRwa, az/ ⓵ adj Bavarian
⓶ nm (Culin) Bavarian cream, bavarois

**bave** /bav/ nf dribble; spittle; slaver; slime

**baver** /bave/ [1] vi (a) ⟨person⟩ to dribble; ⟨animal⟩ to slaver
(b) ⟨pen⟩ to leak; ⟨brush⟩ to drip; ⟨ink, paint⟩ to run
IDIOMS **il leur en a fait** ∼ (colloq) he gave them a hard time

**bavette** /bavɛt/ nf (a) bib
(b) (Culin) flank

**bavoir** /bavwaR/ nm bib

**bavure** /bavyR/ nf (a) smudge
(b) blunder

**bazar** /bazaR/ nm (a) general store
(b) (colloq) mess
(c) (colloq) clutter
(d) bazaar

**bazarder** /bazaRde/ [1] vi (colloq) to throw out

**BCBG** /besebeʒe/ adj (colloq) (abbr = **bon chic bon genre**) chic and conservative, Sloaney (GB)

**BCG** /beseʒe/ nm (abbr = **bacille bilié de Calmette et Guérin**) BCG

**BD** /bede/ nf (colloq): abbr ▶ **BANDE**

**béant**, ∼**e** /beɑ̃, ɑ̃t/ adj gaping

**béat**, ∼**e** /bea, at/ adj ⟨person⟩ blissfully happy; ⟨smile⟩ blissful, beatific

**beau** (**bel** before vowel or mute h), **belle**[1], mpl ∼**x** /bo, bɛl/ ⓵ adj
(a) beautiful; handsome; **se faire** ∼ to do oneself up; **ce n'est pas** ∼ **à voir** (colloq)! it's not a pretty sight!
(b) good; fine; nice; lovely; **un** ∼ **geste** a noble gesture; **fais de** ∼**x rêves!** sweet dreams!; **au** ∼ **milieu de** right in the middle of; **c'est bien** ∼ **tout ça, mais...** (colloq) that's all well and good, but...
(c) ⟨sum⟩ tidy; ⟨salary⟩ very nice
⓶ nm **qu'est-ce que tu as fait de** ∼? done anything interesting?
⓷ **avoir beau** phr **j'ai** ∼ **essayer, je n'y arrive pas** it's no good my trying, I can't do it
⓸ **bel et bien** phr (a) well and truly
(b) definitely
■ ∼ **fixe** fine weather; ∼**x jours** fine weather; palmy days, good days
IDIOMS **faire le** ∼ ⟨dog⟩ to sit up and beg; **c'est du** ∼! (colloq) (ironic) lovely!

**beaucoup** /boku/ ⓵ adv (a) a lot; much; **c'est** ∼ **dire** that's going a bit far; **c'est déjà** ∼ **qu'elle soit venue** it's already quite something that she came; ∼ **moins de livres** far fewer books; **c'est** ∼ **trop** it's far too much; ∼ **trop longtemps** far too long, much too long
(b) ∼ **de** a lot of, a great deal of; much; many; **il ne reste plus** ∼ **de pain** there isn't much bread left; **avec** ∼ **de soin** very carefully; ∼ **d'entre eux** many of them
⓶ **de beaucoup** phr by far
⓷ **pour beaucoup** phr **être pour** ∼ **dans** to have a lot to do with

**beauf** /bof/ nm (colloq) (a) (abbr = **beau-frère**) brother-in-law
(b) (yokel) boor (colloq)

**beau-fils**, pl **beaux-fils** /bofis/ nm
(a) son-in-law
(b) stepson

**beau-frère**, pl **beaux-frères** /bofRɛR/ nm brother-in-law

**beau-père**, pl **beaux-pères** /bopɛR/ nm (a) father-in-law
(b) stepfather

**beauté** /bote/ *nf* beauty; **se faire une ~** to do oneself up; **finir en ~** to end with a flourish

**beaux-arts** /bozaʀ/ *nm pl* fine arts and architecture

**bébé** /bebe/ *nm* baby

**bec** /bɛk/ *nm* **(a)** beak; **donner des coups de ~** to peck; **il a toujours la cigarette au ~** (colloq) he's always got a cigarette stuck in his mouth
**(b)** (of jug) lip; (of teapot) spout; (of wind instrument) mouthpiece; **~ verseur** pourer(-spout)
**IDIOMS clouer le ~ à qn** (colloq) to shut sb up (colloq); **tomber sur un ~** (colloq) to come across a snag

**bécane** /bekan/ *nf* (colloq) bike, bicycle

**bécasse** /bekas/ *nf* woodcock

**bec-de-lièvre**, *pl* **becs-de-lièvre** /bɛkdəljɛvʀ/ *nm* harelip

**bêche** /bɛʃ/ *nf* **(a)** spade
**(b)** garden fork

**bêcher** /beʃe/ [1] *vtr* to dig (with a spade)

**becquée** /beke/ *nf* beakful; **donner la ~ à** to feed ⟨*fledgling*⟩

**bedaine** /bədɛn/ *nf* (colloq) paunch

**bedonnant, ~e** /bədɔnɑ̃, ɑ̃t/ *adj* (colloq) ⟨*person*⟩ paunchy

**bée** /be/ *adj f* **être bouche ~** to stand open-mouthed *or* gaping

**beffroi** /befʀwa/ *nm* belfry

**bégaiement** /begɛmɑ̃/ *nm* stammer, stutter

**bégayer** /begeje/ [21] *vtr, vi* to stammer

**bègue** /bɛg/ *adj* **être ~** to stammer

**béguin** /begɛ̃/ *nm* (colloq) **avoir le ~ pour qn** to have a crush on sb

**beige** /bɛʒ/ *adj, nm* beige

**beignet** /bɛɲɛ/ *nm* **(a)** fritter
**(b)** doughnut, donut (US) (colloq)

**bel** *adj m* ▶ BEAU 1, 4

**bêler** /bele/ [1] *vi* to bleat

**belette** /bəlɛt/ *nf* weasel

**belge** /bɛlʒ/ *adj* Belgian

**Belgique** /bɛlʒik/ *pr nf* Belgium

**bélier** /belje/ *nm* **(a)** ram
**(b)** battering ram

**Bélier** /belje/ *pr nm* Aries

**belle²** /bɛl/ **1** *adj f* ▶ BEAU 1
**2** *nf* decider, deciding game
**3** **de plus belle** *phr* with renewed vigour (GB)
**IDIOMS (se) faire la ~** (colloq) to do a bunk (GB) (colloq), to take a powder (US) (colloq); **en faire voir de ~s à qn** (colloq) to give sb a hard time

**belle-famille**, *pl* **belles-familles** /bɛlfamij/ *nf* in-laws

**belle-fille**, *pl* **belles-filles** /bɛlfij/ *nf*
**(a)** daughter-in-law
**(b)** stepdaughter

**belle-mère**, *pl* **belles-mères** /bɛlmɛʀ/ *nf* **(a)** mother-in-law
**(b)** stepmother

**belle-sœur**, *pl* **belles-sœurs** /bɛlsœʀ/ *nf* sister-in-law

**belligérant** /beliʒeʀɑ̃/ *nm* **(a)** belligerent, warring party
**(b)** combatant

**belliqueux, -euse** /belikø, øz/ *adj* aggressive

**bémol** /bemɔl/ *nm* (Mus) flat; **mi ~** E flat

**bénédiction** /benediksjɔ̃/ *nf* blessing

**bénéfice** /benefis/ *nm* **(a)** profit
**(b)** benefit, beneficial effect
**(c)** advantage

**bénéficiaire** /benefisjɛʀ/ *nmf* beneficiary

**bénéficier** /benefisje/ [2] *v+prep* **~ de** to receive ⟨*help*⟩; to enjoy ⟨*immunity*⟩; to get ⟨*special treatment*⟩

**bénéfique** /benefik/ *adj* beneficial

**Bénélux** /benelyks/ *pr nm* Benelux

**benêt** /bənɛ/ *nm* half-wit

**bénévolat** /benevɔla/ *nm* voluntary work

**bénévole** /benevɔl/ **1** *adj* voluntary
**2** *nmf* voluntary worker

**bénévolement** /benevɔlmɑ̃/ *adv* on a voluntary basis

**bénin, -igne** /benɛ̃, iɲ/ *adj* minor; benign

**béni-oui-oui** /beniwiwi/ *nm inv* (colloq) yes-man

**bénir** /beniʀ/ [3] *vtr* to bless

**bénit, ~e** /beni, it/ *adj* blessed; holy

**bénitier** /benitje/ *nm* holy water font

**benjamin, ~e** /bɛ̃ʒamɛ̃, in/ *nm,f* youngest child

**benne** /bɛn/ *nf* **(a)** skip (GB), dumpster® (US)
**(b)** (colliery) wagon
**(c)** (cable) car

**BEPC** /beapese, bɛps/ *nm* (*abbr* = **Brevet d'études du premier cycle**) *former examination at the end of the first stage of secondary education*

**béquille** /bekij/ *nf* **(a)** crutch
**(b)** kickstand

**bercail** /bɛʀkaj/ *nm* (colloq) home

**berceau**, *pl* **~x** /bɛʀso/ *nm* cradle

**bercer** /bɛʀse/ [12] **1** *vtr* to rock ⟨*baby*⟩
**2** **se bercer** *v refl* (+ *v être*) **se ~ d'illusions** to delude oneself

**berceuse** /bɛʀsøz/ *nf* lullaby

**béret** /beʀe/ *nm* beret

**bergamote** /bɛʀgamɔt/ *nf* bergamot

**berge** /bɛʀʒ/ *nf* (of river, canal) bank

**berger, -ère** /bɛʀʒe, ɛʀ/ *nm,f* shepherd/shepherdess
■ **~ allemand** Alsatian (GB), German shepherd

**bergerie** /bɛʀʒəʀi/ *nf* sheepfold

**berlue** /bɛʀly/ *nf* (colloq) **avoir la ~** to be seeing things

**bermuda** /bɛʀmyda/ *nm* bermudas

**Bermudes** /bɛʀmyd/ *pr nf pl* **les ~s** Bermuda

**berner** /bɛʀne/ [1] *vtr* to fool, to deceive
**besace** /bəzas/ *nf* pouch
**besogne** /bəzɔɲ/ *nf* job
**besoin** /bəzwɛ̃/ **1** *nm* need (de for; de faire to do); **avoir ~ de** to need; **répondre à un ~** to meet a need; **au ~** if need be; **pour les ~s de la cause** for the good of the cause; **être dans le ~** to be in need
**2 besoins** *nm pl* needs; **subvenir aux ~s de qn** to provide for sb
IDIOMS **faire ses ~s** (colloq) ⟨*person*⟩ to relieve oneself; ⟨*animal*⟩ to do its business
**bestial, ~e,** *mpl* **-iaux** /bɛstjal, o/ *adj* brutish, bestial
**bestiaux** /bɛstjo/ *nm pl* **(a)** livestock **(b)** cattle
**bestiole** /bɛstjɔl/ *nf* (colloq) **(a)** creepy-crawly (colloq), bug **(b)** animal
**bétail** /betaj/ *nm* livestock; cattle
**bête** /bɛt/ **1** *adj* stupid, silly; **je suis restée toute ~** I was dumbfounded
**2** *nf* creature; animal
■ **~ à bon Dieu** ladybird (GB), ladybug (US); **~ noire** bête noire (GB), pet hate
IDIOMS **il est ~ comme ses pieds** (colloq) he's as dumb as can be; **chercher la petite ~** (colloq) to nit-pick; **reprendre du poil de la ~** (colloq) to perk up; **travailler comme une ~** (colloq) to work like crazy (colloq)
**bêtement** /bɛtmɑ̃/ *adv* stupidly; **il suffit (tout) ~ de faire** you simply need to do
**bêtise** /betiz/ *nf* **la ~** stupidity; **faire une ~** to do something stupid; **dire des ~s** to talk nonsense; **surtout pas de ~s!** be good now! (colloq)
**bêtisier** /betizje/ *nm* collection of howlers (colloq)
**béton** /betɔ̃/ *nm* concrete; (figurative) watertight
■ **~ armé** reinforced concrete
**bétonnière** /betɔnjɛʀ/ *nf* concrete mixer
**betterave** /bɛtʀav/ *nf* beet; **~ rouge** beetroot; **~ sucrière** sugar beet
**beugler** /bøgle/ [1] *vi* to moo; to bellow
**beur** /bœʀ/ *nmf* (colloq) second-generation North African (*living in France*)
**beurette** /bœʀɛt/ *nf* second-generation North African girl
**beurre** /bœʀ/ *nm* butter; **~ doux** unsalted butter
■ **~ d'escargot** garlic and parsley butter; **~ noir** black butter; **œil au ~ noir** (colloq) black eye
IDIOMS **faire son ~** (colloq) to make a packet (colloq); **compter pour du ~** (colloq) to count for nothing; **vouloir le ~ et l'argent du ~** (colloq) to want to have one's cake and eat it
**beurré, ~e** /bœʀe/ *adj* (colloq) drunk, plastered (colloq)
**beurrer** /bœʀe/ [1] *vtr* to butter
**beurrier** /bœʀje/ *nm* butter dish
**beuverie** /bœvʀi/ *nf* drinking session
**biais** /bjɛ/ **1** *nm inv* **(a)** (of material) bias

**(b)** way; **par le ~ de qn** through sb; **par le ~ de qch** by means of sth
**2 de biais, en biais** *phr* **couper une étoffe en ~** to cut material on the cross
**biaiser** /bjɛze/ [1] *vi* to hedge
**bibelot** /biblo/ *nm* ornament
**biberon** /bibʀɔ̃/ *nm* (baby's) bottle (GB), (nursing) bottle (US)
**bible** /bibl/ *nf* bible; **la Bible** the Bible
**bibliographie** /biblijɔgʀafi/ *nf* bibliography
**bibliographique** /biblijɔgʀafik/ *adj* bibliographical
**bibliothécaire** /biblijɔtekɛʀ/ *nmf* librarian
**bibliothèque** /biblijɔtɛk/ *nf* **(a)** library **(b)** bookcase
**biblique** /biblik/ *adj* biblical
**bic®** /bik/ *nm* biro®
**bicarbonate** /bikaʀbɔnat/ *nm* bicarbonate
**bicentenaire** /bisɑ̃tnɛʀ/ *nm* bicentenary, bicentennial
**biceps** /bisɛps/ *nm inv* biceps
**biche** /biʃ/ *nf* doe
**bichonner** /biʃɔne/ [1] *vtr* (colloq) to pamper
**bicolore** /bikɔlɔʀ/ *adj* ⟨*flag*⟩ two-coloured (GB); ⟨*fabric*⟩ two-tone
**bicoque** /bikɔk/ *nf* (colloq) dump (colloq), house
**bicyclette** /bisiklɛt/ *nf* **(a)** bicycle **(b)** cycling
**bidasse** /bidas/ *nm* (colloq) soldier
**bidet** /bidɛ/ *nm* bidet
**bidon** /bidɔ̃/ **1** *adj inv* (colloq) bogus; phoney (colloq)
**2** *nm* **(a)** can; drum; flask **(b)** (colloq) stomach, paunch **(c)** (colloq) **c'est du ~** it is a load of hogwash (colloq)
**bidonner: se bidonner** /bidɔne/ [1] *v refl* (+ *v être*) (colloq) to laugh, to fall about (colloq)
**bidonville** /bidɔ̃vil/ *nm* shanty town
**bidule** /bidyl/ *nm* (colloq) thingy (GB) (colloq), thingamajig (colloq)
**bielle** /bjɛl/ *nf* connecting rod
**bien** /bjɛ̃/ **1** *adj inv* **(a)** **être ~ dans un rôle** to be good in a part; **être ~ de sa personne** to be good-looking; **ce n'est pas ~ de mentir** it's not nice to lie; **ça fait ~ d'aller à l'opéra** (colloq) it's the done thing to go to the opera **(b)** well; **ne pas se sentir ~** not to feel well; **t'es pas ~** (colloq)**!** you're out of your mind (colloq)**! (c) je suis ~ dans ces bottes** these boots are comfortable; **on est ~ au soleil!** isn't it nice in the sun! **(d)** (colloq) **un quartier ~** a nice district; **des gens ~** respectable people
**2** *adv* **(a)** well; ⟨*function*⟩ properly; ⟨*interpret*⟩ correctly; **~ joué!** well done!; **aller ~** ⟨*person*⟩ to be well; ⟨*business*⟩ to go well;

Oxford
Univ-

**ni** ~ **ni mal** so-so; **j'ai cru** ~ **faire** I thought I was doing the right thing; **c'est** ~ **fait pour elle!** it serves her right!; **tu ferais** ~ **d'y aller** it would be a good idea for you to go
**(b)** ⟨*mix*⟩ thoroughly; ⟨*fill*⟩ completely; ⟨*listen*⟩ carefully
**(c)** ⟨*presented*⟩ well; ⟨*furnished*⟩ tastefully; ⟨*live*⟩ comfortably; **femme** ~ **faite** shapely woman; **aller** ~ **ensemble** to go well together; **aller** ~ **à qn** to suit sb; ~ **prendre une remarque** to take a remark in good part
**(d)** ⟨*nice, sad*⟩ very; ⟨*fear, enjoy*⟩ very much; ⟨*simple, true*⟩ quite; **il y a** ~ **longtemps** a very long time ago; **merci** ~ thank you very much; ~ **rire** to have a good laugh; **c'est** ~ **compris?** is that clear?; ~ **au contraire** on the contrary; ~ **mieux** much *or* far better; ~ **sûr** of course; ~ **entendu** *or* **évidemment** naturally; **il y a** ~ **des années** a good many years ago; ~ **des fois** often, many a time
**(e) je veux** ~ **t'aider** I don't mind helping you; **j'aimerais** ~ **essayer** I would love to try
**(f) il faut** ~ **que ça finisse** it has just got to come to an end
**(g) ça montre** ~ **que** it just goes to show that; **je sais** ~ **que** I know that; **insiste** ~ make sure you insist; **on verra** ~ well, we'll see; **il le fait** ~ **lui, pourquoi pas moi?** if he can do it, why can't I?; **tu peux très** ~ **le faire toi-même** you can easily do it yourself; **que peut-il** ~ **faire à Paris?** what on earth can he be doing in Paris?
**(h)** definitely; **c'est** ~ **ce qu'il a dit** that's exactly what he said; **tu as** ~ **pris les clés?** are you sure you've got the keys?; **c'est** ~ **de lui!** it's just like him!; **c'est** ~ **le moment!** (ironic) great timing!; **c'est** ~ **le moment de partir!** (ironic) what a time to leave!
**(i)** at least; **elle a** ~ **40 ans** she's at least 40
**3** *nm* **(a)** good; **le** ~ **et le mal** good and evil; **ça fait du** ~ **aux enfants** it's good for the children; **vouloir le** ~ **de qn** to have sb's best interests at heart; **vouloir du** ~ **à qn** to wish sb well; **dire du** ~/**le plus grand** ~ **de qn** to speak well/very highly of sb
**(b)** possession; **des** ~**s considérables** substantial assets
**4 bien que** *phr* although
■ ~**s de consommation** consumer goods; ~**s immobiliers** real estate; ~**s mobiliers** personal property; ~**s personnels** private property

**bien-être** /bjɛ̃nɛtʀ/ *nm* **(a)** well-being
**(b)** welfare
**(c)** comforts

**bienfaisance** /bjɛ̃fəzɑ̃s/ *nf* charity

**bienfaisant**, ~**e** /bjɛ̃fəzɑ̃, ɑ̃t/ *adj* beneficial, beneficent

**bienfait** /bjɛ̃fɛ/ *nm* **(a)** kind deed; ~ **du ciel** godsend
**(b)** beneficial effect

**bienfaiteur, -trice** /bjɛ̃fɛtœʀ, tʀis/ *nm,f* benefactor/benefactress

**bien-fondé** /bjɛ̃fɔ̃de/ *nm* (of idea) validity; (of claim) legitimacy

**bien-pensant**, ~**e**, *mpl* ~**s** /bjɛ̃pɑ̃sɑ̃, ɑ̃t/ *adj* **(a)** right-thinking
**(b)** self-righteous

**bienséance** /bjɛ̃seɑ̃s/ *nf* propriety; **les règles de la** ~ the rules of polite society

**bientôt** /bjɛ̃to/ *adv* soon; **à** ~ see you so

**bienveillant**, ~**e** /bjɛ̃vɛjɑ̃, ɑ̃t/ *adj* benevolent

**bienvenu**, ~**e**[1] /bjɛ̃vəny/ *adj* w

**bienvenue**[2] /bjɛ̃vəny/ *nf* wel

**bière** /bjɛʀ/ *nf* **(a)** beer; ~ (
draught (GB) *or* draft (US
**(b)** coffin, casket (US
■ ~ **blonde** lage
brown a

b...

**(c)** (in care...

**bigame** /bigam/ *adj* bigamous

**bigamie** /bigami/ *nf* bigamy

**bigarré**, ~**e** /bigaʀe/ *adj* **(a)** multicoloured (GB)
**(b)** ⟨*crowd*⟩ colourful (GB)

**bigleux, -euse** /biglø, øz/ *adj* (pej) (colloq) poor-sighted; **complètement** ~ as blind as a bat (colloq)

**bigorneau**, *pl* ~**x** /bigɔʀno/ *nm* winkle

**bigot**, ~**e** /bigo, ɔt/ *nm,f* religious zealot

**bigoudi** /bigudi/ *nm* roller, curler

**bijou**, *pl* ~**x** /biʒu/ *nm* **(a)** piece of jewellery (GB) *or* jewelry (US)
**(b)** jewel; (figurative) gem

**bijouterie** /biʒutʀi/ *nf* (shop) jeweller's (GB), jewelry store (US)

**bilan** /bilɑ̃/ *nm* **(a)** balance sheet; **déposer son** ~ to file a petition in bankruptcy
**(b)** outcome
**(c)** (after disaster) toll
**(d)** assessment; ~ **de santé** check-up
**(e)** report

**bilatéral**, ~**e**, *mpl* **-aux** /bilateʀal, o/ *adj* bilateral

**bile** /bil/ *nf* bile
**IDIOMS se faire de la** ~ (colloq) to worry

**bilingue** /bilɛ̃g/ *adj* bilingual

**billard** /bijaʀ/ *nm* **(a)** billiards
**(b)** billiard table
■ ~ **américain** pool; ~ **anglais** snooker
**IDIOMS passer sur le** ~ (colloq) to have an operation

**bille** /bij/ *nf* **(a)** marble
**(b)** (billiard) ball

**billet** /bijɛ/ *nm* **(a)** (bank)note, bill (US)
**(b)** ticket
■ ~ **doux** love letter

**billetterie** /bijɛtʀi/ *nf* cash dispenser

**billion** /biljɔ̃/ *nm* billion (GB), trillion (US)

**bimensuel** /bimɑ̃sɥɛl/ *nm* fortnightly magazine (GB), semimonthly (US)

**bimoteur** /bimɔtœʀ/ *nm* twin-engined plane

**binaire** /binɛʀ/ *adj* binary

**biniou** /binju/ *nm* Breton bagpipes

**binocles** /binɔkl/ *nf pl* (colloq) specs (colloq), glasses

**bio** /bjo/ ☐1 *adj inv* (natural) **aliments** ~ health foods; **produits** ~ organic produce; **yaourt** ~ bio yoghurt
☐2 *nf* (colloq) biography

**biochimie** /bjoʃimi/ *nf* biochemistry

**biodégradable** /bjodegʀadabl/ *adj* biodegradable

**biographie** /bjɔgʀafi/ *nf* biography

**biologie** /bjɔlɔʒi/ *nf* biology

**biophysique** /bjofisik/ *nf* biophysics

**bip** /bip/ *nm* beep; ~ **sonore** tone

**bipède** /bipɛd/ *nm* biped

**biplace** /biplas/ *adj, nm* two-seater

**bique** /bik/ *nf* (colloq) **une vieille** ~ an old bag (colloq)

**biréacteur** /biʀeaktœʀ/ *nm* twin-engined jet

**bis¹** /bis/ *adv* (a) (in address) bis; **33** ~ **rue Juliette Lamber** 33 bis rue Juliette Lamber
(b) (at show, concert) encore

**bis²**, ~**e¹** /bi, biz/ *adj* greyish (GB) *or* grayish (US) brown

**bisannuel, -elle** /bizanɥɛl/ *adj* biennial

**biscornu, ~e** /biskɔʀny/ *adj* quirky

**biscotte** /biskɔt/ *nf* continental toast

**biscuit** /biskɥi/ *nm* biscuit (GB), cookie (US)
∎ ~ **à la cuillère** sponge finger (GB), ladyfinger (US); ~ **salé** cracker

**bise²** /biz/ ☐1 *adj f* ▶ BIS²
☐2 *nf* (a) (colloq) kiss; **faire la** ~ **à qn** to kiss sb on the cheeks
(b) North wind

**biseau, pl ~x** /bizo/ *nm* (a) bevel (edge); **tailler en** ~ to bevel
(b) (tool) bevel

**bison** /bizɔ̃/ *nm* (a) bison
(b) buffalo

**bissextile** /bisɛkstil/ *adj* **année** ~ leap year

**bistouri** /bisturi/ *nm* (Med) bistoury

**bistro(t)** /bistʀo/ *nm* (colloq) bistro, café

**bit** /bit/ *nm* bit

**BIT** /beit/ *nm* (*abbr* = **Bureau international du travail**) ILO

**bitume** /bitym/ *nm* (on road) asphalt

**bivouac** /bivwak/ *nm* bivouac

**bizarre** /bizaʀ/ *adj* odd, strange

**blafard, ~e** /blafaʀ, aʀd/ *adj* pale

**blague** /blag/ *nf* (colloq) (a) joke; ~ **à part** seriously
(b) fib (colloq)
(c) trick; **faire une** ~ **à qn** to play a trick on sb

**blaguer** /blage/ [1] *vi* (colloq) to joke

**blagueur, -euse** /blagœʀ, øz/ *nm,f* (colloq) joker

**blaireau, pl ~x** /blɛʀo/ *nm* (a) badger
(b) shaving brush

**blâmer** /blɑme/ [1] *vtr* to criticize; to blame

**blanc, blanche¹** /blɑ̃, blɑ̃ʃ/ ☐1 *adj* (gen) white; ⟨*page*⟩ blank; ~ **cassé** off-white
☐2 *nm* (a) white; **habillé/peint en** ~ dressed in/painted white
(b) household linen
(c) white meat
(d) (egg) white
(e) blank; gap; **j'ai eu un** ~ my mind went blank
(f) (colloq) correction fluid
(g) **tirer à** ~ to fire blanks
☐3 **blancs** *nm pl* (in chess, draughts) white

**Blanc, Blanche** /blɑ̃, blɑ̃ʃ/ *nm,f* white man/woman

**blanc-bec, pl blancs-becs** /blɑ̃bɛk/ *nm* greenhorn

**blanchâtre** /blɑ̃ʃɑtʀ/ *adj* whitish

**blanche²** /blɑ̃ʃ/ ☐1 *adj f* ▶ BLANC 1
☐2 *nf* (Mus) minim (GB), half note (US)

**blanchiment** /blɑ̃ʃimɑ̃/ *nm* (a) (of money) laundering
(b) (of fabric, paper, pulp) bleaching

**blanchir** /blɑ̃ʃiʀ/ [3] ☐1 *vtr* (a) to whiten ⟨*shoes*⟩
(b) to clear ⟨*name*⟩
(c) to launder ⟨*money*⟩
☐2 *vi* (a) to turn grey (GB) *or* gray (US)
(b) **faire** ~ to blanch ⟨*vegetables*⟩
☐3 **se blanchir** *v refl* (+ *v être*) to clear oneself

**blanchisserie** /blɑ̃ʃisʀi/ *nf* laundry

**blanchisseur** /blɑ̃ʃisœʀ/ *nm* (shop) laundry

**blanchisseuse** /blɑ̃ʃisøz/ *nf* laundress

**blasé, ~e** /blaze/ *adj* blasé

**blason** /blazɔ̃/ *nm* coat of arms
**IDIOMS redorer son** ~ to restore one's reputation

**blasphème** /blasfɛm/ *nm* blasphemy

**blasphémer** /blasfeme/ [14] *vi* to blaspheme

**blatte** /blat/ *nf* cockroach

**blé** /ble/ *nm* wheat; ~ **noir** buckwheat

**bled** /blɛd/ *nm* (colloq) village

**blême** /blɛm/ *adj* pale

**blessant, ~e** /blesɑ̃, ɑ̃t/ *adj* ⟨*remark*⟩ cutting

**blessé, ~e** /blese/ *nm,f* injured *or* wounded man/woman; casualty

**blesser** /blese/ [1] ☐1 *vtr* (a) to injure, to hurt; to wound; **il a été blessé à la tête** he sustained head injuries
(b) to hurt ⟨*person, feelings*⟩; to wound ⟨*pride*⟩
☐2 **se blesser** *v refl* (+ *v être*) to hurt oneself

**blessure** /blesyʀ/ *nf* injury; wound

**blet, blette** /blɛ, blɛt/ *adj* overripe

**bleu**, ~**e** /blø/ [1] adj (a) blue
(b) ⟨steak⟩ very rare
[2] nm (a) blue
(b) bruise
(c) ~ **de travail** overalls
(d) blue cheese
IDIOMS avoir une peur ~**e de qch** to be
scared stiff (colloq) of sth

**bleuâtre** /bløɑtʀ/ adj bluish

**bleuet** /bløɛ/ nm (Bot) cornflower

**blindé**, ~**e** /blɛ̃de/ adj armoured (GB)

**blinder** /blɛ̃de/ [1] vtr to put security
fittings on ⟨door⟩; to armour-plate (GB) ⟨car⟩

**blizzard** /blizaʀ/ nm blizzard

**bloc** /blɔk/ [1] nm (a) block; **faire ~ avec/
contre qn** to side with/unite against sb
(b) notepad; ~ **de papier à lettres** writing
pad
(c) (Comput) block
[2] **à bloc** phr ⟨screw⟩ tightly; ⟨inflate⟩ fully
[3] **en bloc** phr ⟨deny⟩ outright
■ ~ **opératoire** surgical unit

**blocage** /blɔkaʒ/ nm blocking; ~ **des
salaires** wage freeze

**blockhaus** /blɔkos/ nm inv blockhouse

**bloc-notes**, pl **blocs-notes** /blɔknɔt/
nm notepad

**blocus** /blɔkys/ nm inv blockade

**blond**, ~**e** /blɔ̃, ɔ̃d/ [1] adj (a) blonde (GB),
blond (US)
(b) ⟨wheat⟩ golden; ⟨tobacco⟩ light
[2] nm,f (female) blonde (GB), blond (US);
(male) blond

**bloqué**, ~**e** /blɔke/ [1] pp ▶ BLOQUER
[2] pp adj (a) blocked
(b) ⟨mechanism, door⟩ jammed; **elle/la
voiture est** ~**e** she/the car is stuck
(c) **être** ~ ⟨activity⟩ to be at a standstill;
⟨situation⟩ to be deadlocked

**bloquer** /blɔke/ [1] [1] vtr (a) to block
⟨road⟩
(b) to lock ⟨steering wheel⟩; to wedge ⟨door⟩;
(accidentally) to jam ⟨mechanism, door⟩
(c) to stop ⟨vehicle, traveller⟩
(d) to freeze ⟨prices⟩
(e) to stop ⟨project⟩
(f) to lump [sth] together ⟨days⟩
[2] **se bloquer** v refl (+ v être) (a) ⟨brakes,
door⟩ to jam; ⟨wheel⟩ to lock
(b) to retreat

**blottir: se blottir** /blɔtiʀ/ [3] v refl
(+ v être) **se** ~ **contre** to huddle up against;
to snuggle up against

**blouse** /bluz/ nf (a) overall
(b) coat; ~ **blanche** white coat
(c) blouse

**blouson** /bluzɔ̃/ nm (a) blouson;
~ **d'aviateur** bomber jacket
(b) ~ **noir** ≈ rocker

**blue-jean**, pl ~**s** /bludʒin/ nm jeans

**bluffer** /blœfe/ [1] vtr, vi (colloq) to bluff

**BN** /beɛn/ nf (abbr = **Bibliothèque
nationale**) national library in Paris

**boa** /bɔa/ nm boa

**bobard** /bɔbaʀ/ nm (colloq) fib (colloq), tall
story

**bobine** /bɔbin/ nf (of film, cable) reel

**bobo** /bobo/ nm (colloq) (baby talk) (a) pain
(b) scratch

**bocage** /bɔkaʒ/ nm hedged farmland

**bocal**, pl **-aux** /bɔkal, o/ nm jar; bowl

**bœuf**, pl **bœ** /bœf, pl bø/ nm (a) bullock (GB), steer
(US)
(b) ox
(c) beef
IDIOMS faire un effet ~ (colloq) to make a
fantastic (colloq) impression

**bof** /bɔf/ excl (colloq) 'tu préfères la mer ou la
montagne?'—'~!' 'which do you prefer, the
sea or the mountains?'—'I don't mind'

**bogue** /bɔg/ nf or m (Comput) bug; ~ **de l'an
2000** millennium bug

**bohème** /bɔɛm/ [1] adj bohemian
[2] nf la ~ bohemia

**bohémien**, **-ienne** /bɔemjɛ̃, ɛn/ nm,f
Romany, gypsy

**boire** /bwaʀ/ [70] [1] vtr (a) to drink
(b) ⟨paper⟩ to soak up
[2] **se boire** v refl (+ v être) **ce vin se boit
frais** this wine should be drunk chilled
IDIOMS ~ **comme un trou** (colloq) to drink
like a fish (colloq); **il y a à** ~ **et à manger
dans leur théorie** there's both good and bad
in their theory

**bois** /bwa/ [1] nm inv wood; **en** ~ ⟨chair⟩
wooden; ⟨cheque⟩ dud (colloq); ~ **mort**
firewood
[2] nm pl (a) antlers
(b) woodwind section
IDIOMS être de ~ to be insensitive; **il va voir
de quel** ~ **je me chauffe** I'll show him

**boisé**, ~**e** /bwaze/ adj wooded

**boiserie** /bwazʀi/ nf ~(**s**) panelling (GB)

**boisson** /bwasɔ̃/ nf drink

**boîte** /bwat/ nf (a) (container) box
(b) (for food) tin (GB), can; **petits pois en** ~
canned peas
(c) (club) ~ (**de nuit**) nightclub
(d) (colloq) (company) firm; office
■ ~ **crânienne** cranium; ~ **à gants** glove
compartment; ~ **à** or **aux lettres** post box
(GB), mailbox (US); ~ **à** or **aux lettres
électronique** (Comput) electronic mailbox; ~ **à
musique** musical box (GB), music box (US);
~ **à outils** toolbox; ~ **postale, BP** PO Box;
~ **de vitesses** gearbox
IDIOMS mettre qn en ~ (colloq) to tease sb

**boiter** /bwate/ [1] vi to limp

**boiteux**, **-euse** /bwatø, øz/ [1] adj
(a) lame
(b) ⟨chair⟩ wobbly
(c) ⟨argument, alliance⟩ shaky
[2] nm,f lame person

**boîtier** /bwatje/ nm (gen) case; (of camera)
body

**boitiller** /bwatije/ [1] vi to limp slightly

**bol** /bɔl/ nm (a) bowl; ~ **d'air** breath of
fresh air ····⦂

**(b)** (colloq) luck; **coup de** ~ stroke of luck

**bolée** /bɔle/ *nf* ~ **de cidre** bowl of cider

**bolide** /bɔlid/ *nm* high-powered car

**bombage** /bɔ̃baʒ/ *nm* (action) graffiti spraying; (result) (sprayed) graffiti

**bombardement** /bɔ̃baʀdəmɑ̃/ *nm* (Mil) bombardment; bombing; shelling; ~ **aérien** air raid

**bombarder** /bɔ̃baʀde/ [1] *vtr* **(a)** to bombard; to bomb; to shell
**(b)** ~ **qn de questions** to bombard sb with questions
**(c)** (colloq) ~ **qn à un poste** to catapult sb into a job

**bombardier** /bɔ̃baʀdje/ *nm* **(a)** bomber
**(b)** bombardier

**bombe** /bɔ̃b/ *nf* **(a)** bomb; **faire l'effet d'une** ~ to come as a bombshell
**(b)** ~ **(aérosol)** spray
**(c)** riding hat
IDIOMS **partir à toute** ~ (colloq) to rush off

**bombé, ~e** /bɔ̃be/ *adj* **(a)** ⟨forehead⟩ domed; ⟨shape⟩ rounded
**(b)** ⟨road⟩ cambered

**bomber** /bɔ̃be/ [1] ① *vtr* ~ **le torse** to thrust out one's chest; (figurative) to swell with pride
② *vi* **(a)** ⟨plank⟩ to bulge out
**(b)** (colloq) to belt along (colloq)

**bon, bonne¹** /bɔ̃, bɔn/ ① *adj* **(a)** good; **prends un** ~ pull take a warm jumper; **elle est (bien) bonne** (colloq)! that's a good one!; (indignantly) I like that!; **voilà une bonne chose de faite!** that's that out of the way!; **nous sommes ~s derniers** we're well and truly last; **il n'est pas** ~ **à grand-chose** he's pretty useless; **il serait** ~ **qu'elle le sache** she ought to know; **à quoi** ~? what's the point?
**(b)** ⟨person, words⟩ kind; ⟨smile⟩ nice; **avoir** ~ **cœur** to be good-hearted
**(c)** ⟨time, answer⟩ right; **c'est** ~, **vous pouvez y aller** it's OK, you can go
**(d)** ⟨ticket⟩ valid; **tu es** ~ **pour la vaisselle, ce soir!** you're in line for the dishes tonight!
**(e)** **bonne nuit/chance** good night/luck
② *nm,f* **les ~s et les méchants** good people and bad people; (in films) the good guys and the bad guys (colloq)
③ *nm* **(a)** coupon; voucher
**(b)** **il y a du** ~ **dans cet article** there are some good things in this article
④ *adv* **ça sent** ~! that smells good!; **il fait** ~ the weather's mild; **il fait** ~ **dans ta chambre** it's nice and warm in your room
⑤ **pour de bon** *phr* **(a)** really; **tu dis ça pour de** ~? are you serious?
**(b)** for good
■ ~ **de commande** order form; ~ **enfant** good-natured; ~ **de garantie** guarantee slip; ~ **marché** cheap; ~ **mot** witticism; ~ **à rien** good-for-nothing; ~ **sens** common sense; ~ **du Trésor** Treasury bond; ~ **vivant** bon viveur; **bonne action** good deed; **bonne femme** (derogatory) (colloq) woman, (US) (colloq); wife, old lady (colloq); **bonne pâte** good sort; **bonne sœur** (colloq) nun

**bonbon** /bɔ̃bɔ̃/ *nm* sweet (GB), candy (US)

**bonbonne** /bɔ̃bɔn/ *nf* **(a)** demijohn; (bigger) carboy
**(b)** (for gas) cylinder

**bond** /bɔ̃/ *nm* **(a)** leap; **se lever d'un** ~ to leap to one's feet
**(b)** (in time) jump
**(c)** (in profits, exports) leap; (in prices) jump (**de** in); **la médecine a fait un** ~ **en avant avec cette découverte** this discovery was a medical breakthrough
IDIOMS **saisir la balle au** ~ to seize the opportunity; **faire faux** ~ **à qn** to let sb down

**bonde** /bɔ̃d/ *nf* **(a)** (of swimming pool) outlet; (of sink) plughole
**(b)** (stopper) (in pool) outlet cover; (in sink) plug

**bondé, ~e** /bɔ̃de/ *adj* packed (**de** with)

**bondir** /bɔ̃diʀ/ [3] *vi* **(a)** to leap; ~ **de joie** to jump for joy
**(b)** ~ **sur qn/qch** to pounce on sb/sth
**(c)** ⟨animal⟩ to leap about
**(d)** **ça m'a fait** ~ I was absolutely furious (about it)

**bonheur** /bɔnœʀ/ *nm* **(a)** happiness
**(b)** pleasure; **faire le** ~ **de qn** ⟨present⟩ to make sb happy; ⟨event, exhibition⟩ to delight sb
**(c)** **par** ~ fortunately; **au petit** ~ **(la chance)** at random; **tu ne connais pas ton** ~! you don't realize how lucky you are!
IDIOMS **alors, tu as trouvé ton** ~? (colloq) did you find what you wanted?

**bonhomie** /bɔnɔmi/ *nf* good-nature

**bonhomme, *pl* ~s, bonshommes** /bɔnɔm, bɔ̃zɔm/ ① *adj* good-natured
② *nm* (colloq) **(a)** fellow, chap (colloq)
**(b)** husband, old man (colloq)
■ ~ **de neige** snowman
IDIOMS **aller** *or* **suivre son petit** ~ **de chemin** to go peacefully along

**bonification** /bɔnifikɑsjɔ̃/ *nf* **(a)** (in sport) bonus points
**(b)** (financial) bonus

**boniments** /bɔnimɑ̃/ *nm pl* stories; **raconter des** ~ **à qn** to give sb some story (colloq) (**à propos de** about); to smooth-talk sb

**bonjour** /bɔ̃ʒuʀ/ *nm, excl* hello
IDIOMS **être simple comme** ~ (colloq) to be very easy

**bonne²** /bɔn/ ① *adj f* ▶ BON 1
② *nf* **(a)** maid, servant
**(b)** **tu en as de ~s, toi!** you must be joking!
■ ~ **d'enfants** nanny

**bonnement** /bɔnmɑ̃/ *adv* **tout** ~ (quite) simply

**bonnet** /bɔnɛ/ *nm* **(a)** hat; (for baby) bonnet
**(b)** (on bra) cup
■ ~ **de nuit** nightcap; (figurative) wet blanket (colloq)

**bonneterie** /bɔnɛtʀi/ *nf* hosiery

**bonshommes** ▶ BONHOMME

**bonsoir** /bɔ̃swaʀ/ *nm, excl* good evening, good night

**bonté** /bɔ̃te/ *nf* **(a)** kindness
**(b)** (of God) goodness

**bonus** /bɔnys/ *nm inv* no-claims bonus

**boom** /bum/ *nm* boom; **en plein ~** booming

**bord** /bɔʀ/ *nm* **(a)** (of plate, bed) edge; (of road) side; (of river) bank; **au ~ de** on *or* at the edge of ⟨lake, road⟩; (figurative) on the verge of; **au ~ de la mer** at the seaside; by the sea; **~ à ~** edge-to-edge
**(b)** (of cup) rim; (of hat) brim
**(c)** à **~** ⟨work⟩ on board; de **~** ⟨instruments, staff⟩ on board; **on fera** (colloq) **avec les moyens du ~** we'll make do with what we've got
**(d)** side; **être du même ~** to be on the same side

**bordeaux** /bɔʀdo/ **1** *adj inv* burgundy
**2** *nm* Bordeaux; **~ rouge** claret

**border** /bɔʀde/ [1] *vtr* **(a)** to line (de with)
**(b)** ⟨plants⟩ to border ⟨lake⟩
**(c)** to tuck [sb] in
**(d)** to edge ⟨garment⟩ (de with)

**bordereau**, *pl* **~x** /bɔʀdəʀo/ *nm* form, slip

**bordure** /bɔʀdyʀ/ **1** *nf* **(a)** (of sports ground, carpet) border
**(b)** (of road, platform) edge
**2 en bordure de** *phr* **(a)** next to ⟨park, canal, track⟩
**(b)** on the edge of ⟨park⟩; on the side of ⟨road⟩
**(c)** just outside ⟨village⟩

**boréal, ~e**, *mpl* **-aux** /bɔʀeal, o/ *adj* boreal

**borgne** /bɔʀɲ/ *adj* one-eyed

**borne** /bɔʀn/ **1** *nf* **(a) ~ (kilométrique)** kilometre (GB) marker
**(b)** bollard (GB), post (US)
**(c)** (colloq) kilometre (GB)
**(d)** (for electricity) terminal
**2 bornes** *nf pl* **leur ambition est sans ~s** their ambition knows no bounds
■ **~ téléphonique** emergency telephone; taxi stand telephone

**borné, ~e** /bɔʀne/ *adj* narrow-minded

**borner: se borner** /bɔʀne/ [1] *v refl* (+ *v être*) **(a) se ~ à faire** to content oneself with doing
**(b) se ~ à faire** to be limited to doing

**bosquet** /bɔskɛ/ *nm* grove

**bosse** /bɔs/ *nf* **(a)** hump
**(b)** bump
**(c)** dent
IDIOMS **avoir la ~ de** (colloq) to have a flair for; **rouler sa ~** to knock about

**bosseler** /bɔsle/ [19] *vtr* to dent; (in metalwork) to emboss

**bosser** /bɔse/ [1] *vi* (colloq) to work

**bossu, ~e** /bɔsy/ *adj* hunchbacked

**bot** /bo/ *adj m* **pied ~** club foot

**botanique** /bɔtanik/ **1** *adj* botanical
**2** *nf* botany

**botte** /bɔt/ *nf* **(a)** boot
**(b)** (of flowers) bunch; (of hay) bale
■ **~s de caoutchouc** wellington boots

**botter** /bɔte/ [1] *vtr* **(a) ça le botte** (colloq)! he loves it!
**(b)** to kick

**bottin®** /bɔtɛ̃/ *nm* telephone directory

**bottine** /bɔtin/ *nf* ankle-boot

**bouc** /buk/ *nm* **(a)** billy goat
**(b)** goatee
■ **~ émissaire** scapegoat

**boucan** /bukɑ̃/ *nm* (colloq) din, racket (colloq)

**bouche** /buʃ/ *nf* mouth; **faire la fine ~ devant qch** to turn one's nose up at sth
■ **~ d'aération** air vent; **~ d'égout** manhole; **~ d'incendie** fire hydrant; **~ de métro** tube (GB) *or* subway (US) entrance

**bouché, ~e¹** /buʃe/ **1** *pp* ▶ BOUCHER¹
**2** *pp adj* **(a)** blocked
**(b)** ⟨profession⟩ oversubscribed
**(c)** (colloq) dim (colloq), stupid
**(d) cidre ~** bottled cider

**bouche-à-bouche** /buʃabuʃ/ *nm inv* mouth-to-mouth resuscitation

**bouche-à-oreille** /buʃaɔʀɛj/ *nm inv* **le ~** word of mouth

**bouchée²** /buʃe/ *nf* mouthful; **pour une ~ de pain** for next to nothing; **mettre les ~s doubles** to double one's efforts

**boucher¹** /buʃe/ [1] **1** *vtr* **(a)** to cork
**(b)** to block; to clog (up)
**(c)** to fill ⟨crack⟩
**2 se boucher** *v refl* (+ *v être*) **(a) se ~ le nez** to hold one's nose; **se ~ les oreilles** to put one's fingers in one's ears
**(b)** to get blocked
IDIOMS **en ~ un coin à qn** (colloq) to amaze sb

**boucher², -ère** /buʃe, ɛʀ/ *nm,f* butcher

**boucherie** /buʃʀi/ *nf* **(a)** butcher's shop
**(b)** butcher's trade
**(c)** slaughter

**bouchon** /buʃɔ̃/ *nm* **(a)** cork
**(b)** (screw)cap
**(c)** (of wax) plug
**(d)** traffic jam
**(e)** (in fishing) float

**boucle** /bukl/ *nf* **(a)** buckle; **~ d'oreille** earring
**(b)** curl
**(c)** loop
**(d)** (Comput) loop

**bouclé, ~e** /bukle/ *adj* curly

**boucler** /bukle/ [1] *vtr* **(a)** to fasten ⟨belt⟩
**(b)** (colloq) to lock ⟨door⟩
**(c)** (colloq) to cordon off ⟨district⟩
**(d)** (colloq) to complete ⟨investigation⟩
**(e)** (colloq) to lock [sb] up
IDIOMS **la ~** (colloq) to shut up; **~ la boucle** to come full circle

**bouclier** /buklije/ *nm* shield

**bouddhisme** /budism/ *nm* Buddhism

**bouder®** /bude/ [1] *vi* to sulk

**bouderie** /budʀi/ *nf* sulking

**boudin** /budɛ̃/ *nm* ≈ blood sausage

**boudiné, ~e** /budine/ *adj* podgy

**b**

**boudiner** /budine/ [1] *vtr* être boudiné
dans qch to be squeezed into sth

**boue** /bu/ *nf* (a) (gen, figurative) mud
(b) silt

**bouée** /bwe/ *nf* (a) rubber ring
(b) buoy

■ ~ de sauvetage *or* de secours lifebelt (GB),
life preserver (US)

**boueux, -euse** /buø, øz/ *adj* muddy

**bouffant, ~e** /bufã, ãt/ *adj* (a) baggy
(b) ⟨sleeves⟩ puffed
(c) ⟨hairstyle⟩ bouffant

**bouffe** /buf/ *nf* (colloq) (a) eating
(b) food
(c) meal

**bouffée** /bufe/ *nf* (of tobacco, steam) puff; une
~ d'air frais a breath of fresh air

■ ~ de chaleur hot flush (GB), hot flash (US)

**bouffer** (colloq) /bufe/ [1] **1** *vtr* to eat
**2** *vi* to eat; (greedily) to stuff oneself (colloq)

**bouffi, ~e** /bufi/ *adj* puffy

**bouffon** /bufɔ̃/ *nm* (a) clown
(b) jester; buffoon

**bouffonnerie** /bufɔnʀi/ *nf* (a) (actions)
antics
(b) (for comic effect) buffoonery
(c) (intrinsic stupidity) ridiculousness
(d) (in theatre) farce

**bougeoir** /buʒwaʀ/ *nm* (a) candleholder
(b) candlestick

**bougeotte** /buʒɔt/ *nf* (colloq) avoir la ~ to
be restless

**bouger** /buʒe/ [13] **1** *vtr* to move
**2** *vi* (a) to move
(b) (colloq) ⟨sector, company⟩ to be on the
move
(c) (colloq) ville qui bouge lively town
**3** se **bouger** *v refl* (+ *v être*) (colloq) (a) to
get a move on (colloq)
(b) to put some effort in

**bougie** /buʒi/ *nf* (a) candle
(b) (Tech) spark plug

**bougonner** /bugɔne/ [1] *vi* to grumble

**bouillabaisse** /bujabɛs/ *nf* fish soup

**bouillant, ~e** /bujã, ãt/ *adj* boiling (hot)

**bouille** /buj/ *nf* (colloq) face

**bouilli, ~e** /buji/ ▶ BOUILLIR

**bouillie** /buji/ *nf* (a) gruel; en ~ mushy;
mettre qn/qch en ~ to reduce sb/sth to a
pulp
(b) baby cereal

**bouillir** /bujiʀ/ [31] *vi* (a) to boil
(b) to be seething (de with)

**bouilloire** /bujwaʀ/ *nf* kettle

**bouillon** /bujɔ̃/ *nm* (a) broth
(b) (Culin) stock
(c) bouillir à gros ~s to boil fiercely

**bouillonnant, ~e** /bujɔnã, ãt/ *adj*
⟨water⟩ foaming; ⟨person⟩ lively

**bouillonner** /bujɔne/ [1] *vi* (a) to bubble
(b) ~ d'activité to be bustling with activity

**bouillotte** /bujɔt/ *nf* hot-water bottle

**boulanger, -ère** /bulãʒe, ɛʀ/ *nm,f* baker

**boulangerie** /bulãʒʀi/ *nf* bakery

**boulangerie-pâtisserie,** *pl*
**boulangeries-pâtisseries**
/bulãʒʀipatisʀi/ *nf* bakery (*selling cakes and
pastries*)

**boule** /bul/ *nf* (gen) ball; (in bowling) bowl;
mettre qch en ~ to roll sth up into a ball

■ ~ de neige snowball; ~ Quiès® earplug

IDIOMS il a perdu la ~ (colloq) he's gone mad;
mettre qn en ~ (colloq) to make sb furious

**bouleau,** *pl* ~**x** /bulo/ *nm* birch

**bouledogue** /buldɔg/ *nm* bulldog

**boulet** /bulɛ/ *nm* (a) ~ (de canon)
cannonball
(b) ball and chain
(c) (figurative) millstone

**boulette** /bulɛt/ *nf* (a) (of bread, paper) pellet
(b) ~ de viande meatball
(c) (colloq) blunder

**boulevard** /bulvaʀ/ *nm* boulevard

■ ~ périphérique ring road (GB), beltway (US)

**bouleversant, ~e** /bulvɛʀsã, ãt/ *adj*
deeply moving

**bouleversement** /bulvɛʀsəmã/ *nm*
upheaval

**bouleverser** /bulvɛʀse/ [1] *vtr* (a) to
move [sb] deeply
(b) ⟨experience⟩ to shatter
(c) to turn [sth] upside down ⟨house, files⟩
(d) to disrupt ⟨schedule⟩
(e) to change [sth] dramatically ⟨lifestyle⟩

**boulier** /bulje/ *nm* abacus

**boulimie** /bulimi/ *nf* bulimia

**boulon** /bulɔ̃/ *nm* bolt

**boulot, -otte** /bulo, ɔt/ **1** *adj* tubby
**2** *nm* (colloq) (a) work
(b) job

**boulotter** /bulɔte/ [1] *vtr, vi* (colloq) to eat

**boum¹** /bum/ *nm* (a) bang
(b) (colloq) en plein ~ ⟨business⟩ booming;
faire un ~ ⟨birth rates⟩ to soar

**boum²** /bum/ *nf* party

**bouquet** /bukɛ/ *nm* (a) ~ (de fleurs) bunch
of flowers; bouquet
(b) (of firework display) final flourish; c'est le
~! (colloq) (figurative) that's the limit! (colloq)

**bouquin** /bukɛ̃/ *nm* (colloq) book

**bouquiner** /bukine/ [1] *vtr, vi* (colloq) to
read

**bourbier** /buʀbje/ *nm* quagmire

**bourde** /buʀd/ *nf* blunder

**bourdon** /buʀdɔ̃/ *nm* bumblebee

**bourdonnement** /buʀdɔnmã/ *nm*
(of insect) buzzing; (of engine) hum; (of plane)
drone

**bourdonner** /buʀdɔne/ [1] *vi* to buzz; to
hum

**bourg** /buʀ/ *nm* market town

**bourgeois, ~e** /buʀʒwa, az/ **1** *adj*
bourgeois
**2** *nm,f* (a) middle-class person
(b) (in Ancien Regime) bourgeois
(c) burgher

**bourgeoisie** /buʀʒwazi/ *nf* (a) middle classes
(b) bourgeoisie

**bourgeon** /buʀʒɔ̃/ *nm* bud; **en ∼s** in bud

**bourgeonner** /buʀʒɔne/ [1] *vi* to bud

**bourrage** /buʀaʒ/ *nm* **∼ de crâne** brainwashing

**bourrasque** /buʀask/ *nf* (of wind) gust

**bourratif, -ive** /buʀatif, iv/ *adj* very filling, stodgy

**bourre** /buʀ/ *nf* (colloq) **être à la ∼** to be pushed for time

**bourré, ∼e** /buʀe/ *adj* ‹train, museum› packed; ‹case, bag› bulging (**de** with); **∼ de fric** (colloq) stinking rich (colloq)

**bourreau**, *pl* **∼x** /buʀo/ *nm* executioner

**bourrelet** /buʀlɛ/ *nm* roll of fat

**bourrer** /buʀe/ [1] *vtr* (a) to cram [sth] full; to fill ‹pipe›
(b) (colloq) **∼ qn de** to dose sb up with ‹medicine›

**bourricot** /buʀiko/ *nm* donkey

**bourrique** /buʀik/ *nf* (a) donkey
(b) (colloq) pig-headed person

**bourru, ∼e** /buʀy/ *adj* gruff

**bourse** /buʀs/ *nf* (a) grant (GB), scholarship (US)
(b) purse

**Bourse** /buʀs/ *nf* (a) stock exchange
(b) shares; **une société de ∼** a broking (GB) *or* brokerage (US) firm

**boursicoter** /buʀsikɔte/ [1] *vi* to dabble in stocks and shares

**boursier, -ière** /buʀsje, ɛʀ/ ① *adj* **le marché ∼** share prices
② *nm,f* grant holder (GB), scholarship student (US)

**boursouflé, ∼e** /buʀsufle/ *adj*
(a) blistered
(b) puffy
(c) ‹body› bloated

**bousculade** /buskylad/ *nf* (a) jostling; (accidental) crush
(b) rush

**bousculer** /buskyle/ [1] ① *vtr* (a) to push, to jostle ‹person›
(b) to rush
② **se bousculer** *v refl* (+ *v être*) to fall over each other (**pour faire** to do)

**bouse** /buz/ *nf* **une ∼ (de vache)** a cowpat

**bousiller** /buzije/ [1] *vtr* (colloq) to wreck ‹engine›; to smash up ‹car›

**boussole** /busɔl/ *nf* compass

**bout** /bu/ *nm* (a) end; tip; (of shoe) toe; **au ∼ du jardin** at the bottom of the garden; **aller jusqu'au ∼** to go all the way; **aller ( jusqu')**
**au ∼ de** to follow through ‹idea, demand›; **elle est à ∼** she can't take any more; **ne me pousse pas à ∼** don't push me; **être à ∼ d'arguments** to have run out of arguments; **venir à ∼ de** to overcome ‹difficulty›; to get through ‹task, meal›; **au ∼ du compte** in the end; **à ∼ portant** at point-blank range
(b) (of bread, paper) piece; (of land) bit

■ **∼ de chou** (colloq) sweet little thing (colloq); **∼ d'essai** screen test
**IDIOMS tenir le bon ∼** (colloq) to be on the right track; **ne pas être au ∼ de ses peines** not to be out of the woods yet

**boutade** /butad/ *nf* witticism

**boute-en-train** /butɑ̃tʀɛ̃/ *nmf inv* live wire (figurative)

**bouteille** /butɛj/ *nf* (gen) bottle; (of gas) cylinder
**IDIOMS prendre de la ∼** (colloq) to be getting on (a bit)

**boutique** /butik/ *nf* shop (GB), store (US)

**boutiquier, -ière** /butikje, ɛʀ/ *nm,f* shopkeeper

**bouton** /butɔ̃/ *nm* (a) (on clothes) button
(b) knob; button
(c) (Med) spot (GB), pimple (US)
(d) (flower) bud
■ **∼ de fièvre** cold sore; **∼ de manchette** cuff link; **∼ de porte** doorknob; **∼ d'or** buttercup

**boutonner** /butɔne/ [1] *vtr*, **se boutonner** *v refl* (+ *v être*) to button up

**boutonneux, -euse** /butɔnø, øz/ *adj* spotty (GB), pimply (US)

**boutonnière** /butɔnjɛʀ/ *nf* buttonhole

**bouture** /butyʀ/ *nf* cutting

**bovin, ∼e** /bɔvɛ̃, in/ ① *adj* bovine
② *nm* bovine; **des ∼s** cattle

**box**, *pl* **boxes** /bɔks/ *nm* (a) lock-up garage
(b) (for horse) stall
(c) (in bar) alcove
■ **∼ des accusés** (Law) dock

**boxe** /bɔks/ *nf* (Sport) boxing; **∼ française** savate

**boxer** /bɔkse/ [1] *vi* (Sport) to box

**boxeur** /bɔksœʀ/ *nm* (Sport) boxer

**boyau**, *pl* **∼x** /bwajo/ *nm* (a) gut
(b) catgut
(c) (for sausage) casing
(d) tubeless tyre (GB) *or* tire (US)

**boycotter** /bɔjkɔte/ [1] *vtr* to boycott

**BP** *written abbr* ▶ **BOÎTE**

**bracelet** /bʀaslɛ/ *nm* (a) bracelet; bangle
(b) wristband; **∼ de montre** watchstrap

**braconnier** /bʀakɔnje/ *nm* poacher

**brader** /bʀade/ [1] *vtr* (a) to sell cheaply
(b) to sell off

**braderie** /bʀadʀi/ *nf* (a) street market
(b) discount store
(c) clearance sale

**braguette** /bʀagɛt/ *nf* flies (GB), fly (US)

**braille** /bʀaj/ *nm* Braille

**brailler** /bʀaje/ [1] *vi* (colloq) (a) to yell
(b) ‹child, singer› to bawl

**braire** /bʀɛʀ/ [58] *vi* to bray

**braise** /bʀɛz/ *nf* live embers

**brancard** /bʀɑ̃kaʀ/ *nm* stretcher

**branchage** /bʀɑ̃ʃaʒ/ *nm* branches

**branche** /bʀɑ̃ʃ/ *nf* (a) (of tree) branch
(b) **céleri en ∼s** sticks of celery
(c) field, sector ⋯⋗

**(d)** (of family) branch
**(e)** (of candelabra) branch; (of spectacles) arm; (of star) point

**branché, ~e** /bʀɑ̃ʃe/ adj (colloq) trendy (colloq)

**branchement** /bʀɑ̃ʃmɑ̃/ nm **(a)** (electrical) connection
**(b)** (for water) branch pipe; (for electricity) lead (GB), cable (US)

**brancher** /bʀɑ̃ʃe/ [1] vtr **(a)** to plug in
**(b)** to connect (up) ⟨water, electricity⟩
**(c)** (colloq) ~ qn sur to get sb onto ⟨topic⟩
**(d)** (colloq) je vais au cinéma, ça te branche? I'm going to the cinema, are you interested?

**branchie** /bʀɑ̃ʃi/ nf (of fish) gill

**brandir** /bʀɑ̃diʀ/ [3] vtr to brandish

**branlant, ~e** /bʀɑ̃lɑ̃, ɑ̃t/ adj ⟨chair⟩ rickety; ⟨tooth⟩ loose; ⟨argument⟩ shaky

**branle** /bʀɑ̃l/ nm mettre qch en ~ to set [sth] in motion ⟨project, convoy⟩

**branle-bas** /bʀɑ̃lba/ nm inv commotion
■ ~ de combat (Mil) action stations

**branler** /bʀɑ̃le/ [1] vi ⟨wall⟩ to wobble; ⟨chair⟩ to be rickety; ⟨tooth⟩ to be loose

**braquage** /bʀakaʒ/ nm (colloq) robbery

**braquer** /bʀake/ [1] **1** vtr **(a)** to point ⟨gun, camera⟩ (sur, vers at); to turn or fix ⟨eyes⟩ (sur, vers on)
**(b)** ~ à gauche/droite to turn hard left/right
**(c)** (colloq) to point a gun at
**(d)** (colloq) to rob ⟨bank⟩
**(e)** (colloq) ~ qn contre qn/qch to turn sb against sb/sth
**2** vi ⟨driver⟩ to turn the wheel full lock (GB) or all the way (US)
**3** se braquer v refl (+ v être) to dig one's heels in

**bras** /bʀa/ nm inv **(a)** arm; ~ dessus ~ dessous arm in arm; porter qch à bout de ~ (figurative) to keep sth afloat; en ~ de chemise in one's shirtsleeves
**(b)** manpower, labour (GB)
**(c)** (of river) branch; ~ de mer sound
**(d)** (of armchair) arm
■ ~ droit right hand man; ~ de fer arm wrestling; (figurative) trial of strength
IDIOMS les ~ m'en tombent I'm absolutely speechless; avoir le ~ long to have a lot of influence

**brasier** /bʀazje/ nm inferno

**bras-le-corps: à bras-le-corps** /abʀalkɔʀ/ phr ⟨lift⟩ bodily

**brassage** /bʀasaʒ/ nm **(a)** (of beer) brewing
**(b)** (mixing) (of people) intermingling; (of ideas, cultures) cross-fertilization

**brassard** /bʀasaʀ/ nm armband

**brasse** /bʀas/ nf (Sport) breaststroke

**brasser** /bʀase/ [1] vtr **(a)** to toss around ⟨ideas⟩; to shuffle around ⟨papers⟩; to intermingle ⟨population⟩; il brasse des millions he handles big money
**(b)** to brew ⟨beer⟩

**brasserie** /bʀasʀi/ nf **(a)** brasserie
**(b)** brewery

**brasseur, -euse** /bʀasœʀ, øz/ nm,f brewer

**brassière** /bʀasjɛʀ/ nf **(a)** baby's top
**(b)** crop top

**brave** /bʀav/ adj **(a)** nice; un ~ homme a nice man
**(b)** brave; un homme ~ a brave man

**braver** /bʀave/ [1] vtr to defy ⟨person⟩; to brave ⟨storm⟩

**bravo** /bʀavo/ excl bravo!; well done!

**bravoure** /bʀavuʀ/ nf bravery

**break** /bʀɛk/ nm estate car (GB), station wagon (US)

**brebis** /bʀəbi/ nf inv ewe

**brèche** /bʀɛʃ/ nf **(a)** hole, gap
**(b)** (Mil) breach

**bréchet** /bʀeʃɛ/ nm wishbone

**bredouille** /bʀəduj/ adj empty-handed

**bredouiller** /bʀəduje/ [1] vtr, vi to mumble

**bref, brève¹** /bʀɛf, bʀɛv/ **1** adj brief; short
**2** adv (en) ~ in short

**breloque** /bʀəlɔk/ nf (on bracelet) charm

**Brésil** /bʀezil/ pr nm Brazil

**Bretagne** /bʀətaɲ/ pr nf Brittany

**bretelle** /bʀətɛl/ nf **1** **(a)** (gen) strap
**(b)** slip road (GB), ramp (US)
**2** bretelles nf pl braces

**breton, -onne** /bʀətɔ̃, ɔn/ **1** adj Breton
**2** nm (language) Breton

**breuvage** /bʀœvaʒ/ nm beverage

**brève²** /bʀɛv/ **1** adj f ▶ BREF 1
**2** nf news flash

**brevet** /bʀəvɛ/ nm **(a)** ~ (d'invention) patent
**(b)** ~ de secourisme first aid certificate; ~ de pilote pilot's licence (GB)
■ ~ de technicien supérieur, BTS advanced vocational diploma

**breveter** /bʀəvte/ [20] vtr (faire) ~ to patent

**bréviaire** /bʀevjɛʀ/ nm breviary

**bribes** /bʀib/ nf pl (of conversation) snatches

**bric: de bric et de broc** /dəbʀiked(ə)bʀɔk/ phr ⟨furnished⟩ with bits and pieces

**bric-à-brac** /bʀikabʀak/ nm inv bric-à-brac

**bricolage** /bʀikɔlaʒ/ nm DIY (GB), do-it-yourself

**bricole** /bʀikɔl/ nf acheter une ~ to buy a little something; des ~s bits and pieces

**bricoler** /bʀikɔle/ [1] **1** vtr (colloq) **(a)** to tinker with
**(b)** to throw [sth] together
**2** vi to do DIY (GB), to fix things (US)

**bride** /bʀid/ nf **(a)** bridle
**(b)** button loop
IDIOMS partir à ~ abattue to dash off; avoir la ~ sur le cou to have free rein

**bridé, ~e** /bʀide/ adj yeux ~s slanting eyes

**brièvement** /bʀijɛvmɑ̃/ *adv* briefly
**brigade** /bʀigad/ *nf* **(a)** (Mil) brigade
  **(b)** (in police) squad
**brigadier** /bʀigadje/ *nm* **(a)** ≈ corporal
  **(b)** fire chief
**brigand** /bʀigɑ̃/ *nm* brigand, bandit
**brillamment** /bʀijamɑ̃/ *adv* brilliantly
**brillant**, ~**e** /bʀijɑ̃, ɑ̃t/ **1** *adj* **(a)** bright;
  shiny; glistening
  **(b)** brilliant
  **2** *nm* (cut) diamond, brilliant
**briller** /bʀije/ [1] *vi* **(a)** ⟨sun⟩ to shine;
  ⟨flame⟩ to burn brightly; ⟨gem⟩ to sparkle;
  ⟨nose⟩ to be shiny
  **(b)** ~ **de** ⟨eyes⟩ to blaze with ⟨anger⟩
  **(c)** ⟨person⟩ to shine; **elle brille par son
  esprit** she's extremely witty
**brimade** /bʀimad/ *nf* bullying
**brimer** /bʀime/ [1] *vtr* **(a)** to bully
  **(b) se sentir brimé** to feel picked on
**brin** /bʀɛ̃/ *nm* **(a)** (of parsley) sprig; (of straw)
  wisp; (of grass) blade
  **(b) un** ~ **de** a bit of
**brindille** /bʀɛ̃dij/ *nf* twig
**bringue** /bʀɛ̃g/ *nf* (colloq) **(a)** drinking
  party
  **(b)** rave-up (colloq)
  **(c)** (girl) **(grande)** ~ beanpole
**brinquebaler** /bʀɛ̃kbale/ [1] *vi* ⟨load⟩ to
  rattle about; ⟨vehicle⟩ to jolt along
**brio** /bʀijo/ *nm* brilliance; (Mus) brio
**brioche** /bʀijɔʃ/ *nf* **(a)** brioche, (sweet)
  bun
  **(b)** (colloq) paunch
**brioché**, ~**e** /bʀijɔʃe/ *adj* (Culin) brioche
**brique** /bʀik/ *nf* **(a)** brick
  **(b)** (for milk, juice) carton
**briquer** /bʀike/ [1] *vtr* to polish [sth] up
**briquet** /bʀikɛ/ *nm* (cigarette) lighter
**brise** /bʀiz/ *nf* breeze; **bonne** ~ fresh
  breeze
**brise-glace** /bʀizglas/ *nm inv* icebreaker
**briser** /bʀize/ [1] **1** *vtr* **(a)** (gen) to break;
  to break down ⟨resistance⟩
  **(b)** to shatter ⟨dream⟩; to destroy ⟨career,
  person⟩
  **(c)** to shatter ⟨person⟩
  **2 se briser** *v refl* (+ *v être*) **(a)** to break
  **(b)** ⟨dream⟩ to be shattered
  **(c)** ⟨voice⟩ to break
**brise-tout** /bʀiztu/ *nm inv* (person)
  butterfingers
**briseur, -euse** /bʀizœʀ, øz/ *nm,f* wrecker
  ■ ~ **de grève** strike breaker
**brisure** /bʀizyʀ/ *nf* **(a)** crack
  **(b)** fragment
**britannique** /bʀitanik/ *adj* British
**Britannique** /bʀitanik/ *nmf* **un/une** ~ a
  British man/woman; **les** ~**s** the British
  (people)
**broc** /bʀo/ *nm* ewer
**brocante** /bʀɔkɑ̃t/ *nf* **(a)** bric-à-brac trade
  **(b)** flea market

**broche** /bʀɔʃ/ *nf* **(a)** brooch
  **(b)** (for roasting) spit
  **(c)** (in surgery) pin
**brocher** /bʀɔʃe/ [1] *vtr* **(a)** to bind [sth] (with
  paper) ⟨book⟩; **livre broché** paperback
**brochet** /bʀɔʃɛ/ *nm* (Zool) pike
**brochette** /bʀɔʃɛt/ *nf* **(a)** skewer
  **(b)** kebab
**brochure** /bʀɔʃyʀ/ *nf* **(a)** booklet
  **(b)** (travel) brochure
**brocoli** /bʀɔkɔli/ *nm* broccoli
**broder** /bʀɔde/ [1] *vtr, vi* to embroider
**broderie** /bʀɔdʀi/ *nf* embroidery
**bromure** /bʀɔmyʀ/ *nm* bromide
**bronche** /bʀɔ̃ʃ/ *nf* **les** ~**s** the bronchial
  tubes
**broncher** /bʀɔ̃ʃe/ [1] *vi* **sans** ~ without
  turning a hair
**bronchite** /bʀɔ̃ʃit/ *nf* bronchitis
**bronzage** /bʀɔ̃zaʒ/ *nm* (sun)tan
**bronze** /bʀɔ̃z/ *nm* bronze
**bronzé**, ~**e** /bʀɔ̃ze/ *adj* ⟨person⟩
  (sun-)tanned
**bronzer** /bʀɔ̃ze/ [1] *vi* to get a tan, to go
  brown
**brossage** /bʀɔsaʒ/ *nm* (of hair, teeth)
  brushing
**brosse** /bʀɔs/ *nf* brush; **donner un coup de**
  ~ **à qch** to give sth a brush; **avoir les
  cheveux (taillés) en** ~ to have a crew cut
**brosser** /bʀɔse/ [1] **1** *vtr* **(a)** to brush; to
  scrub
  **(b)** to give a quick outline of
  **2 se brosser** *v refl* (+ *v être*) to brush
  oneself down; **se** ~ **les dents** to brush one's
  teeth
**brouette** /bʀuɛt/ *nf* wheelbarrow
**brouhaha** /bʀuaa/ *nm* hubbub
**brouillard** /bʀujaʀ/ *nm* fog
**brouille** /bʀuj/ *nf* **(a)** quarrel
  **(b)** rift
**brouiller** /bʀuje/ [1] **1** *vtr* **(a)** to make
  [sth] cloudy ⟨liquid⟩; to blur ⟨text, vision⟩;
  ~ **les cartes** to confuse *or* cloud the issue
  **(b)** to jam ⟨signal⟩; to interfere with
  ⟨reception⟩
  **2 se brouiller** *v refl* (+ *v être*) **(a)** to fall
  out (avec with)
  **(b)** ⟨liquid⟩ to become cloudy; ⟨vision⟩ to
  become blurred; ⟨mind⟩ to become confused;
  **avoir le teint brouillé** to look ill
**brouillon, -onne** /bʀujɔ̃, ɔn/ **1** *adj*
  **(a)** untidy
  **(b)** disorganized
  **(c)** muddled
  **2** *nm* **(a)** rough draft
  **(b)** rough paper
**broussaille** /bʀusaj/ *nf* **(a)** undergrowth
  **(b)** scrub
  **(c)** bushes
**brousse** /bʀus/ *nf* bush; **en pleine** ~
  (colloq) in the sticks (colloq)
**brouter** /bʀute/ [1] *vtr* to nibble; to graze

**brouteur** , **-euse** /bʀutœʀ øz/ nm,f
browser

**broyer** /bʀwaje/ [23] vtr (a) to grind
⟨wheat⟩
(b) to crush
IDIOMS ∼ **du noir** to brood

**broyeur**, **-euse** /bʀwajœʀ, øz/ nm
(machine) crusher, grinder

**bru** /bʀy/ nf daughter-in-law

**brugnon** /bʀyɲɔ̃/ nm nectarine

**bruiner** /bʀɥine/ [1] v impers to drizzle

**bruissement** /bʀɥismɑ̃/ nm (of leaves)
rustle; (of brook) babbling

**bruit** /bʀɥi/ nm (a) noise; ∼ **étouffé** thud;
**un ∼ de ferraille** a clang
(b) noise, din; ∼ **infernal** or **d'enfer** awful
racket; **sans ∼** silently
(c) **le film a fait beaucoup de ∼** the film
attracted a lot of attention
(d) ∼ **(de couloir)** rumour (GB)

**bruitage** /bʀɥitaʒ/ nm sound effects

**bruiteur** /bʀɥitœʀ/ nm sound effects
engineer

**brûlant**, **∼e** /bʀylɑ̃, ɑ̃t/ adj (a) ⟨tea⟩
boiling hot; ⟨sand, radiator, person⟩ burning
hot; ⟨sun⟩ blazing
(b) ⟨issue⟩ burning
(c) ⟨passion⟩ burning

**brûlé**, **∼e** /bʀyle/ [1] nm,f **un grand ∼** a
third degree burns victim; **service des
grands ∼s** burns unit
[2] nm **ça sent le ∼** there's a smell of
burning

**brûle-parfum(s)** /bʀylpaʀfœ̃/ nm inv
incense burner

**brûle-pourpoint**: **à brûle-pourpoint**
/abʀylpuʀpwɛ̃/ phr point-blank

**brûler** /bʀyle/ [1] [1] vtr (a) to burn
⟨papers⟩; to set fire to ⟨house⟩
(b) to burn ⟨fuel⟩; to use ⟨electricity⟩
(c) ⟨acid⟩ to burn; ⟨water⟩ to scald; **j'ai les
yeux qui me brûlent** my eyes are stinging
(d) (colloq) ∼ **un feu (rouge)** to jump (colloq)
the lights
[2] vi (a) ⟨wood⟩ to burn; ⟨forest, town⟩ to be
on fire
(b) ∼ **(d'envie) de faire** to be longing to do
[3] **se brûler** v refl (+ v être) to burn
oneself

**brûlure** /bʀylyʀ/ nf (a) burn; ∼**s d'estomac**
heartburn
(b) burn mark

**brume** /bʀym/ nf mist; fog; haze

**brumeux**, **-euse** /bʀymø, øz/ adj (a) hazy;
misty
(b) ⟨idea⟩ hazy

**brun**, **∼e** /bʀœ̃, bʀyn/ [1] adj brown, dark;
dark-haired
[2] nm,f dark-haired man/woman
[3] nm brown

**brunir** /bʀyniʀ/ [3] vi (a) ⟨skin⟩ to tan
(b) (Culin) to brown

**brushing** /bʀœʃiŋ/ nm blow-dry

**brusque** /bʀysk/ adj (a) ⟨tone, person⟩
abrupt
(b) ⟨movement⟩ sudden; ⟨bend⟩ sharp

**brusquement** /bʀyskəmɑ̃/ adv
(a) abruptly
(b) suddenly; ⟨brake⟩ sharply

**brusquer** /bʀyske/ [1] vtr (a) to be brusque
with
(b) to rush

**brut**, **∼e¹** /bʀyt/ adj (a) ⟨material⟩ raw;
⟨oil⟩ crude; ⟨stone⟩ rough; ⟨sugar⟩ unrefined
(b) ⟨cider, champagne⟩ dry
(c) ⟨salary⟩ gross

**brutal**, **∼e**, mpl **-aux** /bʀytal, o/ adj
(a) ⟨blow⟩ violent; ⟨pain, death⟩ sudden
(b) ⟨tone⟩ brutal; ⟨gesture, temper⟩ violent
(c) stark

**brutalement** /bʀytalmɑ̃/ adv (a) ⟨repress⟩
brutally; ⟨close⟩ violently
(b) ⟨die, stop⟩ suddenly

**brutaliser** /bʀytalize/ [1] vtr to ill-treat

**brutalité** /bʀytalite/ nf (a) brutality
(b) suddenness

**brute²** /bʀyt/ [1] adj f ▶ BRUT
[2] nf brute; **comme une ∼** ⟨hit⟩ savagely

**Bruxelles** /bʀysɛl/ pr n Brussels

**bruyant**, **∼e** /bʀɥijɑ̃, ɑ̃t/ adj (a) noisy;
loud
(b) resounding

**BTS** /beteɛs/ nm: abbr ▶ BREVET

**bu**, **∼e** /by/ ▶ BOIRE

**buanderie** /bɥɑ̃dʀi/ nf laundry room

**buccal**, **∼e**, mpl **-aux** /bykal, o/ adj oral

**bûche** /byʃ/ nf (a) log (of wood)
(b) (colloq) tumble, fall
(c) (Culin) ∼ **de Noël** yule log

**bûcher¹** /byʃe/ [1] vi (colloq) to slog away
(colloq)

**bûcher²** /byʃe/ nm (a) **le ∼** the stake
(b) (funeral) pyre

**bûcheron** /byʃʀɔ̃/ nm lumberjack

**bûchette** /byʃɛt/ nf (for fire) stick

**bucolique** /bykɔlik/ adj bucolic, pastoral

**budget** /bydʒɛ/ nm budget

**budgétaire** /bydʒetɛʀ/ adj ⟨deficit⟩ budget;
⟨year⟩ financial (GB), fiscal (US)

**budgétiser** /bydʒetize/ [1] vtr to include
[sth] in the budget

**buée** /bɥe/ nf (a) condensation
(b) steam

**buffet** /byfɛ/ nm (a) sideboard
(b) dresser
(c) (station) buffet
(d) (Culin) buffet

**buffle** /byfl/ nm buffalo

**buis** /bɥi/ nm (a) box tree
(b) boxwood

**buisson** /bɥisɔ̃/ nm (a) bush
(b) shrub

**buissonnière** /bɥisɔnjɛʀ/ adj f **faire
l'école ∼** to play truant (GB), to play hooky
(US) (colloq)

**bulbe** /bylb/ nm (Bot) bulb

**bulgare** /bylgaʀ/ *adj, nm* Bulgarian
**Bulgarie** /bylgaʀi/ *pr nf* Bulgaria
**bulldozer** /byldozœʀ/ *nm* bulldozer
**bulle** /byl/ *nf* **(a)** bubble
**(b)** speech bubble
**bulletin** /byltɛ̃/ *nm* **(a)** bulletin, report; ∼ **de santé** medical bulletin
**(b)** certificate; ∼ **de naissance** birth certificate
**(c)** form; ∼ **de salaire** payslip; ∼ **de participation** entry form
**(d)** bulletin, official publication
**(e)** ballot *or* voting paper
**bulletin-réponse**, *pl* **bulletins-réponse** /byltɛ̃ʀepɔ̃s/ *nm* reply coupon
**bulot** /bylo/ *nm* whelk
**buraliste** /byʀalist/ *nmf* **(a)** (for smokers' supplies) tobacconist; (for cigarettes and newspapers) newsagent (GB), newsdealer (US)
**(b)** (counter staff) clerk
**bureau**, *pl* ∼**x** /byʀo/ *nm* **(a)** desk
**(b)** study
**(c)** office
**(d)** board
■ ∼ **d'accueil** reception; ∼ **de poste** post office; ∼ **de tabac** tobacconist's; ∼ **de vote** polling station; **Bureau international du travail, BIT** International Labour Office, ILO
**bureaucratie** /byʀokʀasi/ *nf* bureaucracy
**bureautique** /byʀotik/ *nf* office automation
**burin** /byʀɛ̃/ *nm* chisel
**buriné**, ∼**e** /byʀine/ *adj* ⟨face⟩ craggy
**burlesque** /byʀlɛsk/ *adj* ludicrous; farcical

**bus** /bys/ *nm inv* bus
**buse** /byz/ *nf* **(a)** buzzard
**(b)** (colloq) clot (GB) (colloq), clod (colloq)
**busqué**, ∼**e** /byske/ *adj* ⟨nose⟩ hooked
**buste** /byst/ *nm* **(a)** (in sculpture) bust
**(b)** (Anat) chest
**(c)** bust, breasts
**bustier** /bystje/ *nm* **(a)** long-line bra
**(b)** bustier
**but** /by(t)/ *nm* **(a)** goal; aim, purpose; **aller droit au** ∼ to go straight to the point
**(b)** (in football) goal
**(c)** (in archery) target
**IDIOMS déclarer de** ∼ **en blanc** to declare point-blank
**buté**, ∼**e** /byte/ *adj* stubborn, obstinate
**buter** /byte/ [1] *vi* ∼ **contre qch** to trip over sth; to bump into sth; ∼ **sur** *or* **contre** to come up against ⟨obstacle⟩
**butin** /bytɛ̃/ *nm* (from robbery) haul
**butiner** /bytine/ [1] *vi* to gather pollen
**butte** /byt/ *nf* mound
**IDIOMS être en** ∼ **à** to come up against ⟨difficulties⟩; to be the butt of ⟨jokes⟩
**buvable** /byvabl/ *adj* **(a)** ⟨medicine⟩ to be taken orally
**(b)** drinkable
**buvard** /byvaʀ/ *nm* (papier) ∼ blotting paper
**buvette** /byvɛt/ *nf* refreshment area
**buveur, -euse** /byvœʀ, øz/ *nm,f* drinker; **c'est un gros** ∼ he's a heavy drinker; **un** ∼ **de thé/bière** a tea/beer drinker

# Cc

**c, C** /se/ *nm inv* c, C; **c cédille** c cedilla
**c'** ▶ CE 2
**ça** /sa/ *pron* **(a)** that; this; **c'est pour** ∼ **qu'il est parti** that's why he left; **sans** ∼ otherwise; ∼, **c'est bizarre** that's strange; **la rue a** ∼ **de bien qu'elle est calme** one good thing about the street is that it's quiet
**(b)** it; that; ∼ **fait mal** it hurts; that hurts; ∼ **criait de tous les côtés** there was shouting everywhere
**IDIOMS** ∼ **alors!** well I never! (colloq); ∼, **oui!** definitely!; **elle est bête et méchante avec** ∼ she's stupid and what's more she's nasty; **et avec** ∼? anything else?; **rien que** ∼! (ironic) is that all!; **c'est** ∼! that's right!; ∼ **y est, ∼ recommence!** here we go again!; ∼ **y est, j'ai fini!** that's it, I've finished!
**CA** *written abbr* ▶ CHIFFRE

**caban** /kabɑ̃/ *nm* sailor's jacket
**cabane** /kaban/ *nf* **(a)** hut
**(b)** shed
**(c)** (slang) prison
**cabaret** /kabaʀɛ/ *nm* cabaret
**cabas** /kaba/ *nm* shopping bag
**cabillaud** /kabijo/ *nm* cod
**cabine** /kabin/ *nf* cabin; cab; booth; cubicle
■ ∼ **d'essayage** fitting room; ∼ **de pilotage** cockpit; ∼ **téléphonique** phone box (GB), phone booth
**cabinet** /kabinɛ/ ① *nm* **(a)** (gen) office; (of doctor, dentist) surgery (GB), office (US); (of judge) chambers
**(b)** practice; ∼ **de médecins** medical practice; **ouvrir un** ∼ to set up in practice
**(c)** agency ⋯⋅:

**(d)** (Pol) cabinet; ∼ **ministériel** minister's personal staff

[2] **cabinets** *nm pl* toilet
■ ∼ **de toilette** bathroom

**cabinet-conseil**, *pl* **cabinets-conseil** /kabinɛkɔ̃sɛj/ *nm* firm of consultants

**câble** /kɑbl/ *nm* **(a)** cable; rope
**(b)** cable television

**câbler** /kɑble/ [1] *vtr* **(a)** to install cable television in ⟨*house, town*⟩
**(b)** to cable ⟨*message*⟩

**cabochard**, ∼**e** /kabɔʃaʀ, aʀd/ *adj* (colloq) stubborn

**caboche** /kabɔʃ/ *nf* (colloq) head

**cabosser** /kabose/ [1] *vtr* to dent

**cabot** /kabo/ *nm* (colloq) dog, mutt (colloq)

**cabotin**, ∼**e** /kabɔtɛ̃, in/ *adj* **être** ∼ to like playing to the gallery

**cabrer: se cabrer** /kabʀe/ [1] *v refl* (+ *v être*) **(a)** ⟨*horse*⟩ to rear (**devant** at)
**(b)** ⟨*person*⟩ to jib

**cabri** /kabʀi/ *nm* (Zool) kid

**cabriole** /kabʀijɔl/ *nf* (of clown, child) caper

**CAC®** /kak/ *nm* (*abbr* = **Compagnie des agents de change**) **indice** ∼ **40,** ∼ **40** Paris Stock Exchange index

**caca** /kaka/ *nm* (baby talk) poo (GB) (colloq), poop (US) (colloq)

**cacahuète** /kakawɛt/ *nf* peanut

**cacao** /kakao/ *nm* cocoa

**cacatoès** /kakatɔɛs/ *nm* cockatoo

**cachalot** /kaʃalo/ *nm* sperm whale

**cache**[1] /kaʃ/ *nm* **se servir d'un** ∼ **pour apprendre une liste de vocabulaire** to cover up the answers while learning a list of vocabulary

**cache**[2] /kaʃ/ *nf* ∼ **d'armes** arms cache

**caché**, ∼**e** /kaʃe/ [1] *pp* ▶ CACHER
[2] *pp adj* ⟨*beauty, sense*⟩ hidden; ⟨*pain, desire*⟩ secret

**cache-cache** /kaʃkaʃ/ *nm inv* hide and seek (GB), hide-and-go-seek (US)

**cache-col** /kaʃkɔl/ *nm inv* scarf

**cachemire** /kaʃmiʀ/ *nm* cashmere

**cache-nez** /kaʃne/ *nm inv* scarf, muffler

**cache-pot** /kaʃpo/ *nm inv* flowerpot holder

**cacher** /kaʃe/ [1] [1] *vtr* to hide; ∼ **son jeu** (figurative) to keep one's cards close to one's chest; ∼ **qch à qn** to conceal sth from sb
[2] **se cacher** *v refl* (+ *v être*) **(a)** to hide; (temporarily) to go into hiding; **il ne s'en cache pas** he makes no secret of it
**(b)** ⟨*sun*⟩ to disappear

**cache-sexe** /kaʃsɛks/ *nm inv* G-string

**cachet** /kaʃɛ/ *nm* **(a)** tablet
**(b)** (for letter) stamp; seal; ∼ **de la poste** postmark
**(c)** (of actor) fee

**cacheter** /kaʃte/ [20] *vtr* to seal

**cachette** /kaʃɛt/ *nf* hiding place; **en** ∼ on the sly

**cachot** /kaʃo/ *nm* **(a)** prison cell
**(b)** dungeon

**cachotterie** /kaʃɔtʀi/ *nf* little secret

**cachottier, -ière** /kaʃɔtje, ɛʀ/ *adj* secretive

**cachou** /kaʃu/ *nm* cachou

**cacophonie** /kakɔfɔni/ *nf* cacophony

**cactus** /kaktys/ *nm inv* cactus

**c-à-d** (*written abbr* = **c'est-à-dire**) ie

**cadastre** /kadastʀ/ *nm* **(a)** land register
**(b)** land registry

**cadavérique** /kadaveʀik/ *adj* ⟨*complexion*⟩ deathly pale

**cadavre** /kadavʀ/ *nm* corpse, body

**caddie®** /kadi/ *nm* shopping trolley

**cadeau**, *pl* ∼**x** /kado/ [1] *nm* present, gift; **faire un** ∼ **à qn** to give sb a present; **il ne fait pas de** ∼**x** (examiner, judge) he's very strict
[2] **(-)cadeau** (*combining form*) gift; **papier(-)**∼ wrapping paper

**cadenas** /kadna/ *nm* padlock

**cadence** /kadɑ̃s/ *nf* **(a)** rhythm
**(b)** (of work) rate

**cadet, -ette** /kadɛ, ɛt/ [1] *adj* **(a)** younger
**(b)** youngest
[2] *nm,f* **(a)** younger son/daughter, younger child
**(b)** youngest child
**(c)** younger brother/sister
**(d)** (Sport) *athlete between the ages of 15 and 17*
IDIOMS **c'est le** ∼ **de mes soucis** it's the least of my worries

**cadrage** /kadʀaʒ/ *nm* **(a)** framing
**(b)** composition

**cadran** /kadʀɑ̃/ *nm* (of watch) face; (of meter) dial; ∼ **solaire** sundial

**cadre** /kadʀ/ [1] *nm* **(a)** frame
**(b)** setting; surroundings
**(c) cela sort du** ∼ **de mes fonctions** that's not part of my duties
**(d)** framework
**(e)** executive; ∼ **supérieur** senior executive; **les** ∼**s moyens** middle management
**(f) faire partie des** ∼**s** to be on the company's books
**(g)** (of bicycle) frame
**(h)** (on form) space, box
[2] **dans le cadre de** *phr* **(a)** on the occasion of
**(b)** (of negotiations) within the framework of; (of campaign, plan) as part of

**cadrer** /kadʀe/ [1] [1] *vtr* to centre (GB) ⟨*picture*⟩
[2] *vi* to tally, to fit (**avec** with)

**cadreur** /kadʀœʀ/ *nm* cameraman

**caduc, caduque** /kadyk/ *adj* **(a)** obsolete
**(b)** (Law) null and void
**(c)** ⟨*leaf*⟩ deciduous

**cætera** ▶ ET CÆTERA

**cafard** /kafaʀ/ *nm* **(a)** (colloq) depression; **avoir le** ∼ to be down in the dumps (colloq)
**(b)** cockroach

**cafardeux**, **-euse** /kafaʀdø, øz/ adj
glum; gloomy

**café** /kafe/ nm **(a)** coffee; ~ **en grains**
coffee beans; ~ **soluble** instant coffee
**(b)** café

■ ~ **crème** espresso with milk; ~ **au lait**
coffee with milk; **peau** ~ **au lait** coffee-
coloured (GB) skin

**café-concert**, pl **cafés-concerts**
/kafekɔ̃sɛʀ/ nm café with live music

**caféine** /kafein/ nf caffeine

**cafétéria** /kafeteʀja/ nf cafeteria

**cafetière** /kaftjɛʀ/ nf coffee pot; coffee
maker

**cafouillage** /kafujaʒ/ nm (colloq) bungling
(colloq)

**cafouiller** /kafuje/ [1] vi (colloq) ‹person› to
get flustered; ‹machine› to be on the blink
(colloq); ‹organization› to get in a muddle

**cage** /kaʒ/ nf **(a)** cage
**(b)** (Sport) (colloq) goal

■ ~ **d'ascenseur** lift (GB) or elevator (US)
shaft; ~ **d'escalier** stairwell; ~ **à lapins**
rabbit hutch; ~ **thoracique** rib cage

**cageot** /kaʒo/ nm crate

**cagette** /kaʒɛt/ nf tray

**cagibi** /kaʒibi/ nm store cupboard

**cagnotte** /kaɲɔt/ nf **(a)** kitty
**(b)** jackpot

**cagoule** /kagul/ nf balaclava; hood

**cahier** /kaje/ nm **(a)** notebook; (Sch)
exercise book
**(b)** (in printing) section

■ ~ **de brouillon** rough book; ~ **de textes**
homework notebook

**cahin-caha** /kaɛ̃kaa/ adv (colloq) with
difficulty

**cahot** /kao/ nm jolt

**cahoter** /kaɔte/ [1] vi ‹vehicle› to bounce
along

**cahoteux**, **-euse** /kaɔtø, øz/ adj ‹road›
rough, bumpy

**cahute** /kayt/ nf hut, shack

**caïd** /kaid/ nm (in criminal underworld) boss;
**jouer les** ~**s** to act tough

**caillasse** /kajas/ nf stones

**caille** /kɑj/ nf (Zool) quail

**cailler** /kɑje/ [1] **1 se cailler** v refl
(+ v être) **(a)** ‹milk› to curdle
**(b)** (colloq) ‹person› to be freezing
**2** v impers (colloq) **ça caille** it's freezing

**caillot** /kajo/ nm clot

**caillou**, pl ~**x** /kaju/ nm **(a)** pebble; **gros**
~ **stone**
**(b)** (colloq) nut (colloq); **ne plus avoir un poil
sur le** ~ to be as bald as a coot (colloq)

**caillouteux**, **-euse** /kajutø, øz/ adj
stony

**caïman** /kaimɑ̃/ nm cayman

**Caire** /kɛʀ/ pr n **le** ~ Cairo

**caisse** /kɛs/ nf **(a)** crate
**(b)** (of car) shell, body
**(c)** (slang) car

**(d)** (for money) till; cash register; cash box;
**les** ~**s de l'État** the Treasury coffers; **voler
la** ~ to steal the takings
**(e)** cash desk; (in supermarket) checkout
(counter); (in bank) cashier's desk
**(f)** fund

■ ~ **d'épargne** ≈ savings bank; ~ **noire** slush
fund; ~ **à outils** toolbox

**caissette** /kɛsɛt/ nf small box or case

**caissier**, **-ière** /kesje, ɛʀ/ nm,f cashier

**cajoler** /kaʒɔle/ [1] vtr to cuddle ‹child›

**cajoleur**, **-euse** /kaʒɔlœʀ, øz/ adj
affectionate

**cajou** /kaʒu/ nm **noix de** ~ cashew nut

**cake** /kɛk/ nm fruit cake

**cal** /kal/ nm callus

**calamar** /kalamaʀ/ nm squid

**calamité** /kalamite/ nf disaster, calamity

**calandre** /kalɑ̃dʀ/ nf (Aut) (radiator) grille
(GB)

**calcaire** /kalkɛʀ/ **1** adj ‹water› hard;
‹soil› chalky; ‹rock› limestone
**2** nm **(a)** limestone
**(b)** fur (GB), sediment (US)

**calciner** /kalsine/ [1] vtr **(a)** to char;
(in oven) to burn [sth] to a crisp
**(b)** (in chemistry) to calcine

**calcium** /kalsjɔm/ nm calcium

**calcul** /kalkyl/ nm **(a)** calculation; **faire le**
~ **de qch** to calculate sth
**(b)** arithmetic; ~ **mental** mental arithmetic
**(c)** (scheming) calculation; **agir par** ~ to act
out of self-interest
**(d)** (Med) stone

**calculateur**, **-trice[1]** /kalkylatœʀ, tʀis/
adj calculating

**calculatrice[2]** /kalkylatʀis/ nf (pocket)
calculator

**calculer** /kalkyle/ [1] **1** vtr **(a)** to
calculate, to work out
**(b)** to weigh up ‹advantages, chances›; **tout
bien calculé** all things considered
**(c)** ~ **son coup** to plan one's move
**2** vi to calculate

**calculette** /kalkylɛt/ nf pocket calculator

**cale** /kal/ nf **(a)** wedge; (for wheel) chock; (for
raising vehicle) block
**(b)** (Naut) (ship's) hold

**calé**, **-e** /kale/ adj (colloq) bright; ~ **en**
**qch** brilliant at sth

**calebasse** /kalbas/ nf calabash, gourd

**calèche** /kalɛʃ/ nf barouche, carriage

**caleçon** /kalsɔ̃/ nm **(a)** boxer shorts;
~ **long** long johns (colloq)
**(b)** (for woman) leggings

**calédonien**, **-ienne** /kaledɔnjɛ̃, ɛn/ adj
**(a)** New Caledonian
**(b)** Caledonian

**calembour** /kalɑ̃buʀ/ nm pun, play on
words

**calendrier** /kalɑ̃dʀije/ nm **(a)** calendar
**(b)** schedule
**(c)** dates

**cale-pied**, *pl* ~**s** /kalpje/ *nm* toe clip

**calepin** /kalpɛ̃/ *nm* notebook

**caler** /kale/ [1] **1** *vtr* **(a)** to wedge ⟨*wheel*⟩; to steady ⟨*piece of furniture*⟩; to support ⟨*row of books*⟩; **bien calé dans mon fauteuil** ensconced in my armchair
**(b)** (colloq) **ça cale** it fills you up
**2** *vi* ⟨*car*⟩ to stall
**3 se caler** *v refl* (+ *v être*) to settle ⟨*dans* in⟩

**calfeutrer** /kalføtRe/ [1] **1** *vtr* to stop up ⟨*crack*⟩; to draughtproof ⟨*door*⟩
**2 se calfeutrer** *v refl* (+ *v être*) to shut oneself away

**calibre** /kalibR/ *nm* **(a)** (of gun) bore, calibre (GB); (of pipe, cable) diameter; **arme de gros** ~ large-bore weapon
**(b)** (of eggs, fruit) size, grade
**(c)** gauge

**calibrer** /kalibRe/ [1] *vtr* **(a)** (Tech) to calibrate
**(b)** to grade, to size ⟨*eggs, fruit*⟩

**calice** /kalis/ *nm* chalice

**calife** /kalif/ *nm* caliph

**califourchon: à califourchon** /akalifuRʃɔ̃/ *phr* astride

**câlin**, ~**e** /kɑlɛ̃, in/ **1** *adj* affectionate
**2** *nm* cuddle

**câliner** /kaline/ [1] *vtr* to cuddle

**calleux, -euse** /kalø, øz/ *adj* calloused

**calligraphie** /kaligRafi/ *nf* calligraphy

**calligraphier** /kaligRafje/ [2] *vtr* to write [sth] in a decorative hand

**callosité** /kalozite/ *nf* callus

**calmant**, ~**e** /kalmɑ̃, ɑ̃t/ **1** *adj* soothing
**2** *nm* sedative

**calmar** /kalmaR/ *nm* squid

**calme** /kalm/ **1** *adj* **(a)** ⟨*sea, situation*⟩ calm; ⟨*night*⟩ still; ⟨*place, life*⟩ quiet
**(b)** ⟨*person*⟩ calm
**2** *nm* **(a)** peace (and quiet)
**(b)** calm; (of crowd) calmness; (of night) stillness; **dans le** ~ peacefully
**(c)** composure; **conserver son** ~ to keep calm; **du** ~**!** calm down!; quiet!

**calmement** /kalməmɑ̃/ *adv* calmly

**calmer** /kalme/ [1] **1** *vtr* **(a)** to calm down ⟨*person*⟩; to calm ⟨*stock market*⟩; to defuse ⟨*situation*⟩; to tone down ⟨*discussion*⟩; ~ **les esprits** to calm people down
**(b)** to ease ⟨*pain*⟩; to take the edge off ⟨*hunger*⟩; to quench ⟨*thirst*⟩
**2 se calmer** *v refl* (+ *v être*) **(a)** ⟨*person, situation*⟩ to calm down; ⟨*agitation, storm*⟩ to die down; ⟨*debate*⟩ to quieten (GB) *or* quiet (US) down; ⟨*ardour*⟩ to cool
**(b)** ⟨*pain*⟩ to ease

**calomnie** /kalɔmni/ *nf* slander

**calomnier** /kalɔmnje/ [2] *vtr* to slander

**calorie** /kalɔRi/ *nf* calorie

**calorifère** /kalɔRifɛR/ *adj* heat-conveying

**calorique** /kalɔRik/ *adj* calorie; **ration/valeur** ~ calorie intake/content

**calotte** /kalɔt/ *nf* **(a)** skull cap
**(b)** (colloq) slap
**(c)** ~ **glaciaire** icecap

**calque** /kalk/ *nm* **(a)** tracing
**(b)** tracing paper
**(c)** replica

**calquer** /kalke/ [1] *vtr* **(a)** to copy ⟨*behaviour*⟩
**(b)** to trace ⟨*pattern, design*⟩ ⟨**sur** from⟩

**calumet** /kalymɛ/ *nm* ~ **de la paix** peace pipe

**calvados** /kalvados/ *nm* calvados ⟨*apple brandy distilled in Normandy*⟩

**calvaire** /kalvɛR/ *nm* **(a)** ordeal
**(b)** (monument) wayside cross
**(c)** Calvary

**calvitie** /kalvisi/ *nf* baldness

**camaïeu** /kamajø/ *nm* monochrome

**camarade** /kamaRad/ *nmf* **(a)** friend; ~ **d'atelier** workmate
**(b)** comrade

**camaraderie** /kamaRadRi/ *nf* comradeship

**Cambodge** /kɑ̃bɔdʒ/ *pr nm* Cambodia

**cambouis** /kɑ̃bwi/ *nm* dirty grease

**cambré**, ~**e** /kɑ̃bRe/ *adj* ⟨*back*⟩ arched; ⟨*foot, shoe*⟩ with a high instep

**cambrer** /kɑ̃bRe/ [1] **1** *vtr* to curve, to arch
**2 se cambrer** *v refl* (+ *v être*) to arch one's back

**cambriolage** /kɑ̃bRijɔlaʒ/ *nm* burglary

**cambrioler** /kɑ̃bRijɔle/ [1] *vtr* to burgle (GB), to burglarize (US)

**cambrioleur, -euse** /kɑ̃bRijɔlœR, øz/ *nm,f* burglar

**cambrousse** /kɑ̃bRus/ *nf* (colloq) **la** ~ the sticks (colloq), the country; **en pleine** ~ in the middle of nowhere

**cambrure** /kɑ̃bRyR/ *nf* curve; (of foot) arch
■ ~ **des pieds** instep; ~ **des reins** small of the back

**camée** /kame/ *nm* cameo

**caméléon** /kameleɔ̃/ *nm* chameleon

**camelote** /kamlɔt/ *nf* (colloq) junk (colloq)

**camembert** /kamɑ̃bɛR/ *nm* **(a)** (Culin) Camembert
**(b)** (colloq) pie chart

**camer: se camer** /kame/ [1] *v refl* (+ *v être*) (slang) to be on drugs

**caméra** /kameRa/ *nf* (cine-)camera (GB), movie camera (US)

**caméscope®** /kameskɔp/ *nm* camcorder

**camion** /kamjɔ̃/ *nm* truck

**camion-citerne**, *pl* **camions-citernes** /kamjɔ̃sitɛRn/ *nm* tanker

**camionnette** /kamjɔnɛt/ *nf* van

**camionneur** /kamjɔnœR/ *nm* truck driver

**camisole** /kamizɔl/ *nf* camisole; ~ **de force** straitjacket

**camomille** /kamɔmij/ *nf* camomile

**camouflage** /kamuflaʒ/ *nm* **(a)** (Mil) camouflage
**(b)** (figurative) concealing; disguising ⟨**en** as⟩

**camoufler** /kamufle/ [1] *vtr* **(a)** (Mil) to camouflage
**(b)** to cover up ⟨*crime, mistake, truth*⟩; to conceal ⟨*intention, feelings*⟩
**(c)** to hide ⟨*money*⟩

**camp** /kɑ̃/ *nm* **(a)** (gen) camp
**(b)** (Sport, Pol) side
IDIOMS **ficher** (colloq) **le** ∼ **to split** (colloq), to leave

**campagnard**, ∼**e** /kɑ̃paɲaʀ, aʀd/ **1** *adj* country, rustic
**2** *nm,f* country person

**campagne** /kɑ̃paɲ/ *nf* **(a)** country; (open) countryside
**(b)** campaign; **faire** ∼ to campaign

**campanule** /kɑ̃panyl/ *nf* bellflower

**campement** /kɑ̃pmɑ̃/ *nm* camp, encampment

**camper** /kɑ̃pe/ [1] **1** *vtr* to portray ⟨*character*⟩; to depict ⟨*landscape,scene*⟩
**2** *vi* to camp
**3** **se camper** *v refl* (+ *v être*) **se** ∼ **devant qn/qch** to stand squarely in front of sb/sth

**campeur**, **-euse** /kɑ̃pœʀ, øz/ *nm,f* camper

**camphre** /kɑ̃fʀ/ *nm* camphor

**camping** /kɑ̃piŋ/ *nm* **(a)** camping; **faire du** ∼ **sauvage** to camp rough
**(b)** campsite (GB), campground (US)

**camping-car**, *pl* ∼**s** /kɑ̃piŋkaʀ/ *nm* (controversial) camper

**camping-gaz®** /kɑ̃piŋgaz/ *nm inv* (gas) camping stove

**campus** /kɑ̃pys/ *nm inv* campus

**Canada** /kanada/ *pr nm* Canada

**Canadair®** /kanadɛʀ/ *nm* water bomber

**canadienne** /kanadjɛn/ *nf* **(a)** sheepskin-lined jacket
**(b)** ridge tent

**canal**, *pl* **-aux** /kanal, o/ *nm* **(a)** canal
**(b)** channel
**(c)** (Anat) duct

**canalisation** /kanalizasjɔ̃/ *nf* **(a)** pipe
**(b)** mains

**canaliser** /kanalize/ [1] *vtr* **(a)** to canalize ⟨*river*⟩
**(b)** (figurative) to channel

**canapé** /kanape/ *nm* **(a)** sofa; ∼ **convertible** sofa bed
**(b)** (Culin) canapé

**canaque** /kanak/ *adj* Kanak

**canard** /kanaʀ/ *nm* **(a)** duck; ∼ **laqué** Peking duck
**(b)** (colloq) rag (colloq), newspaper
**(c)** (Mus) wrong note
IDIOMS **ça ne casse pas trois pattes à un** ∼ (colloq) it's nothing to write home about

**canarder** /kanaʀde/ [1] *vtr* (colloq) to snipe at

**canari** /kanaʀi/ *nm* canary

**canasson** /kanasɔ̃/ *nm* (slang) nag (colloq), horse

**cancan** /kɑ̃kɑ̃/ *nm* **(a)** (colloq) gossip
**(b)** cancan

**cancaner** /kɑ̃kane/ [1] *vi* (colloq) to gossip

**cancer** /kɑ̃sɛʀ/ *nm* cancer

**Cancer** /kɑ̃sɛʀ/ *pr nm* Cancer

**cancéreux**, **-euse** /kɑ̃seʀø, øz/ *adj* ⟨*cell*⟩ cancerous; ⟨*person*⟩ with cancer

**cancérigène** /kɑ̃seʀiʒɛn/ *adj* carcinogenic

**cancérologie** /kɑ̃seʀɔlɔʒi/ *nf* cancer research; **service de** ∼ cancer ward

**cancre** /kɑ̃kʀ/ *nm* dunce

**cancrelat** /kɑ̃kʀəla/ *nm* cockroach

**candeur** /kɑ̃dœʀ/ *nf* ingenuousness

**candi** /kɑ̃di/ *adj m* **sucre** ∼ sugar candy

**candidat**, ∼**e** /kɑ̃dida, at/ *nm,f* (Pol) candidate; (for job) applicant; (in competition) contestant; **être** ∼ **aux élections** to stand for election (GB), to run for office (US); **être** ∼ **(à un poste)** to apply (for a post); **pour la vaisselle, il n'y a pas beaucoup de** ∼**s!** (humorous) when it comes to doing the dishes, there aren't many takers

**candidature** /kɑ̃didatyʀ/ *nf*
**(a)** candidature, candidacy; **retirer sa** ∼ to stand down (GB), to drop out (US)
**(b)** (for a post) application; **faire acte de** ∼ to apply

**candide** /kɑ̃did/ *adj* ingenuous

**cane** /kan/ *nf* (female) duck

**caneton** /kantɔ̃/ *nm* duckling

**canette** /kanɛt/ *nf* **(a)** ∼ **(de bière)** (small) bottle of beer
**(b)** can; ∼ **de bière** can of beer
**(c)** (of sewing machine) spool

**canevas** /kanva/ *nm inv* **(a)** canvas
**(b)** tapestry work
**(c)** (figurative) framework

**caniche** /kaniʃ/ *nm* poodle

**canicule** /kanikyl/ *nf* **(a)** scorching heat
**(b)** heatwave

**canif** /kanif/ *nm* penknife

**canin**, ∼**e**[1] /kanɛ̃, in/ *adj* canine

**canine**[2] /kanin/ *nf* canine (tooth)

**caniveau**, *pl* ∼**x** /kanivo/ *nm* gutter

**cannabis** /kanabis/ *nm* cannabis

**canne** /kan/ *nf* **(a)** (walking) stick
**(b)** (Bot) cane
■ ∼ **à pêche** fishing rod

**canneberge** /kanbɛʀʒ/ *nf* cranberry

**cannelle** /kanɛl/ *nf* cinnamon

**cannette** = CANETTE

**cannibale** /kanibal/ *adj, nmf* cannibal

**canoë** /kanɔe/ *nm* **(a)** canoe
**(b)** canoeing

**canoë-kayak** /kanɔekajak/ *nm* canoeing

**canon** /kanɔ̃/ **1** *adj m inv* **droit** ∼ canon law
**2** *nm* **(a)** (big gun; cannon; **tirer un coup de** ∼ to fire a gun; **entendre des coups de** ∼ to hear cannon fire
**(b)** (of firearm) barrel
**(c)** (Mus) canon; **chanter en** ∼ to sing in a round
**(d)** (rule, principle) canon ⋯⋙

**(e)** (in religion) canon

**cañon** /kaɲɔ̃, kaɲɔn/ *nm* canyon

**canonique** /kanɔnik/ *adj* **droit** ~ canon law; **d'âge** ~ (humorous) of a venerable age

**canoniser** /kanɔnize/ [1] *vtr* to canonize

**canot** /kano/ *nm* (small) boat, dinghy; ~ **pneumatique** rubber dinghy; ~ **de sauvetage** (on ship) lifeboat; (on plane) life raft

**canotier** /kanɔtje/ *nm* boater

**canson®** /kɑ̃sɔ̃/ *nm* drawing paper

**cantaloup** /kɑ̃talu/ *nm* cantaloupe melon

**cantate** /kɑ̃tat/ *nf* cantata

**cantatrice** /kɑ̃tatʀis/ *nf* (opera) singer

**cantine** /kɑ̃tin/ *nf* **(a)** canteen (GB), cafeteria; **manger à la** ~ ⟨*child*⟩ to have school dinners
**(b)** tin trunk

**cantique** /kɑ̃tik/ *nm* hymn, canticle

**canton** /kɑ̃tɔ̃/ *nm* canton

**cantonade**: **à la cantonade** /alakɑ̃tɔnad/ *phr* **parler à la** ~ to speak to no-one in particular

**cantonais**, ~**e** /kɑ̃tɔnɛ, ɛz/ **1** *adj* Cantonese
**2** *nm* (language) Cantonese

**cantonal**, ~**e**, *mpl* -**aux** /kɑ̃tɔnal, o/ *adj* cantonal

**cantonner** /kɑ̃tɔne/ [1] *vtr* ~ **qn dans un lieu** to confine sb to a place; ~ **qn dans le rôle de** to reduce sb to the role of

**cantonnier** /kɑ̃tɔnje/ *nm* road-mender

**cantonnière** /kɑ̃tɔnjɛʀ/ *nf* pelmet

**canular** /kanylaʀ/ *nm* hoax

**canule** /kanyl/ *nf* cannula

**canyon** = CAÑON

**caoutchouc** /kautʃu/ *nm* **(a)** rubber
**(b)** rubber plant
**(c)** rubber band

**caoutchouteux**, -**euse** /kautʃutø, øz/ *adj* rubbery

**cap** /kap/ *nm* **(a)** (in geography) cape
**(b)** mark; **passer le** ~ **de la cinquantaine** to pass the fifty mark
**(c)** (direction) course; **maintenir le** ~ to hold one's course; **mettre le** ~ **sur** to head for

**Cap** /kap/ *pr n* **le** ~ Cape Town

**CAP** /seape/ *nm*: *abbr* ▶ CERTIFICAT

**capable** /kapabl/ *adj* capable (**de faire of** doing); **ils sont bien** ~**s de nous mentir** I wouldn't put it past them to lie to us

**capacité** /kapasite/ **1** *nf* **(a)** ability
**(b)** capacity
**2 capacités** *nf pl* (talent) abilities

**cape** /kap/ *nf* cape; cloak
**IDIOMS rire sous** ~ to laugh up one's sleeve

**capeline** /kaplin/ *nf* wide-brimmed hat

**CAPES** /kapɛs/ *nm* (*abbr* = **certificat d'aptitude professionnelle à l'enseignement secondaire**) *secondary school teaching qualification*

**capharnaüm** /kafaʀnaɔm/ *nm* shambles (colloq)

**capillaire** /kapilɛʀ/ **1** *adj* **(a)** capillary
**(b) soins** ~**s** hair care
**2** *nm* capillary

**capitaine** /kapitɛn/ *nm* **(a)** (Mil) (in army, navy) ≈ captain
**(b)** (Sport) captain

**capitainerie** /kapitɛnʀi/ *nf* port authority

**capital**, ~**e¹**, *mpl* -**aux** /kapital, o/ **1** *adj* **(a)** ⟨*importance*⟩ major; ⟨*role, question*⟩ key; **il est** ~ **de faire** it's essential to do
**(b)** ⟨*letter*⟩ capital
**(c) peine** ~**e** capital punishment
**2** *nm* **(a)** capital
**(b) le** ~ **humain/industriel** human/industrial resources
**3 capitaux** *nm pl* capital, funds

**capitale²** /kapital/ *nf* **(a)** capital (city)
**(b)** capital (letter); **en** ~**s d'imprimerie** in block capitals

**capitalisation** /kapitalizasjɔ̃/ *nf* capitalization

**capitaliser** /kapitalize/ [1] *vtr* to capitalize

**capitalisme** /kapitalism/ *nm* capitalism

**capitaliste** /kapitalist/ *adj, nmf* capitalist

**capitonner** /kapitɔne/ [1] *vtr* to pad

**capitulation** /kapitylasjɔ̃/ *nf* capitulation (**devant** to); ~ **sans conditions** unconditional surrender

**capituler** /kapityle/ [1] *vi* to capitulate

**caporal**, *pl* -**aux** /kapɔral, o/ *nm* (Mil) (in army) ≈ corporal

**capot** /kapo/ *nm* (Aut) bonnet (GB), hood (US)

**capotage** /kapɔtaʒ/ *nm* collapse

**capote** /kapɔt/ *nf* **(a)** great-coat
**(b)** (of car, pram) hood (GB), top
**(c)** (colloq) ~ **(anglaise)** condom

**capoter** /kapɔte/ [1] *vi* **(a)** to collapse
**(b)** ⟨*car*⟩ to overturn

**câpre** /kɑpʀ/ *nf* caper

**caprice** /kapʀis/ *nm* **(a)** (of person) whim; **céder aux** ~**s de qn** to indulge sb's whims; **c'est un** ~ **de la nature** ⟨of plant, animal⟩ it's a freak of nature
**(b) faire un** ~ to throw a tantrum

**capricieusement** /kapʀisjøzmɑ̃/ *adv* capriciously; whimsically

**capricieux**, -**ieuse** /kapʀisjø, øz/ *adj* ⟨*person*⟩ capricious; ⟨*machine*⟩ temperamental; ⟨*weather*⟩ changeable; ⟨*destiny*⟩ fickle

**capricorne** /kapʀikɔrn/ *nm* capricorn beetle

**Capricorne** /kapʀikɔrn/ *pr nm* Capricorn

**capsule** /kapsyl/ *nf* **(a)** (of bottle) cap; top
**(b)** (Med) capsule
**(c)** ~ **spatiale** space capsule

**capter** /kapte/ [1] *vtr* **(a)** to get ⟨*channel, programme*⟩; to pick up ⟨*signal*⟩
**(b)** to catch ⟨*attention*⟩
**(c)** to soak up ⟨*light*⟩

**captif**, -**ive** /kaptif, iv/ *adj, nmf* captive

**captivant**, **~e** /kaptivã, ãt/ *adj*
enthralling; gripping; riveting; captivating

**captiver** /kaptive/ [1] *vtr* ‹*beauty*› to
captivate; ‹*music*› to enthrall; ‹*story, person*›
to fascinate

**captivité** /kaptivite/ *nf* captivity

**capture** /kaptyʀ/ *nf* capture

**capturer** /kaptyʀe/ [1] *vtr* to capture

**capuche** /kapyʃ/ *nf* hood; **à ~** with a
hood

**capuchon** /kapyʃõ/ *nm* **(a)** (of garment)
hood
**(b)** (of pen) cap

**capucine** /kapysin/ *nf* nasturtium

**caquet** /kakɛ/ *nm* prattle; **rabattre le ~ à
qn** (colloq) to put sb in his/her place

**caqueter** /kakte/ [20] *vi* ‹*hen*› to cackle

**car¹** /kaʀ/ *conj* because, for

**car²** /kaʀ/ *nm* bus; **~ de police** police van;
**~ (de ramassage) scolaire** school bus

**carabine** /kaʀabin/ *nf* rifle

**carabiné**, **~e** /kaʀabine/ *adj* (colloq)
‹*fever*› raging; ‹*cold*› stinking (colloq)

**caracoler** /kaʀakɔle/ [1] *vi* **(a)** to be well
ahead
**(b)** ‹*horse*› to prance; ‹*rider*› to parade

**caractère** /kaʀaktɛʀ/ *nm* **(a)** (written)
character; **~s d'imprimerie** block capitals;
**en petits/gros ~s** in small/large print
**(b)** nature, temperament; **avoir mauvais ~**
to be bad-tempered
**(c)** (personality) character; **il n'a aucun ~** he's
got no backbone
**(d)** (of house, place) character
**(e)** characteristic
**(f)** nature; **à ~ commercial** of a commercial
nature
**IDIOMS avoir un ~ de cochon** (colloq), **avoir
un sale ~** to have a vile temper

**caractériel**, **-ielle** /kaʀakteʀjɛl/ *adj*
‹*problems*› emotional; ‹*person*› disturbed

**caractériser** /kaʀakteʀize/ [1] **1** *vtr* to
characterize
**2 se caractériser** *v refl* (+ *v être*) to be
characterized

**caractéristique** /kaʀakteʀistik/ **1** *adj*
characteristic
**2** *nf* characteristics

**carafe** /kaʀaf/ *nf* carafe

**caraïbe** /kaʀaib/ *adj* Caribbean

**Caraïbes** /kaʀaib/ *pr nf pl* Caribbean
(islands)

**carambolage** /kaʀãbɔlaʒ/ *nm* pile-up

**caramboler** /kaʀãbɔle/ [1] *vtr* to collide
with

**caramel** /kaʀamɛl/ *nm* **(a)** caramel
**(b)** toffee (GB), toffy (US); **~ mou** ≈ fudge

**carapace** /kaʀapas/ *nf* shell, carapace

**carat** /kaʀa/ *nm* carat; **or 18 ~s** 18-carat
gold

**caravane** /kaʀavan/ *nf* **(a)** caravan (GB),
trailer (US)
**(b)** (convoy) caravan

**caravelle** /kaʀavɛl/ *nf* (boat) caravel

**carbone** /kaʀbɔn/ *nm* **(a)** carbon
**(b)** carbon paper
**(c)** sheet of carbon paper

**carbonique** /kaʀbɔnik/ *adj* carbonic;
**neige ~** dry ice

**carbonisé**, **~e** /kaʀbɔnize/ *adj* burned-
out; charred; burned to a cinder

**carboniser** /kaʀbɔnize/ [1] *vtr* **(a)** to
carbonize
**(b)** to reduce [sth] to ashes

**carburant** /kaʀbyʀã/ *nm* fuel

**carburateur** /kaʀbyʀatœʀ/ *nm*
carburettor (GB), carburetor (US)

**carburer** /kaʀbyʀe/ [1] *vi* **(a)** **il carbure au
vin rouge** he runs on red wine
**(b)** to work flat out

**carcan** /kaʀkã/ *nm* **(a)** (device) iron collar
**(b)** **~ administratif** administrative
constraints

**carcasse** /kaʀkas/ *nf* carcass

**carcéral**, **~e**, *mpl* **-aux** /kaʀseʀal, o/
*adj* prison

**cardan** /kaʀdã/ *nm* universal joint

**cardiaque** /kaʀdjak/ *adj* **être ~** to have a
heart condition; **crise ~** heart attack

**cardinal**, **~e**, *mpl* **-aux** /kaʀdinal, o/
**1** *adj* cardinal
**2** *nm* **(a)** cardinal
**(b)** cardinal number

**cardiologie** /kaʀdjɔlɔʒi/ *nf* cardiology

**cardiologue** /kaʀdjɔlɔg/ *nmf* cardiologist

**carême** /kaʀɛm/ *nm* **le ~** Lent

**carence** /kaʀãs/ *nf* **(a)** (Med) deficiency
**(b)** lack
**(c)** **les ~s de la loi** the shortcomings of the
law

**carène** /kaʀɛn/ *nf* hull (*below the
waterline*)

**caressant**, **~e** /kaʀɛsã, ãt/ *adj*
affectionate; soft

**caresse** /kaʀɛs/ *nf* caress, stroke; **faire
une ~** *or* **des ~s à** to stroke

**caresser** /kaʀese/ [1] *vtr* **(a)** to stroke, to
caress; **~ qn du regard** to look at sb lovingly
**(b)** to entertain ‹*hope, idea*›; to cherish
‹*dream*›
**IDIOMS ~ qn dans le sens du poil** to stay on
the right side of sb

**cargaison** /kaʀgɛzõ/ *nf* **(a)** cargo
**(b)** (colloq) load

**cargo** /kaʀgo/ *nm* (Naut) freighter, cargo
ship

**caricatural**, **~e**, *mpl* **-aux**
/kaʀikatyʀal, o/ *adj* **(a)** grotesque
**(b)** caricatural

**caricature** /kaʀikatyʀ/ *nf* caricature;
**c'est une ~ de procès** it's a mockery of a
trial

**caricaturer** /kaʀikatyʀe/ [1] *vtr* to
caricature

**caricaturiste** /kaʀikatyʀist/ *nmf*
caricaturist

**carie** /kaʀi/ *nf* la ∼ (dentaire) (tooth) decay; **avoir une carie** to have a hole in one's tooth

**carié**, ∼**e** /kaʀje/ *adj* decayed

**carier**: **se carier** /kaʀje/ [2] *v refl* (+ *v être*) ⟨*tooth*⟩ to decay

**carillon** /kaʀijɔ̃/ *nm* (a) (of church) (set of) bells; (tune) chimes
(b) (chiming) clock; (sound) chimes
(c) (door) chimes

**carillonner** /kaʀijɔne/ [1] *vi* (a) ⟨*bells*⟩ to ring out, to peal out
(b) (at door) to ring (loudly)

**caritatif, -ive** /kaʀitatif, iv/ *adj* charitable; **une association caritative** a charity

**carlingue** /kaʀlɛ̃g/ *nf* (of plane) cabin

**carmin** /kaʀmɛ̃/*nm, adj inv* carmine

**carnage** /kaʀnaʒ/ *nm* carnage, massacre

**carnassier, -ière** /kaʀnasje, ɛʀ/ *adj* carnivorous

**carnaval**, *pl* ∼**s** /kaʀnaval/ *nm* carnival

**carnet** /kaʀnɛ/ *nm* (a) notebook
(b) (of tickets, vouchers, stamps) book
■ ∼ **de chèques** chequebook (GB), checkbook (US); ∼ **de correspondance** (Sch) mark book; ∼ **de santé** health record

**carnivore** /kaʀnivɔʀ/ [1] *adj*. carnivorous
[2] *nm* carnivore

**carotide** /kaʀɔtid/ *adj, nf* carotid

**carotte** /kaʀɔt/ *nf* carrot
IDIOMS **manier la** ∼ **et le bâton** to use stick-and-carrot tactics

**caroube** /kaʀub/ *nf* carob

**carpe¹** /kaʀp/ *nm* (Anat) carpus

**carpe²** /kaʀp/ *nf* (fish) carp
IDIOMS **il est resté muet comme une** ∼ he never said a word

**carpette** /kaʀpɛt/ *nf* (a) rug
(b) (colloq) doormat (colloq)

**carré, ∼e** /kaʀe/ [1] *adj* (a) ⟨*shape*⟩ square; **il est** ∼ **d'épaules** he has broad shoulders
(b) ⟨*metre, root*⟩ square
[2] *nm* (a) square
(b) (of sky, ground) patch; (of chocolate) piece; **avoir une coupe au** ∼ to have one's hair cut in a bob; ∼ **blanc** '*suitable for adults only*' *sign on French TV*
(c) (in mathematics) square
(d) ∼ **d'agneau** rack of lamb

**carreau**, *pl* ∼**x** /kaʀo/ *nm* (a) (floor) tile; (wall) tile
(b) window-pane; **faire les** ∼**x** to clean the windows
(c) (on paper) square; (on fabric) check
(d) (in cards) diamonds
IDIOMS **rester sur le** ∼ (colloq) to be left high and dry (colloq); **se tenir à** ∼ (colloq) to watch one's step

**carrefour** /kaʀfuʀ/ *nm* (a) junction; crossroads
(b) (figurative) crossroads

**carrelage** /kaʀlaʒ/ *nm* (a) tiled floor
(b) tiles

**carreler** /kaʀle/ [19] *vtr* to tile

**carrelet** /kaʀlɛ/ *nm* plaice

**carrément** /kaʀemɑ̃/ *adv* (a) **la situation devient** ∼ **inquiétante** quite frankly the situation is becoming worrying; **il vaut** ∼ **mieux les jeter** it would be better just to throw them out
(b) completely; **dans un cas pareil, appelle** ∼ **la police** in such a case, don't hesitate to call the police
(c) ⟨*ask, say*⟩ straight out; ⟨*express*⟩ clearly
(d) **allez-y** ∼! go straight ahead!

**carrière** /kaʀjɛʀ/ *nf* (a) career; **faire** ∼ **dans** to make a career in
(b) quarry; ∼ **de sable** sandpit

**carriole** /kaʀjɔl/ *nf* (a) cart
(b) (colloq) jalopy (colloq), car

**carrossable** /kaʀɔsabl/ *adj* suitable for motor vehicles

**carrosse** /kaʀɔs/ *nm* (horse-drawn) coach

**carrosserie** /kaʀɔsʀi/ *nf* (a) bodywork
(b) coachbuilding
(c) body repair work

**carrossier** /kaʀɔsje/ *nm* coachbuilder

**carrousel** /kaʀusɛl/ *nm* merry-go-round, carousel

**carrure** /kaʀyʀ/ *nf* (a) shoulders
(b) calibre (GB)

**cartable** /kaʀtabl/ *nm* (a) schoolbag, satchel
(b) briefcase

**carte** /kaʀt/ *nf* (a) card; ∼ **à jouer** playing card
(b) pass
(c) map; chart
(d) ∼ **génétique** genetic map
(e) menu; **repas à la** ∼ à la carte meal
■ ∼ **d'abonnement** season ticket; ∼ **d'adhérent** membership card; ∼ **bleue**® credit card; ∼ **de crédit** credit card; ∼ **grise** logbook; ∼ **d'identité** ID card; ∼ **orange**® season ticket (*in the Paris region*); ∼ **postale** postcard; ∼ **à puce** smart card; ∼ **de réduction** discount card; ∼ **de retrait (automatique)** cashcard; ∼ **de séjour** resident's permit; ∼ **vermeil**® senior citizen's railcard; ∼ **des vins** wine list; ∼ **de visite** (social) visiting card; (professional) business card; ∼ **de vœux** greetings card

**cartel** /kaʀtɛl/ *nm* (a) cartel
(b) coalition

**carter** /kaʀtɛʀ/ *nm* (of engine) crankcase; (of gearbox) casing

**cartilage** /kaʀtilaʒ/ *nm* (a) (Anat, Zool) cartilage
(b) (Culin) gristle

**cartomancie** /kaʀtɔmɑ̃si/ *nf* fortune-telling

**cartomancien, -ienne** /kaʀtɔmɑ̃sjɛ̃, ɛn/ *nm,f* fortune-teller

**carton** /kaʀtɔ̃/ *nm* (a) cardboard; **en** ∼ ⟨*folder*⟩ cardboard; ⟨*cups*⟩ paper
(b) (cardboard) box
(c) card
■ ∼ **à dessin** portfolio

IDIOMS faire un ∼ (colloq) to do great (colloq)

**cartonné, ∼e** /kaʀtɔne/ adj **couverture** ∼e (of book) hard cover

**cartonner** (colloq) /kaʀtɔne/ [1] vi to score

**carton-pâte** /kaʀtɔpɑt/ nm inv pasteboard

**cartouche** /kaʀtuʃ/ nf **(a)** cartridge; (of gas) refill
**(b)** ∼ de cigarettes carton of cigarettes

**cas** /kɑ/ 1 nm inv case; **auquel** ∼ in which case; **au** ∼ **où il viendrait** in case he comes; **prends ta voiture, au** ∼ **où** take your car, just in case; **en** ∼ **de besoin** if necessary; **en** ∼ **de décès** in the event of death; **le** ∼ **échéant** if need be; **dans le** ∼ **contraire, vous devrez...** should the opposite occur, you will have to...; **dans le meilleur/pire des** ∼ at best/worst; **en aucun** ∼ under no circumstances; **c'est le** ∼ **de le dire!** you can say that again!; **être dans le même** ∼ **que qn** to be in the same position as sb; **n'aggrave pas ton** ∼ don't make things worse for yourself; **un** ∼ rare a rare occurrence; **c'est un** ∼ **de renvoi** it's grounds for dismissal
2 **en tout cas, en tous les cas** phr
**(a)** in any case, at any rate
**(b)** at least
■ ∼ **de conscience** moral dilemma; ∼ **social** socially disadvantaged person
IDIOMS **il a fait grand** ∼ **de son avancement** he made a big thing of his promotion

**casanier, -ière** /kazanje, ɛʀ/ adj ⟨person⟩ stay-at-home; ⟨existence⟩ unadventurous

**casaque** /kazak/ nf (of jockey) jersey, silk

**cascade** /kaskad/ nf **(a)** waterfall
**(b)** stunt

**cascadeur, -euse** /kaskadœʀ, øz/ nm,f stuntman/stuntwoman

**case** /kɑz/ nf **(a)** hut, cabin
**(b)** (in board games) square
**(c)** (on form) box
■ ∼ **départ** (in board game) start; **retour à la** ∼ **départ** (figurative) back to square one.
IDIOMS **il lui manque une** ∼ (colloq) he's got a screw loose (colloq)

**caser** (colloq) /kɑze/ [1] 1 vtr **(a)** to put, to stick (colloq)
**(b)** to marry off
**(c)** to find a place or job for
2 **se caser** v refl (+ v être) to get married

**caserne** /kazɛʀn/ nf barracks
■ ∼ **de sapeurs-pompiers** fire station

**casher** /kaʃɛʀ/ adj inv kosher

**casier** /kɑzje/ nm **(a)** (in gym) locker
**(b)** pigeonhole
**(c)** ∼ **judiciaire** police record

**casino** /kazino/ nm casino

**casque** /kask/ nm **(a)** helmet; crash helmet; safety helmet
**(b)** headphones
**(c)** hairdryer

**casqué, ∼e** /kaske/ adj helmeted

**casquette** /kaskɛt/ nf cap; **porter plusieurs** ∼s (figurative) to wear several hats

**cassant, ∼e** /kasɑ̃, ɑ̃t/ adj **(a)** brittle
**(b)** curt, abrupt

**casse**[1] /kɑs/ nm (slang) break-in, heist (US) (colloq)

**casse**[2] /kɑs/ nf **(a)** breakage
**(b)** breaker's yard, scrap yard; **mettre à la** ∼ to scrap

**cassé, ∼e** /kɑse/ adj ⟨voice⟩ hoarse

**casse-cou** /kasku/ nmf inv daredevil

**casse-croûte** /kaskʀut/ nm inv snack

**casse-noisettes** /kasnwazɛt/, **casse-noix** /kasnwa/ nm inv nutcrackers

**casser** /kɑse/ [1] 1 vtr to break ⟨object, bone⟩; to crack ⟨nut⟩; ∼ **les prix** to slash prices; ∼ **la figure** (colloq) **à qn** to beat sb up (colloq)
2 vi **(a)** to break
**(b)** (colloq) ⟨couple⟩ to split up
3 **se casser** v refl (+ v être) **(a)** to break
**(b)** **se** ∼ **une** or **la jambe** to break one's leg; **se** ∼ **la figure** (colloq) ⟨pedestrian⟩ to fall over (GB) or down; ⟨venture⟩ to fail; ⟨people⟩ to have a scrap (colloq); **il ne s'est pas cassé la tête** (colloq) he didn't exactly strain himself
**(c)** (colloq) to go away
IDIOMS ∼ **les pieds** (colloq) **à qn** to annoy sb; ∼ **la croûte** to eat; **ça te prendra trois heures, à tout** ∼ (colloq) it'll take you three hours at the very most

**casserole** /kasʀɔl/ nf saucepan, pan
IDIOMS **chanter comme une** ∼ (colloq) to sing atrociously

**casse-tête** /kastɛt/ nm inv **(a)** headache, problem
**(b)** puzzle

**cassette** /kasɛt/ nf **(a)** tape, cassette
**(b)** casket

**casseur** /kasœʀ/ nm **(a)** scrap dealer
**(b)** rioting demonstrator

**cassis** /kasis/ nm inv **(a)** blackcurrant
**(b)** (in road) dip

**cassonade** /kasɔnad/ nf soft brown sugar

**cassoulet** /kasulɛ/ nm: meat and bean stew

**cassure** /kasyʀ/ nf **(a)** break
**(b)** split

**castagnettes** /kastaɲɛt/ nf pl castanets

**caste** /kast/ nf **(a)** caste
**(b)** (derogatory) (social) class

**castor** /kastɔʀ/ nm beaver

**castrer** /kastʀe/ [1] vtr to castrate

**cataclysme** /kataklism/ nm cataclysm

**catacombes** /katakɔ̃b/ nf pl catacombs

**catadioptre** /katadjɔptʀ/ nm reflector

**catalepsie** /katalɛpsi/ nf catalepsy

**catalogue** /katalɔg/ nm catalogue (GB); **acheter sur** ∼ to buy by mail order

**cataloguer** /katalɔge/ [1] vtr **(a)** to catalogue (GB) ⟨objects⟩
**(b)** to label ⟨people⟩

**catalyse** /kataliz/ nf catalysis

**catalytique** /katalitik/ adj catalytic

**catamaran** /katamaʀɑ̃/ *nm* catamaran

**cataplasme** /kataplasm/ *nm* poultice

**catapulter** /katapylte/ [1] *vtr* to catapult

**cataracte** /kataʀakt/ *nf* cataract

**catastrophe** /katastʀɔf/ *nf* disaster; **en ~** in a panic; **atterrissage en ~** crash landing

**catastropher** /katastʀɔfe/ [1] *vtr* to devastate

**catastrophique** /katastʀɔfik/ *adj* disastrous

**catch** /katʃ/ *nm* wrestling

**catcheur, -euse** /katʃœʀ, øz/ *nm,f* wrestler

**catéchisme** /kateʃism/ *nm* catechism

**catégorie** /kategɔʀi/ *nf* **(a)** category; **de première/deuxième ~** top-/low-grade
**(b)** (of staff) grade
**(c)** (in sociology) group
**(d)** (Sport) class

**catégorique** /kategɔʀik/ *adj* categorical

**cathédrale** /katedʀal/ *nf* cathedral

**cathode** /katɔd/ *nf* cathode

**catholicisme** /katɔlisism/ *nm* (Roman) Catholicism

**catholique** /katɔlik/ *adj, nmf* Catholic; **ce n'est pas très ~** (humorous) (colloq) it's a bit unorthodox

**cauchemar** /koʃmaʀ/ *nm* nightmare

**causant, ~e** /kozɑ̃, ɑ̃t/ *adj* (colloq) talkative

**cause** /koz/ *nf* **(a)** cause; **pour la ~ de la liberté** in the cause of freedom
**(b)** reason; **pour ~ de maladie** because of illness; **avoir pour ~ qch** to be caused by sth; **à ~ de** because of
**(c)** case; **être en ~** ⟨system, fact⟩ to be at issue; ⟨person⟩ to be involved; **mettre hors de ~** (gen) to clear; **remettre en ~** to call [sth] into question ⟨policy, right⟩; to cast doubt on ⟨project, efficiency⟩; to undermine ⟨efforts⟩; **remise en ~** (of system) reappraisal; **avoir gain de ~** to win one's case
**IDIOMS en toute connaissance de ~** in full knowledge of the facts

**causer** /koze/ [1] **1** *vtr* **(a)** to cause; **~ des soucis** to give cause for concern
**(b)** (colloq) to talk about; **~ travail** to talk shop
**2 causer de** *v+prep* to talk about
**3** *vi* to talk; to chat

**causette** /kozɛt/ *nf* (colloq) chat; **faire la ~** to have a little chat

**caustique** /kostik/ *adj* caustic

**cautériser** /koteʀize/ [1] *vtr* to cauterize

**caution** /kosjɔ̃/ *nf* **(a)** (when renting) deposit; (in finance) guarantee, security; (Law) bail
**(b)** support

**cautionner** /kosjɔne/ [1] *vtr* **(a)** to give one's support to
**(b)** to stand surety for

**cavalcade** /kavalkad/ *nf* **(a)** stampede, rush
**(b)** cavalcade

**cavale** /kaval/ *nf* (colloq) escape; **en ~** on the run

**cavaler** /kavale/ [1] *vi* (colloq) to rush about

**cavalerie** /kavalʀi/ *nf* cavalry

**cavaleur, -euse** /kavalœʀ, øz/ *adj* (colloq) **être ~** to be a womanizer/man-chaser

**cavalier, -ière** /kavalje, ɛʀ/ **1** *adj* cavalier
**2** *nm,f* **(a)** (horse) rider; **être bon ~** to be a good rider
**(b)** (dancing) partner
**3** *nm* **(a)** cavalryman
**(b)** (in chess) knight
**IDIOMS faire ~ seul** to go it alone

**cave** /kav/ *nf* cellar; **avoir une bonne ~** to have good wines

**caveau**, *pl* **~x** /kavo/ *nm* vault

**caverne** /kavɛʀn/ *nf* cavern

**caviar** /kavjaʀ/ *nm* caviar

**cavité** /kavite/ *nf* cavity

**CCP** /sesepe/ *nm: abbr* ▶ COMPTE

**CD** /sede/ *nm* (*abbr* = **compact disc**) CD

**CD-I** /sedei/ *nm inv* (*abbr* = **compact disc interactif**) CD-I

**ce** /sə/ **1** (**cet** /sɛt/ *before vowel or mute h*, **cette** /sɛt/, *pl* **ces** /se/) *adj* **(a)** this; that; **~ crayon(-ci)** this pencil; **~ livre(-là)** that book; **cette nuit** tonight; last night; **un de ces jours** one of these days
**(b)** (colloq) **cet entretien, ça s'est bien passé?** how did the interview go?
**(c) et pour ces dames?** what are the ladies having?
**(d) elle a eu cette chance que la corde a tenu** she was lucky in that the rope held
**(e) cette arrogance!** what arrogance!; **j'ai un de ces rhumes!** I've got an awful cold!
**2** (**c'** *before e*) *pron* **qui est-~?** who's that?; who is it?; **~ faisant** in so doing; **c'est tout dire** that says it all; **fais ~ que tu veux** do what you like; **c'est ~ à quoi il a fait allusion** that's what he was alluding to; **il a fait faillite, ~ qui n'est pas surprenant** he's gone bankrupt, which is hardly surprising; **il tient à ~ que vous veniez** he's very keen that you should come; **~ que c'est grand!** it's so big!

**CE** /seə/ *nm: abbr* ▶ COURS

**ceci** /səsi/ *pron* this; **à ~ près que** except that; **cet hôtel a ~ de bien que...** one good thing about this hotel is that...

**cécité** /sesite/ *nf* blindness

**céder** /sede/ [14] **1** *vtr* **(a)** to give up ⟨seat, share⟩; to yield ⟨right⟩; to make over ⟨property⟩; **~ le passage** to give way; **~ la place** (figurative) to give way
**(b)** to sell
**2 céder à** *v+prep* to give in to, to yield to
**3** *vi* **(a)** to give in
**(b)** ⟨beam⟩ to give way; ⟨handle⟩ to break off; ⟨door⟩ to yield

**cédille** /sedij/ *nf* cedilla

**cèdre** /sedʀ/ *nm* cedar

**CEE** /seəə/ *nf: abbr* ▶ COMMUNAUTÉ

**CEEA** /seəəa/ *nf* (*abbr* = **Communauté européenne de l'énergie atomique**) EAEC

**CEI** /seəi/ *nf*: *abbr* ▶ COMMUNAUTÉ

**ceinture** /sɛ̃tyʀ/ *nf* **(a)** belt
**(b)** waistband
**(c)** girdle
**(d)** waist; **avoir de l'eau jusqu'à la ~** to be waist-deep in water
**(e)** (Sport) waist hold; **~ noire** black belt
**(f)** ring
■ **~ de sauvetage** lifebelt; **~ de sécurité** safety *or* seat belt
IDIOMS **faire ~** (colloq) to go without; **se serrer la ~** to tighten one's belt

**ceinturer** /sɛ̃tyʀe/ [1] *vtr* to encircle

**ceinturon** /sɛ̃tyʀɔ̃/ *nm* belt

**cela** /səla/ *pron*
■ Note *Cela* and *ça* are equivalent in many cases. See the entry *ça* for more information.
– *Cela* is used in formal contexts and in the expressions shown below.
**(a)** it; that; **quant à ~** as for that; **~ dit** having said that
**(b)** **~ va sans dire** it *or* that goes without saying; **voyez-vous ~!** did you ever hear of such a thing!

**célébration** /selebʀasjɔ̃/ *nf* celebration

**célèbre** /selɛbʀ/ *adj* famous

**célébrer** /selebʀe/ [14] *vtr* **(a)** to celebrate ⟨*event, mass*⟩; to perform ⟨*rite*⟩
**(b)** to praise ⟨*person*⟩

**célébrité** /selebʀite/ *nf* **(a)** fame
**(b)** celebrity

**céleri** /sɛlʀi/ *nm* **(a)** celery
**(b)** celeriac

**céleri-rave**, *pl* **céleris-raves** /selʀiʀav/ *nm* celeriac

**céleste** /selɛst/ *adj* celestial; heavenly; divine

**célibat** /seliba/ *nm* **(a)** single status
**(b)** celibacy

**célibataire** /selibatɛʀ/ **1** *adj* single
**2** *nmf* bachelor/single woman

**celle** ▶ CELUI

**celle-ci** ▶ CELUI-CI

**celle-là** ▶ CELUI-LÀ

**celles-ci** ▶ CELUI-CI

**celles-là** ▶ CELUI-LÀ

**cellier** /selje/ *nm* cellar

**cellophane®** /selɔfan/ *nf* cellophane®

**cellulaire** /selylɛʀ/ *adj* cell; cellular

**cellule** /selyl/ *nf* **(a)** cell
**(b)** unit; **~ familiale** family unit

**cellulite** /selylit/ *nf* **(a)** cellulite
**(b)** cellulitis

**celte** /sɛlt/ *adj, nm* Celtic

**Celte** /sɛlt/ *nmf* Celt

**celui** /səlɥi/, **celle** /sɛl/, *mpl* **ceux** /sø/, *fpl* **celles** /sɛl/ *pron* the one; **le train du matin ou ~ du soir?** the morning train or the evening one?; **ceux, celles** those; the

ones; **ceux d'entre vous qui veulent partir** those of you who want to leave; **ceux qu'il a vendus** the ones he sold; **faire ~ qui n'entend pas** to pretend not to hear

**celui-ci** /səlɥisi/, **celle-ci** /sɛlsi/, *mpl* **ceux-ci** /søsi/, *fpl* **celles-ci** /sɛlsi/ *pron* **(a)** this one; ceux-ci, celles-ci these
**(b)** je n'ai qu'une chose à dire et c'est celle-ci I have only one thing to say and it's this
**(c)** elle essaya la fenêtre mais celle-ci était coincée she tried the window but it was jammed; il entra, suivi de son père et de son frère; **~ portait un paquet** he came in, followed by his father and his brother; the latter was carrying a parcel

**celui-là** /səlɥila/, **celle-là** /sɛlla/, *mpl* **ceux-là** /søla/, *fpl* **celles-là** /sɛlla/ *pron* **(a)** that one; ceux-là, celles-là those (ones)
**(b)** si je n'ai qu'un conseil à te donner, c'est ~ if I only have one piece of advice for you, it's this
**(c)** the former
**(d)** il fit une autre proposition, plus réaliste celle-là he made another proposal, a more realistic one this time
**(e)** (colloq) il exagère, ~! that guy's pushing it a bit! (colloq)
**(f)** (colloq) elle est bien bonne, celle-là! that's a good one!; je ne m'attendais pas à celle-là I didn't expect that!; **~ même** the very one

**cendre** /sɑ̃dʀ/ *nf* ash

**cendré**, **~e** /sɑ̃dʀe/ *adj* blond **~** ash blond

**cendrier** /sɑ̃dʀije/ *nm* ashtray

**Cène** /sɛn/ *nf* **la ~** the Last Supper

**censé**, **~e** /sɑ̃se/ *adj* **être ~ faire** to be supposed to do

**censeur** /sɑ̃sœʀ/ *nm* (Sch) *school official in charge of discipline*

**censure** /sɑ̃syʀ/ *nf* **(a)** censorship
**(b)** board of censors
**(c)** censure

**censurer** /sɑ̃syʀe/ [1] *vtr* **(a)** to censor
**(b)** to ban

**cent** /sɑ̃/ **1** *adj* a hundred, one hundred
**2** *nm* **(a)** hundred
**(b)** (division of euro) cent
**3** **pour cent** *phr* per cent
IDIOMS **faire les ~ pas** to pace up and down; **être aux ~ coups** (colloq) to be worried sick (colloq); **attendre ~ sept ans** (colloq) to wait for ages

**centaine** /sɑ̃tɛn/ *nf* **(a)** hundred
**(b)** about a hundred

**centenaire** /sɑ̃tnɛʀ/ **1** *adj* hundred-year-old, centenarian
**2** *nmf* c'est une ~ she's a hundred years old
**3** *nm* centenary, centennial

**centième** /sɑ̃tjɛm/ *adj* hundredth

**centilitre** /sɑ̃tilitʀ/ *nm* centilitre (GB)

**centime** /sɑ̃tim/ *nm* centime; **~ [d'euro]** cent

**centimètre** /sɑ̃timɛtʀ/ *nm* **(a)** centimetre ···÷

**(b)** ne pas avancer d'un ∼ not to move an inch
**(c)** tape measure

**central**, ∼e¹, *mpl* **-aux** /sɑ̃tʀal, o/
**1** *adj* **(a)** central; **court** ∼ (in tennis) centre (GB) court; **ordinateur** ∼ host computer
**(b)** main
**2** *nm* ∼ **(téléphonique)** (telephone) exchange

**centrale²** /sɑ̃tʀal/ *nf* **(a)** power station
**(b)** prison

**centraliser** /sɑ̃tʀalize/ [1] *vtr* to centralize

**centralisme** /sɑ̃tʀalism/ *nm* centralism

**centre** /sɑ̃tʀ/ *nm* centre (GB); **il se prend pour le** ∼ **du monde** he thinks the whole world revolves around him
∎ ∼ **aéré** children's outdoor activity centre; ∼ **commercial** shopping centre (GB); ∼ **de documentation et d'information, CDI** learning resources centre (GB); ∼ **hospitalier** hospital complex; ∼ **hospitalier universitaire, CHU** ≈ teaching hospital

**centrer** /sɑ̃tʀe/ [1] *vtr* to centre (GB)

**centre-ville**, *pl* **centres-villes** /sɑ̃tʀəvil/ *nm* town centre (GB), city centre (GB)

**centrifuge** /sɑ̃tʀifyʒ/ *adj* centrifugal

**centrifugeuse** /sɑ̃tʀifyʒøz/ *nf* **(a)** juice extractor
**(b)** centrifuge

**centriste** /sɑ̃tʀist/ *adj*, *nmf* centrist

**centuple** /sɑ̃typl/ *nm* **dix mille est le** ∼ **de cent** ten thousand is a hundred times one hundred; **au** ∼ a hundred times over

**cep** /sɛp/ *nm* ∼ **(de vigne)** vine stock

**cépage** /sepaʒ/ *nm* grape variety; ∼ **cabernet** Cabernet grape

**cèpe** /sɛp/ *nm* cep

**cependant** /səpɑ̃dɑ̃/ **1** *conj* yet, however
**2** **cependant que** *phr* whereas, while

**céramique** /seramik/ *nf* **(a)** ceramic
**(b)** ceramics

**cerceau**, *pl* ∼**x** /sɛʀso/ *nm* hoop

**cercle** /sɛʀkl/ *nm* **(a)** circle; **en** ∼ in a circle; **décrire des** ∼**s** ⟨*plane, bird*⟩ to circle (overhead); **le** ∼ **de famille** the family circle
**(b)** circle, society; club
**(c)** hoop

**cercler** /sɛʀkle/ [1] *vtr* to hoop ⟨*barrel*⟩; **les noms cerclés en rouge** the names circled in red

**cercueil** /sɛʀkœj/ *nm* coffin

**céréale** /seʀeal/ *nf* cereal, grain

**céréalier, -ière** /seʀealje, ɛʀ/ *adj* ⟨*production*⟩ cereal; ⟨*region*⟩ cereal-growing

**cérébral**, ∼e, *mpl* **-aux** /seʀebʀal, o/ *adj* **(a)** cerebral
**(b)** intellectual

**cérémonial**, *pl* ∼**s** /seʀemɔnjal/ *nm* ceremonial

**cérémonie** /seʀemɔni/ **1** *nf* ceremony; **tenue** *or* **habit de** ∼ ceremonial dress

**2** **cérémonies** *nf pl* ceremony; **faire des** ∼**s** to stand on ceremony; **sans** ∼**s** ⟨*dinner, invitation*⟩ informal; ⟨*receive*⟩ informally

**cérémonieux, -ieuse** /seʀemɔnjø, øz/ *adj* ceremonious; **d'un air** ∼ ceremoniously

**cerf** /sɛʀ/ *nm* stag

**cerfeuil** /sɛʀfœj/ *nm* chervil

**cerf-volant**, *pl* **cerfs-volants** /sɛʀvɔlɑ̃/ *nm* **(a)** kite
**(b)** stag beetle

**cerise** /s(ə)ʀiz/ *nf* cherry

**cerisier** /s(ə)ʀizje/ *nm* cherry (tree)

**cerne** /sɛʀn/ *nm* ring

**cerné**, ∼**e** /sɛʀne/ *adj* **avoir les yeux** ∼**s** to have rings under one's eyes

**cerner** /sɛʀne/ [1] *vtr* **(a)** to surround
**(b)** to define ⟨*problem*⟩; to figure out ⟨*person*⟩; to determine ⟨*personality*⟩
**(c)** to outline ⟨*drawing*⟩

**certain**, ∼**e** /sɛʀtɛ̃, ɛn/ **1** *adj* **(a)** **être** ∼ **de** to be certain *or* sure of
**(b)** ⟨*fact*⟩ certain, sure; ⟨*date, price, influence*⟩ definite; ⟨*rate*⟩ fixed
**2** *det* **elle restera un** ∼ **temps** she'll stay for some time; **un** ∼ **nombre d'erreurs** a certain number of mistakes; **d'une** ∼**e manière** in a way; **il avait déjà un** ∼ **âge** he was already getting on in years
**3** **certains**, **certaines** *det pl* some; **à** ∼**s moments** sometimes, at times
**4** **certains**, **certaines** *pron pl* some people; ∼**s d'entre eux** some of them

**certainement** /sɛʀtɛnmɑ̃/ *adv* **(a)** most probably
**(b)** certainly; **mais** ∼! certainly!, of course!

**certes** /sɛʀt/ *adv* **ce ne sera** ∼ **pas facile mais...** admittedly it won't be easy but...

**certificat** /sɛʀtifika/ *nm* **(a)** certificate
**(b)** testimonial
∎ ∼ **d'aptitude professionnelle, CAP** *vocational training qualification*; ∼ **de décès** death certificate; ∼ **médical** medical certificate; ∼ **de résidence** proof of residence; ∼ **de scolarité** proof of attendance (*at school or university*); ∼ **de travail** *document from a previous employer giving dates and nature of employment*

**certifié**, ∼**e** /sɛʀtifje/ *adj* **professeur** ∼ fully qualified teacher

**certifier** /sɛʀtifje/ [2] *vtr* **(a)** to certify; **copie certifiée conforme** certified copy
**(b)** **elle m'a certifié que** she assured me that

**certitude** /sɛʀtityd/ *nf* **(a)** certainty; **on sait avec** ∼ **que** we know for certain that
**(b)** **avoir la** ∼ **que** to be certain that

**cérumen** /seʀymɛn/ *nm* earwax

**cerveau**, *pl* ∼**x** /sɛʀvo/ *nm* **(a)** brain
**(b)** mind
**(c)** (person) brain (colloq); **exode** *or* **fuite des** ∼**x** brain drain; **c'est un** ∼ he/she has an outstanding mind
**(d)** brains; nerve centre (GB)
IDIOMS **avoir le** ∼ **dérangé** to be deranged

**cervelas** /sɛʀvəla/ *nm* saveloy

**cervelet** /sɛʀvəlɛ/ *nm* cerebellum

**cervelle** /sɛʀvɛl/ *nf* **(a)** brains; ~ **de veau** (Culin) calf's brains
**(b)** (colloq) **il n'a rien dans la** ~ he's brainless; ~ **d'oiseau** birdbrain (colloq)

**cervical, ~e**, *mpl* **-aux** /sɛʀvikal, o/ *adj* cervical

**ces** ▸ CE 1

**CES** /seəes/ *nm: abbr* ▸ COLLÈGE

**césar** /sezaʀ/ *nm* César (*film award*)

**césarienne** /sezaʀjɛn/ *nf* caesarian (section)

**cessation** /sesasjɔ̃/ *nf* suspension

**cesse** /sɛs/ *nf* **sans** ~ constantly

**cesser** /sese/ [1] **1** *vtr* to stop, to cease; to end; ~ **de faire** to stop doing; to give up doing
**2** *vi* ⟨activity⟩ to cease; ⟨wind⟩ to drop; ⟨rain⟩ to stop; **faire** ~ to put an end *or* a stop to, to end

**cessez-le-feu** /seselfø/ *nm inv* ceasefire

**cession** /sesjɔ̃/ *nf* transfer

**c'est-à-dire** /setadiʀ/ *phr* **(a)** that is (to say)
**(b)** ~ **que** which means (that); **'le travail est trop dur'—'~?'** 'the work is too hard'— 'what do you mean?'

**cet** ▸ CE 1

**CET** /seəte/ *nm: abbr* ▸ COLLÈGE

**cette** ▸ CE 1

**ceux** ▸ CELUI

**ceux-ci** ▸ CELUI-CI

**ceux-là** ▸ CELUI-LÀ

**CFDT** /seɛfdete/ *nf* (*abbr* = **Confédération française démocratique du travail**) CFDT (*French trade union*)

**CGC** /seʒese/ *nf* (*abbr* = **Confédération générale des cadres**) CGC (*French trade union*)

**CGT** /seʒete/ *nf* (*abbr* = **Confédération générale du travail**) CGT (*French trade union*)

**chacal**, *pl* ~**s** /ʃakal/ *nm* jackal

**chacun, ~e** /ʃakœ̃, yn/ *pron* **(a)** each (one); **ils ont** ~ **sa** *or* **leur chambre** they each have their own room
**(b)** everyone; ~ **pour soi** every man for himself

**chagrin, ~e** /ʃagʀɛ̃, in/ **1** *adj* despondent
**2** *nm* grief; **faire du** ~ **à qn** to cause sb grief; **avoir du** ~ to be sad; **avoir un gros** ~ to be very upset; ~ **d'amour** unhappy love affair

**chagriner** /ʃagʀine/ [1] *vtr* **(a)** to pain, to grieve
**(b)** to worry

**chahut** /ʃay/ *nm* racket (colloq)

**chahuter** /ʃayte/ [1] **1** *vtr* to play up ⟨teacher⟩; to heckle ⟨speaker⟩
**2** *vi* to mess around

**chaîne** /ʃɛn/ **1** *nf* **(a)** chain; **attacher qn**

**avec des** ~**s** to chain sb up; **des catastrophes en** ~ a series of disasters; **réaction en** ~ chain reaction
**(b)** assembly line; **produire (qch) à la** ~ to mass-produce (sth)
**(c)** network; ~ **de solidarité** support network
**(d)** ~ **(de télévision)** (television) channel
**(e)** ~ **hi-fi/stéréo** hi-fi/stereo system
**2 chaînes** *nf pl* snow chains
■ ~ **de fabrication** production line

**chaînette** /ʃɛnɛt/ *nf* chain

**chaînon** /ʃɛnɔ̃/ *nm* link; ~ **manquant** missing link

**chair** /ʃɛʀ/ **1** *adj inv* flesh-coloured (GB)
**2** *nf* flesh; meat; **bien en** ~ plump
■ ~ **de poule** gooseflesh, goose pimples; **donner la** ~ **de poule à qn** ⟨cold⟩ to give sb gooseflesh; ⟨fear⟩ to make sb's flesh creep

**chaire** /ʃɛʀ/ *nf* **(a)** pulpit
**(b)** (at university) chair
**(c)** rostrum

**chaise** /ʃɛz/ *nf* chair
■ ~ **haute** high-chair; ~ **longue** deckchair; ~ **roulante** wheelchair
IDIOMS **être assis entre deux** ~**s** to be in an awkward position

**châle** /ʃɑl/ *nm* shawl

**chalet** /ʃalɛ/ *nm* chalet

**chaleur** /ʃalœʀ/ **1** *nf* **(a)** heat; warmth; **coup de** ~ heat stroke; ~ **animale** body heat
**(b)** (of person, welcome, colour) warmth
**(c)** (Zool) **(être) en** ~ (to be) on heat
**2 chaleurs** *nf pl* **les grandes** ~**s** the hot season

**chaleureusement** /ʃalœʀøzmã/ *adv* warmly; wholeheartedly

**chaleureux, -euse** /ʃalœʀø, øz/ *adj* ⟨person, greeting⟩ warm; ⟨audience⟩ enthusiastic

**challenge** /ʃalã̃ʒ/ *nm* **(a)** (Sport) tournament
**(b)** trophy

**challenge(u)r** /ʃalã̃ʒœʀ/ *nm* challenger

**chaloupe** /ʃalup/ *nf* **(a)** rowing boat (GB), rowboat (US)
**(b)** (motor) launch

**chalumeau**, *pl* ~**x** /ʃalymo/ *nm* blowtorch

**chalut** /ʃaly/ *nm* trawl

**chalutier** /ʃalytje/ *nm* **(a)** trawler
**(b)** trawlerman

**chamailler: se chamailler** /ʃamaje/ [1] *v refl* (+ *v être*) (colloq) to squabble

**chamarré, ~e** /ʃamaʀe/ *adj* **(a)** richly ornamented
**(b)** brightly coloured (GB)

**chambard** /ʃã̃baʀ/ *nm* (colloq) din, racket (colloq)

**chambardement** /ʃã̃baʀdəmã/ *nm* (colloq) **(a)** shake-up (colloq)
**(b)** mess

**chambouler** /ʃã̃bule/ [1] *vtr* (colloq) **(a)** to upset ⟨plans, routine⟩ ····✧

**(b)** to turn [sth] upside down ‹*house*›; to mess [sth] up ‹*papers*›

**chambranle** /ʃɑ̃bʀɑl/ *nm* frame

**chambre** /ʃɑ̃bʀ/ *nf* **(a)** bedroom; room; ~ **pour une personne** single room; ~ **à deux lits** twin room; **faire** ~ **à part** to sleep in separate rooms
**(b) musique de** ~ chamber music
**(c)** (in parliament) house
**(d)** (in administration) chamber
■ ~ **à air** inner tube; ~ **d'amis** guest room; ~ **de commerce** chamber of commerce; ~ **à coucher** bedroom; bedroom suite; '~**s d'hôte'** 'bed and breakfast'; ~ **noire** camera obscura; darkroom

**chambrée** /ʃɑ̃bʀe/ *nf* (Mil) soldiers occupying barrack room

**chambrer** /ʃɑ̃bʀe/ [1] *vtr* **(a)** to bring [sth] to room temperature
**(b)** (colloq) (mock) to tease

**chameau,** *pl* ~**x** /ʃamo/ *nm* (Zool) camel

**chamelier** /ʃaməlje/ *nm* camel driver

**chamelle** /ʃamɛl/ *nf* she-camel

**chamois** /ʃamwa/ *nm* (Zool) chamois

**champ** /ʃɑ̃/ 1 *nm* field; (figurative) field, domain; **en pleins** ~**s** in open country; **avoir le** ~ **libre** to have a free hand
2 **à tout bout de champ** *phr* (colloq) all the time
■ ~ **de courses** racetrack

**champagne** /ʃɑ̃paɲ/ *nm* champagne

**champagnisé** /ʃɑ̃paɲize/ *adj* **vin** ~ sparkling wine

**champenois,** ~**e** /ʃɑ̃pənwa, az/ *adj* **(a)** of the Champagne region
**(b) méthode** ~**e** champagne method

**champêtre** /ʃɑ̃pɛtʀ/ *adj* ‹*scene*› rural; **bal** ~ village dance; **déjeuner** ~ country picnic

**champignon** /ʃɑ̃piɲɔ̃/ *nm* **(a)** (Culin) mushroom; ~ **vénéneux** toadstool
**(b)** (Bot, Med) fungus
**(c)** (colloq) throttle, accelerator
■ ~ **atomique** mushroom cloud; ~ **de Paris** button mushroom (GB), champignon (US)

**champion, -ionne** /ʃɑ̃pjɔ̃, ɔn/ *nm,f* champion; **le** ~ **en titre** the titleholder

**championnat** /ʃɑ̃pjɔna/ *nm* championship

**chance** /ʃɑ̃s/ *nf* **(a)** (good) luck; **coup de** ~ stroke of luck; **avoir de la** ~ to be lucky; **avoir la** ~ **de trouver une maison** to be lucky enough to find a house; **par** ~ luckily, fortunately; **tenter** *or* **courir sa** ~ to try one's luck
**(b)** chance (de of); **il y a de fortes** ~**s** ( **pour** ) **que** there's every chance that; **il a ses** ~**s** he stands a good chance; **mettre toutes les** ~**s de son côté** to take no chances; **'il va pleuvoir?'—'il y a des** ~**s'** 'is it going to rain?'—'probably'
**(c)** chance, opportunity

**chancelant,** ~**e** /ʃɑ̃slɑ̃, ɑ̃t/ *adj* **(a)** ‹*gait*› unsteady; ‹*object*› rickety, shaky; ‹*person*› staggering; **d'un pas** ~ unsteadily

**(b)** ‹*courage, faith*› wavering; ‹*empire*› tottering

**chanceler** /ʃɑ̃sle/ [19] *vi* **(a)** ‹*person*› to stagger; ‹*object*› to wobble
**(b)** ‹*courage*› to waver
**(c)** ‹*empire*› to totter; ‹*health*› to be precarious

**chancelier** /ʃɑ̃səlje/ *nm* chancellor

**chancellerie** /ʃɑ̃sɛlʀi/ *nf* Ministry of Justice

**chanceux, -euse** /ʃɑ̃sø, øz/ *adj* lucky

**chandail** /ʃɑ̃daj/ *nm* sweater, jumper (GB)

**chandelier** /ʃɑ̃dəlje/ *nm* candelabra (GB)

**chandelle** /ʃɑ̃dɛl/ *nf* **(a)** candle; **un dîner aux** ~**s** a candlelit dinner
**(b)** (Sport) shoulder stand
**IDIOMS devoir une fière** ~ **à** to be hugely indebted to; **faire des économies de bouts de** ~**s** to make cheeseparing economies

**change** /ʃɑ̃ʒ/ *nm* **(a)** exchange rate
**(b)** (foreign) exchange; **perdre au** ~ (figurative) to lose out

**changeant,** ~**e** /ʃɑ̃ʒɑ̃, ɑ̃t/ *adj* changeable

**changement** /ʃɑ̃ʒmɑ̃/ *nm* change; ~ **en mieux/pire** change for the better/worse

**changer** /ʃɑ̃ʒe/ [13] 1 *vtr* **(a)** to exchange ‹*object*›; to change ‹*secretary, job*›
**(b)** to change ‹*money*›; to cash ‹*traveller's cheque*›
**(c)** to change ‹*purchased item*›
**(d)** ~ **qch de place** to move sth
**(e)** to change ‹*situation, appearance*›; **cette coiffure te change** you look different with your hair like that; **qu'est-ce que ça change?** what difference does it make?; **cela ne change rien au fait que** that doesn't alter the fact that
**(f)** ~ **qn/qch en** to turn sb/sth into
**(g) cela nous change de la pluie** it makes a change from the rain; **pour ne pas** ~ as usual
**(h)** to change ‹*baby*›
2 **changer de** *v+prep* to change; ~ **d'avis** to change one's mind; ~ **de domicile** to move house; ~ **de trottoir** to cross over to the other side of the road; **nous avons changé de route au retour** we came back by a different route
3 *vi* to change
4 **se changer** *v refl* (+ *v être*) **(a)** to get changed
**(b) se** ~ **en** to turn *or* change into

**changeur, -euse** /ʃɑ̃ʒœʀ, øz/ 1 *nm,f* money changer
2 *nm* change machine

**chanoine** /ʃanwan/ *nm* canon

**chanson** /ʃɑ̃sɔ̃/ *nf* **(a)** song; **vedette de la** ~ singing star
**(b) c'est toujours la même** ~ (colloq) it's always the same old story; **je connais la** ~ (colloq) I've heard it all before

**chansonnier, -ière** /ʃɑ̃sɔnje, ɛʀ/ *nm,f* cabaret artist

**chant** /ʃɑ̃/ *nm* **(a)** singing

**(b)** (of bird, whale) song; (of cock) crow(ing); (of cricket) chirp(ing); (of cicada) shrilling
**(c)** song
**(d)** ode; canto
■ ~ **de Noël** Christmas carol

**chantage** /ʃɑ̃taʒ/ *nm* blackmail

**chantant**, **~e** /ʃɑ̃tɑ̃, ɑ̃t/ *adj* singsong

**chanter** /ʃɑ̃te/ [1] **1** *vtr* **(a)** to sing
**(b)** (colloq) **qu'est-ce qu'il nous chante?** what's he talking about?
**2** **chanter à** *v+prep* (colloq) **ça te chante d'y aller?** do you fancy (colloq) going?
**3** *vi* **(a)** to sing; ~ **juste/faux** to sing in tune/out of tune
**(b)** ⟨bird⟩ to sing; ⟨cock⟩ to crow
**(c) faire ~ qn** to blackmail sb

**chanteur**, **-euse** /ʃɑ̃tœʀ, øz/ *nm,f* singer

**chantier** /ʃɑ̃tje/ *nm* **(a)** building site; **en ~** ⟨building⟩ under construction; **notre maison sera en ~ tout l'hiver** the work on our house will go on all winter; **mettre en ~** to undertake ⟨project⟩
**(b)** builder's yard
**(c)** (colloq) mess

**chantonner** /ʃɑ̃tɔne/ [1] *vtr, vi* to hum

**chantre** /ʃɑ̃tʀ/ *nm* eulogist (**de** of); (poet) bard

**chanvre** /ʃɑ̃vʀ/ *nm* hemp

**chaos** /kao/ *nm inv* chaos

**chaotique** /kaɔtik/ *adj* chaotic

**chaparder** /ʃapaʀde/ [1] *vtr* (colloq) to pinch (colloq)

**chape** /ʃap/ *nf* ~ **de béton** concrete screed

**chapeau**, *pl* ~**x** /ʃapo/ **1** *nm* hat
**2** *excl* (colloq) well done!
■ ~ **haut de forme** top hat; ~ **melon** bowler (hat) (GB), derby (hat) (US); ~ **de roue** (Aut) hubcap; **démarrer sur les ~x de roues** (colloq) ⟨car, driver⟩ to shoot off at top speed
IDIOMS **tirer son ~ à** to take one's hat off to

**chapeauter** /ʃapote/ [1] *vtr* (colloq) to head; **le ministère chapeaute notre équipe** our team works under the ministry

**chapelet** /ʃaplɛ/ *nm* **(a)** rosary
**(b)** (of onions, insults, islands) string

**chapelier**, **-ière** /ʃapəlje, ɛʀ/ *nm,f* hatter

**chapelle** /ʃapɛl/ *nf* **(a)** chapel
**(b)** clique, coterie

**chapelure** /ʃaplyʀ/ *nf* breadcrumbs

**chaperon** /ʃapʀɔ̃/ *nm* chaperon(e)

**chapiteau**, *pl* ~**x** /ʃapito/ *nm*
**(a)** marquee (GB), tent; (of circus) big top
**(b)** (of pillar) capital

**chapitre** /ʃapitʀ/ *nm* **(a)** (of book) chapter
**(b)** subject
IDIOMS **avoir voix au ~** to have a say in the matter

**chapka** /ʃapka/ *nf* fur hat

**chaque** /ʃak/ *det* each, every

**char** /ʃaʀ/ *nm* **(a)** (Mil) tank
**(b)** chariot
**(c)** (in carnival) float
■ ~ **d'assaut** (Mil) tank; ~ **à bœufs** oxcart; ~ **à voile** (Sport) sand yacht; ice yacht

**charabia** /ʃaʀabja/ *nm* (colloq) gobbledygook (colloq)

**charade** /ʃaʀad/ *nf* riddle

**charbon** /ʃaʀbɔ̃/ *nm* coal; ~ **de bois** charcoal
IDIOMS **être sur des ~s ardents** to be like a cat on a hot tin roof

**charcuter** /ʃaʀkyte/ [1] *vtr* (colloq) to hack [sb] about

**charcuterie** /ʃaʀkytʀi/ *nf* **(a)** cooked pork meats
**(b)** pork butcher's

**charcutier**, **-ière** /ʃaʀkytje, ɛʀ/ *nm,f* pork butcher

**chardon** /ʃaʀdɔ̃/ *nm* thistle

**charentais**, **~e¹** /ʃaʀɑ̃tɛ, ɛz/ *adj* from the Charente region

**charentaise²** /ʃaʀɑ̃tɛz/ *nf* carpet slipper

**charge** /ʃaʀʒ/ **1** *nf* **(a)** burden, load; (of vehicle) load; (of ship) cargo, freight; **prise en ~** (in taxi) minimum fare
**(b) avoir la ~ de qn/qch** to be responsible for sb/sth; **avoir trois enfants à ~** to have three children to support; **prendre en ~** ⟨guardian⟩ to take charge of ⟨child⟩; ⟨social security system⟩ to accept financial responsibility for ⟨sick person⟩; to take care of ⟨fees⟩
**(c)** ~ **de notaire** ≈ solicitor's office
**(d)** (legal) charge
**(e)** (Mil) charge
**2** **charges** *nf pl* **(a)** expenses, costs
**(b)** (payable by tenant) ~**s** (**locatives**) service charges
■ ~**s patronales** employer's social security contributions.
IDIOMS **revenir à la ~** to try again

**chargé**, **~e** /ʃaʀʒe/ **1** *pp* ▶ CHARGER
**2** *pp adj* **être ~** to be heavy *or* laden (down) with; **un regard ~ de menaces** a threatening look; **être ~ de famille** to have dependents
**3** *adj* ⟨person, vehicle⟩ loaded; ⟨day⟩ busy; **avoir un casier judiciaire ~** to have had several previous convictions
■ ~ **d'affaires** chargé d'affaires; ~ **de cours** part-time lecturer; ~ **de mission** representative

**chargement** /ʃaʀʒəmɑ̃/ *nm* **(a)** (goods) load; cargo
**(b)** (action) loading

**charger** /ʃaʀʒe/ [13] **1** *vtr* **(a)** to load
**(b)** to charge ⟨battery⟩
**(c)** ~ **qn de faire** to give sb the responsibility of doing; **c'est lui qui est chargé de l'enquête** he is in charge of the investigation
**(d)** to bring evidence against ⟨accused⟩
**(e)** ⟨police⟩ to charge at ⟨crowd⟩
**2** **se charger** *v refl* (+ *v être*) **se ~ de** to take responsibility for; **je m'en charge** I'll see to it

**chargeur** /ʃaʀʒœʀ/ *nm* **(a)** (Mil) magazine
**(b)** (of camera) cartridge
**(c)** (Comput) loader

**chariot** /ʃaRjo/ *nm* **(a)** trolley (GB), cart (US)
**(b)** truck
**(c)** waggon (GB)
**(d)** (of typewriter) carriage

**charisme** /kaRism/ *nm* charisma

**charitable** /ʃaRitabl/ *adj* charitable

**charitablement** /ʃaRitabləmɑ̃/ *adv* charitably; kindly

**charité** /ʃaRite/ *nf* **(a)** charity
**(b)** par (pure) ~ out of the kindness of one's heart

**charlatan** /ʃaRlatɑ̃/ *nm* **(a)** quack (colloq)
**(b)** con man
**(c)** (politician) fraud

**charlot** /ʃaRlo/ *nm* (colloq) clown

**charlotte** /ʃaRlɔt/ *nf* **(a)** (Culin) charlotte
**(b)** mobcap

**charmant**, **∼e** /ʃaRmɑ̃, ɑ̃t/ *adj* charming

**charme** /ʃaRm/ **1** *nm* **(a)** charm; faire du ~ à qn to make eyes at sb; cela ne manque pas de ~ (lifestyle, novel) it's not without its charms; (proposition) it's not unattractive
**(b)** spell
**2 charmes** *nm pl* (euphemistic) physical attributes
IDIOMS se porter comme un ~ to be as fit as a fiddle

**charmer** /ʃaRme/ [1] *vtr* to charm

**charmeur**, **-euse** /ʃaRmœR, øz/ **1** *adj* winning, engaging
**2** *nm,f* charmer

**charnel**, **-elle** /ʃaRnɛl/ *adj* carnal

**charnier** /ʃaRnje/ *nm* mass grave

**charnière** /ʃaRnjɛR/ *nf* **(a)** hinge
**(b)** (figurative) bridge; junction; rôle(-)~ pivotal role

**charnu**, **∼e** /ʃaRny/ *adj* (lip) fleshy, thick

**charogne** /ʃaRɔɲ/ *nf* rotting carcass

**charpente** /ʃaRpɑ̃t/ *nf* (of roof) roof structure; (of building) framework; (of person) build

**charpentier** /ʃaRpɑ̃tje/ *nm* carpenter

**charpie** /ʃaRpi/ *nf* réduire *or* mettre qch en ~ to tear sth to shreds

**charretier** /ʃaRtje/ *nm* carter
IDIOMS jurer comme un ~ to swear like a trooper

**charrette** /ʃaRɛt/ *nf* cart; ~ à bras handcart

**charrier** /ʃaRje/ [2] **1** *vtr* **(a)** to carry, to haul
**(b)** (river) to carry [sth] along
**(c)** (colloq) to tease [sb] unmercifully
**2** *vi* (colloq) to go too far

**charrue** /ʃaRy/ *nf* plough (GB), plow (US).
IDIOMS mettre la ~ avant les bœufs to put the cart before the horse

**charte** /ʃaRt/ *nf* charter

**charter** /ʃaRtɛR/ *adj inv* (plane, flight) charter

**chasse** /ʃas/ *nf* **(a)** hunting; shooting; ~ au trésor treasure hunt; la ~ est ouverte it's the open season
**(b)** ~ gardée private hunting (ground); (figurative) preserve
**(c)** donner la ~ à, prendre en ~ to chase
■ ~ à courre hunting; ~ d'eau (toilet) flush; tirer la ~ to pull the chain
IDIOMS qui va à la ~ perd sa place (Proverb) leave your place and you lose it

**chassé-croisé**, *pl* **chassés-croisés** /ʃasekRwaze/ *nm* continual coming and going

**chasse-neige** /ʃasnɛʒ/ *nm inv* snowplough (GB), snowplow (US)

**chasser** /ʃase/ [1] **1** *vtr* **(a)** (animal) to hunt (prey)
**(b)** (hunter) to shoot (GB), to hunt
**(c)** (person) to chase away (animal, intruder); (rain) to drive away (tourists); to fire (domestic servant)
**(d)** to dispel (smoke, doubt)
**2** *vi* to go hunting

**chasseur**, **-euse** /ʃasœR, øz/ **1** *nm,f* hunter
**2** *nm* **(a)** (Mil) fighter (aircraft); fighter pilot
**(b)** (in hotel) bellboy
■ ~ alpin *soldier trained for mountainous terrain*; ~ de têtes head-hunter

**châssis** /ʃasi/ *nm inv* **(a)** (of window) frame
**(b)** (Aut) chassis

**chaste** /ʃast/ *adj* (gen) chaste; (person) celibate

**chasteté** /ʃastəte/ *nf* chastity

**chat** /ʃa/ *nm* cat; tomcat
■ ~ de gouttière ordinary cat; alley cat; ~ perché off-ground tag.
IDIOMS donner sa langue au ~ to give in; il n'y a pas un ~ the place is deserted; avoir un ~ dans la gorge to have a frog in one's throat; il ne faut pas réveiller le ~ qui dort (Proverb) let sleeping dogs lie; s'entendre comme chien et ~ to fight like cat and dog

**châtaigne** /ʃatɛɲ/ *nf* (sweet) chestnut

**châtaignier** /ʃatɛɲe/ *nm* (sweet) chestnut (tree); une table de *or* en ~ a chestnut table

**châtain** /ʃatɛ̃/ *adj m* (hair) brown

**château**, *pl* **∼x** /ʃato/ *nm* **(a)** castle
**(b)** palace
**(c)** mansion
■ ~ de cartes house of cards; ~ d'eau water tower; ~ fort fortified castle
IDIOMS mener la vie de ~ to live the life of Riley (GB), to live like a prince

**châtelain**, **∼e** /ʃatlɛ̃, ɛn/ *nm,f* **(a)** lord/lady of the manor
**(b)** owner of a manor

**châtier** /ʃatje/ [2] *vtr* to punish

**chatière** /ʃatjɛR/ *nf* catflap

**châtiment** /ʃatimɑ̃/ *nm* punishment

**chatoiement** /ʃatwamɑ̃/ *nm* shimmering

**chaton** /ʃatɔ̃/ *nm* **(a)** kitten
**(b)** catkin

**chatouille** /ʃatuj/ *nf* (colloq) tickle

**chatouiller** /ʃatuje/ [1] *vtr* to tickle
IDIOMS ~ **les côtes à qn** (euphemistic) to tan sb's hide

**chatouilleux, -euse** /ʃatujø, øz/ *adj*
(a) ticklish
(b) touchy (**sur** about)

**chatoyant, ~e** /ʃatwajɑ̃, ɑ̃t/ *adj* shimmering; iridescent

**chatoyer** /ʃatwaje/ [23] *vi* to shimmer

**châtrer** /ʃɑtʀe/ [1] *vtr* to castrate

**chatte** /ʃat/ *nf* (female) cat

**chaud, ~e** /ʃo, ʃod/ **1** *adj* (a) hot; warm
(b) ⟨*colour, voice*⟩ warm
(c) **ils n'ont pas été très ~s pour faire** they were not very keen on doing
(d) ⟨*region*⟩ turbulent; ⟨*discussion*⟩ heated; **un des points ~s du globe** one of the flash points of the world
(e) **quartier ~** (colloq) red light district
**2** *adv* **il fait ~** it's warm; it's hot; **ça ne me fait ni ~ ni froid** it doesn't matter one way or the other to me
**3** *nm* heat; **avoir ~** to be warm; to be hot; **nous avons eu ~** (figurative) we had a narrow escape; **se tenir ~** to keep warm
**4** **à chaud** *phr* **à ~** ⟨*analyse*⟩ on the spot; ⟨*reaction*⟩ immediate
■ **~ et froid** (Med) chill

**chaudement** /ʃodmɑ̃/ *adv* (gen) warmly; ⟨*recommend*⟩ heartily

**chaudière** /ʃodjɛʀ/ *nf* boiler

**chaudron** /ʃodʀɔ̃/ *nm* cauldron

**chaudronnerie** /ʃodʀɔnʀi/ *nf* boilermaking industry; boilerworks

**chaudronnier, -ière** /ʃodʀɔnje, ɛʀ/ *nm,f* boilermaker

**chauffage** /ʃofaʒ/ *nm* (a) heating
(b) heater

**chauffagiste** /ʃofaʒist/ *nmf* heating engineer

**chauffant, ~e** /ʃofɑ̃, ɑ̃t/ *adj* heating

**chauffard** /ʃofaʀ/ *nm* (colloq) reckless driver

**chauffe** /ʃof/ *nf* (Tech) fire chamber

**chauffe-eau** /ʃofo/ *nm inv* water-heater

**chauffe-plat** /ʃofpla/ *nm inv* dish warmer

**chauffer** /ʃofe/ [1] **1** *vtr* (a) to heat ⟨*house*⟩; to heat (up) ⟨*object, meal*⟩
(b) ⟨*sun*⟩ to warm
**2** *vi* (a) ⟨*food, oven*⟩ to heat up; ⟨*engine*⟩ to warm up; to overheat
(b) ⟨*radiator*⟩ to give out heat
(c) (colloq) **ça va ~!** there's going to be big trouble!
**3** **se chauffer** *v refl* (+ *v être*) (a) **se ~ au soleil** to bask in the sun
(b) **se ~ au charbon** to have coal-fired heating

**chaufferie** /ʃofʀi/ *nf* (a) boiler room
(b) (in boat) stokehold

**chauffeur** /ʃofœʀ/ *nm* (a) driver
(b) chauffeur

**chauffeuse** /ʃoføz/ *nf* low armless easy chair

**chaume** /ʃom/ *nm* (a) (in field) stubble
(b) thatch

**chaumière** /ʃomjɛʀ/ *nf* (a) thatched cottage
(b) **faire jaser dans les ~s** to cause tongues to wag

**chaussée** /ʃose/ *nf* (a) roadway, highway; (in town) street
(b) (road) surface
(c) causeway

**chausse-pied, pl ~s** /ʃospje/ *nm* shoehorn

**chausser** /ʃose/ [1] **1** *vtr* to put [sth] on ⟨*shoes, spectacles*⟩
**2** *vi* **je chausse du 41** I take a (size) 41
**3** **se chausser** *v refl* (+ *v être*) (a) to put (one's) shoes on
(b) to buy (one's) shoes

**chaussette** /ʃosɛt/ *nf* sock
IDIOMS **laisser tomber qn comme une vieille ~** (colloq) to cast sb off like an old rag

**chausseur** /ʃosœʀ/ *nm* shoe shop manager; shoemaker

**chausson** /ʃosɔ̃/ *nm* (a) slipper
(b) bootee
(c) ballet shoe
■ **~ aux pommes** (Culin) apple turnover

**chaussure** /ʃosyʀ/ *nf* shoe; **~ montante** ankle boot
IDIOMS **trouver ~ à son pied** ⟨*man, woman*⟩ to find the right person

**chauve** /ʃov/ *adj* bald

**chauve-souris, pl chauves-souris** /ʃovsuʀi/ *nf* (Zool) bat

**chauvin, ~e** /ʃovɛ̃, in/ *adj* chauvinistic

**chaux** /ʃo/ *nf* lime

**chavirer** /ʃaviʀe/ [1] **1** *vtr* to overwhelm
**2** *vi* (a) ⟨*boat*⟩ to capsize
(b) **faire ~ les cœurs** to be a heartbreaker
(c) ⟨*objects*⟩ to tip over

**chef** /ʃɛf/ *nm* (a) leader
(b) superior, boss (colloq)
(c) head; (of sales department) manager; **architecte en ~** chief architect
(d) **~ cuisinier** *or* **de cuisine** chef
(e) (colloq) ace; **se débrouiller comme un ~** to manage splendidly
(f) **de mon/leur (propre) ~** on my/their own initiative
(g) **au premier ~** primarily, first and foremost
■ **~ d'accusation** (Law) count of indictment; **~ d'atelier** (shop) foreman; **~ d'équipe** foreman; (Sport) team captain; **~ d'État** head of state; **~ de gare** stationmaster

**chef-d'œuvre, pl chefs-d'œuvre** /ʃɛdœvʀ/ *nm* masterpiece

**chef-lieu, pl chefs-lieux** /ʃɛfljø/ *nm* administrative centre

**chemin** /ʃ(ə)mɛ̃/ *nm* (a) country road; lane; **~ (de terre)** dirt track; path
(b) way; **sur le ~ du retour** on the way back; **reprendre le ~ du bureau** to go back to ⋯⟩

work; **on a fait un bout de ~ ensemble** we walked along together for a while; **~ faisant, en ~** on or along the way; **l'idée fait son ~** the idea is gaining ground; **prendre le ~ de la faillite** to be heading for bankruptcy; **s'arrêter en ~** to stop off on the way; (figurative) to stop
■ **~ de fer** railway, railroad (US); rail

**cheminée** /ʃ(ə)mine/ nf **(a)** chimney; chimney stack
**(b)** fireplace
**(c)** mantelpiece
**(d)** (of ship) funnel

**cheminement** /ʃ(ə)minmɑ̃/ nm **(a)** slow progression
**(b) le ~ de sa pensée** his/her train of thought

**cheminer** /ʃ(ə)mine/ [1] vi **(a)** to walk (along)
**(b)** ⟨idea⟩ to progress, to develop

**cheminot** /ʃ(ə)mino/ nm railway worker (GB), railroader (US)

**chemise** /ʃ(ə)miz/ nf **(a)** shirt
**(b)** folder
■ **~ de nuit** nightgown; (for man) nightshirt
IDIOMS **je m'en moque comme de ma première ~** (colloq) I don't give two hoots (GB) (colloq) or a hoot (US) (colloq); **changer d'avis comme de ~** (colloq) to change one's mind at the drop of a hat

**chemiserie** /ʃ(ə)mizʀi/ nf shirt-making trade; shirt factory; shirt shop

**chemisier** /ʃ(ə)mizje/ nm blouse

**chenal**, pl **-aux** /ʃənal, o/ nm channel, fairway

**chenapan** /ʃənapɑ̃/ nm scallywag (colloq), rascal

**chêne** /ʃɛn/ nm **(a)** oak (tree)
**(b)** oak

**chenet** /ʃənɛ/ nm firedog, andiron

**chenil** /ʃənil/ nm **(a)** (dog) kennel
**(b)** kennels

**chenille** /ʃənij/ nf (Aut, Zool) caterpillar

**cheptel** /ʃɛptɛl/ nm ~ (vif) livestock

**chèque** /ʃɛk/ nm cheque (GB), check (US)
■ **~ en blanc** blank cheque (GB) or check (US); **~ en bois** (colloq) rubber cheque (GB) or check (US); **~ sans provision** bad cheque (GB) or check (US); **~ de voyage** traveller's cheque (GB) or check (US)

**chèque-cadeau**, pl **chèques-cadeaux** /ʃɛkkado/ nm gift token

**chèque-voyage**, pl **chèques-voyage** /ʃɛkvwajaʒ/ nm traveller's cheque

**chéquier** /ʃekje/ nm chequebook (GB), checkbook (US)

**cher, chère**[1] /ʃɛʀ/ [1] adj **(a)** dear; beloved; **un être ~** a loved one
**(b)** (as term of address) dear
**(c)** expensive; **pas ~** cheap
[2] nm,f **mon ~/ma chère** my dear
[3] adv **(a)** a lot (of money); **coûter plus/moins ~** to cost more/less; **acheter ~** to buy at a high price

**(b)** (figurative) ⟨pay, cost⟩ dearly
IDIOMS **ne pas donner ~ de la peau de qn** (colloq) not to rate sb's chances highly

**chercher** /ʃɛʀʃe/ [1] [1] vtr **(a)** to look for ⟨person, object, trouble⟩; to try to find ⟨answer, ideas⟩; to try to remember ⟨name⟩; **~ fortune** to seek one's fortune; **~ qn du regard** to look about for sb
**(b) ~ à faire** to try to do
**(c) aller ~ qn/qch** to go and get sb/sth; to pick sb/sth up
**(d) où est-il allé ~ cela?** what made him think that?
**(e) une maison dans ce quartier, ça va ~ dans les 200 000 euros** a house in this area must fetch (GB) or get (US) about 200,000 euros
[2] **se chercher** v refl (+ v être) **(a)** to try to find oneself
**(b) se ~ des excuses** to try to find excuses for oneself
**(c)** (colloq) to be out to get each other (colloq)

**chercheur, -euse** /ʃɛʀʃœʀ, øz/ nm,f researcher
■ **~ d'or** gold-digger

**chère**[2] /ʃɛʀ/ [1] adj f ▶ **CHER**
[2] nf **faire bonne ~** to eat well

**chèrement** /ʃɛʀmɑ̃/ adv **~ acquise** gained at great cost

**chéri, ~e** /ʃeʀi/ [1] pp ▶ **CHÉRIR**
[2] pp adj beloved
[3] nm,f **(a)** darling
**(b)** (colloq) boyfriend/girlfriend

**chérir** /ʃeʀiʀ/ [3] vtr to cherish ⟨person⟩; to hold [sth] dear ⟨idea⟩

**chérubin** /ʃeʀybɛ̃/ nm cherub

**chétif, -ive** /ʃetif, iv/ adj ⟨child⟩ puny

**cheval**, pl **-aux** /ʃ(ə)val, o/ nm
**(a)** horse; **monter à ~** to ride a horse; **remède de ~** strong medicine; **fièvre de ~** raging fever
**(b)** (Sport) horse-riding
**(c)** horsemeat
[2] **à cheval sur** phr **(a)** astride
**(b)** spanning
**(c)** in between
**(d) être à ~ sur qch** to be a stickler for sth
■ **~ à bascule** rocking horse; **~ de bataille** hobbyhorse; **chevaux de bois** merry-go-round horses

**chevaleresque** /ʃ(ə)valʀɛsk/ adj
**(a)** ⟨literature⟩ courtly
**(b)** ⟨person⟩ chivalrous

**chevalerie** /ʃ(ə)valʀi/ nf chivalry

**chevalet** /ʃ(ə)valɛ/ nm easel

**chevalier** /ʃ(ə)valje/ nm knight

**chevalière** /ʃ(ə)valjɛʀ/ nf signet ring

**cheval-vapeur**, pl **chevaux-vapeur** /ʃ(ə)valvapœʀ, ʃ(ə)vovapœʀ/ nm horsepower

**chevauchée** /ʃ(ə)voʃe/ nf ride

**chevaucher** /ʃ(ə)voʃe/ [1] [1] vtr **(a)** to sit astride ⟨animal, chair⟩
**(b)** to overlap
[2] **se chevaucher** v refl (+ v être) to overlap

**chevelu, ~e** /ʃəvly/ *adj* long-haired

**chevelure** /ʃəvlyʀ/ *nf* hair

**chevet** /ʃəvɛ/ *nm* bedhead; **être au ~ de qn** to be at sb's bedside

**cheveu**, *pl* **~x** /ʃəvø/ **1** *nm* hair; **être à un ~ de** to be within a hair's breadth of; **ne tenir qu'à un ~** to hang by a thread
**2 cheveux** *nm pl* hair
IDIOMS **avoir un ~ sur la langue** to have a lisp; **venir comme un ~ sur la soupe** to come at an awkward moment; **se faire des ~x (blancs)** (colloq) to worry oneself to death; **couper les ~x en quatre** to split hairs; **être tiré par les ~x** to be far-fetched

**cheville** /ʃ(ə)vij/ *nf* **(a)** (Anat) ankle
**(b)** Rawlplug®; peg; dowel
IDIOMS **il n'arrive pas à la ~ de Paul** he can't hold a candle to Paul; **être en ~ avec qn** (colloq) to be in cahoots with sb (colloq)

**chèvre¹** /ʃɛvʀ/ *nm* goat's cheese

**chèvre²** /ʃɛvʀ/ *nf* goat; nanny-goat
IDIOMS **devenir ~** (colloq) to go nuts (slang)

**chevreau**, *pl* **~x** /ʃəvʀo/ *nm* (Zool) kid

**chèvrefeuille** /ʃɛvʀəfœj/ *nm* honeysuckle

**chevreuil** /ʃəvʀœj/ *nm* **(a)** roe (deer); roebuck
**(b)** (Culin) venison

**chevronné, ~e** /ʃəvʀɔne/ *adj* ⟨person⟩ experienced

**chevrotant, ~e** /ʃəvʀɔtɑ̃, ɑ̃t/ *adj* ⟨voice⟩ quavering

**chevroter** /ʃəvʀɔte/ [1] *vtr, vi* to quaver

**chevrotine** /ʃəvʀɔtin/ *nf* buckshot

**chez** /ʃe/ *prep* **(a)** **~ qn** at sb's place; **rentre ~ toi** go home; **de ~ qn** ⟨telephone⟩ from sb's place; **fais comme ~ toi** make yourself at home
**(b)** (referring to shop, office) **aller ~ le boucher** to go to the butcher's; **être convoqué ~ le patron** to be called in before the boss
**(c)** (referring to a region) **~ nous** where I come from; where I live
**(d)** among; **~ l'animal** in animals
**(e)** **ce que j'aime ~ elle, c'est son humour** what I like about her is her sense of humour (GB)
**(f)** in; **~ Cocteau** in Cocteau

**chic** /ʃik/ **1** *adj* **(a)** smart (GB), chic
**(b)** (colloq) fashionable
**(c)** (colloq) ⟨person⟩ nice
**2** *nm* chic; **avoir le ~ pour faire** to have a knack for doing; **avec ~** with style

**chicane** /ʃikan/ *nf* chicane; (on road, ski slope) double bend; **en ~** on alternate sides

**chicaner** /ʃikane/ [1] *vi* to squabble

**chiche** /ʃiʃ/ **1** *adj* **(a)** mean (GB), stingy
**(b)** **être ~ de faire** (colloq) to be quite capable of doing
**2** *excl* **'je vais le faire'—'~!'** (colloq) 'I'll do it'—'I dare you!'

**chichement** /ʃiʃmɑ̃/ *adv* ⟨live⟩ frugally; ⟨give⟩ stingily; ⟨pay⟩ poorly

**chichi** /ʃiʃi/ *nm* fuss

**chicon** /ʃikɔ̃/ *nm* chicory

**chicorée** /ʃikɔʀe/ *nf* **(a)** (plant) chicory; (salad vegetable) endive (GB), chicory (US)
**(b)** (Culin) (powder) chicory; (drink) chicory coffee

**chien, chienne¹** /ʃjɛ̃, ʃjɛn/ **1** *adj* (colloq) **ne pas être ~** not to be too hard
**2** *nm* **(a)** dog
**(b)** (of rifle) hammer
**3 de chien** *phr* (colloq) ⟨job, weather⟩ rotten; **ça me fait un mal de ~** it hurts like hell (colloq)
■ **~ d'aveugle** guide dog; **~ de berger** sheepdog; **~ de garde** guard dog; (figurative) watchdog; **~ de race** pedigree dog
IDIOMS **être couché en ~ de fusil** to be curled up; **ce n'est pas fait pour les ~s** (colloq) it's there to be used

**chiendent** /ʃjɛ̃dɑ̃/ *nm* couch grass; **brosse de ~** scrubbing brush

**chienlit** /ʃjɑ̃li/ *nf* havoc, chaos

**chien-loup**, *pl* **chiens-loups** /ʃjɛ̃lu/ *nm* Alsatian (GB), German shepherd

**chienne²** /ʃjɛn/ **1** *adj f* ▶ CHIEN
**2** *nf* (animal) bitch

**chiffon** /ʃifɔ̃/ *nm* **(a)** rag, (piece of) cloth; **parler ~s** to talk (about) clothes
**(b)** duster

**chiffonné, ~e** /ʃifɔne/ *adj* **(a)** ⟨face⟩ tired-looking
**(b)** (colloq) ⟨person⟩ troubled, ruffled

**chiffonner** /ʃifɔne/ [1] **1** *vtr* **(a)** to crease, to crumple
**(b)** (colloq) to bother ⟨person⟩
**2 se chiffonner** *v refl* (+ *v être*) to crease

**chiffonnier** /ʃifɔnje/ *nm* **se battre comme des ~s** to fight like cat and dog

**chiffrable** /ʃifʀabl/ *adj* calculable; **les pertes ne sont pas ~s** it's impossible to put a figure on the losses

**chiffre** /ʃifʀ/ *nm* **(a)** figure
**(b)** monogram
■ **~ d'affaires, CA** turnover (GB), sales (US); **~ arabe** Arabic numeral; **~ romain** Roman numeral; **~ de vente** sales (figures)

**chiffrer** /ʃifʀe/ [1] **1** *vtr* **(a)** to put a figure on ⟨cost, loss⟩; to cost ⟨job⟩; **~ à** to put the cost of ⟨sth⟩ at ⟨job⟩
**(b)** to encode ⟨message⟩
**2** *vi* (colloq) to add up; **ça chiffre vite** it soon adds up
**3 se chiffrer** *v refl* (+ *v être*) **se ~ à** to amount to, to come to

**chignole** /ʃiɲɔl/ *nf* hand drill

**chignon** /ʃiɲɔ̃/ *nm* bun; chignon

**Chili** /ʃili/ *pr nm* Chile

**chimère** /ʃimɛʀ/ *nf* **(a)** wild dream, pipe dream
**(b)** (in mythology) Chimaera

**chimérique** /ʃimeʀik/ *adj* ⟨hope⟩ wild; ⟨person⟩ fanciful

**chimie** /ʃimi/ *nf* chemistry

**chimiothérapie** /ʃimjoteʀapi/ *nf* chemotherapy

**chimique** /ʃimik/ *adj* **(a)** chemical; ⟨fibre⟩ man-made
**(b)** ⟨food, taste⟩ synthetic
**chimiste** /ʃimist/ *nmf* chemist
**chimpanzé** /ʃɛ̃pɑ̃ze/ *nm* chimpanzee
**chiné, ~e** /ʃine/ *adj* chiné
**Chine** /ʃin/ *pr nf* China
**chiner** /ʃine/ [1] *vi* (colloq) to bargain-hunt, to antique (US)
**chinois, ~e** /ʃinwa, az/ **1** *adj* Chinese **2** *nm* (language) Chinese
IDIOMS **pour moi c'est du ~** it's double-Dutch (GB) *or* Greek to me
**chiot** /ʃjo/ *nm* puppy, pup
**chiper** /ʃipe/ [1] *vtr* (colloq) to pinch (colloq)
**chipie** /ʃipi/ *nf* (colloq) cow (colloq)
**chipoter** /ʃipɔte/ [1] *vi* (colloq) **(a)** to quibble (**sur** over)
**(b)** to pick at one's food
**chipoteur, -euse** /ʃipɔtœʀ, øz/ *adj* (colloq) **(a)** difficult
**(b)** fussy
**chips** /ʃips/ *nf inv* crisp (GB), potato chip (US)
**chique** /ʃik/ *nf* plug (of tobacco)
IDIOMS **couper la ~ à qn** to shut sb up (colloq)
**chiqué** /ʃike/ *nm* (colloq) **(a)** **c'est du ~** it's a put-on
**(b) faire du ~** to put on *or* give oneself airs
**chiquenaude** /ʃiknod/ *nf* flick
**chiquer** /ʃike/ [1] *vtr* **tabac à ~** chewing tobacco
**chiromancie** /kiʀomɑ̃si/ *nf* palmistry
**chirurgical, ~e,** *mpl* **-aux** /ʃiʀyʀʒikal, o/ *adj* surgical
**chirurgie** /ʃiʀyʀʒi/ *nf* surgery
**chirurgien** /ʃiʀyʀʒjɛ̃/ *nm* surgeon
**chlore** /klɔʀ/ *nm* chlorine
**chlorer** /klɔʀe/ [1] *vtr* to chlorinate
**chlorhydrique** /klɔʀidʀik/ *adj* hydrochloric
**chloroforme** /klɔʀofɔʀm/ *nm* chloroform
**chlorophylle** /klɔʀofil/ *nf* chlorophyll
**chlorure** /klɔʀyʀ/ *nm* chloride
**choc** /ʃɔk/ **1** *adj inv* **'prix ~!'** 'huge reductions'
**2** *nm* **(a)** impact, shock; collision; **sous le ~** under the impact
**(b)** (noise) crash, smash; thud; clang; chink
**(c)** (confrontation) (gen, Mil) clash; (Sport) encounter; **de ~** ⟨journalist⟩ ace (colloq)
**(d)** (emotional, physical) shock
**chocolat** /ʃɔkɔla/ *nm* chocolate; **~ noir** *or* **à croquer** plain (GB) *or* dark (US) chocolate
**chœur** /kœʀ/ *nm* **(a)** choir; (in opera, play) chorus; (figurative) chorus (**de** of); **en ~** ⟨say⟩ in unison; ⟨laugh⟩ all together
**(b)** (in church) chancel, choir
**choir** /ʃwaʀ/ [51] *vi* to fall; **laisser ~ qn** to drop sb
**choisir** /ʃwaziʀ/ [3] *vtr* to choose

**choix** /ʃwa/ *nm inv* **(a)** choice; **arrêter son ~ sur** to settle *or* decide on
**(b) de ~** ⟨item⟩ choice; ⟨candidate⟩ first-rate; **les places de ~** the best seats; **un morceau de ~** (of meat) a prime cut; **de second ~** of inferior quality
**choléra** /kɔleʀa/ *nm* cholera
**cholestérol** /kɔlɛsteʀɔl/ *nm* cholesterol
**chômage** /ʃomaʒ/ *nm* unemployment; **mettre qn au ~** to make sb redundant (GB), to lay sb off
■ **~ technique** layoffs
**chômé, ~e** /ʃome/ *adj* **jour ~** day off; **fête ~e** national holiday
**chômer** /ʃome/ [1] *vi* **(a)** to be idle
**(b)** to be out of work
**chômeur, -euse** /ʃomœʀ, øz/ *nm,f* unemployed person
**chope** /ʃɔp/ *nf* beer mug, tankard
**choquant, ~e** /ʃɔkɑ̃, ɑ̃t/ *adj* shocking
**choquer** /ʃɔke/ [1] *vtr* **(a)** to shock ⟨person⟩; to offend ⟨sight, sensibility⟩
**(b)** ⟨news⟩ to shake ⟨person⟩; ⟨accident⟩ to shake [sb] (up)
**chorale** /kɔʀal/ *nf* choir
**chorégraphie** /kɔʀegʀafi/ *nf* choreography
**choriste** /kɔʀist/ *nmf* chorister; member of the choir; member of the chorus
**chorus** /kɔʀys/ *nm inv* chorus; **faire ~ avec qn** (figurative) to join in with sb
**chose** /ʃoz/ *nf* **(a)** (object, abstract) thing; **de deux ~s l'une** it's got to be one thing or the other; **une ~ communément admise** a widely accepted fact; **en mettant les ~s au mieux** at best; **mettre les ~s au point** to clear things up; **avant toute ~** before anything else; above all else
**(b)** matter; **la ~ en question** the matter in hand
**(c) être un peu porté sur la ~** (colloq) to be keen on sex
**chou,** *pl* **~x** /ʃu/ *nm* **(a)** cabbage
**(b)** choux bun (GB), pastry shell (US)
**(c)** dear, darling
■ **~ de Bruxelles** Brussels sprout; **~ à la crème** cream puff; **~ rave** kohlrabi
IDIOMS **bête comme ~** really easy; **faire ~ blanc** (colloq) to draw a blank; **faire ses ~x gras de qch** (colloq) to use sth to one's advantage; **rentrer dans le ~ de qn** (colloq) to beat sb up; to give sb a piece of one's mind
**choucas** /ʃuka/ *nm* jackdaw
**chouchou** /ʃuʃu/ *nm* (colloq) **(a)** (teacher's) pet; (of adoring public) darling
**(b)** (for hair) scrunchie
**chouchouter** /ʃuʃute/ [1] *vtr* (colloq) to pamper
**choucroute** /ʃukʀut/ *nf* sauerkraut
**chouette** /ʃwɛt/ **1** *adj* (colloq) great (colloq), neat (US) (colloq)
**2** *nf* **(a)** owl
**(b) vieille ~** old harridan

75

# chou-fleur ⋯⊱ cinquième ⋯⋯

**chou-fleur**, *pl* **choux-fleurs** /ʃuflœʀ/ *nm* cauliflower

**chourer** /ʃuʀe/ [1] *vtr* (colloq) to pinch (colloq); **se faire ~ qch** to have sth pinched

**choyer** /ʃwaje/ [23] *vtr* to pamper

**chrétien, -ienne** /kʀetjɛ̃, ɛn/ *adj, nm,f* Christian

**chrétienté** /kʀetjɛ̃te/ *nf* **la ~** Christendom

**Christ** /kʀist/ *pr n* **le ~** Christ

**christianisme** /kʀistjanism/ *nm* Christianity

**chromatique** /kʀɔmatik/ *adj* chromatic

**chrome** /kʀom/ *nm* chromium

**chromosome** /kʀomozom/ *nm* chromosome

**chronique** /kʀɔnik/ **1** *adj* chronic **2** *nf* (in newspaper) column, page

**chroniqueur, -euse** /kʀɔnikœʀ, øz/ *nm,f* columnist, editor

**chronologie** /kʀɔnɔlɔʒi/ *nf* chronology

**chronologique** /kʀɔnɔlɔʒik/ *adj* chronological

**chronomètre** /kʀɔnɔmɛtʀ/ *nm* stopwatch

**chronométrer** /kʀɔnɔmetʀe/ [14] *vtr* to time

**chrysalide** /kʀizalid/ *nf* chrysalis

**chu** ▶ CHOIR

**CHU** /seaʃy/ *nm: abbr* ▶ CENTRE

**chuchotement** /ʃyʃɔtmɑ̃/ *nm* whisper

**chuchoter** /ʃyʃɔte/ [1] *vtr, vi* to whisper

**chuintant, ~e** /ʃɥɛ̃tɑ̃, ɑ̃t/ *adj* **bruit ~** hissing sound

**chuinter** /ʃɥɛ̃te/ [1] *vi* (steam) to hiss gently; (tyre) to swish

**chum** /tʃœm/ *nm* (colloq) friend; boyfriend

**chut** /ʃyt/ *excl* shh!, hush!

**chute** /ʃyt/ *nf* (a) (gen) fall; (of empire) collapse; (of hair) loss; (of pressure) drop (b) (of film) ending; (of story) punch line (c) (of cloth) offcut
■ **~ d'eau** waterfall; **la ~ des reins** the small of the back

**Chypre** /ʃipʀ/ *pr nf* Cyprus

**ci** /si/ **1** *det* **cette page-~** this page; **ces jours-~** (past) these last few days; (future) in the next few days; (present) at the moment **2** *pron* this; **~ et ça** this and that

**ci-après** /siapʀɛ/ *adv* below

**cible** /sibl/ *nf* target

**cibler** /sible/ [1] *vtr* to target

**ciboulette** /sibulɛt/ *nf* (Bot) chive; (Culin) chives

**cicatrice** /sikatʀis/ *nf* scar

**cicatrisant, ~e** /sikatʀizɑ̃, ɑ̃t/ *adj* healing

**cicatrisation** /sikatʀizasjɔ̃/ *nf* healing

**cicatriser** /sikatʀize/ [1] *vtr*, **se cicatriser** *v refl* (+ *v être*) to heal

**ci-contre** /sikɔ̃tʀ/ *adv* opposite

**ci-dessous** /sidəsu/ *adv* below

**ci-dessus** /sidəsy/ *adv* above

**cidre** /sidʀ/ *nm* cider

**cidrerie** /sidʀəʀi/ *nf* cider-works

**ciel** /sjɛl/, *pl* **cieux** /sjø/ *nm* (a) sky; **carte du ~** star chart; **à ~ ouvert** (pool) open-air; (sewer) open (b) heaven; **c'est le ~ qui t'envoie** you're a godsend

**cierge** /sjɛʀʒ/ *nm* (church) candle

**cieux** ▶ CIEL

**cigale** /sigal/ *nf* cicada

**cigare** /sigaʀ/ *nm* cigar

**cigarette** /sigaʀɛt/ *nf* cigarette

**ci-gît** /siʒi/ *phr* here lies

**cigogne** /sigɔɲ/ *nf* stork

**ci-inclus, ~e** /siɛ̃kly, yz/ *adj, adv* enclosed

**ci-joint, ~e** /siʒwɛ̃, ɛ̃t/ *adj, adv* enclosed

**cil** /sil/ *nm* eyelash

**ciller** /sije/ [1] *vi* **~ (des yeux)** to blink; **sans ~** without batting an eyelid

**cime** /sim/ *nf* (tree)top

**ciment** /simɑ̃/ *nm* cement

**cimenter** /simɑ̃te/ [1] **1** *vtr* to cement **2** **se cimenter** *v refl* (+ *v être*) (friendship) to grow stronger

**cimenterie** /simɑ̃tʀi/ *nf* cement works

**cimetière** /simtjɛʀ/ *nm* cemetery, graveyard

**cinéaste** /sineast/ *nmf* film director

**ciné-club**, *pl* **~s** /sineklœb/ *nm* film club

**cinéma** /sinema/ *nm* (a) **(salle de) ~** cinema (GB), movie theater (US) (b) cinema; film industry; **faire du ~** to be in films (c) (figurative) (colloq) **arrête ton ~** cut out the play-acting; stop making such a fuss (colloq)
■ **~ d'art et d'essai** cinema showing art films (GB), art house (US)

**cinémathèque** /sinematɛk/ *nf* film archive

**cinématographique** /sinematɔgʀafik/ *adj* film (GB), movie (US)

**cinéphile** /sinefil/ *nmf* cinema enthusiast

**cinglant, ~e** /sɛ̃glɑ̃, ɑ̃t/ *adj* (a) (wind) biting; (rain) driving (b) (remark, irony) scathing

**cinglé, ~e** /sɛ̃gle/ *adj* (colloq) mad (colloq), crazy (colloq)

**cingler** /sɛ̃gle/ [1] *vtr* (a) (rain, wind) to sting (face) (b) (with whip) to lash

**cinoche** /sinɔʃ/ *nm* (colloq) (a) cinema, pictures (colloq) (b) cinema, movie theater (US)

**cinq** /sɛ̃k/ *adj inv, pron, nm inv* five

**cinquantaine** /sɛ̃kɑ̃tɛn/ *nf* about fifty

**cinquante** /sɛ̃kɑ̃t/ *adj inv, pron, nm inv* fifty

**cinquantenaire** /sɛ̃kɑ̃tnɛʀ/ *nm* fiftieth anniversary

**cinquantième** /sɛ̃kɑ̃tjɛm/ *adj* fiftieth

**cinquième** /sɛ̃kjɛm/ **1** *adj* fifth ⋯⊱

**claironner** /klɛʀɔne/ [1] *vtr* to shout [sth] from the rooftops

**clairsemé**, **~e** /klɛʀsəme/ *adj* ⟨*houses*⟩ scattered; ⟨*hair*⟩ thin; ⟨*population*⟩ sparse

**clairvoyance** /klɛʀvwajɑ̃s/ *nf* perceptiveness

**clairvoyant**, **~e** /klɛʀvwajɑ̃, ɑ̃t/ *adj* perceptive

**clamer** /klame/ [1] *vtr* to proclaim

**clameur** /klamœʀ/ *nf* roar

**clan** /klɑ̃/ *nm* clan

**clandestin**, **~e** /klɑ̃dɛstɛ̃, in/ *adj* ⟨*organization*⟩ underground; ⟨*immigration*⟩ illegal; **passager ~** stowaway

**clandestinement** /klɑ̃dɛstinmɑ̃/ *adv* illegally

**clandestinité** /klɑ̃dɛstinite/ *nf* secret *or* clandestine nature; **dans la ~** ⟨*live*⟩ in hiding; ⟨*operate*⟩ in secret

**clap** /klap/ *nm* clapperboard

**clapet** /klapɛ/ *nm* (a) valve
(b) (colloq) mouth, trap (colloq)

**clapier** /klapje/ *nm* rabbit hutch

**clapoter** /klapɔte/ [1] *vi* to lap

**claquage** /klakaʒ/ *nm* pulled *or* strained muscle

**claque** /klak/ *nf* (a) slap
(b) (colloq) slap in the face
(c) (in theatre) claque
**IDIOMS en avoir sa ~** (colloq) to be fed up

**claqué**, **~e** /klake/ *adj* (colloq) knackered (slang), done in (colloq)

**claquement** /klakmɑ̃/ *nm* (of door) bang; (of whip) crack; (of tongue) click; (of flag) flapping

**claquemurer: se claquemurer** /klakmyʀe/ [1] *v refl* (+ *v être*) to shut oneself away (**dans** in)

**claquer** /klake/ [1] **1** *vtr* (a) to slam ⟨*door*⟩
(b) (colloq) to exhaust ⟨*person*⟩
(c) (colloq) to blow (colloq) ⟨*money*⟩
**2** *vi* ⟨*door*⟩ to bang; (closing) to slam shut; ⟨*flag*⟩ to flap; **elle claque des dents** her teeth are chattering
**3 se claquer** *v refl* (+ *v être*) **se ~ un muscle** to pull *or* strain a muscle

**claquettes** /klakɛt/ *nf pl* tap dancing

**clarifier** /klaʀifje/ [2] *vtr* to clarify

**clarinette** /klaʀinɛt/ *nf* clarinet

**clarté** /klaʀte/ *nf* (a) light
(b) (of water) clarity; (of complexion) fairness
(c) (of style) clarity

**classe** /klas/ *nf* (a) (Sch) (group) class, form (GB); (level) year, form (GB), grade (US); **après la ~** after school
(b) (Sch) classroom
(c) (in society, transport) class; **les ~s sociales** social classes
(d) **avoir de la ~** to have class
(e) (Mil) **faire ses ~s** to do one's basic training
■ **~ d'âge** age group; **~ verte** educational schooltrip to the countryside; **~s**

**préparatoires (aux grandes écoles)** *preparatory classes for entrance to Grandes Écoles*

**classement** /klasmɑ̃/ *nm*
(a) classification
(b) filing; **faire du ~ dans ses papiers** to sort one's papers out
(c) grading; **~ trimestriel** (Sch) termly position (in class)
(d) (Sport) ranking; **en tête du ~** in first place
(e) (of hotel) rating

**classer** /klase/ [1] **1** *vtr* (a) to classify
(b) to file (away) ⟨*documents*⟩
(c) (Law) to close ⟨*case*⟩
(d) to list ⟨*old building*⟩
(e) to class ⟨*country, pupils*⟩; to rank ⟨*song, player*⟩
(f) (colloq) to size [sb] up
**2 se classer** *v refl* (+ *v être*) to rank

**classeur** /klasœʀ/ *nm* (a) ring binder
(b) file

**classicisme** /klasisism/ *nm* (a) (in art) classicism
(b) (in clothes, tastes) traditionalism

**classification** /klasifikasjɔ̃/ *nf* classification

**classifier** /klasifje/ [2] *vtr* to classify

**classique** /klasik/ **1** *adj* (a) classical; **faire des études ~s** (Sch) to do classics
(b) classic; ⟨*method*⟩ classic, standard; ⟨*consequence*⟩ usual; **de coupe ~** of classic cut; **c'est ~!** (colloq) it's typical!; **c'est le coup ~!** (colloq) it's the same old story!
**2** *nm* classic

**clause** /kloz/ *nf* clause

**claustrophobie** /klostʀɔfɔbi/ *nf* claustrophobia

**clavecin** /klavsɛ̃/ *nm* harpsichord

**clavicule** /klavikyl/ *nf* collarbone

**clavier** /klavje/ *nm* keyboard; **~ numérique** numeric keypad

**claviste** /klavist/ *nmf* (a) typesetter
(b) (Comput) keyboarder

**clé** /kle/ **1** *nf* (a) (of lock, tin) key; **sous ~** under lock and key; **fermer à ~** to lock; **prix ~s en main** ⟨*car*⟩ on the road price (GB), sticker price (US); **usine ~s en main** turnkey factory
(b) (solution) key (**de** to)
(c) (Mus) key
(c) (spanner (GB), wrench
(d) (of flute) key; (of violin) peg; **~ de fa** bass clef
**2 (-)clé** (*combining form*) **poste/mot(-)~** key post/word
**3 à la clé** *phr* at stake; **avec, à la ~, une récompense** with a reward thrown in
■ **~ anglaise**, **~ à molette** adjustable spanner (GB) *or* wrench (US)

**clef** = CLÉ

**clément**, **~e** /klemɑ̃, ɑ̃t/ *adj* (a) ⟨*judge*⟩ lenient
(b) ⟨*temperature, winter*⟩ mild

**clémentine** /klemɑ̃tin/ *nf* clementine

**cleptomanie** /klɛptɔmani/ *nf* kleptomania

**clerc** /klɛʀ/ *nm* (Law) clerk

**clergé** /klɛʀʒe/ *nm* clergy

**cliché** /kliʃe/ *nm* (a) snapshot
(b) cliché

**client, ~e** /klijã, ãt/ *nm,f* (of shop) customer; (of solicitor) client; (of hotel) guest; (in taxi) fare
IDIOMS **c'est à la tête du ~** it depends whether they like the look of you

**clientèle** /klijãtɛl/ *nf* (of shop) customers; (of solicitor) clients; (of doctor) patients; **se faire une ~** to build up a clientele

**cligner** /kliɲe/ [1] *v+prep* **~ des yeux** to blink; **~ de l'œil** to wink

**clignotant** /kliɲɔtã/ *nm* (Aut) indicator (GB), blinker (US)

**clignoter** /kliɲɔte/ [1] *vi* ‹light› to flash; to flash on and off; ‹star› to twinkle

**climat** /klima/ *nm* climate

**climatique** /klimatik/ *adj* climatic

**climatisation** /klimatizasjõ/ *nf* air-conditioning

**climatiser** /klimatize/ [1] *vtr* to air-condition

**climatiseur** /klimatizœʀ/ *nm* air-conditioner

**clin** /klɛ̃/ *nm* **~ d'œil** wink; (figurative) allusion; **en un ~ d'œil** in a flash

**clinique** /klinik/ **1** *adj* clinical
**2** *nf* private hospital; **~ vétérinaire** veterinary clinic

**clinquant, ~e** /klɛ̃kã, ãt/ *adj* flashy (colloq)

**clip** /klip/ *nm* (a) pop video
(b) clip-on (earring)

**clique** /klik/ *nf* clique; **prendre ses ~s et ses claques** to pack up and go

**cliquer** /klike/ [1] *vi* (Comput) to click (**sur** on)

**cliqueter** /klikte/ [20] *vi* ‹keys› to jingle; ‹chain, machine› to rattle

**clitoris** /klitɔris/ *nm* clitoris

**clivage** /klivaʒ/ *nm* divide; **~ d'opinion** division of opinion

**clochard, ~e** /klɔʃaʀ, aʀd/ *nm,f* tramp

**cloche** /klɔʃ/ *nf* (a) bell
(b) (colloq) clod (colloq), idiot
(c) **~ à fromage** cover of cheese dish
IDIOMS **entendre plusieurs sons de ~** to hear several versions; **sonner les ~s à qn** to bawl sb out (colloq)

**cloche-pied: à cloche-pied** /aklɔʃpje/ *phr* **sauter à ~** to hop

**clocher¹** /klɔʃe/ [1] *vi* (colloq) **il y a quelque chose qui cloche** there's something wrong

**clocher²** /klɔʃe/ *nm* steeple; church *or* bell tower; **querelle de ~** local quarrel

**clochette** /klɔʃɛt/ *nf* (little) bell

**cloison** /klwazõ/ *nf* (a) partition
(b) screen; **~ extensible** folding room-divider

**cloisonner** /klwazɔne/ [1] *vtr* (a) to partition ‹room›; to divide up ‹space›
(b) to divide up ‹society›; to compartmentalize ‹administration›

**cloître** /klwatʀ/ *nm* cloister

**cloîtrer** /klwatʀe/ [1] **1** *vtr* to shut [sb] away
**2 se cloîtrer** *v refl* (+ *v être*) to shut oneself away

**clone** /klon/ *nm* clone

**clope** /klɔp/ *nm or f* (colloq) fag (GB) (colloq), ciggy (colloq), cigarette

**clopin-clopant** /klɔpɛ̃klɔpã/ *phr* (colloq) **aller ~** to hobble along

**cloporte** /klɔpɔʀt/ *nm* woodlouse

**cloque** /klɔk/ *nf* blister

**clore** /klɔʀ/ [79] **1** *vtr* (a) to close ‹debate›
(b) to end, to conclude ‹programme›
(c) to close ‹eyes›
**2 se clore** *v refl* (+ *v être*) to end (**par** with)

**clos, ~e** /klo, oz/ **1** *pp* ▶ CLORE
**2** *pp adj* ‹system› closed; ‹area› enclosed; **monde ~** self-contained world

**clôture** /klotyʀ/ *nf* (a) fence; wire fence; railings
(b) (of debate, session) close; (of subscription) closing; **discours de ~** closing speech

**clôturer** /klotyʀe/ [1] *vtr* (a) to fence in ‹land›
(b) ‹person› to close ‹list›; ‹speech› to end ‹debate›

**clou** /klu/ **1** *nm* (a) nail; stud
(b) (of show) star attraction; (of evening) high point
(c) (Med) boil
**2 clous** *nm pl* (a) pedestrian crossing (GB), crosswalk (US)
(b) (colloq) **des ~s!** no way!
■ **~ de girofle** (Bot, Culin) clove
IDIOMS **enfoncer le ~** to drive the point home

**clouer** /klue/ [1] *vtr* to nail down ‹lid›; to nail together ‹planks›; **~ au sol** (figurative) to pin [sb] down; **être cloué au lit** to be confined to bed

**clown** /klun/ *nm* clown

**clownerie** /kluʀi/ *nf* clowning; **arrête tes ~s** stop clowning about

**club** /klœb/ *nm* (a) club
(b) **~ de vacances** holiday camp

**CM** /seɛm/ *nm: abbr* ▶ COURS

**CNPF** /seɛnpeɛf/ *nm* (*abbr* = **Conseil national du patronat français**) *national council of French employers*

**CNRS** /seɛneɛʀɛs/ *nm* (*abbr* = **Centre national de la recherche scientifique**) *national centre for scientific research*

**coaguler** /kɔagyle/ [1] *vi*, **se coaguler** *v refl* (+ *v être*) to coagulate

**coalition** /kɔalisjõ/ *nf* coalition

**coasser** /kɔase/ [1] *vi* to croak

**cobaye** /kɔbaj/ *nm* guinea pig

**cobra** /kɔbʀa/ *nm* cobra

**cocaïne** /kɔkain/ *nf* cocaine

**cocarde** /kɔkaʀd/ *nf* (a) rosette; (on uniform) cockade
(b) (on vehicle) official badge

**cocasse** /kɔkas/ *adj* comical

**coccinelle** /kɔksinɛl/ *nf* ladybird, ladybug (US)

**coccyx** /kɔksis/ *nm* coccyx

**coche** /kɔʃ/ *nm* (stage)coach
IDIOMS **manquer le** ∼ to miss the boat

**cocher¹** /kɔʃe/ [1] *vtr* to tick (GB), to check (US)

**cocher²** /kɔʃe/ *nm* coachman; cabman

**cochère** /kɔʃɛʀ/ *adj f* **porte** ∼ carriage entrance

**cochon, -onne** /kɔʃɔ̃, ɔn/ [1] *adj* (colloq)
(a) ⟨film⟩ dirty; ⟨person⟩ dirty-minded
(b) ⟨person⟩ messy, dirty
[2] *nm,f* (colloq) (a) pig (colloq), slob (colloq); **de** ∼ ⟨job⟩ botched; ⟨weather⟩ lousy (colloq)
(b) sex maniac
[3] *nm* (a) (Zool) pig, hog
(b) (Culin) pork
■ ∼ **d'Inde** Guinea pig; ∼ **de lait** sucking pig

**cochonnaille** /kɔʃɔnɑj/ *nf* (colloq): products made from pork such as salami, bacon, pâté and ham

**cochonnerie** /kɔʃɔnʀi/ *nf* (colloq) (a) junk (colloq); **il ne mange que des** ∼s he only eats junk food
(b) mess; **faire des** ∼s to make a mess

**cocker** /kɔkɛʀ/ *nm* (cocker) spaniel

**cocktail** /kɔktɛl/ *nm* (a) cocktail
(b) (figurative) mixture
(c) cocktail party

**coco** /koko/ *nm* coconut

**cocon** /kɔkɔ̃/ *nm* cocoon

**cocorico** /kɔkɔʀiko/ *nm* cock-a-doodle-do

**cocotier** /kɔkɔtje/ *nm* coconut palm

**cocotte** /kɔkɔt/ *nf* (a) (colloq) (baby talk) hen
(b) (colloq) **ma** ∼ honey (colloq)
(c) (Culin) casserole (GB), pot

**cocotte-minute®**, *pl* **cocottes-minute** /kɔkɔtminyt/ *nf* pressure cooker

**codage** /kɔdaʒ/ *nm* coding, encoding

**code** /kɔd/ [1] *nm* code
[2] **codes** *nm pl* (of vehicle) dipped (GB) or dimmed (US) (head)lights, low beam
■ ∼ **accès** password; ∼ (**à**) **barres** bar code; ∼ **confidentiel** personal identification number, PIN; ∼ **de la nationalité** regulations as to nationality; ∼ **postal** post code (GB), zip code (US); ∼ **de la route** (Aut) highway code (GB), rules of the road (US); **passer son** ∼ (colloq) to take the written part of a driving test

**coder** /kɔde/ [1] *vtr* to code, to encode

**codétenu, ∼e** /kɔdetny/ *nm,f* fellow prisoner

**codifier** /kɔdifje/ [2] *vtr* to codify ⟨laws⟩; to standardize ⟨language, custom⟩

**codirecteur, -trice** /kɔdiʀɛktœʀ, tʀis/ *nm,f* joint manager; joint director

**coefficient** /kɔefisjɑ̃/ *nm* (a) ratio
(b) margin
(c) weighting factor in an exam; **la chimie est au** ∼ 4 chemistry results are multiplied by 4
(d) (in arithmetic, physics) coefficient

**coéquipier, -ière** /koekipje, ɛʀ/ *nm,f* team mate

**cœur** /kœʀ/ [1] *nm* (a) heart; **il a le** ∼ **malade** he has a heart condition; **serrer qn sur** or **contre son** ∼ to hold sb close; **écouter son** ∼ to go with one's feelings; **aller droit au** ∼ **de qn** to touch sb deeply; **avoir un coup de** ∼ **pour qch** to fall in love with sth; **ça me fait mal au** ∼ **de voir** it sickens me to see; **problème de** ∼ emotional problem; **parler à** ∼ **ouvert** to speak openly; **avoir bon** ∼ to be kind-hearted; **je n'ai plus le** ∼ **à rien** I don't feel like doing anything any more
(b) (Culin) heart
(c) (figurative) (of fruit, rock) core; (of problem, debate) heart; **au** ∼ **de** (of region, town) in the middle of; (of building, problem, system) at the heart of; **au** ∼ **de l'hiver** in the dead of winter
(d) (person) **mon** (**petit**) ∼ sweetheart
(e) courage; **le** ∼ **m'a manqué** my courage failed me; **redonner du** ∼ **à qn** to give sb new heart
(f) (Games) (card) heart; (suit) hearts
[2] **à** ∼ *phr* **avoir à** ∼ **de faire** to be intent on doing; **prendre qch à** ∼ to take sth seriously
[3] **de bon cœur** *phr* willingly; **rire de bon** ∼ to laugh heartily
[4] **par cœur** *phr* by heart; **connaître qn par** ∼ to know sb inside out
IDIOMS **avoir mal au** ∼ to feel sick (GB) or nauseous (US); **avoir du** ∼ **au ventre** to be brave; **avoir le** ∼ **sur la main** to be open-handed; **il ne le porte pas dans son** ∼ he's not his favourite (GB) person; **j'irai mais le** ∼ **n'y est pas** I'll go but my heart isn't in it; **si le** ∼ **t'en dit** if you feel like it; **avoir qch sur le** ∼ to be resentful about sth

**coexister** /kɔegziste/ [1] *vi* to coexist

**coffre** /kɔfʀ/ *nm* (a) chest; ∼ **à jouets** toy box
(b) (for valuables) safe; (individual) safety deposit box; **la salle des** ∼s the strongroom
(c) (of car) boot (GB), trunk (US)
IDIOMS **avoir du** ∼ (colloq) to have a powerful voice

**coffre-fort**, *pl* **coffres-forts** /kɔfʀəfɔʀ/ *nm* safe

**coffret** /kɔfʀɛ/ *nm* (a) casket; ∼ **à bijoux** jewellery (GB) or jewelry (US) box
(b) (of records, cassettes, books) boxed set

**cogérer** /kɔʒeʀe/ [14] *vtr* to co-manage

**cogestion** /kɔʒɛstjɔ̃/ *nf* joint management

**cogiter** /kɔʒite/ [1] *vi* to cogitate, to think

**cognac** /kɔɲak/ *nm* cognac (brandy from the Cognac area)

**cogner** /kɔɲe/ [1] **1** *vtr* to knock

**2** *vi* (a) ~ **contre** ⟨*shutter*⟩ to bang against; ⟨*branch*⟩ to knock against; ⟨*projectile*⟩ to hit; ~ **à la porte** to bang on the door

(b) (colloq) ⟨*boxer*⟩ to hit out

(c) ⟨*heart*⟩ to pound

**3 se cogner** *v refl* (+ *v être*) to bump into something; **se** ~ **le pied contre une pierre** to stub one's toe on a stone

**cognitif, -ive** /kɔɡnitif, iv/ *adj* cognitive

**cohabitation** /kɔabitasjɔ̃/ *nf* (a) living with somebody

(b) *situation where the French President is in political opposition to the government*

**cohabiter** /kɔabite/ [1] *vi* ⟨*people*⟩ to live together; ⟨*things*⟩ to coexist

**cohérence** /kɔeRɑ̃s/ *nf* (a) coherence; consistency

(b) (in physics) cohesion

**cohérent, ~e** /kɔeRɑ̃, ɑ̃t/ *adj* coherent; consistent

**cohéritier, -ière** /kɔeRitje, ɛR/ *nm,f* joint heir

**cohésion** /kɔezjɔ̃/ *nf* cohesion

**cohorte** /kɔɔRt/ *nf* (colloq) crowd, group

**cohue** /kɔy/ *nf* crowd; **c'est la** ~ it's a crush

**coi, coite** /kwa, kwat/ *adj* **se tenir** ~ to remain quiet

**coiffant, ~e** /kwafɑ̃, ɑ̃t/ *adj* **gel** ~ styling gel

**coiffe** /kwaf/ *nf* (gen) headgear; (of nun) wimple

**coiffer** /kwafe/ [1] **1** *vtr* (a) ~ **qn** to do sb's hair; to comb sb's hair

(b) **coiffé d'une casquette** wearing a cap

**2 se coiffer** *v refl* (+ *v être*) (a) to do *or* comb one's hair

(b) **se** ~ **de qch** to put sth on

IDIOMS ~ **qn au poteau** (colloq) *or* **sur le fil** (colloq) to beat sb by a whisker

**coiffeur, -euse**[1] /kwafœR, øz/ *nm,f* hairdresser

**coiffeuse**[2] /kwaføz/ *nf* dressing table

**coiffure** /kwafyR/ *nf* (a) hairstyle

(b) hairdressing

(c) headgear

**coin** /kwɛ̃/ **1** *nm* (a) corner; **à tous les** ~**s de rue** everywhere; **aux quatre** ~**s de la ville** all over the town; **aller au** ~ (as punishment) to go and stand in the corner; **j'ai dû poser mon sac dans un** ~ I must have put my bag down somewhere; **au** ~ **du feu** by the fire

(b) (of eye, mouth) corner; **un sourire en** ~ a half-smile; **un regard en** ~ a sidelong glance

(c) (of ground) plot; (of lawn) patch; **un** ~ **de paradis** an idyllic spot

(d) (in region) **un** ~ **de France** a part of France; **dans le** ~ around here, in these parts; around there, in those parts; **le café du** ~ the local café; **les gens du** ~ the locals; **connaître les bons** ~**s pour manger** to know all the good places to eat

(e) (for photograph) corner; (for file) reinforcing corner

(f) (Tech) wedge

**2 coin(-)** (*combining form*) ~**-repas/-salon** dining/living area

**coincé, ~e** /kwɛ̃se/ **1** *pp* ▶ COINCER

**2** *pp adj* (a) stuck; trapped; ~ **entre** ⟨*house*⟩ wedged between

(b) (colloq) **j'ai le dos** ~, **je suis** ~ my back has gone (colloq)

(c) (figurative) (colloq) stuck (colloq)

(d) (colloq) ill at ease

(e) (colloq) uptight (colloq)

**coincer** /kwɛ̃se/ [12] **1** *vtr* (a) to wedge ⟨*object*⟩; to wedge [sth] open/shut ⟨*door*⟩; ⟨*snow*⟩ to trap ⟨*person*⟩

(b) to jam ⟨*drawer, zip*⟩

(c) (colloq) to catch ⟨*person*⟩; **se faire** ~ **par** to get caught by

(d) (colloq) to catch [sb] out ⟨*person*⟩

**2** *vi* (a) ⟨*zip, drawer*⟩ to stick

(b) (colloq) **ça coince** there's a problem

**3 se coincer** *v refl* (+ *v être*) (a) ⟨*object*⟩ to get stuck *or* jammed

(b) **se** ~ **les doigts** to get one's fingers caught

**coïncidence** /kɔɛ̃sidɑ̃s/ *nf* coincidence

**coïncider** /kɔɛ̃side/ [1] *vi* to coincide

**coing** /kwɛ̃/ *nm* quince

**coite** ▶ COI

**col** /kɔl/ *nm* (a) collar

(b) (in mountains) pass

(c) (of bottle) neck

(d) (Anat) neck

■ ~ **blanc** white-collar worker

**colère** /kɔlɛR/ *nf* (a) anger; **être en** ~ to be angry; **passer sa** ~ **sur qn** to take out *or* vent one's anger on sb; **sous le coup de la** ~ in a fit of anger

(b) **faire** *or* **piquer** (colloq) **une** ~ to have a fit; to throw a tantrum

**coléreux, -euse** /kɔleRø, øz/ *adj* ⟨*person*⟩ quick-tempered

**colifichet** /kɔlifiʃɛ/ *nm* trinket; knick-knack

**colimaçon** /kɔlimasɔ̃/ *nm* snail; **escalier en** ~ spiral staircase

**colin** /kɔlɛ̃/ *nm* (fish) hake; coley

**colin-maillard** /kɔlɛ̃majaR/ *nm* **jouer à** ~ to play blind man's buff

**colique** /kɔlik/ *nf* (a) diarrhoea

(b) stomach pain; (in babies) colic

**colis** /kɔli/ *nm* parcel

■ ~ **piégé** parcel bomb; ~ **postal** parcel sent by mail

**colite** /kɔlit/ *nf* colitis

**collaborateur, -trice** /kɔlabɔRatœR, tRis/ *nm,f* (a) colleague; assistant

(b) employee

(c) (journalist) contributor

(d) (derogatory) collaborator

**collaboration** /kɔlabɔRasjɔ̃/ *nf* (a) (to newspaper) contribution; (work on project) collaboration

(b) (in Second World War) collaboration

**collaborer** /kɔlabɔʀe/ [1] *vi* (a) ~ à to contribute to ‹newspaper›; to collaborate on ‹project›

(b) (as working partner) to collaborate

**collage** /kɔlaʒ/ *nm* collage; (in photography) montage

**collant**, ~**e** /kɔlɑ̃, ɑ̃t/ **1** *adj*
(a) ‹substance, object› sticky
(b) ‹dress› skintight
**2** *nm* tights (GB), panty hose (US)

**collation** /kɔlasjɔ̃/ *nf* light meal

**colle** /kɔl/ *nf* (a) glue; (wallpaper) paste
(b) (colloq) (hard question) poser (colloq); test
(c) (colloq) (students' slang) detention

**collecte** /kɔlɛkt/ *nf* (a) collection; **faire une ~** to raise funds
(b) (prayer) collect

**collecter** /kɔlɛkte/ [1] *vtr* to collect

**collecteur**, -**trice** /kɔlɛktœʀ, tʀis/ *nm,f* collector
■ ~ **de fonds** fundraiser; ~ **d'impôts** tax collector

**collectif**, -**ive** /kɔlɛktif, iv/ **1** *adj* collective; ‹dismissals› mass; ‹heating› shared; ‹ticket› group
**2** *nm* (a) collective
(b) action group

**collection** /kɔlɛksjɔ̃/ *nf* (a) collection; ~ **de timbres** stamp collection
(b) (of books) series; (by same author) set

**collectionner** /kɔlɛksjɔne/ [1] *vtr* (a) to collect
(b) (figurative) ~ **les erreurs** to make one mistake after another

**collectionneur**, -**euse** /kɔlɛksjɔnœʀ, øz/ *nm,f* collector

**collectivement** /kɔlɛktivmɑ̃/ *adv* (gen) collectively; ‹resign› en masse, as a body

**collectivité** /kɔlɛktivite/ *nf* (a) group
(b) community
■ ~ **locale** local authority (GB), local government (US)

**collège** /kɔlɛʒ/ *nm* (a) secondary school (GB), junior high school (US) (*up to age 16*)
(b) college; ~ **électoral** (Pol) electoral college
■ ~ **d'enseignement secondaire**, CES secondary school (GB), junior high school (US); ~ **d'enseignement technique**, CET technical secondary school in France

**collégial**, ~**e**, *mpl* -**iaux** /kɔleʒjal, o/ *adj* ‹church› collegial; ‹system› collegiate

**collégien**, -**ienne** /kɔleʒjɛ̃, ɛn/ *nm,f* schoolboy/schoolgirl

**collègue** /kɔlɛg/ *nmf* colleague

**coller** /kɔle/ [1] **1** *vtr* (a) to stick, to glue ‹wood, paper›; to paste up ‹poster›; to hang ‹wallpaper›; to stick [sth] on ‹label›; to stick down ‹envelope›
(b) ~ **qch contre** *or* **à qch** to press sth against sth; **il la colla contre le parapet** he pushed her up against the parapet
(c) (colloq) to stick (colloq); **je leur ai collé la facture sous le nez** I stuck the bill (right) under their noses; ~ **une amende/une gifle à qn** to fine/slap sb

(d) (colloq) (in exam) **se faire** ~ to fail
(e) (colloq) to give [sb] detention ‹pupil›
**2** *vi* (a) (colloq) to stick
(b) (colloq) ~ **avec** to be consistent *or* fit with
**3** **se coller** *v refl* (+ *v être*) (a) **se** ~ **à** *or* **contre qn/qch** to press oneself against sb/sth
(b) (colloq) **dès qu'il rentre, il se colle devant son ordinateur** as soon as he comes in he's glued (colloq) to his computer

**collerette** /kɔlʀɛt/ *nf* (a) ruff
(b) ruffle

**collet** /kɔlɛ/ *nm* **être** ~ **monté** to be prim

**collier** /kɔlje/ *nm* (a) necklace; ~ **de perles** string of pearls
(b) (of animal) collar
(c) beard
IDIOMS **donner un coup de** ~ to get one's head down; to put one's back into it

**collimateur** /kɔlimatœʀ/ *nm* **avoir qn dans le** ~ (colloq) to have it in for sb (colloq)

**colline** /kɔlin/ *nf* hill

**collision** /kɔlizjɔ̃/ *nf* collision

**colloque** /kɔl(l)ɔk/ *nm* conference, symposium

**collyre** /kɔliʀ/ *nm* eyedrops

**colmater** /kɔlmate/ [1] *vtr* to plug, to seal off ‹leak›; to seal ‹crack›

**colombe** /kɔlɔ̃b/ *nf* dove

**colombier** /kɔlɔ̃bje/ *nm* dovecote

**colon** /kɔlɔ̃/ *nm* colonist

**côlon** /kolɔ̃, kɔlɔ̃/ *nm* colon

**colonel** /kɔlɔnɛl/ *nm* (Mil) (in army) ≈ colonel; (in air force) ≈ group captain (GB), ≈ colonel (US)

**colonial**, ~**e**, *mpl* -**iaux** /kɔlɔnjal, o/ *adj*, *nm,f* colonial

**colonialisme** /kɔlɔnjalism/ *nm* colonialism

**colonie** /kɔlɔni/ *nf* (gen) colony; ~ (**de vacances**) holiday camp (*for children*)

**colonnade** /kɔlɔnad/ *nf* colonnade

**colonne** /kɔlɔn/ *nf* column.
■ ~ **vertébrale** (Anat) spinal column

**colorant**, ~**e** /kɔlɔʀɑ̃, ɑ̃t/ **1** *adj* colouring (GB)
**2** *nm* (a) colouring (GB) agent
(b) dye
(c) (in chemistry) stain
(d) (Culin) colouring (GB)

**coloration** /kɔlɔʀasjɔ̃/ *nf* (a) colouring (GB); dyeing; staining; tinting
(b) colour (GB)

**coloré**, ~**e** /kɔlɔʀe/ *adj* (a) (gen) coloured (GB)
(b) ‹life, crowd› colourful (GB); ‹style› lively

**colorer** /kɔlɔʀe/ [1] *vtr* to colour (GB); to tint; to stain; to dye

**colorier** /kɔlɔʀje/ [2] *vtr* to colour in (GB), to color (US)

**coloris** /kɔlɔʀi/ *nm inv* colour (GB); shade

**colossal**, ~**e**, *mpl* -**aux** /kɔlɔsal, o/ *adj* colossal, huge

**colosse** /kɔlɔs/ *nm* giant

**colporter** /kɔlpɔʀte/ [1] *vtr* **(a)** to spread ‹*news*›
**(b)** to peddle ‹*goods*›

**coltiner: se coltiner** /kɔltine/ [1] *v refl* (+ *v être*) (colloq) **(a)** to lug (colloq) ‹*heavy object*›
**(b)** to get stuck with (colloq) ‹*chore, person*›

**colza** /kɔlza/ *nm* rape

**coma** /kɔma/ *nm* coma

**comateux, -euse** /kɔmatø, øz/ *adj* comatose

**combat** /kɔ̃ba/ *nm* **(a)** (Mil) fighting; ~s aériens air battles; mettre hors de ~ to disable
**(b)** (in politics) struggle; livrer un ~ to campaign
**(c)** (Sport) bout; hors de ~ out of action
■ ~ de coqs cock fight

**combatif, -ive** /kɔ̃batif, iv/ *adj*
**(a)** assertive
**(b)** aggressive

**combativité** /kɔ̃bativite/ *nf* fighting spirit

**combattant, ~e** /kɔ̃batɑ̃, ɑ̃t/ *nm,f* combatant

**combattre** /kɔ̃batʀ/ [61] *vtr, vi* to fight

**combien¹** /kɔ̃bjɛ̃/ **1** *adv* **(a)** ~ mesure le salon? how big is the lounge?; j'aimerais savoir ~ il a payé son costume I'd like to know how much he paid for that suit; ~ êtes-vous? how many of you are there?
**(b)** (to what extent) je ne saurais te dire ~ il me manque I can't tell you how much I miss him
**2 combien de** *det* **(a)** how many, how much
**(b)** ~ de temps faut-il? how long does it take?

**combien²** /kɔ̃bjɛ̃/ *nmf inv* **(a)** tu es le/la ~? (in queue) how many people are before you?
**(b)** le ~ sommes-nous? what's the date today?
**(c)** (for measurements) tu chausses du ~? what size shoes do you take?
**(d)** tu le vois tous les ~? how often do you see him?

**combinaison** /kɔ̃binɛzɔ̃/ *nf* **(a)** combining; combination
**(b)** (of safe) combination
**(c)** (full-length) slip
**(d)** jumpsuit
**(e)** overalls (GB), coveralls (US)
■ ~ de plongée wetsuit

**combine** /kɔ̃bin/ *nf* (colloq) trick (colloq); scheme

**combiné** /kɔ̃bine/ *nm* handset, receiver

**combiner** /kɔ̃bine/ [1] *vtr* **(a)** to combine
**(b)** to work out ‹*plan*›

**comble** /kɔ̃bl/ **1** *adj* ‹*room*› packed
**2** *nm* **(a)** le ~ de l'injustice/du mauvais goût the height of injustice/of bad taste; pour ~ de malchance j'ai... to crown it all, I...; c'est un *or* le ~! (colloq) that's the limit!

**(b)** roof space; de fond en ~ from top to bottom; completely
**3 combles** *nm pl* attic

**combler** /kɔ̃ble/ [1] *vtr* **(a)** to fill (in) ‹*ditch*›
**(b)** to fill in ‹*gaps*›; to make up ‹*deficit*›
**(c)** to fulfil (GB) ‹*need, desire*›; la vie m'a comblé I've had a wonderful life; ~ qn to fill sb with joy

**combustible** /kɔ̃bystibl/ **1** *adj* combustible
**2** *nm* fuel; ~ nucléaire nuclear fuel

**combustion** /kɔ̃bystjɔ̃/ *nf* combustion

**comédie** /kɔmedi/ *nf* **(a)** comedy
**(b)** play-acting; jouer la ~ to put on an act
**(c)** (colloq) scene; faire une ~ to make a scene
■ ~ musicale musical

**comédien, -ienne** /kɔmedjɛ̃, ɛn/ **1** *adj* il est (un peu) ~ (figurative) he puts it on
**2** *nm,f* actor/actress

**comestible** /kɔmɛstibl/ **1** *adj* edible
**2 comestibles** *nm pl* food

**comète** /kɔmɛt/ *nf* comet

**comique** /kɔmik/ **1** *adj* **(a)** comic
**(b)** funny
**2** *nmf* comic actor/actress; comedian
**3** *nm* **(a)** clown
**(b)** comedy

**comité** /kɔmite/ *nm* **(a)** committee
**(b)** group

**commandant** /kɔmɑ̃dɑ̃/ *nm* (in army) ≈ major; (in air force) ≈ squadron leader (GB), ≈ major (US)
■ ~ de bord captain

**commande** /kɔmɑ̃d/ *nf* **(a)** order
**(b)** commission; passer ~ de qch à qn to commission sb to do sth
**(c)** (Tech) control; levier de ~ control lever; être aux *or* tenir les ~s to be at the controls; (figurative) to be in control
**(d)** (Comput) command

**commandement** /kɔmɑ̃dmɑ̃/ *nm* **(a)** (Mil) command
**(b)** (in religion) commandment

**commander** /kɔmɑ̃de/ [1] **1** *vtr* **(a)** to order [sth] (à qn from sb)
**(b)** to commission ‹*book, survey*›
**(c)** (Mil) to command ‹*army*›; to order ‹*attack*›
**(d)** ~ qn to order sb about
**(e)** les circonstances commandent la prudence the circumstances call for caution
**(f)** ‹*machine*› to control ‹*mechanism*›
**2 commander à** *v+prep* **(a)** ~ à to be in command of
**(b)** ~ à to order, to command
**3** *vi* to give the orders, to be in charge
**4 se commander** *v refl* (+ *v être*) ça ne se commande pas it's not something you can control

**commanditer** /kɔmɑ̃dite/ [1] *vtr* **(a)** to finance ‹*company*›
**(b)** to sponsor ‹*project*›
**(c)** to be behind ‹*crime*›

**commando** /kɔmɑ̃do/ *nm* commando

**comme** /kɔm/ **1** *adv* how

**2** *conj* **(a)** as; **ici ~ en Italie** here as in Italy; **il est paresseux, ~ sa sœur d'ailleurs** he's lazy, just like his sister; **jolie ~ tout** really pretty

**(b)** (in comparisons) **il est grand ~ sa sœur** he's as tall as his sister; **c'est tout ~** (colloq) it comes to the same thing; **elle me traite ~ un enfant** she treats me like a child

**(c)** like; **un manteau ~ le tien** a coat like yours; **~ ça** like that; **puisque c'est ~ ça** if that's the way it is

**(d)** as if, as though; **~ pour faire** as if to do

**(e)** (colloq) **elle a eu ~ un évanouissement** she sort of fainted

**(f)** **avare ~ il est, il ne te donnera rien** he's so mean, he won't give you anything

**(g)** as; **travailler ~ jardinier** to work as a gardener

**(h)** as, since; **~ elle était seule** as *or* since she was alone

**(i)** as; **~ il traversait la rue** as he was crossing the road

**IDIOMS ~ quoi!** which just shows!; **~ ci ~ ça** (colloq) so-so (colloq)

**commémoration** /kɔmemɔrasjɔ̃/ *nf* commemoration

**commémorer** /kɔmemɔre/ [1] *vtr* to commemorate

**commencement** /kɔmɑ̃smɑ̃/ *nm* beginning

**commencer** /kɔmɑ̃se/ [12] **1** *vtr* **(a)** to start, to begin

**(b)** **~ à** *or* **de faire** to start *or* begin to do; **ça commence à bien faire!** (colloq) it's getting to be a bit much!

**2** *vi* to start, to begin; **pour ~** for a start; **vous êtes tous coupables à ~ par toi** you're all guilty starting with you

**3** *v impers* **il commence à neiger** it's starting *or* beginning to snow

**comment** /kɔmɑ̃/ *adv* **(a)** how; **~ faire?** how can it be done?; **~ t'appelles-tu?** what's your name?; **~ ça se fait?** (colloq) how come? (colloq)

**(b)** **~?** qu'est-ce que tu dis? pardon? what did you say?; **Paul ~?** Paul who?

**(c)** **~ est leur maison/fils?** what's their house/son like?; **~ trouvez-vous ma robe?** what do you think of my dress?

**(d)** **~ cela?** what do you mean?; **~ donc!** but of course!; **et ~ (donc)!** (colloq) and how! (colloq); **'c'était bon?'—'et ~!'** (colloq) 'was it nice?'—'it certainly was!'

**commentaire** /kɔmɑ̃tɛr/ *nm*

**(a)** comment

**(b)** commentary

**commentateur, -trice** /kɔmɑ̃tatœr, tris/ *nm,f* commentator

**commenter** /kɔmɑ̃te/ [1] *vtr* **(a)** to comment on ⟨*decision, event*⟩

**(b)** to give a commentary on ⟨*film, visit*⟩

**(c)** to commentate on ⟨*match*⟩

**commérage** /kɔmeraʒ/ *nm* gossip

**commerçant, ~e** /kɔmɛrsɑ̃, ɑ̃t/ **1** *adj* ⟨*street*⟩ shopping; ⟨*nation*⟩ trading

**2** *nm,f* shopkeeper, storekeeper (US); retailer

**commerce** /kɔmɛrs/ *nm* **(a)** shop, store (US); **dans le ~** in the shops *or* stores (US)

**(b)** business

**(c)** trade; **faire le ~ de** to trade in; **faire ~ de** to sell; **faire du ~** to be in business

**commercial, ~e, mpl -iaux** /kɔmɛrsjal, o/ **1** *adj* **(a)** commercial; **carrière ~e** career in sales and marketing

**(b)** trade

**2** *nm,f* sales and marketing person

**commercialisation** /kɔmɛrsjalizasjɔ̃/ *nf* marketing

**commercialiser** /kɔmɛrsjalize/ [1] *vtr* to market

**commère** /kɔmɛr/ *nf* gossip

**commettre** /kɔmɛtr/ [60] *vtr* to make ⟨*error*⟩; to commit ⟨*crime*⟩; to carry out ⟨*attack*⟩

**commis** /kɔmi/ *nm* **(a)** (in office) clerk

**(b)** shop assistant (GB), salesclerk (US)

**commissaire** /kɔmisɛr/ *nm* **(a)** **~ (de police)** ≈ police superintendent

**(b)** commissioner

**(c)** (of sports event) steward; (of exhibition) organizer

**commissaire-priseur, pl commissaires-priseurs** /kɔmisɛrprizœr/ *nm* auctioneer

**commissariat** /kɔmisarja/ *nm* **~ (de police)** police station

**commission** /kɔmisjɔ̃/ **1** *nf*

**(a)** committee

**(b)** commission; **payé à la ~** paid on a commission basis

**(c)** errand

**(d)** **faire la ~ à qn** to give sb the message

**2** **commissions** *nf pl* (colloq) shopping

**commissionnaire** /kɔmisjɔnɛr/ *nm* (Econ) agent, broker

**commissure** /kɔmisyr/ *nf* corner

**commode** /kɔmɔd/ **1** *adj* **(a)** (gen) convenient; ⟨*tool*⟩ handy

**(b)** easy

**(c)** **ne pas être (très) ~** to be strict; to be difficult (to deal with)

**2** *nf* chest of drawers

**commodité** /kɔmɔdite/ *nf* convenience

**commotion** /kɔmosjɔ̃/ *nf* **(a)** **~ (cérébrale)** concussion (*of the brain*)

**(b)** (figurative) shock

**commun, ~e¹** /kɔmœ̃, yn/ **1** *adj*

**(a)** common; ⟨*policy, property*⟩ joint; ⟨*friend*⟩ mutual; ⟨*room, memories, experience*⟩ shared; **d'un ~ accord** by mutual agreement; **après dix ans de vie ~e** after living together for ten years

**(b)** ⟨*person, tastes*⟩ common; ⟨*face*⟩ plain

**(c)** **elle est d'une beauté peu ~e** she's uncommonly beautiful

**2** *nm* ordinary; **le ~ des mortels** ordinary mortals; **hors du ~** exceptional

**3** **en commun** *phr* ⟨*work, write*⟩ jointly, ····;·

together; **avoir qch en** ~ to have sth in
common; **nous mettons tout en** ~ we share
everything

**communal**, ~**e**, *mpl* **-aux** /kɔmynal, o/
*adj* ⟨*budget, resources*⟩ local council (GB),
local government (US); ⟨*building*⟩ local
council (GB), community (US)

**communautaire** /kɔmynotɛR/ *adj*
(a) (referring to the EC) ⟨*budget, law*⟩
Community
(b) **la vie** ~ life in a community

**communauté** /kɔmynote/ *nf*
(a) community
(b) commune; **vivre en** ~ to live in a
commune
■ **Communauté économique européenne, CEE**
European Economic Community, EEC;
**Communauté des États indépendants, CEI**
Commonwealth of Independent States, CIS

**commune²** /kɔmyn/ ① *nf* village; town
② **communes** *nf pl* **la Chambre des** ~**s**
the (House of) Commons

**communément** /kɔmynemã/ *adv*
generally

**communicatif, -ive** /kɔmynikatif, iv/
*adj* (a) ⟨*person*⟩ talkative
(b) ⟨*gaiety*⟩ infectious

**communication** /kɔmynikasjɔ̃/ *nf*
(a) ~ **(téléphonique)** (telephone) call; **mettre
qn en** ~ **avec qn** to put sb through to sb
(b) report; (at conference) paper
(c) **demander** ~ **d'un dossier à qn** to ask sb
for a file
(d) (between people) communication, contact
(e) (media) communications
(f) (by phone, radio) **moyens de** ~
communications

**communier** /kɔmynje/ [2] *vi* to receive
Communion

**communion** /kɔmynjɔ̃/ *nf* (a) Communion
(b) (figurative) communion
■ ~ **(privée)** first communion

**communiqué** /kɔmynike/ *nm*
(a) communiqué, press release
(b) statement

**communiquer** /kɔmynike/ [1] ① *vtr*
(a) to announce ⟨*date, result*⟩; to give
⟨*address*⟩
(b) ⟨*person*⟩ to pass on ⟨*document*⟩; to convey
⟨*idea*⟩
② *vi* (a) to communicate
(b) ⟨*rooms*⟩ to be adjoining
③ **se communiquer** *v refl* (+ *v être*)
(a) ⟨*people*⟩ to pass [sth] on to each other
(b) ⟨*fire, disease*⟩ to spread

**communisme** /kɔmynism/ *nm*
communism

**commutateur** /kɔmytatœʀ/ *nm* switch

**commuter** /kɔmyte/ [1] *vtr* to commute

**compact**, ~**e** /kɔ̃pakt/ *adj* (a) ⟨*fog,
crowd*⟩ dense; ⟨*earth*⟩ compact
(b) ⟨*car*⟩ compact

**compagne** /kɔ̃paɲ/ *nf* (a) (female)
companion
(b) (female animal) mate

**compagnie** /kɔ̃paɲi/ *nf* (a) company; **en**
~ **de** together with
(b) **salut la** ~**!** hello everybody!
(c) (commercial) company
(d) theatre company
■ ~ **aérienne** airline; ~ **d'assurance**
insurance company; ~ **pétrolière** oil
company

**compagnon** /kɔ̃paɲɔ̃/ *nm* (a) companion
(b) partner
(c) mate
(d) journeyman
■ ~ **de route** fellow traveller (GB)

**comparable** /kɔ̃paʀabl/ *adj* comparable

**comparaison** /kɔ̃paʀɛzɔ̃/ *nf*
(a) comparison; **c'est sans** ~ **le plus
confortable** it's far and away the most
comfortable
(b) simile
(c) **adjectif de** ~ comparative adjective

**comparaître** /kɔ̃paʀɛtʀ/ [73] *vi* (Law) to
appear

**comparatif, -ive** /kɔ̃paʀatif, iv/ *adj*
comparative

**comparé**, ~**e** /kɔ̃paʀe/ *adj* ⟨*literature,
law*⟩ comparative

**comparer** /kɔ̃paʀe/ [1] ① *vtr* to compare
② **se comparer** *v refl* (+ *v être*) (a) **se** ~ **à
qn/qch** to compare oneself with sb/sth
(b) to be comparable

**comparse** /kɔ̃paʀs/ *nmf* (a) (in theatre)
extra
(b) sidekick (colloq)

**compartiment** /kɔ̃paʀtimã/ *nm*
compartment

**compartimenter** /kɔ̃paʀtimãte/ [1] *vtr*
(a) ~ **un grenier** to divide up a loft with
partitions
(b) (figurative) to compartmentalize
⟨*administration*⟩

**compas** /kɔ̃pa/ *nm* compass

**compassion** /kɔ̃pasjɔ̃/ *nf* compassion

**compatible** /kɔ̃patibl/ *adj* compatible

**compatir** /kɔ̃patiʀ/ [3] *vi* to sympathize

**compatissant**, ~**e** /kɔ̃patisã, ãt/ *adj*
compassionate

**compatriote** /kɔ̃patʀijɔt/ *nmf* fellow-
countryman/-countrywoman, compatriot

**compensation** /kɔ̃pãsasjɔ̃/ *nf*
compensation

**compensé**, ~**e** /kɔ̃pãse/ *adj* (a) **semelle**
~**e** wedge heel
(b) (Med) compensated

**compenser** /kɔ̃pãse/ [1] *vtr* to compensate
for; to make up for; to offset

**compère** /kɔ̃pɛʀ/ *nm* partner; accomplice

**compétence** /kɔ̃petãs/ *nf* (a) ability;
competence, skill
(b) (Law) competence; **relever de la** ~ **de qn**
to fall within the competence of sb
(c) domain

**compétent**, ~**e** /kɔ̃petã, ãt/ *adj*
competent

**compétitif, -ive** /kɔ̃petitif, iv/ *adj*
competitive

**compétition** /kɔ̃petisjɔ̃/ *nf* competition;
**en ~** pour competing for; **faire de la ~** to
compete; **sport de ~** competitive sport

**complaire: se complaire** /kɔ̃plɛʀ/ [59]
*v refl* (+ *v être*) **se ~ à faire** to take pleasure
in doing

**complaisance** /kɔ̃plɛzɑ̃s/ *nf* (a) kindness
(b) (derogatory) soft attitude; **décrire la
situation sans ~** to give an objective
assessment of the situation
(c) (derogatory) complacency

**complaisant, ~e** /kɔ̃plɛzɑ̃, ɑ̃t/ *adj*
(a) obliging
(b) (derogatory) indulgent
(c) (derogatory) complacent, self-satisfied

**complément** /kɔ̃plemɑ̃/ *nm* (a) **~ de
salaire** extra payment
(b) (to funding, programme) supplement
(c) **~ de nom** possessive phrase; **~ d'objet
direct/indirect** direct/indirect object

**complémentaire** /kɔ̃plemɑ̃tɛʀ/ *adj*
(a) ⟨training, information⟩ further; ⟨activity,
amount⟩ supplementary
(b) complementary

**complet, -ète** /kɔ̃plɛ, ɛt/ **1** *adj* (a) (gen)
complete; ⟨failure⟩ total; ⟨inquiry, range⟩
full; ⟨survey⟩ comprehensive
(b) ⟨train, hotel⟩ full; **être (réuni) au (grand)
~** to be all present
**2** *nm* suit; **~ veston** two-/three-piece suit

**complètement** /kɔ̃plɛtmɑ̃/ *adv*
completely; ⟨read⟩ right through; **~ réveillé**
fully awake

**compléter** /kɔ̃plete/ [14] **1** *vtr* (a) to
complete ⟨collection⟩; to top up ⟨sum⟩
(b) ⟨person⟩ to complement ⟨person⟩
(c) to complete ⟨sentence⟩
**2 se compléter** *v refl* (+ *v être*)
⟨elements, people⟩ to complement each other

**complexe** /kɔ̃plɛks/ **1** *adj* complex
**2** *nm* (a) (psychological) complex; **il n'a pas
de ~** he has no inhibitions
(b) (place) complex; **un ~ sportif** a sports
complex

**complexer** /kɔ̃plɛkse/ [1] *vtr* (colloq) to
give [sb] a complex

**complexité** /kɔ̃plɛksite/ *nf* complexity

**complication** /kɔ̃plikasjɔ̃/ *nf*
complication

**complice** /kɔ̃plis/ **1** *adj* (a) **être ~ de
qch** to be a party to sth
(b) ⟨air⟩ of complicity
**2** *nmf* accomplice

**complicité** /kɔ̃plisite/ *nf* (a) complicity
(b) bond

**compliment** /kɔ̃plimɑ̃/ **1** *nm*
compliment
**2 compliments** *nm pl* (gen)
compliments; **(tous) mes ~s!**
congratulations!

**complimenter** /kɔ̃plimɑ̃te/ [1] *vtr* to
compliment

**compliqué, ~e** /kɔ̃plike/ *adj*
complicated; ⟨mind⟩ tortuous

**compliquer** /kɔ̃plike/ [1] **1** *vtr* to
complicate
**2 se compliquer** *v refl* (+ *v être*) (a) to
become more complicated
(b) **se ~ la vie** *or* **l'existence** to make life
difficult for oneself

**complot** /kɔ̃plo/ *nm* plot

**comploter** /kɔ̃plɔte/ [1] *vtr, vi* to plot

**comportement** /kɔ̃pɔʀtəmɑ̃/ *nm* (a) (gen)
behaviour (GB)
(b) (of sportsman, car) performance

**comporter** /kɔ̃pɔʀte/ [1] **1** *vtr* (a) to
include
(b) to comprise, to consist of
(c) to entail, to involve
**2 se comporter** *v refl* (+ *v être*) (a) to
behave, to act
(b) ⟨sportsman, car⟩ to perform

**composant** /kɔ̃pozɑ̃/ *nm* (Tech)
component

**composante** /kɔ̃pozɑ̃t/ *nf* element;
component

**composé, ~e** /kɔ̃poze/ **1** *adj* ⟨salad⟩
mixed
**2** *nm* (in chemistry) compound

**composer** /kɔ̃poze/ [1] **1** *vtr* (a) ⟨elements,
people⟩ to make up
(b) ⟨person⟩ to put [sth] together
⟨programme, menu⟩; to select ⟨team⟩; to
make up ⟨bouquet⟩
(c) ⟨artist⟩ to compose ⟨piece of music⟩; to
paint ⟨picture⟩
(d) to dial ⟨number⟩
**2 se composer** *v refl* (+ *v être*) **se ~ de**
to be made up of

**compositeur, -trice** /kɔ̃pozitœʀ, tʀis/
*nm,f* (a) (Mus) composer
(b) typesetter

**composition** /kɔ̃pozisjɔ̃/ *nf*
(a) (of government, delegation) make-up; (of team)
line-up; (of product) ingredients; (of drug)
composition
(b) (of government) formation; (of team)
selection; (of list, menu) drawing up; **de ma ~**
of my invention
(c) (of piece of music, picture) composition;
(of letter) writing
(d) (Sch) end-of-term test
(e) typesetting
IDIOMS **être de bonne ~** to be good-natured

**composter** /kɔ̃pɔste/ [1] *vtr* to
(date)stamp; to punch ⟨ticket⟩

**compote** /kɔ̃pɔt/ *nf* (Culin) stewed fruit,
compote

**compréhensible** /kɔ̃pʀeɑ̃sibl/ *adj*
(a) understandable
(b) comprehensible

**compréhensif, -ive** /kɔ̃pʀeɑ̃sif, iv/ *adj*
understanding

**compréhension** /kɔ̃pʀeɑ̃sjɔ̃/ *nf*
understanding; comprehension

**comprendre** /kɔ̃pʀɑ̃dʀ/ [52] **1** *vtr* (a) to
understand; **c'est à n'y rien ~** it's ⋯⋗

completely baffling; **mal ∼ to misunderstand;
être compris comme une menace** to be
interpreted as a threat; **se faire ∼** to make
oneself understood
**(b)** to consist of, to comprise
**(c)** to include
**2 se comprendre** *v refl* (+ *v être*)
**(a)** ⟨*people*⟩ to understand each other *or* one
another
**(b) je me comprends** I know what I'm trying
to say
**(c)** ⟨*attitude*⟩ to be understandable

**compresse** /kɔ̃pʀɛs/ *nf* compress

**compresser** /kɔ̃pʀese/ [1] *vtr* to compress

**compression** /kɔ̃pʀɛsjɔ̃/ *nf* **(a)** (Tech)
compression
**(b)** reduction
**(c)** cut; **∼s budgétaires** budget cuts

**comprimé** /kɔ̃pʀime/ *nm* tablet

**comprimer** /kɔ̃pʀime/ [1] *vtr* **(a)** to
constrict; to squeeze ⟨*tube*⟩
**(b)** (Med) to compress
**(c)** (Tech) **air comprimé** compressed air

**compris, ∼e** /kɔ̃pʀi, iz/ **1** *pp* ▶
COMPRENDRE
**2** *pp adj* including; **service ∼/non ∼**
service included/not included
**3 tout compris** *phr* in total, all in (GB)
(colloq)
**4 y compris** *phr* including

**compromettant, ∼e** /kɔ̃pʀɔmetɑ̃, ɑ̃t/
*adj* compromising

**compromettre** /kɔ̃pʀɔmɛtʀ/ [60] **1** *vtr*
**(a)** to endanger, to jeopardize
**(b)** to compromise ⟨*person*⟩; to damage
⟨*reputation*⟩
**2 se compromettre** *v refl* (+ *v être*) to
compromise oneself

**compromis** /kɔ̃pʀɔmi/ *nm* compromise

**comptabiliser** /kɔ̃tabilize/ [1] *vtr* to
count

**comptabilité** /kɔ̃tabilite/ *nf*
**(a)** accountancy
**(b)** bookkeeping; **faire sa ∼** to do one's
accounts
**(c)** accounts department

**comptable** /kɔ̃tabl/ **1** *adj* **(a)** ⟨*year*⟩
accounting; ⟨*department*⟩ accounts
**(b)** ⟨*noun*⟩ countable
**2** *nmf* accountant; bookkeeper

**comptant** /kɔ̃tɑ̃/ *adv* cash

**compte** /kɔ̃t/ **1** *nm* **(a)** count; **faire le ∼
de qch** to work out ⟨*expenditure*⟩; to count
(up) ⟨*objects*⟩; **comment fais-tu ton ∼ pour
faire...?** (figurative) how do you manage to
do...?; **tout ∼ fait** all things considered; **en
fin de ∼** at the end of the day
**(b)** (of money) amount; (of objects, people)
number; **il n'y a pas le ∼** that's not the right
amount; that's not the right number; **il a son
∼** (colloq) he's done for (colloq); (drunk) he's
had a drop too much; **nous avons eu notre ∼
d'ennuis** (figurative) we've had more than our
fair share of problems; **à ce ∼-là** in that case

**(c) prendre qch en ∼, tenir ∼ de qch** to take
sth into account
**(d) être** *or* **travailler à son ∼** to be self-
employed; **pour le ∼ de qn** on behalf of sb;
**y trouver son ∼** to get something out of it
**(e)** account; **∼ en banque** bank account;
**mettre qch sur le ∼ de qn** to charge sth to
sb's account; (figurative) to put sth down to sb
**(f) rendre ∼ de qch à qn** to give an account
of sth to sb; to account for sth to sb; **devoir
rendre des ∼s à qn** to be answerable to sb;
**demander des ∼s à qn** to ask for an
explanation from sb
**(g) se rendre ∼ de** to realize; to notice
**(h) dire qch sur le ∼ de qn** to say sth about
sb
**(i)** (in boxing) count
**2 à bon compte** *phr* **s'en tirer à bon ∼**
to get off lightly
■ **∼ chèques** current account (GB), checking
account (US); **∼ d'épargne** savings account;
**∼ épargne logement** savings account (for
purchasing a property); **∼ chèque postal,
CCP** post office account; **∼ joint** joint
account; **∼ à rebours** countdown

**compte-gouttes** /kɔ̃tgut/ *nm inv*
dropper; **au ∼** (figurative) sparingly

**compter** /kɔ̃te/ [1] **1** *vtr* **(a)** to count; **on
compte deux millions de chômeurs** there is a
total of two million unemployed; **il a toujours
compté ses sous** he has always watched the
pennies; **sans ∼** ⟨*give, spend*⟩ freely; **ses
jours sont comptés** his/her days are
numbered
**(b) ∼ une bouteille pour trois** to allow a
bottle between three people
**(c)** (as fee, price) **∼ qch à qn** to charge sb for
sth
**(d)** to count, to include; **sans ∼ les soucis**
not to mention the worry
**(e)** to have; **notre club compte des gens
célèbres** our club has some well-known
people among its members
**(f) ∼ faire** to intend to do
**(g) il comptait que je lui prête de l'argent** he
expected me to lend him some money
**2** *vi* **(a)** to count; **∼ au nombre de, ∼ parmi**
to be counted among
**(b)** to matter; **c'est l'intention qui compte** it's
the thought that counts; **ça compte
beaucoup pour moi** it means a lot to me
**(c)** to count; **ça ne compte pas, il a triché** it
doesn't count, he cheated
**(d) ∼ avec** to reckon with; to take [sb/sth]
into account; **∼ sans** not to take [sb/sth]
into account
**(e) ∼ sur** to count on ⟨*person, help*⟩; (for
support) to rely on ⟨*person, resource*⟩;
(in anticipation) to reckon on ⟨*sum, income*⟩
**3 se compter** *v refl* (+ *v être*) **leurs
victoires se comptent par douzaines** they
have had dozens of victories
**4 à compter de** *phr* as from
**5 sans compter que** *phr* and what is
more; especially as

**compte(-)rendu**, *pl* **comptes(-) rendus** /kɔ̃tRɑ̃dy/ *nm* (gen) report; (of book) review

**compteur** /kɔ̃tœR/ *nm* meter; clock.
■ ~ **kilométrique** ≈ milometer; ~ **de vitesse** speedometer

**comptine** /kɔ̃tin/ *nf* nursery rhyme

**comptoir** /kɔ̃twaR/ *nm* **(a)** (of café) bar **(b)** (of shop) counter

**comte** /kɔ̃t/ *nm* (title) count; earl

**comtesse** /kɔ̃tɛs/ *nf* countess

**con, conne** /kɔ̃, kɔn/ *nm,f* (vulgar) bloody idiot (GB) (slang), stupid jerk (colloq); **idée à la** ~ lousy idea (colloq)

**concasser** /kɔ̃kase/ [1] *vtr* (Culin, Tech) to crush

**concave** /kɔ̃kav/ *adj* concave

**concéder** /kɔ̃sede/ [14] *vtr* to concede

**concentration** /kɔ̃sɑ̃tRasjɔ̃/ *nf* concentration

**concentré, ~e** /kɔ̃sɑ̃tRe/ [1] *pp* ▶ CONCENTRER
[2] *pp adj* **(a) un air** ~ a look of concentration
**(b)** concentrated; ⟨*lait*⟩ condensed
[3] *nm* (Culin) ~ **de tomate** tomato purée (GB) *or* paste (US)

**concentrer** /kɔ̃sɑ̃tRe/ [1] [1] *vtr* to concentrate
[2] **se concentrer** *v refl* (+ *v être*) to concentrate; ⟨*attention*⟩ to be concentrated

**concept** /kɔ̃sɛpt/ *nm* concept

**conception** /kɔ̃sɛpsjɔ̃/ *nf* **(a)** conception
**(b)** design
**(c)** idea

**concernant** /kɔ̃sɛRnɑ̃/ *prep*
**(a)** concerning
**(b)** as regards, with regard to

**concerner** /kɔ̃sɛRne/ [1] *vtr* **(a)** to concern
**(b)** to affect

**concert** /kɔ̃sɛR/ [1] *nm* (Mus) concert
[2] **de concert** *phr* **ils ont agi de** ~ they worked together

**concertation** /kɔ̃sɛRtasjɔ̃/ *nf*
**(a)** consultation
**(b)** cooperation

**concerté, ~e** /kɔ̃sɛRte/ *adj* concerted

**concerter: se concerter** /kɔ̃sɛRte/ [1] *v refl* (+ *v être*) to consult each other

**concerto** /kɔ̃sɛRto/ *nm* concerto

**concession** /kɔ̃sesjɔ̃/ *nf* **(a)** (compromise) concession; **film sans ~s** uncompromising film
**(b)** (awarding of right) concession (**de** of)
**(c)** (right, contract) (of mine, site) concession; (Aut) dealership

**concessionnaire** /kɔ̃sesjɔnɛR/ *nmf* (commercial) agent; (Aut) dealer

**concevoir** /kɔ̃s(ə)vwaR/ [5] [1] *vtr* **(a)** to design ⟨*product, system*⟩
**(b)** to conceive ⟨*child*⟩
**(c)** to understand ⟨*attitude*⟩
**(d)** to see ⟨*phenomenon, activity*⟩

**(e)** (formal) to conceive ⟨*hatred*⟩
[2] **se concevoir** *v refl* (+ *v être*) **(a)** to be conceivable
**(b)** to be understandable

**concierge** /kɔ̃sjɛRʒ/ *nmf* caretaker (GB), superintendant (US)

**concile** /kɔ̃sil/ *nm* council

**conciliabule** /kɔ̃siljabyl/ *nm* consultation, confab (colloq)

**conciliant, ~e** /kɔ̃siljɑ̃, ɑ̃t/ *adj* conciliatory

**conciliation** /kɔ̃siljasjɔ̃/ *nf* conciliation

**concilier** /kɔ̃silje/ [2] *vtr* to reconcile

**concis, ~e** /kɔ̃si, iz/ *adj* concise

**concision** /kɔ̃sizjɔ̃/ *nf* conciseness

**concitoyen, -enne** /kɔ̃sitwajɛ̃, ɛn/ *nm,f* fellow-citizen

**conclave** /kɔ̃klav/ *nm* conclave

**conclu, ~e** /kɔ̃kly/ ▶ CONCLURE

**concluant, ~e** /kɔ̃klyɑ̃, ɑ̃t/ *adj* conclusive

**conclure** /kɔ̃klyR/ [78] *vtr* **(a)** to conclude (**que** that)
**(b)** to conclude ⟨*deal, agreement*⟩; **'marché conclu!'** 'it's a deal!'
**(c)** ⟨*person*⟩ to conclude ⟨*speech*⟩
**(d)** to bring [sth] to a close ⟨*festival*⟩

**conclusion** /kɔ̃klyzjɔ̃/ *nf*
**(a)** conclusion; **tirer les ~s d'une expérience** to learn from an experience; **ne tire pas de ~s hâtives** don't jump to conclusions
**(b)** (of deal, treaty) conclusion
**(c)** (of speech, session) close
[2] **conclusions** *nf pl* **(a)** (of analysis, autopsy) results; (of inquiry) findings
**(b)** (Law) (of expert) opinion; (of jury) verdict; (of plaintiff) pleadings

**concocter** /kɔ̃kɔkte/ [1] *vtr* (colloq) to concoct ⟨*dish*⟩; to devise ⟨*programme*⟩

**concombre** /kɔ̃kɔ̃bR/ *nm* cucumber

**concordance** /kɔ̃kɔRdɑ̃s/ *nf* concordance; compatibility
■ ~ **des temps** sequence of tenses

**concorder** /kɔ̃kɔRde/ [1] *vi* ⟨*results, evidence*⟩ to tally; ⟨*estimates*⟩ to agree

**concourir** /kɔ̃kuRiR/ [26] [1] *vi* to compete
[2] **concourir à** *v+prep* ~ **à qch/à faire** ⟨*factors*⟩ to combine to bring about sth/to do; ⟨*factor, person*⟩ to help bring about sth/do

**concours** /kɔ̃kuR/ *nm inv* **(a)** (gen) competition; (agricultural) show; ~ **de beauté** beauty contest
**(b)** competitive examination; ~ **d'entrée** entrance examination
**(c)** help, assistance; support; cooperation
■ ~ **de circonstances** combination of circumstances

**concret, -ète** /kɔ̃kRɛ, ɛt/ *adj* **(a)** ⟨*result*⟩ concrete
**(b)** ⟨*mind, person*⟩ practical

**concrètement** /kɔ̃kRɛtmɑ̃/ *adv* **(a)** in concrete terms
**(b)** in practical terms

**concrétisation** /kɔ̃kʀetizasjɔ̃/ *nf*
concrete expression; fulfilment (GB);
achievement

**concrétiser** /kɔ̃kʀetize/ [1] **1** *vtr* to
make [sth] a reality ⟨*plan, project*⟩
**2 se concrétiser** *v refl* (+ *v être*) ⟨*dream*⟩
to become a reality; ⟨*offer*⟩ to materialize

**concubin**, **~e** /kɔ̃kybɛ̃, in/ *nm,f* common
law husband/wife

**concubinage** /kɔ̃kybinaʒ/ *nm*
cohabitation

**concurrence** /kɔ̃kyʀɑ̃s/ *nf* competition;
**prix défiant toute ~** unbeatable price; **jusqu'à
~ de** up to a limit of

**concurrencer** /kɔ̃kyʀɑ̃se/ [12] *vtr* to
compete with

**concurrent**, **~e** /kɔ̃kyʀɑ̃, ɑ̃t/ **1** *adj* rival
**2** *nm,f* (for a job) rival; (Sport) competitor;
(in competitive examination) candidate

**concurrentiel**, **-ielle** /kɔ̃kyʀɑ̃sjɛl/ *adj*
competitive

**condamnable** /kɔ̃danabl/ *adj*
reprehensible

**condamnation** /kɔ̃danasjɔ̃/ *nf* **(a)** (Law)
conviction; sentence
**(b)** condemnation

**condamné**, **~e** /kɔ̃dane/ **1** *adj*
**(a)** ⟨*person*⟩ terminally ill
**(b)** ⟨*door*⟩ sealed up
**2** *nm,f* convicted prisoner

**condamner** /kɔ̃dane/ [1] *vtr* **(a)** (Law) to
sentence; **~ qn à une amende** to fine sb; **~
qn pour vol** to convict sb of theft
**(b)** ⟨*law*⟩ to punish ⟨*thieving, smuggling*⟩
**(c)** ⟨*person, country*⟩ to condemn ⟨*act,
decision*⟩
**(d)** **~ qn à faire** to compel sb to do
**(e)** to seal up ⟨*window*⟩; to shut up ⟨*room*⟩
**(f)** (figurative) to spell death for ⟨*society,
industry*⟩
**(g) les médecins l'ont condamné** the doctors
have given up hope of saving him

**condensation** /kɔ̃dɑ̃sasjɔ̃/ *nf*
condensation

**condensé** /kɔ̃dɑ̃se/ *nm* summary; digest

**condenser** /kɔ̃dɑ̃se/ [1] *vtr*, **se
condenser** *v refl* (+ *v être*) to condense

**condescendance** /kɔ̃desɑ̃dɑ̃s/ *nf*
condescension

**condescendant**, **~e** /kɔ̃desɑ̃dɑ̃, ɑ̃t/ *adj*
condescending

**condiment** /kɔ̃dimɑ̃/ *nm* (Culin) seasoning;
condiment

**condisciple** /kɔ̃disipl/ *nmf* fellow student

**condition** /kɔ̃disjɔ̃/ **1** *nf* **(a)** condition; **à
~ d'avoir le temps** provided (that) one has
the time; **sous ~** ⟨*freed*⟩ conditionally; **sans
~(s)** ⟨*acceptance*⟩ unconditional; ⟨*accept*⟩
unconditionally; **imposer ses ~s** to impose
one's own terms; **~ préalable** precondition
**(b)** (Law) (of contract, treaty) term
**(c) la ~ ouvrière** (the conditions of)
working-class life
**(d) ~ (sociale)** social status

**2 conditions** *nf pl* **(a)** conditions; **dans
ces ~s** in these conditions; in that case
**(b)** terms

**conditionnel**, **-elle** /kɔ̃disjɔnɛl/ **1** *adj*
conditional
**2** *nm* conditional

**conditionnement** /kɔ̃disjɔnmɑ̃/ *nm*
**(a)** conditioning
**(b)** packaging
■ **~ sous vide** vacuum packing

**conditionner** /kɔ̃disjɔne/ [1] *vtr* **(a)** to
condition
**(b)** to package

**condoléances** /kɔ̃dɔleɑ̃s/ *nf pl*
condolences

**condom** /kɔ̃dɔm/ *nm* condom

**condor** /kɔ̃dɔʀ/ *nm* condor

**conducteur**, **-trice** /kɔ̃dyktœʀ, tʀis/
**1** *adj* **(a)** conductive
**(b)** ⟨*principle*⟩ guiding
**2** *nm,f* (of vehicle) driver
**3** *nm* conductor

**conduire** /kɔ̃dɥiʀ/ [69] **1** *vtr* **(a)** to take
⟨*person*⟩; (in car) to drive
**(b)** ⟨*leader, studies*⟩ to lead; **la route qui
conduit à Oxford** the road that goes to
Oxford; **~ qn au désespoir** to drive sb to
despair
**(c)** to drive ⟨*car, train*⟩; to ride ⟨*motorbike*⟩
**(d)** to conduct ⟨*research*⟩; to carry out
⟨*project*⟩; to run ⟨*business*⟩
**(e)** to conduct ⟨*electricity, heat*⟩
**2 se conduire** *v refl* (+ *v être*) to behave

**conduit¹**, **~e** /kɔ̃dɥi, ɥit/ ▶ CONDUIRE

**conduit²** /kɔ̃dɥi/ *nm* **(a)** conduit
**(b)** (Anat) canal
■ **~ de fumée** flue; **~ de ventilation**
ventilation shaft

**conduite** /kɔ̃dɥit/ *nf* **(a)** behaviour (GB);
(of pupil) conduct
**(b)** (of inquiry) conducting; (of building works)
supervision; (of company) management
**(c)** (of vehicle) driving; (of motorbike) riding
**(d)** (Aut) **voiture avec ~ à gauche** left-hand
drive car
**(e)** (exam) driving test
**(f)** pipe

**cône** /kon/ *nm* cone

**confection** /kɔ̃fɛksjɔ̃/ *nf* **(a)** clothing
industry
**(b)** making

**confectionner** /kɔ̃fɛksjɔne/ [1] *vtr* (gen)
to make; to prepare ⟨*meal*⟩

**confédération** /kɔ̃fedeʀasjɔ̃/ *nf*
confederation.
■ **la Confédération helvétique** Switzerland

**confédéré**, **~e** /kɔ̃fedeʀe/ *adj*
confederate

**conférence** /kɔ̃feʀɑ̃s/ *nf* **(a)** lecture
**(b)** conference
**(c)** debate
■ **~ au sommet** summit meeting

**conférencier**, **-ière** /kɔ̃feʀɑ̃sje, ɛʀ/ *nm,f*
speaker; lecturer

**conférer** /kɔ̃feʀe/ [14] *vtr* to give; to confer

**confesser** /kɔ̃fese/ [1] **1** *vtr* **(a)** to confess ⟨*sin*⟩
**(b)** ~ qn to hear sb's confession
**2** **se confesser** *v refl* (+ *v être*) **(a)** to go to confession
**(b)** se ~ à un ami to confide in a friend

**confession** /kɔ̃fesjɔ̃/ *nf* **(a)** confession
**(b)** faith

**confessionnal**, *pl* **-aux** /kɔ̃fesjɔnal, o/ *nm* confessional

**confetti** /kɔ̃feti/ *nm* confetti

**confiance** /kɔ̃fjɑ̃s/ *nf* **(a)** trust; de ~ ⟨*person*⟩ trustworthy; ⟨*mission*⟩ which requires trust; avoir ~ en qn, faire ~ à qn to trust sb; mettre qn en ~ to win sb's trust
**(b)** (in ability, self) confidence ~ en soi (self-)confidence

**confiant**, **~e** /kɔ̃fjɑ̃, ɑ̃t/ *adj* **(a)** confident
**(b)** (self-)confident
**(c)** trusting

**confidence** /kɔ̃fidɑ̃s/ *nf* secret, confidence; être dans la ~ to be in on the secret

**confident**, **~e** /kɔ̃fidɑ̃, ɑ̃t/ *nm,f* confidant/confidante

**confidentialité** /kɔ̃fidɑ̃sjalite/ *nf* confidentiality

**confidentiel**, **-ielle** /kɔ̃fidɑ̃sjɛl/ *adj* confidential

**confier** /kɔ̃fje/ [2] **1** *vtr* **(a)** ~ qch à qn to entrust sb with sth ⟨*mission*⟩; to entrust sth to sb ⟨*money, letters*⟩
**(b)** ~ qch à qn to confide sth to sb ⟨*intentions*⟩
**2** **se confier** *v refl* (+ *v être*) to confide

**configuration** /kɔ̃figyʀasjɔ̃/ *nf* **(a)** shape; la ~ des lieux the layout of the premises
**(b)** configuration
**(c)** set-up

**confiné**, **~e** /kɔ̃fine/ *adj* **(a)** ⟨*atmosphere*⟩ stuffy; ⟨*air*⟩ stale
**(b)** ⟨*space*⟩ confined, restricted

**confiner** /kɔ̃fine/ [1] **1** *vtr* to confine
**2** **confiner à** *v+prep* to border on
**3** **se confiner** *v refl* (+ *v être*) to shut oneself away *or* up

**confins** /kɔ̃fɛ̃/ *nm pl* boundaries

**confirmation** /kɔ̃fiʀmasjɔ̃/ *nf* confirmation

**confirmer** /kɔ̃fiʀme/ [1] **1** *vtr* to confirm ⟨*order, fact*⟩; to uphold ⟨*decision*⟩; to be evidence of ⟨*attitude, quality*⟩; to affirm ⟨*intention*⟩
**2** **se confirmer** *v refl* (+ *v être*) ⟨*news*⟩ to be confirmed; ⟨*testimony*⟩ to be corroborated

**confiserie** /kɔ̃fizʀi/ *nf* **(a)** confectioner's (shop)
**(b)** confectionery

**confisquer** /kɔ̃fiske/ [1] *vtr* to confiscate, to seize

**confit**, **~e** /kɔ̃fi, it/ **1** *adj* ⟨*fruits*⟩ crystallized
**2** *nm* confit; ~ de canard confit of duck

**confiture** /kɔ̃fityʀ/ *nf* (Culin) jam, preserve; marmalade
IDIOMS donner de la ~ aux cochons to cast pearls before swine

**conflictuel**, **-elle** /kɔ̃fliktɥɛl/ *adj* ⟨*subject*⟩ controversial; ⟨*relationship*⟩ confrontational

**conflit** /kɔ̃fli/ *nm* conflict
■ ~ de générations generation gap; ~ social industrial strife

**confluence** /kɔ̃flyɑ̃s/ *nf* confluence; (figurative) convergence

**confluent** /kɔ̃flyɑ̃/ *nm* confluence

**confondre** /kɔ̃fɔ̃dʀ/ [53] **1** *vtr* **(a)** to mix up, to confuse; tous secteurs confondus all sectors taken together
**(b)** to merge
**(c)** (formal) to stagger, to amaze
**(d)** to expose ⟨*traitor*⟩
**2** **se confondre** *v refl* (+ *v être*)
**(a)** ⟨*shapes, colours*⟩ to merge; ⟨*events, facts*⟩ to become confused
**(b)** ⟨*interests, hopes*⟩ to coincide
**(c)** (formal) se ~ en excuses to apologize profusely

**conforme** /kɔ̃fɔʀm/ *adj* **(a)** être ~ à to comply with ⟨*regulations*⟩
**(b)** être ~ à l'original to conform to the original

**conformément** /kɔ̃fɔʀmemɑ̃/ *adv* ~ à in accordance with

**conformer**: **se conformer** /kɔ̃fɔʀme/ [1] *v refl* (+ *v être*) to comply with ⟨*regulations*⟩

**conformisme** /kɔ̃fɔʀmism/ *nm* conformity

**conformiste** /kɔ̃fɔʀmist/ *adj, nmf* conformist

**conformité** /kɔ̃fɔʀmite/ *nf* **(a)** ~ à la loi compliance with the law; en ~ avec ⟨*act*⟩ in accordance with
**(b)** similarity; vérifier la ~ de la traduction à l'original to check that the translation is faithful to the original
**(c)** (of tastes, points of view) correspondence

**confort** /kɔ̃fɔʀ/ *nm* comfort; maison tout ~ house with all mod cons (GB) (colloq) *or* modern conveniences

**confortable** /kɔ̃fɔʀtabl/ *adj* comfortable

**confortablement** /kɔ̃fɔʀtabləmɑ̃/ *adv* comfortably

**conforter** /kɔ̃fɔʀte/ [1] *vtr* to consolidate ⟨*position*⟩; to reinforce ⟨*situation*⟩

**confrère** /kɔ̃fʀɛʀ/ *nm* (at work) colleague; (in association) fellow member

**confrérie** /kɔ̃fʀeʀi/ *nf* brotherhood

**confrontation** /kɔ̃fʀɔ̃tasjɔ̃/ *nf* **(a)** (of ideas, witnesses) confrontation; (of texts) comparison
**(b)** (between people) debate; clash

**confronter** /kɔ̃fʀɔ̃te/ [1] *vtr* **(a)** to confront ⟨*witnesses*⟩
**(b)** to compare ⟨*texts*⟩

**confus**, **~e** /kɔ̃fy, yz/ *adj* **(a)** confused
**(b)** ⟨*feeling, fear*⟩ vague

(c) sorry; embarrassed

**confusément** /kɔ̃fyzemɑ̃/ *adv* ⟨*explain*⟩ confusedly; ⟨*feel*⟩ vaguely

**confusion** /kɔ̃fyzjɔ̃/ *nf* **(a)** confusion
**(b)** embarrassment
**(c)** mix-up

**congé** /kɔ̃ʒe/ *nm* **(a)** leave; **prendre quatre jours de** ~ to take four days off; **être en** ~ **de maladie** to be on sick leave
**(b)** notice; **donner (son)** ~ **à qn** to give sb notice
**(c) prendre** ~ **de qn** to take leave of sb

**congédier** /kɔ̃ʒedje/ [2] *vtr* to dismiss

**congélateur** /kɔ̃ʒelatœʀ/ *nm* freezer; (in refrigerator) freezer compartment

**congelé**, ~**e** /kɔ̃ʒle/ *adj* frozen; **produits** ~**s** frozen foods

**congeler** /kɔ̃ʒle/ [17] **1** *vtr* to freeze
**2 se congeler** *v refl* (+ *v être*) to freeze

**congénital**, ~**e**, *mpl* -**aux** /kɔ̃ʒenital, o/ *adj* congenital

**congère** /kɔ̃ʒɛʀ/ *nf* snowdrift

**congestion** /kɔ̃ʒɛstjɔ̃/ *nf* congestion
■ ~ **cérébrale** stroke

**congestionner** /kɔ̃ʒɛstjɔne/ [1] *vtr* **(a)** **il est tout congestionné** he's all flushed
**(b)** to congest ⟨*street*⟩

**conglomérat** /kɔ̃ɡlɔmeʀa/ *nm*
**(a)** conglomerate
**(b)** (mixture) conglomeration

**congrégation** /kɔ̃ɡʀeɡasjɔ̃/ *nf* congregation; (humorous) assembly

**congrès** /kɔ̃ɡʀɛ/ *nm* conference; **le Congrès** (US) Congress

**congressiste** /kɔ̃ɡʀesist/ *nmf* (conference) delegate

**conifère** /kɔnifɛʀ/ *nm* conifer

**conique** /kɔnik/ *adj* cone-shaped

**conjecture** /kɔ̃ʒɛktyʀ/ *nf* conjecture; **vaines** ~**s** idle speculation

**conjecturer** /kɔ̃ʒɛktyʀe/ [1] *vtr* to speculate

**conjoint**, ~**e** /kɔ̃ʒwɛ̃, ɛ̃t/ **1** *adj* ⟨*action*⟩ joint; ⟨*questions*⟩ linked
**2** *nm,f* spouse; **les** ~**s** the husband and wife

**conjointement** /kɔ̃ʒwɛ̃tmɑ̃/ *adv*
**(a)** jointly
**(b)** at the same time

**conjonction** /kɔ̃ʒɔ̃ksjɔ̃/ *nf* conjunction

**conjonctivite** /kɔ̃ʒɔ̃ktivit/ *nf* conjunctivitis

**conjoncture** /kɔ̃ʒɔ̃ktyʀ/ *nf* situation; circumstances

**conjoncturel**, -**elle** /kɔ̃ʒɔ̃ktyʀɛl/ *adj* ⟨*situation*⟩ economic

**conjugaison** /kɔ̃ʒyɡɛzɔ̃/ *nf* **(a)** (of verb) conjugation
**(b)** (figurative) combination

**conjugal**, ~**e**, *mpl* -**aux** /kɔ̃ʒyɡal, o/ *adj* ⟨*love*⟩ conjugal; ⟨*life*⟩ married

**conjugalement** /kɔ̃ʒyɡalmɑ̃/ *adv* ⟨*live*⟩ as man and wife

**conjuguer** /kɔ̃ʒyɡe/ [1] *vtr* **(a)** to conjugate ⟨*verb*⟩
**(b)** to combine ⟨*efforts*⟩

**conjuration** /kɔ̃ʒyʀasjɔ̃/ *nf* **(a)** conspiracy
**(b)** (of evil spirits) conjuration

**conjurer** /kɔ̃ʒyʀe/ [1] *vtr* **(a)** to avert ⟨*crisis*⟩; to ward off ⟨*danger*⟩
**(b) je vous en conjure** I beg you

**connaissance** /kɔnɛsɑ̃s/ *nf*
**(a)** knowledge; **prendre** ~ **d'un texte** to acquaint oneself with a text; **en** ~ **de cause** with full knowledge of the facts
**(b)** consciousness; **sans** ~ unconscious
**(c)** acquaintance; **faire (plus ample)** ~ **avec qn** to get to know sb (better); **en pays de** ~ among familiar faces; on familiar ground

**connaisseur**, -**euse** /kɔnɛsœʀ, øz/ *nm,f* connoisseur, expert

**connaître** /kɔnɛtʀ/ [73] **1** *vtr* **(a)** to know; **faire** ~ **à qn** to make [sth] known to sb ⟨*decision*⟩; to introduce sb to ⟨*music*⟩; **je l'ai connu en Chine** I met him in China; **tu connais la nouvelle?** have you heard the news?
**(b)** to experience ⟨*hunger, failure*⟩; to enjoy ⟨*success*⟩; to have ⟨*difficulties*⟩; ~ **une forte croissance** to show a rapid growth
**2 se connaître** *v refl* (+ *v être*) **(a)** to know oneself
**(b)** to know each other; **ils se sont connus à Rome** they met in Rome
**(c) s'y** ~ **en vin** to know all about wine
IDIOMS **on connaît la chanson** *or* **musique!** we've heard it all before!; ~ **qch comme sa poche** to know sth like the back of one's hand

**conne** (vulgar) ▶ CON

**connecter** /kɔnɛkte/ [1] *vtr* to connect

**connexion** /kɔnɛksjɔ̃/ *nf* connection

**connivence** /kɔnivɑ̃s/ *nf* connivance; **signe de** ~ sign of complicity

**connotation** /kɔnɔtasjɔ̃/ *nf* connotation

**connu**, ~**e** /kɔny/ ▶ CONNAÎTRE

**conquérant**, ~**e** /kɔ̃keʀɑ̃, ɑ̃t/ *nm,f* conqueror

**conquérir** /kɔ̃keʀiʀ/ [35] *vtr* to conquer; to capture ⟨*market*⟩; to win over ⟨*audience*⟩.
IDIOMS **se croire en pays** *or* **terrain conquis** to lord it over everyone

**conquête** /kɔ̃kɛt/ *nf* conquest

**conquis**, ~**e** ▶ CONQUÉRIR

**consacré**, ~**e** /kɔ̃sakʀe/ *adj* **formule** ~**e** time-honoured (GB) expression; **artiste** ~ recognized artist

**consacrer** /kɔ̃sakʀe/ [1] **1** *vtr* **(a)** to devote; **pouvez-vous me** ~ **un instant?** can you spare me a moment?
**(b)** to sanction
**(c)** to consecrate
**2 se consacrer** *v refl* (+ *v être*) **se** ~ **à** to devote oneself to

**consanguin**, ~**e** /kɔ̃sɑ̃ɡɛ̃, in/ *adj* ⟨*marriage*⟩ between blood relations

**consciemment** /kɔ̃sjamɑ̃/ *adv*
consciously

**conscience** /kɔ̃sjɑ̃s/ *nf* (a) conscience;
**avoir bonne/mauvaise** ~ to have a clear/a
guilty conscience
(b) awareness; **prendre** ~ **de** to become
aware of; **prise de** ~ realization; **perdre** ~ to
lose consciousness
■ ~ **professionnelle** conscientiousness

**consciencieusement** /kɔ̃sjɑ̃sjøzmɑ̃/
*adv* (a) conscientiously
(b) dutifully

**consciencieux, -ieuse** /kɔ̃sjɑ̃sjø, øz/
*adj* conscientious

**conscient,** ~**e** /kɔ̃sjɑ̃, ɑ̃t/ *adj* (a) aware
(b) conscious

**conscrit** /kɔ̃skʀi/ *nm* conscript (GB),
draftee (US)

**consécration** /kɔ̃sekʀasjɔ̃/ *nf* (a) (of author)
recognition
(b) consecration

**consécutif, -ive** /kɔ̃sekytif, iv/ *adj*
consecutive; ~ **à** resulting from; following

**consécutivement** /kɔ̃sekytivmɑ̃/ *adv*
consecutively

**conseil** /kɔ̃sɛj/ *nm* (a) advice; **quelques**
~**s de prudence** a few words of warning; **il
est de bon** ~ he always gives good advice;
~**s d'entretien** cleaning *or* care instructions
(b) council
(c) consultant
■ ~ **d'administration** board of directors; ~ **de
classe** (Sch) staff meeting; ~ **de discipline**
disciplinary committee; ~ **général** *council of
a French department*

**conseiller¹, -ère** /kɔ̃seje, ɛʀ/ [1] *nm,f*
(a) adviser (GB)
(b) counsellor (GB)
[2] *nm* councillor (GB)
■ ~ **commercial** commercial counsellor (GB);
~ **culturel** cultural counsellor (GB); ~ **d'État**
member of the Council of State; ~ **général**
*councillor for a French department*;
~ **municipal** town councillor (GB);
~ **d'orientation** careers adviser

**conseiller²** /kɔ̃seje/ [1] *vtr* to recommend;
to advise; ~ **à qn de faire** to advise sb to do

**consensus** /kɔ̃sɛ̃sys/ *nm inv* consensus

**consentant,** ~**e** /kɔ̃sɑ̃tɑ̃, ɑ̃t/ *adj* willing;
(Law) consenting

**consentement** /kɔ̃sɑ̃tmɑ̃/ *nm* consent

**consentir** /kɔ̃sɑ̃tiʀ/ [30] [1] *vtr* to grant; to
allow
[2] **consentir à** *v+prep* ~ **à qch/à faire** to
agree to sth/to do

**conséquence** /kɔ̃sekɑ̃s/ *nf* consequence;
**être lourd de** ~**s** to have serious
consequences; **sans** ~(**s**) of no consequence;
**ne pas tirer à** ~ to be of no consequence;
**avoir pour** ~ **le chômage** to result in
unemployment; **agir en** ~ to act
accordingly; **avoir des qualifications et un
salaire en** ~ to have qualifications and a
corresponding salary

**conséquent,** ~**e** /kɔ̃sekɑ̃, ɑ̃t/ [1] *adj*
(a) substantial
(b) consistent
[2] **par conséquent** *phr* therefore, as a
result

**conservateur, -trice** /kɔ̃sɛʀvatœʀ,
tʀis/ [1] *adj* (a) conservative
(b) **produit** ~ preservative
[2] *nm,f* (a) conservative
(b) (museum) curator

**conservation** /kɔ̃sɛʀvasjɔ̃/ *nf*
conservation; preservation; **lait longue** ~
long-life milk (GB)

**conservatoire** /kɔ̃sɛʀvatwaʀ/ *nm*
academy; ~ **de musique** conservatoire

**conserve** /kɔ̃sɛʀv/ [1] *nf* (a) **la** ~, **les** ~**s**
canned food; **boîte de** ~ can
(b) preserve
[2] **de conserve** *phr* ⟨act⟩ in concert

**conserver** /kɔ̃sɛʀve/ [1] *vtr* (a) to keep; to
retain; ~ **l'anonymat** to remain anonymous
(b) (Culin) to preserve; (in vinegar) to pickle
(c) ⟨activity⟩ to keep [sb] young

**conserverie** /kɔ̃sɛʀvəʀi/ *nf* (a) cannery,
canning plant
(b) canning industry

**considérable** /kɔ̃sideʀabl/ *adj*
considerable, significant; **l'enjeu est** ~ the
stakes are high

**considération** /kɔ̃sideʀasjɔ̃/ *nf*
(a) consideration; **prendre qch en** ~ to
consider sth, to take sth into account; **en** ~
**de** in view of; **sans** ~ **de** irrespective of
(b) consideration, factor
(c) respect, esteem

**considérer** /kɔ̃sideʀe/ [14] [1] *vtr* (a) to
consider, to take into account
(b) to consider, to regard; ~ **qn/qch comme
(étant)** to consider sb/sth to be, to regard sb/
sth as being; **être bien considéré** to be
highly regarded
[2] **se considérer** *v refl* (+ *v être*) **se** ~
(**comme**) (a) to consider oneself (to be)
(b) to regard one another as being

**consignation** /kɔ̃siɲasjɔ̃/ *nf* (a) deposit
(b) **en** ~ on consignment

**consigne** /kɔ̃siɲ/ *nf* (a) orders,
instructions; **passer la** ~ **à qn** to pass the
word on to sb; '~**s à suivre en cas
d'incendie**' 'fire regulations'
(b) left luggage office (GB), baggage
checkroom (US)
(c) (on bottle) deposit
■ ~ **automatique** left luggage lockers (GB),
baggage lockers (US)

**consigné,** ~**e** /kɔ̃siɲe/ *adj* ⟨bottle⟩
returnable

**consigner** /kɔ̃siɲe/ [1] *vtr* (a) to record, to
write down
(b) to confine ⟨soldier⟩; to give [sb]
detention ⟨pupil⟩

**consistance** /kɔ̃sistɑ̃s/ *nf* (a) consistency;
**avoir de la/manquer de** ~ to be quite thick/
to be too runny ⋯⋗

**(b)** substance, weight; **sans ~** ‹person› spineless; ‹rumour› groundless

**consistant, ~e** /kɔ̃sistɑ̃, ɑ̃t/ *adj* ‹meal, investment› substantial; ‹dish› nourishing

**consister** /kɔ̃siste/ [1] *vi* **(a) ~ en** *or* **dans** to consist in; **~ à faire** to consist in doing **(b) ~ en** to consist of, to be made up of; **en quoi consiste cette aide?** what form does this aid take?

**consœur** /kɔ̃sœʀ/ *nf* **(a)** female colleague **(b)** counterpart

**consolant, ~e** /kɔ̃sɔlɑ̃, ɑ̃t/ *adj* comforting

**consolation** /kɔ̃sɔlasjɔ̃/ *nf* consolation

**console** /kɔ̃sɔl/ *nf* console; **~ de jeu vidéo** games console

**consoler** /kɔ̃sɔle/ [1] **1** *vtr* to console; **si ça peut te ~** if it is any comfort to you **2 se consoler** *v refl* (+ *v être*) to find consolation; **se ~ de** to get over

**consolidable** /kɔ̃sɔlidabl/ *adj* **(a)** ‹debt› fundable **(b)** ‹structure› reinforceable

**consolidation** /kɔ̃sɔlidasjɔ̃/ *nf* **(a)** (of wall) strengthening; (of position) consolidation **(b)** (of debt) consolidation, funding; (of turnover, balance sheet) consolidation; (of currency) strengthening

**consolider** /kɔ̃sɔlide/ [1] **1** *vtr* to consolidate, to strengthen **2 se consolider** *v refl* (+ *v être*) **(a)** to grow stronger, to be strengthened **(b)** to consolidate

**consommable** /kɔ̃sɔmabl/ **1** *adj* edible; drinkable **2 consommables** *nm pl* (Econ, Comput) consumables

**consommateur, -trice** /kɔ̃sɔmatœʀ, tʀis/ *nm,f* **(a)** consumer **(b)** (in bar) customer

**consommation** /kɔ̃sɔmasjɔ̃/ *nf* **(a)** consumption; **faire une grande ~ de** to use a lot of; **de ~** ‹goods, society› consumer **(b)** drink **(c)** consummation

**consommé, ~e** /kɔ̃sɔme/ *nm* consommé

**consommer** /kɔ̃sɔme/ [1] *vtr* **(a)** to consume; to use **(b)** to eat ‹food›; to drink ‹tea›; to take ‹drugs›

**consonance** /kɔ̃sɔnɑ̃s/ *nf* consonance; **mot aux ~s étrangères** foreign-sounding word

**consonne** /kɔ̃sɔn/ *nf* consonant

**conspirateur, -trice** /kɔ̃spiʀatœʀ, tʀis/ *nm,f* conspirator

**conspiration** /kɔ̃spiʀasjɔ̃/ *nf* conspiracy

**conspirer** /kɔ̃spiʀe/ [1] **1** *vi* to conspire, to plot **2 conspirer à** *v+prep* to conspire to bring about; **~ à faire** to conspire to do

**constamment** /kɔ̃stamɑ̃/ *adv* constantly

**constance** /kɔ̃stɑ̃s/ *nf* **(a)** consistency; constancy

**(b)** steadfastness

**constant, ~e¹** /kɔ̃stɑ̃, ɑ̃t/ *adj* **(a)** constant; consistent **(b)** continuous; continual

**constante²** /kɔ̃stɑ̃t/ *nf* constant

**constat** /kɔ̃sta/ *nm* certified *or* official report ■ **~ (à l')amiable:** *accident report drawn up by the parties involved*; **~ d'échec** admission of failure

**constatation** /kɔ̃statasjɔ̃/ *nf* observation

**constater** /kɔ̃state/ [1] *vtr* **(a)** to notice, to note; **~ (par) soi-même** to see for oneself **(b)** to ascertain, to establish **(c)** to record

**constellation** /kɔ̃stɛlasjɔ̃/ *nf* constellation

**constellé, ~e** /kɔ̃stɛlle/ *adj* **~ de** spangled with; riddled with; spotted with

**consternant, ~e** /kɔ̃stɛʀnɑ̃, ɑ̃t/ *adj* **(a)** distressing **(b)** appalling

**consternation** /kɔ̃stɛʀnasjɔ̃/ *nf* consternation

**consterner** /kɔ̃stɛʀne/ [1] *vtr* to fill [sb] with consternation, to dismay

**constipation** /kɔ̃stipasjɔ̃/ *nf* constipation

**constipé, ~e** /kɔ̃stipe/ *adj* constipated

**constiper** /kɔ̃stipe/ [1] *vtr* to make [sb] constipated

**constitué, ~e** /kɔ̃stitɥe/ *adj* **(a) personne bien/mal ~e** person of sound/unsound constitution **(b)** constituted

**constituer** /kɔ̃stitɥe/ [1] **1** *vtr* **(a)** to be, to constitute ‹crime, reason› **(b)** to form, to set up ‹team, commission› **(c)** to make up ‹whole› **(d)** (Law) to settle; **~ qn héritier** to appoint sb as heir **2 se constituer** *v refl* (+ *v être*) **(a)** to build up ‹network, reserve› **(b) se ~ en** to form ‹party› **(c) se ~ prisonnier** to give oneself up

**constitutif, -ive** /kɔ̃stitytif, iv/ *adj* **(a)** (basic) constituent **(b)** (Pol) founding; constitutional

**constitution** /kɔ̃stitysjɔ̃/ *nf* **(a)** (of company) setting up; (of capital) accumulation; (of application) preparing **(b)** constitution

**constructeur, -trice** /kɔ̃stʀyktœʀ, tʀis/ *nm,f* **(a)** (car) manufacturer **(b)** builder

**constructif, -ive** /kɔ̃stʀyktif, iv/ *adj* constructive

**construction** /kɔ̃stʀyksjɔ̃/ *nf* **(a)** construction; building; **en ~** under construction; **de ~ japonaise** Japanese built **(b) la ~** the construction industry; **~ navale** shipbuilding

**construire** /kɔ̃stʀɥiʀ/ [69] **1** *vtr* to build; to construct

**2 se construire** *v refl* (*+ v être*) **(a)** ça s'est beaucoup construit par ici there's been a lot of building here
**(b)** se ~ avec le subjonctif to take the subjunctive
**consul** /kɔ̃syl/ *nm* consul
**consulat** /kɔ̃syla/ *nm* consulate
**consultant**, ~e /kɔ̃syltã, ãt/ *nm,f* consultant
**consultation** /kɔ̃syltasjɔ̃/ *nf*
**(a)** consultation; consulting; ~ électorale election
**(b)** surgery hours (GB), office hours (US)
**consulter** /kɔ̃sylte/ [1] **1** *vtr* to consult; ~ le peuple to hold a general election
**2** *vi* ⟨doctor⟩ to see patients
**3 se consulter** *v refl* (*+ v être*) to consult together; se ~ du regard to exchange glances
**consumer** /kɔ̃syme/ [1] **1** *vtr* ⟨fire⟩ to consume
**2 se consumer** *v refl* (*+ v être*) to burn
**contact** /kɔ̃takt/ *nm* **(a)** contact; garder le ~ to keep in touch; entrer en ~ avec to get in touch with; elle est devenue plus sociable à ton ~ she's become more sociable through spending time with you
**(b)** mettre/couper le ~ to switch on/switch off the ignition
**contacter** /kɔ̃takte/ [1] *vtr* to contact, to get in touch with
**contagieux, -ieuse** /kɔ̃taʒjø, øz/ *adj*
**(a)** contagious
**(b)** ⟨laughter⟩ infectious
**contagion** /kɔ̃taʒjɔ̃/ *nf* contagion
**contamination** /kɔ̃taminasjɔ̃/ *nf* contamination
**contaminer** /kɔ̃tamine/ [1] *vtr* to contaminate; to infect
**conte** /kɔ̃t/ *nm* tale, story
**contemplatif, -ive** /kɔ̃tãplatif, iv/ *adj* contemplative
**contemplation** /kɔ̃tãplasjɔ̃/ *nf* contemplation
**contempler** /kɔ̃tãple/ [1] *vtr* to survey; to contemplate; to look at
**contemporain, ~e** /kɔ̃tãpɔrɛ̃, ɛn/ *adj*, *nm,f* contemporary
**contenance** /kɔ̃t(ə)nãs/ *nf* **(a)** (of container) capacity
**(b)** bearing, attitude; perdre ~ to lose one's composure
**contenant** /kɔ̃t(ə)nã/ *nm* packaging
**conteneur** /kɔ̃t(ə)nœr/ *nm* container
■ ~ vert (for bottles) bottle bank
**contenir** /kɔ̃t(ə)nir/ [36] **1** *vtr* **(a)** to contain ⟨substance, error⟩
**(b)** ⟨container⟩ to hold; ⟨hall⟩ to accommodate ⟨spectators⟩
**(c)** to contain ⟨crowd⟩
**2 se contenir** *v refl* (*+ v être*) to contain oneself
**content, ~e** /kɔ̃tã, ãt/ **1** *adj* happy, pleased, glad; ~ de soi pleased with oneself

**2** *nm* avoir son ~ de to have had one's fill of
**contentement** /kɔ̃tãtmã/ *nm* contentment
**contenter** /kɔ̃tãte/ [1] **1** *vtr* to satisfy ⟨customer, curiosity⟩; facile à ~ easy to please
**2 se contenter** *v refl* (*+ v être*) se ~ de qch to content oneself with sth
**contentieux** /kɔ̃tãsjø/ *nm* **(a)** bone of contention
**(b)** legal department
**(c)** litigation
**contenu, ~e** /kɔ̃t(ə)ny/ **1** *pp* ▶ CONTENIR
**2** *pp adj* restrained; suppressed
**3** *nm* contents; content
**conter** /kɔ̃te/ [1] *vtr* to tell, to recount
**contestable** /kɔ̃tɛstabl/ *adj* questionable
**contestataire** /kɔ̃tɛstatɛr/ **1** *adj* anti-authority
**2** *nmf* protester
**contestation** /kɔ̃tɛstasjɔ̃/ *nf* **(a)** protest
**(b)** challenging; être sujet à ~, prêter à ~ to be questionable; sans ~ possible beyond dispute
**(b)** la ~ dissent
**conteste: sans conteste** /sɑ̃kɔ̃tɛst/ *phr* unquestionably
**contesté, ~e** /kɔ̃tɛste/ *adj* controversial
**contester** /kɔ̃tɛste/ [1] **1** *vtr* to question; to contest; to dispute; to challenge
**2** *vi* **(a)** to raise objections
**(b)** to protest
**contexte** /kɔ̃tɛkst/ *nm* context
**contigu, -uë** /kɔ̃tigy/ *adj* ⟨rooms⟩ adjoining
**continent, ~e** /kɔ̃tinã, ãt/ **1** *adj* continent
**2** *nm* **(a)** continent
**(b)** mainland
**continental, ~e**, *mpl* **-aux** /kɔ̃tinãtal, o/ *adj* **(a)** continental
**(b)** mainland
**contingent** /kɔ̃tɛ̃ʒã/ *nm* **(a)** contingent; (Mil) conscripts, draft (US)
**(b)** quota
**(c)** (Law, figurative) share
**continu, ~e** /kɔ̃tiny/ *adj* continuous
**continuation** /kɔ̃tinɥasjɔ̃/ *nf* continuation
**continuel, -elle** /kɔ̃tinɥɛl/ *adj* continual
**continuer** /kɔ̃tinɥe/ [1] **1** *vtr* to continue
**2** *vi* to continue, to go on
**continuité** /kɔ̃tinɥite/ *nf* continuity
**contondant, ~e** /kɔ̃tɔ̃dã, ãt/ *adj* blunt
**contorsion** /kɔ̃tɔrsjɔ̃/ *nf* contortion
**contorsionner: se contorsionner** /kɔ̃tɔrsjɔne/ [1] *v refl* (*+ v être*) to tie oneself in knots
**contorsionniste** /kɔ̃tɔrsjɔnist/ *nmf* contortionist
**contour** /kɔ̃tur/ *nm* **(a)** outline, contour
**(b)** ~s (of road, river) twists and turns

**contourner** /kɔ̃turne/ [1] *vtr* to go round; to by-pass ⟨*town*⟩; to get round ⟨*problem*⟩

**contraceptif, -ive** /kɔ̃trasɛptif, iv/
**1** *adj* contraceptive
**2** *nm* contraceptive

**contraception** /kɔ̃trasɛpsjɔ̃/ *nf* contraception

**contractant, ~e** /kɔ̃traktɑ̃, ɑ̃t/ **1** *adj* contracting
**2** *nm,f* contracting party

**contracter** /kɔ̃trakte/ [1] **1** *vtr* (a) to tense ⟨*muscle*⟩
**(b)** to incur ⟨*debt*⟩; to take out ⟨*loan*⟩
**(c)** to contract ⟨*disease*⟩
**2 se contracter** *v refl* (+ *v être*) ⟨*muscle, word*⟩ to contract; ⟨*face, person*⟩ to tense up

**contraction** /kɔ̃traksjɔ̃/ *nf* (a) tenseness
**(b)** contraction

**contractuel, -elle** /kɔ̃traktɥɛl/ **1** *adj* contractual; **personnel ~** contract staff
**2** *nm,f* (a) contract employee
**(b)** traffic warden (GB), meter reader (US)

**contradiction** /kɔ̃tradiksjɔ̃/ *nf* contradiction

**contradictoire** /kɔ̃tradiktwar/ *adj* contradictory; **~ à** in contradiction to

**contraignant, ~e** /kɔ̃trɛɲɑ̃, ɑ̃t/ *adj* restrictive

**contraindre** /kɔ̃trɛ̃dr/ [54] **1** *vtr* (a) **~ qn à faire** to force sb to do
**(b)** to restrain, to curb
**2 se contraindre** *v refl* (+ *v être*) **se ~ à** to force oneself to

**contraint, ~e¹** /kɔ̃trɛ̃, ɛ̃t/ *adj* (a) **~ et forcé** (Law) under duress
**(b)** strained, forced

**contrainte²** /kɔ̃trɛ̃t/ *nf* (a) pressure; coercion
**(b)** constraint
**(c) sans ~** without restraint, freely

**contraire** /kɔ̃trɛr/ **1** *adj* (a) opposite; contrary; ⟨*interests*⟩ conflicting; **être ~ aux usages** to be contrary to custom; **dans le cas ~** (should it be) otherwise
**(b)** adverse
**2** *nm* **le ~** the opposite, the contrary; **ne dites pas le ~** don't deny it; **au ~!** on the contrary!

**contrairement** /kɔ̃trɛrmɑ̃/ *adv* **~ à ce qu'on pourrait penser** contrary to what one might think; **~ à qn** unlike sb

**contrariant, ~e** /kɔ̃trarjɑ̃, ɑ̃t/ *adj*
**(a)** ⟨*person*⟩ contrary
**(b)** ⟨*event*⟩ annoying

**contrarier** /kɔ̃trarje/ [2] *vtr* (a) to upset
**(b)** to annoy
**(c)** to frustrate, to thwart

**contrariété** /kɔ̃trarjete/ *nf* vexation

**contraste** /kɔ̃trast/ *nm* contrast

**contrasté, ~e** /kɔ̃traste/ *adj*
**(a)** contrasting
**(b)** ⟨*photo*⟩ with good contrast
**(c)** ⟨*results*⟩ uneven

**contraster** /kɔ̃traste/ [1] **1** *vtr* to contrast ⟨*colours*⟩; to give contrast to ⟨*photo*⟩
**2** *vi* to contrast

**contrat** /kɔ̃tra/ *nm* contract
■ **~ emploi solidarité, CES** part-time low-paid work for the long-term unemployed

**contravention** /kɔ̃travɑ̃sjɔ̃/ *nf*
**(a)** parking ticket; speeding ticket; fine
**(b)** minor offence (GB)

**contre¹** /kɔ̃tr/ **1** *prep* (a) against; **22% ~ 18% hier** 22% as against 18% yesterday; **allongés l'un ~ l'autre** lying side by side
**(b)** versus
**(c)** (in exchange) for; **échange-la ~ une bleue** exchange it for a blue one
**2 par contre** *phr* on the other hand

**contre²** /kɔ̃tr/ **1** *nm* (a) **le pour et le ~** the pros and cons
**(b)** (Sport) counter-attack
**2** *pref* counter

**contre-accusation, pl ~s** /kɔ̃trakyzasjɔ̃/ *nf* counter-charge

**contre-allée, pl ~s** /kɔ̃trale/ *nf* service road; side path

**contre-attaque, pl ~s** /kɔ̃tratak/ *nf* counter-attack

**contrebalancer** /kɔ̃trəbalɑ̃se/ [12] *vtr*
**(a)** to counterbalance
**(b)** to offset

**contrebande** /kɔ̃trəbɑ̃d/ *nf* (a) smuggling
**(b)** smuggled goods, contraband

**contrebandier, -ière** /kɔ̃trəbɑ̃dje, ɛr/ *nm,f* smuggler

**contrebas: en contrebas** /ɑ̃kɔ̃trəba/ *phr* (down) below; **en ~ de** below

**contrebasse** /kɔ̃trəbas/ *nf* double bass

**contrecarrer** /kɔ̃trəkare/ [1] *vtr* to thwart, to foil; to counteract

**contrechamp** /kɔ̃trəʃɑ̃/ *nm* reverse shot

**contrecœur: à contrecœur** /akɔ̃trəkœr/ *phr* reluctantly

**contrecoup** /kɔ̃trəku/ *nm* effects; after-effects; **par ~** as a result

**contre-courant, pl ~s** /kɔ̃trəkurɑ̃/ *nm* counter-current; **nager à ~** to swim against the current; **aller à ~ de la mode** to go against the fashion

**contredire** /kɔ̃trədir/ [65] **1** *vtr* to contradict
**2 se contredire** *v refl* (+ *v être*) (a) to contradict oneself
**(b)** to contradict each other

**contrée** /kɔ̃tre/ *nf* (a) land
**(b)** region

**contre-enquête, pl ~s** /kɔ̃trɑ̃kɛt/ *nf* second enquiry (GB)

**contre-espionnage, pl ~s** /kɔ̃trɛspjɔnaʒ/ *nm* counter-intelligence

**contre-expertise pl ~s** /kɔ̃trɛkspɛrtiz/ *nf* second opinion

**contrefaçon** /kɔ̃trəfasɔ̃/ *nf* (a) forging, counterfeiting
**(b)** forgery, counterfeit

**contrefacteur** /kɔ̃tRəfaktœR/ *nm* (of notes, credit cards, paintings) forger; (of coins) counterfeiter; (of software, invention) pirate

**contrefaire** /kɔ̃tRəfɛR/ [10] *vtr* **(a)** to forge, to counterfeit
**(b)** to imitate
**(c)** to disguise

**contrefort** /kɔ̃tRəfɔR/ *nm* **(a)** foothills
**(b)** buttress
**(c)** (of shoe) back

**contre-indiqué**, **∼e**, *mpl* **∼s** /kɔ̃tRɛ̃dike/ *adj* contra-indicated; inadvisable

**contre-interrogatoire**, *pl* **∼s** /kɔ̃tRɛ̃teRɔgatwaR/ *nm* cross-examination

**contre-jour**, *pl* **∼s** /kɔ̃tRəʒuR/ *nm* backlighting; **à ∼** against *or* into the light

**contremaître**, **-esse** /kɔ̃tRəmɛtR, kɔ̃tRəmɛtRɛs/ *nm,f* foreman/forewoman

**contrepartie** /kɔ̃tRəparti/ *nf*
**(a)** equivalent
**(b)** compensation; **en ∼** in compensation; in return; **mais la ∼ est que le salaire est élevé** but this is offset by the high salary

**contre-pied**, *pl* **∼s** /kɔ̃tRəpje/ *nm* **prendre le ∼ de ce que dit qn** to say the opposite of what sb says

**contreplaqué** /kɔ̃tRəplake/ *nm* plywood

**contrepoids** /kɔ̃tRəpwa/ *nm* counterweight

**contrer** /kɔ̃tRe/ [1] *vtr* to counter; to block

**contresens** /kɔ̃tRəsɑ̃s/ *nm*
**(a)** misinterpretation
**(b)** mistranslation
**(c)** **à ∼** in the opposite direction; the wrong way; against the grain

**contretemps** /kɔ̃tRətɑ̃/ *nm inv*
**(a)** setback, contretemps
**(b)** **à ∼** (Mus) on the off-beat; out of time; (figurative) at the wrong moment

**contre-valeur**, *pl* **∼s** /kɔ̃tRəvalœR/ *nf* exchange value

**contrevenir** /kɔ̃tRəvəniR/ [36] *v+prep* **∼ à** to contravene

**contribuable** /kɔ̃tRibɥabl/ *nmf* taxpayer

**contribuer** /kɔ̃tRibɥe/ [1] *v+prep* **∼ à** to contribute to; to pay one's share of; **cela y a beaucoup contribué** it was a major factor

**contribution** /kɔ̃tRibysjɔ̃/ *nf*
**(a)** contribution; **mettre qn à ∼** to call upon sb's services
**(b)** **∼s** taxes; tax office

**contrit**, **∼e** /kɔ̃tRi, it/ *adj* contrite, apologetic

**contrôle** /kɔ̃tRol/ *nm* **(a)** control
**(b)** check; **∼ de police** police check; **∼ des billets** ticket inspection
**(c)** (Sch) test; **∼ de géographie** geography test
**(d)** check-up
**(e)** monitoring; **sous ∼ médical** under medical supervision
■ **∼ continu** (des **connaissances**) continuous assessment; **∼ fiscal** tax investigation; **∼ technique** (des **véhicules**) MOT (test)

**contrôler** /kɔ̃tRole/ [1] **1** *vtr* **(a)** to control
**(b)** to monitor
**(c)** to check; to inspect; to test
**2 se contrôler** *v refl* (+ *v être*) to control oneself

**contrôleur**, **-euse** /kɔ̃tRolœR, øz/ *nm,f* inspector; **∼ aérien** air-traffic controller

**contrordre** /kɔ̃tRɔRdR/ *nm* **(a)** ordres et **∼s** conflicting orders; **j'irai vendredi, sauf ∼** I'll go on Friday, unless I hear to the contrary
**(b)** counter command

**controverse** /kɔ̃tRɔvɛRs/ *nf* controversy

**controversé**, **∼e** /kɔ̃tRɔvɛRse/ *adj* controversial

**contusion** /kɔ̃tyzjɔ̃/ *nf* bruise

**convaincant**, **∼e** /kɔ̃vɛ̃kɑ̃, ɑ̃t/ *adj*
**(a)** convincing
**(b)** persuasive

**convaincre** /kɔ̃vɛ̃kR/ [57] **1** *vtr* to convince; to persuade
**2 se convaincre** *v refl* (+ *v être*) to convince oneself

**convaincu**, **∼e** /kɔ̃vɛ̃ky/ **1** *pp* ▸ CONVAINCRE
**2** *pp adj* **(a)** convinced; **d'un ton ∼** with conviction
**(b)** ⟨supporter⟩ staunch

**convalescence** /kɔ̃valesɑ̃s/ *nf* convalescence

**convalescent**, **∼e** /kɔ̃valesɑ̃, ɑ̃t/ *adj*, *nm,f* convalescent

**convenable** /kɔ̃vnabl/ *adj* **(a)** suitable
**(b)** reasonable
**(c)** decent; proper; respectable

**convenablement** /kɔ̃vnabləmɑ̃/ *adv* properly; reasonably well; decently

**convenance** /kɔ̃vnɑ̃s/ *nf* **(a)** **pour ∼ personnelle** for personal reasons; **à votre ∼** at your convenience
**(b)** **∼s** (social) conventions

**convenir** /kɔ̃vniR/ [36] **1** *vtr* **(a)** to admit
**(b)** to agree
**2 convenir à** *v+prep* **(a)** to suit; to be suitable for
**3 convenir de** *v+prep* **(a)** **∼ de** to admit, to acknowledge
**(b)** **∼ de** to agree on
**4** *v impers* **(a)** **il convient de faire/que vous fassiez** one/you should do
**(b)** **ce qu'il est convenu d'appeler le réalisme** what is commonly called realism; **comme convenu** as agreed

**convention** /kɔ̃vɑ̃sjɔ̃/ *nf* **(a)** agreement
**(b)** convention; **de ∼** conventional

**conventionné**, **∼e** /kɔ̃vɑ̃sjɔne/ *adj* ⟨doctor, costs⟩ national health service; ⟨clinic⟩ registered; **médecin non ∼** private doctor

**conventionnel**, **-elle** /kɔ̃vɑ̃sjɔnɛl/ *adj*
**(a)** conventional
**(b)** contractual

**convenu**, **∼e** /kɔ̃v(ə)ny/ **1** *pp* ▸ CONVENIR

**2** *pp adj* (a) ‹*date, terms*› agreed
(b) ‹*phrase*› conventional; ‹*smile*› polite

**convergence** /kɔ̃vɛʀʒɑ̃s/ *nf* convergence

**converger** /kɔ̃vɛʀʒe/ [13] *vi* to converge

**conversation** /kɔ̃vɛʀsasjɔ̃/ *nf*
conversation; **avoir de la ∼** to be a good
conversationalist; **dans la ∼ courante** in
everyday speech

**converser** /kɔ̃vɛʀse/ [1] *vi* to converse

**conversion** /kɔ̃vɛʀsjɔ̃/ *nf* conversion

**converti, ∼e** /kɔ̃vɛʀti/ **1** *pp* ▶ CONVERTIR
**2** *nm,f* convert

**convertible** /kɔ̃vɛʀtibl/ *adj* (a) convertible
(b) **canapé ∼** sofa-bed

**convertir** /kɔ̃vɛʀtiʀ/ [3] **1** *vtr* to convert
**2 se convertir** *v refl* (+ *v être*) to convert;
‹*company*› to change products

**convertisseur** /kɔ̃vɛʀtisœʀ/ *nm*
converter

**convexe** /kɔ̃vɛks/ *adj* convex

**conviction** /kɔ̃viksjɔ̃/ *nf* conviction

**convier** /kɔ̃vje/ [2] *vtr* to invite ‹*person*›

**convive** /kɔ̃viv/ *nmf* guest

**convivial, ∼e,** *mpl* **-iaux** /kɔ̃vivjal, o/
*adj* (a) convivial
(b) user-friendly

**convivialité** /kɔ̃vivjalite/ *nf*
(a) friendliness; conviviality
(b) user-friendliness

**convocation** /kɔ̃vɔkasjɔ̃/ *nf* (a) (of meeting)
convening; (of person) summoning; (Mil)
calling up
(b) notice to attend; (Law) summons; (Mil)
call-up papers; **∼ aux examens** notification
of examination timetables

**convoi** /kɔ̃vwa/ *nm* (a) convoy; '**∼
exceptionnel**' (Aut) 'wide *or* dangerous load'
(b) train

**convoiter** /kɔ̃vwate/ [1] *vtr* to covet

**convoitise** /kɔ̃vwatiz/ *nf* **la ∼**
covetousness; **∼ de** lust for

**convoquer** /kɔ̃vɔke/ [1] *vtr* to call, to
convene ‹*meeting*›; to send for ‹*pupil*›; to
summon ‹*witness*›; to call up ‹*soldier*›; **être
convoqué à un examen** to be asked to attend
an exam

**convoyer** /kɔ̃vwaje/ [23] *vtr* to escort

**convoyeur, -euse** /kɔ̃vwajœʀ/ *nm,f*
(a) prison escort
(b) courier; **∼ de fonds** security guard

**convulsif, -ive** /kɔ̃vylsif, iv/ *adj*
(a) convulsive
(b) ‹*laughter*› nervous

**convulsion** /kɔ̃vylsjɔ̃/ *nf* convulsion

**convulsionner** /kɔ̃vylsjɔne/ [1] *vtr* to
convulse

**coopératif, -ive** /kɔɔpeʀatif, iv/ **1** *adj*
cooperative
**2 coopérative** *nf* cooperative

**coopération** /kɔɔpeʀasjɔ̃/ *nf*
(a) cooperation
(b) cultural/technical aid

**coopérer** /kɔɔpeʀe/ [14] *vi* to cooperate

**coordinateur, -trice** /kɔɔʀdinatœʀ,
tʀis/ **1** *adj* coordinating
**2** *nm,f* coordinator

**coordination** /kɔɔʀdinasjɔ̃/ *nf*
(a) coordination
(b) joint committee

**coordonné, ∼e** /kɔɔʀdɔne/ **1** *pp* ▶
COORDONNER
**2** *pp adj* coordinated; coordinating
**3 coordonnés** *nm pl* (in fashion)
coordinates

**coordonnées** /kɔɔʀdɔne/ *nf pl* (a) (on
graph, map) coordinates
(b) information
(c) address and telephone number

**coordonner** /kɔɔʀdɔne/ [1] *vtr* to
coordinate

**copain, copine** /kɔpɛ̃, in/ **1** *adj* pally
(GB) (colloq), chummy (colloq)
**2** *nm,f* (a) friend
(b) boyfriend/girlfriend

**copeau,** *pl* **∼x** /kɔpo/ *nm* shaving

**Copenhague** /kɔpɛnag/ *pr n* Copenhagen

**copie** /kɔpi/ *nf* (a) copying; copy
(b) (Sch) paper

**copier** /kɔpje/ [2] *vtr* (a) to copy
(b) (Sch) **∼ sur qn** to copy *or* crib from sb

**copieur, -ieuse** /kɔpjœʀ, øz/ **1** *nm,f*
(Sch) cheat
**2** *nm* photocopier

**copieusement** /kɔpjøzmɑ̃/ *adv* heartily;
lavishly; copiously

**copieux, -ieuse** /kɔpjø, øz/ *adj* ‹*meal*›
hearty; ‹*portion*› generous; ‹*notes*› copious

**copilote** /kɔpilɔt/ *nmf* co-pilot; co-driver

**copine** ▶ COPAIN

**coprésident, ∼e** /kɔpʀezidɑ̃, ɑ̃t/ *nm,f*
joint president; co-chair

**coproduction** /kɔpʀɔdyksjɔ̃/ *nf* coproduction

**copropriété** /kɔpʀɔpʀijete/ *nf* joint
ownership; co-ownership

**coq** /kɔk/ *nm* cockerel, rooster; cock; **au
chant du ∼** at cockcrow; **le ∼ du village**
(figurative) the local Casanova
∎ **∼ de bruyère** grouse
IDIOMS **être comme un ∼ en pâte** to be in
clover; **sauter du ∼ à l'âne** to hop from one
subject to another

**coque** /kɔk/ *nf* (a) (of boat) hull;
(of hydroplane) fuselage; (of car) body
(b) cockle
(c) (of nut) shell

**coquelicot** /kɔkliko/ *nm* poppy

**coqueluche** /kɔklyʃ/ *nf* (a) whooping-
cough
(b) (colloq) idol

**coquet, -ette** /kɔkɛ, ɛt/ *adj* (a) **être ∼** to
be particular about one's appearance
(b) pretty
(c) (colloq) ‹*sum*› tidy (colloq)

**coquetier** /kɔktje/ *nm* eggcup

**coquetterie** /kɔkɛtʀi/ *nf* interest in one's
appearance; vanity; **par ∼** out of vanity

**coquillage** /kɔkijaʒ/ nm **(a)** shellfish
**(b)** shell

**coquille** /kɔkij/ nf **(a)** shell
**(b)** scallop-shaped dish; ~ **de saumon**
salmon served in a shell
**(c)** misprint
**(d)** (Med) spinal jacket
■ ~ **Saint-Jacques** scallop; scallop shell

**coquillette** /kɔkijɛt/ nf small macaroni

**coquin,** ~**e** /kɔkɛ̃, in/ ⒈ adj
**(a)** mischievous
**(b)** naughty, saucy
⒉ nm,f rascal

**cor** /kɔʀ/ nm **(a)** (Mus) horn
**(b)** (Med) corn
IDIOMS **réclamer** or **demander qch à** ~ **et à cri** to clamour (GB) for sth

**corail,** pl -**aux** /kɔʀaj, o/ adj inv, nm
coral

**Coran** /kɔʀɑ̃/ pr nm **le** ~ the Koran

**corbeau,** pl ~**x** /kɔʀbo/ nm **(a)** crow;
**grand** ~ raven
**(b)** (colloq) writer of a poison-pen letter

**corbeille** /kɔʀbɛj/ nf **(a)** basket
**(b)** dress circle

**corbillard** /kɔʀbijaʀ/ nm hearse

**corde** /kɔʀd/ nf **(a)** rope
**(b)** ~ **(à sauter)** skipping rope
**(c)** (of racket, instrument) string
■ ~ **à linge** clothes line; ~ **raide** tightrope;
~**s vocales** vocal chords
IDIOMS **mériter la** ~ to deserve to be
hanged; **pleuvoir** or **tomber des** ~**s** to be
raining cats and dogs (colloq); **tirer sur la** ~
to push one's luck; **faire jouer la** ~ **sensible**
to tug at the heartstrings; **usé jusqu'à la** ~
threadbare

**cordée** /kɔʀde/ nf roped party (of
climbers)

**cordelière** /kɔʀdəljɛʀ/ nf cord

**cordial,** ~**e,** mpl -**iaux** /kɔʀdjal, o/ adj
cordial; warm-hearted; warm

**cordialement** /kɔʀdjalmɑ̃/ adv warmly;
~ **(vôtre** or **à vous)** yours sincerely

**cordialité** /kɔʀdjalite/ nf warmth;
friendliness

**cordillère** /kɔʀdijɛʀ/ nf cordillera

**cordon** /kɔʀdɔ̃/ nm **(a)** cord; string; lace
**(b)** flex (GB), cord (US)
**(c)** cordon
**(d)** row
**(e)** ribbon
■ ~ **ombilical** umbilical cord

**cordonnerie** /kɔʀdɔnʀi/ nf
**(a)** shoemaking
**(b)** shoe repairing
**(c)** cobbler's

**cordonnier** /kɔʀdɔnje/ nm cobbler
IDIOMS **les** ~**s sont toujours les plus mal
chaussés** it's always the baker's children
who have no bread

**Corée** /kɔʀe/ pr nf Korea

**coriace** /kɔʀjas/ adj tough

**coriandre** /kɔʀjɑ̃dʀ/ nf coriander

**Corinthe** /kɔʀɛ̃t/ pr n **raisins de** ~
currants

**corne** /kɔʀn/ nf **(a)** horn; antler; **à** ~**s**
horned; **blesser d'un coup de** ~ to gore
**(b)** (Mus) horn
**(c)** (colloq) **avoir de la** ~ **aux pieds** to have
calluses on one's feet
■ ~ **d'abondance** horn of plenty, cornucopia;
~ **de brume** foghorn

**cornée** /kɔʀne/ nf cornea

**corneille** /kɔʀnɛj/ nf crow

**cornemuse** /kɔʀnəmyz/ nf bagpipes

**corner** /kɔʀne/ [1] vtr to turn down the
corner of ⟨page⟩; **page cornée** dog-eared
page

**cornet** /kɔʀnɛ/ nm **(a)** (paper) cone
**(b)** (ice-cream) cone, cornet (GB)
■ ~ **à dés** dice cup; ~ **à pistons** cornet

**corniche** /kɔʀniʃ/ nf **(a)** cornice
**(b)** moulding (GB), molding (US)
**(c)** ledge (of rock)
**(d)** cliff road

**cornichon** /kɔʀniʃɔ̃/ nm gherkin

**Cornouailles** /kɔʀnuaj/ pr nf Cornwall

**corollaire** /kɔʀɔlɛʀ/ nm corollary

**corolle** /kɔʀɔl/ nf **(a)** corolla
**(b) en** ~ ⟨skirt⟩ flared

**coron** /kɔʀɔ̃/ nm miners' terraced houses

**corporatif, -ive** /kɔʀpɔʀatif, iv/ adj
corporate

**corporation** /kɔʀpɔʀasjɔ̃/ nf corporation

**corporel, -elle** /kɔʀpɔʀɛl/ adj ⟨needs⟩
bodily; ⟨punishment⟩ corporal

**corps** /kɔʀ/ nm inv body; **(combat)** ~ **à** ~
hand-to-hand combat; **se donner** ~ **et âme à**
to give oneself body and soul to; **faire** ~
**avec** ⟨person⟩ to stand solidly behind;
⟨building⟩ to be joined to; **prendre** ~ to take
shape
■ ~ **enseignant** teaching profession; ~ **et
biens** (to sink) with all hands;
~ **expéditionnaire** expeditionary force;
~ **gras** fatty substance; ~ **médical** medical
profession
IDIOMS **tenir au** ~ to be nourishing

**corpulence** /kɔʀpylɑ̃s/ nf stoutness

**corpulent,** ~**e** /kɔʀpylɑ̃, ɑ̃t/ adj stout,
corpulent

**correct,** ~**e** /kɔʀɛkt/ adj **(a)** ⟨calculation⟩
correct; ⟨copy⟩ accurate
**(b)** ⟨outfit⟩ proper; ⟨conduct⟩ correct
**(c)** (colloq) ⟨result, wine⟩ reasonable, decent
**(d)** ⟨person⟩ polite; fair, correct

**correctement** /kɔʀɛktəmɑ̃/ adv
**(a)** correctly
**(b)** properly
**(c)** decently, reasonably well

**correcteur, -trice** /kɔʀɛktœʀ, tʀis/
⒈ adj corrective
⒉ nm,f **(a)** examiner (GB), grader (US)
**(b)** proofreader

**correction** /kɔʀɛksjɔ̃/ nf **(a)** correcting;
proofreading; marking (GB), grading (US)
**(b)** correction

(c) thrashing
(d) correctness; good manners

**correctionnel, -elle**[1] /kɔʀɛksjɔnɛl/ *adj*
tribunal ∼ magistrate's court

**correctionnelle**[2] /kɔʀɛksjɔnɛl/ *nf*
magistrate's court

**corrélation** /kɔʀelasjɔ̃/ *nf* correlation; être
en ∼ avec qn to be related to sth

**correspondance** /kɔʀɛspɔ̃dɑ̃s/ *nf*
(a) letters; mail; correspondence; **faire sa** ∼
to write some letters; **vendu par** ∼ available
by mail order
(b) correspondence
(c) connection; **trains/vols en** ∼ connecting
trains/flights

**correspondant, ∼e** /kɔʀɛspɔ̃dɑ̃, ɑ̃t/
**1** *adj* corresponding
**2** *nm,f* correspondent; (Sch) pen pal

**correspondre** /kɔʀɛspɔ̃dʀ/ [6]
**1** **correspondre à** *v+prep* to correspond
to; to match; to suit ⟨*tastes*⟩
**2** *vi* to correspond, to write
**3** **se correspondre** *v refl* (+ *v être*) to
correspond

**corrida** /kɔʀida/ *nf* bullfight

**corridor** /kɔʀidɔʀ/ *nm* corridor

**corrigé** /kɔʀiʒe/ *nm* (Sch) correct version

**corriger** /kɔʀiʒe/ [13] **1** *vtr* (a) to correct;
to proofread ⟨*manuscript*⟩; to mark (GB), to
grade (US) ⟨*exam papers*⟩; to redress
⟨*situation*⟩
(b) to adjust ⟨*position*⟩; to modify ⟨*theory*⟩;
∼ **le tir** (Mil) to alter one's aim; (figurative) to
adjust one's tactics
(c) to give [sb] a hiding (colloq); to spank
⟨*child*⟩
**2** **se corriger** *v refl* (+ *v être*) (a) to
correct oneself
(b) **se** ∼ **d'un défaut** to cure oneself of a
fault

**corroborer** /kɔʀɔbɔʀe/ [1] *vtr* to
corroborate

**corroder** /kɔʀɔde/ [1] *vtr* to corrode

**corrompre** /kɔʀɔ̃pʀ/ [53] *vtr* (a) to bribe
(b) to corrupt

**corrompu, ∼e** /kɔʀɔ̃py/ **1** *pp* ▶
CORROMPRE
**2** *pp adj* corrupt

**corrosif, -ive** /kɔʀozif, iv/ *adj*
(a) ⟨*substance*⟩ corrosive
(b) ⟨*humour*⟩ caustic

**corrosion** /kɔʀozjɔ̃/ *nf* corrosion

**corruption** /kɔʀypsjɔ̃/ *nf* (a) corruption
(b) bribery

**corsage** /kɔʀsaʒ/ *nm* (a) blouse
(b) bodice

**corsaire** /kɔʀsɛʀ/ *nm* (a) corsair
(b) pedal pushers

**corse** /kɔʀs/ *adj, nm* Corsican

**corsé, ∼e** /kɔʀse/ *adj* ⟨*coffee*⟩ strong;
⟨*sauce, story*⟩ spicy; ⟨*problem*⟩ tough; ⟨*bill*⟩
steep

**Corse** /kɔʀs/ *pr nf* Corsica

**corser** /kɔʀse/ [1] **1** *vtr* (a) to make [sth]
more difficult; **pour** ∼ **l'affaire** (just) to
complicate matters
(b) to make [sth] spicier ⟨*sauce*⟩
**2** **se corser** *v refl* (+ *v être*) to get more
complicated

**corset** /kɔʀsɛ/ *nm* corset

**corso** /kɔʀso/ *nm* ∼ **fleuri** procession of
floral floats

**cortège** /kɔʀtɛʒ/ *nm* procession

**corvée** /kɔʀve/ *nf* chore; (Mil) fatigue (duty)

**cosmétique** /kɔsmetik/ *adj, nm* cosmetic

**cosmique** /kɔsmik/ *adj* cosmic

**cosmonaute** /kɔsmɔnot/ *nmf* cosmonaut

**cosmopolite** /kɔsmɔpɔlit/ *adj*
cosmopolitan

**cosse** /kɔs/ *nf* (of pea) pod; (of grain) husk

**cossu, ∼e** /kɔsy/ *adj* ⟨*person*⟩ well-to-do;
⟨*interior*⟩ plush; ⟨*house*⟩ smart

**costaud** /kɔsto/ *adj* (colloq) strong, sturdy;
hefty (colloq)

**costume** /kɔstym/ *nm* (a) suit
(b) costume; **répétition en** ∼ dress rehearsal

**costumer: se costumer** /kɔstyme/ [1]
*v refl* (+ *v être*) **se** ∼ **en** to dress up as; **soirée
costumée** fancy-dress party

**cotation** /kɔtasjɔ̃/ *nf* quotation

**cote** /kɔt/ *nf* (a) (of stocks, commodities)
quotation; (stock exchange) list
(b) (of stamp) quoted value
(c) (at races) odds
(d) (of person, film) rating; **avoir la** ∼ **auprès
de** (colloq) to be popular with; to be well
thought of by
(e) (on plan) dimension
(f) (on map) spot height
■ ∼ **d'alerte** flood level; (figurative) danger level;
∼ **de popularité** popularity rating

**coté, ∼e** /kɔte/ **1** *pp* ▶ COTER
**2** *pp adj* être ∼ to be well thought of

**côte** /kot/ **1** *nf* (a) coast
(b) hill; **dans une** ∼ on a hill
(c) rib
(d) chop; ∼ **de bœuf** rib roast
**2** **côte à côte** *phr* side by side
■ **Côte d'Azur** French riviera

**côté** /kote/ **1** *nm* (a) side; **du** ∼ **droit/
gauche** on the righthand/lefthand side;
**chambre** ∼ **rue** room overlooking the street;
**par certains** ∼s in some respects; ∼ **santé**
healthwise; **de mon** ∼, **je pense que...** for
my part, I think that...; **d'un** ∼... **d'un autre**
∼... on the one hand... on the other hand...
(b) way, direction; **de tous** ∼s ⟨*come*⟩ from
all directions; ⟨*run*⟩ all over the place; **du** ∼
**de Nice** ⟨*live*⟩ near Nice; **aller du** ∼ **de Dijon**
to head for Dijon
**2** **à côté** *phr* (a) nearby; **les gens d'à** ∼
the people next door; **à** ∼ **de** next to; **le
ballon est passé à** ∼ **(du but)** the ball went
wide (of the goal); **répondre à** ∼ (by mistake)
to miss the point; (on purpose) to sidestep the
question
(b) by comparison

**(c)** on the side; **elle est étudiante et travaille à ∼** she's a student and works on the side

**③ de côté** *phr* **(a)** sideways
**(b)** aside; **mettre qch de ∼** to put sth aside ⟨*money, object*⟩

**④ aux côtés de** *phr* aux ∼s de qn ⟨*to be*⟩ at sb's side; ⟨*to work*⟩ alongside sb

**coteau**, *pl* ∼**x** /kɔto/ *nm* **(a)** hillside
**(b)** hill
**(c)** (sloping) vineyard

**côtelette** /kotlɛt/ *nf* (Culin) chop

**coter** /kɔte/ [1] *vtr* **(a)** to quote, to list ⟨*shares*⟩; to price ⟨*car*⟩
**(b)** to rate ⟨*film*⟩

**côtier, -ière** /kotje, ɛR/ *adj* coastal; inshore

**cotisation** /kɔtizasjɔ̃/ *nf* **(a)** contribution
**(b)** subscription

**cotiser** /kɔtize/ [1] **①** *vi* **(a)** to pay one's contributions
**(b)** to pay one's subscription (à to)
**② se cotiser** *v refl* (+ *v être*) to club together (GB), to go in together

**coton** /kɔtɔ̃/ *nm* **(a)** cotton
**(b)** thread
**(c)** cotton wool (GB), cotton (US)
IDIOMS **filer un mauvais ∼** to be in a bad way; **élever un enfant dans du ∼** to give a child a very sheltered upbringing; **j'ai les jambes en ∼** (after shock) my legs have turned to jelly

**cotonnade** /kɔtɔnad/ *nf* cotton fabric

**cotonneux, -euse** /kɔtɔnø, øz/ *adj* ⟨*fog*⟩ like cotton-wool; ⟨*cloud*⟩ fleecy

**côtoyer** /kotwaje/ [23] **①** *vtr* to walk alongside ⟨*river*⟩; to move in ⟨*milieu*⟩; to mix with ⟨*people*⟩; to be in close contact with ⟨*death*⟩
**② se côtoyer** *v refl* (+ *v être*) ⟨*people*⟩ to mix

**cotte** /kɔt/ *nf* overalls
■ ∼ **de mailles** coat of mail

**cou** /ku/ *nm* neck; **être endetté jusqu'au ∼** to be up to one's eyes in debt

**couchage** /kuʃaʒ/ *nm* bedding; **un studio avec ∼ pour six** a studio that sleeps six

**couchant** /kuʃɑ̃/ **①** *adj* **au soleil ∼** at sunset
**② nm (a)** sunset
**(b)** west

**couche** /kuʃ/ *nf* **(a)** layer; (of paint) coat
**(b)** nappy (GB), diaper (US)
**(c)** class, sector

**couché, ∼e** /kuʃe/ **①** *pp* ▶ COUCHER
**② pp adj** ⟨*grass*⟩ flattened; ⟨*writing*⟩ sloping

**couche-culotte**, *pl* **couches-culottes** /kuʃkylɔt/ *nf* disposable nappy (GB) *or* diaper (US)

**coucher** /kuʃe/ [1] **①** *nm* bedtime
**② vtr (a)** to put [sb] to bed; to lay out ⟨*wounded person*⟩
**(b)** to lay [sth] on its side; to lay [sth] down
**(c)** to flatten ⟨*grass*⟩
**③ vi** to sleep; **∼ sous les ponts** to sleep rough (GB) *or* outdoors

**④ se coucher** *v refl* (+ *v être*) **(a)** to lie (down)
**(b)** to go to bed
**(c)** ⟨*stem*⟩ to bend; ⟨*boat*⟩ to list; **se ∼ sur** ⟨*cyclist*⟩ to lean forward over ⟨*handlebars*⟩
**(d)** ⟨*sun*⟩ to set
■ ∼ **de soleil** sunset

**couchette** /kuʃɛt/ *nf* couchette, berth

**couci-couça** /kusikusa/ *adv* (colloq) so-so (colloq)

**coucou** /kuku/ **①** *nm* **(a)** cuckoo
**(b)** cowslip
**(c)** (colloq) (old) crate (colloq), plane
**(d)** cuckoo clock
**② excl** (colloq) **(a)** cooee!
**(b)** peekaboo!

**coude** /kud/ *nm* **(a)** elbow; **travailler ∼ à ∼** to work shoulder to shoulder
**(b)** (in river, pipe) bend
IDIOMS **se serrer les ∼s** to stick together

**coudé, ∼e**[1] /kude/ *adj* bent at an angle

**coudée**[2] /kude/ *nf* **avoir les ∼s franches** to have elbow room

**cou-de-pied**, *pl* **cous-de-pied** /kudpje/ *nm* instep

**couder** /kude/ [1] *vtr* to bend

**coudre** /kudR/ [76] *vtr* to sew; to sew [sth] on; to stitch [sth] on; to stitch (up)
IDIOMS **leur histoire est cousue de fil blanc** you can see right through their story

**couenne** /kwan/ *nf* (bacon) rind

**couette** /kwɛt/ *nf* duvet

**couffin** /kufɛ̃/ *nm* Moses basket (GB), bassinet (US)

**couiner** /kwine/ [1] *vi* to squeak, to squeal

**coulant, ∼e** /kulɑ̃, ɑ̃t/ *adj* ⟨*camembert*⟩ runny; ⟨*person*⟩ easy-going

**coulée** /kule/ *nf* (of lava) flow; (of paint) drip

**couler** /kule/ [1] **①** *vtr* **(a)** to cast ⟨*metal, statue*⟩; to pour ⟨*concrete*⟩
**(b)** to sink ⟨*ship*⟩
**(c)** (colloq) to put [sth] out of business; to bring [sb] down
**② vi (a)** ⟨*blood*⟩ to flow; ⟨*paint, cheese*⟩ to run; **faire ∼ qch** to run ⟨*bath*⟩
**(b)** ⟨*tap, pen*⟩ to leak; ⟨*nose*⟩ to run
**(c)** ⟨*boat*⟩ to sink; ⟨*company*⟩ to go under
**③ se couler** *v refl* (+ *v être*) **se ∼ dans/entre** to slip into/between

**couleur** /kulœR/ *nf* **(a)** colour (GB); **de ∼** ⟨*person*⟩ coloured (GB); **sans ∼** colourless (GB); **plein de ∼** colourful (GB)
**(b)** paint
**(c)** **les ∼s** (washing) coloureds (GB); (flag) the colours (GB)
**(d)** (in cards) suit
**(e)** **sous ∼ de faire** while pretending to do
IDIOMS **ne pas voir la ∼ de qch** (colloq) never to get a sniff of sth (colloq); **il m'en a fait voir de toutes les ∼s** (colloq) he put me through the mill

**couleuvre** /kulœvR/ *nf* grass snake
IDIOMS **avaler des ∼s** (colloq) to believe anything one is told

**coulissant**, ~**e** /kulisɑ̃, ɑ̃t/ *adj* sliding

**coulisse** /kulis/ *nf* (a) **les** ~**s, la** ~ the wings; **en** ~ backstage; (figurative) behind the scenes
(b) runner

**coulisser** /kulise/ [1] *vi* to slide

**couloir** /kulwaʀ/ *nm* (a) corridor (GB), hallway; passage; **bruits de** ~**s** rumours (GB)
(b) lane; ~ **aérien** air (traffic) lane

**coup** /ku/ *nm* (a) knock; blow; ~ **à la porte** knock at the door; **à** ~**s de bâton** with a stick; **donner un** ~ **de qch à qn** to hit sb with sth; **donner un** ~ **de poing à qn** to punch sb; **porter un** ~ **(sévère) à** (figurative) to deal [sb/sth] a (severe) blow; **sa fierté en a pris un** ~ it was a blow to his/her pride; **sous le** ~ **de la colère** in (a fit of) anger; **être sous le** ~ **d'une forte émotion** to be in a highly emotional state
(b) (noise) knock; bang; thump, thud; **au douzième** ~ **de minuit** on the last stroke of midnight; **sur le** ~ **de dix heures** (colloq) around ten; ~ **de sifflet** whistle blast
(c) **un (petit)** ~ **de chiffon** a (quick) wipe; **un** ~ **de peinture** a lick of paint
(d) (in tennis, golf, cricket) stroke; shot; (in chess) move; (with dice) throw; (in boxing) punch; **tous les** ~**s sont permis** no holds barred
(e) ~ **de feu/fusil** (gun)shot/(rifle) shot
(f) (colloq) job (colloq), racket (colloq); trick (colloq); **monter un** ~ to plan a job (colloq); **il a raté son** ~ (colloq) he blew it (colloq); **être dans le** ~ to be in on it; to be up to date; **qui a fait le** ~? who did it?
(g) time; **du premier** ~ first time; **à tous les** ~**s** every time; **ce** ~-**ci** this time; **du** ~ (colloq) as a result; **après** ~ afterward(s); ~ **sur** ~ in succession; **tout d'un** ~, **tout à** ~ suddenly, all of a sudden; **d'un** ~, **d'un seul** ~ just like that; **en un seul** ~ in one go (colloq); **sur le** ~ at the time; instantly, on the spot; **pleurer un bon** ~ to have a good cry
(h) **à** ~**s de subventions** by means of subsidies
(i) (colloq) drink
■ ~ **bas** blow below the belt; ~**s et blessures** assault and battery; ~ **dur** blow; ~ **franc** free kick; ~ **monté** put-up job

■ **Note** For translations of expressions such as *coup d'envoi, coup de fil* etc., look up the entries at *envoi, fil* etc.

**IDIOMS tenir le** ~ ⟨shoes⟩ to last out; ⟨repair⟩ to hold; ⟨person⟩ to hold on; **être aux cent** ~**s** (colloq) to be worried sick (colloq); **faire les quatre cents** ~**s** (colloq) to be a real tearaway; **attraper le** ~ **pour faire** (colloq) to get the knack of doing

**coupable** /kupabl/ [1] *adj* guilty; ⟨negligence⟩ culpable; ⟨indifference⟩ shameful
[2] *nmf* culprit

**coupant**, ~**e** /kupɑ̃, ɑ̃t/ *adj* sharp

**coup-de-poing**, *pl* **coups-de-poing** /kudpwɛ̃/ *nm* ~ **américain** knuckle-duster (GB), brass knuckles (US)

**coupe** /kup/ *nf* (a) cutting; cutting out; cut
(b) haircut
(c) (Sport) cup; **la** ~ **du Monde** the World Cup
(d) (fruit) bowl; (champagne) glass
(e) section; ~ **transversale** cross section
■ ~ **en brosse** crew cut
**IDIOMS la** ~ **est pleine** enough is enough; **être sous la** ~ **de qn** to be under sb's control

**coupe-feu** /kupfø/ *nm inv* firebreak

**coupe-gorge** /kupgɔʀʒ/ *nm inv* rough place; rough area

**coupe-papier** /kuppapje/ *nm inv* paper knife

**couper** /kupe/ [1] [1] *vtr* (a) to cut; to cut down; to chop; to cut out; to cut off; ~ **qch en tranches** to slice sth
(b) ⟨road⟩ to cut across; ~ **la route à qn** to cut in on sb
(c) to cut off ⟨road, supplies⟩; to spoil ⟨appetite⟩; to take the edge off ⟨hunger⟩; to turn off ⟨water⟩; ~ **le souffle à qn** to take sb's breath away; ~ **la parole à qn** to interrupt sb
(d) ~ **qn de qn/qch** to cut sb off from sb/sth
(e) to dilute ⟨wine⟩
(f) (in cards) to cut ⟨pack⟩; to trump ⟨card⟩
[2] *vi* **attention ça coupe!** be careful, it's sharp; ~ **à travers champs** to cut across country
[3] **se couper** *v refl* (+ *v être*) to cut oneself
**IDIOMS c'est ton tour de faire à manger, tu n'y couperas pas** it's your turn to cook, you won't get out of it

**couperet** /kupʀɛ/ *nm* cleaver; (of guillotine) blade; **la nouvelle est tombée comme un** ~ the news came as a bolt from the blue

**couperose** /kupʀoz/ *nf* broken veins

**coupe-vent** /kupvɑ̃/ *nm inv*
(a) windcheater (GB), windbreaker (US)
(b) windbreak

**couple** /kupl/ *nm* (a) couple; pair
(b) relationship

**couplet** /kuplɛ/ *nm* (a) verse
(b) couplet

**coupole** /kupɔl/ *nf* cupola, dome

**coupon** /kupɔ̃/ *nm* (a) remnant
(b) ticket voucher
(c) multiuse ticket (*in travel pass*)

**coupon-réponse**, *pl* **coupons-réponses** /kupɔ̃ʀepɔ̃s/ *nm* reply coupon

**coupure** /kupyʀ/ *nf* (a) cut; ~ **d'électricité** *or* **de courant** power cut
(b) break
(c) gap
(d) (bank)note (GB), bill (US)
■ ~ **de journal** *or* **de presse** (newspaper) cutting

**cour** /kuʀ/ *nf* (a) courtyard; (school) playground; (farm) yard
(b) (of sovereign) court; (of celebrity) entourage
(c) courtship
(d) (Law) court
■ ~ **d'arrivée** arrivals area; ~ **de départ** departures area; ~ **martiale** court-martial; ~ **de récréation** playground

**courage** /kuraʒ/ *nm* (a) courage, bravery; **avoir du ~** to be brave
(b) energy; **je n'ai même pas le ~ de me doucher** I don't even have the energy to have a shower; **bon ~!** good luck!; **perdre ~** to lose heart; **je n'ai pas eu le ~ de dire non** I didn't have the heart to say no

**courageusement** /kuraʒøzmɑ̃/ *adv* courageously, bravely

**courageux, -euse** /kuraʒø, øz/ *adj* courageous, brave

**couramment** /kuramɑ̃/ *adv* (a) fluently
(b) ⟨*used*⟩ widely; **cela se fait ~** it's very common

**courant¹** /kurɑ̃/ *prep* **~ janvier** (some time) in January

**courant², ~e** /kurɑ̃, ɑ̃t/ **1** *adj* (a) ⟨*word, practice, mistake*⟩ common
(b) ⟨*language*⟩ everyday; ⟨*procedure*⟩ usual, ordinary; ⟨*size*⟩ standard
(c) ⟨*month, price*⟩ current; **le 15 du mois ~** the 15th of this month
**2** *nm* (a) current; **il n'y a plus de ~** the power has gone off
(b) trend; **un ~ politique** a political trend
(c) **dans le ~ de** in the course of
**3** **au courant** *phr* **être au ~ de** to know about ⟨*news*⟩; to be up to date on ⟨*technique*⟩; **mettre qn au ~** to put sb in the picture; **tenir qn au ~** to keep sb posted
■ **~ d'air** draught (GB), draft (US)

**courbatu, ~e** /kurbaty/ *adj* stiff

**courbature** /kurbatyr/ *nf* ache; **avoir des ~s** to be stiff

**courbaturé, ~e** /kurbatyre/ *adj* stiff; aching

**courbe** /kurb/ **1** *adj* curved
**2** *nf* (a) curve
(b) bend
■ **~ de température** temperature chart

**courber** /kurbe/ [1] *vtr* to bend; **~ le dos** (figurative) to bow down

**courbette** /kurbɛt/ *nf* (low) bow; **faire des ~s** (figurative) to bow and scrape

**courbure** /kurbyr/ *nf* curve

**coureur, -euse** /kurœr, øz/ *nm,f* runner; **~ automobile** racing driver; **~ de jupons** philanderer

**courge** /kurʒ/ *nf* gourd; (vegetable) marrow

**courgette** /kurʒɛt/ *nf* courgette (GB), zucchini (US)

**courir** /kurir/ [26] **1** *vtr* (a) to compete in ⟨*trials*⟩
(b) **~ le monde** to roam the world
(c) **~ les cocktails** to do the round of the cocktail parties; **~ les boutiques** to go round the shops (GB) *or* stores (US)
(d) **~ un (grand) danger** to be in (great) danger; **~ un (gros) risque** to run a (big) risk; **faire ~ un risque à qn** to put sb at risk
(e) (colloq) **~ les filles** to chase after girls
**2** *vi* (a) to run; to race; **~ après qn/qch** to run after sb/sth; to chase after sb/sth; **les**

**voleurs courent toujours** the thieves are still at large; **~ à la catastrophe** to be heading for disaster
(b) ⟨*rumour*⟩ to go around
IDIOMS **tu peux toujours ~!** (colloq) you can go whistle for it! (colloq); **laisser ~** (colloq) to let things ride

**couronne** /kurɔn/ *nf* (a) crown
(b) **~ de fleurs** garland; wreath
(c) ring-shaped loaf
(d) (in Paris) **la petite/grande ~** the inner/outer suburbs

**couronnement** /kurɔnmɑ̃/ *nm* coronation

**couronner** /kurɔne/ [1] *vtr* to crown

**courre** /kur/ *vtr* **chasse à ~** hunting

**courriel** /kurjɛl/ *nm* e-mail

**courrier** /kurje/ *nm* (a) mail, post (GB); **faire son ~** to write letters
(b) **~ des lecteurs** letters to the editor; **~ du cœur** problem page; **~ électronique** electronic mail

**courroie** /kurwa/ *nf* (a) strap
(b) (on machine) belt

**cours** /kur/ *nm inv* (a) lesson, class; **avoir ~** to have a class; **faire ~** to teach
(b) course book, textbook
(c) school; **~ de théâtre** drama school
(d) price; exchange rate
(e) (of river) course
(f) (of tale, events) course; (of ideas) flow; **la vie reprend son ~** life returns to normal; **donner libre ~ à** to give free rein to ⟨*imagination*⟩; **au** *or* **dans le ~ de** in the course of, during; **en ~** ⟨*month*⟩ current; ⟨*project*⟩ under way; ⟨*work*⟩ in progress; **en ~ de journée** in the course of the day
■ **~ d'eau** watercourse; **~ élémentaire première année, CE1** second year of primary school, age 7–8; **~ moyen première année, CM1** fourth year of primary school, age 9–10; **~ particulier(s)** private tuition (GB), private tutoring (US); **~ préparatoire, CP** first year of primary school, age 6–7

**course** /kurs/ *nf* (a) running; run; racing; race; **faire la ~ avec qn** to race sb; **c'est la course tous les matins pour me préparer** I'm always in a rush in the morning to get ready
(b) (in taxi) journey; **c'est 10 euros la ~** the fare is 10 euros
(c) **faire une ~** to run an errand; **faire les ~s** to do the shopping
(d) (of star, planet) path; (of clouds) passage
■ **~ de haies** (in athletics) hurdles; (for horses) steeplechase; **~ d'obstacles** obstacle race; (figurative) obstacle course; **~ de vitesse** (in athletics) sprint; (on motorbikes) speedway race
IDIOMS **ne plus être dans la ~** to be out of touch; **être à bout de ~** to be worn out

**coursier, -ière** /kursje, ɛr/ *nm,f* messenger

**court**, ~**e** /kuʀ, kuʀt/ **1** *adj* (a) short; de ~**e durée** short-lived; short-term; **avoir le souffle** ~ to get out of breath easily
(b) ⟨*defeat, victory, majority*⟩ narrow
**2** *adv* **couper** ~ **à qch** to put paid to sth; **s'arrêter** ~ to stop short
**3** *nm* ~ **de tennis** tennis court
■ ~ **métrage** short (film); ~**e échelle: faire la** ~**e échelle à qn** to give sb a leg up (colloq)
IDIOMS **être à** ~ **de** to be short of ⟨*money*⟩; **prendre qn de** ~ to catch sb unprepared

**court-circuit**, *pl* ~**s** /kuʀsiʀkɥi/ *nm* shortcircuit

**courtier**, **-ière** /kuʀtje, ɛʀ/ *nm,f* broker

**courtiser** /kuʀtize/ [1] *vtr* to woo

**courtois**, ~**e** /kuʀtwa, az/ *adj* ⟨*person, tone*⟩ courteous; ⟨*genre, tradition*⟩ courtly

**courtoisie** /kuʀtwazi/ *nf* courtesy

**couru**, ~**e** /kuʀy/ **1** *pp* ▶ COURIR
**2** *pp adj* ⟨*place*⟩ popular
IDIOMS **c'est** ~ **d'avance** (colloq) it's a foregone conclusion

**cousin**, ~**e** /kuzɛ̃, in/ *nm,f* cousin

**coussin** /kusɛ̃/ *nm* cushion

**cousu**, ~**e** /kuzy/ ▶ COUDRE

**coût** /ku/ *nm* cost; ~ **de la vie** cost of living

**coûtant** /kutã/ *adj m* **prix** ~ cost price

**couteau**, *pl* ~**x** /kuto/ *nm* (a) knife; **donner un coup de** ~ **à qn** to stab sb
(b) razor shell (GB) *or* clam (US)
(c) knife edge
IDIOMS **être à** ~**x tirés avec qn** to be at daggers drawn with sb; **avoir le** ~ **sous la gorge** to have a pistol to one's head

**coûter** /kute/ [1] **1** *vtr* to cost
**2** *vi* to cost; ~ **cher** to be expensive; **ça m'a coûté de m'excuser** it was hard for me to apologize
**3** *v impers* **il t'en coûtera d'avoir fait cela** you will pay for doing this; **coûte que coûte, quoi qu'il en coûte** at all costs
IDIOMS ~ **les yeux de la tête** to cost an arm and a leg (colloq)

**coûteux**, **-euse** /kutø, øz/ *adj* costly

**coutume** /kutym/ *nf* custom; **avoir** ~ **de faire** to be in the habit of doing
IDIOMS **une fois n'est pas** ~ it does no harm just this once

**coutumier**, **-ière** /kutymje, ɛʀ/ *adj* customary

**couture** /kutyʀ/ *nf* (a) sewing; dressmaking; **faire de la** ~ to sew
(b) seam
IDIOMS **sous toutes les** ~**s** from every angle; **battre qn à plates** ~**s** to beat sb hollow

**couturier** /kutyʀje/ *nm* dress designer

**couturière** /kutyʀjɛʀ/ *nf* dressmaker

**couvent** /kuvã/ *nm* convent

**couver** /kuve/ [1] **1** *vtr* (a) to sit on ⟨*eggs*⟩; **la poule couve** the hen is brooding
(b) to overprotect; ~ **qn/qch du regard** to look fondly at sb/sth; to gaze longingly at sb/sth
(c) to be coming down with ⟨*illness*⟩

**2** *vi* ⟨*rebellion*⟩ to brew; ⟨*fire, anger*⟩ to smoulder (GB), to smolder (US)

**couvercle** /kuvɛʀkl/ *nm* (a) lid
(b) screwtop

**couvert**, ~**e** /kuvɛʀ, ɛʀt/ **1** *pp* ▶ COUVRIR
**2** *pp adj* (a) covered (de in, with); **être** ~ **de diplômes** to have a lot of qualifications
(b) ⟨*pool*⟩ indoor; ⟨*market*⟩ covered
(c) ⟨*sky*⟩ overcast
**3** *nm* (a) place setting; **mettre le** ~ to lay the table; **un** ~ **en argent** a silver knife, fork and spoon
(b) cover charge
**4 à couvert** *phr* **se mettre à** ~ to take cover
**5 sous le couvert de** *phr* under the pretence (GB) of; **sous** ~ **de la plaisanterie** under the guise of a joke

**couverture** /kuvɛʀtyʀ/ *nf* (a) blanket; (small) rug (GB), lap robe (US)
(b) (of book, magazine) cover
(c) (media) coverage
IDIOMS **tirer la** ~ **à soi** to turn a situation to one's advantage

**couveuse** /kuvøz/ *nf* incubator

**couvre-feu**, *pl* ~**x** /kuvʀəfø/ *nm* curfew

**couvre-lit**, *pl* ~**s** /kuvʀəli/ *nm* bedspread

**couvreur** /kuvʀœʀ/ *nm* roofer

**couvrir** /kuvʀiʀ/ [32] **1** *vtr* (a) to cover ⟨*furniture, wall, fire, card*⟩; to roof ⟨*house*⟩; ~ **qn de qch** (with blows, jewels, compliments) to shower sb with sth
(b) ⟨*sound*⟩ to drown out
(c) ⟨*transmitter, inspector*⟩ to cover ⟨*region*⟩
(d) to wrap [sb] up; to cover [sb] up
(e) to cover up for ⟨*mistake, person*⟩
(f) (with gun) to cover ⟨*soldier*⟩
(g) to cover ⟨*distance*⟩
(h) ⟨*book, journalist*⟩ to cover ⟨*story, event*⟩
(i) ⟨*sum*⟩ to cover ⟨*expenses*⟩
**2 se couvrir** *v refl* (+ *v être*) (a) to wrap up; to put on a hat
(b) ⟨*sky*⟩ to become overcast
(c) **se** ~ **de** to become covered with
(d) (against accusations) to cover oneself

**CP** /sepe/ *nm*: *abbr* ▶ COURS

**crabe** /kʀab/ *nm* crab

**crachat** /kʀaʃa/ *nm* spit

**crachement** /kʀaʃmã/ *nm* (a) spitting
(b) crackling

**cracher** /kʀaʃe/ [1] **1** *vtr* (a) to spit out; **c'est le portrait de sa mère tout craché** (colloq) she's the spitting image of her mother
(b) to belch (out) ⟨*flames, smoke*⟩
**2** *vi* to spit; **je ne cracherais pas dessus** (colloq) I wouldn't turn up my nose at it

**cracheur** /kʀaʃœʀ/ *nm* ~ **de feu** fire-eater

**crachin** /kʀaʃɛ̃/ *nm* drizzle

**crachoir** /kʀaʃwaʀ/ *nm* spittoon

**crachoter** /kʀaʃɔte/ [1] *vi* (a) to cough and splutter
(b) to crackle

**crack** /kʀak/ *nm* (a) (genius) ace
(b) (colloq) (drug) crack (colloq)

**craie** /kRɛ/ nf chalk

**craindre** /kRɛ̃dR/ [54] vtr (a) to fear, to be afraid of
(b) to be sensitive to ‹cold›; to dislike ‹sun›

**craint**, **~e¹** /kRɛ̃, ɛ̃t/ ▶ CRAINDRE

**crainte²** /kRɛ̃t/ nf fear; **avoir des ~s au sujet de qn** to be worried about sb; **n'ayez ~, soyez sans ~** have no fear

**craintif**, **-ive** /kRɛ̃tif, iv/ adj timorous, timid

**cramoisi**, **~e** /kRamwazi/ adj crimson

**crampe** /kRɑ̃p/ nf cramp

**crampon** /kRɑ̃pɔ̃/ nm crampon; **chaussures à ~s** (for football) boots with studs (GB) or cleats (US); (for running) spiked shoes

**cramponner: se cramponner** /kRɑ̃pɔne/ [1] v refl (+ v être) to hold on tightly

**cran** /kRɑ̃/ ⟦1⟧ nm (a) notch; (in belt) hole; **monter d'un ~** to move up a notch
(b) nick
(c) (colloq) **avoir du ~** to have guts (colloq)
(d) (in hair) wave
⟦2⟧ **à cran** phr **être à ~** to be on edge
■ **~ d'arrêt** flick knife (GB), switchblade (US); **~ de sûreté** safety catch

**crâne** /kRɑn/ nm (a) skull
(b) (colloq) head; **ne rien avoir dans le ~** to have no brains; **bourrer le ~ à qn** (colloq) to brainwash sb

**crânement** /kRɑnmɑ̃/ adv gallantly; proudly

**crânien**, **-ienne** /kRanjɛ̃, ɛn/ adj cranial; **boîte crânienne** cranium

**crapaud** /kRapo/ nm toad

**crapule** /kRapyl/ nf crook

**crapuleux**, **-euse** /kRapylø, øz/ adj villainous

**craqueler: se craqueler** /kRakle/ [19] v refl (+ v être) to crack

**craquement** /kRakmɑ̃/ nm (a) creaking sound, creak
(b) cracking sound, crack

**craquer** /kRake/ [1] ⟦1⟧ vtr (a) to split ‹trousers›
(b) to strike ‹match›
⟦2⟧ vi (a) ‹seam› to split; ‹branch› to crack
(b) ‹floor› to creak
(c) (colloq) ‹person› to crack up (colloq)

**crasse** /kRas/ nf grime, filth

**crasseux**, **-euse** /kRasø, øz/ adj filthy, grimy

**cratère** /kRatɛR/ nm crater

**cravache** /kRavaʃ/ nf whip

**cravate** /kRavat/ nf tie

**crawl** /kRol/ nm crawl

**crayon** /kRɛjɔ̃/ nm pencil; **~ noir** lead pencil; **~ optique** light pen

**créance** /kReɑ̃s/ nf (a) debt (owed by a debtor)
(b) letter of credit

**créancier**, **-ière** /kReɑ̃sje, ɛR/ nm,f creditor

**créateur**, **-trice** /kReatœR, tRis/ nm,f creator; designer

**créatif**, **-ive** /kReatif, iv/ adj creative

**création** /kReasjɔ̃/ nf (a) creation; **la ~ d'une entreprise** the setting up of a company; **la ~ d'un produit nouveau** the development of a new product; **tous les livres de la ~** all the books in the world
(b) (work of art) creation; (play) first production; (commercial) new product

**créativité** /kReativite/ nf creativity

**créature** /kReatyR/ nf creature

**crèche** /kRɛʃ/ nf (a) crèche (GB), day-nursery
(b) (at Christmas) crib (GB), crèche (US)

**crédibilité** /kRedibilite/ nf credibility

**crédible** /kRedibl/ adj credible

**crédit** /kRedi/ nm (a) funds; **les ~s de la recherche** research funding
(b) credit; **accorder un ~** to grant credit terms; **faire ~ à qn** to give sb credit; **porter une somme au ~ d'un compte** to credit sb's account with a sum of money; **mettre or porter qch au ~ de qn** (figurative) to give sb credit for sth

**créditer** /kRedite/ [1] vtr to credit

**créditeur**, **-trice** /kReditœR, tRis/ adj **être ~** to be in credit

**credo** /kRedo/ nm creed

**crédule** /kRedyl/ adj gullible, credulous

**créer** /kRee/ [11] ⟦1⟧ vtr (gen) to create; to develop ‹new product›; to set up ‹company›
⟦2⟧ **se créer** v refl (+ v être) **se ~ des problèmes** to bring trouble on oneself

**crémaillère** /kRemajɛR/ nf **pendre la ~** to have a house-warming (party)

**crémation** /kRemasjɔ̃/ nf cremation

**crématoire** /kRematwaR/ nm crematorium

**crème¹** /kRɛm/ adj inv cream

**crème²** /kRɛm/ nf (a) cream
(b) cream dessert
(c) (colloq) **la ~ des linguistes** the very best linguists
■ **~ Chantilly** whipped cream; **~ glacée** dairy ice cream; **~ de marrons** chestnut spread; **~ renversée** caramel custard

**crémerie** /kRɛmRi/ nf cheese shop (GB) or store (US)

**crémeux**, **-euse** /kRemø, øz/ adj creamy

**créneau**, pl **~x** /kReno/ nm (a) parallel parking
(b) (Econ) market
(c) gap, niche
(d) crenel; **les ~x** crenellations
■ **~ horaire** time slot; **~ publicitaire** advertising slot

**créole** /kReɔl/ adj, nm Creole

**crêpe¹** /kRɛp/ nm (a) crepe
(b) black veil

**crêpe²** /kRɛp/ nf pancake, crêpe

**crêper** /kRepe/ [1] vtr to backcomb (GB), to tease ‹hair›

**crépi** /kʀepi/ *nm* rendering

**crépitement** /kʀepitmɑ̃/ *nm* crackling, crackle; sizzling

**crépiter** /kʀepite/ [1] *vi* ⟨fire⟩ to crackle; ⟨oil⟩ to sizzle; ⟨rain⟩ to patter

**crépon** /kʀepɔ̃/ *nm* crepe paper

**crépu, ~e** /kʀepy/ *adj* frizzy

**crépuscule** /kʀepyskyl/ *nm* twilight, dusk

**crescendo** /kʀeʃɛndo/ **1** *adv* aller ~ ⟨noise⟩ to intensify
**2** *nm* crescendo

**cresson** /kʀesɔ̃, kʀəsɔ̃/ *nm* watercress

**crête** /kʀɛt/ *nf* (a) (of cock) comb; (of bird) crest
(b) (of mountain, wave) crest; (of roof) ridge

**crétin, ~e** /kʀetɛ̃, in/ *nm,f* moron (colloq)

**creuser** /kʀøze/ [1] **1** *vtr* (a) to dig a hole in ⟨ground⟩; to drill a hole in ⟨tooth⟩; to dig into ⟨rock⟩
(b) to dig ⟨hole, canal, grave⟩; to sink ⟨well⟩
(c) ⟨wrinkles⟩ to furrow ⟨face⟩; ~ les reins to arch one's back
(d) to deepen, to increase ⟨deficit, inequalities⟩
(e) to go into [sth] in depth ⟨question, subject⟩
**2** se creuser *v refl* (+ *v être*) ⟨cheeks⟩ to become hollow; ⟨gap⟩ to widen
IDIOMS ça creuse (colloq) it really gives you an appetite; se ~ (la tête *or* la cervelle) (colloq) to rack one's brains

**creux, -euse** /kʀø, øz/ **1** *adj* (a) ⟨trunk, tooth, sound, cheeks⟩ hollow; ⟨stomach, speech⟩ empty; ⟨analysis⟩ shallow; un plat ~ a shallow dish; assiette creuse soup dish
(b) ⟨day, period⟩ slack, off-peak
**2** *adv* sonner ~ to make a hollow sound
**3** *nm* (a) hollow; le ~ des reins the small of the back; le ~ de l'aisselle the armpit; le ~ de la vague the trough of the wave; être au ~ de la vague (figurative) to be at rock bottom
(b) (colloq) avoir un petit ~ to have the munchies (colloq)

**crevaison** /kʀəvɛzɔ̃/ *nf* puncture

**crevasse** /kʀəvas/ *nf* (a) crevasse
(b) crack, fissure
(c) chapped skin

**crève** /kʀɛv/ *nf* (colloq) chill; attraper la ~ to catch a chill *or* one's death (of cold)

**crever** /kʀəve/ [16] **1** *vtr* to puncture, to burst; ~ les yeux de qn to blind sb; to poke sb's eyes out; ça crève les yeux it's blindingly obvious; ça crève le cœur it's heartbreaking
**2** *vi* (a) to burst; to burst open
(b) to die; ~ de faim to be starving
(c) ~ d'envie to be eaten up with envy; ~ d'orgueil to be terribly full of oneself
**3** se crever *v refl* (+ *v être*) il s'est crevé un œil he put his eye out
IDIOMS marche ou crève sink or swim

**crevette** /kʀəvɛt/ *nf* ~ grise shrimp; ~ rose prawn

**cri** /kʀi/ *nm* (a) cry; shout; scream; un ~ aigu a shriek; à grands ~s loudly; pousser les hauts ~s to protest loudly
(b) (of bird) call

**criant, ~e** /kʀijɑ̃, ɑ̃t/ *adj* clear, striking

**criard, ~e** /kʀiaʀ, aʀd/ *adj* ⟨voice⟩ shrill; ⟨colour⟩ garish

**crible** /kʀibl/ *nm* (for minerals) screen; (for sand) riddle; passer au ~ (figurative) to sift through

**cribler** /kʀible/ [1] *vtr* (a) ~ qn/qch de balles to riddle sb/sth with bullets
(b) ~ qn de reproches to heap reproaches on sb

**cric** /kʀik/ *nm* (for car) jack

**criée** /kʀije/ *nf* (vente à la) ~ auction

**crier** /kʀije/ [2] **1** *vtr* (a) to shout
(b) to proclaim; to protest ⟨innocence⟩
**2** crier à *v+prep* on a crié au scandale quand... there was an outcry when...
**3** *vi* (a) to shout; to cry; to scream
(b) ⟨animal⟩ to give a cry; ⟨monkey⟩ to chatter; ⟨gull⟩ to cry; ⟨pig⟩ to squeal

**crieur, -ieuse** /kʀijœʀ, øz/ *nm,f* ~ de journaux news vendor

**crime** /kʀim/ *nm* (a) crime
(b) murder; ~ crapuleux murder for money

**criminalité** /kʀiminalite/ *nf* crime

**criminel, -elle** /kʀiminɛl/ **1** *adj* criminal
**2** *nm,f* (a) criminal
(b) murderer

**crin** /kʀɛ̃/ *nm* horsehair; à tout ~ (figurative) dyed-in-the-wool

**crinière** /kʀinjɛʀ/ *nf* mane

**crique** /kʀik/ *nf* cove

**criquet** /kʀikɛ/ *nm* locust

**crise** /kʀiz/ *nf* (a) crisis; ~ agricole crisis in the agricultural industry; la ~ the economic crisis, the slump
(b) shortage; ~ de l'emploi job shortage
(c) (Med) attack; ~ d'appendicite appendicitis; ~ de toux coughing fit
(d) fit; ~ de colère fit of rage; faire une ~ to have a tantrum; to have a fit (colloq)
■ ~ cardiaque heart attack; ~ de foie indigestion; ~ de nerfs hysterics

**crisper** /kʀispe/ [1] **1** *vtr* l'angoisse crispait son visage his/her face was tense with worry
**2** se crisper *v refl* (+ *v être*) ⟨hands⟩ to clench; ⟨face, person⟩ to tense (up); ⟨smile⟩ to freeze

**crisser** /kʀise/ [1] *vi* ⟨shoes, chalk⟩ to squeak; ⟨snow⟩ to crunch; ⟨tyres, brakes⟩ to screech

**cristal**, *pl* **-aux** /kʀistal, o/ *nm* crystal

**cristallin, ~e** /kʀistalɛ̃, in/ **1** *adj*
(a) crystalline
(b) crystal clear
**2** *nm* (of eye) (crystalline) lens

**cristalliser** /kʀistalize/ [1] *vtr, vi, v refl* (+ *v être*) to crystallize

**critère** /kʀitɛʀ/ *nm* (a) criterion; ~s de

**gestion/de confort** standards of management/comfort; **le ~ déterminant** the crucial factor
**(b)** specification; **remplir les ~s d'âge et de diplôme** to meet the requirements as far as age and qualifications are concerned

**critiquable** /kʀitikabl/ *adj* questionable

**critique¹** /kʀitik/ **1** *adj* critical
**2** *nmf* critic

**critique²** /kʀitik/ *nf* **(a)** criticism; **faire une ~ à** to criticize sb
**(b)** review; **faire la ~ d'un film** to review a film
**(c) la ~ littéraire** literary criticism

**critiquer** /kʀitike/ [1] *vtr* to criticize

**croasser** /kʀɔase/ [1] *vi* to caw

**croc** /kʀo/ *nm* fang

**croche** /kʀɔʃ/ *nf* quaver (GB), eighth note (US); **double ~** semiquaver (GB), sixteenth note (US)

**croche-pied**, *pl* **~s** /kʀɔʃpje/ *nm* (colloq)
**faire un ~ à qn** to trip sb up

**crochet** /kʀɔʃɛ/ *nm* **(a)** hook
**(b)** picklock
**(c)** crochet hook; **faire du ~** to crochet
**(d)** square bracket
**(e) faire un ~** to make a detour
**(f)** (in boxing) hook
**(g)** fang
IDIOMS **vivre aux ~s de qn** (colloq) to sponge off sb (colloq)

**crocheter** /kʀɔʃte/ [18] *vtr* to pick ⟨lock⟩

**crochu**, **~e** /kʀɔʃy/ *adj* ⟨nose⟩ hooked; ⟨hands⟩ clawed

**crocodile** /kʀɔkɔdil/ *nm* crocodile

**croire** /kʀwaʀ/ [71] **1** *vtr* **(a)** to believe; **faire ~ à qn** to make sb believe
**(b)** to think; **je crois savoir que** I happen to know that; **il est malin, faut pas ~!** (colloq) he's clever, believe me!; **tu ne crois pas si bien dire** you don't know how right you are; **on croirait de la soie** it looks *or* feels like silk
**(c) si l'on en croit l'auteur, à en ~ l'auteur** if we are to believe the author; **crois-en mon expérience** take my word for it
**2 croire à** *v+prep* to believe ⟨story⟩; to believe in ⟨ghosts⟩
**3 croire en** *v+prep* to believe in
**4 se croire** *v refl* (+ *v être*) **il se croit beau** he thinks he's handsome

**croisade** /kʀwazad/ *nf* crusade

**croisé**, **~e¹** /kʀwaze/ **1** *pp* ▶ CROISER
**2** *pp adj* **(a)** ⟨legs⟩ crossed; ⟨arms⟩ folded
**(b)** crossbred
**(c)** ⟨agreements⟩ reciprocal

**croisée²** /kʀwaze/ *nf* **(a)** junction; **à la ~ des chemins** at the crossroads
**(b)** window

**croisement** /kʀwazmã/ *nm*
**(a)** crossroads; crossing, junction
**(b)** (of threads, straps) crossing
**(c)** crossbreeding; hybrid, cross(breed)

**croiser** /kʀwaze/ [1] **1** *vtr* **(a)** to cross; **~ les bras** to fold one's arms

**(b) ~ qn/qch** to pass sb/sth (coming the other way)
**(c)** to meet; **mon regard croisa le sien** our eyes met
**(d)** to cross(breed)
**2 se croiser** *v refl* (+ *v être*) ⟨cars⟩ to pass each other; ⟨letters⟩ to cross in the post (GB) *or* mail (US); ⟨roads⟩ to intersect; ⟨lines⟩ to cross

**croisière** /kʀwazjɛʀ/ *nf* cruise

**croissance** /kʀwasãs/ *nf* growth

**croissant** /kʀwasã/ *nm* **(a)** croissant
**(b)** crescent; **~ de lune** crescent moon

**croître** /kʀwatʀ/ [72] *vi* **(a)** to grow; **faire ~** to grow
**(b)** ⟨noise⟩ to get *or* grow louder

**croix** /kʀwa/ *nf* cross; **bras en ~** arms out on either side of the body
IDIOMS **ton argent, tu peux faire une ~ dessus** (colloq) you can kiss your money goodbye; **un jour à marquer d'une ~** a red-letter day

**Croix-Rouge** /kʀwaʀuʒ/ *nf* **la ~** the Red Cross

**croquant**, **~e** /kʀɔkã, ãt/ *adj* crunchy

**croque-madame** /kʀɔkmadam/ *nm inv*: toasted ham and cheese sandwich topped with a fried egg

**croque-monsieur** /kʀɔkməsjø/ *nm inv*: toasted ham and cheese sandwich

**croque-mort**, *pl* **~s** /kʀɔkmɔʀ/ *nm* (colloq) undertaker

**croquer** /kʀɔke/ [1] **1** *vtr* **(a)** to crunch
**(b)** to sketch; **belle à ~** as pretty as a picture
**2** *vi* **(a)** to be crunchy
**(b) ~ dans une pomme** to bite into an apple

**croquette** /kʀɔkɛt/ *nf* croquette

**croquis** /kʀɔki/ *nm* sketch

**crosse** /kʀɔs/ *nf* **(a)** (of rifle) butt
**(b)** (of cane) crook
**(c)** (Sport) stick

**crotte** /kʀɔt/ *nf* dropping; **c'est de la ~ de chien** it's dog mess

**crotter** /kʀɔte/ [1] *vtr* to muddy; **bottes crottées** muddy boots

**crottin** /kʀɔtɛ̃/ *nm* **(a)** dung
**(b)** (small round) goat's cheese

**crouler** /kʀule/ [1] *vi* **(a)** to collapse; to crumble
**(b) ~ sous** to be weighed down by ⟨parcels, debts, work⟩; **~ sous le poids de** ⟨table⟩ to groan under the weight of ⟨books⟩

**croupe** /kʀup/ *nf* (of horse) croup

**croupi**, **~e** /kʀupi/ *adj* stagnant

**croupier** /kʀupje/ *nm* croupier

**croupir** /kʀupiʀ/ [3] *vi* **(a)** ⟨water⟩ to stagnate
**(b) ~ en prison** to rot in jail

**croustillant**, **~e** /kʀustijã, ãt/ *adj*
**(a)** crispy; crunchy
**(b)** ⟨story, details⟩ spicy

**croustiller** /kʀustije/ [1] *vi* ⟨bread⟩ to be crusty; ⟨chocolate⟩ to be crunchy

**croûte** /kʀut/ nf (a) (of bread) crust; (of cheese) rind; **casser la ~** (colloq) to have a bite to eat
(b) (Culin) **pâté en ~** pâté en croute or in pastry
(c) (Med) scab
(d) (colloq) daub, bad painting

**croûton** /kʀutɔ̃/ nm (a) crust
(b) (Culin) crouton

**croyance** /kʀwajãs/ nf belief

**croyant, ~e** /kʀwajã, ãt/ adj **être ~** to be a believer

**CRS** /seeres/ nm (abbr = **compagnie républicaine de sécurité**) **un ~** a member of the French riot police

**cru¹, ~e¹** /kʀy/ ▶ CROIRE

**cru², ~e²** /kʀy/ **1** adj (a) raw; uncooked; ⟨milk⟩ unpasteurized; **se faire manger tout ~** (colloq) to be eaten alive (colloq)
(b) ⟨light, colour⟩ harsh
(c) ⟨language⟩ crude
**2** nm vineyard; vintage; vintage year; **du meilleur ~** ⟨collection⟩ vintage; **du ~** ⟨wine, author⟩ local

**crû, crue³** /kʀy/ ▶CROÎTRE

**cruauté** /kʀyote/ nf cruelty

**cruche** /kʀyʃ/ nf jug (GB), pitcher (US)

**crucial, ~e,** mpl **-iaux** /kʀysjal, o/ adj crucial

**crucifier** /kʀysifje/ [2] vtr to crucify

**crucifix** /kʀysifi/ nm crucifix

**crudité** /kʀydite/ nf **~s** raw vegetables, crudités

**crue⁴** /kʀy/ **1** adj f ▶ CRU² 1
**2** nf rise in water level; flood; **en ~** in spate

**cruel, -elle** /kʀyɛl/ adj cruel

**cruellement** /kʀyɛlmã/ adv (a) cruelly
(b) **manquer ~ de qch** to be desperately short of sth
(c) terribly; **la pénurie de carburant se fait ~ sentir** the fuel shortage is being sorely felt

**crûment** /kʀymã/ adv (a) bluntly
(b) crudely

**crustacé** /kʀystase/ nm shellfish

**crypte** /kʀipt(ə)/ nf crypt

**crypté, ~e** /kʀipte/ adj coded; encrypted

**cube** /kyb/ **1** adj cubic
**2** nm (a) cube
(b) building block

**cubique** /kybik/ adj (a) cubic
(b) cube-shaped

**cucul** /kyky/ adj (colloq) corny (colloq); silly

**cueillette** /kœjɛt/ nf (a) (of fruits, flowers) picking
(b) crop

**cueilli, ~e** /kœji/ ▶ CUEILLIR

**cueillir** /kœjiʀ/ [27] vtr (a) to pick ⟨fruit, flowers⟩
(b) (colloq) to arrest ⟨criminal⟩

**cuiller, cuillère** /kɥijɛʀ/ nf spoon; spoonful; **~ à café** teaspoon; coffee spoon
IDIOMS **il n'y va pas avec le dos de la ~** (colloq) he doesn't do things by halves; **en deux coups de ~ à pot** in two shakes of a lamb's tail (colloq)

**cuillerée** /kɥij(ə)ʀe/ nf spoonful

**cuir** /kɥiʀ/ nm (a) leather
(b) rawhide; hide
■ **~ chevelu** scalp

**cuirassé** /kɥiʀase/ nm battleship

**cuire** /kɥiʀ/ [69] **1** vtr (a) to cook; to bake; to roast; **~ à la vapeur** to steam; **à ~** ⟨apple⟩ cooking
(b) to fire ⟨porcelain⟩
**2** vi (a) ⟨food⟩ to cook; to be cooking; **laissez ~ à petit feu** allow to simmer gently
(b) (colloq) **on cuit sur la plage** it's baking (hot) on the beach
(c) ⟨graze⟩ to sting; **ça me cuit** it stings

**cuisant, ~e** /kɥizã, ãt/ adj (a) ⟨defeat, regret⟩ bitter; ⟨remark⟩ stinging
(b) ⟨pain⟩ burning

**cuisine** /kɥizin/ nf (a) kitchen
(b) galley
(c) kitchen furniture
(d) cooking
(e) (colloq) intrigues

**cuisiner** /kɥizine/ [1] vtr, vi to cook

**cuisinier, -ière¹** /kɥizinje, ɛʀ/ nm,f cook; chef

**cuisinière²** /kɥizinjɛʀ/ nf cooker

**cuissarde** /kɥisaʀd/ nf wader; thighboot

**cuisse** /kɥis/ nf thigh; **des ~s de grenouille** frogs' legs

**cuisson** /kɥisɔ̃/ nf (a) cooking; baking; roasting
(b) (of pottery) firing

**cuistot** /kɥisto/ nm (colloq) cook

**cuit, ~e¹** /kɥi, kɥit/ pp ▶ CUIRE
IDIOMS **c'est ~** (colloq) we've had it (colloq); **c'est du tout ~** (colloq) it's a piece of cake (colloq); it's in the bag (colloq); **elle attend que ça (lui) tombe tout ~** (colloq) she expects things to fall straight into her lap

**cuite²** /kɥit/ nf **tenir une ~** to be plastered (colloq)

**cuivre** /kɥivʀ/ **1** nm (a) **~ (rouge)** copper
(b) **~ (jaune)** brass
**2** **cuivres** nm pl (a) copperware
(b) brass
(c) (Mus) **les ~s** the brass

**cul** /ky/ nm (a) **~** (slang) bottom, arse (GB) (vulgar), ass (US) (slang)
(b) (of bottle) bottom; **~ sec!** (colloq) bottoms up! (colloq)

**culasse** /kylas/ nf (a) cylinder head
(b) breechblock

**culbute** /kylbyt/ nf somersault

**culbuter** /kylbyte/ [1] vi ⟨person⟩ to take a tumble; ⟨vehicle⟩ to overturn

**cul-cul** (colloq) = CUCUL

**cul-de-jatte,** pl **culs-de-jatte** /kydʒat/ nmf person who has had both legs amputated

**cul-de-sac,** pl **culs-de-sac** /kydsak/ nm (a) cul-de-sac

**(b)** dead end

**culinaire** /kylinɛʀ/ *adj* culinary

**culminant, ~e** /kylminɑ̃, ɑ̃t/ *adj* point ~ (of mountain) highest point *or* peak; (of career) peak; (of crisis) height; (of holiday) high point

**culminer** /kylmine/ [1] *vi* **(a)** ~ **au-dessus de qch** to tower above sth
**(b)** ⟨*inflation, unemployment*⟩ to reach its peak

**culot** /kylo/ *nm* (colloq) cheek (colloq); **y aller au** ~ to bluff

**culotte** /kylɔt/ *nf* **(a)** pants (GB), panties (US)
**(b) en ~(s) courte(s)** in short trousers (GB) *or* pants (US)

**culotté, ~e** /kylɔte/ *adj* (colloq) cheeky

**culpabilisation** /kylpabilizasjɔ̃/ *nf* making guilty; feeling of guilt

**culpabiliser** /kylpabilize/ [1] **1** *vtr* to make [sb] feel guilty
**2** *vi* to feel guilty

**culpabilité** /kylpabilite/ *nf* guilt

**culte** /kylt/ *nm* **(a)** cult
**(b)** religion

**cultivateur, -trice** /kyltivatœʀ, tʀis/ *nm,f* farmer

**cultiver** /kyltive/ [1] **1** *vtr* to grow; to cultivate
**2 se cultiver** *v refl* (+ *v être*) to improve one's mind

**culture** /kyltyʀ/ **1** *nf* **(a)** cultivation; **la ~ du blé** wheat growing
**(b)** crop; ~ **d'hiver** winter crop
**(c)** (in biology) culture
**(d)** (of society) culture; ~ **de masse** mass culture
**(e)** knowledge; ~ **classique** classical education
**(f)** arts; **subventionner la** ~ to subsidize the arts
**2 cultures** *nf pl* cultivated land
■ ~ **physique** physical exercise

**culturel, -elle** /kyltyʀɛl/ *adj* cultural

**culturisme** /kyltyʀism/ *nm* body-building

**cumin** /kymɛ̃/ *nm* cumin

**cumul** /kymyl/ *nm* **(a)** ~ **de fonctions** holding of several posts concurrently
**(b)** (Law) ~ **des peines** ≈ sentences to be served consecutively

**cumuler** /kymyle/ [1] *vtr* **(a)** to hold [sth] concurrently ⟨*offices*⟩; to draw [sth] concurrently ⟨*salaries*⟩
**(b)** to accumulate ⟨*handicaps, degrees*⟩
**(c)** to combine ⟨*results*⟩; to add up ⟨*amounts*⟩

**cumulus** /kymylys/ *nm inv* cumulus

**cupide** /kypid/ *adj* grasping

**cupidité** /kypidite/ *nf* avarice, greed, cupidity

**cure** /kyʀ/ *nf* **faire une** ~ to go for a course of treatment in a spa

■ ~ **d'amaigrissement** slimming course (GB), reducing treatment (US); ~ **de sommeil** sleep therapy

**curé** /kyʀe/ *nm* (parish) priest

**cure-dents** /kyʀdɑ̃/ *nm inv* toothpick

**curer** /kyʀe/ [1] **1** *vtr* to clean out ⟨*pipe, pond*⟩
**2 se curer** *v refl* (+ *v être*) **se** ~ **les ongles** to clean one's nails

**curieusement** /kyʀjøzmɑ̃/ *adv* **(a)** oddly, strangely
**(b)** oddly enough

**curieux, -ieuse** /kyʀjø, øz/ **1** *adj*
**(a)** inquisitive, curious
**(b)** strange
**(c) esprit** ~ person with an enquiring mind; **être** ~ **d'apprendre** to be keen to learn
**2** *nm,f* onlooker

**curiosité** /kyʀjozite/ *nf* curiosity

**curriculum vitae** /kyʀikylɔmvite/ *nm inv* curriculum vitae, résumé (US)

**curry** /kyʀi/ *nm* **(a)** curry powder
**(b)** curry

**curseur** /kyʀsœʀ/ *nm* cursor

**cursus** /kyʀsys/ *nm inv* course

**cutané, ~e** /kytane/ *adj* ⟨*irritation*⟩ skin

**cutter** /kytœʀ/ *nm* Stanley knife®

**cuve** /kyv/ *nf* vat; tank

**cuvée** /kyve/ *nf* vatful; **la ~ 1959** the 1959 vintage; ~ **du patron** house wine

**cuvette** /kyvɛt/ *nf* **(a)** bowl; ~ **des wc** lavatory bowl *or* pan
**(b)** (in land) basin

**CV** /seve/ *nm* **(a)** (*abbr* = **curriculum vitae**) CV (GB), résumé (US)
**(b)** (*written abbr* = **cheval-vapeur**) HP

**cybercafé** /sibɛʀkafe/ *nm* cybercafe

**cyberjargon** /sibɛʀʒaʀgɔ̃/ *nm* netspeak

**cyclable** /siklabl/ *adj* **piste** ~ cycle track

**cycle** /sikl/ *nm* **(a)** cycle; ~ **infernal** vicious cycle
**(b)** series
**(c)** (Sch) **premier** ~ *first two years of a university degree course leading to a diploma*; **deuxième** ~ *final two years of a university degree course*; **troisième** ~ postgraduate (GB) *or* graduate (US) studies
**(d)** (bi)cycle

**cyclique** /siklik/ *adj* cyclic

**cyclisme** /siklism/ *nm* cycling; cycle racing

**cycliste** /siklist/ **1** *adj* ⟨*club*⟩ cycling; ⟨*race*⟩ cycle; **coureur** ~ racing cyclist
**2** *nmf* cyclist; **short de** ~ cycling shorts

**cyclone** /siklon/ *nm* **(a)** cyclone
**(b)** (in weather) depression

**cygne** /siɲ/ *nm* swan; ~ **mâle** cob; ~ **femelle** pen; **jeune** ~ cygnet

**cylindre** /silɛ̃dʀ/ *nm* **(a)** cylinder
**(b)** roller

**cylindrée** /silɛ̃dʀe/ *nf* capacity, size; ~ **de 1200 cm³** 1200 cc engine

**cymbale** /sɛ̃bal/ *nm* cymbal

**cynique** /sinik/ *adj* cynical
**cynisme** /sinism/ *nm* cynicism

**cyprès** /sipʀɛ/ *nm* cypress
**cystite** /sistit/ *nf* cystitis

# Dd

**d, D** /de/ *nm inv* d, D
**d'** ▶ DE
**DAB** /deabe/ *nm*: (*abbr* = **distributeur automatique de billets**) automatic teller machine, ATM
**dactylographie** /daktilɔgʀafi/ *nf* typing
**dada** /dada/ *nm* (colloq) **(a)** (baby talk) horsie (colloq)
**(b)** hobby
**(c)** hobbyhorse
**dadais** /dadɛ/ *nm inv* (colloq) clumsy youth; **espèce de grand ~!** you great oaf!
**daigner** /deɲe/ [1] *vtr* to deign (**faire** to do)
**daim** /dɛ̃/ *nm* **(a)** (fallow) deer
**(b)** venison
**(c)** buckskin
**(d)** suede
**dallage** /dalaʒ/ *nm* paving
**dalle** /dal/ *nf* **(a)** slab
**(b)** flagstone
**(c)** concrete foundation slab
**IDIOMS avoir la ~** (colloq) to be ravenous; **que ~** (slang) nothing at all, zilch (colloq)
**daller** /dale/ [1] *vtr* to pave
**daltonien, -ienne** /daltɔnjɛ̃, ɛn/ *adj* colour (GB)-blind
**dam** /dɑ(m)/ *nm* **au grand ~ de** to the great displeasure of
**dame** /dam/ *nf* **(a)** lady
**(b)** (in cards, chess) queen; (in draughts) King
**2 dames** *nf pl* draughts (GB), checkers (US)
**damier** /damje/ *nm* draughtboard (GB), checkerboard (US)
**damnation** /danasjɔ̃/ *nf* damnation
**damner** /dane/ [1] **1** *vtr* to damn
**2 se damner** *v refl* (+ *v être*) to damn oneself; **se ~ pour qch** (colloq) to sell one's soul for sth
**dancing** /dɑ̃siŋ/ *nm* dance hall
**dandiner: se dandiner** /dɑ̃dine/ [1] *v refl* (+ *v être*) (*duck*) to waddle
**Danemark** /danmaʀk/ *pr nm* Denmark
**danger** /dɑ̃ʒe/ *nm* danger
■ **~ public** danger to the public; (figurative) menace
**dangereusement** /dɑ̃ʒʀøzmɑ̃/ *adv* dangerously
**dangereux, -euse** /dɑ̃ʒʀø, øz/ *adj* dangerous
**danois, ~e** /danwa, az/ **1** *adj* Danish

**2** *nm* **(a)** (language) Danish
**(b)** (dog) Great Dane
**dans** /dɑ̃/ *prep* **(a)** in; **être ~ la cuisine** to be in the kitchen; **être ~ un avion/bateau** to be on a plane/boat
**(b)** into; **entrer ~ une pièce** to go into a room; **monter ~ un avion** to get on a plane
**(c)** **boire ~ un verre** to drink out of a glass; **prendre qch ~ un placard** to take sth out of a cupboard
**(d)** **~ deux heures** in two hours; **fait ~ les deux heures** done within two hours; **je t'appellerai ~ la journée** I'll phone you during the day
**(e)** **~ les 30 euros** about 30 euros
**danse** /dɑ̃s/ *nf* **(a)** dance
**(b)** dancing; **faire de la ~** to take dancing classes
■ **~ classique** classical ballet
**danser** /dɑ̃se/ [1] *vtr, vi* to dance
**IDIOMS ne pas savoir sur quel pied ~** not to know what to do
**danseur, -euse** /dɑ̃sœʀ, øz/ *nm,f* dancer; **~ étoile** principal dancer
**dard** /daʀ/ *nm* **(a)** (Zool) sting
**(b)** spear
**dare-dare** /daʀdaʀ/ *adv* (colloq) double quick
**darne** /daʀn/ *nf* (fish) steak
**dartre** /daʀtʀ/ *nf* scurf patch
**date** /dat/ *nf* **(a)** date; **~ limite** deadline; **~ limite de vente** sell-by date
**(b)** time; **depuis cette ~** from that time; **un ami de longue ~** a longstanding friend; **le dernier scandale en ~** the latest scandal
**dater** /date/ [1] **1** *vtr* to date; **à ~ du 31 juillet** as from 31 July
**2** *vi* **(a)** **~ de** to date from
**(b)** to be dated
**dation** /dasjɔ̃/ *nf* **~ (en paiement)** payment in kind
**datte** /dat/ *nf* (Bot, Culin) date
**dattier** /datje/ *nm* date palm
**daube** /dob/ *nf* **bœuf en ~** beef casserole
**dauphin** /dofɛ̃/ *nm* **(a)** dolphin
**(b)** heir apparent
**(c)** dauphin
**daurade** /doʀad/ *nf* (sea) bream
**davantage** /davɑ̃taʒ/ *adv* **(a)** more
**(b)** longer; **rester ~** to stay longer
**DCA** /desea/ *nf* (*abbr* = **défense contre les aéronefs**) antiaircraft defence (GB)

**DDASS** /das/ *nf* (*abbr* = **Direction départementale de l'action sanitaire et sociale**) regional social services department

**de** (**d'** *before vowel or mute h*) /də, d/

■ Note You will find translations for expressions such as *d'abord, de travers, pomme de terre, chemin de fer* etc, at the entries ABORD, TRAVERS, POMME and CHEMIN etc.

[1] *prep* (a) from; **venir ~ Paris** to come from Paris; **il est ~ père italien** his father is Italian
(b) by; **un poème ~ Victor Hugo** a poem by Victor Hugo
(c) of; **les chapeaux ~ Paul** Paul's hats; **le 20 du mois** the 20th of the month; **deux heures d'attente** a two-hour wait; **deux heures ~ libres** two hours free
(d) than; **plus/moins ~ dix** more/less than ten
(e) in; **d'un ton monocorde** in a monotone
(f) with; **pousser qch du pied** to push sth aside with one's foot
(g) **travailler ~ nuit** to work at night; **ne rien faire ~ la journée** to do nothing all day
(h) **être content ~ faire** to be happy to do
[2] *det* **de, de l', de la, du** some; any; **voulez-vous ~ la bière?** would you like some beer?; **je n'ai pas d'argent** I haven't got any money

**dé** /de/ *nm* (a) dice; **les ~s sont jetés** the die is cast
(b) ~ (**à coudre**) thimble

**DEA** /deəa/ *nm* (*abbr* = **diplôme d'études approfondies**) postgraduate certificate (*prior to doctoral thesis*)

**déambulateur** /deɑ̃bylatœʀ/ *nm* zimmer® (frame)

**déambuler** /deɑ̃byle/ [1] *vi* to wander (about)

**débâcle** /debɑkl/ *nf* (a) (Mil) rout
(b) (figurative) collapse

**déballage** /debalaʒ/ *nm* (colloq) jumble; outpouring

**déballer** /debale/ [1] *vtr* (a) to unpack
(b) to display

**débandade** /debɑ̃dad/ *nf* (a) stampede
(b) disarray

**débarbouiller** /debaʀbuje/ [1] [1] *vtr* to wash
[2] **se débarbouiller** *v refl* (+ *v être*) to wash one's face

**débarcadère** /debaʀkadɛʀ/ *nm* landing stage, jetty

**débardeur** /debaʀdœʀ/ *nm* tank top

**débarquement** /debaʀkəmɑ̃/ *nm*
(a) (of goods) unloading
(b) (of passengers) disembarkation
(c) (Mil) landing

**débarquer** /debaʀke/ [1] [1] *vtr* to unload ⟨goods⟩
[2] *vi* (a) to disembark
(b) (Mil) to land
(c) (colloq) to turn up (colloq) (**chez qn** at sb's place)

**débarras** /debaʀa/ *nm inv* (a) junk room
(b) **bon ~!** (colloq) good riddance!

**débarrasser** /debaʀase/ [1] [1] *vtr* (a) to clear (out)
(b) ~ [qn] **de** to free [sb] from ⟨complex⟩; ~ **qn** (**de son manteau**) to take sb's coat
[2] **se débarrasser** *v refl* (+ *v être*) **se ~ de** to get rid of; to dispose of
IDIOMS ~ **le plancher** (colloq) to clear off (colloq)

**débat** /deba/ *nm* debate

**débattre** /debatʀ/ [61] [1] *vtr* to negotiate
[2] **débattre de** *or* **sur** *v+prep* (a) ~ **de** *or* **sur** to discuss
(b) ~ **de** *or* **sur** to debate
[3] **se débattre** *v refl* (+ *v être*) to struggle

**débauche** /deboʃ/ *nf* (a) debauchery
(b) profusion

**débaucher** /deboʃe/ [1] *vtr* (a) to corrupt
(b) to lay [sb] off
(c) (colloq) to tempt [sb] away

**débile** /debil/ [1] *adj* (colloq) daft (colloq)
[2] *nmf* ~ **mental** (Med) retarded person

**débilité** /debilite/ *nf* (a) debility
(b) (colloq) stupidity

**débiner** (colloq) /debine/ [1] [1] *vtr* to badmouth (colloq)
[2] **se débiner** *v refl* (+ *v être*) to clear off (colloq); to make oneself scarce (colloq)

**débit** /debi/ *nm* (a) debit; **la somme est inscrite au ~** the sum has been debited
(b) (when speaking) delivery
(c) (of river) rate of flow
(d) (of liquid) flow; (of gas) output
■ ~ **de boissons** bar

**débiter** /debite/ [1] *vtr* (a) to debit
(b) to reel [sth] off; ~ **des bêtises** to talk a lot of nonsense
(c) to cut [sth] up

**débiteur, -trice** /debitœʀ, tʀis/ [1] *adj* **compte ~** debit account; **pays ~** debtor nation
[2] *nm,f* debtor

**déblayer** /debleje/ [21] *vtr* (a) to clear away ⟨earth, snow⟩
(b) to clear ⟨place⟩

**débloquer** /debloke/ [1] [1] *vtr* (a) to unlock ⟨steering wheel⟩; to unjam ⟨mechanism⟩
(b) to unfreeze ⟨prices⟩; to end the deadlock in ⟨situation⟩
(c) to make [sth] available ⟨credit⟩
[2] *vi* (colloq) to be off one's rocker (colloq)

**déboires** /debwaʀ/ *nm pl*
(a) disappointments
(b) trials, difficulties
(c) setbacks

**déboiser** /debwaze/ [1] *vtr* to deforest

**déboîter** /debwate/ [1] [1] *vtr* to disconnect ⟨tubes⟩
[2] *vi* ⟨car⟩ to pull out
[3] **se déboîter** *v refl* (+ *v être*) **se ~ le genou** to dislocate one's knee

**débonnaire** /debɔnɛʀ/ *adj* good-humoured (GB); kindly

**débordant**, **∼e** /debɔʀdɑ̃, ɑ̃t/ *adj*
(a) ⟨*imagination*⟩ overactive
(b) ∼ **de** brimming with ⟨*energy*⟩; bursting
with ⟨*health*⟩

**débordé**, **∼e** /debɔʀde/ **1** *pp* ▶ DÉBORDER
**2** *pp adj* (a) overwhelmed
(b) overloaded

**débordement** /debɔʀdəmɑ̃/ *nm* (of protest)
flood; (of enthusiasm) excess

**déborder** /debɔʀde/ [1] **1** *vtr* (a) ⟨*problem,
feeling*⟩ to go beyond
(b) **se laisser** ∼ to let oneself be
overwhelmed
(c) (Mil, Sport) to outflank
**2 déborder de** *v+prep* to be brimming
over with; to be bursting with
**3** *vi* (a) ⟨*river*⟩ to overflow
(b) ⟨*liquid*⟩ to overflow; to boil over
(c) to jut out

**débouché** /debuʃe/ *nm* (a) market; ∼**s à
l'exportation** export outlets
(b) job opportunity

**déboucher** /debuʃe/ [1] **1** *vtr* (a) to
unblock
(b) to open; to uncork
**2** *vi* ∼ **sur** ⟨*street*⟩ to open onto; ⟨*talks*⟩ to
lead to
**3 se déboucher** *v refl* (+ *v être*) (a) to
come unblocked
(b) ⟨*ears*⟩ to pop
(c) **se** ∼ **les oreilles/le nez** to unblock one's
ears/nose

**débouler** /debule/ [1] **1** *vtr* to charge
down
**2** *vi* (a) to tumble down
(b) (colloq) to turn up

**déboulonner** /debulɔne/ [1] *vtr* to unbolt

**débourser** /debuʀse/ [1] *vtr* to pay out

**déboussoler** /debusɔle/ [1] *vtr* (colloq) to
confuse

**debout** /dəbu/ **1** *adj inv, adv* (a) standing;
⟨*object*⟩ upright; **se mettre** ∼ to stand up; **je
ne tiens plus** ∼ I'm falling asleep on my feet
(b) **ton histoire tient** ∼ (colloq) your story
seems likely
(c) (out of bed) **être** ∼ to be up
**2** *excl* get up!

**déboutonner** /debutɔne/ [1] **1** *vtr* to
unbutton
**2 se déboutonner** *v refl* (+ *v être*) to
come undone

**débraillé**, **∼e** /debʀɑje/ *adj* ⟨*person*⟩
dishevelled (GB); ⟨*clothes, style*⟩ sloppy

**débrancher** /debʀɑ̃ʃe/ [1] *vtr* to unplug
⟨*appliance*⟩; to disconnect ⟨*alarm system*⟩

**débrayer** /debʀeje/ [21] *vi* (Aut) to declutch

**débridé**, **∼e** /debʀide/ *adj* unbridled

**débris** /debʀi/ *nm inv* (a) fragment; **des** ∼
**de verre** broken glass
(b) piece of wreckage

**débrouillard**, **∼e** /debʀujaʀ, aʀd/ *adj*
resourceful

**débrouiller** /debʀuje/ [1] **1** *vtr* (a) to
disentangle ⟨*threads*⟩
(b) to solve ⟨*riddle*⟩

**2 se débrouiller** *v refl* (+ *v être*) (a) to
manage
(b) to get by; **il se débrouille bien en
espagnol** he speaks good Spanish

**débroussailler** /debʀusaje/ [1] *vtr* to
clear the undergrowth from; (figurative) to do
the groundwork on

**débusquer** /debyske/ [1] *vtr* to flush
[sb/sth] out

**début** /deby/ **1** *nm* beginning; start
**2 débuts** *nm pl* (a) debut
(b) early stages

**débutant**, **∼e** /debytɑ̃, ɑ̃t/ **1** *adj* ⟨*driver,
skier*⟩ novice; ⟨*engineer*⟩ recently qualified
**2** *nm,f* beginner

**débuter** /debyte/ [1] *vi* (a) ⟨*day, novel*⟩ to
begin, to start; ⟨*person*⟩ to start off
(b) to start out (**comme** as)
(c) ⟨*performer*⟩ to make one's debut

**deçà** /dəsa/ **1** *adv* ∼, **delà** here and there
**2 en deçà** *phr* (a) on this side
(b) below

**décacheter** /dekaʃte/ [20] *vtr* to unseal

**décade** /dekad/ *nf* (a) 10-day period
(b) (controversial) decade

**décadence** /dekadɑ̃s/ *nf* decadence;
decline

**décadent**, **∼e** /dekadɑ̃, ɑ̃t/ *adj*
(a) decadent
(b) in decline

**décaféiné**, **∼e** /dekafeine/ *adj*
decaffeinated

**décalage** /dekalaʒ/ *nm* (a) gap
(b) discrepancy
(c) interval, time-lag
(d) shift
■ ∼ **horaire** time difference

**décalcomanie** /dekalkɔmani/ *nf* transfer

**décaler** /dekale/ [1] **1** *vtr* (a) to bring
forward ⟨*date, departure time*⟩
(b) to put (GB) *or* move (US) back ⟨*date,
departure time*⟩
(c) to move [sth] forward ⟨*object*⟩
(d) to move [sth] back ⟨*object*⟩
**2 se décaler** *v refl* (+ *v être*) **se** ∼ **sur la
droite** to move *or* shift to the right

**décalquer** /dekalke/ [1] *vtr* (a) to trace
(**sur** from)
(b) to transfer (**sur** onto)

**décamper** /dekɑ̃pe/ [1] *vi* (colloq) to run off

**décanter** /dekɑ̃te/ [1] **1** *vtr* to allow [sth]
to settle ⟨*liquid*⟩; to clarify ⟨*waste water*⟩
**2 se décanter** *v refl* (+ *v être*) (a) ⟨*liquid*⟩
to settle
(b) ⟨*situation, ideas*⟩ to become clearer

**décapant**, **∼e** /dekapɑ̃, ɑ̃t/ *adj*
(a) scouring
(b) (colloq) ⟨*humour*⟩ abrasive, caustic

**décaper** /dekape/ [1] *vtr* (a) to clean
(b) to strip ⟨*furniture*⟩; ∼ **avec un abrasif** to
scour
(c) (colloq) ⟨*alcohol, soap*⟩ to be harsh

**décapitation** /dekapitasjɔ̃/ *nf*
decapitation; beheading

**décapiter** /dekapite/ [1] *vtr* to behead; to decapitate

**décapotable** /dekapɔtabl/ *adj* une (voiture) ~ a convertible

**décapsuler** /dekapsyle/ [1] *vtr* to take the top off

**décapsuleur** /dekapsylœr/ *nm* bottle-opener

**décathlon** /dekatlɔ̃/ *nm* decathlon

**décéder** /desede/ [14] *vi* (+ *v être*) to die

**décelable** /deslabl/ *adj* detectable

**déceler** /desle/ [17] *vtr* (a) to detect
(b) to reveal ‹anomaly, feeling›
(c) to indicate ‹presence›

**décembre** /desɑ̃bʀ/ *nm* December

**décemment** /desamɑ̃/ *adv* decently

**décence** /desɑ̃s/ *nf* decency

**décennie** /deseni/ *nf* decade

**décent**, **~e** /desɑ̃, ɑ̃t/ *adj* (a) decent
(b) proper

**décentraliser** /desɑ̃tʀalize/ [1] *vtr* to decentralize

**décentrer** /desɑ̃tʀe/ [1] *vtr* to move away from the centre (GB)

**déception** /desɛpsjɔ̃/ *nf* disappointment

**décerner** /desɛʀne/ [1] *vtr* to award

**décès** /desɛ/ *nm inv* death

**décevant**, **~e** /desəvɑ̃, ɑ̃t/ *adj* disappointing

**décevoir** /desəvwaʀ/ [5] *vtr* (a) to disappoint
(b) to fail to fulfil (GB) ‹hope›

**déchaîné**, **~e** /deʃene/ ⊞ *pp* ▶ DÉCHAÎNER
⊟ *pp adj* stirred up; ~ contre furious with

**déchaîner** /deʃene/ [1] ⊞ *vtr* to rouse ‹feelings›; to excite ‹people›
⊟ **se déchaîner** *v refl* (+ *v être*) (a) ‹sea› to rage; ‹feelings› to burst out
(b) to go wild

**déchanter** /deʃɑ̃te/ [1] *vi* to become disenchanted

**décharge** /deʃaʀʒ/ *nf* (a) (of firearm) discharge
(b) ~ municipale (municipal) dump
(c) ~ électrique electric shock
(d) (Law) acquittal

**décharger** /deʃaʀʒe/ [13] ⊞ *vtr* (a) to unload ‹vessel, goods›
(b) to unload ‹firearm›
(c) to fire ‹gun›
(d) ~ qn de to relieve sb of ‹task›
(e) to discharge ‹battery›
(f) to unburden ‹conscience›
⊟ **se décharger** *v refl* (+ *v être*) (a) se ~ de qch to off-load sth
(b) ‹battery› to run down

**décharné**, **~e** /deʃaʀne/ *adj* ‹body› emaciated; ‹finger› bony

**déchausser**: **se déchausser** /deʃose/ [1] *v refl* (+ *v être*) (a) to take off one's shoes
(b) ‹teeth› to work loose due to receding gums

**dèche** /dɛʃ/ *nf* (colloq) être dans la ~ to be broke (colloq)

**déchéance** /deʃeɑ̃s/ *nf* (a) decline
(b) degeneration

**déchet** /deʃɛ/ ⊞ *nm* (a) scrap
(b) waste
(c) wreck
⊟ **déchets** *nm pl* waste material, waste; ~s industriels industrial waste; ~ nucléaires nuclear waste

**déchetterie** /deʃɛtʀi/ *nf* waste reception centre (GB)

**déchiffrer** /deʃifʀe/ [1] *vtr* (a) to decipher
(b) (Mus) to sight-read

**déchiqueté**, **~e** /deʃikte/ ⊞ *pp* ▶ DÉCHIQUETER
⊟ *pp adj* jagged, ragged

**déchiqueter** /deʃikte/ [20] *vtr* (a) to tear [sth] to shreds
(b) ‹machine, animal› to tear to pieces

**déchirant**, **~e** /deʃiʀɑ̃, ɑ̃t/ *adj* (a) heart-rending
(b) agonizing

**déchirer** /deʃiʀe/ [1] ⊞ *vtr* (a) to tear up ‹paper, material›
(b) to tear ‹garment›
(c) to split ‹group›; déchiré entre X et Y torn between X and Y
⊟ **se déchirer** *v refl* (+ *v être*) (a) to tear up
(b) se ~ un muscle to tear a muscle
(c) to tear each other apart

**déchirure** /deʃiʀyʀ/ *nf* (gen, Med) tear

**déchoir** /deʃwaʀ/ [51] *vi* to demean oneself; ~ de son rang to come down in the world

**déchu**, **~e** /deʃy/ *adj* ⊞ *pp* ▶ DÉCHOIR
⊟ *adj* ‹monarch› deposed; ‹angel› fallen

**décibel** /desibɛl/ *nm* decibel

**décidé**, **~e** /deside/ ⊞ *pp* ▶ DÉCIDER
⊟ *pp adj* determined; resolute

**décidément** /desidemɑ̃/ *adv* really

**décider** /deside/ [1] ⊞ *vtr* (a) to decide; c'est décidé it's settled
(b) to persuade (à faire to do)
⊟ **décider de** *v+prep* to decide on; to fix
⊠ **se décider** *v refl* (+ *v être*) (a) to make up one's mind
(b) se ~ pour to decide on

**décideur** /desidœʀ/ *nm* decision-maker

**décimal**, **~e**[1], *mpl* **-aux** /desimal, o/ *adj* decimal

**décimale**[2] /desimal/ *nf* decimal

**décimer** /desime/ [1] *vtr* to decimate

**décisif**, **-ive** /desizif, iv/ *adj* (a) decisive
(b) conclusive

**décision** /desizjɔ̃/ *nf* (a) decision
(b) decisiveness

**déclamer** /deklame/ [1] *vtr* to declaim

**déclaration** /deklaʀasjɔ̃/ *nf* (a) statement; declaration
(b) notification
(c) (Law) statement; ~ de vol/perte report of theft/loss
∎ ~ d'impôts (income-)tax return

**déclaré**, **~e** /deklaʀe/ adj ⟨enemy⟩ avowed; ⟨hatred⟩ professed

**déclarer** /deklaʀe/ [1] **1** vtr (a) to declare; **il a été déclaré coupable** he was found guilty
(b) to declare ⟨goods, revenue⟩; to register ⟨theft⟩; to register ⟨birth⟩; **non déclaré** undeclared; illegal
**2 se déclarer** v refl (+ v être) (a) ⟨fire, epidemic⟩ to break out; ⟨fever⟩ to start
(b) **se ~ pour/contre** to come out for/against

**déclenchement** /deklɑ̃ʃmɑ̃/ nm (of mechanism) release; (of illness) onset; (of reaction) start

**déclencher** /deklɑ̃ʃe/ [1] **1** vtr (a) to spark (off) ⟨protest⟩; to cause ⟨reaction, explosion⟩; to start ⟨avalanche⟩
(b) to launch ⟨offensive⟩; to start ⟨strike, debate⟩
(c) to set off ⟨mechanism⟩
**2 se déclencher** v refl (+ v être) (a) to go off; to be activated
(b) to break out; to begin

**déclic** /deklik/ nm (a) trigger
(b) (of camera) click

**déclin** /deklɛ̃/ nm decline

**déclinaison** /deklinɛzɔ̃/ nf declension

**décliner** /dekline/ [1] **1** vtr (a) to decline; to turn [sth] down
(b) **~ son identité** to give one's name
(c) to decline
**2** vi ⟨light, talent⟩ to fade; ⟨health⟩ to deteriorate; ⟨enthusiasm⟩ to wane; ⟨sun⟩ to go down
**3 se décliner** v refl (+ v être) to decline

**décocher** /dekɔʃe/ [1] vtr to shoot ⟨arrow⟩

**décoder** /dekɔde/ [1] vtr to decode

**décodeur** /dekɔdœʀ/ nm decoder

**décoiffer** /dekwafe/ [1] vtr **~ qn** to ruffle sb's hair

**décoincer** /dekwɛ̃se/ [12] vtr to unjam ⟨mechanism, door⟩; to free ⟨key⟩

**décollage** /dekɔlaʒ/ nm take-off

**décoller** /dekɔle/ [1] **1** vtr to peel off ⟨sticker⟩
**2** vi ⟨plane⟩ to take off
**3 se décoller** v refl (+ v être) to come off

**décolleté**, **~e** /dekɔlte/ **1** adj low-cut
**2** nm low neckline

**décolleuse** /dekɔløz/ nf steam stripper

**décolonisation** /dekɔlɔnizasjɔ̃/ nf decolonization

**décolorant**, **~e** /dekɔlɔʀɑ̃, ɑ̃t/ adj bleaching

**décolorer** /dekɔlɔʀe/ [1] vtr (a) to bleach
(b) to cause to fade

**décombres** /dekɔ̃bʀ/ nm pl rubble

**décommander** /dekɔmɑ̃de/ [1] **1** vtr to call [sth] off
**2 se décommander** v refl (+ v être) to cry off (GB), to beg off

**décomposer** /dekɔ̃poze/ [1] **1** vtr (a) to break down ⟨argument, water⟩
(b) to distort ⟨features⟩

**2 se décomposer** v refl (+ v être) (a) to decompose
(b) to fall apart

**décomposition** /dekɔ̃pozisjɔ̃/ nf
(a) decomposition
(b) disintegration

**décompte** /dekɔ̃t/ nm (a) discount
(b) count; **faire le ~ de** to count [sth] up ⟨votes, points⟩

**décompter** /dekɔ̃te/ [1] vtr (a) to deduct (de from)
(b) to count ⟨votes, points⟩

**déconcentrer** /dekɔ̃sɑ̃tʀe/ [1] vtr to distract

**déconcertant**, **~e** /dekɔ̃sɛʀtɑ̃, ɑ̃t/ adj disconcerting; **d'une facilité ~e** ridiculously easy

**déconcerter** /dekɔ̃sɛʀte/ [1] vtr to disconcert

**déconfit**, **~e** /dekɔ̃fi, it/ adj crestfallen

**déconfiture** /dekɔ̃fityʀ/ nf (a) (of person) failure; (of party, team) defeat
(b) (of company) collapse

**décongeler** /dekɔ̃ʒle/ [17] vtr, vi to defrost

**décongestionner** /dekɔ̃ʒɛstjɔne/ [1]
**1** vtr (a) to ease the pressure on ⟨university, services⟩; to relieve congestion in ⟨motorway⟩; to relieve congestion in ⟨street, town⟩
(b) to clear ⟨nose⟩
**2 se décongestionner** v refl (+ v être) to clear

**déconnecter** /dekɔnɛkte/ [1] vtr (a) to disconnect ⟨appliance⟩
(b) to dissociate

**déconner** /dekɔne/ [1] vi (slang) (a) to kid around (colloq); **faut pas ~!** come off it! (colloq)
(b) to mess around (colloq); to piss around (GB) (slang)
(c) to play up (colloq)

**déconseiller** /dekɔ̃seje/ [1] vtr to advise against

**déconsidérer** /dekɔ̃sidere/ [14] **1** vtr to discredit
**2 se déconsidérer** v refl (+ v être) **tu t'es déconsidéré** it was unworthy of you

**décontenancer** /dekɔ̃tnɑ̃se/ [12] vtr to disconcert

**décontracté**, **~e** /dekɔ̃tʀakte/ **1** pp ▸ DÉCONTRACTER
**2** pp adj (a) relaxed
(b) casual
(c) laid-back (colloq)

**décontracter** /dekɔ̃tʀakte/ [1] vtr, **se décontracter** v refl (+ v être) to relax

**décontraction** /dekɔ̃tʀaksjɔ̃/ nf
(a) relaxation
(b) ease
(c) casual attitude

**déconvenue** /dekɔ̃vəny/ nf disappointment

**décor** /dekɔʀ/ nm (a) decor
(b) setting; **j'ai besoin de changer de ~** I need a change of scene; **partir dans le ~** (colloq) to drive off the road

**(c)** (of film) set; **tourné en ~ naturel** shot on location

**décorateur, -trice** /dekɔratœr, tris/ *nm,f* **(a)** interior decorator
**(b)** set designer

**décoratif, -ive** /dekɔratif, iv/ *adj*
**(a)** ornamental
**(b)** decorative

**décoration** /dekɔrasjɔ̃/ *nf* **(a)** decorating
**(b)** (gen, Mil) decoration
**(c)** interior design

**décorer** /dekɔre/ [1] *vtr* to decorate

**décortiquer** /dekɔrtike/ [1] *vtr* to shell ⟨nut⟩; to peel ⟨prawn⟩

**décote** /dekɔt/ *nf* (Econ) drop

**découcher** /dekuʃe/ [1] *vi* to spend the night away from home

**découdre** /dekudr/ [76] **1** *vtr* to undo, to unpick (GB) ⟨hem, seam⟩
**2** *vi* **en ~** to have a fight **(avec** with)

**découler** /dekule/ [1] *vi* **(a)** to follow **(de** from)
**(b)** to result **(de** from)

**découpage** /dekupaʒ/ *nm* cut-out

**découper** /dekupe/ [1] *vtr* to cut up ⟨tart⟩; to carve ⟨roast⟩; to divide up ⟨land⟩

**découragé, ~e** /dekuraʒe/ *adj* ⟨person⟩ disheartened; ⟨expression⟩ despondent; ⟨tone⟩ dejected

**décourageant, ~e** /dekuraʒɑ̃, ɑ̃t/ *adj* disheartening

**découragement** /dekuraʒmɑ̃/ *nm* discouragement, despondency

**décourager** /dekuraʒe/ [13] *vtr* **(a)** to dishearten
**(b)** to discourage
**(c)** to deter

**décousu, ~e** /dekuzy/ **1** *pp* ▶ DÉCOUDRE
**2** *pp adj* ⟨hem⟩ which has come undone
**3** *adj* ⟨story⟩ rambling; ⟨conversation⟩ casual

**découvert, ~e¹** /dekuvɛr, ɛrt/ **1** *pp* ▶ DÉCOUVRIR
**2** *pp adj* **(a)** bare; **avoir la tête ~e** to be bare-headed
**(b)** ⟨truck⟩ open; ⟨car⟩ open-topped
**3** *nm* overdraft; **être à ~** to be overdrawn

**découverte²** /dekuvɛrt/ *nf* discovery

**découvrir** /dekuvrir/ [32] **1** *vtr* **(a)** to discover; **faire ~ qch à qn** to introduce sb to sth
**(b)** to show ⟨arm, back⟩
**(c)** to leave [sth] exposed ⟨border⟩
**2 se découvrir** *v refl* (+ *v être*) **(a)** to remove one's hat
**(b) elle s'est découvert un talent** she found she had a talent

**décrasser** /dekrase/ *vtr* [1] to get [sb/sth] clean

**décrépit, ~e** /dekrepi, it/ *adj* ⟨person⟩ decrepit; ⟨building⟩ dilapidated; ⟨wall⟩ crumbling

**décrépitude** /dekrepityd/ *nf* degeneration; decay; decrepitude

**décret** /dekrɛ/ *nm* decree

**décréter** /dekrete/ [14] *vtr* **(a)** to order
**(b)** to decree **(que** that)
**(c)** to declare **(que** that)

**décrire** /dekrir/ [67] *vtr* **(a)** to describe
**(b)** to follow

**décrocher** /dekrɔʃe/ [1] **1** *vtr* **(a)** to take down ⟨picture⟩
**(b)** to uncouple ⟨wagon⟩
**(c) ~ son téléphone** to pick up the receiver; to take the phone off the hook
**(d)** (colloq) to get ⟨contract⟩
**2** *vi* to give up
IDIOMS **~ le gros lot** to hit the jackpot

**décroissant, ~e** /dekrwasɑ̃, ɑ̃t/ *adj* fading; lessening; **par** *or* **en ordre ~** in descending order

**décroître** /dekrwatr/ [72] *vi* ⟨level⟩ to fall; ⟨moon⟩ to wane; ⟨day⟩ to get shorter; ⟨light, noise⟩ to fade; ⟨inflation⟩ to go down

**décrypter** /dekripte/ [1] *vtr* **(a)** to decipher ⟨signs⟩
**(b)** to interpret ⟨statement⟩

**déçu, ~e** /desy/ ▶ DÉCEVOIR

**déculpabiliser** /dekylpabilize/ [1] *vtr* to free [sb] of guilt

**décupler** /dekyple/ [1] *vtr, vi* to increase tenfold

**dédaigner** /dedeɲe/ [1] *vtr* to despise

**dédaigneux, -euse** /dedeɲø, øz/ *adj* disdainful, scornful; **être ~ du danger** to be unmindful of danger

**dédain** /dedɛ̃/ *nm* contempt, disdain

**dédale** /dedal/ *nm* **(a)** (of buildings) maze
**(b)** (of laws, formalities) labyrinth

**dedans** /dədɑ̃/ **1** *adv* inside
**2 en dedans** *phr* inside

**dédicace** /dedikas/ *nf* **(a)** dedication **(à qn** to sb)
**(b)** inscription

**dédicacer** /dedikase/ [12] *vtr* **(a)** to dedicate ⟨book⟩ **(à** to)
**(b)** to sign ⟨book, photo⟩

**dédier** /dedje/ [2] *vtr* **(a)** to dedicate ⟨novel⟩ **(à** to)
**(b)** to devote ⟨life⟩ **(à** to)

**dédire: se dédire** /dedir/ [65] *v refl* (+ *v être*) to back out

**dédommagement** /dedɔmaʒmɑ̃/ *nm* compensation

**dédommager** /dedɔmaʒe/ [13] *vtr* **(a)** to compensate
**(b) ~ qn de qch** to make it up to sb for sth

**dédouaner** /dedwane/ [1] *vtr* to clear through customs

**dédoubler: se dédoubler** /deduble/ [1] *v refl* (+ *v être*) ⟨nail⟩ to split; ⟨image⟩ to split in two; ⟨cable⟩ to come apart

**dédramatiser** /dedramatize/ [1] *vi* to play things down

**déductible** /dedyktibl/ *adj* deductible **(de** from); **~ des impôts** tax-deductible

**déduction** /dedyksjɔ̃/ *nf* deduction

**déduire** /dedɥiʀ/ [69] **1** *vtr* **(a)** to deduce
**(b)** to infer
**(c)** to deduct
**2 se déduire** *v refl* (+ *v être*) **(a)** to be inferred
**(b)** to be deduced
**(c)** to be deducted

**déesse** /deɛs/ *nf* goddess

**défaillance** /defajɑ̃s/ *nf* failure

**défaillant, ~e** /defajɑ̃, ɑ̃t/ *adj* **(a)** ⟨*motor, system*⟩ faulty
**(b)** ⟨*organization*⟩ inefficient
**(c)** ⟨*health, memory*⟩ failing; ⟨*person*⟩ fainting

**défaillir** /defajiʀ/ [28] *vi* **(a)** to faint; **se sentir ~** to feel faint
**(b)** ⟨*health, memory*⟩ to fail; **soutenir qn sans ~** to show unflinching support for sb

**défaire** /defɛʀ/ [10] **1** *vtr* to undo; to untie
**2 se défaire** *v refl* (+ *v être*) **(a)** to come undone
**(b) se ~ de** to get rid of; to part with; to rid oneself of
**(c)** ⟨*face*⟩ to fall; **avoir la mine défaite** to look haggard

**défaite** /defɛt/ *nf* defeat

**défaut** /defo/ **1** *nm* **(a)** fault, failing; **prendre qn en ~** to catch sb out
**(b)** defect; flaw; **présenter des ~s** to be faulty; **~ de fabrication** manufacturing fault; **~ de prononciation** speech impediment
**(c)** shortage; **faire ~** ⟨*money, resources*⟩ to be lacking
**2 à défaut de** *phr* **à ~ de (quoi)** failing (which); **à ~ de pouvoir acheter, elle loue** since she can't buy, she has to rent

**défaveur** /defavœʀ/ *nf* **il s'est trompé de 5 euros en ma ~** he overcharged me by 5 euros

**défavorable** /defavɔʀabl/ *adj* ⟨*situation*⟩ unfavourable (GB) (à to); ⟨*person*⟩ opposed (à to)

**défavorisé, ~e** /defavɔʀize/ *adj*
**(a)** underprivileged
**(b)** disadvantaged

**défavoriser** /defavɔʀize/ [1] *vtr* **(a)** to discriminate against
**(b)** to put [sb] at a disadvantage

**défection** /defɛksjɔ̃/ *nf* **(a)** defection
**(b)** non-appearance
**(c)** (of friends) desertion

**défectueux, -euse** /defɛktɥø, øz/ *adj* ⟨*material*⟩ faulty, defective; ⟨*reasoning*⟩ flawed

**défendre** /defɑ̃dʀ/ [6] **1** *vtr* **(a) ~ à qn de faire** to forbid sb to do
**(b)** to defend ⟨*person, country, interests*⟩
**(c)** to fight for ⟨*right*⟩; to stand up for ⟨*friend, principle*⟩; **~ une cause** to champion a cause
**(d)** (Law, Sport) to defend
**2 se défendre** *v refl* (+ *v être*) **(a)** to defend oneself; to stand up for oneself
**(b)** to be tenable
**(c)** to protect oneself

**(d)** (colloq) to get by
**(e) on ne peut se ~ de penser que...** one can't help thinking that...

**défense** /defɑ̃s/ *nf* **(a)** **'~ de fumer'** 'no smoking'; **~ d'en parler devant lui** don't mention it in front of him
**(b)** (Med, Mil, Sport) defence (GB)
**(c)** protection; **sans ~** helpless; unprotected; **la ~ de l'environnement** the protection of the environment; **prendre la ~ de** to stand up for
**(d)** (Zool) tusk

**défenseur** /defɑ̃sœʀ/ *nm* defender

**défensive** /defɑ̃siv/ *nf* **sur la ~** on the defensive

**déférence** /defeʀɑ̃s/ *nf* **marques de ~** marks of respect

**déferler** /defɛʀle/ [1] *vi* **(a)** ⟨*wave*⟩ to break (**sur** on)
**(b)** ⟨*violence*⟩ to erupt
**(c) ~ sur** ⟨*people*⟩ to pour into ⟨*country, town*⟩

**défi** /defi/ *nm* **(a)** challenge; **mettre qn au ~ de faire** to challenge sb to do
**(b) air de ~** defiant look

**défiance** /defjɑ̃s/ *nf* distrust, mistrust

**défiant, ~e** /defjɑ̃, ɑ̃t/ *adj* distrustful, wary

**déficience** /defisjɑ̃s/ *nf* deficiency

**déficit** /defisit/ *nm* **(a)** deficit
**(b)** (Med) deficiency

**déficitaire** /defisitɛʀ/ *adj* showing a deficit; showing a loss; showing a shortfall

**défier** /defje/ [2] *vtr* **(a)** to challenge ⟨*rival*⟩
**(b)** to defy ⟨*danger, death*⟩; **prix défiant toute concurrence** unbeatable price

**défigurer** /defigyʀe/ [1] *vtr* to disfigure

**défilé** /defile/ *nm* **(a)** parade
**(b)** (protest) march
**(c)** (of visitors, candidates) stream
**(d)** gorge
■ **~ aérien** flypast (GB), flyover (US); **~ militaire** march-past; **~ de mode** fashion show

**défiler** /defile/ [1] **1** *vi* **(a)** to parade; ⟨*protesters*⟩ to march
**(b)** ⟨*people*⟩ to come and go
**(c)** ⟨*images, landscape*⟩ to unfold
**(d)** (Comput) to scroll
**2 se défiler** *v refl* (+ *v être*) (colloq) to wriggle out of it

**définir** /definiʀ/ [3] *vtr* to define

**définitif, -ive** /definitif, iv/ **1** *adj* ⟨*accounts, report*⟩ final; ⟨*edition*⟩ definitive; ⟨*refusal*⟩ flat
**2 en définitive** *phr* at the end of the day

**définition** /definisjɔ̃/ *nf* definition

**définitivement** /definitivmɑ̃/ *adv* for good

**défiscalisé, ~e** /defiskalize/ *adj* tax-exempt

**déflagration** /deflagʀasjɔ̃/ *nf* detonation

**défoncer** /defɔ̃se/ [12] *vtr* to break down ⟨*door*⟩; to smash in ⟨*back of a car*⟩

**déformation** /defɔʀmasjɔ̃/ *nf*
(a) distortion
(b) deformity
(c) **c'est de la ~ professionnelle** it's a habit that comes from the job

**déformé**, **~e** /defɔʀme/ *adj* ⟨face, image, truth⟩ distorted; ⟨object, mind⟩ warped; **chaussée ~e** uneven (road) surface

**déformer** /defɔʀme/ [1] **1** *vtr* (a) to bend [sth] (out of shape)
(b) to distort
(c) **on a déformé mes propos** my words have been twisted
**2 se déformer** *v refl* (+ *v être*) to lose its shape

**défoulement** /defulmɑ̃/ *nm* letting off steam

**défouler** /defule/ [1] **1** *vtr* **ça me défoule** it helps me (to) unwind
**2 se défouler** *v refl* (+ *v être*) (a) to let off steam
(b) **se ~ sur qn** to take it out on sb

**défraîchi**, **~e** /defʀeʃi/ *adj* ⟨garment, curtain⟩ worn; ⟨material, beauty⟩ faded

**défrayer** /defʀeje/ [21] *vtr* (a) **~ la chronique** to be the talk of the town
(b) **~ qn** to pay *or* meet sb's expenses

**défricher** /defʀiʃe/ [1] *vtr* to clear, to reclaim

**défriser** /defʀize/ [1] *vtr* to straighten

**défroisser** /defʀwase/ [1] *vtr* to smooth out

**défunt**, **~e** /defœ̃, œ̃t/ **1** *adj* (a) former
(b) late
**2** *nm,f* **le ~** the deceased

**dégagé**, **~e** /degaʒe/ *adj* (a) ⟨road, sky⟩ clear; ⟨forehead⟩ bare
(b) ⟨look⟩ casual

**dégagement** /degaʒmɑ̃/ *nm* (a) clearing
(b) (in football) clearance

**dégager** /degaʒe/ [13] **1** *vtr* (a) to free; **~ qn d'une responsabilité** to relieve sb of a responsibility; **~ des crédits** to make funds available
(b) to unblock ⟨nose⟩
(b) to clear ⟨way⟩; **'dégagez, s'il vous plaît'** 'move along please'; **dégage!** (colloq) get lost! (colloq)
(c) to find ⟨idea, sense⟩
(d) to emit ⟨odour, gas⟩; **~ de la chaleur** to give off heat
**2 se dégager** *v refl* (+ *v être*) (a) to free oneself/itself
(b) ⟨weather, sky⟩ to clear
(c) **se ~ de** to come out of
(d) to become clear

**dégaine** /degɛn/ *nf* (colloq) odd appearance

**dégainer** /degene/ [1] *vtr* to draw ⟨gun⟩

**dégarnir: se dégarnir** /degaʀniʀ/ [3] *v refl* (+ *v être*) to be going bald

**dégât** /dega/ *nm* damage

**dégel** /deʒɛl/ *nm* thaw

**dégeler** /deʒle/ [17] **1** *vtr* (a) to improve ⟨relations⟩

(b) to unfreeze ⟨credit⟩
**2** *vi* to thaw (out)
**3 se dégeler** *v refl* (+ *v être*)
(a) ⟨relations, situation⟩ to thaw
(b) ⟨audience⟩ to warm up

**dégénérer** /deʒenere/ [14] *vi* (a) ⟨incident⟩ to get out of hand; **~ en** to degenerate into
(b) ⟨plant, species⟩ to degenerate

**dégingandé**, **~e** /deʒɛ̃gɑ̃de/ *adj* lanky

**dégivrer** /deʒivʀe/ [1] *vtr* (a) to de-ice ⟨windscreen⟩
(b) to defrost ⟨fridge⟩

**déglingué**, **~e** /deglɛ̃ge/ *adj* (colloq) dilapidated

**déglutir** /deglytiʀ/ [3] *vtr*, *vi* to swallow

**dégonflé**, **~e** /degɔ̃fle/ **1** *adj* ⟨balloon⟩ deflated; ⟨tyre⟩ flat
**2** *nm,f* (colloq) chicken (colloq), coward

**dégonfler** /degɔ̃fle/ [1] **1** *vtr* to deflate ⟨tyre⟩
**2** *vi* ⟨swelling, bump⟩ to go down
**3 se dégonfler** *v refl* (+ *v être*) (a) to deflate; to go down
(b) (colloq) to chicken out (colloq)

**dégot(t)er** /degɔte/ [1] *vtr* (colloq) to find

**dégouliner** /deguline/ [1] *vi* (a) to trickle
(b) to drip (de with)

**dégoupiller** /degupije/ [1] *vtr* **~ une grenade** to pull the pin out of a grenade

**dégourdi**, **~e** /deguʀdi/ *adj* smart

**dégourdir: se dégourdir** /deguʀdiʀ/ [3] *v refl* (+ *v être*) **se ~ les jambes** to stretch one's legs

**dégoût** /degu/ *nm* disgust

**dégoûtant**, **~e** /degutɑ̃, ɑ̃t/ *adj* (a) filthy
(b) (colloq) disgusting; revolting

**dégoûté**, **~e** /degute/ *adj* disgusted; **faire le ~** to turn one's nose up

**dégoûter** /degute/ [1] *vtr* (a) to disgust
(b) to make [sb] feel sick
(c) **~ qn de qch/de faire** to put sb off sth/off doing

**dégradant**, **~e** /degʀadɑ̃, ɑ̃t/ *adj* degrading

**dégradation** /degʀadasjɔ̃/ *nf* (a) damage
(b) deterioration
(c) decline; **la ~ des conditions de vie** the deterioration in the standard of living; **la ~ du pouvoir d'achat** the erosion in purchasing power

**dégradé**, **~e** /degʀade/ **1** *adj* **tons ~s** shaded tones; **coupe ~e** layered cut
**2** *nm* (in colours) gradation

**dégrader** /degʀade/ [1] **1** *vtr* (a) to damage
(b) (Mil) to cashier ⟨officer⟩
(c) to degrade ⟨person⟩
**2 se dégrader** *v refl* (+ *v être*) to deteriorate

**dégrafer** /degʀafe/ [1] **1** *vtr* to undo
**2 se dégrafer** *v refl* (+ *v être*) to come undone

**dégraisser** /degʀese/ [1] *vtr* to trim the fat off

**degré** /dəgʀe/ *nm* (a) degree; **par ~s** gradually; **à un moindre ~** to a lesser extent; **susceptible au plus haut ~** extremely touchy; **brûlures du premier ~** first-degree burns; **~ de parenté** degree of kinship
(b) step; **enseignement du second ~** secondary education; **c'est à prendre au deuxième ~** it is not to be taken literally
(c) **titrer 40° d'alcool** ≈ to be 70% proof
■ **~ Celsius** degree Celsius; **~ Fahrenheit** degree Fahrenheit

**dégressif, -ive** /degʀesif, iv/ *adj* ⟨tax⟩ graduated; **tarifs ~s** tapering charges

**dégringolade** /degʀɛ̃ɡɔlad/ *nf* (colloq)
(a) (gen) fall
(b) (Écon) collapse

**dégringoler** (colloq) /degʀɛ̃ɡɔle/ [1] **1** *vtr* to race down ⟨stairs, hill⟩
**2** *vi* (a) ⟨person⟩ to take a tumble; ⟨books⟩ to tumble down
(b) to drop sharply

**dégriser** /degʀize/ [1] *vtr* (a) to sober [sb] up
(b) to bring [sb] to his/her senses

**déguerpir** /degɛʀpiʀ/ [3] *vi* to leave

**déguisé, ~e** /degize/ *adj* (a) in fancy dress; in disguise
(b) ⟨party⟩ fancy-dress
(c) ⟨attempt⟩ concealed; ⟨compliment⟩ disguised

**déguisement** /degizmɑ̃/ *nm* costume

**déguiser** /degize/ [1] **1** *vtr* (a) to dress [sb] up (en as)
(b) to disguise
**2 se déguiser** *v refl* (+ *v être*) (a) to dress up
(b) to disguise oneself

**dégustation** /degystasjɔ̃/ *nf* tasting

**déguster** /degyste/ [1] *vtr* to savour (GB) ⟨drink, victory⟩; to enjoy ⟨performance⟩

**déhanchement** /deɑ̃ʃmɑ̃/ *nm* (a) swaying hips
(b) lopsidedness

**déhancher: se déhancher** /deɑ̃ʃe/ [1] *v refl* (+ *v être*) to wiggle one's hips

**dehors** /dəɔʀ/ **1** *adv* outside; **mettre qn ~** to throw sb out; to fire sb; to expel sb
**2** *excl* get out!
**3 en dehors de** *phr* (a) outside
(b) apart from

**déjà** /deʒa/ *adv* (a) already
(b) before, already; **je te l'ai ~ dit** I've told you before
(c) (colloq) **il s'est excusé, c'est ~ quelque chose** he apologized, that's something at least; **elle est ~ assez riche!** she's rich enough as it is; **c'est combien, ~?** how much was it again?

**déjà-vu** /deʒavy/ *nm inv* déjà vu; **c'est du ~** (colloq) we've seen it all before

**déjeuner**[1] /deʒœne/ [1] *vi* to have lunch

**déjeuner**[2] /deʒœne/ *nm* lunch

**déjouer** /deʒwe/ [1] *vtr* to frustrate ⟨precaution, manoeuvre⟩; to foil ⟨plan⟩; to evade ⟨inspection⟩

**delà** /dəla/ *adv* **deçà** or **de-ci, ~** here and there

**délabré, ~e** /delabʀe/ *adj* ⟨house, equipment⟩ dilapidated; ⟨health⟩ damaged

**délabrement** /delabʀəmɑ̃/ *nm* dilapidation

**délabrer** /delabʀe/ [1] **1** *vtr* to ruin
**2 se délabrer** *v refl* (+ *v être*) ⟨house⟩ to become run-down; ⟨business, country⟩ to go to rack and ruin; ⟨health⟩ to deteriorate

**délacer** /delase/ [12] *vtr* to undo; to unlace

**délai** /delɛ/ *nm* (a) **dans un ~ de 24 heures** within 24 hours; **respecter un ~** to meet a deadline; **dans les meilleurs ~s** as soon as possible
(b) extension; **demander un ~** to ask for extra time
■ **~ de livraison** delivery or lead time

**délaisser** /delese/ [1] *vtr* (a) to abandon ⟨activity⟩
(b) to neglect ⟨friends⟩

**délassement** /delɑsmɑ̃/ *nm* relaxation

**délasser** /delɑse/ [1] *vtr*, *v refl* (+ *v être*) to relax; **ça délasse** it's relaxing

**délateur, -trice** /delatœʀ, tʀis/ *nm,f* informer

**délation** /delɑsjɔ̃/ *nf* informing

**délavé, ~e** /delave/ *adj* (a) ⟨colour, sky⟩ washed-out; ⟨jeans⟩ faded
(b) waterlogged

**délayer** /deleje/ [21] *vtr* to thin ⟨paint⟩; to mix ⟨flour⟩

**délectation** /delɛktasjɔ̃/ *nf* delight

**délecter: se délecter** /delɛkte/ [1] *v refl* (+ *v être*) **se ~ à faire/en faisant** to delight in doing

**délégation** /delegasjɔ̃/ *nf* delegation

**délégué, ~e** /delege/ *nm,f* delegate
■ **~ syndical** union representative

**déléguer** /delege/ [14] *vtr* (a) to appoint [sb] as a delegate
(b) to delegate ⟨responsibility, power⟩

**délester** /delɛste/ [1] *vtr* (a) to get rid of the ballast from
(b) to divert traffic away from

**délibération** /deliberasjɔ̃/ *nf* deliberation; **mettre qch en ~** to debate sth

**délibéré, ~e** /delibeʀe/ *adj* ⟨act, violation⟩ deliberate; ⟨choice, policy⟩ conscious

**délibérément** /delibeʀemɑ̃/ *adv* ⟨wound, provoke⟩ deliberately; ⟨accept, choose⟩ consciously

**délibérer** /delibeʀe/ [14] **1 délibérer de** or **sur** *v+prep* to discuss
**2** *vi* to be in session

**délicat, ~e** /delika, at/ *adj* (a) ⟨dish⟩ subtle; ⟨person⟩ refined
(b) tactful
(c) thoughtful; **des procédés peu ~s** unscrupulous means
(d) ⟨balance, task⟩ delicate; ⟨business, moment⟩ sensitive; ⟨mission⟩ tricky
(e) ⟨skin⟩ delicate

**délicatement** /delikatmɑ̃/ *adv*
(a) delicately
(b) tactfully

**délicatesse** /delikatɛs/ *nf* (a) delicacy; **la ~ de ses traits** his/her fine features
(b) sensitivity
(c) delicacy, trickiness

**délice** /delis/ *nm* delight

**délicieusement** /delisjøzmɑ̃/ *adv*
(a) deliciously
(b) delightfully

**délicieux, -ieuse** /delisjø, øz/ *adj*
(a) delicious
(b) ⟨*feeling, music*⟩ delightful; ⟨*joy*⟩ exquisite

**délié, ~e** /delje/ *adj* (a) ⟨*waist*⟩ slender
(b) ⟨*movement*⟩ loose
(c) ⟨*mind*⟩ nimble

**délier** /delje/ [2] *vtr* to untie; **~ qn de** to release sb from ⟨*promise*⟩
IDIOMS **~ la langue à qn** to loosen sb's tongue

**délimiter** /delimite/ [1] *vtr* (a) to mark the boundary of
(b) to form the boundary of
(c) to define ⟨*role*⟩; to define the scope of ⟨*subject*⟩

**délinquance** /delɛ̃kɑ̃s/ *nf* crime; **la ~ juvénile** juvenile delinquency

**délinquant, ~e** /delɛ̃kɑ̃, ɑ̃t/ **1** *adj* delinquent
**2** *nm,f* offender

**déliquescence** /delikesɑ̃s/ *nf* decline

**délirant, ~e** /deliRɑ̃, ɑ̃t/ *adj* (a) ⟨*welcome*⟩ ecstatic
(b) (colloq) ⟨*scenario*⟩ crazy (colloq)

**délire** /deliR/ *nm* (a) (Med) delirium
(b) (colloq) madness
(c) frenzy; **salle en ~** ecstatic audience

**délirer** /deliRe/ [1] *vi* (a) (Med) to be delirious
(b) (colloq) to be mad

**délit** /deli/ *nm* offence (GB).
■ **~ de fuite** hit-and-run offence; **~ d'initié** insider dealing

**délivrance** /delivRɑ̃s/ *nf* relief

**délivrer** /delivRe/ [1] *vtr* (a) to free, to liberate; **~ qn de** to relieve sb of
(b) to issue ⟨*passport*⟩

**délocalisation** /delɔkalizasjɔ̃/ *nf* relocation

**déloger** /delɔʒe/ [13] *vtr* (a) to evict ⟨*tenant*⟩
(b) to flush out ⟨*rebels, game*⟩
(c) to remove ⟨*dust*⟩

**déloyal, ~e,** *mpl* **-aux** /delwajal, o/ *adj* ⟨*person*⟩ disloyal; ⟨*competition*⟩ unfair

**deltaplane** /dɛltaplan/ *nm* hang-glider

**déluge** /delyʒ/ *nm* downpour; **~ de** flood of ⟨*tears, complaints*⟩; **le Déluge** the Flood
IDIOMS **après moi le ~** I don't care what happens after I'm gone

**déluré, ~e** /delyRe/ *adj* (a) smart, resourceful
(b) forward

**démagogie** /demagɔʒi/ *nf* demagoguery, demagogy; **faire de la ~** to try to gain popularity

**démagogique** /demagɔʒik/ *adj* demagogic

**demain** /dəmɛ̃/ *adv* tomorrow; **l'Europe de ~** the Europe of the future
IDIOMS **~ il fera jour** tomorrow is another day; **ce n'est pas ~ la veille!** that's not going to happen in a hurry!

**démancher: se démancher** /demɑ̃ʃe/ [1] *v refl* (+ *v être*) ⟨*tool*⟩ to come off its handle

**demande** /dəmɑ̃d/ *nf* (a) request, application, claim (**de** for); **~ de dommages et intérêts** claim for damages; **faire une ~ de mutation** to apply for a transfer
(b) (in economics) demand
(c) application form
■ **~ d'emploi** job application; '**~s d'emploi**' 'situations wanted'; **~ en mariage** marriage proposal

**demandé, ~e** /dəmɑ̃de/ *adj* **très ~** ⟨*destination*⟩ very popular; ⟨*product*⟩ in great demand

**demander** /dəmɑ̃de/ [1] **1** *vtr* (a) to ask for ⟨*advice, money, help*⟩; to apply for ⟨*nationality*⟩; to claim ⟨*damages*⟩; **~ le divorce** to sue for divorce; **~ en mariage** to propose to; '**on demande un plombier**' 'plumber wanted'; **fais ce qu'on te demande!** do as you're told!; **je ne demande pas mieux** there's nothing I would like better
(b) **~ qch à qn** to ask sb sth; **il m'a demandé de tes nouvelles** he asked after you
(c) to send for ⟨*priest*⟩; to dial ⟨*number*⟩; **le patron vous demande** the boss wants to see you
(d) to call for ⟨*reforms*⟩; to require ⟨*effort, qualification*⟩; to need ⟨*attention*⟩
**2 se demander** *v refl* (+ *v être*) to wonder

**demandeur¹, -euse** /dəmɑ̃dœR, øz/ *nm,f* applicant.
■ **~ d'asile** asylum-seeker; **~ d'emploi** job-seeker

**demandeur², -eresse** /dəmɑ̃dœR, d(ə)RES/ *nm,f* (Law) plaintiff

**démangeaison** /demɑ̃ʒɛzɔ̃/ *nf* itch

**démanger** /demɑ̃ʒe/ [13] *vtr* **ça me démange** it itches, it's itching; **l'envie de le gifler me démangeait** I was itching to slap him

**démanteler** /demɑ̃tle/ [17] *vtr* to dismantle; to break up

**démaquillage** /demakijaʒ/ *nm* make-up removal

**démaquillant, ~e** /demakijɑ̃, ɑ̃t/ **1** *adj* ⟨*milk*⟩ cleansing
**2** *nm* make-up remover

**démaquiller: se démaquiller** /demakije/ [1] *v refl* (+ *v être*) to remove one's make-up

**démarcation** /demaRkasjɔ̃/ *nf* demarcation

**démarchage** /demaʀʃaʒ/ *nm* door-to-door selling; ∼ **électoral** canvassing; ∼ **téléphonique** cold calling

**démarche** /demaʀʃ/ *nf* (a) walk
(b) step; **faire une** ∼ **auprès de qn to** approach sb; **faire des** ∼**s pour obtenir qch** to take steps to obtain sth
(c) reasoning; ∼ **de la pensée** thought process

**démarcher** /demaʀʃe/ [1] *vtr* (a) to sell door-to-door
(b) to canvass

**démarque** /demaʀk/ *nf* (of goods) mark-down (**de** of)

**démarquer** /demaʀke/ [1] 1 *vtr* to mark down ⟨*goods*⟩
2 **se démarquer** *v refl* (+ *v être*) (a) **se** ∼ **de** to distance oneself from
(b) (Sport) to get free of one's marker

**démarrage** /demaʀaʒ/ *nm* (a) starting up
(b) spurt
■ ∼ **en côte** hill start

**démarrer** /demaʀe/ [1] 1 *vtr* to start (up)
2 *vi* (a) ⟨*vehicle*⟩ to pull away; ⟨*engine*⟩ to start; ⟨*driver*⟩ to drive off; ⟨*business*⟩ to start up; ⟨*campaign*⟩ to get under way; ⟨*person*⟩ to start off
(b) (Sport) to put on a spurt

**démarreur** /demaʀœʀ/ *nm* (in car) starter

**démasquer** /demaske/ [1] *vtr* to unmask ⟨*person*⟩; to uncover ⟨*plot*⟩

**démazouter** /demazute/ [1] *vtr* to clean the oil from ⟨*beach*⟩

**démêlé** /demele/ *nm* wrangle; **avoir des** ∼**s avec la justice** to get into trouble with the law

**démêler** /demele/ [1] *vtr* (a) to disentangle; to untangle
(b) to sort out ⟨*situation*⟩

**démembrement** /demãbʀəmã/ *nm*
(a) break-up, dismemberment
(b) (of estate) division

**démembrer** /demãbʀe/ [1] *vtr* to divide up, to dismember

**déménagement** /demenaʒmã/ *nm*
(a) moving house; move
(b) removal; **entreprise de** ∼**s** removals firm (GB), moving company (US)

**déménager** /demenaʒe/ [13] 1 *vtr* (a) to move ⟨*furniture*⟩; to relocate ⟨*offices*⟩
(b) to clear ⟨*room*⟩
2 *vi* (a) to move (house)
(b) (colloq) to push off (colloq)
(c) (colloq) to be off one's rocker (colloq)

**déménageur** /demenaʒœʀ/ *nm* removal (GB) *or* moving (US) man

**démence** /demãs/ *nf* (a) insanity
(b) dementia

**démener: se démener** /dem(ə)ne/ [16] *v refl* (+ *v être*) (a) to thrash about
(b) to put oneself out, to exert oneself

**dément**, ∼**e** /demã, ãt/ *adj* (a) insane, mad
(b) (colloq) terrific (colloq)

**démenti** /demãti/ *nm* denial

**démentiel, -ielle** /demãsjɛl/ *adj* insane

**démentir** /demãtiʀ/ [30] *vtr* (a) to deny
(b) ⟨*person*⟩ to refute ⟨*statement*⟩; ⟨*fact*⟩ to give the lie to ⟨*statement*⟩; to belie ⟨*appearance*⟩

**démesure** /demzyʀ/ *nf* (a) (of ambition) excesses
(b) excessive size

**démesuré**, ∼**e** /demzyʀe/ *adj* excessive, immoderate

**démettre** /demɛtʀ/ [60] 1 *vtr* (a) to dislocate ⟨*joint*⟩
(b) to dismiss ⟨*employee*⟩
2 **se démettre** *v refl* (+ *v être*) **se** ∼ **l'épaule** to dislocate one's shoulder

**demeurant: au demeurant** /odəmœʀã/ *phr* as it happens, for all that

**demeure** /dəmœʀ/ *nf* (a) residence
(b) **mettre qn en** ∼ **de faire** to require sb to do
2 **à demeure** *phr* permanently; permanent
IDIOMS **il n'y a pas péril en la** ∼ there's no rush

**demeuré**, ∼**e** /dəmœʀe/ *adj* retarded

**demeurer** /dəmœʀe/ [1] 1 *vi* (a) (+ *v avoir*) to reside, to live
(b) (+ *v être*) to remain
2 *v impers* **il n'en demeure pas moins que** nonetheless, the fact remains that

**demi**, ∼**e**¹ /d(ə)mi/ 1 **et demi, et demie** *phr* and a half; **il est trois heures et** ∼ **e** it's half past three
2 *nm,f* half
3 *nm* (a) glass of beer
(b) (Sport) ∼ **de mêlée/d'ouverture** scrum/stand-off half
4 **à demi** *phr* half; **à** ∼ **éveillé** half awake
5 **demi-** (*combining form*) (a) half; **une** ∼-**pomme** half an apple
(b) partial; **une** ∼-**victoire** a partial victory

**demi-cercle**, *pl* ∼**s** /d(ə)misɛʀkl/ *nm* semicircle

**demie**² /d(ə)mi/ 1 *adj* ▶ DEMI 1,2
2 *nf* **il est déjà la** ∼ it's already half past

**demi-écrémé**, ∼**e**, *mpl* ∼**s** /d(ə)miekʀeme/ *adj* semi-skimmed

**demi-finale**, *pl* ∼**s** /d(ə)mifinal/ *nf* semifinal

**demi-fond**, *pl* ∼**s** /d(ə)mifɔ̃/ *nm* middle-distance running

**demi-frère**, *pl* ∼**s** /d(ə)mifʀɛʀ/ *nm* half-brother; stepbrother

**demi-gros** /d(ə)migʀo/ *nm inv* wholesale direct to the public

**demi-heure**, *pl* ∼**s** /d(ə)mijœʀ/ *nf* half an hour

**demi-journée**, *pl* ∼**s** /d(ə)miʒuʀne/ *nf* half a day; **à la** ∼ on a half-day basis

**démilitariser** /demilitaʀize/ [1] *vtr* to demilitarize

**demi-litre**, *pl* ∼**s** /d(ə)militʀ/ *nm* half a litre (GB)

**demi-mesure**, *pl* ~**s** /d(ə)mim(ə)zyʀ/ *nf* half-measure

**demi-mot**: **à demi-mot** /ad(ə)mimo/ *phr* j'ai compris à ~ I didn't need to have it spelt out

**déminer** /demine/ [1] *vtr* to clear [sth] of mines

**demi-pension** /d(ə)mipɑ̃sjɔ̃/ *nf* half board

**demi-pensionnaire**, *pl* ~**s** /d(ə)mipɑ̃sjɔnɛʀ/ *nmf* (Sch) pupil who has school lunches

**démis**, ~**e** /demi, iz/ **1** *pp* ▶ DÉMETTRE **2** *pp adj* dislocated

**demi-sel** /d(ə)misɛl/ *adj* ⟨butter⟩ slightly salted

**demi-sœur**, *pl* ~**s** /d(ə)misœʀ/ *nf* half-sister; stepsister

**démission** /demisjɔ̃/ *nf* (a) resignation (de from)
(b) (figurative) failure to take responsibility

**démissionner** /demisjone/ [1] *vi* (a) to resign (de from)
(b) to abdicate one's responsibilities

**demi-tarif**, *pl* ~**s** /d(ə)mitaʀif/ **1** *adj* half-price
**2** *adv* half-price
**3** *nm* half-price ticket

**demi-tour**, *pl* ~**s** /d(ə)mituʀ/ *nm* half-turn; **faire** ~ to turn back

**démobiliser** /demɔbilize/ [1] *vtr* (a) to demobilize
(b) to demotivate

**démocrate** /demɔkʀat/ **1** *adj* democratic **2** *nmf* democrat

**démocratie** /demɔkʀasi/ *nf* democracy

**démocratique** /demɔkʀatik/ *adj* democratic

**démocratiser**: **se démocratiser** /demɔkʀatize/ [1] *v refl* (+ *v être*) (a) to become more democratic
(b) to become more accessible

**démodé**, ~**e** /demode/ *adj* old-fashioned

**démoder**: **se démoder** /demode/ [1] *v refl* (+ *v être*) to go out of fashion

**démographie** /demɔgʀafi/ *nf* demography

**démographique** /demɔgʀafik/ *adj* demographic

**demoiselle** /d(ə)mwazɛl/ *nf* (a) young lady
(b) single woman
■ ~ **d'honneur** bridesmaid

**démolir** /demɔliʀ/ [3] *vtr* to demolish; to wreck; to destroy

**démolition** /demɔlisjɔ̃/ *nf* demolition

**démon** /demɔ̃/ *nm* demon, devil
■ ~ **de midi** ≈ middle-age lust

**démoniaque** /demɔnjak/ *adj* demonic

**démonstrateur**, **-trice** /demɔ̃stʀatœʀ, tʀis/ *nm,f* (for products) demonstrator

**démonstratif**, **-ive** /demɔ̃stʀatif, iv/ *adj* demonstrative

**démonstration** /demɔ̃stʀasjɔ̃/ *nf*
(a) display; ~ **de courage** display of courage; ~**s d'amitié** a show of friendship
(b) demonstration
(c) (of theory) demonstration, proof

**démontable** /demɔ̃tabl/ *adj* ⟨furniture⟩ that can be taken apart

**démonté**, ~**e** /demɔ̃te/ *adj* ⟨sea⟩ stormy

**démonte-pneu**, *pl* ~**s** /demɔ̃t(ə)pnø/ *nm* tyre-lever (GB), tire iron (US)

**démonter** /demɔ̃te/ [1] **1** *vtr* (a) to dismantle, to take [sth] to pieces ⟨machine⟩; to remove ⟨wheel⟩
(b) (colloq) to fluster; **ne pas se laisser** ~ to remain unruffled
**2** **se démonter** *v refl* (+ *v être*)
(a) ⟨furniture⟩ to come apart
(b) (colloq) ⟨person⟩ to become flustered

**démontrer** /demɔ̃tʀe/ [1] *vtr* to demonstrate, to prove

**démoralisant**, ~**e** /demɔʀalizɑ̃, ɑ̃t/ *adj* demoralizing

**démoraliser** /demɔʀalize/ [1] *vtr* to demoralize

**démordre** /demɔʀdʀ/ [6] *v+prep* **il n'en démord pas** he sticks by it, he's sticking to it

**démotiver** /demɔtive/ *vtr* to demotivate

**démouler** /demule/ [1] *vtr* to turn [sth] out of the tin (GB) *or* pan (US) ⟨cake⟩; to remove [sth] from the mould (GB) *or* mold (US) ⟨statue⟩

**démultiplier** /demyltiplije/ [2] *vtr* (a) to reduce ⟨speed⟩
(b) to increase ⟨powers, capacity⟩

**démuni**, ~**e** /demyni/ *adj* destitute; penniless; ~ **de** devoid of, without ⟨talent⟩

**démunir** /demyniʀ/ [3] **1** *vtr* to divest (de of)
**2** **se démunir** *v refl* (+ *v être*) **se** ~ **de qch** to leave oneself without sth

**démystifier** /demistifje/ [2] *vtr* (a) ~ **qn** to dispel sb's illusions
(b) to demystify

**démythifier** /demitifje/ [2] *vtr* to demythologize

**dénatalité** /denatalite/ *nf* fall in the birthrate

**dénationaliser** /denasjɔnalize/ [1] *vtr* to denationalize

**dénaturé**, ~**e** /denatyʀe/ *adj* (a) ⟨alcohol⟩ denatured
(b) ⟨tastes⟩ warped; ⟨parents⟩ unnatural

**dénaturer** /denatyʀe/ [1] *vtr* (a) to denature
(b) to distort ⟨facts⟩
(c) to spoil ⟨taste, sauce⟩

**dénicher** /deniʃe/ [1] *vtr* (a) (colloq) to dig out (colloq) ⟨object⟩; to track down ⟨person⟩; to find ⟨right address⟩
(b) to flush out ⟨thief, animal⟩

**dénier** /denje/ [2] *vtr* to deny

**deniers** /dənje/ *nm pl* money; ~**s publics** *or* **de l'État** public funds

**dénigrement** /denigʀəmɑ̃/ *nm*
denigration

**dénigrer** /denigʀe/ [1] *vtr* to denigrate

**dénivellation** /denivɛlasjɔ̃/ *nf*
(a) difference in level
(b) gradient

**dénombrable** /denɔ̃bʀabl/ *adj* countable;
non ~ uncountable

**dénombrement** /denɔ̃bʀəmɑ̃/ *nm* count

**dénombrer** /denɔ̃bʀe/ [1] *vtr* to count

**dénomination** /denɔminasjɔ̃/ *nf* name,
designation

**dénommer** /denɔme/ [1] *vtr* to name

**dénoncer** /denɔ̃se/ [12] [1] *vtr* to denounce
[2] **se dénoncer** *v refl* (+ *v être*) to give
oneself up

**dénonciation** /denɔ̃sjasjɔ̃/ *nf*
denunciation

**dénoter** /denɔte/ [1] *vtr* denote

**dénouement** /denumɑ̃/ *nm*
(a) denouement
(b) outcome

**dénouer** /denwe/ [1] [1] *vtr* (a) to undo
‹knot›
(b) to unravel ‹intrigue›; to resolve ‹crisis›
[2] **se dénouer** *v refl* (+ *v être*) (a) ‹laces›
to come undone
(b) ‹crisis› to resolve itself

**dénoyauter** /denwajote/ [1] *vtr* to stone
(GB), to pit (US)

**denrée** /dɑ̃ʀe/ *nf* (a) foodstuff; ~ **de base**
staple
(b) commodity

**dense** /dɑ̃s/ *adj* dense; concentrated; heavy

**densité** /dɑ̃site/ *nf* (a) density
(b) denseness

**dent** /dɑ̃/ *nf* (a) tooth; **à pleines** *or* **belles**
~s with relish; **ne rien avoir à se mettre**
**sous la** ~ to have nothing to eat
(b) (of comb) tooth; (of fork) prong; **en ~s de**
**scie** ‹blade› serrated; ‹results› which go up
and down
(c) crag
■ ~ **de lait** milk tooth
IDIOMS **avoir une** ~ **contre qn** to bear sb a
grudge; **avoir les** ~s **longues** to be ambitious

**dentaire** /dɑ̃tɛʀ/ *adj* dental

**denté**, ~**e** /dɑ̃te/ *adj* (a) toothed
(b) dentate

**dentelé**, ~**e** /dɑ̃t(ə)le/ *adj* ‹coast›
indented; ‹crest› jagged; ‹stamp› perforated;
‹leaf› dentate

**dentelle** /dɑ̃tɛl/ *nf* lace
IDIOMS **il ne fait pas dans la** ~ he's not one
to bother with niceties

**dentelure** /dɑ̃tlyʀ/ *nf* (of stamp)
perforation; (of crest) jagged outline; (of leaf)
serration

**dentier** /dɑ̃tje/ *nm* dentures

**dentifrice** /dɑ̃tifʀis/ *nm* toothpaste

**dentiste** /dɑ̃tist/ *nmf* dentist

**dentition** /dɑ̃tisjɔ̃/ *nf* dentition

**dénuder** /denyde/ [1] [1] *vtr* to strip

[2] **se dénuder** *v refl* (+ *v être*) (a) to strip
(off)
(b) to become bare

**dénué**, ~**e** /denɥe/ *adj* ~ **de** lacking in;
~ **de sens** senseless

**dénuement** /denymɑ̃/ *nm* destitution;
bareness

**déodorant**, ~**e** /deɔdɔʀɑ̃, ɑ̃t/ [1] *adj*
deodorant
[2] *nm* deodorant

**déontologie** /deɔ̃tɔlɔʒi/ *nf* (professional)
ethics

**dépannage** /depanaʒ/ *nm* repair

**dépanner** /depane/ [1] *vtr* (a) to fix ‹car,
machine›
(b) to tow away
(c) (colloq) to help [sb] out

**dépanneur, -euse¹** /depanœʀ, øz/ *nm,f*
engineer

**dépanneuse²** /depanøz/ *nf* breakdown
truck (GB), tow truck (US)

**dépareillé**, ~**e** /depaʀeje/ *adj* (a) odd;
articles ~s oddments
(b) incomplete

**déparer** /depaʀe/ [1] *vtr* to spoil, to mar

**départ** /depaʀ/ *nm* (a) departure; ~ **des**
**grandes lignes** main line departures;
**téléphone avant ton** ~ phone before you
leave; **être sur le** ~ to be about to leave
(b) resignation; **le** ~ **en retraite** retirement
(c) (gen, Sport) start; **donner le (signal du)** ~
**aux coureurs** to start the race; **prendre un**
**nouveau** ~ (figurative) to make a fresh start;
**au** ~ at first; at the outset; **de** ~ initial;
‹language› source; ‹salary› starting

**départager** /depaʀtaʒe/ [13] *vtr* to decide
between ‹competitors›

**département** /depaʀtəmɑ̃/ *nm*
department

**départemental**, ~**e**, *mpl* **-aux**
/depaʀtəmɑ̃tal, o/ *adj* ‹election› local; ‹road›
secondary

**dépassé**, ~**e** /depase/ *adj* (a) outdated,
outmoded
(b) (colloq) overwhelmed

**dépassement** /depasmɑ̃/ *nm*
(a) overtaking
(b) overrun; ~ **d'horaire** overrunning the
schedule; **le** ~ **de la dose prescrite** exceeding
the stated dose
(c) ~ **de soi** surpassing oneself
■ ~ **budgétaire** cost overrun; ~ **de capacité**
(Comput) overflow

**dépasser** /depase/ [1] [1] *vtr* (a) to
overtake (GB), to pass (US) ‹car, pedestrian›;
to go past ‹place›
(b) to exceed ‹figure, dose, limit›; **elle le**
**dépasse de cinq centimètres** she's five
centimetres (GB) taller than him; **il a**
**dépassé la cinquantaine** he's over *or* past
fifty; ~ **la mesure** *or* **les bornes** to go too far
(c) to be ahead of, to outstrip ‹rival›; **ça me**
**dépasse!** it's beyond me!
[2] *vi* to jut *or* stick out; ‹underskirt› to show

**dépassionner** /depasjɔne/ [1] *vtr* to defuse ⟨*discussion*⟩

**dépatouiller**: **se dépatouiller** /depatuje/ [1] *v refl* (+ *v être*) (colloq) to get by

**dépaysé**, **~e** /depeize/ *adj* **il est complètement ~** he's like a fish out of water; **il n'est pas ~ ici** he feels at home here

**dépaysement** /depeizmɑ̃/ *nm* (a) change of scenery
(b) disorientation

**dépayser** /depeize/ [1] *vtr* (a) to provide [sb] with a pleasant change of scenery
(b) to disorient

**dépecer** /dep(ə)se/ [16] *vtr* to tear apart, to cut up

**dépêche** /depɛʃ/ *nf* dispatch

**dépêcher** /depeʃe/ [16] **1** *vtr* to dispatch (à to)
**2 se dépêcher** *v refl* (+ *v être*) to hurry up

**dépeigné**, **~e** /depeɲe/ *adj* dishevelled (GB)

**dépeindre** /depɛ̃dR/ [55] *vtr* to depict

**dépenaillé**, **~e** /depənaje/ *adj* ragged

**dépénaliser** /depenalize/ [1] *vtr* to decriminalize

**dépendance** /depɑ̃dɑ̃s/ *nf*
(a) dependence, dependency
(b) outbuilding
(c) dependency, dependent territory

**dépendant**, **~e** /depɑ̃dɑ̃, ɑ̃t/ *adj* dependent (de on); **~s l'un de l'autre** interdependent

**dépendre** /depɑ̃dR/ [6] *v+prep* (a) **~ de** to depend on
(b) **~ de** to be dependent on
(c) **~ de** ⟨*organization*⟩ to come under the control of; ⟨*employee*⟩ to be responsible to
(d) **~ de** ⟨*environment*⟩ to be the responsibility of
(e) **~ de** ⟨*territory*⟩ to be a dependency of
(f) **~ de** ⟨*building, land*⟩ to belong to

**dépens** /depɑ̃/ *nm pl* **aux ~ de** at the expense of; **vivre aux ~ des autres** to live off other people

**dépense** /depɑ̃s/ *nf* (a) spending, expenditure; **~s publiques** public expenditure
(b) expense; **réduire ses ~s** to cut down on expenses
(c) outlay; **une ~ de 300 euros** an outlay of 300 euros
(d) consumption; **~ d'énergie physique** expenditure of physical energy

**dépenser** /depɑ̃se/ [1] **1** *vtr* to spend ⟨*money, time*⟩; to use up ⟨*energy, fuel*⟩
**2 se dépenser** *v refl* (+ *v être*) to get (enough) exercise

**dépensier**, **-ière** /depɑ̃sje, ɛR/ *adj* extravagant

**déperdition** /depɛRdisjɔ̃/ *nf* loss

**dépérir** /depeRiR/ [3] *vi* ⟨*person*⟩ to waste away; ⟨*plant*⟩ to wilt; ⟨*economy*⟩ to be on the decline

**dépêtrer**: **se dépêtrer** /depɛtRe/ [1] *v refl* (+ *v être*) **se ~ de** to extricate oneself from

**dépeuplement** /depœpləmɑ̃/ *nm* depopulation

**dépeupler** /depœple/ [1] *vtr* to depopulate ⟨*region*⟩; to reduce the wildlife in ⟨*forest*⟩

**déphasé**, **~e** /defaze/ *adj* (a) (colloq) out of step
(b) out of phase

**dépiauter** /depjote/ [1] *vtr* (colloq) to skin ⟨*animal*⟩

**dépilation** /depilasjɔ̃/ *nf* hair removal

**dépilatoire** /depilatwaR/ *adj* depilatory, hair-removing

**dépistable** /depistabl/ *adj* detectable

**dépistage** /depistaʒ/ *nm* screening (de for); **test de ~ du sida** Aids test

**dépister** /depiste/ [1] *vtr* (a) to track down ⟨*criminal, game*⟩
(b) to detect ⟨*illness*⟩

**dépit** /depi/ **1** *nm* pique; **par ~** out of pique
**2 en dépit de** *phr* in spite of; **en ~ du bon sens** in a very illogical way

**dépité**, **~e** /depite/ *adj* piqued (de at)

**déplacé**, **~e** /deplase/ *adj* inappropriate; **c'est ~** it's out of place; it's uncalled for

**déplacement** /deplasmɑ̃/ *nm* (a) trip; **ça vaut le ~!** it's worth the trip!; **frais de ~** travelling (GB) expenses
(b) moving; shifting; transfer (vers to)
(c) displacement
■ **~ de vertèbre** slipped disc

**déplacer** /deplase/ [12] **1** *vtr* to move ⟨*object, person*⟩; to displace ⟨*population*⟩; to shift ⟨*attention*⟩; to change ⟨*issue*⟩
**2 se déplacer** *v refl* (+ *v être*) (a) to move; **se ~ une vertèbre** to slip a disc
(b) to get about; to travel
(c) ⟨*doctor*⟩ to go out on call

**déplaire** /deplɛR/ [59] **1** *vi* **le spectacle a déplu** the show was not well received
**2 déplaire à** *v+prep* **cela m'a déplu** I didn't like it; **la situation n'est pas pour me ~** the situation quite suits me
**3** *v impers* **ne vous en déplaise** (ironic) whether you like it or not

**déplaisant**, **~e** /deplɛzɑ̃, ɑ̃t/ *adj* unpleasant

**déplâtrer** /deplɑtRe/ [1] *vtr* to remove the cast from ⟨*limb*⟩

**dépliant** /deplijɑ̃/ *nm* (a) leaflet
(b) fold-out page

**déplier** /deplije/ [2] *vtr* to unfold ⟨*newspaper*⟩; to open out ⟨*map*⟩

**déploiement** /deplwamɑ̃/ *nm* (a) display; array
(b) deployment

**déplorable** /deploRabl/ *adj* (a) regrettable
(b) appalling, deplorable

**déplorer** /deploRe/ [1] *vtr* to deplore

**déployer** /deplwaje/ [23] *vtr* **(a)** to display ⟨*talent, wealth*⟩; to expend ⟨*energy*⟩
**(b)** to deploy ⟨*troops*⟩
**(c)** to spread ⟨*wings*⟩; to unfurl ⟨*sail*⟩

**déplumer**: **se déplumer** /deplyme/ [1] *v refl* (+ *v être*) ⟨*bird*⟩ to lose its feathers

**dépoli**, ∼**e** /depɔli/ *adj* **verre** ∼ frosted glass

**dépolitiser** /depɔlitize/ [1] *vtr* to depoliticize

**dépolluer** /depɔlɥe/ [1] *vtr* to rid [sth] of pollution, to clean up

**dépollution** /depɔlysjɔ̃/ *nf* cleanup

**dépopulation** /depɔpylasjɔ̃/ *nf* depopulation

**déportation** /depɔʀtasjɔ̃/ *nf*
**(a)** internment in a concentration camp
**(b)** deportation

**déporté**, ∼**e** /depɔʀte/ *nm,f* **(a)** prisoner interned in a concentration camp
**(b)** transported convict

**déporter** /depɔʀte/ [1] **①** *vtr* **(a)** to send [sb] to a concentration camp
**(b)** to deport
**②** **se déporter** *v refl* (+ *v être*) to swerve

**déposant**, ∼**e** /depozɑ̃, ɑ̃t/ *nm,f*
**(a)** depositor
**(b)** deponent

**déposer** /depoze/ [1] **①** *vtr* **(a)** to dump ⟨*rubbish*⟩; to lay ⟨*wreath*⟩; to drop off, to leave ⟨*parcel, passenger*⟩; to deposit ⟨*money*⟩; ∼ **les armes** to lay down one's arms
**(b)** to register ⟨*trademark*⟩; to submit ⟨*file, offer*⟩; to lodge ⟨*complaint*⟩; ∼ **son bilan** to file a bankruptcy petition
**(c)** ⟨*river*⟩ to deposit ⟨*alluvium*⟩
**②** *vi* (Law) to make a statement, to testify
**③** **se déposer** *v refl* (+ *v être*) ⟨*dust*⟩ to settle; ⟨*deposit*⟩ to collect

**dépositaire** /depoziteʀ/ *nmf* **(a)** agent; ∼ **agréé** authorized dealer
**(b)** trustee

**déposition** /depozisjɔ̃/ *nf* (Law) statement; deposition; evidence

**déposséder** /deposede/ [14] *vtr* to dispossess

**dépôt** /depo/ *nm* **(a)** warehouse; depot
**(b)** outlet; **l'épicerie fait** ∼ **de pain the** grocer's sells bread
**(c)** (of trademark) registration; (of bill) introduction
**(d)** **date limite de** ∼ **des déclarations d'impôt** deadline for income tax returns
**(e)** deposit
**(f)** police cells
■ ∼ **de bilan** voluntary liquidation; ∼ **d'ordures** (rubbish) tip *or* dump (GB), garbage dump (US)

**dépotoir** /depɔtwaʀ/ *nm* **(a)** dump
**(b)** (colloq) shambles (colloq)

**dépôt-vente**, *pl* **dépôts-ventes** /depovɑ̃t/ *nm* secondhand shop (GB) *or* store ⟨*where goods are sold on commission*⟩

**dépouille** /depuj/ *nf* **(a)** skin, hide
**(b)** body; ∼ **mortelle** mortal remains

**(c)** ∼**s** spoils

**dépouillé**, ∼**e** /depuje/ *adj* **(a)** ⟨*style*⟩ spare
**(b)** ⟨*tree*⟩ bare

**dépouillement** /depujmɑ̃/ *nm* **(a)** (of votes) counting, count; (of mail) going through
**(b)** asceticism
**(c)** (of style) sobriety

**dépouiller** /depuje/ [1] *vtr* **(a)** to skin ⟨*animal*⟩
**(b)** to lay [sth] bare ⟨*region*⟩
**(c)** to rob ⟨*person*⟩
**(d)** to count ⟨*votes*⟩; to go through ⟨*mail*⟩

**dépourvu**, ∼**e** /depuʀvy/ **①** *adj* ∼ **de** devoid of ⟨*interest, charm*⟩; without ⟨*heating*⟩
**②** *nm* **prendre qn au** ∼ to take sb by surprise

**dépoussiérer** /depusjeʀe/ [14] *vtr* to dust; (figurative) to revamp

**dépravation** /depʀavasjɔ̃/ *nf* depravity

**dépraver** /depʀave/ [1] *vtr* to deprave

**dépréciation** /depʀesjasjɔ̃/ *nf* depreciation

**déprécier** /depʀesje/ [2] *vtr* **(a)** to depreciate
**(b)** to disparage, to depreciate

**déprédateur -trice** /depʀedatœʀ, tʀis/ *nm,f* vandal

**déprédations** /depʀedasjɔ̃/ *nf pl* damage

**dépressif, -ive** /depʀesif, iv/ *adj, nm,f* depressive

**dépression** /depʀesjɔ̃/ *nf* depression; ∼ **nerveuse** nervous breakdown

**dépressurisation** /depʀesyʀizasjɔ̃/ *nf*
**(a)** depressurization
**(b)** loss of pressure

**déprimant**, ∼**e** /depʀimɑ̃, ɑ̃t/ *adj* depressing

**déprime** /depʀim/ *nf* (colloq) depression

**déprimer** /depʀime/ [1] **①** *vtr* to depress
**②** *vi* (colloq) to be depressed

**déprogrammer** /depʀɔgʀame/ [1] *vtr* to cancel

**depuis** /dəpɥi/ **①** *adv* since; ∼ **je n'ai plus de nouvelles** since then I haven't had any news
**②** *prep* **(a)** since; ∼ **quand vis-tu là-bas?** how long have you been living there?; ∼ **le début jusqu'à la fin** from start to finish
**(b)** for; **il pleut** ∼ **trois jours** it's been raining for three days; ∼ **quand?** how long?; ∼ **peu** recently; ∼ **toujours** always
**(c)** from; ∼ **ma fenêtre** from my window
**③** **depuis que** *phr* since, ever since; **il pleut** ∼ **que nous sommes arrivés** it's been raining ever since we arrived

**député** /depyte/ *nm* **(a)** (in politics) deputy; (in GB) member of Parliament; **être** ∼ **au Parlement européen** to be a Euro-MP *ou* member of the European Parliament
**(b)** representative

**député-maire**, *pl* **députés-maires** /depytemɛʀ/ *nm* deputy and mayor

**déqualifier** /dekalifje/ [2] *vtr* to deskill

**der** /dɛʀ/ *nf* (colloq) last; **la ~ des ~s** the war to end all wars

**déraciné, ~e** /deʀasine/ *nm,f* uprooted person

**déracinement** /deʀasinmɑ̃/ *nm*
(a) uprooting
(b) rootlessness

**déraciner** /deʀasine/ [1] *vtr* (a) to uproot
(b) to eradicate ⟨prejudice⟩

**déraillement** /deʀajmɑ̃/ *nm* derailment

**dérailler** /deʀaje/ [1] *vi* (a) to be derailed; **faire ~ un train** to derail a train
(b) (colloq) to lose one's marbles (colloq); to talk through one's hat (colloq)

**dérailleur** /deʀajœʀ/ *nm* derailleur

**déraisonnable** /deʀɛzɔnabl/ *adj* unrealistic; senseless; unreasonable

**déraisonner** /deʀɛzɔne/ [1] *vi* to talk nonsense

**dérangé, ~e** /deʀɑ̃ʒe/ *adj* (a) upset
(b) (colloq) deranged

**dérangeant, ~e** /deʀɑ̃ʒɑ̃, ɑ̃t/ *adj* disturbing

**dérangement** /deʀɑ̃ʒmɑ̃/ *nm* (a) trouble, inconvenience
(b) ~ intestinal stomach upset
(c) être en ~ ⟨lift, phone⟩ to be out of order

**déranger** /deʀɑ̃ʒe/ [13] **1** *vtr* to disturb ⟨person⟩; to upset ⟨routine, plans⟩; to affect ⟨mind⟩; **excusez-moi de vous ~** (I'm) sorry to bother you; **est-ce que la fumée vous dérange?** do you mind if I smoke?
**2 se déranger** *v refl* (+ *v être*) (a) to go out, to come out; **je me suis dérangé pour rien, c'était fermé** I wasted my time going there, it was shut
(b) to get up; to move
(c) to put oneself out

**dérapage** /deʀapaʒ/ *nm* (a) skid
(b) blunder
(c) loss of control

**déraper** /deʀape/ [1] *vi* (a) ⟨prices, discussion⟩ to get out of control
(b) ⟨knife⟩ to slip
(c) to skid
(d) ⟨skier⟩ to sideslip

**dératisation** /deʀatizasjɔ̃/ *nf* pest control (for rats)

**déréglé, ~e** /deʀegle/ *adj* ⟨mind⟩ unbalanced; ⟨life⟩ irregular; ⟨mechanism⟩ out, disturbed

**dérèglement** /deʀɛɡləmɑ̃/ *nm*
(a) (in machine) fault
(b) disorder

**déréglementer** /deʀegləmɑ̃te/ [1] *vtr* to deregulate

**dérégler** /deʀegle/ [14] *vtr* to affect ⟨weather, organ⟩; to upset ⟨process, mechanism⟩; **~ la radio** to lose the station on the radio; **~ le réveil** to set the alarm clock wrong

**dérider** /deʀide/ [1] **1** *vtr* to cheer [sb] up
**2 se dérider** *v refl* (+ *v être*) to start smiling

**dérision** /deʀizjɔ̃/ *nf* scorn, derision; **tourner qn/qch en ~** to ridicule sb/sth

**dérisoire** /deʀizwaʀ/ *adj* pathetic; trivial

**dérivatif, -ive** /deʀivatif, iv/ **1** *adj* derivative
**2** *nm* (a) diversion (à from)
(b) (Med) derivative

**dérivation** /deʀivasjɔ̃/ *nf* diversion (GB), detour

**dérive** /deʀiv/ *nf* drift; **à la ~** adrift

**dérivé, ~e** /deʀive/ *nm* by-product

**dériver** /deʀive/ [1] **1 dériver de** *v+prep*
(a) ~ de to stem from
(b) ~ de to be derived from
**2** *vi* to drift

**dermatologie** /dɛʀmatɔlɔʒi/ *nf* dermatology

**derme** /dɛʀm/ *nm* dermis

**dernier, -ière**[1] /dɛʀnje, ɛʀ/ **1** *adj*
(a) last; ⟨floor, shelf⟩ top; **je les veux jeudi ~ délai** I want them by Thursday at the latest
(b) latest; **les dernières nouvelles** the latest news; **ces ~ temps** recently
(c) **du ~ ridicule** utterly ridiculous; **c'était la dernière chose à faire** it was the worst possible thing to do
**2** *nm, f* last; **arriver le ~** to arrive last; **c'est bien le ~ de mes soucis** that is the least of my worries; **être le ~ de la classe** to be bottom of the class; **le petit ~** the youngest child; **ce ~** the latter; **le ~ des ~s** the lowest of the low
**3 en dernier** *phr* last; **j'irai chez eux en ~** I'll go to them last
■ **~ cri** latest fashion; **dernières volontés** last requests

**dernière**[2] /dɛʀnjɛʀ/ *nf* (a) **la ~** the latest
(b) last performance

**dernièrement** /dɛʀnjɛʀmɑ̃/ *adv* recently

**dernier-né, dernière-née,** *mpl* **derniers-nés** /dɛʀnjene, dɛʀnjɛʀne/ *nm,f* (a) youngest (child)
(b) latest model

**dérobade** /deʀɔbad/ *nf* evasion

**dérobé, ~e** /deʀɔbe/ **1** *adj* ⟨door, stairs⟩ concealed
**2 à la dérobée** *phr* furtively

**dérober** /deʀɔbe/ [1] **1** *vtr* to steal
**2 se dérober** *v refl* (+ *v être*) (a) to be evasive
(b) to shirk responsibility
(c) **se ~ à** to shirk ⟨duty⟩
(d) ⟨ground, knees⟩ to give way

**dérogation** /deʀɔgasjɔ̃/ *nf* (a) (special) dispensation
(b) infringement (à of)

**dérogatoire** /deʀɔgatwaʀ/ *adj* special; **clause ~** derogation clause

**déroger** /deʀɔʒe/ [13] *v+prep* **~ à** to infringe ⟨law⟩; to depart from ⟨principles⟩; to ignore ⟨obligation⟩; to break with ⟨tradition⟩

**dérouiller** /deʀuje/ [1] (colloq) *vi* to get a hiding (colloq) *or* beating; to suffer

**déroulement** /deʀulmɑ̃/ *nm* (a) le ~ des événements the sequence of events; veiller au bon ~ de to make sure [sth] goes smoothly; ~ de carrière career development
(b) uncoiling, unwinding

**dérouler** /deʀule/ [1] **1** *vtr* to unroll ⟨carpet⟩; to uncoil ⟨rope⟩; to unwind ⟨wire, film⟩
**2** se dérouler *v refl* (+ *v être*) (a) to take place
(b) ⟨negotiations⟩ to proceed; ⟨story⟩ to unfold

**déroutant, ~e** /deʀutɑ̃, ɑ̃t/ *adj* puzzling

**déroute** /deʀut/ *nf* crushing defeat, rout; mettre en ~ to rout; en ~ in disarray

**dérouter** /deʀute/ [1] *vtr* (a) to puzzle
(b) to divert

**derrière¹** /dɛʀjɛʀ/ **1** *prep* behind; ~ les apparences beneath the surface; il faut toujours être ~ son dos you have to keep after him
**2** *adv* behind; (of room) at the back; (in car) in the back

**derrière²** /dɛʀjɛʀ/ *nm* (a) (of house, object) back; de ~ ⟨bedroom⟩ back
(b) (colloq) behind (colloq), backside (colloq)

**des** /de/ **1** *det* ▶ UN 1
**2** *det* ▶ DE

**dès** /dɛ/ **1** *prep* from; ~ (l'âge de) huit ans from the age of eight; ~ maintenant straight away; je vous téléphone ~ mon arrivée I'll phone you as soon as I arrive; ~ Versailles il y a des embouteillages there are traffic jams from Versailles onwards
**2** dès que *phr* as soon as
**3** dès lors *phr* (a) from then on, from that time on, henceforth
(b) therefore, consequently
**4** dès lors que *phr* (a) once, from the moment that
(b) since

**désabusé, ~e** /dezabyze/ *adj* disillusioned; cynical

**désaccord** /dezakɔʀ/ *nm* disagreement; être en ~ to disagree (avec with; sur over)

**désaccordé, ~e** /dezakɔʀde/ *adj* out-of-tune

**désaccoutumer** /dezakutyme/ se désaccoutumer *v refl* se ~ de qch to break one's dependence on sth

**désactiver** /dezaktive/ *vt* to deactivate

**désaffecté, ~e** /dezafɛkte/ *adj* disused

**désaffection** /dezafɛksjɔ̃/ *nf* disaffection (pour with)

**désagréable** /dezagʀeabl/ *adj* unpleasant

**désagrégation** /dezagʀegasjɔ̃/ *nf* disintegration, break-up, collapse

**désagréger: se désagréger** /dezagʀeʒe/ [15] *v refl* (+ *v être*) to disintegrate, to break up

**désagrément** /dezagʀemɑ̃/ *nm* inconvenience

**désaltérant, ~e** /dezalteʀɑ̃, ɑ̃t/ *adj* thirst-quenching

**désaltérer** /dezalteʀe/ [14] **1** *vtr* ~ qn to quench sb's thirst
**2** se désaltérer *v refl* (+ *v être*) to quench one's thirst

**désamorcer** /dezamɔʀse/ [12] *vtr* to defuse ⟨explosive, crisis⟩; to drain ⟨pump⟩

**désappointement** /dezapwɛ̃tmɑ̃/ *nm* disappointment

**désappointer** /dezapwɛ̃te/ [1] *vtr* to disappoint

**désapprobateur, -trice** /dezapʀɔbatœʀ, tʀis/ *adj* disapproving

**désapprobation** /dezapʀɔbasjɔ̃/ *nf* disapproval

**désapprouver** /dezapʀuve/ [1] *vtr* to disapprove of

**désarçonner** /dezaʀsɔne/ [1] *vtr* (a) to throw ⟨rider⟩
(b) to take [sb] aback

**désargenté, ~e** /dezaʀʒɑ̃te/ *adj* (colloq) hard up (colloq), penniless

**désarmant, ~e** /dezaʀmɑ̃, ɑ̃t/ *adj* disarming

**désarmé, ~e** /dezaʀme/ **1** *pp* ▶ DÉSARMER
**2** *pp adj* (a) disarmed
(b) ⟨ship⟩ laid up

**désarmement** /dezaʀməmɑ̃/ *nm*
(a) disarmament
(b) (of ship) laying up

**désarmer** /dezaʀme/ [1] **1** *vtr* (a) to disarm
(b) to lay up ⟨ship⟩
**2** *vi* (a) to disarm
(b) ⟨person⟩ to give up the fight; ⟨anger⟩ to abate

**désarroi** /dezaʀwa/ *nm* distress; confusion

**désarticulé, ~e** /dezaʀtikyle/ *adj* ⟨chair⟩ wrecked; ⟨puppet⟩ with broken joints

**désastre** /dezastʀ/ *nm* disaster

**désastreux, -euse** /dezastʀø, øz/ *adj* disastrous

**désavantage** /dezavɑ̃taʒ/ *nm*
(a) disadvantage
(b) drawback, disadvantage

**désavantager** /dezavɑ̃taʒe/ [13] *vtr* to put [sb/sth] at a disadvantage, to disadvantage

**désavantageux, -euse** /dezavɑ̃taʒø, øz/ *adj* unfavourable (GB), disadvantageous

**désaveu** /dezavø/ *nm* (a) denial
(b) rejection

**désavouer** /dezavwe/ [1] *vtr* (a) to deny
(b) to disown

**désaxé, ~e** /dezakse/ **1** *pp* ▶ DÉSAXER
**2** *pp adj* deranged
**3** *nm,f* deranged person

**désaxer** /dezakse/ [1] *vtr* (a) to put [sth] out of true ⟨wheel⟩
(b) to unbalance ⟨person⟩

**desceller** /desele/ [1] **1** *vtr* to work [sth] free
**2** se desceller *v refl* (+ *v être*) to work loose

**descendance** /desɑ̃dɑ̃s/ *nf* descendants

**descendant, ∼e** /desɑ̃dɑ̃, ɑ̃t/ *nm,f* descendant

**descendre** /desɑ̃dʀ/ [6] **1** *vtr* (+ *v avoir*)
(a) to take [sb/sth] down ⟨à to⟩, to bring [sb/sth] down ⟨de from⟩
(b) to lower ⟨shelf, blind⟩; to wind [sth] down ⟨window ⟩
(c) to go down, to come down ⟨road, steps, river⟩; ∼ **la rivière à la nage** to swim down the river
(d) (colloq) to bump off (colloq) ⟨person⟩; to shoot down ⟨plane⟩
(e) (colloq) to down ⟨bottle⟩
**2** *vi* (+ *v être*) (a) to go down ⟨à to⟩, to come down ⟨de from⟩; ⟨night⟩ to fall; **tu es descendu à pied?** did you walk down?; **la route descend en pente douce** the road slopes down gently
(b) ∼ **de** to step off ⟨step⟩; to get off ⟨train, bike, horse⟩; to get out of ⟨car⟩
(c) ⟨temperature, prices⟩ to drop, to go down; ⟨tide⟩ to go out
(d) ∼ **dans le Midi** to go down to the South (of France)
(e) ∼ **dans un hôtel** to stay at a hotel
(f) ∼ **de** to be descended from

**descente** /desɑ̃t/ *nf* (a) descent; **la** ∼ **a pris une heure** it took an hour to come down
(b) **à ma** ∼ **du train** when I got off the train
(c) ∼ **de police** police raid; **la police a fait une** ∼ **dans l'immeuble** the police raided the building
(d) (in skiing) downhill (event)
■ ∼ **de lit** (bedside) rug

**descriptif, -ive** /deskʀiptif, iv/ *adj* descriptive

**description** /deskʀipsjɔ̃/ *nf* description; **faire une** ∼ **de qch** to describe sth

**désembuer** /dezɑ̃bɥe/ [1] *vtr* to demist (GB), to defog (US)

**désemparé, ∼e** /dezɑ̃paʀe/ **1** *pp* ▶ DÉSEMPARER
**2** *pp adj* distraught, at a loss

**désemparer** /dezɑ̃paʀe/ [1] *vtr* to throw [sb] into confusion

**désemplir** /dezɑ̃pliʀ/ [3] *vi* **ne pas** ∼ to be always full

**désenchanté, ∼e** /dezɑ̃ʃɑ̃te/ *adj* disillusioned, disenchanted (de with)

**désenchantement** /dezɑ̃ʃɑ̃tmɑ̃/ *nm* disillusionment, disenchantment

**désenclaver** /dezɑ̃klave/ [1] *vtr* to open up ⟨region⟩

**désendettement** /dezɑ̃dɛtmɑ̃/ *nm* reduction of the debt

**désenfler** /dezɑ̃fle/ [1] *vi* to become less swollen, to go down

**désengagement** /dezɑ̃ɡaʒmɑ̃/ *nm*
(a) (Econ) disengagement
(b) withdrawal (de from)

**désengager: se désengager** /dezɑ̃ɡaʒe/ [13] *v refl* (+ *v être*) to withdraw (de from)

**désensibiliser** /desɑ̃sibilize/ [1] *vtr* to desensitize

**désenvoûter** /dezɑ̃vute/ [1] *vtr* to break the spell on

**désépaissir** /dezepɛsiʀ/ [3] *vtr* (a) to thin ⟨sauce⟩
(b) to thin [sth] out ⟨hair⟩

**déséquilibre** /dezekilibʀ/ *nm*
(a) unsteadiness; **en** ∼ ⟨table⟩ unstable; ⟨person⟩ off balance
(b) imbalance
(c) derangement

**déséquilibré, ∼e** /dezekilibʀe/ **1** *pp* ▶ DÉSÉQUILIBRER
**2** *pp adj* (Med) unbalanced
**3** *nm,f* lunatic

**déséquilibrer** /dezekilibʀe/ [1] *vtr* (a) to make [sb] lose their balance; to make [sth] unstable
(b) to destabilize ⟨country⟩
(c) (Med) to unbalance

**désert, ∼e** /dezɛʀ, ɛʀt/ **1** *adj*
(a) uninhabited; **île** ∼**e** desert island
(b) deserted
**2** *nm* desert

**déserter** /dezɛʀte/ [1] *vtr, vi* to desert

**déserteur** /dezɛʀtœʀ/ *nm* deserter

**désertion** /dezɛʀsjɔ̃/ *nf* (a) desertion
(b) defection

**désertique** /dezɛʀtik/ *adj* (a) ⟨climate, region⟩ desert
(b) barren

**désespérant, ∼e** /dezɛspeʀɑ̃, ɑ̃t/ *adj* ⟨person, situation⟩ hopeless

**désespéré, ∼e** /dezɛspeʀe/ **1** *pp* ▶ DÉSESPÉRER
**2** *pp adj* ⟨person⟩ in despair; ⟨situation⟩ hopeless; ⟨attempt⟩ desperate; **cri** ∼ cry of despair

**désespérément** /dezɛspeʀemɑ̃/ *adv* despairingly; desperately; hopelessly

**désespérer** /dezɛspeʀe/ [14] **1** *vtr* to drive [sb] to despair
**2 désespérer de** *v+prep* ∼ **de qn** to despair of sb; **il ne désespère pas de le sauver** he hasn't given up hope of saving him
**3** *vi* to despair, to lose hope
**4 se désespérer** *v refl* (+ *v être*) to despair

**désespoir** /dezɛspwaʀ/ *nm* despair; **mettre** *or* **réduire qn au** ∼ to drive sb to despair

**déshabillé** /dezabije/ *nm* negligee

**déshabiller** /dezabije/ [1] **1** *vtr* to undress
**2 se déshabiller** *v refl* (+ *v être*) (a) to undress
(b) to take one's coat off

**déshabituer** /dezabitɥe/ [1] *vtr* ∼ **qn du tabac** to get sb out of the habit of smoking

**désherbant** /dezɛʀbɑ̃/ *nm* weedkiller

**désherber** /dezɛʀbe/ [1] *vtr* to weed

**déshérité** /dezeʀite/ **1** *pp* ▶ DÉSHÉRITER  ⋯⟩

**d**

**[2]** *pp adj* underprivileged; disadvantaged; deprived
**[3]** *nm,f* **les** ~**s** the underprivileged

**déshériter** /dezeʀite/ [1] *vtr* to disinherit

**déshonorant**, ~**e** /dezɔnɔʀɑ̃, ɑ̃t/ *adj* dishonourable (GB), degrading

**déshonorer** /dezɔnɔʀe/ [1] **[1]** *vtr* to bring disgrace on ⟨*family*⟩; to bring [sth] into disrepute ⟨*profession*⟩
**[2] se déshonorer** *v refl* (+ *v être*) to disgrace oneself

**déshumaniser** /dezymanize/ [1] **[1]** *vtr* to dehumanize
**[2] se déshumaniser** *v refl* (+ *v être*) to become dehumanized

**déshydratation** /dezidʀatasjɔ̃/ *nf*
(a) dehydration
(b) drying

**déshydrater** /dezidʀate/ [1] *vtr* to dehydrate

**desiderata** /deziderata/ *nm pl* wishes

**désignation** /deziɲasjɔ̃/ *nf* designation

**désigner** /deziɲe/ [1] *vtr* (a) ⟨*word*⟩ to designate; ⟨*triangle*⟩ to represent
(b) to point out
(c) to choose; **être tout désigné pour** to be just right for

**désillusion** /dezil(l)yzjɔ̃/ *nf* disillusion

**désincarcérer** /dezɛ̃kaʀseʀe/ [14] *vtr* to free

**désincarné**, ~**e** /dezɛ̃kaʀne/ *adj* disembodied

**désinence** /dezinɑ̃s/ *nf* ending

**désinfectant**, ~**e** /dezɛ̃fɛktɑ̃, ɑ̃t/ **[1]** *adj* disinfecting
**[2]** *nm* disinfectant

**désinfecter** /dezɛ̃fɛkte/ [1] *vtr* to disinfect

**désintégrer: se désintégrer** /dezɛ̃tegʀe/ [14] *v refl* (+ *v être*) to disintegrate

**désintéressé**, ~**e** /dezɛ̃teʀese/ **[1]** *pp* ▶ DÉSINTÉRESSER
**[2]** *pp adj* ⟨*person, act*⟩ selfless, unselfish; ⟨*advice*⟩ disinterested

**désintéressement** /dezɛ̃teʀɛsmɑ̃/ *nm*
(a) disinterestedness; **agir avec** ~ to act disinterestedly
(b) (Econ) paying off

**désintéresser: se désintéresser** /dezɛ̃teʀese/ [1] *v refl* (+ *v être*) **se** ~ **de** to lose interest in

**désintérêt** /dezɛ̃teʀɛ/ *nm* lack of interest

**désintoxiquer** /dezɛ̃tɔksike/ [1] *vtr* to detoxify; **se faire** ~ to undergo detoxification

**désinvolte** /dezɛ̃vɔlt/ *adj* casual, offhand

**désinvolture** /dezɛ̃vɔltyʀ/ *nf* casual manner

**désir** /deziʀ/ *nm* wish, desire; **prendre ses** ~**s pour des réalités** to delude oneself

**désirable** /deziʀabl/ *adj* desirable

**désirer** /deziʀe/ [1] *vtr* to want; **effets non** désirés unwanted effects; **que désirez-vous?** what would you like? **laisser à** ~ to leave something to be desired

**désistement** /dezistəmɑ̃/ *nm* withdrawal

**désister: se désister** /deziste/ [1] *v refl* (+ *v être*) to stand down (GB), to withdraw

**désobéir** /dezɔbeiʀ/ [3] *v+prep* to disobey; ~ **à qn** to disobey sb

**désobéissance** /dezɔbeisɑ̃s/ *nf* disobedience

**désobéissant**, ~**e** /dezɔbeisɑ̃, ɑ̃t/ *adj* disobedient

**désobligeant**, ~**e** /dezɔbliʒɑ̃, ɑ̃t/ *adj* discourteous

**désobliger** /dezɔbliʒe/ [13] *vtr* to offend

**désodorisant** /dezɔdɔʀizɑ̃/ *nm* deodorant

**désodoriser** /dezɔdɔʀize/ [1] *vtr* to freshen

**désœuvré**, ~**e** /dezœvʀe/ *adj* at a loose end (GB) (colloq), at loose ends (US) (colloq)

**désœuvrement** /dezœvʀəmɑ̃/ *nm* **par** ~ for lack of anything better to do

**désolation** /dezɔlasjɔ̃/ *nf* (a) grief
(b) desolation

**désolé**, ~**e** /dezɔle/ **[1]** *pp* ▶ DÉSOLER
**[2]** *pp adj* (a) sorry
(b) desolate

**désoler** /dezɔle/ [1] **[1]** *vtr* (a) to upset, to distress
(b) to depress; **tu me désoles!** I despair of you!
**[2] se désoler** *v refl* (+ *v être*) to be upset

**désopilant**, ~**e** /dezɔpilɑ̃, ɑ̃t/ *adj* hilarious

**désordonné**, ~**e** /dezɔʀdɔne/ *adj* ⟨*person*⟩ untidy; ⟨*meeting*⟩ disorderly; ⟨*movements*⟩ uncoordinated; ⟨*existence*⟩ wild

**désordre** /dezɔʀdʀ/ **[1]** *adj inv* (colloq) **faire** ~ to look untidy *or* messy
**[2]** *nm* (a) untidiness; mess; **pièce en** ~ untidy room; **il a tout mis en** ~ he made such a mess
(b) chaos; **semer le** ~ to cause chaos
(c) **dans le** ~ in any order; **gagner dans le** ~ (at races) to win with a combination forecast
(d) disorder; ~**s mentaux** mental disorders

**désorganisation** /dezɔʀganizasjɔ̃/ *nf* disruption; disorganization

**désorganisé**, ~**e** /dezɔʀganize/ *adj* disorganized

**désorienter** /dezɔʀjɑ̃te/ [1] *vtr* (a) to disorientate (GB)
(b) to confuse, to bewilder

**désormais** /dezɔʀmɛ/ *adv* (a) from now on
(b) from then on

**désosser** /dezɔse/ [1] *vtr* (Culin) to bone

**despote** /dɛspɔt/ *nm* despot

**despotique** /dɛspɔtik/ *adj* despotic

**desquelles** ▶ LEQUEL

**desquels** ▶ LEQUEL

**DESS** /deəɛsɛs/ nm (abbr = **diplôme d'études supérieures spécialisées**) *postgraduate degree taken after a Master's*

**dessaisir** /desɛziʀ/ [3] **1** vtr (a) ∼ qn de to relieve sb of ⟨*responsibility*⟩
(b) ∼ qn de to divest sb of ⟨*property*⟩
**2 se dessaisir** v refl (+ v être) se ∼ de to relinquish

**dessaler** /desale/ [1] vtr (a) to desalinate
(b) (Culin) to desalt

**dessécher** /deseʃe/ [14] **1** vtr to dry [sth] out; **arbre desséché** withered tree
**2 se dessécher** v refl (+ v être) ⟨*hair*⟩ to become dry; ⟨*tree*⟩ to wither; ⟨*ground*⟩ to dry out

**dessein** /desɛ̃/ nm design, intention; **à ∼** deliberately

**desserré, ∼e** /deseʀe/ adj loose

**desserrement** /desɛʀmɑ̃/ nm
(a) loosening
(b) (Econ) relaxation; **∼ du crédit** relaxation of credit

**desserrer** /deseʀe/ [1] **1** vtr (a) to loosen; to release; to undo
(b) to relax ⟨*grip, credit*⟩
**2 se desserrer** v refl (+ v être) ⟨*screw*⟩ to work loose; ⟨*knot*⟩ to come undone
IDIOMS **il n'a pas desserré les dents** he never once opened his mouth

**dessert** /desɛʀ/ nm dessert

**desserte** /desɛʀt/ nf (a) (transport) service; **la ∼ d'une ville par les transports en commun** public transport services to and from a city
(b) sideboard

**desservir** /desɛʀviʀ/ [30] vtr (a) ⟨*train*⟩ to serve ⟨*town*⟩
(b) to lead to ⟨*room, floor*⟩
(c) ⟨*hospital*⟩ to serve

**dessin** /desɛ̃/ nm (a) drawing; **tu veux que je te fasse un ∼?** (colloq) do I have to spell it out for you?
(b) design
(c) pattern
(d) outline
■ **∼ animé** cartoon

**dessinateur, -trice** /desinatœʀ, tʀis/ nm,f (a) draughtsman (GB), draftsman (US)
(b) designer
■ **∼ de bande dessinée** (strip) cartoonist

**dessiner** /desine/ [1] **1** vtr (a) to draw
(b) to design ⟨*material, decor*⟩; to draw up ⟨*plans*⟩
**2** vi to draw
**3 se dessiner** v refl (+ v être) (a) ⟨*future*⟩ to take shape
(b) **se ∼ à l'horizon** to appear on the horizon; **il se dessinait nettement dans la lumière** he was clearly outlined in the light

**dessoûler** /desule/ [1] vtr to sober up

**dessous¹** /dəsu/ **1** adv underneath
**2 en dessous** phr (a) underneath; **il habite juste en ∼** he lives on the floor below
(b) **la taille en ∼** the next size down

**3 en dessous de** phr below; **les enfants en ∼ de 13 ans** children under 13

**dessous²** /dəsu/ **1** nm inv (of plate, tongue) underside; (of arm) inside (part); **le ∼ du pied** the sole of the foot; **l'étagère de** or **du ∼** the shelf below; the bottom shelf
**2** nm pl (a) underwear
(b) inside story

**dessous-de-plat** /d(ə)sudpla/ nm inv
(a) table mat
(b) plate stand
(c) trivet

**dessous-de-table** /d(ə)sudtabl/ nm inv backhanders (colloq) (GB), bribes

**dessus¹** /dəsy/ adv on top; **le prix est marqué ∼** the price is on it; **passe ∼** go over it; **compte ∼** count on it; **'ton rapport est fini?'—'non, je travaille** or **suis ∼'** 'is your report finished?'—'no, I'm working on it'

**dessus²** /dəsy/ nm inv (of shoe) upper; (of table, head) top; (of hand) back; **les voisins du ∼** the people who live on the floor above
IDIOMS **reprendre le ∼** to regain the upper hand; (after illness) to get back on one's feet

**dessus-de-lit** /d(ə)sydli/ nm inv bedspread

**déstabiliser** /destabilize/ [1] vtr to unsettle ⟨*person*⟩; to destabilize ⟨*country*⟩

**destin** /dɛstɛ̃/ nm (a) fate
(b) destiny

**destinataire** /dɛstinatɛʀ/ nmf
(a) addressee
(b) beneficiary
(c) payee

**destination** /dɛstinasjɔ̃/ **1** nf destination
**2 à destination de** phr ⟨*train*⟩ bound for

**destinée** /dɛstine/ nf destiny

**destiner** /dɛstine/ [1] **1** vtr (a) ∼ qch à qn to design sth for sb; **être destiné à faire** to be designed or intended to do; to be destined to do
(b) **la lettre ne leur était pas destinée** the letter wasn't for them
**2 se destiner** v refl (+ v être) **elle se destine à une carrière de juriste** she's decided on a legal career

**destituer** /dɛstitɥe/ [1] vtr to discharge ⟨*officer*⟩; to depose ⟨*monarch*⟩

**destitution** /dɛstitysjɔ̃/ nf discharge; deposition

**destructeur, -trice** /dɛstʀyktœʀ, tʀis/ adj destructive

**destruction** /dɛstʀyksjɔ̃/ nf destruction

**désuet, -ète** /dezɥɛ, ɛt/ adj ⟨*decor*⟩ old-world; ⟨*style*⟩ old-fashioned; ⟨*word*⟩ obsolete

**désunion** /dezynjɔ̃/ nf (a) division
(b) discord

**désunir** /dezyniʀ/ [3] vtr to divide, to break up

**détachant** /detaʃɑ̃/ nm stain remover

**détaché, ∼e** /detaʃe/ **1** pp ▶ DÉTACHER
**2** pp adj (a) detached, unconcerned  ····ᐅ

**(b)** ⟨*teacher, diplomat*⟩ on secondment (GB), transferred

**détachement** /detaʃmɑ̃/ *nm*
**(a)** detachment ⟨**de** from⟩
**(b)** (Mil) detachment
**(c)** secondment

**détacher** /detaʃe/ [1] **1** *vtr* **(a)** to untie; to unfasten; to undo
**(b)** to take down ⟨*poster*⟩
**(c)** ~ **les yeux** *or* **le regard de qch** to take one's eyes off sth
**(d)** to second (GB), to transfer
**(e)** to remove the stain(s) from
**2** **se détacher** *v refl* (+ *v être*)
**(a)** ⟨*prisoner, animal*⟩ to break loose; ⟨*boat*⟩ to come untied
**(b)** to come undone
**(c)** ⟨*coupon*⟩ to come out; ⟨*wallpaper*⟩ to come away
**(d)** to grow away from ⟨*person*⟩
**(e)** ⟨*pattern*⟩ to stand out
**(f)** **se ~ de** to detach oneself from; to pull away from

**détail** /detaj/ *nm* **(a)** detail
**(b)** breakdown; **analyse de ~** detailed analysis
**(c)** retail; **acheter (qch) au ~** to buy (sth) retail

**détailler** /detaje/ [1] *vtr* **(a)** to detail; to itemize
**(b)** to scrutinize

**détartrer** /detartre/ [1] *vtr* **(a)** to descale ⟨*kettle*⟩
**(b)** to scale ⟨*teeth*⟩

**détaxe** /detaks/ *nf* **(a)** tax removal
**(b)** tax refund
**(c)** export rebate

**détecter** /detɛkte/ [1] *vtr* to detect

**détecteur** /detɛktœr/ *nm* detector; ~ **de mines** mine detector

**détection** /detɛksjɔ̃/ *nf* detection

**détective** /detɛktiv/ *nm* detective

**déteindre** /detɛ̃dr/ [55] *vi* **(a)** ⟨*garment*⟩ to fade
**(b)** ⟨*colour*⟩ to run
**(c)** (figurative) to rub off

**détendre** /detɑ̃dr/ [6] **1** *vtr* **(a)** to release ⟨*spring*⟩
**(b)** to slacken ⟨*rope, spring*⟩
**(c)** to relax ⟨*muscle*⟩; to calm ⟨*atmosphere, mind*⟩
**2** *vi* **(a)** to be relaxing
**(b)** to be entertaining
**3** **se détendre** *v refl* (+ *v être*) **(a)** ⟨*rope, spring*⟩ to slacken
**(b)** ⟨*person, muscle*⟩ to relax

**détendu**, **~e** /detɑ̃dy/ **1** *pp* ▶ DÉTENDRE
**2** *pp adj* **(a)** relaxed
**(b)** slack

**détenir** /det(ə)nir/ [36] *vtr* **(a)** to keep ⟨*objects*⟩; to hold ⟨*power, record*⟩; to possess ⟨*arms*⟩; to have ⟨*secret, evidence*⟩
**(b)** to detain ⟨*suspect*⟩

**détente** /detɑ̃t/ *nf* **(a)** relaxation
**(b)** détente

**(c)** (on gun) trigger
**IDIOMS être lent** *or* **dur à la ~** (colloq) to be slow on the uptake

**détention** /detɑ̃sjɔ̃/ *nf* **(a)** (of passport, drugs, record) holding; (of arms, secret) possession
**(b)** detention; ~ **préventive** custody

**détenu**, **~e** /det(ə)ny/ *nm,f* prisoner

**détergent** /detɛrʒɑ̃/ *nm* detergent

**détériorer** /deterjɔre/ [1] **1** *vtr* to damage
**2** **se détériorer** *v refl* (+ *v être*)
⟨*situation, weather*⟩ to deteriorate; ⟨*foodstuff*⟩ to go bad

**déterminant**, **~e** /detɛrminɑ̃, ɑ̃t/ *adj*
⟨*role, factor*⟩ decisive

**détermination** /detɛrminasjɔ̃/ *nf* determination

**déterminé**, **~e** /detɛrmine/ **1** *pp* ▶ DÉTERMINER
**2** *pp adj* **(a)** determined
**(b)** given

**déterminer** /detɛrmine/ [1] *vtr* **(a)** to determine ⟨*reason, responsibility*⟩
**(b)** to work out ⟨*policy, terms*⟩
**(c)** to determine ⟨*attitude, decision*⟩
**(d)** ~ **qn à faire** to make sb decide to do

**déterrer** /detere/ [1] *vtr* to dig ⟨*sb/sth*⟩ up

**détestable** /detɛstabl/ *adj* ⟨*style, weather*⟩ appalling; ⟨*habits*⟩ revolting; ⟨*person*⟩ hateful

**détester** /detɛste/ [1] *vtr* **(a)** to detest, to loathe ⟨*person*⟩
**(b)** to hate

**détonateur** /detɔnatœr/ *nm* **(a)** detonator
**(b)** (figurative) catalyst

**détonation** /detɔnasjɔ̃/ *nf* detonation

**détonner** /detɔne/ [1] *vi* to be out of place

**détordre** /detɔrdr/ [6] *vtr* to straighten ⟨*iron bar*⟩; to unwind ⟨*cable*⟩

**détour** /detur/ *nm* **(a)** detour; **ça vaut le ~** it's worth the trip
**(b)** roundabout means
**(c)** circumlocution; **il me l'a dit sans ~s** he told me straight
**(d)** (in road, river) bend

**détourné**, **~e** /deturne/ **1** *pp* ▶ DÉTOURNER
**2** *pp adj* ⟨*reference*⟩ oblique; ⟨*means*⟩ indirect

**détournement** /deturnəmɑ̃/ *nm*
**(a)** misappropriation
**(b)** hijacking
**(c)** (of traffic) diversion
■ ~ **de mineur** (Law) corruption of a minor

**détourner** /deturne/ [1] **1** *vtr* **(a)** to divert ⟨*attention*⟩
**(b)** ~ **les yeux** *or* **le regard** *or* **la tête** to look away
**(c)** to divert ⟨*traffic, river, flight*⟩; ~ **la conversation** to change the subject
**(d)** to hijack ⟨*plane, ship*⟩; to misappropriate ⟨*funds*⟩
**2** **se détourner** *v refl* (+ *v être*) **(a)** **se ~ de** to turn away from ⟨*friend*⟩
**(b)** to look away

**détracteur, -trice** /detʀaktœʀ, tʀis/ *nm,f* detractor

**détraqué, ∼e** /detʀake/ *nm,f* (colloq) deranged person

**détraquer** /detʀake/ [1] **1** *vtr* (a) to bust [sth] (colloq); to make [sth] go wrong
(b) (colloq) ⟨*medicine*⟩ to upset ⟨*stomach*⟩; to damage ⟨*health*⟩
**2 se détraquer** *v refl* (+ *v être*) ⟨*mechanism*⟩ to break down; ⟨*weather*⟩ to break

**détremper** /detʀɑ̃pe/ [1] *vtr* to saturate ⟨*ground*⟩; to soak ⟨*garment*⟩

**détresse** /detʀɛs/ *nf* distress

**détriment: au détriment de** /odetʀimɑ̃də/ *phr* to the detriment of

**détritus** /detʀity(s)/ *nm pl* refuse, rubbish (GB), garbage (US)

**détroit** /detʀwa/ *nm* straits

**détromper** /detʀɔ̃pe/ [1] **1** *vtr* to set [sb] straight
**2 se détromper** *v refl* (+ *v être*) détrompez-vous! don't you believe it!

**détrôner** /detʀone/ [1] *vtr* to dethrone

**détruire** /detʀɥiʀ/ [69] *vtr* to destroy

**dette** /dɛt/ *nf* debt; avoir une ∼ envers qn to be indebted to sb

**DEUG** /dœg/ *nm* (*abbr* = **diplôme d'études universitaires générales**) *university diploma taken after two years' study*

**deuil** /dœj/ *nm* (a) bereavement
(b) mourning, grief
**IDIOMS** faire son ∼ de qch (colloq) to kiss sth goodbye (colloq)

**deux** /dø/ **1** *adj inv* (a) two; ∼ fois twice; des ∼ côtés de la rue on either side *or* both sides of the street; tous les ∼ jours every other day; à nous ∼ I'm all yours; (to enemy) it's just you and me now
(b) a few, a couple of
(c) second; le deux mai the second of May (GB), May second (US)
**2** *pron* elles sont venues toutes les ∼ they both came
**3** *nm inv* two
**IDIOMS** faire ∼ poids, ∼ mesures to have double standards; un tiens vaut mieux que ∼ tu l'auras (Proverb) a bird in the hand is worth two in the bush; en ∼ temps, trois mouvements very quickly; je n'ai fait ni une ni ∼ I didn't have a second's hesitation

**deuxième** /døzjɛm/ **1** *adj* second; dans un ∼ temps nous étudierons... secondly, we will study...
**2** *nmf* second
■ ∼ classe second class, standard class (GB)

**deuxièmement** /døzjɛmmɑ̃/ *adv* secondly

**deux-points** /døpwɛ̃/ *nm inv* colon

**deux-roues** /døʀu/ *nm inv* two-wheeled vehicle

**dévaler** /devale/ [1] *vtr* to hurtle down; to tear down

**dévaliser** /devalize/ [1] *vtr* (a) to rob ⟨*person, bank, safe*⟩
(b) to clean out (colloq) ⟨*shop, larder*⟩

**dévaloriser** /devalɔʀize/ [1] **1** *vtr* (a) to depreciate
(b) to belittle
**2 se dévaloriser** *v refl* (+ *v être*) (a) to lose value; to lose prestige
(b) to put oneself down

**dévaluation** /devaluasjɔ̃/ *nf* devaluation

**dévaluer** /devalɥe/ [1] *vtr* to devalue

**devancer** /dəvɑ̃se/ [12] *vtr* (a) to be ahead of, to outstrip ⟨*competitor*⟩
(b) to anticipate ⟨*demand, desire*⟩; to forestall ⟨*attack, criticisms*⟩

**devant¹** /dəvɑ̃/ **1** *prep* (a) in front of; tous les hommes sont égaux ∼ la loi all men are equal in the eyes of the law; fuir ∼ le danger to run away from danger; le bus est passé ∼ moi sans s'arrêter the bus went straight past me without stopping
(b) outside; il attendait ∼ la porte he was waiting outside the door; he was waiting by the door
(c) ahead of; la voiture ∼ nous the car ahead *or* in front of us; laisser passer quelqu'un ∼ (soi) to let somebody go first; avoir toute la vie ∼ soi to have one's whole life ahead of one
**2** *adv* (a) 'où est la poste?'—'tu es juste ∼' 'where's the post office?'—'you're right in front of it'
(b) pars ∼, je te rejoins go ahead, I'll catch up with you
(c) (of hall, theatre) at the front; (in car) in the front

**devant²** /dəvɑ̃/ *nm* front
**IDIOMS** prendre les ∼s to take the initiative

**devanture** /dəvɑ̃tyʀ/ *nf* (a) (shop)front
(b) shop *or* store (US) window

**dévastation** /devastasjɔ̃/ *nf* devastation

**dévaster** /devaste/ [1] *vtr* (a) ⟨*army*⟩ to lay waste to; ⟨*storm, fire*⟩ to destroy
(b) ⟨*burglar*⟩ to wreck

**déveine** /devɛn/ *nf* (colloq) rotten luck (colloq), bad luck

**développement** /devlɔpmɑ̃/ *nm*
(a) development; pays en voie de ∼ developing nation *or* country
(b) (in photography) developing

**développer** /devlɔpe/ [1] **1** *vtr* to develop
**2 se développer** *v refl* (+ *v être*) ⟨*body, ability*⟩ to develop; ⟨*plant, company, town*⟩ to grow

**devenir¹** /dəvniʀ/ [36] *vi* (+ *v être*) to become; et Paul, qu'est-ce qu'il devient? and what is Paul up to these days?

**devenir²** /dəvniʀ/ *nm* future

**dévergonder: se dévergonder** /devɛʀgɔ̃de/ [1] *v refl* (+ *v être*) to be going to the bad

**déverser** /devɛʀse/ [1] **1** *vtr* to pour ⟨*liquid*⟩; to drop ⟨*bombs*⟩; to dump ⟨*refuse,* ⋯⋮

sand⟩; to discharge ⟨waste⟩; to disgorge
⟨crowd⟩; ~ **du pétrole** to dump oil; to spill oil
**2 se déverser** v refl (+ v être) ⟨river⟩ to
flow; ⟨sewer, crowd⟩ to pour

**dévêtir** /devetiʀ/ [33] **1** vtr to undress
**2 se dévêtir** v refl (+ v être) to get
undressed

**déviation** /devjasjɔ̃/ nf **(a)** diversion (GB),
detour (US)
**(b)** departure, deviation
**(c)** (of compass) deviation
**(d)** (of light) deflection

**dévider** /devide/ [1] vtr to unwind ⟨cable⟩

**dévier** /devje/ [2] **1** vtr to deflect ⟨ball,
trajectory⟩; to divert ⟨traffic⟩
**2** vi **(a)** ⟨bullet, ball⟩ to deflect; ⟨vehicle⟩ to
veer off course
**(b)** ~ **de** to deviate from ⟨plan⟩
**(c)** ⟨tool⟩ to slip
**(d)** ⟨conversation⟩ to drift

**devin** /dəvɛ̃/ nm soothsayer, seer

**deviner** /dəvine/ [1] vtr **(a)** to guess
⟨secret⟩; to foresee, to tell ⟨future⟩
**(b)** to sense ⟨danger⟩
**(c)** to make out, to discern

**devinette** /dəvinɛt/ nf riddle

**devis** /d(ə)vi/ nm inv estimate, quote

**dévisager** /devizaʒe/ [13] vtr to stare at

**devise** /dəviz/ nf **(a)** currency
**(b)** (foreign) currency
**(c)** motto

**deviser** /dəvize/ [1] vi to converse

**dévisser** /devise/ [1] vtr to unscrew

**dévoiler** /devwale/ [1] vtr **(a)** to unveil
**(b)** to reveal; to uncover

**devoir¹** /dəvwaʀ/ [44] **1** v aux **(a)** to have
to; **je dois aller au travail** I've got to or I must
go to work; **il a dû accepter** he had to accept;
**il aurait dû partir** he should have left
**(b) il a dû accepter** he must have accepted;
**elle doit avoir 13 ans** she must be about 13
years old
**(c) cela devait arriver** it was bound to
happen; **un incident qui devait avoir de
graves conséquences** an incident which was
to have serious consequences; **ils doivent
arriver vers 10 heures** they're due to arrive
around 10 o'clock
**2** vtr to owe; **il me doit des excuses** he owes
me an apology
**3 se devoir** v refl (+ v être) **(a) je me dois
de le faire** it's my duty to do it
**(b) les époux se doivent fidélité** spouses owe
it to each other to be faithful
**(c) un homme de son rang se doit d'avoir un
chauffeur** a man of his standing has to have
a chauffeur
**4 comme il se doit** phr **(a) agir comme
il se doit** to behave in the correct way
**(b) comme il se doit, elle est en retard!** as
you might expect, she's late!

**devoir²** /dəvwaʀ/ nm **(a)** duty; **il est de
mon ~ de** it's my duty to
**(b)** test; homework

**dévolu** /devɔly/ nm **jeter son ~ sur** to set
one's heart on ⟨object⟩; to set one's cap at
⟨person⟩

**dévorant, ~e** /devɔʀɑ̃, ɑ̃t/ adj ⟨hunger⟩
voracious; ⟨flames, passion⟩ all-consuming

**dévorer** /devɔʀe/ [1] vtr **(a)** to devour
⟨food, book⟩; ~ **qn de baisers** to smother sb
with kisses
**(b)** ⟨obsession⟩ to consume

**dévot, ~e** /devo, ɔt/ adj devout

**dévotion** /devosjɔ̃/ nf **(a)** devoutness
**(b)** (religious) devotion (**à** to)
**(b)** passion (**pour** for)

**dévoué, ~e** /devwe/ adj devoted (**à** to)

**dévouement** /devumɑ̃/ nm devotion

**dévouer: se dévouer** /devwe/ [1] v refl
(+ v être) **(a)** to devote or dedicate oneself
**(b)** to put oneself out

**dévoyer** /devwaje/ [23] **1** vtr to deprave
[sb], to lead [sb] astray
**2 se dévoyer** v refl (+ v être) to go astray

**dextérité** /dɛksteʀite/ nf dexterity, skill

**dézipper** /dezipe/ vt (Comput) to unzip

**diabète** /djabɛt/ nm diabetes

**diabétique** /djabetik/ adj, nmf diabetic

**diable** /djɑbl/ **1** nm **(a)** devil; **en ~**
diabolically; fiendishly; **un (petit) ~** a little
devil
**(b)** two-wheeled trolley (GB), hand truck (US)
**2** excl my God!; **pourquoi ~** why on earth
IDIOMS **habiter au ~** to live miles from
anywhere; **que le ~ t'emporte!** to hell with
you!; **ce n'est pas le ~!** it's not that difficult!;
**avoir le ~ au corps** to be like someone
possessed; **tirer le ~ par la queue** to live
from hand to mouth

**diablement** /djɑbləmɑ̃/ adv terrifically

**diabolique** /djabɔlik/ adj **(a)** diabolic;
⟨invention⟩ fiendish
**(b)** ⟨person⟩ demonic; ⟨scheme, smile⟩
devilish
**(c)** ⟨precision⟩ uncanny

**diabolo** /djabɔlo/ nm ~ **menthe** mint
cordial and lemonade (GB) or soda (US)

**diadème** /djadɛm/ nm **(a)** tiara
**(b)** diadem

**diagnostic** /djagnɔstik/ nm (gen, Med)
diagnosis

**diagnostiquer** /djagnɔstike/ [1] vtr to
diagnose

**diagonal, ~e¹**, mpl **-aux** /djagɔnal, o/
adj diagonal

**diagonale²** /djagɔnal/ nf diagonal; **lire qch
en ~** to skim through sth

**diagramme** /djagʀam/ nm graph

**dialecte** /djalɛkt/ nm dialect

**dialogue** /djalɔg/ nm dialogue (GB)

**dialoguer** /djalɔge/ [1] vi to have talks

**dialoguiste** /djalɔgist/ nmf screenwriter

**dialyse** /djaliz/ nf dialysis

**diamant** /djamɑ̃/ nm diamond

**diamantaire** /djamɑ̃tɛʀ/ nm **(a)** diamond
cutter

**(b)** diamond merchant

**diamétralement** /djametʀalmɑ̃/ *adv*
diametrically

**diamètre** /djamɛtʀ/ *nm* diameter

**diapason** /djapazɔ̃/ *nm* **(a)** (note) diapason
**(b)** tuning fork
IDIOMS se mettre au ~ to fall in step

**diaphragme** /djafʀagm/ *nm* diaphragm

**diapo** /djapo/ *nf* (colloq) slide

**diaporama** /djapoʀama/ *nm* slide show

**diapositive** /djapozitiv/ *nf* slide,
transparency

**diarrhée** /djaʀe/ *nf* diarrhoea

**dico** /diko/ *nm* (colloq) dictionary

**dictateur** /diktatœʀ/ *nm* dictator

**dictature** /diktatyʀ/ *nf* dictatorship

**dictée** /dikte/ *nf* dictation

**dicter** /dikte/ [1] *vtr* **(a)** to dictate
**(b)** to motivate

**diction** /diksjɔ̃/ *nf* diction; elocution

**dictionnaire** /diksjɔnɛʀ/ *nm* dictionary

**dicton** /diktɔ̃/ *nm* saying

**didacticiel** /didaktisjɛl/ *nm* educational
software program

**didactique** /didaktik/ *adj* **(a)** ⟨work, tone⟩
didactic
**(b)** ⟨term, language⟩ technical, specialist

**dièse** /djɛz/ *adj, nm* sharp; do ~ C sharp

**diesel** /djezɛl/ *nm* diesel

**diète** /djɛt/ *nf* (Med) light diet

**diététicien, -ienne** /djetetisjɛ̃, ɛn/ *nm,f*
dietitian

**diététique** /djetetik/ **1** *adj* dietary;
**produits ~s** health foods; **magasin ~** health-
food shop
**2** *nf* dietetics

**dieu**, *pl* ~**x** /djø/ *nm* **(a)** god
**(b) sur le terrain c'est un ~** he's brilliant on
the sports field
IDIOMS **nager comme un ~** to be a superb
swimmer; **être dans le secret des ~x** to be
privy to the secrets of those on high

**Dieu** /djø/ *nm* God
IDIOMS **se prendre pour ~ le père** to think
one is God Almighty; **chaque jour que ~ fait**
day in, day out; **il vaut mieux s'adresser à ~
qu'à ses saints** (Proverb) always go straight
to the top

**diffamation** /difamasjɔ̃/ *nf* slander; (Law)
libel

**diffamatoire** /difamatwaʀ/ *adj* (in writing)
libellous; (verbally) slanderous; **écrit ~** libel

**diffamer** /difame/ [1] *vtr* (gen) to slander,
to defame; (Law) to libel

**différé, ~e** /difere/ **1** *pp* ▶ DIFFÉRER
**2** *pp adj* **(a)** postponed
**(b)** ⟨payment⟩ deferred
**(c)** ⟨programme⟩ pre-recorded
**3** *nm* (of match, event) recording

**différemment** /difeʀamɑ̃/ *adv* differently

**différence** /difeʀɑ̃s/ *nf* difference; **à la ~
de** unlike; **le droit à la ~** the right to be
different

**différenciation** /difeʀɑ̃sjasjɔ̃/ *nf*
differentiation

**différencier** /difeʀɑ̃sje/ [2] **1** *vtr* **(a)** to
differentiate; **rien ne les différencie** there's
no way of telling them apart
**(b)** to make [sb/sth] different
**2 se différencier** *v refl* (+ *v être*)
**(a)** ⟨person, organization⟩ to differentiate
oneself
**(b)** to differ
**(c)** to become different

**différend** /difeʀɑ̃/ *nm* disagreement

**différent, ~e** /difeʀɑ̃, ɑ̃t/ *adj* different,
various; **pour ~es raisons** for various
reasons

**différentiel, -ielle** /difeʀɑ̃sjɛl/ *adj*
differential

**différer** /difeʀe/ [14] **1** *vtr* to postpone
⟨departure, meeting⟩; to defer ⟨payment⟩
**2** *vi* to differ

**difficile** /difisil/ *adj* **(a)** (gen) difficult;
⟨victory⟩ hard-won; **le plus ~ reste à faire**
the worst is yet to come
**(b)** ⟨person, personality⟩ difficult
**(c)** fussy (sur about); **tu n'es pas ~!** you're
easy to please!

**difficilement** /difisilmɑ̃/ *adv* with
difficulty; ~ **supportable** hard to bear

**difficulté** /difikylte/ *nf* difficulty

**difforme** /difɔʀm/ *adj* ⟨body, limb⟩
deformed; ⟨object⟩ strangely shaped; ⟨tree⟩
twisted

**difformité** /difɔʀmite/ *nf* deformity

**diffus, ~e** /dify, yz/ *adj* ⟨light, heat⟩
diffuse; ⟨feeling⟩ vague

**diffuser** /difyze/ [1] *vtr* **(a)** to broadcast
**(b)** to spread; ~ **le signalement de qn** to
send out a description of sb
**(c)** to distribute ⟨article, book⟩
**(d)** to diffuse ⟨light, heat⟩

**diffusion** /difyzjɔ̃/ *nf* **(a)** broadcasting; **la
~ du film** the showing of the film
**(b)** dissemination, diffusion
**(c)** (commercial) distribution
**(d)** (of newspaper) circulation

**digérer** /diʒeʀe/ [14] *vtr* **(a)** to digest
**(b)** (colloq) to swallow ⟨insult⟩; to stomach
⟨defeat⟩

**digeste** /diʒɛst/ *adj* easily digestible

**digestif, -ive** /diʒɛstif, iv/ **1** *adj*
digestive
**2** *nm* liqueur ⟨taken after dinner⟩; brandy

**digestion** /diʒɛstjɔ̃/ *nf* digestion

**digicode®** /diʒikɔd/ *nm* digital (access)
lock

**digital, ~e**, *mpl* **-aux** /diʒital, o/ *adj*
digital

**digne** /diɲ/ *adj* **(a)** dignified
**(b)** worthy; ~ **de confiance** *or* **de foi**
trustworthy

**dignement** /diɲmɑ̃/ *adv* **(a)** with dignity
**(b)** fittingly

**dignité** /diɲite/ *nf* **(a)** dignity; **avoir sa ~**
to have one's pride    ⋯⟩

**(b)** (title) dignity

**digression** /digʀesjɔ̃/ nf digression

**digue** /dig/ nf **(a)** sea wall
**(b)** dyke (GB), dike (US)
**(c)** harbour (GB) wall

**dilapider** /dilapide/ [1] vtr to squander

**dilatation** /dilatasjɔ̃/ nf **(a)** (of gas) expansion
**(b)** (Med) dilation

**dilater** /dilate/ [1] vtr **(a)** to dilate ⟨pupil, cervix⟩; to distend ⟨stomach⟩
**(b)** to expand ⟨gas⟩

**dilemme** /dilɛm/ nm dilemma

**dilettante** /diletãt/ nmf amateur

**dilettantisme** /diletãtism/ nm amateurism; (pejorative) dilettantism

**diligence** /diliʒãs/ nf **(a)** stagecoach
**(b)** haste

**diligent**, ∼e /diliʒã, ãt/ adj diligent

**diluant** /diluã/ nm thinner

**diluer** /dilue/ [1] vtr **(a)** to dilute
**(b)** to thin [sth] down

**diluvien, -ienne** /dilyvjɛ̃, ɛn/ adj pluies diluviennes torrential rain

**dimanche** /dimãʃ/ nm Sunday.
IDIOMS ce n'est pas tous les jours ∼ not every day is a holiday

**dimension** /dimãsjɔ̃/ nf **(a)** dimension
**(b)** size
**(c)** dimension, aspect
**(d)** (of problem) dimensions

**diminué**, ∼e /diminɥe/ **1** pp ▶ DIMINUER
**2** pp adj ⟨person⟩ weak

**diminuer** /diminɥe/ [1] **1** vtr **(a)** to reduce; to lower
**(b)** to dampen ⟨enthusiasm, courage⟩
**(c)** to belittle ⟨person, achievement⟩
**(d)** to weaken ⟨person⟩; to sap ⟨strength⟩
**2** vi **(a)** to come or go down; to be reduced; to fall; to decrease; les jours diminuent the days are getting shorter
**(b)** ⟨activity, violence⟩ to fall off; ⟨tension⟩ to decrease; ⟨noise, flames, rumours⟩ to die down; ⟨strength⟩ to diminish

**diminutif** /diminytif/ nm **(a)** diminutive
**(b)** pet name

**diminution** /diminysjɔ̃/ nf decrease; reduction; (in production, trade) fall-off

**dinde** /dɛ̃d/ nf turkey (hen)

**dindon** /dɛ̃dɔ̃/ nm turkey (cock)
IDIOMS être le ∼ de la farce to be fooled or duped

**dindonneau**, pl ∼**x** /dɛ̃dɔno/ nm turkey

**dîner¹** /dine/ [1] vi to have dinner
IDIOMS qui dort dîne (Proverb) when you're asleep you don't feel hungry

**dîner²** /dine/ nm dinner

**dînette** /dinɛt/ nf doll's tea set

**dingo** /dɛ̃go/ adj inv (colloq) crazy (colloq)

**dingue** (colloq) /dɛ̃g/ **1** adj **(a)** ⟨person⟩ crazy (colloq)
**(b)** ⟨noise, success⟩ wild; ⟨price, speed⟩ ridiculous

**2** nmf **(a)** nutcase (colloq)
**(b)** un ∼ de musique a music freak (colloq)

**dinosaure** /dinozɔʀ/ nm dinosaur

**diocèse** /djosɛz/ nm diocese

**dioxyde** /dijɔksid/ nm dioxide

**diphtongue** /diftɔ̃g/ nf diphthong

**diplomate** /diplɔmat/ **1** adj diplomatic
**2** nmf diplomat

**diplomatie** /diplɔmasi/ nf diplomacy

**diplomatique** /diplɔmatik/ adj diplomatic

**diplôme** /diplom/ nm **(a)** certificate, diploma; il n'a aucun ∼ he hasn't got any qualifications
**(b)** (at university) degree; diploma
**(c)** (in army, police) staff exam

**diplômé**, ∼**e** /diplome/ **1** adj une infirmière ∼e a qualified nurse
**2** nm,f graduate

**dire¹** /diʀ/ [65] **1** vtr **(a)** to say ⟨words, prayer⟩; to read ⟨lesson⟩; to tell ⟨story, joke⟩; ∼ qch entre ses dents to mutter sth
**(b)** to tell; c'est ce qu'on m'a dit so I've been told; faire ∼ à qn que to let sb know that...; je me suis laissé ∼ que... I heard that...; c'est pas pour ∼, mais.. (colloq) I don't want to make a big deal of it, but (colloq)...; à qui le dites-vous! (colloq) don't I know it!; je ne vous le fais pas ∼! (colloq) you don't need to tell me!; dis donc, où tu te crois? (colloq) hey! where do you think you are?
**(c)** to say (que that); on dit que... it is said that...; si l'on peut ∼ if one might say so; autant ∼ que... you might as well say that...; si j'ose ∼ if I may say so; c'est (tout) ∼! need I say more?; cela dit having said that; tu peux le ∼! (colloq) you can say that again! (colloq); à vrai ∼ actually; entre nous soit dit between you and me; soit dit en passant incidentally; c'est ∼ si j'ai raison it just goes to show I'm right; c'est beaucoup ∼ that's going a bit far; c'est vite dit that's easy for you to say; ce n'est pas dit I'm not that sure; comment ∼? how shall I put it?; pour ainsi ∼ so to speak; autrement dit in other words; comme dirait l'autre (colloq) as they say; il n'y a pas à ∼, elle est belle (colloq) you have to admit, she's beautiful
**(d)** ⟨law⟩ to state; ⟨measuring device⟩ to show; vouloir ∼ to mean
**(e)** ∼ à qn de faire to tell sb to do
**(f)** to think; on dirait de l'estragon it looks or tastes like tarragon; ça ne me dit rien de faire I don't feel like doing; notre nouveau jardinier ne me dit rien (qui vaille) I don't think much of our new gardener
**2** se dire v refl (+ v être) **(a)** to tell oneself; il faut (bien) se ∼ que... one must realize that...
**(b)** to exchange ⟨insults⟩; se ∼ adieu to say goodbye to each other
**(c)** to claim to be
**(d)** ça ne se dit pas you can't say that
**3** se dire v impers il ne s'est rien dit d'intéressant à la réunion nothing of interest was said during the meeting

**dire²** /diʀ/ *nm* au ~ de, selon les ~s de according to

**direct** /diʀɛkt/ **1** *adj* **(a)** ⟨contact, descendant, tax⟩ direct; ⟨superior⟩ immediate
**(b)** ⟨route, access⟩ direct; **ce train est ~ pour Lille** this train is nonstop to Lille
**(c)** direct, frank
**2** *nm* **(a)** live broadcasting; **en ~ de** live from
**(b)** (in boxing) jab; **~ du gauche** left jab
**(c)** express (train)

**directement** /diʀɛktəmɑ̃/ *adv* **(a)** ⟨travel, go⟩ straight
**(b)** directly

**directeur, -trice** /diʀɛktœʀ, tʀis/ **1** *adj* **principe ~** guiding principle; **idée directrice d'un ouvrage** central theme of a book
**2** *nm,f* **(a)** headmaster/headmistress (GB), principal (US); (of private school) principal
**(b)** (of hotel, cinema) manager/manageress
**(c)** director; head
■ **~ de banque** bank manager; **~ général** managing director (GB), chief executive officer (US); **~ de prison** prison governor (GB), warden (US); **~ sportif** (team) manager

**direction** /diʀɛksjɔ̃/ *nf* **(a)** direction; **il a pris la ~ du nord** he headed north; **en ~ de** toward(s); **indiquer la ~ à qn** to tell sb the way; **prenez la ~ Nation** take the train going to 'Nation'
**(b)** (gen) management; supervision; (of newspaper) editorship; (of movement) leadership; **orchestre sous la ~ de** orchestra conducted by
**(c)** management; **la ~ et les ouvriers** management and workers
**(d)** manager's office; head office
**(e)** (Aut) steering

**directive** /diʀɛktiv/ *nf* directive

**directrice** ▶ DIRECTEUR

**dirigeable** /diʀiʒabl/ *adj, nm* dirigible

**dirigeant, -e** /diʀiʒɑ̃, ɑ̃t/ **1** *adj* ⟨class⟩ ruling
**2** *nm* leader

**diriger** /diʀiʒe/ [13] **1** *vtr* **(a)** to be in charge of ⟨people⟩; to run ⟨service, party⟩; to manage ⟨company⟩; to lead ⟨investigation⟩; to direct ⟨operation⟩
**(b)** to steer; to pilot; **il vous dirigera dans la ville** he'll guide you around the town
**(c)** to turn ⟨light, jet⟩ (sur on); to point ⟨gun, telescope⟩ (sur at)
**(d)** to dispatch ⟨goods⟩; to direct ⟨convoy⟩
**(e)** (Mus) to conduct
**(f)** to direct ⟨actors⟩; to manage ⟨theatre company⟩
**2 se diriger** *v refl* (+ *v être*) **se ~ vers** to make for; **avoir du mal à se ~ dans le noir** to have difficulty finding one's way in the dark

**dirigisme** /diʀiʒism/ *nm* planned economy

**discale** /diskal/ *adj f* **hernie ~** slipped disc

**discernement** /disɛʀnəmɑ̃/ *nm* judgment

**discerner** /disɛʀne/ [1] *vtr* **(a)** to detect ⟨sign, smell, expression⟩; to make out ⟨shape, noise⟩
**(b)** to make out ⟨motives⟩; **~ le vrai du faux** to discriminate between truth and untruth

**disciple** /disipl/ *nmf* **(a)** follower
**(b)** disciple

**disciplinaire** /disiplinɛʀ/ *adj* disciplinary

**discipline** /disiplin/ *nf* **(a)** discipline
**(b)** discipline, specialism
**(c)** (Sch) subject
**(d)** sport

**discipliner** /disipline/ [1] *vtr* **(a)** to discipline
**(b)** to control ⟨troops⟩; to discipline ⟨thoughts, feelings⟩
**(c)** to keep [sth] under control ⟨hair⟩

**disco** /disko/ **1** *adj inv* disco
**2** *nm* disco music

**discontinu, ~e** /diskɔ̃tiny/ *adj* ⟨movement⟩ intermittent; ⟨line⟩ broken

**discordance** /diskɔʀdɑ̃s/ *nf* **(a)** (of opinions) conflict
**(b)** (of colours) clash
**(c)** (of sounds) dissonance

**discordant, ~e** /diskɔʀdɑ̃, ɑ̃t/ *adj*
**(a)** ⟨sound, instrument⟩ discordant; ⟨voice⟩ strident
**(b)** ⟨colours⟩ clashing
**(c)** ⟨opinions⟩ conflicting

**discorde** /diskɔʀd/ *nf* discord, dissension

**discothèque** /diskɔtɛk/ *nf* **(a)** music library
**(b)** record collection
**(c)** discotheque

**discourir** /diskuʀiʀ/ [26] *vi* **~ de** *or* **sur qch** to hold forth on sth

**discours** /diskuʀ/ *nm inv* **(a)** speech (sur on)
**(b)** talk; **assez de ~, des actes!** let's have less talk and more action!
**(c)** views; **il tient toujours le même ~** his views haven't changed
**(d)** (in linguistics) speech; discourse

**discrédit** /diskʀedi/ *nm* disrepute; **jeter le ~ sur** to discredit

**discréditer** /diskʀedite/ [1] *vtr* to discredit

**discret, -ète** /diskʀɛ, ɛt/ *adj* **(a)** ⟨person⟩ unassuming; ⟨colour⟩ sober; ⟨charm⟩ subtle; ⟨lighting⟩ subdued; ⟨smile, perfume⟩ discreet; ⟨place⟩ quiet
**(b)** discreet (sur about)
**(c)** not inquisitive

**discrètement** /diskʀɛtmɑ̃/ *adv* discreetly; soberly; quietly

**discrétion** /diskʀesjɔ̃/ **1** *nf* discretion; **dans la plus grande ~** in the greatest secrecy
**2 à discrétion** *phr* **il y avait à boire à ~** you could drink as much as you liked
**3 à la discrétion de** *phr* at the discretion of

**discrimination** /diskʀiminasjɔ̃/ *nf*
discrimination

**discriminatoire** /diskʀiminatwaʀ/ *adj*
discriminatory (**à l'encontre de** against)

**discriminer** /diskʀimine/ [1] *vtr* to
discriminate between ⟨*things, people*⟩

**disculper** /diskylpe/ [1] **1** *vtr* to exculpate
**2 se disculper** *v refl* (+ *v être*) to
vindicate oneself (**auprès de qn** in the eyes
of )

**discussion** /diskysjɔ̃/ *nf* (a) discussion;
**relancer la** ~ to revive the debate
(b) argument

**discutable** /diskytabl/ *adj* debatable;
questionable

**discuté, ~e** /diskyte/ **1** *pp* ▶ DISCUTER
**2** *pp adj* controversial

**discuter** /diskyte/ [1] **1** *vtr* (a) to discuss,
to debate
(b) to question
**2 discuter de** *v+prep* to discuss
**3** *vi* (a) to talk (**avec qn** to sb)
(b) to argue
**4 se discuter** *v refl* (+ *v être*) **ça se
discute, ça peut se** ~ that's debatable

**diseur, -euse** /dizœʀ, øz/ *nm,f* ~ **de
bonne aventure** fortune-teller

**disgrâce** /disgʀɑs/ *nf* disgrace

**disgracieux, -ieuse** /disgʀasjø, øz/ *adj*
ugly; unsightly

**disjoindre** /disʒwɛ̃dʀ/ [56] **1** *vtr* (a) to
loosen
(b) to separate
**2 se disjoindre** *v refl* to come loose

**disjoncter** /disʒɔ̃kte/ [1] *vi* **ça a disjoncté**
the trip switch has gone

**disjoncteur** /disʒɔ̃ktœʀ/ *nm* circuit
breaker

**dislocation** /dislɔkasjɔ̃/ *nf*
(a) dismemberment
(b) ~ (**articulaire**) dislocation (of a joint)

**disloquer** /dislɔke/ [1] *vtr* (a) to
dismember ⟨*empire, state*⟩
(b) to dislocate ⟨*shoulder, arm*⟩

**disparaître** /dispaʀɛtʀ/ [73] *vi* (a) to
disappear; to vanish; **disparaissez!** out of my
sight!; **des centaines de personnes
disparaissent chaque année** hundreds of
people go missing every year
(b) ⟨*pain, smell*⟩ to go; ⟨*stain*⟩ to come out;
⟨*fever*⟩ to subside; **faire** ~ to get rid of ⟨*pain,
dandruff*⟩; to remove ⟨*stain*⟩
(c) (euphemistic) to die; to die out; to become
extinct; **voir** ~ to witness the end of
⟨*civilization*⟩

**disparate** /dispaʀat/ *adj* ill-assorted;
mixed

**disparition** /dispaʀisjɔ̃/ *nf*
(a) disappearance; (of species) extinction; **une
espèce en voie de** ~ an endangered species
(b) (euphemistic) death

**disparu, ~e** /dispaʀy/ **1** *pp* ▶
DISPARAÎTRE

**2** *pp adj* (a) missing; **porté** ~ (Mil) missing
in action
(b) ⟨*civilization, traditions*⟩ lost; ⟨*species*⟩
extinct
(c) (euphemistic) dead
**3** *nm,f* (a) missing person
(b) **les** ~**s** the dead

**dispendieux, -ieuse** /dispɑ̃djø, øz/ *adj*
expensive, extravagant

**dispense** /dispɑ̃s/ *nf* (a) exemption (**de**
from)
(b) certificate of exemption

**dispenser** /dispɑ̃se/ [1] **1** *vtr* (a) to give
⟨*lessons, advice*⟩
(b) ~ **qn de (faire) qch** to exempt sb from
(doing) sth; to excuse sb from (doing) sth; **je
vous dispense de commentaire** I don't need
any comment from you
**2 se dispenser** *v refl* (+ *v être*) **se** ~ **de
(faire) qch** to spare oneself (the trouble of
doing) sth

**disperser** /dispɛʀse/ [1] **1** *vtr* to scatter
⟨*objects, family*⟩; to disperse ⟨*crowd, smoke*⟩;
to break up ⟨*gathering, collection*⟩
**2 se disperser** *v refl* (+ *v être*) to
disperse; to scatter; to break up

**disponibilité** /dispɔnibilite/ **1** *nf*
availability
**2 disponibilités** *nf pl* available funds

**disponible** /dispɔnibl/ *adj* available

**dispos, ~e** /dispo, oz/ *adj* **frais et** ~ fresh
as a daisy

**disposé, ~e** /dispoze/ **1** *pp* ▶ DISPOSER
**2** *pp adj* (a) arranged; laid out
(b) ~ **à faire** willing to do
(c) **être bien** ~ to be in a good mood; **être
bien** ~ **à l'égard de** *or* **envers qn** to be well-
disposed toward(s) sb

**disposer** /dispoze/ [1] **1** *vtr* (a) to
arrange; to position
(b) **les machines dont nous disposons** the
machines we have at our disposal
**2 se disposer** *v refl* (+ *v être*) (a) **se** ~ **à
faire** to be about to do
(b) **se** ~ **en cercle autour de qn** to form a
circle around sb

**dispositif** /dispozitif/ *nm* (a) device;
system
(b) operation; ~ **policier** police operation

**disposition** /dispozisjɔ̃/ **1** *nf*
(a) arrangement; layout; position
(b) disposal; **à la** ~ **du public** for public use
(c) measure, step
**2 dispositions** *nf pl* aptitude

**disproportionné, ~e** /dispʀopɔʀsjone/
*adj* ⟨*effort, demand*⟩ disproportionate; ⟨*head*⟩
out of proportion with one's body

**dispute** /dispyt/ *nf* argument

**disputé, ~e** /dispyte/ *adj* (a) ⟨*title,
match*⟩ keenly contested
(b) ⟨*place, person*⟩ sought-after (**de** by)
(c) ⟨*issue, plan*⟩ controversial

**disputer** /dispyte/ [1] **1** *vtr* (a) to compete
in ⟨*competition*⟩; to compete for ⟨*cup*⟩; to play
⟨*match*⟩; to run ⟨*race*⟩

**(b)** (colloq) to tell [sb] off

**2 se disputer** *v refl* (+ *v être*) **(a)** to argue (**sur** about; **pour** over); **nous nous sommes disputés** we had an argument **(b)** to fight over ⟨*inheritance, bone*⟩ **(c)** ⟨*tournament*⟩ to take place

**disquaire** /diskɛʀ/ *nmf* record dealer

**disqualifier** /diskalifje/ [2] **1** *vtr* to disqualify; **se faire ~ (par)** to be disqualified (by) **2 se disqualifier** *v refl* (+ *v être*) to discredit oneself (**en faisant** by doing)

**disque** /disk/ *nm* **(a)** record; **passer un ~** to play a record **(b)** (gen, Tech) disc; (Comput) disk **(c)** (Sport) discus

■ **~ compact** compact disc; **~ dur** hard disk; **~ souple** flexi-disc; floppy disk; **~ de stationnement** parking disc

**disquette** /diskɛt/ *nf* diskette, floppy disk

**dissection** /disɛksjɔ̃/ *nf* dissection

**dissemblable** /disɑ̃blabl/ *adj* dissimilar, different

**dissémination** /diseminasjɔ̃/ *nf* spread; dispersal; scattering; dissemination

**disséminer** /disemine/ [1] **1** *vtr* to spread ⟨*germs, ideas*⟩; to disband ⟨*pollen*⟩ **2 se disséminer** *v refl* (+ *v être*) ⟨*people*⟩ to scatter; ⟨*germs, ideas*⟩ to spread

**dissension** /disɑ̃sjɔ̃/ *nf* disagreement (**au sein de** within)

**disséquer** /diseke/ [14] *vtr* to dissect

**dissert** /disɛʀ/ *nf* essay

**dissertation** /disɛʀtasjɔ̃/ *nf* essay

**disserter** /disɛʀte/ [1] *vi* to speak (**sur** on)

**dissidence** /disidɑ̃s/ *nf* **(a)** dissent; dissidence; rebellion **(b) la ~** the dissidents

**dissident, ~e** /disidɑ̃, ɑ̃t/ **1** *adj* dissident **2** *nm,f* **(a)** dissident **(b)** dissenter

**dissimulation** /disimylasjɔ̃/ *nf* concealment

**dissimuler** /disimyle/ [1] *vtr* to conceal (**qch à qn** sth from sb)

**dissipation** /disipasjɔ̃/ *nf* **(a)** (of misunderstanding) clearing up **(b)** (of fog, clouds) clearing **(c)** (of attention) wandering **(d)** restlessness

**dissipé, ~e** /disipe/ *adj* ⟨*pupil*⟩ badly-behaved; ⟨*life*⟩ dissipated

**dissiper** /disipe/ [1] **1** *vtr* **(a)** to dispel ⟨*doubt*⟩; to clear up ⟨*misunderstanding*⟩; to disperse ⟨*smoke*⟩ **(b)** to distract ⟨*person*⟩ **2 se dissiper** *v refl* (+ *v être*) **(a)** ⟨*doubt*⟩ to vanish; ⟨*misunderstanding*⟩ to be cleared up; ⟨*mist*⟩ to clear **(b)** to behave badly

**dissocier** /disɔsje/ [2] *vtr* to separate (**de** from)

**dissolu, ~e** /disɔly/ *adj* ⟨*life*⟩ dissolute; ⟨*morals*⟩ loose

**dissolution** /disɔlysjɔ̃/ *nf* dissolution

**dissolvant, ~e** /disɔlvɑ̃, ɑ̃t/ **1** *adj* solvent **2** *nm* **(a)** nail varnish **(b)** solvent

**dissonance** /disɔnɑ̃s/ *nf* dissonance

**dissonant, ~e** /disɔnɑ̃, ɑ̃t/ *adj* ⟨*voice*⟩ dissonant; ⟨*colours*⟩ clashing

**dissoudre** /disudʀ/ [75] **1** *vtr* **(a)** to dissolve ⟨*assembly*⟩; to disband ⟨*movement*⟩ **(b)** to dissolve ⟨*substance*⟩ **2 se dissoudre** *v refl* (+ *v être*) **(a)** ⟨*organization*⟩ to disband **(b)** ⟨*substance*⟩ to dissolve

**dissous, -oute** /disu, ut/ ▶ DISSOUDRE

**dissuader** /disɥade/ [1] *vtr* to dissuade; to put [sb] off; to deter

**dissuasif, -ive** /disɥazif, iv/ *adj* **(a)** dissuasive; deterrent **(b)** prohibitive

**dissuasion** /disɥazjɔ̃/ *nf* (Mil) deterrence

**dissymétrie** /disimetʀi/ *nf* asymmetry

**distance** /distɑ̃s/ *nf* **(a)** distance; **Paris est à quelle ~ de Londres?** how far is Paris from London?; **j'ai couru sur une ~ de deux kilomètres** I ran for two kilometres (GB); **être à faible ~ de** not to be far (away) from; **prendre ses ~s avec** to distance oneself from; **tenir** *or* **garder ses ~s** to stand aloof; **tenir la ~** ⟨*runner*⟩ to stay the course; **à ~** from a distance; **commande à ~** remote control **(b)** gap; **à une semaine de ~** one week apart

**distancer** /distɑ̃se/ [12] *vtr* to outdistance; to outrun; **se laisser ~** to get left behind

**distancier: se distancier** /distɑ̃sje/ [2] *v refl* (+ *v être*) to distance oneself (**de** from)

**distant, ~e** /distɑ̃, ɑ̃t/ *adj* **(a)** ⟨*place, noise*⟩ distant; **~s de trois kilomètres** three kilometres (GB) apart **(b)** ⟨*person*⟩ distant; ⟨*attitude*⟩ reserved; ⟨*relations*⟩ cool

**distendre** /distɑ̃dʀ/ **1** *vtr* **(a)** to distend ⟨*stomach*⟩; to stretch ⟨*skin*⟩, ⟨*cable*⟩ **(b)** to weaken ⟨*bond*⟩, ⟨*tie*⟩ **2 se distendre** *v refl* (+ *v être*) **(a)** to slacken **(b)** to cool

**distiller** /distile/ [1] *vtr* to distil (GB)

**distillerie** /distilʀi/ *nf* **(a)** distillery **(b)** distilling

**distinct, ~e** /distɛ̃, ɛ̃kt/ *adj* **(a)** distinct (**de** from) **(b)** ⟨*sound*⟩ distinct; ⟨*voice*⟩ clear **(c)** ⟨*firm*⟩ separate

**distinctif, -ive** /distɛ̃ktif, iv/ *adj* ⟨*mark*⟩ distinguishing; ⟨*feature*⟩ distinctive

**distinction** /distɛ̃ksjɔ̃/ *nf* **(a)** distinction; **sans ~** without discrimination; indiscriminately **(b)** honour (GB); **~ honorifique** award **(c)** refinement

**distingué**, **~e** /distɛ̃ge/ *adj* distinguished

**distinguer** /distɛ̃ge/ [1] **1** *vtr* **(a)** to distinguish between; **il est difficile de les ~** it's difficult to tell them apart
**(b)** to distinguish, to make out
**(c)** to discern
**(d)** to set [sb] apart; to make [sth] different
**(e)** to single [sb] out for an honour (GB)
**2 se distinguer** *v refl* (+ *v être*) **(a) se ~ de** to differ from; to set oneself apart from
**(b)** to distinguish oneself
**(c)** to be distinguishable
**(d)** to draw attention to oneself

**distordre** /distɔʀdʀ/ **1** *vtr* to contort; **distordu par** contorted with
**2 se distordre** *v refl* to become contorted

**distorsion** /distɔʀsjɔ̃/ *nf* distortion

**distraction** /distʀaksjɔ̃/ *nf* **(a)** leisure, entertainment; **les ~s sont rares ici** there's not much to do around here
**(b)** recreation
**(c)** absent-mindedness

**distraire** /distʀɛʀ/ [58] **1** *vtr* **(a)** to amuse; to entertain
**(b)** **~ qn de qch** to take sb's mind off sth
**(c)** to distract (**de** from; **par** by)
**2 se distraire** *v refl* (+ *v être*) **(a)** to amuse oneself; to enjoy oneself
**(b)** **j'ai besoin de me ~** I need to take my mind off things

**distrait**, **~e** /distʀɛ, ɛt/ *adj* ‹*person*› absent-minded; inattentive; ‹*air*› distracted; ‹*look*› vague

**distraitement** /distʀɛtmɑ̃/ *adv* absent-mindedly; **regarder ~ qch** to look vaguely at sth; **écouter ~** to listen with half an ear

**distrayant**, **~e** /distʀɛjɑ̃, ɑ̃t/ *adj* entertaining

**distribuer** /distʀibɥe/ [1] *vtr* **(a)** to distribute (**à** to); to allocate (**à** to); **~ les cartes** to deal; **~ le courrier** to deliver the mail
**(b)** to supply ‹*water, heat*›

**distributeur, -trice** /distʀibytœʀ, tʀis/ **1** *nm,f* distributor
**2** *nm* **(a)** dispenser; vending machine; **~ de tickets** ticket machine; **~ de billets (de banque)** cash dispenser
**(b)** retailing group
■ **~ automatique de billets**, **DAB** automatic teller machine, ATM

**distribution** /distʀibysjɔ̃/ *nf* **(a)** (sector) retailing
**(b)** (in commerce) distribution
**(c)** (of water, electricity) supply
**(d)** (supplying) distribution, handing out; (of jobs, duties) allocation
**(e)** (geographically) distribution, layout
**(f)** (of actors) casting; cast
■ **~ d'actions gratuites** allocation of bonus shares; **~ automatique** automatic dispensing; **~ du courrier** postal delivery

**dithyrambique** /ditiʀɑ̃bik/ *adj* ‹*speech*›, ‹*comments*› ecstatic; ‹*praise*› extravagant

**diurétique** /djyʀetik/ *adj, nm* diuretic

**divagation** /divagasjɔ̃/ *nf* ravings; rambling

**divaguer** /divage/ [1] *vi* **(a)** to rave; **la fièvre le fait ~** he's delirious with fever
**(b)** to ramble; to talk nonsense
**(c)** to stray

**divan** /divɑ̃/ *nm* divan; couch

**divergence** /divɛʀʒɑ̃s/ *nf* divergence; difference

**divergent**, **~e** /divɛʀʒɑ̃, ɑ̃t/ *adj* divergent

**diverger** /divɛʀʒe/ [13] *vi* to diverge (**de** from); to differ (**de** from)

**divers**, **~e** /divɛʀ, ɛʀs/ *adj* **(a)** various; **les gens les plus ~** all sorts of people
**(b)** miscellaneous

**diversement** /divɛʀsəmɑ̃/ *adv* variously, in different ways

**diversification** /divɛʀsifikasjɔ̃/ *nf* diversification; **une entreprise en voie de ~** a company in the process of diversifying; **une ~ de la clientèle** targeting a wider clientele

**diversifier** /divɛʀsifje/ [2] *vtr* to widen the range of; to diversify

**diversion** /divɛʀsjɔ̃/ *nf* (Mil) diversion

**diversité** /divɛʀsite/ *nf* diversity; variety

**divertir** /divɛʀtiʀ/ [3] **1** *vtr* to entertain; to amuse
**2 se divertir** *v refl* (+ *v être*) to amuse oneself; **pour se ~** for fun

**divertissant**, **~e** /divɛʀtisɑ̃, ɑ̃t/ *adj* amusing; entertaining; enjoyable

**divertissement** /divɛʀtismɑ̃/ *nm* entertainment; recreation

**dividende** /dividɑ̃d/ *nm* dividend

**divin**, **~e** /divɛ̃, in/ *adj* divine

**divinité** /divinite/ *nf* deity; divinity

**diviser** /divize/ [1] **1** *vtr* to divide
**2 se diviser** *v refl* (+ *v être*) **(a)** to become divided (**sur** over)
**(b)** to be divided
**(c)** to be divisible
**(d)** to divide; to fork

**divisible** /divizibl/ *adj* divisible

**division** /divizjɔ̃/ *nf* division

**divisionnaire** /divizjɔnɛʀ/ *adj* **commissaire ~** Chief Superintendent

**divorce** /divɔʀs/ *nm* divorce (**d'avec** from); **prononcer le ~ entre deux époux** to grant a divorce to a couple

**divorcé**, **~e** /divɔʀse/ *nm,f* divorcee

**divorcer** /divɔʀse/ [12] *vi* to get divorced

**divulgation** /divylgasjɔ̃/ *nf* disclosure

**divulguer** /divylge/ [1] *vtr* to disclose

**dix** /dis, *but before consonant* di, *before vowel or mute h* diz/ *adj inv, pron, nm inv* ten
**IDIOMS ne rien savoir faire de ses ~ doigts** to be useless; **un de perdu, ~ de retrouvés** (Proverb) there's plenty more fish in the sea

**dix-huit** /dizɥit/ *adj inv, pron, nm inv* eighteen

**dix-huitième** /dizɥitjɛm/ *adj* eighteenth

**dixième** /dizjɛm/ *adj* tenth

**dix-neuf** /diznœf/ *adj inv, pron, nm inv*
nineteen

**dix-neuvième** /diznœvjɛm/ *adj*
nineteenth

**dix-sept** /dis(s)ɛt/ *adj inv, pron, nm inv*
seventeen

**dix-septième** /dis(s)ɛtjɛm/ *adj*
seventeenth

**dizaine** /dizɛn/ *nf* (a) ten
(b) about ten; des ~s de personnes dozens
of people

**do** /do/ *nm inv* (Mus) (note) C; (in sol-fa) doh

**docile** /dɔsil/ *adj* ⟨animal, person⟩ docile

**dock** /dɔk/ *nm* (a) dock
(b) warehouse

**docteur** /dɔktœr/ *nm* doctor; jouer au ~
to play doctors and nurses

**doctorat** /dɔktɔra/ *nm* PhD, doctorate

**doctrinaire** /dɔktrinɛr/ *adj* ⟨attitude⟩
doctrinaire; ⟨tone⟩ sententious

**doctrine** /dɔktrin/ *nf* doctrine

**document** /dɔkymɑ̃/ *nm* (a) document;
~ sonore audio material; avec ~s à l'appui
with documentary evidence
(b) document, paper

**documentaire** /dɔkymɑ̃tɛr/ [1] *adj*
documentary; à titre ~ for your information
[2] *nm* documentary (sur on, about)

**documentaliste** /dɔkymɑ̃talist/ *nmf*
information officer; (school) librarian

**documentation** /dɔkymɑ̃tasjɔ̃/ *nf*
(a) material (sur on)
(b) research
(c) brochures
(d) centre de ~ resource centre (GB)

**documenter: se documenter**
/dɔkymɑ̃te/ [1] *v refl* (+ *v être*) se ~ sur qch
to research sth

**dodeliner** /dɔdline/ [1] *vi* il dodelinait de
la tête his head was nodding

**dodo** /dodo/ *nm* (baby talk) faire ~ to sleep

**dodu, -e** /dɔdy/ *adj* plump

**dogmatique** /dɔgmatik/ *adj* dogmatic

**dogme** /dɔgm/ *nm* dogma

**dogue** /dɔg/ *nm* mastiff

**doigt** /dwa/ *nm* finger; petit ~ little finger
(GB), pinkie; bout des ~s fingertips; du bout
des ~s (figurative) reluctantly; connaître une
ville sur le bout des ~s to know a city like
the back of one's hand; montrer du ~ to
point at; (figurative) to point the finger at
■ ~ de pied toe
IDIOMS se brûler les ~s to get one's fingers
burned; être à deux ~s de to be a whisker
away from; filer entre les ~s de qn ⟨money,
thief⟩ to slip through sb's fingers; se faire
taper sur les ~s to get one's knuckles
rapped; lever le ~ to put one's hand up

**doigté** /dwate/ *nm* (a) tact
(b) (of pianist) fingering

**doléance** /dɔleɑ̃s/ *nf* complaint

**dollar** /dɔlar/ *nm* dollar

**DOM** /dɔm/ *nm inv* (abbr = **département
d'outre-mer**) *French overseas
(administrative) department*

**domaine** /dɔmɛn/ *nm* (a) estate
(b) field, domain
(c) territory

**domanial, ~e**, *mpl* **-iaux** /dɔmanjal, o/
*adj* state-owned

**dôme** /dom/ *nm* dome

**domestique** /dɔmɛstik/ [1] *adj* (a) ⟨staff,
animal⟩ domestic
(b) ⟨market⟩ domestic, home
[2] *nmf* servant

**domestiquer** /dɔmɛstike/ [1] *vtr* to
domesticate ⟨animal⟩

**domicile** /dɔmisil/ [1] *nm* place of
residence; (of company) registered address
[2] à domicile *phr* travail à ~ working at
*or* from home; 'livraisons à ~' 'home
deliveries'

**domicilié, ~e** /dɔmisilje/ *adj* (a) être ~
à Arras to live in Arras
(b) j'habite à Paris, mais je suis ~e à
Rennes I live in Paris, but my official
address is in Rennes

**dominance** /dɔminɑ̃s/ *nf* dominance

**dominant, ~e**[1] /dɔminɑ̃, ɑ̃t/ *adj*
(a) ⟨colour, gene⟩ dominant; ⟨wind, tendency⟩
prevailing; ⟨feature, idea⟩ main
(b) ⟨class⟩ ruling

**dominante**[2] /dɔminɑ̃t/ *nf* (a) dominant
feature
(b) (Univ) main subject, major

**dominateur, -trice** /dɔminatœr, tris/
*adj* domineering; overbearing; imperious

**domination** /dɔminasjɔ̃/ *nf* domination;
être sous la ~ de to be dominated by

**dominer** /dɔmine/ [1] [1] *vtr* (a) to
dominate; to tower above; de là, on domine
toute la vallée from there you get a view of
the whole valley
(b) to dominate ⟨match, sector⟩
(c) ⟨theme⟩ to dominate
(d) to master ⟨subject⟩; to overcome ⟨fear⟩;
~ la situation to be in control of the
situation
[2] *vi* (a) to rule, to hold sway
(b) to be in the lead
(c) ⟨impression⟩ to prevail; ⟨taste⟩ to stand
out
[3] se dominer *v refl* (+ *v être*) to control
oneself

**dominical, ~e**, *mpl* **-aux** /dɔminikal,
o/ *adj* ⟨walk, mass⟩ Sunday

**domino** /dɔmino/ *nm* domino

**dommage** /dɔmaʒ/ *nm* (a) c'est ~ it's a
shame *or* pity
(b) damage
(c) (Law) tort
■ ~s corporels personal injury; ~s et
intérêts damages

**dommageable** /dɔmaʒabl/ *adj* harmful
(pour to)

**dommages-intérêts** /dɔmaʒɛtɛʀɛ/ *nm pl* damages; **5 000 euros de** ~ 5,000 euros in damages

**dompter** /dɔ̃te/ [1] *vtr* to tame ‹*wild animal*›; to bring [sb] to heel ‹*unruly person*›; to subdue ‹*insurgents*›; to overcome ‹*passion*›

**dompteur, -euse** /dɔ̃tœʀ, øz/ *nm,f* tamer

**DOM-TOM** /dɔmtɔm/ *nm pl* (*abbr* = **départements et territoires d'outre-mer**) *French overseas departments and territories*

**don** /dɔ̃/ *nm* (a) donation; **faire** ~ **de** to give (à to); ~ **de soi** self-sacrifice
(b) gift; **avoir le** ~ **de faire** to have a talent for doing
■ ~ **du sang** blood donation

**donation** /dɔnasjɔ̃/ *nf* (a) donation
(b) (Law) gift

**donc** /dɔ̃k/ *conj* so, therefore; **j'étais** ~ **en train de lire, lorsque…** so I was reading, when…; **je disais** ~ **que…** as I was saying…; **entrez** ~! do come in!; **mais où est-il** ~ **passé?** where on earth has he gone?

**donjon** /dɔ̃ʒɔ̃/ *nm* (of castle) keep

**donne** /dɔn/ *nf* (in cards) deal

**donné, ~e**[1] /dɔne/ ① *pp* ▶ DONNER
② *pp adj* (a) **il n'est pas** ~ **à tout le monde de faire** not everyone can do
(b) given; **à un moment** ~ at one point; all of a sudden
(c) cheap
③ **étant donné (que)** *phr* given (that)

**donnée**[2] /dɔne/ *nf* (a) fact, element
(b) data

**donner** /dɔne/ [1] ① *vtr* (a) to give ‹*present, headache, advice, dinner, lesson*›; ~ **l'heure à qn** to tell sb the time; **je lui donne 40 ans** I'd say he/she was 40; ~ **faim à qn** to make sb feel hungry; **elle donne sa fille à garder à mes parents** she has my parents look after her daughter; **j'ai donné ma voiture à réparer** I've taken my car in to be repaired; **les sondages le donnent en tête** the polls put him in the lead
(b) to show ‹*film*›; to put on ‹*play*›; to give ‹*performance*›
(c) to produce, to yield ‹*fruit, juice*›; to produce ‹*results*›
(d) to show ‹*signs*›
(e) (colloq) to inform on ‹*accomplice*›
② *vi* (a) **le poirier va bien** ~ **cette année** the pear tree will yield a good crop this year
(b) **ne plus savoir où** ~ **de la tête** (figurative) not to know which way to turn
(c) ~ **sur** ‹*room, window*› to overlook; ‹*door*› to give onto; ~ **au nord** to face north; **la cuisine donne dans le salon** the kitchen leads into the living-room
(d) ~ **dans** to tend toward(s)
(e) ~ **de sa personne** to give of oneself
③ **se donner** *v refl* (+ *v être*) (a) **se** ~ **à** to devote oneself to
(b) **se** ~ **le temps de faire** to give oneself time to do

(c) **se** ~ **pour but de faire** to make it one's aim to do
(d) **se** ~ **de grands airs** to put on airs
(e) **se** ~ **des coups** to exchange blows; **se** ~ **le mot** to pass the word on
IDIOMS **donnant donnant: je fais la cuisine, tu fais la vaisselle** fair's fair: I cook, you do the washing-up; **avec lui, c'est donnant donnant** he never does anything for nothing

**donneur, -euse** /dɔnœʀ, øz/ *nm,f* (Med) donor

**dont** /dɔ̃/ *rel pron* (a) whose, of which; **la jeune fille** ~ **on nous disait qu'elle avait 20 ans** the girl who they said was 20; **Sylvaine est quelqu'un** ~ **on se souvient** Sylvaine is somebody (that) you remember; **la maladie** ~ **il souffre** the illness which he's suffering from; **la façon** ~ **il a été traité** the way in which he has been treated
(b) **il y a eu plusieurs victimes** ~ **mon père** there were several victims, one of whom was my father; **des boîtes** ~ **la plupart sont vides** boxes, most of which are empty

**dopage** /dɔpaʒ/ *nm* (a) (of horses) doping
(b) illegal drug-taking

**doper** /dɔpe/ [1] *vtr* to dope

**dorade** /dɔʀad/ *nf* (sea) bream

**doré, ~e** /dɔʀe/ ① *pp* ▶ DORER
② *pp adj* (a) ‹*paint*› gold; ‹*frame*› gilt; ‹*dome*› gilded; ‹*hair*› golden; ‹*skin*› tanned; ‹*bread*› golden brown; ~ **à l'or fin** gilded
(b) ‹*exile*› luxurious; **jeunesse** ~**e** gilded youth
③ *nm* gilt

**dorénavant** /dɔʀenavɑ̃/ *adv* from now on

**dorer** /dɔʀe/ [1] ① *vtr* (a) to gild
(b) (Culin) to glaze
② *vi* (Culin) to brown
③ **se dorer** *v refl* (+ *v être*) **se** ~ **au soleil** to sunbathe

**dorloter** /dɔʀlɔte/ [1] *vtr* to pamper

**dormeur, -euse** /dɔʀmœʀ, øz/ *nm,f* sleeper; **c'est un gros** ~ he sleeps a lot

**dormir** /dɔʀmiʀ/ [30] *vi* (a) to sleep; ~ **debout** (figurative) to be dead on one's feet; **ça m'empêche de** ~ it keeps me awake; **il n'en dort plus** he's losing sleep over it
(b) ‹*money*› to lie idle
IDIOMS **ne** ~ **que d'un œil** to sleep with one eye open; ~ **sur ses deux oreilles, dormir tranquille** to rest easy; ~ **comme un loir** to sleep like a log; ~ **à poings fermés** to be fast asleep

**dorsal, ~e,** *mpl* **-aux** /dɔʀsal, o/ *adj* ‹*pain*› back; ‹*fin*› dorsal

**dortoir** /dɔʀtwaʀ/ ① *nm* dormitory
② **(-)dortoir** (*combining form*) **ville-**~ dormitory town

**dorure** /dɔʀyʀ/ *nf* gilt

**dos** /do/ *nm inv* (a) back; **avoir le** ~ **rond** *or* **voûté** to stoop; **mal de** ~ backache; **voir qn de** ~ to see sb from behind; **robe décolletée dans le** ~ dress with a low back; **il n'a rien sur le** ~ (colloq) he's wearing hardly

anything; **tourner le ~ à** to have one's back
to; to turn one's back to; (figurative) to turn
one's back on
**(b)** (of book) spine; (of blade) blunt edge
**IDIOMS mettre qch sur le ~ de** (colloq) to
blame sth on; **il a bon ~ le réveil!** (colloq) it's
easy to blame it on the alarm-clock!
**dosage** /dozaʒ/ *nm* **(a)** amount;
measurement
**(b)** mix; mixing
**(c)** proportions
**dos-d'âne** /dodɑn/ *nm inv* hump
**dose** /doz/ *nf* **(a)** dose; **forcer la ~** (colloq) to
go a bit far (colloq)
**(b)** measure
**doser** /doze/ [1] *vtr* **(a)** to measure
**(b)** to use [sth] in a controlled way
**dossard** /dosaʀ/ *nm* number (*worn by an
athlete*)
**dossier** /dosje/ *nm* **(a)** file, dossier;
**~ médical** medical records; **~ d'inscription**
(Sch) registration form; **sélection sur ~**
selection by written application
**(b)** (Law) file; case
**(c) le ~ brûlant de la pollution** the
controversial problem of pollution
**(d)** file, folder
**(e)** (of chair) back
**dot** /dɔt/ *nf* dowry
**dotation** /dɔtasjɔ̃/ *nf* allocation;
endowment
**doter** /dote/ [1] *vtr* **(a) ~ qn de qch** to
allocate sth to sb
**(b) ~ qn/qch de** to equip sb/sth with
**(c) ~ qn/qch de** to endow sb/sth with
**douane** /dwan/ *nf* **(a)** customs
**(b)** (on goods) duty
**douanier, -ière** /dwanje, ɛʀ/ [1] *adj*
customs
[2] *nm* customs officer
**double** /dubl/ [1] *adj* double; **l'avantage est
~** the advantage is twofold; **valise à ~ fond**
suitcase with a false bottom; **~ nationalité**
dual nationality; **avoir le don de ~ vue** to
have second sight; **en ~ exemplaire** in
duplicate
[2] *adv* double
[3] *nm* **(a)** double; **leur piscine fait le ~ de la
nôtre** their swimming-pool is twice as big as
ours
**(b)** copy; **un ~ des clés** a spare set of keys
**(c)** (in tennis) doubles
**doublé, ~e** /duble/ [1] *pp* ▶ DOUBLER
[2] *pp adj* **(a)** ⟨*coat*⟩ lined
**(b)** ⟨*film*⟩ dubbed
**doublement** /dubləmɑ̃/ [1] *adv* in two
ways; **il est ~ coupable** he's guilty on two
counts
[2] *nm* (of quantity) doubling
**doubler** /duble/ [1] [1] *vtr* **(a)** to double
**(b)** to line (**de** with)
**(c)** to dub ⟨*film*⟩; to stand in for ⟨*actor*⟩
**(d)** to overtake (GB), to pass (US); **'défense
de ~'** 'no overtaking' (GB), 'no passing' (US)
[2] *vi* to double

[3] **se doubler** *v refl* (+ *v être*) **se ~ de qch**
to be coupled with sth
**doublure** /dublyʀ/ *nf* **(a)** lining
**(b)** (for actor) double
**douce** ▶ DOUX
**douceâtre** /dusɑtʀ/ *adj* sickly sweet
**doucement** /dusmɑ̃/ *adv* **(a)** gently;
**~ avec le vin!** go easy on the wine!
**(b)** quietly
**(c)** slowly
**doucereux, -euse** /dusʀø, øz/ *adj*
⟨*person*⟩ smooth; ⟨*words*⟩ sugary; ⟨*smile*⟩
unctuous
**douceur** /dusœʀ/ [1] *nf* **(a)** softness;
mildness; mellowness; smoothness;
gentleness; **~ de vivre** relaxed rhythm of
life; **avec ~** gently
**(b)** sweet (GB), candy (US)
[2] **en douceur** *phr* **(a)** smoothly;
**atterrissage en ~** smooth landing
**(b) shampooing qui lave en ~** mild
shampoo
**douche** /duʃ/ *nf* shower; **~ froide** cold
shower; (figurative) letdown (colloq)
■ **~ écossaise** alternating hot and cold
shower; (figurative) bucket of cold water
**doucher** /duʃe/ [1] [1] *vtr* **(a)** to give [sb] a
shower
**(b)** (colloq) to dampen ⟨*enthusiasm*⟩
[2] **se doucher** *v refl* (+ *v être*) to take a
shower
**doué, ~e** /dwe/ *adj* **(a)** gifted, talented;
**être ~ pour** to have a gift for
**(b) ~ de** endowed with, gifted with
**douille** /duj/ *nf* **(a)** cartridge (case)
**(b)** (light) socket
**douillet, -ette** /dujɛ, ɛt/ *adj*
**(a)** oversensitive to pain
**(b)** cosy (GB), cozy (US)
**douleur** /dulœʀ/ *nf* **(a)** pain; **médicament
contre la ~** painkiller
**(b)** grief
**douloureuse** ▶ DOULOUREUX
**douloureusement** /duluʀøzmɑ̃/ *adv*
**(a)** grievously; terribly
**(b)** painfully
**douloureux, -euse** /duluʀø, øz/ *adj*
**(a)** painful
**(b)** ⟨*event*⟩ distressing; ⟨*question*⟩ painful
**doute** /dut/ [1] *nm* doubt; **laisser qn dans le
~** to leave sb in a state of uncertainty;
**mettre qch en ~** to call sth into question;
**dans le ~, j'ai préféré ne rien dire** not being
sure I didn't say anything; **il fait peu de ~
que** there's little doubt that; **nul ~ que**
there's no doubt that
[2] **sans doute** *phr* probably; **sans aucun
~** without any doubt
**douter** /dute/ [1] [1] *vtr* **(a) ~ que** to doubt
that *or* whether
**(b) ~ de qch** to have doubts about sth; **elle
l'affirme mais j'en doute** she says it's true
but I have my doubts; **elle ne doute de rien!**
(colloq) (ironic) she's so sure of herself!
[2] *vi* to doubt ⸱⸱⸱⸵

**3** **se douter** *v refl* (+ *v être*) **se ~ de** to suspect; **je m'en doutais!** I thought so!; **je me doute (bien) qu'il devait être furieux** I can (well) imagine that he was furious; **nous étions loin de nous ~ que** we didn't have the least idea that

**douteux, -euse** /dutø, øz/ *adj*
(a) uncertain
(b) ambiguous
(c) dubious
(d) ⟨*deal, character*⟩ shady

**douve** /duv/ *nf* moat

**Douvres** /duvʀ/ *n pr* Dover

**doux, douce** /du, dus/ *adj* ⟨*light, voice, substance*⟩ soft; ⟨*cider*⟩ sweet; ⟨*cheese, shampoo, weather*⟩ mild; ⟨*person, slope*⟩ gentle
**IDIOMS filer ~** (colloq) to keep a low profile; **se la couler douce** (colloq) to take it easy; **en douce** (colloq) on the sly

**douzaine** /duzɛn/ *nf* (a) dozen; **à la ~** by the dozen
(b) about twelve, a dozen or so

**douze** /duz/ *adj inv, pron, nm inv* twelve

**douzième** /duzjɛm/ *adj* twelfth

**doyen, -enne** /dwajɛ̃, ɛn/ *nm,f* (a) oldest person
(b) the (most) senior member
(c) dean

**Dr** (*written abbr* = **docteur**) Dr

**draconien, -ienne** /dʀakɔnjɛ̃, ɛn/ *adj* draconian; very strict

**dragée** /dʀaʒe/ *nf* (a) sugared almond
(b) sugar-coated pill

**dragon** /dʀagɔ̃/ *nm* (a) dragon
(b) (Mil) dragoon

**draguer** /dʀage/ [1] *vtr* (a) (colloq) to come on to (colloq)
(b) to dredge, to drag ⟨*river, canal*⟩

**dragueur, -euse** /dʀagœʀ, øz/ *nm,f* (colloq) **c'est un drôle de ~** (colloq) he's a terrible flirt

**drain** /dʀɛ̃/ *nm* drain

**drainage** /dʀɛnaʒ/ *nm* (a) drainage
(b) (Med) draining (off)

**drainer** /dʀɛne/ [1] *vtr* to drain

**dramatique** /dʀamatik/ *adj* (a) tragic; **ce n'est pas ~** it's not the end of the world
(b) dramatic; **art ~** drama; **auteur ~** playwright

**dramatiquement** /dʀamatikmɑ̃/ *adv* tragically

**dramatiser** /dʀamatize/ [1] *vtr* to dramatize

**dramaturge** /dʀamatyʀʒ/ *nmf* playwright

**drame** /dʀam/ *nm* (a) tragedy; **tourner au ~** to take a tragic turn
(b) drama; play; **~ lyrique** opera

**drap** /dʀa/ *nm* (a) sheet
(b) woollen (GB) cloth
■ **~ de plage** beach towel
**IDIOMS se mettre dans de beaux ~s** to land oneself in a fine mess

**drapeau**, *pl* **~x** /dʀapo/ *nm* flag; **être sous les ~x** to be doing military service

**drap-housse**, *pl* **draps-housses** /dʀaus/ *nm* fitted sheet

**dressage** /dʀɛsaʒ/ *nm* (a) training; (of horse) breaking in
(b) dressage

**dresser** /dʀese/ [1] **1** *vtr* (a) to train ⟨*animal*⟩; to break in ⟨*horse*⟩; to teach [sb] how to behave ⟨*person*⟩
(b) to put up ⟨*scaffolding*⟩
(c) to prick up ⟨*ears*⟩
(d) to lay out ⟨*buffet*⟩
(e) to draw up ⟨*list*⟩; **~ un procès-verbal à qn** to give sb a ticket
(f) **~ qn contre** to set sb against
**2** **se dresser** *v refl* (+ *v être*) (a) to stand up
(b) **se ~ contre** to rebel against
(c) ⟨*statue, obstacle*⟩ to stand; to tower up

**dresseur, -euse** /dʀesœʀ, øz/ *nm,f* trainer

**dribbler** /dʀible/ [1] *vi* to dribble

**drogue** /dʀɔg/ *nf* drug; **la ~** drugs; **c'est devenu une ~** it has become an addiction

**drogué, ~e** /dʀɔge/ *nm,f* drug-addict

**droguer** /dʀɔge/ [1] **1** *vtr* (a) ⟨*doctor*⟩ to dope
(b) to dope ⟨*animal, sportsman*⟩; to drug ⟨*victim*⟩; to doctor ⟨*drink*⟩
**2** **se droguer** *v refl* (+ *v être*) (a) to dope oneself (à, de with)
(b) to take drugs

**droguerie** /dʀɔgʀi/ *nf* hardware shop (GB) or store (US)

**droguiste** /dʀɔgist/ *nmf* owner of a hardware shop

**droit, ~e¹** /dʀwa, at/ **1** *adj* (a) ⟨*line, road, nose*⟩ straight; ⟨*writing*⟩ upright; **se tenir ~** to stand up straight; to sit up strait; **s'écarter du ~ chemin** to stray from the strait and narrow
(b) right; **du côté ~** on the right-hand side
(c) ⟨*person*⟩ straight(forward)
(d) ⟨*skirt*⟩ straight
(e) ⟨*angle*⟩ right
**2** *adv* straight; **continuez tout ~** carry straight on; **marcher ~** to toe the line
**3** *nm* (a) right; **être dans son (bon) ~** to be within one's rights; **cela leur revient de ~** it's theirs by right; **avoir ~ à** to be entitled to; **il a eu ~ à une amende** (ironic) he got a fine; **avoir le ~ de faire** to be allowed to do; to have the right to do; **avoir le ~ de vie ou de mort sur qn** to have power of life and death over sb; **il s'imagine qu'il a tous les ~s** he thinks he can do whatever he likes; **être en ~ de** to be entitled to
(b) **le ~** law; **faire son ~** to study law
(c) fee
(d) (in boxing) right
■ **(prisonnier de) ~ commun** nonpolitical prisoner; **~ d'entrée** entrance fee; **~ de passage** right of way (GB), easement (US); **un ~ de regard sur** a say in; **~s d'auteur**

royalties; ~s de douane customs duties; les ~s de l'homme human rights; ~s de succession inheritance tax

**droite²** /dʀwat/ *nf* (a) right; **la porte de ~** the door on the right; **à ta ~** on your right; **demander à ~ et à gauche** to ask everywhere; to ask everybody
(b) **voter à ~** to vote for the right; **de ~** right-wing
(c) straight line

**droitier, -ière** /dʀwatje, ɛʀ/ *nm,f* right-hander

**droiture** /dʀwatyʀ/ *nf* honesty, uprightness

**drôle** /dʀol/ *adj* (a) funny, odd; **faire (tout) ~ à qn** to give sb a funny feeling; **faire une ~ de tête** to make a bit of a face
(b) funny, amusing
(c) (colloq) **un ~ de courage** a lot of courage
IDIOMS **j'en ai entendu de ~s** I heard some funny things; **en faire voir de ~s à qn** to lead sb a merry dance

**drôlement** /dʀolmã/ *adv* (a) (colloq) really
(b) oddly

**drôlerie** /dʀolʀi/ *nf* **avec ~** amusingly

**dromadaire** /dʀɔmadɛʀ/ *nm* dromedary

**dru, ~e** /dʀy/ ① *adj* ⟨hair⟩ thick
② *adv* (a) ⟨grow⟩ thickly
(b) **la pluie tombait ~** it was raining heavily

**druide** /dʀɥid/ *nm* druid

**DS** /deɛs/ *nf*: Citroen car of the 1950s

**DST** /deɛste/ *nf* (abbr = **Direction de la surveillance du territoire**) French counterintelligence agency

**du** /dy/ *det* ▸ DE

**dû, due,** *mpl* **dus** /dy/ ① *pp* ▸ DEVOIR¹
② *pp adj* (a) owed, owing, due (à to); **en bonne et due forme** in due form
(b) **~ à** due to
③ *nm* **réclamer son ~** to claim one's due

**dualité** /dɥalite/ *nf* duality

**dubitatif, -ive** /dybitatif, iv/ *adj* sceptical (GB), skeptical (US)

**duc** /dyk/ *nm* duke

**duchesse** /dyʃɛs/ *nf* duchess

**duel** /dɥɛl/ *nm* duel (à with); (figurative) battle

**dulcinée** /dylsine/ *nf* lady-love

**dune** /dyn/ *nf* dune

**duo** /dyo, dɥo/ *nm* (a) duet; **en ~** as a duo
(b) double act (GB), duo (US)
(c) (colloq) pair

**dupe** /dyp/ ① *adj* **être ~** to be taken in *or* fooled (de by)
② *nf* dupe; **un marché de ~s** a fool's bargain

**duper** /dype/ [1] *vtr* to fool; **facile à ~** gullible

**duperie** /dypʀi/ *nf* trickery

**duplex** /dyplɛks/ *nm inv* maisonette (GB), duplex apartment (US)

**duplicata** /dyplikata/ *nm inv* duplicate

**duquel** ▸ LEQUEL

**dur, ~e** /dyʀ/ ① *adj* (a) ⟨ground, toothbrush, bread⟩ hard; ⟨meat⟩ tough; ⟨brush, cardboard⟩ stiff; ⟨plastic⟩ rigid
(b) ⟨zip, handle, pedal⟩ stiff; ⟨steering⟩ heavy
(c) ⟨sound, light, colour⟩ harsh
(d) ⟨face, expression⟩ severe
(e) ⟨parents, boss⟩ hard; harsh; ⟨policy⟩ hardline
(f) ⟨living conditions⟩ harsh
(g) ⟨job, sport⟩ hard; tough; ⟨climate, necessity⟩ harsh
(h) ⟨exam⟩ hard, difficult
(i) ⟨water⟩ hard
② *nm,f* (a) tough nut (colloq); **jouer les ~s** to act tough
(b) hardliner
③ *adv* ⟨work, hit⟩ hard
④ *nm* **construction en ~** permanent structure
⑤ **à la dure** *phr* **élevé à la ~e** brought up the hard way
IDIOMS **~ d'oreille** hard of hearing; **avoir la tête ~e** to be stubborn; to be dense; **avoir la vie ~e** ⟨habit⟩ to die hard; **mener la vie ~e à qn** to give sb a hard time

**durable** /dyʀabl/ *adj* ⟨impression⟩ lasting; ⟨interest⟩ enduring; ⟨material⟩ durable

**durablement** /dyʀabləmã/ *adv* on a permanent basis

**durant** /dyʀã/ *prep* (a) for; **des heures ~** for hours and hours
(b) during

**durcir** /dyʀsiʀ/ [3] ① *vtr* (a) to harden ⟨ground, features, position⟩
(b) to step up ⟨strike action⟩; **~ sa politique en matière de** to take a harder line on
② *vi* ⟨clay, artery⟩ to harden; ⟨cement, glue⟩ to set; ⟨bread⟩ to go hard
③ **se durcir** *v refl* (+ *v être*) (a) to harden
(b) to become harsher; to intensify

**durcissement** /dyʀsismã/ *nm*
(a) hardening
(b) intensification

**durée** /dyʀe/ *nf* (a) (of reign, studies) length; (of contract) term; (of cassette) playing time; **séjour d'une ~ de trois mois** three-month stay; **contrat à ~ déterminée** fixed-term contract; **de courte ~** ⟨peace⟩ short-lived; ⟨absence⟩ brief; ⟨loan⟩ short-term
(b) **~ (de vie)** life; **pile longue ~** long-life battery

**durement** /dyʀmã/ *adv* (a) badly
(b) harshly
(c) ⟨look⟩ severely
(d) ⟨hit⟩ hard

**durer** /dyʀe/ [1] *vi* (a) to last
(b) to go on; **ça ne peut plus ~** it can't go on any longer; **faire ~** to prolong ⟨meeting⟩; **faire ~ le plaisir** (ironic) to prolong the agony
(c) ⟨festival⟩ to run

**dures** /dyʀ/ *nf pl* **en faire voir de ~ à ses parents** to give one's parents a hard time

**dureté** /dyʀte/ *nf* (a) (of material, face) hardness; (of meat) toughness; (of brush) stiffness ⋯⟶

**(b)** (of expression, tone, climate) harshness; (of look) severity; **avec ~** ⟨*look*⟩ severely; ⟨*punish*⟩ harshly

**durillon** /dyʀijɔ̃/ *nm* callus

**durite** /dyʀit/ *nf* radiator hose

**DUT** /deyte/ *nm* (*abbr* = **diplôme universitaire de technologie**) *two-year diploma from a university institute of technology*

**duvet** /dyvɛ/ *nm* **(a)** (of bird) down **(b)** sleeping bag

**duveteux**, **-euse** /dyvtø, øz/ *adj* downy

**dynamique** /dinamik/ **1** *adj* dynamic, lively
**2** *nf* **(a)** dynamics

**(b)** process

**dynamiser** /dinamize/ [1] *vtr* to make [sb/sth] more dynamic; to revitalize

**dynamisme** /dinamism/ *nm* dynamism; **être plein de ~** to be very dynamic

**dynamite** /dinamit/ *nf* dynamite

**dynamiter** /dinamite/ [1] *vtr* to dynamite; (figurative) to destroy

**dynastie** /dinasti/ *nf* dynasty

**dysenterie** /disɑ̃tʀi/ *nf* dysentery

**dysfonctionnement** /disfɔ̃ksjɔnmɑ̃/ *nm*
**(a)** (Med) dysfunction
**(b)** malfunctioning

**dyslexie** /dislɛksi/ *nf* dyslexia

# Ee

**e, E** /ə/ *nm inv* e, E; **e dans l'o** o and e joined together

**eau**, *pl* **~x** /o/ **1** *nf* **(a)** water; **l'~ de source** spring water; **prendre l'~** ⟨*shoe*⟩ to let in water; **être en ~** to be dripping with sweat; **mettre à l'~** to launch ⟨*ship*⟩; **se jeter à l'~** to throw oneself into the water; (figurative) to take the plunge; **tomber à l'~** (figurative) to fall through; **nettoyer le sol à grande ~** to sluice the floor down
**(b)** rain
**2** **eaux** *nf pl* **(a)** water; waters
**(b)** (Med) waters
■ **~ bénite** holy water; **~ de chaux** limewater; **~ douce** fresh water; **~ de Javel** ≈ (chloride) bleach; **~ de mer** seawater; **~ oxygénée** hydrogen peroxide; **~ plate** plain water; still mineral water; **~ de rose**: **à l'~ de rose** ⟨*novel*⟩ sentimental; **~x et forêts** forestry commission; **~x usées** waste water
**IDIOMS mettre l'~ à la bouche de qn** to make sb's mouth water; **ou dans ces ~x-là** (colloq) or thereabouts; **vivre d'amour et d'~ fraîche** to live on love alone

**EAU** *written abbr* ▶ ÉMIRATS

**eau-de-vie**, *pl* **eaux-de-vie** /odvi/ *nf* brandy, eau de vie; **à l'~** in brandy

**ébahir** /ebaiʀ/ [3] **1** *vtr* to dumbfound
**2** **s'ébahir** *v refl* (+ *v être*) to be dumbfounded

**ébattre: s'ébattre** /ebatʀ/ [61] *v refl* (+ *v être*) to frolic (about); to frisk about; to splash about

**ébauche** /eboʃ/ *nf* **(a)** (for sculpture) rough shape; (for picture) preliminary sketch; (of novel) preliminary draft; **être encore à l'état d'~** to be still at an early stage
**(b)** **l'~ d'un sourire** a hint of a smile

**ébaucher** /eboʃe/ [1] **1** *vtr* to sketch out ⟨*picture, solution*⟩; to draft ⟨*novel, plan*⟩; to rough-hew ⟨*statue*⟩; to begin ⟨*conversation*⟩
**2** **s'ébaucher** *v refl* (+ *v être*) ⟨*solution, novel*⟩ to begin to take shape; ⟨*friendship*⟩ to begin to develop; ⟨*talks*⟩ to start

**ébène** /ebɛn/ *nf* ebony

**ébéniste** /ebenist/ *nmf* cabinetmaker

**éberluer** /ebɛʀlɥe/ [1] *vtr* to dumbfound

**éblouir** /ebluiʀ/ [3] *vtr* to dazzle

**éblouissement** /ebluismɑ̃/ *nm* **(a)** dazzle
**(b)** dizzy spell

**éborgner** /ebɔʀɲe/ [1] *vtr* **~ qn** to blind sb in one eye; (humorous) to poke sb's eye out

**éboueur** /ebuœʀ/ *nm* dustman (GB), garbageman (US)

**ébouillanter** /ebujɑ̃te/ [1] *vtr* **(a)** to scald
**(b)** to blanch ⟨*vegetables*⟩

**éboulement** /ebulmɑ̃/ *nm* (of wall, cliff) collapse; **~ (de rochers)** rockfall

**éboulis** /ebuli/ *nm inv* mass of fallen rocks; heap of fallen earth

**ébouriffer** /eburife/ [1] *vtr* to tousle; to ruffle

**ébranler** /ebʀɑ̃le/ [1] *vtr* **(a)** to rattle ⟨*windowpane*⟩; to shake ⟨*house*⟩; to weaken ⟨*building*⟩
**(b)** to shake ⟨*person, confidence*⟩

**ébrécher** /ebʀeʃe/ [14] *vtr* to chip ⟨*cup*⟩

**ébriété** /ebʀijete/ *nf* intoxication

**ébrouer: s'ébrouer** /ebʀue/ [1] *v refl* (+ *v être*) **(a)** ⟨*horse*⟩ to snort
**(b)** ⟨*person, dog*⟩ to shake oneself/itself; ⟨*bird*⟩ to flap its wings

**ébruiter** /ebʀɥite/ [1] **1** *vtr* to divulge
**2** **s'ébruiter** *v refl* (+ *v être*) ⟨*news*⟩ to get out

**ébullition** /ebylisjɔ̃/ *nf* (Culin) boiling

**IDIOMS** être en ∼ ⟨*crowd*⟩ to be in a fever of excitement; ⟨*country, brain*⟩ to be in a ferment

**écaille** /ekaj/ *nf* **(a)** (on fish, reptile) scale; (on oyster) shell
**(b)** tortoiseshell; **lunettes en** ∼ horn-rimmed glasses
**(c)** flake

**écailler** /ekaje/ [1] **1** *vtr* **(a)** (Culin) to scale ⟨*fish*⟩; to open ⟨*oyster*⟩
**(b)** ∼ **qch** to chip [sth] off
**2** **s'écailler** *v refl* (+ *v être*) to flake away

**écarlate** /ekaʀlat/ *adj* scarlet

**écart** /ekaʀ/ **1** *nm* **(a)** (between objects) distance, gap; (between dates) interval; (between ideas) gap
**(b)** (between versions, in prices) difference; ∼ **des salaires** pay differential
**(c)** **faire un** ∼ ⟨*horse*⟩ to shy; ⟨*car*⟩ to swerve
**(d)** lapse; ∼**s de langage** bad language
**2** **à l'écart** *phr* **être à l'**∼ to be isolated; **se tenir à l'**∼ to stand apart; to keep oneself to oneself; not to join in; **mettre qn à l'**∼ to push sb aside; to ostracize sb; **entraîner qn à l'**∼ to take sb aside
**3** **à l'écart de** *phr* away from; **tenir qn à l'**∼ **de** to keep sb away from ⟨*place*⟩; to keep sb out of ⟨*activity, talks*⟩

**écarté**, ∼**e** /ekaʀte/ **1** *pp* ▶ ÉCARTER
**2** *pp adj* **(a)** ⟨*fingers*⟩ spread; ⟨*knees, legs*⟩ apart; ⟨*teeth*⟩ widely spaced
**(b)** ⟨*place*⟩ isolated

**écarteler** /ekaʀtəle/ [17] *vtr* (kill) to quarter [sb]

**écartement** /ekaʀtəmɑ̃/ *nm* distance, space

**écarter** /ekaʀte/ [1] **1** *vtr* **(a)** to move [sth] further apart ⟨*objects*⟩; to open ⟨*curtains*⟩; to spread ⟨*fingers, legs*⟩
**(b)** to move [sth] aside ⟨*chair*⟩; to remove ⟨*obstacle*⟩; to push [sb] aside; to move [sb] on
**(c)** to dispel ⟨*suspicion*⟩; to eliminate ⟨*risk, rival*⟩
**(d)** to reject ⟨*idea*⟩; to rule out ⟨*possibility*⟩
**2** **s'écarter** *v refl* (+ *v être*) **(a)** ⟨*crowd, clouds*⟩ to part; ⟨*shutters*⟩ to open
**(b)** to move away; **s'**∼ **de** to move away from ⟨*direction, standard*⟩; to stray from ⟨*path, subject*⟩

**ecchymose** /ekimoz/ *nf* bruise

**ecclésiastique** /eklezjastik/ *nm* cleric

**écervelé**, ∼**e** /esɛʀvəle/ *nm,f* featherbrain

**échafaud** /eʃafo/ *nm* **(a)** scaffold
**(b)** guillotine

**échafaudage** /eʃafodaʒ/ *nm* scaffolding

**échafauder** /eʃafode/ [1] *vtr* to put [sth] together ⟨*plan*⟩; to develop ⟨*theory*⟩

**échalas** /eʃala/ *nm inv* **(a)** cane, stake
**(b)** (colloq) beanpole (colloq)

**échalote** /eʃalɔt/ *nf* shallot

**échancré**, ∼**e** /eʃɑ̃kʀe/ *adj* **(a)** ⟨*dress*⟩ low-cut; ⟨*briefs*⟩ high-cut; **trop** ∼ ⟨*sleeve*⟩ cut too wide

**(b)** ⟨*blouse*⟩ open-necked
**(c)** ⟨*coast*⟩ indented

**échange** /eʃɑ̃ʒ/ **1** *nm* **(a)** exchange; **elles ont fait l'**∼ **de leurs manteaux** they've swapped coats
**(b)** trade; ∼**s commerciaux** trade
**(c)** (cultural, linguistic) exchange
**(d)** (Sport) rally
**2** **en échange** *phr* in exchange, in return
**3** **en échange de** *phr* in exchange for, in return for
■ ∼ **de bons procédés** quid pro quo

**échanger** /eʃɑ̃ʒe/ [13] *vtr* **(a)** to exchange; ∼ **des insultes** to trade insults
**(b)** (Sport) ∼ **des balles** to rally

**échangeur** /eʃɑ̃ʒœʀ/ *nm* interchange (GB), grade separation (US)

**échantillon** /eʃɑ̃tijɔ̃/ *nm* sample

**échappatoire** /eʃapatwaʀ/ *nf* way out (à of)

**échappement** /eʃapmɑ̃/ *nm* (Aut) (**tuyau d'**)∼ exhaust (pipe)

**échapper** /eʃape/ [1] **1** **échapper à** *v+prep* **(a)** ∼ **à** to get away from; (cleverly) to elude
**(b)** ∼ **à** to escape ⟨*death, failure*⟩; (to manage) to avoid ⟨*accident*⟩
**(c)** ∼ **à** to escape from ⟨*social background*⟩; **je sens qu'il m'échappe** ⟨*partner*⟩ I feel he is drifting away from me; ⟨*child*⟩ I feel he's growing away from me
**(d)** ∼ **à qn** *or* **des mains de qn** to slip out of sb's hands
**(e)** **un soupir m'a échappé** I let out a sigh
**(f)** **le titre m'échappe** the title escapes me
**(g)** ∼ **à** to defy ⟨*logic*⟩; ∼ **à la règle** to be an exception to the rule
**2** **s'échapper** *v refl* (+ *v être*) **(a)** to run away; to fly away; to escape; to get away
**(b)** ⟨*gas, smoke*⟩ to escape
**(c)** to get away; **s'**∼ **pour quelques jours** to get away for a few days
**IDIOMS l'**∼ **belle** to have a narrow escape

**écharde** /eʃaʀd/ *nf* splinter

**écharpe** /eʃaʀp/ *nf* **(a)** scarf
**(b)** sash

**échasse** /eʃɑs/ *nf* stilt

**échauder** /eʃode/ [1] *vtr* to put [sb] off.
**IDIOMS chat échaudé craint l'eau froide** (Proverb) once bitten, twice shy

**échauffement** /eʃofmɑ̃/ *nm* (Sport) warm-up

**échauffer** /eʃofe/ [1] *vtr* **(a)** (Sport) to warm up
**(b)** to stir ⟨*imagination*⟩; to stir up ⟨*person, debate*⟩
**(c)** to start [sth] fermenting
**IDIOMS** ∼ **les oreilles de qn** to vex sb

**échéance** /eʃeɑs/ *nf* **(a)** (of debt) due date; (of share, policy) maturity date; (of loan) redemption date; **arriver à** ∼ ⟨*payment*⟩ to fall due; ⟨*investment, policy*⟩ to mature
**(b)** expiry date

(c) à longue/brève ~ ⟨forecast⟩ long-/short-
term; ⟨strengthen, change⟩ in the long/short
term
(d) payment; repayment
(e) date; deadline
**échéancier** /eʃeɑ̃sje/ nm schedule of due
dates; schedule of repayments
**échéant: le cas échéant** /ləkazeʃeɑ̃/
phr if need be, should the case arise
**échec** /eʃɛk/ ① nm (a) failure; setback;
**faire ~ à qn** to thwart sb
(b) (gen, Mil) defeat
(c) **faire ~ au roi** to put the king in check
② **échecs** nm pl **les ~s** chess; chess set
**échelle** /eʃɛl/ nf (a) ladder; **~ coulissante**
extending ladder (GB), extension ladder (US);
**faire la courte ~ à qn** to give sb a leg up
(b) (of map, model) scale; **plan à l'~** scale plan;
**à l'~ mondiale** on a worldwide scale; **~ des
salaires** pay scale
(c) (colloq) (in stocking) ladder
**échelon** /eʃlɔ̃/ nm (a) (of ladder) rung
(b) grade; **sauter les ~s** to get accelerated
promotion
(c) level
**échelonner** /eʃlɔne/ [1] ① vtr (a) to space
[sth] out ⟨objects⟩
(b) to spread ⟨payments, work⟩; to stagger
⟨holidays⟩
(c) to grade ⟨exercises⟩
② **s'échelonner** v refl (+ v être) (a) to be
positioned at intervals
(b) ⟨payments⟩ to be spread; ⟨departures⟩ to
be staggered
**écheveau**, pl **~x** /eʃvo/ nm hank, skein
**échevelé, ~e** /eʃəvle/ adj (a) tousled
(b) ⟨rhythm⟩ frenzied; ⟨romanticism⟩
unbridled
**échine** /eʃin/ nf (a) (Anat) spine
(b) (Culin) ≈ spare rib
**IDIOMS courber l'~ devant** to submit to
**échiquier** /eʃikje/ nm (a) chessboard
(b) chequered (GB) or checkered (US) pattern
**Échiquier** /eʃikje/ pr nm **l'~** the
Exchequer, the Treasury
**écho** /eko/ nm (a) echo; **faire ~ à qch, se
faire l'~ de qch** to echo sth
(b) response; **nous n'avons eu aucun ~ des
pourparlers** we have heard nothing about the
talks
**échographie** /ekoɡRafi/ nf (Med) scan
**échoir** /eʃwaR/ [51] vi (+ v être) ⟨rent⟩ to
fall due; ⟨draft⟩ to be payable
**échoppe** /eʃɔp/ nf stall
**échouer** /eʃwe/ [1] ① vtr to beach ⟨boat⟩
② **échouer à** v+prep to fail ⟨exam, test⟩
③ vi (a) ⟨person, attempt⟩ to fail
(b) to end up (dans in)
④ **s'échouer** v refl (+ v être) ⟨boat⟩ to run
aground; ⟨whale⟩ to be beached
**échu, ~e** /eʃy/ ① pp ▸ ÉCHOIR
② adj expired; **payer à terme ~** to pay in
arrears
**éclabousser** /eklabuse/ [1] vtr (a) to
splash

(b) **il a été éclaboussé par ces rumeurs** the
rumours (GB) have damaged his reputation
**éclair** /eklɛR/ ① adj inv **rencontre ~** brief
meeting; **attaque ~** lightning strike; **guerre
~** blitzkrieg
② nm (a) flash of lightning; **passer comme
un ~** to flash past
(b) (of explosion, diamonds) flash; (of eyes) glint
(c) (of lucidity, triumph) moment; **il a eu un ~ de
génie** he had a brainwave (GB) or
brainstorm (US)
(d) (Culin) éclair
**éclairage** /eklɛRaʒ/ nm lighting; light;
**~ au gaz** gaslight
**éclairagiste** /eklɛRaʒist/ nm (in theatre,
films) electrician
**éclairant, ~e** /eklɛRɑ̃, ɑ̃t/ adj flare
**éclaircie** /eklɛRsi/ nf sunny spell
**éclaircir** /eklɛRsiR/ [3] ① vtr (a) to lighten
⟨colour⟩; to lighten the colour (GB) of ⟨paint,
hair⟩
(b) to shed light on [sth]
② **s'éclaircir** v refl (+ v être) (a) ⟨weather⟩
to clear; **l'horizon s'éclaircit** (figurative) the
outlook is getting brighter
(b) ⟨colour⟩ to fade; ⟨hair⟩ to get lighter
(c) ⟨situation, mystery⟩ to become clearer
(d) ⟨crowd, forest⟩ to thin out
(e) **s'~ les cheveux** to lighten one's hair;
**s'~ la voix** or **la gorge** to clear one's throat
**éclaircissement** /eklɛRsismɑ̃/ nm
(a) explanation
(b) clarification
**éclairé, ~e** /eklɛRe/ adj ⟨person, advice⟩
enlightened; ⟨art lover⟩ well-informed
**éclairer** /eklɛRe/ [1] ① vtr (a) to light
⟨street, room⟩; ⟨sun⟩ to light up ⟨place, object⟩
(b) to give [sb] some light
(c) ⟨remark⟩ to throw light on ⟨text,
situation⟩
(d) to enlighten [sb]
② vi ⟨lamp, candle⟩ to give out light
③ **s'éclairer** v refl (+ v être) (a) ⟨screen,
face⟩ to light up
(b) **s'~ à l'électricité** to have electric lighting
**éclaireur** /eklɛRœR/ nm (a) scout (GB),
Boy Scout (US)
(b) (Mil) scout
**éclaireuse** /eklɛRøz/ nf guide (GB), Girl
Guide (US)
**éclat** /ekla/ nm (a) splinter; **un ~ d'obus** a
piece of shrapnel; **voler en ~s** to shatter
(b) (of light, star) brightness; (of spotlight) glare;
(of snow) sparkle
(c) (of colour, material) brilliance; (of hair,
plumage) shine; (of metal) lustre (GB)
(d) (of face, smile) radiance; (of eyes) sparkle;
**sans ~** ⟨eyes⟩ dull; ⟨beauty⟩ lifeless
(e) splendour (GB); **manquer d'~** ⟨ceremony⟩
to lack sparkle
(f) scene, fuss; **faire un ~** to make a scene
■ **~ de colère** fit of anger; **~ de rire** roar of
laughter; **des ~s de voix** raised voices
**IDIOMS rire aux ~s** to roar with laughter

**éclatant**, **~e** /eklatɑ̃, ɑ̃t/ adj (a) ⟨light⟩ dazzling; ⟨sun⟩ blazing
(b) ⟨colour, plumage⟩ bright; **d'une blancheur ~e** sparkling white
(c) ⟨beauty, smile⟩ radiant; ⟨victory⟩ brilliant
(d) ⟨proof⟩ striking
(e) ⟨laughter⟩ ringing

**éclaté**, **~e** /eklate/ adj (gen) fragmented; ⟨family⟩ divided

**éclatement** /eklatmɑ̃/ nm (a) bursting
(b) explosion
(c) break-up (**en** into)

**éclater** /eklate/ [1] vi (a) ⟨tyre, bubble⟩ to burst; ⟨shell, firework⟩ to explode; ⟨bottle⟩ to shatter; **faire ~** to burst ⟨bubble⟩; to detonate ⟨bomb⟩
(b) ⟨pipe, boil⟩ to burst
(c) ⟨laughter, firing⟩ to break out; ⟨shot⟩ to ring out
(d) ⟨scandal, news⟩ to break; ⟨truth⟩ to come out
(e) ⟨war⟩ to break out; ⟨storm⟩ to break
(f) **laisser ~ sa joie** to be wild with joy
(g) ⟨coalition⟩ to break up (**en** into); ⟨party⟩ to split
(h) to lose one's temper; **~ de rire** to burst out laughing

**éclectique** /eklɛktik/ adj eclectic

**éclipse** /eklips/ nf eclipse

**éclipser** /eklipse/ [1] **1** vtr (a) to eclipse
(b) to obscure
(c) to outshine
**2 s'éclipser** v refl (+ v être) (colloq) to slip away

**éclopé**, **~e** /eklɔpe/ adj injured, lame

**éclore** /eklɔʀ/ [79] vi (a) ⟨chick, egg⟩ to hatch; ⟨flower⟩ to bloom; **faire ~ un œuf** to incubate an egg
(b) ⟨idea⟩ to dawn; ⟨talent⟩ to bloom

**écluse** /eklyz/ nf lock

**écœurant**, **~e** /ekœʀɑ̃, ɑ̃t/ adj (a) ⟨food, smell⟩ sickly
(b) nauseating
(c) (humorous) sickening

**écœurement** /ekœʀmɑ̃/ nm nausea

**écœurer** /ekœʀe/ [1] vtr (a) to make [sb] feel sick
(b) (figurative) to sicken

**éco-guerrier**, **-ière** /ekɔgeʀje, ɛʀ/ nm,f eco-warrior

**école** /ekɔl/ nf (a) school
(b) education system
(c) (**grande**) **~** higher education institution with competitive entrance examination; **une ~ de commerce** a business school
(d) training (**de** in); **être à bonne ~** to be in good hands
(e) (of art) school; **faire ~** to gain a following
■ **~ élémentaire** primary school; **~ d'infirmières** nursing college; **~ maternelle** nursery school; **~ normale** primary teacher training college; **~ primaire** primary school; **École nationale d'administration, ENA**

**Grande École for top civil servants; École normale supérieure, ENS** Grande École from which the educational elite is recruited

**écolier**, **-ière** /ekɔlje, ɛʀ/ nm,f schoolboy/schoolgirl

**écologie** /ekɔlɔʒi/ nf ecology

**écologique** /ekɔlɔʒik/ adj ecological; ⟨speech⟩ on the environment; ⟨interest⟩ environmental; ⟨product⟩ environment-friendly

**écologiste** /ekɔlɔʒist/ **1** adj
(a) ⟨candidate⟩ Green
(b) ⟨measure⟩ ecological
**2** nmf (a) environmentalist
(b) Green (candidate)
(c) ecologist

**écomusée** /ekomyze/ nm ≈ open air museum

**éconduire** /ekɔ̃dɥiʀ/ [69] vtr to turn [sb] away

**économat** /ekɔnɔma/ nm bursar's office

**économe** /ekɔnɔm/ **1** adj thrifty
**2** nm (Culin) potato peeler

**économie** /ekɔnɔmi/ **1** nf (a) (of country) economy
(b) (discipline) economics
(c) (amount saved) saving; **faire l'~ de** to save the cost of ⟨trip⟩
(d) economy, thrift; **par ~** in order to save money; **s'exprimer avec une grande ~ de paroles** to express oneself succinctly
**2 économies** nf pl savings; **faire des ~s** to save up; to save money
■ **~ d'entreprise** managerial economics; **~ de marché** free market (economy)
**IDIOMS il n'y a pas de petites ~s** every little helps

**économique** /ekɔnɔmik/ adj (a) ⟨policy, crisis⟩ economic
(b) economical

**économiser** /ekɔnɔmize/ [1] vtr (a) to save (up) ⟨money⟩; **~ ses forces** to pace oneself
(b) to save ⟨petrol, water, energy⟩
(c) to economize

**économiste** /ekɔnɔmist/ nmf economist

**écoper** /ekɔpe/ [1] vtr to bail out

**écoproduit** /ekɔpʀɔdɥi/ nm eco-product

**écorce** /ekɔʀs/ nf (of tree) bark; (of fruit) peel; (of chestnut) skin
■ **~ terrestre** earth's crust

**écorché**, **~e** /ekɔʀʃe/ adj **~ (vif)** hypersensitive

**écorcher** /ekɔʀʃe/ [1] vtr (a) to skin ⟨animal⟩; to flay ⟨person⟩
(b) to graze ⟨face, leg⟩
(c) to mispronounce ⟨word⟩

**écorchure** /ekɔʀʃyʀ/ nf graze

**écossais**, **~e** /ekɔsɛ, ɛz/ **1** adj Scottish; ⟨whisky⟩ Scotch; ⟨language⟩ Scots; ⟨skirt⟩ tartan
**2** nm (a) (dialect) Scots
(b) (Scottish) Gaelic
(c) tartan (cloth)

**Écossais, ∼e** /ekɔsɛ, ɛz/ *nm,f* Scotsman/
Scotswoman, Scot
**Écosse** /ekɔs/ *pr nf* Scotland
**écosser** /ekɔse/ [1] *vtr* to shell
**écot** /eko/ *nm* share
**écoulement** /ekulmɑ̃/ *nm* **(a)** (of water,
traffic) flow; (of time) passing
**(b)** (Med) discharge
**(c)** (of banknotes, drugs) circulation
**écouler** /ekule/ [1] **1** *vtr* **(a)** to sell
⟨*product*⟩; **les stocks sont écoulés** stocks are
exhausted
**(b)** to fence ⟨*stolen goods*⟩; to pass ⟨*banknote*⟩
**2 s'écouler** *v refl* (+ *v être*) **(a)** ⟨*time, life*⟩
to pass
**(b)** ⟨*river*⟩ to flow
**(c)** ⟨*oil, water*⟩ to escape
**(d)** ⟨*water*⟩ to drain away
**(e)** ⟨*product*⟩ to move
**écourter** /ekurte/ [1] *vtr* to cut short ⟨*stay*⟩
**écoute** /ekut/ *nf* **(a)** **être à l'∼ de** to be
listening to ⟨*programme*⟩; to be (always)
ready to listen to ⟨*problems*⟩
**(b)** audience; **heure de grande ∼** peak
listening time; peak viewing time
**(c)** **un centre d'∼(s)** monitoring centre (GB);
**je suis sur ∼(s)** my phone is being tapped
**écouter** /ekute/ [1] **1** *vtr* **(a)** to listen to
[sb/sth]; **∼ qn chanter** to listen to sb singing;
**∼ aux portes** to eavesdrop
**(b)** **∼ son cœur** to follow one's own
inclination
**2 s'écouter** *v refl* (+ *v être*) **(a)** **s'∼ parler**
to like the sound of one's own voice
**(b)** to cosset oneself
**(c)** **si je m'écoutais** if it was up to me
**écouteur** /ekutœR/ *nm* **(a)** (on phone)
earpiece
**(b)** earphones
**(c)** headphones
**écoutille** /ekutij/ *nf* (Naut) hatch
**écrabouiller** /ekRabuje/ [1] *vtr* (colloq) to
squash
**écran** /ekRɑ̃/ *nm* **(a)** (gen) screen; **crever l'∼**
⟨*actor*⟩ to have a great screen presence; **une
vedette du petit ∼** a TV star
**(b)** cinema (GB), movie theater (US)
**(c)** (on machine) display
**(d)** **crème ∼ total** sun block
■ **∼ antibruit** soundproofing; **∼ de contrôle**
monitor; **∼ à cristaux liquides** liquid crystal
display, LCD; **∼ solaire** sunscreen; **∼ tactile**
touch screen; **∼ de visualisation** VDU screen
**écrasant, ∼e** /ekRazɑ̃, ɑ̃t/ *adj* **(a)** ⟨*weight*⟩
enormous
**(b)** ⟨*heat*⟩ sweltering; ⟨*victory*⟩ resounding;
⟨*responsibility*⟩ heavy
**écraser** /ekRaze/ [1] **1** *vtr* **(a)** to crush
⟨*finger, person*⟩; to squash, to crush ⟨*insect,
hat, fruit, box*⟩; ⟨*driver*⟩ to run over ⟨*person,
animal*⟩; **se faire ∼** to get run over
**(b)** to flatten ⟨*vegetation*⟩
**(c)** (Culin) to mash ⟨*fruit*⟩
**(d)** **∼ sa cigarette** to stub out one's cigarette;
**∼ une larme** to wipe away a tear

**(e)** to press ⟨*nose, face*⟩ (**contre** against)
**(f)** to crush ⟨*rebellion*⟩; to thrash (colloq)
⟨*opponent*⟩
**(g)** to outshine
**(h)** to put [sb] down
**(i)** ⟨*fatigue, heat*⟩ to overcome
**2 s'écraser** *v refl* (+ *v être*) **(a)** ⟨*car,
train*⟩ to crash; ⟨*driver, motorcyclist*⟩ to have
a crash; ⟨*insect*⟩ to splatter (**contre** on)
**(b)** (colloq) to shut up (colloq)
**(c)** (colloq) to keep one's head down
**écrémé, ∼e** /ekReme/ *adj* skimmed
**écrémer** /ekReme/ [14] *vtr* **(a)** to skim
⟨*milk*⟩
**(b)** to cream off the best of ⟨*candidates*⟩
**écrevisse** /ekRəvis/ *nf* crayfish (GB),
crawfish (US)
**écrier: s'écrier** /ekRije/ [2] *v refl* (+ *v être*)
to exclaim
**écrin** /ekRɛ̃/ *nm* (for jewellery) case
**écrire** /ekRiR/ [67] **1** *vtr* **(a)** to write
**(b)** to spell
**2** *vi* to write
**3 s'écrire** *v refl* (+ *v être*) **(a)** to be written
**(b)** to be spelled
**écrit, ∼e** /ekRi, it/ **1** *pp* ▶ ÉCRIRE
**2** *pp adj* written; **c'était ∼** it was bound to
happen
**3** *nm* work, piece of writing
**(b)** document; **par ∼** in writing
**(c)** written examination
IDIOMS **les paroles s'envolent, les ∼s restent**
never put anything in writing; (as security) get
it in writing
**écriteau,** *pl* **∼x** /ekRito/ *nm* sign
**écritoire** /ekRitwaR/ *nf* writing case
**écriture** /ekRityR/ **1** *nf* **(a)** handwriting
**(b)** (in printing) hand
**(c)** (text, activity) writing
**(d)** script; **∼ phonétique** phonetic script
**2 écritures** *nf pl* accounts; **tenir les ∼s** to
do the books
**Écriture** /ekRityR/ *nf* **les (saintes) ∼s** the
Scriptures; **l'∼ sainte** Holy Writ
**écrivain** /ekRivɛ̃/ *nm* writer
**écrou** /ekRu/ *nm* (Tech) nut
**écrouer** /ekRue/ [1] *vtr* (Law) to commit [sb]
to prison
**écroulé, ∼e** /ekRule/ *adj* overwhelmed;
**∼ de rire** (colloq) doubled up with laughter
**écrouler: s'écrouler** /ekRule/ [1] *v refl*
(+ *v être*) to collapse; to fade; to crumble
**écru, ∼e** /ekRy/ *adj* **(a)** ⟨*canvas*⟩
unbleached; ⟨*wool*⟩ undyed; ⟨*silk*⟩ raw
**(b)** (colour) ecru
**écu** /eky/ *nm* **(a)** (in EU) ecu
**(b)** ≈ crown
**(c)** shield
**ECU** /eky/ *nm*: (*abbr* = **European
currency unit**) ECU
**écueil** /ekœj/ *nm* **(a)** reef
**(b)** (figurative) pitfall
**écuelle** /ekɥɛl/ *nf* **(a)** bowl
**(b)** bowlful

**écume** /ekym/ *nf* (a) (on water) foam; (on beer) froth; (on metal) dross
(b) (at mouth) foam, froth

**écumer** /ekyme/ [1] **1** *vtr* (a) to skim
(b) to scour, to search
**2** *vi* ⟨*sea*⟩ to foam; ⟨*wine*⟩ to froth

**écumoire** /ekymwaʀ/ *nf* skimming ladle

**écureuil** /ekyʀœj/ *nm* squirrel

**écurie** /ekyʀi/ *nf* (a) stable
(b) (Sport) stable
(c) (figurative) pigsty

**écusson** /ekysɔ̃/ *nm* (a) (Mil) flash (GB)
(b) (of school) crest, badge; (of club, movement) badge; (of car) insignia
(c) (in heraldry) coat of arms

**écuyer, -ère** /ekɥije, ɛʀ/ **1** *nm,f*
(a) horseman/horsewoman
(b) riding instructor
(c) bareback rider
**2** *nm* (a) squire
(b) equerry

**eczéma** /egzema/ *nm* eczema

**éden** /edɛn/ *nm* paradise

**Éden** /edɛn/ *pr nm* Eden

**édenté, ~e** /edɑ̃te/ *adj* (a) toothless
(b) gap-toothed
(c) ⟨*comb*⟩ broken

**EDF** /œdeɛf/ *nf* (*abbr* = **Électricité de France**) French electricity board

**édicter** /edikte/ [1] *vtr* to enact ⟨*law*⟩

**édifiant, ~e** /edifjɑ̃, ɑ̃t/ *adj* (a) edifying
(b) enlightening

**édifice** /edifis/ *nm* (a) building
(b) structure

**édifier** /edifje/ [2] *vtr* (a) to build [sth]
(b) to build ⟨*empire*⟩
(c) to edify
(d) to enlighten

**Édimbourg** /edɛ̃buʀ/ *pr n* Edinburgh

**édit** /edi/ *nm* edict

**éditer** /edite/ [1] *vtr* (a) to publish ⟨*book, author*⟩; to release ⟨*record*⟩
(b) (Comput) to edit

**éditeur, -trice** /editœʀ, tʀis/ **1** *nm,f*
editor
**2** *nm* (a) publisher
(b) (Comput) editor

**édition** /edisjɔ̃/ **1** *nf* (a) (of book) publication; (of record) release
(b) (book, print) edition; (record) release
(c) publishing; **société d'~** publishing firm
(d) editing
(e) (paper) **~ du soir** evening edition
**2 éditions** *nf pl* **les ~s de la Roulotte** la Roulotte (Publishing Company)

**éditorial, ~e,** *mpl* **-iaux** /editɔʀjal, o/
**1** *adj* ⟨*policy, service*⟩ editorial
**2** *nm* editorial, leader

**édredon** /edʀədɔ̃/ *nm* eiderdown

**éducateur, -trice** /edykatœʀ, tʀis/
**1** *adj* educational
**2** *nm,f* youth worker

**éducatif, -ive** /edykatif, iv/ *adj*
educational

**éducation** /edykasjɔ̃/ *nf* (a) education;
**faire l'~ de qn** to educate sb
(b) training
(c) manners
■ **Éducation nationale, EN** Ministry of Education; (system) state education

**édulcorer** /edylkɔʀe/ [1] *vtr* (a) to sweeten
(b) to tone down ⟨*letter, remark*⟩

**éduquer** /edyke/ [1] *vtr* to educate; to train

**effacé, ~e** /efase/ *adj* retiring

**effacement** /efasmɑ̃/ *nm* (a) deletion;
**touche d'~** (Comput) delete key
(b) (of cassette) erasure
(c) self-effacement

**effacer** /efase/ [12] **1** *vtr* (a) to rub out; to delete; to erase
(b) to wipe ⟨*tape*⟩; to clear ⟨*file*⟩; to clean ⟨*blackboard*⟩
(c) ⟨*rain*⟩ to erase ⟨*tracks*⟩; ⟨*snow*⟩ to cover (up) ⟨*tracks*⟩; ⟨*cream*⟩ to remove ⟨*wrinkles*⟩
(d) to blot out ⟨*memory*⟩; to remove ⟨*differences*⟩
(e) to write off ⟨*debt*⟩
**2 s'effacer** *v refl* (+ *v être*) (a) ça s'efface you can rub it out
(b) ⟨*inscription, drawing, memory*⟩ to fade; ⟨*impression*⟩ to wear off; ⟨*fear*⟩ to disappear
(c) to step aside
(d) to stay in the background

**effaceur** /efasœʀ/ *nm* correction pen

**effarant, ~e** /efaʀɑ̃, ɑ̃t/ *adj* astounding

**effarer** /efaʀe/ [1] *vtr* to alarm

**effaroucher** /efaʀuʃe/ [1] *vtr* (a) to frighten [sb/sth] away
(b) to alarm

**effectif, -ive** /efɛktif, iv/ **1** *adj* real
**2** *nm* (of school) number of pupils; (of university) number of students; (of company) workforce; (of army) strength

**effectivement** /efɛktivmɑ̃/ *adv*
(a) indeed
(b) actually, really

**effectuer** /efɛktɥe/ [1] *vtr* to do ⟨*work, repairs*⟩; to make ⟨*payment, trip*⟩; to carry out ⟨*transaction*⟩; to conduct ⟨*survey*⟩; to serve ⟨*sentence*⟩

**efféminé, ~e** /efemine/ *adj* effeminate

**effervescence** /efɛʀvesɑ̃s/ *nf*
(a) effervescence
(b) turmoil

**effervescent, ~e** /efɛʀvesɑ̃, ɑ̃t/ *adj*
(a) effervescent
(b) (figurative) ⟨*crowd*⟩ seething; ⟨*personality*⟩ effervescent

**effet** /efɛ/ **1** *nm* (a) effect; **prendre ~** ⟨*measure, law*⟩ to take effect; **sous l'~ de l'alcool** under the influence of alcohol; **couper tous ses ~s à qn** to steal sb's thunder
(b) impression; **être du plus mauvais ~** to be in the worst possible taste; **faire un drôle d'~** to make one feel strange; **un ~ de surprise** an element of surprise ⋯⟩

(c) à cet ~ for that purpose
**2** **en effet** *phr* indeed
**3** **effets** *nm pl* things, clothes
■ ~ **de serre** greenhouse effect; ~s
**secondaires** (Med) side effects

**efficace** /efikas/ *adj* effective; efficient

**efficacement** /efikasmɑ̃/ *adv* efficiently;
effectively

**efficacité** /efikasite/ *nf* (of action, remedy)
effectiveness; (of person, device) efficiency

**effigie** /efiʒi/ *nf* (a) effigy; à l'~ de ⟨medal,
stamp⟩ with the head of
(b) logo

**effilé**, ~**e** /efile/ *adj* ⟨almonds⟩ flaked

**effiler** /efile/ [1] **1** *vtr* (a) to sharpen
(b) to string ⟨green beans⟩
**2** **s'effiler** *v refl* (+ *v être*) to fray

**effilocher** /efilɔʃe/ [1] **1** *vtr* to shred
**2** **s'effilocher** *v refl* (+ *v être*) to fray

**efflanqué**, ~**e** /eflɑ̃ke/ *adj* emaciated

**effleurer** /eflœʀe/ [1] *vtr* to touch lightly,
to brush (against); **l'idée ne m'a même pas
effleuré** the idea didn't even cross my mind

**effluent** /eflyɑ̃/ *nm* effluent

**effluve** /eflyv/ *nm* (a) unpleasant smell
(b) fragrance

**effondrement** /efɔ̃dʀəmɑ̃/ *nm* (a) collapse
(b) subsidence

**effondrer: s'effondrer** /efɔ̃dʀe/ [1] *v refl*
(+ *v être*) (a) ⟨roof, person⟩ to collapse;
⟨dream⟩ to crumble; ⟨hopes⟩ to fall
(b) être effondré par la nouvelle to be
distraught at the news

**efforcer: s'efforcer** /efɔʀse/ [12] *v refl*
(+ *v être*) to try hard (**de faire** to do)

**effort** /efɔʀ/ *nm* (a) effort; **fais un petit** ~
**d'imagination!** use a bit of imagination!; **avec
mon dos, je ne peux pas faire d'**~ with this
back of mine, I can't do anything strenuous
(b) (in physics) stress; strain

**effraction** /efʀaksjɔ̃/ *nf* breaking and
entering
■ ~ **informatique** computer hacking

**effrayant**, ~**e** /efʀɛjɑ̃, ɑ̃t/ *adj* ⟨sight,
ugliness⟩ frightening; ⟨thinness, paleness⟩
dreadful

**effrayer** /efʀeje/ [21] *vtr* (a) to frighten; to
alarm
(b) ⟨difficulty, price⟩ to put [sb] off

**effréné**, ~**e** /efʀene/ *adj* ⟨rhythm,
competition⟩ frenzied; ⟨ambition⟩ wild

**effriter** /efʀite/ [1] **1** *vtr* to crumble; to
break up
**2** **s'effriter** *v refl* (+ *v être*) to crumble
(away)

**effroi** /efʀwa/ *nm* dread, terror

**effronté**, ~**e** /efʀɔ̃te/ *adj* cheeky;
shameless

**effroyable** /efʀwajabl/ *adj* dreadful

**effroyablement** /efʀwajabləmɑ̃/ *adv*
(a) horribly
(b) (colloq) terribly

**effusion** /efyzjɔ̃/ *nf* effusion
■ ~ **de sang** bloodshed

**égal**, ~**e**, *mpl* **-aux** /egal, o/ **1** *adj*
(a) equal (à to); **à prix** ~, **je préfère celui-là** if
the price is the same, I'd rather have that
one
(b) ⟨ground⟩ level; ⟨light⟩ even; ⟨colour⟩
uniform; ⟨weather⟩ settled; ⟨pulse, breathing⟩
steady; **d'un pas** ~ at an even pace
(c) **ça m'est** ~ I don't mind (either way); I
don't care
**2** *nm,f* equal; **traiter d'**~ à ~ **avec qn** to
deal with sb as an equal
IDIOMS **rester** ~ à **soi-même** to be one's
usual self; **combattre à armes** ~**es** to be on
an equal footing

**égalable** /egalabl/ *adj* **difficilement** ~
unparalleled; incomparably superior

**également** /egalmɑ̃/ *adv* (a) also, too
(b) equally

**égaler** /egale/ [1] *vtr* to equal ⟨record⟩;
to be as good as ⟨person⟩; to be as high as
⟨price⟩
(b) **trois plus trois égalent six** three plus
three equals six *or* is six

**égalisation** /egalizasjɔ̃/ *nf* (a) levelling
(GB) out
(b) (Sport) **le penalty a permis l'**~ the penalty
evened (GB) *or* tied (US) the score

**égaliser** /egalize/ [1] **1** *vtr* (a) to level
⟨ground⟩
(b) to make [sth] the same size ⟨planks⟩
**2** *vi* (Sport) to equalize (GB), to tie (US)

**égalitaire** /egalitɛʀ/ *adj*, *nmf* egalitarian

**égalité** /egalite/ *nf* (a) equality
(b) (Sport) **être à** ~ to be level (GB), to be tied
(US); ~! deuce!

**égard** /egaʀ/ **1** *nm* (a) consideration; **sans**
~ **pour** without regard for
(b) **à l'**~ **de qn** toward(s) sb; **à cet** ~ in this
respect
**2** **égards** *nm pl* **avec des** ~s with respect;
**être plein d'**~s **envers qn** to be attentive to
sb's every need

**égaré**, ~**e** /egaʀe/ *adj* (a) stray
(b) ⟨look⟩ wild

**égarement** /egaʀmɑ̃/ *nm* (a) distraction,
madness
(b) confusion
(c) erratic behaviour (GB)

**égarer** /egaʀe/ [1] **1** *vtr* (a) to lead [sb]
astray
(b) to mislay
**2** **s'égarer** *v refl* (+ *v être*) (a) to get lost
(b) (figurative) ⟨mind⟩ to wander; ⟨person⟩ to
ramble

**égayer** /egeje/ [21] *vtr* to enliven; to
lighten; to brighten; to cheer [sb] up

**égérie** /eʒeʀi/ *nf* muse

**égide** /eʒid/ *nf* aegis

**églantine** /eglɑ̃tin/ *nf* wild rose, dog-rose

**églefin** /egləfɛ̃/ *nm* haddock

**église** /egliz/ *nf* church

**ego** /ego/ *nm inv* ego

**égocentrique** /egosɑ̃tʀik/ *adj*, *nmf*
egocentric

**égoïsme** /egoism/ *nm* selfishness

**égoïste** /egoist/ *adj* selfish

**égorger** /egɔʀʒe/ [13] *vtr* ~ qn to cut sb's throat

**égosiller: s'égosiller** /egozije/ [1] *v refl* (+ *v être*) **(a)** to shout oneself hoarse
**(b)** to sing at the top of one's voice
**(c)** to yell

**égout** /egu/ *nm* sewer

**égoutter** /egute/ [1] **1** *vtr* to drain
**2 s'égoutter** *v refl* (+ *v être*) ⟨dishes, rice, vegetables⟩ to drain; ⟨washing⟩ to drip dry

**égouttoir** /egutwaʀ/ *nm* draining rack (GB), (dish) drainer (US)

**égratigner** /egʀatiɲe/ [1] **1** *vtr* to scratch, to graze
**2 s'égratigner** *v refl* (+ *v être*) to scratch oneself; to graze oneself

**égratignure** /egʀatiɲyʀ/ *nf* scratch; graze

**égrener** /egʀəne/ [16] *vtr* **(a)** to shell ⟨peas⟩; to remove the seeds from ⟨melon⟩
**(b)** to chime out ⟨notes⟩; ~ son chapelet to tell one's beads

**Égypte** /eʒipt/ *pr nf* Egypt

**égyptien, -ienne** /eʒipsjɛ̃, ɛn/ **1** *adj* Egyptian
**2** *nm* (language) Egyptian

**éhonté, ~e** /eõte/ *adj* ⟨liar, lie⟩ brazen

**Éire** /ɛʀ/ *pr n* Éire, Republic of Ireland

**éjectable** /eʒɛktabl/ *adj* **siège ~** ejector seat (GB), ejection seat (US)

**éjecter** /eʒɛkte/ [1] *vtr* **(a)** (in accident) to throw [sb/sth] out
**(b)** (Tech) to eject

**élaboration** /elabɔʀasjõ/ *nf* development; working out; drafting; putting together

**élaboré, ~e** /elabɔʀe/ *adj* sophisticated; elaborate

**élaborer** /elabɔʀe/ [1] *vtr* to work [sth] out; to draw [sth] up; to put [sth] together

**élaguer** /elage/ [1] *vtr* to prune

**élan** /elã/ *nm* **(a)** (Sport) run up; **saut sans ~** standing jump
**(b)** momentum
**(c)** impetus
**(d)** enthusiasm; **~ patriotique** patriotic fervour (GB)
**(e)** impulse; **~ de tendresse** surge of tenderness
**(f)** (Zool) elk

**élancé, ~e** /elãse/ *adj* slender

**élancement** /elãsmã/ *nm* throbbing pain

**élancer: s'élancer** /elãse/ [12] *v refl* (+ *v être*) **(a)** to dash forward
**(b)** **s'~ vers le ciel** ⟨tree, spire⟩ to soar up toward(s) the sky

**élargi, ~e** /elaʀʒi/ *adj* enlarged; expanded

**élargir** /elaʀʒiʀ/ [3] **1** *vtr* **(a)** to widen ⟨road⟩; to let out ⟨garment⟩
**(b)** to stretch ⟨shoes, sweater⟩
**(c)** to extend ⟨contacts, law⟩; to broaden ⟨knowledge⟩; to increase ⟨majority⟩

**2 s'élargir** *v refl* (+ *v être*) ⟨group⟩ to expand; ⟨gap⟩ to increase; ⟨road⟩ to widen; ⟨person⟩ to fill out; ⟨garment⟩ to stretch

**élastique** /elastik/ **1** *adj* ⟨waistband⟩ elasticated (GB), elasticized (US)
**(b)** ⟨gas, fibre⟩ elastic
**(c)** ⟨rule, timetable⟩ flexible; ⟨budget⟩ elastic
**2** *nm* **(a)** rubber band
**(b)** (in haberdashery) elastic
**(c)** (Sport) bungee cord
**IDIOMS les lâcher avec un ~** (colloq) to be tight-fisted

**élastomère** /elastɔmɛʀ/ *nm* elastomer

**électeur, -trice** /elɛktœʀ, tʀis/ *nm,f* voter

**élection** /elɛksjõ/ *nf* **(a)** election
**(b)** choice; **mon pays d'~** my chosen country

**électoral, ~e, mpl -aux** /elɛktɔʀal, o/ *adj* electoral; election

**électorat** /elɛktɔʀa/ *nm* electorate, voters

**électricien, -ienne** /elɛktʀisjɛ̃, ɛn/ *nm,f* electrician

**électricité** /elɛktʀisite/ *nf* electricity

**électrifier** /elɛktʀifje/ [2] *vtr* to electrify ⟨railtracks⟩

**électrique** /elɛktʀik/ *adj* **(a)** electrical
**(b)** (figurative) ⟨atmosphere⟩ electric

**électriser** /elɛktʀize/ [1] *vtr* to electrify

**électro(-)** /elɛktʀo/ *pref* electro;
**~cardiogramme** electrocardiogram

**électrochoc** /elɛktʀoʃɔk/ *nm* **~s** electroshock therapy, EST

**électrocuter: s'électrocuter** /elɛktʀokyte/ [1] *v refl* (+ *v être*) to be electrocuted

**électrode** /elɛktʀod/ *nf* electrode

**électrogène** /elɛktʀoʒɛn/ *adj* **groupe ~** (electricity) generator

**électromécanicien, -ienne** /elɛktʀomekanisjɛ̃, ɛn/ *nm,f* electrical engineer

**électroménager** /elɛktʀomenaʒe/
**1** *adj m* **appareil ~** household appliance
**2** *nm* **(a)** domestic electrical appliances
**(b)** electrical goods industry

**électron** /elɛktʀõ/ *nm* electron

**électronicien, -ienne** /elɛktʀonisjɛ̃, ɛn/ *nm,f* electronics engineer

**électronique** /elɛktʀonik/ **1** *adj*
**(a)** ⟨circuit⟩ electronic
**(b)** ⟨microscope⟩ electron
**2** *nf* electronics

**électrophone** /elɛktʀofon/ *nm* record player

**élégamment** /elegamã/ *adv* ⟨dress⟩ elegantly

**élégance** /elegãs/ *nf* elegance; **avec ~** ⟨dress⟩ elegantly; ⟨lose⟩ gracefully; ⟨behave⟩ honourably (GB); ⟨resolve problem⟩ neatly

**élégant, ~e** /elegã, ãt/ *adj* elegant; **ce n'est pas très ~ de ta part** it's not very decent of you

**élément** /elemã/ ① *nm* (a) (in structure, ensemble) element; (in device) component; ∼ **moteur** driving force
(b) factor, element; **l'∼-clé de** the key element in
(c) (of furniture) unit
(d) fact; **disposer de tous les ∼s** to have all the facts
(e) (person) **bon ∼** good pupil; good player
(f) (chemical) element
② **éléments** *nm pl* elements

**élémentaire** /elemãtɛR/ *adj* (a) ⟨principle⟩ basic
(b) elementary

**éléphant** /elefã/ *nm* elephant

**éléphanteau**, *pl* ∼**x** /elefãto/ *nm* (elephant) calf

**élevage** /elvaʒ/ *nm* (a) livestock farming; **faire de l'∼ de porcs** to breed pigs; **d'∼** ⟨oysters⟩ farmed; ⟨pheasant⟩ captive-bred
(b) farm; **un ∼ de visons** a mink farm
(c) stock (**de** of)

**élévateur** /elevatœR/ *nm* elevator

**élévation** /elevasjɔ̃/ *nf* (a) rise (**de** in)
(b) (to rank) elevation
(c) (in architecture) elevation

**élevé**, ∼**e** /elve/ *adj* (a) ⟨level, price, rank⟩ high
(b) ⟨plateau⟩ high
(c) ⟨sentiment⟩ fine; ⟨principles⟩ high; ⟨ideal⟩ lofty; ⟨language⟩ elevated

**élève** /elɛv/ *nmf* (gen) student; (Sch) pupil; ∼ **officier** trainee officer

**élever** /elve/ [16] ① *vtr* (a) to put up, to erect
(b) to raise ⟨temperature, level⟩
(c) to lift, to raise ⟨load⟩
(d) **la poésie élève l'âme** poetry is elevating *or* uplifting
(e) to raise ⟨objection⟩
(f) to bring [sb] up; **c'est mal élevé** it's bad manners (**de faire** to do)
(g) to rear ⟨cattle⟩; to keep ⟨bees⟩
② **s'élever** *v refl* (+ *v être*) (a) ⟨rate⟩ to rise
(b) **s'∼ à** ⟨expenses⟩ to come to; ⟨death toll⟩ to stand at
(c) to rise (up); **s'∼ dans les airs** ⟨smoke⟩ to rise up into the air; ⟨bird⟩ to soar into the air
(d) ⟨voice, protests⟩ to be heard
(e) **s'∼ contre qch** to protest against sth
(f) ⟨statue⟩ to stand; **s'∼ au-dessus de qch** to rise above sth

**éleveur**, **-euse** /elvœR, øz/ *nm,f* breeder

**elfe** /ɛlf/ *nm* elf

**élider** /elide/ [1] *vtr* to elide

**éligible** /eliʒibl/ *adj* eligible for office

**élimé**, ∼**e** /elime/ *adj* threadbare

**élimer** /elime/ [1] ① *vtr* to wear [sth] thin
② **s'élimer** *v refl* (+ *v être*) to wear thin

**élimination** /eliminasjɔ̃/ *nf* (a) (gen) elimination, defeat
(b) (of stain) removal ∼ **déchets** waste disposal

**éliminatoire** /eliminatwaR/ *adj* ⟨question, match⟩ qualifying; ⟨mark⟩ eliminatory

**éliminer** /elimine/ [1] *vtr* to eliminate

**élire** /eliR/ [66] *vtr* to elect **se faire ∼** to be elected; ∼ **domicile** to take up residence

**élision** /elizjɔ̃/ *nf* elision

**élite** /elit/ *nf* **l'∼** the elite; **d'∼** ⟨troops⟩ elite, crack; ⟨student⟩ high-flying; ⟨athlete⟩ top

**élitisme** /elitism/ *nm* elitism

**élixir** /eliksiR/ *nm* elixir

**elle** /ɛl/ *pron f* she; it; ∼**s** they; **je les vois plus souvent qu'∼** I see them more often than she does; I see them more often than (I see) her; **le bol bleu est à ∼** the blue bowl is hers

**ellébore** /elebɔR/ *nm* hellebore

**elle-même**, *pl* **elles-mêmes** /ɛlmɛm/ *pron* herself; itself; **elles-mêmes** themselves; '**Mme Roc?**'—'∼' 'Mrs Roc?'—'speaking'

**elles** *pron* ▶ ELLE

**ellipse** /elips/ *nf* ellipsis

**elliptique** /eliptik/ *adj* (a) elliptical
(b) elliptic

**élocution** /elɔkysjɔ̃/ *nf* diction; **défaut d'∼** speech impediment

**éloge** /elɔʒ/ *nm* (a) praise; **être tout à l'∼ de qn** to do sb great credit
(b) eulogy; ∼ **funèbre** funeral oration

**élogieux**, **-ieuse** /elɔʒjø, øz/ *adj* full of praise; laudatory

**éloigné**, ∼**e** /elwaɲe/ *adj* (a) distant; ∼ **de tout** remote; **deux usines ∼es de cinq kilomètres** two factories five kilometres (GB) apart
(b) ⟨memories⟩ distant; ⟨event⟩ remote; ∼ **dans le temps** distant (in time)
(c) ⟨cousin⟩ distant

**éloignement** /elwaɲmã/ *nm* (a) distance
(b) remoteness

**éloigner** /elwaɲe/ [1] ① *vtr* (a) to move [sb/sth] away
(b) **ils font tout pour l'∼ de moi** they are doing everything to drive us apart
② **s'éloigner** *v refl* (+ *v être*) (a) to move away; **ne t'éloigne pas trop** don't go too far away
(b) **s'∼ de** to move away from ⟨party line⟩; to stray from ⟨subject⟩

**élongation** /elɔ̃gasjɔ̃/ *nf* (Med) pulled muscle

**éloquence** /elɔkãs/ *nf* eloquence

**éloquent**, ∼**e** /elɔkã, ãt/ *adj* eloquent

**élu**, ∼**e** /ely/ *nm,f* (a) elected representative
(b) beloved
(c) (in religion) **les ∼s** the Chosen Ones

**élucider** /elyside/ [1] *vtr* to solve ⟨crime, problem⟩; to clarify ⟨circumstances⟩

**élucubrations** /elykybRasjɔ̃/ *nf pl* rantings

**éluder** /elyde/ [1] *vtr* to evade

**Élysée** /elize/ *pr nm* (**palais de**) l'~ *the official residence of the French President*

**émacier: s'émacier** /emasje/ [2] *v refl* (+ *v être*) to become emaciated

**e-mail** /emaj/ *nm* e-mail

**émail**, *pl* **-aux** /emaj, o/ *nm* enamel

**émaillé**, **~e** /emaje/ *adj* ⟨*utensil*⟩ enamel; ⟨*metal*⟩ enamelled

**émanation** /emanasjɔ̃/ *nf* emanation; ~s **de gaz** gas fumes

**émancipation** /emɑ̃sipasjɔ̃/ *nf* emancipation

**émanciper** /emɑ̃sipe/ [1] **[1]** *vtr* to emancipate ⟨*people*⟩; to liberate ⟨*country*⟩
**[2] s'émanciper** *v refl* (+ *v être*) to become emancipated; **femme émancipée** liberated woman

**émaner** /emane/ [1] **[1]** *vi* ~ **de** to emanate from; to come from
**[2]** *v impers* **il émane d'elle un charme fou** she exudes charm

**émaux** ▶ ÉMAIL

**emballage** /ɑ̃balaʒ/ *nm* packaging; wrapping; packing
■ ~ **sous vide** vacuum packing

**emballant**, **~e** /ɑ̃balɑ̃, ɑ̃t/ *adj* (colloq) exciting

**emballer** /ɑ̃bale/ [1] **[1]** *vtr* (**a**) to pack, to wrap
(**b**) (colloq) **être emballé par** to be taken with
**[2] s'emballer** *v refl* (+ *v être*) (**a**) ⟨*horse*⟩ to bolt
(**b**) (colloq) to get carried away
(**c**) (colloq) to get all worked up (colloq)
(**d**) (colloq) ⟨*engine*⟩ to race
(**e**) ⟨*prices, inflation*⟩ to shoot up; ⟨*currency*⟩ to shoot up in value

**embarcadère** /ɑ̃baʀkadɛʀ/ *nm* pier; wharf

**embarcation** /ɑ̃baʀkasjɔ̃/ *nf* boat

**embardée** /ɑ̃baʀde/ *nf* (of car) swerve

**embargo** /ɑ̃baʀgo/ *nm* embargo

**embarquement** /ɑ̃baʀkəmɑ̃/ *nm* boarding

**embarquer** /ɑ̃baʀke/ [1] **[1]** *vtr* (**a**) to load ⟨*goods*⟩; to take [sb] on board
(**b**) (colloq) to take ⟨*object*⟩; ⟨*police*⟩ to pick up ⟨*criminal*⟩
**[2]** *vi* (**a**) to board
(**b**) to sail (**pour** for)
**[3] s'embarquer** *v refl* (+ *v être*) (**a**) to board
(**b**) (colloq) **s'~ dans** to launch into ⟨*explanation*⟩

**embarras** /ɑ̃baʀa/ *nm inv*
(**a**) embarrassment
(**b**) awkward position; difficult situation
(**c**) **n'avoir que l'~ du choix** to have too much to choose from

**embarrassant**, **~e** /ɑ̃baʀasɑ̃, ɑ̃t/ *adj*
(**a**) awkward; embarrassing
(**b**) cumbersome

**embarrassé**, **~e** /ɑ̃baʀase/ **[1]** *pp* ▶ EMBARRASSER

**[2]** *pp adj* (**a**) embarrassed; **être bien ~ pour répondre** to be at a loss for an answer
(**b**) ⟨*room*⟩ cluttered; **~ d'une grosse valise** weighed down with a large suitcase

**embarrasser** /ɑ̃baʀase/ [1] **[1]** *vtr* (**a**) to embarrass
(**b**) to clutter [sth] (up); **cette armoire m'embarrasse plutôt qu'autre chose** this wardrobe is more of a nuisance than anything else
**[2] s'embarrasser** *v refl* (+ *v être*) **s'~ de** to burden oneself with ⟨*baggage, person*⟩

**embauche** /ɑ̃boʃ/ *nf* appointment (GB), hiring (US); **salaire d'~** starting salary

**embaucher** /ɑ̃boʃe/ [1] *vtr* (**a**) to take on (GB), to hire
(**b**) (colloq) to recruit

**embaumer** /ɑ̃bome/ [1] **[1]** *vtr* (**a**) ⟨*smell*⟩ to fill ⟨*place*⟩; ⟨*place*⟩ to smell of ⟨*wax*⟩
(**b**) to embalm
**[2]** *vi* to be fragrant

**embaumeur**, **-euse** /ɑ̃bomœʀ, øz/ *nm,f* embalmer

**embellir** /ɑ̃beliʀ/ [3] **[1]** *vtr* (**a**) to improve [sth]; to make [sb] more attractive
(**b**) to embellish ⟨*story, truth*⟩
**[2]** *vi* to become more attractive

**embellissement** /ɑ̃belismɑ̃/ *nm* (of house) improving; **travaux d'~** improvements

**emberlificoter** /ɑ̃bɛʀlifikɔte/ [1] (colloq)
**[1]** *vtr* (**a**) to entangle
(**b**) to take [sb] in (colloq)
**[2] s'emberlificoter** *v refl* (+ *v être*) to get entangled; to get tangled up (**dans** in)

**embêtant**, **~e** /ɑ̃betɑ̃, ɑ̃t/ *adj*
(**a**) annoying
(**b**) boring

**embêtement** /ɑ̃betmɑ̃/ *nm* problem

**embêter** /ɑ̃bete/ [1] **[1]** *vtr* (**a**) to bother
(**b**) to pester; to annoy
(**c**) to bore
**[2] s'embêter** *v refl* (+ *v être*) (**a**) to be bored
(**b**) **s'~ à faire** to go to the bother of doing

**emblée: d'emblée** /dɑ̃ble/ *phr*
(**a**) straightaway
(**b**) at first sight

**emblématique** /ɑ̃blematik/ *adj* emblematic; symbolic

**emblème** /ɑ̃blɛm/ *nm* emblem

**embobiner** /ɑ̃bɔbine/ [1] *vtr* (colloq) to hoodwink

**emboîter** /ɑ̃bwate/ [1] **[1]** *vtr* to fit [sth] together; **~ qch dans** to fit sth into
**[2] s'emboîter** *v refl* (+ *v être*) ⟨*part*⟩ to fit (**dans** into); ⟨*parts*⟩ to fit together
IDIOMS **~ le pas à qn** to fall in behind sb

**embonpoint** /ɑ̃bɔ̃pwɛ̃/ *nm* stoutness; **avoir de l'~** to be stout

**embouché**, **~e** /ɑ̃buʃe/ *adj* **mal ~** coarse; in a foul mood

**embouchure** /ɑ̃buʃyʀ/ *nf* (of river) mouth; (of instrument) mouthpiece; (of pipe) opening

**embourber**: **s'embourber** /ãbuʀbe/ [1]
*v refl* (+ *v être*) **(a)** to get stuck in the mud
**(b)** to get bogged down

**embourgeoiser**: **s'embourgeoiser**
/ãbuʀʒwaze/ [1] *v refl* (+ *v être*) ⟨*person*⟩ to
become middle-class; ⟨*area*⟩ to become
gentrified

**embout** /ãbu/ *nm* (of cigar, cane) tip;
(of hosepipe) nozzle; (of pipe) mouthpiece

**embouteillage** /ãbutɛjaʒ/ *nm* traffic jam

**emboutir** /ãbutiʀ/ [3] *vtr* **(a)** to stamp, to
press ⟨*part, metal*⟩
**(b)** (colloq) to crash into ⟨*vehicle*⟩

**embranchement** /ãbʀãʃmã/ *nm*
**(a)** junction
**(b)** side road
**(c)** (on railways) branch line

**embrasé**, **~e** /ãbʀaze/ *adj* **(a)** burning
**(b)** glowing

**embrasement** /ãbʀazmã/ *nm* **(a)** blaze
**(b)** dazzling illumination
**(c)** unrest

**embraser** /ãbʀaze/ [1] **1** *vtr* **(a)** to set
[sth] ablaze
**(b)** to set [sth] alight ⟨*country*⟩
**2** **s'embraser** *v refl* (+ *v être*) **(a)** to catch
fire
**(b)** ⟨*country*⟩ to erupt into violence
**(c)** ⟨*sky*⟩ to be set ablaze
**(d)** to burn with desire

**embrasser** /ãbʀase/ [1] **1** *vtr* **(a)** to kiss;
**je t'embrasse** lots of love
**(b)** to embrace; to hug
**(c)** to take up ⟨*career, cause*⟩
**2** **s'embrasser** *v refl* (+ *v être*) **(a)** to kiss
(each other)
**(b)** to embrace; to hug
**IDIOMS ~ qn comme du bon pain** to hug sb
warmly

**embrasure** /ãbʀazyʀ/ *nf* **~ de fenêtre**
window; **~ de porte** doorway

**embrayage** /ãbʀɛjaʒ/ *nm* **(a)** clutch
**(b)** clutch pedal

**embrayer** /ãbʀeje/ [21] *vi* ⟨*driver*⟩ to
engage the clutch; (Tech) to engage

**embrigader** /ãbʀigade/ [1] *vtr* **(a)** to
recruit
**(b)** (Mil) to brigade

**embrouillamini** /ãbʀujamini/ *nm* (colloq)
muddle

**embrouille** /ãbʀuj/ *nf* (colloq) shady
goings-on (colloq)

**embrouiller** /ãbʀuje/ [1] **1** *vtr* **(a)** to
tangle ⟨*wires*⟩
**(b)** to confuse ⟨*matter, person*⟩
**2** **s'embrouiller** *v refl* (+ *v être*) **(a)** to
become tangled
**(b)** ⟨*ideas, person*⟩ to become confused

**embroussaillé**, **~e** /ãbʀusaje/ *adj*
⟨*path*⟩ overgrown; ⟨*hair*⟩ bushy

**embrumé**, **~e** /ãbʀyme/ *adj* **(a)** misty
**(b)** ⟨*mind*⟩ befuddled; ⟨*look*⟩ glazed

**embruns** /ãbʀœ̃/ *nm pl* spray

**embryon** /ãbʀijɔ̃/ *nm* embryo

**embûche** /ãbyʃ/ *nf* **(a)** trap; **dresser des
~s** to set traps
**(b)** hazard; pitfall; **semé d'~s** hazardous;
(figurative) fraught with pitfalls

**embuer** /ãbɥe/ [1] **1** *vtr* to mist up, to fog
up
**2** **s'embuer** *v refl* (+ *v être*) ⟨*window*⟩ to
mist up, to fog up; ⟨*eyes*⟩ to mist over

**embuscade** /ãbyskad/ *nf* ambush

**embusquer**: **s'embusquer** /ãbyske/ [1]
*v refl* (+ *v être*) to lie in ambush

**éméché**, **~e** /emeʃe/ *adj* (colloq) tipsy

**émeraude** /emʀod/ *nf* emerald

**émergence** /emɛʀʒãs/ *nf* emergence

**émerger** /emɛʀʒe/ [13] *vi* to emerge

**émeri** /emʀi/ *nm* emery

**émérite** /emeʀit/ *adj* **(a)** outstanding
**(b)** **professeur ~** emeritus professor

**émerveiller** /emɛʀveje/ [1] **1** *vtr* **~ qn** to
fill sb with wonder
**2** **s'émerveiller** *v refl* (+ *v être*) **s'~ de** or
**devant qch** to marvel at sth

**émetteur, -trice** /emetœʀ, tʀis/ **1** *adj*
**(a)** ⟨*station*⟩ broadcasting
**(b)** ⟨*bank*⟩ issuing
**2** *nm* **(a)** transmitter
**(b)** (of loan, card) issuer

**émettre** /emɛtʀ/ [60] *vtr* **(a)** to express
⟨*opinion, wish*⟩; to put forward ⟨*hypothesis*⟩
**(b)** to utter ⟨*cry*⟩; to produce ⟨*sound, heat*⟩
**(c)** to issue ⟨*document*⟩
**(d)** to broadcast ⟨*programme*⟩
**(e)** to send out ⟨*signal*⟩
**(f)** to emit ⟨*radiation*⟩

**émeute** /emøt/ *nf* riot

**émietter** /emjete/ [1] **1** *vtr* to crumble
[sth]
**2** **s'émietter** *v refl* (+ *v être*) to crumble

**émigrant**, **~e** /emigʀã, ãt/ *nm,f* emigrant

**émigration** /emigʀasjɔ̃/ *nf* emigration

**émigré**, **~e** /emigʀe/ *nm,f* emigrant;
émigré

**émigrer** /emigʀe/ [1] *vi* **(a)** to emigrate
**(b)** ⟨*bird*⟩ to migrate

**émincer** /emɛ̃se/ [12] *vtr* to slice [sth]
thinly

**éminemment** /eminamã/ *adv* eminently

**éminence** /eminãs/ *nf* **(a)** hillock
**(b)** (Anat) protuberance

**Éminence** /eminãs/ *nf* Eminence

**éminent**, **~e** /eminã, ãt/ *adj*
distinguished, eminent

**émirat** /emiʀa/ *nm* emirate

**Émirats** /emiʀa/ *pr nm pl* **~ arabes unis**,
**EAU** United Arab Emirates

**émis**, **~e** /emi, iz/ ▶ ÉMETTRE

**émissaire** /emisɛʀ/ *nm* emissary

**émission** /emisjɔ̃/ *nf* **(a)** programme (GB)
**(b)** (of document) issue
**(c)** (of waves, signals) emission

**emmagasiner** /ãmagazine/ [1] *vtr* **(a)** to
store

**(b)** to stockpile ⟨*goods*⟩; to store up ⟨*knowledge*⟩

**emmanchure** /ɑ̃mɑ̃ʃyʀ/ *nf* armhole

**emmêler** /ɑ̃mɛle/ [1] **1** *vtr* **(a)** to tangle
**(b)** to confuse ⟨*matter*⟩
**2 s'emmêler** *v refl* (+ *v être*) to get
tangled up; **s'~ les pieds dans** to get one's
feet caught in

**emménagement** /ɑ̃menaʒmɑ̃/ *nm*
moving in

**emménager** /ɑ̃menaʒe/ [13] *vi* to move in

**emmener** /ɑ̃mne/ [16] *vtr* **(a)** to take
⟨*person*⟩ (à, jusqu'à to); **veux-tu que je
t'emmène en voiture?** do you want a lift (GB)
*or* a ride (US)?
**(b)** (colloq) (controversial) to take [sth] with one
⟨*object*⟩
**(c)** to take [sb] away

**emmerder** /ɑ̃mɛʀde/ [1] (slang) **1** *vtr* to
annoy, to hassle (colloq); **~ le monde** to be a
pain in the arse (GB) (colloq) *or* ass (US)
(slang)
**2 s'emmerder** *v refl* (+ *v être*) **(a)** to be
bored stiff (colloq)
**(b)** **s'~ à faire** to go to the trouble of doing;
**tu t'emmerdes pas!** you're doing all right for
yourself!; you've got a nerve!

**emmitoufler** /ɑ̃mitufle/ [1] **1** *vtr* to wrap
[sb/sth] up warmly
**2 s'emmitoufler** *v refl* (+ *v être*) to wrap
(oneself) up warmly

**émoi** /emwa/ *nm* agitation, turmoil

**émoluments** /emɔlymɑ̃/ *nm pl*
remuneration

**émonder** /emɔ̃de/ [1] *vtr* to prune

**émotif, -ive** /emɔtif, iv/ *adj* emotional

**émotion** /emɔsjɔ̃/ *nf* emotion

**émotivité** /emɔtivite/ *nf* **enfant d'une
grande ~** highly emotional child

**émousser** /emuse/ [1] **1** *vtr* **(a)** to blunt
**(b)** to dull ⟨*curiosity, sensitivity*⟩
**2 s'émousser** *v refl* (+ *v être*) **(a)** to
become blunt
**(b)** ⟨*curiosity*⟩ to become dulled

**émoustiller** /emustije/ [1] *vtr* **(a)** to
exhilarate
**(b)** to titillate

**émouvant, ~e** /emuvɑ̃, ɑ̃t/ *adj* moving

**émouvoir** /emuvwaʀ/ [43] **1** *vtr* to move,
to touch; **~ l'opinion** to cause a stir
**2 s'émouvoir** *v refl* (+ *v être*) **(a)** to be
touched *or* moved
**(b)** **s'~ de** to become concerned about; to be
bothered by

**empailler** /ɑ̃paje/ [1] *vtr* to stuff

**empailleur, -euse** /ɑ̃pajœʀ, øz/ *nm,f*
taxidermist

**empaler** /ɑ̃pale/ [1] **1** *vtr* to impale
**2 s'empaler** *v refl* (+ *v être*) to become
impaled

**empaqueter** /ɑ̃pakte/ [20] *vtr* to package;
to wrap [sth] up

**emparer: s'emparer** /ɑ̃paʀe/ [1] *v refl*
(+ *v être*) **(a)** **s'~ de** (gen) to get hold of, to
seize; to take over ⟨*town*⟩; to seize ⟨*power*⟩
**(b)** **s'~ de** ⟨*feeling*⟩ to take hold of [sb]

**empâter: s'empâter** /ɑ̃pate/ [1] *v refl*
(+ *v être*) to become puffy; to put on weight

**empêchement** /ɑ̃pɛʃmɑ̃/ *nm* unforeseen
difficulty; **j'ai un ~** something's cropped up

**empêcher** /ɑ̃peʃe/ [1] **1** *vtr* to prevent, to
stop; **~ qn de faire** to prevent sb (from)
doing
**2 s'empêcher** *v refl* (+ *v être*) **je n'ai pas
pu m'~ de rire** I couldn't help laughing
**3** *v impers* **(il) n'empêche** all the same; **il
n'empêche que** the fact remains that

**empereur** /ɑ̃pʀœʀ/ *nm* emperor

**empesé, ~e** /ɑ̃paze/ *adj* ⟨*collar*⟩
starched; ⟨*person, manner*⟩ starchy

**empester** /ɑ̃peste/ [16] **1** *vtr* to stink
[sth] out (GB), to stink up (US)
**2** *vi* to stink

**empêtrer: s'empêtrer** /ɑ̃petʀe/ [1] *v refl*
(+ *v être*) **s'~ dans** to get entangled in
⟨*briars*⟩; to get tangled up in ⟨*lies*⟩

**emphase** /ɑ̃faz/ *nf* **(a)** grandiloquence
**(b)** emphasis

**emphatique** /ɑ̃fatik/ *adj*
**(a)** grandiloquent
**(b)** emphatic

**empiècement** /ɑ̃pjɛsmɑ̃/ *nm* (of garment)
yoke

**empiéter** /ɑ̃pjete/ [14] *vi* to encroach

**empiffrer: s'empiffrer** /ɑ̃pifʀe/ [1] *v refl*
(+ *v être*) (colloq) to stuff oneself

**empiler** /ɑ̃pile/ [1] **1** *vtr* to pile [sth] (up)
**2 s'empiler** *v refl* (+ *v être*) to pile up

**empire** /ɑ̃piʀ/ *nm* empire

**Empire** /ɑ̃piʀ/ *nm* **l'~** the Empire.
■ **l'~ d'Orient** the Byzantine Empire; **l'~
d'Occident** the Western Empire

**empirer** /ɑ̃piʀe/ [1] *vi* to get worse

**empirique** /ɑ̃piʀik/ *adj* empirical

**empirisme** /ɑ̃piʀism/ *nm* empiricism

**emplacement** /ɑ̃plasmɑ̃/ *nm* **(a)** site
**(b)** parking space

**emplette** /ɑ̃plɛt/ *nf* purchase

**emplir** /ɑ̃pliʀ/ [3] *vtr*, **s'emplir** *v refl*
(+ *v être*) to fill (de with)

**emploi** /ɑ̃plwa/ *nm* **(a)** job
**(b)** employment
**(c)** use; **téléviseur couleur à vendre, cause
double ~** colour (GB) TV for sale, surplus to
requirements
**(d)** usage
■ **~ du temps** timetable
IDIOMS **avoir la tête de l'~** to look the part

**employé, ~e** /ɑ̃plwaje/ *nm,f* employee
■ **~ de banque** bank clerk; **~ municipal** local
authority employee

**employer** /ɑ̃plwaje/ [23] **1** *vtr* to employ
⟨*person*⟩; to use ⟨*word, product*⟩
**2 s'employer** *v refl* (+ *v être*) **(a)** to be
used
**(b)** **s'~ à faire** to apply oneself to doing

**employeur, -euse** /ɑ̃plwajœR, øz/ *nm,f* employer

**empocher** /ɑ̃pɔʃe/ [1] *vtr* to pocket

**empoigner** /ɑ̃pwaɲe/ [1] *vtr* to grab (hold of)

**empoisonnant, ~e** /ɑ̃pwazɔnɑ̃, ɑ̃t/ *adj* (colloq) annoying, irritating

**empoisonné, ~e** /ɑ̃pwazɔne/ ① *pp* ▶ EMPOISONNER
② *pp adj* ⟨foodstuff⟩ poisoned; ⟨atmosphere⟩ sour

**empoisonnement** /ɑ̃pwazɔnmɑ̃/ *nm*
(a) poisoning
(b) (colloq) trouble

**empoisonner** /ɑ̃pwazɔne/ [1] ① *vtr* to poison; **~ la vie de qn** to make sb's life a misery
② **s'empoisonner** *v refl* (+ *v être*) to poison oneself; **il s'est empoisonné avec une huître pas fraîche** he got food poisoning from eating a bad oyster

**empoisonneur, -euse** /ɑ̃pwazɔnœR, øz/ *nm,f* (a) poisoner
(b) (colloq) nuisance

**emportement** /ɑ̃pɔRtəmɑ̃/ *nm* fit of anger; **avec ~** angrily

**emporter** /ɑ̃pɔRte/ [1] ① *vtr* (a) to take ⟨object⟩; **pizzas à ~** takeaway pizzas (GB), pizzas to go (US)
(b) ⟨ambulance⟩ to take [sb] away; ⟨plane⟩ to carry [sb] away
(c) ⟨wind, river⟩ to sweep [sb/sth] away; ⟨shell, bullet⟩ to take [sth] off ⟨ear, leg⟩
(d) **une leucémie l'a emporté** he died of leukaemia
(e) to take ⟨position⟩
(f) **l'~** to win; to prevail; **l'~ sur qch** to overcome sth
② **s'emporter** *v refl* (+ *v être*) to lose one's temper

**empoté, ~e** /ɑ̃pɔte/ *adj* (colloq) clumsy, awkward

**empreindre: s'empreindre** /ɑ̃pRɛ̃dR/ [55] *v refl* (+ *v être*) to become marked (de with), to become imbued (de with)

**empreinte** /ɑ̃pRɛ̃t/ *nf* (a) footprint; track
(b) stamp, mark
■ **~s digitales** fingerprints

**empressement** /ɑ̃pRɛsmɑ̃/ *nm*
(a) eagerness; **avec ~** eagerly
(b) attentiveness

**empresser: s'empresser** /ɑ̃pRese/ [1] *v refl* (+ *v être*) **s'~ de faire** to hasten to do; **s'~ autour** or **auprès de qn** to fuss over sb

**emprise** /ɑ̃pRiz/ *nf* hold, influence

**emprisonnement** /ɑ̃pRizɔnmɑ̃/ *nm* imprisonment; **peine d'~** prison sentence

**emprisonner** /ɑ̃pRizɔne/ [1] *vtr* (a) to imprison (à, dans in)
(b) to keep [sb] prisoner

**emprunt** /ɑ̃pRœ̃/ *nm* (a) (money) loan; **faire un ~** to take out a loan
(b) borrowing; **d'~** ⟨car, name⟩ borrowed
(c) ⟨object, book⟩ loan; **c'est un ~ fait à un musée** it's on loan from a museum

(d) (of idea, word) borrowing

**emprunté, ~e** /ɑ̃pRœ̃te/ *adj* awkward

**emprunter** /ɑ̃pRœ̃te/ [1] *vtr* (a) to borrow
(b) to take ⟨road⟩

**empuantir** /ɑ̃pɥɑ̃tiR/ [3] *vtr* to stink out (GB), to stink up (US)

**ému, ~e** /emy/ ① *pp* ▶ ÉMOUVOIR
② *pp adj* moved; touched; nervous; **trop ~ pour parler** too overcome to speak
③ *adj* ⟨words⟩ full of emotion; ⟨memory⟩ fond

**émulation** /emylasjɔ̃/ *nf* competitiveness

**émule** /emyl/ *nmf* imitator; **être l'~ de qn** to model oneself on sb

**émulsifiant** /emylsifjɑ̃/ *nm* emulsifier

**émulsion** /emylsjɔ̃/ *nf* emulsion

**en** /ɑ̃/ ① *prep* (a) in; into; to; **vivre ~ ville** to live in town; **aller ~ Allemagne** to go to Germany; **~ hiver/1991** in winter/1991; **~ semaine** during the week; **voyager ~ train** to travel by train
(b) **il est toujours ~ manteau** he always wears a coat
(c) as; **je vous parle ~ ami** I'm speaking (to you) as a friend
(d) into; **traduire ~ anglais** to translate into English
(e) **c'est ~ or** it's (made of) gold; **le même ~ bleu/plus grand** the same in blue/only bigger; **~ hauteur, le mur fait trois mètres** the wall is three metres (GB) high
(f) (used with gerund) **je l'ai croisé ~ sortant** I met him as I was leaving; **prends un café ~ attendant** have a cup of coffee while you're waiting; **l'enfant se réveilla ~ hurlant** the child woke up screaming; **ouvrez cette caisse ~ soulevant le couvercle** open this box by lifting the lid; **tu aurais moins chaud ~ enlevant ta veste** you'd be cooler if you took your jacket off
② *pron* (a) (indicating means) **il sortit son épée et l'~ transperça** he took out his sword and ran him/her through
(b) (indicating cause) **ça l'a tellement bouleversé qu'il ~ est tombé malade** it distressed him so much that he fell ill (GB) *or* became sick (US)
(c) (representing person) **ils aiment leurs enfants et ils ~ sont aimés** they love their children and they are loved by them
(d) (representing thing) **'veux-tu du vin?'—'oui, j'~ veux'** 'would you like some wine?'—'yes, I'd like some'; **il n'~ reste pas beaucoup** there isn't much (of it) left; there aren't many left; **j'~ suis fier** I'm proud of it
(e) (colloq) **tu ~ as un beau chapeau!** what a nice hat you've got!

**ENA** /ena/ *nf: abbr* ▶ ÉCOLE

**énarque** /enaRk/ *nmf* graduate of the ENA

**encadré** /ɑ̃kadRe/ *nm* (in newspaper) box

**encadrement** /ɑ̃kadRəmɑ̃/ *nm*
(a) supervision
(b) supervisory staff; managerial staff; (Mil) officers
(c) (of picture) frame

**encadrer** /ãkɑdʀe/ [1] *vtr* (a) to supervise ⟨*staff*⟩; to train ⟨*soldier*⟩
(b) to flank ⟨*person*⟩; to frame ⟨*face, window*⟩; ~ **de rouge** to outline [sth] in red
(c) to frame ⟨*picture*⟩

**encaisser** /ãkese/ [1] *vtr* (a) to cash ⟨*cheque, sum of money*⟩
(b) (colloq) to take ⟨*blow, defeat*⟩; **je ne peux pas** ~ **ton frère** I can't stand your brother
IDIOMS ~ **le coup** (colloq) to take it all in one's stride

**encart** /ãkaʀ/ *nm* insert; ~ **publicitaire** promotional insert

**en-cas** /ãka/ *nm inv* snack

**encastrer** /ãkastʀe/ [1] **1** *vtr* to build in ⟨*oven, refrigerator*⟩; to fit ⟨*sink, hotplate*⟩; **baignoire encastrée** sunken bath
**2 s'encastrer** *v refl* (+ *v être*) to fit (**dans** into)

**encaustique** /ãkostik/ *nf* wax polish

**enceinte** /ãsɛ̃t/ **1** *adj f* ⟨*woman*⟩ pregnant
**2** *nf* (a) (mur d')~ surrounding wall
(b) (of prison, palace) compound; (of church) interior

**encens** /ãsã/ *nm inv* incense

**encenser** /ãsãse/ [1] *vtr* to sing the praises of ⟨*person*⟩; to acclaim ⟨*work of art*⟩

**encercler** /ãsɛʀkle/ [1] *vtr* (a) to surround, to encircle
(b) (with pen) to circle

**enchaînement** /ãʃɛnmã/ *nm* (a) (of events) chain
(b) sequence
(c) (in music, sport) transition

**enchaîner** /ãʃɛne/ [1] **1** *vtr* to chain up ⟨*person, animal*⟩; ~ **à** to chain to
**2** *vi* to go on; ~ **avec une nouvelle chanson** to move on to a new song
**3 s'enchaîner** *v refl* (+ *v être*) ⟨*shots, sequences in film*⟩ to follow on

**enchantement** /ãʃãtmã/ *nm* enchantment, spell; **comme par** ~ as if by magic

**enchanter** /ãʃãte/ [1] *vtr* (a) to delight; **ça ne m'enchante guère** it doesn't exactly thrill me; **enchanté (de faire votre connaissance)!** how do you do!
(b) **forêt enchantée** enchanted forest

**enchanteur, -eresse** /ãʃãtœʀ, tʀɛs/
**1** *adj* enchanting
**2** *nm,f* (a) enchanter/enchantress
(b) (figurative) charmer

**enchère** /ãʃɛʀ/ **1** *nf* bid
**2 enchères** *nf pl* **vente aux** ~**s** auction

**enchérir** /ãʃeʀiʀ/ [3] *vi* to bid; ~ **sur qn** to bid more than sb; ~ **sur une offre** to make a higher bid

**enchevêtrement** /ãʃ(ə)vɛtʀəmã/ *nm* (of threads) tangle; (of corridors, streets) labyrinth

**enchevêtrer** /ãʃ(ə)vetʀe/ [1] **1** *vtr* (a) to tangle [sth] up ⟨*threads*⟩
(b) **être enchevêtré** ⟨*sentence, plot*⟩ to be muddled; ⟨*case*⟩ to be complicated

**2 s'enchevêtrer** *v refl* (+ *v être*)
(a) ⟨*branches, threads*⟩ to get tangled
(b) ⟨*phrases, ideas*⟩ to become muddled

**enclave** /ãklav/ *nf* enclave

**enclencher** /ãklãʃe/ [1] **1** *vtr* (a) to set [sth] in motion ⟨*process*⟩
(b) to engage ⟨*mechanism*⟩
**2 s'enclencher** *v refl* (+ *v être*)
(a) ⟨*process*⟩ to get under way
(b) ⟨*mechanism*⟩ to engage

**enclin, ~e** /ãklɛ̃, in/ *adj* inclined (**à** to)

**enclos** /ãklo/ *nm inv* (gen) enclosure; (for animals) pen

**enclume** /ãklym/ *nf* (Tech, Anat) anvil

**encoche** /ãkɔʃ/ *nf* notch

**encoder** /ãkode/ [1] *vtr* to encode

**encodeur** /ãkodœʀ/ *nm* (Comput) encoder

**encolure** /ãkolyʀ/ *nf* (a) (of garment) neckline
(b) collar size
(c) (of animal) neck

**encombrant, ~e** /ãkɔ̃bʀã, ãt/ *adj*
(a) bulky; cumbersome
(b) ⟨*person, matter*⟩ troublesome

**encombre: sans encombre** /sãzãkɔ̃bʀ/ *phr* without a hitch

**encombré, ~e** /ãkɔ̃bʀe/ *adj* ⟨*road, sky*⟩ congested (**de** with); ⟨*room*⟩ cluttered

**encombrement** /ãkɔ̃bʀəmã/ *nm*
(a) traffic congestion
(b) (of switchboard) jamming
(c) (of room) cluttering
(d) (of furniture) bulk

**encombrer** /ãkɔ̃bʀe/ [1] **1** *vtr* (a) ⟨*object, people*⟩ to clutter up ⟨*room*⟩; to obstruct ⟨*road, path*⟩
(b) to jam ⟨*switchboard*⟩; to clutter up ⟨*mind*⟩
**2 s'encombrer** *v refl* (+ *v être*) s'~ **de** to burden oneself with; s'~ **l'esprit** to clutter up one's mind (**de** with)

**encontre: à l'encontre de** /alãkɔ̃tʀədə/ *phr* (a) counter to
(b) against
(c) toward(s)

**encorder: s'encorder** /ãkoʀde/ [1] *v refl* (+ *v être*) to rope up

**encore** /ãkoʀ/ **1** *adv* (a) still; **il n'est** ~ **que midi** it's only midday; **tu en es** ~ **là?** haven't you got (GB) *or* gotten (US) beyond that by now?; **qu'il soit impoli passe** ~, **mais...** the fact that he's rude is one thing, but...
(b) **pas** ~ not yet; **il n'est pas** ~ **rentré** he hasn't come home yet; he still hasn't come home; **cela ne s'est** ~ **jamais vu** it has never been seen before
(c) again; ~ **toi!** you again!; ~**!** encore!, more!; ~ **une fois** once more, once again; **qu'est-ce que j'ai** ~ **fait?** what have I done now?
(d) more; **mange** ~ **un peu** have some more to eat; **c'est** ~ **mieux** it's even better

(e) ∼ un gâteau? another cake?; pendant ∼ trois jours for another three days; qu'est-ce qu'il te faut ∼? what more do you need?

(f) ∼ faut-il qu'elle accepte but she still has to accept; si ∼ il était généreux! if he were at least generous!

(g) only, just; il y a ∼ trois mois only three months ago

**2** **et encore** *phr* if that; c'est tout au plus mangeable, et ∼! it's only just edible, if that!

**3** **encore que** *phr* even though

**encourageant**, ∼**e** /ãkuraʒɑ̃, ɑ̃t/ *adj* encouraging

**encouragement** /ãkuraʒmɑ̃/ *nm* encouragement

**encourager** /ãkuraʒe/ [13] *vtr* **(a)** to encourage (à faire to do)
**(b)** to cheer [sb] on

**encourir** /ãkurir/ [26] *vtr* to incur

**encrasser** /ãkrase/ [1] *vtr* **(a)** to clog [sth] (up) ⟨filter, artery⟩; to make [sth] sooty ⟨chimney⟩
**(b)** to dirty; (Aut) to foul up ⟨spark plugs⟩

**encre** /ãkr/ *nf* ink
■ ∼ de Chine Indian (GB) *or* India (US) ink; ∼ sympathique invisible ink
IDIOMS cela a fait couler beaucoup d'∼ a lot of ink has been spilled over this; se faire un sang d'∼ to be worried sick

**encrier** /ãkrije/ *nm* inkwell; ink pot

**encroûter**: **s'encroûter** /ãkrute/ [1] *v refl* (colloq) to get in a rut

**encyclopédie** /ãsiklɔpedi/ *nf* encyclopedia

**endetté**, ∼**e** /ãdete/ *adj* in debt

**endettement** /ãdɛtmɑ̃/ *nm* debt

**endetter** /ãdete/ [1] **1** *vtr* to put [sb] into debt
**2** **s'endetter** *v refl* (+ *v être*) to get into debt

**endiablé**, ∼**e** /ãdjable/ *adj* ⟨rhythm⟩ furious

**endiguer** /ãdige/ [1] *vtr* to confine ⟨river⟩; to contain ⟨demonstrators⟩; to curb ⟨speculation⟩

**endimanché**, ∼**e** /ãdimɑ̃ʃe/ *adj* in one's Sunday best

**endive** /ãdiv/ *nf* chicory (GB), endive (US)

**endoctriner** /ãdɔktrine/ [1] *vtr* to indoctrinate

**endolori**, ∼**e** /ãdɔlɔri/ *adj* aching

**endolorir** /ãdɔlɔrir/ [3] *vtr* to make [sb/sth] ache

**endommager** /ãdɔmaʒe/ [13] *vtr* to damage

**endormi**, ∼**e** /ãdɔrmi/ *adj* **(a)** ⟨person, animal⟩ sleeping, asleep
**(b)** ⟨village, mind⟩ sleepy

**endormir** /ãdɔrmir/ [30] **1** *vtr* **(a)** to send [sb] to sleep ⟨child⟩; ⟨person, substance⟩ to put [sb] to sleep ⟨patient⟩
**(b)** (from boredom) ⟨person, lecture⟩ to send [sb] to sleep ⟨person⟩
**(c)** to dupe ⟨person, opinion, enemy⟩

**(d)** to allay ⟨suspicion⟩; to numb ⟨faculties⟩
**2** **s'endormir** *v refl* (+ *v être*) **(a)** to fall asleep
**(b)** to get to sleep
**(c)** (figurative) to sit back

**endossable** /ãdosabl/ *adj* ⟨cheque⟩ endorsable

**endosser** /ãdose/ [1] *vtr* **(a)** to take on ⟨role, responsibility⟩
**(b)** to endorse ⟨cheque⟩

**endroit** /ãdrwa/ **1** *nm* **(a)** place; par ∼s in places; à quel ∼? where?
**(b)** (of fabric) right side; à l'∼ (of object) the right way up; (of garment) the right way round (GB) *or* around (US)
**2** **à l'endroit de** *phr* toward(s)

**enduire** /ãdɥir/ [69] **1** *vtr* to coat ⟨de with⟩
**2** **s'enduire** *v refl* (+ *v être*) s'∼ de to put [sth] on

**enduit** /ãdɥi/ *nm* **(a)** coating
**(b)** filler

**endurance** /ãdyrãs/ *nf* **(a)** (of person) stamina; ∼ à resistance to
**(b)** (of engine) endurance

**endurant**, ∼**e** /ãdyrɑ̃, ɑ̃t/ *adj* ⟨person, athlete⟩ tough; ⟨engine, vehicle⟩ hard-wearing

**endurcir** /ãdyrsir/ [3] **1** *vtr* **(a)** ⟨sport, hard work⟩ to strengthen ⟨body, character⟩
**(b)** ⟨ordeal⟩ to harden ⟨person⟩
**2** **s'endurcir** *v refl* (+ *v être*) **(a)** to become stronger
**(b)** to become hardened

**endurer** /ãdyre/ [1] *vtr* **(a)** to endure; faire ∼ qch à qn to put sb through sth
**(b)** to put up with

**énergétique** /enɛrʒetik/ *adj* **(a)** ⟨needs, resources⟩ energy
**(b)** ⟨food⟩ high-calorie

**énergie** /enɛrʒi/ *nf* energy; faire des économies d'∼ to save energy; trouver des ∼s douces to find safe energy sources; avec l'∼ du désespoir driven on by despair; avec ∼ ⟨work⟩ energetically; ⟨protest⟩ strongly
■ ∼ éolienne windpower; ∼ nucléaire nuclear power *ou* energy; ∼ solaire solar power

**énergique** /enɛrʒik/ *adj* **(a)** ⟨person, gesture⟩ energetic; ⟨handshake⟩ vigorous; ⟨face, expression⟩ resolute
**(b)** ⟨action⟩ tough; ⟨protest⟩ strong; ⟨refusal⟩ firm; ⟨intervention⟩ forceful

**énergumène** /enɛrgymɛn/ *nmf* oddball

**énervant**, ∼**e** /enɛrvɑ̃, ɑ̃t/ *adj* irritating

**énervé**, ∼**e** /enɛrve/ *adj* **(a)** irritated
**(b)** nervous; ⟨child⟩ overexcited

**énervement** /enɛrvəmɑ̃/ *nm* **(a)** irritation
**(b)** agitation; elle pleura d'∼ she was so on edge that she cried

**énerver** /enɛrve/ [1] **1** *vtr* **(a)** to put [sb] on edge
**(b)** ∼ qn to get on sb's nerves, to irritate sb
**2** **s'énerver** *v refl* (+ *v être*) to get worked up

**enfance** /ãfãs/ *nf* childhood; la petite ∼ early childhood

**IDIOMS c'est l'~ de l'art** it's child's play

**enfant** /ɑ̃fɑ̃/ *nmf* child; infant; **être ~ unique** to be an only child

■ **~ de chœur** altar boy; **ce n'est pas un ~ de chœur** (figurative) he's no angel

**enfanter** /ɑ̃fɑ̃te/ [1] *vtr* to give birth to

**enfantillage** /ɑ̃fɑ̃tijaʒ/ *nm* childishness

**enfantin**, **~e** /ɑ̃fɑ̃tɛ̃, in/ *adj* (a) simple, easy

(b) **mode ~e** children's fashion

(c) childish

**enfer** /ɑ̃fɛʀ/ *nm* Hell; (figurative) hell; **aller à un train d'~** (colloq) to go hell for leather (colloq); **soirée d'~** (colloq) hell of a party (colloq)

**enfermer** /ɑ̃fɛʀme/ [1] 1 *vtr* (a) to shut [sth] in ⟨*animal*⟩; to lock [sth] up ⟨*money, jewellery*⟩; to lock [sb] up ⟨*person*⟩; **elle est bonne à ~** (colloq) she's stark raving mad (colloq)

(b) **~ qn dans un rôle** to confine sb to a role; **~ qn dans une situation** to trap sb in a situation

2 **s'enfermer** *v refl* (+ *v être*) (a) (gen) to lock oneself in; (accidentally) to get locked in; (in order to be alone) to shut oneself away; **ne reste pas enfermé toute la journée!** don't stay cooped up indoors all day!

(b) **s'~ dans** to retreat into; **s'~ dans le mutisme** to remain obstinately silent

**enfiévré**, **~e** /ɑ̃fjevʀe/ *adj* ⟨*imagination*⟩ fevered; ⟨*atmosphere*⟩ feverish; ⟨*speech*⟩ fiery

**enfilade** /ɑ̃filad/ *nf* (of traps) succession; (of houses, tables) row

**enfiler** /ɑ̃file/ [1] 1 *vtr* (a) to slip on

(b) to thread ⟨*piece of thread, needle*⟩

2 **s'enfiler** *v refl* (+ *v être*) (a) (colloq) to guzzle down

(b) **s'~ dans** to take ⟨*street*⟩

**enfin** /ɑ̃fɛ̃/ *adv* finally; lastly; **~ et surtout** last but not least; **~ seuls!** alone at last!; **mais ~, cessez de vous disputer!** for heaven's sake, stop arguing!; **il pleut tous les jours, ~ presque** it rains every day, well almost

**enflammé**, **~e** /ɑ̃flame/ *adj* (a) burning, on fire

(b) ⟨*person, declaration*⟩ passionate; ⟨*speech*⟩ impassioned

(c) (Med) ⟨*throat, wound*⟩ inflamed

(d) ⟨*sky*⟩ ablaze

**enflammer** /ɑ̃flame/ [1] 1 *vtr* (a) to set fire to [sth]

(b) to inflame ⟨*public opinion, mind*⟩; to fire ⟨*imagination*⟩; to fuel ⟨*anger*⟩

2 **s'enflammer** *v refl* (+ *v être*) (a) ⟨*house, paper*⟩ to go up in flames; ⟨*wood*⟩ to catch fire

(b) ⟨*eyes*⟩ to blaze; ⟨*imagination*⟩ to be fired (**de** with; **à la vue de** by); ⟨*country*⟩ to explode; **s'~ pour qn** to become passionate about sb; **s'~ pour qch** to get carried away by sth

**enfler** /ɑ̃fle/ [1] 1 *vtr* to exaggerate ⟨*story, event*⟩

2 *vi* (a) ⟨*part of body*⟩ to swell (up); ⟨*river, sea*⟩ to swell

(b) ⟨*rumour, anger*⟩ to spread

3 **s'enfler** *v refl* (+ *v être*) ⟨*anger*⟩ to mount; ⟨*voice*⟩ to rise; ⟨*rumour*⟩ to grow

**enfoncement** /ɑ̃fɔ̃smɑ̃/ *nm* (a) recess; dip

(b) **l'~ du pays dans la récession** the country's slide into recession

**enfoncer** /ɑ̃fɔ̃se/ [12] 1 *vtr* (a) to push in ⟨*cork, stake*⟩; **~ ses mains dans ses poches** to dig one's hands into one's pockets; **~ son doigt dans** to stick one's finger into; **~ un clou dans qch** to knock a nail into sth

(b) to break down ⟨*door*⟩; to break through ⟨*enemy lines*⟩; **~ des portes ouvertes** to state the obvious

(c) **ne m'enfonce pas davantage** don't rub it in

2 **s'enfoncer** *v refl* (+ *v être*) (a) **s'~ dans la neige** to sink in the snow; **s'~ dans l'erreur** to make error after error; **les piquets s'enfoncent facilement** the posts go in easily; **s'~ une épine dans le doigt** to get a thorn in one's finger; **s'~ dans la forêt** to go into the forest

(b) (colloq) to make things worse for oneself

**enfouir** /ɑ̃fwiʀ/ [3] 1 *vtr* (a) to bury

(b) **~ qch dans un sac** to shove sth into a bag

2 **s'enfouir** *v refl* (+ *v être*) **s'~ sous les couvertures** to burrow under the blankets

**enfourcher** /ɑ̃fuʀʃe/ [1] *vtr* to mount ⟨*horse*⟩; to get on ⟨*motorbike*⟩

**enfourner** /ɑ̃fuʀne/ [1] *vtr* (a) to put [sth] in the oven

(b) (colloq) to stuff down ⟨*food*⟩

**enfreindre** /ɑ̃fʀɛ̃dʀ/ [55] *vtr* to infringe

**enfuir: s'enfuir** /ɑ̃fɥiʀ/ [9] *v refl* (+ *v être*)

(a) to run away; ⟨*bird*⟩ to fly away

(b) to escape

**enfumer** /ɑ̃fyme/ [1] *vtr* to fill [sth] with smoke; **tu nous enfumes avec tes cigares!** you're smoking us out with your cigars!

**engagé**, **~e** /ɑ̃ɡaʒe/ *nm,f* enlisted man/ woman

**engageant**, **~e** /ɑ̃ɡaʒɑ̃, ɑ̃t/ *adj* ⟨*person, manner*⟩ welcoming; ⟨*dish, place*⟩ inviting

**engagement** /ɑ̃ɡaʒmɑ̃/ *nm*

(a) commitment; **prendre l'~ de faire** to undertake to do

(b) involvement

(c) (Mil) enlistment

**engager** /ɑ̃ɡaʒe/ [13] 1 *vtr* (a) to hire ⟨*staff*⟩; to enlist ⟨*soldier*⟩; to engage ⟨*artist*⟩

(b) to begin ⟨*process, reform policy*⟩; **nous avons engagé la conversation** we struck up a conversation

(c) to commit, to bind ⟨*person*⟩

(d) to stake ⟨*honour*⟩; **~ sa parole** to give one's word

(e) **~ qch dans** to put sth in

(f) to lay out ⟨*capital*⟩

(g) **~ qn à faire** to urge sb to do

⋯⟡

**(h)** (Sport) ∼ qn dans une compétition to
enter sb for a competition
**(i)** to pawn ⟨*valuables*⟩
**2** **s'engager** *v refl* (+ *v être*) **(a)** to
promise (à faire to do); **s'**∼ **vis-à-vis de qn** to
make a commitment to sb
**(b)** **s'**∼ **dans un projet** to embark on a
project
**(c)** to get involved
**(d)** **s'**∼ **sur une route** to go into a road
**(e)** ⟨*lawsuit*⟩ to begin
**(f)** **s'**∼ **dans l'armée** to join the army
**engelure** /ãʒlyʀ/ *nf* chilblain
**engendrer** /ãʒãdʀe/ [1] *vtr* **(a)** to engender
**(b)** ⟨*woman*⟩ to give birth to; ⟨*man*⟩ to father
**engin** /ãʒɛ̃/ *nm* **(a)** device
**(b)** vehicle
**(c)** piece of equipment
**englober** /ãglɔbe/ [1] *vtr* to include
**engloutir** /ãglutiʀ/ [3] *vtr* **(a)** ⟨*sea, storm,
fog*⟩ to engulf, to swallow up
**(b)** (colloq) to gulp [sth] down
**(c)** ⟨*person*⟩ to squander ⟨*money*⟩
**engoncé**, ∼**e** /ãgɔ̃se/ *adj* il était ∼ dans
une veste trop étroite he was squeezed into a
tight jacket
**engorger** /ãgɔʀʒe/ [13] *vtr* **(a)** to block (up)
⟨*pipes, drains*⟩
**(b)** to clog up ⟨*roads*⟩
**engouement** /ãgumã/ *nm* (for thing, activity)
passion; (for person) infatuation
**engouer: s'engouer** /ãgwe/ [1] *v refl*
(+ *v être*) **s'**∼ **de** to develop a passion for
**engouffrer: s'engouffrer** /ãgufʀe/ [1]
*v refl* (+ *v être*) (into a room) to rush; (into a taxi)
to dive
**engourdi**, ∼**e** /ãguʀdi/ *adj* ⟨*limb, body*⟩
numb (**par, de** with); ⟨*person*⟩ drowsy; ⟨*town*⟩
sleepy; ⟨*mind*⟩ dull(ed)
**engourdir: s'engourdir** /ãguʀdiʀ/ [3]
*v refl* (+ *v être*) ⟨*limb*⟩ to go numb; ⟨*mind*⟩ to
grow dull
**engourdissement** /ãguʀdismã/ *nm*
**(a)** ⟨physical⟩ numbness; ⟨mental⟩ drowsiness
**(b)** (of body) numbing; (of mind) dulling
**engrais** /ãgʀɛ/ *nm inv* manure; fertilizer
**engraisser** /ãgʀese/ [1] **1** *vtr* **(a)** to fatten
⟨*cattle*⟩
**(b)** to fertilize ⟨*soil*⟩
**2** *vi* to get fat
**3** **s'engraisser** *v refl* (+ *v être*) (colloq) **s'**∼
(**sur le dos de qn**) to grow fat (off sb's back)
(colloq)
**engranger** /ãgʀãʒe/ [13] *vtr* to gather in
⟨*harvest*⟩; (figurative) to store; to store up
**engrenage** /ãgʀənaʒ/ *nm* **(a)** gears
**(b)** (figurative) (of violence) spiral
**engueuler** (slang) /ãgœle/ [1] **1** *vtr* to tell
[sb] off; to give [sb] an earful (colloq)
**2** **s'engueuler** *v refl* (+ *v être*) to have a
row
**enhardir: s'enhardir** /ãaʀdiʀ/ [3] *v refl*
(+ *v être*) to become bolder
**énième** /ɛnjɛm/ *adj* umpteenth

**énigmatique** /enigmatik/ *adj* enigmatic
**énigme** /enigm/ *nf* **(a)** enigma, mystery
**(b)** riddle; **parler par** ∼**s** to speak in riddles
**enivrant**, ∼**e** /ãnivʀã, ãt/ *adj* intoxicating
**enivrement** /ãnivʀəmã/ *nm* intoxication
**enivrer** /ãnivʀe/ [1] **1** *vtr* **(a)** to make [sb]
drunk
**(b)** ∼ qn ⟨*success*⟩ to go to sb's head
**2** **s'enivrer** *v refl* (+ *v être*) to get drunk
**enjambée** /ãʒãbe/ *nf* stride; **avancer/
s'éloigner à grandes** ∼**s** to stride forward/off
**enjamber** /ãʒãbe/ [1] *vtr* to step over
⟨*obstacle*⟩
**enjeu**, *pl* ∼**x** /ãʒø/ *nm* (Games) stake;
**analyser l'**∼ **des élections** to analyse (GB)
what is at stake in the elections
**enjoindre** /ãʒwɛ̃dʀ/ [56] *vtr* ∼ à qn de faire
to enjoin sb to do
**enjôler** /ãʒole/ [1] *vtr* to beguile
**enjoliver** /ãʒɔlive/ [1] *vtr* to embellish
**enjoliveur** /ãʒɔlivœʀ/ *nm* hubcap
**enjoué**, ∼**e** /ãʒwe/ *adj* ⟨*character*⟩
cheerful; ⟨*tone*⟩ light-hearted
**enlacer** /ãlase/ [12] **1** *vtr* to embrace;
⟨*snake*⟩ to wrap itself around ⟨*prey*⟩
**2** **s'enlacer** *v refl* (+ *v être*) ⟨*people*⟩ to
embrace; ⟨*body*⟩ to intertwine
**enlaidir** /ãlediʀ/ [3] *vtr* to spoil ⟨*landscape*⟩;
to make [sb] look ugly ⟨*person*⟩
**enlevé**, ∼**e** /ãlve/ *adj* lively
**enlèvement** /ãlɛvmã/ *nm* kidnapping
(GB), abduction
**enlever** /ãlve/ [16] **1** *vtr* **(a)** to take [sth]
away, to remove ⟨*piece of furniture, book*⟩; to
take [sth] down ⟨*curtains, pictures*⟩; to take
[sth] off ⟨*garment*⟩; to move, to remove
⟨*vehicle*⟩
**(b)** to remove ⟨*stain, paint*⟩
**(c)** to take ⟨*person, object*⟩ away; ∼ à qn
l'envie de partir to put sb off going
**(d)** to kidnap; to carry [sb] off
**(e)** to carry [sth] off ⟨*trophy*⟩; to capture
⟨*market*⟩
**2** **s'enlever** *v refl* (+ *v être*) **(a)** ⟨*varnish*⟩
to come off; ⟨*stain*⟩ to come out
**(b)** ⟨*part, section*⟩ to be detachable
**(c)** (colloq) **enlève-toi de là** get off (colloq)
**enlisement** /ãlizmã/ *nm* sinking;
(of negotiations) stalemate; (of movement)
collapse
**enliser** /ãlize/ [1] **1** *vtr* to get [sth] stuck
**2** **s'enliser** *v refl* (+ *v être*) **(a)** ⟨*boat,
vehicle*⟩ to get stuck
**(b)** ⟨*inquiry, negotiations*⟩ to drag on
**enluminure** /ãlyminyʀ/ *nf* illumination
**enneigé**, ∼**e** /ãneʒe/ *adj* ⟨*summit*⟩ snowy;
⟨*road*⟩ covered in snow
**enneigement** /ãnɛʒmã/ *nm* bulletin d'∼
snow report
**ennemi**, ∼**e** /ɛnmi/ **1** *adj* **(a)** (Mil) enemy
**(b)** (gen) hostile
**2** *nm,f* enemy
**3** *nm* (Mil) enemy; **passer à l'**∼ to go over to
the enemy

**ennui** /ɑ̃nɥi/ *nm* **(a)** boredom; **tromper l'~** to escape from boredom; **quel ~!** what a bore!
**(b)** problem; **avoir des ~s** to have problems; **j'ai des ~s avec la police** I'm in trouble with the police; **s'attirer des ~s** to get into trouble

**ennuyé**, **~e** /ɑ̃nɥije/ *adj* **(a)** bored
**(b)** embarrassed; **j'étais très ~ de laisser les enfants seuls** I felt awful about leaving the children on their own
**(c) j'aurais été très ~ si je n'avais pas eu la clé** I would have been in real trouble if I hadn't had the key

**ennuyer** /ɑ̃nɥije/ [22] **1** *vtr* **(a)** to bore
**(b)** to bother; **si ça ne vous ennuie pas trop** if you don't mind
**(c)** to annoy
**(d)** to hassle (colloq)
**2 s'ennuyer** *v refl* (+ *v être*) **(a)** to be bored; to get bored
**(b) s'~ de** to miss ⟨friend⟩

**ennuyeux**, **-euse** /ɑ̃nɥijø, øz/ *adj*
**(a)** boring
**(b)** tedious
**(c)** annoying
IDIOMS **être ~ comme la pluie** to be as dull as ditchwater

**énoncé** /enɔ̃se/ *nm* **(a)** (of exam subject) wording ⟨de of⟩; **l'~ d'une théorie** the exposition of a theory
**(b)** (of fact) statement ⟨de of⟩

**énoncer** /enɔ̃se/ [12] *vtr* to pronounce ⟨verdict⟩; to set out, to state ⟨facts⟩; to expound ⟨theory⟩

**enorgueillir: s'enorgueillir** /ɑ̃nɔʀɡœjiʀ/ [3] *v refl* (+ *v être*) to pride oneself ⟨de on⟩

**énorme** /enɔʀm/ *adj* **(a)** ⟨object, person⟩ huge, enormous
**(b)** ⟨success, effort⟩ tremendous; ⟨mistake⟩ terrible; ⟨lie⟩ outrageous

**énormément** /enɔʀmemɑ̃/ *adv* a tremendous amount; a great deal; **~ de temps** a tremendous amount of time; **ça m'a ~ plu** I liked it immensely

**énormité** /enɔʀmite/ *nf* **(a)** (of figure, size) hugeness; (of lie) enormity
**(b)** outrageous remark

**enquérir: s'enquérir** /ɑ̃keʀiʀ/ [35] *v refl* (+ *v être*) **s'~ de** to enquire about

**enquête** /ɑ̃kɛt/ *nf* **(a)** (Law) inquiry, investigation; (into a death) inquest; **~ de police** police investigation
**(b)** (by journalist) investigation
**(c)** (by sociologist) survey

**enquêter** /ɑ̃kete/ [1] *vi* ⟨policeman⟩ to carry out an investigation; ⟨expert⟩ to hold an inquiry

**enquêteur**, **-trice** /ɑ̃ketœʀ, tʀis/ *nm,f*
**(a)** investigating officer
**(b)** pollster
**(c)** interviewer

**enquiquinant**, **~e** /ɑ̃kikinɑ̃, ɑ̃t/ *adj*
(colloq) annoying; boring

**enquiquiner** /ɑ̃kikine/ [1] (colloq) **1** *vtr*
**~ qn** to get on sb's nerves; to pester sb
**2 s'enquiquiner** *v refl* (+ *v être*) **s'~ à faire** to go to the trouble of doing

**enraciner: s'enraciner** /ɑ̃ʀasine/ [1] *v refl* (+ *v être*) **(a)** to take root
**(b)** (figurative) ⟨person⟩ to put down roots; ⟨custom, idea⟩ to take root

**enragé**, **~e** /ɑ̃ʀaʒe/ *adj* **(a)** fanatical
**(b)** enraged
**(c)** (Med) rabid
IDIOMS **manger de la vache ~e** (colloq) to go through hard times

**enrageant**, **~e** /ɑ̃ʀaʒɑ̃, ɑ̃t/ *adj* infuriating

**enrager** /ɑ̃ʀaʒe/ [13] *vi* to be furious; **faire ~ qn** to tease sb

**enrayer** /ɑ̃ʀeje/ [21] **1** *vtr* **(a)** to check ⟨epidemic, development⟩; to curb ⟨inflation⟩; to stop [sth] escalating ⟨crisis⟩
**(b)** to jam ⟨mechanism, gun⟩
**2 s'enrayer** *v refl* (+ *v être*) to get jammed

**enregistrement** /ɑ̃ʀəʒistʀəmɑ̃/ *nm*
**(a)** (of music) recording
**(b)** (of data) recording; (of order) taking down
**(c)** (of baggage) check-in

**enregistrer** /ɑ̃ʀəʒistʀe/ [1] *vtr* **(a)** to record ⟨cassette, album⟩
**(b)** to note ⟨progress, failure⟩; to record ⟨rise, drop⟩
**(c)** to make a record of ⟨expenses⟩; to take ⟨order⟩; to record ⟨data⟩; to set ⟨record⟩
**(d)** to register ⟨birth, claim⟩
**(e)** to check in ⟨baggage⟩
**(f) c'est enregistré, j'enregistre** (colloq) I've made a mental note of it

**enrhumer: s'enrhumer** /ɑ̃ʀyme/ [1] *v refl* (+ *v être*) to catch a cold

**enrichir** /ɑ̃ʀiʃiʀ/ [3] **1** *vtr* **(a)** to make [sb] rich ⟨person⟩; to bring wealth to ⟨country⟩
**(b)** to enrich, to enhance ⟨collection, book⟩
**2 s'enrichir** *v refl* (+ *v être*) **(a)** ⟨person⟩ to become *or* grow rich
**(b)** to be enriched

**enrichissant**, **~e** /ɑ̃ʀiʃisɑ̃, ɑ̃t/ *adj*
⟨experience⟩ rewarding; ⟨relationship⟩ fulfilling

**enrober** /ɑ̃ʀɔbe/ [1] *vtr* **(a)** to coat
**(b)** (figurative) to wrap up ⟨news⟩

**enrôlement** /ɑ̃ʀolmɑ̃/ *nm* (in the army) enlistment; (in political party) enrolment (GB)

**enrôler** /ɑ̃ʀole/ [1] **1** *vtr* to recruit
**2 s'enrôler** *v refl* (+ *v être*) to enlist

**enrouer: s'enrouer** /ɑ̃ʀwe/ [1] *v refl* (+ *v être*) ⟨voice⟩ to go hoarse; ⟨person⟩ to make oneself hoarse; **d'une voix enrouée** hoarsely

**enrouler** /ɑ̃ʀule/ [1] **1** *vtr* **(a)** to wind
**(b)** to wrap
**2 s'enrouler** *v refl* (+ *v être*) **(a)** ⟨thread, tape⟩ to wind
**(b)** ⟨person, animal⟩ to curl up

**ENS** /œɛnɛs/ *nf: abbr* ▶ ÉCOLE

**ensabler: s'ensabler** /ɑ̃sable/ [1] v refl
(+ v être) ⟨vehicle⟩ to get stuck in the sand;
⟨boat⟩ to get stranded ⟨on a sandbank⟩

**ensanglanter** /ɑ̃sɑ̃glɑ̃te/ [1] vtr (a) to
cover [sth] with blood
(b) to bring bloodshed to ⟨country⟩

**enseignant, ~e** /ɑ̃sɛɲɑ̃, ɑ̃t/ **1** adj corps
~ teaching profession
**2** nm,f (Sch) teacher; (at university) lecturer

**enseigne** /ɑ̃sɛɲ/ nf (a) (shop) sign;
~ lumineuse neon sign
(b) (Mil, Naut) ensign
IDIOMS nous sommes logés à la même ~ we
are in the same boat

**enseignement** /ɑ̃sɛɲmɑ̃/ nm
(a) education; l'~ supérieur higher
education
(b) teaching; méthodes d'~ teaching
methods
(c) lesson
■ ~ par correspondance distance learning;
~ professionnel vocational training;
~ religieux religious instruction

**enseigner** /ɑ̃sɛɲe/ [1] vtr to teach

**ensemble** /ɑ̃sɑ̃bl/ **1** adv (a) together
(b) at the same time
**2** nm (a) group; un ~ de personnes a group
of people; une vue d'~ an overall view; plan
d'~ d'une ville general plan of a town; dans
l'~ by and large; dans l'~ de throughout;
dans son or leur ~ as a whole
(b) (of luggage, measures) set
(c) unity, cohesion; former un bel ~ to form
a harmonious whole
(d) (of gestures) coordination; (of sounds)
unison; un mouvement d'~ a coordinated
movement
(e) (in mathematics) set
(f) (Mus) ensemble
(g) (of offices) complex; ~ hôtelier hotel
complex; ~ industriel industrial estate (GB)
or park (US)
(h) (set of clothes) outfit; suit

**ensevelir** /ɑ̃səvəliʀ/ [3] vtr to bury

**ensoleillé, ~e** /ɑ̃sɔleje/ adj sunny

**ensommeillé, ~e** /ɑ̃sɔmeje/ adj sleepy

**ensorcelé, ~e** /ɑ̃sɔʀsəle/ adj enchanted

**ensorceler** /ɑ̃sɔʀsəle/ [19] vtr (a) to cast
or to put a spell on
(b) to bewitch, to enchant

**ensorceleur, -euse** /ɑ̃sɔʀsəlœʀ, øz/
nm,f charmer

**ensuite** /ɑ̃sɥit/ adv (a) then; after; next;
très bien, mais ~? fine, but then what?; il ne
me l'a dit qu'~ he only told me later
(b) secondly

**ensuivre: s'ensuivre** /ɑ̃sɥivʀ/ [19] v refl
(+ v être) to follow, to ensue

**entacher** /ɑ̃taʃe/ [1] vtr to mar ⟨relations⟩

**entaille** /ɑ̃taj/ nf (a) cut; gash
(b) notch

**entailler** /ɑ̃taje/ [1] **1** vtr to cut into;
(deeply) to make a gash in
**2** s'entailler v refl (+ v être) s'~ le doigt
to cut one's finger, to gash one's finger

**entame** /ɑ̃tam/ nf (a) (Culin) first slice
(b) (in cards) lead

**entamer** /ɑ̃tame/ [1] vtr (a) to start ⟨day,
activity⟩; to initiate ⟨procedure⟩; to open
⟨negotiations⟩
(b) to undermine ⟨credibility⟩
(c) to eat into ⟨savings⟩
(d) to cut into ⟨loaf, roast⟩; to open ⟨bottle,
jar⟩; to start eating ⟨dessert⟩
(e) to cut into ⟨skin, wood⟩
(f) to eat into ⟨metal⟩

**entartrer** /ɑ̃taʀtʀe/ [1] **1** vtr to fur up
(GB), to scale up
**2** s'entartrer v refl (+ v être) to scale up;
⟨teeth⟩ to be covered in tartar

**entassement** /ɑ̃tɑsmɑ̃/ nm (a) piling up;
cramming together
(b) pile; heap

**entasser** /ɑ̃tɑse/ [1] **1** vtr (a) to pile
⟨books, clothes⟩
(b) to hoard ⟨money, old things⟩
(c) to pack, to cram ⟨people, objects⟩ (dans
into)
**2** s'entasser v refl (+ v être) ⟨objects⟩ to
pile up; ⟨people⟩ to squeeze (dans into; sur
onto)

**entendement** /ɑ̃tɑ̃dmɑ̃/ nm
understanding; cela dépasse l'~ it's beyond
belief

**entendre** /ɑ̃tɑ̃dʀ/ [6] **1** vtr (a) to hear
⟨noise, word⟩; faire ~ un cri to give a cry; je
n'en ai jamais entendu parler I've never
heard of it; on n'entend plus parler de lui his
name is not mentioned any more
(b) ⟨judge⟩ to hear ⟨witness⟩; à t'~, tout va
bien according to you, everything is fine; elle
ne veut rien ~ she won't listen
(c) to understand; il agit comme il l'entend
he does as he likes; elle a laissé ~ que she
intimated that; ils ne l'entendent pas de cette
oreille they don't see it that way
(d) to mean; qu'entends-tu par là? what do
you mean by that?
(e) ~ faire to intend doing; j'entends qu'on
fasse ce que je dis I expect people to do
what I say
**2** s'entendre v refl (+ v être) (a) to get on
or along
(b) to agree (sur on)
(c) ⟨noise⟩ to be heard
(d) to hear oneself; ⟨two or more people⟩ to
hear each other
(e) phrase qui peut s'~ de plusieurs façons
sentence which can be understood in several
ways

**entendu, ~e** /ɑ̃tɑ̃dy/ **1** pp ▶ ENTENDRE
**2** pp adj (a) 'tu viens demain?'—'~'! 'will
you come tomorrow?'—'OK!' (colloq)
(b) d'un air ~ with a knowing look
**3** bien entendu phr of course

**entente** /ɑ̃tɑ̃t/ nf (a) harmony; vivre en
bonne ~ avec qn to be on good terms with
sb
(b) understanding
(c) arrangement

**entériner** /ɑ̃teʀine/ [1] vtr (a) to ratify

**(b)** to confirm

**enterré**, **~e** /ātɛʀe/ *adj* buried; **mort et ~** dead and buried

**enterrement** /ātɛʀmā/ *nm* **(a)** burial
**(b)** funeral; **faire une tête d'~** (colloq) to look gloomy

**enterrer** /ātɛʀe/ [1] *vtr* to bury
IDIOMS **~ sa vie de garçon** to have a stag party

**entêtant**, **~e** /ātɛtā, āt/ *adj* ⟨*aroma*⟩ heady; ⟨*music*⟩ insistent

**en-tête**, *pl* **~s** /ātɛt/ *nm* heading

**entêtement** /ātɛtmā/ *nm* stubbornness

**entêter**: **s'entêter** /ātete/ [1] *v refl* (+ *v être*) **(a)** to be stubborn
**(b)** to persist

**enthousiasme** /ātuzjasm/ *nm* enthusiasm

**enthousiasmer** /ātuzjasme/ [1] *vtr* to fill [sb] with enthusiasm

**enthousiaste** /ātuzjast/ *adj* enthusiastic

**enticher**: **s'enticher** /ātiʃe/ [1] *v refl* (+ *v être*) **s'~ de** to become infatuated with ⟨*person*⟩

**entier**, **-ière** /ātje, ɛʀ/ [1] *adj* **(a)** whole; **manger un pain ~** to eat a whole loaf; **des heures entières** for hours on end; **lait ~** full-fat milk
**(b)** ⟨*success, satisfaction*⟩ complete; **avoir l'entière responsabilité de qch** to have full responsibility for sth
**(c)** ⟨*object, reputation*⟩ intact; **le mystère reste ~** the mystery remains unsolved
**(d)** **avoir un caractère ~** to be thoroughgoing
[2] *nm* (in mathematics) integer

**entièrement** /ātjɛʀmā/ *adv* entirely, completely; **~ équipé** fully equipped

**entonner** /ātɔne/ [1] *vtr* to start singing ⟨*song*⟩

**entonnoir** /ātɔnwaʀ/ *nm* **(a)** funnel
**(b)** crater

**entorse** /ātɔʀs/ *nf* **(a)** (Med) sprain
**(b)** (figurative) infringement (**à** of); **faire une ~ au règlement** to bend the rules

**entortiller** /ātɔʀtije/ [1] *vtr* **(a)** to wind (**autour de qch** round (GB) sth)
**(b)** to tangle up
[2] **s'entortiller** *v refl* (+ *v être*) ⟨*thread, wool*⟩ to get entangled (**dans** in)

**entourage** /ātuʀaʒ/ *nm* **(a)** family circle
**(b)** circle (of friends); **on dit dans son ~ que** people close to him/her say that

**entouré**, **~e** /ātuʀe/ [1] *pp* ▶ ENTOURER
[2] *adj* **(a)** ⟨*person*⟩ popular
**(b)** **nos patients sont très ~s** our patients are well looked after

**entourer** /ātuʀe/ [1] [1] *vtr* **(a)** to surround
**(b)** **~ qch de qch** to put sth around sth; **~ qch de mystère** to shroud sth in mystery
**(c)** to rally round (GB) *or* around (US) ⟨*sick person*⟩
[2] **s'entourer** *v refl* (+ *v être*) **s'~ d'objets**

to surround oneself with things; **s'~ de précautions** to take every possible precaution

**entracte** /ātʀakt/ *nm* intermission

**entraider**: **s'entraider** /ātʀede/ [1] *v refl* (+ *v être*) to help each other *or* one another

**entrailles** /ātʀaj/ *nf pl* (of animal) innards

**entrain** /ātʀɛ̃/ *nm* **(a)** (of person) spirit, go (GB) (colloq); **retrouver son ~** to cheer up
**(b)** (of party, discussion) liveliness; **sans ~** half-hearted

**entraînant**, **~e** /ātʀɛnā, āt/ *adj* lively

**entraînement** /ātʀɛnmā/ *nm* **(a)** training, coaching
**(b)** practice (GB); **avoir de l'~** to be highly trained; **l'~ à la lecture** reading practice (GB)
**(c)** training session

**entraîner** /ātʀene/ [1] [1] *vtr* **(a)** to lead to; **une panne a entraîné l'arrêt de la production** a breakdown brought production to a standstill
**(b)** ⟨*river, current*⟩ to carry [sb/sth] away ⟨*swimmer, boat*⟩; **il a entraîné qn/qch dans sa chute** he dragged sb/sth down with him
**(c)** to take, to lead ⟨*person*⟩; **~ qn à faire** ⟨*person*⟩ to make sb do; ⟨*circumstances*⟩ to lead sb to do
**(d)** (figurative) to carry [sb] away ⟨*person, group*⟩
**(e)** to train, to coach ⟨*athlete, team*⟩ (**à** for); to train ⟨*horse, soldier*⟩ (**à** for)
**(f)** ⟨*engine, piston*⟩ to drive ⟨*machine, wheel, turbine*⟩
[2] **s'entraîner** *v refl* (+ *v être*) **(a)** ⟨*player, soldiers*⟩ to train
**(b)** to prepare oneself

**entraîneur** /ātʀenœʀ/ *nm* (of athlete) coach

**entrave** /ātʀav/ *nf* hindrance; (on freedom) restriction

**entraver** /ātʀave/ [1] *vtr* to hinder, to impede

**entre** /ātʀ/ *prep*

■ **Note** You will find translations for expressions such as *entre parenthèses*, *entre nous* etc, at the entries PARENTHÈSE, NOUS etc.

**(a)** between; **~ midi et deux** at lunchtime; **'doux ou très épicé?'—'~ les deux'** 'mild or very spicy?'—'in between'; **~ son travail et l'informatique, il n'a pas le temps de sortir** what with work and his computer he doesn't have time to go out
**(b)** among; **organiser une soirée ~ amis** to organize a party among friends; **chacune d'~ elles** each of them; **~ hommes** as one man to another; **~ nous** between you and me; **nous sommes ~ nous** there's just the two of us; we're among friends; **les enfants sont souvent cruels ~ eux** children are often cruel to each other

**entrebâillement** /ātʀəbajmā/ *nm* (in door, shutter, window) gap (**de** in)

**entrebâiller** /ātʀəbaje/ [1] *vtr* to half-open

**entrechoquer** /ãtʀəʃɔke/ [1] **1** *vtr* to clatter ⟨saucepans⟩; to clink ⟨glasses⟩
**2 s'entrechoquer** *v refl* (+ *v être*)
**(a)** ⟨glasses⟩ to clink
**(b)** ⟨ideas, interests⟩ to clash

**entrecôte** /ãtʀəkot/ *nf* **(a)** entrecôte (steak)
**(b)** rib steak

**entrecouper** /ãtʀəkupe/ [1] **1** *vtr* to punctuate
**2 s'entrecouper** *v refl* (+ *v être*) to intersect

**entrecroiser** /ãtʀəkʀwaze/ [1] *vtr* to intertwine

**entre-deux-guerres** /ãtʀədøgɛʀ/ *nm or f inv* interwar period

**entrée** /ãtʀe/ *nf* **(a)** entrance (de to); **se retrouver à l'~ du bureau** to meet outside the office
**(b)** (on motorway) (entry) slip road (GB), on-ramp (US)
**(c)** (in house) hall; (in hotel) lobby; (door) entry
**(d) l'~ dans la récession** the beginning of the recession; **d'~ (de jeu)** from the very start
**(e) l'~ d'un pays dans une organisation** the entry of a country into an organization; **'~ libre'** 'admission free'; **'~ interdite'** 'no entry'
**(f)** ticket; **deux ~s gratuites** two free tickets
**(g)** (of person) entrance; **réussir son ~** ⟨actor⟩ to enter on cue
**(h)** (Culin) starter
**(i)** (in bookkeeping) **~s** receipts
■ **~ des artistes** stage door; **~ en matière** introduction

**entrée-sortie**, *pl* **entrées-sorties** /ãtʀesɔʀti/ *nf* (Comput) input-output

**entrefaites: sur ces entrefaites** /syʀsezãtʀəfɛt/ *phr* at that moment, just then

**entrefilet** /ãtʀəfilɛ/ *nm* brief article

**entrejambes** /ãtʀəʒɑ̃b/ *nm inv* crotch

**entrelacer** /ãtʀəlase/ [12] *vtr*, **s'entrelacer** *v refl* (+ *v être*) to intertwine, to interlace

**entremêler: s'entremêler** /ãtʀəmele/ [1] *v refl* (+ *v être*) (gen) to be mixed; ⟨hair, branches⟩ to get tangled

**entremets** /ãtʀəmɛ/ *nm* dessert

**entremetteur, -euse** /ãtʀəmɛtœʀ, øz/ *nm,f* **(a)** matchmaker
**(b)** go-between

**entremise** /ãtʀəmiz/ *nf* intervention; **il l'a su par mon ~** he heard of it through me

**entreposer** /ãtʀəpoze/ [1] *vtr* to store

**entrepôt** /ãtʀəpo/ *nm* **(a)** warehouse
**(b)** stockroom

**entreprenant, ~e** /ãtʀəpʀənɑ̃, ɑ̃t/ *adj* enterprising

**entreprendre** /ãtʀəpʀɑ̃dʀ/ [52] *vtr* **(a)** to start, to undertake; **~ de faire** to set about doing; to undertake to do
**(b) ~ qn sur un sujet** to engage sb in conversation about sth

**entrepreneur, -euse** /ãtʀəpʀənœʀ, øz/ *nm,f* **(a)** builder
**(b)** contractor
**(c)** owner-manager ⟨of a small firm⟩

**entreprise** /ãtʀəpʀiz/ *nf* **(a)** firm, business; **petites et moyennes ~s** small and medium-sized businesses
**(b)** business, industry; **la libre ~** free enterprise
**(c)** undertaking; venture
■ **~ unipersonnelle à responsabilité limitée**, **EURL** company owned by a sole proprietor

**entrer** /ãtʀe/ [1] **1** *vtr* (+ *v avoir*) **(a)** to bring [sth] in; to take [sth] in
**(b)** (in computing) to enter
**2** *vi* (+ *v être*) **(a)** to get in, to enter; to go in; to come in; **fais-la ~** show her in; **'défense d'~'** (on door) 'no entry'; (on gate) 'no trespassing'; **je ne fais qu'~ et sortir** I can only stay a minute
**(b)** to fit (in); **je n'arrive pas à faire ~ la pièce dans la fente** I can't get the coin into the slot
**(c) ~ dans** to enter ⟨period, debate⟩; to join ⟨company, army, party⟩; **~ à** to enter ⟨school, charts⟩; to get into ⟨university⟩; **~ en** to enter into ⟨negotiations⟩; **~ dans la vie de qn** to come into sb's life; **~ dans la légende** ⟨person⟩ to become a legend; ⟨fact⟩ to become legendary; **cela n'entre pas dans mes attributions** it's not part of my duties; **~ dans une colère noire** to fly into a blind rage

**entresol** /ãtʀəsɔl/ *nm* mezzanine

**entre-temps** /ãtʀətɑ̃/ *adv* meanwhile

**entretenir** /ãtʀətniʀ/ [36] **1** *vtr* **(a)** to look after ⟨garment, house⟩; to maintain ⟨road⟩; **~ sa forme** to keep in shape
**(b)** to support ⟨family⟩; to keep ⟨mistress⟩
**(c)** to keep [sth] going ⟨conversation, fire⟩; to keep [sth] alive ⟨friendship⟩
**(d) ~ qn de qch** to speak to sb about sth
**2 s'entretenir** *v refl* (+ *v être*) **(a)** s'**~ de qch** to discuss sth
**(b)** s'**~ facilement** ⟨house, fabric⟩ to be easy to look after

**entretien** /ãtʀətjɛ̃/ *nm* **(a)** (of house) upkeep; (of car, road) maintenance; (of plant, skin) care
**(b)** cleaning
**(c)** (gen) discussion; (for a job) interview; (in newspaper) interview

**entre-tuer: s'entre-tuer** /ãtʀətɥe/ [1] *v refl* (+ *v être*) to kill each other

**entrevoir** /ãtʀəvwaʀ/ [46] *vtr* **(a)** to catch a glimpse of; (indistinctly) to make out
**(b)** to glimpse ⟨truth, solution⟩
**(c)** to foresee ⟨difficulty⟩; **laisser ~ qch** ⟨result, sign⟩ to point to sth

**entrevue** /ãtʀəvy/ *nf* meeting; (Pol) talks

**entrouvrir** /ãtʀuvʀiʀ/ [32] **1** *vtr* to open [sth] a little
**2 s'entrouvrir** *v refl* (+ *v être*) (gen) ⟨door, country⟩ to half-open; ⟨lips⟩ to part

**énumération** /enymeʀasjɔ̃/ *nf* **(a)** listing
**(b)** catalogue (GB)

**énumérer** /enymeʀe/ [14] *vtr* to enumerate

**envahir** /ɑ̃vaiʀ/ [3] *vtr* (a) ⟨troops, crowd⟩ to invade; ⟨animal⟩ to overrun
(b) to flood ⟨market⟩

**envahissant, ~e** /ɑ̃vaisɑ̃, ɑ̃t/ *adj*
(a) intrusive
(b) pervasive; invasive

**envahisseur** /ɑ̃vaisœʀ/ *nm* invader

**enveloppe** /ɑ̃vlɔp/ *nf* (a) (for letter) envelope; **sous ~** in an envelope
(b) (for parcel) wrapping; (of grains) husk; (of peas, beans) pod
■ **~ budgétaire** budget

**enveloppé, ~e** /ɑ̃vlɔpe/ *adj* ⟨person⟩ plump

**envelopper** /ɑ̃vlɔpe/ [1] **1** *vtr* (a) ⟨person⟩ to wrap [sb/sth] (up); ⟨sheet⟩ to cover
(b) ⟨fog, silence⟩ to envelop; ⟨mystery⟩ to surround
**2 s'envelopper** *v refl* (+ *v être*) to wrap oneself (up)

**envenimer** /ɑ̃vnime/ [1] **1** *vtr* to inflame ⟨debate⟩; to aggravate ⟨situation⟩
**2 s'envenimer** *v refl* (+ *v être*) ⟨dispute⟩ to worsen; ⟨situation⟩ to turn ugly

**envergure** /ɑ̃vɛʀgyʀ/ *nf* (a) (of plane) wingspan
(b) (figurative) (of person) stature; (of project) scale; **un projet d'~** a substantial project; **sans ~** ⟨project⟩ limited; ⟨person⟩ of no account

**envers**¹ /ɑ̃vɛʀ/ *prep* toward(s), to.
IDIOMS **~ et contre tous/tout** in spite of everyone/everything

**envers**² /ɑ̃vɛʀ/ **1** *nm inv* (of sheet of paper) back; (of piece of cloth) wrong side; (of garment) inside; (of coin) reverse
**2 à l'envers** *phr* (a) the wrong way
(b) upside down
(c) inside out
(d) back to front
(e) the wrong way round (GB) *or* around (US); **mettre ses chaussures à l'~** to put one's shoes on the wrong feet
(f) **passer un film à l'~** to run a film backward(s)

**envie** /ɑ̃vi/ *nf* (a) (gen) urge (de faire to do); (for food) craving; **avoir ~ de qch** to feel like sth; **avoir ~ de dormir** to want to go to bed; **mourir d'~ de faire** to be dying to do (colloq); **donner (l')~ à qn de faire** to make sb want to do
(b) envy; **il te fait ~ ce jouet?** would you like that toy?
(c) birthmark

**envier** /ɑ̃vje/ [2] *vtr* to envy

**envieux, -ieuse** /ɑ̃vjø, øz/ **1** *adj* envious
**2** *nm,f* **faire des ~** to make people jealous

**environ** /ɑ̃viʀɔ̃/ *adv* about

**environnant, ~e** /ɑ̃viʀɔnɑ̃, ɑ̃t/ *adj* surrounding

**environnement** /ɑ̃viʀɔnmɑ̃/ *nm* environment

**environner** /ɑ̃viʀɔne/ [1] *vtr* to surround

**environs** /ɑ̃viʀɔ̃/ *nm pl* **être des ~** to be from the area; **aux ~ de** (place) in the vicinity of; (time, moment) around; (amount) in the region of

**envisageable** /ɑ̃vizaʒabl/ *adj* possible

**envisager** /ɑ̃vizaʒe/ [13] *vtr* (a) to plan (de faire to do)
(b) to envisage ⟨hypothesis, situation⟩; to foresee ⟨problem, possibility⟩; **~ le pire** to imagine the worst
(c) to consider

**envoi** /ɑ̃vwa/ *nm* (a) **tous les ~s de colis sont suspendus** parcel post is suspended; **faire un ~ de** to send ⟨flowers, books⟩
(b) **demander l'~ (immédiat) de troupes** to ask for troops to be dispatched (immediately)
(c) **l'~ de la fusée** the rocket launch; **donner le coup d'~ de** to kick off ⟨match⟩; to open ⟨festival⟩
■ **~ recommandé** registered post (GB) *or* mail (US); **~ contre remboursement** cash on delivery

**envol** /ɑ̃vɔl/ *nm* (of bird) flight; (of plane) takeoff

**envolée** /ɑ̃vɔle/ *nf* (a) flight of fancy
(b) (in prices) surge (de in); (of political party) rise.

**envoler: s'envoler** /ɑ̃vɔle/ [1] *v refl* (+ *v être*) (a) ⟨bird⟩ to fly off; ⟨plane, passenger⟩ to take off; ⟨paper, hat⟩ to be blown away
(b) ⟨prices⟩ to soar
(c) to vanish
(d) (colloq) to do a runner (colloq)

**envoûtement** /ɑ̃vutmɑ̃/ *nm*
(a) bewitchment
(b) spell

**envoûter** /ɑ̃vute/ [1] *vtr* to bewitch

**envoyé, ~e** /ɑ̃vwaje/ **1** *adj* **ça c'est (bien) ~!** (colloq) well said!
**2** *nm,f* envoy; **~ spécial** special correspondent

**envoyer** /ɑ̃vwaje/ [24] **1** *vtr* (a) to send; **~ qn étudier à Genève** to send sb off to study in Geneva
(b) to throw ⟨pebble⟩; to fire ⟨missile⟩; **~ qch dans l'œil de qn** to hit sb in the eye with sth; **~ le ballon dans les buts** to put the ball in the net
**2 s'envoyer** *v refl* (+ *v être*) to exchange; **s'~ des baisers** to blow each other kisses
IDIOMS **~ qn promener** (colloq) to send sb packing (colloq); **tout ~ promener** (colloq) to drop the lot (colloq); **il ne me l'a pas envoyé dire** (colloq) and he told me in no uncertain terms

**enzyme** /ɑ̃zim/ *nm or f* enzyme

**éolien, -ienne**¹ /eɔljɛ̃, ɛn/ *adj* ⟨generator⟩ wind

**éolienne**² /eɔlyɛn/ *nf* (aeolian) windmill

**épagneul** /epaɲœl/ *nm* spaniel

**épais, épaisse** /epɛ, ɛs/ **1** adj **(a)** thick; **il n'est pas bien ∼ ce petit!** (colloq) he's a skinny little fellow!
**(b)** ⟨mind⟩ dull
**(c)** ⟨night⟩ deep
**2** adv a lot, much

**épaisseur** /epɛsœʀ/ nf **(a)** thickness; **couper qch dans (le sens de) l'∼** to cut sth sideways
**(b)** layer

**épaissir** /epesiʀ/ [3] **1** vtr **(a)** to thicken
**(b)** to deepen ⟨mystery⟩
**2** vi **(a)** ⟨sauce⟩ to thicken; ⟨jelly⟩ to set
**(b)** to put on weight
**3** **s'épaissir** v refl (+ v être) ⟨sauce, waist, mist⟩ to thicken; ⟨mystery⟩ to deepen

**épancher: s'épancher** /epɑ̃ʃe/ [1] v refl (+ v être) to open one's heart (**auprès de** to)

**épanoui, ∼e** /epanwi/ adj ⟨flower⟩ in full bloom; ⟨smile⟩ beaming; ⟨person⟩ well-adjusted

**épanouir** /epanwiʀ/ [3] **1** vtr **(a)** ⟨sun⟩ to open (out) ⟨flower⟩; ⟨joy⟩ to light up ⟨face⟩
**(b)** (figurative) to make [sb/sth] blossom
**2** **s'épanouir** v refl (+ v être) ⟨flower⟩ to bloom; ⟨face⟩ to light up; ⟨person⟩ to blossom

**épanouissant, ∼e** /epanwisɑ̃, ɑ̃t/ adj fulfilling

**épanouissement** /epanwismɑ̃/ nm
**(a)** (of flower) blooming
**(b)** (of person) development; (of talent) flowering

**épargnant, ∼e** /epaʀɲɑ̃, ɑ̃t/ nm,f saver

**épargne** /epaʀɲ/ nf savings

**épargner** /epaʀɲe/ [1] **1** vtr **(a)** to save ⟨money⟩
**(b)** to spare; **∼ qch à qn** to spare sb sth
**2** vi to save
**3** **s'épargner** v refl (+ v être) to save oneself

**éparpiller** /epaʀpije/ [1] vtr, **s'éparpiller** v refl (+ v être) to scatter

**épars, ∼e** /epaʀ, aʀs/ adj scattered

**épatant, ∼e** /epatɑ̃, ɑ̃t/ adj (colloq) marvellous (GB)

**épate** /epat/ nf (colloq) **faire de l'∼** to show off

**épaté, ∼e** /epate/ adj **(a)** **nez ∼** pug nose, flat nose
**(b)** (colloq) amazed (**de** by)

**épater** /epate/ [1] vtr (colloq) **(a)** to impress; **ça t'épate, hein?** surprised, aren't you?
**(b)** to amaze

**épaule** /epol/ nf shoulder
IDIOMS **changer son fusil d'∼** to change one's tactics; **avoir la tête sur les ∼s** to have one's head screwed on (colloq)

**épauler** /epole/ [1] **1** vtr **(a)** to help
**(b)** to take aim with ⟨rifle⟩
**2** vi to take aim

**épaulette** /epolɛt/ nf **(a)** shoulder-pad
**(b)** (shoulder-)strap
**(c)** (Mil) epaulette

**épave** /epav/ nf **(a)** wreck

**(b)** (car) (gen) wreck; (after accident) write-off (colloq)
**(c)** (person) wreck

**épée** /epe/ nf sword; **c'est un coup d'∼ dans l'eau** it was a complete waste of effort

**épeler** /eple/ [19] vtr to spell ⟨word⟩

**éperdu, ∼e** /epɛʀdy/ adj ⟨need, desire⟩ overwhelming; ⟨glance⟩ desperate; ⟨love⟩ boundless

**éperdument** /epɛʀdymɑ̃/ adv ⟨in love⟩ madly; **je me moque ∼ de ce qu'il pense** I couldn't care less what he thinks

**éperon** /epʀɔ̃/ nm spur

**épervier** /epɛʀvje/ nm (Zool) sparrowhawk

**éphémère** /efemɛʀ/ adj ephemeral; fleeting; short-lived

**épi** /epi/ nm **(a)** (of corn) ear; (of flower) spike; **∼ de maïs** corn cob
**(b)** (unmanageable) tuft of hair (GB), cowlick (US)

**épice** /epis/ nf spice

**épicé, ∼e** /epise/ adj spicy; hot

**épicentre** /episɑ̃tʀ/ nm epicentre (GB)

**épicer** /epise/ [12] vtr to spice; to add spice to

**épicerie** /episʀi/ nf **(a)** grocer's (shop) (GB), grocery (store) (US); **∼ fine** delicatessen
**(b)** grocery trade
**(c)** groceries

**épicier, -ière** /episje, ɛʀ/ nm,f grocer

**épidémie** /epidemi/ nf epidemic

**épiderme** /epidɛʀm/ nm skin

**épidermique** /epidɛʀmik/ adj skin; ⟨sensitivity⟩ extreme; **réaction ∼** gut reaction

**épier** /epje/ [2] vtr **(a)** to spy on ⟨person, behaviour⟩
**(b)** to be on the lookout for

**épilation** /epilasjɔ̃/ nf removal of unwanted hair

**épilepsie** /epilɛpsi/ nf **crise d'∼** epileptic fit

**épiler** /epile/ [1] vtr to remove unwanted hair from; to wax ⟨leg⟩; to pluck ⟨eyebrows⟩

**épilogue** /epilɔg/ nm epilogue (GB)

**épiloguer** /epilɔge/ [1] vi to go on and on (**sur** about)

**épinard** /epinaʀ/ nm spinach
IDIOMS **ça met du beurre dans les ∼s** (colloq) it brings in a nice bit of extra money

**épine** /epin/ nf thorn; **∼ dorsale** spine
IDIOMS **ôter à qn une ∼ du pied** to take a weight off sb's shoulders

**épineux, -euse** /epinø, øz/ adj ⟨stem, character⟩ prickly; ⟨problem⟩ tricky; ⟨question⟩ vexed

**épingle** /epɛ̃gl/ nf pin; **∼ de** or **à nourrice**, **∼ de sûreté** safety pin
IDIOMS **monter qch en ∼** to blow sth up out of proportion; **être tiré à quatre ∼s** (colloq) to be immaculately dressed; **tirer son ∼ du jeu** to get out while the going is good

**épinière** /epinjɛʀ/ adj f **moelle ∼** spinal cord

**épique** /epik/ *adj* epic; **c'était** ∼ (humorous) (colloq) it was quite something (colloq)

**épisode** /epizɔd/ *nm* episode; **roman à** ∼s serialized novel

**épisodique** /epizɔdik/ *adj* sporadic

**épistolaire** /epistɔlɛʀ/ *adj* epistolary; **ils ont des relations** ∼s they correspond

**épitaphe** /epitaf/ *nf* epitaph

**épithète** /epitɛt/ *nf* attributive adjective

**éploré, ∼e** /eplɔʀe/ *adj* **(a)** grief-stricken
**(b)** tearful

**éplucher** /eplyʃe/ [1] *vtr* to peel; (figurative) to go through [sth] with a fine-tooth comb

**épluchure** /eplyʃyʀ/ *nf* ∼s peelings

**éponge** /epɔ̃ʒ/ *nf* **(a)** sponge
**(b)** terry-towelling (GB)
IDIOMS **passer l'**∼ to forget the past

**éponger** /epɔ̃ʒe/ [13] *vtr* **(a)** to mop (up)
**(b)** to absorb ⟨deficit⟩; to pay off ⟨debts⟩

**épopée** /epɔpe/ *nf* **(a)** epic
**(b)** saga

**époque** /epɔk/ *nf* **(a)** time; **vivre avec son** ∼ to move with the times; **quelle** ∼! what's the world coming to!; **à mon** ∼ in my day
**(b)** (historical) era
**(c) en costume d'**∼ in period costume; **des meubles d'**∼ antique furniture

**épouse** /epuz/ *nf* wife, spouse

**épouser** /epuze/ [1] *vtr* **(a)** to marry ⟨person⟩
**(b)** to adopt ⟨cause, idea⟩

**épousseter** /epuste/ [20] *vtr* to dust

**époustoufler** /epustufle/ [1] *vtr* (colloq) to amaze

**épouvantable** /epuvɑ̃tabl/ *adj* **(a)** (gen) dreadful
**(b)** appalling

**épouvantail** /epuvɑ̃taj/ *nm* **(a)** scarecrow
**(b)** (colloq) (ugly person) fright
**(c)** spectre (GB)

**épouvante** /epuvɑ̃t/ *nf* **(a)** terror
**(b)** horror

**épouvanter** /epuvɑ̃te/ [1] *vtr* **(a)** to terrify
**(b)** to horrify

**époux** /epu/ ① *nm inv* husband
② *nm pl* **les** ∼ the (married) couple

**éprendre: s'éprendre** /epʀɑ̃dʀ/ [52] *v refl* (+ *v être*) **s'**∼ **de qn** to become enamoured of sb

**épreuve** /epʀœv/ *nf* **(a)** ordeal
**(b)** test; **mettre à rude** ∼ to put [sb] to a severe test ⟨person⟩; to be very hard on ⟨car, shoes⟩; to tax ⟨patience, nerves⟩; **à toute** ∼ unfailing; **l'**∼ **du feu** ordeal by fire; **à l'**∼ **du feu/des balles** fire-/bullet-proof
**(c)** (part of an) examination; ∼ **écrite** written examination
**(d)** (Sport) ∼ **d'athlétisme** athletics event
**(e)** (photograph, print) proof

**épris, ∼e** /epʀi, iz/ *adj* in love (**de** with)

**éprouvant, ∼e** /epʀuvɑ̃, ɑ̃t/ *adj* gruelling (GB); trying

**éprouver** /epʀuve/ [1] *vtr* **(a)** to feel ⟨regret, love⟩; to have ⟨sensation, difficulty⟩; ∼ **de la jalousie** to be jealous
**(b)** to test
**(c)** ⟨death, event⟩ to distress ⟨person⟩; ⟨storm⟩ to hit ⟨region⟩

**éprouvette** /epʀuvɛt/ *nf* **(a)** test tube
**(b)** sample

**EPS** /œpeɛs/ *nf* (abbr = **éducation physique et sportive**) PE

**épuisant, ∼e** /epɥizɑ̃, ɑ̃t/ *adj* exhausting

**épuisé, ∼e** /epɥize/ ① *pp* ▶ ÉPUISER
② *pp adj* **(a)** exhausted, worn out
**(b)** ⟨publication, livre⟩ out of print; ⟨item⟩ out of stock

**épuisement** /epɥizmɑ̃/ *nm* **(a)** exhaustion
**(b) jusqu'à** ∼ **des stocks** while stocks last

**épuiser** /epɥize/ [1] ① *vtr* **(a)** to exhaust, to wear [sb] out
**(b)** to exhaust ⟨subject, mine⟩
② **s'épuiser** *v refl* (+ *v être*) **(a)** to exhaust oneself
**(b)** ⟨stocks, provisions⟩ to be running out

**épuisette** /epɥizɛt/ *nf* **(a)** landing net
**(b)** shrimp net

**épurateur** /epyʀatœʀ/ *nm* purifier

**épuration** /epyʀasjɔ̃/ *nf* **(a)** (of gas, liquid) purification; (of sewage) treatment
**(b)** purge

**épurer** /epyʀe/ [1] *vtr* **(a)** to purify ⟨water, gas⟩
**(b)** to purge ⟨party⟩
**(c)** to expurgate ⟨text⟩

**équateur** /ekwatœʀ/ *nm* equator

**équation** /ekwɑsjɔ̃/ *nf* equation

**équerre** /ekɛʀ/ *nf* **(a)** set square; **en** or **d'**∼ at right angles
**(b)** flat angle bracket

**équestre** /ekɛstʀ/ *adj* equestrian; **centre** ∼ riding school

**équilibre** /ekilibʀ/ *nm* **(a)** balance; **être en** ∼ **sur** ⟨object⟩ to be balanced on; ⟨person⟩ to balance on
**(b)** equilibrium; **manquer d'**∼ to be unstable; **retrouver son** ∼ to get back to normal

**équilibrer** /ekilibʀe/ [1] *vtr* to balance

**équilibriste** /ekilibʀist/ *nmf* acrobat

**équinoxe** /ekinɔks/ *nm* equinox

**équipage** /ekipaʒ/ *nm* crew

**équipe** /ekip/ *nf* team; crew; shift; **travailler en** ∼ to work as a team; ∼ **de tournage** film crew; **l'**∼ **de nuit** the night shift

**équipé, ∼e**[1] /ekipe/ ① *pp* ▶ ÉQUIPER
② *pp adj* **bien/mal** ∼ well-/ill-equipped; **cuisine** ∼e fitted kitchen

**équipée**[2] /ekipe/ *nf* escapade

**équipement** /ekipmɑ̃/ *nm* **(a)** equipment; kit
**(b)** ∼s facilities

**équiper** /ekipe/ [1] ① *vtr* to equip ⟨hospital, vehicle⟩; to provide ⟨town⟩; to fit out ⟨person⟩

**2 s'équiper** v refl (+ v être) to equip oneself

**équipier, -ière** /ekipje, ɛʀ/ nm,f (a) team member
(b) crew member

**équitable** /ekitabl/ adj fair-minded; fair

**équitablement** /ekitabləmɑ̃/ adv equitably, fairly

**équitation** /ekitasjɔ̃/ nf (horse-)riding

**équité** /ekite/ nf equity

**équivalence** /ekivalɑ̃s/ nf (a) equivalence
(b) titre admis en ∼ recognized qualification

**équivalent, ∼e** /ekivalɑ̃, ɑ̃t/ adj
(a) equivalent
(b) identical

**équivaloir** /ekivalwaʀ/ [45] v+prep ∼ à to be equivalent to ⟨quantity⟩; to amount to ⟨effect⟩

**équivoque** /ekivɔk/ 1 adj (a) ambiguous
(b) ⟨reputation⟩ dubious; ⟨behaviour⟩ questionable
2 nf ambiguity; sans ∼ ⟨reply⟩ unequivocal; ⟨condemn⟩ unequivocally

**érable** /eʀabl/ nm maple (tree)

**érafler** /eʀafle/ [1] 1 vtr to scratch
2 s'érafler v refl (+ v être) to scratch oneself

**érailler: s'érailler** /eʀɑje/ [1] v refl (+ v être) to become hoarse

**ère** /ɛʀ/ nf (a) era; en l'an 10 de notre ∼ in the year 10 AD
(b) age; à l'∼ atomique in the nuclear age

**érection** /eʀɛksjɔ̃/ nf erection

**éreinter** /eʀɛ̃te/ [1] vtr (colloq) to exhaust

**ergot** /ɛʀɡo/ nm (a) (of cock) spur; (of dog) dewclaw
(b) ergot

**ergoter** /ɛʀɡɔte/ [1] vi to split hairs

**ériger** /eʀiʒe/ [13] 1 vtr to erect ⟨statue⟩
2 s'ériger v refl (+ v être) s'∼ en to set oneself up as

**ermite** /ɛʀmit/ nm (a) hermit
(b) recluse

**éroder** /eʀɔde/ [1] vtr to erode

**érosion** /eʀozjɔ̃/ nf erosion

**érotique** /eʀɔtik/ adj erotic

**érotisme** /eʀɔtism/ nm eroticism

**errance** /ɛʀɑ̃s/ nf restless wandering

**errant, ∼e** /eʀɑ̃, ɑ̃t/ adj wandering; rootless; chien ∼ stray dog

**errer** /eʀe/ [1] vi ⟨person, gaze⟩ to wander; ⟨animal⟩ to roam

**erreur** /eʀœʀ/ nf (a) mistake; ∼ de jugement error of judgment; induire qn en ∼ to mislead sb; sauf ∼ de ma part if I'm not mistaken
(b) (Law) error

**erroné, ∼e** /eʀɔne/ adj incorrect, erroneous

**ersatz** /ɛʀzats/ nm ersatz

**érudit, ∼e** /eʀydi, it/ nm,f scholar

**érudition** /eʀydisjɔ̃/ nf erudition, scholarship

**éruption** /eʀypsjɔ̃/ nf eruption

**es** /ɛ/ ▶ ÊTRE¹

**ès** /ɛs/ prep licence ∼ lettres ≈ arts degree, B.A. (degree)

**esbroufe** /ɛzbʀuf/ nf (colloq) faire de l'∼ to swank (colloq), to show off

**escabeau,** pl **∼x** /ɛskabo/ nm stepladder

**escadrille** /ɛskadʀij/ nf squadron

**escadron** /ɛskadʀɔ̃/ nm (Mil) company; ∼ de la mort death squad

**escalade** /ɛskalad/ nf (a) (Sport) climbing; ascent
(b) escalation

**escalader** /ɛskalade/ [1] vtr to scale ⟨wall⟩; to climb ⟨mountain⟩

**escale** /ɛskal/ nf (gen) stopover; (for ship) port of call; ∼ technique (for plane) refuelling (GB) stop; (for ship) overhaul

**escalier** /ɛskalje/ nm (a) staircase
(b) stairs
■ ∼ mécanique or roulant escalator; ∼ de service backstairs

**escalope** /ɛskalɔp/ nf escalope

**escamotable** /ɛskamɔtabl/ adj ⟨landing gear⟩ retractable; ⟨ladder⟩ foldaway

**escamoter** /ɛskamɔte/ [1] vtr
(a) ⟨magician⟩ to make [sth] disappear
(b) to evade ⟨issue⟩

**escampette** /ɛskɑ̃pɛt/ nf (colloq) prendre la poudre d'∼ to scarper (colloq), to skedaddle (colloq)

**escapade** /ɛskapad/ nf escapade

**escargot** /ɛskaʀɡo/ nm snail

**escarpé, ∼e** /ɛskaʀpe/ adj (a) steep
(b) craggy

**escarpement** /ɛskaʀpəmɑ̃/ nm steep slope

**escarpin** /ɛskaʀpɛ̃/ nm court shoe (GB), pump (US)

**escarre** /ɛskaʀ/ nf bedsore

**escient** /ɛsjɑ̃/ nm à bon ∼ wittingly; à mauvais ∼ ill-advisedly

**esclaffer: s'esclaffer** /ɛsklafe/ [1] v refl (+ v être) to guffaw

**esclandre** /ɛsklɑ̃dʀ/ nm scene

**esclavage** /ɛsklavaʒ/ nm slavery; (figurative) tyranny

**esclave** /ɛsklav/ nmf slave

**escompte** /ɛskɔ̃t/ nm discount

**escompter** /ɛskɔ̃te/ [1] vtr to anticipate; ∼ faire to count on doing, to hope to do

**escorte** /ɛskɔʀt/ nf escort

**escorter** /ɛskɔʀte/ [1] vtr to escort

**escrime** /ɛskʀim/ nf fencing

**escrimer: s'escrimer** /ɛskʀime/ [1] v refl (+ v être) (colloq) s'∼ à faire to knock oneself out trying to do (colloq)

**escroc** /ɛskʀo/ nm swindler, crook

**escroquer** /ɛskʀɔke/ [1] vtr to swindle

**escroquerie** /ɛskʀɔkʀi/ nf (a) fraud, swindling; tentative d'∼ attempted fraud
(b) swindle

**ésotérique** /ezɔteʀik/ adj esoteric

**espace** /ɛspas/ nm (a) space
 (b) ~ de loisirs leisure complex
 (c) gap
 (d) en l'~ de in the space of; l'~ d'un instant for a moment
 ■ ~ vert open space; ~ vital living space

**espacer** /ɛspase/ [12] **1** vtr to space [sth] out
 **2** s'espacer v refl (+ v être) to become less frequent

**espadon** /ɛspadɔ̃/ nm swordfish

**espadrille** /ɛspadʀij/ nf espadrille

**Espagne** /ɛspaɲ/ pr nf Spain
 IDIOMS bâtir des châteaux en ~ to build castles in the air

**espagnol, ~e** /ɛspaɲɔl/ **1** adj Spanish
 **2** nm (language) Spanish

**espalier** /ɛspalje/ nm (a) espalier
 (b) fruit-wall

**espèce** /ɛspɛs/ **1** nf (a) species; l'~ humaine mankind
 (b) kind
 **2** espèces nf pl en ~s in cash

**espérance** /ɛspeʀɑ̃s/ nf hope; ~ de vie life expectancy

**espérer** /ɛspeʀe/ [14] **1** vtr (a) ~ qch to hope for sth
 (b) to expect; je n'en espérais pas tant it's more than I expected
 **2** vi to hope

**espiègle** /ɛspjɛɡl/ adj mischievous

**espion, -ionne** /ɛspjɔ̃, ɔn/ nm,f spy

**espionnage** /ɛspjɔnaʒ/ nm espionage, spying

**espionner** /ɛspjɔne/ [1] vtr to spy on

**esplanade** /ɛsplanad/ nf esplanade

**espoir** /ɛspwaʀ/ nm hope; reprendre ~ to feel hopeful again; avec ~ hopefully

**esprit** /ɛspʀi/ nm (a) mind; avoir l'~ mal placé to have a dirty mind (colloq); avoir un ~ de synthèse to be good at synthesizing information; avoir l'~ de contradiction to be contrary; dans mon ~ c'était facile the way I saw it, it was easy; cela ne t'est jamais venu à l'~? didn't it ever occur to you?; avoir l'~ ailleurs to be miles away; les choses de l'~ spiritual matters
 (b) wit; faire de l'~ to try to be witty; ~ d'à-propos ready wit
 (c) dans un ~ de vengeance in a spirit of revenge; ils ont l'~ de famille they're a very close family
 (d) l'un des plus grands ~s de son temps one of the greatest minds of his/her time; calmer les ~s to calm people down; les ~s sont échauffés feelings are running high
 (e) spirit; croire aux ~s to believe in ghosts
 ■ ~ de corps solidarity; ~ d'équipe team spirit
 IDIOMS perdre ses ~s to faint; les grands ~s se rencontrent great minds think alike

**esquimau, -aude**, mpl ~x /ɛskimo, od/ **1** adj Eskimo; chien ~ husky
 **2** nm (a) Eskimo

(b) ®chocolate-covered ice lolly (GB), ice-cream bar (US)

**esquinter** /ɛskɛ̃te/ [1] vtr (colloq) to damage

**esquisse** /ɛskis/ nf (a) sketch
 (b) outline

**esquisser** /ɛskise/ [1] vtr to sketch ‹portrait›; to outline ‹programme›

**esquiver** /ɛskive/ [1] **1** vtr to dodge, to duck ‹blow›; to sidestep ‹issue›
 **2** s'esquiver v refl (+ v être) to slip away

**essai** /esɛ/ **1** nm (a) (Tech, Med) trial; test; être à l'~ to undergo trials; to be tested; ~ sur route road test
 (b) try, attempt; un coup d'~ a try; prendre qn à l'~ to give sb a try-out
 (c) essay
 (d) (in rugby) try
 **2** essais nm pl (Aut) (Sport) qualifying round

**essaim** /esɛ̃/ nm swarm

**essayage** /esɛjaʒ/ nm fitting

**essayer** /eseje/ [21] **1** vtr (a) to try; ~ sa force to test one's strength
 (b) to test ‹weapon, product›; to run trials on ‹car›
 (c) to try on ‹clothes›; to try ‹size, colour›; to try out ‹car›
 **2** vi to try; ~ à la poste to try the post office; j'essaierai que tout se passe bien I'll try to make sure everything goes all right
 **3** s'essayer v refl (+ v être) s'~ à to have a go at, to try one's hand at

**essayiste** /esɛjist/ nmf essayist

**essence** /esɑ̃s/ nf (a) petrol (GB), gasoline (US)
 (b) essential oil
 (c) tree species
 ■ ~ à briquet lighter fuel (GB), lighter fluid (US); ~ ordinaire ≈ 2-star petrol (GB), regular gasoline (US); ~ sans plomb unleaded (petrol) (GB), unleaded gasoline (US); ~ super ≈ 4-star petrol (GB), premium gasoline (US)

**essentiel, -ielle** /esɑ̃sjɛl/ **1** adj essential
 **2** nm c'est l'~ that's the main thing; aller à l'~ to get to the heart of the matter; l'~ des voix the bulk of the vote; pour l'~ mainly; en voyage je n'emporte que l'~ when I travel I only take the bare essentials

**essentiellement** /esɑ̃sjɛlmɑ̃/ adv
 (a) mainly
 (b) essentially

**esseulé, ~e** /esœle/ adj forlorn

**essieu**, pl ~x /esjø/ nm axle

**essor** /esɔʀ/ nm (of technology, area) development; être en plein ~ to be booming

**essorage** /esɔʀaʒ/ nm wringing; spin-drying

**essorer** /esɔʀe/ [1] vtr (a) to wring
 (b) to spin-dry ‹washing›; to spin ‹lettuce›

**essoufflement** /esuflɑ̃mɑ̃/ nm breathlessness; (figurative) loss of impetus

**essouffler** /esufle/ [1] **1** *vtr* to leave [sb]
breathless; **être essoufflé** to be out of breath
**2 s'essouffler** *v refl* (+ *v être*) (a) to get
breathless
(b) to run out of steam

**essuie-glace**, *pl* ~**s** /esɥiglas/ *nm*
windscreen wiper (GB), windshield wiper
(US)

**essuie-mains** /esɥimɛ̃/ *nm inv* hand
towel

**essuie-tout** /esɥitu/ *nm inv* kitchen roll,
kitchen paper

**essuyer** /esɥije/ [22] **1** *vtr* (a) to dry
⟨*glass, hands*⟩; to wipe ⟨*table*⟩; ~ **la vaisselle**
to dry up; ~ **ses larmes** to wipe away one's
tears
(b) to suffer ⟨*defeat, losses*⟩; to meet with
⟨*failure*⟩
**2 s'essuyer** *v refl* (+ *v être*) to dry oneself;
s'~ **les mains** to dry one's hands

**est¹** /ɛ/ ▶ ÊTRE¹

**est²** /ɛst/ **1** *adj inv* east; eastern
**2** *nm* (a) east; **un vent d'**~ an easterly wind
(b) **l'Est the East; de l'Est** eastern

**estafette**® /ɛstafɛt/ *nf* van

**estampe** /ɛstɑ̃p/ *nf* (a) engraving
(b) print

**estamper** /ɛstɑ̃pe/ [1] *vtr* (colloq) to rip [sb]
off (colloq)

**esthète** /ɛstɛt/ *nmf* aesthete

**esthéticienne** /ɛstetisjɛn/ *nf* beautician

**esthétique** /ɛstetik/ **1** *adj* aesthetic;
⟨*decor*⟩ aesthetically pleasing; ⟨*pose*⟩ graceful
**2** *nf* aesthetics

**estimable** /ɛstimabl/ *adj* (a) worthy
(b) laudable
(c) **difficilement** ~ hard to estimate

**estimation** /ɛstimasjɔ̃/ *nf* estimate;
valuation

**estime** /ɛstim/ *nf* respect

**estimer** /ɛstime/ [1] *vtr* (a) to feel;
~ **nécessaire de faire** to consider it
necessary to do
(b) to think highly of ⟨*friend, artist*⟩
(c) to value ⟨*painting*⟩; to assess ⟨*damage*⟩;
**une vitesse estimée à 150 km/h** an estimated
speed of 150 kph
(d) to reckon

**estival**, ~**e**, *mpl* **-aux** /ɛstival, o/ *adj*
(a) summer
(b) summery

**estivant**, ~**e** /ɛstivɑ̃, ɑ̃t/ *nm,f* summer
visitor

**estomac** /ɛstɔma/ *nm* stomach; **avoir l'**~
**bien accroché** to have a strong stomach.
IDIOMS **avoir l'**~ **dans les talons** (colloq) to be
famished

**estomper** /ɛstɔ̃pe/ [1] **1** *vtr* to blur
⟨*shape*⟩; to gloss over ⟨*details*⟩
**2 s'estomper** *v refl* (+ *v être*) ⟨*landscape*⟩
to become blurred; ⟨*hatred, memories*⟩ to
fade

**estrade** /ɛstrad/ *nf* platform

**estragon** /ɛstragɔ̃/ *nm* tarragon

**estropié**, ~**e** /ɛstrɔpje/ *nm,f* cripple

**estropier** /ɛstrɔpje/ [2] **1** *vtr* to maim
**2 s'estropier** *v refl* (+ *v être*) to maim
oneself

**estuaire** /ɛstɥɛr/ *nm* estuary

**esturgeon** /ɛstyrʒɔ̃/ *nm* sturgeon

**et** /e/ *conj* and; ~ **voilà qu'il sort un couteau
de sa poche!** and next thing he whips a
knife out of his pocket!; ~ **alors?** so what?

**étable** /etabl/ *nf* cowshed

**établi**, ~**e** /etabli/ **1** *pp* ▶ ÉTABLIR
**2** *pp adj* (a) ⟨*reputation, use*⟩ established
(b) ⟨*power, regime*⟩ ruling; ⟨*order*⟩
established
**3** *nm* workbench

**établir** /etablir/ [3] **1** *vtr* (a) to set up
⟨*home*⟩
(b) to establish ⟨*rule, link, reputation,
innocence, fact*⟩; to introduce ⟨*tax, discipline*⟩;
to set ⟨*record, standard*⟩
(c) to draw up ⟨*list, plan, budget, file*⟩; to
make out ⟨*cheque, bill*⟩; to prepare ⟨*quote*⟩; to
make ⟨*diagnosis*⟩; to draw ⟨*parallel*⟩
**2 s'établir** *v refl* (+ *v être*) (a) ⟨*person*⟩ to
settle (à, en in); s'~ **à son compte** to set up
one's own business
(b) ⟨*links*⟩ to develop

**établissement** /etablismɑ̃/ *nm*
(a) organization; ~ **bancaire** banking
institution
(b) (of relations, regime) establishment; (of tax,
sanctions) introduction
(c) premises
■ ~ **commercial** commercial establishment;
~ **de crédit** finance company;
~ **d'enseignement supérieur** higher
education institution; ~ **scolaire** school

**étage** /etaʒ/ *nm* (a) floor; **le premier** ~ the
first floor (GB), the second floor (US); **à l'**~
upstairs
(b) (of tower) level; (of aquaduct, cake) tier

**étagère** /etaʒɛr/ *nf* shelf

**étaient** /etɛ/ ▶ ÊTRE¹

**étain** /etɛ̃/ *nm* (a) tin
(b) pewter

**étais** /etɛ/ ▶ ÊTRE¹

**était** /etɛ/ ▶ ÊTRE¹

**étal** /etal/ *nm* (a) (market) stall
(b) butcher's block

**étalage** /etalaʒ/ *nm* (a) window display
(b) display; **faire** ~ **de ses connaissances** to
flaunt one's knowledge

**étalagiste** /etalaʒist/ *nmf* window dresser

**étalement** /etalmɑ̃/ *nm* (of holidays)
staggering; (of payments) spreading

**étaler** /etale/ [1] **1** *vtr* (a) to spread out
⟨*sheet*⟩; to roll [sth] out ⟨*pastry*⟩
(b) to scatter
(c) to spread ⟨*butter, glue*⟩; to apply ⟨*paint,
ointment*⟩
(d) to spread ⟨*work, payments*⟩; to stagger
⟨*departures*⟩

**(e)** to flaunt ⟨*wealth, knowledge*⟩; to display ⟨*merchandise*⟩; **~ qch au grand jour** to bring sth out into the open

**2 s'étaler** *v refl* (+ *v être*) **(a)** ⟨*butter, paint*⟩ to spread

**(b)** ⟨*person*⟩ to sprawl, to spread out

**(c)** (colloq) **s'~ de tout son long** to fall flat on one's face; **s'étaler** *or* **se faire ~ à un examen** to fail an exam

**étalon** /etalɔ̃/ *nm* **(a)** stallion

**(b)** standard

**étalon-or** /etalɔ̃ɔʀ/ *nm inv* gold standard

**étamine** /etamin/ *nf* stamen

**étanche** /etɑ̃ʃ/ *adj* **~ (à l'eau)** waterproof; watertight; **~ (à l'air)** airtight

**étanchéité** /etɑ̃ʃeite/ *nf* waterproofness; watertightness; airtightness

**étancher** /etɑ̃ʃe/ [1] *vtr* to quench ⟨*thirst*⟩

**étang** /etɑ̃/ *nm* pond

**étant** /etɑ̃/ ▶ DONNÉ 3, ÊTRE[1]

**étape** /etap/ *nf* **(a)** stop

**(b)** (in journey) stage; (in race) leg

**(c)** (figurative) stage, step; **brûler les ~s** to go too far too fast

**état** /eta/ **1** *nm* **(a)** condition; **mettre qn hors d'~ de nuire** to put sb out of harm's way; **leur ~ de santé est excellent** they're in excellent health; **maintenir qch en ~ de marche** to keep sth in working order; **hors d'~ de marche** ⟨*car*⟩ off the road; ⟨*machine*⟩ out of order; **j'ai laissé les choses en l'~** I left everything as it was

**(b)** state; **être dans un drôle d'~** (colloq) to be in a hell of a state (colloq); **être dans un ~ second** to be in a trance; **ce n'est encore qu'à l'~ de projet** it's still only at the planning stage

**(c)** statement

**2 faire ~ de** *phr* **(a)** to cite ⟨*document*⟩

**(b)** to mention ⟨*conversation*⟩

**(c)** to state ⟨*preferences*⟩

**(d)** to make a point of mentioning ⟨*success*⟩

■ **~ d'âme** qualm; feeling; **~ civil** registry office (GB); civil status; **~ d'esprit** state of mind; **~ de fait** fact; **~ des lieux** inventory and report on state of repair; **~s de service** service record

IDIOMS **être/se mettre dans tous ses ~s** (colloq) to be in/to get into a state (colloq)

**État** /eta/ *nm* **(a)** state, State

**(b)** state, government

**étatique** /etatik/ *adj* state (GB), public (US)

**état-major**, *pl* **états-majors** /etamaʒɔʀ/ *nm* **(a)** (Mil) staff

**(b)** headquarters

**États-Unis** /etazyni/ *pr nm pl* **~ (d'Amérique)** United States (of America)

**étau**, *pl* **~x** /eto/ *nm* vice (GB), vise (US); (figurative) **l'~ se resserre** the net is tightening

**étayer** /eteje/ [21] *vtr* **(a)** to prop up

**(b)** (figurative) to support ⟨*theory*⟩

**été¹** /ete/ ▶ ÊTRE[1]

**été²** /ete/ *nm* summer

**éteindre** /etɛ̃dʀ/ [55] **1** *vtr* **(a)** to put out ⟨*fire, cigarette*⟩; to blow out ⟨*candle*⟩

**(b)** to switch off ⟨*light, TV, oven*⟩; to turn off ⟨*gas*⟩

**2 s'éteindre** *v refl* (+ *v être*) **(a)** ⟨*cigarette, fire, light*⟩ to go out; ⟨*radio*⟩ to go off

**(b)** (euphemistic) to pass away *or* on

**(c)** ⟨*desire, passion*⟩ to fade

**éteint**, **~e** /etɛ̃, ɛ̃t/ **1** *pp* ▶ ÉTEINDRE

**2** *pp adj* **(a)** ⟨*gaze*⟩ dull

**(b)** ⟨*volcano*⟩ extinct; ⟨*star*⟩ extinct, dead

**étendard** /etɑ̃daʀ/ *nm* standard, flag

**étendre** /etɑ̃dʀ/ [6] **1** *vtr* **(a)** to stretch ⟨*arms, legs*⟩

**(b)** to spread (out) ⟨*cloth*⟩; **~ le linge** to hang out the washing

**(c)** to extend ⟨*embargo*⟩

**2 s'étendre** *v refl* (+ *v être*) **(a)** ⟨*land, forest*⟩ to stretch

**(b)** ⟨*strike, epidemic*⟩ to spread; ⟨*town*⟩ to expand, to grow

**(c)** ⟨*law, measure*⟩ **s'~ à** to apply to

**(d)** ⟨*period, work*⟩ to stretch, to last

**(e)** to lie down

**(f)** **s'~ sur** to dwell on

**étendu**, **~e¹** /etɑ̃dy/ **1** *pp* ▶ ÉTENDRE

**2** *pp adj* ⟨*city*⟩ sprawling; ⟨*region, plain*⟩ vast; ⟨*vocabulary, knowledge, damage*⟩ extensive

**étendue²** /etɑ̃dy/ *nf* **(a)** expanse

**(b)** size

**(c)** scale, extent; range

**éternel**, **-elle** /etɛʀnɛl/ *adj* endless; eternal

**éternellement** /etɛʀnɛlmɑ̃/ *adv* **(a)** forever

**(b)** permanently

**(c)** perpetually

**(d)** eternally

**éterniser: s'éterniser** /etɛʀnize/ [1] *v refl* (+ *v être*) to drag on; ⟨*visitor*⟩ to stay for ages (colloq)

**éternité** /etɛʀnite/ *nf* eternity

**éternuement** /etɛʀnymɑ̃/ *nm* sneeze

**éternuer** /etɛʀnɥe/ [1] *vi* to sneeze

**êtes** /ɛt/ ▶ ÊTRE[1]

**éther** /etɛʀ/ *nm* ether

**éthique** /etik/ **1** *adj* ethical

**2** *nf* **(a)** ethics

**(b)** code of ethics

**ethnie** /ɛtni/ *nf* ethnic group

**ethnique** /ɛtnik/ *adj* ethnic

**ethnologie** /ɛtnɔlɔʒi/ *nf* ethnology

**éthylique** /etilik/ *adj*, *nmf* alcoholic

**éthylisme** /etilism/ *nm* alcoholism

**étiez** /etje/ ▶ ÊTRE[1]

**étincelant**, **~e** /etɛ̃slɑ̃, ɑ̃t/ *adj* ⟨*sun*⟩ blazing; ⟨*star*⟩ twinkling; ⟨*gemstone, glass*⟩ sparkling; ⟨*feathers, colour*⟩ brilliant

**étinceler** /etɛ̃sle/ [19] *vi* to twinkle; to sparkle

**étincelle** /etɛ̃sɛl/ *nf* spark; **jeter des ~s** to glitter; **faire des ~s** to do brilliantly

**étioler**: **s'étioler** /etjɔle/ [1] *v refl* (+ *v être*)
to wilt

**étions** /etjɔ̃/ ▸ ÊTRE¹

**étiquetage** /etiktaʒ/ *nm* labelling (GB)
■ ~ **génétique** gene tagging

**étiqueter** /etikte/ [20] *vtr* to label

**étiquette** /etiket/ *nf* (a) label
(b) tag; **porter une** ~ to be labelled (GB);
**candidat sans** ~ independent candidate
(c) etiquette

**étirer** /etiʀe/ [1] **1** *vtr* to stretch
**2 s'étirer** *v refl* (+ *v être*) (a) ⟨person⟩ to
stretch
(b) ⟨procession, road⟩ to stretch out

**étoffe** /etɔf/ *nf* (a) fabric
(b) (figurative) substance; **avoir l'~ d'un grand
homme** to have the makings of a great man

**étoffer** /etɔfe/ [1] **1** *vtr* to expand
**2 s'étoffer** *v refl* (+ *v être*) to put on
weight

**étoile** /etwal/ *nf* star
■ ~ **filante** shooting star; ~ **de mer** starfish;
~ **polaire** Pole Star
IDIOMS **coucher** *or* **dormir à la belle** ~ to
sleep out in the open

**étoilé**, ~**e** /etwale/ *adj* (a) starry
(b) ⟨glass, windscreen⟩ crazed

**étole** /etɔl/ *nf* stole

**étonnamment** /etɔnamɑ̃/ *adv*
surprisingly

**étonnant**, ~**e** /etɔnɑ̃, ɑ̃t/ *adj*
(a) surprising
(b) amazing

**étonnement** /etɔnmɑ̃/ *nm* surprise

**étonner** /etɔne/ [1] **1** *vtr* to surprise
**2 s'étonner** *v refl* (+ *v être*) to be
surprised

**étouffant**, ~**e** /etufɑ̃, ɑ̃t/ *adj* (a) stifling
(b) oppressive

**étouffé**, ~**e** /etufe/ *adj* (a) ⟨sound, voice⟩
muffled
(b) ⟨sob⟩ choked; ⟨laughter⟩ suppressed

**étouffement** /etufmɑ̃/ *nm* asphyxiation

**étouffer** /etufe/ [1] **1** *vtr* (a) to suppress
⟨protest⟩
(b) to hush up ⟨scandal⟩
(c) to suffocate ⟨person⟩; to choke ⟨plant⟩; **la
générosité ne les étouffe pas** generosity is
not their middle name
(d) to smother ⟨fire⟩
(e) to stifle ⟨yawn⟩; to hold back ⟨sigh⟩
(f) to deaden ⟨noise⟩
**2** *vi* to feel stifled; **on étouffe ici!** (colloq) it's
stifling in here!; **mourir étouffé** to die of
suffocation
**3 s'étouffer** *v refl* (+ *v être*) to choke

**étourderie** /etuʀdəʀi/ *nf* absent-
mindedness

**étourdi**, ~**e** /etuʀdi/ *adj* (a) absent-
minded
(b) unthinking

**étourdir** /etuʀdiʀ/ [3] **1** *vtr* (a) to stun, to
daze
(b) ~ **qn** ⟨noise⟩ to make sb's head spin

**2 s'étourdir** *v refl* (+ *v être*) **s'~ de
paroles** to become intoxicated with words

**étourdissant**, ~**e** /etuʀdisɑ̃, ɑ̃t/ *adj*
⟨noise⟩ deafening; ⟨speed⟩ dizzying

**étourdissement** /etuʀdismɑ̃/ *nm* **avoir
un** ~ to feel dizzy

**étrange** /etʀɑ̃ʒ/ **1** *adj* strange; **chose** ~
**elle n'a pas répondu** strangely enough she
didn't answer
**2** *nm* (a) strangeness
(b) **l'~** the bizarre

**étrangement** /etʀɑ̃ʒmɑ̃/ *adv*
(a) curiously; **vous me rappelez** ~ **un ami**
it's strange but you remind me of a friend
(b) surprisingly

**étranger**, -**ère** /etʀɑ̃ʒe, ɛʀ/ **1** *adj*
(a) foreign
(b) ~ **à** ⟨person⟩ not involved in ⟨case⟩;
outside ⟨group⟩; ⟨fact⟩ with no bearing on
⟨problem⟩; **se sentir** ~ to feel like an
outsider
(c) unfamiliar
**2** *nm,f* (a) foreigner
(b) outsider
(c) stranger
**3** *nm* **à l'~** abroad

**étrangeté** /etʀɑ̃ʒte/ *nf* strangeness

**étranglé**, ~**e** /etʀɑ̃gle/ *adj* (a) ⟨voice⟩
choked; ⟨sound⟩ muffled
(b) ⟨street⟩ narrow

**étranglement** /etʀɑ̃gləmɑ̃/ *nm*
(a) strangulation
(b) (of road, valley) narrow section

**étrangler** /etʀɑ̃gle/ [1] **1** *vtr* (a) to
strangle
(b) to choke
**2 s'étrangler** *v refl* (+ *v être*) (a) to
strangle oneself
(b) to choke

**étrangleur**, -**euse** /etʀɑ̃glœʀ, øz/ *nm,f*
strangler

**être¹** /ɛtʀ/ [7] *vi* (+ *v avoir*)
■ **Note** You will find translations for fixed phrases
using *être* such as *être en train de, être sur le
point de, quoi qu'il en soit, étant donné* etc, at
the entries TRAIN, POINT, QUOI, DONNÉ etc.

(a) to be; **nous sommes pauvres** we are poor
(b) (as auxiliary verb) **elles sont tombées** they
have fallen; they fell; **elle s'était vengée** she
had taken her revenge
(c) (to go) **je n'ai jamais été en Chine** I've
never been to China
(d) (with *ce*) **est-ce leur voiture?** is it their
car?; **c'est grave?** is it serious?; **qui est-ce?**
who is he/she?; who is that?; who is it?; **est-
ce que tu parles russe?** do you speak
Russian?; **qu'est-ce que c'est?** what is it?; **ce
sont mes enfants** these are my children; they
are my children; **c'est cela** that's right; **c'est
à Pierre/lui de choisir** it's Pierre's/his turn to
choose; it's up to Pierre/to him to choose; **il
aurait pu s'excuser, ne serait-ce qu'en
envoyant un mot** he could have apologized if
only by sending a note
(e) (with *il*) **il est facile de critiquer** it is easy

to criticize; **il n'est pas jusqu'à l'Antarctique qui ne soit pollué** even the Antarctic is polluted; **il n'en est rien** this isn't at all the case

**(f)** (with *en*) **où en étais-je?** where was I?; **je ne sais plus où j'en suis** I'm lost; **'où en es-tu de tes recherches?'—'j'en suis à mi-chemin'** 'how far have you got in your research?'—'I'm halfway through'; **j'en suis à me demander si…** I'm beginning to wonder whether…; **∼ en uniforme** to be wearing a uniform

**(g)** (with *y*) **j'y suis** I'm with you, I get it (colloq); **je n'y suis pas** I don't get it (colloq); **nous partons, vous y êtes?** we're leaving, do you understand?; we're leaving, are you ready?

**(h)** (with *à* and *de*) **ce livre est à moi/à mon frère** this book is mine/my brother's; **à qui est ce chien?** whose dog is this?; **je suis à vous tout de suite** I'll be with you right away; **je suis à vous** I'm all yours; **∼ à ce qu'on fait** to have one's mind on what one is doing; **elle est d'un ridicule!** she's so ridiculous!

**être²** /ɛtʀ/ *nm* **(a) ∼ humain** human being; **les ∼s animés et inanimés** animate and inanimate things; **un ∼ sans défense** a defenceless (GB) creature

**(b)** person; **un ∼ cher** a loved one

**(c) de tout son ∼** with one's whole being; **blessé au plus profond de son ∼** hurt to the core

**étreindre** /etʀɛ̃dʀ/ [55] *vtr* to embrace, to hug ⟨*friend*⟩; to clasp ⟨*opponent*⟩

**étreinte** /etʀɛ̃t/ *nf* embrace; grip

**étrenner** /etʀene/ [1] *vtr* to use [sth] for the first time

**étrennes** /etʀɛn/ *nf pl* **(a)** gift
**(b)** money

**étrier** /etʀije/ *nm* stirrup
**IDIOMS mettre à qn le pied à l'∼** (figurative) to get sb started

**étriper** /etʀipe/ [1] *vtr* (figurative) (colloq) **∼ qn** to skin sb alive

**étriqué, ∼e** /etʀike/ *adj* ⟨*jacket*⟩ skimpy; ⟨*life*⟩ restricted

**étroit, ∼e** /etʀwa, at/ **1** *adj* **(a)** narrow; **avoir l'esprit ∼** to be narrow-minded
**(b)** ⟨*links*⟩ close; **en ∼e collaboration** closely
**2 à l'étroit** *phr* **nous sommes un peu à l'∼** we're a bit cramped; **je me sens un peu à l'∼ dans cette jupe** this skirt feels a bit too tight

**étroitement** /etʀwatmɑ̃/ *adv* closely

**étroitesse** /etʀwatɛs/ *nf* narrowness

**étude** /etyd/ **1** *nf* **(a)** study
**(b)** survey
**(c)** (mise à l')**∼** consideration; **à l'∼** under consideration
**(d)** (of lawyer) office
**(e)** (Sch) study room (GB), study hall (US)
**(f)** study period

**2 études** *nf pl* studies; **faire des ∼s** to be a student; **je n'ai pas fait d'∼s (supérieures)** I didn't go to university *or* college
■ **∼ de marché** market research

**étudiant, ∼e** /etydjɑ̃, ɑ̃t/ *nm,f* student

**étudié, ∼e** /etydje/ *adj* **(a)** carefully prepared
**(b)** studied

**étudier** /etydje/ [2] **1** *vtr* to study; to examine ⟨*file, situation*⟩; to learn ⟨*lesson*⟩
**2** *vi* **(a)** to be a student
**(b)** to be studying

**étui** /etɥi/ *nm* case; **∼ à revolver** holster

**étuve** /etyv/ *nf* **(a)** steam room; **le grenier est une ∼** (figurative) the attic is like an oven
**(b)** incubator

**étymologie** /etimɔlɔʒi/ *nf* etymology

**eu, ∼e** /y/ ▶ AVOIR¹

**eucalyptus** /økaliptys/ *nm inv* eucalyptus

**eucharistie** /økaʀisti/ *nf* **(a)** Eucharist
**(b)** Sacrament

**eûmes** /ym/ ▶ AVOIR¹

**eunuque** /ønyk/ *nm* eunuch

**euphémisme** /øfemism/ *nm* euphemism

**euphorie** /øfɔʀi/ *nf* euphoria

**euphorique** /øfɔʀik/ *adj* euphoric

**euphorisant, ∼e** /øfɔʀizɑ̃, ɑ̃t/ **1** *adj* stimulating; uplifting; euphoriant
**2** *nm* (Med) stimulant

**eurasien, -ienne** /øʀazjɛ̃, ɛn/ *adj* Eurasian

**Euratom** /øʀatɔm/ *nf* (*abbr* = **European atomic energy commission**) Euratom

**eurent** /yʀ/ ▶ AVOIR¹

**EURL** /œyɛʀɛl/ *nf*: *abbr* ▶ ENTREPRISE

**euro** /øʀoøʀo/ *nm* (currency) euro

**eurochèque** /øʀoʃɛk/ *nm* Eurocheque

**euroconnecteur** /øʀokɔnɛktœʀ/ *nm* scart socket; scart plug

**eurocrate** /øʀokʀat/ *nmf* eurocrat

**eurodéputé, -e** /øʀodepyte/ *nm,f* Euro MP

**euromarché** /øʀomaʀʃe/ *nm* Euromarket

**Europe** /øʀɔp/ *pr nf* Europe; **l'∼ communautaire** the European community

**européaniser** /øʀopeanize/ [1] **1** *vtr* to europeanize; **∼ un débat** to broaden a debate to a European level
**2 s'européaniser** *v refl* (+ *v être*) ⟨*country*⟩ to become europeanized; ⟨*economy*⟩ to become adapted to a European framework

**européen, -éenne** /øʀopeɛ̃, ɛn/ *adj* European

**eurosceptique** /øʀosɛptik/ *nmf* eurosceptic

**Eurotunnel** /øʀotynɛl/ *nm* Eurotunnel

**eus** /y/ ▶ AVOIR¹

**eusse** /ys/ ▶ AVOIR¹

**eussent** /ys/ ▶ AVOIR¹

**eusses** /ys/ ▶ AVOIR¹

**eussiez** /ysje/ ▶ AVOIR[1]

**eussions** /ysjɔ̃/ ▶ AVOIR[1]

**eut** /y/ ▶ AVOIR[1]

**eût** /yt/ ▶ AVOIR[1]

**eûtes** /yt/ ▶ AVOIR[1]

**euthanasie** /øtanazi/ *nf* euthanasia

**eux** /ø/ *pron* **(a)** they; **je sais que ce n'est pas ~ qui ont fait ça** I know they weren't the ones who did it
**(b)** them; **les inviter, ~, quelle idée!** invite THEM, what an idea!; **c'est à ~** it's theirs

**eux-mêmes** /ømɛm/ *pron* themselves; **les experts ~ reconnaissent que...** even the experts admit that...

**évacuation** /evakчasjɔ̃/ *nf* **(a)** evacuation
**(b)** discharge; **il y a un problème d'~ de l'eau** the water doesn't drain away

**évacuer** /evakчe/ [1] *vtr* **(a)** to evacuate
**(b)** to drain off
**(c)** (figurative) to shrug off ⟨*problem*⟩

**évader**: **s'évader** /evade/ [1] *v refl*
(+ *v être*) **(a)** to escape; **faire ~ qn** to help sb to escape
**(b)** (figurative) to get away (de from)

**évaluable** /evalчabl/ *adj* assessable

**évaluation** /evalчasjɔ̃/ *nf* **(a)** (of collection, house) valuation; **faire l'~ de** to value
**(b)** (of costs, damages) assessment; estimate, appraisal (US)
**(c)** (of staff) appraisal

**évaluer** /evalчe/ [1] *vtr* **(a)** to estimate ⟨*size, length*⟩; to assess ⟨*risks, costs*⟩
**(b)** to value ⟨*inheritance*⟩
**(c)** to assess ⟨*employee, student*⟩

**Évangile** /evãʒil/ *nm* Gospel

**évanouir**: **s'évanouir** /evanwiʀ/ [3] *v refl*
(+ *v être*) **(a)** to faint
**(b)** ⟨*feeling*⟩ to fade

**évanouissement** /evanwismã/ *nm*
**(a)** blackout, fainting fit
**(b)** fading

**évaporation** /evapɔʀasjɔ̃/ *nf* evaporation

**évaporer**: **s'évaporer** /evapɔʀe/ [1] *v refl*
(+ *v être*) **(a)** to evaporate
**(b)** (colloq) to vanish

**évaser** /evaze/ [1] **1** *vtr* to flare
**2 s'évaser** *v refl* (+ *v être*) ⟨*duct*⟩ to open out; ⟨*skirt*⟩ to be flared

**évasif, -ive** /evazif, iv/ *adj* evasive

**évasion** /evazjɔ̃/ *nf* escape

**Ève** /ɛv/ *pr nf* Eve; **en tenue d'~** in her birthday suit
IDIOMS **elle ne le connaît ni d'~ ni d'Adam** she doesn't know him from Adam

**évêché** /eveʃe/ *nm* **(a)** diocese
**(b)** bishop's palace

**éveil** /evɛj/ *nm* awakening

**éveiller** /eveje/ [1] **1** *vtr* **(a)** to arouse ⟨*curiosity, suspicions*⟩; to stimulate ⟨*intelligence*⟩; to awaken ⟨*conscience*⟩; **un enfant éveillé** a bright child
**(b)** to wake (up) ⟨*sleeper*⟩; **être éveillé** to be awake
**2 s'éveiller** *v refl* (+ *v être*) **(a)** to wake up

**(b)** ⟨*imagination*⟩ to start to develop

**événement** /evenmã/ *nm* event

**événementiel, -ielle** /evenmãsjɛl/ *adj* factual

**éventail** /evãtaj/ *nm* **(a)** fan
**(b)** range

**éventaire** /evãtɛʀ/ *nm* stall

**éventer**: **s'éventer** /evãte/ [1] *v refl*
(+ *v être*) ⟨*perfume, coffee*⟩ to go off; ⟨*wine*⟩ to pass its best; ⟨*beer, lemonade*⟩ to go flat

**éventrer** /evãtʀe/ [1] *vtr* **(a)** ⟨*person*⟩ to disembowel; ⟨*bull*⟩ to gore
**(b)** to rip open

**éventualité** /evãtчalite/ *nf* **(a)** eventuality
**(b)** possibility; **dans l'~ de** in the event of

**éventuel, -elle** /evãtчɛl/ *adj* possible

**éventuellement** /evãtчɛlmã/ *adv*
**(a)** possibly
**(b)** if necessary

**évêque** /evɛk/ *nm* bishop (**de** of)

**évertuer**: **s'évertuer** /evɛʀtчe/ [1] *v refl*
(+ *v être*) to try one's best (**à faire** to do)

**éviction** /eviksjɔ̃/ *nf* **(a)** ousting (**de** from)
**(b)** (Law) eviction

**évidemment** /evidamã/ *adv* of course

**évidence** /evidãs/ **1** *nf* **(a)** obviousness
**(b)** obvious fact; **se rendre à l'~** to face the facts; **de toute ~, à l'~** obviously
**2 en évidence** *phr* **laisser qch en ~** to leave sth in an obvious place; **mettre en ~** to highlight ⟨*feature*⟩

**évident, ~e** /evidã, ãt/ *adj* obvious; **ce n'est pas ~** (colloq) not necessarily; it's not so easy

**évider** /evide/ [1] *vtr* to hollow out; to scoop out

**évier** /evje/ *nm* sink

**évincer** /evɛ̃se/ [12] *vtr* to oust ⟨*rival*⟩

**évitable** /evitabl/ *adj* avoidable

**éviter** /evite/ [1] *vtr* **(a)** to avoid; **~ à qn de faire** to save sb (from) doing
**(b)** to dodge ⟨*bullet, blow*⟩

**évocation** /evɔkasjɔ̃/ *nf* **(a)** evocation; reminiscence
**(b)** mention (**de** of)

**évolué, ~e** /evɔlчe/ *adj* **(a)** civilized
**(b)** evolved

**évoluer** /evɔlчe/ [1] *vi* **(a)** to evolve, to change
**(b)** to develop
**(c)** to glide

**évolutif, -ive** /evɔlytif, iv/ *adj* progressive

**évolution** /evɔlysjɔ̃/ *nf* **(a)** evolution
**(b)** development
**(c)** progress
**(d)** progression
**(e)** change; **en pleine ~** undergoing rapid change

**évolutionniste** /evɔlysjɔnist/ *adj* evolutionary

**évoquer** /evɔke/ [1] *vtr* **(a)** to recall
**(b)** to mention, to bring up

(c) to bring back ⟨memory⟩; to be reminiscent of ⟨childhood⟩
(d) to evoke

**ex** /ɛks/ nm (a) (written abbr = **exemple**) eg
(b) (written abbr = **exemplaire**) copy

**ex-** /ɛks/ pref ~**champion** former champion

**exacerber** /ɛgzasɛʀbe/ [1] vtr to exacerbate

**exact, ~e** /ɛgza(kt), akt/ adj (a) correct
(b) accurate
(c) exact
(d) punctual

**exactement** /ɛgzaktəmɑ̃/ adv exactly

**exactitude** /ɛgzaktityd/ nf (a) correctness
(b) accuracy
(c) exactness
(d) punctuality

**ex æquo** /ɛgzeko/ adv ils sont premiers ~ they've tied for first place

**exagération** /ɛgzaʒeʀasjɔ̃/ nf exaggeration

**exagéré, ~e** /ɛgzaʒeʀe/ adj
(a) exaggerated
(b) excessive; d'une sensibilité ~e oversensitive

**exagérément** /ɛgzaʒeʀemɑ̃/ adv excessively

**exagérer** /ɛgzaʒeʀe/ [14] 1 vtr to exaggerate
2 vi to go too far

**exaltant, ~e** /ɛgzaltɑ̃, ɑ̃t/ adj thrilling; inspiring

**exaltation** /ɛgzaltasjɔ̃/ nf (a) elation
(b) stimulation
(c) glorification

**exalté, ~e** /ɛgzalte/ 1 pp ▶ EXALTER
2 pp adj impassioned

**exalter** /ɛgzalte/ [1] vtr (a) to glorify
(b) to heighten
(c) to elate, to thrill

**examen** /ɛgzamɛ̃/ nm (a) (Sch, Univ) examination, exam; passer un ~ to take an exam; ~ de rattrapage retake, resit (GB)
(b) (Med) examination
(c) examination; consideration; review; être en cours d'~ to be under review; to be under consideration
(d) inspection
■ ~ blanc mock (exam), practice exam; ~ de conscience self-examination; ~ spécial d'entrée à l'université, ESEU university entrance exam for students not having the baccalaureate

**examinateur, -trice** /ɛgzaminatœʀ, tʀis/ nm,f examiner

**examiner** /ɛgzamine/ [1] vtr (a) to examine; to review; ~ qch de près to have a close look at sth
(b) (Med) to examine ⟨patient, wound⟩

**exaspération** /ɛgzaspeʀasjɔ̃/ nf
(a) exasperation
(b) intensification

**exaspérer** /ɛgzaspeʀe/ [14] vtr (a) to exasperate, to infuriate
(b) to exacerbate

**exaucer** /ɛgzose/ [12] vtr to grant

**excavatrice** /ɛkskavatʀis/ nf excavator

**excédant, ~e** /ɛksedɑ̃, ɑ̃t/ adj exasperating, infuriating

**excédent** /ɛksedɑ̃/ nm surplus; ~ de bagages excess baggage

**excédentaire** /ɛksedɑ̃tɛʀ/ adj surplus

**excéder** /ɛksede/ [14] vtr (a) to exceed
(b) to infuriate

**excellence** /ɛksɛlɑ̃s/ nf excellence

**Excellence** /ɛksɛlɑ̃s/ nf Son ~ His/Her Excellency

**excellent, ~e** /ɛksɛlɑ̃, ɑ̃t/ adj excellent

**exceller** /ɛksele/ [1] vi to excel

**excentré, ~e** /ɛksɑ̃tʀe/ adj (a) ⟨area⟩ outlying
(b) être ~ ⟨axis⟩ to be off-centre (GB)

**excentricité** /ɛksɑ̃tʀisite/ nf eccentricity

**excentrique** /ɛksɑ̃tʀik/ adj, nmf eccentric

**excepté, ~e** /ɛksɛpte/ 1 pp ▶ EXCEPTER
2 prep except
3 excepté que phr except that

**excepter** /ɛksɛpte/ [1] vtr si l'on excepte except for, apart from

**exception** /ɛksɛpsjɔ̃/ nf exception; faire ~ to be an exception; à l'~ de, à faite de except for; sauf ~ with the occasional exception; d'~ ⟨person⟩ exceptional; ⟨law⟩ emergency

**exceptionnel, -elle** /ɛksɛpsjɔnɛl/ adj (gen) exceptional; ⟨price⟩ bargain; ⟨meeting⟩ extraordinary

**exceptionnellement** /ɛksɛpsjɔnɛlmɑ̃/ adv exceptionally

**excès** /ɛksɛ/ nm inv excess; commettre des ~ to go too far; des ~ de langage bad language; tomber dans l'~ inverse to go to the opposite extreme; ~ de confiance/zèle overconfidence/overzealousness
■ ~ de vitesse speeding

**excessif, -ive** /ɛksesif, iv/ adj
(a) excessive
(b) extreme; il est ~ he is a man of extremes

**excision** /ɛksizjɔ̃/ nf (a) excision
(b) female circumcision

**excitant, ~e** /ɛksitɑ̃, ɑ̃t/ 1 adj
(a) ⟨substance⟩ stimulating
(b) exciting; thrilling
2 nm stimulant

**excitation** /ɛksitasjɔ̃/ nf (a) excitement
(b) arousal
(c) stimulation

**excité, ~e** /ɛksite/ 1 adj (a) ⟨crowd⟩ in a frenzy; ⟨atmosphere⟩ frenzied
(b) ⟨person⟩ thrilled, excited
(c) (sexually) aroused
2 nm,f (a) rowdy
(b) fanatic
(c) neurotic

⋯⋗

IDIOMS être ∼ comme une puce (colloq) to be like a cat on a hot tin roof

**exciter** /ɛksite/ [1] **1** *vtr* (a) to arouse ⟨*anger*⟩; to kindle ⟨*desire*⟩
(b) to thrill
(c) to arouse
(d) to tease ⟨*animal*⟩; to get [sb] excited ⟨*child*⟩; ⟨*coffee*⟩ to get [sb] hyped up
(e) to stimulate ⟨*palate*⟩
**2** **s'exciter** *v refl* (+ *v être*) to get excited

**exclamatif, -ive** /ɛksklamatif, iv/ *adj* exclamatory

**exclamation** /ɛksklamasjɔ̃/ *nf* exclamation

**exclamer: s'exclamer** /ɛksklame/ [1] *v refl* (+ *v être*) to exclaim

**exclu, ∼e** /ɛkskly/ **1** *pp* ▶ EXCLURE
**2** *pp adj* excluded; **c'est exclu!** it's out of the question!; **se sentir ∼** to feel left out

**exclure** /ɛksklyʀ/ [78] *vtr* (a) to exclude ⟨*person*⟩; to rule out ⟨*possibility*⟩
(b) to expel ⟨*member*⟩

**exclusif, -ive** /ɛksklyzif, iv/ *adj* exclusive; **concessionnaire ∼** sole agent

**exclusion** /ɛksklyzjɔ̃/ **1** *nf* (a) exclusion; **∼ sociale** social exclusion
(b) expulsion
(c) suspension
**2** **à l'exclusion de** *phr* with the exception of

**exclusivité** /ɛksklyzivite/ *nf* exclusive rights; **en ∼** ⟨*publish*⟩ exclusively; ⟨*product*⟩ exclusive

**excommunier** /ɛkskɔmynje/ [2] *vtr* to excommunicate

**excrément** /ɛkskʀemɑ̃/ *nm* excrement

**excrétion** /ɛkskʀesjɔ̃/ *nf* excretion

**excroissance** /ɛkskʀwasɑ̃s/ *nf* (a) (Med) growth, excrescence
(b) (in botany) outgrowth

**excursion** /ɛkskyʀsjɔ̃/ *nf* excursion, trip

**excuse** /ɛkskyz/ *nf* (a) excuse
(b) apology

**excuser** /ɛkskyze/ [1] **1** *vtr* to forgive; to pardon; to excuse; **excusez-moi** I'm sorry; **vous êtes tout excusé** it's quite all right
**2** **s'excuser** *v refl* (+ *v être*) to apologize

**exécrable** /ɛgzekʀabl/ *adj* loathsome; dreadful; detestable

**exécrer** /ɛgzekʀe/ [14] *vtr* to loathe

**exécutant, ∼e** /ɛgzekytɑ̃, ɑ̃t/ *nm,f*
(a) performer
(b) **il dit n'avoir été qu'un ∼** he claims he was only obeying orders

**exécuter** /ɛgzekyte/ [1] **1** *vtr* (a) to carry out ⟨*task, mission*⟩; to do ⟨*exercise*⟩
(b) to carry out ⟨*orders, threat*⟩; to fulfil (GB) ⟨*contract*⟩; to enforce ⟨*law, ruling*⟩
(c) to execute ⟨*prisoner*⟩; to kill ⟨*victim*⟩
(d) (Mus) to perform
**2** **s'exécuter** *v refl* (+ *v être*) to comply

**exécutif, -ive** /ɛgzekytif, ive/ *adj* executive

**exécution** /ɛgzekysjɔ̃/ *nf* (a) execution;

carrying out; enforcement; fulfilment (GB); **mettre à ∼** to carry out ⟨*threat*⟩; **travaux en cours d'∼** work in progress; **veiller à la bonne ∼ d'une tâche** to see that a job is done well
(b) execution; **∼ capitale** capital punishment

**exemplaire** /ɛgzɑ̃plɛʀ/ **1** *adj*
(a) exemplary; **élève ∼** model pupil
(b) (Law) exemplary
**2** *nm* (a) copy; print
(b) specimen

**exemplarité** /ɛgzɑ̃plaʀite/ *nf* deterrent nature (**de** of)

**exemple** /ɛgzɑ̃pl/ **1** *nm* (a) example; **sans ∼** unprecedented; **être l'∼ de la gentillesse** to be a model of kindness; **donner qn en ∼** to hold sb up as an example
(b) warning (**pour** to)
**2** **par exemple** *phr* for example; **ça par ∼!** how amazing!; well, honestly!

**exemplifier** /ɛgzɑ̃plifje/ [2] *vtr* to exemplify

**exempt, ∼e** /ɛgzɑ̃, ɑ̃t/ *adj* exempt; **∼ d'impôt** tax-free

**exempter** /ɛgzɑ̃te/ [1] *vtr* to exempt

**exercer** /ɛgzɛʀse/ [12] **1** *vtr* (a) to exercise ⟨*right*⟩; to exert ⟨*authority*⟩
(b) to exercise ⟨*profession*⟩; to practise (GB) ⟨*art*⟩
(c) to exercise ⟨*body*⟩
**2** **s'exercer** *v refl* (+ *v être*) (a) ⟨*athlete*⟩ to train; ⟨*musician*⟩ to practise (GB)
(b) ⟨*influence, force*⟩ to be exerted

**exercice** /ɛgzɛʀsis/ *nm* exercise; **faire de l'∼** to get some exercise; **dans l'∼ de ses fonctions** in the course of one's duty; while at work; **en ∼** ⟨*minister, president*⟩ incumbent; **entrer en ∼** to take up one's duties

**exergue** /ɛgzɛʀg/ *nm* (a) epigraph
(b) inscription

**exhaler** /ɛgzale/ [1] *vtr* to exhale

**exhausser** /ɛgzose/ [1] *vtr* to raise

**exhaustif, -ive** /ɛgzostif, iv/ *adj* exhaustive

**exhiber** /ɛgzibe/ [1] **1** *vtr* to flaunt ⟨*wealth*⟩; to show ⟨*animal*⟩; to expose ⟨*body*⟩
**2** **s'exhiber** *v refl* (+ *v être*) (a) to expose oneself
(b) to flaunt oneself

**exhibition** /ɛgzibisjɔ̃/ *nf* (a) (of animals) show; exhibition
(b) (Sport) demonstration, display
(c) (of wealth) parade; (of emotion) display

**exhibitionniste** /ɛgzibisjɔnist/ *adj, nmf* exhibitionist

**exhortation** /ɛgzɔʀtasjɔ̃/ *nf* exhortation; **∼ au calme** call for calm

**exhorter** /ɛgzɔʀte/ [1] *vtr* to motivate; **∼ qn à faire** to urge *or* exhort sb to do

**exhumer** /ɛgzyme/ [1] *vtr* (a) to exhume
(b) to excavate

**exigeant, ∼e** /ɛgziʒɑ̃, ɑ̃t/ *adj* demanding

**exigence** /ɛgziʒɑ̃s/ *nf* demand (**de** qch for sth)

**exiger** /ɛgziʒe/ [13] *vtr* (a) to demand ⟨*answer, reforms*⟩
(b) to require

**exigibilité** /ɛgziʒibilite/ *nf* (of tax, bill) payability; (of debt) repayability

**exigible** /ɛgziʒibl/ *adj* due

**exigu, -uë** /ɛgzigy/ *adj* ⟨*room*⟩ cramped; ⟨*entrance*⟩ narrow; ⟨*space*⟩ confined

**exil** /ɛgzil/ *nm* exile; **en ~** in exile

**exilé, ~e** /ɛgzile/ *nm,f* exile

**exiler** /ɛgzile/ [1] **1** *vtr* to exile
**2** s'**exiler** *v refl* (+ *v être*) to go into exile

**existence** /ɛgzistɑ̃s/ *nf* (a) existence
(b) (colloq) life

**existentialisme** /ɛgzistɑ̃sjalism/ *nm* existentialism

**exister** /ɛgziste/ [1] *vi* to exist; **si le paradis existe** if there is a heaven; **la maison existe encore** the house is still standing

**exode** /ɛgzɔd/ *nm* exodus; **~ rural** rural depopulation

**exonération** /ɛgzɔneRasjɔ̃/ *nf* exemption

**exonérer** /ɛgzɔneRe/ [14] *vtr* to exempt

**exorbitant, ~e** /ɛgzɔRbitɑ̃, ɑ̃t/ *adj* ⟨*price*⟩ exorbitant; ⟨*demands*⟩ outrageous

**exorbité, ~e** /ɛgzɔRbite/ *adj* bulging

**exorciser** /ɛgzɔRsize/ [1] *vtr* to exorcize

**exotique** /ɛgzɔtik/ *adj* exotic

**exotisme** /ɛgzɔtism/ *nm* exoticism

**expansif, -ive** /ɛkspɑ̃sif, iv/ *adj* communicative, outgoing

**expansion** /ɛkspɑ̃sjɔ̃/ *nf* (a) growth; **en (pleine) ~** (rapidly) growing
(b) expansion

**expansivité** /ɛkspɑ̃sivite/ *nf* expansiveness

**expatriation** /ɛkspatRijasjɔ̃/ *nf* expatriation

**expatrié, ~e** /ɛkspatRije/ *adj, nm,f* expatriate

**expatrier** /ɛkspatRije/ [2] **1** *vtr* to deport
**2** s'**expatrier** *v refl* (+ *v être*) to emigrate

**expectative** /ɛkspɛktativ/ *nf* **rester dans l'~** to wait and see

**expédient** /ɛkspedjɑ̃/ *nm* expedient; **vivre d'~s** to live by one's wits

**expédier** /ɛkspedje/ [2] *vtr* (a) to send; to post (GB), to mail (US); to dispatch; **~ qch à qn** to send sb sth
(b) to get rid of ⟨*person*⟩; to polish off ⟨*work, meal*⟩; **~ un procès en une heure** to get a trial over within one hour

**expéditeur, -trice** /ɛkspeditœR, tRis/ *nm,f* sender

**expéditif, -ive** /ɛkspeditif, iv/ *adj* ⟨*person*⟩ brisk; ⟨*method*⟩ cursory; **une justice expéditive** summary justice

**expédition** /ɛkspedisjɔ̃/ *nf* expedition

**expéditionnaire** /ɛkspedisjɔnɛR/ **1** *adj* expeditionary
**2** *nmf* (a) forwarding agent

(b) copyist

**expérience** /ɛkspeRjɑ̃s/ *nf* (a) experience; **avoir de l'~** to be experienced; **j'en ai fait l'~ à mes dépens** I learned that lesson to my cost
(b) experiment

**expérimental, ~e**, *mpl* **-aux** /ɛkspeRimɑ̃tal, o/ *adj* experimental

**expérimentation** /ɛkspeRimɑ̃tasjɔ̃/ *nf* experimentation
■ **~ animale** experiments on animals

**expérimenté, ~e** /ɛkspeRimɑ̃te/ *adj* experienced

**expérimenter** /ɛkspeRimɑ̃te/ [1] *vtr* to test

**expert** /ɛkspɛR/ *nm* (a) expert (**en** on); **l'avis d'un ~** expert advice
(b) adjuster

**expert-comptable**, *pl* **experts-comptables** /ɛkspɛRkɔ̃tabl/ *nm* ≈ chartered accountant (GB), certified public accountant (US)

**expert-conseil**, *pl* **experts-conseils** /ɛkspɛRkɔ̃sɛj/ *nm* consultant

**expertise** /ɛkspɛRtiz/ *nf* (a) valuation (GB), appraisal (US); assessment
(b) expertise

**expertiser** /ɛkspɛRtize/ [1] *vtr* to value (GB), to appraise (US) ⟨*jewellery*⟩; to assess ⟨*damages*⟩

**expier** /ɛkspje/ [2] *vtr* to atone for, to expiate

**expiration** /ɛkspiRasjɔ̃/ *nf* (a) exhalation
(b) expiry (GB), expiration (US)

**expirer** /ɛkspiRe/ [1] **1** *vtr* to exhale
**2** *vi* (a) ⟨*contract*⟩ to expire
(b) to breathe out

**explicatif, -ive** /ɛksplikatif, iv/ *adj* explanatory

**explication** /ɛksplikasjɔ̃/ *nf* explanation; **nous avons eu une bonne ~** we've talked things through

**explicite** /ɛksplisit/ *adj* ⟨*text, film*⟩ explicit; ⟨*answer*⟩ definite

**explicitement** /ɛksplisitmɑ̃/ *adv* ⟨*mention*⟩ explicitly; ⟨*condemn*⟩ unequivocally; ⟨*ask*⟩ specifically

**expliciter** /ɛksplisite/ [1] *vtr* to clarify

**expliquer** /ɛksplike/ [1] **1** *vtr* (a) to explain
(b) (Sch) to analyse (GB) ⟨*text*⟩
**2** s'**expliquer** *v refl* (+ *v être*) s'**~ qch** to understand sth; **tout finira par s'~** everything will become clear

**exploit** /ɛksplwa/ *nm* exploit, feat

**exploitant, ~e** /ɛksplwatɑ̃, ɑ̃t/ *nm,f* **~ agricole** farmer

**exploitation** /ɛksplwatasjɔ̃/ *nf*
(a) exploitation
(b) **~ agricole** farm; **~ commerciale** business concern
(c) (of land, forest) exploitation; (of airline, shipping line) operation

**e**

**exploiter** /ɛksplwate/ [1] *vtr* **(a)** to exploit ⟨*person*⟩
**(b)** to work ⟨*mine*⟩; to mine ⟨*coal*⟩; to exploit ⟨*forest*⟩; to run ⟨*firm*⟩; to operate ⟨*airline*⟩
**(c)** to make the most of ⟨*gift, knowledge*⟩

**explorateur, -trice** /ɛksplɔʀatœʀ, tʀis/ *nm,f* explorer

**exploration** /ɛksplɔʀasjɔ̃/ *nf* exploration

**explorer** /ɛksplɔʀe/ [1] *vtr* to explore

**exploser** /ɛksploze/ [1] *vi* to explode; to blow up; **faire ~** to blow up; to explode; to cause [sth] to blow up

**explosif, -ive** /ɛksplozif, iv/ **①** *adj* explosive
**②** *nm* explosive; **attentat à l'~** bomb attack

**explosion** /ɛksplozjɔ̃/ *nf* **(a)** explosion
**(b)** outburst
**(c)** (in market) boom

**export** /ɛkspɔʀ/ *nm* export

**exportateur, -trice** /ɛkspɔʀtatœʀ, tʀis/ *nm,f* exporter

**exportation** /ɛkspɔʀtasjɔ̃/ *nf* export

**exporter** /ɛkspɔʀte/ [1] *vtr* to export

**exposé, ~e** /ɛkspoze/ **①** *pp* ▶ EXPOSER
**②** *pp adj* **(a)** exposed; **maison ~e au sud** south-facing house
**(b)** on show; on display
**③** *nm* **(a)** ~ **de** account of; **faire un** *or* **l'~ des faits** to give a statement of the facts
**(b)** (Sch) talk; **faire un ~** to give a talk

**exposer** /ɛkspoze/ [1] **①** *vtr* **(a)** to exhibit ⟨*art*⟩; to display, to put [sth] on display ⟨*goods*⟩
**(b)** to state ⟨*facts*⟩; to outline ⟨*idea, plan*⟩; to explain ⟨*situation*⟩
**(c)** to risk ⟨*life, reputation*⟩
**(d)** to expose ⟨*skin, body*⟩; **ne reste pas exposé au soleil** stay out of the sun
**②** **s'exposer** *v refl* (+ *v être*) **(a)** to put oneself at risk; **s'~ à** to lay oneself open to ⟨*criticsm*⟩
**(b)** **s'~ au soleil** to go out in the sun

**exposition** /ɛkspozisjɔ̃/ *nf* **(a)** (of art) exhibition; (of animals, plants) show; (for trade) fair
**(b)** (in shop) display
**(c)** (of situation, facts) exposition
**(d)** (of house) aspect
**(e)** (to light, radiation) exposure

**exprès¹** /ɛkspʀɛ/ *adv* **(a)** deliberately, on purpose; **comme par un fait ~** as ill-luck would have it
**(b)** specially

**exprès², -esse** /ɛkspʀɛs/ **①** *adj* express
**②** **exprès** *adj inv* **envoyer qch en** *or* **par ~** to send sth special delivery *or* express

**express** /ɛkspʀɛs/ **①** *adj inv* express
**②** *nm inv* **(a)** express (train)
**(b)** espresso

**expressément** /ɛkspʀɛsemɑ̃/ *adv* expressly

**expressif, -ive** /ɛkspʀɛsif, iv/ *adj* expressive

**expression** /ɛkspʀɛsjɔ̃/ *nf* expression; **réduire qch à sa plus simple ~** (figurative) to reduce sth to a minimum
■ **~ corporelle** self-expression through movement

**expressivité** /ɛkspʀɛsivite/ *nf* expressiveness

**exprimable** /ɛkspʀimabl/ *adj* **difficilement ~** hard to express

**exprimer** /ɛkspʀime/ [1] **①** *vtr* to express
**②** **s'exprimer** *v refl* (+ *v être*) **(a)** to express oneself; **si j'ose m'~ ainsi** if I may put it that way
**(b)** to be expressed

**expropriation** /ɛkspʀɔpʀijasjɔ̃/ *nf* compulsory purchase; expropriation

**exproprier** /ɛkspʀɔpʀije/ [2] *vtr* ~ **qn to** put a compulsory purchase order on sb's property

**expulser** /ɛkspylse/ [1] *vtr* **(a)** to evict
**(b)** to deport
**(c)** to expel
**(d)** (Sport) to send [sb] off

**expulsion** /ɛkspylsjɔ̃/ *nf* **(a)** eviction
**(b)** deportation
**(c)** expulsion

**expurger** /ɛkspyʀʒe/ [13] *vtr* to purge

**exquis, ~e** /ɛkski, iz/ *adj* exquisite; delightful

**exsangue** /ɛgzɑ̃g/ *adj* bloodless

**exsuder** /ɛksyde/ [1] **①** *vtr* to exude
**②** *vi* to ooze (**de** from)

**extase** /ɛkstɑz/ *nf* ecstasy

**extasier: s'extasier** /ɛkstazje/ [2] *v refl* (+ *v être*) to go into ecstasy *or* raptures

**extatique** /ɛkstatik/ *adj* ecstatic

**extensible** /ɛkstɑ̃sibl/ *adj* **(a)** extensible
**(b)** extendable

**extensif, -ive** /ɛkstɑ̃sif, iv/ *adj*
**(a)** extensive
**(b)** extended

**extension** /ɛkstɑ̃sjɔ̃/ *nf* extension; **prendre de l'~** ⟨*industry*⟩ to expand; ⟨*strike*⟩ to spread

**exténuer** /ɛkstenɥe/ [1] *vtr* to exhaust

**extérieur, ~e** /ɛksteʀjœʀ/ **①** *adj*
**(a)** outside
**(b)** outer
**(c)** foreign
**(d)** outward
**②** *nm* **(a)** outside; **à l'~** outside, outdoors; **d'~** outdoor
**(b)** exterior, appearance
**(c)** **en ~** ⟨*filmed*⟩ on location

**extérieurement** /ɛksteʀjœʀmɑ̃/ *adv*
**(a)** on the outside
**(b)** outwardly

**extérioriser** /ɛksteʀjɔʀize/ [1] *vtr* to show

**extermination** /ɛkstɛʀminasjɔ̃/ *nf* extermination

**exterminer** /ɛkstɛʀmine/ [1] *vtr* to exterminate; to wipe out

**externat** /ɛkstɛʀna/ *nm* **(a)** (Sch) day school

**(b) préparer l'~** to prepare for medical school entrance exams; **faire son ~** to be a non-resident student doctor (in a hospital)

**externe** /ɛkstɛʀn/ **1** *adj* external; outside; exterior

**2** *nmf* **(a)** (Sch) day pupil

**(b)** (Med) non-residential medical student (GB), extern (US)

**extincteur** /ɛkstɛ̃ktœʀ/ *nm* fire extinguisher

**extinction** /ɛkstɛ̃ksjɔ̃/ *nf* **(a)** (Med) **avoir une ~ de voix** to have lost one's voice

**(b)** extinction; **espèce en voie d'~** endangered species

**(c) après l'~ de l'incendie** after the fire was put out; **après l'~ des feux** after lights out

**extirper** /ɛkstiʀpe/ [1] *vtr* **(a)** to eradicate

**(b)** (colloq) to drag ‹*person*› (**de** out of, from)

**extorquer** /ɛkstɔʀke/ [1] *vtr* to extort

**extorsion** /ɛkstɔʀsjɔ̃/ *nf* extortion

**extra** /ɛkstʀa/ **1** *adj inv* **(a)** (colloq) great (colloq)

**(b)** ‹*product*› of superior quality

**2** *nm inv* **(a)** extra; **se payer un petit ~** to have a little treat

**(b) faire des ~** to do a few extra jobs

**(c)** extra worker

**extracommunautaire**, *pl* **~s** /ɛkstʀakɔmynotɛʀ/ *adj* non-EEC

**extraction** /ɛkstʀaksjɔ̃/ *nf* **(a)** (of oil, gas) extraction; (of coal, diamonds) mining; (of marble, slate) quarrying

**(b)** (of bullet, tooth) extraction

**extrader** /ɛkstʀade/ [1] *vtr* to extradite

**extraire** /ɛkstʀɛʀ/ [58] *vtr* **(a)** to extract ‹*mineral*›; to mine ‹*gold, coal*›; to quarry ‹*slate, marble*›

**(b)** to extract; to pull out; to remove

**extrait** /ɛkstʀɛ/ *nm* **(a)** (from book, film) extract, excerpt; (from speech) extract

**(b)** essence, extract; **~ de viande** meat extract

■ **~ (d'acte) de naissance** birth certificate; **~ de casier judiciaire (de qn)** copy of (sb's) criminal record; **~ de compte** abstract of accounts

**extra-long, -longue**, *mpl* **~s** /ɛkstʀalɔ̃, ɔ̃g/ *adj* ‹*cigarette*› king-size; ‹*clothing*› extra-long

**extralucide** /ɛkstʀalysid/ *adj* clairvoyant

**extraordinaire** /ɛkstʀaɔʀdinɛʀ/ *adj*

**(a)** extraordinary, amazing, remarkable; **c'est quand même ~!** it's incredible!

**(b)** ‹*expenses, measures*› extraordinary

**extraordinairement** /ɛkstʀaɔʀdinɛʀmɑ̃/ *adv* amazingly, extraordinarily

**extrapoler** /ɛkstʀapɔle/ [1] *vtr, vi* to extrapolate

**extrascolaire** /ɛkstʀaskɔlɛʀ/ *adj* extracurricular

**extraterrestre** /ɛkstʀatɛʀɛstʀ/ *nmf* extraterrestrial, alien

**extra-utérin, ~e**, *mpl* **~s** /ɛkstʀayteʀɛ̃, in/ *adj* **grossesse ~e** ectopic pregnancy

**extravagance** /ɛkstʀavagɑ̃s/ *nf*

**(a)** eccentricity

**(b)** extravagance

**extravagant, ~e** /ɛkstʀavagɑ̃, ɑ̃t/ *adj*

**(a)** eccentric

**(b)** extravagant

**(c)** exorbitant

**extraverti, ~e** /ɛkstʀavɛʀti/ *adj, nm,f* extrovert

**extrême** /ɛkstʀɛm/ **1** *adj* **(a)** furthest; **dans l'~ nord/sud du pays** in the extreme North/South of the country

**(b)** extreme

**(c)** drastic

**2** *nm* extreme; **c'est pousser la logique à l'~** that's taking logic to extremes; **à l'~ inverse** at the other extreme

**extrêmement** /ɛkstʀɛmmɑ̃/ *adv* extremely

**Extrême-Orient** /ɛkstʀɛmɔʀjɑ̃/ *pr nm* **l'~** the Far East

**extrémiste** /ɛkstʀemist/ *adj, nmf* extremist

**extrémité** /ɛkstʀemite/ *nf* **(a)** end; (of finger) tip; (of mast) top; (of town, field) edge; **aux deux ~s** at both ends

**(b)** extreme

**exubérance** /ɛgzybeʀɑ̃s/ *nf* exuberance

**exubérant, ~e** /ɛgzybeʀɑ̃, ɑ̃t/ *adj* exuberant

**exultation** /ɛgzyltasjɔ̃/ *nf* exultation

**exulter** /ɛgzylte/ [1] *vi* to be exultant (**de** with), to exult (**de faire** at doing)

**exutoire** /ɛgzytwaʀ/ *nm* outlet

# Ff

**f, F** /ɛf/ *nm inv* **(a)** (letter f, F
**(b)** F3 2-bedroom flat (GB) *or* apartment
**(c)** (*written abbr* = **franc**) 50 F 50 F

**fa** /fa/ *nm inv* (Mus) (note) F; (in sol-fa) fa

**fable** /fabl/ *nf* **(a)** tale
**(b)** fable
**(c)** tall story

**fabricant** /fabʀikɑ̃/ *nm* manufacturer

**fabrication** /fabʀikasjɔ̃/ *nf* making;
manufacture; **~ en série** mass production.
■ **~ assistée par ordinateur, FAO** computer-
aided manufacturing, CAM

**fabrique** /fabʀik/ *nf* factory

**fabriquer** /fabʀike/ [1] *vtr* **(a)** to make; to
manufacture
**(b)** to invent ⟨*alibi*⟩; **qu'est-ce que tu
fabriques?** (colloq) what are you up to?

**fabulateur, -trice** /fabylatœʀ, tʀis/ *nm,f*
compulsive liar

**fabuler** /fabyle/ [1] *vi* **(a)** to make things
up
**(b)** to confabulate

**fabuleusement** /fabyløzmɑ̃/ *adv*
fabulously

**fabuleux, -euse** /fabylø, øz/ *adj* ⟨*beauty*⟩
fabulous; ⟨*sum*⟩ fantastic; ⟨*creature*⟩ mythical

**fac** /fak/ *nf* (colloq) **(a)** faculty
**(b)** university

**façade** /fasad/ *nf* **(a)** (of building) front;
**~ nord** north side
**(b)** façade

**face** /fas/ **1** *nf* **(a)** face
**(b)** side; **le côté ~ d'une pièce** the heads side
of a coin
**(c)** **faire ~** to face up to things; **se faire ~** to
face each other; to be opposite one another;
**faire ~ à** to face ⟨*place*⟩; (figurative) to face
⟨*adversary, challenge*⟩; to cope with
⟨*spending*⟩; to meet ⟨*demand*⟩
**2 de face** *phr* ⟨*photo*⟩ fullface; ⟨*lighting*⟩
frontal
**3 en face** *phr* **il habite en ~** he lives
opposite; **voir les choses en ~** to see things
as they are; **l'équipe d'en ~** the opposing
team
**4 en face de** *phr* **(a)** en ~ de l'église
opposite the church (GB), across from the
church
**(b)** compared with
**5 face à** *phr* **(a)** mon lit est ~ à la fenêtre
my bed faces the window
**(b)** **~ à cette situation** in view of this
situation
**IDIOMS se voiler la ~** not to face facts

**face-à-face** /fasafas/ *nm inv* **(a)** one-to-
one debate (GB), one-on-one debate (US)
**(b)** encounter

**facétie** /fasesi/ *nf* facetious remark;
practical joke

**facétieux, -ieuse** /fasesjø, øz/ *adj*
mischievous

**facette** /fasɛt/ *nf* facet

**fâché, ~e** /fɑʃe/ **1** *pp* ▶ **FÂCHER**
**2** *pp adj* angry; **être ~ avec qn** to have
fallen out with sb

**fâcher: se fâcher** /fɑʃe/ [1] *v refl* (+ *v être*)
**(a)** to get angry
**(b)** to fall out

**fâcheux, -euse** /fɑʃø, øz/ *adj* ⟨*influence*⟩
detrimental; ⟨*delay*⟩ unfortunate; ⟨*news*⟩
distressing

**facial, ~e,** *mpl* **-iaux** /fasjal, o/ *adj*
facial

**faciès** /fasjɛs/ *nm inv* **(a)** facies
**(b)** face

**facile** /fasil/ **1** *adj* **(a)** easy; **avoir la larme
~** to be quick to cry
**(b)** easy-going
**2** *adv* (colloq) easily

**facilement** /fasilmɑ̃/ *adv* **(a)** easily
**(b)** (colloq) **j'ai mis ~ deux heures pour venir**
it took me a good two hours to get here

**facilité** /fasilite/ **1** *nf* **(a)** (of work) easiness;
(of use, maintenance) ease
**(b)** fluency
**2 facilités** *nf pl* **(a)** donner toutes **~s**
pour faire to afford every opportunity to do
**(b)** **~s (de paiement)** easy terms

**faciliter** /fasilite/ [1] *vtr* to make [sth]
easier

**façon** /fasɔ̃/ **1** *nf* **(a)** way; **de toute ~, de
toutes les ~s** anyway; **de ~ à faire** in order
to do; **in such a way as to do; de ~ (à ce)
qu'elle fasse** so (that) she does; **elle nous a
joué un tour à sa ~** she played a trick of her
own on us; **~ de parler** so to speak
**(b)** **un peigne ~ ivoire** an imitation ivory
comb
**(c)** (of garment) making-up
**2 façons** *nf pl* **(a)** en voilà des **~s!** what a
way to behave!; **sans ~s** ⟨*meal*⟩ informal;
⟨*person*⟩ unpretentious

**façonner** /fasone/ [1] *vtr* **(a)** to
manufacture; to make
**(b)** to hew ⟨*wood*⟩; to fashion ⟨*clay*⟩
**(c)** to shape, to mould (GB), to mold (US)

**fac-similé,** *pl* **~s** /faksimile/ *nm*
facsimile

**facteur, -trice** /faktœʀ, tʀis/ **1** *nm,f*
postman/postwoman
**2** *nm* factor

**factice** /faktis/ *adj* ⟨*smile*⟩ forced;
⟨*jewellery*⟩ imitation; ⟨*flower, beauty*⟩
artificial

**faction** /faksjɔ̃/ *nf* **(a)** faction
**(b)** (Mil) guard duty
**factrice** ▶ FACTEUR 1
**factuel, -elle** /faktɥɛl/ *adj* factual
**facturation** /faktyʀasjɔ̃/ *nf* **(a)** invoicing
**(b)** invoicing department
**facture** /faktyʀ/ *nf* bill; invoice
**facturer** /faktyʀe/ [1] *vtr* to invoice
⟨*goods*⟩
**facturette** /faktyʀɛt/ *nf* credit card slip
**facturier, -ière¹** /faktyʀje, ɛʀ/ [1] *nm,f*
invoice clerk
[2] *nm* invoice book
**facturière²** /faktyʀjɛʀ/ *nf* invoicing
machine
**facultatif, -ive** /fakyltatif, iv/ *adj*
optional
**faculté** /fakylte/ *nf* **(a)** (mental) faculty;
ability
**(b)** option
**(c)** (at university) faculty
**(d)** (Law) right
**fade** /fad/ *adj* ⟨*person, book*⟩ dull; ⟨*food,
taste*⟩ tasteless; ⟨*colour*⟩ drab
**fadeur** /fadœʀ/ *nf* blandness; dreariness
**fagot** /fago/ *nm* bundle of firewood
**fagoter** /fagote/ [1] (colloq) [1] *vtr* to do [sb]
up (colloq)
[2] **se fagoter** *v refl* to do oneself up
(colloq); (être) **mal fagoté** (to be) badly
dressed
**faible** /fɛbl/ [1] *adj* **(a)** (gen) weak; ⟨*sight*⟩
poor; ⟨*constitution*⟩ frail; **être ~ avec qn** to
be too soft on sb
**(b)** ⟨*proportion, increase*⟩ small; ⟨*income,
speed*⟩ low; ⟨*means, impact*⟩ limited; ⟨*chance*⟩
slim
**(c)** ⟨*noise, glow*⟩ faint; ⟨*lighting*⟩ dim; ⟨*wind,
rain*⟩ light
**(d)** ⟨*result*⟩ poor; ⟨*argument*⟩ feeble
**(e)** ⟨*pupil, class*⟩ slow; **~ d'esprit** feeble-
minded
**(f) le mot est ~!** that's putting it mildly!
[2] *nmf* weak-willed person
[3] *nm* weakness; **avoir un ~ pour qn** to
have a soft spot for sb
**faiblement** /fɛbləmã/ *adv* weakly;
⟨*influence, increase*⟩ slightly; ⟨*lit*⟩ dimly
**faiblesse** /fɛblɛs/ *nf* **(a)** weakness;
(of invalid) frailty
**(b)** inadequacy
**(c)** (of voice) faintness; (of lighting) dimness
**faiblir** /fɛbliʀ/ [3] *vi* **(a)** ⟨*person, pulse*⟩ to
get weaker; ⟨*sight*⟩ to be failing
**(b)** ⟨*person, currency*⟩ to weaken
**(c)** ⟨*athlete*⟩ to flag; ⟨*plot*⟩ to decline;
⟨*interest*⟩ to wane; ⟨*speed*⟩ to slacken
**(d)** ⟨*storm*⟩ to abate; ⟨*noise*⟩ to grow faint
**faïence** /fajɑ̃s/ *nf* earthenware
**IDIOMS se regarder en chiens de ~** to look
daggers at each other
**faille** /faj/ *nf* **(a)** (in geology) fault
**(b)** flaw; **sans ~** unfailing
**(c)** rift

**faillir** /fajiʀ/ [28] *vi* **(a)** elle a failli le gifler
she almost *or* (very) nearly slapped him
**(b) sans ~** unfailingly
**faillite** /fajit/ *nf* **(a)** bankruptcy
**(b)** failure
**faim** /fɛ̃/ *nf* hunger; **avoir ~** to be hungry;
**mourir de ~** to die of starvation; (figurative) to
be starving; **je suis resté sur ma ~** I was
disappointed
**fainéant, ~e** /feneɑ̃, ɑ̃t/ *adj* lazy
**fainéantise** /feneɑ̃tiz/ *nf* laziness
**faire** /fɛʀ/ [10]

■ **Note** You will find translations for expressions
such as *faire peur, faire semblant* etc., at the
entries PEUR, SEMBLANT etc.

[1] *vtr* **(a)** to make; **~ son lit/une faute** to
make one's bed/a mistake; **~ des jaloux** to
make people jealous; **deux et deux font
quatre** two and two is four
**(b)** to do; **~ de la recherche** to do research;
**j'ai à ~** I have things to do; **que fait-il?** what
does he do?; what is he doing?; **que veux-tu
que j'y fasse?** what do you want me to do
about it?; **~ médecine/du violon** to do *or*
study medicine/to study *or* play the violin;
**~ une école de commerce** to go to business
school; **~ un numéro de téléphone/une lettre**
to dial a number/to write a letter; **~ du
tennis/de la couture** to play tennis/to sew;
**~ un poulet** to do *or* cook a chicken
**(c)** to do ⟨*distance, journey*⟩; to go round
⟨*shops*⟩; to do (colloq) ⟨*region, museums*⟩; **j'ai
fait tous les tiroirs mais je ne l'ai pas trouvé**
I went through all the drawers but I
couldn't find it
**(d)** (colloq) to have ⟨*diabetes, complex*⟩
**(e) ~ le malade** to pretend to be ill
**(f) leur départ ne m'a rien fait** their
departure didn't affect me at all; **ça y fait**
(colloq) it has an effect; **pour ce que ça fait!**
(colloq) for all the good it does!
**(g)** to say; **'bien sûr,' fit-elle** 'of course,' she
said; **le canard fait 'coin-coin'** ducks go
'quack'
**(h) ça m'a fait rire** it made me laugh;
**~ manger un bébé** to feed a baby; **fais voir**
show me; **fais-leur prendre un rendez-vous**
get them to make an appointment;
**~ traverser la rue à un vieillard** to help an
old man across the road
**(i) ~ réparer sa voiture** to have *or* get one's
car repaired
**(j) je n'en ai rien à ~** (colloq) I couldn't care
less; **ça ne fait rien!** it doesn't matter!;
**qu'est-ce que ça peut bien te ~?** (colloq)
what is it to you?; **il sait y ~** he's got the
knack; **il ne fait que pleuvoir** it never stops
raining; **je ne fais qu'obéir aux ordres** I'm
only obeying orders
[2] *vi* **(a)** to do, to act; **fais comme tu veux** do
as you like
**(b)** to look; **~ jeune** to look young
**(c) ça fait 15 ans que j'habite ici** I've been
living here for 15 years; **ça fait 2 mètres de
long** it's 2 metres (GB) long                    ····❯

**(d)** to go (to the toilet); **tu as fait?** have you been?

**(e)** (colloq) ∼ **avec** to make do with; to put up with

**3 se faire** v refl (+ v être) **(a) se** ∼ **un café** to make oneself a coffee; **se** ∼ **comprendre** to make oneself understood

**(b)** to get, to become; **il se fait tard** it's getting late

**(c) s'en** ∼ to worry; **il ne s'en fait pas!** he's not the sort of person to worry about things!; (as criticism) he's got a nerve!

**(d) se** ∼ **à** to get used to

**(e) ça se fait encore ici** it's still done here; **ça ne se fait pas** it's not the done thing

**(f)** ⟨colour, style⟩ to be in (fashion)

**(g) c'est ce qui se fait de mieux** it's the best there is

**(h) comment se fait-il que...?** how is it that...?, how come...?

**faire-part** /fɛʀpaʀ/ nm inv announcement
**faire-valoir** /fɛʀvalwaʀ/ nm inv **être le** ∼ **de** ⟨actor⟩ to be a foil for
**fais** /fɛ/ ▶ FAIRE
**faisaient** /fɛzɛ/ ▶ FAIRE
**faisais** /fɛzɛ/ ▶ FAIRE
**faisait** /fɛzɛ/ ▶ FAIRE
**faisan** /fəzɑ̃/ nm (cock) pheasant
**faisane** /fəzan/ nf (poule) ∼ hen pheasant
**faisant** /fɛzɑ̃/ ▶ FAIRE
**faisceau**, pl ∼**x** /fɛso/ nm **(a)** beam; ∼ **lumineux** beam of light
**(b)** bundle
**faisiez** /fɛzje/ ▶ FAIRE
**faisions** /fɛzjɔ̃/ ▶ FAIRE
**faisons** /fɛzɔ̃/ ▶ FAIRE
**fait**, ∼**e** /fɛ, fɛt/ **1** pp ▶ FAIRE
**2** pp adj **(a)** done; **c'en est** ∼ **de** that's the end of; **c'est bien** ∼ **(pour toi)!** (colloq) it serves you right!
**(b)** ∼ **de** or **en** made (up) of; **idée toute** ∼**e** ready-made idea; **elle est bien** ∼**e** she's got a great figure; **la vie est mal** ∼**e** life is unfair
**(c)** ∼ **pour qch/pour faire** meant for sth/to do
**(d)** ⟨programme, device⟩ designed
**(e)** (colloq) done for
**(f) un fromage bien** ∼ a ripe cheese
**3** nm **(a)** fact; **le** ∼ **est là** or **les** ∼**s sont là**, **il t'a trompé** the fact (of the matter) is that he cheated you; **les** ∼**s et gestes de qn** sb's movements
**(b) de ce** ∼ because of this or that; **être le** ∼ **de qn** to be due to sb
**(c)** event
**(d) aller droit au** ∼ to go straight to the point
**4 au fait** /ofɛt/ phr by the way
**5 de fait** phr **(a)** ⟨situation⟩ de facto
**(b)** ⟨exist, result in⟩ effectively
**(c)** indeed
**6 en fait** phr in fact, actually
**7 en fait de** phr as regards
■ ∼ **divers** (short) news item; ∼ **de société** fact of life

IDIOMS **être au** ∼ **de** to be informed about; **prendre qn sur le** ∼ to catch sb in the act
**faîte** /fɛt/ nm (of mountain) summit; (of house) rooftop; (of tree) top
**faites** /fɛt/ ▶ FAIRE
**falaise** /falɛz/ nf cliff
**fallacieux**, **-ieuse** /falasjø, øz/ adj ⟨argument⟩ fallacious; ⟨pretext⟩ false
**falloir** /falwaʀ/ [50] **1** v impers **(a) il faut qn/qch** we need sb/sth; sb/sth is needed; **il va** ∼ **deux jours/du courage** it will take two days/courage; **il me/te/leur faut qch** I/you/they need sth; **il me faut ce livre!** I've got to have that book!
**(b) il faut faire** we/you etc have (got) to do; we/you etc must do; we/you etc should do; **il ne faut pas la déranger** she mustn't be disturbed; **il fallait le faire** it had to be done; **faut le faire!** (colloq) (admiring) it takes a bit of doing!; (critical) would you believe it?; **comme il faut** ⟨behave⟩ properly
**(c) il faut que tu fasses** you have (got) to do, you must do; you should do
**2 s'en falloir** v refl (+ v être) **peu s'en faut** very nearly; **elle a perdu, mais il s'en est fallu de peu** she lost, but only just
IDIOMS **il faut ce qu'il faut!** there's no point in skimping!; **en moins de temps qu'il ne faut pour le dire** before you could say Jack Robinson
**fallu** /faly/ ▶ FALLOIR
**falsification** /falsifikasjɔ̃/ nf
**(a)** falsification
**(b)** forging
**falsifier** /falsifje/ [2] vtr **(a)** to falsify, to tamper with ⟨document⟩; to distort ⟨facts⟩
**(b)** to forge
**famé**, ∼**e** /fame/ adj **un quartier mal** ∼ **a** disreputable or seedy area
**famélique** /famelik/ adj emaciated, scrawny
**fameux**, **-euse** /famø, øz/ adj **(a)** much talked-about
**(b)** famous
**(c)** excellent
**familial**, ∼**e**, mpl **-iaux** /familjal, o/ adj
**(a)** ⟨meal, life, firm⟩ family
**(b) voiture** ∼**e** estate car (GB), station wagon (US)
**familiariser** /familjaʀize/ [1] vtr to familiarize
**familiarité** /familjaʀite/ nf familiarity
**familier**, **-ière** /familje, ɛʀ/ adj **(a)** ⟨face, landscape⟩ familiar
**(b)** ⟨word⟩ informal, colloquial
**(c)** ⟨attitude⟩ informal; ⟨person, gesture⟩ familiar
**(d) animal** ∼ pet
**familièrement** /familjɛʀmɑ̃/ adv
**(a)** commonly
**(b)** informally
**(c)** with undue familiarity
**famille** /famij/ nf family; **c'est de** ∼ it runs in the family
**famine** /famin/ nf famine

**fanatique** /fanatik/ **1** *adj* ‹believer›
fanatical; ‹admiration, love› ardent
**2** *nmf* **(a)** fanatic
**(b)** (colloq) enthusiast, freak (colloq)
**fanatisme** /fanatism/ *nm* fanaticism
**faner** /fane/ [1] **1** *vi* **(a)** to wither
**(b)** to make hay
**2 se faner** *v refl* (+ *v être*) **(a)** ‹plant› to
wither, to wilt
**(b)** ‹beauty, colour› to fade
**fanfare** /fɑ̃faʀ/ *nf* brass band; **annoncer**
**qch en ~** to trumpet sth
**fanfaron, -onne** /fɑ̃faʀɔ̃, ɔn/ *nm,f*
boaster, swaggerer; **faire le ~** to boast
**fanfaronner** /fɑ̃faʀɔne/ [1] *vi* to boast
**fanion** /fanjɔ̃/ *nm* pennant
**fantaisie** /fɑ̃tɛzi/ *nf* **(a)** imaginativeness;
**manquer de ~** ‹person› to be staid; ‹life› to
be dull
**(b)** whim, fancy
**(c) s'offrir une petite ~** to spoil oneself; **un**
**bijou ~** a piece of costume jewellery (GB) *or*
jewelry (US)
**fantaisiste** /fɑ̃tɛzist/ *adj* **(a)** ‹person›
unreliable; ‹figures› doubtful
**(b)** ‹idea› far-fetched
**fantasme** /fɑ̃tasm/ *nm* fantasy
**fantasque** /fɑ̃task/ *adj* ‹character›
unpredictable; ‹tale› fanciful
**fantassin** /fɑ̃tasɛ̃/ *nm* infantryman,
footsoldier
**fantastique** /fɑ̃tastik/ **1** *adj* fantastic
**2** *nm* **le ~** fantasy
**fantoche** /fɑ̃tɔʃ/ *adj* puppet
**fantôme** /fɑ̃tom/ **1** *nm* ghost
**2** **(-)fantôme** (combining form) ‹train,
city› ghost; **image(-)~** (on screen) ghost;
**société(-)~** (Law) dummy company
**FAO** /ɛfao/ *nf* (Comput) (abbr = **fabrication**
**assistée par ordinateur**) CAM
**faon** /fɑ̃/ *nm* (Zool) fawn
**faramineux, -euse** /faʀaminø, øz/ *adj*
(colloq) colossal, staggering; incredible
**farandole** /faʀɑ̃dɔl/ *nf* (dance) farandole;
≈ conga
**farce** /faʀs/ *nf* **(a)** practical joke; **magasin**
**de ~s et attrapes** joke shop (GB), novelty
store (US)
**(b)** joke
**(c)** (in theatre) farce
**(d)** stuffing, forcemeat
**farceur, -euse** /faʀsœʀ, øz/ *nm,f*
practical joker
**farcir** /faʀsiʀ/ [3] *vtr* (Culin) to stuff
**fard** /faʀ/ *nm* make-up; **sans ~** ‹beauty›
natural; ‹truth› simple
■ **~ à joues** blusher; **~ à paupières** eye-
shadow
IDIOMS **piquer un ~** (colloq) to go as red as a
beetroot (GB), to turn as red as a beet (US)
**fardeau** /faʀdo/ *nm* ~**x** /faʀdo/ *nm* burden
**farder** /faʀde/ [1] **1** *vtr* to disguise ‹truth›
**2 se farder** *v refl* (+ *v être*) ‹actor› to
make up; ‹woman› to use make-up

**farfelu, ~e** /faʀfəly/ *adj* (colloq) ‹idea›
harebrained (colloq); ‹person› scatter-brained
(colloq); ‹show› bizarre
**farfouiller** /faʀfuje/ [1] *vi* (colloq) to
rummage around *or* about (**dans** in)
**farine** /faʀin/ *nf* **(a)** flour
**(b)** baby cereal
■ **~ d'avoine** oatmeal
IDIOMS **se faire rouler dans la ~** (colloq) to be
had (colloq)
**farineux, -euse** /faʀinø, øz/ *adj* ‹food›
starchy; ‹potato› floury
**farniente** /faʀnjɛnte/ *nm* **le ~** lazing
about, lazing around
**farouche** /faʀuʃ/ *adj* **(a)** ‹child, animal›
timid, shy; ‹adult› unsociable
**(b)** ‹look, warrior› fierce
**(c)** ‹enemy, hatred› bitter; ‹adversary› fierce;
‹supporter› staunch; ‹will› iron
**farouchement** /faʀuʃmɑ̃/ *adv* ‹opposed,
independent› fiercely; ‹refuse› doggedly
**fascicule** /fasikyl/ *nm* **(a)** booklet
**(b)** fascicule
**fascinant, ~e** /fasinɑ̃, ɑ̃t/ *adj* ‹person,
film› fascinating; ‹charm, music›
spellbinding
**fascination** /fasinasjɔ̃/ *nf* fascination
**fasciner** /fasine/ [1] *vtr* ‹speaker, music› to
hold [sb] spellbound; ‹sea, person› to
fascinate
**fascisant, ~e** /faʃizɑ̃, ɑ̃t/ *adj* fascistic
**fascisme** /faʃism/ *nm* fascism
**fasse** /fas/ ▶ FAIRE
**fassent** /fas/ ▶ FAIRE
**fasses** /fas/ ▶ FAIRE
**fassiez** /fasje/ ▶ FAIRE
**fassions** /fasjɔ̃/ ▶ FAIRE
**faste** /fast/ **1** *adj* auspicious
**2** *nm* splendour (GB), pomp; **avec ~** with
pomp
**fastidieux, -ieuse** /fastidjø, øz/ *adj*
tedious
**fatal, ~e** /fatal/ *adj* **(a)** inevitable
**(b)** fatal, disastrous
**(c)** ‹moment, day› fateful
**fatalement** /fatalmɑ̃/ *adv* inevitably
**fatalisme** /fatalism/ *nm* fatalism
**fatalité** /fatalite/ *nf* **(a)** **la ~** fate
**(b)** mischance
**(c)** inevitability
**fatidique** /fatidik/ *adj* fateful
**fatigant, ~e** /fatigɑ̃, ɑ̃t/ *adj* **(a)** ‹sport,
journey› tiring; ‹climate› wearing
**(b)** ‹work› arduous
**(c)** ‹person› tiresome; ‹film, conversation›
tedious
**fatigue** /fatig/ *nf* **(a)** tiredness; **être mort**
**de ~, tomber de ~** to be dead tired
**(b)** (Med) fatigue; **~ visuelle** eyestrain
**fatigué, ~e** /fatige/ **1** *pp* ▶ FATIGUER
**2** *pp adj* ‹voice› strained; ‹eyes, smile›
weary

**fatiguer** /fatige/ [1] **1** *vtr* **(a)** to make [sb/sth] tired; to strain ⟨*eyes*⟩
**(b)** to tire [sb] out
**(c)** to wear [sb] out
**(d)** to wear out ⟨*engine*⟩
**2** *vi* **(a)** (colloq) to get tired
**(b)** ⟨*engine, car*⟩ to be labouring (GB)
**3** **se fatiguer** *v refl* (+ *v être*) **(a)** to get tired
**(b)** to tire oneself out
**(c)** se ∼ les yeux to strain one's eyes
**(d)** se ∼ à faire to bother doing

**fatras** /fatʀa/ *nm inv* jumble

**faubourg** /fobuʀ/ *nm* working class area (*on the outskirts*)

**fauché**, ∼**e** /foʃe/ *adj* (colloq) broke (colloq), penniless

**faucher** /foʃe/ [1] *vtr* **(a)** to mow; to scythe
**(b)** ⟨*car, bullet*⟩ to mow [sb] down
**(c)** (colloq) to steal

**faucheuse** /foʃøz/ *nf* mowing machine

**faucille** /fosij/ *nf* sickle

**faucon** /fokɔ̃/ *nm* falcon, hawk (US)

**faudra** ▶ FALLOIR

**faufiler** /fofile/ [1] **1** *vtr* to baste
**2** **se faufiler** *v refl* (+ *v être*) **(a)** se ∼ à l'extérieur to slip out
**(b)** se ∼ dans ⟨*mistakes*⟩ to creep into ⟨*text*⟩
**(c)** ⟨*route*⟩ to snake in and out

**faune** /fon/ *nf* **(a)** wildlife, fauna; la ∼ marine marine life
**(b)** (derogatory) set, crowd

**faussaire** /fosɛʀ/ *nmf* forger

**fausse** ▶ FAUX[1] 1

**faussement** /fosmɑ̃/ *adv* **(a)** falsely, wrongfully
**(b)** deceptively

**fausser** /fose/ [1] *vtr* to distort ⟨*result, mechanism*⟩; to damage ⟨*lock*⟩; to buckle ⟨*blade*⟩
IDIOMS ∼ compagnie à qn to give sb the slip

**faut** ▶ FALLOIR

**faute** /fot/ *nf* **(a)** mistake, error; il a fait un (parcours) sans ∼ he's never put a foot wrong
**(b)** (gen) misdemeanour (GB); (Law) civil wrong; être en ∼ to be at fault; prendre qn en ∼ to catch sb out
**(c)** fault; c'est (de) ma ∼ it's my fault; par la ∼ de qn because of sb; rejeter la ∼ sur qn to lay the blame on sb
**(d)** ∼ de temps through lack of time; ∼ de mieux for want of anything better; ∼ de quoi otherwise, failing which; sans ∼ without fail
**(e)** (Sport) foul; (in tennis) fault

**fauteuil** /fotœj/ *nm* **(a)** chair, armchair
**(b)** (in theatre) seat

**fauteur** /fotœʀ/ *nm* ∼ de troubles troublemaker; ∼ de guerre warmonger

**fautif**, -**ive** /fotif, iv/ **1** *adj* **(a)** at fault
**(b)** ⟨*memory*⟩ faulty; ⟨*reference*⟩ inaccurate
**2** *nm,f* culprit

**fauve** /fov/ **1** *adj* tawny
**2** *nm* **(a)** wild animal

**(b)** big cat
**(c)** (colour) fawn

**fauvette** /fovɛt/ *nf* warbler

**faux[1], fausse** /fo, fos/ **1** *adj* **(a)** ⟨*result, number, idea*⟩ wrong; ⟨*impression, promise, accusation*⟩ false
**(b)** ⟨*beard, tooth, eyelashes*⟩ false
**(c)** ⟨*wood, marble, diamonds*⟩ imitation, fake; ⟨*door, drawer*⟩ false
**(d)** ⟨*passport, money*⟩ forged
**(e)** ⟨*policeman, bishop*⟩ bogus; ⟨*candour, humility*⟩ feigned
**(f)** ⟨*hope*⟩ false; ⟨*fear*⟩ groundless
**(g)** deceitful
**2** *adv* ⟨*play, sing*⟩ out of tune
**3** *nm inv* **(a)** le ∼ falsehood
**(b)** fake; forgery

■ fausse couche (Med) miscarriage; fausse facture bogus invoice; fausse fenêtre blind window; fausse joie ill-founded joy; faire une fausse joie à qn to raise sb's hopes in vain; fausse monnaie forged *or* counterfeit currency; fausse note jarring note; fausse piste wrong track; ∼ ami foreign word which looks deceptively like a word in one's own language; ∼ en écriture(s) falsification of accounts; ∼ frais extras, incidental expenses; ∼ jeton (colloq) two-faced person; ∼ nom assumed name; ∼ pas slip; mistake; faux pas; ∼ pli crease; ∼ témoignage perjury

**faux[2]** /fo/ *nf inv* scythe

**faux-filet**, *pl* ∼**s** /fofilɛ/ *nm* sirloin

**faux-monnayeur**, *pl* ∼**s** /fomɔnɛjœʀ/ *nm* forger, counterfeiter

**faux-semblant**, *pl* ∼**s** /fosɑ̃blɑ̃/ *nm* les ∼s pretence (GB)

**faveur** /favœʀ/ **1** *nf* favour (GB); régime *or* traitement de ∼ preferential treatment; des mesures en ∼ des handicapés measures to help the disabled; intervenir en ∼ de qn to intervene on sb's behalf
**2** à la faveur de *phr* thanks to; à la ∼ de la nuit under cover of darkness

**favorable** /favɔʀabl/ *adj* favourable (GB); être ∼ à qch to be in favour (GB) of sth

**favori**, -**ite** /favɔʀi, it/ **1** *adj*, *nm,f* favourite (GB)
**2** favoris *nm pl* sideburns

**favoriser** /favɔʀize/ [1] *vtr* **(a)** to favour (GB); les milieux favorisés the privileged classes
**(b)** to encourage, to promote

**favorite** ▶ FAVORI 1

**favoritisme** /favɔʀitism/ *nm* favouritism (GB)

**fax** /faks/ *nm inv* **(a)** fax
**(b)** fax machine

**fayot[1]** /fajo/ *nm* (colloq) bean

**fayot[2]**, -**otte** /fajo, ɔt/ *nm,f* (colloq) creep (colloq), crawler (colloq)

**FB** (*written abbr* = **franc belge**) BFr

**fébrile** /febʀil/ *adj* **(a)** ⟨*emotion, gesture*⟩ feverish; ⟨*person*⟩ nervous
**(b)** (Med) feverish

**fébrilité** /febʀilite/ *nf* (a) agitation; **avec ~** agitatedly
(b) nervousness

**fécal, ~e,** *mpl* **-aux** /fekal, o/ *adj* faecal

**fécond, ~e** /fekɔ̃, ɔ̃d/ *adj* (a) fertile
(b) fruitful

**fécondation** /fekɔ̃dasjɔ̃/ *nf* (of female) impregnation; (of plant) pollination; (of egg) fertilization

**féconder** /fekɔ̃de/ [1] *vtr* to impregnate ⟨*female*⟩; to inseminate ⟨*animal*⟩; to pollinate ⟨*plant*⟩; to fertilize ⟨*egg, ovum*⟩

**fécondité** /fekɔ̃dite/ *nf* (a) fertility
(b) (of author) productivity

**fécule** /fekyl/ *nf* starch

**féculent** /fekylã/ *nm* starch; starchy food

**fédéral, ~e,** *mpl* **-aux** /fedeʀal, o/ *adj* federal

**fédéralisme** /fedeʀalism/ *nm* federalism

**fédératif, -ive** /fedeʀatif, iv/ *adj* federal

**fédération** /fedeʀasjɔ̃/ *nf* federation

**fée** /fe/ *nf* fairy; **~ du logis** perfect housewife
IDIOMS **avoir des doigts de ~** to have nimble fingers

**féerie** /fe(e)ʀi/ *nf* (a) **c'est une vraie ~** it's magical
(b) extravaganza

**féerique** /fe(e)ʀik/ *adj* ⟨*beauty*⟩ enchanting; ⟨*landscape, moment*⟩ enchanted

**feignant, ~e** /fɛɲɑ̃, ɑ̃t/ = FAINÉANT

**feindre** /fɛ̃dʀ/ [55] *vtr* to feign; **~ de faire/d'être** to pretend to do/to be

**feinte** /fɛ̃t/ *nf* (a) feint; **faire une ~** (in football, rugby) to dummy (GB), to fake (US)
(b) (colloq) trick, ruse

**fêlé, ~e** /fɛle/ *adj* (colloq) cracked (colloq)

**fêler** /fɛle/ [1] *vtr,* **se fêler** *v refl* (+ *v être*) to crack

**félicitations** /felisitasjɔ̃/ *nf pl* congratulations

**féliciter** /felisite/ [1] **①** *vtr* to congratulate **②** **se féliciter** *v refl* (+ *v être*) **se ~ de qch** to be very pleased about sth

**félin, ~e** /felɛ̃, in/ **①** *adj* (a) feline; **exposition ~e** cat show
(b) ⟨*grace*⟩ feline; ⟨*eyes*⟩ catlike **②** *nm* feline; **les ~s** felines, the cat family

**fêlure** /felyʀ/ *nf* crack

**femelle** /fəmɛl/ **①** *adj* female; **éléphant ~** cow elephant; **moineau ~** hen sparrow **②** *nf* female; (in pair) mate

**féminin, ~e** /feminɛ̃, in/ **①** *adj* ⟨*sex, occupation*⟩ female; ⟨*magazine, record*⟩ women's; ⟨*team, club*⟩ ladies'; ⟨*appearance*⟩ feminine **②** *nm* feminine; **au ~** in the feminine

**féminiser: se féminiser** /feminize/ [1] *v refl* (+ *v être*) ⟨*profession*⟩ to become more open to women; to become predominantly female

**féministe** /feminist/ *adj, nmf* feminist

**féminité** /feminite/ *nf* femininity

**femme** /fam/ *nf* (a) woman
(b) wife
■ **~ d'affaires** businesswoman; **~ de chambre** chambermaid; **~ au foyer** housewife; **~ d'intérieur** homemaker; **~ de service** cleaner, cleaning lady; **~ de tête** assertive woman; ▶ BON, JEUNE
IDIOMS **souvent ~ varie** woman is fickle

**fémur** /femyʀ/ *nm* thighbone; **se casser le col du ~** to break one's hip

**FEN** /fɛn/ *nf* (*abbr* = **Fédération de l'éducation nationale**) FEN (*French teachers' union*)

**fendiller: se fendiller** /fɑ̃dije/ [1] *v refl* (+ *v être*) ⟨*lips*⟩ to chap; ⟨*earth*⟩ to craze over; ⟨*wood*⟩ to crack

**fendre** /fɑ̃dʀ/ [6] **①** *vtr* (a) to chop ⟨*wood*⟩; to slit ⟨*material*⟩
(b) to crack ⟨*wall, stone*⟩; to split ⟨*lip*⟩
(c) **~ le cœur à qn** to break sb's heart
(d) **~ l'air** to slice through the air; **~ la foule** to push one's way through the crowd **②** **se fendre** *v refl* (+ *v être*) (a) to crack
(b) (colloq) to cough up (colloq) ⟨*money*⟩; **tu ne t'es pas fendu!** that didn't break the bank!
IDIOMS **se ~ la pêche** (colloq) to split one's sides (colloq); **avoir la bouche fendue jusqu'aux oreilles** to be grinning from ear to ear

**fenêtre** /fənɛtʀ/ *nf* window
■ **~ à guillotine** sash window
IDIOMS **jeter l'argent par les ~s** to throw money away

**fenouil** /fənuj/ *nm* fennel

**fente** /fɑ̃t/ *nf* (a) slit; (for coin, card) slot; (of jacket) vent
(b) crack; (in wood) split; (in rock) crevice

**féodal, ~e,** *mpl* **-aux** /feɔdal, o/ *adj* feudal

**fer** /fɛʀ/ *nm* (a) iron; **de ~** ⟨*discipline, fist, will*⟩ iron
(b) (on shoe) steel tip
(c) branding iron
(d) **croiser le ~ avec** to cross swords with
■ **~ à cheval** horseshoe; **~ forgé** wrought iron; **~ à repasser** iron
IDIOMS **croire dur comme ~** to believe wholeheartedly; **tomber les quatre ~s en l'air** (colloq) to fall flat on one's back

**fera** /fəʀa/ ▶ FAIRE

**ferai** /fəʀe/ ▶ FAIRE

**feraient** /fəʀɛ/ ▶ FAIRE

**ferais** /fəʀɛ/ ▶ FAIRE

**ferait** /fəʀɛ/ ▶ FAIRE

**feras** /fəʀa/ ▶ FAIRE

**fer-blanc,** *pl* **fers-blancs** /fɛʀblɑ̃/ *nm* tinplate

**ferez** /fəʀe/ ▶ FAIRE

**férié, ~e** /feʀje/ *adj* **jour ~** public holiday (GB), holiday (US)

**feriez** /fəʀje/ ▶ FAIRE

**ferions** /fəʀjɔ̃/ ▶ FAIRE

**ferme¹** /fɛʀm/ **①** *adj* (a) firm                    ⋯⋗

**(b)** (Law) **peine de prison ~** custodial sentence

**2** *adv* ⟨*argue, campaign*⟩ vigorously; ⟨*believe*⟩ firmly; **tenir ~** to stand one's ground

IDIOMS **attendre de pied ~** to be ready and waiting

**ferme²** /fɛʀm/ *nf* farm, farmhouse

**fermement** /fɛʀmǝmɑ̃/ *adv* firmly

**ferment** /fɛʀmɑ̃/ *nm* ferment

**fermenter** /fɛʀmɑ̃te/ [1] *vi* to ferment

**fermer** /fɛʀme/ [1] **1** *vtr* **(a)** to close, to shut ⟨*door, book, eyes*⟩; to clench ⟨*fist*⟩; to draw ⟨*curtain*⟩; to turn off ⟨*tap, gas, radio*⟩; to do up ⟨*jacket*⟩; **~ à clé** to lock (up)
**(b)** to close ⟨*shop, airport, road*⟩; (definitively) to close [sth] down
**2** *vi* to close (down)
**3 se fermer** *v refl* (+ *v être*) **(a)** ⟨*door*⟩ to shut; ⟨*flower*⟩ to close up; ⟨*coat, bracelet*⟩ to fasten
**(b)** ⟨*person*⟩ to clam up; ⟨*face*⟩ to harden
IDIOMS **~ les yeux sur** to turn a blind eye to

**fermeté** /fɛʀmǝte/ *nf* firmness

**fermette** /fɛʀmɛt/ *nf* farmhouse-style cottage

**fermeture** /fɛʀmatyʀ/ *nf* **(a)** (of business, account) closing; (definitive) closure, closing down
**(b)** (on handbag) clasp; (on garment) fastening
■ **~ éclair®, ~ à glissière** zip (GB), zipper (US)

**fermier, -ière** /fɛʀmje, ɛʀ/ **1** *adj* free-range
**2** *nm,f* farmer

**fermoir** /fɛʀmwaʀ/ *nm* (on necklace, bag) clasp

**féroce** /feʀɔs/ *adj* **(a)** fierce; ferocious
**(b)** ⟨*appetite*⟩ voracious

**férocité** /feʀɔsite/ *nf* **(a)** (of animal) ferociousness
**(b)** (of remark) savagery
**(c)** (of person) fierceness

**ferons** /fǝʀɔ̃/ ▶ FAIRE

**feront** /fǝʀɔ̃/ ▶ FAIRE

**ferraille** /feʀaj/ *nf* **(a)** scrap metal
**(b)** scrapheap
**(c)** (colloq) small change

**ferrailleur** /feʀajœʀ/ *nm* scrap (metal) dealer

**ferronnerie** /feʀɔnʀi/ *nf* **(a)** ironworks
**(b)** wrought iron work
**(c)** iron work

**ferroviaire** /feʀɔvjɛʀ/ *adj* ⟨*transport, collision*⟩ rail; ⟨*station, tunnel*⟩ railway (GB), railroad (US)

**fertile** /fɛʀtil/ *adj* fertile; ⟨*year*⟩ productive

**fertilisant** /fɛʀtilizɑ̃/ *nm* fertilizer

**fertilité** /fɛʀtilite/ *nf* fertility

**fervent, ~e** /fɛʀvɑ̃, ɑ̃t/ *adj* ⟨*believer*⟩ fervent; ⟨*admirer*⟩ ardent

**ferveur** /fɛʀvœʀ/ *nf* (of prayer) fervour (GB); (of love) ardour (GB)

**fesse** /fɛs/ *nf* buttock

IDIOMS **coûter la peau des ~s** (colloq) to cost an arm and a leg (colloq)

**fessée** /fese/ *nf* smack on the bottom, spanking

**festin** /fɛstɛ̃/ *nm* feast

**festival** /fɛstival/ *nm* festival

**festivités** /fɛstivite/ *nf pl* festivities

**festoyer** /fɛstwaje/ [23] *vi* to feast

**fêtard, ~e** /fɛtaʀ, aʀd/ *nm,f* (colloq) reveller

**fête** /fɛt/ *nf* **(a)** public holiday (GB), holiday (US)
**(b)** (saint's) name-day; **ça va être ma ~!** (colloq) I'm going to cop it! (colloq)
**(c)** festival
**(d)** (day of) celebration
**(e)** party; **faire la ~** to live it up (colloq)
**(f)** fête, fair, celebrations
■ **~ foraine** funfair; **~ du travail** May Day, Labour Day (GB)
IDIOMS **faire sa ~ à qn** (colloq) to give sb a working over (colloq)

**fêter** /fete/ [1] *vtr* to celebrate ⟨*event*⟩

**fétiche** /fetiʃ/ **1** *adj* lucky
**2** *nm* **(a)** mascot
**(b)** fetish

**fétide** /fetid/ *adj* foul; foul-smelling

**feu¹, ~e** /fø/ *adj* late; **~ la reine, la ~e reine** the late queen

**feu², pl ~x** /fø/ *nm* **(a)** fire; ▶ HUILE
**(b)** light; **sous le ~ des projecteurs** under the glare of the spotlights; (figurative) in the spotlight
**(c)** traffic light; **j'ai le ~ vert de mon patron** my boss has given me the go-ahead
**(d)** (on cooker) ring (GB), burner (US); **faire cuire à petit ~** cook over a gentle heat
**(e)** **avez-vous du ~?** have you got a light?
**(f)** passion; **dans le ~ de la discussion** in the heat of the discussion
**(g)** **~!** (Mil) fire!; **faire ~** to fire; **coup de ~** shot
**(h)** (Mil) action
■ **~ d'artifice** fireworks display; firework; **~ de cheminée** chimney fire; open fire; **~ follet** will-o'-the-wisp; **~ de joie** bonfire; **~ de signalisation, ~ tricolore** traffic light; **~x de croisement** dipped (GB) *or* dimmed (US) headlights; **~x de détresse** warning lights; **~x de route** headlights
IDIOMS **il n'y a pas le ~!** (colloq) there's no rush!; **ne pas faire long ~** (colloq) not to last long; **il n'y a vu que du ~** (colloq) he fell for it; **mourir à petit ~** to die a slow death

**feuillage** /fœjaʒ/ *nm* foliage, leaves

**feuille** /fœj/ *nf* **(a)** (Bot) leaf
**(b)** (of paper, metal) sheet
■ **~ de chou** (colloq) rag (colloq), newspaper; **~ d'impôts** tax return; **~ de maladie** *a form for reclaiming medical expenses from the social security office*; **~ de paie** payslip (GB), pay stub (US)

**feuillet** /fœjɛ/ *nm* **(a)** (in book) leaf
**(b)** page

**feuilleté**, **~e** /fœjte/ adj pâte ~e puff pastry

**feuilleter** /fœjte/ [20] vtr to leaf through [sth]

**feuilleton** /fœjtɔ̃/ nm serial; soap (opera)

**feutre** /føtʀ/ nm (a) felt
(b) felt-tip (pen)

**feutré**, **~e** /føtʀe/ adj ⟨atmosphere⟩ hushed; ⟨sound⟩ muffled

**fève** /fɛv/ nf (a) broad bean
(b) lucky charm (hidden in Twelfth Night cake)

**février** /fevʀije/ nm February

**FF** (written abbr = **franc français**) FFr

**fiabilité** /fjabilite/ nf reliability

**fiable** /fjabl/ adj reliable

**fiançailles** /fjɑ̃saj/ nf pl engagement

**fiancé**, **~e** /fjɑ̃se/ nm,f fiancé/fiancée

**fiancer: se fiancer** /fjɑ̃se/ [12] v refl (+ v être) to get engaged

**fibre** /fibʀ/ nf fibre (GB)

**ficeler** /fisle/ [19] vtr to tie up ⟨parcel⟩

**ficelle** /fisɛl/ nf (a) string
(b) trick; la ~ est un peu grosse it's a bit obvious
(c) thin baguette
IDIOMS tirer sur la ~ to push one's luck

**fiche** /fiʃ/ nf (a) index card; slip
(b) form; ~ d'inscription enrolment (GB) form
(c) plug; prise à trois ~s three-pin plug
■ ~ d'état civil record of personal details for administrative purposes; ~ de paie payslip (GB), pay stub (US)

**ficher** /fiʃe/ [1] **1** vtr (a) to put [sth] on a file; to open a file on [sb]; être fiché (par la police) to be on police files
(b) to drive ⟨stake, nail⟩
(c) (colloq) to do; qu'est-ce que tu fiches? what the heck are you doing? (colloq); n'en avoir rien à ~ not to give a damn (colloq)
(d) (colloq) ~ un coup à qn (figurative) to be a real blow to sb; ~ la paix à qn to leave sb alone
(e) (colloq) ~ qch quelque part to chuck sth somewhere (colloq); ~ qn dehors to kick sb out (colloq)
**2 se ficher** v refl (+ v être) (a) ⟨arrow, knife⟩ to stick
(b) (colloq) se ~ de qn to make fun of sb; se ~ du monde to have a hell of a nerve (colloq)
(c) (colloq) se ~ de ce que qn fait not to give a damn (about) what sb does (colloq)

**fichier** /fiʃje/ nm file; (in library) index

**fichu** (colloq) /fiʃy/ **1** pp ▶ FICHER 1 C, D, E, 2
**2** adj (a) ⟨weather, job⟩ rotten (colloq); ⟨rain⟩ dreadful; ⟨car, TV⟩ damned (colloq)
(b) ⟨person, car⟩ done for (colloq); s'il pleut c'est ~ if it rains that's the end of that
(c) être bien ~ to be well designed; ⟨book⟩ to be well laid out; je suis mal ~ I feel lousy (colloq)

(d) être ~ de faire to be quite capable of doing

**fictif**, **-ive** /fiktif, iv/ adj imaginary; false

**fiction** /fiksjɔ̃/ nf (a) fiction
(b) (on TV) drama

**fidèle** /fidɛl/ **1** adj (a) ⟨person, dog⟩ faithful; être ~ au poste to be always there
(b) loyal
(c) true (à to)
(d) ⟨translation⟩ faithful
**2** nmf (a) loyal supporter
(b) les ~s the faithful

**fidèlement** /fidɛlmɑ̃/ adv (a) faithfully
(b) loyally

**fidéliser** /fidelize/ [1] vtr to secure the loyalty of ⟨clients⟩

**fidélité** /fidelite/ nf (a) fidelity
(b) loyalty
(c) (of translation) accuracy

**fiduciaire** /fidysjɛʀ/ adj fiduciary; société ~ trust company

**fief** /fjɛf/ nm (a) fief
(b) (figurative) territory; (of party) stronghold

**fieffé**, **~e** /fjefe/ adj ~ menteur incorrigible liar

**fier¹**, **fière** /fjɛʀ/ adj proud; avoir fière allure to cut a fine figure

**fier²: se fier** /fje/ [2] v refl (+ v être) (a) se ~ à to trust ⟨person, promise⟩
(b) se ~ à to rely on ⟨person, instrument⟩; to trust to ⟨chance⟩

**fierté** /fjɛʀte/ nf pride

**fièvre** /fjɛvʀ/ nf (a) (high) temperature; avoir de la ~ to have a (high) temperature
(b) frenzy
(c) fervour (GB); ~ électorale election fever
■ ~ de cheval (colloq) raging fever

**fiévreusement** /fjevʀøzmɑ̃/ adv frantically; feverishly

**fiévreux**, **-euse** /fjevʀø, øz/ adj (a) (Med) feverish
(b) (agitated) frantic
(c) ⟨passionate⟩ feverish

**figer** /fiʒe/ [13] **1** vtr to congeal ⟨grease⟩; to thicken ⟨sauce⟩; to clot ⟨blood⟩
**2 se figer** v refl (+ v être) (a) ⟨smile, person⟩ to freeze
(b) ⟨grease⟩ to congeal; ⟨blood⟩ to clot

**fignoler** /fiɲole/ [1] **1** vtr (a) to put the finishing touches to
(b) to take great pains over
**2** vi to fiddle about

**figue** /fig/ nf fig; ~ de Barbarie prickly pear

**figuier** /figje/ nm fig tree

**figurant**, **~e** /figyʀɑ̃, ɑ̃t/ nm,f (in films) extra; (in theatre) bit player

**figuratif**, **-ive** /figyʀatif, iv/ adj figurative, representational; artiste non ~ abstract artist

**figuration** /figyʀasjɔ̃/ nf faire de la ~ (in films) to be an extra; (figurative) to have a token role

**figure** /figyʀ/ nf (a) face

**(b)** faire ∼ d'amateur to look like an amateur; reprendre ∼ humaine to look half-human again
**(c)** (in history, politics) figure
**(d)** (in drawing) figure
IDIOMS prendre ∼ to take shape; faire bonne ∼ to keep an air of composure; to make the right impression; to do well

**figurer** /figyʀe/ [1] **1** *vtr* to represent **2** *vi* ⟨*name, object*⟩ to appear **3** se figurer *v refl* (+ *v être*) to imagine

**figurine** /figyʀin/ *nf* figurine

**fil** /fil/ **1** *nm* **(a)** thread; ▶ COUDRE
**(b)** yarn
**(c)** string; ∼ de fer wire
**(d)** wire; (on appliance) flex (GB), cord (US); (on phone) lead; coup de ∼ (colloq) (phone) call; au bout du ∼ (colloq) on the phone
**(e)** (of conversation, text) thread; perdre le ∼ des événements to lose track of events
**(f)** (of razor) edge
**2** au fil de *phr* in the course of; au ∼ des ans over the years; aller au ∼ de l'eau to go with the flow
■ ∼ conducteur (of heat) conductor; (of novel) thread; (of inquiry) lead; ∼ directeur guiding principle
IDIOMS ne tenir qu'à un ∼ to hang by a thread

**filament** /filamã/ *nm* filament

**filature** /filatyʀ/ *nf* **(a)** textile mill
**(b)** spinning
**(c)** prendre qn en ∼ to tail sb (colloq)

**file** /fil/ *nf* **(a)** ∼ (d'attente) queue (GB), line (US)
**(b)** line; ∼ indienne single file
**(c)** lane; se garer en double ∼ to double-park

**filer** /file/ [1] **1** *vtr* **(a)** to spin ⟨*wool, cotton*⟩
**(b)** to spin ⟨*web, cocoon*⟩
**(c)** to ladder (GB), to get a run in ⟨*tights*⟩
**(d)** to tail [sb] (colloq)
**(e)** (colloq) to give [sth] (à qn to sb)
**2** *vi* (colloq) **(a)** to go off, to leave
**(b)** to rush
**(c)** ⟨*time*⟩ to fly by; ⟨*prisoner*⟩ to get away; ∼ entre les mains to slip through one's fingers

**filet** /file/ *nm* **(a)** net; ∼ à provisions string bag; coup de ∼ (police) raid
**(b)** fillet
**(c)** (of water) trickle; (of smoke) wisp; ∼ de citron dash of lemon juice

**filial**, ∼e¹, *mpl* -iaux /filjal, o/ *adj* filial

**filiale²** /filjal/ *nf* subsidiary

**filiation** /filjasjɔ̃/ *nf* filiation

**filière** /filjɛʀ/ *nf* **(a)** (Sch) course of study
**(b)** (Econ) field
**(c)** suivre la ∼ habituelle to climb up the usual career ladder
**(d)** official channels
**(e)** ∼ (clandestine) de la drogue drugs ring

**filiforme** /filifɔʀm/ *adj* spindly; threadlike

**filigrane** /filigʀan/ *nm* filigree

**filin** /filɛ̃/ *nm* rope

**fille** /fij/ *nf* **(a)** daughter
**(b)** girl; ∼ mère unmarried mother

**fillette** /fijɛt/ *nf* **(a)** little girl
**(b)** (colloq) half bottle

**filleul** /fijœl/ *nm* godson, godchild

**filleule** /fijœl/ *nf* goddaughter, godchild

**film** /film/ *nm* **(a)** film, movie (US)
**(b)** (thin) film
■ ∼ d'animation cartoon

**filmer** /filme/ [1] *vtr* to film

**filmique** /filmik/ *adj* film; cinematic

**filon** /filɔ̃/ *nm* vein, seam

**filou** /filu/ *nm* crook; cheat; rascal

**fils** /fis/ *nm inv* son; Dupont ∼ Dupont Junior

**filtre** /filtʀ/ *nm* filter

**filtrer** /filtʀe/ [1] **1** *vtr* **(a)** to filter
**(b)** to screen ⟨*visitors, calls*⟩
**2** *vi* ⟨*information*⟩ to leak out; ⟨*idea, liquid*⟩ to filter through

**fîmes** /fim/ ▶ FAIRE

**fin¹, fine** /fɛ̃, fin/ **1** *adj* **(a)** ⟨*rain, sand, brush*⟩ fine; ⟨*slice, layer*⟩ thin
**(b)** ⟨*ankle, waist*⟩ slender; ⟨*features*⟩ fine; ⟨*dish*⟩ delicate
**(c)** ⟨*person*⟩ perceptive; ⟨*taste, humour*⟩ subtle; vraiment c'est ∼! that's really clever!; jouer au plus ∼ avec qn to try to outsmart sb; avoir l'air ∼ (colloq) to look a fool
**(d)** avoir l'ouïe ∼e to have a keen sense of hearing
**(e)** au ∼ fond de in the remotest part of ⟨*country*⟩; le ∼ mot de l'histoire the truth of the matter
**2** *adv* **(a)** être ∼ prêt to be all set
**(b)** ⟨*write, grind*⟩ finely; ⟨*slice*⟩ thinly
**3** *nm* le ∼ du ∼ the ultimate
■ ∼e mouche sly customer (colloq); ∼es herbes mixed herbs

**fin²** /fɛ̃/ *nf* **(a)** end, ending; à la ∼ des années 70 in the late '70s; tu vas te taire à la ∼! (colloq) for God's sake, be quiet!; chômeur en ∼ de droits unemployed person no longer entitled to benefit
**(b)** end, death
**(c)** end, aim, purpose
■ ∼ de série oddment

**final**, ∼e¹, *mpl* -aux /final, o/ *adj* final

**finale²** /final/ *nf* (Sport) final

**finalement** /finalmã/ *adv* **(a)** in the end, finally
**(b)** in fact, actually

**finaliser** /finalize/ [1] *vtr* to finalize; to complete

**finalité** /finalite/ *nf* **(a)** purpose, aim
**(b)** finality

**finance** /finãs/ **1** *nf* **(a)** la ∼ finance
**(b)** financiers
**2** finances *nf pl* les ∼s finances; moyennant ∼s for a consideration

**financement** /finãsmã/ *nm* financing

**financer** /finãse/ [12] *vtr* to finance

**financier, -ière** /finãsje, ɛʀ/ **1** *adj* financial

**2** *nm* (a) financier
(b) small cake

**finaud, -e** /fino, od/ *nm,f* (Comput) hacker

**finesse** /finɛs/ *nf* (a) (of thread, writing) fineness; (of layer, paper) thinness
(b) (of dish) delicacy; (of face) fineness; (of waist) slenderness
(c) (of remark, person) perceptiveness; (of actor) sensitivity
(d) (of senses) keenness
(e) **les ~s d'une langue** the subtleties of a language

**fini, ~e** /fini/ **1** *pp* ▶ FINIR
**2** *pp adj* **être ~** to be over, to be finished
**3** *nm* finish

**finir** /finiʀ/ [3] **1** *vtr* (a) to finish (off), to complete; to end ⟨day⟩
(b) to use up ⟨supplies⟩
**2** *vi* to finish, to end; ⟨contract, lease⟩ to run out; **le film finit bien** the film has a happy ending; **ça va mal ~!** it'll end in tears!; **~ par faire** to end up doing; **ils finiront bien par céder** they're bound to give in in the end; **en ~ avec qn/qch** to have done with sb/sth; **finissons-en!** let's get it over with!

**finissant** /finisã/ ▶ FINIR
**finition** /finisjɔ̃/ *nf* (a) finishing
(b) finish

**finlandais, ~e** /fɛ̃lɑ̃dɛ, ɛz/ *adj* Finnish
**Finlandais, ~e** /fɛ̃lɑ̃dɛ, ɛz/ *nm,f* Finn
**Finlande** /fɛ̃lɑ̃d/ *pr nf* Finland

**finnois, ~e** /finwa, az/ **1** *adj* Finnish
**2** *nm* (language) Finnish

**fioriture** /fjɔʀityʀ/ *nf* embellishment
**fioul** /fjul/ *nm* fuel oil
**firent** /fiʀ/ ▶ FAIRE
**firme** /fiʀm/ *nf* firm
**fis** /fi/ ▶ FAIRE
**fisc** /fisk/ *nm* tax office
**fiscal, ~e,** *mpl* **-aux** /fiskal, o/ *adj* fiscal, tax
**fiscaliser** /fiskalize/ [1] *vtr* (a) to tax
(b) to fund [sth] by taxation
**fiscalité** /fiskalite/ *nf* (a) taxation
(b) tax system
**fisse** /fis/ ▶ FAIRE
**fissent** /fis/ ▶ FAIRE
**fisses** /fis/ ▶ FAIRE
**fissible** /fisibl/ *adj* fissionable, fissile
**fissiez** /fisje/ ▶ FAIRE
**fission** /fisjɔ̃/ *nf* fission; **~ nucléaire** nuclear fission
**fissionner** /fisjone/ [1] *vtr, vi* to split
**fissions** /fisjɔ̃/ ▶ FAIRE
**fissure** /fisyʀ/ *nf* (a) crack
(b) (Anat) fissure
**fissurer** /fisyʀe/ [1] *vtr* to crack, to fissure
**fit** /fi/ ▶ FAIRE
**fîtes** /fit/ ▶ FAIRE
**fixation** /fiksasjɔ̃/ *nf* (a) fixing; fastening
(b) (on ski) binding
(c) fixation

**fixe** /fiks/ *adj* (a) fixed
(b) permanent

**fixé, ~e** /fikse/ **1** *pp* ▶ FIXER
**2** *pp adj* (a) **tu es ~ maintenant!** you've got the picture now! (colloq)
(b) **nous ne sommes pas encore très ~s** we haven't really decided yet

**fixer** /fikse/ [1] **1** *vtr* (a) to fix (à to)
(b) to set ⟨date, price⟩; to establish ⟨boundaries⟩; **~ son choix sur** to decide on
(c) to fix ⟨colour, emulsion⟩
(d) to focus ⟨attention⟩; to stare at ⟨person⟩
**2** **se fixer** *v refl* (+ *v être*) (a) ⟨part⟩ to be attached
(b) to set oneself ⟨goal, limit⟩

**flacon** /flakɔ̃/ *nm* (a) (small) bottle
(b) decanter
(c) (in laboratory) flask

**flagada** /flagada/ *adj inv* (colloq) weary
**flageller** /flaʒele/ [1] *vtr* to flog; (as religious punishment) to flagellate
**flageoler** /flaʒɔle/ [1] *vi* **avoir les jambes qui flageolent** to feel wobbly
**flageolet** /flaʒɔlɛ/ *nm* flageolet

**flagrant, ~e** /flagʀɑ̃, ɑ̃t/ *adj* ⟨difference⟩ obvious; ⟨injustice⟩ flagrant; ⟨lie⟩ blatant; **prendre qn en ~ délit** to catch sb red-handed

**flair** /flɛʀ/ *nm* (a) sense of smell, nose
(b) intuition

**flairer** /fleʀe/ [1] *vtr* (a) to sniff ⟨object⟩; **le chien a flairé une piste** the dog has picked up a scent
(b) ⟨animal⟩ to scent; ⟨person⟩ to smell
(c) to sense ⟨danger⟩

**flamand, ~e** /flamɑ̃, ɑ̃d/ **1** *adj* Flemish
**2** *nm* (language) Flemish
**flamant** /flamɑ̃/ *nm* flamingo
**flambant** /flɑ̃bɑ̃/ *adv* **~ neuf** brand new
**flambeau,** *pl* **~x** /flɑ̃bo/ *nm* torch
**flambée** /flɑ̃be/ *nf* (a) fire; **faire une ~** to light a fire
(b) (of hatred) flare-up; (of prices) explosion
**flamber** /flɑ̃be/ [1] **1** *vtr* to flambé ⟨pancake⟩
**2** *vi* to burn
**flamboyant, ~e** /flɑ̃bwajɑ̃, ɑ̃t/ *adj* ⟨fire, light⟩ blazing; ⟨colour⟩ flaming
**flamme** /flam/ *nf* (a) flame; **en ~s** on fire
(b) love, passion
IDIOMS **descendre en ~s** to shoot down; **être tout feu tout ~** to be wildly enthusiastic
**flan** /flɑ̃/ *nm* (Culin) custard tart (GB) *or* flan (US)
IDIOMS **en rester comme deux ronds de ~** (colloq) to be dumbfounded
**flanc** /flɑ̃/ *nm* (of person, mountain) side; (of animal) flank; **être sur le ~** (colloq) to be exhausted
**flancher** /flɑ̃ʃe/ [1] *vi* (colloq) (a) to lose one's nerve
(b) to crack up
(c) ⟨heart, engine⟩ to give out
**flanelle** /flanɛl/ *nf* flannel

**flâner** /flɑne/ [1] *vi* to stroll; to loaf around (colloq)

**flâneur**, **-euse** /flɑnœʀ, øz/ *nm,f*
(a) stroller
(b) loafer (colloq), idler

**flanquer** /flɑ̃ke/ [1] **1** *vtr* (a) to flank; **il est toujours flanqué de son adjoint** his assistant never leaves his side
(b) (colloq) to give ⟨*blow, fine*⟩; ~ **qch par terre** to throw sth to the ground; to drop sth; **to knock sth to the ground**
**2 se flanquer** *v refl* (+ *v être*) (colloq) **se ~ dans** to run into

**flapi**, **~e** /flapi/ *adj* (colloq) worn out

**flaque** /flak/ *nf* ~ (**d'eau**) puddle; ~ **d'huile** pool of oil

**flash**, *pl* **~es** /flaʃ/ *nm* (a) (on camera) flash
(b) ~ (**d'information**) news headlines; ~ **publicitaire** advert (GB), commercial (US)

**flasque**[1] /flask/ *adj* ⟨*skin, flesh*⟩ flabby

**flasque**[2] /flask/ *nf* flask

**flatter** /flate/ [1] **1** *vtr* to flatter
**2 se flatter** *v refl* (+ *v être*) to pride oneself

**flatterie** /flatʀi/ *nf* flattery

**flatteur**, **-euse** /flatœʀ, øz/ *adj*
(a) ⟨*portrait*⟩ flattering
(b) ⟨*person, remarks*⟩ sycophantic

**flatulence** /flatylɑ̃s/ *nf* wind, flatulence

**fléau**, *pl* **~x** /fleo/ *nm* (a) scourge
(b) (figurative) curse, plague
(c) (person) pest

**flèche** /flɛʃ/ *nf* (a) arrow; **partir en ~** to shoot off; **monter en ~** ⟨*prices*⟩ to soar
(b) barbed remark
(c) spire

**flécher** /fleʃe/ [14] *vtr* to signpost

**fléchette** /fleʃɛt/ *nf* (a) dart
(b) (game) darts

**fléchir** /fleʃiʀ/ [3] **1** *vtr* (a) to bend
(b) to sway ⟨*person, opinion*⟩; to weaken ⟨*will*⟩
**2** *vi* (a) ⟨*knees*⟩ to bend; ⟨*legs*⟩ to give way
(b) ⟨*attention*⟩ to flag; ⟨*courage*⟩ to waver; ⟨*will*⟩ to weaken; ⟨*demand*⟩ to fall off

**flegmatique** /flɛgmatik/ *adj* phlegmatic

**flegme** /flɛgm/ *nm* phlegm, composure

**flemmard**, **~e** /flemaʀ, aʀd/ *nm,f* (colloq) lazybones (colloq), lazy devil (colloq)

**flemme** /flɛm/ *nf* (colloq) laziness

**flétan** /fletɑ̃/ *nm* halibut

**flétrir** /fletʀiʀ/ [3] **1** *vtr* to blacken ⟨*reputation*⟩
**2 se flétrir** *v refl* (+ *v être*) ⟨*plant*⟩ to wither; ⟨*flower, beauty*⟩ to fade; ⟨*fruit*⟩ to shrivel

**fleur** /flœʀ/ *nf* (a) flower; **être en ~s** ⟨*garden*⟩ to be full of flowers; ⟨*plant, shrub*⟩ to be in bloom; ⟨*tree, lilac*⟩ to be in blossom; **à ~s** flowery
(b) **à ~ d'eau** just above the water
■ ~ **des champs** wild flower; ~ **de lys** fleur-de-lis

IDIOMS **être ~ bleue** to be romantic; **avoir**

une **sensibilité à ~ de peau** to be hypersensitive; **avoir les nerfs à ~ de peau** to be a bundle of nerves; **faire une ~ à qn** (colloq) to do sb a favour (GB)

**fleuret** /flœʀɛ/ *nm* (sword) foil

**fleurette** /flœʀɛt/ *nf* (Culin) **crème ~** whipping cream

**fleuri**, **~e** /flœʀi/ **1** *pp* ▶ FLEURIR
**2** *pp adj* (a) ⟨*garden*⟩ full of flowers; ⟨*tree*⟩ in blossom; in bloom
(b) ⟨*table*⟩ decorated with flowers
(c) ⟨*wallpaper*⟩ flowery

**fleurir** /flœʀiʀ/ [3] *vi* (a) ⟨*rose bush*⟩ to flower; ⟨*cherry tree*⟩ to blossom
(b) ⟨*new buildings*⟩ to spring up; ⟨*posters*⟩ to appear
(c) to thrive, to flourish

**fleuriste** /flœʀist/ *nm,f* (a) florist
(b) flower shop

**fleuve** /flœv/ **1** *nm* river
**2** (**-)fleuve** (combining form) interminable; ▶ ROMAN-FLEUVE

**flexible** /flɛksibl/ *adj* (a) ⟨*blade, tube*⟩ flexible; ⟨*body*⟩ supple
(b) ⟨*person, timetable*⟩ flexible

**flexion** /flɛksjɔ̃/ *nf* (of object) bending; (of arm, leg) flexing

**flic** /flik/ *nm* (colloq) cop (colloq), policeman

**flipper** /flipœʀ/ *nm* (Games) (a) pinball machine
(b) (device in machine) flipper
(c) (game) pinball

**flirter** /flœʀte/ [1] *vi* to flirt

**flocon** /flɔkɔ̃/ *nm* (of snow) flake; (of dust) speck; (of wool) bit; ~**s d'avoine** oat flakes (GB), oatmeal (US)

**flop** /flɔp/ *nm* (colloq) flop

**flopée** /flɔpe/ *nf* (colloq) (**toute**) **une ~ de gamins** masses of kids (colloq)

**floraison** /flɔʀɛzɔ̃/ *nf* flowering

**floral**, **~e**, *mpl* **-aux** /flɔʀal, o/ *adj* floral

**floralies** /flɔʀali/ *nf pl* flower show

**flore** /flɔʀ/ *nf* flora

**florilège** /flɔʀilɛʒ/ *nm* anthology

**florin** /flɔʀɛ̃/ *nm* (Dutch currency) guilder

**florissant**, **~e** /flɔʀisɑ̃, ɑ̃t/ *adj*
(a) ⟨*activity*⟩ thriving
(b) ⟨*complexion*⟩ ruddy

**flot** /flo/ **1** *nm* (a) (of letters, refugees) flood; (of visitors) stream
(b) **les ~s** the deep, the sea
**2 à flot** *phr* **couler à ~(s)** to flow

**flottant**, **~e** /flɔtɑ̃, ɑ̃t/ *adj* ⟨*wood, line*⟩ floating; ⟨*clothes, hair*⟩ flowing

**flotte** /flɔt/ *nf* (a) fleet
(b) (colloq) rain
(c) (colloq) water

**flottement** /flɔtmɑ̃/ *nm* (a) wavering
(b) (of currency) floating

**flotter** /flɔte/ [1] **1** *vi* (a) to float; ~ **à la dérive** to drift

**(b)** ⟨*mist*⟩ to drift; ⟨*flag*⟩ to fly; **~ au vent** to flutter in the wind; **elle flotte dans ses vêtements** her clothes are hanging off her
**(c)** ⟨*currency*⟩ to float
**2** *v impers* (colloq) to rain

**flotteur** /flɔtœʀ/ *nm* float

**flou, ~e** /flu/ **1** *adj* **(a)** ⟨*outline*⟩ blurred
**(b)** (figurative) vague, hazy
**2** *nm* **(a)** fuzziness
**(b)** (figurative) vagueness
■ **~ artistique** soft focus; (figurative) artistry

**flouer** /flue/ [1] *vtr* (colloq) to cheat; **se faire ~** to be had (colloq)

**fluctuant, ~e** /flyktɥɑ̃, ɑ̃t/ *adj* ⟨*prices, opinions*⟩ fluctuating; ⟨*person*⟩ fickle

**fluet, -ette** /flyɛ, ɛt/ *adj* ⟨*body, person*⟩ slight; ⟨*voice*⟩ thin, reedy

**fluide** /flɥid/ **1** *adj* **(a)** ⟨*oil, paint*⟩ fluid
**(b)** ⟨*style*⟩ fluent; ⟨*traffic*⟩ moving freely
**2** *nm* **(a)** (in physics) fluid
**(b)** (of clairvoyant) (psychic) powers

**fluo** /flyo/ *adj inv* (colloq) fluorescent

**fluor** /flyɔʀ/ *nm* fluorine

**fluorescent, ~e** /flyɔʀɛsɑ̃, ɑ̃t/ *adj* fluorescent

**flûte** /flyt/ **1** *nf* **(a)** (Mus) flute; **petite ~** piccolo
**(b)** (champagne) flute
**(c)** French stick
**2** *excl* (colloq) damn! (colloq), darn it! (colloq)
■ **~ à bec** recorder; **~ de Pan** panpipes

**fluvial, ~e,** *mpl* **-iaux** /flyvjal, o/ *adj* fluvial, river

**flux** /fly/ *nm inv* **(a)** (gen, Econ) flow
**(b)** (in physics) flux
**(c) le ~ et le reflux** flood tide and ebb tide; (figurative) the ebb and flow
**(d)** influx

**FMI** /ɛfɛmi/ *nm*: *abbr* ▶ FONDS

**foc** /fɔk/ *nm* jib

**focal, ~e,** *mpl* **-aux** /fɔkal, o/ *adj* focal

**focaliser** /fɔkalize/ [1] *vtr* to focus ⟨*rays*⟩; to focalize ⟨*electron beam*⟩

**fœtus** /fetys/ *nm inv* foetus

**foi** /fwa/ *nf* **(a)** faith; **avoir la ~** to be a believer
**(b) ma ~ oui** well yes; **en toute bonne ~ je crois que** in all sincerity, I believe that; **il est de mauvaise ~** he doesn't mean a word of it
**(c) sur la ~ de témoins** on the evidence of witnesses; **qui fait** *or* **faisant ~** ⟨*text, signature*⟩ authentic; **sous la ~ du serment** under oath
IDIOMS **sans ~ ni loi** fearing neither God nor man

**foie** /fwa/ *nm* liver; **crise de ~** indigestion

**foin** /fwɛ̃/ *nm* hay; **tas de ~** haystack; **la saison des ~s** the haymaking season

**foire** /fwaʀ/ *nf* **(a)** fair; **~ du livre** book fair
**(b)** fun fair
**(c)** (colloq) bedlam; **faire la ~** (colloq) to live it up (colloq)

**fois** /fwa/ **1** *nf inv* time; **une ~** once; **deux ~ twice; quatre ~ trois font douze** four times three is twelve; **l'autre ~** last time; **une (bonne) ~ pour toutes** once and for all; **une ~ sur deux** half the time; **une ~ sur trois** every third time; **deux ~ sur cinq** two times out of five; **toutes les ~ que** every time (that); **deux ~ plus petit** half as big; **c'est dix ~ trop lourd!** it's far too heavy!; **régler en trois ~** to pay in three instalments (GB); **pour la énième ~** for the hundredth time; **(à) la première ~** the first time; **la première ~ que je vous ai parlé** when I first talked to you
**2 à la fois** *phr* **deux à la ~** two at a time; **elle est à la ~ intelligente et travailleuse** she's both clever and hardworking
**3 des fois** *phr* (colloq) sometimes; **tu n'as pas vu mon chien, des ~?** you wouldn't have seen my dog, by any chance?
**4 des fois que** *phr* (colloq) in case
IDIOMS **il était une ~** once upon a time there was

**foisonner** /fwazɔne/ [1] *vi* to abound

**fol** ▶ FOU 1

**folâtrer** /fɔlɑtʀe/ [1] *vi* to romp about; to frisk

**folichon, -onne** /fɔliʃɔ̃, ɔn/ *adj* (colloq) **pas ~** far from brilliant

**folie** /fɔli/ *nf* **(a)** madness; **aimer qn/qch à la ~** to be mad (GB) *or* crazy about sb/sth
**(b)** act of folly; **elle a fait une ~ en acceptant** she was mad to accept
**(c)** extravagance
■ **~ des grandeurs** delusions of grandeur

**folk** /fɔlk/ *nm* folk music

**folklo** /fɔlklo/ *adj* (colloq) eccentric, crazy (colloq)

**folklore** /fɔlklɔʀ/ *nm* **(a)** folklore
**(b)** (colloq) razzmatazz (colloq)

**folklorique** /fɔlklɔʀik/ *adj* **(a)** ⟨*music*⟩ folk; ⟨*costume*⟩ traditional
**(b)** (colloq) eccentric

**folle** ▶ FOU 1, 2

**follement** /fɔlmɑ̃/ *adv* **s'amuser ~** to have a terrific time

**follet** /fɔlɛ/ *adj m* **feu ~** will-o'-the-wisp

**fomenter** /fɔmɑ̃te/ [1] *vtr* to instigate

**foncé, ~e** /fɔ̃se/ *adj* ⟨*colour*⟩ dark; ⟨*pink*⟩ deep

**foncer** /fɔ̃se/ [12] **1** *vtr* **(a)** to make [sth] darker *or* deeper ⟨*colour*⟩
**(b)** (Culin) to line
**2** *vi* **(a)** (colloq) ⟨*person, vehicle*⟩ to tear along (colloq); **fonce!** get a move on! (colloq); **go for it!** (colloq); **~ vers/dans** to rush toward(s)/into; **~ sur qch/vers la sortie** to make a dash for sth/for the exit; **~ sur qn** to charge at sb; **~ à New York** to dash over to New York
**(b)** ⟨*colour*⟩ (gen) to darken; ⟨*pink, mauve*⟩ to deepen; ⟨*fabric*⟩ to go darker

**fonceur, -euse** /fɔ̃sœʀ, øz/ (colloq) **1** *adj* dynamic
**2** *nm,f* go-getter (colloq)

**foncier, -ière** /fɔ̃sje, ɛʀ/ *adj* ⟨income⟩ from land; **impôt** ∼ property tax

**foncièrement** /fɔ̃sjɛʀmɑ̃/ *adv* fundamentally

**fonction** /fɔ̃ksjɔ̃/ *nf* **(a)** (in administration, company) post; duties; **dans l'exercice de leurs** ∼**s** while carrying out their duties; **occuper la** ∼ **de** to hold the position of; **voiture de** ∼ company car
**(b) en** ∼ **de** according to
**(c)** function; **avoir pour** ∼ **de faire** to be designed to do; **faire** ∼ **de** to serve as
**(d)** profession; ∼ **enseignante** teaching profession
■ ∼ **publique** civil service

**fonctionnaire** /fɔ̃ksjɔnɛʀ/ *nmf* civil servant; (higher ranking) government official

**fonctionnalité** /fɔ̃ksjɔnalite/ *nf* functionality

**fonctionnel, -elle** /fɔ̃ksjɔnɛl/ *adj* functional

**fonctionnement** /fɔ̃ksjɔnmɑ̃/ *nm*
**(a)** (of institution) functioning
**(b)** (of machinery) working; **mauvais** ∼ malfunction; **en** ∼ in service

**fonctionner** /fɔ̃ksjɔne/ [1] *vi* to work; ∼ **à l'essence** to run on petrol (GB) *or* gas (US)

**fond** /fɔ̃/ **1** *nm* **(a)** (of vessel, lake, valley) bottom; (of cupboard, wardrobe) back; ∼ **de la mer** seabed; ∼ **de l'océan** ocean floor; **toucher le** ∼ (in water) to touch the bottom; (figurative) to hit rock bottom
**(b)** (of shop, yard) back; (of corridor, room) far end; **la chambre du** ∼ the back bedroom; **au** ∼ **des bois** deep in the woods; **de** ∼ **en comble** from top to bottom
**(c) les problèmes de** ∼ the basic problems; **un débat de** ∼ an in-depth debate; **au** ∼ *or* **dans le** ∼**, le problème est simple** basically, the problem is simple
**(d)** (of text) content
**(e) regarder qn au** ∼ **des yeux** (suspiciously) to give sb a searching look; **elle a un bon** ∼ she's very good at heart
**(f)** background; ∼ **musical** background music
**(g) un** ∼ **de porto** a drop of port
**(h)** (Naut) **il y a 20 mètres de** ∼ the water is 20 metres (GB) deep
**(i)** (Sport) **épreuve de** ∼ long-distance event
**2 à fond** *phr* **(a) connaître qch à** ∼ to be an expert in sth; **être à** ∼ **pour** (colloq) to support wholeheartedly; **respirer à** ∼ to breathe deeply; **mettre la radio à** ∼ to turn the radio right up
**(b)** (colloq) **rouler à** ∼ to drive at top speed
■ ∼ **d'artichaut** artichoke bottom; ∼ **de teint** foundation (GB), make-up base (US)

**fondamental, ∼e,** *mpl* **-aux** /fɔ̃damɑ̃tal, o/ *adj* **(a)** basic, fundamental
**(b)** essential

**fondamentalement** /fɔ̃damɑ̃talmɑ̃/ *adv*
**(a)** fundamentally
**(b)** radically

**fondant, ∼e** /fɔ̃dɑ̃, ɑ̃t/ *adj* **(a)** ⟨ice⟩ melting
**(b)** ⟨pear⟩ which melts in the mouth

**fondateur, -trice** /fɔ̃datœʀ, tʀis/ *nm,f* founder; **groupe** ∼ founding group

**fondation** /fɔ̃dasjɔ̃/ **1** *nf* foundation
**2 fondations** *nf pl* foundations

**fondé, ∼e** /fɔ̃de/ **1** *pp* ▶ FONDER
**2** *pp adj* justifiable, well-founded, legitimate; **non** ∼**, mal** ∼ ⟨accusation⟩ groundless
■ ∼ **de pouvoir** (of company) authorized representative; (of bank) senior banking executive

**fondement** /fɔ̃dmɑ̃/ *nm* foundation; **être sans** *or* **dénué de** ∼ to be unfounded

**fonder** /fɔ̃de/ [1] **1** *vtr* **(a)** to found
**(b)** to base
**2 se fonder** *v refl* (+ *v être*) **se** ∼ **sur** ⟨theory, method⟩ to be based on; ⟨person⟩ to go on

**fonderie** /fɔ̃dʀi/ *nf* **(a)** foundry
**(b)** casting

**fondre** /fɔ̃dʀ/ [6] **1** *vtr* **(a)** to melt down ⟨metal⟩; to smelt ⟨mineral⟩
**(b)** to cast ⟨statue⟩
**2** *vi* **(a)** ⟨snow, butter⟩ to melt
**(b)** ⟨sugar⟩ to dissolve
**(c)** ⟨savings⟩ to melt away
**(d)** (emotionally) to soften; ∼ **en larmes** to dissolve into tears
**3 se fondre** *v refl* (+ *v être*) **se** ∼ **dans** ⟨person, figure⟩ to blend in with

**fonds** /fɔ̃/ **1** *nm inv* **(a)** (in gallery, museum) collection
**(b)** fund
**2** *nm pl* funds
■ ∼ **d'amortissement** sinking fund; ∼ **bloqués** frozen assets; ∼ **de commerce** business; ∼ **de placement** investment fund; ∼ **de prévoyance** provident fund; ∼ **propres** equity capital; ∼ **de roulement** working capital; ∼ **de solidarité** mutual aid fund; **Fonds monétaire international, FMI** International Monetary Fund, IMF

**fondu, ∼e¹** /fɔ̃dy/ **1** *pp* ▶ FONDRE
**2** *pp adj* ⟨butter⟩ melted; ⟨metal⟩ molten

**fondue²** /fɔ̃dy/ *nf* (Culin) fondue; ∼ **savoyarde** cheese fondue; ∼ **bourguignonne** fondue bourguignonne (*meat dipped in hot oil*)

**font** /fɔ̃/ ▶ FAIRE

**fontaine** /fɔ̃tɛn/ *nf* **(a)** fountain
**(b)** spring

**fonte** /fɔ̃t/ *nf* **(a)** cast iron
**(b)** melting down, smelting
**(c)** thawing; ∼ **des neiges** thaw

**fonts** /fɔ̃/ *nm pl* ∼ **baptismaux** font

**foot** /fut/ *nm* (colloq) = FOOTBALL

**football** /futbol/ *nm* football (GB), soccer

**footballeur, -euse** /futbolœʀ, øz/ *nm,f* football *or* soccer player

**footing** /futiŋ/ *nm* jogging

**forage** /fɔʀaʒ/ *nm* drilling

**forain, -aine** /fɔRɛ̃, ɛn/ **1** *adj* fairground
  **2** *nm* stallkeeper; **les ~s** fairground people

**forçat** /fɔRsa/ *nm* **(a)** convict
  **(b)** galley slave

**force** /fɔRs/ **1** *nf* **(a)** strength; **~s** strength;
**avoir de la ~** to be strong; **c'est au-dessus
de mes ~s** it's too much for me; **de toutes
ses ~s** with all one's might; **ils sont de ~
égale aux échecs** they are evenly matched
at chess
  **(b)** force; **de ~** by force; **faire manger de ~**
to force [sb] to eat; **entrer de ~ dans un lieu**
to force one's way into a place
  **(c)** **~ de vente** sales force; **~s** (Mil) forces;
**d'importantes ~s de police** large numbers of
police
  **2** **à force** *phr* (colloq) **à ~, elle l'a cassé**
she ended up breaking it
  **3** **à force de** *phr* **réussir à ~ de travail** to
succeed by dint of hard work; **il est aphone
à ~ de crier** he's been shouting so much
(that) he's lost his voice
  ■ **~ de dissuasion** (Mil) deterrent force; **~ de
frappe** nuclear weapons; **~s de l'ordre**
forces of law and order

**forcé, ~e** /fɔRse/ **1** *pp* ▶ FORCER
  **2** *pp adj* **(a)** (gen) forced
  **(b)** ‹consequence› inevitable; **c'est ~!** (colloq)
there's no way around it! (colloq)

**forcément** /fɔRsemɑ̃/ *adv* inevitably; **pas
~** not necessarily

**forcené, ~e** /fɔRsəne/ **1** *adj* ‹rhythm›
furious; ‹activity› frenzied
  **2** *nm,f* **(a)** maniac
  **(b)** crazed gunman

**forcer** /fɔRse/ [12] **1** *vtr* **(a)** to force
  **(b)** to break through ‹fence, enclosure›; **~ la
porte de qn** to force one's way into sb's
house; **~ le passage** to force one's way
through
  **2** **forcer sur** *v+prep* to overdo ‹salt,
colour›
  **3** *vi* **(a)** to overdo it
  **(b)** **serrez sans ~** do not tighten too much;
**ne force pas!** don't force it!
  **4** **se forcer** *v refl* (+ *v être*) to force
oneself
  IDIOMS **~ la main à qn** to force sb's hand

**forcing** /fɔRsiŋ/ *nm* (colloq) **faire du ~** to go
all out

**forer** /fɔRe/ [1] *vtr* to drill

**forestier, -ière** /fɔRɛstje, ɛR/ *adj* ‹area›
forested; **chemin ~** forest path; **exploitation
forestière** (place) forestry plantation

**foret** /fɔRɛ/ *nm* drill

**forêt** /fɔRɛ/ *nf* forest; **~ tropicale** rain forest
  IDIOMS **c'est l'arbre qui cache la ~** you can't
see the wood for the trees

**forfait** /fɔRfɛ/ *nm* **(a)** fixed rate; **un ~ de 8
euros** a fixed price of 8 euros
  **(b)** package; **~ avion-auto** fly-drive package
  **(c)** **~ skieur** ski pass
  **(d)** (of player) withdrawal; **déclarer ~** to give
up; (Sport) to withdraw

**forfaitaire** /fɔRfɛtɛR/ *adj* **prix ~** contract
*or* all-inclusive price; **indemnité ~** basic
allowance

**forge** /fɔRʒ/ *nf* **(a)** forge
  **(b)** ironworks

**forgé, ~e** /fɔRʒe/ **1** *pp* ▶ FORGER
  **2** *pp adj* ‹object, metal› wrought

**forger** /fɔRʒe/ [13] *vtr* **(a)** to forge
  **(b)** to form ‹character›

**forgeron** /fɔRʒəRɔ̃/ *nm* blacksmith
  IDIOMS **c'est en forgeant qu'on devient ~**
(Proverb) practice makes perfect

**formaliser: se formaliser** /fɔRmalize/
[1] *v refl* (+ *v être*) to take offence (GB) (**de**
to)

**formalité** /fɔRmalite/ *nf* formality; **les ~s
à accomplir pour obtenir un visa** the
necessary procedure to obtain a visa; **par
pure ~** as a matter of form

**format** /fɔRma/ *nm* format, size

**formatage** /fɔRmataʒ/ *nm* (Comput)
formatting; **faire un ~** to format

**formateur, -trice** /fɔRmatœR, tRis/ *adj*
formative

**formation** /fɔRmasjɔ̃/ *nf* **(a)** education;
training; **avoir une ~ littéraire** to have an
arts background; **en ~** undergoing training
  **(b)** training course
  **(c)** (of government, team) forming
  **(d)** group
  ■ **~ continue, ~ permanente** adult continuing
education; **~ professionnelle** professional
training

**forme** /fɔRm/ **1** *nf* **(a)** shape; form; **en ~
de** in the shape of; **sous ~ de** in the form
of; **sans ~** shapeless; **pour la ~** as a matter
of form
  **(b)** (of payment) method
  **(c)** (physical condition) form; **en pleine ~** in
great shape
  **2** **formes** *nf pl* **(a)** (of person) figure
  **(b)** (of object, building) lines
  **(c)** **faire qch dans les ~s** to do sth in the
correct manner; **y mettre les ~s** to be
tactful

**formé, ~e** /fɔRme/ **1** *pp* ▶ FORMER
  **2** *pp adj* **(a)** made up; formed
  **(b)** educated; trained
  **(c)** ‹writing, sentence› formed

**formel, -elle** /fɔRmɛl/ *adj* **(a)** ‹refusal,
denial, person› categorical; ‹order› strict;
**être ~ sur qch** ‹person› to be definite about
sth
  **(b)** **c'est purement ~** it's just a formality

**formellement** /fɔRmɛlmɑ̃/ *adv*
  **(a)** categorically; strictly
  **(b)** officially; **~ identifié** clearly identified

**former** /fɔRme/ [1] **1** *vtr* **(a)** to form
‹circle, rectangle›
  **(b)** to form, to constitute
  **(c)** to train ‹staff›; to educate ‹person,
tastes›; to develop ‹intelligence›
  **(d)** to form ‹abscess, film›
  **2** **se former** *v refl* (+ *v être*) **(a)** to form
  **(b)** to be formed

⋯⋮

**(c)** to train, to be trained
**(d)** ⟨*character, style*⟩ to develop

**formidable** /fɔʀmidabl/ *adj* **(a)** ⟨*force*⟩ tremendous
**(b)** (colloq) great, marvellous (GB)
**(c)** (colloq) incredible

**formol** /fɔʀmɔl/ *nm* formalin

**formulaire** /fɔʀmylɛʀ/ *nm* form

**formulation** /fɔʀmylasjɔ̃/ *nf* formulation; wording; **la ~ de cette idée est difficile** it's not easy to express that idea

**formule** /fɔʀmyl/ *nf* **(a)** expression; **~ toute faite** set phrase
**(b)** (in travel, tourism) option; **~ à 75F** (in restaurant) set menu at 75F
**(c)** method
**(d)** concept
**(e)** (in science) formula
**(f)** ⟨*of car*⟩ **~ un** Formula One
**(g)** ⟨*of magazine*⟩ format
■ **~ magique** magic words

**formuler** /fɔʀmyle/ [1] *vtr* (gen) to express; to put [sth] into words ⟨*idea*⟩

**fort**, **~e** /fɔʀ, fɔʀt/ **1** *adj* **(a)** strong; **armée ~e de 10 000 hommes** 10,000-strong army; **~ d'un chiffre d'affaires en hausse** boasting an increased turnover
**(b)** ⟨*noise*⟩ loud; ⟨*light*⟩ bright; ⟨*heat, activity*⟩ intense; ⟨*temperature, fever, rate*⟩ high; ⟨*blow, jolt*⟩ hard; ⟨*rain*⟩ heavy; ⟨*spice*⟩ hot; ⟨*majority*⟩ large; ⟨*lack, shortage*⟩ great; ⟨*drop, increase*⟩ sharp; **~e émigration** high level of emigration
**(c)** (at school subject) good
**(d)** ⟨*person*⟩ stout; ⟨*hips*⟩ broad; ⟨*bust*⟩ large; ⟨*thighs*⟩ big
**(e)** (colloq) **c'est un peu ~!** that's a bit much! (colloq)
**2** *adv* **(a)** extremely, very
**(b)** ⟨*doubt*⟩ very much; **avoir ~ à faire** (colloq) to have a lot to do
**(c)** ⟨*hit*⟩ hard; ⟨*squeeze*⟩ tight; ⟨*breathe*⟩ deeply; ⟨*speak*⟩ loudly; **y aller un peu ~** (colloq) to go a bit too far
**(d)** **il ne va pas très ~** he's not very well
**3** *nm* **(a)** fort
**(b)** strong person
**4** **au plus fort de** *phr* **au plus ~ de l'été** at the height of summer
■ **~e tête** rebel
IDIOMS **c'est plus ~ que moi/qu'elle** I/she just can't help it

**fortement** /fɔʀtəmɑ̃/ *adv* ⟨*criticize*⟩ strongly; ⟨*rise*⟩ sharply; ⟨*industrialized*⟩ highly; ⟨*shaken*⟩ deeply; ⟨*damaged*⟩ badly; ⟨*displease, dislike*⟩ greatly; ⟨*armed*⟩ heavily; **il est ~ question de...** it is highly likely that...

**forteresse** /fɔʀtəʀɛs/ *nf* stronghold

**fortiche** /fɔʀtiʃ/ *adj* (colloq) smart, clever (**en a**)

**fortifiant** /fɔʀtifjɑ̃/ *nm* (Med) tonic

**fortification** /fɔʀtifikasjɔ̃/ *nf* fortification

**fortifier** /fɔʀtifje/ [2] *vtr* **(a)** to strengthen ⟨*nails, hair*⟩

**(b)** ⟨*meal*⟩ to fortify; ⟨*holiday, vitamins*⟩ to do [sb] good
**(c)** to reinforce ⟨*construction*⟩

**fortuit**, **~e** /fɔʀtɥi, it/ *adj* ⟨*meeting*⟩ accidental; ⟨*incident, discovery*⟩ fortuitous

**fortune** /fɔʀtyn/ *nf* **(a)** fortune
**(b)** **de ~** makeshift
IDIOMS **faire contre mauvaise ~ bon cœur** to put on a brave face

**fortuné**, **~e** /fɔʀtyne/ *adj* wealthy

**fosse** /fos/ *nf* **(a)** pit
**(b)** grave
**(c)** sandpit
■ **~ commune** communal grave; **~ septique** septic tank

**fossé** /fose/ *nm* **(a)** (gen) ditch; ⟨*of castle*⟩ moat
**(b)** (figurative) gap; rift

**fossette** /fosɛt/ *nf* dimple

**fossile** /fɔsil/ *adj, nm* fossil

**fossiliser** /fɔsilize/ [1] *vtr*, **se fossiliser** *v refl* (+ *v être*) to fossilize

**fossoyeur** /foswajœʀ/ *nm* gravedigger

**fou** (**fol** *before vowel or mute h*), **folle** /fu, fɔl/ **1** *adj* **(a)** (insane) mad; **devenir ~** to go mad; **un tueur ~** a crazed killer
**(b)** ⟨*person, idea*⟩ mad (GB), crazy; ⟨*look*⟩ wild; ⟨*story*⟩ crazy; **être ~ furieux** (colloq) to be raving mad; **être ~ à lier** (colloq) to be stark raving mad (colloq); **entre eux c'est l'amour ~** they're madly in love; **~ de qn** crazy about sb
**(c)** ⟨*success*⟩ huge; **un monde ~** a huge crowd; **avoir un mal ~ à faire** to find it incredibly difficult to do
**(d)** ⟨*vehicle, horse*⟩ runaway; ⟨*lock of hair*⟩ stray; **avoir le ~ rire** to have a fit of the giggles
**2** *nm,f* madman/madwoman; **envoyer qn chez les ~s** (colloq) to send sb to the nuthouse (colloq); **courir comme un ~** to run like mad; **c'est un ~ d'art contemporain** he's mad about contemporary art
**3** *nm* **(a)** fool, court jester
**(b)** (in chess) bishop
IDIOMS **faire les ~s** (colloq) to fool about; **plus on est de ~s plus on rit** (colloq) the more the merrier

**foudre** /fudʀ/ *nf* lightning; **coup de ~** love at first sight; **avoir le coup de ~ pour** to be really taken with

**foudroyant**, **~e** /fudʀwajɑ̃, ɑ̃t/ *adj* ⟨*attack*⟩ lightning; ⟨*look*⟩ furious; ⟨*death*⟩ sudden

**foudroyer** /fudʀwaje/ [23] *vtr* **(a)** to strike ⟨*tree*⟩; **mort foudroyé** struck dead by lightning; **~ qn du regard** to look daggers at sb (colloq)
**(b)** ⟨*bad news*⟩ to devastate

**fouet** /fwɛ/ *nm* **(a)** whip; **dix coups de ~** ten lashes of the whip; **le grand air m'a donné un coup de ~** the fresh air invigorated me; **se heurter de plein ~** to collide head-on
**(b)** (Culin) whisk; **~ mécanique** hand whisk

**fouetter** /fwɛte/ [1] *vtr* (a) to whip, to flog ⟨*person*⟩; to whip ⟨*animal*⟩
(b) **la pluie leur fouettait le visage** the rain lashed their faces
IDIOMS **il n'y a pas de quoi ∼ un chat** (colloq) it's no big deal (colloq); **avoir d'autres chats à ∼** (colloq) to have other fish to fry

**foufou, fofolle** /fufu, fɔfɔl/ *adj* (colloq) scatterbrained

**fougère** /fuʒɛR/ *nf* (a) fern
(b) bracken

**fougue** /fug/ *nf* enthusiasm

**fougueusement** /fugøzmã/ *adv* enthusiastically

**fougueux, -euse** /fugø, øz/ *adj* spirited; enthusiastic

**fouille** /fuj/ *nf* (a) (of place, person, baggage) search
(b) excavation

**fouillé, ∼e** /fuje/ [1] *pp* ▶ FOUILLER
[2] *pp adj* ⟨*study, portrait, piece of work*⟩ detailed; ⟨*style*⟩ elaborate

**fouiller** /fuje/ [1] [1] *vtr* (a) to search; to frisk
(b) to dig ⟨*site*⟩
[2] *vi* ∼ **dans** (gen) to rummage through; to search ⟨*memory*⟩; to delve into ⟨*past*⟩

**fouillis** /fuji/ *nm inv* mess; jumble

**fouine** /fwin/ *nf* (Zool) stone marten

**fouiner** /fwine/ [1] *vi* (a) to forage about
(b) ∼ **dans** to rummage through ⟨*objects, papers*⟩; to poke one's nose into ⟨*life, past*⟩

**foulard** /fulaR/ *nm* scarf, headscarf

**foule** /ful/ *nf* (a) crowd; mob; **il y avait ∼ à la réunion** there were masses of people at the meeting; **venir en ∼ à** to flock to
(b) mass

**foulée** /fule/ *nf* (of horse, athlete) stride; **courir dans la ∼ de qn** (Sport) to tail sb; **dans la ∼ il a… while he was at it, he…**

**fouler** /fule/ [1] [1] *vtr* to tread ⟨*grapes*⟩
[2] **se fouler** *v refl* (+ *v être*) (a) (Med) **se ∼ le poignet** to sprain one's wrist
(b) (colloq) **tu ne t'es pas foulé** you didn't kill yourself (colloq)

**foulure** /fulyR/ *nf* sprain

**four** /fuR/ *nm* (a) oven; **cuire au ∼** to roast, to bake
(b) furnace; kiln
■ **∼ crématoire** crematory (furnace); **∼ à micro-ondes** microwave oven

**fourbu, ∼e** /fuRby/ *adj* exhausted

**fourche** /fuRʃ/ *nf* fork; **faire une ∼** to fork

**fourcher** /fuRʃe/ [1] *vi* **ma langue a fourché** it was a slip of the tongue

**fourchette** /fuRʃɛt/ *nf* (a) fork
(b) (of prices, temperature) range; (of income) bracket; **∼ horaire** period

**fourchu, ∼e** /fuRʃy/ *adj* ⟨*branch*⟩ forked; **cheveux ∼s** split ends

**fourgon** /fuRgɔ̃/ *nm* (a) van
(b) (of train) goods wagon (GB), freight car (US)
■ **∼ à bestiaux** cattle truck

**fourgonnette** /fuRgɔnɛt/ *nf* (small) van

**fourguer** (slang) /fuRge/ [1] *vtr* to flog (colloq) (**à** to), to sell [sth] off (**à** to)

**fourmi** /fuRmi/ *nf* (Zool) ant; **travail de ∼** laborious task
IDIOMS **avoir des ∼s dans les jambes** to have pins and needles in one's legs

**fourmilier** /fuRmilje/ *nm* anteater

**fourmilière** /fuRmiljɛR/ *nf* ant hill

**fourmillement** /fuRmijmã/ *nm* (a) **un ∼ de gens** a mass of people
(b) tingling sensation

**fourmiller** /fuRmije/ [1] [1] **fourmiller de** *v+prep* to be chock-full of ⟨*mistakes*⟩; to be swarming with ⟨*visitors*⟩
[2] *vi* to abound

**fournaise** /fuRnɛz/ *nf* blaze; **la ville est une ∼ en été** the town is baking hot in summer

**fourneau**, *pl* **∼x** /fuRno/ *nm* (a) (Tech) furnace
(b) stove

**fournée** /fuRne/ *nf* batch

**fourni, ∼e** /fuRni/ [1] *pp* ▶ FOURNIR
[2] *pp adj* ⟨*hair*⟩ thick; ⟨*grass*⟩ lush

**fournir** /fuRniR/ [3] [1] *vtr* to supply ⟨*document, equipment*⟩; to provide ⟨*energy*⟩; to contribute ⟨*effort*⟩; to produce ⟨*proof*⟩
[2] **se fournir** *v refl* (+ *v être*) **se ∼ chez** or **auprès de** to get [sth] from

**fournisseur, -euse** /fuRnisœR, øz/
[1] *adj* **pays ∼** exporting country
[2] *nm* supplier; **∼ de drogue** drug dealer
■ **∼ d'accès** (Comput) service provider

**fourniture** /fuRnityR/ *nf* (a) supply, provision
(b) **∼s scolaires/de bureau** school/office stationery; **∼s de laboratoire** laboratory equipment

**fourrage** /fuRaʒ/ *nm* forage; **∼ sec** fodder

**fourré, ∼e** /fuRe/ [1] *pp* ▶ FOURRER
[2] *pp adj* (a) (Culin) filled
(b) fur-lined; lined
(c) (colloq) **toujours ∼ au café** always hanging about at the café
[3] *nm* thicket

**fourrer** /fuRe/ [1] [1] *vtr* (a) (colloq) to stick (colloq); **∼ qch dans la tête de qn** to put sth into sb's head
(b) (Culin) to fill
(c) to line ⟨*garment*⟩
[2] **se fourrer** *v refl* (+ *v être*) (colloq) (a) **se ∼ dans un coin** to get into a corner
(b) **se ∼ une idée dans la tête** to get an idea into one's head

**fourre-tout** /fuRtu/ *adj inv* **sac ∼** holdall (GB), carryall (US)

**fourreur** /fuRœR/ *nm* furrier

**fourrière** /fuRjɛR/ *nf* pound; **mettre une voiture à la ∼** to impound a car

**fourrure** /fuRyR/ *nf* fur, coat

**fourvoyer: se fourvoyer** /fuRvwaje/ [23] *v refl* (+ *v être*) to make a mistake

**foutoir** /futwaʀ/ nm (slang) shambles (colloq); complete chaos

**foutre** /futʀ/ [6] (slang) **1** vtr **(a)** n'en avoir rien à ~ not to give a damn (colloq) **(b)** ~ qch quelque part to stick sth somewhere (colloq)
**2** **se foutre** v refl (+ v être) **(a)** il ne s'est pas foutu de toi! he's been very generous!; se ~ du monde to have a bloody (GB) or hell of a (US) nerve (slang) **(b)** not to give a damn (colloq)
IDIOMS ~ le camp to bugger off (GB) (colloq), to split (US) (colloq)

**foutu, ~e** /futy/ (slang) **1** pp ▶ FOUTRE
**2** pp adj **(a)** (before n) bloody awful (GB) (slang), damned (US) **(b)** être ~ ⟨person, garment⟩ to have had it (colloq) **(c)** être mal ~ to be unattractive; to feel lousy (colloq) **(d)** être ~ de faire to be totally capable of doing

**foyer** /fwaje/ nm **(a)** home; fonder un ~ to get married **(b)** (family) household **(c)** hostel **(d)** club **(e)** (for fire) hearth **(f)** (of resistance) pocket; un ~ d'incendie a fire **(g)** (of rebellion) seat; (of epidemic) source **(h)** (in optics) focus; lunettes à double ~ bifocals
■ ~ fiscal household for tax purposes; ~ de placement foster home

**fracas** /fʀaka/ nm inv (of falling object) crash; (of waves) roar; (of town, battle) din

**fracassant, ~e** /fʀakasɑ̃, ɑ̃t/ adj ⟨noise⟩ deafening; ⟨news⟩ sensational; ⟨success⟩ stunning

**fracasser** /fʀakase/ [1] **1** vtr to smash
**2** **se fracasser** v refl (+ v être) to crash

**fraction** /fʀaksjɔ̃/ nf **(a)** (in mathematics) fraction **(b)** (of sum of money) part; (of company) section; en une ~ de seconde in a split second

**fractionnement** /fʀaksjɔnmɑ̃/ nm division; fragmentation

**fractionner** /fʀaksjɔne/ [1] vtr to divide up ⟨work, group⟩; to split ⟨party⟩

**fracture** /fʀaktyʀ/ nf fracture; ~ du poignet fractured wrist

**fracturer** /fʀaktyʀe/ [1] **1** vtr to break down ⟨door⟩; to break ⟨window⟩; to force ⟨safe⟩
**2** **se fracturer** v refl (+ v être) se ~ la cheville to break one's ankle

**fragile** /fʀaʒil/ adj **(a)** fragile **(b)** ⟨person⟩ frail; ⟨eye⟩ sensitive; ⟨heart⟩ weak

**fragiliser** /fʀaʒilize/ [1] vtr to weaken

**fragilité** /fʀaʒilite/ nf **(a)** fragility **(b)** frailty

**fragment** /fʀagmɑ̃/ nm **(a)** (of cup, bone) fragment

**(b)** (of book, novel) passage

**fragmentaire** /fʀagmɑ̃tɛʀ/ adj patchy; sketchy; sporadic

**fragmentation** /fʀagmɑ̃tasjɔ̃/ nf **(a)** division; splitting up **(b)** fragmentation

**fragmenter** /fʀagmɑ̃te/ [1] vtr to break up ⟨substance⟩; to divide up ⟨work⟩

**fraîche** ▶ FRAIS 1, 5

**fraîchement** /fʀɛʃmɑ̃/ adv **(a)** freshly, newly **(b)** coldly; elle a été ~ accueillie she was given a cool reception

**fraîcheur** /fʀɛʃœʀ/ nf **(a)** coolness; coldness; la ~ du soir the cold evening air **(b)** freshness

**frais, fraîche** /fʀɛ, fʀɛʃ/ **1** adj **(a)** cool; cold; 'servir ~' 'serve chilled' **(b)** ⟨news, snow⟩ fresh; ⟨paint⟩ wet **(c)** ⟨complexion⟩ fresh **(d)** ⟨troops⟩ fresh; de l'argent ~ more money
**2** adv il fait ~ it's cool
**3** nm prendre le ~ to get some fresh air; mettre au ~ to put in a cool place; to put to cool
**4** nm pl **(a)** expenses; aux ~ de l'entreprise paid for by the company; rentrer dans ses ~ to cover one's expenses; faire les ~ de qch to bear the brunt of sth **(b)** fees **(c)** costs
**5** à la fraîche phr in the cool of the morning; in the cool of the evening
■ ~ d'annulation cancellation fees; ~ de déplacement (of employee) travel expenses; (for repairman) call-out charge; ~ divers miscellaneous costs; ~ d'expédition (for parcel) postage and packing; ~ de fonctionnement running costs; ~ de garde childminding fees; ~ d'inscription (gen) registration fees; (for school) school fees (GB), tuition fees (US); (at university) tuition fees; ~ de port postage; ~ professionnels professional expenses; ~ de scolarité tuition fees, school fees (GB)

**fraise** /fʀɛz/ nf **(a)** strawberry; ~ des bois wild strawberry **(b)** (tool, instrument) reamer; milling-cutter; (of dentist) drill
IDIOMS ramener sa ~ (colloq) to stick one's nose in (colloq)

**fraiseur, -euse¹** /fʀɛzœʀ, øz/ nm,f cutter

**fraiseuse²** /fʀɛzøz/ nf milling machine

**fraisier** /fʀɛzje/ nm **(a)** strawberry plant **(b)** strawberry gateau

**framboise** /fʀɑ̃bwaz/ nf **(a)** raspberry **(b)** raspberry liqueur

**framboisier** /fʀɑ̃bwazje/ nm raspberry cane; raspberry bush

**franc, franche** /fʀɑ̃, fʀɑ̃ʃ/ **1** adj **(a)** ⟨person⟩ frank, straight; ⟨reply⟩ straight; ⟨laughter, expression⟩ open, honest; jouer ~ jeu to play fair **(b)** duty-free; ~ de port postage paid
**2** nm (currency) franc; ~ lourd (Hist) new franc

**français**, **~e** /fʀɑ̃sɛ, ɛz/ **1** *adj* French **2** *nm* (language) French

**Français**, **~e** /fʀɑ̃sɛ, ɛz/ *nm,f* Frenchman/Frenchwoman

**France** /fʀɑ̃s/ *pr nf* France

**franche ▸** FRANC 1

**franchement** /fʀɑ̃ʃmɑ̃/ *adv* **(a)** frankly, candidly; **je lui ai demandé ~** I asked him straight out
**(b)** ⟨*lean*⟩ firmly; ⟨*enter*⟩ boldly
**(c)** really; **il m'a franchement agacé** he really annoyed me; **~!** (well) really!

**franchir** /fʀɑ̃ʃiʀ/ [3] *vtr* to cross ⟨*line*⟩; to get over ⟨*fence*⟩; to cover ⟨*distance*⟩

**franchise** /fʀɑ̃ʃiz/ *nf* **(a)** frankness, sincerity
**(b)** exemption
**(c)** (in insurance) excess (GB), deductible (US)
**(d)** (to sell goods) franchise
■ **~ de bagages** baggage allowance; **~ fiscale** tax exemption; **~ postale** 'postage paid'; **en ~ postale** post free

**franchiser** /fʀɑ̃ʃize/ [1] *vtr* to franchise

**franchissement** /fʀɑ̃ʃismɑ̃/ *nm* crossing; clearing; **~ de la ligne continue** crossing the white line

**franciser** /fʀɑ̃size/ [1] *vtr* to gallicize

**franc-jeu** /fʀɑ̃ʒø/ *nm* fair play

**franc-maçon**, **-onne**, *pl* **francs-maçons**, **franc-maçonnes** /fʀɑ̃masɔ̃, ɔn/ *nm,f* Freemason

**franc-maçonnerie**, *pl* **~s** /fʀɑ̃masɔnʀi/ *nf* **la ~** Freemasonry

**franco** /fʀɑ̃ko/ *adv* **(a)** **~ de port** postage paid, carriage paid
**(b)** (colloq) **y aller ~** to go right ahead

**francophone** /fʀɑ̃kɔfɔn/ **1** *adj* French-speaking; ⟨*literature*⟩ in the French language
**2** *nmf* French speaker

**francophonie** /fʀɑ̃kɔfɔni/ *nf* French-speaking world

**franc-parler** /fʀɑ̃paʀle/ *nm* **avoir son ~** to speak one's mind

**frange** /fʀɑ̃ʒ/ *nf* **(a)** (on rug, curtain, garment) fringe
**(b)** (hair) fringe (GB), bangs (US)

**frangin** /fʀɑ̃ʒɛ̃/ *nm* (colloq) brother

**frangine** /fʀɑ̃ʒin/ *nf* (colloq) sister

**franglais** /fʀɑ̃glɛ/ *nm* Franglais

**franquette: à la bonne franquette** /alabɔnfʀɑ̃kɛt/ *phr* (colloq) **recevoir qn à la bonne ~** to have sb over for an informal meal

**frappé**, **~e** /fʀape/ **1** *pp* ▸ FRAPPER
**2** *pp adj* ⟨*cocktail*⟩ frappé; ⟨*coffee*⟩ iced

**frapper** /fʀape/ [1] **1** *vtr* **(a)** (gen) to hit, to strike; **~ à coups de pied** to kick; **~ à coups de poing** to punch; **~ un grand coup** (gen) to hit hard; (on door) to knock
**(b)** to strike ⟨*coin*⟩
**(c)** ⟨*unemployment, epidemic*⟩ to hit ⟨*region*⟩; **les taxes qui frappent les produits français** duties imposed on French goods
**(d)** **ce qui m'a frappé c'est...** what struck me was...; **j'ai été frappé de voir que...** I was amazed to see that...
**2** *vi* **(a)** to hit, to strike; **~ dans ses mains** to clap one's hands
**(b)** to knock; **on a frappé** there was a knock at the door
**(c)** ⟨*criminals*⟩ to strike

**frasque** /fʀask/ *nf* escapade

**fraternel**, **-elle** /fʀatɛʀnɛl/ *adj* fraternal, brotherly

**fraternellement** /fʀatɛʀnɛlmɑ̃/ *adv* in a brotherly fashion

**fraternisation** /fʀatɛʀnizasjɔ̃/ *nf* fraternizing

**fraterniser** /fʀatɛʀnize/ [1] *vi* to fraternize

**fraternité** /fʀatɛʀnite/ *nf* fraternity

**fraude** /fʀod/ *nf* (Law) fraud; **~ fiscale** tax fraud; **~ électorale** vote *or* election rigging; **en ~** ⟨*enter*⟩ illegally

**frauder** /fʀode/ [1] *vi* (on public transport) to travel without a ticket; (in cinema) to slip in without paying

**fraudeur**, **-euse** /fʀodœʀ, øz/ *nm,f* swindler; tax evader; cheat

**frauduleux**, **-euse** /fʀodylø, øz/ *adj* fraudulent

**frayer** /fʀɛje/ [21] **1** *vtr* **~ un passage à qn à travers la foule** to clear a path for sb through the crowd; **~ le chemin** *or* **la voie à qch** (figurative) to pave the way for sth
**2 se frayer** *v refl* (+ *v être*) **se ~ un chemin dans** *or* **à travers** to make one's way through

**frayeur** /fʀɛjœʀ/ *nf* **(a)** fear
**(b)** fright

**fredonner** /fʀədɔne/ [1] *vtr* to hum

**free-lance** /fʀilɑ̃s/ *nmf* freelance, freelancer; **travailler en ~** to work freelance *or* as a freelancer

**freezer** /fʀizœʀ/ *nm* icebox

**frégate** /fʀegat/ *nf* (Naut) frigate

**frein** /fʀɛ̃/ *nm* brake; **donner un coup de ~** to slam on the brakes; **mettre un ~ à** to curb
**IDIOMS ronger son ~** to champ at the bit

**freinage** /fʀɛnaʒ/ *nm* braking

**freiner** /fʀɛne/ [1] **1** *vtr* **(a)** to slow down ⟨*vehicle*⟩
**(b)** to impede ⟨*person*⟩
**(c)** to curb ⟨*inflation*⟩
**2** *vi* **(a)** to brake; **~ à fond** to slam on the brakes
**(b)** (in skiing) to slow down

**frelaté**, **~e** /fʀəlate/ *adj* ⟨*alcohol*⟩ adulterated; ⟨*taste*⟩ unnatural

**frêle** /fʀɛl/ *adj* frail

**frelon** /fʀəlɔ̃/ *nm* hornet

**frémir** /fʀemiʀ/ [3] *vi* **(a)** ⟨*leaf*⟩ to quiver; ⟨*water*⟩ to ripple
**(b)** (with emotion) ⟨*lip*⟩ to tremble; ⟨*person*⟩ to quiver; to shudder
**(c)** (Culin) to start to come to the boil

**frémissant, ~e** /fremisɑ̃, ɑ̃t/ *adj* faire cuire dans l'eau ~e simmer gently in water

**frémissement** /fremismɑ̃/ *nm* **(a)** quiver, tremor **(b)** (of person, hand) quiver, shudder

**frêne** /frɛn/ *nm* ash (tree)

**frénésie** /frenezi/ *nf* frenzy

**frénétique** /frenetik/ *adj* frenzied; frenetic

**frénétiquement** /frenetikmɑ̃/ *adv* ⟨fight⟩ frantically; ⟨dance⟩ frenziedly; ⟨applaud⟩ wildly

**fréquemment** /frekamɑ̃/ *adv* frequently

**fréquence** /frekɑ̃s/ *nf* frequency

**fréquent, ~e** /frekɑ̃, ɑ̃t/ *adj* **(a)** frequent **(b)** common

**fréquentable** /frekɑ̃tabl/ *adj* respectable; ce ne sont pas des gens ~s they are not the sort of people one should associate with

**fréquentation** /frekɑ̃tasjɔ̃/ *nf* **(a)** company; avoir de bonnes/mauvaises ~s to keep good/bad company **(b)** ~ des théâtres theatregoing (GB)

**fréquenté, ~e** /frekɑ̃te/ ☐ *pp* ▶ FRÉQUENTER

☐ *pp adj* popular, busy; lieu bien ~ place that attracts the right sort of people

**fréquenter** /frekɑ̃te/ [1] ☐ *vtr* **(a)** to associate with ⟨person⟩; to move in ⟨milieu⟩ **(b)** to attend ⟨school⟩; to go to ⟨restaurant⟩ ☐ se fréquenter *v refl* (+ *v être*) ⟨friends⟩ to see one another

**frère** /frɛr/ *nm* brother

**fresque** /frɛsk/ *nf* **(a)** fresco **(b)** panorama

**fret** /frɛt/ *nm* freight

**frétiller** /fretije/ [1] *vi* ⟨fish⟩ to wriggle; ~ de la queue ⟨dog⟩ to wag its tail

**freudien, -ienne** /frødjɛ̃, ɛn/ *adj, nm,f* Freudian

**friable** /frijabl/ *adj* ⟨rock, biscuit⟩ crumbly

**friand, ~e** /frijɑ̃, ɑ̃d/ ☐ *adj* être ~ de qch to be very fond of sth ☐ *nm* (Culin) puff; ~ au fromage cheese puff

**friandise** /frijɑ̃diz/ *nf* sweet (GB), candy (US)

**fric** /frik/ *nm* (colloq) dough (colloq), money

**friche** /friʃ/ *nf* waste land

**friction** /friksjɔ̃/ *nf* **(a)** (Med) rub **(b)** friction

**frictionner** /friksjɔne/ [1] ☐ *vtr* to give [sb] a rub ⟨person⟩; to rub ⟨head, feet⟩ ☐ se frictionner *v refl* (+ *v être*) to rub oneself down

**frigidaire®** /friʒidɛr/ *nm* refrigerator

**frigide** /friʒid/ *adj* frigid

**frigo** /frigo/ *nm* (colloq) fridge (colloq)

**frigorifique** /frigɔrifik/ *adj* refrigerated

**frileux, -euse** /frilø, øz/ *adj* **(a)** sensitive to the cold **(b)** ⟨attitude, policy⟩ cautious

**frimas** /frima/ *nm pl* cold weather

**frime** /frim/ *nf* (colloq) pour la ~ for show; c'est de la ~ it's all an act

**frimer** /frime/ [1] *vi* (colloq) to show off (colloq)

**frimousse** /frimus/ *nf* (colloq) little face

**fringale** /frɛ̃gal/ *nf* (colloq) j'ai la ~ I'm absolutely starving (colloq)

**fringuer: se fringuer** /frɛ̃ge/ [1] *v refl* (+ *v être*) (colloq) to dress

**friper** /fripe/ [1] *vtr*, **se friper** *v refl* (+ *v être*) to crease, to crumple

**fripon, -onne** /fripɔ̃, ɔn/ *nm,f* (colloq) rascal

**fripouille** /fripuj/ *nf* (colloq) crook (colloq)

**frire** /frir/ [64] *vtr, vi* to fry

**frisé, ~e¹** /frize/ ☐ *pp* ▶ FRISER ☐ *pp adj* ⟨hair⟩ curly; ⟨person⟩ curly-haired

**frisée²** /frize/ *nf* curly endive

**friser** /frize/ [1] ☐ *vtr* **(a)** to curl; se faire ~ to have one's hair curled **(b)** to border on; cela frise les 10% it's approaching 10% ☐ *vi* to curl; ⟨person⟩ to have curly hair

**frisson** /frisɔ̃/ *nm* shiver, shudder; j'ai des ~s I keep shivering; grand ~ great thrill

**frissonner** /frisɔne/ [1] *vi* **(a)** (with cold) to shiver; (with fear) to shudder **(b)** ⟨leaves⟩ to tremble **(c)** ⟨water, milk⟩ to simmer

**frit** /fri/ ▶ FRIRE

**frite** /frit/ *nf* (Culin) chip (GB), French fry (US)

**friterie** /fritri/ *nf* chip shop (GB), French-fries stall (US)

**friteuse** /fritøz/ *nf* chip pan (GB), deep fat fryer (US)

**friture** /frityr/ *nf* **(a)** frying **(b)** (for frying) fat; oil **(c)** fried food **(d)** (fish) petite ~ ≈ whitebait **(e)** (on radio) crackling

**frivole** /frivɔl/ *adj* frivolous

**froid, ~e** /frwa, frwad/ ☐ *adj* cold; (figurative) cold, cool ☐ *adv* il fait ~ it's cold ☐ *nm* **(a)** cold; coup de ~ chill; prendre ~ to catch a cold **(b)** coldness; ils sont en ~ avec moi relations between them and me are strained; jeter un ~ to cast a chill ☐ à froid *phr* démarrage à ~ cold start IDIOMS il fait un ~ de canard (colloq) it is bitterly cold; donner ~ dans le dos to send a shiver down the spine; ne pas avoir ~ aux yeux to be fearless

**froidement** /frwadmɑ̃/ *adv* **(a)** coolly; abattre ~ to shoot [sb] down in cold blood **(b)** regarder les choses ~ to look at things with a cool head

**froideur** /frwadœr/ *nf* (gen) coldness; (of reception) coolness

**froissement** /frwasmɑ̃/ *nm* **(a)** (of paper, fabric) crumpling; (noise) rustling **(b)** (Med) strain

**froisser** /fʀwɑse/ [1] **1** *vtr* **(a)** to crease ⟨*fabric*⟩; to crumple ⟨*paper*⟩
**(b)** to offend ⟨*person*⟩
**(c)** (Med) to strain
**2 se froisser** *v refl* (+ *v être*) **(a)** to crease
**(b)** to be hurt *or* offended
**(c)** (Med) to strain

**frôlement** /fʀolmɑ̃/ *nm* **(a)** brushing
**(b)** rustling; fluttering

**frôler** /fʀole/ [1] **1** *vtr* **(a)** ⟨*person*⟩ to brush (against)
**(b)** ⟨*bullet, car*⟩ to miss narrowly; **il a frôlé la mort** he came close to dying
**2 se frôler** *v refl* (+ *v être*) ⟨*people*⟩ to brush against each other

**fromage** /fʀomaʒ/ *nm* cheese; ~ **maigre** low-fat cheese; ~ **de tête** brawn (GB), head cheese (US)

**fromager** /fʀomaʒe/ *nm* **(a)** cheesemaker
**(b)** cheese seller

**fromagerie** /fʀomaʒʀi/ *nf* cheese shop

**froment** /fʀomɑ̃/ *nm* wheat

**froncement** /fʀɔ̃smɑ̃/ *nm* **avoir un léger** ~ **de sourcils** to frown slightly

**froncer** /fʀɔ̃se/ [12] *vtr* **(a)** to gather ⟨*pleats*⟩
**(b)** ~ **les sourcils** to frown

**fronde** /fʀɔ̃d/ *nf* **(a)** (weapon) sling
**(b)** (toy) catapult (GB), slingshot (US)
**(c)** revolt

**frondeur, -euse** /fʀɔ̃dœʀ, øz/ *adj* rebellious

**front** /fʀɔ̃/ **1** *nm* **(a)** forehead
**(b)** (Mil) front
**(c)** façade
**2 de front** *phr* **ils marchaient à quatre de** ~ they were walking four abreast; **mener plusieurs tâches de** ~ to have several jobs on the go
**IDIOMS avoir le** ~ **de faire** to have the face *or* effrontery to do

**frontal, ~e,** *mpl* **-aux** /fʀɔ̃tal, o/ *adj* ⟨*attack*⟩ frontal; ⟨*collision*⟩ head-on

**frontalier, -ière** /fʀɔ̃talje, ɛʀ/ **1** *adj* border; **travailleur** ~ person who works across the border
**2** *nm,f* person living near the border

**frontière** /fʀɔ̃tjɛʀ/ *nf* **(a)** frontier, border; ~ **naturelle** natural boundary
**(b)** ~**s entre les disciplines** boundaries between disciplines

**fronton** /fʀɔ̃tɔ̃/ *nm* pediment

**frottement** /fʀɔtmɑ̃/ *nm* **(a)** rubbing
**(b)** friction

**frotter** /fʀɔte/ [1] **1** *vtr* **(a)** to rub
**(b)** to scrub
**2** *vi* to rub
**3 se frotter** *v refl* (+ *v être*) **(a)** se ~ **les yeux** to rub one's eyes
**(b)** to scrub oneself
**(c)** se ~ **à** to take on ⟨*person*⟩
**IDIOMS qui s'y frotte s'y pique** if you go looking for trouble, you'll find it

**frottis** /fʀɔti/ *nm inv* (Med) smear

**froussard, ~e** /fʀusaʀ, aʀd/ *nm,f* (colloq) chicken (colloq), coward

**frousse** /fʀus/ *nf* (colloq) fright

**fructifier** /fʀyktifje/ [2] *vi* ⟨*capital*⟩ to yield a profit; ⟨*business*⟩ to flourish

**fructueux, -euse** /fʀyktɥø, øz/ *adj*
**(a)** ⟨*relationship, meeting*⟩ fruitful; ⟨*attempt, career*⟩ successful
**(b)** (financially) profitable

**frugal, ~e,** *mpl* **-aux** /fʀygal, o/ *adj* frugal

**fruit** /fʀɥi/ *nm* fruit
■ ~ **de la passion** passion fruit; ~ **sec** dried fruit; ~**s de mer** seafood

**fruité, ~e** /fʀɥite/ *adj* ⟨*alcohol, aroma*⟩ fruity

**fruitier, -ière** /fʀɥitje, ɛʀ/ **1** *adj* fruit
**2** *nm,f* fruiterer (GB), fruit seller (US)

**fruste** /fʀyst/ *adj* unsophisticated

**frustrant, ~e** /fʀystʀɑ̃, ɑ̃t/ *adj* frustrating

**frustré, ~e** /fʀystʀe/ *adj* frustrated

**frustrer** /fʀystʀe/ [1] *vtr* **(a)** ~ **qn** to thwart sb
**(b)** ~ **qn de qch** to deprive sb of sth; to cheat sb (out) of sth
**(c)** to frustrate

**fuel** /fjul/ *nm* = FIOUL

**fugace** /fygas/ *adj* fleeting; ⟨*symptom*⟩ elusive

**fugitif, -ive** /fyʒitif, iv/ **1** *adj*
**(a)** ⟨*prisoner*⟩ escaped
**(b)** fleeting, elusive
**2** *nm,f* fugitive

**fugue** /fyg/ *nf* **(a)** **faire une** ~ to run away
**(b)** (Mus) fugue

**fugueur, -euse** /fygœʀ, øz/ *nm,f* runaway ⟨*child*⟩

**fui, ~e** /fɥi/ ▶ FUIR

**fuir** /fɥiʀ/ [29] **1** *vtr* **(a)** to flee ⟨*country, oppression*⟩
**(b)** to avoid ⟨*discussion, person*⟩; to steer clear of ⟨*crowd*⟩; to stay out of ⟨*sun*⟩
**2** *vi* **(a)** ⟨*person*⟩ to flee; ⟨*animal*⟩ to run away; **faire** ~ to scare [sb] off ⟨*person*⟩
**(b)** ⟨*tap, gas, pen*⟩ to leak
**(c)** ~ **devant ses responsabilités** not to face up to one's responsibilities

**fuite** /fɥit/ *nf* **(a)** (gen) flight; (of prisoner) escape; **prendre la** ~ to flee; to escape
**(b)** (of information) leak
**(c)** (of liquid, gas) leak

**fulgurant, ~e** /fylgyʀɑ̃, ɑ̃t/ *adj* ⟨*attack*⟩ lightning; ⟨*progression*⟩ dazzling; ⟨*imagination*⟩ brilliant

**fulminer** /fylmine/ [1] *vi* to fulminate

**fumé, ~e¹** /fyme/ **1** *pp* ▶ FUMER
**2** *pp adj* **(a)** (Culin) smoked
**(b)** ⟨*lenses*⟩ tinted; ⟨*glass*⟩ smoked

**fumée²** /fyme/ *nf* **(a)** smoke; ~**s** (from factory) fumes; **partir en** ~ (figurative) to go up in smoke
**(b)** steam

**fumer** /fyme/ [1] **1** *vtr* to smoke  ····⟩

**2** *vi* **(a)** ⟨*person, chimney*⟩ to smoke
**(b)** ⟨*soup*⟩ to steam; ⟨*acid*⟩ to give off fumes
IDIOMS ∼ comme un pompier *or* sapeur to smoke like a chimney

**fûmes** /fym/ ▸ ÊTRE¹

**fumet** /fymɛ/ *nm* (Culin) (of meat) aroma; (of wine) bouquet

**fumeur, -euse¹** /fymœR, øz/ *nm,f* smoker; zone non ∼s non-smoking area

**fumeux, -euse²** /fymø, øz/ *adj* ⟨*theory, ideas*⟩ woolly (GB), wooly (US)

**fumier** /fymje/ *nm* manure

**fumigène** /fymiʒɛn/ *adj* grenade ∼ smoke grenade

**fumiste** /fymist/ *nm,f* (colloq) **(a)** shirker
**(b)** phoney (colloq)

**fumisterie** /fymistəRi/ *nf* **(a)** (colloq) joke; c'est de la ∼ it's a joke
**(b)** chimney engineering; stove fitting

**fumoir** /fymwaR/ *nm* smoking-room

**funambule** /fynãbyl/ *nmf* tightrope walker

**funèbre** /fynɛbR/ *adj* **(a)** cérémonie/service ∼ funeral ceremony/service
**(b)** gloomy

**funérailles** /fyneRaj/ *nf pl* funeral

**funéraire** /fyneRɛR/ *adj* ⟨*ceremony*⟩ funeral; ⟨*monument*⟩ funerary

**funeste** /fynɛst/ *adj* fatal; fateful

**funiculaire** /fynikylɛR/ *nm* funicular

**fur**: au fur et à mesure /ofyReaməzyR/ *phr* as one goes along; le chemin se rétrécissait au ∼ et à mesure qu'on avançait the path grew progressively narrower as we went along

**furent** /fyR/ ▸ ÊTRE¹

**furet** /fyRɛ/ *nm* ferret

**fureter** /fyRte/ [18] *vi* to rummage

**fureur** /fyRœR/ *nf* **(a)** rage, fury
**(b)** frenzy; avec ∼ frenziedly; ce sport fait ∼ en ce moment that sport is all the rage at the moment

**furibond, ∼e** /fyRibõ, õd/ *adj* furious

**furie** /fyRi/ *nf* rage, fury

**furieusement** /fyRjøzmã/ *adv*
**(a)** furiously, violently
**(b)** (colloq) j'ai ∼ envie de dormir I'm dying to go to sleep

**furieux, -ieuse** /fyRjø, øz/ *adj* **(a)** furious, angry
**(b)** (colloq) ⟨*desire*⟩ terrible
**(c)** ⟨*battle*⟩ intense

**furoncle** /fyRõkl/ *nm* boil

**furtif, -ive** /fyRtif, iv/ *adj* **(a)** furtive; marcher d'un pas ∼ to creep along
**(b)** fleeting

**furtivement** /fyRtivmã/ *adv* furtively

**fus** /fy/ ▸ ÊTRE¹

**fusain** /fyzɛ̃/ *nm* charcoal crayon; charcoal drawing

**fuseau**, *pl* ∼**x** /fyzo/ *nm* **(a)** spindle; en ∼ tapering
**(b)** ski pants
**(c)** ∼ horaire time zone

**fusée** /fyze/ *nf* **(a)** rocket
**(b)** (Aut) stub axle

**fuselage** /fyzlaʒ/ *nm* fuselage

**fuselé, ∼e** /fyzle/ *adj* tapering, spindle-shaped

**fuser** /fyze/ [1] *vi* to ring out; les rires fusaient laughter came from all sides

**fusible** /fyzibl/ *nm* fuse

**fusil** /fyzi/ *nm* **(a)** gun, shotgun; (Mil) rifle
**(b)** sharpening steel
**(c)** gas igniter

**fusillade** /fyzijad/ *nf* **(a)** gunfire
**(b)** shoot-out

**fusiller** /fyzije/ [1] *vtr* **(a)** to shoot
**(b)** (colloq) to wreck
IDIOMS ∼ qn du regard to look daggers at sb

**fusil-mitrailleur**, *pl* **fusils-mitrailleurs** /fyzimitRajœR/ *nm* light machine gun

**fusion** /fyzjõ/ *nf* **(a)** (of metal, ice) melting; roche en ∼ molten rock
**(b)** (in biology, physics) fusion
**(c)** (of companies, parties) merger; (of systems, cultures) fusion; (of peoples) mixing

**fusionner** /fyzjone/ [1] *vtr, vi* to merge

**fusse** /fys/ ▸ ÊTRE¹

**fussent** /fys/ ▸ ÊTRE¹

**fusses** /fys/ ▸ ÊTRE¹

**fussiez** /fysje/ ▸ ÊTRE¹

**fussions** /fysjõ/ ▸ ÊTRE¹

**fut** /fy/ ▸ ÊTRE¹

**fût¹** /fy/ ▸ ÊTRE¹

**fût²** /fy/ *nm* cask, barrel; drum

**futaie** /fytɛ/ *nf* forest of tall trees

**futé, ∼e** /fyte/ **1** *adj* wily, crafty; ce n'est pas très ∼ that isn't *or* wasn't very clever
**2** *nm,f* (petit) ∼ cunning little devil

**fûtes** /fyt/ ▸ ÊTRE¹

**futile** /fytil/ *adj* trivial; superficial

**futilité** /fytilite/ **1** *nf* superficiality
**2** futilités *nf pl* **(a)** banalities
**(b)** trifles; trifling activities
**(c)** trivial details

**futur, ∼e** /fytyR/ **1** *adj* future; mon ∼ mari my husband-to-be
**2** *nm* future

**fuyant, ∼e** /fɥijã, ãt/ *adj* ⟨*look*⟩ shifty

**fuyard, ∼e** /fɥijaR, aRd/ *nm,f* runaway

# Gg

**g, G** /ʒe/ *nm inv* **(a)** (letter) g, G
**(b)** (*written abbr* = **gramme**) 250 g 250 g

**gabarit** /gabaʀi/ *nm* **(a)** (of vehicle) size
**(b)** (colloq) (of person) calibre (GB); (physical) build

**gabonais, ∼e** /gabɔnɛ, ɛz/ *adj* Gabonese

**gâcher** /gɑʃe/ [1] *vtr* **(a)** to waste ⟨*food, talent*⟩; to throw away ⟨*life*⟩
**(b)** to spoil ⟨*party*⟩

**gâchette** /gɑʃɛt/ *nf* **(a)** (of gun) tumbler
**(b)** (controversial) trigger
**(c)** (on lock) tumbler

**gâchis** /gɑʃi/ *nm inv* **(a)** waste
**(b)** mess

**gadget** /gadʒɛt/ *nm* gadget

**gadin** /gadɛ̃/ *nm* (colloq) **ramasser** *or* **prendre un ∼** to fall flat on one's face

**gadoue** /gadu/ *nf* (colloq) mud

**gaélique** /gaelik/ *adj, nm* Gaelic

**gaffe** /gaf/ *nf* (colloq) **(a)** blunder; **faire une ∼** to make a blunder
**(b)** **faire ∼** to watch out

**gag** /gag/ *nm* **(a)** (in film, show) gag
**(b)** joke

**gaga** /gaga/ *adj inv* (colloq) **(a)** gaga (colloq)
**(b)** silly

**gage** /gaʒ/ ⓵ *nm* **(a)** security; **mettre qch en ∼** to pawn sth; **être le ∼ de qch** to be a guarantee of sth
**(b)** (Games) forfeit
**(c)** pledge
⓶ **gages** *nm pl* wages; **tueur à ∼s** hired killer

**gager** /gaʒe/ [13] *vtr* **∼ que** to suppose that, to wager that

**gageure** /gaʒyʀ/ *nf* challenge

**gagnant, ∼e** /gaɲɑ̃, ɑ̃t/ ⓵ *adj* winning
⓶ *nm,f* winner; winning horse; winning ticket

**gagne-pain** /gaɲpɛ̃/ *nm inv* livelihood

**gagne-petit** /gaɲpəti/ *nmf inv* low-wage earner

**gagner** /gaɲe/ [1] ⓵ *vtr* **(a)** to win; **∼ d'une longueur** to win by a length; **c'est gagné!** we've done it!; **à tous les coups on gagne!** every one a winner!
**(b)** to earn; **il gagne bien sa vie** he makes a good living
**(c)** to gain ⟨*reputation, advantage, time*⟩; **∼ de la vitesse** to gather speed
**(d)** to save ⟨*time*⟩; **∼ de la place en faisant** to make more room by doing
**(e)** to win [sb] over
**(f)** to reach ⟨*place*⟩
**(g)** ⟨*blaze, disease*⟩ to spread to ⟨*place*⟩
**(h)** ⟨*fear*⟩ to overcome

**(i)** to beat [sb]; **∼ qn de vitesse** to outstrip sb
⓶ *vi* **(a)** to win
**(b)** **le film gagne à être vu en version originale** the film is best seen in the original version
**(c)** to gain
**(d)** **y ∼** to come off better; **y ∼ en** to gain in ⟨*comfort*⟩
**(e)** ⟨*sea*⟩ to encroach

**gagneur, -euse** /gaɲœʀ, øz/ *nm,f* winner

**gai, ∼e** /gɛ/ *adj* **(a)** ⟨*person*⟩ happy; ⟨*smile, expression*⟩ cheerful; ⟨*conversation*⟩ light-hearted
**(b)** (ironic) **c'est ∼ great!**
**(c)** merry, tipsy

**gaiement** /gɛmɑ̃/ *adv* **(a)** cheerfully, merrily; gaily
**(b)** (ironic) happily

**gaieté** /gete/ *nf* gaiety, cheerfulness

**gaillard, ∼e** /gajaʀ, aʀd/ *nm,f* strapping lad/girl

**gain** /gɛ̃/ *nm* **(a)** earnings; **mes ∼s au jeu** my winnings
**(b)** (on stock exchange) gain
**(c)** saving; **c'est un ∼ de temps considérable** it saves a considerable amount of time

**gaine** /gɛn/ *nf* **(a)** (for dagger) sheath
**(b)** girdle
**(c)** (Tech) sheathing; casing
**(d)** (Bot) sheath

**gainer** /gene/ [1] *vtr* to sheathe

**gala** /gala/ *nm* gala

**galamment** /galamɑ̃/ *adv* gallantly

**galant, ∼e** /galɑ̃, ɑ̃t/ *adj* **(a)** gallant, gentlemanly
**(b)** romantic

**galanterie** /galɑ̃tʀi/ *nf* gallantry

**galaxie** /galaksi/ *nf* galaxy

**galbe** /galb/ *nm* curve

**galbé, ∼e** /galbe/ *adj* shapely

**gale** /gal/ *nf* **(a)** scabies
**(b)** (on dog, cat) mange; (on sheep) scab
**(c)** (Bot) scab

**galère** /galɛʀ/ *nf* **(a)** galley
**(b)** (colloq) hell (colloq)
IDIOMS **être dans la même ∼** to be in the same boat

**galérer** /galeʀe/ [14] *vi* (colloq) to have a hard time

**galerie** /galʀi/ *nf* **(a)** gallery
**(b)** tunnel
■ **∼ marchande** shopping arcade; **∼ de toit** roof rack; **Galerie des Glaces** hall of mirrors ⋯❖

IDIOMS **amuser la ~** (colloq) to play to the gallery; **pour épater la ~** (colloq) to impress the crowd

**galet** /galɛ/ *nm* **(a)** pebble
  **(b)** (Tech) roller

**galette** /galɛt/ *nf* **(a)** round flat biscuit, cookie (US)
  **(b)** pancake
  ■ **~ des Rois** Twelfth Night cake

**Galles** /gal/ *pr nf pl* **le pays de ~** Wales

**gallois, ~e** /galwa, az/ **1** *adj* Welsh
  **2** *nm* (language) Welsh

**Gallois, ~e** /galwa, az/ *nm,f* Welshman/Welshwoman; **les ~** the Welsh

**gallon** /galɔ̃/ *nm* gallon

**galoche** /galɔʃ/ *nf* clog; **menton en ~** protruding chin

**galon** /galɔ̃/ *nm* **(a)** (for trimming) braid
  **(b)** (Mil) stripe; **prendre du ~** to be promoted

**galop** /galo/ *nm* **(a)** gallop; **petit ~** canter; **grand ~** full gallop; **au ~!** (figurative) hurry up!
  **(b)** (Mus) galop
  IDIOMS **chassez le naturel il revient au ~** (Proverb) what's bred in the bone will come out in the flesh

**galopade** /galɔpad/ *nf* **(a)** gallop
  **(b)** (colloq) (figurative) stampede

**galoper** /galɔpe/ [1] *vi* **(a)** to gallop
  **(b)** (colloq) ‹*child*› to charge (around)

**galopin** /galɔpɛ̃/ *nm* rascal

**galvaniser** /galvanize/ [1] *vtr* (lit, fig) to galvanize

**gamba** /gɑ̃ba, *pl* as/ *nf* large (Mediterranean) prawn

**gambader** /gɑ̃bade/ [1] *vi* to gambol

**gamelle** /gamɛl/ *nf* (of soldier) dixie (GB), mess kit; (of camper) billycan (GB), tin dish; (of worker) lunchbox; (for pet) dish
  IDIOMS **prendre une ~** (colloq) to fall flat on one's face (colloq); (figurative) to come a cropper

**gamin, ~e** /gamɛ̃, in/ **1** *adj* ‹*air, look*› youthful; ‹*attitude*› childish
  **2** *nm,f* kid (colloq); **~ des rues** street urchin

**gaminerie** /gaminʀi/ *nf* childish behaviour

**gamme** /gam/ *nf* **(a)** (Mus) scale
  **(b)** range; **produit (de) bas de ~** low quality product; cheap product; **~ de produits** product range

**gammée** /game/ *adj f* **croix ~** swastika

**ganglion** /gɑ̃gliɔ̃/ *nm* ganglion

**gangrène** /gɑ̃gʀɛn/ *nf* **(a)** (Med) gangrene
  **(b)** (figurative) canker

**gangrener** /gɑ̃gʀəne/ [16] **1** *vtr* to corrupt
  **2 se gangrener** *v refl* (+ *v être*) **(a)** (Med) to become gangrenous
  **(b)** (figurative) to become corrupt

**gangster** /gɑ̃gstɛʀ/ *nm* **(a)** gangster
  **(b)** swindler

**gant** /gɑ̃/ *nm* glove
  ■ **~ de boxe** boxing glove; **~ de ménage** rubber glove; **~ de toilette** ≈ (face) flannel (GB), wash cloth (US)

IDIOMS **son tailleur lui va comme un ~** her suit fits her like a glove; **mettre** *or* **prendre des ~s avec qn** to handle sb with kid gloves

**garage** /gaʀaʒ/ *nm* **(a)** garage
  **(b)** garage, filling station
  ■ **~ à vélos** bicycle shed

**garagiste** /gaʀaʒist/ *nmf* **(a)** garage owner
  **(b)** car mechanic

**garant, ~e** /gaʀɑ̃, ɑ̃t/ **1** *adj* **être** *or* **se porter ~ de qn/qch** to vouch for sb/sth
  **2** *nm,f* guarantor

**garanti, ~e¹** /gaʀɑ̃ti/ **1** *pp* ▶ GARANTIR
  **2** *adj* **(a)** with a guarantee
  **(b)** guaranteed

**garantie²** /gaʀɑ̃ti/ *nf* **(a)** (gen, Law) guarantee
  **(b)** (in finance) security; guarantee
  **(c)** (in insurance) cover; **montant des ~s** sum insured

**garantir** /gaʀɑ̃tiʀ/ [3] *vtr* **(a)** to guarantee; **~ qch à qn** to guarantee sb sth
  **(b)** to safeguard ‹*security*›
  **(c)** to guarantee ‹*loan, product*›

**garçon** /gaʀsɔ̃/ *nm* **(a)** boy
  **(b)** young man; **un brave** *or* **gentil ~** a nice chap (GB) *or* guy (US)
  **(c)** bachelor
  **(d) ~ (de café)** waiter
  ■ **~ d'écurie** stableboy; **~ d'honneur** best man; **~ manqué** tomboy

**garçonnet** /gaʀsɔnɛ/ *nm* little boy

**garçonnière** /gaʀsɔnjɛʀ/ *nf* bachelor flat (GB) *or* apartment

**garde¹** /gaʀd/ *nm* **(a)** guard
  **(b)** (for invalid, patient) carer; (in prison) warder
  ■ **~ champêtre** ≈ local policeman (*appointed by the municipality*); **~ du corps** bodyguard; **~ forestier** forest warden; **Garde des Sceaux** French Minister of Justice

**garde²** /gaʀd/ *nf* **(a)** nurse
  **(b)** (gen, Mil, Sport) guard; **la vieille ~** the old guard; **monter la ~** ‹*soldier*› to mount guard; **monter la ~ auprès de qn** to keep watch over sb; to stand guard over sb; **être de ~** ‹*doctor*› to be on call; ‹*soldier*› to be on guard duty
  **(c) mettre qn en ~** to warn sb; **prendre ~** to watch out; to be careful
  **(d)** (of sword) hilt
  **(e)** (page de) **~** endpaper
  ■ **~ à vue** (Law) ≈ police custody

**garde-à-vous** /gaʀdavu/ *nm inv* **se mettre au ~** to stand to attention

**garde-chasse**, *pl* **gardes-chasses** /gaʀdəʃas/ *nm* game warden; gamekeeper

**garde-côte**, *pl* **~s** /gaʀdəkot/ *nm* coastguard ship

**garde-fou**, *pl* **~s** /gaʀdəfu/ *nm* **(a)** parapet
  **(b)** safeguard

**garde-malade**, *pl* **gardes-malades** /gaʀdmalad/ *nmf* home nurse

**garde-manger** /gaʀdmɑ̃ʒe/ *nm inv* meat safe

**garder** /gaʀde/ [1] **1** *vtr* **(a)** to keep ⟨*object*⟩; to keep on ⟨*hat, sweater*⟩; to keep on ⟨*employee*⟩
**(b)** ⟨*soldier*⟩ to guard; ⟨*person*⟩ to look after
**2 se garder** *v refl* (+ *v être*) **(a)** se ~ de faire to be careful not to do
**(b)** ⟨*foodstuff*⟩ to keep

**garderie** /gaʀdəʀi/ *nf* **(a)** day nursery
**(b)** after-school child-minding facility

**garde-robe**, *pl* ~**s** /gaʀdəʀɔb/ *nf* wardrobe

**gardien, -ienne¹** /gaʀdjɛ̃, ɛn/ *nm,f*
**(a)** (in premises) security guard; (in apartment block) caretaker (GB), janitor (US); (in park) keeper; (in prison) warder; (in museum) attendant
**(b)** (Sport) keeper
■ ~ **de but** goalkeeper; ~ **de nuit** night watchman; ~ **de la paix** police officer

**gardiennage** /gaʀdjɛnaʒ/ *nm* (of premises) security; (of apartment block) caretaking

**gardienne²** /gaʀdjɛn/ *nf* **(a)** ▶ GARDIEN
**(b)** ~ **(d'enfant)** childminder (GB), day-care lady (US)

**gardon** /gaʀdɔ̃/ *nm* roach
IDIOMS **être frais comme un** ~ to be as fresh as a daisy

**gare** /gaʀ/ **1** *nf* (railway) station
**2** *excl* ~ **(à toi)!** (threat) careful!, watch it! (colloq)
■ ~ **maritime** harbour (GB) station; ~ **routière** coach station (GB), bus station (US)
IDIOMS **sans crier** ~ without any warning

**garenne** /gaʀɛn/ *nf* (rabbit) warren

**garer** /gaʀe/ [1] **1** *vtr* to park
**2 se garer** *v refl* (+ *v être*) **(a)** to park
**(b)** ⟨*vehicle*⟩ to pull over

**gargariser: se gargariser** /gaʀgaʀize/ [1] *v refl* (+ *v être*) to gargle

**gargarisme** /gaʀgaʀism/ *nm* **(a)** gargling
**(b)** mouthwash

**gargouille** /gaʀguj/ *nf* **(a)** gargoyle
**(b)** waterspout

**gargouiller** /gaʀguje/ [1] *vi* ⟨*water, fountain*⟩ to gurgle; ⟨*stomach*⟩ to rumble

**garnement** /gaʀnəmã/ *nm* brat (colloq)

**garni, ~e** /gaʀni/ **1** *pp* ▶ GARNIR
**2** *adj* **bien** ~ ⟨*wallet*⟩ full; ⟨*fridge*⟩ well-stocked; ⟨*buffet*⟩ copious

**garnir** /gaʀniʀ/ [3] *vtr* **(a)** ⟨*objects*⟩ to fill ⟨*room*⟩; ⟨*person*⟩ to stock ⟨*shelves*⟩
**(b)** to stuff ⟨*cushion*⟩
**(c)** (Culin) to decorate ⟨*cake*⟩; to garnish ⟨*meat*⟩

**garnison** /gaʀnizɔ̃/ *nf* garrison

**garniture** /gaʀnityʀ/ *nf* **(a)** (Culin) side dish; (for dessert) decoration; (for meat, fish) garnish
**(b)** (on hat, garment) trimming
■ ~ **de cheminée** mantelpiece ornaments

**garrigue** /gaʀig/ *nf* garrigue, scrubland (*in southern France*)

**garrot** /gaʀo/ *nm* **(a)** (Med) tourniquet
**(b)** (Zool) withers; **le cheval mesure 1,50 m au** ~ ≈ the horse is 15 hands

**gars** /ga/ *nm inv* (colloq) **(a)** boy
**(b)** chap (GB) (colloq), guy (US) (colloq)

**Gascogne** /gaskɔɲ/ *pr nf* Gascony

**Gascon, -onne** /gaskɔ̃, ɔn/ *nm,f* Gascon
IDIOMS **faire une offre de** ~ to raise false hopes

**gas-oil** /gazwal/ *nm* diesel (GB), fuel oil (US)

**gaspillage** /gaspijaʒ/ *nm* **(a)** wasting; waste
**(b)** squandering

**gaspiller** /gaspije/ [1] *vtr* **(a)** to waste ⟨*time, food*⟩
**(b)** to squander ⟨*resources, talent*⟩

**gastronome** /gastʀɔnɔm/ *nmf* gourmet, gastronome

**gastronomie** /gastʀɔnɔmi/ *nf* gastronomy

**gastronomique** /gastʀɔnɔmik/ *adj* (Culin) gourmet, gastronomic

**gâteau**, *pl* ~**x** /gɑto/ *nm* cake; gâteau
■ ~ **apéritif** cocktail biscuit; ~ **de cire** honeycomb; ~ **de riz** ≈ rice pudding; ~ **sec** biscuit (GB), cookie (US)
IDIOMS **c'est du** ~! (colloq) it's a piece of cake! (colloq); **c'est pas du** ~! (colloq) it's no picnic!

**gâter** /gɑte/ [1] **1** *vtr* to spoil; to ruin ⟨*teeth*⟩
**2 se gâter** *v refl* (+ *v être*) **(a)** to go bad; to rot
**(b)** to take a turn for the worse

**gâterie** /gɑtʀi/ *nf* little treat

**gâteux, -euse** /gɑtø, øz/ *adj* **(a)** senile
**(b)** **il est** ~ **avec sa fille** (colloq) he's dotty about his daughter (colloq)

**gauche¹** /goʃ/ *adj* **(a)** left
**(b)** ⟨*person, manner*⟩ awkward; ⟨*style*⟩ clumsy
IDIOMS **se lever du pied** ~ (colloq) to get out of bed on the wrong side (GB), to get up on the wrong side of the bed (US)

**gauche²** /goʃ/ *nf* **(a)** left; **à** ~ ⟨*drive*⟩ on the left; ⟨*go, look*⟩ to the left; ⟨*turn*⟩ left; **de** ~ ⟨*page*⟩ left-hand
**(b)** Left; **de** ~ left-wing
IDIOMS **passer l'arme à** ~ (colloq) to kick the bucket (colloq); **jusqu'à la** ~ (colloq) completely; **mettre de l'argent à** ~ (colloq) to put money aside

**gauchement** /goʃmã/ *adv* awkwardly

**gaucher, -ère** /goʃe, ɛʀ/ *adj* left-handed

**gaucherie** /goʃʀi/ *nf* awkwardness

**gauchiste** /goʃist/ *adj, nmf* leftist

**gaufre** /gofʀ/ *nf* **(a)** waffle
**(b)** honeycomb

**gaufrette** /gofʀɛt/ *nf* wafer

**gaufrier** /gofʀije/ *nm* waffle iron

**Gaule** /gol/ *pr nf* Gaul

**Gaulois, ~e** /golwa, az/ *nm,f* Gaul

**gaver** /gave/ [1] **1** *vtr* to force-feed ⟨*geese*⟩ ⋯⟩

**2** **se gaver** *v refl* (+ *v être*) **(a)** to stuff oneself
**(b)** se ~ **de** to devour ⟨*novels*⟩

**gay** /gɛ/ *adj inv*, *nm* gay, homosexual

**gaz** /gɑz/ **1** *nm inv* gas
**2** *nm pl* **(a)** (Aut) air-fuel mixture; **rouler à pleins** ~ (colloq) to go at full throttle
**(b)** (Med) wind
■ ~ **d'échappement** exhaust fumes; ~ **de ville** mains gas
IDIOMS **il y a de l'eau dans le** ~ (colloq) there's trouble brewing

**gaze** /gɑz/ *nf* gauze

**gazéifier** /gazeifje/ **[2]** *vtr* to carbonate ⟨*drink*⟩

**gazelle** /gazɛl/ *nf* gazelle

**gazer** /gaze/ **[1]** **1** *vtr* to gas
**2** *vi* (colloq) **ça gaze** things are fine

**gazette** /gazɛt/ *nf* newspaper

**gazeux, -euse** /gazø, øz/ *adj* **(a)** ⟨*drink*⟩ fizzy
**(b)** gaseous

**gazinière** /gazinjɛʀ/ *nf* gas cooker (GB), gas stove

**gazoduc** /gazɔdyk/ *nm* gas pipeline

**gazole** /gazɔl/ *nm* diesel (oil) (GB), fuel oil (US)

**gazon** /gazɔ̃/ *nm* **(a)** grass, turf
**(b)** lawn

**gazouiller** /gazuje/ **[1]** *vi* to twitter; to babble

**GDF** /ʒedeɛf/ (*abbr* = **Gaz de France**) French gas board

**géant, ~e** /ʒeɑ̃, ɑ̃t/ **1** *adj* **(a)** huge
**(b)** giant
**2** *nm,f* giant/giantess

**geignement** /ʒɛɲəmɑ̃/ *nm* moan, groan

**geindre** /ʒɛ̃dʀ/ **[55]** *vi* (in pain) to moan, to groan; to whimper; (complainingly) to whine

**gel** /ʒɛl/ *nm* **(a)** frost; **résistant au** ~ frost-resistant
**(b)** ~ **des prix/salaires** price/wage freeze
**(c)** **après le** ~ **du projet** after the project had been put on ice
**(d)** gel

**gélatine** /ʒelatin/ *nf* gelatine (GB), gelatin (US)

**gelé, ~e**[1] /ʒəle/ **1** *pp* ▸ GELER
**2** *adj* **(a)** ⟨*water, ground*⟩ frozen; ⟨*toe*⟩ frost-bitten; **j'ai les oreilles** ~**es** my ears are frozen
**(b)** ⟨*prices, negotiations*⟩ frozen

**gelée**[2] /ʒəle/ *nf* **(a)** (from fruit) jelly; (from meat, fish) gelatinous stock; **œuf en** ~ egg in aspic
**(b)** gel
**(c)** frost
■ ~ **blanche** hoarfrost

**geler** /ʒəle/ **[17]** **1** *vtr* **(a)** to freeze; to nip ⟨*plant*⟩
**(b)** to freeze ⟨*salaries*⟩; to suspend ⟨*plan*⟩
**2** *vi* ⟨*water, ground, finger, foot*⟩ to freeze; ⟨*plant*⟩ to be frosted
**3** *v impers* **il gèle** it's freezing

**gélule** /ʒelyl/ *nf* capsule

**Gémeaux** /ʒemo/ *pr nm pl* Gemini

**gémir** /ʒemiʀ/ **[3]** *vi* to moan; to whimper

**gémissement** /ʒemismɑ̃/ *nm* moan

**gemme** /ʒɛm/ *nf* **(a)** gem, gemstone
**(b)** resin

**gênant, ~e** /ʒɛnɑ̃, ɑ̃t/ *adj* **(a)** ⟨*box*⟩ cumbersome; ⟨*problem*⟩ annoying
**(b)** embarrassing

**gencive** /ʒɑ̃siv/ *nf* gum

**gendarme** /ʒɑ̃daʀm/ *nm* **(a)** (Mil) gendarme, French policeman
**(b)** dried sausage
■ ~ **couché** road hump

**gendarmerie** /ʒɑ̃daʀm(ə)ʀi/ *nf*
**(a)** ≈ police station
**(b)** ~ **(nationale)** gendarmerie

**gendre** /ʒɑ̃dʀ/ *nm* son-in-law

**gêne** /ʒɛn/ *nf* **(a)** embarrassment
**(b)** discomfort
**(c)** inconvenience
**(d)** poverty

**gêné, ~e** /ʒene/ **1** *pp* ▸ GÊNER
**2** *adj* **(a)** embarrassed
**(b)** short of money

**gène** /ʒɛn/ *nm* gene

**généalogie** /ʒenealɔʒi/ *nf* genealogy

**généalogique** /ʒenealɔʒik/ *adj* genealogical; **arbre** ~ family tree

**gêner** /ʒene/ **[1]** **1** *vtr* **(a)** to disturb, to bother
**(b)** ⟨*smoke, noise*⟩ to bother
**(c)** to embarrass
**(d)** ⟨*belt*⟩ to restrict ⟨*breathing*⟩
**(e)** ⟨*person*⟩ to get in the way of ⟨*progress*⟩
**2** **se gêner** *v refl* (+ *v être*) **(a)** to get in each other's way
**(b)** **je vais me** ~ (colloq) see if I don't; **ne vous gênez pas pour moi** don't mind me

**général, ~e**[1], *mpl* **-aux** /ʒeneʀal, o/
**1** *adj* general; **de l'avis** ~ in most people's opinion; **en** ~, **de façon** ~**e** generally, in general; **en règle** ~**e** as a rule
**2** *nm* general

**générale**[2] /ʒeneʀal/ *nf* **(a)** dress rehearsal
**(b)** general's wife

**généralement** /ʒeneʀalmɑ̃/ *adv* generally

**généralisation** /ʒeneʀalizasjɔ̃/ *nf* widespread use; generalization; spread

**généralisé, ~e** /ʒeneʀalize/ *adj* ⟨*conflict*⟩ widespread; ⟨*process*⟩ general; ⟨*cancer*⟩ generalized

**généraliser** /ʒeneʀalize/ **[1]** **1** *vtr* to bring [sth] into general use
**2** *vi* to generalize
**3** **se généraliser** *v refl* (+ *v être*) ⟨*technique*⟩ to become standard; ⟨*tax*⟩ to become widely applicable; ⟨*strike, illness*⟩ to spread

**généraliste** /ʒeneʀalist/ *adj* non-specialized; **(médecin)** ~ GP, general practitioner

**généralité** /ʒeneʀalite/ *nf* generality

**générateur, -trice** /ʒeneʀatœʀ, tʀis/
**1** adj être ~ de to generate
**2** nm generator

**génération** /ʒeneʀasjɔ̃/ nf generation

**générer** /ʒeneʀe/ [14] vtr to generate

**généreusement** /ʒeneʀøzmɑ̃/ adv
generously; liberally

**généreux, -euse** /ʒeneʀø, øz/ adj
(a) ⟨person, nature⟩ generous; ⟨idea, gesture⟩
noble
(b) ⟨portion⟩ generous; **poitrine généreuse**
large bust

**générique** /ʒeneʀik/ **1** adj generic
**2** nm credits; **le ~ de fin** closing credits

**générosité** /ʒeneʀozite/ nf generosity

**genèse** /ʒənɛz/ nf (a) (of plan) genesis;
(of state) birth
(b) **la Genèse** Genesis

**genêt** /ʒənɛ/ nm (Bot) broom

**généticien, -ienne** /ʒenetisjɛ̃, ɛn/ nm,f
geneticist

**génétique** /ʒenetik/ **1** adj genetic
**2** nf genetics

**génétiquement** /ʒenetikmɑ̃/ adv
genetically; ~ **modifié** genetically modified

**Genève** /ʒənɛv/ pr n Geneva

**genévrier** /ʒənevʀije/ nm juniper

**génial, ~e,** mpl **-iaux** /ʒenjal, o/ adj
(a) brilliant
(b) (colloq) great (colloq)

**génie** /ʒeni/ nm (a) genius; **idée de ~**
brainwave
(b) spirit; genie
(c) engineering

**genièvre** /ʒənjɛvʀ/ nm Dutch gin

**génisse** /ʒenis/ nf heifer

**génital, ~e,** mpl **-aux** /ʒenital, o/ adj
genital

**génocide** /ʒenɔsid/ nm genocide

**génoise** /ʒenwaz/ nf ≈ sponge cake

**genou,** pl **~x** /ʒ(ə)nu/ **1** nm knee; **sur les
~x de qn** on sb's lap
**2** **à genoux** phr **se mettre à ~x** to kneel
down; to go down on one's knees
**IDIOMS faire du ~ à qn** (colloq) to play footsie
with sb (colloq); **mettre qn sur les ~x** (colloq)
to wear sb out

**genouillère** /ʒənujɛʀ/ nf (Sport) knee pad;
(Med) knee support

**genre** /ʒɑ̃ʀ/ nm (a) sort, kind, type; **un peu
dans le ~ de ta robe** a bit like your dress
(b) **pour se donner un ~** (in order) to make
oneself look different
(c) (in grammar) gender
(d) genre
(e) (Bot, Zool) genus
■ **le ~ humain** mankind

**gens** /ʒɑ̃/ nm pl (a) people
(b) servants; retinue
■ **~ d'église** clergymen; **~ de lettres** writers;
**~ de maison** servants; **~ du voyage**
travelling (GB) people

**gentil, -ille** /ʒɑ̃ti, ij/ adj (a) kind, nice
(b) good; **sois ~** be a good boy

(c) **c'est bien ~ tout ça, mais...** that's all
very well, but...

**gentilhomme,** pl **gentilshommes**
/ʒɑ̃tijɔm, ʒɑ̃tizɔm/ nm gentleman;
**~ campagnard** country gentleman

**gentillesse** /ʒɑ̃tijes/ nf (a) kindness
(b) (ironic) **échanger des ~s** to exchange
insults

**gentiment** /ʒɑ̃timɑ̃/ adv (a) kindly
(b) quietly

**géographie** /ʒeɔgʀafi/ nf geography

**geôlier, -ière** /ʒolje, ɛʀ/ nm,f jailer

**géologie** /ʒeɔlɔʒi/ nf geology

**géomètre** /ʒeɔmɛtʀ/ nmf land surveyor

**géométrie** /ʒeɔmetʀi/ nf geometry; **à ~
variable** ⟨doctrine⟩ flexible

**géométrique** /ʒeɔmetʀik/ adj geometric

**Géorgie** /ʒeɔʀʒi/ pr nf (a) (in US) Georgia
(b) (in Europe) Georgia

**gérable** /ʒeʀabl/ adj manageable; **situation
difficilement ~** a situation which is hard to
handle

**gérance** /ʒeʀɑ̃s/ nf management; **mettre
en ~** to appoint a manager for ⟨shop,
company⟩; to appoint a managing agent for
⟨property⟩

**géranium** /ʒeʀanjɔm/ nm geranium

**gérant, ~e** /ʒeʀɑ̃, ɑ̃t/ nm,f manager;
(of property) (managing) agent

**gerbe** /ʒɛʀb/ nf (a) bouquet; wreath
(b) (of water) spray
(c) (of wheat) sheaf

**gercer** /ʒɛʀse/ [12] vi to become chapped

**gerçure** /ʒɛʀsyʀ/ nf (in skin, lips) crack

**gérer** /ʒeʀe/ [14] vtr (a) to manage
⟨production, time⟩; to run ⟨business⟩
(b) to handle ⟨situation⟩

**gériatrie** /ʒeʀjatʀi/ nf geriatrics

**germain, ~e** /ʒɛʀmɛ̃, ɛn/ adj (a) (cousin)
**~ first cousin**
(b) Germanic

**germanique** /ʒɛʀmanik/ adj, nm
Germanic

**germanophone** /ʒɛʀmanɔfɔn/ nmf
German speaker

**germe** /ʒɛʀm/ nm (of embryo, seed) germ;
(of potato) sprout

**germer** /ʒɛʀme/ [1] vi (a) ⟨wheat⟩ to
germinate
(b) ⟨idea, suspicion⟩ to form

**gérondif** /ʒeʀɔ̃dif/ nm gerund, gerundive

**gésier** /ʒezje/ nm gizzard

**gésir** /ʒeziʀ/ [37] vi (formal) **ci-gît Luc Pichon**
here lies Luc Pichon

**geste** /ʒɛst/ nm (a) movement; gesture;
**joindre le ~ à la parole** to suit the action to
the word
(b) gesture, act

**gesticuler** /ʒɛstikyle/ [1] vtr (a) to
gesticulate
(b) to fidget

**gestion** /ʒɛstjɔ̃/ nf (a) management
(b) (of situation) handling      ⋯◇

(c) (of classroom) management
■ ~ **administrative** administration; ~ **des déchets** waste management; ~ **des stocks** stock (GB) or inventory (US) control; ~ **de portefeuille** portfolio management; ~ **de la production assistée par ordinateur** computer-aided production management
**gestionnaire** /ʒɛstjɔnɛʀ/ nmf administrator
■ ~ **de fichiers** (Comput) file-management system; ~ **de portefeuille** portfolio manager
**gestuel, -elle**¹ /ʒɛstɥɛl/ adj gestural
**gestuelle**² /ʒɛstɥɛl/ nf body language
**geyser** /ʒezɛʀ/ nm geyser
**ghetto** /geto/ nm ghetto
**gibecière** /ʒibsjɛʀ/ nf gamebag
**gibier** /ʒibje/ nm game; **gros** ~ big game; (figurative) big-time criminals
**giboulée** /ʒibule/ nf shower
**giclée** /ʒikle/ nf spurt; squirt
**gicler** /ʒikle/ [1] vi to spurt; to squirt
**gifle** /ʒifl/ nf slap in the face
**gifler** /ʒifle/ [1] vtr to slap [sb] across the face
**gigantesque** /ʒigɑ̃tɛsk/ adj huge, gigantic
**gigaoctet** /ʒigaɔktɛ/ nm gigabyte
**GIGN** /ʒeiʒeɛn/ nm (abbr = **Groupe d'intervention de la gendarmerie nationale**) branch of the police specialized in cases of armed robbery, terrorism etc
**gigogne** /ʒigɔɲ/ adj tables ~s nest of tables
**gigot** /ʒigo/ nm leg of lamb
**gigoter** /ʒigɔte/ [1] vi (a) to wriggle (b) to fidget
**gilet** /ʒilɛ/ nm (a) cardigan (b) waistcoat (GB), vest (US)
■ ~ **pare-balles** bulletproof vest; ~ **de sauvetage** lifejacket
**gin** /dʒin/ nm gin; ~ **tonic** gin and tonic
**gingembre** /ʒɛ̃ʒɑ̃bʀ/ nm ginger
**girafe** /ʒiʀaf/ nf (Zool) giraffe
**giratoire** /ʒiʀatwaʀ/ adj gyratory
■ **sens** ~ roundabout (GB), traffic circle (US)
**girofle** /ʒiʀɔfl/ nm un clou de ~ a clove
**girolle** /ʒiʀɔl/ nf chanterelle
**girouette** /ʒiʀwɛt/ nf windvane
**gisement** /ʒizmɑ̃/ nm (of oil, minerals) deposit
**gît** ▶ GÉSIR
**gitan, ~e** /ʒitɑ̃, an/ nm,f Gypsy (GB)
**gîte** /ʒit/ nm (a) shelter (b) (of hare) form
■ ~ **rural** self-catering cottage
**givrant** /ʒivʀɑ̃/ adj m brouillard ~ freezing fog
**givre** /ʒivʀ/ nm frost; ice
**givré, ~e** /ʒivʀe/ adj (a) frosty; frost-covered; frozen (b) (colloq) crazy (c) (Culin) ⟨glass⟩ frosted

**givrer** /ʒivʀe/ [1] vi, **se givrer** v refl (+ v être) to frost over
**glaçage** /glasaʒ/ nm (Culin) (on dessert) icing
**glace** /glas/ nf (a) ice; de ~ ⟨face⟩ stony (b) ice cream (c) mirror (d) sheet of glass; (of shop window) glass; (of car) window
IDIOMS **rester de** ~ to remain unmoved
**glacé, ~e** /glase/ adj (a) ⟨rain⟩ ice-cold; ⟨hands⟩ frozen; **thé** ~ iced tea (b) ⟨cake⟩ iced (c) ⟨atmosphere⟩ frosty; ⟨smile⟩ chilly (d) ⟨paper⟩ glossy
**glacer** /glase/ [12] **1** vtr (a) to freeze ⟨body⟩; to chill [sb] to the bone (b) to intimidate; ~ **le sang de qn** to make sb's blood run cold
**2 se glacer** v refl (+ v être) to freeze
**glaciaire** /glasjɛʀ/ adj glacial
**glacial, ~e, mpl ~s** or **-iaux** /glasjal, o/ adj (a) icy (b) ⟨person, reception⟩ frosty; ⟨silence⟩ stony; ⟨look⟩ icy
**glacier** /glasje/ nm (a) glacier (b) ice-cream maker (c) ice-cream parlour (GB)
**glacière** /glasjɛʀ/ nf coolbox (GB), ice chest (US)
**glaçon** /glasɔ̃/ nm ice cube
**glaire** /glɛʀ/ nf (a) mucus (b) albumen
**glaise** /glɛz/ nf clay
**glaive** /glɛv/ nm double-edged sword
**gland** /glɑ̃/ nm (a) acorn (b) (Anat) glans (c) tassel
**glande** /glɑ̃d/ nf (Anat) gland
**glaner** /glane/ [1] vtr to glean
**glapir** /glapiʀ/ [3] vi (a) ⟨pup⟩ to yap; ⟨fox⟩ to bark (b) ⟨person⟩ to shriek
**glas** /glɑ/ nm inv toll, knell
**glauque** /glok/ adj murky; ⟨street⟩ squalid
**glissade** /glisad/ nf slide; skid
**glissant, ~e** /glisɑ̃, ɑ̃t/ adj slippery
**glissement** /glismɑ̃/ nm (a) sliding (b) (in sense) shift; (among voters) swing; (in prices) fall
**glisser** /glise/ [1] **1** vtr to slip ⟨object⟩ (dans into); to slip in ⟨remark, criticism⟩
**2** vi (a) to be slippery (b) to slip (c) to slide; to glide (d) ~ **sur** to have no effect on
**3 se glisser** v refl (+ v être) se ~ dans to slip into, to sneak into; to creep into
**glissière** /glisjɛʀ/ nf slide; **fermeture à** ~ zip (GB), zipper (US)
**global, ~e, mpl -aux** /glɔbal, o/ adj ⟨sum⟩ total; ⟨result, cost⟩ overall; ⟨agreement, solution⟩ global; ⟨study⟩ comprehensive
**globalement** /glɔbalmɑ̃/ adv on the whole

**globe** /glɔb/ *nm* **(a)** ~ **(terrestre)** earth, globe; **parcourir le** ~ to globe-trot
**(b)** round glass lampshade; glass case
**(c)** (in architecture) dome
■ ~ **oculaire** eyeball

**globule** /glɔbyl/ *nm* globule; blood cell
■ ~ **blanc** white cell; ~ **rouge** red cell

**gloire** /glwaʀ/ *nf* **(a)** glory, fame
**(b)** credit; **faire qch pour la** ~ to do sth (just) for the sake of it
**(c)** glory, praise
**(d) tirer** ~ **de** to pride oneself on
**(e)** celebrity; star

**glorieux, -ieuse** /glɔʀjø, øz/ *adj* glorious

**glorifier** /glɔʀifje/ [2] **1** *vtr* to glorify
**2 se glorifier** *v refl* (+ *v être*) to glory
(**de** in), to boast (**de** about)

**glose** /gloz/ *nf* gloss; note

**gloser** /gloze/ [1] *vi* to ramble on
(**sur** about)

**glossaire** /glɔsɛʀ/ *nm* glossary

**glotte** /glɔt/ *nf* glottis

**gloussement** /glusmɑ̃/ *nm* (of hen) clucking; (of person) chuckle

**glousser** /gluse/ [1] *vi* ⟨hen⟩ to cluck; ⟨person⟩ to chuckle

**glouton, -onne** /glutɔ̃, ɔn/ *adj* ⟨person⟩ gluttonous; ⟨appetite⟩ voracious

**glu** /gly/ *nf* **(a)** bird lime
**(b)** glue

**gluant, ~e** /glyɑ̃, ɑ̃t/ *adj* **(a)** sticky
**(b)** slimy

**glucide** /glysid/ *nm* carbohydrate

**glycémie** /glisemi/ *nf* **taux de** ~ blood sugar level

**glycérine** /gliseʀin/ *nf* glycerin

**gnognotte** /ɲɔɲɔt/ *nf* (colloq) **c'est pas de la** ~! it's not your common or garden variety

**gnome** /gnom/ *nm* gnome

**gnon** /ɲɔ̃/ *nm* (colloq) dent; bruise; **prendre un** ~ to get hit

**go: tout de go** /go/ *phr* ⟨say⟩ straight out

**goal** /gol/ *nm* (colloq) goalkeeper, goalie (colloq)

**gobelet** /gɔblɛ/ *nm* cup; tumbler; beaker; ~ **en carton** paper cup

**gober** /gɔbe/ [1] *vtr* **(a)** to suck ⟨egg⟩; to swallow [sth] whole
**(b)** (colloq) to fall for (colloq) ⟨story⟩

**godasse** /gɔdas/ *nf* (colloq) shoe

**godet** /gɔdɛ/ *nm* **(a)** goblet
**(b)** pot

**goéland** /gɔelɑ̃/ *nm* gull

**goémon** /gɔemɔ̃/ *nm* wrack

**gogo: à gogo** /gogo/ *phr* (colloq) galore; **vin à** ~ wine galore

**goguette: en goguette** /ɑ̃gɔgɛt/ *phr* (colloq) **partir en** ~ to go on a spree

**goinfre** /gwɛ̃fʀ/ *nmf* (colloq) greedy pig (colloq)

**goinfrer: se goinfrer** /gwɛ̃fʀe/ [1] *v refl* (+ *v être*) (colloq) to stuff oneself (colloq) (**de** with)

**goitre** /gwatʀ/ *nm* goitre (GB)

**golden** /gɔldɛn/ *nf inv* Golden Delicious (apple)

**golf** /gɔlf/ *nm* **(a)** golf
**(b)** golf course

**golfe** /gɔlf/ *nm* gulf; bay

**gomme** /gɔm/ **1** *nf* **(a)** eraser, rubber (GB)
**(b)** (substance) gum
**2 à la gomme** *phr* (colloq) ⟨idea⟩ pathetic, useless; ⟨machine⟩ useless; ⟨plan⟩ hopeless
**IDIOMS mettre (toute) la** ~ (colloq) to step on it (colloq); to give it full throttle (colloq); to turn it up full blast

**gommer** /gɔme/ [1] *vtr* **(a)** to rub [sth] out
**(b)** to smooth out ⟨wrinkle⟩; to erase ⟨past, boundaries⟩; to iron out ⟨differences⟩

**gond** /gɔ̃/ *nm* hinge; **sortir de ses** ~s to come off its hinges; to fly off the handle (colloq)

**gondole** /gɔ̃dɔl/ *nf* **(a)** gondola
**(b)** sales shelf

**gondoler: se gondoler** /gɔ̃dɔle/ [1] *v refl* (+ *v être*) ⟨paper⟩ to crinkle; ⟨wood⟩ to warp

**gonflable** /gɔ̃flabl/ *adj* inflatable

**gonflé, ~e** /gɔ̃fle/ **1** *pp* ▶ GONFLER
**2** *adj* **(a)** ⟨tyre, balloon⟩ inflated; ⟨cheeks⟩ puffed out
**(b)** swollen; bloated; puffy; **yeux ~s de sommeil** eyes puffy with sleep
**(c)** (colloq) **être** ~ to have guts (colloq); (critical) to have a nerve (colloq)

**gonfler** /gɔ̃fle/ [1] **1** *vtr* **(a)** to blow up, to inflate ⟨balloon, tyre⟩; to fill ⟨lungs, sail⟩; to puff out ⟨cheeks⟩; **être gonflé à bloc** to be fully inflated; to be raring to go (colloq)
**(b)** to flex ⟨muscle⟩; to make [sth] bulge ⟨pocket, bag⟩; to saturate ⟨sponge⟩; to make [sth] swollen ⟨river⟩; to swell ⟨bud⟩
**(c) il est gonflé d'orgueil** he's full of his own importance
**(d)** to increase ⟨profits⟩; to push up ⟨prices⟩; to inflate ⟨statistics⟩
**2** *vi* (gen) to swell (up); (Culin) to rise

**gonfleur** /gɔ̃flœʀ/ *nm* (air) pump

**gong** /gɔ̃g/ *nm* **(a)** gong
**(b)** (in boxing) bell

**goret** /gɔʀɛ/ *nm* **(a)** piglet
**(b)** (colloq) (child) little pig (colloq)

**gorge** /gɔʀʒ/ *nf* **(a)** throat; **avoir mal à la** ~ to have a sore throat; **tenir qn à la** ~ to have sb by the throat; (figurative) to have a stranglehold over sb; **avoir la** ~ **serrée** or **nouée** to have a lump in one's throat; to have one's heart in one's mouth; **à** ~ **déployée, à pleine** ~ ⟨sing⟩ at the top of one's voice; ⟨laugh⟩ uproariously; **ta remarque m'est restée en travers de la** ~ I found your comment hard to swallow
**(b)** bosom, breast
**(c)** gorge

IDIOMS **faire des ∼s chaudes de qn/qch** to laugh sb/sth to scorn

**gorgé, ∼e¹** /gɔʀʒe/ *adj* **∼ d'eau** ⟨*land*⟩ waterlogged; ⟨*sponge*⟩ saturated with water; **fruit ∼ de soleil** fruit bursting with sunshine

**gorgée²** /gɔʀʒe/ *nf* sip; gulp

**gorger** /gɔʀʒe/ [13] **se gorger** *v refl* (+ *v être*) **se ∼ de nourriture** to gorge oneself

**gorille** /gɔʀij/ *nm* (a) gorilla
(b) (colloq) bodyguard

**gosier** /gozje/ *nm* throat, gullet

**gosse** /gɔs/ *nmf* (colloq) (a) kid (colloq); **sale ∼** brat (colloq)
(b) **il est beau ∼** he's a good-looking fellow

**gothique** /gɔtik/ *adj, nm* Gothic

**gouache** /gwaʃ/ *nf* gouache, poster paint

**gouaille** /gwaj/ *nf* cheek, cheekiness

**goudron** /gudʀɔ̃/ *nm* tar

**goudronner** /gudʀɔne/ [1] *vtr* to tarmac

**gouffre** /gufʀ/ *nm* chasm, abyss; **le ∼ de Padirac** the caves of Padirac

**goujat** /guʒa/ *nm* boor

**goujon** /guʒɔ̃/ *nm* (Zool) gudgeon

**goulée** /gule/ *nf* (colloq) gulp

**goulet** /gule/ *nm* (a) narrows
(b) gully
■ **∼ d'étranglement** bottleneck

**goulot** /gulo/ *nm* (of bottle) neck

**goulu, ∼e** /guly/ *adj* greedy

**goulûment** /gulymã/ *adv* greedily

**goupillon** /gupijɔ̃/ *nm* (a) bottle brush
(b) holy water sprinkler

**gourd, ∼e¹** /guʀ, guʀd/ *adj* numb

**gourde²** /guʀd/ **1** *adj* (colloq) dumb (colloq), gormless (GB) (colloq)
**2** *nf* (a) flask; gourd
(b) (colloq) dope (colloq)

**gourdin** /guʀdɛ̃/ *nm* bludgeon, cudgel

**gourmand, ∼e** /guʀmã, ãd/ *adj* fond of good food; **il est ∼ (de sucreries)** he has a sweet tooth

**gourmandise** /guʀmãdiz/ **1** *nf* weakness for sweet things; weakness for good food
**2** **gourmandises** *nf pl* sweets (GB), candies (US)

**gourmet** /guʀmɛ/ *nm* gourmet

**gourmette** /guʀmɛt/ *nf* chain bracelet

**gourou** /guʀu/ *nm* guru

**gousse** /gus/ *nf* pod; **∼ d'ail** clove of garlic

**gousset** /gusɛ/ *nm* (a) (pocket) fob
(b) gusset

**goût** /gu/ *nm* (a) (gen) taste; palate; **donner du ∼ à qch** to give sth flavour (GB)
(b) **de bon ∼** in good taste; **s'habiller sans ∼** to have no dress sense; **avoir le mauvais ∼ de faire** to be tactless enough to do
(c) liking; **ne pas être du ∼ de tout le monde** not to be to everyone's liking; not to be everyone's cup of tea; **chacun ses ∼s** each to his own; **être au ∼ du jour** to be trendy; **faire qch par ∼** to do sth for pleasure
IDIOMS **tous les ∼s sont dans la nature** (Proverb) it takes all sorts to make a world

**goûter¹** /gute/ [1] **1** *vtr* (a) to taste, to try
(b) to enjoy ⟨*peace, solitude*⟩
**2** **goûter à** *v+prep* (a) **∼ à** to try ⟨*food, drink*⟩
(b) **∼ à** to have a taste of ⟨*freedom, power*⟩

**goûter²** /gute/ *nm* (a) snack
(b) children's party

**goutte** /gut/ **1** *nf* (a) drop (de of); **∼ de pluie** raindrop; **à grosses ∼s** ⟨*rain*⟩ heavily; ⟨*perspire*⟩ profusely
(b) (Med) gout
**2** **gouttes** *nf pl* (Med) drops
IDIOMS **se ressembler comme deux ∼s d'eau** to be as alike as two peas in a pod

**goutte-à-goutte** /gutagut/ *nm inv* (Med) drip

**gouttelette** /gutlɛt/ *nf* droplet

**goutter** /gute/ [1] *vi* to drip

**gouttière** /gutjɛʀ/ *nf* gutter; drainpipe

**gouvernail** /guvɛʀnaj/ *nm* (a) rudder
(b) helm

**gouvernant, ∼e¹** /guvɛʀnã, ãt/ **1** *adj* ruling
**2** **gouvernants** *nm pl* **les ∼s** the government

**gouvernante²** /guvɛʀnãt/ *nf* housekeeper

**gouverne** /guvɛʀn/ *nf* **pour votre ∼** for your information

**gouvernement** /guvɛʀnəmã/ *nm* government

**gouvernemental, ∼e, mpl -aux** /guvɛʀnəmãtal, o/ *adj* government; governmental

**gouverner** /guvɛʀne/ [1] *vtr* (a) to govern, to rule
(b) ⟨*money*⟩ to rule
(c) to steer ⟨*ship*⟩

**gouverneur** /guvɛʀnœʀ/ *nm* governor

**grabataire** /gʀabatɛʀ/ *adj* bedridden

**grabuge** /gʀaby3/ *nm* (colloq) **faire du ∼** to raise hell (colloq)

**grâce** /gʀɑs/ **1** *nf* (a) (of person, gesture) grace; (of landscape) charm
(b) **de bonne ∼** with a (good) grace
(c) favour (GB); **faire à qn la ∼ d'accepter** to do sb the honour (GB) of accepting
(d) mercy; **∼ présidentielle** presidential pardon; **je vous fais ∼ des détails** I'll spare you the details
(e) **∼ à Dieu!** thank God!
**2** **grâce à** *phr* thanks to

**Grâce** /gʀɑs/ *nf* Grace; **votre ∼** your Grace

**gracier** /gʀasje/ [2] *vtr* to pardon, to reprieve

**gracieusement** /gʀasjøzmã/ *adv* (a) free of charge
(b) gracefully

**gracieux, -ieuse** /gʀasjø, øz/ *adj* (a) graceful
(b) gracious

**grade** /gʀad/ *nm* rank; **monter en ∼** to be promoted

**gradé, ∼e** /gʀade/ *nm,f* noncommissioned officer

**gradin** /gʀadɛ̃/ *nm* (in hall) tier; (in arena) terrace

**gradué**, **~e** /gʀadɥe/ *adj* **règle ~e** ruler

**graduer** /gʀadɥe/ [1] *vtr* (a) to increase ⟨*difficulty*⟩
(b) to graduate ⟨*instrument*⟩

**graffiti** /gʀafiti/ *nm pl* graffiti

**graillon** /gʀɑjɔ̃/ *nm* (colloq) **ça sent le ~** it smells of stale fat

**grain** /gʀɛ̃/ *nm* (a) grain; **nourri au ~** corn-fed (GB) *or* grain-fed
(b) grain; **~ de poivre** peppercorn; **~ de café** coffee bean; **~ de moutarde** mustard seed; **~ de raisin** grape
(c) speck
(d) **le ~** the grain; **à gros ~** coarse grained
■ **~ de beauté** beauty spot, mole
IDIOMS **avoir un ~** (colloq) to be loony (colloq); **mettre son ~ de sel** (colloq) to put one's oar in (colloq)

**graine** /gʀɛn/ *nf* seed; birdseed; **monter en ~** ⟨*vegetable*⟩ to run to seed; ⟨*child*⟩ to shoot up
IDIOMS **prends-en de la ~** (colloq) let that be an example to you

**graisse** /gʀɛs/ *nf* (a) (gen) fat; (of seal, whale) blubber
(b) (Tech) grease

**graisser** /gʀese/ [1] *vtr* to grease ⟨*pan*⟩; to lubricate ⟨*mechanism*⟩

**graisseux**, **-euse** /gʀesø, øz/ *adj* (gen) greasy; (Med) fatty

**grammaire** /gʀamɛʀ/ *nf* grammar

**grammatical**, **~e**, *mpl* **-aux** /gʀamatikal, o/ *adj* grammatical

**gramme** /gʀam/ *nm* gram

**grand**, **~e** /gʀɑ̃, gʀɑ̃d/ ⟨1⟩ *adj* (a) ⟨*person, tree, tower*⟩ tall; ⟨*arm, stride, journey*⟩ long; ⟨*margin, angle*⟩ wide; ⟨*place, object, fire*⟩ big
(b) ⟨*crowd, family, fortune*⟩ large, big; **pas ~ monde** not many people; **il fait ~ jour** it's broad daylight; **laver à ~e eau** to wash [sth] in plenty of running water; to wash [sth] down
(c) ⟨*dreamer, collector, friend*⟩ great; ⟨*cheat, gambler*⟩ big; ⟨*drinker, smoker*⟩ heavy; **c'est un ~ timide** he's very shy
(d) ⟨*discovery, news, expedition*⟩ great; ⟨*date*⟩ important; ⟨*role*⟩ major; ⟨*problem, decision*⟩ big
(e) main
(f) ⟨*company, brand*⟩ leading; **les ~es industries** the big industries
(g) ⟨*painter, wine*⟩ great; ⟨*heart, spirit*⟩ noble
(h) ⟨*brother, sister*⟩ elder; ⟨*pupil*⟩ senior (GB), older; **assez ~ pour faire** old enough to do
(i) ⟨*height, length, value, distance*⟩ great; ⟨*size, quantity*⟩ large; ⟨*speed*⟩ high
(j) ⟨*kindness, friendship, danger, interest*⟩ great; ⟨*noise*⟩ loud; ⟨*cold*⟩ severe; ⟨*heat*⟩ intense; ⟨*wind*⟩ strong, high; ⟨*storm*⟩ big, violent; **à ma ~e surprise** much to my surprise

(k) ⟨*family, name*⟩ great; **la ~e bourgeoisie** the upper middle class
(l) ⟨*reception, plan*⟩ grand
(m) ⟨*word*⟩ big; ⟨*phrase*⟩ high-sounding; **faire de ~s gestes** to wave one's arms about; **et voilà, tout de suite les ~s mots** there you go, straight off the deep end
⟨2⟩ *nm,f* big boy/girl; (Sch) senior (GB) *or* older pupil
⟨3⟩ *adv* wide; **ouvrir tout ~ les bras** to throw one's arms open; **ouvrir ~ ses oreilles** to prick up one's ears; **voir ~** to think big
⟨4⟩ *nm* **les ~s de ce monde** the great and the good; the world's leaders
⟨5⟩ **en grand** *phr* ⟨*open*⟩ wide; **faire les choses en ~** to do things on the grand scale
■ **~s axes** main roads; **~ banditisme** organized crime; **le ~ capital** big money; **~ duc** eagle owl; **~ écart** (Sport) splits; **le ~ écran** the big screen; **~ ensemble** high-density housing complex; **le ~ large** the high seas; **~ magasin** department store; **le ~ monde** high society; **le Grand Nord** the Far North; **Grand Pardon** Day of Atonement; **~ prêtre** high priest; **~ prix** grand prix; **le ~ public** the general public; **produit ~ public** consumer product; **la ~e banlieue** the outer suburbs; **la ~e cuisine** haute cuisine; **la Grande Guerre** the First World War; **la ~e muraille de Chine** the Great Wall of China; **~e personne** grown-up, adult; **~e puissance** superpower; **~e roue** big wheel (GB), Ferris wheel (US); **~e surface** supermarket; **~es eaux** fountains; **dès qu'on la gronde, ce sont les ~es eaux** the minute you tell her off, she turns on the waterworks; **~es lignes** main train routes; **~es marées** spring tides; **~es ondes** long wave; **les ~s blessés** the seriously injured; **~s fauves** big cats

**grand-angle**, *pl* **grands-angles** /gʀɑ̃tɑ̃gl, gʀɑ̃zɑ̃gl/ *adj* wide-angle; **un (objectif) ~** a wide-angle lens

**grand-chose** /gʀɑ̃ʃoz/ *pron* **pas ~** not much, not a lot; **il n'y a plus ~ à faire** there isn't much left to do

**Grande-Bretagne** /gʀɑ̃dbʀətaɲ/ *pr nf* Great Britain

**grandement** /gʀɑ̃dmɑ̃/ *adv* greatly; a great deal; extremely

**grandeur** /gʀɑ̃dœʀ/ *nf* (a) size; **~ nature** ⟨*reproduction*⟩ full-scale; ⟨*portrait*⟩ life-size
(b) scale
(c) greatness

**Grand-Guignol** /gʀɑ̃giɲɔl/ *nm* **c'est du ~** it's farcical

**grandiloquence** /gʀɑ̃dilɔkɑ̃s/ *nf* pomposity, grandiloquence

**grandiloquent**, **~e** /gʀɑ̃dilɔkɑ̃, ɑ̃t/ *adj* pompous, grandiloquent

**grandiose** /gʀɑ̃djoz/ *adj* ⟨*site, decor*⟩ grandiose; ⟨*party*⟩ spectacular; ⟨*gesture*⟩ grand

**grandir** /gʀɑ̃diʀ/ [3] ⟨1⟩ *vtr* (a) to magnify
(b) to make [sb] look taller
(c) to exaggerate
⟨2⟩ *vi* (a) to grow; to grow up

····⁝

**(b)** ⟨*company*⟩ to expand; ⟨*crowd, anxiety*⟩ to grow
**3 se grandir** *v refl* (+ *v être*) to make oneself (look) taller

**grandissant, ~e** /gʀɑ̃disɑ̃, ɑ̃t/ *adj* growing

**grand-mère**, *pl* **grands-mères** /gʀɑ̃mɛʀ/ *nf* grandmother

**grand-oncle**, *pl* **grands-oncles** /gʀɑ̃tɔ̃kl, gʀɑ̃zɔ̃kl/ *nm* great-uncle

**grand-peine** /gʀɑ̃pɛn/ **1** *nf* avoir ~ à faire to have great difficulty doing
**2 à grand-peine** *phr* à ~ with great difficulty

**grand-père**, *pl* **grands-pères** /gʀɑ̃pɛʀ/ *nm* grandfather

**grand-route**, *pl* ~**s** /gʀɑ̃ʀut/ *nf* main road

**grand-rue**, *pl* ~**s** /gʀɑ̃ʀy/ *nf* high street

**grands-parents** /gʀɑ̃paʀɑ̃/ *nm pl* grandparents

**grand-tante**, *pl* **grand(s)-tantes** /gʀɑ̃tɑ̃t/ *nf* great-aunt

**grand-voile**, *pl* **grand(s)-voiles** /gʀɑ̃vwal/ *nf* mainsail

**grange** /gʀɑ̃ʒ/ *nf* barn

**granit(e)** /gʀanit/ *nm* granite

**granité, ~e** /gʀanite/ *adj* grained

**granulé** /gʀanyle/ *nm* granule

**graphie** /gʀafi/ *nf* **(a)** written form
**(b)** spelling

**graphique** /gʀafik/ **1** *adj* **(a)** ⟨*work*⟩ graphic
**(b)** ⟨*screen*⟩ graphic; ⟨*software*⟩ graphics
**2** *nm* graph

**graphisme** /gʀafism/ *nm* **(a)** style of drawing
**(b)** handwriting
**(c)** graphic design

**graphologie** /gʀafɔlɔʒi/ *nf* graphology

**grappe** /gʀap/ *nf* (of fruit) bunch; (of flowers) cluster

**grappiller** /gʀapije/ [1] *vtr* to pick up ⟨*fruit*⟩; to glean ⟨*information*⟩

**grappin** /gʀapɛ̃/ *nm* mettre le ~ sur qn (colloq) to get sb in one's clutches

**gras, grasse** /gʀɑ, gʀɑs/ **1** *adj*
**(a)** ⟨*substance*⟩ fatty; ⟨*fish*⟩ oily; ⟨*paper*⟩ greasy
**(b)** coarse, vulgar
**(c)** (in printing) bold
**(d)** loose, phlegmy
**2** *adv* manger ~ to eat fatty foods
**3** *nm* **(a)** (from meat) fat
**(b)** grease
**(c)** (of arm, calf) le ~ the fleshy part

**grassement** /gʀɑsmɑ̃/ *adv* ⟨*pay*⟩ handsomely; ⟨*feed*⟩ lavishly

**grassouillet, -ette** /gʀasujɛ, ɛt/ *adj* (colloq) chubby, plump

**graticiel** /gʀatisjɛl/ *nm* freeware

**gratifiant, ~e** /gʀatifjɑ̃, ɑ̃t/ *adj* gratifying

**gratification** /gʀatifikasjɔ̃/ *nf*
**(a)** gratification
**(b)** bonus

**gratifier** /gʀatifje/ [2] *vtr* ~ qn de qch to give sb sth; se sentir gratifié to feel gratified

**gratin** /gʀatɛ̃/ *nm* **(a)** gratin (*breadcrumbs and cheese*)
**(b)** (colloq) le ~ the upper crust (colloq)

**gratiné, ~e** /gʀatine/ *adj* **(a)** (Culin) au gratin
**(b)** (colloq) ⟨*person*⟩ weird; ⟨*problem*⟩ mind-bending (colloq)

**gratiner** /gʀatine/ [1] *vtr* (faire) ~ un plat to brown a dish

**gratis** /gʀatis/ **1** *adj inv* free
**2** *adv* free (GB), for free

**gratitude** /gʀatityd/ *nf* gratitude; avoir de la ~ pour qn to be grateful to sb

**gratte-ciel** /gʀatsjɛl/ *nm inv* skyscraper

**gratte-papier** /gʀatpapje/ *nm inv* (colloq) pen pusher

**gratter** /gʀate/ [1] **1** *vtr* **(a)** to scratch; to scrape (off)
**(b)** to make [sb] itch; ça me gratte partout I'm itching all over
**2** *vi* ~ à la porte to scratch at the door
**3 se gratter** *v refl* (+ *v être*) to scratch; se ~ la tête to scratch one's head

**grattoir** /gʀatwaʀ/ *nm* **(a)** (tool) scraper
**(b)** (on matchbox) striking strip

**gratuit, ~e** /gʀatɥi, it/ *adj* **(a)** ⟨*place, service*⟩ free
**(b)** ⟨*violence*⟩ gratuitous; ⟨*accusation*⟩ spurious; ⟨*exercise*⟩ pointless

**gratuité** /gʀatɥite/ *nf* la ~ de l'enseignement free education

**gratuitement** /gʀatɥitmɑ̃/ *adv* **(a)** free (GB), for free
**(b)** ⟨*work*⟩ for nothing
**(c)** gratuitously

**gravats** /gʀava/ *nm pl* rubble

**grave** /gʀav/ *adj* **(a)** ⟨*problem, injury*⟩ serious
**(b)** ⟨*expression*⟩ grave, solemn
**(c)** ⟨*voice*⟩ deep; ⟨*note*⟩ low; ⟨*sound*⟩ low-pitched

**gravement** /gʀavmɑ̃/ *adv* **(a)** gravely, solemnly
**(b)** seriously

**graver** /gʀave/ [1] *vtr* to engrave

**graveur, -euse** /gʀavœʀ, øz/ *nm,f* engraver; ~ sur bois wood engraver

**gravier** /gʀavje/ *nm* du ~ gravel

**gravillon** /gʀavijɔ̃/ *nm* grit

**gravir** /gʀaviʀ/ [3] *vtr* to climb up

**gravitation** /gʀavitasjɔ̃/ *nf* gravitation; ~ universelle Newton's law of gravitation

**gravité** /gʀavite/ *nf* **(a)** seriousness
**(b)** solemnity
**(c)** (in physics) gravity

**graviter** /gʀavite/ [1] *vi* to orbit

**gravure** /gʀavyʀ/ *nf* **(a)** la ~ engraving
**(b)** engraving
**(c)** print, reproduction

**gré** /gʀe/ *nm* **(a) contre le ∼ de qn** against sb's will; **de ∼ ou de force** one way or another
**(b)** (formal) **savoir ∼ à qn de qch** to be grateful to sb for sth
**(c) j'ai flâné au ∼ de mon humeur** I strolled where the mood took me

**grec, grecque** /gʀɛk/ 1 *adj* Greek; Grecian
2 *nm* (language) Greek

**Grec, Grecque** /gʀɛk/ *nm,f* Greek

**Grèce** /gʀɛs/ *pr nf* Greece; **∼ antique** Ancient Greece

**grecque** ▶ GREC

**greffe** /gʀɛf/ *nf* **(a)** (of organ) transplant; (of skin) graft
**(b)** (in agriculture) grafting; graft

**greffer** /gʀefe/ [1] 1 *vtr* **(a)** to transplant ⟨organ⟩; to graft ⟨tissue⟩
**(b)** to graft ⟨tree⟩
2 **se greffer** *v refl* (+ *v être*) **se ∼ sur qch** ⟨problem, event⟩ to come along on top of sth

**greffier, -ière** /gʀefje, ɛʀ/ *nm,f* clerk of the court (GB), court clerk (US)

**grégaire** /gʀegɛʀ/ *adj* gregarious

**grège** /gʀɛʒ/ *adj, nm* oatmeal

**grêle** /gʀɛl/ 1 *adj* **(a)** skinny; spindly
**(b)** ⟨voice⟩ reedy; ⟨sound⟩ thin
2 *nf* hail

**grêlé, ∼e** /gʀele/ *adj* pockmarked

**grêler** /gʀele/ [1] *v impers* **il grêle** it's hailing

**grêlon** /gʀelɔ̃/ *nm* hailstone

**grelot** /gʀəlo/ *nm* small bell

**grelotter** /gʀəlɔte/ [1] *vi* to shiver

**grenade** /gʀənad/ *nf* **(a)** grenade
**(b)** pomegranate

**Grenade** /gʀənad/ 1 *pr n* Granada
2 *pr nf* **la ∼** Grenada

**grenadine** /gʀənadin/ *nf* grenadine

**grenaille** /gʀənaj/ *nf* **(a)** steel filings
**(b)** lead shot

**grenat** /gʀəna/ *adj inv* dark red

**grenier** /gʀənje/ *nm* attic, loft; **∼ à grain** granary

**grenouille** /gʀənuj/ *nf* frog

**grès** /gʀɛ/ *nm inv* **(a)** sandstone
**(b)** (piece of) stoneware

**grésillement** /gʀezijmɑ̃/ *nm* **(a)** crackling
**(b)** sizzling

**grésiller** /gʀezije/ [1] *vi* **(a)** ⟨radio⟩ to crackle
**(b)** ⟨butter, oil⟩ to sizzle

**grève** /gʀɛv/ *nf* **(a)** strike; **mouvement de ∼** industrial action
**(b)** shore
■ **∼ de la faim** hunger strike; **∼ sur le tas** sit-down strike; **∼ du zèle** work-to-rule

**grever** /gʀəve/ [16] *vtr* to put a strain on ⟨budget⟩; **l'entreprise est grevée de charges** the company has crippling overheads

**gréviste** /gʀevist/ *nmf* striker

**gribouillage** /gʀibujaʒ/ *nm* (colloq) scribble

**gribouiller** /gʀibuje/ [1] *vtr* (colloq) to scribble

**grief** /gʀijɛf/ *nm* grievance

**grièvement** /gʀijɛvmɑ̃/ *adv* ⟨injured⟩ seriously; ⟨burned⟩ badly; ⟨affected⟩ severely

**griffe** /gʀif/ *nf* **(a)** claw; **tomber entre les ∼s de qn** to fall into sb's clutches
**(b)** (on garment) label
**(c)** signature stamp
**(d)** (in jewellery) claw

**griffer** /gʀife/ [1] 1 *vtr* to scratch
2 **se griffer** *v refl* (+ *v être*) to scratch oneself

**griffonner** /gʀifɔne/ [1] *vtr* **(a)** to scrawl
**(b)** to sketch

**griffure** /gʀifyʀ/ *nf* scratch

**grignoter** /gʀiɲɔte/ [1] 1 *vtr* **(a)** to nibble
**(b)** to encroach on ⟨territory⟩; to conquer ⟨corner of market⟩
**(c)** to fritter away ⟨inheritance⟩
2 *vi* **(a)** ⟨rodent⟩ to gnaw
**(b)** ⟨person⟩ to nibble

**gri-gri,** *pl* **gris-gris** /gʀigʀi/ *nm* lucky charm

**gril** /gʀil/ *nm* grill (GB), broiler (US)

**grillage** /gʀijaʒ/ *nm* wire netting; chicken wire; wire mesh

**grille** /gʀij/ *nf* **(a)** railings; (iron) gate; (of sink, sewer) drain; (of air vent) grille; (in oven, fridge) shelf; (in fireplace, stove) grate
**(b)** (of crossword) grid
**(c)** (on TV, radio) schedule, listings
**(d)** (for assessing results) model
**(e)** (in administration) scale

**grillé, ∼e** /gʀije/ 1 *pp* ▶ GRILLER
2 *pp adj* **(a)** ⟨meat⟩ grilled; ⟨bread⟩ toasted; ⟨almonds⟩ roasted
**(b)** crispy, well-browned
**(c)** burned out; **l'ampoule est ∼e** the bulb has blown
**(d)** (colloq) ⟨spy⟩ exposed

**grille-pain** /gʀijpɛ̃/ *nm inv* toaster

**griller** /gʀije/ [1] 1 *vtr* **(a)** to grill ⟨meat⟩; to toast ⟨bread⟩; to roast ⟨almonds⟩
**(b)** (colloq) to jump (colloq) ⟨light⟩; to ignore ⟨give way sign⟩
**(c)** (colloq) to give the game away about [sb]
**(d)** (colloq) **∼ un adversaire** to manage to get ahead of one's opponent
2 *vi* **(a)** to grill; **faire ∼** to grill; to toast; to roast
**(b)** ⟨bulb⟩ to blow

**grillon** /gʀijɔ̃/ *nm* cricket

**grimaçant, ∼e** /gʀimasɑ̃, ɑ̃t/ *adj* grimacing

**grimace** /gʀimas/ *nf* grimace; funny face

**grimacer** /gʀimase/ [12] *vi* to grimace

**grimer: se grimer** /gʀime/ [1] *v refl* (+ *v être*) to make oneself up

**grimpant, ∼e** /gʀɛ̃pɑ̃, ɑ̃t/ *adj* climbing

**grimper** /gʀɛ̃pe/ [1] 1 *vtr* to climb ⟨stairs⟩ ···⫶

**2** *vi* (a) ~ **aux arbres** to climb (up) trees; **grimpe sur mon dos** get on my back
(b) (colloq) ⟨*road*⟩ to be steep
(c) (colloq) ⟨*prices*⟩ to climb

**grimpeur, -euse** /gʀɛ̃pœʀ, øz/ *nm,f* rock climber

**grinçant, ~e** /gʀɛ̃sɑ̃, ɑ̃t/ *adj* ⟨*tone*⟩ scathing; ⟨*joke*⟩ caustic; ⟨*laugh*⟩ nasty

**grincement** /gʀɛ̃smɑ̃/ *nm* creak(ing); squeak(ing); screech(ing)

**grincer** /gʀɛ̃se/ [12] *vi* ⟨*door*⟩ to creak; ⟨*violin*⟩ to screech; ⟨*chalk*⟩ to squeak; ~ **des dents** to grind one's teeth; (figurative) to gnash one's teeth

**gringalet** /gʀɛ̃galɛ/ *nm* runt

**griotte** /gʀijɔt/ *nf* morello cherry

**grippe** /gʀip/ *nf* flu; ~ **intestinale** gastric flu (GB), intestinal flu (US)
IDIOMS **prendre qn/qch en ~** (colloq) to take a sudden dislike to sb/sth

**gris, ~e** /gʀi, iz/ **1** *adj* (a) grey (GB), gray (US)
(b) dreary; dull
(c) tipsy
**2** *nm inv* grey (GB), gray (US)

**grisaille** /gʀizaj/ *nf* (a) dullness
(b) (of weather) greyness (GB), grayness (US)

**grisant, ~e** /gʀizɑ̃, ɑ̃t/ *adj* (a) ⟨*speed*⟩ exhilarating; ⟨*success*⟩ intoxicating
(b) ⟨*perfume*⟩ heady

**grisâtre** /gʀizɑtʀ/ *adj* ⟨*colour, sky*⟩ greyish (GB), grayish (US); ⟨*morning*⟩ dull

**griser** /gʀize/ [1] *vtr* ⟨*speed*⟩ to exhilarate; ⟨*success*⟩ to intoxicate; **se laisser ~ par le pouvoir** to let power go to one's head

**griserie** /gʀizʀi/ *nf* exhilaration (**de** of)

**grisonnant, ~e** /gʀizɔnɑ̃, ɑ̃t/ *adj* greying

**grisonner** /gʀizɔne/ [1] *vi* to go grey

**grisou** /gʀizu/ *nm* firedamp

**grive** /gʀiv/ *nf* thrush

**grivois, ~e** /gʀivwa, az/ *adj* bawdy; coarse

**grivoiserie** /gʀivwazʀi/ *nf* suggestive remark

**grizzli, grizzly** /gʀizli/ *nm* grizzly bear

**grogne** /gʀɔɲ/ *nf* (colloq) discontent

**grognement** /gʀɔɲəmɑ̃/ *nm* grunt; growl

**grogner** /gʀɔɲe/ [1] *vi* (a) to groan; (figurative) to grumble
(b) ⟨*pig*⟩ to grunt; ⟨*dog*⟩ to growl

**grognon** /gʀɔɲɔ̃/ *adj* grouchy (colloq)

**groin** /gʀwɛ̃/ *nm* snout

**grommeler** /gʀɔmle/ [19] *vi* to grumble

**grondement** /gʀɔ̃dmɑ̃/ *nm* (of torrent, machine) roar; (of crowd) angry murmur

**gronder** /gʀɔ̃de/ [1] **1** *vtr* to tell [sb] off
**2** *vi* (a) ⟨*thunder*⟩ to rumble; ⟨*machine, wind*⟩ to roar
(b) ⟨*rebellion*⟩ to be brewing

**groom** /gʀum/ *nm* bellboy (GB), bellhop (US)

**gros, grosse** /gʀo, gʀos/ **1** *adj* (a) big, large

(b) thick
(c) fat
(d) ⟨*customer, market*⟩ big; ⟨*damage*⟩ considerable
(e) ⟨*problem*⟩ serious, big; ⟨*flaw*⟩ big, major
(f) ⟨*cold*⟩ bad; ⟨*sobs*⟩ loud; ⟨*voice*⟩ deep; ⟨*rain*⟩ heavy; ⟨*smoker*⟩ heavy
**2** *adv* (a) ⟨*write*⟩ big
(b) ⟨*bet, lose*⟩ a lot of money; (figurative) a lot
**3** *nm inv* (a) **le ~ de** the majority of ⟨*spectators*⟩; the bulk of ⟨*work*⟩; most of ⟨*winter*⟩
(b) wholesale trade
(c) **la pêche au ~** game fishing
**4 en ~** *phr* (a) roughly; **en ~ je suis d'accord avec toi** basically, I agree with you
(b) wholesale
(c) in big letters
■ ~ **bonnet** (colloq) big shot (colloq); ~ **lot** first prize; ~ **mot** swearword; ~ **œuvre** shell (of a building); ~ **plan** close-up; ~ **sel** cooking salt; ~ **titre** headline; **grosse caisse** bass drum; **grosse tête** (colloq) brain (colloq)
IDIOMS **en avoir ~ sur le cœur** *or* **la patate** (colloq) to be very upset; **c'est un peu ~ comme histoire!** that's a bit of a tall story!

**groseille** /gʀozɛj/ *nf* redcurrant; ~ **à maquereau** gooseberry

**grosse** ▶ GROS

**grossesse** /gʀosɛs/ *nf* pregnancy
■ ~ **nerveuse** phantom pregnancy (GB), false pregnancy

**grosseur** /gʀosœʀ/ *nf* (a) size
(b) (of thread) thickness
(c) (Med) lump

**grossier, -ière** /gʀosje, ɛʀ/ *adj*
(a) ⟨*person, gesture*⟩ rude; ⟨*language*⟩ bad
(b) ⟨*laugh*⟩ coarse
(c) ⟨*imitation*⟩ crude
(d) ⟨*sketch, idea*⟩ rough; ⟨*work*⟩ crude
(e) ⟨*error*⟩ glaring

**grossièrement** /gʀosjɛʀmɑ̃/ *adv*
(a) ⟨*calculate*⟩ roughly
(b) ⟨*built*⟩ crudely
(c) ⟨*speak*⟩ rudely

**grossièreté** /gʀosjɛʀte/ *nf* (a) rudeness
(b) dirty word
(c) coarseness

**grossir** /gʀosiʀ/ [3] **1** *vtr* (a) to enlarge ⟨*image*⟩
(b) to increase ⟨*numbers*⟩; to boost ⟨*profits*⟩
(c) to exaggerate ⟨*incident*⟩
(d) to make [sb] look fat
**2** *vi* (a) to put on weight
(b) (gen) to grow; ⟨*river*⟩ to swell

**grossissant, ~e** /gʀosisɑ̃, ɑ̃t/ *adj* magnifying

**grossiste** /gʀosist/ *nmf* wholesaler

**grosso modo** /gʀosomodo/ *adv* roughly

**grotesque** /gʀɔtɛsk/ *adj* ridiculous

**grotte** /gʀɔt/ *nf* (a) cave
(b) grotto

**grouiller** /gʀuje/ [1] **1** *vi* to swarm about; to mill about

**2 se grouiller** *v refl* (+ *v être*) (colloq) to get a move on (colloq)

**groupage** /gʀupaʒ/ *nm* bulking; **envoi en ∼** collective shipment

**groupe** /gʀup/ *nm* **(a)** (gen, Econ) group; **par ∼s de deux** in pairs, in twos **(b)** (of objects) group; cluster ■ **∼ d'autodéfense** vigilante group; **∼ électrogène** (electricity) generator; **∼ de pression** pressure group; **∼ sanguin** blood group; **∼ scolaire** school; **∼ des Sept, G7** Group of Seven, G7 countries

**groupement** /gʀupmɑ̃/ *nm* **(a)** association, group **(b)** grouping

**grouper** /gʀupe/ [1] **1** *vtr* to put together **2 se grouper** *v refl* (+ *v être*) to gather (autour de around); to form a group; **se ∼ par trois** to form groups of three; **restez groupés** keep together

**groupuscule** /gʀupyskyl/ *nm* small group

**gruau**, *pl* **∼x** /gʀyo/ *nm* **(a)** gruel **(b)** fine wheat flour

**grue** /gʀy/ *nf* (Tech, Zool) crane IDIOMS **faire le pied de ∼** (colloq) to hang around

**grumeau**, *pl* **∼x** /gʀymo/ *nm* lump

**gruyère** /gʀyjɛʀ/ *nm* Gruyère, Swiss cheese

**Guadeloupe** /gwadlup/ *pr nf* **la ∼** Guadeloupe

**gué** /ge/ *nm* ford; **passer un ruisseau à ∼** to ford a stream

**guenille** /gənij/ *nf* rag; **en ∼s** in rags

**guenon** /gənɔ̃/ *nf* female monkey

**guépard** /gepaʀ/ *nm* cheetah

**guêpe** /gɛp/ *nf* wasp

**guêpier** /gepje/ *nm* **(a)** wasps' nest **(b)** tight corner; **dans quel ∼ es-tu allé te fourrer?** (colloq) what kind of mess have you got (GB) *or* gotten (US) yourself into?

**guêpière** /gepjɛʀ/ *nf* basque, bodyshaper with suspenders (GB) *or* garters (US)

**guère** /gɛʀ/ *adv* hardly; **il n'avait ∼ le choix** he didn't really have a choice

**guéridon** /geʀidɔ̃/ *nm* pedestal table

**guérilla** /geʀija/ *nf* **(a)** guerilla warfare **(b)** guerillas

**guérir** /geʀiʀ/ [3] **1** *vtr* **(a)** to cure ⟨person, disease⟩ **(b)** **∼ qn de** to cure sb of ⟨habit⟩ **2** *vi* to recover; to heal; to get better **3 se guérir** *v refl* (+ *v être*) **se ∼ de** to overcome ⟨shyness⟩

**guérison** /geʀizɔ̃/ *nf* recovery; healing

**guérite** /geʀit/ *nf* **(a)** sentry box **(b)** (on toll road) booth

**guerre** /gɛʀ/ *nf* war; warfare; **les pays en ∼** the warring nations ■ **∼ chimique** chemical war; chemical warfare; **∼ éclair** blitzkrieg, lightning war; **∼ mondiale** world war; **Première/Deuxième Guerre mondiale** World War I/II; **∼ nucléaire** nuclear war; nuclear warfare; **∼ de 14** 1914–18 war; **∼ de Sécession** American Civil War; **∼ d'usure** war of attrition; **∼ des prix** price war IDIOMS **à la ∼ comme à la ∼** in time of hardship you have to make the best of things; **c'est de bonne ∼** it's only fair; **de ∼ lasse, elle renonça** realizing that she was fighting a losing battle, she gave up

**guerrier, -ière** /geʀje, ɛʀ/ *nm,f* warrior

**guet** /gɛ/ *nm* **(a)** lookout; **faire le ∼** to be on the lookout **(b)** (Mil) watch

**guet-apens**, *pl* **guets-apens** /gɛtapɑ̃/ *nm* ambush; (figurative) trap

**guêtre** /gɛtʀ/ *nf* **(a)** (Sport) leggings **(b)** gaiter

**guetter** /gete/ [1] *vtr* **(a)** to watch ⟨prey, criminal, reaction⟩; to watch out for ⟨sign⟩; to look out for ⟨postman⟩ **(b)** to threaten

**guetteur, -euse** /getœʀ, øz/ *nm,f* lookout

**gueule** /gœl/ *nf* **(a)** (slang) face; **il a la ∼ de l'emploi** he really looks the part **(b)** (slang) mouth; **(ferme) ta ∼!** shut your face (GB) *or* mouth! (colloq) **(c)** (of animal) mouth ■ **∼ de bois** (colloq) hangover IDIOMS **faire la ∼** (slang) to be sulking

**gueuler** (slang) /gœle/ [1] **1** *vtr* to yell; to bawl out **2** *vi* to yell, to bawl; to kick up a real fuss; **∼ après qn** to have a go at sb (colloq)

**gui** /gi/ *nm* mistletoe

**guichet** /giʃɛ/ *nm* window; (in bank) counter; (in museum, station) ticket office; (in theatre, cinema) box office; **la pièce se jouera à ∼s fermés** the play is sold out ■ **∼ automatique** automatic teller machine

**guichetier, -ière** /giʃtje, ɛʀ/ *nm,f* ticket clerk

**guide** /gid/ *nm* guide

**guider** /gide/ [1] *vtr* **(a)** (gen) to guide **(b)** to show [sb] the way

**guidon** /gidɔ̃/ *nm* handlebars

**guigne** /giɲ/ *nf* (colloq) bad luck

**guignol** /giɲɔl/ *nm* **(a)** puppet show, ≈ Punch and Judy show **(b)** (derogatory) clown

**guillemets** /gijmɛ/ *nm pl* inverted commas (GB), quotation marks

**guillotine** /gijɔtin/ *nf* guillotine

**guimauve** /gimov/ *nf* **(a)** (Bot) (marsh) mallow **(b)** (confectionery) marshmallow

**guimbarde** /gɛ̃baʀd/ *nf* Jew's harp

**guindé, -e** /gɛ̃de/ *adj* formal

**guingois: de guingois** /dəgɛ̃gwa/ *phr* **être de ∼** to be lopsided

**guirlande** /giʀlɑ̃d/ *nf* garland; tinsel ■ **∼ électrique** set *or* string of fairy lights

**guise** /giz/ *nf* **(a)** '**à votre ∼**' 'just as you like *or* please'

**(b) en ~ de** by way of
**guitare** /gitaʀ/ *nf* guitar
**guitariste** /gitaʀist/ *nmf* guitarist
**gustatif, -ive** /gystatif, iv/ *adj* ⟨organ⟩
taste
**guttural, ~e,** *mpl* **-aux** /gytyʀal, o/ *adj*
guttural
**Guyana** /gɥijana/ *pr nf* Guyana;
**République de ~** Republic of Guyana
**Guyane** /gɥijan/ *pr nf* **~ (française)**
(French) Guyana; **~ hollandaise** Dutch
Guiana

**gym** /ʒim/ *nf* (colloq) (Sch) physical
education; (Sport) gymnastics
**gymnase** /ʒimnɑz/ *nm* gymnasium
**gymnaste** /ʒimnast/ *nmf* gymnast
**gymnastique** /ʒimnastik/ *nf* gymnastics;
exercises
■ **~ corrective** ≈ physiotherapy exercises
**gynécologie** /ʒinekɔlɔʒi/ *nf* gynaecology
**gyrophare** /ʒiʀɔfaʀ/ *nm* flashing light,
emergency rotating light

# H h

**h, H** /aʃ/ *nm inv* **(a)** (letter) h, H; **h muet** mute
h
**(b)** (*written abbr* = **heure**) 9 h 10 9.10
**ha** /ʼa/ (*written abbr* = **hectare**) ha
**habile** /abil/ *adj* clever, skilful (GB)
**habilement** /abilmɑ̃/ *adv* skilfully (GB);
cleverly
**habileté** /abilte/ *nf* skill; skilfulness (GB)
**habillé, ~e** /abije/ *adj* ⟨dress⟩ smart;
⟨dinner⟩ formal
**habillement** /abijmɑ̃/ *nm* clothing
**habiliter** /abilite/ [1] *vtr* to authorize
**habiller** /abije/ [1] **1** *vtr* **(a)** to dress; to
dress [sb] up
**(b)** to clothe; to provide [sb] with clothing
**(c)** to make [sb's] clothes
**(d) un rien l'habille** she looks good in
anything
**2 s'habiller** *v refl* (+ *v être*) **(a)** to get
dressed; to dress up; **s'~ long/court** to wear
long/short skirts
**(b) s'~ chez** to get one's clothes from
**habilleur, -euse** /abijœʀ, øz/ *nmf*
dresser
**habit** /abi/ *nm* **(a) ~s** clothes
**(b)** outfit, costume
**(c)** (of monk, nun) habit
■ **~ de lumière** matador's costume; **~s du
dimanche** Sunday best
**habitable** /abitabl/ *adj* **(a)** habitable
**(b) surface ~** living space
**habitacle** /abitakl/ *nm* **(a)** (aviat) cockpit;
(of rocket) cabin
**(b)** (Aut) interior
**(c)** (Naut) binnacle
**habitant, ~e** /abitɑ̃, ɑ̃t/ *nmf* inhabitant;
resident; **loger chez l'~** to stay as a paying
guest
**habitat** /abita/ *nm* **(a)** (Bot, Zool) habitat
**(b)** housing
**habitation** /abitasjɔ̃/ *nf* **(a)** house,
dwelling; home

**(b)** living; **immeuble d'~** block of flats (GB),
apartment building (US)
■ **~ à loyer modéré, HLM** ≈ (block of) council
flats (GB), low-rent apartment (building) (US)
**habité, ~e** /abite/ *adj* **(a)** inhabited
**(b)** ⟨rocket⟩ manned
**habiter** /abite/ [1] **1** *vtr* to live in
**2** *vi* to live
**habitude** /abityd/ **1** *nf* **(a)** habit; **par ~**
out of habit; **ils ont l'~ de se coucher tôt**
they usually go to bed early; **avoir l'~ de** to
be used to
**(b)** custom
**2 d'habitude** *phr* usually
**habitué, ~e** /abitɥe/ *nmf* regular
**habituel, -elle** /abitɥel/ *adj* usual
**habituellement** /abitɥelmɑ̃/ *adv* usually
**habituer** /abitɥe/ [1] **1** *vtr* **(a) ~ qn à** to
get sb used to
**(b)** to teach
**2 s'habituer** *v refl* (+ *v être*) **s'~ à** to get
used to
**hache** /ʼaʃ/ *nf* axe (GB), ax (US)
**IDIOMS enterrer la ~ de guerre** to bury the
hatchet
**haché, ~e** /ʼaʃe/ *adj* **(a)** ⟨meat⟩ minced
**(b)** ⟨speech⟩ disjointed
**hache-légumes** /ʼaʃlegym/ *nm inv*
vegetable chopper
**hacher** /ʼaʃe/ [1] *vtr* to mince; to chop
**hachette** /ʼaʃɛt/ *nf* hatchet
**hachis** /ʼaʃi/ *nm inv* mince; **~ de persil**
chopped parsley
■ **~ Parmentier** ≈ shepherd's pie
**hachisch** /ʼaʃiʃ/ *nm* hashish
**hachoir** /ʼaʃwaʀ/ *nm* **(a)** mincer
**(b)** chopper
**hachurer** /ʼaʃyʀe/ [1] *vtr* to hatch
**haddock** /ʼadɔk/ *nm* smoked haddock
**hagard, ~e** /ʼagaʀ, aʀd/ *adj* ⟨person⟩
dazed; ⟨eyes⟩ wild

**haï, ~e** /'ai/ ▶ HAÏR

**haie** /'ɛ/ *nf* (a) hedge
(b) (Sport) hurdle; fence; **course de ~s**
hurdle race; steeple chase
(c) line, row; **faire une ~ d'honneur** to form
a guard of honour (GB)

**haillon** /'ɑjɔ̃/ *nm* rag; **en ~s** in rags

**haine** /'ɛn/ *nf* hatred; **s'attirer la ~ de qn** to
earn sb's hatred

**haineux, -euse** /'ɛnø, øz/ *adj* full of
hatred

**haïr** /'aiʀ/ [25] *vtr* to hate

**haïssable** /'aisabl/ *adj* detestable, hateful

**halage** /'alaʒ/ *nm* **chemin de ~** towpath

**hâle** /'ɑl/ *nm* (sun)tan

**hâlé, ~e** /'ɑle/ *adj* tanned

**haleine** /alɛn/ *nf* breath; breathing; **hors
d'~** out of breath; **un travail de longue ~** a
long-drawn-out job

**haler** /'ale/ [1] *vtr* to tow ⟨*boat*⟩; to haul in
⟨*chain*⟩

**haleter** /'alte/ [18] *vi* (a) to gasp for
breath; to pant
(b) ⟨*machine*⟩ to puff; ⟨*chest*⟩ to heave

**hall** /'ol/ *nm* entrance hall (GB), lobby (US);
**~ (de gare)** concourse

**halle** /'al/ *nf* covered market

**hallucination** /alysinasjɔ̃/ *nf*
hallucination; **avoir des ~s** to hallucinate;
to be seeing things

**halluciné, ~e** /alysine/ *adj* ⟨*eyes*⟩ wild

**hallucinogène** /alysinɔʒɛn/ *adj*
hallucinogenic

**halo** /'alo/ *nm* halo; **entouré d'un ~ de
mystère** shrouded in mystery

**halogène** /alɔʒɛn/ *adj* halogen

**halte** /'alt/ ① *nf* (a) stop
(b) stopping place
② *excl* stop!; (Mil) halt!

**halte-garderie**, *pl* **haltes-
garderies** /'altəɡaʀdəʀi/ *nf* ≈ playgroup

**haltère** /altɛʀ/ *nm* dumbbell; barbell; **faire
des ~s** to do weightlifting

**haltérophilie** /alterɔfili/ *nf* weightlifting

**hamac** /'amak/ *nm* hammock

**hameau**, *pl* **~x** /'amo/ *nm* hamlet

**hameçon** /amsɔ̃/ *nm* hook; **mordre à l'~**
to take the bait

**hanche** /'ɑ̃ʃ/ *nf* (of person) hip

**handicap** /'ɑ̃dikap/ *nm* handicap

**handicapé, ~e** /'ɑ̃dikape/ ① *adj*
(a) disabled
(b) **être ~** to be at a disadvantage
② *nm,f* disabled person

**handicaper** /'ɑ̃dikape/ [1] *vtr* to handicap

**hangar** /'ɑ̃ɡaʀ/ *nm* shed; warehouse;
hangar

**hanneton** /'antɔ̃/ *nm* cockchafer (GB),
June bug (US)

**hanter** /'ɑ̃te/ [1] *vtr* to haunt

**hantise** /'ɑ̃tiz/ *nf* dread

**happer** /'ape/ [1] *vtr* to catch ⟨*insect*⟩;
happé par ⟨*arm*⟩ caught up in ⟨*machine*⟩;
⟨*person*⟩ hit by ⟨*train*⟩; (figurative) swallowed
up by ⟨*crowd*⟩

**haranguer** /'aʀɑ̃ɡe/ [1] *vtr* to harangue

**haras** /'aʀa/ *nm inv* stud farm

**harassement** /'aʀasmɑ̃/ *nm* exhaustion

**harasser** /'aʀase/ [1] *vtr* to exhaust

**harcèlement** /'aʀsɛlmɑ̃/ *nm* harassment

**harceler** /'aʀsəle/ [17] *vtr* (a) to pester
(b) to harass

**hardi, ~e** /'aʀdi/ *adj* bold, daring

**hardiesse** /'aʀdjɛs/ *nf* (a) boldness
(b) brazenness

**hareng** /'aʀɑ̃/ *nm* herring

**hargne** /'aʀɲ/ *nf* aggression

**hargneux, -euse** /'aʀɲø, øz/ *adj*
aggressive

**haricot** /'aʀiko/ *nm* (Bot) bean; **~ blanc**
haricot bean; **~ vert** French bean
IDIOMS **c'est la fin des ~s** (colloq) we've had
it (colloq)

**harmonica** /aʀmɔnika/ *nm* mouth organ,
harmonica

**harmonie** /aʀmɔni/ *nf* harmony

**harmonieux, -ieuse** /aʀmɔnjø, øz/ *adj*
harmonious; ⟨*movements*⟩ graceful

**harmoniser** /aʀmɔnize/ [1] ① *vtr* (a) to
coordinate ⟨*colours*⟩
(b) to harmonize; to make [sth] consistent;
to bring into line
(c) (Mus) to harmonize
② **s'harmoniser** *v refl* (+ *v être*) **bien s'~**
⟨*colours*⟩ to go together well

**harnachement** /'aʀnaʃmɑ̃/ *nm* (a) (for
horse) harness
(b) (colloq) (clothes) get-up (colloq)

**harnacher** /'aʀnaʃe/ [1] *vtr* (a) to harness
⟨*horse*⟩
(b) (colloq) to rig out (colloq) ⟨*person*⟩

**harnais** /'aʀnɛ/ *nm inv* harness

**harpe** /'aʀp/ *nf* harp

**harpie** /'aʀpi/ *nf* harpy

**harpon** /'aʀpɔ̃/ *nm* harpoon

**harponner** /'aʀpɔne/ [1] *vtr* to harpoon

**hasard** /'azaʀ/ *nm* chance; **par ~** by
chance; **par un curieux ~** by a curious
coincidence; **par un heureux ~** by a stroke
of luck; **ce n'est pas un ~ si...** it's no
accident that...; **le ~ a voulu que...** as luck
would have it,...; **au ~** ⟨*choose*⟩ at random;
⟨*walk*⟩ aimlessly; ⟨*answer*⟩ off the top of
one's head; **comme par ~, il a oublié son
argent** (ironic) surprise, surprise, he's
forgotten his money; **à tout ~** just in case,
on the off chance; **les ~s de la vie** the
fortunes of life
IDIOMS **le ~ fait bien les choses** fate is a
great provider

**hasarder** /'azaʀde/ [1] ① *vtr* (a) to
venture ⟨*advice*⟩
(b) to risk ⟨*life*⟩
② **se hasarder** *v refl* (+ *v être*) to venture

**hasardeux, -euse** /'azaʀdø, øz/ *adj*
risky

**hâte** /'ɑt/ *nf* (a) haste; **à la ~** hastily
(b) **j'ai ~ de partir/qu'elle parte** I can't wait
to leave/for her to leave

**hâter** /'ɑte/ [1] **1** *vtr* to hasten; **~ le pas** to
quicken one's step
**2 se hâter** *v refl* (+ *v être*) to hurry, to
rush

**hâtif, -ive** /'ɑtif, iv/ *adj* (a) ⟨*judgment*⟩
hasty, hurried
(b) ⟨*plant*⟩ early

**hâtivement** /'ɑtivmã/ *adv* hurriedly,
hastily

**hausse** /'os/ *nf* increase, rise; **être en ~**
⟨*prices*⟩ to be rising; ⟨*goods*⟩ to be going up
in price; **en ~ de 10%** up 10%

**haussement** /'osmã/ *nm* **~ d'épaules**
shrug

**hausser** /'ose/ [1] **1** *vtr* to raise; **~ les
épaules** to shrug one's shoulders
**2 se hausser** *v refl* (+ *v être*) **se ~ sur la
pointe des pieds** to stand on tiptoe

**haut, ~e¹** /'o, 'ot/ **1** *adj* (a) high; tall;
**l'étagère la plus ~e** the top shelf; **à ~e voix**
⟨*speak*⟩ loudly; ⟨*read*⟩ aloud, out loud; **à ~
risque** very risky; **au plus ~ point**
immensely
(b) ⟨*rank, society*⟩ high; ⟨*person, post*⟩ high-
ranking; **~e surveillance** close supervision
(c) (in geography) upper; **la ~e Égypte** Upper
Egypt
(d) **le ~ Moyen Âge** the early Middle Ages
**2** *adv* (a) high; **un personnage ~ placé** a
high-ranking person; **plus ~ sur la page**
higher up on the page; **'voir plus ~'** see
above; **de ~** from above
(b) (in time) far back
(c) loud(ly); **dire qch tout ~** to say sth aloud;
**n'avoir jamais un mot plus ~ que l'autre**
never to raise one's voice
**3** *nm* (a) top; **le ~ du corps** the top half of
the body; **l'étagère du ~** the top shelf; **les
pièces du ~** the upstairs rooms; **parler du ~
d'un balcon** to speak from a balcony
(b) **faire 50 mètres de ~** to be 50 metres (GB)
high
**4 en haut** *phr* upstairs; on an upper floor;
**en ~ de** at the top of
■ **~ en couleur** ⟨*character*⟩ colourful (GB);
**~ fait** heroic deed; **~ lieu de** centre (GB) of
*or* for; **en ~ lieu** in high places; **~e mer** open
sea; **~es sphères** high social circles
IDIOMS **voir les choses de ~** to have a
detached view of things; **tomber de ~** to be
dumbfounded; **connaître des ~s et des bas**
to have one's ups and downs; **~ les mains!**
hands up!; **gagner ~ la main** to win hands
down; **prendre qch de ~** to react indignantly

**hautain, ~e** /'otɛ̃, ɛn/ *adj* haughty

**hautbois** /'obwɑ/ *nm inv* (a) oboe
(b) oboist

**haut-de-forme**, *pl* **hauts-de-
formes** /'odfɔʀm/ *nm* top hat

**haute²** /'ot/ **1** *adj f* ▶ HAUT 1

**2** *nf* (colloq) **les gens de la ~** the upper crust

**haute(-)fidélité**, *pl* **hautes(-)
fidélités** /'otfidelite/ *nf* hi-fi, high fidelity

**hauteur** /'otœʀ/ **1** *nf* (a) height; **prendre
de la ~** ⟨*plane*⟩ to climb; **dans le sens de la
~** upright; **à ~ d'homme** at head height
(b) hill; **gagner les ~s** to reach high
ground
(c) haughtiness
(d) (of voice) pitch
**2 à la hauteur de** *phr* (a) **arriver à la ~
de** to come up to; to draw level with;
**raccourcir une jupe à la ~ des genoux** to
shorten a dress to the knee
(b) (figurative) **être à la ~** to measure up; **être
à la ~ de sa tâche** to be equal to one's job
IDIOMS **tomber de toute sa ~** to fall
headlong

**haut-fond**, *pl* **hauts-fonds** /'ofɔ̃/ *nm*
shallows

**haut(-)fourneau**, *pl* **hauts(-)
fourneaux** /'ofuʀno/ *nm* blast furnace

**haut-le-cœur** /'olkœʀ/ *nm inv* retching,
heaving; **avoir un ~** to retch

**haut-parleur**, *pl* **~s** /'opaʀlœʀ/ *nm*
loudspeaker

**havane** /'avan/ **1** *adj inv* tobacco-brown
**2** *nm* (a) Havana tobacco
(b) Havana cigar

**havre** /'ɑvʀ/ *nm* haven

**Haye** /'ɛ/ *pr n* **la ~** the Hague

**heaume** /'om/ *nm* helmet

**hebdomadaire** /ɛbdɔmadɛʀ/ *adj, nm*
weekly

**hébergement** /ebɛʀʒəmã/ *nm*
(a) accommodation
(b) housing

**héberger** /ebɛʀʒe/ [13] *vtr* to put [sb]
up; to accommodate; to provide shelter
for

**hébété, ~e** /ebete/ *adj* ⟨*look*⟩ stupid

**hébraïque** /ebʀaik/ *adj* Hebrew

**hébreu**, *pl* **~x** /ebʀø/ **1** *adj m* Hebrew
**2** *nm* (language) Hebrew
IDIOMS **pour moi, c'est de l'~** it's all Greek
to me

**HEC** /aʃəse/ *nf* (*abbr* = **Hautes études
commerciales**) *major business school*

**hécatombe** /ekatɔ̃b/ *nf* massacre,
slaughter

**hectare** /ɛktaʀ/ *nm* hectare

**hecto** /ɛkto/ **1** *nm* (*abbr* =
**hectogramme**) hectogram
**2 hecto(-)** (*combining form*) hecto

**hein** /'ɛ̃/ *excl* (colloq) what (colloq)?, sorry?; **ça
t'étonne, ~?** that's surprised you, hasn't it?

**hélas** /'elas/ *excl* alas; **~ non!** unfortunately
not!

**héler** /'ele/ [14] *vtr* to hail

**hélice** /elis/ *nf* (a) (screw) propeller
(b) helix

**hélicoptère** /elikɔptɛʀ/ *nm* helicopter

**héliporté**, **~e** /elipɔʀte/ adj helicopter-borne

**hellène** /ellɛn/ adj Hellenic

**helvétique** /ɛlvetik/ adj Helvetic, Swiss; **la Confédération ~** Switzerland

**helvétisme** /ɛlvetism/ nm Swiss French expression

**hématologie** /ematɔlɔʒi/ nf haematology

**hématome** /ematom/ nm bruise

**hémicycle** /emisikl/ nm semicircular auditorium

**hémisphère** /emisfɛʀ/ nm hemisphere

**hémoglobine** /emɔglɔbin/ nf haemoglobin

**hémophile** /emɔfil/ **1** adj haemophilic
**2** nmf haemophiliac

**hémorragie** /emɔʀaʒi/ nf
(a) haemorrhage, bleeding
(b) (of capital) outflow

**hémorroïdes** /emɔʀɔid/ nf pl piles, haemorrhoids

**henné** /'ene/ nm henna

**hennir** /'eniʀ/ [3] vi to neigh, to whinny

**hépatique** /epatik/ **1** adj hepatic
**2** nmf person with a liver complaint

**hépatite** /epatit/ nf hepatitis

**héraldique** /eʀaldik/ adj heraldic

**herbacé**, **~e** /ɛʀbase/ adj herbaceous

**herbage** /ɛʀbaʒ/ nm pasture

**herbe** /ɛʀb/ **1** nf (a) grass; **mauvaise ~** weed
(b) (Culin) herb
**2 en herbe** phr (a) ⟨wheat⟩ in the blade
(b) ⟨musician⟩ budding
**IDIOMS couper l'~ sous le pied de qn** to pull the rug from under sb's feet

**herbeux**, **-euse** /ɛʀbø, øz/ adj grassy

**herbier** /ɛʀbje/ nm herbarium

**herbivore** /ɛʀbivɔʀ/ **1** adj herbivorous
**2** nm herbivore

**herboriste** /ɛʀbɔʀist/ nmf herbalist

**herboristerie** /ɛʀbɔʀistəʀi/ nf (a) herb trade
(b) herbalist's shop (GB) or store (US)

**héréditaire** /eʀeditɛʀ/ adj hereditary; (figurative) ⟨enemy⟩ traditional

**hérédité** /eʀedite/ nf (a) heredity
(b) (of title) hereditary nature

**hérésie** /eʀezi/ nf (a) heresy
(b) (humorous) sacrilege

**hérétique** /eʀetik/ **1** adj heretical
**2** nmf heretic

**hérissé**, **~e** /'eʀise/ adj ⟨hair⟩ bristling, standing up on end; **~ de** spiked with ⟨nails⟩

**hérisser** /'eʀise/ [1] **1** vtr (a) ⟨bird⟩ to ruffle (up) ⟨feathers⟩
(b) **~ qch de** to spike sth with
(c) (colloq) **ça me hérisse** it makes my hackles rise
**2 se hérisser** v refl (+ v être) ⟨hair⟩ to stand on end

**hérisson** /'eʀisɔ̃/ nm hedgehog

**héritage** /eʀitaʒ/ nm (a) inheritance; **laisser qch en ~** to bequeath sth; **recevoir qch en ~** to inherit sth
(b) heritage

**hériter** /eʀite/ [1] **1** vtr to inherit
**2 hériter de** v+prep to inherit
**3** vi to inherit; to come into an inheritance; **~ de qn** to receive an inheritance from sb

**héritier**, **-ière** /eʀitje, ɛʀ/ nm,f heir/heiress

**hermétique** /ɛʀmetik/ adj (a) hermetic; airtight; watertight
(b) ⟨milieu⟩ impenetrable; ⟨poetry, author⟩ abstruse; ⟨face⟩ inscrutable

**hermétiquement** /ɛʀmetikmɑ̃/ adv
(a) ⟨sealed⟩ hermetically
(b) ⟨speak⟩ abstrusely

**hermine** /ɛʀmin/ nf (a) stoat
(b) ermine

**hernie** /'ɛʀni/ nf (a) hernia
(b) (in tyre) bulge

**héroïne** /eʀɔin/ nf (a) heroine
(b) heroin

**héroïque** /eʀɔik/ adj heroic; epic

**héroïsme** /eʀɔism/ nm heroism

**héron** /'eʀɔ̃/ nm heron

**héros** /'eʀo/ nm inv hero

**herse** /'ɛʀs/ nf (a) harrow
(b) portcullis

**hertzien**, **-ienne** /ɛʀtzjɛ̃, ɛn/ adj ⟨wave⟩ Hertzian; ⟨station⟩ radio-relay

**hésitant**, **~e** /ezitɑ̃, ɑ̃t/ adj (a) hesitant
(b) ⟨start⟩ shaky

**hésitation** /ezitasjɔ̃/ nf (a) indecision, hesitancy
(b) hesitation

**hésiter** /ezite/ [1] vi to hesitate; **elle hésite encore** she's still undecided; **il n'y a pas à ~** it's got to be done; **j'hésite sur le chemin à prendre** I'm not sure which path to take; **~ à faire** to be hesitant to do

**hétéroclite** /eteʀɔklit/ adj ⟨population, work⟩ heterogeneous; ⟨objects⟩ miscellaneous

**hétérogène** /eteʀɔʒɛn/ adj mixed, heterogeneous

**hétérosexuel**, **-elle** /eteʀɔsɛksɥel/ adj, nm,f heterosexual

**hêtre** /'ɛtʀ/ nm (a) beech (tree)
(b) beechwood

**heure** /œʀ/ nf (a) hour; **24 ~s sur 24** 24 hours a day; **dans l'~ qui a suivi** within the hour; **d'~ en ~** ⟨increase⟩ by the hour; **à trois ~s d'avion de Paris** three hours from Paris by plane; **à trois ~s de marche de Paris** a three-hour walk from Paris; **faire du 60 à l'~** (colloq) to do 60 km per hour; **payé à l'~** paid by the hour; **une petite ~** an hour at the most
(b) time; **quelle ~ est-il?** what time is it?; **il est 10 ~s** it's 10 (o'clock); **il est 10 ~s 20** it's 20 past 10; **il est 10 ~s moins 20** it's 20 to 10; **mettre sa montre à l'~** to set one's watch; ⋯⋗

l'∼ **tourne** time is passing; ∼s **d'ouverture** opening times; **être à l'∼** to be on time; **à une ∼ avancée (de la nuit)** late at night; **de bonne ∼** early; **c'est son ∼** it's his/her usual time; **à l'∼ où je te parle** as we speak; **de la première ∼** from the very beginning; **à la première ∼** at first light; **ta dernière ∼ est arrivée** your time has come; **à l'∼ actuelle, pour l'∼** at the present time; **l'∼ du déjeuner** lunchtime; **l'∼ est grave** the situation is serious; **il est peintre à ses ∼s** he paints in his spare time; **à la bonne ∼!** well done!
(c) era, age; **vivre à l'∼ des satellites** to live in the satellite era
■ ∼ **d'affluence** peak hour; ∼ **d'été** summer time (GB), daylight saving(s) time; ∼ **H** (Mil, figurative) zero hour; ∼ **d'hiver** winter time (GB), standard time; ∼ **de pointe** rush hour; ∼s **supplémentaires** overtime

**heureusement** /œʀøzmɑ̃/ *adv* fortunately

**heureux, -euse** /œʀø, øz/ *adj* (a) happy; ∼ **en ménage** happily married; **très ∼ de faire votre connaissance** (very) pleased to meet you
(b) ⟨*ending*⟩ happy; ⟨*proportions*⟩ pleasing; ⟨*choice*⟩ fortunate; ⟨*surprise*⟩ pleasant
(c) ⟨*winner*⟩ lucky; **'il a réussi!'—'encore ∼!'** he succeeded!'—'just as well!'
IDIOMS **attendre un ∼ événement** to be expecting a baby

**heurt** /œʀ/ *nm* (a) collision
(b) (figurative) (between people) clash; **sans ∼s** ⟨*do*⟩ smoothly; ⟨*relationship*⟩ smooth

**heurter** /'œʀte/ [1] **1** *vtr* (a) ⟨*object*⟩ to hit; ⟨*person*⟩ to collide with, to bump into
(b) (figurative) to go against ⟨*convention*⟩; to hurt ⟨*feelings*⟩
**2** *vi* ∼ **contre** to strike
**3 se heurter** *v refl* (+ *v être*) to collide; (figurative) to clash; **se ∼ à** to bump into ⟨*table*⟩; to come up against ⟨*refusal, problem*⟩

**hévéa** /evea/ *nm* rubber tree

**hexagonal, ∼e, mpl -aux** /ɛgzagɔnal, o/ *adj* (a) hexagonal
(b) (colloq) ⟨*policy*⟩ inward-looking

**hexagone** /ɛgzagon/ *nm* (a) hexagon
(b) (colloq) **l'Hexagone** France

**hiberner** /ibɛʀne/ [1] *vi* to hibernate

**hibou, pl ∼x** /'ibu/ *nm* owl

**hic** /'ik/ *nm* (colloq) snag; **voilà le ∼** there's the snag

**hideux, -euse** /'idø, øz/ *adj* hideous

**hier** /jɛʀ/ *adv* yesterday; **ça ne date pas d'∼** it's nothing new

**hiérarchie** /'jeʀaʀʃi/ *nf* hierarchy

**hiérarchique** /'jeʀaʀʃik/ *adj* hierarchical; **mon supérieur ∼** my immediate superior; **par la voie ∼** through the correct channels

**hiérarchiser** /'jeʀaʀʃize/ [1] *vtr* to organize [sth] into a hierarchy ⟨*structure*⟩

**hiératique** /jeʀatik/ *adj* hieratic

**hiéroglyphe** /'jeʀoɡlif/ *nm* hieroglyph; **les ∼s** hieroglyphics

**hi-fi** /'ifi/ *adj inv, nf inv* hi-fi

**hilarant, ∼e** /ilaʀɑ̃, ɑ̃t/ *adj* hilarious; **gaz ∼** laughing gas

**hilare** /ilaʀ/ *adj* **être ∼** to be laughing

**hilarité** /ilaʀite/ *nf* mirth, hilarity

**hindou, ∼e** /ɛ̃du/ *adj, nm,f* Hindu

**hindouisme** /ɛ̃duism/ *nm* Hinduism

**hippique** /ipik/ *adj* equestrian; **concours ∼** showjumping event (GB), horse show

**hippocampe** /ipokɑ̃p/ *nm* sea horse

**hippodrome** /ipodʀom/ *nm* racecourse (GB), racetrack (US)

**hippopotame** /ipopotam/ *nm* hippopotamus

**hirondelle** /iʀɔ̃dɛl/ *nf* swallow

**hirsute** /'iʀsyt/ *adj* dishevelled (GB), unkempt

**hispanique** /ispanik/ *adj, nmf* Hispanic

**hispano-américain, ∼e, mpl ∼s** /ispanoameʀikɛ̃, ɛn/ *adj* Hispanic-American, Spanish-American

**hispanophone** /ispanofon/ *nmf* Spanish speaker

**hisse** /'is/ *excl* **oh ∼!** heave-ho!

**hisser** /'ise/ [1] **1** *vtr* to hoist ⟨*flag*⟩
**2 se hisser** *v refl* (+ *v être*) to heave oneself up

**histoire** /istwaʀ/ *nf* (a) history; **l'∼ jugera** posterity will be the judge
(b) story; **tout ça, c'est des ∼s!** (colloq) that's all fiction!; **une ∼ à dormir debout** a tall story; **raconter des ∼s** to tell fibs
(c) matter, business; ∼ **d'amour** love affair; ∼ **de famille** family matter; **il m'est arrivé une drôle d'∼** a funny thing happened to me
(d) fuss; trouble; **elle fait toujours des ∼s** she's always making a fuss; **ça va faire des ∼s** it will cause trouble; **c'est une femme à ∼s** she's a troublemaker; **une vie sans ∼s** an uneventful life; **ça a été toute une ∼ pour faire** it was a terrible job doing; **au travail, et pas d'∼s!** (colloq) get on with it, no messing about! (colloq)
(e) (colloq) ∼ **de rire** just for fun

**historien, -ienne** /istoʀjɛ̃, ɛn/ *nm,f* historian

**historique** /istoʀik/ *adj* (a) historical
(b) historic
(c) **passé ∼** past historic

**hit-parade, pl ∼s** /'itpaʀad/ *nm* charts

**hiver** /ivɛʀ/ *nm* winter

**hivernage** /ivɛʀnaʒ/ *nm* wintering

**hivernal, ∼e, mpl -aux** /ivɛʀnal, o/ *adj*
(a) winter
(b) wintry

**hiverner** /ivɛʀne/ [1] *vi* ⟨*animals*⟩ to winter

**HLM** /aʃɛlɛm/ *nm or f: abbr* ▶ HABITATION

**hochement** /'ɔʃmɑ̃/ *nm* nod; shake of the head

**hocher** /'ɔʃe/ [1] *vtr* ∼ **la tête** to nod; to shake one's head

**hochet** /'ɔʃɛ/ *nm* rattle

**hockey** /'ɔkɛ/ *nm* hockey

**holà** /'ɔla/ *excl* hey (there)!

**IDIOMS mettre le ∼ à qch** to put an end *or* a stop to sth

**holding** /'ɔldiŋ/ *nm or f* holding company

**hold-up,** *pl* ∼ *or* ∼**s** /'ɔldœp/ *nm* hold-up

**hollandais, ∼e** /'ɔlɑ̃dɛ, ɛz/ **[1]** *adj* Dutch **[2]** *nm* (language) Dutch

**Hollandais, ∼e** /'ɔlɑ̃dɛ, ɛz/ *nm,f* Dutchman/Dutchwoman; **les ∼** the Dutch

**Hollande** /'ɔlɑ̃d/ *pr nf* Holland

**holocauste** /ɔlɔkost/ *nm* holocaust

**homard** /'ɔmaʀ/ *nm* lobster

**homéopathie** /ɔmeɔpati/ *nf* homeopathy

**homéopathique** /ɔmeɔpatik/ *adj* homeopathic; **à doses ∼s** (figurative) in small doses

**homicide** /ɔmisid/ *nm* homicide; manslaughter; murder

**hommage** /ɔmaʒ/ *nm* homage, tribute; **présenter ses ∼s** to pay one's respects

**hommasse** /ɔmas/ *adj* mannish

**homme** /ɔm/ *nm* man; **l'∼** man; mankind; **un ∼ à la mer!** man overboard!; **comme un seul ∼** as one; **leur ∼ de confiance** their right-hand man; **il n'est pas ∼ à se venger** he's not the type to want revenge
■ **∼ d'affaires** businessman; **∼ des cavernes** caveman; **∼ d'esprit** wit; **∼ d'État** statesman; **∼ à femmes** womanizer; **∼ au foyer** house-husband; **∼ de main** hired hand; **∼ de paille** front, straw man (US); **∼ de terrain** man with practical experience; **∼ à tout faire** handyman; **∼ de troupe** private; **∼s en blanc** surgeons
**IDIOMS un ∼ averti en vaut deux** (Proverb) forewarned is forearmed

**homme-grenouille,** *pl* **hommes-grenouilles** /ɔmgʀənuj/ *nm* frogman

**homme-orchestre,** *pl* **hommes-orchestres** /ɔmɔʀkɛstʀ/ *nm* one-man band

**homogène** /ɔmɔʒɛn/ *adj* homogeneous

**homogénéité** /ɔmɔʒeneite/ *nf* homogeneity

**homologue** /ɔmɔlɔg/ **[1]** *adj* homologous **[2]** *nmf* counterpart, opposite number

**homologuer** /ɔmɔlɔge/ [1] *vtr* (a) to approve ⟨*product*⟩ (b) (Sport) to recognize officially

**homonyme** /ɔmɔnim/ *nm* (a) homonym (b) namesake

**homosexualité** /ɔmɔsɛksɥalite/ *nf* homosexuality

**homosexuel, ∼elle** /ɔmɔsɛksɥɛl/ *adj*, *nm,f* homosexual

**Hongrie** /'ɔ̃gʀi/ *pr nf* Hungary

**honnête** /ɔnɛt/ *adj* (a) honest (b) decent; respectable (c) fair, reasonable

**honnêtement** /ɔnɛtmɑ̃/ *adv* (a) ⟨*say, manage*⟩ honestly; ⟨*reply*⟩ frankly; ⟨*behave*⟩ properly; ⟨*judge*⟩ fairly (b) fairly, reasonably; **s'acquitter ∼ d'une tâche** to do a decent job

**honnêteté** /ɔnɛtte/ *nf* honesty

**honneur** /ɔnœʀ/ *nm* (a) honour (GB); **à toi l'∼!** you do the honours (GB)!; **j'ai l'∼ de vous informer que** I beg to inform you that; **j'ai l'∼ de solliciter** I would respectfully request; **d'∼** ⟨*stairs*⟩ main (b) credit; **c'est tout à leur ∼** it's all credit to them (c) **mettre qn à l'∼** to honour (GB) sb; **être à l'∼ en** to be in favour (GB); **faire ∼ à un repas** to do justice to a meal; **faire les ∼s de la maison à qn** to show sb around the house; **avoir les ∼s de la presse** to be mentioned in the press; **en quel ∼?** (colloq) (ironic) any particular reason why?
**IDIOMS en tout bien tout ∼** with no hidden motive

**honnir** /'ɔniʀ/ [3] *vtr* **honni soit qui mal y pense** evil unto him who evil thinks

**honorabilité** /ɔnɔʀabilite/ *nf* integrity

**honorable** /ɔnɔʀabl/ *adj* (a) honourable (GB) (b) ⟨*score*⟩ creditable; ⟨*salary*⟩ decent

**honorablement** /ɔnɔʀabləmɑ̃/ *adv* (a) honourably (GB) (b) decently

**honoraire** /ɔnɔʀɛʀ/ **[1]** *adj* ⟨*member*⟩ honorary **[2] honoraires** *nm pl* fee, fees

**honorer** /ɔnɔʀe/ [1] *vtr* (a) to honour (GB) ⟨*god, person, memory*⟩ (b) to honour (GB) ⟨*promise, debt*⟩ (c) to be a credit to ⟨*country, profession*⟩

**honorifique** /ɔnɔʀifik/ *adj* honorary

**honoris causa** /ɔnɔʀiskoza/ *phr* **être nommé docteur ∼** to be awarded an honorary doctorate

**honte** /'ɔ̃t/ *nf* (a) shame; **avoir ∼ de** to be ashamed of; **sans fausse ∼** quite openly (b) disgrace; **faire la ∼ de** to be a disgrace to; **quelle ∼!** what a disgrace!

**honteusement** /'ɔ̃tøzmɑ̃/ *adv* (a) shamefully (b) shamelessly

**honteux, -euse** /'ɔ̃tø, øz/ *adj* (a) disgraceful (b) ashamed

**hôpital,** *pl* **-aux** /ɔpital, o/ *nm* hospital **IDIOMS c'est l'∼ qui se moque de la charité** it's the pot calling the kettle black

**hoquet** /'ɔkɛ/ *nm* **avoir le ∼** to have hiccups

**hoqueter** /'ɔkte/ [20] *vi* ⟨*person*⟩ to hiccup

**horaire** /ɔʀɛʀ/ **[1]** *adj* per hour, hourly; **tranche** *or* **plage ∼** time-slot **[2]** *nm* timetable, schedule; **les ∼s libres** *or* **à la carte** flexitime

**horde** /'ɔʀd/ *nf* horde

**horizon** /ɔʀizɔ̃/ *nm* horizon

**horizontal, ∼e¹,** *mpl* **-aux** /ɔʀizɔ̃tal, o/ *adj* horizontal

**horizontale²** /ɔʀizɔ̃tal/ *nf* horizontal

**horloge** /ɔʀlɔʒ/ *nf* clock

**horloger, -ère** /ɔRlɔʒe, ɛR/ nm,f
watchmaker
**horlogerie** /ɔRlɔʒRi/ nf (a) watchmaking
(b) watchmaker's (shop)
**hormis** /'ɔRmi/ prep (formal) save, except
(for)
**hormonal, ～e,** mpl **-aux** /ɔRmɔnal, o/
adj ⟨problem⟩ hormonal; ⟨treatment⟩
hormone
**hormone** /ɔRmon/ nf hormone
**horodateur** /ɔRɔdatœR/ nm parking ticket
machine
**horoscope** /ɔRɔskɔp/ nm horoscope
**horreur** /ɔRœR/ nf (a) horror; **quelle ～!**
how horrible!
(b) dire des ～s de or sur qn to say awful
things about sb
(c) loathing; **avoir ～ de qn/de faire** to loathe
sb/doing
**horrible** /ɔRibl/ adj (a) horrible
(b) revolting
(c) hideous
**horriblement** /ɔRibləmɑ̃/ adv ⟨damaged⟩
horribly; ⟨cold⟩ terribly
**horrifier** /ɔRifje/ [2] vtr to horrify
**horripiler** /ɔRipile/ [1] vtr to exasperate
**hors** /'ɔR/

■ **Note** You will find translations for expressions
such as *hors série, hors d'usage* etc., at the
entries SÉRIE, USAGE etc.

**1** prep outside; **longueur ～ tout** overall
length
**2** hors de phr out of, outside; **～ d'ici!** get
out of here!
IDIOMS **être ～ de soi** to be beside oneself
**hors-bord** /'ɔRbɔR/ nm inv speedboat
**hors-d'œuvre** /'ɔRdœvR/ nm inv starter,
hors d'oeuvre
**hors-jeu** /'ɔRʒø/ nm inv **(pour) ～ for**
offside
**hors-la-loi** /'ɔRlalwa/ nm inv outlaw
**hors-piste** /'ɔRpist/ nm inv off-piste skiing
**hortensia** /ɔRtɑ̃sja/ nm hydrangea
**horticulteur, -trice** /ɔRtikyltœR, tRis/
nm,f horticulturist
**hospice** /ɔspis/ nm home; **～ de vieillards**
old people's home
**hospitalier, -ière** /ɔspitalje, ɛR/ adj
(a) hospital; **centre ～** hospital
(b) hospitable
**hospitalisation** /ɔspitalizasjɔ̃/ nf
hospitalization; **～ à domicile** home (medical)
care
**hospitaliser** /ɔspitalize/ [1] vtr to
hospitalize
**hospitalité** /ɔspitalite/ nf hospitality
**hostie** /ɔsti/ nf Host
**hostile** /ɔstil/ adj hostile
**hostilité** /ɔstilite/ nf hostility
**hôte** /ot/ **1** nm (a) host
(b) occupant
**2** nmf guest

**hôtel** /otɛl/ nm hotel
■ **～ particulier** town house; **～ de passe** hotel
used by prostitutes; **～ des ventes** saleroom;
**～ de ville** ≈ town hall
**hôtelier, -ière** /otəlje, ɛR/ **1** adj
⟨industry⟩ hotel; ⟨school⟩ hotel management
**2** nm,f hotelier
**hôtellerie** /otɛlRi/ nf hotel business
**hôtesse** /otɛs/ nf (at home, at exhibition)
hostess; (in company) receptionist; (in boat)
stewardess
■ **～ d'accueil** receptionist; **～ de l'air** air
hostess
**hotte** /'ɔt/ nf (a) basket
(b) hood
■ **～ aspirante** extractor hood (GB), ventilator
(US); **la ～ du Père Noël** Santa Claus's sack
**houblon** /'ublɔ̃/ nm hop, hops
**houille** /'uj/ nf coal
**houiller, -ère** /'uje, ɛR/ adj ⟨industry⟩
coal; ⟨area⟩ coalmining
**houle** /'ul/ nf swell
**houlette** /'ulɛt/ nf (of shepherd) crook; **sous
la ～ de** (figurative) under the leadership of
**houleux, -euse** /'ulø, øz/ adj (a) ⟨sea⟩
rough
(b) ⟨meeting⟩ stormy
**houppe** /'up/ nf (a) (of hair) tuft; (of threads)
tassel
(b) powder puff
**houppette** /'upɛt/ nf powder puff
**hourra** /'uRa/ nm cheer
**houspiller** /'uspije/ [1] vtr to scold
**housse** /'us/ nf cover, slipcover; dustcover;
garment bag
**houx** /'u/ nm inv holly
**HT** (written abbr = **hors taxes**) exclusive
of tax
**hublot** /'yblo/ nm (in plane) window; (in boat)
porthole
**huche** /'yʃ/ nf (a) chest
(b) **～ à pain** bread bin
**huer** /'ɥe/ [1] vtr to boo
**huile** /ɥil/ nf (a) oil
(b) oil painting
■ **～ de coude** (humorous) elbow grease;
**～ solaire** suntan oil
IDIOMS **tout/ça baigne dans l'～** (colloq)
everything/it is going smoothly; **jeter** or
**verser de l'～ sur le feu** to add fuel to the fire
**huiler** /ɥile/ [1] vtr to oil
**huileux, -euse** /ɥilø, øz/ adj oily
**huis** /'ɥi/ nm inv **à ～ clos** (Law) in camera;
(figurative) behind closed doors
**huissier** /ɥisje/ nm (a) **～ (de justice)**
bailiff
(b) porter; usher
**huit** /'ɥit, but before consonant 'ɥi/ **1** adj
inv eight; **mardi en ～ a** week on Tuesday
**2** pron eight
**3** nm inv (a) eight
(b) a figure of eight

**huitaine** /ˈɥitɛn/ *nf* (a) about a week; **sous ~** within a week
(b) about eight

**huitième** /ˈɥitjɛm/ [1] *adj* eighth
[2] *nf* (Sch) *fourth year of primary school, age 9–10*

**huître** /ɥitʀ/ *nf* oyster

**hululement** /ˈylylmɑ̃/ *nm* hooting

**hululer** /ˈylyle/ [1] *vi* to hoot

**humain, ~e** /ymɛ̃, ɛn/ [1] *adj* (a) human; **pertes ~es** loss of life
(b) ⟨regime⟩ humane; ⟨person⟩ human, understanding
[2] *nm* human (being)

**humainement** /ymɛnmɑ̃/ *adv*
(a) humanly
(b) humanely

**humaniser** /ymanize/ [1] [1] *vtr* to humanize
[2] **s'humaniser** *v refl* (+ *v être*) to become more human

**humanitaire** /ymanitɛʀ/ *adj* humanitarian

**humanité** /ymanite/ *nf* humanity

**humble** /œ̃bl/ *adj* humble

**humblement** /œ̃bləmɑ̃/ *adv* humbly

**humecter** /ymɛkte/ [1] *vtr* to moisten

**humer** /ˈyme/ [1] *vtr* to sniff; to smell

**humeur** /ymœʀ/ *nf* (a) mood; **être de bonne/mauvaise ~** to be in a good/bad mood
(b) temperament; **être d'~ égale** to be even-tempered; **être d'~ inégale** to be moody; **elle est connue pour sa bonne ~** she's known for her good humour
(c) bad temper; **geste d'~** bad-tempered gesture; **avec ~** bad-temperedly

**humide** /ymid/ *adj* (a) damp
(b) ⟨climate⟩ humid; ⟨season⟩ rainy; **il fait froid et ~** it's cold and damp; **il fait une chaleur ~** it's muggy

**humidifier** /ymidifje/ [2] *vtr* to humidify

**humidité** /ymidite/ *nf* (a) dampness, damp
(b) humidity

**humiliant, ~e** /ymiljɑ̃, ɑ̃t/ *adj* humiliating

**humiliation** /ymiljasjɔ̃/ *nf* humiliation

**humilier** /ymilje/ [2] *vtr* to humiliate

**humilité** /ymilite/ *nf* (a) humility
(b) (of task) humble nature

**humoriste** /ymɔʀist/ *nmf* (a) humorist
(b) joker

**humoristique** /ymɔʀistik/ *adj* humorous; **dessin ~** cartoon

**humour** /ymuʀ/ *nm* humour (GB); **avoir de l'~** to have a sense of humour (GB); **faire de l'~** to make jokes

**huppé, ~e** /ˈype/ *adj* (a) (colloq) ⟨person⟩ upper-crust
(b) ⟨bird⟩ crested

**hurlement** /ˈyʀləmɑ̃/ *nm* (of animal) howl, howling; (of person) yell, howl; (of siren) wail, wailing

**hurler** /ˈyʀle/ [1] [1] *vtr* to yell
[2] *vi* (a) to yell; (with pain, anger) to howl
(b) ⟨siren⟩ to wail; ⟨wind⟩ to roar; ⟨radio⟩ to blare
**IDIOMS ~ avec les loups** to follow the crowd; **~ à la mort** to bay at the moon

**hurluberlu, ~e** /yʀlybɛʀly/ *nm,f* oddball (colloq)

**hutte** /ˈyt/ *nf* hut

**hybride** /ibʀid/ *adj, nm* hybrid

**hydratant, ~e** /idʀatɑ̃, ɑ̃t/ *adj* moisturizing

**hydratation** /idʀatasjɔ̃/ *nf* (a) hydration
(b) moisturizing

**hydrate** /idʀat/ *nm* **~ de carbone** carbohydrate

**hydrater** /idʀate/ [1] [1] *vtr* (a) to hydrate
(b) to moisturize ⟨skin⟩
[2] **s'hydrater** *v refl* (+ *v être*) **bien s'~** to take plenty of fluids

**hydraulique** /idʀolik/ *adj* hydraulic

**hydravion** /idʀavjɔ̃/ *nm* seaplane, hydroplane

**hydro** /idʀo/ *pref* hydro; **~électrique** hydroelectric

**hydrocarbure** /idʀɔkaʀbyʀ/ *nm* hydrocarbon

**hydrocution** /idʀɔkysjɔ̃/ *nf* immersion hypothermia

**hydrofuge** /idʀɔfyʒ/ *adj* water-repellent

**hydrogène** /idʀɔʒɛn/ *nm* hydrogen

**hydroglisseur** /idʀɔglisœʀ/ *nm* hydroplane

**hydrophile** /idʀɔfil/ *adj* absorbent

**hydroxyde** /idʀɔksid/ *nm* hydroxide

**hyène** /ˈjɛn/ *nf* hyena

**hygiaphone®** /iʒjafɔn/ *nm* grill (*perforated communication panel*)

**hygiène** /iʒjɛn/ *nf* hygiene; **bonne ~ alimentaire** healthy diet
■ **~ corporelle** personal hygiene

**hygiénique** /iʒjenik/ *adj* (a) hygienic
(b) ⟨lifestyle⟩ healthy

**hymen** /imɛn/ *nm* (a) hymen
(b) nuptial bond

**hymne** /imn/ *nm* hymn; **~ national** national anthem

**hyperactif, -ive** /ipɛʀaktif, iv/ *adj* hyperactive

**hyperclassique** /ipɛʀklasik/ *adj* ⟨reaction⟩ absolutely classic; **roman ~** great classic

**hypermarché** /ipɛʀmaʀʃe/ *nm* hypermarket (GB), large supermarket

**hypermétrope** /ipɛʀmetʀɔp/ *adj* longsighted

**hypernerveux, -euse** /ipɛʀnɛʀvø, øz/ *adj* highly strung

**hypersensible** /ipɛʀsɑ̃sibl/ *adj* hypersensitive

**hypersophistiqué**, **~e** /ipɛʀsɔfistike/ *adj* very sophisticated

**hyperspécialisé**, **~e** /ipɛʀspesjalize/ *adj* highly specialized

**hypertension** /ipɛʀtɑ̃sjɔ̃/ *nf* **~ (artérielle)** high blood pressure

**hypertexte** /ipɛʀtɛkst/ *nm* hypertext

**hypertoile** /ipɛʀtwal/ *nf* World Wide Web

**hypertrophie** /ipɛʀtʀɔfi/ *nf* **(a)** (Med) enlargement
**(b)** (of town) overdevelopment

**hypertrophier: s'hypertrophier** /ipɛʀtʀɔfje/ [2] *v refl* (+ *v être*) **(a)** (Med) to hypertrophy
**(b)** ⟨*town*⟩ to become overdeveloped

**hypnose** /ipnoz/ *nf* hypnosis

**hypnotique** /ipnɔtik/ *adj, nm* hypnotic

**hypnotiser** /ipnɔtize/ [1] *vtr* to hypnotize; (figurative) to mesmerize

**hypnotiseur, -euse** /ipnɔtizœʀ, øz/ *nm,f* hypnotist

**hypocalorique** /ipɔkalɔʀik/ *adj* low-calorie

**hypocondriaque** /ipɔkɔ̃dʀijak/ *adj, nmf* hypochondriac

**hypocrisie** /ipɔkʀizi/ *nf* hypocrisy

**hypocrite** /ipɔkʀit/ **1** *adj* hypocritical
**2** *nmf* hypocrite

**hypodermique** /ipɔdɛʀmik/ *adj* hypodermic

**hypokhâgne** /ipɔkaɲ/ *nf: first year preparatory class in humanities for entrance to École normale supérieure*

**hypotension** /ipɔtɑ̃sjɔ̃/ *nf* **~ (artérielle)** low blood pressure

**hypothécaire** /ipɔtekɛʀ/ *adj* mortgage; **créancier/débiteur ~** mortgagee/mortgager

**hypothèque** /ipɔtɛk/ *nf* mortgage

**hypothéquer** /ipɔteke/ [14] *vtr* to mortgage

**hypothèse** /ipɔtɛz/ *nf* hypothesis

**hypothétique** /ipɔtetik/ *adj* hypothetical

**hystérie** /isteʀi/ *nf* hysteria

**hystérique** /isteʀik/ *adj* hysterical

# I i

**i, I** /i/ *nm inv* i, I
IDIOMS **mettre les points sur les i** to make things crystal clear

**ibérique** /ibeʀik/ *adj* Iberian

**iceberg** /ajsbɛʀg, isbɛʀg/ *nm* iceberg

**ici** /isi/ *adv* **(a)** here; **c'est ~ que...** this is where...; **par ~** this way; around here; **les gens d'~** the locals; **je vois ça d'~!** I can just picture it!
**(b) jusqu'~** until now; until then; **d'~ peu** shortly; **d'~ deux jours** two days from now; **d'~ là** by then; **il l'aime bien, mais d'~ à ce qu'il l'épouse...** he likes her, but as for marrying her...

**ici-bas** /isiba/ *adv* here below

**icône** /ikon/ *nf* icon

**id.** *written abbr* = IDEM

**idéal**, **~e**, *mpl* **-aux** /ideal, o/ **1** *adj* ideal
**2** *nm* ideal; **dans l'~** ideally

**idéalisme** /idealism/ *nm* idealism

**idée** /ide/ *nf* idea; thought; **avoir de l'~** to be inventive; **avoir une ~ derrière la tête** to have something in mind; **se faire des ~s** to imagine things; **avoir les ~s larges** to be broad-minded; **changer d'~** to change one's mind; **avoir de la suite dans les ~s** to be single-minded; not to be easily deterred; **avoir dans l'~ de faire** to plan to do; **tu ne**

**m'ôteras pas de l'~ que...** I still think that...; **ça ne m'est pas venu à l'~** it never occurred to me
■ **~ fixe** obsession; **~ de génie** brainwave (colloq); **~ noire** dark thought; **~ reçue** received idea

**idem** /idɛm/ *adv* ditto

**identification** /idɑ̃tifikasjɔ̃/ *nf* identification

**identifier** /idɑ̃tifje/ [2] **1** *vtr* to identify
**2 s'identifier** *v refl* (+ *v être*) **(a)** to become identified
**(b)** to identify

**identique** /idɑ̃tik/ *adj* **(a)** identical
**(b)** unchanged

**identité** /idɑ̃tite/ *nf* **(a)** identity
**(b)** similarity

**idéologie** /ideɔlɔʒi/ *nf* ideology

**idiomatique** /idjɔmatik/ *adj* idiomatic

**idiome** /idjom/ *nm* idiom

**idiot**, **~e** /idjo, ɔt/ **1** *adj* stupid
**2** *nm* idiot; **faire l'~** to behave like an idiot

**idiotie** /idjɔsi/ *nf* **(a)** stupid thing
**(b)** stupidity

**idolâtrer** /idɔlatʀe/ [1] *vtr* to idolize

**idole** /idɔl/ *nf* idol

**idylle** /idil/ *nf* **(a)** love affair
**(b)** (in literature) idyll

**idyllique** /idilik/ *adj* idyllic

**if** /if/ *nm* **(a)** yew (tree)

**(b)** yew (wood)

**IFOP** /ifɔp/ *nm* (*abbr* = **Institut français d'opinion publique**) French institute for opinion polls

**ignare** /iɲaʀ/ *adj* ignorant

**ignifuge** /iɲifyʒ/ *adj* fireproofing

**ignifuger** /iɲifyʒe/ [13] *vtr* to fireproof

**ignoble** /iɲɔbl/ *adj* **(a)** ⟨*person, conduct*⟩ vile
**(b)** ⟨*place*⟩ squalid; ⟨*food*⟩ revolting

**ignominie** /iɲɔmini/ *nf* **(a)** ignominy
**(b)** dreadful thing

**ignorance** /iɲɔʀɑ̃s/ *nf* ignorance

**ignorant, ～e** /iɲɔʀɑ̃, ɑ̃t/ *adj* ignorant

**ignoré, ～e** /iɲɔʀe/ *adj* unknown; ignored

**ignorer** /iɲɔʀe/ [1] *vtr* **(a)** **j'ignore comment/si** I don't know how/whether; **～ tout de qch** to know nothing of *or* about sth; **～ l'existence de** to be unaware of the existence of
**(b)** to ignore ⟨*person*⟩

**iguane** /igwan/ *nm* iguana

**il** /il/ **1** *pron sg* he; it; they
**2** *pron impers* it; **～s** they
**2** *pron impers* it; **～ pleut** it's raining

**île** /il/ *nf* island
■ **l'～ de Beauté** Corsica

**illégal, ～e,** *mpl* **-aux** /ilegal, o/ *adj* illegal

**illégalité** /ilegalite/ *nf* illegality; **être dans l'～** to be in breach of the law

**illégitime** /ileʒitim/ *adj* ⟨*child*⟩ illegitimate

**illégitimité** /ileʒitimite/ *nf* (of child) illegitimacy; (of love) illicitness

**illettré, ～e** /iletʀe/ *adj, nm,f* illiterate

**illicite** /ilisit/ *adj* illicit; unlawful

**illico** /iliko/ *adv* (colloq) straightaway

**illimité, ～e** /ilimite/ *adj* unlimited

**illisible** /ilizibl/ *adj* **(a)** illegible
**(b)** unreadable

**illogique** /ilɔʒik/ *adj* illogical

**illumination** /ilyminasjɔ̃/ **1** *nf*
**(a)** floodlighting
**(b)** flash of inspiration
**2** **illuminations** *nf pl* (in town) illuminations

**illuminé, ～e** /ilymine/ **1** *adj*
**(a)** ⟨*monument*⟩ floodlit
**(b)** ⟨*face*⟩ radiant
**2** *nm,f* **(a)** visionary
**(b)** crank

**illuminer** /ilymine/ [1] *vtr* **(a)** to illuminate; to floodlight
**(b)** ⟨*smile*⟩ to light up ⟨*face*⟩
**2** **s'illuminer** *v refl* (+ *v être*) to light up

**illusion** /ilyzjɔ̃/ *nf* illusion; **se faire des ～s** to delude oneself; **il ne fait pas ～** he doesn't fool anyone

**illusionner: s'illusionner** /ilyzjɔne/ *v refl* (+ *v être*) to delude oneself (**sur qch/qn** about sth/sb)

**illusionniste** /ilyzjɔnist/ *nmf* conjurer

**illusoire** /ilyzwaʀ/ *adj* illusory

**illustrateur, -trice** /ilystʀatœʀ, tʀis/ *nm,f* illustrator

**illustration** /ilystʀasjɔ̃/ *nf* illustration

**illustre** /ilystʀ/ *adj* illustrious

**illustré** /ilystʀe/ *nm* comic

**illustrer** /ilystʀe/ [1] **1** *vtr* to illustrate
**2** **s'illustrer** *v refl* (+ *v être*) to distinguish oneself

**îlot** /ilo/ *nm* **(a)** islet
**(b)** **～s de végétation** isolated patches of vegetation

**ils ▶** IL 1

**image** /imaʒ/ *nf* **(a)** picture
**(b)** (on film) frame
**(c)** reflection, image
**(d)** **à l'～ de ses prédécesseurs…** just like his/her predecessors…
**(e)** image; **les ～s d'un poème** the imagery of a poem
■ **～ d'Épinal** *simplistic print of traditional French life*; (figurative) clichéd image; **～ de marque** brand image; corporate image; (public) image

**imagé, ～e** /imaʒe/ *adj* ⟨*style*⟩ colourful (GB)

**imagerie** /imaʒʀi/ *nf* **(a)** imagery
**(b)** print trade
**(c)** imaging

**imaginable** /imaʒinabl/ *adj* conceivable, imaginable

**imaginaire** /imaʒinɛʀ/ *adj* imaginary

**imaginatif, -ive** /imaʒinatif, iv/ *adj* imaginative

**imagination** /imaʒinasjɔ̃/ *nf* imagination

**imaginer** /imaʒine/ [1] **1** *vtr* **(a)** to imagine, to picture
**(b)** to suppose
**(c)** to devise, to think up
**2** **s'imaginer** *v refl* (+ *v être*) **(a)** to imagine, to picture
**(b)** to picture oneself; **s'～ à 60 ans** to picture oneself at 60
**(c)** to think

**imbattable** /ɛ̃batabl/ *adj* unbeatable

**imbécile** /ɛ̃besil/ **1** *adj* idiotic
**2** *nmf* fool; **faire l'～** to play the fool

**imberbe** /ɛ̃bɛʀb/ *adj* beardless

**imbiber** /ɛ̃bibe/ [1] **1** *vtr* to soak
**2** **s'imbiber** *v refl* (+ *v être*) **s'～ de** to become soaked with

**imbriquer: s'imbriquer** /ɛ̃bʀike/ [1] *v refl* (+ *v être*) **(a)** ⟨*slates*⟩ to overlap
**(b)** ⟨*issues*⟩ to be interlinked; ⟨*parts*⟩ to interlock

**imbu, ～e** /ɛ̃by/ *adj* full; **～ de sa personne** full of oneself

**imbuvable** /ɛ̃byvabl/ *adj* **(a)** undrinkable
**(b)** (colloq) unbearable

**imitateur, -trice** /imitatœʀ, tʀis/ *nm,f*
**(a)** impressionist
**(b)** (of painting) imitator

**imitation** /imitasjɔ̃/ *nf* imitation; (of person) impression

**imiter** /imite/ [1] *vtr* (a) to imitate; to forge ⟨*signature*⟩
(b) to do an impression of [sb]
(c) il part, je vais l'∼ he's leaving and I'm going to do the same

**immaculé**, ∼**e** /imakyle/ *adj* immaculate

**immangeable** /ɛ̃mɑ̃ʒabl/ *adj* inedible

**immanquablement** /ɛ̃mɑ̃kabləmɑ̃/ *adv* inevitably

**immatriculation** /imatʀikylasjɔ̃/ *nf* registration; **numéro d'**∼ registration (GB) or license (US) number

**immatriculer** /imatʀikyle/ [1] *vtr* to register; to register (GB) or license (US) ⟨*car*⟩

**immédiat**, ∼**e** /imedja, at/ **1** *adj* immediate
**2** *nm* **dans l'**∼ for the time being

**immédiatement** /imedjatmɑ̃/ *adv* immediately

**immense** /imɑ̃s/ *adj* (gen) huge; ⟨*pain, regret*⟩ immense; ⟨*joy, courage*⟩ great

**immensité** /imɑ̃site/ *nf* (of place) immensity; (of knowledge) breadth

**immerger** /imɛʀʒe/ [13] *vtr* to immerse ⟨*object*⟩; to bury [sth] at sea

**immersion** /imɛʀsjɔ̃/ *nf* (a) (of body, object) immersion; (of corpse) burial at sea
(b) flooding

**immettable** /ɛ̃metabl/ *adj* (colloq) unwearable

**immeuble** /imœbl/ *nm* (a) building
(b) real asset

**immigrant**, ∼**e** /imigʀɑ̃, ɑ̃t/ *adj, nm,f* immigrant

**immigration** /imigʀasjɔ̃/ *nf* immigration

**immigré**, ∼**e** /imigʀe/ *adj, nm,f* immigrant

**immigrer** /imigʀe/ [1] *vi* to immigrate

**imminent**, ∼**e** /iminɑ̃, ɑ̃t/ *adj* imminent

**immiscer: s'immiscer** /imise/ [12] *v refl* (+ *v être*) to interfere

**immobile** /imɔbil/ *adj* (gen) motionless; ⟨*vehicle*⟩ stationary; ⟨*stare*⟩ fixed

**immobilier** /imɔbilje/ *nm* **l'**∼ property (GB), real estate (US)

**immobiliser** /imɔbilize/ [1] **1** *vtr* (a) to bring [sth] to a standstill ⟨*vehicle*⟩; to stop ⟨*machine*⟩
(b) to immobilize ⟨*person*⟩
(c) to tie up ⟨*capital*⟩
**2** **s'immobiliser** *v refl* (+ *v être*) to come to a halt; to stop

**immobilisme** /imɔbilism/ *nm* opposition to change

**immobilité** /imɔbilite/ *nf* (a) immobility
(b) stillness

**immodéré**, ∼**e** /imɔdeʀe/ *adj*
(a) excessive
(b) immoderate

**immoler** /imɔle/ [1] *vtr* to sacrifice (à to)

**immonde** /imɔ̃d/ *adj* (a) filthy
(b) revolting

**immondices** /imɔ̃dis/ *nf pl* refuse (GB), trash (US)

**immoral**, ∼**e**, *mpl* **-aux** /imɔʀal, o/ *adj* immoral

**immortaliser** /imɔʀtalize/ [1] *vtr* to immortalize

**immortel, -elle¹** /imɔʀtɛl/ *adj* immortal

**immortelle²** /imɔʀtɛl/ *nf* everlasting (flower)

**immuable** /imɥabl/ *adj* (a) immutable
(b) unchanging
(c) perpetual

**immuniser** /imynize/ [1] *vtr* to immunize

**immunitaire** /imynitɛʀ/ *adj* (Med) immune

**immunité** /imynite/ *nf* immunity

**impact** /ɛ̃pakt/ *nm* impact; mark

**impair**, ∼**e** /ɛ̃pɛʀ/ **1** *adj* ⟨*number*⟩ odd; ⟨*day, year*⟩ odd-numbered
**2** *nm* indiscretion, faux pas

**imparable** /ɛ̃paʀabl/ *adj* (a) unstoppable
(b) unanswerable
(c) irrefutable

**impardonnable** /ɛ̃paʀdɔnabl/ *adj* unforgivable

**imparfait**, ∼**e** /ɛ̃paʀfɛ, ɛt/ **1** *adj* imperfect
**2** *nm* **l'**∼ the imperfect (tense)

**impartial**, ∼**e**, *mpl* **-iaux** /ɛ̃paʀsjal, o/ *adj* impartial

**impartir** /ɛ̃paʀtiʀ/ [3] *vtr* to give; **dans les temps impartis** within the given time

**impasse** /ɛ̃pas/ *nf* (a) dead end
(b) deadlock

**impassible** /ɛ̃pasibl/ *adj* impassive

**impatience** /ɛ̃pasjɑ̃s/ *nf* impatience

**impatient**, ∼**e** /ɛ̃pasjɑ̃, ɑ̃t/ *adj* impatient

**impatienter** /ɛ̃pasjɑ̃te/ [1] **1** *vtr* to irritate
**2** **s'impatienter** *v refl* (+ *v être*) to get impatient

**impayable** /ɛ̃pɛjabl/ *adj* (colloq) priceless

**impayé**, ∼**e** /ɛ̃pɛje/ *adj* unpaid

**impeccable** /ɛ̃pɛkabl/ *adj* perfect; impeccable; spotless

**impénétrable** /ɛ̃penetʀabl/ *adj*
(a) impenetrable
(b) inscrutable

**impénitent**, ∼**e** /ɛ̃penitɑ̃, ɑ̃t/ *adj* ⟨*drinker*⟩ inveterate; ⟨*bachelor*⟩ confirmed

**impensable** /ɛ̃pɑ̃sabl/ *adj* unthinkable

**imper** /ɛ̃pɛʀ/ *nm* (colloq) raincoat, mac (GB) (colloq)

**impératif, -ive** /ɛ̃peʀatif, iv/ **1** *adj* imperative
**2** *nm* (a) (of situation) imperative; (for quality) necessity
(b) (in grammar) imperative

**impératrice** /ɛ̃peʀatʀis/ *nf* empress

**imperceptible** /ɛ̃pɛʀsɛptibl/ *adj* imperceptible

**imperfection** /ɛ̃pɛʀfɛksjɔ̃/ *nf* imperfection

**impérial**, ∼e¹, *mpl* **-iaux** /ɛ̃peʀjal, o/
*adj* imperial

**impériale²** /ɛ̃peʀjal/ *nf* **autobus à** ∼
double-decker bus

**impérialisme** /ɛ̃peʀjalism/ *nm*
imperialism

**impérieux, -ieuse** /ɛ̃peʀjø, øz/ *adj*
**(a)** imperious
**(b)** pressing

**impérissable** /ɛ̃peʀisabl/ *adj*
imperishable

**imperméable** /ɛ̃pɛʀmeabl/ 1 *adj*
**(a)** ⟨*material*⟩ waterproof; ⟨*ground*⟩
impermeable
**(b)** impervious
2 *nm* raincoat

**impertinence** /ɛ̃pɛʀtinɑ̃s/ *nf*
**(a)** impertinence
**(b)** impertinent remark

**impertinent**, ∼e /ɛ̃pɛʀtinɑ̃, ɑ̃t/ *adj*
impertinent

**imperturbable** /ɛ̃pɛʀtyʀbabl/ *adj*
imperturbable; unruffled

**imperturbablement** /ɛ̃pɛʀtyʀbabləmɑ̃/
*adv* ⟨*continue, listen*⟩ unperturbed

**impétueux, -euse** /ɛ̃petɥø, øz/ *adj* (gen)
impetuous; ⟨*torrent*⟩ raging

**impie** /ɛ̃pi/ *adj* impious

**impitoyable** /ɛ̃pitwajabl/ *adj* merciless,
pitiless; relentless; ruthless

**implacable** /ɛ̃plakabl/ *adj* implacable;
tough; harsh

**implacablement** /ɛ̃plakabləmɑ̃/ *adv*
relentlessly; ruthlessly

**implantation** /ɛ̃plɑ̃tasjɔ̃/ *nf*
establishment; setting up; installation;
settlement

**implanté**, ∼e /ɛ̃plɑ̃te/ *adj* **(a)** ⟨*factory,
party*⟩ established; ⟨*population*⟩ settled
**(b)** ⟨*roots*⟩ established; **dents mal** ∼**es**
crooked teeth

**implanter** /ɛ̃plɑ̃te/ [1] 1 *vtr* **(a)** to
establish ⟨*factory*⟩; to build ⟨*supermarket*⟩;
to open ⟨*agency*⟩; to introduce ⟨*product,
fashion*⟩; to instil (GB) ⟨*ideas*⟩
**(b)** (Med) to implant
2 **s'implanter** *v refl* (+ *v être*) ⟨*company,
product*⟩ to establish itself; ⟨*factory*⟩ to be
built; ⟨*person*⟩ to settle; ⟨*party*⟩ to gain a
following

**implication** /ɛ̃plikasjɔ̃/ *nf* **(a)** involvement
**(b)** implication
**(c)** commitment

**implicite** /ɛ̃plisit/ *adj* implicit

**implicitement** /ɛ̃plisitmɑ̃/ *adv*
implicitly; (Comput) by default

**impliquer** /ɛ̃plike/ [1] *vtr* **(a)** to implicate
**(b)** to involve ⟨*staff*⟩
**(c)** to involve (**de faire** doing)
**(d)** to mean

**implorer** /ɛ̃plɔʀe/ [1] *vtr* **(a)** to beseech, to
implore
**(b)** to beg for

**imploser** /ɛ̃ploze/ [1] *vi* to implode

**impoli**, ∼e /ɛ̃pɔli/ *adj* rude, impolite

**impolitesse** /ɛ̃pɔlitɛs/ *nf* rudeness

**impondérable** /ɛ̃pɔ̃deʀabl/ *nm*
imponderable

**impopulaire** /ɛ̃pɔpylɛʀ/ *adj* unpopular

**importance** /ɛ̃pɔʀtɑ̃s/ *nf* **(a)** importance;
**quelle** ∼**?** what does it matter?
**(b)** size; (of damage) extent; **prendre de l'**∼ to
increase in size
**(c) prendre de l'**∼ ⟨*person*⟩ to become more
important

**important**, ∼e /ɛ̃pɔʀtɑ̃, ɑ̃t/ 1 *adj*
**(a)** important
**(b)** significant; considerable; sizeable; large;
lengthy
**(c) prendre un air** ∼ to adopt a self-
important manner
2 *nm,f* **jouer les** ∼**s** to act important (colloq)

**importateur, -trice** /ɛ̃pɔʀtatœʀ, tʀis/
1 *adj* importing
2 *nm,f* importer

**importation** /ɛ̃pɔʀtasjɔ̃/ *nf* **(a)** importation
**(b)** import

**importer** /ɛ̃pɔʀte/ [1] 1 *vtr* to import
2 *v impers* **peu importe** *or* **qu'importe que**...
it doesn't matter *or* what does it matter if...;
**n'importe quel enfant** any child; **n'importe
qui** anybody, anyone; **n'importe lequel** any;
**n'importe où** anywhere; **prends n'importe
quoi** take anything; **elle dit n'importe quoi**
she talks nonsense

**importun**, ∼e /ɛ̃pɔʀtœ̃, yn/ 1 *adj*
**(a)** troublesome; tiresome; **visiteur** ∼
unwelcome visitor
**(b)** ⟨*visit*⟩ ill-timed; ⟨*remark*⟩ ill-chosen
2 *nm,f* unwelcome visitor; tiresome
individual

**importuner** /ɛ̃pɔʀtyne/ [1] *vtr* **(a)** to
bother
**(b)** to disturb

**imposable** /ɛ̃pozabl/ *adj* ⟨*person*⟩ liable to
tax; ⟨*income*⟩ taxable

**imposant**, ∼e /ɛ̃pozɑ̃, ɑ̃t/ *adj* imposing

**imposer** /ɛ̃poze/ [1] 1 *vtr* **(a)** ⟨*person*⟩ to
impose ⟨*sanctions, deadline*⟩; to lay down
⟨*rule*⟩; **elle nous a imposé le silence** she
made us be quiet
**(b)** to impose ⟨*idea, opinion*⟩; to set ⟨*fashion*⟩
**(c)** to command ⟨*respect*⟩
**(d)** to tax
2 **en imposer** *v+prep* **elle en impose à
ses élèves** she inspires respect in her pupils
3 **s'imposer** *v refl* (+ *v être*) **(a)** ⟨*choice,
solution*⟩ to be obvious; ⟨*change*⟩ to be called
for; **une visite au Louvre s'impose** a visit to
the Louvre is a must
**(b)** to impose ⟨*sth*⟩ on oneself; **s'**∼ **de
travailler le soir** to make it a rule to work in
the evening
**(c)** to impose (**à qn** on sb)
**(d) s'**∼ **comme leader** to establish oneself/
itself as the leader; **s'**∼ **sur un marché** to
establish itself in a market
**(e)** ⟨*person*⟩ to make one's presence felt;
⟨*will*⟩ to impose itself

**imposition** /ɛ̃pozisjɔ̃/ *nf* taxation

**impossibilité** /ɛ̃pɔsibilite/ *nf*
impossibility; **être dans l'~ de faire** to be
unable to do

**impossible** /ɛ̃pɔsibl/ ⟦1⟧ *adj* impossible
⟦2⟧ *nm* **l'~** the impossible; **faire** or **tenter l'~**
to do everything one can

**imposteur** /ɛ̃pɔstœʀ/ *nm* impostor

**imposture** /ɛ̃pɔstyʀ/ *nf* **(a)** deception
**(b)** fraud

**impôt** /ɛ̃po/ *nm* tax; **après ~** after tax
■ **~ sur le revenu** income tax

**impotent, ~e** /ɛ̃pɔtɑ̃, ɑ̃t/ ⟦1⟧ *adj* infirm
⟦2⟧ *nm,f* person with impaired mobility

**impraticable** /ɛ̃pʀatikabl/ *adj* impassable

**imprécis, ~e** /ɛ̃pʀesi, iz/ *adj* ⟨outline,
memory⟩ vague; ⟨concept⟩ hazy; ⟨aim⟩
inaccurate; ⟨results⟩ imprecise; ⟨person⟩
vague

**imprécision** /ɛ̃pʀesizjɔ̃/ *nf* imprecision;
vagueness; inaccuracy

**imprégner** /ɛ̃pʀeɲe/ [14] ⟦1⟧ *vtr* to
impregnate
⟦2⟧ **s'imprégner** *v refl* (+ *v être*) **s'~ de** to
become soaked with ⟨water⟩; to immerse
oneself in ⟨language⟩

**imprenable** /ɛ̃pʀənabl/ *adj* **avec vue ~**
with unobstructed view guaranteed

**imprésario** /ɛ̃pʀesaʀjo/ *nm* agent,
impresario

**impression** /ɛ̃pʀesjɔ̃/ *nf* **(a)** impression;
**faire bonne ~** to make a good impression;
**j'ai l'~ d'être surveillé** I feel I am being
watched
**(b)** printing; **faute d'~** misprint
**(c)** pattern

**impressionnant, ~e** /ɛ̃pʀesjɔnɑ̃, ɑ̃t/
*adj* **(a)** impressive
**(b)** disturbing

**impressionner** /ɛ̃pʀesjɔne/ [1] *vtr* **(a)** to
impress
**(b)** ⟨image⟩ to disturb
**(c)** to act on ⟨retina⟩

**impressionnisme** /ɛ̃pʀesjɔnism/ *nm*
Impressionism

**impressionniste** /ɛ̃pʀesjɔnist/ *nmf*
Impressionist

**imprévisible** /ɛ̃pʀevizibl/ *adj*
unpredictable

**imprévu, ~e** /ɛ̃pʀevy/ ⟦1⟧ *adj*
**(a)** unforeseen
**(b)** unexpected
⟦2⟧ *nm* **(a)** hitch
**(b) l'~** the unexpected; **plein d'~** ⟨person,
film⟩ quirky; ⟨trip⟩ with a few surprises
**(c)** unforeseen expense

**imprimante** /ɛ̃pʀimɑ̃t/ *nf* printer
■ **~ à jet d'encre** ink-jet printer; **~ (à) laser**
laser printer; **~ à marguerite** daisywheel
printer; **~ matricielle** dot matrix printer

**imprimé, ~e** /ɛ̃pʀime/ ⟦1⟧ *pp* ▶ IMPRIMER
⟦2⟧ *pp adj* printed (**de** with)
⟦3⟧ *nm* **(a)** form
**(b)** printed matter

**(c)** print; **un ~ à fleurs** a floral print

**imprimer** /ɛ̃pʀime/ [1] *vtr* **(a)** to print
⟨text⟩
**(b)** to put ⟨stamp, seal⟩
**(c)** to leave an imprint of [sth]

**imprimerie** /ɛ̃pʀimʀi/ *nf* **(a)** printing;
**atelier d'~** printing shop
**(b)** printing works
**(c)** printers, print workers

**imprimeur** /ɛ̃pʀimœʀ/ *nm* printer

**improbable** /ɛ̃pʀɔbabl/ *adj* unlikely

**improductif, -ive** /ɛ̃pʀɔdyktif, iv/ *adj*
unproductive; **capitaux ~s** idle capital

**impromptu, ~e** /ɛ̃pʀɔ̃pty/ ⟦1⟧ *adj*
impromptu
⟦2⟧ *adv* impromptu

**impropre** /ɛ̃pʀɔpʀ/ *adj* ⟨term, usage⟩
incorrect; **~ à** unfit for ⟨human
consumption⟩

**improvisation** /ɛ̃pʀɔvizasjɔ̃/ *nf*
improvisation

**improvisé, ~e** /ɛ̃pʀɔvize/ *adj* ⟨speech⟩
improvised; ⟨meal⟩ impromptu; ⟨means⟩
makeshift; ⟨solution⟩ ad hoc; ⟨cook⟩ stand-in

**improviser** /ɛ̃pʀɔvize/ [1] ⟦1⟧ *vtr* to
improvise ⟨meal, speech⟩; to concoct ⟨excuse,
alibi⟩
⟦2⟧ *vi* to improvise
⟦3⟧ **s'improviser** *v refl* (+ *v être*) **(a) s'~
cuisinier** to act as a cook
**(b) un camp pour réfugiés ne s'improvise
pas** you can't create a refugee camp just like
that

**improviste: à l'improviste** /alɛ̃pʀɔvist/
*phr* unexpectedly

**imprudemment** /ɛ̃pʀydamɑ̃/ *adv* ⟨speak⟩
carelessly; ⟨act⟩ unwisely

**imprudence** /ɛ̃pʀydɑ̃s/ *nf* **(a)** carelessness
**(b) commettre une ~** to do something foolish

**imprudent, ~e** /ɛ̃pʀydɑ̃, ɑ̃t/ *adj* ⟨person,
words⟩ careless; ⟨action⟩ rash

**impudence** /ɛ̃pydɑ̃s/ *nf* impudence

**impudent, ~e** /ɛ̃pydɑ̃, ɑ̃t/ *adj* impudent

**impudeur** /ɛ̃pydœʀ/ *nf* immodesty;
shamelessness

**impuissance** /ɛ̃pɥisɑ̃s/ *nf* (gen, Med)
impotence; **~ à faire** inability to do

**impuissant, ~e** /ɛ̃pɥisɑ̃, ɑ̃t/ *adj*
**(a)** powerless, helpless
**(b)** (Med) impotent

**impulsif, -ive** /ɛ̃pylsif, iv/ *adj* impulsive

**impulsion** /ɛ̃pylsjɔ̃/ *nf* **(a)** (gen) impulse;
(Tech) pulse
**(b)** (figurative) impetus

**impunément** /ɛ̃pynemɑ̃/ *adv* with
impunity; **on ne joue pas ~ avec sa santé**
you don't play fast and loose with your
health and get away with it

**impuni, ~e** /ɛ̃pyni/ *adj* unpunished

**impunité** /ɛ̃pynite/ *nf* impunity

**impur, ~e** /ɛ̃pyʀ/ *adj* **(a)** ⟨thoughts⟩
impure
**(b)** ⟨air⟩ dirty; ⟨blood⟩ tainted
**(c)** ⟨ore⟩ impure

**impureté** /ɛ̃pyʀte/ *nf* impurity

**imputable** /ɛ̃pytabl/ *adj* (a) attributable (à to)
(b) chargeable (**sur** to)

**imputer** /ɛ̃pyte/ [1] *vtr* to attribute, to impute

**inabordable** /inabɔʀdabl/ *adj* (a) ⟨*coast*⟩ inaccessible
(b) ⟨*prices*⟩ prohibitive

**inacceptable** /inaksɛptabl/ *adj* unacceptable

**inaccessible** /inaksesibl/ *adj*
(a) inaccessible
(b) ⟨*person*⟩ unapproachable

**inaccoutumé** /inakutyme/ *adj* unusual

**inachevé, ~e** /inaʃve/ *adj* unfinished

**inactif, -ive** /inaktif, iv/ ❶ *adj* idle; ⟨*person*⟩ inactive; ⟨*population*⟩ non-working
❷ *nm,f* non-worker; **les ~s** the non-working population

**inactivité** /inaktivite/ *nf* inactivity

**inadaptation** /inadaptasjɔ̃/ *nf* (a) (of law, equipment) inappropriateness (**à** for)
(b) (emotional, social) maladjustment (**à** to)

**inadapté, ~e** /inadapte/ *adj* (a) ⟨*child*⟩ maladjusted
(b) ⟨*means*⟩ inappropriate; ⟨*tool*⟩ unsuitable; ⟨*law*⟩ ill-adapted

**inadéquat, ~e** /inadekwa, at/ *adj* inadequate; unsuitable

**inadmissible** /inadmisibl/ *adj*
(a) intolerable
(b) unacceptable

**inadvertance**: **par inadvertance** /paʀinadvɛʀtɑ̃s/ *phr* inadvertently

**inaltérable** /inalteʀabl/ *adj*
(a) ⟨*substance*⟩ unalterable, non-corroding; ⟨*colour*⟩ fade-resistant
(b) ⟨*character*⟩ constant; ⟨*principle*⟩ immutable; ⟨*hope*⟩ steadfast

**inaltéré, ~e** /inalteʀe/ *adj* ⟨*substance*⟩ unaltered; ⟨*sky, air*⟩ pure

**inamovible** /inamɔvibl/ *adj* irremovable

**inanimé, ~e** /inanime/ *adj* ⟨*matter*⟩ inanimate; ⟨*person*⟩ unconscious; lifeless

**inanition** /inanisjɔ̃/ *nf* starvation

**inaperçu, ~e** /inapɛʀsy/ *adj* **passer ~** to go unnoticed

**inapte** /inapt/ *adj* unfit

**inaptitude** /inaptityd/ *nf* unfitness

**inarticulé, ~e** /inaʀtikyle/ *adj* inarticulate

**inassouvi, ~e** /inasuvi/ *adj* ⟨*appetite*⟩ insatiable; ⟨*person, desire*⟩ unsatisfied

**inattaquable** /inatakabl/ *adj* (a) (Mil) unassailable
(b) irreproachable
(c) irrefutable

**inattendu, ~e** /inatɑ̃dy/ *adj* unexpected

**inattentif, -ive** /inatɑ̃tif, iv/ *adj*
(a) inattentive; distracted
(b) heedless

**inattention** /inatɑ̃sjɔ̃/ *nf* inattention; **faute d'~** careless mistake

**inaudible** /inodibl/ *adj* inaudible

**inaugural, ~e, mpl -aux** /inogyʀal, o/ *adj* (a) ⟨*ceremony*⟩ inauguration
(b) ⟨*flight*⟩ maiden

**inauguration** /inogyʀasjɔ̃/ *nf* (of building) inauguration; (of exhibition) opening

**inaugurer** /inogyʀe/ [1] *vtr* (a) to unveil ⟨*statue, plaque*⟩; to open ⟨*motorway, school*⟩
(b) to open ⟨*conference*⟩
(c) to mark the start of ⟨*period*⟩

**inavouable** /inavwabl/ *adj* shameful

**inavoué, ~e** /inavwe/ *adj* ⟨*crime, vice*⟩ unconfessed; ⟨*aim*⟩ undisclosed; ⟨*fear*⟩ hidden

**incalculable** /ɛ̃kalkylabl/ *adj*
(a) innumerable
(b) incalculable

**incandescent, ~e** /ɛ̃kɑ̃dɛsɑ̃, ɑ̃t/ *adj* incandescent; white-hot; glowing

**incapable** /ɛ̃kapabl/ *adj* (a) **~ de faire** incapable of doing; unable to do
(b) incompetent

**incapacité** /ɛ̃kapasite/ *nf* (a) inability; **être dans l'~ de faire** to be unable to do
(b) incompetence
(c) disability
(d) (Law) incapacity

**incarcération** /ɛ̃kaʀseʀasjɔ̃/ *nf* imprisonment

**incarcérer** /ɛ̃kaʀseʀe/ [14] *vtr* to imprison

**incarnation** /ɛ̃kaʀnasjɔ̃/ *nf* incarnation

**incarné, ~e** /ɛ̃kaʀne/ *adj* (a) **c'est la bêtise ~e** he/she is stupidity itself
(b) ⟨*nail*⟩ ingrowing

**incarner** /ɛ̃kaʀne/ [1] ❶ *vtr* (a) to embody
(b) to play, to portray
❷ **s'incarner** *v refl* (+ *v être*) to become incarnate

**incartade** /ɛ̃kaʀtad/ *nf* (a) misdemeanour (GB)
(b) (in riding) shy; **faire une ~** to shy

**incassable** /ɛ̃kasabl/ *adj* unbreakable

**incendiaire** /ɛ̃sɑ̃djɛʀ/ ❶ *adj* (a) ⟨*bomb*⟩ incendiary
(b) ⟨*statement*⟩ inflammatory
❷ *nmf* arsonist

**incendie** /ɛ̃sɑ̃di/ *nm* fire; **~ criminel** arson

**incendier** /ɛ̃sɑ̃dje/ [2] *vtr* (a) to burn (down), to torch
(b) (colloq) to haul [sb] over the coals

**incertain, ~e** /ɛ̃sɛʀtɛ̃, ɛn/ *adj* ⟨*person, date, result*⟩ uncertain; ⟨*effect*⟩ unknown; ⟨*colour*⟩ indeterminate; ⟨*smile*⟩ vague; ⟨*weather*⟩ unsettled; ⟨*step*⟩ hesitant

**incertitude** /ɛ̃sɛʀtityd/ *nf* uncertainty

**incessamment** /ɛ̃sesamɑ̃/ *adv* very shortly

**incessant, ~e** /ɛ̃sesɑ̃, ɑ̃t/ *adj* ⟨*noise, rain*⟩ incessant; ⟨*activity*⟩ unceasing

**inceste** /ɛ̃sɛst/ *nm* incest

**incestueux, -euse** /ε̃sεstɥ∅, ∅z/ *adj*
incestuous

**inchangé, ~e** /ε̃ʃãʒe/ *adj* unchanged

**incidemment** /ε̃sidamã/ *adv* **(a)** in
passing
**(b)** by chance

**incidence** /ε̃sidãs/ *nf* **(a)** impact
**(b)** incidence

**incident, ~e** /ε̃sidã, ãt/ *nm* incident; ~ de
parcours hitch; **l'~ est clos** the matter is
closed

**incinérateur** /ε̃sineratœr/ *nm*
**(a)** incinerator
**(b)** crematorium (GB), crematory (US)

**incinération** /ε̃sinerasjɔ̃/ *nf*
**(a)** incineration
**(b)** cremation

**incinérer** /ε̃sinere/ [14] *vtr* **(a)** to burn; to
incinerate
**(b)** to cremate

**inciser** /ε̃size/ [1] *vtr* to make an incision
in

**incisif, -ive¹** /ε̃sizif, iv/ *adj* ⟨*criticism*⟩
incisive; ⟨*portrait*⟩ telling; ⟨*look*⟩ piercing

**incision** /ε̃sizjɔ̃/ *nf* incision

**incisive²** /ε̃siziv/ ⏹1 *adj f* ▶ INCISIF
⏹2 *nf* incisor

**incitation** /ε̃sitasjɔ̃/ *nf* **(a)** incentive
**(b)** (Law) incitement

**inciter** /ε̃site/ [1] *vtr* ⟨*person, situation*⟩ to
encourage; ⟨*event, decision*⟩ to prompt; ~ qn
à la prudence to make sb cautious

**inclassable** /ε̃klasabl/ *adj* unclassifiable

**inclinable** /ε̃klinabl/ *adj* adjustable

**inclinaison** /ε̃klinεzɔ̃/ *nf* (of hill) incline;
(of wall, seat) angle; (of roof) slope; (of boat) list

**inclination** /ε̃klinasjɔ̃/ *nf* inclination

**incliné, ~e** /ε̃kline/ *adj* **(a)** ⟨*ground*⟩
sloping; ⟨*roof*⟩ steep
**(b)** ⟨*wall*⟩ leaning

**incliner** /ε̃kline/ [1] ⏹1 *vtr* to tilt
⟨*sunshade*⟩; to tip up ⟨*bottle*⟩; ~ le buste to
lean forward
⏹2 s'incliner *v refl* (+ *v être*) **(a)** to lean
forward; ( politely) to bow
**(b)** s'~ devant qch to bow to sth, to accept
sth
**(c)** to give in (colloq)
**(d)** s'~ devant le courage de qn to admire
sb's courage

**inclure** /ε̃klyr/ [78] *vtr* **(a)** to include
**(b)** to enclose

**inclus, ~e** /ε̃kly, yz/ ⏹1 *pp* ▶ INCLURE
⏹2 *pp adj* **(a)** jusqu'à jeudi ~ up to and
including Thursday (GB), through Thursday
(US)
**(b)** enclosed

**inclusion** /ε̃klyzjɔ̃/ *nf* inclusion

**inclusivement** /ε̃klyzivmã/ *adv* jusqu'au
4 mai ~ till 4 May inclusive

**incognito** /ε̃kɔnito/ ⏹1 *adv* incognito
⏹2 *nm* garder l'~ to remain incognito

**incohérence** /ε̃kɔerãs/ *nf* **(a)** incoherence
**(b)** discrepancy

**incohérent, ~e** /ε̃kɔerã, ãt/ *adj* ⟨*talk,
behaviour*⟩ incoherent; ⟨*attitude*⟩ illogical

**incollable** /ε̃kɔlabl/ *adj* **(a)** (colloq) elle est
~ en latin you can't catch her out in Latin
**(b)** riz ~ easy-cook rice

**incolore** /ε̃kɔlɔr/ *adj* colourless (GB);
⟨*glass*⟩ clear

**incomber** /ε̃kɔ̃be/ [1] *v+prep* ~ à ⟨*task*⟩ to
fall to; ⟨*responsibility*⟩ to lie with

**incommode** /ε̃kɔmɔd/ *adj*
**(a)** inconvenient; awkward
**(b)** uncomfortable

**incommodé, ~e** /ε̃kɔmɔde/ ⏹1 *pp* ▶
INCOMMODER
⏹2 *pp adj* unwell, indisposed

**incommoder** /ε̃kɔmɔde/ [1] *vtr* to bother

**incomparable** /ε̃kɔ̃parabl/ *adj*
incomparable

**incompatible** /ε̃kɔ̃patibl/ *adj*
incompatible

**incompétence** /ε̃kɔ̃petãs/ *nf* (gen)
incompetence; (Law) incompetency

**incompétent, ~e** /ε̃kɔ̃petã, ãt/ *adj*
incompetent

**incomplet, -ète** /ε̃kɔ̃plε, εt/ *adj*
incomplete

**incompréhensible** /ε̃kɔ̃preãsibl/ *adj*
incomprehensible

**incompréhension** /ε̃kɔ̃preãsjɔ̃/ *nf*
**(a)** incomprehension
**(b)** lack of understanding

**incompressible** /ε̃kɔ̃presibl/ *adj*
**(a)** incompressible
**(b)** ⟨*costs*⟩ fixed

**incompris, ~e** /ε̃kɔ̃pri, iz/ *nm,f*
misunderstood person

**inconcevable** /ε̃kɔ̃svabl/ *adj*
inconceivable

**inconditionnel, -elle** /ε̃kɔ̃disjɔnεl/
⏹1 *adj* unconditional
⏹2 *nm,f* devoted admirer; fan

**inconfortable** /ε̃kɔ̃fɔrtabl/ *adj*
**(a)** uncomfortable
**(b)** awkward

**incongru, ~e** /ε̃kɔ̃gry/ *adj* ⟨*behaviour*⟩
unseemly; ⟨*remark*⟩ incongruous

**incongruité** /ε̃kɔ̃grɥite/ *nf* incongruity

**inconnu, ~e** /ε̃kɔny/ ⏹1 *adj* unknown;
⟨*territories*⟩ unexplored
⏹2 *nm,f* **(a)** unknown ( person)
**(b)** stranger

**inconsciemment** /ε̃kɔ̃sjamã/ *adv*
**(a)** subconsciously
**(b)** unintentionally, unconsciously

**inconscience** /ε̃kɔ̃sjãs/ *nf*
**(a)** recklessness
**(b)** (Med) unconsciousness

**inconscient, ~e** /ε̃kɔ̃sjã, ãt/ ⏹1 *adj*
**(a)** unthinking; foolhardy
**(b)** (Med) unconscious
**(c)** ⟨*act, gesture*⟩ unconscious, automatic
⏹2 *nm,f* c'est un ~ he's irresponsible
⏹3 *nm* l'~ the unconscious

**inconséquent**, **~e** /ɛ̃kɔ̃sekɑ̃, ɑ̃t/ *adj*
⟨*person, behaviour*⟩ inconsistent
**inconsidéré**, **~e** /ɛ̃kɔ̃sidere/ *adj*
(a) ⟨*remark, act*⟩ ill-considered
(b) ⟨*consumption*⟩ excessive
**inconsidérément** /ɛ̃kɔ̃sideremɑ̃/ *adv*
⟨*drink*⟩ to excess; ⟨*spend*⟩ wildly
**inconsistant**, **~e** /ɛ̃kɔ̃sistɑ̃, ɑ̃t/ *adj*
⟨*argument, plot*⟩ flimsy; ⟨*programme*⟩
lacking in substance; ⟨*person*⟩ characterless
**inconstant**, **~e** /ɛ̃kɔ̃stɑ̃, ɑ̃t/ *adj* fickle
**incontestable** /ɛ̃kɔ̃tɛstabl/ *adj*
unquestionable, indisputable
**incontesté**, **~e** /ɛ̃kɔ̃tɛste/ *adj* ⟨*victory*⟩
undisputed; ⟨*fact*⟩ uncontested
**incontinent**, **~e** /ɛ̃kɔ̃tinɑ̃, ɑ̃t/ *adj*
incontinent
**incontournable** /ɛ̃kɔ̃turnabl/ *adj* ⟨*facts*⟩
that cannot be ignored
**incontrôlable** /ɛ̃kɔ̃trolabl/ *adj*
(a) unverifiable
(b) uncontrollable
**inconvenance** /ɛ̃kɔ̃vnɑ̃s/ *nf* impropriety
**inconvenant**, **~e** /ɛ̃kɔ̃vnɑ̃, ɑ̃t/ *adj*
unsuitable; improper, unseemly
**inconvénient** /ɛ̃kɔ̃venjɑ̃/ *nm* drawback,
disadvantage; **si vous n'y voyez pas d'~** if
you have no objection
**incorporer** /ɛ̃kɔrpɔre/ [1] *vtr* (a) (Culin) to
blend
(b) to incorporate
**incorrect**, **~e** /ɛ̃kɔrɛkt/ *adj* (a) incorrect;
faulty; inaccurate
(b) ⟨*behaviour*⟩ improper; ⟨*term*⟩ unsuitable;
⟨*person*⟩ impolite
(c) unfair
**incorrection** /ɛ̃kɔrɛksjɔ̃/ *nf* (of style,
language) incorrectness; (of behaviour)
impropriety
**incorrigible** /ɛ̃kɔriʒibl/ *adj* incorrigible
**incrédule** /ɛ̃kredyl/ *adj* incredulous
**incrédulité** /ɛ̃kredylite/ *nf* incredulity
**incriminer** /ɛ̃krimine/ [1] *vtr* ⟨*person*⟩ to
accuse; ⟨*evidence*⟩ to incriminate; **l'article
incriminé** the offending article
**incroyable** /ɛ̃krwajabl/ *adj* incredible,
unbelievable; **~ mais vrai** strange but true
**incrustation** /ɛ̃krystasjɔ̃/ *nf* (a) inlaying
(b) inlay
(c) encrustation
**incruster** /ɛ̃kryste/ [1] **1** *vtr* (a) to inlay
(b) **incrusté de diamants** encrusted with
diamonds
**2 s'incruster** *v refl* (+ *v être*) ⟨*pebble,
shell*⟩ to become embedded
**incubation** /ɛ̃kybasjɔ̃/ *nf* incubation
**incuber** /ɛ̃kybe/ [1] *vtr* to incubate, to
hatch
**inculpation** /ɛ̃kylpasjɔ̃/ *nf* (Law) charge
**inculpé**, **~e** /ɛ̃kylpe/ *nm,f* **l'~** ≈ the
accused
**inculper** /ɛ̃kylpe/ [1] *vtr* (Law) to charge
**inculquer** /ɛ̃kylke/ [1] *vtr* to inculcate

**inculte** /ɛ̃kylt/ *adj* uncultivated
**incurable** /ɛ̃kyrabl/ *adj, nmf* incurable
**incursion** /ɛ̃kyrsjɔ̃/ *nf* incursion, foray
**incurver** /ɛ̃kyrve/ [1] *vtr*, **s'incurver**
*v refl* (+ *v être*) to curve, to bend
**Inde** /ɛ̃d/ *pr nf* India
**indécence** /ɛ̃desɑ̃s/ *nf* (gen) indecency;
(of remark) impropriety
**indécent**, **~e** /ɛ̃desɑ̃, ɑ̃t/ *adj* indecent;
⟨*luxury*⟩ obscene
**indéchiffrable** /ɛ̃deʃifrabl/ *adj*
(a) indecipherable
(b) ⟨*mystery*⟩ incomprehensible
**indécis**, **~e** /ɛ̃desi, iz/ **1** *adj* (a) **il est
encore ~** he hasn't decided yet
(b) indecisive
**2** *nm,f* (a) indecisive person
(b) (in opinion poll) 'don't know'; (in election)
floating voter
**indécision** /ɛ̃desizjɔ̃/ *nf* (a) indecision,
uncertainty
(b) indecisiveness
**indécrottable** /ɛ̃dekrɔtabl/ *adj* (colloq)
hopeless (colloq)
**indéfini**, **~e** /ɛ̃defini/ *adj* (a) ⟨*number*⟩
indeterminate
(b) ⟨*sadness*⟩ undefined; ⟨*duration*⟩
indefinite
(c) (in grammar) indefinite
**indéfiniment** /ɛ̃definimɑ̃/ *adv*
indefinitely
**indéfinissable** /ɛ̃definisabl/ *adj*
undefinable
**indélébile** /ɛ̃delebil/ *adj* indelible
**indélicatesse** /ɛ̃delikatɛs/ *nf*
(a) indelicacy, tactlessness
(b) dishonesty
(c) act of dishonesty
**indemne** /ɛ̃dɛmn/ *adj* unscathed,
unharmed
**indemnisation** /ɛ̃dɛmnizasjɔ̃/ *nf*
(a) indemnification
(b) indemnity, compensation
**indemniser** /ɛ̃dɛmnize/ [1] *vtr* to
indemnify
**indemnité** /ɛ̃dɛmnite/ *nf* (a) (Law)
indemnity, compensation
(b) allowance
■ **~ de chômage** unemployment benefit;
**~ journalière** sick pay; **~ de licenciement**
severance pay
**indéniable** /ɛ̃denjabl/ *adj* undeniable
**indentation** /ɛ̃dɑ̃tasjɔ̃/ *nf* indentation
**indépendamment** /ɛ̃depɑ̃damɑ̃/ **1** *adv*
independently
**2 indépendamment de** *phr*
(a) regardless of
(b) in addition to
**indépendance** /ɛ̃depɑ̃dɑ̃s/ *nf*
independence
**indépendant**, **~e** /ɛ̃depɑ̃dɑ̃, ɑ̃t/ **1** *adj*
(a) independent
(b) ⟨*room*⟩ separate; **maison ~e** detached
house                                                  ⋯⟡

**2** *nm,f* freelance, self-employed person

**indépendantiste** /ɛ̃depɑ̃dɑ̃tist/ **1** *adj* ⟨organization⟩ (pro-)independence
**2** *nmf* **(a)** freedom fighter
**(b)** member of an independence movement

**indescriptible** /ɛ̃dɛskʀiptibl/ *adj* indescribable

**indésirable** /ɛ̃deziʀabl/ *adj* ⟨person⟩ undesirable; **effets ~s** (Med) adverse reactions

**indéterminé, ~e** /ɛ̃detɛʀmine/ *adj* ⟨form, quantity⟩ indeterminate; ⟨reason⟩ unspecified

**index** /ɛ̃dɛks/ *nm inv* **(a)** index; **mettre qn/ qch à l'~** to blacklist sb/sth
**(b)** forefinger

**indexer** /ɛ̃dɛkse/ [1] *vtr* **(a)** to index-link; **~ qch sur qch** to index sth to sth
**(b)** to index

**indicateur, -trice** /ɛ̃dikatœʀ, tʀis/ **1** *adj* **panneau** *or* **poteau ~** signpost
**2** *nm* **(a)** informer
**(b)** indicator
**(c)** gauge, indicator

**indicatif, -ive** /ɛ̃dikatif, iv/ **1** *adj* indicative
**2** *nm* **(a)** (in grammar) indicative
**(b)** **~ (téléphonique)** dialling (GB) code
**(c)** theme tune

**indication** /ɛ̃dikasjɔ̃/ *nf* **(a)** indication
**(b)** information; **sauf ~ contraire** unless otherwise indicated
**(c)** (for use) instruction
**(d)** indication, clue

**indice** /ɛ̃dis/ *nm* **(a)** sign, indication
**(b)** (in inquiry) clue
**(c)** (Econ) index; **~ du coût de la vie** cost of living index
**(d)** **l'~ d'écoute** audience ratings

**indicible** /ɛ̃disibl/ *adj* inexpressible

**indien, -ienne** /ɛ̃djɛ̃, ɛn/ *adj* **(a)** Indian
**(b)** (North American) Indian

**indifféremment** /ɛ̃difeʀamɑ̃/ *adv* **(a)** equally
**(b)** **servir ~ de salon ou de bureau** to be used either as a living room or a study

**indifférence** /ɛ̃difeʀɑ̃s/ *nf* indifference

**indifférent, ~e** /ɛ̃difeʀɑ̃, ɑ̃t/ *adj* **(a)** indifferent
**(b)** irrelevant

**indifférer** /ɛ̃difeʀe/ [14] *vtr* to leave [sb] indifferent

**indigence** /ɛ̃diʒɑ̃s/ *nf* destitution, extreme poverty

**indigène** /ɛ̃diʒɛn/ **1** *adj* **(a)** ⟨fauna, flora⟩ indigenous
**(b)** ⟨population, custom⟩ local; native
**2** *nmf* local; native

**indigeste** /ɛ̃diʒɛst/ *adj* indigestible

**indigestion** /ɛ̃diʒɛstjɔ̃/ *nf* **(a)** indigestion
**(b)** **avoir une ~ de qch** to be fed up with sth (colloq)

**indignation** /ɛ̃diɲasjɔ̃/ *nf* indignation

**indigne** /ɛ̃diɲ/ *adj* **(a)** ⟨conduct⟩ disgraceful; ⟨mother, son⟩ bad
**(b)** **~ de qn** unworthy of sb

**indigné, ~e** /ɛ̃diɲe/ *adj* indignant

**indigner** /ɛ̃diɲe/ [1] **1** *vtr* to make [sb] indignant, to outrage [sb]
**2** **s'indigner** *v refl* (+ *v être*) to be indignant

**indignité** /ɛ̃diɲite/ *nf* **(a)** despicableness
**(b)** despicable act, disgraceful act

**indigo** /ɛ̃digo/ *adj inv, nm* indigo

**indiqué, ~e** /ɛ̃dike/ **1** *pp* ▶ INDIQUER
**2** *pp adj* **(a)** ⟨treatment⟩ recommended
**(b)** **à l'heure ~e** at the specified time; **le village est très mal ~** the village is very badly signposted

**indiquer** /ɛ̃dike/ [1] *vtr* **(a)** ⟨person⟩ to point out, to point to; ⟨signpost⟩ to show the way to; **pouvez-vous m'~ la banque la plus proche?** can you tell me where the nearest bank is?
**(b)** to indicate **(que that)**
**(c)** **je peux t'~ un bon médecin** I can give you the name of a good doctor
**(d)** to give; **l'heure indiquée sur le programme est fausse** the time given on the programme (GB) is wrong
**(e)** ⟨meter, map⟩ to show; **le restaurant n'est pas indiqué** there are no signs to the restaurant

**indirect, ~e** /ɛ̃diʀɛkt/ *adj* indirect

**indiscipline** /ɛ̃disiplin/ *nf* lack of discipline

**indiscipliné, ~e** /ɛ̃disipline/ *adj* undisciplined, unruly

**indiscret, -ète** /ɛ̃diskʀɛ, ɛt/ *adj* **(a)** ⟨person⟩ inquisitive; **à l'abri des regards ~s** away from prying eyes
**(b)** ⟨person, question⟩ indiscreet; **il est ~** he can't keep a secret

**indiscrétion** /ɛ̃diskʀesjɔ̃/ *nf* **(a)** inquisitiveness; **sans ~, combien gagnez-vous?** if you don't mind my asking, how much do you earn?
**(b)** lack of discretion
**(c)** indiscreet remark

**indiscutable** /ɛ̃diskytabl/ *adj* indisputable, unquestionable

**indispensable** /ɛ̃dispɑ̃sabl/ **1** *adj* essential; **être ~ à qn** to be indispensable to sb
**2** *nm* **l'~** the essentials

**indisposé, ~e** /ɛ̃dispoze/ *adj* unwell, indisposed

**indisposer** /ɛ̃dispoze/ [1] *vtr* **(a)** to annoy
**(b)** to upset [sb], to make [sb] feel ill

**indisposition** /ɛ̃dispozisjɔ̃/ *nf* indisposition

**indissociable** /ɛ̃disɔsjabl/ *adj* inseparable

**indistinct, ~e** /ɛ̃distɛ̃, ɛ̃kt/ *adj* indistinct

**individu** /ɛ̃dividy/ *nm* **(a)** individual
**(b)** human being, person

(c) un sinistre ∼ a sinister individual *or* character; un ∼ armé an armed man
(d) (in scientific study) subject

**individualiser** /ɛ̃dividɥalize/ [1] **1** *vtr*
(a) to tailor [sth] to individual needs
(b) to individualize
**2 s'individualiser** *v refl* (+ *v être*) to become more individual

**individualiste** /ɛ̃dividɥalist/ *adj* individualistic

**individuel, -elle** /ɛ̃dividɥɛl/ *adj* (gen) individual; ⟨*responsibility*⟩ personal; ⟨*room*⟩ single; **maison individuelle** (detached) house

**indivisible** /ɛ̃divizibl/ *adj* indivisible

**Indochine** /ɛ̃dɔʃin/ *pr nf* Indochina

**indo-européen, -éenne** /ɛ̃dooʀopeɛ̃, ɛn/ *adj* Indo-European

**indolence** /ɛ̃dɔlɑ̃s/ *nf* laziness, indolence

**indolent, ∼e** /ɛ̃dɔlɑ̃, ɑ̃t/ *adj* lazy, indolent

**indolore** /ɛ̃dɔlɔʀ/ *adj* painless

**indomptable** /ɛ̃dɔ̃tabl/ *adj* ⟨*person, courage*⟩ indomitable; ⟨*anger, passion, person*⟩ uncontrollable; ⟨*animal*⟩ untamable; **avec une énergie ∼** with tireless energy

**Indonésie** /ɛ̃dɔnezi/ *pr nf* Indonesia

**indu, ∼e** /ɛ̃dy/ *adj* ⟨*hour*⟩ ungodly (colloq), unearthly; ⟨*remark, reaction*⟩ inappropriate

**indubitable** /ɛ̃dybitabl/ *adj* indubitable

**indubitablement** /ɛ̃dybitabləmɑ̃/ *adv* undoubtedly

**induction** /ɛ̃dyksjɔ̃/ *nf* induction

**induire** /ɛ̃dɥiʀ/ [69] *vtr* (a) ⟨*event, measures*⟩ to lead to, to bring about
(b) to infer, to conclude
(c) to induce; ∼ **qn en erreur** to mislead sb
(d) to induce ⟨*current*⟩

**indulgence** /ɛ̃dylʒɑ̃s/ *nf* (a) (of parent, audience) indulgence
(b) (of jury) leniency

**indulgent, ∼e** /ɛ̃dylʒɑ̃, ɑ̃t/ *adj* (a) ⟨*parent, audience*⟩ indulgent
(b) ⟨*jury*⟩ lenient

**industrialisation** /ɛ̃dystʀializasjɔ̃/ *nf* industrialization

**industrialiser** /ɛ̃dystʀialize/ [1] **1** *vtr* to industrialize
**2 s'industrialiser** *v refl* (+ *v être*) to become industrialized

**industrie** /ɛ̃dystʀi/ *nf* (a) industry; **l'∼ hôtelière** the hotel trade
(b) industrial concern

**industriel, -ielle** /ɛ̃dystʀijɛl/ **1** *adj* industrial; **pain ∼** factory-baked bread
**2** *nm,f* industrialist, manufacturer

**inébranlable** /inebʀɑ̃labl/ *adj*
(a) unshakeable, unwavering
(b) immovable

**inédit, ∼e** /inedi, it/ *adj* ⟨*book*⟩ (previously) unpublished; ⟨*situation*⟩ (totally) new

**ineffable** /inefabl/ *adj* ineffable, unutterable

**inefficace** /inefikas/ *adj* (a) ineffective
(b) inefficient

**inefficacité** /inefikasite/ *nf*
(a) ineffectiveness, inefficacy
(b) inefficiency

**inégal, ∼e,** *mpl* **-aux** /inegal, o/ *adj* unequal; uneven; irregular; ⟨*mood*⟩ changeable, erratic

**inégalable** /inegalabl/ *adj* incomparable

**inégalé, ∼e** /inegale/ *adj* unequalled (GB), unrivalled (GB)

**inégalement** /inegalmɑ̃/ *adv*
(a) unequally
(b) unevenly

**inégalité** /inegalite/ *nf* (a) disparity
(b) inequality
(c) (of mood) changeability; (of surface) unevenness

**inéluctable** /inelyktabl/ *adj, nm* inevitable

**inénarrable** /inenaʀabl/ *adj* hilarious

**inepte** /inɛpt/ *adj* ⟨*person*⟩ inept; ⟨*judgment*⟩ inane; ⟨*remark*⟩ idiotic

**ineptie** /inɛpsi/ *nf* (a) inanity
(b) idiotic remark
(c) (action) stupid thing

**inépuisable** /inepɥizabl/ *adj* inexhaustible

**inerte** /inɛʀt/ *adj* (a) inert
(b) apathetic

**inertie** /inɛʀsi/ *nf* (a) inertia
(b) apathy, inertia

**inespéré, ∼e** /inɛspeʀe/ *adj* ⟨*victory*⟩ unhoped for; **c'est une occasion ∼e de faire** this is a heaven-sent opportunity to do

**inestimable** /inɛstimabl/ *adj* ⟨*value*⟩ inestimable; ⟨*help*⟩ invaluable

**inévitable** /inevitabl/ *adj* inevitable; unavoidable

**inexact, ∼e** /inɛgza, akt/ *adj* inaccurate

**inexactitude** /inɛgzaktityd/ *nf*
(a) inaccuracy
(b) unpunctuality

**inexcusable** /inɛkskyzabl/ *adj* inexcusable

**inexistant, ∼e** /inɛgzistɑ̃, ɑ̃t/ *adj* ⟨*means, help*⟩ nonexistent

**inexpérience** /inɛkspeʀjɑ̃s/ *nf* inexperience

**inexpérimenté, ∼e** /inɛkspeʀimɑ̃te/ *adj* inexperienced

**inexplicable** /inɛksplikabl/ *adj* inexplicable

**inexpressif, -ive** /inɛkspʀesif, iv/ *adj* inexpressive

**inexprimable** /inɛkspʀimabl/ *adj* inexpressible

**in extremis** /inɛkstʀemis/ *phr* at the last minute

**infaillible** /ɛ̃fajibl/ *adj* infallible

**infaisable** /ɛ̃fəzabl/ *adj* unfeasible, impossible

**infamant, ∼e** /ɛ̃famɑ̃, ɑ̃t/ *adj*
(a) ⟨*remark*⟩ defamatory

···⟶

**(b)** ⟨act⟩ infamous
**infâme** /ɛ̃fɑm/ adj **(a)** ⟨food, smell⟩
revolting
**(b)** ⟨person⟩ despicable; ⟨crime⟩ odious
**infamie** /ɛ̃fami/ nf **(a)** infamy
**(b)** infamous act
**(c)** slanderous remark
**infanterie** /ɛ̃fɑ̃tʀi/ nf infantry
**infantile** /ɛ̃fɑ̃til/ adj **(a)** ⟨illness⟩ childhood;
⟨mortality⟩ infant; ⟨psychology⟩ child
**(b)** ⟨person, behaviour⟩ infantile, childish
**infantilisme** /ɛ̃fɑ̃tilism/ nm childishness
**infarctus** /ɛ̃faʀktys/ nm inv heart attack
**infatigable** /ɛ̃fatigabl/ adj tireless
**infatué**, **∼e** /ɛ̃fatɥe/ adj être ∼ de sa
personne to be full of oneself
**infect**, **∼e** /ɛ̃fɛkt/ adj foul; revolting
**infecter** /ɛ̃fɛkte/ [1] **1** vtr **(a)** (Med) to
infect
**(b)** (figurative) to poison
**2** **s'infecter** v refl (+ v être) to become
infected, to go septic
**infectieux**, **-ieuse** /ɛ̃fɛksjø, øz/ adj
infectious
**infection** /ɛ̃fɛksjɔ̃/ nf **(a)** (Med) infection
**(b)** (figurative) c'est une ∼! it stinks to high
heaven! (colloq)
**inférieur**, **∼e** /ɛ̃feʀjœʀ/ **1** adj **(a)** lower;
⟨size⟩ smaller; ⟨length⟩ shorter; ∼ à la
moyenne below average; être en nombre ∼
to be fewer in number
**(b)** inferior
**(c)** (in mathematics) si a est ∼ à b if a is less
than b
**2** nm,f inferior
**infériorité** /ɛ̃feʀjɔʀite/ nf inferiority
**infernal**, **∼e**, mpl **-aux** /ɛ̃fɛʀnal, o/ adj
**(a)** ⟨noise, heat⟩ infernal; cycle ∼
unstoppable chain of events
**(b)** ⟨situation⟩ diabolical; ce gosse est ∼
(colloq) that child is a monster
**infertile** /ɛ̃fɛʀtil/ adj barren, infertile
**infester** /ɛ̃fɛste/ [1] vtr to infest, to
overrun; infesté de puces flea-ridden
**infidèle** /ɛ̃fidɛl/ **1** adj unfaithful; disloyal
**2** nm,f infidel
**infidélité** /ɛ̃fidelite/ nf **(a)** infidelity; faire
des ∼s à to be unfaithful to
**(b)** disloyalty
**infiltration** /ɛ̃filtʀasjɔ̃/ nf **(a)** ∼s d'eau
water seepage
**(b)** (of spies) infiltration
**(c)** (Med) injection
**infiltrer** /ɛ̃filtʀe/ [1] **1** vtr to infiltrate
**2** **s'infiltrer** v refl (+ v être) **(a)** ⟨liquid⟩ to
seep; ⟨light, cold⟩ to filter in
**(b)** ⟨person⟩ s'∼ dans to infiltrate ⟨group,
place⟩
**infime** /ɛ̃fim/ adj tiny, minute
**infini**, **∼e** /ɛ̃fini/ **1** adj infinite
**2** nm l'∼ infinity
**infiniment** /ɛ̃finimɑ̃/ adv immensely;
∼ plus infinitely more

**infinité** /ɛ̃finite/ nf l'∼ infinity; une ∼ de
an endless number of
**infinitif** /ɛ̃finitif/ nm infinitive
**infirme** /ɛ̃fiʀm/ **1** adj (gen) disabled;
(because of age) infirm
**2** nmf disabled person; les ∼s the disabled
**infirmer** /ɛ̃fiʀme/ [1] vtr (gen, Law) to
invalidate
**infirmerie** /ɛ̃fiʀməʀi/ nf (gen) infirmary;
sick room; sick bay
**infirmier** /ɛ̃fiʀmje/ nm male nurse
**infirmière** /ɛ̃fiʀmjɛʀ/ nf nurse
**infirmité** /ɛ̃fiʀmite/ nf (gen) disability;
(through old age) infirmity
**inflammable** /ɛ̃flamabl/ adj flammable
**inflammation** /ɛ̃flamasjɔ̃/ nf (Med)
inflammation
**inflammatoire** /ɛ̃flamatwaʀ/ adj (Med)
inflammatory
**inflation** /ɛ̃flasjɔ̃/ nf inflation
**infléchir** /ɛ̃fleʃiʀ/ [3] vtr, **s'infléchir**
v refl (+ v être) to soften; to deflect
**inflexible** /ɛ̃flɛksibl/ adj inflexible
**infliger** /ɛ̃fliʒe/ [13] vtr to impose ⟨fine⟩
**influençable** /ɛ̃flyɑ̃sabl/ adj
impressionable
**influence** /ɛ̃flyɑ̃s/ nf influence
**influencer** /ɛ̃flyɑ̃se/ [12] vtr to influence
⟨person⟩; to affect ⟨situation⟩
**influent**, **∼e** /ɛ̃flyɑ̃, ɑ̃t/ adj influential
**influer** /ɛ̃flye/ [1] v+prep ∼ sur to have an
influence on
**informateur**, **-trice** /ɛ̃fɔʀmatœʀ, tʀis/
nm,f **(a)** (gen) informant
**(b)** (police) informer
**informaticien**, **-ienne** /ɛ̃fɔʀmatisjɛ̃, ɛn/
nm,f computer scientist
**information** /ɛ̃fɔʀmasjɔ̃/ nf
**(a)** information; une ∼ a piece of
information
**(b)** (in newspaper, on television) une ∼ a piece of
news; écouter les ∼s to listen to the news;
contrôler l'∼ to control the media
**(c)** (Comput) data, information
**informatique** /ɛ̃fɔʀmatik/ **1** adj
computer
**2** nf computer science, computing
**informatisation** /ɛ̃fɔʀmatizasjɔ̃/ nf
computerization
**informatiser** /ɛ̃fɔʀmatize/ [1] **1** vtr to
computerize
**2** **s'informatiser** v refl (+ v être) to
become computerized
**informe** /ɛ̃fɔʀm/ adj shapeless
**informer** /ɛ̃fɔʀme/ [1] **1** vtr to inform
**2** **s'informer** v refl (+ v être) **(a)** to keep
oneself informed
**(b)** s'∼ de qch to enquire about sth
**(c)** s'∼ sur qn to make enquiries about sb
**infortune** /ɛ̃fɔʀtyn/ nf misfortune
**infortuné**, **∼e** /ɛ̃fɔʀtyne/ **1** adj ill-fated
**2** nm,f unfortunate
**infra** /ɛ̃fʀa/ adv below; voir ∼ see below

**infraction** /ɛ̃fʀaksjɔ̃/ *nf* offence (GB); être en ~ to be in breach of the law

**infranchissable** /ɛ̃fʀɑ̃ʃisabl/ *adj* ⟨obstacle⟩ insurmountable; ⟨border⟩ impassable

**infrarouge** /ɛ̃fʀaʀuʒ/ *adj, nm* infrared; missile guidé par ~ heat-seeking missile

**infrastructure** /ɛ̃fʀastʀyktyʀ/ *nf*
(a) facilities
(b) (Econ) infrastructure

**infructueux, -euse** /ɛ̃fʀyktɥø, øz/ *adj* fruitless

**infuser** /ɛ̃fyze/ [1] *vi* ⟨tea⟩ to brew, to infuse

**infusion** /ɛ̃fyzjɔ̃/ *nf* (a) herbal tea
(b) infusion

**ingénier: s'ingénier** /ɛ̃ʒenje/ [2] *v refl* (+ *v être*) to do one's utmost (à faire to do)

**ingénierie** /ɛ̃ʒeniʀi/ *nf* engineering

**ingénieur** /ɛ̃ʒenjœʀ/ *nm* engineer

**ingénieur-conseil,** *pl* **ingénieurs-conseils** /ɛ̃ʒenjœʀkɔ̃sɛj/ *nm* consulting engineer

**ingénieux, -ieuse** /ɛ̃ʒenjø, øz/ *adj* ingenious

**ingéniosité** /ɛ̃ʒenjozite/ *nf* ingenuity

**ingénu, ~e** /ɛ̃ʒeny/ *adj* ingenuous

**ingénuité** /ɛ̃ʒenɥite/ *nf* ingenuousness; en toute ~ in all innocence

**ingérence** /ɛ̃ʒeʀɑ̃s/ *nf* interference (dans in)

**ingérer** /ɛ̃ʒeʀe/ [14] **1** *vtr* to ingest
**2** **s'ingérer** *v refl* (+ *v être*) to interfere

**ingestion** /ɛ̃ʒɛstjɔ̃/ *nf* ingestion

**ingrat, ~e** /ɛ̃gʀa, at/ *adj* (a) ungrateful
(b) ⟨face, landscape⟩ unattractive
(c) ⟨task, role⟩ thankless; ⟨land, soil⟩ unproductive

**ingratitude** /ɛ̃gʀatityd/ *nf* ingratitude

**ingrédient** /ɛ̃gʀedjɑ̃/ *nm* ingredient

**ingurgiter** /ɛ̃gyʀʒite/ [1] *vtr* to gulp down

**inhabitable** /inabitabl/ *adj* uninhabitable

**inhabité, ~e** /inabite/ *adj* uninhabited

**inhabituel, -elle** /inabitɥɛl/ *adj* unusual

**inhalation** /inalasjɔ̃/ *nf* inhalation

**inhaler** /inale/ [1] *vtr* to inhale

**inhérent, ~e** /ineʀɑ̃, ɑ̃t/ *adj* inherent

**inhibition** /inibisjɔ̃/ *nf* inhibition

**inhumain, ~e** /inymɛ̃, ɛn/ *adj* inhuman

**inhumation** /inymasjɔ̃/ *nf* (a) burial
(b) funeral

**inhumer** /inyme/ [1] *vtr* to bury

**inimaginable** /inimaʒinabl/ *adj*
(a) unimaginable
(b) unthinkable

**inimitable** /inimitabl/ *adj* inimitable

**ininflammable** /inɛ̃flamabl/ *adj* nonflammable

**inintéressant, ~e** /inɛ̃teʀesɑ̃, ɑ̃t/ *adj* uninteresting

**ininterrompu, ~e** /inɛ̃teʀɔ̃py/ *adj*
(a) ⟨process⟩ uninterrupted; ⟨drop⟩ continuous; ⟨traffic⟩ endless
(b) ⟨procession⟩ unbroken

**initial, ~e¹,** *mpl* **-iaux** /inisjal, o/ *adj* initial

**initiale²** /inisjal/ *nf* initial

**initiateur, -trice** /inisjatœʀ, tʀis/ *nm,f*
(a) originator; instigator
(b) instructor

**initiation** /inisjasjɔ̃/ *nf* (a) introduction
(b) initiation

**initiative** /inisjativ/ *nf* initiative; avoir l'esprit d'~ to have initiative

**initié, ~e** /inisje/ **1** *adj* (Comput) ~ à l'informatique computer literate
**2** *nm,f* (a) initiate
(b) insider trader
(c) (Comput) ~ à l'informatique computer-literate person

**initier** /inisje/ [2] **1** *vtr* (a) to introduce
(b) to initiate
**2** **s'initier** *v refl* (+ *v être*) s'~ à qch to learn sth

**injecter** /ɛ̃ʒɛkte/ [2] *vtr* to inject

**injection** /ɛ̃ʒɛksjɔ̃/ *nf* injection

**injonction** /ɛ̃ʒɔ̃ksjɔ̃/ *nf* injunction, command

**injure** /ɛ̃ʒyʀ/ *nf* insult, abuse

**injurier** /ɛ̃ʒyʀje/ [1] *vtr* to insult, to swear at

**injurieux, -ieuse** /ɛ̃ʒyʀjø, øz/ *adj* ⟨remark⟩ abusive; ⟨attitude⟩ insulting

**injuste** /ɛ̃ʒyst/ *adj* unfair

**injustement** /ɛ̃ʒystəmɑ̃/ *adv* unjustly; unfairly

**injustice** /ɛ̃ʒystis/ *nf* injustice; unfairness; réparer une ~ to right a wrong

**injustifié, ~e** /ɛ̃ʒystifje/ *adj* unjustified

**inlassable** /ɛ̃lasabl/ *adj* ⟨person⟩ tireless; ⟨curiosity⟩ insatiable; ⟨efforts⟩ unremitting

**inlassablement** /ɛ̃lasabləmɑ̃/ *adv* tirelessly

**inné, ~e** /inne/ *adj* innate

**innocemment** /inɔsamɑ̃/ *adv* innocently; pas ~ disingenuously

**innocence** /inɔsɑ̃s/ *nf* innocence

**innocent, ~e** /inɔsɑ̃, ɑ̃t/ *adj* innocent

**innocenter** /inɔsɑ̃te/ [1] *vtr* to prove [sb] innocent

**innombrable** /innɔ̃bʀabl/ *adj*
(a) countless
(b) ⟨crowd⟩ vast

**innommable** /innɔmabl/ *adj* unspeakable

**innovateur, -trice** /inɔvatœʀ, tʀis/ *nm,f* innovator

**innover** /inɔve/ [1] *vi* to innovate

**inoculer** /inɔkyle/ [1] *vtr* to inoculate

**inodore** /inɔdɔʀ/ *adj* ⟨substance⟩ odourless (GB)

**inoffensif, -ive** /inɔfɑ̃sif, iv/ *adj* harmless

**inondation** /inɔ̃dasjɔ̃/ *nf* (a) flood ⋯⋗

**(b)** flooding

**inonder** /inɔ̃de/ [1] *vtr* to flood

**inopérant, ~e** /inɔpeʀɑ̃, ɑ̃t/ *adj* ineffective

**inopiné, ~e** /inɔpine/ *adj* unexpected

**inopportun, ~e** /inɔpɔʀtœ̃, yn/ *adj*
**(a)** inappropriate
**(b)** ill-timed

**inoubliable** /inublijabl/ *adj* unforgettable

**inouï, ~e** /inwi/ *adj* ⟨event⟩ unprecedented; ⟨success⟩ incredible; **c'est ~** that's unheard of

**inox** /inɔks/ *nm inv* stainless steel

**inoxydable** /inɔksidabl/ *adj* ⟨metal⟩ non-oxidizing; **acier ~** stainless steel

**inqualifiable** /ɛ̃kalifjabl/ *adj* unspeakable

**inquiet, -iète** /ɛ̃kjɛ, ɛt/ *adj* **(a)** anxious
**(b)** worried

**inquiétant, ~e** /ɛ̃kjetɑ̃, ɑ̃t/ *adj*
**(a)** worrying
**(b)** frightening

**inquiéter** /ɛ̃kjete/ [14] **1** *vtr* **(a)** to worry
**(b)** **les douaniers ne l'ont pas inquiété** the customs officers didn't bother him
**2** **s'inquiéter** *v refl* (+ *v être*) **(a)** to worry
**(b)** **s'~ de qch** to enquire about sth

**inquiétude** /ɛ̃kjetyd/ *nf* **(a)** anxiety, concern
**(b)** worry; **il n'y a pas d'~ à avoir** there's nothing to worry about

**inquisiteur, -trice** /ɛ̃kizitœʀ, tʀis/
**1** *adj* inquisitive
**2** *nm,f* inquisitor

**inquisition** /ɛ̃kizisjɔ̃/ *nf* inquisition

**insaisissable** /ɛ̃sɛzisabl/ *adj* ⟨person, character⟩ elusive; ⟨nuance⟩ imperceptible

**insalubre** /ɛ̃salybʀ/ *adj* insanitary

**insanité** /ɛ̃sanite/ *nf* **(a)** rubbish, nonsense
**(b)** insanity

**insatiable** /ɛ̃sasjabl/ *adj* insatiable

**insatisfaction** /ɛ̃satisfaksjɔ̃/ *nf* dissatisfaction

**insatisfait, ~e** /ɛ̃satisfɛ, ɛt/ *adj* dissatisfied (**de** with); unsatisfied

**inscription** /ɛ̃skʀipsjɔ̃/ *nf* **(a)** (in school) enrolment (GB); (at university) registration
**(b)** **l'~ au club coûte 40 euros** the membership fee for the club is 40 euros; **~ électorale** registration as a voter
**(c)** inscription; graffiti

**inscrire** /ɛ̃skʀiʀ/ [67] **1** *vtr* **(a)** to enrol (GB) ⟨pupil⟩; to register ⟨student⟩
**(b)** to write down ⟨name, date⟩
**2** **s'inscrire** *v refl* (+ *v être*) **(a)** to enrol (GB); to register; **s'~ au chômage** to register as unemployed; **s'~ à un parti** to join a party
**(b)** **s'~ dans le cadre de** to be in line with
**(c)** **s'~ en faux contre qch** to dispute the validity of sth

**inscrit, ~e** /ɛ̃skʀi, it/ **1** *pp* ▸ **INSCRIRE**
**2** *nm,f* registered student; registered voter

**insecte** /ɛ̃sɛkt/ *nm* insect

**insecticide** /ɛ̃sɛktisid/ *nm* insecticide

**insécurité** /ɛ̃sekyʀite/ *nf* insecurity

**INSEE** *nm* (*abbr* **Institut National de la Statistique et des Études Économiques**) French national institute of statistics and economic studies

**insémination** /ɛ̃seminasjɔ̃/ *nf* insemination; **~ artificielle** artificial insemination

**insensé, ~e** /ɛ̃sɑ̃se/ *adj* **(a)** insane
**(b)** (colloq) ⟨crowd, traffic jam⟩ phenomenal

**insensibiliser** /ɛ̃sɑ̃sibilize/ [1] *vtr* (Med) to anaesthetize

**insensibilité** /ɛ̃sɑ̃sibilite/ *nf* insensitivity

**insensible** /ɛ̃sɑ̃sibl/ *adj* **(a)** impervious
**(b)** insensitive

**insensiblement** /ɛ̃sɑ̃sibləmɑ̃/ *adv* imperceptibly

**inséparable** /ɛ̃sepaʀabl/ *adj* inseparable

**insérer** /ɛ̃seʀe/ [14] **1** *vtr* to insert
**2** **s'insérer** *v refl* (+ *v être*) (gen) to be inserted

**insertion** /ɛ̃sɛʀsjɔ̃/ *nf* **(a)** insertion
**(b)** integration

**insidieux, -ieuse** /ɛ̃sidjø, øz/ *adj* insidious

**insigne** /ɛ̃siɲ/ **1** *adj* ⟨honour, favour⟩ great
**2** *nm* badge

**insignifiant, ~e** /ɛ̃siɲifjɑ̃, ɑ̃t/ *adj* insignificant

**insinuation** /ɛ̃sinɥasjɔ̃/ *nf* insinuation

**insinuer** /ɛ̃sinɥe/ [1] **1** *vtr* to insinuate
**2** **s'insinuer** *v refl* (+ *v être*) **s'~ dans** ⟨person⟩ to worm one's way into; ⟨liquid⟩ to seep into

**insipide** /ɛ̃sipid/ *adj* insipid

**insistance** /ɛ̃sistɑ̃s/ *nf* insistence

**insistant, ~e** /ɛ̃sistɑ̃, ɑ̃t/ *adj* insistent

**insister** /ɛ̃siste/ [1] *vi* **(a)** to insist; **'ça ne répond pas'—'insiste'** 'there's no reply!'—'keep trying'
**(b)** **~ sur** to stress ⟨danger, need⟩; to put the emphasis on ⟨spelling⟩
**(c)** **~ sur** to pay particular attention to ⟨stain⟩

**insolation** /ɛ̃sɔlasjɔ̃/ *nf* sunstroke

**insolence** /ɛ̃sɔlɑ̃s/ *nf* **(a)** insolence
**(b)** insolent remark

**insolent, ~e** /ɛ̃sɔlɑ̃, ɑ̃t/ *adj* **(a)** ⟨child, tone⟩ insolent
**(b)** ⟨rival, winner⟩ arrogant

**insolite** /ɛ̃sɔlit/ *adj, nm* unusual

**insoluble** /ɛ̃sɔlybl/ *adj* insoluble

**insolvable** /ɛ̃sɔlvabl/ *adj* insolvent

**insomniaque** /ɛ̃sɔmnjak/ *adj, nmf* insomniac

**insomnie** /ɛ̃sɔmni/ *nf* insomnia

**insondable** /ɛ̃sɔ̃dabl/ *adj* unfathomable

**insonorisation** /ɛ̃sɔnɔʀizasjɔ̃/ *nf* soundproofing

**insonoriser** /ɛ̃sɔnɔʀize/ [1] *vtr* to soundproof

**insouciance** /ɛ̃susjɑ̃s/ *nf* carefreeness

**insouciant**, ∼**e** /ɛ̃susjɑ̃, ɑ̃t/ *adj* carefree

**insoumission** /ɛ̃sumisjɔ̃/ *nf*
**(a)** insubordination
**(b)** (Mil) draft-dodging

**insoupçonné**, ∼**e** /ɛ̃supsɔne/ *adj*
unsuspected

**insoutenable** /ɛ̃sutnabl/ *adj* **(a)** ⟨*pain*⟩
unbearable
**(b)** ⟨*opinion*⟩ untenable

**inspecter** /ɛ̃spɛkte/ [1] *vtr* to inspect

**inspecteur, -trice** /ɛ̃spɛktœʀ, tʀis/ *nm,f*
inspector
■ ∼ **de police** ≈ detective constable (GB);
∼ **du travail** health and safety inspector

**inspection** /ɛ̃spɛksjɔ̃/ *nf* **(a)** inspection
**(b)** inspectorate

**inspiration** /ɛ̃spiʀasjɔ̃/ *nf* inspiration

**inspirer** /ɛ̃spiʀe/ [1] **1** *vtr* **(a)** to inspire
⟨*person*⟩; **être bien/mal inspiré de faire** to be
well-/ill-advised to do; **un roman inspiré des
vieux contes populaires** a novel based on old
folk tales
**(b)** to appeal to; **ça ne m'inspire pas** that
doesn't appeal to me
**(c)** ∼ **la méfiance à qn** to inspire distrust in
sb
**2** *vi* to breathe in, to inhale
**3 s'inspirer** *v refl* (+ *v être*) **s'**∼ **de** to
draw one's inspiration from

**instabilité** /ɛ̃stabilite/ *nf* (gen) instability

**instable** /ɛ̃stabl/ *adj* (gen) unstable;
⟨*weather*⟩ unsettled

**installateur, -trice** /ɛ̃stalatœʀ, tʀis/
*nm,f* fitter

**installation** /ɛ̃stalasjɔ̃/ **1** *nf*
**(a)** installation, putting in
**(b)** system; ∼ **électrique** (electric) wiring
**(c)** move; **depuis mon** ∼ **à Paris** since I
moved to Paris
**2 installations** *nf pl* facilities

**installé**, ∼**e** /ɛ̃stale/ **1** *pp* ▶ INSTALLER
**2** *pp adj* ⟨*person*⟩ living (à in); ⟨*company*⟩
based; **être bien** ∼ **dans un fauteuil** to be
ensconced in an armchair; **ils sont bien** ∼**s
dans leur nouvelle maison** they're very snug
in their new home; **c'est un homme** ∼
(figurative) he's very nicely set up

**installer** /ɛ̃stale/ [1] **1** *vtr* **(a)** to install, to
put in ⟨*central heating, sink*⟩; to put up
⟨*shelves*⟩; to connect ⟨*gas*⟩
**(b)** to put ⟨*guest*⟩ (dans in); ∼ **qn dans un
fauteuil** to sit sb in an armchair; ∼ **qn à un
poste** to appoint sb to a post
**2 s'installer** *v refl* (+ *v être*) **(a)** ⟨*recession*⟩
to set in; ⟨*illness*⟩ to take hold; **le doute
commence à s'**∼ **dans leur esprit** they're
beginning to have doubts
**(b) s'**∼ **à son compte** to set up one's own
business
**(c)** to settle; **partir s'**∼ **à l'étranger** to go and
live abroad; **je viendrai te voir quand tu
seras installé** I'll come and see you when
you're settled in; **s'**∼ **au soleil** to sit in the

sun; **s'**∼ **à son bureau** to settle down at
one's desk; **installe-toi, j'arrive!** make
yourself at home, I'm coming!

**instamment** /ɛ̃stamɑ̃/ *adv* insistently

**instance** /ɛ̃stɑ̃s/ *nf* **(a)** authority; **les** ∼**s
d'un parti politique** the leaders of a political
party
**(b) être en** ∼ **de divorce** to be engaged in
divorce proceedings

**instant**, ∼**e** /ɛ̃stɑ̃, ɑ̃t/ *nm* moment,
instant; **à tout** *or* **chaque** ∼ all the time; **par**
∼**s** at times; **pour l'**∼ for the moment; **il
devrait arriver d'un** ∼ **à l'autre** he should
arrive any minute now; **à l'**∼ **même où** just
when

**instantané**, ∼**e** /ɛ̃stɑ̃tane/ **1** *adj*
instantaneous; ⟨*drink, soup*⟩ instant
**2** *nm* snapshot

**instar: à l'instar de** /alɛ̃staʀdə/ *phr*
following the example of

**instaurer** /ɛ̃stɔʀe/ [1] *vtr* to establish
⟨*regime, dialogue*⟩; to impose ⟨*curfew*⟩

**instigateur, -trice** /ɛ̃stigatœʀ, tʀis/
*nm,f* **(a)** instigator
**(b)** originator

**instigation** /ɛ̃stigasjɔ̃/ *nf* **à l'**∼ **de qn** at
sb's instigation

**instiller** /ɛ̃stile/ [1] *vtr* to instil (GB)

**instinct** /ɛ̃stɛ̃/ *nm* instinct; **d'**∼
instinctively

**instinctif, -ive** /ɛ̃stɛ̃ktif, iv/ *adj*
instinctive

**instituer** /ɛ̃stitɥe/ [1] *vtr* to institute

**institut** /ɛ̃stity/ *nm* **(a)** institute
**(b)** ∼ **de beauté** beauty salon *or* parlour
(GB)
■ **Institut universitaire de formation des
maîtres, IUFM** *primary teacher training
college*; **Institut universitaire de technologie,
IUT** university institute of technology

**instituteur, -trice** /ɛ̃stitytœʀ, tʀis/ *nm,f*
(primary school) teacher

**institution** /ɛ̃stitysjɔ̃/ *nf* **(a)** institution
**(b)** private school

**institutrice** ▶ INSTITUTEUR

**instructeur** /ɛ̃stʀyktœʀ/ *nm* (gen, Mil)
instructor

**instructif, -ive** /ɛ̃stʀyktif, iv/ *adj* (gen)
instructive; ⟨*experience*⟩ enlightening

**instruction** /ɛ̃stʀyksjɔ̃/ **1** *nf* **(a)** (gen)
education; (Mil) training
**(b)** (Law) *preparation of a case for trial*
**2 instructions** *nf pl* instructions
■ ∼ **civique** civics; ∼ **religieuse** religious
instruction

**instruire** /ɛ̃stʀɥiʀ/ [69] **1** *vtr* **(a)** to teach
⟨*child*⟩; to train ⟨*soldiers*⟩
**(b)** (Law) ∼ **une affaire** to prepare a case for
trial
**2 s'instruire** *v refl* (+ *v être*) to learn

**instruit**, ∼**e** /ɛ̃stʀɥi, it/ *adj* educated

**instrument** /ɛ̃stʀymɑ̃/ *nm* (gen, Mus)
instrument; ∼ **à cordes/à percussion/à vent** ⋯⟶

string/percussion/wind instrument; **jouer
d'un ~** to play an instrument; **être l'~ de qn**
to be sb's tool
■ **~s de bord** controls

**insu: à l'insu de** /alɛ̃sydə/ *phr* **à l'~ de qn**
without sb knowing

**insubordination** /ɛ̃sybɔRdinasjɔ̃/ *nf*
insubordination

**insubordonné, ~e** /ɛ̃sybɔRdɔne/ *adj*
rebellious; insubordinate

**insuffisamment** /ɛ̃syfizamɑ̃/ *adv*
insufficiently; inadequately

**insuffisance** /ɛ̃syfizɑ̃s/ *nf*
(a) insufficiency, shortage
(b) poor standard; **l'~ de la production** the
shortfall in production
(c) (Med) insufficiency

**insuffisant, ~e** /ɛ̃syfizɑ̃, ɑ̃t/ *adj*
(a) insufficient
(b) inadequate

**insuffler** /ɛ̃syfle/ [1] *vtr* to instil (GB); **~ la
vie à qn** to breathe life into sb

**insulaire** /ɛ̃sylɛR/ *adj* ⟨*population*⟩ island;
⟨*mentality*⟩ insular

**insultant, ~e** /ɛ̃syltɑ̃, ɑ̃t/ *adj* insulting

**insulte** /ɛ̃sylt/ *nf* insult

**insulter** /ɛ̃sylte/ [1] *vtr* to insult; to shout
abuse at; ⟨*attitude*⟩ to be an insult to

**insupportable** /ɛ̃sypɔRtabl/ *adj*
unbearable

**insurgé, ~e** /ɛ̃syRʒe/ *nm,f* insurgent,
rebel

**insurger: s'insurger** /ɛ̃syRʒe/ [13] *v refl*
(+ *v être*) (a) to rise up
(b) to protest

**insurmontable** /ɛ̃syRmɔ̃tabl/ *adj*
insurmountable; insuperable; unconquerable

**insurrection** /ɛ̃syRɛksjɔ̃/ *nf* insurrection

**intact, ~e** /ɛ̃takt/ *adj* intact

**intarissable** /ɛ̃taRisabl/ *adj* ⟨*imagination*⟩
inexhaustible; ⟨*source*⟩ never-ending

**intégral, ~e,** *mpl* **-aux** /ɛ̃tegRal, o/ *adj*
(a) ⟨*payment*⟩ full, in full
(b) ⟨*tan*⟩ all-over
(c) ⟨*text*⟩ unabridged; **version ~e** uncut
version

**intégralement** /ɛ̃tegRalmɑ̃/ *adv* ⟨*pay*⟩ in
full

**intégralité** /ɛ̃tegRalite/ *nf* **l'~ de leur
salaire** their entire salary

**intégrante** /ɛ̃tegRɑ̃t/ *adj f* **faire partie ~ de
qch** to be an integral part of sth

**intégration** /ɛ̃tegRasjɔ̃/ *nf* integration

**intègre** /ɛ̃tɛgR/ *adj* ⟨*person, life*⟩ honest

**intégrer** /ɛ̃tegRe/ [14] **1** *vtr* (a) to insert
(b) to integrate ⟨*population*⟩
(c) (colloq) **il vient d'~ Harvard** he has just
got into Harvard
**2 s'intégrer** *v refl* (+ *v être*)
(a) ⟨*population*⟩ to integrate
(b) ⟨*building*⟩ to fit in

**intégrisme** /ɛ̃tegRism/ *nm*
fundamentalism

**intégrité** /ɛ̃tegRite/ *nf* integrity

**intellect** /ɛ̃telɛkt/ *nm* intellect

**intellectuel, -elle** /ɛ̃telɛktɥel/ **1** *adj*
⟨*work*⟩ intellectual; ⟨*effort*⟩ mental
**2** *nm,f* intellectual

**intelligence** /ɛ̃teliʒɑ̃s/ *nf* (a) intelligence
(b) **agir d'~ avec qn** to act in agreement
with sb

**intelligent, ~e** /ɛ̃teliʒɑ̃, ɑ̃t/ *adj*
intelligent; clever

**intelligible** /ɛ̃teliʒibl/ *adj* intelligible

**intempéries** /ɛ̃tɑ̃peRi/ *nf pl* bad weather

**intempestif, -ive** /ɛ̃tɑ̃pɛstif, iv/ *adj*
untimely; ⟨*curiosity, zeal*⟩ misplaced

**intemporel, -elle** /ɛ̃tɑ̃pɔRɛl/ *adj* timeless

**intenable** /ɛ̃t(ə)nabl/ *adj* (a) ⟨*situation*⟩
unbearable
(b) ⟨*child*⟩ difficult

**intendance** /ɛ̃tɑ̃dɑ̃s/ *nf* (Sch)
administration

**intendant, ~e** /ɛ̃tɑ̃dɑ̃, ɑ̃t/ **1** *nm,f* (Sch)
bursar
**2** *nm* (Mil) quartermaster; paymaster

**intense** /ɛ̃tɑ̃s/ *adj* (gen) intense; ⟨*red, green*⟩
vivid; ⟨*traffic*⟩ heavy

**intensif, -ive** /ɛ̃tɑ̃sif, iv/ *adj* intensive

**intensification** /ɛ̃tɑ̃sifikasjɔ̃/ *nf*
intensification

**intensifier** /ɛ̃tɑ̃sifje/ [2] *vtr*,
**s'intensifier** *v refl* (+ *v être*) to intensify

**intensité** /ɛ̃tɑ̃site/ *nf* intensity

**intensivement** /ɛ̃tɑ̃sivmɑ̃/ *adv*
intensively

**intenter** /ɛ̃tɑ̃te/ [1] *vtr* **~ un procès à qn** to
sue sb

**intention** /ɛ̃tɑ̃sjɔ̃/ *nf* intention; **c'est l'~
qui compte** it's the thought that counts; **à l'~
de qn** ⟨*remark*⟩ aimed at sb

**intentionné, ~e** /ɛ̃tɑ̃sjɔne/ *adj* **bien/mal
~** well-/ill-intentioned

**intentionnel, -elle** /ɛ̃tɑ̃sjɔnɛl/ *adj*
intentional

**interaction** /ɛ̃teRaksjɔ̃/ *nf* interaction

**interbancaire** /ɛ̃teRbɑ̃kɛR/ *adj* interbank

**intercalaire** /ɛ̃teRkalɛR/ **1** *adj* **feuille** *or*
**feuillet ~** insert
**2** *nm* divider

**intercaler** /ɛ̃teRkale/ [1] *vtr* to insert

**intercéder** /ɛ̃teRsede/ [14] *vi* to intercede

**intercepter** /ɛ̃teRsɛpte/ [1] *vtr* to intercept

**interchangeable** /ɛ̃teRʃɑ̃ʒabl/ *adj*
interchangeable

**interclasse** /ɛ̃teRklas/ *nm* break (between
classes)

**interdiction** /ɛ̃teRdiksjɔ̃/ *nf* (a) banning;
'**~ de dépasser**' 'no overtaking' (GB), 'no
passing' (US)
(b) ban; **lever une ~** to lift a ban
■ **~ de séjour** prohibition on residence

**interdire** /ɛ̃teRdiR/ [65] *vtr* to ban; **~ à qn
de faire, ~ que qn fasse** to forbid sb to do

**interdisciplinaire** /ɛ̃teRdisiplinɛR/ *adj*
(Sch) cross-curricular; (Univ) interdisciplinary

**interdit**, **∼e** /ɛ̃tɛʀdi, it/ **1** *pp* ▶
INTERDIRE
**2** *pp adj* prohibited, forbidden; **entrée** ∼e
no entry *or* admittance; **film** ∼ **aux moins de
13 ans** film unsuitable for children under 13
**3** *adj* dumbfounded
**4** *nm* proscription; taboo

**intéressant**, **∼e** /ɛ̃teʀɛsɑ̃, ɑ̃t/ **1** *adj*
(a) interesting
(b) ⟨*prices, conditions*⟩ attractive; **il est plus
∼ de payer au comptant qu'à crédit** it's
better to pay in cash rather than by credit
**2** *nm,f* **faire l'∼** *or* **son ∼** to show off

**intéressé**, **∼e** /ɛ̃teʀese/ **1** *pp* ▶
INTÉRESSER
**2** *pp adj* (a) interested
(b) attentive
(c) **les parties** ∼**es** those concerned; **les
personnes** ∼**es aux bénéfices** people with a
share in the profits
(d) ⟨*person*⟩ self-interested; ⟨*action*⟩
motivated by self-interest; **ses conseils
étaient** ∼**s** he/she had a selfish motive for
giving that advice
**3** *nm,f* person concerned

**intéressement** /ɛ̃teʀɛsmɑ̃/ *nm* share in
the profits

**intéresser** /ɛ̃teʀese/ [1] **1** *vtr* (a) to
interest; **ça ne m'intéresse pas** I'm not
interested
(b) ⟨*problem, decision*⟩ to concern
(c) ∼ **les salariés aux bénéfices** to offer a
profit-sharing scheme to employees
**2** **s'intéresser** *v refl* (+ *v être*) **s'∼ à** (gen)
to be interested in; to take an interest in

**intérêt** /ɛ̃teʀɛ/ *nm* (a) interest; **recherche
digne d'∼** worthwhile research; **l'∼
supérieur de la nation** the higher good of the
country; **je ne vois pas l'∼ de cette réforme**
I can't see the point of this reform; **par ∼**
⟨*act*⟩ out of self-interest; ⟨*marry*⟩ for money
(b) (financial) interest

**interférence** /ɛ̃tɛʀfeʀɑ̃s/ *nf* interference

**interférer** /ɛ̃tɛʀfeʀe/ [14] *vi* to interfere

**intérieur**, **∼e** /ɛ̃teʀjœʀ/ **1** *adj*
(a) internal, interior; ⟨*sea*⟩ inland; ⟨*pocket*⟩
inside; **le côté ∼** the inside
(b) domestic; **sur le plan ∼** on the domestic
front
(c) ⟨*regulations*⟩ internal
**2** *nm* (of box, newspaper) inside; (of car, house)
interior; **à l'∼** inside; indoors; **à l'∼ des
terres** inland; **d'∼** ⟨*game*⟩ indoor; **être fier de
son ∼** to be proud of one's home

**intérim** /ɛ̃teʀim/ *nm* (a) interim (period);
**président par ∼** acting president; **assurer
l'∼ de** to stand in for
(b) temporary work; **travailler en ∼** to temp
(colloq)

**intérimaire** /ɛ̃teʀimɛʀ/ *adj* ⟨*committee*⟩
interim; ⟨*minister*⟩ acting; ⟨*job, staff*⟩
temporary

**intérioriser** /ɛ̃teʀjɔʀize/ [1] *vtr* to
internalize

**interjection** /ɛ̃tɛʀʒɛksjɔ̃/ *nf* interjection

**interligne** /ɛ̃tɛʀliɲ/ *nm* line space

**interlocuteur**, **-trice** /ɛ̃tɛʀlɔkytœʀ,
tʀis/ *nm,f* (a) **mon ∼** the person I am/was
talking to
(b) (in negotiations) representative
(c) **Louis est notre seul ∼** Louis is our only
contact

**interloquer** /ɛ̃tɛʀlɔke/ [1] *vtr* to take [sb]
aback

**interlude** /ɛ̃tɛʀlyd/ *nm* interlude

**intermède** /ɛ̃tɛʀmɛd/ *nm* interlude

**intermédiaire** /ɛ̃tɛʀmedjɛʀ/ **1** *adj* ⟨*rate,
stage*⟩ intermediate
**2** *nmf* (in negotiations) go-between; (in industry)
middleman
**3** *phr* **par l'∼ de** through

**interminable** /ɛ̃tɛʀminabl/ *adj*
(a) interminable, never-ending
(b) endless

**intermittence** /ɛ̃tɛʀmitɑ̃s/ *nf* **par ∼**
⟨*rain*⟩ on and off; ⟨*work*⟩ intermittently

**intermittent**, **∼e** /ɛ̃tɛʀmitɑ̃, ɑ̃t/ *adj*
⟨*rain, fever*⟩ intermittent; ⟨*noise, efforts*⟩
sporadic

**internat** /ɛ̃tɛʀna/ *nm* boarding school

**international**, **∼e**, *mpl* **-aux**
/ɛ̃tɛʀnasjɔnal, o/ *adj* international

**interne** /ɛ̃tɛʀn/ **1** *adj* (gen) internal;
⟨*training*⟩ in-house; ⟨*ear*⟩ inner
**2** *nmf* (a) (Sch) boarder
(b) ∼ **(en médecine)** houseman (GB), intern
(US)

**internement** /ɛ̃tɛʀnəmɑ̃/ *nm* (Med)
committal (to a psychiatric institution)

**interner** /ɛ̃tɛʀne/ [1] *vtr* to commit ⟨*mental
patient*⟩

**Internet** /ɛ̃tɛʀnɛt/ *nm* Internet; **naviguer
sur (l') ∼** to surf the Internet

**interpellation** /ɛ̃tɛʀpelasjɔ̃/ *nf* **procéder
à des ∼s** to take people in for questioning

**interpeller** /ɛ̃tɛʀpəle/ [1] *vtr* (a) to call
out to; to shout at
(b) to question; (in police station) to take [sb]
in for questioning

**interphone®** /ɛ̃tɛʀfɔn/ *nm* (a) intercom
(b) entry phone

**interposer: s'interposer** /ɛ̃tɛʀpoze/ [1]
*v refl* (+ *v être*) to intervene; **par personne
interposée** through an intermediary

**interprétariat** /ɛ̃tɛʀpʀetaʀja/ *nm*
interpreting

**interprétation** /ɛ̃tɛʀpʀetasjɔ̃/ *nf* (a) (gen,
Mus) interpretation
(b) (profession) interpreting

**interprète** /ɛ̃tɛʀpʀɛt/ *nmf* (a) interpreter
(b) performer
(c) spokesperson

**interpréter** /ɛ̃tɛʀpʀete/ [14] *vtr* (a) to play
⟨*role, sonata*⟩; to sing ⟨*song*⟩
(b) to interpret

**interpréteur** /ɛ̃tɛʀpʀetœʀ/ *nm* (Comput)
interpreter

**interrogateur**, **-trice** /ɛ̃tɛʀɔgatœʀ,
tʀis/ *adj* enquiring; **d'un air ∼** enquiringly

**interrogatif, -ive** /ɛ̃tɛʀɔgatif, iv/ *adj*
interrogative

**interrogation** /ɛ̃tɛʀɔgasjɔ̃/ *nf* (a) (of witness)
questioning
(b) (in grammar) question
(c) (Sch) test; ~ **orale** oral test

**interrogatoire** /ɛ̃tɛʀɔgatwaʀ/ *nm* (gen)
interrogation; (by police) questioning

**interroger** /ɛ̃tɛʀɔʒe/ [13] **1** *vtr* (a) (gen) to
question; to ask; (figurative) to examine
⟨conscience⟩; **être interrogé comme témoin**
(Law) to be called as a witness
(b) ~ **son répondeur** to check one's calls
(c) (Sch) to test
**2 s'interroger** *v refl* (+ *v être*) **s'~ sur** to
wonder about

**interrompre** /ɛ̃tɛʀɔ̃pʀ/ [53] **1** *vtr* (a) to
interrupt; to break off ⟨dialogue⟩; ⟨person⟩ to
cease ⟨activity⟩; ~ **son repas pour faire** to
stop eating to do
(b) to put an end to ⟨holiday⟩; to stop
⟨treatment⟩; to terminate ⟨pregnancy⟩
**2 s'interrompre** *v refl* (+ *v être*)
(a) ⟨person, conversation⟩ to break off
(b) ⟨rain⟩ to stop

**interrupteur** /ɛ̃tɛʀyptœʀ/ *nm* switch

**interruption** /ɛ̃tɛʀypsjɔ̃/ *nf* (a) break;
**sans** ~ continuously
(b) ending; **l'~ du dialogue entre** the
breaking off of the dialogue (GB) between

**intersection** /ɛ̃tɛʀsɛksjɔ̃/ *nf* intersection

**interstice** /ɛ̃tɛʀstis/ *nm* (in floor) crack;
(in shutters, blinds) chink

**intervalle** /ɛ̃tɛʀval/ *nm* (a) space; **à ~s
réguliers** at regular intervals
(b) interval; **dans l'~** meanwhile, in the
meantime

**intervenir** /ɛ̃tɛʀvəniʀ/ [36] *vi* (a) ⟨changes⟩
to take place; ⟨agreement⟩ to be reached
(b) ⟨speaker⟩ to speak
(c) (in emergency) ⟨police⟩ to intervene
(d) ~ **auprès de qn pour qn** to intercede
with sb on sb's behalf

**intervention** /ɛ̃tɛʀvɑ̃sjɔ̃/ *nf*
(a) intervention
(b) speech; lecture
(c) (Med) ~ **(chirurgicale)** operation

**intervertir** /ɛ̃tɛʀvɛʀtiʀ/ [3] *vtr* to invert

**interviewer** /ɛ̃tɛʀvjuve/ [1] *vtr* to
interview

**intestin** /ɛ̃tɛstɛ̃/ *nm* bowel, intestine

**intestinal, ~e, *mpl* -aux** /ɛ̃tɛstinal, o/
*adj* intestinal

**intime** /ɛ̃tim/ **1** *adj* (a) ⟨life, diary⟩
private; ⟨friend, relationship⟩ intimate;
⟨hygiene⟩ personal
(b) ⟨gathering⟩ intimate; ⟨conversation⟩
private; ⟨dinner⟩ quiet
(c) ⟨room⟩ cosy (GB), cozy (US)
(d) ⟨knowledge⟩ intimate
**2** *nmf* close friend

**intimement** /ɛ̃timmɑ̃/ *adv* intimately; **je
suis ~ convaincu que...** I'm absolutely
convinced that...

**intimidation** /ɛ̃timidasjɔ̃/ *nf* intimidation;
**d'~** ⟨measures, remarks⟩ intimidatory

**intimider** /ɛ̃timide/ [1] *vtr* to intimidate

**intimité** /ɛ̃timite/ *nf* (a) intimacy
(b) privacy; **dans la plus stricte ~** in the
strictest privacy
(c) private life
(d) (of house, setting) cosiness

**intitulé** /ɛ̃tityle/ *nm* title, heading

**intituler** /ɛ̃tityle/ [1] **1** *vtr* to call
**2 s'intituler** *v refl* (+ *v être*) to be called,
to be entitled

**intolérable** /ɛ̃tɔleʀabl/ *adj* intolerable;
deeply shocking

**intolérance** /ɛ̃tɔleʀɑ̃s/ *nf* intolerance

**intolérant, ~e** /ɛ̃tɔleʀɑ̃, ɑ̃t/ *adj*
intolerant

**intonation** /ɛ̃tɔnasjɔ̃/ *nf* intonation

**intoxication** /ɛ̃tɔksikasjɔ̃/ *nf* (a) (Med)
poisoning
(b) (figurative) disinformation

**intoxiquer** /ɛ̃tɔksike/ [1] **1** *vtr* to poison
**2 s'intoxiquer** *v refl* (+ *v être*) to poison
oneself

**intraitable** /ɛ̃tʀɛtabl/ *adj* inflexible

**intra-muros** /ɛ̃tʀamyʀos/ *adj inv* **Paris ~**
Paris itself

**intransigeance** /ɛ̃tʀɑ̃ziʒɑ̃s/ *nf*
intransigence

**intransigeant, ~e** /ɛ̃tʀɑ̃ziʒɑ̃, ɑ̃t/ *adj*
⟨attitude⟩ uncompromising; ⟨person⟩
intransigent

**intraveineuse** /ɛ̃tʀavɛnøz/ *nf*
intravenous injection

**intrépide** /ɛ̃tʀepid/ *adj* intrepid, bold

**intrépidité** /ɛ̃tʀepidite/ *nf* boldness

**intrigant, ~e** /ɛ̃tʀigɑ̃, ɑ̃t/ *nm,f* schemer

**intrigue** /ɛ̃tʀig/ *nf* (a) intrigue
(b) plot; **une ~ policière** a detective story

**intriguer** /ɛ̃tʀige/ [1] *vtr* to intrigue

**intrinsèque** /ɛ̃tʀɛ̃sɛk/ *adj* intrinsic

**introduction** /ɛ̃tʀɔdyksjɔ̃/ *nf* (a) (gen)
introduction
(b) (of key, probe) insertion

**introduire** /ɛ̃tʀɔdɥiʀ/ [69] **1** *vtr* (a) to
insert ⟨object⟩
(b) to usher [sb] in ⟨visitor⟩; (surreptitiously) to
smuggle [sb] in
(c) to introduce ⟨person⟩
(d) to introduce ⟨product, idea⟩
**2 s'introduire** *v refl* (+ *v être*) **s'~ dans** to
get into

**introduit, ~e** /ɛ̃tʀɔdɥi, it/ ▶ INTRODUIRE

**introspection** /ɛ̃tʀɔspɛksjɔ̃/ *nf*
introspection

**introverti, ~e** /ɛ̃tʀɔvɛʀti/ *nm,f* introvert

**intrus, ~e** /ɛ̃tʀy, yz/ *nm,f* intruder

**intrusion** /ɛ̃tʀyzjɔ̃/ *nf* (a) (gen) intrusion
(b) interference

**intuitif, ~ive** /ɛ̃tɥitif, iv/ *adj* intuitive

**intuition** /ɛ̃tɥisjɔ̃/ *nf* intuition

**inusable** /inyzabl/ *adj* hardwearing

**inusité, ~e** /inyzite/ *adj* uncommon

**inutile** /inytil/ *adj* useless; pointless; needless; (**il est**) ∼ **de faire** there's no point in doing; ∼ **de dire que** needless to say; **sans risques** ∼**s** without unnecessary risks

**inutilement** /inytilmã/ *adv* unnecessarily; needlessly; in vain

**inutilisable** /inytilizabl/ *adj* unusable

**inutilité** /inytilite/ *nf* (of expense, action) pointlessness

**invalide** /ɛ̃valid/ **1** *adj* disabled **2** *nmf* disabled person

**invalidité** /ɛ̃validite/ *nf* (Med) disability

**invariable** /ɛ̃vaʀjabl/ *adj* invariable

**invasion** /ɛ̃vazjɔ̃/ *nf* invasion

**invendable** /ɛ̃vãdabl/ *adj* unsaleable

**invendu, ∼e** /ɛ̃vãdy/ *adj* unsold

**inventaire** /ɛ̃vãtɛʀ/ *nm* (a) stocktaking (GB), inventory (US) **(b)** stocklist (GB), inventory (US) **(c)** (of wardrobe, suitcase) list of contents

**inventer** /ɛ̃vãte/ [1] **1** *vtr* to invent; to devise; **je n'invente rien** I'm not making it up **2 s'inventer** *v refl* (+ *v être*) **ça ne s'invente pas** that has to be true **IDIOMS il n'a pas inventé la poudre** (colloq) he is not very bright

**inventeur, -trice** /ɛ̃vãtœʀ, tʀis/ *nmf* inventor

**inventif, -ive** /ɛ̃vãtif, iv/ *adj* (a) inventive **(b)** resourceful

**invention** /ɛ̃vãsjɔ̃/ *nf* (a) invention **(b)** fabrication; **c'est de l'**∼ **pure** it's a complete fabrication

**inventorier** /ɛ̃vãtɔʀje/ [2] *vtr* to make out an inventory of

**inverse** /ɛ̃vɛʀs/ **1** *adj* (gen) opposite; **dans l'ordre** ∼ (referring to list) in reverse order **2** *nm* (gen) **l'**∼ the opposite; **à l'**∼ conversely; **à l'**∼ **de ce qu'il croyait** contrary to what he thought

**inversement** /ɛ̃vɛʀsəmã/ *adv* (gen) conversely

**inverser** /ɛ̃vɛʀse/ [1] *vtr* (a) to invert ⟨*position*⟩; to reverse ⟨*roles*⟩; **image inversée** mirror image **(b)** to reverse ⟨*electric current*⟩

**inversion** /ɛ̃vɛʀsjɔ̃/ *nf* inversion; reversal

**invertébré, ∼e** /ɛ̃vɛʀtebʀe/ *adj* invertebrate

**invertir** /ɛ̃vɛʀtiʀ/ [3] *vtr* to reverse; to switch [sth] round ⟨*words*⟩

**investigation** /ɛ̃vɛstigasjɔ̃/ *nf* investigation; **d'**∼ investigative

**investir** /ɛ̃vɛstiʀ/ [3] **1** *vtr* (a) to invest ⟨*capital*⟩ **(b)** to invest ⟨*person, ambassador*⟩ **(c)** ⟨*police*⟩ to go into; ⟨*tourists, demonstrators*⟩ to take over **(d)** ⟨*army*⟩ to besiege **2 s'investir** *v refl* (+ *v être*) **s'**∼ **dans** to put a lot of oneself into; to invest emotionally in

**investissement** /ɛ̃vɛstismã/ *nm* (gen) investment; (Mil) investing

**investisseur** /ɛ̃vɛstisœʀ/ *nm* investor

**investiture** /ɛ̃vɛstityʀ/ *nf* investiture

**invétéré, ∼e** /ɛ̃vetere/ *adj* ⟨*drinker, thief*⟩ inveterate; ⟨*liar*⟩ compulsive

**invincible** /ɛ̃vɛ̃sibl/ *adj* ⟨*people*⟩ invincible

**inviolable** /ɛ̃vjɔlabl/ *adj* (gen) inviolable; ⟨*door, safe*⟩ impregnable

**invisible** /ɛ̃vizibl/ *adj* (a) invisible; **la route était** ∼ **depuis la maison** the road could not be seen from the house **(b)** ⟨*danger*⟩ unseen

**invitation** /ɛ̃vitasjɔ̃/ *nf* invitation

**invité, ∼e** /ɛ̃vite/ *nm,f* guest

**inviter** /ɛ̃vite/ [1] *vtr* to invite; **ceci invite à penser que...** this suggests that...

**invivable** /ɛ̃vivabl/ *adj* unbearable

**invocation** /ɛ̃vɔkasjɔ̃/ *nf* invocation

**involontaire** /ɛ̃vɔlɔ̃tɛʀ/ *adj* ⟨*reaction*⟩ involuntary; ⟨*mistake*⟩ unintentional

**invoquer** /ɛ̃vɔke/ [1] *vtr* to invoke

**invraisemblable** /ɛ̃vʀɛsãblabl/ *adj* **(a)** ⟨*story*⟩ unlikely; ⟨*explanation*⟩ implausible **(b)** (colloq) fantastic, incredible

**invraisemblance** /ɛ̃vʀɛsãblãs/ *nf* **(a)** unlikelihood **(b)** improbability

**invulnérable** /ɛ̃vylneʀabl/ *adj* invulnerable

**iode** /jɔd/ *nm* iodine

**iota** /jɔta/ *nm inv* iota **IDIOMS ne pas changer d'un** ∼ not to change one iota; **ne pas bouger d'un** ∼ not to move an inch

**ira** /iʀa/ ▶ ALLER[1]

**irai** /iʀe/ ▶ ALLER[1]

**iraient** /iʀe/ ▶ ALLER[1]

**irais** /iʀe/ ▶ ALLER[1]

**irait** /iʀe/ ▶ ALLER[1]

**iras** /iʀa/ ▶ ALLER[1]

**irascible** /iʀasibl/ *adj* ⟨*person*⟩ quick-tempered

**irez** /iʀe/ ▶ ALLER[1]

**iriez** /iʀje/ ▶ ALLER[1]

**irions** /iʀjɔ̃/ ▶ ALLER[1]

**iris** /iʀis/ *nm inv* (a) (flower) iris **(b)** (of eye) iris

**irisé, ∼e** /iʀize/ *adj* iridescent

**irlandais, ∼e** /iʀlãdɛ, ɛz/ **1** *adj* Irish **2** *nm* (language) Irish

**Irlandais, ∼e** /iʀlãdɛ, ɛz/ *nm,f* Irishman/Irishwoman

**Irlande** /iʀlãd/ *pr nf* Ireland; **la République d'**∼ the Republic of Ireland; **l'**∼ **du Nord** Northern Ireland

**ironie** /iʀɔni/ *nf* irony; **faire de l'**∼ to be ironic

**ironique** /iʀɔnik/ *adj* ironic

**ironiser** /iʀɔnize/ [1] *vi* to be ironic (**sur** about)

**irons** /iʁɔ̃/ ▶ ALLER[1]

**iront** /iʁɔ̃/ ▶ ALLER[1]

**irradier** /iʁadje/ [2] [1] *vtr* to irradiate [2] *vi* to radiate

**irrattrapable** /iʁatʁapabl/ *adj* irretrievable

**irréalisable** /iʁealizabl/ *adj* ⟨dream⟩ impossible; ⟨plan⟩ unworkable

**irrécupérable** /iʁekypeʁabl/ *adj*
(a) irrecoverable
(b) damaged beyond repair
(c) ⟨delinquent⟩ beyond help

**irréductible** /iʁedyktibl/ *nmf* diehard

**irréel, -elle** /iʁeɛl/ *adj* unreal

**irréfléchi, ~e** /iʁefleʃi/ *adj* ill-considered

**irréfutable** /iʁefytabl/ *adj* irrefutable

**irrégularité** /iʁegylaʁite/ *nf* irregularity

**irrégulier, -ière** /iʁegylje, ɛʁ/ *adj*
(a) irregular; uneven
(b) ⟨procedure⟩ irregular; **immigré en situation irrégulière** illegal immigrant
(c) ⟨athlete⟩ whose performance is uneven

**irrégulièrement** /iʁegyljɛʁmɑ̃/ *adv*
(a) illegally
(b) irregularly; unevenly; erratically

**irrémédiable** /iʁ(ʁ)emedjabl/ *adj* irreparable

**irremplaçable** /iʁɑ̃plasabl/ *adj* irreplaceable

**irréparable** /iʁepaʁabl/ [1] *adj* ⟨car⟩ beyond repair; ⟨damage, crime⟩ irreparable [2] *nm* **commettre l'~** to go beyond the point of no return

**irrépressible** /iʁepʁesibl/ *adj* (gen) irrepressible; ⟨tears⟩ uncontrollable

**irréprochable** /iʁepʁoʃabl/ *adj* ⟨life, employee⟩ beyond reproach; ⟨work⟩ perfect

**irrésistible** /iʁezistibl/ *adj* irresistible; ⟨person, joke⟩ hilarious

**irrésolu, ~e** /iʁezɔly/ *adj* ⟨person⟩ indecisive; ⟨problem, mystery⟩ unsolved

**irrespirable** /iʁɛspiʁabl/ *adj* ⟨air⟩ unbreathable; ⟨atmosphere⟩ stifling

**irresponsable** /iʁɛspɔ̃sabl/ *adj* irresponsible

**irrévérencieux, -ieuse** /iʁeveʁɑ̃sjø, øz/ *adj* irreverent

**irréversible** /iʁevɛʁsibl/ *adj* irreversible

**irrévocable** /iʁevɔkabl/ *adj* irrevocable

**irrigation** /iʁigasjɔ̃/ *nf* (a) (of land) irrigation
(b) (Med) supply of blood

**irriguer** /iʁige/ [1] *vtr* to irrigate

**irritation** /iʁitasjɔ̃/ *nf* (gen, Med) irritation

**irriter** /iʁite/ [1] [1] *vtr* (a) to irritate, to annoy
(b) (Med) to irritate

[2] **s'irriter** *v refl* (+ *v être*) (a) to get angry
(b) (Med) to become irritated

**irruption** /iʁypsjɔ̃/ *nf* **faire ~ dans** to burst into ⟨room⟩

**islam** /islam/ *nm* **l'~** Islam

**islamique** /islamik/ *adj* Islamic

**islamisme** /islamism/ *nm* Islam

**Islande** /islɑ̃d/ *pr nf* Iceland

**isolant, ~e** /izɔlɑ̃, ɑ̃t/ *adj* insulating

**isolation** /izɔlasjɔ̃/ *nf* insulation

**isolement** /izɔlmɑ̃/ *nm* (a) (of village) remoteness; (of house) isolated location
(b) (of patient, politician) isolation; (of prisoner) solitary confinement

**isoler** /izɔle/ [1] [1] *vtr* (a) to isolate ⟨sick person, dissident⟩; to put [sb] in solitary confinement ⟨prisoner⟩
(b) to isolate ⟨gene, substance⟩
(c) to soundproof; to insulate
(d) to insulate ⟨wire⟩
[2] **s'isoler** *v refl* (+ *v être*) to isolate oneself

**isoloir** /izɔlwaʁ/ *nm* voting *or* polling (GB) booth

**isotherme** /izotɛʁm/ *adj* refrigerated; **boîte ~** ice box; **sac ~** cool bag

**issu, ~e**[1] /isy/ *adj* **être ~ de** to come from; to result from

**issue**[2] /isy/ *nf* (a) exit; **'sans ~'** 'no exit'
(b) solution; **situation sans ~** situation with no solution
(c) outcome; **à l'~ de** at the end of; **à l'~ de trois jours de pourparlers** at the close of three days of talks
■ **~ de secours** emergency exit

**Italie** /itali/ *pr nf* Italy

**italien, -ienne** /italjɛ̃, ɛn/ [1] *adj* Italian [2] *nm* (language) Italian

**italique** /italik/ *nm* italics

**itinéraire** /itineʁɛʁ/ *nm* (a) (gen) route; (detailed) itinerary
(b) (figurative) career
■ **~ bis** alternative route; **~ de délestage** relief route

**itinérant, ~e** /itineʁɑ̃, ɑ̃t/ *adj* ⟨exhibition⟩ touring; ⟨life⟩ peripatetic; ⟨circus⟩ travelling (GB)

**IUFM** /iyɛfɛm/ *nm*: *abbr* ▶ INSTITUT

**IUT** /iyte/ *nm*: *abbr* ▶ INSTITUT

**ivoire** /ivwaʁ/ *adj inv, nm* ivory

**ivoirien, -ienne** /ivwaʁjɛ̃, ɛn/ *adj* of the Ivory Coast

**ivre** /ivʁ/ *adj* (a) drunk, intoxicated
(b) **~ de rage** wild with rage

**ivresse** /ivʁɛs/ *nf* (a) intoxication
(b) exhilaration

**ivrogne** /ivʁɔɲ/ *nmf* drunkard

# Jj

**j, J** /ʒi/ *nm inv* j, J; **le jour J** D-day

**j'** ▶ JE

**jabot** /ʒabo/ *nm* **(a)** (of bird) crop
**(b)** (of shirt) jabot

**jacasser** /ʒakase/ [1] *vi* to chatter

**jachère** /ʒaʃɛʀ/ *nf* **(terre en)** ~ fallow land

**jacinthe** /ʒasɛ̃t/ *nf* hyacinth

**jackpot** /(d)ʒakpɔt/ *nm* **(a)** jackpot
**(b)** slot machine

**jacquet** /ʒakɛ/ *nm* backgammon

**jacter** /ʒakte/ [1] *vi* (slang) to jaw (colloq), to talk

**jade** /ʒad/ *nm* jade

**jadis** /ʒadis/ *adv* formerly, in the past

**jaguar** /ʒagwaʀ/ *nm* jaguar

**jaillir** /ʒajiʀ/ [3] *vi* ‹liquid› to gush out; ‹tears› to flow; ‹flame› to shoot up; ‹truth› to emerge

**jais** /ʒɛ/ *nm inv* **(a)** jet
**(b)** (noir) de ~ jet-black

**jalon** /ʒalɔ̃/ *nm* **(a)** marker
**(b)** (figurative) **poser les** ~**s de** to prepare the ground for

**jalonner** /ʒalɔne/ [1] *vtr* **(a)** ‹trees› to line ‹road›; ‹incidents› to punctuate ‹career›
**(b)** to mark out ‹road›

**jalousement** /ʒaluzmɑ̃/ *adv* jealously; enviously

**jalouser** /ʒaluze/ [1] *vtr* to be jealous of

**jalousie** /ʒaluzi/ *nf* **(a)** jealousy
**(b)** slatted blind

**jaloux, -ouse** /ʒalu, uz/ **1** *adj* jealous
**2** *nm,f* jealous man/woman

**jamais** /ʒamɛ/ *adv* **(a)** never; **rien n'est** ~ **certain** nothing is ever certain; **sait-on** ~? you never know; ~ **de la vie!** never!
**(b)** ever; **plus belle que** ~ prettier than ever; **si** ~ if
**(c)** **à tout** ~ forever
**(d)** **ne...** ~ **que** only; **il ne fait** ~ **que son devoir** he is only doing his duty

**jambe** /ʒɑ̃b/ *nf* leg; **avoir de bonnes** ~**s** to have strong legs; **courir à toutes** ~**s** to run as fast as one's legs can carry one; **j'ai les** ~**s comme du coton** (colloq) I feel weak at the knees; **traîner la** ~ (colloq) to trudge along

**IDIOMS cela me fait une belle** ~ (colloq) a fat lot of good that does me (colloq); **il ne tient plus sur ses** ~**s** he can hardly stand up; **prendre ses** ~**s à son cou** to take to one's heels; **tenir la** ~ **à qn** to keep talking to sb; **par-dessus** *or* **par-dessous la** ~ in a slipshod manner

**jambon** /ʒɑ̃bɔ̃/ *nm* ham

■ ~ **blanc** *or* **de Paris** cooked ham; ~ **de pays** cured ham

**jambonneau**, *pl* ~**x** /ʒɑ̃bɔno/ *nm* knuckle of ham

**jante** /ʒɑ̃t/ *nf* **(a)** rim
**(b)** wheel

**janvier** /ʒɑ̃vje/ *nm* January

**Japon** /ʒapɔ̃/ *pr nm* Japan

**japonais, ~e** /ʒapɔnɛ, ɛz/ **1** *adj* Japanese
**2** *nm* (language) Japanese

**jappement** /ʒapmɑ̃/ *nm* yapping

**japper** /ʒape/ [1] *vi* to yap

**jaquette** /ʒakɛt/ *nf* **(a)** morning coat
**(b)** dust jacket
**(c)** (on tooth) crown

**jardin** /ʒaʀdɛ̃/ *nm* garden (GB), yard (US); **chaise de** ~ garden chair (GB), patio chair (US)

■ ~ **d'acclimatation** = ~ ZOOLOGIQUE; ~ **d'agrément** ornamental garden; ~ **d'enfants** kindergarten; ~ **potager** vegetable garden; ~ **public** park; ~ **zoologique** zoo

**jardinage** /ʒaʀdinaʒ/ *nm* gardening

**jardiner** /ʒaʀdine/ [1] *vi* to do some gardening

**jardinier, -ière¹** /ʒaʀdinje, ɛʀ/ **1** *adj* garden
**2** *nm,f* gardener

**jardinière²** /ʒaʀdinjɛʀ/ *nf* jardinière

**jargon** /ʒaʀgɔ̃/ *nm* **(a)** jargon; ~ **administratif** officialese
**(b)** gibberish

**jarre** /ʒaʀ/ *nf* (earthenware) jar

**jarret** /ʒaʀɛ/ *nm* **(a)** (of human) ham, hollow of the knee
**(b)** (of animal) hock
**(c)** (Culin) ~ **de veau** knuckle of veal

**jarretelle** /ʒaʀtɛl/ *nf* suspender (GB), garter (US)

**jars** /ʒaʀ/ *nm inv* gander

**jaser** /ʒaze/ [1] *vi* to gossip

**jasmin** /ʒasmɛ̃/ *nm* jasmine

**jatte** /ʒat/ *nf* bowl, basin

**jauge** /ʒoʒ/ *nf* gauge; ~ **d'huile** dipstick

**jaunâtre** /ʒonɑtʀ/ *adj* yellowish

**jaune** /ʒon/ **1** *adj* yellow; ~ **d'or** golden yellow; ~ **paille** straw-coloured (GB); ~ **poussin** bright yellow; **teint** ~ sallow complexion
**2** *nm* **(a)** yellow
**(b)** ~ **(d'œuf)** (egg) yolk
**(c)** blackleg (GB), scab

**IDIOMS rire** ~ (colloq) to give a forced laugh

**jaunir** /ʒoniʀ/ [3] **1** *vtr* to turn [sth] yellow, to make [sth] go yellow
**2** *vi* to go yellow

**jaunisse** /ʒonis/ *nf* jaundice; **il va en faire une ~!** (colloq) that'll put his nose out of joint!

**java** /ʒava/ *nf* (a) popular dance
(b) (colloq) booze-up (colloq)

**Javel** /ʒavɛl/ *nf* (**eau de**) **~** ≈ bleach

**javelliser** /ʒavelize/[1] *vtr* to chlorinate

**javelot** /ʒavlo/ *nm* javelin

**J.-C.** (*written abbr* = **Jésus-Christ**) **avant ~ BC; après ~ AD**

**je** (**j'** *before vowel or mute h*) /ʒ(ə)/ *pron* I

**jean** /dʒin/ *nm* (a) (pair of) jeans
(b) denim

**jeannette** /ʒanɛt/ *nf* ≈ Brownie

**je-ne-sais-quoi** /ʒənsɛkwa/ *nm inv* **avoir un ~** to have a certain something

**jérémiades** /ʒeʀemjad/ *nf pl* moaning

**jerrican** /ʒeʀikan/ *nm* jerrycan

**jersey** /ʒɛʀzɛ/ *nm* (a) jersey
(b) stocking stitch

**jésuite** /ʒezɥit/ *adj, nm* Jesuit

**Jésus** /ʒezy/ *pr n* Jesus

**jet¹** /ʒɛ/ *nm* (a) throwing; throw
(b) jet; spurt; burst; **passer au ~** to hose down; **premier ~** (figurative) first sketch; **d'un seul ~** ⟨*write*⟩ in one go
■ **~ d'eau** fountain; hosepipe

**jet²** /dʒɛt/ *nm* jet (plane)

**jetable** /ʒətabl/ *adj* disposable

**jetée** /ʒəte/ *nf* pier; jetty

**jeter** /ʒəte/ [20] **1** *vtr* (a) to throw; to hurl; to throw away *or* out; **~ qch à qn** to throw sth to sb ⟨*ball*⟩; to throw sth at sb ⟨*stone*⟩; **~ qn dehors** to throw sb out; **~ quelques idées sur le papier** (figurative) to jot down a few ideas; **bon à ~** fit for the bin (GB) *or* the garbage (US)
(b) to give ⟨*cry, light*⟩; to cast ⟨*glance, shadow*⟩
(c) to create ⟨*confusion, terror*⟩; **~ l'émoi dans la ville** to throw the town into turmoil
**2 se jeter** *v refl* (+ *v être*) (a) **se ~ du haut d'un pont** to throw oneself off a bridge; **se ~ sur** to fall upon ⟨*opponent*⟩; to pounce on ⟨*prey, newspaper*⟩; **se ~ au cou de qn** to fling oneself around sb's neck; **se ~ à l'eau** to jump into the water; (figurative) to take the plunge; **(aller) se ~ contre un arbre** to crash into a tree
(b) ⟨*river*⟩ to flow

**jeton** /ʒ(ə)tɔ̃/ *nm* (for machine) token; (in board games) counter; (at casino) chip

**jeu**, *pl* **~x** /ʒø/ *nm* (a) **le ~** play; **un ~** a game; **faire un ~** to play a game; **par ~** for fun; **entrer en ~** to come into the picture; **se prendre** *or* **se piquer au ~** to get hooked; **mettre en ~** to bring [sth] into play; to stake; **hors ~** offside; **ils ont beau ~ de me critiquer** it's easy for them to criticize me
(b) **le ~** gambling; **ton avenir est en ~** your future is at stake

(c) (in cards) hand; **cacher bien son ~** (figurative) to keep it quiet
(d) (of cards) deck; **~ d'échecs** chess set
(e) (of actor) acting; (of musician) playing; (of sportsman) game
(f) (of keys, spanners) set
■ **~ d'argent** game played for money; **~ de construction** construction set; **~ électronique** computer game; **~ de massacre** ≈ coconut shy (GB); **~ de mots** pun; **~ de l'oie** ≈ snakes and ladders (GB); **~ de société** board game; party game; **~ télévisé** (TV) game show; **~x Olympiques**, **JO** Olympic Games IDIOMS **jouer le ~** to play the game; **c'est pas de** *or* **du ~!** (colloq) that's not fair!; **faire le ~ de qn** to play into sb's hands

**jeu-concours**, *pl* **jeux-concours** /ʒøkɔ̃kuʀ/ *nm* competition

**jeudi** /ʒødi/ *nm* Thursday
IDIOMS **ça aura lieu la semaine des quatre ~s!** (colloq) it won't happen, not in a month of Sundays!

**jeun: à jeun** /aʒœ̃/ *phr* (a) on an empty stomach
(b) (colloq) sober

**jeune** /ʒœn/ **1** *adj* (a) (gen) young; ⟨*industry*⟩ new; ⟨*face, hairstyle*⟩ youthful; **nos ~s années** our youth; **le ~ âge** youth; **le ~ marié** the groom; **la ~ mariée** the bride
(b) younger; **mon ~ frère** my younger brother
**2** *nmf* young person; **les ~s** young people
**3** *adv* **s'habiller ~** to wear young styles; **faire ~** to look young
■ **~ femme** young woman; **~ fille** girl; **~ homme** young man; **~ loup** up-and-coming executive; **~ premier** romantic lead

**jeûne** /ʒøn/ *nm* (a) fasting; fast
(b) period of fasting

**jeûner** /ʒøne/ [1] *vi* to fast

**jeunesse** /ʒœnɛs/ *nf* (a) youth; **une seconde ~** a new lease of life; **une erreur de ~** a youthful indiscretion
(b) young people
IDIOMS **il faut que ~ se passe** youth will have its fling; **les voyages forment la ~** travel broadens the mind

**jf** *written abbr* = **JEUNE FEMME** *or* **FILLE**; ▶ **JEUNE**

**jh** *written abbr* = **JEUNE HOMME**; ▶ **JEUNE**

**JO** /ʒio/ *nm pl*: *abbr* ▶ **JEU**

**joaillerie** /ʒoajʀi/ *nf* (a) jeweller's shop (GB), jewelry store (US)
(b) jewellery (GB), jewelry (US)

**joaillier, -ière** /ʒoalje, ɛʀ/ *nm,f* jeweller (GB), jeweler (US)

**Joconde** /ʒokɔ̃d/ *n pr* **la ~** the Mona Lisa

**joggeur, -euse** /dʒɔgœʀ, øz/ *nm,f* jogger

**joie** /ʒwa/ *nf* joy; **au comble de la ~** overjoyed; **se faire une ~ de faire** to look forward to doing; to be delighted to do
IDIOMS **s'en donner à cœur ~** to enjoy oneself to the full; (figurative) to have a field day

**joignable** /ʒwaɲabl/ *adj* il n'est pas ~ en ce moment he's not available at the moment

**joindre** /ʒwɛ̃dʀ/ [56] **1** *vtr* **(a)** to get hold of ⟨*person*⟩
**(b)** to enclose ⟨*cheque*⟩; to attach ⟨*card*⟩
**(c)** to link ⟨*points*⟩; to put [sth] together ⟨*planks, feet*⟩; ~ l'intelligence à la simplicité to be intelligent without being pretentious
**2 se joindre** *v refl* (+ *v être*) **(a)** se ~ à to join ⟨*person, group*⟩; to join in ⟨*conversation*⟩
**(b)** ⟨*lips*⟩ to meet; ⟨*hands*⟩ to join
IDIOMS ~ les deux bouts (colloq) to make ends meet

**joint¹**, ~e /ʒwɛ̃, ɛ̃t/ ▶ JOINDRE

**joint²** /ʒwɛ̃/ *nm* (in wood) joint; (on pipes) seal

**jointure** /ʒwɛ̃tyʀ/ *nf* joint

**jojo** (colloq) /ʒoʒo/ **1** *adj inv* il n'est pas ~ ton chapeau your hat isn't very nice; ce n'est pas ~ ce qu'ils lui ont fait what they did to him/her wasn't very nice
**2** *nm* un affreux ~ a horrible brat (colloq); a weirdo (colloq)

**joli**, ~e /ʒɔli/ **1** *adj* (gen) nice; ⟨*face*⟩ pretty; ⟨*sum*⟩ tidy; faire ~ to look nice
**2** *nm* c'est du ~! (ironic) very nice!
■ ~ cœur smooth talker; faire le ~ cœur to play Romeo
IDIOMS être ~ à croquer *or* comme un cœur to be as pretty as a picture

**joliment** /ʒɔlimɑ̃/ *adv* **(a)** prettily, nicely
**(b)** (colloq) ⟨*happy, well*⟩ really; ⟨*handle*⟩ nicely

**jonc** /ʒɔ̃/ *nm* rush

**joncher** /ʒɔ̃ʃe/ [1] *vtr* ⟨*papers, leaves*⟩ to be strewn over ⟨*ground*⟩

**jonction** /ʒɔ̃ksjɔ̃/ *nf* **(a)** junction
**(b)** link-up

**jongler** /ʒɔ̃gle/ [1] *vi* to juggle

**jonque** /ʒɔ̃k/ *nf* junk

**jonquille** /ʒɔ̃kij/ *nf* daffodil

**jouable** /ʒwabl/ *adj* **(a)** feasible; le pari est ~ the gamble might pay off
**(b)** ⟨*piece of music*⟩ playable; une pièce qui n'est pas ~ a play that's impossible to stage

**joue** /ʒu/ *nf* **(a)** cheek
**(b)** (Mil) en ~! aim!; mettre qn en ~ to take aim at sb

**jouer** /ʒwe/ [1] **1** *vtr* **(a)** ⟨*children, musician*⟩ to play
**(b)** to back ⟨*horse*⟩; to stake ⟨*money*⟩; to risk ⟨*reputation, life*⟩; c'est joué d'avance it's a foregone conclusion; tout n'est pas encore joué the game isn't over yet; ~ le tout pour le tout to go for broke (colloq)
**(c)** qu'est-ce qu'on joue au théâtre/cinéma? what's on at the theatre/cinema?
**(d)** ~ les imbéciles to play dumb
**2 jouer à** *v+prep* to play ⟨*tennis, game*⟩; to play with ⟨*doll*⟩; ~ à qui perd gagne to play 'loser takes all'; ~ à la marchande to play shops
**3 jouer de** *v+prep* **(a)** ~ de to play ⟨*instrument*⟩
**(b)** ~ de to use ⟨*influence*⟩

**4** *vi* **(a)** to play; arrête de ~ avec ta bague! stop fiddling with your ring!; à toi de ~! your turn!; (figurative) the ball's in your court!; bien joué! well played!; (figurative) well done!
**(b)** to gamble; ~ avec to gamble with ⟨*life, health*⟩; ~ aux courses to bet on the horses; ~ sur to bank on ⟨*credulity*⟩
**(c)** to act; il joue bien he's a good actor
**(d)** ⟨*argument, clause*⟩ to apply; ⟨*age*⟩ to matter; faire ~ ses relations to make use of one's connections
**5 se jouer** *v refl* (+ *v être*) **(a)** ⟨*future, peace*⟩ to be at stake; ⟨*drama*⟩ to be played out
**(b)** se ~ de to make light work of ⟨*obstacle*⟩

**jouet** /ʒwɛ/ *nm* **(a)** toy
**(b)** plaything

**joueur**, **-euse** /ʒwœʀ, øz/ **1** *adj*
**(a)** playful
**(b)** être ~/joueuse to be a gambling man/woman
**2** *nm,f* **(a)** player; être beau/mauvais ~ to be a good/bad loser
**(b)** gambler

**joufflu**, ~e /ʒufly/ *adj* ⟨*person*⟩ chubby-cheeked; ⟨*face*⟩ chubby

**joug** /ʒu/ *nm* yoke

**jouir** /ʒwiʀ/ [3] *v+prep* ~ de to enjoy; to enjoy the use of ⟨*property*⟩; ⟨*place*⟩ to have ⟨*view, climate*⟩

**jouissance** /ʒwisɑ̃s/ *nf* **(a)** (Law) use
**(b)** pleasure

**joujou**, *pl* ~**x** /ʒuʒu/ *nm* (baby talk) toy

**jour** /ʒuʀ/ *nm* **(a)** day; quel ~ sommes-nous? what day is it today?; un ~ ou l'autre some day; ~ pour ~ to the day; à ce ~ to date; à ~ up to date; mettre à ~ to bring up to date ⟨*work*⟩; to revise ⟨*edition*⟩; mise à ~ updating; de nos ~s nowadays; d'un ~ à l'autre ⟨*expected*⟩ any day now; ⟨*change*⟩ from one day to the next; du ~ au lendemain overnight; d'un ~ ⟨*fashion*⟩ passing; ⟨*queen*⟩ for a day; vivre au ~ le ~ to live one day at a time; le ~ se lève it's getting light; au lever du ~ at daybreak; le petit ~ the early morning; de ~ ⟨*work*⟩ days; ⟨*travel*⟩ in the daytime
**(b)** daylight; light; en plein ~ in broad daylight; se faire ~ ⟨*truth*⟩ to come to light; éclairer qch d'un ~ nouveau to shed new light on sth; je t'ai vu sous ton vrai ~ I saw you in your true colours (GB)
**(c)** (figurative) donner le ~ à qn to bring sb into the world; voir le ~ ⟨*person*⟩ to come into the world; ⟨*work of art*⟩ to see the light of day; mes ~s sont comptés my days are numbered; des ~s difficiles hard times; les beaux ~s reviennent spring will soon be here
**(d)** (in wall) gap; ~s openwork (embroidery)
■ ~ de l'An New Year's Day; ~ férié bank holiday (GB), legal holiday (US); ~ de fermeture closing day; ~ ouvrable working day

**journal**, *pl* **-aux** /ʒuʀnal, o/ *nm*
**(a)** newspaper
**(b)** magazine
**(c)** news (bulletin)

 ⋯⋯

**(d)** journal

■ ~ **de bord** logbook; ~ **intime** diary; **Journal officiel** *government publication listing new acts, laws etc*

**journalier, -ière** /ʒuʀnalje, ɛʀ/ *adj* daily

**journalisme** /ʒuʀnalism/ *nm* journalism

**journaliste** /ʒuʀnalist/ *nmf* journalist

**journalistique** /ʒuʀnalistik/ *adj* journalistic

**journée** /ʒuʀne/ *nf* day; ~ **de repos** day off; **dans la** ~ during the day; **la** ~ **d'hier/de mardi** yesterday/Tuesday; **faire des** ~s **de huit heures** to work an eight-hour day

**joute** /ʒut/ *nf* **(a)** (figurative) jousting, battle; ~ **oratoire** *or* **verbale** sparring match **(b)** joust

**jouvence** /ʒuvɑ̃s/ *nf* **fontaine de** ~ Fountain of Youth

**jouxter** /ʒukste/ [1] *vtr* to adjoin

**jovial, ~e,** *mpl* ~**s** *or* **-iaux** /ʒɔvjal, o/ *adj* jovial

**jovialité** /ʒɔvjalite/ *nf* joviality

**joyau,** *pl* ~**x** /ʒwajo/ *nm* jewel, gem

**joyeusement** /ʒwajøzmɑ̃/ *adv* merrily, cheerfully

**joyeux, -euse** /ʒwajø, øz/ *adj* merry, cheerful

**jubilation** /ʒybilasjɔ̃/ *nf* joy, jubilation

**jubilé** /ʒybile/ *nm* jubilee

**jubiler** /ʒybile/ [1] *vi* to be jubilant

**jucher** /ʒyʃe/ [1] *vtr*, **se jucher** *v refl* (+ *v être*) to perch

**judaïsme** /ʒydaism/ *nm* Judaism

**judas** /ʒyda/ *nm inv* peephole

**judiciaire** /ʒydisjɛʀ/ *adj* judicial

**judicieux, -ieuse** /ʒydisjø, øz/ *adj* judicious, sensible

**judo** /ʒydo/ *nm* judo

**juge** /ʒyʒ/ *nm* judge; **être à la fois** ~ **et partie** to be judge and jury

■ ~ **d'instruction** examining magistrate; ~ **de touche** linesman

**jugé: au jugé** /oʒyʒe/ *phr* ⟨*value*⟩ by guesswork; ⟨*shoot*⟩ blind

**jugement** /ʒyʒmɑ̃/ *nm* judgment; **passer en** ~ ⟨*case*⟩ to come to court

**jugeote** /ʒyʒɔt/ *nf* (colloq) common sense

**juger** /ʒyʒe/ [13] **1** *vtr* **(a)** to judge ⟨*person, competition*⟩; **mal** ~ **qn** to misjudge sb **(b)** to consider; ~ **utile de faire** to consider it useful to do **(c)** (Law) to try ⟨*case*⟩; to judge ⟨*case*⟩; **le tribunal jugera** the court will decide **2 juger de** *v+prep* to assess; **j'en jugerai par moi-même** I'll judge for myself; **à en** ~ **par** judging by

**juguler** /ʒygyle/ [1] *vtr* to stamp out ⟨*epidemic, uprising*⟩; to curb ⟨*inflation*⟩

**juif, juive** /ʒɥif, ʒɥiv/ **1** *adj* Jewish **2** *nm,f* Jew

**juillet** /ʒɥijɛ/ *nm* July; **le 14** ~ Bastille Day

**juin** /ʒɥɛ̃/ *nm* June

**juive** ▶ JUIF

**jumeau, -elle¹,** *mpl* ~**x** /ʒymo, ɛl/ *adj, nm,f* twin

**jumelage** /ʒymlaʒ/ *nm* twinning

**jumeler** /ʒymle/ [19] *vtr* to twin

**jumelle²** /ʒymɛl/ *nf,* **jumelles** *nf pl* binoculars; ~**s de théâtre** opera glasses

**jument** /ʒymɑ̃/ *nf* mare

**jungle** /ʒœ̃gl/ *nf* jungle

**junte** /ʒœ̃t/ *nf* junta

**jupe** /ʒyp/ *nf* skirt

IDIOMS **il est toujours dans les** ~**s de sa mère** he's tied to his mother's apron strings

**jupe-culotte,** *pl* **jupes-culottes** /ʒypkylɔt/ *nf* culottes, divided skirt

**jupette** /ʒypɛt/ *nf* short skirt

**jupon** /ʒypɔ̃/ *nm* petticoat

IDIOMS **courir le** ~ to womanize

**juré, ~e** /ʒyʀe/ **1** *pp* ▶ JURER **2** *pp adj* **(a)** on oath; sworn-in **(b)** ⟨*enemy*⟩ sworn **3** *nm* juror; **les** ~**s** the members of the jury

**jurer** /ʒyʀe/ [1] **1** *vtr* to swear; **on leur a fait** ~ **le secret** they were sworn to secrecy; ~ **de tuer qn** to vow to kill sb; **ah mais je te jure!** (colloq) honestly! (colloq) **2 jurer de** *v+prep* to swear to **3** *vi* **(a)** to swear **(b)** ⟨*colours*⟩ to clash **(c) ne** ~ **que par** to swear by **4 se jurer** *v refl* (+ *v être*) **(a)** to swear [sth] to one another **(b)** to vow

IDIOMS **il ne faut** ~ **de rien** (Proverb) never say never

**juridiction** /ʒyʀidiksjɔ̃/ *nf* **(a)** jurisdiction **(b)** courts

**juridique** /ʒyʀidik/ *adj* legal; **vide** ~ gap in the law

**jurisprudence** /ʒyʀispʀydɑ̃s/ *nf* case law

**juriste** /ʒyʀist/ *nmf* **(a)** jurist **(b)** lawyer

**juron** /ʒyʀɔ̃/ *nm* swearword

**jury** /ʒyʀi/ *nm* **(a)** jury **(b)** panel of judges **(c)** board of examiners

**jus** /ʒy/ *nm inv* **(a)** juice **(b)** (from meat) juices; gravy **(c)** electricity; **prendre le** ~ to get a shock

**jusque** (**jusqu'** *before vowel*) /ʒysk/ **1** *prep* **(a) aller jusqu'à Paris** to go as far as Paris; to go all the way to Paris; **courir jusqu'au bout du jardin** to run right down to the bottom of the garden (GB) *or* the end of the yard (US); **suivre qn** ~ **dans sa chambre** to follow sb right into his/her room; **la nouvelle est arrivée jusqu'à nous** the news has reached us; **jusqu'où comptez-vous aller?** how far do you intend to go? **(b) jusqu'à, jusqu'en** until, till; **jusqu'à présent, jusqu'ici** (up) until now **(c) monter jusqu'à 20°** to go up to 20° **(d)** to the point of; **aller jusqu'à faire** to go so far as to do

243

## jusque-là ⋯⟶ kidnapper ⋯⋯

(e) even; des détritus ~ sous la table rubbish everywhere, even under the table
[2] **jusqu'à ce que** phr until
**jusque-là** /ʒyskəla/ adv (a) until then, up to then
(b) up to here; up to there
IDIOMS **en avoir ~ de qn/qch** (colloq) to have had it up to here with sb/sth (colloq); **s'en mettre ~** (colloq) to stuff one's face (colloq)
**justaucorps** /ʒystokɔʀ/ nm inv leotard
**juste** /ʒyst/ [1] adj (a) ⟨person⟩ just, fair
(b) ⟨cause⟩ just; ⟨anger⟩ righteous; ⟨word, answer⟩ right, correct
(c) ⟨balance, watch⟩ accurate; ~ **milieu** happy medium; **à ~ titre** with good reason; **dire des choses ~s** to make some valid points; **apprécier qn à sa ~ valeur** to get a fair picture of sb
(d) (Mus) ⟨piano, voice⟩ in tune; ⟨note⟩ true
(e) **c'est un peu ~** (in width, time) it's a bit tight; (in quantity) it's barely enough
[2] adv (a) ⟨sing⟩ in tune; ⟨guess⟩ right; **elle a vu ~** she was right; **viser ~** to aim straight
(b) just; ~ **à temps** just in time
(c) (tout) ~ only just; **j'arrive ~** I've only just arrived; **c'est tout ~ s'il sait lire** he can hardly read
[3] **au juste** phr exactly
[4] nm righteous man; **les ~s** the righteous
**justement** /ʒystəmɑ̃/ adv (a) precisely
(b) just
(c) correctly
(d) justifiably
**justesse** /ʒystɛs/ [1] nf (a) correctness; **avec ~** correctly
(b) accuracy; **avec ~** accurately

[2] **de justesse** phr ⟨succeed⟩ only just
**justice** /ʒystis/ nf (a) justice; **rendre la ~** to dispense justice; **il faut leur rendre cette ~ qu'ils sont...** one has to acknowledge that they are...; **ce n'est que ~** it is only fair; **se faire ~** to take the law into one's own hands; to take one's own life
(b) **la ~** the law; the legal system; the courts; **action en ~** legal action
**justicier, -ière** /ʒystisje, ɛʀ/ nm,f righter of wrongs
**justificatif, -ive** /ʒystifikatif, iv/ nm documentary evidence; ~ **de domicile** proof of domicile; ~ **de frais** receipt
**justification** /ʒystifikasjɔ̃/ nf
(a) justification
(b) explanation; documentary evidence
**justifié, ~e** /ʒystifje/ [1] pp ▶ JUSTIFIER
[2] pp adj (a) justified; **non ~** unjustified
**justifier** /ʒystifje/ [2] [1] vtr to justify ⟨method, absence⟩; to vindicate ⟨guilty party⟩; to explain ⟨ignorance⟩; **les faits ont justifié nos craintes** events proved our fears to have been justified; **tu essaies toujours de la ~** you are always making excuses for her
[2] **justifier de** v+prep to give proof of
[3] **se justifier** v refl (+ v être) (a) to make excuses; (in court) to clear oneself
(b) ⟨decision⟩ to be justified (by)
**jute** /ʒyt/ nm jute; (toile de) ~ hessian
**juteux, -euse** /ʒytø, øz/ adj ⟨fruit⟩ juicy
**juvénile** /ʒyvenil/ adj youthful; juvenile
**juxtaposer** /ʒykstapoze/ [1] vtr to juxtapose
**juxtaposition** /ʒykstapozisjɔ̃/ nf juxtaposition

k

# Kk

**k, K** /ka/ nm inv k, K
**kafkaïen, -ïenne** /kafkajɛ̃, ɛn/ adj Kafkaesque
**kakatoès** /kakatɔɛs/ nm inv cockatoo
**kaki** /kaki/ [1] adj inv khaki
[2] nm (a) persimmon
(b) khaki
**kaléidoscope** /kaleidɔskɔp/ nm kaleidoscope
**kanak** = CANAQUE
**kangourou** /kɑ̃guʀu/ [1] adj inv **poche ~** front pocket; **slip ~** pouch-front briefs
[2] nm (a) kangaroo
(b) ®baby carrier
**karaté** /kaʀate/ nm karate
**karité** /kaʀite/ nm shea; **beurre de ~** shea butter
**kart** /kaʀt/ nm go-kart

**karting** /kaʀtiŋ/ nm go-karting; **faire du ~** to go karting
**kasher** /kaʃɛʀ/ adj inv kosher
**kayak** /kajak/ nm kayak; **faire du ~** to go kayaking
**képi** /kepi/ nm kepi
**kératine** /keʀatin/ nf keratin
**kermesse** /kɛʀmɛs/ nf fete
**kérosène** /keʀozɛn/ nm kerosene
**kF** written abbr = KILOFRANC
**kg** (written abbr = **kilogramme**) kg
**kibboutz**, pl **-tzim** /kibuts, kibutsim/ nm kibbutz
**kick** /kik/ nm kick-start
**kidnapper** /kidnape/ [1] vtr to kidnap; **se faire ~** to be kidnapped

**kidnappeur, -euse** /kidnapœʀ, øz/ nm,f kidnapper

**kif-kif** /kifkif/ adj inv (colloq) **c'est** ~ **(bourricot)** it's all the same

**kilo¹** /kilo/ pref kilo

**kilo²** /kilo/ nm (abbr = **kilogramme**) kilo; **prendre des** ~**s** to put on weight

**kilofranc** /kilofʀɑ̃/ nm 1,000 French francs

**kilogramme** /kilogʀam/ nm kilogram

**kilométrage** /kilometʀaʒ/ nm ≈ mileage

**kilomètre** /kilomɛtʀ/ nm kilometre (GB)

**kilomètre-heure** pl **kilomètres-heure** /kilomɛtʀœʀ/ nm kilometre (GB) per hour

**kilométrique** /kilometʀik/ adj ⟨distance⟩ in kilometres (GB); ⟨price⟩ per kilometre (GB)

**kilo-octet** /kiloɔktɛ/ nm kilobyte

**kilotonne** /kilotɔn/ nf kiloton

**kilowattheure** /kilowatœʀ/ nm kilowatt-hour

**kimono** /kimono/ nm (a) kimono
(b) judo suit

**kinésithérapeute** /kineziteʀapøt/ nmf physiotherapist (GB), physical therapist (US)

**kinésithérapie** /kineziteʀapi/ nf physiotherapy (GB), physical therapy (US)

**kiosque** /kjɔsk/ nm kiosk
■ ~ **à musique** bandstand

**kiwi** /kiwi/ nm kiwi

**klaxon®** /klaksɔn/ nm (car) horn

**klaxonner** /klaksɔne/ [1] vi to sound one's horn (GB), to honk the horn

**kleptomane** /klɛptɔman/ adj, nmf kleptomaniac

**knock-out** /nɔkaut/ ① adj inv knocked out
② nm knockout

**Ko** (written abbr = **kilo-octet**) KB

**KO** /kao/ ① adj inv (abbr = **knocked out**)
(a) KO'd (colloq); **mettre qn** ~ to KO sb (colloq)
(b) (colloq) exhausted
② nm (abbr = **knockout**) KO (colloq)

**koala** /kɔala/ nm koala (bear)

**kopeck** /kɔpɛk/ nm kopeck; **ça ne vaut pas un** ~ it's not worth a penny

**krach** /kʀak/ nm (on stock exchange) crash

**kraft** /kʀaft/ nm (**papier**) ~ brown paper

**kurde** /kyʀd/ adj, nm Kurdish

**Kurde** /kyʀd/ nmf Kurd

**kW** (written abbr = **kilowatt**) kW

**K-way®** /kawe/ nm windcheater (GB), windbreaker (US)

**kyrielle** /kiʀjɛl/ nf **une** ~ **de** a string of

**kyste** /kist/ nm cyst

# L l

**l, L** /ɛl/ nm inv (a) (letter) l, L
(b) (written abbr = **litre**) 20 l 20 l

**l'** ▶ LE

**la¹** det, pron ▶ LE

**la²** /la/ nm (Mus) (note) A; (in sol-fa) lah; **donner le** ~ to give an A; (figurative) to set the tone

**là** /la/ adv (a) there; here; **viens** ~ come here; ~ **où je travaille** where I work; **pas par ici, par** ~ not this way, that way; **de** ~ **au village** from there to the village
(b) then; **d'ici** ~ between now and then; by then; **et** ~, **le téléphone a sonné** and then the phone rang; **en ce temps-**~ in those days; **ce jour-**~ that day
(c) **s'il en est (arrivé)** ~, **c'est que...** if he's got to that point, it's because...; **alors** ~ **tu exagères!** now you're going too far!; **que vas-tu chercher** ~? what are you thinking of?; **il a fallu en passer par** ~ there was no alternative; **qu'entendez-vous par** ~? what do you mean by that?; **si tu vas par** ~ if you are saying that; **de** ~ hence; from that

**là-bas** /labɑ/ adv over there

**labeur** /labœʀ/ nm hard work

**labo** /labo/ nm (colloq) lab (colloq)

**laboratoire** /labɔʀatwaʀ/ nm laboratory
■ ~ **d'analyses médicales** medical laboratory; ~ **de langues** language laboratory; ~ **pharmaceutique** pharmaceutical company

**laborieusement** /labɔʀjøzmɑ̃/ adv laboriously

**laborieux, -ieuse** /labɔʀjø, øz/ adj
(a) ⟨work, process⟩ arduous; ⟨style⟩ laboured (GB)
(b) **les classes laborieuses** the working classes

**labour** /labuʀ/ nm ploughing; **cheval de** ~ plough horse

**labourer** /labuʀe/ [1] vtr to plough (GB), to plow (US)

**labyrinthe** /labiʀɛ̃t/ nm maze; labyrinth

**lac** /lak/ nm (a) lake
(b) reservoir

**lacer** /lase/ [12] vtr to lace up ⟨shoes, corset⟩

**lacérer** /laseʀe/ [14] vtr to lacerate; to slash

**lacet** /lasɛ/ nm (a) lace; **chaussures à** ~**s** lace-up shoes; **nouer ses** ~**s** to do up one's laces
(b) (in road) **une route en** ~**s** a twisting road

**lâche** /lɑʃ/ ⊟ adj (a) ⟨person, crime⟩ cowardly
(b) ⟨belt⟩ loose
(c) ⟨regulation⟩ lax
⊡ nmf coward

**lâchement** /lɑʃmã/ adv ils se sont ~ enfuis they fled like cowards; il a été ~ assassiné he was foully murdered

**lâcher¹** /lɑʃe/ [1] ⊟ vtr (a) to drop ⟨object⟩; to let go of ⟨rope⟩; lâche-moi let go of me; (figurative) (colloq) give me a break (colloq); ~ prise to lose one's grip
(b) to reveal ⟨information⟩; to let out ⟨scream⟩
(c) to let [sb/sth] go ⟨person, animal⟩
(d) to drop ⟨friend, activity⟩; la peur ne la lâche plus depuis she's been living in constant terror ever since
⊡ vi ⟨rope⟩ to give way; ⟨brakes⟩ to fail; ses nerfs ont lâché he/she went to pieces

**lâcher²** /lɑʃe/ nm (of balloons, birds) release

**lâcheté** /lɑʃte/ nf (a) cowardice; par ~ out of cowardice
(b) cowardly act

**laconique** /lakɔnik/ adj laconic; terse

**lacrymal, ~e,** mpl **-aux** /lakʀimal, o/ adj lachrymal

**lacrymogène** /lakʀimɔʒɛn/ adj ⟨grenade, bomb⟩ teargas; gaz ~ teargas

**lacté, ~e** /lakte/ adj (a) ⟨product⟩ milk
(b) ⟨liquid⟩ milky; la voie ~e the Milky Way

**lacune** /lakyn/ nf (in knowledge, law) gap

**là-dedans** /lad(ə)dã/ adv in here; in there; et moi ~ qu'est-ce que je fais? (colloq) and where do I come in?

**là-dessous** /lad(ə)su/ adv under here; under there; il y a qch de louche ~ (colloq) there's something fishy about all this (colloq)

**là-dessus** /lad(ə)sy/ adv (a) on here; on there
(b) qu'as-tu à dire ~? what have you got to say about it?
(c) ~ il a raccroché with that he hung up

**ladite** ▶ LEDIT

**lagon** /lagɔ̃/ nm lagoon

**lagune** /lagyn/ nf lagoon

**là-haut** /lao/ adv (a) up here; up there; tout ~ (all the) way up there
(b) upstairs
(c) in heaven

**laïc** /laik/ nm layman

**laïcité** /laisite/ nf secularism; secularity

**laid, ~e** /lɛ, lɛd/ adj (a) ugly
(b) disgusting

**laideur** /lɛdœʀ/ nf ugliness

**lainage** /lɛnaʒ/ nm (a) woollen (GB) material
(b) woollen (GB) garment

**laine** /lɛn/ nf wool; de or en ~ woollen (GB), wool
■ ~ peignée worsted; ~ de verre glass wool; ~ vierge new wool (GB), virgin wool

**laïque** /laik/ ⊟ adj ⟨school⟩ nondenominational (GB), public (US); ⟨state, mind⟩ secular
⊡ nmf layman/laywoman; les ~s lay people

**laisse** /lɛs/ nf (for dog) lead (GB), leash (US)

**laissé-pour-compte, laissée-pour-compte,** mpl **laissés-pour-compte** /lesepuʀkɔ̃t/ nm,f les laissés-pour-compte (gen) the forgotten people; les laissés-pour-compte de la révolution technologique the casualties of the technological revolution

**laisser** /lese/ [1] ⊟ vtr to leave; ~ la liberté à qn to let sb go free; je te laisse I must go; ~ le choix à qn to give sb the choice; laisse ce jouet à ton frère let your brother have the toy; laisse-le, ça lui passera ignore him, he'll get over it; cela me laisse sceptique I'm sceptical (GB) or skeptical (US)
⊡ v aux ~ qn/qch faire to let sb/sth do; laisse-moi faire let me do it; leave it to me; laisse faire! so what!
⊟ se **laisser** v refl (+ v être) se ~ bercer par les vagues to be lulled by the waves; il se laisse insulter he puts up with insults; elle n'est pas du genre à se ~ faire she won't be pushed around; il ne veut pas se ~ faire he won't let you touch him; se ~ aller to let oneself go

**laisser-aller** /leseale/ nm inv
(a) scruffiness
(b) sloppiness

**laissez-passer** /lesepase/ nm inv pass

**lait** /lɛ/ nm milk
■ ~ de chaux whitewash; ~ concentré non sucré evaporated milk; ~ demi-écrémé low-fat milk; ~ écrémé skimmed milk (GB), skim or nonfat milk (US); ~ maternel breastmilk; ~ de poule eggnog

**laitage** /lɛtaʒ/ nm dairy product

**laitance** /lɛtãs/ nf (Culin, Zool) soft roe

**laiterie** /lɛtʀi/ nf (a) dairy
(b) dairy industry

**laiteux, -euse** /lɛtø, øz/ adj ⟨liquid, white⟩ milky; ⟨complexion⟩ creamy

**laitier, -ière** /lɛtje, ɛʀ/ ⊟ adj ⟨industry, product⟩ dairy; ⟨production, cow⟩ milk
⊡ nm,f milkman/milkwoman

**laiton** /lɛtɔ̃/ nm brass

**laitue** /lɛty/ nf lettuce

**laïus** /lajys/ nm inv (colloq) speech

**lama** /lama/ nm (a) (animal) llama
(b) (religious leader) lama

**lambda** /lãbda/ adj inv (colloq) average

**lambeau,** pl ~**x** /lãbo/ nm (of cloth) rag; (of paper, hide) strip; (of flesh) bit

**lambris** /lãbʀi/ nm inv panelling (GB); marble walls; (on ceiling) mouldings (GB), moldings (US)

**lambrisser** /lãbʀise/ [1] vtr to panel

**lame** /lam/ nf (a) (of knife, saw) blade
(b) knife
(c) sword; une fine ~ an expert swordsman ····⫶·

**(d)** (of metal, wood) strip; (on blind) slat
■ ~ **de fond** ground swell; (figurative) upheaval;
~ **de rasoir** razor blade

**lamé** /lame/ *nm* lamé; **en** ~ lamé

**lamelle** /lamɛl/ *nf* **(a)** (of wood, metal) small
strip
**(b)** (Culin) sliver; **découper en fines** ~**s to**
slice thinly
**(c)** (Bot) (of mushroom) gill

**lamentable** /lamɑ̃tabl/ *adj* pathetic, awful

**lamentablement** /lamɑ̃tabləmɑ̃/ *adv*
⟨*fail*⟩ miserably; ⟨*cry*⟩ piteously

**lamentation** /lamɑ̃tasjɔ̃/ *nf* wailing

**lamenter: se lamenter** /lamɑ̃te/ [1] *v refl*
(+ *v être*) to moan; **se** ~ **sur son propre sort**
to feel sorry for oneself

**lampadaire** /lɑ̃padɛʀ/ *nm* **(a)** standard
(GB) *or* floor (US) lamp
**(b)** streetlight

**lampe** /lɑ̃p/ *nf* **(a)** lamp, light
**(b)** (light) bulb
■ ~ **à bronzer** sun lamp; ~ **de chevet** bedside
light; ~ **électrique** torch (GB), flashlight (US);
~ **de poche** pocket torch (GB), flashlight
(US); ~ **témoin** indicator light; ~ **tempête**
hurricane lamp

**lampée** /lɑ̃pe/ *nf* (colloq) gulp

**lampion** /lɑ̃pjɔ̃/ *nm* paper lantern

**lance** /lɑ̃s/ *nf* (gen) spear; (in jousting) lance
■ ~ **d'incendie** fire hose nozzle

**lancée** /lɑ̃se/ *nf* **sur ma** ~ while I was at it;
**continuer sur sa** ~ to continue to forge
ahead

**lancement** /lɑ̃smɑ̃/ *nm* **(a)** (of ship,
company) launching; (of process) setting up
**(b)** (of product, book) launch; (of loan) floating;
(of actor) promotion
**(c)** (of missile) launching; launch

**lance-pierres** /lɑ̃spjɛʀ/ *nm inv* catapult
IDIOMS **payer qn avec un** ~ (colloq) to pay sb
peanuts (colloq)

**lancer¹** /lɑ̃se/ [12] **1** *vtr* **(a)** to throw ⟨*ball,
pebble, javelin*⟩; ~ **le poids** to put the shot
**(b)** to launch ⟨*rocket, ship*⟩; to fire ⟨*arrow*⟩;
to drop ⟨*bomb*⟩; to start up ⟨*engine*⟩
**(c)** to throw out ⟨*smoke, flames*⟩; to give
⟨*look*⟩; to put about ⟨*rumour*⟩; to issue
⟨*ultimatum*⟩; to send out ⟨*invitation*⟩
**(d)** to hurl ⟨*insult*⟩; to make ⟨*accusation*⟩;
**lança-t-il** he said
**2** *vi* (colloq) to throb; **mon doigt me lance** my
finger is throbbing
**3 se lancer** *v refl* (+ *v être*) **(a) se** ~ **dans
des dépenses** to get involved in expense; **se**
~ **dans les affaires** to go into business
**(b) se** ~ **dans le vide** to jump
**(c)** to throw [sth] to each other ⟨*ball*⟩; to
exchange ⟨*insults*⟩

**lancer²** /lɑ̃se/ *nm* **(a)** (Sport) ~ **du disque**
discus event; ~ **du poids** shot put (event)
**(b) le** ~, **la pêche au** ~ rod and reel fishing

**lance-roquettes** /lɑ̃sʀɔkɛt/ *nm inv*
rocket launcher

**lancinant**, ~**e** /lɑ̃sinɑ̃, ɑ̃t/ *adj* ⟨*pain*⟩
shooting; ⟨*music, rhythm*⟩ insistent

**landau** /lɑ̃do/ *nm* pram (GB), baby carriage
(US)

**lande** /lɑ̃d/ *nf* moor

**langage** /lɑ̃gaʒ/ *nm* language
■ ~ **administratif** official jargon; ~ **des
sourds-muets** sign language

**lange** /lɑ̃ʒ/ *nm* **(a)** swaddling clothes
**(b)** nappy (GB), diaper (US)

**langer** /lɑ̃ʒe/ [13] *vtr* **(a)** to wrap [sb] in
swaddling clothes ⟨*baby*⟩
**(b)** to put a nappy (GB) *or* diaper (US) on
⟨*baby*⟩

**langoureux, -euse** /lɑ̃guʀø, øz/ *adj*
languorous

**langouste** /lɑ̃gust/ *nf* spiny lobster

**langoustine** /lɑ̃gustin/ *nf* langoustine

**langue** /lɑ̃g/ *nf* **(a)** tongue; **tirer la** ~ to
stick out one's tongue; (for doctor) to put out
one's tongue; (figurative) to be dying of thirst;
to struggle financially
**(b)** language; speech
**(c) mauvaise** ~ malicious gossip
**(d)** ~ **de terre** spit of land
■ ~ **de bois** political cant; ~ **maternelle**
mother tongue; ~ **verte** slang
IDIOMS **avoir la** ~ **bien pendue** (colloq) to be
very talkative; **avoir qch sur le bout de la** ~
to have sth on the tip of one's tongue

**languette** /lɑ̃gɛt/ *nf* (on shoe) tongue; (on
satchel, bag) strap; (of ham) long narrow strip

**langueur** /lɑ̃gœʀ/ *nf* languor

**languir** /lɑ̃giʀ/ [3] **1** *vi* ⟨*conversation*⟩
to languish; ⟨*economy*⟩ to be sluggish
**(b) je languis de vous revoir** I'm longing to
see you; **faire** ~ **qn** to keep sb in suspense
**2 se languir** *v refl* (+ *v être*) to pine

**languissant**, ~**e** /lɑ̃gisɑ̃, ɑ̃t/ *adj*
⟨*economy*⟩ sluggish; ⟨*conversation*⟩ desultory

**lanière** /lanjɛʀ/ *nf* (gen) strap; (of whip) lash

**lanterne** /lɑ̃tɛʀn/ *nf* **(a)** lantern
**(b)** (Aut) sidelight (GB), parking light (US)
IDIOMS **éclairer la** ~ **de qn** to enlighten sb

**laper** /lape/ [1] *vtr* to lap (up) ⟨*soup, milk*⟩

**lapider** /lapide/ [1] *vtr* **(a)** to stone [sb] to
death
**(b)** to throw stones at

**lapin** /lapɛ̃/ *nm* **(a)** rabbit; ~ **de garenne**
wild rabbit; **coup du** ~ rabbit punch;
(in accident) whiplash injury; **cage** *or* **cabane à**
~**s** rabbit hutch; (figurative) (colloq) tower
block
**(b)** rabbit(skin)
IDIOMS **poser un** ~ **à qn** (colloq) to stand sb
up; **se faire tirer comme des** ~**s** (colloq) to be
picked off like flies; **c'est un chaud** ~ (colloq)
he's a randy devil

**lapine** /lapin/ *nf* doe rabbit

**laps** /laps/ *nm inv* ~ **de temps** period of
time

**lapsus** /lapsys/ *nm inv* slip

**laquais** /lakɛ/ *nm inv* lackey

**laque** /lak/ *nf* **(a)** hairspray
**(b)** lacquer; gloss paint (GB), enamel (US)

**laqué**, ~**e** /lake/ *adj* ⟨*paint*⟩ gloss

**laquelle** ▶ LEQUEL

**laquer** /lake/ [1] *vtr* to lacquer; to paint [sth] in gloss (GB) *or* enamel (US)

**larbin** /laʀbɛ̃/ *nm* (derogatory) (colloq) servant

**lard** /laʀ/ *nm* ≈ fat streaky bacon

**larder** /laʀde/ [1] *vtr* (Culin) to lard; ~ qn de coups de couteau (figurative) to stab sb repeatedly

**lardon** /laʀdɔ̃/ *nm* (Culin) bacon cube

**large** /laʀʒ/ **1** *adj* (a) ⟨shoulders, hips⟩ broad; ⟨avenue, bed⟩ wide; ⟨coat⟩ loose-fitting; ⟨trousers⟩ loose; ⟨skirt⟩ full; ⟨jumper⟩ big; ⟨smile⟩ broad; ⟨curve⟩ long; ~ de trois mètres three metres (GB) wide
(b) ⟨advance, profit⟩ substantial; ⟨choice, public⟩ wide; ⟨majority⟩ large; au sens ~ in a broad sense
(c) ⟨person⟩ generous
(d) ⟨life⟩ comfortable
(e) avoir les idées ~s, être ~ d'esprit to be broad-minded
**2** *adv* (a) ⟨plan⟩ on a generous scale; ⟨calculate, measure⟩ on the generous side
(b) s'habiller ~ to wear loose-fitting clothes
**3** *nm* (a) faire quatre mètres de ~ to be four metres (GB) wide
(b) open sea; au ~ offshore
IDIOMS ne pas en mener ~ (colloq) to be worried sick (colloq)

**largement** /laʀʒəmɑ̃/ *adv* (a) widely
(b) largely, to a large extent; être ~ responsable de qch to be largely responsible for sth
(c) arriver ~ en tête to be a clear winner; ~ en dessous de la limite well under the limit
(d) tu as ~ le temps you've got plenty of time
(e) easily; une chaîne en or vaudrait ~ le double a gold chain would easily be worth twice as much
(f) ⟨contribute⟩ generously

**largesse** /laʀʒes/ *nf* generous gift

**largeur** /laʀʒœʀ/ *nf* (a) width, breadth; dans le sens de la ~ widthwise
(b) ~ d'esprit broad-mindedness

**largué, ~e** /laʀge/ *adj* (colloq) (a) lost, out of one's depth
(b) out of touch

**larguer** /laʀge/ [1] *vtr* (a) (Mil) to drop ⟨bomb, missile⟩; to drop ⟨parachutist⟩; to release ⟨satellite⟩
(b) to unfurl ⟨sail⟩; ~ les amarres to cast off; (figurative) to set off
(c) (colloq) to give up ⟨studies⟩; to chuck (colloq) ⟨boyfriend, girlfriend⟩

**larme** /laʀm/ *nf* (a) tear; elle a ri aux ~s she laughed till she cried; avoir la ~ à l'œil to be a bit weepy
(b) (colloq) drop

**larmoyant, ~e** /laʀmwajɑ̃, ɑ̃t/ *adj*
(a) ⟨eyes⟩ full of tears
(b) ⟨voice⟩ whining; ⟨speech⟩ maudlin

**larmoyer** /laʀmwaje/ [23] *vi* (a) ⟨eyes⟩ to water

(b) ⟨person⟩ to whine

**larron** /laʀɔ̃/ *nm* (a) (humorous) scoundrel
(b) thief
IDIOMS s'entendre comme ~s en foire to be as thick as thieves

**larvaire** /laʀvɛʀ/ *adj* ⟨state⟩ embryonic

**larve** /laʀv/ *nf* (a) (Zool) larva
(b) ⟨person⟩ wimp (colloq)

**larvé, ~e** /laʀve/ *adj* latent

**laryngite** /laʀɛ̃ʒit/ *nf* laryngitis

**larynx** /laʀɛ̃ks/ *nm inv* larynx

**las, lasse** /lɑ, lɑs/ *adj* weary

**lasagnes** /lazaɲ/ *nf pl* lasagna

**lascar** /laskaʀ/ *nm* (colloq) fellow

**lascif, -ive** /lasif, iv/ *adj* ⟨person, look⟩ lascivious; ⟨temperament⟩ lustful

**laser** /lazɛʀ/ *nm* laser

**lassant, ~e** /lasɑ̃, ɑ̃t/ *adj* (a) ⟨speech⟩ tedious; ⟨reproaches⟩ tiresome
(b) tiring

**lasser** /lase/ [1] **1** *vtr* (a) to bore ⟨person, audience⟩
(b) to weary ⟨person, audience⟩
**2** se lasser *v refl* (+ *v être*) ⟨person⟩ to grow tired; sans se ~ without tiring; patiently

**lassitude** /lasityd/ *nf* weariness

**lasso** /laso/ *nm* lasso; prendre au ~ to lasso

**latence** /latɑ̃s/ *nf* latency

**latent, ~e** /latɑ̃, ɑ̃t/ *adj* ⟨danger, illness⟩ latent; ⟨anxiety, jealousy⟩ underlying

**latéral, ~e, mpl -aux** /lateʀal, o/ *adj* ⟨door, exit⟩ side; ⟨tunnel, aisle⟩ lateral

**latéralement** /lateʀalmɑ̃/ *adv* sideways

**latin, ~e** /latɛ̃, in/ **1** *adj* (a) ⟨texts⟩ Latin
(b) ⟨temperament⟩ Latin; ⟨culture⟩ Mediterranean
(c) langues ~es Romance languages
**2** *nm* (language) Latin
IDIOMS c'est à y perdre son ~ you can't make head or tail of it

**latino-américain, ~e, mpl ~s** /latinoameʀikɛ̃, ɛn/ *adj* Latin-American

**latitude** /latityd/ *nf* latitude
IDIOMS avoir toute ~ de faire to be entirely free to do

**latte** /lat/ *nf* (a) lath; (of floor) board
(b) (of bed base) slat

**laudatif, -ive** /lodatif, iv/ *adj* laudatory

**lauréat, ~e** /loʀea, at/ *nm,f*
(a) (of competition) winner
(b) (in exam) successful candidate

**laurier** /loʀje/ **1** *nm* (a) (Bot) laurel; ~ commun bay (tree)
(b) (Culin) feuille de ~ bay leaf
**2** lauriers *nm pl* laurels; s'endormir sur ses ~s to rest on one's laurels

**laurier-rose, pl lauriers-roses** /loʀjeʀoz/ *nm* oleander

**lavable** /lavabl/ *adj* washable

**lavabo** /lavabo/ *nm* washbasin, washbowl

**lavage** /lavaʒ/ *nm* (a) washing; cleaning  ····▷

**(b)** (washing machine cycle) wash
■ ~ **de cerveau** brainwashing; **faire un ~ d'estomac à qn** to pump sb's stomach (out)

**lavande** /lavɑ̃d/ *adj inv, nf* lavender

**lave** /lav/ *nf* lava; **coulée de ~** lava flow

**lave-glace**, *pl* **~s** /lavglas/ *nm* windscreen (GB) *or* windshield (US) washer

**lave-linge** /lavlɛ̃ʒ/ *nm inv* washing machine

**lavement** /lavmɑ̃/ *nm* (Med) enema

**laver** /lave/ [1] **1** *vtr* **(a)** to wash ‹clothes, child, car›; **~ son linge** to do one's washing; **~ la vaisselle** to do the dishes; **~ qch à grande eau** to wash sth down
**(b)** to clean ‹wound›
**(c)** to clear; **~ qn d'une accusation** to clear sb of an accusation
**2 se laver** *v refl* (+ *v être*) **(a)** to wash; **se ~ les mains** to wash one's hands; **se ~ les dents** to brush one's teeth
**(b)** to be washable
**(c) se ~ d'un affront** to take revenge for an insult
IDIOMS **je m'en lave les mains** I'm washing my hands of it

**laverie** /lavʀi/ *nf* **~ (automatique)** launderette, laundromat® (US)

**lave-vaisselle** /lavvɛsɛl/ *nm inv* dishwasher

**lavis** /lavi/ *nm inv* wash drawing

**lavoir** /lavwaʀ/ *nm* wash house

**laxatif** /laksatif/ *nm* laxative

**laxisme** /laksism/ *nm* laxity

**laxiste** /laksist/ *adj* lax

**layette** /lɛjɛt/ *nf* baby clothes, layette

**le, la¹** (**l'** *before vowel or mute h*), *pl* **les** /lə, la, l, lɛ/ **1** *det* **(a)** the; **la table de la cuisine** the kitchen table; **les Dupont** at the Duponts; **elle aime les chevaux** she likes horses; **arriver sur** *or* **vers les 11 heures** to arrive at about 11 o'clock
**(b) elle s'est cogné ~ bras** she banged her arm
**(c)** a, an; **9 euros ~ kilo** 9 euros a kilo
**(d) (oh) la jolie robe!** what a pretty dress!
**2** *pron* him; her; it; them; **je ne les comprends pas** I don't understand them
**3** *pron neutre* **je ~ savais** I knew; I knew it; **je ~ croyais aussi, mais...** I thought so too, but...; **espérons-~!** let's hope so!

**lé** /le/ *nm* (of cloth, wallpaper) width

**LEA** /ɛlaa/ *nf pl* (*abbr* = **langues étrangères appliquées**) *university language course with emphasis on business and management*

**leadership** /lidœʀʃip/ *nm* **(a)** leading role
**(b)** supremacy

**lèche-bottes** (colloq) /lɛʃbɔt/ **1** *nmf inv* crawler (GB) (colloq), bootlicker (colloq)
**2** *nm* crawling (GB) (colloq), bootlicking (colloq)

**lécher** /leʃe/ [1] **1** *vtr* **(a)** to lick ‹spoon, plate›
**(b)** ‹flames› to lick; ‹sea› to lap against

**2 se lécher** *v refl* (+ *v être*) **se ~ les doigts** to lick one's fingers

**lèche-vitrines** /lɛʃvitʀin/ *nm inv* window-shopping

**leçon** /ləsɔ̃/ *nf* lesson; **~ particulière** private lesson; **cela lui servira de ~** that'll teach him a lesson

**lecteur, -trice** /lɛktœʀ, tʀis/ **1** *nm,f* **(a)** reader
**(b)** teaching assistant
**2** *nm* **(a)** (Comput) reader; **~ optique** optical scanner *or* reader; **~ de disquettes** disk drive
**(b)** player; **~ laser** CD player

**lecture** /lɛktyʀ/ *nf* **(a)** (of book, newspaper) reading; **faire la ~ à qn** to read to sb
**(b)** reading, interpretation
**(c)** reading material; **tu as pris de la ~?** have you brought something to read?
**(d)** (of music, X-ray, disk) reading
**(e)** (of cassette, CD) play; playing

**ledit, ladite**, *pl* **lesdits, lesdites** /lədi, ladit, ledi, ledit/ *adj* the aforementioned

**légal, ~e**, *mpl* **-aux** /legal, o/ *adj* legal; lawful

**légalement** /legalmɑ̃/ *adv* legally; lawfully

**légaliser** /legalize/ [1] *vtr* to legalize

**légalité** /legalite/ *nf* **(a)** legality
**(b)** lawfulness

**légataire** /legatɛʀ/ *nmf* legatee

**légendaire** /leʒɑ̃dɛʀ/ *adj* legendary

**légende** /leʒɑ̃d/ *nf* **(a)** legend
**(b)** (accompanying picture) caption; (on map) key
**(c)** tall story

**léger, -ère** /leʒe, ɛʀ/ **1** *adj* **(a)** light; **se sentir plus ~** (figurative) to have a great weight off one's mind
**(b)** (Culin) ‹meal› light
**(c)** ‹person› nimble; ‹step› light
**(d)** ‹laugh› gentle; ‹blow, knock› soft; ‹error, delay› slight; ‹taste, hope› faint; ‹wind, rain› light; ‹injury› minor
**(e)** ‹tea, drink› weak; ‹perfume, wine› light; ‹tobacco› mild (GB), light (US)
**(f)** ‹action› ill-considered; ‹remark› thoughtless; ‹argument, proof› weak
**(g)** (colloq) **c'est un peu ~** it's a bit skimpy
**(h)** ‹woman, way of life› loose; ‹husband, mood› fickle
**(i)** (Mil) light
**2** *adv* ‹travel› light; **cuisiner/manger ~** to cook/to eat light meals
**3 à la légère** *phr* (gen) without thinking; ‹accuse› rashly; **prendre qch à la légère** not to take sth seriously

**légèrement** /leʒɛʀmɑ̃/ *adv* **(a)** ‹move› gently; ‹perfume› lightly; ‹tremble, injured› slightly
**(b)** (Culin) ‹eat› lightly
**(c)** ‹walk, run› lightly, nimbly
**(d)** ‹act, speak› without thinking

**légèreté** /leʒɛʀte/ *nf* **(a)** lightness; nimbleness

**(b)** thoughtlessness; fickleness; **la ~ de ses mœurs** his/her loose morals

**légiférer** /leʒifeʀe/ [14] *vi* to legislate

**légion** /leʒjɔ̃/ *nf* **(a)** (Mil) legion
**(b)** army
■ **la Légion (étrangère)** the Foreign Legion

**légionnaire** /leʒjɔnɛʀ/ *nm* (Roman) legionary; (in Foreign Legion) legionnaire

**législateur, -trice** /leʒislatœʀ, tʀis/ *nm,f* legislator, law-maker

**législatif, -ive** /leʒislatif, iv/ *adj* legislative; **élections législatives** ≈ general election

**législation** /leʒislasjɔ̃/ *nf* legislation

**législature** /leʒislatyʀ/ *nf* **(a)** term of office
**(b)** legislature

**légiste** /leʒist/ *nm* jurist

**légitime** /leʒitim/ *adj* **(a)** ‹child, right› legitimate; ‹union, heir› lawful
**(b)** ‹action› legitimate; ‹anger› justifiable
**(c)** ‹reward› just
■ **~ défense** self-defence (GB)

**légitimité** /leʒitimite/ *nf* **(a)** legitimacy
**(b)** (of an act) lawfulness

**legs** /lɛg/ *nm inv* (Law, gen) legacy; (of personal belongings) bequest

**léguer** /lege/ [14] *vtr* **(a)** (in one's will) to leave
**(b)** to hand down ‹traditions›; to pass on ‹flaw›

**légume** /legym/ *nm* vegetable; **~s secs** pulses

**leitmotiv** /lajtmɔtiv/ *nm* leitmotiv

**Léman** /lemɑ̃/ *n pr* **le lac ~** Lake Geneva

**lendemain** /lɑ̃dəmɛ̃/ **1** *nm* **(a)** **le ~, la journée du ~** the following day; **dès le ~** the (very) next day; **le ~ de l'accident** the day after the accident; **du jour au ~** overnight
**(b)** **au ~ de** (in the period) after; **au ~ de la guerre** just after the war
**(c)** **le ~** tomorrow, the future; **sans ~** ‹happiness, success› short-lived
**2** **lendemains** *nm pl* **(a)** outcome; consequences
**(b)** future; **des ~s difficiles** difficult days ahead

**lénifiant, ~e** /lenifjɑ̃, ɑ̃t/ *adj* soothing

**lent, ~e1** /lɑ̃, ɑ̃t/ *adj* slow; ‹film, vehicle› slow-moving; ‹poison› slow-acting

**lente2** /lɑ̃t/ *nf* (Zool) nit

**lentement** /lɑ̃t(ə)mɑ̃/ *adv* slowly

**lenteur** /lɑ̃tœʀ/ *nf* slowness; **avec ~** slowly

**lentille** /lɑ̃tij/ *nf* **(a)** (Bot, Culin) lentil
**(b)** lens; **~s de contact** contact lenses

**léopard** /leɔpaʀ/ *nm* **(a)** leopard
**(b)** leopardskin

**lèpre** /lɛpʀ/ *nf* leprosy

**lépreux, -euse** /lepʀø, øz/ *nm,f* leper

**lequel** /ləkɛl/, **laquelle** /lakɛl/, lesquels *mpl*, **lesquelles** *fpl* /lekɛl/, (with *à*) **auquel, auxquels** *mpl*,

**auxquelles** *fpl* /okɛl/, (with *de*) **duquel** /dykɛl/, **desquels** *mpl*, **desquelles** *fpl* /dekɛl/ **1** **lequel, laquelle,** lesquels, **lesquelles** *adj* who; which; **il m'a présenté son cousin, ~ cousin vit en Grèce** he introduced me to his cousin, who lives in Greece; **auquel cas** in which case
**2** *rel prón* who; which; **les gens contre lesquels ils luttaient** the people (who) they were fighting against
**3** *pron* which; **lesquels sont les plus compétents?** which are the most competent?

**les ▶ LE**

**lesbienne** /lɛsbjɛn/ *nf* lesbian

**lesdites ▶ LEDIT**

**lesdits ▶ LEDIT**

**lèse-majesté** /lɛzmaʒɛste/ *nf inv* lese-majesty

**léser** /leze/ [14] *vtr* to wrong ‹person›; to prejudice ‹interests›

**lésiner** /lezine/ [1] *vi* **ne pas ~ sur** to be liberal with ‹ingredients, money, compliments›

**lésion** /lezjɔ̃/ *nf* (Med) lesion

**lesquels, lesquelles ▶ LEQUEL**

**lessive** /lesiv/ *nf* **(a)** washing powder; washing liquid
**(b)** washing

**lessiver** /lesive/ [1] *vtr* **(a)** to wash
**(b)** (colloq) **être lessivé** to be washed out (colloq)

**lessiveuse** /lesivøz/ *nf* boiler, copper (GB)

**lest** /lɛst/ *nm* **(a)** ballast; **jeter** *or* **lâcher du ~** to jettison ballast
**(b)** (on fishing net) weight

**leste** /lɛst/ *adj* **(a)** ‹person, animal› agile, nimble
**(b)** ‹joke, remark› risqué

**lestement** /lɛstəmɑ̃/ *adv* nimbly

**lester** /lɛste/ [1] *vtr* **(a)** to ballast
**(b)** (colloq) to stuff sth

**létal, ~e,** *mpl* **-aux** /letal, o/ *adj* lethal

**léthargie** /letaʀʒi/ *nf* lethargy

**léthargique** /letaʀʒik/ *adj* **(a)** ‹person› lethargic; ‹industry› sluggish
**(b)** (Med) lethargic

**lettre** /lɛtʀ/ **1** *nf* **(a)** (of alphabet) letter; **~ majuscule** *or* **capitale** capital letter; **~ d'imprimerie** block letter; **en toutes ~s** in full; **c'est écrit en toutes ~s dans le rapport** it's down in black and white in the report; **les Romains furent des urbanistes avant la ~** the Romans were city planners before the concept was invented; **à la ~, au pied de la ~** to the letter; **il prend tout ce qu'on lui dit à la ~** he takes everything you say literally
**(b)** (message) letter; **~ de rupture** letter ending a relationship
**2** **lettres** *nf pl* **(a)** (university subject) French; (more general) arts (GB), humanities (US)
**(b)** letters; **femme de ~s** woman of letters; **avoir des ~s** to be well read
■ **~ explicative** covering letter; **~ de** ⋯⟶

recommandation letter of recommendation;
~ **recommandée** registered letter; **~s
classiques** French and Latin; **~s modernes**
French language and literature
**IDIOMS passer comme une ~ à la poste**
(colloq) ⟨reform⟩ to go through smoothly;
⟨excuse⟩ to be accepted without any
questions

**lettré, ~e** /letʀe/ nm,f man/woman of
letters

**leu: à la queue leu leu** /alakølølø/ phr
in single file

**leucémie** /løsemi/ nf leukaemia

**leur** /lœʀ/ **1** pron them; **il ~ a écrit** he
wrote to them; **il ~ a fallu faire** they had to
do
  **2** det (pl **leurs**) their; **un de ~s amis** a
friend of theirs; **pendant ~ absence** while
they were away
  **3 le leur, la leur, les leurs** pron theirs;
**c'est le ~** it's theirs; **il est des ~s** he's one
of them; **ils m'ont demandé d'être des ~s**
they asked me to come along; **ils vivent loin
des ~s** they live far away from their
families

**leurre** /lœʀ/ nm **(a)** illusion
  **(b)** (in fishing, hunting) lure
  **(c)** (Mil) decoy

**leurrer** /lœʀe/ [1] **1** vtr to delude
  **2 se leurrer** v refl (+ v être) to delude
oneself

**levain** /ləvɛ̃/ nm (fermenting agent) starter; (for
bread) leaven (GB), sourdough (US)

**levant** /ləvɑ̃/ **1** adj m **soleil ~** rising sun
  **2** nm east; **au ~** in the east; **du ~ au
couchant** from east to west

**levé, ~e**[1] /ləve/ **1** pp ▶ **LEVER**[1]
  **2** pp adj **(a) voter à main ~e** to vote by a
show of hands
  **(b)** up; **elle est toujours la première ~e** she's
always the first up

**levée**[2] /ləve/ nf **(a)** (of embargo, sentence,
martial law) lifting; (of diplomatic immunity)
removal; (of secrecy, taboo) ending; (of session)
close
  **(b)** (of mail) collection
  **(c)** (embankment) levee
  ■ **~ de boucliers** outcry

**lever**[1] /ləve/ [16] **1** vtr **(a)** to raise; **~ la
main** or **le doigt** (for permission to speak) to put
up one's hand; **~ la main sur qn** to raise a
hand to sb; **~ les bras au ciel** to throw up
one's hands; **lève les pieds quand tu
marches!** don't drag your feet!; **~ les yeux** or
**la tête** to look up
  **(b)** to lift ⟨object⟩; to raise ⟨barrier⟩; **~ son
verre** to raise one's glass
  **(c)** (out of bed) to get [sb] up ⟨child, sick
person⟩
  **(d)** to lift ⟨embargo, restriction⟩; to raise
⟨siege⟩; to end ⟨taboo, secret⟩; to remove
⟨obstacle⟩; to close ⟨session⟩
  **(e)** to levy ⟨tax⟩
  **(f)** to flush out ⟨game, partridges⟩
  **2** vi **(a)** (Culin) ⟨dough⟩ to rise

  **(b)** ⟨seedlings, corn⟩ to come up
  **3 se lever** v refl (+ v être) **(a)** to get up
  **(b)** to stand up; **se ~ de table** to leave the
table
  **(c)** ⟨person, people⟩ to rise up
  **(d)** ⟨sun⟩ to rise; **le jour se lève** it's getting
light
  **(e)** ⟨wind⟩ to rise
  **(f)** ⟨fog, mist⟩ to clear; ⟨weather⟩ to clear up

**lever**[2] /ləve/ nm **(a) être là au ~ des
enfants** to be there when the children get up
  **(b) au ~ du jour** at daybreak

**lève-tard** /lɛvtaʀ/ nmf inv late riser

**lève-tôt** /lɛvto/ nmf inv early riser

**levier** /ləvje/ nm lever; **soulever qch avec
un ~** to lever sth up.
  ■ **~ de changement de vitesse** (Aut) gear lever
(GB), gear stick (US); **~ de commande**
control stick

**lévitation** /levitasjɔ̃/ nf levitation

**lèvre** /lɛvʀ/ nf lip; **avoir le sourire aux ~s** to
be smiling; **du bout des ~s** ⟨eat⟩ half-
heartedly; ⟨reply⟩ grudgingly
  **IDIOMS être suspendu aux ~s de qn** to hang
on sb's every word

**lévrier** /levʀije/ nm greyhound

**levure** /ləvyʀ/ nf yeast; **~ chimique** baking
powder

**lexical, ~e, mpl -aux** /lɛksikal, o/ adj
lexical

**lexique** /lɛksik/ nm **(a)** glossary; (bilingual)
vocabulary (book)
  **(b)** lexicon, lexis

**lézard** /lezaʀ/ nm **(a)** lizard
  **(b)** lizardskin

**lézarde** /lezaʀd/ nf crack

**lézarder** /lezaʀde/ [1] **1** vtr to crack
  **2** vi (colloq) **~ au soleil** to bask in the sun
  **3 se lézarder** v refl (+ v être) to crack

**liaison** /ljɛzɔ̃/ nf **(a)** link; **la ~ Calais–
Douvres** the Calais–Dover line
  **(b) ~ radio** radio contact; **~ satellite**
satellite link
  **(c) assurer la ~ entre différents services** to
liaise between different services
  **(d)** (love) affair
  **(e)** (between words) liaison

**liane** /ljan/ nf creeper, liana

**liant, ~e** /ljɑ̃, ɑ̃t/ adj sociable

**liasse** /ljas/ nf (of banknotes) wad; (of letters,
papers, documents) bundle

**Liban** /libɑ̃/ pr nm Lebanon

**libellé** /libelle/ nm wording

**libeller** /libɛlle/ [1] vtr **(a)** to draw up
⟨contract⟩
  **(b)** to word ⟨article⟩
  **(c)** to make out ⟨cheque⟩

**libellule** /libɛllyl/ nf dragonfly

**libéral, ~e, mpl -aux** /libeʀal, o/ adj
  **(a)** liberal
  **(b)** (in politics) Liberal
  **(c)** free-market

**libéralisation** /libeʀalizasjɔ̃/ *nf*
liberalization; ~ **des mœurs** relaxation of
moral standards

**libéraliser** /libeʀalize/ [1] **1** *vtr* to
liberalize
**2 se libéraliser** *v refl* (+ *v être*) ⟨*country,
attitudes*⟩ to become more liberal

**libéralisme** /libeʀalism/ *nm* liberalism

**libéralité** /libeʀalite/ *nf* liberality

**libérateur, -trice** /libeʀatœʀ, tʀis/
**1** *adj* liberating
**2** *nm,f* (de pays, ville, personne) liberator

**libération** /libeʀasjɔ̃/ *nf* (a) (of prisoner,
hostage) release
**(b)** (of country, population) liberation; ~ **des
femmes** women's liberation
**(c)** relief
**(d)** (of prices) deregulation

**Libération** /libeʀasjɔ̃/ *nf* (of 1944) **la** ~ the
Liberation

**libéré, ~e** /libeʀe/ **1** *pp* ▶ LIBÉRER
**2** *pp adj* **(a)** ⟨*man, woman*⟩ liberated
**(b)** ⟨*country, area, town*⟩ free
**(c)** ⟨*post, premises*⟩ vacant

**libérer** /libeʀe/ [14] **1** *vtr* **(a)** to liberate
⟨*country, town*⟩; to free ⟨*companion, hostage*⟩
**(b)** to release ⟨*prisoner, hostage*⟩; to free
⟨*slave, animal*⟩
**(c)** to allow [sb] to go ⟨*employee*⟩
**(d)** to liberate ⟨*person, imagination*⟩; (of post,
duties) to relieve ⟨*minister*⟩; ~ **qn de
l'emprise de qn** to get sb away from sb's
influence
**(e)** to release ⟨*emotion*⟩; to give free rein to
⟨*imagination*⟩
**(f)** to relieve ⟨*mind, person*⟩; ~ **sa
conscience** to unburden oneself
**(g)** to vacate ⟨*apartment, office*⟩; ~ **la
chambre avant midi** (in hotel) to check out
before noon
**(h)** to free ⟨*arm, hand*⟩; to release ⟨*spring,
catch*⟩
**(i)** to liberalize ⟨*economy, trade*⟩; to
deregulate ⟨*prices*⟩; ~ **les loyers** to lift rent
controls
**(j)** to release ⟨*gas, energy*⟩
**2 se libérer** *v refl* (+ *v être*) **(a)** to free
oneself/itself; **se ~ d'une dette** to pay a debt
**(b) j'essaierai de me ~ mercredi** I'll try and
be free on Wednesday

**libertaire** /libɛʀtɛʀ/ *adj, nmf* libertarian

**liberté** /libɛʀte/ *nf* **(a)** (gen) freedom; **être
en ~** to be free; **élever des animaux en ~** to
raise animals in a natural habitat; **espèce
vivant en ~** species in the wild; **l'assassin
est toujours en ~** the killer is still at large;
**prendre la ~ de faire** to take the liberty of
doing; ~ **de pensée** freedom of thought
**(b)** (Law) **mettre qn en ~ conditionnelle** to
release sb on parole; **mise en ~ surveillée**
release on probation

**libertin, ~e** /libɛʀtɛ̃, in/ *adj, nm,f*
libertine

**libido** /libido/ *nf* libido

**libraire** /libʀɛʀ/ *nmf* bookseller

**librairie** /libʀɛʀi/ *nf* **(a)** bookshop (GB),
bookstore
**(b)** bookselling business

**librairie-papeterie,** *pl* **librairies-
papeteries** /libʀɛʀipapɛtʀi/ *nf*
stationer's and bookshop

**libre** /libʀ/ *adj* **(a)** ⟨*person, country*⟩ free;
~ **à elle de partir** it's up to her whether she
goes or not; **être ~ de ses actes** to do as one
wishes
**(b)** ⟨*person*⟩ free and easy; ⟨*manner*⟩ free;
⟨*opinion*⟩ candid; ⟨*morality*⟩ easygoing
**(c)** ⟨*hand, thumb*⟩ free; ⟨*road, way*⟩ clear
**(d)** ⟨*person, room*⟩ available; ⟨*seat*⟩ free
**(e)** ⟨*WC*⟩ vacant; **la ligne n'est pas ~** (on
telephone) the number is engaged (GB) *or*
busy (US)
■ ~ **arbitre** free will; ~ **circulation** freedom of
movement
**IDIOMS être ~ comme l'air** to be as free as a
bird

**libre-échange** /libʀeʃɑ̃ʒ/ *nm* free trade

**librement** /libʀəmɑ̃/ *adv* freely

**libre-service,** *pl* **libres-services**
/libʀəsɛʀvis/ **1** *adj inv* self-service
**2** *nm* **(a) le** ~ self-service
**(b)** self-service shop (GB) *or* store (US); self-
service restaurant
■ ~ **bancaire** automatic teller

**lice** /lis/ *nf* **être en ~** to have entered the
lists

**licence** /lisɑ̃s/ *nf* **(a)** (bachelor's) degree;
~ **en droit** law degree
**(b)** (Law) licence (GB); **produit sous ~**
licensed product

**licencié, ~e** /lisɑ̃sje/ **1** *pp* ▶ LICENCIER
**2** *pp adj* ⟨*student*⟩ graduate
**3** *nm,f* **(a)** graduate (GB), college graduate
(US)
**(b)** ~ **(économique)** redundant employee
(GB), laid-off worker

**licenciement** /lisɑ̃simɑ̃/ *nm* dismissal;
~ **(économique)** redundancy (GB), lay-off;
~ **abusif** unfair dismissal; ~ **collectif** mass
redundancy; ~ **sec** compulsory redundancy
(*without compensation*)

**licencier** /lisɑ̃sje/ [2] *vtr* **(a)** to make [sb]
redundant (GB), to lay [sb] off
**(b)** to dismiss (GB), to let [sb] go

**licencieux, -ieuse** /lisɑ̃sjø, øz/ *adj*
licentious

**lichen** /likɛn/ *nm* lichen

**licite** /lisit/ *adj* lawful

**licorne** /likɔʀn/ *nf* unicorn

**lie** /li/ *nf* **(a)** dregs, lees
**(b)** (figurative) dregs

**lie-de-vin** /lidvɛ̃/ *adj inv* wine-coloured
(GB)

**liège** /ljɛʒ/ *nm* cork; **bouchon en ~** cork

**liégeois, ~e** /ljeʒwa, az/ *adj* of Liège;
**café ~** *iced coffee topped with whipped cream*

**lien** /ljɛ̃/ *nm* **(a)** strap; string
**(b)** connection, link (**entre** between)    ⸱⸱⸱⸱⸱⸱⸱

(c) (gen) link, tie (**avec** with); (emotional) tie, bond; **~s économiques** economic links; **~s de parenté** family ties

**lier** /lje/ [1] **1** *vtr* (a) to tie [sb/sth] up; **il avait les mains liées** his hands were tied
(b) to bind; **ils sont très liés** they are very close
(c) to link ⟨*ideas, events*⟩
(d) **~ amitié avec qn** to strike up a friendship with sb
(e) (Mus) to slur ⟨*notes*⟩
**2 se lier** *v refl* (+ *v être*) to make friends

**lierre** /ljɛʀ/ *nm* ivy

**liesse** /ljɛs/ *nf* jubilation; **en ~** jubilant

**lieu** /ljø/ **1** *nm* (a) (*pl* **~x**) place; **~ de passage** thoroughfare; **en tous ~x** everywhere; **en ~ et place de qn** ⟨*sign, act*⟩ on behalf of sb; **en dernier ~** lastly; **avoir ~** to take place; **tenir ~ de** to serve as ⟨*bedroom, study*⟩; **il y a ~ de s'inquiéter** there is cause for anxiety; **s'il y a ~** if necessary; **donner ~ à** to cause ⟨*scandal*⟩
(b) (*pl* **~s**) coley
**2 au lieu de** *phr* instead of
**3 lieux** *nm pl* (a) **sur les ~x** at or on the scene; on the spot; **repérer les ~x** to have a scout around
(b) premises; **visiter les ~x** to visit the premises
■ **~ commun** platitude; **~ public** public place

**lieue** /ljø/ *nf* league; **~ marine** marine league
IDIOMS **j'étais à cent** *or* **mille ~s d'imaginer** I never for a moment imagined

**lieutenant** /ljøtnɑ̃/ *nm* (a) (Mil) (in army) ≈ lieutenant (GB), ≈ first lieutenant (US); (in air force) ≈ flying officer (GB), ≈ first lieutenant (US)
(b) (on boat) first officer

**lièvre** /ljɛvʀ/ *nm* (Zool) hare
IDIOMS **courir plusieurs ~s à la fois** to try to do too many things at once

**lifting** /liftiŋ/ *nm* face-lift

**ligament** /ligamɑ̃/ *nm* ligament

**ligaturer** /ligatyʀe/ [1] *vtr* (Med) to tie

**lignage** /liɲaʒ/ *nm* lineage

**ligne** /liɲ/ *nf* (a) (gen) line; **lire les ~s de la main de qn** to read sb's palm; **~ droite** straight line; (driving) straight piece of road; **la dernière ~ droite avant l'arrivée** the home straight; **je vous écris ces quelques ~s pour vous dire...** this is just a quick note to tell you...; **à la ~!** new paragraph!
(b) (in public transport) service; route; (of train, underground) line; **~ de chemin de fer** railway line; **~s intérieures** domestic flights
(c) cable; **~ aérienne** overhead cable
(d) (telephone) line
(e) figure; **garder la ~** to stay slim
(f) (of body) contours; (of face) shape; (of hills) outline; **la ~ aérodynamique d'une voiture** the aerodynamic lines of a car
(g) (of clothes, furniture, style) look
(h) outline; **raconter un événement dans ses grandes ~s** to give an outline of events
(i) fishing line; **pêche à la ~** angling

(j) line; row; **les ~s ennemies** (Mil) the enemy lines
(k) (Comput) **en ~** on line
■ **~ de conduite** line of conduct; **se donner comme ~ de conduite de faire** to make it a rule to do; **~ de démarcation** (Mil) demarcation line; **~ de mire** line of sight; **~ de tir** line of fire
IDIOMS **être en première ~** to be in the front line; (figurative) to be in the firing line; **entrer en ~ de compte** to be taken into account

**lignée** /liɲe/ *nf* (a) descendants; lineage; **de haute ~** of noble descent
(b) tradition

**lignite** /liɲit/ *nm* brown coal, lignite

**ligoter** /ligɔte/ [1] *vtr* to truss ⟨*person*⟩ up

**ligue** /lig/ *nf* league

**liguer: se liguer** /lige/ [1] *v refl* (+ *v être*) ⟨*people*⟩ to join forces

**lilas** /lila/ *adj inv*, *nm* lilac

**lilliputien, -ienne** /lilipysjɛ̃, ɛn/ *adj*, *nm,f* Lilliputian

**limace** /limas/ *nf* (Zool) slug

**limaçon** /limasɔ̃/ *nm* snail

**limaille** /limaj/ *nf* filings

**limande** /limɑ̃d/ *nf* (Zool) dab

**limande-sole**, *pl* **limandes-soles** /limɑ̃dsɔl/ *nf* (Zool) lemon sole

**lime** /lim/ *nf* (a) (Tech) file; **~ à ongles** nail file
(b) (Bot) lime
(c) (Zool) lima

**limer** /lime/ [1] **1** *vtr* (a) to file ⟨*nail, metal*⟩; to file down ⟨*key*⟩
(b) to file through ⟨*bars of cage*⟩
**2 se limer** *v refl* (+ *v être*) **se ~ les ongles** to file one's nails

**limier** /limje/ *nm* (a) bloodhound
(b) (colloq) sleuth

**limitatif, -ive** /limitatif, iv/ *adj* limiting, restrictive

**limitation** /limitasjɔ̃/ *nf* (of power, liberty) limitation, restriction; (of prices, interest rates) control; **~ de vitesse** (Aut) speed limit

**limite** /limit/ **1** *nf* (a) border
(b) (of estate, piece of land) boundary; (of sea, forest, village) edge
(c) limit; **connaître ses ~s** to know one's (own) limitations; **vraiment, il dépasse les ~s!** he's really going too far!; **à la ~, je préférerais qu'il refuse** I'd almost prefer it if he refused
(d) **à la ~ de** on the verge of; **activités à la ~ de la légalité** activities bordering on the illegal
(e) **dans une certaine ~** up to a point, to a certain extent; **dans la ~ de, dans les ~s de** within the limits of
**2 (-)limite** (*combining form*) **date(-)~** deadline; **date(-)~ de vente** sell-by date; **vitesse(-)~** maximum speed
■ **~ d'âge** age limit

**limiter** /limite/ [1] **1** *vtr* to limit, to

restrict ⟨*power, duration, number*⟩; **cela limite nos possibilités** that rather limits our scope
**2 se limiter** *v refl* (+ *v être*) **(a) se ~ à deux verres de bière par jour** to limit oneself to two glasses of beer a day; **je me limiterai à quelques observations** I'll confine myself to a few observations
**(b) se ~ à** to be limited to; **la vie ne se limite pas au travail** there's more to life than work

**limitrophe** /limitʁɔf/ *adj* ⟨*country, region*⟩ adjacent; ⟨*city*⟩ border

**limoger** /limɔʒe/ [13] *vtr* to dismiss

**limon** /limɔ̃/ *nm* **(a)** silt
**(b)** (on horse-drawn carriage) shaft

**limonade** /limɔnad/ *nf* lemonade (GB), lemon soda (US)

**limousine** /limuzin/ *nf* (Aut) limousine

**limpide** /lɛ̃pid/ *adj* **(a)** clear, limpid
**(b)** (figurative) ⟨*explanation, style*⟩ clear, lucid

**limpidité** /lɛ̃pidite/ *nf* clarity

**lin** /lɛ̃/ *nm* **(a)** flax
**(b)** linen

**linceul** /lɛ̃sœl/ *nm* shroud

**linéaire** /lineɛʁ/ *adj* linear

**linge** /lɛ̃ʒ/ *nm* **(a)** linen; **~ sale** dirty linen
**(b)** washing; **corde** *or* **fil à ~** clothes line
**(c) ~ (de corps)** underwear
**(d)** cloth
■ **~ de maison** household linen; **~ de toilette** bathroom linen

**lingère** /lɛ̃ʒɛʁ/ *nf* laundry woman

**lingerie** /lɛ̃ʒʁi/ *nf* **(a)** linen room
**(b)** lingerie

**lingot** /lɛ̃go/ *nm* ingot

**linguiste** /lɛ̃gɥist/ *nmf* linguist

**linguistique** /lɛ̃gɥistik/ **1** *adj* linguistic
**2** *nf* linguistics

**linotte** /linɔt/ *nf* linnet

**linteau**, *pl* **~x** /lɛ̃to/ *nm* lintel

**lion** /ljɔ̃/ *nm* lion; **~ de mer** sealion
IDIOMS **avoir mangé du ~** (colloq) to be full of beans (GB) (colloq), to be full of pep (US) (colloq)

**Lion** /ljɔ̃/ *pr nm* Leo

**lionceau**, *pl* **~x** /ljɔ̃so/ *nm* lion cub

**lionne** /ljɔn/ *nf* lioness

**lipide** /lipid/ *nm* lipid

**liquéfier** /likefje/ [2] *vtr*, **se liquéfier** *v refl* (+ *v être*) to liquefy

**liquette** /likɛt/ *nf* (colloq) shirt

**liqueur** /likœʁ/ *nf* liqueur

**liquidation** /likidasjɔ̃/ *nf* **(a)** (Law) (of property) liquidation; (of debts) settlement
**(b)** clearance; **~ totale (du stock)** total clearance

**liquide** /likid/ **1** *adj* **(a)** liquid; **miel ~** clear honey
**(b) argent ~** cash
**2** *nm* **(a)** liquid
**(b)** cash

■ **~ correcteur** correction fluid, white-out (fluid) (US); **~ de frein** brake fluid

**liquider** /likide/ [1] *vtr* **(a)** to settle ⟨*accounts*⟩; to liquidate ⟨*company, business*⟩
**(b)** to clear ⟨*goods, stock*⟩
**(c)** (colloq) to liquidate (colloq) ⟨*enemy, witness*⟩
**(d)** (colloq) to demolish ⟨*meal*⟩; to empty ⟨*glass*⟩

**liquidité** /likidite/ *nf* **des ~s** liquid assets

**lire**[1] /liʁ/ [66] *vtr* to read; **~ qch en diagonale** to skim through sth; **~ sur les lèvres de qn** to lip-read what sb is saying; **~ dans les pensées de qn** to read sb's mind

**lire**[2] /liʁ/ *nf* lira

**lis** /lis/ *nm inv* lily

**liseré** /lizʁe/ *nm*, **liséré** /lizeʁe/ *nm* (on dress) edging; piping

**liseron** /lizʁɔ̃/ *nm* bindweed, convolvulus

**liseuse** /lizøz/ *nf* **(a)** bed jacket
**(b)** small reading lamp

**lisible** /lizibl/ *adj* **(a)** legible
**(b)** readable

**lisière** /lizjɛʁ/ *nf* **(a)** (of wood, field) edge; (of village) outskirts
**(b)** (on piece of fabric) selvage

**lisse** /lis/ *adj* ⟨*skin, surface*⟩ smooth; ⟨*tyre*⟩ worn

**lisser** /lise/ [1] *vtr* to smooth ⟨*hair, garment*⟩; to stroke ⟨*beard*⟩

**liste** /list/ *nf* (gen) list; (at election) list (of candidates) (GB), ticket (US)
■ **~ d'attente** waiting list; **~ électorale** electoral roll; **~ de mariage** wedding list
IDIOMS **être sur ~ rouge** to be ex-directory (GB), to have an unlisted number (US)

**lister** /liste/ [1] *vtr* to list

**lit** /li/ *nm* **(a)** bed; **~ à une place** *or* **d'une personne** single bed; **~ à deux places** *or* **de deux personnes** double bed; **aller** *or* **se mettre au ~** to go to bed; **garder le ~** to stay in bed; **tirer qn du ~** to drag sb out of bed; **au ~!** bedtime!; **~ métallique** iron bedstead; **le ~ n'était pas défait** the bed had not been slept in
**(b)** (Law) marriage
**(c)** (of river) bed; **la rivière est sortie de son ~** the river has overflowed its banks
■ **~ de camp** camp bed (GB), cot (US); **~ pliant** folding bed; **~s superposés** bunk beds

**litanie** /litani/ *nf* litany

**literie** /litʁi/ *nf* bedding

**lithographie** /litɔgʁafi/ *nf* **(a)** lithography
**(b)** lithograph

**litière** /litjɛʁ/ *nf* **(a)** (for cattle) litter; (for horses) bedding; (for cats) cat litter
**(b)** (mode of transport) litter

**litige** /litiʒ/ *nm* dispute; **point de ~** bone of contention; **point at issue; les parties en ~** the litigants

**litigieux, -ieuse** /litiʒjø, øz/ *adj* ⟨*case, point, argument*⟩ contentious

**litre** /litʁ/ *nm* **(a)** (measure) litre (GB)
**(b)** litre (GB) bottle

**littéraire** /liteʀɛʀ/ **1** adj ‹work, criticism›
literary; **études ∿s** arts studies
**2** nm,f **(a)** literary person
**(b)** arts or liberal arts (US) student

**littéral**, **∿e**, mpl **-aux** /literal, o/ adj
literal

**littéralement** /literalmã/ adv literally;
verbatim

**littérature** /literatyʀ/ nf literature

**littoral**, **∿e**, mpl **-aux** /litɔral, o/ **1** adj
coastal
**2** nm coast

**liturgie** /lityʀʒi/ nf liturgy

**livide** /livid/ adj deathly pale

**living** /liviŋ/ nm living-room

**livraison** /livʀɛzõ/ nf delivery; **'∿s à
domicile'** 'we deliver'; **il est venu prendre ∿
de la commande** he came to pick up the
order

**livre¹** /livʀ/ nm book; **c'est mon ∿ de
chevet** it's my bedside book; (figurative) it's my
bible
■ **∿ blanc** blue book; **∿ de bord** logbook;
**∿ d'or** visitors' book; **∿ de poche®**
paperback; **∿ scolaire** schoolbook

**livre²** /livʀ/ nf **(a)** pound; **∿ sterling** pound
sterling; **∿ irlandaise** Irish pound, punt
**(b)** (unit of weight) half a kilo; (in UK) pound

**livrée** /livʀe/ nf livery

**livrer** /livʀe/ [1] **1** vtr **(a)** to deliver
‹goods›; **∿ qn** to deliver sb's order
**(b)** to hand [sb] over ‹criminal›; to betray
‹accomplice, secret›
**(c) être livré à soi-même** to be left to one's
own devices
**(d) il nous livre un peu de lui-même** he
reveals something of himself
**2 se livrer** v refl ( + v être) **(a) se ∿ à un
trafic de drogue** to engage in drug trafficking
**(b) se ∿ à** ‹criminal› to give oneself up to
**(c) se ∿ à un ami** to confide in a friend

**livret** /livʀɛ/ nm **(a)** booklet
**(b)** libretto
■ **∿ de caisse d'épargne** ≈ savings book (GB),
bankbook (for a savings account) (US); **∿ de
famille** family record book (of births,
marriages and deaths)

**livreur**, **-euse** /livʀœʀ, øz/ nm,f delivery
man/woman

**lobe** /lɔb/ nm lobe; **∿ de l'oreille** ear lobe

**local**, **∿e**, pl **-aux** /lɔkal, o/ **1** adj
‹newspaper, authorities› local; ‹pain,
showers› localized
**2** nm **(a)** place; **les scouts ont besoin d'un
∿** the scouts need a place to meet
**(b) ∿ commercial** commercial premises; **les
locaux du journal** the newspaper offices

**localement** /lɔkalmã/ adv on a local
level; **appliquer la crème ∿** apply the cream
locally

**localisation** /lɔkalizasjõ/ nf **(a)** location
**(b) la ∿ d'un incendie** localizing a fire

**localiser** /lɔkalize/ [1] vtr **(a)** to locate
‹person, noise›

**(b)** to confine, to localize ‹fire›

**localité** /lɔkalite/ nf locality

**locataire** /lɔkatɛʀ/ nm,f tenant

**locatif**, **-ive** /lɔkatif, iv/ adj rental

**location** /lɔkasjõ/ nf **(a)** (by owner) renting
out; (by tenant) renting; **agence de ∿** rental
agency
**(b)** rented accommodation
**(c)** rent
**(d)** (of equipment) hire; **∿ de voitures** car hire,
car rental; **contrat de ∿** rental agreement;
**∿ de vidéos** video rental
**(e)** (of theatre seats) reservation, booking (GB)

**location-vente**, pl **locations-
ventes** /lɔkasjõvãt/ nf 100% mortgage
scheme

**locomotion** /lɔkɔmɔsjõ/ nf locomotion

**locomotive** /lɔkɔmɔtiv/ nf engine,
locomotive; **∿ à vapeur** steam engine

**locuteur**, **-trice** /lɔkytœʀ, tʀis/ nm,f
speaker

**locution** /lɔkysjõ/ nf phrase; idiom

**logarithme** /lɔgaʀitm/ nm logarithm, log

**loge** /lɔʒ/ nf **(a)** (caretaker's dwelling) lodge
**(b)** (of actor) dressing room; (in theatre) box
**(c)** (in freemasonry) Lodge
**(d)** loggia

**logé**, **∿e** /lɔʒe/ **1** pp ▶ LOGER
**2** pp adj housed; **être ∿, nourri, blanchi** to
have bed, board and one's laundry done

**logement** /lɔʒmã/ nm **(a)** accommodation;
**∿ individuel** flat (GB), apartment (US); house
**(b)** housing; **la crise du ∿** the housing crisis

**loger** /lɔʒe/ [13] **1** vtr **(a)** to house ‹student›
**(b)** to put [sb] up ‹friend›; to provide
accommodation for ‹refugees›
**(c)** ‹hotel› to have accommodation for
**(d)** to put; **je n'ai pas pu ∿ tous mes
meubles dans le salon** I couldn't fit all my
furniture in the living room
**(e) ∿ une balle dans la tête de qn** to shoot sb
in the head
**2** vi **(a)** to live
**(b)** to stay; **∿ à l'hôtel** to stay at a hotel
**3 se loger** v refl ( + v être) **(a)** to find
accommodation; **se nourrir et se ∿** to pay for
food and accommodation
**(b) se ∿ dans qch** to get stuck in sth; ‹dust›
to collect in sth; **la balle est venue se ∿ dans
le genou** the bullet lodged in his/her knee

**logeur**, **-euse** /lɔʒœʀ, øz/ nm,f lodger

**loggia** /lɔdʒja/ nf loggia

**logiciel** /lɔʒisjɛl/ nm **(a)** software; **∿ de
base** system(s) software
**(b)** program
**(c)** (Comput) **∿ de navigation** browser

**logique** /lɔʒik/ **1** adj **(a)** logical; **il n'est
pas ∿ avec lui-même** he is not consistent
**(b)** (colloq) reasonable; **ce serait ∿ qu'ils
soient en colère** one could understand why
they would be angry
**2** nf logic; **manquer de ∿** to be illogical;
**c'est dans la ∿ des choses** it's in the nature
of things; **en toute ∿** logically

**logiquement** /lɔʒikmɑ̃/ *adv* logically

**logis** /lɔʒi/ *nm inv* home, dwelling

**logistique** /lɔʒistik/ *nf* logistics

**logo** /lɔgo/ *nm* logo

**loi** /lwa/ *nf* (a) law; **voter une ~** to pass a law

(b) **la ~** the law; **enfreindre la ~** to break the law; **tomber sous le coup de la ~** to be *or* constitute an offence (GB); **faire la ~** (figurative) to lay down the law

(c) rule; law; **la ~ du milieu** the law of the underworld; **c'est la ~ des séries** things always happen in a row

■ **~ d'amnistie** *act granting amnesty to some offenders*; **~ communautaire** community law; **~ informatique et libertés** data protection act; **~ de la jungle** law of the jungle

**loin** /lwɛ̃/ **1** *adv* (a) a long way, far (away); **c'est ~** it's a long way; **c'est trop ~** it's too far; **il habite plus ~** he lives further *or* farther away; **du plus ~ qu'il m'aperçut** as soon as he saw me; **voir plus ~** (in text) see below

(b) (in time) **tout cela est bien ~** that was all a long time ago; **aussi ~ que je me souvienne** as far back as I can remember; **l'été n'est plus très ~ maintenant** summer isn't far off now

(c) (figurative) **de là à dire qu'il est incompétent, il n'y a pas ~** that comes close to saying he's incompetent; **il n'est pas bête, ~ s'en faut!** he's not stupid, far from it!; **ça va beaucoup plus ~** it goes much further

**2 loin de** *phr* (a) (in space) far from; **est-ce encore ~ d'ici?** is it much further *or* farther from here?

(b) (in time) far from; **cela ne fait pas ~ de quatre ans que je suis ici** I've been here for almost four years now

(c) (figurative) far from, a long way from; **~ de moi cette idée!** nothing could be further from my mind!; **avec l'imprimante, il faut compter pas ~ de 8 000 euros** if you include the printer, you're talking about 8,000 euros or thereabouts

**3 de loin** *phr* from a distance; **je ne vois pas très bien de ~** I can't see very well at a distance; **c'est de ~ ton meilleur roman** it's by far your best novel

**4 au loin** *phr* **au ~** in the distance

**5 de loin en loin** *phr* (a) on pouvait voir **des maisons de ~ en ~** you could see houses scattered here and there

(b) every now and then

IDIOMS **~ des yeux, ~ du cœur** (Proverb) out of sight, out of mind

**lointain, ~e** /lwɛ̃tɛ̃, ɛn/ **1** *adj*
(a) ⟨*country, past*⟩ distant
(b) ⟨*link*⟩ remote
(c) ⟨*person*⟩ distant
**2** *nm* background; **dans le ~** ⟨*see, hear*⟩ in the distance

**loir** /lwaʀ/ *nm* (edible) dormouse

**loisir** /lwaziʀ/ *nm* (a) spare time; **(tout) à ~** at (great) leisure

(b) **avoir tout ~ de faire** to have plenty of time to do
(c) leisure activity

**lombaire** /lɔ̃bɛʀ/ *nf* lumbar vertebra

**londonien, -ienne** /lɔ̃dɔnjɛ̃, ɛn/ *adj* (of) London

**Londres** /lɔ̃dʀ/ *pr n* London

**long, longue** /lɔ̃, lɔ̃g/ **1** *adj* long; **plus/trop ~ de deux mètres** two metres (GB) longer/too long; **être ~ (à faire)** ⟨*person*⟩ to be slow (to do); **être en longue maladie** to be on extended sick leave; **il guérira, mais ce sera ~** he will get better, but it's going to take a long time; **être ~ à la détente** (colloq) to be slow on the uptake (colloq)

**2** *adv* (a) **en dire ~/trop ~/plus ~** to say a lot/too much/more (**sur qn/qch** about sb/sth)

(b) **s'habiller ~** to wear longer skirts

**3** *nm* (a) **un câble de six mètres de ~** a cable six metres (GB) long, a six-metre (GB) long cable; **en ~** lengthwise; **en ~ et en large** ⟨*tell*⟩ in great detail; **marcher de ~ en large** to pace up and down; **en ~, en large et en travers** (colloq) ⟨*tell*⟩ at great length; **le ~ du mur** along the wall; up *or* down the wall; **tomber de tout son ~** to fall flat (on one's face)

**4 à la longue** *phr* in the end, eventually

■ **~ métrage** feature-length film

**long-courrier**, *pl* **~s** /lɔ̃kuʀje/ *nm*
(a) ocean-going ship
(b) long-haul aircraft

**longer** /lɔ̃ʒe/ [13] *vtr* (a) ⟨*person, train*⟩ to go along ⟨*forest, coast*⟩; to follow ⟨*river*⟩

(b) ⟨*garden, road*⟩ to run alongside ⟨*lake, field*⟩

**longévité** /lɔ̃ʒevite/ *nf* longevity

**longiligne** /lɔ̃ʒiliɲ/ *adj* lanky, rangy

**longitude** /lɔ̃ʒityd/ *nf* longitude

**longitudinal, ~e**, *mpl* **-aux** /lɔ̃ʒitydinal, o/ *adj* longitudinal, lengthwise

**longtemps** /lɔ̃tɑ̃/ *adv* ⟨*wait, sleep*⟩ (for) a long time; **il t'a fallu ~?** did it take you long?; **~ avant/après** long before/after; **je peux le garder plus ~?** can I keep it a bit longer?; **il n'y a pas ~ qu'il travaille ici** he hasn't worked here long; **il y a** *or* **ça fait ~ qu'il n'a pas téléphoné** he hasn't phoned for ages (colloq); **il est mort depuis ~** he died a long time ago; **il n'y a pas si ~ c'était encore possible** it was still possible until quite recently

**longue** ▶ LONG 1, 4

**longuement** /lɔ̃gmɑ̃/ *adv* ⟨*hesitate, talk*⟩ for a long time; ⟨*explain, interview*⟩ at length

**longueur** /lɔ̃gœʀ/ **1** *nf* (a) (in space, time) length; **la maison est tout en ~** the house is long and narrow; **traîner en ~** ⟨*film, book*⟩ to go on forever

(b) (in race, swimming) length; **avoir une ~ d'avance sur qn** (Sport) to be one length ahead of sb; (figurative) to be ahead of sb; **le saut en ~** the long *or* broad (US) jump

(d) length

**2** **longueurs** nf pl (in film, book, speech) overlong passages

**3** **à longueur de** phr à ~ de journée all day long; à ~ d'année all year round; à ~ d'émissions programme (GB) after programme (GB)

■ ~ d'onde wavelength

**longue-vue**, pl **longues-vues** /lɔ̃gvy/ nf telescope

**look** /luk/ nm (colloq) look; image

**looping** /lupiŋ/ nm loop

**lopin** /lɔpɛ̃/ nm ~ (de terre) patch of land

**loquace** /lɔkas/ adj talkative, loquacious

**loque** /lɔk/ **1** nf ~ (humaine) (human) wreck

**2** **loques** nf pl rags

**loquet** /lɔkɛ/ nm latch

**lorgner** /lɔʀɲe/ [1] vtr (colloq) to give [sb] the eye ⟨person⟩ (colloq); to cast longing glances at ⟨jewel, cake⟩; to have one's eye on ⟨inheritance, job⟩

**lorgnette** /lɔʀɲɛt/ nf (a) opera-glasses
(b) spy-glass

**lorgnon** /lɔʀɲɔ̃/ nm (a) lorgnette
(b) pince-nez

**lors**: **lors de** /lɔʀ/ phr (a) during
(b) at the time of

**lorsque** (**lorsqu'** before vowel or mute h) /lɔʀsk(ə)/ conj when

**losange** /lɔzɑ̃ʒ/ nm (shape) lozenge; en ~ diamond-shaped

**lot** /lo/ nm (a) (of inheritance) share; (of land) plot
(b) (in lottery) prize; gagner le gros ~ to hit the jackpot
(c) (of objects for sale) batch; (at auction) lot
(d) (of person) être au-dessus du ~ to be above the average
(e) fate, lot

**loterie** /lɔtʀi/ nf raffle; (in fair) tombola (GB), raffle (US); (large scale) lottery

**loti**, ~**e** /lɔti/ adj bien/mal ~ well/badly off

**lotion** /losjɔ̃/ nf lotion

**lotir** /lɔtiʀ/ [3] vtr terrain(s) à ~ plots for sale

**lotissement** /lɔtismɑ̃/ nm housing estate (GB), subdivision (US)

**loto** /lɔto/ nm lotto; le ~ national national lottery

**lotte** /lɔt/ nf monkfish; (freshwater) burbot

**lotus** /lɔtys/ nm inv lotus

**louable** /luabl/ adj commendable, praiseworthy

**louage** /luaʒ/ nm voiture de ~ rented car (GB), rental car (US)

**louange** /luɑ̃ʒ/ nf praise

**loubard** /lubaʀ/ nm (colloq) hooligan, delinquent youth

**louche** /luʃ/ **1** adj ⟨person, past, affair⟩ shady; ⟨place⟩ seedy
**2** nf ladle; ladleful

**loucher** /luʃe/ [1] vi to have a squint

**louer** /lue/ [1] vtr (a) ⟨owner, landlord⟩ to

let (GB), to rent out ⟨house⟩; to hire out ⟨premises⟩; to rent out ⟨equipment⟩; 'à ~' 'for rent', 'to let' (GB)
(b) ⟨tenant⟩ to rent ⟨house⟩; to hire ⟨room⟩; to rent ⟨equipment, film⟩
(c) to hire ⟨staff⟩
(d) to praise; Dieu soit loué thank God

**loufoque** /lufɔk/ adj (colloq) crazy (colloq)

**louis** /lwi/ nm inv ~ d'or (gold) louis

**loukoum** /lukum/ nm Turkish delight

**loulou** /lulu/ nm (a) spitz
(b) (colloq) hooligan, delinquent youth
(c) (colloq) pet (GB) (colloq), honey (US)

**loup** /lu/ nm (a) wolf; le grand méchant ~ the big bad wolf; à pas de ~ stealthily
(b) ~ (de mer) (sea) bass
(c) domino, mask

■ (vieux) ~ de mer old salt, old tar

IDIOMS avoir une faim de ~ to be ravenous; être connu comme le ~ blanc to be known to everybody; hurler avec les ~s to follow the herd or crowd; se jeter dans la gueule du ~ to stick one's head in the lion's mouth; les ~s ne se mangent pas entre eux (Proverb) (there is) honour (GB) among thieves; quand on parle du ~ (on en voit la queue) (Proverb) speak of the devil; l'homme est un ~ pour l'homme (Proverb) dog eat dog

**loupe** /lup/ nf magnifying glass

**louper** (colloq) /lupe/ [1] **1** vtr (a) to miss ⟨train, opportunity, visitor⟩; il n'en loupe pas une he's always opening his big mouth
(b) to flunk (colloq) ⟨exam⟩; to screw up (colloq) ⟨sauce, piece of work⟩
**2** vi j'avais dit que ça se casserait, ça n'a pas loupé I said it would break, and sure enough it did; tu vas tout faire ~ you'll mess everything up

**loup-garou**, pl **loups-garous** /lugaʀu/ nm werewolf

**loupiote** /lupjɔt/ nf (colloq) small lamp

**lourd**, ~**e** /luʀ, luʀd/ **1** adj (a) ⟨person, object, metal⟩ heavy
(b) ⟨stomach, head, steps⟩ heavy; ⟨gesture⟩ clumsy
(c) ⟨meal, food⟩ heavy; ⟨wine⟩ heady; ~ à digérer heavy on the stomach
(d) ⟨equipment, weapons⟩ heavy
(e) ⟨fine, taxation⟩ heavy
(f) ⟨defeat, responsibility⟩ heavy; ⟨mistake⟩ serious
(g) ⟨administration, structure⟩ unwieldy; ⟨staff numbers⟩ large
(h) ⟨person, animal⟩ ungainly; ⟨body, object, architecture⟩ heavy; ⟨building⟩ cumbersome, ponderous
(i) ⟨joke⟩ flat; ⟨style⟩ clumsy
(j) ⟨atmosphere, silence⟩ heavy; ⟨heat⟩ sultry
(k) être ~ de dangers to be fraught with danger
**2** adv (a) peser ~ to weigh a lot; (figurative) to carry a lot of weight
(b) (of weather) il fait ~ it's close
(c) (colloq) pas ~ not a lot, not much; dix personnes, ça ne fait pas ~ ten people, that's not a lot

IDIOMS **avoir la main** ~**e** to be heavy-handed; **avoir la main** ~**e avec le sel/le parfum** to overdo the salt/the perfume

**lourdement** /luʀdəmɑ̃/ *adv* (a) heavily; **se tromper** ~ to be gravely mistaken
(b) **marcher** ~ to walk clumsily; **insister** ~ **sur** to keep going on about

**lourdeur** /luʀdœʀ/ *nf* (a) (of organization) complexity
(b) heaviness
(c) (of style) clumsiness; (in a text) clumsy expression
(d) weight
(e) (of person) oafishness; (of joke) poorness; (of architecture) ungainliness
(f) (of weather) closeness

**loutre** /lutʀ/ *nf* (a) otter
(b) otterskin

**louve** /luv/ *nf* she-wolf

**louveteau**, *pl* ~**x** /luvto/ *nm* (Zool) wolf cub

**louvoyer** /luvwaje/ [23] *vi* (a) ⟨ship⟩ to tack
(b) (figurative) to manoeuvre (GB), to maneuver (US)

**lover: se lover** /lɔve/ [1] *v refl* (+ *v être*) ⟨snake⟩ to coil itself up; ⟨person⟩ to curl up

**loyal**, ~**e**, *mpl* **-aux** /lwajal, o/ *adj*
(a) ⟨friend⟩ true; ⟨servant⟩ loyal, faithful
(b) ⟨procedure, conduct⟩ honest; ⟨competition, game⟩ fair

**loyalisme** /lwajalism/ *nm* loyalty

**loyaliste** /lwajalist/ *adj, nmf* loyalist

**loyauté** /lwajote/ *nf* (a) loyalty
(b) honesty

**loyer** /lwaje/ *nm* rent

**lu**, ~**e** /ly/ ▶ LIRE¹

**lubie** /lybi/ *nf* whim

**lubricité** /lybʀisite/ *nf* lechery; lewdness

**lubrifiant** /lybʀifjɑ̃/ *nm* lubricant

**lubrifier** /lybʀifje/ [2] *vtr* to lubricate

**lubrique** /lybʀik/ *adj* ⟨person⟩ lecherous; ⟨look, dance⟩ lewd

**lucarne** /lykaʀn/ *nf* (small) window; (in roof) skylight

**lucide** /lysid/ *adj* clear-sighted; lucid

**lucidité** /lysidite/ *nf* lucidity; clear-headedness; clarity; **juger en toute** ~ to judge without any illusions

**luciole** /lysjɔl/ *nf* firefly

**lucratif**, **-ive** /lykʀatif, iv/ *adj* lucrative

**ludique** /lydik/ *adj* ⟨activity⟩ play

**ludothèque** /lydɔtɛk/ *nf* toy library

**luette** /lɥɛt/ *nf* uvula

**lueur** /lɥœʀ/ *nf* (faint) light; **les** ~**s de la ville** the city lights; **à la** ~ **d'une bougie** by candlelight; **à la** ~ **des événements d'hier** in the light of yesterday's events; **les dernières** ~**s du soleil couchant** the dying glow of the sunset

**luge** /lyʒ/ *nf* (a) toboggan (GB), sled (US)
(b) (Sport) luge

**lugubre** /lygybʀ/ *adj* gloomy; mournful

**lui¹** /lɥi/ *pron* **1** *pron m* (a) he; **elle lit,** ~ **regarde la télévision** she's reading, he's watching TV; ~ **seul a le droit de parler** he alone has the right to talk
(b) him; **à cause de** ~ because of him; **je les vois plus souvent que** ~ I see them more often than he does; I see them more often than I see him; **c'est à** ~ it's his, it belongs to him; it's his turn; **c'est à** ~ **de choisir** it's up to him to choose
**2** *pron mf* it; **le parti lance un appel, apportez-**~ **votre soutien** the party is launching an appeal—give it your support; **l'Espagne a signé, le Portugal,** ~, **n'a pas encore donné son accord** Spain has signed while Portugal hasn't yet agreed
**3** *pron f* her; **je** ~ **ai annoncé la nouvelle** I told her the news

**lui²** /lɥi/ ▶ LUIRE

**lui-même** /lɥimɛm/ *pron* (a) (referring to person) himself; '**M. Greiner?**'—'~' (on phone) 'Mr Greiner?'—'speaking'
(b) (referring to object, concept) itself

**luire** /lɥiʀ/ [69] *vi* to shine; to glow; **leur regard luisait de colère** their eyes blazed with anger

**luisant,** ~**e** /lɥizɑ̃, ɑ̃t/ *adj* shining; glistening

**lumbago** /lœbago/ *nm* back pain

**lumière** /lymjɛʀ/ **1** *nf* (a) light; ~ **naturelle/électrique** natural/electric light; **la** ~ **du jour** daylight; **il y a une** ~ **très particulière dans cette région** there's a very special quality to the light in this region; **les** ~**s de la ville** the city lights; **à la** ~ **d'une chandelle** by candlelight; **à la** ~ **des récents événements** in the light of recent events
(b) (person) **ce n'est pas une** ~ he'll never set the world on fire
**2 lumières** *nf pl* (a) (of vehicle) lights
(b) (colloq) **j'ai besoin de vos** ~**s** I need to pick your brains

**Lumières** /lymjɛʀ/ *nf pl* **le siècle des** ~ the Age of Enlightenment

**luminaire** /lyminɛʀ/ *nm* light (fitting)

**lumineux, -euse** /lyminø, øz/ *adj*
(a) luminous; **panneau** ~ electronic display (board); **enseigne lumineuse** neon sign; **rayon** ~ ray of light
(b) **idée lumineuse** brilliant idea
(c) ⟨smile, gaze⟩ radiant

**luminosité** /lyminozite/ *nf* brightness, luminosity

**lump** /lœmp/ *nm* **œufs de** ~ lumpfish roe

**lunaire** /lynɛʀ/ *adj* lunar

**lunatique** /lynatik/ *nmf* moody person

**lunch** /lœʃ/ *nm* buffet (lunch); buffet (supper)

**lundi** /lœdi/ *nm* Monday

**lune** /lyn/ *nf* moon; **pleine** ~ full moon.
■ ~ **de miel** honeymoon; ~ **rousse** ≈ April moon
IDIOMS **être dans la** ~ (colloq) to have one's head in the clouds; **avoir l'air de tomber de la** ~ to look blank; **demander la** ~ (colloq) to ····⊹

cry for the moon; **promettre la** ~ (colloq) to promise the earth; **décrocher la** ~ to do the impossible

**luné, ~e** /lyne/ *adj* (colloq) **mal** ~ grumpy

**lunette** /lynɛt/ ⊡ *nf* lavatory seat
⊡ **lunettes** *nf pl* **(a)** glasses
**(b)** (protective) goggles; ~**s de natation** swimming goggles
■ ~ **arrière** (Aut) rear window; ~**s noires** dark glasses; ~**s de soleil** sunglasses

**lunule** /lynyl/ *nf* (on nail) half-moon

**lurette** /lyrɛt/ *nf* (colloq) **il y a** *or* **cela fait belle** ~ **que je ne l'ai pas vue** it's been ages since I last saw her (colloq)

**luron** /lyrɔ̃/ *nm* fellow

**lustre** /lystr/ ⊡ *nm* **(a)** (gen) (decorative) ceiling light; (made of glass) chandelier
**(b)** sheen
**(c)** (of place, institution) prestigious image; **donner un nouveau** ~ **à** to give fresh appeal to
⊡ **lustres** *nm pl* (colloq) **depuis des** ~**s** for ages (colloq)

**lustré, ~e** /lystre/ *adj* **(a)** glossy; (through wear) shiny
**(b)** ⟨fabric⟩ glazed

**lustrer** /lystre/ [1] *vtr* to polish ⟨shoes, mirror⟩

**luth** /lyt/ *nm* **(a)** (Mus) lute
**(b)** (Zool) leatherback

**luthier** /lytje/ *nm* stringed instrument maker

**lutin** /lytɛ̃/ *nm* goblin

**lutte** /lyt/ *nf* **(a)** conflict; struggle; fight; ~ **d'influence** power struggle; **la** ~ **contre le cancer** the fight against cancer
**(b)** (Sport) wrestling
■ ~ **armée** armed conflict; ~ **de classes** class war; ~ **d'intérêts** clash of interests

**lutter** /lyte/ [1] *vi* to struggle; to fight; ~ **contre qn** to fight against sb; ~ **contre** to fight against ⟨crime, unemployment, illness⟩; to fight against ⟨violence⟩; to contend with ⟨noise, bad weather⟩; **Louis luttait contre le sommeil** Louis was struggling to stay awake

**lutteur, -euse** /lytœr, øz/ *nm,f* (gen) fighter; (Sport) wrestler

**luxation** /lyksasjɔ̃/ *nf* dislocation

**luxe** /lyks/ *nm* luxury; **s'offrir le** ~ **de faire** to afford the luxury of doing; (figurative) to give oneself the satisfaction of doing; **je l'ai nettoyé et ce n'était pas du** ~ (colloq) I gave it a much needed clean; **avoir des goûts de** ~ to have expensive tastes

**Luxembourg** /lyksɑ̃bur/ *pr nm* Luxembourg

**Luxembourgeois, ~e** /lyksɑ̃burʒwa, az/ *nm,f* **(a)** native of Luxembourg
**(b)** inhabitant of Luxembourg

**luxer: se luxer** /lykse/ *v refl* (+ *v être*) **se** ~ **l'épaule** to dislocate one's shoulder

**luxueux, -euse** /lyksɥø, øz/ *adj* luxurious

**luxure** /lyksyr/ *nf* lust

**luxuriant, ~e** /lyksyrjɑ̃, ɑ̃t/ *adj* luxuriant

**luzerne** /lyzɛrn/ *nf* alfalfa, lucerne (GB)

**lycée** /lise/ *nm* secondary school (*preparing students aged 15–18 for the baccalaureate*)

**lycéen, -éenne** /liseɛ̃, ɛn/ *nm,f* secondary school student

**lymphatique** /lɛ̃fatik/ *adj* **(a)** lethargic
**(b)** lymphatic

**lyncher** /lɛ̃ʃe/ [1] *vtr* to lynch

**lynx** /lɛ̃ks/ *nm inv* lynx
IDIOMS **avoir un œil** *or* **des yeux de** ~ to have very keen eyesight

**lyonnais, ~e**[1] /ljɔnɛ, ɛz/ *adj* of Lyons

**lyonnaise**[2] /ljɔnɛz/ *nf* **(a)** (Culin) **à la** ~ à la lyonnaise
**(b)** *regional game of boules*

**lyophiliser** /ljɔfilize/ [1] *vtr* to freeze-dry

**lyre** /lir/ *nf* lyre

**lyrique** /lirik/ *adj* **(a)** (Mus) ⟨song, composer⟩ operatic; ⟨singer, season⟩ opera
**(b)** ⟨poetry, poet⟩ lyric; ⟨content, tone⟩ lyrical

**lyrisme** /lirism/ *nm* lyricism

**lys** /lis/ *nm inv* lily

# M m

**m, M** /ɛm/ *nm inv* **(a)** (letter) m, M
**(b)** (*written abbr* = **mètre**) 30 m 30 m

**m'** ▶ ME

**M.** (*written abbr* = **Monsieur**) Mr

**ma** ▶ MON

**macabre** /makabʀ/ *adj* macabre

**macadam** /makadam/ *nm* tarmac®

**macaque** /makak/ *nm* macaque

**macaron** /makaʀɔ̃/ *nm* **(a)** macaroon
**(b)** lapel badge; sticker

**macédoine** /masedwan/ *nf* mixed diced
vegetables

**macérer** /maseʀe/ [14] *vi* ⟨plant, fruit⟩ to
soak, to steep; ⟨meat⟩ to marinate

**mâche** /mɑʃ/ *nf* corn salad, lamb's lettuce

**mâcher** /mɑʃe/ [1] *vtr* to chew
IDIOMS ∼ **la besogne** *or* **le travail à qn** to
break the back of the work for sb; **il ne
mâche pas ses mots** he doesn't mince his
words

**machette** /maʃɛt/ *nf* machete

**machiavélique** /makjavelik/ *adj*
Machiavellian

**machin** /maʃɛ̃/ *nm* (colloq) **(a)** thing,
thingummy (colloq), whatsit (colloq)
**(b)** old fogey

**Machin, ∼e** /maʃɛ̃, in/ *nm,f* (colloq)
what's-his-name (colloq)/what's-her-name
(colloq)

**machinal, ∼e,** *mpl* **-aux** /maʃinal, o/
*adj* ⟨gesture, reaction⟩ mechanical

**machination** /maʃinasjɔ̃/ *nf* plot

**machine** /maʃin/ *nf* **(a)** machine; **taper à
la ∼** to type; **coudre à la ∼** to machine-sew;
**faire deux ∼s (de linge)** (colloq) to do two
loads of washing
**(b)** (Naut) engine; **faire ∼ arrière** to go astern;
(figurative) to back-pedal
■ **∼ à calculer** calculating machine; **∼ à
coudre** sewing machine; **∼ à écrire**
typewriter; **∼ à laver** washing machine; **∼ à
laver la vaisselle** dishwasher; **∼ à sous** slot
machine, one-armed bandit

**machinerie** /maʃinʀi/ *nf* **(a)** machinery
**(b)** machine room; (Naut) engine room

**machiste** /ma(t)ʃist/ *adj, nm* male
chauvinist

**mâchoire** /mɑʃwaʀ/ *nf* jaw

**mâchouiller** /mɑʃuje/ [1] *vtr* (colloq) to
chew (on)

**maçon** /masɔ̃/ *nm* bricklayer; builder;
mason

**maçonnerie** /masɔnʀi/ *nf* building;
bricklaying; masonry work

**maculer** /makyle/ [1] *vtr* to smudge; **∼ qch
de sang** to spatter sth with blood

**madame,** *pl* **mesdames** /madam,
medam/ *nf* **(a)** (addressing a woman whose name
you do not know) **Madame** (in letter) Dear
Madam; **bonsoir ∼!** good evening!;
**mesdames et messieurs bonsoir** good
evening ladies and gentlemen
**(b)** (addressing a woman whose name you know, for
example Bon) Mrs, Ms; (in a letter) **Madame**
Dear Ms Bon; **bonjour, ∼** good morning,
Mrs Bon
**(c)** (polite form of address) madam; '**∼ a
sonné?**' 'you rang, Madam?'

**Madeleine** /madlɛn/ *pr n* **pleurer comme
une ∼** to cry one's eyes out

**mademoiselle,** *pl*
**mesdemoiselles** /madmwazɛl,
medmwazɛl/ *nf* **(a)** (addressing a woman whose
name you do not know) **Mademoiselle** (in letter)
Dear Madam; **bonjour, ∼!** good morning!;
**mesdames, mesdemoiselles, messieurs**
ladies and gentlemen
**(b)** (addressing a woman whose name you know, for
example Bon) Miss, Ms; (in a letter)
**Mademoiselle** Dear Miss Bon; **bonjour, ∼**
good morning, Miss Bon
**(c)** (polite form of address) madam; '**∼ a
sonné?**' 'you rang, Madam?'

**madone** /madɔn/ *nf* madonna

**madrier** /madʀije/ *nm* beam

**maestria** /maɛstʀija/ *nf* brilliance,
panache

**maf(f)ia** /mafja/ *nf* mafia; **la Mafia** the
Mafia

**maf(f)ieux, -ieuse** /mafjø, øz/ *adj*
mafia

**magasin** /magazɛ̃/ *nm* **(a)** shop, store;
**grand ∼** department store; **faire les ∼s** to go
shopping
**(b)** **avoir en ∼** to have in stock

**magasinier, -ière** /magazinje, ɛʀ/ *nm,f*
**(a)** stock controller
**(b)** warehouse keeper

**magazine** /magazin/ *nm* magazine

**mage** /maʒ/ *nm* magus; **les rois ∼s** the
(Three) Wise Men

**maghrébin, ∼e** /magʀebɛ̃, in/ *adj* North
African, Maghrebi

**magicien, -ienne** /maʒisjɛ̃, ɛn/ *nm,f*
**(a)** magician/enchantress
**(b)** conjuror
**(c)** (figurative) wizard

**magie** /maʒi/ *nf* **(a)** magic
**(b)** conjuring

**magique** /maʒik/ *adj* **(a)** magic; **formule
∼** magic words
**(b)** (figurative) magical

**m**

**magistère** /maʒistɛʀ/ *nm*: high-level
University degree

**magistral, ~e,** *mpl* **-aux** /maʒistʀal, o/
*adj* **(a)** brilliant; **réussir un coup ~** to bring
off a masterstroke
**(b)** magisterial

**magistrat** /maʒistʀa/ *nm* magistrate

**magistrature** /maʒistʀatyʀ/ *nf*
**(a)** magistracy
**(b)** public office

**magma** /magma/ *nm* **(a)** magma
**(b)** (figurative) jumble

**magnanime** /maɲanim/ *adj*
magnanimous

**magnat** /maɲa/ *nm* magnate, tycoon

**magner: se magner** /maɲe/ [1] *v refl*
(+ *v être*) (slang) to get a move on (colloq)

**magnésie** /maɲezi/ *nf* magnesia

**magnétique** /maɲetik/ *adj* magnetic

**magnétiser** /maɲetize/ [1] *vtr* **(a)** to
magnetize
**(b)** to hypnotize, to mesmerize

**magnétiseur, -euse** /maɲetizœʀ, øz/
*nm,f* healer

**magnétisme** /maɲetism/ *nm* magnetism

**magnéto(phone)** /maɲeto(fɔn)/ *nm* tape
recorder

**magnétoscope** /maɲetɔskɔp/ *nm* VCR,
video recorder

**magnificence** /maɲifisɑ̃s/ *nf*
magnificence, splendour (GB)

**magnifier** /maɲifje/ [1] *vtr* **(a)** to idealize
⟨memory⟩, ⟨feeling⟩
**(b)** to glorify ⟨heroism⟩, ⟨act⟩

**magnifique** /maɲifik/ *adj* gorgeous,
magnificent

**magot** /mago/ *nm* (colloq) pile (of money)
(colloq)

**magouille** /maguj/ *nf* (colloq) **(a)** wangling
(colloq), fiddling (colloq)
**(b)** trick; **~s politiques** political
skulduggery; **~s électorales** election rigging

**magret** /magʀɛ/ *nm* **~ de canard** duck
breast

**Mahomet** /maɔme/ *pr n* Mohammed

**mai** /mɛ/ *nm* May; **le premier ~** May Day

**maigre** /mɛgʀ/ **1** *adj* **(a)** ⟨person⟩ thin
**(b)** ⟨meat⟩ lean; ⟨cheese⟩ low-fat
**(c)** ⟨day⟩ without meat; **faire** or **manger ~** to
abstain from meat
**(d)** ⟨talents, savings⟩ meagre (GB); ⟨applause⟩
scant
**(e)** ⟨lawn, hair⟩ sparse
**2** *nmf* thin man/woman; **c'est une fausse ~**
she looks thinner than she is

**maigrement** /mɛgʀəmɑ̃/ *adv* ⟨paid⟩
poorly

**maigreur** /mɛgʀœʀ/ *nf* **(a)** thinness
**(b)** meagreness (GB)

**maigrichon, -onne** /mɛgʀiʃɔ̃, ɔn/ *adj*
skinny

**maigrir** /mɛgʀiʀ/ [3] *vi* to lose weight

**mail** /maj/ *nm* **(a)** mall

**(b)** (game) pall-mall
**(c)** e-mail (message)

**mailer** /majle/ *vt* to e-mail

**mailing** /mɛliŋ/ *nm* (controversial) **(a)** direct
mail advertising
**(b)** mail shot
**(c)** mailing pack

**maille** /maj/ *nf* **(a)** stitch; **une ~ qui file**
(in tights) a ladder
**(b)** mesh; **passer à travers les ~s** to slip
through the net
**(c)** (in fence) link
**IDIOMS avoir ~ à partir avec qn** to have a
brush with sb

**maillet** /majɛ/ *nm* mallet

**maillon** /majɔ̃/ *nm* (in chain) link

**maillot** /majo/ *nm* **(a)** ~ (de corps) vest
(GB), undershirt (US)
**(b)** (of footballer) shirt; (of cyclist) jersey
**(c)** swimsuit
■ **~ de bain** swimsuit; **le ~ jaune** the leader
in the Tour de France

**main** /mɛ̃/ *nf* **(a)** hand; **se donner** or **se tenir
la ~** to hold hands; **saluer qn de la ~** to
wave at sb; **haut les ~s!** hands up!;
**demander la ~ de qn** to ask for sb's hand in
marriage; **avoir qch bien en ~(s)** to hold sth
firmly; (figurative) to have sth well in hand; **si
tu lèves la ~ sur elle** if you lay a finger on
her; **à la ~** ⟨sew⟩ by hand; ⟨adjust⟩ manually;
**fait ~** handmade; **vol à ~ armée** armed
robbery; **donner un coup de ~ à qn** to give
sb a hand
**(b)** **une ~ secourable** a helping hand; **une ~
criminelle** someone with criminal intentions
**(c)** **avoir qch sous la ~** to have sth to hand;
**cela m'est tombé sous la ~** I just happened
to come across it; **mettre la ~ sur qch** to get
one's hands on sth; **je n'arrive pas à mettre la
~ dessus** I can't lay my hands on it; **je l'ai
eu entre les ~s mais** I did have it but; **être
entre les ~s de qn** ⟨power⟩ to be in sb's
hands; **prendre qn/qch en ~s** to take sb/sth
in hand; **à ne pas mettre entre toutes les ~s**
⟨book⟩ not for general reading; **tomber entre
les ~s de qn** to fall into sb's hands; **les ~s
vides** empty-handed; **je le lui ai remis en ~s
propres** I gave it to him/her in person; **de la
~ à la ~** ⟨sell⟩ privately; ⟨be paid⟩ cash (in
hand)
**(d)** **écrit de la ~ du président** written by the
president himself; **de ma plus belle ~** in my
best handwriting
**(e)** **avoir le coup de ~** to have the knack; **se
faire la ~** to practise (GB)
**(f)** (in cards) hand; deal
**(g)** **à ~ droite/gauche** on the right/left
■ **~ courante** handrail
**IDIOMS j'en mettrais ma ~ au feu** or **à
couper** I'd swear to it; **d'une ~ de fer** with
an iron rod; **il n'y est pas allé de ~ morte!**
(colloq) he didn't pull his punches!; **avoir la ~
leste** to be always ready with a slap; **faire ~
basse sur** to help oneself to ⟨goods⟩; to take

over ⟨*market, country*⟩; **en venir aux ~s** to come to blows; **avoir la ~ heureuse** to be lucky

**mainate** /mɛnat/ *nm* mynah bird

**main-d'œuvre**, *pl* **mains-d'œuvre** /mɛ̃dœvʀ/ *nf* labour (GB)

**main-forte** /mɛ̃fɔʀt/ *nf inv* **prêter ~ à qn** to come to sb's aid

**mainmise** /mɛ̃miz/ *nf* seizure

**maint**, **~e** /mɛ̃, mɛ̃t/ *det* many, many a; **à ~es reprises** many times

**maintenance** /mɛ̃tnɑ̃s/ *nf* maintenance

**maintenant** /mɛ̃t(ə)nɑ̃/ *adv* now; nowadays; **commence dès ~** start straightaway

**maintenir** /mɛ̃t(ə)niʀ/ [36] **1** *vtr* **(a)** to keep; to maintain; to keep up; **~ qch debout** to keep sth upright
**(b)** to support ⟨*wall, ankle*⟩
**(c)** to stand by ⟨*decision*⟩; **~ que** to maintain that; **~ sa candidature** ⟨*politician*⟩ not to withdraw one's candidacy
**2 se maintenir** *v refl* (+ *v être*) ⟨*trend*⟩ to persist; ⟨*price*⟩ to remain stable; ⟨*weather*⟩ to remain fair; ⟨*political system*⟩ to remain in force; ⟨*currency*⟩ to hold steady

**maintien** /mɛ̃tjɛ̃/ *nm* **(a)** maintaining; **assurer le ~ de l'ordre** to maintain order
**(b)** support
**(c)** deportment

**maire** /mɛʀ/ *nm* mayor
■ **~ adjoint** deputy mayor

**mairie** /meʀi/ *nf* **(a)** town council (GB) *or* hall (US); **être élu à la ~ de** to be elected mayor of
**(b)** town hall

**mais** /mɛ/ *conj* but; **incroyable ~ vrai** strange but true; **il est bête, ~ bête!** (colloq) he's so incredibly stupid!; **~, vous pleurez!** good heavens, you're crying!; **~ j'y pense** now that I come to think of it

**maïs** /mais/ *nm inv* **(a)** maize (GB), corn (US)
**(b)** sweetcorn; **épi de ~** corn on the cob

**maison** /mɛzɔ̃/ **1** *adj inv* ⟨*product*⟩ home-made
**2** *nf* **(a)** house
**(b)** home
**(c)** family, household; **gens de ~** domestic staff
**(d)** firm; **avoir 15 ans de ~** to have been with the firm for 15 years
■ **~ d'arrêt** prison; **~ bourgeoise** *imposing town house*; **~ de campagne** house in the country; **~ close** brothel; **~ de correction** institution for young offenders; **~ de la culture** ≈ community arts centre (GB); **~ des jeunes et de la culture, MJC** ≈ youth club; **~ de maître** manor; **~ mère** headquarters; main branch; **~ de passe** brothel; **~ de retraite** old people's *or* retirement home; **~ de santé** nursing home; **la Maison Blanche** the White House
IDIOMS **c'est gros comme une ~** (colloq) it sticks out a mile

**maisonnée** /mɛzɔne/ *nf* household; family

**maître, -esse¹** /mɛtʀ, ɛs/ **1** *adj* **(a)** être **~ de soi** to have self-control; **être ~ chez soi** to be master in one's own house; **être ~ de son véhicule** to be in control of one's vehicle
**(b)** main; key; major
**2** *nm,f* **(a)** teacher
**(b)** (of house) master/mistress
**(c)** (of animal) owner
**3** *nm* **(a)** ruler; **être (le) seul ~ à bord** to be in sole command; **être son propre ~** to be one's own master/mistress; **régner en ~ absolu** to reign supreme
**(b)** master; **être passé ~ dans l'art de qch/ de faire** to be a past master of sth/at doing; **en ~** masterfully
**(c)** (*also* **Me**) Maître (*form of address given to members of the legal profession*)
■ **~ d'hôtel** maître d'hôtel (GB), maître d' (US); **~ à penser** mentor; **maîtresse femme** strong-minded woman
IDIOMS **trouver son ~** to meet one's match

**maître-assistant**, **~e**, *mpl* **maîtres-assistants** /mɛtʀasistɑ̃, ɑ̃t/ *nm,f* ≈ senior lecturer (GB), senior instructor (US)

**maître-chanteur**, *pl* **maîtres-chanteurs** /mɛtʀəʃɑ̃tœʀ/ *nm* blackmailer

**maître-nageur**, *pl* **maîtres-nageurs** /mɛtʀənaʒœʀ/ *nm* **(a)** swimming instructor
**(b)** pool attendant

**maîtresse²** /mɛtʀɛs/ **1** *adj f* ▶ MAÎTRE 1
**2** *nf* **(a)** ▶ MAÎTRE 2
**(b)** mistress

**maîtrise** /mɛtʀiz/ *nf* **(a)** mastery
**(b)** perfect command
**(c)** ~ (**de soi**) self-control
**(d)** master's degree

**maîtriser** /mɛtʀize/ [1] **1** *vtr* **(a)** to control ⟨*feelings*⟩; to bring [sth] under control ⟨*fire*⟩; to overcome ⟨*opponent*⟩
**(b)** to master ⟨*language*⟩
**2 se maîtriser** *v refl* (+ *v être*) to have self-control

**maïzena®** /maizena/ *nf* cornflour

**majesté** /maʒɛste/ *nf* majesty

**majestueux, -euse** /maʒɛstɥø, øz/ *adj* majestic; stately

**majeur, ~e** /maʒœʀ/ **1** *adj* **(a)** être **~** to be over 18 *or* of age
**(b)** main, major; **en ~e partie** for the most part
**(c)** (Mus) major
**2** *nm* middle finger

**majoration** /maʒɔʀasjɔ̃/ *nf* increase

**majordome** /maʒɔʀdom/ *nm* butler

**majorer** /maʒɔʀe/ [1] *vtr* to increase

**majoritaire** /maʒɔʀitɛʀ/ *adj* majority

**majoritairement** /maʒɔʀitɛʀmɑ̃/ *adv*
**(a)** by a majority (vote)                        ···❖

(b) **province ∼ catholique** predominantly Catholic province

**majorité** /maʒɔʀite/ *nf* (a) majority; **ils sont en ∼** they are in the majority; **ce sont, en ∼, des enfants** they are, for the most part, children
(b) **la ∼** the government, the party in power

**majuscule** /maʒyskyl/ ⓵ *adj* capital ⓶ *nf* capital (letter)

**mal**, *mpl* **maux** /mal, mo/ ⓵ *adj inv*
(a) wrong; **qu'a-t-elle fait de ∼?** what has she done wrong?
(b) bad; **ce ne serait pas ∼ de déménager** it wouldn't be a bad idea to move out
(c) (colloq) **il n'est pas mal** ⟨*film*⟩ it's not bad; ⟨*man*⟩ he's not bad(-looking)
⓶ *nm* (a) trouble, difficulty; **avoir du ∼ à faire** to find it difficult to do; **se donner du ∼** to go to a lot of trouble; **ne te donne pas ce ∼!** don't bother!
(b) pain; **faire ∼** to hurt, to be painful; **se faire ∼** to hurt oneself; **j'ai ∼** it hurts; **avoir ∼ partout** to ache all over; **elle avait très ∼** she was in pain; **avoir ∼ à la tête** to have a headache; **avoir ∼ à la gorge** to have a sore throat; **j'ai ∼ au genou** my knee hurts; **j'ai ∼ au cœur** I feel sick (GB) *or* nauseous
(c) illness, disease
(d) **être en ∼ de** to be short of ⟨*inspiration*⟩; to be lacking in ⟨*affection*⟩
(e) harm; **faire du ∼ à** to harm, to hurt; **une douche ne te ferait pas de ∼** (humorous) a shower wouldn't do you any harm
(f) **le ∼** evil; **qu'elle parte, est-ce vraiment un ∼?** is it really a bad thing that she is leaving?; **sans penser à ∼** without meaning any harm; **dire du ∼ de qn/qch** to speak ill of sb/sth
⓷ *adv* (a) badly; not properly; **elle travaille ∼** her work isn't good; **je t'entends ∼** I can't hear you very well
(b) with difficulty; **on voit ∼ comment** it's difficult to see how
(c) ⟨*diagnosed, addressed*⟩ wrongly; **j'avais ∼ compris** I had misunderstood; **∼ informé** ill-informed
(d) **se trouver ∼** to faint; **être ∼** ⟨*assis or couché or installé*⟩ not to be comfortable; **être au plus ∼** to be critically ill
⓸ **pas mal** *phr* (a) ⟨*travel, read*⟩ quite a lot
(b) **il ne s'en est pas ∼ tiré** (in exam) he coped quite well; (in dangerous situation) he got off lightly
∎ **∼ de l'air** airsickness; **∼ de mer** seasickness; **∼ du pays** homesickness; **∼ du siècle** world-weariness; **∼ des transports** travel sickness

**malade** /malad/ ⓵ *adj* ⟨*person*⟩ ill, sick; ⟨*animal*⟩ sick; ⟨*organ, plant*⟩ diseased; **tomber ∼** to fall ill *or* sick, to get sick (US); **être ∼ en voiture/en avion** to get carsick/airsick; **j'en suis ∼** (figurative) (colloq) it makes me sick; **∼ d'inquiétude** worried sick
⓶ *nmf* (a) sick man/woman
(b) patient

∎ **∼ imaginaire** hypochondriac; **∼ mental** mentally ill person

**maladie** /maladi/ *nf* illness, disease; **il va en faire une ∼** (colloq) (figurative) he'll have a fit (colloq)
∎ **∼ sexuellement transmissible, MST** sexually transmitted disease, STD; **∼ du sommeil** sleeping sickness

**maladif, -ive** /maladif, iv/ *adj* ⟨*child*⟩ sickly; ⟨*jealousy*⟩ pathological

**maladresse** /maladʀɛs/ *nf* (a) clumsiness, awkwardness
(b) tactlessness
(c) blunder

**maladroit, ∼e** /maladʀwa, wat/ ⓵ *adj*
(a) clumsy
(b) tactless
⓶ *nm,f* (a) clumsy person
(b) tactless person

**maladroitement** /maladʀwatmã/ *adv*
(a) clumsily, awkwardly
(b) tactlessly; ineptly

**malaise** /malɛz/ *nm* (a) dizzy turn; **avoir un ∼** to feel faint
(b) (figurative) uneasiness; unrest
∎ **∼ cardiaque** mild heart attack

**malaxer** /malakse/ [1] *vtr* (a) to cream ⟨*butter*⟩; to knead ⟨*dough*⟩
(b) to mix ⟨*cement*⟩

**malchance** /malʃɑ̃s/ *nf* bad luck, misfortune; **par ∼** as ill luck would have it

**malchanceux, -euse** /malʃɑ̃sø, øz/ *adj* unlucky

**maldonne** /maldɔn/ *nf* misunderstanding

**mâle** /mɑl/ ⓵ *adj* (a) male; ⟨*elephant*⟩ bull; ⟨*antelope, rabbit*⟩ buck; ⟨*sparrow*⟩ cock; **cygne ∼** cob; **canard ∼** drake
(b) manly
⓶ *nm* (a) male
(b) (humorous) he-man (colloq)

**malédiction** /malediksjɔ̃/ *nf* curse

**maléfice** /malefis/ *nm* evil spell

**maléfique** /malefik/ *adj* evil

**malencontreusement** /malɑ̃kɔ̃tʀøzmã/ *adv* inopportunely; unfortunately

**malencontreux, -euse** /malɑ̃kɔ̃tʀø, øz/ *adj* unfortunate

**malentendant, ∼e** /malɑ̃tɑ̃dɑ̃, ɑ̃t/ *nm,f* **les ∼s** the hearing-impaired

**malentendu** /malɑ̃tɑ̃dy/ *nm* misunderstanding

**malfaçon** /malfasɔ̃/ *nf* defect

**malfaisant, ∼e** /malfəzɑ̃, ɑ̃t/ *adj* evil; harmful

**malfaiteur** /malfɛtœʀ/ *nm* criminal

**malformation** /malfɔʀmasjɔ̃/ *nf* malformation

**malgache** /malgaʃ/ *adj, nm* Malagasy

**malgré** /malgʀe/ *prep* in spite of, despite; **∼ cela, ∼ tout** nevertheless; **∼ moi** against my wishes; reluctantly

**malhabile** /malabil/ *adj* clumsy

**malheur** /malœʀ/ *nm* (a) le ~ misfortune, adversity; **faire le ~ de qn** to bring sb nothing but unhappiness
(b) misfortune; accident; **un grand ~** a tragedy; **un ~ est si vite arrivé!** accidents can so easily happen!
(c) misfortune; **ceux qui ont le ~ de faire** those who are unfortunate enough to do; **j'ai eu le ~ de le leur dire** I made the mistake of telling them; **par ~** as bad luck would have it; **si par ~ la guerre éclatait** if, God forbid, war should break out; **porter ~** to be bad luck
**IDIOMS faire un ~** (colloq) to be a sensation; to go wild; **à quelque chose ~ est bon** (Proverb) every cloud has a silver lining

**malheureusement** /maløʀøzmɑ̃/ *adv* unfortunately

**malheureux, -euse** /maløʀø, øz/ ① *adj*
(a) ⟨*person, life*⟩ unhappy, miserable; ⟨*victim, choice, word*⟩ unfortunate; ⟨*candidate*⟩ unlucky; **c'est ~ que** it's a pity *or* shame that
(b) (colloq) ⟨*sum*⟩ paltry, pathetic
② *nm,f* (a) poor wretch; **le ~!** poor man!
(b) poor person; **les ~** the poor
**IDIOMS être ~ comme les pierres** to be as miserable as sin

**malhonnête** /malɔnɛt/ *adj* dishonest

**malhonnêteté** /malɔnɛtte/ *nf* dishonesty

**malice** /malis/ *nf* (a) mischief
(b) malice; **être sans ~** to be harmless

**malicieux, -ieuse** /malisjø, øz/ *adj* mischievous

**malin, maligne** /malɛ̃, maliɲ/ ① *adj*
(a) clever; **j'ai eu l'air ~!** (ironic) I looked like a total fool!
(b) malicious
(c) (Med) malignant
② *nm,f* **c'est un ~** he's a crafty one
**IDIOMS à ~, ~ et demi** (Proverb) there's always someone who will outwit you

**malingre** /malɛ̃gʀ/ *adj* ⟨*person, tree*⟩ sickly

**malintentionné, ~e** /malɛ̃tɑ̃sjone/ *adj* malicious

**malle** /mal/ *nf* trunk

**malléabilité** /maleabilite/ *nf* malleability

**mallette** /malɛt/ *nf* briefcase

**malmener** /malmәne/ [16] *vtr* (a) to manhandle
(b) to give [sb] a rough ride

**malnutrition** /malnytʀisjɔ̃/ *nf* malnutrition

**malodorant, ~e** /malɔdɔʀɑ̃, ɑ̃t/ *adj* foul-smelling

**malotru, ~e** /malɔtʀy/ *nm,f* boor

**Malouines** /malwin/ *pr nf pl* **les (îles) ~** the Falklands

**malpoli, ~e** /malpoli/ *adj* rude

**malpropre** /malpʀɔpʀ/ ① *adj* dirty
② *nm,f* **se faire renvoyer comme un ~** to be chucked out (colloq)

**malsain, ~e** /malsɛ̃, ɛn/ *adj* unhealthy

**Malte** /malt/ *pr nf* Malta

**malthusianisme** /maltyzjanism/ *nm* Malthusianism

**maltraiter** /maltʀɛte/ [1] *vtr* to mistreat

**malus** /malys/ *nm inv* loaded premium

**malveillance** /malvɛjɑ̃s/ *nf* malice

**malveillant, ~e** /malvɛjɑ̃, ɑ̃t/ *adj* malicious

**malvenu, ~e** /malvәny/ *adj* out of place

**malversation** /malvɛʀsasjɔ̃/ *nf*
(a) malpractice
(b) embezzlement

**malvoyant, ~e** /malvwajɑ̃, ɑ̃t/ *nmf* partially sighted person

**maman** /mamɑ̃/ *nf* mum (GB) (colloq), mom (US) (colloq)

**mamelle** /mamɛl/ *nf* udder; teat

**mamelon** /mamlɔ̃/ *nm* (a) nipple
(b) hillock

**mamie** /mami/ *nf* (colloq) granny (colloq), grandma (colloq)

**mammifère** /mamifɛʀ/ *nm* mammal

**mammouth** /mamut/ *nm* mammoth

**mamy** = MAMIE

**manager¹, manageur** /manaʒœʀ/ *nm* manager

**manager²** /manaʒe/ [13] *vtr* to manage

**manche¹** /mɑ̃ʃ/ *nm* (a) (of tool) handle; (of violin) neck
(b) (colloq) clumsy idiot
■ ~ **à balai** broomhandle; broomstick; joystick

**manche²** /mɑ̃ʃ/ *nf* (a) sleeve; **sans ~s** sleeveless
(b) (Sport) round; (in cards) hand; (in bridge) game; (in tennis) set
**IDIOMS avoir qn dans la ~** to have sb in one's pocket; **c'est une autre paire de ~s** (colloq) it's a different ball game (colloq)

**Manche** /mɑ̃ʃ/ *pr nf* **la ~** the (English) Channel

**manchette** /mɑ̃ʃɛt/ *nf* (a) (double) cuff
(b) oversleeve
(c) headline

**manchot, -otte** /mɑ̃ʃo, ɔt/ ① *adj* one-armed; one-handed; **il est ~** he's only got one arm; **ne pas être ~** (colloq) to be pretty good with one's hands (colloq)
② *nm* penguin

**mandarine** /mɑ̃daʀin/ *nf* mandarin orange

**mandat** /mɑ̃da/ *nm* (a) ~ **(postal)** money order
(b) term of office; **exercer son ~** to be in office
(c) mandate
■ ~ **d'arrêt** (arrest) warrant; ~ **d'expulsion** expulsion order; eviction order; ~ **de perquisition** search warrant

**mandataire** /mɑ̃datɛʀ/ *nmf*
(a) representative, agent
(b) proxy

**mandater** /mɑ̃date/ [1] *vtr* to appoint [sb] as one's representative; to give a mandate to

**mandat-lettre**, pl **mandats-lettres** /mãdalɛtʀ/ nm postal order

**mandibule** /mãdibyl/ nf mandible

**mandoline** /mãdɔlin/ nf mandolin

**manège** /manɛʒ/ nm (a) merry-go-round
(b) riding school
(c) (little) trick, (little) game; **j'ai bien observé ton ~** I know what you are up to

**manette** /manɛt/ nf (a) lever; joystick
(b) (figurative) **~s** controls

**mangeable** /mãʒabl/ adj edible

**mangeoire** /mãʒwaʀ/ nf manger; trough; feeding tray

**manger¹** /mãʒe/ [13] **1** vtr (a) to eat; **il n'y a rien à ~ dans la maison** there's no food in the house
(b) to use up ⟨savings⟩; to go through ⟨inheritance⟩; to take up ⟨time⟩
(c) ⟨rust, acid⟩ to eat away
(d) **~ ses mots** to mumble
**2** vi to eat; **~ au restaurant** to eat out; **~ à sa faim** to eat one's fill; **donner à ~ à qn** to feed sb; to give sb something to eat; **faire à ~** to cook; **inviter qn à ~** to invite sb for a meal; **~ chinois** to have a Chinese meal; **on mange mal ici** the food is not good here
**3** **se manger** v refl (+ v être) **ça se mange?** can you eat it?; **le gaspacho se mange froid** gazpacho is served cold

**manger²** /mãʒe/ nm food

**mangeur, -euse** /mãʒœʀ, øz/ nm,f **bon/ gros ~** good/big eater
■ **mangeuse d'hommes** man-eater

**mangouste** /mãɡust/ nf (a) mongoose
(b) mangosteen

**mangue** /mãɡ/ nf mango

**maniable** /manjabl/ adj ⟨object, car⟩ easy to handle; ⟨book⟩ manageable in size

**maniaque** /manjak/ **1** adj particular, fussy
**2** nmf (a) fusspot (GB), fussbudget (US)
(b) fanatic; **c'est un ~ de l'ordre** he's obsessive about tidiness
(c) maniac
(d) (Med) manic

**maniaquerie** /manjakʀi/ nf fussiness

**manichéen, -éenne** /manikeɛ̃, ɛn/ adj Manichean; dualistic

**manie** /mani/ nf (a) habit; **c'est une vraie ~** it's an absolute obsession
(b) quirk, idiosyncrasy
(c) (Med) mania

**maniement** /manimã/ nm handling; (of machine) operation; (of language) command
■ **~ d'armes** arms drill

**manier** /manje/ [2] **1** vtr to handle
**2** **se manier** v refl (+ v être) **se ~ aisément** ⟨tool⟩ to be easy to handle; ⟨car⟩ to handle well
IDIOMS **~ la fourchette avec entrain** (colloq) (humorous) to have a hearty appetite

**maniéré, -e** /manjeʀe/ adj affected

**manière** /manjɛʀ/ nf (a) way; **d'une certaine ~** in a way; **leur ~ de vivre/penser**

their way of life/thinking; **de toutes les ~s possibles** in every possible way; **de telle ~ que** in such a way that; **de ~ à faire** so as to do; **de ~ à ce que** so that; **à ma ~** my (own) way; **de quelle ~?** how?; **de toute ~, de toutes ~s** anyway, in any case; **la ~ forte** strong-arm tactics, force
(b) style; **à la ~ de qn/qch** in the style of sb/sth
(c) manners; **faire des ~s** to stand on ceremony

**manifestant, ~e** /manifɛstã, ãt/ nm,f demonstrator

**manifestation** /manifɛstasjɔ̃/ nf
(a) demonstration
(b) event; **~s sportives** sporting events
(c) (of phenomenon) appearance
(d) (of feeling) expression, manifestation
■ **~ silencieuse** vigil; **~ de soutien** rally

**manifeste** /manifɛst/ **1** adj obvious, manifest
**2** nm manifesto

**manifester** /manifɛste/ [1] **1** vtr to show ⟨courage⟩; to express ⟨desire, fears⟩; **~ sa présence** to make one's presence known
**2** vi to demonstrate; **appeler à ~ le 5 juin** to call a demonstration for 5 June
**3** **se manifester** v refl (+ v être)
(a) ⟨symptom⟩ to manifest itself; ⟨phenomenon⟩ to appear; ⟨worry⟩ to show itself
(b) ⟨witness⟩ to come forward; ⟨person⟩ to appear; to get in touch

**manigance** /manigãs/ nf little scheme

**manigancer** /manigãse/ [12] vtr
**~ quelque chose** to be up to something; **~ un mauvais coup** to hatch up a scheme

**manipulateur, -trice** /manipylatœʀ, tʀis/ nm,f (a) technician
(b) (pejorative) manipulator

**manipulation** /manipylasjɔ̃/ nf
(a) (of object) handling
(b) manipulation
(c) (Sch) experiment

**manipuler** /manipyle/ [1] vtr (a) to handle ⟨object⟩; to use ⟨words⟩
(b) to manipulate ⟨person⟩

**manitou** /manitu/ nm (colloq) big noise (colloq); **un grand ~ de la finance** a big noise in the financial world

**manivelle** /manivɛl/ nf handle
IDIOMS **donner le premier tour de ~** to start filming

**manne** /man/ nf godsend

**mannequin** /mankɛ̃/ nm (a) (fashion) model
(b) dummy

**manœuvre¹** /manœvʀ/ nm unskilled worker

**manœuvre²** /manœvʀ/ nf manoeuvre (GB), maneuver (US); **champ de ~** military training area; **fausse ~** mistake

**manœuvrer** /manœvʀe/ [1] **1** vtr (a) to manoeuvre (GB), to maneuver (US) ⟨vehicle⟩
(b) to operate ⟨machine⟩

**(c)** to manipulate ⟨*person*⟩
**2** *vi* to manoeuvre (GB), to maneuver (US)

**manoir** /manwaʀ/ *nm* manor (house)

**manomètre** /manɔmɛtʀ/ *nm* pressure gauge

**manquant, ~e** /mɑ̃kɑ̃, ɑ̃t/ *adj* missing

**manque** /mɑ̃k/ **1** *nm* **(a)** ~ de lack of; shortage of; ~ de chance, il est tombé malade just his luck, he fell ill
**(b)** gap; en ~ d'affection in need of affection; être en ~ ⟨*drug addict*⟩ to be suffering from withdrawal symptoms
**2** à la manque *phr* (colloq) une idée à la ~ a useless idea

**manqué, ~e** /mɑ̃ke/ **1** *pp* ▶ MANQUER
**2** *pp adj* ⟨*attempt*⟩ failed; ⟨*opportunity*⟩ missed

**manquer** /mɑ̃ke/ **1** **1** *vtr* **(a)** to miss; un film à ne pas ~ a film not to be missed; tu l'as manquée de cinq minutes you missed her/it by five minutes
**(b)** ~ son coup (colloq) to fail
**(c)** (colloq) la prochaine fois je ne le manquerai pas next time I won't let him get away with it
**2** **manquer à** *v+prep* **(a)** ~ à qn to be missed by sb; ma tante me manque I miss my aunt
**(b)** ~ à sa parole to break one's word
**3** **manquer de** *v+prep* **(a)** ~ de to lack; on ne manque de rien we don't want for anything; elle ne manque pas de charme she's not without charm; on manque d'air ici it's stuffy in here
**(b)** je ne manquerai pas de vous le faire savoir I'll be sure to let you know; et évidemment, ça n'a pas manqué! (colloq) and sure enough that's what happened!
**(c)** il a manqué (de) casser un carreau he almost broke a windowpane
**4** *vi* **(a)** les vivres vinrent à ~ the supplies ran out; le courage leur manqua their courage failed them; ce n'est pas l'envie qui m'en manque it's not that I don't want to
**(b)** ⟨*person*⟩ to be absent; to be missing
**5** *v impers* il lui manque un doigt he's got a finger missing; il nous manque deux joueurs pour former une équipe we're two players short of a team; il ne manquerait plus que ça! (colloq) that would be the last straw!
**6** **se manquer** *v refl* (+ *v être*) to miss each other

**mansarde** /mɑ̃saʀd/ *nf* attic room

**mansardé, ~e** /mɑ̃saʀde/ *adj* ⟨*room*⟩ attic

**mansuétude** /mɑ̃sɥetyd/ *nf* indulgence

**manteau,** *pl* **~x** /mɑ̃to/ *nm* coat
■ ~ de cheminée mantelpiece
IDIOMS sous le ~ illicitly

**manucure** /manykyʀ/ **1** *nmf* manicurist
**2** *nf* manicure

**manuel, -elle** /manɥɛl/ **1** *adj* manual
**2** *nm* manual; (Sch) textbook
■ ~ de conversation phrase book

**manuellement** /manɥɛlmɑ̃/ *adv* manually

**manufacture** /manyfaktyʀ/ *nf* **(a)** factory
**(b)** manufacture

**manufacturer** /manyfaktyʀe/ [1] *vtr* to manufacture

**manu militari** /manymilitaʀi/ *adv* forcibly.

**manuscrit, ~e** /manyskʀi, it/ **1** *adj* handwritten
**2** *nm* manuscript

**manutention** /manytɑ̃sjɔ̃/ *nf* handling

**manutentionnaire** /manytɑ̃sjɔnɛʀ/ *nm* warehouseman

**mappemonde** /mapmɔ̃d/ *nf* **(a)** map of the world (in two hemispheres)
**(b)** globe

**maquereau,** *pl* **~x** /makʀo/ *nm* mackerel

**maquette** /makɛt/ *nf* scale model

**maquillage** /makijaʒ/ *nm* **(a)** making-up
**(b)** make-up

**maquiller** /makije/ [1] **1** *vtr* **(a)** to make [sb] up
**(b)** to doctor ⟨*truth*⟩; ~ un crime en accident to disguise a crime as an accident
**2** **se maquiller** *v refl* (+ *v être*) **(a)** to put make-up on
**(b)** to wear make-up

**maquilleur, -euse** /makijœʀ, øz/ *nm,f* make-up artist

**maquis** /maki/ *nm inv* maquis; prendre le ~ to go underground

**maquisard, ~e** /makizaʀ, aʀd/ *nm,f* member of the Resistance

**marabout** /maʀabu/ *nm* **(a)** marabou
**(b)** marabout

**maraîchage** /maʀɛʃaʒ/ *nm* market gardening (GB), truck farming (US)

**maraîcher, -ère** /maʀɛʃe, ɛʀ/ **1** *adj* produits ~s market garden produce (GB), truck (US)
**2** *nm,f* market gardener (GB), truck farmer (US)

**marais** /maʀɛ/ *nm inv* marsh; swamp
■ ~ salant saltern

**marasme** /maʀasm/ *nm* stagnation

**marathon** /maʀatɔ̃/ *nm* marathon

**marathonien, -ienne** /maʀatɔnjɛ̃, ɛn/ *nm,f* marathon runner

**marâtre** /maʀɑtʀ/ *nf* cruel mother

**maraude** /maʀod/ *nf* pilfering; en ~ ⟨*person*⟩ on the prowl

**marauder** /maʀode/ [1] *vi* **(a)** to pilfer
**(b)** to prowl around

**maraudeur, -euse** /maʀodœʀ, øz/ *nm,f* petty thief

**marbre** /maʀbʀ/ *nm* **(a)** marble
**(b)** marble top
**(c)** marble statue
IDIOMS rester de ~ to remain stony-faced; la nouvelle les laissa de ~ they were completely unmoved by the news

m

**marbrer** /maʀbʀe/ [1] *vtr* to marble

**marbrerie** /maʀbʀəʀi/ *nf* marble industry; marble masonry

**marbrier, -ière**[1] /maʀbʀije, ɛʀ/ *nm* marble mason

**marbrière**[2] /maʀbʀijɛʀ/ *nf* marble quarry

**marbrure** /maʀbʀyʀ/ *nf* marbling

**marc** /maʀ/ *nm* marc.
∎ ~ **de café** coffee grounds

**marcassin** /maʀkasɛ̃/ *nm* young wild boar

**marchand, ~e** /maʀʃɑ̃, ɑ̃d/ **1** *adj* ⟨*quality*⟩ marketable; ⟨*sector*⟩ trade; ⟨*value*⟩ market
**2** *nm,f* shopkeeper; stallholder; ~ **d'armes/de bestiaux** arms/cattle dealer; ~ **de charbon/vins** coal/wine merchant
∎ ~ **ambulant** hawker; ~ **de couleurs** ironmonger (GB), hardware merchant; ~ **de glaces** ice cream vendor; ~ **en gros** wholesaler; ~ **de journaux** newsagent; news vendor; ~ **des quatre saisons** costermonger (GB), fruit and vegetable merchant; ~ **de sable** sandman; ~ **de tapis** carpet salesman

**marchandage** /maʀʃɑ̃daʒ/ *nm* haggling

**marchander** /maʀʃɑ̃de/ [1] *vtr* (a) to haggle over
(b) (figurative) ~ **sa peine** not to put oneself out

**marchandise** /maʀʃɑ̃diz/ *nf* goods, merchandise; **tromper qn sur la** ~ to swindle sb

**marche** /maʀʃ/ *nf* (a) walking; walk; pace, step; **faire de la** ~ to go walking; **à 10 minutes de** ~ 10 minutes' walk away
(b) march; **fermer la** ~ to bring up the rear; **ouvrir la** ~ to be at the head of the march
(c) (of vehicle) progress; (of events) course; (of time) march; **bus en** ~ moving bus; **dans le sens contraire de la** ~ facing backward(s)
(d) (of mechanism) operation; (of organization) running; **en état de** ~ in working order; **mettre en** ~ to start (up) ⟨*machine*⟩; to switch on ⟨*TV*⟩
(e) step; **les** ~**s** the stairs
∎ ~ **arrière** reverse; **faire** ~ **arrière** to reverse; (figurative) to backpedal; ~ **avant** forward; ~ **à suivre** procedure
IDIOMS **prendre le train en** ~ to join halfway through; to climb onto the bandwagon

**marché** /maʀʃe/ *nm* (a) market; **faire son** ~ to do one's shopping at the market
(b) deal; **conclure un** ~ **avec qn** to strike a deal with sb; ~ **conclu!** it's a deal!; **bon/meilleur** ~ cheap/cheaper; **par-dessus le** ~ (colloq) to top it all
∎ ~ **de l'emploi** job market; ~ **libre** free market; ~ **noir** black market; ~ **aux puces** flea market; ~ **du travail** labour (GB) market; **Marché commun** Common Market

**marchepied** /maʀʃəpje/ *nm* (a) step
(b) steps

**marcher** /maʀʃe/ [1] *vi* (a) to walk; ⟨*demonstrators*⟩ to march

(b) to tread; **se laisser** ~ **sur les pieds** (figurative) to let oneself be walked over
(c) ⟨*mechanism, system*⟩ to work; **ma radio marche mal** my radio doesn't work properly; **faire** ~ **qch** to get sth to work; ~ **au gaz** to run on gas; **les bus ne marchent pas le soir** the buses don't run in the evenings
(d) (colloq) ~ **(bien)/**~ **mal** ⟨*work, relationship*⟩ to go well/not to go well; ⟨*film, student*⟩ to do well/not to do well; ⟨*actor*⟩ to go down well/not to go down well
(e) (colloq) **c'est trop risqué, je ne marche pas** it's too risky, count me out; **ça marche!** it's a deal!
(f) (colloq) to fall for it
(g) (colloq) **faire** ~ **qn** to pull sb's leg; **faire** ~ **son monde** (colloq) to be good at giving orders
IDIOMS **il ne marche pas, il court!** (colloq) he's as gullible as they come

**marcheur, -euse** /maʀʃœʀ, øz/ *nm,f* walker

**mardi** /maʀdi/ *nm* Tuesday

**mare** /maʀ/ *nf* (a) pond
(b) ~ **de** pool of ⟨*blood*⟩

**marécage** /maʀekaʒ/ *nm* marsh, swamp

**marécageux, -euse** /maʀekaʒø, øz/ *adj* ⟨*ground*⟩ marshy, swampy; ⟨*plant*⟩ marsh

**maréchal, pl -aux** /maʀeʃal, o/ *nm* ≈ field marshal (GB), general of the army (US)

**maréchal-ferrant, pl maréchaux-ferrants** /maʀeʃalferɑ̃, maʀeʃoferɑ̃/ *nm* farrier

**marée** /maʀe/ *nf* tide; **la** ~ **monte/descend** the tide is coming in/is going out; **à** ~ **haute/basse** at high/low tide
∎ ~ **noire** oil slick
IDIOMS **contre vents et** ~**s** come hell or high water; against all odds

**marelle** /maʀɛl/ *nf* hopscotch

**marémoteur, -trice** /maʀemɔtœʀ, tʀis/ *adj* tidal; **usine marémotrice** tidal power station

**mareyeur, -euse** /maʀɛjœʀ, øz/ *nm,f* fish wholesaler

**margarine** /maʀgaʀin/ *nf* margarine

**marge** /maʀʒ/ **1** *nf* (a) margin
(b) leeway; **on a 10 minutes de** ~ we've got 10 minutes to spare
(c) scope; **tu devrais me laisser plus de** ~ **de décision** you should allow me more scope for making decisions
(d) profit margin; mark-up
**2 en marge de** *phr* **vivre en** ~ **de la loi** to live outside the law; **se sentir en** ~ to feel like an outsider
∎ ~ **bénéficiaire** profit margin; ~ **commerciale** gross profit; ~ **d'erreur** margin of error; ~ **de sécurité** safety margin

**marginal, ~e, mpl -aux** /maʀʒinal, o/ **1** *adj* (a) marginal
(b) ⟨*artist*⟩ fringe
(c) on the margins of society
**2** *nm,f* dropout; **les marginaux** the fringe elements of society

**marginaliser** /maʀʒinalize/ [1] *vtr* to marginalize

**marguerite** /maʀɡəʀit/ *nf* daisy

**mari** /maʀi/ *nm* husband

**mariage** /maʀjaʒ/ *nm* (a) marriage; **né d'un premier ~** from a previous marriage; **~ de raison** marriage of convenience; **faire un riche ~** to marry into money
(b) wedding
(c) (figurative) (of colours) marriage; (of companies) merger; (of parties) alliance; (of techniques) fusion
■ **~ blanc** marriage in name only; **~ civil** civil wedding; **~ religieux** church wedding

**Marianne** /maʀjan/ *pr n* Marianne (*female figure personifying the French Republic*)

**marié, ~e** /maʀje/ **1** *pp* ▶ MARIER
**2** *pp adj* married
**3** *nm,f* **le (jeune) ~** the (bride)groom; **la (jeune) ~e** the bride; **les ~s** the newlyweds

**marier** /maʀje/ [2] **1** *vtr* to marry
**2 se marier** *v refl* (+ *v être*) (a) to get married
(b) (*colours*) to blend

**marijuana** /maʀiʀwana/ *nf* marijuana

**marin, ~e**[1] /maʀɛ̃, in/ **1** *adj* (a) (*life*) marine; (*salt*) sea; (*drilling*) offshore
(b) **pull ~** seaman's jersey; **costume ~** sailor suit
**2** *nm* sailor
■ **~ d'eau douce** fair-weather sailor; **~ pêcheur** fisherman
IDIOMS **avoir le pied ~** not to get seasick

**marine**[2] /maʀin/ **1** *adj inv* navy (blue)
**2** *nm* marine

**marine**[3] /maʀin/ *nf* navy; **de ~** nautical

**mariner** /maʀine/ [1] *vtr, vi* to marinate

**marinière** /maʀinjɛʀ/ *nf* smock

**marionnette** /maʀjɔnɛt/ *nf* (a) puppet
(b) **~s** puppet show
■ **~ à fils** marionette

**marionnettiste** /maʀjɔnetist/ *nmf* puppeteer

**maritalement** /maʀitalmɑ̃/ *adv* (*live*) as man and wife

**maritime** /maʀitim/ *adj* (*climate, commerce*) maritime; (*area*) coastal; (*company*) shipping

**marivaudage** /maʀivodaʒ/ *nm* (a) gallant banter
(b) refined affectation (*in the style of Marivaux*)

**marjolaine** /maʀʒɔlɛn/ *nf* marjoram

**marmaille** (colloq) /maʀmaj/ *nf* rabble of kids (colloq)

**marmelade** /maʀməlad/ *nf* stewed fruit

**marmite** /maʀmit/ *nf* (a) (cooking-)pot
(b) potful
IDIOMS **faire bouillir la ~** (colloq) to bring home the bacon

**marmiton** /maʀmitɔ̃/ *nm* chef's assistant

**marmonner** /maʀmɔne/ [1] *vtr* to mumble, to mutter

**marmot** /maʀmo/ *nm* (colloq) kid (colloq), brat (colloq)

**marmotte** /maʀmɔt/ *nf* (a) marmot
(b) (figurative) sleepyhead (colloq)

**maroquinerie** /maʀɔkinʀi/ *nf* (a) leather shop
(b) leather industry; leather trade; (**articles de**) **~** leather goods

**marotte** /maʀɔt/ *nf* (a) pet subject, hobby horse; pet *or* favourite (GB) hobby
(b) puppet

**marquant, ~e** /maʀkɑ̃, ɑ̃t/ *adj* (*fact*) memorable; (*memory*) lasting

**marque** /maʀk/ *nf* (a) brand, make; **de ~** (*product*) branded; (*guest*) distinguished; (*person*) eminent
(b) mark; sign; **~ de doigts** fingermarks; **on voit encore les ~s (de coups)** you can still see the bruises; **~ du pluriel** plural marker; **laisser sa ~** to make one's mark
(c) (Sport) score; **à vos ~s, prêts, partez!** on your marks, get set, go!
■ **~ déposée** registered trademark; **~ de fabrication** manufacturer's brand name; **~ de fabrique** trademark

**marqué, ~e** /maʀke/ **1** *pp* ▶ MARQUER
**2** *pp adj* (a) **il a le corps ~ de traces de coups** he's bruised all over; **elle est restée ~e par la guerre** the war left its mark on her; **visage ~** worn face
(b) (*difference*) marked

**marquer** /maʀke/ [1] **1** *vtr* (a) to mark (*goods*); to brand (*cattle*)
(b) to mark, to signal (*beginning, end*)
(c) to mark (*body, object*)
(d) (figurative) (*event, work*) to leave its mark on (*person*); **c'est quelqu'un qui m'a beaucoup marqué** he/she was a strong influence on me
(e) to write [sth] down (*information*); to mark (*price*); **qu'est-ce qu'il y a de marqué?** what does it say?
(f) to show; **~ la mesure** (Mus) to beat time; **il faut ~ le coup** let's celebrate
(g) **~ un temps (d'arrêt)** to pause
(h) (Sport) to score (*goal*); to mark (*opponent*)
**2** *vi* (a) to leave a mark
(b) (Sport) to score

**marqueur** /maʀkœʀ/ *nm* marker pen

**marquis, ~e** /maʀki, iz/ *nm,f* marquis/ marchioness

**marraine** /maʀɛn/ *nf* (a) godmother
(b) sponsor
■ **~ de guerre** *soldier's wartime female penfriend*

**marrant, ~e** /maʀɑ̃, ɑ̃t/ *adj* (colloq) funny

**marre** /maʀ/ *adv* (colloq) **en avoir ~** to be fed up (colloq)

**marrer: se marrer** /maʀe/ [1] *v refl* (+ *v être*) (colloq) (a) to have a great time
(b) to have a good laugh

**marron, -onne** /maʀɔ̃, ɔn/ **1** *adj* crooked
⋯⟡

2 *adj inv* brown; ~ **clair/foncé** light/dark brown
3 *nm* (a) chestnut
(b) brown
■ ~ **glacé** marron glacé; ~**s chauds** roast chestnuts

**marronnier** /maʀɔnje/ *nm* chestnut (tree)

**mars** /maʀs/ *nm inv* March
IDIOMS **arriver comme** ~ **en carême** to come as sure as night follows day

**Marseillaise** /maʀsɛjɛz/ *nf* Marseillaise (*French national anthem*)

**marsouin** /maʀswɛ̃/ *nm* porpoise

**marteau**, *pl* ~**x** /maʀto/ *nm* hammer; (*of judge*) gavel; (*on door*) knocker

**marteler** /maʀtəle/ [17] *vtr* (a) to hammer, to pound
(b) to rap out ⟨*words*⟩

**martial**, ~**e**, *mpl* **-iaux** /maʀsjal, o/ *adj* ⟨*art, law*⟩ martial; ⟨*music, step*⟩ military

**martinet** /maʀtinɛ/ *nm* (a) (Zool) swift
(b) whip

**martingale** /maʀtɛ̃gal/ *nf* (a) (on jacket) half belt
(b) (for horse) martingale

**martre** /maʀtʀ/ *nf* (a) marten
(b) sable

**martyr**, ~**e**[1] /maʀtiʀ/ 1 *adj* martyred; **enfant** ~ battered child
2 *nm,f* martyr

**martyre**[2] /maʀtiʀ/ *nm* (a) martyrdom
(b) agony; **souffrir le** ~ to suffer agony

**martyriser** /maʀtiʀize/ [1] *vtr* (a) to torment ⟨*victim, animal*⟩; to batter ⟨*child*⟩
(b) to martyr

**marxisme** /maʀksism/ *nm* Marxism

**mas** /ma/ *nm inv* farmhouse (*in Provence*)

**mascarade** /maskaʀad/ *nf* (a) farce; ~ **de justice** travesty of justice
(b) masked ball

**mascotte** /maskɔt/ *nf* mascot

**masculin**, ~**e** /maskylɛ̃, in/ 1 *adj* ⟨*population, sex, part*⟩ male; ⟨*sport*⟩ man's; ⟨*magazine, team*⟩ men's; ⟨*face, noun*⟩ masculine
2 *nm* masculine

**masochisme** /mazɔʃism/ *nm* masochism

**masochiste** /mazɔʃist/ *nmf* masochist

**masque** /mask/ *nm* (a) mask
(b) face-pack
(c) expression
■ ~ **à gaz** gas mask; ~ **de plongée** diving mask; ~ **de soudeur** face shield
IDIOMS **jeter le** ~ to show one's true colours (GB)

**masqué**, ~**e** /maske/ *adj* (a) ⟨*bandit*⟩ masked
(b) (figurative) concealed

**masquer** /maske/ [1] 1 *vtr* (a) to conceal ⟨*defect*⟩; to mask ⟨*problem*⟩
(b) to block ⟨*opening, light*⟩
2 **se masquer** *v refl* (+ *v être*) to hide [sth] from oneself ⟨*truth*⟩

**massacrante** /masakʀɑ̃t/ *adj f* **être d'humeur** ~ to be in a foul mood

**massacre** /masakʀ/ *nm* massacre, slaughter

**massacrer** /masakʀe/ [1] *vtr* (a) to massacre, to slaughter
(b) (figurative) (colloq) to slaughter (colloq) ⟨*opponent*⟩; to massacre ⟨*piece of music*⟩; to botch ⟨*job*⟩; to criticize ⟨*play, actor*⟩

**massage** /masaʒ/ *nm* massage

**masse** /mas/ *nf* (a) mass; ~ **rocheuse** rocky mass; **une** ~ **humaine** a mass of humanity
(b) **une** ~ **de** a lot of; **des** ~**s de** (colloq) masses of; **départs en** ~ mass exodus
(c) **la** ~, **les** ~**s** the masses; **culture de** ~ mass culture
■ ~ **d'armes** mace; ~ **monétaire** money supply; ~ **salariale** (total) wage bill
IDIOMS (**se laisser**) **tomber comme une** ~ to collapse; **dormir comme une** ~ to sleep like a log (colloq)

**massepain** /maspɛ̃/ *nm* marzipan cake

**masser** /mase/ [1] 1 *vtr* to massage
2 **se masser** *v refl* (+ *v être*) (a) to mass
(b) **se** ~ **les jambes** to massage one's legs

**masseur**, **-euse** /masœʀ, øz/ *nm,f* masseur/masseuse

**massicot** /masiko/ *nm* (for paper) guillotine

**massif**, **-ive** /masif, iv/ 1 *adj*
(a) ⟨*features*⟩ heavy; ⟨*silhouette*⟩ massive
(b) ⟨*dose*⟩ massive; ⟨*redundancies*⟩ mass
(c) ⟨*gold, oak*⟩ solid
2 *nm* (a) massif
(b) (flower) bed

**massivement** /masivmɑ̃/ *adv* ⟨*demonstrate*⟩ in great numbers; ⟨*inject*⟩ in massive doses; ⟨*approve*⟩ overwhelmingly

**mass media** /masmedja/ *nm pl* mass media

**massue** /masy/ *nf* (gen, Sport) club, bludgeon

**mastic** /mastik/ 1 *adj inv* putty-coloured (GB)
2 *nm* (for windows) putty; (for holes) filler

**mastiquer** /mastike/ [1] *vtr* to chew

**mastoc** /mastɔk/ *adj inv* (colloq) huge

**mastodonte** /mastodɔ̃t/ *nm* (a) mastodon
(b) (figurative) (person) colossus, hulk (colloq); (animal) monster

**masturber** /mastyʀbe/ [1] *vtr*, **se masturber** *v refl* (+ *v être*) to masturbate

**m'as-tu-vu** /matyvy/ *nmf inv* (colloq) show-off

**mat**, ~**e** /mat/ 1 *adj* (a) ⟨*paint*⟩ matt (GB), matte (US)
(b) ⟨*complexion*⟩ olive
(c) ⟨*sound*⟩ dull
2 *nm* (échec et) ~! checkmate!

**mât** /ma/ *nm* (a) mast
(b) pole; climbing pole; ~ **de drapeau** flagpole

**matador** /matadɔʀ/ *nm* matador

**match** /matʃ/ *nm* match; (in team sports) match (GB), game (US);~ **nul** draw (GB), tie (US); **faire** ~ **nul** to draw (GB), to tie (US)
■ ~ **de classement** league match

**matelas** /matla/ *nm inv* mattress; ~ **pneumatique** air bed

**matelassé, ~e** /matlase/ *adj* ‹*material*› quilted; ‹*door*› padded

**matelot** /matlo/ *nm* (a) sailor
(b) ≈ ordinary seaman (GB), ≈ seaman apprentice (US)

**mater** /mate/ [1] *vtr* to bring [sb/sth] into line ‹*rebels*›; to take [sb/sth] in hand ‹*child, horse*›

**matérialiser** /materjalize/ [1] **1** *vtr*
(a) to realize ‹*dream*›; to make [sth] happen ‹*plan*›
(b) to mark; ‘**chaussée non matérialisée sur 3 km**’ ‘no road markings for 3 km’
**2 se matérialiser** *v refl* (+ *v être*) to materialize

**matérialisme** /materjalism/ *nm* materialism

**matérialiste** /materjalist/ *adj* materialistic

**matériau**, *pl* ~**x** /materjo/ *nm* material; ~**x de construction** building materials

**matériel, -ielle** /materjel/ **1** *adj* ‹*cause, conditions*› material; ‹*means*› practical
**2** *nm* (a) equipment; ~ **agricole** farm machinery
(b) material
■ ~ **informatique** hardware

**matériellement** /materjelmã/ *adv*
(a) **c'est** ~ **possible** it can be done
(b) financially

**maternel, -elle**[1] /maternel/ *adj*
(a) ‹*instinct*› maternal; ‹*love*› motherly
(b) ‹*aunt*› maternal; **du côté** ~ on the mother's side

**maternelle**[2] /maternel/ *nf* nursery school

**maternellement** /maternelmã/ *adv* in a motherly way

**materner** /materne/ [1] *vtr* (a) to mother
(b) to mollycoddle

**maternité** /maternite/ *nf* (a) motherhood
(b) pregnancy; **de** ~ ‹*leave*› maternity
(c) maternity hospital

**mathématicien, -ienne** /matematisjɛ̃, ɛn/ *nm,f* mathematician

**mathématiquement** /matematikmã/ *adv* (a) mathematically
(b) logically

**mathématiques** /matematik/ *nf pl* mathematics

**matheux, -euse** /matø, øz/ *nm,f* (colloq) mathematician

**maths** /mat/ *nf pl* (colloq) maths (GB) (colloq), math (US) (colloq)

**matière** /matjer/ *nf* (a) material; **fournir la** ~ **d'un roman** to provide the material for a novel
(b) matter; **en** ~ **d'emploi** as far as employment is concerned; ~ **à réflexion** food for thought
(c) (Sch) subject
■ ~**s fécales** faeces; ~**s grasses** fat; ~ **grise** grey (GB) *or* gray (US) matter; ~ **première** raw material

**Matignon** /matiɲɔ̃/ *pr n: offices of the French Prime Minister*

**matin** /matɛ̃/ *nm* morning; **de bon** ~ early in the morning
IDIOMS **être du** ~ to be a morning person

**matinal, ~e**, *mpl* **-aux** /matinal, o/ *adj* ‹*walk*› morning; ‹*hour*› early; **être** ~ to be an early riser, to be up early

**mâtiné, ~e** /matine/ *adj* **un anglais** ~ **de français** a mixture of English and French

**matinée** /matine/ *nf* (a) morning
(b) matinée
IDIOMS **faire la grasse** ~ to sleep in

**matines** /matin/ *nf pl* matins

**matraquage** /matrakaʒ/ *nm*
(a) bludgeoning
(b) (figurative) ~ **publicitaire** hype (colloq)

**matraque** /matrak/ *nf* club; truncheon (GB), billy (US); **c'est le coup de** ~ (figurative) (colloq) it costs a fortune

**matraquer** /matrake/ [1] *vtr* (a) to club
(b) ‹*media*› to bombard ‹*public*›

**matriarcal, ~e**, *mpl* **-aux** /matrijarkal, o/ *adj* matriarchal

**matrice** /matris/ *nf* (a) matrix
(b) (Tech) die

**matricule** /matrikyl/ *nm* reference number; (Mil) service number

**matrimonial, ~e**, *mpl* **-iaux** /matrimɔnjal, o/ *adj* marriage, matrimonial

**matrone** /matron/ *nf* matronly woman

**maturation** /matyrasjɔ̃/ *nf* ripening; maturing

**maturité** /matyrite/ *nf* maturity

**maudire** /modir/ [80] *vtr* to curse

**maudit, ~e** /modi, it/ **1** *pp* ▶ MAUDIRE
**2** *adj* (colloq) blasted (colloq)
**3** *nm,f* damned soul; **les** ~**s** the damned

**maugréer** /mogree/ [11] *vi* to grumble (**contre** about)

**maure** /mor/ *adj* Moorish

**maussade** /mosad/ *adj* ‹*mood*› sullen; ‹*weather*› dull; ‹*landscape*› bleak

**mauvais, ~e** /move, ez/ **1** *adj* (a) bad, poor; ‹*lawyer, doctor*› incompetent; ‹*wage*› low; **du** ~ **tabac** cheap tobacco
(b) ‹*address*› wrong
(c) ‹*day, moment*› bad; ‹*method*› wrong
(d) bad; ‹*surprise*› nasty; ‹*taste, smell*› unpleasant; **par** ~ **temps** in bad weather; **ça a** ~ **goût** it tastes horrible
(e) ‹*cold, wound*› nasty; ‹*sea*› rough
(f) ‹*person, smile*› nasty; ‹*intentions, thoughts*› evil; **préparer un** ~ **coup** to be up to mischief
**2** *adv* **sentir** ~ to smell; **sentir très** ~ to stink; **il fait** ~ the weather is bad

····❖

**m**

3 *nm* il n'y a pas que du ~ dans le projet the project isn't all bad

■ ~ esprit scoffing person; scoffing attitude; ~ garçon tough guy; ~ traitements ill-treatment; ~e herbe weed; ~es rencontres bad company

IDIOMS l'avoir ~e (colloq) to be furious

**mauve¹** /mov/ *adj, nm* mauve

**mauve²** /mov/ *nf* mallow

**mauviette** /movjɛt/ *nf* wimp (colloq)

**maux** ▶ MAL

**maxi-** /maksi/ *pref* ~-jupe maxi-skirt; ~-bouteille one-and-a-half litre (GB) bottle

**maxillaire** /maksilɛR/ *nm* jawbone

**maxima** ▶ MAXIMUM

**maximal**, ~e, *mpl* -aux /maksimal, o/ *adj* maximum

**maxime** /maksim/ *nf* maxim

**maximum**, *pl* ~s *or* **maxima** /maksimɔm, maksima/ 1 *adj* maximum
2 *nm* (a) maximum; **10 euros au grand** ~ 10 euros at the very most; **au** ~ ⟨*work*⟩ to the maximum; ⟨*reduce*⟩ as much as possible; **obtenir le** ~ **d'avantages** to get as many advantages as possible; **faire le** ~ to do one's utmost
(b) (Law) maximum sentence

**mayonnaise** /majɔnɛz/ *nf* mayonnaise

**mazagran** /mazagRã/ *nm*: *thick china goblet for coffee*

**mazout** /mazut/ *nm* (fuel) oil

**me** (**m'** *before vowel or mute h*) /m(ə)/ *pron*
(a) me; **tu ne m'as pas fait mal** you didn't hurt me
(b) myself; **je** ~ **lave** (**les mains**) I wash (my hands)

**Me** *written abbr* = MAÎTRE 3 c

**méandre** /meãdR/ *nm* meander; **les** ~s **de l'administration** the maze of officialdom; **les** ~s **de ta pensée** the rambling development of your ideas

**mec** /mɛk/ *nm* (colloq) guy (colloq); **mon** ~ my man (colloq)

**mécanicien, -ienne** /mekanisjɛ̃, ɛn/
1 *adj* mechanical
2 *nm,f* mechanic
3 *nm* (of train) engine driver (GB), (locomotive) engineer (US); (of plane) flight engineer; (of boat) engineer

**mécanique** /mekanik/ 1 *adj* mechanical; ⟨*toy*⟩ clockwork; ⟨*razor*⟩ hand
2 *nf* (a) mechanics; **une merveille de** ~ a marvel of engineering
(b) (colloq) machine

**mécaniquement** /mekanikmã/ *adv* mechanically; **fabriqué** ~ machine-made

**mécaniser** /mekanize/ [1] *vtr*, **se mécaniser** *v refl* (+ *v être*) to mechanize

**mécanisme** /mekanism/ *nm* mechanism

**mécano** /mekano/ *nm* (colloq) mechanic

**mécénat** /mesena/ *nm* patronage

**mécène** /mesɛn/ *nm* patron of the arts

**méchamment** /meʃamã/ *adv*
(a) spitefully, maliciously; viciously; **traiter qn** ~ to treat sb badly
(b) (colloq) ⟨*damage*⟩ badly; ⟨*good*⟩ terribly

**méchanceté** /meʃãste/ *nf* (a) nastiness; **par pure** ~ out of pure spite
(b) maliciousness, viciousness
(c) malicious act; malicious remark

**méchant**, ~e /meʃã, ãt/ 1 *adj*
(a) ⟨*person*⟩ nasty, malicious; ⟨*animal*⟩ vicious; ⟨*flu, business*⟩ nasty, bad
(b) (colloq) fantastic (colloq), terrific (colloq)
2 *nm,f* (a) villain, baddie (colloq)
(b) naughty boy/girl

**mèche** /mɛʃ/ *nf* (a) (of hair) lock
(b) (in hair) streak
(c) (of candle) wick
(d) (Med) packing
(e) (of explosive) fuse
(f) (drill) bit

IDIOMS **être de** ~ **avec qn** (colloq) to be in cahoots with sb (colloq); **vendre la** ~ to let the cat out of the bag

**méchoui** /meʃwi/ *nm* North African style barbecue; spit-roast lamb

**méconnaissable** /mekɔnɛsabl/ *adj* unrecognizable

**méconnaissance** /mekɔnɛsãs/ *nf*
(a) ignorance
(b) misreading

**méconnaître** /mekɔnɛtR/ [73] *vtr* to misread; to be mistaken about

**méconnu**, ~e /mekɔny/ *adj* ⟨*artist, work*⟩ neglected; ⟨*value*⟩ unrecognized

**mécontent**, ~e /mekɔ̃tã, ãt/ *adj* dissatisfied; ⟨*voter*⟩ discontented; **pas** ~ rather pleased

**mécontentement** /mekɔ̃tãtmã/ *nm*
(a) dissatisfaction
(b) discontent
(c) annoyance

**mécontenter** /mekɔ̃tãte/ [1] *vtr* to annoy; to anger

**Mecque** /mɛk/ *pr n* **la** ~ Mecca

**médaille** /medaj/ *nf* (a) medal; ~ **d'or** gold medal
(b) coin
(c) medallion

**médaillon** /medajɔ̃/ *nm* (a) locket
(b) (in art, architecture) medallion

**médecin** /medsɛ̃/ *nm* doctor; ~ **traitant** general practitioner, GP (GB)
■ ~ **de garde** duty doctor, doctor on duty; ~ **légiste** forensic surgeon

**médecine** /medsin/ *nf* medicine
■ ~ **scolaire** ≈ school health service; ~ **du travail** ≈ occupational medicine; ~s **douces** *or* **parallèles** alternative medicine

**média** /medja/ 1 *nm* medium
2 **médias** *nm pl* **les** ~s the media

**médiateur, -trice** /medjatœR, tRis/
1 *adj* mediatory
2 *nm* mediator; ombudsman

**médiathèque** /medjatɛk/ *nf* multimedia library

**médiation** /medjasjɔ̃/ *nf* mediation

**médiatique** /medjatik/ *adj* ⟨*exploitation*⟩ by the media; ⟨*success*⟩ media

**médiatisation** /medjatizasjɔ̃/ *nf* media coverage

**médiatiser** /medjatize/ [1] *vtr* to give [sth] publicity in the media

**médical**, **∼e**, *mpl* **-aux** /medikal, o/ *adj* medical

**médicament** /medikamɑ̃/ *nm* medicine, drug

**médication** /medikasjɔ̃/ *nf* medication

**médicinal**, **∼e**, *mpl* **-aux** /medisinal, o/ *adj* medicinal

**médico-légal**, **∼e**, *mpl* **-aux** /medikolegal, o/ *adj* forensic; **certificat ∼** autopsy report

**médico-pédagogique**, *pl* **∼s** /medikopedagɔʒik/ *adj* **institut ∼** special school

**médiéval**, **∼e**, *mpl* **-aux** /medjeval, o/ *adj* medieval

**médiocre** /medjɔkʀ/ *adj* mediocre; ⟨*pupil, intelligence*⟩ below average; ⟨*soil, light, return, food*⟩ poor; ⟨*interest, success*⟩ limited; ⟨*income*⟩ meagre (GB)

**médiocrement** /medjɔkʀəmɑ̃/ *adv* rather badly

**médiocrité** /medjɔkʀite/ *nf* **(a)** mediocrity **(b)** meagreness (GB)

**médire** /mediʀ/ [65] *v+prep* **∼ de** to speak ill of

**médisance** /medizɑ̃s/ *nf* malicious gossip

**médisant**, **∼e** /medizɑ̃, ɑ̃t/ *adj* malicious

**médit** /medi/ ▶ MÉDIRE

**méditation** /meditasjɔ̃/ *nf* meditation

**méditer** /medite/ [1] **1** *vtr* to mull over; **longuement médité** ⟨*plan*⟩ carefully considered
**2** *vi* to meditate; **∼ sur** to meditate on ⟨*existence*⟩; to ponder on *or* over ⟨*problem*⟩

**Méditerranée** /mediteʀane/ *pr nf* **la (mer) ∼** the Mediterranean (Sea)

**méditerranéen**, **-éenne** /mediteʀaneɛ̃, ɛn/ *adj* Mediterranean

**médium** /medjɔm/ *nm* medium

**méduse** /medyz/ *nf* jellyfish

**méduser** /medyze/ [1] *vtr* to dumbfound

**meeting** /mitiŋ/ *nm* meeting

**méfait** /mefɛ/ **1** *nm* misdemeanour (GB); crime
**2 méfaits** *nm pl* detrimental effect

**méfiance** /mefjɑ̃s/ *nf* mistrust, suspicion; **∼ de qn envers qn/qch** sb's wariness of sb/ sth

**méfiant**, **∼e** /mefjɑ̃, ɑ̃t/ *adj* suspicious; **elle est d'un naturel ∼** she's always very wary

**méfier**: **se méfier** /mefje/ [2] *v refl* (+ *v être*) **(a) se ∼ de qn/qch** not to trust sb/ sth; **sans se ∼** quite trustingly

**(b) se ∼ de qch** to be wary of sth; **méfie-toi!** be careful!; watch it!

**méga** /mega/ *pref* mega; **∼hertz** megahertz

**mégalomane** /megalɔman/ *adj, nmf* megalomaniac

**mégaoctet** /megaɔktɛ/ *nm* megabyte

**mégarde**: **par mégarde** /paʀmegaʀd/ *phr* inadvertently

**mégère** /meʒɛʀ/ *nf* shrew

**mégot** /mego/ *nm* cigarette butt

**meilleur**, **∼e¹** /mɛjœʀ/ **1** *adj* **(a)** better (**que** than)
**(b)** best; **au ∼ prix** ⟨*buy*⟩ at the lowest price; ⟨*sell*⟩ at the highest price
**2** *nm,f* **le ∼**, **la ∼e** the best one
**3** *adv* better; **il fait ∼ qu'hier** the weather is better than it was yesterday
**4** *nm* **le ∼** the best bit; **pour le ∼ et pour le pire** for better or for worse

**meilleure²** /mɛjœʀ/ *nf* **ça c'est la ∼!** that's the best one yet!

**mélancolie** /melɑ̃kɔli/ *nf* (gen) melancholy; (Med) melancholia

**mélancolique** /melɑ̃kɔlik/ **1** *adj* melancholy
**2** *nmf* melancholic

**mélancoliquement** /melɑ̃kɔlikmɑ̃/ *adv* melancholically, in a melancholy fashion

**mélange** /melɑ̃ʒ/ *nm* (of teas, tobaccos) blend; (of products, ideas) combination; (of colours) mixture; **c'est un ∼** (coton et synthétique) it's a mix (of cotton and synthetic fibres (GB))

**mélanger** /melɑ̃ʒe/ [13] **1** *vtr* **(a)** to blend ⟨*teas, oils, tobaccos*⟩; to mix ⟨*colours, shades*⟩
**(b)** to put together ⟨*styles, people, objects*⟩
**(c)** to mix up; **∼ les cartes** to shuffle (the cards)
**2 se mélanger** *v refl* (+ *v être*) **(a)** ⟨*teas, oils, tobaccos*⟩ to blend; ⟨*colours, shades*⟩ to mix, to blend together
**(b)** ⟨*ideas*⟩ to get muddled

**mélangeur** /melɑ̃ʒœʀ/ *nm* mixer

**mélasse** /melas/ *nf* black treacle (GB), molasses

**mêlée** /mele/ *nf* **(a)** mêlée; **∼ générale** free-for-all
**(b)** (Sport) scrum
**(c)** (figurative) fray

**mêler** /mele/ [1] **1** *vtr* **(a)** to mix ⟨*products, colours*⟩; to blend ⟨*ingredients, cultures*⟩; to combine ⟨*influences*⟩
**(b) être mêlé à un scandale** to be involved in a scandal
**2 se mêler** *v refl* (+ *v être*) **(a)** ⟨*cultures, religions*⟩ to mix; ⟨*smells, voices*⟩ to mingle
**(b) se ∼ à** to mingle with ⟨*crowd*⟩; to mix with ⟨*people*⟩; to join in ⟨*conversation*⟩
**(c) se ∼ de** to meddle in; **mêle-toi de tes affaires** (colloq) mind your own business

**méli-mélo**, *pl* **mélis-mélos** /melimelo/ *nm* jumble, mess

**mélo** /melo/ *adj* (colloq) slushy (colloq), schmaltzy (colloq)

m

**mélodie** /melɔdi/ *nf* **(a)** melody, tune
**(b)** melodiousness
**mélodrame** /melɔdʀam/ *nm* melodrama
**mélomane** /melɔman/ *nmf* music lover
**melon** /məlɔ̃/ *nm* **(a)** melon
**(b)** bowler (hat) (GB), derby (hat) (US)
**membrane** /mɑ̃bʀan/ *nf* (Anat) membrane
**membre** /mɑ̃bʀ/ *nm* **(a)** member; **les pays
~s** the member countries
**(b)** limb; **~ postérieur** hind limb
**mémé** /meme/ *nf* (colloq) gran (colloq),
granny (colloq)
**même** /mɛm/ **1** *adj* **(a)** same
**(b) c'est l'intelligence ~** he's/she's
intelligence itself
**(c) le jour ~ où** the very same day that;
**c'est cela ~** that's it exactly
**2** *adv* **(a)** even; **je ne m'en souviens ~ plus**
I can't even remember now
**(b)** very; **c'est ici ~ que je l'ai rencontré**
I met him at this very place
**3** **de même** *phr* **agir** *or* **faire de ~** to do
the same; **il en va de ~ pour** the same is
true of
**4** **de même que** *phr* **le prix du café, de
~ que celui du tabac, a augmenté de 10%** the
price of coffee, as well as that of tobacco, has
risen by 10%
**5** **même si** *phr* even if
**6** *pron* **le ~, la ~, les ~s** the same; **ce sac
est le ~ que celui de Pierre** this bag is the
same as Pierre's
**mémento** /memɛ̃to/ *nm* guide
**mémo** /memo/ *nm* (colloq) note
**Mémo-Appel** /memoapɛl/ *nm* reminder
call service
**mémoire¹** /memwaʀ/ **1** *nm* **(a)** memo
**(b)** dissertation
**2** **mémoires** *nm pl* memoirs
**mémoire²** /memwaʀ/ *nf* **(a)** memory; **si
j'ai bonne ~** if I remember rightly; **ne pas
avoir de ~** to have a bad memory; **de ~
d'homme** in living memory; **en ~ de** to the
memory of, in memory of; **pour ~** for the
record; for reference
**(b)** (Comput) memory; storage; **mettre des
données en ~** to input data
■ **~ centrale** main storage *or* memory;
**~ morte** read-only memory, ROM; **~ vive**
random access memory, RAM
**Mémophone** /memofɔn/ *nm* public
voicemail service
**mémorable** /memɔʀabl/ *adj* memorable
**mémorial**, **~e**, *mpl* **-iaux** /memɔʀjal, o/
*nm* memorial
**mémoriser** /memɔʀize/ [1] *vtr* to
memorize
**menaçant**, **~e** /mənasɑ̃, ɑ̃t/ *adj*
menacing
**menace** /mənas/ *nf* threat; **sous la ~**
under duress; **sous la ~ d'une arme** at
gunpoint
**menacer** /mənase/ [12] *vtr* **(a)** to threaten
⟨*person*⟩

**(b)** to pose a threat to; **être menacé** ⟨*stability,
economy*⟩ to be in jeopardy; ⟨*life*⟩ to be in
danger; ⟨*population*⟩ to be at risk
**ménage** /menaʒ/ *nm* **(a)** household; **se
mettre en ~ avec qn** to set up home with sb;
**scènes de ~** domestic rows; **monter son ~**
to buy the household goods
**(b)** housework; **faire le ~** to do the cleaning;
**faire des ~s** to do domestic cleaning work
IDIOMS **faire bon ~** to be compatible
**ménagement** /menaʒmɑ̃/ *nm* **avec ~s**
gently; **sans ~s** ⟨*say*⟩ bluntly; ⟨*push*⟩
roughly
**ménager¹** /menaʒe/ [13] **1** *vtr* **(a)** to
handle [sb] carefully; to deal carefully with
[sb]; to be gentle with [sb]; to be careful with
[sth]; **~ la susceptibilité de qn** to humour
(GB) sb
**(b)** to be careful with ⟨*clothes, savings*⟩; **il ne
ménage pas sa peine** he spares no effort
**2** **se ménager** *v refl* (+ *v être*) to take it
easy
**ménager²**, **-ère¹** /menaʒe, ɛʀ/ *adj* ⟨*jobs*⟩
domestic; ⟨*equipment*⟩ household; **appareils
~s** domestic appliances; **travaux ~s**
housework
**ménagère²** /menaʒɛʀ/ *nf* **(a)** housewife
**(b)** canteen of cutlery
**ménagerie** /menaʒʀi/ *nf* menagerie
**mendiant**, **~e** /mɑ̃djɑ̃, ɑ̃t/ *nm,f* beggar
**mendicité** /mɑ̃disite/ *nf* begging
**mendier** /mɑ̃dje/ [2] **1** *vtr* to beg for
**2** *vi* to beg
**mener** /məne/ [16] **1** *vtr* **(a) ~ qn quelque
part** to take sb somewhere; to drive sb
somewhere
**(b)** to lead ⟨*people, country*⟩; to run
⟨*company*⟩; **il ne se laisse pas ~ par sa
grande sœur** he won't be bossed about by his
sister (colloq)
**(c) ~ au village** ⟨*road*⟩ to go or lead to the
village
**(d) ~ à** to lead to; **cette histoire peut te ~
loin** it could be a very nasty business; **~ à
bien** to complete [sth] successfully; to bring
[sth] to a successful conclusion; to handle
[sth] successfully
**(e)** to carry out ⟨*study, reform*⟩; to run
⟨*campaign*⟩; **~ une enquête** to hold an
investigation; **~ sa vie comme on l'entend** to
live as one pleases
**2** *vi* (Sport) to be in the lead
IDIOMS **~ la danse** *or* **le jeu** to call the tune
**ménestrel** /menɛstʀɛl/ *nm* minstrel
**meneur**, **-euse** /mənœʀ, øz/ *nm,f* leader
**menhir** /meniʀ/ *nm* menhir
**méninge** /menɛ̃ʒ/ **1** *nf* (Anat) meninx
**2** **méninges** *nf pl* (colloq) brains (colloq)
**méningite** /menɛ̃ʒit/ *nf* meningitis
**ménisque** /menisk/ *nm* meniscus
**ménopause** /menopoz/ *nf* menopause
**menotte** /mənɔt/ **1** *nf* tiny hand
**2** **menottes** *nf pl* handcuffs
**mensonge** /mɑ̃sɔ̃ʒ/ *nm* **(a)** lie

**(b) le ~** lying
**mensonger, -ère** /mɑ̃sɔ̃ʒe, ɛʀ/ adj
⟨accusations⟩ false; ⟨advertising⟩ misleading
**mensualité** /mɑ̃sɥalite/ nf monthly
instalment (GB)
**mensuel, -elle** /mɑ̃sɥɛl/ ①  adj monthly
②  nm monthly magazine
**mensuellement** /mɑ̃sɥɛlmɑ̃/ adv once a
month, monthly
**mensurations** /mɑ̃syʀasjɔ̃/ nf pl
measurements
**mental, ~e, mpl -aux** /mɑ̃tal, o/ adj
mental; **handicapé ~** mentally handicapped
person
**mentalité** /mɑ̃talite/ nf mentality
**menteur, -euse** /mɑ̃tœʀ, øz/ ①  adj
⟨person⟩ untruthful; ⟨statement⟩ full of lies
②  nm,f liar
**menthe** /mɑ̃t/ nf (a) mint; **~ poivrée**
peppermint; **~ verte** spearmint
(b) mint tea
(c) **~ (à l'eau)** mint cordial
**menthol** /mɑ̃tɔl/ nm menthol
**mentholé, ~e** /mɑ̃tɔle/ adj mentholated;
menthol
**mention** /mɑ̃sjɔ̃/ nf (a) mention; **faire ~
de qch** to mention sth
(b) (Sch) **~ passable** pass with 50 to 60%;
**~ très bien** pass with 80% upward(s)
(c) note; **rayer la ~ inutile** or **les ~s inutiles**
delete as appropriate
**mentionner** /mɑ̃sjɔne/ [1] vtr to mention
**mentir** /mɑ̃tiʀ/ [30] ①  vi (a) to lie, to tell
lies
(b) ⟨figures⟩ to be misleading
②  **se mentir** v refl (+ v être) (a) to fool
oneself
(b) to lie to one another
**menton** /mɑ̃tɔ̃/ nm chin
**menu, ~e** /məny/ ①  adj (a) ⟨person⟩
slight; ⟨foot, piece⟩ tiny; ⟨writing⟩ small
(b) ⟨jobs⟩ small; ⟨details⟩ minute; **~ fretin**
small fry
②  adv ⟨write⟩ small; ⟨chop⟩ finely
③  nm menu
④  **par le menu** phr in (great) detail
■ **~ fretin** small fry; **~e monnaie** small
change
**menuiserie** /mənɥizʀi/ nf woodwork
**menuisier** /mənɥizje/ nm joiner (GB),
finish carpenter
**méprendre: se méprendre** /mepʀɑ̃dʀ/
[52] v refl (+ v être) to be mistaken
**mépris** /mepʀi/ nm inv contempt; **au ~ de
la loi** regardless of the law
**méprisable** /mepʀizabl/ adj contemptible
**méprisant, ~e** /mepʀizɑ̃, ɑ̃t/ adj
⟨gesture⟩ contemptuous; ⟨person⟩ disdainful
**méprise** /mepʀiz/ nf mistake
**mépriser** /mepʀize/ [1] vtr to despise
⟨person, wealth⟩; to scorn ⟨danger, offer⟩
**mer** /mɛʀ/ nf (a) sea; **une ~ d'huile** a glassy
sea; **en pleine ~** out at sea; **la ~ monte** the
tide is coming in

**(b)** seaside
**IDIOMS ce n'est pas la ~ à boire** it's not all
that difficult
**mercantile** /mɛʀkɑ̃til/ adj mercenary
**mercenaire** /mɛʀsənɛʀ/ adj, nmf
mercenary
**mercerie** /mɛʀsəʀi/ nf haberdasher's shop
(GB), notions store (US)
**merci¹** /mɛʀsi/ nm, excl thank you
**merci²** /mɛʀsi/ nf mercy; **on est toujours à
la ~ d'un accident** there's always the risk of
an accident
**mercredi** /mɛʀkʀədi/ nm Wednesday
**mercure** /mɛʀkyʀ/ nm mercury
**mercurochrome®** /mɛʀkyʀokʀom/ nm
Mercurochrome®, antiseptic
**merde** /mɛʀd/ nf, excl (vulgar) shit (slang)
**mère** /mɛʀ/ ①  nf (a) mother
(b) **~ supérieure** Mother Superior
②  **(-)mère** (combining form) **cellule/maison
~** parent cell/company
■ **~ célibataire** single mother; **~ de famille**
mother; housewife; **~ porteuse** surrogate
mother; **~ poule** mother hen
**merguez** /mɛʀgɛz/ nf inv spicy sausage
**méridien** /meʀidjɛ̃/ nm meridian
**méridional, ~e, mpl -aux** /meʀidjɔnal,
o/ ①  adj southern
②  nm,f Southerner
**meringue** /məʀɛ̃g/ nf meringue
**mérite** /meʀit/ nm merit; credit; **au ~**
according to merit; **vanter les ~s de** to sing
the praises of
**mériter** /meʀite/ [1] ①  vtr to deserve;
**~ réflexion** to be worth considering
②  **se mériter** v refl (+ v être) **ça se mérite**
it's something that has to be earned
**merlan** /mɛʀlɑ̃/ nm whiting
**merle** /mɛʀl/ nm blackbird
**mérou** /meʀu/ nm grouper
**merveille** /mɛʀvɛj/ ①  nf marvel, wonder
②  **à merveille** phr wonderfully
**merveilleux, -euse** /mɛʀvɛjø, øz/ adj
marvellous (GB), wonderful
**mes ▶ MON**
**mésaventure** /mezavɑ̃tyʀ/ nf
misadventure
**mesdames ▶ MADAME**
**mesdemoiselles ▶ MADEMOISELLE**
**mésentente** /mezɑ̃tɑ̃t/ nf dissension;
disagreement
**mésestimer** /mezɛstime/ [1] vtr to
underrate; to underestimate
**mesquin, ~e** /mɛskɛ̃, in/ adj (a) petty-
minded; petty
(b) ⟨person⟩ mean (GB), cheap (US) (colloq)
**mesquinerie** /mɛskinʀi/ nf (a) meanness
(b) stinginess
(c) mean trick; mean remark
**message** /mesaʒ/ nm message;
**~ publicitaire** commercial
**messager, -ère** /mesaʒe, ɛʀ/ nm,f
(a) messenger ···⁛

(b) envoy

**messagerie** /mesaʒʀi/ nf (a) freight
forwarding
■ ~ **électronique** electronic mail service,
e-mail; ~ **vocale** voice messaging

**messe** /mɛs/ nf mass; ~**s basses** (colloq)
whispering

**messie** /mesi/ nm messiah

**messieurs** ▶ MONSIEUR

**mesure** /məzyʀ/ nf (a) measure; **prendre
des ~s** to take measures; to take steps
(b) measurement; **c'est du sur ~** it's made to
measure; **tu as un emploi sur ~** the job is
tailor-made for you; **c'est une adversaire à ta
~** she is a match for you
(c) **unité de ~** unit of measurement;
**instrument de ~** measuring device; **deux ~s
de lait pour une ~ d'eau** two parts milk to
one of water
(d) moderation; **dépasser la ~** to go too far
(e) (Mus) bar; **battre la ~** to beat time
(f) **être en ~ de rembourser** to be in a
position to reimburse; **dans la ~ du possible**
as far as possible; **dans la ~ où** insofar as

**mesurer** /məzyʀe/ [1] **1** vtr (a) to
measure; ~ **le tour de cou de qn** to take sb's
neck measurement
(b) to measure ⟨productivity, gap⟩; to assess
⟨difficulties, risks, effects⟩; to consider
⟨consequences⟩; ~ **ses paroles** to weigh one's
words
**2** vi ~ **20 mètres carrés** to be 20 metres (GB)
square; **elle mesure 1,60 m** she's 1.60 m tall
**3** **se mesurer** v refl (+ v être) (a) **se ~ en
mètres** to be measured in metres (GB)
(b) **se ~ à** or **avec qn** to pit one's strength
against sb

**métal,** pl **-aux** /metal, o/ nm metal; **pièce
de** or **en ~** metal coin; ~ **jaune** gold

**métallique** /metalik/ adj (a) metal; **c'est
~** it's made of metal
(b) metallic

**métallisé, ~e** /metalize/ adj ⟨green, blue⟩
metallic

**métallurgie** /metalyʀʒi/ nf
(a) metalworking industry
(b) metallurgy

**métallurgique** /metalyʀʒik/ adj
metallurgical

**métamorphose** /metamɔʀfoz/ nf
metamorphosis

**métamorphoser** /metamɔʀfoze/ [1]
**1** vtr to transform [sb/sth] completely
**2** **se métamorphoser** v refl (+ v être) **se
~ en** to metamorphose into

**métaphore** /metafɔʀ/ nf metaphor

**métayage** /metejaʒ/ nm tenant farming,
sharecropping

**métayer, -ère** /meteje, ɛʀ/ nm,f tenant
farmer (GB), sharecropper (US)

**météo** /meteo/ nf weather forecast

**météore** /meteɔʀ/ nm meteor

**météorite** /meteɔʀit/ nm or nf meteorite

**météorologie** /meteɔʀɔlɔʒi/ nf
meteorology

**météorologique** /meteɔʀɔlɔʒik/ adj
meteorological; **conditions ~s** weather
conditions

**météorologiste** /meteɔʀɔlɔʒist/,
**météorologue** /meteɔʀɔlɔg/ nmf
meteorologist

**métèque** /metɛk/ nm (offensive) foreigner,
dago (offensive)

**méthane** /metan/ nm methane

**méthode** /metɔd/ nf (a) method
(b) (for languages) course book (GB), textbook
(US)
(c) way; **j'ai ma ~ pour le convaincre** I've got
a way of convincing him

**méthodique** /metɔdik/ adj methodical

**méthodiquement** /metɔdikmɑ̃/ adv
methodically; **procédons ~** let's take things
step by step

**méticuleux, -euse** /metikylø, øz/ adj
meticulous; painstaking

**métier** /metje/ nm (a) job; profession;
trade; craft; **avoir 20 ans de ~** to have 20
years' experience; **c'est le ~ qui rentre!** you
learn by your mistakes!
(b) ~ **à tisser** weaving loom

**métis, -isse** /metis/ nm,f person of mixed
race

**métissage** /metisaʒ/ nm (of people)
miscegenation; (of plants, animals) crossing

**métrage** /metʀaʒ/ nm (a) (of material) length
(b) **long ~** feature(-length) film

**mètre** /mɛtʀ/ nm (a) metre (GB); **le 60 ~s**
the 60 metres (GB); **piquer un cent ~s** (colloq)
to break into a run
(b) rule (GB), yardstick (US); ~ **ruban** or **de
couturière** tape measure

**métrique** /metʀik/ adj metric

**métro** /metʀo/ nm underground (GB),
subway (US).
IDIOMS ~, **boulot, dodo** (colloq) the daily
grind

**métronome** /metʀɔnɔm/ nm metronome

**métropole** /metʀɔpɔl/ nf (a) metropolis
(b) major city
(c) Metropolitan France

**métropolitain, ~e** /metʀɔpɔlitɛ̃, ɛn/ adj
(a) ⟨network⟩ underground (GB), subway (US)
(b) from Metropolitan France

**métropolite** /metʀɔpɔlit/ nm
metropolitan

**mets** /mɛ/ nm inv dish, delicacy

**mettable** /mɛtabl/ adj wearable

**metteur** /mɛtœʀ/ nm ~ **en scène** director

**mettre** /mɛtʀ/ [60] **1** vtr (a) to put; to put
in ⟨heating, shower⟩; to put up ⟨curtains,
shelves⟩; **je mets les enfants à la crèche**
I send the children to a creche; **mets ton
écharpe** put your scarf on; ~ **le linge à
sécher** to put the washing out to dry; **faire ~
le téléphone** to have a telephone put in
(b) to wear
(c) ~ **qn en colère** to make sb angry

**(d)** to put on ⟨*radio, TV, heating*⟩; **mets moins fort!** turn it down!; **~ le réveil** to set the alarm
**(e)** to put up ⟨*sign*⟩; **qu'est-ce que je dois ~?** what shall I put?; **je t'ai mis un mot** I've left you a note; **~ en musique** to set to music; **~ en anglais** to put into English
**(f) y ~ du sien** to put oneself into it; **combien pouvez-vous ~?** how much can you afford?; **how much can you put in?; elle a mis une heure** it took her an hour (**pour faire** to do)
**(g)** (Sch) **je vous ai mis trois sur vingt** I've given you three out of twenty
**(h)** (colloq) **mettons qu'il vienne, qu'est-ce que vous ferez?** supposing he comes, what will you do?
[2] *vi* **~ bas** ⟨*animal*⟩ to give birth; to calve
[3] **se mettre** *v refl* (+ *v être*) **(a)** se **~ devant la fenêtre** to stand in front of the window; **se ~ au lit** to go to bed; **se ~ debout** to stand up; **où est-ce que ça se met?** where does this go?
**(b)** to spill [sth] on oneself
**(c) je ne sais pas quoi me ~** I don't know what to put on
**(d) se ~ à l'anglais** to take up English; **il va se ~ à pleuvoir** it's going to start raining
**(e) je préfère me ~ bien avec lui** I prefer to get on the right side of him; **se ~ à l'aise** to make oneself comfortable

**meuble** /mœbl/ [1] *adj* ⟨*soil*⟩ loose
[2] *nm* **un ~** a piece of furniture
**IDIOMS sauver les ~s** to salvage something
**meublé** /mœble/ *nm* furnished apartment
**meubler** /mœble/ [1] *vtr* to furnish; **la plante meuble bien la pièce** the plant makes the room look more cosy (GB) *or* cozy (US)
**meugler** /møgle/ [1] *vi* to moo
**meule** /møl/ *nf* **(a)** millstone
**(b)** grindstone
**(c) ~ de foin** haystack
**meunier, -ière** /mønje, ɛʀ/ *nm,f* miller
**meurtre** /mœʀtʀ/ *nm* murder
**meurtrier, -ière** /mœʀtʀije, ɛʀ/ [1] *adj* ⟨*fighting, repression*⟩ bloody; ⟨*explosion, accident*⟩ fatal; ⟨*epidemic*⟩ deadly; ⟨*arm*⟩ lethal
[2] *nm,f* murderer
**meurtrir** /mœʀtʀiʀ/ [3] *vtr* **(a)** to hurt
**(b)** to bruise
**(c)** to wound ⟨*self-esteem*⟩
**meute** /møt/ *nf* pack of hounds
**mexicain, ~e** /mɛksikɛ̃, ɛn/ *adj* Mexican
**Mexico** /mɛksiko/ *pr n* Mexico City
**Mexique** /mɛksik/ *pr nm* Mexico
**mezzanine** /medzanin/ *nf* mezzanine
**MF** /ɛmɛf/ *nf* (*abbr* = **modulation de fréquence**) frequency modulation, FM
**mi** /mi/ *nm inv* (Mus) (note) E; (in sol-fa) mi, me
**mi-** /mi/ *pref* **à la ~-mai/saison** in mid-May/-season; **~-chinois, ~-français** half Chinese, half French

**miam-miam** /mjammjam/ *excl* (colloq) yum-yum! (colloq)
**miauler** /mjole/ [1] *vi* to miaow (GB), to meow
**mi-bas** /miba/ *nm inv* knee sock, long sock
**miche** /miʃ/ *nf* round loaf
**mi-chemin: à mi-chemin** /amiʃmɛ̃/ *phr* halfway; (figurative) halfway through
**mi-clos, ~e** /miklo, oz/ *adj* half-closed
**micmac** /mikmak/ *nm* (colloq) shady goings-on (colloq)
**mi-côte: à mi-côte** /amikot/ *phr* halfway up; halfway down
**mi-course: à mi-course** /amikuʀs/ *phr* halfway through the race; (figurative) halfway through
**micro¹** /mikʀo/ *pref* micro
**micro²** /mikʀo/ *nm* microphone, mike (colloq); **~ caché** bug
**microbe** /mikʀɔb/ *nm* germ, microbe
**microclimat** /mikʀoklima/ *nm* microclimate
**microcosme** /mikʀɔkɔsm/ *nm* microcosm
**micro-cravate,** *pl* **micros-cravates** /mikʀokʀavat/ *nm* lapel-microphone
**micro-édition** /mikʀoedisjɔ̃/ *nf* desktop publishing
**microfilm** /mikʀɔfilm/ *nm* microfilm
**micro-informatique** /mikʀoɛ̃fɔʀmatik/ *nf* microcomputing
**micro-ondes** /mikʀoɔ̃d/ *nm inv* microwave (colloq)
**micro-ordinateur,** *pl* **~s** /mikʀoɔʀdinatœʀ/ *nm* microcomputer
**microphone** /mikʀɔfɔn/ *nm* microphone
**microprocesseur** /mikʀopʀɔsɛsœʀ/ *nm* microprocessor
**microscope** /mikʀɔskɔp/ *nm* microscope
**microscopique** /mikʀɔskɔpik/ *adj* microscopic; (figurative) tiny
**microsillon** /mikʀɔsijɔ̃/ *nm* (disque) **~** microgroove record
**mi-cuisse: à mi-cuisse** /amikɥis/ *phr* above one's knees
**midi** /midi/ *nm* **(a)** twelve o'clock, midday, noon; **je fais mes courses entre ~ et deux** (colloq) I go shopping in my lunch hour
**(b)** lunchtime
**(c) le Midi** the South of France
**midinette** /midinɛt/ *nf* bimbo (colloq)
**mi-distance: à mi-distance** /amidistɑ̃s/ *phr* halfway
**mie** /mi/ *nf* bread without the crusts
**miel** /mjɛl/ *nm* honey
**IDIOMS être tout sucre tout ~** to be as nice as pie (colloq)
**mielleux, -euse** /mjɛlø, øz/ *adj* ⟨*tone*⟩ unctuous, honeyed; ⟨*person*⟩ fawning
**mien, mienne** /mjɛ̃, mjɛn/ [1] *det* **ces idées, je les ai faites miennes** I adopted these ideas

⋯⋟

**2** **le mien**, **la mienne**, **les miens**, **les miennes** *pron* mine

**miette** /mjɛt/ *nf* crumb; **réduire en ~s** to smash [sth] to bits ⟨*vase*⟩; to shatter ⟨*hopes*⟩; **elle n'en perd pas une ~** (colloq) she's taking it all in

**mieux** /mjø/ **1** *adj inv* better; **le ~, la ~, les ~** the best; the nicest; the most attractive; **ce qu'il y a de ~** the best
**2** *adv* (a) better; **je ne peux pas te dire ~** that's all I can tell you; **qui dit ~?** any other offers?; any advance on that bid?; **de ~ en ~** better and better; **on la critiquait à qui ~ ~** each person criticized her more harshly than the last
(b) **le ~, la ~, les ~** the best; (of two) the better
**3** *nm inv* **le ~ est de refuser** the best thing is to refuse; **il y a un/du ~** there is an/some improvement; **je ne demande pas ~ que de rester ici** I'm perfectly happy staying here; **fais pour le ~, fais au ~** do whatever is best; **tout va pour le ~** everything's fine; **elle est au ~ avec sa voisine** she is on very good terms with her neighbour (GB)

**mièvre** /mjɛvʀ/ *adj* vapid; soppy

**mièvrerie** /mjɛvʀəʀi/ *nf* vapidity; soppiness

**mi-figue** /mifig/ *adj inv* **~ mi-raisin** ⟨*smile*⟩ half-hearted; ⟨*compliment*⟩ ambiguous

**mignon, -onne** /miɲõ, ɔn/ *adj* (a) cute
(b) sweet, kind

**migraine** /migʀɛn/ *nf* splitting headache

**migration** /migʀasjõ/ *nf* migration

**migratoire** /migʀatwaʀ/ *adj* migratory

**migrer** /migʀe/ [1] *vi* to migrate

**mi-hauteur**: **à mi-hauteur** /amiotœʀ/ *phr* halfway up; halfway down

**mi-jambe**: **à mi-jambe** /amiʒɑ̃b/ *phr* (up) to one's knees

**mijaurée** /miʒoʀe/ *nf* **ne fais pas ta ~** don't put on such airs

**mijoter** /miʒɔte/ [1] **1** *vtr* (Culin) to prepare
**2** *vi* (Culin) to simmer

**mijoteuse®** /miʒɔtøz/ *nf* slow cooker

**mikado** /mikado/ *nm* spillikins

**mil** /mil/ *adj inv* = MILLE 1

**milice** /milis/ *nf* militia; **~ de quartier** local vigilante group

**Milice** /milis/ *nf* **la ~** the Milice (*French wartime paramilitary organization which collaborated with the Germans against the Resistance*)

**milicien, -ienne** /milisjɛ̃, ɛn/ *nm,f*
(a) militiaman/militiawoman
(b) member of the Milice

**milieu**, *pl* **~x** /miljø/ **1** *nm* (a) middle; **au beau** *or* **en plein ~** right in the middle; **au ~ de la nuit** halfway through the night
(b) middle ground
(c) environment; **en ~ rural** in the country
(d) background, milieu; **le ~** the underworld
**2 au milieu de** *phr* (a) among; **être au ~ de ses amis** to be with one's friends

(b) surrounded by; **au ~ du désastre** in the midst of disaster

**militaire** /militɛʀ/ **1** *adj* military; army
**2** *nm* serviceman

**militairement** /militɛʀmɑ̃/ *adv* (a) by military means; **zone occupée ~** military occupied zone
(b) with military efficiency; along military lines

**militant, ~e** /militɑ̃, ɑ̃t/ **1** *adj* militant
**2** *nm,f* (of organization) active member, activist; (for cause) campaigner

**militantisme** /militɑ̃tism/ *nm* political activism

**militariste** /militaʀist/ *adj* militaristic

**militer** /milite/ [1] *vi* (a) to campaign
(b) to be a political activist

**mille** /mil/ **1** *adj inv* a thousand, one thousand; **deux/trois ~** two/three thousand
**2** *nm inv* (a) a thousand, one thousand
(b) bull's eye; **taper dans le ~** to hit the bull's-eye; (figurative) to hit the nail on the head
**3** *nm* (a) **~ (marin** *or* **nautique)** (nautical) mile
(b) (air) mile
**4 pour mille** *phr* per thousand
IDIOMS **je vous le donne en ~** you'll never guess (in a million years)

**millénaire** /milenɛʀ/ **1** *adj* (a) **un arbre ~** a one-thousand-year-old tree
(b) ⟨*tradition*⟩ age-old
**2** *nm* (a) **pendant des ~s** for thousands of years
(b) millennium, millenary

**mille-pattes** /milpat/ *nm inv* centipede, millipede

**millésime** /milezim/ *nm* vintage, year

**milli** /mili/ *pref* milli; **~mètre** millimetre (GB)

**milliard** /miljaʀ/ *nm* billion

**milliardaire** /miljaʀdɛʀ/ *nmf* multimillionaire, billionaire

**millième** /miljɛm/ *adj* thousandth

**millier** /milje/ *nm* (a) thousand
(b) **un ~** about a thousand

**million** /miljõ/ *nm* million

**millionième** /miljɔnjɛm/ *adj* millionth

**millionnaire** /miljɔnɛʀ/ **1** *adj* **être ~** ⟨*firm*⟩ to be worth millions; ⟨*person*⟩ to be a millionaire
**2** *nmf* millionaire

**mime** /mim/ *nm* mime

**mimer** /mime/ [1] *vtr* (a) to mime
(b) to mimic

**mimétisme** /mimetism/ *nm* (a) (Zool) mimicry
(b) **par ~** through unconscious imitation

**mimique** /mimik/ *nf* funny face

**minable** /minabl/ *adj* (colloq) (a) ⟨*salary, person*⟩ pathetic
(b) ⟨*place*⟩ crummy (colloq); ⟨*existence*⟩ miserable

**minage** /minaʒ/ *nm* mining

**minaret** /minaʀɛ/ *nm* minaret
**minauder** /minode/ [1] *vi* **(a)** to mince about
**(b)** to simper
**mince** /mɛ̃s/ *adj* **(a)** slim, slender; ⟨*face, slice*⟩ thin
**(b)** ⟨*consolation*⟩ small; ⟨*chance*⟩ slim
**minceur** /mɛ̃sœʀ/ *nf* slimness; slenderness; thinness
**mincir** /mɛ̃siʀ/ [3] *vi* to lose weight
**mine** /min/ *nf* **(a)** expression; **faire ~ d'accepter** to pretend to accept; **elle nous a dit, ~ de rien, que** (colloq) she told us, casually, that; **il est doué, ~ de rien** (colloq) it may not be obvious, but he's very clever
**(b) avoir bonne ~** ⟨*person*⟩ to look well
**(c)** (in pencil) lead
**(d)** mine; **~ d'or** gold mine
**(e)** (Mil) mine
IDIOMS **ne pas payer de ~** (colloq) not to look anything special (colloq)
**miner** /mine/ [1] *vtr* **(a)** to sap ⟨*morale, energy*⟩; to undermine ⟨*health*⟩
**(b)** (Mil) to mine
**minerai** /minʀɛ/ *nm* ore; **~ de fer** iron ore
**minéral, ~e, mpl -aux** /mineʀal, o/
1 *adj* ⟨*water*⟩ mineral; ⟨*chemistry*⟩ inorganic
2 *nm* mineral
**minéralogique** /mineʀalɔʒik/ *adj* **plaque ~** number plate (GB), license plate (US)
**minerve** /minɛʀv/ *nf* (Med) surgical collar (GB), neck brace (US)
**minet** /minɛ/ *nm* **(a)** pussycat
**(b)** (colloq) pretty boy (colloq)
**minette** /minɛt/ *nf* **(a)** pussycat
**(b)** (colloq) cool chick (colloq)
**mineur, ~e** /minœʀ/ 1 *adj* **(a)** (Law) under 18
**(b)** ⟨*detail*⟩ minor
**(c)** (Mus) **en ré ~** in D minor
2 *nm,f* (Law) person under 18
3 *nm* miner; **~ de fond** pit worker
**mini-** /mini/ *pref* mini
**miniature** /minjatyʀ/ *adj, nf* miniature
**miniaturisation** /minjatyʀizasjɔ̃/ *nf* miniaturization
**minibus** /minibys/ *nm inv* minibus
**minicassette®** /minikasɛt/ *nf* mini-cassette®
**minier, -ière** /minje, ɛʀ/ *adj* mining
**mini-informatique** /miniɛ̃fɔʀmatik/ *nf* minicomputing
**mini-jupe, pl ~s** /miniʒyp/ *nf* mini-skirt
**minimal, ~e, mpl -aux** /minimal, o/ *adj* minimal, minimum
**minimalisme** /minimalism/ *nm* minimalism
**minime** /minim/ 1 *adj* negligible
2 *nmf* (Sport) junior (*7 to 13 years old*)
**minimiser** /minimize/ [1] *vtr* to minimize
**minimum, pl ~s or minima** /minimɔm, minima/ 1 *adj* minimum

2 *nm* **(a)** minimum; **un ~ de bon sens** a certain amount of common sense; **il faut au ~ deux heures pour faire le trajet** the journey takes at least two hours
**(b)** (Law) minimum sentence
■ **~ vital** subsistence level
**mini-ordinateur, pl ~s** /miniɔʀdinatœʀ/ *nm* minicomputer
**minipilule** /minipilyl/ *nf* low-dose combined pill
**ministère** /ministɛʀ/ *nm* ministry; (in UK, US) department
**ministériel, -ielle** /ministeʀjɛl/ *adj* ministerial, cabinet
**ministre** /ministʀ/ *nm* **(a)** minister; (in UK) Secretary of State; (in US) Secretary
**(b)** (of religion) minister
**Minitel®** /minitɛl/ *nm* Minitel (*terminal linking phone users to a database*)
**minitéler** /minitele/ [14] *vtr* to contact via Minitel
**minitéliste** /minitelist/ *n* Minitel user
**minivague** /minivag/ *nf* soft perm
**minois** /minwa/ *nm inv* fresh young face
**minoration** /minɔʀasjɔ̃/ *nf*
**(a)** undervaluation; underestimation
**(b)** reduction; **~ des prix** cut in prices
**minorer** /minɔʀe/ [1] *vtr* **(a)** to reduce (de by)
**(b)** to undervalue; to underestimate
**minoritaire** /minɔʀitɛʀ/ *adj* minority
**minorité** /minɔʀite/ *nf* **(a)** minority; **être mis en ~** to be defeated
**(b)** (age) minority
■ **~ de blocage** blocking minority
**minoterie** /minɔtʀi/ *nf* **(a)** flour mill
**(b)** flour-milling
**minou** /minu/ *nm* pussycat
**minuit** /minɥi/ *nm* midnight
**minuscule** /minyskyl/ 1 *adj* ⟨*person, thing*⟩ tiny; ⟨*quantity*⟩ tiny, minute
2 *nf* small letter; (in printing) lower-case letter
**minutage** /minytaʒ/ *nm* (precise) timing
**minute** /minyt/ *nf* minute; **la ~ de vérité** the moment of truth
**minuter** /minyte/ [1] *vtr* **(a)** to time
**(b)** to work out the timing of
**minuterie** /minytʀi/ *nf* **(a)** time-switch
**(b)** automatic lighting
**minuteur** /minytœʀ/ *nm* timer
**minutie** /minysi/ *nf* meticulousness
**minutieusement** /minysjøzmɑ̃/ *adv* with meticulous care; in great detail
**minutieux, -ieuse** /minysjø, øz/ *adj* meticulous; ⟨*description*⟩ detailed
**mioche** /mjɔʃ/ *nmf* (colloq) kid (colloq)
**mirabelle** /miʀabɛl/ *nf* **(a)** mirabelle (*small yellow plum*)
**(b)** plum brandy
**miracle** /miʀakl/ 1 *adj inv* **un médicament ~** a wonder drug; **une méthode ~** a magic formula     ⋯⟶

**2** nm (a) miracle; **faire un** ∼ to work a miracle; (figurative) to work miracles; **comme par** ∼ as if by magic
(b) miracle play

**miraculeux, -euse** /miʀakylø, øz/ adj miraculous; ⟨product, remedy⟩ which works wonders

**mirador** /miʀadɔʀ/ nm watchtower

**mirage** /miʀaʒ/ nm mirage

**mi-raisin** /miʀɛzɛ̃/ adj inv ▶ MI-FIGUE

**miraud, ∼e** /miʀo, od/ adj (colloq) shortsighted

**mirobolant, ∼e** /miʀɔbɔlɑ̃, ɑ̃t/ adj (colloq) fabulous (colloq)

**miroir** /miʀwaʀ/ nm mirror

**miroitement** /miʀwatmɑ̃/ nm sparkling; shimmering

**miroiter** /miʀwate/ [1] vi to shimmer; **faire** ∼ **qch à qn** to hold out the prospect of sth to sb

**mis, ∼e¹** /mi, miz/ ▶ METTRE

**misanthrope** /mizɑ̃tʀɔp/ **1** adj misanthropic
**2** nmf misanthropist, misanthrope

**mise²** /miz/ nf **une** ∼ **de cinq euros** a five-euro bet
■ ∼ **de fonds** investment; ∼ **en plis** set
IDIOMS **être de** ∼ ⟨conduct⟩ to be proper

**miser** /mize/ [1] **1** vtr to bet
**2** vi (a) ∼ **sur** to bet on, to place a bet on
(b) ∼ **sur qn** to place all one's hopes in sb

**misérabilisme** /mizeʀabilism/ nm
(a) sordid realism
(b) tendency to dwell on the dark side

**misérable** /mizeʀabl/ **1** adj (a) ⟨person⟩ destitute, poor; ⟨life⟩ poor
(b) ⟨salary⟩ meagre (GB)
**2** nmf (a) pauper
(b) scoundrel

**misère** /mizeʀ/ nf (a) destitution; **réduire qn à la** ∼ to reduce sb to poverty
(b) misery, wretchedness
(c) trouble, woe; **on a tous nos petites** ∼s we all have our troubles
(d) **être payé une** ∼ to be paid a pittance

**miséreux, -euse** /mizeʀø, øz/ nm,f destitute person; **les** ∼ the destitute

**miséricorde** /mizeʀikɔʀd/ nf, excl mercy

**misogyne** /mizɔʒin/ adj misogynous

**misogynie** /mizɔʒini/ nf misogyny

**missel** /misɛl/ nm missal

**missile** /misil/ nm missile

**mission** /misjɔ̃/ nf mission

**missionnaire** /misjɔnɛʀ/ adj, nmf missionary

**missive** /misiv/ nf missive

**mistral** /mistʀal/ nm mistral

**mitaine** /mitɛn/ nf fingerless mitten

**mite** /mit/ nf (clothes) moth

**mi-temps¹** /mitɑ̃/ nm inv part-time job

**mi-temps²** /mitɑ̃/ nf inv (Sport) half-time

**miteux, -euse** /mitø, øz/ adj seedy; shabby

**mitigé, ∼e** /mitiʒe/ adj ⟨reception⟩ lukewarm; ⟨success⟩ qualified

**mitonner** /mitɔne/ [1] vtr to cook [sth] lovingly

**mitoyen, -enne** /mitwajɛ̃, ɛn/ adj ⟨hedge⟩ dividing; **mur** ∼ party wall

**mitraille** /mitʀaj/ nf hail of bullets

**mitrailler** /mitʀaje/ [1] vtr (a) to machine-gun
(b) ∼ **qn de questions** to fire questions at sb
(c) (colloq) to take photo after photo of [sb/sth]

**mitraillette** /mitʀajɛt/ nf submachine gun

**mitrailleuse** /mitʀajøz/ nf machine gun

**mi-voix: à mi-voix** /amivwa/ phr in a low voice

**mixage** /miksaʒ/ nm sound mixing

**mixer¹** /mikse/ [1] vtr to mix

**mixer²** /miksɛʀ/ = MIXEUR

**mixeur** /miksœʀ/ nm (a) mixer
(b) blender

**mixité** /miksite/ nf (gen) mixing of sexes; (Sch) coeducation

**mixte** /mikst/ adj (a) ⟨school⟩ coeducational; ⟨class⟩ mixed
(b) ⟨couple, marriage⟩ mixed; ⟨economy⟩ mixed; **société** ∼ joint venture

**mixture** /mikstyʀ/ nf (a) concoction
(b) (in pharmacy) mixture
(c) mishmash (colloq)

**MJC** /ɛmʒise/ nf (abbr = **maison des jeunes et de la culture**) ≈ youth club

**MLF** /ɛmɛlɛf/ nm (abbr = **mouvement de libération des femmes**) ≈ Women's Lib

**Mlle** (written abbr = **Mademoiselle**) Ms, Miss

**mm** (written abbr = **millimètre**) mm

**MM.** (written abbr = **Messieurs**) Messrs

**Mme** (written abbr = **Madame**) Ms, Mrs

**mnémotechnique** /mnemɔtɛknik/ adj mnemonic

**Mo** (written abbr = **mégaoctet**) Mb, MB

**mobile** /mɔbil/ **1** adj (gen) mobile; ⟨leaf⟩ loose
**2** nm (a) motive
(b) mobile

**mobilier, -ière** /mɔbilje, ɛʀ/ **1** adj **biens** ∼s movable property
**2** nm furniture

**mobilisation** /mɔbilizasjɔ̃/ nf mobilization

**mobiliser** /mɔbilize/ [1] **1** vtr to mobilize ⟨soldier⟩; to call up ⟨civilian⟩
**2** se mobiliser v refl (+ v être) to rally

**mobilité** /mɔbilite/ nf mobility

**mobylette®** /mɔbilɛt/ nf moped

**mocassin** /mɔkasɛ̃/ nm moccasin, loafer

**moche** /mɔʃ/ adj (colloq) (a) ⟨person⟩ ugly; ⟨garment⟩ ghastly
(b) ⟨incident⟩ dreadful
(c) ⟨act⟩ nasty

**modalité** /mɔdalite/ **1** nf modality
**2** modalités nf pl terms; practical details

**mode¹** /mɔd/ *nm* **(a)** way, mode; ~ de paiement method of payment
**(b)** (in grammar) mood
■ ~ d'emploi instructions for use

**mode²** /mɔd/ *nf* **(a)** fashion; lancer une ~ to start a trend; à la ~ ⟨garment, club⟩ fashionable; ⟨singer⟩ popular
**(b)** fashion industry

**modèle** /mɔdɛl/ **1** *adj* (gen) model; ⟨conduct⟩ perfect, exemplary
**2** *nm* **(a)** (gen) model; prendre ~ sur qn to do as sb does/did; ~ à suivre somebody to look up to; la tente grand ~ large-size tent; le ~ au-dessus the next size up; ~ de signature specimen signature
**(b)** pattern; ~ déposé registered pattern
■ ~ réduit scale model

**modeler** /mɔdle/ [17] *vtr* to model ⟨clay⟩; to mould (GB) or mold (US) ⟨character⟩

**modélisme** /mɔdelism/ *nm* modelling

**modération** /mɔdeʀasjɔ̃/ *nf*
**(a)** moderation
**(b)** (in price, tax) reduction

**modéré, ~e** /mɔdeʀe/ *adj* ⟨party, speed, words⟩ moderate; ⟨price⟩ reasonable; ⟨temperament⟩ even; ⟨enthusiasm⟩ mild

**modérément** /mɔdeʀemɑ̃/ *adv*
**(a)** relatively
**(b)** slightly

**modérer** /mɔdeʀe/ [14] *vtr* to curb ⟨expenses⟩; to moderate ⟨language⟩; to reduce ⟨speed⟩

**moderne** /mɔdɛʀn/ *adj* modern

**moderniser** /mɔdɛʀnize/ [1] *vtr* to modernize; to update

**modernité** /mɔdɛʀnite/ *nf* modernity

**modeste** /mɔdɛst/ *adj* ⟨sum, apartment, person⟩ modest; ⟨cost⟩ moderate; ⟨background⟩ humble

**modestement** /mɔdɛstəmɑ̃/ *adv* modestly

**modestie** /mɔdɛsti/ *nf* modesty

**modification** /mɔdifikasjɔ̃/ *nf* modification

**modifier** /mɔdifje/ [2] *vtr* to change; to alter, to modify

**modique** /mɔdik/ *adj* ⟨sum, resources⟩ modest

**modiste** /mɔdist/ *nf* milliner

**modulation** /mɔdylasjɔ̃/ *nf* modulation
■ ~ de fréquence, MF frequency modulation, FM

**module** /mɔdyl/ *nm* (gen, Sch) module

**moduler** /mɔdyle/ [1] *vtr* **(a)** to modulate
**(b)** to adjust ⟨price⟩; to adapt ⟨policy⟩

**moelle** /mwal/ *nf* marrow
■ ~ épinière spinal cord

**moelleux, -euse** /mwalø, øz/ *adj*
**(a)** ⟨carpet⟩ thick; ⟨bed⟩ soft
**(b)** ⟨wine⟩ mellow

**mœurs** /mœʀ(s)/ *nf pl* **(a)** customs; habits; lifestyle; l'évolution des ~ the change in attitudes

**(b)** morals; des ~ dissolues loose morals; la police des ~, les Mœurs (colloq) the vice squad
**(c)** (of animals) behaviour
IDIOMS autres temps, autres ~ other days, other ways

**mohair** /mɔɛʀ/ *nm* mohair

**moi¹** /mwa/ *pron* **(a)** I, me; c'est ~ it's me
**(b)** me; pour ~ for me; des amis à ~ friends of mine; c'est à ~ it's mine; it's my turn

**moi²** /mwa/ *nm* le ~ the self

**moignon** /mwaɲɔ̃/ *nm* stump

**moi-même** /mwamɛm/ *pron* myself

**moindre** /mwɛ̃dʀ/ *adj* **(a)** lesser; à ~ prix more cheaply
**(b)** le ~ the least; je n'en ai pas la ~ idée I haven't got the slightest idea

**moine** /mwan/ *nm* monk
IDIOMS l'habit ne fait pas le ~ (Proverb) you can't judge a book by its cover

**moineau,** *pl* **~x** /mwano/ *nm* sparrow

**moins¹** /mwɛ̃/ **1** *prep* **(a)** minus
**(b)** il est huit heures ~ dix it's ten (minutes) to eight; il était à ~ une (colloq) it was a close shave (colloq)
**2** *adv* (comparative) less; (superlative) le ~ the least; le ~ difficile the less difficult; the least difficult; de ~ en ~ less and less; ~ je sors, ~ j'ai envie de sortir the less I go out, the less I feel like going out; il n'en est pas ~ vrai que it's nonetheless true that; il ressemble à son frère en ~ gros he looks like his brother, only thinner; à tout le ~, pour le ~ to say the least; il y avait deux fourchettes en ~ dans la boîte there were two forks missing from the box
**3** moins de *quantif* ~ de livres fewer books; ~ de sucre less sugar; les ~ de 20 ans people under 20
**4** à moins de *phr* unless
**5** à moins que *phr* unless
**6** au moins *phr* at least
**7** du moins *phr* at least

**moins²** /mwɛ̃/ *nm inv* minus
■ ~ que rien good-for-nothing, nobody

**moiré, ~e** /mwaʀe/ *adj* moiré; watered

**mois** /mwa/ *nm inv* month

**moisi** /mwazi/ *nm* mould (GB), mold (US)

**moisir** /mwaziʀ/ [3] *vi* ⟨foodstuff⟩ to go mouldy (GB) or moldy (US); ⟨object, plant⟩ to become mildewed

**moisissure** /mwazisyʀ/ *nf* **(a)** mould (GB), mold (US)
**(b)** mildew

**moisson** /mwasɔ̃/ *nf* harvest

**moissonner** /mwasɔne/ [1] *vtr* to harvest

**moissonneuse** /mwasɔnøz/ *nf* reaper

**moite** /mwat/ *adj* ⟨heat⟩ muggy; ⟨skin⟩ sweaty

**moiteur** /mwatœʀ/ *nf* (of air) mugginess; (of skin) sweatiness

**moitié** /mwatje/ *nf* half; à ~ vide half empty

m

**moitié-moitié** /mwatjemwatje/ *adv* half-and-half

**moka** /mɔka/ *nm* **(a)** mocha
**(b)** mocha cake

**molaire** /mɔlɛR/ *nf* molar

**molécule** /mɔlekyl/ *nf* molecule

**moleskine** /mɔleskin/ *nf* **(a)** imitation leather
**(b)** moleskin

**molester** /mɔleste/ [1] *vtr* to manhandle

**molette** /mɔlɛt/ *nf* (of spanner) adjusting knob

**mollasson, -onne** /mɔlasõ, ɔn/ *adj* (colloq) sluggish

**molle** ▶ MOU 1

**mollement** /mɔlmã/ *adv* **(a)** idly
**(b)** ⟨*work*⟩ without much enthusiasm; ⟨*protest*⟩ half-heartedly

**mollet** /mɔlɛ/ ⓵ *adj m* œuf ∼ soft-boiled egg
⓶ *nm* (Anat) calf

**molleton** /mɔltõ/ *nm* **(a)** flannel; flannelette
**(b)** (table) felt
**(c)** (ironing board) cover

**molletonner** /mɔltɔne/ [1] *vtr* to line with fleece

**mollir** /mɔliR/ [3] *vi* **(a)** ⟨*courage*⟩ to fail; ⟨*resistance*⟩ to grow weaker; ⟨*person*⟩ to soften
**(b)** ⟨*knees*⟩ to give way; ⟨*arm*⟩ to go weak

**mollusque** /mɔlysk/ *nm* mollusc (GB), mollusk (US)

**molosse** /mɔlɔs/ *nm* huge dog

**môme** /mom/ *nmf* (colloq) kid (colloq); brat (colloq)

**moment** /mɔmã/ *nm* moment; le ∼ venu when the time comes/came; il devrait arriver d'un ∼ à l'autre he should arrive any minute now; à un ∼ donné at some point; at a given moment; à ce ∼-là at that time; just then; in that case; au ∼ où at the time (when); au ∼ où il quittait son domicile as he was leaving his home; jusqu'au ∼ où until; du ∼ que as long as, provided; il arrive toujours au bon or mauvais ∼! he certainly picks his moment to call!; un ∼! just a moment!; ça va prendre un ∼ it will take a while; au bout d'un ∼ after a while; par ∼s at times; les ∼s forts du film the film's highlights; dans ses meilleurs ∼s, il fait penser à Orson Welles at his best, he reminds one of Orson Welles; à mes ∼s perdus in my spare time

**momentané, ∼e** /mɔmãtane/ *adj* momentary

**momentanément** /mɔmãtanemã/ *adv* for a moment, momentarily

**momie** /mɔmi/ *nf* mummy

**mon, ma,** *pl* **mes** /mõ, ma, mɛ/ *det* my; j'ai ∼ idée I have my own ideas about that

**monacal, ∼e,** *mpl* **-aux** /mɔnakal, o/ *adj* monastic

**monarchie** /mɔnaRʃi/ *nf* monarchy

**monarchiste** /mɔnaRʃist/ *adj, nmf* monarchist

**monarque** /mɔnaRk/ *nm* monarch

**monastère** /mɔnastɛR/ *nm* monastery

**monceau,** *pl* ∼**x** /mõso/ *nm* (of rubbish) pile

**mondain, ∼e** /mõdɛ̃, ɛn/ ⓵ *adj* ⟨*life, ball*⟩ society; ⟨*conversation*⟩ polite
⓶ *nm,f* socialite

**monde** /mõd/ *nm* **(a)** world; pas le moins du ∼ not in the least; aller or voyager de par le ∼ to travel the world; c'est le bout du ∼! it's in the back of beyond!; ce n'est pas le bout du ∼! it's not such a big deal!; à la face du ∼ for all the world to see; en ce bas ∼ here below; elle n'est plus de ce ∼ she's no longer with us; je n'étais pas encore au ∼ I wasn't yet born; le ∼ médical the medical world; le ∼ animal the animal kingdom; un ∼ nous sépare we are worlds apart
**(b)** people; tout le ∼ everybody; tout mon petit ∼ my family and friends
**(c)** society; le beau or grand ∼ high society
IDIOMS se faire un ∼ de qch to get all worked up about sth; depuis que le ∼ est ∼ since the beginning of time; c'est un ∼! (colloq) that's a bit much!

**mondial, ∼e,** *mpl* **-iaux** /mõdjal, o/ *adj* world; ⟨*success*⟩ worldwide; seconde guerre ∼e Second World War

**mondialement** /mõdjalmã/ *adv* être ∼ connu to be world famous

**mondialisation** /mõdjalizasjõ/ *nf* globalization

**mondialiser** /mõdjalize/ [1] *vtr* to globalize; to cause [sth] to spread worldwide

**mondialisme** /mõdjalism/ *nm* internationalism

**mondovision** /mõdɔvizjõ/ *nf* satellite broadcasting

**monétaire** /mɔnetɛR/ *adj* ⟨*system, stability*⟩ monetary; ⟨*market*⟩ money

**monétariste** /mɔnetaRist/ *adj, nmf* monetarist

**monétique** /mɔnetik/ *nf* electronic banking

**monétiser** /mɔnetize/ [1] *vtr* to monetize

**Mongolie** /mõgɔli/ *pr nf* Mongolia

**mongolien, -ienne** /mõgɔljɛ̃, ɛn/ (controversial) *nm,f* Down's syndrome child

**moniteur, -trice** /mɔnitœR, tRis/ ⓵ *nm,f*
**(a)** (Aut, Sport) instructor
**(b)** (in holiday camp) group leader (GB), counselor (US)
⓶ *nm* **(a)** (TV) monitor
**(b)** (Comput) monitor system

**monitorat** /mɔnitɔRa/ *nm* tutoring; tutorial system

**monnaie** /mɔnɛ/ *nf* **(a)** currency; fausse ∼ forged or counterfeit currency
**(b)** change; faire de la ∼ to get some change
**(c)** coin; battre ∼ to mint or strike coins; l'hôtel de la Monnaie, la Monnaie the Mint
**(d)** (Econ) money

■ ~ **d'échange** trading currency; bargaining chip; ~ **de papier** paper money
**IDIOMS rendre à qn la ~ de sa pièce** to pay sb back in his/her own coin; **c'est ~ courante** it's commonplace

**monnayable** /mɔnɛjabl/ *adj* **(a)** (in finance) convertible
**(b)** ⟨*skill*⟩, ⟨*qualification*⟩ marketable

**monnayer** /mɔnɛje/ [21] *vtr* **(a)** to convert [sth] into cash
**(b)** to capitalize on ⟨*talent, experience*⟩;
~ **qch contre qch** to exchange sth for sth

**mono¹** /mono/ *pref* mono; ~**chrome** monochrome; ~**lingue** monolingual

**mono²** /mono/ *nf* (in hi-fi) mono

**monocellulaire** /mɔnosɛlylɛʁ/ *adj*
**famille** ~ nuclear family

**monocle** /mɔnɔkl/ *nm* monocle

**monocorde** /mɔnɔkɔʁd/ *adj* ⟨*voice, speech*⟩ monotonous; ⟨*instrument*⟩ single-string

**monogame** /mɔnɔgam/ *adj* monogamous

**monogamie** /mɔnɔgami/ *nf* monogamy

**monoï** /mɔnɔj/ *nm inv* coconut oil (*used in cosmetics*)

**monologue** /mɔnɔlɔg/ *nm* monologue (GB)
■ ~ **intérieur** stream of consciousness

**mononucléose** /mɔnonykleoz/ *nf* mononucleosis; ~ **infectieuse** glandular fever

**monoparental, ~e,** *mpl* **-aux** /mɔnoparɑ̃tal, o/ *adj* **famille** ~**e** single-parent family

**monopole** /mɔnɔpɔl/ *nm* monopoly

**monopoliser** /mɔnɔpɔlize/ [1] *vtr* to monopolize

**monoprocesseur** /mɔnopʁɔsɛsœʁ/ *nm* single-chip computer

**monoski** /mɔnɔski/ *nm* **(a)** monoski
**(b)** monoskiing

**monothéiste** /mɔnɔteist/ *adj* monotheistic

**monotone** /mɔnɔtɔn/ *adj* monotonous

**monotonie** /mɔnɔtɔni/ *nf* monotony

**monoxyde** /mɔnɔksid/ *nm* monoxide

**Monseigneur,** *pl* **Messeigneurs** /mɔ̃sɛɲœʁ, mesɛɲœʁ/ *nm* Your Highness; Your Eminence; ~ **le duc de Parme** His Grace, the duke of Parma

**monsieur,** *pl* **messieurs** /məsjø, mesjø/ *nm* **(a)** (addressing a man whose name you do not know) **Monsieur** (in a letter) Dear Sir; **bonjour** ~! good morning!
**(b)** (addressing a man whose name you know, for instance Hallé) **Monsieur** (in a letter) Dear Mr Hallé; **bonjour** ~! good morning, Mr Hallé
**(c)** ( polite form of address) **'Monsieur a sonné?'** 'you rang, sir?'
**(d)** man; **le double messieurs** the men's doubles; **c'était un (grand)** ~! he was a (true) gentleman!
■ ~ **Tout le Monde** the man in the street

**monstre** /mɔ̃stʁ/ **1** *adj* (colloq) ⟨*task, success, publicity*⟩ huge; ⟨*nerve*⟩ colossal
**2** *nm* **(a)** monster
**(b)** freak (of nature)
■ ~ **marin** sea monster

**monstrueux, -euse** /mɔ̃stʁyø, øz/ *adj*
**(a)** ⟨*crime, cruelty*⟩ monstrous
**(b)** hideous; **d'une laideur monstrueuse** hideously ugly
**(c)** ⟨*error*⟩ colossal

**monstruosité** /mɔ̃stʁyozite/ *nf*
**(a)** (of conduct) monstrousness
**(b)** atrocity
**(c)** monstrosity; **dire des** ~**s** to say preposterous things

**mont** /mɔ̃/ *nm* mountain
■ **le** ~ **Blanc** Mont Blanc

**montage** /mɔ̃taʒ/ *nm* **(a)** set-up
**(b)** (of machine) assembly; (of tent) putting up; **chaîne de** ~ assembly line
**(c)** (of film) editing; **salle de** ~ cutting room
**(d)** (of gem) setting
■ ~ **photo** photomontage; ~ **sonore** sound montage

**montagnard, ~e** /mɔ̃taɲaʁ, aʁd/ **1** *adj* ⟨*people, plant*⟩ mountain; ⟨*custom*⟩ highland
**2** *nm,f* mountain dweller

**montagne** /mɔ̃taɲ/ *nf* **(a)** mountain
**(b) la** ~ the mountains; **de** ~ ⟨*road, animal*⟩ mountain; **il neige en haute** ~ it's snowing on the upper slopes
■ ~**s russes** big dipper, roller coaster
**IDIOMS se faire une** ~ **de qch** to get really worked up about sth

**montagneux, -euse** /mɔ̃taɲø, øz/ *adj* mountainous

**montant, ~e** /mɔ̃tɑ̃, ɑ̃t/ **1** *adj* **(a)** ⟨*cabin, group*⟩ going up
**(b)** ⟨*road*⟩ uphill
**(c)** ⟨*neck*⟩ high; ⟨*socks*⟩ long; **chaussures** ~**es** ankle boots
**2** *nm* **(a)** sum; **le** ~ **des pertes** the total losses; **d'un** ~ **de** ⟨*deficit, savings*⟩ amounting to; ⟨*cheque*⟩ to the amount of; ⟨*goods*⟩ for a total of
**(b)** (of door, window) upright, jamb; transom; (of scaffolding) pole; (of ladder) upright

**mont-de-piété,** *pl* **monts-de-piété** /mɔ̃dpjete/ *nm* pawnshop, pawnbroker's

**monte-charge** /mɔ̃tʃaʁʒ/ *nm inv* goods lift (GB) *or* elevator (US)

**montée** /mɔ̃te/ *nf* **(a)** (up slope) climb; (of mountain) ascent
**(b)** (of plane) climb
**(c)** rising; rise; **la** ~ **des eaux** the rise in the water level; **une brusque** ~ **d'adrénaline** a rush of adrenaline
**(d)** (in prices) rise; (in danger) increase
**(e)** hill; **une légère** ~ a slight slope

**monter** /mɔ̃te/ [1] **1** *vtr* (+ *v avoir*) **(a)** to take [sb/sth] up; to take [sb/sth] upstairs; to bring [sb/sth] up; to bring [sb/sth] upstairs; **impossible de** ~ **le piano par l'escalier** it's impossible to get the piano up the stairs
**(b)** to put [sth] up; to raise ⟨*shelf*⟩

⋯∴

m

(c) to go up [sth]; to come up [sth]; ~ **la colline à bicyclette** to cycle up the hill
(d) to turn up ‹*volume, gas*›
(e) ~ **les blancs en neige** beat *or* whisk the eggwhites until stiff
(f) ~ **qn contre qn** to set sb against sb
(g) to ride ‹*horse*›
(h) (Zool) to mount
(i) to assemble ‹*appliance, unit*›; to put up ‹*tent, scaffolding*›; ~ **un film** to edit a film
(j) to hatch ‹*plot*›; to set up ‹*company*›; to stage ‹*play*›; **monté de toutes pièces** ‹*story*› fabricated from beginning to end

**2** *vi* (+ *v être*) (a) to go up; to go upstairs; to come up; to come upstairs; ‹*plane*› to climb; ‹*bird*› to fly up; ‹*sun, mist*› to rise; **tu es monté à pied?** did you walk up?; did you come up on foot?; ~ **sur** to get onto ‹*footpath*›; to climb onto ‹*stool*›; ~ **à l'échelle** to climb (up) the ladder; **faites-les** ~ send them up
(b) ~ **dans une voiture/dans un train** to get in a car/on a train; ~ **sur** to get on ‹*bike, horse*›
(c) ‹*road*› to go uphill, to climb; ‹*ground*› to rise; ~ **jusqu'à** ‹*path, wall*› to go up to; ~ **en lacets** to wind its way up
(d) ‹*garment, water*› to come up (**jusqu'à** to)
(e) ‹*temperature, price*› to rise, to go up; ‹*tide*› to come in
(f) ~ **à** *or* **sur Paris** to go up to Paris
(g) ~ (**à cheval**) to ride
(h) (Mil) ~ **à l'assaut** *or* **l'attaque** to mount an attack
(i) ‹*employee*› to rise, to move up; ‹*artist*› to rise
(j) ‹*anger, emotion*› to mount; ‹*tears*› to well up; **le ton monta** the discussion became heated
(k) ~ **à la tête de qn** to go to sb's head
(l) (Aut, Tech) ~ **à 250 km/h** to go up to 250 km/h

IDIOMS **se** ~ **la tête** (colloq) to get worked up (colloq)

**monteur, -euse** /mɔ̃tœʀ, øz/ *nm,f*
(a) fitter
(b) (in film-making) editor
(c) paste-up artist

**montgolfière** /mɔ̃ɡɔlfjɛʀ/ *nf* hot-air balloon

**monticule** /mɔ̃tikyl/ *nm* (a) hillock
(b) mound

**montrable** /mɔ̃tʀabl/ *adj* ‹*person*› presentable; ‹*images*› suitable for viewing

**montre** /mɔ̃tʀ/ *nf* watch; **trois heures** ~ **en main** three hours exactly

**Montréal** /mɔ̃ʀeal/ *pr n* Montreal

**montrer** /mɔ̃tʀe/ [1] **1** *vtr* (a) to show; ~ **qch à qn** to show sb sth
(b) to show ‹*feelings, knowledge*›
(c) ‹*person*› to point out ‹*track, place, object*›; ‹*survey, table*› to show ‹*trend, results*›; ~ **qn du doigt** to point at sb; to point the finger at sb

**2 se montrer** *v refl* (+ *v être*) (a) to show oneself to be; to prove (to be); **il faut se** ~ **optimiste** we must try to be optimistic
(b) ‹*person*› to show oneself; ‹*sun*› to show out

IDIOMS ~ **les dents** to bare one's teeth; ~ **le bout de son nez** to show one's face; to peep through

**monture** /mɔ̃tyʀ/ *nf* (a) (for rider) mount
(b) (of glasses) frames; (of ring) setting

**monument** /mɔnymɑ̃/ *nm* (a) monument
(b) (historic) building; **visiter les** ~**s de Paris** to see the sights of Paris
(c) **un des** ~**s de la littérature européenne** a masterpiece of European literature
■ ~ **historique** ancient monument; ~ **aux morts** war memorial

**monumental, ~e,** *mpl* **-aux** /mɔnymɑ̃tal, o/ *adj* monumental

**moquer: se moquer** /mɔke/ [1] *v refl* (+ *v être*) (a) **se** ~ **de** to make fun of
(b) **se** ~ **de** not to care about
(c) **se** ~ **du monde** to take people for fools

**moquerie** /mɔkʀi/ *nf* (a) mocking remark
(b) mockery

**moquette** /mɔkɛt/ *nf* wall-to-wall carpet

**moqueur, -euse** /mɔkœʀ, øz/ *adj* mocking

**moral, ~e¹,** *mpl* **-aux** /mɔʀal, o/ **1** *adj*
(a) moral; **n'avoir aucun sens** ~ to have no sense of right and wrong
(b) ‹*torture*› mental; ‹*support*› moral
(c) ‹*person*› moral; ‹*conduct*› ethical
**2** *nm* (a) morale; **avoir le** ~ to be in good spirits; **avoir le** ~ **à zéro** (colloq) to feel very down; **remonter le** ~ **de qn** to raise sb's spirits
(b) mind; **au** ~ **comme au physique** mentally and physically

**morale²** /mɔʀal/ *nf* (a) morality; **leur** ~ their moral code
(b) moral; **faire la** ~ **à qn** to give sb a lecture
(c) **la** ~ moral philosophy, ethics

**moralement** /mɔʀalmɑ̃/ *adv* (a) morally, ethically
(b) psychologically

**moralisant, ~e** /mɔʀalizɑ̃, ɑ̃t/ *adj* moralizing

**moralisateur, -trice** /mɔʀalizatœʀ, tʀis/ *adj* moralizing, moralistic

**moraliser** /mɔʀalize/ [1] *vtr* to clean up; to reform

**moraliste** /mɔʀalist/ *nmf* moralist

**moralité** /mɔʀalite/ *nf* (a) morals
(b) (of action) morality
(c) moral; ~**, ne faites confiance à personne** the moral is: don't trust anybody

**morbide** /mɔʀbid/ *adj* morbid

**morbidité** /mɔʀbidite/ *nf* morbidity

**morceau,** *pl* ~**x** /mɔʀso/ *nm* (a) piece, bit; ~ **de sucre** sugar lump; **manger un** ~ (colloq) to have a snack
(b) (of meat) cut; **bas** ~ cheap cut
(c) (Mus) piece; ~ **de piano** piano piece
(d) (from book) extract

**IDIOMS recoller les ∼x** to patch things up
**morceler** /mɔʁsəle/ [19] *vtr* to divide [sth] up
**mordant, ∼e** /mɔʁdɑ̃, ɑ̃t/ **1** *adj*
(a) caustic, scathing
(b) ⟨*cold*⟩ biting
**2** *nm* (a) sarcasm
(b) ⟨colloq⟩ (of person, team) zip ⟨colloq⟩
**mordiller** /mɔʁdije/ [1] *vtr* to nibble at
**mordoré, ∼e** /mɔʁdɔʁe/ *adj* golden brown
**mordre** /mɔʁdʁ/ [6] **1** *vtr* to bite
**2 mordre à** *v+prep* **∼ à l'appât** *or* **l'hameçon** to take the bait
**3** *vi* (a) **∼ dans une pomme** to bite into an apple
(b) **∼ sur** to go over ⟨*white line*⟩; to encroach on ⟨*territory*⟩
(c) ⟨colloq⟩ to fall for it ⟨colloq⟩
**4 se mordre** *v refl* (+ *v être*) **se ∼ la langue** to bite one's tongue
**IDIOMS je m'en suis mordu les doigts** I could have kicked myself
**mordu, ∼e** /mɔʁdy/ **1** *adj* ⟨colloq⟩ (a) **être ∼ de qch** to be mad about sth ⟨colloq⟩
(b) smitten
**2** *nm,f* ⟨colloq⟩ fan; **les ∼s du ski** skiing fans
**morfondre: se morfondre** /mɔʁfɔ̃dʁ/ [6] *v refl* (+ *v être*) (a) **se ∼ à attendre** *or* **en attendant** to wait dejectedly
(b) to pine
**morgue** /mɔʁg/ *nf* (a) morgue; (hospital) mortuary
(b) arrogance
**moribond, ∼e** /mɔʁibɔ̃, ɔ̃d/ **1** *adj* ⟨*person*⟩ dying; ⟨*civilization*⟩ moribund
**2** *nm,f* dying man/woman
**morille** /mɔʁij/ *nf* morel (mushroom)
**morne** /mɔʁn/ *adj* (a) gloomy; ⟨*face*⟩ glum
(b) ⟨*landscape, life*⟩ dreary
**morose** /mɔʁoz/ *adj* morose; gloomy
**morosité** /mɔʁozite/ *nf* gloom
**morphine** /mɔʁfin/ *nf* morphine
**morphologie** /mɔʁfɔlɔʒi/ *nf* morphology
**morpion** /mɔʁpjɔ̃/ *nm* noughts and crosses (GB), tick-tack-toe (US)
**mors** /mɔʁ/ *nm inv* bit; **prendre le ∼ aux dents** to take the bit between its/one's teeth
**morse** /mɔʁs/ *nm* (a) walrus
(b) (code) **∼** Morse code
**morsure** /mɔʁsyʁ/ *nf* (a) bite; **∼ de chien** dogbite
(b) **la ∼ du froid** the biting cold
**mort¹** /mɔʁ/ *nf* death; **mourir de sa belle ∼** to die peacefully in old age; **il n'y a pas eu ∼ d'homme** there were no fatalities; **trouver la ∼** to die; **mise à ∼** (of condemned) killing; (of bull) dispatch; **à ∼** ⟨*fight*⟩ to the death; ⟨*war*⟩ ruthless; ⟨*brake, squeeze*⟩ like mad ⟨colloq⟩
■ **∼ cérébrale** brain death
**IDIOMS la ∼ dans l'âme** with a heavy heart
**mort², ∼e** /mɔʁ, mɔʁt/ **1** *pp* ▶ MOURIR
**2** *pp adj* (a) dead

(b) **je suis ∼ de froid** I'm freezing to death; **je suis ∼** ⟨colloq⟩ I'm dead tired
(c) ⟨*district*⟩ dead; ⟨*season*⟩ slack
(d) ⟨*civilization*⟩ dead; ⟨*city*⟩ lost
**3** *nm,f* dead person, dead man/woman
**4** *nm* (a) fatality; **il y a eu 12 ∼s** there were 12 dead
(b) **jouer; faire le ∼** to play dead; to lie low
**IDIOMS ne pas y aller de main ∼e** ⟨colloq⟩ not to pull any punches
**mortalité** /mɔʁtalite/ *nf* mortality
**mort-aux-rats** /mɔʁoʁa/ *nf inv* rat poison
**mortel, -elle** /mɔʁtɛl/ **1** *adj* (a) ⟨*blow, illness*⟩ fatal; ⟨*poison*⟩ lethal; ⟨*venom*⟩ deadly
(b) ⟨*cold*⟩ deathly
(c) ⟨*enemy*⟩ mortal
(d) ⟨*person, meeting*⟩ deadly boring
(e) ⟨*being*⟩ mortal
**2** *nm,f* mortal
**mortellement** /mɔʁtɛlmɑ̃/ *adv*
(a) ⟨*injured*⟩ fatally
(b) ⟨*boring*⟩ deadly
**mortier** /mɔʁtje/ *nm* mortar
**mort-né, ∼e,** *mpl* **∼s** /mɔʁne/ *adj*
(a) stillborn
(b) ⟨*plan*⟩ abortive
**mortuaire** /mɔʁtɥɛʁ/ *adj* **cérémonie ∼** funeral ceremony; **veillée ∼** wake
**morue** /mɔʁy/ *nf* cod
**morve** /mɔʁv/ *nf* nasal mucus, snot (slang)
**mosaïque** /mɔzaik/ *nf* mosaic
**Moscou** /mɔsku/ *pr n* Moscow
**mosquée** /mɔske/ *nf* mosque
**mot** /mo/ *nm* (a) word; **à ∼s couverts** in veiled terms; **au bas ∼** at least; **il est bête et le ∼ est faible!** he's stupid and that's putting it mildly!; **dire un ∼ à qn** to have a word with sb; **il ne dit jamais un ∼ plus haut que l'autre** he never raises his voice; **avoir son ∼ à dire** to be entitled to one's say
(b) note; **je t'ai laissé un ∼** I left you a note
■ **∼ d'esprit** witticism; **∼ d'ordre** watchword; **∼ d'ordre de grève** strike call; **∼ de passe** password; **∼s croisés** crossword; **∼s doux** sweet nothings
**IDIOMS ne pas avoir peur des ∼s** to call a spade a spade; **manger ses ∼s** to mumble; **se donner le ∼** to pass the word around
**motard, ∼e** /mɔtaʁ, aʁd/ **1** *nm,f* ⟨colloq⟩ biker ⟨colloq⟩
**2** *nm* police motorcyclist
**mot-clé,** *pl* **mots-clés** /mokle/ *nm* key word
**moteur, -trice** /mɔtœʁ, tʁis/ **1** *adj*
(a) ⟨*force, principle*⟩ driving; **la voiture a quatre roues motrices** the car has four-wheel drive
(b) (Med) **troubles ∼s** motor problems
**2** *nm* (a) motor
(b) engine
(c) **être le ∼ de qch** to be the driving force behind sth
**motif** /mɔtif/ *nm* (a) grounds; **des ∼s d'espérer** grounds for hope    ⋯◈

**(b)** reason
**(c)** motive
**(d)** pattern; à ~ floral with a floral pattern
**motion** /mɔsjɔ̃/ *nf* motion
**motivant**, ~**e** /mɔtivɑ̃, ɑ̃t/ *adj* ‹salary› attractive; ‹work› rewarding
**motivation** /mɔtivasjɔ̃/ *nf* **(a)** motivation **(b)** motive; ~**s profondes** deeper motives
**motivé**, ~**e** /mɔtive/ *adj* **(a)** motivated **(b)** ‹complaint› justifiable
**motiver** /mɔtive/ [1] *vtr* **(a)** to motivate **(b)** to lead to ‹decision, action›; **motivé par** caused by
**moto** /mɔto/ *nf* **(a)** (motor)bike **(b)** motorcycling
**motocyclette** /mɔtosiklɛt/ *nf* motorcycle
**motocyclisme** /mɔtosiklism/ *nm* motorcycle racing
**motocycliste** /mɔtosiklist/ **1** *adj* motorcycle **2** *nmf* motorcyclist
**motoneige** /mɔtonɛʒ/ *nf* snowmobile
**motoriser** /mɔtɔrize/ [1] *vtr* to motorize; **être motorisé** (colloq) to have transport (GB) *or* transportation (US)
**motrice** ▶ MOTEUR 1
**motte** /mɔt/ *nf* ~ **(de terre)** clod (of earth); ~ **de gazon** sod, piece of turf; ~ **(de beurre)** slab of butter
**motus** /mɔtys/ *excl* (colloq) ~ **(et bouche cousue)**! keep it under your hat!
**mou** (**mol** *before vowel or mute h*), **molle** /mu, mɔl/ **1** *adj* **(a)** ‹substance, cushion› soft; ‹blow› dull **(b)** ‹stomach› flabby **(c)** ‹person› listless; ‹growth› sluggish **(d)** ‹parent› soft **(e)** ‹speech› feeble **2** *nm* **(a)** wimp (colloq) **(b)** (in butchery) lights (GB), lungs (US) **(c)** (in rope) slack; **donner du** ~ **à qn** (colloq) to give sb a bit of leeway
**mouchard**, ~**e** /muʃaʀ, aʀd/ **1** *nm,f* (colloq) **(a)** grass (colloq) (GB), informer **(b)** sneak (colloq) **2** *nm* **(a)** tachograph **(b)** spyhole
**moucharder** /muʃaʀde/ [1] *vtr* (colloq) **(a)** ~ **qn** to inform on sb; to squeal (colloq) on sb **(b)** to sneak (colloq)
**mouche** /muʃ/ *nf* **(a)** fly **(b)** patch, beauty spot **(c)** bull's eye; **faire** ~ to hit the bull's eye; (figurative) to be right on target **(d)** (Sport) (on foil) button
■ ~ **verte** greenbottle; ~ **du vinaigre** fruit fly
IDIOMS **quelle** ~ **les a piqués?** (colloq) what's got (GB) *or* gotten (US) into them?; **prendre la** ~ to fly off the handle
**moucher** /muʃe/ [1] **1** *vtr* ~ **qn** to blow sb's nose; (colloq) to put sb in their place

**2 se moucher** *v refl* (+ *v être*) to blow one's nose
IDIOMS **il ne se mouche pas du pied** *or* **du coude** (colloq) he's full of airs and graces
**moucheron** /muʃʀɔ̃/ *nm* midge
**moucheté**, ~**e** /muʃte/ *adj* **(a)** ‹material› flecked; ‹plumage, fish› speckled; ‹coat› spotted; ‹horse› dappled **(b)** (Sport) ‹foil› buttoned
**mouchoir** /muʃwaʀ/ *nm* handkerchief; tissue
**moudre** /mudʀ/ [77] *vtr* to grind
**moue** /mu/ *nf* pout; **faire la** ~ to pout; (doubtfully) to pull a face
**mouette** /mwɛt/ *nf* (sea)gull
**moufle** /mufl/ *nf* mitten
**mouiller** /muje/ [1] **1** *vtr* **(a)** to wet; to get [sth] wet **(b)** to drop ‹anchor›; to lay ‹mine› **2** *vi* to anchor, to drop anchor **3 se mouiller** *v refl* (+ *v être*) to get wet
**mouillette** /mujɛt/ *nf* (colloq) soldier (colloq), finger of bread (eaten with a boiled egg)
**moulage** /mulaʒ/ *nm* **(a)** casting; **faire un** ~ **de qch** to take a cast of sth **(b)** (of grain) milling
**moulant**, ~**e** /mulɑ̃, ɑ̃t/ *adj* tight-fitting
**moule**[1] /mul/ *nm* **(a)** mould (GB), mold (US) **(b)** tin, pan (US); ~ **à gaufre** waffle iron
**moule**[2] /mul/ *nf* mussel
**mouler** /mule/ [1] *vtr* **(a)** to mould (GB), to mold (US) ‹substance›; to cast ‹bronze›; to mint ‹medal› **(b)** to take a cast of **(c)** ‹garment› to hug
**moulin** /mulɛ̃/ *nm* mill
■ ~ **à paroles** (colloq) chatterbox; ~ **à vent** windmill
IDIOMS **apporter de l'eau au** ~ **de qn** to fuel sb's arguments; **on ne peut être à la fois au four et au** ~ one can't be in two places at once; **on y entre comme dans un** ~ (colloq) one can just slip in
**mouliner** /muline/ [1] *vtr* to grind, to mill
**moulinet** /muline/ *nm* **faire des** ~**s avec les bras** to wave one's arms about
**moulu**, ~**e** /muly/ **1** *pp* ▶ MOUDRE **2** *pp adj* ‹coffee, pepper› ground **3** *adj* (colloq) ~ **(de fatigue)** worn out
**moumoute** /mumut/ *nf* (colloq) **(a)** toupee **(b)** sheepskin jacket
**mourant**, ~**e** /muʀɑ̃, ɑ̃t/ *adj* ‹person, animal› dying; ‹light› fading; ‹voice› faint
**mourir** /muʀiʀ/ [34] *vi* (+ *v être*) to die; ~ **de froid** to die of exposure; to die of cold; **je meurs de soif/de froid** I'm dying of thirst/ freezing to death; **c'était à** ~ **(de rire)**! it was hilarious!; ~ **debout** to be active to the end
IDIOMS **partir c'est** ~ **un peu** to say goodbye is to die a little; **je ne veux pas** ~ **idiot** (colloq) I want to know
**mouroir** /muʀwaʀ/ *nm* (derogatory) old people's home, twilight home

**mousquetaire** /muskətɛʀ/ nm
musketeer
**mousqueton** /muskətɔ̃/ nm snap clasp
**moussant, ~e** /musɑ̃, ɑ̃t/ adj ⟨gel⟩
foaming
**mousse¹** /mus/ nm ship's apprentice
**mousse²** /mus/ nf (a) moss
(b) foam; (from soap) lather; (on milk) froth; (on
beer) head
(c) ~ au chocolat chocolate mousse
(d) foam rubber
■ ~ carbonique fire foam; ~ à raser shaving
foam
**mousseline** /muslin/ nf (a) muslin
(b) chiffon
**mousser** /muse/ [1] vi to foam; to lather
IDIOMS se faire ~ (colloq) to blow one's own
trumpet
**mousseux, -euse** /musø, øz/ adj
(a) ⟨wine⟩ sparkling; ⟨beer⟩ fizzy
(b) ⟨lace⟩ frothy
**mousson** /musɔ̃/ nf monsoon
**moustache** /mustaʃ/ [1] nf moustache
(GB), mustache (US)
[2] **moustaches** nf pl (Zool) whiskers
**moustachu, ~e** /mustaʃy/ adj ⟨person⟩
with a moustache (GB) or mustache (US)
**moustiquaire** /mustikɛʀ/ nf mosquito
net
**moustique** /mustik/ nm mosquito
**moutarde** /mutaʀd/ adj inv, nf mustard
IDIOMS la ~ me monte au nez! (colloq) I'm
beginning to see red!
**mouton** /mutɔ̃/ [1] nm (a) sheep
(b) mutton
(c) sheepskin
(d) (derogatory) sheep
[2] **moutons** nm pl (a) small fleecy clouds
(b) whitecaps
(c) fluff
■ ~ à cinq pattes rare bird
IDIOMS revenons à nos ~s (colloq) let's get
back to the point
**mouture** /mutyʀ/ nf (a) (of coffee) grind
(b) première/nouvelle ~ first/new version
**mouvant, ~e** /muvɑ̃, ɑ̃t/ adj (a) ⟨ground⟩
unstable
(b) ⟨group⟩ shifting
(c) ⟨opinion⟩ changing
**mouvement** /muvmɑ̃/ nm (a) (gen)
movement; faire un ~ to move; ~ perpétuel
perpetual motion; accélérer le ~ to speed up
(b) bustle; suivre le ~ (figurative) to follow the
crowd
(c) impulse, reaction; un ~ de colère a
surge of anger
(d) le ~ étudiant the student protest
movement; ~ de grève strike, industrial
action
(e) le ~ des idées the evolution of ideas; un
milieu en ~ a changing environment
(f) (Econ) le ~ du marché market
fluctuations; ~ de hausse upward trend
**mouvementé, ~e** /muvmɑ̃te/ adj
(a) ⟨life, week, trip⟩ eventful, hectic

(b) ⟨terrain⟩ rough
**mouvoir: se mouvoir** /muvwaʀ/ [43]
v refl (+ v être) to move
**moyen, -enne¹** /mwajɛ̃, ɛn/ [1] adj
(a) medium; medium-sized
(b) ⟨income⟩ middle; ⟨level⟩ intermediate
(c) average, mean; le Français ~ the
average Frenchman
[2] nm (a) means, way (de faire of doing);
employer les grands ~s to resort to drastic
measures; (il n'y a) pas ~ de lui faire
comprendre qu'il a tort it's impossible to
make him realize he's wrong
(b) (of expression, production) means;
(of investigation, payment) method
[3] **au moyen de** phr by means of
[4] **par le moyen de** phr by means of
[5] **moyens** nm pl (a) means; faute de ~s
through lack of money; avoir de petits ~s
not to be very well off
(b) resources; donner à qn les ~s de faire to
give sb the means to do
(c) ability; perdre ses ~s to go to pieces
■ ~ de locomotion or transport means of
transport (GB) or transportation (US); Moyen
Âge Middle Ages
**moyenâgeux, -euse** /mwajɛnɑʒø, øz/
adj (a) medieval
(b) antiquated
**moyen-courrier, pl ~s** /mwajɛ̃kuʀje/
nm medium-haul airliner
**moyennant** /mwajɛnɑ̃/ prep ~ finances
for a fee; ~ quoi in view of which; in return
for which
**moyenne²** /mwajɛn/ [1] adj f ▶ MOYEN
[2] nf (a) average; la ~ d'âge the average
age; en ~ on average
(b) half marks (GB), 50%
(c) (Aut) average speed
**moyennement** /mwajɛnmɑ̃/ adv
⟨intelligent, wealthy⟩ moderately; ⟨like⟩ to a
certain extent
**Moyen-Orient** /mwajɛnɔʀjɑ̃/ pr nm
Middle East
**moyeu, pl ~x** /mwajø/ nm hub
**MST** /ɛmɛste/ nf: abbr ▶ MALADIE
**mû, mue¹** /my/ ▶ MOUVOIR
**mucoviscidose** /mykovisidoz/ nf cystic
fibrosis
**mucus** /mykys/ nm inv mucus
**mue²** /my/ nf (a) (of insect) metamorphosis;
(of reptile) sloughing of the skin; (of bird,
mammal) moulting (GB), molting (US); (of stag)
casting
(b) (of snake, insect) slough, sloughed skin
(c) breaking (GB) or changing (US) of voice
**muer** /mɥe/ [1] [1] vi (a) ⟨insect⟩ to
metamorphose; ⟨snake⟩ to slough its skin;
⟨bird, mammal⟩ to moult (GB), to molt (US)
(b) sa voix mue, il mue his voice is breaking
(GB) or changing (US)
[2] **se muer** v refl (+ v être) (a) to be
transformed
(b) to transform oneself

**muet, -ette** /mɥɛ, ɛt/ ① *adj* (a) dumb; speechless
(b) ⟨*witness*⟩ silent
(c) ⟨*vowel, consonant*⟩ mute
(d) ⟨*film*⟩ silent; ⟨*role*⟩ non-speaking
② *nm,f* mute

**mufle** /myfl/ ① *adj* boorish, loutish
② *nm* (a) (Zool) muffle; muzzle
(b) boor, lout

**muflerie** /myfləʀi/ *nf* boorishness

**mugir** /myʒiʀ/ [3] *vi* (a) to low; to bellow
(b) ⟨*wind*⟩ to howl; ⟨*siren*⟩ to wail; ⟨*torrent*⟩ to roar

**mugissement** /myʒismɑ̃/ *nm* (a) (of cow) lowing; (of bull, ox) bellowing
(b) (of wind) howling; (of waves) roar

**muguet** /mygɛ/ *nm* lily of the valley

**mulâtre** /mylɑtʀ/ *adj* mulatto

**mule** /myl/ *nf* (a) female mule
(b) (slipper) mule

**mulet** /mylɛ/ *nm* (male) mule

**mulot** /mylo/ *nm* fieldmouse

**multi** /mylti/ *pref* multi; ~colore multicoloured (GB); ~media multimedia; ~programmation multiple programming

**multicarte** /myltikaʀt/ *adj inv* représentant ~ representative for several firms

**multifonction** /myltifɔ̃ksjɔ̃/ *adj inv* multipurpose; (Comput) multifunction

**multipare** /myltipaʀ/ *adj* multiparous

**multiple** /myltipl/ ① *adj* (a) ⟨*reasons, occasions*⟩ numerous, many; ⟨*births*⟩ multiple; à choix ~ multiple-choice
(b) ⟨*causes, facets*⟩ many, various
(c) (in science) multiple
② *nm* multiple

**multipliable** /myltiplijabl/ *adj* multiplicable

**multiplication** /myltiplikasjɔ̃/ *nf* (a) ~ de increase in the number of
(b) (in mathematics, science) multiplication

**multiplicité** /myltiplisite/ *nf* multiplicity

**multiplier** /myltiplije/ [2] ① *vtr* (a) to multiply
(b) to increase ⟨*risks, fortune*⟩; to increase the number of ⟨*trains, accidents*⟩
② **se multiplier** *v refl* (+ *v être*)
(a) ⟨*branches, villas*⟩ to grow in number; ⟨*incidents*⟩ to be on the increase; ⟨*difficulties*⟩ to increase
(b) ⟨*animals, germs*⟩ to multiply

**multipropriété** /myltipʀɔpʀijete/ *nf* time-sharing

**multirisque** /myltiʀisk/ *adj* assurance ~ comprehensive insurance

**multisalle** /myltisal/ *adj inv* cinéma ~ cinema complex, multiplex

**multitude** /myltityd/ *nf* (a) une ~ de a mass of ⟨*tourists, objects*⟩; a lot of ⟨*reasons, ideas*⟩
(b) multitude, throng

**municipal, ~e,** *mpl* **-aux** /mynisipal, o/ *adj* ⟨*council*⟩ local, town; city; ⟨*park, pool*⟩ municipal; arrêté ~ bylaw

**municipales** /mynisipal/ *nf pl* local elections

**municipalité** /mynisipalite/ *nf*
(a) municipality
(b) town council; city council

**munir** /myniʀ/ [3] ① *vtr* to provide; ~ un bâtiment d'un escalier de secours to put a fire escape on a building; **muni de** fitted with
② **se munir** *v refl* (+ *v être*) se ~ de to bring; to take

**munitions** /mynisjɔ̃/ *nf pl* ammunition

**muqueuse** /mykøz/ *nf* mucous membrane

**mur** /myʀ/ ① *nm* wall; faire les pieds au ~ to do a handstand against the wall; (figurative) to tie oneself up in knots
② **murs** *nm pl* (of business) premises; (of palace, embassy) confines; être dans ses ~s to own one's own house
■ ~ portant *or* porteur load-bearing wall; ~ du son sound barrier; **Mur des lamentations** Wailing Wall
IDIOMS faire le ~ to go over the wall; mettre qn au pied du ~ to call sb's bluff; être au pied du ~ to be up against the wall

**mûr, ~e¹** /myʀ/ *adj* (a) ripe
(b) mature; l'âge ~ middle age; après ~e réflexion after careful consideration
(c) ready; il est ~ pour des aveux he's ready to confess
(d) ⟨*situation*⟩ at a decisive stage
IDIOMS en voir des vertes et des pas ~es (colloq) to go through a lot

**muraille** /myʀɑj/ *nf* great wall

**mural, ~e,** *mpl* **-aux** /myʀal, o/ *adj* ⟨*covering, map*⟩ wall; ⟨*plant*⟩ climbing

**mûre²** /myʀ/ ① *adj f* ▶ MÛR
② *nf* blackberry

**mûrement** /myʀmɑ̃/ *adv* ~ réfléchi carefully thought through

**murer** /myʀe/ [1] *vtr* to build a wall around [sth]; to brick [sth] up; to block [sth] off

**muret** /myʀɛ/ *nm* low wall

**mûrier** /myʀje/ *nm* mulberry tree

**mûrir** /myʀiʀ/ [3] ① *vtr* (a) to ripen ⟨*fruit*⟩
(b) to mature ⟨*person*⟩; to develop ⟨*plan*⟩
② *vi* (a) ⟨*fruit*⟩ to ripen
(b) ⟨*person, talent*⟩ to mature; ⟨*plan, idea*⟩ to evolve; ⟨*passion*⟩ to develop
(c) ⟨*abscess*⟩ to come to a head

**murmure** /myʀmyʀ/ *nm* (a) murmur
(b) ~s mutterings
(c) (of wind) whisper

**murmurer** /myʀmyʀe/ [1] ① *vtr* (a) to murmur
(b) to say; on murmure qu'il est riche he is rumoured (GB) to be rich
② *vi* (a) ⟨*person*⟩ to murmur; ⟨*wind*⟩ to whisper

**musaraigne** /myzaʀɛɲ/ *nf* (Zool) shrew

**musc** /mysk/ *nm* musk

**muscade** /myskad/ *nf* nutmeg

**muscle** /myskl/ nm muscle
**musclé**, **∼e** /myskle/ adj (a) muscular
(b) ⟨music, speech⟩ powerful; ⟨reaction⟩ strong; ⟨intervention⟩ tough
(c) (Econ) competitive
**muscler** /myskle/ [1] **1** vtr (a) ∼ les bras to develop the arm muscles
(b) to strengthen
**2 se muscler** v refl (+ v être) to develop one's muscles
**musculaire** /myskylɛR/ adj muscle; muscular
**musculation** /myskylasjɔ̃/ nf (exercices de) ∼ (gen) bodybuilding; (Med) exercises to strengthen the muscles; **salle de** ∼ weights room
**musculature** /myskylatyR/ nf musculature
**muse** /myz/ nf (a) Muse
(b) (figurative) muse
**museau**, pl **∼x** /myzo/ nm (a) muzzle; snout; nose
(b) (colloq) face
**musée** /myze/ nm museum; art gallery (GB), art museum (US); **une ville** ∼ a city of great historical and artistic importance
**museler** /myzale/ [19] vtr to muzzle
**muselière** /myzəljɛR/ nf muzzle
**musette**[1] /myzɛt/ nm accordion music
**musette**[2] /myzɛt/ nf (a) haversack
(b) lunchbag
**muséum** /myzeɔm/ nm ∼ (d'histoire naturelle) natural history museum
**musical**, **∼e**, mpl **-aux** /myzikal, o/ adj ⟨event⟩ musical; ⟨critic⟩ music; ⟨choice⟩ of music
**music-hall**, pl **∼s** nm /mysikol/ music hall
**musicien**, **-ienne** /myzisjɛ̃, ɛn/ **1** adj musical
**2** nm,f musician
**musique** /myzik/ nf music; **travailler en** ∼ to work with music in the background; **mettre en** ∼ to set [sth] to music; **faire de la** ∼ to play an instrument; **une** ∼ **de film** a film score
**IDIOMS connaître la** ∼ (colloq) to know the score (colloq); **je ne peux pas aller plus vite que la** ∼ (colloq) I can't go any faster than I'm already going; **être réglé comme du papier à** ∼ (colloq) ⟨person⟩ to be as regular as clockwork; ⟨conference, project⟩ to go very smoothly

**musulman**, **∼e** /myzylmɑ̃, an/ adj, nm,f Muslim
**mutabilité** /mytabilite/ nf mutability
**mutant**, **∼e** /mytɑ̃, ɑ̃t/ adj, nm,f mutant
**mutation** /mytasjɔ̃/ nf (a) transfer
(b) transformation; **en pleine** ∼ undergoing radical transformation
(c) mutation
**muter** /myte/ [1] vtr to transfer ⟨official⟩
**mutilation** /mytilasjɔ̃/ nf mutilation
**mutilé**, **∼e** /mytile/ nm,f disabled person; ∼ **de guerre** disabled war veteran
**mutiler** /mytile/ [1] vtr to mutilate
**mutin**, **∼e** /mytɛ̃, in/ **1** adj mischievous
**2** nm mutineer; rioter
**mutiner: se mutiner** /mytine/ [1] v refl (+ v être) to mutiny; to riot
**mutinerie** /mytinRi/ nf mutiny; riot
**mutisme** /mytism/ nm silence
**mutuel**, **-elle**[1] /mytɥɛl/ adj mutual
**mutuelle**[2] /mytɥɛl/ nf mutual insurance company
**mutuellement** /mytɥɛlmɑ̃/ adv mutually; **s'aider** ∼ to help each other
**myope** /mjɔp/ adj short-sighted
**myopie** /mjɔpi/ nf short-sightedness
**myosotis** /mjɔzɔtis/ nm inv forget-me-not
**myriade** /miRjad/ nf myriad (**de** of)
**myrrhe** /miR/ nf myrrh
**myrtille** /miRtij/ nf bilberry, blueberry
**mystère** /mistɛR/ nm (a) mystery
(b) secrecy
(c) rite
**mystérieusement** /misteRjøzmɑ̃/ adv mysteriously
**mystérieux**, **-ieuse** /misteRjø, øz/ adj mysterious
**mysticisme** /mistisism/ nm mysticism
**mystification** /mistifikasjɔ̃/ nf (a) hoax
(b) myth
**mystique** /mistik/ **1** adj mystical
**2** nf (a) mysticism
(b) mystique
(c) blind belief
**mythe** /mit/ nm myth
**mythique** /mitik/ adj mythical
**mythologie** /mitɔlɔʒi/ nf mythology
**mythologique** /mitɔlɔʒik/ adj mythological
**mythomane** /mitɔman/ adj, nm,f mythomaniac

# N n

**n, N** /ɛn/ [1] *nm inv* (a) (letter) n, N
  (b) **n°** (*written abbr* = **numéro**) no
  [2] **N** *nf* (*abbr* = **nationale**) **la N7** the N7
**n'** ▶ NE

**nabot, ~e** /nabo, ɔt/ *nm,f* (offensive) dwarf

**nacelle** /nasɛl/ *nf* (a) (of hot-air balloon) gondola
  (b) carrycot (GB), carrier (US)
  (c) (of worker) cradle

**nacre** /nakʀ/ *nf* mother-of-pearl

**nacré, ~e** /nakʀe/ *adj* pearly

**nage** /naʒ/ *nf* (a) swimming; **200 mètres quatre ~s** 200 metres (GB) medley; **traverser à la ~** to swim across
  (b) **être en ~** to be in a sweat
  ■ **~ indienne** sidestroke; **~ libre** freestyle

**nageoire** /naʒwaʀ/ *nf* (a) (of fish) fin
  (b) (of seal) flipper

**nager** /naʒe/ [13] [1] *vtr* to swim
  [2] *vi* (a) to swim
  (b) (figurative) **~ dans le bonheur** to bask in contentment; **elle nage dans sa robe** her dress is far too big for her
  (c) (colloq) to be absolutely lost
  IDIOMS **~ entre deux eaux** to run with the hare and hunt with the hounds

**nageur, -euse** /naʒœʀ, øz/ *nm,f* swimmer

**naguère** /nagɛʀ/ *adv* (a) quite recently
  (b) formerly

**naïf, naïve** /naif, iv/ *adj* naïve

**nain, ~e** /nɛ̃, nɛn/ [1] *adj* ⟨tree⟩ dwarf; ⟨dog⟩ miniature
  [2] *nm,f* dwarf

**naissance** /nɛsɑ̃s/ *nf* (a) (gen) birth; (of rumour) start; **de ~** ⟨Italian, French⟩ by birth; ⟨deaf⟩ from birth; **à ma ~** when I was born
  (b) **à la ~ du cou** at the base of the neck

**naissant, ~e** /nɛsɑ̃, ɑ̃t/ *adj* new

**naître** /nɛtʀ/ [74] *vi* (+ *v être*) (a) to be born; **elle est née le 5 juin** she was born on 5 June; **le bébé doit ~ à la fin du mois** the baby is due at the end of the month; **l'enfant à ~** the unborn baby *or* child; **je l'ai vu ~** (figurative) I have known him since he was a baby
  (b) (figurative) ⟨idea⟩ to be born; ⟨company⟩ to come into existence; ⟨love⟩ to spring up; ⟨day⟩ to break; **faire ~** to give rise to ⟨hope⟩; **voir ~** to see the birth of ⟨newspaper, century⟩

**naïve** ▶ NAÏF

**naïvement** /naivmɑ̃/ *adv* naively; artlessly

**naïveté** /naivte/ *nf* naivety

**nanisme** /nanism/ *nm* dwarfism

**nantir** /nɑ̃tiʀ/ [3] *vtr* **~ qn de** to provide sb with; to award [sth] to sb

**nantis** /nɑ̃ti/ *nm pl* **les ~** the well-off

**naphtaline** /naftalin/ *nf* mothballs

**nappe** /nap/ *nf* (a) tablecloth
  (b) (of oil, gas) layer; (of water, fire) sheet; (of fog) blanket

**napper** /nape/ [1] *vtr* (Culin) to coat; to glaze

**napperon** /napʀɔ̃/ *nm* mat

**narcisse** /naʀsis/ *nm* (flower) narcissus

**narcissisme** /naʀsisism/ *nm* narcissism

**narco(-)** /naʀko/ *pref* drug; **~-dollars/-trafiquant** drug money/trafficker

**narcotique** /naʀkɔtik/ *adj, nm* narcotic

**narguer** /naʀge/ [1] *vtr* to taunt ⟨person⟩

**narine** /naʀin/ *nf* nostril

**narquois, ~e** /naʀkwa, az/ *adj* mocking

**narrateur, -trice** /naʀatœʀ, tʀis/ *nm,f* narrator

**narratif, -ive** /naʀatif, iv/ *adj* narrative

**narration** /naʀasjɔ̃/ *nf* narration

**narrer** /naʀe/ [1] *vtr* to relate

**nasal, ~e, mpl -aux** /nazal, o/ *adj* nasal; **hémorragie ~e** heavy nosebleed

**naseau, pl ~x** /nazo/ *nm* nostril

**nasillard, ~e** /nazijaʀ, aʀd/ *adj* ⟨voice⟩ nasal; ⟨instrument⟩ tinny

**nasillement** /nazijmɑ̃/ *nm* nasal twang

**nasiller** /nazije/ [1] *vi* (a) to speak with a nasal voice
  (b) ⟨duck⟩ to quack

**nasse** /nas/ *nf* (a) keepnet
  (b) (figurative) net

**natal, ~e, mpl ~s** /natal/ *adj* native

**nataliste** /natalist/ *adj* ⟨policy⟩ pro-birth

**natalité** /natalite/ *nf* **(taux de) ~** birthrate

**natation** /natasjɔ̃/ *nf* swimming

**natif, -ive** /natif, iv/ *adj* **~ de** native of

**nation** /nasjɔ̃/ *nf* nation
  ■ **les Nations unies** the United Nations

**national, ~e[1], mpl -aux** /nasjɔnal, o/ *adj* national

**nationale[2]** /nasjɔnal/ *nf* ≈ A road (GB), highway (US)

**nationalisation** /nasjɔnalizasjɔ̃/ *nf* nationalization

**nationaliser** /nasjɔnalize/ [1] *vtr* to nationalize

**nationalisme** /nasjɔnalism/ *nm* nationalism

**nationalité** /nasjɔnalite/ *nf* nationality

**nativité** /nativite/ *nf* nativity

**natte** /nat/ *nf* (a) plait, braid (US)
  (b) mat

**natter** /nate/ [1] *vtr* to plait

**naturalisation** /natyʀalizasjɔ̃/ *nf* naturalization

**naturalisé, ~e** /natyʀalize/ *adj* naturalized

**naturaliser** /natyʀalize/ [1] *vtr* to naturalize ⟨foreigner, species⟩; to assimilate ⟨word, custom⟩

**naturalisme** /natyʀalism/ *nm* naturalism

**nature** /natyʀ/ **1** *adj inv* (a) ⟨yoghurt⟩ plain; ⟨tea⟩ black
(b) (colloq) ⟨person⟩ natural
**2** *nf* (a) nature; **protection de la ~** protection of the environment; **en pleine ~** in the heart of the countryside; **lâcher qn dans la ~** to leave sb in the middle of nowhere; (figurative) to let sb loose
(b) **de ~ à faire** likely to do; **des offres de toute ~** offers of all kinds
(c) **peindre d'après ~** to paint from life; **plus vrai que ~** larger than life
(d) **en ~** ⟨pay⟩ in kind
■ **~ humaine** human nature; **~ morte** still life; ▶ PETIT

**naturel, -elle** /natyʀɛl/ **1** *adj* natural
**2** *nm* (a) nature, disposition; **être d'un ~ craintif** to be timid by nature
(b) **il manque de ~** he's not very natural
(c) **au ~** ⟨rice⟩ plain; ⟨tuna⟩ in brine

**naturisme** /natyʀism/ *nm* nudism

**naturiste** /natyʀist/ *nmf* naturist (GB), nudist

**naufrage** /nofʀaʒ/ *nm* shipwreck, sinking; **faire ~** ⟨ship⟩ to be wrecked; ⟨sailor⟩ to be shipwrecked; ⟨company⟩ to collapse

**naufragé, ~e** /nofʀaʒe/ **1** *adj* shipwrecked
**2** *nm,f* survivor (of a shipwreck); castaway

**nauséabond, ~e** /nozeabɔ̃, ɔ̃d/ *adj* sickening, nauseating

**nausée** /noze/ *nf* nausea

**nautique** /notik/ *adj* ⟨science⟩ nautical; ⟨sports⟩ water

**nautisme** /notism/ *nm* water sports

**naval, ~e, mpl ~s** /naval/ *adj*
(a) ⟨industry⟩ shipbuilding
(b) (Mil) naval

**navet** /navɛ/ *nm* (a) turnip
(b) rubbishy film (GB), turkey (US) (colloq)

**navette** /navɛt/ *nf* shuttle; shuttle service; **faire la ~** (to work) to commute
■ **~ spatiale** space shuttle

**navigable** /navigabl/ *adj* navigable

**navigant, ~e** /navigɑ̃, ɑ̃t/ *adj* **personnel ~** (on plane) flight personnel; (Naut) seagoing personnel; **mécanicien ~** flight engineer

**navigateur, -trice** /navigatœʀ, tʀis/ *nm,f* (a) navigator
(b) sailor
(c) (Comput) browser

**navigation** /navigasjɔ̃/ *nf* navigation
■ **~ de plaisance** boating; yachting

**naviguer** /navige/ [1] *vi* (a) ⟨ship, sailor⟩ to sail; ⟨pilot, plane⟩ to fly; **en état de ~** ⟨ship⟩ seaworthy

(b) to navigate
(c) (Comput) to browse; **~ sur l'Internet** to surf the Internet

**navire** /naviʀ/ **1** *nm* ship
**2** **navire-** (combining form) **~-école/-usine** training/factory ship; **~s-citernes** tankers
■ **~ amiral** flagship; **~ de guerre** warship

**navrant, ~e** /navʀɑ̃, ɑ̃t/ *adj*
(a) depressing
(b) distressing

**navré, ~e** /navʀe/ *adj* **je suis vraiment ~** I am terribly sorry; **avoir l'air ~** to look sad

**nazi, ~e** /nazi/ *adj, nm,f* Nazi

**nazisme** /nazism/ *nm* Nazism

**ne** /nə/ (**n'** before vowel or mute h) *adv*

■ **Note** In cases where *ne* is used with *pas, jamais, guère, rien, plus, aucun, personne* etc, one should consult the corresponding entry.
– *ne + verb + que* is treated in the entry below.

**je n'ai que 20 euros** I've only got 20 euros; **il n'y a que lui pour être aussi désagréable** only he can be so unpleasant; **tu n'es qu'un raté** you're nothing but a loser (colloq); **je n'ai que faire de tes conseils** you can keep your advice

**né, ~e** /ne/ **1** *pp* ▶ NAÎTRE
**2** *pp adj* **bien ~** highborn; **Madame Masson ~e Roux** Mrs Masson née Roux
**3** (**-)né** (combining form) **musicien(-)/ écrivain(-)~** born musician/writer

**néanmoins** /neɑ̃mwɛ̃/ *adv* nevertheless

**néant** /neɑ̃/ *nm* (a) **le ~** nothingness; **réduire à ~** to destroy ⟨argument, hopes⟩
(b) 'revenus: ~' 'income: nil'

**nébuleux, -euse** /nebylø, øz/ *adj*
(a) ⟨sky⟩ cloudy
(b) ⟨idea⟩ vague, nebulous

**nécessaire** /neseseʀ/ **1** *adj* necessary (à for); **plus qu'il n'est ~** more than is necessary; **les voix ~s pour renverser le gouvernement** the votes needed in order to overthrow the government
**2** *nm* (a) **faire le ~** to do what is necessary
(b) essentials; **le strict ~** the bare essentials
■ **~ de couture** sewing kit; **~ à ongles** manicure set; **~ de toilette** toiletries

**nécessairement** /neseseʀmɑ̃/ *adv* necessarily; **passe-t-on ~ par Oslo?** do you have to go via Oslo?

**nécessité** /nesesite/ *nf* (a) necessity; **~ urgente** urgent need; **~ de qch/de faire/ d'être** need for sth/to do/to be; **de première ~** vital; **par ~** out of necessity; **être dans la ~ de faire** to have no choice but to do
(b) need; **être dans la ~** to be in need
IDIOMS **~ fait loi** (Proverb) necessity knows no law

**nécessiter** /nesesite/ [1] *vtr* to require

**nécessiteux, -euse** /nesesitø, øz/ *nm,f* needy person; **les ~** the needy

**nec plus ultra** /nɛkplyzyltʀa/ *nm inv* **le ~** the last word (**de** in)

**nécrologie** /nekʀɔlɔʒi/ *nf* deaths column

**nécrologique** /nekʀɔlɔʒik/ *adj* obituary

**nectar** /nɛktaʀ/ nm nectar

**néerlandais, ～e** /neɛʀlɑ̃dɛ, ɛz/ ⌐1⌐ adj
Dutch
⌐2⌐ nm (language) Dutch

**Néerlandais, ～e** /neɛʀlɑ̃dɛ, ɛz/ nm,f
Dutchman/Dutchwoman; **les ～** the Dutch

**nef** /nɛf/ nf nave; **～ latérale** side aisle

**néfaste** /nefast/ adj harmful

**négatif, -ive¹** /negatif, iv/ ⌐1⌐ adj negative
⌐2⌐ nm negative

**négation** /negasjɔ̃/ nf (a) negation
(b) (in grammar) negative

**négative²** /negativ/ ⌐1⌐ adj f ▶ NÉGATIF 1
⌐2⌐ nf **répondre par la ～** to reply in the
negative

**négativement** /negativmɑ̃/ adv
negatively

**négligé, ～e** /negliʒe/ ⌐1⌐ adj ⟨person⟩
sloppy; ⟨house⟩ neglected; ⟨injury⟩ untreated
⌐2⌐ nm negligée

**négligeable** /negliʒabl/ adj ⟨amount⟩
negligible; ⟨person⟩ insignificant

**négligemment** /negliʒamɑ̃/ adv
(a) nonchalantly
(b) carelessly

**négligence** /negliʒɑ̃s/ nf (a) negligence
(b) oversight

**négligent, ～e** /negliʒɑ̃, ɑ̃t/ adj
⟨employee⟩ negligent, careless; ⟨glance⟩
casual

**négliger** /negliʒe/ [13] ⌐1⌐ vtr (gen) to
neglect; to leave untreated ⟨cold⟩; to ignore
⟨rule⟩; **une offre qui n'est pas à ～** an offer
that's worth considering; **～ de faire** to fail to
do
⌐2⌐ **se négliger** v refl (+ v être) (a) not to
take care over one's appearance
(b) not to look after oneself

**négoce** /negɔs/ nm trade (**avec** with)

**négociable** /negɔsjabl/ adj negotiable

**négociant, ～e** /negɔsjɑ̃, ɑ̃t/ nm,f
merchant; wholesaler

**négociateur, -trice** /negɔsjatœʀ, tʀis/
nm,f negotiator

**négociation** /negɔsjasjɔ̃/ nf negotiation

**négocier** /negɔsje/ [2] vtr, vi to negotiate

**nègre** /nɛgʀ/ nm (a) (offensive) Negro
(b) ghostwriter

**négresse** /negʀɛs/ nf (offensive) Negress

**négritude** /negʀityd/ nf black identity,
negritude

**négroïde** /negʀɔid/ adj Negroid

**neige** /nɛʒ/ nf snow; **～ fondue** slush; sleet;
**aller à la ～** to go skiing; **blancs battus en ～**
stiffly beaten eggwhites
IDIOMS **être blanc comme ～** to be completely
innocent

**neiger** /neʒe/ [13] v impers to snow

**nénuphar** /nenyfaʀ/ nm waterlily

**néo** /neo/ pref neo

**néologisme** /neɔlɔʒism/ nm neologism

**néon** /neɔ̃/ nm (a) neon
(b) neon light

**néo-zélandais, ～e** /neozelɑ̃dɛ, ɛz/ adj
New Zealand

**Néo-Zélandais, ～e** /neozelɑ̃dɛ, ɛz/ nm,f
New Zealander

**népotisme** /nepɔtism/ nm nepotism

**nerf** /nɛʀ/ (a) nerve; **être malade des ～s** to
suffer from nerves
(b) spirit, go (colloq); **redonner du ～ à qn** to
put new heart into sb
IDIOMS **jouer avec les ～s de qn** to be
deliberately annoying; **ses ～s ont lâché** he/
she went to pieces; **avoir les ～s à fleur de
peau** to have frayed nerves; **avoir les ～s en
pelote** (colloq) or **en boule** (colloq) or **à vif** to be
really wound up; **être sur les ～s, avoir ses
～s** (colloq) to be on edge; **taper** (colloq) or
**porter sur les ～s de qn** to get on sb's nerves;
**être à bout de ～s** to be at the end of one's
tether or rope (US); **passer ses ～s sur** (colloq)
**qn/qch** to take it out on sb/sth; **l'argent est le
～ de la guerre** money is the sinews of war

**nerveusement** /nɛʀvøzmɑ̃/ adv (a) ⟨wait⟩
nervously
(b) **être épuisé ～** to be suffering from
nervous exhaustion

**nerveux, -euse** /nɛʀvø, øz/ ⌐1⌐ adj
(a) ⟨person⟩ tense
(b) ⟨engine⟩ responsive; ⟨horse⟩ vigorous
(c) (Anat) ⟨cell⟩ nerve; ⟨system⟩ nervous
⌐2⌐ nm,f nervous person

**nervosité** /nɛʀvozite/ nf (a) nervousness
(b) excitability
(c) (of engine) responsiveness

**nervure** /nɛʀvyʀ/ nf (of leaf) nervure

**n'est-ce pas** /nɛspa/ adv **c'est joli, ～?**
it's pretty, isn't it?; **～ qu'il est gentil?** isn't
he nice?

**net, nette** /nɛt/ ⌐1⌐ adj (a) ⟨price, weight⟩
net
(b) ⟨change⟩ marked; ⟨tendency⟩ distinct
(c) ⟨victory, memory⟩ clear; ⟨situation⟩
clearcut; ⟨handwriting⟩ neat; ⟨break⟩ clean;
**en avoir le cœur ～** to be clear in one's
mind about it
(d) ⟨house, hands⟩ clean; (figurative)
⟨conscience⟩ clear; **faire place nette** to clear
everything away
⌐2⌐ adv ⟨stop⟩ dead; ⟨kill⟩ outright; ⟨refuse⟩
flatly; **la corde a cassé ～** the rope snapped

**Net** /nɛt/ nm **le ～** the Net

**netiquette** /netikɛt/ nf netiquette

**nettement** /nɛtmɑ̃/ adv (a) ⟨increase,
deteriorate⟩ markedly; ⟨dominate⟩ clearly;
⟨prefer⟩ definitely
(b) ⟨see, say⟩ clearly; ⟨refuse⟩ flatly;
⟨remember⟩ distinctly

**netteté** /nɛtte/ nf (a) (of image, features)
sharpness; (of result, statement) definite nature
(b) (of place) cleanness; (of work) neatness

**nettoyage** /netwajaʒ/ nm (a) clean(up);
**～ de printemps** spring-cleaning
(b) cleaning; (of skin) cleansing; **～ à sec** dry-
cleaning
(c) **opération de ～** (colloq) (by army, police)
mopping-up operation

**nettoyant** /nɛtwajɑ̃/ *nm* cleaning agent

**nettoyer** /netwaje/ [23] *vtr* **(a)** (gen) to clean; to clean up ⟨*garden*⟩; to clean out ⟨*river*⟩; to clean off ⟨*stain*⟩ **(b)** (figurative) ⟨*police*⟩ to clean up ⟨*town*⟩

**neuf¹** /nœf/ *adj inv, pron, nm inv* nine

**neuf², neuve** /nœf, nœv/ ⓵ *adj* new; **tout ~ brand new; 'état ~' 'as new'** ⓶ *nm inv* new; **quoi de ~?** what's new?; **habillé de ~** dressed in new clothes; **faire du ~ avec du vieux** to revamp things **IDIOMS faire peau neuve** to undergo a transformation

**neurasthénie** /nøʀasteni/ *nf* depression

**neurasthénique** /nøʀastenik/ *nmf* depressive

**neuro** /nøʀo/ *pref* neuro

**neurone** /nøʀɔn/ *nm* neurone

**neutralisation** /nøtʀalizasjɔ̃/ *nf* neutralization

**neutraliser** /nøtʀalize/ [1] *vtr* to neutralize

**neutralité** /nøtʀalite/ *nf* neutrality

**neutre** /nøtʀ/ *adj* neutral; neuter

**neutron** /nøtʀɔ̃/ *nm* neutron

**neuvième** /nœvjɛm/ ⓵ *adj* ninth ⓶ *nf* (Sch) *third year of primary school, age 8–9*

**neveu**, *pl* **~x** /n(ə)vø/ *nm* nephew

**névralgie** /nevʀalʒi/ *nf* neuralgia

**névralgique** /nevʀalʒik/ *adj* **(a)** neuralgic **(b) point ~** key point

**névrose** /nevʀoz/ *nf* neurosis

**névrosé, ~e** /nevʀoze/ *adj, nm,f* neurotic

**New York** /njujɔʀk/ *pr n* **(a)** New York City **(b) l'État de ~** New York (State)

**nez** /ne/ *nm* nose; **~ en trompette** turned-up nose; **ça sent le parfum à plein ~** (colloq) there's a strong smell of perfume; **je n'ai pas mis le ~ dehors** (colloq) I didn't set foot outside; **mettre le ~ à la fenêtre** (colloq) to show one's face at the window; **lever le ~** to look up; **tu as le ~ dessus** (colloq) it's staring you in the face; **avoir du ~, avoir le ~ fin** (figurative) to be shrewd **IDIOMS mener qn par le bout du ~** (colloq) to have sb under one's thumb; **avoir qn dans le ~** (colloq) to have it in for sb; **avoir un coup** *or* **verre dans le ~** (colloq) to have had one too many (colloq); **au ~ (et à la barbe) de qn** right under sb's nose; **filer** *or* **passer sous le ~ de qn** to slip through sb's fingers; **se casser le ~** (colloq) to fail

**NF** /ɛnɛf/ *adj, nf (abbr = norme française)* French manufacturing standard

**ni** /ni/ *conj* nor, or; **elle ne veut ~ ne peut changer** she doesn't want to change, nor can she; **elle ne veut pas le voir ~ lui parler** she doesn't want to see him or talk to him; **~...~** neither... nor; **~ l'un ~ l'autre** neither of them; **il ne m'a dit ~ oui ~ non** he didn't say yes or no

**IDIOMS ~ vu ~ connu** (colloq) on the sly (colloq); **c'est ~ fait ~ à faire** (colloq) it's a botched job (colloq); **il n'a fait ~ une ~ deux** (colloq) he didn't have a second's hesitation

**niais, ~e** /njɛ, njɛz/ *adj* stupid

**niaiserie** /njɛzʀi/ *nf* **(a)** stupidity **(b)** stupid *or* inane remark

**nicaraguayen, -enne** /nikaʀagwajɛ̃, ɛn/ *adj* Nicaraguan

**niche** /niʃ/ *nf* **(a)** kennel, doghouse (US) **(b)** recess; (for statue) niche **(c)** (colloq) trick

**nichée** /niʃe/ *nf* (of birds) brood; (of mice) litter

**nicher** /niʃe/ [1] ⓵ *vi* **(a)** ⟨*bird*⟩ to nest **(b)** (colloq) ⟨*person*⟩ to live ⓶ **se nicher** *v refl* (+ *v être*) **(a)** ⟨*bird*⟩ to nest **(b)** ⟨*person, cottage*⟩ to nestle

**nickel** /nikɛl/ ⓵ *adj* (colloq) spotless ⓶ *nm* nickel

**nicotine** /nikɔtin/ *nf* nicotine

**nid** /ni/ *nm* nest ■ **~ d'aigle** eyrie; **~ d'ange** snuggle suit; **~ à poussière** dust trap; **~ de résistance** pocket of resistance

**nid-d'abeilles**, *pl* **nids-d'abeilles** /nidabɛj/ *nm* honeycomb weave

**nid-de-poule**, *pl* **nids-de-poule** /nidpul/ *nm* pothole

**nièce** /njɛs/ *nf* niece

**nième** /ɛnjɛm/ = **ÉNIÈME**

**nier** /nje/ [2] *vtr* to deny ⟨*fact, existence*⟩

**nigaud, ~e** /nigo, od/ *adj* silly

**nigérian, ~e** /niʒeʀjɑ̃, an/ *adj* Nigerian

**nigérien, -ienne** /niʒeʀjɛ̃, ɛn/ *adj* of Niger

**nihiliste** /niilist/ *adj, nmf* nihilist

**nîmois, ~e** /nimwa, az/ *adj* of Nîmes

**nipper: se nipper** /nipe/ [1] *v refl* (+ *v être*) (colloq) to get rigged out in one's Sunday best (colloq)

**nippes** /nip/ *nf pl* (colloq) rags (colloq), old clothes

**nippon, -onne** /nipɔ̃, ɔn/ *adj* Japanese

**niveau**, *pl* **~x** /nivo/ *nm* (gen) level; (of knowledge, education) standard; **au ~ du sol** at ground level; **être de ~** to be level; **arrivé au ~ du bus, il...** when he drew level with the bus he...; **bâtiment sur deux ~x** two-storey (GB) *or* two-story (US) building; '**~ bac + 3**' baccalauréat or equivalent plus 3 years' higher education; **de haut ~** ⟨*athlete*⟩ top; ⟨*candidate*⟩ high-calibre (GB); **au plus haut ~** ⟨*discussion*⟩ top-level ■ **~ de langue** register; **~ social** social status; **~ sonore** sound level; **~ de vie** standard of living

**nivelage** /nivlaʒ/ *nm* standardization

**niveler** /nivle/ [19] *vtr* **(a)** to level ⟨*ground*⟩ **(b)** to bring [sth] to the same level ⟨*salaries*⟩; **~ par le bas/haut** to level down/up

**nobiliaire** /nɔbiljɛʀ/ *adj* nobiliary

**noble** /nɔbl/ **1** *adj* (gen) noble; ⟨family⟩ aristocratic; ⟨person⟩ of noble birth
**2** *nmf* nobleman/noblewoman

**noblement** /nɔbləmɑ̃/ *adv* (a) nobly
(b) handsomely

**noblesse** /nɔblɛs/ *nf* nobility; **la petite ∼** the gentry

**noce** /nɔs/ *nf* (a) (colloq) party; **faire la ∼** (figurative) (colloq) to live it up (colloq), to party (colloq)
(b) wedding party
(c) ∼s wedding

**noceur, -euse** /nɔsœʀ, øz/ *nm,f* (colloq) party animal (colloq)

**nocif, -ive** /nɔsif, iv/ *adj* noxious, harmful

**noctambule** /nɔktɑ̃byl/ *nmf* night owl

**nocturne¹** /nɔktyʀn/ *adj* ⟨attack⟩ night; ⟨animal⟩ nocturnal; **la vie ∼** nightlife

**nocturne²** /nɔktyʀn/ *nf* (a) (in sport) evening fixture
(b) (of shop) late-night opening

**Noël** /nɔɛl/ *nm* Christmas; **'Joyeux ∼'** 'Merry Christmas'; **de ∼** ⟨tree, gift⟩ Christmas

**nœud** /nø/ *nm* (a) (gen) knot; **faire un ∼ de cravate** to tie a tie
(b) (of matter) crux; (of play) core
∎ **∼ coulant** slipknot; **∼ papillon** bow tie; **∼ de vipères** nest of vipers

**noir, ∼e¹** /nwaʀ/ **1** *adj* (a) (gen) black; ⟨eyes⟩ dark; ⟨person, race⟩ black; **être ∼ de coups** to be black and blue; **être ∼ de monde** to be swarming with people
(b) ⟨street⟩ dark; **il fait ∼** it's dark
(c) ⟨year⟩ bad, bleak; ⟨poverty⟩ dire; ⟨idea⟩ gloomy, dark
(d) ⟨look⟩ black; ⟨plot, design⟩ evil, dark; **se mettre dans une colère ∼e** to fly into a towering rage
**2** *nm* (a) (colour) black
(b) **avoir du ∼ sur le visage** to have a black mark on one's face
(c) darkness
(d) **au ∼** ⟨sell⟩ on the black market; **travailler au ∼** to work without declaring one's earnings; to moonlight (colloq)
(e) (colloq) **un (petit) ∼** an espresso
**IDIOMS voir tout en ∼** to look on the black side (of things)

**Noir, ∼e** /nwaʀ/ *nm,f* black man/woman

**noirâtre** /nwaʀɑtʀ/ *adj* blackish

**noiraud, ∼e** /nwaʀo, od/ *adj* swarthy

**noirceur** /nwaʀsœʀ/ *nf* (gen) blackness; (of hair, night, eyes) darkness

**noircir** /nwaʀsiʀ/ [3] **1** *vtr* (a) ⟨coal⟩ to make [sth] dirty; ⟨smoke⟩ to blacken
(b) (figurative) **∼ du papier** to scribble away; **∼ la situation** to paint a black picture of the situation
**2** *vi* ⟨banana⟩ to go black; ⟨wall⟩ to get dirty; ⟨metal⟩ to tarnish; ⟨person⟩ to get brown
**3 se noircir** *v refl* (+ *v être*) ⟨sky⟩ to darken; **se ∼ le visage** to blacken one's face

**noire** /nwaʀ/ **1** *adj f* ▶ NOIR 1
**2** *nf* (Mus) crotchet (GB), quarter note (US)

**noise** /nwaz/ *nf* **chercher ∼ or des ∼s à qn** to pick a quarrel with sb

**noisetier** /nwaztje/ *nm* hazel (tree)

**noisette** /nwazɛt/ *nf* (a) hazelnut
(b) **∼ de beurre** small knob of butter

**noix** /nwa/ *nf inv* (a) walnut (GB), English walnut (US)
(b) **∼ de beurre** knob of butter
∎ **∼ de cajou** cashew nut; **∼ de coco** coconut; **∼ (de) muscade** nutmeg

**nom** /nɔ̃/ **1** *nm* (a) name; **petit ∼** first name; **∼ et prénom** full name; **donner un ∼ à to name; sans ∼** unspeakable; **George Sand, de son vrai ∼ Aurore Dupin** George Sand, whose real name was Aurore Dupin; **parler en son propre ∼** to speak for oneself
(b) noun
**2 au nom de** *phr* (a) in the name of
(b) on behalf of
∎ **∼ de baptême** Christian name; **∼ d'emprunt** pseudonym; **∼ de famille** surname; **∼ de jeune fille** maiden name
**IDIOMS traiter qn de tous les ∼s** (colloq) to call sb all the names under the sun; **appeler les choses par leur ∼** to call a spade a spade

**nomade** /nɔmad/ *nmf* nomad

**nombre** /nɔ̃bʀ/ *nm* number; **un ∼ à deux chiffres** a two-digit number; **un certain ∼ de** some; **être en ∼ inférieur** ⟨players⟩ to be fewer in number; ⟨group⟩ to be smaller; **ils étaient au ∼ de 30** there were 30 of them; **écrasé sous le ∼** (of people) overcome by sheer weight of numbers; (of letters) overwhelmed by the sheer volume; **bon ∼ de** a good many; **∼ de fois** many times

**nombreux, -euse** /nɔ̃bʀø, øz/ *adj* ⟨population, collection⟩ large; ⟨people, objects⟩ numerous, many; **ils étaient peu ∼** there weren't many of them; **ils ont répondu ∼ à l'appel** a great many people responded to the appeal; **les touristes deviennent trop ∼** the number of tourists is becoming excessive

**nombril** /nɔ̃bʀil/ *nm* navel; **elle se prend pour le ∼ du monde** (colloq) she thinks she's God's gift to mankind

**nombrilisme** /nɔ̃bʀilism/ *nm* (colloq) navel-gazing (colloq)

**nombriliste** *adj* (colloq) egocentric

**nomenclature** /nɔmɑ̃klatyʀ/ *nf* nomenclature; (in dictionary) word list

**nominal, ∼e, mpl -aux** /nɔminal, o/ *adj* (gen) nominal; ⟨list⟩ of names

**nominatif, -ive** /nɔminatif, iv/ **1** *adj* ⟨list⟩ of names; ⟨invitation⟩ personal; ⟨share⟩ registered
**2** *nm* nominative

**nomination** /nɔminasjɔ̃/ *nf*
(a) appointment
(b) letter of appointment
(c) (controversial) nomination

**nominativement** /nɔminativmɑ̃/ *adv* by name

**nominer** /nɔmine/ [1] *vtr* to nominate

**nommément** /nɔmemã/ *adv* specifically, by name

**nommer** /nɔme/ [1] **1** *vtr* **(a)** to appoint; **être nommé à Paris** to be posted to Paris **(b)** to name ⟨*person*⟩; to call ⟨*thing*⟩; **pour ne ~ personne** to mention no names
**2 se nommer** *v refl* (+ *v être*) **(a)** to be called
**(b)** to give one's name

**non** /nɔ̃/ **1** *adv* **(a)** no; **'tu y vas?'—'~'** 'are you going?'—'no, I'm not'; **ah, ça ~!** definitely not!; **faire ~ de la tête** to shake one's head; **je pense que ~** I don't think so; **je te dis que ~** no, I tell you; **il paraît que ~** apparently not; **tu trouves ça drôle? moi ~** do you think that's funny? I don't; **~ sans raison** not without reason; **~ moins difficile** just as difficult; **qu'il soit d'accord ou ~** whether he agrees or not; **tu viens, oui ou ~?** are you coming or not?; **sois un peu plus poli, ~ mais!** (colloq) be a bit more polite, for heaven's sake!
**(b)** non; **~ alcoolisé** nonalcoholic; **~ négligeable** considerable
**2** *nm inv* **(a)** no
**(b)** 'no' vote
**3 non plus** *phr* **je ne suis pas d'accord ~ plus** I don't agree either; **il n'a pas aimé le film, moi ~ plus** he didn't like the film and neither did I
**4 non(-)** (/nɔn/ *before vowel or mute h*) (combining form) **~-fumeur** nonsmoker; **~-syndiqué** non union member

**nonagénaire** /nɔnaʒenɛʀ/ *adj* **être ~** to be in one's nineties

**non-aligné, ~e**, *mpl* **~s** /nɔnaliɲe/ *nm,f* nonaligned country

**nonante** /nɔnɑ̃t/ *adj inv, pron* ninety

**non-assistance** /nɔnasistɑ̃s/ *nf* **~ à personne en danger** failure to render assistance

**nonchalance** /nɔ̃ʃalɑ̃s/ *nf* nonchalance

**nonchalant, ~e** /nɔ̃ʃalɑ̃, ɑ̃t/ *adj* nonchalant

**non-dit** /nɔ̃di/ *nm inv* **le ~** what is left unsaid

**non-figuratif, -ive**, *mpl* **~s** /nɔ̃fiɡyʀatif, iv/ *adj* abstract

**non-fonctionnement** /nɔ̃fɔ̃ksjɔnmɑ̃/ *nm* failure to operate

**non-initié, ~e**, *mpl* **~s** /nɔninisje/ *nm,f* layman, lay person

**non-inscrit, ~e**, *mpl* **~s** /nɔnɛ̃skʀi, it/ *nm,f* independent

**non-lieu**, *pl* **~x** /nɔ̃ljø/ *nm* (Law) dismissal (of a charge); **il y a eu ~** the case was dismissed

**nonne** /nɔn/ *nf* nun

**nonnette** /nɔnɛt/ *nf* small iced gingerbread

**non-recevoir** /nɔ̃ʀəsəvwaʀ/ *nm* **fin de ~** flat refusal

**non-reconduction**, *pl* **~s** /nɔ̃ʀəkɔ̃dyksjɔ̃/ *nf* (of contract) nonrenewal

**non-respect** /nɔ̃ʀɛspɛ/ *nm* **~ de** failure to comply with ⟨*clause*⟩; failure to respect ⟨*person*⟩

**non-sens** /nɔ̃sɑ̃s/ *nm inv* nonsense

**non-spécialiste**, *pl* **~s** /nɔ̃spesjalist/ *nmf* layman

**non-violent, ~e**, *mpl* **~s** /nɔ̃vjɔlɑ̃, ɑ̃t/ *nm,f* advocate of nonviolence

**non-voyant, ~e**, *mpl* **~s** /nɔ̃vwajɑ̃, ɑ̃t/ *nm,f* visually handicapped person

**nord** /nɔʀ/ **1** *adj inv* north; northern
**2** *nm* **(a)** north; **le vent du ~** the north wind; **le ~ de l'Europe** northern Europe **(b) le Nord** the North; **la Corée du Nord** North Korea
IDIOMS **il ne perd pas le ~!** (colloq) he's got his head screwed on! (colloq)

**nord-africain, ~e**, *mpl* **~s** /nɔʀafʀikɛ̃, ɛn/ *adj* North African

**nord-américain, ~e**, *mpl* **~s** /nɔʀamerikɛ̃, ɛn/ *adj* North American

**nord-est** /nɔʀ(d)ɛst/ **1** *adj inv* northeast; northeastern
**2** *nm* northeast

**nordique** /nɔʀdik/ *adj* Nordic

**nord-ouest** /nɔʀ(d)wɛst/ **1** *adj inv* northwest; northwestern
**2** *nm* northwest

**Nord-Sud** /nɔʀsyd/ *adj inv* North-South

**normal, ~e¹**, *mpl* **-aux** /nɔʀmal, o/ *adj* normal; **il est ~ que** it is natural that; **il n'est pas ~ que** it is not right that

**normale²** /nɔʀmal/ *nf* **(a)** average **(b)** norm; **retour à la ~** return to normal

**normalement** /nɔʀmalmɑ̃/ *adv* normally

**normalisation** /nɔʀmalizasjɔ̃/ *nf* **(a)** normalization
**(b)** standardization

**normaliser** /nɔʀmalize/ [1] *vtr* **(a)** to normalize ⟨*relations*⟩
**(b)** to standardize ⟨*sizes*⟩

**normalité** /nɔʀmalite/ *nf* normality

**normand, ~e** /nɔʀmɑ̃, ɑ̃d/ **1** *adj* **(a)** ⟨*conquest*⟩ Norman
**(b)** ⟨*coast*⟩ Normandy; ⟨*team*⟩ from Normandy
**2** *nm* Norman (French)

**Normand, ~e** /nɔʀmɑ̃, ɑ̃d/ *nm,f* Norman
IDIOMS **une réponse de ~** a noncommittal reply

**normatif, -ive** /nɔʀmatif, iv/ *adj* normative

**norme** /nɔʀm/ *nf* (gen) norm; (Tech) standard

**Norvège** /nɔʀvɛʒ/ *pr nf* Norway

**norvégien, -ienne** /nɔʀveʒjɛ̃, ɛn/ **1** *adj* Norwegian
**2** *nm* (language) Norwegian

**nos** ▸ NOTRE

**nostalgie** /nɔstalʒi/ *nf* nostalgia

**nostalgique** /nɔstalʒik/ *adj* nostalgic

**notable** /nɔtabl/ **1** *adj* ⟨*fact*⟩ notable; ⟨*progress*⟩ significant ····⫶

**2** *nm* notable

**notaire** /nɔtɛʀ/ *nm* notary public

**notamment** /nɔtamɑ̃/ *adv* (a) notably
(b) in particular

**notation** /nɔtasjɔ̃/ *nf* (a) notation
(b) (of pupil) marking (GB), grading (US);
(of staff) grading

**note** /nɔt/ *nf* (a) bill (GB), check (US); **faire
la ~ de qn** to write out sb's bill (GB) *or*
check (US)
(b) (Mus) note; (figurative) note, touch; **forcer la
~** to overdo it
(c) mark (GB), grade (US); **~ éliminatoire** fail
mark (GB) *or* grade (US)
(d) (written) note; **prendre qch en ~** to make a
note of sth; **prendre (bonne) ~ de qch**
(figurative) to take (due) note of sth
■ **~ de frais** expense account; **~ d'honoraires**
bill; **~ de service** memorandum

**noter** /nɔte/ [1] *vtr* (a) to write down ⟨*idea,
address*⟩
(b) to notice ⟨*change*⟩; **notez (bien) que je
n'ai rien à lui reprocher** mind you I haven't
got anything particular against him; **il faut
quand même ~** it has to be said
(c) to mark (GB), to grade (US) ⟨*exercise*⟩; to
give a mark (GB) *or* grade (US) to ⟨*pupil*⟩; to
grade ⟨*employee*⟩

**notice** /nɔtis/ *nf* (a) note
(b) instructions

**notifier** /nɔtifje/ [2] *vtr* **~ qch à qn** (gen) to
notify sb of sth; (Law) to give sb notice of sth

**notion** /nɔsjɔ̃/ *nf* (a) notion; **perdre la ~ de**
to lose all sense of
(b) **~s** basic knowledge

**notoire** /nɔtwaʀ/ *adj* ⟨*fact, position*⟩ well-
known; ⟨*swindler, stupidity*⟩ notorious

**notoirement** /nɔtwaʀmɑ̃/ *adv* manifestly;
notoriously

**notoriété** /nɔtɔʀjete/ *nf* (a) fame; (of product)
reputation; **il est de ~ (publique) que** it's
common knowledge that
(b) (person) celebrity

**notre**, *pl* **nos** /nɔtʀ, no/ *det* our; **à nos
âges** at our age; **c'était ~ avis à tous** we all
felt the same; **nos enfants à nous** (colloq) our
children

**nôtre** /notʀ/ **1** *det* **nous avons fait ~s ces
idées** we've adopted these ideas
**2** **le nôtre, la nôtre, les nôtres** *pron*
ours; **soyez des ~s!** won't you join us?; **les
~s** our own people; (team, group) our side

**nouer** /nwe/ [1] **1** *vtr* (a) (gen) to tie; to
knot ⟨*tie*⟩; to tie up ⟨*parcel*⟩; **avoir la gorge
nouée** to have a lump in one's throat
(b) to establish ⟨*relations*⟩; to engage in
⟨*dialogue*⟩
**2** **se nouer** *v refl* (+ *v être*) (a) ⟨*plot*⟩ to
take shape
(b) ⟨*diplomatic relations*⟩ to be established;
⟨*dialogue, friendship*⟩ to begin

**nougat** /nuga/ *nm* nougat

**nouilles** /nuj/ *nf pl* noodles, pasta

**nounou** /nunu/ *nf* (colloq) nanny (GB), nurse

**nounours** /nunuʀs/ *nm inv* (colloq) teddy
bear

**nourrice** /nuʀis/ *nf* (a) childminder (GB),
babysitter (US)
(b) wet nurse

**nourrir** /nuʀiʀ/ [3] **1** *vtr* (a) to feed
⟨*person, animal*⟩; to nourish ⟨*skin, leather*⟩;
**bien nourri** well-fed; **~ au sein/au biberon** to
breast-/to bottle-feed; **mon travail ne me
nourrit pas** I don't make enough to live on
(b) (figurative) to harbour (GB) ⟨*hopes*⟩; to feed
⟨*fire*⟩; to fuel ⟨*passion*⟩
**2** **se nourrir** *v refl* (+ *v être*) ⟨*animal*⟩ to
feed; ⟨*person*⟩ to eat; **se ~ de** to live on
⟨*vegetables*⟩; to feed on ⟨*illusions*⟩

**nourrissant**, **~e** /nuʀisɑ̃, ɑ̃t/ *adj*
nourishing

**nourrisson** /nuʀisɔ̃/ *nm* infant

**nourriture** /nuʀityʀ/ *nf* (a) food
(b) diet

**nous** /nu/ *pron* (a) (subject) we; (object) us;
**~ sommes en avance** we're early; **donne-~
l'adresse** give us the address; **entre ~, il
n'est pas très intelligent** between you and
me, he isn't very intelligent; **une maison à ~**
a house of our own; **pensons à ~** let's think
of ourselves
(b) (with reflexive verb) **~ soignons** we look
after ourselves; **~ ~ aimons** we love each
other

**nous-même**, *pl* **nous-mêmes**
/numɛm/ *pron* ourselves

**nouveau** (**nouvel** *before vowel or mute
h*), **nouvelle¹**, *mpl* **~x** /nuvo, nuvɛl/
**1** *adj* (gen) new; ⟨*attempt, attack*⟩ fresh; **tout
~** brand-new; **se faire faire un ~ costume** to
have a new suit made; to have another suit
made; **une nouvelle fois** once again; **les ~x
élus** the newly-elected members; **les ~x
mariés** the newlyweds
**2** *nm,f* (in school) new boy/girl; (in company)
new employee; (in army) new recruit
**3** *nm* **téléphone-moi s'il y a du ~** give me a
call if there is anything new to report; **j'ai du
~ pour toi** I've got some news for you
**4** **à nouveau**, **de nouveau** *phr* (once)
again

**nouveau-né**, **~e**, *mpl* **~s** /nuvone/
*nm,f* newborn baby

**nouveauté** /nuvote/ *nf* (a) novelty; **ce
n'est pas une ~!** that's nothing new!
(b) (gen) new thing; (book) new publication;
(record) new release; (car, machine) new model

**nouvel** ▶ NOUVEAU 1

**nouvelle²** /nuvɛl/ **1** *adj f* ▶ NOUVEAU 1
**2** *nf* (a) ▶ NOUVEAU 2
(b) news; **une ~** a piece of news; **tu connais
la ~?** have you heard the news?; **recevoir
des ~s de qn** to hear from sb; (through
somebody else) to hear news of sb; **il m'a
demandé de tes ~s** he asked after you; **aux
dernières ~s, il se porte bien** (colloq) the last
I heard he was doing fine; **il aura de mes ~s!**

(colloq) he'll be hearing from me!; **goûte ce petit vin, tu m'en diras des** ∼**s** (colloq) have a taste of this wine, it's really good!
(c) short story

**nouvellement** /nuvɛlmɑ̃/ *adv* recently

**Nouvelle-Zélande** /nuvɛlzelɑ̃d/ *pr nf* New Zealand

**nouvelliste** /nuvelist/ *nmf* short-story writer

**novateur, -trice** /nɔvatœʀ, tʀis/ 1 *adj* innovative
2 *nm,f* innovator, pioneer

**novembre** /nɔvɑ̃bʀ/ *nm* November

**novice** /nɔvis/ 1 *adj* inexperienced, green
2 *nmf* novice

**noyade** /nwajad/ *nf* drowning

**noyau,** *pl* ∼**x** /nwajo/ *nm* (a) stone (GB), pit (US)
(b) small group; ∼**x de résistance** pockets of resistance
(c) nucleus

**noyauter** /nwajote/ [1] *vtr* to infiltrate

**noyé, ∼e** /nwaje/ *nm,f* drowned person

**noyer¹** /nwaje/ [23] 1 *vtr* (gen) to drown; to flood ⟨*village, engine*⟩; ∼ **qn sous un flot de paroles** to talk sb's head off (colloq)
2 **se noyer** *v refl* (+ *v être*) to drown; (suicide) to drown oneself; **mourir noyé** to drown
IDIOMS **se ∼ dans un verre d'eau** to make a mountain out of a molehill

**noyer²** /nwaje/ *nm* walnut (tree)

**nu, ∼e** /ny/ 1 *adj* ⟨*person*⟩ naked; ⟨*wall, tree, coastline*⟩ bare; ⟨*truth*⟩ plain; **pieds ∼s** barefoot; **torse ∼** stripped to the waist
2 *nm* (in art) nude
3 **à nu** *phr* **être à ∼** to be exposed; **mettre son cœur à ∼** to open one's heart

**nuage** /nɥaʒ/ *nm* cloud; **sans ∼s** ⟨*sky*⟩ cloudless; ⟨*happiness*⟩ unclouded; ∼ **de lait** dash of milk
IDIOMS **descendre de son ∼** to come back to earth

**nuageux, -euse** /nɥaʒø, øz/ *adj* ⟨*sky*⟩ cloudy

**nuance** /nɥɑ̃s/ *nf* (a) (of colour) shade
(b) (of meaning) nuance; **sans ∼** ⟨*commentary*⟩ clearcut; ⟨*personality*⟩ straightforward
(c) slight difference; **à cette ∼ près que** with the small reservation that
(d) (Mus) nuance

**nuancer** /nɥɑ̃se/ [12] *vtr* (a) to qualify ⟨*opinion*⟩; to modify ⟨*view of situation*⟩; **peu nuancé** unsubtle
(b) to moderate ⟨*remarks, statements*⟩

**nucléaire** /nykleɛʀ/ 1 *adj* nuclear
2 *nm* **le ∼** nuclear energy; nuclear technology

**nudité** /nydite/ *nf* (a) nakedness, nudity
(b) (of place, wall) bareness

**nuée** /nɥe/ *nf* (of insects) swarm; (of people) horde

**nues** /ny/ *nf pl* **tomber des ∼** (colloq) to be flabbergasted (colloq); **porter qn aux ∼** to praise sb to the skies

**nui** /nɥi/ ▶ NUIRE

**nuire** /nɥiʀ/ [69] 1 **nuire à** *v+prep* to harm ⟨*person*⟩; to be harmful to ⟨*health, interests, reputation*⟩; to damage ⟨*crops*⟩
2 **se nuire** *v refl* (+ *v être*) (a) to do each other a lot of harm
(b) to do oneself a lot of harm

**nuisance** /nɥizɑ̃s/ *nf* nuisance

**nuisible** /nɥizibl/ *adj* ⟨*substance, waste*⟩ dangerous; ⟨*influence*⟩ harmful; **insecte ∼** (insect) pest; ∼ **à** detrimental to

**nuit** /nɥi/ *nf* night; **cette ∼** last night; tonight; **voyager de ∼** to travel by night; **avant la ∼** before dark; **à la tombée de la ∼** at nightfall; **il fait ∼** it's dark; **il faisait ∼ noire** it was pitch dark; **ça se perd dans la ∼ des temps** it is lost in the mists of time
■ ∼ **blanche** sleepless night; ∼ **bleue** *night of terrorist bomb attacks*
IDIOMS **c'est le jour et la ∼** they're as different as chalk and cheese; **attends demain pour donner ta réponse: la ∼ porte conseil** wait till tomorrow to give your answer: sleep on it first

**nuitée** /nɥite/ *nf* (in a hotel) overnight stay

**nul, nulle** /nyl/ 1 *adj* (a) (colloq) ⟨*person*⟩ hopeless; ⟨*piece of work*⟩ worthless; ⟨*film*⟩ trashy (colloq)
(b) (Law) ⟨*contract*⟩ void; ⟨*will*⟩ invalid; ⟨*elections*⟩ null and void; ⟨*vote*⟩ spoiled
(c) (Sport) **match ∼** tie, draw (GB); nil-all draw
(d) ⟨*difference*⟩ nil
(e) ∼ **homme/pays** no man/country; ∼ **autre que vous** no-one else but you
2 *nm,f* (colloq) idiot (colloq); **c'est un ∼** he's a dead loss (colloq)
3 *pron* no-one
4 **nulle part** *phr* nowhere

**nullement** /nylmɑ̃/ *adv* not at all

**nullité** /nylite/ *nf* (a) (Law) nullity; **frapper de ∼** to render void
(b) (of argument) invalidity; (of book, film) (colloq) worthlessness
(c) (colloq) (person) idiot (colloq)

**numéraire** /nymeʀɛʀ/ *nm* cash

**numéral, ∼e,** *mpl* **-aux** /nymeʀal, o/
1 *adj* numeral
2 *nm* numeral

**numération** /nymeʀasjɔ̃/ *nf* (Math) numeration
■ ∼ **globulaire** blood count

**numérique** /nymeʀik/ *adj* (gen) numerical; ⟨*display*⟩ digital; **clavier ∼** keypad

**numéro** /nymeʀo/ *nm* (a) number; ∼ **de téléphone** telephone number
(b) (magazine) issue; **suite au prochain ∼** to be continued
(c) (in show) act
(d) (colloq) **quel ∼!** what a character!

∼∻

■ ~ **d'abonné** customer's number; ~ **d'appel gratuit** freefone number (GB), toll-free number (US); ~ **vert** = ~ D'APPEL GRATUIT  IDIOMS **tirer le bon** ~ to be lucky

**numérotation** /nymeʀɔtasjɔ̃/ nf numbering

**numéroter** /nymeʀɔte/ [1] vtr to number

**numerus clausus** /nymeʀysklozys/ nm inv quota

**nunuche** /nynyʃ/ adj (colloq) bird-brained (colloq), silly

**nu-pied**, pl ~**s** /nypje/ nm sandal

**nuptial**, ~**e**, mpl **-iaux** /nypsjal, o/ adj ⟨mass⟩ nuptial; ⟨room⟩ bridal; **cérémonie** ~**e** wedding

**nuque** /nyk/ nf nape (of the neck)

**nurse** /nœʀs/ nf nanny (GB), nurse

**nutritif, -ive** /nytʀitif, iv/ adj ⟨skin cream⟩ nourishing; ⟨value⟩ nutritive

**nutrition** /nytʀisjɔ̃/ nf nutrition

**nymphe** /nɛ̃f/ nf nymph

**nymphéa** /nɛ̃fea/ nm waterlily

**nymphomane** /nɛ̃fɔman/ adj, nf nymphomaniac

# Oo

**o, O** /o/ nm inv o, O

**oasis** /ɔazis/ nf inv oasis

**obéir** /ɔbeiʀ/ [3] v+prep **(a)** to obey; ~ **à** to obey ⟨order⟩  **(b)** ⟨brakes, vehicle⟩ to respond

**obéissance** /ɔbeisɑ̃s/ nf obedience

**obéissant, ~e** /ɔbeisɑ̃, ɑ̃t/ adj obedient

**obélisque** /ɔbelisk/ nm obelisk

**obèse** /ɔbɛz/ adj obese

**objecter** /ɔbʒɛkte/ [1] vtr to object

**objectif, -ive** /ɔbʒɛktif, iv/ 1 adj objective  2 nm **(a)** objective  **(b)** lens  **(c)** target

**objection** /ɔbʒɛksjɔ̃/ nf objection

**objectivité** /ɔbʒɛktivite/ nf objectivity

**objet** /ɔbʒɛ/ 1 nm **(a)** object; ~ **fragile** fragile item; ~**s personnels** personal possessions  **(b)** (of debate, research) subject; (of hatred, desire) object; **faire l'**~ **de** to be the subject of ⟨inquiry, research⟩; to be subjected to ⟨surveillance⟩; to be the object of ⟨desire, hatred⟩  **(c)** purpose, object; '~: **réponse à votre lettre du...'** 're: your letter of...'  **(d)** (Law) ~ **d'un litige** matter at issue  2 **-objet** (combining form) as an object; **femme-**~ woman as an object  ■ ~**s trouvés** lost property; ~ **volant non identifié, ovni** unidentified flying object, UFO

**obligataire** /ɔbligatɛʀ/ (Fin) adj ⟨market, issue⟩ bond; **emprunt** ~ bond issue

**obligation** /ɔbligasjɔ̃/ nf **(a)** obligation, responsibility; duty  **(b)** necessity; **se voir** or **se trouver dans l'**~ **de faire** to be forced to do  **(c)** (Econ) bond  **(d)** (Law) obligation  ■ ~**s militaires, OM** military service

**obligatoire** /ɔbligatwaʀ/ adj  **(a)** compulsory  **(b)** (colloq) inevitable

**obligatoirement** /ɔbligatwaʀmɑ̃/ adv inevitably, necessarily

**obligé, ~e** /ɔbliʒe/ 1 pp ▶ OBLIGER  2 pp adj **(a)** (constrained) **se voir** ~ **de faire** to be forced to do  **(b)** (indebted) **être** ~ **à qn de** to be obliged or grateful to sb for  **(c)** (necessary) essential; **un passage** ~ ( **pour**) (figurative) a prerequisite (for)  3 nm,f **(a) être l'**~ **de qn** to be obliged or indebted to sb  **(b)** (in law) obligor

**obligeamment** /ɔbliʒamɑ̃/ adv obligingly

**obligeance** /ɔbliʒɑ̃s/ nf **avoir l'**~ **de** to be kind enough to

**obligeant, ~e** /ɔbliʒɑ̃, ɑ̃t/ adj obliging; kind

**obliger** /ɔbliʒe/ [13] 1 vtr **(a)** ~ **qn à faire** to force sb to do; ⟨rules⟩ to make it compulsory for sb to; ⟨duty⟩ to compel sb to; **je suis obligé de partir** I have to go  **(b)** ~ **qn** to oblige sb  2 **s'obliger** v refl (+ v être) **s'**~ **à faire** to force oneself to do

**oblique** /ɔblik/ adj slanting; sidelong; oblique

**obliquement** /ɔblikmɑ̃/ adv at an angle; diagonally

**oblitération** /ɔbliteʀasjɔ̃/ nf (of stamp) cancelling (GB); ⟨cachet d'⟩~ postmark

**oblitérer** /ɔbliteʀe/ [14] vtr to cancel, to obliterate ⟨stamp⟩

**oblong, -ongue** /ɔblɔ̃, ɔ̃g/ adj oblong

**obnubiler** /ɔbnybile/ [1] vtr to obsess

**obscène** /ɔpsɛn/ adj obscene

**obscur, ~e** /ɔpskyʀ/ adj **(a)** dark  **(b)** obscure  **(c)** lowly  **(d)** vague

**obscurcir** /ɔpskyʀsiʀ/ [3] **1** *vtr* **(a)** to make [sth] dark ⟨*place*⟩
**(b)** to obscure ⟨*view*⟩
**2 s'obscurcir** *v refl* (+ *v être*) **(a)** ⟨*sky, place*⟩ to darken
**(b)** ⟨*situation*⟩ to become confused

**obscurément** /ɔpskyʀemɑ̃/ *adv* **(a)** ⟨*feel*⟩ vaguely
**(b)** ⟨*live*⟩ in obscurity

**obscurité** /ɔpskyʀite/ *nf* darkness

**obsédant, ~e** /ɔpsedɑ̃, ɑ̃t/ *adj* ⟨*memory, dream, music*⟩ haunting; ⟨*rhythm*⟩ insistent

**obsédé, ~e** /ɔpsede/ *nm,f* **~ (sexuel)** sex maniac

**obséder** /ɔpsede/ [14] *vtr* ⟨*memory, dream*⟩ to haunt; ⟨*idea, problem*⟩ to obsess

**obsèques** /ɔpsɛk/ *nf pl* funeral

**obséquieux, -ieuse** /ɔpsekjø, øz/ *adj* obsequious

**observateur, -trice** /ɔpsɛʀvatœʀ, tʀis/ **1** *adj* observant
**2** *nm,f* observer

**observation** /ɔpsɛʀvasjɔ̃/ *nf*
**(a)** observation
**(b)** observation, remark; comment
**(c)** reproach

**observatoire** /ɔpsɛʀvatwaʀ/ *nm*
**(a)** observatory
**(b)** look-out post

**observer** /ɔpsɛʀve/ [1] **1** *vtr* **(a)** to watch, to observe
**(b)** to notice, to observe ⟨*phenomenon, reaction*⟩
**(c)** to observe ⟨*rules, treaty*⟩; to keep to ⟨*diet*⟩; to maintain ⟨*strategy*⟩; **~ le silence** to keep quiet
**2 s'observer** *v refl* (+ *v être*) **(a)** to watch each other
**(b)** to keep a check on oneself

**obsession** /ɔpsɛsjɔ̃/ *nf* obsession

**obsolète** /ɔpsɔlɛt/ *adj* obsolete

**obstacle** /ɔpstakl/ *nm* **(a)** obstacle
**(b)** (in horseriding) fence

**obstétricien, -ienne** /ɔpstetʀisjɛ̃, ɛn/ *nm,f* obstetrician

**obstétrique** /ɔpstetʀik/ *nf* obstetrics

**obstination** /ɔpstinasjɔ̃/ *nf* obstinacy

**obstiné, ~e** /ɔpstine/ **1** *pp* ▶ OBSTINER
**2** *pp adj* **(a)** stubborn
**(b)** dogged

**obstinément** /ɔpstinemɑ̃/ *adv* obstinately

**obstiner: s'obstiner** /ɔpstine/ [1] *v refl* (+ *v être*) to persist

**obstruction** /ɔpstʀyksjɔ̃/ *nf* obstruction

**obstruer** /ɔpstʀye/ [1] **1** *vtr* to obstruct
**2 s'obstruer** *v refl* (+ *v être*) to get blocked

**obtempérer** /ɔptɑ̃peʀe/ [14] *v+prep* to comply; **~ à** to comply with ⟨*order*⟩

**obtenir** /ɔptəniʀ/ [36] *vtr* to get, to obtain

**obtention** /ɔptɑ̃sjɔ̃/ *nf* getting, obtaining

**obturation** /ɔptyʀasjɔ̃/ *nf* **(a)** blocking (up)
**(b) vitesse d'~** shutter speed

**obturer** /ɔptyʀe/ [1] *vtr* to block up

**obtus, ~e** /ɔpty, yz/ *adj* obtuse

**obus** /ɔby/ *nm inv* shell

**occasion** /ɔkazjɔ̃/ *nf* **(a)** occasion; **à l'~** some time; **à or en plusieurs ~s** on several occasions; **les grandes ~s** special occasions
**(b)** opportunity, chance; **être l'~ de qch** to give rise to sth
**(c)** second-hand buy
**(d)** bargain

**occasionnel, -elle** /ɔkazjɔnɛl/ *adj* occasional

**occasionner** /ɔkazjɔne/ [1] *vtr* to cause

**occident** /ɔksidɑ̃/ *nm* **(a)** west
**(b) l'Occident** the West

**occidental, ~e, mpl -aux** /ɔksidɑ̃tal, o/ *adj* western

**Occidental, ~e, mpl -aux** /ɔksidɑ̃tal, o/ *nm,f* Westerner

**occitan** /ɔksitɑ̃/ *nm* langue d'oc

**occulte** /ɔkylt/ *adj* **(a)** occult
**(b)** secret

**occulter** /ɔkylte/ [1] *vtr* **(a)** to eclipse
**(b)** to obscure ⟨*issue*⟩; to conceal ⟨*truth*⟩

**occultisme** /ɔkyltism/ *nm* occultism

**occupant, ~e** /ɔkypɑ̃, ɑ̃t/ **1** *adj* occupying
**2** *nm,f* (of house) occupier; (of vehicle) occupant

**occupation** /ɔkypasjɔ̃/ *nf* **(a)** (pastime) occupation
**(b)** occupation, job
**(c)** occupancy
**(d)** (of country, factory) occupation

**occupé, ~e** /ɔkype/ **1** *pp* ▶ OCCUPER
**2** *pp adj* **(a)** ⟨*person, life*⟩ busy
**(b)** ⟨*seat*⟩ taken; ⟨*phone*⟩ engaged (GB), busy; ⟨*toilet*⟩ engaged
**(c)** (Mil) ⟨*country*⟩ occupied

**occuper** /ɔkype/ [1] **1** *vtr* **(a)** to live in, to occupy ⟨*flat, house*⟩; to be in ⟨*shower, cell*⟩; to sit in ⟨*seat*⟩
**(b)** to take up ⟨*space, time*⟩
**(c)** to occupy ⟨*person, mind*⟩; **ça m'occupe!** it keeps me busy!; **le sujet qui nous occupe** the matter which we are dealing with
**(d)** to have ⟨*employment*⟩; to hold ⟨*job, office*⟩
**(e)** ⟨*strikers, army*⟩ to occupy ⟨*place*⟩; **~ les locaux** to stage a sit-in
**2 s'occuper** *v refl* (+ *v être*) **(a)** to keep oneself busy *or* occupied
**(b) s'~ de** to see to, to take care of ⟨*dinner, tickets*⟩; to be dealing with ⟨*file, matter*⟩; to take care of ⟨*child, animal, plant*⟩; to attend to ⟨*customer*⟩; to be in charge of ⟨*finance, library*⟩; **occupe-toi de tes affaires** (colloq) *or* **de ce qui te regarde!** (colloq) mind your own business! (colloq)

**occurrence** /ɔkyʀɑ̃s/ *nf* **(a)** case, instance; **en l'~** in this case
**(b)** occurrence

**OCDE** /ɔsedeə/ *nf* (*abbr* = **Organisation de coopération et de développement économiques**) OECD

**océan** /ɔseã/ *nm* ocean

**océanique** /ɔseanik/ *adj* oceanic

**océanographe** /ɔseanɔgRaf/ *nmf* oceanographer

**ocre** /ɔkR/ *adj inv*, *nm* ochre (GB)

**octante** /ɔktãt/ *adj inv*, *pron* (in Belgian, Canadian, Swiss, French) eighty

**octave** /ɔktav/ *nf* octave

**octet** /ɔktɛt/ *nm* (a) (Comput) byte
(b) (in physics) octet

**octobre** /ɔktɔbR/ *nm* October

**octogénaire** /ɔktɔʒenɛR/ *nmf* octogenarian

**octogonal, ~e**, *mpl* **-aux** /ɔktɔgɔnal, o/ *adj* octagonal

**octroi** /ɔktRwa/ *nm* (a) granting
(b) octroi

**octroyer** /ɔktRwaje/ [23] *vtr* **~ à qn** to grant sb ⟨*pardon, favour*⟩; to allocate sb sth ⟨*budget*⟩

**oculaire** /ɔkylɛR/ *adj* **troubles ~s** eye trouble; **témoin ~** eyewitness

**oculiste** /ɔkylist/ *nmf* oculist, ophthalmologist

**ode** /ɔd/ *nf* ode

**odeur** /ɔdœR/ *nf* smell

**odieux, -ieuse** /ɔdjø, øz/ *adj* horrible

**odorant, ~e** /ɔdɔRã, ãt/ *adj* which has a smell

**odorat** /ɔdɔRa/ *nm* sense of smell

**OECE** /ɔesea/ *nf* (*abbr* = **Organisation européenne de coopération économique**) OEEC

**œdème** /edɛm/ *nm* (Med) oedema

**œdipe** /edip/ *nm* Oedipus complex

**œil**, *pl* **yeux** /œj, jø/ *nm* eye; **ouvrir l'~** to keep one's eyes open; **fermer les yeux sur qch** to turn a blind eye to sth; **acheter qch les yeux fermés** to buy sth with complete confidence; **avoir l'~ à tout** to be vigilant; **jeter un ~ à** *or* **sur qch** to have a quick look at sth; **aux yeux de tous** openly; **jeter un coup d'~ à qch** to glance at sth; **avoir le coup d'~** to have a good eye; **regarder qch d'un ~ neuf** to see sth in a new light; **voir qch d'un mauvais ~** to take a dim view of sth; **à mes yeux** in my opinion
■ **~ de verre** glass eye
IDIOMS **mon ~!** (colloq) my eye! (colloq), my foot! (colloq); **à l'~** (colloq) for nothing, for free (colloq); **faire les gros yeux à qn** to glare at sb; **dévorer qn/qch des yeux** to gaze longingly at sb/sth; **faire les yeux doux à qn** to make eyes at sb; **tourner de l'~** (colloq) to faint; **cela me sort par les yeux** (colloq) I've had it up to here (colloq); **avoir bon pied bon ~** to be as fit as a fiddle; **sauter aux yeux** to be obvious

**œillade** /œjad/ *nf* (a) wink
(b) glance

**œillère** /œjɛR/ *nf* blinker

**œillet** /œjɛ/ *nm* (a) carnation
(b) (in shoe, tarpaulin) eyelet; (in belt) hole; (made of metal) grommet

**œilleton** /œjtɔ̃/ *nm* (in door) peephole

**œnologie** /enɔlɔʒi/ *nf* oenology

**œsophage** /ezɔfaʒ/ *nm* oesophagus

**œstrogène** /ɛstRɔʒɛn/ *nm* oestrogen

**œuf** /œf, *pl* ø/ *nm* egg; **~s de cabillaud** cod's roe
■ **~ à la coque** boiled egg; **~ dur** hard-boiled egg; **~ sur le plat** fried egg; **~s brouillés** scrambled eggs

**œuvre** /œvR/ *nf* (a) (artistic, literary) work; **~s complètes** complete works
(b) **être à l'~** to be at work; **voir qn à l'~** to see sb in action; **mettre en ~** to implement ⟨*reform*⟩; to display ⟨*ingenuity*⟩; **tout mettre en ~ pour faire** to make every effort to do
■ **~ d'art** work of art; **~ de bienfaisance** *or* **de charité** charity

**off** /ɔf/ *adj inv* (colloq) **voix ~** voice-over

**offensant, ~e** /ɔfãsã, ãt/ *adj* offensive (**pour à**)

**offense** /ɔfãs/ *nf* insult

**offenser** /ɔfãse/ [1] **1** *vtr* to offend
**2 s'offenser** *v refl* (+ *v être*) to take offence (GB)

**offensif, -ive¹** /ɔfãsif, iv/ *adj* (Mil) offensive

**offensive²** /ɔfãsiv/ *nf* (Mil, figurative) offensive

**offert, -e** /ɔfɛR, ɛRt/ ▶ OFFRIR

**office** /ɔfis/ **1** *nm* (a) **faire ~ de table** to serve as a table
(b) **~ religieux** service
(c) butlery
**2 d'office** *phr* **d'~** without consultation; **nos propositions ont été rejetées d'~** our proposals were dismissed out of hand; **commis d'~** ⟨*lawyer*⟩ appointed by the court
■ **~ du tourisme** tourist information office

**officiel, -ielle** /ɔfisjɛl/ **1** *adj* official; **être en visite officielle** to be on a state visit
**2** *nm* official

**officier¹** /ɔfisje/ [2] *vi* to officiate

**officier²** /ɔfisje/ *nm* officer

**officieusement** /ɔfisjøzmã/ *adv* unofficially

**officieux, -ieuse** /ɔfisjø, øz/ *adj* unofficial

**officine** /ɔfisin/ *nf* dispensary; pharmacy

**offrande** /ɔfRãd/ *nf* offering

**offrant** /ɔfRã/ **1** *pres p* ▶ OFFRIR
**2** *nm* **vendre qch au plus ~** to sell sth to the highest bidder

**offre** /ɔfR/ *nf* (a) offer; **répondre à une ~ d'emploi** to reply to a job advertisement
(b) (Écon) supply
■ **~ d'achat** bid; **~ publique d'achat, OPA** takeover bid

**offrir** /ɔfRiR/ [4] **1** *vtr* (a) **~ qch à qn** to give sth to sb
(b) to buy (**à qn** for sb)

(c) to offer ‹*choice*›; to offer ‹*resignation*›; to present ‹*problems*›
2 **s'offrir** *v refl* (+ *v être*) **(a)** **s'~** to buy oneself ‹*flowers*›; **ils ne peuvent pas s'~ le théâtre** they can't afford to go to the theatre (GB); **s'~ un jour de vacances** to give oneself a day off
(b) ‹*solution*› to present itself; **s'~ en spectacle** to make an exhibition of oneself

offusquer /ɔfyske/ [1] **1** *vtr* to offend
2 **s'offusquer** *v refl* (+ *v être*) to be offended

ogive /ɔʒiv/ *nf* rib

ogre /ɔɡʀ/ *nm* ogre

oh /o/ *excl* oh!; **~ hisse!** heave-ho!

oie /wa/ *nf* goose; **~ blanche** naïve young girl

oignon /ɔɲɔ̃/ *nm* **(a)** onion
(b) (of flower) bulb
IDIOMS occupe-toi de tes ~s (colloq) mind your own business (colloq)

oiseau, *pl* **~x** /wazo/ *nm* bird; **un (drôle d')~** an oddball (colloq)
IDIOMS trouver l'~ rare (colloq) to find the one person in a million

oiseau-mouche, *pl* **oiseaux-mouches** /wazomuʃ/ *nm* hummingbird

oiseleur /wazlœʀ/ *nm* bird-catcher

oisellerie /wazɛlʀi/ *nf* bird shop

oisif, **-ive** /wazif, iv/ **1** *adj* idle
2 *nm,f* idler; **les ~s** the idle rich

oisillon /wazijɔ̃/ *nm* fledgling

oisiveté /wazivte/ *nf* idleness
IDIOMS l'~ est mère de tous les vices (Proverb) the devil makes work for idle hands

olé: **olé olé** /ɔleɔle/ *phr* (colloq) ‹*joke*› naughty

oléagineux, **-euse** /ɔleaʒinø, øz/ **1** *adj* oleaginous
2 *nm inv* oleaginous plant

oléiculture /ɔleikyltyʀ/ *nf* olive-growing

oléoduc /ɔleɔdyk/ *nm* (oil) pipeline

olfactif, **-ive** /ɔlfaktif, iv/ *adj* olfactory

oligo-élément, *pl* **~s** /ɔligoelemɑ̃/ *nm* trace element

olivâtre /ɔlivɑtʀ/ *adj* olive-greenish; sallow

olive /ɔliv/ *nf* olive

oliveraie /ɔlivʀɛ/ *nf* olive grove

olivier /ɔlivje/ *nm* **(a)** olive tree
(b) olive wood

olympiade /ɔlɛ̃pjad/ **1** *nf* Olympiad
2 **olympiades** *nf pl* Olympics

olympique /ɔlɛ̃pik/ *adj* Olympic

ombilic /ɔ̃bilik/ *nm* umbilicus, navel

ombrage /ɔ̃bʀaʒ/ *nm* shade
IDIOMS porter ~ à qn to offend sb; **prendre ~ de qch** to take umbrage at sth

ombrager /ɔ̃bʀaʒe/ [13] *vtr* to shade

ombrageux, **-euse** /ɔ̃bʀaʒø, øz/ *adj* tetchy

ombre /ɔ̃bʀ/ *nf* **(a)** shade; **tu leur fais de l'~** you're (standing) in their light; (figurative) you put them in the shade; **rester dans l'~ de qn** to be in sb's shadow
(b) shadow
(c) darkness
(d) **laisser certains détails dans l'~** to be deliberately vague about certain details
(e) hint; **une ~ de tristesse passa dans son regard** a look of sadness crossed his/her face
■ **~ chinoise** shadow puppet; **~ à paupières** eye shadow
IDIOMS jeter une ~ au tableau to spoil the picture

ombrelle /ɔ̃bʀɛl/ *nf* parasol, sunshade

omelette /ɔmlɛt/ *nf* omelette

omettre /ɔmɛtʀ/ [60] *vtr* to leave out, to omit

omission /ɔmisjɔ̃/ *nf* omission

omnibus /ɔmnibys/ *nm inv* slow *or* local train

omniprésent, **~e** /ɔmnipʀezɑ̃, ɑ̃t/ *adj* omnipresent

omnisports /ɔmnispɔʀ/ *adj inv* **salle ~** sports hall; **club ~** (multi-)sports club

omnivore /ɔmnivɔʀ/ *nmf* omnivore

omoplate /ɔmɔplat/ *nf* shoulder blade

OMS /oɛmɛs/ *nf* (*abbr* = **Organisation mondiale de la santé**) WHO

on /ɔ̃/ *pron* **(a)** **~ a refait la route** the road was resurfaced; **~ a prétendu que** it was claimed that; **il pleut des cordes, comme ~ dit** it's raining cats and dogs, as they say
(b) we; **mon copain et moi, ~ va en Afrique** my boyfriend and I are going to Africa
(c) you; **alors, ~ se promène?** so you're taking a stroll then?
(d) **~ fait ce qu'~ peut!** one does what one can!; **toi, ~ ne t'a rien demandé** nobody asked you for your opinion; **~ ne m'a pas demandé mon avis** they didn't ask me for my opinion

once /ɔ̃s/ *nf* ounce

oncle /ɔ̃kl/ *nm* uncle

onctueux, **-euse** /ɔ̃ktɥø, øz/ *adj* **(a)** smooth, creamy
(b) unctuous

onde /ɔ̃d/ *nf* wave; **grandes ~s** long wave; **sur les ~s** on the air

ondée /ɔ̃de/ *nf* shower

on-dit /ɔ̃di/ *nm inv* **les ~** hearsay

ondoyant, **~e** /ɔ̃dwajɑ̃, ɑ̃t/ *adj* rippling; lithe; swaying

ondoyer /ɔ̃dwaje/ [23] *vi* to undulate; to sway

ondulant, **~e** /ɔ̃dylɑ̃, ɑ̃t/ *adj* swaying; undulating

ondulation /ɔ̃dylasjɔ̃/ *nf* **(a)** undulation; swaying
(b) curves; wave

ondulé, **~e** /ɔ̃dyle/ *adj* ‹*hair, shape*› wavy; ‹*cardboard*› corrugated

onéreux, **-euse** /ɔneʀø, øz/ *adj* expensive

**ONG** /ɔɛnʒe/ nf (abbr = **organisation non gouvernementale**) NGO

**ongle** /ɔ̃gl/ nm nail
IDIOMS **jusqu'au bout des ~s** through and through

**onglet** /ɔ̃glɛ/ nm (a) tab; **avec ~s** with thumb-index
(b) (Culin) prime cut of beef

**onirique** /ɔniʀik/ adj dream-like

**onomatopée** /ɔnɔmatɔpe/ nf onomatopoeia

**ont** /ɔ̃/ ▶ AVOIR¹

**ONU** /ɔny, oɛny/ nf (abbr = **Organisation des Nations unies**) UN, UNO

**onyx** /ɔniks/ nm inv onyx

**onze** /ɔ̃z/ adj inv, pron, nm inv eleven

**onzième** /ɔ̃zjɛm/ [1] adj eleventh
[2] nf (Sch) first year of primary school, age 6–7

**OPA** /opea/ nf (abbr = **offre publique d'achat**) takeover bid

**opaque** /ɔpak/ adj (a) opaque
(b) (figurative) ⟨text⟩ opaque; ⟨night⟩ dark; ⟨wood, fog⟩ impenetrable

**OPEP** /ɔpɛp/ nf (abbr = **Organisation des pays producteurs de pétrole**) OPEC

**opéra** /ɔpeʀa/ nm (a) opera
(b) opera house

**opérateur, -trice** /ɔpeʀatœʀ, tʀis/ nm,f operator; **~ de saisie** keyboarder

**opération** /ɔpeʀasjɔ̃/ nf (a) **~ (chirurgicale)** operation, surgery
(b) calculation
(c) (Tech) operation
(d) process
(e) transaction

**opératoire** /ɔpeʀatwaʀ/ adj (a) ⟨technique⟩ surgical; ⟨risk⟩ in operating
(b) operative

**opercule** /ɔpɛʀkyl/ nm (a) (Bot, Zool) operculum
(b) lid

**opéré, ~e** /ɔpeʀe/ nm,f person who has had an operation

**opérer** /ɔpeʀe/ [14] [1] vtr (a) to operate on; **~ qn de l'appendicite** to remove sb's appendix; **se faire ~** to have an operation, to have surgery
(b) to bring about ⟨change⟩
[2] vi (a) (Med) to operate
(b) ⟨cure, charm⟩ to work
(c) to proceed
(d) ⟨thief⟩ to operate

**opérette** /ɔpeʀɛt/ nf operetta, light opera

**ophtalmologiste** /ɔftalmɔlɔʒist/ nmf ophthalmologist

**opiner** /ɔpine/ [1] vi **~ du bonnet** or **de la tête** to nod in agreement

**opiniâtre** /ɔpinjatʀ/ adj ⟨resistance⟩ dogged; ⟨work⟩ relentless; ⟨person⟩ tenacious

**opinion** /ɔpinjɔ̃/ nf (a) opinion; **mon ~ est faite** my mind is made up
(b) **l'~ (publique)** public opinion

**opium** /ɔpjɔm/ nm opium

**opportun, ~e** /ɔpɔʀtœ̃, yn/ adj appropriate

**opportuniste** /ɔpɔʀtynist/ nmf opportunist

**opportunité** /ɔpɔʀtynite/ nf
(a) appropriateness
(b) opportunity

**opposant, ~e** /ɔpozɑ̃, ɑ̃t/ nm,f opponent

**opposé, ~e** /ɔpoze/ [1] adj (a) ⟨direction⟩ opposite
(b) ⟨opinion⟩ opposite; ⟨parties, sides⟩ opposing; ⟨interests⟩ conflicting
(c) opposed
[2] **à l'opposé** phr (a) **à l'~ de mes frères** in contrast to my brothers
(b) **il est parti à l'~** he went off in the opposite direction

**opposer** /ɔpoze/ [1] [1] vtr (a) to put up ⟨resistance, argument⟩
(b) **~ à** to match or pit [sb] against ⟨person, team⟩
(c) ⟨problem⟩ to divide ⟨people⟩
(d) to compare
[2] **s'opposer** v refl (+ v être) (a) **s'~ à qch** to be opposed to sth
(b) **s'~ à** to stand in the way of ⟨change⟩
(c) to contrast
(d) ⟨ideas, opinions⟩ to conflict; ⟨people⟩ to disagree
(e) ⟨teams⟩ to confront each other

**opposition** /ɔpozisjɔ̃/ nf (a) opposition; **par ~ à** in contrast with or to
(b) **faire ~ à un chèque** to stop a cheque (GB) or check (US)

**oppressant, ~e** /ɔpʀesɑ̃, ɑ̃t/ adj oppressive

**oppresser** /ɔpʀese/ [1] vtr to oppress; **se sentir oppressé** to feel breathless

**oppression** /ɔpʀesjɔ̃/ nf oppression

**opprimer** /ɔpʀime/ [1] vtr to oppress ⟨people⟩

**opter** /ɔpte/ [1] vi to opt

**opticien, -ienne** /ɔptisjɛ̃, ɛn/ nm,f optician

**optimal, ~e, mpl -aux** /ɔptimal, o/ adj optimum

**optimiser** /ɔptimize/ [1] vtr to optimize

**optimisme** /ɔptimism/ nm optimism

**optimiste** /ɔptimist/ adj optimistic

**option** /ɔpsjɔ̃/ nf option; **en ~** optional

**optique** /ɔptik/ [1] adj (a) (Anat) optic
(b) optical
[2] nf (a) optics
(b) perspective

**opulence** /ɔpylɑ̃s/ nf opulence

**or¹** /ɔʀ/ conj and yet; **~, ce jour-là, il...** now, on that particular day, he...

**or²** /ɔʀ/ [1] adj inv gold; ⟨hair⟩ golden
[2] nm (a) gold; **en ~** gold; ⟨husband⟩ marvellous (GB); ⟨opportunity⟩ golden
(b) gilding

**oracle** /ɔʀakl/ nm oracle

**orage** /ɔʀaʒ/ nm storm

**orageux, -euse** /ɔʀaʒø, øz/ *adj* stormy

**oraison** /ɔʀɛzõ/ *nf* prayer; ~ **funèbre** funeral oration

**oral, ~e,** *mpl* **-aux** /ɔʀal, o/ ⬜1 *adj*
(a) oral
(b) (Med) **par voie ~e** orally
⬜2 *nm* (Sch) oral (examination)

**oralement** /ɔʀalmã/ *adv* (a) (Med) orally
(b) verbally

**orange¹** /ɔʀãʒ/ *adj inv* orange; ⟨light⟩ amber (GB), yellow (US)

**orange²** /ɔʀãʒ/ *nf* orange

**orangeade** /ɔʀãʒad/ *nf* orangeade

**oranger** /ɔʀãʒe/ *nm* orange tree

**orangerie** /ɔʀãʒʀi/ *nf* orangery

**orateur, -trice** /ɔʀatœʀ, tʀis/ *nm,f*
(a) speaker
(b) orator

**orbite** /ɔʀbit/ *nf* (a) orbit
(b) eye-socket

**orchestral, ~e,** *mpl* **-aux** /ɔʀkɛstʀal, o/ *adj* orchestral

**orchestration** /ɔʀkɛstʀasjõ/ *nf* orchestration

**orchestre** /ɔʀkɛstʀ/ *nm* (a) orchestra
(b) band
(c) orchestra stalls (GB), orchestra (US)

**orchestrer** /ɔʀkɛstʀe/ [1] *vtr* to orchestrate

**orchidée** /ɔʀkide/ *nf* orchid

**ordinaire** /ɔʀdinɛʀ/ ⬜1 *adj* (a) ordinary; ⟨quality⟩ standard; ⟨reader, tourist⟩ average; **journée peu ~** unusual day
(b) **très ~** ⟨meal, wine⟩ very average; ⟨person⟩ very ordinary
⬜2 *nm* **sortir de l'~** to be out of the ordinary
⬜3 **à l'ordinaire, d'ordinaire** *phr* usually

**ordinal, ~e,** *mpl* **-aux** /ɔʀdinal, o/ *adj* ordinal

**ordinateur** /ɔʀdinatœʀ/ *nm* computer

**ordination** /ɔʀdinasjõ/ *nf* ordination

**ordonnance** /ɔʀdɔnãs/ *nf* prescription

**ordonner** /ɔʀdɔne/ [1] *vtr* (a) to order
(b) to put [sth] in order
(c) to ordain

**ordre** /ɔʀdʀ/ *nm* (a) (command) order; **j'ai des ~s** I'm acting under orders; **à vos ~s!** (Mil) yes, sir!; **jusqu'à nouvel ~** until further notice
(b) (sequence) order; **par ~ alphabétique** in alphabetical order
(c) tidiness, orderliness
(d) (orderly state) order; **rappeler qn à l'~** to reprimand sb; **tout est rentré dans l'~** everything is back to normal; **rétablir l'~ (public)** to restore law and order
(e) nature; **c'est dans l'~ des choses** it's in the nature of things; **de l'~ de 30%** in the order of 30% (GB), on the order of 30% (US); **de premier ~** first-rate
(f) (in religion) order; **entrer dans les ~s** to take (holy) orders

(g) **libellez le chèque à l'~ de X** make the cheque (GB) *or* check (US) payable to X
■ **~ du jour** agenda

**ordure** /ɔʀdyʀ/ ⬜1 *nf* filth
⬜2 **ordures** *nf pl* refuse (GB), garbage (US)

**ordurier, -ière** /ɔʀdyʀje, ɛʀ/ *adj* filthy

**orée** /ɔʀe/ *nf* (a) edge
(b) (figurative) start

**oreille** /ɔʀɛj/ *nf* (a) ear; **n'écouter que d'une ~** to half-listen; **ouvre-bien les ~s!** listen carefully
(b) hearing; **avoir l'~ fine** to have keen hearing
(c) **à l'abri des ~s indiscrètes** where no-one can hear
IDIOMS **tirer les ~s à qn** to tell sb off

**oreiller** /ɔʀɛje/ *nm* pillow

**oreillons** /ɔʀɛjõ/ *nm pl* mumps

**ores: d'ores et déjà** /dɔʀzedeʒa/ *phr* already

**orfèvre** /ɔʀfɛvʀ/ *nmf* goldsmith; **être ~ en la matière** to be an expert in the field

**orfèvrerie** /ɔʀfɛvʀəʀi/ *nf* (a) goldsmith's art
(b) goldsmith's and silversmith's

**organe** /ɔʀgan/ *nm* organ

**organigramme** /ɔʀganigʀam/ *nm* organization chart

**organique** /ɔʀganik/ *adj* organic

**organisation** /ɔʀganizasjõ/ *nf* organization

**organiser** /ɔʀganize/ [1] ⬜1 *vtr* to organize
⬜2 **s'organiser** *v refl* (+ *v être*)
(a) ⟨opposition⟩ to get organized
(b) to organize oneself
(c) ⟨fight, help⟩ to be organized

**organisme** /ɔʀganism/ *nm* (a) body
(b) organism
(c) organization, body

**orgasme** /ɔʀgasm/ *nm* orgasm

**orge** /ɔʀʒ/ *nf* barley

**orgie** /ɔʀʒi/ *nf* orgy

**orgue** /ɔʀg/ *nm* (Mus) organ

**orgueil** /ɔʀgœj/ *nm* pride

**orgueilleux, -euse** /ɔʀgœjø, øz/ *adj* overproud

**orient** /ɔʀjã/ *nm* (a) east
(b) **l'Orient** the East

**oriental, ~e,** *mpl* **-aux** /ɔʀjãtal, o/ *adj* eastern; oriental

**Oriental, ~e,** *mpl* **-aux** /ɔʀjãtal, o/ *nm,f* Asian; **les Orientaux** Asians

**orientation** /ɔʀjãtasjõ/ *nf* (a) (of house) aspect; (of aerial) angle
(b) (of inquiry) direction
(c) (Sch) **changer d'~** to change courses

**orienter** /ɔʀjãte/ [1] ⬜1 *vtr* (a) to adjust ⟨aerial, lamp⟩
(b) **~ la conversation sur** to bring the conversation around to
(c) to direct ⟨person⟩
(d) (Sch) to give [sb] career advice

⋯⟶

**s'orienter** *v refl* (+ *v être*) **(a)** to get *or* find one's bearings
**(b)** s'~ vers ⟨person⟩ to turn toward(s); s'~ vers les carrières scientifiques to go in for a career in science
**orifice** /ɔʀifis/ *nm* **(a)** orifice
**(b)** (of pipe) mouth; (of tube) neck
**originaire** /ɔʀiʒinɛʀ/ *adj* ⟨plant, animal⟩ native; famille ~ d'Asie Asian family
**original, ~e,** *mpl* **-aux** /ɔʀiʒinal, o/
1 *adj* **(a)** original
**(b)** eccentric
2 *nm* original
**originalité** /ɔʀiʒinalite/ *nf* originality
**origine** /ɔʀiʒin/ *nf* origin; être d'~ modeste to come from a modest background; dès l'~ right from the start; à l'~ originally
**originel, -elle** /ɔʀiʒinɛl/ *adj* original
**orme** /ɔʀm/ *nm* **(a)** elm (tree)
**(b)** elm (wood)
**ornement** /ɔʀnəmɑ̃/ *nm* **(a)** ornament
**(b)** decorative detail
**orner** /ɔʀne/ [1] *vtr* to decorate
**ornière** /ɔʀnjɛʀ/ *nf* rut
**ornithologie** /ɔʀnitɔlɔʒi/ *nf* ornithology
**ornithorynque** /ɔʀnitɔʀɛ̃k/ *nm* (duck-billed) platypus, duckbill (US)
**orphelin, ~e** /ɔʀfəlɛ̃, in/ *nm,f* orphan
**orphelinat** /ɔʀfəlina/ *nm* orphanage
**orque** /ɔʀk/ *nm or f* killer whale
**orteil** /ɔʀtɛj/ *nm* toe; gros ~ big toe
**orthodoxe** /ɔʀtɔdɔks/ *adj, nmf* Orthodox
**orthographe** /ɔʀtɔgʀaf/ *nf* spelling
**orthographier** /ɔʀtɔgʀafje/ [2] *vtr* to spell
**orthopédie** /ɔʀtɔpedi/ *nf* orthopedics
**orthophoniste** /ɔʀtɔfɔnist/ *nmf* speech therapist
**ortie** /ɔʀti/ *nf* (stinging) nettle
**orvet** /ɔʀvɛ/ *nm* slowworm, blindworm
**os** /ɔs, *pl* o/ *nm inv* bone; en chair et en ~ in the flesh
IDIOMS il y a un ~ (colloq) there's a hitch; tomber sur un ~ (colloq) to come across a snag; être trempé jusqu'aux ~ (colloq) to be soaked to the skin (colloq)
**osciller** /ɔsile/ [1] *vi* **(a)** ⟨pendulum⟩ to swing; ⟨boat⟩ to rock; ⟨head⟩ to roll from side to side
**(b)** ⟨currency⟩ to fluctuate
**(c)** to vacillate
**osé, ~e** /oze/ *adj* **(a)** risqué
**(b)** ⟨behaviour⟩ daring; ⟨words⟩ outspoken
**oseille** /ozɛj/ *nf* **(a)** sorrel
**(b)** (colloq) dough (colloq), money
**oser** /oze/ [1] *vtr* to dare; si j'ose dire if I may say so
**osier** /ozje/ *nm* **(a)** (tree) osier
**(b)** wicker, osier
**osmose** /ɔsmoz/ *nf* osmosis
**ossature** /ɔsatyʀ/ *nf* skeleton; ~ du visage bone structure
**ossements** /ɔsmɑ̃/ *nm pl* remains

**osseux, -euse** /ɔsø, øz/ *adj* **(a)** bony
**(b)** ⟨disease⟩ bone
**ostentatoire** /ɔstɑ̃tatwaʀ/ *adj* ostentatious
**ostéopathe** /ɔsteɔpat/ *nmf* osteopath
**ostracisme** /ɔstʀasism/ *nm* ostracism
**ostréiculture** /ɔstʀeikyltyʀ/ *nf* oyster farming
**otage** /ɔtaʒ/ *nm* hostage
**OTAN** /ɔtɑ̃/ *nf* (abbr = **Organisation du traité de l'Atlantique Nord**) NATO
**otarie** /ɔtaʀi/ *nf* eared seal, otary
**ôter** /ote/ [1] 1 *vtr* **(a)** to take off ⟨clothes, glasses⟩; to remove ⟨bones, stain⟩
**(b)** ~ qch à qn to take sth away from sb
**(c)** (in mathematics) 4 ôté de 9, il reste 5 9 minus *or* take away 4 leaves 5
2 **s'ôter** *v refl* (+ *v être*) s'~ qch de l'esprit to get sth out of one's mind *or* head
**otite** /ɔtit/ *nf* inflammation of the ear
**oto-rhino-laryngologiste,** *pl* ~s /otoʀinolaʀɛ̃gɔlɔʒist/ *nmf* ENT specialist
**ou** /u/ *conj* or; ~ (bien)... ~ (bien)... either... or...
**où** /u/ 1 *adv* where; je l'ai perdu je ne sais ~ I've lost it somewhere or other; par ~ êtes-vous passés pour venir? which way did you come?; ~ en êtes-vous? where have you got to?; ~ allons-nous? what are things coming to!
2 *rel pron* **(a)** where; le quartier ~ nous habitons the area we live in; d'~ s'élevait de la fumée out of which smoke was rising; ~ qu'ils aillent wherever they go
**(b)** la misère ~ elle se trouvait the poverty in which she was living; au train *or* à l'allure ~ vont les choses (at) the rate things are going; le travail s'est accumulé, d'~ ce retard there is a backlog of work, hence the delay
**(c)** when; le matin ~ je l'ai rencontré the morning I met him
**ouate** /wat/ *nf* **(a)** cotton wool (GB), cotton (US)
**(b)** wadding
**oubli** /ubli/ *nm* **(a)** l'~ de qch forgetting sth; (of duty) neglect of sth
**(b)** omission
**(c)** oblivion; tomber dans l'~ to be completely forgotten
**oublier** /ublije/ [2] 1 *vtr* **(a)** to forget ⟨name, date, fact⟩; to forget about ⟨worries, incident⟩; se faire ~ to keep a low profile
**(b)** to leave out ⟨person, detail⟩
**(c)** to neglect ⟨duty, friend⟩
2 **s'oublier** *v refl* (+ *v être*) **(a)** to be forgotten
**(b)** to leave oneself out
**oubliettes** /ublijɛt/ *nf pl* oubliette
**oued** /wɛd/ *nm* wadi
**ouest** /wɛst/ 1 *adj inv* west; western
2 *nm* **(a)** west
**(b)** l'Ouest the West
**ouf** /uf/ 1 *nm* faire ~ to breathe a sigh of relief

**2** *excl* phew!

**oui** /wi/ **1** *adv* yes; **alors c'est ~?** so the answer is yes?; **découvrir si ~ ou non** to discover whether or not; **dire ~ à qch** to welcome sth; **to agree to sth; faire ~ de la tête** to nod; **lui, prudent? un lâche, ~!** him, cautious? a coward, more like! (colloq); **je crois que ~** I think so
**2** *nm inv* **(a)** yes
**(b)** 'yes' vote; **le ~ l'a emporté** the ayes have it
IDIOMS **pour un ~ (ou) pour un non** ‹*get angry*› for the slightest thing; ‹*change one's mind*› at the drop of a hat

**ouï**, **~e** /wi/ ▶ OUÏR

**ouï-dire** /widir/ *nm inv* **par ~** by hearsay

**ouïe** /wi/ *nf* **(a)** hearing; **être tout ~** to be all ears
**(b)** (of fish) gill

**ouïr** /wir/ [38] *vtr* to hear; **j'ai ouï dire que** word has reached me that

**ouistiti** /wistiti/ *nm* marmoset

**ouragan** /uragɑ̃/ *nm* hurricane

**ourler** /urle/ [1] *vtr* to hem

**ourlet** /urlɛ/ *nm* hem

**ours** /urs/ *nm inv* **(a)** bear
**(b) il est un peu ~** he's a bit surly
■ **~ blanc** polar bear; **~ en peluche** teddy bear; **~ polaire** = **~ BLANC**
IDIOMS **vendre la peau de l'~ avant de l'avoir tué** (Proverb) to count one's chickens before they're hatched

**ourse** /urs/ *nf* she-bear

**oursin** /ursɛ̃/ *nm* (sea) urchin

**ourson** /ursɔ̃/ *nm* bear cub

**outil** /uti/ *nm* tool; **~ de travail** work tool

**outrage** /utraʒ/ *nm* insult
■ **~ à agent** verbal assault of a policeman

**outrager** /utraʒe/ [13] *vtr* to offend

**outrance** /utrɑ̃s/ *nf* **à ~** excessively

**outrancier**, **-ière** /utrɑ̃sje, ɛr/ *adj* extreme

**outre** /utr/ **1** *prep* in addition to
**2** *adv* **passer ~** to pay no heed
**3** **outre mesure** *phr* unduly
**4** **en outre** *phr* in addition

**outre-Atlantique** /utratlɑ̃tik/ *adv* across the Atlantic; **d'~** American

**outre-Manche** /utrəmɑ̃ʃ/ *adv* across the Channel; **d'~** British

**outremer** /utrəmɛr/ *adj inv, nm* ultramarine

**outre-mer** /utrəmɛr/ *adv* overseas

**outrer** /utre/ [1] *vtr* **(a)** to outrage
**(b)** to exaggerate

**outre-tombe** /utrətɔ̃b/ *adv* **une voix d'~** a voice from beyond the grave

**ouvert**, **~e** /uvɛr, ɛrt/ **1** *pp* ▶ OUVRIR
**2** *pp adj* **(a)** open; **grand ~** wide open; **être ~ aux idées nouvelles** to be open to new ideas
**(b)** ‹*gas*› on; ‹*tap*› running
**(c)** ‹*question*› open-ended

**ouvertement** /uvɛrtəmɑ̃/ *adv* openly; blatantly

**ouverture** /uvɛrtyr/ *nf* **(a)** opening; **heures d'~** opening hours
**(b)** openness; **~ d'esprit** open-mindedness; **~ à l'Ouest** opening-up to the West
**(c)** (Mus) overture

**ouvrable** /uvrabl/ *adj* ‹*day*› working; ‹*hours*› business

**ouvrage** /uvraʒ/ *nm* **(a)** work
**(b)** book, work
**(c)** piece of work; **~ de broderie** piece of embroidery
IDIOMS **avoir du cœur à l'~** to work with a will

**ouvragé**, **~e** /uvraʒe/ *adj* finely wrought

**ouvrant**, **~e** /uvrɑ̃, ɑ̃t/ *adj* **toit ~** sunroof

**ouvré**, **~e** /uvre/ *adj* **jour ~** working day

**ouvre-boîtes** /uvrəbwat/ *nm inv* can-opener

**ouvreur**, **-euse** /uvrœr, øz/ *nm,f* usher/usherette

**ouvrier**, **-ière** /uvrije, ɛr/ **1** *adj* of the workers; **classe ouvrière** working class
**2** *nm,f* worker; workman

**ouvrir** /uvrir/ [32] **1** *vtr* (gen) to open; to undo ‹*collar, shirt, zip*›; to initiate ‹*dialogue*›; to open up ‹*possibilities, market*›; **ne pas ~ la bouche** not to say a word; **~ les bras à qn** to welcome sb with open arms; **~ l'esprit à qn** to open sb's mind
**2** *vi* **(a)** to open the door; **ouvre-moi!** let me in!
**(b)** to open
**(c)** to be opened
**3** **s'ouvrir** *v refl* (+ *v être*) (gen) to open; ‹*shirt, dress*› to come undone; ‹*dialogue, process*› to be initiated; ‹*country, economy*› to open up; ‹*ground, scar*› to open up; ‹*person*› to cut open ‹*head*›; **s'~ les veines** to slash one's wrists; **s'~ à qn** to open one's heart to sb

**ovaire** /ovɛr/ *nm* ovary

**ovale** /oval/ *adj, nm* oval

**ovation** /ovasjɔ̃/ *nf* **(a)** ovation
**(b)** accolade

**ovationner** /ovasjone/ [1] *vtr* to greet [sb/sth] with wild applause

**ovni** /ovni/ *nm* (*abbr* = **objet volant non identifié**) unidentified flying object, UFO

**ovulation** /ovylasjɔ̃/ *nf* ovulation

**ovule** /ovyl/ *nm* **(a)** (Anat) ovum
**(b)** (Bot) ovule

**oxyde** /oksid/ *nm* oxide; **~ de carbone** carbon monoxide

**oxyder** /okside/ [1] *vtr*, **s'oxyder** *v refl* (+ *v être*) to oxidize

**oxygène** /oksiʒɛn/ *nm* **(a)** oxygen
**(b)** air

**oxygéner** /oksiʒene/ [14] **1** *vtr* to oxygenate ┄┄┊>

**2 s'oxygéner** *v refl* (+ *v être*) ⟨*person*⟩ to get some fresh air

**ozone** /ozon/ *nf* ozone; **la couche d'~** the ozone layer

# Pp

**p, P** /pe/ *nm inv* p, P

**PAC** *nf* (*abbr* **politique agricole commune**) CAP

**pacha** /paʃa/ *nm* pasha

**pachyderme** /paʃidɛʀm/ *nm* (Zool) pachyderm; **de ~** (figurative) heavy

**pacifier** /pasifje/ [1] *vtr* to establish peace in

**pacifique** /pasifik/ **1** *adj* peaceful
**2** *nmf* peace-loving person

**Pacifique** /pasifik/ *pr nm* **le ~** the Pacific

**pacifiste** /pasifist/ *adj, nmf* pacifist

**pacotille** /pakɔtij/ *nf* **de la ~** cheap rubbish

**pacte** /pakt/ *nm* pact

**PAF** /paf/ **1** *nm: abbr* ▶ PAYSAGE
**2** *nf: abbr* ▶ POLICE

**pagaie** /pagɛ/ *nf* (Naut) paddle

**pagaille** (colloq) /pagɑj/ **1** *nf* mess; **semer la ~** to cause chaos
**2 en pagaille** *phr* in a mess

**paganisme** /paganism/ *nm* paganism

**pagayer** /pageje/ [21] *vi* to paddle

**page**[1] /paʒ/ *nm* page (boy)

**page**[2] /paʒ/ *nf* page; **en première ~** on the front page; **tourner la ~** (figurative) to turn over a new leaf
■ **~ d'accueil** (Comput) home page; **~ de publicité** commercial break
IDIOMS **être à la ~** to be up to date

**pagination** /paʒinasjɔ̃/ *nf* pagination

**paginer** /paʒine/ [1] *vtr* to paginate

**pagne** /paɲ/ *nm* (a) loincloth
(b) grass skirt

**pagode** /pagɔd/ *nf* pagoda

**paie** /pɛ/ *nf* pay; **bulletin** *or* **fiche de ~** payslip
IDIOMS **ça fait une ~ que je ne l'ai pas vu** (colloq) it's ages since I saw him (colloq)

**paiement** /pɛmɑ̃/ *nm* payment

**païen, -ïenne** /pajɛ̃, ɛn/ *adj, nm,f* pagan

**paillard, ~e** /pajaʀ, aʀd/ *adj* bawdy

**paillasse** /pajas/ *nf* (a) straw mattress
(b) lab bench
(c) draining board

**paillasson** /pajasɔ̃/ *nm* doormat

**paille** /pɑj/ **1** *adj inv* **jaune ~** straw yellow
**2** *nf* straw; **~ de fer** steel wool
IDIOMS **être sur la ~** (colloq) to be penniless; **tirer à la courte ~** to draw lots

**paillette** /pajɛt/ *nf* (a) sequin, spangle (US); **robe à ~s** sequined *or* spangled (US) dress
(b) glitter
(c) **savon en ~s** soap flakes

**pain** /pɛ̃/ *nm* (a) bread; **des miettes de ~** breadcrumbs
(b) loaf; **un petit ~** a (bread) roll
(c) **~ de viande** meat loaf
(d) (of soap) bar
■ **~ blanc** white bread; **~ de campagne** farmhouse bread; **~ complet** wholemeal bread; **~ d'épices** gingerbread; **~ grillé** toast; **~ au lait** milk roll; **~ de mie** sandwich loaf; **~ de seigle** rye bread; **~ de son** bran bread
IDIOMS **se vendre comme des petits ~s** to sell like hot cakes; **ça ne mange pas de ~** (colloq) it doesn't cost anything; **je ne mange pas de ce ~-là** (colloq) I won't have anything to do with it

**pair, ~e**[1] /pɛʀ/ **1** *adj* ⟨*number*⟩ even
**2** *nm* (a) peer; **c'est une cuisinière hors ~** she's an excellent cook
(b) **aller** *or* **marcher de ~ avec qch** to go hand in hand with sth
**3 au pair** *phr* **travailler au ~** to work as an au pair

**paire**[2] /pɛʀ/ *nf* pair; **donner une ~ de gifles à qn** to box sb's ears
IDIOMS **les deux font la ~!** they're two of a kind!

**paisible** /pɛzibl/ *adj* peaceful, quiet, calm

**paisiblement** /pɛziblǝmɑ̃/ *adv* peacefully

**paître** /pɛtʀ/ [74] *vi* to graze
IDIOMS **envoyer ~ qn** (colloq) to send sb packing (colloq)

**paix** /pɛ/ *nf inv* peace; **avoir la ~** to get some peace; **laisser qn en ~** to leave sb alone; **la ~!** (colloq) be quiet!

**pakistanais, ~e** /pakistanɛ, ɛz/ *adj* Pakistani

**palabrer** /palabʀe/ [1] *vi* to discuss endlessly

**palace** /palas/ *nm* luxury hotel

**palais** /palɛ/ *nm inv* (a) palate
(b) palace
(c) (Law) **~ (de justice)** law courts
■ **~ des sports** sports centre (GB)

**palan** /palɑ̃/ *nm* hoist

**pale** /pal/ *nf* (of propeller, oar) blade

**pâle** /pɑl/ *adj* pale; **vert ~** pale green
IDIOMS **faire ~ figure à côté de** to pale into insignificance beside

**palefrenier, -ière** /palfʀənje, ɛʀ/ nm,f
groom
**paléolithique** /paleɔlitik/ adj, nm
Paleolithic
**paléontologie** /paleɔ̃tɔlɔʒi/ nf
paleontology
**palet** /palɛ/ nm (a) (in ice hockey) puck
(b) quoit
**paletot** /palto/ nm jacket
IDIOMS tomber sur le ∼ de qn (colloq) to lay
into sb (colloq)
**palette** /palɛt/ nf (a) palette
(b) range; une ∼ d'activités a range of
activities
(c) (of pork, mutton) ≈ shoulder
**pâleur** /pɑlœʀ/ nf paleness; pallor
**palier** /palje/ nm (a) landing; mon voisin
de ∼ my neighbour (GB) on the same floor
(b) level; plateau
(c) (in diving) ∼ (de décompression)
(decompression) stage
**palière** /paljɛʀ/ adj f porte ∼ entry door
**pâlir** /pɑliʀ/ [3] vi (a) to fade
(b) to grow pale
**palissade** /palisad/ nf fence
**palliatif** /paljatif/ nm palliative
**pallier** /palje/ [2] vtr to compensate for
**palmarès** /palmaʀɛs/ nm inv (a) honours
(GB) list; list of (award) winners
(b) record of achievements
(c) hit parade
(d) bestsellers list
**palme** /palm/ nf (a) palm leaf
(b) palm (tree)
(c) (for diver) flipper
(d) (Mil) ≈ bar
(e) prize
**palmé, ∼e** /palme/ adj (a) ⟨feet⟩ webbed
(b) ⟨leaf⟩ palmate
**palmier** /palmje/ nm palm (tree)
**palombe** /palɔ̃b/ nf wood pigeon
**palourde** /paluʀd/ nf clam
**palpable** /palpabl/ adj palpable; tangible
**palper** /palpe/ [1] vtr (a) (Med) to palpate
(b) to feel
**palpitant, ∼e** /palpitɑ̃, ɑ̃t/ adj thrilling
**palpitation** /palpitasjɔ̃/ nf (a) (Med)
palpitation
(b) twitching
**palpiter** /palpite/ [1] vi ⟨heart⟩ to beat; to
flutter; ⟨vein⟩ to pulse
**paludisme** /palydism/ nm malaria
**pâmer: se pâmer** /pɑme/ [1] v refl
(+ v être) se ∼ devant qch to swoon over sth
**pamphlet** /pɑ̃flɛ/ nm satirical tract
**pamphlétaire** /pɑ̃fletɛʀ/ nmf
pamphleteer
**pamplemousse** /pɑ̃pləmus/ nm
grapefruit
**pan** /pɑ̃/ 1 nm (a) (of cliff, house) section;
(of life) part
(b) (of tower) side; ∼s d'un manteau coat-tails

2 excl (also onomatopoeic) bang!; thump!;
whack!
**pan-** /pɑ̃, pan/ pref Pan; ∼-russe Pan-
Russian; ∼-européen Pan-European
**panacée** /panase/ nf panacea
**panache** /panaʃ/ nm (a) panache
(b) plume
**panaché, ∼e** /panaʃe/ 1 adj ⟨bouquet,
salad⟩ mixed; ⟨tulip, ivy⟩ variegated
2 nm shandy (GB), shandygaff (US)
**panacher** /panaʃe/ [1] vtr to mix
**panama** /panama/ nm panama (hat)
**panaris** /panaʀi/ nm inv whitlow
**pancarte** /pɑ̃kaʀt/ nf (a) notice (GB), sign
(US)
(b) placard (GB), sign (US)
**pancréas** /pɑ̃kʀeas/ nm inv pancreas
**panda** /pɑ̃da/ nm panda
**paner** /pane/ [1] vtr to coat with
breadcrumbs
**panier** /panje/ nm (a) basket
(b) (in dishwasher) rack
(c) (Sport) basket
■ ∼ à linge linen basket; ∼ à salade salad
shaker; Black Maria (GB), paddy wagon (US)
IDIOMS être un ∼ percé (colloq) to spend
money like water; ils sont tous à mettre
dans le même ∼ (colloq) they are all about
the same; le dessus du ∼ (colloq) the pick of
the bunch; mettre au ∼ to throw [sth] out; to
get rid of [sth]
**panique** /panik/ nf panic; semer or jeter la
∼ to spread panic; être pris de ∼ to be
panic-stricken
**paniquer** /panike/ [1] vi (colloq) to panic
**panne** /pan/ nf (of vehicle, machine)
breakdown; (of engine) failure; ∼ de courant
power failure; tomber en ∼ sèche or
d'essence to run out of petrol (GB) or gas
(US); être en ∼ de (colloq) to be out of
⟨coffee⟩; to have run out of ⟨ideas⟩
**panneau, pl ∼x** /pano/ nm (a) sign;
board
(b) notice board
(c) panel
■ ∼ indicateur signpost; ∼ publicitaire
hoarding (GB), billboard; ∼ de signalisation
routière road sign; ∼ solaire solar panel
IDIOMS tomber dans le ∼ (colloq) to fall for it
(colloq)
**panonceau, pl ∼x** /panɔ̃so/ nm sign;
board
**panoplie** /panɔpli/ nf (a) outfit
(b) display of weapons
**panorama** /panɔʀama/ nm (a) panorama
(b) (of art, culture) survey
**panoramique** /panɔʀamik/ adj (a) ⟨view,
visit⟩ panoramic
(b) ⟨windscreen⟩ wrap-around
(c) ⟨screen⟩ wide
**panse** /pɑ̃s/ nf (a) (of cow) paunch
(b) (colloq) belly (colloq)
(c) (of jug) belly

**p**

**pansement** /pɑ̃smɑ̃/ *nm* dressing; ~ **(adhésif)** plaster (GB), Band-Aid®

**panser** /pɑ̃se/ [1] *vtr* to dress ⟨*wound*⟩; to put a dressing on ⟨*arm, leg*⟩

**pantalon** /pɑ̃talɔ̃/ *nm* trousers (GB), pants (US); ~ **de pyjama** pyjama (GB) *or* pajama (US) bottoms

**panthère** /pɑ̃tɛʀ/ *nf* panther

**pantin** /pɑ̃tɛ̃/ *nm* puppet

**pantois, ~e** /pɑ̃twa, az/ *adj* flabbergasted

**pantomime** /pɑ̃tɔmim/ *nf* **(a)** mime
**(b)** mime show

**pantouflard, ~e** /pɑ̃tuflaʀ, aʀd/ *adj* (colloq) **qu'est-ce que tu es ~!** what a stay-at-home you are!

**pantoufle** /pɑ̃tufl/ *nf* slipper

**panure** /panyʀ/ *nf* breadcrumbs

**PAO** /peao/ *nf* **(a)** *abbr* ▶ PRODUCTION
**(b)** *abbr* ▶ PUBLICATION

**paon** /pɑ̃/ *nm* peacock

**paonne** /pan/ *nf* peahen

**papa** /papa/ *nm* dad (colloq), daddy (colloq), father; **fils** *or* **fille à ~** spoiled little rich kid (colloq)

**pape** /pap/ *nm* **(a)** pope
**(b)** (figurative) high priest

**paperasse** /papʀas/ *nf* (colloq) **(a)** bumph (GB) (colloq), documents
**(b)** paperwork

**papeterie** /papɛtʀi/ *nf* **(a)** stationer's (shop), stationery shop (GB) *or* store (US)
**(b)** stationery
**(c)** papermaking industry
**(d)** paper mill

**papi** /papi/ *nm* (colloq) granddad (colloq), grandpa (colloq)

**papier** /papje/ *nm* **(a)** paper
**(b)** ~**s (d'identité)** (identity) papers *or* documents
**(c)** (colloq) (newspaper) article, piece (colloq)
■ ~ **alu** (colloq), ~ **(d')aluminium** aluminium (GB) *or* aluminum (US) foil, kitchen foil; ~ **brouillon** rough paper (GB), scrap paper; ~ **cadeau** gift wrap; ~ **d'emballage** wrapping paper; ~ **hygiénique** toilet paper; ~ **journal** newsprint; ~ **à lettres** writing paper; ~ **peint** wallpaper; ~ **de verre** sandpaper; ~**s gras** litter
IDIOMS **être dans les petits ~s de qn** (colloq) to be in sb's good books; ▶ MUSIQUE

**papier-calque**, *pl* **papiers-calque** /papjekalk/ *nm* tracing paper

**papillon** /papijɔ̃/ *nm* **(a)** butterfly; ~ **de nuit** moth
**(b)** (brasse) ~ butterfly (stroke)

**papillonner** /papijɔne/ [1] *vi* **(a)** to flit about
**(b)** to flirt incessantly

**papillote** /papijɔt/ *nf* **(a)** (Culin) foil parcel
**(b)** (for hair) curlpaper

**papoter** /papɔte/ [1] *vi* (colloq) to chatter

**paprika** /papʀika/ *nm* paprika

**papy** = PAPI

**Pâque** /pɑk/ *nf* **la ~ juive** Passover

**paquebot** /pakbo/ *nm* liner

**pâquerette** /pakʀɛt/ *nf* daisy
IDIOMS **être au ras des ~s** (colloq) to be very basic

**Pâques** /pɑk/ *nm*, *nf pl* Easter

**paquet** /pakɛ/ *nm* **(a)** packet (GB), package (US); (of cigarettes, coffee) packet (GB), pack (US)
**(b)** parcel
**(c)** (of clothes) bundle
**(d)** (colloq) masses
**(e)** (colloq) packet (GB) (colloq), bundle (US) (colloq)
■ ~ **de muscles** (colloq) muscleman
IDIOMS **mettre le ~** (colloq) to pull out all the stops

**paquet-cadeau**, *pl* **paquets-cadeaux** /pakɛkado/ *nm* gift-wrapped present

**par** /paʀ/ **1** *prep* **(a)** **elle est arrivée ~ la droite** she came from the right; **le peintre a terminé** *or* **fini ~ la cuisine** the painter did the kitchen last
**(b)** ~ **le passé** in the past; ~ **une belle journée d'été** on a beautiful summer's day; **ils sortent même ~ moins 40°** they go outdoors even when it's minus 40°
**(c)** per; ~ **jour/an** a day/year; ~ **personne** per person
**(d)** by; **payer ~ carte de crédit** to pay by credit card; **être pris ~ son travail** to be taken up with one's work; **deux ~ deux** ⟨*work*⟩ in twos; ⟨*walk*⟩ two by two
**(e)** in; ~ **étapes** in stages; ~ **endroits** in places
**(f)** **l'accident est arrivé ~ sa faute** it was his/her fault that the accident happened; ~ **jalousie** out of jealousy
**(g)** through; **tu peux me faire passer le livre ~ ta sœur** you can get the book to me via your sister; **entre ~ le garage** come in through the garage
**2** **de par** *phr* (formal) **(a)** **voyager de ~ le monde** to travel all over the world
**(b)** **de ~ leurs origines** by virtue of their origins

**parabole** /paʀabɔl/ *nf* **(a)** parable
**(b)** parabola

**parachever** /paʀaʃve/ [16] *vtr* **(a)** to complete
**(b)** to put the finishing touches to

**parachutage** /paʀaʃytaʒ/ *nm* airdrop

**parachute** /paʀaʃyt/ *nm* parachute

**parachuter** /paʀaʃyte/ [1] *vtr* to parachute

**parachutisme** /paʀaʃytism/ *nm* parachuting

**parachutiste** /paʀaʃytist/ *nmf*
**(a)** parachutist
**(b)** paratrooper

**parade** /paʀad/ *nf* **(a)** (Mil) parade
**(b)** (in fencing) parry
**(c)** (by animal) display

**parader** /paʀade/ [1] *vi* to strut about

**p**

**paradis** /paʀadi/ nm inv **(a)** heaven
**(b)** paradise
■ ~ **terrestre** Garden of Eden
**IDIOMS tu ne l'emporteras pas au** ~ (colloq)
you'll live to regret it

**paradisiaque** /paʀadizjak/ adj heavenly

**paradoxal,** ~**e,** mpl **-aux** /paʀadɔksal,
o/ adj paradoxical

**paradoxe** /paʀadɔks/ nm paradox

**paraffine** /paʀafin/ nf **(a)** paraffin (GB),
kerosene (US)
**(b)** paraffin wax

**parages** /paʀaʒ/ nm pl neighbourhood
(GB); **elle est dans les** ~ she is around
somewhere

**paragraphe** /paʀagʀaf/ nm paragraph

**paraître** /paʀɛtʀ/ [73] **1** vi **(a)** to come
out, to be published; **'à** ~**'** 'forthcoming
titles'
**(b)** to appear, to seem, to look
**(c)** to appear; to show; **elle ne laisse rien** ~
**de ses sentiments** she doesn't let her
feelings show at all; ~ **en public** to appear
in public; ~ **à son avantage** to look one's
best
**2** v impers **il paraît qu'il a menti** apparently
he lied; **oui, il paraît** so I hear

**parallèle¹** /paʀalɛl/ **1** adj **(a)** parallel
**(b)** ⟨market⟩ unofficial; ⟨medicine⟩
alternative
**2** nm parallel

**parallèle²** /paʀalɛl/ nf parallel line

**parallèlement** /paʀalɛlmã/ adv **(a)** ~ **à**
parallel to
**(b)** at the same time

**paralyser** /paʀalize/ [1] vtr **(a)** (Med) to
paralyse (GB)
**(b)** to paralyse (GB) [sth]; to bring [sth] to a
halt

**paralysie** /paʀalizi/ nf paralysis

**paralytique** /paʀalitik/ adj, nmf paralytic

**paramédical,** ~**e,** mpl **-aux**
/paʀamedikal, o/ adj paramedical

**paramètre** /paʀamɛtʀ/ nm parameter

**paranoïaque** /paʀanɔjak/ adj, nmf
paranoiac

**paranormal,** ~**e,** mpl **-aux**
/paʀanɔʀmal, o/ adj paranormal

**parapente** /paʀapãt/ nm **(a)** paraglider
**(b)** paragliding

**paraphe** /paʀaf/ nm **(a)** initials
**(b)** signature

**paraphrase** /paʀafʀɑz/ nf paraphrase

**paraplégique** /paʀapleʒik/ adj, nmf
paraplegic

**parapluie** /paʀaplɥi/ nm umbrella

**parascolaire** /paʀaskɔlɛʀ/ adj
extracurricular

**parasitaire** /paʀazitɛʀ/ adj parasitic(al)

**parasite** /paʀazit/ **1** adj ⟨organism⟩
parasitic(al); ⟨idea⟩ intrusive
**2** nm **(a)** parasite
**(b)** (on TV, radio) ~**s** interference

**parasol** /paʀasɔl/ nm beach umbrella; sun
umbrella

**paratonnerre** /paʀatɔnɛʀ/ nm lightning
rod

**paravent** /paʀavã/ nm screen

**parc** /paʀk/ nm **(a)** park
**(b)** playpen
**(c)** (for animals) pen
**(d)** (of facilities) (total) number; (of capital goods)
stock; ~ **automobile** fleet of cars; (nationwide)
number of cars (on the road); ~ **immobilier**
housing stock
■ ~ **d'attractions** amusement or theme park;
~ **de loisirs** theme park; ~ **national** national
park; ~ **naturel** nature park

**parce: parce que** /paʀs(ə)k(ə)/ phr
because

**parcelle** /paʀsɛl/ nf **(a)** plot (of land)
**(b)** une ~ **de bonheur** a bit of happiness

**parchemin** /paʀʃəmɛ̃/ nm parchment

**par-ci** /paʀsi/ adv ~ **par-là** here and there

**parcimonie** /paʀsimɔni/ nf parsimony

**parcmètre** /paʀkmɛtʀ/ nm parking meter

**parcourir** /paʀkuʀiʀ/ [26] vtr **(a)** to travel
all over ⟨country⟩; ~ **la ville** to go all over
town
**(b)** to cover ⟨distance⟩
**(c)** to glance through ⟨letter⟩; to scan
⟨horizon⟩

**parcours** /paʀkuʀ/ nm inv **(a)** (of bus,
traveller) route; (of river) course; ~ **fléché**
waymarked trail
**(b)** (Sport) course; ~ **de golf** round of golf
**(c)** career; **son** ~ (of artist) the development
of his/her art; **incident de** ~ hitch

**par-delà** /paʀdəla/ prep beyond

**par-derrière** /paʀdɛʀjɛʀ/ adv **(a)** passer
~ to go round (GB) or to the back; **ils m'ont
attaqué** ~ they attacked me from behind
**(b)** critiquer qn ~ to criticize sb behind his/
her back

**par-dessous** /paʀdəsu/ prep, adv
underneath

**pardessus** /paʀdəsy/ nm inv overcoat

**par-dessus** /paʀdəsy/ **1** adv **(a)** pose
**ton sac dans un coin et mets ton manteau** ~
put your bag in a corner and put your coat
on top of it
**(b)** le mur n'est pas haut, passe ~ the wall
isn't high, climb over it
**2** prep **(a)** saute ~ le ruisseau jump over
the stream
**(b)** ce que j'aime ~ tout what I like best of
all

**par-devant** /paʀdəvã/ adv **(a)** passer ~
to come round by the front
**(b)** il te fait des sourires ~ mais dit du mal
de toi dans ton dos he's all smiles to your
face but says nasty things about you behind
your back

**pardon** /paʀdɔ̃/ nm **(a)** forgiveness;
pardon; **je te demande** ~ I'm sorry
**(b)** ~**!** sorry!; ~ **madame/monsieur, je
cherche...** excuse me please, I'm looking
for...

p

**pardonnable** /paʁdɔnabl/ *adj* forgivable;
**ils ne sont pas ~s** it's unforgivable of them

**pardonner** /paʁdɔne/ [1] **1** *vtr* to forgive;
**pardonnez-moi, mais...** excuse me, but...
**2** *vi* **ne pas ~** ⟨*illness, error*⟩ to be fatal

**pare-balles** /paʁbal/ *adj inv* bulletproof

**pare-brise** /paʁbʁiz/ *nm inv* windscreen
(GB), windshield (US)

**pare-chocs** /paʁʃɔk/ *nm inv* bumper

**pareil, -eille** /paʁɛj/ **1** *adj* **(a)** similar;
**c'est toujours ~ avec toi** it's always the
same with you; **à nul autre ~** without equal
**(b)** such; **je n'ai jamais dit une chose pareille**
I never said any such thing
**2** *nm,f* equal; **d'un dynamisme sans ~**
incredibly dynamic; **pour moi c'est du ~ au
même** (colloq) it makes no difference to me
**3** *adv* (colloq) **faire ~** to do the same

**parent, ~e** /paʁɑ̃, ɑ̃t/ **1** *adj* ⟨*languages*⟩
similar; **~ avec** ⟨*person*⟩ related to
**2** *nm,f* **(a)** relative, relation
**(b)** (Zool) parent
**3** *nm* **(a)** parent
**(b)** **~s** forebears
■ **~ pauvre** poor relation

**parental, ~e**, *mpl* **-aux** /paʁɑ̃tal, o/ *adj*
parental

**parenté** /paʁɑ̃te/ *nf* **(a)** (between people)
blood relationship
**(b)** (between stories) connection

**parenthèse** /paʁɑ̃tɛz/ *nf* **(a)** bracket;
**ouvrir une ~** (figurative) to digress; **entre ~s**
(figurative) incidentally
**(b)** interlude

**parer** /paʁe/ [1] **1** *vtr* **(a)** to ward off
**(b)** to protect
**(c)** to adorn
**(d)** **~ qn/qch de qch** to attribute sth to sb/
sth
**2** **parer à** *v+prep* **~ à toute éventualité** to
be prepared for all contingencies; **~ au plus
pressé** to deal with the most urgent matters
first

**pare-soleil** /paʁsɔlɛj/ *nm inv* visor

**paresse** /paʁɛs/ *nf* laziness

**paresser** /paʁese/ [1] *vi* to laze (around)

**paresseux, -euse** /paʁesø, øz/ **1** *adj*
lazy
**2** *nm,f* lazy person
**3** *nm* (Zool) sloth

**parfaire** /paʁfɛʁ/ [10] *vtr* to complete
⟨*education, works*⟩; to perfect ⟨*technique*⟩

**parfait, ~e** /paʁfɛ, ɛt/ **1** *adj* **(a)** perfect
**(b)** ⟨*likeness*⟩ exact; ⟨*discretion*⟩ absolute
**(c)** ⟨*tourist*⟩ archetypal; ⟨*example*⟩ classic
**2** *nm* (in grammar) perfect

**parfaitement** /paʁfɛtmɑ̃/ *adv* ⟨*happy,
capable*⟩ perfectly; ⟨*tolerate, accept*⟩ fully

**parfois** /paʁfwa/ *adv* sometimes

**parfum** /paʁfœ̃/ *nm* **(a)** perfume
**(b)** (of flower, fruit) scent; (of bath salts)
fragrance; (of wine) bouquet; (of coffee) aroma
**(c)** flavour (GB)

IDIOMS **mettre qn au ~** (colloq) to put sb in
the picture

**parfumé, ~e** /paʁfyme/ **1** *pp* ▶
PARFUMER
**2** *pp adj* **(a)** ⟨*flower*⟩ sweet-scented; ⟨*fruit,
air*⟩ fragrant
**(b)** ⟨*handkerchief*⟩ scented
**(c)** **glace ~e au café** coffee-flavoured (GB) ice
cream

**parfumer** /paʁfyme/ [1] **1** *vtr* **(a)** **les
fleurs parfument la pièce** the room is
fragrant with flowers
**(b)** to put scent on ⟨*handkerchief*⟩; to put
scent in ⟨*bath*⟩
**(c)** to flavour (GB)
**2** **se parfumer** *v refl* (+ *v être*) **(a)** to
wear perfume
**(b)** to put perfume on

**parfumerie** /paʁfymʁi/ *nf* perfumery

**pari** /paʁi/ *nm* **(a)** bet
**(b)** betting
**(c)** gamble

**parier** /paʁje/ [2] *vtr* to bet; **il y a fort** *or*
**gros à ~ que** it's a safe bet that; **je l'aurais
parié!** I knew it!

**Paris** /paʁi/ *pr n* Paris

**parisien, -ienne** /paʁizjɛ̃, ɛn/ *adj*
Parisian, Paris

**parité** /paʁite/ *nf* parity; **à ~** at parity

**parjure** /paʁʒyʁ/ *nm* perjury

**parking** /paʁkiŋ/ *nm* car park (GB),
parking lot (US)

**par-là** /paʁla/ *adv* **par-ci ~** here and there

**parlant, ~e** /paʁlɑ̃, ɑ̃t/ *adj* **(a)** ⟨*gesture*⟩
eloquent; ⟨*evidence, figure*⟩ which speaks for
itself
**(b)** **le cinéma ~** the talkies (colloq); **un film ~**
a talking picture

**Parlement** /paʁləmɑ̃/ *nm* Parliament

**parlementaire** /paʁləmɑ̃tɛʁ/ **1** *adj*
parliamentary
**2** *nmf* **(a)** Member of Parliament
**(b)** negotiator

**parlementer** /paʁləmɑ̃te/ [1] *vi* to
negotiate

**parler** /paʁle/ [1] **1** *vtr* **(a)** to speak;
**~ (l')italien** to speak Italian
**(b)** **~ affaires/politique** to talk (about)
business/politics
**2** **parler à** *v+prep* **~ à qn** to talk *or* speak
to sb
**3** **parler de** *v+prep* **(a)** **~ de qn/qch** to
talk about sb/sth; to mention sb/sth; **~ de
tout et de rien, ~ de choses et d'autres** to
talk about this and that; **les journaux en ont
parlé** it was in the papers; **faire ~ de soi** to
get oneself talked about; to make the news;
**qui parle de vous expulser?** who said
anything about throwing you out?; **ta
promesse, parlons-en!** some promise!; **n'en
parlons plus!** let's drop it; that's the end of
it; **on m'a beaucoup parlé de vous** I've heard
a lot about you
**(b)** **~ de** ⟨*book, film*⟩ to be about
**4** *vi* to talk, to speak; **parle plus fort** speak

up, speak louder; ~ **en connaissance de
cause** to know what one is talking about;
**une prime? tu parles!** (colloq) a bonus? you
must be joking! (colloq); **il s'écoute** ~ he
loves the sound of his own voice
**5 se parler** *v refl* (+ *v être*) **(a)** to talk *or*
speak (to each other)
**(b)** to be on speaking terms
**(c)** ‹*language, dialect*› to be spoken
IDIOMS **trouver à qui** ~ to meet one's match
**parloir** /paʀlwaʀ/ *nm* (in school) visitors'
room; (in prison) visiting room; (in convent)
parlour (GB)
**parme** /paʀm/ *adj inv, nm* mauve
**Parmentier** /paʀmɑ̃tje/ *pr n* **hachis** ~
cottage pie, shepherd's pie
**parmi** /paʀmi/ *prep* **(a)** among, amongst
**(b)** **demain il sera** ~ **nous** he'll be with us
tomorrow
**(c)** **choisir** ~ **huit destinations** to choose
from eight destinations
**parodie** /paʀɔdi/ *nf* **(a)** parody
**(b)** mockery
**parodier** /paʀɔdje/ [2] *vtr* to parody
**paroi** /paʀwa/ *nf* **(a)** (of tunnel) side; (of cave)
wall; (of tube, pipe) inner surface
**(b)** (of house) wall
**(c)** ~ **rocheuse** rock face
**(d)** (Anat) wall
**paroisse** /paʀwas/ *nf* parish
**paroissial**, ~**e**, *mpl* -**iaux** /paʀwasjal,
o/ *adj* parish
**parole** /paʀɔl/ *nf* **(a)** speech; **avoir la** ~
**facile** to have the gift of the gab (colloq)
**(b)** **laisser la** ~ **à qn** to let sb speak; **temps
de** ~ speaking time
**(c)** word; ~**s en l'air** empty words; **une** ~
**blessante** a hurtful remark
**(d)** (promise) word; **donner sa** ~ to give one's
word; ~ **d'honneur!** cross my heart!,
I promise!; **ma** ~**!** (upon) my word!
**(e)** words; **c'est** ~ **d'évangile** it's gospel
truth; ~**s** words, lyrics; **film sans** ~**s** silent
film
**parolier**, -**ière** /paʀɔlje, ɛʀ/ *nm,f* **(a)** lyric
writer
**(b)** librettist
**paroxysme** /paʀɔksism/ *nm* (of pleasure)
paroxysm; (of battle) climax; (of ridiculousness)
height
**parpaing** /paʀpɛ̃/ *nm* breeze-block, cinder
block
**parquer** /paʀke/ [1] *vtr* **(a)** to pen ‹*cattle*›
**(b)** to coop up ‹*people*›
**(c)** to park ‹*car*›
**parquet** /paʀkɛ/ *nm* **(a)** parquet (floor)
**(b)** (Law) **le** ~ ≈ the prosecution
**parrain** /paʀɛ̃/ *nm* **(a)** godfather
**(b)** (of candidate) sponsor; (of organization)
patron
**parrainer** /paʀene/ [1] *vtr* **(a)** to be patron
of ‹*organization*›
**(b)** to sponsor ‹*programme, race*›
**parricide** /paʀisid/ *nm* parricide

**parsemer** /paʀsəme/ [16] *vtr* **une pelouse
parsemée de fleurs** a lawn dotted with
flowers
**part** /paʀ/ **1** *nf* **(a)** (of cake) slice; (of meat,
rice) helping; (of market, legacy) share; **avoir sa**
~ **de misères** to have one's (fair) share of
misfortunes
**(b)** proportion; **une grande** ~ **de** a high
proportion *or* large part of; **pour une bonne**
~ to a large *or* great extent; **à** ~ **entière**
‹*member*› full; ‹*science*› in its own right
**(c)** share; **faire sa** ~ **de travail** to do one's
share of the work; **prendre** ~ **à** to take part
in; **il m'a fait** ~ **de ses projets** he told me
about his plans
**(d)** **de toute(s)** ~(**s**) from all sides; **de** ~ **et
d'autre** on both sides, on either side; **de** ~
**en** ~ ‹*pierce*› right *or* straight through
**(e)** **pour ma/notre** ~ for my/our part; **d'une**
~..., **d'autre** ~... on (the) one hand... on the
other hand...; **prendre qch en mauvaise** ~ to
take sth badly
**2 à part** *phr* **(a)** ‹*file*› separately; **mettre
qch à** ~ to put sth to one side; **prendre qn à**
~ to take sb aside; **une salle à** ~ a separate
room; **blague à** ~ joking aside
**(b)** **être un peu à** ~ ‹*person*› to be out of the
ordinary; **un cas à** ~ a special case
**(c)** apart from; **à** ~ **ça** apart from that
**3 de la part de** *phr* **(a)** **de la** ~ **de**
‹*write, act*› on behalf of
**(b)** **de la** ~ **de qn** from sb; **donne-leur le
bonjour de ma** ~ say hello to them for me;
**de leur** ~, **rien ne m'étonne** nothing they do
surprises me
IDIOMS **faire la** ~ **des choses** to put things
in perspective
**partage** /paʀtaʒ/ *nm* **(a)** dividing, sharing;
**recevoir qch en** ~ to be left sth (in a will)
**(b)** distribution
**(c)** sharing, division; **régner sans** ~ to reign
absolutely; **une victoire sans** ~ a total
victory
**(d)** division, partition
**partagé**, ~**e** /paʀtaʒe/ **1** *pp* ▸ PARTAGER
**2** *pp adj* **(a)** ‹*opinion, unions*› divided
**(b)** ‹*reactions, feelings*› mixed
**(c)** **être** ~ to be torn
**(d)** ‹*grief*› shared; **les torts sont** ~**s** they are
both to blame
**(e)** ‹*affection*› mutual
**partager** /paʀtaʒe/ [13] **1** *vtr* **(a)** to share;
**faire** ~ **qch à qn** to let sb share in sth; **il sait
nous faire** ~ **ses émotions** he knows how to
get his feelings across
**(b)** to divide ‹*country, room*›
**(c)** to divide [sth] (up), to split ‹*inheritance,
work*›
**2 se partager** *v refl* (+ *v être*) **(a)** to
share ‹*money, work, responsibility*›
**(b)** to be divided, to be shared
**(c)** ‹*costs, responsibility*› to be shared; ‹*cake*›
to be cut (up)
**partance** /paʀtɑ̃s/ *nf* **en** ~ about to take
off; about to sail; about to leave; **être en** ~
**pour** *or* **vers** to be bound for

**partenaire** /paʀtənɛʀ/ *nmf* partner; **qui était le ~ d'Arletty?** who played opposite Arletty?
■ **~s sociaux** ≈ unions and management

**partenariat** /paʀtənaʀja/ *nm* partnership

**parterre** /paʀtɛʀ/ *nm* **(a)** (in garden) bed
**(b)** stalls (GB), orchestra (US)

**parti, ~e¹** /paʀti/ **⓵** *adj* (colloq) **être ~** to be tight (colloq)
**⓶** *nm* **(a)** group; party; **les ~s de l'opposition** the opposition parties
**(b)** option; **prendre ~** to commit oneself; **prendre le ~ de qn** to side with sb
**(c) bon ~** suitable match
■ **~ pris** bias
IDIOMS **prendre son ~ de qch** to come to terms with sth; **tirer ~ de** to take advantage of [sth]; to turn [sth] to good account

**partial, ~e,** *mpl* **-iaux** /paʀsjal, o/ *adj* biased (GB)

**partialité** /paʀsjalite/ *nf* bias

**participant, ~e** /paʀtisipɑ̃, ɑ̃t/ *nm,f* participant

**participation** /paʀtisipasjɔ̃/ *nf*
**(a)** participation; involvement
**(b)** contribution; **~ aux frais** (financial) contribution

**participe** /paʀtisip/ *nm* participle; **~ passé** past participle

**participer** /paʀtisipe/ [1] *v+prep* **(a) ~ à** to participate in, to take part in; to be involved in
**(b) ~ à** to contribute to

**particularisme** /paʀtikylaʀism/ *nm* distinctive identity

**particularité** /paʀtikylaʀite/ *nf* **(a)** special feature
**(b)** (of disease, situation) particular nature

**particule** /paʀtikyl/ *nf* particle; **nom à ~** aristocratic name

**particulier, -ière** /paʀtikylje, ɛʀ/ **⓵** *adj*
**(a)** particular
**(b)** ⟨rights, privileges, role⟩ special; ⟨example, objective⟩ specific
**(c)** ⟨car, secretary⟩ private
**(d)** ⟨case, situation⟩ unusual; ⟨talent, effort⟩ special; ⟨habits⟩ odd; ⟨accent, style⟩ distinctive, unusual; **c'est quelqu'un de très ~** he's/she's somebody out of the ordinary; he's/she's weird
**⓶ en particulier** *phr* **(a)** in private
**(b)** individually
**(c)** in particular, particularly
**⓷** *nm* (simple) ~ private individual

**particulièrement** /paʀtikyljɛʀmɑ̃/ *adv*
**(a)** particularly, exceptionally
**(b)** in particular

**partie²** /paʀti/ **⓵** *adj f* ▶ PARTI 1
**⓶** *nf* **(a)** part; (of amount, salary) proportion, part; **la majeure ~ des gens** most people; **en ~** partly, in part; **faire ~ des premiers** to be among the first; **cela fait ~ de leurs avantages** that's one of their advantages
**(b)** line (of work); **il est de la ~** it's in his line (of work)

**(c)** game; **faire une ~** to have a game; **gagner la ~** to win the game; (figurative) to win the day; **j'espère que tu seras de la ~** I hope you can come; **ce n'est que ~ remise** maybe next time
**(d)** (in contract, negotiations) party; **les ~s en présence** the parties involved; **être ~ prenante dans** to be actively involved in
**(e)** (Mus) part
■ **~ civile** plaintiff; **~ de pêche** fishing trip; **~ de plaisir** fun
IDIOMS **avoir affaire à forte ~** to have a tough opponent; **prendre qn à ~** to take sb to task

**partiel, -ielle** /paʀsjɛl/ *adj* ⟨payment⟩ part; ⟨destruction, agreement⟩ partial

**partir** /paʀtiʀ/ [30] **⓵** *vi* (+ *v* être) **(a)** to leave, to go; **~ à pied** to leave on foot; **~ en courant** to run off; **~ sans laisser d'adresse** to disappear without trace; **~ loin/à Paris** to go far away/to Paris; **~ en week-end** to go away for the weekend; **~ à la pêche** to go fishing; **~ en tournée** to set off on tour (GB) or on a tour; **~ en retraite** to retire
**(b)** ⟨vehicle, train⟩ to leave; ⟨plane⟩ to take off; ⟨motor⟩ to start; **les coureurs sont partis** the runners are off; **à vos marques, prêts, partez!** on your marks, get set, go!
**(c)** ⟨bullet⟩ to be fired; ⟨cork⟩ to shoot out; ⟨capsule⟩ to shoot off; ⟨retort⟩ to slip out; **le coup de feu est parti** the gun went off; **il était tellement énervé que la gifle est partie toute seule** he was so angry that he slapped him/her before he could stop himself
**(d)** ⟨path, road⟩ to start; **~ favori** to start favourite (GB); **~ battu d'avance** to be doomed from the start; **~ de rien** to start from nothing; **c'est parti** go!; **et voilà, c'est parti, il pleut!** (colloq) here we go, it's raining!; **être bien parti** to have got (GB) or gotten (US) off to a good start; **être bien parti pour gagner** to seem all set to win; **c'est mal parti** (colloq) things don't look too good
**(e)** **~ de** to start from ⟨idea⟩; **~ du principe que** to work on the assumption that; **~ d'une bonne intention** to be well-meant
**(f)** ⟨stain⟩ to come out; ⟨smell⟩ to go; ⟨enamel, button⟩ to come off
**(g)** ⟨parcel, application⟩ to be sent (off)
**(h) quand il est parti on ne l'arrête plus** (colloq) once he starts or gets going there's no stopping him
**⓶ à partir de** *phr* from; **à ~ de 16 heures/de 2 000 euros** from 4 o'clock onwards/2,000 euros; **à ~ du moment où** as soon as; as long as; **fabriqué à ~ d'un alliage** made from an alloy

**partisan, ~e** /paʀtizɑ̃, an/ **⓵** *adj*
**(a)** partisan
**(b) ~ de qch/de faire** in favour (GB) of sth/of doing; **être ~ du moindre effort** (colloq) to be lazy
**⓶** *nm,f* (gen) supporter, partisan; (Mil) partisan

**partition** /paʀtisjɔ̃/ *nf* (Mus) score

**partout** /paʀtu/ *adv* **(a)** everywhere; **avoir**

**mal** ∼ to ache all over; **un peu** ∼ **dans le monde** more or less all over the world; ∼ **où je vais** wherever I go
**(b)** (Sport) **trois** (**points** or **buts**) ∼ three all
IDIOMS **fourrer son nez** ∼ (colloq) to stick one's nose into everything (colloq)

**parure** /paʀyʀ/ nf **(a)** finery
**(b)** set of jewels

**parution** /paʀysjɔ̃/ nf publication

**parvenir** /paʀvəniʀ/ [36] v+prep (+ v être)
**(a)** ∼ **à** to reach ⟨place, person⟩; **faire** ∼ **qch à qn** to send sth to sb; to get sth to sb
**(b)** ∼ **à** to reach ⟨agreement⟩; to achieve ⟨balance⟩
**(c)** ∼ **à faire** to manage to do

**parvenu, ∼e** /paʀvəny/ nm,f upstart

**parvis** /paʀvi/ nm inv (of church) square

**pas¹** /pa/ adv **(a)** **je ne prends** ∼ **de sucre** I don't take sugar; **ils n'ont** ∼ **le téléphone** they haven't got a phone; **je ne pense** ∼ I don't think so; **elle a aimé le film, mais lui** ∼ she liked the film but he didn't
**(b)** (in expressions, exclamations) ∼ **du tout** not at all; ∼ **le moins du monde** not in the least; ∼ **tant que ça,** ∼ **plus que ça** not all that much; ∼ **d'histoires!** I don't want any arguments or fuss!; ∼ **de chance!** hard luck!; ∼ **possible!** I can't believe it!; ∼ **vrai?** (colloq) isn't that so?

**pas²** /pa/ nm inv **(a)** step; **marcher à** ∼ **feutrés** to walk softly; **faire ses premiers** ∼ to take one's first steps; **faire le premier** ∼ to make the first move; **suivre qn** ∼ **à** ∼ to follow sb everywhere; **de là à dire qu'il s'en fiche** (colloq), **il n'y a qu'un** ∼ there's only a fine line between that and saying he doesn't care; **j'habite à deux** ∼ (d'ici) I live very near here; **l'hiver arrive à grands** ∼ winter is fast approaching; **apprendre les** ∼ **du tango** to learn how to tango
**(b)** pace; **marcher d'un bon** ∼ to walk at a brisk pace; **marcher au** ∼ to march; (on horseback) **'roulez au** ∼' 'dead slow' (GB), '(very) slow' (US); **mettre qn au** ∼ to bring sb to heel; **partir au** ∼ **de course** to rush off; **j'y vais de ce** ∼ I'm on my way now
**(c)** footstep
**(d)** footprint; **revenir sur ses** ∼ to retrace one's steps
IDIOMS **se tirer d'un mauvais** ∼ to get out of a tight corner; **sauter le** ∼ to take the plunge; **prendre le** ∼ **sur qch** to overtake sth

**pascal, ∼e,** mpl ∼**s** or -**aux** /paskal, o/ adj ⟨weekend⟩ Easter; ⟨candle, lamb⟩ paschal

**pas-de-porte** /padpɔʀt/ nm inv key money

**passable** /pasabl/ adj **(a)** ⟨film⟩ fairly good; ⟨results⟩ reasonable
**(b)** (Sch) fair

**passablement** /pasabləmɑ̃/ adv ⟨drunk, annoyed⟩ rather; ⟨drink, worry⟩ quite a lot

**passade** /pasad/ nf fad

**passage** /pasaʒ/ nm **(a)** traffic; **interdire le** ∼ **des camions dans la ville** to ban lorries from (driving through) the town
**(b)** stay; **ton** ∼ **dans la ville a été bref** your stay in the town was brief
**(c)** **attendre le** ∼ **du boulanger** to wait for the baker's van to come; **je peux te prendre au** ∼ I can pick you up on the way; **des hôtes de** ∼ short-stay guests; **se servir au** ∼ (figurative) to take a cut (of the profits); to pocket some of the profits
**(d)** '∼ **interdit, voie privée**' 'no entry, private road'; **pour céder le** ∼ **à l'ambulance** in order to let the ambulance go past
**(e)** **chaque** ∼ **de votre chanson à la radio** every time your song is played on the radio
**(f)** way, path; **prévoir le** ∼ **de câbles** to plan the route of cables
**(g)** ∼ **(de qch) à qch** transition (from sth) to sth
**(h)** alley; passageway
**(i)** (in novel) passage; (in film) sequence
■ ∼ **à l'acte** acting out; ∼ **à niveau** level crossing (GB), grade crossing (US); ∼ **pour piétons** pedestrian crossing; ∼ **à tabac** beating; ∼ **à vide** bad patch; unproductive period

**passager, -ère** /pasaʒe, ɛʀ/ **1** adj ⟨situation, crisis⟩ temporary; ⟨feeling⟩ passing; ⟨shower⟩ brief; ⟨unease⟩ slight, short-lived
**2** nm,f passenger; ∼ **clandestin** stowaway

**passant, ∼e** /pasɑ̃, ɑ̃t/ **1** adj ⟨street⟩ busy
**2** nm,f passer-by
**3** nm (on belt, watchstrap) loop

**passation** /pasasjɔ̃/ nf ∼ **des pouvoirs** transfer of power

**passe¹** /pas/ nm (colloq) **(a)** master key
**(b)** pass

**passe²** /pas/ nf **(a)** (Sport) pass
**(b)** **être dans une** ∼ **difficile** to be going through a difficult patch; **être en** ∼ **de faire** to be (well) on the way to doing

**passé, ∼e** /pase/ **1** pp ▸ PASSER
**2** pp adj **(a)** ⟨years, experiences⟩ past; ∼ **de mode** dated
**(b)** **l'année passée** last year
**(c)** ⟨colour, material⟩ faded
**3** nm **(a)** past
**(b)** past (tense)
**4** prep after; ∼ **8 heures il s'endort dans son fauteuil** come eight o'clock he goes to sleep in his armchair
■ ∼ **antérieur** past anterior; ∼ **composé** present perfect; ∼ **simple** past historic

**passéisme** /paseism/ nm attachment to the past

**passe-montagne,** pl ∼**s** /pasmɔ̃taɲ/ nm balaclava

**passe-partout** /paspaʀtu/ adj inv ⟨expression⟩ catch-all; ⟨garment⟩ for all occasions

**passe-passe** /paspas/ nm inv **tour de** ∼ conjuring trick; (figurative) sleight of hand

**passeport** /paspɔʀ/ *nm* passport

**passer** /pase/ [1] **1** *vtr* **(a)** to cross ⟨*river, border*⟩; to go through ⟨*door, customs*⟩; to get over ⟨*hedge, obstacle*⟩; **il m'a fait ∼ la frontière** he got me across the border; **∼ qch à la douane** to get sth through customs
**(b)** to go past, to pass; **quand vous aurez passé le feu, tournez à droite** turn right after the lights; **le malade ne passera pas la nuit** the patient won't last the night
**(c)** **∼ le doigt sur la table** to run one's finger over the table-top; **∼ la tête à la fenêtre** to stick one's head out of the window
**(d)** to pass ⟨*object*⟩; to pass [sth] on ⟨*instructions, disease*⟩; **∼ sa colère sur ses collègues** to take one's anger out on one's colleagues
**(e)** to lend; to give
**(f)** (on phone) **tu peux me ∼ Chris?** can you put Chris on?; **je vous le passe** I'm putting you through
**(g)** to take, to sit ⟨*examination*⟩; to have ⟨*interview*⟩; **faire ∼ un test à qn** to give sb a test
**(h)** to spend ⟨*time*⟩; **dépêche-toi, on ne va pas y ∼ la nuit!** (colloq) hurry up, or we'll be here all night!
**(i)** **elle leur passe tout** she lets them get away with murder
**(j)** to skip ⟨*page, paragraph*⟩; **je vous passe les détails** I'll spare you the details
**(k)** **∼ l'aspirateur** to vacuum
**(l)** to filter ⟨*coffee*⟩; to strain ⟨*fruit juice, sauce*⟩; to purée ⟨*vegetables*⟩
**(m)** to slip [sth] on ⟨*garment, ring*⟩; to slip into ⟨*dress*⟩
**(n)** to play ⟨*record, cassette*⟩; to show ⟨*film, slides*⟩; to place ⟨*ad*⟩
**(o)** to enter into ⟨*agreement*⟩; to place ⟨*order*⟩
**(p)** (Aut) **∼ la troisième** to go into third gear
**(q)** (Games) **∼ son tour** to pass
**2** *vi* (+ *v être*) **(a)** to go past or by, to pass; **∼ sur un pont** to go over a bridge; **le facteur n'est pas encore passé** the postman hasn't been yet; **∼ à côté de** ⟨*person*⟩ to pass; ⟨*road*⟩ to run alongside; **∼ à pied/à bicyclette** to walk/cycle past
**(b)** **je ne fais que ∼** I've just popped in (GB) *or* dropped by for a minute; **∼ dans la matinée** ⟨*plumber*⟩ to come by in the morning; **∼ prendre qn/qch** to pick sb/sth up
**(c)** to go; **passons au salon** let's go into the lounge; **les contrebandiers sont passés en Espagne** the smugglers have crossed into Spain
**(d)** to get through; **tu ne passeras pas, c'est trop étroit** you'll never get through, it's too narrow; **il m'a fait signe de ∼** he waved me on; **vas-y, ça passe!** go on, there's plenty of room!; **∼ par-dessus bord** to fall overboard; **il est passé par la fenêtre** he fell out of the window; he got in through the window
**(e)** **∼ par** to go through; **∼ par le standard** to go through the switchboard; **je ne sais jamais ce qui se passe par la tête** I never know what's going on in your head
**(f)** (colloq) **il accuse le patron, ses collègues,**

**bref, tout le monde y passe** he's accusing the boss, his colleagues—basically, everyone in sight; **que ça te plaise ou non, il va falloir y ∼** whether you like it or not, there's no alternative; **on ne peut pas faire autrement que d'en ∼ par là** there is no other way around it
**(g)** **∼ sur** to pass over ⟨*question, mistake*⟩; **∼ à côté d'une question** to miss the point; **laisser ∼ une occasion** to miss an opportunity
**(h)** **soit dit en ∼** incidentally
**(i)** ⟨*comments, speech*⟩ to go down well; ⟨*law, measure, candidate*⟩ to get through; ⟨*attitude, doctrine*⟩ to be accepted; **j'ai mangé quelque chose qui n'est pas passé** I ate something which didn't agree with me; **que je sois critiqué, passe encore, mais calomnié, non!** criticism is one thing, but I draw the line at slander; **∼ au premier tour** to be elected in the first round; **∼ dans la classe supérieure** to move up to the year above; **(ça) passe pour cette fois** (colloq) I'll let it go this time
**(j)** **∼ à l'ennemi** to go over to the enemy; **∼ de main en main** to be passed around; **∼ constamment d'un sujet à l'autre** to flit from one subject to another; **∼ à un taux supérieur** to go up to a higher rate
**(k)** **∼ pour un imbécile** to look a fool; **∼ pour un génie** to pass as a genius; **il passe pour l'inventeur de l'ordinateur** he's supposed to have invented computers; **il se fait ∼ pour mon frère** he passes himself off as my brother
**(l)** ⟨*pain, crisis*⟩ to pass; **quand l'orage sera** *or* **aura passé** when the storm is over; **ça passera** ⟨*bad mood*⟩ it'll pass; ⟨*hurt*⟩ you'll get over it; **∼ de mode** to go out of fashion; **faire ∼ à qn l'envie de faire** to cure sb of the desire to do; **ce médicament fait ∼ les maux d'estomac** this medicine relieves stomach ache
**(m)** ⟨*performer, group*⟩ (on stage) to be appearing; (on TV, radio) to be on; ⟨*show, film*⟩ to be on; ⟨*music*⟩ to be playing
**(n)** **∼ avant/après** to come before/after; **il fait ∼ sa famille avant ses amis** he puts his family before his friends
**(o)** (colloq) **où étais-tu passé?** where did you get to?; **où est passé mon livre?** where has my book got to?
**(p)** ⟨*time*⟩ to pass, to go by; **je ne vois pas le temps ∼** I don't know where the time goes
**(q)** to turn to; **∼ à l'étape suivante** to move on to the next stage; **nous allons ∼ au vote** let's vote now
**(r)** **∼ de père en fils** to be handed down from father to son; **l'expression est passée dans la langue** the expression has become part of the language
**(s)** to be promoted to; **elle est passée maître dans l'art de mentir** she's an accomplished liar
**(t)** ⟨*money, amount*⟩ to go on *or* into; ⟨*product, material*⟩ to go into
**(u)** (colloq) **y ∼** to die
**(v)** ⟨*colour, material*⟩ to fade
**(w)** ⟨*coffee*⟩ to filter

**(x)** ~ **en marche arrière** to go into reverse; **la troisième passe mal** third gear is a bit stiff
**(y)** (in bridge, poker) to pass
**3 se passer** v refl (+ v être) **(a)** to happen; **tout s'est passé très vite** it all happened very fast; **tout se passe comme si le yen avait été dévalué** it's as if the yen had been devalued
**(b)** to take place; **la scène se passe au Viêt Nam** the scene is set in Vietnam
**(c)** ⟨examination, negotiations⟩ to go; **ça ne se passera pas comme ça!** I won't leave it at that!
**(d)** ⟨period⟩ to go by, to pass; **deux ans se sont passés depuis** that was two years ago
**(e) se** ~ **de** to do without ⟨object, activity, person⟩; to go without ⟨meal, sleep⟩; **se** ~ **de commentaires** to speak for itself
**(f) se** ~ **la langue sur les lèvres** to run one's tongue over one's lips; **se** ~ **la main sur le front** to put a hand to one's forehead
**(g) ils se sont passé des documents** they exchanged some documents
**IDIOMS qu'est-ce qu'elle nous a passé!** (colloq) she really went for us! (colloq)
**passerelle** /pasʀɛl/ nf **(a)** footbridge
**(b)** link
**(c)** (to boat) gangway; (to plane) steps
**passe-temps** /pastɑ̃/ nm inv pastime, hobby
**passeur, -euse** /pasœʀ, øz/ nmf
**(a)** ferryman/ferrywoman
**(b)** smuggler; (for drugs) courier
**passible** /pasibl/ adj (Law) ~ **de** ⟨crime⟩ punishable by; ⟨person⟩ liable to
**passif, -ive** /pasif, iv/ **1** adj passive
**2** nm **(a)** passive (voice)
**(b)** debit; **mettre qch au** ~ **de qn** to count sth amongst sb's failures
**passion** /pasjɔ̃/ nf passion
**passionnant, ~e** /pasjɔnɑ̃, ɑ̃t/ adj exciting, fascinating, riveting
**passionné, ~e** /pasjɔne/ **1** adj ⟨love⟩ passionate; ⟨debate, argument⟩ impassioned; **être** ~ **de** or **pour qch** to have a passion for sth
**2** nmf enthusiast
**passionnel, -elle** /pasjɔnɛl/ adj ⟨debate⟩ passionate; ⟨crime⟩ of passion
**passionner** /pasjɔne/ [1] **1** vtr **(a)** to fascinate; **la botanique le passionne** he has a passion for botany
**(b)** to inflame ⟨debate⟩
**2 se passionner** v refl (+ v être) to have a passion (**pour** for)
**passivité** /pasivite/ nf passivity
**passoire** /paswaʀ/ nf **(a)** colander
**(b)** strainer
**pastel** /pastɛl/ **1** adj inv ⟨shade⟩ pastel
**2** nm pastel
**pastèque** /pastɛk/ nf watermelon
**pasteur** /pastœʀ/ nm **(a)** minister, pastor
**(b)** priest
**(c)** shepherd

**pasteuriser** /pastœʀize/ [1] vtr to pasteurize
**pastiche** /pastiʃ/ nm pastiche
**pastille** /pastij/ nf **(a)** pastille, lozenge; ~ **contre la toux** cough drop
**(b)** ~ **de menthe** peppermint
**(c)** spot
**(d)** (of cloth, rubber) patch; (of plastic) disc
**pastoral, ~e[1], mpl -aux** /pastɔʀal, o/ adj pastoral
**pastorale[2]** /pastɔʀal/ nf (Mus) pastoral
**patachon** /pataʃɔ̃/ nm (colloq) **mener une vie de** ~ to live in the fast lane
**patata** /patata/ excl (colloq) ▸ PATATI
**patate** /patat/ nf (colloq) **(a)** spud (colloq); ~ **douce** sweet potato
**(b)** blockhead (colloq), idiot
**patati** /patati/ excl (colloq) ~, **patata** and so on and so forth
**pataud, ~e** /pato, od/ adj clumsy
**patauger** /patɔʒe/ [13] vi **(a)** to splash about; to paddle
**(b)** to flounder
**pâte** /pat/ **1** nf **(a)** pastry; dough; batter
**(b)** paste
**2 pâtes** nf pl ~**s (alimentaires)** pasta
■ ~ **d'amandes** marzipan; ~**s de fruit(s)** fruit jellies; ~ **à modeler** Plasticine®; ~ **à tartiner** spread
**IDIOMS mettre la main à la** ~ to pitch in
**pâté** /pate/ nm **(a)** pâté
**(b)** pie; ~ **en croûte** ≈ pie
**(c)** ~ **de maisons** block (of houses)
**(d)** (ink)blot
**(e)** sandcastle
**pâtée** /pate/ nf dog food; cat food; swill
**patelin** /patlɛ̃/ nm (colloq) small village
**patente** /patɑ̃t/ nf: licence (GB) to exercise a trade or profession
**patère** /pateʀ/ nf peg, hook
**paternalisme** /patɛʀnalism/ nm paternalism
**paternaliste** /patɛʀnalist/ adj paternalistic
**paternel, -elle** /patɛʀnɛl/ adj **(a)** paternal
**(b)** fatherly
**paternité** /patɛʀnite/ nf **(a)** fatherhood; (Law) paternity
**(b)** authorship
**pâteux, -euse** /patø, øz/ adj
**(a)** ⟨substance⟩ doughy; ⟨gruel⟩ mushy
**(b)** ⟨voice⟩ thick
**pathétique** /patetik/ adj moving
**pathologique** /patɔlɔʒik/ adj pathological
**patiemment** /pasjamɑ̃/ adv patiently
**patience** /pasjɑ̃s/ nf patience
**IDIOMS prendre son mal en** ~ to resign oneself to one's fate
**patient, ~e** /pasjɑ̃, ɑ̃t/ adj, nmf patient
**patienter** /pasjɑ̃te/ [1] vi to wait
**patin** /patɛ̃/ nm **(a)** skate ⋯▸

**(b)** (Tech) (on helicopter) skid; (on sledge) runner
■ ~ **à glace** ice skate; ice-skating; ~ **à roulettes** roller skate; roller-skating

**patinage** /patinaʒ/ *nm* skating

**patine** /patin/ *nf* patina; finish, sheen

**patiner** /patine/ [1] **1** *vtr* to apply a finish to
**2** *vi* **(a)** to skate
**(b)** (Aut) ⟨wheel⟩ to spin; ⟨clutch⟩ to slip; **faire ~ l'embrayage** to slip the clutch
**3 se patiner** *v refl* (+ *v être*) to acquire a patina

**patineur, -euse** /patinœʀ, øz/ *nm,f* skater

**patinoire** /patinwaʀ/ *nf* ice rink

**pâtir** /pɑtiʀ/ [3] *vi* ~ **de** to suffer as a result of

**pâtisserie** /pɑtisʀi/ *nf* **(a)** cake shop, pâtisserie
**(b)** pastry, cake

**pâtissier, -ière** /pɑtisje, ɛʀ/ *nm,f* confectioner, pastry cook

**patois** /patwa/ *nm inv* patois, dialect

**patraque** /patʀak/ *adj* (colloq) **être ~** to be under the weather (colloq)

**patriarche** /patʀijaʀʃ/ *nm* patriarch

**patrie** /patʀi/ *nf* homeland, country

**patrimoine** /patʀimwan/ *nm* **(a)** (of person, family) patrimony; (of firm) capital
**(b)** heritage
■ ~ **génétique** gene pool

**patriote** /patʀijɔt/ **1** *adj* patriotic
**2** *nm,f* patriot; **en ~** patriotically

**patriotisme** /patʀijɔtism/ *nm* patriotism

**patron, -onne** /patʀɔ̃, ɔn/ **1** *nm,f* boss (colloq)
**2** *nm* (sewing) pattern
■ ~ **de pêche** skipper, master

**patronal, ~e,** *mpl* **-aux** /patʀɔnal, o/ *adj* ⟨organization⟩ employers'

**patronat** /patʀɔna/ *nm* employers

**patronne** ▶ PATRON 1

**patronner** /patʀɔne/ [1] *vtr* to sponsor

**patronyme** /patʀɔnim/ *nm* patronymic

**patrouille** /patʀuj/ *nf* patrol

**patrouiller** /patʀuje/ [1] *vi* to be on patrol

**patte** /pat/ *nf* **(a)** leg; paw; foot; **donner la ~** to give its paw; **retomber sur ses ~s** to fall on its feet
**(b)** (colloq) leg, foot; **tu es toujours dans mes ~s** you are always getting under my feet; **marcher à quatre ~s** to walk on all fours; to crawl; **traîner la ~** to limp
**(c)** (colloq) hand; **bas les ~s!** (colloq) keep your hands to yourself!; hands off! (colloq)
**(d)** tab; (on shelving unit) lug; (on garment) flap
**(e)** sideburn
■ ~**s d'éléphant** flares; ~ **folle** (colloq) gammy leg (GB), game leg (US); ~**s de mouche** spidery scrawl
IDIOMS **faire ~ de velours** ⟨cat⟩ to draw in its claws; ⟨person⟩ to switch on the charm;

**montrer ~ blanche** to prove one is acceptable; **se tirer dans les ~s** to pull dirty tricks on each other

**patte-d'oie,** *pl* **pattes-d'oie** /patdwa/ *nf* **(a)** crow's-foot
**(b)** junction

**pâturage** /pɑtyʀaʒ/ *nm* pasture

**pâture** /pɑtyʀ/ *nf* **(a)** feed; **être jeté en ~** (figurative) to be thrown to the lions
**(b)** pasture

**paume** /pom/ *nf* palm (of the hand)

**paumé, ~e** /pome/ *adj* (colloq) **(a)** ⟨person⟩ mixed up (GB), out of it (US) (colloq)
**(b)** ⟨place⟩ godforsaken

**paumer** (colloq) /pome/ [1] **1** *vtr, vi* to lose
**2 se paumer** *v refl* (+ *v être*) to get lost

**paupière** /popjɛʀ/ *nf* eyelid

**paupiette** /popjɛt/ *nf* ~ **de veau** stuffed escalope of veal

**pause** /poz/ *nf* **(a)** break; **faire une ~** to take a break
**(b)** (in process) pause
**(c)** (Mus) rest

**pauvre** /povʀ/ **1** *adj* **(a)** poor
**(b)** sparse; ~ **en sucre** low in sugar; lacking sugar
**(c) un ~ type** (colloq) a poor guy (colloq); a dead loss (colloq)
**2** *nm,f* (colloq) **le/la ~!** poor man/woman!; poor thing!
**3** *nm* **un ~** a poor man; ~ **d'esprit** half-wit

**pauvrement** /povʀəmɑ̃/ *adv* poorly

**pauvresse** /povʀɛs/ *nf* poor wretch, pauper

**pauvreté** /povʀəte/ *nf* **(a)** poverty
**(b)** shabbiness

**pavage** /pavaʒ/ *nm* paving

**pavaner: se pavaner** /pavane/ [1] *v refl* (+ *v être*) to strut (about)

**pavé** /pave/ *nm* cobblestone; **se retrouver sur le ~** to find oneself out on the street
IDIOMS **lancer un ~ dans la mare** to set the cat among the pigeons; **tenir le haut du ~** to head the field

**paver** /pave/ [1] *vtr* to lay [sth] with cobblestones

**pavillon** /pavijɔ̃/ *nm* **(a)** (detached) house
**(b)** (for exhibition) pavilion; (of hospital) wing
**(c)** (of ear) auricle
**(d)** (of loudspeaker) horn
**(e)** (Naut) flag

**pavillonnaire** /pavijɔnɛʀ/ *adj* **zone ~** residential area; **banlieue ~** suburb consisting of houses (*as opposed to high-rise buildings*)

**pavoiser** /pavwaze/ [1] *vi* (colloq) to crow

**pavot** /pavo/ *nm* poppy

**payable** /pɛjabl/ *adj* payable; ~ **à la commande** cash with order

**payant, ~e** /pɛjɑ̃, ɑ̃t/ *adj* **(a)** ⟨person⟩ paying
**(b)** ⟨show⟩ not free
**(c)** (colloq) lucrative, profitable

**paye** /pɛj/ = PAIE

**payement** /pɛjmã/ = PAIEMENT

**payer** /peje/ [21] **1** *vtr* **(a)** to pay; to pay for; **il est payé pour le savoir!** he knows that to his cost!; **faire ~ qch à qn** to charge sb for sth; **~ qch à qn** (colloq) to buy sb sth **(b)** to pay for ⟨*mistake, carelessness*⟩ **2** *vi* **(a)** ⟨*efforts, sacrifice*⟩ to pay off; ⟨*profession, activity*⟩ to pay **(b)** (colloq) to be funny **3 se payer** *v refl* (+ *v être*) **(a)** ⟨*service, goods*⟩ to have to be paid for **(b)** (colloq) to treat oneself to ⟨*holiday*⟩; to get ⟨*cold, bad mark*⟩; to get landed with ⟨*job*⟩; **se ~ un arbre** to crash into a tree **IDIOMS se ~ du bon temps** (colloq) to have a good time; **se ~ la tête de qn** (colloq) to take the mickey out of sb (GB) (colloq), to razz sb (US) (colloq)

**pays** /pei/ *nm* **(a)** country **(b) la Bourgogne est le ~ du bon vin** Burgundy is the home of good wine; **gens du ~** local people **IDIOMS voir du ~** to do some travelling (GB)

**paysage** /peiza3/ *nm* landscape, scenery ■ **~ audiovisuel français, PAF** French radio and TV scene

**paysager, -ère** /peiza3e, ɛʀ/ *adj* **(a)** environmental **(b)** ⟨*garden*⟩ landscaped

**paysagiste** /peiza3ist/ *nmf* **(jardinier) ~** landscape gardener

**paysan, -anne** /peizã, an/ **1** *adj* ⟨*life*⟩ rural; ⟨*ways*⟩ peasant; ⟨*soup, bread*⟩ country **2** *nm,f* **(a)** ≈ small farmer **(b)** (derogatory) peasant

**paysannerie** /peizanʀi/ *nf* small farmers; peasantry

**Pays-Bas** /peibɑ/ *pr nm pl* **les ~** The Netherlands

**PC** /pese/ *nm* **(a)** (Pol) (*abbr* = **parti communiste**) CP, Communist Party **(b)** (*abbr* = **personal computer**) PC

**PCF** /peseɛf/ *nm* (*abbr* = **parti communiste français**) French Communist Party

**PCV** /peseve/ *nm* (*abbr* = **paiement contre vérification**) reverse charge call (GB), collect call (US)

**PDG** /pede3e/ *nm* (*abbr* = **président-directeur général**) chief executive officer

**péage** /pea3/ *nm* **(a)** toll **(b)** tollbooth

**peau**, *pl* **~x** /po/ *nf* **(a)** skin; **n'avoir que la ~ sur les os** to be all skin and bone **(b)** leather; **gants de ~** leather gloves **(c)** peel **(d)** (colloq) life; **risquer sa ~** to risk one's life; **faire la ~ à qn** to kill sb; **vouloir la ~ de qn** to want sb dead **IDIOMS être bien dans sa ~** (colloq) to feel good about oneself; **avoir qn dans la ~** (colloq) to be crazy about sb (colloq); **prendre une balle dans la ~** (colloq) to be shot

**peaufiner** /pofine/ [1] *vtr* to put the finishing touches to ⟨*work, text*⟩

**Peau-Rouge**, *pl* **Peaux-Rouges** /poʀu3/ *nmf* Red Indian

**péché** /peʃe/ *nm* sin; **ce serait un ~ de rater ça** (colloq) it would be a crime to miss that; **le chocolat, c'est mon ~ mignon** I've got a weakness for chocolate

**pêche** /pɛʃ/ *nf* **(a)** peach **(b)** fishing; **aller à la ~** to go fishing **(c)** (colloq) clout (colloq) **(d)** (colloq) **avoir la ~** to be feeling great ■ **~ à la ligne** angling

**pécher** /peʃe/ [14] *vi* to sin; **~ par excès de confiance** to be overconfident; **le roman pèche sur un point** the novel has one shortcoming

**pêcher¹** /pɛʃe/ [1] **1** *vtr* to go fishing for **2** *vi* to fish; **~ à la mouche** to fly-fish; **~ à la ligne** to angle

**pêcher²** /pɛʃe/ *nm* peach tree

**pécheresse** /peʃʀɛs/ *nf* sinner

**pêcherie** /pɛʃʀi/ *nf* **(a)** fish factory **(b)** fishing ground

**pécheur** /peʃœʀ/ *nm* sinner

**pêcheur** /pɛʃœʀ/ *nm* fisherman

**pectoral**, *pl* **-aux** /pɛktɔʀal, o/ *nm* pectoral muscle

**pécule** /pekyl/ *nm* savings, nest egg (colloq)

**pécuniaire** /pekynjɛʀ/ *adj* financial

**pédagogie** /pedagɔ3i/ *nf* **(a)** education, pedagogy **(b)** teaching skills **(c)** teaching method

**pédagogique** /pedagɔ3ik/ *adj* ⟨*activity*⟩ educational; ⟨*system*⟩ education; ⟨*method*⟩ teaching

**pédagogue** /pedagɔg/ *nmf* educationalist

**pédale** /pedal/ *nf* pedal **IDIOMS perdre les ~s** (colloq) to lose one's grip

**pédaler** /pedale/ [1] *vi* to pedal

**pédalier** /pedalje/ *nm* (of bicycle) chain transmission; (of piano) pedals

**pédalo®** /pedalo/ *nm* pedalo (GB), pedal boat

**pédant, ~e** /pedã, ãt/ *adj* pedantic

**pédérastie** /pedeʀasti/ *nf* **(a)** pederasty **(b)** homosexuality

**pédestre** /pedɛstʀ/ *adj* **randonnée ~** ramble

**pédiatre** /pedjatʀ/ *nmf* paediatrician

**pédiatrie** /pedjatʀi/ *nf* paediatrics

**pédicure** /pedikyʀ/ *nmf* chiropodist (GB), podiatrist (US)

**pedigree** /pedigʀe/ *nm* pedigree

**pédologue** /pedɔlɔg/ *nmf* pedologist

**pédophilie** /pedɔfili/ *nf* paedophilia

**pègre** /pɛgʀ/ *nf* underworld

**peigne** /pɛɲ/ *nm* comb

**peigner** /peɲe/ [1] **1** *vtr* to comb ⟨*hair, wool*⟩

 ⋯⋗

**2 se peigner** *v refl* (+ *v être*) to comb one's hair

**peignoir** /pɛɲwaʀ/ *nm* dressing gown (GB), robe (US); ~ **de bain** bathrobe

**peinard**, **~e** /penaʀ, aʀd/ *adj* (colloq) ⟨*job*⟩ cushy (colloq); ⟨*place*⟩ snug

**peindre** /pɛ̃dʀ/ [55] **1** *vtr* (a) to paint
  (b) to depict
  **2** *vi* to paint

**peine** /pɛn/ **1** *nf* (a) sorrow, grief; **avoir de la ~** to feel sad; **faire de la ~ à qn** ⟨*person*⟩ to hurt sb; ⟨*event, remark*⟩ to upset sb
  (b) effort, trouble; **c'est ~ perdue** it's a waste of effort; **il n'est pas au bout de ses ~s** his troubles are far from over; **il n'a pas encore got a long way to go; ce n'est pas la ~ de crier** there's no need to shout; **pour ta ~** for your trouble
  (c) difficulty; **sans ~** easily; **avec ~** with difficulty
  (d) (Law) penalty, sentence; **~ de prison** prison sentence; **'défense de fumer sous ~ d'amende'** 'no smoking, offenders will be fined'
  **2 à peine** *phr* hardly; **il était à ~ arrivé qu'il pensait déjà à repartir** no sooner had he arrived than he was thinking of leaving again
  ■ **~ capitale** capital punishment; **~ de cœur** heartache; **~ de mort** death penalty

**peiner** /pene/ [1] **1** *vtr* to sadden, to upset
  **2** *vi* ⟨*person*⟩ to struggle; ⟨*car*⟩ to labour (GB)

**peint**, **~e** /pɛ̃, ɛ̃t/ ▶ PEINDRE

**peintre** /pɛ̃tʀ/ *nm* painter

**peinture** /pɛ̃tyʀ/ *nf* (a) paint
  (b) paintwork
  (c) painting; **je ne peux pas le voir en ~** (colloq) I can't stand the sight of him
  (d) portrayal

**peinturlurer** /pɛ̃tyʀlyʀe/ [1] *vtr* to daub

**péjoratif**, **-ive** /peʒɔʀatif, iv/ *adj* pejorative

**Pékin** /pekɛ̃/ *pr n* Beijing, Peking

**PEL** /peœɛl/ *nm: abbr* ▶ PLAN

**pelage** /pəlaʒ/ *nm* coat, fur

**pelé**, **~e** /pəle/ *adj* ⟨*animal*⟩ mangy; ⟨*hill*⟩ bare

**pêle-mêle** /pɛlmɛl/ *adv* higgledy-piggledy

**peler** /pəle/ [17] **1** *vtr* to peel
  **2** *vi* (a) ⟨*skin, nose*⟩ to peel
  (b) (colloq) **~ (de froid)** to freeze

**pèlerin** /pɛlʀɛ̃/ *nm* pilgrim

**pèlerinage** /pɛlʀinaʒ/ *nm* pilgrimage

**pélican** /pelikɑ̃/ *nm* pelican

**pelisse** /pəlis/ *nf* fur-trimmed coat, pelisse

**pelle** /pɛl/ *nf* shovel; spade; **à la ~** (colloq) by the dozen.
  ■ **~ à tarte** cake slice

**pelleteuse** /pɛltøz/ *nf* mechanical digger

**pellicule** /pelikyl/ **1** *nf* film
  **2 pellicules** *nf pl* dandruff

**pelote** /p(ə)lɔt/ *nf* (of wool) ball

**peloton** /p(ə)lɔtɔ̃/ *nm* (a) platoon; **~ d'exécution** firing squad
  (b) (in cycling) pack; **dans le ~ de tête** in the leading pack

**pelotonner: se pelotonner** /p(ə)lɔtɔne/ [1] *v refl* (+ *v être*) (a) to snuggle up
  (b) to huddle up

**pelouse** /p(ə)luz/ *nf* lawn; **'~ interdite'** 'keep off the grass'

**peluche** /p(ə)lyʃ/ *nf* (a) plush; **jouet en ~** cuddly toy (GB), stuffed animal (US)
  (b) fluff

**pelucher** /p(ə)lyʃe/ [1] *vi* to become fluffy

**pelure** /p(ə)lyʀ/ *nf* (of vegetable, fruit) peel; (of onion) skin

**pelvis** /pɛlvis/ *nm inv* pelvis

**pénal**, **~e**, *mpl* **-aux** /penal, o/ *adj* criminal

**pénaliser** /penalize/ [1] *vtr* to penalize

**pénalité** /penalite/ *nf* penalty

**penaud**, **~e** /pəno, od/ *adj* sheepish

**penchant** /pɑ̃ʃɑ̃/ *nm* (a) fondness
  (b) weakness
  (c) tendency

**penché**, **~e** /pɑ̃ʃe/ **1** *pp* ▶ PENCHER
  **2** *pp adj* ⟨*tree*⟩ leaning; ⟨*writing*⟩ slanting

**pencher** /pɑ̃ʃe/ [1] **1** *vtr* to tilt; to tip [sth] up; **~ la tête en avant** to bend one's head forward(s)
  **2** *vi* (a) ⟨*tower, tree*⟩ to lean; ⟨*boat*⟩ to list; ⟨*picture*⟩ to slant
  (b) **~ pour** to incline toward(s) ⟨*theory*⟩; to be in favour (GB) of ⟨*solution*⟩
  **3 se pencher** *v refl* (+ *v être*) (a) to lean
  (b) to bend down
  (c) **se ~ sur** to look into ⟨*problem*⟩

**pendable** /pɑ̃dabl/ *adj* **jouer un tour ~ à qn** to play a rotten trick on sb

**pendaison** /pɑ̃dɛzɔ̃/ *nf* hanging

**pendant** /pɑ̃dɑ̃/ **1** *prep* for; **je t'ai attendu ~ des heures** I waited for you for hours; **~ combien de temps avez-vous vécu à Versailles?** how long did you live in Versailles?; **il a été malade ~ tout le trajet** he was sick throughout the journey; **~ ce temps(-là)** meanwhile
  **2 pendant que** *phr* while

**pendeloque** /pɑ̃dlɔk/ *nf* pendant, drop (on earring)

**pendentif** /pɑ̃dɑ̃tif/ *nm* pendant

**penderie** /pɑ̃dʀi/ *nf* (a) wardrobe
  (b) walk-in cupboard (GB) *or* closet

**pendouiller** /pɑ̃duje/ [1] *vi* (colloq) to dangle down

**pendre** /pɑ̃dʀ/ [6] **1** *vtr* (a) to hang ⟨*person*⟩
  (b) to hang ⟨*picture, curtains*⟩; to hang up ⟨*clothes*⟩
  **2** *vi* (a) ⟨*object, clothes*⟩ to hang; ⟨*arms, legs*⟩ to dangle
  (b) ⟨*strips, lock of hair*⟩ to hang down; ⟨*cheek, breasts*⟩ to sag
  **3 se pendre** *v refl* (+ *v être*) (a) to hang oneself

**(b)** se ~ à to hang from ⟨*branch*⟩; se ~ au cou de qn to throw one's arms around sb's neck

IDIOMS ça te pend au nez (colloq) you've got it coming to you

**pendu, ~e** /pɑ̃dy/ [1] *pp* ▶ PENDRE
[2] *pp adj* **(a)** ⟨*person*⟩ hanged
**(b)** ⟨*object*⟩ hung, hanging; être ~ aux lèvres de qn to hang on sb's every word; être toujours ~ au téléphone to spend all one's time on the telephone
[3] *nm,f* hanged man/woman

**pendulaire** /pɑ̃dylɛʀ/ *adj* pendular

**pendule¹** /pɑ̃dyl/ *nm* pendulum

**pendule²** /pɑ̃dyl/ *nf* clock

IDIOMS remettre les ~s à l'heure to set the record straight

**pénétrant, ~e** /penetʀɑ̃, ɑ̃t/ *adj* ⟨*wind*⟩ penetrating; ⟨*cold*⟩ piercing; ⟨*comment*⟩ shrewd; ⟨*mind, look*⟩ penetrating

**pénétration** /penetʀasjɔ̃/ *nf* penetration

**pénétré, ~e** /penetʀe/ [1] *pp* ▶ PÉNÉTRER
[2] *pp adj* earnest, intense; être ~ de to be imbued with ⟨*feeling*⟩

**pénétrer** /penetʀe/ [14] [1] *vtr* **(a)** ⟨*rain*⟩ to soak *or* seep into ⟨*ground*⟩; ⟨*sun*⟩ to penetrate ⟨*foliage*⟩
**(b)** to fathom ⟨*secret, thoughts*⟩
**(c)** to penetrate
**(d)** ⟨*idea, fashion*⟩ to reach ⟨*group*⟩
[2] *vi* ~ dans to enter, to get into; to penetrate; faire ~ la pommade en massant doucement rub the ointment into your skin

**pénible** /penibl/ *adj* ⟨*effort*⟩ painful; ⟨*work*⟩ hard; ⟨*journey*⟩ difficult; ⟨*person*⟩ tiresome

**péniblement** /penibləmɑ̃/ *adv* ⟨*walk*⟩ with difficulty; ⟨*reach*⟩ barely

**péniche** /peniʃ/ *nf* barge

**pénicilline** /penisilin/ *nf* penicillin

**péninsulaire** /penɛ̃sylɛʀ/ *adj* peninsular

**péninsule** /penɛ̃syl/ *nf* peninsula

**pénis** /penis/ *nm inv* penis

**pénitence** /penitɑ̃s/ *nf* **(a)** penance
**(b)** punishment

**pénitencier** /penitɑ̃sje/ *nm* prison

**pénitentiaire** /penitɑ̃sjɛʀ/ *adj* ⟨*institution*⟩ penal; ⟨*regime*⟩ prison

**pénombre** /penɔ̃bʀ/ *nf* half-light

**pensable** /pɑ̃sabl/ *adj* thinkable; ce n'est pas ~ it's unthinkable

**pense-bête**, *pl* **pense-bêtes** /pɑ̃sbɛt/ *nm* reminder

**pensée** /pɑ̃se/ *nf* **(a)** thought; être perdu dans ses ~s to be lost in thought
**(b)** mind; nous serons avec vous par la ~ we'll be with you in spirit
**(c)** thinking
**(d)** (Bot) pansy

**penser** /pɑ̃se/ [1] [1] *vtr* **(a)** to think; ~ du bien de qn to think well of sb; je n'en pense rien I have no opinion about it; c'est bien ce que je pensais! I thought as much!; tu penses vraiment ce que tu dis? do you

really mean what you're saying?; tout porte à ~ que there's every indication that; vous pensez si j'étais content! you can imagine how pleased I was!; 'il s'est excusé?'— 'penses-tu!' 'did he apologize?'—'you must be joking!'
**(b)** ça me fait ~ qu'il faut que je leur écrive that reminds me that I must write to them
**(c)** ~ faire to be thinking of doing, to intend to do
**(d)** to think [sth] up ⟨*plan, device*⟩
[2] **penser à** *v+prep* **(a)** ~ à to think of, to think about; ne pensez à rien empty your mind; sans ~ à mal without meaning any harm; tu n'y penses pas! you can't be serious!; n'y pensons plus! let's forget about it!
**(b)** ~ à to remember; il me fait ~ à mon père he reminds me of my father
**(c)** ~ à faire to be thinking of doing
[3] *vi* to think; je lui ai dit ma façon de ~! I gave him/her a piece of my mind!; ~ tout haut to think out loud

**penseur** /pɑ̃sœʀ/ *nm* thinker

**pensif, -ive** /pɑ̃sif, iv/ *adj* pensive, thoughtful

**pension** /pɑ̃sjɔ̃/ *nf* **(a)** pension
**(b)** boarding house
**(c)** boarding school
■ ~ alimentaire alimony; ~ complète full board; ~ de famille family hotel

**pensionnaire** /pɑ̃sjɔnɛʀ/ *nmf* **(a)** (in hotel) resident
**(b)** (in prison) inmate
**(c)** (Sch) boarder

**pensionnat** /pɑ̃sjɔna/ *nm* boarding school

**pensionné, ~e** /pɑ̃sjɔne/ *nm,f* pensioner

**pensivement** /pɑ̃sivmɑ̃/ *adv* pensively

**pentagone** /pɛ̃tagɔn/ *nm* pentagon

**pente** /pɑ̃t/ *nf* slope; toit en ~ sloping roof
IDIOMS être sur la mauvaise ~ ⟨*person*⟩ to be going astray; ⟨*company*⟩ to be going downhill; remonter la ~ to get back on one's feet

**Pentecôte** /pɑ̃tkot/ *nf* Pentecost; à la ~ at Whitsun

**pénurie** /penyʀi/ *nf* shortage

**pépé** /pepe/ *nm* (colloq) **(a)** grandpa (colloq)
**(b)** old man

**pépère** /pepɛʀ/ *adj* (colloq) ⟨*life*⟩ cushy (colloq); ⟨*place*⟩ nice

**pépin** /pepɛ̃/ *nm* **(a)** pip; sans ~s seedless
**(b)** (colloq) slight problem
**(c)** (colloq) umbrella

**pépinière** /pepinjɛʀ/ *nf* (for trees, plants) nursery

**pépite** /pepit/ *nf* nugget

**péquenaud, ~e** /pɛkno, od/ *nm,f* (colloq) country bumpkin (colloq)

**perçant, ~e** /pɛʀsɑ̃, ɑ̃t/ *adj* **(a)** ⟨*cry, voice*⟩ shrill; ⟨*gaze*⟩ piercing
**(b)** ⟨*vision*⟩ sharp

**percée** /pɛʀse/ *nf* **(a)** opening

···❖

**(b)** breakthrough

**perce-neige** /pɛʀsənɛʒ/ *nm inv or* nf inv
snowdrop

**perce-oreille**, *pl* **~s** /pɛʀsɔʀɛj/ *nm*
earwig

**percepteur** /pɛʀsɛptœʀ/ *nm* tax inspector

**perceptible** /pɛʀsɛptibl/ *adj* **(a)** ⟨*sound*⟩
perceptible
**(b)** ⟨*tax*⟩ payable

**perception** /pɛʀsɛpsjɔ̃/ *nf* **(a)** tax office
**(b)** perception

**percer** /pɛʀse/ [12] **1** *vtr* **(a)** to pierce
⟨*body, surface*⟩; to burst ⟨*abscess, eardrum*⟩
**(b)** to make ⟨*door*⟩; to bore ⟨*tunnel*⟩; to build
⟨*road*⟩; ~ **un trou dans** to make a hole in
**(c)** to pierce ⟨*silence, air*⟩; to break through
⟨*clouds*⟩
**(d)** to penetrate ⟨*secret*⟩; ~ **qn à jour** to see
through sb
**(e)** ~ **ses dents** to be teething
**2** *vi* **(a)** ⟨*sun*⟩ to break through; ⟨*plant*⟩ to
come up; ⟨*tooth*⟩ to come through
**(b)** (Mil, Sport) to break through
**(c)** ⟨*actor*⟩ to become known

**perceuse** /pɛʀsøz/ *nf* drill

**percevable** /pɛʀsəvabl/ *adj* ⟨*tax*⟩ payable

**percevoir** /pɛʀsəvwaʀ/ [5] *vtr* **(a)** to collect
⟨*tax*⟩; to receive ⟨*rent*⟩
**(b)** to perceive ⟨*change*⟩; to feel ⟨*vibration*⟩;
**être perçu comme** to be seen as

**perche** /pɛʀʃ/ *nf* **(a)** (gen) pole; (of ski tow) T-
bar; (for microphone) boom
**(b)** (colloq) (grande) ~ beanpole (colloq)
**(c)** (Zool) perch
IDIOMS **tendre la ~ à qn** to throw sb a line

**perché**, **~e** /pɛʀʃe/ *pp adj* perched; **voix
haut ~e** high-pitched voice; **ma valise est ~e
en haut de l'armoire** my suitcase is on top of
the wardrobe

**percher** /pɛʀʃe/ [1] **1** *vtr* ~ **qch sur une
étagère** to stick sth up on a shelf
**2** *vi* to perch; to roost
**3** **se percher** *v refl* (+ *v être*) to perch

**perchoir** /pɛʀʃwaʀ/ *nm* **(a)** perch
**(b)** (Pol) (colloq) Speaker's Chair

**perclus**, **~e** /pɛʀkly, yz/ *adj* crippled

**percolateur** /pɛʀkɔlatœʀ/ *nm* (espresso)
coffee machine

**percussions** /pɛʀkysjɔ̃/ *nf pl* **les ~**
percussion instruments; percussion section;
drums

**percutant**, **~e** /pɛʀkytɑ̃, ɑ̃t/ *adj*
⟨*criticism*⟩ hard-hitting; ⟨*slogan*⟩ punchy
(colloq)

**percuter** /pɛʀkyte/ [1] **1** *vtr* ⟨*car, driver*⟩
to hit
**2** *vi* ~ **contre** ⟨*vehicle*⟩ to crash into; ⟨*shell*⟩
to explode against
**3** **se percuter** *v refl* (+ *v être*) to collide

**perdant**, **~e** /pɛʀdɑ̃, ɑ̃t/ **1** *adj* losing;
**être ~** to have lost out
**2** *nm,f* loser

**perdition** /pɛʀdisjɔ̃/ *nf* **(a)** **lieu de ~** den of
iniquity

**(b) en ~** ⟨*ship*⟩ in distress

**perdre** /pɛʀdʀ/ [6] **1** *vtr* **(a)** to lose; ~ **de
vue** to lose sight of; **leurs actions ont perdu
9%** their shares have dropped 9%
**(b)** to shed ⟨*leaves, flowers*⟩
**(c)** to miss ⟨*chance*⟩
**(d)** to waste ⟨*day, years*⟩; **perdre son temps**
to waste one's time
**(e) je perds mes chaussures** my shoes are
too big; **je perds mon pantalon** my trousers
are falling down
**(f)** to bring [sb] down; **cet homme te perdra**
that man will be your undoing
**2** *vi* to lose; **j'y perds** I lose out
**3** **se perdre** *v refl* (+ *v être*) **(a)** to get lost;
**se ~ dans ses pensées** to be lost in thought
**(b)** ⟨*tradition*⟩ to die out
IDIOMS ~ **la raison** or **l'esprit** to go out of
one's mind

**perdrix** /pɛʀdʀi/ *nf inv* partridge

**perdu**, **~e** /pɛʀdy/ **1** *pp* ▶ PERDRE
**2** *pp adj* **(a)** lost; **chien ~** stray dog; **balle
~e** stray bullet; **c'est ~ d'avance** it's
hopeless
**(b)** ⟨*day, opportunity*⟩ wasted; **c'est du temps
~** it's a waste of time
**(c)** ⟨*harvest*⟩ ruined; **il est ~** there's no hope
for him
**(d)** ⟨*person*⟩ lost
**3** *adj* remote, isolated
IDIOMS **se lancer à corps ~ dans** to throw
oneself headlong into; **ce n'est pas ~ pour
tout le monde** somebody will do all right out
of it

**père** /pɛʀ/ *nm* father; **Dupont ~** Dupont
senior; **le ~ Dupont** (colloq) old Dupont (colloq)
■ **le ~ Noël** Santa Claus

**péremption** /peʀɑ̃psjɔ̃/ *nf* **date de ~** use-
by date

**péremptoire** /peʀɑ̃ptwaʀ/ *adj* peremptory

**perfection** /pɛʀfɛksjɔ̃/ *nf* perfection

**perfectionnement** /pɛʀfɛksjɔnmɑ̃/ *nm*
improvement

**perfectionner** /pɛʀfɛksjɔne/ [1] **1** *vtr* to
perfect ⟨*technique*⟩; to refine ⟨*art*⟩
**2** **se perfectionner** *v refl* (+ *v être*) to
improve

**perfectionniste** /pɛʀfɛksjɔnist/ *adj, nmf*
perfectionist

**perfide** /pɛʀfid/ *adj* perfidious, treacherous

**perfidie** /pɛʀfidi/ *nf* perfidy, treachery

**perforation** /pɛʀfɔʀasjɔ̃/ *nf* perforation

**perforer** /pɛʀfɔʀe/ [1] *vtr* **(a)** to pierce; to
perforate
**(b)** to punch; **carte perforée** punch card

**performance** /pɛʀfɔʀmɑ̃s/ *nf* **(a)** result,
performance
**(b)** achievement

**performant**, **~e** /pɛʀfɔʀmɑ̃, ɑ̃t/ *adj* ⟨*car,
equipment*⟩ high-performance; ⟨*person,
techniques*⟩ efficient; ⟨*company*⟩ competitive

**perfusion** /pɛʀfyzjɔ̃/ *nm* (Med) drip (GB),
IV (US)

**péricliter** /peʀiklite/ [1] *vi* to be going
downhill

**péridurale** /peʀidyʀal/ *nf* epidural

**péril** /peʀil/ *nm* peril, danger; **à ses risques et ∼s** at his/her own risk; **il n'y a pas ∼ en la demeure** what's the hurry?

**périlleux, -euse** /peʀijø, øz/ *adj* perilous

**périmé, ∼e** /peʀime/ *adj* (a) out-of-date; **son passeport est ∼** his/her passport has expired
(b) ‹*idea, custom*› outdated

**périmètre** /peʀimɛtʀ/ *nm* (a) perimeter
(b) area

**périnée** /peʀine/ *nm* perineum

**période** /peʀjɔd/ *nf* period; era

**périodique** /peʀjɔdik/ ⒈ *adj* (a) ‹*fever*› recurring
(b) **serviette ∼** sanitary towel (GB), sanitary napkin (US)
⒉ *nm* periodical

**péripétie** /peʀipesi/ *nf* (a) incident
(b) event
(c) adventure
(d) **les ∼s d'une intrigue** the twists and turns of a plot

**périphérie** /peʀifeʀi/ *nf* periphery

**périphérique** /peʀifeʀik/ ⒈ *adj* (gen) peripheral; ‹*area*› outlying; **radio ∼** broadcasting station situated outside the territory to which it transmits
⒉ *nm* ring road (GB), beltway (US)

**périphrase** /peʀifʀaz/ *nf* circumlocution

**périple** /peʀipl/ *nm* journey; voyage

**périr** /peʀiʀ/ [3] *vi* to die, to perish

**périscolaire** /peʀiskɔlɛʀ/ *adj* extracurricular

**périscope** /peʀiskɔp/ *nm* periscope

**périssable** /peʀisabl/ *adj* perishable

**Péritel®** /peʀitɛl/ *nf* **prise ∼** scart socket; scart plug

**perle** /pɛʀl/ *nf* (a) pearl; **∼ fine** real pearl
(b) (figurative) gem; **∼ rare** real treasure
(c) (colloq) howler (colloq)

**perler** /pɛʀle/ [1] *vi* ‹*drop, tear*› to appear

**permanence** /pɛʀmanɑ̃s/ ⒈ *nf*
(a) permanence
(b) persistence
(c) **∼ téléphonique** manned line; **assurer** *or* **tenir une ∼** to be on duty; to hold a surgery (GB), to have office hours (US)
(d) permanently manned office
(e) (Sch) (private) study room (GB), study hall (US)
⒉ **en permanence** *phr* (a) permanently
(b) constantly

**permanent, ∼e¹** /pɛʀmanɑ̃, ɑ̃t/ *adj*
(a) ‹*staff, exhibition*› permanent; ‹*committee*› standing
(b) ‹*tension, danger*› constant; ‹*show*› continuous

**permanente²** /pɛʀmanɑ̃t/ *nf* perm

**perméable** /pɛʀmeabl/ *adj* permeable

**permettre** /pɛʀmɛtʀ/ [60] ⒈ *vtr* (a) **∼ à qn de faire** to allow sb to do, to give sb permission to do; **(vous) permettez!** j'étais là

avant! excuse me! I was here first!; **il est menteur comme c'est pas permis** (colloq) he's an incredible liar
(b) **∼ à qn de faire** to allow *or* enable sb to do, to give sb the opportunity to do; **leurs moyens ne le leur permettent pas** they can't afford it; **autant qu'il est permis d'en juger** as far as one can tell
⒉ **se permettre** *v refl* (+ *v être*) (a) **je peux me ∼ ce genre de plaisanterie avec lui** I can get away with telling him that kind of joke; **se ∼ de faire** to take the liberty of doing
(b) **je ne peux pas me ∼ d'acheter une nouvelle voiture** I can't afford to buy a new car

**permis, ∼e** /pɛʀmi, iz/ ⒈ *pp* ▶
PERMETTRE
⒉ *pp adj* permitted
⒊ *nm inv* permit, licence (GB)
■ **∼ de conduire** driver's licence (GB); driving test; **∼ de séjour** residence permit; **∼ de travail** work permit

**permission** /pɛʀmisjɔ̃/ *nf* (a) permission
(b) (Mil) leave; **partir en ∼** to go on leave

**permutable** /pɛʀmytabl/ *adj* interchangeable

**permuter** /pɛʀmyte/ [1] *vtr* to switch [sth] around ‹*letters, labels*›

**pernicieux, -ieuse** /pɛʀnisjø, øz/ *adj* pernicious

**Pérou** /peʀu/ *pr nm* Peru
**IDIOMS ce n'est pas le ∼** it's not a fortune

**perpendiculaire** /pɛʀpɑ̃dikylɛʀ/ *adj, nf* perpendicular

**perpète** /pɛʀpɛt/ *nf* (colloq) **être condamné à ∼** ‹prisoners' slang› to get life (colloq); **habiter à ∼** to live miles away

**perpétrer** /pɛʀpetʀe/ [14] *vtr* to perpetrate

**perpétuel, -elle** /pɛʀpetɥɛl/ *adj* perpetual

**perpétuellement** /pɛʀpetɥɛlmɑ̃/ *adv* constantly, perpetually

**perpétuer** /pɛʀpetɥe/ [1] *vtr* to perpetuate

**perpétuité** /pɛʀpetɥite/ *nf* perpetuity; **à ∼** (Law) ‹imprisonment› life

**perplexe** /pɛʀplɛks/ *adj* perplexed, baffled

**perplexité** /pɛʀplɛksite/ *nf* perplexity

**perquisition** /pɛʀkizisjɔ̃/ *nf* search

**perquisitionner** /pɛʀkizisjɔne/ [1] *vtr* to search ‹house›

**perron** /peʀɔ̃/ *nm* flight of steps

**perroquet** /peʀɔkɛ/ *nm* parrot

**perruche** /peʀyʃ/ *nf* budgerigar (GB), parakeet (US)

**perruque** /peʀyk/ *nf* wig

**persan, ∼e** /pɛʀsɑ̃, an/ *adj* Persian

**perse** /pɛʀs/ *adj* Persian

**persécuter** /pɛʀsekyte/ [1] *vtr* to persecute

**persécution** /pɛʀsekysjɔ̃/ *nf* persecution

**persévérance** /pɛʀseveʀɑ̃s/ *nf* perseverance

**p**

**persévérer** /pɛʀseveʀe/ [14] *vi* (a) to persevere
(b) to persist
**persienne** /pɛʀsjɛn/ *nf* (louvred (GB)) shutter
**persiflage** /pɛʀsiflaʒ/ *nm* mockery
**persifleur, -euse** /pɛʀsiflœʀ, øz/ *adj* ⟨tone, comment⟩ mocking
**persil** /pɛʀsi(l)/ *nm* parsley
**persistance** /pɛʀsistɑ̃s/ *nf* persistence
**persistant, ~e** /pɛʀsistɑ̃, ɑ̃t/ *adj* ⟨heat, problem⟩ continuing; ⟨smell, snow⟩ lingering; ⟨cough, symptom⟩ persistent
**persister** /pɛʀsiste/ [1] *vi* ⟨symptom, pain⟩ to persist; ⟨inflation⟩ to continue; **je persiste à croire que** I still think that
**personnage** /pɛʀsɔnaʒ/ *nm* (a) character
(b) figure; **un ~ public** a public figure
**personnaliser** /pɛʀsɔnalize/ [1] *vtr* to add a personal touch to
**personnalité** /pɛʀsɔnalite/ *nf*
(a) personality
(b) important person
**personne¹** /pɛʀsɔn/ *pron* anyone, anybody; no-one, nobody; **~ n'est parfait** nobody's perfect
**personne²** /pɛʀsɔn/ *nf* person; **dix ~s** ten people; **les ~s âgées** the elderly; **bien fait de sa ~** good-looking; **le respect de la ~** respect for the individual; **il s'en occupe en ~** he's dealing with it personally; **c'est la cupidité en ~** he/she is greed personified
■ **~ à charge** dependant; **~ civile** *or* **morale** artificial person, legal entity
**personnel, -elle** /pɛʀsɔnɛl/ **1** *adj*
(a) ⟨friend, effects⟩ personal; ⟨papers⟩ private
(b) individual
(c) selfish
(d) ⟨pronoun⟩ personal
**2** *nm* staff; workforce; employees, personnel
**personnellement** /pɛʀsɔnɛlmɑ̃/ *adv* personally
**personnifier** /pɛʀsɔnifje/ [2] *vtr* to personify
**perspective** /pɛʀspɛktiv/ *nf* (a) (in art) perspective
(b) view
(c) perspective, angle
(d) prospect
**perspicace** /pɛʀspikas/ *adj* perceptive
**perspicacité** /pɛʀspikasite/ *nf* insight, perspicacity
**persuader** /pɛʀsɥade/ [1] *vtr* to persuade
**persuasif, -ive** /pɛʀsɥazif, iv/ *adj* persuasive
**persuasion** /pɛʀsɥazjɔ̃/ *nf* persuasion
**perte** /pɛʀt/ *nf* (a) loss; **à ~ de vue** as far as the eye can see
(b) waste
(c) ruin; **courir** *or* **aller à sa ~** to be heading for a fall
**pertinemment** /pɛʀtinamɑ̃/ *adv*
(a) perfectly well
(b) pertinently

**pertinence** /pɛʀtinɑ̃s/ *nf* pertinence
**pertinent, ~e** /pɛʀtinɑ̃, ɑ̃t/ *adj* pertinent
**perturbant, ~e** /pɛʀtyʀbɑ̃, ɑ̃t/ *adj* disturbing
**perturbation** /pɛʀtyʀbasjɔ̃/ *nf*
(a) disruption
(b) disturbance
(c) upheaval
**perturber** /pɛʀtyʀbe/ [1] *vtr* to disrupt ⟨traffic, market, meeting⟩; to interfere with ⟨development⟩; to disturb ⟨sleep⟩
**pervenche** /pɛʀvɑ̃ʃ/ *nf* (a) periwinkle
(b) (colloq) (female) traffic warden (GB), meter maid (US) (colloq)
**pervers, ~e** /pɛʀvɛʀ, ɛʀs/ **1** *adj*
(a) wicked
(b) perverted
(c) ⟨effect⟩ pernicious
**2** *nm,f* pervert
**perversion** /pɛʀvɛʀsjɔ̃/ *nf* perversion
**perversité** /pɛʀvɛʀsite/ *nf* perversity
**pervertir** /pɛʀvɛʀtiʀ/ [3] *vtr* to corrupt
**pesant, ~e** /pəzɑ̃, ɑ̃t/ *adj* (a) heavy
(b) cumbersome
(c) ⟨atmosphere, silence⟩ oppressive
IDIOMS **valoir son ~ d'or** to be worth its weight in gold
**pesanteur** /pəzɑ̃tœʀ/ *nf* (a) (of style) heaviness; (of bureaucracy) inertia
(b) gravity
**pèse-personne**, *pl* **~s** /pɛzpɛʀsɔn/ *nm* bathroom scales
**peser** /pəze/ [16] **1** *vtr* (a) to weigh
(b) to weigh up; **~ ses mots** to choose one's words carefully; **tout bien pesé** all things considered
**2** *vi* (a) to weigh; **je pèse 70 kg** I weigh 70 kg; **~ lourd** to weigh a lot
(b) to carry weight; **~ dans/sur une décision** to have a decisive influence in/on a decision
(c) **~ sur** ⟨suspicion⟩ to hang over ⟨person⟩
(d) ⟨tax, debts⟩ to weigh [sb/sth] down ⟨person, country⟩
(e) ⟨person, decision⟩ to influence (greatly) ⟨policy⟩
**peseta** /pezeta/ *nf* peseta
**pessimisme** /pesimism/ *nm* pessimism
**pessimiste** /pesimist/ **1** *adj* pessimistic
**2** *nmf* pessimist
**peste** /pɛst/ *nf* (a) plague
(b) (colloq) pest (colloq)
IDIOMS **je me méfie de lui comme de la ~** (colloq) I don't trust him an inch
**pester** /pɛste/ [1] *vi* **~ contre qn/qch** to curse sb/sth
**pesticide** /pɛstisid/ *nm* pesticide
**pet** /pɛ/ *nm* (colloq) fart (colloq)
**pétale** /petal/ *nm* petal
**pétanque** /petɑ̃k/ *nf* petanque
**pétarader** /petaʀade/ [1] *vi* to backfire
**pétard** /petaʀ/ *nm* banger (GB), firecracker (US); **être en ~** (colloq) to be hopping mad (GB) (colloq), to be real mad (US) (colloq)
**péter** /pete/ [14] *vi* (a) (slang) to fart (colloq)

**(b)** (colloq) ⟨*balloon*⟩ to burst; ⟨*situation*⟩ to blow up; ⟨*thread*⟩ to snap

**pétillant**, ~**e** /petijã, ãt/ *adj* sparkling

**pétiller** /petije/ [1] *vi* ⟨*drink*⟩ to fizz; ⟨*firewood*⟩ to crackle; ⟨*eyes*⟩ to sparkle

**petit**, ~**e** /p(ə)ti, it/ **1** *adj* **(a)** small, little; short; **une toute** ~**e pièce** a tiny room; **se faire tout** ~ (figurative) to try to make oneself inconspicuous
**(b)** ⟨*walk, distance*⟩ short
**(c)** young, little; **c'est notre** ~ **dernier** he's our youngest
**(d)** ⟨*eater*⟩ light; ⟨*wage*⟩ low; ⟨*cry, worry*⟩ little; ⟨*hope*⟩ slight; ⟨*detail, defect*⟩ minor; ⟨*job*⟩ modest
**(e) une** ~**e trentaine de personnes** under thirty people
**2** *adv* **tailler** ~ to be small-fitting; ~ **à** ~ little by little
■ ~ **ami** boyfriend; ~ **bois** kindling; ~ **coin** (colloq) (euphemistic) loo (GB) (colloq), bathroom (US); ~ **déjeuner** breakfast; ~ **noir** (colloq) coffee; ~ **nom** (colloq) first name; ~ **pois** (garden) pea, petit pois; ~ **pot** jar of baby food; ~ **rat** (de l'Opéra) pupil at Paris Opéra's ballet school; ~ **salé** streaky salted pork; ~**e amie** girlfriend; ~**e annonce** classified advertisement; ~**e nature** weakling; ~**e reine** cycling; ~**e voiture** toy car; ~**s chevaux** ≈ ludo

**petit-beurre**, *pl* **petits-beurre** /p(ə)tibœr/ *nm* petit beurre biscuit

**petit-cousin**, **petite-cousine**, *mpl* **petits-cousins** /p(ə)tikuzɛ̃, p(ə)titkuzin/ *nm,f* second cousin

**petite-fille**, *pl* **petites-filles** /p(ə)titfij/ *nf* granddaughter

**petitesse** /p(ə)titɛs/ *nf* **(a)** pettiness
**(b)** small size

**petit-fils**, *pl* **petits-fils** /p(ə)tifis/ *nm* grandson

**pétition** /petisjɔ̃/ *nf* petition

**petit-lait** /p(ə)tilɛ/ *nm* **ça se boit comme du** ~**!** (colloq) it slips down nicely!

**petit-nègre** /p(ə)tinɛgr/ *nm inv* (colloq) pidgin French

**petits-enfants** /p(ə)tizɑ̃fɑ̃/ *nm pl* grandchildren

**pétrifiant**, ~**e** /petrifjã, ãt/ *adj* petrifying

**pétrifier** /petrifje/ [2] *vtr* **(a)** to petrify
**(b)** (figurative) to transfix

**pétrin** /petrɛ̃/ *nm* dough trough
**IDIOMS être dans le** ~ to be in a fix (colloq)

**pétrir** /petrir/ [3] *vtr* **(a)** to knead ⟨*dough*⟩
**(b)** to mould (GB), to mold (US) ⟨*personality*⟩

**pétrole** /petrɔl/ *nm* oil, petroleum

**pétrolette** /petrɔlɛt/ *nf* (colloq) moped

**pétrolier**, -**ière** /petrɔlje, ɛr/ **1** *adj* oil
**2** *nm* oil tanker

**pétulant**, ~**e** /petylã, ãt/ *adj* exuberant

**peu** /pø/
■ **Note** See the entries *avant, depuis, d'ici* and *sous* for the use of *peu* with these words.

**1** *adv* **(a)** not much; **il parle** ~ he doesn't talk much; **elle gagne très** ~ she earns very little; **deux semaines c'est trop** ~ two weeks isn't long enough; **si** ~ **que ce soit** however little; **très** ~ **pour moi!** (colloq) thanks, but no thanks!
**(b)** not very; **assez** ~ **connu** little-known; **elle n'est pas** ~ **fière** she's more than a little proud
**2** *pron* few, not many
**3 de peu** *phr* only just
**4 peu de** *quantif* ~ **de mots** few words; ~ **de temps** little time
**5** *nm* **le** ~ **de** the little ⟨*trust, freedom*⟩; the few ⟨*books, friends*⟩; the lack of ⟨*interest*⟩
**6 un peu** *phr* **(a)** a little, a bit; **reste encore un** ~ stay a little longer; **parle un** ~ **plus fort** speak a little louder; **un** ~ **plus de** a few more ⟨*books*⟩; **a little more** ⟨*time*⟩; **un** ~ **beaucoup** more than a bit
**(b)** just; **répète un** ~ **pour voir!** (colloq) you just try saying that again!; **pour un** ~ **ils se seraient battus** they very nearly had a fight
**7 peu à peu** *phr* gradually, little by little
**8 pour peu que** *phr* if; **pour** ~ **qu'il ait bu, il va nous raconter sa vie** one drink, and he'll tell us his life story

**peuplade** /pœplad/ *nf* small tribe

**peuple** /pœpl/ *nm* people

**peuplement** /pœpləmã/ *nm* population

**peupler** /pœple/ [1] **1** *vtr* **(a)** to populate ⟨*country*⟩; to stock ⟨*forest, pond*⟩
**(b)** ⟨*animals, plants*⟩ to colonize ⟨*region*⟩; ⟨*students*⟩ to fill ⟨*street*⟩
**2 se peupler** *v refl* (+ *v être*) to fill up

**peuplier** /pøplije/ *nm* poplar

**peur** /pœr/ *nf* fear; fright; scare; **être mort** *or* **vert** (colloq) **de** ~ to be scared to death; **une** ~ **panique s'empara de lui** he was panic-stricken; **avoir** ~ to be afraid; **j'en ai bien** ~ I'm afraid so; **faire** ~ **à qn** to frighten sb; **maigre à faire** ~ terribly thin

**peureusement** /pœrøzmã/ *adv* fearfully

**peureux**, -**euse** /pœrø, øz/ *adj* fearful

**peut-être** /pøtɛtr/ *adv* perhaps, maybe

**phalange** /falɑ̃ʒ/ *nf* phalanx

**phallocrate** /falɔkrat/ *nm* male chauvinist

**phalloïde** /falɔid/ *adj* **amanite** ~ death cap

**phallus** /falys/ *nm inv* phallus

**pharaon** /faraɔ̃/ *nm* pharaoh

**phare** /far/ *nm* **(a)** headlight
**(b)** lighthouse

**pharmacie** /farmasi/ *nf* **(a)** chemist's (shop) (GB), drugstore (US), pharmacy
**(b)** medicine cabinet
**(c)** (science) pharmacy

**pharmacien**, -**ienne** /farmasjɛ̃, ɛn/ *nm,f* (dispensing) chemist (GB), pharmacist

**pharyngite** /farɛ̃ʒit/ *nf* pharyngitis

**pharynx** /faʀɛks/ *nm inv* pharynx
**phase** /faz/ *nf* **(a)** stage
 **(b)** phase
**phénoménal, ~e**, *mpl* **-aux**
 /fenɔmenal, o/ *adj* phenomenal
**phénomène** /fenɔmɛn/ *nm*
 **(a)** phenomenon
 **(b)** (colloq) **c'est un ~** he/she's quite a
 character
**philanthropie** /filɑ̃tʀɔpi/ *nf* philanthropy
**philatélie** /filateli/ *nf* stamp collecting
**philatéliste** /filatelist/ *nmf* philatelist
**philosophe** /filɔzɔf/ *nmf* philosopher
**philosophie** /filɔzɔfi/ *nf* philosophy
**philosophique** /filɔzɔfik/ *adj*
 philosophical
**phobie** /fɔbi/ *nf* phobia
**phonétique** /fɔnetik/ **1** *adj* phonetic
 **2** *nf* phonetics
**phonographe** /fɔnɔgʀaf/ *nm* gramophone
 (GB), phonograph (US)
**phoque** /fɔk/ *nm* **(a)** seal
 **(b)** sealskin
**phosphate** /fɔsfat/ *nm* phosphate
**phosphore** /fɔsfɔʀ/ *nm* phosphorus
**phosphorescent, ~e** /fɔsfɔʀesɑ̃, ɑ̃t/
 *adj* phosphorescent
**photo** /fɔto/ *nf* **(a)** photography
 **(b)** photo
 ■ **~ d'identité** passport photo
**photocomposition** /fɔtokɔ̃pozisjɔ̃/ *nf*
 filmsetting (GB), photocomposition (US)
**photocopie** /fɔtokɔpi/ *nf* photocopy
**photocopier** /fɔtokɔpje/ [2] *vtr* to
 photocopy
**photocopieur** /fɔtokɔpjœʀ/ *nm*
 photocopier
**photocopieuse** /fɔtokɔpjøz/ *nf*
 photocopier
**photogénique** /fɔtoʒenik/ *adj* photogenic
**photographe** /fɔtogʀaf/ *nmf*
 photographer
**photographie** /fɔtogʀafi/ *nf*
 **(a)** photography
 **(b)** photograph, picture
**photographier** /fɔtogʀafje/ [2] *vtr* to
 photograph, to take a photo of
**photographique** /fɔtogʀafik/ *adj*
 photographic
**photomaton®** /fɔtomatɔ̃/ *nm* photo booth
**photosynthèse** /fɔtosɛ̃tɛz/ *nf*
 photosynthesis
**photothèque** /fɔtotɛk/ *nf* picture library
**phrase** /fʀaz/ *nf* **(a)** sentence
 **(b)** phrase; **avoir une ~ malheureuse** to say
 the wrong thing; **~ toute faite** stock phrase
 **(c)** (Mus) phrase
**phréatique** /fʀeatik/ *adj* **nappe ~** ground
 water
**physicien, -ienne** /fizisjɛ̃, ɛn/ *nm,f*
 physicist
**physiologie** /fizjɔlɔʒi/ *nf* physiology

**physiologique** /fizjɔlɔʒik/ *adj*
 physiological
**physionomie** /fizjɔnɔmi/ *nf* **(a)** face
 **(b)** (figurative) (of country) face; (of area)
 appearance, look
**physiothérapie** /fizjoteʀapi/ *nf*
 physiotherapy (GB), physical therapy (US)
**physique¹** /fizik/ **1** *adj* physical
 **2** *nm* **(a)** physical appearance
 **(b)** physique; **avoir un ~ séduisant** to look
 attractive
 IDIOMS **avoir le ~ de l'emploi** to look the
 part
**physique²** /fizik/ *nf* physics
**piaf** /pjaf/ *nm* (colloq) little bird
**piaffer** /pjafe/ [1] *vi* **(a)** ⟨horse⟩ to paw the
 ground
 **(b)** ⟨person⟩ to be impatient; **~ d'impatience**
 to be champing at the bit
**piailler** /pjɑje/ [1] *vi* ⟨bird⟩ to chirp
**pianiste** /pjanist/ *nmf* pianist
**piano** /pjano/ **1** *nm* piano; **jouer qch au ~**
 to play sth on the piano
 **2** *adv* (Mus) piano
 ■ **~ à queue** grand piano
**pianoter** /pjanɔte/ [1] *vi* to tinkle on the
 piano
**PIB** /peibe/ *nm: abbr* ▶ PRODUIT
**pic** /pik/ **1** *nm* **(a)** peak
 **(b)** pick
 **(c)** woodpecker
 **2 à pic** *phr* ⟨cliff⟩ sheer; ⟨ravine⟩ very
 steep
 IDIOMS **tomber à ~** to come just at the right
 time
**pichenette** /piʃnɛt/ *nf* flick
**pichet** /piʃɛ/ *nm* jug (GB), pitcher
**pick-up** /pikœp/ *nm inv* (colloq) record
 player
**picorer** /pikɔʀe/ [1] *vi* ⟨bird⟩ to peck about
**picotement** /pikɔtmɑ̃/ *nm* tingling;
 tickling
**picoter** /pikɔte/ [1] **1** *vtr* to sting ⟨eyes,
 nose, skin⟩; to tickle ⟨throat⟩
 **2** *vi* ⟨throat⟩ to tickle; ⟨eyes⟩ to sting
**pie** /pi/ *nf* **(a)** magpie
 **(b)** (colloq) chatterbox (colloq)
**pièce** /pjɛs/ **1** *nf* **(a)** room
 **(b)** coin; **~ de monnaie** coin
 **(c)** play; **~ de théâtre** play
 **(d)** bit, piece; **en ~s** in bits; **mettre qn/qch
 en ~s** to pull sb/sth to pieces
 **(e)** part; **~ de rechange** spare part
 **(f)** patch
 **(g)** document; **juger sur ~s** to judge on the
 actual evidence; **c'est inventé de toutes ~s**
 (figurative) it's a complete fabrication
 **(h)** piece, item; (in chess set, puzzle) piece; **~ de
 collection** collector's item; **on n'est pas aux
 ~s** (colloq) we're not in a sweat-shop
 **2 -pièces** (*combining form*) **(a) un trois-
 ~s cuisine** a three-roomed apartment with
 kitchen
 **(b) un deux-~s** a two-piece swimsuit

■ ~ **à conviction** exhibit; ~ **détachée** spare part; **en** ~**s détachées** in kit form; dismantled; ~ **d'identité** identity papers; ~ **maîtresse** showpiece; key element; ~ **montée** layer cake

**piécette** /pjesεt/ *nf* small coin

**pied** /pje/ *nm* **(a)** foot; **être** ~**s nus** to be barefoot(ed); **les** ~**s joints** with one's feet together; (figurative) to jump in with both feet; **coup de** ~ kick; **à** ~ on foot; **promenade à** ~ walk; **taper du** ~ to stamp one's foot; to tap one's foot; **de la tête aux** ~**s** from head to foot; **portrait en** ~ full-length portrait; **avoir conscience de là où on met les** ~**s** (colloq) to know what one is letting oneself in for; **sur un** ~ **d'égalité** on an equal footing
**(b)** (of hill, stairs) foot, bottom; (of glass) stem; (of lamp) base; (of camera) stand
**(c)** (of celery, lettuce) head; ~ **de vigne** vine
**(d)** (measurement) foot
■ ~ **à coulisse** calliper rule
IDIOMS **être sur** ~ (*person*) to be up and about; (*business*) to be up and running; **mettre sur** ~ to set up; **j'ai** ~ I can touch the bottom; **perdre** ~ to go out of one's depth; to lose ground; **être à** ~ **d'œuvre** to be ready to get down to work; **elle joue au tennis comme un** ~ (colloq) she's hopeless at tennis; **faire un** ~ **de nez à qn** to thumb one's nose at sb; **faire du** ~ **à qn** to play footsy with sb (colloq); **faire des** ~**s et des mains** (colloq) **pour obtenir** to work really hard at getting; **ça lui fera les** ~**s** (colloq) that will teach him a lesson; **c'est le** ~ (colloq) that's terrific (colloq); **mettre à** ~ to suspend; **lever le** ~ (colloq) to slow down

**pied-à-terre** /pjetatεʀ/ *nm inv* pied-à-terre

**pied-bot**, *pl* **pieds-bots** /pjebo/ *nm* person with a club foot

**piédestal**, *pl* **-aux** /pjedεstal, o/ *nm* pedestal

**pied-noir**, *pl* **pieds-noirs** /pjenwaʀ/ *nmf* (colloq): *French colonial born in Algeria*

**piège** /pjεʒ/ *nm* **(a)** trap; **il s'est laissé prendre au** ~ he walked into the trap
**(b)** pitfall

**piéger** /pjeʒe/ [15] *vtr* **(a)** to trap (*animal, criminal*)
**(b)** to trick, to trap (*person*)
**(c)** to booby-trap (*letter, parcel, car*)

**piercing** /piʀsiŋ/ *nm* **le** ~ body piercing; **elle a un** ~ **au nombril** she has a pierced navel

**pierre** /pjεʀ/ *nf* stone; rock; **poser la première** ~ to lay the foundation stone
IDIOMS **jeter la** ~ **à qn** to accuse sb; **faire d'une** ~ **deux coups** to kill two birds with one stone

**pierreries** /pjεʀʀi/ *nf pl* gems

**pierreux, -euse** /pjεʀø, øz/ *adj* stony

**piété** /pjete/ *nf* piety; **de** ~ devotional

**piétiner** /pjetine/ [1] **1** *vtr* **(a)** to trample [sth] underfoot

**(b)** to trample on
**2** *vi* **(a)** ~ **d'impatience** to hop up and down with impatience
**(b)** to shuffle along; to trudge along
**(c)** to make no headway

**piéton, -onne** /pjetɔ̃, ɔn/ **1** *adj* pedestrianized
**2** *nm,f* pedestrian

**piétonnier, -ière** /pjetɔnje, εʀ/ *adj* pedestrianized

**piètre** /pjεtʀ/ *adj* (*actor, writer*) very mediocre; (*health, results*) very poor; **c'est une** ~ **consolation** that's small comfort

**pieu, pl** ~**x**[1] /pjø/ *nm* stake

**pieuvre** /pjœvʀ/ *nf* octopus

**pieux**[2], **pieuse** /pjø, øz/ *adj* **(a)** pious, religious
**(b)** (*affection, silence*) reverent
■ ~ **mensonge** white lie

**pif** /pif/ *nm* (colloq) **(a)** nose, conk (GB) (colloq), schnozzle (US) (colloq)
**(b)** intuition; **j'ai eu du** ~ I had a hunch (colloq); **au** ~ (*measure*) roughly; (*decide*) just like that

**pige** /piʒ/ *nf* **travailler à la** ~, **faire des** ~**s** to do freelance work

**pigeon** /piʒɔ̃/ *nm* **(a)** pigeon
**(b)** (colloq) sucker (colloq)
■ ~ **voyageur** carrier pigeon

**pigeonnier** /piʒɔnje/ *nm* pigeon house; pigeon loft; dovecote

**piger** /piʒe/ [13] *vtr* (colloq) to understand

**pigiste** /piʒist/ *nmf* freelance

**pigment** /pigmɑ̃/ *nm* pigment

**pigmenter** /pigmɑ̃te/ [1] *vtr* to alter the pigmentation of

**pignon** /piɲɔ̃/ *nm* **(a)** gable
**(b)** gearwheel
**(c)** pine kernel
IDIOMS **avoir** ~ **sur rue** to be well-established

**pilaf** /pilaf/ *nm* pilau; **riz** ~ pilau rice

**pile**[1] /pil/ *adv* (colloq) **(a)** **s'arrêter** ~ to stop dead
**(b)** exactly; **à 10 heures et demie** ~ at ten-thirty sharp; ~ **à l'heure** right on time; **tu tombes** ~ you're just the person I wanted to see

**pile**[2] /pil/ *nf* **(a)** pile; stack
**(b)** ~ (*électrique*) battery; **à** ~**s** battery-operated
**(c)** pier
**(d)** (of coin) **le côté** ~ the reverse side; **jouer à** ~ **ou face** to play heads or tails
■ ~ **bouton** button battery; ~ **solaire** solar cell

**piler** /pile/ [1] **1** *vtr* to grind; to crush
**2** *vi* (colloq) (*car*) to pull up short; (*driver*) to slam on the brakes

**pileux, -euse** /pilø, øz/ *adj* **système** ~ hair

**pilier** /pilje/ *nm* **(a)** pillar
**(b)** (figurative) mainstay
**(c)** (in rugby) prop forward

p

**pillage** /pijaʒ/ nm pillage, plundering; looting

**pillard**, **~e** /pijaʀ, aʀd/ nm,f looter; pillager

**piller** /pije/ [1] vtr to pillage ⟨town⟩; to loot ⟨shop⟩; to plunder ⟨temple⟩

**pilleur**, **-euse** /pijœʀ, øz/ nm,f looter; plunderer

**pilon** /pilɔ̃/ nm (a) pestle
(b) (of poultry) drumstick

**pilonnage** /pilɔnaʒ/ nm (Mil) bombardment

**pilotage** /pilotaʒ/ nm piloting

**pilote** /pilɔt/ ⊡ nm pilot
⊡ (-)**pilote** (combining form) projet(-)~ pilot project; hôpital(-)~ experimental hospital
■ ~ **automobile** racing driver

**piloter** /pilote/ [1] vtr to pilot ⟨plane, ship⟩; to drive ⟨car⟩

**pilotis** /piloti/ nm inv stilts

**pilule** /pilyl/ nf pill
IDIOMS **avaler la ~** (colloq) to grin and bear it; **faire passer la ~** (colloq) to sweeten the pill

**pimbêche** /pɛ̃bɛʃ/ nf stuck-up madam (colloq)

**piment** /pimɑ̃/ nm (a) hot pepper
(b) spice
■ ~ **rouge** hot red pepper, chilli; ~ **vert** green chilli pepper

**pimpant**, **~e** /pɛ̃pɑ̃, ɑ̃t/ adj spruce, smart

**pin** /pɛ̃/ nm pine (tree); **pomme de ~** pine cone

**pinailler** /pinaje/ [1] vi (slang) to split hairs

**pince** /pɛ̃s/ nf (a) (pair of) pliers; (pair of) tongs
(b) (in garment) dart; **un pantalon à ~s** pleat front trousers (GB) or pants (US)
(c) (of crab) pincer, claw
■ ~ **à cheveux** hair grip; ~ **coupante** wire cutters; ~ **à dessin** bulldog clip; ~ **à épiler** tweezers; ~ **à linge** clothes peg; ~ **à sucre** sugar tongs; ~ **à vélo** bicycle clip

**pincé**, **~e**[1] /pɛ̃se/ adj ⟨smile⟩ tight-lipped; **prendre un air ~** to become stiff or starchy

**pinceau**, pl **~x** /pɛ̃so/ nm (paint) brush

**pincée**[2] /pɛ̃se/ ⊡ adj f ▶ PINCÉ
⊡ nf (of pepper, salt) pinch

**pincement** /pɛ̃smɑ̃/ nm pinch; **avoir un ~ de cœur** to feel a twinge of sadness

**pince-monseigneur**, pl **pinces-monseigneur** /pɛ̃smɔ̃sɛɲœʀ/ nf jemmy, slim jim

**pince-nez** /pɛ̃sne/ nm inv pince-nez

**pincer** /pɛ̃se/ [12] ⊡ vtr (a) ⟨person⟩ to pinch; ⟨crab⟩ to nip
(b) (colloq) to nab (colloq), to catch ⟨thief⟩
(c) ~ **les lèvres** to purse one's lips
(d) to pluck ⟨string⟩
(e) ⟨wind, cold⟩ to sting ⟨face⟩
⊡ **se pincer** v refl (+ v être) to pinch oneself; **se ~ le nez** to hold one's nose; **elle s'est pincée en refermant le tiroir** she caught her fingers closing the drawer

IDIOMS **en ~ pour qn** (colloq) to be stuck on sb (colloq)

**pince-sans-rire** /pɛ̃ssɑ̃ʀiʀ/ nmf inv **c'est un ~** he has a deadpan sense of humour (GB)

**pincettes** /pɛ̃sɛt/ nf pl **il n'est pas à prendre avec des ~** (colloq) he's like a bear with a sore head (colloq)

**pinède** /pinɛd/ nf pine forest

**pingouin** /pɛ̃gwɛ̃/ nm (a) auk
(b) penguin

**ping-pong**®, pl **~s** /piŋpɔ̃/ nm table tennis, ping-pong®

**pingre** /pɛ̃gʀ/ adj stingy, niggardly

**pingrerie** /pɛ̃gʀəʀi/ nf stinginess

**pin-pon** /pɛ̃pɔ̃/ nm: sound of a two-tone siren

**pin's** /pins/ nm inv lapel badge

**pintade** /pɛ̃tad/ nf guinea fowl

**pintadeau**, pl **~x** /pɛ̃tado/ nm young guinea fowl

**pinte** /pɛ̃t/ nf (a) pint (GB) (= 0,57 litre)
(b) ≈ quart (US) (= 0,94 litre)
(c) pot, tankard

**pinter**: **se pinter** /pɛ̃te/ [1] v refl (+ v être) (colloq) to get plastered (colloq) or drunk

**pin-up** /pinœp/ nf inv (colloq) glamour (GB) girl

**pioche** /pjɔʃ/ nf (a) mattock; pickaxe (GB), pickax (US)
(b) (Games) stack

**piocher** /pjɔʃe/ [1] vtr (a) to dig [sth] over ⟨soil⟩
(b) (Games) to take [sth] from the stack ⟨card⟩

**piolet** /pjɔlɛ/ nm ice axe (GB), ice pick (US)

**pion**, **pionne** /pjɔ̃, pjɔn/ ⊡ nm,f (colloq) (Sch) student paid to supervise pupils
⊡ nm (a) (in games) counter; (in chess) pawn; (in draughts) draught (GB), checker (US)
(b) (figurative) pawn

**pionnier**, **-ière** /pjɔnje, ɛʀ/ adj, nm,f pioneer

**pipe** /pip/ nf pipe
IDIOMS **casser sa ~** (colloq) to kick the bucket (colloq)

**pipeau**, pl **~x** /pipo/ nm (reed-)pipe
IDIOMS **c'est du ~** (colloq) it's no great shakes (colloq); **c'est pas du ~** (colloq) it's for real (colloq)

**pipelette** /piplɛt/ nf (colloq) gossip(monger)

**piper** /pipe/ [1] vtr (a) (colloq) **ne pas ~** (**mot**) not to say a word
(b) to load ⟨dice⟩

**pipi** /pipi/ nm (colloq) pee (colloq); wee-wee (colloq)

**piquant**, **~e** /pikɑ̃, ɑ̃t/ ⊡ adj (a) ⟨stem, thistle⟩ prickly; ⟨nail⟩ sharp
(b) ⟨mustard, sauce⟩ hot; ⟨cheese⟩ sharp
⊡ nm (a) (of stem, thistle) prickle; (of hedgehog, cactus) spine; (of barbed wire) spike, barb
(b) (of story) spiciness; (of situation) piquancy

**pique**[1] /pik/ nm (Games) spades

**pique²** /pik/ nf **(a)** cutting remark
**(b)** pike; (of picador) lance

**piqué, ~e** /pike/ adj ⟨wood⟩ worm-eaten;
⟨linen, mirror, fruit⟩ spotted; ⟨paper⟩ foxed

**pique-assiette** /pikasjɛt/ nmf inv (colloq)
sponger (colloq)

**pique-nique,** pl **~s** /piknik/ nm picnic

**piquer** /pike/ [1] **1** vtr **(a)** to sting; to bite;
to prick
**(b)** (colloq) to give [sb] an injection; **faire ~
un animal** to have an animal put down
**(c)** ⟨mildew, rust⟩ to spot ⟨linen, mirror⟩; to
fox ⟨paper, book⟩
**(d) ses yeux la piquaient** her eyes were
stinging; **ça me pique partout** I'm itchy all
over
**(e)** (colloq) to pinch (GB) (colloq), to steal
⟨book, idea⟩; to borrow ⟨pencil, pullover⟩
**(f)** to catch; **ils se sont fait ~ à tricher
pendant l'examen** they got caught cheating
in the exam
**(g) ~ qn au vif** to cut sb to the quick
**(h)** to arouse ⟨curiosity⟩
**(i)** (colloq) **~ un fou rire** to have a fit of the
giggles; **~ une crise de nerfs** to throw a fit
(colloq); **~ un cent mètres** to break into a run
**(j) ~ une tête** to dive
**2** vi **(a)** ⟨beard⟩ to be bristly; ⟨wool⟩ to be
scratchy; ⟨throat, eyes⟩ to sting
**(b)** ⟨bird⟩ to swoop down; ⟨plane⟩ to dive;
**~ du nez** ⟨person⟩ to nod off; ⟨plane⟩ to go
into a nosedive
**(c)** (colloq) **arrête de ~ dans le plat** stop
picking (things out of the dish)
**3 se piquer** v refl (+ v être) **(a)** to prick
oneself; **se ~ aux orties** to get stung by
nettles
**(b)** to inject oneself
**(c) se ~ de pouvoir réussir seul** to claim
that one can manage on one's own
**IDIOMS quelle mouche t'a piqué?** (colloq)
what's eating you? (colloq); **son article n'était
pas piqué des hannetons** (colloq) his/her
article didn't pull any punches

**piquet** /pikɛ/ nm **(a)** stake
**(b)** peg
**(c)** (in skiing) gate pole
**(d)** (of sunshade) pole
**(e)** picket; **~ de grève** (strike) picket, picket
line

**piquette** /pikɛt/ nf (colloq) plonk (GB)
(colloq), cheap wine

**piqûre** /pikyʀ/ nf **(a)** injection, shot
**(b)** (of thorn, pin) prick; (of nettle, bee) sting;
(of mosquito) bite
**(c)** stitch; stitching

**pirate** /piʀat/ nm pirate
■ **~ de l'air** hijacker, skyjacker

**pirater** /piʀate/ [1] vtr to pirate

**piraterie** /piʀatʀi/ nf piracy
■ **~ aérienne** hijacking, skyjacking;
**~ informatique** computer hacking

**pire** /piʀ/ **1** adj **(a)** worse (**que** than)
**(b)** worst; **les ~s mensonges** the most
wicked lies

**2** nm **le ~** the worst; **au ~** at the very
worst

**pirogue** /piʀɔg/ nf dugout canoe

**pirouette** /piʀwɛt/ nf pirouette; **s'en tirer
par une ~** to dodge the question skilfully
(GB)

**pis** /pi/ **1** adj inv worse
**2** adv worse; **tant ~** too bad
**3** nm inv (of cow) udder

**pis-aller** /pizale/ nm inv makeshift
solution

**pisciculteur, -trice** /pisikyltœʀ, tʀis/
nm,f fish farmer

**pisciculture** /pisikyltyʀ/ nf fish farming

**piscine** /pisin/ nf swimming pool

**pisse** /pis/ nf (slang) piss (slang)

**pissenlit** /pisɑ̃li/ nm dandelion
**IDIOMS manger les ~s par la racine** (slang) to
be pushing up the daisies (colloq)

**pisser** (slang) /pise/ [1] **1** vtr **~ le sang**
⟨person, nose, injury⟩ to pour with blood
**2** vi to pee (colloq), to piss (slang)
**IDIOMS il pleut comme vache qui pisse** it's
pissing down (slang); **laisse ~!** forget it!

**pissotière** /pisɔtjɛʀ/ nf (colloq) street
urinal

**pistache** /pistaʃ/ nf pistachio

**piste** /pist/ nf **(a)** trail; **être sur une fausse
~** to be on the wrong track
**(b)** (in police investigation) lead
**(c)** (in stadium) track; (in horseracing)
racecourse (GB), racetrack (US); (in motor
racing) racetrack; (in circus) ring; (in skiing)
slope; (in cross-country skiing) trail; **~ de danse**
dance floor; **entrer en ~** (at circus) to come
into the ring; (figurative) to enter the fray
**(d)** track, path; (in desert) trail
**(e)** (in airport) runway
**(f)** (on record, cassette) track
■ **~ cyclable** cycle lane; cycle path

**pister** /piste/ [1] vtr to trail, to track

**pistil** /pistil/ nm pistil

**pistolet** /pistɔlɛ/ nm **(a)** pistol, gun; **tirer
au ~** to fire a pistol
**(b)** (Tech) gun; **~ à peinture** spray gun

**pistolet-mitrailleur,** pl **pistolets-
mitrailleurs** /pistɔlɛmitʀajœʀ/ nm
submachine gun

**piston** /pistɔ̃/ nm **(a)** (Tech) piston
**(b)** (colloq) contacts; **avoir du ~** to have
connections in the right places

**pistonner** /pistɔne/ [1] vtr (colloq) to pull
strings for

**pitance** /pitɑ̃s/ nf fare

**piteusement** /pitøzmɑ̃/ adv pitifully,
pathetically

**piteux, -euse** /pitø, øz/ adj **(a)** ⟨results⟩
poor, pitiful
**(b)** ⟨air⟩ crestfallen

**pitié** /pitje/ nf pity; mercy; **prendre qn en ~**
to take pity on sb; **il fait ~** he's a pitiful
sight; **par ~, tais-toi!** for pity's sake, be
quiet!

**piton** /pitɔ̃/ nm **(a)** hook ⋯⋙

**(b)** (in climbing) piton
**(c)** (of mountain) peak
**pitoyable** /pitwajabl/ adv **(a)** pitiful
**(b)** pathetic
**pitoyablement** /pitwajabləmã/ adv
**(a)** pitifully
**(b)** ⟨fail⟩ miserably; ⟨sing⟩ pathetically
**pitre** /pitʀ/ nm clown, buffoon
**pitrerie** /pitʀəʀi/ nf clowning
**pittoresque** /pitɔʀɛsk/ adj picturesque;
colourful (GB)
**pivert** /pivɛʀ/ nm green woodpecker
**pivoine** /pivwan/ nf peony
**pivot** /pivo/ nm **(a)** (Tech) pivot
**(b)** (of economy, strategy, group) linchpin; (of plot)
kingpin
**(c)** (Sport) (player) pivot, post
**(d)** (of tooth) post and core
**pivotant**, **~e** /pivɔtã, ãt/ adj ⟨chair⟩
swivel; ⟨sign⟩ pivoting; ⟨door⟩ revolving
**pivoter** /pivɔte/ [1] vi ⟨person, animal,
panel⟩ to pivot; ⟨door⟩ to revolve; ⟨chair⟩ to
swivel
**PJ** /peʒi/ nf **(a)** (abbr = **police judiciaire**)
detective division of the French police force
**(b)** (abbr = **pièce(s) jointe(s)**) enc
**PL** (written abbr = **poids lourd**) HGV (GB),
heavy truck (US)
**placard** /plakaʀ/ nm **(a)** cupboard; **mettre
au ~** (figurative) to put [sth] on ice ⟨plan⟩; to
shunt [sb] aside ⟨person⟩
**(b)** poster, bill
**placarder** /plakaʀde/ [1] vtr **(a)** to post, to
stick
**(b)** to cover [sth] with posters
**place** /plas/ nf **(a)** room, space
**(b)** (in theatre, cinema, bus) seat; **payer sa ~**
(in cinema, theatre) to pay for one's ticket; (on
train) to pay one's fare
**(c)** place; **remettre qch à sa ~** to put sth
back in its place; **être en bonne ~ pour
gagner** to be well-placed or in a good
position to win; **la ~ d'un mot dans une
phrase** the position of a word in a sentence;
**sur ~** to/on the spot; **on the spot; il faut
savoir rester à sa ~** you must know your
place; **tenir une grande ~ dans la vie de qn**
to play a large part in sb's life
**(d)** **à la ~ de** instead of, in place of; **(si
j'étais) à ta ~** if I were in your position
**(e)** **en ~** ⟨system, structure⟩ in place; ⟨troops⟩
in position; ⟨leader, party, regime⟩ ruling; **ne
plus tenir en ~** to be restless; **mettre en ~** to
put [sth] in place ⟨programme⟩; to put [sth]
in position ⟨team⟩; to establish, to set up
⟨network, institution⟩
**(f)** (in town) square; **la ~ du village** the
village square
**(g)** (Econ) market; **~ financière** financial
market
**(h)** job; **perdre sa ~** to lose one's job
**(i)** **être dans la ~** to be on the inside; **avoir
un pied dans la ~** to have a foot in the door
**placé**, **~e** /plase/ **1** pp ▶ PLACER
**2** pp adj **(a)** (located) **être ~** ⟨object, tap,

*window⟩* to be; ⟨chair, table, statue⟩ to be
placed; ⟨person⟩ (gen) to be; (at the theatre,
cinema) to be sitting; **être bien/mal ~**
⟨building, shop⟩ to be well/badly situated;
⟨person⟩ (at table, at a function) to have a good/
bad place
**(b)** (in a hierarchy) **être bien ~ sur une liste** to
have a good position on the list; **il est bien ~
pour le poste** he's a likely candidate for the
job; **avoir des amis haut ~s** to have friends
in high places
**(c)** **être bien/mal ~ pour faire** (to succeed) to
be well/badly placed to do; (to know, judge) to
be in a (good)/in no position to do
**placebo** /plasebo/ nm placebo
**placement** /plasmã/ nm **(a)** investment
**(b)** **assurer le ~ des diplômés** to ensure that
graduates find employment
**(c)** (of child) fostering
**placenta** /plasɛ̃ta/ nm placenta
**placer** /plase/ [12] **1** vtr **(a)** to put, to place
⟨object⟩; to seat ⟨person⟩; **~ sa confiance en
qn** to put one's trust in sb; **~ ses espoirs en
qn** to pin one's hopes on sb; **mal placé**
⟨pride⟩ misplaced
**(b)** to place, to find a job for ⟨person⟩
**(c)** to invest ⟨money⟩
**(d)** to slip in ⟨remark, anecdote⟩; **je n'arrive
pas à en ~ une avec elle!** (colloq) I can't get a
word in edgeways (GB) or edgewise (US) with
her!
**(e)** to place [sb] in care ⟨child⟩
**2** **se placer** v refl (+ v être) **(a)** **se ~ près
de** to sit next to
**(b)** **se ~ premier** to come first
**placeur**, **-euse** /plasœʀ, øz/ nm,f usher/
usherette
**placide** /plasid/ adj placid, calm
**placier**, **-ière** /plasje, ɛʀ/ nm,f **(a)** sales
representative
**(b)** market superintendent
**plafond** /plafɔ̃/ nm **(a)** ceiling; (of tent,
vehicle, tunnel) roof
**(b)** ceiling, limit
**plafonnement** /plafɔnmã/ nm **(a)** setting
a ceiling on ⟨pay⟩; setting a limit on
⟨spending⟩
**(b)** (on pay) ceiling (**de** on); (on spending)
limitation (**de** of)
**plafonnier** /plafɔnje/ nm (gen) flush-fitting
ceiling light; (in car) interior light
**plage** /plaʒ/ nf beach
■ **~ arrière** rear window shelf; **~ horaire** time
slot
**plagiaire** /plaʒjɛʀ/ nmf plagiarist
**plagiat** /plaʒja/ nm plagiarism
**plagier** /plaʒje/ [2] vtr to plagiarize
**plaid** /plɛd/ nm tartan rug (GB), plaid
blanket (US)
**plaidant**, **~e** /plɛdã, ãt/ adj litigant
**plaider** /plede/ [1] **1** vtr to plead ⟨case⟩
**2** vi **(a)** to plead
**(b)** **~ en faveur de qn** ⟨circumstances⟩ to
speak in favour (GB) of sb
**plaidoirie** /plɛdwaʀi/ nf plea

**plaidoyer** /plɛdwaje/ *nm* **(a)** speech for the defence (GB)
**(b)** plea

**plaie** /plɛ/ *nf* **(a)** wound; sore; cut
**(b)** (colloq) **cet enfant, quelle ∼!** (colloq) that child is such a pain! (colloq)

**plaignant, ∼e** /plɛɲɑ̃, ɑ̃t/ *nm,f* plaintiff

**plaindre** /plɛ̃dʀ/ [54] **1** *vtr* to pity
**2 se plaindre** *v refl* (+ *v être*) **(a)** to complain
**(b)** ⟨*injured person*⟩ to moan

**plaine** /plɛn/ *nf* plain

**plain-pied: de plain-pied** /dəplɛ̃pje/ *phr* **une maison de ∼** a single-storey (GB) *or* single-story (US) house

**plainte** /plɛ̃t/ *nf* **(a)** (gen, Law) complaint
**(b)** moan, groan

**plaintif, -ive** /plɛ̃tif, iv/ *adj* plaintive

**plaintivement** /plɛ̃tivmɑ̃/ *adv* plaintively, dolefully

**plaire** /plɛʀ/ [59] **1** **plaire à** *v+prep*
**(a)** **elle plaît aux hommes** men find her attractive; **elle m'a plu tout de suite** I liked her straight away
**(b)** **mon travail me plaît** I like my job; **un modèle qui plaît beaucoup** a very popular model
**2 se plaire** *v refl* (+ *v être*) **(a)** ⟨*people, couple*⟩ to like each other
**(b)** **ils se plaisent ici** they like it here
**(c)** **il se plaît à dire qu'il est issu du peuple** he likes to say that he's a son of the people
**3** *v impers* **s'il te plaît, s'il vous plaît** please

**plaisamment** /plɛzamɑ̃/ *adv*
**(a)** agreeably
**(b)** amusingly

**plaisance** /plɛzɑ̃s/ *nf* **la navigation de ∼** boating; **bateau de ∼** pleasure boat

**plaisancier, -ière** /plɛzɑ̃sje, ɛʀ/ *nm,f* amateur sailor

**plaisant, ∼e** /plɛzɑ̃, ɑ̃t/ *adj* **(a)** pleasant
**(b)** amusing, funny

**plaisanter** /plɛzɑ̃te/ [1] *vi* to joke

**plaisanterie** /plɛzɑ̃tʀi/ *nf* joke

**plaisir** /plɛziʀ/ *nm* pleasure; **prendre un malin ∼ à faire** to take a wicked delight in doing; **faire ∼ à qn** to please sb; **faites-moi le ∼ de vous taire!** would you please shut up! (colloq); **faire durer le ∼** to make the pleasure last; (ironic) to prolong the agony

**plan** /plɑ̃/ *nm* **(a)** (of town, underground) map; (in building) plan, map
**(b)** (for building) plan; **tirer des ∼s** to draw up plans
**(c)** (of machine) blueprint
**(d)** (of essay, book) outline, framework
**(e)** (in cinematography) shot; **premier ∼** foreground
**(f)** level; **au premier ∼ de l'actualité** at the forefront of the news; **sur le ∼ politique** from a political point of view
**(g)** plan; **c'est le bon ∼** (colloq) it's a good idea
■ **∼ d'eau** artificial lake; **∼ d'épargne** savings plan; **∼ d'épargne-logement, PEL** savings scheme entitling depositor to a cheap mortgage.
**IDIOMS laisser qn en ∼** (colloq) to leave sb in the lurch; **laisser qch en ∼** (colloq) to leave sth unfinished

**planche** /plɑ̃ʃ/ *nf* **(a)** (gen) plank; (for kneading dough) board; **faire la ∼** to float on one's back
**(b)** plate
■ **∼ à roulettes** (Sport) skateboard; **∼ de salut** lifeline; **∼ à voile** windsurfing board
**IDIOMS monter sur les ∼s** to go on the stage; **avoir du pain sur la ∼** (colloq) to have one's work cut out

**plancher¹** /plɑ̃ʃe/ [1] *vi* (students' slang) to work

**plancher²** /plɑ̃ʃe/ *nm* **(a)** floor
**(b)** (Econ) floor; **atteindre le ∼** to bottom out

**planchiste** /plɑ̃ʃist/ *nmf* windsurfer

**plancton** /plɑ̃ktɔ̃/ *nm* plankton

**plané** /plane/ *adj m* **vol ∼** glide; **faire un vol ∼** (figurative) to go flying

**planer** /plane/ [1] *vi* **(a)** ⟨*plane, bird*⟩ to glide
**(b)** **laisser ∼ le doute** to allow uncertainty to persist
**(c)** (colloq) to have one's head in the clouds

**planétaire** /planetɛʀ/ *adj* planetary; (figurative) global

**planète** /planɛt/ *nf* planet

**planeur** /planœʀ/ *nm* **(a)** glider
**(b)** gliding

**planifier** /planifje/ [2] *vtr* to plan

**planning** /planiŋ/ *nm* (controversial) (colloq) schedule
■ **∼ familial** family planning service

**planque** /plɑ̃k/ *nf* (colloq) (for person) hideout

**planquer** (colloq) /plɑ̃ke/ [1] **1** *vtr* to hide ⟨*person*⟩; to hide [sth] away ⟨*object*⟩
**2 se planquer** *v refl* (+ *v être*) to hide

**plan-séquence,** *pl* **plans-séquences** /plɑ̃sekɑ̃s/ *nm* sequence shot

**plant** /plɑ̃/ *nm* young plant

**plantaire** /plɑ̃tɛʀ/ *adj* (Anat) plantar; **voûte ∼** arch of the foot

**plantation** /plɑ̃tasjɔ̃/ *nf* **(a)** plantation
**(b)** (of flowers) bed; (of vegetables) patch

**plante** /plɑ̃t/ *nf* **(a)** plant; **∼ verte** houseplant; **∼ grasse** succulent
**(b)** ∼ (des pieds) sole (of the foot)

**planter** /plɑ̃te/ [1] **1** *vtr* **(a)** to plant ⟨*flowers, shrub*⟩
**(b)** to drive in ⟨*stake*⟩; to knock in ⟨*nail*⟩; **∼ un couteau dans** to stick a knife into
**(c)** to pitch ⟨*tent*⟩; **∼ le décor** to set the scene
**(d)** ∼ (là) to drop ⟨*tool*⟩; to abandon ⟨*car*⟩
**2 se planter** *v refl* (+ *v être*) **(a)** (colloq) **aller se ∼ devant qch** to go and stand in front of sth
**(b)** (colloq) to crash

**(c)** (colloq) to get it wrong; **il s'est planté en histoire** he made a mess of the history exam

**plantureux, -euse** /plɑ̃tyʀø, øz/ adj ⟨bosom⟩ ample; ⟨woman⟩ buxom

**plaque** /plak/ nf (of ice) patch; (on skin) blotch; (of glass) plate; (of marble) slab; (on door of surgery) brass plate; (of policeman) badge
■ ~ **d'égout** manhole cover; ~ **d'immatriculation** number plate (GB), license plate (US)
IDIOMS **être à côté de la** ~ (colloq) to be completely mistaken

**plaqué, ~e** /plake/ adj ~ **or** gold-plated

**plaquer** /plake/ [1] ① vtr **(a)** ~ **qn contre qch** to pin sb against sth
**(b)** (colloq) to leave ⟨job, spouse⟩
② **se plaquer** v refl (+ v être) **se** ~ **contre un mur** to flatten oneself against a wall

**plaquette** /plaket/ nf **(a)** (of butter) packet
**(b)** (of pills) ≈ blister strip
■ ~ **de frein** brake shoe

**plastic** /plastik/ nm plastic explosive

**plasticage** /plastikaʒ/ nm bomb attack (de on)

**plastifier** /plastifje/ [2] vtr to coat [sth] with plastic

**plastique¹** /plastik/ nm plastic

**plastique²** /plastik/ nf (of object, statue) formal beauty; (of person) physique

**plastiquer** /plastike/ [1] vtr to carry out a bomb attack on

**plastron** /plastʀɔ̃/ nm shirt front

**plat, ~e** /pla, plat/ ① adj **(a)** flat
**(b)** ⟨boat⟩ flat-bottomed; ⟨watch, lighter⟩ slimline; ⟨hair⟩ limp
**(c)** ⟨style, description⟩ lifeless
② nm **(a)** dish
**(b)** course
③ **à plat** phr **(a)** **poser qch à** ~ to lay sth down flat; **à** ~ **ventre** flat on one's stomach; **tomber à** ~ ⟨joke⟩ to fall flat
**(b)** ⟨tyre⟩ flat; ⟨battery⟩ (GB), dead
**(c)** (colloq) **être à** ~ ⟨person⟩ to be run down
■ ~ **de résistance** main course
IDIOMS **mettre les pieds dans le** ~ (colloq) to put one's foot in it; **faire tout un** ~ **de qch** (colloq) to make a big deal about sth

**platane** /platan/ nm plane tree

**plateau, pl ~x** /plato/ nm **(a)** tray
**(b)** ~ **de tournage** film set
**(c)** (in geography) plateau
**(d)** (of weighing scales) pan

**plate-bande, pl plates-bandes** /platbɑ̃d/ nf border, flower bed

**platée** /plate/ nf (colloq) plateful (**de** of)

**plate-forme, pl plates-formes** /platfɔʀm/ nf platform; ~ **pétrolière** oil rig

**platine¹** /platin/ adj inv, nm platinum

**platine²** /platin/ nf (record player) turntable

**platitude** /platityd/ nf platitude

**platonique** /platɔnik/ adj platonic

**plâtre** /plɑtʀ/ nm **(a)** plaster
**(b)** (Med) plaster cast

IDIOMS **essuyer les** ~**s** to put up with the initial problems

**plâtrer** /plɑtʀe/ [1] vtr **(a)** to plaster ⟨wall⟩
**(b)** (Med) ~ **le bras de qn** to put sb's arm in plaster

**plâtreux, -euse** /plɑtʀø, øz/ adj chalky

**plâtrier, -ière** /plɑtʀije, ɛʀ/ nm,f plasterer

**plausible** /plozibl/ adj plausible

**playback** /plɛbak/ nm inv miming, lip syncing; **chanter en** ~ to lip-sync (a song)

**plébiscite** /plebisit/ nm plebiscite

**plébisciter** /plebisite/ [1] vtr **(a)** to elect [sb] with a huge majority
**(b)** to vote overwhelmingly in favour (GB) of

**pléiade** /plejad/ nf galaxy, pleiad

**plein, ~e** /plɛ̃, plɛn/ ① adj **(a)** full
**(b)** **un** ~ **panier** a basketful; **prendre à** ~**es mains** to pick up a handful of ⟨earth, sand, coins⟩
**(c)** ⟨brick, wall⟩ solid; ⟨cheeks, face⟩ plump; ⟨shape⟩ rounded
**(d)** ⟨power, effect⟩ full; ⟨satisfaction, confidence⟩ complete
**(e)** ⟨day, month⟩ whole, full; ⟨moon⟩ full
**(f)** **en** ~**e poitrine/réunion/forêt** (right) in the middle of the chest/meeting/forest; **en** ~ **jour** in broad daylight; **en** ~ **été** at the height of summer
**(g)** (Zool) ~**e** ⟨animal⟩ pregnant; ⟨cow⟩ in calf
**(h)** (colloq) sloshed (colloq), drunk
**(i) veste** ~**e peau** jacket made out of full skins
② adv **(a) avoir des billes** ~ **les poches** to have one's pockets full of marbles; **il a des idées** ~ **la tête** he's full of ideas
**(b) être orienté** ~ **sud** to face due south
③ nm **faire le** ~ **de** to fill up with ⟨water, petrol⟩; **le** ~ **s'il vous plaît** fill it up please
④ **plein de** (colloq) quantif ~ **de** lots of, loads (colloq) of
⑤ **à plein** phr fully
⑥ **tout plein** phr (colloq) really
IDIOMS **en avoir** ~ **le dos** (colloq) to be fed up

**plein-air** /plɛnɛʀ/ nm inv (Sch) (outdoor) games

**pleinement** /plɛnmɑ̃/ adv fully

**plein-emploi** /plɛnɑ̃plwa/ nm inv full employment

**plein-temps, pl pleins-temps** /plɛ̃tɑ̃/ nm full-time job

**plénier, -ière** /plenje, ɛʀ/ adj plenary

**pléonasme** /pleɔnasm/ nm pleonasm

**pleurer** /plœʀe/ [1] ① vtr to mourn ⟨friend⟩
② vi **(a)** to cry, to weep
**(b)** ⟨eyes⟩ to water
**(c)** ~ **sur qn/qch** to shed tears over sb/sth; **arrête de** ~ **sur ton sort!** stop feeling sorry for yourself!
**(d)** (colloq) ⟨person⟩ to whine
IDIOMS **elle n'a plus que ses yeux pour** ~ all she can do is cry

**pleureur** /plœʀœʀ/ adj m **saule** ~ weeping willow

**pleureuse** /plœʀøz/ nf (hired) mourner

**pleurnicher** /plœRniʃe/ [1] *vi* (colloq) to snivel

**pleurnicheur, -euse** /plœRniʃœR, øz/ *nm,f* (colloq) sniveller

**pleurs** /plœR/ *nm pl* tears; **en ~** in tears

**pleuvoir** /pløvwaR/ [39] [1] *v impers* to rain; **il pleut** it's raining; **il pleut à torrents** it's pouring with rain
[2] *vi* ⟨*blows, bombs*⟩ to rain down

**pli** /pli/ *nm* (a) (gen) fold; (in trousers) crease; (in skirt) pleat
(b) (Games) trick
(c) letter; **sous ~ cacheté** in a sealed envelope
IDIOMS **ça ne fait pas un ~** (colloq) there's no doubt about it; **c'est un ~ à prendre** it's something you've got to get used to

**pliage** /plijaʒ/ *nm* folding

**pliant, ~e** /plijã, ãt/ [1] *adj* folding
[2] *nm* folding stool, campstool

**plier** /plije/ [2] [1] *vtr* (a) to fold; to fold up
(b) to bend ⟨*stem, arm*⟩
(c) to submit
[2] *vi* (a) ⟨*tree, branch, joint*⟩ to bend; ⟨*plank, floor*⟩ to sag
(b) to give in
[3] **se plier** *v refl* (+ *v être*) (a) to fold
(b) **se ~ à** to submit to
IDIOMS **être plié (en deux** *or* **quatre)** (colloq) to be doubled up with laughter

**plinthe** /plɛ̃t/ *nf* skirting board (GB), baseboard (US)

**plisser** /plise/ [1] [1] *vtr* (a) to pleat ⟨*cloth*⟩
(b) to crease ⟨*garment*⟩
(c) **~ le front** to knit one's brows; **~ les yeux** to screw up one's eyes
[2] *vi* ⟨*stocking*⟩ to wrinkle; ⟨*skirt*⟩ to be creased

**pliure** /plijyR/ *nf* fold; **la ~ du genou** the back of the knee

**plomb** /plɔ̃/ *nm* (a) lead; **sans ~** ⟨*petrol*⟩ unleaded; **soleil de ~** burning sun; **ciel de ~** leaden sky
(b) (in hunting) **un ~** a lead pellet; **du ~** lead shot
(c) fuse
IDIOMS **avoir du ~ dans l'aile** (colloq) to be in a bad way (colloq); **cela va leur mettre du ~ dans la cervelle** (colloq) that will knock some sense into them

**plombage** /plɔ̃baʒ/ *nm* (in dentistry) filling

**plomber** /plɔ̃be/ [1] *vtr* to fill ⟨*tooth*⟩

**plombier** /plɔ̃bje/ *nm* plumber

**plonge** /plɔ̃ʒ/ *nf* (colloq) washing up, dishwashing (US)

**plongée** /plɔ̃ʒe/ *nf* (a) (skin) diving
(b) scuba diving
(c) snorkelling (GB); **~ sous-marine** deep-sea diving; **faire de la ~** to go diving

**plongeoir** /plɔ̃ʒwaR/ *nm* (a) diving-board
(b) springboard

**plongeon** /plɔ̃ʒɔ̃/ *nm* (a) dive
(b) fall

**plonger** /plɔ̃ʒe/ [13] [1] *vtr* to plunge

[2] *vi* (a) to dive
(b) ⟨*bird*⟩ to swoop down
[3] **se plonger** *v refl* (+ *v être*) (a) to plunge
(b) to bury oneself

**plongeur, -euse** /plɔ̃ʒœR, øz/ *nm,f*
(a) diver
(b) dishwasher

**plot** /plo/ *nm* (a) (electrical) contact
(b) (of wood) block

**plouc** /pluk/ *nm* (colloq) country bumpkin (colloq)

**plouf** /pluf/ [1] *nm inv* splash; **faire un ~** to go splash
[2] *excl* splash!

**ployer** /plwaje/ [23] *vi* ⟨*branch, person*⟩ to bend; **~ sous un fardeau** to be weighed down by a burden

**plu** /ply/ ▶ PLAIRE; PLEUVOIR

**pluie** /plɥi/ *nf* (a) rain; **sous une ~ battante** in driving rain
(b) (of missiles, insults) hail; (of sparks, compliments) shower
■ **~s acides** acid rain
IDIOMS **il n'est pas né de la dernière ~** (colloq) he wasn't born yesterday (colloq); **faire la ~ et le beau temps** to call the shots (colloq)

**plume** /plym/ *nf* (a) (Zool) feather
(b) (pen) nib; **écrire au fil de la ~** to write as the thoughts come into one's head
IDIOMS **voler dans les ~s de qn** (colloq) to fly at sb

**plumeau**, *pl* **~x** /plymo/ *nm* (a) feather duster
(b) tuft

**plumer** /plyme/ [1] *vtr* to pluck ⟨*bird*⟩

**plumier** /plymje/ *nm* pencil box

**plupart: la plupart** /laplypaR/ *nf inv* **la ~ des gens** most people; **la ~ du temps** most of the time, mostly

**pluridisciplinaire** /plyRidisiplinɛR/ *adj* multidisciplinary

**pluriel, -elle** /plyRjɛl/ [1] *adj* plural
[2] *nm* plural

**plus¹** /ply, plys, plyz/ [1] *prep* plus
[2] *adv* (a) (comparative) more; (superlative) **le ~** the most; **il travaille ~ (que moi)** he works more (than I do); **~ j'y pense, moins je comprends** the more I think about it, the less I understand; **~ ça va** as time goes on; **qui ~ est** furthermore; **de ~ en ~** more and more; **~ petit** smaller; **le ~ petit** the smallest; **trois heures ~ tôt** three hours earlier; **deux fois ~ cher** twice as expensive; **il est on ne peut ~ désagréable** he's as unpleasant as can be; **il est ~ ou moins artiste** he's an artist of sorts; **il a été ~ ou moins poli** he wasn't particularly polite
(b) (in negative constructions) **elle ne fume ~** she doesn't smoke any more; **il n'y a ~ d'œufs** there are no more eggs; **~ jamais ça!** never again!; **~ que trois jours avant Noël!** only three days to go until Christmas!
[3] **plus de** *quantif* **deux fois ~ de livres** ⋯✧

que twice as many books as; **il a gagné le ~ d'argent** he won the most money; **les gens de ~ de 60 ans** people over 60
**4 au plus** *phr* at the most
**5 de plus** *phr* **(a)** furthermore, what's more
**(b) donnez-moi deux pommes de ~** give me two more apples; **une fois de ~** once more
**6 en plus** *phr* **en ~ (de cela)** on top of that; **les taxes en ~** plus tax

**plus²** /plys/ *nm inv* **(a) le signe ~** the plus sign
**(b)** (colloq) plus (colloq)

**plusieurs** /plyzjœʀ/ **1** *adj* several; **une ou ~ personnes** one or more people
**2** *pron* **~ ont déjà signé** several people have already signed

**plus-value**, *pl* **~s** /plyvaly/ *nf*
**(a)** (of property) increase in value; (sales profit) capital gain
**(b)** surcharge
**(c)** (Econ) surplus value

**plutôt** /plyto/ *adv* rather; instead; **passe ~ le matin** call round (GB) *or* come by (US) in the morning preferably; **~ mourir!** I'd rather die!; **demande ~ à Corinne** ask Corinne instead; **dis ~ que tu n'as pas envie de le faire** why don't you just say that you don't want to do it?; **la nouvelle a été ~ bien accueillie** the news went down rather well

**pluvieux, -ieuse** /plyvjø, øz/ *adj* wet, rainy

**PME** /peɛmə/ *nf pl* (*abbr* = **petites et moyennes entreprises**) small and medium-sized enterprises, SMEs

**PMI** /peɛmi/ *nf pl* (*abbr* = **petites et moyennes industries**) small and medium-sized industries

**PMU** /peɛmy/ *nm* (*abbr* = **Pari mutuel urbain**) *French state-controlled betting system*

**PNB** /peɛnbe/ *nm* (*abbr* = **produit national brut**) gross national product, GNP

**pneu** /pnø/ *nm* tyre (GB), tire (US)

**pneumatique** /pnømatik/ *adj* inflatable

**pneumonie** /pnømɔni/ *nf* pneumonia

**poche¹** /pɔʃ/ *nm* (**livre de**) ~ paperback

**poche²** /pɔʃ/ *nf* **(a)** (in garment, bag) pocket; **en ~** in one's pocket; **il avait 200 euros en ~** he had 200 euros on him; **s'en mettre plein** *or* **se remplir les ~s** (colloq) to line one's pockets; **faire les ~s de qn** to pick sb's pocket
**(b) ~ de gaz/d'air** gas/air pocket
**(c) avoir des ~s sous les yeux** to have bags under one's eyes
**(d)** (Zool) (of kangaroo) pouch
■ **~ revolver** hip pocket
IDIOMS **c'est dans la ~** (colloq) it's in the bag (colloq); **en être de sa ~** (colloq) to be out of pocket; **ne pas avoir les yeux dans sa ~** (colloq) not to miss a thing (colloq); **connaître un endroit comme sa ~** (colloq) to know a place like the back of one's hand

**pocher** /pɔʃe/ [1] *vtr* (Culin) to poach

**pochette** /pɔʃɛt/ *nf* **(a)** (for pencils) case; (for credit cards) wallet; (for make-up, glasses) pouch; (for document) folder; (for record) sleeve
**(b)** (of matches) book
**(c)** clutch bag

**pochoir** /pɔʃwaʀ/ *nm* stencil

**podium** /pɔdjɔm/ *nm* podium

**poêle¹** /pwal/ *nm* **(a)** stove
**(b)** (on coffin) pall

**poêle²** /pwal/ *nf* frying pan

**poème** /pɔɛm/ *nm* poem; **c'est tout un ~** (colloq) it's quite something

**poésie** /pɔezi/ *nf* **(a)** poetry
**(b)** poem

**poète** /pɔɛt/ *nm* **(a)** poet
**(b)** dreamer

**poétique** /pɔetik/ *adj* poetic

**poids** /pwa/ *nm inv* **(a)** weight; **peser son ~** to be very heavy; **adversaire de ~** opponent to be reckoned with
**(b)** burden; **être un ~ pour qn** to be a burden on sb; **avoir un ~ sur la conscience** to have a guilty conscience
**(c)** influence
**(d) des ~ en laiton** brass weights
**(e)** (in athletics) shot; **lancer le ~** to put the shot
■ **~ et haltères** weightlifting; **~ lourd** (Sport) heavyweight; heavy truck
IDIOMS **avoir** *or* **faire deux ~ deux mesures** to have double standards

**poignant, ~e** /pwaɲɑ̃, ɑ̃t/ *adj* **(a)** poignant
**(b)** heart-rending, harrowing

**poignard** /pwaɲaʀ/ *nm* dagger; **coup de ~** stab

**poignarder** /pwaɲaʀde/ [1] *vtr* to stab

**poigne** /pwaɲ/ *nf* **avoir de la ~** to have a strong grip; **homme à ~** strong man

**poignée** /pwaɲe/ *nf* **(a)** handful
**(b)** (of door, drawer, bag) handle; (of sword) hilt
■ **~ de main** handshake

**poignet** /pwaɲɛ/ *nm* **(a)** wrist
**(b)** (of shirt) cuff

**poil** /pwal/ *nm* **(a)** (on body, animal) hair; **à ~** (slang) stark naked; **caresser dans le sens du ~** to stroke [sth] the way the fur lies; to butter [sb] up (colloq); **ça marche au ~** (colloq) it works like a dream
**(b)** (colloq) (of irony) touch; (of commonsense) shred; **à un ~ près** by a whisker
**(c)** (of cloth) nap; (of brush) bristle
■ **~ à gratter** itching powder
IDIOMS **être de bon/mauvais ~** (colloq) to be in a good/bad mood; **hérisser le ~ de qn** (colloq) to put sb's back up (colloq); **avoir un ~ dans la main** (colloq) to be bone idle

**poilu, ~e** /pwaly/ *adj* hairy

**poinçon** /pwɛ̃sɔ̃/ *nm* **(a)** (tool) punch
**(b)** (on gold) die, stamp; hallmark

**poinçonner** /pwɛ̃sɔne/ [1] *vtr* **(a)** to punch, to clip
**(b)** to hallmark

**poinçonneur, -euse** /pwɛ̃sɔnœʀ, øz/ *nm,f* ticket-puncher

**poindre** /pwɛ̃dʀ/ [56] *vi* ‹*day*› to break

**poing** /pwɛ̃/ *nm* fist; **coup de ∼** punch; **montrer le ∼** to shake one's fist; **être pieds et ∼s liés** (figurative) to have one's hands tied
IDIOMS **dormir à ∼s fermés** to sleep like a log

**point** /pwɛ̃/ ⚀ *nm* **(a)** point; **un ∼ de rencontre** a meeting point; **∼ de vente** (sales) outlet
**(b)** (at sea) position; **faire le ∼** to take bearings; (figurative) to take stock of the situation
**(c)** **être sur le ∼ de faire** to be just about to do; **au ∼ où j'en suis, ça n'a pas d'importance!** I'm past caring!
**(d)** **il m'agace au plus haut ∼** he annoys me intensely; **je ne le pensais pas bête à ce ∼** I didn't think he was that stupid; **à tel ∼ que** to such an extent that; **douloureux au ∼ que** so painful that
**(e)** (on agenda) item, point; **un ∼ de détail** a minor point; **en tout ∼, en tous ∼s** in every respect *or* way
**(f)** dot; **un ∼ de colle** a spot of glue; **un ∼ de rouille** a speck of rust; **∼ d'intersection** point of intersection
**(g)** (Games, Sport) point; **compter les ∼s** to keep (the) score
**(h)** (Sch) mark (GB), point (US); **être un bon ∼ pour** to be a plus point for
**(i)** full stop (GB), period (US); **mettre un ∼ final à qch** (figurative) to put a stop to sth; **tu vas te coucher un ∼ c'est tout!** (colloq) you're going to bed and that's final!
**(j)** (Med) pain; **avoir un ∼ à la poitrine** to have a pain in one's chest
**(k)** (in sewing, knitting) stitch
⚁ **à point** *phr* **(a)** **à ∼ nommé** just at the right moment
**(b)** **à ∼** ‹*meat*› medium rare
⚂ **au point** *phr* **être au ∼** ‹*system, machine*› to be well designed; ‹*show*› to be well put together; **mettre au ∼** to perfect ‹*system, method*›; to develop ‹*vaccine, machine*›; **faire la mise au ∼** (in photography) to focus; **faire une mise au ∼** (figurative) to set the record straight
■ **∼ argent** cash point; **∼ chaud** trouble *or* hot spot; **∼ de côté** (pain) stitch; **∼ de départ** starting point; **nous revoilà à notre ∼ de départ** (figurative) we're back to square one; **∼ d'eau** water tap (GB) *or* faucet (US); **∼ d'exclamation** exclamation mark; **∼ faible** weak point; **∼ fort** strong point; **∼ d'interrogation** question mark; **∼ de mire** (Mil) target; (figurative) focal point; **∼ mort** neutral; **être au ∼ mort** (in car) to be in neutral; ‹*business, trade*› to be at a standstill; **∼ noir** (Med) blackhead; (of situation) problem; **∼ de repère** landmark; point of reference; **∼ de suture** (Med) stitch; **∼ de vue** point of view; viewpoint; **du ∼ de vue du sens** as far as meaning is concerned; **∼s de suspension** suspension points
IDIOMS **être mal en ∼** to be in a bad way

**pointage** /pwɛ̃taʒ/ *nm* **(a)** (on list) ticking off (GB), checking off (US)
**(b)** (of employee) clocking in

**pointe** /pwɛ̃t/ ⚀ *nf* **(a)** (of knife) point; (of shoe) toe; (of hair) end; (of railing) spike; (of spear) tip; **en ∼** pointed
**(b)** **de ∼** ‹*technology*› advanced, state-of-the-art; ‹*sector, industry*› high-tech; **à la ∼ du progrès** state-of-the-art
**(c)** high; **une vitesse de ∼ de 200 km/h** a maximum *or* top speed of 200 km/h; **heure de ∼** rush hour; **aux heures de ∼** at peak time
**(d)** (of garlic) touch; (of accent) hint
**(e)** blocked shoe
⚁ **pointes** *nf pl* **faire des ∼s** to dance on points
■ **∼ du pied** tiptoe

**pointer** /pwɛ̃te/ [1] ⚀ *vtr* **(a)** to tick off (GB), to check off (US) ‹*names, figures*›; to check ‹*list*›
**(b)** to point ‹*weapon*›; **∼ le doigt vers** to point at; **∼ son nez** (colloq) to show one's face
⚁ *vi* **(a)** ‹*employee*› to clock in; **∼ à l'agence pour l'emploi** to sign on at the unemployment office
**(b)** ‹*sun, plant*› to come up; ‹*day*› to break
⚂ **se pointer** *v refl* (+ *v être*) (colloq) to turn up

**pointillé, ∼e** /pwɛ̃tije/ ⚀ *adj* dotted
⚁ *nm* dotted line

**pointilleux, -euse** /pwɛ̃tijø, øz/ *adj* ‹*person*› fussy, pernickety

**pointu, ∼e** /pwɛ̃ty/ *adj* **(a)** (gen) pointed; ‹*scissors*› with a sharp point
**(b)** ‹*check*› close, thorough
**(c)** ‹*question, approach*› precise

**pointure** /pwɛ̃tyʀ/ *nf* (of glove, shoe) size

**point-virgule**, *pl* **points-virgules** /pwɛ̃viʀgyl/ *nm* semicolon

**poire** /pwaʀ/ *nf* **(a)** pear
**(b)** (colloq) sucker (colloq)
IDIOMS **couper la ∼ en deux** to split the difference; **garder une ∼ pour la soif** to save something for a rainy day

**poireau**, *pl* **∼x** /pwaʀo/ *nm* leek

**poirier** /pwaʀje/ *nm* **(a)** pear (tree)
**(b)** **faire le ∼** to do a headstand

**pois** /pwa/ *nm inv* **(a)** (Bot, Culin) pea; **petit ∼** (garden) pea
**(b)** dot; **à ∼** polka dot, spotted
■ **∼ cassé** split pea; **∼ chiche** chickpea

**poison** /pwazɔ̃/ *nm* poison

**poisse** /pwas/ *nf* (colloq) **(a)** rotten luck (colloq)
**(b)** drag (colloq)

**poisseux, -euse** /pwasø, øz/ *adj* ‹*hands, table*› sticky; ‹*atmosphere*› muggy; ‹*restaurant*› greasy

**poisson** /pwasɔ̃/ *nm* fish; **les ∼s d'eau douce/de mer** freshwater/saltwater fish
■ **∼ rouge** goldfish
IDIOMS **être comme un ∼ dans l'eau** to be in one's element

p

**poissonnerie** /pwasɔnʀi/ *nf* fishmonger's (shop) (GB), fish shop (US)

**poissonnier, -ière** /pwasɔnje, ɛʀ/ *nm,f* fishmonger (GB), fish vendor (US)

**Poissons** /pwasɔ̃/ *pr nm pl* Pisces

**poitrail** /pwatʀaj/ *nm* breast

**poitrine** /pwatʀin/ *nf* **(a)** chest; **tour de ~** chest size
**(b)** breasts; **tour de ~** bust size
■ **~ fumée** ≈ smoked streaky bacon

**poivre** /pwavʀ/ *nm* pepper

**poivré, ~e** /pwavʀe/ *adj* ⟨*sauce*⟩ peppery

**poivrer** /pwavʀe/ [1] *vtr* to add pepper to

**poivron** /pwavʀɔ̃/ *nm* sweet pepper, capsicum

**poivrot, ~e** /pwavʀo, ɔt/ *nm,f* (colloq) drunk

**poker** /pɔkɛʀ/ *nm* poker; **coup de ~** gamble

**polaire** /pɔlɛʀ/ *adj* polar; arctic

**polar** /pɔlaʀ/ *nm* (colloq) detective novel

**polariser** /pɔlaʀize/ [1] *vtr*, **se polariser** *v refl* (+ *v être*) **(a)** to polarize
**(b)** to focus

**pôle** /pol/ *nm* **(a)** pole
**(b)** centre (GB)

**polémique** /pɔlemik/ *nf* debate

**poli, ~e** /pɔli/ [1] *pp* ▶ POLIR
[2] *pp adj* ⟨*metal, style*⟩ polished
[3] *adj* polite
[4] *nm* shine

**police** /pɔlis/ *nf* **(a)** police; police force
**(b)** security service
**(c) faire la ~** to keep order
**(d)** (in insurance) policy
■ **~ judiciaire, PJ** *detective division of the French police force*; **~ de l'air et des frontières, PAF** border police; **~ des mœurs** *or* **mondaine** vice squad; **~ secours** ≈ emergency services

**policier, -ière** /pɔlisje, ɛʀ/ [1] *adj* (gen) police; ⟨*novel*⟩ detective
[2] *nm* policeman; **femme ~** policewoman

**poliment** /pɔlimɑ̃/ *adv* politely

**polir** /pɔliʀ/ [3] *vtr* to polish ⟨*stone, metal*⟩

**polisson, -onne** /pɔlisɔ̃, ɔn/ *nm,f* naughty child

**politesse** /pɔlitɛs/ *nf* politeness; **rendre la ~ à qn** to return the compliment

**politicien, -ienne** /pɔlitisjɛ̃, ɛn/ *nm,f* politician

**politique¹** /pɔlitik/ *adj* (gen) political; ⟨*behaviour, act*⟩ calculating

**politique²** /pɔlitik/ *nf* **(a)** politics; **faire de la ~** ⟨*militant*⟩ to be involved in politics
**(b)** policy; **notre ~ des prix** our pricing policy
IDIOMS **pratiquer la ~ de l'autruche** to stick one's head in the sand; **pratiquer la ~ du pire** to envisage the worst-case scenario

**politiser** /pɔlitize/ [1] *vtr* to politicize

**pollen** /pɔl(l)ɛn/ *nm* pollen

**polluant, ~e** /pɔl(l)yɑ̃, ɑ̃t/ [1] *adj* polluting

[2] *nm* pollutant

**polluer** /pɔl(l)ɥe/ [1] *vtr* to pollute

**pollution** /pɔl(l)ysjɔ̃/ *nf* pollution

**polo** /pɔlo/ *nm* **(a)** polo shirt
**(b)** (Sport) polo

**polochon** /pɔlɔʃɔ̃/ *nm* (colloq) bolster; **bataille de ~s** pillow fight

**Pologne** /pɔlɔɲ/ *pr nf* Poland

**polonais, ~e** /pɔlɔnɛ, ɛz/ [1] *adj* Polish
[2] *nm* (language) Polish

**Polonais, ~e** *nm,f* Pole

**poltronnerie** /pɔltʀɔnʀi/ *nf* cowardice

**polycopier** /pɔlikɔpje/ [2] *vtr* to duplicate

**polyculture** /pɔlikyltyʀ/ *nf* mixed farming

**polygame** /pɔligam/ *adj* polygamous

**polyglotte** /pɔliglɔt/ *adj, nmf* polyglot

**Polytechnique** /pɔliteknik/ *nf*: *Grande École of Science and Technology*

**polyvalence** /pɔlivalɑ̃s/ *nf* **(a)** versatility
**(b)** (of employee) flexibility

**polyvalent, ~e** /pɔlivalɑ̃, ɑ̃t/ *adj* ⟨*equipment*⟩ multipurpose; ⟨*employee*⟩ who does several jobs

**pommade** /pɔmad/ *nf* (Med) ointment
IDIOMS **passer de la ~ à qn** (colloq) to butter sb up (colloq)

**pomme** /pɔm/ *nf* **(a)** apple
**(b)** (of watering can) rose; (of shower) shower-head; (of walking stick) pommel, knob
**(c)** (colloq) mug (GB) (colloq), sucker (colloq); **ça va encore être pour ma ~** I'm in for it again (colloq)
■ **~ d'Adam** Adam's apple; **~ de pin** pine cone; **~ de terre** potato; **~s frites** chips (GB), (French) fries
IDIOMS **tomber dans les ~s** (colloq) to faint

**pommeau, pl ~x** /pɔmo/ *nm* knob; pommel

**pommette** /pɔmɛt/ *nf* cheekbone

**pommier** /pɔmje/ *nm* apple tree

**pompe** /pɔ̃p/ *nf* **(a)** pump
**(b)** (slang) shoe
**(c)** pomp
**(d)** (Sport) (colloq) press-up (GB), push-up
■ **~ à essence** petrol pump, gas pump (US); **~s funèbres** undertaker's (GB), funeral director's
IDIOMS **avoir un coup de ~** (colloq) to be knackered (GB) (slang) *or* pooped (colloq)

**pomper** /pɔ̃pe/ [1] *vtr* **(a)** to pump ⟨*liquid, air*⟩
**(b)** (students' slang) to copy
IDIOMS **~ l'air à qn** (colloq) to get on sb's nerves

**pompette** /pɔ̃pɛt/ *adj* (colloq) tipsy (colloq), drunk

**pompeux, -euse** /pɔ̃pø, øz/ *adj* pompous

**pompier, -ière** /pɔ̃pje, ɛʀ/ [1] *adj* pompous
[2] *nm* fireman, firefighter; **appeler les ~s** to call the fire brigade (GB) *or* department (US)

p

**pompiste** /pɔ̃pist/ *nmf* petrol (GB) *or* gas (US) pump attendant

**pompon** /pɔ̃pɔ̃/ *nm* (on hat) pompom, bobble; (on slipper) pompom
IDIOMS **décrocher le** ~ (colloq) to win first prize

**pomponner: se pomponner** /pɔ̃pɔne/ [1] *v refl* (+ *v être*) to get dolled up

**ponce** /pɔ̃s/ *nf* **pierre** ~ pumice stone

**poncer** /pɔ̃se/ [12] *vtr* (a) (Tech) to sand
(b) to pumice

**ponceuse** /pɔ̃søz/ *nf* sander

**ponction** /pɔ̃ksjɔ̃/ *nf* (a) (Med) puncture
(b) levy

**ponctualité** /pɔ̃ktɥalite/ *nf* punctuality

**ponctuation** /pɔ̃ktɥasjɔ̃/ *nf* punctuation

**ponctuel, -elle** /pɔ̃ktɥɛl/ *adj* (a) ⟨*person*⟩ punctual
(b) ⟨*action*⟩ limited; ⟨*problem*⟩ isolated

**ponctuer** /pɔ̃ktɥe/ [1] *vtr* to punctuate

**pondéré, ~e** /pɔ̃deRe/ *adj* (a) ⟨*person*⟩ levelheaded
(b) ⟨*factor*⟩ weighted

**pondre** /pɔ̃dR/ [6] *vtr* (a) to lay ⟨*egg*⟩
(b) (colloq) to churn out (colloq) ⟨*poetry, articles*⟩

**poney** /pɔnɛ/ *nm* pony

**pont** /pɔ̃/ ① *nm* (a) bridge
(b) link, tie; **couper les** ~**s** to break off all contact
(c) extended weekend (*including days between a public holiday and a weekend*)
(d) deck
② **ponts** *nm pl* ~**s** (**et chaussées**) highways department
■ ~ **aérien** airlift; ~ **à péage** toll bridge
IDIOMS **coucher sous les** ~**s** to sleep rough, to be a tramp; **il coulera beaucoup d'eau sous les** ~**s avant que...** it will be a long time before...; **faire un** ~ **d'or à qn** to offer sb a large sum to accept a job

**pontife** /pɔ̃tif/ *nm* (a) pontiff; **le souverain** ~ the pope
(b) (colloq) pundit (colloq)

**pontificat** /pɔ̃tifika/ *nm* pontificate

**pontifier** /pɔ̃tifje/ [2] *vi* to pontificate

**pont-levis**, *pl* **ponts-levis** /pɔ̃ləvi/ *nm* drawbridge

**ponton** /pɔ̃tɔ̃/ *nm* (a) landing stage
(b) pontoon

**pope** /pɔp/ *nm* pope, orthodox priest

**popote** /pɔpɔt/ *nf* (colloq) cooking

**populace** /pɔpylas/ *nf* **la** ~ the masses

**populaire** /pɔpylɛR/ *adj* (a) ⟨*suburb*⟩ working-class; ⟨*art, novel*⟩ popular; ⟨*edition*⟩ cheap; ⟨*restaurant*⟩ basic; **classe** ~ working class
(b) ⟨*tradition*⟩ folk; **culture** ~ folklore
(c) popular
(d) ⟨*revolt*⟩ popular; ⟨*will*⟩ of the people
(e) ⟨*expression, term*⟩ vulgar
(f) **République** ~ People's Republic

**popularité** /pɔpylaRite/ *nf* popularity

**population** /pɔpylasjɔ̃/ *nf* population

**populeux, -euse** /pɔpylø, øz/ *adj* densely populated, populous

**porc** /pɔR/ *nm* (a) pig, hog (US)
(b) pork
(c) pigskin

**porcelaine** /pɔRsəlɛn/ *nf* porcelain, china

**porcelet** /pɔRsəlɛ/ *nm* piglet

**porc-épic**, *pl* ~**s** /pɔRkepik/ *nm* porcupine

**porche** /pɔRʃ/ *nm* porch

**porcherie** /pɔRʃəRi/ *nf* pigsty

**porcin, ~e** /pɔRsɛ̃, in/ *adj* porcine

**pore** /pɔR/ *nm* pore

**poreux, -euse** /pɔRø, øz/ *adj* porous

**porno** /pɔRno/ *adj, nm* (colloq) porn (colloq)

**pornographique** /pɔRnɔgRafik/ *adj* pornographic

**port** /pɔR/ *nm* (a) harbour (GB); port
(b) haven
(c) wearing; carrying
(d) bearing
(e) (transport) carriage; postage
■ ~ **d'attache** port of registry; home base; ~ **de pêche** fishing harbour (GB); fishing port; ~ **de plaisance** marina
IDIOMS **arriver à bon** ~ to arrive safe and sound

**portable** /pɔRtabl/ ① *adj* portable; **ordinateur** ~ laptop computer
② *nm* mobile (phone)

**portail** /pɔRtaj/ *nm* (of park) gate; (of church) great door

**portant, ~e** /pɔRtɑ̃, ɑ̃t/ *adj* (a) ⟨*wall*⟩ load-bearing
(b) **bien** ~ in good health
IDIOMS **à bout** ~ at point-blank range

**portatif, -ive** /pɔRtatif, iv/ *adj* portable

**porte** /pɔRt/ *nf* (a) door; gate; **devant la** ~ **de l'hôpital** outside the hospital; **aux** ~**s du désert** at the edge of the desert; **ouvrir sa** ~ **à qn** to let sb in; **c'est la** ~ **ouverte à la criminalité** it's an open invitation to crime; **mettre à la** ~ to expel; to fire; **ce n'est pas la** ~ **à côté** (colloq) it's quite far
(b) gateway; **la victoire leur ouvre la** ~ **de la finale** the victory clears the way to the final for them
(c) (in airport) gate
(d) (car) door
■ ~ **battante** swing door; ~ **d'écluse** lock gate; ~ **d'entrée** front door; main entrance; ~ **de service** service entrance; ~ **de sortie** exit; escape route
IDIOMS **prendre la** ~ to leave; **entrer par la petite/grande** ~ to start at the bottom/top

**porté, ~e¹** /pɔRte/ *adj* **être** ~ **sur qch** to be keen on sth

**porte-à-faux** /pɔRtafo/ *nm inv* **être en** ~ ⟨*wall*⟩ to be out of plumb; ⟨*construction*⟩ to be cantilevered; ⟨*person*⟩ to be in an awkward position

**porte-à-porte** /pɔRtapɔRt/ *nm inv*
(a) door-to-door selling
(b) door-to-door canvassing

p

**porte-avions** /pɔʀtavjõ/ *nm inv* aircraft carrier

**porte-bagages** /pɔʀt(ə)bagaʒ/ *nm inv* carrier; luggage rack; roof rack

**porte-bébé** /pɔʀt(ə)bebe/ *nm inv* baby carrier

**porte-bonheur** /pɔʀt(ə)bɔnœʀ/ *nm inv* lucky charm

**porte-clés**, **porte-clefs** /pɔʀt(ə)kle/ *nm inv* key ring

**porte-documents** /pɔʀt(ə)dɔkymã/ *nm inv* briefcase, attaché case

**portée²** /pɔʀte/ **1** *adj f* ▶ PORTÉ
**2** *nf* **(a)** range; être à ~ de main *or* à la ~ de la main to be within reach; to be to hand **(b)** c'est à la ~ de n'importe qui anybody can do it; anybody can understand it; se mettre à la ~ de qn to come down to sb's level **(c)** impact **(d)** (of kittens) litter **(e)** (Mus) staff, stave (GB)

**porte-fenêtre**, *pl* **portes-fenêtres** /pɔʀt(ə)fənɛtʀ/ *nf* French window

**portefeuille** /pɔʀt(ə)fœj/ **1** *adj* jupe ~ wrap-over skirt **2** *nm* **(a)** wallet, billfold (US) **(b)** portfolio

**porte-jarretelles** /pɔʀt(ə)ʒaʀtɛl/ *nm inv* suspender belt (GB), garter belt (US)

**portemanteau**, *pl* **-x** /pɔʀt(ə)mãto/ *nm* **(a)** coat rack **(b)** coat stand **(c)** coat hanger

**portemine** /pɔʀt(ə)min/ *nm* propelling (GB) *or* mechanical (US) pencil

**porte-monnaie** /pɔʀt(ə)mɔnɛ/ *nm inv* purse (GB), coin purse (US)

**porte-parapluies** /pɔʀt(ə)paʀaplɥi/ *nm inv* umbrella stand

**porte-parole** /pɔʀt(ə)paʀɔl/ *nm inv* spokesperson, spokesman/spokeswoman

**porte-plume** /pɔʀt(ə)plym/ *nm inv* penholder

**porter** /pɔʀte/ [1] **1** *vtr* **(a)** to carry **(b)** ~ qch quelque part to take sth somewhere; ~ qch à qn to take sb sth **(c)** ⟨wall, chair⟩ to carry, to bear ⟨weight⟩ **(d)** to wear ⟨dress, contact lenses⟩; to have ⟨moustache⟩ **(e)** to have ⟨initials, date, name⟩; to bear ⟨seal⟩; il porte bien son nom the name suits him **(f)** to bear ⟨flowers⟩ **(g)** ~ qch à to bring sth up to, to put sth up to ⟨rate, number⟩; ~ la température de l'eau à 80°C to heat the water to 80°C **(h)** ~ son regard vers to look at; si tu portes la main sur elle if you lay a finger on her; ~ un jugement sur qch to pass judgment on sth **(i)** ~ qch sur un registre to enter sth on a register; se faire ~ malade to report sick; ~ plainte to lodge a complaint

**(j)** tout nous porte à croire que everything leads us to believe that **(k)** ~ bonheur *or* chance to be lucky **2** **porter sur** *v+prep* ⟨debate⟩ to be about; ⟨measure⟩ to concern; ⟨ban⟩ to apply to **3** *vi* une voix qui porte a voice that carries; le coup a porté the blow hit home **4** **se porter** *v refl* (+ *v être*) **(a)** se ~ bien/ mal ⟨person⟩ to be well/ill; ⟨business⟩ to be going well/badly **(b)** se ~ sur ⟨suspicion⟩ to fall on; ⟨infection⟩ to spread to

**porte-savon** /pɔʀt(ə)savõ/ *nm inv* soapdish

**porte-serviettes** /pɔʀt(ə)sɛʀvjɛt/ *nm inv* towel rail

**porteur, -euse** /pɔʀtœʀ, øz/ **1** *adj* **(a)** être ~ d'un virus to carry a virus **(b)** mur ~ load-bearing wall **(c)** ⟨market, sector⟩ expanding **(d)** ⟨current, wave, frequency⟩ carrier **2** *nm,f* holder, bearer **3** *nm* **(a)** porter; messenger **(b)** (of cheque) bearer; ~ d'actions shareholder ■ ~ sain (Med) symptom-free carrier

**porte-voix** /pɔʀt(ə)vwa/ *nm inv* megaphone

**portier** /pɔʀtje/ *nm* porter

**portière** /pɔʀtjɛʀ/ *nf* (of car) door

**portillon** /pɔʀtijõ/ *nm* gate

**portion** /pɔʀsjõ/ *nf* **(a)** (Culin) portion; helping **(b)** part, portion; (of road) stretch
IDIOMS réduire qn à la ~ congrue to give sb the strict minimum

**portique** /pɔʀtik/ *nm* **(a)** portico **(b)** (in gym) frame **(c)** swing frame

**porto** /pɔʀto/ *nm* port

**portoricain**, **~e** /pɔʀtɔʀikɛ̃, ɛn/ *adj* Puerto Rican

**portrait** /pɔʀtʀɛ/ *nm* **(a)** portrait **(b)** description, picture **(c)** tu es tout le ~ de ton père you're the spitting image of your father **(d)** (colloq) face; se faire tirer le ~ to have one's photo taken

**portrait-robot**, *pl* **portraits-robots** /pɔʀtʀɛʀɔbo/ *nm* photofit®, identikit®

**portuaire** /pɔʀtɥɛʀ/ *adj* port

**portugais**, **~e** /pɔʀtygɛ, ɛz/ **1** *adj* Portuguese **2** *nm* (language) Portuguese

**Portugal** /pɔʀtygal/ *pr nm* Portugal

**pose** /poz/ *nf* **(a)** (of window) putting in; (of cupboard) fitting; (of carpet) laying **(b)** pose; prendre une ~ to strike a pose **(c)** (in photography) exposure

**posé**, **~e** /poze/ *adj* ⟨air, person⟩ composed; ⟨gesture, voice⟩ controlled

**posément** /pozemã/ *adv* calmly, carefully

**poser** /poze/ [1] **1** *vtr* **(a)** to put down ⟨book, glass⟩

**(b)** to put in ‹*window*›; to install ‹*radiator*›; to fit ‹*lock*›; to lay ‹*tiling, cable*›; to plant ‹*bomb*›; to put up ‹*wallpaper, curtains*›
**(c)** to assert ‹*theory*›; ∼ **sa candidature à un poste** to apply for a job; ∼ **une addition** to write a sum down
**(d)** to ask ‹*question*›; to set ‹*riddle*›; **ça ne pose aucun problème** that's no problem at all
**(e)** (Mus) to place ‹*voice*›
**2** *vi* **(a)** to pose
**(b)** to put on airs
**3 se poser** *v refl* (+ *v être*) **(a)** ‹*bird, insect*› to settle
**(b)** ‹*plane*› to land
**(c)** ‹*eyes*› to fall
**(d) se** ∼ **en** to claim to be; to present oneself as
**(e) se** ∼ **des questions** to ask oneself questions
**(f)** ‹*problem, case*› to arise; **la question ne se pose pas** there's no question of it; it goes without saying

**poseur, -euse** /pozœR, øz/ *nm,f* poser (colloq)
■ ∼ **de bombes** bomber; ∼ **de moquette** carpet fitter

**positif, -ive** /pozitif, iv/ *adj* **(a)** ‹*reply*› affirmative
**(b)** ‹*interview*› constructive; ‹*outcome*› positive
**(c)** ‹*reaction*› favourable (GB)
**(d)** ‹*person, attitude*› positive
**(e)** ‹*number*› positive

**position** /pozisjõ/ *nf* **(a)** position; **en** ∼ **horizontale** horizontally; **placer qn dans une** ∼ **difficile** to put sb in a difficult *or* an awkward position
**(b)** (in ranking) place, position
**(c)** position, stance; **prendre** ∼ **sur un problème** to take a stand on an issue; **camper sur ses** ∼**s** to stand one's ground
**(d)** (bank) balance

**positivement** /pozitivmã/ *adv* ‹*answer*› positively; ‹*react, judge*› favourably (GB)

**posologie** /pozɔlɔʒi/ *nf* dosage

**possédant, ∼e** /posedã, ãt/ *nm,f* **les** ∼**s** the rich, the wealthy

**possédé, ∼e** /posede/ *nm,f* **les** ∼**s** the possessed

**posséder** /posede/ [14] *vtr* **(a)** to own, to possess ‹*property, army*›; to hold ‹*responsibility*›
**(b)** to have ‹*skill, quality*›
**(c)** to speak [sth] fluently; to have a thorough knowledge of [sth]
**(d)** ‹*anger, pain*› to overwhelm
**(e)** (colloq) **il nous a bien possédés** he really had us there (colloq)

**possesseur** /posesœR/ *nm* (of property) owner; (of diploma) holder; (of passport) bearer

**possessif, -ive** /posesif, iv/ *adj* possessive

**possession** /posesjõ/ *nf* possession

**possibilité** /posibilite/ **1** *nf*
**(a)** possibility
**(b)** opportunity; ∼ **d'embauche** job opportunity
**2 possibilités** *nf pl* **(a)** (of person) abilities; (of device) potential uses
**(b)** resources

**possible** /posibl/ **1** *adj* **(a)** possible; **dès que** ∼ as soon as possible; **tout le courage** ∼ the utmost courage; **tous les cas** ∼**s et imaginables** every conceivable case; **le plus cher** ∼ ‹*sell*› at the highest possible price; **autant que** ∼ as much as possible; **il n'y a pas d'erreur** ∼**, c'est lui** it's him, without a shadow of a doubt; **tout est** ∼ anything is possible; **pas** ∼**!** (colloq) I don't believe it!; you're joking!; **'tu vas acheter une voiture?'—'**∼**'** 'are you going to buy a car?'—'maybe'
**(b)** (colloq) **il a une chance pas** ∼ he's incredibly lucky
**2** *nm* **faire (tout) son** ∼ to do one's best

**post(-)** /post/ *pref* post(-)

**postal, ∼e,** *mpl* **-aux** /postal, o/ *adj* ‹*van*› post office (GB), mail (US); ‹*services*› postal

**poste**[1] /post/ *nm* **(a)** position, job; post; ∼**s vacants** *or* **à pourvoir** vacancies
**(b)** (Sport) position
**(c)** ∼ **(de travail)** work station; **il est toujours fidèle au** ∼ you can always rely on him
**(d)** ∼ **de police** police station
**(e)** ∼ **de radio** radio set
**(f)** (tele)phone; extension
**(g)** shift
**(h)** (in accountancy) item
■ ∼ **d'aiguillage** signal box; ∼ **de douane** customs post; ∼ **de pilotage** flight deck; ∼ **de secours** first-aid station

**poste**[2] /post/ *nf* post office; **envoyer par la** ∼ to send [sth] by post (GB), to mail (US)
■ ∼ **aérienne** airmail; ∼ **restante** poste restante (GB), general delivery (US)

**poster**[1] /poste/ [1] **1** *vtr* **(a)** to post (GB), to mail (US)
**(b)** to post ‹*guard*›; to put [sb] in place ‹*spy*›
**2 se poster** *v refl* (+ *v être*) **se** ∼ **devant** to station oneself in front of

**poster**[2] /postɛR/ *nm* poster

**postérieur, ∼e** /posterjœR/ *adj* **(a)** ‹*date*› later; ‹*event*› subsequent; **un écrivain** ∼ **à Flaubert** a writer who came after Flaubert
**(b)** ‹*part, section*› posterior; ‹*legs*› hind

**postérité** /posterite/ *nf* posterity; **passer à la** ∼ ‹*person*› to go down in history; ‹*work*› to become part of the cultural heritage

**posthume** /postym/ *adj* posthumous

**postiche** /postiʃ/ **1** *adj* ‹*beard*› false
**2** *nm* **(a)** hairpiece; toupee; wig
**(b)** false moustache (GB) *or* mustache (US)
**(c)** false beard

**postier, -ière** /postje, ɛR/ *nm,f* postal worker

**postillon** /pɔstijɔ̃/ nm (colloq) drop of saliva

**postillonner** /pɔstijɔne/ [1] vi (colloq) to spit (saliva)

**post-scriptum** /pɔstskʀiptɔm/ nm inv postscript

**postsynchroniser** /pɔstsɛ̃kʀɔnize/ [1] vtr to dub, to add the soundtrack to

**postulant, ~e** /pɔstylɑ̃, ɑ̃t/ nm,f candidate

**postulat** /pɔstyla/ nm premise; postulate

**postuler** /pɔstyle/ [1] vi to apply

**posture** /pɔstyʀ/ nf (a) posture
(b) position

**pot** /po/ nm (a) container; jar; carton, tub; (earthenware) pot; jug; un ~ de peinture a tin of paint
(b) (chamber) pot
(c) (colloq) drink
(d) (colloq) do (GB) (colloq), drinks party
(e) (colloq) avoir du ~ to be lucky
■ ~ catalytique catalytic converter; ~ d'échappement (Aut) silencer (GB), muffler (US); exhaust
IDIOMS payer les ~s cassés to pick up the pieces; tourner autour du ~ (colloq) to beat about the bush

**potable** /pɔtabl/ adj (a) eau ~ drinking water
(b) (colloq) decent

**potage** /pɔtaʒ/ nm soup

**potager** /pɔtaʒe/ nm kitchen garden

**pot-au-feu** /pɔtofø/ nm inv (a) boiled beef (with vegetables)
(b) boiling beef

**pot-de-vin,** pl **pots-de-vin** /podvɛ̃/ nm bribe, backhander (GB) (colloq)

**pote** /pɔt/ nm (colloq) mate (GB) (colloq), pal (US) (colloq)

**poteau,** pl **~x** /pɔto/ nm post; goalpost
■ ~ électrique electricity pole (supplying domestic power lines)

**potelé, ~e** /pɔtle/ adj chubby

**potence** /pɔtɑ̃s/ nf gallows

**potentiel, -ielle** /pɔtɑ̃sjɛl/ ⃞1 adj potential
⃞2 nm potential

**poterie** /pɔtʀi/ nf (a) pottery
(b) piece of pottery

**potiche** /pɔtiʃ/ nf vase

**potier, -ière** /pɔtje, ɛʀ/ nm,f potter

**potin** /pɔtɛ̃/ nm (colloq) (a) gossip
(b) din (colloq)

**potion** /posjɔ̃/ nf potion

**potiron** /pɔtiʀɔ̃/ nm pumpkin (GB), winter squash (US)

**pot-pourri,** pl **pots-pourris** /popuʀi/ nm (a) (Mus) medley
(b) potpourri

**pou,** pl **~x** /pu/ nm louse
IDIOMS chercher des ~x (colloq) to nitpick (colloq); être laid comme un ~ (colloq) to be as ugly as sin

**poubelle** /pubɛl/ nf bin (GB), trash can (US); dustbin (GB), garbage can (US)

**pouce** /pus/ nm (a) thumb
(b) big toe
(c) inch; ne pas bouger d'un ~ not to budge an inch
IDIOMS se tourner or rouler les ~s (colloq) to twiddle one's thumbs; manger sur le ~ to have a quick bite to eat; donner un coup de ~ à qn to help sb get started

**poudre** /pudʀ/ nf (gen) powder; ~ (à canon) gunpowder; ~ à récurer scouring powder
IDIOMS mettre le feu aux ~s to bring things to a head; jeter de la ~ aux yeux to try to impress

**poudrer** /pudʀe/ [1] vtr to powder

**poudreux, -euse** /pudʀø, øz/ adj powdery

**poudrier** /pudʀije/ nm powder compact

**poudrière** /pudʀijɛʀ/ nf (a) powder magazine
(b) (figurative) time bomb

**pouf** /puf/ nm (a) pouffe
(b) faire ~ to fall with a soft thud

**pouffer** /pufe/ [1] vi ~ (de rire) to burst out laughing

**pouilleux, -euse** /pujø, øz/ adj (a) (colloq) seedy
(b) flea-ridden

**poulailler** /pulaje/ nm (a) henhouse; hen run
(b) hens
(c) (colloq) (in theatre) le ~ the Gods (GB), the gallery

**poulain** /pulɛ̃/ nm (a) colt; foal
(b) protégé

**poularde** /pulaʀd/ nf fattened chicken

**poule** /pul/ nf (a) hen
(b) boiling fowl
(c) (colloq) ma ~ my pet (colloq), honey (US) (colloq)
■ ~ d'eau moorhen; ~ faisane hen pheasant; ~ mouillée (colloq) wimp (colloq); ~ naine bantam; ~ au pot boiled chicken
IDIOMS quand les ~s auront des dents (colloq) pigs might fly; tuer la ~ aux œufs d'or to kill the goose that lays the golden egg

**poulet** /pulɛ/ nm chicken
■ ~ d'élevage ≈ battery chicken; ~ fermier ≈ free-range chicken

**pouliche** /puliʃ/ nf filly

**poulie** /puli/ nf pulley

**poulpe** /pulp/ nm octopus

**pouls** /pu/ nm inv pulse

**poumon** /pumɔ̃/ nm lung; ~ d'acier or artificiel iron lung; à pleins ~s ⟨shout⟩ at the top of one's voice; ⟨breathe⟩ deeply

**poupe** /pup/ nf stern; avoir le vent en ~ to have the wind in one's sails

**poupée** /pupe/ nf doll

**poupon** /pupɔ̃/ nm (a) tiny baby
(b) baby doll

**pouponner** /pupɔne/ [1] vi (colloq) to play the doting father/mother

**pour¹** /puʀ/ *prep* **(a)** (in order) to; ~ **faire** to do; in order to do; **pour ne pas faire** so as not to do; **c'était** ~ **rire** *or* **plaisanter** it was a joke; ~ **que** so that; ~ **ainsi dire** so to speak **(b)** for; **le train** ~ **Paris** the train for Paris *or* to Paris; **ce sera prêt** ~ **vendredi?** will it be ready by Friday?; ~ **toujours** forever; **le bébé c'est** ~ **quand?** when is the baby due?; **se battre** ~ **une femme** to fight over a woman; **c'est fait** *or* **étudié** ~**!** (colloq) that's what it's for; **je suis** ~ (colloq) I'm in favour (GB) **(c)** about; as regards; **se renseigner** ~ to find out about; ~ **l'argent** as regards the money, as for the money; ~ **moi, il a tort** as far as I am concerned, he's wrong **(d) elle a** ~ **ambition d'être pilote** her ambition is to be a pilot **(e) elle avait** ~ **elle de savoir écouter** she had the merit of being a good listener **(f)** ~ **autant que je sache** as far as I know; ~ **être intelligente, ça elle l'est!** she really is intelligent! **(g) j'ai mis** ~ **40 euros d'essence** I've put in 40 euros' worth of petrol (GB) *or* gas (US); **merci** ~ **tout** thank you for everything; **je n'y suis** ~ **rien** I had nothing to do with it; **je n'en ai pas** ~ **longtemps** it won't take long **(h) dix** ~ **cent** ten per cent; **une cuillère de vinaigre** ~ **quatre d'huile** one spoonful of vinegar to four of oil; ~ **une large part** to a large extent

**pour²** /puʀ/ *nm* **le** ~ **et le contre** the pros and the cons

**pourboire** /puʀbwaʀ/ *nm* tip

**pourcentage** /puʀsɑ̃taʒ/ *nm* **(a)** percentage **(b)** commission **(c)** cut (colloq)

**pourchasser** /puʀʃase/ [1] *vtr* **(a)** to hunt ⟨*animal, criminal*⟩ **(b)** to pursue ⟨*person*⟩

**pourparlers** /puʀpaʀle/ *nm pl* talks; **être en** ~ ⟨*people*⟩ to be engaged in talks

**pourpre** /puʀpʀ/ *adj, nm* crimson

**pourquoi** /puʀkwa/ **1** *adv, conj* why; ~ **donc?** but why?; ~ **pas** *or* **non?** why not?; ~ **pas un week-end à Paris?** what *or* how about a weekend in Paris?; **va donc savoir** ~! God knows why! **2** *nm inv* **le** ~ **et le comment** the why and the wherefore

**pourri, ~e** /puʀi/ **1** *pp* ▶ POURRIR **2** *pp adj* **(a)** (gen) rotten; ⟨*vegetation*⟩ rotting **(b)** (colloq) ⟨*weather, car*⟩ rotten (colloq); ⟨*person*⟩ crooked (colloq) **3** *nm* rotten part; **ça sent le** ~ it smells rotten

**pourrir** /puʀiʀ/ [3] **1** *vtr* **(a)** to rot ⟨*wood*⟩ **(b)** to spoil ⟨*person*⟩ **(c)** (colloq) to spoil [sb] rotten (colloq) **2** *vi* **(a)** ⟨*food*⟩ to go bad **(b)** ⟨*wood*⟩ to rot **(c)** ⟨*person*⟩ to rot; ⟨*situation*⟩ to deteriorate

**pourriture** /puʀityʀ/ *nf* **(a)** rot, decay **(b)** corruption, rottenness

**poursuite** /puʀsɥit/ *nf* **(a)** pursuit; **être à la** ~ **de** to be in pursuit of **(b)** chase **(c)** continuation **(d)** ~ **(judiciaire)** (judicial) proceedings

**poursuivre** /puʀsɥivʀ/ [62] **1** *vtr* **(a)** to chase **(b)** ⟨*person*⟩ to hound; ⟨*nightmare*⟩ to haunt; ~ **qn de ses assiduités** to force one's attentions on sb **(c)** to seek (after) ⟨*honours, truth*⟩; to pursue ⟨*goal*⟩ **(d)** to continue ⟨*journey, studies*⟩; to pursue ⟨*talks*⟩ **(e)** (Law) ~ **qn (en justice** *or* **devant les tribunaux)** to sue sb **2** *vi* to continue; ~ **sur un sujet** to continue talking on a subject **3** **se poursuivre** *v refl* (+ *v être*) ⟨*talks, conflict, journey*⟩ to continue

**pourtant** /puʀtɑ̃/ *adv* though; **et** ~ and yet; **techniquement** ~**, le film est parfait** technically, however, the film is perfect

**pourtour** /puʀtuʀ/ *nm* **(a)** perimeter; circumference **(b)** surrounding area

**pourvoir** /puʀvwaʀ/ [40] **1** *vtr* **(a)** to fill ⟨*post*⟩ **(b)** ~ **qn de** to endow sb with **2** **pourvoir à** *v+prep* to provide for **3** **se pourvoir** *v refl* (+ *v être*) **se** ~ **de** to provide oneself with ⟨*currency*⟩; to equip oneself with ⟨*boots*⟩

**pourvoyeur, -euse** /puʀvwajœʀ, øz/ *nm,f* ~ **de** source of ⟨*jobs, funding*⟩

**pourvu, ~e** /puʀvy/ **1** *pp* ▶ POURVOIR **2** **pourvu que** *phr* **(a)** provided (that), as long as **(b)** let's hope; ~ **que ça dure!** let's hope it lasts!

**pousse** /pus/ *nf* **(a)** (Bot) shoot **(b)** growth

**poussé, ~e¹** /puse/ **1** *pp* ▶ POUSSER **2** *pp adj* ⟨*inquiry*⟩ thorough; ⟨*studies*⟩ advanced

**poussée²** /puse/ *nf* **(a)** (of water, crowd) pressure; (of wind) force **(b)** thrust **(c)** (Med) attack; ~ **de fièvre** sudden high temperature **(d)** (in price) (sharp) rise; (in racism, violence) upsurge

**pousser** /puse/ [1] **1** *vtr* **(a)** to push ⟨*wheelbarrow, person*⟩; to move *or* shift [sth] (out of the way), to push [sth] aside; ~ **une porte** to push a door to; to push a door open; ~ **qn du coude** to give sb a dig *or* to nudge sb with one's elbow **(b)** ~ **qn à faire** to encourage sb to do; to urge sb to do; ⟨*hunger, despair*⟩ to drive sb to do; ~ **à la consommation** to encourage people to buy more; to encourage people to drink more ····❯

**(c)** to push ⟨*pupil*⟩; to keep [sb] at it ⟨*employee*⟩; to drive [sth] hard ⟨*car*⟩
**(d)** to push ⟨*product, protégé*⟩
**(e)** to pursue ⟨*studies, research*⟩; **c'est ~ un peu loin la plaisanterie** that's taking the joke a bit far
**(f)** to let out ⟨*cry*⟩; to heave ⟨*sigh*⟩
**2** *vi* **(a)** ⟨*child*⟩ to grow; ⟨*plant*⟩ to grow; to sprout; ⟨*tooth*⟩ to come through; ⟨*buildings*⟩ to spring up; **je fais ~ des légumes** I grow vegetables; **se laisser ~ les cheveux** to grow one's hair
**(b) ~ plus loin** to go on further
**(c)** (colloq) to overdo it, to go too far
**3 se pousser** *v refl* (+ *v être*) to move over
**IDIOMS à la va comme je te pousse** (colloq) any old how

**poussette** /pusɛt/ *nf* pushchair (GB), stroller (US)

**poussière** /pusjɛʀ/ *nf* **(a)** dust; **tomber en ~** to crumble away; to fall to bits
**(b)** speck of dust
**IDIOMS 10 euros/20 ans et des ~s** (colloq) just over 10 euros/20 years

**poussiéreux, -euse** /pusjeʀø, øz/ *adj*
**(a)** dusty
**(b)** outdated, fossilized

**poussin** /pusɛ̃/ *nm* chick

**poussoir** /puswaʀ/ *nm* (push) button

**poutre** /putʀ/ *nf* **(a)** beam
**(b)** girder

**pouvoir¹** /puvwaʀ/ [49] **1** *v aux* **(a)** to be able to; **peux-tu soulever cette boîte?** can you lift this box?; **dès que je pourrai** as soon as I can; **je n'en peux plus** I've had it (colloq); I'm full (colloq); **tout peut arriver** anything could happen; **il ne peut pas ne pas gagner** he's bound to win; **on peut toujours espérer** there's no harm in wishing; **qu'est-ce que cela peut (bien) te faire?** (colloq) what business is it of yours?
**(b)** to be allowed to; **est-ce que je peux me servir de ta voiture?** can I use your car?; **on peut dire que** it can be said that; **on peut ne pas faire l'accord** the agreement is optional
**(c) pouvez-vous/pourriez-vous me tenir la porte s'il vous plaît?** can you/could you hold the door (open) for me please?
**(d) puisse cette nouvelle année exaucer vos vœux les plus chers** may the new year bring you everything you could wish for; **s'il croit que je vais payer il peut toujours attendre** if he thinks I'm going to pay he's got another think coming; **ce qu'il peut être grand!** how tall he is!
**2** *vtr* **que puis-je pour vous?** what can I do for you?; **je fais ce que je peux** I'm doing my best
**3** *v impers* **il peut faire très froid en janvier** it can get very cold in January; **ce qu'il a pu pleuvoir!** you wouldn't believe how much it rained!
**4 il se peut** *v impers* **il se peut que les**

prix augmentent en juin prices may *or* might rise in June; **cela se pourrait qu'il soit fâché** he might be angry
**5 on ne peut plus** *phr* **il est on ne peut plus timide** he is as shy as can be
**6 on ne peut mieux** *phr* **ils s'entendent on ne peut mieux** they get on extremely well
**IDIOMS autant que faire se peut** as far as possible

**pouvoir²** /puvwaʀ/ *nm* **(a)** (gen) power; **~ d'achat** purchasing power; **avoir le ~ de faire** to be able to do, to have the power to do; **je n'ai pas le ~ de décider** it's not up to me to decide
**(b)** (Pol) power; **avoir tous ~s** to have *or* exercise full powers; **le ~ en place** the government in power
■ **le ~ judiciaire** the judiciary; **~ législatif** legislative power; **~s publics** authorities

**pragmatisme** /pʀagmatism/ *nm* pragmatism

**praire** /pʀɛʀ/ *nf* clam

**prairie** /pʀeʀi/ *nf* meadow

**praline** /pʀalin/ *nf* sugared (GB) *or* sugar-coated (US) almond

**praliné, ~e** /pʀaline/ **1** *adj* praline
**2** *nm* praline

**praticable** /pʀatikabl/ *adj* ⟨*road*⟩ passable

**praticien, -ienne** /pʀatisjɛ̃, ɛn/ *nm,f*
**(a)** general practitioner, GP
**(b)** practitioner

**pratiquant, ~e** /pʀatikɑ̃, ɑ̃t/ *adj* practising (GB); **être très ~** to be very devout

**pratique** /pʀatik/ **1** *adj* practical; ⟨*device*⟩ handy; ⟨*place, route*⟩ convenient
**2** *nf* **(a) la ~ des arts martiaux est très répandue** many people practise (GB) martial arts; **cela nécessite de longues heures de ~** it takes hours of practice; **avoir une bonne ~ de l'anglais** to have a good working knowledge of English
**(b)** practical experience
**(c)** practice; **mettre qch en ~** to put sth into practice
**(d) les ~s religieuses** religious practices

**pratiquement** /pʀatikmɑ̃/ *adv* **(a)** in practice
**(b)** practically, virtually; **~ jamais** hardly ever

**pratiquer** /pʀatike/ [1] **1** *vtr* **(a)** to play ⟨*tennis*⟩; to do ⟨*yoga*⟩; to take part in ⟨*activity*⟩; to practise (GB) ⟨*language*⟩; **il est croyant mais ne pratique pas** he believes in God but doesn't practise (GB) his religion
**(b)** to use ⟨*method, blackmail*⟩; to pursue ⟨*policy*⟩; to charge ⟨*rate of interest*⟩
**(c)** to carry out ⟨*examination, graft*⟩
**2 se pratiquer** *v refl* (+ *v être*) ⟨*sport*⟩ to be played; ⟨*technique, policy, strategy*⟩ to be used; ⟨*price, tariff*⟩ to be charged

**pré** /pʀe/ *nm* meadow

**pré-** /pʀe/ *pref* pre(-); **~-accord** preliminary agreement

**préalable** /pʀealabl/ **1** *adj* ⟨*notice*⟩ prior; ⟨*study*⟩ preliminary

**2** *nm* precondition; preliminary
**3** **au préalable** *phr* first, beforehand
**préalablement** /pʀealabləmɑ̃/ *adv* beforehand
**préambule** /pʀeɑ̃byl/ *nm* **(a)** preamble **(b)** forewarning
**préau**, *pl* **~x** /pʀeo/ *nm* (of school) covered playground; (of prison) exercise yard
**préavis** /pʀeavi/ *nm inv* notice
**précaire** /pʀekɛʀ/ *adj* ⟨existence⟩ precarious; ⟨job⟩ insecure; ⟨construction⟩ flimsy
**précariser** /pʀekaʀize/ [1] *vtr* **~ l'emploi** to casualize labour (GB)
**précarité** /pʀekaʀite/ *nf* precariousness; **la ~ de l'emploi** job insecurity
**précaution** /pʀekosjɔ̃/ *nf* precaution; caution; **par ~** as a precaution
**précédemment** /pʀesedamɑ̃/ *adv* previously
**précédent, ~e** /pʀesedɑ̃, ɑ̃t/ **1** *adj* previous
**2** *nm,f* **le ~, la ~e** the previous one
**3** *nm* precedent; **sans ~** unprecedented
**précéder** /pʀesede/ [14] *vtr* **(a)** ⟨person⟩ to go in front of, to precede; ⟨vehicle⟩ to be in front of
**(b) il m'avait précédé de cinq minutes** he'd got there five minutes ahead of me
**(c)** ⟨paragraph, crisis⟩ to precede; **la semaine qui a précédé votre départ** the week before you left
**précepte** /pʀesɛpt/ *nm* precept
**précepteur, -trice** /pʀesɛptœʀ, tʀis/ *nm,f* (private) tutor
**prêcher** /pʀeʃe/ [1] **1** *vtr* **(a)** to preach **(b)** to advocate
**2** *vi* to preach
IDIOMS **~ le faux pour savoir le vrai** to tell a lie in order to get at the truth
**précieusement** /pʀesjøzmɑ̃/ *adv* carefully
**précieux, -ieuse** /pʀesjø, øz/ *adj* **(a)** ⟨stone, book⟩ precious; ⟨piece of furniture⟩ valuable
**(b)** ⟨information⟩ very useful; ⟨collaborator⟩ valued
**(c)** ⟨friendship, right⟩ precious; ⟨friend⟩ very dear
**(d)** ⟨style, language⟩ precious
**précipice** /pʀesipis/ *nm* precipice
**précipitamment** /pʀesipitamɑ̃/ *adv* hurriedly
**précipitation** /pʀesipitasjɔ̃/ **1** *nf* haste
**2 précipitations** *nf pl* rainfall, precipitation
**précipité, ~e** /pʀesipite/ *adj* **(a)** rapid **(b)** hasty, precipitate
**précipiter** /pʀesipite/ [1] **1** *vtr* **(a) ~ qn dans le vide** (from roof) to push sb off; (out of window) to push sb out
**(b)** to hasten ⟨departure, decision⟩; **~ les choses** to rush things

**2 se précipiter** *v refl* (+ *v être*) **(a) il s'est précipité dans le vide** he jumped off
**(b)** to rush; **se ~ au secours de qn** to rush to sb's aid; **se ~ sur** to rush at ⟨person⟩; to rush for ⟨object⟩
**(c)** to rush
**(d)** ⟨action⟩ to move faster
**précis, ~e** /pʀesi, iz/ **1** *adj*
**(a)** ⟨programme, criterion⟩ specific; ⟨idea, date⟩ definite; ⟨moment⟩ particular
**(b)** ⟨person, gesture⟩ precise; ⟨figure, data⟩ accurate; ⟨place⟩ exact
**2** *nm inv* handbook
**précisément** /pʀesizemɑ̃/ *adv* precisely
**préciser** /pʀesize/ [1] **1** *vtr* **(a)** to add; **faut-il le** *or* **est-il besoin de ~** needless to say
**(b)** to state; **~ ses intentions** to state one's intentions
**(c)** to specify; **pouvez-vous ~?** could you be more specific?
**(d)** to clarify ⟨ideas⟩
**2 se préciser** *v refl* (+ *v être*) **(a)** ⟨danger, future⟩ to become clearer; ⟨plan, trip⟩ to take shape
**(b)** ⟨shape, reality⟩ to become clear
**précision** /pʀesizjɔ̃/ *nf* **(a)** precision
**(b)** accuracy; **localiser avec ~** to pinpoint; **instrument de ~** precision instrument
**(c)** detail
**précité, ~e** /pʀesite/ *adj* aforementioned
**précoce** /pʀekɔs/ *adj* **(a)** precocious
**(b)** ⟨season⟩ early
**(c)** ⟨senility⟩ premature
**précompte** /pʀekɔ̃t/ *nm* deduction; **~ de l'impôt** deduction of tax at source
**préconçu, ~e** /pʀekɔ̃sy/ *adj* preconceived
**préconiser** /pʀekɔnize/ [1] *vtr* to recommend
**précuit, ~e** /pʀekɥi, it/ *adj* precooked
**précurseur** /pʀekyʀsœʀ/ **1** *adj m* precursory; **signes ~s de l'orage** signs that herald a storm
**2** *nm* pioneer; **~ de** precursor of
**prédateur** /pʀedatœʀ/ *nm* **(a)** predator
**(b)** hunter-gatherer
**prédécesseur** /pʀedesesœʀ/ *nm* predecessor
**prédestiner** /pʀedɛstine/ [1] *vtr* to predestine
**prédicateur, -trice** /pʀedikatœʀ, tʀis/ *nm,f* preacher
**prédiction** /pʀediksjɔ̃/ *nf* prediction
**prédilection** /pʀedilɛksjɔ̃/ *nf* predilection, liking; **de ~** favourite (GB)
**prédire** /pʀediʀ/ [65] *vtr* to predict
**prédisposer** /pʀedispoze/ [1] *vtr* to predispose
**prédominant, ~e** /pʀedɔminɑ̃, ɑ̃t/ *adj* predominant
**prédominer** /pʀedɔmine/ [1] *vi* to predominate

**préétablir** /pʀeetabliʀ/ [3] *vtr* to pre-establish

**préexister** /pʀeɛɡziste/ [1] *vi* to pre-exist

**préfabriqué** /pʀefabʀike/ *nm*
(a) prefabricated material
(b) prefab (colloq)

**préface** /pʀefas/ *nf* preface

**préfacer** /pʀefase/ [12] *vtr* to write a *or* the preface to

**préfectoral**, **~e**, *mpl* **-aux** /pʀefɛktɔʀal, o/ *adj* ⟨level, authorization⟩ prefectorial; ⟨administration, building⟩ prefectural

**préfecture** /pʀefɛktyʀ/ *nf* (a) prefecture
(b) main city of a French department
■ **~ de police** police headquarters (*in some large French cities*)

**préférable** /pʀefeʀabl/ *adj* preferable

**préféré**, **~e** /pʀefeʀe/ *adj*, *nm,f* favourite (GB)

**préférence** /pʀefeʀɑ̃s/ *nf* preference; **achète cette marque de ~** if you can, buy this brand

**préférentiel**, **-ielle** /pʀefeʀɑ̃sjɛl/ *adj* preferential

**préférer** /pʀefeʀe/ [14] *vtr* to prefer; **j'aurais préféré ne jamais l'apprendre** I wish I'd never found out

**préfet** /pʀefɛ/ *nm* prefect

**préfigurer** /pʀefiɡyʀe/ [1] *vtr* to prefigure

**préfixe** /pʀefiks/ *nm* prefix

**préhistoire** /pʀeistwaʀ/ *nf* prehistory

**préjudice** /pʀeʒydis/ *nm* harm, damage; **~ moral** moral wrong; **porter ~ à qn** to harm sb; **au ~ de qn** to the detriment of sb

**préjugé** /pʀeʒyʒe/ *nm* prejudice; **~(s) en faveur de qn** bias in favour (GB) of sb

**préjuger** /pʀeʒyʒe/ [13] *vtr*, **préjuger de** *v+prep* to prejudge

**prélasser**: **se prélasser** /pʀelase/ [1] *v refl* (+ *v être*) to lounge

**prélat** /pʀela/ *nm* prelate

**prélavage** /pʀelavaʒ/ *nm* prewash

**prêle** /pʀɛl/ *nf* (Bot) horsetail

**prélèvement** /pʀelɛvmɑ̃/ *nm*
(a) sampling; sample; **faire un ~ de sang** to take a blood sample
(b) **faire un ~ bancaire de 100 euros** to make a debit of 100 euros
■ **~ automatique** direct debit; **~ à la source** deduction at source

**prélever** /pʀelve/ [16] *vtr* (a) to take a sample of ⟨blood, water⟩; to remove ⟨organ⟩
(b) to debit
(c) to deduct ⟨tax⟩
(d) to take ⟨percentage⟩

**préliminaire** /pʀeliminɛʀ/ ① *adj* preliminary
② **préliminaires** *nm pl* preliminaries

**prélude** /pʀelyd/ *nm* prelude

**préluder** /pʀelyde/ [1] *v+prep* **~ à** to be a prelude to

**prématuré**, **~e** /pʀematyʀe/ ① *adj* premature

② *nm,f* premature baby

**préméditation** /pʀemeditasjɔ̃/ *nf* premeditation

**préméditer** /pʀemedite/ [1] *vtr* to premeditate

**premier**, **-ière**[1] /pʀəmje, ɛʀ/ ① *adj*
(a) first; **(dans) les ~s temps** at first
(b) ⟨artist, power⟩ leading; ⟨student⟩ top; **être ~** to be top; to be first; **c'est le ~ prix** it's the cheapest
(c) ⟨impression⟩ first, initial
(d) ⟨quality⟩ prime; ⟨objective⟩ primary
② *nm,f* first; **je préfère le ~** I prefer the first one; **arriver le ~** to come first; **être le ~ de la classe** to be top of the class
③ *nm* (a) first floor (GB), second floor (US)
(b) first; **le ~ de l'an** New Year's Day
(c) first arrondissement
④ **en premier** *phr* first
■ **~ âge** ⟨clothes⟩ for babies up to six months; **~ de cordée** (Sport) leader; **~ ministre** prime minister; **le ~ venu** just anybody; the first person to come along; **~s secours** first aid

**première**[2] /pʀəmjɛʀ/ ① ▶ PREMIER 1, 2
② *nf* (a) first; **~ mondiale** world first
(b) première
(c) (Sch) sixth year of secondary school, age 16–17
(d) (Aut) first (gear)
(e) (colloq) first class
③ **de première** *phr* (colloq) first-rate

**premièrement** /pʀəmjɛʀmɑ̃/ *adv*
(a) firstly, first
(b) for a start, for one thing

**prémisse** /pʀemis/ *nf* premise, premiss (GB)

**prémolaire** /pʀemɔlɛʀ/ *nf* premolar

**prémonition** /pʀemɔnisjɔ̃/ *nf* premonition

**prémonitoire** /pʀemɔnitwaʀ/ *adj* premonitory

**prémunir** /pʀemyniʀ/ [3] ① *vtr* to protect
② **se prémunir** *v refl* (+ *v être*) to protect oneself

**prenant**, **~e** /pʀənɑ̃, ɑ̃t/ *adj* ⟨film⟩ fascinating; ⟨voice⟩ captivating; ⟨work⟩ absorbing

**prendre** /pʀɑ̃dʀ/ [52]
■ Note Prendre is very often translated by *to take* but see the entry below for a wide variety of usages.
– For translations of certain fixed phrases such as *prendre froid*, *prendre soin de*, *prendre parti* etc, refer to the entries FROID, SOIN, PARTI.

① *vtr* (a) to take; **~ un vase dans le placard** to take a vase out of the cupboard; **prenez donc une chaise** take a seat; **~ un congé** to take time off; **~ le train/l'avion** to take the train/plane; **on m'a pris tous mes bijoux** I had all my jewellery (GB) *or* jewelry (US) stolen; **la guerre leur a pris deux fils** they lost two sons in the war; **~ les mensurations de qn** to take sb's measurements; **~ les choses comme elles sont** to take things as they

come; **ne le prends pas mal** don't take it the wrong way; **je vous ai pris pour quelqu'un d'autre** I thought you were someone else
**(b)** ~ **un accent** to pick up an accent; to put on an accent
**(c)** to bring; **n'oublie pas de** ~ **des bottes** don't forget to bring a pair of boots
**(d)** to get ⟨*food, petrol*⟩; ~ **de l'argent au distributeur** to get some money out of the cash dispenser
**(e)** to have ⟨*drink, meal*⟩; to take ⟨*medicine*⟩; **aller** ~ **une bière** to go for a beer
**(f)** to choose ⟨*topic, question*⟩
**(g)** to charge; **il prend 15% au passage** (colloq) he takes a cut of 15%
**(h)** to take up ⟨*space, time*⟩
**(i)** to take [sb] on; to engage [sb]
**(j)** to pick [sb/sth] up; ~ **les enfants à l'école** to collect the children from school
**(k)** to catch; **elle s'est fait** ~ **en train de voler** she got caught stealing
**(l)** (colloq) **qu'est-ce qui te prend?** what's the matter with you?; **ça te/leur prend souvent?** are you/they often like this?
**(m)** to involve ⟨*spectator, reader*⟩; **être pris par un livre/film** to get involved in a book/film
**(n)** to get ⟨*slap, sunburn*⟩; to catch ⟨*cold*⟩
**(o) il est très gentil quand on sait le** ~ he's very nice when you know how to handle him
**(p)** to take [sth] down ⟨*address*⟩
**(q) où a-t-il pris qu'ils allaient divorcer?** where did he get the idea they were going to get divorced?
**(r)** to take over ⟨*management, power*⟩; to assume ⟨*control*⟩; **je prends ça sur moi** I'll see to it; **elle a pris sur elle de leur parler** she took it upon herself to talk to them
**(s)** to put on ⟨*weight*⟩; to gain ⟨*lead*⟩
**(t)** to take on ⟨*lease*⟩; to take ⟨*job*⟩
**(u)** to take on ⟨*rival*⟩
**(v)** to take, to seize ⟨*town*⟩; to capture ⟨*ship, tank*⟩; to take ⟨*chesspiece, card*⟩
**2** *vi* **(a)** ~ **à gauche/vers le nord** to go left/north
**(b)** ⟨*wood*⟩ to catch; ⟨*fire*⟩ to break out
**(c)** ⟨*jelly, glue*⟩ to set; ⟨*mayonnaise*⟩ to thicken
**(d)** ⟨*strike, innovation*⟩ to be a success; ⟨*idea, fashion*⟩ to catch on; ⟨*dye, cutting*⟩ to take
**(e)** ~ **sur son temps libre pour traduire un roman** to translate a novel in one's spare time
**(f)** ~ **sur soi** to take a hold on oneself, to get a grip on oneself
**(g)** (colloq) **ça ne prend pas!** it won't work!
**(h)** (colloq) **c'est toujours moi qui prends!** I'm always the one who gets it in the neck!
(colloq); **il en a pris pour 20 ans** he got 20 years
**3** **se prendre** *v refl* (+ *v être*) **(a) en Chine le thé se prend sans sucre** in China they don't put sugar in their tea
**(b) les mauvaises habitudes se prennent vite** bad habits are easily picked up

**(c) se** ~ **par la taille** to hold each other around the waist
**(d) se** ~ **les doigts dans la porte** to catch one's fingers in the door
**(e)** (colloq) **il s'est pris une gifle** he got a slap in the face
**(f) se** ~ **à faire** to find oneself doing; **se** ~ **de sympathie pour qn** to take to sb
**(g) pour qui est-ce que tu te prends?** who do you think you are?
**(h) s'en** ~ **à** to attack ⟨*person, press*⟩; to take it out on [sb]; to go for [sb]
**(i) savoir s'y** ~ **avec** to have a way with ⟨*children*⟩
**(j) il faut s'y** ~ **à l'avance pour avoir des places** you have to book ahead to get seats; **tu t'y es pris trop tard** you left it too late; **il s'y est pris à plusieurs fois** he tried several times; **elle s'y prend mal** she goes about it the wrong way
**IDIOMS c'est à** ~ **ou à laisser** take it or leave it

**preneur, -euse** /pʀənœʀ, øz/ *nm,f* **il n'y a pas** ~ there are no takers; **trouver** ~ to attract a buyer; to find a buyer

**prénom** /pʀenɔ̃/ *nm* first name, forename

**prénommer** /pʀenɔme/ [1] **1** *vtr* to name, to call
**2** **se prénommer** *v refl* (+ *v être*) to be called

**prénuptial, ~e**, *pl* **-iaux** /pʀenypsjal, o/ *adj* prenuptial; prior to marriage

**préoccupant, ~e** /pʀeɔkypɑ̃, ɑ̃t/ *adj* worrying

**préoccupation** /pʀeɔkypasjɔ̃/ *nf* worry

**préoccuper** /pʀeɔkype/ [1] **1** *vtr* **(a)** to worry; **avoir l'air préoccupé** to look worried
**(b)** to preoccupy
**(c)** to concern
**2** **se préoccuper** *v refl* (+ *v être*) **se** ~ **de** to be concerned about ⟨*situation*⟩; to think about ⟨*future*⟩

**préparateur, -trice** /pʀepaʀatœʀ, tʀis/ *nm,f* ~ **en pharmacie** pharmacist's assistant

**préparatifs** /pʀepaʀatif/ *nm pl* preparations

**préparation** /pʀepaʀasjɔ̃/ *nf*
**(a)** preparation
**(b)** training

**préparatoire** /pʀepaʀatwaʀ/ *adj* preliminary

**préparer** /pʀepaʀe/ [1] **1** *vtr* **(a)** (gen) to prepare; to make ⟨*meal*⟩; to get [sth] ready ⟨*clothes, file*⟩; to plan ⟨*holidays, future*⟩; to draw up ⟨*plan*⟩; to hatch ⟨*plot*⟩; **il est en train de** ~ **le dîner** he's getting dinner ready; **des plats préparés** ready-to-eat meals
**(b)** ~ **qn à qch** (gen) to prepare sb for sth; to coach sb for sth ⟨*race, examination*⟩; **essaie de la** ~ **avant de lui annoncer la nouvelle** try and break the news to her gently
**2** **se préparer** *v refl* (+ *v être*) **(a)** to get ready
**(b)** to prepare
**(c)** ⟨*storm, trouble*⟩ to be brewing; ⟨*changes*⟩ ┈┈▷

to be in the offing; **un coup d'État se prépare
dans le pays** a coup d'état is imminent in
the country
**(d) se ~ une tasse de thé** to make or fix (US)
oneself a cup of tea

**prépondérance** /pʀepɔ̃deʀɑ̃s/ nf
predominance

**prépondérant, ~e** /pʀepɔ̃deʀɑ̃, ɑ̃t/ adj
predominant

**préposé, ~e** /pʀepoze/ nm,f **(a)** official;
**~ des douanes** customs official; **~ au
vestiaire** cloakroom attendant
**(b)** postman/postwoman

**préposition** /pʀepozisjɔ̃/ nf preposition

**prépuce** /pʀepys/ nm foreskin

**préretraite** /pʀeʀətʀɛt/ nf early
retirement

**prérogative** /pʀeʀɔɡativ/ nf prerogative;
**~ de qn/qch sur** primacy of sb/sth over

**près** /pʀɛ/ **1** adv **(a)** close; **ce n'est pas tout
~** it's quite a way; **se raser de ~** to have a
close shave
**(b)** ça pèse 10 kg, à quelques grammes ~ it
weighs 10 kg, give or take a few grams; **à
ceci** or **cela ~ que** except that; **il m'a
remboursé au centime ~** he paid me back to
the very last penny; **gagner à deux voix ~** to
win by two votes; **à une exception ~** with
only one exception
**2** **près de** phr **(a)** near; être **~ du but** to
be close to achieving one's goal; **j'aimerais
être ~ de toi** I'd like to be with you
**(b)** near, nearly; **je ne suis pas ~ de
recommencer** I'm not about to do that again;
**le problème n'est pas ~ d'être résolu** the
problem is nowhere near solved
**(c)** close; **ils sont très ~ l'un de l'autre** they
are very close
**(d)** nearly, almost; **cela coûte ~ de 1000
euros** it costs nearly 1,000 euros
**3** **de près** phr closely; **se suivre de ~**
⟨competitors⟩ to be close together; ⟨siblings⟩
to be close in age
**4** **à peu près** phr **~ vide** practically
empty; **~ 200 euros** about 200 euros; **à peu
~ de la même façon** in much the same way

**présage** /pʀezaʒ/ nm **(a)** omen
**(b)** harbinger
**(c)** prediction

**présager** /pʀezaʒe/ [13] vtr ⟨event⟩ to
presage; ⟨person⟩ to predict; **laisser ~** to
suggest

**presbyte** /pʀɛsbit/ adj longsighted (GB),
farsighted (US)

**presbytère** /pʀɛsbitɛʀ/ nm presbytery

**presbytie** /pʀɛsbisi/ nf longsightedness
(GB), farsightedness (US)

**préscolaire** /pʀeskɔlɛʀ/ adj preschool

**prescription** /pʀɛskʀipsjɔ̃/ nf
prescription; 'se conformer aux ~s du
médecin' 'to be taken in accordance with
doctor's instructions'

**prescrire** /pʀɛskʀiʀ/ [67] vtr **(a)** (Med) to
prescribe
**(b)** to stipulate

**présélection** /pʀeselɛksjɔ̃/ nf
**(a)** shortlisting
**(b)** (Tech) presetting

**présélectionner** /pʀeselɛksjɔne/ [1] vtr
**(a)** to shortlist
**(b)** to preselect; to preset

**présence** /pʀezɑ̃s/ nf (gen) presence; (at
work) attendance; **il fait de la ~, c'est tout**
he's present and not much else; **les forces en
~ dans le conflit** the forces involved in the
conflict; **il a besoin d'une ~** he needs
company; **avoir beaucoup de ~ (sur scène)**
to have great stage presence
■ **~ d'esprit** presence of mind

**présent, ~e¹** /pʀezɑ̃, ɑ̃t/ **1** adj
**(a)** present; **M. Maquanne, ici ~** Mr
Maquanne, who is here with us; **avoir qch ~
à l'esprit** to have [sth] in mind ⟨advice⟩; to
have [sth] fresh in one's mind ⟨memory⟩
**(b)** actively involved; **un chanteur très ~ sur
scène** a singer with a strong stage presence
**2** nm,f **la liste des ~s** the list of those
present
**3** nm **(a)** **le ~** the present
**(b)** (in grammar) present (tense)
**(c)** gift, present
**4** **à présent** phr at present; now

**présentable** /pʀezɑ̃tabl/ adj presentable

**présentateur, -trice** /pʀezɑ̃tatœʀ, tʀis/
nm,f presenter; newsreader (GB), newscaster
(US)

**présentation** /pʀezɑ̃tasjɔ̃/ nf
**(a)** introduction; **faire les ~s** to make the
introductions
**(b)** appearance
**(c)** (of dish, letter) presentation; (of products)
display
**(d)** show, showing; **~ de mode** fashion show
**(e)** (of programme) presentation
**(f)** (of card, ticket) production; (of cheque)
presentation
**(g)** presentation, exposé

**présente²** /pʀezɑ̃t/ **1** adj f ▶ PRÉSENT 1
**2** nf **(a)** **par la ~** hereby
**(b)** ▶ PRÉSENT 2

**présenter** /pʀezɑ̃te/ [1] **1** vtr **(a)** to
introduce; to present
**(b)** to show ⟨ticket, card, menu⟩
**(c)** to present ⟨programme, show, collection⟩;
to display ⟨goods⟩
**(d)** to present ⟨receipt, bill⟩; to submit
⟨estimate, report⟩; to introduce ⟨proposal,
bill⟩; **~ une liste pour les élections** to put
forward a list (of candidates) for the
elections
**(e)** to present ⟨situation, budget, theory⟩; to
set out ⟨objections, point of view⟩; **~ qn
comme (étant) un monstre** to portray sb as a
monster
**(f)** to offer ⟨condolences⟩; **~ des excuses** to
apologize
**(g)** to involve ⟨risk, difficulty⟩; to show
⟨differences⟩; to offer ⟨advantage⟩; to have
⟨aspect, feature⟩
**2** vi **~ bien** to have a smart appearance
**3** **se présenter** v refl (+ v être) **(a)** il faut

se ∼ à la réception you must go to reception; **présentez-vous à 10 heures** come at 10 o'clock
**(b)** to introduce oneself
**(c) se ∼ à** to take ⟨*examination*⟩; to stand for ⟨*election*⟩
**(d)** ⟨*opportunity*⟩ to arise; ⟨*solution*⟩ to emerge
**(e) se ∼ en, se ∼ sous forme de** ⟨*product*⟩ to come in the form of
**(f)** l'affaire se présente bien things are looking good

**présentoir** /pʀezɑ̃twaʀ/ *nm* **(a)** display stand *or* unit
**(b)** display shelf

**préservatif** /pʀezɛʀvatif/ *nm* condom

**préservation** /pʀezɛʀvasjɔ̃/ *nf* protection; preservation

**préserver** /pʀezɛʀve/ [1] *vtr* **(a)** to preserve
**(b)** to protect

**présidence** /pʀezidɑ̃s/ *nf* **(a)** presidency; chairmanship
**(b)** presidential palace

**président** /pʀezidɑ̃/ *nm* president; chairman
■ ∼ de la République President of the Republic

**président-directeur**, *pl* **présidents-directeurs**
/pʀezidiʀɛktœʀ/ *nm* ∼ **général** chairman and managing director (GB), chief executive officer

**présidente** /pʀezidɑ̃t/ *nf* **(a)** president; chairwoman, chairperson; chairman
**(b)** First Lady

**présidentiel, -ielle** /pʀezidɑ̃sjɛl/ *adj* presidential

**présidentielles** /pʀezidɑ̃sjɛl/ *nf pl* presidential election

**présider** /pʀezide/ [1] *vtr* **(a)** to chair
**(b)** to be the president of; to be the chairman/chairwoman of; to preside over

**présomption** /pʀezɔ̃psjɔ̃/ *nf* **(a)** (Law) presumption
**(b)** assumption
**(c) plein de** ∼ presumptuous

**présomptueux, -euse** /pʀezɔ̃ptɥø, øz/ *adj* arrogant; presumptuous

**presque** /pʀɛsk/ *adv* almost, nearly; **il y a trois ans** ∼ **jour pour jour** it's nearly three years to the day; **c'était le bonheur ou** ∼ it was as close to happiness as one can get; **il ne reste** ∼ **rien** there's hardly anything left

**presqu'île** /pʀɛskil/ *nf* peninsula

**pressant, ∼e** /pʀɛsɑ̃, ɑ̃t/ *adj* ⟨*need*⟩ pressing; ⟨*appeal*⟩ urgent; ⟨*salesman*⟩ insistent

**presse** /pʀɛs/ *nf* **(a)** press; newspapers; **avoir bonne** ∼ to be well thought of
**(b)** (gen) press; (printing) press; **mettre sous** ∼ to send [sth] to press; **'sous** ∼' 'in preparation'

**pressé, ∼e** /pʀɛse/ *adj* **(a)** ⟨*person*⟩ in a hurry; ⟨*steps*⟩ hurried

**(b)** ∼ **de faire** keen to do
**(c)** ⟨*business*⟩ urgent; **parer au plus** ∼ to do the most urgent thing(s) first

**presse-ail** /pʀɛsaj/ *nm inv* garlic press

**presse-citron** /pʀɛsitʀɔ̃/ *nm inv* lemon squeezer

**pressentiment** /pʀesɑ̃timɑ̃/ *nm* premonition

**pressentir** /pʀesɑ̃tiʀ/ [30] *vtr* to have a premonition about

**presse-papiers** /pʀɛspapje/ *nm inv* paperweight

**presser** /pʀɛse/ [1] **1** *vtr* **(a)** ∼ **qn de faire** to urge sb to do
**(b)** to press ⟨*debtor*⟩; to harry ⟨*enemy*⟩
**(c)** ⟨*hunger, necessity*⟩ to drive [sb] on
**(d)** to increase ⟨*rhythm*⟩; ∼ **le pas** *or* **mouvement** to hurry
**(e)** to press ⟨*button*⟩
**(f)** to squeeze ⟨*hand, object*⟩
**(g)** to squeeze ⟨*orange, sponge*⟩; to press ⟨*grapes*⟩
**(h)** to press ⟨*record*⟩
**2** *vi* ⟨*matter*⟩ to be pressing; ⟨*work*⟩ to be urgent; **le temps presse** time is running out
**3** **se presser** *v refl* (+ *v être*) **(a)** se ∼ **autour de qn/qch** to press around sb/sth
**(b)** to hurry up
**(c)** to flock

**pressing** /pʀɛsiŋ/ *nm* dry-cleaner's

**pression** /pʀɛsjɔ̃/ *nf* **(a)** (gen) pressure; ∼ **artérielle** blood pressure; **sous** ∼ under pressure; pressurized; **faire** ∼ **sur** to press on ⟨*surface*⟩; to put pressure on ⟨*person*⟩
**(b)** snap (fastener)

**pressoir** /pʀɛswaʀ/ *nm* **(a)** pressing shed
**(b)** press; ∼ **à pommes** cider press

**pressurer** /pʀɛsyʀe/ [1] *vtr* **(a)** to press ⟨*fruit, seeds*⟩
**(b)** (colloq) (exploiter) to milk (colloq)

**pressuriser** /pʀɛsyʀize/ [1] *vtr* to pressurize

**prestance** /pʀɛstɑ̃s/ *nf* **avoir de la** ∼ to have great presence

**prestataire** /pʀɛstatɛʀ/ *nm* **(a)** ∼ **de service** (service) contractor, service provider
**(b)** recipient (*of a state benefit*)

**prestation** /pʀɛstasjɔ̃/ *nf* **(a)** benefit
**(b)** provision; ∼ **de service** (provision of a) service
**(c)** service
**(d)** performance; ∼ **télévisée** televised appearance

**prestidigitation** /pʀɛstidiʒitasjɔ̃/ *nf* conjuring

**prestige** /pʀɛstiʒ/ *nm* prestige; **le** ∼ **de l'uniforme** the glamour (GB) of a uniform

**prestigieux, -ieuse** /pʀɛstiʒjø, øz/ *adj* prestigious

**présumer** /pʀezyme/ [1] **1** *vtr* to presume; **le présumé terroriste** the alleged terrorist
**2** **présumer de** *v+prep* (trop) ∼ **de ses forces** to overestimate one's strength

p

**présupposer** /pʀesypoze/ [1] *vtr* to presuppose

**prêt**, **~e** /pʀɛ, pʀɛt/ **1** *adj* ready; être fin ~ to be all set; il est ~ à tout he will stop at nothing
**2** *nm* (a) le service de ~ de la bibliothèque the library loans service
(b) loan
■ ~ immobilier property loan; ~ personnalisé personal loan

**prêt-à-porter** /pʀɛtapɔʀte/ *nm* ready-to-wear

**prétendant**, **~e** /pʀetɑ̃dɑ̃, ɑ̃t/ **1** *nm,f*
(a) candidate
(b) pretender
**2** *nm* suitor

**prétendre** /pʀetɑ̃dʀ/ [6] **1** *vtr* to claim; à ce qu'il prétend according to him; on le prétend très spirituel he is said to be very witty
**2 prétendre à** *v+prep* to claim ⟨damages⟩; to aspire to ⟨job⟩
**3 se prétendre** *v refl* (+ *v être*) il se prétend artiste he makes out *or* claims he is an artist

**prétendu**, **~e** /pʀetɑ̃dy/ *adj* ⟨culprit⟩ alleged; ⟨doctor⟩ would-be

**prétendument** /pʀetɑ̃dymɑ̃/ *adv* supposedly

**prête-nom**, *pl* **~s** /pʀɛtnɔ̃/ *nm* frontman, man of straw; société ~ dummy (US) company

**prétentieux**, **-ieuse** /pʀetɑ̃sjø, øz/
**1** *adj* pretentious
**2** *nm,f* pretentious person

**prétention** /pʀetɑ̃sjɔ̃/ **1** *nf*
(a) pretentiousness; être sans ~ to be unpretentious
(b) avoir la ~ de faire to claim to do
**2 prétentions** *nf pl* quelles sont vos ~s? what salary are you asking for?

**prêter** /pʀete/ [1] **1** *vtr* (a) to lend ⟨money, object⟩; ~ sur gages to loan against security
(b) ~ attention à to pay attention to; ~ la main à qn to lend sb a hand; ~ l'oreille to listen; ~ serment to take an oath
(c) ~ à qn to attribute [sth] to sb
**2 prêter à** *v+prep* to give rise to ⟨confusion⟩; son attitude prête à rire his/her attitude is ridiculous; tout prête à croire *or* penser que all the indications would suggest that
**3 se prêter** *v refl* (+ *v être*) (a) se ~ à to take part in
(b) roman qui se prête à une adaptation cinématographique novel which lends itself to a film adaptation

**prétérit** /pʀeteʀit/ *nm* preterite

**prêteur**, **-euse** /pʀetœʀ, øz/ **1** *adj* il n'est pas ~ he's very possessive about his belongings
**2** *nm,f* ~ sur gages pawnbroker

**prétexte** /pʀetɛkst/ *nm* excuse, pretext;

donner qch comme ~, prendre ~ de qch to use sth as an excuse; sous aucun ~ on no account

**prétexter** /pʀetɛkste/ [1] **1** *vtr* to use [sth] as an excuse, to plead
**2 prétexter de** *v+prep* ~ de qch pour faire to use sth as an excuse for doing

**prêtre** /pʀɛtʀ/ *nm* priest

**prêtresse** /pʀɛtʀɛs/ *nf* priestess

**preuve** /pʀœv/ *nf* (a) proof; une ~ a piece of evidence; apporter la ~ de/que to offer proof of/that; la ~ est faite de/que now there is proof of/that; ~ en main with concrete proof; faire ses ~s to prove oneself
(b) demonstration; faire ~ de to show; ~ de bonne volonté gesture of goodwill

**prévaloir** /pʀevalwaʀ/ [45] **1** *vi* to prevail
**2 se prévaloir** *v refl* (+ *v être*) se ~ de son ancienneté to claim seniority

**prévenance** /pʀevnɑ̃s/ *nf* consideration

**prévenant**, **~e** /pʀevnɑ̃, ɑ̃t/ *adj* considerate

**prévenir** /pʀevniʀ/ [36] *vtr* (a) to tell
(b) to call ⟨doctor, police⟩
(c) to warn
(d) to prevent ⟨disaster⟩
(e) to anticipate ⟨wishes⟩
IDIOMS mieux vaut ~ que guérir (Proverb) prevention is better than cure

**préventif**, **-ive** /pʀevɑ̃tif, iv/ *adj* preventive

**prévention** /pʀevɑ̃sjɔ̃/ *nf* prevention; faire de la ~ to take preventive action

**prévenu**, **~e** /pʀevny/ *nm,f* (Law) defendant

**prévisible** /pʀevizibl/ *adj* predictable

**prévision** /pʀevizjɔ̃/ *nf* (a) forecasting; en ~ de in anticipation of
(b) prediction; forecast; ~s météorologiques weather forecast

**prévisionnel**, **-elle** /pʀevizjɔnɛl/ *adj* projected

**prévisionniste** /pʀevizjɔnist/ *nmf* forecaster

**prévoir** /pʀevwaʀ/ [42] *vtr* (a) to predict ⟨change⟩; to foresee ⟨event, victory⟩; to anticipate ⟨reaction⟩; to forecast ⟨result, weather⟩; c'était à ~! that was predictable!
(b) to plan ⟨meeting, journey, building⟩; to set the date for ⟨return, move⟩; (Law) to make provision for ⟨case, eventuality⟩; ce n'était pas prévu! that wasn't meant to happen!; remplissez le formulaire prévu à cet effet fill in the appropriate form; tout a été prévu all the arrangements have been made
(c) to make sure one takes ⟨coat, umbrella⟩
(d) to expect ⟨visitor, shortage, strike⟩
(e) to allow ⟨sum of money, time⟩

**prévoyance** /pʀevwajɑ̃s/ *nf* foresight

**prévoyant**, **~e** /pʀevwajɑ̃, ɑ̃t/ *adj* far-sighted

**prévu**, **~e** /pʀevy/ ▶ PRÉVOIR

**prier** /pʀije/ [2] **1** *vtr* (a) ~ qn de faire to ask sb to do; je vous prie d'excuser mon

**retard** I'm so sorry I'm late; **je vous prie de vous taire** will you kindly be quiet; **elle ne s'est pas fait ~** she didn't have to be asked twice
**(b)** to pray to ⟨god⟩; **~ que** to pray that
**2** *vi* to pray

**prière** /prijɛr/ *nf* **(a)** prayer; **faire sa ~** to say one's prayers
**(b)** request; plea, entreaty; **~ de ne pas fumer** no smoking please

**prieuré** /prijœre/ *nm* **(a)** priory
**(b)** priory church

**primaire** /primɛr/ **1** *adj* **(a)** primary
**(b)** ⟨person⟩ limited; ⟨reasoning⟩ simplistic
**2** *nm* **(a)** (Sch) **le ~** primary education
**(b)** (Econ) **le ~** the primary sector
**(c) le ~** the palaeozoic era

**primate** /primat/ *nm* primate

**primauté** /primote/ *nf* primacy

**prime** /prim/ **1** *adj* **(a) de ~ abord** at first, initially
**(b) A ~** A prime
**2** *nf* **(a)** bonus; free gift
**(b)** allowance
**(c)** subsidy
**(d)** (in insurance) premium
■ **~ d'ancienneté** seniority bonus; **~ de risque** danger money

**primer** /prime/ [1] **1** *vtr* **(a)** to take precedence over, to prevail over
**(b)** to award a prize to
**2 primer sur** *v+prep* (controversial) ▶ PRIMER 1A
**3** *vi* **pour moi, c'est la qualité qui prime** what counts for me is quality

**primeur** /primœr/ **1** *nf* **avoir la ~ de l'information** to be the first to hear sth
**2 primeurs** *nf pl* early fruit and vegetables

**primevère** /primvɛr/ *nf* primrose

**primitif, -ive** /primitif, iv/ *adj* (gen) primitive; ⟨budget⟩ initial; ⟨project, state⟩ original

**primordial, ~e, mpl -iaux** /primɔrdjal, o/ *adj* essential, vital

**prince** /prɛ̃s/ *nm* prince
IDIOMS **être bon ~** to be magnanimous

**princesse** /prɛ̃sɛs/ *nf* princess
IDIOMS **aux frais de la ~** (colloq) at the company's expense; at sb's expense

**princier, -ière** /prɛ̃sje, ɛr/ *adj* ⟨title, tastes, sum⟩ princely; ⟨luxury⟩ dazzling

**principal, ~e, mpl -aux** /prɛ̃sipal, o/
**1** *adj* **(a)** ⟨factor⟩ main; ⟨task⟩ principal
**(b)** ⟨country, role⟩ leading
**(c)** ⟨inspector⟩ chief
**2** *nm* **(a) le ~** the main thing
**(b)** (Sch) principal

**principalement** /prɛ̃sipalmɑ̃/ *adv* mainly

**principauté** /prɛ̃sipote/ *nf* principality

**principe** /prɛ̃sip/ **1** *nm* **(a)** principle; **par ~** on principle
**(b)** assumption

**(c)** (concept) principle; **quel est le ~ de la machine à vapeur?** how does a steam engine work?
**2 en principe** *phr* **(a)** as a rule
**(b)** in theory

**printanier, -ière** /prɛ̃tanje, ɛr/ *adj* ⟨sun⟩ spring; ⟨weather⟩ spring-like

**printemps** /prɛ̃tɑ̃/ *nm inv* **(a)** spring
**(b)** (colloq) **mes 60 ~** my 60 summers

**prion** /prijɔ̃/ *nm* prion

**priori** ▶ A PRIORI

**prioritaire** /prijɔritɛr/ *adj* ⟨file, project⟩ priority; **être ~** to have priority

**priorité** /prijɔrite/ *nf* priority; **avoir la ~** to have right (GB) or the right (US) of way

**pris, ~e¹** /pri, priz/ **1** *pp* ▶ PRENDRE
**2** *pp adj* **(a)** busy; **j'ai les mains ~es** I've got my hands full; **les places sont toutes ~es** all the seats are taken
**(b)** ⟨nose⟩ stuffed up; ⟨lungs⟩ congested
**(c) ~ de** overcome with; **~ de panique** panic-stricken

**prise²** /priz/ *nf* **(a)** storming; **la ~ de la Bastille** the storming of the Bastille
**(b)** catching; **une belle ~** a fine catch
**(c)** (in judo, wrestling) hold
**(d) n'offrir aucune ~** to have no handholds; to have no footholds; **avoir ~ sur qn** to have a hold over sb; **donner ~ à** to lay oneself open to
**(e)** socket (GB), outlet (US); plug; jack; **~ multiple** (multiplug) adaptor; trailing socket
■ **~ de bec** (colloq) row, argument; **~ en charge** (of expenses) payment; **~ de conscience** realization; **~ de contact** initial contact; **~ de courant** socket (GB), outlet (US); **~ d'eau** water supply point; **~ de sang** blood test; **~ de vue** shooting; shot
IDIOMS **être aux ~s avec des difficultés** to be grappling with difficulties

**priser** /prize/ [1] *vtr* **(a)** to hold [sth] in esteem
**(b) ~ (du tabac)** to take snuff

**prisme** /prism/ *nm* prism

**prison** /prizɔ̃/ *nf* prison; **condamné à trois ans de ~** sentenced to three years' imprisonment

**prisonnier, -ière** /prizɔnje, ɛr/ **1** *adj* **il est ~** he is a prisoner
**2** *nm,f* prisoner

**privatif, -ive** /privatif, iv/ *adj* private

**privation** /privasjɔ̃/ *nf* **(a)** (of rights) deprivation
**(b)** want; **s'imposer des ~s** to make sacrifices

**privatisation** /privatizasjɔ̃/ *nf* privatization

**privatiser** /privatize/ [1] *vtr* to privatize

**privé, ~e** /prive/ **1** *pp* ▶ PRIVER
**2** *pp adj* **~ de** deprived of; **tu seras ~ de dessert!** you'll go without dessert!
**3** *adj* (gen) private; ⟨interview⟩ unofficial
**4** *nm* **(a)** (Econ) private sector
**(b)** (Sch) **le ~** private schools ⋯⟶

**(c)** en ∼ in private

**priver** /pʀive/ [1] **1** *vtr* ∼ qn/qch de to deprive sb/sth of; ∼ qn de sorties to forbid sb to go out

**2 se priver** *v refl* (+ *v être*) **pourquoi se ∼?** why deprive ourselves?; **se ∼ de qch/de faire** to go *or* do without sth/doing

**privilège** /pʀivilɛʒ/ *nm* privilege

**privilégié, ∼e** /pʀivileʒje/ **1** *pp* ▶ PRIVILÉGIER

**2** *pp adj* **(a)** privileged

**(b)** fortunate

**(c)** ⟨*moment, links*⟩ special; ⟨*treatment*⟩ preferential

**privilégier** /pʀivileʒje/ [2] *vtr* **(a)** to favour (GB)

**(b)** to give priority to

**prix** /pʀi/ *nm inv* **(a)** price; **à** *or* **au ∼ coûtant** at cost price; **acheter qch à ∼ d'or** to pay a small fortune for sth; **il faut être prêt à y mettre le ∼** you have to be prepared to pay for it; **mettre qch à ∼ à 50 euros** to start the bidding for sth at 50 euros

**(b)** (figurative) price; **à tout ∼** at all costs; **attacher beaucoup de ∼ à** to value [sth] highly ⟨*friendship*⟩

**(c)** prize

**pro(-)** /pʀo/ *pref* pro(-)

**probabilité** /pʀobabilite/ *nf* **(a)** probability, likelihood

**(b)** les ∼s probability theory

**probable** /pʀobabl/ *adj* probable, likely

**probablement** /pʀobabləmã/ *adv* probably

**probant, ∼e** /pʀobã, ãt/ *adj* ⟨*argument, demonstration*⟩ convincing; ⟨*force, proof*⟩ conclusive

**probatoire** /pʀobatwaʀ/ *adj* **examen ∼** assessment test; **épreuve ∼** aptitude test

**probité** /pʀobite/ *nf* integrity, probity

**problématique** /pʀoblematik/ *adj* ⟨*situation*⟩ problematic; ⟨*outcome*⟩ uncertain

**problème** /pʀoblɛm/ *nm* problem

**procédé** /pʀosede/ *nm* **(a)** process

**(b)** practice (GB); **échange de bons ∼s** exchange of courtesies

**procéder** /pʀosede/ [14] **1 procéder à** *v+prep* to carry out ⟨*check, survey*⟩; to undertake ⟨*reform*⟩; **∼ à un tirage au sort/un vote** to hold a draw/a vote

**2 procéder de** *v+prep* to be a product of

**3** *vi* to go about things; **∼ par élimination** to use a process of elimination

**procédure** /pʀosedyʀ/ *nf* **(a)** proceedings

**(b)** procedure

**procès** /pʀosɛ/ *nm inv* **(a)** trial

**(b)** lawsuit, case; **intenter un ∼ à qn** to sue sb

**(c)** indictment; **faire le ∼ de qn/qch** to put sb/sth in the dock

**IDIOMS sans autre forme de ∼** without further ado

**processeur** /pʀosesœʀ/ *nm* processor

**procession** /pʀosesjõ/ *nf* procession

**processus** /pʀosesys/ *nm inv* **(a)** process

**(b)** (Med) evolution

**procès-verbal,** *pl* **-aux** /pʀosɛvɛʀbal, o/ *nm* **(a)** (of meeting) minutes

**(b)** statement of offence (GB)

**prochain, ∼e** /pʀoʃɛ̃, ɛn/ **1** *adj* **(a)** next; **en juin ∼** next June; **à la ∼e!** (colloq) see you! (colloq)

**(b)** ⟨*meeting*⟩ coming, forthcoming; ⟨*departure, war*⟩ imminent; **un jour ∼** one day soon

**2** *nm* fellow man; **aime ton ∼** love thy neighbour (GB)

**prochainement** /pʀoʃɛnmã/ *adv* soon

**proche** /pʀoʃ/ **1** *adj* **(a)** nearby; **∼ de** close to, near

**(b)** ⟨*departure*⟩ imminent; **la victoire est ∼** victory is at hand; **la fin est ∼** the end is (drawing) near

**(c)** ⟨*event*⟩ recent; ⟨*memory*⟩ real, vivid

**(d)** similar; **∼ de** ⟨*figure, language*⟩ close to; ⟨*attitude*⟩ verging on

**(e)** ⟨*people*⟩ close; (on form) (plus) **∼ parent** next of kin

**2** *nm* **(a)** close relative

**(b)** close friend

**Proche-Orient** /pʀoʃoʀjã/ *pr nm* **le ∼** the Near East

**proclamation** /pʀoklamasjõ/ *nf* proclamation

**proclamer** /pʀoklame/ [1] *vtr* **(a)** to proclaim

**(b)** to declare

**procréer** /pʀokʀee/ [11] *vi* to procreate

**procuration** /pʀokyʀasjõ/ *nf* **(a)** power of attorney

**(b)** proxy; proxy form

**procurer** /pʀokyʀe/ [1] **1** *vtr* to bring; to give

**2 se procurer** *v refl* (+ *v être*) **(a)** to obtain

**(b)** to buy

**procureur** /pʀokyʀœʀ/ *nm* prosecutor

**prodige** /pʀodiʒ/ *nm* **(a)** prodigy

**(b)** feat; **faire des ∼s** to work wonders; **∼ technique** technical miracle

**prodigieux, -ieuse** /pʀodiʒjø, øz/ *adj* ⟨*quantity*⟩ prodigious; ⟨*person*⟩ wonderful

**prodigue** /pʀodig/ *adj* **(a)** extravagant

**(b)** être **∼ de** to be lavish with

**prodiguer** /pʀodige/ [1] *vtr* **(a)** to give lots of ⟨*advice*⟩

**(b)** to give ⟨*treatment, first aid*⟩

**producteur, -trice** /pʀodyktœʀ, tʀis/ **1** *adj* **pays ∼ de pétrole** oil-producing country

**2** *nm,f* producer

**productif, -ive** /pʀodyktif, iv/ *adj* ⟨*work*⟩ productive; ⟨*investment*⟩ profitable

**production** /pʀodyksjõ/ *nf* **(a)** (gen) production; (of energy) generation

**(b)** (gen) products, goods

■ **∼ assisteé par ordinateur, PAO** computer aided manufacturing, CAM

**productivité** /pʀɔdyktivite/ *nf*
productivity

**produire** /pʀɔdɥiʀ/ [69] **1** *vtr* **(a)** (gen) to
produce; **cette usine produit peu** this factory
has a low output; **un artiste/écrivain qui
produit beaucoup** a prolific artist/writer
**(b)** to bring in ⟨*money, wealth*⟩; to yield
⟨*interest*⟩
**(c)** to produce, to have ⟨*effect, result*⟩; to
create, to make ⟨*impression*⟩; to cause
⟨*sensation, emotion*⟩
**2 se produire** *v refl* (+ *v être*) **(a)** ⟨*event*⟩
to occur, to happen
**(b)** ⟨*singer*⟩ to perform

**produit** /pʀɔdɥi/ *nm* **(a)** product; **des ~s**
goods, products; **~s alimentaires** foodstuffs;
**~s agricoles** agricultural produce
**(b)** income; yield, return; profit; **vivre du ~
de sa terre** to live off the land; **le ~ de la
vente** the proceeds of the sale
**(c)** (of research) result; (of activity) product
■ **~ chimique** chemical; **~ d'entretien**
cleaning product, household product;
**~ intérieur brut, PIB** gross domestic product,
GDP; **~ national brut, PNB** gross national
product, GNP

**proéminent, ~e** /pʀɔeminɑ̃, ɑ̃t/ *adj*
prominent

**profanateur, -trice** /pʀɔfanatœʀ, tʀis/
*nm,f* profaner

**profanation** /pʀɔfanasjɔ̃/ *nf* desecration;
defilement; debasement

**profane** /pʀɔfan/ **1** *adj* secular
**2** *nmf* **(a)** layman/laywoman
**(b)** nonbeliever
**3** *nm* **le ~ et le sacré** the sacred and the
profane

**profaner** /pʀɔfane/ [1] *vtr* to desecrate
⟨*temple*⟩; to defile ⟨*memory*⟩; to debase
⟨*institution*⟩

**proférer** /pʀɔfeʀe/ [14] *vtr* to hurl
⟨*insults*⟩; to make ⟨*threats*⟩; to utter ⟨*words*⟩

**professer** /pʀɔfese/ [1] *vtr* to profess

**professeur** /pʀɔfesœʀ/ *nm* (in school)
teacher; (in higher education) lecturer (GB),
professor (US); (holding university chair)
professor; **~ des écoles** primary school
teacher

**profession** /pʀɔfesjɔ̃/ *nf* **(a)** occupation;
profession; **exercer la ~ d'infirmière** to be a
nurse by profession; **être sans ~** to have no
occupation
**(b)** declaration, profession
■ **~ libérale** profession

**professionnalisme** /pʀɔfesjɔnalism/
*nm* professionalism

**professionnel, -elle** /pʀɔfesjɔnɛl/
**1** *adj* **(a)** ⟨*qualifications*⟩ professional; ⟨*life,
environment*⟩ working; ⟨*disease*⟩
occupational; ⟨*training*⟩ vocational
**(b)** ⟨*player*⟩ professional
**2** *nm,f* professional; **le salon est réservé
aux ~s** the fair is restricted to people in the
trade

**professionnellement** /pʀɔfesjɔnɛlmɑ̃/
*adv* professionally

**professoral, ~e,** *mpl* **-aux** /pʀɔfesɔʀal,
o/ *adj* professorial

**profil** /pʀɔfil/ *nm* profile; **être de ~** to be in
profile; **se mettre de ~** to turn sideways

**profiler** /pʀɔfile/ [1] **1** *vtr* **la tour profile sa
silhouette dans le ciel** the tower is
silhouetted *or* outlined against the sky
**2 se profiler** *v refl* (+ *v être*) ⟨*shape*⟩ to
stand out; ⟨*problem*⟩ to emerge; ⟨*events*⟩ to
approach

**profit** /pʀɔfi/ *nm* **(a)** benefit, advantage; **au
~ des handicapés** in aid of the
handicapped; **mettre à ~** to make the most
of ⟨*free time, course*⟩; to turn [sth] to good
account ⟨*situation*⟩; to make good use of
⟨*idea*⟩
**(b)** profit; **être une source de ~ pour** to be a
source of wealth for

**profitable** /pʀɔfitabl/ *adj* **(a)** beneficial
**(b)** profitable

**profiter** /pʀɔfite/ [1] **1 profiter à** *v+prep*
**~ à qn** to benefit sb
**2 profiter de** *v+prep* to use ⟨*advantage*⟩;
to make the most of ⟨*holiday, situation*⟩; to
take advantage of ⟨*visit, weakness, person*⟩
**3** *vi* (colloq) ⟨*person*⟩ to grow; ⟨*plant*⟩ to
thrive

**profiteur, -euse** /pʀɔfitœʀ, øz/ *nm,f*
profiteer

**profond, ~e** /pʀɔfɔ̃, ɔ̃d/ **1** *adj* **(a)** deep;
**peu ~** shallow
**(b)** ⟨*boredom*⟩ acute; ⟨*sigh*⟩ heavy; ⟨*feeling,
sleep, colour*⟩ deep
**(c)** ⟨*change, ignorance*⟩ profound
**(d)** ⟨*mind, remark*⟩ profound; ⟨*gaze*⟩
penetrating
**(e)** **la France ~e** provincial France;
**l'Amérique ~e** small-town America
**2** *adv* deeply, deep down

**profondément** /pʀɔfɔ̃demɑ̃/ *adv* **(a)** ⟨*dig*⟩
deep
**(b)** deeply; greatly; profoundly; **détester ~**
to loathe

**profondeur** /pʀɔfɔ̃dœʀ/ *nf* **(a)** depth; **avoir
une ~ de 3 mètres** to be 3 metres (GB) deep
**(b)** (of feeling) depth; (of remark, work)
profundity; **en ~** ⟨*analysis*⟩ in-depth; ⟨*work*⟩
thorough

**profusion** /pʀɔfyzjɔ̃/ *nf* profusion;
abundance

**progéniture** /pʀɔʒenityʀ/ *nf* progeny

**progiciel** /pʀɔʒisjɛl/ *nm* software package

**programmateur, -trice**
/pʀɔgʀamatœʀ, tʀis/ **1** *nm,f* programme
(GB) planner
**2** *nm* timer

**programmation** /pʀɔgʀamasjɔ̃/ *nf*
programming

**programme** /pʀɔgʀam/ *nm*
**(a)** programme (GB)
**(b)** (of action) plan; (of work) programme (GB);
**c'est tout un ~!** (humorous) that'll take some
doing!

⋯⋙

(c) (Sch) syllabus

(d) (Comput) program

**programmer** /pRɔgʀame/ [1] *vtr* (a) to schedule ⟨*broadcast*⟩; to plan ⟨*work*⟩

(b) (Comput) to program

**programmeur, -euse** /pRɔgʀamœʀ, øz/ *nm,f* (computer) programmer

**progrès** /pRɔgʀɛ/ *nm inv* (a) progress; les ∼ de la médecine advances in medicine; être en ∼ ⟨*person*⟩ to be making progress; ⟨*results*⟩ to be improving

(b) increase; être en ∼ de 10% to be up by 10%

(c) (of illness) progression

**progresser** /pRɔgʀese/ [1] *vi* (a) to rise; to increase; ∼ de 3% ⟨*rate*⟩ to rise by 3%; ⟨*party*⟩ to gain 3%

(b) ⟨*politician*⟩ to make gains; ⟨*illness*⟩ to spread; ⟨*crime*⟩ to be on the increase

(c) ⟨*pupil, inquiry, country*⟩ to make progress; ⟨*relations*⟩ to improve; ⟨*technology*⟩ to progress

(d) ⟨*climber*⟩ to make progress; ⟨*army*⟩ to advance

**progressif, -ive** /pRɔgʀesif, iv/ *adj* progressive

**progression** /pRɔgʀɛsjɔ̃/ *nf* (a) progress; advance; spread; increase

(b) (in mathematics, music) progression

**progressiste** /pRɔgʀesist/ *adj* progressive

**prohibé, ∼e** /pRɔibe/ *adj* ⟨*goods, substance, weapon*⟩ prohibited; ⟨*trade, action*⟩ illegal; port d'arme ∼ illegal possession of a firearm

**prohiber** /pRɔibe/ [1] *vtr* to prohibit

**prohibitif, -ive** /pRɔibitif, iv/ *adj*

(a) ⟨*price*⟩ prohibitive

(b) ⟨*law*⟩ prohibition

**prohibition** /pRɔibisjɔ̃/ *nf* prohibition

**proie** /pRwa/ *nf* prey; être en ∼ à l'angoisse to be racked by anxiety; pays en ∼ à la guerre civile country in the grip of civil war

**projecteur** /pRɔʒɛktœʀ/ *nm*

(a) searchlight; floodlight; être sous les ∼s to be in the spotlight

(b) projector

**projectile** /pRɔʒɛktil/ *nm* missile; projectile

**projection** /pRɔʒɛksjɔ̃/ *nf* (a) l'éruption commença par une ∼ de cendres the eruption began with a discharge of ashes

(b) le cuisinier a reçu des ∼s d'huile bouillante the cook got spattered with scalding oil

(c) projection; showing; salle de ∼ screening room

**projectionniste** /pRɔʒɛksjɔnist/ *nmf* projectionist

**projet** /pRɔʒɛ/ *nm* (a) plan; en ∼, à l'état de ∼ at the planning stage

(b) project

(c) (rough) draft

(d) (in architecture) execution plan

■ ∼ de loi (government) bill

**projeter** /pRɔʒte/ [20] *vtr* (a) to throw; le choc l'a projeté par terre the shock sent him hurtling to the ground

(b) to cast ⟨*shadow*⟩

(c) to show ⟨*film*⟩

(d) to plan (de faire to do)

**prolétaire** /pRɔletɛʀ/ *adj, nmf* proletarian

**prolétariat** /pRɔletaʀja/ *nm* proletariat

**proliférer** /pRɔlifeʀe/ [14] *vi* to proliferate

**prolifique** /pRɔlifik/ *adj* prolific

**prolixe** /pRɔliks/ *adj* verbose, prolix

**prologue** /pRɔlɔg/ *nm* prologue

**prolongation** /pRɔlɔ̃gasjɔ̃/ *nf* continuation; extension; (Sport) extra time

**prolongé, ∼e** /pRɔlɔ̃ʒe/ *adj* ⟨*effort*⟩ sustained; ⟨*stay*⟩ extended; ⟨*exhibition*⟩ prolonged

**prolongement** /pRɔlɔ̃ʒmɑ̃/ *nm* (a) (of road, stay) extension

(b) la rue Berthollet se trouve dans le ∼ de la rue de la Glacière Rue de la Glacière becomes Rue Berthollet

**prolonger** /pRɔlɔ̃ʒe/ [13] **1** *vtr* to extend ⟨*stay*⟩; to prolong ⟨*meeting, life*⟩

**2** se prolonger *v refl* (+ *v être*) (a) to persist; to go on

(b) ⟨*street*⟩ se ∼ jusqu'à to go as far as

**promenade** /pRɔmnad/ *nf* (a) walk; ride; drive

(b) walkway; promenade

**promener** /pRɔmne/ [16] **1** *vtr* (a) to take [sb] out ⟨*person*⟩; to take [sth] out for a walk ⟨*animal*⟩; ça te promènera (colloq) it'll get you out

(b) to carry ⟨*object*⟩

(c) to show [sb] around

**2** se promener *v refl* (+ *v être*) to go for a walk/drive/ride

**promeneur, -euse** /pRɔmnœʀ, øz/ *nm,f* walker

**promesse** /pRɔmɛs/ *nf* (a) promise; avoir la ∼ de qn to have sb's word; tenir ses ∼s to keep one's promises

(b) ∼ de vente agreement to sell

■ ∼ en l'air *or* de Gascon *or* d'ivrogne empty *or* idle promise

**prometteur, -euse** /pRɔmɛtœʀ, øz/ *adj* promising

**promettre** /pRɔmɛtʀ/ [60] **1** *vtr* (a) ∼ qch à qn to promise sb sth; je te promets qu'il le regrettera he'll regret it, I guarantee you

(b) une soirée qui promet bien des surprises an evening that holds a few surprises in store

**2** *vi* ⟨*pupil*⟩ (a) to show promise; un film qui promet a film which sounds interesting

(b) (colloq) cet enfant promet! that child is going to be a handful!; ça promet! that promises to be fun!

**3** se promettre *v refl* (+ *v être*) (a) to promise oneself

(b) se ∼ de faire to resolve to do

**promiscuité** /pRɔmiskɥite/ *nf* lack of privacy

**promontoire** /pʀɔmɔ̃twaʀ/ *nm*
promontory

**promoteur, -trice** /pʀɔmɔtœʀ, tʀis/
*nm,f* ∼ (immobilier) property developer

**promotion** /pʀɔmɔsjɔ̃/ *nf* (a) promotion
(b) (special) offer; **en** ∼ on (special) offer

**promotionnel, -elle** /pʀɔmɔsjɔnɛl/ *adj*
promotional

**promouvoir** /pʀɔmuvwaʀ/ [43] *vtr* to
promote

**prompt, ∼e** /pʀɔ̃, pʀɔ̃t/ *adj* ⟨reaction⟩
prompt; ⟨gesture, glance⟩ swift; ⟨return⟩
sudden

**promulguer** /pʀɔmylge/ [1] *vtr* to
promulgate

**prôner** /pʀone/ [1] *vtr* to advocate

**pronom** /pʀɔnɔ̃/ *nm* pronoun

**pronominal, ∼e, mpl -aux**
/pʀɔnɔminal, o/ *adj* pronominal

**prononcé, ∼e** /pʀɔnɔ̃se/ *adj* ⟨accent,
taste⟩ strong; ⟨wrinkles⟩ deep; **avoir un goût**
∼ **pour** to be particularly fond of

**prononcer** /pʀɔnɔ̃se/ [12] **1** *vtr* (a) to
pronounce ⟨word⟩
(b) to mention ⟨name⟩; to say ⟨phrase⟩
(c) to deliver ⟨speech⟩
(d) to pronounce ⟨death penalty⟩; ∼ **le
divorce** to grant a divorce
**2 se prononcer** *v refl* (+ *v être*) (a) to be
pronounced
(b) **se** ∼ **contre/en faveur de qch** to declare
oneself against/in favour (GB) of sth; **se** ∼
**sur qch** to give one's opinion on sth

**prononciation** /pʀɔnɔ̃sjasjɔ̃/ *nf*
pronunciation

**pronostic** /pʀɔnɔstik/ *nm* (a) forecast
(b) prediction
(c) (medical) prognosis

**pronostiquer** /pʀɔnɔstike/ [1] *vtr* (in sport)
to forecast ⟨result⟩; to herald ⟨defeat, victory⟩

**propagande** /pʀɔpagɑ̃d/ *nf* propaganda

**propagateur, -trice** /pʀɔpagatœʀ, tʀis/
*nm,f* proponent

**propagation** /pʀɔpagasjɔ̃/ *nf* spread;
propagation

**propager** /pʀɔpaʒe/ [13] **1** *vtr* to spread
⟨rumour, disease⟩; to propagate ⟨species,
sound⟩
**2 se propager** *v refl* (+ *v être*) to spread;
to propagate

**propane** /pʀɔpan/ *nm* propane

**propension** /pʀɔpɑ̃sjɔ̃/ *nf* propensity

**prophète** /pʀɔfɛt/ *nm* prophet

**prophétie** /pʀɔfesi/ *nf* prophecy

**prophétiser** /pʀɔfetize/ [1] *vtr* to
prophesy

**propice** /pʀɔpis/ *adj* favourable (GB);
**trouver le moment** ∼ to find the right
moment

**proportion** /pʀɔpɔʀsjɔ̃/ *nf* proportion; **en**
∼, **ils sont mieux payés** they are
proportionately better paid; **être sans** ∼
**avec** to be out of (all) proportion to; **toutes**
∼**s gardées** relatively speaking

**proportionnel, -elle¹** /pʀɔpɔʀsjɔnɛl/
*adj* proportional

**proportionnelle²** /pʀɔpɔʀsjɔnɛl/ *nf*
proportional representation

**proportionner** /pʀɔpɔʀsjɔne/ [1] *vtr* ∼
**qch à qch** to make sth proportional to sth;
**proportionné à** proportional to

**propos** /pʀɔpo/ **1** *nm inv* (a) **à** ∼, **je...** by
the way, I...; **à** ∼ **de** about; **à** ∼ **de qui?**
about who?; **à ce** ∼, **je voudrais...** in this
connection, I would like...
(b) **à** ∼ at the right moment; **mal à** ∼ at
(just) the wrong moment
**2** *nm pl* comments; '∼ **recueillis par J.
Brun'** 'interview by J. Brun'

**proposer** /pʀɔpoze/ [1] **1** *vtr* (a) to
suggest
(b) to offer ⟨drink, dish⟩
(c) to put forward ⟨solution⟩; to propose
⟨strategy⟩
**2 se proposer** *v refl* (+ *v être*) (a) **se** ∼
**pour faire** to offer to do
(b) **se** ∼ **de faire** to intend to do

**proposition** /pʀɔpozisjɔ̃/ *nf* (a) suggestion
(b) proposal
(c) clause
∎ ∼ **de loi** ≈ bill

**propre** /pʀɔpʀ/ **1** *adj* (a) clean; **nous voilà**
∼**s!** (figurative) we're in a fine mess now!
(b) tidy, neat
(c) ⟨person, life⟩ decent; **des affaires pas très**
∼**s** unsavoury (GB) business
(d) own; **ma** ∼ **voiture** my own car; **ce sont
tes** ∼**s paroles** you said so yourself; those
were your very words
(e) of one's own; **chaque pays a des lois qui
lui sont** ∼**s** each country has its own
particular laws
(f) ⟨baby⟩ toilet-trained; ⟨animal⟩
housetrained (GB), housebroken (US)
**2 propre à** *phr* (a) ∼ à peculiar to
(b) ∼ à **faire** likely to do; liable to do
(c) ∼ à appropriate for; **produit déclaré** ∼ à
**la consommation** product fit for
consumption
**3** *nm* (a) **mettre qch au** ∼ to make a fair
copy of sth
(b) **c'est du** ∼! (ironic) that's very nice!
(c) **le** ∼ **de cette nouvelle technologie est de
faire** what is peculiar to this new technology
is that it does; ∼ à **rien** good-for-nothing

**proprement** /pʀɔpʀəmɑ̃/ *adv* (a) purely;
**à** ∼ **parler** strictly speaking
(b) absolutely
(c) really
(d) literally; **l'air est devenu** ∼ **irrespirable**
the air has become literally unbreathable
(e) specifically
(f) well and truly; **le professeur l'a** ∼ **remis
à sa place** he was well and truly put in his
place by the teacher
(g) neatly
(h) ⟨earn living⟩ honestly; ⟨live⟩ decently

**propreté** /pʀɔpʀəte/ *nf* (a) cleanliness;
**d'une** ∼ **douteuse** not very clean
(b) honesty

**p**

**propriétaire** /pʀɔpʀijetɛʀ/ *nmf* **(a)** owner; un petit ~ a small-scale property owner; ils sont ~s de leur maison they own their own house; faire le tour du ~ to look round (GB) *or* around the house
**(b)** landlord/landlady
**propriété** /pʀɔpʀijete/ *nf* **(a)** ownership
**(b)** property; ~ privée private property
**(c)** (of substance) property
**(d)** (of term) aptness
■ ~ artistique et littéraire copyright
**propulser** /pʀɔpylse/ [1] *vtr* to propel
**propulseur** /pʀɔpylsœʀ/ ① *adj m* propellent
② *nm* engine; ~ (de fusée) (rocket) engine
■ ~ à hélice propeller
**propulsion** /pʀɔpylsjɔ̃/ *nf* propulsion; à ~ nucléaire nuclear-powered
**prorata** /pʀɔʀata/ *nm inv* proportion
**proroger** /pʀɔʀɔʒe/ [13] *vtr* **(a)** to defer ⟨date⟩; to renew ⟨passport⟩
**(b)** to adjourn ⟨meeting⟩
**prosaïque** /pʀɔzaik/ *adj* prosaic
**proscription** /pʀɔskʀipsjɔ̃/ *nf*
**(a)** proscription
**(b)** banishment; frapper qn de ~ to banish sb
**proscrire** /pʀɔskʀiʀ/ [67] *vtr* to ban; to banish
**proscrit, ~e** /pʀɔskʀi, it/ *nm,f* outcast
**prose** /pʀoz/ *nf* **(a)** prose; poème en ~ prose poem
**(b)** (humorous) distinctive prose
**prosélytisme** /pʀɔzelitism/ *nm* proselytizing
**prospecter** /pʀɔspɛkte/ [1] *vtr* **(a)** to canvass
**(b)** to prospect
**prospecteur, -trice** /pʀɔspɛktœʀ, tʀis/ *nm,f* **(a)** canvasser
**(b)** prospector
**prospectif, -ive** /pʀɔspɛktif, iv/ *adj* long-term
**prospection** /pʀɔspɛksjɔ̃/ *nf*
**(a)** canvassing
**(b)** prospecting
**prospectus** /pʀɔspɛktys/ *nm inv* leaflet
**prospère** /pʀɔspɛʀ/ *adj* thriving; prosperous
**prospérer** /pʀɔspeʀe/ [14] *vi* to thrive; to prosper
**prospérité** /pʀɔspeʀite/ *nf* prosperity
**prostate** /pʀɔstat/ *nf* prostate (gland)
**prosternation** /pʀɔstɛʀnasjɔ̃/ *nf*
**(a)** prostration
**(b)** (figurative) self-abasement
**prosternement** /pʀɔstɛʀnəmã/ *nm*
**(a)** prostrate position
**(b)** prostration
**prosterner: se prosterner** /pʀɔstɛʀne/ [1] *v refl* (+ *v être*) **(a)** to prostrate oneself
**(b)** (figurative) to grovel
**prostitué** /pʀɔstitɥe/ *nm* (male) prostitute

**prostituée** /pʀɔstitɥe/ *nf* prostitute
**prostituer: se prostituer** /pʀɔstitɥe/ [1] *v refl* (+ *v être*) to prostitute oneself
**prostitution** /pʀɔstitysjɔ̃/ *nf* prostitution
**prostration** /pʀɔstʀasjɔ̃/ *nf* prostration
**protagoniste** /pʀɔtagɔnist/ *nmf* protagonist
**protecteur, -trice** /pʀɔtɛktœʀ, tʀis/
① *adj* **(a)** protective
**(b)** patronizing
② *nm,f* protector
**protection** /pʀɔtɛksjɔ̃/ *nf* **(a)** protection; être sous haute ~ to be under tight security; de ~ ⟨screen, measures⟩ protective; ⟨zone, system⟩ protection
**(b)** protective device
■ ~ sociale social welfare system
**protectionnisme** /pʀɔtɛksjɔnism/ *nm* protectionism
**protectionniste** /pʀɔtɛksjɔnist/ *adj, nmf* protectionist
**protégé, ~e** /pʀɔteʒe/ *nm,f* protégé
**protéger** /pʀɔteʒe/ [15] ① *vtr* to protect
② **se protéger** *v refl* (+ *v être*) to protect oneself
**protège-slip**, *pl* ~s /pʀɔtɛʒslip/ *nm* panty-liner
**protège-tibia**, *pl* ~s /pʀɔtɛʒtibja/ *nm* shinpad
**protéine** /pʀɔtein/ *nf* protein
**protestant, ~e** /pʀɔtɛstã, ãt/ *adj, nm,f* Protestant
**protestantisme** /pʀɔtɛstãtism/ *nm* Protestantism
**protestataire** /pʀɔtɛstatɛʀ/ *nmf* protester
**protestation** /pʀɔtɛstasjɔ̃/ *nf* protest
**protester** /pʀɔtɛste/ [1] ① **protester de** *v+prep* ~ de son innocence to protest one's innocence
② *vi* to protest
**prothèse** /pʀɔtɛz/ *nf* prosthesis; artificial limb; dentures; ~ auditive hearing aid
**prothésiste** /pʀɔtezist/ *nmf* prosthetist
**protocolaire** /pʀɔtɔkɔlɛʀ/ *adj* formal; official; question ~ question of protocol
**protocole** /pʀɔtɔkɔl/ *nm* **(a)** formalities; protocol
**(b)** ~ d'accord draft agreement
**prototype** /pʀɔtɔtip/ *nm* prototype
**protubérance** /pʀɔtybeʀãs/ *nf* protuberance
**protubérant, ~e** /pʀɔtybeʀã, ãt/ *adj* protruding
**prou** /pʀu/ *adv* peu ou ~ more or less
**proue** /pʀu/ *nf* prow, bow(s)
**prouesse** /pʀuɛs/ *nf* feat; (ironic) exploit
**prouver** /pʀuve/ [1] ① *vtr* **(a)** to prove
**(b)** to show
**(c)** to demonstrate
② **se prouver** *v refl* (+ *v être*) **(a)** to prove to oneself
**(b)** ils se sont prouvé qu'ils s'aimaient they proved their love for each other

**IDIOMS n'avoir plus rien à ~** to have proved oneself

**provenance** /pʀɔvnɑ̃s/ *nf* origin; **en ~ de** from

**provençal, ~e,** *mpl* **-aux** /pʀɔvɑ̃sal, o/ *adj* Provençal; **à la ~e** (Culin) (à la) provençale

**provenir** /pʀɔvniʀ/ [36] *vi* **(a)** to come (**de** from); **provenant de** from
**(b)** to stem (**de** from)

**proverbe** /pʀɔvɛʀb/ *nm* proverb

**proverbial, ~e,** *mpl* **-iaux** /pʀɔvɛʀbjal, o/ *adj* proverbial

**providence** /pʀɔvidɑ̃s/ **1** *nf* **(a)** salvation
**(b)** providence
**2** **(-)providence** (*combining form*) État(-) ~ welfare state

**providentiel, -ielle** /pʀɔvidɑ̃sjɛl/ *adj* providential

**province** /pʀɔvɛ̃s/ *nf* **(a)** province
**(b) la ~** the provinces; **ville de ~** provincial town

**provincial, ~e,** *mpl* **-iaux** /pʀɔvɛ̃sjal, o/ *adj, nm,f* provincial

**proviseur** /pʀɔvizœʀ/ *nm* headteacher (GB) *or* principal (US) (*of a lycée*)

**provision** /pʀɔvizjɔ̃/ **1** *nf* **(a)** stock; supply
**(b)** deposit; credit (balance)
**2 provisions** *nf pl* food shopping

**provisoire** /pʀɔvizwaʀ/ *adj* provisional; temporary

**provisoirement** /pʀɔvizwaʀmɑ̃/ *adv* provisionally

**provocant, ~e** /pʀɔvɔkɑ̃, ɑ̃t/ *adj* provocative

**provocateur, -trice** /pʀɔvɔkatœʀ, tʀis/ *nm,f* agitator

**provocation** /pʀɔvɔkasjɔ̃/ *nf* provocation

**provoquer** /pʀɔvɔke/ [1] *vtr* **(a)** to cause ‹*accident*›; to provoke ‹*reaction, anger*›; **~ l'accouchement** to induce labour (GB)
**(b)** to provoke; **~ qn en duel** to challenge sb to a duel
**(c)** (sexually) to arouse

**proxénète** /pʀɔksenɛt/ *nm* procurer, pimp

**proxénétisme** /pʀɔksenetism/ *nm* procuring

**proximité** /pʀɔksimite/ *nf* **(a)** nearness, proximity; **à ~** nearby; **à ~ de** near
**(b)** imminence; **à cause de la ~ de Noël** because it is/was so close to Christmas

**prude** /pʀyd/ *adj* prudish

**prudemment** /pʀydamɑ̃/ *adv* **(a)** carefully
**(b)** cautiously

**prudence** /pʀydɑ̃s/ *nf* caution; **avec ~** cautiously; with caution; **par ~** as a precaution; **redoubler de ~** to be doubly careful

**prudent, ~e** /pʀydɑ̃, ɑ̃t/ *adj* **(a)** careful; **ce n'est pas ~ de faire** it isn't safe to do
**(b)** cautious
**(c)** wise

**prud'homme** /pʀydɔm/ *nm* **Conseil des ~s** ≈ industrial tribunal (GB), labor relations board (US)

**prune** /pʀyn/ *nf* **(a)** plum
**(b)** plum brandy
**IDIOMS pour des ~s** (colloq) for nothing

**pruneau,** *pl* **~x** /pʀyno/ *nm* prune

**prunelle** /pʀynɛl/ *nf* **(a)** sloe; ≈ sloe gin
**(b)** (of eye) pupil

**prunier** /pʀynje/ *nm* plum tree

**Prusse** /pʀys/ *pr nf* Prussia

**PS** /pɛɛs/ *nm* (*abbr* = **post-scriptum**) PS

**psalmodier** /psalmɔdje/ [2] *vi* to chant psalms

**psaume** /psom/ *nm* psalm

**pseudo-** /psødo/ *pref* pseudo; **~-équilibre** so-called balance; **~-savant** self-styled scientist

**pseudonyme** /psødɔnim/ *nm* pseudonym

**psy** /psi/ *nmf* (colloq) shrink (colloq), therapist

**psychanalyse** /psikanaliz/ *nf* psychoanalysis

**psychanalyser** /psikanalize/ [1] *vtr* to psychoanalyse (GB)

**psyché** /psiʃe/ *nf* **(a)** cheval glass
**(b)** psyche

**psychiatrie** /psikjatʀi/ *nf* psychiatry

**psychiatrique** /psikjatʀik/ *adj* psychiatric

**psychique** /psiʃik/ *adj* mental

**psychisme** /psiʃism/ *nm* psyche

**psychologie** /psikɔlɔʒi/ *nf* **(a)** psychology
**(b)** (psychological) insight

**psychologique** /psikɔlɔʒik/ *adj* psychological

**psychologue** /psikɔlɔg/ **1** *adj* **être ~** to understand people very well
**2** *nmf* psychologist

**psychopathe** /psikɔpat/ *nmf* psychopath

**psychose** /psikoz/ *nf* **(a)** psychosis
**(b) ~ de la guerre** obsessive fear of war

**psychosomatique** /psikosɔmatik/ *adj* psychosomatic

**psychothérapeute** /psikoteʀapøt/ *nmf* psychotherapist

**psychothérapie** /psikoteʀapi/ *nf* psychotherapy

**PTT** /petete/ *nf pl* (*abbr* = **Administration des postes et télécommunications et de la télédiffusion**) *former French postal and telecommunications service*

**pu** /py/ ▶ POUVOIR[1]

**puant, ~e** /pɥɑ̃, ɑ̃t/ *adj* **(a)** stinking; smelly
**(b)** (colloq) **un type ~** an incredibly arrogant guy (colloq)

**puanteur** /pɥɑ̃tœʀ/ *nf* stench

**pub** /pyb/ *nf* (colloq): *abbr* ▶ PUBLICITÉ

**pubère** /pybɛʀ/ *adj* pubescent

**puberté** /pybɛʀte/ *nf* puberty

**pubis** /pybis/ *nm inv* pubes; pubis

p

**public, -ique** /pyblik/ ① *adj* public;
⟨*education*⟩ state (GB), public (US); ⟨*company*⟩
state-owned; **la dette publique** the national
debt
② *nm* (a) public; **'interdit au** ∼**'** 'no
admittance'; **'avis au** ∼**'** 'public notice'
(b) audience; spectators; **tous** ∼**s** for all ages
(c) readership
(d) **avoir un** ∼ to have a following
(e) **le** ∼ the public sector

**publication** /pyblikasjɔ̃/ *nf* publication
■ ∼ **assistée par ordinateur, PAO** desktop
publishing, DTP

**publicitaire** /pyblisitɛʀ/ ① *adj*
⟨*campaign*⟩ advertising; ⟨*gift*⟩ promotional
② *nmf* **il/elle est** ∼ he/she's in advertising
③ *nm* advertising agency

**publicité** /pyblisite/ *nf* (a) advertising;
**faire de la** ∼ **pour** to advertise
(b) (*also* **pub** (colloq)) advertisement, advert
(GB), ad (colloq)
(c) publicity; **faire une mauvaise** ∼ **à qn/qch**
to give sb/sth a bad press
■ ∼ **comparative** knocking copy (colloq);
∼ **mensongère** misleading advertising

**publier** /pyblije/ [2] *vtr* to publish

**publiquement** /pyblikmɑ̃/ *adv* publicly

**puce** /pys/ *nf* (a) flea
(b) (silicon) chip; ∼ **à mémoire** memory chip
IDIOMS **ça m'a mis la** ∼ **à l'oreille** that set me
thinking; **secouer les** ∼ **à qn** (colloq) to bawl
sb out (colloq)

**puceau**, *pl* ∼**x** /pyso/ *adj m* (colloq) **il est
encore** ∼ he's still a virgin

**pucelle** /pysɛl/ *adj f* (colloq) **être** ∼ to be a
virgin

**puceron** /pysʀɔ̃/ *nm* aphid

**pudeur** /pydœʀ/ *nf* (a) sense of modesty;
**sans** ∼ shamelessly
(b) decency; sense of propriety

**pudibond**, ∼**e** /pydibɔ̃, ɔ̃d/ *adj* prudish

**pudique** /pydik/ *adj* (a) modest
(b) discreet

**pudiquement** /pydikmɑ̃/ *adv* (a) modestly
(b) discreetly

**puer** /pɥe/ [1] ① *vtr* to stink of
② *vi* to stink; **il puait des pieds** his feet
stank

**puéricultrice** /pɥeʀikyltʀis/ *nf* pediatric
nurse

**puériculture** /pɥeʀikyltyʀ/ *nf* childcare

**puéril**, ∼**e** /pɥeʀil/ *adj* childish; puerile

**puis** /pɥi/ *adv* (a) then; **des poires et** ∼ **des
pêches** pears and peaches; **et** ∼ **quoi encore!**
(colloq) what next?
(b) **il va être en colère? et** ∼ **(après)?** (colloq)
so what if he's angry!

**puisard** /pɥizaʀ/ *nm* soakaway (GB), sink
hole (US)

**puiser** /pɥize/ [1] *vtr* ∼ **qch dans qch** to
draw sth from sth

**puisque** ( **puisqu'** *before vowel or mute
h*) /pɥisk(ə)/ *conj* since; ∼ **c'est comme ça,
je m'en vais** if that's how it is, I'm off

**puissance** /pɥisɑ̃s/ *nf* (a) power; **la** ∼
**militaire** military strength *or* might
(b) (country) power; **une grande** ∼ a
superpower
(c) (of light) intensity; (of sound) volume
(d) (in algebra) power; **dix** ∼ **trois** ten to the
power (of) three

**puissant**, ∼**e** /pɥisɑ̃, ɑ̃t/ ① *adj* powerful;
strong
② **puissants** *nm pl* **les** ∼**s** the powerful

**puits** /pɥi/ *nm* (a) well; ∼ **de pétrole** oil
well
(b) shaft
■ ∼ **de science** fount of knowledge

**pull** /pyl/ *nm* (colloq) sweater

**pull-over**, *pl* ∼**s** /pylɔvɛʀ/ *nm* sweater

**pullulement** /pylylmɑ̃/ *nm*
(a) proliferation
(b) multitude

**pulluler** /pylyle/ [1] *vi* (a) to proliferate
(b) **les touristes pullulent dans la région** the
area is swarming with tourists

**pulmonaire** /pylmɔnɛʀ/ *adj* ⟨*disease*⟩
lung; ⟨*artery*⟩ pulmonary

**pulpe** /pylp/ *nf* (of fruit) pulp; (of potato) flesh

**pulpeux, -euse** /pylpø, øz/ *adj* ⟨*body,
lips*⟩ luscious; ⟨*fruit*⟩ fleshy

**pulsation** /pylsasjɔ̃/ *nf* beat; ∼**s
cardiaques** heartbeat; heartbeats

**pulsion** /pylsjɔ̃/ *nf* impulse, urge

**pulvérisation** /pylveʀizasjɔ̃/ *nf* (a) (liquid)
spraying
(b) (of solid) pulverization (GB)

**pulvériser** /pylveʀize/ [1] *vtr* (a) to spray
(b) to pulverize
(c) to shatter (colloq) ⟨*record*⟩

**puma** /pyma/ *nm* puma

**punaise** /pynɛz/ *nf* (a) drawing pin (GB),
thumbtack (US)
(b) (Zool) bug

**punaiser** /pynɛze/ [1] *vtr* (colloq) to pin *ou*
tack (US) [sth] up

**punch**[1] /pɔ̃ʃ/ *nm* (drink) punch

**punch**[2] /pœnʃ/ *nm* (a) punch
(b) energy; **avoir du** ∼ ⟨*slogan*⟩ to be punchy
(colloq); ⟨*person*⟩ to have drive

**punching-ball**, *pl* ∼**s** /pœnʃiŋbol/ *nm*
punchball (GB), punching bag (US)

**punir** /pyniʀ/ [3] *vtr* to punish

**punitif, -ive** /pynitif, iv/ *adj* punitive

**punition** /pynisjɔ̃/ *nf* (a) punishment
(b) **il n'a pas fait sa** ∼ he hasn't done the
task he was given as punishment

**pupille**[1] /pypij/ *nmf* ward; ∼ **de l'État** child
in care; ∼ **de la Nation** war orphan

**pupille**[2] /pypij/ *nf* (of eye) pupil

**pupitre** /pypitʀ/ *nm* (a) control panel;
console
(b) music stand; music rest
(c) desk
(d) lectern

**pupitreur, -euse** /pypitʀœʀ, øz/ *nm,f*
computer operator

**pur**, **∼e** /pyʀ/ [1] *adj* **(a)** (gen) pure; ‹*diamond*› flawless; ‹*voice, sky*› clear **(b)** ‹*truth*› pure; ‹*coincidence, madness*› sheer; **en ∼e perte** to no avail; **c'est de la paresse ∼e et simple** it's laziness, pure and simple; **∼ et dur** hardline **(c)** ‹*tradition*› true; **un ∼ produit de** a typical product of; **à l'état ∼** ‹*genius*› sheer [2] *nm,f* virtuous person

**purée** /pyʀe/ *nf* purée; **∼ (de pommes de terre)** mashed potatoes ∎ **∼ de pois** pea souper (GB), fog

**purement** /pyʀmɑ̃/ *adv* purely

**pureté** /pyʀte/ *nf* purity

**purgatif, -ive** /pyʀɡatif, iv/ *adj* purgative

**purgatoire** /pyʀɡatwaʀ/ *nm* **le ∼** purgatory

**purge** /pyʀʒ/ *nf* **(a)** purgative **(b)** purge

**purger** /pyʀʒe/ [13] *vtr* **(a)** (Med) to purge **(b)** to bleed ‹*radiator*›; to drain ‹*pipe*›; to purify ‹*metal*› **(c)** (Law) to serve ‹*sentence*›

**purificateur** /pyʀifikatœʀ/ *nm* **∼ d'atmosphère** *or* **d'air** air purifier

**purification** /pyʀifikasjɔ̃/ *nf* purification

**purifier** /pyʀifje/ [2] *vtr* to purify; to cleanse

**purin** /pyʀɛ̃/ *nm* slurry

**puriste** /pyʀist/ *nmf* purist

**puritain**, **∼e** /pyʀitɛ̃, ɛn/ [1] *adj* puritanical; Puritan [2] *nm,f* puritan; Puritan

**pur-sang** /pyʀsɑ̃/ *nm inv* thoroughbred

**pus** /py/ *nm inv* pus

**pustule** /pystyl/ *nf* pustule

**putois** /pytwa/ *nm inv* **(a)** polecat **(b)** skunk (fur)

**putréfaction** /pytʀefaksjɔ̃/ *nf* putrefaction; **en état de ∼** decomposing

**putsch** /putʃ/ *nm* putsch

**puzzle** /pœzl, pyzl/ *nm* jigsaw puzzle

**PV** /peve/ *nm* (colloq) (*abbr* = **procès-verbal**) fine; parking ticket; speeding ticket

**PVC** /pevese/ *nm* (*abbr* = **chlorure de polyvinyle**) PVC

**pygmée** /piɡme/ *nmf* pygmy

**pyjama** /piʒama/ *nm* (pair of) pyjamas (GB), (pair of) pajamas (US)

**pylône** /pilon/ *nm* pylon; (for radio, TV transmitter) mast; (of bridge) tower

**pyramide** /piʀamid/ *nf* pyramid

**pyrénéen, -éenne** /piʀeneɛ̃, ɛn/ *adj* Pyrenean

**pyrex®** /piʀɛks/ *nm inv* Pyrex®

**pyrogravure** /piʀoɡʀavyʀ/ *nf* pokerwork

**pyromane** /piʀɔman/ *nmf* pyromaniac; (Law) arsonist

**python** /pitɔ̃/ *nm* python

# Qq

**q**, **Q** /ky/ *nm inv* q, Q

**qcm** /kyseɛm/ *nm* (*abbr* = **questionnaire à choix multiple**) multiple-choice questionnaire, mcq

**QG** /kyʒe/ *nm: abbr* ▶ QUARTIER

**QI** /kyi/ *nm: abbr* ▶ QUOTIENT

**qu'** ▶ QUE

**quadragénaire** /kwadʀaʒenɛʀ/ *nmf* forty-year-old

**quadrature** /kwadʀatyʀ/ *nf* quadrature; **c'est la ∼ du cercle** it's like squaring the circle

**quadriennal**, **∼e**, *mpl* **-aux** /kwadʀijenal, o/ *adj* **(a)** ‹*plan*› four-year **(b)** quadrennial

**quadrillage** /kadʀijaʒ/ *nm* cross-ruling

**quadrillé**, **∼e** /kadʀije/ *adj* ‹*paper*› squared

**quadriller** /kadʀije/ [1] *vtr* **(a)** ‹*police*› to spread one's net over **(b)** to cross-rule ‹*paper*›

**quadrimoteur** /k(w)adʀimɔtœʀ/ *nm* four-engined plane

**quadrupède** /k(w)adʀypɛd/ *adj, nm* quadruped

**quadruple** /k(w)adʀypl/ *nm* **le ∼ de cette quantité** four times this amount

**quadruplé**, **∼e** /k(w)adʀyple/ *nm,f* quadruplet, quad

**quai** /kɛ/ *nm* **(a)** quay; **le navire est à ∼** the ship has docked **(b)** (of river) bank **(c)** (station) platform ∎ **∼ d'embarquement** loading dock; **Quai des Orfèvres** *criminal investigation department of the French police force*; **Quai d'Orsay** French Foreign Office

**qualificatif, -ive** /kalifikatif, iv/ [1] *adj* qualifying [2] *nm* **(a)** (in grammar) qualifier **(b)** term, word

**qualification** /kalifikasjɔ̃/ *nf* **(a)** qualification **(b)** skills; **sans ∼** unskilled

**qualifié**, **∼e** /kalifje/ *adj* ‹*staff, labour*› skilled; qualified

**qualifier** /kalifje/ [2] [1] *vtr* **(a)** to describe ···ᐅ

**(b)** to qualify
**2 se qualifier** *v refl* (+ *v être*) (Sport) to qualify

**qualitatif, -ive** /kalitatif, iv/ *adj* qualitative

**qualité** /kalite/ *nf* **(a)** quality; **de première ~** of the highest quality; **avoir beaucoup de ~s** to have many qualities
**(b) en (sa) ~ de représentant** in his/her capacity as a representative; **nom, prénom et ~** surname, first name and occupation

**quand** /kɑ̃, kɑ̃t/ **1** *conj* **(a)** when; **~ il arrivera, vous lui annoncerez la nouvelle** when he gets here, you can tell him the news; **~ je pense que ma fille va avoir dix ans!** to think that my daughter's almost ten!; **~ je vous le disais!** I told you so!
**(b)** whenever; **~ il pleut plus de trois jours la cave est inondée** whenever it rains for more than three days, the cellar floods
**(c)** even if; **~ (bien même) la terre s'écroulerait, il continuerait à dormir** he'd sleep through an earthquake
**2** *adv* when; **de ~ date votre dernière réunion?** when was your last meeting?; **depuis ~ habitez-vous ici?** how long have you been living here?; **à ~ la semaine de 30 heures?** (colloq) when will we get a 30-hour working week?
**3 quand même** *phr* still; **ils ne veulent pas de moi, mais j'irai ~ même!** they don't want me, but I'm still going!; **~ même, tu exagères!** (colloq) come on, that's going too far!

**quant: quant à** /kɑ̃ta/ *phr* **(a)** as for; **la France, ~ à elle,... as for France, it...
**(b)** about, concerning

**quantifier** /kɑ̃tifje/ [2] *vtr* to quantify

**quantitatif, -ive** /kɑ̃titatif, iv/ *adj* quantitative

**quantité** /kɑ̃tite/ *nf* **(a)** quantity, amount
**(b) des ~s de** scores of ⟨people⟩; a lot of ⟨things⟩; **du pain/vin en ~** plenty of bread/wine

**quarantaine** /kaʀɑ̃tɛn/ *nf* **(a)** about forty
**(b) être en ~** to be in quarantine; to be ostracized

**quarante** /kaʀɑ̃t/ *adj inv, pron, nm inv* forty

**quarante-cinq** /kaʀɑ̃tsɛ̃k/ *adj inv, pron, nm inv* forty-five
■ **~ tours** single

**quarantième** /kaʀɑ̃tjɛm/ *adj* fortieth

**quart** /kaʀ/ *nm* **(a)** quarter; **un ~ d'heure** a quarter of an hour; **les trois ~s du temps** (colloq) most of the time
**(b)** a quarter-litre (GB) bottle; a quarter-litre (GB) pitcher
**(c)** (Naut) **être de ~** to be on watch
■ **~ de cercle** quadrant; **~ de tour** 90° turn; **faire qch au ~ de tour** (colloq) to do sth immediately

**quartier** /kaʀtje/ *nm* **(a)** area, district; **de ~** ⟨cinema, grocer⟩ local

**(b)** quarter; **un ~ de pommes** a slice of apple; **un ~ d'orange** an orange segment
**(c)** (of moon) quarter
**(d)** (Mil) **~s** quarters; **avoir ~ libre** to be off duty; to have time off
■ **~ général, QG** headquarters, HQ
IDIOMS **ne pas faire de ~** to show no mercy

**quart-monde** /kaʀmɔ̃d/ *nm inv* underclass

**quartz** /kwaʀts/ *nm* quartz

**quasi** /kazi/ **1** *adv* almost
**2 quasi-** (*combining form*) **~-indifférence** virtual indifference; **la ~-totalité de** almost all of; **à la ~-unanimité** almost unanimously

**quasiment** /kazimɑ̃/ *adv* (colloq) practically

**quaternaire** /kwatɛʀnɛʀ/ *adj, nm* Quaternary

**quatorze** /katɔʀz/ *adj inv, pron, nm inv* fourteen
IDIOMS **chercher midi à ~ heures** (colloq) to complicate matters

**quatorzième** /katɔʀzjɛm/ *adj* fourteenth

**quatrain** /katʀɛ̃/ *nm* quatrain

**quatre** /katʀ/ *adj inv, pron, nm inv* four
IDIOMS **faire les ~ volontés de qn** to give in to sb's every whim; **être tiré à ~ épingles** to be dressed up to the nines (colloq); **ne pas y aller par ~ chemins** not to beat about the bush; **je vais leur parler entre ~ yeux** I'm going to talk to them face to face; **monter un escalier ~ à ~** to go up the stairs four at a time; **être entre ~ planches** (colloq) to be six feet under

**quatre-heures** /katʀœʀ/ *nm inv* afternoon snack (*for children*)

**quatre-quarts** /kat(ʀə)kaʀ/ *nm inv* pound cake

**quatre-vingt(s)** /katʀəvɛ̃/ *adj, pron, nm* eighty

**quatre-vingt-dix** /katʀəvɛ̃dis/ *adj inv, pron, nm inv* ninety

**quatre-vingt-dixième** /katʀəvɛ̃dizjɛm/ *adj* ninetieth

**quatre-vingtième** /katʀəvɛ̃tjɛm/ *adj* eightieth

**quatrième** /katʀijɛm/ **1** *adj* fourth
**2** *nf* **(a)** (Sch) *third year of secondary school, age 13–14*
**(b)** (Aut) fourth (gear)
■ **le ~ âge** very old people
IDIOMS **en ~ vitesse** (colloq) in double quick time (colloq)

**quatuor** /kwatɥɔʀ/ *nm* quartet

**que** (**qu'** *before vowel or mute h*) /kə/ **1** *conj* **(a)** that; **je pense qu'il a raison** I think he's right; **je veux ~ tu m'accompagnes** I want you to come with me
**(b)** so (that); **approche, ~ je te regarde** come closer so I can look at you
**(c)** whether; **~ cela vous plaise ou non** whether you like it or not
**(d) si vous venez et ~ vous ayez le temps** if you come and (if you) have the time

**(e)** il n'était pas sitôt parti qu'elle appela la **police** no sooner had he left than she called the police

**(f)** ~ tout le monde sorte! everyone must leave!; ~ ceux qui n'ont pas compris le **disent** let anyone who hasn't understood say so; **qu'il crève!** (slang) let him rot! (colloq)

**(g)** than; as; **plus gros** ~ **moi** fatter than me; **aussi grand** ~ **mon frère** as tall as my brother

**2** *pron* what; ~ **dire?** what can you say?; **je ne sais pas ce qu'il a dit** I don't know what he said; **qu'est-ce que c'est que ça?** what's that?

**3** *rel pron* that; who(m); which; **je n'aime pas la voiture** ~ **tu as achetée** I don't like the car (that) you've bought

**4** *adv* ~ **c'est joli** it's so pretty; ~ **de monde** what a lot of people

**Québec** /kebɛk/ **1** *pr nm* **le** ~ Quebec **2** *pr n* Quebec

**québécois**, ~**e** /kebekwa, az/ *adj* of Quebec

**Québécois**, ~**e** /kebekwa, az/ *nm,f* Quebecois, Quebecker

**quel**, **quelle** /kɛl/ **1** *det* who; what; which; **je me demande quelle est la meilleure solution** I wonder what the best solution is; **de ces deux médicaments,** ~ **est le plus efficace?** which of these two medicines is more effective?

**2** *adj* **(a)** what; which; **quelle heure est-il?** what time is it?; **dans** ~ **tiroir l'as-tu mis?** which drawer did you put it in?; ~ **âge as-tu?** how old are you?

**(b)** what; how; **quelle coïncidence!** what a coincidence!

**(c)** **quelle que soit la route que l'on prenne** whatever *or* whichever road we take; ~ **que soit le vainqueur** whoever the winner may be

**quelconque** /kɛlkɔ̃k/ **1** *adj* ⟨person⟩ ordinary; ordinary-looking; ⟨novel, actor⟩ poor; ⟨restaurant⟩ second-rate; ⟨place⟩ characterless

**2** *adj* any; **si pour une raison** ~ if for some reason or other; **si le livre avait un intérêt** ~ if the book was in any way interesting

**quelle** ▸ QUEL

**quelque** /kɛlk/ **1** *quantif* some; a few; any; **depuis** ~ **temps** for some time; **je voudrais ajouter** ~**s mots** I'd like to add a few words; **ça dure trois heures et** ~**s** it lasts over three hours; **si pour** ~ **raison que ce soit** if for whatever reason

**2** *adv* **(a)** **les** ~ **deux mille spectateurs** the two thousand odd spectators

**(b)** however; ~ **admirable que soit son attitude** however admirable his/her attitude may be

**3** **quelque chose** *pron* something; anything; **il y a** ~ **chose qui ne va pas** something's wrong; **si** ~ **chose leur arrive** if anything should happen to them; **il a** ~

**chose de son grand-père** he's got a look of his grandfather about him; **ça me dit** ~ **chose** it rings a bell

**4** **quelque part** *phr* somewhere; anywhere

**5** **quelque peu** *phr* somewhat

**quelquefois** /kɛlkəfwa/ *adv* sometimes

**quelques-uns**, **quelques-unes** /kɛlkəzœ̃, yn/ *pron* some, a few

**quelqu'un** /kɛlkœ̃/ *pron* someone, somebody; anyone, anybody; ~ **d'autre** someone else; **c'est** ~ **de compétent** he/she is competent

**quémander** /kemɑ̃de/ [1] *vtr* to beg

**qu'en-dira-t-on** /kɑ̃diratɔ̃/ *nm inv* gossip

**quenelle** /kənɛl/ *nf: dumpling made of flour and egg, flavoured with meat or fish*

**quenotte** /kənɔt/ *nf* (colloq) toothy-peg (colloq), tooth

**quenouille** /kənuj/ *nf* distaff

**querelle** /kəʀɛl/ *nf* **(a)** quarrel; **chercher** ~ **à qn** to pick a quarrel with sb

**(b)** dispute

**quereller: se quereller** /kəʀɛle/ [1] *v refl* (+ *v être*) to quarrel

**question** /kɛstjɔ̃/ *nf* **(a)** question; **je ne me suis jamais posé la** ~ I've never really thought about it; **pose-leur la** ~ ask them

**(b)** matter, question; issue; ~ **d'habitude!** it's a matter of habit; **en** ~ in question; at issue; **(re)mettre en** ~ to reappraise; to reassess; **se remettre en** ~ to take a new look at oneself; **la** ~ **n'est pas là** that's not the point; **il est** ~ **d'elle dans l'article** she's mentioned in the article; **il n'est pas** ~ **que tu partes** you can't possibly leave; **pas** ~**!** no way! (colloq)

**(c)** (colloq) ~ **santé, ça va** where health is concerned, things are OK

**questionnaire** /kɛstjɔnɛʀ/ *nm* questionnaire

**questionner** /kɛstjɔne/ [1] *vtr* to question

**quête** /kɛt/ *nf* **(a)** collection; **faire la** ~ to take the collection; to pass the hat round; to collect for charity

**(b)** search; **la** ~ **du Graal** the quest for the Holy Grail

**quêter** /kete/ [1] *vi* to take the collection; ~ **pour une œuvre** to collect for a charity

**quetsche** /kwɛtʃ/ *nf* (sweet purple) plum

**queue** /kø/ *nf* **(a)** tail

**(b)** (of flower) stem; (of apple) stalk (GB), stem (US)

**(c)** (of pot) handle

**(d)** (Sport) cue

**(e)** (of procession) tail(-end); (of train) rear, back; **ils arrivent en** ~ **(de peloton) des grandes entreprises** they come at the bottom of the league table of companies

**(f)** **faire la** ~ to stand in a queue (GB), to stand in line (US)

**IDIOMS une histoire sans** ~ **ni tête** (colloq) a cock and bull story; **la** ~ **basse** with one's tail between one's legs; **il n'y en avait pas la** ⋯⟡

**q**

∼ **d'un(e)** (colloq) there were none to be seen; **faire une** ∼ **de poisson à qn** to cut in front of sb; **finir en** ∼ **de poisson** to fizzle out

**queue-de-cheval,** pl **queues-de-cheval** /kødʃəval/ nf ponytail

**queue-de-pie,** pl **queues-de-pie** /kødpi/ nf (colloq) tails, tailcoat

**queux** /kø/ nm inv **maître** ∼ **chef**

**qui** /ki/ **1** pron who; whom; ∼ **veut-elle voir?** who does she want to speak to?
**2** rel pron (a) who; that; which; **est-ce vous** ∼ **venez d'appeler?** was it you who called just now?; **ce** ∼ **me plaît chez lui** what I like about him
(b) ∼ **que vous soyez** whoever you are; **je n'ai jamais frappé** ∼ **que ce soit** I've never hit anybody

**quiche** /kiʃ/ nf quiche, flan

**quiconque** /kikɔ̃k/ **1** rel pron whoever, anyone who
**2** pron anyone, anybody

**quiétude** /kjetyd/ nf tranquillity

**quignon** /kiɲɔ̃/ nm crusty end (of a loaf)

**quille** /kij/ nf (a) skittle
(b) (Naut) keel
IDIOMS **être reçu comme un chien dans un jeu de** ∼**s** (colloq) to be given a very unfriendly welcome

**quincaillerie** /kɛ̃kajʀi/ nf (a) hardware shop (GB) or store (US)
(b) hardware
(c) hardware business

**quinconce** /kɛ̃kɔ̃s/ nm **en** ∼ in staggered rows

**quinquagénaire** /kɛ̃kaʒenɛʀ/ nmf fifty-year-old

**quinquennal,** ∼**e,** mpl **-aux** /kɛ̃kenal, o/ adj (a) ⟨plan⟩ five-year
(b) five-yearly

**quintal,** pl **-aux** /kɛ̃tal, o/ nm quintal

**quinte** /kɛ̃t/ nf (a) (Mus) fifth
(b) **une** ∼ **(de toux)** a coughing fit

**quintette** /kɛ̃tɛt/ nm quintet

**quintuple** /kɛ̃typl/ nm **le** ∼ **de cette quantité** five times the amount

**quintuplé,** ∼**e** /kɛ̃typle/ nm,f quintuplet, quin (GB), quint (US)

**quinzaine** /kɛ̃zɛn/ nf (a) fortnight (GB), two weeks; **sous** ∼ within 2 weeks
(b) about fifteen

**quinze** /kɛ̃z/ adj inv, pron, nm inv fifteen

**quinzième** /kɛ̃zjɛm/ adj fifteenth

**quiproquo** /kipʀɔko/ nm misunderstanding

**quittance** /kitɑ̃s/ nf (a) receipt
(b) bill

**quitte** /kit/ **1** adj (a) **nous sommes** ∼**s, je suis** ∼ **avec lui** we're quits
(b) **en être** ∼ **pour la peur/un rhume** to get off with a fright/a cold
**2** **quitte à** phr ∼ **à aller à Londres, autant que ce soit pour quelques jours** if you're going to London anyway, you might as well go for a few days
■ ∼ **ou double** double or quits

**quitter** /kite/ [1] **1** vtr (a) to leave ⟨place, person, road⟩
(b) to leave ⟨job, organization⟩; ∼ **la scène** to give up acting; **il ne l'a pas quittée des yeux de tout le repas** he didn't take his eyes off her throughout the meal; **ne quittez pas** hold the line
(c) ⟨company⟩ to move from ⟨street⟩; to move out of ⟨building⟩
(d) **un grand homme nous a quittés** a great man has passed away
(e) to take off ⟨garment, hat⟩
**2** **se quitter** v refl (+ v être) to part; **ils ne se quittent plus** they're inseparable now

**qui-vive** /kiviv/ nm inv **être sur le** ∼ to be on the alert

**quoi** /kwa/ **1** pron (a) what; **à** ∼ **penses-tu?** what are you thinking about?; **à** ∼ **bon recommencer?** what's the point of starting again?
(b) ∼ **qu'elle puisse en dire** whatever she may say; ∼ **qu'il en soit** be that as it may
**2** rel pron **il n'y a rien sur** ∼ **vous puissiez fonder vos accusations** there's nothing on which to base your accusations; **à** ∼ **il a répondu** to which he replied; **après** ∼ **ils sont partis** after which they left; **(il n'y a) pas de** ∼**!** my pleasure; **il n'y a pas de** ∼ **se fâcher** there's no reason to get angry; **il n'a (même) pas de** ∼ **s'acheter un livre** he hasn't (even) got enough money to buy a book

**quoique** (**quoiqu'** before vowel or mute h) /kwak(ə)/ conj although, though; **nous sommes mieux ici qu'à Paris,** ∼ we're better off here than in Paris, but then (again)

**quota** /kɔta/ nm quota (**sur on**)

**quote-part,** pl **quotes-parts** /kɔtpaʀ/ nf share

**quotidien, -ienne** /kɔtidjɛ̃, ɛn/ **1** adj
(a) daily
(b) everyday
**2** nm (a) daily (paper)
(b) everyday life

**quotidiennement** /kɔtidjɛnmɑ̃/ adv every day, daily

**quotient** /kɔsjɑ̃/ nm quotient
■ ∼ **intellectuel, QI** intelligence quotient, IQ

# Rr

**r, R** /ɛR/ *nm inv* r, R

**rab** /Rab/ *nm* (colloq) **(a)** extra; **faire du ~ to** do extra hours
**(b) demander du ~** to ask for seconds

**rabâcher** /Rabɑʃe/ [1] **1** *vtr* to keep repeating
**2** *vi* to keep harping on

**rabais** /Rabɛ/ *nm inv* discount

**rabaisser** /Rabese/ [1] **1** *vtr* to belittle
**2 se rabaisser** *v refl* (+ *v être*) to demean oneself

**rabat** /Raba/ *nm* (of bag, table, pocket) flap

**rabat-joie** /Rabaʒwa/ *adj inv* **être ~** to be a killjoy

**rabattre** /RabatR/ [61] **1** *vtr* **(a)** ⟨person⟩ to shut ⟨lid⟩; to put *or* fold up ⟨foldaway seat, tray⟩
**(b)** to turn [sth] down ⟨collar, sheet⟩
**(c)** ⟨player⟩ to smash ⟨ball⟩
**(d) ~ le gibier** to beat the undergrowth for game
**2 se rabattre** *v refl* (+ *v être*) **(a)** ⟨lid⟩ to shut; ⟨leaf of table⟩ to fold up
**(b)** ⟨driver, vehicle⟩ to pull back in
**(c) se ~ sur** to make do with

**rabbin** /Rabɛ̃/ *nm* rabbi; **grand ~** chief rabbi

**râblé, ~e** /Rable/ *adj* **(a)** ⟨animal⟩ sturdy
**(b)** ⟨person⟩ stocky

**rabot** /Rabo/ *nm* (tool) plane

**raboter** /Rabote/ [1] *vtr* to plane

**rabougri, ~e** /RabugRi/ *adj* ⟨tree⟩ stunted

**rabrouer** /RabRue/ [1] *vtr* to snub

**racaille** /Rakaj/ *nf* scum

**raccommoder** /Rakɔmɔde/ [1] *vtr* **(a)** to darn ⟨socks⟩
**(b)** (colloq) to reconcile ⟨people⟩

**raccompagner** /Rakɔ̃paɲe/ [1] *vtr* **~ qn chez lui** to walk/to drive sb (back) home

**raccord** /RakɔR/ *nm* **(a)** (in wallpaper) join
**(b)** (in painting) touch-up
**(c)** (in film) link shot

**raccordement** /RakɔRdəmɑ̃/ *nm* link road

**raccorder** /RakɔRde/ [1] *vtr* to connect

**raccourci** /RakuRsi/ *nm* (road) shortcut

**raccourcir** /RakuRsiR/ [3] **1** *vtr* **(a)** (gen) to shorten
**(b)** to cut ⟨text, speech⟩
**2** *vi* ⟨days⟩ to get shorter, to draw in
**IDIOMS tomber sur qn à bras raccourcis** (colloq) to lay into sb

**raccrocher** /RakRɔʃe/ [1] **1** *vtr* to hang [sth] back up
**2** *vi* to hang up

**3 se raccrocher** *v refl* (+ *v être*) **se ~ à** to grab hold of ⟨rail⟩; (figurative) to cling to ⟨person, excuse⟩

**race** /Ras/ *nf* **(a)** race
**(b)** (Zool) breed; **chien de ~** pedigree (dog)

**racheter** /Raʃte/ [18] **1** *vtr* **(a)** to buy [sth] back
**(b)** to buy some more ⟨wine⟩
**(c)** to buy new ⟨sheets⟩
**(d)** to buy out ⟨company, factory⟩; **je rachète votre voiture 1 000 euros** I'll buy your car off you for 1,000 euros
**(e)** to redeem ⟨sinner⟩
**2 se racheter** *v refl* (+ *v être*) to redeem oneself

**rachitique** /Raʃitik/ *adj* ⟨animal, plant, person⟩ scrawny

**rachitisme** /Raʃitism/ *nm* rickets

**racial, ~e,** *mpl* **-iaux** /Rasjal, o/ *adj* racial; **émeutes ~es** race riots

**racine** /Rasin/ *nf* root

**racisme** /Rasism/ *nm* racism

**raciste** /Rasist/ *adj, nmf* racist

**racket** /Rakɛt/ *nm* extortion racket; racketeering

**raclée** /Rakle/ *nf* (colloq) hiding (colloq)

**racler** /Rakle/ [1] **1** *vtr* **(a)** to scrape [sth] clean ⟨plate⟩
**(b)** to scrape off ⟨rust⟩
**(c)** to scrape against
**2 se racler** *v refl* (+ *v être*) **se ~ la gorge** to clear one's throat

**raclette** /Raklɛt/ *nf* **(a)** raclette (Swiss cheese dish)
**(b)** scraper

**racolage** /Rakɔlaʒ/ *nm* touting (**de** for); soliciting (**de** for)

**racoler** /Rakɔle/ [1] *vtr* ⟨prostitute⟩ to solicit

**racontar** /Rakɔ̃taR/ *nm* (colloq) **des ~s** idle gossip

**raconter** /Rakɔ̃te/ [1] *vtr* to tell ⟨story⟩; to describe ⟨incident⟩; **~ qch à qn** to tell sb sth; **qu'est-ce que tu racontes?** what are you talking about?

**racornir** /RakɔRniR/ [3] *vtr*, **se racornir** *v refl* (+ *v être*) **(a)** to harden
**(b)** to shrivel (up)

**radar** /RadaR/ *nm* radar

**rade** /Rad/ *nf* harbour (GB); **rester en ~** (colloq) ⟨person⟩ to be left stranded

**radeau,** *pl* **~x** /Rado/ *nm* raft

**radiateur** /Radjatœʀ/ *nm* radiator; **~ électrique** electric heater

**radiation** /Radjasjɔ̃/ *nf* radiation

**radical**, ∼**e**, *mpl* **-aux** /ʀadikal, o/ *adj*,
*nm,f* radical

**radicalement** /ʀadikalmɑ̃/ *adv* radically;
completely

**radier** /ʀadje/ [2] *vtr* ∼ **un médecin** to
strike off a doctor (GB), to take away a
doctor's license (US); ∼ **un avocat** to disbar a
lawyer

**radieux**, **-ieuse** /ʀadjø, øz/ *adj* (a) ⟨*sun*⟩
dazzling
 **(b)** ⟨*weather*⟩ glorious
 **(c)** ⟨*face, smile*⟩ radiant; ⟨*person*⟩ radiant
with joy

**radin**, ∼**e** /ʀadɛ̃, in/ *adj* (colloq) stingy
(colloq)

**radinerie** /ʀadinʀi/ *nf* (colloq) stinginess
(colloq)

**radio¹** /ʀadjo/ **1** *adj inv* ⟨*contact, signal*⟩
radio
 **2** *nm* radio operator

**radio²** /ʀadjo/ *nf* (a) radio
 **(b)** X-ray

**radioactivité** /ʀadjoaktivite/ *nf*
radioactivity

**radiocassette** /ʀadjokasɛt/ *nm* radio
cassette player

**radiodiffuser** /ʀadjodifyze/ [1] *vtr* to
broadcast

**radiographie** /ʀadjoɡʀafi/ *nf*
 **(a)** radiography
 **(b)** X-ray (photograph)

**radiologue** /ʀadjolɔɡ/ *nmf* radiologist

**radiophonique** /ʀadjofɔnik/ *adj* radio

**radio-réveil**, *pl* **radios-réveils**
/ʀadjoʀevɛj/ *nm* clock radio

**radioscopie** /ʀadjoskɔpi/ *nf* fluoroscopy

**radiothérapie** /ʀadjoteʀapi/ *nf*
radiotherapy

**radis** /ʀadi/ *nm inv* radish; **je n'ai plus un**
∼ (colloq) I haven't got a penny

**radoter** /ʀadote/ [1] *vi* (a) to talk nonsense
 **(b)** to repeat oneself

**radoucir: se radoucir** /ʀadusiʀ/ [3] *v refl*
(+ *v être*) ⟨*person*⟩ to soften up; ⟨*weather*⟩ to
turn milder

**radoucissement** /ʀadusismɑ̃/ *nm* **la
météo annonce un** ∼ the forecast is for
milder weather

**rafale** /ʀafal/ *nf* (a) (of wind, rain) gust;
(of snow) flurry
 **(b)** (of gunfire) burst

**raffermir** /ʀafɛʀmiʀ/ [3] *vtr* (a) to tone
⟨*skin*⟩; to tone up ⟨*muscles*⟩
 **(b)** to strengthen ⟨*position*⟩; to steady
⟨*market*⟩

**raffinage** /ʀafinaʒ/ *nm* refining

**raffiné**, ∼**e** /ʀafine/ *adj* refined; ⟨*food*⟩
sophisticated

**raffinement** /ʀafinmɑ̃/ *nm* (a) refinement
 **(b)** elegance

**raffiner** /ʀafine/ [1] *vtr* to refine

**raffinerie** /ʀafinʀi/ *nf* refinery; ∼ **de
pétrole** oil refinery

**raffoler** /ʀafɔle/ [1] *v+prep* ∼ **de** to be
crazy about (colloq)

**raffut** /ʀafy/ *nm* (colloq) (a) racket (colloq)
 **(b)** stink (colloq), row

**rafiot** /ʀafjo/ *nm* (colloq) boat, (old) tub
(colloq)

**rafistoler** /ʀafistɔle/ [1] *vtr* (colloq) to patch
up

**rafle** /ʀafl/ *nf* (a) raid
 **(b)** roundup

**rafler** /ʀafle/ [1] *vtr* (colloq) (a) to make off
with, to swipe (colloq)
 **(b)** to walk off with ⟨*medal, reward*⟩

**rafraîchir** /ʀafʀɛʃiʀ/ [3] **1** *vtr* ⟨*rain*⟩ to
cool ⟨*atmosphere*⟩; **le thé glacé te rafraîchira**
the iced tea will cool you down
 **2** **se rafraîchir** *v refl* (+ *v être*) ⟨*weather*⟩
to get cooler; ⟨*person*⟩ to refresh oneself
**IDIOMS** ∼ **la mémoire de qn** (colloq) to refresh
sb's memory

**rafraîchissant**, ∼**e** /ʀafʀɛʃisɑ̃, ɑ̃t/ *adj*
refreshing

**rafraîchissement** /ʀafʀɛʃismɑ̃/ *nm*
refreshment

**ragaillardir** /ʀaɡajaʀdiʀ/ [3] *vtr* to cheer
[sb] up

**rage** /ʀaʒ/ *nf* (a) rabies
 **(b)** rage; **être fou de** ∼ to be in a mad rage;
**faire** ∼ ⟨*disease*⟩ to be rife; ⟨*epidemic, fire*⟩ to
rage
 ∎ ∼ **de dents** raging toothache

**rageant**, ∼**e** /ʀaʒɑ̃, ɑ̃t/ *adj* (colloq)
infuriating

**rageusement** /ʀaʒøzmɑ̃/ *adv* furiously;
angrily

**ragot** /ʀaɡo/ *nm* (colloq) malicious gossip

**ragoût** /ʀaɡu/ *nm* stew, ragout

**rai** /ʀɛ/ *nm* ∼ **de lumière** ray of light

**raï** /ʀaj/ *nm: music from the Maghreb with
Western influences*

**raid** /ʀɛd/ *nm* (a) (Mil) raid
 **(b)** (Sport) trek

**raide** /ʀɛd/ *adj* (a) (gen) stiff; ⟨*hair*⟩ straight;
⟨*rope*⟩ taut
 **(b)** steep
 **(c)** (colloq) **je trouve ça un peu** ∼ that's a bit
steep
**IDIOMS être** ∼ **comme un piquet** to be stiff as
a ramrod; **tomber** ∼ to be flabbergasted

**raideur** /ʀɛdœʀ/ *nf* (a) stiffness
 **(b)** steepness

**raidir** /ʀɛdiʀ/ [3] **1** *vtr* to tense ⟨*arm, body*⟩
 **2** **se raidir** *v refl* (+ *v être*) ⟨*body*⟩ to tense
up; **se** ∼ **contre la douleur** to brace oneself
against pain

**raie** /ʀɛ/ *nf* (a) (in hair) parting (GB), part
(US)
 **(b)** scratch
 **(c)** (Zool) skate

**rail** /ʀaj/ *nm* rail, track
 ∎ ∼ **de sécurité** crash barrier

**raillerie** /ʀajʀi/ *nf* mockery

**rainette** /ʀɛnɛt/ *nf* tree frog

**rainure** /ʀenyʀ/ *nf* groove

**raisin** /ʀɛzɛ̃/ *nm* grapes; ~s secs raisins

**raison** /ʀɛzɔ̃/ *nf* (a) reason; ~ d'agir reason for action; en ~ d'une panne owing to a breakdown; à plus forte ~ even more so, especially; avec ~ justifiably; comme de ~ as one might expect
(b) avoir ~ to be right; donner ~ à qn to agree with sb
(c) reason; se rendre à la ~ to see reason; ramener qn à la ~ to bring sb to his/her senses; se faire une ~ de qch to resign oneself to sth; plus que de ~ more than is sensible; avoir ~ de qn/qch to get the better of sb/sth; à ~ de at the rate of

**raisonnable** /ʀɛzɔnabl/ *adj* reasonable; moderate; sensible

**raisonné, ~e** /ʀɛzɔne/ **1** *pp* ▶ RAISONNER
**2** *pp adj* (a) ⟨*attitude*⟩ cautious; ⟨*decision*⟩ carefully thought out
(b) ⟨*enthusiasm*⟩ measured

**raisonnement** /ʀɛzɔnmɑ̃/ *nm* reasoning; selon le même ~ by the same token; il tient le ~ suivant his argument is as follows; je ne tiens pas le même ~ I look at it differently

**raisonner** /ʀɛzɔne/ [1] **1** *vtr* to reason with
**2** *vi* to think
**3** **se raisonner** *v refl* (+ *v être*) ⟨*person*⟩ to be more sensible, to pull oneself together

**rajeunir** /ʀaʒœniʀ/ [3] **1** *vtr* (a) to make [sb] look/feel younger
(b) ~ qn to make sb out to be younger
(c) to bring *or* inject new blood into
**2** *vi* to look/to feel younger

**rajeunissement** /ʀaʒœnismɑ̃/ *nm*
(a) nous avons enregistré un ~ de la population we see that the population is getting younger
(b) modernization
(c) updating
(d) rejuvenation

**rajouter** /ʀaʒute/ [1] *vtr* to add; en ~ (colloq) to exaggerate

**rajuster** /ʀaʒyste/ [1] *vtr* to straighten ⟨*clothing*⟩

**râle** /ʀɑl/ *nm* (a) rale
(b) groan
(c) death rattle

**ralenti, ~e** /ʀalɑ̃ti/ **1** *pp* ▶ RALENTIR
**2** *pp adj* ⟨*gesture, rhythm, growth*⟩ slower
**3** *nm* slow motion

**ralentir** /ʀalɑ̃tiʀ/ [3] *vtr, vi,* **se ralentir** *v refl* (+ *v être*) to slow down

**ralentissement** /ʀalɑ̃tismɑ̃/ *nm*
(a) slowing down
(b) tailback

**ralentisseur** /ʀalɑ̃tisœʀ/ *nm* speed ramp

**râler** /ʀɑle/ [1] *vi* (a) (colloq) to moan (colloq); ça me fait ~ it annoys me
(b) to groan

**râleur, -euse** /ʀɑlœʀ, øz/ *nm,f* (colloq) moaner (colloq)

**ralliement** /ʀalimɑ̃/ *nm* rallying

**rallier** /ʀalje/ [2] **1** *vtr* ~ qn à sa cause to win sb over
**2** **se rallier** *v refl* (+ *v être*) se ~ à to rally to ⟨*republicans*⟩; to come round to ⟨*opinion*⟩

**rallonge** /ʀalɔ̃ʒ/ *nf* (a) extension cord, extension lead (GB)
(b) (of table) leaf

**rallonger** /ʀalɔ̃ʒe/ [13] **1** *vtr* to extend; to lengthen
**2** *vi* les jours rallongent the days are drawing out

**rallye** /ʀali/ *nm* (car) rally

**ramadan** /ʀamadɑ̃/ *nm* Ramadan; faire le ~ to keep Ramadan

**ramage** /ʀamaʒ/ **1** *nm* (of bird) song
**2** **ramages** *nm pl* foliage pattern

**ramassage** /ʀamasaʒ/ *nm* car de ~ (for employees) works *or* company bus; (for pupils) school bus

**ramassé, ~e** /ʀamase/ **1** *pp* ▶ RAMASSER
**2** *pp adj* (a) stocky, squat
(b) être ~ sur soi-même to be hunched up

**ramasser** /ʀamase/ [1] **1** *vtr* to collect; to pick up; to dig up ⟨*potatoes*⟩; se faire ~ dans une rafle (colloq) to get picked up in a (police) raid
**2** **se ramasser** *v refl* (+ *v être*) (a) to huddle up
(b) (colloq) to come a cropper (colloq); se faire ~ à un examen to fail an exam

**ramassis** /ʀamasi/ *nm inv* (derogatory) (of people) bunch; (of ideas, objects) jumble

**rambarde** /ʀɑ̃baʀd/ *nf* guardrail

**rame** /ʀam/ *nf* (a) oar
(b) (of paper) ream
(c) une ~ de métro a metro train

**rameau,** *pl* ~**x** /ʀamo/ *nm* (Bot) branch

**ramener** /ʀamne/ [16] **1** *vtr*
(a) ~ l'inflation à 5% to reduce inflation to 5 per cent
(b) to restore ⟨*order*⟩; ~ qn à la réalité to bring sb back to reality; ~ qn à la vie to bring sb round; ~ toujours tout à soi always to relate everything to oneself
(c) to take [sb/sth] back
(d) to bring back; to return
**2** **se ramener** *v refl* (+ *v être*) se ~ à to come down to, to boil down to

**ramequin** /ʀamkɛ̃/ *nm* ramekin

**ramer** /ʀame/ [1] *vi* to row

**rameur, -euse** /ʀamœʀ, øz/ *nm,f* rower

**rameuter** /ʀamøte/ [1] *vtr* to round up

**ramification** /ʀamifikasjɔ̃/ *nf* (a) network
(b) ramification

**ramifier: se ramifier** /ʀamifje/ [2] *v refl* (+ *v être*) ⟨*stem, nerve*⟩ to branch; ⟨*branch*⟩ to divide

**ramollir** /ʀamɔliʀ/ [3] **1** *vtr* to soften
**2** **se ramollir** *v refl* (+ *v être*) (a) to become soft
(b) (colloq) ⟨*person*⟩ to get soft

**ramollissement** /ʀamɔlismɑ̃/ *nm*
softening

**ramoner** /ʀamɔne/ [1] *vtr* to sweep
⟨*chimney*⟩

**ramoneur** /ʀamɔnœʀ/ *nm* chimney sweep

**rampant, ~e** /ʀɑ̃pɑ̃, ɑ̃t/ *adj* (a) ⟨*animal*⟩
crawling; ⟨*plant*⟩ creeping
**(b)** ⟨*inflation*⟩ creeping

**rampe** /ʀɑ̃p/ *nf* (a) banister; hand-rail
**(b)** (in theatre) **la ~** the footlights
■ **~ d'accès** (for motorway) sliproad (GB),
entrance ramp (US); (of building) ramp

**ramper** /ʀɑ̃pe/ [1] *vi* (a) to crawl
**(b)** to creep

**ramure** /ʀamyʀ/ *nf* (a) (of tree) branches
**(b)** antlers

**rancard** /ʀɑ̃kaʀ/ *nm* (slang) (a) ⟨rendezvous⟩
date
**(b)** (information) tip

**rancart** /ʀɑ̃kaʀ/ *nm* (colloq) **mettre au ~** to
shunt [sb] aside

**rance** /ʀɑ̃s/ *adj* rancid

**rancœur** /ʀɑ̃kœʀ/ *nf* resentment

**rançon** /ʀɑ̃sɔ̃/ *nf* (a) ransom
**(b) la ~ de la gloire** the price of fame

**rancune** /ʀɑ̃kyn/ *nf* (a) resentment
**(b)** grudge; **sans ~!** no hard feelings

**rancunier, -ière** /ʀɑ̃kynje, ɛʀ/ *adj* **être ~**
to be a person who holds grudges

**randonnée** /ʀɑ̃dɔne/ *nf* hiking

**randonneur, -euse** /ʀɑ̃dɔnœʀ, øz/ *nm,f*
hiker, rambler

**rang** /ʀɑ̃/ *nm* (a) row; (in necklace) strand; **se
mettre en ~s** ⟨*children*⟩ to get into (a) line
**(b)** (Mil, figurative) rank; **sortir du ~** to rise *or*
come up through the ranks; **serrer les ~s** to
close ranks
**(c)** (in a hierarchy) rank; **être au 5ᵉ ~ mondial
des exportateurs** to be the 5th largest
exporter in the world; **acteur de second ~**
second-rate actor; **des personnes de son ~**
people of one's own station

**rangé, ~e¹** /ʀɑ̃ʒe/ 1 *pp* ▶ RANGER¹
2 *pp adj* ⟨*life*⟩ orderly; ⟨*person*⟩ well-
behaved

**rangée²** /ʀɑ̃ʒe/ *nf* row

**rangement** /ʀɑ̃ʒmɑ̃/ *nm* (a) **c'est un
maniaque du ~** he's obsessively tidy
**(b)** storage space

**ranger¹** /ʀɑ̃ʒe/ [13] 1 *vtr* (a) to put away;
**où ranges-tu tes verres?** where do you keep
the glasses?
**(b)** to arrange, to put into order; **~ un
animal dans les mammifères** to class an
animal as a mammal
**(c)** to tidy
2 **se ranger** *v refl* (+ *v être*) (a) to line up
**(b)** ⟨*vehicle, driver*⟩ to pull over
**(c) se ~ à l'avis de qn** to go along with sb
**(d)** to settle down

**ranger²** /ʀɑ̃dʒɛʀ/ *nm* (a) ranger
**(b)** heavy-duty boot

**ranimer** /ʀanime/ [1] *vtr* (a) to revive
⟨*person*⟩

**(b)** to rekindle ⟨*fire, hope*⟩; to stir up
⟨*quarrel*⟩

**rapace** /ʀapas/ 1 *adj* ⟨*person*⟩ rapacious
2 *nm* bird of prey

**rapacité** /ʀapasite/ *nf* (a) (of an animal)
ferocity
**(b)** (of trader) greed

**rapatrié, ~e** /ʀapatʀije/ *nm,f* repatriate
(de from)

**rapatrier** /ʀapatʀije/ [2] *vtr* to repatriate

**râpe** /ʀɑp/ *nf* (Culin) grater

**râper** /ʀɑpe/ [1] *vtr* to grate ⟨*cheese, carrot*⟩;
**c'est râpé** (figurative) (colloq) it's off (colloq)

**rapetisser** /ʀap(ə)tise/ [1] *vi* to shrink

**râpeux, -euse** /ʀɑpø, øz/ *adj* rough

**raphia** /ʀafja/ *nm* raffia

**rapide** /ʀapid/ 1 *adj* quick, rapid; fast
2 *nm* (a) rapids; **descendre un ~** to shoot
the rapids
**(b)** (train) express

**rapidement** /ʀapidmɑ̃/ *adv* quickly; fast

**rapidité** /ʀapidite/ *nf* speed

**rapiécer** /ʀapjese/ [14] *vtr* to patch

**rappel** /ʀapɛl/ *nm* (a) reminder; **~ à l'ordre**
call to order
**(b)** (lettre de) **~** reminder
**(c)** back pay
**(d)** (of ambassador) recall; (of actors) curtain
call
**(e)** (Med) booster

**rappeler** /ʀaple/ [19] 1 *vtr* (a) **~ qch à qn**
to remind sb of sth; **rappelons-le** let's not
forget; **~ qn à l'ordre** to call sb to order
**(b)** to call [sb] back
**(c)** (on phone) to call *or* ring [sb] back
2 **se rappeler** *v refl* (+ *v être*) to
remember

**rappliquer** /ʀaplike/ [1] *vi* (colloq) (a) to
turn up (colloq)
**(b)** to come back

**rapport** /ʀapɔʀ/ 1 *nm* (a) connection, link;
**être sans ~ avec, n'avoir aucun ~ avec** to
have nothing to do with
**(b) ~s** relations; **avoir *or* entretenir de bons
~s avec qn** to be on good terms with sb
**(c) être en ~ avec qn** to be in touch with sb
**(d) sous tous les ~s** in every respect
**(e)** report
**(f)** return, yield; **immeuble de ~** block of
flats (GB) *or* apartment block (US) that is
rented out
**(g)** ratio; **bon ~ qualité prix** good value for
money
2 **par rapport à** *phr* (a) compared with;
**par ~ au dollar** against the dollar
**(b) le nombre de voitures par ~ au nombre
d'habitants** the number of cars per head of
the population
**(c)** with regard to, toward(s); **l'attitude de la
population par ~ à l'immigration** people's
attitudes to immigration
■ **~ de force** power struggle; **~s sexuels**
sexual relations

**rapporter** /ʀapɔʀte/ [1] 1 *vtr* (a) to bring
back; to take back

(b) to bring in ⟨income⟩; ∼ **10%** to yield or return 10%

(c) to report; **on m'a rapporté que** I was told that

**2** vi (a) to bring in money

(b) (colloq) to tell tales

**3 se rapporter** v refl (+ v être) **se ∼ à** to relate to, to bear a relation to

**rapproché, ∼e** /RapRɔʃe/ **1** pp ▶ RAPPROCHER

**2** pp adj close together

**rapprochement** /RapRɔʃmã/ nm

(a) rapprochement

(b) connection

**rapprocher** /RapRɔʃe/ [1] **1** vtr (a) to move [sth] closer

(b) to bring [sth] forward(s) ⟨date⟩

(c) to bring [sb] (closer) together ⟨people⟩

(d) to compare

**2 se rapprocher** v refl (+ v être) to get closer, to get nearer; **leurs peintures se rapprochent des fresques antiques** their paintings are similar to classical frescoes

**rapt** /Rapt/ nm kidnapping (GB), abduction

**raquette** /Rakɛt/ nf (a) (for tennis) racket; (for table-tennis) bat (GB), paddle (US)

(b) snowshoe

**rare** /RɑR/ adj (a) (not common) (gen) rare; ⟨job⟩ unusual; ⟨intelligence⟩ exceptional; **il est ∼ qu'il vienne en train** it's unusual for him to come by train

(b) (not numerous) few, rare; ⟨visits⟩ infrequent; (not abundant) (gen) scarce; ⟨hair⟩ thin; ⟨vegetation⟩ sparse; **se faire ∼** ⟨product⟩ to become scarce; **vous vous faites ∼ ces temps-ci** you are not around much these days

**raréfier** /RaRefje/ [2] **1** vtr (a) to rarefy ⟨air, gas⟩

(b) to make [sth] rare

**2 se raréfier** v refl (+ v être) ⟨air⟩ to become thinner; ⟨gas⟩ to rarefy; ⟨food, money⟩ to become scarce; ⟨species⟩ to become rare

**rarement** /RaRmã/ adv rarely, seldom

**rareté** /RɑRte/ nf shortage, scarcity; rarity

**rarissime** /RaRisim/ adj extremely rare

**ras, ∼e** /Rɑ, Rɑz/ **1** adj ⟨hair⟩ close-cropped; ⟨fur⟩ short; **à poil ∼** ⟨animal⟩ short-haired; ⟨carpet⟩ short-piled; **en ∼e campagne** in (the) open country; **une cuillère à café ∼e** a level teaspoonful; **à ∼ bord** to the brim

**2** adv short; **couper (à) ∼** to cut [sth] very short ⟨hair, lawn⟩

**3 au ras de** phr **au ∼ du sol** at ground level

IDIOMS **faire table ∼e de** to make a clean sweep of

**RAS** /ɛRɑɛs/ (abbr = **rien à signaler**) nothing to report

**rasade** /Razad/ nf (a) glassful

(b) swig (colloq)

**rasage** /Razaʒ/ nm (a) (action) shaving

(b) (result) shave

**ras-de-cou** /Radku/ nm inv (a) crew-neck sweater

(b) choker

**rase-mottes** /Razmɔt/ nm inv **faire du ∼, voler en ∼** to fly low

**raser** /Raze/ [1] **1** vtr (a) to shave; to shave off; **∼ de près** to give [sb] a close shave

(b) to demolish; to raze [sth] to the ground

(c) ⟨bullet⟩ to graze; ⟨plane, bird⟩ to skim

**2 se raser** v refl (+ v être) to shave

IDIOMS **∼ les murs** to hug the walls

**ras-le-bol** /Ralbɔl/ nm inv (colloq) discontent

**rasoir** /RazwaR/ **1** adj inv (colloq) boring

**2** nm **∼ mécanique** razor; **∼ électrique** electric shaver

**rassasier** /Rasazje/ [2] **1** vtr ⟨food⟩ to fill [sb] up

**2 se rassasier** v refl (+ v être) to eat one's fill

**rassemblement** /Rasãbləmã/ nm

(a) rally

(b) gathering

(c) meeting

**rassembler** /Rasãble/ [1] **1** vtr to gather [sb/sth] together ⟨people⟩; to round up ⟨sheep, herd⟩; to unite ⟨citizens, nation⟩; to gather ⟨information, proof⟩; **∼ ses forces** to summon up one's strength

**2 se rassembler** v refl (+ v être) (a) to gather

(b) to assemble

**rasseoir: se rasseoir** /RaswaR/ [41] v refl (+ v être) to sit down (again)

**rasséréner** /RaseRene/ [14] vtr to calm [sb] down ⟨person⟩

**rassis, ∼e** /Rasi, iz/ adj ⟨bread⟩ stale

**rassurant, ∼e** /Rasyrã, ãt/ adj reassuring

**rassurer** /RasyRe/ [1] **1** vtr to reassure

**2 se rassurer** v refl (+ v être) to reassure oneself; **rassure-toi** don't worry; **je suis rassuré** I'm relieved

**rat** /Ra/ nm (a) rat

(b) skinflint, cheapskate (colloq)

**ratatiner: se ratatiner** /Ratatine/ [1] vpr (a) ⟨fruit⟩ to shrivel

(b) ⟨face, person⟩ to become wizened

**ratatouille** /Ratatuj/ nf ratatouille

**rate** /Rat/ nf (a) (Zool) female rat

(b) (Anat) spleen

**raté, ∼e** /Rate/ **1** pp ▶ RATER

**2** pp adj (a) ⟨actor, painter⟩ failed; **une vie ∼e** a wasted life

(b) ⟨opportunity⟩ missed

**3** nm,f (person) failure

**4 ratés** nm pl (in negotiations, system) hiccups

**râteau**, pl **∼x** /Rɑto/ nm rake

**râtelier** /Rɑtəlje/ nm hayrack

IDIOMS **manger à tous les ∼s** to run with the hare and hunt with the hounds

**rater** /ʀate/ [1] **1** *vtr* (a) to fail ‹*exam*›; to spoil ‹*sauce*›; **elle a raté son coup** (colloq) she has failed
(b) to miss ‹*train, target*›
**2** *vi* ‹*plan*› to fail; **il dit toujours des bêtises, ça ne rate jamais** (colloq) he can always be relied upon to say something stupid

**ratifier** /ʀatifje/ [2] *vtr* (a) to ratify ‹*treaty, contract*›
(b) to confirm ‹*plan, proposal*›

**ration** /ʀasjɔ̃/ *nf* (a) ration
(b) share

**rationaliser** /ʀasjɔnalize/ [1] *vtr* to rationalize

**rationnel, -elle** /ʀasjɔnɛl/ *adj* rational

**rationnement** /ʀasjɔnmɑ̃/ *nm* rationing

**rationner** /ʀasjɔne/ [1] **1** *vtr* to ration ‹*petrol*›; to impose rationing on ‹*population*›
**2 se rationner** *v refl* (+ *v être*) to cut down

**ratisser** /ʀatise/ [1] *vtr* (a) to rake over; to rake up
(b) to comb ‹*area*›

**raton** /ʀatɔ̃/ *nm* young rat
■ ~ **laveur** racoon

**rattachement** /ʀataʃmɑ̃/ *nm* (a) (of country) unification
(b) (of person) **demander son** ~ **à** to ask to be posted to

**rattacher** /ʀataʃe/ [1] *vtr* (a) to attach ‹*region*›; to post ‹*employee*›
(b) to retie; to fasten [sth] again
(c) **plus rien ne la rattache à Lyon** she no longer has any ties with Lyons

**rattrapage** /ʀatʀapaʒ/ *nm* (a) (Econ) adjustment
(b) catching up; **cours de** ~ remedial lesson

**rattraper** /ʀatʀape/ [1] **1** *vtr* (a) to catch up with ‹*competitor*›
(b) to catch ‹*fugitive*›
(c) to make up for ‹*lost time, deficit*›; to make up ‹*points, distance*›; ~ **son retard** to catch up
(d) to put right ‹*error*›; to smooth over ‹*blunder*›; to save ‹*situation*›
(e) to catch ‹*object*›
**2 se rattraper** *v refl* (+ *v être*) (a) to redeem oneself
(b) to make up for it
(c) (Sch) to catch up
(d) to make up one's losses
(e) **se** ~ **de justesse** to stop oneself just in time; **se** ~ **à une branche** to save oneself by catching hold of a branch

**rature** /ʀatyʀ/ *nf* crossing-out; deletion

**raturer** /ʀatyʀe/ [1] *vtr* to cross out

**rauque** /ʀok/ *adj* (a) husky
(b) hoarse

**ravage** /ʀavaʒ/ *nm* **les** ~**s de la guerre** the ravages of war; **faire des** ~**s** to wreak havoc; ‹*epidemic*› to take a terrible toll; **tu vas faire des** ~**s avec ta mini-jupe** (humorous) you'll knock them dead in that mini-skirt

**ravagé, ~e** /ʀavaʒe/ *adj* (colloq) crazy

**ravager** /ʀavaʒe/ [13] *vtr* (a) ‹*fire, war*› to devastate, to ravage
(b) ‹*disease*› to ravage ‹*face*›; ‹*grief*› to tear [sb] apart

**ravalement** /ʀavalmɑ̃/ *nm* (a) cleaning
(b) refacing
(c) (figurative) facelift

**ravaler** /ʀavale/ [1] *vtr* (a) to clean; to reface; to renovate ‹*building*›
(b) to revamp ‹*image*›
(c) to suppress ‹*anger*›; ~ **ses larmes** to hold back one's tears

**ravier** /ʀavje/ *nm* small dish (*for hors-d'œuvre*)

**ravigoter** /ʀavigɔte/ [1] *vtr* (colloq) ‹*fresh air*› to invigorate; ‹*drink*› to perk [sb] up

**ravin** /ʀavɛ̃/ *nm* ravine

**ravir** /ʀaviʀ/ [3] *vtr* (a) to delight; **ça te va à** ~ it really suits you
(b) to steal

**raviser: se raviser** /ʀavize/ [1] *v refl* (+ *v être*) to change one's mind

**ravissant, ~e** /ʀavisɑ̃, ɑ̃t/ *adj* beautiful

**ravisseur, -euse** /ʀavisœʀ, øz/ *nm,f* kidnapper (GB), abductor

**ravitaillement** /ʀavitajmɑ̃/ *nm* supplies

**ravitailler** /ʀavitaje/ [1] **1** *vtr* (a) to provide [sb] with fresh supplies ‹*town*›
(b) to refuel
**2 se ravitailler** *v refl* (+ *v être*) to obtain fresh supplies

**raviver** /ʀavive/ [1] *vtr* to rekindle; to revive

**rayé, ~e** /ʀeje/ **1** *pp* ▶ RAYER
**2** *pp adj* (a) ‹*fabric*› striped
(b) ‹*record*› scratched

**rayer** /ʀeje/ [21] *vtr* (a) to cross [sth] out; '~ **la mention inutile**' 'delete whichever does not apply'
(b) **la ville a été rayée de la carte** the town was wiped off the map
(c) to scratch

**rayon** /ʀejɔ̃/ *nm* (a) radius; **dans un** ~ **de 10 km** within a 10 km radius; ~ **d'action** range; (figurative) sphere of activity
(b) ray; beam; **les** ~**s X** X-rays; **être soigné aux** ~**s** to undergo radiation treatment
(c) (of wheel) spoke
(d) shelf; ~ **de bibliothèque** (book)shelf
(e) (in big store) department; (in small shop) section; **tous nos modèles sont en** ~ all our styles are on display
(f) (colloq) **c'est mon** ~ that's my department (colloq); **il en connaît un** ~ **à ce sujet** he knows a lot about it

**rayonnage** /ʀejɔnaʒ/ *nm* shelves

**rayonnant, ~e** /ʀejɔnɑ̃, ɑ̃t/ *adj* radiant

**rayonne** /ʀejɔn/ *nf* rayon

**rayonnement** /ʀejɔnmɑ̃/ *nm* (a) radiation
(b) radiance
(c) (of country) influence

**rayonner** /ʀejɔne/ [1] *vi* (a) ‹*light, heat*› to radiate
(b) ‹*star*› to shine

**(c)** ⟨*person*⟩ to glow
**(d)** ⟨*city*⟩ to exert its influence
**(e)** ⟨*soldiers*⟩ to patrol; ⟨*tourists*⟩ to tour around
**(f)** ⟨*streets*⟩ to radiate
**rayure** /ʀɛjyʀ/ *nf* **(a)** stripe
**(b)** scratch
**raz-de-marée** /ʀadmaʀe/ *nm inv* tidal wave
**razzia** /ʀazja/ *nf* raid
**ré** /ʀe/ *nm inv* (note) D; (in sol-fa) re
**réabonner** /ʀeabɔne/ [1] *vtr* ∼ qn to renew sb's subscription (à to)
**réaccoutumer** /ʀeakutyme/ [1] *vtr* ∼ qn à qch to get sb used to sth again
**réacheminer** /ʀeaʃ(ə)mine/ *vt* to redirect
**réacteur** /ʀeaktœʀ/ *nm* **(a)** ∼ (nucléaire) (nuclear) reactor
**(b)** jet engine
**réaction** /ʀeaksjɔ̃/ *nf* **(a)** reaction; response
**(b)** avion à ∼ jet aircraft
**réactionnaire** /ʀeaksjɔnɛʀ/ *adj, nmf* reactionary
**réactualiser** /ʀeaktɥalize/ [1] *vtr* (gen) to update; to relaunch ⟨*debate*⟩
**réadapter: se réadapter** /ʀeadapte/ [1] *v refl* to readjust (à qch to sth)
**réaffirmer** /ʀeafiʀme/ [1] *vtr* to reaffirm, to reassert
**réagir** /ʀeaʒiʀ/ [3] *vi* to react; to respond
**réalisable** /ʀealizabl/ *adj* feasible; workable
**réalisateur, -trice** /ʀealizatœʀ, tʀis/ *nm,f* director
**réalisation** /ʀealizasjɔ̃/ *nf* **(a)** (of dream) fulfilment (GB)
**(b)** (of study) carrying out
**(c)** achievement
**(d)** (of film) production
**réaliser** /ʀealize/ [1] **1** *vtr* **(a)** to fulfil (GB) ⟨*ambition*⟩; to achieve ⟨*ideal, feat*⟩
**(b)** to make ⟨*model*⟩; to carry out ⟨*survey, study*⟩
**(c)** to direct ⟨*film*⟩
**(d)** to realize
**2 se réaliser** *v refl* (+ *v être*) **(a)** ⟨*dream*⟩ to come true; ⟨*predictions*⟩ to be fulfilled
**(b)** se ∼ (dans qch) to find fulfilment (GB) (in sth)
**réalisme** /ʀealism/ *nm* realism
**réaliste** /ʀealist/ *adj* (gen) realistic; (in art) realist
**réalité** /ʀealite/ *nf* la ∼ reality; en ∼ in reality; tenir compte des ∼s to take the facts into consideration
**réanimation** /ʀeanimasjɔ̃/ *nf* **(a)** (service de) ∼ intensive care (unit)
**(b)** resuscitation
**réapparaître** /ʀeapaʀɛtʀ/ [73] *vi* ⟨*sun*⟩ to come out again; ⟨*illness*⟩ to recur
**réapprovisionner** /ʀeapʀɔvizjɔne/ [1] *vtr* to restock ⟨*shop*⟩
**réarmer** /ʀeaʀme/ [1] *vtr* **(a)** to rearm

**(b)** to reload ⟨*gun*⟩
**réassortir** /ʀeasɔʀtiʀ/ [3] *vtr* to replenish
**rébarbatif, -ive** /ʀebaʀbatif, iv/ *adj* off-putting; forbidding
**rebâtir** /ʀ(ə)batiʀ/ [3] *vtr* to rebuild
**rebattre** /ʀ(ə)batʀ/ [61] *vtr* ∼ les oreilles de qn avec une histoire to go on (and on) about something
**rebattu, ∼e** /ʀ(ə)baty/ **1** *pp* ▶ REBATTRE
**2** *pp adj* ⟨*joke, story*⟩ hackneyed
**rebelle** /ʀəbɛl/ **1** *adj* **(a)** rebel
**(b)** rebellious
**(c)** ⟨*curl, lock of hair*⟩ stray; ⟨*stain*⟩ stubborn
**2** *nmf* rebel
**rebeller: se rebeller** /ʀəbɛle/ [1] *v refl* (+ *v être*) to rebel
**rébellion** /ʀebɛljɔ̃/ *nf* rebellion
**rebiffer: se rebiffer** /ʀ(ə)bife/ [1] *vpr* (colloq) to rebel
**rebiquer** /ʀ(ə)bike/ [1] *vi* (colloq) to stick up
**reboiser** /ʀ(ə)bwaze/ [1] *vtr* to reafforest
**rebond** /ʀ(ə)bɔ̃/ *nm* **(a)** bounce
**(b)** recovery
**rebondi, ∼e** /ʀ(ə)bɔ̃di/ *adj* **(a)** ⟨*shape*⟩ round, rounded; ⟨*cheek*⟩ chubby; ⟨*stomach*⟩ fat; ⟨*buttocks*⟩ rounded
**(b)** (figurative) ⟨*wallet*⟩ bulging
**rebondir** /ʀ(ə)bɔ̃diʀ/ [3] *vi* **(a)** to bounce
**(b)** to start up again; to take a new turn
**rebondissement** /ʀ(ə)bɔ̃dismɑ̃/ *nm* (of controversy) sudden revival; (in trial) new development
**rebord** /ʀ(ə)bɔʀ/ *nm* **(a)** ledge; ∼ de fenêtre windowsill
**(b)** rim
**(c)** edge
**rebours: à rebours** /ʀ(ə)buʀ/ *phr* ⟨*count, walk*⟩ backward(s)
**rebouteux, -euse** /ʀ(ə)butø, øz/ *nm,f* (colloq) bonesetter
**rebrousse-poil: à rebrousse-poil** /aʀ(ə)bʀuspwal/ *phr* the wrong way
**rebrousser** /ʀ(ə)bʀuse/ [1] *vtr* ∼ chemin to turn back
**rébus** /ʀebys/ *nm inv* rebus
**rebut** /ʀ(ə)by/ *nm* rubbish; mettre qch au ∼ to throw sth on the scrapheap
**rebuter** /ʀ(ə)byte/ [1] *vtr* **(a)** to disgust; to repel
**(b)** to put [sb] off
**récalcitrant, ∼e** /ʀekalsitʀɑ̃, ɑ̃t/ *adj* recalcitrant
**recaler** /ʀ(ə)kale/ [1] *vtr* (colloq) to fail ⟨*candidate*⟩
**récapitulatif** /ʀekapitylatif/ *nm* summary of the main points
**récapituler** /ʀekapityle/ [1] *vtr* to sum up
**receler** /ʀəs(ə)le, ʀsəle/ [17] *vtr* **(a)** ∼ des marchandises to possess stolen goods
**(b)** to contain
**receleur, -euse** /ʀ(ə)s(ə)lœʀ, ʀsəlœʀ, øz/ *nm,f* possessor of stolen goods

r

**récemment** /ʀesamã/ *adv* recently

**recensement** /ʀ(ə)sãsmã/ *nm* **(a)** census **(b)** inventory

**recenser** /ʀ(ə)sãse/ [1] *vtr* **(a)** to take a census of ⟨*population*⟩ **(b)** to list ⟨*objects*⟩

**récent, ~e** /ʀesã, ãt/ *adj* recent; ⟨*house*⟩ new

**recentrer** /ʀəsãtʀe/ [1] *vtr*, **se recentrer** *v refl* (+ *v être*) to refocus

**récépissé** /ʀesepise/ *nm* receipt

**réceptacle** /ʀeseptakl/ *nm* container; **~ à verre** bottle bank

**récepteur** /ʀeseptœʀ/ *nm* receiver

**réceptif, -ive** /ʀeseptif, iv/ *adj* receptive

**réception** /ʀesɛpsjɔ̃/ *nf* **(a)** reception **(b)** welcome **(c) s'occuper de la ~ des marchandises** to take delivery of the goods

**réceptionner** /ʀesɛpsjɔne/ [1] *vtr* **(a)** to take delivery of ⟨*goods*⟩ **(b)** to catch ⟨*ball*⟩

**réceptionniste** /ʀesɛpsjɔnist/ *nmf* receptionist

**récession** /ʀesesjɔ̃/ *nf* recession

**recette** /ʀ(ə)sɛt/ *nf* **(a) ~ (de cuisine)** recipe **(b)** formula, recipe **(c)** takings; **faire ~** to bring in money; (figurative) to be a success; **les ~s et (les) dépenses** receipts and expenses

**receveur, -euse** /ʀəs(ə)vœʀ, øz/ *nm,f* (on bus) conductor ■ **~ des postes** postmaster

**recevoir** /ʀəsvwaʀ, ʀ(ə)səvwaʀ/ [5] *vtr* **(a)** to receive, to get; **il a reçu une tuile sur la tête** he got hit on the head by a tile; **je n'ai d'ordre à ~ de personne** I don't take orders from anyone **(b)** to welcome ⟨*guests*⟩; **être bien reçu** to be well received; to get a good reception; **ils reçoivent beaucoup** they do a lot of entertaining; **Laval reçoit Caen** (Sport) Laval is playing host to Caen **(c)** to see ⟨*patients*⟩ **(d)** to receive ⟨*radio signal*⟩ **(e)** (Sch) to pass ⟨*candidate*⟩; **être reçu à un examen** to pass an exam

**rechange: de rechange** /dəʀ(ə)ʃãʒ/ *phr* ⟨*part*⟩ spare; ⟨*solution*⟩ alternative

**réchapper** /ʀeʃape/ [1] *v+prep* **~ de** to come through ⟨*illness, accident*⟩

**recharge** /ʀ(ə)ʃaʀʒ/ *nf* refill; reload

**rechargeable** /ʀ(ə)ʃaʀʒabl/ *adj* ⟨*lighter, pen*⟩ refillable; ⟨*battery, appliance*⟩ rechargeable

**recharger** /ʀ(ə)ʃaʀʒe/ [13] *vtr* to reload; to refill; to recharge ⟨*battery*⟩

**réchaud** /ʀeʃo/ *nm* stove; **~ électrique** electric ring (GB), hotplate

**réchauffé, ~e** /ʀeʃofe/ ① *pp* ▶ RÉCHAUFFER
② *pp adj* ⟨*joke, story*⟩ hackneyed

**③** *nm* **c'est du ~** there's nothing new about it

**réchauffement** /ʀeʃofmã/ *nm* warming (up); **le ~ de la planète** global warming

**réchauffer** /ʀeʃofe/ [1] ① *vtr* **(a)** (Culin) to reheat, to heat [sth] up **(b)** to warm up ⟨*person, hands, room*⟩
② **se réchauffer** *v refl* (+ *v être*) to warm up

**rêche** /ʀɛʃ/ *adj* ⟨*hands, fabric*⟩ rough

**recherche** /ʀ(ə)ʃɛʀʃ/ *nf* **(a)** research **(b)** search; **être à la ~ de** to be looking for **(c) ~ de** pursuit of ⟨*happiness*⟩ **(d) sans ~** without affectation ■ **~ d'emploi** job-hunting

**recherché, ~e** /ʀ(ə)ʃɛʀʃe/ ① *pp* ▶ RECHERCHER
② *pp adj* **(a)** sought-after **(b)** in demand **(c)** ⟨*dress*⟩ meticulous; ⟨*style*⟩ original **(d)** ⟨*aim*⟩ intended

**rechercher** /ʀ(ə)ʃɛʀʃe/ [1] *vtr* **(a)** to look for; **il est recherché par la police** he's wanted by the police; **'recherchons vendeuse qualifiée'** 'qualified sales assistant (GB) or clerk (US) required' **(b)** to seek ⟨*security*⟩; to fish for ⟨*compliments*⟩

**rechigner** /ʀ(ə)ʃiɲe/ [1] ① *v+prep* **~ à faire** to balk at doing
② *vi* to grumble

**rechute** /ʀəʃyt/ *nf* relapse

**rechuter** /ʀ(ə)ʃyte/ [1] *vi* **(a)** (Med) to have a relapse **(b)** (Econ) ⟨*price, currency*⟩ to fall again

**récidive** /ʀesidiv/ *nf* **(a)** (Law) second offence (GB) **(b)** (figurative) repetition **(c)** (Med) recurrence

**récidiver** /ʀesidive/ [1] *vi* (Law) to reoffend

**récidiviste** /ʀesidivist/ *nmf* second offender, recidivist; habitual offender

**récif** /ʀesif/ *nm* reef

**récipient** /ʀesipjã/ *nm* container

**réciprocité** /ʀesipʀɔsite/ *nf* reciprocity

**réciproque** /ʀesipʀɔk/ ① *adj* reciprocal
② *nf* reverse; **la ~ est vraie** the reverse is true

**réciproquement** /ʀesipʀɔkmã/ *adv* **et ~** and vice versa

**récit** /ʀesi/ *nm* **(a)** story **(b)** narrative

**récital** /ʀesital/ *nm* recital

**récitation** /ʀesitasjɔ̃/ *nf* **apprendre une ~** to learn a text (off) by heart

**réciter** /ʀesite/ [1] *vtr* to recite

**réclamation** /ʀeklamasjɔ̃/ *nf* **(a)** complaint **(b)** claim; **sur ~** on request

**réclame** /ʀeklam/ *nf* **(a)** publicity **(b)** advertisement **(c) 'en ~'** 'on offer' (GB), 'on sale'

**réclamer** /ʀeklame/ [1] ① *vtr* to ask for ⟨*person, thing, money*⟩; to call for ⟨*reform,*

*inquiry*⟩; to claim ⟨*compensation*⟩; **travail qui réclame de l'attention** work that requires attention
2 **se réclamer** *v refl* (+ *v être*) **se ~ de** ⟨*person, group*⟩ to claim to be representative of

**reclasser** /Rəklase/ [1] *vtr* **(a)** to reclassify ⟨*documents*⟩
**(b)** to redeploy

**reclus, ~e** /Rəkly, yz/ *adj* reclusive; **vivre ~ to** live as a recluse

**réclusion** /Reklyzjɔ̃/ *nf* **(a)** (Law) imprisonment
**(b)** reclusion

**recoin** /Rəkwɛ̃/ *nm* corner; (figurative) recess

**récolte** /Rekɔlt/ *nf* harvest; crop

**récolter** /Rekɔlte/ [1] *vtr* **(a)** to harvest ⟨*corn*⟩; to dig up ⟨*potatoes*⟩
**(b)** ⟨*bee*⟩ to collect ⟨*pollen*⟩; ⟨*person*⟩ to win ⟨*points*⟩; to collect ⟨*information*⟩

**recommandable** /Rəkɔmɑ̃dabl/ *adj* **un individu peu ~** a disreputable individual

**recommandation** /Rəkɔmɑ̃dasjɔ̃/ *nf* recommendation

**recommandé, ~e** /Rəkɔmɑ̃de/ 1 *pp* ▸
RECOMMANDER
2 *pp adj* ⟨*letter*⟩ registered

**recommander** /Rəkɔmɑ̃de/ [1] 1 *vtr*
**(a)** to advise
**(b)** to recommend
2 **se recommander** *v refl* (+ *v être*) **se ~ de qn** to give sb's name as a reference

**recommencement** /Rəkɔmɑ̃smɑ̃/ *nm* **l'histoire est un éternel ~** history is constantly repeating itself

**recommencer** /Rəkɔmɑ̃se/ [12] *vtr* **(a)** to start [sth] again
**(b)** to do [sth] again

**récompense** /Rekɔ̃pɑ̃s/ *nf* **(a)** reward
**(b)** award

**récompenser** /Rekɔ̃pɑ̃se/ [1] *vtr* to reward

**réconciliation** /Rekɔ̃siljasjɔ̃/ *nf* reconciliation

**réconcilier** /Rekɔ̃silje/ [2] 1 *vtr* **~ Pierre avec Paul** to bring Pierre and Paul back together; **~ morale et politique** to reconcile morality with politics
2 **se réconcilier** *v refl* (+ *v être*) ⟨*friends*⟩ to make up; ⟨*nations*⟩ to be reconciled

**reconduction** /R(ə)kɔ̃dyksjɔ̃/ *nf* renewal

**reconduire** /R(ə)kɔ̃dɥiR/ [69] *vtr* **(a)** to see [sb] out; **~ qn chez lui** to take sb home
**(b)** to extend ⟨*strike, ceasefire*⟩; to renew ⟨*mandate*⟩

**réconfort** /Rekɔ̃fɔR/ *nm* comfort

**réconfortant, ~e** /Rekɔ̃fɔRtɑ̃, ɑ̃t/ *adj*
**(a)** comforting
**(b)** cheering
**(c)** fortifying

**réconforter** /Rekɔ̃fɔRte/ [1] *vtr* **(a)** to comfort; to console
**(b) ~ qn** to cheer sb up

**(c)** to fortify

**reconnaissance** /R(ə)kɔnɛsɑ̃s/ *nf*
**(a)** gratitude; **en ~ de** in appreciation of
**(b)** recognition
**(c)** (of wrongs) admission, admitting; (of qualities) recognition, recognizing
**(d)** (Mil) reconnaissance

**reconnaissant, ~e** /R(ə)kɔnɛsɑ̃, ɑ̃t/ *adj* grateful

**reconnaître** /R(ə)kɔnɛtR/ [73] 1 *vtr* **(a)** to recognize ⟨*person*⟩
**(b)** to identify; **je reconnais bien là leur générosité** it's just like them to be so generous
**(c)** to admit ⟨*facts, errors*⟩
**(d)** to recognize ⟨*trade union, regime*⟩; **~ un enfant** to recognize a child legally
**(e)** to acknowledge
2 **se reconnaître** *v refl* (+ *v être*) **se ~ à qch** to be recognizable by sth

**reconnu, ~e** /R(ə)kɔny/ 1 *pp* ▸
RECONNAÎTRE
2 *pp adj* ⟨*fact*⟩ recognized

**reconquérir** /R(ə)kɔ̃keRiR/ [35] *vtr* to reconquer, to recover ⟨*territory*⟩; (figurative) to regain ⟨*esteem*⟩; to win back ⟨*person, right*⟩

**reconstituer** /R(ə)kɔ̃stitɥe/ [1] *vtr* to re-form ⟨*association*⟩; to reconstruct ⟨*crime*⟩; to recreate ⟨*era, decor*⟩; to piece [sth] together again ⟨*broken object*⟩; to build up again ⟨*reserves*⟩

**reconstitution** /R(ə)kɔ̃stitysjɔ̃/ *nf* (of crime, event) reconstruction

**reconstruire** /R(ə)kɔ̃stRɥiR/ [69] *vtr* **(a)** to reconstruct
**(b)** to rebuild

**reconversion** /R(ə)kɔ̃vɛRsjɔ̃/ *nf* (of worker) redeployment; (of region) redevelopment; (of economy) restructuring; (of factory) conversion

**reconvertir** /R(ə)kɔ̃vɛRtiR/ [3] 1 *vtr* to redeploy ⟨*staff*⟩; to convert ⟨*factory*⟩; to adapt ⟨*equipment*⟩
2 **se reconvertir** *v refl* (+ *v être*) ⟨*staff*⟩ to switch to a new type of employment; ⟨*company*⟩ to switch to a new type of production

**recopier** /R(ə)kɔpje/ [2] *vtr* **(a)** to copy out
**(b)** to write up ⟨*notes*⟩

**record** /R(ə)kɔR/ 1 *adj inv* record
2 *nm* (Sport, figurative) record

**recoudre** /R(ə)kudR/ [76] *vtr* **(a)** to sew [sth] back on ⟨*button*⟩
**(b)** (Med) to stitch up ⟨*wound*⟩

**recoupement** /R(ə)kupmɑ̃/ *nm* cross-check

**recouper** /R(ə)kupe/ [1] 1 *vtr* to cut [sth] again ⟨*hair, hedge*⟩; to recut ⟨*garment*⟩
2 **se recouper** *v refl* (+ *v être*)
**(a)** ⟨*versions*⟩ to tally; ⟨*results*⟩ to add up
**(b)** ⟨*lines*⟩ to intersect

**recourbé, ~e** /R(ə)kuRbe/ *adj* (gen) curved; ⟨*nose, beak*⟩ hooked

**recourir** /R(ə)kuRiR/ [26] *v+prep* **~ à** to use ⟨*remedy*⟩; to resort to ⟨*strategy*⟩

r

**recours** /ʀ(ə)kuʀ/ *nm inv* **(a)** recourse; resort; **sans autre ∼ que** with no other way out but; **avoir ∼ à** to have recourse to ⟨*remedy*⟩; to resort to ⟨*strategy*⟩; to go to ⟨*expert*⟩
**(b)** (Law) appeal

**recouvrement** /ʀ(ə)kuvʀəmã/ *nm* (of tax, contributions) collection; (of sum, debt) recovery

**recouvrer** /ʀ(ə)kuvʀe/ [1] *vtr* to recover; to collect ⟨*tax*⟩

**recouvrir** /ʀ(ə)kuvʀiʀ/ [32] *vtr* **(a)** to cover
**(b)** to re-cover
**(c)** to hide, to conceal

**recracher** /ʀ(ə)kʀaʃe/ [1] *vtr* to spit out

**récréation** /ʀekʀeasjɔ̃/ *nf* **(a)** playtime (GB), break (GB), recess (US)
**(b)** recreation

**recréer** /ʀ(ə)kʀee/ [11] *vtr* to recreate

**récrier**: **se récrier** /ʀekʀije/ [2] *v refl* (+ *v être*) to exclaim

**récrimination** /ʀekʀiminasjɔ̃/ *nf* recrimination

**récriminer** /ʀekʀimine/ [1] *vi* to rail

**recroqueviller**: **se recroqueviller** /ʀ(ə)kʀɔkvije/ [1] *v refl* (+ *v être*) **(a)** ⟨*person*⟩ to huddle up
**(b)** ⟨*leaf, petal*⟩ to shrivel up

**recrudescence** /ʀ(ə)kʀydesãs/ *nf* (of violence, interest) fresh upsurge; (of bombing, demands) new wave; (of fire) renewed outbreak

**recrudescent, ∼e** /ʀ(ə)kʀydesã, ãt/ *adj* **être ∼** to be on the increase

**recrue** /ʀəkʀy/ *nf* recruit

**recrutement** /ʀ(ə)kʀytmã/ *nm* recruitment

**recruter** /ʀ(ə)kʀyte/ [1] *vtr* to recruit

**rectangle** /ʀɛktãgl/ *nm* rectangle

**rectangulaire** /ʀɛktãgylɛʀ/ *adj* rectangular

**recteur** /ʀɛktœʀ/ *nm* (Sch, Univ) chief education officer

**rectificatif, -ive** /ʀɛktifikatif, iv/ *nm* **(a)** (in newspaper) correction
**(b)** (to law) amendment

**rectification** /ʀɛktifikasjɔ̃/ *nf* correction; rectification; adjustment

**rectifier** /ʀɛktifje/ [2] *vtr* to correct, to rectify; to adjust

**rectiligne** /ʀɛktiliɲ/ *adj* straight

**recto** /ʀɛkto/ *nm* front; **∼ verso** on both sides

**rectorat** /ʀɛktɔʀa/ *nm* ≈ local education authority (GB), ≈ board of education (US)

**rectum** /ʀɛktɔm/ *nm* rectum

**reçu, ∼e** /ʀ(ə)sy/ **1** *pp* ▶ RECEVOIR
**2** *pp adj* ⟨*candidate*⟩ successful
**3** *nm* receipt

**recueil** /ʀ(ə)kœj/ *nm* collection; anthology

**recueillement** /ʀəkœjmã/ *nm*
**(a)** contemplation
**(b)** reverence

**recueilli, ∼e** /ʀəkœji/ **1** *pp* ▶ RECUEILLIR

**2** *pp adj* ⟨*air*⟩ rapt; ⟨*person*⟩ rapt in prayer; ⟨*crowd, silence*⟩ reverential

**recueillir** /ʀəkœjiʀ/ [27] **1** *vtr* **(a)** to collect ⟨*donations, anecdotes*⟩; to gather ⟨*evidence, testimonies*⟩
**(b)** to get ⟨*votes, news*⟩; to gain ⟨*consensus*⟩; to win ⟨*praise*⟩
**(c)** to collect ⟨*water, resin*⟩; to gather ⟨*honey*⟩
**(d)** to take in ⟨*orphan*⟩
**(e)** to record ⟨*impressions, opinions*⟩
**2 se recueillir** *v refl* (+ *v être*) to engage in private prayer

**recul** /ʀ(ə)kyl/ *nm* **(a)** detachment; **avec le ∼** with hindsight, in retrospect; **prendre du ∼** to stand back
**(b)** (in production) drop, fall; (of doctrine) decline
**(c)** (of army) pulling back; (of tide, floodwaters) recession; **avoir un mouvement de ∼** to recoil; **feu de ∼** reversing light

**reculé, ∼e** /ʀəkyle/ *adj* remote

**reculer** /ʀ(ə)kyle/ [1] **1** *vtr* **(a)** to move back ⟨*object*⟩
**(b)** (in car) to reverse (GB), to back up
**(c)** to put off ⟨*event, decision*⟩; to put back ⟨*date*⟩
**2** *vi* **(a)** ⟨*person*⟩ to move back; to stand back; ⟨*driver, car*⟩ to reverse
**(b)** ⟨*army*⟩ to pull *or* draw back
**(c)** ⟨*forest*⟩ to be gradually disappearing; ⟨*river*⟩ to go down; ⟨*sea*⟩ to recede
**(d)** ⟨*currency, exports*⟩ to fall; ⟨*doctrine*⟩ to decline; **faire ∼ le chômage** to reduce unemployment
**(e)** to back down; **ne ∼ devant rien** to stop at nothing
**3 se reculer** *v refl* (+ *v être*) (gen) to move back; to stand back

**reculons**: **à reculons** /aʀ(ə)kylɔ̃/ *phr* **aller à ∼** to go backward(s)

**récupérable** /ʀekypeʀabl/ *adj*
**(a)** ⟨*material*⟩ reusable
**(b)** ⟨*object*⟩ which can be made good again
**(c)** ⟨*delinquent*⟩ who can be rehabilitated

**récupération** /ʀekypeʀasjɔ̃/ *nf*
**(a)** salvage; recycling
**(b)** recovery
**(c)** appropriation

**récupérer** /ʀekypeʀe/ [14] **1** *vtr* **(a)** to get back ⟨*money, strength*⟩
**(b)** to retrieve
**(c)** to salvage ⟨*scrap iron*⟩; to reclaim ⟨*rags*⟩
**(d)** to save ⟨*boxes*⟩
**(e)** to make up ⟨*days*⟩
**(f)** to appropriate ⟨*ideas*⟩
**2** *vi* to recover

**récurer** /ʀekyʀe/ [1] *vtr* to scour; to scrub

**récurrent, ∼e** /ʀekyʀã, ãt/ *adj* recurrent

**récuser** /ʀekyze/ [1] **1** *vtr* to challenge ⟨*jury*⟩
**2 se récuser** *v refl* (+ *v être*) ⟨*judge*⟩ to decline to act in a case

**recyclable** /ʀ(ə)siklabl/ *adj* recyclable

**recyclage** /ʀ(ə)siklaʒ/ *nm* **(a)** recycling
**(b)** retraining

**recycler** /R(ə)sikle/ [1] **1** *vtr* **(a)** to recycle ⟨*material*⟩
**(b)** ∼ **le personnel** to retrain the staff
**2 se recycler** *v refl* (+ *v être*) **(a)** to retrain
**(b)** to change jobs

**rédacteur, -trice** /Redaktœr, tris/ *nm,f*
**(a)** author, writer
**(b)** editor

**rédaction** /Redaksjɔ̃/ *nf* **(a)** writing
**(b)** editing
**(c)** editorial offices
**(d)** editorial staff
**(e)** (Sch) essay (GB), theme (US)

**reddition** /Rɛdisjɔ̃/ *nf* surrender

**rédemption** /Redɑ̃psjɔ̃/ *nf* redemption

**redescendre** /Rədɛsɑ̃dR/ [6] **1** *vtr* (gen) to take [sb/sth] back down; ⟨*person*⟩ to go/come back down ⟨*stairs*⟩
**2** *vi* (+ *v être*) to go (back) down; to go down again

**redevable** /Rədvabl, R(ə)dəvabl/ *adj* **être** ∼ **de qch à qn** to owe sth to sb; **être** ∼ **de l'impôt** to be liable for tax

**redevance** /Rədvɑ̃s, R(ə)dəvɑ̃s/ *nf* **(a)** (gen) charge; (for television) licence (GB) *or* license (US) fee; (for telephone) rental charge
**(b)** royalty

**rédhibitoire** /RedibitwaR/ *adj* ⟨*cost*⟩ prohibitive; ⟨*obstacle*⟩ insurmountable

**rediffuser** /R(ə)difyze/ [1] *vtr* to repeat, to rerun ⟨*programme*⟩

**rédiger** /Rediʒe/ [13] *vtr* to write ⟨*article*⟩; to write up ⟨*notes*⟩; to draft ⟨*contract*⟩

**redingote** /R(ə)dɛ̃gɔt/ *nf* (for man) frock coat; (for woman) fitted coat

**redire** /RədiR/ [65] *vtr* to repeat; **trouver quelque chose à** ∼ **à qch** to find fault with sth

**redite** /R(ə)dit/ *nf* (needless) repetition

**redondance** /R(ə)dɔ̃dɑ̃s/ *nf* redundancy

**redondant, ∼e** /R(ə)dɔ̃dɑ̃, ɑ̃t/ *adj*
**(a)** superfluous
**(b)** redundant

**redonner** /R(ə)dɔne/ [1] *vtr* ∼ **qch à qn** to give sb sth again

**redorer** /R(ə)dɔRe/ [1] *vtr* to regild; ∼ **son blason** ⟨*person*⟩ to restore one's image

**redoublant, ∼e** /R(ə)dublɑ̃, ɑ̃t/ *nm,f* student repeating a year

**redoublement** /R(ə)dubləmɑ̃/ *nm* intensification

**redoubler** /R(ə)duble/ [1] **1** *vtr* (Sch) ∼ **une classe** to repeat a year
**2 redoubler de** *v+prep* ∼ **de prudence** to be twice as careful; **la tempête a redoublé de violence** the storm has become even fiercer
**3** *vi* **(a)** to repeat a year
**(b)** to intensify

**redoutable** /R(ə)dutabl/ *adj* ⟨*weapon, exam*⟩ formidable; ⟨*disease*⟩ dreadful

**redouter** /R(ə)dute/ [1] *vtr* to fear

**redressement** /RədRɛsmɑ̃/ *nm* **maison de** ∼ reformatory

**redresser** /R(ə)dRese/ [1] **1** *vtr* **(a)** to straighten (up); to put [sth] up again; ∼ **la tête** to lift one's head up
**(b)** to put [sth] back on its feet ⟨*economy*⟩; to turn [sth] around ⟨*company*⟩; to aid the recovery of ⟨*currency*⟩
**(c)** to straighten up ⟨*glider, steering wheel*⟩; ∼ **la barre** to right the helm; (figurative) to put things back on an even keel
**(d)** to rectify ⟨*error*⟩
**2 se redresser** *v refl* (+ *v être*) **(a)** to stand up; to sit up; to stand up straight; to sit up straight
**(b)** ⟨*economy, plant*⟩ to recover; ⟨*country*⟩ to get back on its feet

**redresseur** /RədRɛsœR/ *nm* ∼ **de torts** righter of wrongs

**réductible** /Redyktibl/ *adj* ⟨*costs*⟩ which can be reduced *or* cut

**réduction** /Redyksjɔ̃/ *nf* **(a)** discount, reduction; ∼ **étudiants** concession for students
**(b)** cutting, reducing
**(c)** reduction, cut; ∼s **d'effectifs** staff cuts
**(d)** (of statue) small replica

**réduire** /Reduir/ [68] **1** *vtr* **(a)** to reduce; to cut ⟨*tax*⟩; to cut down on ⟨*staff, spending*⟩
**(b)** to reduce ⟨*photograph*⟩; to scale down ⟨*drawing*⟩; to cut ⟨*text*⟩
**(c)** ∼ **qch en poudre** to crush sth to powder; **être réduit en cendres** ⟨*city*⟩ to be reduced to ashes; ⟨*dreams*⟩ to turn to ashes
**(d)** ∼ **à** to reduce to; **voilà à quoi j'en suis réduit!** this is what I've been reduced to!
**(e)** to reduce ⟨*sauce*⟩
**2** *vi* ⟨*sauce*⟩ to reduce; ⟨*spinach*⟩ to shrink
**3 se réduire** *v refl* (+ *v être*) **(a)** ⟨*costs*⟩ to be reduced; ⟨*imports*⟩ to be cut
**(b)** **cela se réduit à bien peu de chose** it doesn't amount to very much

**réduit, ∼e** /Redui, it/ **1** *pp* ▸ RÉDUIRE
**2** *pp adj* **(a)** ⟨*rate, speed*⟩ reduced, lower; ⟨*time*⟩ shorter; ⟨*activity*⟩ reduced; ⟨*group*⟩ smaller; **visibilité** ∼**e** restricted visibility
**(b)** ⟨*means, choice*⟩ limited; ⟨*group*⟩ small
**(c)** ⟨*size*⟩ small
**3** *nm* cubbyhole

**rééditer** /Reedite/ [1] *vtr* to reprint ⟨*book*⟩

**rééducation** /Reedykasjɔ̃/ *nf*
**(a)** physiotherapy; ∼ **de la parole** speech therapy
**(b)** rehabilitation

**rééduquer** /Reedyke/ [1] *vtr* to restore normal functioning to ⟨*limb*⟩; to rehabilitate

**réel, réelle** /Reɛl/ **1** *adj* (gen) real; ⟨*fact*⟩ true
**2** *nm* **le** ∼ the real

**réellement** /Reɛlmɑ̃/ *adv* really

**réembaucher** /Reɑ̃boʃe/ [1] *vtr* to take [sb] on again

**réemployer** /Reɑ̃plwaje/ [23] *vtr* to reinvest ⟨*funds*⟩; to re-employ ⟨*staff*⟩

**rééquilibrer** /ReekilibRe/ [1] *vtr* **(a)** (Aut) to balance ⟨*wheels*⟩
**(b)** to balance ⟨*budget*⟩

r

**réévaluer** /ʀeevalɥe/ [1] *vtr* **(a)** to revalue ⟨*currency*⟩; to revise ⟨*tax*⟩
**(b)** to reappraise

**réexpédier** /ʀeɛkspedje/ [2] *vtr* **(a)** to forward, to redirect
**(b)** to send [sth] back

**réf** (*written abbr* = **référence**) ref

**refaire** /ʀəfɛʀ/ [10] **1** *vtr* **(a)** to do [sth] again ⟨*exercise*⟩; to make [sth] again ⟨*journey, mistake*⟩; ∼ **le même chemin** to go back the same way; ∼ **un numéro de téléphone** to redial a number
**(b)** **je vais** ∼ **de la soupe** I'll make some more soup
**(c)** **vouloir** ∼ **le monde** to want to change the world; **se faire** ∼ **le nez** to have one's nose re-modelled (GB); ∼ **sa vie** to start all over again
**(d)** to redo ⟨*roof*⟩; to redecorate ⟨*room*⟩; to resurface ⟨*road*⟩
**2 se refaire** *v refl* (+ *v être*) **(a) se** ∼ **une santé** to recuperate; **se** ∼ **une beauté** to redo one's make-up
**(b) se** ∼ **à** to get used to [sth] again
**(c) on ne se refait pas** a person can't change

**réfection** /ʀefɛksjɔ̃/ *nf* repairing

**réfectoire** /ʀefɛktwaʀ/ *nm* refectory; (Mil) mess

**référence** /ʀefeʀɑ̃s/ **1** *nf* **(a)** reference; **en** *or* **par** ∼ **à** in reference to; **faire** ∼ **à** to refer to; **lui? ce n'est pas une** ∼! who, him? well, he's not much of an example!
**(b)** reference number
**2 références** *nf pl* references

**référendum** /ʀefeʀɛ̃dɔm/ *nm* referendum

**référer** /ʀefeʀe/ [14] **1 référer à** *v+prep* **en** ∼ **à** to consult
**2 se référer** *v refl* (+ *v être*) **(a) se** ∼ **à** to refer to
**(b) se** ∼ **à** to consult

**refermer** /ʀ(ə)fɛʀme/ [1] **1** *vtr* **(a)** to close
**(b)** to close [sth] again
**2 se refermer** *v refl* (+ *v être*) ⟨*door*⟩ to close; ⟨*wound*⟩ to close up

**réfléchi, ∼e** /ʀefleʃi/ *adj* **(a)** ⟨*person*⟩ reflective, thoughtful
**(b)** ⟨*decision*⟩ considered; ⟨*action*⟩ well-considered; **c'est tout** ∼ my mind is made up
**(c)** ⟨*image*⟩ reflected
**(d)** ⟨*verb*⟩ reflexive

**réfléchir** /ʀefleʃiʀ/ [3] **1** *vtr* to reflect ⟨*heat*⟩
**2 réfléchir à** *v+prep* to think about
**3** *vi* to think; **mais réfléchis donc un peu!** use your brain!
**4 se réfléchir** *v refl* (+ *v être*) to be reflected

**réflecteur** /ʀeflɛktœʀ/ *nm* reflector

**reflet** /ʀ(ə)flɛ/ *nm* **(a)** reflection
**(b)** glint; shimmer; sheen; **cheveux châtains aux** ∼**s roux** brown hair with auburn highlights

**refléter** /ʀ(ə)flete/ [14] **1** *vtr* to reflect; **son visage reflétait son émotion** his/her emotion showed in his/her face

**2 se refléter** *v refl* (+ *v être*) to be reflected

**réflexe** /ʀeflɛks/ **1** *adj* reflex
**2** *nm* **(a)** reflex
**(b)** reaction; **manquer de** ∼ to be slow to react; **par** ∼ automatically
■ ∼ **conditionné** conditioned reflex

**réflexion** /ʀeflɛksjɔ̃/ *nf* **(a)** thought, reflection
**(b)** thinking, reflection; ∼ **faite** *or* **à la** ∼, **je n'irai pas** on second thoughts, I won't go; **donner matière à** ∼ to be food for thought
**(c)** remark, comment; **s'attirer des** ∼**s** to attract criticism
**(d)** study; **document de** ∼ discussion paper
**(e)** (of image) reflection

**refluer** /ʀ(ə)flɥe/ [1] *vi* ⟨*liquid*⟩ to flow back

**reflux** /ʀ(ə)fly/ *nm inv* ebb tide

**refonte** /ʀ(ə)fɔ̃t/ *nf* **(a)** overhaul
**(b)** (of contract) rewriting

**reforestation** /ʀ(ə)fɔʀɛstasjɔ̃/ *nf* reafforestation

**réformateur, -trice** /ʀefɔʀmatœʀ, tʀis/ *nm,f* reformer

**réforme** /ʀefɔʀm/ *nf* **(a)** reform
**(b)** (Mil) discharge
**(c) la Réforme** the Reformation

**réformé, ∼e** /ʀefɔʀme/ *nm,f* Calvinist

**reformer** /ʀ(ə)fɔʀme/ [1] *vtr* to re-form

**réformer** /ʀefɔʀme/ [1] *vtr* **(a)** to reform
**(b)** (Mil) to declare [sb] unfit for service ⟨*conscript*⟩; to discharge ⟨*soldier*⟩

**refoulé, ∼e** /ʀ(ə)fule/ *nm,f* repressed *or* inhibited person

**refoulement** /ʀ(ə)fulmɑ̃/ *nm* **(a)** (of impulse) repression
**(b)** pushing back; turning back; driving back; forcing back

**refouler** /ʀ(ə)fule/ [1] *vtr* **(a)** to suppress ⟨*memory*⟩; to repress ⟨*tendency*⟩; to hold back ⟨*tears*⟩
**(b)** to force [sth] back ⟨*liquid*⟩; to push back ⟨*enemy*⟩; to turn back ⟨*immigrant*⟩

**réfractaire** /ʀefʀaktɛʀ/ *adj* **(a)** ∼ **à** resistant to ⟨*influence*⟩; impervious to ⟨*music*⟩
**(b)** refractory

**réfracter** /ʀefʀakte/ [1] *vtr* to refract

**réfraction** /ʀefʀaksjɔ̃/ *nf* refraction

**refrain** /ʀ(ə)fʀɛ̃/ *nm* **(a)** chorus
**(b)** (old) refrain

**refréner** /ʀ(ə)fʀene/, **réfréner** /ʀefʀene/ [14] *vtr* to curb

**réfrigérant, ∼e** /ʀefʀiʒeʀɑ̃, ɑ̃t/ *adj* cooling

**réfrigérateur** /ʀefʀiʒeʀatœʀ/ *nm* refrigerator

**réfrigérer** /ʀefʀiʒeʀe/ [14] *vtr* to refrigerate ⟨*food*⟩; to cool ⟨*place*⟩

**refroidir** /ʀəfʀwadiʀ/ [3] **1** *vtr* **(a)** to cool down; to cool
**(b)** ∼ **qn** to dampen sb's spirits
**2** *vi* **(a)** to cool down
**(b)** to get cold

**3 se refroidir** *v refl* (+ *v être*) ⟨*weather*⟩ to get colder; ⟨*joint*⟩ to stiffen up; ⟨*person*⟩ to get cold

**refroidissement** /ʀəfʀwadismɑ̃/ *nm*
(a) drop in temperature
(b) cooling
(c) (Med) chill

**refuge** /ʀ(ə)fyʒ/ *nm* (a) refuge
(b) (mountain) refuge
(c) (for animals) sanctuary
(d) traffic island

**réfugié, ~e** /ʀefyʒje/ *nm,f* refugee

**réfugier: se réfugier** /ʀefyʒje/ [2] *v refl* (+ *v être*) to take refuge

**refus** /ʀ(ə)fy/ *nm inv* refusal; **ce n'est pas de ~** (colloq) I wouldn't say no (colloq)
■ **~ de priorité** failure to give way

**refuser** /ʀ(ə)fyze/ [1] **1** *vtr* (a) (gen) to refuse; to turn down ⟨*offer*⟩; **~ de faire** to refuse to do
(b) to reject ⟨*budget, manuscript, racism*⟩; to refuse to accept ⟨*fact*⟩; to turn away ⟨*spectator*⟩
**2 se refuser** *v refl* (+ *v être*) (a) **ça ne se refuse pas** it's too good to pass up (colloq); I wouldn't say no (colloq)
(b) to deny oneself ⟨*pleasure*⟩; **on ne se refuse rien!** (colloq) you're certainly not stinting yourself!
(c) **se ~ à** to refuse to accept ⟨*evidence*⟩; to refuse to adopt ⟨*solution*⟩

**réfuter** /ʀefyte/ [1] *vtr* to refute

**regagner** /ʀ(ə)gaɲe/ [1] *vtr* (a) to get back to ⟨*place*⟩
(b) to regain ⟨*esteem*⟩

**regain** /ʀ(ə)gɛ̃/ *nm* **~ de** rise in ⟨*inflation*⟩; revival of ⟨*interest*⟩; resurgence of ⟨*violence*⟩

**régal** /ʀegal/ *nm* (a) culinary delight; **c'est un ~!** it's delicious!
(b) (figurative) delight; **un ~ pour les yeux** a feast for the eyes

**régalade** /ʀegalad/ *nf* **boire à la ~** *to drink without letting one's lips touch the bottle*

**régaler: se régaler** /ʀegale/ [1] *v refl* (+ *v être*) (a) **je me régale** it's delicious; **les enfants se sont régalés avec ton dessert** the children really enjoyed your dessert
(b) (figurative) **se ~ avec** to enjoy [sth] thoroughly ⟨*film*⟩; **se ~ de** to love ⟨*anecdote*⟩

**regard** /ʀ(ə)gaʀ/ **1** *nm* (a) look; **porter son ~ sur qch** to look at sth; **détourner le ~** to look away; **j'ai croisé son ~** our eyes met; **à l'abri des ~s indiscrets** far from prying eyes
(b) expression; **son ~ triste** his/her sad expression; **sous le ~ amusé de qn** under the amused eye of sb; **jeter un ~ noir à qn** to give sb a black look
(c) **le ~ des autres** other people's opinion; **porter un ~ nouveau sur qch** to take a fresh look at sth
**2 au regard de** *phr* (formal) **au ~ de la loi** in the eyes of the law
**3 en regard** *phr* **avec une carte en ~** with a map on the opposite page

**regardant, ~e** /ʀəgaʀdɑ̃, ɑ̃t/ *adj* **ne pas être très ~** not to be very particular *or* fussy

**regarder** /ʀ(ə)gaʀde/ [1] **1** *vtr* (a) to look at ⟨*person, scene, landscape*⟩; **~ qch méchamment/fixement/longuement** to glare/stare/gaze at sth; **~ qn en face** to look sb in the face; **~ la réalité *or* les choses en face** to face facts; **~ qn de haut** to look down one's nose at sb
(b) to watch ⟨*film, TV*⟩; **regarde bien comment je fais** watch what I do carefully
(c) to look at ⟨*watch, map*⟩; to have a look at ⟨*tyres, oil*⟩; **~ qch dans** to look sth up in ⟨*dictionary*⟩; **~ si** to have a look and see if
(d) to look at ⟨*situation*⟩; **~ pourquoi/si/qui** to see why/if/who
(e) (colloq) to concern ⟨*person*⟩; **ça ne vous regarde pas** it's none of your business
(f) **elle ne regarde que ses intérêts** she thinks only of her own interests
**2 regarder à** *v+prep* to think about; **ne pas ~ à la dépense** to spare no expense; **à y ~ de plus près** on closer examination
**3** *vi* to look; **~ en l'air/par terre** to look up/down; **regarde où tu mets les pieds** watch where you put your feet
**4 se regarder** *v refl* (+ *v être*) (a) to look at oneself
(b) to look at one another

**régate** /ʀegat/ *nf* regatta

**régence** /ʀeʒɑ̃s/ *nf* (a) regency
(b) **la Régence** the Regency

**régénérer** /ʀeʒeneʀe/ [14] **1** *vtr* (a) to regenerate
(b) to reactivate
**2 se régénérer** *v refl* (+ *v être*) (a) ⟨*cells*⟩ to regenerate
(b) (figurative) to regain one's strength

**régent, ~e** /ʀeʒɑ̃, ɑ̃t/ *nm,f* regent

**régenter** /ʀeʒɑ̃te/ [1] *vtr* (a) to rule
(b) to regulate

**régie** /ʀeʒi/ *nf* (a) state control; local government control
(b) **~ d'État** state-owned company
(c) stage management; production department
(d) central control room

**regimber** /ʀ(ə)ʒɛ̃be/ [1] *vi* (a) ⟨*person*⟩ to balk (contre at)
(b) ⟨*horse*⟩ to jib

**régime** /ʀeʒim/ *nm* (a) diet; **être au ~** to be on a diet
(b) (Pol) system (of government); government; regime
(c) (in administration) system, regime; **~ de faveur** preferential treatment
(d) (Law) **~ matrimonial** marriage settlement
(e) (of engine) (running) speed; **tourner à plein ~** ⟨*engine*⟩ to run at top speed; ⟨*factory*⟩ to work at full capacity
(f) (of bananas) bunch

**régiment** /ʀeʒimɑ̃/ *nm* regiment

**région** /ʀeʒjɔ̃/ *nf* region; area

r

**régional**, **∼e**, *mpl* **-aux** /ʀeʒjɔnal, o/ *adj*
regional

**régionalisme** /ʀeʒjɔnalism/ *nm*
regionalism

**régir** /ʀeʒiʀ/ [3] *vtr* to govern

**régisseur** /ʀeʒisœʀ/ *nm* **(a)** (of estate)
steward, manager
**(b)** stage manager

**registre** /ʀ(ə)ʒistʀ/ *nm* **(a)** register; **les ∼s
de la police** police records
**(b)** (of novel) style
**(c)** (of language, voice) register; **cet acteur a un
∼ limité** this actor has a limited range

**réglable** /ʀeglabl/ *adj* **(a)** adjustable
**(b)** payable

**réglage** /ʀeglaʒ/ *nm* regulating; setting;
adjustment

**réglé**, **∼e** /ʀegle/ *adj* **(a)** ruled, lined
**(b)** ⟨*life*⟩ well-ordered
**(c)** **l'affaire est ∼e** the matter is settled

**règle** /ʀegl/ **1** *nf* **(a)** ruler
**(b)** rule; **∼s de sécurité** safety regulations;
**respecter les ∼s du jeu** to play by the rules;
**dans les ∼s de l'art** by the rule book; **en ∼
générale** as a rule
**2 règles** *nf pl* period
**3 en règle** *phr* ⟨*request*⟩ formal; ⟨*papers,
accounts*⟩ in order; **subir un interrogatoire en
∼** to be given a grilling; **pour passer la
frontière, il faut être en ∼** to cross the
border, your papers must be in order

**règlement** /ʀɛɡləmã/ *nm* **(a)** regulations,
rules
**(b)** payment
**(c)** settlement
■ **∼ de comptes** settling of scores

**réglementaire** /ʀɛɡləmãtɛʀ/ *adj*
⟨*uniform*⟩ regulation; ⟨*format*⟩ prescribed;
⟨*procedure*⟩ statutory

**réglementation** /ʀɛɡləmãtasjɔ̃/ *nf*
**(a)** rules, regulations
**(b)** regulation, control

**réglementer** /ʀɛɡləmãte/ [1] *vtr* to
regulate

**régler** /ʀegle/ [14] *vtr* **(a)** to settle ⟨*debt*⟩; to
pay ⟨*bill*⟩; to pay for ⟨*purchase, work*⟩; **avoir
des comptes à ∼ avec qn** (figurative) to have a
score to settle with sb; **∼ son compte à qn**
(colloq) to sort sb out
**(b)** to settle, to sort out ⟨*problem*⟩
**(c)** to settle ⟨*details, terms*⟩
**(d)** to adjust ⟨*height*⟩; to regulate ⟨*speed*⟩; to
tune ⟨*engine*⟩; to set ⟨*pressure*⟩
**(e)** **∼ sa conduite sur celle de qn** to model
one's behaviour (GB) on sb's
**(f)** to rule (lines on) ⟨*paper*⟩

**réglisse** /ʀeglis/ *nf* liquorice (GB), licorice
(US)

**régnant**, **∼e** /ʀeɲã, ãt/ *adj* ⟨*dynasty*⟩
reigning; ⟨*ideology*⟩ prevailing

**règne** /ʀɛɲ/ *nm* **(a)** reign; rule
**(b)** (figurative) reign
**(c)** (in biology) kingdom

**régner** /ʀeɲe/ [14] *vi* **(a)** ⟨*sovereign*⟩ to
reign, to rule

**(b)** ⟨*boss*⟩ to be in control; **∼ en maître sur**
to reign supreme over
**(c)** ⟨*confusion, fear*⟩ to reign; ⟨*smell*⟩ to
prevail; **la confiance règne!** (ironic) there's
trust for you!; **faire ∼** to give rise to
⟨*insecurity*⟩; to impose ⟨*order*⟩

**regonfler** /ʀ(ə)ɡɔ̃fle/ [1] *vtr* **(a)** to reinflate
⟨*tyre*⟩; to blow [sth] up again ⟨*balloon*⟩
**(b)** (colloq) to increase ⟨*staff*⟩; to boost ⟨*sales,
profits*⟩

**regorger** /ʀ(ə)ɡɔʀʒe/ [13] *vi* **∼ de** ⟨*shop*⟩ to
be packed with; ⟨*region*⟩ to have an
abundance of

**régresser** /ʀegʀese/ [1] *vi* **(a)** ⟨*waters*⟩ to
recede; ⟨*unemployment*⟩ to go down
**(b)** ⟨*industry*⟩ to be in decline
**(c)** ⟨*epidemic*⟩ to die out

**régressif**, **-ive** /ʀegʀesif, iv/ *adj*
regressive

**régression** /ʀegʀesjɔ̃/ *nf* **(a)** decline
**(b)** regression

**regret** /ʀəɡʀɛ/ *nm* regret; **j'apprends avec
∼ que** I'm sorry to hear that; **j'ai le ∼ de
vous annoncer** I regret to inform you

**regrettable** /ʀəɡʀɛtabl/ *adj* regrettable

**regretter** /ʀəɡʀete/ [1] *vtr* **(a)** to be sorry
about, to regret ⟨*situation, action*⟩; **je regrette
de ne pas pouvoir t'aider** I'm sorry I can't
help you
**(b)** to regret ⟨*decision*⟩; **∼ d'avoir fait** to
regret doing; **je ne regrette rien** I have no
regrets
**(c)** to miss ⟨*person, place*⟩; **notre regretté
collègue** (formal) our late colleague

**regroupement** /ʀ(ə)ɡʀupmã/ *nm*
**(a)** grouping; pooling; bringing together
**(b)** merger
**(c)** getting [sb/sth] back together; rounding
up

**regrouper** /ʀ(ə)ɡʀupe/ [1] **1** *vtr* **(a)** to
group [sth] together; to bring [sth] together;
to pool ⟨*interests*⟩; **∼ deux chapitres en un
seul** to merge two chapters into one
**(b)** to reassemble ⟨*pupils*⟩; to round up
⟨*animals*⟩
**2 se regrouper** *v refl* (+ *v être*)
**(a)** ⟨*companies*⟩ to group together;
⟨*malcontents*⟩ to gather
**(b)** ⟨*runners*⟩ to bunch together again

**régularisation** /ʀegylaʀizasjɔ̃/ *nf*
**(a)** (of situation) sorting out, regularization
**(b)** (of watercourse) regulation

**régulariser** /ʀegylaʀize/ [1] *vtr* **(a)** to sort
out, to regularize ⟨*position, situation*⟩
**(b)** to regulate ⟨*flow*⟩; to stabilize ⟨*price,
market*⟩

**régularité** /ʀegylaʀite/ *nf* **(a)** regularity
**(b)** (of rhythm, production, progress) steadiness;
(of features) regularity; (of writing) neatness;
(of surface) evenness; (of quantity) consistency
**(c)** legality

**régulateur**, **-trice** /ʀegylatœʀ, tʀis/
**1** *adj* regulating
**2** *nm* regulator

**régulation** /ʀegylasjɔ̃/ *nf* regulation,
control

**régulier, -ière** /ʀegylje, ɛʀ/ *adj* **(a)** (gen)
regular; ⟨*flow, rise, effort*⟩ steady; ⟨*quality*⟩
consistent; ⟨*thickness*⟩ even; ⟨*writing*⟩ neat;
⟨*life*⟩ (well-)ordered; **vol** ～ scheduled flight
**(b)** ⟨*person*⟩ honest; ⟨*papers, ballot*⟩ in
order; ⟨*government*⟩ legitimate
**(c)** ⟨*verb*⟩ regular

**régulièrement** /ʀegyljɛʀmɑ̃/ *adv*
**(a)** regularly
**(b)** steadily
**(c)** evenly
**(d)** normally

**régurgiter** /ʀegyʀʒite/ [1] *vtr* to
regurgitate

**réhabiliter** /ʀeabilite/ [1] **1** *vtr* **(a)** to
rehabilitate
**(b)** to renovate
**2 se réhabiliter** *v refl* (+ *v être*) to
redeem oneself

**réhabituer** /ʀeabitɥe/ [1] *vtr* to
reaccustom ⟨qn à qch sb to sth; qn à faire sb
to doing⟩

**rehausser** /ʀəose/ [1] *vtr* **(a)** to raise
**(b)** to enhance ⟨*prestige*⟩
**(c)** to set off ⟨*pattern*⟩

**réimplanter** /ʀeɛ̃plɑ̃te/ [1] *vtr* to re-
establish ⟨*factory, industry*⟩

**réimprimer** /ʀeɛ̃pʀime/ [1] *vtr* to reprint

**rein** /ʀɛ̃/ (Anat) **1** *nm* kidney; ～ **artificiel**
kidney machine
**2 reins** *nm pl* **les** ～**s** the small of the
back; **une serviette autour des** ～**s** a towel
around one's waist

**réincarner: se réincarner** /ʀeɛ̃kaʀne/
[1] *v refl* (+ *v être*) to be reincarnated

**reine** /ʀɛn/ *nf* **(a)** queen
**(b)** (figurative) **être la** ～ **des imbéciles** (colloq)
to be a prize idiot

**reine-claude**, *pl* **reines-claudes**
/ʀɛnklod/ *nf* greengage

**reinette** /ʀɛnɛt/ *nf* rennet apple

**réinscrire: se réinscrire** /ʀeɛ̃skʀiʀ/
[67] *v refl* (+ *v être*) to re-enrol

**réinsérer** /ʀeɛ̃seʀe/ [14] *vtr* **(a)** to
reintegrate
**(b)** to reinsert

**réinstaller** /ʀeɛ̃stale/ [1] **1** *vtr* to put
[sth] back
**2 se réinstaller** *v refl* (+ *v être*) **se** ～
**dans un fauteuil** to settle (oneself) back into
an armchair

**réintégrer** /ʀeɛ̃tegʀe/ [14] *vtr* **(a)** to
return to ⟨*place, group, system*⟩
**(b)** ～ qn ⟨dans ses fonctions⟩ to reinstate
sb

**réitérer** /ʀeiteʀe/ [14] *vtr* to repeat

**rejaillir** /ʀ(ə)ʒajiʀ/ [3] *vi* **(a)** ⟨*liquid*⟩ to
splash back; to spurt back
**(b)** ～ **sur** qn ⟨*success*⟩ to reflect on sb;
⟨*scandal*⟩ to affect sb adversely

**rejaillissement** /ʀ(ə)ʒajismɑ̃/ *nm*
(of scandal) adverse effect; (of success)
reflection

**rejet** /ʀ(ə)ʒɛ/ *nm* **(a)** (gen) rejection;
(of complaint) dismissal; (of motion) defeat;
(of request) denial
**(b)** (of waste) discharge; disposal; ～**s** waste

**rejeter** /ʀəʒte, ʀʒəte/ [20] **1** *vtr* **(a)** to
reject ⟨*advice, candidacy, outsider*⟩; to turn
down ⟨*offer*⟩; to deny ⟨*request*⟩; to set aside
⟨*decision*⟩
**(b)** ～ qch sur qn to shift sth onto sb
⟨*blame*⟩
**(c)** ⟨*factory*⟩ to discharge ⟨*waste*⟩; to eject
⟨*smoke*⟩
**(d)** ⟨*person, company*⟩ to dispose of ⟨*waste*⟩;
⟨*sea*⟩ to wash up ⟨*body, debris*⟩
**(e)** ～ [qch] **en arrière** to throw back ⟨*head,
hair*⟩
**2 se rejeter** *v refl* (+ *v être*) **se** ～ **la faute**
to blame each other

**rejeton** /ʀəʒtɔ̃, ʀʒətɔ̃/ *nm* **(a)** offshoot
**(b)** (colloq) offspring

**rejoindre** /ʀ(ə)ʒwɛ̃dʀ/ [56] **1** *vtr* **(a)** to
meet up with
**(b)** to catch up with
**(c)** to join; to rejoin
**(d)** to get to; to get back to, to return to
**(e)** ～ qn sur qch to concur with sb on sth
**2 se rejoindre** *v refl* (+ *v être*) ⟨*people*⟩ to
meet up; ⟨*roads*⟩ to meet

**rejouer** /ʀ(ə)ʒwe/ [1] *vtr* (gen) to play [sth]
again; to replay ⟨*match, point*⟩

**réjoui, ～e** /ʀeʒwi/ *adj* cheerful

**réjouir** /ʀeʒwiʀ/ [3] **1** *vtr* **(a)** to delight
⟨*person*⟩; to gladden ⟨*heart*⟩
**(b)** to amuse
**2 se réjouir** *v refl* (+ *v être*) to rejoice; **se**
～ **de** qch to be delighted at ⟨*news*⟩; to be
delighted with ⟨*success*⟩

**réjouissance** /ʀeʒwisɑ̃s/ **1** *nf* rejoicing
**2 réjouissances** *nf pl* celebrations; **quel
est le programme des** ～**s?** (colloq) what
delights are in store for us?

**réjouissant, ～e** /ʀeʒwisɑ̃, ɑ̃t/ *adj*
**(a)** heartening, delightful
**(b)** amusing

**relâche** /ʀ(ə)lɑʃ/ *nf* **(a)** (of theatre, cinema)
closure; **faire** ～ to be closed
**(b)** break, rest; **sans** ～ relentlessly

**relâchement** /ʀ(ə)lɑʃmɑ̃/ *nm*
**(a)** (of discipline, effort) slackening; (of morals)
loosening
**(b)** (of muscle) slackening

**relâcher** /ʀ(ə)lɑʃe/ [1] **1** *vtr* **(a)** to loosen
⟨*hold*⟩
**(b)** to release ⟨*captive*⟩
**(c)** to relax ⟨*discipline*⟩; ～ **son attention** to
let one's attention wander; ～ **ses efforts** to
let up
**2 se relâcher** *v refl* (+ *v être*) **(a)** ⟨*hold,
tie*⟩ to loosen; ⟨*muscle*⟩ to relax
**(b)** ⟨*effort*⟩ to slacken; ⟨*zeal*⟩ to flag; ⟨*pupil*⟩
to grow slack

r

**relais** /R(ə)lɛ/ *nm inv* **(a)** intermediary; **prendre le ~ (de qn/qch)** to take over (from sb/sth)
**(b)** (Sport) relay
**(c)** restaurant; hotel
**(d)** (Tech) relay; **~ hertzien** radio relay station

**relance** /R(ə)lɑ̃s/ *nf* (of industry, idea) revival; (of economy) reflation; (in inflation) rise; **mesures de ~** reflationary measures

**relancer** /R(ə)lɑ̃se/ [12] *vtr* **(a)** to throw [sth] again ⟨ball⟩; to throw [sth] back (again) ⟨ball⟩
**(b)** to restart ⟨engine⟩; to relaunch ⟨company⟩; to revive ⟨idea⟩; to reopen ⟨debate⟩; to boost ⟨investment⟩; to reflate ⟨economy⟩
**(c)** ⟨creditor⟩ to chase [sb] up; ⟨person⟩ to pester

**relater** /R(ə)late/ [1] *vtr* (formal) to recount

**relatif, -ive**¹ /R(ə)latif, iv/ **1** *adj* relative; **le risque est très ~** there is relatively little risk
**2** *nm* relative (pronoun)

**relation** /R(ə)lasjɔ̃/ **1** *nf* **(a)** connection
**(b)** acquaintance; **~s d'affaires** business acquaintances
**(c)** relationship; **avoir de bonnes ~s avec qn** to have a good relationship with sb; **entrer en ~ avec qn** to get in touch with sb
**2 relations** *nf pl* relations
■ **~s extérieures** foreign affairs; **~s publiques** public relations

**relative**² /R(ə)lativ/ **1** *adj f* ▸ RELATIF 1
**2** *nf* relative (clause)

**relativement** /R(ə)lativmɑ̃/ **1** *adv* relatively
**2 relativement à** *phr* in relation to

**relativiser** /R(ə)lativize/ [1] *vtr* to put [sth] into perspective

**relativité** /R(ə)lativite/ *nf* relativity

**relax** /Rəlaks/ *adj inv* (colloq) ⟨person⟩ laid-back (colloq); ⟨clothes⟩ casual; ⟨party⟩ informal

**relaxant, ~e** /Rəlaksɑ̃, ɑ̃t/ *adj* relaxing

**relaxation** /Rəlaksasjɔ̃/ *nf* relaxation

**relaxer** /Rəlakse/ [1] **1** *vtr* **(a)** to discharge ⟨defendant⟩
**(b)** to relax ⟨muscle, person⟩
**2 se relaxer** *v refl* (+ *v être*) to relax

**relayer** /R(ə)leje/ [21] **1** *vtr* **(a)** to take over from, to relieve
**(b)** to relay ⟨broadcast⟩
**2 se relayer** *v refl* (+ *v être*) **(a)** to take turns
**(b)** to take over from each other

**reléguer** /R(ə)lege/ [14] *vtr* (gen) to relegate; to consign ⟨object⟩; **~ qn/qch au second plan** to push sb/sth into the background

**relent** /R(ə)lɑ̃/ *nm* **(a)** lingering odour (GB)
**(b)** (figurative) whiff

**relevé, ~e** /Rəlve, Rləve/ **1** *adj* spicy
**2** *nm* **(a)** noting down; **faire le ~ de** to list ⟨mistakes⟩; to make a note of ⟨expenses⟩; to read ⟨meter⟩

**(b)** ~ **bancaire** bank statement

**relève** /R(ə)lɛv/ *nf* **(a)** **la ~ s'effectue à 20 heures** the changeover takes place at 8 pm; **la ~ de la garde** the changing of the guard; **prendre la ~** to take over
**(b)** relief; relief team

**relever** /Rəlve, Rləve/ [16] **1** *vtr* **(a)** to pick up ⟨person, stool⟩; to put [sth] back up (again)
**(b)** to raise ⟨lever⟩
**(c)** ~ **la tête** to raise one's head; to look up; (figurative) to refuse to accept defeat
**(d)** to turn up ⟨collar⟩; to lift ⟨skirt⟩; to wind up ⟨car window⟩; to raise ⟨sail, blind⟩; ~ **ses cheveux** to put one's hair up
**(e)** to note, to notice; to point out; ~ **la moindre inexactitude** to seize on the slightest inaccuracy
**(f)** to take down ⟨date, name⟩; to take ⟨prints⟩; ~ **le compteur** to read the meter
**(g)** to take in ⟨exam papers⟩
**(h)** to react to ⟨remark⟩; ~ **le défi/un pari** to take up the challenge/a bet
**(i)** to rebuild ⟨wall⟩; to put [sth] back on its feet ⟨country, economy⟩
**(j)** to raise ⟨standard, price⟩; to increase ⟨productivity⟩
**(k)** to relieve ⟨team⟩; ~ **la garde** to change the guard
**(l)** to spice up ⟨dish, story⟩
**(m)** ~ **qn de ses fonctions** to relieve sb of their duties
**2 relever de** *v+prep* **(a)** ~ **de** ⟨department⟩ to come under ⟨Ministry⟩; **cela ne relève pas de mes fonctions** that's not part of my duties
**(b)** **cela relève de la gageure** this comes close to being impossible
**3 se relever** *v refl* (+ *v être*) **(a)** to pick oneself up; to get up again
**(b)** **se ~ automatiquement** to be raised automatically
**(c)** ⟨blind⟩ to be raised
**(d)** **se ~ de** to recover from

**relief** /Rəljɛf/ *nm* **(a)** relief; (on medal, coin) raised pattern; **en ~** ⟨globe of the world⟩ in relief; ⟨letters⟩ raised; **cinéma en ~** three-dimensional cinema; **mettre qch en ~** to accentuate sth; **un ~ accidenté** a hilly landscape
**(b)** depth; **l'effet de ~** the effect of depth

**relier** /Rəlje/ [2] *vtr* **(a)** to link; to link up; to link together; to join up; to connect
**(b)** to bind ⟨book⟩; **relié cuir** leather-bound

**religieuse**¹ /Rəliʒjøz/ **1** *adj f* ▸ RELIGIEUX 1
**2** *nf* **(a)** nun
**(b)** (Culin) religieuse

**religieusement** /Rəliʒjøzmɑ̃/ *adv*
**(a)** religiously
**(b)** ⟨listen⟩ with rapt attention
**(c)** ⟨get married⟩ in church

**religieux, -ieuse**² /Rəliʒjø, øz/ **1** *adj*
**(a)** religious; ⟨school, wedding⟩ church; ⟨music⟩ sacred
**(b)** (figurative) ⟨silence⟩ reverent

2 *nm* monk

**religion** /ʀ(ə)liʒjɔ̃/ *nf* **(a)** religion
**(b)** faith
**(c)** entrer en ~ to enter the Church

**reliquaire** /ʀ(ə)likɛʀ/ *nm* reliquary

**reliquat** /ʀ(ə)lika/ *nm* (of sum) remainder;
(of account) balance

**relique** /ʀ(ə)lik/ *nf* relic

**relire** /ʀ(ə)liʀ/ [66] *vtr* to reread; to read
[sth] over

**reliure** /ʀəljyʀ/ *nf* **(a)** binding
**(b)** bookbinding

**reloger** /ʀ(ə)lɔʒe/ [13] *vtr* to rehouse

**reluire** /ʀ(ə)lɥiʀ/ [69] *vi* to shine; to glisten
IDIOMS il sait passer la brosse à ~ he's a
real flatterer

**reluisant**, **~e** /ʀ(ə)lɥizɑ̃, ɑ̃t/ *adj* shiny;
glistening; **peu ~** (figurative) far from brilliant

**remâcher** /ʀ(ə)mɑʃe/ [1] *vtr* **(a)** to chew
[sth] again
**(b)** (colloq) to ruminate over ⟨*problem, past*⟩

**remaniement** /ʀ(ə)manimɑ̃/ *nm*
modification; revision; reorganization

**remanier** /ʀ(ə)manje/ [2] *vtr* to modify; to
redraft; to reorganize; to reshuffle

**remarier**: **se remarier** /ʀ(ə)maʀje/ [2]
*v refl* (+ *v être*) to remarry

**remarquable** /ʀ(ə)maʀkabl/ *adj*
**(a)** remarkable
**(b)** striking
**(c)** noteworthy

**remarquablement** /ʀ(ə)maʀkabləmɑ̃/
*adv* remarkably

**remarque** /ʀ(ə)maʀk/ *nf* **(a)** remark; **faire
des ~s** to comment
**(b)** (written) comment
**(c)** critical remark, criticism

**remarqué**, **~e** /ʀ(ə)maʀke/ *adj*
⟨*initiative*⟩ noteworthy; ⟨*increase*⟩ noticeable

**remarquer** /ʀ(ə)maʀke/ [1] *vtr* **(a)** to
point out
**(b)** to observe
**(c)** to notice; **remarque, ce n'est pas très
important** mind you, it's not very important;
**se faire ~** to draw attention to oneself
**(d)** **~ un visage dans la foule** to spot a face
in the crowd
2 **se remarquer** *v refl* (+ *v être*) **(a)** to
attract attention
**(b)** to show

**remballer** /ʀɑ̃bale/ [1] *vtr* to pack [sth] up
again

**rembarrer** /ʀɑ̃baʀe/ [1] *vtr* (colloq) to send
[sb] packing (colloq)

**remblai** /ʀɑ̃blɛ/ *nm* **(a)** embankment; **route
en ~** raised road
**(b)** filling in; banking up
**(c)** (terre de) **~** (for railway, road) ballast; (for
ditch) fill; (for excavation) backfill

**rembobiner** /ʀɑ̃bɔbine/ [1] *vtr* to rewind

**rembourrer** /ʀɑ̃buʀe/ [1] *vtr* to stuff
⟨*chair*⟩; to pad ⟨*shoulders*⟩

**remboursable** /ʀɑ̃buʀsabl/ *adj* ⟨*loan,
debt*⟩ repayable; ⟨*ticket, medicine, treatment*⟩
refundable

**remboursement** /ʀɑ̃buʀsəmɑ̃/ *nm*
**(a)** repayment
**(b)** refund
**(c)** reimbursement

**rembourser** /ʀɑ̃buʀse/ [1] *vtr* **(a)** to pay
off, to repay ⟨*loan, debt*⟩
**(b)** to give a refund to ⟨*customer*⟩; to refund
the price of ⟨*item*⟩
**(c)** to reimburse ⟨*expenses, employee*⟩; **~ un
ami** to pay a friend back

**rembrunir**: **se rembrunir** /ʀɑ̃bʀyniʀ/ [3]
*v refl* (+ *v être*) ⟨*face*⟩ to darken, to cloud
over

**remède** /ʀ(ə)mɛd/ *nm* medicine; remedy,
cure
■ **~ de bonne femme** folk remedy; **~ de
cheval** strong medicine
IDIOMS aux grands maux les grands **~s**
desperate times call for desperate measures

**remédier** /ʀ(ə)medje/ [2] *v+prep* **~ à** to
remedy

**remembrement** /ʀ(ə)mɑ̃bʀəmɑ̃/ *nm*
regrouping of lands

**remémorer**: **se remémorer**
/ʀ(ə)memɔʀe/ [1] *v refl* (+ *v être*) to recall, to
recollect

**remerciement** /ʀ(ə)mɛʀsimɑ̃/ *nm*
thanks; **je n'ai pas eu un seul ~** I didn't get
a word of thanks; **lettre de ~** thank-you
letter

**remercier** /ʀ(ə)mɛʀsje/ [2] *vtr* **(a)** to
thank; **je vous remercie** thank you
**(b)** (ironic) to dismiss

**remettre** /ʀ(ə)mɛtʀ/ [60] 1 *vtr* **(a)** **~ qch
dans/sur** to put sth back in/on; **~ qch en
mémoire à qn** to remind sb of sth
**(b)** **~ à qn** to hand [sth] over to sb ⟨*keys*⟩; to
hand [sth] in to sb ⟨*letter*⟩; to present [sth]
to sb ⟨*reward*⟩
**(c)** **~ qch droit** *or* **d'aplomb** to put sth
straight again
**(d)** to postpone ⟨*visit*⟩
**(e)** to put [sth] on again ⟨*heating*⟩; to play
[sth] again ⟨*record*⟩
**(f)** **~ une vis** to put a new screw in
**(g)** **~** to add some more ⟨*salt*⟩; to add another
⟨*nail*⟩
**(h)** to put [sth] back on ⟨*coat*⟩
**(i)** (Med) to put [sth] back in place ⟨*joint*⟩
**(j)** ⟨*medicine*⟩ to make [sb] feel better
**(k)** **~ qn/le visage de qn** to remember sb/
sb's face
**(l)** (colloq) **~ ça** to start again; **on s'est bien
amusé, quand est-ce qu'on remet ça?** that
was fun, when are we going to do it again?
2 **se remettre** *v refl* (+ *v être*) **(a)** **se ~ à
un endroit** to go or get back to a place
**(b)** **se ~ au travail** to go back to work; **se ~
au dessin** to start drawing again
**(c)** **se ~ en jean** to wear jeans again
**(d)** **se ~ de** to recover from ⟨*illness*⟩; to get
over ⟨*shock*⟩   ···❯

**(e) s'en ~ à qn** to leave it to sb; **s'en ~ à la décision de qn** to accept sb's decision
**(f) se ~ avec qn** to get back together with sb

**réminiscence** /ʀeminisɑ̃s/ *nf*
**(a)** reminiscence
**(b)** recollection

**remise** /ʀ(ə)miz/ *nf* **(a) attendre la ~ des clés** to wait for the keys to be handed over; **~ des prix** prizegiving; **~ des médailles** medals ceremony
**(b)** discount
**(c) une ~ de peine** a remission
**(d) ~ de fonds** remittance of funds
**(e)** shed

**remiser** /ʀ(ə)mize/ [1] *vtr* to put [sth] away (**dans in**)

**rémission** /ʀemisjɔ̃/ *nf* remission; **sans ~** ⟨*punish*⟩ mercilessly; ⟨*rain*⟩ without stopping

**remmener** /ʀɑ̃mne/ [16] *vtr* to take [sb] back

**remodeler** /ʀəmɔdle/ [17] *vtr* to restructure; to reshape; to replan

**remontant** /ʀ(ə)mɔ̃tɑ̃/ *nm* pick-me-up (colloq), tonic

**remontée** /ʀ(ə)mɔ̃te/ *nf* **(a)** climb up; **la ~ de la Saône en péniche** going up the Saône by barge
**(b)** (in price) rise; (in violence) increase
■ **~ mécanique** (Sport) ski lift

**remonte-pente**, *pl* **~s** /ʀ(ə)mɔ̃tpɑ̃t/ *nm* ski-tow

**remonter** /ʀəmɔ̃te/ [1] **1** *vtr* (+ *v avoir*)
**(a) ~ qch** to take sth back up/upstairs; to bring sth back up/upstairs
**(b)** to put [sth] back up; **~ un seau d'un puits** to pull a bucket up from a well
**(c)** to raise ⟨*shelf, blind*⟩; to wind [sth] back up ⟨*car window*⟩; to roll up ⟨*sleeves*⟩; to turn up ⟨*collar*⟩; to pull up ⟨*socks*⟩
**(d)** to go/to come back up; to climb back up; to drive back up
**(e)** to sail up ⟨*river*⟩; to go up ⟨*road*⟩; **~ une filière** *or* **piste** to follow a trail
**(f) ~ qn** *or* **le moral de qn** to cheer sb up
**(g)** to put [sth] back together again; to put [sth] back ⟨*wheel*⟩
**(h)** to wind [sth] up; **être remonté à bloc** (colloq) to be full of energy
**(i)** to revive ⟨*play, show*⟩
**2** *vi* (+ *v être*) **(a)** ⟨*person*⟩ to go/to come back up; ⟨*tide*⟩ to come in again; ⟨*price, temperature*⟩ to rise again; **~ sur** to step back onto ⟨*pavement*⟩; to climb back onto ⟨*wall*⟩; **~ à la surface** ⟨*diver*⟩ to surface; ⟨*oil, object*⟩ to rise to the surface; **~ dans les sondages** to move up in the opinion polls
**(b) ~ dans le temps** to go back in time; **~ à** ⟨*historian*⟩ to go back to; ⟨*event*⟩ to date back to; **faire ~** to trace (back) ⟨*origins*⟩
**(c)** ⟨*skirt*⟩ to ride up
**(d) les odeurs d'égout remontent dans la maison** the smell from the drains reaches our house

**3 se remonter** *v refl* (+ *v être*) **se ~ le moral** to cheer oneself up; to cheer each other up

**remontoir** /ʀ(ə)mɔ̃twaʀ/ *nm* winder

**remontrance** /ʀəmɔ̃tʀɑ̃s/ *nf* reprimand

**remontrer** /ʀəmɔ̃tʀe/ [1] *vi* **en ~ à qn** to teach sb a thing or two

**remords** /ʀəmɔʀ/ *nm inv* remorse

**remorquage** /ʀəmɔʀkaʒ/ *nm* towing

**remorque** /ʀəmɔʀk/ *nf* **(a)** towrope; **prendre en ~** to tow ⟨*car*⟩
**(b)** trailer

**remorquer** /ʀəmɔʀke/ [1] *vtr* to tow ⟨*vehicle*⟩

**remorqueur** /ʀəmɔʀkœʀ/ *nm* tug

**remous** /ʀ(ə)mu/ *nm inv* **(a)** eddy
**(b)** backwash; wash
**(c)** (of ideas) turmoil; (in crowd) stir

**rempailler** /ʀɑ̃paje/ [1] *vtr* to reseat ⟨*chair*⟩

**rempart** /ʀɑ̃paʀ/ *nm* **(a)** rampart; battlements; **les ~s de la ville** the city walls
**(b)** defence (GB)

**remplaçable** /ʀɑ̃plasabl/ *adj* replaceable

**remplaçant, ~e** /ʀɑ̃plasɑ̃, ɑ̃t/ *nm,f*
**(a)** (gen) substitute; (at school) supply (GB) *or* substitute (US) teacher; (actor) stand-in
**(b)** successor

**remplacement** /ʀɑ̃plasmɑ̃/ *nm* replacement; **faire des ~s** ⟨*teacher*⟩ to do supply (GB) *or* substitute (US) teaching; ⟨*temp*⟩ to do temporary work; **produit de ~** substitute

**remplacer** /ʀɑ̃plase/ [12] *vtr* **(a)** to stand in for, to cover for ⟨*colleague*⟩
**(b)** to replace; **on peut ~ le vinaigre par du jus de citron** you can use lemon juice instead of vinegar

**remplir** /ʀɑ̃pliʀ/ [3] *vtr* **(a)** to fill (up) ⟨*container*⟩; to fill in ⟨*form*⟩; **~ qch à moitié** to half fill sth; **~ qn de joie** to fill sb with joy; **une vie bien remplie** a full life
**(b)** to carry out ⟨*role, mission*⟩; to fulfil (GB) ⟨*duty, role*⟩

**remplissage** /ʀɑ̃plisaʒ/ *nm* **(a)** filling
**(b)** (derogatory) **faire du ~** to pad out one's work

**remplumer: se remplumer** /ʀɑ̃plyme/ [1] *v refl* (colloq) (financially) to get back on one's feet; (physically) to put some weight back on

**rempocher** /ʀɑ̃pɔʃe/ [1] *vtr* to put [sth] back in one's pocket

**remporter** /ʀɑ̃pɔʀte/ [1] *vtr* to win ⟨*seat, title, victory*⟩; **~ un vif succès** to be a great success

**rempoter** /ʀɑ̃pɔte/ [1] *vtr* to repot

**remuant, ~e** /ʀ(ə)mɥɑ̃, ɑ̃t/ *adj* **(a)** rowdy
**(b)** boisterous; energetic

**remue-ménage** /ʀ(ə)mymenaʒ/ *nm inv*
**(a)** commotion
**(b)** bustle

**remuer** /ʀ(ə)mɥe/ [1] **1** *vtr* **(a)** to move ⟨*hand, head*⟩; to wiggle ⟨*toe, hips*⟩; to wag ⟨*tail*⟩
**(b)** to shake ⟨*object*⟩
**(c)** to move ⟨*object*⟩
**(d)** to stir ⟨*soup*⟩; to toss ⟨*salad*⟩
**(e)** to turn over ⟨*earth*⟩; to poke ⟨*ashes*⟩
**(f)** (figurative) to rake up ⟨*past*⟩; to stir up ⟨*memories*⟩
**(g)** to upset ⟨*person*⟩
**2** *vi* ⟨*person*⟩ to move; ⟨*leaves*⟩ to flutter; ⟨*boat*⟩ to bob up and down
**3 se remuer** *v refl* (+ *v être*) (colloq) **(a)** to get a move on (colloq)
**(b) se ~ pour obtenir** to make an effort to get

**rémunérateur, -trice** /ʀemyneʀatœʀ, tʀis/ *adj* lucrative

**rémunération** /ʀemyneʀasjɔ̃/ *nf* pay; payment

**rémunérer** /ʀemyneʀe/ [14] *vtr* to pay ⟨*person*⟩; to pay for ⟨*work*⟩

**renâcler** /ʀ(ə)nɑkle/ [1] *vi* **(a)** ⟨*person*⟩ to show reluctance
**(b)** ⟨*animal*⟩ to snort

**renaissance** /ʀ(ə)nɛsɑ̃s/ *nf* rebirth; revival

**Renaissance** /ʀ(ə)nɛsɑ̃s/ *nf* Renaissance

**renaître** /ʀ(ə)nɛtʀ/ [74] *vi* (+ *v être*) **(a)** to come back to life
**(b)** ⟨*hope, desire*⟩ to return; **faire ~ l'espoir** to bring new hope

**rénal, ~e,** *mpl* **-aux** /ʀenal, o/ *adj* ⟨*artery*⟩ renal; ⟨*infection*⟩ kidney

**renard** /ʀ(ə)naʀ/ *nm* **(a)** fox
**(b)** wily old fox

**renarde** /ʀ(ə)naʀd/ *nf* vixen

**renardeau,** *pl* **~x** /ʀ(ə)naʀdo/ *nm* fox cub

**renchérir** /ʀɑ̃ʃeʀiʀ/ [3] *vi* **(a)** to add; **~ sur ce que dit qn** to add something to what sb says
**(b)** to go one step further
**(c)** to raise the bidding

**rencontre** /ʀɑ̃kɔ̃tʀ/ *nf* **(a)** meeting; encounter; **faire la ~ de qn** to meet sb
**(b)** (Sport) match (GB), game (US); **~ d'athlétisme** athletics meeting (GB), track meet (US)
■ **~ au sommet** summit meeting

**rencontrer** /ʀɑ̃kɔ̃tʀe/ [1] **1** *vtr* **(a)** to meet ⟨*person*⟩; **~ qn sur son chemin** to come across sb
**(b)** to encounter, to meet with ⟨*problem, opposition*⟩
**(c)** to come across ⟨*object, word*⟩
**(d)** to meet ⟨*player, team*⟩
**2 se rencontrer** *v refl* (+ *v être*) **(a)** to meet
**(b)** ⟨*quality, object, person*⟩ to be found

**rendant** /ʀɑ̃dɑ̃/ ▸ RENDRE

**rendement** /ʀɑ̃dmɑ̃/ *nm* **(a)** (from land, investment) yield; (of machine, worker) output
**(b)** (of factory) productivity; (of machine, worker) efficiency

**(c)** (of sportsman, pupil) performance

**rendez-vous** /ʀɑ̃devu/ *nm inv*
**(a)** appointment; date; **sur ~** by appointment; **j'ai ~ avec un ami** I'm meeting a friend; **le soleil n'était pas au ~** the sun didn't shine
**(b)** meeting
**(c)** gathering; meeting place

**rendormir: se rendormir** /ʀɑ̃dɔʀmiʀ/ [30] *v refl* (+ *v être*) to go back to sleep

**rendre** /ʀɑ̃dʀ/ [6] **1** *vtr* **(a)** (gen) to give back, to return; to repay, to pay back ⟨*loan*⟩; to return ⟨*greeting, invitation, goods*⟩; **~ la pareille à qn** to pay sb back; **il la déteste mais elle le lui rend bien** he hates her and she feels the same about him
**(b) ~ la santé/vue à qn** to restore sb's health/sight
**(c) ~ qch possible** to make sth possible; **~ qn fou** to drive sb mad
**(d)** to hand in ⟨*homework*⟩
**(e)** ⟨*land*⟩ to yield ⟨*crop, quantity*⟩
**(f)** to convey ⟨*atmosphere, nuance*⟩; **ça ne rendra rien en couleurs** it won't come out in colour (GB)
**(g)** (colloq) to bring up ⟨*food, bile*⟩
**(h)** to pronounce ⟨*sentence*⟩; to return ⟨*verdict*⟩
**(i) les tomates rendent de l'eau (à la cuisson)** tomatoes give out water during cooking
**2** *vi* **(a)** ⟨*land*⟩ to be productive; ⟨*plant*⟩ to produce a good crop
**(b)** (colloq) to throw up (colloq)
**3 se rendre** *v refl* (+ *v être*) **(a) se ~ à Rome/en ville** to go to Rome/to town
**(b) se ~ indispensable/malade** to make oneself indispensable/ill
**(c)** to give oneself up; to surrender
**(d) se ~ à qch** to bow to ⟨*argument*⟩
IDIOMS **~ l'âme** *or* **l'esprit** to pass away

**rendu, -e** ▸ /ʀɑ̃dy/ RENDRE

**rêne** /ʀɛn/ *nf* rein

**renfermé, ~e** /ʀɑ̃fɛʀme/ **1** *pp* ▸ RENFERMER
**2** *pp adj* ⟨*person*⟩ withdrawn; ⟨*feeling*⟩ hidden
**3** *nm* **odeur de ~** musty smell

**renfermer** /ʀɑ̃fɛʀme/ [1] **1** *vtr* to contain
**2 se renfermer** *v refl* (+ *v être*) to become withdrawn

**renflé, ~e** /ʀɑ̃fle/ *adj* ⟨*vase*⟩ rounded; ⟨*dome*⟩ bulbous; ⟨*stomach*⟩ bulging

**renflement** /ʀɑ̃fləmɑ̃/ *nm* bulge

**renflouer** /ʀɑ̃flue/ [1] *vtr* **(a)** to raise ⟨*ship*⟩
**(b)** to bail out ⟨*person, company*⟩

**renfoncement** /ʀɑ̃fɔ̃smɑ̃/ *nm* recess; **~ de porte** doorway

**renforcer** /ʀɑ̃fɔʀse/ [12] **1** *vtr* to reinforce; to strengthen
**2 se renforcer** *v refl* (+ *v être*) ⟨*power*⟩ to increase; ⟨*control*⟩ to become tighter; ⟨*team, numbers*⟩ to grow; ⟨*sector*⟩ to grow stronger

**renfort** /ʀɑ̃fɔʀ/ *nm* **(a)** (Mil) reinforcement ⋯⁝

**(b)** support; annoncé à grand ∼ de publicité well-publicized
**(c)** (Sport) substitute

**renfrogné**, ∼**e** /ʀɑ̃fʀɔɲe/ adj sullen

**renfrogner: se renfrogner** /ʀɑ̃fʀɔɲe/ [1] v refl (+ v être) to become sullen

**rengaine** /ʀɑ̃gɛn/ nf c'est toujours la même ∼ (figurative) it's the same old thing every time

**rengainer** /ʀɑ̃gene/ [1] vtr to sheathe ⟨sword⟩; to put [sth] back in its holster ⟨pistol⟩

**rengorger: se rengorger** /ʀɑ̃gɔʀʒe/ [13] v refl (+ v être) ⟨bird⟩ to puff out its breast; ⟨person⟩ to swell with conceit

**reniement** /ʀ(ə)nimɑ̃/ nm disavowal

**renier** /ʀənje/ [2] **1** vtr to renounce ⟨religion, opinion⟩; to disown ⟨child, work, friend⟩
**2 se renier** v refl (+ v être) to go back on what one has said or promised

**reniflement** /ʀ(ə)nifləmɑ̃/ nm **(a)** sniffing
**(b)** sniff

**renifler** /ʀ(ə)nifle/ [1] vtr, vi to sniff

**renne** /ʀɛn/ nm reindeer

**renom** /ʀənɔ̃/ nm **(a)** fame
**(b)** reputation

**renommé**, ∼**e¹** /ʀənɔme/ adj famous

**renommée²** /ʀənɔme/ nf **(a)** reputation
**(b)** fame

**renoncement** /ʀ(ə)nɔ̃smɑ̃/ nm renunciation

**renoncer** /ʀ(ə)nɔ̃se/ [12] v+prep to give up; ∼ à to give up; to abandon; to renounce; ∼ à faire to abandon the idea of doing

**renonciation** /ʀ(ə)nɔ̃sjasjɔ̃/ nf giving up

**renouer** /ʀənwe/ [1] **1** vtr **(a)** to retie ⟨laces⟩
**(b)** to pick up the thread of ⟨conversation⟩
**2** ∼ **avec** v+prep to get back in touch with ⟨person⟩; to revive ⟨tradition⟩; to go back to ⟨past⟩

**renouveau**, pl ∼**x** /ʀənuvo/ nm revival

**renouveler** /ʀənuvle/ [19] **1** vtr **(a)** (gen) to renew; to repeat ⟨suggestion, experience⟩; to replace ⟨equipment, team⟩; to change ⟨water⟩
**(b)** to revitalize ⟨genre, style⟩
**2 se renouveler** v refl (+ v être) **(a)** une pièce où l'air ne se renouvelle pas a room which isn't aired
**(b)** ⟨artist⟩ to try out new ideas
**(c)** ⟨experience⟩ to be repeated

**renouvellement** /ʀənuvɛlmɑ̃/ nm
**(a)** renewal
**(b)** replacement
**(c)** revitalization

**rénovateur, -trice** /ʀenɔvatœʀ, tʀis/ nm,f reformer

**rénovation** /ʀenɔvasjɔ̃/ nf renovation

**rénover** /ʀenɔve/ [1] vtr **(a)** to renovate ⟨area, house⟩; to restore ⟨furniture⟩
**(b)** to reform ⟨institution, policy⟩; to revamp ⟨project⟩

**renseignement** /ʀɑ̃sɛɲmɑ̃/ **1** nm
**(a)** information; est-ce que je peux vous demander un ∼? can I ask you something?; ∼s pris upon investigation; 'pour tous ∼s, s'adresser à...' 'all enquiries to...'
**(b)** (Mil) intelligence
**2 renseignements** nm pl **(a)** information
**(b)** directory enquiries (GB) or assistance (US)

**renseigner** /ʀɑ̃seɲe/ [1] **1** vtr ∼ qn to give information to sb
**2 se renseigner** v refl (+ v être) to find out, to enquire; to make enquiries

**rentabilisation** /ʀɑ̃tabilizasjɔ̃/ nf la ∼ de l'entreprise est notre premier objectif our primary aim is to make the company profitable

**rentabiliser** /ʀɑ̃tabilize/ [1] vtr to secure a return on ⟨investment⟩; to make a profit on ⟨product⟩; to make [sth] profitable ⟨business⟩

**rentabilité** /ʀɑ̃tabilite/ nf **(a)** profitability
**(b)** return

**rentable** /ʀɑ̃tabl/ adj profitable

**rente** /ʀɑ̃t/ nf **(a)** private income
**(b)** annuity; ∼ viagère life annuity
**(c)** government stock

**rentrée** /ʀɑ̃tʀe/ nf **(a)** (general) return to work (after the slack period of the summer break in France); ∼ (des classes or scolaire) start of the (new) school year; mon livre sera publié à la ∼ my book will be published in the autumn (GB) or fall (US)
**(b)** return (to work)
**(c)** comeback; ∼ politique political comeback
**(d)** receipts; ∼ (d'argent) income; takings
■ ∼ parlementaire reassembly of Parliament

**rentrer** /ʀɑ̃tʀe/ [1] **1** vtr **(a)** to bring [sth] in; to take [sth] in
**(b)** to raise ⟨landing gear⟩; to draw in ⟨claws⟩; rentrez le ventre! hold your stomach in!
**(c)** to tuck ⟨shirt⟩ (dans into)
**2** vi (+ v être) **(a)** to go in; to get in; to fit; ∼ dans un arbre (colloq) to hit a tree
**(b)** ∼ dans to go back into; to come back into
**(c)** ∼ (chez soi) to get (or go or come) back (home); to return (home)
**(d)** ∼ dans ses frais to recoup one's money
**(e)** ⟨money⟩ to come in
**(f)** faire ∼ qch dans la tête de qn to get sth into sb's head
IDIOMS il m'est rentré dedans (slang) he bumped or ran into me; he crashed into me

**renversant**, ∼**e** /ʀɑ̃vɛʀsɑ̃, ɑ̃t/ adj astounding, astonishing

**renverse** /ʀɑ̃vɛʀs/ nf tomber à la ∼ to fall flat on one's back

**renversement** /ʀɑ̃vɛʀsəmɑ̃/ nm
**(a)** reversal
**(b)** overthrow; removal from office

**renverser** /ʀɑ̃vɛʀse/ [1] **1** vtr **(a)** to knock over; to knock down
**(b)** to spill
**(c)** to turn [sth] upside down

**(d)** to reverse
**(e)** to overthrow; to vote [sb/sth] out of office
  **2 se renverser** *v refl* (+ *v être*) ⟨*boat*⟩ to capsize; ⟨*bottle*⟩ to fall over; ⟨*liquid*⟩ to spill

**renvoi** /ʀɑ̃vwa/ *nm* **(a)** expulsion; dismissal
**(b)** return; **~ d'un colis** return of a parcel
**(c)** postponement
**(d)** cross-reference
**(e)** belch, burp (colloq)

**renvoyer** /ʀɑ̃vwaje/ [24] *vtr* **(a)** to throw [sth] back ⟨*ball*⟩; to reflect ⟨*light, heat*⟩; to echo ⟨*sound*⟩
**(b)** to return ⟨*mail*⟩
**(c)** to send [sb] back; **~ qn chez lui** to send sb home
**(d)** to expel; to dismiss
**(e)** to postpone ⟨*debate*⟩; to adjourn ⟨*case*⟩
**(f)** **~ à** to refer to

**réorganisation** /ʀeɔʀɡanizasjɔ̃/ *nf* reorganization

**réorienter** /ʀeɔʀjɑ̃te/ [1] *vtr* to reorientate ⟨*pupil*⟩, ⟨*student*⟩ (**vers** toward(s)); to reshape ⟨*policy*⟩

**réouverture** /ʀeuvɛʀtyʀ/ *nf* reopening

**repaire** /ʀ(ə)pɛʀ/ *nm* den; hideout

**répandre** /ʀepɑ̃dʀ/ [6] **1** *vtr* **(a)** to spread ⟨*substance*⟩; to pour ⟨*liquid*⟩; to spill ⟨*liquid*⟩
**(b)** to scatter ⟨*seeds, rubbish*⟩
**(c)** to spread ⟨*news, religion*⟩; to give off ⟨*heat, smoke, smell*⟩
  **2 se répandre** *v refl* (+ *v être*) to spread

**répandu, ~e** /ʀepɑ̃dy/ *adj* widespread

**réparable** /ʀepaʀabl/ *adj* **(a)** ⟨*object*⟩ repairable
**(b)** ⟨*mistake*⟩ which can be put right

**reparaître** /ʀ(ə)paʀɛtʀ/ [73] *vi* **(a)** = RÉAPPARAÎTRE
**(b)** ⟨*magazine*⟩ to be back in print

**réparateur, -trice** /ʀepaʀatœʀ, tʀis/
  **1** *adj* refreshing
  **2** *nm,f* engineer (GB), fixer (US)

**réparation** /ʀepaʀasjɔ̃/ *nf* **(a)** repairing, mending; repair
**(b)** compensation
**(c)** redress

**réparer** /ʀepaʀe/ [1] *vtr* **(a)** to repair, to mend, to fix
**(b)** to put [sth] right ⟨*error*⟩; to make up for ⟨*oversight*⟩
**(c)** to compensate for ⟨*damage*⟩

**reparler** /ʀ(ə)paʀle/ [1] *vtr* **(a)** **~ de** to discuss [sth] again (**à qn, avec qn** with sb)
**(b)** **~ à qn** to be back on speaking terms with sb

**repartie** /ʀepaʀti/ *nf* rejoinder; **elle a de la ~** she always has a ready reply

**repartir** /ʀ(ə)paʀtiʀ/ [30] *vi* (+ *v être*) **(a)** to leave (again); to go back
**(b)** ⟨*person*⟩ to set off again; ⟨*machine*⟩ to start again; ⟨*sector*⟩ to pick up again
**(c)** **~ à zéro** to start again from scratch

**répartir** /ʀepaʀtiʀ/ [3] **1** *vtr* **(a)** to share [sth] out; to split ⟨*profits, expenses*⟩; to distribute ⟨*weight*⟩

**(b)** to spread ⟨*payments*⟩
  **2 se répartir** *v refl* (+ *v être*) **(a)** to share out, to split
**(b)** ⟨*work, votes*⟩ to be split; **se ~ en** ⟨*people, objects*⟩ to divide (up) into

**répartition** /ʀepaʀtisjɔ̃/ *nf* **(a)** sharing out; dividing up
**(b)** distribution

**repas** /ʀ(ə)pɑ/ *nm inv* meal

**repassage** /ʀ(ə)pasaʒ/ *nm* ironing

**repasser** /ʀ(ə)pase/ [1] **1** *vtr* **(a)** to iron
**(b)** to cross [sth] again ⟨*river, border*⟩
**(c)** to take [sth] again ⟨*exam*⟩
**(d)** to pass [sth] again ⟨*tool, salt*⟩; **je te repasse Jean** (on phone) I'll put you back on to Jean
**(e)** (colloq) **~ qch à qn** to give sb sth ⟨*cold*⟩
  **2** *vi* (+ *v être*) **(a)** to go past again; **si tu repasses à Lyon, viens me voir** if you're ever back in Lyons, come and see me
**(b)** ⟨*film*⟩ to be showing again
**(c)** **quand elle fait la vaisselle, je dois ~ derrière elle** I always have to do the dishes again after she's done them

**repêchage** /ʀ(ə)pɛʃaʒ/ *nm* **(a)** recovery ⟨*from water*⟩
**(b)** **épreuve de ~** resit (GB), retest (US)

**repêcher** /ʀ(ə)peʃe/ [1] *vtr* to recover; to fish out

**repeindre** /ʀ(ə)pɛ̃dʀ/ [55] *vtr* to repaint

**repenser** /ʀ(ə)pɑ̃se/ [1] **1** *vtr* to rethink
  **2** *vi* **à** v+prep to think back to ⟨*childhood*⟩; to think again about ⟨*anecdote*⟩

**repenti, ~e** /ʀ(ə)pɑ̃ti/ *adj* repentant

**repentir¹: se repentir** /ʀ(ə)pɑ̃tiʀ/ [30] *v refl* (+ *v être*) **(a)** to regret
**(b)** to repent

**repentir²** /ʀ(ə)pɑ̃tiʀ/ *nm* repentance

**repérable** /ʀ(ə)peʀabl/ *adj* that can be spotted

**repérage** /ʀ(ə)peʀaʒ/ *nm* (Mil) location (**de of**)

**répercussion** /ʀepɛʀkysjɔ̃/ *nf* repercussion

**répercuter** /ʀepɛʀkyte/ [1] **1** *vtr* **(a)** to pass [sth] on ⟨*increase*⟩
**(b)** to send back ⟨*sound*⟩
  **2 se répercuter** *v refl* (+ *v être*) ⟨*sound*⟩ to echo; ⟨*increase*⟩ to be reflected (**sur** in)

**repère** /ʀ(ə)pɛʀ/ *nm* **(a)** marker; (reference) mark
**(b)** ⟨*event*⟩ landmark; ⟨*date*⟩ reference point

**repérer** /ʀ(ə)peʀe/ [14] **1** *vtr* **(a)** (colloq) to spot; **~ les lieux** to check out a place
**(b)** to locate ⟨*target*⟩
  **2 se repérer** *v refl* (+ *v être*) to get one's bearings

**répertoire** /ʀepɛʀtwaʀ/ *nm* **(a)** notebook with thumb index
**(b)** **~ téléphonique** telephone book
**(c)** repertoire

**répertorier** /ʀepɛʀtɔʀje/ [2] *vtr* **(a)** to list; to index
**(b)** to identify

**répéter** /Repete/ [14] **1** *vtr* **(a)** to repeat; ~ qch à qn to say sth to sb again; **je te répète que tu as tort** I'm telling you, you're wrong **(b)** to rehearse ⟨*play*⟩; to rehearse for ⟨*concert*⟩
**2 se répéter** *v refl* (+ *v être*) **(a)** to repeat oneself
**(b)** **j'ai beau me ~ que** no matter how often I tell myself that
**(c)** ⟨*incident*⟩ to be repeated

**répétitif, -ive** /Repetitif, iv/ *adj* repetitive

**répétition** /Repetisjɔ̃/ *nf* **(a)** repetition
**(b)** rehearsal; ~ **générale** dress rehearsal

**repeupler** /R(ə)pœple/ [1] *vtr* **(a)** to repopulate
**(b)** to restock
**(c)** to reforest

**repiquer** /R(ə)pike/ [1] *vtr* to transplant ⟨*rice*⟩; to prick out ⟨*seedlings*⟩

**répit** /Repi/ *nm* respite

**replacer** /R(ə)plase/ [12] *vtr* ~ qch dans son contexte to set sth back in context

**replanter** /R(ə)plɑ̃te/ [1] *vtr* **(a)** to transplant
**(b)** to replant

**replâtrer** /R(ə)plɑtRe/ [1] *vtr* **(a)** to replaster
**(b)** to patch up ⟨*group*⟩

**replet, -ète** /Rəplɛ, ɛt/ *adj* plump, chubby

**repli** /R(ə)pli/ *nm* **(a)** double fold
**(b)** fold
**(c)** (Mil) withdrawal
**(d)** ~ **sur soi(-même)** withdrawal

**replier** /R(ə)plije/ [2] **1** *vtr* **(a)** to fold up ⟨*map*⟩
**(b)** to fold [sth] back ⟨*sheet*⟩
**(c)** to fold up ⟨*deckchair, fan*⟩; to close ⟨*umbrella, penknife*⟩
**(d)** **elle replia ses jambes** she tucked her legs under her; ~ **ses ailes** ⟨*bird*⟩ to fold its wings
**2 se replier** *v refl* (+ *v être*) **(a)** ⟨*blade*⟩ to fold up
**(b)** ⟨*army*⟩ to withdraw
**(c)** **se ~ sur soi-même** ⟨*person*⟩ to become withdrawn

**réplique** /Replik/ *nf* **(a)** retort, rejoinder; **il a la ~ facile** he's always ready with an answer
**(b)** line; **donner la ~ à qn** to play opposite sb
**(c)** replica; **elle est la ~ de sa mère** she is the image of her mother

**répliquer** /Replike/ [1] **1** *vtr* to retort
**2 répliquer à** *v+prep* to argue with ⟨*person*⟩; to respond to ⟨*criticism*⟩
**3** *vi* **(a)** to answer back
**(b)** to retaliate, to respond

**répondant, -e** /Repɔ̃dɑ̃, ɑ̃t/ *nm,f* referee; (Law) surety, guarantor

**répondeur** /Repɔ̃dœR/ *nm* ~ **(téléphonique)** (telephone) answering machine

**répondre** /Repɔ̃dR/ [6] **1** *vtr* to answer, to reply; **il m'a été répondu que** I was told that; **qu'as-tu à ~?** what's your answer?

**2 répondre à** *v+prep* **(a)** ~ **à** to reply to, to answer ⟨*person, question, letter*⟩; to answer ⟨*phone*⟩
**(b)** ~ **à** to talk back to
**(c)** ~ **à** to answer, to meet ⟨*needs*⟩; to fulfil (GB) ⟨*wishes*⟩; to fit ⟨*description*⟩; to come up to ⟨*expectations*⟩
**(d)** ~ **à** to respond to ⟨*appeal, criticism*⟩; to return ⟨*greeting*⟩; ~ **à un sourire** to smile back; **les freins ne répondent plus** the brakes have failed
**3 répondre de** *v+prep* ~ **de qn** to vouch for sb; ~ **de ses actes** to answer for one's actions

**réponse** /Repɔ̃s/ *nf* **(a)** answer, reply
**(b)** response

**report** /RəpɔR/ *nm* **(a)** adjournment; postponement; deferment
**(b)** transfer

**reportage** /R(ə)pɔRtaʒ/ *nm* **(a)** report
**(b)** reporting

**reporter¹** /R(ə)pɔRte/ [1] **1** *vtr* **(a)** to put back ⟨*date*⟩; to postpone ⟨*event*⟩; to defer ⟨*judgment*⟩
**(b)** to carry forward ⟨*result*⟩; to copy out ⟨*name*⟩
**(c)** to take [sth] back ⟨*goods*⟩
**(d)** to transfer ⟨*affection*⟩; ~ **son agressivité sur qn** to take one's aggression out on sb
**2 se reporter** *v refl* (+ *v être*) **se ~ à** to refer to; to think back to

**reporter²** /RəpɔRtɛR/ *nm* reporter

**repos** /Rəpo/ *nm inv* rest; **mon jour de ~** my day off

**reposant, ~e** /Rəpozɑ̃, ɑ̃t/ *adj* peaceful, restful; soothing; relaxing

**repose-pieds** /R(ə)pozpje/ *nm inv* footrest

**reposer** /Rəpoze/ [1] **1** *vtr* **(a)** to rest; **avoir le visage reposé** to look rested; **lire qch à tête reposée** to read sth at one's leisure
**(b)** to put [sth] down ⟨*phone*⟩; to put [sth] down again
**(c)** to ask [sth] again ⟨*question*⟩
**2** *vi* **(a)** to rest; **'ici repose le Dr Grunard'** 'here lies Dr Grunard'; **laisser ~ la terre** to rest the land; **'laisser ~ la pâte'** 'let the dough stand'
**(b)** ~ **sur** to be based on; **la poutre repose sur...** the beam is supported by...
**3 se reposer** *v refl* (+ *v être*) **(a)** to have a rest, to rest
**(b)** **se ~ sur qn** to rely on sb

**repose-tête** /Rəpoztɛt/ *nm inv* head rest

**repoussant, ~e** /Rəpusɑ̃, ɑ̃t/ *adj* hideous

**repousser** /R(ə)puse/ [1] **1** *vtr* **(a)** to push [sth] to ⟨*door*⟩; to push back ⟨*object*⟩
**(b)** to push away ⟨*objects*⟩; to push back ⟨*lock of hair*⟩
**(c)** to push *or* drive back ⟨*crowd, animal*⟩; (Mil) to repel ⟨*attack*⟩
**(d)** to dismiss ⟨*objection*⟩; to decline ⟨*help*⟩; to turn down ⟨*request*⟩
**(e)** to revolt
**(f)** to postpone ⟨*event*⟩; to move [sth] back ⟨*date*⟩

**2** *vi* to grow again; to grow back

**répréhensible** /ʀepʀeɑ̃sibl/ *adj*
reprehensible

**reprendre** /ʀ(ə)pʀɑ̃dʀ/ [52] **1** *vtr* (a) ~ du
**pain/vin** to have some more bread/wine; **j'en
ai repris deux fois** I had three helpings
**(b)** to pick [sth] up again ⟨*object, tool*⟩; to
take [sth] back ⟨*present*⟩; to collect ⟨*person,
car*⟩
**(c)** to take [sb] on again ⟨*employee*⟩; ⟨*shop*⟩
to take [sth] back ⟨*item*⟩; **si on me reprend
ma vieille voiture** if I can trade in my old car
**(d)** to resume ⟨*walk, story*⟩; to take up [sth]
again ⟨*studies*⟩; to revive ⟨*play, tradition*⟩;
~ **le travail** to go back to work; **tu reprends
le train à quelle heure?** what time is your
train back?; ~ **une histoire au début** to go
back to the beginning of a story
**(e)** to take over ⟨*business, shop*⟩
**(f)** **on ne me reprendra plus à lui rendre
service!** you won't catch me doing him/her
any favours (GB) again!
**(g)** ~ **confiance** to regain one's confidence
**(h)** to alter ⟨*clothes*⟩; ~ **le travail de qn** to
correct sb's work
**(i)** to take up ⟨*idea, thesis, policy*⟩
**(j)** to repeat ⟨*argument*⟩; to take up ⟨*slogan,
news*⟩
**(k)** to correct ⟨*pupil*⟩
**(l)** **mon mal de dents m'a repris** my
toothache has come back
**2** *vi* (a) ⟨*business*⟩ to pick up again; ⟨*plant*⟩
to recover
**(b)** to start again
**(c)** **'c'est étrange,' reprit-il** 'it's strange,' he
continued
**3** **se reprendre** *v refl* (+ *v être*) **(a)** to
correct oneself
**(b)** to pull oneself together
**(c)** **s'y** ~ **à trois fois pour faire** to make
three attempts to do *or* at doing

**représailles** /ʀ(ə)pʀezɑj/ *nf pl* reprisals;
retaliation

**représentant, ~e** /ʀ(ə)pʀezɑ̃tɑ̃, ɑ̃t/ *nm,f*
**(a)** representative
**(b)** ~ **(de commerce)** sales representative

**représentatif, -ive** /ʀəpʀezɑ̃tatif, iv/
*adj* representative

**représentation** /ʀəpʀezɑ̃tasjɔ̃/ *nf*
**(a)** representation
**(b)** performance
**(c)** commercial travelling (GB); ~ **exclusive**
sole agency

**représenter** /ʀəpʀezɑ̃te/ [1] **1** *vtr*
**(a)** (in painting) to depict; to portray
**(b)** to represent; to mean; **les enfants
représentent les deux tiers de la population**
children make up two thirds of the
population
**(c)** to represent ⟨*person, company*⟩
**(d)** to perform ⟨*play*⟩
**2** **se représenter** *v refl* (+ *v être*) **(a)** to
imagine ⟨*scene*⟩
**(b)** ⟨*opportunity*⟩ to arise again
**(c)** **se** ~ **à un examen** to retake an
examination

**répressif, -ive** /ʀepʀesif, iv/ *adj*
repressive

**répression** /ʀepʀesjɔ̃/ *nf* suppression

**réprimande** /ʀepʀimɑ̃d/ *nf* reprimand

**réprimander** /ʀepʀimɑ̃de/ [1] *vtr* to
reprimand

**réprimer** /ʀepʀime/ [1] *vtr* to suppress; to
repress ⟨*desire*⟩

**repris** /ʀ(ə)pʀi/ *nm inv* ~ **de justice** ex-
convict

**reprise** /ʀəpʀiz/ *nf* **(a)** (of work, negotiations)
resumption; (of play, film) rerun; **à plusieurs
*or* maintes** ~**s** on several occasions,
repeatedly
**(b)** (of demand, production) increase; (of business)
revival; (of economy) upturn
**(c)** (of goods) return, taking back; trade-in;
(of company) takeover
**(d)** key money
**(e)** (Aut) acceleration
**(f)** mend; darn
**(g)** (in boxing) round; (in football) start of
second half

**repriser** /ʀəpʀize/ [1] *vtr* to mend; to darn

**réprobation** /ʀepʀɔbasjɔ̃/ *nf* disapproval

**reproche** /ʀ(ə)pʀɔʃ/ *nm* reproach; **j'ai un
ou deux** ~**s à vous faire** I've one or two
criticisms to make; **sans** ~ beyond reproach

**reprocher** /ʀəpʀɔʃe/ [1] **1** *vtr* **(a)** ~ **qch
à qn** to criticize *or* reproach sb for sth; **on
ne peut rien lui** ~ he's/she's beyond
reproach; **elle me reproche de ne jamais lui
écrire** she complains that I never write to
her
**(b)** **les faits qui lui sont reprochés** the
charges against him/her
**2** **se reprocher** *v refl* (+ *v être*) **se** ~ **qch**
to blame *or* reproach oneself for sth

**reproducteur, -trice** /ʀəpʀɔdyktœʀ,
tʀis/ *adj* **(a)** reproductive
**(b)** ⟨*animal*⟩ breeding

**reproduction** /ʀ(ə)pʀɔdyksjɔ̃/ *nf*
**(a)** reproduction
**(b)** reproduction, copy; **droit de** ~ copyright

**reproduire** /ʀ(ə)pʀɔdɥiʀ/ [69] **1** *vtr* (gen)
to reproduce; to recreate ⟨*conditions*⟩
**2** **se reproduire** *v refl* (+ *v être*) **(a)** ⟨*man,
plants*⟩ to reproduce
**(b)** ⟨*situation*⟩ to recur

**réprouver** /ʀepʀuve/ [1] *vtr* to condemn

**reptile** /ʀɛptil/ *nm* reptile

**repu, ~e** /ʀəpy/ *adj* full

**républicain, ~e** /ʀepyblikɛ̃, ɛn/ *adj,
nm,f* republican

**république** /ʀepyblik/ *nf* republic; **on est
en** ~ it's a free country

**répudier** /ʀepydje/ [2] *vtr* **(a)** to repudiate
⟨*spouse*⟩
**(b)** to renounce ⟨*right, faith*⟩

**répugnance** /ʀepyɲɑ̃s/ *nf* **(a)** revulsion
**(b)** reluctance; **avec** ~ reluctantly

**répugnant, ~e** /ʀepyɲɑ̃, ɑ̃t/ *adj*
**(a)** revolting
**(b)** disgusting ⋯⟶

(c) loathsome

**répugner** /ʀepyɲe/ [1] *v+prep* **(a)** ~ à
⟨food⟩ to disgust ⟨person⟩
**(b)** ~ à ⟨person⟩ to be averse to ⟨work⟩; ~ à
faire to be reluctant to do

**répulsion** /ʀepylsjɔ̃/ *nf* repulsion

**réputation** /ʀepytasjɔ̃/ *nf* reputation; **se
faire une** ~ to make a name for oneself

**réputé, ~e** /ʀepyte/ *adj* **(a)** ⟨company⟩
reputable; ⟨writer⟩ of repute; ⟨product⟩ well-
known; ~ **pour qch** renowned for sth;
**l'avocat le plus** ~ **de Paris** the best lawyer in
Paris
**(b)** ~ **cher** reputed to be expensive

**requérir** /ʀəkeʀiʀ/ [35] *vtr* **(a)** to request
**(b)** to require

**requête** /ʀəkɛt/ *nf* **(a)** request
**(b)** (Law) petition

**requiem** /ʀekwijɛm/ *nm inv* requiem

**requin** /ʀ(ə)kɛ̃/ *nm* (Zool, figurative) shark

**requis, ~e** /ʀəki, iz/ **1** *pp* ▶ REQUÉRIR
**2** *pp adj* ⟨patience⟩ necessary; ⟨age⟩
required

**réquisition** /ʀekizisjɔ̃/ *nf* requisitioning

**réquisitionner** /ʀekizisjɔne/ [1] *vtr* **(a)** to
requisition
**(b)** to commandeer ⟨premises⟩; to conscript
⟨workers⟩

**réquisitoire** /ʀekizitwaʀ/ *nm* closing
speech for the prosecution

**RER** /ɛʀəɛʀ/ *nm* (*abbr* = **réseau express
régional**) *rapid-transit rail system in the
Paris region*

**rescapé, ~e** /ʀɛskape/ **1** *adj* surviving
**2** *nm,f* survivor

**rescousse: à la rescousse** /alaʀɛskus/
*phr* **aller à la** ~ **de qn** to go to sb's rescue

**réseau**, *pl* ~**x** /ʀezo/ *nm* network

**réservation** /ʀezɛʀvasjɔ̃/ *nf* reservation,
booking (GB)

**réserve** /ʀezɛʀv/ *nf* **(a)** reservation; **sous
~ de changement** subject to alteration; **'sous
(toute)** ~**'** (in a programme) 'to be confirmed'
**(b)** stock; **des** ~**s de sucre** a stock of sugar;
~**(s) d'argent** money in reserve
**(c)** (Econ) ~**s de charbon** coal reserves; ~**s
d'eau** water supply
**(d)** (of person, manner) reserve
**(e)** stockroom
**(f)** (in museum) storeroom
**(g)** ~ **naturelle** nature reserve
**(h)** ~ **indienne** Indian reservation
**(i)** (Mil) **officier de** ~ reserve officer

**réservé, ~e** /ʀezɛʀve/ **1** *pp* ▶ RÉSERVER
**2** *pp adj* **(a)** ⟨fishing⟩ private
**(b)** ~ **à la clientèle** for patrons only; **voie** ~**e
aux autobus** bus lane; **'tous droits** ~**s'** 'all
rights reserved'
**(c)** ⟨person⟩ reserved

**réserver** /ʀezɛʀve/ [1] **1** *vtr* **(a)** to
reserve, to book ⟨seat, ticket⟩
**(b)** to put aside ⟨goods⟩
**(c)** to set aside ⟨money, time⟩
**(d)** ~ **un bon accueil à qn** to give sb a warm

welcome; **sans savoir ce que l'avenir nous
réserve** without knowing what the future
has in store for us
**(e)** ~ **son jugement** to reserve judgment
**2 se réserver** *v refl* (+ *v être*) **se** ~ **les
meilleurs morceaux** to save the best bits for
oneself; **se** ~ **le droit de faire** to reserve the
right to do; **il se réserve pour la candidature
à la présidence** he's saving himself for the
presidential race

**réserviste** /ʀezɛʀvist/ *nmf* reservist

**réservoir** /ʀezɛʀvwaʀ/ *nm* **(a)** tank
**(b)** reservoir

**résidant, ~e** /ʀezidɑ̃, ɑ̃t/ *adj* resident

**résidence** /ʀezidɑ̃s/ *nf* **(a)** residence
**(b)** place of residence; **assigné à** ~ under
house arrest
■ ~ **principale/secondaire** main/second home;
~ **universitaire** (university) hall of residence
(GB), residence hall (US)

**résident, ~e** /ʀezidɑ̃, ɑ̃t/ *nm,f* resident

**résidentiel, -ielle** /ʀezidɑ̃sjɛl/ *adj*
residential

**résider** /ʀezide/ [1] *vi* **(a)** to live
**(b)** ~ **dans qch** to lie in sth

**résidu** /ʀezidy/ *nm* **(a)** residue
**(b)** remnant
**(c)** waste

**résignation** /ʀeziɲasjɔ̃/ *nf* resignation
(à to)

**résigner: se résigner** /ʀeziɲe/ [1] *v refl*
(+ *v être*) to resign oneself

**résiliation** /ʀeziljasjɔ̃/ *nf* (of contract)
termination

**résilier** /ʀezilje/ [2] *vtr* to terminate
⟨contract⟩

**résine** /ʀezin/ *nf* resin

**résineux** /ʀezinø/ *nm* conifer

**résistance** /ʀezistɑ̃s/ *nf* **(a)** resistance;
**manquer de** ~ ⟨person⟩ to lack stamina
**(b)** (in electricity) (gen) resistance; (of household
appliance) element

**résistant, ~e** /ʀezistɑ̃, ɑ̃t/ **1** *adj*
**(a)** ⟨person⟩ tough, resilient; ⟨plant⟩ hardy
**(b)** ⟨metal⟩ resistant; ⟨fabric, garment⟩ hard-
wearing
**2** *nm,f* Resistance fighter

**résister** /ʀeziste/ [1] *v+prep* (gen) to resist;
~ **à** to resist ⟨offer⟩; to stand ⟨strain⟩; to
withstand ⟨pressure⟩; to get through ⟨ordeal⟩;
**le mur n'a pas résisté** the wall collapsed; ~ **à
l'épreuve du temps** to stand the test of time;
**il ne supporte pas qu'on lui résiste** he doesn't
like it when people stand up to him

**résolu, ~e** /ʀezɔly/ **1** *pp* ▶ RÉSOUDRE
**2** *pp adj* resolute, determined

**résolument** /ʀezɔlymɑ̃/ *adv* resolutely

**résolution** /ʀezɔlysjɔ̃/ *nf* **(a)** (gen, Pol)
resolution
**(b)** resolve
**(c)** solution

**résonance** /ʀezɔnɑ̃s/ *nf* (gen) resonance

**résonner** /rezɔne/ [1] *vi* **(a)** ⟨*step, laughter*⟩ to ring out; ⟨*alarm*⟩ to resound; ⟨*cymbals*⟩ to clash
**(b)** ⟨*room*⟩ to echo; ∼ **de** to resound with

**résorber** /rezɔrbe/ [1] **1** *vtr* to absorb ⟨*deficit, surplus*⟩; to reduce ⟨*inflation*⟩
**2 se résorber** *v refl* (+ *v être*) **(a)** ⟨*deficit*⟩ to be reduced
**(b)** (Med) to be resorbed

**résorption** /rezɔrpsjɔ̃/ *nf* (of unemployment, inflation) reduction (**de** of)

**résoudre** /rezudʀ/ [75] **1** *vtr* to solve ⟨*equation, problem*⟩; to resolve ⟨*crisis*⟩
**2 se résoudre** *v refl* (+ *v être*) **se** ∼ **à faire** to resolve *or* make up one's mind to do; **être résolu à faire** to be determined to do

**respect** /ʀɛspɛ/ *nm* (gen) respect; **manquer de** ∼ **à qn** to be disrespectful to sb; **le** ∼ **de soi** self-respect
**IDIOMS sauf votre** ∼ with all due respect; **tenir qn en** ∼ to keep sb at bay

**respectabilité** /ʀɛspɛktabilite/ *nf* respectability

**respectable** /ʀɛspɛktabl/ *adj* respectable

**respecter** /ʀɛspɛkte/ [1] **1** *vtr* (gen) to respect; to treat [sth] with respect; to honour (GB) ⟨*commitment*⟩; **faire** ∼ **l'ordre/la loi** to enforce order/the law
**2 se respecter** *v refl* (+ *v être*) to respect oneself; **tout homme qui se respecte** any self-respecting man

**respectif, -ive** /ʀɛspɛktif, iv/ *adj* respective

**respectueux, -euse** /ʀɛspɛktɥø, øz/ *adj* respectful; ∼ **de la loi** law-abiding; **salutations respectueuses** yours faithfully

**respirable** /ʀɛspiʀabl/ *adj* **(a)** breathable
**(b)** ⟨*atmosphere*⟩, ⟨*mood*⟩ bearable

**respiration** /ʀɛspiʀasjɔ̃/ *nf* **(a)** breathing; **avoir une** ∼ **difficile** to have breathing difficulties
**(b)** breath; **retenir sa** ∼ to hold one's breath

**respiratoire** /ʀɛspiʀatwaʀ/ *adj* respiratory

**respirer** /ʀɛspiʀe/ [1] **1** *vtr* **(a)** to breathe in ⟨*air, dust*⟩
**(b)** to smell ⟨*perfume*⟩
**(c)** ⟨*person, place*⟩ to exude
**2** *vi* **(a)** to breathe
**(b)** (figurative) to catch one's breath; **laisse-moi** ∼ let me get my breath back

**resplendir** /ʀɛsplɑ̃diʀ/ [3] *vi* **(a)** ⟨*light*⟩ to shine brightly; ⟨*snow*⟩ to sparkle
**(b)** ∼ **de santé** to be glowing with health

**resplendissant, -e** /ʀɛsplɑ̃disɑ̃, ɑ̃t/ *adj* **(a)** ⟨*light*⟩ brilliant
**(b)** ⟨*beauty*⟩ radiant

**responsabiliser** /ʀɛspɔ̃sabilize/ [1] *vtr* to give [sb] a sense of responsibility

**responsabilité** /ʀɛspɔ̃sabilite/ *nf* (gen) responsibility; (Law) liability; **avoir la** ∼ to be responsible for; **engageant la** ∼ **de la société** for which the company is liable
■ ∼ **civile** (in insurance) personal liability

**responsable** /ʀɛspɔ̃sabl/ **1** *adj*
**(a)** ⟨*person, error*⟩ responsible
**(b)** accountable; (Law) liable
**(c)** **être** ∼ **de qn/qch** to be in charge of sb/sth
**(d)** ⟨*person, attitude, act*⟩ responsible
**2** *nm,f* **(a)** (gen) person in charge; (of shop, project) manager; (of party) leader; (of department) head
**(b)** **les** ∼**s de la catastrophe** the people responsible for the catastrophe
**(c)** **le grand** ∼ **c'est le tabac** smoking is the main cause

**resquiller** /ʀɛskije/ [1] *vi* (colloq) (on train) not to pay the fare; (at show) to sneak in (colloq)

**resquilleur, -euse** /ʀɛskijœʀ, øz/ *nm,f* (colloq) fare dodger

**ressac** /ʀəsak/ *nm* backwash

**ressaisir: se ressaisir** /ʀ(ə)seziʀ/ [3] *v refl* (+ *v être*) to pull oneself together

**ressasser** /ʀ(ə)sase/ [1] *vtr* to brood over ⟨*failure*⟩; to dwell on ⟨*misfortunes*⟩

**ressemblance** /ʀ(ə)sɑ̃blɑ̃s/ *nf*
**(a)** resemblance, likeness
**(b)** (between things) similarity

**ressemblant, -e** /ʀ(ə)sɑ̃blɑ̃, ɑ̃t/ *adj* **un portrait** ∼ a portrait which is a good likeness

**ressembler** /ʀ(ə)sɑ̃ble/ [1]
**1 ressembler à** *v+prep* to look like, to resemble; to be like
**2 se ressembler** *v refl* (+ *v être*) **(a)** to look alike
**(b)** to be alike

**ressemeler** /ʀ(ə)səmle/ [19] *vtr* to resole

**ressentiment** /ʀ(ə)sɑ̃timɑ̃/ *nm* resentment

**ressentir** /ʀ(ə)sɑ̃tiʀ/ [30] **1** *vtr* to feel
**2 se ressentir** *v refl* (+ *v être*) **se** ∼ **de** to feel the effects of; to suffer from

**resserrer** /ʀ(ə)seʀe/ [1] **1** *vtr* **(a)** to tighten ⟨*knot, screw, grip*⟩
**(b)** **resserrez les rangs!** close up a bit!
**(c)** to tighten up on ⟨*discipline, supervision*⟩
**2 se resserrer** *v refl* (+ *v être*) **(a)** ⟨*road*⟩ to narrow
**(b)** ⟨*friendship*⟩ to become stronger
**(c)** ⟨*link, knot, grip*⟩ to tighten
**(d)** ⟨*gap*⟩ to close
**(e)** ⟨*group of people*⟩ to draw closer together
**(f)** ⟨*discipline*⟩ to become stricter

**resservir** /ʀ(ə)seʀviʀ/ [30] **1** *vtr* **(a)** to serve [sth] (up) again
**(b)** to give [sb] another helping
**2 se resservir** *v refl* (+ *v être*) to take another helping

**ressort** /ʀ(ə)sɔʀ/ *nm* **(a)** (Tech) spring
**(b)** **avoir du** ∼ to have resilience
**(c)** **être du** ∼ **de qn** to be within sb's province; (Law) to fall within the jurisdiction of ⟨*court*⟩; **en premier** ∼ in the first resort

**ressortir** /ʀ(ə)sɔʀtiʀ/ [30] **1** *vtr* **(a)** to take [sth] out again ····⟶

**(b)** to bring [sth] out again; to dig out (colloq) ⟨affair, scandal⟩
**2** vi (+ v être) **(a)** ⟨person⟩ to go out again
**(b)** ⟨bullet⟩ to come out
**(c)** to stand out; **voici ce qui ressort de l'étude** the results of the study are as follows; **faire ~** to bring to light ⟨contradiction⟩; ⟨make-up⟩ to accentuate ⟨eyes⟩
**(d)** ⟨film, record⟩ to be re-released
**3** v impers (+ v être) **il ressort que** it emerges that

**ressortissant, ~e** /ʀ(ə)sɔʀtisɑ̃, ɑ̃t/ nm,f national

**ressouder** /ʀ(ə)sude/ [1] vtr to solder [sth] again

**ressource** /ʀ(ə)suʀs/ nf **(a)** resource; **les ~s énergétiques** energy resources
**(b)** option; **en dernière ~** as a last resort
**(c) avoir de la ~** (colloq) to be resourceful
**(d) ~s** means; **être sans ~s** to have no means of support

**ressourcer: se ressourcer** /ʀ(ə)suʀse/ [12] v refl (+ v être) to recharge one's batteries

**ressusciter** /ʀesysite/ [1] **1** vtr **(a)** to revive ⟨tradition⟩; to resurrect ⟨past⟩
**(b)** to raise [sb] from the dead; (figurative) to bring [sb] back to life
**2** vi ⟨dead person⟩ to rise from the dead

**restant, ~e** /ʀɛstɑ̃, ɑ̃t/ **1** adj remaining
**2** nm **(a) le ~** the remainder; the rest
**(b) un ~ de poulet** some left-over chicken

**restaurant** /ʀɛstɔʀɑ̃/ nm restaurant
■ **~ universitaire, RU** university canteen (GB), cafeteria

**restaurateur, -trice** /ʀɛstɔʀatœʀ, tʀis/ nm,f **(a)** restaurant owner
**(b)** restorer

**restauration** /ʀɛstɔʀasjɔ̃/ nf **(a)** catering; **~ rapide** fast-food industry
**(b)** restoration

**restaurer** /ʀɛstɔʀe/ [1] **1** vtr **(a)** to feed
**(b)** to restore
**2 se restaurer** v refl (+ v être) to have something to eat

**reste** /ʀɛst/ **1** nm **le ~** the rest; the remainder; **un ~ de tissu** some left-over material; **au ~, du ~** besides
**2 restes** nm pl **(a)** remains
**(b)** leftovers
**IDIOMS sans demander son ~** without further ado; **être en ~ avec qn** to feel indebted to sb; **pour ne pas être en ~** so as not to be outdone

**rester** /ʀɛste/ [1] (+ v être) **1** vi **(a)** to stay, to remain; **que ça reste entre nous!** this is strictly between you and me!
**(b)** to remain; **restez assis!** remain seated!; don't get up!; **~ sans manger** to go without food; **~ paralysé** to be left paralysed; **~ les bras croisés** (figurative) to stand idly by
**(c)** to be left, to remain
**(d)** ⟨memory, work of art⟩ to live on

**(e) ~ sur une bonne impression** to be left with a good impression
**(f) en ~ à** to go no further than; **je compte bien ne pas en ~ là** I won't let the matter rest there; **restons-en là pour le moment** let's leave it at that for now
**2** v impers **il reste une minute** there is one minute left; **il ne me reste plus que lui** he's all I've got left; **il reste que, il n'en reste pas moins que** the fact remains that

**restituer** /ʀɛstitɥe/ [1] vtr **(a)** to restore
**(b)** to reconstruct ⟨text⟩; to reproduce ⟨sound⟩

**restitution** /ʀɛstitysjɔ̃/ nf **(a)** return; restoration
**(b)** reproduction

**restreindre** /ʀɛstʀɛ̃dʀ/ [55] **1** vtr to curb, to cut back on; to limit; to restrict
**2 se restreindre** v refl (+ v être)
**(a)** ⟨possibilities⟩ to become restricted; ⟨influence⟩ to wane
**(b) se ~** ⟨dans ses dépenses⟩ to cut back (on one's expenses)

**restreint, ~e** /ʀɛstʀɛ̃, ɛ̃t/ adj ⟨public, vocabulary⟩ limited; ⟨team⟩ small

**restrictif, -ive** /ʀɛstʀiktif, iv/ adj restrictive

**restriction** /ʀɛstʀiksjɔ̃/ nf **(a)** restriction; **~s salariales** wage restraints; **sans ~** freely
**(b) sans ~** ⟨approve⟩ without reservations; ⟨support⟩ unreservedly

**restructurer** /ʀəstʀyktyʀe/ [1] vtr to restructure; to redevelop ⟨area⟩

**résultat** /ʀezylta/ nm (gen) result; (of research) results, findings; (of negotiations, inquiry) result, outcome; **sans ~** without success

**résulter** /ʀezylte/ [1] **1 résulter de** v+prep to be the result of, to result from
**2** v impers **il résulte de ce que vous venez de dire que** it follows from what you have just said that; **il en résulte que** as a result

**résumé** /ʀezyme/ nm summary, résumé; **en ~** to sum up; **faire un ~ de qch (à qn)** to give (sb) a rundown of or on sth

**résumer** /ʀezyme/ [1] **1** vtr **(a)** to summarize ⟨text⟩
**(b)** to sum up ⟨news⟩
**2 se résumer** v refl (+ v être) **(a)** to sum up
**(b) se ~ à** to come down to

**résurgence** /ʀezyʀʒɑ̃s/ nf resurgence; revival

**resurgir** /ʀ(ə)syʀʒiʀ/ [3] vi to reappear

**résurrection** /ʀezyʀɛksjɔ̃/ nf
**(a)** resurrection
**(b)** revival
**(c)** rebirth

**rétablir** /ʀetabliʀ/ [3] **1** vtr **(a)** to restore; **~ la circulation** to get the traffic moving again
**(b)** to re-establish ⟨truth, facts⟩
**(c) ~ qn dans ses fonctions** to reinstate sb in his/her job

**2 se rétablir** *v refl* (+ *v être*) **(a)** to recover
**(b)** ⟨*calm*⟩ to return; ⟨*situation*⟩ to return to normal

**rétablissement** /ʀetablismɑ̃/ *nm*
**(a)** restoration
**(b)** re-establishment
**(c)** recovery

**rétamer** (colloq) /ʀetame/ [1] **1** *vtr* (tire) to wear [sb] out; (beat) to hammer (colloq)
**2 se rétamer** *v refl* (+ *v être*) (colloq) to fall, to come a cropper (colloq)

**retape** /ʀ(ə)tap/ *nf* (slang) **faire de la ~ pour qch** to beat the drum for sth

**retaper** /ʀ(ə)tape/ [1] *vtr* (colloq) **(a)** to do up ⟨*house*⟩
**(b)** to put [sb] on his/her feet again

**retard** /ʀ(ə)taʀ/ *nm* **(a)** lateness
**(b)** delay; **avoir du ~** to be late; **nous sommes en ~ sur l'emploi du temps** we're behind schedule; **prendre du ~** to fall *or* get behind; **avoir du courrier en ~** to have a backlog of mail; **sans ~** without delay
**(c)** backwardness; **il a deux ans de ~** (Sch) he's two years behind at school

**retardataire** /ʀ(ə)taʀdatɛʀ/ *nmf* latecomer

**retardé**, **~e** /ʀətaʀde/ *adj* ⟨*person*⟩ backward

**retardement**: **à retardement** /aʀ(ə)taʀdəmɑ̃/ *phr* ⟨*mechanism, device*⟩ delayed-action; **bombe à ~** time-bomb; ⟨*act, get angry*⟩ after the event

**retarder** /ʀ(ə)taʀde/ [1] **1** *vtr* **(a)** to make [sb] late; **être retardé** ⟨*train*⟩ to be delayed
**(b)** to hold [sb] up
**(c)** to put off, to postpone ⟨*departure, operation*⟩
**(d)** to put back ⟨*clock*⟩
**2** *vi* ⟨*clock*⟩ to be slow

**retenir** /ʀət(ə)niʀ, ʀtəniʀ/ [36] **1** *vtr* **(a)** to keep ⟨*person*⟩; **~ qn prisonnier** to hold sb captive; **~ qn à dîner** to ask sb to stay for dinner
**(b)** to hold [sb] up, to detain ⟨*person*⟩
**(c)** to hold ⟨*object, attention*⟩; to hold back ⟨*hair, dog, crowd*⟩; to stop ⟨*person*⟩; **~ sa langue** to hold one's tongue; **~ qn par la manche** to catch hold of sb's sleeve; **votre réclamation a retenu toute notre attention** your complaint is receiving our full attention
**(d)** to hold back ⟨*tears*⟩; to hold ⟨*breath*⟩; to stifle ⟨*scream, yawn*⟩; to contain, to suppress ⟨*anger*⟩
**(e)** to retain ⟨*heat, water, odour*⟩
**(f)** to reserve, to book ⟨*table, room*⟩; to set ⟨*date*⟩
**(g)** to deduct ⟨*sum*⟩
**(h)** to remember; **toi, je te retiens!** (colloq) I won't forget this!
**(i)** to accept ⟨*argument, plan*⟩; (Law) to uphold ⟨*charge*⟩
**(j)** (in mathematics) **je pose 5 et je retiens 2** I put down 5 and carry 2

**2 se retenir** *v refl* (+ *v être*) **(a)** to stop oneself; **se ~ à qch** to hang on to sth
**(b)** **se ~ de pleurer** to hold back the tears
**(c)** (colloq) to control oneself

**rétention** /ʀetɑ̃sjɔ̃/ *nf* **(a)** (Med) retention
**(b)** withholding

**retentir** /ʀ(ə)tɑ̃tiʀ/ [3] *vi* to ring out; to resound

**retentissant**, **~e** /ʀ(ə)tɑ̃tisɑ̃, ɑ̃t/ *adj*
**(a)** ⟨*failure*⟩ resounding; ⟨*trial, film*⟩ sensational
**(b)** ⟨*cry, noise*⟩ ringing; resounding

**retentissement** /ʀ(ə)tɑ̃tismɑ̃/ *nm* (gen) effect; (of book, artist) impact

**retenue** /ʀət(ə)ny/ *nf* **(a)** restraint; **perdre toute ~** to lose one's inhibitions; **boire sans ~** to drink to excess
**(b)** deduction
**(c)** (Sch) detention
**(d)** **tu as oublié la ~ des dizaines** you forgot to carry over from the tens column

**réticence** /ʀetisɑ̃s/ *nf* **(a)** reluctance
**(b)** **ses ~s en ce qui concerne le passé** his/her reticence about the past

**réticent**, **~e** /ʀetisɑ̃, ɑ̃t/ *adj* **(a)** hesitant
**(b)** reluctant

**rétif, -ive** /ʀetif, iv/ *adj* restive; rebellious

**rétine** /ʀetin/ *nf* retina

**retiré**, **~e** /ʀətiʀe/ *adj* ⟨*life*⟩ secluded
**(b)** ⟨*place*⟩ remote

**retirer** /ʀətiʀe/ [1] **1** *vtr* **(a)** to take off ⟨*garment, piece of jewellery*⟩
**(b)** to take out, to remove; **~ ses troupes d'un pays** to withdraw its troops from a country
**(c)** to withdraw ⟨*foot, hand*⟩; **retire ta main** move your hand away
**(d)** to withdraw ⟨*permission, privilege*⟩; to take away ⟨*right, property*⟩; **~ un produit de la vente** to recall a product; **~ une pièce de l'affiche** to close a play
**(e)** to withdraw ⟨*complaint, offer, support*⟩; **je retire ce que j'ai dit** I take back what I said
**(f)** to collect, to pick up ⟨*ticket, luggage*⟩; to withdraw ⟨*money*⟩
**(g)** to get, to derive ⟨*profits*⟩; **il en retire 2 000 euros par an** he gets 2,000 euros a year out of it
**2 se retirer** *v refl* (+ *v être*) **(a)** to withdraw, to leave; **un homme retiré de la politique** a man retired from political life
**(b)** **la mer se retire** the tide is going out

**retombées** /ʀətɔ̃be/ *nf pl*
**(a)** **~ radioactives** radioactive fallout
**(b)** effects, consequences
**(c)** (of invention) spin-offs

**retomber** /ʀətɔ̃be/ [1] *vi* (+ *v être*) **(a)** to fall again; **~ en enfance** to regress to childhood
**(b)** ⟨*person, cat, projectile*⟩ to land; ⟨*ball, curtain*⟩ to come down; ⟨*fog*⟩ to set in again; **ça va te ~ sur le nez** (figurative) (colloq) it'll come down on your head
**(c)** ⟨*anger*⟩ to subside; ⟨*interest*⟩ to wane ⋯⟶

(d) ⟨currency, temperature⟩ to fall
(e) ~ sur qn ⟨responsibility⟩ to fall on sb; faire ~ la responsabilité sur qn to pass the buck to sb ⟨colloq⟩

**retordre** /ʀ(ə)tɔʀdʀ/ [6] *vtr* donner du fil à ~ à qn to give sb a hard time

**rétorquer** /ʀetɔʀke/ [1] *vtr* to retort

**retors, ~e** /ʀətɔʀ, ɔʀs/ *adj* ⟨person⟩ crafty; ⟨argument⟩ devious

**rétorsion** /ʀetɔʀsjɔ̃/ *nf* retaliation

**retouche** /ʀ(ə)tuʃ/ *nf* alteration; (of photograph, picture) retouching

**retoucher** /ʀ(ə)tuʃe/ [1] *vtr* to make alterations to; to touch up

**retour** /ʀ(ə)tuʀ/ *nm* return; (billet de) ~ return ticket (GB), round trip (ticket) (US); au ~ on the way back; être de ~ (à la maison) to be back (home); on attend le ~ au calme people are waiting for things to calm down; il connaît maintenant le succès et c'est un juste ~ des choses he's successful now, and deservedly so; elle s'engage, en ~, à payer la facture she undertakes for her part to pay the bill; 'sans ~ ni consigne' 'no deposit or return'; par ~ du courrier by return of post (GB), by the next mail (US)
■ ~ d'âge change of life; ~ en arrière flashback; ~ de bâton ⟨colloq⟩ backlash
IDIOMS être sur le ~ ⟨colloq⟩ to be over the hill ⟨colloq⟩

**retournement** /ʀ(ə)tuʀnəmɑ̃/ *nm* reversal; un ~ de l'opinion publique a turn around in public opinion

**retourner** /ʀ(ə)tuʀne/ [1] **1** *vtr* (+ *v avoir*)
(a) to turn [sth] over; to turn ⟨mattress⟩
(b) to turn [sth] inside out
(c) to turn over ⟨earth⟩; to toss ⟨salad⟩
(d) to return ⟨compliment, criticism⟩; ~ la situation to reverse the situation
(e) to turn [sth] upside down ⟨room⟩; ⟨news, film⟩ to shake ⟨person⟩
(f) to send [sth] back, to return
**2** *vi* (+ *v être*) (a) to turn back, to return
**3 se retourner** *v refl* (+ *v être*) (a) to turn around
(b) to turn over; il n'a pas arrêté de se ~ (dans son lit) he kept tossing and turning
(c) ⟨colloq⟩ to get organized
(d) se ~ contre qn ⟨person⟩ to turn against sb; ⟨arguments⟩ to backfire on sb
(e) elle s'est retourné le doigt she bent back her finger
(f) s'en ~ (chez soi) to go back (home)
**4** *v impers* j'aime savoir de quoi il retourne I like to know what's going on
IDIOMS ~ qn comme une crêpe ⟨colloq⟩ to make sb change their mind completely

**retracer** /ʀətʀase/ [12] *vtr* (a) to redraw ⟨line⟩
(b) to recount ⟨event⟩

**rétractable** /ʀetʀaktabl/ *adj* retractable

**rétracter** /ʀetʀakte/ [1] *vtr*, **se rétracter** *v refl* (+ *v être*) to retract

**retrait** /ʀ(ə)tʀɛ/ **1** *nm* (gen) withdrawal; (of suitcase, packet) collection; ~ du permis (de conduire) disqualification from driving
**2 en retrait** *phr* maison en ~ de house set back from ⟨road⟩; se tenir en ~ to stand back; rester en ~ to stay in the background

**retraite** /ʀ(ə)tʀɛt/ *nf* (a) retirement; prendre sa ~ to retire
(b) pension
(c) (Mil) retreat
(d) (place) retreat; (of bandits) hiding place
■ ~ par capitalisation loanback pension; ~ complémentaire private pension

**retraité, ~e** /ʀətʀete/ *nm,f* retired person

**retraiter** /ʀətʀete/ [1] *vtr* to reprocess ⟨plutonium⟩

**retranché, ~e** /ʀ(ə)tʀɑ̃ʃe/ *adj* entrenched

**retranchement** /ʀ(ə)tʀɑ̃ʃmɑ̃/ *nm* entrenchment; pousser qn dans ses derniers ~s to drive sb into a corner

**retrancher** /ʀ(ə)tʀɑ̃ʃe/ [1] **1** *vtr* (a) to cut out ⟨word⟩
(b) to subtract ⟨amount⟩; to deduct ⟨costs⟩
**2 se retrancher** *v refl* (+ *v être*) (Mil, gen) to take up position; to entrench oneself

**retransmettre** /ʀətʀɑ̃smɛtʀ/ [60] *vtr* (a) to broadcast; retransmis par satellite relayed by satellite
(b) to retransmit

**retransmission** /ʀətʀɑ̃smisjɔ̃/ *nf*
(a) broadcast
(b) relay
(c) retransmission

**rétrécir** /ʀetʀesiʀ/ [3] *vi*, se rétrécir *v refl* (+ *v être*) (a) to narrow
(b) to shrink

**rétrécissement** /ʀetʀesismɑ̃/ *nm*
(a) shrinkage
(b) narrowing
(c) contraction

**rétribuer** /ʀetʀibɥe/ [1] *vtr* to remunerate

**rétribution** /ʀetʀibysjɔ̃/ *nf* remuneration

**rétro** /ʀetʀo/ *nm* (a) nostalgic style
(b) retro fashions

**rétroactif, -ive** /ʀetʀoaktif, iv/ *adj* (Law, gen) retroactive

**rétrograde** /ʀetʀogʀad/ *adj* ⟨person⟩ reactionary; ⟨policy, measure⟩ retrograde

**rétrograder** /ʀetʀogʀade/ [1] **1** *vtr* (a) to demote
(b) (Sport) to relegate
**2** *vi* (Aut) to change down (GB), to downshift (US)

**rétrospectif, -ive¹** /ʀetʀɔspɛktif, iv/ *adj* retrospective

**rétrospective²** /ʀetʀɔspɛktiv/ *nf* (gen) retrospective; (of films) festival

**rétrospectivement** /ʀetʀɔspɛktivmɑ̃/ *adv* in retrospect; looking back

**retroussé, ~e** /ʀ(ə)tʀuse/ *adj* ⟨nose⟩ turned up; ⟨lip⟩ curling

**retrousser** /ʀ(ə)tʀuse/ [1] *vtr* to hitch up (GB), to hike up (US) ⟨skirt⟩; to roll up ⟨sleeves⟩

**retrouvailles** /RǝtRuvɑj/ *nf pl* **(a)** reunion
**(b)** reconciliation

**retrouver** /Rǝtruve/ [1] **1** *vtr* **(a)** to find
⟨*lost object*⟩
**(b)** to find [sth] again ⟨*work, object*⟩
**(c)** to regain ⟨*strength, health*⟩
**(d)** to remember ⟨*name, tune*⟩
**(e)** to be back in ⟨*place*⟩
**(f)** to recognize ⟨*person, style*⟩; **je retrouve sa
mère en elle** I can see her mother in her
**(g)** to join, to meet ⟨*person*⟩
**2 se retrouver** *v refl* (+ *v être*) **(a)** to
meet (again); **on s'est retrouvé en famille** the
family got together; **comme on se retrouve!**
fancy seeing you here!
**(b) se ∼ enceinte** to find oneself pregnant;
**se ∼ sans argent** to be left penniless
**(c) se** *or* **s'y ∼ dans** to find one's way
around in ⟨*place, mess*⟩; to follow, to
understand ⟨*explanation*⟩; **il y a trop de
changements, on ne s'y retrouve plus** there
are too many changes, we don't know if
we're coming or going
**(d)** (colloq) **s'y ∼** to break even; (making profit)
to do well
**(e)** ⟨*quality*⟩ to be found; ⟨*problem*⟩ to occur
**(f) se ∼ dans qn/qch** to see *or* recognize
oneself in sb/sth

**rétroviseur** /RetRovizœR/ *nm* **(a)** rear-
view mirror
**(b)** wing mirror (GB), outside rear-view
mirror (US)

**réunification** /Reynifikasjɔ̃/ *nf*
reunification

**réunifier** /Reynifje/ [2] **1** *vtr* to reunify
**2 se réunifier** *v refl* (+ *v être*) to be
reunified

**réunion** /Reynjɔ̃/ *nf* **(a)** meeting; **être en ∼**
⟨*person*⟩ to be at a meeting
**(b)** gathering
**(c)** reunion
**(d)** (of different talents) combination; (of poems)
collection
**(e)** union

**réunir** /ReyniR/ [3] **1** *vtr* **(a)** ⟨*conference*⟩ to
bring together ⟨*participants*⟩; ⟨*organizer*⟩ to
get [sb] together ⟨*participants*⟩
**(b)** to call [sb] together ⟨*delegates*⟩; to
convene ⟨*assembly*⟩
**(c)** to have [sb] round (GB) *or* over ⟨*friends*⟩
**(d)** to join ⟨*edges*⟩
**(e)** to unite ⟨*provinces*⟩
**(f) ∼ les conditions nécessaires** to fulfil
(GB) all the necessary conditions
**(g)** to raise ⟨*funds*⟩
**(h)** to assemble ⟨*elements, evidence*⟩; to
gather [sth] together ⟨*documents*⟩
**(i)** ⟨*road, canal*⟩ to connect
**2 se réunir** *v refl* (+ *v être*) to meet; to get
together

**réussir** /ReysiR/ [3] **1** *vtr* to achieve
⟨*unification*⟩; to carry out [sth] successfully
⟨*operation*⟩; to make a success of ⟨*life*⟩
**2 réussir à** *v+prep* **(a) ∼ à faire** to
succeed in doing; **∼ à un examen** to pass an
exam

**(b) ∼ à qn** ⟨*life, method*⟩ to turn out well for
sb; ⟨*rest*⟩ to do sb good
**3** *vi* **(a)** to succeed
**(b)** ⟨*attempt*⟩ to be successful
**(c)** ⟨*person*⟩ to do well

**réussite** /Reysit/ *nf* (gen) success

**revaloir** /R(ǝ)valwaR/ [45] *vtr* **je te
revaudrai ça** (vengefully) I'll get even with you
for that; (in gratitude) I'll return the favour
(GB)

**revalorisation** /R(ǝ)valɔRizasjɔ̃/ *nf*
**(a)** (increase) **une ∼ des salaires de 3%** a 3%
wage increase
**(b)** (renewed esteem) **la ∼ des enseignants** the
enhanced prestige of teachers

**revaloriser** /R(ǝ)valɔRize/ [1] *vtr* **(a)** to
increase ⟨*salary*⟩; to revalue ⟨*currency*⟩
**(b)** to reassert the value of ⟨*traditions*⟩
**(c)** to renovate ⟨*area*⟩

**revanche** /R(ǝ)vɑ̃ʃ/ **1** *nf* **(a)** revenge
**(b)** (Sport) return match (GB) *or* game (US)
**2 en revanche** *phr* on the other hand

**rêvasser** /Revase/ [1] *vi* to daydream

**rêve** /Rɛv/ *nm* **(a)** dreaming
**(b)** dream; **fais de beaux ∼s!** sweet dreams!
**(c) une maison de ∼** a dream house
**(d) c'est le ∼** this is just perfect

**rêvé, -e** /Reve/ *adj* ideal, perfect

**revêche** /Rǝvɛʃ/ *adj* ⟨*manner, tone*⟩ sour;
⟨*person*⟩ crabby

**réveil** /Revɛj/ *nm* **(a)** waking (up)
**(b)** (after anaesthetic) **j'ai eu des nausées au ∼**
I felt nauseous when I regained
consciousness
**(c)** (of movement) resurgence; (of pain) return;
(of volcano) return to activity
**(d)** (Mil) reveille
**(e)** alarm clock

**réveille-matin** /Revɛjmatɛ̃/ *nm inv*
alarm clock

**réveiller** /Reveje/ [1] **1** *vtr* **(a)** to wake
[sb] up, to wake
**(b)** to revive ⟨*person*⟩; to awaken ⟨*feeling*⟩;
to arouse ⟨*curiosity*⟩; to stir up ⟨*memory*⟩
**2 se réveiller** *v refl* (+ *v être*) **(a)** to wake
up; to awaken
**(b)** to regain consciousness
**(c)** ⟨*volcano*⟩ to become active again
**(d)** ⟨*pain, appetite*⟩ to come back; ⟨*memory*⟩
to be reawakened

**réveillon** /Revɛjɔ̃/ *nm* **∼ du Nouvel An**
New Year's Eve party

**réveillonner** /Revɛjɔne/ [1] *vi* to celebrate
Christmas Eve; to see the New Year in

**révélateur, -trice** /RevelatœR, tRis/
**1** *adj* ⟨*detail, fact*⟩ revealing, telling
**2** *nm* (in photography) developer

**révélation** /Revelasjɔ̃/ *nf* revelation

**révéler** /Revele/ [14] **1** *vtr* **(a)** to reveal; to
give away ⟨*secret*⟩
**(b)** to show
**(c)** to discover ⟨*artist*⟩
**(d)** (in photography) to develop
**2 se révéler** *v refl* (+ *v être*) **se ∼ faux** to
turn out to be wrong

**revenant**, **~e** /Rəv(ə)nã, ãt/ *nm,f* ghost

**revendeur**, **-euse** /R(ə)vãdœR, øz/ *nm,f*
(a) stockist
(b) un ~ de drogue a drug dealer
(c) seller (of stolen goods)

**revendicatif**, **-ive** /R(ə)vãdikatif, iv/ *adj*
protest; **journée revendicative** day of protest

**revendication** /R(ə)vãdikasjõ/ *nf*
(of workers) demand; (of country) claim

**revendiquer** /R(ə)vãdike/ [1] *vtr* (a) to
demand ⟨*pay rise*⟩; to claim ⟨*territory*⟩
(b) to claim responsibility for ⟨*attack*⟩
(c) to proclaim ⟨*origins*⟩

**revendre** /R(ə)vãdR/ [6] *vtr* (a) to sell [sth]
retail, to retail
(b) to resell ⟨*car, house*⟩; to sell on ⟨*stolen
object*⟩; **avoir de l'énergie à ~** to have energy
to spare

**revenir** /Rəvnir, Rvənir/ [36] (+ *v être*) **1** *vi*
(a) to come back; to come again
(b) ⟨*person, animal, vehicle*⟩ to come back, to
return; **~ de loin** (figurative) to have had a
close shave; **mon chèque m'est revenu** my
cheque (GB) *or* check (US) was returned
(c) **~ à** to return to, to come back to
⟨*method, story*⟩
(d) ⟨*appetite, memory*⟩ to come back; ⟨*sun*⟩ to
come out again; ⟨*season*⟩ to return; ⟨*idea,
theme*⟩ to recur; **~ à la mémoire** *or* **l'esprit de
qn** to come back to sb; **ça me revient!** now I
remember!
(e) **~ à 100 euros** to come to 100 euros; **ça
revient cher** it works out expensive
(f) **~ sur** to go back over ⟨*question, past*⟩; to
go back on ⟨*decision, promise*⟩; to retract
⟨*confession*⟩
(g) **~ de** to get over ⟨*illness, surprise*⟩; to
lose ⟨*illusion*⟩; **la vie à la campagne, j'en suis
revenu** as for life in the country, I've seen it
for what it is; **je n'en reviens pas des
progrès que tu as faits** (colloq) I'm amazed at
the progress you've made
(h) **~ aux oreilles de qn** ⟨*remark*⟩ to reach
sb's ears
(i) **~ à qn** ⟨*property*⟩ to go to sb; ⟨*honour*⟩ to
fall to sb; **ça leur revient de droit** it's theirs
by right; **la décision revient au rédacteur** it is
the editor's decision
(j) (Culin) **faire ~** to brown
**2** *v impers* **c'est à vous qu'il revient de
trancher** it is for you to decide
IDIOMS **il a une tête qui ne me revient pas**
I don't like the look of him

**revenu** /Rəv(ə)ny, Rvəny/ *nm* income;
(of state) revenue
■ **~ minimum d'insertion, RMI** *minimum
benefit paid to those with no other source of
income*

**rêver** /Reve/ [1] **1** *vtr* (a) to dream
(b) to dream of ⟨*success, revenge*⟩
**2** *vi* to dream

**réverbération** /ReveRbeRasjõ/ *nf* (a) glare
(b) reflection
(c) reverberation

**réverbère** /ReveRbeR/ *nm* street lamp *or*
light

**réverbérer** /ReveRbeRe/ [14] **1** *vtr* to
reflect
**2** **se réverbérer** *v refl* (+ *v être*) ⟨*light,
heat*⟩ to be reflected; ⟨*sound*⟩ to reverberate

**révérence** /ReveRãs/ *nf* (a) curtsey; bow
(b) reverence
IDIOMS **tirer sa ~** (colloq) to take one's leave

**révérencieux**, **-ieuse** /ReveRãsjø, øz/
*adj* deferential (envers to); **attitude peu
révérencieuse** irreverent attitude

**révérend**, **~e** /ReveRã, ãd/ *nm,f*
(a) Father/Mother Superior
(b) reverend

**révérer** /ReveRe/ [14] *vtr* to revere

**rêverie** /RevRi/ *nf* (a) daydreaming
(b) daydream

**revers** /R(ə)veR/ *nm inv* (a) (of hand) back;
(of cloth) wrong side; (of coin) reverse; **le ~ de
la médaille** (figurative) the downside (colloq)
(b) (on jacket) lapel; (of trousers) turn-up (GB),
cuff (US)
(c) (in tennis) backhand (stroke)
(d) setback

**réversibilité** /ReveRsibilite/ *nf*
reversibility; (in law) reversion

**réversible** /ReveRsibl/ *adj* (gen) reversible

**revêtement** /R(ə)vɛtmã/ *nm* (a) (of road)
surface
(b) coating; covering

**revêtir** /R(ə)vetiR/ [33] **1** *vtr* (a) to assume
⟨*gravity, solemnity*⟩; to have ⟨*disadvantage*⟩;
to take on ⟨*significance*⟩; **~ la forme de** to
take the form of
(b) to put on ⟨*garment*⟩
(c) **~ qch de** to cover sth with ⟨*carpet, tiles*⟩
**2** **se revêtir** *v refl* (+ *v être*) **se ~ de** to
put on ⟨*cloak*⟩; to become covered with
⟨*snow*⟩

**rêveur**, **-euse** /RevœR, øz/ **1** *adj* dreamy
**2** *nm,f* dreamer

**revient** /R(ə)vjɛ̃/ *nm* **prix de ~** cost price

**revigorer** /R(ə)vigɔRe/ [1] *vtr* to revive

**revirement** /R(ə)viRmã/ *nm* turnaround

**réviser** /Revize/ [1] *vtr* (a) to revise
⟨*position, prices*⟩; to review ⟨*constitution*⟩
(b) to overhaul ⟨*car, boiler*⟩; to revise
⟨*manuscript*⟩
(c) (Sch) to revise (GB), to review (US)

**révision** /Revizjõ/ *nm* (a) revision; review
(b) (of car) service; (of manuscript) revision;
(of accounts) audit
(c) (Sch) revision (GB), review (US)

**revitaliser** /R(ə)vitalize/ [1] *vtr* to
revitalize

**revivifier** /R(ə)vivifje/ [2] *vtr* to revive; to
revivify

**revivre** /R(ə)vivR/ [63] **1** *vtr* (a) to go over,
to relive ⟨*event, past*⟩; **faire ~ qch à qn** to
bring back memories of sth to sb
(b) to live through [sth] again ⟨*war*⟩
**2** *vi* (a) to come alive again
(b) to be able to breathe again
(c) **faire ~** to revive ⟨*tradition*⟩

**révocation** /Revɔkasjɔ̃/ *nf* (of will)
revocation; (of person) dismissal

**revoici** /R(ə)vwasi/ *prep* (colloq) ~ **Marianne!**
here's Marianne again!

**revoilà** /R(ə)vwala/ = REVOICI

**revoir¹** /R(ə)vwaR/ [46] *vtr* **(a)** to see [sb/
sth] again
**(b)** to go over ⟨*exercise, lesson*⟩; to review
⟨*method*⟩; to check through ⟨*accounts*⟩

**revoir²: au revoir** /ɔR(ə)vwaR/ *phr*
goodbye

**révoltant, ~e** /Revɔltɑ̃, ɑ̃t/ *adj* appalling

**révolte** /Revɔlt/ *nf* **(a)** revolt
**(b)** rebellion

**révolté, ~e** /Revɔlte/ *adj* **(a)** (insubordinate)
rebellious
**(b)** (shocked) appalled

**révolter** /Revɔlte/ [1] **1** *vtr* to appal (GB)
**2 se révolter** *v refl* (+ *v être*) **(a)** to rebel
**(b)** to be appalled

**révolu, ~e** /Revɔly/ *adj* **(a)** ce temps est
~ those days are over *or* past
**(b) avoir 12 ans ~s** to be over 12 years of
age

**révolution** /Revɔlysjɔ̃/ *nf* **(a)** revolution
**(b)** turmoil
**(c)** (of planet) revolution

**révolutionnaire** /RevɔlysjɔnɛR/ *adj, nmf*
revolutionary

**révolutionner** /Revɔlysjɔne/ [1] *vtr* to
revolutionize

**revolver** /RevɔlvɛR/ *nm* **(a)** revolver
**(b)** handgun; **coup de ~** gunshot

**révoquer** /Revɔke/ [1] *vtr* **(a)** to revoke
⟨*will*⟩
**(b)** to dismiss ⟨*person*⟩

**revue** /R(ə)vy/ *nf* **(a)** (gen) magazine;
(academic) journal
**(b)** (Mil) parade; **passer en ~** to review
⟨*troops*⟩; to inspect ⟨*equipment*⟩
**(c)** revue
**(d)** examination; **passer qch en ~** to go
over sth
■ **~ de presse** review of the papers

**révulser** /Revylse/ [1] **1** *vtr* to appal (GB)
**2 se révulser** *v refl* (+ *v être*) ⟨*eyes*⟩ to
roll (upward(s)); ⟨*face*⟩ to contort

**révulsion** /Revylsjɔ̃/ *nf* (Med, gen)
revulsion

**rez-de-chaussée** /REdʃose/ *nm inv*
ground floor (GB), first floor (US)

**RF** (*written abbr* = **République
française**) French Republic

**rhabiller: se rhabiller** /Rabije/ [1] *v refl*
(+ *v être*) to get dressed again
**IDIOMS il peut aller se ~!** (slang) he can go
back where he came from!

**rhapsodie** /Rapsɔdi/ *nf* rhapsody

**rhésus** /Rezys/ *nm inv* **(a) facteur ~**
rhesus factor
**(b)** rhesus monkey

**rhétorique** /RetɔRik/ **1** *adj* rhetorical
**2** *nf* rhetoric

**Rhin** /Rɛ̃/ *pr nm* **le ~** the Rhine

**rhinocéros** /RinɔseRɔs/ *nm inv*
rhinoceros

**rhubarbe** /RybaRb/ *nf* rhubarb

**rhum** /Rɔm/ *nm* rum

**rhumatisme** /Rymatism/ *nm* rheumatism

**rhume** /Rym/ *nm* cold; **~ des foins** hay
fever

**ri** /Ri/ ▶ RIRE¹

**ribambelle** /Ribɑ̃bɛl/ *nf* (colloq) (of children)
flock; (of friends) host; (of names) whole string

**Ricain, ~e** (colloq) /Rikɛ̃, ɛn/ (offensive or
humorous) *nm,f* Yank (colloq)

**ricaner** /Rikane/ [1] *vi* **(a)** to snigger
**(b)** to giggle

**riche** /Riʃ/ **1** *adj* (gen) rich; ⟨*person*⟩ rich,
wealthy; ⟨*library*⟩ well-stocked; ⟨*decor*⟩
elaborate; **une ~ idée** an excellent idea
**2** *nmf* rich man/woman; **les ~s** the rich

**richement** /Riʃmɑ̃/ *adv* richly, lavishly
⟨*furnished, decorated*⟩

**richesse** /Riʃɛs/ **1** *nf* **(a)** wealth; **c'est
toute notre ~** it's all we have
**(b)** (of jewellery) magnificence; (of garment)
richness
**(c)** (of foodstuff) richness
**(d)** (of fauna, vocabulary) richness;
(of documentation) wealth
**2 richesses** *nf pl* wealth; **~s naturelles**
natural resources

**richissime** /Riʃisim/ *adj* (colloq)
fabulously rich

**ricin** /Risɛ̃/ *nm* **huile de ~** castor oil

**ricocher** /Rikɔʃe/ [1] *vi* ⟨*bullet*⟩ to ricochet
(**sur** off); (off an obstacle) to rebound (**sur** off)

**ricochet** /Rikɔʃɛ/ *nm* (of bullet) ricochet;
(of stone) bounce; **faire des ~s** to skim stones

**rictus** /Riktys/ *nm inv* (fixed) grin, rictus

**ride** /Rid/ *nf* (on face, fruit) wrinkle; (on lake)
ripple

**rideau,** *pl* **~x** /Rido/ *nm* **(a)** curtain
**(b)** (of shop) roller shutter
**(c)** (of flames) wall
■ **~ de fumée** blanket of smoke

**rider** /Ride/ [1] **1** *vtr* **(a)** to wrinkle ⟨*face,
skin*⟩
**(b)** to ripple ⟨*surface, lake*⟩
**2 se rider** *v refl* (+ *v être*) **(a)** ⟨*skin*⟩ to
wrinkle
**(b)** ⟨*lake*⟩ to ripple

**ridicule** /Ridikyl/ **1** *adj* **(a)** ridiculous
**(b)** ⟨*wage*⟩ ridiculously low, pathetic
**2** *nm* **(a)** ridicule
**(b)** (of situation) absurdity

**ridiculiser** /Ridikylize/ [1] **1** *vtr* to
ridicule; to wipe the floor with ⟨*competitor*⟩
**2 se ridiculiser** *v refl* (+ *v être*) ⟨*person*⟩
to make a fool of oneself

**ridule** /Ridyl/ *nf* fine wrinkle

**rien¹** /Rjɛ̃/ **1** *pron* **(a)** nothing; **il n'y a plus
~** there's nothing left; **~ n'y fait!** nothing's
any good!; **~ d'autre** nothing else;
**'pourquoi?'—'pour ~'** 'why?'—'no reason';
**'merci'—'de ~'** 'thank you'—'you're
welcome' *or* 'not at all'; **en moins de ~** in ⋯⊱

no time at all; **ça ou ~, c'est pareil** it makes no odds; **c'est trois fois ~** (colloq) it's next to nothing
**(b) ~ que la bouteille pèse deux kilos** the bottle alone weighs two kilos; **elle voudrait un bureau ~ qu'à elle** (colloq) she would like an office all to herself; **~ que ça?** (colloq) is that all?; **ils habitent un château, ~ que ça!** (ironic) they live in a castle, no less! *or* if you please!
**(c)** anything; **sans que j'en sache ~** without my knowing anything about it
**(d)** (Sport, gen) nil; (in tennis) love
**2 de rien (du tout)** *phr* **un petit bleu de ~ (du tout)** a tiny bruise
**3 en rien** *phr* at all, in any way
IDIOMS **~ à faire!** it's no good *or* use!; **ce n'est pas ~!** (exploit) it's quite something!; (task) it's no joke!; (sum of money) it's not exactly peanuts! (colloq)

**rien²** /ʀjɛ̃/ **1** *nm* **un ~ le fâche** the slightest thing annoys him; **se disputer pour un ~** to quarrel over nothing; **les petits ~s qui rendent la vie agréable** the little things which make life pleasant; **un/une ~ du tout** a worthless person
**2 un rien** *phr* (colloq) a (tiny) bit

**rieur, rieuse** /ʀijœʀ, øz/ *adj* (person, tone) cheerful; (face, eyes) laughing

**rigide** /ʀiʒid/ *adj* **(a)** rigid
**(b)** stiff

**rigidité** /ʀiʒidite/ *nf* rigidity

**rigolade** /ʀiɡɔlad/ *nf* (colloq) **(a) quelle ~!** what a laugh! (colloq)
**(b)** joke
**(c) réparer ça, c'est de la ~!** repairing this is a piece of cake (colloq)

**rigole** /ʀiɡɔl/ *nf* **(a)** channel
**(b)** rivulet

**rigoler** /ʀiɡɔle/ [1] *vi* (colloq) **(a)** to laugh
**(b)** to have fun
**(c)** to joke, to kid (colloq)

**rigolo, -ote** /ʀiɡɔlo, ɔt/ (colloq) **1** *adj*
**(a)** funny
**(b)** odd
**2** *nm,f* **(a)** joker
**(b) c'est un petit ~** he's quite a little comedian

**rigoriste** /ʀiɡɔʀist/ *adj* (attitude) unbending, rigoristic; (morals) strict

**rigoureusement** /ʀiɡuʀøzmɑ̃/ *adv* completely; carefully

**rigoureux, -euse** /ʀiɡuʀø, øz/ *adj*
**(a)** (discipline, person) strict
**(b)** (climate, working conditions) harsh, severe
**(c)** (research, demonstration) meticulous; (analysis) rigorous

**rigueur** /ʀiɡœʀ/ **1** *nf* **(a)** strictness
**(b)** harshness
**(c)** rigour (GB)
**(d)** (Econ) austerity
**2 de rigueur** *phr* obligatory

**3 à la rigueur** *phr* **à la ~ je peux te prêter 50 euros** at a pinch (GB) *or* in a pinch (US) I can lend you 50 euros
IDIOMS **tenir ~ à qn de qch** to bear sb a grudge for sth

**rillettes** /ʀijɛt/ *nf pl* ≈ potted meat

**rime** /ʀim/ *nf* rhyme

**rimer** /ʀime/ [1] *vi* **(a)** to rhyme
**(b) cela ne rime à rien** it makes no sense

**rimmel®** /ʀimɛl/ *nm* mascara

**rinçage** /ʀɛ̃saʒ/ *nm* **(a)** rinsing
**(b)** rinse

**rince-doigts** /ʀɛ̃sdwa/ *nm inv* **(a)** finger bowl
**(b)** finger wipe

**rincer** /ʀɛ̃se/ [12] **1** *vtr* **(a)** to rinse
**(b)** to rinse [sth] out
**2 se rincer** *v refl* (+ *v être*) **se ~ les mains/les cheveux** to rinse one's hands/hair

**ring** /ʀiŋ/ *nm* (boxing) ring

**ringard, ~e** /ʀɛ̃ɡaʀ, aʀd/ *adj* (colloq) out of date

**riper** /ʀipe/ [1] *vi* (foot) to slip; (bicycle) to skid

**riposte** /ʀipɔst/ *nf* **(a)** reply, riposte
**(b)** response
**(c)** (Sport) (in fencing) riposte; (in boxing) counter

**riposter** /ʀipɔste/ [1] **1** *vtr* to retort
**2** *vi* **(a)** to retort; **~ à qn/qch par** to counter sb/sth with
**(b)** to respond
**(c)** (Mil) to return fire, to shoot back
**(d)** (in sport) to ripost

**ripou**, *pl* **~x** /ʀipu/ *adj* (slang) crooked (colloq), bent (colloq)

**riquiqui** /ʀikiki/ *adj inv* (colloq) (room, car) poky (colloq); (portion) measly (colloq)

**rire¹** /ʀiʀ/ [68] **1** *vi* **(a)** to laugh; **tu nous feras toujours ~!** you're a real scream! (colloq)
**(b)** to have fun; **il faut bien ~ un peu** you need a bit of fun now and again; **fini de ~** the fun's over; **c'était pour ~** it was a joke; **sans ~** (colloq) seriously; **laisse-moi ~** (colloq), **ne me fais pas ~** (colloq) don't make me laugh
**(c) ~ de qn/qch** to laugh at sb/sth
**2 se rire** *v refl* (+ *v être*) **se ~ de qn** (formal) to laugh at sb; **se ~ des difficultés** (formal) to make light of difficulties
IDIOMS **rira bien qui rira le dernier** (Proverb) he who laughs last laughs longest; **être mort de ~** (colloq) to be doubled up (with laughter)

**rire²** /ʀiʀ/ *nm* laughter; **un ~** a laugh; **il a eu un petit ~** he chuckled
■ **~s préenregistrés** canned laughter

**ris** /ʀi/ *nm inv* **(a)** (Culin) **~ (de veau)** calf's sweetbread
**(b)** (Naut) reef

**risée** /ʀize/ *nf* **être la ~ de** to be the laughing stock of

**risette** /ʀizɛt/ *nf* (colloq) smile

**risible** /ʀizibl/ *adj* ridiculous, laughable

**risque** /ʀisk/ *nm* risk; **c'est sans ∼** it's safe; **à ∼s** ⟨*group, loan*⟩ high-risk
■ **les ∼s du métier** occupational hazards

**risqué, ∼e** /ʀiske/ *adj* **(a)** risky; ⟨*investment*⟩ high-risk
**(b)** ⟨*joke*⟩ risqué; ⟨*hypothesis*⟩ daring

**risquer** /ʀiske/ [1] **1** *vtr* **(a)** to face ⟨*accusation, condemnation*⟩
**(b)** to risk ⟨*death, criticism*⟩; **vas-y, tu ne risques rien** go ahead, you're safe; (figurative) go ahead, you've got nothing to lose; **∼ gros** to take a major risk
**(c)** to risk ⟨*life, reputation, job*⟩
**(d)** to venture ⟨*look, question*⟩; **∼ un œil** to venture a glance; **∼ le coup** (colloq) to risk it
**2 risquer de** *v+prep* **(a)** **tu risques de te brûler** you might burn yourself
**(b)** **il ne veut pas ∼ de perdre son travail** he doesn't want to risk losing his job
**3 se risquer** *v refl* (+ *v être*) **(a)** to venture; **je ne m'y risquerais pas** I wouldn't risk it
**(b)** **se ∼ à dire** to dare to say
**4** *v impers* **il risque de pleuvoir** it might rain; **il risque d'y avoir du monde** there may well be a lot of people there
**IDIOMS ∼ le tout pour le tout** to stake *or* risk one's all

**risque-tout** /ʀiskatu/ *adj inv* daredevil

**rissoler** /ʀisɔle/ [1] *vtr, vi* (Culin) to brown

**ristourne** /ʀistuʀn/ *nf* discount, rebate

**rite** /ʀit/ *nm* rite

**rituel, -elle** /ʀitɥɛl/ *adj, nm* ritual

**rivage** /ʀivaʒ/ *nm* shore

**rival, ∼e**, *mpl* **-aux** /ʀival, o/ *adj, nm,f* rival

**rivaliser** /ʀivalize/ [1] *vi* to compete with; **∼ avec qch** to rival sth

**rivalité** /ʀivalite/ *nf* rivalry

**rive** /ʀiv/ *nf* **(a)** (of river) bank
**(b)** (of sea, lake) shore

**river** /ʀive/ [1] *vtr* to clinch ⟨*nail, rivet*⟩; **être rivé à** (figurative) to be tied to ⟨*one's work*⟩; **avoir les yeux rivés sur** to have one's eyes riveted on

**riverain, ∼e** /ʀivʀɛ̃, ɛn/ *nm,f* (of street) resident; (beside river) riverside resident

**rivet** /ʀivɛ/ *nm* rivet

**rivière** /ʀivjɛʀ/ *nf* river
■ **∼ de diamants** diamond necklace

**rixe** /ʀiks/ *nf* brawl

**riz** /ʀi/ *nm* rice

**rizière** /ʀizjɛʀ/ *nf* paddy field

**RMI** /ɛʀɛmi/ *nm* (abbr = **revenu minimum d'insertion**) *minimum benefit paid to those with no other source of income*

**RN** /ɛʀɛn/ *nf* (abbr = **route nationale**) ≈ A road (GB), highway (US)

**robe** /ʀɔb/ *nf* **(a)** (gen) dress
**(b)** (of lawyer) gown
**(c)** (of horse) coat; (of wine) colour (GB)
■ **∼ de chambre** dressing gown, robe (US)

**robinet** /ʀɔbinɛ/ *nm* (for water) tap (GB), faucet (US); (for gas) tap (GB), valve (US)

**robot** /ʀɔbo/ *nm* robot; **∼ ménager** food processor

**robotique** /ʀɔbɔtik/ *nf* robotics

**robotisation** /ʀɔbɔtizasjɔ̃/ *nf* automation

**robotiser** /ʀɔbɔtize/ [1] *vtr* to automate

**robuste** /ʀɔbyst/ *adj* robust, sturdy; ⟨*appetite*⟩ healthy; ⟨*faith*⟩ strong

**robustesse** /ʀɔbystɛs/ *nf* **(a)** robustness, sturdiness
**(b)** soundness

**roc** /ʀɔk/ *nm* rock

**rocade** /ʀɔkad/ *nf* bypass; ring road

**rocaille** /ʀɔkaj/ *nf* **(a)** loose stones
**(b)** rock garden

**rocailleux, -euse** /ʀɔkajø, øz/ *adj* **(a)** ⟨*terrain*⟩ rocky, stony
**(b)** ⟨*voice*⟩ harsh, grating

**rocambolesque** /ʀɔkɑ̃bɔlɛsk/ *adj* fantastic, incredible

**roche** /ʀɔʃ/ *nf* rock

**rocher** /ʀɔʃe/ *nm* rock

**rocheux, -euse** /ʀɔʃø, øz/ *adj* rocky

**rock** /ʀɔk/ *nm* **(a)** rock (music)
**(b)** jive

**rockeur, -euse** /ʀɔkœʀ, øz/ *nm,f* **(a)** rock musician
**(b)** rock fan

**rococo** /ʀɔkoko/ *adj inv* ⟨*art, style*⟩ rococo

**rodage** /ʀɔdaʒ/ *nm* (of vehicle, engine) running in (GB), breaking in (US)

**rodéo** /ʀɔdeo/ *nm* rodeo

**roder** /ʀɔde/ [1] *vtr* **(a)** to run in (GB), to break in (US) ⟨*engine*⟩
**(b)** to polish up ⟨*show*⟩; **être (bien) rodé** ⟨*department*⟩ to be running smoothly

**rôder** /ʀode/ [1] *vi* to prowl; **∼ autour de qn** to hang around sb

**rôdeur, -euse** /ʀodœʀ, øz/ *nm,f* prowler

**rogne** /ʀɔɲ/ *nf* (colloq) **se mettre en ∼** to get mad (colloq)

**rogner** /ʀɔɲe/ [1] *vtr* **(a)** to trim ⟨*angle*⟩; to clip ⟨*nails*⟩
**(b)** **∼ sur** to cut down on ⟨*budget*⟩

**rognon** /ʀɔɲɔ̃/ *nm* (Culin) kidney

**roi** /ʀwa/ *nm* king
■ **les ∼s mages** the (three) wise men
**IDIOMS tirer les Rois** to eat Twelfth Night cake

**roitelet** /ʀwatlɛ/ *nm* **(a)** wren
**(b)** kinglet

**rôle** /ʀol/ *nm* **(a)** (for actor) part, role; **premier ∼** lead, leading role
**(b)** (gen) role; (of heart, part of body) function, role; **à tour de ∼** in turn
**IDIOMS avoir le beau ∼** (colloq) to have the easy job

**romain, ∼e¹** /ʀɔmɛ̃, ɛn/ *adj* **(a)** Roman
**(b)** **l'Église ∼e** the Roman Catholic Church
**(c)** **caractères ∼s** roman typeface

**romaine²** /ʀɔmɛn/ *nf* cos lettuce

**roman, ~e** /ʀɔmɑ̃, an/ **1** adj **(a)** ⟨church, style⟩ Romanesque; (in England) Norman
**(b)** ⟨language⟩ Romance
**2** nm **(a)** novel; **~ courtois** courtly romance
**(b)** (style) **le ~ the** Romanesque
■ **~ policier** detective story

**romance** /ʀɔmɑ̃s/ nf **(a)** love song
**(b)** romance

**romancer** /ʀɔmɑ̃se/ [12] vtr **(a)** to romanticize
**(b)** to fictionalize

**romanche** /ʀɔmɑ̃ʃ/ nm, adj Romans(c)h

**romancier, -ière** /ʀɔmɑ̃sje, ɛʀ/ nm,f novelist

**romand, ~e** /ʀɔmɑ̃, ɑ̃d/ adj ⟨Swiss person⟩ French-speaking

**romanesque** /ʀɔmanɛsk/ **1** adj
**(a)** ⟨person⟩ romantic
**(b)** ⟨narrative, story⟩ fictional
**2** nm **(a)** **le ~** fiction
**(b)** **le ~ d'une situation** the fantastical aspect of a situation

**roman-feuilleton, pl romans-feuilletons** /ʀɔmɑ̃fœjtɔ̃/ nm serial

**roman-fleuve, pl romans-fleuves** /ʀɔmɑ̃flœv/ nm roman-fleuve, saga

**roman-photo, pl romans-photos** /ʀɔmɑ̃foto/ nm photo-story

**romantique** /ʀɔmɑ̃tik/ adj, nmf romantic

**romantisme** /ʀɔmɑ̃tism/ nm romanticism

**romarin** /ʀɔmaʀɛ̃/ nm rosemary

**rombière** /ʀɔ̃bjɛʀ/ nf (slang) **une ~** an old bag (colloq)

**rompre** /ʀɔ̃pʀ/ [53] **1** vtr (gen) to break, to break off ⟨relationship⟩; to upset ⟨equilibrium⟩; to disrupt ⟨harmony⟩; to end ⟨isolation⟩
**2** vi **~ avec** to break with ⟨habit, tradition⟩; to make a break from ⟨past⟩; to break away from ⟨background⟩; to break up with ⟨fiancé⟩
**3** **se rompre** v refl (+ v être) to break

**rompu, ~e** /ʀɔ̃py/ **1** pp ▶ ROMPRE
**2** pp adj **~ (de fatigue)** worn-out

**romsteck** /ʀɔmstɛk/ nm rump steak

**ronce** /ʀɔ̃s/ nf bramble

**ronchon, -onne** /ʀɔ̃ʃɔ̃, ɔn/ adj (colloq) grumpy (colloq)

**ronchonner** /ʀɔ̃ʃɔne/ [1] vi (colloq) to grumble

**rond, ~e¹** /ʀɔ̃, ʀɔ̃d/ **1** adj **(a)** ⟨object, hole⟩ round
**(b)** ⟨writing⟩ rounded; ⟨face⟩ round; ⟨person⟩ plump
**(c)** ⟨number⟩ round
**(d)** (colloq) drunk
**2** nm circle; **faire des ~s dans l'eau** to make ripples in the water
■ **~ de serviette** napkin ring
IDIOMS **ouvrir des yeux ~s** to be wide-eyed with astonishment

**ronde²** /ʀɔ̃d/ **1** adj f ▶ ROND 1
**2** nf **(a)** round dance; **entrer dans la ~** to join the dance
**(b)** (of policeman) patrol; (of soldiers) watch

**(c)** (Mus) semibreve (GB), whole note (US)
**3** **à la ronde** phr around

**rondelle** /ʀɔ̃dɛl/ nf **(a)** slice
**(b)** (Tech) washer

**rondement** /ʀɔ̃dmɑ̃/ adv promptly

**rondeur** /ʀɔ̃dœʀ/ nf **(a)** roundness
**(b)** curve

**rondin** /ʀɔ̃dɛ̃/ nm log

**rondouillard, ~e** /ʀɔ̃dujaʀ, aʀd/ adj (colloq) tubby (colloq)

**rond-point, pl ronds-points** /ʀɔ̃pwɛ̃/ nm roundabout (GB), traffic circle (US)

**ronflant, ~e** /ʀɔ̃flɑ̃, ɑ̃t/ adj **(a)** ⟨stove⟩ roaring
**(b)** ⟨style⟩ high-flown

**ronflement** /ʀɔ̃fləmɑ̃/ nm **(a)** snore
**(b)** (of engine) purr

**ronfler** /ʀɔ̃fle/ [1] vi **(a)** ⟨sleeper⟩ to snore; ⟨engine⟩ to purr
**(b)** (colloq) to be fast asleep

**ronger** /ʀɔ̃ʒe/ [13] **1** vtr **(a)** ⟨mouse, dog⟩ to gnaw; ⟨worms⟩ to eat into; ⟨caterpillar⟩ to eat away
**(b)** ⟨acid, rust⟩ to erode
**(c)** ⟨disease⟩ to wear down
**2** **se ronger** v refl (+ v être) **se ~ les ongles** to bite one's nails
IDIOMS **se ~ les sangs** (colloq) to worry oneself sick

**rongeur** /ʀɔ̃ʒœʀ/ nm rodent

**ronronnement** /ʀɔ̃ʀɔnmɑ̃/ nm (of cat, engine) purring

**ronronner** /ʀɔ̃ʀɔne/ [1] vi to purr

**roquet** /ʀɔkɛ/ nm **(a)** yappy little dog
**(b)** (colloq) bad-tempered little runt (colloq)

**roquette** /ʀɔkɛt/ nf rocket

**rosace** /ʀozas/ nf **(a)** rosette
**(b)** rose window
**(c)** (decorative motif) rose

**rosaire** /ʀozɛʀ/ nm rosary

**rosâtre** /ʀozɑtʀ/ adj pinkish

**rosbif** /ʀɔsbif/ nm joint of beef (GB), roast of beef (US); (meal) roast beef

**rose¹** /ʀoz/ adj (gen) pink; ⟨cheeks⟩ rosy
IDIOMS **la vie n'est pas ~** life isn't a bed of roses

**rose²** /ʀoz/ nf (Bot) rose
■ **~ des sables** gypsum flower; **~ trémière** hollyhock
IDIOMS **envoyer qn sur les ~s** (colloq) to send sb packing (colloq); **découvrir le pot aux ~s** (colloq) to find out what is going on

**rosé** /ʀoze/ nm rosé

**roseau, pl ~x** /ʀozo/ nm (Bot) reed

**rosée** /ʀoze/ nf dew

**roseraie** /ʀozʀɛ/ nf rose garden

**rosier** /ʀozje/ nm (Bot) rosebush, rose

**rosir** /ʀoziʀ/ [3] vi ⟨sky⟩ to turn pink; ⟨face⟩ to go pink

**rosse** /ʀɔs/ **1** adj (colloq) nasty, mean
**2** nf **(a)** nag (colloq)
**(b)** meanie (colloq), nasty person

**rosser** /ʀɔse/ [1] *vtr* (colloq) to give ⟨person⟩ a good thrashing; to beat ⟨animal⟩

**rosserie** /ʀɔsʀi/ *nf* **(a)** nasty remark; mean trick
**(b)** meanness; nastiness

**rossignol** /ʀɔsiɲɔl/ *nm* nightingale

**rot** /ʀo/ *nm* (colloq) burp (colloq); **faire un ∼** to burp (colloq)

**rotation** /ʀɔtasjɔ̃/ *nf* **(a)** (movement) rotation
**(b)** (Mil) turnaround
**(c)** (of crops, staff, shift) rotation

**roter** /ʀɔte/ [1] *vtr* (colloq) to burp (colloq), to belch

**rôti** /ʀɔti/ *nm* **(a)** joint
**(b)** roast

**rotin** /ʀɔtɛ̃/ *nm* rattan

**rôtir** /ʀɔtiʀ/ [3] *vtr* to roast ⟨meat⟩; to toast, to grill ⟨bread⟩

**rôtisseur, -euse** /ʀɔtisœʀ, øz/ *nm,f* seller of roast meat

**rôtissoire** /ʀɔtiswaʀ/ *nf* rotisserie, roasting spit

**rotonde** /ʀɔtɔ̃d/ *nf* (building) rotunda

**rotondité** /ʀɔtɔ̃dite/ *nf* roundness

**rotule** /ʀɔtyl/ *nf* (Anat) kneecap
IDIOMS **être sur les ∼s** (colloq) to be on one's last legs

**roturier, -ière** /ʀɔtyʀje, ɛʀ/ *nm,f* commoner

**rouage** /ʀwaʒ/ *nm* **(a)** (of machine) (cog)wheel; **les ∼s** the parts *or* works
**(b)** (of administration) machinery; **les ∼s bureaucratiques** the wheels of bureaucracy

**roublard, ∼e** /ʀublaʀ, aʀd/ *adj* (colloq) crafty, cunning

**roublardise** /ʀublaʀdiz/ *nf* (colloq) craftiness, cunning

**rouble** /ʀubl/ *nm* rouble

**roucouler** /ʀukule/ [1] *vi* **(a)** ⟨bird⟩ to coo
**(b)** ⟨lovers⟩ to bill and coo

**roue** /ʀu/ *nf* wheel; **∼ dentée** cogwheel
■ **∼ motrice** driving wheel; **∼ de secours** spare wheel *or* tyre (GB), spare tire (US)
IDIOMS **être la cinquième ∼ du carrosse** to feel unwanted; **pousser qn à la ∼** to be behind sb; **faire la ∼** ⟨peacock⟩ to spread its tail, to display; ⟨person⟩ to strut around; (in gymnastics) to do a cartwheel

**rouer** /ʀwe/ [1] *vtr* **∼ qn de coups** to beat sb up

**rouerie** /ʀuʀi/ *nf* **(a)** cunning
**(b)** cunning trick

**rouet** /ʀwɛ/ *nm* spinning wheel

**rouge** /ʀuʒ/ [1] *adj* **(a)** (gen) red; ⟨person, face⟩ flushed
**(b)** ⟨beard, hair, fur⟩ ginger
**(c)** red-hot
[2] *nmf* (communist) Red
[3] *nm* **(a)** red; **le ∼ lui monta au visage** he/she went red in the face
**(b)** **∼ à joues** blusher, rouge; **∼ à lèvres** lipstick

**(c)** **le feu est au ∼** the (traffic) lights are red; **passer au ∼** to jump the lights (GB) *or* a red light
**(d)** (colloq) red (wine); **gros ∼** (colloq) cheap red wine; **un coup de ∼** (colloq) a glass of red wine
IDIOMS **être ∼ comme une tomate** *or* **une écrevisse** (from embarrassment) to be as red as a beetroot (GB) *or* a beet (US); (from running) to be red in the face

**rougeâtre** /ʀuʒɑtʀ/ *adj* reddish

**rougeaud, ∼e** /ʀuʒo, od/ *adj* ⟨person⟩ ruddy-faced; ⟨face, complexion⟩ ruddy

**rouge-gorge, pl rouges-gorges** /ʀuʒgɔʀʒ/ *nm* robin (redbreast)

**rougeoiement** /ʀuʒwamɑ̃/ *nm* red glow

**rougeole** /ʀuʒɔl/ *nf* measles

**rougeoyer** /ʀuʒwaje/ [23] *vi* ⟨sun⟩ to glow fiery red; ⟨fire⟩ to glow red

**rouget** /ʀuʒɛ/ *nm* red mullet, goatfish (US)

**rougeur** /ʀuʒœʀ/ *nf* **(a)** redness
**(b)** redness; flushing
**(c)** red blotch

**rougir** /ʀuʒiʀ/ [3] [1] *vtr* to redden
[2] *vi* **(a)** to blush; to flush; to go red; **ne ∼ de rien** to have no shame
**(b)** ⟨fruit, sky⟩ to turn red
**(c)** ⟨metal⟩ to become red hot

**rougissant, ∼e** /ʀuʒisɑ̃, ɑ̃t/ *adj* ⟨person⟩ blushing; ⟨sky⟩ reddening

**rouille** /ʀuj/ [1] *adj inv* red-brown
[2] *nf* rust

**rouiller** /ʀuje/ [1] [1] *vtr* to rust
[2] *vi* to rust, to go rusty
[3] **se rouiller** *v refl* (+ *v être*) to get rusty

**roulade** /ʀulad/ *nf* (Sport) roll

**roulant, ∼e** /ʀulɑ̃, ɑ̃t/ *adj* **table ∼e** trolley; **personnel ∼** train crew

**roulé** /ʀule/ *nm* (Culin) roll

**rouleau, pl ∼x** /ʀulo/ *nm* **(a)** roll
**(b)** breaker, roller
**(c)** (Tech) roller
**(d)** roller, curler
■ **∼ compresseur** steamroller; **∼ à pâtisserie** rolling pin

**roulement** /ʀulmɑ̃/ *nm* **(a)** (of thunder) rumble; (of drum) roll
**(b)** (of capital) circulation
**(c)** rotation; **travailler par ∼** to work (in) shifts
**(d)** (Tech) **∼ à billes** ball bearing

**rouler** /ʀule/ [1] [1] *vtr* **(a)** to roll ⟨barrel, tyre⟩; to wheel ⟨cart⟩
**(b)** to roll up ⟨carpet, sleeve, paper⟩; to roll ⟨cigarette⟩
**(c)** **∼ les épaules** to roll one's shoulders
**(d)** (colloq) **∼ qn** to cheat sb
[2] *vi* **(a)** ⟨ball, person⟩ to roll
**(b)** ⟨vehicle⟩ to go; **∼ à gauche** to drive on the left; **les bus ne roulent pas le dimanche** the buses don't run on Sundays
[3] **se rouler** *v refl* (+ *v être*) **se ∼ dans** to roll in ⟨grass, mud⟩

**roulette** /ʀulɛt/ *nf* **(a)** caster

⋯⋗

(b) roulette
(c) (dentist's) drill
IDIOMS **marcher comme sur des** ~**s** (colloq) to go smoothly *or* like a dream

**roulis** /ʀuli/ *nm* (of boat) rolling; (of car, train) swaying

**roulotte** /ʀulɔt/ *nf* (horse-drawn) caravan (GB), trailer (US)

**Roumanie** /ʀumani/ *pr nf* Romania

**roupie** /ʀupi/ *nf* rupee

**roupiller** /ʀupije/ [1] *vtr* (colloq) to sleep

**roupillon** /ʀupijɔ̃/ *nm* (colloq) snooze (colloq), nap

**rouquin, ~e** /ʀukɛ̃, in/ *nm,f* (colloq) redhead

**rouspéter** /ʀuspete/ [14] *vi* (colloq) to grumble

**rousse** /ʀus/ *adj f* ▶ ROUX

**rousseur** /ʀusœʀ/ *nf* (of hair, foliage) redness; (of shade) russet colour (GB)

**roussi** /ʀusi/ *nm* **ça sent le** ~ there's a smell of burning; (figurative) there's trouble brewing

**roussir** /ʀusiʀ/ [3] **1** *vtr* to turn [sth] brown
**2** *vi* (a) to go brown
(b) (Culin) **faire** ~ to brown

**routage** /ʀutaʒ/ *nm* sorting and mailing

**routard, ~e** /ʀutaʀ, aʀd/ *nm,f* (colloq) backpacker

**route** /ʀut/ *nf* (a) road, highway (US); **tenir la** ~ ⟨car⟩ to hold the road; (figurative) (colloq) ⟨argument⟩ to hold water; ⟨equipment⟩ to be well-made
(b) road; **il y a six heures de** ~ it's a six-hour drive; **faire de la** ~ (colloq) to do a lot of mileage
(c) route; ~**s maritimes** sea routes
(d) way; **la** ~ **sera longue** it will be a long journey; **j'ai changé d'avis en cours de** ~ I changed my mind along the way; **être en** ~ ⟨person⟩ to be on one's way; ⟨dish⟩ to be cooking; **être en** ~ **pour** to be en route to; **faire fausse** ~ to go off course; (figurative) to be mistaken; **se mettre en** ~ to set off; **en** ~**!** let's go!; **mettre en** ~ to start ⟨machine, car⟩; to get [sth] going ⟨project⟩
■ ~ **départementale** secondary road; ~ **nationale** trunk road (GB), ≈ A road (GB), national highway (US)

**routier, -ière** /ʀutje, ɛʀ/ **1** *adj* road
**2** *nm* (a) lorry driver (GB), truck driver
(b) transport café (GB), truck stop (US)

**routine** /ʀutin/ *nf* routine

**routinier, -ière** /ʀutinje, ɛʀ/ *adj* ⟨person⟩ set in one's ways; ⟨work, life⟩ routine

**rouvrir: se rouvrir** /ʀuvʀiʀ/ [32] *v refl* (+ *v être*) ⟨door⟩ to open (again); ⟨wound⟩ to open up (again)

**roux, rousse** /ʀu, ʀus/ **1** *adj* ⟨leaves⟩ russet; ⟨hair⟩ red; ⟨person⟩ red-haired; ⟨fur⟩ ginger
**2** *nm,f* red-haired person, redhead

**royal, ~e**, *mpl* **-aux** /ʀwajal, o/ *adj*
(a) royal
(b) ⟨present⟩ fit for a king; ⟨tip, salary⟩ princely
(c) ⟨indifference⟩ supreme; ⟨peace⟩ blissful

**royalement** /ʀwajalmɑ̃/ *adv* (a) royally; **être payé** ~ to be paid handsomely
(b) (colloq) **il se moque** ~ **de son travail** he really couldn't care less about his work

**royaliste** /ʀwajalist/ *adj, nmf* royalist.
IDIOMS **être plus** ~ **que le roi** to be more Catholic than the pope

**royaume** /ʀwajom/ *nm* kingdom

**Royaume-Uni** /ʀwajomyni/ *pr nm* **le** ~ the United Kingdom

**royauté** /ʀwajote/ *nf* (a) kingship
(b) monarchy

**RSVP** (*written abbr* = **répondez s'il vous plaît**) RSVP

**ruade** /ʀyad/ *nf* (a) (by horse) buck
(b) (by person, party) attack

**ruban** /ʀybɑ̃/ *nm* ribbon; ~ **adhésif** adhesive tape, sticky tape (GB)

**rubéole** /ʀybeɔl/ *nf* German measles

**rubis** /ʀybi/ *nm inv* (a) ruby
(b) ruby (red)

**rubrique** /ʀybʀik/ *nf* (a) (of newspaper) section; ~ **mondaine** social column
(b) category

**ruche** /ʀyʃ/ *nf* (a) beehive
(b) hive of activity

**rude** /ʀyd/ *adj* (a) ⟨job, day⟩ hard, tough; ⟨winter⟩ harsh; ⟨ordeal⟩ severe
(b) ⟨material, beard⟩ rough
(c) ⟨features⟩ coarse
(d) **c'est un** ~ **gaillard** he's a strapping fellow
(e) ⟨opponent⟩ tough

**rudement** /ʀydmɑ̃/ *adv* (a) roughly
(b) (colloq) really

**rudesse** /ʀydɛs/ *nf* (a) harshness, severity
(b) coarseness

**rudimentaire** /ʀydimɑ̃tɛʀ/ *adj* (a) basic
(b) (Anat) rudimentary

**rudiments** /ʀydimɑ̃/ *nm pl* **avoir quelques** ~ **de** to have a rudimentary knowledge of

**rudoyer** /ʀydwaje/ [23] *vtr* to bully

**rue** /ʀy/ *nf* street
IDIOMS **ça ne court pas les** ~**s** (colloq) it's pretty thin on the ground; **descendre dans la** ~ to take to the street

**ruée** /ʀųe/ *nf* rush; ~ **vers l'or** gold rush

**ruelle** /ʀųɛl/ *nf* alleyway, back street

**ruer** /ʀųe/ [1] **1** *vi* ⟨horse⟩ to kick
**2 se ruer** *v refl* (+ *v être*) to rush
IDIOMS ~ **dans les brancards** to rebel

**rugby** /ʀygbi/ *nm* rugby; ~ **à treize** rugby league; ~ **à quinze** rugby union

**rugbyman**, *pl* **rugbymen** /ʀygbiman, mɛn/ *nm* rugby player

**rugir** /ʀyʒiʀ/ [3] **1** *vtr* to bellow (out), to growl
**2** *vi* ⟨animal, engine⟩ to roar; ⟨wind⟩ to howl

393

**rugissement** /ʁyʒismɑ̃/ *nm* (of animal, person) roar; (of wind) howling
**rugosité** /ʁyɡozite/ *nf* roughness
**rugueux, -euse** /ʁyɡø, øz/ *adj* rough
**ruine** /ʁɥin/ *nf* (a) (of building, person, reputation, company) ruin; (of civilization) collapse; (of hope) death; **en ∼(s)** ruined; **ce n'est pas la ∼** (colloq) it's not that expensive
(b) ruin
(c) wreck
**ruiner** /ʁɥine/ [1] **1** *vtr* (a) to ruin ⟨person, economy⟩; **∼ qn** to be a drain on sb's resources
(b) to destroy ⟨health, happiness⟩
(c) to ruin ⟨life⟩; to shatter ⟨hopes⟩
**2 se ruiner** *v refl* (+ *v être*) to be ruined, to lose everything; to ruin oneself
**ruineux -euse** /ʁɥinø, øz/ *adj* very expensive
**ruisseau**, *pl* **∼x** /ʁɥiso/ *nm* (a) stream, brook
(b) **∼ de larmes** stream of tears
**ruisseler** /ʁɥisle/ [19] *vi* (a) ⟨water⟩ to stream; ⟨grease⟩ to drip
(b) to be streaming; **∼ de sueur** to be dripping with sweat
**ruissellement** /ʁɥisɛlmɑ̃/ *nm* (of rain) streaming; (of grease) dripping
**rumeur** /ʁymœʁ/ *nf* (a) rumour (GB)
(b) (of voices, wind) murmur
**ruminant** /ʁyminɑ̃/ *nm* ruminant
**ruminer** /ʁymine/ [1] **1** *vtr* (a) to ruminate
(b) to brood on ⟨misery⟩; to chew over (colloq) ⟨idea, plan⟩
**2** *vi* (a) to ruminate
(b) ⟨person⟩ to brood
**rumsteck** /ʁɔmstɛk/ *nm* rump steak
**rupestre** /ʁypɛstʁ/ *adj* (a) ⟨plants⟩ rock
(b) ⟨paintings⟩ cave, rock

**rupture** /ʁyptyʁ/ *nf* (a) (of relations) breaking-off
(b) breakdown
(c) break-up; **lettre de ∼** letter ending a relationship
(d) (of dam, dyke) breaking; (of pipe) fracture
**rural, ∼e**, *mpl* **-aux** /ʁyʁal, o/ *adj* ⟨exodus, environment⟩ rural; ⟨road, life⟩ country
**ruse** /ʁyz/ *nf* (a) trick, ruse; **∼ de guerre** (humorous) cunning stratagem
(b) cunning, craftiness
**rusé, ∼e** /ʁyze/ *adj* cunning, crafty
**ruser** /ʁyze/ [1] *vi* (a) to be crafty
(b) **∼ avec** to trick ⟨enemy, police⟩
**rush**, *pl* **rushes** /ʁœʃ/ **1** *nm* (in race) final burst
**2 rushes** *nm pl* (of film) rushes
**russe** /ʁys/ *adj, nm* Russian
**Russie** /ʁysi/ *pr nf* Russia
**rustaud, ∼e** /ʁysto, od/ *adj* rustic
**rusticité** /ʁystisite/ *nf* rustic character
**rustine®** /ʁystin/ *nf* (puncture-repair) patch
**rustique** /ʁystik/ *adj* rustic, country
**rustre** /ʁystʁ/ **1** *adj* uncouth
**2** *nm* lout
**rut** /ʁyt/ *nm* rutting season
**rutilant, ∼e** /ʁytilɑ̃, ɑ̃t/ *adj* sparkling; gleaming
**Ruanda** /ʁwɑ̃da/ *pr nm* Rwanda
**rythme** /ʁitm/ *nm* (a) rhythm; **marquer le ∼** to beat time
(b) (of growth) rate; (of life) pace
■ **∼ cardiaque** heart rate
**rythmer** /ʁitme/ [1] *vtr* (a) to give rhythm to
(b) to regulate ⟨life, work⟩
**rythmique** /ʁitmik/ *adj* rhythmic

# Ss

**s, S** /ɛs/ *nm inv* s, S
**s'** (a) ▸ SE
(b) ▸ SI¹ 2
**sa** ▸ SON¹
**sabbat** /saba/ *nm* (a) Sabbath
(b) witches' Sabbath
**sabbatique** /sabatik/ *adj* (Univ) sabbatical
**sable** /sɑbl/ *nm* sand; **∼s mouvants** quicksands
**sablé, ∼e** /sable/ **1** *adj* **pâte ∼e** shortcrust pastry
**2** *nm* shortbread biscuit (GB) *or* cookie (US)
**sabler** /sable/ [1] *vtr* to grit ⟨roadway⟩

IDIOMS **∼ le champagne** to crack open some champagne
**sablier** /sablije/ *nm* hourglass; egg timer
**sablonneux, -euse** /sablɔnø, øz/ *adj* sandy
**sabot** /sabo/ *nm* (a) clog
(b) (Zool) hoof
**sabotage** /sabotaʒ/ *nm* sabotage
**saboter** /sabote/ [1] *vtr* to sabotage
**saboteur, -euse** /sabotœʁ, øz/ *nm,f* (of equipment) saboteur
**sabre** /sɑbʁ/ *nm* (a) sword
(b) sabre (GB)

**sabrer** /sɑbʀe/ [1] *vtr* (colloq) to cut chunks out of ‹*article*›

**sac** /sak/ *nm* (a) (gen) bag
**(b)** sack
**(c)** bag(ful), sack(ful)
**(d) mettre à ~** to sack ‹*city, region*›; to ransack ‹*shop, house*›
■ **~ de couchage** sleeping bag; **~ à dos** rucksack, backpack; **~ à main** handbag, purse (US); **~ postal** mail sack; **~ à provisions** shopping bag, carry-all (US)
**IDIOMS l'affaire est dans le ~** (colloq) it's in the bag (colloq); **avoir plus d'un tour dans son ~** to have more than one trick up one's sleeve; **vider son ~** (colloq) to get it off one's chest; **se faire prendre la main dans le ~** to be caught red-handed; **mettre dans le même ~** (colloq) to lump together

**saccade** /sakad/ *nf* jerk

**saccadé, ~e** /sakade/ *adj* ‹*movement*› jerky; ‹*rhythm*› staccato; ‹*voice*› clipped

**saccager** /sakaʒe/ [13] *vtr* **(a)** to wreck, to devastate ‹*region*›; to vandalize ‹*building*›
**(b)** to sack

**saccharine** /sakaʀin/ *nf* saccharin

**SACEM** /sasɛm/ *nf* (abbr = **Société des auteurs, compositeurs et éditeurs de musique**) *association of composers and music publishers to protect copyright and royalties*

**sacerdoce** /sasɛʀdɔs/ *nm* priesthood

**sachet** /saʃɛ/ *nm* (of powder) packet; (of herbs, spices) sachet; **~ de thé** tea bag

**sacoche** /sakɔʃ/ *nf* **(a)** bag
**(b)** (on bicycle) pannier (GB), saddlebag (US)

**sacquer** /sake/ [1] *vtr* (colloq) **(a)** to sack (colloq), to fire (colloq)
**(b)** ‹*teacher*› to mark [sb] strictly
**(c) je ne peux pas le ~** I can't stand the sight of him

**sacre** /sakʀ/ *nm* (of king) coronation; (of bishop) consecration

**sacré, ~e** /sakʀe/ *adj* **(a)** ‹*art, object, place*› sacred; ‹*cause*› holy
**(b)** ‹*rule, right*› sacred
**(c)** (colloq) **être un ~ menteur** to be a hell of a liar (colloq)
**(d)** (colloq) **~ Paul, va!** Paul, you old devil!
**IDIOMS avoir le feu ~** to be full of zeal

**sacrement** /sakʀəmɑ̃/ *nm* sacrament; **les derniers ~s** the last rites

**sacrément** /sakʀemɑ̃/ *adv* (colloq) incredibly (colloq)

**sacrer** /sakʀe/ [1] *vtr* to crown ‹*king*›; to consecrate ‹*bishop*›

**sacrifice** /sakʀifis/ *nm* sacrifice

**sacrifier** /sakʀifje/ [1] **1** *vtr* to sacrifice
**2 sacrifier à** *v+prep* to conform to ‹*fashion*›
**3 se sacrifier** *v refl* (+ *v être*) **(a)** to sacrifice oneself
**(b)** (colloq) to make sacrifices

**sacrilège** /sakʀilɛʒ/ *nm* sacrilege

**sacristie** /sakʀisti/ *nf* (of catholic church) sacristy; (of protestant church) vestry

**sacro-saint, ~e, mpl ~s** /sakʀosɛ̃, ɛ̃t/ *adj* sacrosanct

**sadique** /sadik/ **1** *adj* sadistic
**2** *nmf* sadist

**sadisme** /sadism/ *nm* sadism

**sadomasochisme** /sadomazɔʃism/ *nm* sadomasochism

**safari** /safaʀi/ *nm* safari

**safran** /safʀɑ̃/ *adj inv, nm* saffron

**saga** /saga/ *nf* saga

**sagacité** /sagasite/ *nf* sagacity, shrewdness

**sage** /saʒ/ **1** *adj* **(a)** wise, sensible
**(b)** good, well-behaved
**(c)** ‹*tastes, fashion*› sober
**2** *nm* **(a)** wise man, sage
**(b)** expert

**sage-femme, pl sages-femmes** /saʒfam/ *nf* midwife

**sagement** /saʒmɑ̃/ *adv* **(a)** wisely
**(b)** ‹*sit, listen*› quietly
**(c)** ‹*dress*› soberly

**sagesse** /saʒɛs/ *nf* **(a)** wisdom, common sense; (of advice) soundness; **la voix de la ~** the voice of reason
**(b)** good behaviour (GB)

**Sagittaire** /saʒitɛʀ/ *pr nm* Sagittarius

**Sahara** /saaʀa/ *pr nm* Sahara

**saignant, ~e** /sɛɲɑ̃, ɑ̃t/ *adj* **(a)** ‹*meat*› rare
**(b)** (figurative) (colloq) ‹*criticism*› savage

**saignée** /sɛɲe/ *nf* **(a)** (Med) bloodletting, bleeding
**(b)** (in budget) hole
**(c)** (in tree) cut

**saignement** /sɛɲ(ə)mɑ̃/ *nm* bleeding

**saigner** /sɛɲe/ [1] **1** *vtr* **(a)** (Med) to bleed
**(b)** to kill ‹*animal*› (by slitting its throat); **~ un cochon** to stick a pig
**2** *vi* to bleed; **~ du nez** to have a nosebleed
**IDIOMS ~ qn à blanc** to bleed sb dry; **se ~ (aux quatre veines) pour qn** to make big sacrifices for sb

**saillant, ~e** /sajɑ̃, ɑ̃t/ *adj* **(a)** ‹*jaw*› prominent; ‹*muscle, eyes*› bulging; ‹*angle*› salient
**(b)** ‹*fact, episode*› salient

**saillie** /saji/ *nf* **(a)** projection; **le balcon est en ~** the balcony juts out
**(b)** (Zool) covering

**saillir** /sajiʀ/ [28] *vi* **(a)** to jut out
**(b)** ‹*ribs, muscles*› to bulge

**sain, ~e** /sɛ̃, sɛn/ *adj* (gen) healthy, sound; ‹*wound*› clean; **~ d'esprit** sane; **~ de corps et d'esprit** sound in body and mind; **~ et sauf** ‹*return*› safe and sound

**saindoux** /sɛ̃du/ *nm inv* lard

**sainement** /sɛnmɑ̃/ *adv* **(a)** ‹*live*› healthily
**(b)** ‹*reason*› soundly

**saint, ~e** /sɛ̃, sɛ̃t/ **1** *adj* **(a)** holy; **vendredi ~** Good Friday

**(b)** ~ **Paul** Saint Paul
**2** *nm,f* saint
■ ~**e nitouche** goody-goody (colloq); **la Sainte Vierge** the Virgin Mary

**Saint-Barthélémy** /sɛ̃baʀtelemi/ *nf* **la** ~ the St Bartholomew's Day massacre

**saint-bernard** /sɛ̃bɛʀnaʀ/ *nm inv* St Bernard

**Saint-Esprit** /sɛ̃tɛspʀi/ *pr nm* Holy Spirit

**sainteté** /sɛ̃te/ *nf* saintliness

**saint-glinglin**: **à la saint-glinglin** /alasɛ̃glɛ̃glɛ̃/ *phr* (colloq) probably never; **rester/attendre jusqu'à la** ~ to stay/to wait till the cows come home (colloq)

**saint-honoré** /sɛ̃tɔnɔʀe/ *nm inv*: cream-filled tart topped with choux and caramel

**Saint-Jacques** /sɛ̃ʒak/ *pr n* **coquille** ~ scallop

**Saint-Jean** /sɛ̃ʒɑ̃/ *nf* **la** ~ Midsummer Day

**Saint-Sylvestre** /sɛ̃silvɛstʀ/ *nf* **la** ~ New Year's Eve

**saisie** /sezi/ *nf* **(a)** (gen, Law) seizure
**(b)** keyboarding; ~ **de données** data capture

**saisir** /seziʀ/ [3] **1** *vtr* **(a)** to grab; to seize; ~ **au vol** to catch ⟨*ball*⟩; **'affaire à** ~' 'amazing bargain'
**(b)** to understand
**(c)** to catch ⟨*name, bits of conversation*⟩
**(d)** ⟨*emotion, cold*⟩ to grip ⟨*person*⟩
**(e)** to strike, to impress ⟨*person*⟩
**(f)** (Law) to seize ⟨*property*⟩; ~ **la justice d'une affaire** to refer a matter to a court
**(g)** (Comput) to capture ⟨*data*⟩; to key ⟨*text*⟩
**2 se saisir** *v refl* (+ *v être*) **se** ~ **de** to catch *or* grab hold of ⟨*object*⟩

**saisissant, ~e** /sezisɑ̃, ɑ̃t/ *adj* **(a)** ⟨*cold*⟩ piercing
**(b)** ⟨*effect, resemblance*⟩ striking

**saison** /sɛzɔ̃/ *nf* (gen) season; **en cette** ~ at this time of year; **en toute** ~ all (the) year round; **la haute/morte** ~ the high/slack season; **prix hors** ~ off-season prices

**saisonnier, -ière** /sɛzɔnje, ɛʀ/ **1** *adj* seasonal
**2** *nm,f* (worker) seasonal worker

**salace** /salas/ *adj* salacious

**salade** /salad/ *nf* **(a)** lettuce
**(b)** salad
**(c)** (colloq) muddle; **raconter des** ~**s** to spin yarns (colloq)

**saladier** /saladje/ *nm* salad bowl

**salaire** /salɛʀ/ *nm* salary; wages

**salaison** /salɛzɔ̃/ *nf* salt meat

**salamandre** /salamɑ̃dʀ/ *nf* salamander

**salant** /salɑ̃/ *adj m* **marais** ~ saltern

**salarial, ~e,** *mpl* **-iaux** /salaʀjal, o/ *adj*
**(a)** ⟨*policy, rise*⟩ wage
**(b) cotisation** ~**e** employee's contribution

**salarié, ~e** /salaʀje/ **1** *adj* ⟨*worker*⟩ wage-earning; ⟨*job*⟩ salaried
**2** *nm,f* **(a)** wage earner
**(b)** salaried employee

---

**salaud** /salo/ *nm* (offensive) (slang) bastard (slang)

**sale** /sal/ **1** *adj* **(a)** (*after n*) dirty
**(b)** (*before n*) (colloq) ⟨*person*⟩ horrible; ⟨*animal, illness, habit*⟩ nasty; ⟨*weather*⟩ foul, horrible; ⟨*work, place*⟩ rotten; ~ **menteur!** you dirty liar!; **il a une** ~ **tête** he looks dreadful; **faire une** ~ **tête** to look annoyed; **un** ~ **coup** a very nasty blow; **un** ~ **caractère** a foul temper
**2** *nm* **mettre qch au** ~ to put sth in the wash

**salé, ~e** /sale/ *adj* **(a)** salt, salty
**(b)** salted; ⟨*snack*⟩ savoury (GB)
**(c)** (colloq) ⟨*bill*⟩ steep

**salement** /salmɑ̃/ *adv* **(a) manger** ~ to be a messy eater
**(b)** (colloq) badly, seriously

**saler** /sale/ [1] *vtr* **(a)** to salt ⟨*food*⟩; ~ **et poivrer** to add salt and pepper
**(b)** to grit (GB), to salt (US) ⟨*road*⟩

**saleté** /salte/ *nf* **(a)** dirtiness; dirt; filth; **ramasser les** ~**s** to pick up the rubbish (GB) *or* trash (US); **faire des** ~**s** to make a mess
**(b)** (colloq) **c'est de la** ~ (gadget, goods) it's rubbish; **c'est une vraie** ~ **ce virus!** it's a rotten bug!

**salière** /saljɛʀ/ *nf* saltcellar, saltshaker (US)

**salir** /saliʀ/ [3] **1** *vtr* **(a)** to dirty; to soil
**(b)** to sully ⟨*reputation*⟩
**2** *vi* ⟨*industry, coal*⟩ to pollute
**3 se salir** *v refl* (+ *v être*) to get dirty, to dirty oneself

**salissant, ~e** /salisɑ̃, ɑ̃t/ *adj* **(a)** ⟨*colour*⟩ which shows the dirt
**(b)** ⟨*work*⟩ dirty

**salive** /saliv/ *nf* saliva

**saliver** /salive/ [1] *vi* to salivate; ~ **devant qch** to drool over sth

**salle** /sal/ *nf* **(a)** (gen) room; hall; (in restaurant) (dining) room; (in hospital) ward; (in theatre) auditorium; **faire** ~ **comble** ⟨*show*⟩ to be packed; **en** ~ ⟨*sport*⟩ indoor
**(b)** audience
■ ~ **d'attente** waiting room; ~ **de bains** bathroom; ~ **de cinéma** cinema (GB), movie theater (US); ~ **de classe** classroom; ~ **de concert** concert hall; ~ **d'eau** shower room; ~ **d'embarquement** departure lounge; ~ **des fêtes** village hall; community centre (GB); ~ **de garde** (in hospital) staff room; ~ **de gymnastique** gymnasium; ~ **de jeu(x)** (in casino) gaming room; (for children) playroom; ~ **à manger** dining room; dining-room suite; ~ **de séjour** living room; ~ **des ventes** auction room

**salon** /salɔ̃/ *nm* **(a)** (gen) lounge; drawing room
**(b)** sitting-room suite; ~ **de jardin** garden furniture
**(c)** (trade) show; fair; exhibition; ~ **du livre** book fair
**(d)** (of intellectuals) salon
**(e)** (Comput) chatroom ⋯⧫

**S**

■ ~ **de beauté** beauty salon; ~ **de coiffure** hairdressing salon; ~ **d'essayage** fitting room; ~ **de thé** tearoom

**salopette** /salɔpɛt/ *nf* overalls

**salpêtre** /salpɛtʀ/ *nm* saltpetre (GB)

**salsifis** /salsifi/ *nm inv* salsify

**saltimbanque** /saltɛ̃bɑ̃k/ *nmf* **(a)** street acrobat
**(b)** entertainer

**salubre** /salybʀ/ *adj* ⟨*lodgings*⟩ salubrious

**salubrité** /salybʀite/ *nf* (of air, climate) healthiness; (of dwelling) salubrity
■ ~ **publique** public health

**saluer** /salɥe/ [1] *vtr* **(a)** to greet ⟨*person*⟩; ~ **qn de la tête** to nod to sb
**(b)** to say goodbye to ⟨*person*⟩
**(c)** (Mil) to salute
**(d)** to welcome ⟨*decision, news*⟩
**(e)** to pay tribute to ⟨*memory*⟩

**salut** /saly/ *nm* **(a)** greeting; ~**!** hello!, hi!; bye!; ~ **de la tête** nod
**(b)** salute
**(c)** salvation

**salutaire** /salytɛʀ/ *adj* ⟨*experience*⟩ salutary; ⟨*effect*⟩ beneficial; ⟨*air*⟩ healthy

**salutation** /salytasjɔ̃/ *nf* greeting

**salvateur, -trice** /salvatœʀ, tʀis/ *adj* saving

**salve** /salv/ *nf* **(a)** salvo; **tirer une** ~ **d'honneur** to fire a salute
**(b)** ~ **d'applaudissements** burst of applause

**samedi** /samdi/ *nm* Saturday

**SAMU** /samy/ *nm* (*abbr* = **Service d'assistance médicale d'urgence**) ≈ mobile accident unit (GB), emergency medical service, EMS (US)

**sanatorium** /sanatɔʀjɔm/ *nm* sanatorium (GB), sanitarium (US)

**sanctifier** /sɑ̃ktifje/ [1] *vtr* to sanctify

**sanction** /sɑ̃ksjɔ̃/ *nf* (Law) penalty, sanction; disciplinary measure; (Sch) punishment

**sanctionner** /sɑ̃ksjɔne/ [1] *vtr* **(a)** to punish
**(b)** to give official recognition to ⟨*training*⟩

**sanctuaire** /sɑ̃ktɥɛʀ/ *nm* **(a)** shrine
**(b)** sanctuary

**sandale** /sɑ̃dal/ *nf* sandal

**sandwich**, *pl* ~**s** *or* ~**es** /sɑ̃dwitʃ/ *nm* sandwich; (**pris**) **en** ~ sandwiched

**sang** /sɑ̃/ *nm* **(a)** blood; **être en** ~ to be covered with blood; **se terminer dans le** ~ to end in bloodshed
**(b) de** ~ ⟨*brother, ties*⟩ blood; **être du même** ~ to be kin
**IDIOMS il a ça dans le** ~ it's in his blood; **mettre qch à feu et à** ~ to put sth to fire and sword; **mon** ~ **n'a fait qu'un tour** my heart missed a beat; I saw red; **se faire du mauvais** ~ (colloq) to worry; **bon** ~**!** for God's sake! (colloq)

**sang-froid** /sɑ̃fʀwa/ *nm inv* composure; **garde ton** ~**!** keep calm!; **de** ~ in cold blood

**sanglant**, ~**e** /sɑ̃glɑ̃, ɑ̃t/ *adj* bloody

**sangle** /sɑ̃gl/ *nf* **(a)** (gen) strap
**(b)** (of saddle) girth
**(c)** (of seat, bed) webbing

**sangler** /sɑ̃gle/ [1] *vtr* to girth ⟨*horse*⟩

**sanglier** /sɑ̃glije/ *nm* wild boar

**sanglot** /sɑ̃glo/ *nm* sob

**sangloter** /sɑ̃glɔte/ [1] *vi* to sob

**sangsue** /sɑ̃sy/ *nf* leech

**sanguin**, ~**e¹** /sɑ̃gɛ̃, in/ *adj* blood

**sanguinaire** /sɑ̃ginɛʀ/ *adj* ⟨*crime*⟩ bloody; ⟨*person*⟩ bloodthirsty

**sanguine²** /sɑ̃gin/ **1** *adj f* ▶ SANGUIN
**2** *nf* **(a)** blood orange
**(b)** red chalk drawing

**sanguinolent**, ~**e** /sɑ̃ginɔlɑ̃, ɑ̃t/ *adj* blood-stained

**sanisette®** /sanizɛt/ *nf* automatic public toilet

**sanitaire** /sanitɛʀ/ **1** *adj* ⟨*regulations*⟩ health; ⟨*conditions*⟩ sanitary
**2 sanitaires** *nm pl* **les** ~**s** (in house) the bathroom; (in campsite) the toilet block

**sans** /sɑ̃/ **1** *adv* without
**2** *prep* **(a)** without; **un couple** ~ **enfant** a childless couple; ~ **cela** otherwise
**(b) il est resté trois mois** ~ **téléphoner** he didn't call for three months; **il est poli,** ~ **plus** he's polite, but that's as far as it goes
**(c) on sera dix** ~ **les enfants** there'll be ten of us not counting the children; **500 euros** ~ **l'hôtel** 500 euros not including accommodation
**3 sans que** *phr* without; **pars** ~ **qu'on te voie** leave without anyone seeing you
■ ~ **domicile fixe, SDF** of no fixed abode, NFA

**sans-abri** /sɑ̃zabri/ *nmf inv* **un** ~ a homeless person; **les** ~ the homeless

**sans-emploi** /sɑ̃zɑ̃plwa/ *nmf inv* unemployed person

**sans-faute** /sɑ̃fot/ *nm inv* faultless performance

**sans-gêne** /sɑ̃ʒɛn/ *adj inv* bad-mannered

**santal** /sɑ̃tal/ *nm* sandalwood

**santé** /sɑ̃te/ *nf* health; **avoir la** ~ to enjoy good health; **se refaire une** ~ to build up one's strength; **avoir une petite** ~ to be frail; **à votre** ~**!** cheers!; **à la** ~ **de Janet!** here's to Janet!

**santon** /sɑ̃tɔ̃/ *nm* Christmas crib figure

**saoul**, ~**e** = SOÛL

**saper** /sape/ [1] **1** *vtr* to undermine
**2 se saper** *v refl* (+ *v être*) (colloq) to dress

**sapeur** /sapœʀ/ *nm* sapper
**IDIOMS fumer comme un** ~ to smoke like a chimney

**sapeur-pompier**, *pl* **sapeurs-pompiers** /sapœʀpɔ̃pje/ *nm* fireman

**saphir** /safiʀ/ *nm* **(a)** sapphire
**(b)** (on record player) stylus

**sapin** /sapɛ̃/ *nm* **(a)** fir tree; ~ **de Noël** Christmas tree
**(b)** deal

**saquer** /sake/ [1] *vtr* (colloq) = SACQUER

**sarbacane** /saʀbakan/ *nf* blowpipe

**sarcasme** /saʀkasm/ *nm* **(a)** sarcasm
**(b)** sarcastic remark

**sarcastique** /saʀkastik/ *adj* sarcastic

**sarcophage** /saʀkɔfaʒ/ *nm* sarcophagus

**sardine** /saʀdin/ *nf* **(a)** (Zool) sardine
**(b)** (colloq) tent peg

**sarment** /saʀmɑ̃/ *nm* vine shoot

**sarrasin** /saʀazɛ̃/ *nm* buckwheat

**sarrau** /saʀo/ *nm* smock

**sas** /sas/ *nm inv* **(a)** airlock
**(b)** (on canal) lock
**(c)** (in bank) security double door system

**satanique** /satanik/ *adj* **(a)** ⟨smile, ruse⟩ fiendish
**(b)** ⟨cult⟩ Satanic

**satellite** /satɛlit/ *nm* satellite

**satiété** /sasjete/ [1] *nf* satiation, satiety
[2] **à satiété** *phr* **(a)** manger à ∼ to eat one's fill
**(b)** ⟨say, repeat⟩ ad nauseam

**satin** /satɛ̃/ *nm* satin

**satiné**, **∼e** /satine/ *adj* ⟨fabric, cloth⟩ satiny; ⟨paint⟩ satin-finish

**satire** /satiʀ/ *nf* satire

**satirique** /satiʀik/ *adj* satirical

**satisfaction** /satisfaksjɔ̃/ *nf* satisfaction; **la ∼ de nos besoins** the fulfilment (GB) of our needs

**satisfaire** /satisfɛʀ/ [10] [1] *vtr* (gen) to satisfy; to fulfil (GB) ⟨aspiration, requirement⟩
[2] **satisfaire à** *v+prep* to fulfil (GB) ⟨obligation⟩; to meet ⟨norm, standard⟩
[3] **se satisfaire** *v refl* (+ *v être*) **se ∼ de** to be satisfied with ⟨explanation⟩; to be content with ⟨low salary⟩

**satisfaisant**, **∼e** /satisfəzɑ̃, ɑ̃t/ *adj*
**(a)** satisfactory
**(b)** satisfying

**satisfait**, **∼e** /satisfɛ, ɛt/ *adj* ⟨customer, need, smile⟩ satisfied; ⟨desire⟩ gratified; ⟨person⟩ happy

**saturation** /satyʀasjɔ̃/ *nf* (of market) saturation; (in trains, hotels) overcrowding; (of network) overloading; **arriver à ∼** ⟨market, network⟩ to reach saturation point; ⟨person⟩ to have had as much as one can take

**saturé**, **∼e** /satyʀe/ *adj* ⟨market⟩ saturated; ⟨profession⟩ overcrowded

**saturer** /satyʀe/ [1] *vtr* to saturate

**satyre** /satiʀ/ *nm* **(a)** satyr
**(b)** lecher

**sauce** /sos/ *nf* (Culin) sauce; **(r)allonger la ∼** (figurative) (colloq) to spin things out
IDIOMS **mettre qch à toutes les ∼s** to adapt sth to any purpose

**saucière** /sosjɛʀ/ *nf* sauceboat

**saucisse** /sosis/ *nf* sausage; **chair à ∼** sausage meat
■ **∼ de Francfort** frankfurter

**saucisson** /sosisɔ̃/ *nm* (slicing) sausage; **∼ à l'ail** garlic sausage; **∼ sec** ≈ salami

**sauf¹** /sof/ [1] *prep* **(a)** except, but
**(b)** **∼ contrordre** failing an order to the contrary; **∼ avis contraire** unless otherwise stated; **∼ erreur de ma part** if I'm not mistaken
[2] **sauf si** *phr* unless
[3] **sauf que** *phr* except that

**sauf²**, **sauve** /sof, sov/ *adj* **(a)** safe; **laisser la vie sauve à qn** to spare sb's life
**(b)** ⟨honour, reputation⟩ intact

**sauf-conduit**, *pl* **∼s** /sofkɔ̃dɥi/ *nm* safe-conduct

**sauge** /soʒ/ *nf* sage

**saugrenu**, **∼e** /sogʀəny/ *adj* crazy, potty (GB) (colloq)

**saule** /sol/ *nm* willow

**saumâtre** /somɑtʀ/ *adj* ⟨water⟩ brackish; ⟨taste⟩ bitter and salty

**saumon** /somɔ̃/ *nm* salmon

**saumure** /somyʀ/ *nf* brine

**sauna** /sona/ *nm* sauna

**saupoudrer** /supudʀe/ [1] *vtr* **(a)** to sprinkle
**(b)** (figurative) to give [sth] sparingly

**saur** /sɔʀ/ *adj m* **hareng ∼** kippered herring

**saut** /so/ *nm* **(a)** jump; **faire un petit ∼ to skip**; **au ∼ du lit** first thing in the morning
**(b)** (Sport) **le ∼** jumping
**(c)** (colloq) **faire un ∼ chez qn** to pop in and see sb
■ **∼ à la corde** skipping; **∼ à l'élastique** bungee jumping; **∼ en hauteur** high jump; **∼ à la perche** pole vault; **∼ périlleux** mid-air somersault

**saute** /sot/ *nf* **∼ de température** sudden change in temperature; **∼ d'humeur** mood swing

**sauté**, **∼e** /sote/ [1] *adj* (Culin) sautéed
[2] *nm* (Culin) **∼ d'agneau** sautéed lamb

**saute-mouton** /sotmutɔ̃/ *nm inv* leapfrog

**sauter** /sote/ [1] [1] *vtr* **(a)** to jump ⟨distance, height⟩; to jump over ⟨stream⟩
**(b)** to skip ⟨meal, paragraph⟩; to leave out ⟨details⟩; (Sch) **∼ une classe** to skip a year
**(c)** to miss ⟨word, turn⟩
[2] *vi* **(a)** to jump; **∼ à pieds joints** to jump with one's feet together; **∼ à la corde** to skip; **faire ∼ un enfant sur ses genoux** to dandle a child on one's knee; **∼ sur qn** to pounce on sb; **∼ à la gorge de qn** to go for sb's throat; **∼ au cou de qn** to greet sb with a kiss
**(b)** **∼ dans un taxi** to jump *or* hop into a taxi
**(c)** **∼ d'un sujet à l'autre** to skip from one subject to another
**(d)** (colloq) **faire ∼ une réunion** to cancel a meeting; **faire ∼ une contravention** to get out of paying a parking ticket
**(e)** ⟨bicycle chain, fan belt⟩ to come off
**(f)** **faire ∼ une serrure** to force a lock; **faire ∼ les boutons** to burst one's buttons ⋯⋗

S

**(g)** ⟨bridge, building⟩ to be blown up, to go up; **faire ∼ les plombs** to blow the fuses **(h)** (Culin) **faire ∼ to sauté** ⟨onions⟩ IDIOMS **∼ aux yeux** to be blindingly obvious; **et que ça saute!** (colloq) make it snappy! (colloq); **∼ au plafond** (colloq) to jump for joy; to hit the roof (colloq); to be staggered

**sauterelle** /sotʀɛl/ nf grasshopper

**sauterie** /sotʀi/ nf party

**sautillant, ∼e** /sotijɑ̃, ɑ̃t/ adj ⟨rhythm, gait⟩ bouncy; ⟨bird⟩ hopping

**sautiller** /sotije/ [1] vi **(a)** ⟨bird⟩ to hop **(b)** ⟨child⟩ to skip along; to jump up and down

**sauvage** /sovaʒ/ **1** adj **(a)** ⟨animal, plant⟩ wild; ⟨tribe⟩ primitive **(b)** ⟨behaviour⟩ savage, wild; ⟨struggle⟩ fierce **(c)** unsociable **(d)** illegal **2** nmf **(a)** savage **(b)** unsociable person, loner

**sauvagement** /sovaʒmɑ̃/ adv savagely

**sauvageon, -onne** /sovaʒɔ̃, ɔn/ nm,f wild child

**sauvagerie** /sovaʒʀi/ nf savagery

**sauve** ▶ SAUF²

**sauvegarde** /sovɡaʀd/ nf (of heritage, peace, values) maintenance; (of rights) protection

**sauvegarder** /sovɡaʀde/ [1] vtr **(a)** to safeguard **(b)** (Comput) to save; to back [sth] up ⟨file⟩

**sauve-qui-peut** /sovkipø/ nm inv stampede

**sauver** /sove/ [1] **1** vtr **(a)** (gen) to save; **∼ la vie à qn** to save sb's life; **elle est sauvée** ⟨ill person⟩ she has pulled through (colloq) **(b)** to salvage ⟨goods⟩ **(c) ce qui le sauve à mes yeux, c'est sa générosité** his redeeming feature for me is his generosity **2 se sauver** v refl (+ v être) **(a)** to escape; to run away; (from danger) to run **(b)** (colloq) **il faut que je me sauve** I've got to rush off now IDIOMS **∼ la situation** to save the day; **sauve qui peut!** run for your life!

**sauvetage** /sovtaʒ/ nm rescue; **cours de ∼** life-saving training

**sauveteur** /sovtœʀ/ nm rescuer

**sauvette: à la sauvette** /alasovɛt/ phr **(a)** ⟨prepare, sign⟩ in a rush **(b)** ⟨film, record⟩ on the sly

**sauveur** /sovœʀ/ nm saviour (GB)

**savamment** /savamɑ̃/ adv **(a)** learnedly, eruditely **(b)** skilfully (GB)

**savane** /savan/ nf savannah

**savant, ∼e** /savɑ̃, ɑ̃t/ **1** adj **(a)** ⟨person⟩ learned, erudite **(b)** ⟨study⟩ scholarly; ⟨calculation⟩ complicated **(c)** ⟨manoeuvre⟩ clever; ⟨direction⟩ skilful (GB) **(d)** ⟨animal⟩ performing

**2** nm,f scholar **3** nm scientist

**savate** /savat/ nf (colloq) **(a)** old slipper **(b)** old shoe

**saveur** /savœʀ/ nf flavour (GB); **sans ∼** tasteless

**savoir¹** /savwaʀ/ [47] **1** vtr **(a)** to know ⟨truth, answer⟩; **vous n'êtes pas sans ∼ que** you are no doubt aware that; **va or allez ∼!** who knows!; **est-ce que je sais, moi!** how should I know!; **pour autant que je sache** as far as I know; **comment l'as-tu su?** how did you find out?; **je l'ai su par elle** she told me about it; **ne ∼ que faire pour...** to be at a loss as to how to...; **sachant que** knowing that; given that; **qui vous savez** you-know-who; **je ne sais qui** somebody or other; **tu en sais des choses!** you really know a thing or two! **(b) ∼ faire** to know how to do; **je sais conduire** I can drive; **∼ écouter** to be a good listener; **elle sait y faire avec les hommes** she knows how to handle men **2 se savoir** v refl (+ v être) **ça se saurait** people would know about it **3 à savoir** phr that is to say IDIOMS **ne pas ∼ où donner de la tête** not to know whether one is coming or going

**savoir²** /savwaʀ/ nm **(a)** learning **(b)** knowledge **(c)** body of knowledge

**savoir-faire** /savwaʀfɛʀ/ nm inv know-how

**savoir-vivre** /savwaʀvivʀ/ nm inv manners

**savon** /savɔ̃/ nm **(a)** soap; **∼ de Marseille** household soap **(b)** (bar of) soap IDIOMS **passer un ∼ à qn** (colloq) to give sb a telling-off

**savonner** /savɔne/ [1] vtr to soap

**savonnette** /savɔnɛt/ nf small cake of soap

**savourer** /savuʀe/ [1] vtr to savour (GB)

**savoureux, -euse** /savuʀø, øz/ adj ⟨dish⟩ tasty; ⟨anecdote⟩ juicy

**saxophone** /saksɔfɔn/ nm saxophone

**saxophoniste** /saksɔfɔnist/ nmf saxophonist

**scabreux, -euse** /skabʀø, øz/ adj obscene

**scalp** /skalp/ nm **(a)** scalp **(b)** scalping

**scalpel** /skalpɛl/ nm scalpel

**scalper** /skalpe/ [1] vtr to scalp

**scandale** /skɑ̃dal/ nm scandal; **faire (un or du) ∼** (gen) to cause a scandal; ⟨person⟩ to cause a fuss; **la presse à ∼** the gutter press; **c'est un ∼!** it's scandalous!

**scandaleux, -euse** /skɑ̃dalø, øz/ adj scandalous, outrageous

**scandaliser** /skɑ̃dalize/ [1] **1** vtr to outrage **2 se scandaliser** v refl (+ v être) to be shocked

**scander** /skɑ̃de/ [1] *vtr* **(a)** to scan
**(b)** to chant ⟨*slogan, name*⟩

**scandinave** /skɑ̃dinav/ *adj* Scandinavian

**scanneur** /skanœʀ/ *nm* scanner

**scaphandre** /skafɑ̃dʀ/ *nm* **(a)** deep-sea
diving suit
**(b)** spacesuit

**scaphandrier** /skafɑ̃dʀije/ *nm* deep-sea
diver

**scarabée** /skaʀabe/ *nm* **(a)** beetle
**(b)** scarab

**scarlatine** /skaʀlatin/ *nf* scarlet fever

**scatologie** /skatɔlɔʒi/ *nf* scatology

**sceau**, *pl* ∼**x** /so/ *nm* **(a)** seal; **sous le** ∼
**du secret** in strictest secrecy
**(b)** stamp, hallmark

**scélérat**, ∼**e** /seleʀa, at/ *nm,f* villain

**scellé** /sele/ *nm* seal; **apposer les** ∼**s** to
affix seals

**sceller** /sele/ [1] *vtr* **(a)** to seal
**(b)** to fix [sth] securely ⟨*shelf, bar*⟩

**scénario** /senaʀjo/ *nm* **(a)** screenplay,
script
**(b)** scenario; ∼ **catastrophe** nightmare
scenario

**scénariste** /senaʀist/ *nmf* scriptwriter

**scène** /sɛn/ *nf* **(a)** (in theatre) stage; **entrer
en** ∼ to come on
**(b)** scene; **la** ∼ **se passe à Paris** the scene is
set in Paris
**(c)** quitter **la** ∼ to give up the stage; **mettre
en** ∼ to stage ⟨*play*⟩; to direct ⟨*film*⟩
**(d)** scene; **occuper le devant de la** ∼
(figurative) to be in the news
**(e)** faire une ∼ to throw a fit (colloq)
**(f)** scene; ∼**s de panique** scenes of panic
■ ∼ **de ménage** domestic dispute

**scepticisme** /sɛptisism/ *nm* scepticism
(GB), skepticism (US)

**sceptique** /sɛptik/ **1** *adj* sceptical (GB),
skeptical (US); **laisser qn** ∼ to leave sb
unconvinced
**2** *nmf* sceptic (GB), skeptic (US)

**sceptre** /sɛptʀ/ *nm* sceptre (GB)

**schéma** /ʃema/ *nm* **(a)** diagram
**(b)** outline
**(c)** pattern

**schématique** /ʃematik/ *adj* **(a)** ⟨*vision,
argument*⟩ simplistic
**(b)** schematic

**schématiser** /ʃematize/ [1] *vtr* to
simplify

**schizophrénie** /skizɔfʀeni/ *nf*
schizophrenia

**sciatique** /sjatik/ **1** *adj* **nerf** ∼ sciatic
nerve
**2** *nf* **avoir une** ∼ to have sciatica

**scie** /si/ *nf* saw; ∼ **sauteuse** jigsaw

**sciemment** /sjamɑ̃/ *adv* knowingly

**science** /sjɑ̃s/ *nf* **(a)** science
**(b)** knowledge
■ ∼**s naturelles** ≈ biology (*sg*); ∼**s occultes**
black arts; **Sciences Po** (colloq) *Institute of
Political Science*

**science-fiction** /sjɑ̃sfiksjɔ̃/ *nf* science
fiction

**scientifique** /sjɑ̃tifik/ **1** *adj* scientific
**2** *nmf* scientist

**scier** /sje/ [2] *vtr* **(a)** to saw
**(b)** (colloq) to stun

**scierie** /siʀi/ *nf* sawmill

**scinder** /sɛ̃de/ [1] **1** *vtr* to split ⟨*group*⟩
**2** **se scinder** *v refl* (+ *v être*) to split up

**scintillant**, ∼**e** /sɛ̃tijɑ̃, ɑ̃t/ *adj* twinkling

**scintiller** /sɛ̃tije/ [1] *vi* ⟨*diamond*⟩ to
sparkle; ⟨*star*⟩ to twinkle; ⟨*water*⟩ to glisten

**scission** /sisjɔ̃/ *nf* **(a)** split, schism
**(b)** fission

**sciure** /sjyʀ/ *nf* ∼ **(de bois)** sawdust

**sclérose** /skleʀoz/ *nf* **(a)** (Med) sclerosis
**(b)** fossilization, ossification
■ ∼ **en plaques** multiple sclerosis, MS

**scléroser** /skleʀoze/ [1] **1** *vtr* (Med) to
sclerose
**2** **se scléroser** *v refl* (+ *v être*)
**(a)** ⟨*institution, person*⟩ to become fossilized
**(b)** (Med) ⟨*tissue*⟩ to become hardened

**scolaire** /skɔlɛʀ/ *adj* ⟨*holidays, book*⟩
school; ⟨*reform, publication*⟩ educational;
⟨*failure*⟩ academic; **établissement** ∼ school

**scolarisation** /skɔlaʀizasjɔ̃/ *nf* schooling

**scolariser** /skɔlaʀize/ [1] *vtr* to send [sb]
to school

**scolarité** /skɔlaʀite/ *nf* **(a)** schooling;
**durant ma** ∼ when I was at school; **la** ∼
**obligatoire** compulsory education
**(b)** (in university) registrar's office

**scoliose** /skɔljoz/ *nf* scoliosis

**scooter** /skutœʀ/ *nm* (motor) scooter

**score** /skɔʀ/ *nm* **(a)** (Sch, Sport) score; ∼ **nul**
draw (GB), tie (US)
**(b)** results

**scorie** /skɔʀi/ *nf* **(a)** scoria
**(b)** slag

**scorpion** /skɔʀpjɔ̃/ *nm* (Zool) scorpion

**Scorpion** /skɔʀpjɔ̃/ *pr nm* Scorpio

**scotch**, *pl* ∼**es** /skɔtʃ/ *nm* **(a)** Scotch
(whisky)
**(b)** ®Sellotape® (GB), Scotch® tape (US)

**scotcher** /skɔtʃe/ [1] *vtr* to Sellotape®
(GB), to Scotch-tape® (US)

**scout**, ∼**e** /skut/ **1** *adj* scout
**2** *nm,f* boy scout/girl scout

**scribe** /skʀib/ *nm* scribe

**scribouillard**, ∼**e** /skʀibujaʀ, aʀd/ *nm,f*
(colloq) pen pusher (GB) (colloq), pencil pusher
(US)

**script** /skʀipt/ *nm* **(a)** écrire en ∼ to print
**(b)** script

**scripte** /skʀipt/ *nmf* continuity man/girl

**scrupule** /skʀypyl/ *nm* scruple

**scrupuleusement** /skʀypyløzmɑ̃/ *adv*
scrupulously

**scrupuleux, -euse** /skʀypylø, øz/ *adj*
scrupulous; **peu** ∼ unscrupulous

**scrutateur, -trice** /skʀytatœʀ, tʀis/ *adj*
searching

**scruter** /skʀyte/ [1] *vtr* to scan ⟨*horizon*⟩; to scrutinize ⟨*object*⟩; to examine ⟨*ground, person*⟩

**scrutin** /skʀytɛ̃/ *nm* **(a)** ballot; dépouiller le ~ to count the votes
**(b)** polls; jour du ~ polling day; mode de ~ electoral system
■ ~ **majoritaire** election by majority vote

**sculpter** /skylte/ [1] *vtr* to sculpt, to carve

**sculpteur** /skyltœʀ/ *nm* sculptor

**sculptural, ~e**, *mpl* **-aux** /skyltyʀal, o/ *adj* ⟨*art*⟩ sculptural; ⟨*shape, beauty*⟩ statuesque

**sculpture** /skyltyʀ/ *nf* sculpture; la ~ sur bois woodcarving

**SDF** /ɛsdeɛf/ ▸ SANS

**se** (**s'** *before vowel or mute h*) /sə, s/ *pron*
**(a)** oneself; himself; herself; itself; il ~ regarde he's looking at himself
**(b)** each other; ils ~ regardaient they were looking at each other
**(c)** ~ ronger les ongles to bite one's nails; il ~ lave les pieds he's washing his feet
**(d)** elle ~ comporte honorablement she behaves honourably (GB); l'écart ~ creuse the gap is widening
**(e)** les exemples ~ comptent sur les doigts de la main the examples can be counted on the fingers of ones hand
**(f)** comment ~ fait-il que...? how come...?, how is it that...?

**séance** /seɑ̃s/ *nf* **(a)** (of court, parliament) session; (of committee) meeting; ~ tenante immediately
**(b)** (in cinema) show
■ ~ **de spiritisme** séance

**seau**, *pl* **~x** /so/ *nm* bucket, pail

**sébile** /sebil/ *nf* begging bowl

**sec, sèche** /sɛk, sɛʃ/ **1** *adj* **(a)** ⟨*weather, hair*⟩ dry; ⟨*fruit*⟩ dried
**(b)** ⟨*wine, cider*⟩ dry; boire son gin ~ to like one's gin straight
**(c)** ⟨*person, statement*⟩ terse; ⟨*letter*⟩ curt
**(d)** ⟨*noise*⟩ sharp
**2** *nm* être à ~ ⟨*river*⟩ to have dried up; (figurative) ⟨*person*⟩ to have no money
**3** *adv* **(a)** se briser ~ to snap
**(b)** (colloq) ⟨*rain, drink*⟩ a lot
**IDIOMS aussi ~** (colloq) immediately

**sécateur** /sekatœʀ/ *nm* clippers

**sécession** /sesesjɔ̃/ *nf* secession

**sèche** /sɛʃ/ *adj f* ▸ SEC 1

**sèche-cheveux** /sɛʃʃəvø/ *nm inv* hairdrier (GB), blow-dryer

**sèche-linge** /sɛʃlɛ̃ʒ/ *nm inv* tumble-drier (GB), tumble-dryer

**sèchement** /sɛʃmɑ̃/ *adv* drily, coldly

**sécher** /seʃe/ [1] **1** *vtr* **(a)** (gen) to dry
**(b)** (colloq) to skip ⟨*class*⟩
**2** *vi* ⟨*hair, clothes*⟩ to dry; ⟨*mud*⟩ to dry up; fleur séchée dried flower; mettre des vêtements à ~ to hang clothes up to dry

**sécheresse** /seʃʀɛs/ *nf* **(a)** drought
**(b)** dryness

**(c)** curt manner

**séchoir** /seʃwaʀ/ *nm* **(a)** clothes airer, clothes horse
**(b)** tumble-drier (GB), tumble-dryer

**second, ~e¹** /səgɔ̃, ɔ̃d/ **1** *adj*
**(a)** (in sequence, series) second; chapitre ~ chapter two; en ~ lieu secondly; dans un ~ temps... subsequently...; c'est à prendre au ~ degré it is not to be taken literally
**(b)** (in hierarchy) second; de ~ ordre second-rate; politicien de ~ plan minor politician; jouer un ~ rôle (in theatre) to play a supporting role; jouer les ~s rôles (figurative) to play second fiddle
**2** *nm,f* second one
**3** *nm* **(a)** second-in-command
**(b)** second floor (GB), third floor (US)
**4** **en second** *phr* ⟨*arrive, leave*⟩ second

**secondaire** /səgɔ̃dɛʀ/ **1** *adj* **(a)** secondary
**(b)** minor
**(c)** (Sch) école ~ secondary school (GB), high school (US)
**(d)** effets ~s side effects
**2** *nm* (Sch) secondary school (GB) *or* high school (US) education

**seconde²** /səgɔ̃d/ **1** *adj f* ▸ SECOND 1
**2** *nf* **(a)** ▸ SECOND 2
**(b)** second; en une fraction de ~ in a split second
**(c)** (Sch) *fifth year of secondary school, age 15–16*
**(d)** billet de ~ second-class ticket
**(e)** (Aut) second (gear)

**seconder** /səgɔ̃de/ [1] *vtr* ⟨*person*⟩ to assist

**secouer** /səkwe/ [1] **1** *vtr* **(a)** to shake ⟨*bottle, branch, person*⟩; to shake out ⟨*rug, umbrella*⟩; ~ la tête to shake one's head; être un peu secoué (in car, plane) to have rather a bumpy ride
**(b)** to shake off ⟨*dust, snow, yoke*⟩
**(c)** ⟨*crisis*⟩ to shake ⟨*person, country*⟩
**(d)** (colloq) to get [sb] going (colloq)
**2** **se secouer** *v refl* (+ *v être*) **(a)** to give oneself a shake
**(b)** (colloq) to pull oneself together
**(c)** (colloq) to wake up, to get moving (colloq)

**secourable** /səkuʀabl/ *adj* ⟨*person*⟩ helpful

**secourir** /səkuʀiʀ/ [26] *vtr* **(a)** to help
**(b)** to rescue
**(c)** to give first aid to

**secourisme** /səkuʀism/ *nm* first aid

**secouriste** /səkuʀist/ *nmf* first-aid worker

**secours** /səkuʀ/ **1** *nm inv* help; au ~! help!; appeler *or* crier au ~ to shout for help; porter ~ à qn to help sb; le ~ en mer sea rescue operations; de ~ ⟨*wheel*⟩ spare; ⟨*exit*⟩ emergency; ⟨*kit*⟩ first-aid; ⟨*team*⟩ rescue; ⟨*battery*⟩ back-up
**2** *nm pl* **(a)** rescuers; reinforcements
**(b)** relief supplies; supplies; premiers ~ first aid

**secousse** /səkus/ *nf* jolt; ~ (sismique) (earth) tremor

**secret, -ète** /səkRɛ, ɛt/ [1] *adj* **(a)** secret
**(b)** ⟨*person*⟩ secretive
[2] *nm* **(a)** secret; **ne pas avoir de ∼s pour
qn** to have no secrets from sb; **il n'en fait
pas un ∼ he** makes no secret of it
**(b)** secrecy; **mettre qn dans le ∼** to let sb in
on the secret; **en ∼** in secret; **encore une de
ces gaffes dont il a le ∼** another of those
blunders that only he knows how to make
**(c)** solitary confinement
■ **∼ bancaire** bank confidentiality; **∼ de
fabrication** industrial secret; **∼ de
Polichinelle** open secret; **∼ professionnel**
professional confidentiality

**secrétaire** /s(ə)kRetɛR/ [1] *nmf* secretary
[2] *nm* ( piece of furniture) secretaire (GB),
secretary (US)
■ **∼ de direction** personal assistant; **∼ d'État**
(in France) minister; (in Great Britain, America)
Secretary of State; **∼ de rédaction** sub-editor
(GB), copy-editor

**secrétariat** /s(ə)kRetaRja/ *nm*
**(a)** secretarial work
**(b)** secretariat

**secrète** ▸ SECRET 1

**secrètement** /səkRɛtmã/ *adv* secretly

**sécréter** /sekRete/ [14] *vtr* **(a)** to secrete
⟨*sap, bile*⟩
**(b)** to exude ⟨*liquid*⟩

**sécrétion** /sekResjɔ̃/ *nf* secretion

**sectaire** /sɛktɛR/ *adj, nmf* sectarian

**secte** /sɛkt/ *nf* sect; faction

**secteur** /sɛktœR/ *nm* **(a)** (Econ) sector;
**∼ tertiaire** service sector; **∼ d'activité** sector
**(b)** area, territory; (Mil) sector
**(c)** (electrical) **le ∼** the mains; **appareil
fonctionnant sur ∼** mains-operated
appliance; **panne de ∼** power failure

**section** /sɛksjɔ̃/ *nf* **(a)** section; (of party,
trade union) branch; (of book) part
**(b)** (Sch) stream (GB), track (US)
■ **∼ d'autobus** fare stage

**sectionner** /sɛksjone/ [1] *vtr* **(a)** to sever
**(b)** to divide up ⟨*organization*⟩

**sectoriel, -ielle** /sɛktɔRjɛl/ *adj* sectoral

**sectorisation** /sɛktɔRizasjɔ̃/ *nf* division

**sectoriser** /sɛktɔRize/ [1] *vtr* to divide
[sth] into sectors

**Sécu** /seky/ *nf* National Health Service

**séculaire** /sekylɛR/ *adj* **(a)** ⟨*tradition*⟩
ancient
**(b)** ⟨*house, tree*⟩ hundred-year-old

**séculier, -ière** /sekylje, ɛR/ *adj* secular

**secundo** /səgɔ̃do/ *adv* secondly

**sécuriser** /sekyRize/ [1] *vtr* **(a)** to
reassure
**(b)** to make [sb] feel secure

**sécurité** /sekyRite/ *nf* **(a)** security; **∼ de
l'emploi** job security; **de ∼** ⟨*system*⟩ security;
⟨*reasons*⟩ of security
**(b)** safety; **se sentir en ∼** to feel secure *or*
safe
■ **∼ routière** road safety; **∼ sociale** *French
national health and pensions organization*

**sédatif** /sedatif/ *nm* sedative

**sédentaire** /sedâtɛR/ *adj* sedentary

**sédentariser** /sedâtaRize/ [1] *vtr* to settle

**sédentarité** /sedâtaRite/ *nf* (of population)
settled way of life; (of job) sedentary nature

**sédiment** /sedimã/ *nm* sediment

**sédimentation** /sedimãtasjɔ̃/ *nf*
sedimentation

**séducteur, -trice** /sedyktœR, tRis/
[1] *adj* seductive, attractive
[2] *nm,f* **(a)** charmer
**(b)** seducer/seductress

**séduction** /sedyksjɔ̃/ *nf* **(a)** charm
**(b)** seduction; **pouvoir de ∼** (of person) power
of seduction; (of money) lure; (of words)
seductive power

**séduire** /sedɥiR/ [1] *vtr* **(a)** ⟨*person*⟩ to
captivate; **il aime ∼** he likes to charm
people
**(b)** to appeal to ⟨*person*⟩
**(c)** ⟨*person*⟩ to win over
**(d)** to seduce

**séduisant, ∼e** /sedɥizã, ãt/ *adj* ⟨*person*⟩
attractive; ⟨*idea*⟩ appealing

**segment** /sɛgmã/ *nm* segment

**segmenter** /sɛgmãte/ [1] *vtr*, **se
segmenter** *v refl* (+ *v être*) to segment

**ségrégation** /segRegasjɔ̃/ *nf* segregation

**seiche** /sɛʃ/ *nf* cuttlefish

**seigle** /sɛgl/ *nm* rye; **pain de ∼** rye bread

**seigneur** /sɛɲœR/ *nm* lord; **être grand ∼**
to be full of largesse
■ **∼ de la guerre** warlord
IDIOMS **à tout ∼ tout honneur** (Proverb) credit
where credit is due

**Seigneur** /sɛɲœR/ *nm* Lord; **∼!** Good
Lord!

**seigneurial, ∼e,** *mpl* **-iaux** /sɛɲœRjal,
o/ *adj* ⟨*home*⟩ stately; ⟨*manner*⟩ lordly

**sein** /sɛ̃/ *nm* **(a)** (Anat) breast; **les ∼s nus**
topless; **nourrir (son enfant) au ∼** to breast-
feed (one's baby)
**(b)** **au ∼ de** within

**séisme** /seism/ *nm* earthquake, seism

**seize** /sɛz/ *adj inv, pron, nm inv* sixteen

**seizième** /sɛzjɛm/ *adj* sixteenth

**séjour** /seʒuR/ *nm* **(a)** stay; **∼s à l'étranger**
(on CV) time spent abroad
**(b)** (salle de) **∼** living room
**(c)** **un ∼ champêtre** a rural retreat
■ **∼ linguistique** language study vacation

**séjourner** /seʒuRne/ [1] *vi* **(a)** ⟨*person*⟩ to
stay
**(b)** ⟨*liquid*⟩ to remain; ⟨*snow*⟩ to lie

**sel** /sɛl/ *nm* **(a)** salt; **gros ∼** coarse salt
**(b)** (figurative) **la situation ne manque pas de
∼** the situation has a certain piquancy
■ **∼s de bain** bath salts

**sélect, ∼e** /selɛkt/ *adj* (colloq) ⟨*club, bar*⟩
exclusive; ⟨*clientele*⟩ select

**sélecteur, -trice** /selɛktœR, tRis/ [1] *adj*
selective
[2] *nm* **(a)** (Comput) selector     ⋯⟶

**(b)** (Aut) gear lever, gearshift

**sélectif, -ive** /selɛktif, iv/ *adj* selective

**sélection** /selɛksjɔ̃/ *nf* (gen) selection; (for a job) selection process; **~ à l'entrée** selective entry

**sélectionner** /selɛksjɔne/ [1] *vtr* to select

**self-service,** *pl* **~s** /sɛlfsɛʀvis/ *nm* self-service restaurant

**selle** /sɛl/ **1** *nf* saddle; **remis en ~** ⟨*player, regime*⟩ firmly (re)established
**2 selles** *nf pl* (Med) stools

**seller** /sele/ [1] *vtr* to saddle

**sellette** /selɛt/ *nf* **être sur la ~** to be in the hot seat

**selon** /səlɔ̃/ *prep* **(a)** according to; **~ moi, il va pleuvoir** in my opinion, it's going to rain; **~ les termes du président** in the President's words; **l'idée ~ laquelle** the idea that
**(b)** depending on ⟨*time, circumstances*⟩; **la situation varie ~ les régions** the situation varies from region to region; **c'est ~** (colloq) it all depends

**semailles** /səmɑj/ *nf pl* **(a)** sowing season
**(b)** seeds
**(c)** **faire les ~** to sow

**semaine** /s(ə)mɛn/ *nf* **(a)** week
**(b)** week's wages
**IDIOMS vivre à la petite ~** to live from day to day

**sémantique** /semɑ̃tik/ **1** *adj* semantic
**2** *nf* semantics

**semblable** /sɑ̃blabl/ **1** *adj* **(a)** similar
**(b)** identical
**2** *nmf* fellow creature; **eux et leurs ~s** they and their kind

**semblant** /sɑ̃blɑ̃/ *nm* **un ~ de légalité** a semblance of legality; **faire ~ d'être triste** to pretend to be sad

**sembler** /sɑ̃ble/ [1] **1** *vi* to seem
**2** *v impers* **il semble bon de faire** it seems appropriate to do; **le problème est réglé à ce qu'il me semble** the problem has been solved, or so it seems to me; **faites comme bon vous semble** do whatever you think best; **elle a, semble-t-il, refusé** apparently, she refused

**semelle** /s(ə)mɛl/ *nf* sole
■ **~ compensée** wedge heel; **~ intérieure** insole
**IDIOMS être dur comme de la ~** (colloq) to be as tough as old boots (GB) (colloq) *or* leather (US)

**semence** /s(ə)mɑ̃s/ *nf* seed

**semer** /s(ə)me/ [16] *vtr* **(a)** to sow ⟨*seeds*⟩
**(b)** to sow ⟨*discord, doubt*⟩; to spread ⟨*confusion, panic*⟩
**(c)** to scatter ⟨*objects*⟩; **semé de difficultés** plagued with difficulties; **ciel semé d'étoiles** star-spangled sky; **on récolte ce qu'on a semé** as you sow so shall you reap
**(d)** (colloq) to drop ⟨*purse, keys*⟩
**(e)** (colloq) to shake off ⟨*pursuer*⟩

**semestre** /s(ə)mɛstʀ/ *nm* (Sch) semester

**semestriel, -ielle** /səmɛstʀijɛl/ *adj*
**(a)** twice-yearly; half-yearly
**(b)** (at university) ⟨*exam*⟩ end-of-semester (GB), final (US); ⟨*class*⟩ one-semester

**semeur, -euse** /səmœʀ, øz/ *nm,f* sower; **~ de troubles** troublemaker

**semi** /səmi/ *pref* **~-automatique** semiautomatic; **~-liberté** relative freedom; **~-remorque** articulated lorry (GB), tractor-trailer (US)

**semi-échec,** *pl* **~s** /səmieʃɛk/ *nm* partial failure

**sémillant, ~e** /semijɑ̃, ɑ̃t/ *adj* spirited

**séminaire** /seminɛʀ/ *nm* **(a)** seminar
**(b)** seminary

**séminariste** /seminaʀist/ *nm* seminarist

**sémiologie** /semjɔlɔʒi/ *nf* semiology

**sémiotique** /semjɔtik/ **1** *adj* semiotic
**2** *nf* semiotics

**semis** /s(ə)mi/ *nm inv* **(a)** sowing
**(b)** seedling
**(c)** seedbed

**semonce** /səmɔ̃s/ *nf* reprimand; **coup de ~** warning shot

**semoule** /səmul/ *nf* semolina; **sucre ~** caster sugar

**sempiternel, -elle** /sɑ̃pitɛʀnɛl/ *adj* perpetual

**sénat** /sena/ *nm* senate

**sénateur** /senatœʀ/ *nm* senator

**sénile** /senil/ *adj* senile

**sénilité** /senilite/ *nf* senility

**sens** /sɑ̃s/ **1** *nm inv* **(a)** direction, way; **dans le ~ de la largeur** widthways, across; **être dans le bon ~** to be the right way up; **retourner un problème dans tous les ~** to consider a problem from every angle; **courir dans tous les ~** to run all over the place; **~ dessus dessous** /sɑ̃d(ə)sydəsu/ upside down; (figurative) very upset; **aller dans le bon ~** ⟨*reforms*⟩ to be a step in the right direction; **le ~ de l'histoire** the tide of history; **nous travaillons dans ce ~** that's what we are working toward(s)
**(b)** meaning; **le ~ figuré d'un mot** the figurative sense of a word; **employer un mot au ~ propre** to use a word literally; **cela n'a pas de ~** it doesn't make sense; it's absurd
**(c)** sense; **retrouver l'usage de ses ~** to regain consciousness; **avoir le ~ pratique** to be practical; **ne pas avoir le ~ du ridicule** not to realize when one looks silly; **avoir le ~ des affaires** to have a flair for business; **n'avoir aucun ~ des réalités** to live in a dream world
**2** *nm pl* senses; **plaisirs des ~** sensual pleasures
■ **~ giratoire** roundabout (GB), traffic circle (US); **~ interdit** no-entry sign; one-way street; **~ obligatoire** one-way sign; **~ unique** one-way sign; one-way street

**sensation** /sɑ̃sasjɔ̃/ *nf* feeling, sensation; **aimer les ~s fortes** to like one's thrills; **la décision a fait ~** the decision caused a sensation; **un journal à ~** a tabloid

**s**

**sensationnel, -elle** /sãsasjɔnɛl/ *adj*
(a) (colloq) fantastic (colloq)
(b) sensational, astonishing

**sensé, ∼e** /sãse/ *adj* sensible

**sensément** /sãsemã/ *adv* sensibly

**sensibilisation** /sãsibilizasjɔ̃/ *nf*
(a) campagne de ∼ awareness campaign
(b) (Med) sensitizing

**sensibiliser** /sãsibilize/ [1] *vtr* (a) ∼ le public à un problème to increase public awareness of an issue
(b) (Med) to sensitize

**sensibilité** /sãsibilite/ *nf* (a) sensibility
(b) (in photography) sensitivity

**sensible** /sãsibl/ *adj* (a) (gen) sensitive; être ∼ aux compliments to like compliments; je suis ∼ au fait que I am aware that; un être ∼ a sentient being; je suis très ∼ au froid I really feel the cold
(b) ⟨skin⟩ sensitive; (because of injury) tender; ⟨limb⟩ sore; j'ai la gorge ∼ I often get a sore throat
(c) ⟨rise, difference⟩ appreciable; ⟨effort⟩ real; la différence est à peine ∼ the difference is hardly noticeable

**sensiblement** /sãsibləmã/ *adv*
(a) ⟨reduce, increase⟩ appreciably, noticeably; ⟨different⟩ perceptibly
(b) ⟨alike⟩ roughly

**sensiblerie** /sãsibləʀi/ *nf* sentimentality

**sensitif, -ive** /sãsitif, iv/ *adj* sensory

**sensoriel, -ielle** /sãsɔʀjɛl/ *adj* sensory; organe ∼ sense organ

**sensualité** /sãsɥalite/ *nf* sensuality

**sensuel, -elle** /sãsɥɛl/ *adj* sensual

**sentence** /sãtãs/ *nf* (a) sentence
(b) maxim

**sentencieux, -ieuse** /sãtãsjø, øz/ *adj* sententious

**senteur** /sãtœʀ/ *nf* scent

**senti, ∼e** /sãti/ *adj* bien ∼ ⟨words⟩ well-chosen; ⟨answer⟩ blunt; ⟨speech⟩ forthright

**sentier** /sãtje/ *nm* path, track; hors des ∼s battus off the beaten track

**sentiment** /sãtimã/ *nm* feeling; il est incapable de ∼ he's incapable of emotion; faire du ∼ to sentimentalize; prendre qn par les ∼s to appeal to sb's better nature; les beaux *or* bons ∼s fine sentiments; être animé de mauvais ∼s to have bad intentions; ∼s affectueux *or* amicaux best wishes

**sentimental, ∼e, mpl -aux** /sãtimãtal, o/ *adj* sentimental; romantic; vie ∼e lovelife

**sentinelle** /sãtinɛl/ *nf* sentry

**sentir** /sãtiʀ/ [30] **1** *vtr* (a) to smell
(b) to feel; je ne sens rien I can't feel anything; je ne sens plus mes pieds my feet are numb
(c) to be conscious of ⟨importance⟩; to feel ⟨beauty, force⟩; to appreciate ⟨difficulties⟩; to sense ⟨danger, disapproval⟩; je sens qu'il est

sincère I feel that he's sincere; je te sens inquiet I can tell you're worried; se faire ∼ ⟨need⟩ to be felt

**2** *vi* (a) to smell; ça sent l'ail it smells of garlic
(b) le poisson commence à ∼ the fish is beginning to smell
(c) to smack of; ciel nuageux qui sent l'orage cloudy sky that heralds a storm

**3** **se sentir** *v refl* (+ *v être*) (a) to feel; se ∼ mieux to feel better
(b) ⟨effect⟩ to be felt

IDIOMS je ne peux pas le ∼ I can't stand him

**seoir** /swaʀ/ [41] **1** seoir à *vtr* ⟨dress⟩ to suit

**2** *v impers* il sied de faire it is appropriate to do

**sépale** /sepal/ *nm* sepal

**séparable** /sepaʀabl/ *adj* separable

**séparation** /sepaʀasjɔ̃/ *nf* (a) (gen, Law) separation
(b) (between gardens) boundary; (figurative) boundary, dividing line
■ ∼ de biens (Law) matrimonial division of property; ∼ de corps (Law) judicial separation

**séparatisme** /sepaʀatism/ *nm* separatism

**séparé, ∼e** /sepaʀe/ *adj* (a) vivre ∼ to live apart
(b) separate

**séparément** /sepaʀemã/ *adv* separately

**séparer** /sepaʀe/ [1] **1** *vtr* (a) (gen) to separate; to pull [sb] apart ⟨fighters⟩; c'est un malentendu qui les a séparés they parted because of a misunderstanding
(b) to distinguish between ⟨concepts, areas⟩
(c) to divide; tout les sépare they are worlds apart

**2** **se séparer** *v refl* (+ *v être*) (a) ⟨guests⟩ to part; ⟨partners, lovers⟩ to split up
(b) se ∼ de to leave ⟨friend, group⟩; to split up with; (Law) to separate from ⟨husband, wife⟩
(c) se ∼ de to let [sb] go ⟨employee⟩; to part with ⟨personal possession⟩
(d) to divide; la route se sépare (en deux) the road forks

**sépia** /sepja/ *adj inv* sepia

**sept** /sɛt/ *adj inv, pron, nm inv* seven
■ les ∼ Familles (Games) Happy Families
IDIOMS tourne ∼ fois ta langue dans ta bouche avant de parler think before you speak

**septante** /sɛptãt/ *adj inv, pron* seventy

**septembre** /sɛptãbʀ/ *nm* September

**septennat** /sɛptena/ *nm* seven-year term (of office)

**septentrional, ∼e, mpl -aux** /sɛptãtʀijonal, o/ *adj* northern

**septicémie** /sɛptisemi/ *nf* blood-poisoning

**septième** /sɛtjɛm/ **1** *adj* seventh

**2** *nf* (Sch) *fifth year of primary school, age 10–11*

■ le ~ *art* cinematography

**septuagénaire** /sɛptɥaʒenɛʀ/ *adj* être ~ to be in one's seventies

**septuor** /sɛptɥɔʀ/ *nm* septet

**sépulture** /sepyltyʀ/ *nf* **(a)** grave
**(b)** burial

**séquelle** /sekɛl/ *nf* **(a)** after-effect
**(b)** repercussion
**(c)** consequence

**séquence** /sekãs/ *nf* sequence

**séquestrer** /sekɛstʀe/ [1] *vtr* (gen) to hold ⟨*hostage*⟩; (Law) to confine [sb] illegally

**sera** /səʀa/ ▶ ÊTRE[1]

**serai** /səʀɛ/ ▶ ÊTRE[1]

**seraient** /səʀɛ/ ▶ ÊTRE[1]

**sérail** /seʀaj/ *nm* **(a)** seraglio
**(b)** innermost circle

**serais** /səʀɛ/ ▶ ÊTRE[1]

**serait** /səʀɛ/ ▶ ÊTRE[1]

**seras** /səʀa/ ▶ ÊTRE[1]

**serein, ~e** /səʀɛ̃, ɛn/ *adj* ⟨*sky*⟩ clear; ⟨*person, face*⟩ serene; ⟨*criticism*⟩ objective

**sereinement** /səʀɛnmã/ *adv* ⟨*look*⟩ serenely; ⟨*speak*⟩ calmly; ⟨*judge*⟩ dispassionately

**sérénade** /seʀenad/ *nf* **(a)** serenade
**(b)** (colloq) racket (colloq), din

**sérénité** /seʀenite/ *nf* **(a)** (of face, mind) serenity; (of person) equanimity
**(b)** (of judge, verdict) impartiality
**(c)** (of sky, weather) calmness

**serez** /səʀe/ ▶ ÊTRE[1]

**serf, serve** /sɛʀ, sɛʀv/ *nm,f* serf

**sergent** /sɛʀʒã/ *nm* (Mil) (in army) ≈ sergeant

**série** /seʀi/ *nf* **(a)** series; catastrophes en ~ a series of catastrophes
**(b)** numéro de ~ serial number; ~ limitée limited edition; modèle de ~ (gen) mass-produced model; (car) production model; numéro hors ~ special issue
**(c)** set, collection
**(d)** (on television) series
**(e)** (Sport) division

■ ~ noire series of disasters

**sérieusement** /seʀjøzmã/ *adv* seriously; considerably

**sérieux, -ieuse** /seʀjø, øz/ **1** *adj*
**(a)** serious; être ~ dans son travail to be serious about one's work; avoir des lectures sérieuses to read serious books
**(b)** ⟨*situation, threat*⟩ serious; ⟨*clue, lead*⟩ important; ⟨*offer*⟩ genuine; 'pas ~ s'abstenir' 'genuine enquiries only'
**(c)** reliable
**(d)** responsible; cela ne fait pas très ~ that doesn't make a very good impression
**(e)** ⟨*effort, need*⟩ real; ⟨*progress*⟩ considerable; ⟨*handicap*⟩ serious

**2** *nm* seriousness; garder son ~ to keep a straight face; perdre son ~ to start to laugh; se prendre au ~ to take oneself seriously

**seriez** /səʀje/ ▶ ÊTRE[1]

**sérigraphie** /seʀigʀafi/ *nf* **(a)** silkscreen printing
**(b)** silkscreen print

**serin** /səʀɛ̃/ *nm* (Zool) canary

**seriner** /səʀine/ [1] *vtr* (colloq) ~ qch à qn to drum sth into sb

**seringue** /səʀɛ̃g/ *nf* syringe

**serions** /səʀjɔ̃/ ▶ ÊTRE[1]

**serment** /sɛʀmã/ *nm* **(a)** oath; prêter ~ to take the oath
**(b)** vow

■ un ~ d'ivrogne an empty promise

**sermon** /sɛʀmɔ̃/ *nm* **(a)** sermon
**(b)** lecture

**sermonner** /sɛʀmɔne/ [1] *vtr* to lecture, to give [sb] a talking-to

**séronégatif, -ive** /seʀonegatif, iv/ *adj* HIV negative

**serons** /səʀɔ̃/ ▶ ÊTRE[1]

**seront** /səʀɔ̃/ ▶ ÊTRE[1]

**séropositif, -ive** /seʀopozitif, iv/ *adj*
**(a)** (gen) seropositive
**(b)** HIV positive

**séropositivité** /seʀopozitivite/ *nf* (HIV antibody) seropositivity

**serpe** /sɛʀp/ *nf* billhook

**serpent** /sɛʀpã/ *nm* (Zool) snake; ~ à sonnette rattlesnake

**serpenter** /sɛʀpãte/ [1] *vi* ⟨*road, river*⟩ to wind

**serpentin** /sɛʀpãtɛ̃/ *nm* streamer

**serpillière** /sɛʀpijɛʀ/ *nf* floorcloth

**serre** /sɛʀ/ *nf* **(a)** greenhouse
**(b)** talon, claw

**serré, ~e** /seʀe/ **1** *adj* **(a)** ⟨*screw, nut*⟩ tight; ⟨*skirt, trousers*⟩ tight; trop serré too tight
**(b)** ⟨*grass*⟩ thick; ⟨*writing*⟩ cramped
**(c)** ⟨*deadlines, budget*⟩ tight; ⟨*bend*⟩ sharp; ⟨*control*⟩ strict; ⟨*struggle*⟩ hard; ⟨*debate*⟩ heated; ⟨*match*⟩ close
**(d)** ⟨*coffee*⟩ very strong

**2** *adv* ⟨*write*⟩ in a cramped hand; ⟨*knit*⟩ tightly; il va falloir jouer ~ si... we can't take any chances if...

**serre-livres** /sɛʀlivʀ/ *nm inv* book end

**serrement** /sɛʀmã/ *nm* **(a)** ~ de main handshake
**(b)** avoir *or* ressentir un ~ de cœur to feel a pang

**serrer** /seʀe/ [1] **1** *vtr* **(a)** to grip ⟨*steering wheel, rope*⟩; ~ qn/qch dans ses bras to hug sb/sth; ~ la main de qn to shake hands with sb; ~ les poings to clench one's fists; ça me serre le cœur de voir ça it wrings my heart to see that
**(b)** to tighten ⟨*knot, screw*⟩; to turn [sth] off tightly ⟨*tap*⟩; sans ~ ⟨*attach, screw*⟩ loosely
**(c)** ⟨*shoes, clothes*⟩ to be too tight
**(d)** ~ à droite to get *or* stay in the right-hand lane; ~ qn de près to be hot on sb's tail

**(e)** to push [sth] closer together ⟨*objects, tables*⟩; to squeeze ⟨*person*⟩; **être serrés** to be packed together
**(f)** to cut ⟨*expenses, prices*⟩
**2 se serrer** *v refl* (+ *v être*) **(a)** to squeeze up; **ils se sont serrés les uns contre les autres** they huddled together
**(b) se ~ dans une jupe** to squeeze oneself into a skirt; **nous nous sommes serré la main** we shook hands
**(c) avoir la gorge qui se serre** to have a lump in one's throat

**serrure** /sɛʀyʀ/ *nf* lock; **trou de ~** keyhole

**serrurerie** /sɛʀyʀʀi/ *nf* locksmith's

**serrurier** /sɛʀyʀje/ *nm* locksmith

**sertir** /sɛʀtiʀ/ [3] *vtr* to set ⟨*stone*⟩

**sérum** /seʀɔm/ *nm* serum; **~ de vérité** truth drug

**servage** /sɛʀvaʒ/ *nm* serfdom

**servante** /sɛʀvɑ̃t/ *nf* maidservant

**serve ▶** SERF

**serveur, -euse** /sɛʀvœʀ, øz/ *nm,f* waiter/ waitress

**servi, ~e** /sɛʀvi/ **1** *pp* ▶ SERVIR
**2** *pp adj* **(a) 'prends de la viande'—'merci je suis déjà ~'** 'have some meat'—'I already have some, thank you'
**(b)** (colloq) **nous voulions du soleil, nous sommes ~s** we wanted some sunshine and we've certainly got it

**serviable** /sɛʀvjabl/ *adj* obliging, helpful

**service** /sɛʀvis/ **1** *nm* **(a)** favour (GB); **rendre un ~ à qn** to do sb a favour (GB)
**(b)** (in transport) service; **~ de bus** bus service
**(c) être en ~** ⟨*lift*⟩ to be in working order; ⟨*motorway*⟩ to be open; ⟨*bus*⟩ to be running
**(d) rendre ~ à qn** ⟨*machine*⟩ to be a help to sb; ⟨*shop*⟩ to be convenient (for sb)
**(e)** service; **être au ~ de son pays** to serve one's country; **travailler au ~ de la paix** to work for peace; **'à votre ~!'** 'don't mention it!', 'not at all!'; **avoir 20 ans de ~ dans une entreprise** to have been with a firm 20 years; **être de** *or* **en ~** to be on duty; **état de ~(s)** record of service; **pharmacie de ~** duty chemist
**(f)** (at table) service; **faire le ~** to serve; to act as waiter
**(g)** (domestic) service; **entrer au ~ de qn** to go to work for sb; **prendre qn à son ~** to take sb on; **escalier de ~** back stairs
**(h)** department; **~ du personnel** personnel department; **~ des urgences** casualty department (GB), emergency room (US); **les ~s de sécurité** the security services; **chef de ~** (in administration) section head; (in hospital) senior consultant
**(i)** (Mil) **~ (militaire)** military *or* national service
**(j)** set; **un ~ à thé** a tea set; **~ de table** dinner service
**(k)** (in church) service
**(l)** (Sport) service, serve; **être au ~** to serve

**2** **services** *nm pl* services; **se passer des ~s de qn** to dispense with sb's services
■ **~ après-vente** after-sales service; **~ d'ordre** stewards; **~ de presse** press office; press and publicity department; **~ public** public service

**serviette** /sɛʀvjɛt/ *nf* **(a) ~ (de toilette)** towel; **~ (de table)** (table) napkin
**(b)** briefcase
■ **~ de bain** bath towel; **~ hygiénique** sanitary towel (GB), sanitary napkin (US)

**serviette-éponge**, *pl* **serviettes-éponges** /sɛʀvjɛtepɔ̃ʒ/ *nf* terry towel

**servile** /sɛʀvil/ *adj* servile; slavish

**servilement** /sɛʀvilmɑ̃/ *adv* ⟨*obey, imitate*⟩ slavishly; ⟨*flatter*⟩ obsequiously

**servilité** /sɛʀvilite/ *nf* servility

**servir** /sɛʀviʀ/ [30] **1** *vtr* **(a)** to serve; **qu'est-ce que je vous sers (à boire)?** what would you like to drink?; **tu es mal servi** you haven't got much; **'Madame est servie'** 'dinner is served, Madam'; **au moment de ~** before serving
**(b)** ⟨*situation*⟩ to help ⟨*person, cause*⟩; to serve ⟨*interests*⟩; ⟨*person*⟩ to further ⟨*ambition*⟩
**(c)** to deal ⟨*cards*⟩
**2 servir à** *v+prep* **~ à qn** to be used by sb; **~ à qch** to be used for sth; **les exercices m'ont servi à comprendre la règle** the exercises helped me to understand the rule
**(b)** to come in useful; **cela ne sert à rien de faire** there's no point in doing
**3 servir de** *v+prep* **~ d'intermédiaire à qn** to act as an intermediary for sb; **~ d'arme** to be used as a weapon
**4** *vi* **(a)** (Mil) **~ dans** to serve in
**(b)** (Sport) to serve
**(c) il a servi dix ans chez nous** he was in our service for ten years
**(d)** ⟨*object*⟩ to be used
**5 se servir** *v refl* (+ *v être*) **(a)** (at table) to help oneself; **se ~ un verre de vin** to pour oneself a glass of wine
**(b)** (in shop) to serve oneself
**(c) se ~ de qn/qch** to use sb/sth; **se ~ d'une situation** to make use of a situation
**(d)** (Culin) to be served

**serviteur** /sɛʀvitœʀ/ *nm* servant

**servitude** /sɛʀvityd/ *nf* **(a)** servitude
**(b)** (figurative) constraint

**ses ▶** SON¹

**sésame** /sezam/ *nm* sesame

**session** /sɛsjɔ̃/ *nf* **(a)** session
**(b)** examination session; **~ de rattrapage** retakes
**(c)** course

**set** /sɛt/ *nm* (Sport) set
■ **~ de table** place mat

**seuil** /sœj/ *nm* **~ (de la porte)** doorstep; doorway, threshold

**seul, ~e** /sœl/ **1** *adj* **(a)** alone, on one's own; **vous êtes ~ dans la vie?** are you

single?; **elle veut vous parler ~ à ~** or **~e à ~(e)** she wants to speak to you in private; **parler tout ~** to talk to oneself
**(b)** by oneself, on one's own; **il a mangé un poulet à lui tout ~** he ate a whole chicken all by himself; **ça va tout ~** it's really easy; things are running smoothly
**(c)** only; **la ~e et unique personne** the one and only person; **pas un ~ client** not a single customer; **l'espion et l'ambassadeur sont une ~e et même personne** the spy and the ambassador are one and the same person; **d'une ~e pièce** in one piece; **à la ~e idée de faire** at the very idea of doing; **ils ont parlé d'une ~e voix** they were unanimous; **elle ~e pourrait vous le dire** only she could tell you
**(d)** lonely; **c'est un homme ~** he's a lonely man
**2** *nm,f* **le ~, la ~e** the only one; **les ~s, les ~es** the only ones; **ils sont les ~s à croire que** they're alone in thinking that

**seulement** /sœlmã/ *adv* **(a)** only; **nous étions ~ deux** there were only the two of us; **'nous étions dix'—'~?'** 'there were ten of us'—'is that all?'; **elle revient ~ demain** she's not coming back until tomorrow
**(b) c'est possible, ~ je veux y réfléchir** it's possible, only or but I'd like to think about it
**(c) si ~** if only

**sève** /sɛv/ *nf* **(a)** sap
**(b)** (figurative) vigour (GB)

**sévère** /sevɛʀ/ *adj* ⟨look, tone, punishment⟩ severe; ⟨person, upbringing⟩ strict; ⟨selection⟩ rigorous; ⟨judgment⟩ harsh; ⟨losses⟩ heavy

**sévèrement** /sevɛʀmã/ *adv* severely; harshly; strictly

**sévérité** /severite/ *nf* **(a)** strictness, harshness
**(b)** sternness, severity

**sévices** /sevis/ *nm pl* physical abuse

**sévir** /seviʀ/ [3] *vi* **(a)** to clamp down
**(b)** ⟨storm, war⟩ to rage; ⟨poverty⟩ to be rife
**(c)** (figurative) ⟨doctrine⟩ to hold sway; ⟨phenomenon⟩ to be rife

**sevrage** /səvʀaʒ/ *nm* weaning

**sevrer** /səvʀe/ [16] *vtr* to wean

**sexagénaire** /sɛksaʒenɛʀ/ *nmf* sixty-year 1-old

**sexe** /sɛks/ *nm* **(a)** sex; **indépendamment du ~, de l'ethnie, de l'âge** irrespective of gender, race or age; **un bébé de ~ féminin** a female baby
**(b)** genitals

**sexiste** /sɛksist/ *adj, nmf* sexist

**sexologue** /sɛksɔlɔg/ *nmf* sex therapist

**sextuor** /sɛkstɥɔʀ/ *nm* sextet

**sextuplé, ~e** /sɛkstyple/ *nm,f* sextuplet

**sexualité** /sɛksɥalite/ *nf* sexuality

**sexué, ~e** /sɛksɥe/ *adj* sexed; sexual

**sexuel, -elle** /sɛksɥɛl/ *adj* (gen) sexual; ⟨education, gland⟩ sex

**seyant, ~e** /sɛjã, ãt/ *adj* becoming

**SF** /ɛsɛf/ *nf* (abbr = **science-fiction**) sci-fi

**SFP** /ɛsɛfpe/ *nf* (abbr = **Société française de production et de création audiovisuelles**) *TV and video production company*

**shaker** /ʃekœʀ/ *nm* cocktail shaker

**shampooing** /ʃãpwɛ̃/ *nm* shampoo

**shampouiner** /ʃãpwine/ [1] *vtr* to shampoo

**shampouineur, -euse** /ʃãpwinœʀ, øz/ *nm,f*: trainee hairdresser (who washes hair)

**shérif** /ʃeʀif/ *nm* sheriff

**shetland** /ʃɛtlãd/ *nm* **(a)** Shetland wool
**(b)** Shetland pony

**shoot** /ʃut/ *nm* **(a)** (Sport) shot
**(b)** (colloq) (of drug) fix (colloq)

**shooter** /ʃute/ [1] **1** *vi* to shoot
**2 se shooter** *v refl* (+ *v être*) (colloq) to shoot up (colloq)

**short** /ʃɔʀt/ *nm* shorts

**si¹** /si/ **1** *adv* **(a)** yes; **'tu ne le veux pas?'—'~!'** 'don't you want it?'—'yes I do!'; **il n'ira pas, moi ~** he won't go, but I will
**(b)** so; **c'est un homme ~ agréable** he's such a pleasant man; **~ bien que** so; so much so that; **rien n'est ~ beau qu'un coucher de soleil** there's nothing so beautiful as a sunset; **est-elle ~ bête qu'on le dit?** is she as stupid as people say (she is)?
**2** *conj* (**s'** before **il** or **ils**) **(a)** if; **~ j'étais riche** if I were rich; **~ j'avais su!** if only I'd known!; **vous pensez ~ j'étais content!** you can imagine how happy I was!; **~ ce n'est (pas) toi, qui est-ce?** if it wasn't you, who was it?; **il n'a rien pris avec lui ~ ce n'est un livre** he didn't take anything with him apart from a book; **à quoi servent ces réunions ~ ce n'est à nous faire perdre notre temps?** what purpose do these meetings serve other than to waste our time?; **~ tant est qu'une telle distinction ait un sens** if such a distinction makes any sense
**(b) ~ tu venais avec moi?** how about coming with me?
**(c)** whereas

**si²** /si/ *nm inv* (note) B; (in sol-fa) ti

**siamois, ~e** /sjamwa, az/ **1** *adj* **(a)** ⟨cat⟩ Siamese
**(b) des frères ~** male Siamese twins
**2** *nm inv* **(a)** (language) Siamese
**(b)** Siamese cat

**sibylle** /sibil/ *nf* sibyl

**SICAV** /sikav/ *nf* (abbr = **société d'investissement à capital variable**) unit trust, mutual fund

**sida** /sida/ *nm* (abbr = **syndrome immunodéficitaire acquis**) Aids

**side-car**, *pl* **~s** /sidkaʀ/ *nm* **(a)** sidecar
**(b)** motorcycle combination

**sidéral, ~e**, *mpl* **-aux** /sideʀal, o/ *adj* sidereal

**sidérer** /sideʀe/ [14] *vtr* (colloq) to stagger (colloq)

**sidérurgie** /sideʀyʀʒi/ *nf* steel industry

**sidérurgique** /sideʀyʀʒik/ *adj* steel

**siècle** /sjɛkl/ *nm* **(a)** century; **au Vᵉ ~ après J.-C.** in the 5th century AD; **d'ici la fin du ~** by the turn of the century; **il y a des ~s** (colloq) **que je ne suis venu ici** I haven't been here for ages
**(b)** age; **le ~ de Louis XIV** the age of Louis XIV

**sied ▶** SEOIR

**siège** /sjɛʒ/ *nm* **(a)** seat
**(b)** **~ (social)** (of company) head office; (of organization) headquarters
**(c)** (of MP) seat
**(d)** (Mil) siege
**(e)** (Anat) seat

**siéger** /sjeʒe/ [15] *vi* **(a)** to sit
**(b)** to be in session
**(c)** to have its headquarters

**sien, sienne** /sjɛ̃, sjɛn/ ⎡**1**⎤ *det* **cette maison est sienne à présent** the house is now his/hers
⎡**2**⎤ **le sien, la sienne, les siens, les siennes** *pron* his/hers; **être de retour parmi les ~s** to be back with one's family; to be back among one's own friends; **faire des siennes** ⟨person⟩ to be up to mischief; ⟨computer⟩ to act up

**sieste** /sjɛst/ *nf* nap, siesta

**sifflant, ~e** /siflɑ̃, ɑ̃t/ *adj* **(a)** hissing; wheezing
**(b)** sibilant

**sifflement** /sifləmɑ̃/ *nm* (of person, train) whistle; (of kettle, wind) whistling; (of bird, insect) chirping; (of snake) hissing

**siffler** /sifle/ [1] ⎡**1**⎤ *vtr* **(a)** to whistle ⟨tune⟩; to whistle for ⟨dog⟩; to whistle at ⟨person⟩
**(b)** ⟨referee⟩ to blow one's whistle for ⟨foul⟩
**(c)** to hiss, to boo
⎡**2**⎤ *vi* **(a)** (gen) to whistle; ⟨projectile⟩ to whistle through the air; ⟨bird⟩ to chirp; ⟨snake⟩ to hiss
**(b)** to blow one's whistle

**sifflet** /siflɛ/ *nm* **(a)** whistle; **coup de ~** whistle
**(b)** (of train) whistle; (of kettle) whistling
**(c)** hiss, boo
IDIOMS **couper le ~ à qn** (colloq) to shut sb up (colloq)

**sifflotement** /siflotmɑ̃/ *nm* whistling

**siffloter** /siflote/ [1] *vi* to whistle away to oneself

**sigle** /sigl/ *nm* acronym

**signal,** *pl* **-aux** /siɲal, o/ *nm* signal
■ **~ d'alarme** alarm signal; **~ sonore** (on answerphone) tone

**signalement** /siɲalmɑ̃/ *nm* description

**signaler** /siɲale/ [1] ⎡**1**⎤ *vtr* **(a)** **~ qch à qn** to point sth out to sb; to inform sb of sth
**(b)** **~ à qn que** to remind sb that
**(c)** to indicate ⟨roadworks, danger⟩
**(d)** to report ⟨fact⟩
⎡**2**⎤ **se signaler** *v refl* (+ *v être*) **se ~ par qch** to distinguish oneself by sth

**signalétique** /siɲaletik/ *adj* descriptive; **fiche ~** specification sheet

**signalisation** /siɲalizasjɔ̃/ *nf*
**(a)** signalling (GB)
**(b)** signals
■ **~ routière** roadsigns and markings

**signaliser** /siɲalize/ [1] *vtr* to signpost ⟨road⟩; to mark out and light ⟨runway⟩

**signataire** /siɲatɛʀ/ *nmf* signatory

**signature** /siɲatyʀ/ *nf* **(a)** signature
**(b)** signing

**signe** /siɲ/ *nm* sign; **~ astral** star sign; **~ précurseur** omen; **~ distinctif** *or* **particulier** distinguishing feature; **c'était un ~ du destin** it was fate; **~s de ponctuation** punctuation marks; **faire ~ à qn** to wave to sb; (figurative) to get in touch with sb; **d'un ~ de la main/tête, elle m'a montré la cuisine** she pointed to/nodded her head in the direction of the kitchen; **faire ~ que oui** to indicate agreement
IDIOMS **il n'a pas donné ~ de vie depuis six mois** there's been no sign of him for six months

**signer** /siɲe/ [1] ⎡**1**⎤ *vtr* to sign; **il signe son troisième roman** he's written his third novel
⎡**2**⎤ **se signer** *v refl* (+ *v être*) to cross oneself

**signet** /siɲɛ/ *nm* (Comput) bookmark; **créer un ~ sur** to bookmark ⟨site⟩

**signifiant, ~e** /siɲifjɑ̃, ɑ̃t/ *adj* significant

**significatif, -ive** /siɲifikatif, iv/ *adj* significant

**signification** /siɲifikasjɔ̃/ *nf* **(a)** meaning
**(b)** importance

**signifié** /siɲifje/ *nm* signified

**signifier** /siɲifje/ [1] *vtr* **(a)** to mean
**(b)** **~ qch à qn** to inform sb of sth

**silence** /silɑ̃s/ *nm* **(a)** silence; **'un peu de ~ s'il vous plaît'** 'quiet please'; **passer qch sous ~** to say nothing about sth
**(b)** (Mus) rest

**silencieusement** /silɑ̃sjøzmɑ̃/ *adv* silently

**silencieux, -ieuse** /silɑ̃sjø, øz/ ⎡**1**⎤ *adj* silent; quiet
⎡**2**⎤ *nm* **(a)** (on gun) silencer
**(b)** (on exhaust) silencer (GB), muffler (US)

**silex** /silɛks/ *nm inv* flint; **en** *or* **de ~** flint

**silhouette** /silwɛt/ *nf* **(a)** silhouette; outline
**(b)** figure; shape

**silice** /silis/ *nf* silica

**silicium** /silisjɔm/ *nm* silicon

**silicone** /silikon/ *nf* silicone

**sillage** /sijaʒ/ *nm* **(a)** (of ship) wake; (of plane) vapour (GB) trail; slipstream
**(b)** (of person) wake

**sillon** /sijɔ̃/ *nm* **(a)** furrow
**(b)** line
**(c)** fissure
**(d)** groove

**sillonner** /sijone/ [1] *vtr* **(a)** ⟨roads⟩ to criss-cross; ⟨police⟩ to patrol; **~ la France en voiture** to drive all over France
**(b)** to furrow

**S**

**silo** /silo/ nm silo

**simagrée** /simagʀe/ nf play-acting

**simiesque** /simjɛsk/ adj ape-like

**similaire** /similɛʀ/ adj similar

**similarité** /similaʀite/ nf similarity

**similicuir** /similikɥiʀ/ nm imitation
leather

**similitude** /similityd/ nf similarity

**simple** /sɛ̃pl/ ① adj (a) (gen) simple; **c'est
(bien) ~, il ne fait plus rien** he simply doesn't
do anything any more
(b) ⟨decor⟩ plain; ⟨person, air⟩ unaffected
(c) ⟨origins⟩ modest
(d) ⟨worker⟩ ordinary; **c'est un ~
avertissement** it's just a warning; **le ~ fait de
poser la question** the mere fact of asking the
question; **par ~ curiosité** out of pure
curiosity; **sur ~ présentation du passeport**
on presentation of one's passport
(e) ⟨ice-cream cone, knot⟩ single
② nm (a) **le prix varie du ~ au double** the
price can turn out to be twice as high
(b) (Sport) **~ dames/messieurs** ladies'/men's
singles
■ **~ d'esprit** simple-minded

**simplement** /sɛ̃pləmɑ̃/ adv (a) simply,
merely, just; **vas-y, ~ fais attention** you can
go, only be careful
(b) ⟨dress, live⟩ simply
(c) easily

**simplet, -ette** /sɛ̃plɛ, ɛt/ adj simple

**simplicité** /sɛ̃plisite/ nf (a) simplicity;
**c'est d'une ~ enfantine** it's so easy a child
could do it
(b) (of person) unpretentiousness; (of thing)
simplicity; **avec ~** simply

**simplification** /sɛ̃plifikasjɔ̃/ nf
simplification

**simplifier** /sɛ̃plifje/ [2] ① vtr to simplify
② **se simplifier** v refl (+ v être) **se ~ la
vie** to make life easier for oneself

**simpliste** /sɛ̃plist/ adj simplistic

**simulacre** /simylakʀ/ nm (a) pretence
(GB); **~ de procès** mock trial
(b) sham; **~ de justice** travesty of justice

**simulateur, -trice** /simylatœʀ, tʀis/
① nm,f (a) shammer, faker
(b) malingerer
② nm (Tech) simulator

**simulation** /simylasjɔ̃/ nf (a) simulation
(b) malingering

**simuler** /simyle/ [1] vtr to feign; to
simulate

**simultané, ~e** /simyltane/ adj
simultaneous

**sincère** /sɛ̃sɛʀ/ adj (gen) sincere; ⟨friend⟩
true; ⟨emotion, offer⟩ genuine; ⟨opinion⟩
honest

**sincèrement** /sɛ̃sɛʀmɑ̃/ adv ⟨think⟩
really; ⟨regret, thank, speak⟩ sincerely
(b) frankly

**sincérité** /sɛ̃seʀite/ nf sincerity; honesty;
genuineness

**sinécure** /sinekyʀ/ nf sinecure

**sine qua non** /sinekwanɔn/ phr **condition
~** sine qua non

**singe** /sɛ̃ʒ/ nm (a) monkey; ape; **les grands
~s** the apes
(b) mimic; **faire le ~** to clown around

**singer** /sɛ̃ʒe/ [13] vtr to ape; to feign

**singeries** /sɛ̃ʒʀi/ nf pl antics; **faire des ~**
to monkey around; to pull funny faces

**singulariser: se singulariser**
/sɛ̃gylaʀize/ [1] v refl (+ v être) to draw
attention to oneself

**singularité** /sɛ̃gylaʀite/ nf (a) peculiarity,
singularity
(b) uniqueness

**singulier, -ière** /sɛ̃gylje, ɛʀ/ ① adj
(a) peculiar, unusual
(b) **combat ~** single combat
② nm (a) singular
(b) singularity

**singulièrement** /sɛ̃gyljɛʀmɑ̃/ adv
(a) oddly
(b) radically

**sinistre** /sinistʀ/ ① adj sinister; ⟨place,
future⟩ bleak; ⟨evening⟩ dreary
② nm disaster; accident; blaze

**sinistré, ~e** /sinistʀe/ ① adj stricken;
**région ~e** disaster area
② nm,f disaster victim

**sinon** /sinɔ̃/ ① conj (a) otherwise, or else
(b) except, apart from
(c) not to say; **c'est devenu difficile ~
impossible** it has become difficult if not
impossible
② **sinon que** phr except that, other than
that

**sinueux, -euse** /sinɥø, øz/ adj sinuous;
winding; tortuous

**sinus** /sinys/ nm inv sinus

**sinusite** /sinyzit/ nf sinusitis

**siphon** /sifɔ̃/ nm (a) (gen) siphon
(b) U-bend

**siphonné, ~e** /sifɔne/ adj (colloq) nuts
(colloq), crazy (colloq)

**sire** /siʀ/ nm Sire

**sirène** /siʀɛn/ nf (a) (gen) siren; (of boat)
foghorn
(b) mermaid, siren
■ **~ d'alarme** fire alarm

**sirop** /siʀo/ nm (a) syrup (GB), sirup (US);
cordial
(b) (medicine) syrup (GB), sirup (US), mixture;
**~ pectoral** cough mixture

**siroter** /siʀote/ [1] vtr (colloq) to sip

**sirupeux, -euse** /siʀypø, øz/ adj syrupy
(GB), sirupy (US)

**sis, ~e** /si, siz/ adj located

**sismique** /sismik/ adj seismic

**sismographie** /sismɔgʀafi/ nf
seismography

**site** /sit/ nm (a) area; **~ touristique** place of
interest; **~ archéologique** archaeological site
(b) site
■ **~ de bavardage** (Comput) chatroom; **~ vierge**
green-field site; **~ Web** Web site

**sitôt** /sito/ **1** *adv* ∼ **rentrés** as soon as we/they get back; as soon as we/they got back; **je n'y retournerai pas de** ∼ I won't go back there in a hurry (colloq)
**2** *conj* ∼ **que** as soon as
IDIOMS ∼ **dit,** ∼ **fait** no sooner said than done

**situation** /situɑsjɔ̃/ *nf* **(a)** situation
**(b)** job, position
**(c)** location
■ ∼ **de famille** marital status

**situer** /situe/ [1] **1** *vtr* **(a)** (in space and time) to place; **l'hôtel est bien situé** the hotel is in a good location
**(b)** ∼ **une histoire en 2001/à Palerme** to set a story in 2001/in Palermo
**2** **se situer** *v refl* (+ *v être*) **(a)** **se** ∼ **à Paris en 1900** to be set in Paris in 1900
**(b) politiquement, je me situe plutôt à gauche** politically, I'm more to the left

**six** /sis, *but before consonant* si, *and before vowel or mute h* siz/ *adj inv, pron, nm inv* six

**sixième** /sizjɛm/ **1** *adj* sixth
**2** *nf* (Sch) *first year of secondary school, age 11–12*

**skaï®** /skaj/ *nm* imitation leather
**skate-board,** *pl* ∼**s** /skɛtbɔʀd/ *nm*
**(a)** skateboard
**(b)** skateboarding

**sketch,** *pl* ∼**es** /skɛtʃ/ *nm* sketch

**ski** /ski/ *nm* **(a)** ski
**(b) le** ∼ skiing
■ ∼ **de fond** cross-country skiing; ∼ **nautique** water skiing; ∼ **de piste** downhill skiing

**skier** /skje/ [2] *vi* to ski

**skieur, -ieuse** /skjœʀ, øz/ *nm,f* skier

**slalom** /slalɔm/ *nm* slalom

**slalomer** /slalɔme/ [1] *vi* **(a)** (Sport) to slalom
**(b)** (figurative) to zigzag

**slave** /slav/ *adj* Slavonic

**Slave** /slav/ *nmf* Slav

**slip** /slip/ *nm* **(a)** underpants
**(b)** slipway

**slogan** /slɔɡɑ̃/ *nm* slogan

**slow** /slo/ *nm* slow dance

**smala** /smala/ *nf* (colloq) tribe (colloq)

**SME** /ɛsɛmə/ *nm: abbr* ▶ SYSTÈME

**SMIC** /smik/ *nm* (*abbr* = **salaire minimum interprofessionel de croissance**) guaranteed minimum wage

**smoking** /smɔkiŋ/ *nm* dinner jacket (GB), tuxedo

**SNCF** /ɛsɛnseɛf/ *nf* (*abbr* = **Société nationale des chemins de fer français**) *French national railway company*

**snob** /snɔb/ **1** *adj* ⟨person⟩ stuck-up (colloq); ⟨restaurant⟩ posh
**2** *nmf* snob; **c'est un** ∼ he's a snob

**snober** /snɔbe/ [1] *vtr* to snub

**snobisme** /snɔbism/ *nm* snobbery

**sobre** /sɔbʀ/ *adj* **(a)** ⟨person⟩ abstemious; sober; temperate; ⟨life⟩ simple
**(b)** ⟨style⟩ plain, sober

**sobrement** /sɔbʀəmɑ̃/ *adv* soberly; in moderation; ⟨live⟩ frugally

**sobriété** /sɔbʀijete/ *nf* sobriety, temperance; restraint; moderation

**sobriquet** /sɔbʀikɛ/ *nm* nickname

**soc** /sɔk/ *nm* ploughshare (GB), plowshare (US)

**sociabilité** /sɔsjabilite/ *nf* sociability

**sociable** /sɔsjabl/ *adj* **(a)** sociable
**(b)** social

**social,** ∼**e,** *mpl* **-iaux** /sɔsjal, o/ **1** *adj*
**(a)** social; **le milieu** ∼ **de qn** sb's social background
**(b) conflit** ∼ industrial dispute
**2** *nm* **le** ∼ social issues

**socialement** /sɔsjalmɑ̃/ *adv* socially; **être** ∼ **pris en charge** to be in the care of the social services

**socialiser** /sɔsjalize/ [1] *vtr* **(a)** to socialize
**(b)** to collectivize

**socialisme** /sɔsjalism/ *nm* socialism

**socialiste** /sɔsjalist/ *adj, nmf* socialist

**sociétaire** /sɔsjetɛʀ/ *nmf* member

**société** /sɔsjete/ *nf* **(a)** society; **la haute** ∼ high society
**(b)** company; ∼ **de nettoyage** cleaning company
**(c)** (formal) **rechercher la** ∼ **de qn** to seek sb's company

**socioculturel, -elle** /sɔsjokyltyʀɛl/ *adj* sociocultural; **centre** ∼ recreation centre (GB)

**socio-démocrate,** *pl* ∼**s** /sɔsjodemɔkʀat/ **1** *adj* social democratic
**2** *nmf* social democrat

**socio-éducatif, -ive,** *mpl* ∼**s** /sɔsjoedykatif, iv/ *adj* socioeducational

**sociologie** /sɔsjɔlɔʒi/ *nf* sociology

**sociologue** /sɔsjɔlɔɡ/ *nmf* sociologist

**socioprofessionnel, -elle** /sɔsjopʀɔfɛsjɔnɛl/ *adj* social and occupational

**socle** /sɔkl/ *nm* pedestal, plinth; base; stand

**socque** /sɔk/ *nm* clog

**socquette** /sɔkɛt/ *nf* ankle sock, anklet (US)

**soda** /sɔda/ *nm* fizzy drink (GB), soda (US)

**sodium** /sɔdjɔm/ *nm* sodium

**sodomiser** /sɔdɔmize/ [1] *vtr* to sodomize, to bugger

**sœur** /sœʀ/ *nf* sister; ∼ **jumelle** twin sister

**sofa** /sɔfa/ *nm* sofa

**soi** /swa/ *pron* **(a)** **autour de** ∼ around one; **laisser la porte se refermer derrière** ∼ to let the door shut behind one; **trouver en** ∼ **les ressources nécessaires** to find the necessary inner resources; **garder qch pour** ∼ to keep sth to oneself ⋯⟫

**S**

**(b)** la logique n'est pas un objectif en ~ logic is not an end in itself; cela va de ~ it goes without saying

**soi-disant** /swadizã/ **1** adj inv **(a)** self-styled
**(b)** (controversial) so-called
**2** adv supposedly; **elle a** ~ **la migraine** she has a migraine, or so she says

**soie** /swa/ nf **(a)** silk
**(b)** bristle

**soient** /swa/ ▶ ÊTRE[1]

**soierie** /swaʀi/ nf **(a)** silk
**(b)** silk industry

**soif** /swaf/ nf **(a)** thirst; **avoir** ~ to be thirsty
**(b)** ~ **de** thirst for; hunger for; lust for; **avoir** ~ **d'affection** to crave affection

**soignant**, ~**e** /swaɲɑ̃, ɑ̃t/ adj medical; **médecin** ~ doctor, GP

**soigné**, ~**e** /swaɲe/ **1** pp ▶ SOIGNER
**2** pp adj **(a)** ⟨nails⟩ well-manicured; ⟨hair, clothes⟩ immaculate
**(b)** ⟨publication⟩ carefully produced; ⟨work⟩ meticulous; **peu** ~ ⟨work⟩ careless

**soigner** /swaɲe/ [1] **1** vtr **(a)** ⟨doctor⟩ to treat
**(b)** to look after ⟨person, customer⟩
**(c)** to take care over ⟨appearance⟩; to look after ⟨hands⟩
**2** **se soigner** v refl (+ v être) **(a)** to treat oneself; to look after oneself
**(b)** ⟨illness⟩ to be treatable
**(c)** to take care over one's appearance

**soigneusement** /swaɲøzmɑ̃/ adv carefully; meticulously; neatly

**soigneux, -euse** /swaɲø, øz/ adj
**(a)** ⟨work⟩ conscientious; ⟨examination⟩ careful
**(b)** ⟨person⟩ neat, tidy

**soi-même** /swamɛm/ pron oneself

**soin** /swɛ̃/ **1** nm **(a)** care; **prendre** ~ **de qch** to take care of sth; **prendre** ~ **de qn/sa santé** to look after sb/one's health; **prendre** ~ **de sa petite personne** to coddle oneself; **laisser à qn le** ~ **de faire** to leave it to sb to do
**(b)** product; ~ **antipelliculaire** dandruff treatment
**2** **soins** nm pl **(a)** (Med) treatment; care; **recevoir des** ~**s** to receive treatment; ~ **dentaires** dental care; **les premiers** ~**s à donner aux brûlés** first-aid treatment for burns; ~**s à domicile** homecare
**(b)** care; ~**s corporels** or **du corps** body care
**(c)** 'aux bons ~**s de**' 'care of', 'c/o'
IDIOMS **être aux petits** ~**s pour qn** to attend to sb's every need

**soir** /swaʀ/ nm evening; night; **le** ~ **du 3**, **3 au** ~ on the evening of the 3rd; **il sort tous les samedis** ~ he goes out every Saturday night; **6 heures du** ~ 6 pm; **à ce** ~! see you tonight!

**soirée** /sware/ nf **(a)** evening; **dans** or **pendant la** ~, **en** ~ in the evening
**(b)** party; **aller dans une** ~ to go to a party
**(c)** evening performance or show

**sois** /swa/ ▶ ÊTRE[1]

**soit[1]** /swa/ **1** ▶ ÊTRE[1]
**2** conj **(a)** ~, ~ either, or; ~ **du fromage**, ~ **un gâteau** either cheese, or a cake
**(b)** that is, ie; **toutes mes économies**, ~ **200 euros** all my savings, ie or that is, 200 euros
**(c)** (in mathematics) ~ **un triangle ABC** let ABC be a triangle

**soit[2]** /swat/ adv very well; **je me suis trompé**, ~, **mais là n'est pas la question** all right, so I was wrong, but that's not the point

**soixantaine** /swasɑ̃tɛn/ nf **(a)** about sixty
**(b)** **avoir la** ~ to be about sixty

**soixante** /swasɑ̃t/ adj inv, pron, nm inv sixty

**soixante-dix** /swasɑ̃tdis/ adj inv, pron, nm inv seventy

**soixante-dixième** /swasɑ̃tdizjɛm/ adj seventieth

**soixantième** /swasɑ̃tjɛm/ adj sixtieth

**soja** /sɔʒa/ nm soya bean (GB), soybean (US); **sauce de** ~ soy sauce

**sol** /sɔl/ nm **(a)** ground; floor
**(b)** soil
**(c)** (Mus) (note) G; (in sol-fa) soh

**solaire** /sɔlɛʀ/ adj ⟨energy⟩ solar; ⟨engine⟩ solar-powered; ⟨cream⟩ sun

**soldat** /sɔlda/ nm soldier, serviceman

**solde[1]** /sɔld/ **1** nm balance; **faire le** ~ **d'un compte** to settle an account
**2** **en solde** phr **acheter une veste en** ~ to buy a jacket in a sale
**3** **soldes** nm pl sales; sale

**solde[2]** /sɔld/ nf (Mil) pay; **avoir qn à sa** ~ (figurative) to have sb in one's pay

**solder** /sɔlde/ [1] **1** vtr **(a)** to sell off ⟨merchandise⟩
**(b)** to settle the balance of ⟨account⟩
**2** **se solder** v refl (+ v être) **se** ~ **par qch** to end in sth

**solderie** /sɔldəʀi/ nf discount shop

**sole** /sɔl/ nf (Zool) sole

**soleil** /sɔlɛj/ nm sun; ~ **de minuit** midnight sun; **en plein** ~ ⟨sit⟩ in (the) hot sun; ⟨leave something⟩ in direct sunlight; **quand il y a du** ~ when it's sunny; **attraper un coup** or **des coups de** ~ to get sunburned

**solennel, -elle** /sɔlanɛl/ adj (gen) solemn; ⟨appeal, declaration⟩ formal

**solennité** /sɔlanite/ nf solemnity

**solfège** /sɔlfɛʒ/ nm **(a)** music theory; ~ **chanté** sol-fa
**(b)** music theory book

**solidaire** /sɔlidɛʀ/ adj ⟨team, group⟩ united
**(b)** (Tech) ⟨parts⟩ interdependent

**solidariser: se solidariser** /sɔlidaʀize/ [1] v refl (+ v être) **se** ~ **avec qn/qch** to stand by sb/sth

**solidarité** /sɔlidaʀite/ nf solidarity

**solide** /sɔlid/ **1** adj **(a)** ⟨food, matter⟩ solid

(b) ⟨*house, friendship*⟩ solid; ⟨*shoes, bag*⟩ sturdy; ⟨*link, fastening, blade*⟩ strong; ⟨*position, base*⟩ firm
(c) ⟨*person, constitution, heart*⟩ strong; **avoir la tête ~** (figurative) to have one's head screwed on (right)
(d) ⟨*business, experience, reasons*⟩ sound; ⟨*guarantees*⟩ firm
**2** *nm* (a) solid; **manger du ~** to eat solids
(b) **ce qu'il te dit, c'est du ~** what he says is sound
(c) **les meubles anciens, c'est du ~** antique furniture is solidly built

**solidement** /sɔlidmɑ̃/ *adv* ⟨*attach, establish*⟩ firmly; ⟨*barricaded*⟩ securely; **un rapport ~ documenté** a well-documented report

**solidifier** /sɔlidifje/ [2] *vtr*, **se solidifier** *v refl* (+ *v être*) to solidify

**solidité** /sɔlidite/ *nf* (a) (of construction) solidity; (of machine) strength; (of link) firmness; (of clothes) hard-wearing quality; **d'une grande ~** well-built; sturdy; strong; hard-wearing
(b) (of argument) soundness

**soliloque** /sɔlilɔk/ *nm* soliloquy

**soliste** /sɔlist/ *nmf* soloist

**solitaire** /sɔlitɛʀ/ **1** *adj* (a) ⟨*person, life*⟩ solitary; ⟨*old age, childhood*⟩ lonely; **navigateur ~** single-handed yachtsman
(b) ⟨*house*⟩ isolated
**2** *nmf* solitary person, loner; **en ~** ⟨*live*⟩ alone; ⟨*sail*⟩ single-handed
**3** *nm* (a) (diamond) solitaire
(b) rogue boar
(c) (Games) solitaire

**solitude** /sɔlityd/ *nf* (a) solitude
(b) loneliness

**solliciter** /sɔlisite/ [1] *vtr* (a) (formal) to seek ⟨*interview, post, advice*⟩
(b) to approach ⟨*person, organization*⟩; to canvass ⟨*customer, voter*⟩; **être très sollicité** to be assailed by requests; to be very much in demand

**sollicitude** /sɔlisityd/ *nf* concern, solicitude

**solstice** /sɔlstis/ *nm* solstice

**soluble** /sɔlybl/ *adj* soluble

**solution** /sɔlysjɔ̃/ *nf* (a) solution, solving; resolution
(b) solution; **une ~ de facilité** an easy way out
(c) (in chemistry) solution

**solutionner** /sɔlysjɔne/ [1] *vtr* to solve

**solvabilité** /sɔlvabilite/ *nf* (a) solvency
(b) creditworthiness

**solvable** /sɔlvabl/ *adj* solvent; creditworthy

**solvant** /sɔlvɑ̃/ *nm* solvent

**somatiser** /sɔmatize/ [1] *vtr* to have a psychosomatic reaction to

**sombre** /sɔ̃bʀ/ *adj* (a) dark; **il fait ~** it's dark
(b) ⟨*thought, future*⟩ dark, black; ⟨*conclusion*⟩ depressing; ⟨*air, person*⟩ solemn

(c) (*before n*) (colloq) ⟨*idiot*⟩ absolute; ⟨*affair*⟩ murky

**sombrer** /sɔ̃bʀe/ [1] *vi* (a) ⟨*ship*⟩ to sink
(b) **~ dans** ⟨*person*⟩ to sink into ⟨*despair, alcoholism*⟩

**sommaire** /sɔmɛʀ/ **1** *adj* ⟨*explanation*⟩ cursory; ⟨*description*⟩ rough; ⟨*installation, meal*⟩ rough and ready; ⟨*execution*⟩ summary
**2** *nm* (a) contents; **au ~ de notre numéro de juillet** featured in our July issue
(b) (colloq) **au ~ : un débat sur le chômage** a debate on unemployment is on the programme (GB)

**sommairement** /sɔmɛʀmɑ̃/ *adv* summarily

**sommation** /sɔmasjɔ̃/ *nf* (from police) warning; (from guard) challenge

**somme¹** /sɔm/ *nm* nap, snooze (colloq)

**somme²** /sɔm/ *nf* (a) sum, amount
(b) sum total; **la ~ de nos connaissances** the sum total of our knowledge; **il a fourni une grosse ~ de travail** he did a great deal of work; **en ~, ~ toute** all in all

**sommeil** /sɔmɛj/ *nm* sleep; **avoir le ~ agité** to sleep fitfully; **avoir le ~ léger** to be a light sleeper

**sommeiller** /sɔmeje/ [1] *vi* (a) to doze
(b) to lie dormant

**sommelier, -ière** /sɔmǝlje, ɛʀ/ *nm,f* wine waiter, sommelier

**sommer** /sɔme/ [1] *vtr* **~ qn de faire** to command sb to do

**sommes** /sɔm/ ▶ ÊTRE¹

**sommet** /sɔmɛ/ *nm* (a) (of mountain) peak; summit
(b) (gen) top; (of wave) crest; (of curve, career) peak
(c) (of glory, stupidity) height; **atteindre des ~s** ⟨*prices, sales*⟩ to peak
(d) summit; **conférence au ~** summit meeting
(e) (of triangle, angle) apex; (of cone) vertex

**sommier** /sɔmje/ *nm* (bed) base

**somnambule** /sɔmnɑ̃byl/ **1** *adj* **être ~** to sleepwalk
**2** *nmf* sleepwalker

**somnifère** /sɔmnifɛʀ/ **1** *adj* soporific
**2** *nm* (a) soporific
(b) sleeping pill

**somnolence** /sɔmnɔlɑ̃s/ *nf* drowsiness

**somnolent, ~e** /sɔmnɔlɑ̃, ɑ̃t/ *adj*
(a) drowsy
(b) ⟨*town*⟩ sleepy; ⟨*industry, country*⟩ lethargic

**somnoler** /sɔmnɔle/ [1] *vi* (a) to drowse
(b) ⟨*town*⟩ to be sleepy; ⟨*industry, country*⟩ to be lethargic

**somptueux, -euse** /sɔ̃ptɥø, øz/ *adj* sumptuous

**somptuosité** /sɔ̃ptɥozite/ *nf* sumptuousness

**son¹, sa,** *pl* **ses** /sɔ̃, sa, sɛ/ *det* his/her/ its; **ses enfants** his/her children; **ses pattes** ⋯⟶

its paws; **elle a ~ lundi** she's off on Monday; she gets Mondays off; **~ étourdie de sœur** (colloq) his/her absent-minded sister

**son²** /sɔ̃/ *nm* **(a)** sound; **ingénieur du ~** engineer
**(b)** volume; **baisser le ~** to turn the volume down
**(c)** bran; **pain au ~** bran loaf
■ **~ et lumière** son et lumière

**sonar** /sɔnaʀ/ *nm* sonar

**sonate** /sɔnat/ *nf* sonata

**sondage** /sɔ̃daʒ/ *nm* **(a)** poll; survey
**(b)** (Med) catheterization; probe
**(c)** (Naut) sounding

**sonde** /sɔ̃d/ *nf* **(a)** (Med) catheter; probe
**(b)** sounding lead; sounding line
**(c)** drill
**(d)** taster

**sonder** /sɔ̃de/ [1] *vtr* **(a)** to poll; to survey; to sound out
**(b)** to probe
**(c)** (Med) to catheterize; to probe
**(d)** (Naut) to sound

**songe** /sɔ̃ʒ/ *nm* dream

**songer** /sɔ̃ʒe/ [13] *v+prep* **à qch/à faire** to think of sth/of doing; **tu n'y songes pas!** you can't be serious!

**songeur, -euse** /sɔ̃ʒœʀ, øz/ *adj* pensive

**sonnant, ~e** /sɔnɑ̃, ɑ̃t/ *adj* **à trois heures ~es** on the stroke of three

**sonné, ~e** /sɔne/ **1** *pp* ▶ SONNER
**2** *pp adj* **(a)** groggy; shattered
**(b)** **elle a quarante ans bien ~s** (colloq) she's well into her forties

**sonner** /sɔne/ [1] **1** *vtr* **(a)** to ring ⟨bell⟩
**(b)** ⟨clock⟩ to strike ⟨hour⟩; ⟨person⟩ to sound ⟨retreat, alarm⟩; to ring out ⟨vespers⟩
**(c)** to ring for; **on ne t'a pas sonné!** (colloq) did anyone ask you?
**(d)** (colloq) ⟨blow⟩ to make [sb] dizzy; ⟨news⟩ to stagger
**2 sonner de** *v+prep* to sound ⟨horn⟩; to play ⟨bagpipes⟩
**3** *vi* **(a)** ⟨bell, phone⟩ to ring; ⟨hour⟩ to strike; ⟨alarm clock⟩ to go off; ⟨alarm, trumpet⟩ to sound; **leur dernière heure a sonné** their last hour has come
**(b)** ⟨word, expression⟩ to sound

**sonnerie** /sɔnʀi/ *nf* **(a)** ringing; chimes; **système qui déclenche une ~** system that sets off an alarm
**(b)** (of horn) sounding

**sonnet** /sɔnɛ/ *nm* sonnet

**sonnette** /sɔnɛt/ *nf* bell; doorbell; **tirer la ~ d'alarme** to pull the emergency cord; (figurative) to sound the alarm

**sonore** /sɔnɔʀ/ *adj* **(a)** ⟨laugh, kiss, slap⟩ resounding
**(b)** resonant; echoing; hollow-sounding
**(c)** ⟨vibrations⟩ sound; **le volume ~ est tel que...** the noise level is so high that...; **effets ~s** sound effects; **un document ~** a recording
**(d)** ⟨consonant⟩ voiced

**sonorisation** /sɔnɔʀizasjɔ̃/ *nf* public address system, PA system

**sonorité** /sɔnɔʀite/ *nf* **(a)** (of instrument, voice) tone; **les ~s de l'italien** the sound of Italian
**(b)** (of hi-fi) sound quality
**(c)** resonance

**sont** /sɔ̃/ ▶ ÊTRE¹

**sophistication** /sɔfistikasjɔ̃/ *nf* sophistication

**sophistiqué, ~e** /sɔfistike/ *adj*
**(a)** sophisticated
**(b)** artificial, mannered

**sophrologie** /sɔfʀɔlɔʒi/ *nf* relaxation therapy

**soporifique** /sɔpɔʀifik/ *adj, nm* soporific

**soprano** /sɔpʀano/ *nmf* soprano

**sorbet** /sɔʀbɛ/ *nm* sorbet

**sorcellerie** /sɔʀsɛlʀi/ *nf* witchcraft; sorcery

**sorcier** /sɔʀsje/ **1** *adj m* (colloq) **ce n'est (pourtant) pas ~!** (but) it's dead easy! (colloq)
**2** *nm* **(a)** wizard; sorcerer
**(b)** witch doctor

**sorcière** /sɔʀsjɛʀ/ *nf* witch; sorceress

**sordide** /sɔʀdid/ *adj* squalid; sordid

**sornettes** /sɔʀnɛt/ *nf pl* tall stories

**sort** /sɔʀ/ *nm* **(a)** lot; **être satisfait de son ~** to be satisfied with one's lot
**(b)** fate; **le ~ est contre moi** I'm ill-fated; **tirer qch au ~** to draw lots for sth
**(c)** curse, spell; **jeter un ~ à qn** to put a curse on sb; **le ~ en est jeté** the die is cast

**sortable** /sɔʀtabl/ *adj* **mon mari n'est pas ~** I can't take my husband anywhere

**sorte** /sɔʀt/ **1** *nf* sort, kind
**2 de la sorte** *phr* in this way
**3 de sorte que** *phr* **(a)** so that
**(b)** **la toile est peinte de ~ que** the canvas is painted in such a way that
**(c)** **de ~ que je n'ai pas pu venir** with the result that I couldn't come
**4 en quelque sorte** *phr* in a way
**5 en sorte de** *phr* **fais en ~ d'être à l'heure** try to be on time
**6 en sorte que** *phr* **fais en ~ que tout soit en ordre** make sure everything is tidy

**sortie** /sɔʀti/ *nf* **(a)** exit; **je t'attendrai à la ~** I'll wait for you outside (the building); **à la ~ de la ville** on the outskirts of the town; on the edge of the town
**(b)** **à ma ~ du tribunal** when I left the court; **se retrouver à la ~ de l'école** to meet after school; **à la ~ de l'hiver** at the end of winter
**(c)** **faire une ~ fracassante** to make a dramatic exit; **la ~ de la récession/crise** the end of the recession/crisis
**(d)** outing; **faire une ~ avec l'école** to go on a school outing; **ce soir, c'est mon soir de ~** tonight is my night out; **priver qn de ~** to keep sb in, ground sb (colloq)
**(e)** (of new product) launching; (of film) release; (of book) publication; (of fashion collection) showing

**(f)** (Tech) output; **faire une ∼ sur imprimante** to print

■ **∼ des artistes** stage-door; **∼ d'autoroute** exit; **∼ de bain** bathrobe

**sortilège** /sɔʀtilɛʒ/ *nm* spell

**sortir¹** /sɔʀtiʀ/ [30] **1** *vtr* **(a)** to take [sb/ sth] out ⟨*person, dog*⟩
**(b)** to get [sb/sth] out; **∼ les mains de ses poches** to take one's hands out of one's pockets; **∼ la poubelle** to put the bin out; **∼ sa langue** to stick one's tongue out
**(c)** (colloq) to chuck (colloq) [sb] out ⟨*person*⟩; to send [sb] out ⟨*pupil*⟩
**(d)** **∼ qn de** to get sb out of ⟨*situation*⟩
**(e)** to bring out ⟨*book*⟩; to release ⟨*film*⟩; to show ⟨*collection*⟩
**(f)** to turn out ⟨*book, record, film, product*⟩
**(g)** to bring [sth] out ⟨*newspaper*⟩
**(h)** (colloq) to come out with (colloq) ⟨*remarks*⟩; **∼ une blague** to crack a joke
**2** *vi* (+ *v être*) **(a)** to go out; to come out; **∼ déjeuner** to go out for lunch; **être sorti** to be out; **∼ en courant** to run out; **faire ∼ qn** to get sb outside; **laisser ∼ qn** to allow sb out
**(b)** to go out; **∼ avec qn** to go out with sb; **inviter qn à sortir** to ask sb out
**(c)** **∼ de** to leave; **∼ de chez qn** to leave sb's house; **sortez d'ici!** get out of here!; **∼ de son lit** to get out of bed; **∼ tout chaud du four** to be hot from the oven; **∼ de chez le médecin** to come out of the doctor's
**(d)** **∼ d'un rêve** to wake up from a dream; **∼ de la récession** to pull out of the recession; **∼ de l'hiver** to reach the end of winter
**(e)** **∼ à peine de l'enfance** to be just emerging from childhood; **∼ d'une guerre** to emerge from a war
**(f)** ⟨*water, smoke, cork*⟩ to come out; **faire ∼** to squeeze [sth] out ⟨*juice*⟩; to eject ⟨*cassette*⟩
**(g)** ⟨*bud, insect*⟩ to come out; ⟨*tooth*⟩ to come through
**(h)** to stick out
**(i)** ⟨*film, book, new model*⟩ to come out; **∼ tous les jours/tous les mois** ⟨*paper*⟩ to be published daily/monthly
**(j)** **∼ de** ⟨*person, product*⟩ to come from; **∼ de Berkeley** to have graduated from Berkeley; **d'où sors-tu à cette heure?** (colloq) where have you been?
**(k)** **∼ du sujet** ⟨*remark*⟩ to be beside the point; **cela sort de mes fonctions** that's not within my authority
**(l)** ⟨*number*⟩ to come up
**(m)** (Comput) to exit
**3** **se sortir** *v refl* (+ *v être*) **(a)** **se ∼ de la pauvreté** to escape from poverty; **s'en ∼** to get out of it; to get over it; **s'en ∼ vivant** to escape with one's life
**(b)** **s'en ∼** to pull through; to cope; to manage; **s'en ∼ à peine** to scrape a living

**sortir²** /sɔʀtiʀ/ *nm* **au ∼ de** at the end of

**SOS** /ɛsoɛs/ *nm* **(a)** SOS
**(b)** emergency service; **∼ médecins** emergency medical service

**(c)** helpline; **∼ enfants battus** child abuse helpline

**sosie** /sɔzi/ *nm* double; **c'est ton ∼!** he/ she's the spitting image of you!

**sot, sotte** /so, sɔt/ **1** *adj* silly
**2** *nm,f* silly thing; **petit ∼!** you silly thing!

**sottement** /sɔtmã/ *adv* foolishly, stupidly

**sottise** /sɔtiz/ *nf* **(a)** silliness, foolishness
**(b)** silly remark; **dire des ∼s** to talk rubbish
**(c)** **faire des ∼s** ⟨*children*⟩ to be naughty

**sou** /su/ *nm* **(a)** (colloq) penny (GB), cent (US); **il est près de ses ∼s** he's a penny-pincher; **c'est une affaire de gros ∼s** there's big money involved
**(b)** (colloq) **il n'a pas un ∼ de bon sens** he hasn't got a scrap of common sense
**(c)** (former unit of French currency) sou

**soubassement** /subasmã/ *nm*
**(a)** (of building, pillar) base
**(b)** bedrock

**soubresaut** /subʀəso/ *nm* start; jolt

**soubrette** /subʀɛt/ *nf* maid

**souche** /suʃ/ *nf* **(a)** (tree) stump; (vine) stock
**(b)** stock; **de ∼ paysanne** of peasant stock
**(c)** (of chequebook) stub
IDIOMS **dormir comme une ∼** to sleep like a log

**souci** /susi/ *nm* **(a)** **se faire du ∼** to worry
**(b)** problem; **j'ai d'autres ∼s (en tête)** I've got other things to worry about
**(c)** (formal) **avoir le ∼ de qch** to care about sth; **avoir le ∼ de faire** to be anxious to do; **dans le seul ∼ de faire plaisir** with the sole intention of pleasing
**(d)** marigold

**soucier: se soucier** /susje/ [2] *v refl* (+ *v être*) to care (**de** about); **sans se ∼ de qch/faire** without concerning oneself with sth/doing

**soucieux, -ieuse** /susjø, øz/ *adj* worried

**soucoupe** /sukup/ *nf* saucer
■ **∼ volante** flying saucer

**soudain, ∼e** /sudɛ̃, ɛn/ **1** *adj* sudden
**2** *adv* suddenly, all of a sudden

**soudainement** /sudɛnmã/ *adv* suddenly

**soude** /sud/ *nf* **∼ caustique** caustic soda

**souder** /sude/ [1] **1** *vtr* **(a)** to weld
**(b)** to join ⟨*edges*⟩; to bind [sb] together ⟨*people*⟩
**2** **se souder** *v refl* (+ *v être*) ⟨*vertebrae*⟩ to fuse; ⟨*bone*⟩ to knit together

**soudoyer** /sudwaje/ [23] *vtr* to bribe

**soudure** /sudyʀ/ *nf* weld; join; welding

**soufflant, ∼e** /suflã, ãt/ *adj* **(a)** machine **∼e** blowing apparatus
**(b)** (colloq) stunning

**souffle** /sufl/ *nm* **(a)** breath; **couper le ∼ à qn** to wind sb; (figurative) to take sb's breath away; **(en) avoir le ∼ coupé** to be winded; (figurative) to be speechless; **être à bout de ∼** ⟨*person*⟩ to be out of breath; ⟨*country, economy*⟩ to be running out of steam; **donner** ⋯❖

un second *or* nouveau ∼ à qn/qch to put new life into sb/sth; avoir du ∼ ⟨*saxophonist*⟩ to have good lungs; ⟨*singer*⟩ to have a powerful voice; ⟨*sportsman*⟩ to be fit; (figurative) ⟨*person*⟩ to have staying power
(b) breathing
(c) breeze; **pas un** ∼ **d'air** not a breath of air
(d) spirit; ∼ **révolutionnaire** revolutionary spirit
(e) inspiration
(f) (from fan, explosion) blast
(g) (Med) ∼ **au cœur** heart murmur

**soufflé**, **∼e** /sufle/ ⓵ *adj* (colloq) flabbergasted
⓶ *nm* (Culin) soufflé

**souffler** /sufle/ [1] ⓵ *vtr* (a) to blow out ⟨*candle*⟩
(b) to blow ⟨*air, smoke, dust*⟩
(c) to whisper ⟨*words*⟩; ∼ **qch à l'oreille de qn** to whisper sth in sb's ear; ∼ **la réplique à un acteur** to prompt an actor
(d) to suggest ⟨*idea*⟩
(e) to blow ⟨*glass*⟩; to blast ⟨*metal*⟩
(f) ⟨*explosion*⟩ to blow out ⟨*window*⟩; to blow up ⟨*building*⟩
(g) (colloq) to flabbergast
⓶ *vi* (a) ⟨*wind*⟩ to blow; **le vent souffle fort** there's a strong wind
(b) ⟨*person*⟩ to get one's breath back; ⟨*horse*⟩ to get its wind back
(c) to puff; **suant et soufflant** huffing and puffing
(d) ⟨*person, animal*⟩ to blow; ∼ **dans une trompette** to blow into a trumpet
(e) to tell sb the answer; **on ne souffle pas!** no prompting!
IDIOMS ∼ **comme un bœuf** *or* **un phoque** *or* **une locomotive** to puff and pant

**soufflerie** /sufləʀi/ *nf* (a) blower; blower house
(b) glassblower; glassblowing company

**soufflet** /suflɛ/ *nm* (a) bellows
(b) gusset

**souffleur**, **-euse** /suflœʀ, øz/ *nm,f*
(a) prompter
(b) ∼ **(de verre)** glassblower

**souffrance** /sufʀɑ̃s/ *nf* suffering

**souffrant**, **∼e** /sufʀɑ̃, ɑ̃t/ *adj* unwell

**souffre-douleur** /sufʀədulœʀ/ *nm inv* punch-bag (GB), punching-bag (US)

**souffrir** /sufʀiʀ/ [4] ⓵ *vtr* (a) ∼ **tout de qn** to put up with anything from sb; **il ne souffre pas la critique** he can't take criticism
(b) **cette affaire ne peut** ∼ **aucun retard** this matter brooks no delay
⓶ *vi* (a) ⟨*person*⟩ to suffer; ∼ **de** to suffer from; **ma cheville me fait** ∼ my ankle hurts; **est-ce qu'il souffre?** is he in pain?; **faire** ∼ ⟨*person*⟩ to make [sb] suffer; ⟨*situation*⟩ to upset; ∼ **du racisme** to be a victim of racism
(b) ⟨*crops, economy*⟩ to be badly affected; ⟨*country, city*⟩ to suffer

**soufre** /sufʀ/ *nm* sulphur (GB)

**souhait** /swɛ/ *nm* wish
IDIOMS **à vos ∼s!** bless you!

**souhaitable** /swɛtabl/ *adj* desirable

**souhaiter** /swete/ [1] *vtr* (a) to hope for
(b) ∼ **qch à qn** to wish sb sth; ∼ **la bienvenue à qn** to welcome sb; **je vous souhaite d'obtenir très bientôt votre diplôme** I hope you get your degree very soon
(c) **il souhaite se rendre là-bas en voiture** he would like to go by car

**souiller** /suje/ [1] *vtr* (a) to soil, to make [sth] dirty; **être souillé de** to be stained with
(b) to defile ⟨*place, person*⟩; to sully ⟨*memory*⟩

**souillon** /sujɔ̃/ *nf* slattern

**souillure** /sujyʀ/ *nf* stain

**souk** /suk/ *nm* (a) souk
(b) (colloq) mess; racket (colloq)

**soûl**, **∼e** /su, sul/ ⓵ *adj* drunk
⓶ **tout son soûl** *phr* ⟨*drink, eat*⟩ one's fill

**soulagement** /sulaʒmɑ̃/ *nm* relief

**soulager** /sulaʒe/ [13] *vtr* (gen) to relieve; to ease ⟨*conscience*⟩; **le comprimé m'a soulagé** the tablet made me feel better; **tu m'as soulagé d'un grand poids** you've taken a great weight off my shoulders

**soûlant**, **∼e** /sulɑ̃, ɑ̃t/ *adj* (colloq) **elle est ∼e!** she makes my head spin!

**soûler** /sule/ [1] ⓵ *vtr* (a) ⟨*person*⟩ to get [sb] drunk; ⟨*alcohol*⟩ to make [sb] drunk
(b) ⟨*perfume*⟩ to intoxicate
(c) (colloq) **tu me soûles avec tes histoires** you're making my head spin!
⓶ **se soûler** *v refl* (+ *v être*) to get drunk

**soulèvement** /sulɛvmɑ̃/ *nm* uprising

**soulever** /sulve/ [16] ⓵ *vtr* (a) to lift ⟨*object*⟩; to raise ⟨*dust*⟩; ∼ **qn/qch de terre** to pick sb/sth up
(b) to arouse ⟨*enthusiasm, anger*⟩; to stir up ⟨*crowd*⟩; to raise ⟨*problems*⟩
⓶ **se soulever** *v refl* (+ *v être*) (a) to raise oneself up
(b) to rise up
IDIOMS **ça me soulève le cœur** it turns my stomach; it makes me sick

**soulier** /sulje/ *nm* shoe
IDIOMS **être dans ses petits ∼s** to feel uncomfortable

**souligner** /suliɲe/ [1] *vtr* (a) to underline ⟨*word*⟩; to outline ⟨*eyes*⟩
(b) to emphasize

**soumettre** /sumɛtʀ/ [60] ⓵ *vtr* (a) to bring [sb/sth] to heel ⟨*person, group, region*⟩; to subdue ⟨*rebels*⟩
(b) ∼ **qn/qch à** to subject sb/sth to
(c) to submit
(d) ∼ **un produit à une température élevée** to subject a product to a high temperature
⓶ **se soumettre** *v refl* (+ *v être*) (a) to submit
(b) **se** ∼ **à** to accept ⟨*rule*⟩

**soumis**, **∼e** /sumi, iz/ ⓵ *pp* ▶ soumettre
⓶ *adj* submissive

**soumission** /sumisjɔ̃/ *nf* submission

**soupape** /supap/ *nf* valve

**soupçon** /supsɔ̃/ *nm* (a) suspicion

**(b)** (colloq) (of milk, wine) drop; (of salt) pinch; (of flavour) hint

**soupçonner** /supsɔne/ [1] *vtr* to suspect

**soupçonneux, -euse** /supsɔnø, øz/ *adj* suspicious, mistrustful

**soupe** /sup/ *nf* **(a)** soup; **à la ~!** (colloq) (humorous) grub's up! (colloq)
**(b)** (colloq) slush
■ **~ populaire** soup kitchen
IDIOMS **être ~ au lait** (colloq) to be quick-tempered; **cracher dans la ~** (colloq) to look a gift horse in the mouth

**soupente** /supɑ̃t/ *nf* **(a)** loft, garret
**(b)** cupboard under the stairs

**souper¹** /supe/ [1] *vi* to have late dinner

**souper²** /supe/ *nm* late dinner, supper

**soupeser** /supəze/ [16] *vtr* **(a)** to feel the weight of
**(b)** to weigh up ⟨arguments⟩

**soupière** /supjɛʀ/ *nf* soup tureen

**soupir** /supiʀ/ *nm* sigh

**soupirail**, *pl* **-aux** /supiʀaj, o/ *nm* cellar window

**soupirer** /supiʀe/ [1] *vi* to sigh

**souple** /supl/ *adj* **(a)** ⟨body⟩ supple; ⟨stalk⟩ flexible; ⟨hair⟩ soft
**(b)** ⟨step, style⟩ flowing; ⟨shape⟩ smooth
**(c)** ⟨rule⟩ flexible

**souplesse** /suplɛs/ *nf* **(a)** (of stalk) flexibility; (of hair) softness; (of body) suppleness
**(b)** (of step) litheness; (of gesture) grace; (of car) smoothness; (of style) fluidity
**(c)** (of rule) flexibility

**source** /suʀs/ *nf* **(a)** spring
**(b)** source; **prendre sa ~ dans** *or* **à** ⟨river⟩ to rise in *or* at; **citer ses ~s** to give one's sources
IDIOMS **ça coule de ~** it's obvious; **retour aux ~s** return to basics

**sourcil** /suʀsi/ *nm* eyebrow

**sourciller** /suʀsije/ [1] *vi* to raise one's eyebrows; **sans ~** without batting an eyelid

**sourd, ~e** /suʀ, suʀd/ 1 *adj* **(a)** deaf; **~ à** deaf to ⟨pleas⟩
**(b)** ⟨noise⟩ dull; ⟨voice⟩ muffled
**(c)** ⟨pain⟩ dull
**(d)** ⟨consonant⟩ voiceless, surd
2 *nm,f* deaf person; **les ~s** the deaf
IDIOMS **faire la ~e oreille** to turn a deaf ear; **comme un ~** ⟨shout⟩ at the top of one's voice; **comme un ~** like one possessed; **ce n'est pas tombé dans l'oreille d'un ~** it didn't go unheard

**sourdine** /suʀdin/ *nf* (Mus) mute; (on piano) soft pedal; **écouter la radio en ~** to have the radio on quietly

**sourd-muet, sourde-muette**, *pl* **sourds-muets, sourdes-muettes** /suʀmɥɛ, suʀdmɥɛt/ 1 *adj* deaf and dumb
2 *nm,f* deaf-mute

**souriant, ~e** /suʀjɑ̃, ɑ̃t/ *adj* smiling

**souriceau**, *pl* **~x** /suʀiso/ *nm* young mouse

**souricière** /suʀisjɛʀ/ *nf* **(a)** mousetrap
**(b)** trap

**sourire¹** /suʀiʀ/ [68] *vi* **(a)** to smile; **~ jusqu'aux oreilles** to grin from ear to ear
**(b)** **~ à qn** ⟨fate, fortune⟩ to smile on sb

**sourire²** /suʀiʀ/ *nm* smile; **le ~ aux lèvres** with a smile on one's face

**souris** /suʀi/ *nf inv* mouse

**sournois, ~e** /suʀnwa, az/ *adj* ⟨person, look⟩ sly; ⟨behaviour⟩ underhand; ⟨pain⟩ insidious

**sous** /su/ *prep* **(a)** under, underneath; **un journal ~ le bras** a newspaper under one's arm; **~ la pluie** in the rain
**(b)** under; **~ le numéro 4757** under number 4757
**(c)** during; **~ la présidence de Mitterrand** during Mitterrand's presidency
**(d)** within; **~ peu** before long
**(e)** **~ traitement** undergoing treatment; **~ antibiotiques** on antibiotics

**sous-alimenté, ~e, mpl ~s** /suzalimɑ̃te/ *adj* undernourished

**sous-bois** /subwa/ *nm inv* undergrowth

**sous-catégorie**, *pl* **~s** /sukategɔʀi/ *nf* subcategory

**sous-chef**, *pl* **~s** /suʃɛf/ *nm* second-in-command

**souscripteur, -trice** /suskʀiptœʀ, tʀis/ *nm,f* subscriber **(de** to**)**

**souscription** /suskʀipsjɔ̃/ *nf*
**(a)** subscription
**(b)** **~ d'un contrat d'assurances** taking out an insurance policy

**souscrire** /suskʀiʀ/ [67] 1 *vtr* to take out ⟨insurance⟩; to sign ⟨contract⟩; to subscribe ⟨sum of money⟩
2 **souscrire à** *v+prep* to subscribe to

**souscrit, ~e** /suskʀi, it/ 1 *pp* ▶ SOUSCRIRE
2 *pp adj* **(a)** subscribed
**(b)** subscript

**sous-cutané, ~e, mpl ~s** /sukytane/ *adj* subcutaneous

**sous-développé, ~e, mpl ~s** /sudevlɔpe/ *adj* underdeveloped

**sous-directeur, -trice, mpl ~s** /sudiʀɛktœʀ, tʀis/ *nm,f* assistant manager

**sous-direction**, *pl* **~s** /sudiʀɛksjɔ̃/ *nf* division; **~ des affaires économiques et financières** economic and financial affairs division

**sous-effectif**, *pl* **~s** /suzefɛktif/ *nm* understaffing; **ils sont en ~** they're understaffed

**sous-employer** /suzɑ̃plwaje/ [23] *vtr* to underemploy

**sous-entendre** /suzɑ̃tɑ̃dʀ/ [6] *vtr* to imply

**sous-entendu, ~e, mpl ~s** /suzɑ̃tɑ̃dy/
1 *pp* ▶ SOUS-ENTENDRE
2 *pp adj* understood

····⁑

**S**

**3** *nm* innuendo

**sous-équipé**, **~e**, *mpl* **~s** /suzekipe/ *adj* underequipped

**sous-estimer** /suzestime/ [1] *vtr* to underestimate

**sous-évaluer** /suzevalɥe/ [1] *vtr* to underestimate; to undervalue

**sous-fifre**, *pl* **~s** /sufifʀ/ *nm* (colloq) underling

**sous-jacent**, **~e**, *mpl* **~s** /suʒasɑ̃, ɑ̃t/ *adj* (a) ⟨idea, problem, tension⟩ underlying
(b) subjacent

**sous-lieutenant**, *pl* **~s** /suljøtnɑ̃/ *nm* (in the army) ≈ second lieutenant; (in the air force) ≈ pilot officer

**sous-louer** /sulwe/ [1] *vtr* to sublet; to sublease

**sous-main** /sumɛ̃/ **1** *nm inv* desk blotter
**2 en sous-main** *phr* secretly

**sous-marin**, **~e**, *mpl* **~s** /sumaʀɛ̃, in/ **1** *adj* submarine, underwater; deep-sea
**2** *nm* (a) submarine
(b) (colloq) spy

**sous-marque**, *pl* **~s** /sumaʀk/ *nf* sub-brand

**sous-officier**, *pl* **~s** /suzɔfisje/ *nm* noncommissioned officer

**sous-ordre**, *pl* **~s** /suzɔʀdʀ/ *nm* suborder

**sous-payer** /supeje/ [21] *vtr* to underpay

**sous-préfecture**, *pl* **~s** /supʀefɛktyʀ/ *nf*: administrative subdivision of a department in France

**sous-produit**, *pl* **~s** /supʀɔdɥi/ *nm* (a) by-product
(b) second-rate product

**sous-prolétariat**, *pl* **~s** /supʀɔletaʀja/ *nm* underclass

**sous-pull**, *pl* **~s** /supyl/ *nm* thin polo-neck jumper

**soussigné**, **~e** /susiɲe/ *adj, nm,f* undersigned

**sous-sol**, *pl* **~s** /susɔl/ *nm* (a) basement
(b) subsoil

**sous-tasse**, *pl* **~s** /sutas/ *nf* saucer

**sous-titrage**, *pl* **~s** /sutitʀaʒ/ *nm* subtitling

**sous-titre**, *pl* **~s** /sutitʀ/ *nm* subtitle

**sous-titrer** /sutitʀe/ [1] *vtr* to subtitle

**soustraction** /sustʀaksjɔ̃/ *nf* subtraction

**soustraire** /sustʀɛʀ/ [58] **1** *vtr* (a) to subtract
(b) to steal
(c) to take away ⟨person⟩; **~ qn/qch à la vue de qn** to hide sb/sth from sb
(d) to shield ⟨person⟩; **~ qn à la mort** to save sb's life
**2 se soustraire** *v refl* (+ *v être*) (a) **se ~ à** to escape from
(b) **se ~ à la justice** to escape justice

**sous-traitance**, *pl* **~s** /sutʀɛtɑ̃s/ *nf* subcontracting; **travail donné en ~** work contracted out

**sous-verre** /suvɛʀ/ *nm inv* (a) clip-frame
(b) coaster

**sous-vêtement**, *pl* **~s** /suvɛtmɑ̃/ *nm* underwear

**soutane** /sutan/ *nf* cassock

**soute** /sut/ *nf* hold; **~ à bagages** baggage hold

**soutenable** /sutnabl/ *adj* (a) bearable; **pas ~** unbearable
(b) tenable

**soutenance** /sutnɑ̃s/ *nf* viva (voce) (GB), orals (US)

**soutènement** /sutɛnmɑ̃/ *nm* retaining structure; (in mine) props

**souteneur** /sutnœʀ/ *nm* pimp (colloq), procurer

**soutenir** /sutniʀ/ [36] **1** *vtr* (a) (gen) to support ⟨person, team, currency⟩; **~ à bout de bras** to keep [sb/sth] afloat ⟨person, project⟩; **~ qn contre qn** to side with sb against sb; **~ le moral de qn** to keep sb's spirits up
(b) to maintain ⟨contrary⟩; to defend ⟨paradox⟩; to uphold ⟨opinion⟩
(c) to keep [sb] going
(d) to keep [sth] going ⟨conversation⟩; to keep up ⟨effort, pace⟩
(e) to withstand ⟨shock, attack, stares⟩; to bear ⟨comparison⟩
(f) **~ sa thèse** to have one's viva (voce) (GB) or defense (US)
**2 se soutenir** *v refl* (+ *v être*) to support each other

**soutenu**, **~e** /sutny/ **1** *pp* ▶ SOUTENIR
**2** *pp adj* ⟨effort, activity⟩ sustained; ⟨attention⟩ close; ⟨rhythm⟩ steady
**3** *adj* (a) ⟨market⟩ firm; ⟨colour⟩ deep; ⟨language⟩ formal
(b) (Mus) ⟨note⟩ sustained

**souterrain**, **~e** /sutɛʀɛ̃, ɛn/ **1** *adj* (a) underground
(b) **économie ~e** black economy
**2** *nm* underground passage, tunnel

**soutien** /sutjɛ̃/ *nm* support

**soutien-gorge**, *pl* **soutiens-gorge** /sutjɛ̃gɔʀʒ/ *nm* bra

**soutirer** /sutire/ [1] *vtr* **~ qch à qn** to squeeze sth out of sb ⟨money⟩; to extract sth from sb ⟨confession⟩

**souvenance** /suvnɑ̃s/ *nf* **à ma ~** as far as I recall; **avoir ~ de qch** to remember sth

**souvenir¹: se souvenir** /suvniʀ/ [36] *v refl* (+ *v être*) **se ~ de qn/qch** to remember sb/sth

**souvenir²** /suvniʀ/ *nm* (a) memory; **garder un bon ~ de qch** to have happy memories of sth; **ne pas avoir ~ de** to have no recollection of
(b) memory; **s'effacer du ~ de qn** to fade from sb's memory
(c) souvenir; memento; **en ~** as a souvenir; as a memento; as a keepsake; **boutique de ~s** souvenir shop (GB) or store (US)
(d) **mon bon ~ à** remember me to

**souvent** /suvɑ̃/ *adv* often

**souverain**, **∼e** /suvʀɛ̃, ɛn/ **1** *adj*
(a) ⟨state⟩ sovereign; ⟨authority⟩ supreme
(b) ⟨happiness, scorn⟩ supreme
(c) ⟨remedy⟩ sovereign; ⟨advice, virtue⟩ sterling
(d) ⟨person⟩ haughty
**2** *nm,f* sovereign, monarch

**souverainement** /suvʀɛnmɑ̃/ *adv* **votre attitude me déplaît ∼** I dislike your attitude intensely

**souveraineté** /suvʀɛnte/ *nf* sovereignty

**soviet** /sɔvjɛt/ *nm* soviet; **Soviet suprême** Supreme Soviet

**soviétique** /sɔvjetik/ *adj* Soviet

**soyeux**, **-euse** /swajø, øz/ *adj* silky

**soyez** /swaje/ ▶ ÊTRE¹

**soyons** /swajɔ̃/ ▶ ÊTRE¹

**SPA** /ɛspea/ *nf* (*abbr* = **Société protectrice des animaux**) society for the prevention of cruelty to animals

**spacieux**, **-ieuse** /spasjø, øz/ *adj* spacious

**spaghetti** /spageti/ *nm inv* **des ∼** spaghetti

**sparadrap** /spaʀadʀa/ *nm* (a) surgical *or* adhesive tape
(b) (sticking) plaster (GB), Band-aid®

**spartiate** /spaʀsjat/ *adj, nmf* Spartan

**spasme** /spasm/ *nm* spasm

**spasmophilie** /spasmɔfili/ *nf* spasmophilia

**spatial**, **∼e**, *mpl* **-iaux** /spasjal, o/ *adj*
(a) spatial
(b) space; **vaisseau ∼** spaceship

**spatule** /spatyl/ *nf* (a) spatula
(b) filling-knife

**speaker**, **speakerine** /spikœʀ, spikʀin/ *nm,f* announcer

**spécial**, **∼e**, *mpl* **-iaux** /spesjal, o/ *adj*
(a) special
(b) odd

**spécialement** /spesjalmɑ̃/ *adv*
(a) specially
(b) especially; **pas ∼** not especially

**spécialiser**: **se spécialiser** /spesjalize/ [1] *v refl* (+ *v être*) to specialize

**spécialiste** /spesjalist/ *nmf* specialist

**spécialité** /spesjalite/ *nf* speciality (GB), specialty (US)

**spécificité** /spesifisite/ *nf* (a) specificity
(b) characteristic
(c) uniqueness

**spécifier** /spesifje/ [2] *vtr* to specify

**spécifique** /spesifik/ *adj* specific

**spécimen** /spesimɛn/ *nm* (a) specimen
(b) (free) sample
(c) (colloq) odd specimen (colloq)

**spectacle** /spɛktakl/ *nm* (a) sight; **se donner** *or* **s'offrir en ∼** to make an exhibition of oneself
(b) show; **∼ de danse** dance show; **'∼s'** 'entertainment'; **film à grand ∼** spectacular
(c) show business

**spectaculaire** /spɛktakylɛʀ/ *adj* spectacular

**spectateur**, **-trice** /spɛktatœʀ, tʀis/ *nm,f* (a) member of the audience
(b) spectator

**spectre** /spɛktʀ/ *nm* (a) ghost
(b) spectre (GB)
(c) **∼ lumineux** spectrum of light

**spéculateur**, **-trice** /spekylatœʀ, tʀis/ *nm,f* speculator

**spéculatif**, **-ive** /spekylatif, iv/ *adj* speculative

**spéculation** /spekylasjɔ̃/ *nf* (a) (Econ) speculation; **∼ sur** speculation in
(b) (gen) speculation (**sur** on, about)

**spéculer** /spekyle/ [1] *vi* to speculate; **∼ à la hausse/baisse** to bull/bear

**spéléologie** /speleɔlɔʒi/ *nf* (a) caving, potholing (GB), spelunking (US)
(b) speleology

**spermatozoïde** /spɛʀmatɔzɔid/ *nm* **des ∼s** spermatozoa

**sperme** /spɛʀm/ *nm* sperm

**sphère** /sfɛʀ/ *nf* sphere

**sphérique** /sferik/ *adj* spherical

**sphincter** /sfɛ̃ktɛʀ/ *nm* sphincter

**sphinx** /sfɛ̃ks/ *nm inv* (a) Sphinx
(b) hawkmoth

**spirale** /spiʀal/ *nf* spiral

**spiritisme** /spiʀitism/ *nm* spiritualism

**spiritualité** /spiʀitɥalite/ *nf* spirituality

**spirituel**, **-elle** /spiʀitɥɛl/ *adj*
(a) spiritual
(b) witty

**spiritueux**, **-euse** /spiʀitɥø, øz/ *nm inv* spirit

**splendeur** /splɑ̃dœʀ/ *nf* (of scenery, site) splendour (GB); (of era, reign) glory

**splendide** /splɑ̃did/ *adj* splendid; stunning

**spolier** /spɔlje/ [2] *vtr* to despoil (**de** of)

**spongieux**, **-ieuse** /spɔ̃ʒjø, øz/ *adj* spongy

**sponsoriser** /spɔ̃sɔʀize/ [1] *vtr* to sponsor

**spontané**, **∼e** /spɔ̃tane/ *adj* spontaneous

**spontanéité** /spɔ̃taneite/ *nf* spontaneity

**sporadique** /spɔʀadik/ *adj* sporadic

**spore** /spɔʀ/ *nf* spore

**sport** /spɔʀ/ *nm* sport; sports; **aller aux ∼s d'hiver** to go on a winter sports holiday (GB) *or* vacation (US)

**sportif**, **-ive** /spɔʀtif, iv/ **1** *adj* (a) ⟨event⟩ sports; **je ne suis pas ∼** I'm not the sporty type
(b) ⟨appearance⟩ athletic, sporty (colloq)
**2** *nm,f* sportsman/sportswoman; **c'est un ∼** he's athletic

**spot** /spɔt/ *nm* (a) spotlight
(b) **∼** ( publicitaire) commercial

**squale** /skwal/ *nm* shark

**square** /skwaʀ/ *nm* small public garden

**squash** /skwaʃ/ *nm* squash

S

**squatter¹** /skwate/ [1] *vtr* to squat in

**squatter²** /skwatœʀ/ *nm* squatter

**squelette** /skəlɛt/ *nm* **(a)** skeleton
**(b)** (colloq) bag of bones (colloq)
**(c)** framework

**squelettique** /skəlɛtik/ *adj* ⟨*person, legs*⟩
scrawny; ⟨*tree*⟩ skeletal; ⟨*report*⟩ sketchy

**stabiliser** /stabilize/ [1] **1** *vtr* to stabilize;
to consolidate
**2 se stabiliser** *v refl* (+ *v être*)
⟨*unemployment*⟩ to stabilize; ⟨*person*⟩ to
become stable

**stabilité** /stabilite/ *nf* stability

**stable** /stabl/ *adj* stable

**stade** /stad/ *nm* **(a)** (Sport) stadium
**(b)** stage; **à ce ~** at this stage

**stage** /staʒ/ *nm* **(a)** professional training
**(b)** work experience; **~ pratique** period of
work experience
**(c)** course; **suivre un ~ de formation** to go on
a training course

**stagiaire** /staʒjɛʀ/ *nmf* **(a)** trainee
**(b)** student teacher

**stagnation** /stagnasjɔ̃/ *nf* stagnation

**stagner** /stagne/ [1] *vi* to stagnate

**stalactite** /stalaktit/ *nf* stalactite

**stalagmite** /stalagmit/ *nf* stalagmite

**stalle** /stal/ *nf* stall

**stand** /stɑ̃d/ *nm* stand; stall
■ **~ de tir** shooting range; shooting gallery

**standard** /stɑ̃daʀ/ **1** *adj inv* standard
**2** *nm* switchboard

**standardisation** /stɑ̃daʀdizasjɔ̃/ *nf*
standardization

**standardiste** /stɑ̃daʀdist/ *nmf*
switchboard operator

**standing** /stɑ̃diŋ/ *nm* **(a) de ~**
⟨*apartment*⟩ luxury
**(b)** standard of living

**star** /staʀ/ *nf* star

**starter** /staʀtɛʀ/ *nm* (Aut) choke

**station** /stasjɔ̃/ *nf* **(a)** station; taxi-rank
(GB), taxi stand; **c'est à deux ~s d'ici** it's two
stops from here
**(b) ~ (de radio)** (radio) station
**(c) ~ balnéaire** seaside resort; **~ thermale**
spa
**(d) ~ debout** *or* **verticale** upright posture *or*
position
**(f)** stop, pause

**stationnaire** /stasjɔnɛʀ/ *adj* **(a)** stationary
**(b)** stable

**stationnement** /stasjɔnmɑ̃/ *nm* parking

**stationner** /stasjɔne/ [1] *vi* to park

**station-service**, *pl* **stations-
service** /stasjɔ̃sɛʀvis/ *nf* service *or* filling
station

**statique** /statik/ *adj* static

**statistique** /statistik/ *nf* **(a)** statistics
**(b)** statistic

**statue** /staty/ *nf* statue

**statuer** /statye/ [1] *vi* to give a ruling

**statuette** /statyɛt/ *nf* statuette

**statu quo** /statykwo/ *nm inv* status quo

**stature** /statyʀ/ *nf* **(a)** stature
**(b)** height

**statut** /staty/ *nm* **(a)** statute
**(b)** status

**statutaire** /statytɛʀ/ *adj* statutory

**steak** /stɛk/ *nm* steak; **un ~ haché** a
hamburger

**sténodactylo** /stenodaktilo/ **1** *nmf*
shorthand typist (GB), stenographer (US)
**2** *nf* shorthand typing (GB), stenography
(US)

**sténographier** /stenɔgʀafje/ [2] *vtr* to
take [sth] down in shorthand

**sténotypiste** /stenɔtipist/ *nmf*
stenotypist

**steppe** /stɛp/ *nf* steppe

**stéréo** /steʀeo/ *adj inv*, *nf* stereo

**stéréophonique** /steʀeɔfɔnik/ *adj*
stereophonic

**stéréotype** /steʀeɔtip/ *nm* **(a)** stereotype
**(b)** cliché

**stérile** /steʀil/ *adj* (gen) sterile; ⟨*land*⟩
barren; ⟨*discussion*⟩ fruitless

**stérilet** /steʀilɛ/ *nm* coil, IUD

**stériliser** /steʀilize/ [1] *vtr* to sterilize

**stérilité** /steʀilite/ *nf* **(a)** sterility;
barrenness
**(b)** fruitlessness

**sterling** /stɛʀliŋ/ *adj inv* sterling; **livre ~**
pound sterling

**sternum** /stɛʀnɔm/ *nm* breastbone,
sternum

**stéthoscope** /stetɔskɔp/ *nm* stethoscope

**stigmate** /stigmat/ *nm* **(a)** scar
**(b)** mark

**stimulant, ~e** /stimylɑ̃, ɑ̃t/ *adj*
invigorating; bracing; stimulating

**stimulation** /stimylasjɔ̃/ *nf* stimulation

**stimuler** /stimyle/ [1] **1** *vtr* **(a)** to
stimulate ⟨*organ, function*⟩
**(b)** to spur [sb] on
**2** *vi* **(a)** to be bracing
**(b)** (colloq) to act as a spur

**stimulus**, *pl* **stimuli** /stimylys, stimyli/
*nm* stimulus

**stipuler** /stipyle/ [1] *vtr* to stipulate

**stock** /stɔk/ *nm* stock; **avoir qch en ~** to
have sth in stock

**stockage** /stɔkaʒ/ *nm* **(a)** stocking;
stockpiling
**(b)** (Comput) storage

**stocker** /stɔke/ [1] *vtr* **(a)** to stock
**(b)** to stockpile
**(c)** to store ⟨*data*⟩

**stoïque** /stɔik/ *adj* stoical

**stop** /stɔp/ *nm* **(a)** stop sign
**(b)** (colloq) hitch-hiking (colloq); **prendre qn en
~** to give sb a lift (GB) *or* ride (US)

**stopper** /stɔpe/ [1] **1** *vtr* **(a)** to stop; to
halt ⟨*development*⟩
**(b)** to mend
**2** *vi* to stop

**store** /stɔʀ/ *nm* **(a)** blind
**(b)** awning

**strabisme** /stʀabism/ *nm* squint

**strapontin** /stʀapɔ̃tɛ̃/ *nm* foldaway seat

**stratagème** /stʀataʒɛm/ *nm* stratagem

**strate** /stʀat/ *nf* stratum

**stratégie** /stʀateʒi/ *nf* strategy

**stratégique** /stʀateʒik/ *adj* strategic

**stratifié, ~e** /stʀatifje/ *adj* **(a)** stratified
**(b)** laminated

**stratosphère** /stʀatɔsfɛʀ/ *nf*
stratosphere

**stress** /stʀɛs/ *nm inv* stress

**stressant, ~e** /stʀɛsɑ̃, ɑ̃t/ *adj* stressful

**stresser** /stʀese/ [1] *vtr* to put [sb] on
edge; to put [sb] under stress

**strict, ~e** /stʀikt/ *adj* **(a)** (gen) strict; **au
sens ~** in the strict sense of the word
**(b)** ⟨hairstyle, outfit⟩ severe

**strident, ~e** /stʀidɑ̃, ɑ̃t/ *adj* ⟨noise⟩
piercing; ⟨voice⟩ strident

**strie** /stʀi/ *nf* **(a)** streak
**(b)** groove
**(c)** (in geology) **des ~s** striation

**strip-tease** /stʀiptiz/ *nm* striptease

**strophe** /stʀɔf/ *nf* stanza, verse

**structure** /stʀyktyʀ/ *nf* **(a)** structure
**(b)** organization; **~ d'accueil** shelter, refuge

**structurer** /stʀyktyʀe/ [1] *vtr* to structure

**stuc** /styk/ *nm* stucco

**studieux, -ieuse** /stydjø, øz/ *adj* ⟨pupil⟩
studious; ⟨holiday⟩ study

**studio** /stydjo/ *nm* **(a)** studio flat (GB),
studio apartment (US)
**(b)** studio

**stupéfaction** /stypefaksjɔ̃/ *nf*
stupefaction

**stupéfait, ~e** /stypefɛ, ɛt/ *adj* astounded

**stupéfiant, ~e** /stypefjɑ̃, ɑ̃t/ ① *adj*
stunning
② *nm* drug, narcotic

**stupéfier** /stypefje/ [2] *vtr* to astound

**stupeur** /stypœʀ/ *nf* **(a)** astonishment
**(b)** (Med) stupor

**stupide** /stypid/ *adj* stupid

**stupidité** /stypidite/ *nf* stupidity

**style** /stil/ *nm* **(a)** style; **~ de vie** lifestyle;
**c'est bien ton ~ de faire** it's just like you to
do
**(b)** **meubles de ~** (reproduction) period
furniture
**(c)** speech form; **~ indirect** indirect *or*
reported speech

**stylé, ~e** /stile/ *adj* well-trained

**styliser** /stilize/ [1] *vtr* to stylize

**styliste** /stilist/ *nmf* fashion designer

**stylo** /stilo/ *nm* (fountain) pen; **~ bille** ballpoint pen; **~ feutre** felt-tip pen

**su¹, ~e** /sy/ ▶ SAVOIR

**su²** /sy/ *nm* **au vu et au ~ de tous** openly

**suaire** /sɥɛʀ/ *nm* shroud

**suant, ~e** /sɥɑ̃, ɑ̃t/ *adj* **(a)** sweaty

**(b)** (colloq) deadly dull

**suave** /sɥav/ *adj* ⟨perfume, music, smile⟩
sweet; ⟨voice⟩ mellifluous; ⟨person, manner⟩
suave

**subalterne** /sybaltɛʀn/ *nmf* subordinate;
(Mil) low-ranking officer, subaltern

**subconscient** /sybkɔ̃sjɑ̃/ *nm*
subconscious

**subdiviser** /sybdivize/ [1] *vtr* to subdivide

**subir** /sybiʀ/ [3] *vtr* **(a)** to be subjected to
⟨violence, pressure⟩; to suffer ⟨defeat,
damage⟩
**(b)** to take ⟨examination⟩; to have
⟨operation, test⟩; **~ l'influence de qn** to be
under sb's influence
**(c)** to put up with
**(d)** to undergo

**subit, ~e** /sybi, it/ *adj* sudden

**subitement** /sybitmɑ̃/ *adv* suddenly

**subjectif, -ive** /sybʒɛktif, iv/ *adj*
subjective

**subjectivité** /sybʒɛktivite/ *nf*
subjectivity

**subjonctif** /sybʒɔ̃ktif/ *nm* subjunctive

**subjuguer** /sybʒyge/ [1] *vtr* **(a)** to
captivate, to enthral (GB)
**(b)** to subjugate

**sublime** /syblim/ *adj* sublime

**sublimer** /syblime/ [1] *vtr*, *vi* to sublimate

**submerger** /sybmɛʀʒe/ [13] *vtr* **(a)** to
submerge
**(b)** to flood ⟨market, switchboard⟩
**(c)** ⟨crowd, emotion⟩ to overwhelm
**(d)** **~ qn de travail** to inundate sb with
work

**subodorer** /sybodɔʀe/ [1] *vtr* to detect

**subordination** /sybɔʀdinasjɔ̃/ *nf*
subordination

**subordonné, ~e¹** /sybɔʀdɔne/ *nm,f*
subordinate

**subordonnée²** /sybɔʀdɔne/ *nf*
subordinate clause; **~ relative** relative
clause

**subordonner** /sybɔʀdɔne/ [1] *vtr* **(a)** **être
subordonné à qn** to be subordinate to sb
**(b)** **être subordonné à qch** to be subject to
sth

**suborner** /sybɔʀne/ [1] *vtr* to bribe
⟨witness⟩

**subreptice** /sybʀɛptis/ *adj* surreptitious

**subside** /sybsid/ *nm* **(a)** grant
**(b)** allowance

**subsidiaire** /sybzidjɛʀ/ *adj* subsidiary;
**question ~** tiebreaker

**subsistance** /sybzistɑ̃s/ *nf* subsistence;
(moyens de) **~** means of support

**subsister** /sybziste/ [1] *vi* **(a)** to remain
**(b)** ⟨custom⟩ to survive
**(c)** **ça leur suffit à peine pour ~** it's barely
enough for them to live on

**substance** /sypstɑ̃s/ *nf* substance

**substantif** /sypstɑ̃tif/ *nm* noun,
substantive

**S**

**substituer** /sypstitɥe/ [1] **1** *vtr* to substitute

**2 se substituer** *v refl* (+ *v être*) **se ~ à** to take the place of

**substitut** /sypstity/ *nm* substitute

**substitution** /sypstitysjɔ̃/ *nf* substitution; **produit de ~ du sucre** sugar substitute

**subterfuge** /syptɛrfyʒ/ *nm* ploy, subterfuge

**subtil, ~e** /syptil/ *adj* subtle; skilful (GB)

**subtiliser** /syptilize/ [1] *vtr* **~ qch à qn** to steal sth from sb

**subtilité** /syptilite/ *nf* subtlety

**subvenir** /sybvənir/ [36] *v+prep* **~ à** to meet ⟨*expenses, needs*⟩; **~ aux besoins de sa famille** to provide for one's family

**subvention** /sybvɑ̃sjɔ̃/ *nf* **(a)** grant **(b)** subsidy

**subventionner** /sybvɑ̃sjɔne/ [1] *vtr* to subsidize

**subversif, -ive** /sybvɛrsif, iv/ *adj* subversive

**subversion** /sybvɛrsjɔ̃/ *nf* subversion

**suc** /syk/ *nm* (of fruit) juice; (of plant) sap; **~s digestifs** *or* **gastriques** gastric juices

**succédané** /syksedane/ *nm* substitute, ersatz

**succéder** /syksede/ [14] **1 succéder à** *v+prep* **(a)** **~ à** to succeed ⟨*person*⟩ **(b)** **~ à** to follow

**2 se succéder** *v refl* (+ *v être*) to succeed *or* follow one another

**succès** /syksɛ/ *nm inv* success; **avoir du ~, être un ~** to be a success; ⟨*record*⟩ to be a hit; **à ~** ⟨*actor, film*⟩ successful

**successeur** /syksesœr/ *nm* successor

**successif, -ive** /syksesif, iv/ *adj* successive

**succession** /syksesjɔ̃/ *nf* **(a)** series, succession **(b)** (Law) succession; **prendre la ~ de** to succeed **(c)** inheritance, estate

**succinct, ~e** /syksɛ̃, ɛ̃t/ *adj* ⟨*essay*⟩ succinct; ⟨*speech*⟩ brief; ⟨*meal*⟩ frugal

**succomber** /sykɔ̃be/ [1] *vi* **(a)** to die **(b)** to give way, to yield; **~ sous le poids** to collapse under the weight **(c)** **~ à** to succumb to ⟨*charm, despair*⟩; to give in to ⟨*temptation*⟩

**succulent, ~e** /sykylɑ̃, ɑ̃t/ *adj* delicious

**succursale** /sykyrsal/ *nf* branch, outlet

**sucer** /syse/ [12] *vtr* to suck

**sucette** /sysɛt/ *nf* lollipop, lolly (colloq)

**suçoter** /sysɔte/ [1] *vtr* to suck

**sucre** /sykr/ *nm* **(a)** sugar **(b)** sugar lump

■ **~ cristallisé** granulated sugar; **~ glace** icing sugar (GB), powdered sugar (US); **~ en poudre** caster sugar (GB), superfine sugar (US); **~ roux** brown sugar

IDIOMS **casser du ~ sur le dos de qn** to run sb down, to badmouth sb (colloq)

**sucré, ~e** /sykre/ *adj* sweet; sweetened

**sucrer** /sykre/ [1] *vtr* to put sugar in; to sweeten

**sucrerie** /sykrəri/ *nf* **(a)** sugar refinery **(b)** **~s** sweets (GB)

**sucrier** /sykrije/ *nm* sugar bowl

**sud** /syd/ **1** *adj inv* south; southern **2** *nm* **(a)** south; **exposé au ~** south-facing **(b)** **le Sud** the South

**sudation** /sydasjɔ̃/ *nf* sweating

**sud-est** /sydɛst/ **1** *adj inv* southeast; southeastern **2** *nm* southeast; **le Sud-Est asiatique** South East Asia

**sudiste** /sydist/ *adj, nmf* Confederate

**sud-ouest** /sydwɛst/ **1** *adj inv* southwest; southwestern **2** *nm* southwest

**Suède** /sɥɛd/ *pr nf* Sweden

**suédois, ~e** /sɥedwa, az/ **1** *adj* Swedish **2** *nm* (language) Swedish

**Suédois, ~e** /sɥedwa, az/ *nm,f* Swede

**suer** /sɥe/ [1] **1** *vtr* to sweat; **~ sang et eau** to sweat blood and tears **2** *vi* to sweat; **faire ~ qn** (colloq) to bore sb stiff (colloq)

**sueur** /sɥœr/ *nf* sweat; **j'en avais des ~s froides** I was in a cold sweat about it

**suffi** /syfi/ ▶ SUFFIRE

**suffire** /syfir/ [64] **1** *vi* to be enough; **un rien suffit à le mettre en colère** it only takes the slightest thing to make him lose his temper **2 se suffire** *v refl* (+ *v être*) **se ~ (à soi-même)** to be self-sufficient **3** *v impers* **il suffit de me téléphoner** all you have to do is phone me; **il suffit d'une lampe pour éclairer la pièce** one lamp is enough to light the room; **il suffit que je sorte sans parapluie pour qu'il pleuve!** every time I go out without my umbrella, it's guaranteed to rain; **ça suffit (comme ça)!** that's enough!

**suffisamment** /syfizamɑ̃/ *adv* enough

**suffisance** /syfizɑ̃s/ *nf* self-importance

**suffisant, ~e** /syfizɑ̃, ɑ̃t/ *adj* **(a)** sufficient **(b)** self-important

**suffixe** /syfiks/ *nm* suffix

**suffocant, ~e** /syfɔkɑ̃, ɑ̃t/ *adj* **(a)** suffocating **(b)** staggering

**suffocation** /syfɔkasjɔ̃/ *nf* suffocation; choking

**suffoquer** /syfɔke/ [1] **1** *vtr* to suffocate **2** *vi* **(a)** to suffocate **(b)** to choke

**suffrage** /syfraʒ/ *nm* suffrage; **~s exprimés** recorded votes

**suggérer** /sygʒere/ [14] *vtr* to suggest

**suggestif, -ive** /sygʒɛstif, iv/ *adj* ⟨*music*⟩ evocative; ⟨*pose*⟩ suggestive; ⟨*dress*⟩ provocative

**suggestion** /sygʒɛstjɔ̃/ *nf* suggestion

**suicidaire** /sɥisidɛr/ *adj* suicidal

**suicide** /sɥisid/ *nm* suicide
**suicider: se suicider** /sɥiside/ [1] *v refl*
(+ *v être*) to commit suicide
**suie** /sɥi/ *nf* soot
**suinter** /sɥɛ̃te/ [1] *vi* **(a)** ⟨*liquid*⟩ to seep; to
ooze
**(b)** ⟨*walls*⟩ to sweat; ⟨*wound*⟩ to weep
**suis** /sɥi/ ▶ ÊTRE¹
**suisse** /sɥis/ **1** *adj* Swiss
**2** *nm* **(a)** Swiss Guard
**(b)** verger
**Suisse** /sɥis/ *pr nf* Switzerland
**suite** /sɥit/ **1** *nf* **(a)** rest; la ∼ des
événements what happens next
**(b)** (of story) continuation; (of series) next
instalment (GB); (of meal) next course
**(c)** sequel
**(d)** result; les ∼s (of action) the
consequences; (of incident) the repercussions;
(of illness) the after-effects
**(e)** donner ∼ à to follow up ⟨*complaint*⟩; to
deal with ⟨*order*⟩; rester sans ∼ ⟨*plan*⟩ to be
dropped
**(f)** faire ∼ à to follow upon ⟨*incident*⟩;
prendre la ∼ de qn to take over from sb
**(g)** avoir de la ∼ dans les idées to be single-
minded
**(h)** (of incidents) series; (of successes) run
**(i)** (hotel) suite
**(j)** (of monarch) suite
**(k)** (Mus) suite
**2 de suite** *phr* in succession, in a row; et
ainsi de ∼ and so on
**3 par la suite** *phr* **(a)** afterward(s)
**(b)** later
**4 par suite de** *phr* due to
**5 à la suite de** *phr* **(a)** following
**(b)** behind
**suivant¹** /sɥivɑ̃/ *prep* **(a)** in accordance
with ⟨*tradition*⟩; ∼ leur habitude as they
usually do
**(b)** depending on
**(c)** according to
**suivant², ∼e** /sɥivɑ̃, ɑ̃t/ **1** *adj*
**(a)** following
**(b)** next
**2** *nm,f* le ∼ the following one; the next one
**3 le suivant, la suivante** *phr* as
follows
**suivi, ∼e** /sɥivi/ **1** *pp* ▶ SUIVRE
**2** *pp adj* **(a)** ⟨*work*⟩ steady; ⟨*effort*⟩
sustained; ⟨*correspondence*⟩ regular
**(b)** ⟨*policy*⟩ coherent
**3** *nm* **(a)** monitoring
**(b)** follow-up; ∼ des malades follow-up care
for patients
**suivre** /sɥivʀ/ [62] **1** *vtr* **(a)** to follow
⟨*person, car*⟩; suivez le guide! this way,
please!
**(b)** to follow, to come after ⟨*period,
incident*⟩; 'à ∼' 'to be continued'
**(c)** to follow ⟨*route, coast*⟩; ⟨*road*⟩ to run
alongside ⟨*railway line*⟩; ∼ le droit chemin
to keep to the straight and narrow
**(d)** to follow ⟨*example*⟩; to obey ⟨*impulse*⟩

**(e)** to follow ⟨*lesson, match*⟩; to follow the
progress of ⟨*pupil, patient*⟩; ∼ l'actualité to
keep up with the news
**(f)** to do ⟨*course*⟩
**(g)** to follow ⟨*explanation, logic*⟩; je vous
suis I'm with you
**(h)** to keep pace with [sb/sth]
**2** *vi* faire ∼ son courrier to have one's mail
forwarded; faire ∼ please forward
**3 se suivre** *v refl* (+ *v être*) **(a)** ⟨*numbers,
pages*⟩ to be in order; ⟨*cards*⟩ to be
consecutive
**(b)** to happen one after the other
**4** *v impers* comme suit as follows
**sujet, -ette** /syʒɛ, ɛt/ **1** *adj* être ∼ à to
be prone to ⟨*migraine*⟩
**2** *nm* **(a)** subject; un ∼ d'actualité a topical
issue; c'est à quel ∼? what is it about?; au
∼ de about
**(b)** (Sch) question; ∼ libre topic of one's own
choice; hors ∼ off the subject
**(c)** cause; c'est un ∼ d'étonnement it is
amazing
**(d)** c'est un brillant ∼ he's a brilliant
student
**(e)** (of kingdom) subject
**sulfate** /sylfat/ *nm* sulphate (GB)
**sulfureux, -euse** /sylfyʀø, øz/ *adj*
⟨*vapour*⟩ sulphurous (GB); ⟨*bath*⟩ sulphur
(GB)
**sultan** /syltɑ̃/ *nm* sultan
**sultane** /syltan/ *nf* sultana
**summum** /sɔm(m)ɔm/ *nm* height
**sumo** /sumo, symo/ *nm inv* sumo wrestling
**super¹** /sypɛʀ/ *pref* super
**super²** /sypɛʀ/ **1** *adj inv* (colloq) great
(colloq)
**2** *nm* four-star (petrol) (GB), super
**superbe** /sypɛʀb/ *adj* superb, magnificent
**superbement** /sypɛʀbəmɑ̃/ *adv*
**(a)** superbly
**(b)** haughtily
**supercarburant** /sypɛʀkaʀbyʀɑ̃/ *nm*
four-star petrol, super
**supercherie** /sypɛʀʃəʀi/ *nf* **(a)** deception
**(b)** hoax
**supérette** /sypeʀɛt/ *nf* minimarket
**superficie** /sypɛʀfisi/ *nf* area
**superficiel, -ielle** /sypɛʀfisjɛl/ *adj* (gen)
superficial; ⟨*layer*⟩ surface
**superflu, ∼e** /sypɛʀfly/ *adj*
**(a)** superfluous
**(b)** unnecessary
**supérieur, ∼e** /sypeʀjœʀ/ **1** *adj*
**(a)** ⟨*jaw, lip, floor*⟩ upper
**(b)** ⟨*ranks, classes*⟩ upper
**(c)** higher (à than); ⟨*size*⟩ bigger (à than);
⟨*length*⟩ longer (à than)
**(d)** ⟨*work, quality*⟩ superior (à to)
**(e)** ⟨*air, tone*⟩ superior
**2** *nm,f* **(a)** superior; ∼ hiérarchique
immediate superior
**(b)** (in monastery, convent) Superior
**3** *nm* higher education

**S**

**supérieurement** /syperjœrmɑ̃/ *adv*
exceptionally

**supériorité** /syperjɔrite/ *nf* superiority

**superlatif, -ive** /sypɛrlatif, iv/ **1** *adj*
superlative
**2** *nm* superlative

**supermarché** /sypɛrmarʃe/ *nm*
supermarket

**superposer** /sypɛrpoze/ [1] *vtr* **(a)** to
stack [sth] (up); **lits superposés** bunk beds
**(b)** to superimpose ‹*drawings*›

**superposition** /sypɛrpozisjɔ̃/ *nf*
superposition

**superproduction** /sypɛrprɔdyksjɔ̃/ *nf*
blockbuster (colloq)

**superpuissance** /sypɛrpɥisɑ̃s/ *nf*
superpower

**superstitieux, -ieuse** /sypɛrstisjø, øz/
*adj* superstitious

**superstition** /sypɛrstisjɔ̃/ *nf* superstition

**superviser** /sypɛrvize/ [1] *vtr* to supervise

**supplanter** /syplɑ̃te/ [1] *vtr* to supplant

**suppléant, ~e** /sypleɑ̃, ɑ̃t/ *nm,f*
replacement; (for judge) deputy; (for teacher)
supply (GB) *or* substitute (US) teacher; (for
doctor) locum

**suppléer** /syplee/ [11] *v+prep* ~ **à** to make
up for, to compensate for

**supplément** /syplemɑ̃/ *nm* **(a)** extra
charge; supplement; **le vin est en** ~ the wine
is extra
**(b)** ~ **d'informations** additional information
**(c)** (newspaper) supplement

**supplémentaire** /syplemɑ̃tɛr/ *adj*
additional, extra; **train** ~ relief train

**suppliant, ~e** /syplijɑ̃, ɑ̃t/ *adj* ‹*voice*›
pleading; ‹*look*› imploring

**supplice** /syplis/ *nm* torture

**supplicier** /syplisje/ [2] *vtr* **(a)** to torture
**(b)** to execute

**supplier** /syplije/ [2] *vtr* to beg, to beseech

**support** /sypɔr/ *nm* **(a)** support; **servir de**
~ **à qch** to serve as a support for sth
**(b)** (for ornaments) stand
**(c)** back-up; ~ **audiovisuel** audio-visual aid

**supportable** /sypɔrtabl/ *adj* bearable

**supporter¹** /sypɔrte/ [1] **1** *vtr* **(a)** to
support, to bear the weight of ‹*structure*›
**(b)** to bear ‹*costs*›
**(c)** to put up with ‹*misery, behaviour,
person*›; to bear ‹*suffering*›; ‹*plant*› to
withstand ‹*cold*›; **elle ne supporte pas
d'attendre** she can't stand waiting
**2 se supporter** *v refl* (+ *v être*) **ils ne
peuvent plus se** ~ they can't stand each
other any more

**supporter²** /sypɔrtœr/ *nmf* supporter

**supposer** /sypoze/ [1] *vtr* **(a)** to suppose
**(b)** to assume
**(c)** to presuppose

**supposition** /sypozisjɔ̃/ *nf* supposition

**suppositoire** /sypozitwar/ *nm*
suppository

**suppôt** /sypo/ *nm* ~ **de Satan** fiend

**suppression** /sypresjɔ̃/ *nf* removal;
abolition; withdrawal; suppression;
elimination; breaking, ending, deletion; ~**s
d'emplois** job cuts

**supprimer** /syprime/ [1] *vtr* **(a)** to cut
‹*job*›; to stop ‹*aid, vibration*›; to abolish ‹*tax,
law*›; to remove ‹*effect, obstacle*›; to do away
with ‹*class*›; to withdraw ‹*licence*›; to break
‹*monopoly*›; to suppress ‹*evidence*›; to cut out
‹*sugar, salt*›; to delete ‹*word*›; ~ **un train** to
cancel a train
**(b)** to eliminate ‹*person*›

**suppurer** /sypyre/ [1] *vi* to suppurate

**supputer** /sypyte/ [1] *vtr* to calculate, to
work out

**supranational, ~e, *mpl* -aux**
/sypranasjɔnal, o/ *adj* supranational

**suprématie** /sypremasi/ *nf* supremacy

**suprême** /syprɛm/ *adj* supreme

**sur¹** /syr/ *prep* **(a)** on; ~ **la table** on the
table; **prends un verre** ~ **la table** take a glass
from the table; **appliquer la lotion** ~ **vos
cheveux** apply the lotion to your hair; **la clé
est** ~ **la porte** the key is in the door; **écrire**
~ **du papier** to write on paper; **elle est** ~ **la
photo** she's in the photograph
**(b)** over; **un pont** ~ **la rivière** a bridge across
*or* over the river
**(c)** **une table d'un mètre** ~ **deux** a table that
measures one metre (GB) by two; ~ **150
hectares** over an area of 150 hectares
**(d)** **se diriger** ~ **Valence** to head for Valence
**(e)** ‹*debate, essay, thesis*› on; ‹*poem*› about
**(f)** **être** ~ **une affaire** to be involved in a
business deal
**(g)** **une personne** ~ **dix** one person out of *or*
in ten; **un mardi** ~ **deux** every other Tuesday
**(h)** **faire proposition** ~ **proposition** to make
one offer after another
**(i)** **ils se sont quittés** ~ **ces mots** with these
words, they parted; ~ **le moment** at the time;
~ **ce, je vous laisse** with that, I must leave
you

**sur², ~e** /syr/ *adj* (slightly) sour

**sûr, ~e** /syr/ **1** *adj* **(a)** ‹*information,
service, person*› reliable; ‹*opinion, investment*›
sound; **d'une main** ~**e** with a steady hand
**(b)** safe
**(c)** certain; **c'est** ~ **et certain** it's definite; **à
coup** ~ definitely
**(d)** sure; **j'en suis** ~ **et certain** I'm positive; **il
est** ~ **de lui** he's self-confident; **j'en étais** ~**!** I
knew it!
**2** *adv* **bien** ~ **(que oui)** of course
**IDIOMS être** ~ **de son coup** (colloq) to be
confident of success

**surabondance** /syrabɔ̃dɑ̃s/ *nf*
overabundance

**surabonder** /syrabɔ̃de/ [1] *vi* to abound

**surajouter: se surajouter** /syraʒute/
[1] *v refl* to be added on (**à** to)

**suranné, ~e** /syrane/ *adj* ‹*ideas*›
outmoded; ‹*style*› outdated

**surcharge** /syʁʃaʁʒ/ *nf* excess load, overload; **une ~ de travail** extra work

**surchargé, ~e** /syʁʃaʁʒe/ *adj* ⟨*day*⟩ overloaded; ⟨*class*⟩ overcrowded

**surcharger** /syʁʃaʁʒe/ [13] *vtr* to overload; **~ qn de travail** to overburden sb with work

**surchauffer** /syʁʃofe/ [1] *vtr* to overheat

**surclasser** /syʁklase/ [1] *vtr* to outclass

**surconsommation** /syʁkɔ̃sɔmasjɔ̃/ *nf* (Econ) overconsumption; **~ de médicaments** excessive drug consumption

**surcroît** /syʁkʁwa/ *nm* increase; **un ~ de travail** extra work; **de ~** moreover

**surdité** /syʁdite/ *nf* deafness

**surdoué, ~e** /syʁdwe/ *adj* (exceptionally) gifted

**sureau,** *pl* **~x** /syʁo/ *nm* elder (tree)

**sureffectif** /syʁefɛktif/ *nm* excess staff

**surélever** /syʁelve/ [16] *vtr* to raise the height of ⟨*house, road*⟩

**sûrement** /syʁmɑ̃/ *adv* **(a)** most probably
**(b)** **~ pas** certainly not
**(c)** safely

**surenchère** /syʁɑ̃ʃɛʁ/ *nf* **(a)** higher bid
**(b)** **faire de la ~** to try to go one better

**surenchérir** /syʁɑ̃ʃeʁiʁ/ [3] *vi* **(a)** to make a higher bid
**(b)** to add; to chime in

**surendetté, ~e** /syʁɑ̃dete/ *adj* deeply in debt; overextended

**surendettement** /syʁɑ̃dɛtmɑ̃/ *nm* excessive debt

**surestimer** /syʁɛstime/ [1] **1** *vtr* to overvalue ⟨*property*⟩; to overrate ⟨*qualities*⟩
**2** **se surestimer** *v refl* (+ *v être*) to rate oneself too highly

**sûreté** /syʁte/ *nf* **(a)** (of place, person) safety; (of country) security
**(b)** (of judgment) soundness; (of gesture) steadiness
**(c)** (on gun) safety catch; (on door) safety lock

**surévaluer** /syʁevalɥe/ [1] *vtr* to overvalue ⟨*currency*⟩; to overestimate ⟨*cost*⟩

**surexciter** /syʁɛksite/ [1] *vtr* to overexcite

**surf** /sœʁf/ *nm* surfing

**surface** /syʁfas/ *nf* **(a)** surface; **de ~** ⟨*installations*⟩ above ground; ⟨*friendliness*⟩ superficial; **faire ~** to surface
**(b)** surface area; **en ~** in area

**surfait, ~e** /syʁfɛ, ɛt/ *adj* overrated

**surfer** /sœʁfe/ [1] *vi* **(a)** to go surfing
**(b)** (Comput) **~ sur l'Internet** to surf the Internet

**surfiler** /syʁfile/ [1] *vtr* to oversew

**surgelé, ~e** /syʁʒəle/ *adj* deep-frozen; **les produits ~s** frozen food

**surgeler** /syʁʒəle/ [17] *vtr* to deep-freeze

**surgénérateur** /syʁʒeneʁatœʁ/ *nm* fast-breeder reactor

**surgir** /syʁʒiʁ/ [3] *vi* ⟨*person*⟩ to appear suddenly; ⟨*difficulty*⟩ to crop up; **faire ~ la vérité** to bring the truth to light

**surhomme** /syʁɔm/ *nm* superman

**surhumain, ~e** /syʁymɛ̃, ɛn/ *adj* superhuman

**surimpression** /syʁɛ̃pʁesjɔ̃/ *nf* double exposure; **en ~** superimposed

**surinformation** /syʁɛ̃fɔʁmasjɔ̃/ *nf* surfeit of information

**sur-le-champ** /syʁləʃɑ̃/ *adv* right away

**surlendemain** /syʁlɑ̃d(ə)mɛ̃/ *nm* **le ~** two days later

**surligner** /syʁliɲe/ [1] *vtr* to highlight

**surligneur** /syʁliɲœʁ/ *nm* highlighter (pen)

**surmenage** /syʁmənaʒ/ *nm* overwork

**surmener** /syʁmene/ [16] **1** *vtr* to overwork
**2** **se surmener** *v refl* (+ *v être*) to push oneself too hard

**surmontable** /syʁmɔ̃tabl/ *adj* surmountable

**surmonter** /syʁmɔ̃te/ [1] *vtr* to overcome

**surmultiplié, ~e** /syʁmyltiplije/ *adj* **vitesse ~e** overdrive

**surnager** /syʁnaʒe/ [13] *vi* to float

**surnaturel, -elle** /syʁnatyʁɛl/ *adj*
**(a)** supernatural
**(b)** eerie

**surnom** /syʁnɔ̃/ *nm* nickname

**surnombre** /syʁnɔ̃bʁ/ *nm* **en ~** ⟨*objects*⟩ surplus; ⟨*staff*⟩ excess; ⟨*passenger*⟩ extra

**surnommer** /syʁnɔme/ [1] *vtr* to nickname

**surnuméraire** /syʁnymeʁɛʁ/ *adj, nmf* supernumerary

**surpasser** /syʁpase/ [1] **1** *vtr* to surpass
**2** **se surpasser** *v refl* (+ *v être*) to surpass oneself, to excel oneself

**surpeuplé, ~e** /syʁpœple/ *adj*
**(a)** overpopulated
**(b)** overcrowded

**surplace** /syʁplas/ *nm inv* **faire du ~** (in traffic jam) to be stuck; (in work, inquiry) to be getting nowhere; (in cycling) to do a track stand

**surplomb** /syʁplɔ̃/ *nm* **en ~** overhanging

**surplomber** /syʁplɔ̃be/ [1] *vtr* to overhang

**surplus** /syʁply/ *nm inv* (of goods) surplus

**surpopulation** /syʁpɔpylasjɔ̃/ *nf* overpopulation

**surprenant, ~e** /syʁpʁənɑ̃, ɑ̃t/ *adj* surprising; amazing

**surprendre** /syʁpʁɑ̃dʁ/ [52] **1** *vtr* **(a)** to surprise
**(b)** to take [sb] by surprise; **se laisser ~ par la pluie** to get caught in the rain
**(c)** to catch ⟨*thief*⟩
**(d)** to overhear ⟨*conversation*⟩; to intercept ⟨*smile*⟩ ⋯⋫

**2** *vi* ⟨*behaviour*⟩ to be surprising; ⟨*show*⟩ to surprise; ⟨*person*⟩ to surprise people

**surprise** /syʀpʀiz/ *nf* surprise; **créer la ~** to cause a stir; **il m'a fait la ~ de venir me voir** he came to see me as a surprise; **avoir la bonne ~ d'apprendre que** to be pleasantly surprised to hear that; **voyage sans ~** uneventful trip; **gagner sans ~** to win as expected

**surproduction** /syʀpʀɔdyksjɔ̃/ *nf* overproduction

**surqualifié, ~e** /syʀkalifje/ *adj* overqualified

**surréalisme** /suʀ(ʀ)ealism/ *nm* surrealism

**surréaliste** /suʀ(ʀ)ealist/ **1** *adj*
(a) surrealist
(b) ⟨*landscape, vision*⟩ surreal
**2** *nmf* surrealist

**surrégénérateur** /syʀʀeʒeneʀatœʀ/ *nm* fast-breeder reactor

**sursaut** /syʀso/ *nm* (a) start; **en ~** with a start
(b) (of energy, enthusiasm) sudden burst; (of pride, indignation) flash; **dans un dernier ~** in a final spurt of effort

**sursauter** /syʀsote/ [1] *vi* to jump, to start

**sursis** /syʀsi/ *nm inv* (a) respite
(b) (Law) suspended sentence
(c) (Mil) deferment of military service

**surtaxe** /syʀtaks/ *nf* surcharge

**surtaxer** /syʀtakse/ [1] *vtr* to surcharge

**surtout** /syʀtu/ *adv* above all; **~ quand/que** especially when/as; **~ pas!** certainly not!

**surveillance** /syʀvɛjɑ̃s/ *nf* (a) watch; (police) surveillance; **déjouer la ~ de qn** to escape detection by sb
(b) supervision; **sous ~ médicale** under medical supervision

**surveillant, ~e** /syʀvɛjɑ̃, ɑ̃t/ *nm,f*
(a) (Sch) supervisor
(b) **~ de prison** prison warder (GB) *or* guard
(c) store detective

**surveiller** /syʀveje/ [1] **1** *vtr* (a) (gen) to watch; to keep watch on ⟨*building*⟩
(b) to supervise ⟨*work, pupils*⟩; to monitor ⟨*progress*⟩
(c) **~ sa santé** to take care of one's health
**2 se surveiller** *v refl* (+ *v être*) to watch oneself

**survenir** /syʀvəniʀ/ [36] *vi* (+ *v être*) ⟨*death, storm*⟩ to occur; ⟨*difficulty, conflict*⟩ to arise

**survêtement** /syʀvɛtmɑ̃/ *nm* tracksuit

**survie** /syʀvi/ *nf* survival

**survivant, ~e** /syʀvivɑ̃, ɑ̃t/ *nm,f* survivor

**survivre** /syʀvivʀ/ [63] **1 survivre à** *v+prep* ⟨*person*⟩ to survive ⟨*event, injuries*⟩; to outlive ⟨*person*⟩; ⟨*work, influence*⟩ to outlast ⟨*person*⟩
**2** *vi* to survive

**survol** /syʀvɔl/ *nm* (a) flying over

(b) synopsis

**survoler** /syʀvɔle/ [1] *vtr* (a) to fly over ⟨*place*⟩
(b) to do a quick review of ⟨*problem*⟩

**survolté, ~e** /syʀvɔlte/ *adj* (colloq) overexcited

**sus**: **en sus** /ɑ̃sys/ *phr* **être en ~** to be extra; **en ~ de** on top of; in addition to

**susceptibilité** /sysɛptibilite/ *nf* touchiness

**susceptible** /sysɛptibl/ *adj* (a) touchy
(b) **~ de faire** likely to do

**susciter** /sysite/ [1] *vtr* (a) to spark off ⟨*reaction, debate*⟩; to create ⟨*problem*⟩
(b) to arouse ⟨*enthusiasm, interest*⟩; to give rise to ⟨*fear*⟩

**susmentionné, ~e** *adj* aforementioned

**suspect, ~e** /syspɛ, ɛkt/ **1** *adj* suspicious; ⟨*information, logic*⟩ dubious; ⟨*foodstuff, honesty*⟩ suspect; ⟨*person*⟩ suspicious-looking
**2** *nm,f* suspect

**suspecter** /syspɛkte/ [1] *vtr* to suspect

**suspendre** /syspɑ̃dʀ/ [6] **1** *vtr* (a) to hang up; **être suspendu aux lèvres de qn** to be hanging on sb's every word
(b) to suspend ⟨*programme, payment*⟩; to end ⟨*strike*⟩; to adjourn ⟨*session, inquiry*⟩
(c) to suspend ⟨*official, athlete*⟩
**2 se suspendre** *v refl* (+ *v être*) to hang; **se ~ à une corde** to hang from a rope

**suspens**: **en suspens** /ɑ̃syspɑ̃/ *phr*
(a) **laisser qch en ~** to leave sth unresolved ⟨*question*⟩; to leave sth unfinished ⟨*work*⟩
(b) **tenir qn en ~** to keep sb in suspense

**suspense** /syspɛns/ *nm* suspense; **film** *or* **roman à ~** thriller

**suspension** /syspɑ̃sjɔ̃/ *nf* (a) (gen, Tech) suspension
(b) (of aid, work) suspension; (of session, trial) adjournment
(c) **en ~** ⟨*particles*⟩ in suspension
(d) pendant, ceiling light

**suspicieux, -ieuse** /syspisjø, øz/ *adj* suspicious

**suspicion** /syspisjɔ̃/ *nf* suspicion

**sustenter**: **se sustenter** /systɑ̃te/ [1] *v refl* (+ *v être*) to have a little snack

**susurrer** /sysyʀe/ [1] *vtr, vi* to whisper

**suture** /sytyʀ/ *nf* suture; **point de ~** stitch

**suzerain, ~e** /syzʀɛ̃, ɛn/ *nm,f* suzerain

**svelte** /svɛlt/ *adj* slender

**sveltesse** /svɛltɛs/ *nf* slenderness

**SVP** (*written abbr* = **s'il vous plaît**) please

**syllabe** /sil(l)ab/ *nf* syllable

**sylviculture** /silvikyltyʀ/ *nf* forestry

**symbiose** /sɛ̃bjoz/ *nf* symbiosis

**symbole** /sɛ̃bɔl/ *nm* (a) symbol
(b) creed

**symbolique** /sɛ̃bɔlik/ *adj* (a) symbolic
(b) ⟨*gesture*⟩ token; ⟨*price*⟩ nominal

**symboliser** /sɛ̃bɔlize/ [1] *vtr* to symbolize

**S**

**symétrie** /simetʀi/ *nf* symmetry

**symétrique** /simetʀik/ *adj* **(a)** ‹*design, face*› symmetrical
**(b)** ‹*relation*› symmetric

**sympa** /sɛpa/ *adj inv* (colloq) nice

**sympathie** /sɛpati/ *nf* **(a)** avoir de la ~ pour qn to like sb
**(b)** sympathy; croyez à toute ma ~ you have my deepest sympathy

**sympathique** /sɛpatik/ *adj* nice; pleasant

**sympathisant, ~e** /sɛpatizɑ̃, ɑ̃t/ *nm,f* sympathizer

**sympathiser** /sɛpatize/ [1] *vi* to get on well

**symphonie** /sɛfɔni/ *nf* symphony

**symphonique** /sɛfɔnik/ *adj* symphonic

**symptomatique** /sɛptɔmatik/ *adj* symptomatic

**symptôme** /sɛptom/ *nm* symptom

**synagogue** /sinagɔg/ *nf* synagogue

**synchronique** /sɛkʀɔnik/ *adj* synchronic

**synchronisation** /sɛkʀɔnizasjɔ̃/ *nf* synchronization

**synchroniser** /sɛkʀɔnize/ [1] *vtr* to synchronize

**syncope** /sɛkɔp/ *nf* **(a)** fainting fit; tomber en ~ to faint
**(b)** (Mus) syncopation

**syndic** /sɛdik/ *nm* property manager

**syndical, ~e, mpl -aux** /sɛdikal, o/ *adj* (trade) union

**syndicalisme** /sɛdikalism/ *nm* **(a)** trade unionism
**(b)** union activities

**syndicaliste** /sɛdikalist/ *nmf* union activist

**syndicat** /sɛdika/ *nm* **(a)** trade union
**(b)** (employers') association
■ ~ d'initiative tourist information office

**syndiqué, ~e** /sɛdike/ *adj* être ~ to be a union member

**syndrome** /sɛdʀom/ *nm* syndrome
■ ~ immunodéficitaire acquis acquired immunodeficiency syndrome

**synergie** /sinɛʀʒi/ *nf* synergy (entre between)

**synonyme** /sinɔnim/ ⓵ *adj* synonymous
⓶ *nm* synonym; dictionnaire de ~s ≈ thesaurus

**syntaxe** /sɛtaks/ *nf* syntax

**synthèse** /sɛtɛz/ *nf* **(a)** synthesis
**(b)** produit de ~ synthetic product
**(c)** images de ~ computer-generated images

**synthétique** /sɛtetik/ *adj* **(a)** synthetic
**(b)** ‹*vision*› global

**synthétiseur** /sɛtetizœʀ/ *nm* synthesizer

**syphilis** /sifilis/ *nf inv* syphilis

**systématique** /sistematik/ *adj* systematic

**système** /sistɛm/ *nm* **(a)** system; ~ de canaux canal system *or* network
**(b)** ~ pileux hair
■ le ~ D (colloq) resourcefulness; ~ monétaire européen, SME European Monetary System, EMS
IDIOMS taper sur le ~ de qn (colloq) to get on sb's nerves

# Tt

**t, T** /te/ *nm inv* t, T; en (forme de) T T-shaped

**t'** ▶ TE

**ta** ▶ TON¹

**tabac** /taba/ *nm* **(a)** tobacco
**(b)** tobacconist's (GB), smoke shop (US)
**(c)** (colloq) big hit
■ ~ blond Virginia tobacco; ~ brun dark tobacco; ~ à priser snuff
IDIOMS passer qn à ~ (colloq) to beat sb up

**tabagie** /tabaʒi/ *nf* c'est une vraie ~ ici! it's really smoky in here!

**tabagisme** /tabaʒism/ *nm* tobacco addiction

**tabernacle** /tabɛʀnakl/ *nm* tabernacle

**table** /tabl/ *nf* **(a)** table; mettre *or* dresser la ~ to set *or* lay the table; nous étions toujours à ~ quand... we were still eating when...; passer *or* se mettre à ~ to sit down at the table; (figurative) (colloq) to spill the beans (colloq)
**(b)** ~ des négociations negotiating table
**(c)** ~ de logarithmes log table
■ ~ basse coffee table; ~ de chevet bedside table (GB), night stand (US); ~ d'écoute wiretapping set; être mis sur ~ d'écoute to have one's phone tapped; ~ des matières (table of) contents; ~ de mixage mixing desk; ~ de nuit = ~ de chevet; ~ ronde round table
IDIOMS mettre les pieds sous la ~ to let others wait on you

**tableau, pl ~x** /tablo/ *nm* **(a)** picture; painting
**(b)** (description) picture; en plus, il était ivre, tu vois un peu le ~! (colloq) on top of that he was drunk, you can just imagine!
**(c)** table, chart                                  ⋯▸

**(d)** (Sch) blackboard
**(e)** (displaying information) (gen) board; (for trains) indicator board; ~ **horaire** timetable
**(f)** (in play) short scene
■ ~ **d'affichage** notice board; ~ **de bord** (in car) dashboard; (on plane, train) instrument panel; ~ **de chasse** (in hunting) total number of kills; (figurative) list of conquests
IDIOMS **jouer sur les deux** ~**x** to hedge one's bets

**tablée** /table/ *nf* table; **une grande** ~ a large party

**tabler** /table/ [1] *vi* ~ **sur** to bank on (colloq)

**tablette** /tablɛt/ *nf* **(a)** (of chocolate) bar; (of chewing-gum) stick
**(b)** shelf

**tablier** /tablije/ *nm* **(a)** apron
**(b)** roadway
IDIOMS **rendre son** ~ to give in (GB) *or* give (US) one's notice

**tabloïd** /tablɔid/ *adj, nm* tabloid

**tabou** /tabu/ **1** *adj* **(a)** taboo
**(b)** sacred
**2** *nm* taboo

**tabouret** /taburɛ/ *nm* stool

**tac** /tak/ *nm* **répondre du** ~ **au** ~ to answer as quick as a flash

**tache** /taʃ/ *nf* **(a)** stain; ~ **d'humidité** damp patch
**(b)** (figurative) stain, blot; **sans** ~ (reputation) spotless
**(c)** (on fruit) mark; (on skin) blotch, mark
**(d)** (of colour) spot; patch
■ ~**s de rousseur** freckles
IDIOMS **faire** ~ **d'huile** to spread like wildfire

**tâche** /taʃ/ *nf* task, job; **tu ne me facilites pas la** ~! you're not making my job any easier!; **les** ~**s ménagères** household chores

**tacher** /taʃe/ [1] **1** *vtr* **(a)** (substance) to stain; (person) to get a stain on (garment)
**(b)** to tarnish, to stain (reputation)
**2** *vi* to stain; **ça ne tache pas** it doesn't stain

**tâcher** /taʃe/ [1] *v+prep* ~ **de faire** to try to do

**tacheté** /taʃte/ *adj* (fur) speckled

**tacite** /tasit/ *adj* tacit

**taciturne** /tasityʀn/ *adj* taciturn

**tact** /takt/ *nm* tact; **avec** ~ tactfully

**tactile** /taktil/ *adj* (sense) tactile

**tactique** /taktik/ **1** *adj* (gen, Mil) tactical
**2** *nf* tactic; **la** ~ tactics

**taie** /tɛ/ *nf* ~ **(d'oreiller)** pillowcase; ~ **(de traversin)** bolstercase

**taillader** /tajade/ [1] *vtr* to slash

**taille** /taj/ *nf* **(a)** waist, waistline
**(b)** size; **de grande/petite** ~ large/small; **de** ~ (problem, ambition) considerable; (event, question) very important; **être de** ~ **à faire** to be up to *or* capable of doing
**(c)** (of garment) size; '~ **unique**' 'one size'; **essaie la** ~ **au-dessus** try the next size up
**(d)** height; **être de grande/petite** ~ to be tall/ short

**(e)** (of tree, shrub) pruning; (of hedge) clipping, trimming; (of diamond, glass) cutting

**taillé, ~e** /taje/ **1** *pp* ▶ TAILLER
**2** *pp adj* **(a)** ~ **en athlète** built like an athlete
**(b)** **être** ~ **pour faire** to be cut out to do
**(c)** **cristal** ~ cut glass

**taille-crayons** /tajkʀɛjɔ̃/ *nm inv* pencil sharpener

**tailler** /taje/ [1] **1** *vtr* **(a)** to cut (glass, marble); to sharpen (pencil); to prune (tree, shrub); to trim (hair, beard)
**(b)** to cut (steak); to carve (sculpture); to cut out (garment); **taillé sur mesure** (garment) custom-made; (figurative) (role) tailor-made
**2** *vi* ~ **grand/petit** (garment) to be cut on the large/small side
**3** **se tailler** *v refl* (+ *v être*) **(a)** to carve out [sth] for oneself (career, empire); to make [sth] for oneself (reputation)
**(b)** (slang) to beat it (colloq)

**tailleur** /tajœʀ/ *nm* **(a)** (woman's) suit
**(b)** tailor; **s'asseoir en** ~ to sit down cross-legged
■ ~ **de pierre** stone-cutter

**taillis** /taji/ *nm inv* **(a)** undergrowth
**(b)** coppice

**tain** /tɛ̃/ *nm* **miroir sans** ~ two-way mirror

**taire** /tɛʀ/ [59] **1** *vtr* **(a)** not to reveal (name, secret); to hush up (truth)
**(b)** to keep [sth] to oneself (sadness, resentment)
**2** **se taire** *v refl* (+ *v être*) **(a)** (person) to be silent
**(b)** (person) to stop talking; (bird, journalist) to fall silent; **faire** ~ to make [sb] be quiet (pupils); to silence (opponent, media); to put a stop to (rumours); **tais-toi!** be quiet!
**(c)** (noise) to stop; (orchestra) to fall silent

**talc** /talk/ *nm* talc, talcum powder

**talent** /talɑ̃/ *nm* talent; **de** ~ talented

**talentueux, -euse** /talɑ̃tɥø, øz/ *adj* talented

**talisman** /talismɑ̃/ *nm* talisman

**talkie-walkie**, *pl* **talkies-walkies** /tokiwoki/ *nm* walkie-talkie

**taloche** /talɔʃ/ *nf* (colloq) clout (colloq)

**talon** /talɔ̃/ *nm* **(a)** (of foot, shoe) heel
**(b)** (of cheque, ticket) stub
**(c)** (in cards) pile
■ ~ **aiguille** stiletto heel
IDIOMS **être sur les** ~**s de qn** to be hard *or* hot on sb's heels

**talonner** /talɔne/ [1] *vtr* **(a)** ~ **qn** to be hot on sb's heels
**(b)** (person) to badger (person); (hunger, anxiety) to torment (person)

**talonnette** /talɔnɛt/ *nf* lift (in a shoe)

**talus** /taly/ *nm inv* **(a)** embankment
**(b)** bank, slope

**tamanoir** /tamanwaʀ/ *nm* anteater

**tambouille** /tɑ̃buj/ *nf* (colloq) grub (colloq)

**tambour** /tɑ̃buʀ/ *nm* drum; **mener qch** ~ **battant** to deal with sth briskly

**tambourin** /tãbuʀɛ̃/ *nm* tambourine

**tambouriner** /tãbuʀine/ [1] *vi* ~ **à la porte de qn** to hammer on sb's door

**tamis** /tami/ *nm inv* sieve

**Tamise** /tamiz/ *pr nf* **la** ~ the Thames

**tamiser** /tamize/ [1] *vtr* to sieve, to sift ⟨*sand, flour*⟩; to filter ⟨*light, colours*⟩

**tampon** /tãpɔ̃/ *nm* **(a)** (in office) stamp; ~ (encreur) (ink) pad
**(b)** (for sponging) (gen) pad; (Med) swab; ~ **à récurer** scouring pad
**(c)** ~ **hygiénique** tampon

**tamponner** /tãpone/ [1] *vtr* **(a)** to swab ⟨*wound, cut*⟩; to mop ⟨*forehead*⟩
**(b)** to stamp ⟨*document*⟩
**(c)** to crash into ⟨*vehicle*⟩

**tamponneuse** /tãpɔnøz/ *adj f* **auto** ~ bumper car, dodgem

**tam-tam**, *pl* ~**s** /tamtam/ *nm* tomtom

**tanche** /tãʃ/ *nf* tench

**tandem** /tãdɛm/ *nm* **(a)** tandem
**(b)** (figurative) duo

**tandis**: **tandis que** /tãdi(s)k(ə)/ *phr* while

**tangent**, ~**e**[1] /tãʒã, ãt/ *adj* **(a)** tangent, tangential
**(b)** (colloq) **elle a été reçue, mais c'était** ~ she got through, but only by the skin of her teeth (colloq)

**tangente**[2] /tãʒãt/ *nf* tangent

**tangible** /tãʒibl/ *adj* tangible

**tanguer** /tãge/ [1] *vi* ⟨*ship, plane*⟩ to pitch

**tanière** /tanjɛʀ/ *nf* **(a)** den
**(b)** lair

**tank** /tãk/ *nm* tank

**tanner** /tane/ [1] *vtr* **(a)** to tan ⟨*leather, hides*⟩
**(b)** ⟨*sun*⟩ to make [sth] leathery ⟨*face, skin*⟩

**tannerie** /tanʀi/ *nf* **(a)** tannery
**(b)** tanning

**tant** /tã/ **1** *adv* **(a)** (so) much; **il a** ~ **insisté que** he was so insistent that; **vous m'en direz** ~! (colloq) you don't say!; **le moment** ~ **attendu** the long-awaited moment
**(b)** **n'aimer rien** ~ **que...** to like nothing so much as...; ~ **bien que mal** ⟨*repair, lead*⟩ after a fashion; ⟨*manage*⟩ more or less; **essayer** ~ **bien que mal de s'adapter** to be struggling to adapt
**(c)** ~ **que** as long as; **je ne partirai pas** ~ **qu'il ne m'aura pas accordé un rendez-vous** I won't leave until he's given me an appointment; **traite-moi de menteur** ~ **que tu y es!** (colloq) go ahead and call me a liar!
**(d)** (replacing number) **gagner** ~ **par mois** to earn so much a month
**2** **tant de** *quantif* **Loulou, Pivachon et** ~ **d'autres** Loulou, Pivachon and so many others; ~ **de travail** so much work
**3** (in phrases) ~ **pis** too bad; ~ **mieux** so much the better; ~ **mieux pour toi** good for you; ~ **et plus** a great deal; a great many; ~ **et si bien que** so much so that; **s'il avait un** ~ **soit peu de bon sens** if he had the slightest bit of common sense; ~ **qu'à faire, autant repeindre toute la pièce** we may as well repaint the whole room while we're at it; **en** ~ **que** as; **en** ~ **que tel** as such; **si** ~ **est qu'il puisse y aller** that is if he can go at all; **je ne l'aime pas** ~ **que ça** I don't like him/her all that much

**tante** /tãt/ *nf* aunt

**tantôt** /tãto/ *adv* sometimes

**taon** /tã/ *nm* horsefly

**tapage** /tapaʒ/ *nm* **(a)** din, racket (colloq)
**(b)** furore (GB), furor (US)
**(c)** hype; ~ **médiatique** media hype
■ ~ **nocturne** disturbance of the peace at night

**tapageur, -euse** /tapaʒœʀ, øz/ *adj*
**(a)** ⟨*person*⟩ rowdy
**(b)** ⟨*luxury*⟩ showy; ⟨*campaign*⟩ hyped-up

**tapant**, ~**e** /tapã, ãt/ *adj* **à trois heures** ~**es** at three o'clock sharp *or* on the dot

**tape** /tap/ *nf* pat; slap

**tape-à-l'œil** /tapalœj/ *adj inv* (colloq) ⟨*colour*⟩ loud; ⟨*jewellery, decor*⟩ garish

**taper** /tape/ [1] **1** *vtr* **(a)** to hit ⟨*person, dog*⟩
**(b)** to type ⟨*letter*⟩
**2** **taper sur** *v+prep* to hit; ~ **sur l'épaule de qn** to tap sb on the shoulder
**3** *vi* **(a)** ~ **des mains** to clap one's hands; ~ **à la porte** to knock at the door; **le soleil tape aujourd'hui** (colloq) the sun is beating down today
**(b)** ~ **(à la machine)** to type
**4** **se taper** *v refl* (+ *v être*) **(a)** (colloq) **se** ~ **dessus** to knock each other about
**(b)** **c'est à se** ~ **la tête contre les murs** (figurative) it's enough to drive you up the wall
**(c)** (colloq) to get stuck with (colloq) ⟨*chore, person*⟩
IDIOMS **elle m'a tapé dans l'œil** (colloq) I thought she was striking

**tapette** /tapɛt/ *nf* **(a)** carpet beater
**(b)** fly swatter
**(c)** mousetrap

**tapeur, -euse** /tapœʀ, øz/ *nm,f* (colloq) scrounger (colloq)

**tapioca** /tapjɔka/ *nm* tapioca

**tapir**[1]: **se tapir** /tapiʀ/ [3] *v refl* (+ *v être*)
**(a)** ⟨*person, animal*⟩ to hide
**(b)** to crouch

**tapir**[2] /tapiʀ/ *nm* (Zool) tapir

**tapis** /tapi/ *nm inv* rug; carpet; mat; **mettre qch sur le** ~ (figurative) to bring sth up; **mettre** *or* **envoyer qn au** ~ to throw sb
■ ~ **de bain(s)** bathmat; ~ **roulant** moving walkway; (for luggage) carousel; (in factory, supermarket) conveyor belt

**tapisser** /tapise/ [1] *vtr* **(a)** to wallpaper; to decorate ⟨*room*⟩; to cover ⟨*armchair*⟩
**(b)** ⟨*snow*⟩ to carpet ⟨*ground*⟩; ⟨*residue*⟩ to line ⟨*bottom of container*⟩

**tapisserie** /tapisʀi/ *nf* **(a)** tapestry
**(b)** wallpaper
**(c)** tapestry work

····❖·

IDIOMS faire ~ to be a wallflower

tapissier, **-ière** /tapisje, ɛʀ/ *nm,f*
(a) upholsterer
(b) tapestry-maker

tapoter /tapɔte/ [1] *vtr* to tap ‹*table, object*›; to pat ‹*cheeks, back*›

taquin, **~e** /takɛ̃, in/ *adj* ‹*person*› teasing

taquiner /takine/ [1] *vtr* ‹*person*› to tease

tarabiscoté, **~e** /taʀabiskɔte/ *adj* ‹*design*› over-ornate; ‹*reasoning*› convoluted

tarama /taʀama/ *nm* taramasalata

taratata /taʀatata/ *excl* (colloq) nonsense!, rubbish! (colloq)

tard /taʀ/ **1** *adv* late; **plus ~** later; **bien plus ~** much later (on); **au plus ~** at the latest; **pas plus ~ qu'hier** only yesterday
2 **sur le tard** *phr* ‹*marry*› late in life

tarder /taʀde/ [1] **1** *vi* **(a) ~ à faire** to take a long time doing; to put off *or* delay doing
(b) ‹*reaction*› to be a long time coming; **les enfants ne vont pas ~** the children won't be long
2 *v impers* **il me tarde de la revoir** I'm longing to see her again

tardif, **-ive** /taʀdif, iv/ *adj* late; belated

tardivement /taʀdivmɑ̃/ *adv* ‹*arrive*› late; ‹*react*› rather belatedly

tare /taʀ/ *nf* **(a)** tare
(b) defect

taré, **~e** /taʀe/ *adj* (colloq) crazy (colloq)

targette /taʀʒɛt/ *nf* bolt

targuer: **se targuer** /taʀge/ [1] *v refl* (+ *v être*) to claim, to boast

tarif /taʀif/ *nm* **(a)** (gen) rate; (on bus, train) fare; (for consultation) fee; **payer plein ~** to pay full price; to pay full fare; **~ de nuit** night-time rate
(b) price list
■ **~ douanier** customs tariff

tarification /taʀifikasjɔ̃/ *nf* price setting; tariff

tarir /taʀiʀ/ [23] **1** *vtr* to dry up ‹*source, well*›; to sap ‹*strength*›
2 *vi* **ne pas ~ d'éloges sur qn/qch** to be full of praise for sb/sth
3 **se tarir** *v refl* (+ *v être*) to dry up

tarot /taʀo/ *nm* tarot (*card game*)

tartare /taʀtaʀ/ *adj* **(a)** Tartar
(b) (Culin) **sauce ~** tartare sauce

tarte /taʀt/ *nf* **(a)** (Culin) tart
(b) (slang) wallop (colloq)
IDIOMS c'est pas de la ~ (colloq) it's no picnic (colloq)

tartelette /taʀtəlɛt/ *nf* (small) tart

tartine /taʀtin/ *nf* **(a)** slice of bread and butter
(b) (colloq) **il en a écrit une ~** he wrote reams about it

tartiner /taʀtine/ [1] *vtr* to spread

tartre /taʀtʀ/ *nm* (in kettle) scale; (on teeth) tartar

tartufe /taʀtyf/ *nm* hypocrite

tas /tɑ/ **1** *nm inv* **(a)** heap, pile; **en ~** ‹*put, place*› in a heap *or* pile; **~ de ferraille** scrap heap; (figurative) (colloq) wreck
(b) (colloq) **un ~**, **des ~** loads (colloq)
2 **dans le tas** *phr* (colloq) **tirer dans le ~** to fire into the crowd
3 **sur le tas** *phr* **apprendre sur le ~** to learn on the job; **grève sur le ~** sit-down strike

tasse /tɑs/ *nf* cup; **~ à thé** teacup
IDIOMS boire la ~ (colloq) to swallow a mouthful of water (when swimming)

tassement /tɑsmɑ̃/ *nm* contraction; **~ de vertèbres** compression of the vertebrae

tasser /tɑse/ [1] **1** *vtr* to press down ‹*earth*›; to pack down ‹*hay*›; to pack ‹*clothes, people*› (**dans** into); **il a la cinquantaine bien tassée** (colloq) he's well over fifty
2 **se tasser** *v refl* (+ *v être*) **(a)** (with age) to shrink
(b) (in train, car) ‹*people*› to squash up
(c) (colloq) ‹*rumour, conflict*› to die down

tata /tata/ *nf* (colloq) auntie

tâter /tɑte/ [1] **1** *vtr* to feel; **~ le sol du pied** to test the ground
2 **se tâter** *v refl* (+ *v être*) (colloq) **je me tâte** I'm thinking about it
IDIOMS ~ le terrain to put out feelers

tatillon, **-onne** /tɑtijɔ̃, ɔn/ *adj* nit-picking

tâtonnement /tɑtɔnmɑ̃/ *nm* **~s dans l'obscurité** groping around in the dark; **les ~s des chercheurs** tentative research; **après dix années de ~s** after ten years of trial and error

tâtonner /tɑtɔne/ [1] *vi* to grope about *or* around

tâtons: **à tâtons** /atɑtɔ̃/ *phr* **avancer à ~** to feel one's way along

tatouage /tatwaʒ/ *nm* tattoo

tatouer /tatwe/ [1] *vtr* to tattoo

tatoueur, **-euse** /tatwœʀ, øz/ *nm,f* tattooist

taudis /todi/ *nm inv* **(a)** hovel
(b) pigsty

taule /tol/ *nf* (slang) prison

taupe /top/ *nf* **(a)** (Zool) mole
(b) moleskin

taupinière /topinjɛʀ/ *nf* **(a)** molehill
(b) (mole) tunnels

taureau, *pl* **~x** /tɔʀo/ *nm* (Zool) bull
IDIOMS prendre le ~ par les cornes to take the bull by the horns

Taureau /tɔʀo/ *pr nm* Taurus

tauromachie /tɔʀɔmaʃi/ *nf* bullfighting

taux /to/ *nm inv* **(a)** (gen) rate; **~ de chômage** unemployment rate
(b) (Med) (of alcohol, albumen, sugar) level; (of bacteria, sperm) count

taxation /taksasjɔ̃/ *nf* **(a)** taxation
(b) assessment

taxe /taks/ *nf* tax; **boutique hors ~s** duty-free shop (GB) *or* store (US); **1 000 euros toutes ~s comprises** 1,000 euros inclusive of tax

■ ~ **de douane** customs duty; ~ **foncière**
property tax; ~ **d'habitation** ≈ council tax
(*paid by residents to cover local services*); ~ **à**
**la valeur ajoutée** value added tax

**taxer** /takse/ [1] *vtr* **(a)** (Econ) to tax
**(b)** ~ **qn de laxisme** to accuse sb of being
lax

**taxi** /taksi/ *nm* taxi, cab (US)

**taxidermiste** /taksidɛrmist/ *nmf*
taxidermist

**Tchad** /tʃad/ *pr nm* Chad

**tchador** /tʃadɔr/ *nm* chador

**tchao** /tʃao/ *excl* (colloq) bye! (colloq), see
you! (colloq)

**tchèque** /tʃɛk/ **1** *adj* Czech; **République**
~ Czech Republic
**2** *nm* (Ling) Czech

**tchin(-tchin)** /tʃin(tʃin)/ *excl* (colloq)
cheers!

**TD** /tede/ *nm pl* (colloq) (*abbr* = **travaux**
**dirigés**) (Sch) practical

**te** (**t'** *before vowel or mute h*) /t(ə)/ *pron*
**(a)** (direct or indirect object) you
**(b)** (reflexive pronoun) yourself; **va** ~ **laver les**
**mains** go and wash your hands

**té** /te/ *nm* T-square; **en** ~ T-shaped

**technicien, -ienne** /tɛknisjɛ̃, ɛn/ *nm,f*
**(a)** technician
**(b)** technical expert
**(c)** engineer
■ ~ **de surface** cleaner

**technique¹** /tɛknik/ **1** *adj* technical
**2** *nm* technical subjects

**technique²** /tɛknik/ *nf* **(a)** technique
**(b)** technology

**technocrate** /tɛknɔkrat/ *nmf* technocrat

**technologie** /tɛknɔlɔʒi/ *nf* technology

**teck** /tɛk/ *nm* teak; **en** ~ teak

**teckel** /tekɛl/ *nm* dachshund

**tee-shirt,** *pl* ~**s** /tiʃœrt/ *nm* T-shirt

**teigne** /tɛɲ/ *nf* **(a)** (Med) ringworm
**(b)** moth
**(c)** (colloq) **être méchant comme une** ~ to be
a nasty (GB) *or* real (US) piece of work
(colloq)

**teigneux, -euse** /tɛɲø, øz/ *adj* (colloq)
cantankerous

**teindre** /tɛ̃dr/ [73] **1** *vtr* to dye; to stain
**2 se teindre** *v refl* (+ *v être*) to dye one's
hair

**teint,** ~**e¹** /tɛ̃, tɛ̃t/ **1** *pp* ▶ TEINDRE
**2** *pp adj* dyed; stained
**3** *nm* complexion; **avoir le** ~ **rose** *or* **frais**
to have a healthy glow to one's cheeks

**teinte²** /tɛ̃t/ *nf* **(a)** shade
**(b)** colour (GB)

**teinter** /tɛ̃te/ [1] **1** *vtr* **(a)** to tint; to stain;
to dye
**(b)** ~ **qch de** to tinge sth with
**2 se teinter** *v refl* (+ *v être*) **se** ~ **de** to
become tinged with

**teinture** /tɛ̃tyr/ *nf* dye; (for wood) stain

**teinturerie** /tɛ̃tyrri/ *nf* (dry-)cleaner's

**teinturier, -ière** /tɛ̃tyrje, ɛr/ *nm,f*
**(a)** dry-cleaner
**(b)** dyer

**tel, telle** /tɛl/ *adj* **(a)** such; **une telle**
**conduite** such behaviour (GB)
**(b)** like; ~ **père,** ~ **fils** like father like son
**(c) telle est la vérité** that is the truth;
**comme** ~, **en tant que** ~ as such; **ses**
**affaires étaient restées telles quelles** his/her
things were left as they were
**(d) avec un** ~ **enthousiasme** with such
enthusiasm; **de telle sorte** *or* **façon** *or*
**manière que** in such a way that; so that
**(e) admettons qu'il arrive** ~ **jour, à telle**
**heure** suppose that he arrives on such and
such a day, at such and such a time

**télé** /tele/ *adj inv, nf* (colloq) TV

**télé-achat** /teleaʃa/ *nm* teleshopping

**téléchargeable** /teleʃarʒabl/ *adj*
(Comput) downloadable; uploadable

**téléchargement** /teleʃarʒmɑ̃/ *nm*
(Comput) download; upload

**télécharger** /teleʃarʒe/ *vt* (Comput) to
download; upload

**télécommande** /telekɔmɑ̃d/ *nf* remote
control

**télécommander** /telekɔmɑ̃de/ [1] *vtr*
**(a)** to operate [sth] by remote control;
**voiture télécommandée** remote-controlled
car
**(b)** (figurative) to mastermind

**télécommunication** /telekɔmynikasjɔ̃/
*nf* telecommunications

**téléconférence** /telekɔ̃ferɑ̃s/ *nf*
**(a)** conference call
**(b)** teleconference

**télécopie** /telekɔpi/ *nf* fax

**télécopier** /telekɔpje/ [2] *vtr* to fax

**télécopieur** /telekɔpjœr/ *nm* fax
machine, fax

**télédiffuser** /teledifyze/ [1] *vtr* to
broadcast

**télé-enseignement,** *pl* ~**s**
/teleɑ̃sɛɲəmɑ̃/ *nm* distance learning

**téléfilm** /telefilm/ *nm* TV film, TV movie

**télégramme** /telegram/ *nm* telegram

**télégraphier** /telegrafje/ [1] *vtr* to
telegraph

**télégraphique** /telegrafik/ *adj* ⟨*pole,*
*message*⟩ telegraph; ⟨*style*⟩ telegraphic

**téléguidage** /telegidaʒ/ *nm* radio control

**téléguider** /telegide/ [1] *vtr* **(a)** to control
[sth] by radio
**(b)** (figurative) to mastermind

**télématique** /telematik/ **1** *adj* ⟨*service,*
*network*⟩ viewdata (GB), videotex⊕
**2** *nf* telematics

**téléobjectif** /teleɔbʒɛktif/ *nm* telephoto
lens

**télépathie** /telepati/ *nf* telepathy

**téléphérique** /teleferik/ *nm* cable car

**téléphone** /telefɔn/ *nm* phone     ····❖

■ ∼ **arabe** (colloq) grapevine, bush telegraph; ∼ **portable** mobile phone; ∼ **portatif** pocket car phone; **le** ∼ **rouge** the hotline

**téléphoner** /telefɔne/ [1] *vi* to phone; to make a phone call; ∼ **à qn** to phone sb

**téléphonique** /telefɔnik/ *adj* (tele)phone

**télescope** /telɛskɔp/ *nm* telescope

**télescoper** /telɛskɔpe/ [1] **1** *vtr* ⟨*truck, juggernaut*⟩ to crush ⟨*car*⟩
**2** **se télescoper** *v refl* (+ *v être*)
(a) ⟨*vehicles*⟩ to collide
(b) ⟨*notions, tendencies*⟩ to overlap

**télescopique** /telɛskɔpik/ *adj* telescopic

**téléscripteur** /teleskriptœr/ *nm* teleprinter, teletypewriter

**télésiège** /telesjɛʒ/ *nm* chair lift

**téléski** /teleski/ *nm* ski tow

**téléspectateur, -trice** /telespɛktatœr, tris/ *nm,f* viewer

**télésurveillance** /telesyrvɛjãs/ *nf* electronic surveillance

**télétransmission** /teletrãsmisjɔ̃/ *nf* transmission

**télétravail** /teletravaj/ *nm* teleworking

**télévente** /televãt/ *nf* telesales

**télévisé, ∼e** /televize/ *adj* television; televised

**téléviseur** /televizœr/ *nm* television (set)

**télévision** /televizjɔ̃/ *nf* television, TV

**télex** /telɛks/ *nm inv* telex; **par** ∼ by telex

**télexer** /telɛkse/ [1] *vtr* to telex

**tellement** /tɛlmã/ **1** *adv* (modifying an adjective or adverb) so; (modifying a verb or comparative) so much; **pas** ∼ not much; **il n'aime pas** ∼ **lire** he doesn't like reading much; **j'ai de la peine à suivre** ∼ **c'est compliqué** it's so complicated that I find it hard to follow
**2** **tellement de** *quantif* (colloq) **il y a** ∼ **de choses à voir** there's so much to see; **il a eu** ∼ **de chance** he was so lucky; **il y en a un** ∼ **qui aimeraient le faire** so many people would like to do it

**téméraire** /temerɛr/ *adj* ⟨*person, plan*⟩ reckless; ⟨*judgment*⟩ rash; **courageux mais pas** ∼ brave but not foolhardy

**témérité** /temerite/ *nf* recklessness; rashness; **avoir la** ∼ **de faire** to have the temerity to do

**témoignage** /temwaɲaʒ/ *nm* (a) story
(b) account; ∼**s recueillis auprès de** accounts given by
(c) evidence; testimony; **des** ∼**s contradictoires/qui concordent** conflicting/ corroborating evidence
(d) ∼ **d'amitié** (gift) token of friendship; **les** ∼**s de sympathie** expressions of sympathy

**témoigner** /temwaɲe/ [1] **1** *vtr* (a) (Law) to testify
(b) ∼ **de l'affection** to show affection
**2** **témoigner de** *v+prep* (a) ∼ **de** to show
(b) ∼ **du courage de qn** to vouch for sb's courage
**3** *vi* (a) (Law) to give evidence

(b) **'il était toujours poli', témoignent les voisins** neighbours (GB) say he was always polite

**témoin** /temwɛ̃/ *nm* (a) (gen, Law) witness; ∼ **oculaire** eyewitness
(b) (at duel) second
(c) (Tech) indicator *or* warning light

**tempe** /tɑ̃p/ *nf* temple

**tempérament** /tɑ̃peramã/ *nm* disposition; **avoir du** ∼ to have a strong character

**tempérance** /tɑ̃perãs/ *nf* temperance

**température** /tɑ̃peratyr/ *nf* temperature

**tempéré, ∼e** /tɑ̃pere/ *adj* temperate

**tempérer** /tɑ̃pere/ [14] *vtr* to temper; to moderate ⟨*argument*⟩

**tempête** /tɑ̃pɛt/ *nf* (a) gale; storm
(b) uproar; **déclencher une** ∼ **de protestations** to trigger a wave of protest

**tempêter** /tɑ̃pete/ [1] *vi* to rage

**temple** /tɑ̃pl/ *nm* (a) (gen) temple; (protestant) church
(b) (figurative) temple

**tempo** /tɛmpo/ *nm* (Mus) tempo

**temporaire** /tɑ̃pɔrɛr/ *adj* temporary

**temporel, -elle** /tɑ̃pɔrɛl/ *adj* (gen) temporal

**temporisateur, -trice** /tɑ̃pɔrizatœr, tris/ **1** *adj* temporizing
**2** *nm,f* temporizer

**temporiser** /tɑ̃pɔrize/ [1] *vi* to stall

**temps** /tɑ̃/ *nm inv* (a) weather; **un beau** ∼ fine weather; **le** ∼ **est à la pluie** it looks like rain; **quel** ∼ **fait-il?** what's the weather like?; **par tous les** ∼ in all weathers
(b) time; **le** ∼ **arrangera les choses** time will take care of everything; **peu de** ∼ **avant** shortly before; **en peu de** ∼ in a short time; **dans peu de** ∼ shortly; **dans quelque** ∼ before long; **pendant ce** ∼(**-là**) meanwhile; **qu'as-tu fait tout ce** ∼(**-là**)? what have you been doing all this time?; **en un rien de** ∼ in no time at all; **les trois quarts du** ∼ most of the time; **le** ∼ **de ranger mes affaires et j'arrive** just let me put my things away and I'll be with you; **on a (tout) le** ∼ we've got (plenty of) time; **avoir dix** *or* **cent fois le** ∼ to have all the time in the world; **laisser à qn le** ∼ **de faire** to give sb time to do; **mettre** *or* **prendre du** ∼ to take time; **beaucoup de** ∼ a long time; **tu y as mis le** ∼!, **tu en as mis du** ∼! you (certainly) took your time!; **le** ∼ **passe vite** time flies; **faire passer le** ∼ to while away the time; **avoir du** ∼ **à perdre** to have time on one's hands; **c'est du** ∼ **perdu, c'est une perte de** ∼ it's a waste of time; **le** ∼ **presse!** time is short!; **j'ai trouvé le** ∼ **long** (the) time seemed to drag; **finir dans les** ∼ to finish in time; **à** ∼ ⟨*leave, finish*⟩ in time; **juste à** ∼ just in time; **de** ∼ **en** ∼, **de** ∼ **à autre** from time to time; **il était** ∼! (impatiently) (and) about time too!; (with relief) just in the nick of time!; **en** ∼ **utile** in time; **en** ∼ **voulu** in due course; at the right time; **ne durer qu'un** ∼ to be short-lived

**(c)** au *or* du ~ des Grecs in the time of the Greeks; au *or* du ~ où in the days when; le bon vieux ~ the good old days; ces derniers ~ recently; ces ~-ci lately; de mon ~ in my day; dans le ~ in those days; en ~ normal usually; en d'autres ~ at any other time
**(d)** stage; en deux ~ in two stages; dans un premier ~ first; dans un deuxième ~ subsequently; dans un dernier ~ finally
**(e)** (of verb) tense
**(f)** avoir un travail à ~ partiel/plein to have a part-/full-time job
**(g)** (Sport) time; il a réalisé le meilleur ~ he got the best time; améliorer son ~ d'une seconde to knock a second off one's time
**(h)** (of engine) stroke
**(i)** (Mus) time; mesure à deux ~ two-four time
■ ~ d'antenne airtime; ~ fort (Mus) forte; (figurative) high point; ~ mort slack period; ~ universel Greenwich Mean Time, GMT IDIOMS au ~ pour moi! my mistake!; par les ~ qui courent with things as they are; se payer du bon ~ (colloq) to have a whale of a time (colloq)

**tenable** /tənabl/ *adj* **(a)** bearable; la situation n'est pas ~ the situation is unbearable
**(b)** (defendable) tenable
**(c)** les élèves ne sont pas ~s aujourd'hui the pupils are being impossible today

**tenace** /tənas/ *adj* **(a)** ⟨stain, headache⟩ stubborn; ⟨perfume⟩ long-lasting; ⟨fog, cough, memory⟩ persistent
**(b)** ⟨person⟩ tenacious; persistent; ⟨will⟩ tenacious

**ténacité** /tenasite/ *nf* tenacity; persistence

**tenaille** /tənɑj/ *nf* pincers

**tenailler** /tənɑje/ [1] *vtr* il était tenaillé par le remords he was racked with remorse

**tenancier, -ière** /tənɑ̃sje, ɛʀ/ *nm,f* (of café) landlord/landlady; (of hotel, casino) manager/manageress

**tenant, ~e** /tənɑ̃, ɑ̃t/ ① *nm,f* (Sport) ~ du titre titleholder
② *nm* d'un seul ~ all in one piece
IDIOMS les ~s et les aboutissants de qch the ins and outs of sth

**tendance** /tɑ̃dɑ̃s/ *nf* **(a)** tendency
**(b)** (in politics) tendency; toutes ~s politiques confondues across party lines
**(c)** trend

**tendancieux, -ieuse** /tɑ̃dɑ̃sjø, øz/ *adj* biased (GB), tendentious

**tendeur** /tɑ̃dœʀ/ *nm* **(a)** (of tent) guy rope
**(b)** (for roof rack) elastic strap

**tendon** /tɑ̃dɔ̃/ *nm* tendon

**tendre¹** /tɑ̃dʀ/ [6] ① *vtr* **(a)** to tighten ⟨rope, cable⟩; to stretch ⟨elastic, skin⟩; to extend ⟨spring⟩; ~ le bras to reach out; ~ les bras à qn to greet sb with open arms; ~ la main to reach out; to hold out one's hand; ~ la main à qn to hold one's hand out to sb; (figurative) to lend sb a helping hand

**(b)** to spread ⟨cloth, sheet⟩
**(c)** to set ⟨trap⟩; to put up ⟨clothes line⟩
**(d)** ~ qch à qn to hold sth out to sb
② **tendre à** *v+prep* ~ à faire to tend to do
③ *vi* **(a)** ~ vers to strive for
**(b)** ~ vers to approach ⟨value⟩; to tend to ⟨zero⟩
④ **se tendre** *v refl* (+ *v être*) **(a)** to tighten
**(b)** to become strained

**tendre²** /tɑ̃dʀ/ ① *adj* **(a)** ⟨wood, fibre⟩ soft; ⟨skin, vegetables⟩ tender
**(b)** ⟨shoot, grass⟩ new; ~ enfance earliest childhood
**(c)** ⟨pink, green⟩ soft
**(d)** ⟨person⟩ loving; ⟨love, smile, words⟩ tender; ⟨temperament⟩ gentle; ne pas être ~ avec qn/qch to be hard on sb/sth
**(e)** ⟨husband, wife⟩ dear
② *nmf* soft-hearted person

**tendrement** /tɑ̃dʀəmɑ̃/ *adv* tenderly

**tendresse** /tɑ̃dʀɛs/ *nf* **(a)** tenderness
**(b)** affection

**tendu, ~e** /tɑ̃dy/ ① *pp* ▶ TENDRE¹
② *pp adj* ⟨rope⟩ tight
③ *adj* ⟨person, meeting⟩ tense

**ténèbres** /tenɛbʀ/ *nf pl* les ~ darkness

**ténébreux, -euse** /tenebʀø, øz/ *adj*
**(a)** dark
**(b)** obscure

**teneur** /tənœʀ/ *nf* **(a)** (of solid) content; (of gas, liquid) level
**(b)** (of report) import

**ténia** /tenja/ *nm* tapeworm

**tenir** /təniʀ/ [36] ① *vtr* **(a)** to hold; ~ qn par la main to hold sb's hand; tiens! (giving sth to sb) here you are!; tiens, regarde! hey, look!; si je le tenais! if I could get my hands on him!
**(b)** to keep [sb] under control; il nous tient he's got a hold on us
**(c)** (Mil) to hold ⟨hill, bridge, city⟩
**(d)** to hold ⟨captive, animal⟩; je te tiens! I've caught you!
**(e)** to have ⟨information⟩
**(f)** to hold ⟨job⟩; to run ⟨shop, house, business⟩; to be in charge of ⟨switchboard, reception⟩
**(g)** to keep; '~ hors de portée des enfants' 'keep out of reach of children'
**(h)** ~ sa tête droite to hold one's head upright; ~ les yeux baissés to keep one's eyes lowered
**(i)** to hold down ⟨load, cargo⟩; to hold up ⟨trousers, socks⟩
**(j)** to keep to ⟨itinerary⟩
**(k)** ~ la mer ⟨ship⟩ to be seaworthy; ~ le coup to hold out; ~ le choc ⟨person⟩ to stand the strain
**(l)** ⟨object⟩ to take up ⟨room⟩; ⟨person⟩ to hold ⟨role, position⟩
**(m)** ~ qn/qch pour responsable to hold sb/sth responsible; ~ qn pour mort to give sb up for dead
② **tenir à** *v+prep* **(a)** ~ à to be fond of, to like; ~ à la vie to value one's life ⋯⋗

**(b) j'y tiens** I insist; **~ à ce que qn fasse** to insist that sb should do
**3 tenir de** v+prep **~ de qn** to take after sb
**4 vi (a)** ⟨rope, shelf, dam⟩ to hold; ⟨stamp, glue⟩ to stick; ⟨bandage, structure⟩ to stay in place; ⟨hairstyle⟩ to stay tidy
**(b) ~ (bon)** (gen) to hang on; (Mil) to hold out
**(c) la neige tient** the snow is settling; **les fleurs n'ont pas tenu** the flowers didn't last long
**(d)** ⟨theory⟩ to hold good; ⟨alibi⟩ to stand up
**(e)** ⟨people, objects⟩ to fit; **~ à six dans une voiture** to fit six into a car; **mon article tient en trois pages** my article takes up only three pages
**5 se tenir** v refl (+ v être) **(a) se ~ la tête à deux mains** to hold one's head in one's hands
**(b) se ~ par le bras** to be arm in arm; **se ~ par la main** to hold hands
**(c) se ~ à qch** to hold onto sth; **tiens-toi** or **tenez-vous bien** (figurative) (colloq) prepare yourself for a shock
**(d) se ~ accroupi** to be squatting; **se ~ au milieu** to be standing in the middle; **se ~ prêt** to be ready
**(e)** to behave; **se ~ bien/mal** to behave well/badly
**(f) se ~ bien/mal** to have (a) good posture/(a) bad posture; **tiens-toi droit!** stand up straight!
**(g)** ⟨demonstration, exhibition⟩ to be held
**(h)** ⟨argument, book⟩ to hold together; **ça se tient** it makes sense
**(i) tenez-vous le pour dit!** (colloq) I don't want to have to tell you again!
**(j) s'en ~ à** to keep to; **s'en ~ aux ordres** to stick to orders; **ne pas savoir à quoi s'en ~** not to know what to make of it
**6 v impers il ne tient qu'à toi de partir** it's up to you to decide whether to leave; **qu'à cela ne tienne!** never mind!

**tennis** /tenis/ **1** nm inv tennis; **~ de table** table tennis
**2** nm inv or nf inv tennis shoe
**tennisman**, pl **tennismen** /tenisman, mɛn/ nm (male) tennis player
**ténor** /tenɔʀ/ nm tenor
**tension** /tɑ̃sjɔ̃/ nf **(a)** (of cable, muscle) tension
**(b)** (Med) **~ (artérielle)** blood pressure; **être sous ~** to be under stress
**(c)** (in electricity) tension; **basse ~** low voltage; **sous ~** ⟨wire⟩ live; ⟨machine⟩ switched on
**(d)** (between people) tension
**tentacule** /tɑ̃takyl/ nm tentacle
**tentateur, -trice** /tɑ̃tatœʀ, tʀis/ nm,f tempter/temptress
**tentation** /tɑ̃tasjɔ̃/ nf temptation
**tentative** /tɑ̃tativ/ nf attempt; **~ de meurtre** (gen) murder attempt; (Law) attempted murder
**tente** /tɑ̃t/ nf tent
**tenter** /tɑ̃te/ [1] vtr **(a)** to attempt; **~ sa chance** to try one's luck; **~ le tout pour le tout** to risk one's all

**(b)** to tempt; **cela ne la tente guère** that doesn't appeal to her very much; **laisse-toi ~!** be a devil!; **~ le diable** to court disaster
**tenture** /tɑ̃tyʀ/ nf **(a)** curtain; **~s** draperies
**(b)** fabric wall covering
**tenu, ~e¹** /təny/ **1** pp ▸ TENIR
**2** pp adj **(a) bien/mal ~** ⟨child⟩ well/badly cared for; ⟨house⟩ well/badly kept
**(b) ~ de faire** required to do; **~ à** bound by
**tenue²** /təny/ nf **(a) ~ (vestimentaire)** dress, clothes; **être en ~ légère** to be scantily dressed; **en ~** (Mil) uniformed
**(b) avoir de la ~** to have good manners; **un peu de ~!** mind your manners!
**(c)** posture
**ter** /tɛʀ/ adv **(a)** (in address) ter; **15 ~ rue du Rocher** 15 ter rue du Rocher
**(b)** three times
**térébenthine** /teʀebɑ̃tin/ nf turpentine
**tergal®** /tɛʀgal/ nm Terylene®
**tergiversation** /tɛʀʒivɛʀsasjɔ̃/ nf equivocation
**tergiverser** /tɛʀʒivɛʀse/ [1] vi **(a)** to dither
**(b)** to shilly-shally
**terme** /tɛʀm/ **1** nm **(a)** term, word
**(b)** end; **mettre un ~ à qch** to put an end to sth; **toucher à son ~** to come to an end; **arriver à ~** ⟨period, contract⟩ to expire; **accoucher avant ~** to give birth prematurely
**(c) passé ce ~ vous paierez des intérêts** after this date, you will pay interest; **à moyen ~** ⟨loan⟩ medium-term
**(d) trouver un moyen ~** to find a compromise
**2 termes** nm pl terms; **~s de l'échange** terms of trade; **en bons ~s** on good terms
**terminaison** /tɛʀminɛzɔ̃/ nf ending
**terminal, ~e¹**, mpl **-aux** /tɛʀminal, o/
**1** adj ⟨year⟩ final; **phase ~e** (of operation) concluding phase; (of illness) terminal phase
**2** nm terminal
**terminale²** /tɛʀminal/ nf (Sch) final year (of secondary school)
**terminer** /tɛʀmine/ [1] **1** vtr to finish; to end
**2** vi to finish; **en ~ avec** to be through with; **pour ~** in conclusion
**3 se terminer** v refl (+ v être) **(a)** to end; **être terminé** to be over
**(b) se ~ par** ⟨word, number, object⟩ to end in
**terminologie** /tɛʀminɔlɔʒi/ nf terminology
**terminus** /tɛʀminys/ nm inv (of train) end of the line; (of bus) terminus
**termite** /tɛʀmit/ nm termite
**ternaire** /tɛʀnɛʀ/ adj (in maths, physics) ternary; (Mus) compound
**terne** /tɛʀn/ adj ⟨hair, life⟩ dull; ⟨colour⟩ drab; ⟨eyes, expression⟩ lifeless
**ternir** /tɛʀniʀ/ [3] **1** vtr **(a)** to tarnish ⟨metal⟩; to fade ⟨fabric⟩
**(b)** to tarnish ⟨image, reputation⟩

**2 se ternir** *v refl* (+ *v être*) to tarnish

**terrain** /tɛʁɛ̃/ *nm* (a) (gen) ground; (Mil) field
**(b)** plot of land
**(c)** land
**(d)** (for football, rugby, cricket) pitch, field; ground; (for volley-ball, handball, tennis) court; (in golf) course
**(e)** (figurative) nous ne vous suivrons pas sur ce ~ we won't go along with you there; un ~ d'entente common ground; travailler sur le ~ to do fieldwork; ~ favorable (Med) predisposing factors; (in sociology) favourable (GB) environment; déblayer le ~ to clear the ground; préparer le ~ to pave the way; tâter le ~ to put out feelers
■ ~ d'atterrissage landing strip; ~ d'aviation airfield; ~ de camping campsite; ~ de jeu(x) playground; ~ de sport(s) sports ground; ~ vague wasteland

**terrasse** /tɛʁas/ *nf* (a) terrace; s'installer à la ~ d'un café to sit at a table outside a café
**(b)** flat roof
**(c)** large balcony

**terrassement** /tɛʁasmɑ̃/ *nm* excavation; faire des travaux de ~ to carry out excavation work

**terrasser** /tɛʁase/ [1] *vtr* ⟨illness⟩ to strike down; terrassé par (by heat, grief) prostrated by

**terrassier** /tɛʁasje/ *nm* building labourer

**terre** /tɛʁ/ **1** *nf* (a) ground; sous ~ underground
**(b)** earth; soil; sortir de ~ ⟨plant⟩ to come up
**(c)** land; le retour à la ~ the movement back to the land; aller à ~ to go ashore; s'enfoncer à l'intérieur des ~s to go deep inland
**(d)** earth; il croit que la ~ entière est contre lui he thinks the whole world is against him; redescends sur ~! come back to earth!
**(e)** de la ~ ⟨glaise⟩ clay; un pot en ~ an earthenware pot
**(f)** (in electricity) earth (GB), ground (US)
**2 terre à terre** *phr* ⟨question⟩ basic; ⟨conversation, person⟩ pedestrian
**3 par terre** *phr* on the ground; on the floor; c'est à se rouler par ~ (colloq) it's hilarious; ça a fichu tous nos projets par ~ (colloq) it messed up all our plans (colloq)
■ ~ d'asile country of refuge; ~ battue trodden earth; sur ~ battue on a clay court
IDIOMS avoir les pieds sur ~ (colloq) to have one's feet firmly planted on the ground

**Terre** /tɛʁ/ *nf* Earth; sur la ~ on Earth

**terreau**, *pl* ~x /tɛʁo/ *nm* compost; ~ de feuilles leaf mould (GB), leaf mold (US)

**terre-plein**, *pl* **terres-pleins** /tɛʁplɛ̃/ *nm* (of road) central reservation (GB), median strip (US)

**terrer: se terrer** /tɛʁe/ [1] *v refl* (+ *v être*)
**(a)** ⟨rabbit⟩ to disappear into its burrow; ⟨fox⟩ to go to earth
**(b)** ⟨fugitive⟩ to hide

**terrestre** /tɛʁɛstʁ/ *adj* (a) ⟨surface, diameter⟩ of the Earth
**(b)** ⟨animals⟩ land
**(c)** ⟨war, transport⟩ land; la vie/le paradis ~ life/heaven on earth

**terreur** /tɛʁœʁ/ *nf* terror; c'est ma grande ~ it's my greatest fear

**terrible** /tɛʁibl/ *adj* (a) (gen) terrible; ⟨thirst, desire⟩ tremendous; il est ~, il ne veut jamais avoir tort (colloq) it's terrible the way he never wants to admit that he's wrong
**(b)** (colloq) terrific (colloq)

**terriblement** /tɛʁibləmɑ̃/ *adv* terribly; il a ~ grandi he's grown an awful lot

**terrien, -ienne** /tɛʁjɛ̃, ɛn/ *adj* propriétaire ~ landowner

**terrier** /tɛʁje/ *nm* (a) (gen) hole; un ~ de renard a fox's earth
**(b)** (Zool) terrier

**terrifiant, ~e** /tɛʁifjɑ̃, ɑ̃t/ *adj* terrifying

**terrifier** /tɛʁifje/ [2] *vtr* to terrify

**terrine** /tɛʁin/ *nf* (gen) terrine; (round) earthenware bowl

**territoire** /tɛʁitwaʁ/ *nm* territory.
■ ~ d'outre-mer, TOM French overseas (administrative) territory

**territorial, ~e**, *mpl* **-iaux** /tɛʁitɔʁjal, o/ *adj* (a) ⟨waters, integrity⟩ territorial
**(b)** ⟨administration⟩ divisional; regional

**terroir** /tɛʁwaʁ/ *nm* land; vin du ~ local wine

**terroriser** /tɛʁɔʁize/ [1] *vtr* (a) to terrorize
**(b)** to terrify

**terrorisme** /tɛʁɔʁism/ *nm* terrorism

**terroriste** /tɛʁɔʁist/ *adj, nmf* terrorist

**tertiaire** /tɛʁsjɛʁ/ *adj* (a) (Econ) ⟨sector, industry⟩ service
**(b)** (in geology) Tertiary

**tertio** /tɛʁsjo/ *adv* thirdly

**tes** ▶ TON¹

**tesson** /tesɔ̃/ *nm* shard, fragment

**test** /tɛst/ *nm* test; ~ (de dépistage) du sida Aids test; faire passer des ~s à qn (gen) to give sb tests; (Med) to carry out tests on sb

**testament** /tɛstamɑ̃/ *nm* (Law) will; (figurative) legacy

**testamentaire** /tɛstamɑ̃tɛʁ/ *adj* of a will

**tester** /tɛste/ [1] *vtr* to test

**testicule** /tɛstikyl/ *nm* testicle

**tétanos** /tetanos/ *nm inv* tetanus

**têtard** /tɛtaʁ/ *nm* (Zool) tadpole

**tête** /tɛt/ *nf* (a) head; en pleine ~ (right) in the head; ~ baissée ⟨rush⟩ headlong; la ~ en bas ⟨hang⟩ upside down; se laver la ~ to wash one's hair; au-dessus de nos ~s overhead; être tombé sur la ~ (figurative) (colloq) to have gone off one's rocker (colloq); ma ~ est mise à prix there's a price on my head; vouloir la ~ de qn to want sb's head; to be after sb's head; risquer sa ~ to risk one's neck (colloq); des ~s vont tomber (figurative) heads will roll ⋯⟩

(b) face; **une bonne/sale ∼** a nice/nasty face; **tu en fais une ∼!** what a face!; **quelle ∼ va-t-il faire?** how's he going to react?; **il (me) fait la ∼** he's sulking; **il a une ∼ à tricher** he looks like a cheat; **tu as une ∼ à faire peur, aujourd'hui!** you look dreadful today!

(c) **de ∼** ‹quote, recite› from memory; ‹calculate› in one's head; **tu n'as pas de ∼!** you have a mind like a sieve!; **avoir qch en ∼** to have sth in mind; **où avais-je la ∼?** whatever was I thinking of?; **ça (ne) va pas, la ∼?** (colloq) are you out of your mind or what?; **mets-lui ça dans la ∼** drum it into him/her; **passer par la ∼ de qn** ‹idea› to cross sb's mind; **monter la ∼ à Pierre contre Paul** to turn Pierre against Paul; **j'ai la ∼ qui tourne** my head's spinning; **monter à la ∼ de qn** ‹alcohol, success› to go to sb's head; **il a encore toute sa ∼ (à lui)** he's still got all his faculties; **n'en faire qu'à sa ∼** to go one's own way; **tenir ∼ à qn** to stand up to sb

(d) ( person) **avoir ses ∼s** to have one's favourites (GB); **un dîner en ∼ à ∼** an intimate dinner for two; **par ∼** (gen) a head, each; (in statistics) per capita

(e) (measurement) head; **avoir une ∼ d'avance sur qn** to be a short length in front of sb

(f) **il a été nommé à la ∼ du groupe** he was appointed head of the group; **prendre la ∼ des opérations** to take charge of operations; **être à la ∼ d'une immense fortune** to be the possessor of a huge fortune

(g) top; **être en ∼ (de** ‹list, category›) to be at the top; (in election, race, survey) to be in the lead; **en ∼ de phrase** at the beginning of a sentence

(h) (of train) front; (of convoy) head; (of tree, mast) top; (of screw, nail) head; **en ∼ de file** first in line

(i) (Sport) (in football) **faire une ∼** to head the ball

(j) (Mil) (of missile) warhead

(k) **∼ de lecture** (in tape recorder, video recorder) head

■ **∼ en l'air** scatterbrain; **∼ brûlée** daredevil; **∼ à claques** (colloq) pain (colloq); **∼ de linotte = ∼ EN L'AIR; ∼ de mort** skull; death's head; skull and crossbones; **∼ de mule** (colloq) mule; **être une vraie ∼ de mule** (colloq) to be as stubborn as a mule; **∼ de Turc** (colloq) whipping boy

IDIOMS **j'en mettrais ma ∼ à couper** I'd swear to it; **en avoir par-dessus la ∼** (colloq) to be fed up to the back teeth (colloq); **ça me prend la ∼** (colloq) it's a real drag (colloq)

**tête-à-queue** /tɛtakø/ *nm inv* **faire un ∼** to slew round *or* around

**tête-à-tête** /tɛtatɛt/ *nm inv* (a) tête-à-tête
(b) private meeting

**tête-bêche** /tɛtbɛʃ/ *adv* (a) top-to-tail
(b) head-to-tail

**tétée** /tete/ *nf* (a) feeding
(b) feed

**téter** /tete/ [14] **1** *vtr* to suck at ‹breast›; to feed from ‹bottle›; to suck ‹milk›
**2** *vi* to suckle; **donner à ∼ à** to feed ‹baby›

**tétine** /tetin/ *nf* (a) teat (GB), nipple (US)
(b) dummy (GB), pacifier (US)
(c) (of animal) teat

**têtu, ∼e** /tety/ *adj* stubborn

**texte** /tɛkst/ *nm* (a) text; '**∼ intégral**' 'unabridged'
(b) (Law) **∼ de loi** bill; law

**textile** /tɛkstil/ **1** *adj* textile
**2** *nm* (a) textile industry
(b) **∼s synthétiques** synthetic fibres (GB)

**texto** /tɛksto/ (colloq) = TEXTUELLEMENT

**textuellement** /tɛkstɥɛlmɑ̃/ *adv* ‹recount› word for word

**texture** /tɛkstyʀ/ *nf* (a) (of fabric, material) texture
(b) (of novel) structure

**TGV** /teʒeve/ *nm* (abbr = **train à grande vitesse**) TGV, high-speed train

**thé** /te/ *nm* (a) tea
(b) tea party

**théâtral, ∼e,** *mpl* **-aux** /teɑtʀal, o/ *adj*
(a) ‹performance› stage; ‹season, company› theatre (GB); ‹production, technique› theatrical; **l'œuvre ∼e de Racine** the plays of Racine
(b) ‹gesture› histrionic; ‹tone› melodramatic

**théâtre** /teɑtʀ/ *nm* theatre (GB); **le ∼ antique** Greek classical drama; **de ∼** ‹actor, director, ticket› theatre (GB); ‹decor, costume› stage; **coup de ∼** coup de théâtre; (figurative) dramatic turn of events; **faire du ∼** (as profession) to be an actor; (at school) to do drama; **être le ∼ d'affrontements** (figurative) to be the scene of fighting
■ **∼ de Boulevard** farce

**théière** /tejɛʀ/ *nf* teapot

**théine** /tein/ *nf* theine

**thématique** /tematik/ **1** *adj* thematic
**2** *nf* themes

**thème** /tɛm/ *nm* (a) topic, subject; (of film) theme
(b) (translation) prose
(c) (Mus) theme
■ **∼ astral** birth chart

**théologie** /teɔlɔʒi/ *nf* theology

**théorème** /teɔʀɛm/ *nm* theorem

**théoricien, -ienne** /teɔʀisjɛ̃, ɛn/ *nm,f* theoretician

**théorie** /teɔʀi/ *nf* theory; **en ∼** in theory

**théorique** /teɔʀik/ *adj* theoretical

**thérapeute** /teʀapøt/ *nmf* therapist

**thérapeutique** /teʀapøtik/ *adj* ‹effect› therapeutic; **choix ∼** choice of treatment

**thérapie** /teʀapi/ *nf* (a) (Med) treatment
(b) (in psychology) therapy

**thermal, ∼e,** *mpl* **-aux** /tɛʀmal, o/ *adj* ‹spring› thermal; **station ∼e** spa

**thermalisme** /tɛʀmalism/ *nm*
(a) balneology
(b) hydrotherapy industry

**thermes** /tɛʀm/ *nm pl* (a) (Roman) thermae
(b) thermal baths

**thermique** /tɛʀmik/ *adj* thermal

**thermo** /tɛʀmo/ *pref* thermo; ~**nucléaire** thermonuclear

**thermomètre** /tɛʀmɔmɛtʀ/ *nm* thermometer

**thermostat** /tɛʀmɔsta/ *nm* thermostat

**thèse** /tɛz/ *nf* **(a)** (for doctorate) thesis (GB), dissertation (US)
**(b)** thesis, argument
**(c) avancer la** ~ **de l'accident** to put forward the theory that it was an accident

**thon** /tɔ̃/ *nm* tuna

**thonier** *nm* tuna boat

**thoracique** /tɔʀasik/ *adj* **cage** ~ ribcage

**thorax** /tɔʀaks/ *nm inv* thorax

**thym** /tɛ̃/ *nm* thyme

**thyroïde** /tiʀɔid/ *adj, nf* thyroid

**tibia** /tibja/ *nm* shinbone, tibia

**tic** /tik/ *nm* **(a)** tic; **être plein de** ~**s** to be constantly twitching
**(b)** ~ **de langage** verbal tic

**ticket** /tikɛ/ *nm* (for train, platform) ticket; ~ **de caisse** till receipt (GB), sales slip (US); ~ **modérateur** *patient's contribution towards the cost of medical treatment*

**ticket-restaurant®**, *pl* **tickets-restaurant** /tikɛʀɛstɔʀɑ̃/ *nm* luncheon voucher, meal ticket

**tic-tac** /tiktak/ *nm inv* **faire** ~ to tick

**tiède** /tjɛd/ *adj* **(a)** lukewarm; warm; mild
**(b)** (figurative) lukewarm

**tièdement** /tjɛdmɑ̃/ *adv* half-heartedly

**tiédeur** /tjedœʀ/ *nf* **(a)** (of season) mildness; (of air, room) warmth
**(b)** (figurative) half-heartedness

**tiédir** /tjediʀ/ [3] *vi* **(a) faire** ~ to warm *or* heat (up); **laisser** ~ to allow [sth] to cool
**(b)** ⟨feelings⟩ to cool; ⟨enthusiasm⟩ to wane

**tien, tienne** /tjɛ̃, tjɛn/ **le tien, la tienne, les tiens, les tiennes** *pron* yours; **un métier comme le** ~ a job like yours; **à la tienne!** cheers!; (ironic) good luck to you!

**tiens** ▸ TENIR

**tierce¹** /tjɛʀs/ *adj f* ▸ TIERS 1

**tiercé** /tjɛʀse/ *nm* (Games) **jouer au** ~ to bet on the horses

**tiers, tierce²** /tjɛʀ, tjɛʀs/ **1** *adj* third; **un pays** ~ (gen) another country; a non-member country; **une tierce personne** a third party
**2** *nm inv* **(a)** third; **le** ~**/les deux** ~ **du travail** one third/two thirds of the work
**(b)** (person) outsider; (Law) third party
■ **le Tiers État** the Third Estate

**tiers-monde** /tjɛʀmɔ̃d/ *nm* Third World

**tiers-mondisme** /tjɛʀmɔ̃dism/ *nm* support for the Third World

**tiers-mondiste** /tjɛʀmɔ̃dist/ **1** *adj* in support of the Third World
**2** *nmf* supporter of the Third World

**tige** /tiʒ/ *nf* (of plant) (gen) stem, stalk

**tigre** /tigʀ/ *nm* (Zool) tiger

**tigré, ~e** /tigʀe/ *adj* **(a)** striped

**(b)** spotted

**tigresse** /tigʀɛs/ *nf* (Zool, figurative) tigress

**tilleul** /tijœl/ *nm* **(a)** limetree
**(b)** limewood
**(c)** lime-blossom tea

**tilt** /tilt/ *nm* (colloq) **ça a fait** ~ **(dans mon esprit)** (colloq) the penny dropped (colloq)

**timbale** /tɛ̃bal/ *nf* **(a)** (metal) tumbler
**(b)** (Mus) kettledrum; ~**s** timpani
**(c)** (Culin) timbale

**timbre** /tɛ̃bʀ/ *nm* **(a)** stamp
**(b)** postmark
**(c)** (of voice) tone, timbre
**(d)** (Med) patch

**timbre-poste**, *pl* **timbres-poste** /tɛ̃bʀəpɔst/ *nm* postage stamp

**timbrer** /tɛ̃bʀe/ [1] *vtr* to stamp

**timide** /timid/ *adj* ⟨person⟩ shy, timid; ⟨criticism⟩ timid; ⟨success⟩ limited

**timidement** /timidmɑ̃/ *adv* shyly; timidly; (without conviction) half-heartedly

**timidité** /timidite/ *nf* shyness

**timoré, ~e** /timɔʀe/ *adj* timorous

**tintamarre** /tɛ̃tamaʀ/ *nm* din; **faire du** ~ to make a din

**tintement** /tɛ̃tmɑ̃/ *nm* chiming; tinkling

**tinter** /tɛ̃te/ [1] *vi* ⟨bells⟩ to chime; ⟨doorbell⟩ to ring; ⟨small bell⟩ to tinkle; ⟨glass, coins⟩ to clink; ⟨keys⟩ to jingle; (Mus) ⟨triangle⟩ to ring

**tintinnabuler** /tɛ̃tinabyle/ [1] *vi* to tinkle

**tipi** /tipi/ *nm* te(e)pee

**tique** /tik/ *nf* (Zool) tick

**tiquer** /tike/ [1] *vi* (colloq) to wince; **sans** ~ without batting an eyelid (GB) *or* eyelash (US)

**tir** /tiʀ/ *nm* **(a)** (Mil) fire; **déclencher le** ~ to open fire
**(b)** (Sport) shooting
**(c)** ~ **de grenades** grenade firing
**(d)** (in games, sports) (with ball) shot
**(e)** shooting

**tirade** /tiʀad/ *nf* **(a)** declamation
**(b)** tirade

**tirage** /tiʀaʒ/ *nm* **(a)** ~ **(au sort)** draw; **désigner par** ~ **(au sort)** to draw ⟨name, winner⟩
**(b)** impression
**(c)** edition; ~ **limité** limited edition
**(d)** (of book) run; (of newspaper) circulation

**tiraillement** /tiʀajmɑ̃/ *nm* **(a)** pulling, tugging
**(b)** nagging pain; ~**s d'estomac** hunger pangs
**(c)** friction

**tirailler** /tiʀaje/ [1] *vtr* to tug (at), to pull (at) ⟨rope, sleeve⟩; **être tiraillé entre son travail et sa famille** to be torn between one's work and one's family

**tire-au-flanc** /tiʀoflɑ̃/ *nm inv* (colloq) shirker, skiver (colloq)

**tire-bouchon**, *pl* ~**s** /tiʀbuʃɔ̃/ *nm* corkscrew; **en** ~ ⟨tail⟩ curly

**tire-d'aile**: **à tire-d'aile** /atiʀdɛl/ *phr* in a flurry of wings; (figurative) hurriedly

**tirelire** /tiʀliʀ/ *nf* piggy bank

**tirer** /tiʀe/ [1] **1** *vtr* (a) to pull ⟨*vehicle*⟩; to pull up ⟨*chair, armchair*⟩; to pull away ⟨*rug*⟩
(b) to pull ⟨*hair*⟩; to pull on ⟨*rope*⟩; to tug at ⟨*sleeve*⟩; ~ **qn par le bras** to pull sb's arm
(c) ~ **ses cheveux en arrière** to pull back one's hair; **avoir les traits tirés** to look drawn
(d) to draw ⟨*bolt, curtain*⟩; to pull down ⟨*blind*⟩; to close ⟨*door, shutter*⟩
(e) to fire off ⟨*bullet, grenade*⟩; to fire ⟨*missile*⟩; to shoot ⟨*arrow*⟩
(f) (Sport) ~ **un penalty** to take a penalty
(g) ~ **(au sort)** to draw ⟨*card, name, winner*⟩; to draw for ⟨*partner*⟩
(h) (in astrology) ~ **les cartes à qn** to tell the cards for sb
(i) to draw ⟨*wine*⟩; to withdraw ⟨*money*⟩; ~ **qch de sa poche** to pull sth out of one's pocket
(j) ~ **le pays de la récession** to get the country out of recession; **tire-moi de là!** get me out of this!
(k) ~ **[qch] de qn** to get [sth] from sb ⟨*information, confession*⟩; ~ **[qch] de qch** to draw [sth] from sth ⟨*strength, resources*⟩; to derive [sth] from sth ⟨*pride, satisfaction*⟩; to make [sth] out of sth ⟨*money*⟩
(l) ~ **de qch** to base [sth] on sth ⟨*story, film*⟩; to get [sth] from sth ⟨*name*⟩
(m) to print ⟨*book, negative*⟩; to run off ⟨*proofs, copies*⟩
(n) to draw ⟨*line*⟩
(o) (colloq) **plus qu'une semaine à** ~ only one more week to go
(p) ~ **un chèque** to draw a cheque (GB) *or* check (US)
**2** *vi* (a) to pull; ~ **sur qch** to pull on sth; to tug at sth
(b) (with firearm) to shoot; to fire
(c) (in football) to shoot; (in handball, basketball) to take a shot
(d) ~ **(au sort)** to draw lots
(e) **la cheminée tire bien** the chimney draws well
(f) ~ **à mille exemplaires** ⟨*periodical*⟩ to have a circulation of one thousand
(g) ~ **sur le jaune/l'orangé** ⟨*colour*⟩ to be yellowish/orangy
**3** **se tirer** *v refl* (+ *v être*) (a) **se** ~ **de** to come through ⟨*situation, difficulties*⟩
(b) **se** ~ **une balle** to shoot oneself; **se** ~ **dessus** to shoot at one another
(c) (colloq) **s'en** ~ to cope; (from accident) to escape; (from illness) to pull through; **s'en** ~ **à bon prix** to get off lightly

**tiret** /tiʀɛ/ *nm* dash

**tirette** /tiʀɛt/ *nf* pull tab; cord

**tireur, -euse** /tiʀœʀ, øz/ *nm,f* (a) (Mil, Sport) marksman/markswoman
(b) gunman

**tiroir** /tiʀwaʀ/ *nm* (in piece of furniture) drawer; **à** ~**s** (figurative) ⟨*novel, play*⟩ episodic
**IDIOMS racler les fonds de** ~ to scrape some money together

**tiroir-caisse**, *pl* **tiroirs-caisses** /tiʀwaʀkɛs/ *nm* cash register

**tisane** /tizan/ *nf* herbal tea, tisane

**tison** /tizɔ̃/ *nm* (fire) brand

**tisonnier** /tizɔnje/ *nm* poker

**tissage** /tisaʒ/ *nm* (a) weaving
(b) weave

**tisser** /tise/ [1] *vtr* (a) ⟨*person, machine*⟩ to weave
(b) ⟨*spider*⟩ to spin ⟨*web*⟩

**tisserand, -e** /tisʀɑ̃, ɑ̃d/ *nm,f* weaver

**tissu** /tisy/ *nm* (a) material, fabric
(b) (Anat) ~ **osseux** bone tissue
(c) (of intrigue) web; (of lies) pack; (of insults) string; ~ **social** social fabric

**titan** /titɑ̃/ *nm* titan; **de** ~ titanic

**titane** /titan/ *nm* titanium

**titiller** /titije/ [1] *vtr* to titillate

**titre** /titʀ/ *nm* (a) (of book, film, chapter) title; (in newspaper) headline; **avoir pour** ~ to be entitled; **les** ~**s de l'actualité** the headlines
(b) (rank) title; ~ **mondial** world title; ~ **nobiliaire** *or* **de noblesse** title; **le** ~ **d'ingénieur** the status of qualified engineer; **en** ~ ⟨*professor, director*⟩ titular; ⟨*supplier*⟩ appointed; ⟨*mistress, rival*⟩ official; ~**s universitaires** university qualifications
(c) **à juste** ~ quite rightly; **à** ~ **d'exemple** as an example; **à** ~ **définitif** on a permanent basis; **à** ~ **privé** in a private capacity; **à** ~ **gracieux** free; **à** ~ **indicatif** as a rough guide; **à quel** ~ **a-t-il été invité?** why was he invited?
(d) (Law) deed; ~ **de propriété** title deed
(e) (on stock exchange) security
(f) (Econ) item; ~ **budgétaire** budgetary item
(g) (of solution) titre (GB); (of wines, spirits) strength; (of precious metal) fineness
■ ~ **de gloire** claim to fame; ~ **de transport** ticket

**titré, -e** /titʀe/ *adj* titled; **être** ~ to be titled

**tituber** /titybe/ [1] *vi* to stagger

**titulaire** /titylɛʀ/ **1** *adj* (gen) permanent; ⟨*lecturer*⟩ tenured
**2** *nmf* (a) (gen) permanent staff member; tenured lecturer (GB) *or* professor (US)
(b) holder; **être** ~ **de** to hold ⟨*degree, post*⟩; to have ⟨*bank account*⟩

**titularisation** /titylaʀizasjɔ̃/ *nf* confirmation in a post; (Univ) granting of tenure

**titulariser** /titylaʀize/ [1] *vtr* to give permanent status to ⟨*staff*⟩; to grant tenure to ⟨*professor*⟩

**toast** /tost/ *nm* toast

**toboggan** /tɔbɔgɑ̃/ *nm* (a) slide
(b) ® flyover (GB), overpass (US)
(c) (Tech) (for rubble) chute

**toc** /tɔk/ **1** *nm* (colloq) **c'est du** ~ it's fake
**2** *excl* ~**! ** ~**!** knock! knock!

**tocsin** /tɔksɛ̃/ *nm* alarm (bell), tocsin

**toge** /tɔʒ/ *nf* (a) (of academic) gown; (of judge) robe

**(b)** toga

**toi** /twa/ *pron* **(a)** you; ∼, **ne dis rien** don't say anything; **elle est plus âgée que** ∼ she's older than you; **à** ∼ (in game) your turn; **c'est à** ∼ it's yours; **c'est** ∼ **de choisir** it's your turn to choose; it's up to you to choose **(b)** yourself; **reprends-**∼ pull yourself together

**toile** /twal/ *nf* **(a)** cloth; ∼ **de lin** linen (cloth); **de la grosse** ∼ canvas
**(b)** (in art) canvas; painting; ∼ **de maître** master painting
**(c)** (Naut) canvas
■ ∼ **d'araignée** spider's web; cobweb; ∼ **cirée** oilcloth; ∼ **de jute** hessian; ∼ **de tente** canvas; tent

**toilettage** /twalɛtaʒ/ *nm* (of animal) grooming

**toilette** /twalɛt/ ⓵ *nf* **(a) faire sa** ∼ ⟨*person*⟩ to have a wash; ⟨*animal*⟩ to wash itself; **faire la** ∼ **d'un mort** to lay out a corpse
**(b)** outfit; **en grande** ∼ all dressed up
⓶ **toilettes** *nf pl* toilet (GB), bathroom (US)

**toiletter** /twalete/ [1] *vtr* to groom ⟨*dog*⟩

**toi-même** /twamɛm/ *pron* yourself

**toise** /twaz/ *nf* height gauge

**toiser** /twaze/ [1] *vtr* to look [sb] up and down

**toit** /twa/ *nm* roof
■ **le** ∼ **du Monde** the roof of the world; ∼ **ouvrant** sunroof
IDIOMS **crier qch sur (tous) les** ∼**s** to shout sth from the rooftops

**toiture** /twatyʀ/ *nf* **(a)** roof
**(b)** roofing

**tôle** /tol/ *nf* **(a)** sheet metal
**(b)** metal sheet *or* plate
**(c)** (slang) = TAULE

**tolérable** /tɔleʀabl/ *adj* bearable; tolerable

**tolérance** /tɔleʀɑ̃s/ *nf* **(a)** tolerance; indulgence
**(b) ce n'est pas un droit, c'est une** ∼ it isn't legal but it is tolerated
**(c)** (of medicine, noise) tolerance

**tolérant, ∼e** /tɔleʀɑ̃, ɑ̃t/ *adj* tolerant

**tolérer** /tɔleʀe/ [14] *vtr* to tolerate

**tôlerie** /tolʀi/ *nf* sheet-metal working; sheet-metal trade; sheet-metal works

**tollé** /tɔle/ *nm* outcry, hue and cry

**TOM** /tɔm/ *nm: abbr* ▶ TERRITOIRE

**tomate** /tɔmat/ *nf* **(a)** tomato
**(b)** tomato plant
**(c)** pastis with a dash of grenadine

**tombal, ∼e,** *mpl* **-aux** /tɔ̃bal, o/ *adj* **inscription** ∼**e** gravestone inscription

**tombant, ∼e** /tɔ̃bɑ̃, ɑ̃t/ *adj* ⟨*shoulders*⟩ sloping; ⟨*moustache, eyelids*⟩ drooping; ⟨*ears*⟩ floppy

**tombe** /tɔ̃b/ *nf* **(a)** grave
**(b)** gravestone

**tombeau,** *pl* ∼**x** /tɔ̃bo/ *nm* **(a)** tomb; **mettre qn au** ∼ to lay sb in their grave

**(b) c'est un** ∼ ⟨*person*⟩ he/she will keep quiet

**tombée** /tɔ̃be/ *nf* **à la** ∼ **du jour** at close of day; **la** ∼ **de la nuit** nightfall

**tomber¹** /tɔ̃be/ [1] *vi* (+ *v être*) **(a)** (gen) to fall; ⟨*person, chair*⟩ to fall over; ⟨*tree, wall*⟩ to fall down; (from height) ⟨*person, vase*⟩ to fall off; ⟨*hair, teeth*⟩ to fall out; ⟨*plaster, covering*⟩ to come off; ∼ **du lit/de ma poche** to fall out of bed/out of my pocket; **le vent a fait** ∼ **une tuile du toit** the wind blew a tile off the roof; **se laisser** ∼ **dans un fauteuil** to flop into an armchair; **laisser** ∼ **un gâteau sur le tapis** to drop a cake on the carpet
**(b)** ⟨*rain, snow, theatre curtain*⟩ to fall; ⟨*fog*⟩ to come down; **qu'est-ce que ça tombe!** (colloq) it's pouring down!; **la foudre est tombée sur un arbre** the lightning struck a tree
**(c)** ⟨*price, temperature*⟩ to fall; ⟨*anger*⟩ to subside; ⟨*fever*⟩ to come down; ⟨*wind*⟩ to drop; ⟨*day*⟩ to draw to a close; ⟨*conversation*⟩ to die down; **faire** ∼ to bring down ⟨*price, temperature*⟩; to dampen ⟨*enthusiasm*⟩; **je tombe de sommeil** I can't keep my eyes open
**(d)** ⟨*dictator, regime, city*⟩ to fall; ⟨*obstacle*⟩ to vanish; **faire** ∼ to bring down ⟨*regime, dictator*⟩; (figurative) to break down ⟨*barriers*⟩
**(e)** ⟨*belly*⟩ to sag; ⟨*shoulders*⟩ to slope
**(f)** ⟨*lock of hair*⟩ to fall; ∼ **bien/mal** ⟨*garment, curtain*⟩ to hang well/badly
**(g)** ∼ **dans un piège** (figurative) to fall into a trap; ∼ **sous le coup d'une loi** to fall within the provisions of a law; ∼ **aux mains** *or* **entre les mains de qn** ⟨*document, power*⟩ to fall into sb's hand; ∼ **malade/amoureux** to fall ill/in love
**(h)** ⟨*decision, verdict*⟩ to be announced; ⟨*news*⟩ to break; ⟨*reply*⟩ to be given
**(i)** ∼ **sur** to come across ⟨*stranger, object*⟩; to run into ⟨*friend*⟩; ∼ **sur la bonne page** to hit on the right page; **si tu prends cette rue, tu tomberas sur la place** if you follow this street, you'll come to the square
**(j) c'est tombé juste au bon moment** it came just at the right time; **tu ne pouvais pas mieux** ∼! you couldn't have come at a better time!; you couldn't have done better!; **tu tombes mal, j'allais partir** you're unlucky, I was just about to leave; **il faut toujours que ça tombe sur moi!** (colloq) (decision, choice) why does it always have to be me?; (misfortune) why does it always have to happen to me?
**(k)** ⟨*birthday*⟩ to fall on ⟨*day*⟩
**(l) laisser** ∼ to give up ⟨*job, activity*⟩; to drop ⟨*plan, habit*⟩; **laisse** ∼! forget it!; **laisser** ∼ **qn** to drop sb; to let sb down
**(m)** ∼ **sur qn** ⟨*soldiers, thugs*⟩ to fall on sb; ⟨*raiders, police*⟩ to descend on sb

**tomber²** /tɔ̃be/ *nm* hang; **ce velours a un beau** ∼ this velvet hangs well

**tombeur** /tɔ̃bœʀ/ *nm* (colloq) lady-killer

**tombola** /tɔ̃bɔla/ *nf* tombola (GB), lottery

**tome¹** /tom/ *nm* **(a)** volume
**(b)** part, book

**tome²** /tɔm/ *nf* = TOMME

**tomme** /tɔm/ *nf* tomme *or* tome (cheese)

**tommette** /tɔmɛt/ *nf* hexagonal floor tile

**ton¹, ta**, *pl* **tes** /tɔ̃, ta, te/ *det* your; **un de tes amis** a friend of yours

**ton²** /tɔ̃/ *nm* **(a)** pitch; tone; **~ grave/aigu** low/high pitch; **d'un ~ dédaigneux** scornfully; **baisser le ~** to lower one's voice; (figurative) to moderate one's tone; **eh bien, si tu le prends sur ce ~** well, if you're going to take it like that
**(b)** (in linguistics) tone; **langue à ~s** tone language
**(c)** **donner le ~** to set the tone; to set the fashion; **de bon ~** in good taste
**(d)** (Mus) pitch; key; tone; (instrument) pitch pipe
**(e)** (of colour) shade; **~ sur ~** in matching tones

**tonalité** /tɔnalite/ *nf* **(a)** (Mus) key; tonality
**(b)** (of vowel) tone
**(c)** (of voice) tone
**(d)** (of colours) tonality
**(e)** dialling tone (GB), dial tone (US)

**tondeuse** /tɔ̃døz/ *nf* **(a)** (for sheep) shears
**(b)** (for cutting hair) clippers
**(c)** **~ (à gazon)** lawnmower

**tondre** /tɔ̃dʀ/ [6] *vtr* to shear ‹sheep›; to clip ‹dog›; to mow ‹lawn›; **~ qn** to shave sb's head

**tongs** /tɔ̃g/ *nf pl* flip-flops, thongs (US)

**tonicité** /tɔnisite/ *nf* **(a)** bracing effect
**(b)** tone

**tonifiant, ~e** /tɔnifjɑ̃, ɑ̃t/ *adj* **(a)** ‹climate, air› bracing
**(b)** ‹exercise, lotion› toning

**tonifier** /tɔnifje/ [2] *vtr* to tone up

**tonique¹** /tɔnik/ *adj* **(a)** ‹drink› tonic; (figurative) ‹air› bracing; ‹book› stimulating
**(b)** **lotion ~** toning lotion
**(c)** ‹accent› tonic

**tonique²** /tɔnik/ *nf* (Mus) tonic

**tonitruant, ~e** /tɔnitʀyɑ̃, ɑ̃t/ *adj* booming

**tonitruer** /tɔnitʀye/ [1] *vi* to thunder

**tonnage** /tɔnaʒ/ *nm* tonnage

**tonnant, ~e** /tɔnɑ̃, ɑ̃t/ *adj* booming; thunderous

**tonne** /tɔn/ *nf* (1,000 kg) tonne, metric ton; **des ~s de choses à faire** (colloq) loads of things to do (colloq)

**tonneau**, *pl* **~x** /tɔno/ *nm* **(a)** barrel
**(b)** (of car) somersault
**(c)** (of plane) barrel roll
**(d)** (Naut) ton
IDIOMS **du même ~** (colloq) of the same kind

**tonnelle** /tɔnɛl/ *nf* arbour (GB)

**tonner** /tɔne/ [1] *vi*, *v impers* to thunder

**tonnerre** /tɔnɛʀ/ *nm* thunder; **un coup de ~** a clap of thunder; (figurative) a thunderbolt
**(b)** (of cannons, artillery) thundering; **un ~ d'applaudissements** thunderous applause

**(c)** (colloq) **ça marche du ~** it's going fantastically well

**tonsure** /tɔ̃syʀ/ *nf* (of monk) tonsure

**tonte** /tɔ̃t/ *nf* **(a)** **~ (des moutons)** shearing
**(b)** fleece

**tonton** /tɔ̃tɔ̃/ *nm* (colloq) uncle; **~ Pierre** Uncle Pierre

**tonus** /tɔnys/ *nm inv* **(a)** (of person) energy, dynamism
**(b)** (of muscle) tone, tonus

**top** /tɔp/ *nm* pip, beep; **donner le ~ de départ** to give the starting signal

**topaze** /tɔpaz/ *nf* topaz

**toper** /tɔpe/ [1] *vi* **topons là!** let's shake on it!

**topo** /tɔpo/ *nm* (colloq) short talk; short piece; **c'est toujours le même ~** it's always the same old story (colloq)

**topographie** /tɔpɔgʀafi/ *nf* topography

**toquade** /tɔkad/ *nf* (colloq) **(a)** (for thing) passion
**(b)** (on person) crush (colloq)

**toque** /tɔk/ *nf* **(a)** (of woman) toque; (of chef) chef's hat; (of judge) hat; **~ en fourrure** fur cap
**(b)** (of jockey) cap

**toqué, ~e** /tɔke/ *adj* (colloq) crazy (colloq)

**torche** /tɔʀʃ/ *nf* torch
■ **~ électrique** torch (GB), flashlight

**torcher** /tɔʀʃe/ [1] *vtr* (colloq) **(a)** to wipe
**(b)** to dash off (colloq) ‹article, report›; to cobble [sth] together

**torchis** /tɔʀʃi/ *nm inv* cob (for walls)

**torchon** /tɔʀʃɔ̃/ *nm* **(a)** (gen) cloth; **~ (de cuisine)** tea towel (GB), dish towel (US)
**(b)** (newspaper) (derogatory) rag (colloq)
**(c)** (colloq) messy piece of work
IDIOMS **le ~ brûle** (colloq) it's war

**tordant, ~e** /tɔʀdɑ̃, ɑ̃t/ *adj* (colloq) hilarious

**tordre** /tɔʀdʀ/ [6] **1** *vtr* **(a)** to twist ‹arm, wrist›; to wring ‹neck›
**(b)** to bend ‹nail, bar, bumper›
**(c)** to wring out ‹washing›
**2** **se tordre** *v refl* (+ *v être*) **(a)** ‹person› **se ~ la cheville** to twist one's ankle; **se ~ de douleur** to writhe in pain
**(b)** ‹bumper› to bend

**tordu, ~e** /tɔʀdy/ *adj* **(a)** ‹nose, legs› crooked; ‹branches, trunk, iron bar› twisted
**(b)** (figurative) ‹idea› weird, strange; ‹logic, reasoning› twisted

**tornade** /tɔʀnad/ *nf* tornado

**torpeur** /tɔʀpœʀ/ *nf* torpor

**torpille** /tɔʀpij/ *nf* torpedo

**torpiller** /tɔʀpije/ [1] *vtr* to torpedo

**torréfier** /tɔʀefje/ [2] *vtr* to roast

**torrent** /tɔʀɑ̃/ *nm* torrent; **pleuvoir à ~s** to rain very heavily

**torrentiel, -ielle** /tɔʀɑ̃sjɛl/ *adj* torrential

**torride** /tɔʀid/ *adj* ‹sun› scorching

**tors, torse¹** /tɔʀ, tɔʀs/ *adj* (gen) twisted

**torsade** /tɔʀsad/ *nf* **(a)** twist, coil

**(b)** cable stitch

**(c)** (in architecture) cable moulding (GB), cable molding (US)

**torsader** /tɔʀsade/ [1] *vtr* to twist; **une colonne torsadée** a cable column

**torse²** /tɔʀs/ *nm* **(a)** (gen) chest; **se mettre ∼ nu** to strip to the waist
**(b)** (Anat) torso

**torsion** /tɔʀsjɔ̃/ *nf* **(a)** twisting
**(b)** torsion

**tort** /tɔʀ/ **1** *nm* **(a)** **avoir ∼** to be wrong; **j'aurais bien ∼ de m'inquiéter!** it would be silly of me to worry!; **être en ∼** to be in the wrong; **donner ∼ à qn** ⟨*referee, judge*⟩ to blame sb; ⟨*facts*⟩ to prove sb wrong
**(b)** fault; **les ∼s sont partagés** there are faults on both sides; **avoir des ∼s envers qn** to have wronged sb
**(c)** mistake; **j'ai eu le ∼ de le croire** I made the mistake of believing him
**(d)** **faire du ∼ à qn/qch** to harm sb/sth
**2** **à tort** *phr* ⟨*accuse*⟩ wrongly; **à ∼ et à travers** ⟨*spend*⟩ wildly; **parler à ∼ et à travers** to talk a lot of nonsense

**torticolis** /tɔʀtikɔli/ *nm inv* stiff neck

**tortillard** /tɔʀtijaʀ/ *nm* (colloq) small local train

**tortiller** /tɔʀtije/ [1] **1** *vtr* to twist ⟨*fibres, strands*⟩; to twiddle ⟨*handkerchief*⟩
**2** **se tortiller** *v refl* (+ *v être*) to wriggle

**tortionnaire** /tɔʀsjɔnɛʀ/ *nmf* torturer

**tortue** /tɔʀty/ *nf* **(a)** (sea) turtle
**(b)** tortoise, turtle (US)
**(c)** (butterfly) tortoiseshell

**tortueux, -euse** /tɔʀtɥø, øz/ *adj*
**(a)** ⟨*road, staircase*⟩ winding
**(b)** (figurative) ⟨*behaviour*⟩ devious; ⟨*mind, reasoning*⟩ tortuous

**torture** /tɔʀtyʀ/ *nf* torture

**torturer** /tɔʀtyʀe/ [1] **1** *vtr* **(a)** to torture ⟨*person*⟩
**(b)** ⟨*thought, feeling*⟩ to torment
**(c)** to distort ⟨*text*⟩; **style torturé** tortured style
**2** **se torturer** *v refl* (+ *v être*) to torment oneself; **se ∼ l'esprit** to rack one's brains

**torve** /tɔʀv/ *adj* ⟨*look*⟩ menacing, baleful

**tôt** /to/ *adv* **(a)** ⟨*start*⟩ early; **∼ le matin** early in the morning
**(b)** soon, early; **le plus ∼ serait le mieux** the sooner the better; **∼ ou tard** sooner or later; **on ne m'y reprendra pas de si ∼** I won't do that again in a hurry.

**total, ∼e,** *mpl* **-aux** /tɔtal, o/ **1** *adj* complete, total
**2** *nm* total
**3** **au total** *phr* **au ∼ cela fait 350 euros** altogether that comes to 350 euros

**totalement** /tɔtalmɑ̃/ *adv* totally, completely

**totaliser** /tɔtalize/ [1] *vtr* **(a)** to total ⟨*profits*⟩
**(b)** to have a total of ⟨*points, votes*⟩

**totalitaire** /tɔtalitɛʀ/ *adj* **(a)** ⟨*regime, state*⟩ totalitarian

**(b)** ⟨*doctrine*⟩ all-embracing

**totalitarisme** /tɔtalitaʀism/ *nm* totalitarianism

**totalité** /tɔtalite/ *nf* **la ∼ du personnel** all the staff; **la ∼ des dépenses** the total expenditure; **nous vous rembourserons en ∼** we will refund you in full

**totem** /tɔtɛm/ *nm* **(a)** totem
**(b)** totem pole

**toubib** /tubib/ *nm* (colloq) doctor, quack (colloq)

**toucan** /tukɑ̃/ *nm* toucan

**touchant, ∼e** /tuʃɑ̃, ɑ̃t/ *adj* moving; touching

**touche** /tuʃ/ *nf* **(a)** (gen) button; (on keyboard) key; (on stringed instrument) fret
**(b)** (of paintbrush) stroke; (of paint) dash; (of artist) touch
**(c)** (Sport) sideline, touchline; **mettre qn sur la ∼** (figurative) to push sb aside
**(d)** (in fencing) hit
**(e)** (in fishing) bite

**touche-à-tout** /tuʃatu/ *adj inv* **être ∼** to be into everything; to be a jack of all trades

**toucher¹** /tuʃe/ [1] **1** *vtr* **(a)** **∼ (de la main)** to touch ⟨*object, surface, person*⟩; **∼ du bois** (superstitiously) to touch wood; **∼ le front de qn** to feel sb's forehead
**(b)** to be touching ⟨*wall, ceiling, bottom of sth*⟩; **∼ le sol** to land
**(c)** to hit ⟨*opponent, car, kerb*⟩
**(d)** to touch, to move ⟨*person*⟩; **ça me touche beaucoup** I am very touched
**(e)** ⟨*event, crisis*⟩ to affect ⟨*person, country*⟩; ⟨*storm*⟩ to hit ⟨*region, city*⟩
**(f)** ⟨*country, house*⟩ to be next to
**(g)** ⟨*person*⟩ to get ⟨*money*⟩; to cash ⟨*cheque*⟩
**2** **toucher à** *v+prep* **(a)** **∼ à** to touch ⟨*object*⟩; **∼ à tout** to be into everything; (figurative) to be a jack of all trades; **avec son air de ne pas y ∼, c'est un malin** (colloq) he looks as if butter wouldn't melt in his mouth, but he's a sly one
**(b)** **∼ à** to concern ⟨*activity, issue*⟩
**(c)** **∼ à** to infringe on ⟨*right, freedom*⟩
**(d)** **∼ à** to get on to ⟨*problem*⟩
**3** **se toucher** *v refl* (+ *v être*) ⟨*houses, gardens*⟩ to be next to each other

**toucher²** /tuʃe/ *nm* **(a)** **le ∼** touch, the sense of touch
**(b)** (of pianist) touch

**touche-touche**: **à touche-touche** /atuʃtuʃ/ *phr* (colloq) **être à ∼** ⟨*cars*⟩ to be bumper to bumper; ⟨*people*⟩ to be on top of each other (colloq)

**touffe** /tuf/ *nf* (of hair, grass) tuft

**touffu, ∼e** /tufy/ *adj* **(a)** ⟨*eyebrows, beard*⟩ bushy; ⟨*vegetation*⟩ dense; ⟨*bush*⟩ thick; **au poil ∼** with thick fur
**(b)** ⟨*text*⟩ dense

**touiller** /tuje/ [1] *vtr* (colloq) to stir ⟨*sauce*⟩

**toujours** /tuʒuʀ/ *adv* **(a)** always; **comme ∼** as always; **de ∼** ⟨*friend*⟩ very old; ⟨*friendship*⟩ long-standing; **∼ plus vite** faster and faster ⋯⟶

**(b)** still; **il n'est ~ pas levé?** is he still not up?
**(c)** anyway; **on peut ~ essayer** we can always try; **c'est ~ ça de pris** *or* **de gagné** that's something at least; **~ est-il que** the fact remains that

**toupet** /tupɛ/ *nm* **(a)** (colloq) cheek (colloq), nerve (colloq)
**(b)** (of hair) tuft; quiff (GB), forelock (US)

**toupie** /tupi/ *nf* top; **faire tourner une ~** to spin a top

**tour¹** /tuʀ/ *nm* **(a)** (gen) turn; (around axis) revolution; **donner un ~ de clé** to turn the key; **faire un ~ de manège** to have a go on the merry-go-round; **faire un ~ sur soi-même** ⟨*dancer*⟩ to spin around; ⟨*planet*⟩ to rotate; **fermer qch à double ~** to double-lock sth; **à ~ de bras** (colloq) ⟨*invest, buy up*⟩ left, right and centre (GB) (colloq)
**(b) faire le ~ de qch** (gen) to go around sth; to drive around sth; **la nouvelle a vite fait le ~ du village** the news spread rapidly through the village
**(c)** (of pond) edges; (of pipe, tree trunk) circumference; (of head, hips) measurement; (standard measurement) size
**(d)** walk, stroll; (on bicycle) ride; (in car) drive, spin; **je suis allé faire un ~ à Paris** I went to Paris
**(e)** look; **faire le ~ d'un problème** to have a look at a problem; **faire le ~ de ses relations** to go through one's acquaintances; **ce roman, on en a vite fait le ~** (colloq) there's not much to this novel
**(f)** (gen) turn; (in competition) round; **à qui le ~?** whose turn is it?; **chacun son ~** each one in his turn; **il perd plus souvent qu'à son ~** he loses more often than he would like; he loses more often than he should; **~ à ~** by turns; in turn
**(g) ~ de scrutin** ballot, round of voting
**(h)** trick; **jouer un ~ à qn** to play a trick on sb; **ça te jouera des ~s** it's going to get you into trouble one of these days
**(i)** trick; **~ de cartes** card trick; **~ d'adresse** feat of skill
**(j)** (in situation) turn; **donner un ~ nouveau à qch** to give a new twist to sth
**(k)** (Tech) lathe
■ **~ de chant** song recital; **~ de garde** turn of duty; **~ de potier** potter's wheel; **~ de rein(s)** back strain

**tour²** /tuʀ/ *nf* **(a)** tower
**(b)** tower block (GB), high rise (US)
**(c)** (in chess) rook, castle
**(d)** siege-tower

**tourbe** /tuʀb/ *nf* peat

**tourbière** /tuʀbjɛʀ/ *nf* peat bog

**tourbillon** /tuʀbijɔ̃/ *nm* **(a)** whirlwind; whirlpool; **~ de poussière** whirl of dust
**(b)** (of memories) swirl; (of reforms) whirlwind

**tourbillonner** /tuʀbijɔne/ [1] *vi* ⟨*snow, leaves*⟩ to swirl, to whirl; ⟨*dancers*⟩ to twirl

**tourelle** /tuʀɛl/ *nf* (of building, tank) turret; (of submarine) conning tower

**tourisme** /tuʀism/ *nm* tourism

■ **~ vert** countryside holidays

**touriste** /tuʀist/ *nmf* tourist

**touristique** /tuʀistik/ *adj* ⟨*brochure, menu, season*⟩ tourist; ⟨*influx*⟩ of tourists; ⟨*town, area*⟩ which attracts tourists

**tourment** /tuʀmɑ̃/ *nm* torment

**tourmente** /tuʀmɑ̃t/ *nf* **(a)** storm
**(b)** turmoil

**tourmenté, ~e** /tuʀmɑ̃te/ *adj* ⟨*person, face*⟩ tormented; ⟨*soul*⟩ tortured
**(b)** ⟨*era, life*⟩ turbulent
**(c)** ⟨*landscape*⟩ rugged

**tourmenter** /tuʀmɑ̃te/ [1] **1** *vtr* **(a)** to worry
**(b)** to torment
**(c)** ⟨*creditors*⟩ to harass
**2 se tourmenter** *v refl* (+ *v être*) to worry

**tournage** /tuʀnaʒ/ *nm* **(a)** shooting, filming
**(b)** film set

**tournant, ~e** /tuʀnɑ̃, ɑ̃t/ **1** *adj* **(a)** ⟨*seat*⟩ swivel; ⟨*sprinkler*⟩ rotating; ⟨*door*⟩ revolving
**(b)** ⟨*presidency*⟩ rotating; ⟨*strike*⟩ staggered
**2** *nm* **(a)** (in road) bend
**(b)** turning point
**(c)** turn; **au ~ du siècle** at the turn of the century
**(d)** change of direction

**tourné, ~e¹** /tuʀne/ *adj* **(a)** **~ vers** ⟨*eyes, look, person*⟩ turned toward(s); ⟨*activity, policy*⟩ oriented toward(s); **~ vers le passé/ l'avenir** backward-/forward-looking; **porte ~e vers la mer** gate facing the sea
**(b)** **bien ~** ⟨*compliment, letter*⟩ nicely phrased
**(c)** ⟨*milk*⟩ off

**tourne-disque**, *pl* **~s** /tuʀnədisk/ *nm* record player

**tournée²** /tuʀne/ *nf* **(a)** (of postman) round
**(b)** (of team, singer) tour
**(c)** (colloq) (of drinks) round

**tournemain: en un tournemain** /ɑ̃nœ̃tuʀnəmɛ̃/ *phr* in no time

**tourner** /tuʀne/ [1] **1** *vtr* **(a)** to turn; **~ la tête vers** to turn to look at; **~ les yeux vers** to look at
**(b)** to shoot ⟨*film*⟩
**(c)** to get around ⟨*difficulty, law*⟩
**(d)** to phrase ⟨*letter, criticism*⟩
**(e)** **~ qn/qch en dérision** to deride sb/sth
**(f)** **~ et retourner qch dans son esprit** to mull sth over
**(g)** to stir ⟨*sauce*⟩; to toss ⟨*salad*⟩
**2** *vi* **(a)** (gen) to turn; ⟨*planet*⟩ to rotate; ⟨*rotating door*⟩ to revolve; ⟨*dancer*⟩ to spin; **faire ~** to turn; to spin; **faire ~ les tables** (in spiritualism) to do table-turning
**(b)** **~ autour de** (gen) to turn around; ⟨*planet*⟩ to revolve around; ⟨*plane*⟩ to circle
**(c)** **~ (en rond)** ⟨*person*⟩ to go round and round; ⟨*driver*⟩ to drive round and round; **~ en rond** (figurative) ⟨*discussion*⟩ to go round in circles

(d) ~ **autour de** ⟨*sum of money*⟩ to be (somewhere) in the region of
(e) ⟨*engine, factory*⟩ to run; ~ **rond** ⟨*engine*⟩ to run smoothly; ⟨*business*⟩ to be doing well; **faire** ~ to run ⟨*business, company*⟩; **mon frère ne tourne pas rond depuis quelque temps** (colloq) my brother has been acting strangely for some time
(f) **les choses ont bien/mal tourné pour lui** things turned out well/badly for him
(g) ⟨*director*⟩ to shoot; ~ **(dans un film)** ⟨*actor*⟩ to make a film (GB) *or* movie (US)
(h) ⟨*milk, meat*⟩ to go off
(i) ~ **autour de qn** to hang around sb
**3** **se tourner** *v refl* (+ *v être*) (a) **se** ~ **vers qn/qch** to turn to sb/sth
(b) **se** ~ **vers qn/qch** to turn toward(s) sb/sth
(c) to turn around

**tournesol** /tuʀnəsɔl/ *nm* sunflower
**tournevis** /tuʀnəvis/ *nm inv* screwdriver
**tourniquet** /tuʀnikɛ/ *nm* (a) turnstile
(b) revolving stand
(c) sprinkler
**tournoi** /tuʀnwa/ *nm* tournament
**tournoyer** /tuʀnwaje/ [23] *vi* (a) ⟨*leaves, papers*⟩ to swirl around; ⟨*vultures*⟩ to wheel; ⟨*flies*⟩ to fly around in circles
(b) ⟨*dancers*⟩ to whirl; **faire** ~ to twirl ⟨*stick, skirt*⟩
**tournure** /tuʀnyʀ/ *nf* (a) turn; **prendre** ~ ⟨*plan*⟩ to take shape
(b) ~ **(de phrase)** turn of phrase
■ ~ **d'esprit** frame of mind
**tourte** /tuʀt/ *nf* pie; ~ **à la viande** meat pie
**tourteau**, *pl* ~**x** /tuʀto/ *nm* (Culin, Zool) crab
**tourtereau**, *pl* ~**x** /tuʀtəʀo/ **1** *nm* (Zool) young turtle dove
**2** **tourtereaux** *nm pl* (humorous) lovebirds
**tourterelle** /tuʀtəʀɛl/ *nf* turtle dove
**tous** ▶ TOUT
**Toussaint** /tusɛ̃/ *nf* **la** ~ All Saints' Day
**tousser** /tuse/ [1] *vi* ⟨*person*⟩ to cough
**toussotement** /tusɔtmɑ̃/ *nm* cough; splutter
**toussoter** /tusɔte/ [1] *vi* ⟨*person*⟩ to have a slight cough; ⟨*engine*⟩ to splutter
**tout** /tu/, ~**e** /tut/, *mpl* **tous** /tu *adj*, tus *pron*/, *fpl* **toutes** /tut/

■ **Note** You will find translations for expressions such as *à tout hasard, tout compte fait, tout neuf* etc, at the entries HASARD, COMPTE, NEUF etc.

**1** *pron* (a) **tout** everything; all; anything; ~ **est prétexte à querelle(s)** any pretext will do to start a quarrel; ~ **n'est pas perdu** all is not lost; **en** ~ in all; in every respect; **en** ~ **et pour** ~ all told; ~ **bien compté** *or* **pesé** *or* **considéré** all in all
(b) **tous** /tus/, **toutes** all; all of them/us/you; **tous ensemble** all together; **est-ce que ça conviendra à tous?** will it suit everybody?
**2** *adj* (a) **bois** ~ **ton lait** drink all your

milk; ~ **le reste** everything else; ~ **le monde** everybody; **manger** ~ **un pain** to eat a whole loaf; **il a plu** ~**e la journée** it rained all day (long)
(b) **c'est** ~ **un travail** it's quite a job
(c) all; everything; anything; ~ **ce qui compte** all that matters; ~ **ce qu'il dit n'est pas vrai** not all of what he says is true; **être** ~ **ce qu'il y a de plus serviable** to be most obliging
(d) any; **à** ~ **moment** at any time; constantly; ~ **autre que lui/toi aurait abandonné** anybody else would have given up
(e) **en** ~**e franchise** in all honesty; **il aurait** ~ **intérêt à placer cet argent** it would be in his best interests to invest this money
(f) **il a souri pour** ~**e réponse** his only reply was a smile
(g) **tous, toutes** all, every; **j'ai** ~**es les raisons de me plaindre** I have every reason to complain; **nous irons tous les deux** we'll both go; **je les prends tous les trois** I'm taking all three
(h) **tous/toutes les** every; **tous les deux jours** every other day; **tous les combien?** how often?
**3** *adv* (a) very, quite; all; **être** ~ **étonné** to be very surprised; ~ **seul** all by oneself; ~ **en haut** right at the top; **la colline est** ~ **en fleurs** the hill is a mass of flowers; **veste** ~ **cuir** all leather jacket
(b) ~ **prêt** ready-made
(c) while; although; **il lisait** ~ **en marchant** he was reading as he walked; **elle le défendait** ~ **en le sachant coupable** she defended him although she knew he was guilty
(d) ~ **malin/roi qu'il est, il...** he may be clever/a king, but he...
**4** **du tout** *phr* (*pas*) **du** ~ not at all
**5** *nm* (*pl* ~**s**) whole; the (whole) lot; the main thing; **former un** ~ to make up *or* form a whole
**6** **Tout-** (*combining form*) **le Tout-Paris/-Londres** the Paris/London smart set
■ ~ **à coup** suddenly; ~ **d'un coup** suddenly; all at once; ~ **à fait** quite, absolutely; ~ **à l'heure** in a moment; a little while ago, just now; **à** ~ **à l'heure!** see you later!; ~ **de même** all the same, even so; ~ **de même!** really!; ~ **de suite** at once
IDIOMS **être** ~ **yeux** ~ **oreilles** to be very attentive

**tout-à-l'égout** /tutalegu/ *nm inv* main drainage, main sewer
**toutefois** /tutfwa/ *adv* however
**toute-puissance** /tutpɥisɑ̃s/ *nf* omnipotence; supremacy
**toutou** /tutu/ *nm* (colloq) doggie (colloq), dog
**tout-petit**, *pl* ~**s** /tup(ə)ti/ *nm* (a) baby
(b) toddler
**Tout-Puissant** /tupɥisɑ̃/ *nm* **le** ~ the Almighty, God Almighty
**tout-venant** /tuv(ə)nɑ̃/ *nm inv* all and sundry

**toux** /tu/ *nf inv* cough

**toxicité** /tɔksisite/ *nf* toxicity

**toxicodépendance** /tɔksikodepɑ̃dɑ̃s/ *nf* drug dependency

**toxicologie** /tɔksikɔlɔʒi/ *nf* toxicology

**toxicomane** /tɔksikɔman/ *nmf* drug addict

**toxicomanie** /tɔksikɔmani/ *nf* drug addiction

**toxine** /tɔksin/ *nf* toxin

**toxique** /tɔksik/ *adj* toxic, poisonous

**TP** /tepe/ *nm pl: abbr* ▶ TRAVAIL

**trac** /tʀak/ *nm* (colloq) (of actor) stage fright; (before exam, conference) nerves; **avoir le ~** (gen) to feel nervous; ‹*actor, performer*› to have stage fright

**traçage** /tʀasaʒ/ *nm* (a) marking out; laying-out
(b) (Comput) tracing

**tracas** /tʀaka/ *nm inv* (a) trouble
(b) problems; **~ quotidiens** everyday problems
(c) worries; **se faire du ~ pour qn/qch** to worry about sb/sth

**tracasser** /tʀakase/ [1] **1** *vtr* to bother ‹*person*›
**2 se tracasser** *v refl* (+ *v être*) to worry

**tracasserie** /tʀakasʀi/ *nf* (a) hassle (colloq)
(b) harassment

**trace** /tʀas/ *nf* (a) trail; **suivre qn à la ~** to track sb; (figurative) to follow sb's trail
(b) **~s** tracks; **~s d'ours/de ski** bear's/ski tracks; **~s de pas** footprints; **sur les ~s de Van Gogh** in the footsteps of Van Gogh
(c) (of burn) mark; (of wound) scar; (of paint) mark; (of blood, dampness) trace; **~s de doigts** fingermarks; **~s de coups** bruises
(d) (of activity) sign; (of presence) trace; **des ~s d'effraction** signs of a break-in

**tracé** /tʀase/ *nm* (a) (of town) layout; (of road) plan
(b) (of road, railway) route; (of river) course; (of border, coast) line
(c) (on graph, in sketch) line

**tracer** /tʀase/ [12] *vtr* (a) to draw ‹*line, map, portrait*›; (on graph) to plot ‹*curve*›; to write ‹*word, letters*›
(b) **à 15 ans son avenir était déjà tout tracé** at 15, his/her future was already mapped out
(c) **~ le chemin à qn** (figurative) to show sb the way

**trachée** /tʀaʃe/ *nf* windpipe

**trachée-artère**, *pl* **trachées-artères** /tʀaʃeaʀtɛʀ/ *nf* windpipe, trachea

**trachéite** /tʀakeit/ *nf* tracheitis

**tract** /tʀakt/ *nm* pamphlet, tract

**tractation** /tʀaktasjɔ̃/ *nf* negotiation

**tracter** /tʀakte/ [1] *vtr* ‹*vehicle*› to tow ‹*trailer*›; ‹*cable*› to pull up ‹*cable car*›

**tracteur** /tʀaktœʀ/ *nm* tractor

**traction** /tʀaksjɔ̃/ *nf* (a) traction; **à ~ mécanique** mechanically drawn
(b) (Tech) tension

■ **~ arrière** (Aut) rear-wheel drive; **~ avant** (Aut) front-wheel drive

**tradition** /tʀadisjɔ̃/ *nf* (a) tradition
(b) legend; **la ~ veut que…** legend has it that…

**traditionaliste** /tʀadisjɔnalist/ *adj, nmf* traditionalist

**traditionnel, -elle** /tʀadisjɔnɛl/ *adj* traditional

**traducteur, -trice** /tʀadyktœʀ, tʀis/ *nm,f* translator

**traduction** /tʀadyksjɔ̃/ *nf* translation; **faire des ~s** to do translation work

**traduire** /tʀadɥiʀ/ [69] **1** *vtr* (a) to translate
(b) ‹*word, artist, book*› to convey; ‹*rebellion, violence*› to be the expression of; ‹*price rise*› to be the result of
(c) (Law) **~ qn en justice** to bring sb to justice
**2 se traduire** *v refl* (+ *v être*) (a) ‹*joy, fear*› to show
(b) ‹*crisis, instability*› to result; **se ~ par un échec** to result in failure

**traduisible** /tʀadɥizibl/ *adj* translatable

**trafic** /tʀafik/ *nm* (a) traffic; **~ d'armes** arms dealing; **~ de drogue** drug trafficking
(b) **~ (routier)** (road) traffic; **~ aérien** air traffic

**trafiquant, -e** /tʀafikɑ̃, ɑ̃t/ *nm,f* trafficker, dealer; **~ de drogue** drugs dealer

**trafiquer** /tʀafike/ [1] *vtr* (a) to fiddle with ‹*car, meter*›
(b) (colloq) **je me demande ce qu'il trafique** I wonder what he's up to

**tragédie** /tʀaʒedi/ *nf* tragedy

**tragédien, -ienne** /tʀaʒedjɛ̃, ɛn/ *nm,f* tragic actor

**tragique** /tʀaʒik/ **1** *adj* tragic
**2** *nm* tragedy

**trahir** /tʀaiʀ/ [3] **1** *vtr* (a) to betray; to break ‹*promise*›
(b) ‹*writing, words*› to betray ‹*thoughts*›
(c) ‹*translator, words*› to misrepresent
(d) ‹*strength, legs*› to fail ‹*person*›
**2 se trahir** *v refl* (+ *v être*) to give oneself away, to betray oneself

**trahison** /tʀaizɔ̃/ *nf* (a) treachery; **~ de qn/qch** betrayal of sb/sth
(b) treason

**train** /tʀɛ̃/ **1** *nm* (a) train; **par le** *or* **en ~** ‹*travel*› by train
(b) (convoy) train; **~ de péniches** train of barges
(c) series (**de** of)
(d) pace; **aller bon ~** to walk briskly; **aller bon ~** ‹*rumours*› to be flying around; ‹*sales*› to be going well; ‹*conversation*› to flow easily; **au ~ où vont les choses** (at) the rate things are going; **à fond de ~** (colloq) at top speed
(e) (Zool) **~ de derrière** hindquarters; **~ de devant** forequarter
**2 en train** *phr* (a) **être en ~** to be full of energy

**(b) mettre en ∼** to get [sth] started ⟨*process*⟩
**(c) être en ∼ de faire** to be (busy) doing;
**j'étais en ∼ de dormir** I was sleeping
■ **∼ d'atterrissage** undercarriage; **∼ électrique**
(toy) train set; **∼ de vie** lifestyle

**traînant**, **∼e** /tʀɛnɑ̃, ɑ̃t/ *adj* shuffling;
**voix ∼e** drawl

**traînard**, **∼e** /tʀɛnaʀ, aʀd/ *nm,f* (colloq)
slowcoach, slowpoke; straggler

**traînasser** (colloq) /tʀɛnase/ [1] *vi* **(a)** to
loaf about (colloq)
**(b)** to take ages

**traîne** /tʀɛn/ *nf* **(a)** (of dress) train
**(b)** seine (net)
IDIOMS **être à la ∼** to lag behind

**traîneau**, *pl* **∼x** /tʀɛno/ *nm* **(a)** sleigh
**(b)** (of vacuum cleaner) cylinder

**traînée** /tʀɛne/ *nf* **(a)** streak; **∼ de sang**
streak of blood
**(b)** trail

**traîner** /tʀɛne/ [1] **1** *vtr* **(a)** to drag [sb/
sth] (along) ⟨*person, suitcase*⟩; to drag [sth]
across the floor ⟨*chair*⟩
**(b)** (colloq) to lug [sth] around (colloq) ⟨*object*⟩;
to drag [sth] around ⟨*object*⟩
**(c) ∼ qn chez le médecin** to drag sb off to
the doctor's
**(d) il traîne un rhume depuis deux semaines**
for two weeks now he's had a cold that he
can't shake off; **∼ les pieds** to drag one's
feet
**2** *vi* **(a) ∼ dans les rues** to hang around on
the streets; **j'ai traîné au lit** I slept in
**(b)** to take forever; **ne traîne pas, on doit
terminer à 4 heures** get a move on (colloq),
we've got to finish at four
**(c)** to dawdle
**(d)** ⟨*building work, illness*⟩ to drag on
**(e) ∼ par terre** ⟨*skirt*⟩ to trail on the ground;
⟨*curtains*⟩ to trail on the floor
**(f) ∼ derrière qch** to be trailing behind sth
**(g)** ⟨*clothes, toys*⟩ to be lying about *or*
around; **laisser ∼ qch** to leave sth lying
about *or* around ⟨*chequebook*⟩
**3** **se traîner** *v refl* (+ *v être*) **(a)** ⟨*injured
person*⟩ **se ∼ par terre** to drag oneself along
the ground
**(b) se ∼ jusqu'à la cuisine** to drag oneself
through to the kitchen
**(c)** ⟨*train*⟩ to crawl along; ⟨*negotiations*⟩ to
drag on
IDIOMS **∼ la jambe** *or* **la patte** (colloq) to
limp; **∼ ses guêtres** (colloq) *or* **ses bottes**
(colloq) to knock around (colloq)

**train(-)train** /tʀɛ̃tʀɛ̃/ *nm inv* (derogatory)
(colloq) daily routine

**traire** /tʀɛʀ/ [58] *vtr* to milk ⟨*cow, goat*⟩

**trait¹**, **∼e** /tʀɛ, ɛt/ ▶ TRAIRE

**trait²** /tʀɛ/ **1** *nm* **(a)** line; stroke; **souligner
un mot d'un ∼ rouge** to underline a word in
red; **∼ pour ∼** ⟨*replica*⟩ line for line;
⟨*reproduce*⟩ line by line
**(b)** (of style, book) feature; (of person) trait;
**∼ caractéristique** characteristic; **∼ de
caractère** trait, characteristic

**(c) ∼ d'humour** *or* **d'esprit** witticism; **∼ de
génie** stroke of genius
**(d) avoir ∼ à** to relate to
**(e) d'un (seul) ∼** (gen) at one go
**(f) de ∼** ⟨*animal*⟩ draught (GB) *or* draft (US)
**2** **traits** *nm pl* features
■ **∼ d'union** hyphen; (figurative) link
IDIOMS **tirer un ∼ sur qch** to put sth firmly
behind one

**traitant** /tʀɛtɑ̃/ *adj m* **médecin ∼** doctor,
GP

**traite** /tʀɛt/ **1** *nf* **(a)** (Econ) draft, bill
**(b) la ∼ des Blanches** the white slave trade
**(c)** milking; **la ∼ des vaches** milking cows
**2** **d'une traite** *phr* **d'une ∼**
⟨*recite*⟩ in one breath; ⟨*drink*⟩ in one go

**traité** /tʀɛte/ *nm* **(a)** (Law) treaty;
**∼ commercial** trade agreement
**(b)** treatise

**traitement** /tʀɛtmɑ̃/ *nm* **(a)** (Med)
treatment
**(b)** salary
**(c)** handling; **il faut accélérer le ∼ des
demandes** applications must be dealt with
more quickly
**(d)** (of data) processing
**(e)** (Tech) (of water, waste) processing; (of wood)
treatment
■ **∼ de faveur** preferential treatment; **∼ de
texte** word-processing (package)

**traiter** /tʀɛte/ [1] **1** *vtr* **(a)** to treat
⟨*person, animal, object*⟩
**(b)** (Med) to treat ⟨*sick person, infection*⟩
**(c)** to deal with ⟨*question, problem*⟩
**(d)** to treat ⟨*wood, textile*⟩; to process ⟨*waste*⟩
**(e)** to process ⟨*data*⟩
**(f) ∼ qn de qch** to call sb sth
**2** **traiter de** *v+prep* to deal with
**3** *vi* to negotiate, to do (GB) *or* make a deal
**4** **se traiter** *v refl* (+ *v être*) **ils se sont
traités de tous les noms** they called each
other all sorts of names

**traiteur** /tʀɛtœʀ/ *nm* caterer

**traître**, **traîtresse** /tʀɛtʀ, tʀɛtʀɛs/ *nm,f*
traitor; **en ∼** by surprise

**traîtrise** /tʀɛtʀiz/ *nf* **(a)** act of treachery
**(b)** (of person) treachery

**trajectoire** /tʀaʒɛktwaʀ/ *nf* **(a)** (of bullet,
missile) trajectory
**(b)** (of planet, satellite) path
**(c)** career

**trajet** /tʀaʒɛ/ *nm* **(a)** journey, trip; (by sea)
crossing
**(b)** route

**trame** /tʀam/ *nf* **(a)** (of fabric) weft
**(b)** (of story) framework

**tramer**: **se tramer** /tʀame/ [1] *v refl*
(+ *v être*) ⟨*plot*⟩ to be hatched

**trampoline** /tʀɑ̃pɔlin/ *nm* trampoline

**tramway** /tʀamwɛ/ *nm* **(a)** tram (GB),
streetcar (US)
**(b)** tramway (GB), streetcar line (US)

**tranchant**, **∼e** /tʀɑ̃ʃɑ̃, ɑ̃t/ **1** *adj*
**(a)** sharp
**(b)** ⟨*person*⟩ forthright; ⟨*tone*⟩ curt

2 *nm* (of blade) sharp edge, cutting edge

**tranche** /tʀɑ̃ʃ/ *nf* **(a)** (of bread, meat, cheese) slice; (of lard, bacon) rasher
**(b)** (of operation) phase; (in timetable) period, time slot
**(c)** (of book, coin) edge
■ ~ **d'âge** age bracket

**tranché, ~e¹** /tʀɑ̃ʃe/ 1 *pp* ▶ TRANCHER
2 *pp adj* ⟨salmon⟩ pre-sliced
3 *adj* **(a)** ⟨opinion, position, reply⟩ cut-and-dried; ⟨inequalities⟩ marked
**(b)** ⟨colours⟩ bold

**tranchée²** /tʀɑ̃ʃe/ *nf* **(a)** (Mil) trench
**(b)** (of road) cutting

**trancher** /tʀɑ̃ʃe/ [1] 1 *vtr* to slice, to cut ⟨bread, meat⟩; to cut through ⟨rope⟩; to cut [sth] off ⟨head⟩; to slit ⟨throat⟩
2 *vi* **(a)** ⟨colour, outline⟩ to stand out
**(b)** to come to a decision

**tranquille** /tʀɑ̃kil/ *adj* **(a)** quiet; calm; peaceful; **tiens-toi ~!** keep still!; be quiet!; **il s'est tenu ~ pendant quelques mois** he behaved himself for a few months
**(b)** **être ~** to be or feel easy in one's mind; **sa mère n'est pas ~ quand il sort** his mother worries when he goes out
**(c)** **avoir la conscience ~** to have a clear conscience

**tranquillement** /tʀɑ̃kilmɑ̃/ *adv* **(a)** **elle dort ~** she's sleeping peacefully; **j'aimerais pouvoir travailler ~** I wish I could work in peace
**(b)** quietly
**(c)** **nous avons marché ~** we walked along at a leisurely pace
**(d)** **nous étions ~ en train de discuter** we were chatting away happily

**tranquillisant, ~e** /tʀɑ̃kilizɑ̃, ɑ̃t/ 1 *adj* reassuring, comforting
2 *nm* tranquillizer (GB)

**tranquilliser** /tʀɑ̃kilize/ [1] *vtr* to reassure

**tranquillité** /tʀɑ̃kilite/ *nf* **(a)** calmness; calm
**(b)** ~ **(d'esprit)** peace of mind

**transaction** /tʀɑ̃zaksjɔ̃/ *nf* transaction

**transalpin, ~e** /tʀɑ̃zalpɛ̃, in/ *adj*
**(a)** transalpine
**(b)** Italian

**transat¹** /tʀɑ̃zat/ *nm* (colloq) **(a)** deckchair
**(b)** baby chair

**transat²** /tʀɑ̃zat/ *nf* (Sport) transatlantic race

**transatlantique** /tʀɑ̃zatlɑ̃tik/ *adj* transatlantic

**transborder** /tʀɑ̃sbɔʀde/ [1] *vtr* to transship ⟨goods⟩; to transfer ⟨passengers⟩

**transbordeur** /tʀɑ̃sbɔʀdœʀ/ *nm*
**(a)** transporter bridge
**(b)** traverser
**(c)** ferry

**transcendant, ~e** /tʀɑ̃sɑ̃dɑ̃, ɑ̃t/ *adj*
**(a)** (in philosophy) transcendent
**(b)** (colloq) wonderful

**transcender** /tʀɑ̃sɑ̃de/ [1] *vtr* to transcend

**transcription** /tʀɑ̃skʀipsjɔ̃/ *nf* transcription

**transcrire** /tʀɑ̃skʀiʀ/ [67] *vtr* to transcribe

**transe** /tʀɑ̃s/ *nf* trance

**transférer** /tʀɑ̃sfeʀe/ [14] *vtr* **(a)** (gen) to transfer; to relocate ⟨offices⟩
**(b)** (Law) to transfer, to convey ⟨property⟩

**transfert** /tʀɑ̃sfɛʀ/ *nm* **(a)** (of person, data, money, property) transfer; (of offices) relocation
**(b)** (psychological) transference

**transfigurer** /tʀɑ̃sfigyʀe/ [1] *vtr* to transform

**transformable** /tʀɑ̃sfɔʀmabl/ *adj* convertible

**transformateur** /tʀɑ̃sfɔʀmatœʀ/ *nm* transformer

**transformation** /tʀɑ̃sfɔʀmasjɔ̃/ *nf* transformation; (of mineral, energy) conversion

**transformer** /tʀɑ̃sfɔʀme/ [1] 1 *vtr* **(a)** to alter ⟨garment, façade⟩; to change ⟨person, landscape⟩
**(b)** ~ **qn/qch en** (gen) to turn sb/sth into; to transform sb/sth into; ~ **un garage en bureau** to convert a garage into an office
2 **se transformer** *v refl* (+ *v être*)
**(a)** ⟨person⟩ to transform oneself; to be transformed
**(b)** **se ~ en** ⟨embryo, larva, bud⟩ to turn into

**transfrontalier, -ière** /tʀɑ̃sfʀɔ̃talje, ɛʀ/ *adj* cross-border

**transfuge** /tʀɑ̃sfyʒ/ 1 *nmf* defector
2 *nm* (Mil) deserter

**transfusé, ~e** /tʀɑ̃sfyze/ 1 *pp* ▶ TRANSFUSER
2 *pp adj* ⟨blood⟩ transfused; ⟨person⟩ who has been given a blood transfusion

**transfuser** /tʀɑ̃sfyze/ [1] *vtr* to give a blood transfusion to

**transfusion** /tʀɑ̃sfyzjɔ̃/ *nf* transfusion

**transgresser** /tʀɑ̃sgʀese/ [1] *vtr* to break ⟨law, rule, taboo⟩; to defy ⟨ban⟩

**transhumance** /tʀɑ̃zymɑ̃s/ *nf* transhumance, seasonal migration of livestock to summer pastures

**transi, ~e** /tʀɑ̃zi/ 1 *pp* ▶ TRANSIR
2 *pp adj* chilled; ~ **de peur** paralysed (GB) with fear; **un amoureux ~** a bashful lover

**transiger** /tʀɑ̃ziʒe/ [13] *vi* to compromise

**transir** /tʀɑ̃ziʀ/ [3] *vtr* to chill; to paralyse

**transistor** /tʀɑ̃zistɔʀ/ *nm* transistor

**transit** /tʀɑ̃zit/ *nm* transit; **en ~** in transit

**transitaire** /tʀɑ̃zitɛʀ/ 1 *adj* transit; **pays ~** transit point
2 *nmf* forwarding agent

**transiter** /tʀɑ̃zite/ [1] *vi* ~ **par** ⟨goods, passengers⟩ to pass through, to go via

**transitif, -ive** /tʀɑ̃zitif, iv/ *adj* transitive

**transition** /tʀɑ̃zisjɔ̃/ *nf* transition

**transitoire** /tʀɑ̃zitwaʀ/ *adj* transitional

**translucide** /tʀɑ̃slysid/ *adj* translucent

**transmanche** /tʀɑ̃smɑ̃ʃ/ *adj inv* cross-Channel

**transmetteur** /tʀɑ̃smɛtœʀ/ *nm* transmitter

**transmettre** /tʀɑ̃smɛtʀ/ [60] **1** *vtr* **(a)** to pass [sth] on, to convey ⟨*information, order, news*⟩; to pass [sth] on ⟨*story, knowledge*⟩; to pass [sth] down ⟨*culture, fortune*⟩; **transmettez-leur mes félicitations** give them my congratulations
**(b)** to transmit ⟨*image, signal, data*⟩
**(c)** to broadcast ⟨*news, programme*⟩
**(d)** to hand [sth] on ⟨*property, land*⟩; to hand over ⟨*power*⟩
**(e)** (Med) to transmit ⟨*virus, illness*⟩
**2 se transmettre** *v refl* (+ *v être*) **(a)** to pass [sth] on to each other ⟨*message, data*⟩
**(b)** ⟨*signals, data*⟩ to be transmitted
**(c)** ⟨*tradition, culture*⟩ to be handed down; ⟨*story*⟩ to be passed on
**(d)** ⟨*virus, illness*⟩ to be transmitted

**transmissible** /tʀɑ̃smisibl/ *adj* transmissible, transmittable

**transmission** /tʀɑ̃smisjɔ̃/ *nf*
**(a)** transmission, passing on; **la ~ des connaissances** the communication of knowledge
**(b)** (of data, signals) transmission
**(c)** (of programme) broadcasting
**(d)** (of tradition, secret, culture) handing down; (of fortune, property) transfer
**(e)** (Aut, Med) transmission
■ **~ de pensées** thought transference

**transparaître** /tʀɑ̃spaʀɛtʀ/ [73] *vi* to show through; **laisser ~** ⟨*face, words*⟩ to betray; ⟨*person*⟩ to let [sth] show ⟨*emotions*⟩

**transparence** /tʀɑ̃spaʀɑ̃s/ *nf* **(a)** (of glass, fabric) transparency; (of water) clearness; **on voyait ses jambes en ~ (à travers sa jupe)** you could see her legs through her skirt
**(b)** (of skin) translucency; (of colour) limpidity
**(c)** (of person) transparency; (of policy) openness

**transparent, ~e** /tʀɑ̃spaʀɑ̃, ɑ̃t/ **1** *adj*
**(a)** transparent; ⟨*water*⟩ clear
**(b)** ⟨*complexion*⟩ translucent
**(c)** ⟨*person*⟩ transparent
**2** *nm* (for overhead projector) transparency

**transpercer** /tʀɑ̃spɛʀse/ [12] *vtr*
**(a)** ⟨*sword, arrow*⟩ to pierce ⟨*body*⟩; ⟨*bullet*⟩ to go through
**(b)** ⟨*rain*⟩ to go through
**(c)** ⟨*pain*⟩ to shoot through

**transpiration** /tʀɑ̃spiʀasjɔ̃/ *nf*
**(a)** sweating, perspiration
**(b)** sweat
**(c)** (Bot) transpiration

**transpirer** /tʀɑ̃spiʀe/ [1] *vi* **(a)** to sweat, to perspire
**(b)** ⟨*secret*⟩ to leak out

**transplantation** /tʀɑ̃splɑ̃tasjɔ̃/ *nf*
**(a)** transplant; **~ d'organes** organ transplants
**(b)** transplantation

**transplanter** /tʀɑ̃splɑ̃te/ [1] *vtr* to transplant

**transport** /tʀɑ̃spɔʀ/ **1** *nm* transport, transportation (US)
**2 transports** *nm pl* **~s en commun** public transport *or* transportation (US)

**transportable** /tʀɑ̃spɔʀtabl/ *adj* transportable; **il n'est pas ~** (injured person) he cannot be moved

**transporter** /tʀɑ̃spɔʀte/ [1] *vtr* **(a)** to carry ⟨*person, object*⟩; to transport ⟨*passengers, goods*⟩; **être transporté à l'hôpital** to be taken to hospital
**(b)** to carry ⟨*pollen, virus, disease*⟩
**(c)** **être transporté dans un monde féerique** to be transported into a magical world

**transporteur** /tʀɑ̃spɔʀtœʀ/ *nm* carrier; **~ aérien** air carrier; **~ routier** road haulier (GB), road haulage contractor (GB), trucking company (US)

**transposer** /tʀɑ̃spoze/ [1] *vtr* to transpose

**transsexuel, -elle** /tʀɑ̃ssɛksɥɛl/ *adj, nm,f* transsexual

**transsibérien, -ienne** /tʀɑ̃ssibeʀjɛ̃, ɛn/ **1** *adj* trans-Siberian
**2** *nm* **le Transsibérien** the Trans-Siberian Railway

**transvaser** /tʀɑ̃svaze/ [1] *vtr* to decant ⟨*liquid*⟩

**transversal, ~e, mpl -aux** /tʀɑ̃svɛʀsal, o/ *adj* transverse; **rue ~e** side street

**trapèze** /tʀapɛz/ *nm* **(a)** (Sport) trapeze
**(b)** (in geometry) trapezium (GB), trapezoid (US)

**trapéziste** /tʀapezist/ *nmf* trapeze artist

**trappe** /tʀap/ *nf* (gen) trap door

**trappeur** /tʀapœʀ/ *nm* trapper

**trapu, ~e** /tʀapy/ *adj* ⟨*man, outline*⟩ stocky

**traquenard** /tʀaknaʀ/ *nm* trap

**traquer** /tʀake/ [1] *vtr* (gen) to track down; ⟨*photographer*⟩ to hound ⟨*film star*⟩

**traumatisant, ~e** /tʀomatizɑ̃, ɑ̃t/ *adj* traumatic

**traumatiser** /tʀomatize/ [1] *vtr* to traumatize

**traumatisme** /tʀomatism/ *nm* **(a)** (Med) traumatism
**(b)** (psychological) trauma

**travail, pl -aux** /tʀavaj, o/ **1** *nm* **(a)** (gen) work; job; **se mettre au ~** to get down to work; **avoir du ~** to have work to do; **les gros travaux** the heavy work; **(félicitations) c'est du beau ~!** you've done a great job on that!; **qu'est-ce que c'est que ce ~?** what do you call this?; **ne me téléphone pas à mon ~** don't call me at work; **chercher du/un ~** to look for work/a job; **être sans ~** to be out of work; **le ~ temporaire** temporary work; **le ~ de nuit** nightwork
**(b)** (Econ) labour (GB); **entrer dans le monde du ~** to enter the world of work
**(c)** **le ~ musculaire** muscular effort　　···⟩

(d) **le ~ de** working with *or* in ⟨*metal, wood, stone*⟩

(e) workmanship; **un ~ superbe** a superb piece of workmanship

(f) (of water, erosion) action

(g) (of wine) fermentation; (of wood) warping

(h) (of woman in childbirth) labour (GB)

**2 travaux** *nm pl* (a) (gen) work; (on road) roadworks (GB), roadwork (US); **faire faire des travaux dans sa maison** to have work done in one's house

(b) (of researcher) work

(c) (of commission) deliberations

(d) **les travaux agricoles** agricultural work; **travaux de couture** needlework

■ **~ à la chaîne** assembly-line work; **~ à domicile** working at *or* from home; **~ au noir** (gen) *work for which no earnings are declared*; (holding two jobs) moonlighting; **travaux manuels** handicrafts; **travaux pratiques, TP** practical work; lab work; **travaux publics, TP** civil engineering

**travaillé, ~e** /tʀavaje/ **1** *pp* ▶ TRAVAILLER

**2** *pp adj* ⟨*jewel*⟩ finely-worked; ⟨*carving*⟩ elaborate; ⟨*gold, silver*⟩ wrought; ⟨*style*⟩ polished

**travailler** /tʀavaje/ [1] **1** *vtr* (a) to work on ⟨*style, school subject, voice, muscles*⟩; to practise (GB) ⟨*sport, instrument*⟩

(b) to work ⟨*wood, metal*⟩; (Culin) to knead ⟨*dough*⟩; to cultivate ⟨*land*⟩

(c) **~ qn** ⟨*idea, affair*⟩ to be on sb's mind; ⟨*jealousy, pain*⟩ to plague sb; **un doute me travaillait** I had a nagging doubt

**2 travailler à** *v+prep* to work on ⟨*project, essay*⟩; to work toward(s) ⟨*objective*⟩

**3** *vi* (a) ⟨*person, machine, muscles*⟩ to work; **faire ~ son cerveau** to apply one's mind; **~ en équipes** to work shifts

(b) ⟨*shop, hotel, shopkeeper*⟩ to do business; **~ à perte** ⟨*company, business*⟩ to run at a loss

(c) **nous voulons la paix et c'est dans ce sens que nous travaillons** we want peace and we are working toward(s) it

(d) ⟨*athlete*⟩ to train; ⟨*musician*⟩ to practise (GB)

(e) ⟨*wood*⟩ to warp

**travailleur, -euse** /tʀavajœʀ, øz/ **1** *adj*

(a) ⟨*pupil*⟩ hardworking

(b) ⟨*classes*⟩ working

**2** *nm,f* worker

**travailliste** /tʀavajist/ **1** *adj* Labour

**2** *nmf* Labour MP

**travée** /tʀave/ *nf* (a) row

(b) (Tech) span

**travelling** /tʀavliŋ/ *nm* (in cinema) tracking; tracking shot

**travers** /tʀavɛʀ/ **1** *nm inv* (a) foible, quirk

(b) (Naut) beam

(c) (Culin) **~ de porc** sparerib

**2 à travers** *phr* (a) ⟨*see, look*⟩ through

(b) ⟨*walk*⟩ across; **voyager à ~ le monde** to travel all over the world

(c) **voyager à ~ le temps** to travel through time

(d) through; **à ~ ces informations** through this information

**3 au travers** *phr* through; **passer au ~ de** (figurative) to escape ⟨*inspection*⟩

**4 de travers** *phr* (a) askew; **ta veste est boutonnée de ~** your jacket is buttoned up wrongly; **il a le nez de ~** he has a twisted nose; **j'ai avalé de ~** it went down the wrong way; **regarder qn de ~** to give sb filthy looks

(b) wrong; **comprendre de ~** to misunderstand

**5 en travers** *phr* across; **un bus était en ~ de la route** a bus was stuck across the road; **se mettre en ~ de la route** ⟨*people*⟩ to stand in the middle of the road; **rester en ~ de la gorge de qn** (colloq) to be hard to swallow

**traverse** /tʀavɛʀs/ *nf* (on railway line) sleeper (GB), tie (US)

**traversée** /tʀavɛʀse/ *nf* (a) crossing; **la ~ du désert** crossing the desert; (figurative) (of company) a difficult period

(b) (of city) **évitez la ~ de Paris** avoid going through Paris

**traverser** /tʀavɛʀse/ [1] *vtr* (a) to cross ⟨*road, bridge, border, town, ocean, room*⟩; to go through ⟨*town, forest, tunnel*⟩; to make one's way through ⟨*group, crowd*⟩; **il traversa le jardin en courant** he ran across the garden (GB) *or* yard (US)

(b) ⟨*river*⟩ to run through ⟨*region*⟩; ⟨*road*⟩ to go through ⟨*region*⟩; ⟨*bridge, river*⟩ to cross ⟨*railway line, town*⟩

(c) ⟨*rain*⟩ to soak through ⟨*clothes*⟩; **la balle lui a traversé le bras** the bullet went right through his/her arm

(d) to go through ⟨*crisis*⟩; to live through ⟨*war*⟩

(e) **~ l'esprit de qn** to cross sb's mind

**traversin** /tʀavɛʀsɛ̃/ *nm* bolster

**travesti, ~e** /tʀavɛsti/ **1** *pp* ▶ TRAVESTIR

**2** *pp adj* in disguise; **rôle ~** role played by a member of the opposite sex

**3** *nm* (a) transvestite

(b) (actor) actor playing a female role; (in cabaret) drag artist (colloq)

**travestir** /tʀavɛstiʀ/ [3] **1** *vtr* (a) to dress [sb] up ⟨*person*⟩

(b) to distort ⟨*truth*⟩

**2 se travestir** *v refl* (+ *v être*) (a) to dress up

(b) to cross-dress

**trébucher** /tʀebyʃe/ [1] *vi* to stumble

**trèfle** /tʀɛfl/ *nm* (a) clover

(b) (Games) (card) club; (suit) clubs

(c) shamrock

**tréfonds** /tʀefɔ̃/ *nm inv* **le ~ de** the very depths of

**treillage** /tʀɛjaʒ/ *nm* (a) trellis

(b) lattice fence

**treille** /tʀɛj/ *nf* (a) (vine) arbour (GB)

(b) climbing vine

**treillis** /tʀeji/ *nm inv* (a) (Mil) fatigues

**(b)** canvas
**(c)** trellis; ~ **métallique** wire grille
**treize** /tʀɛz/ *adj inv, pron, nm inv* thirteen
**treizième** /tʀɛzjɛm/ *adj* thirteenth
**tréma** /tʀema/ *nm* diaeresis; **i ~ i** diaeresis
**tremblant, ~e** /tʀɑ̃blɑ̃, ɑ̃t/ *adj*
**(a)** ‹person, hands› shaking
**(b)** ‹voice› trembling
**(c)** ‹image, light› flickering; ‹sound› tremulous
**tremble** /tʀɑ̃bl/ *nm* aspen
**tremblement** /tʀɑ̃bləmɑ̃/ *nm* **(a)** (of person, hands) shaking, trembling; (of lips) trembling
**(b)** (of voice) trembling
**(c)** (of leaves) quivering
■ ~ **de terre** earthquake
**trembler** /tʀɑ̃ble/ [1] *vi* **(a)** ‹person, legs› to shake, to tremble
**(b)** ‹voice› to tremble; ‹sound, note› to waver
**(c)** ‹building, floor› to shake
**(d)** (be afraid) to tremble; ~ **pour qn** to fear for sb
**(e)** ‹light, image› to flicker
**(f)** ‹leaves› to quiver
**trembloter** /tʀɑ̃blɔte/ [1] *vi* **(a)** ‹person, hands› to tremble slightly
**(b)** ‹voice› to tremble
**trémolo** /tʀemɔlo/ *nm* **(a)** (of voice) quaver
**(b)** (of instrument) tremolo
**trémousser: se trémousser**
/tʀemuse/ [1] *v refl* (+ *v être*) **(a)** to fidget
**(b)** to wiggle around
**trempe** /tʀɑ̃p/ *nf* **avoir la ~ d'un dirigeant** to have the makings of a leader
**trempé, ~e** /tʀɑ̃pe/ **1** *pp* ▶ TREMPER
**2** *pp adj* **(a)** ‹person, garments› soaked (through); ‹grass› sodden
**(b)** (Tech) ‹steel› tempered; ‹glass› toughened
**tremper** /tʀɑ̃pe/ [1] **1** *vtr* **(a)** ‹rain, person› to soak ‹person, garment›
**(b)** to dip; **j'ai juste trempé mes lèvres** I just had a sip
**(c)** to soak ‹hands›
**(d)** (Tech) to temper
**2** *vi* **(a)** ‹clothes, vegetables› to soak; **faire ~ qch** to soak sth
**(b)** (colloq) ~ **dans qch** to be mixed up in sth
**tremplin** /tʀɑ̃plɛ̃/ *nm* **(a)** springboard
**(b)** ski jump; water-ski jump
**trentaine** /tʀɑ̃tɛn/ *nf* **(a)** about thirty
**(b)** **avoir la ~** to be about thirty
**trente** /tʀɑ̃t/ *adj inv, pron, nm inv* thirty
**trente-et-un** /tʀɑ̃teœ̃/ *nm* **être sur son ~** (colloq) to be dressed up to the nines
**trentenaire** /tʀɑ̃tənɛʀ/ *adj* ‹person› in his/her thirties; ‹tree, building› around thirty years old
**trente-six** /tʀɑ̃tsis/ *adj inv, pron, nm inv* thirty-six
**IDIOMS voir ~ chandelles** (colloq) to see stars
**trente-trois** /tʀɑ̃tʀwa/ *adj inv, pron, nm inv* thirty-three
■ ~ **tours** LP
**trentième** /tʀɑ̃tjɛm/ *adj* thirtieth

**trépas** /tʀepɑ/ *nm* demise
**trépidant, ~e** /tʀepidɑ̃, ɑ̃t/ *adj* ‹rhythm, speed› pulsating; ‹life› hectic; ‹story› exciting
**trépied** /tʀepje/ *nm* (gen) tripod
**trépigner** /tʀepiɲe/ [1] *vi* (with anger, impatience) to stamp one's feet
**très** /tʀɛ/ *adv* very; ~ **connu** very well-known; **être ~ amoureux** to be very much in love; ~ **en avance** very early; ~ **volontiers** gladly; **'tu vas bien?'—'non, pas ~'** 'are you well?'—'no, not terribly'; **elle a ~ envie de partir** she's dying to leave (colloq)
**trésor** /tʀezɔʀ/ *nm* **(a)** treasure
**(b)** **déployer des ~s d'inventivité** to show infinite inventiveness
**(c)** (person) **mon ~** precious
**trésorerie** /tʀezɔʀʀi/ *nf* **(a)** funds; cash
**(b)** (of company) accounts
**(c)** government finance
**trésorier, -ière** /tʀezɔʀje, ɛʀ/ *nm,f* treasurer
**tressaillement** /tʀɛsajmɑ̃/ *nm* **(a)** (from surprise, fear) start; (of hope, pleasure) quiver; (from pain) wince
**(b)** (of person, muscle, animal) twitch; (of machine, ground) vibration
**tressaillir** /tʀɛsajiʀ/ [28] *vi* **(a)** (with surprise) to start; (with pleasure) to quiver
**(b)** ‹person, muscle› to twitch
**tresse** /tʀɛs/ *nf* **(a)** plait
**(b)** (of thread) braid
**tresser** /tʀɛse/ [1] *vtr* to plait ‹hair, threads›; to weave ‹straw, string›
**tréteau**, *pl* ~**x** /tʀeto/ *nm* trestle
**treuil** /tʀœj/ *nm* winch
**trêve** /tʀɛv/ *nf* **(a)** (Mil) truce
**(b)** respite; ~ **de plaisanteries!** that's enough joking!
**tri** /tʀi/ *nm* sorting; sorting out; **centre de ~** (postal) sorting office; **faire le ~ de** to sort ‹mail›; to sort out ‹documents, clothes›; **faire un ~ parmi des choses** to select among things
**triage** /tʀijaʒ/ *nm* **gare de ~** marshalling (GB) yard
**triangle** /tʀijɑ̃gl/ *nm* triangle
■ ~ **des Bermudes** Bermuda Triangle
**triangulaire** /tʀijɑ̃gylɛʀ/ *adj*
**(a)** triangular
**(b)** ‹agreement, partnership› three-way
**triathlon** /tʀiatlɔ̃/ *nm* triathlon
**tribal, ~e**, *mpl* -**aux** /tʀibal, o/ *adj* tribal
**tribord** /tʀibɔʀ/ *nm* starboard
**tribu** /tʀiby/ *nf* tribe
**tribulations** /tʀibylasjɔ̃/ *nf pl* tribulations
**tribun** /tʀibœ̃/ *nm* **(a)** tribune
**(b)** great orator
**tribunal**, *pl* -**aux** /tʀibynal, o/ *nm* (Law) court; **traîner qn devant les tribunaux** to take sb to court

**tribune** /tʀibyn/ *nf* **(a)** (in stadium) stand; (in court) gallery
**(b)** (of speaker) platform, rostrum
**(c)** (in newspaper) comments column

**tribut** /tʀiby/ *nm* tribute

**tributaire** /tʀibytɛʀ/ *adj* être ∼ de ⟨*country, person*⟩ to depend on

**tricentenaire** /tʀisɑ̃tnɛʀ/ *adj* three-hundred-year-old

**triche** /tʀiʃ/ *nf* (colloq) c'est de la ∼ that's cheating

**tricher** /tʀiʃe/ [1] *vi* to cheat; ∼ sur son âge to lie about one's age

**tricherie** /tʀiʃʀi/ *nf* cheating

**tricheur, -euse** /tʀiʃœʀ, øz/ *nm,f* cheat

**tricolore** /tʀikɔlɔʀ/ *adj* **(a)** three-coloured (GB); feux ∼s traffic lights
**(b)** (colloq) French; l'équipe ∼ the French team

**tricot** /tʀiko/ *nm* **(a)** knitting; faire du ∼ to knit
**(b)** knitwear; en ∼ knitted

**tricoter** /tʀikɔte/ [1] *vtr* to knit; tricoté (à la) main handknitted

**tricycle** /tʀisikl/ *nm* tricycle

**trident** /tʀidɑ̃/ *nm* trident

**tridimensionnel, -elle** /tʀidimɑ̃sjɔnɛl/ *adj* three-dimensional

**triennal, ∼e, mpl -aux** /tʀijenal, o/ *adj*
**(a)** ⟨*mandate*⟩ three-year
**(b)** ⟨*vote*⟩ three-yearly

**trier** /tʀije/ [2] *vtr* **(a)** to sort ⟨*mail*⟩
**(b)** to sort [sth] out ⟨*information*⟩; to select ⟨*clients*⟩
IDIOMS ∼ sur le volet to handpick

**trifouiller** /tʀifuje/ [1] *vi* (colloq) ∼ dans to rummage through; to tinker with

**trilingue** /tʀilɛ̃g/ *adj* trilingual

**trilogie** /tʀilɔʒi/ *nf* trilogy

**trimbal(l)er** /tʀɛ̃bale/ [1] *vtr* (colloq) to lug [sth] around; to drag [sb] around

**trimer** /tʀime/ [1] *vi* (colloq) to slave away

**trimestre** /tʀimɛstʀ/ *nm* **(a)** (period) quarter; (Sch) term
**(b)** quarterly income; quarterly payment

**trimestriel, -ielle** /tʀimɛstʀijɛl/ *adj* (gen) quarterly; ⟨*exam*⟩ end-of-term

**trimoteur** /tʀimɔtœʀ/ *nm* three-engined plane

**tringle** /tʀɛ̃gl/ *nf* **(a)** (gen) rail
**(b)** (Tech) rod

**trinité** /tʀinite/ *nf* trinity

**trinquer** /tʀɛ̃ke/ [1] *vi* to clink glasses; ∼ à qch to drink to sth

**trio** /tʀi(j)o/ *nm* trio

**triomphal, ∼e, mpl -aux** /tʀijɔ̃fal, o/ *adj* triumphant

**triomphalisme** /tʀijɔ̃falism/ *nm* triumphalism

**triomphant, ∼e** /tʀijɔ̃fɑ̃, ɑ̃t/ *adj* triumphant

**triomphateur, -trice** /tʀijɔ̃fatœʀ, tʀis/ *adj* triumphant

**triomphe** /tʀijɔ̃f/ *nm* triumph; faire un ∼ à qn to give sb a triumphal reception

**triompher** /tʀijɔ̃fe/ [1] **1** triompher de *v+prep* to triumph over ⟨*enemy*⟩; to overcome ⟨*resistance*⟩
**2** *vi* **(a)** ⟨*fighter*⟩ to triumph; ⟨*truth*⟩ to prevail
**(b)** to be triumphant

**tripartisme** /tʀipaʀtism/ *nm* tripartite *or* three-party system

**tripatouiller** /tʀipatuje/ [1] *vtr* (colloq) to fiddle with (colloq) ⟨*object*⟩; to paw (colloq) ⟨*person*⟩

**triperie** /tʀipʀi/ *nf* **(a)** tripe shop
**(b)** tripe trade

**tripes** /tʀip/ *nf pl* **(a)** (Culin) tripe
**(b)** (colloq) guts, innards

**triplace** /tʀiplas/ *adj* three-seater

**triple** /tʀipl/ **1** *adj* triple; l'avantage est ∼ the advantages are threefold; en ∼ exemplaire in triplicate; ∼ idiot! (colloq) prize idiot! (colloq)
**2** *nm* coûter le ∼ to cost three times as much

**triplé, ∼e** /tʀiple/ *nm,f* triplet

**triplement** /tʀipləmɑ̃/ *adv* **(a)** in three respects
**(b)** trebly

**tripler** /tʀiple/ [1] **1** *vtr* to treble ⟨*quantity, price*⟩
**2** *vi* to treble (de in)

**triporteur** /tʀipɔʀtœʀ/ *nm* delivery tricycle

**tripot** /tʀipo/ *nm* **(a)** gambling joint (colloq)
**(b)** dive (colloq)

**tripotée** /tʀipɔte/ *nf* (colloq) **(a)** (good) hiding (colloq)
**(b)** une ∼ de hordes of

**tripoter** /tʀipɔte/ [1] *vtr* (colloq) to fiddle with ⟨*object*⟩

**trique** /tʀik/ *nf* cudgel; battre à coups de ∼ to cudgel
IDIOMS être maigre *or* sec comme un coup de ∼ to be as thin as a rake

**trisaïeul, ∼e** /tʀizajœl/ *nm,f* great-great-grandfather/grandmother

**trisannuel, -elle** /tʀizanɥɛl/ *adj* triennial

**trisomie** /tʀizɔmi/ *nf* trisomy; ∼ 21 Down's Syndrome

**trisomique** /tʀizɔmik/ *adj* enfant ∼ Down's Syndrome child

**triste** /tʀist/ *adj* **(a)** (gen) sad; ⟨*town, existence*⟩ dreary; ⟨*weather, day*⟩ gloomy; ⟨*colour*⟩ drab
**(b)** ⟨*end, business, reputation*⟩ dreadful; ⟨*show, state*⟩ sorry; ⟨*character*⟩ unsavoury (GB); c'est la ∼ vérité unfortunately, that's the truth of the matter; faire la ∼ expérience de qch to learn about sth to one's cost

**tristement** /tʀistəmɑ̃/ *adv* sadly

**tristesse** /tʀistɛs/ *nf* (gen) sadness; (of place, evening) dreariness; (of weather, day) gloominess

**triton** /tritɔ̃/ *nm* (Zool) **(a)** (mollusc) triton
 **(b)** newt

**triturer** /trityʀe/ [1] *vtr* to fiddle with
⟨button⟩; to knead ⟨*dough*⟩
 IDIOMS se ∼ la cervelle (colloq) *or* les
 méninges (colloq) to rack one's brains (colloq)

**trivial**, ∼**e**, *mpl* **-iaux** /trivjal, o/ *adj*
 **(a)** coarse
 **(b)** ordinary, everyday; ⟨*style*⟩ mundane

**trivialité** /trivjalite/ *nf* **(a)** coarseness
 **(b)** triteness, triviality
 **(c)** platitude

**troc** /trɔk/ *nm* barter; **faire du** ∼ to barter

**troène** /trɔɛn/ *nm* privet

**troglodyte** /trɔglɔdit/ *nm* cave-dweller

**trogne** /trɔɲ/ *nf* (colloq) mug (colloq), face

**trognon** /trɔɲɔ̃/ *nm* (of apple) core

**trois** /trwa/ *adj inv, pron, nm inv* three
 IDIOMS **être haut comme** ∼ **pommes** to be
 kneehigh to a grasshopper; **jamais deux
 sans** ∼ bad luck comes in threes

**trois-huit** /trwaɥit/ *nm pl* system of three
 eight-hour shifts

**troisième** /trwazjɛm/ ⓵ *adj* third
 ⓶ *nf* **(a)** (Sch) *fourth year of secondary
 school, age 14–15*
 **(b)** (Aut) third (gear)
 ■ **le** ∼ **âge** the elderly

**troisièmement** /trwazjɛmmɑ̃/ *adv*
 thirdly

**trois-mâts** /trwamɑ/ *nm inv* three-master

**trois-quarts** /trwakaʀ/ ⓵ *nm inv*
 **(a)** three-quarter length coat
 **(b)** (rugby player) three-quarter
 ⓶ **de trois-quarts** *phr* ⟨*portrait*⟩ three-
 quarter length

**trombe** /trɔ̃b/ *nf* **(a)** (caused by whirlwind)
 waterspout; **partir en** ∼ to go hurtling off
 **(b)** ∼**s d'eau** masses of water; torrential
 rain

**trombone** /trɔ̃bɔn/ *nm* **(a)** trombone
 **(b)** trombonist
 **(c)** paperclip

**trompe** /trɔ̃p/ *nf* **(a)** (Zool) (of elephant)
 trunk; (of insect) proboscis
 **(b)** (Mus) horn

**trompe-la-mort** /trɔ̃plamɔʀ/ *nmf inv*
 daredevil

**trompe-l'œil** /trɔ̃plœj/ *nm inv* **(a)** (painting)
 trompe l'œil
 **(b)** (figurative) smokescreen

**tromper** /trɔ̃pe/ [1] ⓵ *vtr* **(a)** (gen) to
 deceive; to be unfaithful to ⟨husband, wife⟩;
 ∼ **les électeurs** to mislead the voters
 **(b)** ∼ **la vigilance de qn** to slip past sb's
 guard
 **(c) pour** ∼ **l'attente** to while away the time
 ⓶ **se tromper** *v refl* (+ *v être*) **(a)** to be
 mistaken; **se** ∼ **sur qn** to be wrong about sb;
 **il ne faut pas s'y** ∼, **qu'on ne s'y trompe pas**
 make no mistake about it
 **(b)** to make a mistake; **se** ∼ **de bus** to take
 the wrong bus

**tromperie** /trɔ̃pʀi/ *nf* deceit

**trompette¹** /trɔ̃pɛt/ *nm* (in army) bugler

**trompette²** /trɔ̃pɛt/ *nf* trumpet

**trompettiste** /trɔ̃petist/ *nmf* trumpet
 (player)

**trompeur, -euse** /trɔ̃pœʀ, øz/ *adj*
 ⟨*promise*⟩ misleading; ⟨*appearance*⟩
 deceptive

**tronc** /trɔ̃/ *nm* **(a)** (of tree, body) trunk;
 (of column) shaft
 **(b)** collection box
 ■ ∼ **commun** (of species) common origin;
 (of disciplines) (common) core curriculum

**tronche** /trɔ̃ʃ/ *nf* (slang) mug (colloq), face

**tronçon** /trɔ̃sɔ̃/ *nm* section

**tronçonneuse** /trɔ̃sɔnøz/ *nf* chain saw

**trône** /tron/ *nm* throne

**trôner** /trone/ [1] *vi* **le professeur trônait au
 milieu de ses étudiants** the professor was
 holding court among his students; ∼ **sur**
 ⟨*photograph*⟩ to have pride of place on

**tronquer** /trɔ̃ke/ [1] *vtr* to truncate

**trop** /tro/ ⓵ *adv* too; too much; **beaucoup**
 *or* **bien** ∼ **lourd** far *or* much too heavy; **j'ai**
 ∼ **mangé** I've had too much to eat; **j'ai** ∼
 **dormi** I've slept too long; **nous sommes** ∼
 **peu nombreux** there are too few of us; **12
 francs c'est** ∼ **peu** 12 francs is too little; **ce
 serait** ∼ **beau!** one should be so lucky!; **c'est**
 ∼ **bête!** how stupid!; ∼ **enthousiaste**
 overenthusiastic; ∼ **c'est** ∼**!** enough is
 enough!; **c'était** ∼ **drôle** it was so funny
 ⓶ **trop de** *quantif* ∼ **de pression/meubles**
 too much pressure/furniture; ∼ **de livres/
 monde** too many books/people
 ⓷ **de trop, en trop** *phr* **il y a une assiette
 en** ∼ there's one plate too many; **il y a a 12
 euros de** ∼ there's 12 euros too much; **ta
 remarque était de** ∼ your remark was
 uncalled for; **se sentir de** ∼ to feel one is in
 the way

**trophée** /trɔfe/ *nm* trophy

**tropical**, ∼**e**, *mpl* **-aux** /trɔpikal, o/ *adj*
 tropical

**tropique** /trɔpik/ *nm* tropic

**trop-perçu**, *pl* ∼**s** /tropɛʀsy/ *nm*
 **(a)** excess payment
 **(b)** overpayment of tax; **remboursement d'un**
 ∼ tax refund

**trop-plein**, *pl* ∼**s** /troplɛ̃/ *nm* **(a)** (of energy)
 excess
 **(b)** (Tech) (from bath) overflow

**troquer** /trɔke/ [1] *vtr* (gen) ∼ **qch contre
 qch** to swap sth for sth; to barter sth for sth

**troquet** /trɔke/ *nm* (colloq) bar

**trot** /tro/ *nm* trot

**trotte** /trɔt/ *nf* (colloq) **ça fait une** ∼ it's a
 fair walk

**trotter** /trɔte/ [1] *vi* **(a)** ⟨horse, rider⟩ to
 trot
 **(b)** ⟨person, mouse⟩ to scurry (about)
 **(c)** (figurative) ∼ **dans la tête** ⟨thought⟩ to go
 through one's mind; ⟨music⟩ to go through
 one's head

**trotteur** /trɔtœʀ/ *nm* **(a)** trotter                  ⋯⋮⋗

(b) *shoe with a low, broad heel*

**trotteuse** /tʀɔtøz/ *nf* (on watch) second
hand

**trottiner** /tʀɔtine/ [1] *vi* (a) ⟨*horse*⟩ to jog
  (b) ⟨*person, mouse*⟩ to scurry along

**trottinette** /tʀɔtinɛt/ *nf* scooter

**trottoir** /tʀɔtwaʀ/ *nm* pavement (GB),
sidewalk (US); **le bord du** ∼ the kerb (GB) *or*
curb (US)

**trou** /tʀu/ *nm* (a) hole
  (b) (in timetable) (gen) gap; (in budget) deficit;
  (in savings) hole
  (c) (colloq) ⟨*perdu*⟩ dump (colloq)
  ■ ∼ **d'aération** airhole; ∼ **d'air** air pocket;
  ∼ **de mémoire** memory lapse; ∼ **normand**
  *glass of spirits between courses to aid
  digestion*; ∼ **de serrure** keyhole

**troublant**, ∼**e** /tʀublɑ̃, ɑ̃t/ *adj*
  (a) disturbing; disconcerting
  (b) (sexually) unsettling

**trouble** /tʀubl/ **1** *adj* (a) ⟨*liquid*⟩ cloudy;
  ⟨*glasses*⟩ smudgy
  (b) ⟨*picture, outline*⟩ blurred
  (c) ⟨*feeling*⟩ confused; ⟨*business, milieu*⟩
  shady
  **2** *adv* **je vois** ∼ my eyes are blurred
  **3** *nm* (a) unrest; ∼**s ethniques** ethnic
  unrest
  (b) trouble; **jeter le** ∼ to stir up trouble
  (c) confusion; embarrassment
  (d) emotion; **ressentir un** ∼ to feel a thrill of
  emotion
  (e) (Med) ∼**s** disorders

**trouble-fête** /tʀubləfɛt/ *nmf inv*
spoilsport

**troubler** /tʀuble/ [1] **1** *vtr* (a) to make
[sth] cloudy ⟨*liquid*⟩; to blur ⟨*sight, picture*⟩
  (b) to disturb ⟨*sleep, person*⟩; to disrupt
  ⟨*plans*⟩; **en ces temps troublés** in these
  troubled times
  (c) to disconcert ⟨*person*⟩
  **2 se troubler** *v refl* (+ *v être*) (a) ⟨*person*⟩
  to become flustered
  (b) ⟨*liquid*⟩ to become cloudy; **ma vue se
  troubla** my eyes became blurred

**trouée** /tʀue/ *nf* (a) gap
  (b) (Mil) breach

**trouer** /tʀue/ [1] *vtr* to make a hole (*or*
holes) in; to wear a hole (*or* holes) in;
**semelle trouée** sole with a hole (*or* holes) in
it

**troufion** /tʀufjɔ̃/ *nm* (slang) soldier

**trouillard**, ∼**e** /tʀujaʀ, aʀd/ (slang) **1** *adj*
cowardly
  **2** *nm,f* chicken (colloq), coward

**trouille** /tʀuj/ *nf* (slang) **avoir la** ∼ to be
scared

**troupe** /tʀup/ *nf* (a) (Mil) troops
  (b) (of actors) company; (on tour) troupe
  (c) (of deer) herd; (of birds) flock; (of tourists)
  troop; (of children) band

**troupeau**, *pl* ∼**x** /tʀupo/ *nm* (of buffalo,
cattle) herd; (of sheep) flock; (of geese) gaggle

**trousse** /tʀus/ *nf* (a) (little) case
  (b) kit

■ ∼ **d'écolier** pencil case; ∼ **de médecin**
doctor's bag; ∼ **de secours** first-aid kit; ∼ **de
toilette** toilet bag
  **IDIOMS être aux** ∼**s de qn** to be hot on sb's
  heels

**trousseau**, *pl* ∼**x** /tʀuso/ *nm* (a) (of keys)
bunch
  (b) (of bride) trousseau; (of baby) clothes

**trouvaille** /tʀuvaj/ *nf* (a) (object) find
  (b) bright idea, brainwave

**trouvé**, ∼**e** /tʀuve/ **1** *pp* ▶ TROUVER
  **2** *pp adj* **réplique bien** ∼**e** neat riposte; **tout**
  ∼ ⟨*solution*⟩ ready-made; ⟨*culprit*⟩ obvious

**trouver** /tʀuve/ [1] **1** *vtr* (a) (gen) to find;
  ∼ **qch par hasard** to come across sth; ∼ **un
  intérêt à qch** to find sth interesting; ∼ **à
  redire** to find fault; ∼ **le moyen de faire** to
  manage to do; **j'ai trouvé!** I've got it!; **tu as
  trouvé ça tout seul?** (ironic) did you work that
  out all by yourself?; **si tu continues tu vas
  me** ∼! (colloq) don't push your luck! (colloq);
  ∼ **du plaisir à faire** to get pleasure out of
  doing; **aller** ∼ **qn** to go and see sb
  (b) **je trouve ça drôle** I think it's funny; **j'ai
  trouvé bon de vous prévenir** I thought it
  right to warn you; **je me demande ce qu'elle
  te trouve!** I wonder what she sees in you!; **je
  te trouve bien calme, qu'est-ce que tu as?**
  you're very quiet, what's the matter?
  **2 se trouver** *v refl* (+ *v être*) (a) to be; **se**
  ∼ **à Rome** to be in Rome; **se** ∼ **dans
  l'impossibilité de faire** to be unable to do
  (b) to feel; **j'ai failli me** ∼ **mal** I nearly passed
  out
  (c) **il se** ∼ **beau** he thinks he's good-looking
  (d) to find ⟨*excuse*⟩
  **3** *v impers* **il se trouve qu'elle ne leur avait
  rien dit** as it happened, she hadn't told them
  anything; **si ça se trouve ça te plaira** (colloq)
  you might like it

**truand** /tʀyɑ̃/ *nm* (a) gangster
  (b) crook

**trublion** /tʀyblijɔ̃/ *nm* troublemaker

**truc** /tʀyk/ *nm* (a) (colloq) knack; trick; **avoir
un** ∼ **pour gagner de l'argent** to know a good
way of making money; **un** ∼ **du métier** a
trick of the trade
  (b) thing; **il y a un tas de** ∼**s à faire dans la
  maison** there are loads of things to do in the
  house (colloq); **il y a un** ∼ **qui ne va pas**
  there's something wrong
  (c) (colloq) thingummy (colloq), whatsit (colloq)
  (d) (person) what's-his-name/what's-her-
  name, thingy (colloq)

**trucage** /tʀykaʒ/ *nm* (in cinema) special
effect

**truchement** /tʀyʃmɑ̃/ *nm* **par le** ∼ **de qch**
through sth; **par le** ∼ **de qn** through the
intervention of sb

**truculent**, ∼**e** /tʀykylɑ̃, ɑ̃t/ *adj* earthy

**truelle** /tʀyɛl/ *nf* trowel

**truffe** /tʀyf/ *nf* (a) (Culin) truffle
  (b) (of dog) nose

**truffer** /tʀyfe/ [1] *vtr* **ta lettre est truffée de
fautes** your letter is riddled with mistakes

**truie** /tʀɥi/ *nf* sow

**truite** /tʀɥit/ *nf* trout

**truquage** = TRUCAGE

**truquer** /tʀyke/ [1] *vtr* (a) to fiddle (colloq) ⟨*accounts*⟩
(b) to mark ⟨*cards*⟩
(c) to fix ⟨*elections, match*⟩

**trust** /tʀœst/ *nm* trust

**tsar** /tsaʀ/ *nm* tsar

**tsé-tsé** /tsetse/ *nf inv* (**mouche**) ∼ tsetse (fly)

**tsigane** = TZIGANE

**TTC** (*abbr* = **toutes taxes comprises**) inclusive of tax

**tu** /ty/ *pron* you
IDIOMS être à ∼ et à toi avec qn to be on familiar terms with sb

**tuant**, ∼**e** /tɥɑ̃, ɑ̃t/ *adj* (colloq) exhausting

**tuba** /tyba/ *nm* (a) (Mus) tuba
(b) (of swimmer) snorkel

**tube** /tyb/ ① *nm* (a) tube; pipe
(b) (colloq) (song) hit
② **à pleins tubes** *phr* (colloq) **mettre le son à pleins** ∼**s** to turn the sound right up (colloq)
■ ∼ **cathodique** cathode ray tube; ∼ **digestif** digestive tract; ∼ **à essai** test tube

**tubercule** /tybɛʀkyl/ *nm* (a) (Bot) tuber
(b) (Anat) tuberosity

**tuberculeux**, **-euse** /tybɛʀkylø, øz/ *adj* tubercular; être ∼ to have TB

**tuberculose** /tybɛʀkyloz/ *nf* tuberculosis, TB

**tubulaire** /tybylɛʀ/ *adj* tubular

**TUC** /tyk/ *nm pl* (*abbr* = **travaux d'utilité collective**) paid community service (*for the young unemployed*)

**tué** /tɥe/ *nm* person killed; **sept** ∼**s, cinq blessés** seven people killed, five injured

**tuer** /tɥe/ [1] ① *vtr* (a) (gen) to kill
(b) (colloq) to wear [sb] out
② **se tuer** *v refl* (+ *v être*) (a) (accidentally) to be killed
(b) to kill oneself
(c) se ∼ **au travail** to work oneself to death

**tuerie** /tyʀi/ *nf* killings

**tue-tête**: **à tue-tête** /atytɛt/ *phr* at the top of one's voice

**tueur**, **-euse** /tɥœʀ, øz/ *nm,f* (a) killer
(b) slaughterman/slaughterwoman
■ ∼ **à gages** hired *or* professional killer

**tuile** /tɥil/ *nf* (a) tile
(b) (colloq) blow; **quelle** ∼! what a blow!
(c) (Culin) *thin almond biscuit*

**tulipe** /tylip/ *nf* tulip

**tuméfier** /tymefje/ [2] *vtr* to make [sth] swell up

**tumeur** /tymœʀ/ *nf* tumour (GB)

**tumulte** /tymylt/ *nm* (a) uproar
(b) turmoil

**tumultueux**, **-euse** /tymyltɥø, øz/ *adj* turbulent; tempestuous; stormy

**tungstène** /tœ̃gstɛn/ *nm* tungsten

**tunique** /tynik/ *nf* tunic

**tunisien**, **-ienne** /tynizjɛ̃, ɛn/ *adj* Tunisian

**tunnel** /tynɛl/ *nm* tunnel; **le** ∼ **sous la Manche** the Channel Tunnel
IDIOMS **voir le bout du** ∼ to see light at the end of the tunnel

**turban** /tyʀbɑ̃/ *nm* turban

**turbin** /tyʀbɛ̃/ *nm* (slang) daily grind (colloq), work

**turbine** /tyʀbin/ *nf* turbine

**turboréacteur** /tyʀbɔʀeaktœʀ/ *nm* turbojet (engine)

**turbot** /tyʀbo/ *nm* turbot

**turbulence** /tyʀbylɑ̃s/ *nf* (a) turbulence
(b) unruliness
(c) unrest

**turbulent**, ∼**e** /tyʀbylɑ̃, ɑ̃t/ *adj* ⟨*child*⟩ unruly; ⟨*class*⟩ rowdy; ⟨*teenager*⟩ rebellious; être ∼ **en classe** to be disruptive in class

**turc, turque** /tyʀk/ ① *adj* Turkish
② *nm* (language) Turkish

**Turc, Turque** /tyʀk/ *nm,f* Turk

**turfiste** /tœʀfist/ *nmf* racegoer, punter (colloq)

**turlupiner** /tyʀlypine/ [1] *vtr* (colloq) to bother

**turpitude** /tyʀpityd/ *nf* (a) turpitude, depravity
(b) base act; low remark

**turque** ▶ TURC 1

**Turquie** /tyʀki/ *pr nf* Turkey

**turquoise** /tyʀkwaz/ *adj inv*, *nf* turquoise

**tutelle** /tytɛl/ *nf* guardianship

**tuteur**, **-trice** /tytœʀ, tʀis/ ① *nm,f*
(a) (Law) guardian
(b) tutor
② *nm* (Bot) stake

**tutoiement** /tytwamɑ̃/ *nm* using the 'tu' form

**tutoyer** /tytwaje/ [23] *vtr* to address [sb] using the 'tu' form

**tutu** /tyty/ *nm* tutu

**tuyau**, *pl* ∼**x** /tɥijo/ *nm* (a) (Tech) pipe
(b) (colloq) tip (colloq)
■ ∼ **d'arrosage** hose; ∼ **d'échappement** exhaust

**tuyauterie** /tɥijotʀi/ *nf* (Tech) piping

**TVA** /tevea/ *nf* (*abbr* = **taxe à la valeur ajoutée**) VAT

**tympan** /tɛ̃pɑ̃/ *nm* eardrum

**type** /tip/ ① *nm* (a) type, kind; **plusieurs accidents de ce** ∼ several accidents of this kind
(b) (classic) example; **elle est le** ∼ **même de la femme d'affaires** she's the classic example of a business woman
(c) (physical) type
(d) (colloq) guy (colloq); **sale** ∼! swine! (colloq); **brave** ∼ nice chap (colloq)
② (**-)type** (*combining form*) typical, classic

**typer** /tipe/ [1] *vtr* to portray [sb] as a type; to play [sb] as a type

**typhoïde** /tifɔid/ *adj, nf* typhoid

**typhon** /tifɔ̃/ *nm* typhoon

**typique** /tipik/ *adj* typical

**typiquement** /tipikmã/ *adv* typically; **une famille ~ américaine** a typically American family

**typographie** /tipɔgʀafi/ *nf* typography

**typographique** /tipɔgʀafik/ *adj* typographical

**tyran** /tiʀã/ *nm* tyrant

**tyrannie** /tiʀani/ *nf* tyranny

**tyrannique** /tiʀanik/ *adj* tyrannical

**tyranniser** /tiʀanize/ [1] *vtr* to tyrannize

**tzigane** /dzigan, tsigan/ ① *adj, nmf* gypsy ② *nm* (language) Romany

# U u

**u, U** /y/ *nm inv* u, U; **en (forme de) U** U-shaped

**ubac** /ybak/ *nm* north-facing side

**ubiquité** /ybikɥite/ *nf* ubiquity; **je n'ai pas le don d'~!** I can't be everywhere at once!

**ubuesque** /ybyɛsk/ *adj* grotesque

**ulcère** /ylsɛʀ/ *nm* ulcer

**ulcérer** /ylseʀe/ [14] *vtr* **(a)** to sicken, to revolt
**(b)** (Med) to ulcerate

**ulcéreux, -euse** /ylseʀø, øz/ *adj* ⟨wound⟩ ulcerated

**ULM** /yɛlɛm/ *nm inv* (abbr = **ultraléger motorisé**) microlight; microlighting; **faire de l'~** to go microlighting

**ultérieur, ~e** /ylteʀjœʀ/ *adj* subsequent; **une date ~e** a later date

**ultérieurement** /ylteʀjœʀmã/ *adv*
**(a)** subsequently
**(b)** later

**ultimatum** /yltimatɔm/ *nm* ultimatum

**ultime** /yltim/ *adj* **(a)** final
**(b)** ultimate

**ultra** /yltʀa/ *adj, nmf* extremist

**ultraconfidentiel, -ielle** /yltʀakɔ̃fidãsjɛl/ *adj* top secret

**ultrafin, ~e** /yltʀafɛ̃, in/ *adj* ⟨slice⟩ wafer-thin; ⟨stocking⟩ sheer; ⟨fibre⟩ ultra-fine

**ultraléger, -ère** /yltʀaleʒe, ɛʀ/ *adj* ⟨material, cigarette⟩ ultra light; ⟨clothing, fabric, equipment⟩ very light

**ultramoderne** /yltʀamɔdɛʀn/ *adj* (gen) ultramodern; ⟨system, technology⟩ state-of-the-art

**ultrarapide** /yltʀaʀapid/ *adj* high-speed

**ultrasecret, -ète** /yltʀasəkʀɛ, ɛt/ *adj* top secret

**ultrasensible** /yltʀasãsibl/ *adj* ⟨person⟩ hypersensitive; ⟨film⟩ ultrasensitive; ⟨issue⟩ highly sensitive

**ultrason** /yltʀasɔ̃/ *nm* ultrasound

**ultraviolet, -ette** /yltʀavjɔlɛ, ɛt/ ① *adj* ultraviolet ② *nm* ultraviolet ray; **séance d'~s** session on a sunbed

**ululer** /ylyle/ [1] *vi* to hoot

**un, une¹** /œ̃(n), yn/ ① *det* (*pl* **des**) **(a)** a, an; one; **un homme** a man; **une femme** a woman; **avec ~ sang-froid remarquable** with remarkable self-control; **il n'y avait pas ~ arbre** there wasn't a single tree; **~ accident est vite arrivé** accidents soon happen
**(b)** **il y avait des roses et des lis** there were roses and lilies; **il y a des gens qui trichent** there are some people who cheat
**(c)** **il fait ~ froid** *or* **~ de ces froids!** it's so cold!; **elle m'a donné une de ces gifles!** she gave me such a slap!; **il y a ~ monde aujourd'hui!** there are so many people today!
② *pron* (*pl* **uns, unes**) one; **(l')~ de** *or* **d'entre nous** one of us; **les ~s pensent que...** some think that...
③ *adj* one, a, an; **trente et une personnes** thirty-one people; **~ jour sur deux** every other day
④ *nm,f* one; **~ par personne** one each; **les deux villes n'en font plus qu'une** the two cities have merged into one; **~ à** *or* **par ~** one by one
⑤ *nm* one; **page ~** page one
IDIOMS **fière comme pas une** extremely proud; **il est menteur comme pas ~** he's the biggest liar; **~ pour tous et tous pour ~** all for one and one for all; ▶ DIX

**unanime** /ynanim/ *adj* unanimous

**unanimement** /ynanimmã/ *adv*
**(a)** ⟨adopted, elected⟩ unanimously
**(b)** (figurative) ⟨admired⟩ universally

**unanimité** /ynanimite/ *nf* unanimity; **à l'~** ⟨elected⟩ unanimously; **à l'~ moins deux voix** with only two votes against; **faire l'~** to have unanimous support *or* backing

**une²** /yn/ ① *det, pron, adj* ▶ UN 1, 2, 3, 4 ② *nf* **la ~** the front page; **être à la ~** to be in the headlines

**uni, ~e** /yni/ ① *pp* ▶ UNIR
② *pp adj* **(a)** ⟨family⟩ close-knit; ⟨couple⟩ close; ⟨people, rebels⟩ united
**(b)** ⟨fabric, colour⟩ plain
**(c)** ⟨surface⟩ smooth, even

**unicité** /ynisite/ *nf* uniqueness

u

**unidirectionnel, -elle** /ynidiʀɛksjɔnɛl/ *adj* ‹*transmitter*› unidirectional; ‹*receiver*› one-way

**unième** /ynjɛm/ *adj* first; **vingt et ~** twenty-first

**unification** /ynifikasjɔ̃/ *nf* unification

**unifier** /ynifje/ [2] **1** *vtr* **(a)** to unify ‹*country, market*›
**(b)** to standardize ‹*procedure, system*›
**2 s'unifier** *v refl* (+ *v être*) ‹*countries, groups*› to unite

**uniforme** /ynifɔʀm/ **1** *adj* (gen) uniform; ‹*buildings, streets, existence*› monotonous; ‹*regulation*› across-the-board
**2** *nm* uniform; **en ~** uniformed

**uniformément** /ynifɔʀmemɑ̃/ *adv* uniformly

**uniformiser** /ynifɔʀmize/ [1] *vtr* to standardize ‹*rate*›; to make [sth] uniform ‹*colour*›

**uniformité** /ynifɔʀmite/ *nf* (of tastes) uniformity; (of life, buildings) monotony

**unijambiste** /yniʒãbist/ **1** *adj* **être ~** to have only one leg
**2** *nmf* one-legged person

**unilatéral, ~e,** *mpl* **-aux** /ynilateʀal, o/ *adj* unilateral; ‹*parking*› on one side only

**unilingue** /ynilɛ̃g/ *adj* unilingual, monolingual

**uninominal, ~e,** *mpl* **-aux** /yninɔminal, o/ *adj* (Pol) ‹*ballot*› for a single candidate

**union** /ynjɔ̃/ *nf* **(a)** union
**(b)** association; **~ de consommateurs** consumers' association
**(c)** marriage
■ **~ libre** cohabitation; **~ sportive,** US sports club; **Union européenne** European Union
IDIOMS **l'~ fait la force** (Proverb) united we stand, divided we fall

**unique** /ynik/ *adj* **(a)** only; **il est l'~ témoin** he's the only witness; **être fille** *or* **fils ~** to be an only child
**(b)** single; **parti ~** single party; **système à parti ~** one-party system; **‘prix ~’** 'all at one price'
**(c)** unique; **une occasion ~** a unique opportunity; **~ en son genre** ‹*person, object*› one of a kind; ‹*event*› one-off (GB), one-shot (US)
**(d)** (colloq) **ce type est ~!** that guy's priceless! (colloq)

**uniquement** /ynikmɑ̃/ *adv* (gen) only; **en vente ~ par correspondance** available by mail order only; **c'était ~ pour te taquiner** it was only to tease you; **il pense ~ à s'amuser** all he thinks about is having fun; **~ dans un but commercial** purely for commercial ends

**unir** /yniʀ/ [3] **1** *vtr* **(a)** to unite ‹*people, country*›; **des hommes unis par les mêmes idées** men brought together by the same ideas
**(b)** to combine ‹*qualities, resources*›
**(c)** to join [sb] in matrimony

**2 s'unir** *v refl* (+ *v être*) **(a)** to unite
**(b)** to marry

**unisexe** /ynisɛks/ *adj* unisex

**unisson** /ynisɔ̃/ *nm* unison; **à l'~** (Mus) in unison; (figurative) in accord

**unitaire** /ynitɛʀ/ *adj* ‹*cost*› unit

**unité** /ynite/ *nf* **(a)** unity; **film qui manque d'~** film lacking in cohesion; **il y a ~ de vues entre eux** they share the same viewpoint
**(b)** unit; **~ monétaire** unit of currency; **20 euros l'~** 20 euros each; **vendre qch à l'~** to sell sth singly
■ **~ centrale (de traitement)** (Comput) central processing unit, CPU; **~ de disque** (Comput) disk drive

**univers** /ynivɛʀ/ *nm inv* **(a)** universe
**(b)** whole world
**(c)** world; **l'~ de Kafka** Kafka's world

**universaliser** /ynivɛʀsalize/ [1] *vtr* to universalize

**universalité** /ynivɛʀsalite/ *nf* universality

**universel, -elle** /ynivɛʀsɛl/ *adj* ‹*language, theme*› universal; ‹*history*› world; ‹*remedy*› all-purpose

**universitaire** /ynivɛʀsitɛʀ/ **1** *adj* ‹*town*› university; ‹*work*› academic
**2** *nmf* academic

**université** /ynivɛʀsite/ *nf* university (GB), college (US)
■ **~ d'été** summer school

**uns** *pron* ▶ **UN 2**

**Untel, Unetelle** /œ̃tɛl, yntɛl/ *nm,f* **Monsieur ~** Mr so-and-so; **Madame Unetelle** Mrs so-and-so

**urbain, ~e** /yʀbɛ̃, ɛn/ *adj* **(a)** urban; **vie ~e** city life
**(b)** (formal) urbane

**urbanisation** /yʀbanizasjɔ̃/ *nf* urbanization

**urbaniser** /yʀbanize/ [1] *vtr* to urbanize ‹*region*›; **zone urbanisée** built-up area

**urbanisme** /yʀbanism/ *nm* town planning (GB), city planning (US)

**urbaniste** /yʀbanist/ *nmf* town planner (GB), city planner (US)

**urée** /yʀe/ *nf* urea

**urètre** /yʀɛtʀ/ *nm* urethra

**urgence** /yʀʒɑ̃s/ *nf* **(a)** urgency; **il y a ~** it's urgent, it's a matter of urgency; **d'~** ‹*act*› immediately; ‹*summon*› urgently; ‹*measures, treatment*› emergency; **de toute** *or* **d'extrême ~** as a matter of great urgency; **transporter qn d'~ à l'hôpital** to rush sb to hospital; **en ~** as a matter of urgency
**(b)** (Med) **une ~** an emergency; **le service des ~s, les ~s** the casualty department

**urgent, ~e** /yʀʒɑ̃, ɑ̃t/ *adj* urgent

**urinaire** /yʀinɛʀ/ *adj* urinary; **appareil ~** urinary tract

**urinal,** *pl* **-aux** /yʀinal, o/ *nm* urinal

**urine** /yʀin/ *nf* urine

**uriner** /yʀine/ [1] *vi* to urinate

**urinoir** /yʀinwaʀ/ nm urinal

**urne** /yʀn/ nf **(a)** ~ (**électorale**) ballot box; **se rendre aux ~s** to go to the polls
**(b)** urn

**urologie** /yʀɔlɔʒi/ nf urology

**urologue** /yʀɔlɔɡ/ nmf urologist

**URSS** /yɛʀɛsɛs, yʀs/ pr nf (abbr = **Union des Républiques socialistes soviétiques**) USSR

**urticaire** /yʀtikɛʀ/ nf hives

**uruguayen, -enne** /yʀygwejɛ̃, ɛn/ adj Uruguayan

**us** /ys/ nm pl **les ~ et coutumes** the ways and customs

**US** /yɛs/ nf (abbr = **union sportive**) sports club

**USA** /yɛsa/ nm pl (abbr = **United States of America**) USA

**usage** /yzaʒ/ nm **(a)** use; **à l'~, par l'~** with use; **en ~** in use; **faire ~ de** to use ⟨product⟩; **to exercise** ⟨authority⟩; **faire bon/mauvais ~ de qch** to put sth to good/bad use; **faire de l'~** ⟨garment⟩ to last; **à ~ privé** for private use; **à ~s multiples** ⟨appliance⟩ multipurpose; **il a perdu l'~ d'un œil/l'~ de la parole** he's lost the use of one eye/the power of speech; **hors d'~** ⟨garment⟩ unwearable; ⟨machine⟩ out of order
**(b)** (in a language) usage; **en ~** in usage
**(c)** custom; **l'~ est de faire** the custom is to do; it's usual practice to do; **entrer dans l'~** ⟨word⟩ to come into common use; ⟨behaviour⟩ to become common practice; ⟨politeness⟩ customary; ⟨precautions⟩ usual
■ ~ **de faux** (Law) use of false documents; **faux et ~ de faux** forgery and use of false documents

**usagé, ~e** /yzaʒe/ adj **(a)** ⟨garment⟩ well-worn; ⟨tyre⟩ worn
**(b)** ⟨syringe⟩ used

**usager** /yzaʒe/ nm (of service) user; (of language) speaker; ~ **de la route** road-user

**usant, ~e** /yzɑ̃, ɑ̃t/ adj exhausting, wearing

**usé, ~e** /yze/ **1** pp ▶ USER
**2** pp adj ⟨object⟩ worn; ⟨person⟩ worn-down; ⟨heart, eyes⟩ worn-out; ⟨joke⟩ hackneyed; ~ **jusqu'à la corde** ⟨carpet⟩ threadbare; ⟨tyre⟩ worn down to the tread; (figurative) ⟨joke⟩ hackneyed

**user** /yze/ **1** vtr to wear out ⟨shoes⟩; to wear down ⟨person⟩; **les piles sont usées** the batteries have run down or out; ~ **ses vêtements jusqu'à la corde** to wear one's clothes out; ~ **sa santé** to ruin one's health
**2** **user de** v+prep (gen) to use; to exercise ⟨right⟩; to take ⟨precautions⟩; ~ **de diplomatie** to be diplomatic
**3** **s'user** v refl (+ v être) **(a)** ⟨shoes⟩ to wear out

**(b)** ⟨person⟩ **s'~ à la tâche** or **au travail** to wear oneself out with overwork; **s'~ la santé** to ruin one's health

**usinage** /yzinaʒ/ nm **(a)** (with a machine tool) machining
**(b)** (industrial production) manufacture

**usine** /yzin/ nf factory, plant
■ ~ **de traitement** recycling plant; ~ **métallurgique** ironworks; ~ **sidérurgique** steelworks

**usiner** /yzine/ [1] vtr **(a)** to machine
**(b)** to manufacture

**usité, ~e** /yzite/ adj commonly used

**ustensile** /ystɑ̃sil/ nm utensil

**usuel, -elle** /yzɥɛl/ adj ⟨object⟩ everyday; ⟨word⟩ common

**usufruit** /yzyfʀɥi/ nm (Law) usufruct

**usufruitier, -ière** /yzyfʀɥitje, ɛʀ/ nm,f tenant for life

**usure** /yzyʀ/ nf **(a)** (of clothes) wear and tear; (of tyre, machine) wear; **résister à l'~** to wear well
**(b)** (of energy, enemy) wearing down
**(c)** ~ **du temps** wearing effect of time
**(d)** usury

**usurier, -ière** /yzyʀje, ɛʀ/ nm,f usurer

**usurpateur, -trice** /yzyʀpatœʀ, tʀis/ nm,f usurper

**usurpation** /yzyʀpasjɔ̃/ nf usurpation

**usurper** /yzyʀpe/ [1] vtr to usurp

**ut** /yt/ nm (Mus) C

**utérus** /yteʀys/ nm inv womb

**utile** /ytil/ **1** adj (gen) useful; **être ~** ⟨person, book⟩ to be helpful; ⟨umbrella⟩ to come in handy; **il est ~ de signaler** it's worth pointing out; **il n'a pas jugé ~ de me prévenir** he didn't think it necessary to let me know; **en quoi puis-je vous être ~?** how can I help you?
**2** nm **joindre l'~ à l'agréable** to mix business with pleasure

**utilement** /ytilmɑ̃/ adv ⟨intervene⟩ effectively; ⟨occupy oneself⟩ usefully

**utilisable** /ytilizabl/ adj usable

**utilisateur, -trice** /ytilizatœʀ, tʀis/ nm,f user

**utilisation** /ytilizasjɔ̃/ nf use

**utiliser** /ytilize/ [1] vtr (gen) to use; to make use of ⟨resources⟩

**utilitaire** /ytilitɛʀ/ adj ⟨role⟩ practical; ⟨object⟩ functional, utilitarian; ⟨vehicle⟩ commercial

**utilité** /ytilite/ nf **(a)** usefulness; **d'une grande ~** ⟨book, machine⟩ very useful; ⟨person⟩ very helpful; **d'aucune ~** of no use
**(b)** use; **je n'en ai pas l'~** I have no use for it

**utopie** /ytɔpi/ nf **(a)** Utopia
**(b)** wishful thinking

**utopique** /ytɔpik/ adj utopian

**UV** /yve/ nm pl (abbr = **ultraviolets**) ultraviolet rays; **séance d'~** session on a sunbed

**uvule** /yvyl/ nf uvula

# Vv

**v, V** /ve/ *nm inv* v, V; **en (forme de) V** V-shaped; **pull en V** V-necked sweater
**va** /va/ ▶ ALLER[1]
**vacance** /vakɑ̃s/ [1] *nf* vacancy
[2] **vacances** *nf pl* holiday (GB), vacation (US); **être en ~s** to be on holiday (GB) *or* vacation (US)
■ **~s scolaires** (Sch) school holidays (GB) *or* vacation (US)
**vacancier, -ière** /vakɑ̃sje, ɛʀ/ *nm,f* holidaymaker (GB), vacationer (US)
**vacant, ~e** /vakɑ̃, ɑ̃t/ *adj* vacant
**vacarme** /vakaʀm/ *nm* din, racket (colloq)
**vacataire** /vakatɛʀ/ *nmf* (a) temporary employee
(b) supply teacher (GB), substitute teacher (US)
**vaccin** /vaksɛ̃/ *nm* (Med) vaccine
**vaccination** /vaksinasjɔ̃/ *nf* vaccination
**vacciner** /vaksine/ [1] *vtr* (a) to vaccinate
(b) (humorous) **je suis vacciné!** (colloq) I've learned my lesson!
**vache** /vaʃ/ [1] *adj* (colloq) mean, nasty
[2] *nf* (a) cow
(b) cowhide
■ **~ à eau** water bottle; **~ à lait** (figurative) money-spinner (colloq); **années de ~s maigres** lean years
IDIOMS **parler français comme une ~ espagnole** (colloq) to speak very bad French
**vachement** /vaʃmɑ̃/ *adv* (colloq) really
**vacherie** /vaʃʀi/ *nf* (colloq) (a) meanness
(b) bitchy remark (colloq)
(c) dirty trick
(d) **c'est une vraie ~ ce virus** this virus is a damned nuisance (colloq)
**vachette** /vaʃɛt/ *nf* (a) young cow
(b) calfskin
**vacillant, ~e** /vasijɑ̃, ɑ̃t/ *adj* (a) ⟨legs⟩ unsteady; ⟨person⟩ unsteady on one's legs; ⟨light, flame⟩ flickering
(b) ⟨power, majority⟩ shaky
**vaciller** /vasije/ [1] *vi* (a) ⟨person⟩ to be unsteady on one's legs; ⟨legs⟩ to be unsteady
(b) ⟨person, object⟩ to sway; ⟨light, flame⟩ to flicker
(c) ⟨health⟩ to fail; ⟨majority⟩ to weaken
**vadrouille** /vadʀuj/ *nf* (colloq) stroll; **être en ~** to be wandering about
**vadrouiller** /vadʀuje/ [1] *vi* (colloq) to wander around
**va-et-vient** /vaevjɛ̃/ *nm inv* (a) comings and goings; **faire le ~** to go to and fro; to go back and forth
(b) two-way switch
**vagabond, ~e** /vagabɔ̃, ɔ̃d/ [1] *adj* ⟨dog⟩ stray; ⟨mood⟩ ever-changing

[2] *nm,f* vagrant
**vagabondage** /vagabɔ̃daʒ/ *nm*
(a) wandering
(b) (Law) vagrancy
**vagabonder** /vagabɔ̃de/ [1] *vi* to wander
**vagin** /vaʒɛ̃/ *nm* vagina
**vagissement** /vaʒismɑ̃/ *nm* wail
**vague¹** /vag/ [1] *adj* vague; **ce sont de ~s parents** they're distant relatives
[2] *nm* (a) **il regardait dans le ~** he was staring into space
(b) **avoir du ~ à l'âme** to feel melancholic
**vague²** /vag/ *nf* wave; **faire des ~s** ⟨wind⟩ to make ripples; (figurative) ⟨scandal⟩ to cause a stir
■ **~ de chaleur** heatwave; **~ de froid** cold spell
IDIOMS **être au creux de la ~** to be at a low ebb
**vaguement** /vagmɑ̃/ *adv* vaguely
**vaillamment** /vajamɑ̃/ *adv* courageously, valiantly
**vaillance** /vajɑ̃s/ *nf* courage; **avec ~** courageously
**vaillant, ~e** /vajɑ̃, ɑ̃t/ *adj* (a) courageous
(b) strong
**vain, ~e** /vɛ̃, vɛn/ [1] *adj* (a) futile; **mes efforts ont été ~s** my efforts were in vain
(b) ⟨promises⟩ empty; ⟨hopes⟩ vain
(c) ⟨person⟩ vain
[2] **en vain** *phr* in vain
**vaincre** /vɛ̃kʀ/ [57] [1] *vtr* (a) to defeat ⟨opponent⟩
(b) to overcome ⟨prejudices, complex⟩; to beat ⟨unemployment, illness⟩
[2] *vi* to win
**vaincu, ~e** /vɛ̃ky/ ▶ VAINCRE
**vainement** /vɛnmɑ̃/ *adv* in vain
**vainqueur** /vɛ̃kœʀ/ [1] *adj m* victorious
[2] *nm* victor; winner; prizewinner; conqueror
**vais** /vɛ/ ▶ ALLER[1]
**vaisseau, pl ~x** /veso/ *nm* (a) (Anat, Bot) vessel
(b) (Naut) vessel; warship
■ **~ spatial** spaceship
**vaisselier** /vesəlje/ *nm* dresser
**vaisselle** /vesɛl/ *nf* (a) crockery, dishes
(b) dishes; **faire la ~** to do the dishes
**val, pl ~s** *or* **vaux** /val, vo/ *nm* valley
IDIOMS **être toujours par monts et par vaux** to be always on the move
**valable** /valabl/ *adj* (a) ⟨explanation⟩ valid; ⟨solution⟩ viable
(b) ⟨document⟩ valid
(c) (colloq) ⟨work, project⟩ worthwhile

**valdinguer** /valdɛ̃ge/ [1] *vi* (colloq) to go flying (colloq)

**valet** /valɛ/ *nm* (a) manservant
(b) (in cards) jack
■ ~ **de chambre** valet; ~ **de ferme** farm hand; ~ **de nuit** rack, valet (US)

**valeur** /valœʀ/ *nf* (a) value; **prendre de la** ~ to go up in value; **les objets de** ~ valuables
(b) (of person, artist) worth; (of work) value, merit; (of method, discovery) value; **attacher de la** ~ **à qch** to value sth; **mettre qch en** ~ to emphasize ⟨*fact, talent*⟩; to set off ⟨*eyes, painting*⟩; **se mettre en** ~ to make the best of oneself; to show oneself to best advantage
(c) validity
(d) value; **nous n'avons pas les mêmes** ~s we don't share the same values
(e) (on stock exchange) security; ~s securities, stock, stocks and shares
■ ~ **sûre** gilt-edged security (GB), blue chip; (figurative) safe bet; ~s **mobilières** securities

**valeureux, -euse** /valøʀø, øz/ *adj* valorous

**validation** /validasjɔ̃/ *nf* (a) validation
(b) stamping

**valide** /valid/ *adj* (a) valid
(b) able-bodied; fit

**valider** /valide/ [1] *vtr* to stamp ⟨*ticket*⟩; **faire** ~ to have [sth] recognized ⟨*diploma*⟩

**validité** /validite/ *nf* validity

**valise** /valiz/ *nf* suitcase; **faire ses** ~s to pack
IDIOMS **avoir des** ~s **sous les yeux** (colloq) to have bags under one's eyes

**vallée** /vale/ *nf* valley

**vallon** /valɔ̃/ *nm* dale, small valley

**vallonné, ~e** /valɔne/ *adj* ⟨*landscape*⟩ undulating; ⟨*country*⟩ hilly

**valoir** /valwaʀ/ [45] **1** *vtr* ~ **qch à qn** to earn sb sth ⟨*praise, criticism*⟩; to win sb sth ⟨*friendship*⟩; to bring sb sth ⟨*problems*⟩
**2** *vi* (a) ~ **une fortune/cher** to be worth a fortune/a lot; **ça vaut combien?** how much is it worth?; ~ **de l'or** (figurative) to be very valuable
(b) **que vaut ce film/vin?** what's that film/wine like?; **il ne vaut pas mieux que son frère** he's no better than his brother; **ne rien** ~ to be rubbish; to be useless; to be worthless; **la chaleur ne me vaut rien** the heat doesn't suit me; **ça ne me dit rien qui vaille** I don't like the sound of it
(c) to be as good as; **ton travail vaut bien/largement le leur** your work is just as good/every bit as good as theirs; **rien ne vaut la soie** nothing beats silk
(d) to be worth; **le musée vaut le détour** the museum is worth a detour; **ça vaut la peine** *or* **le coup** (colloq) it's worth it
(e) ⟨*rule, criticism*⟩ to apply
(f) **faire** ~ to put [sth] to work ⟨*money*⟩; to point out ⟨*necessity*⟩; to emphasize ⟨*quality*⟩; to assert ⟨*right*⟩; **faire** ~ **que** to point out that; **se faire** ~ to push oneself forward

**3 se valoir** *v refl* (+ *v être*) to be the same
**4** *v impers* **il vaut mieux faire, mieux vaut faire** it's better to do; **il vaut mieux que tu y ailles** you'd better go

**valorisation** /valɔʀizasjɔ̃/ *nf* (a) (of product) promotion
(b) (of region, resources) development

**valoriser** /valɔʀize/ [1] *vtr* (a) to promote ⟨*product*⟩; to make [sth] attractive ⟨*profession, course*⟩
(b) to develop ⟨*region, resources*⟩

**valse** /vals/ *nf* waltz

**valse-hésitation,** *pl* **valses-hésitations** /valsezitasjɔ̃/ *nf* shilly-shallying (colloq)

**valser** /valse/ [1] *vi* to waltz

**valseur, -euse** /valsœʀ, øz/ *nm,f* waltzer

**valu, ~e** /valy/ ▶ VALOIR

**valve** /valv/ *nf* valve

**vamp** /vɑ̃p/ *nf* (colloq) vamp

**vampire** /vɑ̃piʀ/ *nm* (a) vampire
(b) (figurative) bloodsucker
(c) (Zool) vampire bat

**vampiriser** /vɑ̃piʀize/ [1] *vtr* (figurative) to cannibalize

**van** /vɑ̃/ *nm* (a) horsebox (GB), horse-car (US)
(b) van

**vandale** /vɑ̃dal/ *nmf* vandal

**vandalisme** /vɑ̃dalism/ *nm* vandalism

**vanille** /vanij/ *nf* vanilla; **une gousse de** ~ a vanilla pod

**vanité** /vanite/ *nf* (a) vanity; **tirer** ~ **de qch** to pride oneself on sth
(b) (of efforts) futility; (of promise) emptiness; (of undertaking) uselessness

**vaniteux, -euse** /vanitø, øz/ *adj* vain

**vanne** /van/ *nf* (a) gate; sluice gate; floodgate
(b) (colloq) dig (colloq)
IDIOMS **fermer les** ~s (colloq) to cut funding

**vanner** /vane/ [1] *vtr* (colloq) to tire [sb] out

**vannerie** /vanʀi/ *nf* basket-making; **objets en** ~ wickerwork

**vantardise** /vɑ̃taʀdiz/ *nf* (a) boastfulness
(b) boast

**vanter** /vɑ̃te/ [1] **1** *vtr* to praise, to extol
**2 se vanter** *v refl* (+ *v être*) to boast
(b) **se** ~ **de faire** to pride oneself on doing

**va-nu-pieds** /vanypje/ *nmf inv* tramp, bum (US) (colloq)

**vapeur** /vapœʀ/ **1** *nf* steam; **bateau à** ~ steamboat; **renverser la** ~ (figurative) to backpedal; **faire cuire qch à la** ~ to steam sth
**2 vapeurs** *nf pl* fumes

**vaporeux, -euse** /vapɔʀø, øz/ *adj* diaphanous

**vaporisateur** /vapɔʀizatœʀ/ *nm* spray

**vaporisation** /vapɔʀizasjɔ̃/ *nf* spraying

**vaporiser** /vapɔʀize/ [1] *vtr* to spray

**vaquer** /vake/ [1] *v+prep* ~ **à ses occupations** to attend to one's business

**varappe** /vaʀap/ *nf* rock-climbing

**varappeur, -euse** /vaʀapœʀ, øz/ *nm,f*
rock climber

**varech** /vaʀɛk/ *nm* kelp

**vareuse** /vaʀøz/ *nf* **(a)** jersey
**(b)** (Mil) uniform jacket

**variable** /vaʀjabl/ **1** *adj* **(a)** variable
**(b)** ⟨*weather*⟩ changeable; ⟨*mood*⟩
unpredictable
**2** *nf* variable

**variante** /vaʀjɑ̃t/ *nf* variant

**variation** /vaʀjasjɔ̃/ *nf* variation;
**connaître de fortes ~s** to fluctuate
considerably

**varice** /vaʀis/ *nf* varicose vein

**varicelle** /vaʀisɛl/ *nf* chicken pox

**varié, ~e** /vaʀje/ *adj* **(a)** varied
**(b)** various

**varier** /vaʀje/ **2** **1** *vtr* to vary; **pour ~ les
plaisirs** just for a (pleasant) change
**2** *vi* to vary; **l'inflation varie de 4% à 6%**
inflation fluctuates between 4% and 6%

**variété** /vaʀjete/ **1** *nf* **(a)** variety; **une
grande ~ d'articles** a wide range of items
**(b)** (Bot) variety
**(c)** sort
**2** **variétés** *nf pl* **spectacle de ~s** variety
show; **les ~s françaises** French popular
music

**variole** /vaʀjɔl/ *nf* smallpox

**Varsovie** /vaʀsɔvi/ *pr n* Warsaw

**vas** /va/ ▶ ALLER¹

**vase¹** /vaz/ *nm* vase
IDIOMS **c'est la goutte d'eau qui fait
déborder le ~** it's the last straw

**vase²** /vaz/ *nf* silt, sludge

**vasectomie** /vazɛktɔmi/ *nf* vasectomy

**vaseux, -euse** /vazø, øz/ *adj* **(a)** muddy
**(b)** (colloq) **je me sens plutôt ~** I'm not really
with it (colloq)
**(c)** (colloq) ⟨*speech, explanation*⟩ woolly

**vasistas** /vazistas/ *nm inv* louvre (GB)
window

**vasque** /vask/ *nf* **(a)** (of fountain) basin
**(b)** bowl

**vassal, ~e,** *mpl* **-aux** /vasal, o/ *nm,f*
vassal

**vaste** /vast/ *adj* **(a)** ⟨*estate, sector*⟩ vast;
⟨*market*⟩ huge
**(b)** ⟨*audience, choice*⟩ large
**(c)** ⟨*fraud*⟩ massive; ⟨*campaign*⟩ extensive;
⟨*movement, attack*⟩ large-scale; ⟨*work*⟩ wide-
ranging

**va-t-en-guerre** /vatɑ̃gɛʀ/ *nm inv*
warmonger

**va-tout** /vatu/ *nm inv* **jouer/tenter son ~**
to stake/to risk everything

**vaudeville** /vodvil/ *nm* light comedy;
**tourner au ~** to turn into a farce

**vaudou** /vodu/ *adj inv, nm* voodoo

**vaurien, -ienne** /voʀjɛ̃, ɛn/ *nm,f*
**(a)** rascal
**(b)** lout, yobbo (GB) (colloq), hoodlum (colloq)

**vautour** /votuʀ/ *nm* vulture

**vautrer: se vautrer** /votʀe/ [1] *v refl*
(+ *v être*) **(a) se ~ sur** to sprawl on
**(b) se ~ dans un fauteuil** to loll in an
armchair

**va-vite: à la va-vite** /alavavit/ *phr* in a
rush

**veau,** *pl* **~x** /vo/ *nm* **(a)** calf
**(b)** (Culin) veal
**(c)** calfskin

**vecteur** /vɛktœʀ/ *nm* **(a)** vector
**(b)** (figurative) vehicle
**(c)** (of disease) carrier

**vécu, ~e** /veky/ **1** *pp* ▶ VIVRE
**2** *pp adj* ⟨*drama, story*⟩ real-life
**3** *nm* personal experiences

**vedette** /vədɛt/ *nf* **(a)** star; **avoir la ~** to
have top billing
**(b)** (Naut) launch

**végétal, ~e,** *mpl* **-aux** /veʒetal, o/
**1** *adj* vegetable
**2** *nm* vegetable

**végétalien, -ienne** /veʒetaljɛ̃, ɛn/ *adj,
nm,f* vegan

**végétarien, -ienne** /veʒetaʀjɛ̃, ɛn/ *adj,
nm,f* vegetarian

**végétatif, -ive** /veʒetatif, iv/ *adj*
vegetative

**végétation** /veʒetasjɔ̃/ **1** *nf* vegetation
**2** **végétations** *nf pl* (Med) adenoids

**végéter** /veʒete/ [14] *vi* ⟨*person*⟩ to
vegetate; ⟨*project*⟩ to stagnate

**véhémence** /veemɑ̃s/ *nf* vehemence

**véhicule** /veikyl/ *nm* vehicle
■ **~ utilitaire** commercial vehicle

**véhiculer** /veikyle/ [1] *vtr* to carry
⟨*people, goods, substance*⟩; **~ une image** to
promote an image

**veille** /vɛj/ *nf* **(a) la ~** the day before; **la ~
au soir** the night before; **à la ~ de** on the
eve of
**(b) être en état de ~** to be awake
**(c)** vigil

**veillée** /veje/ *nf* **(a)** evening; **à la ~** in the
evening
**(b)** vigil; **~ funèbre** wake

**veiller** /veje/ [1] **1** *vtr* to watch over ⟨*ill
person*⟩; to keep watch over ⟨*dead person*⟩
**2** **veiller à** *v+prep* to look after ⟨*health*⟩;
**~ à ce que** to see to it that, to make sure
that
**3** **veiller sur** *v+prep* to watch over ⟨*child*⟩
**4** *vi* **(a)** to stay up
**(b)** to be on watch
**(c)** to be watchful
IDIOMS **~ au grain** to be on one's guard

**veilleur** /vɛjœʀ/ *nm,f* **~ de nuit** night
watchman

**veilleuse** /vɛjøz/ *nf* **(a)** night light
**(b)** pilot light
**(c)** side light (GB), parking light (US)

**veinard, ~e** /venaʀ, aʀd/ *nm,f* (colloq)
lucky devil (colloq)

**veine** /vɛn/ *nf* **(a)** vein
**(b)** (in wood) grain

····⋮·

**(c)** (of coal) seam
**(d)** inspiration; **dans la même ~** in the same vein; **en ~ de générosité** in a generous mood
**(e)** (colloq) luck; **il a de la ~** he's lucky
**veiné, ~e** /vene/ *adj* ‹skin, hand, marble› veined; ‹wood› grained
**veinure** /venyʀ/ *nf* (in wood) grain; (in marble) veining
**vêler** /vɛle/ [1] *vi* ‹cow› to calve
**velléité** /vɛlleite/ *nf* **(a)** vague desire
**(b)** vague attempt
**vélo** /velo/ *nm* (colloq) bike; **faire du ~** to cycle
■ **~ d'appartement** exercise bike; **~ tout terrain, VTT** mountain bike
**vélo-cross** /velokʀɔs/ *nm inv* **(a)** cyclo-cross
**(b)** cyclo-cross bike
**vélomoteur** /velomɔtœʀ/ *nm* moped
**velours** /vəluʀ/ *nm inv* **(a)** velvet
**(b)** corduroy
IDIOMS **une main de fer dans un gant de ~** an iron fist in a velvet glove; **faire patte de ~** to switch on the charm
**velouté, ~e** /vəlute/ **1** *adj* ‹skin, voice› velvety; ‹wine› smooth
**2** *nm* **(a)** (Culin) **~ de champignons** cream of mushroom soup
**(b)** softness; smoothness
**velu, ~e** /vəly/ *adj* **(a)** hairy
**(b)** (Bot) villous
**vénal, ~e**, *mpl* **-aux** /venal, o/ *adj* ‹person› venal; ‹behaviour› mercenary
**vendable** /vɑ̃dabl/ *adj* saleable (GB)
**vendange** /vɑ̃dɑ̃ʒ/ *nf* grape harvest
**vendanger** /vɑ̃dɑ̃ʒe/ [13] **1** *vtr* to harvest ‹grapes›; to pick the grapes from ‹vine›
**2** *vi* to harvest the grapes
**vendeur, -euse** /vɑ̃dœʀ, øz/ *nm,f* **(a)** shop assistant
**(b)** salesman/saleswoman
■ **~ ambulant** pedlar (GB), peddler (US); **~ de journaux** news vendor
**vendre** /vɑ̃dʀ/ [6] **1** *vtr* **(a)** to sell; **~ à crédit** to sell on credit; **~ en gros** to wholesale; **~ au détail** to retail; **'à ~'** 'for sale'
**(b)** to betray ‹person›; to sell ‹secrets›
**2 se vendre** *v refl* (+ *v être*) **(a)** to be sold
**(b)** **se ~ bien** to sell well
**(c)** to sell oneself; **se ~ à l'ennemi** to sell out to the enemy
**vendredi** /vɑ̃dʀədi/ *nm* Friday; **~ saint** Good Friday
**vendu, ~e** /vɑ̃dy/ **1** *pp* ▶ VENDRE
**2** *pp adj* bribed
**3** *nm,f* traitor
**vénéneux, -euse** /venenø, øz/ *adj* poisonous
**vénérable** /veneʀabl/ *adj* ‹person› venerable; ‹tree, object› ancient
**vénération** /veneʀasjɔ̃/ *nf* veneration
**vénérer** /veneʀe/ [14] *vtr* to venerate; to revere

**vénérien, -ienne** /veneʀjɛ̃, ɛn/ *adj* venereal
**vengeance** /vɑ̃ʒɑ̃s/ *nf* revenge
**venger** /vɑ̃ʒe/ [13] **1** *vtr* to avenge
**2 se venger** *v refl* (+ *v être*) to get one's revenge; **se ~ sur qn/qch** to take it out on sb/sth
**vengeur, vengeresse** /vɑ̃ʒœʀ, vɑ̃ʒʀɛs/ *adj* vengeful; avenging; vindictive
**véniel, -ielle** /venjɛl/ *adj* ‹sin› venial
**venimeux, -euse** /vənimø, øz/ *adj* venomous
**venin** /vənɛ̃/ *nm* venom
**venir** /vəniʀ/ [36] **1** *v aux* **(a)** venir de faire to have just done; **elle vient de partir** she's just left; **'vient de paraître'** (of book) 'new!'
**(b)** **~ aggraver la situation** to make the situation worse
**(c)** **le ballon est venu rouler sous mes pieds** the ball rolled up to my feet
**(d)** **s'il venait à pleuvoir** if it should rain
**2** *vi* (+ *v être*) **(a)** to come; **~ de** to come from; **~ après/avant** to come after/before; **allez, viens!** come on!; **viens voir** come and see; **j'en viens** I've just been there; **je viens de sa part** he/she sent me to see you; **faire ~ qn** to send for sb; to get sb to come; **faire ~ le médecin** to call the doctor; **ça ne m'est jamais venu à l'idée** it never crossed my mind; **dans les jours à ~** in the next few days
**(b)** **en ~ à** to come to; **en ~ aux mains** to come to blows
**vent** /vɑ̃/ *nm* **(a)** wind; **~ d'est** east wind; **~ du large** seaward wind; **grand ~** gale, strong wind; **il fait** *or* **il y a du ~** it's windy; **en plein ~** exposed to the wind; in the open; **passer en coup de ~** (figurative) to rush through; **faire du ~** (with fan) to create a breeze; **~ favorable, bon ~** favourable (GB) wind; **avoir le ~ en poupe** to sail *or* run before the wind; (figurative) to have the wind in one's sails; **coup de ~** fresh gale
**(b)** **un ~ de liberté** a wind of freedom; **un ~ de folie** a wave of madness
**(c)** (euphemistic) wind
IDIOMS **c'est du ~!** it's just hot air!; **du ~!** (colloq) get lost! (colloq); **quel bon ~ vous amène?** to what do I owe the pleasure (of your visit)?; **être dans le ~** to be trendy; **avoir ~ de qch** to get wind of sth; **contre ~s et marées** come hell or high water; against all odds
**vente** /vɑ̃t/ *nf* sale; **en ~ libre** (gen) freely available; ‹medicines› available over the counter; **mettre qch en ~** to put [sth] up for sale
■ **~ par correspondance** mail order selling; **~ au détail** retailing; **~ aux enchères** auction (sale); **~ en gros** wholesaling
**ventilateur** /vɑ̃tilatœʀ/ *nm* fan; ventilator
**ventilation** /vɑ̃tilasjɔ̃/ *nf* ventilation (system)
**ventiler** /vɑ̃tile/ [1] *vtr* **(a)** to ventilate
**(b)** to break down ‹expenses, profits›

**(c)** to assign ⟨staff⟩; to allocate ⟨tasks, equipment⟩

**ventouse** /vãtuz/ *nf* **(a)** suction pad (GB), suction cup (US); **faire ∼** to stick
**(b)** plunger
**(c)** (Med) cupping glass

**ventral, ∼e,** *mpl* **-aux** /vãtral, o/ *adj* ventral; **parachute ∼** lap-pack parachute

**ventre** /vãtr/ *nm* **(a)** stomach; **avoir mal au ∼** to have stomach ache; **ça me donne mal au ∼ de voir ça** (figurative) (colloq) it makes me sick to see that sort of thing
**(b)** (of animal) (under)belly
**(c) ne rien avoir dans le ∼** (colloq) to have no guts (colloq); **avoir la peur au ∼** to feel sick with fear
**(d)** (of pot, boat, plane) belly
IDIOMS **courir ∼ à terre** to run flat out

**ventricule** /vãtrikyl/ *nm* ventricle

**ventriloque** /vãtrilɔk/ *nmf* ventriloquist

**ventripotent, ∼e** /vãtripɔtã, ãt/ *adj* (colloq) portly, fat-bellied

**ventru, ∼e** /vãtry/ *adj* ⟨man⟩ paunchy, pot-bellied; ⟨pot, piece of furniture⟩ rounded; ⟨wall⟩ bulging

**venu, ∼e¹** /vəny/ ①*pp* ▶ VENIR
② *pp adj* **bien ∼** apt; **mal ∼** badly timed; **il serait mal ∼ de le leur dire** it wouldn't be a good idea to tell them
③ *nm,f* **nouveau ∼** newcomer

**venue²** /vəny/ *nf* visit; **∼ au monde** birth

**vêpres** /vɛpr/ *nf pl* vespers

**ver** /vɛr/ *nm* worm; woodworm; maggot
■ **∼ à soie** silkworm; **∼ solitaire** tapeworm; **∼ de terre** earthworm
IDIOMS **tirer les ∼s du nez à qn** (colloq) to worm information out of sb

**véracité** /verasite/ *nf* truthfulness

**véranda** /verãda/ *nf* veranda

**verbal, ∼e,** *mpl* **-aux** /vɛrbal, o/ *adj* verbal; verb

**verbaliser** /vɛrbalize/ [1] *vi* to record an offence (GB)

**verbe** /vɛrb/ *nm* **(a)** verb
**(b)** language; **avoir le ∼ haut** to be arrogant in one's speech

**verdâtre** /vɛrdɑtr/ *adj* greenish

**verdeur** /vɛrdœr/ *nf* sprightliness

**verdict** /vɛrdikt/ *nm* verdict

**verdir** /vɛrdir/ [3] *vi* **(a)** (gen) to turn green; ⟨copper⟩ to tarnish
**(b)** to turn pale

**verdoyant, ∼e** /vɛrdwajã, ãt/ *adj* green

**verdure** /vɛrdyr/ *nf* **(a)** greenery
**(b)** green vegetables

**véreux, -euse** /verø, øz/ *adj* **(a)** ⟨fruit⟩ worm-eaten
**(b)** ⟨politician, lawyer⟩ bent (colloq), crooked

**verge** /vɛrʒ/ *nf* **(a)** penis
**(b)** switch, birch

**vergé** /vɛrʒe/ *nm* laid paper

**verger** /vɛrʒe/ *nm* orchard

**vergeture** /vɛrʒətyr/ *nf* stretch mark

**verglacé, ∼e** /vɛrɡlase/ *adj* icy

**verglas** /vɛrɡla/ *nm inv* black ice

**vergogne: sans vergogne** /sãvɛrɡɔɲ/ *phr* shamelessly

**véridique** /veridik/ *adj* true

**vérifiable** /verifjabl/ *adj* **être facilement ∼** to be easy to check *or* verify

**vérification** /verifikasjɔ̃/ *nf* (on equipment, identity) check; (of alibi, fact) verification

**vérifier** /verifje/ [2] ① *vtr* to check; to verify
② **se vérifier** *v refl* (+ *v être*) ⟨hypothesis, theory⟩ to be borne out

**véritable** /veritabl/ *adj* real; true; genuine

**véritablement** /veritabləmã/ *adv* really

**vérité** /verite/ *nf* **(a)** truth; **l'épreuve de ∼** the acid test; **à la ∼** to tell the truth
**(b) énoncer des ∼s premières** to state the obvious
**(c)** sincerity

**verlan** /vɛrlã/ *nm*: French slang formed by inverting the syllables

**vermeil, -eille** /vɛrmɛj/ ① *adj* **(a)** bright red
**(b)** ⟨wine⟩ ruby
② *nm* vermeil

**vermicelle** /vɛrmisɛl/ *nm* **du ∼, des ∼s** vermicelli

**vermifuge** /vɛrmifyʒ/ *nm* wormer

**vermillon** /vɛrmijɔ̃/ *adj inv* bright red

**vermine** /vɛrmin/ *nf* **(a)** vermin
**(b)** (figurative) scum

**vermoulu, ∼e** /vɛrmuly/ *adj* worm-eaten

**verni, ∼e** /vɛrni/ ① *pp* ▶ VERNIR
② *pp adj* varnished; patent-leather; glazed
③ *adj* (colloq) lucky; **il n'est pas ∼** he's unlucky

**vernir** /vɛrnir/ [3] ① *vtr* to varnish; to glaze
② **se vernir** *v refl* (+ *v être*) **se ∼ les ongles** to paint one's nails

**vernis** /vɛrni/ *nm inv* **(a)** varnish; glaze
**(b)** (figurative) veneer; **si on gratte le ∼, on voit que...** if you scratch the surface, you'll see that...
■ **∼ à ongles** nail varnish (GB) *or* polish

**vernissage** /vɛrnisaʒ/ *nm* **(a)** (of art exhibition) preview, private view
**(b)** varnishing; glazing

**vernissé, ∼e** /vɛrnise/ *adj* **(a)** glazed
**(b)** glossy

**verre** /vɛr/ *nm* **(a)** glass; **de** *or* **en ∼** glass; **un ∼ à eau/vin** a water/wine glass; **∼s et couverts** glassware and cutlery; **lever son ∼ à la santé de qn** to raise one's glass to sb
**(b)** glass, glassful; **un ∼ d'eau/de vin** a glass of water/wine
**(c)** drink
**(d)** lens; **∼ grossissant** magnifying glass
■ **∼ de contact** contact lens; **∼ à pied** stemmed glass

**verrerie** /vɛrri/ *nf* **(a)** glassmaking
**(b)** glassworks, glass factory

**verrière** /vɛRjɛR/ nf (a) glass roof
  (b) glass wall
**verroterie** /vɛRɔtRi/ nf glass jewellery (GB)
  or jewelry (US)
**verrou** /vɛRu/ nm bolt
  IDIOMS **être sous les ~s** to be behind bars
**verrouillage** /vɛRujaʒ/ nm bolting;
  locking; locking mechanism
  ■ ~ **central** or **centralisé (des portes)** central
  locking
**verrouiller** /vɛRuje/ [1] vtr to bolt
  ⟨window, door⟩; to lock ⟨car door, gun⟩
**verrue** /vɛRy/ nf wart; ~ **plantaire** verruca
**vers¹** /vɛR/ prep

  ■ **Note** When vers is part of an expression such
  as se tourner vers, tendre vers etc, you will find
  the translation at the entries TOURNER, TENDRE¹
  3 etc.
  – See below for other uses of vers.

  (a) toward(s); **se déplacer de la gauche ~ la**
  **droite** to move from left to right
  (b) near, around; about; toward(s); ~ **cinq**
  **heures** at about five o'clock; ~ **le soir**
  toward(s) evening
**vers²** /vɛR/ nm inv line (of verse)
**versant** /vɛRsɑ̃/ nm side
**versatile** /vɛRsatil/ adj unpredictable,
  volatile
**verse**: **à verse** /avɛRs/ phr **il pleut à ~** it's
  pouring down
**Verseau** /vɛRso/ pr nm Aquarius
**versement** /vɛRsəmɑ̃/ nm (a) payment;
  ~ **comptant** cash payment
  (b) instalment (GB)
  (c) deposit; **faire un ~ sur son compte** to pay
  money into one's account
**verser** /vɛRse/ [1] **1** vtr (a) to pour
  (b) to pay ⟨sum, pension⟩
  (c) to shed ⟨tear, blood⟩
  (d) ~ **une pièce à un dossier** to add a
  document to a file
  **2** vi (a) to overturn
  (b) to lapse
  (c) ⟨jug⟩ to pour
**verset** /vɛRsɛ/ nm (in Bible, Koran) verse
**verseur, -euse** /vɛRsœR, øz/ adj pouring;
  **flacon ~** bottle with a pouring spout
**versifier** /vɛRsifje/ [2] vtr to put [sth] into
  verse
**version** /vɛRsjɔ̃/ nf (a) translation (into
  one's own language)
  (b) version
  ■ ~ **originale, vo** (of film) original version
**verso** /vɛRso/ nm back; **voir au ~** see
  over(leaf)
**vert, ~e** /vɛR, vɛRt/ **1** adj (a) green; **être**
  ~ **de peur** to be white with fear
  (b) ⟨fruit⟩ green, unripe; ⟨wine⟩ immature
  (c) sprightly
  (d) (before n) ⟨reprimand⟩ sharp, stiff
  **2** nm green
  **3** **verts** nm pl **les ~s** the Greens

  IDIOMS **avoir la main ~e** to have green
  fingers (GB) or a green thumb (US)
**vert-de-gris** /vɛRdəgRi/ **1** adj inv blue-
  green
  **2** nm inv verdigris
**vertébral, ~e**, mpl **-aux** /vɛRtebRal, o/
  adj vertebral
**vertébré** /vɛRtebRe/ nm vertebrate
**vertèbre** /vɛRtɛbR/ nf vertebra
**vertement** /vɛRtəmɑ̃/ adv sharply
**vertical, ~e¹**, mpl **-aux** /vɛRtikal, o/ adj
  vertical; upright
**verticale²** /vɛRtikal/ nf vertical
**verticalement** /vɛRtikalmɑ̃/ adv
  (a) vertically
  (b) (in crossword) down
**vertige** /vɛRtiʒ/ nm (a) dizziness; vertigo;
  **avoir le ~** to suffer from vertigo; to feel
  dizzy
  (b) **avoir des ~s** to have dizzy or giddy
  spells
**vertigineux, -euse** /vɛRtiʒinø, øz/ adj
  dizzy, giddy; breathtaking; staggering
**vertu** /vɛRty/ **1** nf (a) virtue; **de petite ~** of
  easy virtue
  (b) (of plant, remedy) property
  **2** **en vertu de** phr by virtue of ⟨law⟩; in
  accordance with ⟨agreement⟩
**vertueux, -euse** /vɛRtɥø, øz/ adj
  virtuous
**verve** /vɛRv/ nf eloquence
**verveine** /vɛRvɛn/ nf verbena (tea)
**vésicule** /vezikyl/ nf vesicle; ~ **biliaire** gall
  bladder
**vespéral, ~e**, mpl **-aux** /vɛspeRal, o/
  adj evening
**vessie** /vesi/ nf bladder
  IDIOMS **prendre des ~s pour des lanternes**
  (colloq) to think the moon is made of green
  cheese
**veste** /vɛst/ nf jacket; ~ **de survêtement**
  tracksuit top
  IDIOMS **retourner sa ~** (colloq) to change
  sides
**vestiaire** /vɛstjɛR/ nm (in gym) changing
  room (GB), locker room; (in theatre)
  cloakroom; **laisser sa fierté au ~** to forget
  one's pride
**vestibule** /vɛstibyl/ nm hall; foyer (GB),
  lobby
**vestige** /vɛstiʒ/ nm (a) relic; **des ~s**
  **archéologiques** archaeological remains
  (b) vestige
**vestimentaire** /vɛstimɑ̃tɛR/ adj **tenue ~**
  way of dressing; **mode ~** fashion
**veston** /vɛstɔ̃/ nm (man's) jacket
**vêtement** /vɛtmɑ̃/ nm piece of clothing;
  **des ~s** clothes; '~s **pour hommes**'
  'menswear'; ~s **de sport** sportswear
**vétéran** /veteRɑ̃/ nm veteran
**vétérinaire** /veteRinɛR/ **1** adj veterinary
  **2** nmf veterinary surgeon (GB), veterinarian
  (US)

**vétille** /vetij/ *nf* trifle

**vêtir** /vɛtiʀ/ [33] **1** *vtr* to dress ⟨person, doll⟩

**2 se vêtir** *v refl* (+ *v être*) to dress (oneself)

**veto** /veto/ *nm* veto; **mettre** *or* **opposer son ∼ à qch** to veto sth

**vêtu, ∼e** /vɛty/ ▶ VÊTIR

**vétuste** /vetyst/ *adj* (a) dilapidated
(b) outdated

**vétusté** /vetyste/ *nf* dilapidation (de of), run-down state (de of); outdated state (de of)

**veuf, veuve** /vœf, vœv/ **1** *adj* widowed
**2** *nm,f* widower/widow

**veule** /vøl/ *adj* weak, spineless

**veuvage** /vœvaʒ/ *nm* widowhood

**veuve** *adj, nf* ▶ VEUF

**vexant, ∼e** /vɛksɑ̃, ɑ̃t/ *adj* (a) hurtful
(b) tiresome, vexing

**vexation** /vɛksasjɔ̃/ *nf* humiliation

**vexer** /vɛkse/ [1] **1** *vtr* (a) to offend
(b) to annoy
**2 se vexer** *v refl* (+ *v être*) to take offence (GB)

**via** /vja/ *prep* via; through

**viabilité** /vjabilite/ *nf* (a) viability
(b) (of road) suitability for vehicles

**viable** /vjabl/ *adj* (a) viable
(b) ⟨project⟩ feasible; ⟨situation⟩ bearable, tolerable

**viaduc** /vjadyk/ *nm* viaduct

**viager** /vjaʒe/ *nm* life annuity

**viande** /vjɑ̃d/ *nf* meat; **∼ de bœuf/mouton** beef/mutton
■ **∼ des Grisons** dried beef

**vibrant, ∼e** /vibʀɑ̃, ɑ̃t/ *adj* (a) vibrating
(b) ⟨voice⟩ resonant; ⟨speech⟩ vibrant; ⟨praise⟩ glowing; ⟨plea⟩ impassioned; ⟨crowd⟩ excited

**vibration** /vibʀasjɔ̃/ *nf* vibration; **traitement par ∼s** vibromassage

**vibrer** /vibʀe/ [1] *vi* (a) to vibrate
(b) ⟨voice⟩ to quiver; ⟨heart⟩ to thrill

**vibromasseur** /vibʀomasœʀ/ *nm* vibrator

**vicaire** /vikɛʀ/ *nm* curate

**vice** /vis/ *nm* (a) vice; **vivre dans le ∼ to** lead a dissolute life
(b) vice; **mon ∼, c'est le tabac** my vice is smoking
(c) fault, defect; **∼ de fabrication** manufacturing defect

**vice-président, ∼e,** *mpl* **∼s**
/vispʀezidɑ̃, ɑ̃t/ *nm,f* (of state) vice-president; (of committee, company) vice-chair(man), vice-president (US)

**vice-roi,** *pl* **∼s** /visʀwa/ *nm* viceroy

**vice(-)versa** /visvɛʀsa/ *adv* vice versa

**vichy** /viʃi/ *nm* (a) gingham
(b) vichy water

**vicier** /visje/ [2] *vtr* to pollute ⟨air⟩; to contaminate ⟨blood⟩

**vicieux, -ieuse** /visjø, øz/ *adj*
(a) lecherous; **il faut être ∼ pour aimer ça** you've got to be perverted to like that
(b) ⟨person⟩ sly; ⟨attack⟩ well-disguised; ⟨question⟩ trick; ⟨argument⟩ deceitful
(c) **un cercle ∼** a vicious circle

**vicinal, ∼e,** *mpl* **-aux** /visinal, o/ *adj*
**chemin ∼** byroad

**vicomte** /vikɔ̃t/ *nm* viscount

**vicomtesse** /vikɔ̃tɛs/ *nf* viscountess

**victime** /viktim/ *nf* (a) victim, casualty; **être ∼ d'un infarctus** to suffer a heart attack
(b) sacrificial victim

**victoire** /viktwaʀ/ *nf* (gen) victory; (Sport) win

**victorien, -ienne** /viktɔʀjɛ̃, ɛn/ *adj* Victorian

**victorieux, -ieuse** /viktɔʀjø, øz/ *adj* ⟨army⟩ victorious; ⟨athlete⟩ winning; ⟨smile⟩ of victory

**victuailles** /viktɥaj/ *nf pl* provisions, victuals

**vidange** /vidɑ̃ʒ/ *nf* (a) emptying
(b) oil change; **huile de ∼** waste oil
(c) (of washing machine) waste pipe

**vidanger** /vidɑ̃ʒe/ [13] **1** *vtr* (a) to empty, to drain ⟨tank, ditch⟩
(b) to drain off ⟨liquid⟩
**2** *vi* ⟨washing machine⟩ to empty

**vide** /vid/ **1** *adj* empty; ⟨tape, page⟩ blank; ⟨flat⟩ vacant; **tu l'as loué ∼ ou meublé?** are you renting it unfurnished or furnished?
(b) ⟨mind, day⟩ empty; ⟨look⟩ vacant
**2** *nm* (a) space; **sauter** *or* **se jeter dans le ∼** to jump; (figurative) to leap into the unknown; **parler dans le ∼** to talk to oneself; to talk at random
(b) vacuum; void; **emballé sous ∼** vacuum-packed; **faire le ∼ autour de soi** to drive everybody away; **j'ai besoin de faire le ∼ dans ma tête** I need to forget about everything
(c) emptiness; **le ∼ de l'existence** the emptiness of life
(d) gap; **combler un** *or* **le ∼** to fill in a gap; (figurative) to fill a gap
**3 à vide** *phr* (a) empty
(b) with no result

**vidéaste** /videast/ *nmf* video director

**vidéo** /video/ **1** *adj inv* video
**2** *nf* video; **tourner un film en ∼** to make a video

**vidéocassette** /videokasɛt/ *nf* videotape

**vidéoclip** /videoklip/ *nm* (music) video

**vidéoclub** /videoklœb/ *nm* video store

**vidéoconférence** /videokɔ̃feʀɑ̃s/ *nf*
(a) videoconference
(b) videoconferencing

**vidéodisque** /videodisk/ *nm* videodisc

**vide-ordures** /vidɔʀdyʀ/ *nm inv* rubbish (GB) *or* garbage (US) chute

**vidéothèque** /videotɛk/ *nf* (a) video library

···⦂

(b) video collection

**vide-poches** /vidpɔʃ/ *nm inv* tidy

**vider** /vide/ [1] **1** *vtr* (a) to empty; to drain ⟨*tank, pond*⟩
(b) to empty [sth] (out) ⟨*water, rubbish*⟩
(c) (colloq) to throw [sb] out (colloq)
(d) (Culin) to gut ⟨*fish*⟩; to draw ⟨*game*⟩
(e) (colloq) to wear [sb] out; to drain
**2 se vider** *v refl* (+ *v être*) to empty; **en été, Paris se vide de ses habitants** in the summer all Parisians leave town

**videur, -euse** /vidœʀ, øz/ *nm,f* (colloq) bouncer

**vie** /vi/ *nf* (gen) life; **être en** ～ to be alive; **il y a laissé sa** ～ that was how he lost his life; **donner la** ～ **à qn** to bring sb into the world; **la** ～ **est chère** the cost of living is high; **mode de** ～ lifestyle; **notre** ～ **de couple** our relationship; **donner de la** ～ **à une fête** to liven up a party; **sans** ～ lifeless
■ ～ **active** working life
IDIOMS **c'est la belle** ～! this is the life!; **avoir la** ～ **dure** ⟨*prejudices*⟩ to be ingrained; **mener la** ～ **dure à qn** to make life hard for sb; **faire la** ～ (colloq) to have a wild time; to live it up (colloq); **à la** ～, **à la mort!** till death us do part!

**vieil** ▶ VIEUX

**vieillard, -e** /vjɛjaʀ, aʀd/ *nm,f* old man/woman; **les** ～**s** old people

**vieille** ▶ VIEUX

**vieillesse** /vjɛjɛs/ *nf* (of person) old age; (of building, tree) great age

**vieilli, -e** /vjeji/ **1** *pp* ▶ VIEILLIR
**2** *pp adj* (a) old-looking
(b) ⟨*equipment*⟩ outdated; ⟨*expression*⟩ dated
(c) **vin** ～ **en fût** wine matured in the cask

**vieillir** /vjejiʀ/ [3] **1** *vtr* (a) ⟨*hairstyle*⟩ to make [sb] look older
(b) ⟨*illness*⟩ to age ⟨*person*⟩
**2** *vi* (a) to get older; **je vieillis** I'm getting old; **j'ai vieilli** I'm older; **notre population vieillit** we have an ageing population
(b) ⟨*body, building*⟩ to show signs of age; ⟨*person*⟩ to age; **il vieillit mal** he's losing his looks
(c) ⟨*wine*⟩ to mature
(d) ⟨*work*⟩ to become outdated
**3 se vieillir** *v refl* (+ *v être*) (a) to make oneself look older
(b) to make oneself out to be older

**vieillissant, -e** /vjejisɑ̃, ɑ̃t/ *adj* ageing

**vieillissement** /vjejismɑ̃/ *nm* ageing

**vieillot, -otte** /vjejo, ɔt/ *adj* quaint; old-fashioned

**viennois, -e** /vjɛnwa, az/ *adj* (a) (in Austria) Viennese; (in France) of Vienne
(b) (Culin) ⟨*chocolate, coffee*⟩ Viennese

**viennoiserie** /vjɛnwazʀi/ *nf* Viennese pastry

**vierge** /vjɛʀʒ/ **1** *adj* (a) virgin
(b) blank; unused; clean
(c) ⟨*wool*⟩ new; ⟨*olive oil*⟩ virgin
**2** *nf* virgin

**Vierge** /vjɛʀʒ/ **1** *nf* (a) **la (Sainte)** ～ the (Blessed) Virgin
(b) madonna
**2** *pr nf* Virgo

**Viêt Nam** /viɛtnam/ *pr nm* Vietnam

**vietnamien, -ienne** /vjɛtnamjɛ̃, ɛn/
**1** *adj* Vietnamese
**2** *nm* (language) Vietnamese

**vieux (vieil** *before vowel or mute h*), **vieille,** *mpl* **vieux** /vjø, vjɛj/ **1** *adj* old; **être** ～ **avant l'âge** to be old before one's time; **une institution vieille de 100 ans** a 100-year-old institution; **il est très vieille France** he's a gentleman of the old school
**2** *nm,f* (a) old person; **un petit** ～ a little old man; **les** ～ old people; **mes** ～ (colloq) my parents
(b) (colloq) **mon pauvre** ～ you poor old thing
**3** *adv* **vivre** ～ to live to a ripe old age; **il s'habille** ～ he dresses like an old man
**4** *nm* **prendre un coup de** ～ to age; **faire du neuf avec du** ～ to revamp things
■ **vieille fille** old maid; ～ **beau** ageing Romeo; ～ **garçon** old bachelor; ～ **jeu** old-fashioned; ～ **rose** dusty pink
IDIOMS ～ **comme le monde,** ～ **comme Hérode** as old as the hills

**vif, vive¹** /vif, viv/ **1** *adj* (a) ⟨*colour, light*⟩ bright
(b) ⟨*person*⟩ lively, vivacious; ⟨*imagination*⟩ vivid
(c) ⟨*protests*⟩ heated; ⟨*opposition*⟩ fierce; **sa réaction a été un peu vive** he/she reacted rather strongly
(d) ⟨*contrast*⟩ sharp; ⟨*interest, desire*⟩ keen; ⟨*pain*⟩ acute; ⟨*success*⟩ notable
(e) ⟨*pace, movement*⟩ brisk; **à vive allure** ⟨*drive*⟩ at high speed; **avoir l'esprit** ～ to be very quick
(f) ⟨*cold, wind*⟩ biting; ⟨*edge*⟩ sharp; **air** ～ fresh air; **cuire à feu** ～ to cook over a high heat
(g) **de vive voix** in person
**2** *nm* **à** ～ ⟨*flesh*⟩ bared; ⟨*knee*⟩ raw; ⟨*wire*⟩ exposed; **avoir les nerfs à** ～ to be on edge; **la plaie est à** ～ it's an open wound; **piquer qn au** ～ to cut sb to the quick

**vigie** /viʒi/ *nf* (Naut) (a) lookout
(b) crow's nest

**vigilance** /viʒilɑ̃s/ *nf* vigilance; **échapper à la** ～ **de qn** to escape sb's attention

**vigilant, -e** /viʒilɑ̃, ɑ̃t/ *adj* ⟨*person*⟩ vigilant; ⟨*eye*⟩ watchful

**vigile** /viʒil/ *nm* (a) night watchman
(b) security guard

**vigne** /viɲ/ *nf* (a) vine
(b) vineyard
■ ～ **vierge** Virginia creeper

**vigneron, -onne** /viɲ(ə)ʀɔ̃, ɔn/ *nm,f* winegrower

**vignette** /viɲɛt/ *nf* (a) *detachable label on medicines for reimbursement by social security*
(b) tax disc (GB)
(c) label

**(d)** vignette

**vignoble** /viɲɔbl/ *nm* vineyard

**vigoureux, -euse** /viguʀø, øz/ *adj*
**(a)** ⟨*person, handshake*⟩ vigorous; ⟨*athlete, body*⟩ strong; ⟨*plant*⟩ sturdy
**(b)** ⟨*resistance, style*⟩ vigorous

**vigueur** /vigœʀ/ **1** *nf* **(a)** vigour (GB)
**(b)** strength
**2** **en vigueur** *phr* ⟨*law, system*⟩ in force; ⟨*regime, conditions*⟩ current; **entrer en ~** to come into force

**VIH** /veiaʃ/ *nm* (*abbr* = **virus immunodéficitaire humain**) HIV

**viking** /vikiɲ/ *adj* Viking

**vil, ~e** /vil/ *adj* ⟨*person*⟩ base; ⟨*deed*⟩ vile, base

**vilain, ~e** /vilɛ̃, ɛn/ **1** *adj* **(a)** ugly
**(b)** (colloq) ⟨*germ, creature*⟩ nasty; ⟨*child*⟩ naughty
**(c)** ⟨*fault*⟩ bad; ⟨*word*⟩ dirty
**2** *nm,f* naughty boy/girl

**vilenie** /vileni/ *nf* **(a)** baseness (**de** of)
**(b)** vile *or* base act

**villa** /villa/ *nf* **(a)** ≈ detached house
**(b)** villa

**village** /vilaʒ/ *nm* village

**villageois, ~e** /vilaʒwa, az/ *nm,f* villager

**ville** /vil/ *nf* **(a)** town; city; **la vieille ~** the old town; **aller en ~** to go into town
**(b)** town *or* city council
■ **~ d'eau(x)** spa town; **~ franche** free city; **~ nouvelle** new town

**ville-dortoir**, *pl* **villes-dortoirs**
/vildɔʀtwaʀ/ *nf* dormitory town (GB)

**villégiature** /vileʒjatyʀ/ *nf* holiday (GB), vacation (US)

**vin** /vɛ̃/ *nm* wine; **~ blanc/rouge** white/red wine; **~ de pays** *or* **de terroir** *quality wine produced in a specific region*; **couper son ~** to add water to one's wine
■ **~ d'appellation d'origine contrôlée** appellation contrôlée wine (*with a guarantee of origin*); **~ cuit** *wine which has undergone heating during maturation*; **~ d'honneur** reception
IDIOMS **avoir le ~ gai/triste** to get happy/maudlin after one has had a few drinks; **mettre de l'eau dans son ~** to mellow; **quand le ~ est tiré, il faut le boire** (Proverb) once you have started something, you have to see it through

**vinaigre** /vinɛɡʀ/ *nm* vinegar
IDIOMS **tourner au ~** to turn sour

**vinaigrette** /vinɛɡʀɛt/ *nf* French dressing

**vinasse** (colloq) /vinas/ *nf* plonk (GB) (colloq), cheap wine

**vindicatif, -ive** /vɛ̃dikatif, iv/ *adj* vindictive

**vingt** /vɛ̃, vɛ̃t/ **1** *adj inv* twenty
**2** *pron* twenty; (Sch) **j'ai eu ~ sur ~** ≈ I got full marks (GB) *or* full credit (US)
**3** *nm inv* twenty

**vingtaine** /vɛ̃tɛn/ *nf* about twenty

**vingtième** /vɛ̃tjɛm/ *adj* twentieth

**vinicole** /vinikɔl/ *adj* ⟨*sector, region*⟩ wine-producing; ⟨*cellar, trade*⟩ wine

**vinyle** /vinil/ *nm* vinyl

**viol** /vjɔl/ *nm* **(a)** rape
**(b)** (of law, temple) violation

**violacé, ~e** /vjɔlase/ *adj* purplish

**violation** /vjɔlasjɔ̃/ *nf* **(a)** (of law, territory) violation
**(b)** (of agreement, confidentiality) breach
■ **~ de domicile** forcible entry (*into a person's home*)

**violemment** /vjɔlamã/ *adv* violently

**violence** /vjɔlɑ̃s/ *nf* **(a)** violence; **~ verbale** verbal abuse; **par la ~** through violence; **with violence; se faire ~** to force oneself
**(b)** act of violence; **~s à l'enfant** child abuse

**violent, ~e** /vjɔlɑ̃, ɑ̃t/ *adj* violent; ⟨*colour*⟩ harsh

**violenter** /vjɔlɑ̃te/ [1] *vtr* to assault sexually

**violer** /vjɔle/ [1] *vtr* **(a)** to rape; **se faire ~** to be raped
**(b)** to desecrate ⟨*tomb*⟩; **~ l'intimité de qn** to invade sb's privacy
**(c)** to infringe ⟨*law*⟩

**violet, -ette¹** /vjɔlɛ, ɛt/ **1** *adj* purple
**2** *nm* purple

**violette²** /vjɔlɛt/ *nf* violet

**violeur** /vjɔlœʀ/ *nm* rapist

**violon** /vjɔlɔ̃/ *nm* violin
■ **~ d'Ingres** hobby
IDIOMS **accorder ses ~s** to agree on which line to take

**violoncelle** /vjɔlɔ̃sɛl/ *nm* cello

**violoncelliste** /vjɔlɔ̃selist/ *nmf* cellist

**violoniste** /vjɔlɔnist/ *nmf* violinist

**vipère** /vipɛʀ/ *nf* viper; **avoir une langue de ~** to have a wicked tongue

**virage** /viʀaʒ/ *nm* **(a)** bend
**(b)** change of direction
**(c)** (in skiing) turn

**virago** /viʀago/ *nf* virago

**viral, ~e, *mpl* -aux** /viʀal, o/ *adj* viral

**virement** /viʀmã/ *nm* transfer; **faire un ~** to make a transfer.
■ **~ automatique** standing order

**virer** /viʀe/ [1] **1** *vtr* **(a)** to transfer ⟨*money*⟩
**(b)** (colloq) to fire ⟨*employee*⟩; **se faire ~** to get fired
**2** **virer à** *v+prep* **~ au rouge** to turn red
**3** *vi* **(a)** ⟨*vehicle*⟩ to turn; **~ de bord** (figurative) to do a U-turn, to do a flip-flop (US)
**(b)** to change colour (GB); ⟨*colour*⟩ to change

**virevolter** /viʀvɔlte/ [1] *vi* to twirl

**virginité** /viʀʒinite/ *nf* virginity

**virgule** /viʀɡyl/ *nf* **(a)** comma; **à la ~ près** down to the last comma
**(b)** (decimal) point

**viril, ~e** /viʀil/ *adj* manly, virile; masculine

**virilité** /viʀilite/ *nf* virility

**virtualité** /viʀtɥalite/ nf (a) virtuality
(b) potentiality

**virtuel, -elle** /viʀtɥɛl/ adj (a) potential
(b) (in science) virtual

**virtuellement** /viʀtɥɛlmã/ adv
(a) virtually
(b) potentially

**virtuose** /viʀtɥoz/ 1 adj virtuoso
2 nmf (a) (Mus) virtuoso
(b) master

**virtuosité** /viʀtɥozite/ nf (a) (Mus)
virtuosity
(b) brilliance

**virulence** /viʀylãs/ nf virulence

**virulent, ~e** /viʀylã, ãt/ adj virulent

**virus** /viʀys/ nm inv (Med, Comput) virus
(b) bug (colloq), craze

**vis** /vis/ nf inv screw
IDIOMS **serrer la ~ à qn** to tighten the
screws on sb

**visa** /viza/ nm visa
■ ~ **de censure** (censor's) certificate

**visage** /vizaʒ/ nm face; **à ~ découvert**
openly

**vis-à-vis** /vizavi/ 1 nm inv (a) **maison
sans ~** house with an open outlook
(b) **assis en ~** sitting opposite each other
(c) (Sport) opponent
(d) meeting, encounter
2 **vis-à-vis de** phr (a) **~ de qch** in
relation to sth; **~ de qn** toward(s) sb
(b) beside

**viscéral, ~e,** mpl **-aux** /viseʀal, o/ adj
(a) **réaction ~e** gut reaction
(b) visceral

**viscéralement** /viseʀalmã/ adv
violently, virulently

**viscère** /viseʀ/ nm (a) internal organ
(b) **les ~s** viscera

**viscosité** /viskozite/ nf viscosity

**visée** /vize/ nf (a) aim
(b) design
(c) sighting; aiming

**viser** /vize/ [1] 1 vtr (a) to aim at ⟨target⟩;
to aim for ⟨heart, middle⟩
(b) to aim for ⟨job, results⟩; to aim at
⟨market⟩
(c) ⟨law, campaign⟩ to be aimed at; ⟨remark,
allusion⟩ to be meant for
2 **viser à** v+prep **~ à qch/à faire** to aim at
sth/to do
3 vi to aim; **~ (trop) haut** (figurative) to set
one's sights (too) high

**viseur** /vizœʀ/ nm (a) viewfinder
(b) (of gun) sight

**visibilité** /vizibilite/ nf visibility

**visible** /vizibl/ adj (a) visible
(b) obvious

**visiblement** /vizibləmã/ adv visibly

**visière** /vizjɛʀ/ nf (a) (of cap) peak
(b) eyeshade

**vision** /vizjõ/ nf (a) eyesight, vision
(b) view; **~ globale** global view
(c) sight

(d) **avoir des ~s** to see things, to have
visions

**visionnaire** /vizjɔnɛʀ/ adj, nmf visionary

**visionner** /vizjɔne/ [1] vtr to view ⟨film,
slides⟩

**visionneuse** /vizjɔnøz/ nf viewer

**visite** /vizit/ nf visit; call; **rendre ~ à qn** to
pay sb a call; **avoir de la ~** to have visitors
■ ~ **de contrôle** (Med) follow-up visit;
~ **médicale** medical (examination)

**visiter** /vizite/ [1] vtr (a) to visit ⟨museum,
town⟩
(b) to view ⟨apartment⟩
(c) to visit ⟨patient⟩

**visiteur, -euse** /vizitœʀ, øz/ nm,f visitor

**vison** /vizõ/ nm (a) mink
(b) mink (coat)

**visqueux, -euse** /viskø, øz/ adj
(a) viscous, viscid
(b) sticky, gooey (colloq)

**visser** /vise/ [1] vtr (a) to screw [sth] on
(b) **être vissé sur sa chaise** to be glued to
one's chair

**visualisation** /vizɥalizasjõ/ nf
visualization; (Comput) display

**visualiser** /vizɥalize/ [1] vtr to visualize

**visuel, -elle** /vizɥɛl/ adj visual

**vital, ~e,** mpl **-aux** /vital, o/ adj vital

**vitalité** /vitalite/ nf vitality; energy

**vitamine** /vitamin/ nf vitamin

**vitaminé, ~e** /vitamine/ adj with added
vitamins

**vite** /vit/ adv (a) quickly; **~!** quick!; **ça ira
~** it'll soon be over; it won't take long; **on a
pris un verre ~ fait** (colloq) we had a quick
drink
(b) **j'ai parlé trop ~** I spoke too hastily; I
spoke too soon; **c'est ~ dit!** that's easy to
say!

**vitesse** /vitɛs/ nf (a) speed; **partir à toute
~** to rush away; **à deux ~s** ⟨system⟩ two-tier;
**faire de la ~** to drive fast; **prendre qn de ~**
to outstrip sb; **en ~** quickly; in a rush
(b) gear
IDIOMS **à la ~ grand V, en quatrième ~** at
top speed

**viticole** /vitikɔl/ adj wine; wine-producing

**viticulteur, -trice** /vitikyltœʀ, tʀis/ nm,f
wine-grower

**viticulture** /vitikyltyʀ/ nf wine-growing

**vitrage** /vitʀaʒ/ nm windows; **double ~**
double glazing

**vitrail,** pl **-aux** /vitʀaj, o/ nm stained glass
window

**vitre** /vitʀ/ nf (a) windowpane
(b) pane of glass
(c) (of car, train) window

**vitrerie** /vitʀəʀi/ (a) glazier's
(b) glasswork

**vitrier** /vitʀije/ nm glazier

**vitrifier** /vitʀifje/ [2] vtr (a) to varnish
⟨floor⟩
(b) (Tech) to vitrify

**vitrine** /vitʀin/ *nf* **(a)** (shop *or* store) window; **faire les ∼s** to go window-shopping **(b)** display cabinet (GB), curio cabinet (US) **(c)** (show)case

**vitriol** /vitʀijɔl/ *nm* vitriol

**vitupérer** /vitypeʀe/ [14] *vi* to rail

**vivable** /vivabl/ *adj* bearable; **ce n'est pas ∼ ici** it is impossible to live here

**vivace** /vivas/ *adj* enduring

**vivacité** /vivasite/ *nf* **(a)** (of person) vivacity; (of feeling) intensity **(b)** (of intelligence) keenness; (of reaction, movement) swiftness; **avec ∼** ⟨*move, react*⟩ swiftly **(c)** (of memory, colour, impression) vividness; (in eyes) spark; (of light) brightness

**vivant, ∼e** /vivã, ãt/ **1** *adj* **(a)** living; **il est ∼** he is alive; **un homard ∼** a live lobster **(b)** ⟨*person, style*⟩ lively; ⟨*description*⟩ vivid **(c)** **être encore ∼** ⟨*custom*⟩ to be still alive **2** *nm* **(a)** living being; **les ∼s** the living **(b)** **du ∼ de mon père** while my father was alive

**vive²** /viv/ **1** *adj f* ▶ VIF 1 **2** *nf* weever

**vivement** /vivmã/ *adv* ⟨*encourage, react*⟩ strongly; ⟨*contrast, speak*⟩ sharply; ⟨*move, feel, regret*⟩ deeply; ⟨*rise*⟩ swiftly

**vivier** /vivje/ *nm* **(a)** fishpond **(b)** fish-tank

**vivifiant, ∼e** /vivifjã, ãt/ *adj* **(a)** invigorating **(b)** stimulating

**vivifier** /vivifje/ [2] *vtr* to invigorate

**vivisection** /viviseksjɔ̃/ *nf* vivisection

**vivoter** /vivɔte/ [1] *vi* to struggle along

**vivre** /vivʀ/ [63] **1** *vtr* **(a)** to live through ⟨*era*⟩; to go through ⟨*difficult times*⟩; to experience ⟨*love*⟩ **(b)** to cope with ⟨*divorce, failure, change*⟩ **2** *vi* **(a)** to live; **∼ vieux** to live to a great age; **vive la révolution!** long live the revolution!; **∼ à la campagne** to live in the country; **être facile à ∼** to be easy to live with; to be easy to get on with; **∼ avec son temps** to move with the times; **se laisser ∼** to take things easy; **apprendre à ∼ à qn** (colloq) to teach sb some manners (colloq); **∼ aux dépens de qn** to live off sb **(b)** ⟨*fashion*⟩ to last; **avoir vécu** ⟨*person*⟩ to have seen a great deal of life; (humorous) ⟨*object*⟩ to have had its day **(c)** ⟨*town*⟩ to be full of life IDIOMS **qui vivra verra** what will be will be

**vivres** /vivʀ/ *nm pl* **(a)** food, supplies **(b)** **couper les ∼ à qn** to cut off sb's allowance

**vizir** /viziʀ/ *nm* vizier; **le Grand ∼** the Grand Vizier

**vo** /veo/ *nf: abbr* ▶ VERSION

**vocable** /vɔkabl/ *nm* term

**vocabulaire** /vɔkabylɛʀ/ *nm* vocabulary

**vocal, ∼e,** *mpl* **-aux** /vɔkal, o/ *adj* vocal

**vocalement** /vɔkalmã/ *adv* vocally

**vocalise** /vɔkaliz/ *nf* singing exercise

**vocation** /vɔkasjɔ̃/ *nf* **(a)** vocation, calling **(b)** purpose; **région à ∼ agricole** farming area

**vociférer** /vɔsifeʀe/ [14] *vtr, vi* to shout

**vodka** /vɔdka/ *nf* vodka

**vœu,** *pl* **∼x** /vø/ *nm* **(a)** wish; **faire un ∼** to make a wish **(b)** New Year's greetings; **adresser ses ∼x à qn** to wish sb a happy New Year **(c)** vow; **∼x de pauvreté** vows of poverty

**vogue** /vɔg/ *nf* fashion, vogue

**voguer** /vɔge/ [1] *vi* ⟨*ship*⟩ to sail IDIOMS **et vogue la galère!** come what may!

**voici** /vwasi/ **1** *prep* here is, this is; here are, these are; **∼ mes clés** here are my keys; **∼ un mois** a month ago; **∼ bientôt deux mois qu'elle travaille chez nous** she's been working with us for nearly two months **2 voici que** *phr* all of a sudden

**voie** /vwa/ *nf* **(a)** way; **montrer la ∼ à qn** to show sb the way; **ouvrir la ∼ à** to pave the way for; **être sur la bonne ∼** ⟨*person*⟩ to be on the right track; **les travaux sont en bonne ∼** the work is progressing; **par ∼ de conséquence** consequently; **espèce en ∼ de disparition** endangered species **(b)** channels; **par des ∼ détournées** by roundabout means **(c)** lane; **route à trois ∼s** three-lane road **(d)** (of railway) track; **le train entre en gare ∼ 2** the train is arriving at platform 2 **(e)** **par ∼ buccale** *or* **orale** orally ■ **∼ aérienne** air route; **∼ ferrée** railway track (GB), railroad track (US); **∼ de garage** siding; **mettre qn sur une ∼ de garage** (figurative) to shunt sb onto the sidelines; **Voie lactée** Milky Way; **∼ privée** private road; **∼ publique** public highway; **∼ rapide** expressway; **∼ sans issue** dead end; no through road; **∼s respiratoires** respiratory tract

**voilà** /vwala/ **1** *prep* here is, this is; here are, these are; **voici mon fils et ∼ ma fille** this is my son and this is my daughter; **me ∼!** I'm coming!; here I am!; **le ∼ qui se remet à rire!** there he goes again laughing!; **∼ tout** that's all; **∼ un mois** a month ago **2 en voilà** *phr* **tu veux des fraises? en ∼** you'd like some strawberries? here you are **3 voilà que** *phr* (colloq) **et ∼ qu'une voiture arrive** and the next thing you know, a car pulls up **4** *excl* **∼! j'arrive!** (I'm) coming!; **(et) ∼! il remet ça!** there he goes again! IDIOMS **il a de l'argent, en veux-tu en ∼!** he has as much money as he could wish for!

**voilage** /vwalaʒ/ *nm* net curtain (GB), sheer curtain (US)

**voile¹** /vwal/ *nm* **(a)** veil; **lever le ∼ sur qch** to bring sth out in the open **(b)** voile

■ ~ **islamique** yashmak; ~ **du palais** soft palate, velum

**voile²** /vwal/ *nf* (Naut) (a) sail; **faire** ~ **vers** to sail toward(s)
(b) sailing

**voilé, ~e** /vwale/ *adj* (a) ⟨person, object⟩ veiled
(b) ⟨sun, sky⟩ hazy; ⟨eyes⟩ misty; ⟨voice⟩ with a catch in it; ⟨photo⟩ fogged
(c) ⟨threat, criticism⟩ veiled
(d) ⟨wheel⟩ buckled

**voiler** /vwale/ [1] **1** *vtr* (a) to veil ⟨landscape, sun⟩; ⟨person, fact⟩ to conceal ⟨event, fact⟩
(b) to buckle ⟨wheel⟩
(c) to mist ⟨eyes⟩
(d) to cover ⟨face, nudity⟩; to veil ⟨statue⟩
**2 se voiler** *v refl* (+ *v être*) (a) ⟨sky⟩ to cloud over; ⟨sun⟩ to become hazy; ⟨eyes⟩ to become misty
(b) ⟨person⟩ to wear a veil
IDIOMS **se ~ la face** to look the other way

**voilette** /vwalɛt/ *nf* veil

**voilier** /vwalje/ *nm* (a) sailing boat (GB), sailboat (US)
(b) yacht, sailing ship

**voilure** /vwalyʀ/ *nf* sails; **une ~ de 500m²** 500m² of sail

**voir** /vwaʀ/ [46] **1** *vtr* (a) to see; **faire ~ qch à qn** to show sb sth; **laisser ~ qch** to show sth; **~ si/pourquoi** to find out *or* to see if/why; **on l'a vue entrer** she was seen going in; **je le vois** *or* **verrais bien enseignant** I can just see him as a teacher; **aller ~ qn** to go to see sb; **le film est à ~** the film is worth seeing; **~ du pays** to see the world; **on voit bien qu'elle n'a jamais travaillé!** you can tell she's never worked!; **on n'a jamais vu ça!** it's unheard of!
(b) **avoir quelque chose à ~ avec** to have something to do with
**2 voir à** *v+prep* to see to; **voyez à ce que tout soit prêt** see to it that everything is ready
**3** *vi* (a) **~, y ~** to be able to see; **~ double** to see double
(b) **~ clair dans qch** to have a clear understanding of sth; **il faut ~** we'll have to see
**4 se voir** *v refl* (+ *v être*) (a) to see oneself
(b) ⟨stain⟩ to show; **la tour se voit de loin** the tower can be seen from far away; **ça ne s'est jamais vu!** it's unheard of!
(c) **se ~ obligé** *or* **dans l'obligation de faire** to find oneself forced to do
(d) **se ~ l'un l'autre** to see each other; **ils ne peuvent pas se ~ (en peinture)** (colloq) they can't stand each other
IDIOMS **ne pas ~ plus loin que le bout de son nez** to see no further than the end of one's nose; **j'en ai vu d'autres** I've seen worse; **en faire ~ à qn** to give sb a hard time

**voire** /vwaʀ/ *adv* or even, not to say

**voirie** /vwaʀi/ *nf* road, road and waterways network

**voisin, ~e** /vwazɛ̃, in/ **1** *adj* (a) ⟨house, town⟩ neighbouring (GB); ⟨lake, forest⟩ nearby; ⟨room⟩ next; **les régions ~es de la Manche** the regions bordering the English Channel
(b) ⟨date, result⟩ close (**de** to)
(c) ⟨feelings, ideas⟩ similar; ⟨species⟩ (closely) related
**2** *nm,f* neighbour (GB); **ma ~e de palier** the woman across the landing; **mon ~ de table** the man next to me at table

**voisinage** /vwazinaʒ/ *nm*
(a) neighbourhood (GB); **entretenir des rapports de bon ~** to maintain neighbourly (GB) relations
(b) proximity; **vivre dans le ~ d'une usine** to live close to a factory

**voiture** /vwatyʀ/ *nf* (a) car, automobile (US)
(b) carriage (GB), car (US); **en ~!** all aboard!
■ **~ à bras** hand-drawn cart; **~ de tourisme** saloon (car) (GB), sedan (US)

**voiture-balai**, *pl* **voitures-balais** /vwatyʀbalɛ/ *nf* support vehicle

**voiture-lit**, *pl* **voitures-lits** /vwatyʀli/ *nf* sleeper, sleeping car

**voix** /vwa/ *nf inv* (a) (gen) voice; **élever la ~** to raise one's voice; **à ~ haute** out loud; **rester sans ~** to remain speechless; **à portée de ~** within earshot; **faire entendre sa ~** (figurative) to make oneself heard
(b) vote
(c) **à la ~ active/passive** in the active/passive voice

**vol** /vɔl/ **1** *nm* (a) (of bird, plane) flight; **prendre son ~** to fly off; **à ~ d'oiseau** as the crow flies; **il y a trois heures de ~** it's a three-hour flight; **de ~** ⟨conditions⟩ flying; ⟨plan⟩ flight
(b) **un ~ de** a flock of ⟨birds⟩; a cloud of ⟨insects⟩; **de haut ~** (figurative) ⟨diplomat⟩ high-flying; ⟨burglar⟩ big-time
(c) theft, robbery
**2 au vol** *phr* **attraper une balle au ~** to catch a ball in mid-air; **saisir des bribes de conversation au ~** to catch snatches of conversation
■ **~ à l'arraché** bag snatching; **~ avec effraction** burglary; **~ à l'étalage** shoplifting; **~ à la tire** pickpocketing

**volage** /vɔlaʒ/ *adj* fickle

**volaille** /vɔlaj/ *nf* (a) poultry
(b) fowl

**volant, ~e** /vɔlɑ̃, ɑ̃t/ **1** *adj* flying
**2** *nm* (a) steering wheel; **être au ~** to be at the wheel; **un brusque coup de ~** a sharp turn of the wheel; **un as du ~** an ace driver; **la sécurité au ~** safe driving
(b) flounce; **à ~s** flounced
(c) shuttlecock

**volatil, ~e¹** /vɔlatil/ *adj* volatile

**volatile²** /vɔlatil/ *nm* (a) fowl
(b) bird

**volatiliser: se volatiliser** /vɔlatilize/ [1] *v refl* (+ *v être*) (a) to volatilize
(b) (humorous) to vanish into thin air

**volcan** /vɔlkɑ̃/ *nm* volcano

**volcanique** /vɔlkanik/ *adj* (a) ⟨*region*⟩ volcanic

(b) ⟨*temperament*⟩ explosive

**volée** /vɔle/ **1** *nf* (a) (of birds) flock, flight

(b) (of blows, stones) volley; **donner une ~ à qn** to give sb a good thrashing

(c) flight (of stairs)

(d) (Sport) volley

**2** **à toute volée** *phr* **les cloches sonnaient à toute ~** the bells were pealing out

**voler** /vɔle/ [1] **1** *vtr* (a) **~ qch à qn** to steal sth from sb; **tu ne l'as pas volé!** (figurative) it serves you right!

(b) **~ qn** to rob sb; **~ le client** to rip the customer off (colloq)

**2** *vi* (a) to fly; **~ au secours de qn** to rush to sb's aid

(b) **~ en éclats** ⟨*window*⟩ to shatter

**volet** /vɔlɛ/ *nm* (a) shutter

(b) (of leaflet, brochure) (folding) section; (of plan) part, component

**voleter** /vɔlte/ [20] *vi* to flutter

**voleur, -euse** /vɔlœʀ, øz/ **1** *adj* **être ~** ⟨*cat*⟩ to be a thief; ⟨*shopkeeper*⟩ to be dishonest

**2** *nm,f* thief; swindler

**IDIOMS se sauver comme un ~** to slip away like a thief in the night

**volière** /vɔljɛʀ/ *nf* aviary

**volley(-ball)** /vɔlɛ(bɔl)/ *nm* volleyball

**volontaire** /vɔlɔ̃tɛʀ/ **1** *adj* (a) ⟨*work*⟩ voluntary; ⟨*omission*⟩ deliberate

(b) ⟨*person, air*⟩ determined; ⟨*child*⟩ self-willed

**2** *nmf* volunteer; **se porter ~** to volunteer

**volonté** /vɔlɔ̃te/ **1** *nf* (a) will; **bonne ~** goodwill; **aller contre la ~ de qn** to go against sb's wishes; **manifester la ~ de faire** to show one's willingness to do

(b) willpower; **avoir une ~ de fer** to have an iron will

**2** **à volonté** *phr* (a) **'vin/pain à ~'** 'unlimited wine/bread'

(b) ⟨*modifiable*⟩ as required

**volontiers** /vɔlɔ̃tje/ *adv* (a) gladly; **j'irais ~ à Paris** I'd love to go to Paris; **'tu me le prêtes?'—'~'** 'will you lend it to me?'—'certainly'

(b) ⟨*admit*⟩ readily

**volt** /vɔlt/ *nm* volt

**voltage** /vɔltaʒ/ *nm* voltage

**volte-face** /vɔlt(ə)fas/ *nf inv* (a) **faire ~** to turn around

(b) (figurative) volte-face, U-turn

**voltige** /vɔltiʒ/ *nf* (haute) **~** acrobatics

**voltiger** /vɔltiʒe/ [13] *vi* (a) to flutter

(b) to go flying

**volubilité** /vɔlybilite/ *nf* volubility

**volume** /vɔlym/ *nm* (gen) volume; **donner du ~ à ses cheveux** to give one's hair body; **~ sonore** sound level

**volumineux, -euse** /vɔlyminø, øz/ *adj* voluminous, bulky

**volupté** /vɔlypte/ *nf* voluptuousness

**voluptueux, -euse** /vɔlyptɥø, øz/ *adj* voluptuous

**volute** /vɔlyt/ *nf* (on pillar, column) volute; (of violin) scroll; (of smoke) curl

**vomi** /vɔmi/ *nm* (colloq) vomit

**vomir** /vɔmiʀ/ [3] **1** *vtr* to bring up ⟨*meal*⟩; to vomit ⟨*bile*⟩

**2** *vi* ⟨*person*⟩ to be sick

**vomissement** /vɔmismɑ̃/ *nm* vomiting

**vont** /vɔ̃/ ▸ ALLER[1]

**vorace** /vɔʀas/ *adj* voracious

**voracité** /vɔʀasite/ *nf* voracity, voraciousness

**vos** ▸ VOTRE

**votant, ~e** /vɔtɑ̃, ɑ̃t/ *nm,f* voter

**vote** /vɔt/ *nm* (a) voting; (of law) passing

(b) vote

**voter** /vɔte/ [1] **1** *vtr* to vote ⟨*budget*⟩; to pass ⟨*parliamentary bill*⟩; to vote for ⟨*amnesty*⟩

**2** *vi* to vote; **~ blanc** to cast a blank vote

**votre**, *pl* **vos** /vɔtʀ, vo/ *det* your; **c'est pour ~ bien** it's for your own good; **à ~ arrivée** when you arrive; when you arrived

**vôtre** /votʀ/ **1** *det* **mes biens sont ~s** all I have is yours; **'amicalement ~'** 'best wishes'

**2** **le vôtre, la vôtre, les vôtres** *pron* yours; **à la ~!** (colloq) cheers!

**vouer** /vwe/ [1] **1** *vtr* (a) **~ une reconnaissance éternelle à qn** to be eternally grateful to sb; **~ un véritable culte à qn** to worship sb

(b) to doom; **film voué à l'échec** film doomed to failure

(c) **~ sa vie à qch** to devote one's life to sth

**2** **se vouer** *v refl* (+ *v être*) (a) **se ~ à qch** to devote oneself to sth

(b) **ils se vouent une haine féroce** they hate each other intensely

**vouloir**[1] /vulwaʀ/ [48] **1** *vtr* (a) (gen) to want; **qu'est-ce qu'ils nous veulent encore?** (colloq) what do they want now?; **il en veut 2 000 euros** he wants 2,000 euros for it; **comme le veut la loi** as the law demands; **que veux-tu boire?** what do you want to drink?; what would you like to drink?; **je voudrais un kilo de poires** I'd like a kilo of pears; **je comprends très bien que tu ne veuilles pas répondre** I can quite understand that you may not wish to reply; **sans le ~** ⟨*knock over, reveal*⟩ by accident; ⟨*annoy*⟩ without meaning to; **que tu le veuilles ou non** whether you like it or not; **elle fait ce qu'elle veut de son mari** she twists her husband around her little finger; **je ne vous veux aucun mal** I don't wish you any harm; **tu ne voudrais pas me faire croire que** you're not trying to tell me that; **tu voudrais que je leur fasse confiance?** do you expect me to trust them?; **comment veux-tu que je le sache?** how should I know?; **j'aurais voulu** ····⟶

**t'y voir!** (colloq) I'd like to have seen you in the same position!; **tu l'auras voulu!** it'll be all your own fault!

**(b) voulez-vous fermer la fenêtre?** would you mind closing the window?; **voudriez-vous avoir l'obligeance de faire** (formal) would you be so kind as to do; **veuillez patienter** (on phone) please hold the line; **si vous voulez bien me suivre** if you'd like to follow me; **veux-tu te taire!** will you be quiet!; **ils ont bien voulu nous prêter leur voiture** they were kind enough to lend us their car; **je veux bien te croire** I'm quite prepared to believe you; **je veux bien qu'il soit malade mais** I know he's ill, but; **'ce n'est pas cher'—'si on veut!'** 'it's not expensive'—'or so you say!'

**(c)** ~ **dire** to mean; **qu'est-ce que ça veut dire?** what does that mean?; what's all this about?

**(d) comme le veut la tradition** as tradition has it

**2 en vouloir** *v+prep* **(a)** en ~ **à qn** to bear a grudge against sb; **je leur en veux de m'avoir trompé** I hold it against them for not being honest with me; **ne m'en veux pas** please forgive me

**(b)** en ~ **à qch** to be after sth

**3 se vouloir** *v refl* (+ *v être*) **(a)** ⟨*person*⟩ to like to think of oneself as; ⟨*book, method*⟩ to be meant to be

**(b) s'en** ~ to be cross with oneself; **s'en** ~ **de** to regret; **je m'en serais voulu de ne pas vous avoir prévenu** I would never have forgiven myself if I hadn't warned you

IDIOMS ~ **c'est pouvoir** (Proverb) where there's a will there's a way

**vouloir²** /vulwaR/ *nm* will

**voulu,** ~**e** /vuly/ **1** *pp* ▶ VOULOIR¹

**2** *pp adj* **(a)** required; **on n'obtient jamais les renseignements** ~**s** you never get the information you want; **en temps** ~ in time; **au moment** ~ at the right time

**(b)** ⟨*omission*⟩ deliberate; ⟨*meeting*⟩ planned

**vous** /vu/ *pron* **(a)** you; **je sais que ce n'est pas** ~ I know it wasn't you; **c'est** ~ **qui avez gagné** you have won; ~ **aussi,** ~ **avez l'air malade** you don't look very well either; **ce sont des amis à** ~? are they friends of yours?; **c'est à** ~ it's yours, it belongs to you; it's your turn

**(b)** yourself; yourselves; **allez** ~ **laver les mains** go and wash your hands; **pensez à** ~ **deux** think of yourselves

**vous-même,** *pl* **vous-mêmes** /vumɛm/ *pron* **(a)** yourself; **vous me l'avez dit** ~ you told me yourself

**(b) allez-y** ~**s** go yourselves; **vous verrez par** ~**s** you'll see for yourselves

**voûte** /vut/ *nf* (gen) vault; (of porch) archway; (of tunnel) roof; (figurative) (of leaves, branches) arch

■ **la** ~ **céleste** the sky; the heavens; ~ **du palais** roof of the mouth; ~ **plantaire** arch of the foot

**voûté,** ~**e** /vute/ *adj* **(a)** ⟨*cellar*⟩ vaulted

**(b)** ⟨*back*⟩ bent; **il est** ~ he has a stoop

**voûter** /vute/ [1] **1** *vtr* **(a)** (in architecture) to vault ⟨*room*⟩

**(b)** to give [sb] a stoop

**2 se voûter** *v refl* (+ *v être*) ⟨*person*⟩ to develop a stoop; ⟨*back*⟩ to become bent

**vouvoiement** /vuvwamɑ̃/ *nm* using the 'vous' or polite form

**vouvoyer** /vuvwaje/ [23] *vtr* to address [sb] using the 'vous' form

**voyage** /vwajaʒ/ *nm* trip; journey; **partir en** ~ to go on a trip; **le** ~ **aller** the outward journey; **aimer les** ~**s** to love travelling (GB)

■ ~ **d'affaires** business trip; **être en** ~ **d'affaires** to be on a business trip; ~ **d'études** study trip; ~ **de noces** honeymoon; ~ **organisé** package tour

**voyager** /vwajaʒe/ [13] *vi* to travel

**voyageur, -euse** /vwajaʒœR, øz/ *nm,f* **(a)** passenger; **'réservé aux** ~**s munis de billets'** 'ticketholders only'

**(b)** traveller (GB)

■ ~ **de commerce** travelling (GB) salesman

**voyagiste** /vwajaʒist/ *nmf* tour operator

**voyance** /vwajɑ̃s/ *nf* clairvoyance

**voyant,** ~**e** /vwajɑ̃, ɑ̃t/ **1** *adj* ⟨*colour*⟩ loud

**2** *nm,f* **(a)** clairvoyant

**(b)** sighted person

**3** *nm* light; ~ **d'huile** (Aut) oil warning light

**voyelle** /vwajɛl/ *nf* vowel

**voyeur, -euse** /vwajœR, øz/ *nm,f* voyeur

**voyeurisme** /vwajœRism/ *nm* voyeurism

**voyou** /vwaju/ *nm* lout

**vrac: en vrac** /ɑ̃vRak/ *phr* **(a)** loose, unpackaged

**(b)** in bulk

**(c) jeter ses idées en** ~ **sur le papier** to jot down one's ideas as they come

**vrai,** ~**e** /vRɛ/ **1** *adj* true; real, genuine; **il n'y a rien de** ~ **dans ses déclarations** there's no truth in his statements; **la** ~**e raison de mon départ** the real reason for my leaving; **des** ~**s jumeaux** identical twins; **plus** ~ **que nature** ⟨*picture, scene*⟩ larger than life

**2** *nm* truth; **il y a du** ~ **dans ce que tu dis** there's some truth in what you say; **être dans le** ~ to be in the right; **pour de** ~ for real; **à** ~ **dire, à dire** ~ to tell the truth

**3** *adv* **faire** ~ to look real; **son discours sonne** ~ his speech has the ring of truth

**vraiment** /vRɛmɑ̃/ *adv* really

**vraisemblable** /vRɛsɑ̃blabl/ *adj* ⟨*excuse*⟩ convincing; ⟨*scenario*⟩ plausible; ⟨*hypothesis*⟩ likely; **il est** ~ **que** it is likely that

**vraisemblablement** /vRɛsɑ̃blabləmɑ̃/ *adv* probably

**vraisemblance** /vRɛsɑ̃blɑ̃s/ *nf* (of hypothesis) likelihood; (of situation, explanation) plausibility

**vrille** /vRij/ *nf* **(a)** spiral; (of airplane) tailspin; **descendre en** ~ ⟨*airplane*⟩ to go into a spiral dive

**(b)** (Bot) tendril

**(c)** (Tech) gimlet

**vrombir** /vʀɔ̃biʀ/ [3] *vi* ⟨*engine*⟩ to roar; **faire ∼ un moteur** to rev up an engine

**VRP** /veɛʀpe/ *nm* (*abbr* = **voyageur représentant placier**) representative, rep (colloq)

**VTT** /vetete/ ▶ VÉLO

**vu, ∼e¹** /vy/ **1** *pp* ▶ VOIR
 **2** *pp adj* **(a) être bien/mal ∼** ⟨*person*⟩ to be/ not to be well thought of; **c'est bien ∼ de faire** it's good form to do that; **ce serait plutôt mal ∼** it wouldn't go down well
 **(b) bien ∼!** good point!; **c'est tout ∼** my mind is made up
 **(c) ∼?** got it? (colloq)
 **3** *prep* in view of
 **4** **vu que** *phr* in view of the fact that

**vue²** /vy/ *nf* **(a)** sight; **avoir une bonne ∼** to have good eyesight; **don de double ∼** gift of second sight; **perdre qn de ∼** (figurative) to lose touch with sb; **à ∼** ⟨*shoot*⟩ on sight; ⟨*fly plane*⟩ without instruments; ⟨*payable*⟩ on demand
 **(b)** view; **à ma ∼, il s'enfuit** he took to his heels when he saw me; **avoir ∼ sur le lac** to look out onto the lake
 **(c)** (opinion) view; **∼s** views; **∼ optimiste des choses** optimistic view of things
 **(d) avoir des ∼s sur qn/qch** to have designs on sb/sth
 **(e) en ∼** in sight; ⟨*person*⟩ prominent; **mettre une photo bien en ∼** to display a photo prominently; **c'est quelqu'un de très en ∼** he's/she's very much in the public eye; **j'ai un terrain en ∼** I have a plot of land in mind; I've got my eye on a piece of land; **en ∼ de faire** with a view to doing
 ■ **∼ d'ensemble** overall view
 IDIOMS **à ∼ d'œil** *or* **de nez** (colloq) at a rough guess; **vouloir en mettre plein la ∼ à qn** to try to dazzle sb

**vulcanologue** /vylkanɔlɔg/ *nmf* volcanologist

**vulgaire** /vylgɛʀ/ *adj* **(a)** vulgar, coarse
 **(b)** common, ordinary; **c'est un ∼ employé** he's just a lowly employee

**vulgairement** /vylgɛʀmɑ̃/ *adv* **(a)** ⟨*speak*⟩ coarsely
 **(b)** commonly

**vulgarisation** /vylgaʀizasjɔ̃/ *nf* popularization; **revue de ∼ scientifique** scientific review for the general public

**vulgariser** /vylgaʀize/ [1] **1** *vtr* to popularize; to bring [sth] into general use
 **2** **se vulgariser** *v refl* (+ *v être*) ⟨*technology*⟩ to become generally accessible; ⟨*expression*⟩ to come into general use

**vulgarité** /vylgaʀite/ *nf* vulgarity, coarseness

**vulnérable** /vylneʀabl/ *adj* vulnerable

**vulve** /vylv/ *nf* vulva

# Ww

**w, W** /dubləve/ *nm inv* **(a)** (letter) w, W
 **(b) W** (*written abbr* = **watt**) 60 W 60 W

**wagon** /vagɔ̃/ *nm* **(a)** wagon (GB), car (US); (for passengers) carriage (GB), car (US)
 **(b)** wagonload (GB), carload (US)
 ■ **∼ à bestiaux** cattle truck (GB), cattle car (US); **∼ de marchandises** goods wagon (GB), freight car (US)

**wagon-bar**, *pl* **wagons-bars** /vagɔ̃baʀ/ *nm* buffet car

**wagon-citerne**, *pl* **wagons-citernes** /vagɔ̃sitɛʀn/ *nm* tanker

**wagon-lit**, *pl* **wagons-lits** /vagɔ̃li/ *nm* sleeper, sleeping car (US)

**wagonnet** /vagɔnɛ/ *nm* trolley (GB), cart (US)

**wagon-restaurant**, *pl* **wagons-restaurants** /vagɔ̃ʀɛstɔʀɑ̃/ *nm* restaurant car (GB), dining car (US)

**wallon, -onne** /walɔ̃, ɔn/ **1** *adj* Walloon
 **2** *nm* (language) Walloon

**Wallonie** /walɔni/ *pr nf* Walloon area of Belgium

**waters** /watɛʀ/ *nm pl* (colloq) toilets

**watt-heure**, *pl* **watts-heures** /watœʀ/ *nm* watt-hour

**WC** /(dublə)vese/ *nm pl* toilet; **aller aux ∼** to go to the toilet

**winchester** /winʃɛstɛʀ/ *nf* Winchester® rifle

**wishbone** /wiʃbon/ *nm* (Naut, Sport) wishbone boom

# Xx

**x, X** /iks/ *nm inv* (letter) x, X; **il y a x temps que c'est fini** it's been over for ages; **porter plainte contre X** (Law) to take an action against person or persons unknown; **film classé X** X-rated movie

**xénophobe** /gzenɔfɔb/ **1** *adj* xenophobic **2** *nmf* xenophobe

**xénophobie** /gzenɔfɔbi/ *nf* xenophobia

**xérès** /kseʀɛs/ *nm inv* sherry

**xylographe** /ksilɔgʀaf/ *nm* xylographer

**xylophène®** /ksilɔfɛn/ *nm* wood preservative

# Yy

**y¹, Y** /igʀɛk/ *nm inv* (letter) y, Y

**y²** /i/ *pron* **(a)** it; **tu t'~ attendais?** were you expecting it?; **il n'~ connaît rien** he knows nothing about it; **j'~ pense parfois** I sometimes think about it; **elle n'~ peut rien** there's nothing she can do about it; **j'~ viens** I'm coming to that; **rien n'~ fait** it's no use; **je n'~ comprends rien** I don't understand a thing; **tu ~ as gagné** you got the best deal; **plus difficile qu'il n'~ paraît** harder than it seems
**(b)** there; **j'~ ai mangé une fois** I ate there once; **n'~ va pas** don't go
**(c)** **il ~ a** there is/are; **du vin? il n'~ en a plus** wine? there's none left; **il n'~ a qu'à téléphoner** just phone

IDIOMS **~ mettre du sien** to work at it

**ya(c)k** /'jak/ *nm* yak

**yaourt** /'jauʀ(t)/ *nm* yoghurt

**yaourtière** /'jauʀtjɛʀ/ *nf* yoghurt-maker

**yéménite** /'jemenit/ *adj* Yemeni

**yen** /'jɛn/ *nm* yen

**yéti** /'jeti/ *nm* yeti

**yeux** *nm pl* ▶ ŒIL

**yoga** /'jɔga/ *nm* yoga

**yole** /'jɔl/ *nf* skiff

**yougoslave** /'jugɔslav/ *adj* Yugoslavian

**youpi** /'jupi/ *excl* (colloq) yippee!

**youyou** /'juju/ *nm* **(a)** ululation **(b)** dinghy

# Zz

**z, Z** /zɛd/ *nm inv* z, Z

**zaïrois, ~e** /zaiʀwa, az/ *adj* Zairean

**zambien, -ienne** /zãbjɛ̃, ɛn/ *adj* Zambian

**zapper** /zape/ [1] *vi* to flick through the TV channels

**zébré, ~e** /zebʀe/ *adj* ⟨fabric⟩ zebra-striped; **~ de** streaked with

**zèbre** /zɛbʀ/ *nm* **(a)** zebra **(b)** (figurative) (colloq) bloke (GB) (colloq), guy (colloq)

**zébrure** /zebʀyʀ/ *nf* stripe

**zébu** /zeby/ *nm* zebu

**zélé, ~e** /zele/ *adj* enthusiastic, zealous

**zèle** /zɛl/ *nm* zeal, enthusiasm; **faire du ~** or **de l'excès de ~** to be overzealous

**zénith** /zenit/ *nm* zenith; **à son ~** ⟨career⟩ at its height

**zéphyr** /zefiʀ/ *nm* zephyr

**zéro** /zeʀo/ **1** *adj* **~ heure** midnight, twenty-four hundred (hours); **il sera exactement ~ heure vingt minutes dix secondes** the time will be twelve twenty and ten seconds; **j'ai eu ~ faute dans ma dictée** I didn't make a single mistake in my dictation; **niveau/croissance ~** zero level/growth
**2** *nm* **(a)** zero, nought (GB); **avoir un ~ en latin** to get zero or nought in Latin; **remettre**

**un compteur à** ∼ to reset a counter to zero; **avoir le moral à** ∼ (figurative) to be down in the dumps (colloq); **c'est beau à regarder mais question goût c'est** ∼ (colloq) it's nice to look at, but no marks for flavour (GB)
**(b)** (in sport) (gen) nil; (in tennis) love; **trois (buts) à** ∼ three nil
■ ∼ **de conduite** (Sch) bad mark for behaviour (GB)
**IDIOMS partir de** ∼ to start from scratch; **tout reprendre à** ∼ to start all over again

**zeste** /zɛst/ nm un ∼ **de citron** the zest of a lemon

**zézayer** /zezeje/ [21] vi to lisp

**zibeline** /ziblin/ nf sable

**zieuter** /zjøte/ [1] vtr (colloq) to get a load of (colloq), to take a look at

**zigoto** /zigɔto/ nm (colloq) guy (colloq); **faire le** ∼ to clown around

**zigue** /zig/ nm (colloq) guy (colloq)

**zigzag** /zigzag/ nm zigzag; **route en** ∼ winding road; **faire des** ∼s to zigzag (**parmi** through); **partir en** ∼ to zigzag off

**zinc** /zɛ̃g/ nm **(a)** zinc; **toiture de** or **en** ∼ tin roofing
**(b)** (colloq) counter, bar

**zingueur** /zɛ̃gœʀ/ nm roofer

**zinzin** (colloq) /zɛ̃zɛ̃/ **1** adj inv cracked (colloq)
**2** nm thingamajig (colloq)

**zip** /zip/ nm zip (GB), zipper (US)

**zippé, ∼e** /zipe/ adj zip-up

**zipper** /zipe/ vt (Comput) to zip

**zizanie** /zizani/ nf ill-feeling, discord

**zizi** /zizi/ nm (colloq) willy (GB) (colloq), penis

**zodiac®** /zɔdjak/ nm inflatable dinghy

**zodiaque** /zɔdjak/ nm zodiac

**zona** /zona/ nm shingles

**zonage** /zonaʒ/ nm zoning

**zonard, ∼e** /zonaʀ, aʀd/ nm,f (colloq) dropout (colloq)

**zone** /zon/ nf **(a)** zone, area; ∼ **interdite** off-limits area; (on signpost) no entry
**(b) la** ∼ (colloq) the slum belt; **de seconde** ∼ second-rate
■ ∼ **d'activités** business park; ∼ **artisanale** small industrial estate (GB) or park; ∼ **bleue** restricted parking zone; ∼ **industrielle** industrial estate (GB) or park

**zoner** /zone/ [1] vi (colloq) to hang about (colloq)

**zoo** /zo/ nm zoo

**zoologie** /zɔɔlɔʒi/ nf zoology

**zoom** /zum/ nm **(a)** zoom lens
**(b)** zoom

**zouave** /zwav/ nm **(a)** (colloq) clown, comedian; **faire le** ∼ to clown around (colloq)
**(b)** (soldier) zouave

**zoulou, ∼e** /zulu/ adj Zulu

**zozo** /zozo/ nm (colloq) ninny (GB) (colloq), jerk (colloq)

**zozoter** /zɔzɔte/ [1] vi to lisp

**zut** /zyt/ excl (colloq) damn! (colloq)

• • • • • • • • • • • • • • • • • • • • • • • • • • • • • • • • • • • • • • • • • • • • • • • • •

**Calendar**
**Culture**
**Letters**

# Calendar of French traditions, festivals, and holidays

## January
1  8  15  22  29
2  9  16  23  30
3  10  17  24  31
4  11  18  25
5  12  19  26
6  13  20  27
7  14  21  28

## February
1  8  15  22
2  9  16  23
3  10  17  24
4  11  18  25
5  12  19  26
6  13  20  27
7  14  21  28

## March
1  8  15  22  29
2  9  16  23  30
3  10  17  24  31
4  11  18  25
5  12  19  26
6  13  20  27
7  14  21  28

## April
1  8  15  22  29
2  9  16  23  30
3  10  17  24
4  11  18  25
5  12  19  26
6  13  20  27
7  14  21  28

## May
1  8  15  22  29
2  9  16  23  30
3  10  17  24  31
4  11  18  25
5  12  19  26
6  13  20  27
7  14  21  28

## June
1  8  15  22  29
2  9  16  23  30
3  10  17  24
4  11  18  25
5  12  19  26
6  13  20  27
7  14  21  28

## July
1  8  15  22  29
2  9  16  23  30
3  10  17  24  31
4  11  18  25
5  12  19  26
6  13  20  27
7  14  21  28

## August
1  8  15  22  29
2  9  16  23  30
3  10  17  24  31
4  11  18  25
5  12  19  26
6  13  20  27
7  14  21  28

## September
1  8  15  22  29
2  9  16  23  30
3  10  17  24
4  11  18  25
5  12  19  26
6  13  20  27
7  14  21  28

## October
1  8  15  22  29
2  9  16  23  30
3  10  17  24  31
4  11  18  25
5  12  19  26
6  13  20  27
7  14  21  28

## November
1  8  15  22  29
2  9  16  23  30
3  10  17  24
4  11  18  25
5  12  19  26
6  13  20  27
7  14  21  28

## December
1  8  15  22  29
2  9  16  23  30
3  10  17  24  31
4  11  18  25
5  12  19  26
6  13  20  27
7  14  21  28

• • • • • • • • • • • • • • • • • • • • • • • • • • • • • • • •

**1 January**
**le jour de l'an** (New Year's Day) is a
public holiday and a day of family
celebration, with a large lunch,
traditionally featuring seafood of
various kinds.

**6 January**
**la Fête des Rois** (Epiphany or Twelfth
night). Around this time, most families
have a *galette des Rois*, a rich pastry
cake filled with *frangipane* (almond
paste). The cake contains a *fève*, literally
a bean, as this is what was originally
used. Nowadays the *fève* takes the form
of a tiny plastic or ceramic figure. The
person who gets the *fève* in their portion
puts on the cardboard crown which
comes with the cake.

**2 February**
**la Chandeleur** (Candlemas) is
celebrated in the church but is not a
public holiday. However, it is traditional
to eat *crêpes* (pancakes) on this day.

**14 February**
**la Saint Valentin** (St Valentine's Day).
As in many other countries, people
celebrate a romantic relationship with
gifts of flowers or chocolates.

**1 April**
**le premier avril** (April Fool's Day).
The French also take advantage of this
occasion to play tricks on one another,
calling out *poisson d'avril!* (literally
'April fish').

**1 May**
**La Fête du Travail** (International
Labour Day) is a public holiday.

**8 May**
**le 8 mai** or **la Fête de la Victoire** is a
public holiday commemorating Victory
in Europe on 8 May 1945.

**24 June**
**la Saint-Jean** (Midsummer's Day).
In many areas, bonfires (*les feux de la
Saint-Jean*) are lit on Midsummer's
Night. People are supposed to jump over
these, re-enacting a pagan custom
intended to ward off the cold of winter.

**14 July**
**la Fête Nationale** or **le 14 juillet** is
usually called Bastille Day in English
and is a public holiday in France. It
commemorates the taking of the
Bastille prison in Paris and the
liberation of its prisoners by the people
of Paris in 1789, one of the first events of
the Revolution. All over France there
are parades on the day of the 14th and
firework displays and *bals* (local
dances) either on the night of the 13th
or of the 14th.

**15 August**
**l'Assomption** (Feast of the
Assumption) is a public holiday. Many
people in France are either setting off
on holiday around the 15th or else
returning home, so this is traditionally
a very busy time on the roads.

**1 November**
**la Toussaint** (All Saints' Day) is a
public holiday and the day when people
remember their dead relatives and
friends, although properly speaking it is
All Souls' Day the following day that is
set aside for this in the church. People
take flowers to the cemetery,
particularly chrysanthemums, as these
are in bloom at this time. Because of
this association, it is best to avoid
taking chrysanthemums as a gift for
someone. Schoolchildren have a two-
week holiday around this time.

**11 November**
**le 11 novembre** is a public holiday to
commemorate the Armistice of 1918
and a day of remembrance for those
who died in the two world wars and in
subsequent conflicts. All towns and
villages hold parades in which war
veterans accompany local officials and a
brass band to lay wreaths on the war
memorial. In Paris, the President lays a
wreath on the tomb of the unknown
soldier beneath the *Arc de Triomphe* on
the *Champs-Élysées*.

**8 December**
**la fête de l'Immaculée Conception**
(Feast of the Immaculate Conception).
In the city of Lyons, this is celebrated as

**Calendar**

la **Fête de la Lumière** (Festival of
Light) said to commemorate the Virgin's
intervention to prevent the plague
reaching Lyons in the Middle Ages.
People put rows of candles in coloured
glass jars on the outsides of their
windowsills, so that all the buildings in
the centre of the city are illuminated.

### 24 December
la veille de Noël (Christmas Eve) is
the time when most people exchange
presents. Many people go to *la messe de
minuit* (midnight mass).

### 25 December
**Noël** (Christmas) is a public holiday
and a day of eating and drinking. Lunch
will often start with a variety of
seafood, oysters being particularly
popular. Turkey is often eaten as a main
course, sometimes with chestnut
stuffing. A variety of cheeses will be
followed by *la bûche de Noël*, a rich
chocolate cake in the form of a snow-
covered log. French people do not
usually send Christmas cards, the
custom being to send wishes for the
coming year to more distant friends and
relatives during the month of January.

### 26 December
There is no particular name for the day
after Christmas Day and it is not a
public holiday.

### 31 December
la **Saint-Sylvestre** (New Year's Eve).
Many people have parties to celebrate
*le réveillon du Nouvel An* (New Year's
Eve Party). Once again, food plays a
major part and, as at Christmas, this is a
time to splash out on luxury foods such
as *foie gras*. There will often be dancing
and the New Year will be welcomed in
with champagne.

## Movable feasts

### Mardi gras
Shrove Tuesday, the last day of carnival
before the beginning of Lent on Ash
Wednesday. Traditionally, *crêpes*
(pancakes) are eaten for supper. In many
areas of France, sugared fritters called
*bugnes* in and around Lyons and
*oreillettes* farther south, are eaten
between *la fête des Rois* and *mardi gras*.

### le Vendredi saint
Good Friday is celebrated in the church,
but is not a public holiday.

### Pâques
Easter Sunday, *le dimanche de Pâques*,
is for many people the occasion for a big
family lunch. Easter hunts are
organised for children, with chocolate
eggs, rabbits, hens, or fish traditionally
hidden in the family garden. *Le lundi de
Pâques* (Easter Monday) is a public
holiday.

l'**Ascension**, the Thursday forty days
after Easter, is a public holiday in
France.

la **Pentecôte** (Whitsun) on the seventh
Sunday after Easter represents for
many people the first long weekend of
the summer, as *le lundi de la Pentecôte*
(Whit Monday) is a public holiday.
Many families go to stay with friends
or relatives in the country.

la **Fête des mères** (Mother's Day) is the
Sunday after *Pentecôte*. This is another
occasion for a big family meal, with
presents for the mother. **La fête des
pères** (Father's Day) is celebrated in
similar fashion two weeks later.

# A–Z of French Life and Culture

### Académie française
A learned body whose main role nowadays is to monitor new developments in the French language and to make decisions as to what is acceptable and what is not, although these decisions are not always taken entirely seriously by the public at large. Its 40 members are elected for life on the basis of their contribution to scholarship or literature.

### agrégation
A qualification awarded by **CONCOURS** for entry to the limited number of highest level teaching posts in secondary and higher education.

### Alliance Française
A private organization which aims to spread awareness of French language and culture. It has centres in cities throughout the world, providing classes and a variety of cultural activities.

### année scolaire
The French school year starts with the **RENTRÉE DES CLASSES** in early September and ends in early July. There is a week's holiday in late October/early November around *la Toussaint* (All Saints' Day, 1 November), two weeks around Christmas and New Year, two weeks in February, and two weeks in April. Many families go on skiing holidays during the February break.

### ANPE - Agence nationale pour l'emploi
The national agency which assists jobseekers. The unemployed must register with *ANPE* to claim benefit and receive training.

### Antenne 2 ▶ FRANCE 2

### arrondissement
The three largest cities in France - Paris, Lyons, and Marseilles – are divided into numbered administrative areas called *arrondissements*. Each has its own mayor and council, and the number of the *arrondissement* is usually part of the postcode. The system makes for a convenient way for people to talk about which part of the city they live in e.g. '*le neuvième arrondissement*' or simply '*le neuvième*'.
An *arrondissement* is also a sub-division of a **DÉPARTEMENT**.

### ARTE
A television channel, run jointly by France and Germany, which provides a high standard of cultural programmes.

## Assemblée Nationale

The lower house of the French parliament, also called the **Chambre des députés**. There are 577 **DÉPUTÉS**, elected for a five-year term, often after two rounds of voting as at least 50% of the vote must be obtained.

## Astérix

A hugely popular comic-book character invented by cartoonists Goscinny and Uderzo. *Astérix* is a tiny but invincible village leader in the ancient province of Gaul whose fictional adventures with his fellow-villagers often involve fighting and outwitting the occupying Romans and make for gentle mockery of cultures outside Gaul. The *Astérix* books have been translated into 40 languages.

## autoroute

France has an extensive motorway system, which is largely financed by tolls calculated according to the distance travelled and the vehicle type. Tickets are obtained and tolls paid at *péages* (tollgates). There is a speed limit for standard vehicles of 130 km/h (approx. 80 mph) and 110 km/h (approx. 70 mph) in wet weather.

## baccalauréat

The *baccalauréat*, generally known informally as the *Bac*, is the examination sat in the final year of the **LYCÉE** (*la terminale*), so usually at age 17 or 18. Students sit exams in a fairly broad range of subjects in a particular category: the *Bac S* places emphasis on the sciences, for example, whilst the *Bac L* has a literary bias. Some categories cater for students specializing in more directly job-based subjects such as agriculture. The final result is given as a single overall mark or grade out of 20, although the scores for individual subjects are also given. It is common to use the *Bac* as a point of reference in job adverts, so that *Bac + 4* would mean a person who had completed 4 years of full-time study after the *Bac*, with appropriate diplomas to show for it.

## bachelier

The holder of the **BACCALAURÉAT**, entitled to enrol for university courses.

## bande dessinée (BD)

Comic books of all sorts and for a wide variety of age and interest groups are immensely popular in France and form an important part of French culture. Cartoon characters such as *Astérix, Lucky Luke*, and *Tintin* are household names and older comic books are often collectors' items.

## Basque

The Basque country extends on both sides of the Pyrenees with about one quarter of a million Basques living in France and ten times that number in Spain. The French Basque region (*le Pays basque français*) does not have any autonomous status nor is Basque recognized as an official language. It is, however, taught in some schools, and there are an estimated 40,000 Basque speakers in France.

## BCBG

The letters *BCBG* stand for *bon chic bon genre,* although the full form is hardly ever used. *BCBG* is used to sum up a person, style of dress, lifestyle etc. as reflecting conventional upper middle-class or *bourgeois* values and tastes. In most cases, this is not intended as a compliment.

## beur

A second-generation North African from the **MAGHREB** living in France.

## boules

A type of bowls, also called **pétanque**, played all over France, using metal *boules* and a jack known as a *cochonnet.* Special areas (*terrains de boules*) are set aside for the game in towns and villages, although one of the obvious attractions of the game is that it can be played virtually anywhere, so a family lunch in the summer will often end in a game of *boules* (*une partie de boules*). There are some regional variations, notably in the size and form of the playing area and the size of the bowls.

## brasserie

The original meaning of *brasserie* is 'brewery', and although the word is still used in this sense, it has come also to mean a type of bar-restaurant, usually serving simple, traditional French food at reasonable prices. Most *brasseries* offer a fixed-price menu, especially at lunchtime.

## Breton

The ancient Celtic language of Brittany (*Bretagne*). It is related to Welsh, Irish, Scottish Gaelic, and Cornish. Recent decades have seen a revival of interest in the language going hand in hand with the assertion of a regional cultural identity and a movement for independence from France. Breton is fairly widely spoken and is taught in secondary schools in the region, although it is not recognized as an official language in France.

## Brevet d'études professionnelles (BEP)

A vocational qualification awarded at the end of a two-year, practically-based course in a **LYCÉE** specializing in providing teaching directly related to the workplace.

## Brevet de technicien (BT)

A vocational qualification awarded at the end of a three-year course in a special section of a **LYCÉE**. There is considerable competition for entry to courses, and the standards required result in a high dropout rate.

## Brevet de technicien supérieur (BTS)

A vocational qualification awarded at the end of a two-year course after

Culture

. . . . . . . . . . . . . . . . . . . . . . . . . . . . . . . . . . . . . . . . . . . . . . .

the **BACCALAURÉAT** in a specific professional field.

### Brevet des collèges
A general educational qualification taken in a range of subjects by students aged around 15 in the final year of **COLLÈGE**.

### bureau de tabac
Tobacconists are either individual shops or else are to be found in a *bar-tabac* or *café-tabac*. They are also often combined with a newsagents (*marchand de journaux*). As well as being licensed to sell tobacco and cigarettes, they have a state licence to sell stamps, **LOTO** tickets, the **VIGNETTE** (road tax disc for motor vehicles), and certain other official documents.

### Canal Plus (Canal+)
A privately-owned French television channel broadcasting mainly feature films. Viewers pay a subscription and access the channel using a decoder.

### canton
A *canton* is an administrative unit of French local government which contains several **COMMUNES**. It elects a member of the **CONSEIL GÉNÉRAL**.

### CAPES - certificat d'aptitude au professorat de l'enseignement du second degré
The qualification normally required in order to teach in a secondary school. Qualification is by means of a competitive examination (**CONCOURS**) usually at the end of a two-year course in a specialist teacher-training institute (*IUFM: Institut universitaire pour la formation des maîtres*).

### Carte bleue
A credit card issued by French banks as part of the international Visa network.

### Carte grise
The registration document for a motor vehicle. It is an offence not to carry it when driving the vehicle, and police checks are frequent. Vehicle registration numbers depend on the **DÉPARTEMENT** in which the owner lives and have to be changed if the owner moves to a different one.

### Carte nationale d'identité
Although not obligatory, most French citizens possess a *carte nationale d'identité* (national identity card), obtained from their local **MAIRIE**, **PRÉFECTURE**, or *commissariat de police* (police station), as proof of identity is often required, for example when paying by cheque. It is also accepted as a travel document by all EC countries.

### Catalan
The language spoken by 25 per cent of people in Spain and by some people

• • • • • • • • • • • • • • • • • • • • • • • • • • • • • • • • • • •

in the Perpignan area of southwest France. It is taught in schools in the area but is not recognized as an official language in France.

### CDI - Centre de documentation et d'information

A resource and information centre providing library and IT facilities in a school or college. The term has largely replaced *bibliothèque* (library) in this context.

### CE - cycle élémentaire

Also called *cours élémentaire*, this is the programme for the two years of primary school for children aged 7 to 9 (*CE1* and *CE2*).

### Césars

Prizes awarded annually for achievements in the film industry, so the French equivalent of the Oscars.

### CFDT

A large and influential trade union which is close to the **PARTI SOCIALISTE**, but which has a much wider membership.

### CGT

A large and influential trade union which has a tradition of association with the **PARTI COMMUNISTE**, but which has a much wider membership.

### Chambre des députés ▶ ASSEMBLÉE NATIONALE

### champignons

The French use the word *champignons* (mushrooms) to refer to any of the types of mushroom-like fungi that are to be found in the countryside, whether edible or not. Cultivated button mushrooms are called *champignons de Paris*. Hunting for edible *champignons* is almost a national leisure activity, and many varieties are highly prized. Advice on whether a *champignon* is edible or not can usually be obtained in a **PHARMACIE**.

### Champs-Élysées

The world-famous avenue in central Paris, known for its luxury shops, hotels, and clubs. At one end is the *Arc de Triomphe*, the scene of the remembrance ceremony each year for the Armistice of 1918 and under which is the tomb of an unknown soldier, killed in World War I.

### charcuterie

A shop or supermarket counter selling a wide variety of pork products. As well as cuts of pork, *charcutiers* usually sell chicken both raw and ready-cooked, and there will be various types of raw and cooked ham, a variety of pâtés, often homemade in small shops, and a selection of *saucissons*. Most *charcuteries* also offer a variey of salads, various types of savoury pastries, and a number of dishes, different every day, which can be reheated at home or on the premises. Some *charcuteries* also offer a catering service, in which case the shop will probably call itself a *charcutier-traiteur*. The word *charcuterie* is also used to mean pork products such as ham and *saucisson*.

### chasse

*La chasse* (hunting) is a widely practised sport in France. Legislation as to the rights of hunters to hunt over privately-owned land varies according to the region and the amount of land concerned. During the hunting season, hunting is permitted on Thursdays, Saturdays, and Sundays. It is advisable not to stray from public footpaths when walking in the countryside on these days. The hunters (*les chasseurs*) are a powerful political lobby and are represented in the **ASSEMBLÉE NATIONALE**.

### CHU - centre hospitalier universitaire

A teaching hospital attached to the medical faculty of a university.

### Cinquième

*La Cinquième* is an educational television channel which broadcasts on the **ARTE** channel during the day.

### Cinquième république

This is the present régime in France. The constitution was established in 1958 according to principles put forward by Charles de Gaulle.

### classes

In French schools, after **CM**, classes go in reverse order, starting at age 11-12 in *sixième* and progressing through *cinquième, quatrième, troisième, seconde, première*, and ending in *terminale* at age 17 or 18, the year in which the **BACCALAURÉAT** is taken. Education in France is compulsory up to the end of *seconde*.

### classe de neige

A period, generally a week, which a school class, usually of under-twelves, spends in a mountain area. Ski tuition is integrated with normal school work.

### classe préparatoire

An intensive two-year course, provided by some prestigious **LYCÉES**, which prepares students for the competitive examinations (**CONCOURS**) by means of which students are selected for the **GRANDES ÉCOLES**.

### CM - Cycle moyen

Also called *Cours moyen* this is the programme for the two years of primary school for children aged 9 to 11 (*CM1* and *CM2*).

### cohabitation

A period of power sharing between opposing political parties which can occur since the presidential mandate lasts for seven years, but legislative elections are five-yearly.

Culture

### collège

A state school for pupils between the ages of 11 and 15, between the **ÉCOLE PRIMAIRE** and the **LYCÉE**. The organisation of the school and the curriculum followed are laid down at national level.

### colonie de vacances

A holiday village or summer camp for children. Originally set up as a means of giving poorer city children a means of getting out into the countryside, these are still largely state-subsidized. The informal word for them is *colo*.

### commune

The *commune* is the smallest administrative unit of French local government. Each has its own **MAIRE** (mayor) and **CONSEIL MUNICIPAL** and with other *communes* forms a **CANTON**.

### concours

Entry into many areas of the public services, including the teaching profession, as well as the most prestigious institutes of higher education, depends on succeeding in a competitive examination or *concours*. The number of candidates admitted depends on the number of posts or places available in a given year.

### conduite accompagnée (CA)

A learner driver who has passed the theory part of the driving test (*code de la route*) in a state-approved driving school is allowed to practise driving a vehicle accompanied by a qualified driver over the age of 28. Such drivers are not allowed to drive on **AUTOROUTES** and are required to have a white sticker with a red 'A' displayed on the rear of their vehicle.

### conseil de classe

A committee representing each class in a **COLLÈGE** or **LYCÉE** consisting of the class teachers, two elected parent members, and two elected class members. It is chaired by the head teacher. The *conseil de classe* meets regularly to discuss the progress of the class and any problems that have arisen.

### conseil général

The body of representatives elected every six years to implement public policy in each **DÉPARTEMENT**.

### conseil municipal

The *conseil municipal* is the local council elected for a 6-year term by the inhabitants of a **COMMUNE**. The *conseil municipal* then elects the **MAIRE** (mayor). It is responsible for the management of local public services and amenities.

Culture

. . . . . . . . . . . . . . . . . . . . . . . . . . . . . . . . . . . . . . . . . . . . . . . .

### conseil régional

Each member of a *conseil régional* is elected for a term of six years to represent a **DÉPARTEMENT**. The *conseillers régionaux* then appoint a president and an executive team.

### CP - Cycle préparatoire

Also called *Cours préparatoire*, this is the first year of primary school, starting a child's formal education off at the statutory age of 6.
Most children will have already attended an **ÉCOLE MATERNELLE**.

### CRS – compagnies républicaines de sécurité

Special police units trained in public order techniques and riot control. They also police the **AUTOROUTES** and support mountain rescue and lifeguard work.

### département

An administrative unit of government in France. Each *département* has a number and this appears as the first two digits in postcodes for addresses within the *département* and as the two-digit number at the end of registration numbers on motor vehicles.

### député

An elected member of the **ASSEMBLÉE NATIONALE**.

### DEUG - diplôme d'études universitaires générales

A qualification awarded after two years of university education in non-scientific subject areas. Students are required to pass this in order to go on to study for the **LICENCE**, and the **DEUG** is also accepted as a qualification for entry into professional life.

### DEUST - Diplôme d'études universitaires de sciences et techniques

The equivalent of the **DEUG** in science and technology.

### DOM - Département d'outre-mer

An overseas **DÉPARTEMENT** which also has the status of a region. At present there are four of these: Guadeloupe, Guyane, Martinique, and Réunion.

### droguerie

As a shop or supermarket section, there seems little connection between the name, which might be literally translated as 'drugstore', and the merchandise displayed. However, *drogue* can also mean the raw ingredients of dyes, and *droguistes* were originally dye merchants. Nowadays you will find not only dyes but household products and cleaning utensils, candles, and a variety of other useful household items.

• • • • • • • • • • • • • • • • • • • • • • • • • • • • • • • • • • • • • • • • • •

### DUT - diplôme universitaire de technologie
A qualification awarded after two years of higher education in an **IUT**. Courses are vocationally based and include a compulsory period of work experience.

### école libre
Private sector school education, provided predominantly by the Catholic church.

### école maternelle
A school providing free nursery education from age 2 to 6. Many children start at 2 and virtually all children attend between the ages of 4 and 6, which is the statutory school starting age and the time at which children move into the **ÉCOLE PRIMAIRE**

### école primaire
A primary school for children between the ages of 6, the statutory minimum age for starting school, and 11.

### école secondaire
Secondary education in France consists of two phases: **COLLÈGE** (11–15 years) and **LYCEE** (15/16–17/18 years).

### EDF-GDF - Électricité de France-Gaz de France
The state-owned utility combining electricity generation and distribution of gas and electricity.

### Élysée ▶ PALAIS DE L' ÉLYSÉE

### Emmaüs
A charitable organization founded in 1954 by the Abbé Pierre, a Catholic priest and well-known public figure. The organisation, which has wide public support, aims to help underprivileged people. It has centres throughout France, run by volunteers who collect and sell secondhand furniture, clothes, and bric-à-brac.

### Europe 1
A popular commercial French-language radio station, which broadcasts news, popular music, sport, and light entertainment from the Saarland in Germany.

### Événement du jeudi - l' Événement du jeudi
A popular weekly news magazine.

### Express - l'Express
A weekly news magazine offering in-depth coverage of political and cultural matters.

Culture

### faculté
*La faculté* - and more usually and informally *la fac* - is the way that students refer to their university, particularly the location itself, so that *aller à la fac* would be the equivalent of 'to go into college'.

### Figaro - le Figaro
A right-wing national daily newspaper with a wide circulation.

### France 2
This is the main publicly-owned television channel and aims to provide a wide range of quality programmes.

### France 3
A state-owned television channel which is regionally based and is required to promote regional diversity and to cover a wide range of beliefs and opinions.

### France Culture
A 24-hour **RADIO FRANCE** radio station featuring serious talk programmes on a wide variety of cultural and social topics.

### France Info
A 24-hour radio news station run by **RADIO FRANCE**.

### France Inter
A **RADIO FRANCE** radio station broadcasting mainly light entertainment, including a considerable proportion of studio comedy shows, but also offering good news coverage.

### France Musiques
A 24-hour **RADIO FRANCE** radio station. Its main focus is classical music but it also provides considerable coverage of jazz and world music.

### France Télécom
The state-owned telephone company. It no longers holds a monopoly.

### Front National
An extreme right-wing political party, founded in 1972 by Jean-Marie Le Pen.

### Gendarmerie nationale
A section of the military which provides police services outside the major towns.

### gîte rural
A farmhouse or other building in the country which has been turned into a holiday cottage. Houses displaying the official *gîte de France* sign must conform to certain standards.

. . . . . . . . . . . . . . . . . . . . . . . . . . . . . . . . . . . . . .

### grande école

A prestigious higher education establishment admitting students on the results of a **CONCOURS**. They have different areas of specialization and competition for entry is fierce, as they are widely believed to offer the highest level of education available and thus a guarantee of subsequent career success.

### HLM - habitation à loyer modéré

Public housing, usually apartments, for which the rent is considerably lower than the average for private-sector housing. Tenants have the right to buy their homes, provided they undertake not to sell them within 5 years.

### hôtel de ville ▶ MAIRIE

### Humanité - l'Humanité

The communist national daily newspaper.

### Internet

A wealth of useful information on French culture, society, and current affairs can be obtained on the Internet. All the main French newspapers have websites (e.g. http://www.lemonde.fr), as do the television channels (e.g. http://www.france3.fr and http://www.tf1.fr). The *Louvre* museum has an interesting site at http://web.culture.fr/louvre.

### immatriculation ▶ PLAQUE D'IMMATRICULATION

### IUT - Institut universitaire de technologie

An institute of technology attached to a university, which provides vocationally-based courses leading to the **DUT**.

### Libération

A left-wing national daily newspaper published in Paris. A separate edition is published for Lyons.

### licence

A university degree awarded after a year's study following the **DEUG**.

### Loto

The French national lottery. People play the Loto using special machines which can be found in **BUREAUX DE TABAC** throughout France.

### Luxembourg ▶ PALAIS DU LUXEMBOURG

### lycée

A school providing the last three years of secondary education after **COLLÈGE**. The first year is *seconde* at the age of 15/16, going through *première*, and ending with *terminale* at age 17/18. As well as those which provide a conventional academic education, there are a number of different types of *lycée* offering a more vocationally-based education.

Culture

. . . . . . . . . . . . . . . . . . . . . . . . . . . . . . . . . . . . . . . . . . .

### M6

A popular, privately-owned, commercial television channel.

### magasins

Opening and closing times of shops (*les magasins*) vary according to the type of shop and the location. Department stores (*les grands magasins*) are generally open all day from 9 a.m. to 7 p.m. In larger towns, most other shops, with the exception of small food shops, are also open all day. Privately-owned food shops such as butchers and fishmongers generally open at 8 a.m. and do not close in the evening until 7 or 7.30. Most, however, are closed between midday and 2 or 3 p.m. In small towns, all the shops, with the exception of bakers, generally close for 2 or 3 hours in the middle of the day. In both small and large towns, it is always possible to find all types of food shops open on Sunday mornings until midday. In smaller towns, however, many of the shops are closed on Mondays.

### Maghreb

The region of Islamic North Africa which covers the former French colony of Algeria and the former French protectorates of Morocco and Tunisia.

### maire

The chief officer of a **COMMUNE** elected by the **CONSEIL MUNICIPAL**. He or she represents state authority locally, officiates at marriages, and supervises local elections.

### mairie

The *mairie* (town hall) is the administrative headquarters of the **CONSEIL MUNICIPAL**. In larger towns the *mairie* is often called the **HÔTEL DE VILLE**.

### marchés

All towns in France have a weekly market with stalls selling a variety of produce, and some areas in big cities have a market every day. Many stalls are held by local people selling their own produce. Despite supermarkets, many people do much of their food shopping *au marché*.

### Marianne

The symbolic female figure often used to represent the French Republic. There are statues of her in public places all over France, and she also appears on the standard French stamp. She is always depicted wearing the Phrygian bonnet, a pointed cap which became one of the symbols of liberty as represented by the 1789 Revolution.

### Marseillaise

The French national anthem, so called because it was the marching song of a group of republican volunteers from Marseilles a few years after the 1789 revolution.

## Matignon

The *Hôtel Matignon* in the rue de Varenne in Paris is the official residence and office of the prime minister. *Hôtel* is used here in the sense of a large private town house, which would have been its original use in the eighteenth century.

## Médecins du monde

A charitable organization which provides medical and humanitarian aid in areas stricken by war, famine, or natural disaster.

## Médecins sans frontières

A charitable organisation which sends medical teams anywhere in the world where they are needed to cope with the effects on people of war and disaster.

## Minitel

A computer terminal available in a variety of models to the subscribers of **FRANCE TÉLÉCOM**. It gives users access to the *Télétel* network, which has a huge variety of services, payable at different rates, including the telephone directory. It can now be accessed via the Internet.

## MJC - Maison des jeunes et de la culture

A community youth centre offering a wide variety of services and activities.

## Monde - le Monde

A national daily newspaper. Its political stance is left of centre, and it is entirely owned by its staff. It provides full coverage of national and international news and is known for its in-depth analysis of current issues. It is unusual in publishing virtually no photographs of current events.

## Nouvel Observateur - le Nouvel Observateur

A left-wing weekly magazine providing in-depth articles on current political issues and good coverage of culture and the arts.

## Occitan

The old language of the southern half of France. It is still spoken in a number of different dialects by an estimated four million people, and recent years have seen an immense revival of interest in promoting its survival. It can now be learned in many schools in the south, although it has no status as an official language in France.

## Palais Bourbon

A large eighteenth-century residence on the left bank of the Seine which is now the seat of the **ASSEMBLÉE NATIONALE**.

## Palais de l'Élysée

The official residence and office of the French President, situated just off the **CHAMPS-ÉLYSÉES** in Paris.

Culture

### Palais des Congrès

A huge conference centre. Several large cities have one of these, notably Paris and Lyons. As well as supplying luxury conference facilities, they have a large amount of exhibition space, and auditoriums where concerts and performances are held.

### Palais du Luxembourg

A seventeenth century palace in the *jardin du Luxembourg* in Paris. It is now the seat of the **SÉNAT**.

### paysan

Since *paysan* can be used in French to mean both 'small farmer' and, more offensively, 'peasant', small farmers are generally referred to as *agriculteurs*. However, many small farmers take pride in their identity as *paysans*, particularly in the more remote areas of the country, where small farms are still the usual form of cultivation. The difficulty of making a living with a limited amount of land has, however, led to many such farms being abandoned or amalgamated into larger units and a general movement of the traditional rural population towards the towns.

### Parti communiste français (PCF)

The French Communist Party still has a significant following, but support for it has been decreasing steadily in recent years.

### Parti socialiste (PS)

The main political party of the left.

### permis de conduire

A driving licence can be issued to a person over the age of 18 who has passed both parts of the driving test. The first part is the theory test (*code de la route*) and consists of forty questions based on the highway code. This can be sat from the age of 16 onwards and gives the right to **CONDUITE ACCOMPAGNÉE**. The practical driving test has to be taken within two years of the theory test. It is compulsory to carry your driving licence with you when you are driving a vehicle.

### pétanque ▶ BOULES

### pharmacie

Pharmacies in France generally sell only medicines and closely related products such as toiletries and some brands of make-up and perfume. The products of the major perfume houses are to be found in *parfumeries*. Pharmacists traditionally play an active paramedical role, and people will often consult a pharmacist rather than a doctor in the case of minor ailments or accidents such as snake bites. Pharmacies are easily spotted by the green cross, which is lit up when the pharmacy is open. A *pharmacie de garde* (duty chemist) can dispense medicines outside normal opening hours as part of a local rota.

. . . . . . . . . . . . . . . . . . . . . . . . . . . . . . . . . . . . . . . . . . . .

### plaque d'immatriculation
A vehicle's registration plate. The last two figures indicate the number of the **DÉPARTEMENT** in which the owner lives. If you move into another *département*, you are obliged by law to change your registration plate accordingly.

### PMU – pari mutuel urbain
The *PMU* sign is to be seen outside many **BUREAUX DE TABAC**. It indicates a state-regulated horse-race betting outlet. The most popular form of betting is the *tiercé*, in which punters have to predict the first three places in a given race.

### Point – le Point
A centre-right weekly news magazine offering in-depth coverage of politics and economics.

### police
There are three principal police forces: the *police municipale* who are responsible for routine local policing such as traffic offences, who are locally organized and are not armed, the *police nationale* who are nationally organized and generally armed, and the **GENDARMERIE NATIONALE** which is a branch of the military.

### Poste – La Poste
The state monopoly postal service. Postboxes in France are yellow.

### préfet
The most senior offical responsible for representing the state within the **DÉPARTEMENT**.

### préfecture
The administrative headquarters of a **DÉPARTEMENT**.

### Premier ministre
The chief minister of the government, appointed by the **PRÉSIDENT DE LA RÉPUBLIQUE** and responsible for the overall management of government affairs.

### Président de la République
The president is the head of state and is elected for a term of 7 years. Under the constitution of the **CINQUIÈME RÉPUBLIQUE** the president plays a strong executive role in the governing of the country.

### Prix Fémina
A literary prize awarded in November each year by a jury of women.

### Prix Goncourt
A literary prize awarded each November for a novel published in that year. The event attracts considerable media coverage and speculation.

Culture

**Prix Médicis**
A literary prize awarded in November each year for an innovative novel or book of short stories.

**Quai d'Orsay**
The *ministère des Affaires étrangères* (ministry of Foreign Affairs) is situated here, so *Quai d'Orsay* is often used by journalists to mean the ministry.

**Radio France**
The state-owned radio broadcasting company.

**région**
The largest administrative unit in France, consisting of a number of **DÉPARTEMENTS**. Each has its own **CONSEIL RÉGIONAL** (regional council) which has responsibilities in education and economic planning.

**rentrée**
The week at the beginning of September when the new school year starts and around which much of French administrative life revolves. The preceding weeks see intensive advertising of associated merchandise, from books and stationery to clothes and sports equipment. Many stores and supermarkets have have a range of special purchases at bargain prices.
*La rentrée littéraire* marks the start of the literary year and *la rentrée parlementaire* signals the reassembly of parliament after the recess.

**repas**
Traditionally the midday meal was the big meal of the day, and for people who live in country areas this is still largely the case. Even in big cities many people continue to eat a big meal in the middle of the day, either in a family restaurant near their place of work or by buying a freshly cooked hot dish from a **CHARCUTERIE**. However, people living and working in the larger cities are tending more and more to have a snack lunch and to eat their main meal in the evening. In either case, the main meal virtually always consists of a number of courses, typically a starter such as *pâté, saucisson*, or salad, then meat or fish with a vegetable dish, followed by cheese and dessert. Cheese is virtually always eaten, as one might expect in a country that boasts a huge variety of different cheeses, and is always served before the dessert. In town and country alike, Sunday is the day for a big family meal in the middle of the day, and the **PÂTISSERIES** are usually crowded on Sunday mornings as people queue up to buy a large tart or cake for their hosts or guests.

. . . . . . . . . . . . . . . . . . . . . . . . . . . . . . . . . . . . . . . . . . . . . . . . .

## restaurants

France is rightly famed for the quality of its restaurants, from the small family-run business to the grand establishments. It is always possible to find restaurants and **BRASSERIES** offering fixed-price menus which are generally good value for money. A basket of bread is usually included in the price of the meal, and most restaurants will have several inexpensive house wines, available in *pichets* (jugs) of ¼, ½, and 1 litre. Service is included in the bill, although many people do leave a tip if the meal and the service have been good.

## restaurants du coeur

A charitable organization, widely publicized by virtue of having been set up by a much loved humourist called Coluche, who died in a motorcycle accident in 1986. It serves meals to the poor and homeless, particularly in the winter.

## route départementale

These are signalled on French road maps as 'D' followed by a number and are marked in yellow. They are roads maintained by the **DÉPARTEMENT** and are secondary roads, not intended to be used for fast travel from place to place. Many of them have stretches marked in green on maps to highlight areas or views of particular beauty.

## route nationale

A *route nationale* forms part of the state-maintained road network, outside the **AUTOROUTES** but providing fast roads for travel between towns and cities. They are signalled by 'N' followed by the road number and are marked in red on French road maps.

## RPR - Rassemblement pour la République

The largest political party on the right, founded by Jacques Chirac in 1976.

## SAMU – service d'aide médicale d'urgence

A 24 hour service coordinated by each **DÉPARTMENT** to provide mobile medical services and staff, ambulances, and helicopters to accident scenes and emergencies.

## Sénat

The upper house of parliament which meets in the **PALAIS DU LUXEMBOURG**. It consists of 321 elected *sénateurs*. It votes laws and the state budget.

## SNCF – Société nationale des chemins de fer français

The state-owned railway company, which also has access to private finance.

## tabac ▶ BUREAU DE TABAC

Culture

**télécarte**

A phone card for use in telephone kiosks, widely available from **FRANCE TÉLÉCOM**, *bureaux de poste, tabacs* and *marchands de journaux.*

**TF1 - Télévision française 1**

Originally a state-controlled television channel, now privately-owned, *TF1* has an obligation to ensure that 50% of its programmes are of French origin.

**TGV - train à grande vitesse**

The new-generation high-speed electric train. It runs on special tracks and can reach speeds of up to 300 km/h.

**Tintin**

A comic-book character invented by the Belgian cartoonist Hergé in 1929. *Tintin's* adventures with the irrepressible *Capitaine Haddock* are still bestsellers and have been translated into more than 40 languages.

**TOM - territoire d'outre-mer**

An overseas territory, constitutionally part of the French Republic and whose citizens have French nationality.

**Tour de France**

Probably the most famous cycle race in the world, the *Tour de France* takes place over a different route each year but always ends around July 14 on the **CHAMPS ÉLYSÉES**. The overall winner after each section of the race is entitled to wear *le maillot jaune* (yellow jersey).

**UDF - Union pour la démocratie française**

A political grouping, allowing various centre-right parties to work together at times of elections.

**verlan**

A type of slang in which syllables are reversed so that for example *l'envers = verlan, pourri = ripou.*

**Verts - Les Verts**

A political party committed to the protection of the environment.

**vignette**

The disc which by law must be displayed on the windscreen of a motor vehicle to certify that the road tax has been paid. This must be renewed every November, and is obtainable from a **BUREAU DE TABAC** on payment of the tax. Older vehicles pay a lower rate.

Culture

# Letter-writing in French

## Holiday postcard

- *Beginnings (informal):* Cher *is used for a man,* Chère *for a woman. A letter to two males or to a male and female begins with* Chers. *For two female correspondents* Chères Madeleine et Hélène. *For friends and relatives:* Chers amis, Chers cousins, *etc. For a family:* Chers tous.

- *Address: On an envelope Mr, Mrs and Miss can be abbreviated to M., Mme, Mlle, although the full forms are considered preferable in more formal letters. There is no direct equivalent for Ms. If you do not know a woman's marital status use* Madame (Mme).

  *Road names such as* rue, avenue, place *are not generally given capital letters.*

  *The name of the town comes after the postcode and on the same line.*

14. 7. 2003

Cher Alexandre,

Grosses bises d'Edimbourg! Cela fait trois jours que nous sommes ici et nous n'avons pas encore vu la pluie! Espérons que ça va durer. La vieille ville est très belle et du château on a une vue splendide jusqu'à l'estuaire. Et en Normandie, comment ça va?

A bientôt pour des retrouvailles parisiennes,

Marie et Dominique

M. A. Pilnard

38 rue Glacière

75013 Paris

- *Endings (informal):*
  Bien amicalement,
  Amitiés; A bientôt =
  *see you soon.*

. . . . . . . . . . . . . . . . . . . . . . . . . . . . . . . . . . . . . . . . . . .

## Christmas and New Year wishes (informal)

- On most personal letters French speakers do not put their address at the top of the letter. The date is given preceded by *le*. For the first day of the month *le 1er* is used. Generally, the name of the town in which the letter is written is placed before the date.

① The tradition of Christmas cards is much less widespread in France than in Great Britain. While Christmas greetings may be sent, it is more customary to send best wishes for the New Year in January.

② In the year 2003/2004 etc. = *en l'an 2003/2004 etc.*, but *bonne année 2003/2004 etc.*

le 18 décembre 2003 ①

Chers Steve et Michelle,

Nous vous souhaitons un Joyeux Noël ① et une très bonne année 2004 ②! En espérant que cette nouvelle année vous apportera tout ce que vous désirez et que nous trouverons une occasion pour nous revoir!

Bises à vous deux,

Gérard

## New Year wishes (formal)

le 5 janvier 2004

Je vous ① présente mes meilleurs vœux pour l'année 2004. Que cette année vous apporte, à vous et à votre famille, bonheur et prospérité.

Pierre Carlier

① Note the use of the formal form *vous*.

**Letters**

## Invitation (informal)

*Invitations to parties are usually by word of mouth, but for more formal events such as weddings, invitations are sent out.*

① *Note the use of the informal form* tu *betweeen good friends.*

---

*Paris, le 28/04/03*

Cher Denis,

Que fais-tu ① cet été? Pascal et moi avons décidé d'inviter tous les copains d'Orléans à nous rejoindre dans notre maison de Dordogne pour le weekend du 14 juillet. Il y aura fête au village avec bal populaire et feu d'artifice. Le petit vin du pays n'est pas mal non plus!

Nous comptons sur toi pour venir trinquer avec nous,

Bises,

Martine

---

**Letters**

■ *Endings (informal):* Bises *(= lots of love) is very informal and is appropriate for very good friends and family. Alternatives for close friends and family include* Bien à toi, Bons baisers *or affectionately* Je t'embrasse. *If the letter is addressed to more than one person use* Bien à vous *or* Je vous embrasse.

**Invitation (formal)**

Christine et Félix Prévost
81 rue Esque moise
59000 Lille

Lille, le 28 avril 2003

Chers amis,

Nous avons l'immense plaisir de vous annoncer le mariage de notre fils Victor et de mademoiselle Stéphanie Heusdens.

La cérémonie aura lieu à l'Hôtel de Ville à 15 heures le samedi 7 juin. Vous recevrez bientôt un faire-part et une invitation à dîner mais nous tenions à vous prévenir suffisamment tôt pour que vous puissiez arranger votre voyage. Nous espérons qu'il vous sera possible de vous joindre à nous.

Amicalement,①

Christine et Félix

■ *In a more formal letter, especially where a reply is generally required, the sender's address is written on the left-hand side of the page. An alternative is in the centre of the page, particularly on printed stationery.*

① *Endings: Alternatives could be* Amitiés, Bien amicalement.

. . . . . . . . . . . . . . . . . . . . . . . . . . . . . . . . . . . . . .

## Accepting an invitation

> *Emilie Joly*
> *2 rue de la Pompe*
> *75016 Paris*
>
> *le 16 mars 2003*
>
> *Chère Madame Dubois,*
>
> *Je vous ① remercie de bien vouloir me recevoir pour les deux premières semaines de juillet. Je serai très heureuse de vous revoir ainsi que Natalie, bien entendu. Nous avons passé un si bon séjour linguistique à Manchester l'été dernier que nous avions très envie de nous retrouver. Mes parents ne pouvant m'envoyer en Angleterre cette année, c'est avec un immense plaisir que j'accepte votre invitation.*
>
> *Je vous prie de bien vouloir accepter, Madame, l'expression de mes sentiments les meilleurs.*
>
> *Emilie*

- *In a more formal social letter where the correspondent is known personally by name it can be used in the opening greeting.*

- *The title of the person receiving the letter must be repeated in the closing formula. These formulas are more elaborate than in English, with a number of possible variations. Some of these are shown in the following letters in this section.*

① *Since the letter is from a young person to the mother of a friend, she uses the formal* vous *form and writes to her as Madame Dubois. Madame Dubois would address Emilie using* tu.

. . . . . . . . . . . . . . . . . . . . . . . . . . . . . . . . . . . . . . . . . . . . . . .

## Replying to a job advertisement

- *Address: The sender's address may be written or printed in the middle of the page or on the left-hand side. The address of the person receiving the letter is on the right-hand side or beneath the sender's address if it is in the central position. Where the name or job title of the person is known it is used in their address.*

- *Beginnings (formal): the standard opening for a business letter when the recipient is not personally known to you is* Monsieur, Madame, Mademoiselle *or* Messieurs *in the case of general correspondence to a company.*

  *If the person holds a very important position this can be used, e.g.* Monsieur le Maire, Madame le Consul.

Alexander Smith
5, Winchester Drive
Stoke Gifford
Bristol BS34 8DP

Bristol, le 4 février 2004

Madame la Directrice
MEDIAPHOT
6 rue de la Victoire
62100 Calais

Madame,

L'annonce parue en page 13 dans 'Courrier Photo' concernant un poste de tireur m'a vivement intéressé. Je suis actuellement photographe indépendant mais je serais heureux de travailler à nouveau au sein d'une équipe d'entreprise. Je pense posséder l'expérience et les qualités requises pour vous donner toute satisfaction dans ce poste, comme vous pourrez le constater au vu de mon CV. Je suis de nationalité britannique mais je me débrouille bien en français. Je souhaite travailler à Calais car je vais prochainement me marier avec une Calaisienne.

Je me tiens à votre disposition pour un entretien éventuel, et vous prie d'agréer, Madame, l'expression de mes sentiments distingués.

A. Smith

P.J. **(1)** : un CV avec photo **(2)**

- *Endings (formal): the form of address used in the opening should be inserted into the closing formula e.g.* Madame, Monsieur le Maire, *etc*

  **(1)** *P.J. (pièce(s) jointe(s)) = enclosures (encl).*

  **(2)** *In France prospective employers generally request a handwritten letter* (lettre manuscrite) *and a photograph to accompany an application or curriculum vitae.*

• • • • • • • • • • • • • • • • • • • • • • • • • • • • • • • • • • • • • • • • • • •

## Curriculum Vitae

David Baker
67 Whiteley Avenue
St George
Bristol
BS5 6TW
Grande-Bretagne

Téléphone +44 (0)117 945 3421; Fax +44 (0)117 945 7225

e-mail dbaker@hotmail.com

Nationalité britannique

Né ① le 30.06.1982 à Londres

### FORMATION ET DIPLÔMES

1998: GCSEs dans sept matières (équivalent à un niveau de fin de Seconde)
John Radcliffe School, Croydon

2000: 'A Levels' en Mathématiques, Informatique, Allemand et Français
(équivalent au Baccalauréat)

### EXPERIENCE PROFESSIONNELLE

2001: Stage de quatre mois à Sempo-Informatik, Francfort au département
médias

2002: Contrat de formation de six mois à MEDIALAB, Paris (conception
d'images de synthèse)

### DIVERS

Très bonne connaissance de l'outil informatique

Allemand et français courants

Permis de conduire

① The feminine form née is used for a woman.

■ Where appropriate a heading 'Situation de famille' could give relevant personal details e.g.
marié/e, deux/trois enfants etc.; divorcé/e, deux enfants; célibataire.

**Letters**

. . . . . . . . . . . . . . . . . . . . . . . . . . . . . . . . . . . . . . . . . .

## Seeking a job as an au pair

Letters

> Sally Paledra
> 5 Avon Crescent
> Kenilworth
> Warwickshire
> CV8 2PQ
>
> le 3 mars 2003
>
> Madame,
>
> Vos coordonnées m'ont été communiquées par l'agence `Au Pair International', qui m'a demandé de vous écrire directement. Je suis en effet à la recherche d'un emploi au pair pour une période de neuf à dix mois à partir de septembre prochain.
>
> J'aime beaucoup les enfants et ils apprécient également ma compagnie. J'ai une grande expérience du baby-sitting. J'ai aussi fait un stage d'un mois dans une crèche privée ①.
>
> Je suis enthousiaste, discrète et je sais prendre des initiatives. J'ai étudié le français au lycée pendant cinq ans et je connais un peu la France pour y avoir passé des vacances à plusieurs reprises. J'ai aussi mon permis de conduire.
>
> Dans l'espoir d'une réponse positive de votre part, je vous prie d'agréer, Madame, l'expression de mes salutations respectueuses.
>
> S. Paledra
>
> P.J. : un CV avec photo

① Or be more specific, e.g. pour des enfants de 3 mois à 3 ans.

■ To supply references: Vous trouverez également ci-joint les adresses de personnes pouvant fournir une lettre de recommandation or pouvant me recommander.

## Enquiry to a tourist office

M. et Mme Baude
13 La Faverolle
45000 Orléans

Syndicat d'initiative
de St Gervais
74170 Saint-Gervais-les-Bains

Orléans, le 24 mars 2003

Monsieur,

Nous vous serions reconnaissants de bien vouloir nous faire parvenir
toute la documentation dont vous disposez sur les villas de location à
proximité de la station thermale. Nous désirons également recevoir des
informations sur les activités de loisirs durant l'été.
Vous trouverez ci-joint une enveloppe timbrée ① pour la réponse.

Dans l'attente de votre réponse, je vous prie d'agréer, Monsieur,
l'expression de nos salutations distinguées.

J. Baude

**Letters**

① enveloppe timbrée = *stamped addressed envelope.*

■ *Note that, unlike in English, a reference or the purpose of a business letter is placed, where required, above the opening greeting. e.g.* Objet: commande 03/08/21 *or* Réf: 000/23.

# Letter-writing in French

**Booking a hotel room**

Miss Sylvia Daley
The Willows
49 North Terrace
Kings Barton
Nottinghamshire
NG8 4LQ
England

Hôtel Beauséjour
Chemin des Mimosas
06100 Grasse

le 8 avril 2003

J'ai bien reçu le dépliant de votre hôtel et je vous en remercie.

Je souhaite réserver une chambre calme avec salle de bains, en pension complète ① pour la période du 7 au 18 juin. Pour les arrhes, je vous prie de m'informer de leur montant et des modalités de paiement possibles depuis la Grande-Bretagne.

En vous remerciant d'avance, je vous prie de croire, Madame, en mes sentiments les meilleurs.

① *Or* une chambre avec douche en demi-pension *or* avec petit déjeuner. *The term en suite does not exist for bathroom facilities in French.*

## Booking a campsite

Frances Good
22 Daniel Avenue
Caldwood
Leeds LS8 7RR
tel. 0113 2998767

Camping 'Les Embruns'
18 allée des Capucins
29350 Moëlan-sur-Mer

le 25 avril 2003

Monsieur,

Nous souhaitons réserver dans votre camping, pour la période du 2 au 15 juillet, deux emplacements de tente côte à côte① et, si possible, pas trop loin de la plage② . Il s'agit de deux tentes de deux personnes. Nous aurons également deux motos de 1000cc chacune.

Dès que nous aurons confirmation de votre part, nous vous adresserons le montant de la réservation.

Pouvez-vous nous indiquer à cet effet, les possibilités de paiement depuis l'étranger.

Veuillez croire, Monsieur, en l'expression de nos sentiments les meilleurs.

F. Good

① Or if you have a caravan un emplacement de caravane.

② Other requirements might be ombragé (shady), or abrité (sheltered).

**Letters**

. . . . . . . . . . . . . . . . . . . . . . . . . . . . . . . . . . . . . . . . . . . . . . . . . . . . . . . . . .

**Cancelling a reservation**

Mrs J. Warrington
Downlands
Steyning
West Sussex
BN44 6LZ

Hôtel des Voyageurs
9 cours Gambetta
91940 Les Ulis

le 15 février 2003

Monsieur,

Je suis au regret de devoir annuler la réservation de chambre pour deux personnes
pour la nuit du 24 au 25 mars, que j'avais effectuée par téléphone le 18 janvier
dernier. ①

Je vous remercie de votre compréhension et vous prie d'agréer, Monsieur,
l'expression de mes sentiments distingués.

J. Warrington

① *If reasons for the cancellation are specified these could include:* pour raisons de santé/de
famille, en raison d'un décès dans la famille, *etc.*

**Sending
an e-mail**

File    Edit    View  Text    Mail    Attach    User    Tools  Window

Fichier  Edition  Vue  Texte  Message  Rattacher  Agent  Outil  Fenêtre

To: toothild@scene.co.uk
Cc: itumoran@ecosse.ac.uk
Subject: tu es connectée?

Cher Daniel,

J'ai bien reçu ton mél①. Je suis ravie que nous puissions communiquer
par Internet. N'oublie pas de joindre à ton prochain message le fichier sur
l'argot que tu m'as promis!

Salut, ②

Clare

① *Note that* mél *is an abbreviated form of* message électronique. *To send an attachment =* joindre
un fichier.

② *Endings (informal): An alternative could be* A bientôt *or simply* Bises *to a close friend in an
informal context.*

Letters

**a¹, A** *n* **(a)** (letter) a, A *m*
**(b)** A (Mus) la *m*

**a², an** *det* un/une

■ **Note** The determiner or indefinite article *a* or
*an* is translated by *un* + *masculine noun* and by
*une* + *feminine noun*: *a tree* = un arbre; *a chair*
= une chaise. There are, however, some cases
where the article is not translated:
– with professions and trades: *her mother is a
teacher* = sa mère est professeur;
– with other nouns used in apposition: *he's a
widower* = il est veuf;
– with *what a*: *what a pretty house* = quelle jolie
maison.
– When expressing prices in relation to weight,
the definite article *le/la* is used in French: *ten
euros a kilo* = dix euros le kilo. In other
expressions where *a/an* means *per* the French
translation is *par*. *twice a day* = deux fois par
jour; but: *50 kilometres an hour* = 50 kilomètres/
heure.

**aback** *adv* **to be taken ~** être déconcerté/-e

**abandon** *vtr* abandonner ⟨*person, hope*⟩;
renoncer à ⟨*activity, attempt*⟩

**abbey** *n* abbaye *f*

**abbreviate** *vtr* abréger (**to** en)

**abbreviation** *n* abréviation *f*

**abdomen** *n* abdomen *m*

**abduct** *vtr* enlever

**abide** *vi* **to ~ by** respecter ⟨*rule, decision*⟩

**ability** *n* **(a)** (capability) capacité *f*; **to the
best of one's ~** de son mieux
**(b)** (talent) talent *m*

**able** *adj*

■ **Note** *to be able to* meaning *can* is usually
translated by the verb *pouvoir*. *I was not able to
help him* = je ne pouvais pas l'aider.
– When *to be able to* implies the acquiring of a
skill, *savoir* is used: *he's nine and he's still not
able to read* = il a neuf ans et il ne sait toujours
pas lire.

**(a) to be ~ to do** pouvoir faire; **she was ~
to play the piano at the age of four** elle
savait jouer du piano à quatre ans
**(b)** ⟨*lawyer, teacher*⟩ compétent/-e; ⟨*child*⟩
doué/-e

**able-bodied** *adj* robuste, fort/-e

**abnormal** *adj* anormal/-e

**abnormality** *n* anomalie *f*

**aboard** ① *adv* à bord
② *prep* à bord de ⟨*plane*⟩; dans ⟨*train*⟩; **~
ship** à bord

**abolish** *vtr* abolir ⟨*law, right*⟩; supprimer
⟨*service, allowance*⟩

**abolition** *n* (of law, right) abolition *f*; (of
service) suppression *f*

**abominable** *adj* abominable

**aborigine** *n* aborigène *mf*

**abort** *vtr* faire avorter ⟨*foetus*⟩; interrompre
⟨*plan*⟩; abandonner ⟨*computer program*⟩

**abortion** *n* avortement *m*; **to have an ~** se
faire avorter

**abortive** *adj* ⟨*attempt, project*⟩ avorté/-e;
⟨*coup, raid*⟩ manqué/-e

**about** ① *adj* **to be ~ to do** être sur le
point de faire
② *adv* **(a)** environ, à peu près; **~ an hour**
environ une heure; **it's ~ the same** c'est à
peu près pareil; **at ~ 6 pm** vers 18 h; **it's just
~ ready** c'est presque prêt
**(b) there was no-one ~** il n'y avait
personne; **there is a lot of flu ~** il y a
beaucoup de grippes en ce moment; **he's
somewhere ~** il est dans les parages
③ *prep* **(a)** (concerning) **a book ~ France** un
livre sur la France; **what's it ~?** (of book, film)
ça parle de quoi?; **may I ask what it's ~?**
pourriez-vous me dire de quoi il s'agit?; **it's
~ my son** c'est au sujet de mon fils
**(b) there's something odd ~ him** il a
quelque chose de bizarre; **what I like ~ her
is her honesty** ce que j'aime chez elle c'est
sa franchise
**(c)** (around) **to wander ~ the streets** errer
dans les rues
**(d) how or what ~ some tea?** et si on
prenait un thé?; **how ~ going into town?** et
si on allait en ville?
**(e) what ~ the legal costs?** et les frais de
justice?; **what ~ you?** et toi?
IDIOMS **it's ~ time (that) somebody made an
effort** il serait temps que quelqu'un fasse un
effort; **~ time too!** ce n'est pas trop tôt!
(colloq)

**about-face** *n* volte-face *f inv*

**above** ① *prep* au-dessus de; **~ the painting**
au-dessus du tableau; **~ it** au-dessus;
**children ~ the age of 12** les enfants âgés de
plus de 12 ans; **~ all else** par-dessus tout; **to
hear sth ~ the shouting** entendre qch au
milieu des cris
② *adj* **the ~ items** les articles
susmentionnés *or* figurant ci-dessus
③ *adv* **(a)** au-dessus; **a desk with a shelf ~**
un bureau avec une étagère au-dessus; **the
apartment ~** l'appartement du dessus
**(b)** (in text) **see ~** voir ci-dessus
**(c)** (more) plus; **children of 12 and ~** les
enfants âgés de 12 ans et plus
④ **above all** *phr* surtout

**above-mentioned** *adj* susmentionné/-e

**abrasive** *adj* ⟨*person, manner*⟩ mordant/-e

**abreast** *adv* to walk three ∼ marcher à trois de front; **to keep** ∼ **of** se tenir au courant de

**abroad** *adv* à l'étranger; **from** ∼ de l'étranger

**abrupt** *adj* brusque

**ABS** *n* (*abbr* = **anti-lock braking system**) ABS; ∼ **brakes** freins *mpl* ABS

**abscess** *n* abcès *m*

**abseiling** *n* (GB) descente *f* en rappel

**absence** *n* absence *f*

**absent** *adj* absent/-e (**from** de)

**absentee** *n* absent/-e *m/f*

**absent-minded** *adj* distrait/-e

**absolute** *adj* absolu/-e

**absolutely** *adv* absolument

**absorb** *vtr* absorber; ∼**ed in one's work** plongé/-e dans son travail

**absorbent** *adj* absorbant/-e

**abstain** *vi* s'abstenir (**from** de)

**abstract** *adj* abstrait/-e

**absurd** *adj* absurde, ridicule

**abundant** *adj* abondant/-e

**abuse** ⌐1⌐ *n* (a) (maltreatment) mauvais traitement *m*; (sexual) sévices *mpl* (sexuels) (b) (of alcohol, power) abus *m*; **drug** ∼ usage *m* des stupéfiants (c) (insults) injures *fpl* ⌐2⌐ *vtr* (a) (hurt) maltraiter; (sexually) abuser de ⟨*woman*⟩; exercer des sévices sexuels sur ⟨*child*⟩ (b) abuser de ⟨*position, power, trust*⟩ (c) (insult) injurier

**abusive** *adj* ⟨*person*⟩ grossier/-ière; ⟨*words*⟩ injurieux/-ieuse

**abyss** *n* abîme *m*

**academic** ⌐1⌐ *n* universitaire *mf* ⌐2⌐ *adj* (a) ⟨*career, book*⟩ universitaire; ⟨*year*⟩ académique (b) (theoretical) théorique

**academy** *n* (school) école *f*; (learned society) académie *f*

**accelerate** *vi* accélérer

**accelerator** *n* accélérateur *m*

**accent** *n* accent *m*

**accentuate** *vtr* souligner

**accept** *vtr* (gen) accepter; (tolerate) admettre

**acceptable** *adj* acceptable

**acceptance** *n* acceptation *f*

**access** ⌐1⌐ *n* accès *m*; **to have** ∼ **to** avoir accès à ⟨*information, funds, place*⟩ ⌐2⌐ *vtr* accéder à ⟨*database, information*⟩

**accessible** *adj* accessible (**to** à)

**accessory** *n* accessoire *m*; (on car) extra *m*

**accident** *n* accident *m*; **car/road** ∼ accident de voiture/de la route; **by** ∼ accidentellement; (by chance) par hasard

**accidental** *adj* (a) ⟨*death*⟩ accidentel/-elle (b) ⟨*mistake*⟩ fortuit/-e

**accidentally** *adv* (a) (by accident) accidentellement (b) (by chance) par hasard

**accident-prone** *adj* sujet/-ette aux accidents

**accommodate** *vtr* (a) (put up) loger (b) (hold, provide space for) contenir (c) (adapt to) s'adapter à ⟨*change, view*⟩ (d) (satisfy) satisfaire ⟨*need*⟩

**accommodating** *adj* accommodant/-e (**to** envers)

**accommodation** *n* (*also* ∼**s** (US)) logement *m*

**accommodation officer** *n* responsable *mf* de l'hébergement

**accompany** *vtr* accompagner

**accomplice** *n* complice *mf*

**accomplish** *vtr* accomplir ⟨*task, mission*⟩; réaliser ⟨*objective*⟩

**accomplishment** *n* réussite *f*

**accord** *n* accord *m*; **of my own** ∼ de moi-même

**accordance: in accordance with** *phr* ⟨*act*⟩ conformément à ⟨*rules, instructions*⟩; ⟨*be*⟩ conforme à ⟨*law, agreement*⟩

**according: according to** *phr* (a) ⟨*act*⟩ selon ⟨*law, principles*⟩; ∼ **to plan** comme prévu (b) d'après ⟨*newspaper, person*⟩

**accordingly** *adv* en conséquence

**accordion** *n* accordéon *m*

**accost** *vtr* (approach) aborder; (sexually) accoster

**account** ⌐1⌐ *n* (a) (in bank, post office, shop) compte *m* (**at, with** à); **in my** ∼ sur mon compte (b) **to take sth into** ∼, **to take** ∼ **of sth** tenir compte de qch (c) (description) compte-rendu *m* (d) **on** ∼ **of** à cause de; **on no** ∼ sous aucun prétexte; **on my** ∼ à cause de moi ⌐2⌐ **accounts** *n pl* (a) (records) comptabilité *f*, comptes *mpl* (b) (department) (service *m*) comptabilité *f* ∎ **account for** (a) (explain) expliquer ⟨*fact, behaviour*⟩; justifier ⟨*expense*⟩ (b) (represent) représenter ⟨*proportion, percentage*⟩

**accountable** *adj* responsable (**to** devant; **for** de)

**accountancy** *n* comptabilité *f*

**accountant** *n* comptable *mf*

**account holder** *n* titulaire *mf*

**account number** *n* numéro *m* de compte

**accumulate** ⌐1⌐ *vtr* accumuler ⌐2⌐ *vi* s'accumuler

**accuracy** *n* (of figures, watch) justesse *f*; (of map, aim) précision *f*; (of forecast) exactitude *f*

**accurate** *adj* ⟨*figures, watch, information*⟩ juste; ⟨*report, map, forecast*⟩ exact/-e

**accurately** *adv* ⟨*calculate*⟩ exactement; ⟨*report*⟩ avec exactitude; ⟨*assess*⟩ précisément

**accusation** *n* accusation *f*

**accuse** *vtr* accuser (**of** de)

**accused** n the ~ l'accusé/-e m/f

**accuser** n accusateur/-trice m/f

**accustomed** adj (a) to be ~ to sth/to doing avoir l'habitude de qch/de faire
(b) (usual) habituel/-elle

**ace** n as m

**ache** ①n douleur f (in à)
②vi ⟨person⟩ avoir mal; my back ~s j'ai mal au dos

**achieve** vtr atteindre ⟨aim⟩; atteindre à ⟨perfection⟩; obtenir ⟨result⟩; réaliser ⟨ambition⟩

**achievement** n réussite f

**aching** adj ⟨body, limbs⟩ douloureux/-euse

**acid** n, adj acide (m)

**acid rain** n pluies fpl acides

**acknowledge** vtr admettre ⟨fact⟩; reconnaître ⟨error, problem, authority⟩; accuser réception de ⟨letter⟩

**acknowledgement** ①n (a) (of error, guilt) aveu m
(b) (confirmation of receipt) accusé m de réception
②**acknowledgements** n pl (in book) remerciements mpl

**acne** n acné f

**acorn** n gland m

**acoustic** adj acoustique

**acoustic guitar** n guitare f sèche

**acoustics** n pl the ~ are good l'acoustique f est bonne

**acquaintance** n connaissance f (with de)

**acquainted** adj to be ~ se connaître; to get or become ~ with sb faire la connaissance de qn; to get or become ~ with sth découvrir qch

**acquiesce** vi accepter; to ~ in sth donner son accord tacite à qch

**acquire** vtr acquérir ⟨expertise⟩; obtenir ⟨information⟩; faire l'acquisition de ⟨possessions⟩; acheter ⟨company⟩

**acquit** vtr (Law) acquitter; to be ~ted être disculpé/-e (of de)

**acre** n acre f, ≈ demi-hectare m

**acrobat** n acrobate mf

**acrobatics** n pl acrobaties fpl

**across** ①prep (a) a journey ~ the desert un voyage à travers le désert; the bridge ~ the river le pont qui traverse la rivière; to go or travel ~ sth traverser qch; she leaned ~ the table elle s'est penchée au-dessus de la table
(b) (on the other side of) de l'autre côté de; ~ the street (from me) de l'autre côté de la rue
②adv to help sb ~ aider qn à traverser; to go ~ to sb aller vers qn; to look ~ at sb regarder dans la direction de qn
③**across from** phr en face de

**acrylic** n acrylique m

**act** ①n (a) acte m; an ~ of kindness un acte de bonté
(b) (Law) loi f; **Act of Parliament** loi votée par le Parlement

(c) (in show) numéro m
(d) to put on an ~ jouer la comédie
②vtr jouer ⟨part, role⟩
③vi (a) (take action) agir
(b) (behave) agir, se comporter
(c) ⟨actor⟩ jouer, faire du théâtre
(d) (pretend) jouer la comédie, faire semblant
(e) (take effect) ⟨drug⟩ agir
(f) to ~ as ⟨person, object⟩ servir de
■ **act out** jouer ⟨role, part⟩; réaliser ⟨fantasy⟩

**acting** ①n (performance) jeu m, interprétation f; (occupation) métier m d'acteur; I've done some ~ j'ai fait du théâtre
②adj ⟨director, manager⟩ intérimaire

**action** n (a) (gen) action f; (steps) mesures fpl; to take ~ agir, prendre des mesures (against contre); to put a plan into ~ mettre un projet à exécution ~s speak louder than words mieux vaut agir que parler
(b) (fighting) action f, combat m; killed in ~ tué/-e au combat
(c) (in filming) action f; ~! moteur!

**action film** n film m d'action

**action group** n groupe m de pression

**action-packed** adj ⟨film⟩ plein/-e d'action; ⟨holiday⟩ bien rempli/-e

**action replay** n (GB) répétition f d'une séquence

**activate** vtr faire démarrer ⟨system⟩; actionner ⟨switch⟩; déclencher ⟨alarm⟩

**active** adj ⟨person, life⟩ actif/-ive; ⟨volcano⟩ en activité

**activist** n activiste mf

**activity** n activité f

**activity holiday** n (GB) ≈ vacances fpl sportives

**actor** n acteur m, comédien m

**actress** n actrice f, comédienne f

**actual** adj ⟨circumstances⟩ réel/réelle; ⟨words⟩ exact/-e; in ~ fact en fait; the ~ problem le problème lui-même

**actually** adv (a) (in fact) en fait; their profits have ~ risen en fait, leurs bénéfices ont augmenté; ~, I don't feel like it à vrai dire je n'en ai pas envie
(b) (really) vraiment; yes, it ~ happened! mais oui, c'est vraiment arrivé!

**acupuncture** n acupuncture f

**acute** adj (a) ⟨anxiety, pain⟩ vif/vive; ⟨boredom⟩ profond/-e
(b) ⟨illness⟩ aigu/aiguë
(c) ⟨mind⟩ pénétrant/-e
(d) ⟨accent, angle⟩ aigu/aiguë

**ad** n (abbr = **advertisement**) (a) (small) ~ (petite) annonce f (for pour)
(b) (on radio, TV) pub f (colloq) (for pour)

**AD** (abbr = **Anno Domini**) ap J.-C.

**adamant** adj catégorique (about sur); he is ~ that il maintient que

**adapt** ①vtr adapter (to à; for pour; from de)
②vi ⟨person⟩ s'adapter (to à)

**adaptable** *adj* souple

**adapter, adaptor** *n* adaptateur *m*

**add** *vtr* (a) ajouter, rajouter (**onto, to** à)
(b) (*also* ~ **together**) additionner
⟨*numbers*⟩; **to** ~ **sth to** ajouter qch à ⟨*figure, total*⟩
■ **add up**: ¶ ~ **up** ⟨*facts, figures*⟩ s'accorder;
**to** ~ **up to** s'élever à ⟨*total*⟩; ¶ ~ **up [sth]**
additionner ⟨*cost, numbers*⟩

**adder** *n* (snake) vipère *f*

**addict** *n* (a) (drug-user) toxicomane *mf*
(b) (of TV, coffee) accro *mf* (colloq) (**of** de)

**addicted** *adj* **to be** ~ (to alcohol, drugs) avoir
une dépendance (**to** à); (to TV, coffee) être
accro (colloq) (**to** de)

**addiction** *n* dépendance *f* (**to** à)

**addictive** *adj* ⟨*drug, substance*⟩ qui crée
une dépendance; **to be** ~ ⟨*chocolate, power*⟩
être comme une drogue

**addition** ⌐1⌐ *n* (a) (to list, house) ajout *m*
(b) (in mathematics) addition *f*
⌐2⌐ **in addition** *phr* en plus

**additional** *adj* supplémentaire

**additive** *n* additif *m*

**add-on** *adj* supplémentaire

**address** ⌐1⌐ *n* adresse *f*; **to change (one's)**
~ changer d'adresse
⌐2⌐ *vtr* (a) mettre l'adresse sur ⟨*parcel, letter*⟩;
**to** ~ **sth to sb** adresser qch à qn
(b) (speak to) s'adresser à ⟨*group*⟩
(c) (aim) adresser ⟨*remark, complaint*⟩ (**to** à)

**address book** *n* carnet *m* d'adresses

**adenoids** *n pl* végétations *fpl* (adénoïdes)

**adept** *adj* expert/-e (**at** en)

**adequate** *adj* (a) (sufficient) suffisant/-e
(b) (satisfactory) satisfaisant/-e

**adhere** *vi* adhérer (**to** à)

**adhesive** ⌐1⌐ *n* colle *f*, adhésif *m*
⌐2⌐ *adj* collant/-e; ~ **tape** papier *m* collant,
Scotch® *m*

**adjacent** *adj* contigu/contiguë; ~ **to sth**
attenant à qch

**adjective** *n* adjectif *m*

**adjourn** *vtr* ajourner ⟨*trial*⟩ (**for** pour; **until**
à)

**adjudicate** *vtr* juger ⟨*contest*⟩; examiner
⟨*case, claim*⟩

**adjust** ⌐1⌐ *vtr* régler ⟨*component, level,
position, speed*⟩; ajuster ⟨*price, rate*⟩; rajuster
⟨*clothing*⟩; modifier ⟨*figures*⟩
⌐2⌐ *vi* ⟨*person*⟩ s'adapter (**to** à)

**adjustable** *adj* réglable

**adjustment** *n* (a) (of rates) rajustement *m*
(**of** de); (of controls, machine) réglage *m* (**of** de)
(b) (mental) adaptation *f* (**to** à)
(c) (modification) modification *f*; **to make** ~**s to**
apporter des modifications à ⟨*system,
machine*⟩

**ad-lib** *vtr, vi* improviser

**administer** *vtr* (*also* **administrate**)
gérer ⟨*company, affairs, estate*⟩; gouverner
⟨*territory*⟩

**administration** *n* (gen) administration *f*;
(paperwork) travail *m* administratif

**administrative** *adj* administratif/-ive

**administrator** *n* administrateur/-trice
*m/f*

**admirable** *adj* admirable

**admiral** *n* amiral *m*

**admiration** *n* admiration *f* (**for** pour)

**admire** *vtr* admirer

**admirer** *n* admirateur/-trice *m/f*

**admission** *n* (a) (entry) entrée *f*, admission
*f* (**to** dans); **'no** ~**'** 'entrée interdite'
(b) (fee) (droit *m* d')entrée *f*
(c) (confession) aveu *m*; **an** ~ **of guilt** un aveu
de culpabilité

**admissions office** *n* (Univ) service *m*
d'inscriptions

**admit** *vtr* (a) reconnaître, admettre
⟨*mistake, fact*⟩; **to** ~ **that...** reconnaître
que...; **to** ~ **to** reconnaître, admettre
⟨*mistake, fact*⟩
(b) (confess) reconnaître ⟨*guilt*⟩; **to** ~ **to
sth/doing** avouer qch/avoir fait
(c) (let in) laisser entrer ⟨*person*⟩ (**into** dans);
**to be** ~**ted to hospital** être hospitalisé/-e

**admittance** *n* accès *m*, entrée *f*; **'no** ~**'**
'accès interdit au public'

**admittedly** *adv* il est vrai, il faut en
convenir

**adolescent** ⌐1⌐ *n* adolescent/-e *m/f*
⌐2⌐ *adj* (a) (gen) adolescent/-e; ⟨*crisis,
rebellion*⟩ d'adolescent; ⟨*problem*⟩ des
adolescents
(b) (childish) puéril/-e

**adopt** *vtr* adopter

**adopted** *adj* ⟨*child*⟩ adopté/-e; ⟨*son,
daughter*⟩ adoptif/-ive

**adoption** *n* adoption *f*

**adorable** *adj* adorable

**adore** *vtr* adorer (**doing** faire)

**adoring** *adj* ⟨*husband*⟩ épris/-e; ⟨*fan*⟩
passionné/-e

**adrenalin(e)** *n* adrénaline *f*

**Adriatic (Sea)** *pr n* **the** ~ la mer *f*
Adriatique, l'Adriatique *f*

**adrift** *adj, adv* ⟨*person, boat*⟩ à la dérive; **to
come** ~ se détacher (**of, from** de)

**adult** ⌐1⌐ *n* adulte *mf*
⌐2⌐ *adj* (gen) adulte; ⟨*life*⟩ d'adulte; ⟨*film,
magazine*⟩ pour adultes

**adultery** *n* adultère *m* (**with** avec)

**adulthood** *n* âge *m* adulte

**advance** ⌐1⌐ *n* (a) (forward movement) avance
*f*; (progress) progrès *m*
(b) (sum of money) avance *f*, acompte *m* (**on**
sur)
(c) **to make** ~**s to sb** (gen) faire des
démarches auprès de qn; (sexually) faire des
avances à qn
⌐2⌐ *vtr* (a) avancer ⟨*sum of money*⟩
(b) faire avancer ⟨*career, research*⟩; servir
⟨*cause, interests*⟩

**3** *vi* **(a)** (move forward) ⟨*person*⟩ avancer, s'avancer (**on, towards** vers); (Mil) ⟨*army*⟩ avancer (**on** sur)
**(b)** (progress) progresser, faire des progrès
**4** **in advance** *phr* à l'avance

**advanced** *adj* ⟨*course, class*⟩ supérieur/-e; ⟨*student, stage*⟩ avancé/-e; ⟨*equipment, technology*⟩ de pointe, perfectionné/-e

**advance warning** *n* préavis *m*

**advantage** *n* **(a)** avantage *m*; **it is to our ∼ to do** il est dans notre intérêt de faire
**(b)** (asset) atout *m*
**(c) to take ∼ of** utiliser, profiter de ⟨*situation, offer, service*⟩; exploiter ⟨*person*⟩

**advantageous** *adj* avantageux/-euse

**advent** *n* (gen) apparition *f* (**of** de); **Advent** (prior to Christmas) l'Avent *m*

**adventure** *n* aventure *f*

**adventure holiday** *n* vacances *fpl* 'aventure'

**adventurous** *adj* aventureux/-euse

**adverb** *n* adverbe *m*

**adverse** *adj* ⟨*reaction, conditions, publicity*⟩ défavorable; ⟨*effect, consequences*⟩ négatif/-ive

**advert** *n* (GB) (colloq) (in paper) annonce *f*; (small ad) petite annonce *f*; (on TV, radio) pub *f* (colloq), spot *m* publicitaire

**advertise** **1** *vtr* faire de la publicité pour ⟨*product, event, service*⟩; mettre *or* passer une annonce pour ⟨*car, house, job*⟩
**2** *vi* **(a)** (for publicity) faire de la publicité
**(b)** (in small ads) passer une annonce

**advertisement** *n* **(a)** (for product, event) publicité *f* (**for** pour); **a good/bad ∼ for** une bonne/mauvaise publicité pour
**(b)** (to sell house, get job) annonce *f*; (in small ads) petite annonce *f*

**advertising** *n* publicité *f*

**advertising agency** *n* agence *f* de publicité

**advertising campaign** *n* campagne *f* publicitaire

**advice** *n* conseils *mpl* (**on** sur; **about** à propos de); **a piece of ∼** un conseil; **it was good ∼** c'était un bon conseil

**advisable** *adj* **it is ∼ to do** il est recommandé de faire

**advise** *vtr* **(a)** conseiller, donner des conseils à (**about** sur); **to ∼ sb to do** conseiller à qn de faire; **to ∼ sb against doing** déconseiller à qn de faire
**(b)** recommander ⟨*rest, course of action*⟩
**(c)** (inform) **to ∼ sb (of)** aviser qn (de)

**adviser, advisor** *n* conseiller/-ère *m/f* (**to** auprès de)

**advisory service** *n* service *m* d'aide et de conseil

**Aegean (Sea)** *pr n* **the ∼** la mer Égée

**aerial** **1** *n* antenne *f*
**2** *adj* aérien/-ienne

**aerobics** *n* aérobic *m*

**aeroplane** *n* (GB) avion *m*

**aerosol** *n* bombe *f* aérosol

**aesthetic, esthetic** (US) *adj* esthétique

**affair** *n* **(a)** affaire *f*; **state of ∼s** situation *f*
**(b)** (relationship) liaison *f* (**with** avec)

**affect** *vtr* **(a)** (have effect on) avoir une incidence sur ⟨*price*⟩; affecter, avoir des conséquences pour ⟨*career, environment*⟩; affecter, toucher ⟨*region, population*⟩; influer sur ⟨*decision, outcome*⟩
**(b)** (emotionally) émouvoir
**(c)** (Med) atteindre ⟨*person*⟩; affecter ⟨*health, heart*⟩

**affection** *n* affection *f* (**for sb** pour qn)

**affectionate** *adj* affectueux/-euse

**affinity** *n* **(a)** (attraction) attirance *f* (**with, for** pour)
**(b)** (resemblance) ressemblance *f*

**affinity card** *n* carte *f* de fidélité

**affluence** *n* richesse *f*

**afford** *vtr* **(a)** (financially) **to be able to ∼ sth** avoir les moyens d'acheter qch; **if I can ∼ it** si j'ai les moyens; **I can't ∼ to pay the rent** je n'ai pas les moyens de payer le loyer
**(b)** (spare) **to be able to ∼** disposer de ⟨*time*⟩
**(c)** (risk) **to be able to ∼ sth/to do** se permettre qch/de faire; **he can't ∼ to wait** il ne peut pas se permettre d'attendre

**affordable** *adj* ⟨*price*⟩ abordable

**afield** *adv* **far ∼** loin; **further ∼** plus loin

**afloat** *adj, adv* **to stay ∼** ⟨*person, object*⟩ rester à la surface (de l'eau); ⟨*boat*⟩ rester à flot

**afraid** *adj* **(a)** (scared) **to be ∼** avoir peur (**of** de; **to do, of doing** de faire)
**(b)** (anxious) **she was ∼ (that) there would be an accident** elle craignait un accident; **I'm ∼ it might rain** je crains qu'il (ne) pleuve
**(c) I'm ∼ I can't come** je suis désolé mais je ne peux pas venir; **I'm ∼ so/not** je crains que oui/non

**afresh** *adv* à nouveau

**Africa** *pr n* Afrique *f*; **to ∼** en Afrique

**African** **1** *n* Africain/-e *m/f*
**2** *adj* africain/-e; ⟨*elephant*⟩ d'Afrique

**African-American** *n* Afro-américain/-e *m/f*

**Afro-Caribbean** *adj* antillais/-e

**after** **1** *adv* après; **soon** *or* **not long ∼** peu après; **the year ∼** l'année suivante *or* d'après; **the day ∼** le lendemain
**2** *prep* **(a)** après; **shortly ∼ the strike** peu après la grève; **∼ that** après (cela); **the day ∼ tomorrow** après-demain; **to tidy up ∼ sb** ranger derrière qn; **to ask ∼ sb** demander des nouvelles de qn; **∼ you!** après vous!
**(b) that's the house they're ∼** c'est la maison qu'ils veulent acheter; **the police are ∼ him** il est recherché par la police
**(c) year ∼ year** tous les ans; **it was one disaster ∼ another** on a eu catastrophe sur catastrophe
**(d) we called her Kate ∼ my mother** nous l'avons appelée Kate comme ma mère     ⋯‡

**(e)** (US) **it's twenty ~ eleven** il est onze heures vingt

**3** *conj* **(a)** (in the past) après avoir *or* être (+ *pp*), après que (+ *indicative*); **~ he had consulted Bill, he left** après avoir consulté Bill, il est parti; **~ he had changed she brought him to the office** après qu'il se fut changé, elle le conduisit au bureau; **~ we married/he left** après notre mariage/son départ

**(b)** (in the future) quand, une fois que

**(c) why did he do that ~ we'd warned him?** pourquoi a-t-il fait ça alors que nous l'avions prévenu?

**4 after all** *phr* après tout

**after-effect** *n* (Med) contrecoup *m*; (figurative) répercussion *f*

**aftermath** *n* conséquences *fpl*; **in the ~ of** à la suite de ‹*war, scandal, election*›

**afternoon** *n* après-midi *m or f inv*; **in the ~** (dans) l'après-midi; **on Friday ~(s)** le vendredi après-midi; **good ~!** bonjour!

**after-sales service** *n* service *m* après-vente

**after-shave** *n* après-rasage *m*

**aftershock** *n* secousse *f* secondaire

**after-sun** *adj* après-soleil *inv*

**aftertaste** *n* arrière-goût *m*

**afterthought** *n* pensée *f* après coup

**afterwards**, **afterward** (US) *adv* **(a)** (after) après; **straight ~** tout de suite après

**(b)** (later) plus tard

**again** *adv* encore;

■ Note When used with a verb, *again* is often translated by adding the prefix *re* to the verb in French: *to start again* = recommencer; *to marry again* = se remarier; *I'd like to read that book again* = j'aimerais relire ce livre; *she never saw them again* = elle ne les a jamais revus. You can check *re+* verbs by consulting the French side of the dictionary.

– For other uses of *again*, see below.

**sing it ~!** chante-le encore!; **once ~** encore une fois; **yet ~ he refused** il a encore refusé; **when you are well ~** quand tu seras rétabli; **I'll never go there ~** je n'y retournerai jamais; **~ and ~** à plusieurs reprises

**against** *prep* contre; **~ the wall** contre le mur; **I'm ~ it** je suis contre; **to be ~ doing** être contre l'idée de faire; **the pound fell ~ the dollar** la livre a baissé par rapport au dollar; **~ a background of** sur un fond de; **~ the light** à contre-jour

**age 1** *n* **(a)** âge *m*; **to come of ~** atteindre la majorité; **to be under ~** (Law) être mineur/-e

**(b)** (era) ère *f*, époque *f* (of de); **the video ~** l'ère de la vidéo; **in this day and ~** à notre époque

**(c)** (colloq) **it's ~s since I've played golf** ça fait une éternité que je n'ai pas joué au golf; **I've been waiting for ~s** j'attends depuis des heures

**2** *vtr, vi* vieillir

**aged** *adj* **(a) ~ between 20 and 25** âgé/-e de 20 à 25 ans; **a boy ~ 12** un garçon de 12 ans

**(b)** (old) âgé/-e

**age group** *n* tranche *f* d'âge

**ageism** *n* discrimination *f* en raison de l'âge

**agency** *n* agence *f*

**agenda** *n* ordre *m* du jour

**agent** *n* agent *m* (**for sb** de qn)

**aggravate** *vtr* (make worse) aggraver; (annoy) exaspérer

**aggression** *n* (gen) agression *f*; (of person) agressivité *f*

**aggressive** *adj* agressif/-ive

**aggro** *n* (colloq) (violence) violence *f*; (hostility) hostilité *f*

**agile** *adj* agile

**agitate** *vi* faire campagne (**for** pour)

**agitated** *adj* agité/-e, inquiet/-iète

**AGM** *n* (*abbr* = **annual general meeting**) assemblée *f* générale annuelle

**agnostic** *n, adj* agnostique (*mf*)

**ago** *adv* **three weeks ~** il y a trois semaines; **long ~** il y a longtemps; **how long ~?** il y a combien de temps?; **not long ~** il y a peu de temps

**agonize** *vi* se tourmenter (**over, about** à propos de)

**agonizing** *adj* ‹*pain, death*› atroce; ‹*choice*› déchirant/-e

**agony** *n* (physical) douleur *f* atroce; (mental) angoisse *f*

**agony aunt** *n* journaliste *mf* responsable du courrier du cœur

**agony column** *n* courrier *m* du cœur

**agree 1** *vtr* **(a)** (concur) être d'accord (**that** sur le fait que)

**(b)** (admit) convenir (**that** que)

**(c)** (consent) **to ~ to do** accepter de faire; **she ~d to speak to me** elle a accepté de me parler

**(d)** (settle on, arrange) se mettre d'accord sur ‹*date, price*›; **to ~ to do** convenir de faire

**2** *vi* **(a)** (hold same opinion) être d'accord (**with** avec; **about, on** sur; **about doing** pour faire); **'I ~!'** 'je suis bien d'accord!'

**(b)** (reach mutual understanding) se mettre d'accord (**about, on** sur)

**(c)** (consent) accepter; **to ~ to** consentir à ‹*suggestion, terms*›

**(d)** (hold with, approve) **to ~ with** approuver ‹*belief, idea, practice*›

**(e)** (tally) ‹*stories, statements, figures*› concorder (**with** avec)

**(f)** (suit) **to ~ with sb** ‹*climate*› être bon/bonne pour qn; ‹*food*› réussir à qn

**(g)** (in grammar) s'accorder (**with** avec; **in** en)

**3 agreed** *pp adj* convenu/-e; **is that ~d?** c'est entendu?

**agreeable** *adj* agréable

**agreement** *n* **(a)** accord *m* (**to do** pour faire); **to reach an ~** parvenir à un accord

**(b)** (undertaking) engagement *m*

**(c)** (contract) contrat *m*

**(d)** (in grammar) accord *m*

**agricultural** *adj* agricole

**agriculture** *n* agriculture *f*

**aground** *adv* **to run ∼** s'échouer

**ahead** ⟦1⟧ *adv* **(a)** ⟨*run*⟩ en avant; **to send sb on ∼** envoyer qn en éclaireur; **to send one's luggage on ∼** faire envoyer ses bagages; **a few kilometres ∼** à quelques kilomètres
**(b)** (in time) **in the months ∼** pendant les mois à venir
**(c)** (in leading position) **to be ∼ in the polls** être en tête des sondages; **to be 30 points ∼** avoir 30 points d'avance
⟦2⟧ **ahead of** *phr* **(a)** (in front of) devant ⟨*person, vehicle*⟩; **to be three metres ∼ of sb** avoir trois mètres d'avance sur qn
**(b) to be ∼ of sb** (in polls, ratings) avoir un avantage sur qn; **to be ∼ of the others** ⟨*pupil*⟩ être plus avancé/-e que les autres

**aid** ⟦1⟧ *n* aide *f* (**from** de; **to, for** à); **in ∼ of** au profit de ⟨*charity*⟩
⟦2⟧ *adj* ⟨*organization*⟩ d'entraide
⟦3⟧ *vtr* aider ⟨*person*⟩ (**to do** à faire); faciliter ⟨*digestion, recovery*⟩

**aid agency** *n* organisation *f* humanitaire

**aide** *n* aide *mf*, assistant/-e *m/f*

**Aids** *n* (*abbr* = **Acquired Immune Deficiency Syndrome**) sida *m*

**Aids sufferer** *n* sidéen/-éenne *m/f*

**aid worker** *n* employé/-e *m/f* d'une organisation humanitaire

**aim** ⟦1⟧ *n* **(a)** (purpose) but *m*
**(b)** (with weapon) **to take ∼ at sb/sth** viser qn/qch
⟦2⟧ *vtr* **(a) to be ∼ed at sb** ⟨*campaign, product, remark*⟩ viser qn
**(b)** braquer ⟨*gun, camera*⟩ (**at** sur); lancer ⟨*ball, stone*⟩ (**at** sur)
⟦3⟧ *vi* **to ∼ for sth, to ∼ at sth** viser qch; **to ∼ at doing, to ∼ to do** avoir l'intention de faire

**air** ⟦1⟧ *n* **(a)** air *m*; **in the open ∼** en plein air, au grand air; **to let the ∼ out of sth** dégonfler qch; **he threw the ball up into the ∼** il a jeté le ballon en l'air
**(b) to travel by ∼** voyager par avion
**(c)** (on radio, TV) **to be/go on the ∼** être/passer à l'antenne
⟦2⟧ *vtr* **(a)** aérer ⟨*garment, room, bed*⟩
**(b)** exprimer ⟨*opinion, view*⟩; **to ∼ one's grievances** exposer ses griefs
IDIOMS **to put on ∼s** se donner de grands airs; **to vanish into thin ∼** se volatiliser

**air ambulance** *n* avion *m* sanitaire

**airbag** *n* airbag *m*

**air bed** *n* (GB) matelas *m* pneumatique

**air-conditioned** *adj* climatisé/-e

**air-conditioning** *n* climatisation *f*, air *m* conditionné

**aircraft** *n* avion *m*, aéronef *m*

**aircrew** *n* équipage *m* d'un avion

**airfare** *n* tarif *m* d'avion

**airfield** *n* aérodrome *m*, terrain *m* d'aviation

**air force** *n* armée *f* de l'air, forces *fpl* aériennes

**air-freshener** *n* désodorisant *m* d'atmosphère

**air gun** *n* fusil *m* à air comprimé

**airhead** *n* (colloq) évaporé/-e *m/f*

**air hostess** *n* hôtesse *f* de l'air

**airline** *n* compagnie *f* aérienne

**airmail** *n* poste *f* aérienne; **by ∼** par avion

**airplane** *n* (US) avion *m*

**airport** *n* aéroport *m*

**air raid** *n* attaque *f* aérienne, raid *m* (aérien)

**airstrike** *n* frappe *f* aérienne

**air terminal** *n* (at airport) aérogare *f*; (in town) terminal *m*

**airtight** *adj* étanche à l'air

**air-traffic controller** *n* contrôleur/-euse *m/f* aérien/-ienne, aiguilleur *m* du ciel

**air travel** *n* voyages *mpl* aériens

**airwaves** *n pl* ondes *fpl*

**airy** *adj* **(a)** ⟨*room*⟩ clair/-e et spacieux/-ieuse
**(b)** ⟨*manner*⟩ désinvolte, insouciant/-e

**aisle** *n* **(a)** (in church) (side passage) bas-côté *m*; (centre passage) allée *f* centrale
**(b)** (in train, plane) couloir *m*; (in cinema, shop) allée *f*

**ajar** *adj, adv* entrouvert/-e, entrebaillé/-e

**alarm** ⟦1⟧ *n* **(a)** (warning) alarme *f*; **smoke ∼** détecteur *m* de fumée
**(b)** (fear) frayeur *f*; (concern) inquiétude *f*
⟦2⟧ *vtr* inquiéter ⟨*person*⟩

**alarm clock** *n* réveille-matin *m*, réveil *m*

**alarmed** *adj* effrayé/-e

**album** *n* album *m*

**alcohol** *n* alcool *m*; **∼-free** sans alcool; **∼ content** teneur *f* en alcool

**alcoholic** ⟦1⟧ *n* alcoolique *mf*
⟦2⟧ *adj* ⟨*drink*⟩ alcoolisé/-e; ⟨*stupor*⟩ alcoolique

**alcoholism** *n* alcoolisme *m*

**alcopop** *n* soda *m* alcoolisé

**alcove** *n* renfoncement *m*

**ale** *n* bière *f*

**alert** ⟦1⟧ *n* alerte *f*
⟦2⟧ *adj* **(a)** (lively) ⟨*child*⟩ éveillé/-e; ⟨*adult*⟩ alerte
**(b)** (attentive) vigilant/-e
⟦3⟧ *vtr* **(a)** alerter ⟨*authorities*⟩
**(b) to ∼ sb to** mettre qn en garde contre ⟨*danger*⟩; attirer l'attention de qn sur ⟨*fact, situation*⟩

**A-levels** *n pl* (GB) (Sch) ≈ baccalauréat *m*

**algebra** *n* algèbre *f*

**Algeria** *pr n* Algérie *f*

**alibi** *n* **(a)** (Law) alibi *m*
**(b)** (excuse) excuse *f*

**alien** *n* **(a)** (gen, Law) étranger/-ère *m/f* (**to** à) ⋯▸

**(b)** (from space) extraterrestre *mf*

**alienate** *vtr* éloigner ⟨supporters, colleagues⟩

**alight** **1** *adj* to set sth ~ mettre le feu à qch
**2** *vi* ⟨passenger⟩ descendre (from de)

**alike** **1** *adj* (identical) pareil/-eille; (similar) semblable; to look ~ se ressembler
**2** *adv* ⟨dress, think⟩ de la même façon

**alimony** *n* pension *f* alimentaire

**alive** *adj* **(a)** vivant/-e, en vie; to be burnt ~ être brûlé/-e vif/vive
**(b)** to come ~ ⟨party, place⟩ s'animer; ⟨history⟩ prendre vie
**(c)** to be ~ ⟨tradition⟩ être vivant/-e; ⟨interest⟩ être vif/vive
**(d)** ~ with grouillant/-e de ⟨insects⟩

**alkaline** *adj* alcalin/-e

**all**

■ **Note** When *all* is used as a pronoun, it is generally translated by *tout*.
– When *all* is followed by a *that* clause, *all that* is translated by *tout ce que*: *after all (that) we've done* = après tout ce que nous avons fait.
– When referring to a specified group of people or objects, the translation of *all* reflects the number and gender of the people or objects referred to; *tous* is used for a group of people or objects of masculine or mixed or unspecified gender and *toutes* for a group of feminine gender: *we were all delighted* = nous étions tous ravis; *'where are the cups?'—'they're all in the kitchen'* = 'où sont les tasses?'—'elles sont toutes dans la cuisine'. ▶ 1
– In French, determiners agree in gender and number with the noun that follows: *all the time* = tout le temps; *all the family* = toute la famille; *all men* = tous les hommes; *all the books* = tous les livres; *all women* = toutes les femmes; *all the chairs* = toutes les chaises. ▶ 2
– As an adverb meaning *completely*, *all* is generally translated by *tout*: *he was all alone* = il était tout seul; *the girls were all excited* = les filles étaient tout excitées.
– However, when the adjective that follows is in the feminine and begins with a consonant the translation is *toute/toutes*: *she was all alone* = elle était toute seule; *the girls were all alone* = les filles étaient toutes seules. ▶ 3A
– For more examples and particular usages see the entry below.

**1** *pron* tout; that's ~ I want c'est tout ce que je veux; I spent it ~, I spent ~ of it j'ai tout dépensé; ~ of our things toutes nos affaires
**2** *det* tout/toute (+ *sg*); tous/toutes (+ *pl*); ~ those who came (men, mixed group) tous ceux qui sont venus; (women) toutes celles qui sont venues; ~ his life toute sa vie; ~ the time tout le temps
**3** *adv* **(a)** tout; she's ~ wet elle est toute mouillée; ~ in white tout en blanc; ~ along the canal tout le long du canal; to be ~ for sth être tout à fait pour qch; tell me ~ about it! raconte-moi tout!
**(b)** (Sport) (they are) six ~ (il y a) six partout

**4** **all along** *phr* ⟨know⟩ depuis le début, toujours
**5** **all the** *phr* ~ the more difficult d'autant plus difficile; ~ the better! tant mieux!
**6** **all too** *phr* ⟨easy, often⟩ bien trop
**7** **at all** *phr* not at ~! (acknowledging thanks) de rien!; (answering query) pas du tout!; it is not at ~ certain ce n'est pas du tout certain; nothing at ~ rien du tout
**8** **of all** *phr* the easiest of ~ le plus facile; first of ~ pour commencer

**all clear** *n* to give sb the ~ donner le feu vert à qn (to do pour faire); ⟨doctor⟩ déclarer qn guéri/-e

**allegation** *n* allégation *f*

**allege** *vtr* to ~ that (claim) prétendre que (+ *conditional*); (publicly) déclarer que (+ *conditional*); it was ~d that il a été dit que

**allegedly** *adv* prétendument

**allegiance** *n* allégeance *f*

**allergic** *adj* allergique (to à)

**allergist** *n* allergologue *mf*

**allergy** *n* allergie *f* (to à)

**alleviate** *vtr* soulager ⟨boredom, pain⟩; réduire ⟨overcrowding, stress⟩

**alley** *n* (walkway) allée *f*; (for vehicles) ruelle *f*

**alliance** *n* alliance *f*

**allied** *adj* ⟨group⟩ allié/-e

**all-important** *adj* essentiel/-ielle

**all-inclusive** *adj* ⟨fee, price⟩ tout compris

**all-in-one** *adj* ⟨garment⟩ d'une seule pièce

**all-night** *adj* ⟨party, meeting⟩ qui dure toute la nuit; ⟨service⟩ ouvert/-e toute la nuit; ⟨radio station⟩ qui émet 24 heures sur 24

**allocate** *vtr* affecter ⟨funds⟩ (for, to à); accorder ⟨time⟩ (to à); assigner ⟨tasks⟩ (to à)

**allot** *vtr* attribuer ⟨money⟩ (to à); in the ~ted time dans le temps imparti

**allotment** *n* (GB) parcelle *f* de terre

**all-out** *adj* ⟨strike⟩ total/-e; ⟨attack⟩ en règle; ⟨effort⟩ acharné/-e

**all over** **1** *adj* fini/-e; when it's ~ quand tout sera fini
**2** *adv* (everywhere) partout; to be trembling ~ trembler de partout
**3** *prep* partout dans ⟨room, town⟩; ~ China partout en Chine

**allow** *vtr* **(a)** (authorize) permettre à, autoriser ⟨person, organization⟩ (to do à faire); it isn't ~ed c'est interdit; she isn't ~ed to go out elle n'a pas le droit de sortir
**(b)** (let) laisser; he ~ed the situation to get worse il a laissé la situation s'aggraver
**(c)** (enable) to ~ sb/sth to do permettre à qn/qch de faire; it would ~ the company to expand cela permettrait à la société de s'agrandir
**(d)** (allocate) prévoir; to ~ two days for the job prévoir deux jours pour faire le travail
**(e)** ⟨referee⟩ accorder ⟨goal⟩; ⟨insurer⟩ agréer ⟨claim⟩
**(f)** (condone) tolérer ⟨rudeness, swearing⟩
■ **allow for** tenir compte de

**allowance** *n* (a) (gen) allocation *f*; (from employer) indemnité *f*
(b) (tax) ∼ abattement *m* fiscal
(c) (spending money) (for child) argent *m* de poche; (for student) argent *m* (pour vivre); (from trust, guardian) rente *f*
(d) your baggage ∼ is 40 kg vous avez droit à 40 kg de bagages
(e) to make ∼(s) for sth tenir compte de qch; to make ∼(s) for sb essayer de comprendre qn

**alloy wheel** *n* jante *f* en alliage léger

**all right, alright** ⟦1⟧ *adj* ⟨film, garment, place⟩ pas mal (colloq); is my hair ∼? ça va mes cheveux?; are you ∼? ça va?; I'm ∼ thanks ça va merci; is it ∼ if…? est-ce que ça va si…?
⟦2⟧ *adv* (a) (giving agreement) d'accord
(b) ⟨work⟩ comme il faut; ⟨see, hear⟩ bien

**all-round** *adj* ⟨athlete⟩ complet/-ète; ⟨improvement⟩ général/-e

**all-rounder** *n* to be a good ∼ être bon/ bonne en tout

**all-time** *adj* ⟨record⟩ absolu/-e; the ∼ greats (people) les grands *mpl*; ∼ high record *m* absolu

**all told** *adv* en tout

**allusion** *n* allusion *f* (to à)

**ally** ⟦1⟧ *n* allié/-e *m/f*
⟦2⟧ *v refl* to ∼ oneself with s'allier avec

**almond** *n* (a) (nut) amande *f*
(b) (also ∼ **tree**) amandier *m*

**almost** *adv* (a) (practically) presque; we're ∼ there nous sommes presque arrivés; it's ∼ dark il fait presque nuit
(b) he ∼ died/forgot il a failli mourir/ oublier

**alone** ⟦1⟧ *adj* seul/-e; all ∼ tout seul/toute seule; to leave sb ∼ laisser qn seul/-e; (in peace) laisser qn tranquille; leave that bike ∼! ne touche pas à ce vélo!
⟦2⟧ *adv* (a) ⟨work, live, travel⟩ seul/-e
(b) for this reason ∼ rien que pour cette raison
IDIOMS to go it ∼ (colloq) faire cavalier seul

**along**

■ Note When *along* is used as a preposition meaning *all along* it can usually be translated by *le long de*: *there were trees along the road* = il y avait des arbres le long de la route. For particular usages see the entry below.
– *along* is often used after verbs of movement. If the addition of *along* does not change the meaning of the verb, *along* will not be translated: *as he walked along* = tout en marchant.

⟦1⟧ *adv* to push sth ∼ pousser qch; to be running ∼ courir; I'll be ∼ in a second j'arrive tout de suite
⟦2⟧ *prep* (a) (all along) le long de; there were chairs ∼ the wall il y avait des chaises contre le mur
(b) to walk ∼ the beach marcher sur la plage; to look ∼ the shelves chercher dans les rayons; halfway ∼ the path à mi-chemin

⟦3⟧ **along with** *phr* (accompanied by) accompagné/-e de; (at same time as) en même temps que

**alongside** ⟦1⟧ *prep* (a) (all along) le long de
(b) to draw up ∼ sb ⟨vehicle⟩ s'arrêter à la hauteur de qn
⟦2⟧ *adv* à côté

**aloud** *adv* ⟨read⟩ à haute voix; ⟨think⟩ tout haut

**alphabet** *n* alphabet *m*

**alphabetically** *adv* par ordre alphabétique

**alpine** *adj* (also **Alpine**) alpin/-e

**Alps** *pr n pl* the ∼ les Alpes *fpl*

**already** *adv* déjà; it's 10 o'clock ∼ il est déjà 10 heures; he's ∼ left il est déjà parti

**alright** = ALL RIGHT

**Alsatian** *n* (GB) (dog) berger *m* allemand

**also** *adv* aussi

**alter** ⟦1⟧ *vtr* (a) changer ⟨person⟩; (radically) transformer ⟨person⟩; changer ⟨opinion, rule, timetable⟩; modifier ⟨amount, document⟩; affecter ⟨value, climate⟩
(b) retoucher ⟨dress, shirt⟩
⟦2⟧ *vi* changer

**alteration** ⟦1⟧ *n* modification *f* (to, in de)
⟦2⟧ **alterations** *n pl* (building work) travaux *mpl*

**alternate** ⟦1⟧ *adj* (a) (successive) ⟨chapters, layers⟩ en alternance
(b) (every other) on ∼ days un jour sur deux
(c) (US) (other) autre
⟦2⟧ *vtr* to ∼ sth and or with sth alterner qch et qch
⟦3⟧ *vi* ⟨people⟩ se relayer; ⟨colours, patterns, seasons⟩ alterner (with avec)

**alternately** *adv* alternativement

**alternative** ⟦1⟧ *n* (from two) alternative *f*, autre possibilité *f*; (from several) possibilité *f*; to have no ∼ ne pas avoir le choix
⟦2⟧ *adj* (a) ⟨date, flight, plan⟩ autre; ⟨accommodation, product⟩ de remplacement; ⟨solution⟩ de rechange
(b) (unconventional) alternatif/-ive

**alternatively** *adv* sinon; ∼, you can book by phone vous avez aussi la possibilité de réserver par téléphone

**alternative medicine** *n* médecines *fpl* parallèles *or* douces

**although** *conj* bien que (+ *subjunctive*); ∼ he is shy bien qu'il soit timide

**altitude** *n* altitude *f*

**alto** *n* (voice) (of female) contralto *m*; (of male) haute-contre *f*

**altogether** *adv* (a) (completely) complètement; not ∼ true pas complètement vrai
(b) (in total) en tout; how much is that ∼? ça fait combien en tout?

**aluminium foil** *n* papier *m* aluminium

**always** *adv* toujours; he's ∼ complaining il n'arrête pas de se plaindre

**Alzheimer's disease** *n* maladie *f* d'Alzheimer

**am** adv (abbr = **ante meridiem**) three ~ trois heures (du matin)

**amalgamate** ① vtr (merge) fusionner ‹companies, schools› (with avec; into en) ② vi ‹company, union› fusionner (with avec)

**amateur** ① n amateur m ② adj ‹sportsperson, musician› amateur; ‹sport› en amateur

**amaze** vtr surprendre; (stronger) stupéfier

**amazed** adj stupéfait/-e; I'm ~ (that) ça m'étonne que (+ subjunctive)

**amazement** n stupéfaction f

**amazing** adj extraordinaire

**Amazon** pr n Amazone m

**ambassador** n ambassadeur m

**amber** n (a) (resin, colour) ambre m (b) (GB) (traffic signal) orange m

**ambiguous** adj ambigu/ambiguë

**ambition** n ambition f (to do de faire)

**ambitious** adj ambitieux/-ieuse

**ambulance** n ambulance f; ~ crew équipe f d'ambulanciers/-ières

**ambush** ① n embuscade f ② vtr tendre une embuscade à

**amenable** adj ~ to ‹person› sensible à ‹reason, advice›

**amend** vtr amender ‹law›; modifier ‹document›

**amendment** n (to law) amendement m (to à); (to contract) modification f (to à)

**amends** n pl to make ~ se racheter; to make ~ for réparer ‹damage›; to make ~ to sb (financially) dédommager qn

**amenities** n pl (of hotel) équipements mpl; (of house, sports club) installations fpl

**America** pr n Amérique f

**American** ① n (a) (person) Américain/-e m/f (b) (also ~ **English**) américain m ② adj américain/-e; ‹embassy› des États-Unis

**American Indian** n Indien/-ienne m/f d'Amerique du Nord

**amiable** adj aimable (to avec)

**amicable** adj (friendly) amical/-e; an ~ settlement un arrangement à l'amiable

**amiss** ① adj there is something ~ il y a quelque chose qui ne va pas ② adv to take sth ~ prendre qch de travers

**ammunition** n munitions fpl

**amnesty** n amnistie f

**among**, **amongst** prep (a) (amidst) parmi; ~ the crowd parmi la foule; to be ~ friends être entre amis (b) (one of) ~ the world's poorest countries un des pays les plus pauvres du monde; she was ~ those who survived elle faisait partie des survivants; to be ~ the first être dans les premiers (c) (between) entre

**amount** n (of goods, food) quantité f; (of people, objects) nombre m; (of money) somme f; a large ~ of beaucoup de; the full ~ le montant total ■ **amount to** (a) s'élever à ‹total› (b) (be equivalent to) revenir à ‹confession, betrayal›; it ~s to the same thing cela revient au même

**amp** n (a) (abbr = **ampere**) ampère m (b) (colloq) (abbr = **amplifier**) ampli m (colloq)

**amphetamine** n amphétamine f

**ample** adj (a) ‹provisions, resources› largement suffisant/-e (for pour); there's ~ room il y a largement la place (b) ‹proportions, bust› généreux/-euse

**amplifier** n amplificateur m

**amputate** vtr amputer; to ~ sb's leg amputer qn de la jambe

**amuse** ① vtr (a) (cause laughter) amuser; to be ~d at or by s'amuser de (b) (entertain) ‹game, story› distraire (c) (occupy) ‹activity, hobby› occuper ② v refl to ~ oneself (a) (entertain) se distraire (b) (occupy) s'occuper

**amusement** n (a) (mirth) amusement m (at face à) (b) (diversion) distraction f

**amusement arcade** n (GB) salle f de jeux électroniques

**amusement park** n parc m d'attractions

**amusing** adj amusant/-e

**an** ▶ A²

**anachronism** n anachronisme m

**anaemic** adj (Med) anémique

**anaesthetic** (GB), **anesthetic** (US) n, adj anesthésique (m)

**anaesthetize** (GB), **anesthetize** (US) vtr anesthésier

**analogy** n analogie f

**analyse** (GB), **analyze** (US) vtr analyser

**analysis** n analyse f

**analytic(al)** adj analytique

**anarchist** n, adj anarchiste (mf)

**anarchy** n anarchie f

**anatomy** n anatomie f

**ancestor** n ancêtre mf

**anchor** n ancre f; to drop ~ jeter l'ancre

**anchovy** n anchois m

**ancient** adj (dating from BC) antique; (very old) ancien/-ienne; ~ Greek grec ancien; ~ Greece la Grèce antique; ~ monument monument m historique

**and** conj et; cups ~ plates des tasses et des assiettes; he stood up ~ went out il s'est levé et il est sorti; come ~ see viens voir; two hundred ~ sixty-two deux cent soixante-deux; faster ~ faster de plus en plus vite

**Andorra** pr n Andorre f

**angel** n ange m

**anger** 1 *n* colère *f* (**at** devant; **towards** contre)
2 *vtr* mettre [qn] en colère ⟨*person*⟩

**angle** 1 *n* angle *m*
2 *vi* (**a**) (fish) pêcher (à la ligne)
(**b**) (colloq) **to ~ for sth** chercher à obtenir qch

**Anglo-French** *adj* anglo-français/-e, franco-britannique

**angrily** *adv* ⟨*react, speak*⟩ avec colère

**angry** *adj* ⟨*person, expression*⟩ furieux/-ieuse; ⟨*scene, words*⟩ de colère; **to be ~** (**at** *or* **with sb**) être en colère (contre qn); **to get ~** se fâcher; **to make sb ~** mettre qn en colère

**animal** 1 *n* animal *m*, bête *f*
2 *adj* animal/-e

**animal activist** *n* militant/-e *m/f* pour les droits des animaux

**animal experiment** *n* expérience *f* sur les animaux

**animal rights** *n pl* droits *mpl* des animaux

**animal testing** *n* expérimentation *f* animale

**animated** *adj* animé/-e

**animator** *n* (cartoonist) animateur/-trice *m/f*

**ankle** *n* cheville *f*

**ankle chain** *n* chaîne *f* de cheville

**ankle sock** *n* socquette *f*

**annex** 1 *n* (*also* **annexe** (GB)) annexe *f*
2 *vtr* annexer ⟨*territory, land, country*⟩ (**to** à)

**annihilate** *vtr* anéantir

**anniversary** *n* anniversaire *m* (**of** de)

**annotate** *vtr* annoter

**announce** *vtr* annoncer (**that** que)

**announcement** *n* (**a**) (spoken) annonce *f*
(**b**) (written) avis *m*; (of birth, death) faire-part *m inv*

**announcer** *n* (on TV) speaker/-erine *m/f*; **radio ~** présentateur/-trice *m/f* de radio

**annoy** *vtr* ⟨*person*⟩ (by behaviour) agacer; (by opposing wishes) contrarier; ⟨*noise*⟩ gêner

**annoyance** *n* agacement *m* (**at** devant), contrariété *f* (**at** à cause de)

**annoyed** *adj* contrarié/-e (**at, by** par); (stronger) agacé/-e, fâché/-e (**at, by** par); **~ with sb** fâché/-e contre qn

**annoying** *adj* agaçant/-e (**to do** de faire)

**annual** 1 *n* (**a**) (book) album *m* (annuel)
(**b**) (plant) plante *f* annuelle
2 *adj* annuel/-elle

**annually** *adv* ⟨*earn, produce*⟩ par an; ⟨*do, inspect*⟩ tous les ans

**anomaly** *n* anomalie *f*

**anonymous** *adj* anonyme

**anorak** *n* anorak *m*

**anorexia (nervosa)** *n* anorexie *f* mentale

**another**

■ Note *Another* is translated by *un autre* or *une autre* according to the gender of the noun it

refers to: *another book* = un autre livre; *another chair* = une autre chaise.
– Note that *en* is always used with *un/une autre* in French to represent a noun that is understood: *that cake was delicious, can I have another (one)?* = ce gâteau était délicieux, est-ce que je peux en prendre un autre? For more examples and particular usages, see the entry below.

1 *det* (**a**) (an additional) un/-e autre, encore un/-e; **would you like ~ drink?** est-ce que tu veux un autre verre?; **I've broken ~ plate** j'ai encore cassé une assiette; **that will cost you ~ £5** cela vous coûtera 5 livres sterling de plus; **in ~ five weeks** dans cinq semaines
(**b**) (a different) un/-e autre; **~ time** une autre fois; **he has ~ job now** il a un nouveau travail maintenant
2 *pron* un/-e autre; **she had ~** elle en a pris un/-e autre; **one after ~** l'un/l'une après l'autre; **in one way or ~** d'une façon ou d'une autre

**answer** 1 *n* (gen) réponse *f* (**to** à); (to problem, puzzle) solution *f* (**to** à); **there's no ~** (to door) il n'y a personne; (on phone) ça ne répond pas; **the right/wrong ~** la bonne/mauvaise réponse
2 *vtr* répondre à; **to ~ the door** aller *or* venir ouvrir la porte; **to ~ the phone** répondre au téléphone
3 *vi* (**a**) répondre; **to ~ to** répondre *or* correspondre à ⟨*description*⟩
(**b**) (be accountable) **to ~ to sb** être responsable devant qn

■ **answer back** répondre

■ **answer for** répondre de ⟨*action, person*⟩; **they have a lot to ~ for!** ils ont beaucoup de comptes à rendre!

**answerable** *adj* responsable (**to sb** devant qn; **for sth** de qch)

**answering machine**, **answerphone** *n* répondeur *m* (téléphonique)

**ant** *n* fourmi *f*

**antagonize** *vtr* (annoy) contrarier; (stronger) éveiller l'hostilité de

**Antarctic** 1 *pr n* **the ~** l'Antarctique *m*
2 *adj* antarctique

**antelope** *n* antilope *f*

**antenatal** *adj* prénatal/-e

**antenatal class** *n* (GB) cours *m* de préparation à l'accouchement

**antenna** *n* antenne *f*

**anthropology** *n* anthropologie *f*

**anti** 1 *prep* contre
2 **anti(-)** *pref* anti(-)

**antibacterial** *adj* antibactérien/-ienne

**antibiotic** *n* antibiotique *m*; **on ~s** sous antibiotiques

**anticipate** *vtr* (**a**) (foresee) prévoir, s'attendre à ⟨*problem, delay*⟩; **as ~d** comme prévu
(**b**) (guess in advance) anticiper ⟨*needs, result*⟩ ···✧

**(c)** (pre-empt) devancer ⟨*person, act*⟩

**anticipation** *n* **(a)** (excitement) excitation *f*; (pleasure in advance) plaisir *m* anticipé
**(b)** (expectation) prévision *f* (**of** de)

**anticlimax** *n* déception *f*

**anticlockwise** *adj, adv* (GB) dans le sens inverse des aiguilles d'une montre

**antidepressant** *n* antidépresseur *m*

**antidote** *n* antidote *m* (**to, for** contre, à)

**antihistamine** *n* antihistaminique *m*

**antique** **1** *n* (object) objet *m* ancien *or* d'époque; (furniture) meuble *m* ancien *or* d'époque
**2** *adj* ancien/-ienne

**antique shop** *n* magasin *m* d'antiquités

**anti-Semitism** *n* antisémitisme *m*

**antiseptic** *n, adj* antiseptique (*m*)

**antisocial** *adj* ~ **behaviour** comportement *m* incorrect; (criminal behaviour) comportement *m* délinquant
**(b)** (reclusive) sauvage

**anti-theft** *adj* ⟨*lock, device*⟩ antivol *inv*

**anti-virus software** *n* logiciel *m* antivirus

**antlers** *n pl* bois *mpl* de cerf

**anxiety** *n* **(a)** (worry) grandes inquiétudes *fpl* (**about** à propos de; **for** pour); **to be in a state of** ~ être angoissé/-e
**(b)** (eagerness) désir *m* ardent (**to do** de faire)
**(c)** (in psychology) anxiété *f*

**anxiety attack** *n* crise *f* d'angoisse

**anxious** *adj* **(a)** (worried) très inquiet/-iète (**about** à propos de; **for** pour); **to be** ~ **about doing** s'inquiéter de faire
**(b)** ⟨*moment, time*⟩ angoissant/-e
**(c)** (eager) très désireux/-euse (**to do** de faire)

**anxiously** *adv* **(a)** (worriedly) avec inquiétude
**(b)** (eagerly) avec impatience

**any**

■ **Note** When *any* is used as a determiner in questions and conditional sentences it is translated by *du, de l', de la* or *des* according to the gender and number of the noun that follows: *is there any soap? = y a-t-il du savon?; is there any flour? = y a-t-il de la farine?; are there any questions? = est-ce qu'il y a des questions?*
– In negative sentences *any* is translated by *de* or *d'* (before a vowel or mute 'h'): *we don't have any money = nous n'avons pas d'argent.*
– When *any* is used as a pronoun in negative sentences and in questions it is translated by *en*: *we don't have any = nous n'en avons pas; have you got any? = est-ce que vous en avez?*
– For more examples and other uses see the entry below.

**1** *det* **(a)** (in questions, conditional sentences) du/ de l'/de la/des; **is there** ~ **tea?** est-ce qu'il y a du thé?; **if you have** ~ **money** si vous avez de l'argent
**(b)** (with negative) de, d'; **I don't need** ~ **advice** je n'ai pas besoin de conseils
**(c)** (no matter which) n'importe quel/quelle;

tout; ~ **pen will do** n'importe quel stylo fera l'affaire; **you can have** ~ **cup you like** vous pouvez prendre n'importe quelle tasse; **I'm ready to help in** ~ **way I can** je suis prêt à faire tout ce que je peux pour aider; **come round and see me** ~ **time** passe me voir quand tu veux
**2** *pron, quantif* **(a)** (in questions, conditional sentences) **have you got** ~? est-ce que vous en avez?; **have** ~ **of you got a car?** est-ce que l'un/-e d'entre vous a une voiture?
**(b)** (with negative) **he hasn't got** ~ il n'en a pas; **there is hardly** ~ **left** il n'en reste presque pas; **she doesn't like** ~ **of them** (people) elle n'aime aucun d'entre eux/elles; (things) elle n'en aime aucun/-e
**(c)** (no matter which) n'importe lequel/laquelle; 'which colour would you like?'—'~' 'quelle couleur veux-tu?'—'n'importe laquelle'; ~ **of those pens** n'importe lequel de ces stylos; ~ **of them could do it** n'importe qui d'entre eux/elles pourrait le faire
**3** *adv* **have you got** ~ **more of these?** est-ce que vous en avez d'autres?; **do you want** ~ **more wine?** voulez-vous encore du vin?; **he doesn't live here** ~ **more** il n'habite plus ici

**anybody** *pron* (*also* **anyone**) **(a)** (in questions, conditional sentences) quelqu'un; **is there** ~ **in the house?** est-ce qu'il y a quelqu'un dans la maison?; **if** ~ **asks, tell them I've gone out** si quelqu'un me cherche, dis que je suis sorti
**(b)** (with negative) personne; **there wasn't** ~ **in the house** il n'y avait personne dans la maison; **I didn't have** ~ **to talk to** il n'y avait personne avec qui j'aurais pu parler
**(c)** (no matter who) n'importe qui; ~ **could do it** n'importe qui pourrait le faire; ~ **who wants to, can go** tous ceux qui le veulent, peuvent y aller; ~ **can make a mistake** ça arrive à tout le monde de faire une erreur; ~ **would think you were deaf** c'est à croire que tu es sourd

**anyhow** *adv* **(a)** = ANYWAY A
**(b)** (carelessly) n'importe comment

**anyone** = ANYBODY

**anything** *pron* **(a)** (in questions, conditional sentences) quelque chose; **is there** ~ **to be done?** peut-on faire quelque chose?
**(b)** (with negative) rien; **she didn't say** ~ elle n'a rien dit; **he didn't have** ~ **to do** il n'avait rien à faire; **don't believe** ~ **he says** ne crois pas un mot de ce qu'il dit
**(c)** (no matter what) tout; ~ **is possible** tout est possible; **she'll eat** ~ elle mange tout; **he was** ~ **but happy** il n'était pas du tout heureux

**anytime** *adv* (*also* **any time**) n'importe quand; ~ **after 2 pm** n'importe quand à partir de 14 heures; ~ **you like** quand tu veux; **he could arrive** ~ **now** il pourrait arriver d'un moment à l'autre

**anyway** *adv* **(a)** (in any case) (*also* **anyhow**) de toute façon
**(b)** (all the same) quand même; **I don't really like hats, but I'll try it on** ~ je n'aime pas

vraiment les chapeaux, mais je vais quand même l'essayer; **thanks** ∼ merci quand même

**(c)** (at any rate) en tout cas; **we can't go out, not yet** ∼ nous ne pouvons pas sortir, pas pour l'instant en tout cas

**(d)** (well) '∼, **we arrived at the station...**' 'bref, nous sommes arrivés à la gare...'

**anywhere** *adv* **(a)** (in questions, conditional sentences) quelque part; **we're going to Spain, if** ∼ si on va quelque part, ce sera en Espagne

**(b)** (with negative) nulle part; **you can't go** ∼ tu ne peux aller nulle part; **there isn't** ∼ **to sit** il n'y a pas de place pour s'asseoir; **you won't get** ∼ **if you don't pass your exams** tu n'arriveras à rien si tu ne réussis pas tes examens; **crying isn't going to get you** ∼ ça ne t'avancera à rien de pleurer

**(c)** (no matter where) n'importe où; ∼ **you like** où tu veux; ∼ **in England** partout en Angleterre

**apart** ①*adj, adv* **(a)** trees planted 10 **metres** ∼ des arbres plantés à 10 mètres d'intervalle

**(b)** (separated) séparé/-e; **we hate being** ∼ nous détestons être séparés; **they need to be kept** ∼ il faut les garder séparés

**(c)** (to one side) **he stood** ∼ **(from the group)** il se tenait à l'écart (du groupe)

②**apart from** *phr* **(a)** (separate from) à l'écart de; **it stands** ∼ **from the other houses** elle est à l'écart des autres maisons; **he lives** ∼ **from his wife** il vit séparé de sa femme

**(b)** (leaving aside) en dehors de, à part; ∼ **from being illegal, it's also dangerous** (mis) à part que c'est illégal, c'est aussi dangereux

**apartheid** *n* apartheid *m*

**apartment** *n* appartement *m*

**apartment block** *n* immeuble *m*

**apartment house** *n* (US) résidence *f*

**apathetic** *adj* (by nature) amorphe; (from illness, depression) apathique

**apex** *n* sommet *m*

**APEX** *n* (*abbr* = **Advance Purchase Excursion**) APEX *m*

**apologetic** *adj* ‹*gesture, letter*› d'excuse; **to be** ∼ **(about)** s'excuser (de)

**apologize** *vi* s'excuser (**to sb** auprès de qn; **for sth** de qch; **for doing** d'avoir fait)

**apology** *n* excuses *fpl* (**for sth** pour qch; **for doing** pour avoir fait); **to make an** ∼ s'excuser

**apostrophe** *n* apostrophe *f*

**appal** (GB), **appall** (US) *vtr* (shock) scandaliser; (horrify, dismay) horrifier

**appalling** *adj* **(a)** ‹*crime, conditions*› épouvantable

**(b)** ‹*manners, joke, taste*› exécrable; ‹*noise, weather*› épouvantable

**apparatus** *n* (gen) appareil *m*; (in gym) agrès *mpl*

**apparent** *adj* **(a)** (seeming) ‹*contradiction, willingness*› apparent/-e

**(b)** (clear) évident/-e; **for no** ∼ **reason** sans raison apparente

**apparently** *adv* apparemment

**appeal** ①*n* **(a)** (gen, Law) appel *m* (**for** à; **on behalf of** en faveur de)

**(b)** (attraction) charme *m*; (interest) intérêt *m*

②*vi* **(a)** (Law) faire appel (**against** de)

**(b)** (Sport) **to** ∼ **to** demander l'arbitrage de ‹*referee*›; **to** ∼ **against** contester ‹*decision*›

**(c)** **to** ∼ **for** lancer un appel à ‹*order, tolerance*›; faire appel à ‹*witnesses*›; **to** ∼ **for help** demander de l'aide

**(d)** (attract) **to** ∼ **to sb** ‹*idea*› tenter qn; ‹*person*› plaire à qn; ‹*place*› attirer qn

**appeal fund** *n* fonds *m* d'aide

**appealing** *adj* **(a)** (attractive) ‹*child*› attachant/-e; ‹*idea*› séduisant/-e; ‹*modesty*› charmant/-e

**(b)** ‹*look*› suppliant/-e

**appear** *vi* **(a)** (become visible) apparaître

**(b)** (turn up) arriver

**(c)** (seem) **to** ∼ **to be/to do** ‹*person*› avoir l'air d'être/de faire; **to** ∼ **depressed** avoir l'air déprimé; **it** ∼**s that** il semble que

**(d)** ‹*book, article, name*› paraître

**(e)** **to** ∼ **on stage** paraître en scène; **to** ∼ **on TV** passer à la télévision

**(f)** (Law) **to** ∼ **in court** comparaître devant le tribunal

**appearance** *n* **(a)** (arrival) (of person, vehicle) arrivée *f*; (of development, invention) apparition *f*; **to put in an** ∼ faire une apparition

**(b)** (on TV, in play, film) passage *m*

**(c)** (look) (of person) apparence *f*; (of district, object) aspect *m*; **to judge** *or* **go by** ∼**s** se fier aux apparences

**appendicitis** *n* appendicite *f*

**appendix** *n* appendice *m*; **to have one's** ∼ **removed** se faire opérer de l'appendicite

**appetite** *n* appétit *m*

**appetite suppressant** *n* anorexigène *m*

**appetizer** *n* (biscuit, olive etc) amuse-gueule *m inv*; (starter) hors-d'œuvre *m*

**appetizing** *adj* appétissant/-e

**applaud** *vtr, vi* applaudir

**applause** *n* applaudissements *mpl*; **there was a burst of** ∼ les applaudissements ont éclaté

**apple** *n* pomme *f*

**applecore** *n* trognon *m* de pomme

**applet** *n* (Comput) applet *m*, applette *f*

**apple tree** *n* pommier *m*

**appliance** *n* appareil *m*; **household** ∼ appareil électroménager

**applicant** *n* (for job, membership) candidat/-e *m/f* (**for** à); (for passport, benefit, loan) demandeur/-euse *m/f* (**for** de); (for citizenship) postulant/-e *m/f* (**for** à)

**application** *n* **(a)** (for job) candidature *f* (**for** à); (for membership, passport, loan) demande *f* (**for** de)

**(b)** (of ointment) application *f* (**to** à)

**(c)** (of law, penalty, rule) application *f*

**application form** n (gen) formulaire m
de demande; (for job) formulaire m de
candidature; (for membership) demande f
d'inscription

**apply** ⊞ vtr (gen) appliquer; exercer
⟨pressure⟩ (to sur)
⊠ vi (a) to ∼ (for) faire une demande (de)
⟨passport, loan, visa, permit⟩; poser sa
candidature à ⟨job⟩; to ∼ to faire une
demande d'inscription à ⟨college⟩
(b) (be valid) ⟨definition, term⟩ s'appliquer (to
à); ⟨ban, rule, penalty⟩ être en vigueur
③ v refl to ∼ oneself s'appliquer

**appoint** vtr nommer ⟨person⟩ (to sth à qch;
to do pour faire; as comme); fixer ⟨date,
place⟩

**appointment** n (a) (meeting) rendez-vous
m (at chez; with avec; to do pour faire);
business ∼ rendez-vous m d'affaires; to
make an ∼ prendre rendez-vous
(b) (to post) nomination f

**appraisal** n évaluation f

**appreciate** ⊞ vtr (a) apprécier ⟨help,
effort⟩; être sensible à ⟨favour⟩; être
reconnaissant/-e de ⟨kindness, sympathy⟩; I'd
∼ it if you could reply soon je vous serais
reconnaissant de répondre sans tarder
(b) (realize) se rendre (bien) compte de, être
conscient/-e de
(c) (enjoy) apprécier ⟨music, art, food⟩
⊠ vi ⟨object⟩ prendre de la valeur; ⟨value⟩
monter

**appreciation** n (a) (gratitude)
remerciement m (for pour)
(b) (enjoyment) appréciation f (of de)
(c) (increase) hausse f (of, in de)

**appreciative** adj (a) (grateful)
reconnaissant/-e (of de)
(b) (admiring) admiratif/-ive

**apprehensive** adj inquiet/-iète; to be ∼
about sth/doing appréhender qch/de faire

**apprentice** n apprenti/-e m/f (to de)

**apprenticeship** n apprentissage m

**approach** ⊞ n (a) (route of access) voie f
d'accès
(b) (arrival) approche f
(c) (to problem) approche f
(d) to make ∼es to sb faire des démarches
auprès de qn
⊠ vtr (a) (draw near to) s'approcher de
⟨person, place⟩; (verge on) approcher de
(b) (deal with) aborder ⟨problem, subject⟩
(c) to ∼ sb (about sth) s'adresser à qn (au
sujet de qch); (more formally) faire des
démarches auprès de qn (pour qch)
③ vi ⟨person, car⟩ (s')approcher; ⟨event,
season⟩ approcher

**approachable** adj abordable, d'un abord
facile

**appropriate** ⊞ adj (a) ⟨behaviour, choice,
place⟩ approprié/-e (for pour); ⟨dress, gift⟩
qui convient (after n) (for à); ⟨punishment⟩
juste (for à); ⟨name⟩ bien choisi/-e
(b) (relevant) ⟨authority⟩ compétent/-e

⊠ vtr s'approprier ⟨property, document⟩;
affecter ⟨funds, land⟩ (for à)

**appropriately** adv (a) ⟨behave, speak⟩
avec à-propos; ⟨dress⟩ convenablement
(b) ⟨designed, chosen, sited⟩ judicieusement

**approval** n approbation f (of de; to do pour
faire); on ∼ à l'essai

**approve** ⊞ vtr approuver ⟨product, plan⟩;
accepter ⟨person⟩
⊠ vi to ∼ of sb/sth apprécier qn/qch; he
doesn't ∼ of drinking il est contre l'alcool

**approving** adj approbateur/-trice

**approximate** adj approximatif/-ive

**approximately** adv (a) (about) environ; at
∼ four o'clock vers quatre heures
(b) ⟨equal, correct⟩ à peu près

**apricot** n (fruit) abricot m

**April** n avril m

**April Fools' Day** n le premier avril

**apron** n tablier m

**apt** adj ⟨choice, description⟩ heureux/-euse;
⟨title, style⟩ approprié/-e (to, for à)

**aptitude** n aptitude f

**aquarium** n aquarium m

**Aquarius** n Verseau m

**aquarobics** n aquagym f

**aquatic** adj (gen) aquatique; ⟨sport⟩
nautique

**aqueduct** n aqueduc m

**Arab** ⊞ n (person) Arabe mf
⊠ adj arabe

**Arabic** ⊞ n (language) arabe m
⊠ adj arabe; ⟨lesson, teacher⟩ d'arabe

**Arab-Israeli** adj israélo-arabe

**arbitrary** adj arbitraire

**arbitration** n arbitrage m; to go to ∼ ≈
aller aux prud'hommes

**arcade** n arcade f; shopping ∼ galerie f
marchande

**arch** ⊞ n arche f
⊠ vtr arquer; to ∼ one's back ⟨person⟩
cambrer le dos; ⟨cat⟩ faire le dos rond
③ arch(-) pref par excellence; ∼-enemy
ennemi/-e m/f juré/-e; ∼-rival grand rival

**archaeologist** (GB), **archeologist**
(US) n archéologue mf

**archaeology** (GB), **archeology** (US) n
archéologie f

**archery** n tir m à l'arc

**architect** n architecte mf

**architecture** n architecture f

**archive** n archive f

**Arctic** ⊞ pr n the ∼ l'Arctique m
⊠ adj arctique

**ardent** adj ⟨defence, opposition, lover⟩
passionné/-e; ⟨supporter⟩ fervent/-e

**area** n (a) (region) région f; (of city) zone f;
(district) quartier m; in the London ∼ dans la
région de Londres; residential ∼ zone f
résidentielle

**(b)** (in building) dining ∼ coin *m* salle-à-manger; **no-smoking** ∼ zone *f* non-fumeurs; **waiting** ∼ salle *f* d'attente **(c)** (of knowledge) domaine *m*; (of business) secteur *m*
**(d)** (in geometry) aire *f*; (of land) superficie *f*

**area code** *n* indicatif *m* de zone

**arena** *n* arène *f*

**Argentina** *pr n* Argentine *f*

**argue** ①️ *vtr* (debate) discuter (de), débattre (de); **to** ∼ **that** (maintain) soutenir que
②️ *vi* **(a)** (quarrel) se disputer (**with** avec; **about**, **over** sur, pour)
**(b)** (debate) discuter (**about** de)
**(c)** (put one's case) argumenter (**for** en faveur de; **against** contre)

**argument** *n* **(a)** (quarrel) dispute *f* (**about** à propos de); **to have an** ∼ se disputer
**(b)** (discussion) débat *m*, discussion *f* (**about** à propos de)
**(c)** (case) argument *m* (**for** en faveur de; **against** contre)

**argumentative** *adj* ergoteur/-euse

**Aries** *n* Bélier *m*

**arise** *vi* **(a)** ⟨problem⟩ survenir; ⟨question⟩ se poser; **if the need** ∼**s** si le besoin se fait sentir
**(b)** (be the result of) résulter (**from** de)

**aristocrat** *n* aristocrate *mf*

**arithmetic** *n* arithmétique *f*

**arm** ①️ *n* bras *m*; (of chair) accoudoir *m*; ∼ **in** ∼ bras dessus bras dessous; **to have sth over/under one's** ∼ avoir qch sur/sous le bras; **to fold one's** ∼**s** croiser les bras
②️ **arms** *n pl* (weapons) armes *fpl*
③️ *vtr* (Mil) armer
IDIOMS **to keep sb at** ∼**'s length** tenir qn à distance

**armaments** *n pl* armements *mpl*

**armband** *n* (for swimmer) bracelet *m* de natation; (for mourner) crêpe *m* de deuil

**armchair** *n* fauteuil *m*

**armed** *adj* armé/-e (**with** de); ⟨raid, robbery⟩ à main armée

**armed forces**, **armed services** *n pl* forces *fpl* armées

**armour** (GB), **armor** (US) *n* armure *f*

**armoured** (GB), **armored** (US) *adj* blindé/-e

**armour-plated** (GB), **armor-plated** (US) *adj* ⟨vehicle⟩ blindé/-e; ⟨ship⟩ cuirassé/-e

**armpit** *n* aisselle *f*

**arms control** *n* contrôle *m* des armements

**arms race** *n* course *f* aux armements

**arms treaty** *n* traité *m* sur le contrôle des armements

**army** ①️ *n* armée *f*; **to join the** ∼ s'engager
②️ *adj* militaire

**aroma** *n* arôme *m*

**aromatherapy** *n* aromathérapie *f*

**around** ①️ *adv* **(a)** (approximately) environ, à peu près; **at** ∼ **3 pm** vers 15 heures

**(b)** (in the vicinity) **to be (somewhere)** ∼ être dans les parages; **are they** ∼? est-ce qu'ils sont là?
**(c)** (in circulation) **CDs have been** ∼ **for years** ça fait des années que les CD existent; **one of the most gifted musicians** ∼ un des musiciens les plus doués du moment
**(d)** **all** ∼ tout autour; **the only garage for miles** ∼ le seul garage à des kilomètres à la ronde; **to ask sb (to come)** ∼ dire à qn de passer
②️ *prep* **(a)** autour de ⟨fire, table⟩; **the villages** ∼ **Dublin** les villages des environs de Dublin; **clothes scattered** ∼ **the room** des vêtements éparpillés partout dans la pièce; **(all)** ∼ **the world** partout dans le monde; **to walk** ∼ **the town** se promener dans la ville; **the people** ∼ **here** les gens d'ici
**(b)** (at) vers; ∼ **midnight** vers minuit

**arouse** *vtr* éveiller ⟨interest, suspicion⟩; exciter ⟨anger, jealousy⟩; **to be** ∼**d** ⟨person⟩ être excité/-e

**arrange** ①️ *vtr* **(a)** disposer ⟨chairs, ornaments⟩; arranger ⟨room, hair, clothes⟩; arranger, disposer ⟨flowers⟩
**(b)** (organize) organiser ⟨party, meeting, holiday⟩; fixer ⟨date, appointment⟩; **to** ∼ **to do** s'arranger pour faire
**(c)** convenir de ⟨loan⟩
②️ *vi* **to** ∼ **for sth** prendre des dispositions pour qch; **to** ∼ **for sb to do** prendre des dispositions pour que qn fasse

**arrangement** *n* **(a)** (of objects, chairs) disposition *f*; (of flowers) composition *f*
**(b)** (agreement) entente *f*, accord *m*; **to come to an** ∼ s'arranger
**(c)** (preparations) ∼**s** préparatifs *mpl*; **to make** ∼**s to do** s'arranger pour faire

**array** *n* gamme *f*

**arrears** *n pl* arriéré *m*; **I am in** ∼ **with my payments** j'ai du retard dans mes paiements

**arrest** ①️ *n* arrestation *f*; **to be under** ∼ être en état d'arrestation
②️ *vtr* arrêter

**arrival** *n* arrivée *f*; **on sb's** ∼ à l'arrivée de qn

**arrival(s) lounge** *n* salon *m* d'arrivée

**arrivals board** *n* tableau *m* d'arrivée

**arrival time** *n* heure *f* d'arrivée

**arrive** *vi* **(a)** arriver (**at** à; **from** de)
**(b)** **to** ∼ **at** parvenir à ⟨decision, solution⟩

**arrogant** *adj* arrogant/-e

**arrow** *n* flèche *f*

**arson** *n* incendie *m* criminel

**arsonist** *n* pyromane *mf*

**art** *n* art *m*; **I'm bad at** ∼ je suis mauvais en dessin

**artefact** *n* objet *m* (fabriqué)

**artery** *n* artère *f*

**art exhibition** *n* (paintings) exposition *f* de tableaux; (sculpture) exposition *f* de sculpture

**art gallery** *n* (museum) musée *m* d'art; (commercial) galerie *f* d'art

**arthritis** *n* arthrite *f*

**artichoke** *n* artichaut *m*

**article** *n* article *m* (**about, on** sur)

**artificial** *adj* artificiel/-ielle

**artificial limb** *n* prothèse *f*, membre *m* artificiel

**artificial respiration** *n* respiration *f* artificielle

**artillery** *n* artillerie *f*

**artisan** *n* artisan *m*

**artist** *n* artiste *mf*

**artistic** *adj* ‹*talent*› artistique; ‹*temperament, person*› artiste

**arts** *n pl* (a) (culture) **the ~** les arts *mpl* (b) (Univ) lettres *fpl* (c) **~ and crafts** artisanat *m*

**art school** *n* école *f* des beaux-arts

**arts student** *n* étudiant/-e *m/f* en lettres

**art student** *n* étudiant/-e *m/f* des beaux-arts

**as** ⓵ *conj* (a) comme; **~ you know** comme vous le savez; **~ usual** comme d'habitude; **do ~ I say** fais ce que je te dis; **leave it ~ it is** laisse-le tel quel; **~ she was coming down the stairs** comme elle descendait l'escalier; **~ she grew older** au fur et à mesure qu'elle vieillissait; **~ a child, he…** (quand il était) enfant, il… (b) (because, since) comme, puisque; **~ you were out, I left a note** comme *or* puisque tu étais sorti, j'ai laissé un petit mot (c) (although) **strange ~ it may seem** aussi curieux que cela puisse paraître; **try ~ he might, he could not forget it** il avait beau essayer, il ne pouvait pas oublier (d) **the same…~** le/la même…que; **I've got a jacket the same ~ yours** j'ai la même veste que toi (e) **so ~ to do** pour faire, afin de faire ⓶ *prep* comme, en; **dressed ~ a sailor** habillé/-e en marin; **he works ~ a pilot** il travaille comme pilote; **a job ~ a teacher** un poste d'enseignant/-e; **to treat sb ~ an equal** traiter qn en égal ⓷ *adv* (in comparisons) **he is ~ intelligent ~ you** il est aussi intelligent que toi; **~ fast ~ you can** aussi vite que possible; **he's twice ~ strong ~ me** il est deux fois plus fort que moi; **I have ~ much** *or* **many ~ she has** j'en ai autant qu'elle; **~ much ~ possible** autant que possible; **~ little ~ possible** le moins possible; **~ soon ~ possible** dès que possible; **he has a house in Nice ~ well ~ an apartment in Paris** il a une maison à Nice ainsi qu'un appartement à Paris ⓸ **as for** *phr* quant à, pour ce qui est de ⓹ **as from, as of** *phr* à partir de ⓺ **as if** *phr* comme (si); **it looks ~ if we've lost** on dirait que nous avons perdu ⓻ **as long as** *phr* du moment que (+ *indicative*), pourvu que (+ *subjunctive*) ⓼ **as such** *phr* en tant que tel

**asbestos** *n* amiante *m*

**ascend** *vtr* gravir ‹*steps, hill*›

**ascent** *n* ascension *f*

**ascertain** *vtr* établir (**that** que)

**ash** *n* (a) cendre *f* (b) (*also* **~ tree**) frêne *m*

**ashamed** *adj* honteux/-euse; **to be ~** avoir honte (**of** de; **to do** de faire; **that** que (+ *subjunctive*))

**ashen** *adj* ‹*complexion*› terreux/-euse

**ashore** *adv* **to go ~** débarquer; **washed ~** rejeté/-e sur le rivage

**ashtray** *n* cendrier *m*

**Asia** *pr n* Asie *f*

**Asian** ⓵ *n* (from Far East) Asiatique *mf*; (in UK) personne *f* originaire du sous-continent indien ⓶ *adj* asiatique

**aside** ⓵ *n* **to say sth in an ~** dire qch en aparté ⓶ *adv* **to stand ~** s'écarter; **to put sth ~** (save) mettre qch de côté; (in shop) réserver qch; **to take sb ~** prendre qn à part ⓷ **aside from** *phr* à part

**ask** ⓵ *vtr* (a) demander; **to ~ a question** poser une question; **to ~ sb sth** demander qch à qn; **to ~ sb to do** demander à qn de faire (b) (invite) inviter ‹*person*› (**to** à); **to ~ sb to dinner** inviter qn à dîner ⓶ *vi* (a) (request) demander (b) (make enquiries) se renseigner; **to ~ about sb** s'informer au sujet de qn ⓷ *v refl* **to ~ oneself** se demander ■ **ask after** demander des nouvelles de ‹*person*› ■ **ask for**: ¶ **~ for [sth]** demander ‹*drink, money, help*›; ¶ **~ for [sb]** demander à voir; (on phone) demander à parler à

**askance** *adv* **to look ~ at sb/sth** considérer qn/qch avec méfiance

**askew** *adj, adv* de travers

**asking price** *n* prix *m* demandé

**asleep** *adj* **to be ~** dormir; **to fall ~** s'endormir; **to be sound** *or* **fast ~** dormir à poings fermés

**asparagus** *n* asperge *f*

**aspect** *n* (a) aspect *m* (b) (of house) orientation *f*

**asphalt** *n* bitume *m*

**aspic** *n* aspic *m*

**aspiration** *n* aspiration *f* (**to** à)

**aspire** *vi* aspirer (**to** à; **to do** à faire)

**aspirin** *n* aspirine® *f*

**ass** *n* (a) (donkey) âne *m* (b) (colloq) (fool) idiot/-e *m/f*

**assassin** *n* assassin *m*

**assassinate** *vtr* assassiner

**assassination** *n* assassinat *m*

**assault** ⓵ *n* (a) (Law) agression *f* (**on** sur) (b) (Mil) assaut *m* (**on** de) ⓶ *vtr* (a) (Law) agresser; **to be indecently ~ed** être victime d'une agression sexuelle (b) (Mil) assaillir

**assemble** ⓵ *vtr* (a) (gather) rassembler (b) (construct) assembler; **easy to ~** facile à monter

**2** *vi* ⟨*passengers, marchers*⟩ se rassembler; ⟨*parliament, team, family*⟩ se réunir

**assembly** *n* (a) (gen) assemblée *f*
(b) (Sch) rassemblement *m*
(c) (of components, machines) assemblage *m*

**assembly line** *n* chaîne *f* de montage

**assent** **1** *n* assentiment *m* (to à)
**2** *vi* donner son assentiment (to à)

**assert** *vtr* (a) (state) affirmer (that que); to ∼ oneself s'affirmer
(b) revendiquer ⟨*right, claim*⟩

**assertion** *n* déclaration *f* (that selon laquelle)

**assertive** *adj* assuré/-e

**assess** *vtr* (a) évaluer ⟨*person, problem*⟩; estimer ⟨*damage, value*⟩
(b) fixer ⟨*tax*⟩
(c) (Sch) contrôler ⟨*pupil*⟩

**assessment** *n* (a) (evaluation) appréciation *f* (of de); (of damage, value) estimation *f* (of de)
(b) (for tax) imposition *f*
(c) (Sch) contrôle *m*

**asset** *n* atout *m*; ∼s (private) avoir *m*; (of company) actif *m*

**assign** *vtr* (a) assigner ⟨*resources*⟩ (to à)
(b) to ∼ a task to sb confier une tâche à qn
(c) (attribute) attribuer (to à)
(d) (appoint) nommer (to à)

**assignment** *n* (a) (specific duty) mission *f*
(b) (academic) devoir *m*

**assimilate** **1** *vtr* assimiler
**2** *vi* s'assimiler (into dans)

**assist** **1** *vtr* (a) (help) aider; (in organization) assister (to do, in doing à faire)
(b) (facilitate) faciliter ⟨*development, process*⟩
**2** *vi* aider (in doing à faire); to ∼ in prendre part à ⟨*operation, rescue*⟩

**assistance** *n* aide *f* (to à); (more formal) assistance *f* (to à)

**assistant** **1** *n* (a) (helper) assistant/-e *m/f*; (in hierarchy) adjoint/-e *m/f*
(b) (also **shop** ∼) vendeur/-euse *m/f*
(c) (GB) (foreign language) ∼ (in school) assistant/-e *m/f*; (in university) lecteur/-trice *m/f*
**2** *adj* ⟨*editor, manager*⟩ adjoint/-e

**associate** **1** *n* associé/-e *m/f*
**2** *vtr* (a) associer ⟨*idea, memory*⟩ (with à)
(b) to be ∼d with ⟨*person*⟩ faire partie de ⟨*movement, group*⟩; être mêlé/-e à ⟨*shady deal*⟩
**3** *vi* to ∼ with sb fréquenter qn

**association** *n* association *f*

**assorted** *adj* ⟨*objects, colours*⟩ varié/-e; ⟨*foodstuffs*⟩ assorti/-e

**assortment** *n* (of objects, colours) assortiment *m* (of de); (of people) mélange *m* (of de)

**assume** *vtr* (a) (suppose) supposer (that que)
(b) prendre ⟨*control, identity, office*⟩; assumer ⟨*responsibility*⟩; affecter ⟨*expression, indifference*⟩; under an ∼d name sous un nom d'emprunt

**assumption** *n* supposition *f*

**assurance** *n* assurance *f*

**assure** *vtr* assurer; to ∼ sb that assurer à qn que

**asterisk** *n* astérisque *m*

**asthma** *n* asthme *m*

**asthmatic** *n, adj* asthmatique ⟨*mf*⟩

**astonish** *vtr* surprendre, étonner

**astonished** *adj* étonné/-e (by, at par; to do de faire)

**astonishing** *adj* étonnant/-e

**astonishment** *n* étonnement *m*

**astound** *vtr* stupéfier

**astounding** *adj* incroyable

**astray** *adv* (a) to go ∼ (go missing) se perdre
(b) to lead sb ∼ (confuse) induire qn en erreur; (corrupt) détourner qn du droit chemin

**astride** **1** *adv* à califourchon
**2** *prep* à califourchon sur

**astrologer, astrologist** *n* astrologue *mf*

**astrology** *n* astrologie *f*

**astronaut** *n* astronaute *mf*

**astronomer** *n* astronome *mf*

**astronomic, astronomical** *adj* astronomique

**astronomy** *n* astronomie *f*

**astute** *adj* astucieux/-ieuse

**asylum** *n* asile *m*; **lunatic** ∼ asile de fous

**asylum-seeker** *n* demandeur/-euse *m/f* d'asile

**at** *prep*

■ Note *at* is often translated by *à*: *at the airport* = à l'aéroport; *at midnight* = à minuit; *at the age of 50* = à l'âge de 50 ans.
– Remember that *à* + *le* always becomes *au* and *à* + *les* always becomes *aux* (*au bureau, aux bureaux*).
– When *at* means *at the house, shop,* etc *of*, it is translated by *chez*: *at Amanda's* = chez Amanda; *at the hairdresser's* = chez le coiffeur.
– For examples and other usages, see the entry below.
– *At* is used with many verbs, adjectives and nouns (*look at, good at, at last*) etc. For translations consult the appropropriate verb, adjective or noun entry.

(a) à; ∼ **school** à l'école; ∼ **4 o'clock** à quatre heures; ∼ **Easter** à Pâques; ∼ **night** la nuit; ∼ **the moment** en ce moment
(b) chez; ∼ **my house** chez moi; ∼ **home** à la maison, chez soi

**atheist** *n, adj* athée ⟨*mf*⟩

**Athens** *pr n* Athènes

**athlete** *n* athlète *mf*

**athlete's foot** *n* mycose *f*

**athletic** *adj* athlétique

**athletics** *n* (GB) athlétisme *m*; (US) sports *mpl*

**Atlantic** **1** *pr n* the ∼ l'Atlantique *m*  ⋯▸

**a**

**2** *adj* ‹coast› atlantique

**atlas** *n* atlas *m*

**ATM** *n* (*abbr* = **automated teller machine**) guichet *m* automatique

**atmosphere** *n* (a) (air) atmosphère *f*
(b) (mood) ambiance *f*; (bad) atmosphère *f*

**atom** *n* atome *m*

**atom bomb** *n* bombe *f* atomique

**atomic** *adj* atomique, nucléaire

**atrocious** *adj* atroce

**atrocity** *n* atrocité *f*

**attach** *vtr* attacher (**to** à)

**attaché** *n* attaché/-e *m/f*

**attaché case** *n* attaché-case *m*

**attached** *adj* (a) (fond) **to be ~ to** être attaché/-e à
(b) ‹document› ci-joint/-e

**attachment** *n* (a) (affection) attachement *m*
(b) (device) accessoire *m*
(c) (in e-mail) pièce-jointe *f*

**attack** **1** *n* (a) (gen) attaque *f* (**on** contre); (criminal) agression *f* (**against, on** contre); (terrorist) attentat *m*
(b) (of illness) crise *f* (**of** de)
**2** *vtr* (a) (gen) attaquer; (criminally) agresser ‹victim›
(b) s'attaquer à ‹task, problem›

**attacker** *n* (gen) agresseur *m*; (Mil, Sport) attaquant/-e *m/f*

**attempt** **1** *n* (a) tentative *f* (**to do** de faire); **to make an ~ to do** *or* **at doing** tenter de faire
(b) **to make an ~ on sb's life** attenter à la vie de qn
**2** *vtr* tenter (**to do** de faire); **~ed murder** tentative de meurtre

**attend** **1** *vtr* assister à ‹ceremony, meeting›; aller à ‹church, school›; suivre ‹class, course›
**2** *vi* être présent/-e
■ **attend to** s'occuper de ‹person, problem›

**attendance** *n* présence *f* (**at** à)

**attendant** *n* (in cloakroom, museum, car park) gardien/-ienne *m/f*; (at petrol station) pompiste *mf*; (at pool) surveillant/-e *m/f*

**attention** *n* (a) attention *f*; **to draw ~ to sth** attirer l'attention sur qch
(b) (Mil) **to stand to** *or* **at ~** être au garde-à-vous; **~!** garde-à-vous!

**attention deficit disorder** *n* troubles *mpl* chroniques de l'attention

**attentive** *adj* (alert) attentif/-ive; (solicitous) attentionné/-e (**to** à)

**attic** *n* grenier *m*; **the toys are in the ~** les jouets sont au grenier

**attic room** *n* mansarde *f*

**attitude** *n* attitude *f* (**to, towards** (GB) à l'égard de)

**attorney** *n* (US) avocat *m*

**attract** *vtr* attirer

**attraction** *n* (a) (favourable feature) attrait *m* (**of** de; **for** pour)
(b) (entertainment, sight) attraction *f*

(c) (sexual) attirance *f* (**to** pour)

**attractive** *adj* ‹person, offer› séduisant/-e; ‹child› charmant/-e; ‹place› attrayant/-e

**attribute** **1** *n* attribut *m*
**2** *vtr* attribuer (**to** à)

**aubergine** *n* (GB) aubergine *f*

**auburn** *adj* auburn *inv*

**auction** **1** *n* enchères *fpl*
**2** *vtr* (*also* **~ off**) vendre [qch] aux enchères

**auctioneer** *n* commissaire-priseur *m*

**auction house** *n* société *f* de commissaires-priseurs

**audacity** *n* audace *f*

**audible** *adj* audible

**audience** *n* (in cinema, concert, theatre) public *m*, salle *f*; (of radio programme) auditeurs *mpl*; (of TV programme) téléspectateurs *mpl*

**audience ratings** *n pl* indice *m* d'écoute

**audio** *adj* audio *inv*

**audiobook** *n* livre-cassette *m*

**audiovisual, AV** *adj* audiovisuel/-elle

**audit** **1** *n* audit *m*
**2** *vtr* auditer, vérifier

**audition** **1** *n* audition *f* (**for** pour)
**2** *vtr, vi* auditionner (**for** pour)

**auditor** *n* (a) commissaire *m* aux comptes
(b) (US) (student) auditeur/-trice *m/f*

**auditorium** *n* salle *f*

**augur** *vi* **to ~ well** être de bon augure

**August** *n* août *m*

**aunt** *n* tante *f*

**au pair** *n* (jeune) fille *f* au pair

**aura** *n* (of place) atmosphère *f*; (of person) aura *f*

**aural** *adj* (a) (gen) auditif/-ive
(b) (Sch) ‹comprehension, test› oral/-e

**auspicious** *adj* prometteur/-euse

**austere** *adj* austère

**austerity** *n* austérité *f*

**Australia** *pr n* Australie *f*

**Australian** **1** *n* Australien/-ienne *m/f*
**2** *adj* australien/-ienne; ‹embassy› d'Australie

**Austria** *pr n* Autriche *f*

**Austrian** **1** *n* Autrichien/-ienne *m/f*
**2** *adj* autrichien/-ienne; ‹embassy› d'Autriche

**authentic** *adj* authentique

**author** *n* auteur *m*

**authoritarian** *adj* autoritaire

**authoritative** *adj* (a) (forceful) autoritaire
(b) (reliable) ‹work› qui fait autorité; ‹source› bien informé/-e

**authority** *n* (a) autorité *f*; **the authorities** les autorités
(b) (permission) autorisation *f*

**authorization** *n* autorisation *f*

**authorize** *vtr* autoriser (**to do** à faire)

**autism** *n* autisme *m*

**autobiographical** *adj* autobiographique

**autobiography** *n* autobiographie *f*

**Autocue**® *n* prompteur *m*

**autograph** 1 *n* autographe *m*
2 *vtr* dédicacer

**automatic** 1 *n* (a) (washing machine) machine *f* à laver automatique
(b) (car) voiture *f* (à changement de vitesse) automatique
(c) (gun) automatique *m*
2 *adj* automatique

**automatically** *adv* automatiquement

**automatic pilot** *n* (device) pilote *m* automatique

**automation** *n* automatisation *f*

**automobile** *n* automobile *f*

**autonomy** *n* autonomie *f*

**autopsy** *n* autopsie *f*

**autumn** *n* automne *m*; **in ~** en automne

**auxiliary** *n*, *adj* auxiliaire (*mf*)

**availability** *n* (of option, service) existence *f*; **subject to ~** (of holidays, rooms, theatre seats) dans la limite des places disponibles

**available** *adj* disponible (**for** pour; **to** à)

**avalanche** *n* avalanche *f*

**avarice** *n* cupidité *f*

**avenge** *vtr* venger

**avenue** *n* (a) (street, road) avenue *f*
(b) (path, driveway) allée *f*

**average** 1 *n* moyenne *f* (**of** de); **on (the) ~** en moyenne; **above/below (the) ~** au-dessus de/au-dessous de la moyenne
2 *adj* moyen/-enne
3 *vtr* faire en moyenne

**averse** *adj* opposé/-e (**to** à); **to be ~ to doing** répugner à faire

**aversion** *n* aversion *f* (**to** pour)

**avert** *vtr* éviter; **to ~ one's eyes from sth** détourner les yeux de qch

**aviary** *n* volière *f*

**aviation** *n* aviation *f*

**avid** *adj* ⟨collector, reader⟩ passionné/-e; **to be ~ for sth** être avide de qch

**avocado** *n* (also **~ pear**) avocat *m*

**avoid** *vtr* (gen) éviter; esquiver ⟨issue, question⟩; **to ~ doing** éviter de faire

**await** *vtr* attendre

**awake** 1 *adj* (not yet asleep) éveillé/-e; (after sleeping) réveillé/-e; **wide ~** bien réveillé/-e; **the noise kept me ~** le bruit m'a empêché de dormir
2 *vtr* réveiller ⟨person⟩
3 *vi* ⟨person⟩ se réveiller

**award** 1 *n* (prize) prix *m* (**for** de)
2 *vtr* décerner ⟨prize⟩; attribuer ⟨grant⟩; accorder ⟨points, penalty⟩

**award ceremony** *n* cérémonie *f* de remise de prix

**award-winning** *adj* ⟨book, film⟩ primé/-e; ⟨writer⟩ lauréat/-e

**aware** *adj* (conscious) conscient/-e (**of** de); (informed) au courant (**of** de)

**awareness** *n* conscience *f* (**of** de; **that** que)

**away**

■ Note *away* often appears after a verb in English to show that an action is continuous or intense. If *away* does not change the basic meaning of the verb only the verb is translated: *he was snoring away* = il ronflait.

1 *adj* (Sport) ⟨goal, match, win⟩ à l'extérieur; **the ~ team** les visiteurs *mpl*
2 *adv* (a) **to be ~** être absent/-e (**from** de); **to be ~ on business** être en voyage d'affaires; **to be ~ from home** ne pas être chez soi, être absent/-e de chez soi; **she's ~ in Paris** elle est à Paris; **to crawl ~** partir en rampant; **3 km ~** à 3 km; **London is two hours ~** Londres est à deux heures d'ici; **my birthday is two months ~** mon anniversaire est dans deux mois
(b) (Sport) ⟨play⟩ à l'extérieur

**awe** *n* crainte *f* mêlée d'admiration; **to listen in ~** écouter impressionné/-e; **to be in ~ of sb** avoir peur de qn

**awe-inspiring** *adj* impressionnant/-e

**awful** *adj* (a) affreux/-euse, atroce; (in quality) exécrable
(b) **I feel ~** (ill) je ne me sens pas bien du tout; (guilty) je culpabilise
(c) (colloq) **an ~ lot (of)** énormément (de)

**awfully** *adv* extrêmement

**awkward** *adj* (a) ⟨tool⟩ peu commode; ⟨shape, design⟩ difficile
(b) (clumsy) ⟨person, gesture⟩ maladroit/-e
(c) ⟨issue, choice⟩ difficile; **at an ~ time** au mauvais moment
(d) (embarrassing) ⟨question⟩ embarrassant/-e; ⟨situation⟩ délicat/-e; ⟨silence⟩ gêné/-e
(e) (uncooperative) ⟨person⟩ difficile (**about** à propos de)

**awning** *n* (on shop) banne *f*, auvent *m*; (on tent, house) auvent *m*; (on market stall) bâche *f*

**awry** 1 *adj* de travers *inv*
2 *adv* **to go ~** mal tourner

**axe, ax** (US) 1 *n* hache *f*
2 *vtr* virer (colloq) ⟨employee⟩; supprimer ⟨jobs⟩; abandonner ⟨plan⟩

**axis** *n* axe *m*

**axle** *n* essieu *m*

# Bb

**b**, **B** *n* (a) (letter) b, B *m*
(b) B (Mus) si *m*

**BA** *n* (*abbr* = **Bachelor of Arts**) (degree)
diplôme *m* universitaire de lettres

**babe** *n* (colloq) super nana *f* (colloq)

**baby** ⊡ *n* bébé *m*
⊡ *adj* ⟨*clothes, food*⟩ pour bébés; ⟨*brother, sister*⟩ petit/-e (*before n*); **~ seal** bébé phoque

**babysit** *vi* faire du babysitting

**babysitter** *n* baby-sitter *mf*

**babysitting** *n* baby-sitting *m*

**baccalaureate** *n* European/International Baccalaureate baccalauréat *m* européen/international

**bachelor** *n* célibataire *m*

**Bachelor of Arts** *n* (person) licencié/-e *m/f* ès lettres

**back** ⊡ *n* (a) (of person, animal) dos *m*; **to turn one's ~ on sb/sth** tourner le dos à qn/qch; **behind sb's ~** dans le dos de qn
(b) (of page, cheque, hand, envelope, coat) dos *m*; (of vehicle, plane, building, head) arrière *m*; (of chair, sofa) dossier *m*; (of cupboard, drawer, fridge, bus) fond *m*; **the ones at the ~ couldn't see** ceux qui étaient derrière ne pouvaient pas voir; **the steps at the ~ of the building** l'escalier à l'arrière de l'immeuble; **at the ~ of the drawer** au fond du tiroir; **at the ~ of the plane/bus** à l'arrière de l'avion/au fond du bus; **in the ~ (of the car)** à l'arrière
(c) (Sport) arrière *m*; **left ~** arrière gauche
⊡ *adj* ⟨*paw, wheel*⟩ arrière; ⟨*bedroom*⟩ du fond; ⟨*page*⟩ dernier/-ière (*before n*); ⟨*garden, gate*⟩ de derrière
⊡ *adv* (a) **to be ~** être de retour; **I'll be ~ in five minutes** je reviens dans cinq minutes; **to come ~** rentrer (**from** de); **to come ~ home** rentrer chez soi
(b) **to give/put sth ~** rendre/remettre qch; **to phone ~** rappeler; **I'll write ~ (to him)** je lui répondrai
(c) ⟨*look, jump, lean*⟩ en arrière
(d) **~ in 1964/April** en 1964/avril
(e) **to travel to London and ~** faire un aller-retour à Londres
⊡ *vtr* (a) (support) soutenir ⟨*candidate, bill*⟩; apporter son soutien à ⟨*project*⟩; justifier ⟨*claim*⟩ (**with** à l'aide de); financer ⟨*venture*⟩
(b) **to ~ the car into the garage** rentrer la voiture au garage en marche arrière
(c) (bet on) parier sur ⟨*favourite, winner*⟩
⊡ **back and forth** *phr* **to go** *or* **travel ~ and forth** (commute) ⟨*person, bus*⟩ faire la navette (**between** entre); **to go** *or* **walk ~ and forth** faire des allées et venues (**between** entre); **to sway ~ and forth** se balancer

■ **back away** reculer; **to ~ away from** s'éloigner de ⟨*person*⟩; chercher à éviter ⟨*confrontation*⟩
■ **back down** céder
■ **back out:** ¶ **~ out (a)** ⟨*car, driver*⟩ sortir en marche arrière
(b) ⟨*person*⟩ se désister; **to ~ out of** annuler ⟨*deal*⟩
¶ **~ [sth] out: to ~ the car out of the garage** faire sortir la voiture du garage en marche arrière
■ **back up** confirmer ⟨*claims, theory*⟩; soutenir ⟨*person*⟩; (Comput) sauvegarder

**backache** *n* **to have ~** avoir mal au dos

**backbencher** *n* (GB Pol) député *m* (sans portefeuille ministériel)

**backbone** *n* colonne *f* vertébrale

**back cover** *n* dos *m*

**backdate** *vtr* antidater ⟨*cheque, letter*⟩

**back door** *n* (of car) portière *f* arrière; (of building) porte *f* de derrière

**backdrop** *n* toile *f* de fond

**backer** *n* (a) (supporter) allié/-e *m/f*
(b) (of project) commanditaire *m*; (of business) bailleur *m* de fonds

**backfire** *vi* (a) ⟨*scheme*⟩ avoir l'effet inverse; **to ~ on sb** se retourner contre qn
(b) ⟨*car*⟩ pétarader

**backgammon** *n* jaquet *m*

**background** ⊡ *n* (a) (of person) (social) milieu *m*; (family) origines *fpl*; (professional) formation *f*
(b) (of events, situation) contexte *m*; **against a ~ of violence** dans un climat de violence; **to remain in the ~** rester au second plan; **voices in the ~** des voix en bruit de fond
(c) (of painting, photo, scene) arrière-plan *m*; **in the ~** à l'arrière-plan
⊡ *adj* (a) ⟨*information*⟩ sur les origines de la situation; **~ reading** lectures *fpl* complémentaires
(b) ⟨*music, lighting*⟩ d'ambiance; ⟨*noise*⟩ de fond

**backhand** *n* (Sport) revers *m*

**backhander** *n* (colloq) (bribe) pot-de-vin *m*

**backing** *n* (a) (support) soutien *m*
(b) (reverse layer) revêtement *m* intérieur

**backing singer** *n* chanteur/-euse *m/f* d'accompagnement

**backing vocals** *n pl* chœurs *mpl*

**backlash** *n* réaction *f* violente (**against** contre)

**backlog** *n* retard *m*; **I've got a huge ~ (of work)** j'ai plein de travail en retard

**back number** *n* ancien numéro *m*

**backpack** ⊡ *n* sac *m* à dos

**2** *vi* to go ~ing partir en voyage avec son sac à dos

**backpacker** *n* routard/-e *m/f*

**back pay** *n* rappel *m* de salaire

**back-pedal** *vi* (figurative) faire marche arrière

**back rest** *n* dossier *m*

**back seat** *n* siège *m* arrière; **to take a ~** (figurative) s'effacer

**backside** *n* (colloq) derrière *m* (colloq)

**backstage** *adv* dans les coulisses

**backstreet** **1** *n* petite rue *f*
**2** *adj* ⟨*loanshark, abortionist*⟩ clandestin/-e

**backstroke** *n* dos *m* crawlé

**back to back** *adv* **to stand ~** ⟨*two people*⟩ se mettre dos à dos

**back to front** *adj, adv* à l'envers

**backtrack** *vi* rebrousser chemin; (figurative) faire marche arrière

**backup** **1** *n* (gen) soutien *m*; (Mil) renforts *mpl*; (Comput) sauvegarde *f*
**2** *adj* ⟨*copy, disk, file*⟩ de sauvegarde

**backward** **1** *adj* **(a)** ⟨*look, step*⟩ en arrière
**(b)** ⟨*nation*⟩ arriéré/-e
**(c)** ⟨*person*⟩ arriéré/-e
**2** *adv* (*also* **backwards**) **(a)** ⟨*walk*⟩ à reculons; ⟨*lean, step, fall*⟩ en arrière; **to move ~** reculer; **to walk ~ and forward** faire des allées et venues
**(b)** ⟨*count*⟩ à rebours; ⟨*play*⟩ à l'envers

**backwards** = BACKWARD 2

**backwater** *n* village *m* tranquille, trou *m* (colloq)

**backyard** *n* **(a)** (GB) (courtyard) arrière-cour *f*
**(b)** (US) (back garden) jardin *m* de derrière

**bacon** *n* bacon *m*, ≈ lard *m*; **~ and egg(s)** des œufs au bacon

**bacteria** *n pl* bactéries *fpl*

**bad** **1** *n* **the good and the ~** le bon et le mauvais; **there is good and ~ in everyone** il y a du bon et du mauvais dans chacun
**2** *adj* **(a)** (gen) mauvais/-e (*before n*); ⟨*joke*⟩ stupide; ⟨*language*⟩ grossier/-ière; **to be ~ at** être mauvais/-e en ⟨*subject*⟩; **not ~** (colloq) pas mal (colloq); **too ~ !** (sympathetic) pas de chance!; (hard luck) tant pis!; **it will look ~** cela fera mauvais effet; **to feel ~** avoir mauvaise conscience (**about** à propos de)
**(b)** (serious) ⟨*accident, injury, mistake*⟩ grave; **a ~ cold** un gros rhume
**(c) it's ~ for you** *or* **your health** c'est mauvais pour la santé
**(d) to have a ~ back** souffrir du dos; **to have a ~ chest** être malade des poumons; **to be in a ~ way** (colloq) aller très mal
**(e)** ⟨*fruit*⟩ pourri/-e; **to go ~** pourrir

**badge** *n* (gen) badge *m*; (official) insigne *m*

**badly** *adv* **(a)** ⟨*begin, behave, sleep*⟩ mal; ⟨*made, worded*⟩ mal; **to go ~** mal se passer; ⟨*exam, interview*⟩ mal se passer; **to do ~** ⟨*candidate, company*⟩ obtenir de mauvais résultats; **to take sth ~** mal prendre qch

**(b)** ⟨*suffer*⟩ beaucoup; ⟨*affect*⟩ sérieusement; ⟨*hurt, damaged*⟩ gravement
**(c) to want/need sth ~** avoir très envie de/grand besoin de qch

**badly behaved** *adj* désobéissant/-e

**badly off** *adj* pauvre

**bad-mannered** *adj* ⟨*person*⟩ mal élevé/-e

**badminton** *n* badminton *m*

**bad-tempered** *adj* (temporarily) irrité/-e; (habitually) irritable

**baffle** *vtr* rendre [qn] perplexe, confondre

**baffled** *adj* perplexe (**by** devant)

**bag** **1** *n* sac *m* (**of** de)
**2 bags** *n pl* bagages *mpl*; **to pack one's ~s** faire ses bagages; (figurative) faire ses valises
**IDIOMS to have ~s under one's eyes** avoir des valises sous les yeux (colloq)

**baggage** *n* bagages *mpl*

**baggage allowance** *n* franchise *f* de bagages

**baggage reclaim** *n* réception *f* des bagages

**baggy** *adj* large, ample

**bagpipes** *n* cornemuse *f*

**bail** *n* caution *f*; **to be (out) on ~** être libéré/-e sous caution
■ **bail out**: ¶ ~ **out** (of plane) sauter; ¶ ~ [sb] **out** (gen) tirer [qn] d'affaire ⟨*person*⟩; (Law) payer la caution pour ⟨*person*⟩

**bailiff** *n* huissier *m*

**bait** *n* appât *m*

**bake** **1** *vtr* faire cuire [qch] au four ⟨*dish, vegetable*⟩; faire ⟨*bread, cake*⟩
**2** *vi* **(a)** (make bread) faire du pain; (make cakes) faire de la pâtisserie
**(b)** (cook) ⟨*food*⟩ cuire

**baked beans** *n pl* haricots *mpl* blancs à la sauce tomate

**baked potato** *n* pomme *f* de terre en robe des champs (au four)

**baker** *n* boulanger/-ère *m/f*

**bakery** *n* boulangerie *f*

**balance** **1** *n* **(a)** équilibre *m* (**between** entre); **to lose one's ~** perdre l'équilibre; **the right ~** le juste milieu
**(b)** (scales) balance *f*; **to hang in the ~** être en jeu
**(c)** (of account) solde *m*; **to pay the ~** verser le surplus
**2** *vtr* **(a)** mettre [qch] en équilibre ⟨*ball, plate*⟩ (**on** sur)
**(b)** (compensate for) (*also* ~ **out**) compenser, équilibrer
**(c)** (counterbalance) contrebalancer ⟨*weights*⟩
**(d)** (adjust) équilibrer ⟨*diet, budget*⟩; **to ~ the books** dresser le bilan
**3** *vi* **(a)** ⟨*person*⟩ se tenir en équilibre (**on** sur); ⟨*object*⟩ tenir en équilibre (**on** sur)
**(b)** (*also* ~ **out**) s'équilibrer
**(c)** ⟨*books, figures*⟩ être en équilibre
**4 balanced** *pp adj* ⟨*person, view, diet*⟩ équilibré/-e; ⟨*article, report*⟩ objectif/-ive

**balance of payments** *n* balance *f* des paiements

**balance of power** *n* équilibre *m* des forces

**balance of trade** *n* balance *f* du commerce extérieur

**balance sheet** *n* bilan *m*

**balcony** *n* **(a)** (in house, hotel) balcon *m*
**(b)** (in theatre) deuxième balcon *m*

**bald** *adj* **(a)** ⟨*man, head*⟩ chauve
**(b)** ⟨*tyre*⟩ lisse

**Balkan** ⟨1⟩ **Balkans** *pr n pl* the ~s les Balkans *mpl*
⟨2⟩ *adj* balkanique

**ball** ⟨1⟩ *n* **(a)** (gen) balle *f*; (in football, rugby) ballon *m*; (in billiards) bille *f*
**(b)** (of dough, clay) boule *f* (of de); (of wool, string) pelote *f* (of de)
**(c)** (dance) bal *m*
⟨2⟩ **balls** *n pl* (slang) **(a)** (testicles) couilles *fpl* (slang)
**(b)** (rubbish) conneries *fpl* (slang)

**ballet** *n* ballet *m*

**ball gown** *n* robe *f* de bal

**balloon** *n* **(a)** ballon *m*
**(b)** (*also* **hot air ~**) montgolfière *f*

**ballot** ⟨1⟩ *n* **(a)** scrutin *m*
**(b)** (*also* **~ paper**) bulletin *m* de vote
⟨2⟩ *vtr* consulter [qn] (par vote) (on sur)

**ballot box** *n* urne *f* (électorale)

**ballpark figure** *n* (colloq) chiffre *m* approximatif

**ballpoint (pen)** *n* stylo *m* (à) bille

**ballroom** *n* salle *f* de danse

**ballroom dancing** *n* danse *f* de salon

**Baltic** *adj* the ~ Sea la mer *f* Baltique

**ban** ⟨1⟩ *n* interdiction *f* (on de)
⟨2⟩ *vtr* (gen) interdire; suspendre ⟨*athlete*⟩; to ~ **sb from doing** interdire à qn de faire

**banal** *adj* banal/-e

**banana** *n* banane *f*

**band** *n* **(a)** (of people) groupe *m* (of de); (of musicians) (rock) groupe (de rock); (municipal) fanfare *f*; **jazz ~** orchestre *m* de jazz
**(b)** (strip) bande *f*
**(c)** (GB) (of age, income tax) tranche *f*
**(d)** (around arm) brassard *m*; **(hair) ~** bandeau *m*

■ **band together** se réunir (to do pour faire)

**bandage** ⟨1⟩ *n* bandage *m*
⟨2⟩ *vtr* bander ⟨*head, limb, wound*⟩

**bandit** *n* bandit *m*

**bandwagon** *n*
IDIOMS **to jump** *or* **climb on the ~** prendre le train en marche

**bang** ⟨1⟩ *n* **(a)** (of explosion) détonation *f*, boum *m*; (of door, window) claquement *m*
**(b)** (knock) coup *m*
⟨2⟩ *adv* (colloq) ~ **in the middle** en plein centre
⟨3⟩ *vtr* **(a)** taper sur ⟨*drum, saucepan*⟩; to ~ **sth down on the table** poser bruyamment

qch sur la table; **to ~ one's head** se cogner la tête (**on** contre); **to ~ one's fist on the table** taper du poing sur la table
**(b)** (slam) claquer ⟨*door, window*⟩
⟨4⟩ *vi* ⟨*door, shutter*⟩ claquer
IDIOMS ~ **goes** (colloq) **my holiday/my promotion** je peux dire adieu à mes vacances/mon avancement

■ **bang into**: ¶ ~ **into** [sb/sth] heurter

**bangle** *n* bracelet *m*

**banish** *vtr* bannir (**from** de)

**banister, bannister** (GB) *n* rampe *f* (d'escalier)

**bank** ⟨1⟩ *n* **(a)** banque *f*
**(b)** (of river, lake) rive *f*; (of major river) bord *m*; (of canal) berge *f*
**(c)** (mound) talus *m*; (of snow) congère *f*; (of flowers) massif *m*; (of fog, mist) banc *m*
⟨2⟩ *vi* **to ~ with the National** avoir un compte (bancaire) à la Nationale

■ **bank on** compter sur ⟨*person*⟩ (**to do** pour faire); **to ~ on doing** escompter faire

**bank account** *n* compte *m* bancaire

**bank card** *n* carte *f* bancaire

**bank charges** *n pl* frais *mpl* bancaires

**bank clerk** *n* employé/-e *m/f* de banque

**banker** *n* banquier/-ière *m/f*

**banker's draft** *n* traite *f* bancaire

**banker's order** *n* virement *m* bancaire

**bank holiday** *n* (GB) jour *m* férié; (US) jour *m* de fermeture des banques

**banking** *n* **(a)** (business) opérations *fpl* bancaires
**(b)** (profession) la banque

**banking hours** *n pl* heures *fpl* d'ouverture des banques

**bank manager** *n* directeur/-trice *m/f* d'agence bancaire

**banknote** *n* billet *m* de banque

**bank robber** *n* cambrioleur/-euse *m/f* de banque

**bank robbery** *n* cambriolage *m* de banque

**bankroll** *vtr* (colloq) financer

**bankrupt** *adj* ⟨*person*⟩ ruiné/-e; ⟨*economy*⟩ en faillite; **to go ~** faire faillite

**bankruptcy** *n* faillite *f*

**bank statement** *n* relevé *m* de compte

**banner** *n* banderole *f*

**baptism** *n* baptême *m*

**baptize** *vtr* baptiser

**bar** ⟨1⟩ *n* **(a)** (of metal, wood) barre *f*; (on cage, window) barreau *m*
**(b)** (pub) bar *m*; (counter) comptoir *m*
**(c)** ~ **of soap** savonnette *f*; ~ **of chocolate** tablette *f* de chocolat
**(d)** (Law) (profession) the ~ le barreau
**(e)** (Sport) barre *f*
**(f)** (Mus) mesure *f*
⟨2⟩ *prep* sauf; **all ~ one** tous sauf un seul/une seule
⟨3⟩ *vtr* **(a)** barrer ⟨*way, path*⟩; **to ~ sb's way** barrer le passage à qn

**(b)** (ban) exclure ⟨person⟩ (**from sth** de qch); **to ~ sb from doing** interdire à qn de faire

**barbaric** adj barbare

**barbecue** n barbecue m

**barbed wire, barbwire** (US) n (fil m de fer) barbelé m

**barber** n coiffeur m (pour hommes)

**Barcelona** pr n Barcelone

**bar chart** n histogramme m

**bar code** n code m à barres

**bare** ⓵ adj (gen) nu/-e; ⟨cupboard, room⟩ vide; **with one's ~ hands** à mains nues; **the ~ minimum** le strict nécessaire
⓶ vtr **to ~ one's teeth** montrer les dents

**bareback** adv ⟨ride⟩ à cru

**barefoot** ⓵ adj **to be ~** être nu-pieds
⓶ adv ⟨run, walk⟩ pieds nus

**barely** adv à peine

**bargain** ⓵ n **(a)** (deal) marché m (**between** entre)
**(b)** (good buy) affaire f
⓶ vi **(a)** (for deal) négocier (**with** avec)
**(b)** (over price) marchander (**with** avec)
■ **bargain for, bargain on** s'attendre à

**bargaining** ⓵ n négociations fpl
⓶ adj ⟨position, power⟩ de négociation

**barge** ⓵ n péniche f; (for freight) chaland m
⓶ vi **to ~ past sb** passer devant qn en le bousculant
■ **barge in** (enter noisily) faire irruption; (interrupt) interrompre brutalement

**bark** ⓵ n **(a)** (of tree) écorce f
**(b)** (of dog) aboiement m
⓶ vi aboyer (**at sb/sth** après qn/qch)

**barley** n orge f

**barmaid** n serveuse f de bar

**barman** n barman m

**barn** n (for crops) grange f; (for cattle) étable f

**baron** n baron m

**barracks** n caserne f

**barrage** n (gen) barrage m; (Mil) tir m de barrage

**barrel** n **(a)** (for beer, wine) tonneau m, fût m; (for oil) baril m
**(b)** (of gun) canon m

**barricade** n barricade f

**barrier** n barrière f

**barrier cream** n crème f protectrice

**barring** prep à moins de

**barrister** n (GB) avocat/-e m/f

**barter** vi (exchange) faire du troc; (haggle) marchander

**base** ⓵ n (gen, Mil) base f; (of tree, lamp) pied m
⓶ adj ignoble
⓷ vtr fonder (**on** sur); **the film is ~d on a true story** le film est tiré d'une histoire vraie; **to be ~d in Paris** ⟨person, company⟩ être basé/-e à Paris

**baseball** n base-ball m

**basement** n sous-sol m; **in the ~** au sous-sol

**bash** ⓵ n (colloq) **(a)** (blow) coup m
**(b)** (attempt) tentative f; **to have a ~ at sth, to give sth a ~** s'essayer à qch
**(c)** (party) grande fête f
⓶ vtr cogner ⟨person⟩; rentrer dans ⟨tree, wall, kerb⟩
■ **bash into**: **~ into [sth]** rentrer dans

**bashful** adj timide

**basic** adj **(a)** (gen) essentiel/-ielle; ⟨problem, principle⟩ fondamental/-e
**(b)** (in bathroom) lavabo m; (portable) cuvette f
**(b)** (elementary) ⟨knowledge, skill⟩ élémentaire; ⟨wage, training⟩ de base

**basically** adv fondamentalement

**basics** n pl essentiel m; **to get down to ~** aborder l'essentiel

**basil** n basilic m

**basin** n **(a)** (bowl) bol m
**(b)** (in bathroom) lavabo m; (portable) cuvette f

**basis** n base f (**for, of** de); **on a regular/temporary ~** régulièrement/à titre provisoire

**basket** n panier m

**basketball** n (game) basket(-ball) m; (ball) ballon m de basket

**bass** n basse f

**bass drum** n grosse caisse f

**bass guitar** n basse f

**bastard** n **(a)** (illegitimate child) bâtard/-e m/f
**(b)** (slang) salaud m (slang)

**baste** vtr (Culin) arroser

**bastion** n bastion m

**bat** ⓵ n **(a)** (in cricket, baseball) batte f; (in table tennis) raquette f
**(b)** (Zool) chauve-souris f
⓶ vi (be batsman) être le batteur; (handle a bat) manier la batte

**batch** n (of loaves) fournée f; (of goods) lot m

**bated** adj **with ~ breath** en retenant son souffle

**bath** ⓵ n bain m; (GB) (tub) baignoire f; **to have a ~** prendre un bain
⓶ **baths** n pl **(a)** (for swimming) piscine f
**(b)** (in spa) thermes mpl
⓷ vtr (GB) baigner

**bathe** ⓵ vtr laver ⟨wound⟩ (**in** dans; **with** à)
⓶ vi **(a)** (swim) se baigner
**(b)** (US) (take bath) prendre un bain
**(c) to be ~d in** ruisseler de ⟨sweat⟩; être inondé/-e de ⟨light⟩

**bather** n baigneur/-euse m/f

**bathing** n baignade f

**bathing cap** n bonnet m de bain

**bathing costume** n costume m de bain

**bath mat** n tapis m de bain

**bathrobe** n sortie f de bain

**bathroom** n **(a)** salle f de bains
**(b)** (US) (lavatory) toilettes fpl

**bathroom cabinet** n armoire f de toilette

**bathroom scales** n pl pèse-personne m

**bath towel** n serviette f de bain

**bathtub** n baignoire f

**baton** n (GB) (policeman's) matraque f; (traffic policeman's) bâton m; (Mus) baguette f; (in relay race) témoin m

**batsman** n batteur m

**batter** 1 n pâte f
  2 vtr battre

**battered** adj (a) ⟨kettle, hat⟩ cabossé/-e; ⟨suitcase⟩ très abîmé/-e
  (b) ⟨wife⟩ battu/-e

**battery** n pile f; (in car) batterie f

**battery charger** n chargeur m de batteries

**battery farming** n élevage m en batterie

**battery powered** adj à piles

**battle** 1 n bataille f; (figurative) lutte f
  2 vi (gen, Mil) combattre (with sb contre qn); to ~ for sth/to do lutter pour qch/pour faire

**battlefield** n champ m de bataille

**battleship** n cuirassé m

**bawdy** adj ⟨song⟩ grivois/-e; ⟨person⟩ paillard/-e

**bawl** vi (weep) brailler; (shout) hurler

**bay** 1 n (a) (on coast) baie f
  (b) (Bot) (also ~ **tree**) laurier(-sauce) m
  (c) loading/parking ~ aire f de chargement/stationnement
  2 vi ⟨dog⟩ aboyer (at contre, après)
  IDIOMS to hold sb/sth at ~ tenir qn/qch à distance

**bay leaf** n feuille f de laurier

**bayonet** n baïonnette f

**BC** (abbr = **Before Christ**) av. J.-C.

**be**
  ■ Note for translations of there is, there are, here is and here are, see the entries THERE and HERE

  1 vi (a) être; she is French elle est française; we are late nous sommes en retard; he is a doctor/widower il est médecin/veuf; it is Monday c'est lundi; it's me! c'est moi!; ~ good! sois sage!
  (b) (physical and mental states) avoir; I am cold/hot j'ai froid/chaud; are you hungry/thirsty? as-tu faim/soif?; his hands were cold il avait froid aux mains
  (c) (weather) faire; it is cold/windy il fait froid/du vent; it is 40° il fait 40°
  (d) (health) aller; how are you? (polite) comment allez-vous?; (more informally) comment vas-tu?; (very informally) ça va?; how is your son? comment va votre fils?; ▶ WELL[1], FINE, BETTER
  (e) (visit) I've never been to Sweden je ne suis jamais allé en Suède; have you ever been to Africa? tu es déjà allé en Afrique?; has the postman been? est-ce que le facteur est passé?
  (f) (age) avoir; how old are you? quel âge as-tu?; I am 23 j'ai 23 ans
  (g) (in mathematics) faire; 2 plus 2 is 4 2 et 2 font 4
  (h) (cost) coûter; how much is it? combien ça coûte?
  (i) (phrases) so ~ it d'accord; if I were you à ta place

  2 v aux (a) (in passives) être; the doors have been repainted les portes ont été repeintes, on a repeint les portes; it is said that... on dit que...
  (b) (in continuous tenses) we are going to London tomorrow nous allons à Londres demain; it is raining il pleut; he is reading il lit, il est en train de lire; ▶ FOR, SINCE
  (c) (with infinitive) devoir; you are to do it at once tu dois le faire tout de suite; they are to ~ married ils vont se marier; it was to ~ expected il fallait s'y attendre; it was nowhere to ~ found il était introuvable
  (d) (in tag questions) it's a lovely house, isn't it? c'est une très belle maison, n'est-ce pas?; they're not in the garden, are they? ils ne sont pas dans le jardin, par hasard?; today is Tuesday, isn't it? c'est bien mardi aujourd'hui?
  (e) (in short answers) 'you are not going out'—'yes I am!' 'tu ne sors pas'—'si!'; 'are you English?'—'yes, I am' 'vous êtes anglais?'—'oui', 'oui, je suis anglais'

**beach** n plage f

**beach ball** n ballon m de plage

**beach buggy** n buggy m

**beacon** n (a) (on runway) balise f
  (b) (lighthouse) phare m
  (c) (also **radio** ~) radiobalise f

**bead** n (a) perle f; (string of) ~s collier m
  (b) (of sweat, dew) goutte f

**beak** n bec m

**beam** 1 n (a) (of light, torch) rayon m; (of car lights, lighthouse) faisceau m
  (b) (wooden) poutre f
  2 vtr transmettre ⟨signal⟩
  3 vi rayonner

**bean** n haricot m

**beansprout** n germe m de soja

**bear** 1 n ours m
  2 vtr (a) (carry) porter; to ~ a resemblance to ressembler à; to ~ no relation to n'avoir aucun rapport avec; to ~ sth in mind tenir compte de qch
  (b) (endure) supporter; I can't ~ to watch je ne veux pas voir ça
  (c) (stand up to) résister à ⟨scrutiny, inspection⟩
  (d) (yield) donner ⟨fruit, crop⟩; ⟨investment⟩ rapporter ⟨interest⟩
  3 vi (a) to ~ left/right ⟨person⟩ prendre à gauche/à droite
  (b) to bring pressure to ~ on sb exercer une pression sur qn
  ■ **bear out** confirmer ⟨claim, story⟩; appuyer ⟨person⟩
  ■ **bear up** ⟨person⟩ tenir le coup; ⟨structure⟩ résister
  ■ **bear with**: ~ with [sb] être indulgent/-e avec; ~ with me for a minute pardonnez-moi un instant

**bearable** adj supportable

**beard** n barbe f

**bearded** adj barbu/-e

**bearer** *n* (of news, gift, letter) porteur/-euse *m/f*; (of passport) titulaire *mf*

**bearing** *n* **(a)** (of person) allure *f*
**(b) to have no/little ~ on sth** n'avoir aucun rapport/avoir peu de rapport avec qch
**(c) to take a compass ~** faire un relevé au compas

**bearings** *n pl* **to get one's ~** se repérer

**beast** *n* **(a)** (animal) bête *f*
**(b)** (colloq) (person) brute *f*

**beat** 1 *n* **(a)** (of drum, heart) battement *m*
**(b)** (rhythm) rythme *m*
**(c)** (of policeman) ronde *f*
2 *vtr* **(a)** battre; **to ~ sb with a stick** donner des coups de bâton à qn; **to ~ sb at tennis** battre qn au tennis; **to ~ time** (Mus) battre la mesure; **she beat me to it** elle a été plus rapide que moi
**(b) it ~s walking** c'est mieux que marcher; **you can't ~ Italian shoes** rien ne vaut les chaussures italiennes
3 *vi* ⟨waves, rain⟩ battre (**against** contre); ⟨person⟩ cogner (**at, on** à); ⟨heart, drum, wings⟩ battre
■ **beat back** repousser ⟨group, flames⟩
■ **beat down** ⟨rain⟩ tomber à verse (**on** sur); ⟨sun⟩ taper (**on** sur)
■ **beat off** repousser ⟨attacker⟩
■ **beat up** tabasser (colloq) ⟨person⟩

**beating** *n* **(a)** (punishment) raclée *f* (colloq), correction *f*
**(b)** (of drum, heart, wings) battement *m*

**beautician** *n* esthéticien/-ienne *m/f*

**beautiful** *adj* beau/belle (*before n*); ⟨weather, shot⟩ superbe; **a ~ place** un bel endroit.

──────────
■ **Note** the irregular form *bel* of the adjective *beau, belle* is used before masculine nouns beginning with a vowel or a mute 'h'.
──────────

**beautifully** *adv* **(a)** ⟨play, write⟩ admirablement
**(b)** ⟨furnished⟩ magnifiquement; **~ dressed** habillé/-e avec beaucoup de goût

**beauty** *n* beauté *f*

**beauty parlour** (GB), **beauty parlor** (US) *n* salon *m* de beauté

**beauty queen** *n* reine *f* de beauté

**beauty salon** *n* salon *m* de beauté

**beauty spot** *n* **(a)** (on skin) grain *m* de beauté; (fake) mouche *f*
**(b)** (place) beau site *m or* coin *m*

**beaver** *n* castor *m*

**because** 1 *conj* parce que
2 **because of** *phr* à cause de

**beckon** 1 *vtr* faire signe à; **to ~ sb in** faire signe à qn d'entrer
2 *vi* faire signe (**to sb to do** à qn de faire)

**become** 1 *vi* devenir; **to ~ ill** tomber malade
2 *v impers* **what has ~ of your brother?** qu'est-ce que ton frère est devenu?

**becoming** *adj* ⟨behaviour⟩ convenable; ⟨garment, haircut⟩ seyant/-e

**bed** *n* **(a)** lit *m*; **to go to ~** aller au lit
**(b)** (of flowers) parterre *m*
**(c)** (of sea) fond *m*; (of river) lit *m*

**bed and breakfast, B and B** *n* chambre *f* avec petit déjeuner, ≈ chambre *f* d'hôte

**bedclothes** *n pl* couvertures *fpl*

**bedraggled** *adj* dépenaillé/-e

**bedridden** *adj* alité/-e, cloué/-e au lit

**bedroom** *n* chambre *f* (à coucher)

**bedside** *n* chevet *m*

**bedsit, bedsitter** *n* (GB) chambre *f* meublée

**bedspread** *n* dessus *m* de lit

**bedtime** *n* **it's ~** c'est l'heure d'aller se coucher

**bee** *n* abeille *f*

**beech** *n* hêtre *m*

**beef** *n* bœuf *m*; **roast ~** rôti *m* de bœuf

**beefburger** *n* hamburger *m*

**beehive** *n* ruche *f*

**beeline** *n*
IDIOMS **to make a ~ for** se diriger tout droit vers

**beep** 1 *n* (of electronic device) bip *m*; (of car) coup *m* de klaxon®
2 *vi* ⟨device⟩ faire bip *or* bip-bip; ⟨car⟩ klaxonner

**beer** *n* bière *f*

**bee sting** *n* piqûre *f* d'abeille

**beet** *n* betterave *f*

**beetle** *n* scarabée *m*

**beetroot** *n* (GB) betterave *f*

**before** 1 *prep* **(a)** avant; **the day ~ yesterday** avant-hier; **the day ~ the exam** la veille de l'examen
**(b)** (in front of) devant
**(c)** (US) (in telling time) **ten ~ six** six heures moins dix
2 *adj* précédent/-e, d'avant; **the day ~** la veille; **the week ~** la semaine précédente **(a)** (beforehand)
3 *adv* **(a)** (beforehand) avant; **long ~** bien avant; (previously) auparavant
**two months ~** deux mois auparavant
**(b)** (already) déjà; **have you been to India ~?** est-ce que tu es déjà allé en Inde?; **I've never seen him ~ in my life** c'est la première fois que je le vois; **you never told me ~** tu ne m'as jamais dit ça
4 *conj* avant de (+ *infinitive*), avant que (+ *subj*); **~ I go, I would like to say that** avant de partir, je voudrais dire que; **~ he goes, I must remind him that** avant qu'il parte, il faut que je lui rappelle que

**beforehand** *adv* (ahead of time) à l'avance; (earlier) auparavant, avant

**befriend** *vtr* (look after) prendre [qn] sous son aile; (make friends with) se lier d'amitié avec

**beg** 1 *vtr* demander (**from** à); **to ~ sb for sth** demander qch à qn; **I ~ your pardon** je vous demande pardon ···>

**2** *vi* ⟨person⟩ mendier (**from** à); ⟨dog⟩ faire le beau; **to ~ for help** demander de l'aide

**beggar** *n* mendiant/-e *m/f*

**begin** **1** *vtr* commencer ⟨journey, meeting, meal, game⟩ (**with** par, avec); provoquer ⟨debate, dispute⟩; lancer ⟨campaign, trend⟩; déclencher ⟨war⟩; **to ~ doing** commencer à faire
**2** *vi* commencer; **to ~ with sth** commencer par qch; **to ~ again** recommencer
**3 to begin with** *phr* (at first) au début, au départ; (firstly) d'abord, premièrement

**beginner** *n* débutant/-e *m/f*

**beginning** *n* début *m*, commencement *m*; **in** *or* **at the ~** au début, au départ; **to go back to the ~** reprendre au début

**beginnings** *n pl* (of person, business) débuts *mpl*; (of movement) origines *fpl*

**behalf**: **on ~ of** (GB), **in ~ of** (US) *phr* ⟨act, speak⟩ au nom de, pour; ⟨phone, write⟩ de la part de; ⟨negotiate⟩ pour le compte de

**behave** **1** *vi* se comporter, se conduire (**towards** envers)
**2** *v refl* **to ~ oneself** bien se comporter; **~ yourself!** tiens-toi bien!

**behaviour** (GB), **behavior** (US) *n* (gen) comportement *m* (**towards** envers); (Sch) conduite *f*; **to be on one's best ~** bien se tenir

**behead** *vtr* décapiter

**behind** **1** *n* (colloq) derrière *m* (colloq)
**2** *adj* **to be ~ with** avoir du retard dans ⟨work⟩; **to be too far ~** avoir trop de retard
**3** *adv* ⟨follow on⟩ derrière; ⟨look, glance⟩ en arrière; **the car ~** la voiture de derrière
**4** *prep* (a) derrière; **~ my back** derrière le dos; (figurative) derrière mon dos; **~ the scenes** en coulisses
(b) (supporting) **to be (solidly) ~ sb** soutenir qn (à fond)

**beige** *n*, *adj* beige (*m*)

**Beijing** *pr n* Pékin, Bei-jing

**being** *n* (a) (human) ~ être *m* (humain)
(b) **to come into ~** prendre naissance

**Beirut** *pr n* Beyrouth

**Belarus** *pr n* Bélarus *f*

**belch** **1** *n* renvoi *m*, rot *m*
**2** *vtr* (also **~ out**) vomir, cracher ⟨smoke, fire⟩
**3** *vi* avoir un renvoi

**belfry** *n* beffroi *m*, clocher *m*

**Belgian** **1** *n* Belge *mf*
**2** *adj* belge; ⟨embassy⟩ de Belgique

**Belgium** *pr n* Belgique *f*

**belie** *vtr* démentir

**belief** *n* (a) (opinion) conviction *f* (**about** sur, à propos de)
(b) (confidence) confiance *f*, foi *f* (**in** dans)
(c) (religious faith) foi *f*

**believable** *adj* crédible

**believe** **1** *vtr* croire; **I don't ~ you!** ce n'est pas vrai!
**2** *vi* **to ~ in** croire à ⟨promises, ghosts⟩; croire en ⟨God⟩

**believer** *n* (in God) croyant/-e *m/f*; (in progress, liberty) adepte *mf* (**in** de)

**belittle** *vtr* rabaisser

**bell** *n* (in church) cloche *f*; (handbell) clochette *f*; (on toy, cat) grelot *m*; (on bicycle) sonnette *f*; **door ~** sonnette *f*
IDIOMS **that name rings a ~** ce nom me dit quelque chose

**belligerent** **1** *n* belligérant *m*
**2** *adj* ⟨person⟩ agressif/-ive; ⟨country⟩ belligérant/-e

**bellow** *vi* ⟨bull⟩ mugir (**with** de); ⟨person⟩ hurler

**bellows** *n pl* soufflet *m*

**belly** *n* ventre *m*

**bellyache** *n* (colloq) mal *m* au ventre

**bellybutton** *n* (colloq) nombril *m*

**belong** *vi* **to ~ to** ⟨property⟩ appartenir à ⟨person⟩; ⟨person⟩ faire partie de ⟨club, society, set⟩; **where do these books ~?** où vont ces livres?

**belongings** *n pl* affaires *fpl*; **personal ~** effets *mpl* personnels

**beloved** *n*, *adj* bien-aimé/-e (*m/f*)

**below** **1** *prep* au-dessous de; **~ freezing** au-dessous de zéro; **~ the surface** sous la surface
**2** *adv* **the apartment ~** l'appartement du dessous; **the people (in the street) ~** les gens en bas (dans la rue); **the village ~** le village en contrebas; **100 metres ~** 100 mètres plus bas; **see ~** (on page) voir ci-dessous

**belt** **1** *n* (a) (gen) ceinture *f*
(b) (Tech) courroie *f*
**2** *vtr* (colloq) (hit) flanquer une beigne à (colloq) ⟨person⟩
IDIOMS **to tighten one's ~** se serrer la ceinture; **that was below the ~** c'était un coup bas
■ **belt out**: **~ out** [sth], **~** [sth] **out** chanter [qch] à pleins poumons ⟨song⟩
■ **belt up** (a) (colloq) (shut up) la fermer (colloq), se taire
(b) (Aut) attacher sa ceinture de sécurité

**bemused** *adj* perplexe

**bench** *n* (a) (gen) banc *m*; (workbench) établi *m*
(b) (Law) (also **Bench**) (judges collectively) magistrature *f* (assise); (judges hearing a case) Cour *f*

**benchmark** **1** *n* (a) (gen) point *m* de référence
(b) (Comput) test *m* de performance
**2** *vtr* évaluer les performances de ⟨computer system⟩

**bend** **1** *n* (in road) tournant *m*, virage *m*; (in river) courbe *f*
**2** *vtr* plier ⟨arm, leg⟩; pencher ⟨head⟩; tordre ⟨pipe, nail, wire⟩
**3** *vi* (a) ⟨road, path⟩ tourner; ⟨branch⟩ ployer
(b) ⟨person⟩ se pencher; **to ~ forward** se pencher en avant
■ **bend down**, **bend over** se pencher

**beneath** [1] *prep* (a) sous; ∼ **the calm exterior** sous des apparences calmes
(b) **it is ∼ you to do** c'est indigne de toi de faire
[2] *adv* en dessous; **the apartment ∼** l'appartement en dessous

**benefactor** *n* bienfaiteur *m*

**beneficial** *adj* ⟨*effect, influence*⟩ bénéfique; ⟨*change*⟩ salutaire

**beneficiary** *n* bénéficiaire *mf*

**benefit** [1] *n* (a) (advantage) avantage *m* (from de)
(b) (financial aid) allocation *f*; **to be on ∼(s)** (GB) toucher les allocations
[2] *adj* ⟨*concert, match*⟩ de bienfaisance
[3] *vtr* profiter à ⟨*person*⟩; être avantageux/-euse pour ⟨*group, nation*⟩
[4] *vi* profiter; **to ∼ from** tirer profit de; **to ∼ from doing** gagner à faire
IDIOMS **to give sb the ∼ of the doubt** accorder à qn le bénéfice du doute

**benevolent** *adj* bienveillant/-e

**benign** *adj* (a) ⟨*person, smile*⟩ bienveillant/-e
(b) (Med) bénin/-igne

**bent** *adj* (a) ⟨*nail, wire, stick*⟩ tordu/-e; ⟨*person*⟩ (stooped) courbé/-e
(b) **to be ∼ on doing** vouloir à tout prix faire

**bereaved** *adj* endeuillé/-e, en deuil

**bereavement** *n* deuil *m*

**berry** *n* baie *f*

**berserk** *adj* **to go ∼** être pris/-e de folie furieuse

**berth** [1] *n* (a) (bunk) couchette *f*
(b) (at dock) mouillage *m*
[2] *vtr* faire mouiller ⟨*ship*⟩
[3] *vi* ⟨*ship*⟩ venir à quai
IDIOMS **to give sb/sth a wide ∼** (colloq) éviter qn/qch

**beset** *adj* **a country ∼ by strikes** un pays en proie aux grèves

**beside** *prep* (a) (next to) à côté de; ∼ **the sea** au bord de la mer
(b) (in comparison with) par rapport à
IDIOMS **to be ∼ oneself (with anger)** être hors de soi; **to be ∼ oneself (with joy)** être fou/folle de joie

**besides** [1] *adv* (a) (moreover) d'ailleurs
(b) (in addition) en plus, aussi
[2] *prep* en plus de

**besiege** *vtr* (Mil) assiéger; (figurative) assaillir

**besotted** *adj* follement épris/-e (with de)

**best** [1] *n* **the ∼** le meilleur/la meilleure *m/f*; **the ∼ of friends** les meilleurs amis/meilleures amies du monde; **at ∼** au mieux; **to make the ∼ of sth** s'accommoder de qch; **to do one's ∼ to do** faire de son mieux *or* faire (tout) son possible pour faire; **all the ∼!** (good luck) bonne chance!; (cheers) à ta santé!
[2] *adj* meilleur/-e; **the ∼ book I've ever read** le meilleur livre que j'aie jamais lu; **my ∼ dress** ma plus belle robe
[3] *adv* le mieux; ∼ **of all** mieux que tout

**best friend** *n* meilleur ami/meilleure amie *m/f*

**best man** *n* témoin *m*

**bestow** *vtr* accorder ⟨*honour*⟩ (on à); conférer ⟨*title*⟩ (on à)

**bestseller** *n* bestseller *m*

**best-selling** *adj* ⟨*product*⟩ le/la plus vendu/-e; **the ∼ novelist of 1999** le romancier qui s'est vendu le plus en 1999

**bet** [1] *n* pari *m*; (in casino) mise *f*
[2] *vtr* parier (on sur)
[3] *vi* parier (on sur); (in casino) miser

**betray** *vtr* trahir

**betrayal** *n* trahison *f*

**better**

■ Note When *better* is used as an adjective, it is translated by *meilleur* or *mieux* depending on the context (see 2 below, and note that *meilleur* is the comparative form of *bon*, *mieux* the comparative form of *bien*).

[1] *n* **the ∼ of the two** le meilleur/la meilleure *or* le/la mieux des deux; **so much the ∼** tant mieux
[2] *adj* meilleur/-e; mieux; **this wine is ∼** ce vin est meilleur; **to get ∼** ⟨*situation, weather*⟩ s'améliorer; ⟨*ill person*⟩ aller mieux; **things are getting ∼** ça va mieux; **to be ∼** ⟨*patient, cold*⟩ aller mieux; **to be a ∼ swimmer than sb** nager mieux que qn; **to be ∼ at** être meilleur/-e en ⟨*subject, sport*⟩; **it's ∼ than nothing** c'est mieux que rien; **the bigger/sooner the ∼** le plus grand/vite possible; **the less said about that the ∼** mieux vaut ne pas parler de ça
[3] *adv* mieux; **you had ∼ do, you'd ∼ do** (advising) tu ferais mieux de faire; (warning) tu as intérêt à faire; **we'd ∼ leave** on ferait mieux de partir
[4] *vtr* améliorer
IDIOMS **for ∼ (or) for worse** advienne que pourra; (in wedding vow) pour le meilleur et pour le pire; **to get the ∼ of** triompher de ⟨*opponent*⟩; **his curiosity got the ∼ of him** sa curiosité a pris le dessus; **to go one ∼** faire encore mieux (than que); **to think ∼ of it** changer d'avis

**better off** *adj* (a) (more wealthy) plus riche (than que)
(b) (in better situation) mieux

**betting** *n* paris *mpl*

**betting shop** *n* (GB) bureau *m* de PMU

**between** [1] *prep* (a) entre; ∼ **you and me, ∼ ourselves** entre nous; ∼ **now and next year** d'ici l'année prochaine
(b) **they drank the whole bottle ∼ (the two of) them** ils ont bu toute la bouteille à eux deux
[2] *adv* (*also* **in ∼**) (in space) au milieu, entre les deux; (in time) entre-temps; **the two main roads and the streets (in) ∼** les deux rues principales et les petites rues situées entre elles; **neither red nor orange, but somewhere in ∼** ni rouge ni orange mais entre les deux

**beverage** n boisson f, breuvage m

**beware** ① excl prenez garde!, attention!
② vi se méfier (**of** de); ~ **of...** attention à...

**bewildered** adj ⟨person⟩ déconcerté/-e (**at**, **by** par); ⟨look⟩ perplexe

**bewildering** adj déconcertant/-e

**bewitch** vtr ensorceler

**beyond** ① prep (a) (in space and time)
au-delà de
(b) ~ **one's means** au-dessus de ses moyens;
~ **all hope** au-delà de toute espérance; ~
**one's control** hors de son contrôle; **he is** ~
**help** on ne peut rien faire pour lui; **it's** ~ **me**
ça me dépasse
(c) (other than) en dehors de, à part
② adv au-delà
③ conj à part (+ infinitive)
IDIOMS **to be in the back of** ~ être au bout
du monde

**bias** ① n (a) (prejudice) parti m pris
(b) (tendency) tendance f
② vtr **to** ~ **sb against/in favour of** prévenir
qn contre/en faveur de

**biased, biassed** adj ⟨person⟩ partial/-e;
⟨report⟩ manquant d'objectivité; **to be** ~
⟨person⟩ avoir des partis pris; **to be** ~
**against** avoir un préjugé défavorable envers

**bib** n (baby's) bavoir m; (of apron, dungarees)
bavette f

**Bible** n Bible f

**biblical** adj biblique

**bibliography** n bibliographie f

**bicarbonate of soda** n bicarbonate m
de soude

**bicentenary, bicentennial** n
bicentenaire m

**biceps** n biceps m

**bicker** vi se chamailler (**about** au sujet de)

**bickering** n chamailleries fpl

**bicycle** ① n bicyclette f, vélo m; **on a/by** ~
à bicyclette
② adj ⟨pump⟩ à bicyclette; ⟨bell, lamp⟩ de
bicyclette; ⟨race⟩ cycliste

**bicycle clip** n pince f à vélo

**bicycle lane** n piste f cyclable

**bid** ① n (a) (at auction) enchère f (**for** sur; **of**
de)
(b) (for contract) soumission f
(c) (attempt) tentative f (**to do** pour faire)
② vtr (a) offrir ⟨money⟩ (**for** pour)
(b) (say) **to** ~ **sb good morning** dire bonjour
à qn
③ vi (at auction) enchérir (**for** sur); (for contract)
soumissionner (**for** pour)

**bidder** n (at auction) enchérisseur/-euse m/f;
**to go to the highest** ~ être adjugé/-e au plus
offrant/-e

**bidding** n (at auction) enchères fpl

**bide** vi
IDIOMS **to** ~ **one's time** attendre le bon
moment

**bidet** n bidet m

**bifocals** n pl verres mpl à double foyer

**big** adj (gen) grand/-e (before n); (bulky, fat)
gros/grosse (before n); ⟨meal⟩ copieux/-ieuse;
**to get** ~**(ger)** (taller) grandir; (fatter) grossir; **a**
~ **book** (thick) un gros livre; (large-format) un
grand livre; **his** ~ **brother** son grand frère,
son frère aîné; **a** ~ **mistake** une grave
erreur; **to be in** ~ **trouble** être dans le pétrin
(colloq); **to have** ~ **ideas, to think** ~ voir
grand

**bigamy** n bigamie f

**big business** n (a) les grandes
entreprises fpl
(b) **to be** ~ rapporter gros

**big dipper** n (GB) (at fair) montagnes fpl
russes

**big game** n gros gibier m

**bigheaded** adj (colloq) prétentieux/-ieuse

**bigmouth** n (colloq) **he's such a** ~ ! il ne
sait pas tenir sa langue!

**big name** n (in music, art) grand nom m; (in
film, sport) star f; **to be a** ~ être connu/-e (**in**
dans le monde de)

**bigoted** adj intolérant/-e, sectaire

**bigotry** n intolérance f, sectarisme m

**big screen** n grand écran m

**big shot** n (colloq) gros bonnet m (colloq)

**big toe** n gros orteil m

**big top** n (tent) grand chapiteau m

**bike** n (cycle) vélo m; (motorbike) moto f

**biker** n (colloq) motard m (colloq)

**bikini** n bikini® m

**bilingual** adj bilingue

**bill** ① n (a) (in restaurant) addition f; (for
services, electricity) facture f; (from hotel, doctor,
dentist) note f
(b) (Pol) projet m de loi
(c) (poster) affiche f
(d) (US) dollar ~ billet m d'un dollar
(e) (beak) bec m
② vtr **to** ~ **sb for sth** facturer qch à qn
IDIOMS **to fit** or **fill the** ~ faire l'affaire

**billboard** n panneau m d'affichage

**billet** vtr cantonner (**on, with** chez)

**billiards** n billard m

**billion** n (a thousand million) milliard m; (GB)
(a million million) billion m

**billionaire** n milliardaire mf

**billow** vi ⟨clouds, smoke⟩ s'élever en
tourbillons
■ **billow out** ⟨skirt, sail⟩ se gonfler; ⟨steam⟩
s'élever

**billy goat** n bouc m

**bimbo** n (colloq) ravissante idiote f
(derogatory)

**bin** n (GB) (for rubbish) poubelle f

**bind** vtr (a) (tie up) attacher (**to** à)
(b) **to be bound by** être tenu/-e par ⟨law,
oath⟩
(c) (also ~ **together**) unir ⟨people,
community⟩
(d) relier ⟨book⟩

**binder** n (for papers, lecture notes) classeur m

**binding** ① n reliure f

**2** adj ⟨agreement, contract⟩ qui engage
**binge** n (colloq) **to go on a ~** faire la noce
**bingo** n bingo m
**bin liner** n (GB) sac m poubelle
**binoculars** n pl jumelles fpl
**biochemist** n biochimiste mf
**biochemistry** n biochimie f
**biodegradable** adj biodégradable
**biodiversity** n diversité f biologique
**bioengineering** n génie m biologique
**biographical** adj biographique
**biography** n biographie f
**biological** adj biologique
**biological clock** n horloge f biologique
**biological warfare** n guerre f
biologique
**biologist** n biologiste mf
**biology** n biologie f
**biopsy** n biopsie f
**biotechnology** n biotechnologie f
**birch** n bouleau m
**bird** n **(a)** (Zool) oiseau m
**(b)** (GB) (colloq) (girl) nana f (colloq)
IDIOMS **to kill two ~s with one stone** faire
d'une pierre deux coups
**bird of prey** n oiseau m de proie
**bird's eye view** n vue f d'ensemble
**birdsong** n chant m des oiseaux
**bird-watching** n **to go ~** observer les
oiseaux
**biro®** n (GB) stylo-bille m, bic® m
**birth** n naissance f **(of** de)
**birth certificate** n certificat m de
naissance
**birth control** n (in society) contrôle m des
naissances; (by couple) contraception f
**birthday** n anniversaire m; **Happy
Birthday!** Bon or Joyeux Anniversaire!
**birthday party** n (for child) goûter m
d'anniversaire; (for adult) soirée f
d'anniversaire
**birthing pool** n piscine f d'accouchement
**birthmark** n tache f de naissance
**birth mother** n mère f biologique
**birthplace** n lieu m de naissance
**birthrate** n taux m de natalité
**birth sign** n signe m du zodiaque
**biscuit** n **(a)** (GB) biscuit m, petit gâteau m
**(b)** (US) pain m au lait
**bisexual** n, adj bisexuel/-elle (m/f)
**bishop** n **(a)** évêque m
**(b)** (in chess) fou m
**bit** **1** n **(a)** (gen) morceau m (**of** de); (of paper,
string, land) bout m (**of** de); (of book, film)
passage m
**(b)** (colloq) **a ~ (of)** un peu (de); **a little ~** un
petit peu
**(c)** (of horse) mors m
**2 a bit** phr (colloq) un peu; **a ~ early** un
peu trop tôt; **she isn't a ~ like me** elle ne me
ressemble pas du tout

IDIOMS **~ by ~** petit à petit; **~s and pieces**
(fragments) morceaux mpl; (belongings) affaires
fpl
**bitch** n **(a)** (dog) chienne f
**(b)** (colloq derogatory) garce f (colloq)
**bite** **1** n **(a)** morsure f; (from insect) piqûre f
**(b)** (mouthful) bouchée f; **to have a ~ to eat**
manger un morceau
**2** vtr ⟨animal, person⟩ mordre; ⟨insect⟩
piquer; **to ~ one's nails** se ronger les ongles
**3** vi ⟨fish⟩ mordre
■ **bite off**: **~ off [sth]**, **~ [sth] off** arracher
[qch] d'un coup de dent
**biting** adj **(a)** ⟨wind⟩ cinglant/-e
**(b)** ⟨comment⟩ mordant/-e
**bitter** adj **(a)** (gen) amer/-ère; ⟨wind⟩ glacial/-e;
⟨disappointment, truth⟩ cruel/-elle
IDIOMS **to the ~ end** jusqu'au bout
**bitterly** adv ⟨complain, speak⟩ amèrement;
⟨regret⟩ profondément; **it's ~ cold** il fait un
froid terrible
**bitterness** n amertume f
**bizarre** adj bizarre
**black** **1** n **(a)** (colour) noir m
**(b)** (also **Black**) (person) Noir/-e m/f
**(c) to be in the ~** être créditeur/-trice
**2** adj **(a)** (gen) noir/-e; ⟨night⟩ obscur/-e;
⟨tea⟩ nature; **to turn ~** noircir
**(b)** (also **Black**) ⟨community, culture⟩
noir/-e
■ **black out** ⟨person⟩ s'évanouir
**black and white** **1** n noir et blanc m
**2** adj ⟨TV, camera film⟩ noir et blanc inv;
⟨movie, photography⟩ (en) noir et blanc inv
**blackberry** n mûre f
**blackbird** n merle m
**blackboard** n tableau m (noir); **on the ~**
au tableau
**black box** n boîte f noire
**blackcurrant** n cassis m
**blacken** vtr noircir
**black eye** n œil m poché
**blackhead** n point m noir
**black ice** n verglas m
**blacklist** **1** n liste f noire
**2** vtr mettre [qn] à l'index
**blackmail** **1** n chantage m
**2** vtr faire chanter ⟨victim⟩
**blackmailer** n maître-chanteur m
**black market** n **on the ~** au marché
noir
**blackout** n **(a)** (power cut) panne f de
courant; (in wartime) black-out m
**(b)** (faint) étourdissement m
**Black Sea** pr n mer f Noire
**black sheep** n brebis f galeuse
**blacksmith** n forgeron m
**black tie** n (on invitation) '~' 'tenue f de
soirée'
**bladder** n vessie f
**blade** n (of knife, sword, axe) lame f; (of fan,
propeller, oar) pale f; (of grass) brin m
**blame** **1** n responsabilité f (**for** de)   ⋯⋮

**b**

2 *vtr* I ~ **you** c'est ta faute; **to ~ sb for sth** reprocher qch à qn; **to ~ sth on sb** tenir qn responsable de qch; **to be to ~ for sth** être responsable de qch
3 *v refl* **to ~ oneself for sth** se sentir responsable de qch

**blameless** *adj* irréprochable

**blancmange** *n* blanc-manger *m*

**bland** *adj* ⟨*food, flavour*⟩ fade; ⟨*person*⟩ terne

**blank** 1 *n* (a) (empty space) blanc *m*; **my mind's a ~** j'ai la tête vide
(b) (cartridge) cartouche *f* à blanc
2 *adj* (a) ⟨*paper, page*⟩ blanc/blanche; ⟨*screen*⟩ vide; ⟨*cassette*⟩ vierge
(b) ⟨*expression*⟩ ébahi/-e; **my mind went ~** j'ai eu un trou de mémoire
■ **blank out:** ~ **[sth] out,** ~ **out [sth]** rayer [qch] de sa mémoire

**blank cheque** (GB), **blank check** (US) *n* chèque *m* en blanc; (figurative) carte *f* blanche

**blanket** *n* (a) couverture *f*
(b) (of snow) couche *f*; (of cloud, fog) nappe *f*

**blare** *v* ■ **blare out:** ¶ ~ **out** ⟨*music, radio*⟩ jouer à plein volume; ¶ ~ **out [sth]** déverser ⟨*music*⟩

**blasphemous** *adj* ⟨*person*⟩ blasphémateur/-trice; ⟨*statement*⟩ blasphématoire

**blasphemy** *n* blasphème *m*

**blast** 1 *n* (a) (explosion) explosion *f*
(b) (of air) souffle *m*
(c) **at full ~** ⟨*play music*⟩ à plein volume
2 *vtr* (blow up) faire sauter; **to ~ a hole in the wall** percer un mur à l'explosif
■ **blast off** ⟨*rocket*⟩ décoller

**blast-off** *n* lancement *m*

**blatant** *adj* ⟨*lie, disregard*⟩ éhonté/-e; ⟨*abuse*⟩ flagrant/-e

**blatantly** *adv* ouvertement; **to be ~ obvious** sauter aux yeux

**blaze** 1 *n* (fire) incendie *m*; (in hearth) feu *m*, flambée *f*; **in a ~ of publicity** sous les feux des médias
2 *vtr* **to ~ a trail** faire œuvre de pionnier
3 *vi* (*also* ~ **away**) (a) ⟨*fire, house*⟩ brûler
(b) ⟨*lights*⟩ briller

**blazer** *n* blazer *m*

**blazing** *adj* (violent) ⟨*argument*⟩ violent/-e; ⟨*fire*⟩ ronflant/-e; ⟨*building, car*⟩ embrasé/-e

**bleach** 1 *n* (a) (disinfectant) eau *f* de javel
(b) (for hair) décolorant *m*
2 *vtr* décolorer ⟨*hair*⟩; blanchir ⟨*linen*⟩

**bleak** *adj* ⟨*landscape*⟩ désolé/-e; ⟨*weather*⟩ maussade; ⟨*outlook, future*⟩ sombre

**bleary** *adj* ⟨*eyes*⟩ bouffi/-e; **to be ~-eyed** avoir les yeux bouffis

**bleat** *vi* ⟨*sheep, goat*⟩ bêler

**bleed** 1 *vtr* **to ~ sb dry** saigner qn à blanc
2 *vi* saigner; **my finger's ~ing** j'ai le doigt qui saigne

**bleep** 1 *n* (signal) bip *m*, bip-bip *m*
2 *vtr* **to ~ sb** appeler qn (au bip), biper qn

**bleeper** *n* (GB) bip *m*

**blemish** *n* (gen) imperfection *f*; (on fruit) tache *f*; (pimple) bouton *m*

**blend** 1 *n* mélange *m* (**of** de)
2 *vtr* mélanger ⟨*ingredients, colours, styles*⟩
3 *vi* **to ~ (together)** ⟨*colours, tastes, styles*⟩ se fondre; **to ~ with** ⟨*colours, tastes, sounds*⟩ se marier à; ⟨*smells*⟩ se mêler à
■ **blend in:** ¶ ~ **in** s'harmoniser (**with** avec); ¶ ~ **[sth] in** incorporer ⟨*ingredient*⟩

**blender** *n* mixeur *m*, mixer *m*

**bless** *vtr* bénir; ~ **you!** (after sneeze) à vos souhaits!; **to be ~ed with** jouir de ⟨*health, beauty*⟩

**blessing** *n* (a) bénédiction *f*
(b) (good thing) bienfait *m*; **a ~ in disguise** un bienfait caché

**blight** *n* (on society) plaie *f* (**on** de); **urban ~** délabrement *m* urbain

**blind** 1 *n* (a) **the ~** les aveugles *mpl*
(b) (on window) store *m*
2 *adj* ⟨*person*⟩ aveugle; **to go ~** perdre la vue; ~ **in one eye** borgne
3 *vtr* (a) ⟨*injury, accident*⟩ rendre aveugle
(b) ⟨*sun, light*⟩ éblouir
(c) ⟨*pride, love*⟩ aveugler
IDIOMS **to turn a ~ eye** fermer les yeux (**to** sur)

**blind alley** *n* voie *f* sans issue

**blind date** *n* rendez-vous *m* avec un/-e inconnu/-e

**blindfold** 1 *n* bandeau *m*
2 *adj* (*also* ~**ed**) aux yeux bandés
3 *adv* les yeux bandés
4 *vtr* bander les yeux à ⟨*person*⟩

**blinding** *adj* ⟨*light*⟩ aveuglant/-e; ⟨*headache*⟩ atroce

**blindly** *adv* ⟨*obey, follow*⟩ aveuglément

**blindness** *n* cécité *f*; (figurative) aveuglement *m*

**blind spot** *n* (a) (in eye) point *m* aveugle
(b) (in car, on hill) angle *m* mort

**blink** *vi* ⟨*person*⟩ cligner des yeux; ⟨*light*⟩ clignoter

**blinker** *n* (a) (Aut) clignotant *m*
(b) ~**s** œillères *fpl*

**blinkered** *adj* ⟨*attitude, approach*⟩ borné/-e

**blip** *n* (on screen) spot *m*; (on graph) accident *m* (d'une courbe)

**bliss** *n* bonheur *m* parfait

**blissfully** *adv* ~ **happy** au comble du bonheur; ~ **ignorant** dans la plus parfaite ignorance

**blister** 1 *n* (on skin) ampoule *f*
2 *vi* ⟨*skin, paint*⟩ cloquer

**blister pack** *n* blister *m*, habillage *m* transparent

**blithely** *adv* (nonchalantly) avec insouciance; (cheerfully) allègrement

**blitz** 1 *n* bombardement *m* aérien
2 *vtr* bombarder

**blizzard** *n* tempête *f* de neige; (in Arctic regions) blizzard *m*

**bloated** adj ⟨face, body⟩ bouffi/-e; ⟨stomach⟩ ballonné/-e

**blob** n (a) (drop) grosse goutte f
(b) (shape) forme f floue

**block** ⬛1 n (a) (slab) bloc m
(b) ~ of flats immeuble m (d'habitation); office ~ immeuble de bureaux
(c) (of houses) pâté m de maisons
(d) (for butcher, executioner) billot m
⬛2 vtr bloquer ⟨exit, road, ball⟩; boucher ⟨drain, hole, artery, view⟩; to have a ~ed nose avoir le nez bouché
■ **block out**: ~ out [sth], ~ [sth] out (a) (hide) boucher ⟨view⟩; cacher ⟨light, sun⟩
(b) (suppress) refouler ⟨memory, problem⟩

**blockade** ⬛1 n blocus m
⬛2 vtr bloquer, faire le blocus de ⟨port⟩

**blockage** n obstruction f

**blockbook** vtr louer [qch] en groupe ⟨seats⟩

**blockbuster** n (colloq) (a) (book) livre m à succès, bestseller m
(b) (film) superproduction f

**block capitals, block letters** n pl in ~ (on form) en caractères mpl or capitales fpl d'imprimerie

**bloke** n (colloq) type m (colloq), mec m (colloq)

**blonde** ⬛1 n blonde f
⬛2 adj blond/-e

**blood** n sang m
IDIOMS in cold ~ de sang-froid

**blood bank** n banque f du sang

**bloodcurdling** adj à vous figer le sang dans les veines

**blood donor** n donneur/-euse m/f de sang

**blood group** n groupe m sanguin

**blood pressure** n tension f artérielle; high ~ hypertension f

**blood relation** n parent/-e m/f par le sang

**bloodshed** n effusion f de sang

**bloodshot** adj injecté/-e de sang

**blood sport** n sport m sanguinaire

**bloodstained** adj taché/-e de sang

**bloodstream** n sang m

**blood test** n analyse f de sang

**bloodthirsty** adj sanguinaire

**blood type** n groupe m sanguin

**bloody** ⬛1 adj (a) ⟨hand, body⟩ ensanglanté/-e; ⟨battle⟩ sanglant/-e
(b) (GB) (colloq) sacré/-e ⟨before n⟩; ~ fool! espèce d'idiot!
⬛2 adv (GB) (slang) sacrément (colloq)

**bloom** ⬛1 n (flower) fleur f; in ~ en fleur
⬛2 vi (a) (be in flower) être fleuri/-e; (come into flower) fleurir
(b) to be ~ing with health être resplendissant/-e de santé

**blossom** ⬛1 n (flower) fleur f; (flowers) fleurs fpl
⬛2 vi fleurir; (figurative) s'épanouir

**blot** ⬛1 n (gen) tache f; (of ink) pâté m; (figurative) ombre f

⬛2 vtr (a) (dry) sécher [qch] au buvard ⟨ink⟩
(b) (stain) tacher
■ **blot out** effacer ⟨memories⟩; masquer ⟨view⟩

**blotch** n (on skin) plaque f rouge; (of ink, colour) tache f

**blotchy** adj ⟨complexion⟩ marbré/-e

**blotting paper** n papier m buvard

**blouse** n chemisier m

**blow** ⬛1 n coup m
⬛2 vtr (a) the wind blew the door shut un coup de vent a fermé la porte; to be blown off course ⟨ship⟩ être dévié/-e par le vent
(b) ⟨person⟩ faire ⟨bubble, smoke ring⟩; souffler ⟨glass⟩; to ~ one's nose se moucher; to ~ one's whistle donner un coup de sifflet
(c) ⟨explosion⟩ faire ⟨hole⟩ (in dans); to be blown to pieces or bits by être réduit/-e en poussière par
(d) faire sauter ⟨fuse⟩; griller ⟨light bulb⟩
⬛3 vi (a) ⟨wind⟩ souffler; ⟨person⟩ souffler (into dans; on sur)
(b) to ~ in the wind ⟨flag, clothes⟩ voler au vent
(c) ⟨fuse⟩ sauter; ⟨bulb⟩ griller; ⟨tyre⟩ éclater
■ **blow away**: ¶ ~ away s'envoler; ¶ ~ [sth] away, ~ away [sth] ⟨wind⟩ emporter ⟨object⟩
■ **blow down** ⟨wind⟩ faire tomber ⟨tree⟩
■ **blow off**: ¶ ~ off ⟨hat⟩ s'envoler; ¶ ~ [sth] off ⟨wind⟩ emporter ⟨hat⟩; ⟨explosion⟩ emporter ⟨roof⟩
■ **blow out** souffler ⟨candle⟩; éteindre ⟨flames⟩
■ **blow over** ⟨storm⟩ s'apaiser; ⟨affair⟩ être oublié/-e
■ **blow up**: ¶ ~ up ⟨building⟩ sauter; ⟨bomb⟩ exploser
¶ ~ [sb/sth] up (a) faire sauter ⟨building, person⟩; faire exploser ⟨bomb⟩
(b) gonfler ⟨tyre⟩
(c) agrandir ⟨photograph⟩

**blow-dry** ⬛1 n brushing m
⬛2 vtr to ~ sb's hair faire un brushing à qn

**blowout** n (a) (electrical) court-circuit m
(b) (of tyre) crevaison f
(c) (colloq) (meal) gueuleton m (colloq)

**blowtorch** n lampe f à souder

**blubber** n graisse f de baleine

**bludgeon** vtr to ~ sb to death tuer qn à coups de matraque

**blue** ⬛1 n bleu m
⬛2 adj (a) bleu/-e
(b) (colloq) ⟨movie⟩ porno (colloq); ⟨joke⟩ cochon/-onne (colloq)
IDIOMS to appear/happen out of the ~ apparaître/se passer à l'improviste

**bluebell** n jacinthe f des bois

**blueberry** n (US) myrtille f

**blue cheese** n (fromage m) bleu m

**blue chip** adj ⟨company, share⟩ de premier ordre

**blue collar worker** n ouvrier m, col m bleu

**blue jeans** n pl jean m

**blueprint** n bleu m; (figurative) projet m (**for** pour; **for doing** pour faire)

**blues** n pl (a) (Mus) **the** ~ le blues m (b) (colloq) **to have the** ~ avoir le cafard (colloq)

**bluff** vtr, vi bluffer (colloq) IDIOMS **to call sb's** ~ prendre qn au mot

**blunder** ① n bourde f ② vi (a) (make mistake) faire une bourde (b) (move clumsily) **to** ~ **into sth** se cogner à qch

**blunt** ① adj (a) ⟨knife, scissors⟩ émoussé/-e; ⟨pencil⟩ mal taillé/-e; ⟨instrument⟩ contondant/-e (b) ⟨person, manner⟩ abrupt/-e; ⟨criticism⟩ direct/-e ② vtr émousser ⟨knife⟩

**bluntly** adv franchement

**blur** ① n image f floue ② vtr brouiller

**blurb** n (on book cover) texte m de présentation; (derogatory) baratin m

**blurred** adj indistinct/-e; ⟨image, idea⟩ flou/-e; ⟨memory⟩ confus/-e; **to have** ~ **vision** avoir des troubles de la vue

**blurt** v ■ **blurt out** laisser échapper ⟨truth, secret⟩

**blush** vi rougir (**at** devant; **with** de)

**blusher** n fard m à joues

**blustery** adj ~ **wind** bourrasque f

**blu-tak®** n patafix® m

**BO** n (colloq) (abbr = **body odour**) odeur f corporelle; **he's got** ~ il sent mauvais

**boar** n (also **wild** ~) sanglier m

**board** ① n (a) (plank) planche f; **bare** ~**s** plancher nu (b) (committee) conseil m; ~ **of directors** conseil d'administration (c) (for chess, draughts) tableau m (d) (in classroom) tableau m (noir) (e) (notice board) panneau m d'affichage; (to advertise) panneau m (f) (Comput) plaquette f (g) (accommodation) **full** ~ pension f complète; **half** ~ demi-pension f; ~ **and lodging** le gîte et le couvert ② vtr monter à bord de ⟨plane, ship⟩; monter dans ⟨bus, train⟩; ⟨pirates⟩ aborder ⟨vessel⟩ ③ **on board** phr à bord IDIOMS **above** ~ légal/-e; **across the** ~ à tous les niveaux ■ **board up** boucher [qch] avec des planches ⟨window⟩; barricader [qch] avec des planches ⟨house⟩

**boarder** n (a) (lodger) pensionnaire m (b) (school pupil) interne mf

**board game** n jeu m de société (à damier)

**boarding** n embarquement m

**boarding card** n carte f d'embarquement

**boarding school** n école f privée avec internat

**board meeting** n réunion f du conseil d'administration

**boardroom** n salle f du conseil

**boast** ① n vantardise f ② vtr s'enorgueillir de ③ vi se vanter (**about** de)

**boastful** adj vantard/-e

**boat** n (gen) bateau m; (sailing) voilier m; (rowing) barque f; (liner) paquebot m IDIOMS **to be in the same** ~ (colloq) être tous/ toutes dans la même galère

**boater** n (hat) canotier m

**boathouse** n abri m à bateaux

**boating** ① n navigation f de plaisance ② adj ⟨accident, enthusiast⟩ de bateau; ⟨trip⟩ en bateau

**boatyard** n chantier m de construction de bateaux

**bob** ① n (haircut) coupe f au carré ② vi (also ~ **up and down**) ⟨boat, float⟩ danser

**bobsled, bobsleigh** n bobsleigh m

**bode** vi **to** ~ **well/ill** être de bon/mauvais augure

**bodily** adj ⟨function⟩ physiologique; ⟨fluid⟩ organique

**body** n (a) (of person, animal) corps m (b) (corpse) corps m, cadavre m (c) (of car) carrosserie f (d) (of water) étendue f (e) (organization) organisme m (f) (of wine) corps m; (of hair) volume m

**bodybuilder** n culturiste mf

**body-building** n culturisme m

**bodyguard** n garde m du corps

**body language** n langage m corporel

**body piercing** n piercing m

**body warmer** n gilet m matelassé

**bodywork** n carrosserie f

**bog** n (a) (marshy ground) marais m (b) (also **peat** ~) tourbière f IDIOMS **to get** ~**ged down in sth** s'enliser dans qch

**boggle** vi **the mind** ~**s!** c'est époustouflant!

**bog-standard** adj (colloq) ordinaire

**bogus** adj ⟨doctor, document⟩ faux/fausse (before n); ⟨claim⟩ bidon inv; ⟨company⟩ factice

**bohemian** adj ⟨lifestyle⟩ de bohème; ⟨person⟩ bohème

**boil** ① n (a) **to bring sth to the** ~ porter qch à ébullition (b) (on skin) furoncle m ② vtr faire bouillir; **to** ~ **an egg** faire cuire un œuf ③ vi bouillir; **the kettle is** ~**ing** l'eau bout (dans la bouilloire); **to make sb's blood** ~ faire sortir qn de ses gonds ■ **boil down to** (figurative) se ramener à ■ **boil over** déborder

**boiled egg** n œuf m à la coque

**boiled potatoes** n pl pommes fpl de terre à l'anglaise

**boiler** n chaudière f

**boiler suit** n (GB) bleu m de travail

**boiling** adj ⟨liquid⟩ bouillant/-e; **it's ~ !**
(colloq) il fait une chaleur infernale!

**boiling point** n point m d'ébullition;
(figurative) point m limite

**boisterous** adj ⟨adult, game⟩ bruyant/-e;
⟨child⟩ turbulent/-e

**bold** adj (a) (daring) ⟨person⟩ intrépide;
⟨attempt, plan⟩ audacieux/-ieuse
(b) (cheeky) ⟨person⟩ effronté/-e
(c) ⟨colour⟩ vif/vive; ⟨design⟩ voyant/-e; **~
print** caractères mpl gras

**bollard** n balise f

**bolster** 1 n traversin m
2 vtr (also **~ up**) soutenir

**bolt** 1 n (a) (lock) verrou m
(b) **~ of lightning** coup m de foudre
2 vtr (a) (lock) verrouiller
(b) (also **~ down**) engloutir ⟨food⟩
3 vi ⟨horse⟩ s'emballer; ⟨person⟩ détaler
(colloq)
4 **bolt upright** phr droit/-e comme un i
IDIOMS **a ~ out of the blue** un coup de
tonnerre

**bomb** 1 n bombe f
2 vtr bombarder ⟨town, house⟩

**bombard** vtr bombarder (**with** de)

**bomb blast** n explosion f

**bomb disposal unit** n équipe f de
déminage m

**bomber** n (a) (plane) bombardier m
(b) (terrorist) poseur/-euse m/f de bombes

**bomber jacket** n blouson m d'aviateur

**bombing** n bombardement m; (by terrorists)
attentat m à la bombe

**bomb scare** n alerte f à la bombe

**bombshell** n obus m; (figurative) bombe f

**bombsite** n zone f touchée par une
explosion

**Bomb Squad** n brigade f antiterroriste

**bona fide** adj ⟨attempt⟩ sincère; ⟨member⟩
vrai/-e (before n); ⟨contract⟩ de bonne foi

**bond** 1 n (a) (link) liens mpl (**of** de;
**between** entre)
(b) (in finance) obligation f; **savings ~** bon m
d'épargne
2 vtr (stick) faire adhérer
3 vi ⟨person⟩ s'attacher (**with** à)

**bone** 1 n os m; (of fish) arête f
2 vtr désosser ⟨joint, chicken⟩; enlever les
arêtes de ⟨fish⟩
IDIOMS **~ of contention** sujet m de dispute;
**to have a ~ to pick with sb** avoir un compte
à régler avec qn

**bone china** n porcelaine f tendre or à l'os

**bone dry** adj complètement sec/sèche

**bone idle** adj flemmard/-e

**bone-marrow transplant** n greffe f
de moelle osseuse

**bonfire** n (of rubbish) feu m de jardin; (for
celebration) feu m de joie

**Bonfire Night** n (GB) la soirée du 5
novembre (fêtée avec feux de joie et feux
d'artifice)

**bonnet** n (a) (hat) bonnet m
(b) (GB) (Aut) capot m

**bonus** n (a) (payment) prime f
(b) (advantage) avantage m

**bony** adj ⟨person, body⟩ anguleux/-euse;
⟨finger, arm⟩ osseux/-euse

**boo** 1 n huée f
2 excl (to give sb a fright) hou!; (to jeer) hou!
hou!
3 vtr huer ⟨actor, speaker⟩
4 vi pousser des huées

**booby trap** 1 n (a) mécanisme m piégé
(b) (practical joke) traquenard m
2 vtr piéger

**booing** n huées fpl

**book** 1 n (a) (to read) livre m (**about** sur; **of** de);
**history ~** livre d'histoire
(b) (exercise book) cahier m
(c) (of cheques, tickets, stamps) carnet m; **~ of
matches** pochette f d'allumettes
2 **books** n pl (accounts) livres mpl de
comptes
3 vtr (a) réserver ⟨table, room, taxi, ticket⟩;
faire les réservations pour ⟨holiday⟩; **to be
fully ~ed** être complet/-ète
(b) ⟨policeman⟩ dresser un procès-verbal or
un P.V. (colloq) à ⟨motorist, offender⟩; (US)
(arrest) arrêter ⟨suspect⟩
(c) ⟨referee⟩ donner un carton jaune à
⟨player⟩
4 vi réserver
IDIOMS **to be in sb's good ~s** être dans les
petits papiers de qn (colloq); **to be in sb's bad
~s** ne pas avoir la cote avec qn

**bookcase** n bibliothèque f

**book club** n club m du livre

**booking** n (GB) réservation f

**booking form** n bon m de réservation

**booking office** n (GB) bureau m de
location

**bookkeeping** n comptabilité f

**booklet** n brochure f

**booklist** n liste f de livres

**bookmaker** n bookmaker m

**bookmark** 1 n (for page) marque-pages
m, signet m; (Comput) signet m
2 vtr créer un signet sur ⟨website⟩

**bookseller** n libraire mf

**bookshelf** n (single) étagère f; (in bookcase)
rayon m

**bookshop, book store** (US) n
librairie f

**book token** n (GB) chèque-livre m

**bookworm** n mordu/-e m/f (colloq) de la
lecture

**boom** 1 n (a) (of cannon, thunder)
grondement m; (of drum) boum m; (of
explosion) détonation f; **~!** badaboum!
(b) (Econ) boom m; (in prices, sales) explosion f
(**in** de)
2 vi (a) ⟨cannon, thunder⟩ gronder; ⟨voice⟩
retentir ⋯⋯

**(b)** ⟨economy⟩ prospérer; ⟨exports, sales⟩ monter en flèche; **business is** ∼**ing** les affaires vont bien

**boon** n **(a)** (asset) aide f précieuse **(to** à) **(b)** (stroke of luck) aubaine f **(for** pour)

**boost** **1** n **to give sb/sth a** ∼ encourager qn/stimuler qch
**2** vtr stimuler ⟨economy, sales⟩; encourager ⟨investment⟩; augmenter ⟨profit⟩; **to** ∼ **sb's confidence** redonner confiance à qn; **to** ∼ **morale** remonter le moral

**booster** n (Med) vaccin m de rappel

**boot** n **(a)** botte f; (of climber, hiker) chaussure f; (for workman, soldier) brodequin m; **football** ∼ (GB) chaussure f de football
**(b)** (GB) (of car) coffre m
■ **boot up** (Comput) ∼ **[sth] up,** ∼ **up [sth]** amorcer ⟨computer⟩

**booth** n (in language lab) cabine f; (at fair) baraque f; **polling** ∼ isoloir m; **telephone** ∼ cabine f (téléphonique)

**bootlace** n lacet m (de chaussure)

**booze** n (colloq) bibine f (colloq); (wine only) pinard m (colloq)

**border** **1** n **(a)** (frontier) frontière f; **to cross the** ∼ passer la frontière
**(b)** (edge) bord m
**(c)** (flower bed) plate-bande f
**2** vtr **(a)** (frontier) longer ⟨lake, forest⟩; ⟨country⟩ border ⟨ocean⟩; avoir une frontière commune avec ⟨country⟩
**(b)** (surround) border
**3** adj frontalier/-ière
■ **border on:** ∼ **on [sth] (a)** ⟨country⟩ être limitrophe de; ⟨garden, land⟩ toucher
**(b)** (verge on) friser ⟨rudeness, madness⟩

**border dispute** n différend m frontalier

**borderline** n frontière f, limite f (**between** entre); **a** ∼ **case** un cas limite

**bore** **1** n **(a)** (person) raseur/-euse m/f (colloq)
**(b)** (situation) **what a** ∼**!** quelle barbe!
**(c)** (of gun) calibre m
**2** vtr **(a)** ennuyer ⟨person⟩
**(b)** (drill) percer ⟨hole⟩; creuser ⟨well, tunnel⟩

**bored** adj ⟨expression⟩ ennuyé/-e; **to be** or **get** ∼ s'ennuyer (**with** de)
IDIOMS **to be** ∼ **stiff** or ∼ **to tears** s'ennuyer à mourir

**boredom** n ennui m

**boring** adj ennuyeux/-euse

**born** adj né/-e; **to be** ∼ naître; **she was** ∼ **in** May elle est née en mai

**borough** n arrondissement m urbain

**borrow** vtr emprunter (**from** à)

**borrower** n emprunteur/-euse m/f

**borrowing** n emprunt m

**Bosnia** pr n Bosnie f

**Bosnian** adj bosniaque, bosnien/-ienne; ∼ **Serb/Muslim** Serbe/Musulman de Bosnie

**bosom** n poitrine f; **in the** ∼ **of one's family** au sein de sa famille; ∼ **friend** ami/-e m/f intime

**boss** n (colloq) patron/-onne m/f, chef m

■ **boss about** (colloq), **boss around** (colloq) mener [qn] par le bout du nez ⟨person⟩

**bossy** adj (colloq) autoritaire

**botanic(al)** adj botanique; ∼ **gardens** jardin m botanique

**botany** n botanique f

**botch** vtr (colloq) bâcler

**both** **1** det ∼ **sides of the road** les deux côtés de la rue; ∼ **children** came les enfants sont venus tous les deux; ∼ **her parents** ses deux parents
**2** conj ∼ **here and abroad** ici comme à l'étranger
**3** pron, quantif (of things) les deux; (of people) tous les deux; **let's take** ∼ **of them** prenons les deux; ∼ **of you are wrong** vous avez tort tous les deux

**bother** **1** n **(a)** (inconvenience) ennui m, embêtement m (colloq); **without any** ∼ sans aucune difficulté
**(b)** (GB) (colloq) (trouble) ennuis mpl; **to be in a spot of** ∼ avoir des ennuis
**2** vtr **(a)** (worry) tracasser; **don't let it** ∼ **you** ne te tracasse pas avec ça
**(b)** (disturb) déranger; **I'm sorry to** ∼ **you** je suis désolé de vous déranger
**3** vi **(a)** (take trouble) **please don't** ∼ s'il te plaît, ne te dérange pas; **don't** ∼ **doing** ce n'est pas la peine de faire
**(b)** (worry) **it's not worth** ∼**ing about** ça ne vaut pas la peine qu'on s'en occupe

**bottle** **1** n (gen) bouteille f; (for perfume, medicine) flacon m; (for baby) biberon m
**2** vtr **(a)** embouteiller ⟨milk, wine⟩
**(b)** (GB) mettre [qch] en conserve ⟨fruit⟩
**3** **bottled** pp adj ⟨beer, gas⟩ en bouteille; ∼**d water** eau f minérale
■ **bottle up** étouffer ⟨anger, grief⟩

**bottle bank** n réceptacle m à verre

**bottle feed** vtr nourrir [qn] au biberon

**bottleneck** n **(a)** (traffic jam) embouteillage m
**(b)** (narrow part of road) rétrécissement m de la chaussée

**bottle-opener** n décapsuleur m

**bottle top** n capsule f (de bouteille)

**bottom** **1** n **(a)** (of hill, steps, wall) pied m; (of page, list) bas m; (of bag, bottle, hole, river, sea, garden) fond m; (of boat) carène f; (of vase, box) dessous m; (of league) dernière place f; **at the** ∼ **of the pile** sous le tas; **to be** ∼ **of the class** être dernier/-ière de la classe
**(b)** (colloq) (buttocks) derrière m (colloq)
**2** adj ⟨layer, shelf⟩ du bas; ⟨sheet⟩ de dessous; ⟨bunk⟩ inférieur/-e; ⟨division, half⟩ dernier/-ière (before n)
**3** (colloq) **bottoms** n pl pyjama ∼s pantalon m de pyjama; **bikini** ∼s bas m de maillot de bain
IDIOMS **to get to the** ∼ **of a matter** découvrir le fin fond d'une affaire

**bottom line** n (decisive factor) **the** ∼ **is that** la vérité c'est que; **that's the** ∼ ça c'est le vrai problème

**boulder** n rocher m

**bounce** ① n (a) (of ball) rebond m
(b) (of mattress, material) élasticité f; (of hair) souplesse f
② vtr faire rebondir ⟨ball⟩
③ vi (a) ⟨ball, object⟩ rebondir (off sur; over au dessus de); **to ~ up and down on sth** ⟨person⟩ sauter sur qch
(b) (colloq) ⟨cheque⟩ être sans provision
■ **bounce back** (after illness) se remettre; (in career) faire un retour en force

**bouncer** n (colloq) videur m

**bound** ① **bounds** n pl limites fpl; **to be out of ~s** être interdit/-e d'accès
② adj (a) **to be ~ to do sth** aller sûrement faire qch; **it was ~ to happen** cela devait arriver
(b) (obliged) (by promise, rules, terms) tenu/-e (**by** par; **to do** de faire)
(c) **~ for** ⟨person, bus, train⟩ en route pour; ⟨aeroplane⟩ à destination de
③ vi bondir; **to ~ into the room** entrer dans la pièce en coup de vent

**boundary** n (gen) limite f (**between** entre); (of sports field) limites fpl du terrain

**bouquet** n bouquet m

**bourgeois** adj bourgeois/-e

**bout** n (a) (of fever, malaria) accès m; (of insomnia) crise f; **drinking ~** soûlerie f
(b) (in boxing) combat m
(c) (period of activity) période f

**boutique** n boutique f

**bow¹** n (a) (weapon) arc m
(b) (for violin) archet m
(c) (knot) nœud m

**bow²** ① n (a) (movement) salut m; **to take a ~** saluer
(b) (of ship) avant m, proue f
② vtr baisser ⟨head⟩; courber ⟨branch⟩; incliner ⟨tree⟩
③ vi (a) saluer; **to ~ to sb** saluer qn
(b) **to ~ to pressure** céder à la pression

**bowel** n intestin m; **the ~s of the earth** les entrailles fpl de la terre

**bowl** ① n (for food) bol m; (for salad) saladier m; (for soup) assiette f creuse; (for washing) cuvette f; (of lavatory) cuvette f
② vtr lancer ⟨ball⟩
③ vi (a) lancer; **to ~ to sb** lancer la balle à qn
(b) (US) (go bowling) aller au bowling
■ **bowl over** (a) (knock down) renverser ⟨person⟩
(b) **to be ~ed over** (by news) être stupéfait/-e; (by beauty, generosity) être bouleversé/-e

**bowlegged** adj ⟨person⟩ aux jambes arquées

**bowler** n (a) (in cricket) lanceur m
(b) (also **~ hat**) chapeau m melon

**bowling** n (also **tenpin ~**) bowling m

**bowling alley** n bowling m

**bowling green** n terrain m de boules (sur gazon)

**bowls** n jeu m de boules (sur gazon)

**bow tie** n nœud-papillon m

**box** ① n (a) (cardboard) boîte f; (crate) caisse f; **~ of matches** boîte d'allumettes
(b) (on page, form) case f
(c) (in theatre) loge f; (in stadium) tribune f
(d) (also **PO Box**) boîte f postale
② vtr (a) (pack) mettre [qch] en caisse
(b) **to ~ sb's ears** gifler qn
③ vi (Sport) boxer

**boxer** n (a) (fighter) boxeur m
(b) (dog) boxer m

**boxer shorts** n pl caleçon m (court)

**boxing** n boxe f

**Boxing Day** n (GB) lendemain m de Noël

**box number** n numéro m de boîte postale

**box office** n guichet m

**boy** n garçon m

**boy band** n boys band m

**boycott** ① n boycottage m (**against, of, on** de)
② vtr boycotter

**boyfriend** n (petit) copain m or ami m

**bra** n soutien-gorge m

**brace** ① n (a) (for teeth) appareil m dentaire
(b) (for broken limb) attelle f
② **braces** n pl (GB) bretelles fpl
③ vtr ⟨person⟩ arc-bouter ⟨body, back⟩ (**against** contre)
④ v refl **to ~ oneself** (physically) s'arc-bouter; (mentally) se préparer (**for** à; **to do** à faire)

**bracelet** n bracelet m

**bracing** adj vivifiant/-e, tonifiant/-e

**bracken** n fougère f

**bracket** ① n (a) (round) parenthèse f; (square) crochet m; **in ~s** entre parenthèses or crochets
(b) (for shelf) équerre f; (for lamp) applique f
(c) (category) **age ~** tranche f d'âge
② vtr (a) (put in brackets) (round) mettre [qch] entre parenthèses; (square) mettre [qch] entre crochets
(b) (also **~ together**) mettre [qn] dans le même groupe ⟨people⟩

**brag** vi se vanter (**to** auprès de; **about** de)

**braid** n (a) (of hair) tresse f, natte f
(b) (trimming) galon m

**brain** n cerveau m; **~s** cervelle f

**brainchild** n grande idée f

**brain damage** n lésions fpl cérébrales

**brain dead** adj dans un coma dépassé

**brain drain** n fuite f des cerveaux

**brain surgery** n neurochirurgie f

**brain teaser** n (colloq) casse-tête m inv

**brainwash** vtr faire subir un lavage de cerveau à

**brainwashing** n (of prisoners) lavage m de cerveau; (of public) bourrage m (colloq) de crâne

**brainwave** n idée f géniale, illumination f

**brainy** adj (colloq) doué/-e

**braise** vtr braiser

**brake** ① n frein m
② vi freiner

**brake pad** n plaquette f de frein
**bramble** n (a) ronce f
(b) (GB) (berry) mûre f
**bran** n son m
**branch** n (a) (of tree) branche f; (of road, railway) embranchement m
(b) (of shop) succursale f; (of bank) agence f; (of company) filiale f
■ **branch off** bifurquer
■ **branch out** se diversifier
**brand** ⟨1⟩ n marque f
⟨2⟩ vtr (a) marquer (au fer) ⟨animal⟩
(b) to ~ **sb as sth** désigner qn comme qch
**branded** adj ⟨goods⟩ de marque inv
**brandish** vtr brandir
**brand leader** n leader m du marché
**brand name** n marque f déposée
**brand-new** adj tout neuf/toute neuve
**brandy** n eau-de-vie f; (cognac) cognac m
**brash** adj ⟨person, manner⟩ bravache
**brass** n (a) (metal) laiton m, cuivre m jaune
(b) (Mus) (also ~ **section**) cuivres mpl
**brass band** n fanfare f
**brat** n (colloq) marmot m (colloq), môme mf (colloq)
**bravado** n bravade f
**brave** ⟨1⟩ n (Indian) brave m
⟨2⟩ adj (gen) courageux/-euse; ⟨smile⟩ brave; to put on a ~ **face** faire bonne contenance
⟨3⟩ vtr braver
**bravely** adv courageusement
**bravery** n courage m, bravoure f
**brawl** ⟨1⟩ n bagarre f
⟨2⟩ vi se bagarrer (with avec)
**bray** vi ⟨donkey⟩ braire; ⟨person⟩ brailler
**brazen** adj éhonté/-e
■ **brazen out**: ~ it out payer d'audace
**Brazil** pr n Brésil m
**breach** ⟨1⟩ n (a) (of rule) infraction f (of à); (of discipline, duty) manquement m (of à); (of copyright) violation f; to be in ~ of enfreindre ⟨law⟩; violer ⟨agreement⟩
(b) (gap) brèche f
⟨2⟩ vtr faire une brèche dans ⟨defence⟩
**breach of contract** n rupture f de contrat
**breach of the peace** n atteinte f à l'ordre public
**bread** n pain m
**bread and butter** n tartine f de pain beurré; (figurative) gagne-pain m
**breadbin** n (GB) boîte f or huche f à pain
**breadboard** n planche f à pain
**breadcrumbs** n pl miettes fpl de pain; (Culin) chapelure f
**breadline** n to be on the ~ être au seuil de l'indigence
**bread roll** n petit pain m
**breadth** n largeur f; (figurative) (of experience, knowledge) étendue f
**breadwinner** n soutien m de famille

**break** ⟨1⟩ n (a) (gap) (in wall) brèche f; (in row, line) espace m; (in circuit) rupture f
(b) (pause) (gen) pause f; (at school) récréation f; to take a ~ faire une pause; the Christmas ~ les vacances de Noël; to have a ~ from work arrêter de travailler; a ~ with the past une rupture avec le passé
(c) (also **commercial** ~) page f de publicité
(d) a lucky ~ un coup de veine (colloq)
⟨2⟩ vtr (a) (gen) casser; briser ⟨seal⟩; rompre ⟨silence, monotony, spell⟩; to ~ one's leg se casser la jambe
(b) enfreindre ⟨law⟩; to ~ one's promise manquer à sa promesse
(c) dépasser ⟨speed limit⟩; battre ⟨record⟩
(d) ⟨branches⟩ freiner ⟨fall⟩; ⟨hay⟩ amortir ⟨fall⟩
(e) débourrer ⟨horse⟩
(f) (in tennis) to ~ sb's serve faire le break
(g) to ~ the news to sb apprendre la nouvelle à qn
⟨3⟩ vi (a) (gen) se casser; ⟨arm, bone, leg⟩ se fracturer; ⟨bag⟩ se déchirer; to ~ in two se casser en deux
(b) ⟨waves⟩ se briser
(c) ⟨good weather⟩ se gâter; ⟨heatwave⟩ cesser
(d) ⟨storm, scandal, story⟩ éclater
(e) to ~ with sb rompre les relations avec qn; to ~ with tradition rompre avec la tradition
(f) ⟨boy's voice⟩ muer
■ **break away** (a) se détacher (from de)
(b) (escape) s'échapper
■ **break down**: ¶ ~ down (a) ⟨car, machine⟩ tomber en panne
(b) ⟨person⟩ s'effondrer, craquer (colloq); to ~ down in tears fondre en larmes
¶ ~ ⟨sth⟩ down (a) enfoncer ⟨door⟩; (figurative) faire tomber ⟨barriers⟩; vaincre ⟨resistance⟩
(b) (analyse) ventiler ⟨cost, statistics⟩; décomposer ⟨data, findings⟩ (into par)
■ **break even** rentrer dans ses frais
■ **break free** s'échapper
■ **break in**: ¶ ~ in (a) ⟨thief⟩ entrer (par effraction); ⟨police⟩ entrer de force
(b) (interrupt) interrompre
¶ ~ ⟨sth⟩ in débourrer ⟨horse⟩; assouplir ⟨shoe⟩
■ **break into** (a) entrer dans [qch] (par effraction) ⟨building⟩; forcer ⟨safe⟩
(b) entamer ⟨new packet, savings⟩
(c) to ~ into song/into a run se mettre à chanter/courir
■ **break off**: ¶ ~ off (a) ⟨end⟩ se casser; ⟨handle, piece⟩ se détacher
(b) ⟨speaker⟩ s'interrompre
~ ⟨sth⟩ off (a) casser ⟨branch, piece⟩
(b) rompre ⟨engagement⟩; interrompre ⟨conversation⟩
■ **break out** (a) ⟨epidemic, fire⟩ se déclarer; ⟨fight, riot, storm⟩ éclater; to ~ out in a rash avoir une éruption de boutons
(b) ⟨prisoner⟩ s'échapper (of de)
■ **break up**: ¶ ~ up (a) ⟨couple⟩ se séparer

**(b)** ⟨crowd, cloud⟩ se disperser; ⟨meeting⟩ se terminer
**(c)** (GB Sch) **schools ∼ up on Friday** les cours finissent vendredi
¶ **∼ [sth] up** démanteler ⟨drugs ring⟩; séparer ⟨couple⟩; désunir ⟨family⟩; briser ⟨marriage⟩; mettre fin à ⟨demonstration⟩

**breakaway** n ⟨faction, group, state⟩ séparatiste

**breakdown** n **(a)** (of vehicle, machine) panne f
**(b)** (of communications, negotiations) rupture f; (of discipline, order) effondrement m
**(c) to have a (nervous) ∼** faire une dépression (nerveuse)
**(d)** (of figures, statistics) ventilation f

**breakfast** n petit déjeuner m

**breakfast television** n télévision f à l'heure du petit déjeuner

**break-in** n cambriolage m

**breaking point** n (figurative) **to be at ∼** être à bout

**breakneck** adj ⟨pace, speed⟩ fou/folle, insensé/-e

**breakthrough** n (gen) percée f; (in negotiations, investigation) progrès m

**break-up** n (of alliance, relationship) rupture f; (of political party, family, group) éclatement m; (of marriage) échec m

**breakwater** n brise-lames m inv

**breast** n **(a)** (woman's) sein m; (chest) poitrine f
**(b)** (Culin) (of poultry) blanc m, filet m

**breast-feed** vtr, vi allaiter

**breast stroke** n brasse f

**breath** n **(a)** souffle m; **out of ∼** à bout de souffle; **to hold one's ∼** retenir sa respiration; (figurative) retenir son souffle
**(b)** (from mouth) haleine f; (visible) respiration f; **to have bad ∼** avoir (une) mauvaise haleine
IDIOMS **to take sb's ∼ away** couper le souffle à qn

**breathalyse** (GB), **breathalyze** (US) vtr faire subir un alcootest à ⟨driver⟩

**Breathalyzer**® n alcootest m

**breathe** ① vtr **(a)** respirer ⟨oxygen⟩
**(b)** souffler ⟨germs⟩ (**on** sur)
**(c) don't ∼ a word!** pas un mot!
② vi **(a)** ⟨person, animal⟩ respirer; **to ∼ heavily** souffler fort, haleter
**(b)** ⟨wine⟩ s'aérer
■ **breathe in**: ¶ **∼ in** inspirer; ¶ **∼ [sth] in** inhaler
■ **breathe out**: ¶ **∼ out** expirer; ¶ **∼ out, ∼ [sth] out** exhaler

**breather** n pause f; **take a ∼** faire une pause

**breathing** n respiration f

**breathing space** n **(a)** (respite) répit m
**(b)** ( postponement) délai m

**breathless** adj ⟨runner⟩ hors d'haleine; ⟨asthmatic⟩ haletant/-e

**breathtaking** adj ⟨feat, skill⟩ stupéfiant/-e; ⟨scenery⟩ à vous couper le souffle

**breath test** ① n alcootest m
② vtr faire subir un alcootest à ⟨driver⟩

**breed** ① n race f
② vtr élever ⟨animals⟩; (figurative) engendrer
③ vi se reproduire
④ **bred** pp adj **ill-/well-∼** mal/bien élevé/-e

**breeder** n (of animals) éleveur m

**breeding** n **(a)** (of animals) reproduction f
**(b)** (good manners) bonnes manières fpl

**breeding ground** n (figurative) foyer m (**for** de)

**breeze** ① n brise f
② vi **to ∼ in/out** entrer/sortir d'un air dégagé; **to ∼ through an exam** réussir un examen sans difficulté

**brevity** n brièveté f

**brew** ① vtr brasser ⟨beer⟩; préparer ⟨tea⟩; **freshly ∼ed coffee** du café fraîchement passé
② vi **(a)** ⟨beer⟩ fermenter; ⟨tea⟩ infuser
**(b)** ⟨storm, crisis⟩ se préparer

**brewer** n brasseur m

**brewery** n brasserie f

**bribe** ① n pot-de-vin m
② vtr soudoyer ⟨police⟩; suborner ⟨witness⟩; acheter ⟨servant, voter⟩

**bribery** n corruption f

**brick** n brique f

**bricklayer** n maçon m

**bridal** adj ⟨gown⟩ de mariée; ⟨car⟩ des mariés; ⟨suite⟩ nuptial/-e

**bride** n (jeune) mariée f; **the ∼ and groom** les (jeunes) mariés mpl

**bridegroom** n jeune marié m

**bridesmaid** n demoiselle f d'honneur

**bridge** ① n **(a)** pont m (**over** sur; **across** au-dessus de); (figurative) (link) rapprochement m
**(b)** (on ship) passerelle f
**(c)** (of nose) arête f; (of spectacles) arcade f
**(d)** (on guitar, violin) chevalet m
**(e)** (for teeth) bridge m
**(f)** (game) bridge m
② vtr **(a) to ∼ a gap in [sth]** combler un vide dans ⟨conversation⟩; combler un trou dans ⟨budget⟩
**(b)** (span) enjamber ⟨two eras⟩

**bridle** ① n bride f
② vtr brider
③ vi se cabrer (**at** contre; **with** sous l'effet de)

**bridle path** n piste f cavalière

**brief** ① n **(a)** (GB) (remit) attributions fpl; (role) tâche f
**(b)** (Law) dossier m
② **briefs** n pl slip m
③ adj bref/brève; **in ∼** en bref
④ vtr (inform) informer (**on** de); (instruct) donner des instructions à (**on** sur)

**briefcase** n serviette f; (without handle) porte-documents m inv

**briefing** n briefing m (on sur)

**briefly** adv (a) (gen) brièvement; ⟨look, pause⟩ un bref instant
(b) (in short) en bref

**brigade** n brigade f

**bright** adj (a) ⟨colour⟩ vif/vive; ⟨garment⟩ aux couleurs vives; ⟨sunshine⟩ éclatant/-e; ⟨room, day⟩ clair/-e; ⟨star, eye, metal⟩ brillant/-e
(b) (clever) intelligent/-e; a ∼ idea une idée lumineuse
(c) to look on the ∼ side voir le bon côté des choses

**brighten** v ■ brighten up: ¶ ∼ up (a) ⟨person⟩ s'égayer (at à); ⟨face⟩ s'éclairer (at à)
(b) ⟨weather⟩ s'éclaircir; ¶ ∼ [sth] up égayer ⟨room, decor⟩

**brightly** adv (a) ⟨dressed⟩ de couleurs vives
(b) ⟨shine, burn⟩ d'un vif éclat

**brightness** n (a) (of colour, light, smile) éclat m
(b) (of room) clarté f

**bright spark** n (GB) (colloq) petit/-e futé/-e m/f (colloq)

**brilliance** n éclat m

**brilliant** adj (a) ⟨student, career, success⟩ brillant/-e
(b) (bright) éclatant/-e
(c) (GB) (colloq) (fantastic) super (colloq), génial/-e (colloq); to be ∼ at sth être doué/-e en qch

**brilliantly** adv (a) (very well) brillamment
(b) (very brightly) ⟨shine⟩ avec éclat

**brim** n bord m

**brine** n (a) (sea water) eau f de mer
(b) (for pickling) saumure f

**bring** vtr (a) apporter ⟨present, object, message⟩; amener ⟨person, animal, car⟩; to ∼ sth with one apporter qch; to ∼ sb/sth into the room entrer qn/qch dans la pièce
(b) apporter ⟨happiness, rain, change, hope⟩; to ∼ a smile to sb's face faire sourire qn
■ **bring about** provoquer ⟨change, disaster⟩; entraîner ⟨success, defeat⟩
■ **bring along** apporter ⟨object⟩; amener, venir avec ⟨friend, partner⟩
■ **bring back** (a) rapporter ⟨souvenir⟩ (from de); to ∼ back memories ranimer des souvenirs
(b) rétablir ⟨custom⟩; restaurer ⟨monarchy⟩
■ **bring down** (a) renverser ⟨government⟩
(b) réduire ⟨inflation, expenditure⟩; faire baisser ⟨price, temperature⟩
(c) (shoot down) abattre
■ **bring forward** avancer ⟨date⟩
■ **bring in** rapporter ⟨money, interest⟩; introduire ⟨legislation, measure⟩; rentrer ⟨harvest⟩; faire appel à ⟨expert, army⟩
■ **bring off** réussir ⟨feat⟩; conclure ⟨deal⟩
■ **bring on** (a) provoquer ⟨attack, migraine⟩
(b) faire entrer ⟨substitute player⟩
■ **bring out** (a) sortir ⟨edition, new model⟩
(b) (highlight) faire ressortir ⟨flavour, meaning⟩

■ **bring round** (a) (revive) faire revenir [qn] à soi
(b) (convince) convaincre
■ **bring up** (a) aborder, parler de ⟨subject⟩
(b) vomir, rendre ⟨food⟩
(c) élever ⟨child⟩; well brought up bien élevé/-e

**brink** n bord m

**brisk** adj (a) (efficient) ⟨manner, tone⟩ vif/ vive; ⟨person⟩ efficace
(b) (energetic) ⟨trot⟩ rapide; at a ∼ pace à vive allure
(c) ⟨business, trade⟩ florissant/-e; business was ∼ les affaires marchaient bien
(d) ⟨air⟩ vivifiant/-e; ⟨wind⟩ vif/vive

**bristle** [1] n (gen) poil m; (on pig) soie f
[2] vi (a) ⟨hairs⟩ se dresser
(b) ⟨person⟩ se hérisser (at à; with de)

**Britain** pr n (also **Great** ∼) Grande-Bretagne f

**British** [1] n pl the ∼ les Britanniques mpl
[2] adj britannique; the ∼ embassy l'ambassade f de Grande-Bretagne

**British Isles** pr n pl îles fpl Britanniques

**Briton** n Britannique mf

**Brittany** pr n Bretagne f

**brittle** adj ⟨twig⟩ cassant/-e; ⟨nails, hair⟩ fragile

**broach** vtr aborder ⟨subject⟩

**broad** adj (a) (wide) large; to have ∼ shoulders être large d'épaules
(b) ⟨meaning⟩ large; ⟨outline⟩ général/-e
(c) ⟨accent⟩ fort/-e (before n); in ∼ daylight en plein jour

**broad-based** adj ⟨approach, campaign⟩ global/-e; ⟨education⟩ généralisé/-e

**broad bean** n fève f

**broadcast** [1] n émission f
[2] vtr diffuser ⟨programme⟩ (to à)
[3] vi ⟨station, channel⟩ émettre (on sur)

**broadcaster** n animateur/-trice m/f

**broadcasting** n (field) communication f audiovisuelle; (action) diffusion f; to work in ∼ travailler dans l'audiovisuel

**broaden** [1] vtr étendre ⟨appeal, scope⟩; élargir ⟨horizons, knowledge⟩; travel ∼s the mind les voyages ouvrent l'esprit
[2] vi s'élargir

**broadminded** adj ⟨person⟩ large d'esprit; ⟨attitude⟩ libéral/-e

**broadsheet** n journal m de grand format

**brocade** n brocart m

**broccoli** n (Bot) brocoli m; (Culin) brocolis mpl

**brochure** n (booklet) brochure f; (leaflet) dépliant m; (for hotel) prospectus m

**broil** vtr (US) faire griller ⟨meat⟩

**broke** adj (colloq) ⟨person⟩ fauché/-e (colloq)

**broken** adj (a) (gen) cassé/-e; ⟨glass, window, line⟩ brisé/-e; ⟨radio, machine⟩ détraqué/-e
(b) ⟨man, woman⟩ brisé/-e
(c) ⟨French⟩ mauvais/-e (before n)

**broken-down** adj ⟨machine⟩ en panne

**broken-hearted** adj to be ~ avoir le cœur brisé

**broken home** n famille f désunie

**broken marriage** n foyer m désuni

**broker** n courtier m; **insurance** ~ courtier m d'assurance; **real-estate** ~ (US) agent m immobilier

**brolly** n (GB) (colloq) parapluie m

**bronchitis** n bronchite f

**bronze** n bronze m

**brooch** n broche f

**brood** ① n (of birds) couvée f; (of mammals) nichée f
② vi (a) (ponder) broyer du noir; to ~ about ressasser, ruminer ⟨problem⟩
(b) ⟨bird⟩ couver

**brook** n ruisseau m

**broom** n balai m

**broth** n bouillon m

**brothel** n maison f close

**brother** n frère m

**brother-in-law** n beau-frère m

**brotherly** adj fraternel/-elle

**brow** n (a) (forehead) front m; (eyebrow) sourcil m
(b) (of hill) sommet m

**brown** ① n (of object) marron m; (of hair, skin, eyes) brun m
② adj (a) ⟨shoes, leaves, paint, eyes⟩ marron inv; ⟨hair⟩ châtain inv; **light/dark** ~ marron clair/foncé
(b) (tanned) bronzé/-e; **to go** ~ bronzer
③ vtr faire roussir ⟨sauce⟩; faire dorer ⟨meat, onions⟩
④ vi ⟨meat, potatoes⟩ dorer

**brown bread** n pain m complet

**brown envelope** n enveloppe f kraft

**Brownie** n jeannette f

**brown paper** n papier m kraft

**brown rice** n riz m complet

**brown sugar** n sucre m brun, cassonade f

**browse** vi (a) (in shop) regarder
(b) (graze) brouter

■ **browse through** feuilleter ⟨book⟩

**browser** n navigateur m

**bruise** ① n (on skin) bleu m, ecchymose f (on sur); (on fruit) tache f (on sur)
② vtr meurtrir ⟨person⟩; taler, abîmer ⟨fruit⟩; **to** ~ **one's arm** se faire un bleu sur le bras

**brunette** n brune f

**brunt** n **to bear the** ~ **of** être le plus touché/la plus touchée par ⟨disaster⟩; subir tout le poids de ⟨anger⟩

**brush** ① n (a) (for hair, clothes, shoes) brosse f; (small, for sweeping up) balayette f; (broom) balai m; (for paint) pinceau m
(b) **to have a** ~ **with death** frôler la mort; **to have a** ~ **with the law** avoir des démêlés avec la justice
② vtr brosser ⟨carpet, clothes⟩; **to** ~ **one's hair/teeth** se brosser les cheveux/les dents
③ vi **to** ~ **against** frôler; **to** ~ **past sb** frôler qn en passant

■ **brush aside** repousser ⟨criticism, person⟩

■ **brush up (on)** se remettre à ⟨subject⟩

**brushwood** n (firewood) brindilles fpl; (brush) broussailles fpl

**brusque** adj brusque (**with** avec)

**Brussels** pr n Bruxelles

**Brussels sprout** n chou m de Bruxelles

**brutal** adj brutal/-e

**brutality** n brutalité f (**of** de)

**brute** ① n (a) (man) brute f
(b) (animal) bête f
② adj ⟨strength⟩ simple (before n); **by** ~ **force** par la force

**BSc** n (GB) (Univ) (abbr = **Bachelor of Science**) diplôme m universitaire en sciences

**BSE** n (abbr = **Bovine Spongiform Encephalopathy**) ESB f, encéphalopathie f spongiforme bovine

**bubble** ① n bulle f (**in** dans); **to blow** ~s faire des bulles
② vi ⟨fizzy drink⟩ pétiller; ⟨boiling liquid⟩ bouillonner; **to** ~ (**over**) **with** déborder de ⟨enthusiasm, ideas⟩

**bubble bath** n bain m moussant

**bubblewrap** n bulle-pack® m

**buck** ① n (a) (US) (colloq) dollar m
(b) (male animal) mâle m
② vi ⟨horse⟩ ruer
IDIOMS **to pass the** ~ refiler (colloq) la responsabilité à quelqu'un d'autre

**bucket** n seau m (**of** de)

**buckle** ① n boucle f
② vtr (a) attacher, boucler ⟨belt, shoe⟩
(b) (damage) gondoler
③ vi (a) ⟨metal, surface⟩ se gondoler; ⟨wheel⟩ se voiler
(b) ⟨belt, shoe⟩ s'attacher, se boucler
(c) ⟨knees, legs⟩ céder

**bud** ① n (of leaf) bourgeon m; (of flower) bouton m
② vi (a) (develop leaf buds) bourgeonner; (develop flower buds) boutonner
(b) ⟨flower, breast⟩ pointer

**Buddha** pr n Bouddha m

**Buddhism** n bouddhisme m

**Buddhist** n, adj bouddhiste (mf)

**budding** adj ⟨athlete, champion⟩ en herbe; ⟨talent, career, romance⟩ naissant/-e

**buddy** n (colloq) copain m, pote m (colloq)

**budge** ① vtr (a) (move) bouger
(b) (persuade) faire changer d'avis à
② vi (a) (move) bouger (**from, off** de)
(b) (give way) changer d'avis (**on** sur)

■ **budge over** (colloq), **budge up** (colloq) se pousser

**budgerigar** n perruche f

**budget** ① n budget m (**for** pour)
② vi **to** ~ **for** budgétiser ses dépenses en fonction de ⟨increase, needs⟩

**buff** n (a) (colloq) (enthusiast) mordu/-e m/f
(b) (colour) chamois m

**buffalo** n (GB) buffle m; (US) bison m

**buffer** n tampon m

**buffet¹** n buffet m

**buffet²** vtr ⟨wind⟩ ballotter ⟨ship⟩; battre
⟨coast⟩

**buffoon** n bouffon/-onne m/f

**bug** ① n (a) (colloq) (insect) (gen) bestiole f;
(bedbug) punaise f
(b) (colloq) (also **stomach** ∼) ennuis mpl
gastriques
(c) (germ) microbe m
(d) (fault) (gen) défaut m; (Comput) bogue f or
m, bug m
(e) (hidden microphone) micro m caché
② vtr (a) poser des micros dans ⟨room,
building⟩; **the room is** ∼**ged** il y a un micro
(caché) dans la pièce
(b) (colloq) (annoy) embêter ⟨person⟩

**buggy** n (a) (GB) (pushchair) poussette f
(b) (US) (pram) landau m
(c) (carriage) boghei m

**bugle** n clairon m

**build** ① n (of person) carrure f
② vtr (gen) construire; édifier ⟨church,
monument⟩; bâtir ⟨career, future⟩; fonder
⟨empire⟩; créer ⟨software, interface⟩; **to be
well built** ⟨person⟩ être bien bâti/-e
③ vi construire; **to** ∼ **on** tirer parti de
⟨popularity, success⟩
■ **build up**: ¶ ∼ **up** ⟨gas, deposits⟩
s'accumuler; ⟨traffic⟩ s'intensifier; ⟨business,
trade⟩ se développer; ⟨tension, excitement⟩
monter; ¶ ∼ **[sth] up** accumuler ⟨wealth⟩;
établir ⟨trust⟩; constituer ⟨collection⟩; créer
⟨business⟩; établir ⟨picture, profile⟩; se faire
⟨reputation⟩; affermir ⟨muscles⟩; **to** ∼ **oneself
up, to** ∼ **up one's strength** prendre des
forces

**builder** n (contractor) entrepreneur m en
bâtiment; (worker) ouvrier/-ière m/f du
bâtiment

**building** n (gen) bâtiment m; (with offices,
apartments) immeuble m; (palace, church) édifice
m

**building contractor** n entrepreneur m
en bâtiment

**building site** n chantier m (de
construction)

**building society** n (GB) société f
d'investissement et de crédit immobilier

**build-up** n (a) (in traffic, pressure)
intensification f (of de); (in weapons, stocks)
accumulation f (of de); (in tension)
accroissement m (of de)
(b) (publicity) **the** ∼ **to sth** les préparatifs de
qch

**built-in** adj ⟨wardrobe⟩ encastré/-e;
(figurative) intégré/-e

**built-up** adj ⟨region⟩ urbanisé/-e; ∼ **area**
agglomération f

**bulb** n (a) (electric) ampoule f (électrique)
(b) (of plant) bulbe m

**Bulgaria** pr n Bulgarie f

**Bulgarian** ① n (a) (person) Bulgare mf
(b) (language) bulgare m
② adj bulgare

**bulge** ① n (in clothing, carpet) bosse f; (in pipe,
tube) renflement m; (in tyre) hernie f; (in wall)
bombement m; (in cheek) gonflement m
② vi ⟨bag, pocket, cheeks⟩ être gonflé/-e;
⟨wallet⟩ être bourré/-e; ⟨surface⟩ se
boursoufler; ⟨stomach⟩ ballonner; **his eyes
were bulging** les yeux lui sortaient de la tête

**bulimia (nervosa)** n boulimie f

**bulimic** n, adj boulimique (mf)

**bulk** n (a) (of package, correspondence) volume
m; (of building, vehicle) masse f; **the** ∼ **of** la
majeure partie de
(b) **in** ∼ ⟨buy, sell⟩ en gros; ⟨transport⟩ en
vrac

**bulk-buying** n achat m en gros

**bulky** adj ⟨person⟩ corpulent/-e; ⟨package⟩
volumineux/-euse; ⟨book⟩ épais/-aisse

**bull** n (ox) taureau m; (elephant, whale) mâle m

**bull bar** n pare-buffle(s) m

**bulldog** n bouledogue m

**bulldozer** n bulldozer m, bouteur m

**bullet** n balle f

**bulletin** n bulletin m; **news** ∼ bulletin
d'informations

**bulletin board** n (gen) tableau m
d'affichage; (Comput) messagerie f
électronique

**bulletproof** adj ⟨glass, vehicle, door⟩
blindé/-e

**bulletproof vest** n gilet m pare-balles
inv

**bullfight** n corrida f

**bullfighter** n torero m

**bullfighting** n (gen) corridas fpl; (art)
tauromachie f

**bullion** n lingots mpl

**bullock** n bœuf m

**bullring** n arène f

**bull's-eye** n mille m

**bully** ① n (child) petite brute f; (adult) tyran
m
② vtr intimider; (stronger) tyranniser

**bum** n (colloq) (a) (GB) (buttocks) derrière m
(colloq)
(b) (US) (vagrant) clochard m

**bumbag** n (sacoche f) banane f

**bumblebee** n bourdon m

**bumf, bumph** n (GB) (colloq) paperasserie f
(colloq)

**bump** ① n (a) (lump) (on body) bosse f (on à);
(on road) bosse f (on, in sur)
(b) (jolt) secousse f
(c) (sound) bruit m sourd
② vtr cogner (**against, on** contre); **to** ∼ **one's
head** se cogner la tête
■ **bump into** rentrer dans ⟨person, object⟩;
(meet) tomber sur (colloq) ⟨person⟩

**bumper** ① n pare-chocs m inv

**2** adj ⟨crop, sales, year⟩ record (after n); ⟨edition⟩ exceptionnel/-elle

**bumper car** n auto f tamponneuse

**bumpkin** n (colloq) (also **country ~**) péquenaud/-e m/f (colloq)

**bumpy** adj ⟨road⟩ accidenté/-e; ⟨wall⟩ irrégulier/-ière; ⟨landing⟩ agité-e

**bun** n **(a)** (cake) petit pain m sucré **(b)** (hairstyle) chignon m

**bunch** n (of flowers) bouquet m; (of vegetables) botte f; (of grapes) grappe f; (of bananas) régime m; (of keys) trousseau m; (of people) groupe m

**bundle** **1** n (of clothes) ballot m; (of papers, notes) liasse f; (of books) paquet m; (of straw) botte f; **~ of sticks** fagot m de bois; **~ of nerves** boule f de nerfs
**2** vtr **to ~ sb/sth into** fourrer (colloq) qn/qch dans

**bundled software** n ensemble m de logiciels complémentaires (livré avec un ordinateur)

**bungalow** n pavillon m (sans étage)

**bungee jumping** n saut m à l'élastique

**bungle** vtr rater (colloq) ⟨attempt, burglary⟩

**bunion** n oignon m

**bunk** n **(a)** (on ship, train) couchette f **(b)** (also **~ bed**) lits mpl superposés
■ **bunk off** (colloq): **to ~ off school** sécher l'école

**bunker** n **(a)** (Mil) bunker m **(b)** (in golf) bunker m **(c)** (for coal) soute f

**bunny** n **(a)** (also **~ rabbit**) (Jeannot) lapin m **(b)** (also **~ girl**) hôtesse f

**bunting** n guirlandes fpl

**buoy** **1** n (gen) bouée f; (for marking) balise f (flottante)
**2** vtr (also **~ up**) **(a)** revigorer ⟨person, morale⟩ **(b)** stimuler ⟨prices, economy⟩ **(c)** (keep afloat) maintenir à flot

**buoyant** adj **(a)** ⟨object⟩ qui flotte **(b)** ⟨person⟩ vif/vive; ⟨mood, spirits⟩ enjoué-e; ⟨step⟩ allègre **(c)** ⟨market, prices⟩ ferme; ⟨economy⟩ en expansion

**burden** **1** n fardeau m (**to sb** pour qn)
**2** vtr **(a)** (also **~ down**) encombrer (**with** de) **(b)** (figurative) (with work, taxes) accabler (**with** de); **I don't want to ~ you with my problems** je ne veux pas vous ennuyer avec mes problèmes

**bureau** n **(a)** (office) bureau m **(b)** (US) (government department) service m **(c)** (GB) (desk) secrétaire m **(d)** (US) (chest of drawers) commode f

**bureaucracy** n bureaucratie f

**bureaucrat** n bureaucrate mf

**bureaucratic** adj bureaucratique

**burgeoning** adj ⟨talent, love, industry, crime⟩ croissant/-e; ⟨population, industries⟩ en plein essor

**burger** n hamburger m

**burger bar** n fast-food m

**burglar** n cambrioleur/-euse m/f

**burglar alarm** n sonnerie f d'alarme

**burglary** n (gen) cambriolage m; (Law) vol m avec effraction

**burgle** vtr cambrioler

**burgundy** **1** **Burgundy** pr n Bourgogne f
**2** n **(a)** (also **Burgundy**) (wine) bourgogne m **(b)** (colour) (couleur f) bordeaux m

**burial** n enterrement m

**burly** adj ⟨person⟩ solidement charpenté/-e

**Burma** pr n Birmanie f

**burn** **1** n brûlure f
**2** vtr (gen) brûler; laisser brûler ⟨food⟩
**3** vi brûler
■ **burn down**: **¶ ~ down** ⟨house⟩ être détruit/-e par le feu; **¶ ~ [sth] down** réduire [qch] en cendres ⟨house⟩
■ **burn up** brûler ⟨calories⟩; dépenser ⟨energy⟩

**burner** n (on cooker) brûleur m
IDIOMS **to put sth on the back ~** mettre qch en veilleuse

**burning** **1** n **there's a smell of ~** ça sent le brûlé
**2** adj **(a)** (on fire) en flammes, en feu; (alight) ⟨candle, lamp, fire⟩ allumé/-e **(b)** ⟨desire⟩ brûlant/-e; ⟨passion⟩ ardent/-e

**burnt-out** adj ⟨building, car⟩ calciné/-e; ⟨person⟩ usé/-e (par le travail)

**burp** (colloq) **1** n rot m (colloq), renvoi m
**2** vi ⟨person⟩ roter (colloq); ⟨baby⟩ faire son rot (colloq)

**burrow** **1** n terrier m
**2** vi ⟨animal⟩ creuser un terrier; **to ~ into/ under sth** creuser dans/sous qch

**bursary** n (GB) (grant) bourse f (d'études)

**burst** **1** n (of flame) jaillissement m; (of gunfire) rafale f; (of activity, enthusiasm) accès m; **a ~ of laughter** un éclat de rire; **a ~ of applause** un tonnerre d'applaudissements
**2** vtr (gen) crever; rompre ⟨blood vessel⟩; **to ~ its banks** ⟨river⟩ déborder
**3** vi (gen) crever; ⟨pipe⟩ éclater; ⟨dam⟩ rompre; **to be ~ing with health/pride** déborder de santé/fierté
■ **burst into (a)** faire irruption dans ⟨room⟩ **(b) to ~ into flames** s'enflammer; **to ~ into tears** fondre en larmes
■ **burst out**: **to ~ out laughing** éclater de rire; **to ~ out crying** fondre en larmes
■ **burst through** rompre ⟨barricade⟩; **to ~ through the door** entrer violemment

**bury** vtr enterrer

**bus** n autobus m, bus m; (long-distance) autocar m, car m; **by ~** en (auto)bus, par le bus; **on the ~** dans le bus

**bus conductor** n receveur m d'autobus

**b**

**bus driver** n conducteur/-trice m/f
d'autobus

**bush** n (a) buisson m
(b) (bushland) the ~ la brousse f
IDIOMS don't beat about the ~ cessez de
tourner autour du pot

**bushfire** n feu m de brousse

**bushy** adj ⟨hair, tail⟩ touffu/-e; ⟨beard⟩
épais/-aisse; ⟨eyebrows⟩ broussailleux/-euse

**business** 1 n (a) (commerce) affaires fpl; to
go into ~ se lancer dans les affaires; she's
gone to Brussels on ~ elle est allée à
Bruxelles en voyage d'affaires; to mix ~ with
pleasure joindre l'utile à l'agréable; he's in
the insurance ~ il travaille dans les
assurances
(b) (company, firm) affaire f, entreprise f; (shop)
commerce m, boutique f; small ~es les
petites entreprises
(c) let's get down to ~ passons aux choses
sérieuses; to go about one's ~ vaquer à ses
occupations
(d) (concern) that's her ~ ça la regarde; it's
none of your ~! ça ne te regarde pas!; mind
your own ~! (colloq) occupe-toi de tes affaires!
(colloq)
2 adj ⟨address, letter, transaction⟩
commercial/-e; ⟨meeting⟩ d'affaires
IDIOMS she means ~! elle ne plaisante pas!;
to work like nobody's ~ (colloq) travailler
d'arrache-pied

**business associate** n associé/-e m/f

**business card** n carte f de visite

**business class** n (on plane) classe f
affaires

**business hours** n pl (in office) heures fpl
de bureau; (of shop) heures fpl d'ouverture

**businesslike** adj sérieux/-ieuse

**businessman** n homme m d'affaires

**business park** n parc m d'affaires or
d'activités

**business plan** n projet m commercial

**business school** n école f de commerce

**business studies** n pl études fpl de
commerce

**business trip** n voyage m d'affaires

**businesswoman** n femme f d'affaires

**busker** n (GB) musicien/-ienne m/f
ambulant/-e

**bus lane** n couloir m d'autobus

**bus pass** n carte f de bus

**bus shelter** n abribus® m

**bus station** n gare f routière

**bus stop** n arrêt m de bus

**bust** 1 n (a) (breasts) poitrine f
(b) (statue) buste m
2 adj (colloq) (a) (broken) fichu/-e (colloq)
(b) (bankrupt) to go ~ faire faillite

**bustle** 1 n (activity) affairement m (of de);
hustle and ~ grande animation f
2 vi ⟨person, crowd⟩ s'affairer; to ~ in/out
entrer/sortir d'un air affairé

**bustling** adj ⟨street, shop, town⟩ animé/-e

**busy** 1 adj (a) ⟨person⟩ occupé/-e (with
avec; doing à faire)
(b) ⟨shop⟩ où il y a beaucoup de monde;
⟨junction, airport⟩ où le trafic est intense;
⟨road⟩ très fréquenté/-e; ⟨street, town⟩
animé/-e; ⟨day, week⟩ chargé/-e
(c) (engaged) ⟨line⟩ occupé/-e
2 v refl to ~ oneself doing s'occuper à faire

**busybody** n (colloq) he's a real ~ il se mêle
de tout

**but** 1 conj mais
2 prep sauf; anybody ~ him n'importe qui
sauf lui; nobody ~ me knows how to do it il
n'y a que moi qui sache le faire; nothing
~ a coward ce n'est qu'un lâche; the
last ~ one l'avant-dernier
3 adv one can't help ~ admire her on ne
peut pas s'empêcher de l'admirer
4 but for phr ~ for you, I would have died
sans toi je serais mort; he would have gone
~ for me si je n'avais pas été là il serait
parti

**butane** n butane m

**butcher** 1 n boucher m; ~'s (shop)
boucherie f
2 vtr abattre ⟨animal⟩; massacrer ⟨people⟩

**butchery** n (a) (trade) boucherie f
(b) (slaughter) massacre m

**butler** n maître m d'hôtel, majordome m

**butt** 1 n (a) (of rifle) crosse f; (of cigarette)
mégot m (colloq)
(b) (US) (colloq) (buttocks) derrière m (colloq)
(c) to be the ~ of sb's jokes être la cible des
blagues de qn
2 vtr ⟨person⟩ donner un coup de tête à;
⟨animal⟩ donner un coup de corne à
■ **butt in** interrompre

**butter** 1 n beurre m
2 vtr beurrer ⟨bread⟩
■ **butter up** (colloq): ~ [sb] up, ~ up [sb]
passer de la pommade à (colloq)

**buttercup** n bouton d'or m

**butterfingers** n empoté/-e m/f

**butterfly** n papillon m
IDIOMS to have butterflies (in one's stomach)
avoir le trac (colloq)

**butterfly stroke** n brasse f papillon

**buttock** n fesse f

**button** 1 n (a) (on coat, switch) bouton m
(b) (US) (badge) badge m
(c) (Comput) bouton m
2 vi ⟨dress⟩ se boutonner
■ **button up** boutonner ⟨garment⟩

**buttonhole** 1 n (a) (on garment)
boutonnière f
(b) (GB) (flower) (fleur f de) boutonnière f
2 vtr (colloq) accrocher (colloq) ⟨person⟩

**buttress** n (a) contrefort m; (figurative)
soutien m
(b) (also flying ~) arc-boutant m

**buxom** adj ⟨woman⟩ à la poitrine
généreuse

**buy** 1 n a good ~ une bonne affaire
2 vtr acheter (from sb à qn); to ~ sth from
the supermarket/from the baker's acheter qch

au supermarché/chez le boulanger; **to ~ sb
sth** acheter qch à qn; **to ~ some time** gagner
du temps

■ **buy off** acheter ⟨*person, witness*⟩
■ **buy out** racheter la part de ⟨*co-owner*⟩
■ **buy up** acheter systématiquement ⟨*shares,
property*⟩

**buyer** *n* acheteur/-euse *m/f*

**buyout** *n* rachat *m* d'entreprise

**buzz** ①① *n* **(a)** (of insect) bourdonnement *m*
**(b)** (colloq) (phone call) **to give sb a ~** passer
un coup de fil à qn
**(c)** (colloq) (thrill) **it gives me a ~** (from alcohol)
ça me fait planer (colloq); **to get a ~ out of
doing** prendre son pied (colloq) en faisant
②② *vtr* **to ~ sb** appeler qn au bip, biper qn
③③ *vi* ⟨*bee, fly*⟩ bourdonner; ⟨*buzzer*⟩ sonner

**buzzard** *n* buse *f*

**buzzer** *n* (gen) sonnerie *f*; (on pocket) bip *m*

**buzzword** *n* (colloq) mot *m* à la mode

**by** ①① *prep* **(a)** (with passive verbs) par; **he was
bitten ~ a snake** il a été mordu par un
serpent
**(b)** (with present participle) en; **~ working extra
hours** en faisant des heures
supplémentaires; **to learn French ~ listening
to the radio** apprendre le français en
écoutant la radio; **to begin ~ doing**
commencer par faire
**(c)** (by means of) par; **to pay ~ cheque** payer
par chèque; **to travel to Rome ~ Venice** aller à
Rome en passant par Venise; **to travel ~
bus/train** voyager en bus/train; **~ bicycle** à
bicyclette, en vélo; **~ candlelight** ⟨*dine*⟩ aux
chandelles; ⟨*read*⟩ à la bougie
**(d)** (from) à; **I could tell ~ the look on her
face that** rien qu'à la regarder je savais que
**(e)** (near) à côté de, près de; **~ the window** à
côté de la fenêtre; **~ the sea** au bord de la
mer
**(f)** (showing authorship) de; **a film ~ Claude
Chabrol** un film de Claude Chabrol; **who is it
~?** c'est de qui?
**(g)** (in time expressions) avant; **~ midnight**
avant minuit; **~ this time next week** d'ici la
semaine prochaine; **~ the time she had got
downstairs he was gone** le temps qu'elle
descende, il était parti; **he should be here ~
now** il devrait être déjà là
**(h)** (according to) selon; **to play ~ the rules**
jouer selon les règles; **~ my watch** à ma
montre
**(i)** (showing amount) de; **prices have risen ~
20%** les prix ont augmenté de 20%; **he's
taller than me ~ two centimetres** il fait deux
centimètres de plus que moi
**(j)** (in measurements) sur; **20 metres ~ 10
metres** 20 mètres sur 10
**(k)** (showing rate, quantity) à; **paid ~ the hour**
payé à l'heure
**(l)** little **~ little** peu à peu; **day ~ day** jour
après jour; **one ~ one** un par un, une par
une; **~ oneself** tout seul/toute seule; **to go**
*or* **pass ~ sb/sth** passer devant qn/qch
**(m)** (in compass directions) quart; **south ~
south-west** sud quart sud-ouest
②② *adv* **(a)** (past) **to go ~** passer; **the people
walking ~** les gens qui passent/passaient,
les passants; **as time goes ~** avec le temps
**(b)** (near) près; **he lives close ~** il habite
tout près
**(c)** (aside) **to put money ~** mettre de l'argent
de côté

**bye** *excl* (colloq) (*also* **~-bye**) au revoir!

**by(e)-election** *n* (GB) élection *f* partielle

**bygone** *adj* ⟨*days, years, scene*⟩ d'antan; **a
~ era** une époque révolue
IDIOMS **to let ~s be ~s** enterrer le passé

**by(e)law** *n* arrêté *m* municipal

**bypass** ①① *n* **(a)** (road) rocade *f*
**(b)** (pipe, channel) by-pass *m inv*
**(c)** (in electricity) dérivation *f*
**(d)** (Med) (*also* **~ operation**) pontage *m*
②② *vtr* contourner ⟨*town, city*⟩

**by-product** *n* dérivé *m*; (figurative) effet *m*
secondaire

**bystander** *n* spectateur/-trice *m/f*

**byte** *n* (Comput) octet *m*

**byword** *n* **to be a ~ for** être synonyme de

# Cc

**c, C** *n* **(a)** (letter) c, C *m*
**(b)** C (Mus) do *m*

**cab** *n* **(a)** (taxi) taxi *m*
**(b)** (for driver) cabine *f*

**cabbage** *n* chou *m*

**cab-driver** *n* chauffeur *m* de taxi

**cabin** *n* **(a)** (hut) cabane *f*; (in holiday camp)
chalet *m*
**(b)** (in boat, plane) cabine *f*

**cabin crew** *n* personnel *m* de bord

**cabinet** *n* **(a)** (cupboard) petit placard *m*;
**display ~** vitrine *f*; **cocktail ~** meuble *m* bar
**(b)** (GB) (Pol) cabinet *m*

**cabinet minister** *n* (GB) ministre *m*

**cable** ①① *n* câble *m*
②② *adj* ⟨*channel, network*⟩ câblé/-e

**cable car** *n* téléphérique *m*

**cable TV** *n* télévision *f* par câble

**cab-rank**, **cab stand** n station f de taxis

**cackle** vi ⟨hen⟩ caqueter; ⟨person⟩ (talk) caqueter; (laugh) ricaner

**CAD** n (abbr = **computer-aided design**) CAO f

**CADCAM** n (abbr = **computer-aided design and computer-aided manufacture**) CFAO f

**caddy** n caddie m

**cadet** n (Mil) élève mf officier

**cadge** vtr (colloq) to ~ sth off or from sb taper (colloq) qch à qn ⟨cigarette, money⟩; to ~ a meal/a lift se faire inviter/emmener en voiture

**Caesarean**, **Caesarian** n (also ~ section) césarienne f

**café** n (a) ≈ snack-bar m; **pavement** ~, **sidewalk** ~ café m
(b) (US) bistro m

**cafeteria** n (gen) cafétéria f; (Sch) cantine f; (Univ) restaurant m universitaire

**caffein(e)** n caféine f; ~-free décaféiné/-e

**cage** ⟨1⟩ n cage f
⟨2⟩ vtr mettre [qch] en cage ⟨animal⟩; a ~d animal un animal en cage

**cagoule** n (GB) K-way® m

**cahoots** n pl (colloq) to be in ~ être de mèche (colloq) (**with** avec)

**Cairo** pr n Le Caire

**cajole** vtr cajoler

**cake** n (a) (Culin) gâteau m; (sponge) génoise f
(b) (of soap, wax) pain m
IDIOMS it's a piece of ~ (colloq) c'est du gâteau (colloq)

**cake shop** n ≈ pâtisserie f

**calcium** n calcium m

**calculate** vtr (a) calculer ⟨cost, distance, price⟩
(b) évaluer ⟨effect, probability⟩
(c) to be ~d to do avoir été conçu/-e pour faire

**calculated** adj ⟨crime⟩ prémédité/-e; ⟨attempt, insult⟩ délibéré/-e; ⟨risk⟩ calculé/-e

**calculating** adj ⟨manner, person⟩ calculateur/-trice

**calculation** n calcul m

**calculator** n calculatrice f, calculette f

**calendar** n calendrier m

**calf** n (a) (Zool) veau m
(b) (also ~skin) vachette f
(c) (Anat) mollet m

**calibre** (GB), **caliber** (US) n calibre m

**California** pr n Californie f

**call** ⟨1⟩ n (a) (also **phone** ~) appel m (téléphonique) (**from** de); to make a ~ appeler, téléphoner
(b) (cry) (human) appel m (**for** à); (animal) cri m
(c) (summons) appel m
(d) (visit) visite f
(e) (demand) demande f (**for** de)

(f) (need) there's no ~ **for sth** il n'y a pas de raison pour qch
(g) (Sport) décision f
(h) **to be on** ~ ⟨doctor⟩ être de garde; ⟨engineer⟩ être de service
⟨2⟩ vtr (a) (gen) appeler; **what is he** ~ed? comment s'appelle-t-il?; **the boss** ~ed me **into his office** le chef m'a fait venir dans son bureau
(b) organiser ⟨strike⟩; convoquer ⟨meeting⟩; fixer ⟨election⟩
(c) (waken) réveiller ⟨person⟩
(d) (describe as) **to** ~ **sb stupid** traiter qn d'imbécile; **I wouldn't** ~ **it spacious** je ne dirais pas que c'est spacieux
⟨3⟩ vi (a) (gen) appeler; **who's** ~ing? qui est à l'appareil?
(b) (visit) passer; **to** ~ **at** passer chez ⟨person, shop⟩; passer à ⟨bank, library⟩; ⟨train⟩ s'arrêter à ⟨town, station⟩
■ **call back**: ¶ ~ **back** (on phone) rappeler; ¶ ~ [sb] **back** rappeler ⟨person⟩
■ **call for**: ~ **for** [sth] (a) (demand) appeler ⟨ambulance, doctor⟩; **to** ~ **for help** appeler à l'aide
(b) (demand) réclamer
(c) (require) exiger ⟨treatment, skill⟩; nécessiter ⟨change⟩
■ **call in**: ¶ ~ **in** (visit) passer; ¶ ~ [sb] **in** faire entrer ⟨client, patient⟩; faire appel à ⟨expert⟩
■ **call off** abandonner ⟨investigation⟩; annuler ⟨deal, wedding⟩; rompre ⟨engagement⟩
■ **call on** (a) (visit) rendre visite à ⟨relative, friend⟩; visiter ⟨patient, client⟩
(b) **to** ~ **on sb to do** demander à qn de faire
■ **call out**: ¶ ~ **out** appeler; (louder) crier ¶ ~ [sb] **out** (a) appeler ⟨doctor, troops⟩
(b) ⟨union⟩ lancer un ordre de grève à ⟨members⟩
~ [sth] **out** appeler ⟨name, number⟩
■ **call up**: ¶ ~ **up** appeler ¶ ~ [sb/sth] **up** (a) (on phone) appeler
(b) (Mil) appeler [qn] sous les drapeaux ⟨soldier⟩

**call box** n (GB) cabine f téléphonique; (US) poste m téléphonique

**call centre** n centre m d'appels

**caller** n (a) (on phone) personne f qui appelle
(b) (visitor) visiteur/-euse m/f

**callous** adj inhumain/-e

**call-out charge** n frais mpl de déplacement

**calm** ⟨1⟩ n calme m; (in adversity) sang-froid m
⟨2⟩ adj calme; **keep** ~! du calme!
⟨3⟩ vtr calmer
■ **calm down**: ¶ ~ **down** se calmer ¶ ~ [sb/sth] **down** calmer

**calmly** adv ⟨act, speak⟩ calmement; ⟨sleep, smoke⟩ tranquillement

**Calor gas**® n (GB) butane m

**calorie** n calorie f

**camcorder** n caméscope® m

**camel** n chameau m

**camera** *n* **(a)** (for photos) appareil *m* photo **(b)** (for movies) caméra *f*

**camera crew** *n* équipe *f* de télévision

**cameraman** *n* cadreur *m*, cameraman *m*

**camisole** *n* caraco *m*

**camouflage** ⒈ *n* camouflage *m* ⒉ *vtr* camoufler (**with** avec)

**camp** ⒈ *n* camp *m* ⒉ *vi* camper; **to go ~ing** faire du camping

**campaign** ⒈ *n* campagne *f* ⒉ *vi* faire campagne (**for** pour; **against** contre)

**campaigner** *n* militant/-e *m/f* (**for** pour; **against** contre); (Pol) candidat/-e *m/f* en campagne (électorale)

**camp bed** *n* lit *m* de camp

**camper** *n* **(a)** (person) campeur/-euse *m/f* **(b)** (also ~ **van**) camping-car *m*

**campfire** *n* feu *m* de camp

**camping** *n* camping *m*; **to go ~** faire du camping

**campsite** *n* terrain *m* de camping, camping *m*

**campus** *n* campus *m*

**can¹** *modal aux* **(a)** (be able to) pouvoir; **~ you come?** est-ce que tu peux venir?, peux-tu venir?; **we will do all we ~** nous ferons tout ce que nous pouvons *or* tout notre possible **(b)** (know how to) savoir; **she ~ swim** elle sait nager; **I can't drive** je ne sais pas conduire; **he ~ speak French** il parle français **(c)** (permission, requests, offers, suggestions) pouvoir; **~ we park here?** est-ce que nous pouvons nous garer ici?; **you can't turn right** vous ne pouvez pas *or* vous n'avez pas le droit de tourner à droite; **~ you do me a favour?** peux-tu *or* est-ce que tu peux me rendre un service? **(d)** (with verbs of perception) **~ they see us?** est-ce qu'ils nous voient?; **I can't feel a thing** je ne sens rien; **she can't understand English** elle ne comprend pas l'anglais **(e)** (in expressions) **you can't be hungry!** tu ne peux pas avoir faim!; **you can't be serious!** tu veux rire!; **this can't be right** il doit y avoir une erreur; **~ you believe it!** tu te rends compte?; **what ~ she want from me?** qu'est-ce qu'elle peut bien me vouloir?

**can²** ⒈ *n* (of food) boîte *f*; (of drink) cannette *f*; (aerosol) bombe *f*; (for petrol) bidon *m*; (of paint) pot *m* ⒉ *vtr* mettre (qch) en conserve

**Canada** *pr n* Canada *m*

**Canadian** ⒈ *n* Canadien/-ienne *m/f* ⒉ *adj* canadien/-ienne; (embassy) du Canada

**canal** *n* canal *m*

**canal boat**, **canal barge** *n* péniche *f*

**Canaries** *pr n pl* (also **Canary Islands**) **the ~** les Canaries *fpl*

**cancel** *vtr* (gen) annuler; mettre une opposition à (cheque)

**cancellation** *n* annulation *f*

**cancer** *n* cancer *m*; **to have ~** avoir un cancer; **lung ~** cancer du poumon

**Cancer** *n* Cancer *m*

**cancer patient** *n* cancéreux/-euse *m/f*

**cancer research** *n* cancérologie *f*

**candid** *adj* franc/franche

**candidate** *n* candidat/-e *m/f*

**candle** *n* bougie *f*; (in church) cierge *m*

**candlelight** *n* lueur *f* de bougie

**candlelit dinner** *n* dîner *m* aux chandelles

**candlestick** *n* bougeoir *m*; (ornate) chandelier *m*

**candy** *n* (US) (sweets) bonbons *mpl*; (sweet) bonbon *m*

**candyfloss** *n* (GB) barbe *f* à papa

**cane** *n* **(a)** (material) rotin *m*; **~ furniture** meubles en rotin **(b)** (of sugar, bamboo) canne *f* **(c)** (for walking) canne *f*; (for plant) tuteur *m*; (GB) (for punishment) badine *f*

**canine** *n* canine *f*

**canister** *n* boîte *f* métallique; **a tear gas ~** une bombe lacrymogène

**cannabis** *n* cannabis *m*

**canned** *adj* **(a)** (food) en boîte **(b)** (colloq) (laughter) enregistré/-e

**cannibal** *n* cannibale *mf*

**cannon** *n* canon *m*

**canoe** ⒈ *n* (gen) canoë *m*; (dugout) pirogue *f*; (Sport) canoë-kayac *m* ⒉ *vi* faire du canoë

**canoeing** *n* **to go ~** faire du canoë-kayac

**can-opener** *n* ouvre-boîtes *m inv*

**cantankerous** *adj* acariâtre

**canteen** *n* **(a)** (GB) (dining room) cantine *f* **(b)** (Mil) (flask) bidon *m*; (mess tin) gamelle *f* **(c)** **a ~ of cutlery** une ménagère

**canter** *vi* (rider) faire un petit galop; (horse) galoper

**canvas** *n* toile *f*

**canvass** *vtr* **(a)** **to ~ voters** faire du démarchage électoral auprès des électeurs **(b)** **to ~ opinion on sth** sonder l'opinion au sujet de qch **(c)** (for business) prospecter (area)

**canvasser** *n* agent *m* électoral

**canyon** *n* cañon *m*

**canyoning** *n* canyoning *m*

**cap** ⒈ *n* **(a)** casquette *f*; **baseball ~** casquette de baseball **(b)** (of pen) capuchon *m*; (of bottle) capsule *f* **(c)** (for tooth) couronne *f* ⒉ *vtr* **(a)** (limit) imposer une limite budgétaire à (local authority); plafonner (budget) **(b)** (cover) couronner (**with** de) IDIOMS **to ~ it all** pour couronner le tout

**capability** *n* **(a)** (capacity) capacité *f* (**to do** de faire) **(b)** (aptitude) aptitude *f*; **outside my capabilities** au-delà de mes compétences

**capable** *adj* **(a)** (competent) compétent/-e ⋯‣

**(b)** (able) capable (**of** de)

**capacity** n **(a)** (of box, bottle) contenance f; (of building) capacité f d'accueil; **full to ~** comble
**(b)** (of factory) capacité f de production
**(c)** (role) **in my ~ as a doctor** en ma qualité de médecin
**(d)** (ability) **to have a ~ for** avoir des facilités pour ⟨learning, mathematics⟩; **a ~ for doing** une aptitude à faire

**cape** n **(a)** (cloak) cape f
**(b)** (on coast) cap m

**caper** n **(a)** (Culin) câpre f
**(b)** (colloq) (scheme) combine f
**(c)** (colloq) (antic) pitrerie f

**Cape Town** pr n Le Cap

**capital** ⓵ n **(a)** (letter) majuscule f
**(b)** (also ~ **city**) capitale f
**(c)** (money) capital m
⓶ adj **(a)** ⟨letter⟩ majuscule; **~ A** A majuscule
**(b)** (Law) ⟨offence⟩ capital/-e

**capital expenditure** n dépenses fpl d'investissement

**capital investment** n dépenses fpl d'investissement

**capitalism** n capitalisme m

**capitalist** n, adj capitaliste (mf)

**capitalize** vi **to ~ on** tirer parti de ⟨situation, advantage⟩

**capital punishment** n peine f capitale

**capitulate** vi capituler (**to** devant)

**Capricorn** n Capricorne m

**capsize** vi chavirer

**captain** ⓵ n capitaine m
⓶ vtr être le capitaine de ⟨team⟩; commander ⟨ship, platoon⟩

**caption** n légende f

**captivate** vtr captiver, fasciner

**captive** n captif/-ive m/f

**captivity** n captivité f

**captor** n (of person) geôlier/-ière m/f

**capture** ⓵ n (of person, animal) capture f; (of stronghold) prise f
⓶ vtr **(a)** capturer ⟨person, animal⟩; prendre ⟨stronghold⟩
**(b)** saisir ⟨likeness⟩; rendre ⟨feeling⟩

**car** ⓵ n **(a)** (Aut) voiture f
**(b)** (on train) wagon m; **restaurant ~** wagon-restaurant m
⓶ adj ⟨industry, insurance⟩ automobile; ⟨journey, chase⟩ en voiture; ⟨accident⟩ de voiture

**caramel** n caramel m

**carat** n carat m; **18 ~ gold** or 18 carats

**caravan** ⓵ n caravane f; (horse-drawn) roulotte f
⓶ vi **to go ~ning** (GB) faire du caravanage

**caravan site** n camping m pour caravanes

**carbohydrate** n hydrate m de carbone

**car bomb** n bombe f dissimulée dans une voiture

**carbon** n carbone m

**carbon copy** n copie f carbone; (figurative) réplique f exacte

**carbon dioxide** n dioxyde m de carbone

**carbon monoxide** n monoxyde m de carbone

**car boot sale** n (GB) brocante f (d'objets apportés dans le coffre de sa voiture)

**carburettor** (GB), **carburetor** (US) n carburateur m

**card** n carte f
**IDIOMS to play one's ~s right** bien jouer son jeu (colloq)

**cardboard** n carton m

**cardboard box** n (boîte f en) carton m

**cardboard city** n: zone urbaine où les sans-abri logent dans des cartons

**card game** n partie f de cartes

**cardiac** adj cardiaque

**cardiac arrest** n arrêt m du cœur

**cardigan** n cardigan m

**card key** n carte f magnétique

**cardphone** n téléphone m à carte

**card trick** n tour m de cartes

**care** ⓵ n **(a)** (attention) attention f, soin m; **to take ~ to do** prendre soin de faire; **'take ~!'** (be careful) 'fais attention!'; (goodbye) 'à bientôt!'; **'handle with ~'** 'fragile'
**(b)** (looking after) (of person, animal) soins mpl; (of car, plant, clothes) entretien m (of de); **to take ~ of** (deal with) s'occuper de ⟨child, client, garden, details⟩; (be careful with) prendre soin de ⟨machine, car⟩; (keep in good condition) entretenir ⟨car, teeth⟩; (look after) garder ⟨shop, watch⟩; **to take ~ of oneself** (look after oneself) prendre soin de soi; (cope) se débrouiller tout seul/toute seule; (defend oneself) se défendre
**(c)** (Med) soins mpl
**(d)** (GB) **to be in ~** ⟨child⟩ être (placé/-e) en garde
**(e)** (worry) souci m
⓶ vi **(a)** (be concerned) **to ~ about** s'intéresser à ⟨art, environment⟩; se soucier du bien-être de ⟨pupils, the elderly⟩; **I don't ~!** ça m'est égal!; **she couldn't ~ less about...** elle se moque or se fiche (colloq) complètement de...; **I'm past caring** je m'en moque
**(b)** (love) **to ~ about sb** aimer qn
■ **care for**: ¶ **~ for** [sth] **(a)** (like) aimer; **would you ~ for a drink?** voulez-vous boire quelque chose?
**(b)** (maintain) entretenir ⟨car, garden⟩; prendre soin de ⟨skin, plant⟩
¶ **~ for** [sb/sth] s'occuper de ⟨child, animal⟩; soigner ⟨patient⟩

**care assistant** n aide-soignant/-e m/f

**career** n carrière f

**career break** n interruption f de carrière

**careers adviser**, **careers officer** n conseiller/-ère m/f d'orientation

**careers office** n service m d'orientation professionnelle

**carefree** *adj* insouciant/-e

**careful** *adj* ⟨*person, driving*⟩ prudent/-e; ⟨*planning, preparation*⟩ minutieux/-ieuse; ⟨*research, examination*⟩ méticuleux/-euse; **to be ∼ to do** *or* **about doing** prendre soin de faire; **to be ∼ with sth** faire attention à qch; **be ∼!** (fais) attention!

**carefully** *adv* ⟨*walk, open, handle*⟩ prudemment; ⟨*write*⟩ soigneusement; ⟨*listen, read, look*⟩ attentivement

**careless** *adj* ⟨*person*⟩ négligent/-e, imprudent/-e; ⟨*work*⟩ bâclé/-e; ⟨*writing*⟩ négligé/-e; ⟨*driving*⟩ négligent/-e; **∼ mistake** faute d'étourderie; **it was ∼ of me to do** ça a été de la négligence de ma part de faire

**carelessness** *n* négligence *f*

**carer** *n* (relative) *personne ayant un parent handicapé ou malade à charge*; (professional) aide *f* familiale

**caress** *vtr* caresser

**caretaker** *n* concierge *mf*

**care worker** *n* assistant/-e *m/f* social/-e

**car ferry** *n* ferry *m*

**cargo** *n* chargement *m*

**cargo ship** *n* cargo *m*

**car hire** *n* location *f* de voitures

**car hire company** *n* société *f* de location de voitures

**Caribbean** *pr n* **the ∼ (sea)** la mer des Antilles *or* des Caraïbes

**caricature** *n* caricature *f*

**caring** *adj* **(a)** (loving) ⟨*parent*⟩ affectueux/-euse
**(b)** (compassionate) ⟨*person, attitude*⟩ compréhensif/-ive; ⟨*society*⟩ humain/-e

**carjacking** *n* vol *m* de voiture (avec agression du conducteur)

**carnage** *n* carnage *m*

**carnation** *n* œillet *m*

**carnival** *n* **(a)** carnaval *m*
**(b)** (US) (funfair) fête *f* foraine

**carol** *n* chant *m* de Noël

**carousel** *n* **(a)** (merry-go-round) manège *m*
**(b)** (for luggage, slides) carrousel *m*

**car park** *n* (GB) parc *m* de stationnement

**carpenter** *n* menuisier *m*

**carpentry** *n* menuiserie *f*

**carpet** *n* (fitted) moquette *f*; (loose) tapis *m*

**carpet sweeper** *n* balai *m* mécanique

**car phone** *n* téléphone *m* de voiture

**car radio** *n* autoradio *m*

**carriage** *n* **(a)** (ceremonial) carrosse *m*
**(b)** (of train) wagon *m*, voiture *f*
**(c)** (of goods) transport *m*; **∼ paid** port *m* payé
**(d)** (of typewriter) chariot *m*

**carriageway** *n* chaussée *f*

**carrier** *n* **(a)** (transport company) transporteur *m*; (airline) compagnie *f* aérienne
**(b)** (of disease) porteur/-euse *m/f*
**(c)** (GB) (*also* **∼ bag**) sac *m* (en plastique)

**carrot** *n* carotte *f*

**carry** ⟨1⟩ *vtr* **(a)** ⟨*person*⟩ porter; **to ∼ sth in/out** apporter/emporter qch
**(b)** ⟨*vehicle, pipe, vein*⟩ transporter; ⟨*tide, current*⟩ emporter
**(c)** comporter ⟨*warning*⟩
**(d)** comporter ⟨*risk, responsibility*⟩; être passible de ⟨*penalty*⟩
**(e)** ⟨*bridge, road*⟩ supporter ⟨*load, traffic*⟩
**(f)** faire voter ⟨*bill*⟩; **the motion was carried by 20 votes to 13** la motion l'a emporté par 20 votes contre 13
**(g)** (Med) être porteur/-euse de ⟨*disease, virus*⟩
**(h)** (in mathematics) retenir
**(i)** (hold) porter ⟨*head*⟩
⟨2⟩ *vi* ⟨*sound, voice*⟩ porter
**IDIOMS to get carried away** (colloq) s'emballer (colloq), se laisser emporter
■ **carry forward** reporter ⟨*balance, total*⟩
■ **carry off** (gen) emporter; remporter ⟨*prize*⟩; **to ∼ it off** (colloq) réussir, y arriver
■ **carry on**: ¶ **∼ on (a)** (continue) continuer ⟨*doing* à faire⟩
**(b)** (colloq) (behave) se conduire
¶ **∼ on [sth]** maintenir ⟨*tradition*⟩; poursuivre ⟨*activity, discussion*⟩
■ **carry out** réaliser ⟨*study*⟩; effectuer ⟨*experiment, reform, attack, repairs*⟩; exécuter ⟨*plan, orders*⟩; mener ⟨*investigation, campaign*⟩; accomplir ⟨*mission*⟩; remplir ⟨*duties*⟩; mettre [qch] à exécution ⟨*threat*⟩; tenir ⟨*promise*⟩

**carryall** *n* (US) fourre-tout *m inv*

**carrycot** *n* (GB) porte-bébé *m*

**carry-on** *n* (colloq) cirque *m* (colloq)

**carryout** *n* repas *m* à emporter

**car seat** *n* siège-auto *m*

**carsick** *adj* **to be ∼** avoir le mal de la route

**cart** ⟨1⟩ *n* charrette *f*
⟨2⟩ *vtr* (colloq) (*also* **∼ around**, **∼ about**) (colloq) trimballer (colloq) ⟨*bags*⟩

**cartel** *n* cartel *m*; **drug ∼** cartel *m* de la drogue

**car theft** *n* vol *m* de voitures

**carton** *n* (of juice, milk) carton *m*, brique *f*; (of yoghurt, cream) pot *m*; (of cigarettes) cartouche *f*; (US) (for house removals) carton *m*

**cartoon** *n* **(a)** (film) dessin *m* animé
**(b)** (drawing) dessin *m* humoristique; (comic strip) bande *f* dessinée

**cartridge** *n* (for pen, gun, video) cartouche *f*; (for camera) chargeur *m*

**cartwheel** *n* **to do a ∼** faire la roue

**carve** ⟨1⟩ *vtr* **(a)** tailler, sculpter ⟨*wood, stone, figure*⟩ (out of dans)
**(b)** graver ⟨*letters, name*⟩ (onto sur)
**(c)** découper ⟨*meat*⟩
⟨2⟩ *vi* découper
■ **carve out (a)** se faire ⟨*niche, name*⟩; se tailler ⟨*reputation, market*⟩
**(b)** creuser ⟨*gorge, channel*⟩
■ **carve up**: **∼ up [sth]**, **∼ [sth] up** partager ⟨*proceeds*⟩; morceler ⟨*estate, territory*⟩

**carving** *n* sculpture *f*

**carving knife** n couteau m à découper
**car wash** n lavage m automatique
**case**¹ ① n (a) (gen) cas m; **in that ~** en ce cas, dans ce cas-là; **in 7 out of 10 ~s** 7 fois sur 10, dans 7 cas sur 10; **a ~ in point** un cas d'espèce, un exemple typique
(b) (Law) affaire f; procès m; **the ~ for the Crown** (GB), **the ~ for the State** (US) l'accusation f; **the ~ for the defence** la défense
(c) (argument) arguments mpl
② **in any case** phr (a) (besides, anyway) de toute façon
(b) (at any rate) en tout cas
③ **in case** phr au cas où (+ conditional); **just in ~** au cas où
④ **in case of** phr en cas de ⟨fire, accident⟩
**case**² n (a) (suitcase) valise f; (crate, chest) caisse f
(b) (display cabinet) vitrine f
(c) (for spectacles, binoculars, weapon) étui m; (for camera, watch) boîtier m
**CASE** n (abbr = **computer-aided software engineering**) CPAO f
**case study** n étude f de cas
**cash** ① n (a) (notes and coin) espèces fpl, argent m liquide; **to pay in ~** payer en espèces; **I haven't got any ~ on me** je n'ai pas d'argent liquide
(b) (money in general) argent m
(c) ( payment) comptant m; **discount for ~** remise f pour paiement comptant
② vtr encaisser ⟨cheque⟩
■ **cash in**: ¶ **to ~ in on** tirer profit de, profiter de; ¶ **~ [sth] in** se faire rembourser, réaliser ⟨bond, policy⟩; (US) encaisser ⟨check⟩
**cash-and-carry** n libre-service m de vente en gros
**cash card** n carte f de retrait
**cash desk** n caisse f
**cash dispenser** n (also **cashpoint**) distributeur m automatique de billets de banque, billetterie f
**cashew nut** n cajou m
**cash flow** n marge f brute d'auto-financement, MBA f
**cashier** n caissier/-ière m/f
**cashless** adj ⟨society⟩ sans argent liquide
**cashmere** n (lainage m en) cachemire m
**cash on delivery**, **COD** n envoi m contre remboursement
**cashpoint** = CASH DISPENSER
**cash register** n caisse f enregistreuse
**casino** n casino m
**cask** n fût m, tonneau m
**casserole** n (a) (container) daubière f, cocotte f
(b) (GB) (food) ragoût m cuit au four
**cassette** n cassette f
**cassette deck** n platine f à cassettes
**cassette player** n lecteur m de cassettes
**cast** ① n (a) (list of actors) distribution f; (actors) acteurs mpl

(b) (Med) (also **plaster ~**) plâtre m
(c) (mould) moule m
② vtr (a) jeter, lancer ⟨stone, fishing line⟩; projeter ⟨shadow⟩; **to ~ doubt on** émettre des doutes sur; **to ~ light on** éclairer; **to ~ a spell on** jeter un sort à
(b) jeter ⟨glance⟩ (at sur)
(c) distribuer les rôles de ⟨play, film⟩; **she was cast as Blanche** elle a joué Blanche
(d) couler ⟨plaster, metal⟩
(e) **to ~ one's vote** voter
**castaway** n naufragé/-e m/f
**caste** n caste f
**caster sugar** n (GB) sucre m en poudre
**casting** n distribution f
**casting vote** n voix f prépondérante
**cast iron** n fonte f; **a ~ alibi** un alibi en béton (colloq)
**castle** n (a) château m
(b) (in chess) tour f
**cast-offs** n pl vêtements mpl dont on n'a plus besoin, vieux vêtements
**castrate** vtr castrer
**casual** adj (a) (informal) ⟨clothes, person⟩ décontracté/-e
(b) ⟨acquaintance, relationship⟩ de passage; **~ sex** relations fpl sexuelles non suivies
(c) ⟨attitude, gesture, remark⟩ désinvolte
(d) ⟨glance⟩ superficiel/-ielle
(e) ⟨work⟩ (temporary) temporaire; (occasional) occasionnel/-elle
**casualize** vtr **to ~ labour** précariser l'emploi
**casually** adv (a) ⟨enquire, remark⟩ d'un air détaché
(b) ⟨dressed⟩ simplement
**casualty** ① n (a) (person) victime f
(b) (hospital ward) urgences fpl; **in ~** aux urgences
② **casualties** n pl (soldiers) pertes fpl; (civilians) victimes fpl
**casual wear** n vêtements mpl sport
**cat** n (domestic) chat m; (female) chatte f; **the big ~s** les grands félins mpl
IDIOMS **to let the ~ out of the bag** vendre la mèche; **to rain ~s and dogs** pleuvoir des cordes
**catalogue**, **catalog** (US) n catalogue m
**catalyst** n catalyseur m
**catalytic converter** n pot m catalytique
**catapult** n (hand-held) lance-pierres m inv
**catarrh** n catarrhe m
**catastrophe** n catastrophe f
**catch** ① n (a) (on purse, door) fermeture f
(b) (drawback) piège m
(c) (act of catching) prise f; **to play ~** jouer à la balle
(d) (in fishing) pêche f; (one fish) prise f
② vtr (a) ⟨person⟩ attraper ⟨ball, fish, person⟩; **to ~ hold of sth** attraper qch; **to ~ sb's attention** or **eye** attirer l'attention de qn; **to ~ sight of sb/sth** apercevoir qn/qch
(b) (take by surprise) prendre, attraper; **to ~ sb**

doing surprendre qn en train de faire; **we got caught in the rain** nous avons été surpris par la pluie
**(c)** prendre ⟨*bus, plane*⟩
**(d)** (grasp) prendre ⟨*hand, arm*⟩; agripper ⟨*branch, rope*⟩; captiver, éveiller ⟨*interest*⟩
**(e)** (hear) saisir (colloq), comprendre
**(f) to ∼ one's fingers in** se prendre les doigts dans ⟨*drawer, door*⟩; **to get one's shirt caught on** accrocher sa chemise à ⟨*nail*⟩; **to get caught in** se prendre dans ⟨*barbed wire, thorns*⟩
**(g)** attraper ⟨*cold, disease, flu*⟩
**(h) to ∼ fire** prendre feu, s'enflammer
**3** *vi* **(a) to ∼ on** ⟨*shirt*⟩ s'accrocher à ⟨*nail*⟩; ⟨*wheel*⟩ frotter contre ⟨*frame*⟩
**(b)** ⟨*wood, fire*⟩ prendre
■ **catch on (a)** (become popular) devenir populaire (**with** auprès de)
**(b)** (understand) comprendre, saisir
■ **catch out (a)** (take by surprise) prendre [qn] de court; (doing something wrong) prendre [qn] sur le fait
**(b)** (trick) attraper, jouer un tour à
■ **catch up:** ¶ ∼ **up** (in race) regagner du terrain; (in work) rattraper son retard; **to ∼ up on** rattraper ⟨*work, sleep*⟩; se remettre au courant de ⟨*news*⟩; ¶ ∼ **[sb/sth] up** rattraper
**catch-22 situation** *n* situation *f* inextricable
**catching** *adj* contagieux/-ieuse
**catchphrase** *n* formule *f* favorite, rengaine *f*
**catchy** *adj* ⟨*tune*⟩ entraînant/-e; ⟨*slogan*⟩ accrocheur/-euse
**categorical** *adj* catégorique
**categorize** *vtr* classer (**by** d'après)
**category** *n* catégorie *f*
**cater** *vi* **(a)** ⟨*caterer*⟩ organiser des réceptions
**(b) to ∼ for** (GB) *or* **to** (US) accueillir ⟨*children, guests*⟩; pourvoir à ⟨*needs*⟩; ⟨*programme*⟩ s'adresser à ⟨*audience*⟩
**caterer** *n* traiteur *m*
**catering** *n* (provision) approvisionnement *m*; (trade, industry, career) restauration *f*
**caterpillar** *n* chenille *f*
**cathedral** *n* cathédrale *f*
**Catholic** *n, adj* catholique (*mf*)
**Catholicism** *n* catholicisme *m*
**catnap** *vi* faire un somme, sommeiller
**Catseye®** *n* (GB) plot *m* rétroréfléchissant
**cattle** *n* bétail *m*
**catwalk** *n* podium *m*; ∼ **show** défilé *m* de mode
**cauliflower** *n* chou-fleur *m*
**cause 1** *n* cause *f* (**of** de); **there is ∼ for concern** il y a des raisons de s'inquiéter; **to have ∼ to do** avoir des raisons de faire; **with good ∼** à juste titre
**2** *vtr* causer, occasionner ⟨*damage, grief, problem*⟩; provoquer ⟨*chaos, disease, controversy*⟩; entraîner ⟨*suffering*⟩; amener

⟨*confusion*⟩; **to ∼ sb problems** causer des problèmes à qn; **to ∼ trouble** créer des problèmes
**caustic** *adj* caustique
**caution 1** *n* **(a)** (care) prudence *f*
**(b)** (wariness) circonspection *f*
**(c)** (warning) avertissement *m*
**2** *vtr* **(a)** (warn) avertir (**that** que)
**(b)** (Sport) donner un avertissement à ⟨*player*⟩
**IDIOMS to throw** *or* **cast ∼ to the wind(s)** oublier toute prudence
**cautionary** *adj* ⟨*look, gesture*⟩ d'avertissement; **a ∼ tale** un conte moral
**cautious** *adj* **(a)** (careful) prudent/-e
**(b)** (wary) ⟨*person, reception, response*⟩ réservé/-e; ⟨*optimism*⟩ prudent/-e
**cave** *n* grotte *f*
■ **cave in (a)** ⟨*tunnel, roof*⟩ s'effondrer
**(b)** ⟨*person*⟩ céder
**caveman** *n* homme *m* des cavernes
**caviar(e)** *n* caviar *m*
**caving** *n* spéléologie *f*; **to go ∼** faire de la spéléologie
**cavity** *n* cavité *f*
**cavort** *vi* faire des cabrioles
**caw** *vi* croasser
**cc** *n* (*abbr* = **cubic centimetre**) cm³
**CCTV** *n* (*abbr* = **closed-circuit television**) télévision *f* en circuit fermé
**CD** *n* (*abbr* = **compact disc**) CD *m*
**CD player**, **CD system** *n* platine *f* laser
**CD-ROM** *n* CD-ROM *m*, disque *m* optique compact
**cease** *vtr, vi* cesser
**cease-fire** *n* cessez-le-feu *m inv*
**cedar** *n* cèdre *m*
**cede** *vtr, vi* céder (**to** à)
**cedilla** *n* cédille *f*
**ceiling** *n* plafond *m*
**celebrate 1** *vtr* fêter; (more formally) célébrer
**2** *vi* faire la fête
**celebrated** *adj* célèbre (**for** pour)
**celebration** *n* **(a)** (celebrating) célébration *f*
**(b)** (party) fête *f*
**(c)** (public festivities) ∼**s** cérémonies *fpl*
**celebrity 1** *n* célébrité *f*
**2** *adj* ⟨*guest*⟩ célèbre; ⟨*panel*⟩ de célébrités
**celery** *n* céleri *m*
**celibate** *adj* (chaste) chaste
**cell** *n* cellule *f*
**cellar** *n* cave *f*
**cello** *n* violoncelle *m*
**cellphone**, **cellular phone** *n* radiotéléphone *m*
**cellulite** *n* cellulite *f*
**Celsius** *adj* Celsius *inv*
**Celt** *n* Celte *mf*
**Celtic** *adj* celtique, celte
**cement** *n* ciment *m*

**cement mixer** n bétonnière f

**cemetery** n cimetière m

**censor** [1] n censeur mf
[2] vtr censurer

**censorship** n censure f (of de)

**censure** [1] n censure f
[2] vtr critiquer

**census** n recensement m

**cent** n (of dollar) cent m; (of euro) cent m, centime m [d'euro]

**centenary** n centenaire m

**center** (US) = CENTRE

**centigrade** adj in degrees ∼ en degrés Celsius

**centimetre** (GB), **centimeter** (US) n centimètre m

**central** adj (a) central/-e; ∼ **London** le centre de Londres
(b) (in the town centre) situé/-e en centre-ville
(c) (key) principal/-e

**Central America** pr n Amérique f centrale

**central heating** n chauffage m central

**centralize** vtr centraliser

**central locking** n verrouillage m central or centralisé

**central reservation** n (GB) (Aut) terre-plein m central

**centre** (GB), **center** (US) [1] n centre m; in the ∼ au centre; town ∼, city ∼ centre-ville m; the ∼ of attention le centre de l'attention; the ∼ of power le siège du pouvoir; shopping/sports ∼ centre m commercial/sportif
[2] vtr, vi centrer
■ **centre around**, **centre on** ⟨activities, person⟩ se concentrer sur; ⟨people, industry⟩ se situer autour de ⟨town⟩; ⟨life, thoughts⟩ être centré/-e sur ⟨person, work⟩

**centre-forward** n (Sport) avant-centre m

**centre ground** n centre m; to occupy the ∼ être au centre

**centre-half** n (Sport) demi-centre m

**centrepiece** (GB), **centerpiece** (US) n (of table) décoration f centrale; (of exhibition) clou m

**centre-stage** to take/occupy ∼ devenir/être le point de mire

**century** n siècle m; in the 20th ∼ au XXᵉ siècle; at the turn of the ∼ au début du siècle

**ceramic** adj en céramique

**ceramics** n céramiques fpl

**cereal** n céréale f; breakfast ∼ céréales pour le petit déjeuner

**cerebral palsy** n paralysie f motrice centrale

**ceremony** n cérémonie f; to stand on ∼ faire des cérémonies

**cert** n (colloq) it's a (dead) ∼! (colloq) ça ne fait pas un pli! (colloq)

**certain** adj (a) (sure) certain/-e, sûr/-e (about, of de); I'm ∼ (of it) j'en suis certain

or sûr; absolutely ∼ sûr et certain; I'm ∼ that I checked je suis sûr d'avoir vérifié; I'm ∼ that he refused je suis sûr qu'il a refusé
(b) (specific) ⟨amount, number, conditions⟩ certain/-e (before n); ∼ **people** certains mpl; to a ∼ extent dans une certaine mesure

**certainly** adv certainement

**certainty** n certitude f

**certificate** n (gen) certificat m; (of birth, death, marriage) acte m; 18-∼ film film interdit aux moins de 18 ans

**certified** adj certifié/-e

**certified mail** n (US) to send by ∼ envoyer en recommandé

**certified public accountant** n (US) expert-comptable m

**certify** vtr (a) (confirm) certifier
(b) (authenticate) authentifier

**cervical cancer** n cancer m du col de l'utérus

**cervical smear** n frottis m vaginal

**CFC** n (abbr = **chlorofluorocarbon**) CFC m

**chafe** vi frotter (on, against sur)

**chain** [1] n (a) (metal links) chaîne f
(b) (on lavatory) chasse f (d'eau)
(c) (on door) chaîne f de sûreté
(d) (of shops, hotels) chaîne f (of de)
(e) (of events) série f; (of ideas) enchaînement m
[2] vtr enchaîner ⟨person, animal⟩; to ∼ a bicycle to sth attacher une bicyclette à qch avec une chaîne

**chain reaction** n réaction f en chaîne

**chain saw** n tronçonneuse f

**chain-smoke** vi fumer comme un sapeur (colloq), fumer sans arrêt

**chain-smoker** n gros fumeur/grosse fumeuse m/f

**chain store** n (single shop) magasin m faisant partie d'une chaîne; (retail group) magasin m à succursales multiples

**chair** [1] n (a) chaise f; (armchair) fauteuil m
(b) (chairperson) président/-e m/f
(c) (Univ) chaire f (of, in de)
[2] vtr présider ⟨meeting⟩

**chair lift** n télésiège m

**chairman** n président/-e m/f; Mr Chairman monsieur le Président; Madam Chairman madame la Présidente

**chairperson** n président/-e m/f

**chalet** n (mountain) chalet m; (in holiday camp) bungalow m

**chalk** n craie f

**challenge** [1] n (a) défi m; to take up a ∼ relever un défi
(b) (challenging task) challenge m; to rise to the ∼ relever le challenge
[2] vtr (a) défier ⟨person⟩ (to à; to do de faire)
(b) débattre ⟨ideas⟩; contester ⟨statement, authority⟩

**challenger** n challenger m (for de)

**challenging** adj (a) ⟨work⟩ stimulant/-e
(b) ⟨look⟩ provocateur/-trice

**chamber** [1] n chambre f
[2] **chambers** n pl (Law) cabinet m; (GB Pol)
the upper/lower ∼ la Chambre des lords/des
communes

**chambermaid** n femme f de chambre

**chamber music** n musique f de
chambre

**Chamber of Commerce** n chambre f
de commerce et d'industrie

**chameleon** n caméléon m

**champagne** n, adj champagne (m) inv

**champion** n champion/-ionne m/f

**championship** n championnat m

**chance** [1] n (a) (opportunity) occasion f; to
have or get the ∼ to do avoir l'occasion de
faire; **you've missed your** ∼ tu as laissé
passer l'occasion
(b) (likelihood) chance f; there is a ∼ that
she'll get a job in Paris il y a des chances
qu'elle trouve un travail à Paris; she has a
good ∼ elle a de bonnes chances
(c) (luck) hasard m; by ∼ par hasard
(d) (risk) risque m; to take a ∼ prendre un
risque
(e) (possibility) chance f; not to stand a ∼
n'avoir aucune chance; by any ∼ par hasard
[2] vtr to ∼ doing courir le risque de faire;
to ∼ it tenter sa chance
IDIOMS no ∼! (colloq) pas question! (colloq)

**chancellor** n chancelier m; (Univ)
président m

**Chancellor of the Exchequer** n
(GB) Chancelier m de l'Échiquier

**chandelier** n lustre m

**change** [1] n (a) (gen) changement m;
(adjustment) modification f; the ∼ in the
schedule la modification du programme; ∼
of plan changement de programme; a ∼ of
clothes des vêtements de rechange; a ∼ for
the better un changement en mieux; that
makes a nice ∼ ça change agréablement;
she needs a ∼ elle a besoin de se changer
les idées; to need a ∼ of air avoir besoin de
changer d'air; for a ∼ pour changer
(b) (cash) monnaie f; small ∼ petite
monnaie; she gave me 10 euros ∼ elle m'a
rendu 10 euros; have you got ∼ for 50
euros? pouvez-vous me changer un billet de
50 euros?
[2] vtr (a) (alter) changer; (in part) modifier; to
∼ sb/sth into transformer qn/qch en; to ∼
one's mind changer d'avis; to ∼ one's mind
about doing abandonner l'idée de faire; to ∼
colour changer de couleur
(b) changer de ⟨clothes, name, car, job, TV
channel⟩; (in shop) échanger ⟨item⟩ (for pour);
to ∼ places (seats) changer de place (with
avec)
(c) changer ⟨battery, tyre⟩; to ∼ a bed
changer les draps
(d) changer ⟨cheque, currency⟩ (into, for en)

[3] vi (a) ⟨situation, person⟩ changer; ⟨wind⟩
tourner; the lights ∼d from red to orange les
feux sont passés du rouge à l'orange
(b) (into different clothes) se changer; to ∼ into
passer ⟨garment⟩; to ∼ out of ôter, enlever
⟨garment⟩
(c) (from bus, train) changer
[4] **changed** pp adj ⟨man, woman⟩ autre
(before n)
■ **change round** déplacer ⟨large objects⟩;
changer [qn/qch] de place ⟨workers, objects,
words⟩

**changeable** adj ⟨condition, weather⟩
changeant/-e; ⟨price⟩ variable

**changeover** n passage m (to à)

**changing** adj ⟨colours, environment⟩
changeant/-e; ⟨attitude, world⟩ en évolution

**changing room** n (at sports centre)
vestiaire m; (US) (in shop) cabine f d'essayage

**channel** [1] n (a) (TV station) chaîne f; (radio
band) canal m
(b) (groove) rainure f
(c) (in sea, river) chenal m
(d) through the proper ∼s par la voie
normale; to go through official ∼s passer
par la voie officielle
[2] vtr canaliser (to, into dans)

**Channel** pr n the (English) ∼ la Manche

**channel ferry** n ferry m trans-Manche

**channel-hop** vi zapper (colloq)

**Channel Islands** pr n pl îles fpl
Anglo-Normandes

**Channel Tunnel** pr n tunnel m sous la
Manche

**chant** [1] n (a) (of crowd) chant m scandé
(b) (of devotees) mélopée f
[2] vi ⟨crowd⟩ scander des slogans; ⟨choir,
monks⟩ psalmodier

**chaos** n (gen) pagaille f (colloq); (economic,
cosmic) chaos m; in a state of ∼ ⟨house⟩ sens
dessus dessous; ⟨country⟩ en plein chaos

**chaotic** adj désordonné/-e

**chap** [1] n (GB) (colloq) type m (colloq)
[2] vtr gercer; ∼ped lips lèvres gercées

**chapel** n chapelle f

**chaperone** [1] n chaperon m
[2] vtr chaperonner

**chaplain** n aumônier m

**chapter** n chapitre m; in ∼ 3 au chapitre 3

**character** n (a) (gen) caractère m
(b) (in book, play, film) personnage m (from de)
(c) a real ∼ un sacré numéro (colloq); a local
∼ une figure locale

**characteristic** [1] n (gen) caractéristique
f; (of person) trait m de caractère
[2] adj caractéristique (of de)

**characterize** vtr (a) (depict) dépeindre
(as comme)
(b) (typify) caractériser; to be ∼d by se
caractériser par

**character reference** n références fpl

**charade** n comédie f

**charades** n pl (game) charades fpl

**charcoal** [1] n (a) (fuel) charbon m de bois ⋯⋙

**(b)** (for drawing) fusain m
**2** adj (also ~ **grey**) (gris) anthracite inv

**charge** **1** n **(a)** (fee) frais mpl; additional or extra ~ supplément m; **to reverse the ~s** (on phone) appeler en PCV
**(b)** (accusation) accusation f (of de); (Law) inculpation f; **murder ~ inculpation** d'assassinat; **to press ~s against sth** engager des poursuites contre qch
**(c)** (attack) charge f (against contre)
**(d) to be in ~** (gen) être responsable (of de); (Mil) commander; **the person in ~** le/la responsable; **to take ~** prendre les choses en main
**(e)** (child) enfant mf dont on s'occupe; (pupil) élève mf; (patient) malade mf
**(f)** (explosive, electrical) charge f
**2** vtr **(a)** prélever ⟨commission⟩; percevoir ⟨interest⟩ (on sur); **to ~ sb for sth** faire payer qch à qn; **how much do you ~?** vous prenez combien?; **I ~ £20 an hour** je prends 20 livres sterling de l'heure
**(b) to ~ sth to** mettre qch sur ⟨account⟩
**(c)** ⟨police⟩ inculper ⟨suspect⟩ (with de)
**(d)** (rush at) charger ⟨enemy⟩; ⟨bull⟩ foncer sur ⟨person⟩
**(e)** charger ⟨battery⟩
**3** vi **to ~ into/out of** se précipiter dans/de ⟨room⟩

**charge account** n (US) compte-client m

**charge card** n (credit card) carte f de crédit; (store card) carte f d'achat

**char-grilled** adj ⟨steak⟩ grillé/-e au charbon de bois

**charisma** n charisme m

**charismatic** adj charismatique

**charitable** adj ⟨person, act, explanation⟩ charitable (to envers); ⟨organization⟩ caritatif/-ive

**charity** n **(a)** (virtue) charité f
**(b)** (organization) organisation f caritative; **to give to/collect money for ~** donner à/collecter des fonds pour des œuvres de bienfaisance

**charity shop** n magasin m d'articles d'occasion ⟨vendus au profit d'une œuvre de bienfaisance⟩

**charity work** n travail m bénévole ⟨au profit d'une œuvre de bienfaisance⟩

**charm** n **(a)** charme m
**(b)** lucky ~ porte-bonheur m inv

**charming** adj ⟨person, place⟩ charmant/-e; ⟨child, animal⟩ adorable

**charred** adj carbonisé/-e

**chart** **1** n **(a)** (graph) graphique m
**(b)** (table) tableau m
**(c)** (map) carte f
**(d) the ~s** le hit-parade
**2** vtr **(a)** (on map) tracer ⟨route⟩
**(b)** enregistrer ⟨progress⟩

**charter** **1** n charte f
**2** vtr affréter ⟨plane⟩

**chartered accountant, CA** n (GB) ≈ expert-comptable m

**charter flight** n (GB) vol m charter

**chase** **1** n poursuite f (after de)
**2** vtr **(a)** pourchasser ⟨person, animal⟩; **to ~ sb/sth up** or **down the street** courir après qn/qch dans la rue
**(b)** (also ~ **after**) courir après ⟨woman, man, success⟩
■ **chase away, chase off** chasser ⟨person, animal⟩

**chassis** n châssis m

**chastity** n chasteté f

**chat** **1** n conversation f; **to have a ~** bavarder (with avec; about sur)
**2** vi bavarder (with, to avec)
■ **chat up** (GB) (colloq) draguer (colloq)

**chatline** n réseau m téléphonique; (sexual) ≈ téléphone m rose

**chatroom** n site m de bavardage, salon m virtuel

**chat show** n (GB) talk-show m

**chatter** **1** n (of person) bavardage m; (of birds) gazouillis m
**2** vi ⟨person⟩ bavarder; ⟨birds⟩ gazouiller; **her teeth were ~ing** elle claquait des dents

**chatterbox** n moulin m à paroles (colloq)

**chatty** adj ⟨person⟩ ouvert/-e; ⟨letter⟩ vivant/-e

**chauffeur** **1** n chauffeur m; **a ~-driven car** une voiture avec chauffeur
**2** vtr conduire

**chauvinist** n, adj **(a)** (gen) chauvin/-e (m/f)
**(b)** (also **male ~**) macho (m) (colloq)

**cheap** adj **(a)** bon marché inv; **to be ~** être bon marché, ne pas coûter cher inv; **~er** moins cher/-ère
**(b)** (shoddy) de mauvaise qualité
**(c)** ⟨joke⟩ facile; ⟨trick⟩ sale (before n)

**cheapen** vtr rabaisser

**cheaply** adv ⟨produce, sell⟩ à bas prix; **to eat ~** manger pour pas cher

**cheap rate** adj, adv à tarif réduit

**cheat** **1** n tricheur/-euse m/f
**2** vtr tromper; **to feel ~ed** se sentir lésé/-e; **to ~ sb (out) of** dépouiller qn de
**3** vi tricher (in à); **to ~ at cards** tricher aux cartes; **to ~ on sb** tromper qn

**Chechnya** pr n Tchétchénie f

**check** **1** n **(a)** (for quality, security) contrôle m (on sur)
**(b)** (medical) examen m
**(c)** (restraint) frein m (on à)
**(d)** (in chess) ~! échec au roi!; **in ~** en échec
**(e)** (also ~ **fabric**) tissu m à carreaux; (also ~ **pattern**) carreaux mpl
**(f)** (US) (cheque) chèque m
**(g)** (US) (bill) addition f
**(h)** (US) (receipt) ticket m
**(i)** (US) (tick) croix f
**2** adj ⟨shirt, skirt⟩ à carreaux
**3** vtr **(a)** (gen) vérifier; contrôler ⟨ticket, area, work⟩; prendre ⟨temperature⟩; examiner ⟨watch, map, pocket⟩
**(b)** (curb) contrôler ⟨prices, inflation⟩; freiner ⟨growth⟩; maîtriser ⟨emotions⟩

**4** *vi* (a) vérifier; **to ~ with sb** demander à
qn; **to ~ for** dépister ⟨*problems*⟩; chercher
⟨*leaks, flaws*⟩
(b) **to ~ into** arriver à ⟨*hotel*⟩
■ **check in**: ¶ ~ **in** (at airport) enregistrer; (at
hotel) arriver (at à); ¶ ~ **[sb/sth] in**
enregistrer ⟨*baggage, passengers*⟩
■ **check off** cocher ⟨*items*⟩
■ **check out**: ¶ ~ **out** (leave) partir; **to ~
out of** quitter ⟨*hotel*⟩; ¶ ~ **[sth] out** vérifier
⟨*information*⟩; examiner ⟨*package, building*⟩;
se renseigner sur ⟨*club, scheme*⟩
■ **check up on** faire une enquête sur
⟨*person*⟩; vérifier ⟨*story, details*⟩
**checkbook** *n* (US) carnet *m* de chèques,
chéquier *m*
**checkered** (US) = CHEQUERED
**checkers** (US) = CHEQUERS
**check-in** *n* enregistrement *m*
**checking account** *n* (US) compte *m*
courant
**checklist** *n* liste *f* de contrôle
**checkmate** *n* échec *m* et mat
**checkout** *n* caisse *f*
**checkout assistant** *n* caissier/-ière
*m/f*
**checkpoint** *n* poste *m* de contrôle
**checkroom** *n* (US) (cloakroom) vestiaire *m*;
(for baggage) consigne *f*
**checkup** *n* (a) (at doctor's) examen *m*
médical, bilan *m* de santé; **to have a ~**
passer *or* se faire faire un examen médical
(b) (at dentist's) visite *f* de routine
**cheek** *n* (a) (of face) joue *f*; **~ to ~** joue
contre joue
(b) culot *m* (colloq); **what a ~!** quel culot!
**cheekbone** *n* pommette *f*
**cheeky** *adj* ⟨*person*⟩ effronté/-e,
insolent/-e; ⟨*question*⟩ impoli/-e; ⟨*grin*⟩
espiègle, coquin/-e
**cheer** **1** *n* acclamation *f*; **to get a ~** être
acclamé/-e
**2 cheers** *excl* (a) (toast) à la vôtre! (colloq);
(to close friend) à la tienne! (colloq)
(b) (GB) (colloq) (thanks) merci!
(c) (GB) (colloq) (goodbye) salut!
**3** *vtr, vi* applaudir
■ **cheer up**: ¶ ~ **up** reprendre courage; **~
up!** courage!; ¶ ~ **[sb] up** remonter le moral
à ⟨*person*⟩; ¶ ~ **[sth] up** égayer ⟨*room*⟩
**cheerful** *adj* ⟨*person, mood, music*⟩
joyeux/-euse; ⟨*tone*⟩ enjoué/-e; ⟨*colour*⟩ gai/-e
**cheerleader** *n* majorette *f*
**cheese** *n* fromage *m*; **~ sandwich**
sandwich *m* au fromage
**cheeseboard** *n* (object) plateau *m* à
fromage; (selection) plateau *m* de fromages
**cheetah** *n* guépard *m*
**chef** *n* chef *m* cuisinier
**chemical** **1** *n* produit *m* chimique
**2** *adj* chimique
**chemist** *n* (a) (GB) pharmacien/-ienne *m/f*;
**~'s (shop)** pharmacie *f*
(b) (scientist) chimiste *mf*

**chemistry** *n* chimie *f*
**chemotherapy** *n* chimiothérapie *f*
**cheque** (GB), **check** (US) *n* chèque *m*; **to
make out** *or* **write a ~ for £20** faire un
chèque de 20 livres sterling
**chequebook** (GB), **checkbook** (US) *n*
chéquier *m*, carnet *m* de chèques
**cheque card** *n* (GB) carte *f* de garantie
bancaire
**chequered** (GB), **checkered** (US) *adj*
(a) ⟨*cloth*⟩ à damiers
(b) ⟨*career, history*⟩ en dents de scie
**chequers** (GB), **checkers** (US) *n* jeu *m*
de dames
**cherish** *vtr* caresser ⟨*hope*⟩; chérir
⟨*memory, person*⟩
**cherry** **1** *n* (a) (fruit) cerise *f*
(b) (*also* **~ tree**) cerisier *m*
**2** *adj* (*also* **~-red**) rouge cerise *inv*
**chess** *n* échecs *mpl*; **a game of ~** une
partie d'échecs
**chessboard** *n* échiquier *m*
**chess set** *n* jeu *m* d'échecs
**chest** *n* (a) (of person) poitrine *f*; **~
measurement** tour *m* de poitrine
(b) (furniture) coffre *m*; **~ of drawers**
commode *f*
(c) (crate) caisse *f*
IDIOMS **to get something off one's ~** (colloq)
vider son sac (colloq)
**chestnut** **1** *n* (a) (nut) marron *m*,
châtaigne *f*
(b) (*also* **~ tree**) (horse) marronnier *m*
(d'Inde); (sweet) châtaignier *m*
**2** *adj* ⟨*hair*⟩ châtain *inv*; **a ~ horse** un
(cheval) alezan
**chew** *vtr* mâcher ⟨*food, gum*⟩; mordiller
⟨*pencil*⟩; ronger ⟨*bone*⟩
**chewing gum** *n* chewing-gum *m*
**chewy** *adj* difficile à mâcher
**chick** *n* (fledgling) oisillon *m*; (of fowl) poussin
*m*
**chicken** *n* (a) (fowl) poulet *m*, poule *f*
(b) (meat) poulet *m*
(c) (colloq) (coward) poule *f* mouillée
■ **chicken out** (colloq) se dégonfler (colloq)
**chicken pox** *n* varicelle *f*
**chicken wire** *n* grillage *m* (à mailles
fines)
**chickpea** *n* pois *m* chiche
**chicory** *n* (a) (vegetable) endive *f*
(b) (in coffee) chicorée *f*
**chief** **1** *n* chef *m*
**2** *adj* (a) ⟨*reason*⟩ principal/-e
(b) ⟨*editor*⟩ en chef
**chief executive** *n* directeur *m* général
**chiefly** *adv* notamment, surtout
**chief of police** *n* ≈ préfet *m* de police
**Chief of Staff** *n* (Mil) chef *m* d'état-major;
(of White House) secrétaire *m* général
**chiffon** *n* mousseline *f*
**chilblain** *n* engelure *f*

**child** *n* enfant *mf*; **when I was a** ~ quand j'étais enfant

**child abuse** *n* mauvais traitements *mpl* infligés à un enfant; (sexual) sévices *mpl* sexuels exercés sur l'enfant

**childbirth** *n* accouchement *m*

**childcare** *n* (nurseries etc) structures *fpl* d'accueil pour les enfants d'âge préscolaire; (bringing up children) éducation *f* des enfants

**childcare facilities** *n pl* crèche *f*

**childhood** ⓵ *n* enfance *f*; **in (his) early** ~ dans sa prime enfance
⓶ *adj* ⟨friend, memory⟩ d'enfance; ⟨illness⟩ infantile

**childish** *adj* puéril/-e

**childless** *adj* sans enfants

**childlike** *adj* enfantin/-e

**childminder** *n* (GB) nourrice *f*

**children's home** *n* maison *f* d'enfants

**Chile** *pr n* Chili *m*

**chill** ⓵ *n* (a) (coldness) fraîcheur *f*; **there is a** ~ **in the air** le fond de l'air est frais; **to send a** ~ **down sb's spine** donner des frissons à qn
(b) (illness) coup *m* de froid
⓶ *adj* (a) ⟨wind⟩ frais/fraîche
(b) ⟨reminder, words⟩ brutal/-e
⓷ *vtr* (a) mettre [qch] à refroidir ⟨dessert, soup⟩; rafraîchir ⟨wine⟩
(b) (make cold) faire frissonner ⟨person⟩; **to** ~ **sb's** *or* **the blood** glacer le sang à qn
⓸ *vi* ⟨dessert⟩ refroidir; ⟨wine⟩ rafraîchir
■ **chill out** (colloq) décompresser (colloq); ~ **out!** laisse faire!

**chilli, chili** *n* (a) (also ~ **pepper**) piment *m* rouge
(b) (also ~ **powder**) chili *m*
(c) (also ~ **con carne**) chili *m* con carne

**chilly** *adj* froid; **it's** ~ il fait froid

**chime** *n* carillon *m*

**chimney** *n* cheminée *f*

**chimpanzee** *n* chimpanzé *m*

**chin** *n* menton *m*

**china** ⓵ *n* porcelaine *f*
⓶ *adj* ⟨cup, plate⟩ en porcelaine

**China** *pr n* Chine *f*

**Chinese** ⓵ *n* (a) (person) Chinois/-oise *m/f*
(b) (language) chinois *m*
⓶ *adj* chinois/-oise; ⟨embassy⟩ de Chine

**chink** *n* (a) (in wall) fente *f*; (in curtain) entrebâillement *m*
(b) (sound) tintement *m*

**chip** ⓵ *n* (a) (fragment) fragment *m* (of de); (of wood) copeau *m*; (of glass) éclat *m*
(b) (in wood, china) ébréchure *f*
(c) (microchip) puce *f* (électronique)
⓶ **chips** *n pl* (a) (GB) (fried potatoes) frites *fpl*
(b) (US) (crisps) chips *fpl*
⓷ *vtr* ébrécher ⟨glass, plate⟩; écailler ⟨paint⟩; **to** ~ **a tooth** se casser une dent
IDIOMS **to have a** ~ **on one's shoulder** être amer/-ère

■ **chip in** (GB) (colloq) (financially) donner un peu d'argent

**chipboard** *n* aggloméré *m*

**chip shop** *n* marchand *m* de frites

**chiropodist** *n* pédicure *mf*

**chiropractor** *n* chiropraticien/-ienne *m/f*, chiropracteur *m*

**chirp** *vi* ⟨bird⟩ pépier

**chisel** ⓵ *n* ciseau *m*
⓶ *vtr* ciseler

**chitchat** *n* (colloq) bavardage *m*

**chivalry** *n* (a) chevalerie *f*
(b) (courtesy) galanterie *f*

**chive** *n* ciboulette *f*

**chlorine** *n* chlore *m*

**choc-ice** *n* (GB) esquimau *m*

**chock-a-block** *adj* plein à craquer

**chocolate** ⓵ *n* chocolat *m*
⓶ *adj* ⟨sweets⟩ en chocolat; ⟨biscuit, cake, ice cream⟩ au chocolat

**choice** *n* choix *m* (**between, of** entre); **to make a** ~ faire un choix, choisir; **to be spoilt for** ~ avoir l'embarras du choix; **out of** *or* **from** ~ par choix

**choir** *n* (of church, school) chorale *f*; (professional) chœur *m*

**choirboy** *n* petit chanteur *m*, jeune choriste *m*

**choke** ⓵ *n* (Aut) starter *m*
⓶ *vtr* (a) (throttle) étrangler ⟨person⟩
(b) ⟨fumes, smoke⟩ étouffer
⓷ *vi* s'étouffer
■ **choke back** étouffer ⟨cough, sob⟩; **to** ~ **back one's tears** retenir ses larmes

**cholera** *n* choléra *m*

**cholesterol** *n* cholestérol *m*

**choose** ⓵ *vtr* (a) (select) choisir (**from** parmi)
(b) (decide) décider (**to do** de faire)
⓶ *vi* (a) (select) choisir (**between** entre)
(b) (prefer) **to** ~ **to do** préférer faire

**choosy** *adj* difficile (**about** en ce qui concerne)

**chop** ⓵ *n* (Culin) côtelette *f*; **pork** ~ côtelette *f* de porc
⓶ *vtr* (a) (also ~ **up**) couper ⟨wood⟩; couper, émincer ⟨vegetable, meat⟩; hacher ⟨parsley, onion⟩; **to** ~ **sth finely** hacher qch
(b) réduire ⟨service, deficit⟩
IDIOMS **to** ~ **and change** ⟨person⟩ changer d'avis comme de chemise
■ **chop down** abattre ⟨tree⟩
■ **chop off** couper ⟨branch, end⟩; trancher ⟨head, hand, finger⟩

**chopping board** *n* planche *f* à découper

**chopping knife** *n* couteau *m* de cuisine

**choppy** *adj* ⟨sea, water⟩ agité/-e

**chopstick** *n* baguette *f* (chinoise)

**chord** *n* accord *m*

**chore** *n* tâche *f*; **to do the** ~**s** faire le ménage

**choreograph** *vtr* chorégraphier

**chorus** *n* (a) (singers) chœur *m*

**(b)** (piece of music) chœur *m*
**(c)** (refrain) refrain *m*
**Christ** *pr n* le Christ, Jésus-Christ
**christen** *vtr* baptiser
**christening** *n* baptême *m*
**Christian** ① *n* chrétien/-ienne *m/f*
② *adj* chrétien/-ienne; ⟨*attitude*⟩ charitable
**Christianity** *n* christianisme *m*
**Christian name** *n* nom *m* de baptême
**Christmas** *n* ∼ (day) (jour *m* de) Noël; **at**
∼ à Noël; **Merry** ∼!, **Happy** ∼! Joyeux Noël!
**Christmas card** *n* carte *f* de Noël
**Christmas eve** *n* veille *f* de Noël
**Christmas tree** *n* sapin *m* de Noël
**chrome** *n* chrome *m*
**chronic** *adj* **(a)** ⟨*illness*⟩ chronique
**(b)** ⟨*liar*⟩ invétéré/-e; ⟨*problem, shortage*⟩
chronique
**chronicle** *n* chronique *f*
**chronological** *adj* chronologique
**chubby** *adj* ⟨*child, finger*⟩ potelé/-e; ⟨*cheek*⟩
rebondi/-e; ⟨*face*⟩ joufflu/-e; ⟨*adult*⟩
rondelet/-ette
**chuck** *vtr* (colloq) **(a)** (*also* ∼ **away**)
balancer (colloq), jeter
**(b)** larguer (colloq) ⟨*boyfriend, girlfriend*⟩
**chuckle** *vi* glousser; **to** ∼ **at sth** rire de
qch
**chuffed** *adj* (GB) (colloq) vachement (colloq)
content/-e (**about, at, with** de)
**chum** *n* (colloq) copain/copine *m/f* (colloq),
pote *m* (colloq)
**chunk** *n* **(a)** (of meat, fruit) morceau *m*; (of
wood) tronçon *m*; (of bread) quignon *m*;
**pineapple** ∼**s** ananas *m* en morceaux
**(b)** (of population, text, day) partie *f* (**of** de)
**church** ① *n* (Catholic, Anglican) église *f*;
(Protestant) temple *m*
② *adj* ⟨*bell, choir, steeple*⟩ d'église; ⟨*fête*⟩
paroissial/-e; ⟨*wedding*⟩ religieux/-ieuse
**churchgoer** *n* pratiquant/-e *m/f*
**church hall** *n* salle *f* paroissiale
**churchyard** *n* cimetière *m*
**churn** ① *n* **(a)** (for butter) baratte *f*
**(b)** (GB) (for milk) bidon *m*
② *vtr* **to** ∼ **butter** baratter
■ **churn out** pondre [qch] en série ⟨*novels*⟩;
produire [qch] en série ⟨*goods*⟩
■ **churn up** faire des remous dans ⟨*water*⟩
**chute** *n* **(a)** (slide) toboggan *m*
**(b)** (for rubbish) vide-ordures *m inv*
**(c)** (for toboggan) piste *f* de toboggan
**cicada** *n* cigale *f*
**cider** *n* cidre *m*
**cigar** *n* cigare *m*
**cigarette** ① *n* cigarette *f*
② *adj* ⟨*ash, smoke*⟩ de cigarette; ⟨*case,
paper*⟩ à cigarettes
**cigarette lighter** *n* (portable) briquet *m*;
(in car) allume-cigares *m inv*
**cinder** *n* (glowing) braise *f*; (ash) cendre *f*
**Cinderella** *pr n* Cendrillon

**cinecamera** *n* caméra *f* (d'amateur)
**cine film** *n* pellicule *f* cinématographique
**cinema** *n* cinéma *m*
**cinemagoer** *n* (regular) cinéphile *mf*,
amateur *m* de cinéma; (spectator)
spectacteur/-trice *m/f*
**cinnamon** *n* cannelle *f*
**circle** ① *n* **(a)** (gen) cercle *m*; **to go round
in** ∼**s** tourner en rond; **to have** ∼**s under
one's eyes** avoir les yeux cernés
**(b)** (in theatre) balcon *m*; **in the** ∼ au balcon
② *vtr* **(a)** ⟨*plane*⟩ tourner autour de
⟨*airport*⟩; ⟨*person, animal, vehicle*⟩ faire le
tour de ⟨*building*⟩; tourner autour de
⟨*person, animal*⟩
**(b)** (surround) encercler
③ *vi* tourner en rond (**around** autour de)
**circuit** *n* **(a)** (gen) circuit *m*
**(b)** (lap) tour *m*
**circuit breaker** *n* disjoncteur *m*
**circular** ① *n* (newsletter) circulaire *f*;
(advertisement) prospectus *m*
② *adj* ⟨*object*⟩ rond/-e; ⟨*argument*⟩
circulaire
**circulate** ① *vtr* faire circuler
② *vi* **(a)** (gen) circuler
**(b)** (at party) **let's** ∼ on va aller faire
connaissance
**circulation** *n* **(a)** (gen) circulation *f*
**(b)** (of newspaper) tirage *m*
**circulation figures** *n pl* chiffres *mpl* de
tirage
**circumcision** *n* (of boy) circoncision *f*; (of
girl) excision *f*
**circumference** *n* circonférence *f*
**circumflex** *n* accent *m* circonflexe
**circumstances** *n pl* **(a)** circonstances
*fpl*; **in** *or* **under the** ∼ dans ces
circonstances; **under no** ∼ en aucun cas
**(b)** (financial position) situation *f*
**circumstantial** *adj* ⟨*evidence*⟩ indirect/-e
**circus** *n* cirque *m*
**CIS** *pr n* (*abbr* = **Commonwealth of
Independent States**) CEI *f*
**cistern** *n* (of lavatory) réservoir *m* de chasse
d'eau; (in loft or underground) citerne *f*
**citizen** *n* **(a)** (of state) citoyen/-enne *m/f*;
(when abroad) ressortissant/-e *m/f*
**(b)** (of town) habitant/-e *m/f*
**citizenship** *n* nationalité *f*
**citrus fruit** *n* agrume *m*
**city** *n* (grande) ville *f*; **the City** (GB) la City
**city centre** (GB), **city center** (US) *n*
centre-ville *m*
**civic** *adj* ⟨*administration, official*⟩
municipal/-e; ⟨*pride, responsibility*⟩ civique
**civic centre** (GB), **civic center** (US)
*n* centre *m* municipal (culturel et
administratif)
**civil** *adj* **(a)** ⟨*case, court, offence*⟩ civil/-e
**(b)** (polite) courtois/-e
**civil engineering** *n* génie *m* civil
**civilian** *n* civil/-e *m/f*

**civilization** *n* civilisation *f*
**civilized** *adj* civilisé/-e
**civil law** *n* droit *m* civil
**civil liberty** *n* libertés *fpl* individuelles
**civil rights** *n pl* droits *mpl* civils
**civil servant** *n* fonctionnaire *mf*
**civil service** *n* fonction *f* publique
**civil war** *n* guerre *f* civile
**claim** ⓵ *n* (a) (demand) revendication *f*
(b) (in insurance) (against a person) réclamation
*f*; (for fire, theft) demande *f* d'indemnisation
(c) (for welfare benefit) demande *f* d'allocation
(d) (assertion) affirmation *f*
⓶ *vtr* (a) (maintain) prétendre
(b) revendiquer ⟨money, property,
responsibility, right⟩
(c) faire une demande de ⟨benefit⟩; faire une
demande de remboursement de ⟨expenses⟩
⓷ *vi* (a) to ~ for damages faire une
demande pour dommages et intérêts
(b) (apply for benefit) faire une demande
d'allocation
**claimant** *n* (a) (for benefit, compensation)
demandeur/-euse *m/f* (to à)
(b) (to title, estate) prétendant/-e *m/f* (to à)
**claim form** *n* déclaration *f* de sinistre
**clairvoyant** *n* voyant/-e *m/f*, extralucide
*mf*
**clam** *n* palourde *f*
■ **clam up** ne plus piper mot (on sb à qn)
**clammy** *adj* moite
**clamour** (GB), **clamor** (US) ⓵ *n* (shouting)
clameur *f*
⓶ *vi* (a) (demand) to ~ for sth réclamer qch;
to ~ for sb to do réclamer à qn de faire
(b) (rush, fight) se bousculer (for pour avoir; to
do pour faire)
**clamp** ⓵ *n* (a) (on bench) valet *m*
(b) (also **wheel~**) sabot *m* de Denver
⓶ *vtr* (a) cramponner ⟨two parts⟩; (at bench)
fixer [qch] à l'aide d'un valet (onto à)
(b) serrer ⟨jaw, teeth⟩
(c) (also **wheel~**) mettre un sabot de
Denver à ⟨car⟩
■ **clamp down:** ¶ ~ down on faire de la
répression contre ⟨crime⟩; mettre un frein à
⟨extravagance⟩
**clampdown** *n* mesures *fpl* de répression
(on sb contre qn; on sth de qch)
**clan** *n* clan *m*
**clandestine** *adj* clandestin/-e
**clang** ⓵ *n* fracas *m*, bruit *m* métallique
⓶ *vi* ⟨gate⟩ claquer avec un son métallique;
⟨bell⟩ retentir
**clap** ⓵ *n* to give sb a ~ applaudir qn; a ~
of thunder un coup de tonnerre
⓶ *vtr* to ~ one's hands battre *or* taper des
mains, frapper dans ses mains
⓷ *vi* applaudir
**clapping** *n* applaudissements *mpl*
**claret** ⓵ *n* (wine) bordeaux *m* (rouge)
(b) (colour) bordeaux *m*
**clarification** *n* éclaircissement *m*,
clarification *f*

**clarify** *vtr* éclaircir, clarifier
**clarinet** *n* clarinette *f*
**clarity** *n* clarté *f*
**clash** ⓵ *n* (a) (confrontation) affrontement *m*
(b) (of cultures, interests, personalities) conflit *m*
(c) a ~ of cymbals un coup de cymbales
⓶ *vtr* entrechoquer ⟨bin lids⟩; frapper
⟨cymbals⟩
⓷ *vi* (a) (fight, disagree) s'affronter; to ~ with
sb (fight) se heurter à qn; (disagree) se
quereller avec qn (on, over au sujet de)
(b) (be in conflict) ⟨interests, beliefs⟩ être
incompatibles
(c) (coincide) ⟨meetings⟩ avoir lieu en même
temps (with que)
(d) ⟨colours⟩ jurer
**clasp** *n* (on bracelet, bag, purse) fermoir *m*; (on
belt) boucle *f*
**class** ⓵ *n* (gen) classe *f*; (lesson) cours *m* (in
de); to be in a ~ of one's own être hors
catégorie; to travel first/second ~ voyager en
première/deuxième classe; first/second ~
degree ≈ licence *f* avec mention très bien/
bien
⓶ *vtr* classer
**class conscious** *adj* soucieux/-ieuse des
distinctions sociales
**classic** *n*, *adj* classique (*m*)
**classical** *adj* classique
**classics** *n* lettres *fpl* classiques
**classification** *n* (a) (category)
classification *f*, catégorie *f*
(b) (categorization) classement *m*
**classified** ⓵ *n* (also ~ **ad**) petite
annonce *f*
⓶ *adj* (secret) confidentiel/-ielle
**classify** *vtr* (a) (file) classer
(b) (declare secret) classer [qch]
confidentiel/-ielle
**classmate** *n* camarade *mf* de classe
**classroom** *n* salle *f* de classe
**class system** *n* système *m* de classes
**classy** *adj* (colloq) ⟨person, dress⟩ qui a de la
classe; ⟨car, hotel⟩ de luxe; ⟨actor,
performance⟩ de grande classe
**clatter** ⓵ *n* cliquetis *m*; (loud) fracas *m*
⓶ *vi* ⟨typewriter⟩ cliqueter; ⟨dishes⟩
s'entrechoquer
**clause** *n* (a) (in grammar) proposition *f*
(b) (in contract, treaty) clause *f*; (in will, act of
Parliament) disposition *f*
**claustrophobia** *n* claustrophobie *f*
**claw** *n* (a) (gen) griffe *f*; (of bird of prey) serre
*f*; (of crab, lobster) pince *f*
(b) (on hammer) arrache-clou *m*, pied-de-biche
*m*
**clay** *n* argile *f*
**clean** ⓵ *adj* (a) (gen) propre; ⟨air, water⟩
pur/-e; my hands are ~ j'ai les mains
propres; ~ and tidy d'une propreté
irréprochable; a ~ sheet of paper une feuille
blanche
(b) ⟨joke⟩ anodin/-e

(c) ⟨*reputation*⟩ sans tache; ⟨*record, licence*⟩ vierge

(d) (Sport) ⟨*tackle*⟩ sans faute; ⟨*hit*⟩ précis/-e

(e) (neat) ⟨*lines, profile*⟩ pur/-e

**2** *vtr* nettoyer; **to ~ one's teeth** se brosser les dents

■ **clean out** nettoyer [qch] à fond ⟨*cupboard, room*⟩

■ **clean up**: ¶ **~ up (a)** tout nettoyer
**(b)** (wash oneself) se débarbouiller
¶ **~ [sth] up** nettoyer

**clean-cut** *adj* ⟨*image, person*⟩ soigné/-e

**cleaner** *n* **(a)** (woman) femme *f* de ménage; (man) agent *m* de nettoyage
**(b)** (detergent) produit *m* de nettoyage
**(c)** (shop) **cleaner's** pressing *m*

**cleaning** *n* (domestic) ménage *m*; (commercial) nettoyage *m*, entretien *m*

**cleaning product** *n* produit *m* d'entretien

**cleanliness** *n* propreté *f*

**cleanse** *vtr* nettoyer ⟨*skin, wound*⟩

**cleanser** *n* **(a)** (for face) démaquillant *m*
**(b)** (household) produit *m* d'entretien

**clean-shaven** *adj* **he's ~** il n'a ni barbe ni moustache

**clear** **1** *adj* **(a)** (transparent) ⟨*glass, liquid*⟩ transparent/-e; ⟨*blue*⟩ limpide; ⟨*lens, varnish*⟩ incolore; ⟨*honey*⟩ liquide; **~ soup** consommé *m*
**(b)** (distinct) ⟨*image, outline*⟩ net/nette; ⟨*sound, voice*⟩ clair/-e
**(c)** (comprehensible) ⟨*description, instruction*⟩ clair/-e; **to make sth ~ to sb** faire comprendre qch à qn; **is that ~?** est-ce que c'est clair?
**(d)** (obvious) ⟨*need, sign*⟩ évident/-e; ⟨*advantage*⟩ net/nette (*before n*); ⟨*majority*⟩ large (*before n*); **it is ~ that** il est clair que
**(e)** (not confused) ⟨*idea, memory*⟩ clair/-e; ⟨*plan*⟩ précis/-e; **to keep a ~ head** garder les idées claires
**(f)** (empty) ⟨*view*⟩ dégagé/-e; ⟨*table*⟩ débarrassé/-e; ⟨*space*⟩ libre
**(g)** ⟨*conscience*⟩ tranquille
**(h)** ⟨*skin*⟩ net/nette; ⟨*sky*⟩ sans nuage; ⟨*day, night*⟩ clair/-e; **on a ~ day** par temps clair/-e

**2** *adv* **to jump ~ of** sth éviter qch en sautant sur le côté; **to pull sb ~ of** extraire qn de ⟨*wreckage*⟩; **to stay** *or* **steer ~ of** éviter ⟨*town centre, troublemakers*⟩

**3** *vtr* **(a)** enlever ⟨*rubbish, papers, mines*⟩; dégager ⟨*snow*⟩ (**from, off** de)
**(b)** déboucher ⟨*drains*⟩; débarrasser ⟨*table, room*⟩; vider ⟨*desk*⟩; évacuer ⟨*area, building*⟩; effacer ⟨*screen*⟩; défricher ⟨*land*⟩; **to ~ one's throat** se racler la gorge; **to ~ a path through sth** se frayer un chemin à travers qch
**(c)** dissiper ⟨*fog, smoke*⟩; disperser ⟨*crowd*⟩
**(d)** s'acquitter de ⟨*debt*⟩
**(e)** ⟨*bank*⟩ compenser ⟨*cheque*⟩
**(f)** innocenter ⟨*accused*⟩ (**of** de); **to ~ one's name** blanchir son nom
**(g)** approuver ⟨*request*⟩; **to ~ sth with sb** obtenir l'accord de qn pour qch

**(h)** franchir ⟨*hurdle, wall*⟩
**(i) to ~ customs** passer à la douane
**4** *vi* **(a)** ⟨*liquid, sky*⟩ s'éclaircir
**(b)** ⟨*smoke, fog, cloud*⟩ se dissiper
**(c)** ⟨*air*⟩ se purifier
**(d)** ⟨*rash*⟩ disparaître
**(e)** ⟨*cheque*⟩ être compensé/-e

■ **clear away**: ¶ **~ away** débarrasser; ¶ **~ [sth] away** balayer ⟨*leaves*⟩; enlever ⟨*rubbish*⟩; ranger ⟨*papers, toys*⟩

■ **clear up**: ¶ **~ up (a)** (tidy up) faire du rangement
**(b)** ⟨*weather*⟩ s'éclaircir; ⟨*infection*⟩ disparaître
¶ **~ [sth] up (a)** ranger ⟨*mess, room, toys*⟩; ramasser ⟨*litter*⟩
**(b)** résoudre ⟨*problem*⟩; dissiper ⟨*misunderstanding*⟩

**clearance** *n* **(a)** (of rubbish) enlèvement *m*; **land ~** défrichement *m* du terrain
**(b)** (permission) autorisation *f*
**(c)** (also **~ sale**) liquidation *f*

**clear-cut** *adj* ⟨*plan, division*⟩ précis/-e; ⟨*difference*⟩ net/nette (*before n*); ⟨*problem, rule*⟩ clair/-e

**clear-headed** *adj* lucide

**clearing** *n* (glade) clairière *f*

**clearly** *adv* **(a)** ⟨*speak, hear, think, write*⟩ clairement; ⟨*see*⟩ bien; ⟨*visible*⟩ bien; ⟨*labelled*⟩ clairement
**(b)** (obviously) manifestement

**clear-out** *n* (colloq) **to have a ~** faire du rangement

**cleavage** *n* décolleté *m*

**cleaver** *n* fendoir *m*

**clef** *n* clef *f*; **in the treble ~** en clef de fa

**cleft** *adj* ⟨*chin*⟩ marqué/-e d'un sillon; ⟨*palate*⟩ fendu/-e

**clench** *vtr* serrer

**clergy** *n* clergé *m*

**clergyman** *n* ecclésiastique *m*

**clerical** *adj* **(a)** (of clergy) clérical/-e
**(b)** ⟨*staff*⟩ de bureau; **~ work** travail *m* de bureau

**clerk** *n* **(a)** (in office, bank) employé/-e *m/f*
**(b)** (GB) (to lawyer) ≈ clerc *m*; (in court) greffier/-ière *m/f*
**(c)** (US) (in hotel) réceptionniste *mf*; (in shop) vendeur/-euse *m/f*

**clever** *adj* **(a)** (intelligent) intelligent/-e
**(b)** (ingenious) ⟨*solution, gadget, person*⟩ astucieux/-ieuse, futé/-e
**(c)** (skilful) habile, adroit/-e

**cliché** *n* cliché *m*, lieu *m* commun

**clichéd** *adj* ⟨*expression*⟩ rebattu/-e; ⟨*idea, technique*⟩ éculé/-e; ⟨*art, music*⟩ bourré/-e (colloq) de clichés

**click** **1** *n* **(a)** (of machine, lock) déclic *m*
**(b)** (of fingers, heels, tongue) claquement *m*
**(c)** (Comput) clic *m*
**2** *vtr* **to ~ one's fingers** faire claquer ses doigts; **to ~ one's heels** claquer des talons  ⋯⇨

**3** vi ⟨camera, lock⟩ faire un déclic; ⟨door⟩ faire un petit bruit sec; **to ~ on** cliquer sur ⟨icon⟩

**client** n client/-e m/f

**clientele** n clientèle f

**cliff** n (by sea) falaise f; (inland) escarpement m

**climate** n climat m

**climax** n (of war, conflict) paroxysme m; (of plot, speech, play) point m culminant; (of career) apogée m

**climb** **1** n (up hill) escalade f; (up tower) montée f; (up mountain) ascension f
**2** vtr grimper ⟨hill⟩; faire l'ascension de ⟨mountain⟩; escalader ⟨lamppost, wall⟩; grimper à ⟨ladder, tree⟩; monter ⟨staircase⟩
**3** vi (a) ⟨person⟩ grimper; **to ~ down** descendre ⟨rock face⟩; **to ~ over** enjamber ⟨stile⟩; passer par-dessus ⟨fence, wall⟩; escalader ⟨debris, rocks⟩; **to ~ up** grimper à ⟨ladder, tree⟩; monter ⟨steps⟩
(b) ⟨aircraft⟩ monter
(c) ⟨road⟩ monter
(d) (increase) monter
■ **climb down** revenir sur sa décision

**climber** n grimpeur/-euse m/f, alpiniste mf

**climbing** n escalade f

**clinch** vtr (a) **to ~ a deal** conclure une affaire
(b) décider de ⟨argument⟩

**cling** vi (a) **to ~ (on) to sb/sth** se cramponner à qn/qch; **to ~ together** se cramponner l'un à l'autre
(b) ⟨clothes⟩ coller (**to** à)
(c) ⟨smell⟩ résister

**clingfilm** n (GB) scellofrais® m

**clinic** n centre m médical

**clinical** adj (a) ⟨medicine⟩ clinique; ⟨approach⟩ objectif/-ive
(b) (unfeeling) froid/-e

**clink** **1** vtr faire tinter ⟨glass, keys⟩; **to ~ glasses with** trinquer avec
**2** vi ⟨glass, keys⟩ tinter

**clip** **1** n (a) (on earring) clip m; (for hair) barrette f
(b) (from film) extrait m
**2** vtr (a) tailler ⟨hedge⟩; couper ⟨nails, moustache⟩; tondre ⟨dog, sheep⟩
(b) accrocher ⟨microphone⟩ (**to** à); fixer ⟨brooch⟩ (**to** à)
IDIOMS **to ~ sb's wings** rogner les ailes à qn

**clipart** n clip-art m

**clipboard** n (gen) porte-bloc m inv à pince; (Comput) presse-papiers m inv

**clip frame** n sous-verre m inv

**clip-ons** n pl clips mpl

**clippers** n pl (for nails) coupe-ongles m inv; (for hair, hedge) tondeuse f

**clipping** n (from paper) coupure f de presse

**cloak** **1** n cape f
**2** vtr (a) **~ed in** enveloppé/-e dans ⟨darkness⟩; enveloppé/-e de ⟨secrecy⟩
(b) (disguise) masquer

**cloakroom** n (a) (for coats) vestiaire m

(b) (GB) (lavatory) toilettes fpl

**clock** n (large) horloge f; (small) pendule f; (Sport) chronomètre m; **to put the ~s forward/back one hour** avancer/reculer les pendules d'une heure; **to work around the ~** travailler 24 heures sur 24
■ **clock off** (GB) pointer (à la sortie)
■ **clock on** (GB) pointer

**clock radio** n radio-réveil m

**clock tower** n beffroi m

**clockwise** adj, adv dans le sens des aiguilles d'une montre

**clockwork** adj ⟨toy⟩ mécanique
IDIOMS **to go like ~** aller comme sur des roulettes

**clog** n sabot m

**cloister** n cloître m

**clone** **1** n clone m
**2** vtr cloner

**cloning** n clonage m

**close¹** **1** adj (a) (near) proche (**to** de), voisin/-e (**to** de)
(b) ⟨relative, friend⟩ proche; ⟨resemblance⟩ frappant/-e
(c) ⟨contest, result⟩ serré/-e
(d) ⟨scrutiny⟩ minutieux/-ieuse; ⟨supervision⟩ étroit/-e; **to pay ~ attention to sth** faire une attention toute particulière à qch; **to keep a ~ watch or eye on sb/sth** surveiller étroitement qn/qch
(e) ⟨print, formation⟩ serré/-e
(f) ⟨weather⟩ lourd/-e; **it's ~** il fait lourd
**2** adv **to live quite ~ (by)** habiter tout près; **to move sth ~r** approcher qch; **to follow ~ behind** suivre de près; **to hold sb ~** serrer qn; **~ together** serrés les uns contre les autres; **Christmas is ~** Noël approche
**3 close by** phr près de ⟨wall, bridge⟩; **the ambulance is ~ by** l'ambulance n'est pas loin
**4 close to** phr (a) (near) près de
(b) (on point of) au bord de ⟨tears, hysteria⟩; **to be ~ to doing** être sur le point de faire
(c) (almost) près de; **to come ~ to doing** faillir faire
IDIOMS **it was a ~ call** (colloq) or **shave** (colloq) or **thing** je l'ai/tu l'as etc échappé belle

**close²** **1** n fin f
**2** vtr (a) fermer ⟨door, book⟩
(b) fermer ⟨border, port⟩; barrer ⟨road⟩; interdire l'accès à ⟨area⟩
(c) mettre fin à ⟨meeting⟩; fermer ⟨account⟩
(d) **to ~ the gap** réduire l'écart
(e) conclure ⟨deal⟩
**3** vi (a) ⟨airport, polls, shop⟩ fermer; ⟨door, container, eyes, mouth⟩ se fermer
(b) (cease to operate) fermer définitivement
(c) ⟨meeting, play⟩ prendre fin; **to ~ with** se terminer par ⟨song⟩
(d) ⟨currency, index⟩ clôturer (**at** à)
(e) ⟨gap⟩ se réduire
**4 closed** pp adj fermé/-e; **behind ~d doors** à huis clos

■ **close down**: ¶ ~ **down** fermer définitivement; ¶ ~ **[sth] down** fermer [qch] définitivement

■ **close up**: ¶ ~ **up (a)** ⟨flower, wound⟩ se refermer; ⟨group⟩ se serrer **(b)** ⟨shopkeeper⟩ fermer ¶ ~ **[sth] up (a)** fermer ⟨shop⟩ **(b)** boucher ⟨hole⟩

**closed-circuit television, CCTV** n télévision f en circuit fermé

**close-fitting** adj ⟨garment⟩ ajusté/-e, près du corps

**close-knit** adj ⟨family, group⟩ très uni/-e

**closely** adv ⟨follow, watch⟩ de près; ⟨resemble⟩ beaucoup; **to be ~ related** ⟨people⟩ être proches parents

**close-run** adj très serré/-e

**closet** ⟨1⟩ n (US) (cupboard) placard m; (for clothes) penderie f
⟨2⟩ adj ⟨alcoholic, fascist⟩ inavoué/-e

**close-up** ⟨1⟩ n gros plan m; **in ~** en gros plan
⟨2⟩ **close up** adv (from) ~ de près

**closing** ⟨1⟩ n fermeture f
⟨2⟩ adj ⟨minutes, words⟩ dernier/-ière (before n); ⟨scene, stage⟩ final/-e; ⟨speech⟩ de clôture

**closing date** n date f limite (**for** de)

**closing-down sale, closing-out sale** (US) n liquidation f

**closing time** n heure f de fermeture

**closure** n fermeture f

**clot** ⟨1⟩ n caillot m
⟨2⟩ vtr, vi coaguler, cailler

**cloth** n **(a)** (fabric) tissu m
**(b)** (for polishing, dusting) chiffon m; (for floor) serpillière f; (for drying dishes) torchon m; (for table) nappe f

**clothes** n pl vêtements mpl; **to put on/take off one's ~** s'habiller/se déshabiller

**clothes brush** n brosse f à habits

**clotheshanger** n cintre m

**clothes line** n corde f à linge

**clothes peg** n pince f à linge

**clothes shop** n magasin m de vêtements

**clothing** n vêtements mpl; **an item** or **article of ~** un vêtement

**cloud** ⟨1⟩ n nuage m; **to cast a ~ over sth** jeter une ombre sur qch
⟨2⟩ vtr **(a)** ⟨steam, breath⟩ embuer ⟨mirror⟩; ⟨tears⟩ brouiller ⟨vision⟩
**(b)** obscurcir ⟨judgment⟩; brouiller ⟨memory⟩; **to ~ the issue** brouiller les cartes
IDIOMS **to be living in ~-cuckoo-land** croire au père Noël

■ **cloud over** ⟨sky⟩ se couvrir (de nuages); ⟨face⟩ s'assombrir

**cloudy** adj **(a)** ⟨weather⟩ couvert/-e
**(b)** ⟨liquid⟩ trouble

**clout** n **(a)** (blow) claque f, coup m
**(b)** (influence) influence f (**with** auprès de, sur)

**clove** n **(a)** (spice) clou m de girofle
**(b)** (of garlic) gousse f

**clover** n trèfle m

**clown** n clown m
■ **clown around** (GB) faire le clown or le pitre

**club** n **(a)** (association) club m
**(b)** (colloq) (nightclub) boîte f de nuit
**(c)** (in cards) trèfle m
**(d)** (for golf) club m
**(e)** (weapon) massue f
■ **club together** cotiser

**club car** n (US) wagon-bar m de première classe

**club class** n classe f club or affaires

**cluck** vi ⟨hen⟩ glousser

**clue** n indication f (**to, as to** quant à); (in police investigation) indice m (**to** quant à); (in crossword) définition f; **I haven't (got) a ~** (colloq) je n'ai aucune idée

**clued-up** adj (colloq) calé/-e (colloq) (**about** sur)

**clueless** adj (colloq) nul/nulle (colloq) (**about** en)

**clump** n (of flowers, grass) touffe f; (of trees) massif m; (of earth) motte f

**clumsiness** n (carelessness) maladresse f; (awkwardness) gaucherie f; (of system) côté m peu pratique

**clumsy** adj ⟨person, attempt⟩ maladroit/-e; ⟨object⟩ grossier/-ière; ⟨animal⟩ pataud/-e; ⟨tool⟩ peu maniable; ⟨style⟩ lourd/-e

**cluster** ⟨1⟩ n (of flowers, berries) grappe f; (of people, islands, trees) groupe m; (of houses) ensemble m; (of diamonds) entourage m; (of stars) amas m
⟨2⟩ vi ⟨people⟩ se rassembler (**around** autour de)

**clutch** ⟨1⟩ n (Aut) embrayage m
⟨2⟩ vtr tenir fermement
■ **clutch at** tenter d'attraper ⟨branch, rail, person⟩; saisir ⟨arm⟩

**clutch bag** n pochette f

**clutches** n pl **to fall into the ~ of** tomber sous les griffes or la patte (colloq) de

**clutter** ⟨1⟩ n désordre m
⟨2⟩ vtr (also ~ **up**) encombrer

**c/o** prep (abbr = **care of**) chez

**Co** n (abbr = **company**) Cie

**coach** ⟨1⟩ n **(a)** (bus) (auto)car m
**(b)** (GB) (of train) wagon m
**(c)** (Sport) entraîneur/-euse m/f
**(d)** (for drama, voice) répétiteur/-trice m/f
**(e)** (horse-drawn) carrosse m
⟨2⟩ vtr **(a)** (Sport) entraîner ⟨team⟩
**(b)** (teach) **to ~ sb** donner des leçons particulières à qn (**in** en)

**coach station** n gare f routière

**coach trip** n excursion f en autocar

**coal** n charbon m
IDIOMS **to haul sb over the ~s** (colloq) passer un savon à qn (colloq)

**coalfield** n bassin m houiller

**coal fire** n cheminée f (où brûle un feu de charbon)

**coalition** n coalition f

**coalmine** n mine f de charbon

**coalminer** n mineur m

**coarse** adj (a) ⟨texture⟩ grossier/-ière; ⟨skin⟩ épais/-aisse; ⟨sand, salt⟩ gros/grosse (before n)
(b) ⟨manners⟩ grossier/-ière; ⟨language, joke⟩ cru/-e

**coast** ⟦1⟧ n côte f; **off the ~** près de la côte
⟦2⟧ vi ⟨car, bicycle⟩ descendre en roue libre

**coastal** adj côtier/-ière

**coaster** n (mat) dessous-de-verre m inv

**coastguard** n (a) (person) garde-côte m
(b) (organization) gendarmerie f maritime

**coastline** n littoral m

**coat** ⟦1⟧ n (a) (garment) manteau m
(b) (of dog, cat) pelage m; (of horse, leopard) robe f
(c) (layer) couche f
⟦2⟧ vtr **to ~ sth with** enduire qch de ⟨paint, adhesive⟩; couvrir qch de ⟨dust, oil⟩; enrober qch de ⟨breadcrumbs, chocolate, sauce⟩

**coat hanger** n cintre m

**coat of arms** n blason m, armoiries fpl

**coat rack** n portemanteau m

**coax** vtr cajoler; **to ~ sb into doing** persuader qn (gentiment) de faire

**cobbler** n cordonnier m

**cobblestones** n pl pavés mpl

**cobweb** n toile f d'araignée

**cocaine** n cocaïne f

**cock** ⟦1⟧ n (a) (rooster) coq m
(b) (male bird) (oiseau m) mâle m
⟦2⟧ vtr (a) **to ~ an eyebrow** hausser les sourcils; **to ~ a leg** ⟨dog⟩ lever la patte; **to ~ an ear** dresser l'oreille
(b) (tilt) pencher
(c) (Mil) armer ⟨gun⟩

**cock-and-bull story** n histoire f abracadabrante or à dormir debout

**cockatoo** n cacatoès m

**cockerel** n jeune coq m

**cockle** n coque f

**cockpit** n cockpit m, poste m de pilotage

**cockroach** n cafard m

**cocktail** n cocktail m

**cocktail bar** n bar m

**cocky** adj impudent/-e

**cocoa** n cacao m; (drink) chocolat m

**coconut** n noix f de coco

**cocoon** n cocon m

**cod** n morue f

**COD** n (abbr = **cash on delivery**) envoi m contre remboursement

**code** ⟦1⟧ n (a) (gen) code m
(b) (also **dialling ~**) indicatif m
⟦2⟧ vtr coder

**codeine** n codéine f

**code name** n nom m de code

**codeword** n (password) mot m de passe

**coeducational** adj mixte

**coerce** vtr exercer des pressions sur; **to ~ sb into doing** contraindre qn à faire

**coexist** vi coexister (with avec)

**coffee** ⟦1⟧ n café m; **a black/white ~** un café (noir)/au lait
⟦2⟧ adj ⟨dessert⟩ au café; ⟨cup, filter, spoon⟩ à café

**coffee break** n pause(-)café f

**coffee pot** n cafetière f

**coffee table** n table f basse

**coffin** n cercueil m

**cog** n (tooth) dent f d'engrenage; (wheel) pignon m

**cohabit** vi cohabiter (with avec)

**coherent** adj cohérent/-e

**coil** ⟦1⟧ n (a) (of rope, barbed wire) rouleau m; (of electric wire) bobine f; (of hair) boucle f; (of snake) anneau m
(b) (contraceptive) stérilet m
⟦2⟧ vtr (also **~ up**) enrouler ⟨hair, rope, wire⟩
⟦3⟧ vi s'enrouler (**round** autour de)

**coin** ⟦1⟧ n pièce f (de monnaie); **a pound ~** une pièce d'une livre
⟦2⟧ vtr forger ⟨term⟩

**coin box** n (pay phone) cabine f (téléphonique) à pièces

**coincide** vi coïncider (with avec)

**coincidence** n coïncidence f, hasard m; **it is a ~ that** c'est par coïncidence que; **by ~** par hasard

**coincidental** adj fortuit/-e

**coin operated** adj qui marche avec des pièces

**coke** n (a) (fuel) coke m
(b) (colloq) (cocaine) coke f (colloq)

**Coke®** n coca m

**colander** n passoire f

**cold** ⟦1⟧ n (a) (chilliness) froid m; **to feel the ~** être sensible au froid, être frileux/-euse
(b) (Med) rhume m; **to have a ~** être enrhumé/-e, avoir un rhume
⟦2⟧ adj (a) (chilly) froid; **to be** or **feel ~** ⟨person⟩ avoir froid; **the room was ~** il faisait froid dans la pièce; **it's** or **the weather's ~** il fait froid; **to go ~** ⟨food, water⟩ se refroidir
(b) ⟨manner⟩ froid/-e; **to be ~ to** or **towards sb** être froid/-e avec qn
IDIOMS **in ~ blood** de sang-froid; **to be out ~** être sans connaissance

**cold-blooded** adj ⟨animal⟩ à sang froid; ⟨killer⟩ sans pitié

**cold calling** n démarchage m par téléphone

**coldness** n froideur f

**cold shoulder** n **to give sb the ~** snober qn, battre froid à qn

**cold sore** n bouton m de fièvre

**cold sweat** n **to bring sb out in a ~** donner des sueurs froides à qn

**cold turkey** n (colloq) (treatment) sevrage m; (reaction) réaction f de manque; **to be ~** être en manque

**Cold War** n guerre f froide

**coleslaw** n salade f à base de chou cru

**colic** *n* coliques *fpl*

**collaborate** *vi* collaborer (**on, in** à; **with** avec)

**collaboration** *n* collaboration *f*

**collaborator** *n* collaborateur/-trice *m/f*

**collapse** ① *n* **(a)** (of regime, economy) effondrement *m* (**of, in** de)
**(b)** (of deal, talks) échec *m*
**(c)** (of company) faillite *f* (**of** de)
**(d)** (of person) (physical) écroulement *m*; (mental) effondrement *m*
**(e)** (of building, bridge) effondrement *m*; (of tunnel, wall) écroulement *m*
**(f)** (Med) (of lung) collapsus *m*
② *vi* **(a)** ⟨regime, economy⟩ s'effondrer; ⟨deal, talks⟩ échouer
**(b)** ⟨company⟩ faire faillite
**(c)** ⟨person⟩ s'écrouler
**(d)** ⟨building, bridge⟩ s'effondrer; ⟨tunnel, wall⟩ s'écrouler; ⟨chair⟩ s'affaisser (**under** sous)
**(e)** (Med) ⟨lung⟩ se dégonfler
**(f)** (fold) ⟨bike, pushchair⟩ se plier

**collapsible** *adj* pliant/-e

**collar** *n* **(a)** (on garment) col *m*
**(b)** (for animal) collier *m*
**IDIOMS to get hot under the** ∼ se mettre en rogne (colloq)

**collarbone** *n* clavicule *f*

**collar size** *n* encolure *f*

**collate** *vtr* collationner

**colleague** *n* collègue *mf*

**collect** ① *adv* (US) **to call sb** ∼ appeler qn en PCV
② *vtr* **(a)** ramasser ⟨wood, litter, rubbish⟩; rassembler ⟨information⟩; recueillir ⟨signatures⟩
**(b)** (as hobby) collectionner, faire collection de ⟨stamps, coins⟩
**(c)** ⟨objects⟩ prendre, ramasser ⟨dust⟩
**(d)** percevoir ⟨rent⟩; encaisser ⟨fares, money⟩; recouvrer ⟨debt⟩; toucher ⟨pension⟩; percevoir ⟨tax, fine⟩
**(e)** faire la levée de ⟨mail, post⟩
**(f)** (pick up) aller chercher ⟨person⟩; récupérer ⟨keys, book⟩
③ *vi* **(a)** ⟨dust, leaves⟩ s'accumuler; ⟨people⟩ se rassembler
**(b) to** ∼ **for charity** faire la quête pour des bonnes œuvres
④ **collected** *pp adj* **(a)** ⟨person⟩ calme
**(b)** (assembled) **the** ∼**ed works of Dickens** les œuvres complètes de Dickens

**collection** *n* **(a)** (of coins, records) collection *f*; (anthology) recueil *m*; **art** ∼ collection *f* (de tableaux)
**(b)** (money) collecte *f* (**for** pour); (in church) quête *f*
**(c)** (of mail) levée *f*

**collective** *adj* collectif/-ive

**collective ownership** *n* copropriété *f*

**collector** *n* **(a)** (of coins, stamps) collectionneur/-euse *m/f*
**(b)** (of taxes) percepteur *m*; (of rent, debts) encaisseur *m*

**collector's item** *n* pièce *f* de collection

**college** *n* établissement *m* d'enseignement supérieur; (school, part of university) collège *m*; (US Univ) faculté *f*; **to go to** ∼, **to be at** *or* **in** (US) ∼ faire des études supérieures

**college of further education, CFE** *n* (GB) *école ouverte aux adultes et aux jeunes pour terminer un cycle d'études secondaires*

**collide** *vi* ⟨vehicle, plane⟩ entrer en collision (**with** avec)

**collie** *n* (dog) colley *m*

**colliery** *n* houillère *f*

**collision** *n* collision *f*

**colloquial** *adj* familier/-ière

**colon** *n* **(a)** (Anat) côlon *m*
**(b)** (punctuation) deux points *mpl*

**colonel** *n* colonel *m*

**colonialist** *n, adj* colonialiste (*mf*)

**colonization** *n* colonisation *f*

**colonize** *vtr* coloniser

**colonizer** *n* colon *m*

**colony** *n* colonie *f*

**colour** (GB), **color** (US) ① *n* **(a)** couleur *f*; **what** ∼ **is it?** de quelle couleur est-il/elle?; **to put** ∼ **into sb's cheeks** redonner des couleurs à qn
**(b)** (dye) (for food) colorant *m*; (for hair) teinture *f*
② *vtr* **(a)** (with paints, crayons) colorier; (with food dye) colorer
**(b)** (prejudice) fausser ⟨judgment⟩
③ *vi* ⟨person⟩ rougir
**IDIOMS to be off** ∼ ne pas être en forme; **to show one's true** ∼**s** se montrer sous son vrai jour

**colour blind** *adj* daltonien/-ienne

**coloured** (GB), **colored** (US) *adj* ⟨pen, paper, bead⟩ de couleur; ⟨picture⟩ en couleur; ⟨light, glass⟩ coloré/-e

**colour film** *n* (for camera) pellicule *f* couleur

**colourful** (GB), **colorful** (US) *adj* **(a)** ⟨dress, shirt⟩ aux couleurs vives
**(b)** ⟨story, life⟩ haut en couleur; ⟨character⟩ pittoresque

**colouring** (GB), **coloring** (US) *n* **(a)** (of animal) couleurs *fpl*; (of person) teint *m*
**(b)** (for food) colorant *m*

**colour scheme** *n* couleurs *fpl*, coloris *m*

**colour supplement** *n* supplément *m* illustré

**colour television** *n* télévision *f* (en) couleur

**colt** *n* poulain *m*

**column** *n* **(a)** (pillar) colonne *f*
**(b)** (on page, list) colonne *f*
**(c)** (newspaper article) rubrique *f*; **sports** ∼ rubrique sportive

**columnist** *n* journaliste *mf*

**coma** *n* coma *m*; **in a** ∼ dans le coma

**comatose** *adj* (Med) comateux/-euse; (figurative) abruti/-e

**comb** ① *n* peigne *m*    ···⊹

**2** *vtr* **to** ~ **sb's hair** peigner qn; **to** ~ **one's hair** se peigner

**combat** **1** *n* combat *m*
**2** *vtr* lutter contre, combattre

**combat jacket** *n* veste *f* de treillis

**combination** *n* combinaison *f*

**combine** **1** *n* groupe *m*
**2** *vtr* **(a)** combiner ⟨*activities, colours, items*⟩ (**with** avec); associer ⟨*ideas, aims*⟩ (**with** à); **to** ~ **forces** (merge) s'allier; (cooperate) collaborer
**(b)** (Culin) mélanger (**with** avec)
**3** *vi* **(a)** ⟨*activities, colours, elements*⟩ se combiner
**(b)** ⟨*people, groups*⟩ s'associer; ⟨*firms*⟩ fusionner

**combined** *adj* **(a)** (joint) ~ **operation** collaboration *f*; **a** ~ **effort** une collaboration
**(b)** (total) ⟨*salary, age*⟩ total/-e
**(c)** ⟨*effects*⟩ combiné/-e

**combine harvester** *n*
moissonneuse-batteuse *f*

**come** *vi* **(a)** ⟨*person, day*⟩ venir; ⟨*bus, news, winter, war*⟩ arriver; ⟨*dustman, postman*⟩ passer; **to** ~ **down** descendre ⟨*stairs, street*⟩; **to** ~ **up** monter ⟨*stairs, street*⟩; **to** ~ **into** entrer dans ⟨*house, room*⟩; **when the time** ~**s** lorsque le moment sera venu; (**I'm**) **coming!** j'arrive!; **to** ~ **to sb for** venir demander [qch] à qn ⟨*money, advice*⟩; **don't** ~ **any closer** ne vous approchez pas (plus); **to** ~ **as a shock/ surprise** être un choc/une surprise
**(b)** (reach) **to** ~ **up/down to** ⟨*water*⟩ venir jusqu'à; ⟨*dress, curtain*⟩ arriver à
**(c)** (happen) **how** ~? comment ça se fait?; **to take things as they** ~ prendre les choses comme elles viennent; ~ **what may** advienne que pourra
**(d)** (begin) **to** ~ **to do** finir par faire
**(e)** **to** ~ **from** ⟨*person*⟩ être originaire de, venir de ⟨*city, country*⟩; ⟨*word, legend*⟩ venir de ⟨*language, country*⟩; ⟨*stamps, painting*⟩ provenir de ⟨*place*⟩; ⟨*smell, sound*⟩ venir de ⟨*place*⟩
**(f)** (in order) **to** ~ **after** suivre, venir après; **to** ~ **before** (in time, list, queue) précéder; (in importance) passer avant; **to** ~ **first/last** (in race) arriver premier/dernier
**(g) when it** ~**s to sth/to doing** lorsqu'il s'agit de qch/de faire
**(h) to** ~ **true** se réaliser; **to** ~ **undone** se défaire

■ **come across**: ¶ ~ **across** ⟨*meaning, message*⟩ passer; ⟨*feelings*⟩ transparaître; ~ **across as** donner l'impression d'être ⟨*liar, expert*⟩; paraître ⟨*honest*⟩; ¶ ~ **across [sth]** tomber sur ⟨*article*⟩

■ **come along (a)** ⟨*bus, person*⟩ arriver; ⟨*opportunity*⟩ se présenter
**(b)** (hurry up) ~ **along!** dépêche-toi!
**(c)** (attend) venir (**to** à)
**(d)** (progress) ⟨*pupil*⟩ faire des progrès; ⟨*book, work, project*⟩ avancer; ⟨*painting, tennis*⟩ progresser

■ **come apart (a)** (accidentally) ⟨*book, box*⟩ se déchirer; ⟨*toy, camera*⟩ se casser

**(b)** (intentionally) ⟨*components*⟩ se séparer; ⟨*machine*⟩ se démonter

■ **come around** (US) = COME ROUND

■ **come away** partir

■ **come back (a)** (return) revenir (**from** de; **to** à); (to one's house) rentrer
**(b)** ⟨*law, system*⟩ être rétabli/-e; ⟨*trend*⟩ revenir à la mode

■ **come down (a)** ⟨*person, lift, blind*⟩ descendre; ⟨*curtain*⟩ tomber
**(b)** ⟨*price, inflation, temperature*⟩ baisser; ⟨*cost*⟩ diminuer
**(c)** ⟨*snow, rain*⟩ tomber
**(d)** ⟨*ceiling, wall*⟩ s'écrouler; ⟨*hem*⟩ se défaire
**(e) to** ~ **down with** attraper ⟨*flu*⟩

■ **come forward (a)** (step forward) s'avancer
**(b)** (volunteer) se présenter

■ **come in (a)** (enter) entrer (**through** par)
**(b)** ⟨*tide*⟩ monter
**(c) to** ~ **in useful** être utile
**(d) to** ~ **in for criticism** ⟨*person*⟩ être critiqué/-e; ⟨*plan*⟩ faire l'objet de nombreuses critiques

■ **come into (a)** hériter de ⟨*money*⟩; entrer en possession de ⟨*inheritance*⟩
**(b) luck doesn't** ~ **into it** ce n'est pas une question de hasard

■ **come off (a)** ⟨*button, handle*⟩ se détacher; ⟨*lid*⟩ s'enlever; ⟨*paint*⟩ s'écailler
**(b)** ⟨*ink*⟩ s'effacer; ⟨*stain*⟩ partir
**(c)** ⟨*plan, trick*⟩ réussir

■ **come on (a)** ~ **on!** allez!
**(b)** ⟨*person, patient*⟩ faire des progrès; ⟨*bridge, novel*⟩ avancer; ⟨*plant*⟩ pousser
**(c)** ⟨*light*⟩ s'allumer; ⟨*heating, fan*⟩ se mettre en route
**(d)** ⟨*actor*⟩ entrer en scène

■ **come out (a)** ⟨*person, animal, vehicle*⟩ sortir (**of** de); ⟨*star*⟩ apparaître; ⟨*sun, moon*⟩ se montrer
**(b)** (strike) faire la grève; **to** ~ **out on strike** faire la grève
**(c)** ⟨*contact lens, tooth*⟩ tomber; ⟨*contents*⟩ sortir; ⟨*cork*⟩ s'enlever
**(d)** ⟨*water, smoke*⟩ sortir (**through** par)
**(e)** ⟨*stain*⟩ s'en aller, partir
**(f)** ⟨*magazine, novel*⟩ paraître; ⟨*album, film, product*⟩ sortir
**(g)** ⟨*details, facts*⟩ être révélé/-e; ⟨*results*⟩ être connu/-e
**(h)** ⟨*photo, photocopy*⟩ être réussi/-e
**(i) to** ~ **out with** sortir ⟨*excuse*⟩; raconter ⟨*nonsense*⟩; **to** ~ **straight out with it** le dire franchement
**(j)** ⟨*homosexual*⟩ déclarer publiquement son homosexualité

■ **come over**: ¶ ~ **over** venir (**to do** faire); ¶ **what's** ~ **over you?** qu'est-ce qui te prend?

■ **come round** (GB), **come around** (US)
**(a)** (regain consciousness) reprendre connaissance
**(b)** (visit) venir
**(c)** (change mind) changer d'avis

■ **come through**: ¶ ~ **through (a)** (survive) s'en tirer

(b) ⟨*heat, ink*⟩ traverser; ⟨*light*⟩ passer
¶ ∼ **through** [sth] se tirer de ⟨*crisis*⟩; survivre à ⟨*operation, ordeal*⟩
■ **come to:** ¶ ∼ **to** reprendre connaissance; ¶ ∼ **to** [sth] ⟨*shopping*⟩ revenir à; ⟨*bill, total*⟩ s'élever à; **that** ∼**s to £40** cela fait 40 livres sterling; **it may not** ∼ **to that** nous n'en arriverons peut-être pas là
■ **come under (a) to** ∼ **under threat** être menacé/-e
(b) (be classified under) être classé/-e dans le rayon ⟨*reference, history*⟩
■ **come up (a)** ⟨*problem, issue*⟩ être soulevé/-e; ⟨*name*⟩ être mentionné/-e
(b) ⟨*opportunity*⟩ se présenter; **something urgent has** ∼ **up** j'ai quelque chose d'urgent à faire
(c) ⟨*sun, moon*⟩ sortir; ⟨*daffodils*⟩ sortir
(d) (in law) ⟨*case*⟩ passer au tribunal
(e) **to** ∼ **up against** se heurter à ⟨*problem*⟩
(f) **to** ∼ **up with** trouver ⟨*answer, idea*⟩

**comeback** n come-back m; **to make a** ∼ ⟨*person*⟩ faire un come-back; ⟨*trend*⟩ revenir à la mode

**comedian** n (male) comique m

**comedienne** n actrice f comique

**comedy** n comédie f

**comet** n comète f

**comeuppance** n (colloq) **to get one's** ∼ avoir ce qu'on mérite

**comfort** ⨐1⨑ n (a) confort m; **to live in** ∼ vivre dans l'aisance; **home** ∼**s** le confort du foyer
(b) (consolation) réconfort m, consolation f
⨐2⨑ vtr consoler; (stronger) réconforter

**comfortable** adj (a) ⟨*chair, clothes, journey*⟩ confortable; ⟨*temperature*⟩ agréable
(b) ⟨*person*⟩ à l'aise

**comfortably** adv (gen) confortablement; (easily) facilement, aisément; **to be** ∼ **off** être à l'aise

**comforting** adj réconfortant/-e

**comic** ⨐1⨑ n (a) = COMEDIAN
(b) (magazine) bande f dessinée
⨐2⨑ adj comique

**comical** adj cocasse, comique

**comic strip** n bande f dessinée

**coming** ⨐1⨑ n arrivée f; ∼**s and goings** allées et venues fpl
⨐2⨑ adj ⟨*election, event*⟩ prochain/-e (*before* n); ⟨*months, weeks*⟩ à venir

**comma** n virgule f

**command** ⨐1⨑ n (a) (order) ordre m
(b) (military control) commandement m; **to be in** ∼ commander
(c) (of language) maîtrise f; **to be in** ∼ **of the situation** avoir la situation en main
(d) (Comput) commande f
⨐2⨑ vtr (a) ordonner à ⟨*person*⟩ (**to do** de faire)
(b) inspirer ⟨*affection, respect*⟩
(c) (Mil) commander ⟨*regiment*⟩

**commander** n (gen) chef m; (Mil) commandant m

**commanding** adj ⟨*manner, voice*⟩ impérieux/-ieuse; ⟨*presence*⟩ imposant/-e

**commanding officer, CO** n commandant m

**commando** n commando m

**commemorate** vtr commémorer

**commence** vtr, vi commencer

**commend** vtr louer (**on** pour)

**comment** ⨐1⨑ n (a) (public) commentaire m (**on** sur); (in conversation) remarque f (**on** sur); (written) annotation f
(b) **to be a** ∼ **on** en dire long sur
⨐2⨑ vi faire des commentaires (**on** sur)

**commentary** n commentaire m (**on** de)

**commentator** n (sports) commentateur/-trice m/f; (current affairs) journaliste mf

**commerce** n commerce m

**commercial** ⨐1⨑ n annonce f publicitaire
⨐2⨑ adj commercial/-e

**commercial break** n publicité f

**commercial traveller** n voyageur m de commerce

**commiserate** vi compatir (**with** avec; **about, over** à propos de)

**commission** ⨐1⨑ n (a) (fee) commission f
(b) (order) commande f (**for** de)
(c) (committee) commission f (**on** sur)
⨐2⨑ vtr (a) commander ⟨*work*⟩ (**from** à); **to** ∼ **sb to do** charger qn de faire
(b) (Mil) **to be** ∼**ed (as) an officer** être nommé/-e officier

**commissioner** n (a) (gen) membre m d'une commission
(b) (GB) (in police) ≈ préfet m de police
(c) (in the EC) membre m de la Commission européenne

**commit** vtr (a) commettre ⟨*crime, error, sin*⟩; **to** ∼ **suicide** se suicider
(b) **to** ∼ **oneself** s'engager (**to** à)
(c) consacrer ⟨*money, time*⟩ (**to** à)

**commitment** n (a) (obligation) engagement m (**to do** à faire)
(b) (sense of duty) attachement m (**to** à)

**committed** adj (a) (devoted) ⟨*parent, teacher*⟩ dévoué/-e; ⟨*Christian, Socialist*⟩ fervent/-e; **to be** ∼ **to/to doing** se consacrer à/à faire
(b) (with commitments) pris/-e

**committee** n comité m; (to investigate, report) commission f

**commodity** n article m; (food) denrée f

**common** ⨐1⨑ n terrain m communal
⨐2⨑ **Commons** n pl (GB) (Pol) **the Commons** les Communes fpl
⨐3⨑ adj (a) (frequent) courant/-e, fréquent/-e; **in** ∼ **use** d'un usage courant
(b) (shared) commun/-e (**to** à); **in** ∼ en commun; **it is** ∼ **knowledge** c'est de notoriété publique
(c) **the** ∼ **people** le peuple; **a** ∼ **criminal** un criminel ordinaire
(d) (low-class) commun/-e; **it looks/sounds** ∼ ça fait commun

**common-law husband** n concubin m
**common-law marriage** n concubinage m
**common-law wife** n concubine f
**commonly** adv communément
**Common Market** n Marché m commun
**commonplace** adj (common) commun/-e; (trite) banal/-e
**common room** n salle f de détente
**common sense** n bon sens m, sens m commun
**Commonwealth** n the ~ le Commonwealth
**Commonwealth of Independent States** pr n Communauté f des États indépendants
**commotion** n (a) (noise) vacarme m, brouhaha m
(b) (disturbance) émoi m, agitation f
**communal** adj ⟨property, area, showers⟩ commun/-e; ⟨garden⟩ collectif/-ive; ⟨life⟩ communautaire
**commune** n communauté f
**communicate** [1] vtr communiquer ⟨ideas, feelings⟩ (to à); transmettre ⟨information⟩ (to à)
[2] vi communiquer
**communication** n communication f
**communication cord** n (GB) sonnette f d'alarme
**communications** n pl (GB) communications fpl, liaison f
**communications company** n société f de communications
**communication studies** n pl études fpl en communication
**communion** n communion f
**communism** n communisme m
**communist** n, adj communiste (mf)
**community** n communauté f
**community care** n soins mpl en dehors du milieu hospitalier
**community centre** (GB), **community center** (US) n maison f de quartier
**community service** n travail m d'intérêt public
**commute** vi to ~ between Oxford and London faire le trajet entre Oxford et Londres tous les jours
**commuter** n navetteur/-euse m/f, migrant/-e m/f journalier/-ière
**compact** [1] n poudrier m
[2] adj compact/-e
**compact disc** n disque m compact
**companion** n compagnon/compagne m/f
**companionship** n compagnie f
**company** n (a) (firm) société f; airline ~ compagnie f aérienne
(b) theatre ~ troupe f de théâtre, compagnie f théâtrale
(c) (Mil) compagnie f

(d) (companionship) compagnie f; to keep sb ~ tenir compagnie à qn
(e) (visitors) visiteurs mpl
**company car** n voiture f de fonction
**company director** n directeur/-trice m/f général/-e
**company pension scheme** n régime m de retraite de l'enterprise
**company secretary** n secrétaire mf général/-e
**comparable** adj comparable (to, with à)
**comparative** adj (a) (in grammar) comparatif/-ive
(b) (relative) relatif/-ive; in ~ terms en termes relatifs
(c) ⟨study⟩ comparatif/-ive
**comparatively** adv relativement
**compare** [1] vtr comparer (with, to avec, à)
[2] vi être comparable (with à)
[3] **compared with** prep phr ~d with sb/sth par rapport à qn/qch
[4] v refl to ~ oneself with or to se comparer à
**comparison** n comparaison f; in or by ~ with par rapport à
**compartment** n compartiment m
**compass** n boussole f; (also ship's ~) compas m; the points of the ~ les points mpl cardinaux
**compasses** n pl (a pair of) ~ un compas
**compassion** n compassion f (for pour)
**compassionate** adj compatissant/-e; on ~ grounds pour raisons fpl personnelles
**compatible** adj compatible (with avec)
**compel** vtr contraindre (to do à faire), obliger (to do de faire)
**compelling** adj ⟨reason, argument⟩ convaincant/-e; ⟨speaker⟩ fascinant/-e
**compensate** [1] vtr dédommager, indemniser
[2] vi to ~ for compenser
**compensation** n (a) (gen) compensation f (for de)
(b) (financial) indemnisation f
**compete** [1] vi (a) (gen) rivaliser; to ~ against or with rivaliser avec (for pour obtenir)
(b) (commercially) ⟨companies⟩ se faire concurrence; to ~ with faire concurrence à (for pour obtenir)
(c) (in sport) être en compétition (against, with avec); to ~ in participer à ⟨Olympics, race⟩
[2] **competing** pres p adj rival/-e
**competence** n (a) (ability) compétence f
(b) (skill) compétences fpl
**competent** adj compétent/-e, capable
**competition** n (a) (gen) concurrence f
(b) (contest) concours m; (race) compétition f
(c) (competitors) concurrence f
**competitive** adj (a) ⟨person⟩ qui a l'esprit de compétition; ⟨environment⟩ compétitif/-ive
(b) ⟨price, product⟩ compétitif/-ive
(c) ⟨sport⟩ de compétition

**competitor** *n* concurrent/-e *m/f*

**compilation** *n* **(a)** (collection) compilation *f*
**(b)** (act of compiling) (of reference book) rédaction *f*; (of dossier) constitution *f*

**compile** *vtr* **(a)** dresser ⟨*list, catalogue*⟩; établir ⟨*report*⟩
**(b)** (Comput) compiler

**complacent** *adj* suffisant/-e; **to be ∼ about** être trop confiant/-e de ⟨*success, future*⟩

**complain** *vi* se plaindre (**to** à; **about** de; **of** de); (officially) se plaindre (**to** auprès de)

**complaint** *n* plainte *f*; (official) réclamation *f*; **there have been ∼s about the noise** on s'est plaint du bruit; **to have grounds** *or* **cause for ∼** avoir lieu de se plaindre

**complement** ⒈ *n* complément *m*
⒉ *vtr* compléter

**complementary** *adj* complémentaire (**to** de)

**complementary medicine** *n* médecine *f* parallèle

**complete** ⒈ *adj* **(a)** complet/-ète
**(b)** (finished) achevé/-e
⒉ *vtr* **(a)** (finish) terminer ⟨*building, course, exercise*⟩; achever ⟨*task, journey*⟩
**(b)** compléter ⟨*collection, phrase*⟩
**(c)** remplir ⟨*form*⟩

**completely** *adv* complètement

**completion** *n* achèvement *m*

**complex** ⒈ *n* complexe *m*; **sports ∼** complexe sportif; **he's got a ∼ about his weight** son poids le complexe
⒉ *adj* complexe

**complexion** *n* teint *m*

**complexity** *n* complexité *f*

**compliance** *n* conformité (**with** à)

**compliant** *adj* conciliant/-e

**complicate** *vtr* compliquer

**complicated** *adj* compliqué/-e

**complication** *n* **(a)** (problem) inconvénient *m*, problème *m*
**(b)** (Med) complication *f*

**compliment** ⒈ *n* compliment *m*; **to pay sb a ∼** faire un compliment à qn
⒉ *vtr* complimenter, faire des compliments à

**complimentary** *adj* **(a)** ⟨*remark*⟩ flatteur/-euse
**(b)** (free) gratuit/-e

**compliments** *n pl* compliments *mpl* (**to** à)

**comply** *vi* **to ∼ with** se conformer à ⟨*orders*⟩; respecter, observer ⟨*rules*⟩

**component** *n* (gen) composante *f*; (in car, machine) pièce *f*; (electrical) composant *m*

**compose** *vtr* **(a)** (gen) composer; **∼d of** composé/-e de
**(b)** **to ∼ oneself** se ressaisir

**composed** *adj* calme

**composer** *n* compositeur/-trice *m/f*

**composition** *n* **(a)** (gen) composition *f*
**(b)** (essay) rédaction *f* (**about, on** sur)

**compost** *n* compost *m*

**composure** *n* calme *m*

**compound** ⒈ *n* **(a)** (enclosure) enceinte *f*
**(b)** (in chemistry) composé *m* (**of** de)
**(c)** (word) mot *m* composé
⒉ *adj* **(a)** (gen) composé/-e
**(b)** (Med) ⟨*fracture*⟩ multiple

**comprehend** *vtr* comprendre

**comprehensible** *adj* compréhensible, intelligible

**comprehension** *n* compréhension *f*

**comprehensive** ⒈ *n* (GB Sch) (*also* **∼ school**) école *f* (publique) secondaire
⒉ *adj* ⟨*report, list*⟩ complet/-ète, détaillé/-e; ⟨*knowledge*⟩ étendu/-e; **∼ insurance policy** assurance *f* tous risques

**compress** ⒈ *n* compresse *f*
⒉ *vtr* comprimer

**comprise** *vtr* comprendre; **to be ∼d of** être composé/-e de

**compromise** ⒈ *n* compromis *m*
⒉ *vtr* compromettre
⒊ *vi* transiger, arriver à un compromis; **to ∼ on sth** trouver un compromis sur qch

**compromising** *adj* compromettant/-e

**compulsive** *adj* **(a)** (inveterate) invétéré/-e; (psychologically) compulsif/-ive
**(b)** (fascinating) fascinant/-e

**compulsory** *adj* obligatoire

**computer** *n* ordinateur *m*

**computer-aided design, CAD** *n* conception *f* assistée par ordinateur, CAO *f*

**computer-aided learning, CAL** *n* enseignement *m* assisté par ordinateur

**computer crime** *n* piratage *m* informatique

**computer dating** *n* organisation *f* de rencontres (en utilisant un ordinateur)

**computer game** *n* jeu *m* informatique

**computer graphics** *n* infographie *f*

**computer hacker** *n* pirate *m* informatique

**computerize** *vtr* mettre [qch] sur ordinateur ⟨*accounts*⟩; informatiser ⟨*list*⟩

**computer literate** *adj* **to be ∼** avoir des notions d'informatique

**computer program** *n* programme *m* informatique

**computer programmer** *n* programmeur/-euse *m/f*

**computer science** *n* informatique *f*

**computer scientist** *n* informaticien/-ienne *m/f*

**computing** *n* informatique *f*

**comrade** *n* camarade *mf*

**comradeship** *n* camaraderie *f*

**con** (colloq) ⒈ *n* escroquerie *f*, arnaque *f* (slang)
⒉ *vtr* tromper, rouler (colloq), arnaquer (slang)

**conceal** *vtr* dissimuler (**from** à)

**concede** ⒈ *vtr* concéder
⒉ *vi* céder

**conceit** *n* suffisance *f*

**conceited** *adj* ⟨person⟩ vaniteux/-euse; ⟨remark⟩ suffisant/-e

**conceive** *vtr, vi* concevoir

**concentrate** ⟨1⟩ *vtr* concentrer ⟨effort⟩; employer ⟨resources⟩; centrer ⟨attention⟩
⟨2⟩ *vi* (a) ⟨person⟩ se concentrer (on sur); to ~ on doing s'appliquer à faire
(b) to ~ on ⟨film, journalist⟩ s'intéresser surtout à

**concentration** *n* concentration *f* (on sur); to lose one's ~ se déconcentrer

**concentration camp** *n* camp *m* de concentration

**concept** *n* concept *m*

**conception** *n* conception *f*

**concern** ⟨1⟩ *n* (a) (worry) inquiétude *f* (about à propos de); to cause ~ être inquiétant/-e
(b) (preoccupation) préoccupation *f*; environmental ~s des préoccupations écologiques
(c) (company) entreprise *f*; a going ~ une affaire rentable
⟨2⟩ *vtr* (a) (worry) inquiéter
(b) (affect, interest) concerner, intéresser; to whom it may ~ à qui de droit; (in letter) Monsieur; as far as the pay is ~ed en ce qui concerne le salaire
(c) (be about) ⟨book, programme⟩ traiter de; ⟨fax, letter⟩ concerner

**concerned** *adj* (a) (anxious) inquiet/-ète (about à propos de); to be ~ for sb se faire du souci pour qn
(b) (involved) concerné/-e; all (those) ~ toutes les personnes concernées

**concerning** *prep* concernant

**concert** *n* concert *m*

**concerted** *adj* ⟨action, campaign⟩ concerté/-e; to make a ~ effort to do faire un sérieux effort pour faire

**concert hall** *n* salle *f* de concert

**concertina** ⟨1⟩ *n* concertina *m*
⟨2⟩ *vi* se plier en accordéon

**concerto** *n* concerto *m*

**concession** *n* (a) (compromise) concession *f* (on sur; to à)
(b) (discount) réduction *f*; '~s' 'tarif réduit'

**conciliatory** *adj* ⟨gesture, terms⟩ conciliant/-e; ⟨measures⟩ conciliatoire

**concise** *adj* concis/-e

**conclude** ⟨1⟩ *vtr* conclure
⟨2⟩ *vi* ⟨story, event⟩ se terminer (with par, sur); ⟨speaker⟩ conclure (with par)

**concluding** *adj* final/-e

**conclusion** *n* (a) (end) fin *f*
(b) (opinion, resolution) conclusion *f*

**conclusive** *adj* concluant/-e

**concoct** *vtr* concocter

**concrete** ⟨1⟩ *n* béton *m*
⟨2⟩ *adj* (a) ⟨block⟩ de béton; ⟨base⟩ en béton
(b) (real) concret/-ète

**concuss** *vtr* to be ~ed être commotionné/-e

**concussion** *n* commotion *f* cérébrale

**condemn** ⟨1⟩ *vtr* (a) (gen) condamner
(b) déclarer [qch] inhabitable ⟨building⟩
⟨2⟩ **condemned** *pp adj* ⟨cell⟩ des condamnés à mort; ~ed man/woman condamné/-e *m/f* à mort

**condensation** *n* (on walls) condensation *f*; (on windows) buée *f*

**condense** ⟨1⟩ *vtr* condenser
⟨2⟩ *vi* se condenser

**condensed milk** *n* lait *m* concentré sucré

**condescend** *vtr* to ~ to do condescendre à faire

**condescending** *adj* condescendant/-e

**condition** *n* (a) (gen) condition *f*; on ~ that you come à condition que tu viennes
(b) (state) état *m*, condition *f*; to be in good/bad ~ ⟨house, car⟩ être en bon/mauvais état
(c) (disease) maladie *f*

**conditional** *adj* conditionnel/-elle

**conditioner** *n* après-shampooing *m*, démêlant *m*

**condolences** *n pl* condoléances *fpl*

**condom** *n* préservatif *m*

**condominium** *n* (US) (also ~ unit) appartement *m* (dans une copropriété)

**condone** *vtr* tolérer

**conducive** *adj* ~ to favorable à

**conduct** ⟨1⟩ *n* conduite *f* (towards envers)
⟨2⟩ *vtr* (a) mener ⟨business, campaign⟩
(b) mener ⟨experiment, inquiry⟩; célébrer ⟨ceremony⟩
(c) (Mus) diriger ⟨orchestra⟩
(d) conduire ⟨electricity, heat⟩

**conductor** *n* (a) (Mus) chef *m* d'orchestre
(b) (on bus) receveur *m*; (on train) chef *m* de train

**conductress** *n* receveuse *f*

**cone** *n* (a) (shape) cône *m*
(b) (also ice-cream ~) cornet *m*
(c) (for traffic) balise *f*

**confectioner** *n* (of sweets) confiseur/-euse *m/f*; (of cakes) pâtissier-confiseur *m*; ~'s (shop) pâtisserie-confiserie *f*

**confectionery** *n* (sweets) confiserie *f*; (cakes) pâtisserie *f*

**confer** ⟨1⟩ *vtr* conférer (on à)
⟨2⟩ *vi* conférer (about de; with avec)

**conference** *n* (academic, business) conférence *f*; (political) congrès *m*; peace ~ conférence pour la paix

**confess** ⟨1⟩ *vtr* (a) avouer (that que)
(b) confesser ⟨sins⟩
⟨2⟩ *vi* avouer; to ~ to a crime avouer (avoir commis) un crime

**confession** *n* (a) (gen, Law) aveu *m* (of de)
(b) (in religion) confession *f*; to go to ~ se confesser

**confetti** *n* confettis *mpl*

**confide** *vi* to ~ in se confier à ⟨person⟩

**confidence** *n* (a) (faith) confiance *f* (**in** en); **to have (every)** ~ **in sb/sth** avoir (pleine) confiance en qn/qch
(b) (in politics) **vote of** ~ vote *m* de confiance; **motion of no** ~ motion *f* de censure
(c) (self-assurance) assurance *f*, confiance *f* en soi
(d) **to tell sb sth in** ~ dire qch à qn confidentiellement

**confidence trick** *n* escroquerie *f*

**confident** *adj* (a) (sure) sûr/-e, confiant/-e
(b) (self-assured) assuré/-e, sûr/-e de soi

**confidential** *adj* confidentiel/-ielle

**confine** *vtr* (a) confiner ⟨person⟩ (**in, to** dans); enfermer ⟨animal⟩ (**in** dans)
(b) (limit) limiter (**to** à)

**confined** *adj* (gen) confiné/-e; ⟨space⟩ restreint/-e

**confinement** *n* (in prison) détention *f*

**confirm** *vtr* confirmer; **to** ~ **receipt of sth** accuser réception de qch

**confirmation** *n* confirmation *f*

**confirmed** *adj* ⟨smoker, liar⟩ invétéré/-e; ⟨bachelor, sinner⟩ endurci/-e

**confiscate** *vtr* confisquer (**from** à)

**conflict** ① *n* conflit *m*
② *vi* être en contradiction (**with** avec)

**conflicting** *adj* contradictoire

**conform** ① *vtr* conformer (**to** à)
② *vi* ⟨person⟩ se conformer (**with, to** à)

**conformist** *n*, *adj* conformiste (*mf*)

**confront** *vtr* affronter ⟨danger, enemy⟩; faire face à ⟨problem⟩

**confrontation** *n* affrontement *m*

**confrontational** *adj* provocateur/-trice

**confuse** *vtr* (a) (bewilder) troubler ⟨person⟩
(b) (mistake) confondre (**with** avec)
(c) (complicate) compliquer ⟨argument⟩; **to** ~ **the issue** compliquer les choses

**confused** *adj* ⟨person⟩ troublé/-e; ⟨account, thoughts, mind⟩ confus/-e; **to get** ~ s'embrouiller

**confusing** *adj* déroutant/-e, peu clair/-e

**confusion** *n* confusion *f*

**congeal** *vi* ⟨fat⟩ se figer; ⟨blood⟩ se coaguler

**congenial** *adj* agréable

**congenital** *adj* congénital/-e

**congested** *adj* (a) ⟨road⟩ embouteillé/-e; ⟨district⟩ surpeuplé/-e
(b) ⟨lungs⟩ congestionné/-e

**congestion** *n* (a) traffic ~ embouteillages *mpl*
(b) (of lungs) congestion *f*

**conglomerate** *n* conglomérat *m*

**congratulate** *vtr* féliciter (**on** de)

**congratulations** *n pl* félicitations *fpl*; ~ **on the birth of your new baby** félicitations à l'occasion de la naissance de votre bébé

**congregate** *vi* se rassembler

**congregation** *n* assemblée *f* des fidèles

**congress** *n* congrès *m* (**on** sur)

**Congress** *n* (US) Congrès *m*

**congressman** *n* (US) membre *m* du Congrès

**conifer** *n* conifère *m*

**conjugal** *adj* conjugal/-e

**conjugate** ① *vtr* conjuguer
② *vi* ⟨verb⟩ se conjuguer

**conjunctivitis** *n* conjonctivite *f*

**conjure** *vi* faire des tours de prestidigitation
∎ **conjure up** évoquer ⟨image⟩

**conjurer** *n* prestidigitateur/-trice *m/f*

**con man** *n* arnaqueur *m* (slang), escroc *m*

**connect** *vtr* (a) raccorder ⟨end, hose⟩ (**to** à); accrocher ⟨coach⟩ (**to** à)
(b) ⟨road, railway⟩ relier ⟨place, road⟩ (**to, with** à)
(c) brancher ⟨appliance⟩ (**to** à)
(d) raccorder ⟨phone, subscriber⟩

**connected** *adj* (a) ⟨idea, event⟩ lié/-e (**to, with** à); **everything** ~ **with music** tout ce qui se rapporte à la musique
(b) (in family) apparenté/-e (**to** à)

**connecting** *adj* (a) ⟨flight⟩ de correspondance
(b) ⟨room⟩ attenant/-e

**connection** *n* (a) (link) (between events) rapport *m*; (of person) lien *m* (**between** entre; **with** avec); **in** ~ **with** au sujet de, à propos de
(b) (contact) relation *f*; **to have useful** ~**s** avoir des relations
(c) (to mains) branchement *m*
(d) (to telephone network) raccordement *m*; (to number) mise *f* en communication (**to** avec); **bad** ~ mauvaise communication *f*
(e) (in travel) correspondance *f*
(f) (Comput) connexion *f*; **Internet** ~ connexion Internet

**connive** *vi* **to** ~ **at** contribuer délibérément à; **to** ~ (**with sb**) **to do** être de connivence *or* de mèche (colloq) (avec qn) pour faire

**connoisseur** *n* connaisseur/-euse *m/f*

**connotation** *n* connotation *f* (**of** de)

**conquer** *vtr* conquérir ⟨territory, people⟩; vaincre ⟨enemy, unemployment⟩

**conqueror** *n* conquérant/-e *m/f*

**conquest** *n* conquête *f*

**conscience** *n* conscience *f*; **they have no** ~ ils n'ont aucun sens moral; **to have a guilty** ~ avoir mauvaise conscience; **to have a clear** ~ avoir la conscience tranquille

**conscientious** *adj* consciencieux/-ieuse

**conscientious objector, CO** *n* objecteur *m* de conscience

**conscious** *adj* (a) (aware) conscient/-e (**of** de; **that** du fait que)
(b) (deliberate) ⟨decision⟩ réfléchi/-e; ⟨effort⟩ consciencieux/-ieuse
(c) (awake) réveillé/-e

**consciousness** *n* **to lose/regain** ~ perdre/reprendre connaissance

**conscript** *n* appelé *m*

**conscription** n (system) conscription f
**consecrate** vtr consacrer
**consecutive** adj consécutif/-ive
**consensus** n consensus m (**among** au sein de; **about** quant à; **on** sur)
**consent** ⟨1⟩ n consentement m; **age of** ∼ âge m légal; **by common** or **mutual** ∼ d'un commun accord
⟨2⟩ vi consentir (**to** à); **to** ∼ **to sb doing** consentir à ce que qn fasse
**consequence** n (a) conséquence f; **as a** ∼ **of** du fait de ⟨change, process⟩; à la suite de ⟨event⟩
(b) (importance) importance f
**consequently** adv par conséquent
**conservation** n (a) (of nature) protection f (**of** de); **energy** ∼ maîtrise f de l'énergie
(b) (of heritage) conservation f
**conservation area** n zone f protégée
**conservationist** n défenseur m des ressources naturelles
**conservative** ⟨1⟩ n conservateur/-trice m/f
⟨2⟩ adj (a) ⟨party⟩ conservateur/-trice
(b) ⟨taste, style⟩ classique
**Conservative Party** n (GB) parti m conservateur
**conservatory** n (a) (for plants) jardin m d'hiver
(b) (academy) conservatoire m
**conserve** ⟨1⟩ n confiture f
⟨2⟩ vtr (a) protéger ⟨forest⟩; sauvegarder ⟨wildlife⟩; conserver ⟨remains, ruins⟩
(b) économiser ⟨resources⟩; ménager ⟨energy⟩
**consider** vtr (a) (give thought to) considérer ⟨options, facts⟩; examiner ⟨evidence, problem⟩; étudier ⟨offer⟩
(b) (take into account) prendre [qch] en considération ⟨risk, cost⟩; songer à ⟨person⟩; faire attention à ⟨person's feelings⟩
(c) (envisage) **to** ∼ **doing** envisager de faire; **to** ∼ **sb/sth as sth** penser à qn/qch comme qch
(d) (regard) **to** ∼ **that** considérer or estimer que; **to** ∼ **oneself (to be) a genius** se considérer comme un génie
**considerable** adj considérable
**considerate** adj ⟨person⟩ attentionné/-e; ⟨behaviour⟩ courtois/-e; **to be** ∼ **towards sb** avoir des égards pour qn
**consideration** n (a) considération f (**for** envers); **to give sth careful** ∼ réfléchir longuement à qch; **to take sth into** ∼ prendre qch en considération; **out of** ∼ par considération
(b) (fee) **for a** ∼ moyennant finance
**considering** prep, conj étant donné, compte tenu de
**consign** vtr expédier ⟨goods⟩ (**to** à)
**consignment** n (sending) expédition f; (goods) lot m, livraison f
**consist** vi **to** ∼ **of** se composer de; **to** ∼ **in** résider dans; **to** ∼ **in doing** consister à faire
**consistency** n (a) (texture) consistance f

(b) (of view, policy) cohérence f
**consistent** adj (a) ⟨growth, level, quality⟩ régulier/-ière
(b) ⟨attempts, demands⟩ répété/-e
(c) ⟨argument⟩ cohérent/-e; ∼ **with** en accord avec ⟨account, belief⟩
**consistently** adv (invariably) systématiquement; (repeatedly) à maintes reprises
**consolation** n consolation f (**to** pour)
**console** ⟨1⟩ n (a) (control panel) console f
(b) (for hi-fi) meuble m hi-fi; (for video) meuble m vidéo
⟨2⟩ vtr consoler (**for, on** de; **with** avec)
**consolidate** vtr (a) consolider ⟨position⟩
(b) réunir ⟨resources⟩; fusionner ⟨companies⟩
**consonant** n consonne f
**consortium** n consortium m
**conspicuous** adj ⟨feature, sign⟩ visible; ⟨garment⟩ voyant/-e; **to be** ∼ se remarquer
**conspiracy** n conspiration f
**conspirator** n conspirateur/-trice m/f
**conspire** vi conspirer; **to** ∼ **to do** ⟨people⟩ conspirer en vue de faire; ⟨events⟩ conspirer à faire
**constable** n (GB) agent m de police
**constant** adj ⟨problem, reminder, threat⟩ permanent/-e; ⟨care, temperature⟩ constant/-e; ⟨disputes, questions⟩ incessant/-e; ⟨attempts⟩ répété/-e; ⟨companion⟩ éternel/-elle
**constantly** adv constamment
**constellation** n constellation f
**constipated** adj constipé/-e
**constipation** n constipation f
**constituency** n (district) circonscription f électorale; (voters) électeurs mpl
**constituent** n (a) (Pol) électeur/-trice m/f
(b) (of character) trait m; (of event, work of art) élément m
**constitute** vtr constituer
**constitution** n constitution f
**constitutional** adj constitutionnel/-elle
**constraint** n contrainte f
**constrict** vtr comprimer ⟨flow, blood vessel⟩; gêner ⟨breathing, movement⟩
**construct** vtr construire (**of** avec; **in** en)
**construction** n construction f
**construction site** n chantier m
**construction worker** n ouvrier/-ière m/f du bâtiment
**constructive** adj constructif/-ive
**consul** n consul m
**consulate** n consulat m
**consult** ⟨1⟩ vtr consulter (**about** sur)
⟨2⟩ vi s'entretenir (**about** sur; **with** avec)
**consultancy** n (also ∼ **firm**) cabinet-conseil m
**consultant** n (a) (expert) consultant/-e m/f, conseiller/-ère m/f (**on, in** en)
(b) (GB) (doctor) spécialiste mf

**consultation** n (for advice) consultation f (about sur); (for discussion) entretien m (about sur); after ∼ with après avoir consulté

**consumables** n pl consommables mpl

**consume** vtr (a) (use up) consommer ⟨fuel, food, drink⟩
(b) to be ∼d by or with être dévoré/-e par ⟨envy⟩; brûler de ⟨desire⟩; être rongé/-e par ⟨guilt⟩

**consumer** n consommateur/-trice m/f; (of electricity, gas) abonné/-e m/f

**consumer advice** n conseils mpl au consommateurs

**consumer goods** n pl biens mpl de consommation

**consumer protection** n défense f du consommateur

**consumer society** n société f de consommation

**consummate** vtr consommer ⟨marriage⟩

**consumption** n consommation f

**contact** ① n (a) (gen) contact m (between entre; with avec); to be in/make ∼ être en/se mettre en contact
(b) (acquaintance) connaissance f; (professional) contact m
② vtr contacter, se mettre en rapport avec

**contact lens** n lentille f or verre m de contact

**contagious** adj contagieux/-ieuse

**contain** vtr (a) contenir ⟨amount, ingredients⟩; contenir, comporter ⟨information, mistakes⟩
(b) (curb) maîtriser ⟨blaze⟩; enrayer ⟨epidemic⟩; limiter ⟨costs, problem⟩; retenir ⟨flood⟩

**container** n (for food, liquids) récipient m; (for plants) bac m; (for waste, for transporting) conteneur m

**contaminate** vtr contaminer

**contamination** n contamination f

**contemplate** vtr (a) (consider) envisager ⟨doing de faire⟩
(b) (look at) contempler

**contemporary** ① n contemporain/-e m/f
② adj (present-day) contemporain/-e; (up-to-date) moderne; (of same period) de l'époque

**contempt** n mépris m (for de); to hold sb/ sth in ∼ mépriser qn/qch; ∼ of court (Law) outrage m à magistrat

**contemptible** adj méprisable

**contemptuous** adj méprisant/-e

**contend** ① vtr soutenir (that que)
② vi (a) (deal with) to ∼ with affronter
(b) (compete) to ∼ with sb for sth disputer qch à qn

**contender** n (a) (in competition) concurrent/-e m/f
(b) (for post) candidat/-e m/f (for à)

**content** ① n (a) (quantity) teneur f
(b) (of book, essay) fond m
② adj satisfait/-e (with de)

**contented** adj ⟨person⟩ content/-e (with de); ⟨feeling⟩ de bien-être

**contention** n (a) (opinion) assertion f
(b) (dispute) dispute f

**contentment** n contentement m

**contents** n pl (gen) contenu m; (of house, for insurance) biens mpl mobiliers; list or table of ∼ table f des matières

**contest** ① n (a) (competition) concours m
(b) (struggle) lutte f
② vtr (a) contester ⟨decision, will⟩
(b) (compete for) disputer ⟨match⟩

**contestant** n (in competition, game) concurrent/-e m/f; (in fight) adversaire mf; (for job, in election) candidat/-e m/f

**context** n contexte m

**continent** n (a) continent m
(b) the Continent (GB) l'Europe f continentale

**continental** adj (a) continental/-e
(b) (GB) ⟨holiday⟩ en Europe continentale

**continental breakfast** n petit déjeuner m (avec café, pain, beurre et confiture)

**continental quilt** n (GB) couette f

**contingency** n imprévu m

**contingency fund** n fonds m de secours

**contingency plan** n plan m de réserve

**continual** adj continuel/-elle

**continually** adv continuellement

**continuation** n (a) (gen) continuation f
(b) (of story) suite f; (of route) prolongement m

**continue** ① vtr continuer
② vi ⟨person⟩ continuer (doing, to do à or de faire); ⟨noise, debate, strike⟩ se poursuivre; to ∼ with continuer, poursuivre ⟨task, treatment⟩

**continuity** n continuité f

**continuous** adj (a) ⟨growth, decline, noise⟩ continu/-e; ⟨care⟩ constant/-e; ⟨line⟩ ininterrompu/-e; ∼ assessment (GB) contrôle m continu
(b) ⟨tense⟩ progressif/-ive

**continuously** adv (without a break) sans interruption; (repeatedly) continuellement

**contort** vtr tordre

**contortion** n contorsion f

**contour** n (a) (outline) contour m
(b) (also ∼ line) courbe f hypsométrique or de niveau

**contraband** n contrebande f

**contraception** n contraception f

**contraceptive** ① n contraceptif m
② adj contraceptif/-ive

**contract** ① n contrat m
② vtr (a) (gen) contracter
(b) to be ∼ed to do être tenu/-e par contrat de faire
③ vi (a) to ∼ to do s'engager par contrat à faire
(b) ⟨muscle, wood⟩ se contracter

**contraction** n contraction f

**contract killer** n tueur/-euse m/f à gages
**contractor** n (a) (business) entrepreneur/-euse m/f
(b) (worker) contractuel/-elle m/f
**contradict** vtr, vi contredire
**contradiction** n contradiction f
**contradictory** adj contradictoire (to à)
**contraflow** n (GB) circulation f à sens alterné
**contraindication** n contre-indication f
**contrary** ① n contraire m; on the ~ (bien) au contraire; unless you hear anything to the ~ sauf contrordre
② adj (a) ⟨idea, view⟩ contraire
(b) ⟨person⟩ contrariant/-e
③ **contrary to** phr contrairement à
**contrast** ① n contraste m; in ~ to sth, by ~ with sth par contraste avec qch; in ~ to sb à la différence de qn; by or in ~ par contre
② vtr to ~ X with Y faire ressortir le contraste (qui existe) entre X et Y
③ vi contraster (with avec)
**contrasting** adj ⟨examples⟩ opposé/-e; ⟨colour⟩ contrasté/-e; ⟨views⟩ très différent/-e
**contribute** ① vtr (a) verser ⟨sum⟩ (to à); to ~ £5m contribuer pour 5 millions de livres sterling
(b) (to gift, charity) donner (to à; towards pour)
(c) apporter ⟨ideas⟩ (to à); écrire ⟨article⟩ (to pour)
② vi (a) to ~ to or towards contribuer à ⟨change, decline⟩
(b) (to community life, research) participer (to à); (to programme, magazine) collaborer (to à)
(c) to ~ to cotiser à ⟨pension fund⟩
(d) (to charity) donner (de l'argent) (to à)
**contribution** n (a) (to tax, pension, profits, cost) contribution f (towards à)
(b) (to charity, campaign) don m; to make a ~ faire un don (to à)
(c) sb's ~ le rôle que qn a joué dans ⟨success, undertaking⟩; ce que qn a apporté à ⟨science, sport⟩
(d) (to programme) participation f; (to magazine) article m
**contributor** n (to charity) donateur/-trice m/f; (in discussion) participant/-e m/f; (to magazine, book) collaborateur/-trice m/f
**con trick** n (colloq) escroquerie f, duperie f
**contrive** vtr (arrange) organiser; to ~ to do parvenir à faire
**contrived** adj (a) ⟨incident, meeting⟩ non fortuit/-e
(b) ⟨plot⟩ tiré/-e par les cheveux; ⟨style, effect⟩ étudié/-e
**control** ① n (a) (gen) contrôle m (of de); (of operation, project) direction f (of de); (of life, emotion, self) maîtrise f (of, over de); to be in ~ of contrôler ⟨territory⟩; diriger ⟨operation, organization⟩; maîtriser ⟨problem⟩; avoir le contrôle de ⟨ball, vehicle⟩ to be in ~ (of oneself) se maîtriser; to bring or keep [sth] under ~ maîtriser; to lose ~ (of sth) perdre le contrôle (de qch)

(b) (on vehicle, equipment) commande f; (on TV) bouton m de réglage; to be at the ~s être aux commandes
② vtr (a) dominer ⟨organization, situation⟩; contrôler ⟨territory⟩; diriger ⟨traffic, project⟩; être majoritaire dans ⟨company⟩
(b) maîtriser ⟨person, animal, inflation, fire⟩; endiguer ⟨epidemic⟩; dominer ⟨emotion⟩; retenir ⟨laughter⟩; to ~ oneself se contrôler
(c) commander ⟨machine⟩; manœuvrer ⟨boat, vehicle⟩; piloter ⟨plane⟩; contrôler ⟨ball⟩
(d) régler ⟨speed, temperature⟩; contrôler ⟨immigration, prices⟩
**control panel** n (on plane) tableau m de bord; (on machine) tableau m de contrôle; (on TV) (panneau m de) commandes fpl
**control room** n poste m de commande; (TV) (salle f de) régie f
**control tower** n tour f de contrôle
**controversial** adj (gen) controversé/-e; (open to criticism) qui prête à controverse
**controversy** n controverse f
**conundrum** n énigme f
**convalesce** vi se remettre
**convene** vtr organiser ⟨meeting⟩; convoquer ⟨group⟩
**convenience** n avantage m (of doing de faire); (of device, food, shop) commodité f; for (the sake of) ~ pour raisons de commodité; at your ~ quand cela vous conviendra
**convenience foods** n pl plats mpl (tout) préparés
**convenient** adj (a) ⟨place, time⟩ pratique; to be ~ for sb convenir à qn
(b) (useful, practical) pratique, commode
(c) ⟨shops⟩ situé/-e tout près; ⟨chair⟩ à portée de main
**convent** n couvent m
**convention** n (a) (gen) convention f
(b) (social norms) convenances fpl, conventions fpl
**conventional** adj (gen) conventionnel/-elle; ⟨person⟩ conformiste; ⟨medicine⟩ traditionnel/-elle
**converge** vi converger
**conversant** adj to be ~ with être versé/-e dans
**conversation** n conversation f
**converse** vi converser (with avec; in en)
**conversion** n (of currency, measurement) conversion f (from de; to en); (of building) aménagement m (to, into en); (to new beliefs) conversion f (from de; to à); (in rugby) transformation f
**conversion rate** n taux m de change
**convert** ① n converti/-e m/f (to à)
② vtr (a) (change into sth else) transformer; (modify) adapter
(b) convertir ⟨currency, measurement⟩ (from de; to, into en)
(c) aménager ⟨building, loft⟩ (to, into en)
(d) (to new beliefs) convertir (to à; from de)
(e) (in rugby) transformer ⟨try⟩

**3** *vi* (a) ⟨*sofa, device*⟩ être convertible (**into** en)
(b) ⟨*person*⟩ se convertir (**to** à; **from** de)

**convertible** *n* décapotable *f*

**convex** *adj* convexe

**convey** *vtr* (a) ⟨*person*⟩ transmettre ⟨*information*⟩ (**to** à); exprimer ⟨*condolences, feeling, idea*⟩ (**to** à)
(b) ⟨*words, images*⟩ traduire ⟨*mood, impression*⟩
(c) ⟨*vehicle*⟩ transporter; ⟨*pipes*⟩ amener

**conveyancing** *n* rédaction *f* des actes de propriété

**conveyor belt** *n* (in factory) transporteur *m* à bande *or* à courroie; (for luggage) tapis *m* roulant

**convict** **1** *n* (imprisoned criminal) détenu/-e *m/f*; (deported criminal) bagnard *m*
**2** *vtr* reconnaître *or* déclarer [qn] coupable (**of** de; **of doing** d'avoir fait)

**conviction** *n* (a) (Law) condamnation *f* (**for** pour)
(b) (belief) conviction *f* (**that** que)

**convince** *vtr* convaincre ⟨*person*⟩ (**to do** de faire)

**convincing** *adj* ⟨*account, evidence*⟩ convaincant/-e; ⟨*victory, lead*⟩ indiscutable

**convoy** *n* convoi *m*

**convulsion** *n* convulsion *f*

**coo** *vi* roucouler

**cook** **1** *n* cuisinier/-ière *m/f*
**2** *vtr* faire cuire ⟨*vegetables, pasta, eggs*⟩; préparer ⟨*meal*⟩ (**for** pour)
**3** *vi* ⟨*person*⟩ cuisiner, faire la cuisine; ⟨*vegetable, meat, meal*⟩ cuire

**cook-chill foods** *n pl* plats *mpl* préparés, plats *mpl* cuisinés

**cooker** *n* (GB) cuisinière *f*

**cookery book** *n* (GB) livre de cuisine

**cookie** *n* (a) (biscuit) gateau *m* sec, biscuit *m*
(b) (Comput) cookie *m*

**cooking** *n* cuisine *f*

**cooking apple** *n* pomme *f* à cuire

**cooking chocolate** *n* chocolat *m* pâtissier

**cool** **1** *n* (a) (coldness) fraîcheur *f*
(b) (colloq) (calm) sang-froid *m*; **to keep one's** ~ (not get angry) ne pas s'énerver; (stay calm) garder son sang-froid; **to lose one's** ~ (get angry) s'énerver; (panic) perdre son sang-froid
**2** *adj* (a) ⟨*day, drink, water, weather*⟩ frais/fraîche; ⟨*dress*⟩ léger/-ère; ⟨*colour*⟩ froid/-e
(b) (calm) calme
(c) (unfriendly) froid/-e
(d) (casual) décontracté/-e, cool *inv* (colloq)
(e) (colloq) (trendy) branché/-e (colloq)
**3** *vtr* (a) refroidir ⟨*soup*⟩; rafraîchir ⟨*wine, room*⟩
(b) calmer ⟨*anger, ardour*⟩
**4** *vi* (a) (get colder) refroidir
(b) ⟨*enthusiasm*⟩ faiblir; ⟨*friendship*⟩ se dégrader

■ **cool down** ⟨*engine, water*⟩ refroidir; ⟨*person, situation*⟩ se calmer

**cool bag** *n* sac *m* isotherme

**cool box** *n* (GB) glacière *f*

**cooling-off period** *n* (in industrial relations) délai *m* de conciliation; (in contract) délai *m* de réflexion

**coop** *n* poulailler *m*

■ **coop up**: ¶ ~ [sb/sth] up enfermer, cloîtrer

**cooperate** *vi* coopérer (**with** avec; **in** à; **in doing** pour faire)

**cooperation** *n* coopération *f* (**on** à)

**cooperative** **1** *n* (a) (organization) coopérative *f*
(b) (US) (apartment house) immeuble *m* en copropriété
**2** *adj* coopératif/-ive

**coordinate** **1** *n* (on map, graph) coordonnée *f*
**2** *vtr* coordonner (**with** avec)

**coordinates** *n pl* (clothes) ensemble *m*

**coordination** *n* coordination *f*

**coordinator** *n* coordinateur/-trice *m/f*

**cope** *vi* s'en sortir (colloq), se débrouiller; **to** ~ **with** s'occuper de ⟨*person, work*⟩; faire face à ⟨*demand, disaster, problem*⟩; supporter ⟨*death, depression, difficult person*⟩

**Copenhagen** *pr n* Copenhague

**copious** *adj* (a) (plentiful) ⟨*supply*⟩ abondant/-e
(b) (generous) ⟨*quantity, serving*⟩ copieux/-ieuse

**cop-out** *n* (colloq) (excuse) excuse *f* bidon (colloq)

**copper** *n* (a) (metal) cuivre *m*
(b) (GB) (colloq) (coin) petite monnaie *f*
(c) (GB) (colloq) (policeman) flic *m* (colloq)
(d) (colour) couleur *f* cuivre

**copy** **1** *n* (a) (gen) copie *f*
(b) (of book, newspaper, report) exemplaire *m*
**2** *vtr* copier (**from** sur)
**3** *vi* copier

■ **copy down, copy out** recopier ⟨*quote, address*⟩

**copyright** *n* copyright *m*, droit *m* d'auteur

**coral** *n* corail *m*

**cord** **1** *n* cordon *m*
**2** *n pl* (colloq) (*also* **corduroys**) pantalon *m* en velours (côtelé)

**cordial** **1** *n* (a) (fruit drink) sirop *m* de fruits
(b) (US) (liqueur) liqueur *m*
**2** *adj* cordial/-e (**to, with** avec)

**cordless** *adj* ⟨*telephone, kettle*⟩ sans fil

**cordon** *n* cordon *m*

■ **cordon off** boucler ⟨*street, area*⟩; contenir ⟨*crowd*⟩

**corduroy** *n* velours *m* côtelé

**core** *n* (a) (of apple) trognon *m*
(b) (of problem) cœur *m*
(c) rotten to the ~ pourri/-e jusqu'à l'os; English to the ~ anglais/-e jusqu'au bout des ongles

⋯⋗

**(d)** (of nuclear reactor) cœur m
**(e)** (small group) noyau m; **hard ∼** noyau dur
**core curriculum** n tronc m commun
**Corfu** pr n Corfou f
**cork** n **(a)** (substance) liège m
**(b)** (object) bouchon m
**corkscrew** n tire-bouchon m
**corn** n **(a)** (GB) (wheat) blé m
**(b)** (US) (maize) maïs m
**(c)** (on foot) cor m
**cornea** n cornée f
**corner** ⌐1⌐ n **(a)** (gen) coin m; **the house on the ∼** la maison qui fait l'angle; **at the ∼ of the street** au coin de la rue; **to go round the ∼** tourner au coin de la rue; **just around the ∼** (nearby) tout près; (around the bend) juste après le coin; **out of the ∼ of one's eye** du coin de l'œil
**(b)** (bend) virage m
**(c)** (in boxing) coin m (de repos); (in football, hockey) corner m
⌐2⌐ vtr **(a)** acculer ⟨animal, enemy⟩; coincer (colloq) ⟨person⟩
**(b)** accaparer ⟨market⟩
**IDIOMS in a tight ∼** dans une impasse; **to cut ∼s** (financially) faire des économies
**corner shop** n petite épicerie f
**cornerstone** n pierre f angulaire
**cornflour** n farine f de maïs
**cornflower** n bleuet m, barbeau m
**corn on the cob** n maïs m en épi
**Cornwall** pr n (comté m de) Cornouailles f
**corny** adj (colloq) ⟨joke⟩ (old) éculé/-e; (feeble) faiblard/-e (colloq); ⟨film, story⟩ à la guimauve
**coronary** n infarctus m
**coronation** n couronnement m
**coroner** n coroner m
**corporal** n (gen) caporal m; (in artillery) brigadier m
**corporal punishment** n châtiment m corporel
**corporate** adj **(a)** ⟨accounts, funds⟩ appartenant/-e à une société; ⟨clients, employees⟩ d'une société (or de sociétés)
**(b)** ⟨action⟩ commun/-e; ⟨decision⟩ collectif/-ive
**corporate identity, corporate image** n image f de marque (d'une société)
**corporate raider** n raider m (organisateur d'OPA)
**corporation** n (grande) société f
**corps** n corps m
**corpse** n cadavre m
**correct** ⌐1⌐ adj **(a)** ⟨amount, answer, decision⟩ correct/-e; ⟨figure, time⟩ exact/-e
**(b)** ⟨behaviour⟩ correct/-e, convenable
⌐2⌐ vtr corriger
**correcting fluid** n liquide m correcteur
**correction** n correction f
**correspond** vi **(a)** (match) concorder, correspondre (**with** à)
**(b)** (be equivalent) être équivalent/-e (**to** à)

**(c)** (exchange letters) correspondre (**with** avec; **about** au sujet de)
**correspondence** n correspondance f
**correspondence course** n cours m par correspondance
**correspondent** n **(a)** (journalist) journaliste mf; (abroad) correspondant/-e m/f
**(b)** (letter writer) correspondant/-e m/f
**corresponding** adj (matching) correspondant/-e; (similar) équivalent/-e
**corridor** n **(a)** couloir m
**(b)** (of land) corridor m
**corroborate** vtr corroborer
**corrode** ⌐1⌐ vtr corroder
⌐2⌐ vi se corroder
**corrosion** n corrosion f
**corrugated** adj ondulé/-e
**corrugated iron** n tôle f ondulée
**corrupt** ⌐1⌐ adj corrompu/-e
⌐2⌐ vtr corrompre
**corruption** n corruption f
**Corsica** pr n Corse f
**cosh** n (GB) matraque f
**cosmetic** ⌐1⌐ n produit m de beauté
⌐2⌐ adj (figurative) superficiel/-ielle
**cosmetic surgery** n chirurgie f esthétique
**cosmonaut** n cosmonaute mf
**cosmopolitan** n, adj cosmopolite (mf)
**cost** ⌐1⌐ n **(a)** (price) coût m, prix m (**of** de); (expense incurred) frais mpl; **at ∼** au prix coûtant
**(b)** (figurative) prix m; **at all ∼s** à tout prix; **he knows to his ∼ that** il a appris à ses dépens que
⌐2⌐ vtr **(a)** coûter; **how much does it ∼?** combien ça coûte?; **the TV will ∼ £100 to repair** la réparation de la télé coûtera 100 livres sterling
**(b)** (estimate price of) calculer le prix de revient de ⟨product⟩; calculer le coût de ⟨project, work⟩
**co-star** ⌐1⌐ n co-vedette f
⌐2⌐ vtr **a film ∼ring X and Y** un film avec X et Y
**cost-cutting** n réduction f des frais
**cost-effective** adj rentable
**costly** adv coûteux/-euse
**cost of living** n coût m de la vie
**cost price** n (for producer) prix m de revient; (for consumer) prix m coûtant
**costume** n **(a)** (clothes) costume m
**(b)** (GB) (also **swimming ∼**) maillot m de bain
**costume jewellery** (GB), **costume jewelry** (US) n bijoux mpl fantaisie
**cosy** (GB), **cozy** (US) adj (comfortable) douillet/-ette; (intimate) intime; **it's ∼ here** on est bien ici
**cot** n **(a)** (GB) (for baby) lit m de bébé
**(b)** (US) (bed) lit m de camp
**cot death** n (GB) mort f subite du nourrisson

**cottage** n maisonnette f; (thatched) chaumière f

**cottage cheese** n fromage m blanc à gros grains

**cotton** n (a) ( plant, material) coton m (b) (thread) fil m de coton

**cotton bud** n Coton-Tige® m

**cotton wool** n ouate f (de coton)

**couch** n (a) (sofa) canapé m (b) (doctor's) lit m; ( psychoanalyst's) divan m

**couch potato** n (colloq) pantouflard/-e m/f (colloq) (qui passe son temps devant la télé)

**cough** ⓵ n toux f; **to have a** ~ tousser ⓶ vi tousser

**cough mixture** n (sirop m) antitussif m

**could** modal aux (a) (be able to) pouvoir; **I couldn't move** je ne pouvais pas bouger; **she couldn't come yesterday** elle n'a pas pu venir hier (b) (know how to) savoir; **he couldn't swim** il ne savait pas nager; **she** ~ **speak four languages** elle parlait quatre langues (c) ( permission, requests, suggestions) pouvoir; **we** ~ **only go out at weekends** nous ne pouvions sortir or nous n'avions le droit de sortir que le week-end; ~ **I speak to Annie?** est-ce que je pourrais parler à Annie?; ~ **you help me?** pourrais-tu m'aider? (d) (with verbs of perception) **I couldn't see a thing** je n'y voyais rien; **they couldn't understand me** ils ne me comprenaient pas; **we** ~ **hear them laughing** on les entendait rire (e) **you** ~ **have died** tu aurais pu mourir; **they** ~ **have warned us** ils auraient pu nous prévenir; **I** ~ **be wrong** je me trompe peut-être; **if only I** ~ **start again** si seulement je pouvais tout recommencer

**council** n conseil m; **the town** ~ le conseil municipal; **the Council of Europe** le Conseil de l'Europe

**council estate** n lotissement m de logements sociaux

**council house** n habitation f à loyer modéré

**council housing** n logements mpl sociaux

**councillor, councilor** (US) n conseiller/-ère m/f

**council tax** n (GB) ≈ impôts mpl locaux

**counsel** ⓵ n (lawyer) avocat/-e m/f ⓶ vtr conseiller ⟨person⟩ (**about, on** sur)

**counselling** (GB), **counseling** (US) n (advice) assistance f; ( psychological) aide f psychosociale; **debt** ~ assistance aux personnes endettées; **bereavement** ~ aide psychosociale aux personnes endeuillées

**counsellor, counselor** (US) n conseiller/-ère m/f

**count** ⓵ n (a) (numerical record) décompte m; (at election) dépouillement m; **at the last** ~ au dernier décompte; **to keep (a)** ~ **of** tenir compte de; **to lose** ~ ne plus savoir où on en est dans ses calculs; **to be out for the** ~ (colloq) être KO (colloq) (b) (level) taux m; **cholesterol** ~ taux de cholestérol (c) (figure) chiffre m (d) (Law) chef m d'accusation; **on three** ~s pour trois chefs d'accusation (e) (nobleman) comte m ⓶ vtr (a) compter ⟨points, people, objects⟩; énumérer ⟨reasons, causes⟩; ~**ing the children** en comptant les enfants; **not** ~**ing my sister** sans compter ma sœur (b) (consider) **to** ~ **sb as sth** considérer qn comme qch ⓷ vi compter; **it's the thought that** ~s c'est l'intention qui compte
■ **count against** jouer contre ⟨person⟩
■ **count on** compter sur ⟨person, event⟩; **don't** ~ **on it!** ne comptez pas dessus!
■ **count up** calculer ⟨cost, hours⟩; compter ⟨money, boxes⟩

**countdown** n compte m à rebours (**to** avant)

**counter** ⓵ n (a) (in shop, snack bar) comptoir m; (in bank, post office) guichet m; (in pub, bar) bar m (b) (in game) jeton m ⓶ vtr répondre à ⟨threat⟩; neutraliser ⟨effet⟩; parer ⟨blow⟩; enrayer ⟨inflation⟩ ⓷ vi riposter (**with sth** par qch) ⓸ **counter to** phr (gen) contrairement à; ⟨be, go, run⟩ à l'encontre de

**counteract** vtr contrebalancer ⟨influence⟩; contrecarrer ⟨negative effects⟩

**counter-attack** n contre-attaque f (**against** sur)

**counter-clockwise** adj, adv (US) dans le sens inverse des aiguilles d'une montre

**counterfeit** ⓵ adj ⟨signature, note⟩ contrefait/-e; ~ **money** fausse monnaie f ⓶ vtr contrefaire

**counterfoil** n talon m, souche f

**counterpart** n (of person) homologue mf; (of company, institution) équivalent m

**counter-productive** adj contre-productif/-ive

**countersign** vtr contresigner

**countess** n comtesse f

**countless** adj ~ **letters** un nombre incalculable de lettres; **on** ~ **occasions** je ne sais combien de fois

**country** n (a) pays m; **developing/third world** ~ pays en voie de développement/du tiers monde; ~ **of birth** pays natal (b) (countryside) campagne f; **in the** ~ à la campagne; **open** ~ rase campagne; **across** ~ à travers la campagne

**country club** n club m de loisirs

**country dancing** n danse f folklorique

**country house** n manoir m

**country music** n country music f

**countryside** n campagne f

**county** n comté m

**county council** n (GB) ≈ conseil m régional

**coup** n (a) (also ~ **d'état**) coup m d'État
(b) **to pull off a** ~ réussir un beau coup

**couple** n (a) couple m
(b) **a** ~ **(of)** (two) deux; (a few) deux ou trois; **a** ~ **of times** deux ou trois fois

**coupon** n (a) (voucher) bon m; **petrol** ~ (GB) bon d'essence
(b) (in ad) coupon m; **reply** ~ coupon-réponse m

**courage** n courage m

**courageous** adj courageux/-euse

**courgette** n courgette f

**courier** n (a) (also **travel** ~) accompagnateur/-trice m/f
(b) (for parcels, documents) coursier m; (for drugs) transporteur m

**course** ⬚1 n (a) (gen) cours m (**of** de); **in the** ~ **of time** au cours de; **in the** ~ **of time** avec le temps; **in due** ~ en temps utile; ~ **of action** moyen m d'action, parti m
(b) (route) cours m; (of boat, plane) cap m; **to be on** ~ (boat, plane) tenir le cap; **to go off** ~ (ship) dévier de son cap; **to change** ~ (gen) changer de direction; (boat, plane) changer de cap
(c) (classes) cours m (**in** en; **of** de)
(d) (Med) **a** ~ **of treatment** un traitement
(e) (Sport) (in golf) terrain m de golf m; (in racing) champ m de courses
(f) (part of meal) plat m; **the main** ~ le plat principal; **five-**~ **meal** repas m de cinq plats
⬚2 **of course** phr bien sûr, évidemment

**course book** n méthode f

**coursework** n devoirs mpl (de contrôle continu)

**court** ⬚1 n (a) (Law) cour f, tribunal m; **to go to** ~ aller devant les tribunaux (**over** pour); **to take sb to** ~ poursuivre qn en justice
(b) (for tennis, squash) court m; (for basketball) terrain m
(c) (of sovereign) cour f
(d) (courtyard) cour f
⬚2 vtr courtiser (woman, voters)

**court case** n procès m, affaire f

**courteous** adj courtois/-e (**to** envers)

**courtesy** n courtoisie f

**courthouse** n (Law) palais m de justice

**court-martial** vtr faire passer [qn] en cour martiale

**courtroom** n salle f d'audience

**courtyard** n cour f

**cousin** n cousin/-e m/f

**cove** n (bay) avise f

**cover** ⬚1 n (a) (lid) couvercle m; (for duvet, typewriter, cushion, furniture) housse f; (of record) pochette f; (blanket) couverture f
(b) (shelter) abri m; **to take** ~ se mettre à l'abri; **under** ~ à l'abri
(c) (for teacher, doctor) remplacement m
(d) (insurance) assurance f (**for** pour; **against** contre)

⬚2 vtr (a) (gen) couvrir (**with** avec); recouvrir (cushion, sofa, surface, person, cake) (**with** de)
(b) (deal with) (article, speaker) traiter; (journalist) couvrir
(c) (insure) assurer, couvrir (**for, against** contre; **for doing** pour faire)
■ **cover for** remplacer (employee)
■ **cover up:** ¶ **to** ~ **up for** couvrir (friend); ¶ ~ **[sth] up** recouvrir (object); dissimuler (mistake, truth); étouffer (scandal)

**coverage** n (gen) couverture f; **newspaper** ~ couverture par les journaux; **live** ~ reportage m en direct

**cover charge** n prix m de couvert

**covering** n (a) (for wall, floor) revêtement m
(b) (layer of snow, moss) couche f

**covering letter** n lettre f d'accompagnement

**cover note** n (from insurance company) attestation f d'assurance

**covert** adj (operation) secret/-ète; (glance) furtif/-ive; (threat) voilé-e

**cover-up** n opération f de camouflage

**cover version** n version f

**covetous** adj cupide

**cow** n vache f

**coward** n lâche mf

**cowardice** n lâcheté f

**cowardly** adj lâche

**cowboy** n (a) (US) cowboy m
(b) (incompetent worker) fumiste m

**cower** vi se recroqueviller

**cox** ⬚1 n barreur m
⬚2 vtr, vi barrer

**coy** adj (a) (smile, look) de fausse modestie
(b) (reticent) réservé/-e (**about** à propos de)

**cozy** (US) = cosy

**crab** n crabe m

**crack** ⬚1 n (a) (in rock) fissure f; (in varnish, ground) craquelure f; (in wall, cup, bone) fêlure f
(b) (in door) entrebâillement m; (in curtains) fente f
(c) (also ~ **cocaine**) crack m
(d) (noise) craquement m
(e) (colloq) (attempt) essai m, tentative f; **to have a** ~ **at doing** essayer de faire
⬚2 adj (player) de première; (troops, shot) d'élite
⬚3 vtr (a) fêler (bone, wall, cup)
(b) casser (nut, egg); **to** ~ **a safe** fracturer un coffre-fort; **to** ~ **sth open** ouvrir qch; ~ **one's head open** se fendre le crâne
(c) déchiffrer (code)
(d) faire claquer (whip); faire craquer (knuckles, joints)
⬚4 vi (a) (bone, cup, wall, ice) se fêler; (varnish) se craqueler; (skin) se crevasser; (ground) se fendre
(b) (person) craquer (colloq)
(c) (knuckles, twig) craquer; (whip) claquer
(d) (voice) se casser
■ **crack down** prendre des mesures énergiques, sévir (**on** contre)

**crackdown** n mesure f sévère (**on** contre); **the ~ on drugs** l'action f antidrogue

**cracker** n (**a**) (biscuit) cracker m, biscuit m salé

(**b**) (for Christmas) diablotin m

**crackle** 1 n crépitement m

2 vi ⟨fire, radio⟩ crépiter; ⟨hot fat⟩ grésiller

**cradle** 1 n berceau m

2 vtr bercer ⟨baby⟩; tenir [qch] délicatement ⟨object⟩

**craft** n (**a**) (skill) métier m

(**b**) (craftwork) artisanat m; **arts and ~s** artisanat (d'art)

(**c**) (boat) embarcation f

**craftsman** n artisan m

**crafty** adj astucieux/-ieuse

**crag** n rocher m escarpé

**cram** 1 vtr **to ~ sth into** enfoncer or fourrer (colloq) qch dans ⟨bag, car⟩; **~med full** plein à craquer

2 vi ⟨student⟩ bachoter (**for** pour)

**cramp** 1 n crampe f

2 vtr gêner

**cramped** adj ⟨house, office⟩ exigu/-uë

**cranberry** n canneberge f

**crane** n grue f

**crank** n (**a**) (colloq) (freak) fanatique mf, fana mf (colloq)

(**b**) (handle) manivelle f

**crash** 1 n (**a**) (noise) fracas m

(**b**) (accident) accident m; **car ~** accident de voiture; **train ~** catastrophe f ferroviaire

(**c**) (of stock market) krach m

2 vtr **to ~ one's car** avoir un accident de voiture

3 vi (**a**) ⟨car, plane⟩ s'écraser; ⟨vehicles, planes⟩ se rentrer dedans, se percuter; **to ~ into sth** rentrer dans or percuter qch

(**b**) ⟨share prices⟩ s'effondrer

■ **crash out** (colloq) (go to sleep) pioncer (slang); (collapse) s'écrouler (colloq)

**crash course** n cours m intensif

**crash diet** n régime m d'amaigrissement intensif

**crash helmet** n casque m

**crash landing** n atterrissage m en catastrophe

**crass** adj grossier/-ière; **~ ignorance** ignorance f crasse

**crate** n (for bottles, china) caisse f; (for fruit, vegetables) cageot m

**crater** n (of volcano) cratère m; (caused by explosion) entonnoir m

**cravat** n foulard m (pour homme)

**crave** vtr (also **~ for**) avoir un besoin maladif de ⟨drug⟩; avoir soif de ⟨affection⟩; avoir envie de ⟨food⟩

**crawl** 1 n (**a**) (in swimming) crawl m

(**b**) **at a ~** au pas; **to go at a ~** ⟨vehicle⟩ rouler au pas

2 vi (**a**) ⟨insect, snake, person⟩ ramper

(**b**) ⟨baby⟩ marcher à quatre pattes

(**c**) ⟨vehicle⟩ rouler au pas

(**d**) ⟨time⟩ se traîner

(**e**) **to be ~ing with** fourmiller de ⟨insects, tourists⟩

(**f**) (colloq) (flatter) faire du lèche-bottes (colloq) (**to** à)

**crayfish** n (**a**) (freshwater) écrevisse f

(**b**) (spiny lobster) langouste f

**crayon** n (wax) craie f grasse; (pencil) crayon m de couleur

**craze** n vogue f; **to be the latest ~** faire fureur

**crazy** adj (colloq) (gen) fou/folle; ⟨idea⟩ insensé/-e; **~ about** fou/folle de ⟨person⟩; passionné/-e de ⟨activity⟩

**crazy golf** n (GB) mini-golf m

**creak** vi ⟨hinge⟩ grincer; ⟨floorboard⟩ craquer

**cream** 1 n crème f; **strawberries and ~** fraises à la crème

2 adj (**a**) (couleur) crème inv

(**b**) ⟨cake, bun⟩ à la crème

■ **cream off**: **~ off [sth]**, **~ [sth] off** prélever ⟨best pupils⟩; ramasser ⟨profits⟩

**cream cheese** n fromage m à tartiner

**cream soda** n soda m parfumé à la vanille

**crease** 1 n (intentional) pli m; (accidental) faux pli m

2 vtr froisser ⟨paper, cloth⟩

3 vi ⟨cloth⟩ se froisser

**create** vtr (gen) créer; provoquer ⟨interest⟩; poser ⟨problem⟩; faire ⟨good impression⟩

**creation** n création f

**creative** adj (**a**) ⟨person⟩ créatif/-ive

(**b**) ⟨process, imagination⟩ créateur/-trice

**creator** n créateur/-trice m/f (**of** de)

**creature** n (**a**) (living being) créature f

(**b**) (animal) animal m

**crèche** n (GB) (nursery) crèche f; (in shopping centre) halte-garderie f; **workplace ~** crèche f d'entreprise

**credentials** n pl (**a**) (reputation) qualifications fpl

(**b**) (reference) pièce f d'identité

**credibility** n crédibilité f

**credible** adj crédible

**credit** 1 n (**a**) (merit) mérite m (**for** de); **to get/take the ~** se voir attribuer/s'attribuer le mérite (**for** de); **to be a ~ to sb/sth** faire honneur à qn/qch

(**b**) (in business) crédit m; **to buy sth on ~** acheter qch à crédit; **to be in ~** être créditeur/-trice

2 vtr (**a**) **to ~ sb with** attribuer à qn ⟨achievement⟩

(**b**) créditer ⟨account⟩ (**with** de)

**credit card** n carte f de crédit

**credit facilities** n pl facilités fpl de crédit

**credit note** n avoir m

**creditor** n créancier/-ière m/f

**credits** n pl générique m

**creditworthy** adj solvable

**credulous** adj crédule, naïf/naïve

**creed** n (religious persuasion) croyance f; (opinions) principes mpl, credo m

**creek** n (a) (GB) crique f
(b) (US) (stream) ruisseau m

**creep** vi (a) to ~ in/out ⟨person⟩ entrer/sortir à pas de loup; to ~ under sth se glisser sous qch; to ~ along ⟨vehicle⟩ avancer lentement; ⟨insect, cat⟩ ramper
(b) ⟨plant⟩ grimper

**creeper** n (in jungle) liane f; (climbing plant) plante f grimpante

**creepy** adj (colloq) qui donne la chair de poule

**creepy-crawly** n (colloq) bestiole f (colloq)

**cremate** vtr incinérer

**cremation** n (a) (ceremony) crémation f
(b) (practice) incinération f

**crematorium** n (GB) crématorium m

**crepe, crêpe** n crêpe m

**crescent** n croissant m

**crescent moon** n croissant m de (la) lune

**cress** n cresson m

**crest** n (a) (ridge) crête f
(b) (coat of arms) armoiries fpl

**Crete** pr n Crète f

**Creutzfeldt-Jacob disease, CJD** n maladie f de Creutzfeldt-Jacob

**crevice** n fissure f

**crew** n (a) (on ship, plane) équipage m
(b) (on film, radio) équipe f

**crewcut** n coupe f (de cheveux) en brosse

**crew neck sweater** n pull m ras du cou

**crib** 1 n (cot) lit m d'enfant
2 vi copier (from sur)

**crick** n a ~ in one's neck un torticolis

**cricket** n (a) (insect) grillon m
(b) (game) cricket m

**cricketer** n joueur m de cricket

**crime** n (a) (minor) délit m; (serious) crime m (against contre)
(b) (phenomenon) criminalité f

**criminal** n, adj criminel/-elle (m/f)

**criminal record** n casier m judiciaire; to have a/no ~ avoir un casier judiciaire chargé/vierge

**crimson** 1 n cramoisi m
2 adj pourpre

**cringe** vi (a) (in fear) avoir un mouvement de recul
(b) (with embarrassment) avoir envie de rentrer sous terre

**cripple** 1 n impotent/-e m/f
2 vtr (a) estropier; ~d for life infirme à vie
(b) paralyser ⟨country, industry⟩

**crisis** n crise f (in dans; over à cause de)

**crisp** adj ⟨biscuit⟩ croustillant/-e; ⟨fruit⟩ croquant/-e; ⟨garment⟩ frais/fraîche; ⟨banknote, snow⟩ craquant/-e; ⟨air⟩ vif/vive; ⟨manner⟩ brusque

**crispbread** n pain m grillé suédois

**crisps** n pl (also **potato** ~) chips fpl

**crisscross** 1 adj ⟨pattern⟩ en croisillons
2 vi s'entrecroiser

**criterion** n critère m (for de)

**critic** n (a) (reviewer) critique m
(b) (opponent) détracteur/-trice m/f

**critical** adj ⟨point, condition, remark⟩ critique; ⟨stage⟩ crucial/-e; ⟨moment⟩ décisif/-ive; to be ~ of sb/sth critiquer qn/qch

**critically** adv (a) ⟨examine⟩ d'un œil critique
(b) ⟨ill⟩ très gravement

**criticism** n critique f

**criticize** vtr, vi critiquer

**croak** vi ⟨frog⟩ coasser

**Croatia** pr n Croatie f

**crochet** vtr faire [qch] au crochet; a ~(ed) sweater un pull au crochet

**crockery** n vaisselle f

**crocodile** n crocodile m

**croissant** n croissant m

**crony** n (petit-e) copain/copine m/f

**crook** n (a) (person) escroc m
(b) (shepherd's) houlette f
(c) (of arm) creux m
IDIOMS by hook or by ~ coûte que coûte

**crooked** adj (a) ⟨line⟩ brisé/-e; ⟨picture, teeth, beam⟩ de travers
(b) (colloq) (dishonest) malhonnête

**crop** n (a) (produce) culture f; (harvest) récolte f
(b) (whip) cravache f
■ **crop up** ⟨matter, problem⟩ surgir; ⟨name⟩ être mentionné/-e; ⟨opportunity⟩ se présenter

**cross** 1 n (a) croix f; to put a ~ against cocher ⟨name, item⟩
(b) (hybrid) croisement m
2 adj (angry) fâché/-e (with contre); to get ~ se fâcher
3 vtr (a) (gen) traverser; franchir ⟨border, line⟩; it ~ed his mind that il lui est venu à l'esprit or l'idée que; to ~ one's legs croiser les jambes
(b) (intersect) couper
(c) barrer ⟨cheque⟩
4 vi se croiser
■ **cross off, cross out** barrer, rayer ⟨name, item⟩

**cross-border** adj trans-frontalier/-ière

**cross-Channel** adj trans-Manche

**cross-check** vtr, vi revérifier

**cross-country** n (a) (running) cross m
(b) (skiing) ski m de fond

**cross cultural** adj inter-culturel/-elle

**cross-examine** vtr (gen) interroger; (Law) faire subir un contre-interrogatoire à

**cross-eyed** adj ⟨person⟩ atteint/-e de strabisme; to be ~ loucher, avoir un strabisme

**crossfire** n feux mpl croisés; to get caught in the ~ être pris/-e entre deux feux

**crossing** n (a) (journey) traversée f

**(b)** (on road) passage *m* clouté; (level crossing) passage *m* à niveau

**cross-legged** *adv* ⟨sit⟩ en tailleur

**cross-purposes** *n pl* **we are at ~** il y a un malentendu; (disagreement) nous sommes en désaccord

**cross-reference** *n* renvoi *m* **(to** à)

**crossroads** *n* carrefour *m*

**cross-section** *n* échantillon *m* **(of** de)

**crossword** *n* (*also* **~ puzzle**) mots *mpl* croisés

**crotch** *n* **(a)** (of body) entrecuisse *m*
**(b)** (in trousers) entrejambe *m*

**crotchet** *n* (GB) noire *f*

**crouch** *vi* (*also* **~ down**) ⟨person⟩ s'accroupir; (to spring) ⟨animal⟩ se ramasser

**crow** ⏻ *n* corbeau *m*
⏼ *vi* **(a)** (exult) exulter
**(b)** ⟨cock⟩ chanter
IDIOMS **as the ~ flies** à vol d'oiseau

**crowbar** *n* pince-monseigneur *f*

**crowd** ⏻ *n* foule *f*; (watching sport, play) spectateurs *mpl*
⏼ *vtr* **(a)** entasser ⟨people, furniture⟩ **(into** dans)
**(b)** encombrer ⟨room, house⟩ **(with** de)
⏽ *vi* **to ~ into** s'entasser dans ⟨room, lift, vehicle⟩

**crowded** *adj* **(a)** ⟨place⟩ plein/-e de monde; (jam-packed) bondé/-e; **to be ~ with** être plein/-e de
**(b)** ⟨schedule⟩ chargé/-e

**crowd-puller** *n* (event) grosse attraction *f*

**crown** ⏻ *n* **(a)** (of monarch) couronne *f*
**(b)** (of hill) crête *f*; (of head) crâne *m*
**(c)** (on tooth) couronne *f*
⏼ *vtr* couronner

**Crown court** *n* (GB) ≈ cour *f* d'assises

**crown jewels** *n pl* joyaux *mpl* de la Couronne

**crown prince** *n* prince *m* héritier

**crow's nest** *n* nid *m* de pie

**crucial** *adj* crucial/-e

**crucifix** *n* crucifix *m*

**crude** *adj* **(a)** ⟨method⟩ rudimentaire; ⟨estimate⟩ approximatif/-ive
**(b)** ⟨joke⟩ grossier/-ière; ⟨person⟩ vulgaire
**(c)** (unprocessed) brut/-e; **~ oil** pétrole *m* brut

**cruel** *adj* cruel/-elle

**cruelty** *n* cruauté *f* **(to** envers)

**cruise** ⏻ *n* croisière *f*; **to go on a ~** faire une croisière
⏼ *vtr* ⟨driver, taxi⟩ parcourir ⟨street, city⟩
⏽ *vi* ⟨ship⟩ croiser; ⟨plane⟩ voler

**cruise missile** *n* missile *m* de croisière

**cruiser** *n* **(a)** (cabin cruiser) petit bateau *m* de croisière
**(b)** (Mil) croiseur *m*

**crumb** *n* miette *f*

**crumble** ⏻ *vtr* émietter ⟨bread⟩
⏼ *vi* **(a)** ⟨rock⟩ s'effriter; ⟨building⟩ se délabrer

**(b)** ⟨relationship, economy⟩ se désagréger; ⟨opposition⟩ s'effondrer

**crummy** *adj* (colloq) **(a)** (substandard) minable (colloq)
**(b)** (unwell) **to feel ~** se sentir patraque (colloq)

**crumple** *vtr* froisser ⟨paper⟩; **to ~ sth into a ball** rouler qch en boule

**crunch** *vtr* croquer ⟨apple, biscuit⟩
IDIOMS **when** *or* **if it comes to the ~** au moment crucial

**crunchy** *adj* croquant/-e

**crusade** *n* croisade *f*

**crush** ⏻ *n* bousculade *f*
⏼ *vtr* **(a)** écraser ⟨can, fruit, person, vehicle⟩ **(against** contre); broyer ⟨arm, leg⟩; piler ⟨ice⟩
**(b)** écraser ⟨enemy, uprising⟩; étouffer ⟨protest⟩
**(c)** chiffonner ⟨garment, fabric⟩

**crushing** *adj* ⟨defeat, weight⟩ écrasant/-e; ⟨blow⟩ percutant/-e; **a ~ setback** un revers cuisant

**crust** *n* (gen) croûte *f*; **the earth's ~** l'écorce *f* terrestre

**crutch** *n* béquille *f*

**crux** *n* **the ~ of the matter** le point crucial

**cry** ⏻ *n* cri *m*
⏼ *vi* pleurer **(about** à cause de); **to ~ with laughter** rire aux larmes
■ **cry out (a)** (with pain, grief) pousser un cri *or* des cris
**(b)** (call) crier, s'écrier
■ **cry off** (GB) (cancel) se décommander

**cryogenics** *n* cryogénie *f*

**crypt** *n* crypte *f*

**cryptic** *adj* ⟨remark⟩ énigmatique; ⟨crossword⟩ crypté/-e

**crystal** *n* cristal *m*

**crystal ball** *n* boule *f* de cristal

**crystal clear** *adj* **(a)** ⟨water⟩ cristallin/-e be a
**(b)** (obvious) clair/-e comme de l'eau de roche

**CS gas** *n* gaz *m* lacrymogène

**cub** *n* (Zool) petit *m*

**Cuba** *pr n* Cuba *f*

**cubby-hole** *n* (colloq) cagibi *m* (colloq)

**cube** ⏻ *n* (gen) cube *m*; **ice ~** glaçon *m*
⏼ *vtr* couper [qch] en cubes ⟨meat⟩

**cubic** *adj* **(a)** cubique
**(b)** ⟨metre, centimetre⟩ cube

**cubicle** *n* (in changing room) cabine *f*; (in public toilets) cabinet *m*

**cuckoo** *n* coucou *m*

**cucumber** *n* concombre *m*

**cuddle** ⏻ *n* câlin *m*; **to give sb a ~** faire un câlin à qn
⏼ *vtr* câliner

**cuddly toy** *n* (GB) peluche *f*

**cue** *n* **(a)** (line) réplique *f*; (action) signal *m*
**(b)** (Sport) queue *f* de billard

**cuff** *n* **(a)** poignet *m*
**(b)** (US) (on trousers) revers *m*

⋯⋯⟩

IDIOMS off the ~ au pied levé

**cuff link** *n* bouton *m* de manchette

**cul-de-sac** *n* impasse *f*, cul-de-sac *m*

**culinary** *adj* culinaire

**cull** ① *n* massacre *m*
② *vtr* massacrer ⟨seals, whales⟩

**culminate** *vtr* aboutir (**in** à)

**culottes** *n pl* jupe-culotte *f*

**culprit** *n* coupable *mf*

**cult** ① *n* culte *m*; (contemporary religion) secte *f*
② *adj* a ~ **film** un film-culte; **to be a** ~
**figure** faire l'objet d'un culte

**cultivate** *vtr* cultiver

**cultural** *adj* culturel/-elle

**cultural attaché** *n* attaché/-e *m/f*
culturel/-elle

**culture** *n* culture *f*

**cultured** *adj* cultivé/-e; ⟨pearl⟩ de culture

**culture shock** *n* choc *m* culturel

**culture vulture** *n* (colloq) fana *mf* de
culture (colloq)

**cumbersome** *adj* encombrant/-e

**cumulative** *adj* cumulatif/-ive

**cunning** ① *n* (a) (of person) ruse *f*; (nastier)
fourberie *f*
② *adj* (a) ⟨person⟩ rusé/-e; (nastier) fourbe
(b) ⟨trick⟩ habile; ⟨device⟩ astucieux/-ieuse

**cup** ① *n* (a) tasse *f*
(b) (trophy) coupe *f*
② *vtr* **to** ~ **sth in one's hands** prendre qch
dans le creux de ses mains

**cupboard** *n* placard *m*

**curable** *adj* guérissable

**curate** *n* vicaire *m*

**curator** *n* conservateur/-trice *m/f*

**curb** ① *n* (a) restriction *f* (**on** à)
(b) (US) (sidewalk) bord *m* du trottoir
② *vtr* refréner ⟨desires⟩; limiter ⟨powers⟩;
juguler ⟨spending⟩; restreindre
⟨consumption⟩

**curdle** *vi* ⟨milk⟩ se cailler; ⟨sauce⟩ tourner

**cure** ① *n* remède *m* (**for** à)
② *vtr* (a) (gen) guérir (**of** de)
(b) (Culin) (dry) sécher; (salt) saler; (smoke)
fumer

**cure-all** *n* panacée *f* (**for** contre)

**curfew** *n* couvre-feu *m*; **ten o'clock** ~
couvre-feu à partir de dix heures

**curio** *n* curiosité *f*, objet *m* rare

**curiosity** *n* curiosité *f* (**about** sur, au sujet
de); **out of** ~ par curiosité

**curious** *adj* curieux/-ieuse

**curiously** *adv* ⟨silent, detached⟩
étrangement; ~ **enough** chose assez curieuse

**curl** ① *n* boucle *f*
② *vtr* friser ⟨hair⟩
③ *vi* (a) ⟨hair⟩ friser
(b) (also ~ **up**) ⟨paper⟩ (se) gondoler; ⟨edges,
leaf⟩ se racornir
■ **curl up** ⟨person⟩ se pelotonner; ⟨cat⟩ se
mettre en rond; **to** ~ **up in bed** se blottir
dans son lit

**curler** *n* bigoudi *m*

**curly** *adj* ⟨hair⟩ (tight curls) frisé/-e; (loose
curls) bouclé/-e; ⟨tail, eyelashes⟩ recourbé/-e

**currant** *n* raisin *m* de Corinthe

**currency** *n* monnaie *f*, devise *f*

**current** ① *n* courant *m*
② *adj* ⟨leader, situation, policy⟩ actuel/-elle;
⟨year, research⟩ en cours

**current account** *n* (GB) compte *m*
courant

**current affairs** *n* actualité *f*

**currently** *adv* actuellement, en ce moment

**curriculum** *n* programme *m*; **in the** ~ au
programme

**curriculum vitae** *n* curriculum vitae *m*

**curry** ① *n* curry *m*; **chicken** ~ curry de
poulet
② *vtr* **to** ~ **favour** chercher à se faire bien
voir (**with sb** de qn)

**curse** ① *n* (a) (scourge) fléau *m*
(b) (swearword) juron *m*
(c) (spell) malédiction *f*
② *vtr* maudire
③ *vi* jurer (**at** après)

**cursor** *n* curseur *m*

**curt** *adj* sec/sèche

**curtail** *vtr* (restrict) mettre une entrave à; (cut
back) réduire

**curtain** *n* rideau *m*

**curtsey** ① *n* révérence *f*
② *vi* faire la révérence (**to** à)

**curve** ① *n* courbe *f*
② *vi* ⟨line, wall⟩ s'incurver; ⟨road, railway⟩
faire une courbe

**cushion** ① *n* coussin *m*
② *vtr* amortir

**cushy** *adj* (colloq) peinard/-e (colloq)

**custard** *n* (GB) (creamy) ≈ crème *f* anglaise

**custodial sentence** *n* peine *f* de prison

**custodian** *n* (of collection) gardien/-ienne
*m/f*; (in museum) conservateur/-trice *m/f*

**custody** *n* (a) (detention) détention *f*; **to take
sb into** ~ arrêter qn
(b) (of child) garde *f*

**custom** *n* (a) coutume *f*, usage *m*
(b) (customers) clientèle *f*

**customary** *adj* habituel/-elle; (more formal)
coutumier/-ière

**customer** *n* client/-e *m/f*

**customer services** *n* service *m*
clientèle

**customize** *vtr* fabriquer [qch] sur
commande ⟨car⟩

**custom-made** *adj* ⟨clothes⟩ fait/-e sur
mesure

**customs** *n* douane *f*; **to go through** ~
passer à la douane

**customs duties** *n pl* droits *mpl* de
douane

**customs hall** *n* douane *f*

**customs officer**, **customs official**
*n* douanier/-ière *m/f*

**cut** ① *n* **(a)** (incision) entaille *f*; (in surgery) incision *f*
**(b)** (wound) coupure *f*
**(c)** (hairstyle) coupe *f*
**(d)** (colloq) (share) part *f*
**(e)** (reduction) réduction *f* (in de); **job** ∼**s** suppression *f* d'emplois; **a** ∼ **in salary** une baisse de salaire
② *vtr* **(a)** (gen) couper; **to** ∼ **oneself** se couper; **to** ∼ **one's finger** se couper le doigt; **to have one's hair cut** se faire couper les cheveux
**(b)** tailler ⟨*gem, suit, marble*⟩; ⟨*locksmith*⟩ faire ⟨*key*⟩
**(c)** (edit) couper ⟨*article, film*⟩; supprimer ⟨*scene*⟩
**(d)** (reduce) réduire ⟨*cost, inflation, list*⟩ (**by** de); baisser ⟨*price*⟩
**(e) to** ∼ **a tooth** percer une dent
**(f)** (record) faire, graver ⟨*album*⟩
**(g)** (Comput) couper ⟨*text*⟩
③ *vi* **(a)** (with knife, scissors) couper; **to** ∼ **into** entamer ⟨*cake*⟩; couper ⟨*fabric, paper*⟩; inciser ⟨*flesh*⟩
**(b) to** ∼ **down a sidestreet** couper par une petite rue
**IDIOMS to** ∼ **sb dead** ignorer complètement qn
■ **cut back**: ¶ ∼ **back** faire des économies
¶ ∼ **[sth] back (a)** (reduce) réduire (**to** à)
**(b)** ( prune) tailler
■ **cut down**: ¶ ∼ **down** réduire sa consommation; **to** ∼ **down on smoking** fumer moins; ¶ ∼ **[sth] down (a)** (chop down) abattre
**(b)** (reduce) réduire
■ **cut off (a)** couper ⟨*hair, piece, corner*⟩; enlever ⟨*excess, crusts*⟩; amputer ⟨*limb*⟩
**(b)** (disconnect) couper ⟨*mains service*⟩
**(c) to** ∼ **off sb's allowance** couper les vivres à qn
**(d) to** ∼ **sb off** (on phone) couper qn; (interrupt) interrompre qn
**(e) to feel** ∼ **off** se sentir isolé/-e
■ **cut out**: ¶ ∼ **out** ⟨*engine, fan*⟩ s'arrêter
¶ ∼ **[sth] out (a)** découper ⟨*article, picture*⟩ (**from** dans)
**(b)** (colloq) ∼ **it out!** ça suffit!
■ **cut short** abréger ⟨*holiday, discussion*⟩
■ **cut up** couper
**cut and paste** *n* couper-coller *m*
**cutback** *n* réduction *f*; ∼**s in** réductions dans le budget de ⟨*defence, health*⟩; **government** ∼**s** réductions budgétaires du gouvernement

**cute** *adj* (colloq) **(a)** mignon/-onne
**(b)** (US) (clever) malin/-igne
**cutlery** *n* couverts *mpl*
**cutlet** *n* côtelette *f*
**cut-off** ① *n* (upper limit) limite *f*
② **cut-offs** *n pl* jean *m* coupé
**cut-price** (GB), **cut-rate** (US) *adj* à prix réduit
**cut-throat** *adj* ⟨*competition*⟩ acharné/-e; **a** ∼ **business** un milieu très dur
**cutting** ① *n* **(a)** (from newspaper) coupure *f* (**from** de)
**(b)** (in film-making) montage *m*
② *adj* ⟨*tone*⟩ cassant/-e; ⟨*remark*⟩ désobligeant/-e
**cutting edge** *n* **to be at the** ∼ **of** être à l'avant-garde de
**CV**, **cv** *n* (*abbr* = **curriculum vitae**) cv, CV *m*
**cyanide** *n* cyanure *m*
**cybercafe** *n* cybercafé *m*
**cyberculture** *n* cyberculture *f*
**cyberspace** *n* cyberespace *m*
**cycle** ① *n* **(a)** cycle *m*
**(b)** (bicycle) vélo *m*
② *vi* faire du vélo
**cycle lane** *n* piste *f* cyclable
**cycle race** *n* course *f* cycliste
**cycling** *n* cyclisme *m*
**cycling shorts** *n pl* cuissard *m*
**cyclist** *n* (gen) cycliste *mf*; (Sport) coureur/-euse *m/f* cycliste
**cyclone** *n* cyclone *m*
**cygnet** *n* jeune cygne *m*
**cylinder** *n* **(a)** (in engine) cylindre *m*
**(b)** (of gas) bouteille *f*
**(c)** (GB) (*also* **hot water** ∼) ballon *m* d'eau chaude
**cynic** *n* cynique *mf*
**cynical** *adj* cynique
**cynicism** *n* cynisme *m*
**Cyprus** *pr n* Chypre *f*
**cyst** *n* kyste *m*
**Czech** ① *n* **(a)** (person) Tchèque *mf*
**(b)** (language) tchèque *m*
② *adj* tchèque
**Czech Republic** *pr n* République *f* tchèque

# Dd

**d**, **D** *n* **(a)** (letter) d, D *m*
**(b)** **D** (Mus) ré *m*
**dab** ① *n* (of paint) touche *f*; (of butter) petit
morceau *m*
  ② *vtr* tamponner ⟨*stain*⟩ (**with** de); **to ~**
  **one's eyes** se tamponner les yeux
**dabble** *v* ■ **dabble in** faire [qch] en
amateur ⟨*painting, politics*⟩
**dachshund** *n* teckel *m*
**dad, Dad** *n* (colloq) papa *m* (colloq) ; père *m*
**daddy, Daddy** *n* (colloq) papa *m* (colloq)
**daffodil** *n* jonquille *f*
**daft** *adj* (colloq)  bête
**dagger** *n* poignard *m*
  IDIOMS **to look ~s at sb** fusiller qn du
  regard
**daily** ① *n* (newspaper) quotidien *m*
  ② *adj* **(a)** ⟨*visit, routine*⟩ quotidien/-ienne;
  **on a ~ basis** tous les jours
  **(b)** ⟨*wage, rate*⟩ journalier/-ière
  ③ *adv* quotidiennement; **twice ~** deux fois
  par jour
**dainty** *adj* ⟨*porcelain, handkerchief*⟩
délicat/-e; ⟨*shoe, hand, foot*⟩ mignon/-onne
**dairy** ① *n* **(a)** (on farm) laiterie *f*; (shop)
crémerie *f*
  **(b)** (company) société *f* laitière
  ② *adj* ⟨*butter*⟩ fermier/-ière; ⟨*cow, farm,
  product, cream*⟩ laitier/-ière
**daisy** *n* (common) pâquerette *f*; (garden)
marguerite *f*
  IDIOMS **to be as fresh as a ~** être frais/
  fraîche comme un gardon
**dam** *n* barrage *m*
**damage** ① *n* **(a)** (gen) dégâts *mpl* (**to**
causés à)
  **(b)** (Med) **brain ~** lésions *fpl* cérébrales
  **(c)** (figurative) **to do ~ to** porter atteinte à; **the**
  **~ is done** le mal est fait
  ② *vtr* **(a)** endommager ⟨*building*⟩; nuire à
  ⟨*environment, health*⟩; **to ~ one's eyesight**
  s'abîmer les yeux
  **(b)** porter atteinte à ⟨*reputation*⟩
**damages** *n pl* (Law) dommages-intérêts
*mpl*
**damaging** *adj* (to reputation, person)
préjudiciable (**to** à, **pour**); ⟨*effect*⟩
préjudiciable; (to health, environment) nuisible
(**to** pour)
**damn** (colloq) ① *n* **not to give a ~ about sb/**
**sth** se ficher (colloq) éperdument de qn/qch
  ② *adj* (*also* **damned**) ⟨*key, car*⟩ fichu/-e
  (colloq) (*before n*)
  ③ *excl* merde! (colloq), zut! (colloq)
**damp** ① *n* humidité *f*
  ② *adj* ⟨*clothes, house*⟩ humide; ⟨*skin*⟩ moite
**dampen** *vtr* **(a)** humecter ⟨*cloth*⟩

**(b)** refroidir ⟨*enthusiasm*⟩
**damson** *n* prune *f* (de Damas)
**dance** ① *n* (gen) danse *f*; (social occasion)
soirée *f* dansante
  ② *vi* **(a)** ⟨*person*⟩ danser (**with** avec)
  **(b)** ⟨*eyes*⟩ briller (**with** de)
  ■ **dance about, dance up and down**
  sautiller sur place
**dancer** *n* danseur/-euse *m/f*
**dancing** *n* danse *f*
**dandruff** *n* pellicules *fpl*
**danger** *n* danger *m* (**of** de; **to** pour); **to be in**
**~** être en danger; **to be in ~ of doing**
risquer de faire
**danger list** *n* **on the ~** dans un état
critique
**dangerous** *adj* dangereux/-euse (**for** pour;
**to do** de faire)
  IDIOMS **to be on ~ ground** avancer en
  terrain miné
**dangerously** *adv* (gen) dangereusement;
⟨*ill*⟩ gravement; **to live ~** prendre des
risques
**danger signal** *n* signal *m* de danger
**dangle** ① *vtr* balancer ⟨*puppet, keys*⟩;
laisser pendre ⟨*legs*⟩
  ② *vi* ⟨*puppet, keys*⟩ se balancer (**from** à);
  ⟨*earrings*⟩ pendiller; ⟨*legs*⟩ pendre
**Danish** ① *n* (language) danois *m*
  ② *adj* (gen) danois/-e; ⟨*embassy*⟩ du
  Danemark
**dare** ① *n* défi *m*
  ② *modal aux* oser; **to ~ (to) do** oser faire; **I**
  **~ say** c'est bien possible
  ③ *vtr* **to ~ sb to do** défier qn de faire; **I ~**
  **you!** chiche que tu ne le fais pas! (colloq)
**daredevil** *n, adj* casse-cou (*mf*) *inv*
**daring** *adj* **(a)** (courageous, novel)
audacieux/-ieuse
  **(b)** ⟨*suggestion, dress*⟩ osé/-e
**dark** ① *n* **in the ~** dans le noir *or*
l'obscurité; **before ~** avant la (tombée de la)
nuit; **after ~** après la tombée de la nuit
  ② *adj* **(a)** ⟨*room, alley, day, sky*⟩ sombre; **it is**
  **getting ~** il commence à faire noir *or* nuit;
  **it's ~** il fait noir *or* nuit
  **(b)** ⟨*colour, suit*⟩ sombre; **a ~ blue dress** une
  robe bleu foncé
  **(c)** ⟨*hair, complexion*⟩ brun/-e
  **(d)** ⟨*secret, thought*⟩ noir/-e (*before n*)
  IDIOMS **to be in the ~** être dans le noir; **to**
  **leave sb in the ~** laisser qn dans
  l'ignorance; **to keep sb in the ~ about sth**
  cacher qch à qn
**darken** ① *vtr* **(a)** obscurcir ⟨*sky,
landscape*⟩; assombrir ⟨*house*⟩
  **(b)** foncer ⟨*colour*⟩

**2** *vi* **(a)** ⟨*sky, room*⟩ s'obscurcir
**(b)** (in colour) foncer; ⟨*skin*⟩ brunir

**dark glasses** *n pl* lunettes *fpl* noires

**darkness** *n* obscurité *f*; **in ~** dans l'obscurité

**darkroom** *n* chambre *f* noire

**dark-skinned** *adj* basané/-e

**darling** *n* **(a)** (my) **~** (to loved one) chéri/-e *m/f*; (to child) mon chou (colloq); (to acquaintance) mon cher/ma chère *m/f*
**(b)** (kind, lovable person) amour *m*, ange *m*

**darn** *vtr* repriser

**dart** *n* fléchette *f*; **to play ~s** jouer aux fléchettes

**dartboard** *n* cible *f*

**dash** **1** *n* **(a)** (rush) course *f* folle; **it was a mad ~** on a dû se presser
**(b)** (small amount) (of liquid) goutte *f*; (of powder) pincée *f*; (of colour) touche *f*
**(c)** (punctuation) tiret *m*
**2** *vtr* **(a) to ~ sth against** projeter qn/qch contre ⟨*rocks*⟩
**(b)** anéantir ⟨*hopes*⟩
**3** *vi* se précipiter (into dans); **to ~ out of** sortir en courant de ⟨*shop, room*⟩
■ **dash off:** ¶ **~ off** se sauver; ¶ **~ [sth] off** écrire [qch] en vitesse

**dashboard** *n* tableau *m* de bord

**data** *n pl* données *fpl*

**database** *n* base *f* de données

**data entry** *n* introduction *f* de données

**data processing** *n* (procedure) traitement *m* des données; (career) informatique *f*; (department) service *m* informatique

**data protection** *n* protection *f* de l'information

**data security** *n* sécurité *f* des données

**data storage device** *n* périphérique *m* de stockage

**date** **1** *n* **(a)** date *f*; **~ of birth** date de naissance; **what's the ~ today?** on est le combien aujourd'hui?; **at a later ~, at some future ~** plus tard
**(b)** (on coin) millésime *m*
**(c)** (meeting) rendez-vous *m*; **to have a lunch ~** être pris/-e à déjeuner
**(d) who's your ~ for tonight?** avec qui sors-tu ce soir?
**(e)** (fruit) datte *f*
**2** *vtr* **(a)** (gen) dater
**(b)** sortir avec ⟨*person*⟩
**3** *vi* **to ~ from** *or* **back to** ⟨*building*⟩ dater de; ⟨*problem, friendship*⟩ remonter à
**4 to date** *phr* à ce jour, jusqu'ici

**dated** *adj* ⟨*clothes, style*⟩ démodé/-e; ⟨*idea, custom*⟩ dépassé/-e; ⟨*language*⟩ vieilli/-e; **the film seems ~ now** le film a mal vieilli

**date rape** *n* viol *m* (*au cours d'une sortie en tête à tête*)

**dating agency** *n* club *m* de rencontres

**daughter** *n* fille *f*

**daughter-in-law** *n* belle-fille *f*, bru *f*

**daunting** *adj* ⟨*task, prospect*⟩ décourageant/-e; ⟨*person*⟩ intimidant/-e

**dawdle** *vi* flâner, traînasser (colloq)

**dawn** **1** *n* aube *f*; **at ~** à l'aube; **at the crack of ~** à l'aube
**2** *vi* **(a)** ⟨*day*⟩ se lever
**(b) it ~ed on me that** je me suis rendu compte que; **it suddenly ~ed on her why** elle a soudain compris pourquoi

**dawn raid** *n* descente *f* de police très tôt le matin

**day** *n* **(a)** jour *m*; **what ~ is it today?** quel jour sommes-nous aujourd'hui? **every ~** tous les jours; **every other ~** tous les deux jours; **from ~ to ~** ⟨*live*⟩ au jour le jour; ⟨*change*⟩ d'un jour à l'autre; **the ~ when** *or* **that** le jour où; **the ~ after** le lendemain; **the ~ before** la veille; **the ~ before yesterday** avant-hier; **the ~ after tomorrow** après-demain
**(b)** (with emphasis on duration) journée *f*; **all ~** toute la journée; **during the ~** pendant la journée
**(c)** (age, period) époque *f*; **in those ~s** à cette époque; **these ~s** ces temps-ci
**IDIOMS those were the ~s** c'était le bon temps; **that'll be the ~!** je voudrais voir ça!; **to call it a ~** s'arrêter là; **to save the ~** sauver la situation

**daybreak** *n* aube *f*

**day-care** *n* (for children) service *m* de garderie

**daydream** **1** *n* rêves *mpl*
**2** *vi* rêvasser

**daylight** *n* **(a)** (light) jour *m*, lumière *f* du jour; **it was still ~** il faisait encore jour
**(b)** (dawn) lever *m* du jour, point *m* du jour

**daylight robbery** *n* (colloq) **it's ~!** c'est de l'arnaque! (colloq)

**day nursery** *n* garderie *f*

**day release** *n* formation *f* permanente

**day return** *n* (GB) aller-retour *m* valable une journée

**daytime** *n* journée *f*

**day-to-day** *adj* quotidien/-ienne

**day-trip** *n* excursion *f* pour la journée

**daze** *n* **in a ~** (from news) ahuri/-e; (from blow) étourdi/-e; (from drugs) hébété/-e

**dazed** *adj* (by news) ahuri/-e; (by blow) étourdi/-e

**dazzle** *vtr* éblouir; **to ~ sb with** éblouir qn par ⟨*beauty, knowledge*⟩

**dazzling** *adj* éblouissant/-e

**D-day** *n* **(a)** (important day) jour *m* J
**(b)** (Mil) le 6 juin 1944 ⟨*jour du débarquement des Alliés en Normandie*⟩

**dead** **1** *n* **(a) the ~** les morts *mpl*
**(b) at ~ of night** en pleine nuit; **in the ~ of winter** en plein hiver
**2** *adj* mort/-e; **the ~ man/woman** le mort/la morte; **to drop (down) ~** tomber raide mort/-e; **the phone went ~** la ligne a été coupée
**3** *adv* (GB) ⟨*certain, straight*⟩ absolument; ····⟶

~ **on time** pile (colloq) à l'heure; ~ **easy** (colloq) simple comme bonjour (colloq); **they were ~ lucky!** (colloq) ils ont eu du pot! (colloq); ~ **tired** (colloq) crevé/-e (colloq), claqué/-e (colloq); **to be ~ set on doing** être tout à fait décidé/-e à faire; **to stop ~** s'arrêter net

**deaden** *vtr* calmer ⟨*pain*⟩; amortir ⟨*blow*⟩; assourdir ⟨*sound*⟩

**dead end** ⟦1⟧ *n* impasse *f*
⟦2⟧ **dead-end** *adj* ⟨*job*⟩ sans perspectives

**dead heat** *n* (in athletics) arrivée *f* ex-aequo; (in horseracing) dead-heat *m inv*

**deadline** *n* date *f* or heure *f* limite, délai *m*; **to meet a ~** respecter un délai

**deadlock** *n* impasse *f*; **to reach (a) ~** aboutir à une impasse

**dead loss** *n* (colloq) **to be a ~** être nul/ nulle (colloq)

**deadly** ⟦1⟧ *adj* **(a)** ⟨*poison, enemy*⟩ mortel/-elle
**(b) in ~ earnest** avec le plus grand sérieux
⟦2⟧ *adv* ⟨*dull, boring*⟩ terriblement

**deadpan** *adj* ⟨*humour*⟩ pince-sans-rire *inv*

**deaf** ⟦1⟧ *n* **the ~** les sourds *mpl*, les malentendants *mpl*
⟦2⟧ *adj* **(a)** sourd/-e; **to go ~** devenir sourd/-e
**(b) to turn a ~ ear to** faire la sourde oreille à, rester sourd/-e à

**deaf aid** *n* (GB) prothèse *f* auditive

**deafening** *adj* assourdissant/-e

**deaf without speech** *adj* sourd-muet/ sourde-muette

**deal** ⟦1⟧ *n* **(a)** (agreement) accord *m*; (in business) affaire *f*; (with friend) marché *m*; **it's a ~!** marché conclu!
**(b) a great** *or* **good ~** beaucoup (of de)
⟦2⟧ *vtr* **(a)** porter ⟨*blow*⟩ (**to** à)
**(b)** distribuer ⟨*cards*⟩; donner ⟨*hand*⟩
⟦3⟧ *vi* **to ~ in** être dans le commerce de ⟨*commodity, shares*⟩
■ **deal with (a)** s'occuper de ⟨*problem, request*⟩
**(b)** traiter de ⟨*topic*⟩

**dealer** *n* **(a)** (in business) marchand/-e *m/f*; (large-scale) négociant/-e *m/f*
**(b)** (on stock exchange) opérateur/-trice *m/f*
**(c)** (in drugs) revendeur/-euse *m/f* de drogue, dealer *m* (colloq)
**(d)** (in cards) donneur/-euse *m/f*

**dealing** ⟦1⟧ *n* **(a)** (trading) vente *f*; **foreign exchange ~** opérations *fpl* de change; **share ~** transactions *fpl* boursières
**(b)** (trafficking) trafic *m*; **drug ~** le trafic de drogue
⟦2⟧ **dealings** *n pl* relations *fpl* (**with** avec)

**dear** ⟦1⟧ *n* **(my) ~** mon chéri/ma chérie *m/f*; (more formal) mon cher/ma chère *m/f*
⟦2⟧ *adj* **(a)** (gen) cher/chère; **he's my ~est friend** c'est mon meilleur ami; **to hold sb/sth ~** être attaché/-e à qn/qch, chérir qn/qch
**(b)** (in letter) cher/chère; **Dear Sir/Madam** Monsieur, Madame; **Dear Sirs** Messieurs;

**Dear Mr Jones** Cher Monsieur; **Dear Mr and Mrs Jones** Cher Monsieur, Chère Madame; **Dear Anne and Paul** Chers Anne et Paul
⟦3⟧ *excl* **oh ~!** (dismay, surprise) oh mon Dieu!; (less serious) aïe!, oh là là!

**death** *n* mort *f*; (more formally) décès *m*; **to drink/to work oneself to ~** se tuer en buvant/au travail
IDIOMS **to be at ~'s door** être à l'article de la mort; **to frighten sb to ~** faire une peur bleue à qn (colloq); **to be bored to ~** (colloq) s'ennuyer à mourir; **I'm sick to ~ of this!** (colloq) j'en ai par-dessus la tête!

**death camp** *n* camp *m* de la mort

**death penalty** *n* peine *f* de mort

**death row** *n* quartier *m* des condamnés à mort

**death sentence** *n* condamnation *f* à mort

**death threat** *n* menaces *fpl* de mort

**death toll** *n* nombre *m* de morts

**death trap** *n* **to be a ~** être très dangereux/-euse

**debar** *vtr* **to be ~red from doing** ne pas avoir le droit de faire

**debatable** *adj* discutable

**debate** *n* débat *m* (**on, about** sur); (informal discussion) discussion *f* (**about** à propos de); **to hold a ~ on** débattre de ⟨*issue*⟩

**debauchery** *n* débauche *f*

**debit** ⟦1⟧ *n* débit *m*
⟦2⟧ *vtr* débiter ⟨*account*⟩ (**with** de)

**debit card** *n* carte *f* bancaire (*sans paiement différé*)

**debrief** *vtr* interroger; **to be ~ed** ⟨*diplomat, agent*⟩ rendre compte (oralement) d'une mission; ⟨*defector, freed hostage*⟩ être interrogé/-e

**debris** *n* (of plane) débris *mpl*; (of building) décombres *mpl*; (rubbish) déchets *mpl*

**debt** *n* dette *f* (**to** envers); **to get into ~** s'endetter

**debt collector** *n* agent *m* de recouvrement

**debtor** *n* débiteur/-trice *m/f*

**debug** *vtr* déboguer ⟨*software*⟩

**debut** *n* débuts *mpl*

**decade** *n* décennie *f*

**decadent** *adj* décadent/-e

**decaffeinated** *adj* décaféiné/-e

**decanter** *n* (for wine, port) carafe *f* (à décanter); (for whisky) flacon *m* à whisky

**decathlon** *n* décathlon *m*

**decay** ⟦1⟧ *n* **(a)** (of vegetation, body) pourriture *f*; (of building) délabrement *m*
**(b) tooth ~** carie *f* dentaire
**(c)** (of society) décadence *f*
⟦2⟧ *vi* ⟨*timber, vegetation*⟩ pourrir; ⟨*tooth*⟩ se carier; ⟨*building*⟩ se détériorer

**deceased** ⟦1⟧ *n* **the ~** le défunt/la défunte *m/f*
⟦2⟧ *adj* décédé/-e, défunt/-e

**deceit** *n* malhonnêteté *f*

**deceitful** *adj* malhonnête

**deceive** ① *vtr* (a) tromper, duper ⟨*friend*⟩; **to be** ∼**d** être dupe
(b) tromper ⟨*spouse, lover*⟩
② *v refl* **to** ∼ **oneself** se faire des illusions

**December** *n* décembre *m*

**decency** *n* (a) (good manners) politesse *f*
(b) (propriety) convenances *fpl*

**decent** *adj* (a) ⟨*family, man, woman*⟩ comme il faut, bien *inv* (colloq); **it's** ∼ **of him** c'est très gentil à lui
(b) (adequate) convenable
(c) (good) ⟨*camera, education, result*⟩ bon/bonne (*before n*); ⟨*profit*⟩ appréciable; **to make a** ∼ **living** bien gagner sa vie
(d) ⟨*behaviour, clothes, language*⟩ décent/-e, correct/-e

**decentralize** *vtr* décentraliser

**deception** *n* duplicité *f*

**deceptive** *adj* trompeur/-euse

**decide** ① *vtr* (a) **to** ∼ **to do** décider de faire; (after much hesitation) se décider à faire
(b) (settle) régler ⟨*matter*⟩; décider de ⟨*fate, outcome*⟩
② *vi* décider; **to** ∼ **against** écarter ⟨*plan, idea*⟩; **to** ∼ **between** choisir, faire un choix entre ⟨*applicants, books*⟩
■ **decide on** (a) se décider pour ⟨*hat, wallpaper*⟩; fixer ⟨*date*⟩
(b) décider de ⟨*course of action, size, budget*⟩

**deciduous** *adj* ⟨*tree*⟩ à feuilles caduques

**decimal** *adj* ⟨*system, currency*⟩ décimal/-e; ∼ **point** virgule *f*

**decipher** *vtr* déchiffrer

**decision** *n* décision *f*; **to make** *or* **take a** ∼ prendre une décision

**decision-maker** *n* décideur/-euse *m/f*

**decision-making** *n* **to be good/bad at** ∼ savoir/ne pas savoir prendre les décisions

**decisive** *adj* (a) ⟨*manner, tone*⟩ ferme
(b) ⟨*battle, factor*⟩ décisif/-ive; ⟨*argument*⟩ concluant/-e

**deck** *n* (a) (on ship) pont *m*; **on** ∼ sur le pont; **below** ∼**(s)** sur le pont inférieur
(b) (US) (terrace) terrasse *f*
(c) ∼ **of cards** jeu *m* de cartes
**IDIOMS to clear the** ∼**s** déblayer le terrain

**deckchair** *n* chaise *f* longue, transat *m*

**declaration** *n* déclaration *f*

**declare** *vtr* (a) déclarer (**that** que); annoncer ⟨*intention, support*⟩
(b) déclarer ⟨*war*⟩ (**on** à); proclamer ⟨*independence*⟩
(c) déclarer ⟨*income*⟩

**decline** ① *n* (a) (waning) déclin *m* (**of** de); **to be in** ∼ être sur le déclin
(b) (drop) baisse *f* (**in, of** de); **to be on the** *or* **in** ∼ être en baisse
② *vi* (a) (drop) ⟨*demand, quality*⟩ baisser (**by** de); ⟨*support*⟩ être en baisse
(b) (wane) être sur le déclin
(c) (refuse) refuser

**decode** *vtr* décoder ⟨*code, message, signal*⟩

**decompose** *vi* se décomposer

**decompress** *vtr* décomprimer, décompresser

**decor** *n* décoration *f*; (in theatre) décor *m*

**decorate** ① *vtr* (a) décorer ⟨*cake, tree*⟩ (**with** de, avec)
(b) **to** ∼ **a room** (paint) peindre une pièce; (paper) tapisser une pièce
② *vi* faire des travaux de décoration

**decoration** *n* décoration *f*

**decorative** *adj* décoratif/-ive

**decorator** *n* peintre *m*, décorateur/-trice *m/f*

**decoy** ① *n* leurre *m*
② *vtr* attirer [qn] dans un piège

**decrease** ① *n* diminution *f* (**in** de); (in price) baisse *f* (**in** de)
② *vi* ⟨*population*⟩ diminuer; ⟨*price, popularity, rate*⟩ baisser, diminuer

**decreasing** *adj* décroissant/-e

**decree** *n* (a) (order) décret *m*
(b) (judgment) jugement *m*, arrêt *m*

**decrepit** *adj* ⟨*building*⟩ délabré/-e; ⟨*horse, old person*⟩ décrépit/-e

**decriminalize** *vtr* décriminaliser, légaliser

**dedicate** *vtr* dédier ⟨*book*⟩ (**to** à); consacrer ⟨*life*⟩ (**to** à)

**dedicated** *adj* ⟨*teacher, mother, fan*⟩ dévoué/-e; ⟨*worker*⟩ zélé/-e

**dedication** *n* (a) (devotion) dévouement *m* (**to** à); ∼ **to duty** dévouement
(b) (in a book, on music programme) dédicace *f*

**deduce** *vtr* déduire (**that** que)

**deduct** *vtr* prélever ⟨*subscription, tax*⟩ (**from** sur); déduire ⟨*sum*⟩ (**from** de)

**deduction** *n* (a) (from wages) retenue *f* (**from** sur); (of tax) prélèvement *m*
(b) (conclusion) déduction *f*, conclusion *f*

**deed** *n* (a) (action) action *f*; **to do one's good** ∼ **for the day** faire sa bonne action *or* sa BA (colloq)
(b) (for property) acte *m* de propriété

**deep** ① *adj* (a) (gen) profond/-e; ⟨*snow*⟩ épais/épaisse; **a** ∼**pile carpet** une moquette de haute laine; **how** ∼ **is the lake?** quelle est la profondeur du lac?; **the lake is 13 m** ∼ le lac fait 13 m de profondeur
(b) (dark) ⟨*colour*⟩ intense; ⟨*tan*⟩ prononcé/-e; ∼ **blue eyes** des yeux d'un bleu profond
(c) **to be** ∼ **in thought** être plongé/-e dans ses pensées; **to be** ∼ **in conversation** être en grande conversation
② *adv* (a) ⟨*dig, bury, cut*⟩ profondément
(b) ∼ **down** *or* **inside she was frightened** dans son for intérieur elle avait peur

**deepen** ① *vtr* (a) creuser ⟨*channel*⟩
(b) approfondir ⟨*knowledge, understanding*⟩
② *vi* (a) ⟨*concern, love*⟩ augmenter; ⟨*knowledge*⟩ s'approfondir; ⟨*crisis*⟩ s'aggraver; ⟨*mystery*⟩ s'épaissir; ⟨*silence*⟩ se faire plus profond
(b) ⟨*voice*⟩ devenir plus grave
(c) ⟨*colour*⟩ foncer

····▷

**3 deepening** *pres p adj* ⟨*mystery, need, rift*⟩ croissant/-e; ⟨*crisis*⟩ de plus en plus grave; ⟨*confusion*⟩ de plus en plus grand/-e

**deep-(fat-)fryer** *n* friteuse *f*

**deep-freeze** *n* congélateur *m*

**deep-fry** *vtr* faire frire

**deeply** *adv* profondément

**deep-rooted** *adj* ⟨*anxiety, prejudice*⟩ profondément enraciné/-e

**deep-sea** *adj* ⟨*diver, diving*⟩ sous-marin/-e; ⟨*fisherman, fishing*⟩ hauturier/-ière

**deer** *n* (red) cerf *m*; (roe) chevreuil *m*; (fallow) daim *m*; (doe) biche *f*

**de-escalate** *vtr* faire baisser ⟨*tension, violence*⟩; désamorcer ⟨*crisis*⟩

**deface** *vtr* abîmer ⟨*wall*⟩; couvrir [qch] d'inscriptions, dégrader ⟨*monument*⟩

**default** **1** *vi* ne pas régler ses échéances **2 by default** *phr* par défaut; **to win by ~** gagner par forfait

**defeat** **1** *n* défaite *f*; **to admit ~** ⟨*team, troops*⟩ concéder la défaite; ⟨*person*⟩ avouer son échec **2** *vtr* (a) vaincre ⟨*enemy*⟩; battre ⟨*team, opposition, candidate*⟩; **the government was ~ed** le gouvernement a été mis en échec (b) rejeter ⟨*bill, proposal*⟩ (c) **it ~s me** ça me dépasse

**defeatist** *n, adj* défaitiste ⟨*mf*⟩

**defect** **1** *n* (flaw) défaut *m*; (minor) imperfection *f*; **a speech ~** un défaut d'élocution **2** *vi* faire défection; **to ~ to the West** passer à l'Ouest

**defective** *adj* défectueux/-euse

**defector** *n* transfuge *mf* (**from** de)

**defence** (GB), **defense** (US) *n* (gen, Law, Sport) défense *f*; **in her ~** à sa décharge

**defenceless** (GB), **defenseless** (US) *adj* ⟨*person, animal*⟩ sans défense; ⟨*town, country*⟩ sans défenses

**defend** *vtr* défendre ⟨*fort, freedom, interests, title*⟩; justifier ⟨*behaviour, decision*⟩

**defendant** *n* accusé/-e *m/f*

**defender** *n* défenseur *m*

**defensive** *adj* ⟨*reaction, behaviour*⟩ de défense; **to be (very) ~** être sur la défensive

**defer** **1** *vtr* reporter ⟨*meeting, decision*⟩ (**until** à); remettre [qch] à plus tard ⟨*departure*⟩; différer ⟨*payment*⟩ **2** *vi* **to ~ to sb** s'incliner devant qn

**deference** *n* déférence *f*; **in ~ to** par déférence pour

**defiance** *n* attitude *f* de défi

**defiant** *adj* ⟨*person*⟩ rebelle; ⟨*behaviour*⟩ provocant/-e

**deficiency** *n* (a) (shortage) insuffisance *f* (**of**, **in** de); (of vitamins) carence *f* (**of** en) (b) (weakness) faiblesse *f*

**deficient** *adj* déficient/-e (**in** en)

**deficit** *n* déficit *m*

**define** *vtr* définir

**definite** *adj* ⟨*plan, amount*⟩ précis/-e;

⟨*feeling, improvement, increase*⟩ net/nette; ⟨*decision, agreement*⟩ ferme; **a ~ answer** une réponse claire et nette; **nothing is ~ yet** rien n'est encore sûr; **to be ~ (sure)** être certain/-e (**about** de); (unyielding) être formel/-elle (**about** sur)

**definitely** *adv* sans aucun doute; **he ~ said he wasn't coming** il a bien dit qu'il ne viendrait pas

**definition** *n* définition *f*

**definitive** *adj* définitif/-ive

**deflate** *vtr* dégonfler

**deflationary** *adj* déflationniste

**deflect** *vtr* (a) défléchir, dévier ⟨*missile*⟩ (b) détourner ⟨*blame, criticism, attention*⟩

**deformed** *adj* déformé/-e; (from birth) difforme

**defraud** *vtr* escroquer ⟨*client, employer*⟩; frauder ⟨*tax office*⟩

**defrost** **1** *vtr* décongeler ⟨*food*⟩; dégivrer ⟨*refrigerator*⟩ **2** *vi* ⟨*refrigerator*⟩ dégivrer; ⟨*food*⟩ décongeler

**deft** *adj* adroit/-e de ses mains, habile

**defunct** *adj* défunt/-e

**defuse** *vtr* désamorcer

**defy** *vtr* (a) défier ⟨*authority, person*⟩ (b) **to ~ sb to do** mettre qn au défi de faire (c) défier ⟨*description*⟩; résister à ⟨*efforts*⟩

**degenerate** **1** *adj* dégénéré/-e **2** *vi* dégénérer

**degrade** *vtr* humilier ⟨*person*⟩

**degrading** *adj* ⟨*conditions, film*⟩ dégradant/-e; ⟨*job*⟩ avilissant/-e; ⟨*treatment*⟩ humiliant/-e

**degree** *n* (a) (measurement) degré *m* (b) (from university) diplôme *m* universitaire; **first** *or* **bachelor's ~** ≈ licence *f* (c) **to such a ~ that** à tel point que; **to a ~, to some ~** dans une certaine mesure; **by ~s** petit à petit (d) (US) **first ~ murder** homicide *m* volontaire avec préméditation

**degree ceremony** *n* (GB Univ) cérémonie *f* de remise des diplômes

**degree course** *n* (GB Univ) programme *m* d'études universitaires

**dehydrated** *adj* déshydraté/-e; ⟨*milk*⟩ en poudre; **to become ~** se déshydrater

**de-icer** *n* dégivrant *m*

**deign** *vtr* **to ~ to do** condescendre à faire, daigner faire

**deity** *n* divinité *f*

**dejected** *adj* découragé/-e

**delay** **1** *n* (gen) retard *m* (**of** de; **to, on** sur); **a few minutes' ~** un délai de quelques minutes; **without (further) ~** sans (plus) tarder **2** *vtr* (a) différer ⟨*decision, publication*⟩; **to ~ doing** attendre pour faire (b) retarder ⟨*train, arrival, post*⟩

**delayed** *adj* **to be ~** être retardé/-e

**delegate** **1** *n* délégué/-e *m/f*

2 *vtr* déléguer ⟨*responsibility, task*⟩ (**to** à)

**delegation** *n* délégation *f*

**delete** *vtr* supprimer (**from** de); (with pen) barrer; (on computer) effacer

**delete key** *n* touche *f* effacement

**deliberate** *adj* (a) (intentional) délibéré/-e; **it was** ∼ il/elle l'a fait etc exprès
(b) (measured) ⟨*movement*⟩ mesuré/-e

**deliberately** *adv* ⟨*do, say*⟩ exprès; ⟨*sarcastic, provocative*⟩ délibérément

**delicacy** *n* (a) (of object, situation) délicatesse *f*; (of mechanism) sensibilité *f*
(b) (food) (savoury) mets *m* raffiné; (sweet) friandise *f*

**delicate** *adj* (gen) délicat/-e; ⟨*features*⟩ fin/-e

**delicatessen** *n* (a) (shop) épicerie *f* fine
(b) (US) (eating-place) restaurant-traiteur *m*

**delicious** *adj* délicieux/-ieuse

**delight** 1 *n* joie *f*, plaisir *m*; **to take** ∼ **in sth/in doing** prendre plaisir à qch/à faire
2 *vtr* ravir ⟨*person*⟩ (**with** par)

**delighted** *adj* ravi/-e (**at, by, with** de; **to do** de faire); ∼ **to meet you** enchanté

**delightful** *adj* charmant/-e

**delinquency** *n* délinquance *f*

**delinquent** *n, adj* délinquant/-e (*m/f*)

**delirious** *adj* **to be** ∼ délirer

**deliver** 1 *vtr* (a) livrer ⟨*goods, groceries*⟩ (**to** à); distribuer ⟨*mail*⟩ (**to** à); remettre ⟨*note*⟩ (**to** à)
(b) mettre au monde ⟨*baby*⟩; délivrer ⟨*baby animal*⟩
(c) faire ⟨*speech*⟩; donner ⟨*ultimatum*⟩; rendre ⟨*verdict*⟩
2 *vi* ⟨*tradesman*⟩ livrer; ⟨*postman*⟩ distribuer le courrier

**delivery** *n* (a) (of goods, milk) livraison *f*; (of mail) distribution *f*; **on** ∼ à la livraison
(b) (of baby) accouchement *m*

**delude** *vtr* tromper; **to** ∼ **oneself** se faire des illusions

**deluge** *n* déluge *m*

**delusion** *n* illusion *f*

**demand** 1 *n* (a) (gen) demande *f* (**for** de); **on** ∼ (gen) à la demande; ⟨*payable*⟩ à vue; **to be in** ∼ être très demandé/-e
(b) (pressure) exigence *f*
2 *vtr* (a) (request) demander ⟨*reform*⟩; (forcefully) exiger ⟨*ransom*⟩; réclamer ⟨*inquiry*⟩
(b) (require) demander ⟨*skill, time, patience*⟩ (of sb de qn); (more imperatively) exiger

**demanding** *adj* (a) ⟨*person*⟩ exigeant/-e
(b) ⟨*work, course*⟩ ardu/-e; ⟨*schedule*⟩ chargé/-e

**demean** *v refl* **to** ∼ **oneself** s'abaisser

**demeaning** *adj* humiliant/-e

**demented** *adj* fou/folle

**dementia** *n* démence *f*

**demerara (sugar)** *n* sucre *m* roux cristallisé

**demilitarize** *vtr* démilitariser

**demister** *n* (GB) dispositif *m* antibuée

**demo** *n* (colloq) (a) (protest) manif *f* (colloq)
(b) (sample version) démo *f* (colloq), version *f* de démonstration

**demobilize** *vtr* démobiliser

**democracy** *n* démocratie *f*

**democrat** *n* démocrate *mf*

**democratic** *adj* démocratique

**demolish** *vtr* démolir

**demolition** *n* démolition *f*

**demon** *n* démon *m*

**demonstrate** 1 *vtr* (a) démontrer ⟨*theory, truth*⟩
(b) manifester ⟨*concern, support*⟩; montrer ⟨*skill*⟩
(c) faire la démonstration de ⟨*machine, product*⟩; **to** ∼ **how to do** montrer comment faire
2 *vi* manifester (**for** en faveur de; **against** contre)

**demonstration** *n* (a) (march) manifestation *f* (**against** contre; **for** en faveur de)
(b) (of machine, theory) démonstration *f*

**demonstrative** *adj* démonstratif/-ive

**demonstrator** *n* manifestant/-e *m/f*

**demoralize** *vtr* démoraliser

**demote** *vtr* rétrograder

**den** *n* (a) (of lion) antre *m*; (of fox) tanière *f*
(b) (room) tanière *f*

**denial** *n* (of accusation, rumour) démenti *m*; (of guilt, rights, freedom) négation *f*

**denim** 1 *n* jean *m*; ∼**s** jean *m*
2 *adj* ⟨*jacket, skirt*⟩ en jean; ∼ **jeans** jean *m*

**Denmark** *pr n* Danemark *m*

**denomination** *n* (a) (name) dénomination *f*
(b) (faith) confession *f*
(c) (value) valeur *f*

**denounce** *vtr* (a) (inform on, criticize) dénoncer
(b) (accuse) accuser

**dense** *adj* dense

**density** *n* densité *f*

**dent** 1 *n* (in metal) bosse *f*
2 *vtr* cabosser ⟨*car*⟩

**dental** *adj* dentaire

**dental floss** *n* fil *m* dentaire

**dental surgeon** *n* chirurgien-dentiste *m*

**dental surgery** *n* (GB) (premises) cabinet *m* dentaire

**dentist** *n* dentiste *mf*

**dentistry** *n* médecine *f* dentaire

**dentures** *n pl* dentier *m*

**deny** *vtr* (a) démentir ⟨*rumour*⟩; nier ⟨*accusation*⟩; **to** ∼ **doing** *or* **having done** nier avoir fait
(b) **to** ∼ **sb sth** refuser qch à qn

**deodorant** *n* (personal) déodorant *m*; (for room) déodorisant *m*

**depart** *vi* (a) partir (**from** de; **for** pour)
(b) (deviate) **to** ∼ **from** s'éloigner de

**department** n (a) (of company) service m
(b) (governmental) ministère m; (administrative)
service m; **social services** ~ services sociaux
(c) (in store) rayon m; **toy** ~ rayon jouets
(d) (in hospital) service m
(e) (in university) département m
(f) (in school) section f

**departmental** adj ⟨head, meeting⟩ de
service

**department store** n grand magasin m

**departure** n (of person, train) départ m; (from
truth, regulation) entorse f (**from** à); (from policy,
tradition) rupture f (**from** par rapport à)

**departure gate** n porte f de départ

**departures board** n tableau m des
départs

**departure time** n heure f de départ

**depend** vi to ~ **on** dépendre de, compter
sur (**for** pour); to ~ **on sb/sth to do** compter
sur qn/qch pour faire; **that** ~s cela dépend;
~**ing on the season** suivant la saison

**dependable** adj ⟨person⟩ digne de
confiance; ⟨machine⟩ fiable

**dependant** n personne f à charge

**dependence, dependance** (US) n (a)
(reliance) dépendance f (**on** vis-à-vis de)
(b) (addiction) dépendance f (**on** à)

**dependent** adj ⟨relative⟩ à charge; **to be**
~ (**up)on** (gen) dépendre de; (financially) vivre
à la charge de

**depict** vtr (visually) représenter; (in writing)
dépeindre (**as** comme)

**depiction** n peinture f, représentation f

**deplete** vtr réduire

**deplorable** adj déplorable

**deplore** vtr déplorer

**deploy** vtr déployer

**depopulation** n dépeuplement m

**deport** vtr expulser (**to** vers)

**deportation** n expulsion f

**depose** vtr déposer

**deposit** ① n (a) (to bank account) dépôt m;
**on** ~ en dépôt
(b) (on house, hire purchase goods) versement m
initial (**on** sur); (on holiday, goods) acompte m,
arrhes fpl (**on** sur)
(c) (against damage, breakages) caution f
(d) (on bottle) consigne f
(e) (of silt, mud) dépôt m; (of coal, mineral)
gisement m
② vtr déposer ⟨money⟩; **to** ~ **sth with sb**
confier qch à qn

**deposit account** n (GB) compte m de
dépôt

**depot** n (a) (gen) dépôt m
(b) (US) (station) (bus) gare f routière; (rail)
gare f ferroviaire

**depress** vtr (a) déprimer ⟨person⟩
(b) appuyer sur ⟨button⟩
(c) faire baisser ⟨prices⟩; affaiblir ⟨trading⟩

**depressed** adj (a) ⟨person⟩ déprimé/-e
(b) ⟨region, industry⟩ en déclin

**depressing** adj déprimant/-e

**depression** n dépression f; **to suffer from**
~ être dépressif/-ive

**deprivation** n (poverty) privations fpl

**deprive** vtr priver (**of** de)

**deprived** adj ⟨area, family⟩ démuni/-e;
⟨childhood⟩ malheureux/-euse

**depth** ① n (a) (of hole, water) profondeur f;
(of layer) épaisseur f; **to be out of one's** ~ (in
water) ne plus avoir pied; (in situation) être
complètement perdu/-e
(b) (of colour, emotion) intensité f; (of crisis)
gravité f
(c) (of knowledge) étendue f; (of analysis, novel)
profondeur f; **to examine sth in** ~ examiner
qch en détail
② **depths** n pl (of sea) profondeurs fpl; **in
the** ~**s of winter** au plus profond de l'hiver;
**to be in the** ~**s of despair** toucher le fond du
désespoir

**deputize** vi to ~ **for sb** remplacer qn

**deputy** ① n (a) (aide) adjoint/-e m/f;
(replacement) remplaçant/-e m/f
(b) (politician) député m
② adj adjoint/-e

**deputy chairman** n vice-président m

**deputy president** n vice-président m

**derail** vtr faire dérailler

**deranged** adj dérangé/-e

**deregulate** vtr libérer ⟨prices⟩; déréguler
⟨market⟩

**derelict** adj ⟨building⟩ délabré/-e

**derision** n moqueries fpl

**derive** vtr tirer ⟨benefit, income⟩ (**from** de)

**derogatory** adj désobligeant/-e (**about**
envers); ⟨term⟩ péjoratif/-ive

**descend** ① vtr descendre ⟨steps, slope,
path⟩
② vi (a) ⟨person, plane⟩ descendre (**from** de)
(b) ⟨rain, darkness, mist⟩ tomber (**on, over**
sur)
(c) to ~ **on sb** débarquer chez qn (colloq)
(d) **to be** ~**ed from** descendre de

**descendant** n descendant/-e m/f (**of** de)

**descent** n (a) descente f (**on, upon** sur)
(b) (extraction) descendance f

**describe** vtr décrire

**description** n description f (**of** de); (for
police) signalement m (**of** de)

**descriptive** adj descriptif/-ive

**desecrate** vtr profaner ⟨altar, shrine⟩

**desert** ① n désert m
② vtr abandonner ⟨person⟩ (**for** pour);
déserter ⟨cause⟩; abandonner ⟨post⟩
③ vi ⟨soldier⟩ déserter
**IDIOMS to get one's just** ~**s** avoir ce qu'on
mérite

**desert boot** n bottine f en croûte de cuir,
clarks® f inv

**deserted** adj désert/-e

**deserter** n déserteur m (**from** de)

**desert island** n île f déserte

**deserve** vtr mériter (**to do** de faire)

**deserving** adj ⟨winner⟩ méritant/-e; ⟨cause⟩ louable

**design** ① n (a) (development) (of object, appliance) conception f; (of building, room) agencement m; (of clothing) création f (b) (drawing, plan) plan m (for de) (c) (art of designing) design m; (fashion) stylisme m (d) (pattern) motif m; **a leaf** ~ un motif de feuilles (e) (subject of study) arts mpl appliqués ② vtr (a) concevoir ⟨building, appliance⟩; **to be** ~**ed for sth/to do** être conçu/-e pour qch/ pour faire (b) ⟨designer⟩ créer ⟨costume, garment⟩; dessiner ⟨building, appliance⟩

**designate** vtr **to** ~ **sb (as) sth** désigner qn (comme) qch; **to** ~ **sth (as) sth** classer qch (comme) qch; **to** ~ **sth for** destiner qch à

**designer** ① n (gen) concepteur/-trice m/f; (of furniture, in fashion) créateur/-trice m/f; (of sets) décorateur/-trice m/f; **costume** ~ costumier/-ière m/f ② adj ~ **clothes,** ~ **labels** vêtements mpl griffés; ~ **label** griffe f

**design fault** n faute f de conception

**desirable** adj (a) ⟨outcome, solution⟩ souhaitable; ⟨area, position⟩ convoité/-e; ⟨job, gift⟩ séduisant/-e (b) (sexually) désirable

**desire** ① n désir m (for de); **to have no** ~ **to do** n'avoir aucune envie de faire ② vtr désirer; **it leaves a lot to be** ~**d** cela laisse beaucoup à désirer

**desk** n (a) bureau m; **writing** ~ secrétaire m (b) (in classroom) (pupil's) table f; (teacher's) bureau m (c) **reception** ~ réception f; **information** ~ bureau m de renseignements; **cash** ~ caisse f

**desktop** n (also ~ **computer**) ordinateur m de bureau

**desktop publishing, DTP** n micro-édition f, PAO f

**desolate** adj désolé/-e

**despair** ① n désespoir m; **in** or **out of** ~ de désespoir ② vi désespérer (**of** de; **of doing** de faire)

**desperate** adj ⟨person, plea, situation⟩ désespéré/-e; ⟨criminal⟩ prêt/-e à tout; **to be** ~ **for** avoir désespérément besoin de ⟨affection, help⟩; attendre désespérément ⟨news⟩

**desperately** adv (a) ⟨plead, look, fight⟩ désespérément; **to need sth** ~ avoir très besoin de qch (b) ⟨poor⟩ terriblement; ⟨ill⟩ très gravement

**desperation** n désespoir m

**despicable** adj méprisable

**despise** vtr mépriser

**despite** prep malgré

**despondent** adj abattu/-e, découragé/-e

**despot** n despote m

**dessert** n dessert m

**dessertspoon** n cuillère f à dessert

**dessert wine** n vin m doux

**destabilize** vtr déstabiliser

**destination** n destination f

**destined** adj (a) destiné/-e (**for, to** à; **to do** à faire) (b) (bound for) ~ **for Paris** à destination de Paris

**destiny** n destin m, destinée f

**destitute** adj sans ressources

**destroy** vtr (a) détruire ⟨building, evidence⟩; briser ⟨career, person⟩ (b) (kill) abattre ⟨animal⟩; détruire, anéantir ⟨population, enemy⟩

**destruction** n destruction f

**destructive** adj destructeur/-trice

**detach** vtr détacher (**from** de)

**detachable** adj ⟨coupon, section, strap⟩ détachable; ⟨lever, collar⟩ amovible

**detached** adj détaché/-e

**detached house** n maison f (individuelle)

**detachment** n détachement m

**detail** ① n détail m; **in (more)** ~ (plus) en détail; **to go into** ~**s** entrer dans les détails; **to have an eye for** ~ prêter attention aux détails ② vtr exposer ⟨qch⟩ en détail ⟨plans⟩; énumérer ⟨items⟩

**detain** vtr (a) (delay) retenir (b) (keep in custody) placer ⟨qn⟩ en détention

**detainee** n détenu/-e m/f

**detect** vtr déceler ⟨error, traces⟩; détecter ⟨crime, leak, sound⟩; sentir ⟨mood⟩

**detectable** adj discernable

**detection** n (of disease, error) détection f; **crime** ~ la lutte contre la criminalité; **to escape** ~ ⟨criminal⟩ ne pas être découvert/-e; ⟨error⟩ ne pas être décelé/-e

**detective** n ≈ inspecteur/-trice m/f (de police); **private** ~ détective m

**detective story** n roman m policier

**detector** n détecteur m

**detention** n (a) (confinement) détention f (b) (in school) retenue f, colle f (colloq)

**detention centre** n centre m de détention pour mineurs

**deter** vtr dissuader (**from doing** de faire)

**detergent** n détergent m

**deteriorate** vi se détériorer

**determination** n détermination f

**determine** vtr déterminer; **to** ~ **how** établir comment

**determined** adj ⟨person⟩ fermement décidé/-e (**to do** à faire); ⟨air⟩ résolu/-e

**deterrent** n (gen) moyen m de dissuasion; (Mil) force f de dissuasion

**detest** vtr détester (**doing** faire)

**detonate** vtr faire exploser ⟨bomb⟩

**detour** n détour m

**d**

**detox** (colloq) [1] n to be in ~ être en cure de désintoxication
[2] adj ⟨centre, treatment⟩ de désintoxication
**detract** vi to ~ from porter atteinte à ⟨success, value⟩; nuire à ⟨image⟩; diminuer ⟨pleasure⟩
**detriment** n to the ~ of au détriment de
**detrimental** adj nuisible (to à)
**deuce** n (in tennis) ~! égalité!
**devaluation** n (of currency) dévaluation f
**devastated** adj ⟨land, region⟩ ravagé/-e; ⟨person⟩ anéanti/-e
**devastation** n dévastation f
**develop** [1] vtr (a) attraper ⟨illness⟩; prendre ⟨habit⟩; présenter ⟨symptom⟩
(b) élaborer ⟨plan⟩; mettre au point ⟨technique⟩; développer ⟨argument⟩
(c) développer ⟨mind, business, market⟩
(d) mettre en valeur ⟨land, site⟩; aménager ⟨city centre⟩
(e) (in photography) développer
[2] vi (a) (evolve) ⟨child, society, country, plot⟩ se développer; ⟨skills⟩ s'améliorer; to ~ into devenir
(b) (come into being) ⟨friendship, difficulty⟩ naître; ⟨crack⟩ se former; ⟨illness⟩ se déclarer
(c) (progress, advance) ⟨friendship⟩ se développer; ⟨difficulty, illness⟩ s'aggraver; ⟨crack, fault⟩ s'accentuer; ⟨game, story⟩ se dérouler
(d) (in size) ⟨town, business⟩ se développer
**developer** n (also **property** ~) promoteur m (immobilier)
**developing country** n pays m en voie de développement
**development** n (a) (gen) développement m
(b) (of product) mise f au point; (of housing, industry) création f
(c) (of land) mise f en valeur; (of site, city centre) aménagement m
(d) (innovation) progrès m; **major** ~s des découvertes fpl majeures (**in** dans le domaine de)
(e) (event) changement m; **recent** ~s in Europe les derniers événements en Europe
**deviate** vi (a) (from norm) s'écarter (**from** de)
(b) (from course) dévier (**from** de)
**device** n (a) (household) appareil m
(b) (Tech) dispositif m
(c) (also **explosive** ~, **incendiary** ~) engin m explosif
(d) (means) moyen m (**for doing, to do** or pour faire)
IDIOMS **to be left to one's own** ~s être laissé/-e à soi-même
**devil** n (a) (also **Devil**) the ~ le Diable
(b) (evil spirit) démon m
IDIOMS **speak of the** ~! quand on parle du loup (on en voit la queue)! (colloq)
**devil's advocate** n avocat m du diable
**devious** adj retors/-e
**devise** vtr concevoir ⟨scheme, course⟩; inventer ⟨product, machine⟩
**devoid** adj ~ of dépourvu/-e de

**devolution** n (a) (of powers) transfert m (**from** de; **to** à)
(b) (policy) régionalisation f
**devote** vtr consacrer (**to** à; **to doing** à faire); **to** ~ **oneself** se consacrer (**to** à)
**devoted** adj ⟨person, animal⟩ dévoué/-e (**to** à); ⟨fan⟩ fervent/-e
**devotion** n (to person, work) dévouement m (**to** à); (to cause) attachement m (**to** à); (to God) dévotion f (**to** à)
**devour** vtr dévorer
**devout** adj ⟨Catholic, prayer⟩ fervent/-e; ⟨person⟩ pieux/pieuse
**dew** n rosée f
**diabetes** n diabète m
**diabetic** n, adj diabétique (mf)
**diagnose** vtr diagnostiquer
**diagnosis** n diagnostic m
**diagonal** [1] n diagonale f
[2] adj diagonal/-e
**diagonally** adv en diagonale
**diagram** n schéma m; (in mathematics) figure f
**dial** [1] n cadran m
[2] vtr faire, composer ⟨number⟩; appeler ⟨person⟩; **to** ~ **999** (for police, ambulance) ≈ appeler police secours; (for fire brigade) ≈ appeler les pompiers
**dialect** n dialecte m
**dialling code** n (GB) indicatif m
**dialling tone** (GB), **dial tone** (US) n tonalité f
**dialogue** n dialogue m
**dialogue box** n boîte f de dialogue
**dialysis** n dialyse f
**diameter** n diamètre m
**diamond** n (a) (gem) diamant m
(b) (shape) losange m
(c) (in cards) carreau m
**diaper** n (US) couche f (de bébé)
**diaphragm** n diaphragme m
**diarrhoea** (GB), **diarrhea** (US) n diarrhée f
**diary** n (a) (for appointments) agenda m; **to put sth in one's** ~ noter qch dans son agenda
(b) (journal) journal m intime
**dice** [1] n (object) dé m; (game) dés mpl
[2] vtr couper [qch] en cubes ⟨vegetable, meat⟩
**dictate** [1] vtr (a) dicter ⟨letter⟩
(b) imposer ⟨terms⟩ (**to** à); déterminer ⟨outcome⟩
[2] vi (a) **to** ~ **to one's secretary** dicter une lettre (or un texte) à sa secrétaire
(b) **to** ~ **to sb** imposer sa volonté à qn
**dictation** n dictée f
**dictator** n dictateur m
**dictatorship** n dictature f
**dictionary** n dictionnaire m
**die** vi mourir (**of, from** de); **to be dying** être

mourant/-e, se mourir; **to be dying to do** mourir d'envie de faire; **to be dying for** avoir une envie folle de

■ **die down** ⟨*emotion, row*⟩ s'apaiser; ⟨*fighting*⟩ s'achever; ⟨*storm*⟩ se calmer; ⟨*laughter*⟩ diminuer; ⟨*applause*⟩ se calmer

■ **die out** ⟨*species*⟩ disparaître

**diesel** n (a) (*also* ∼ **fuel**, ∼ **oil**) gazole m (b) (*also* ∼ **car**) diesel m

**diesel engine** n (moteur m) diesel m

**diet** n (a) (normal food) alimentation f (of à base de) (b) (slimming food) régime m; **to go on a** ∼ se mettre au régime

**dietician** n diététicien/-ienne m/f

**differ** vi (a) (be different) différer (**from** de; **in** par) (b) (disagree) différer (d'opinion) (**on** sur; **from sb** à qn)

**difference** n (a) différence f (**in, of** de); **to tell the** ∼ **between** faire la différence entre; **it won't make any** ∼ ça ne changera rien; **it makes no** ∼ **to me** cela m'est égal (b) (disagreement) différend m (**over** à propos de; **with** avec); **a** ∼ **of opinion** une divergence d'opinion

**different** adj différent/-e (**from, to** (GB), **than** (US) de)

**differentiate** ①️ vtr différencier (**from** de) ②️ vi (a) (tell the difference) faire la différence (**between** entre) (b) (show the difference) faire la distinction (**between** entre)

**differently** adv (in another way) autrement (**from** que); (in different ways) différemment (**from** de)

**difficult** adj difficile; **to find it** ∼ **to do** avoir du mal à faire; **to be** ∼ **to get on with** être difficile à vivre

**difficulty** n difficulté f; **to have** ∼ (**in**) **doing** avoir du mal à faire

**diffident** adj ⟨*person*⟩ qui manque d'assurance; ⟨*smile, gesture*⟩ timide

**dig** ①️ n (a) (with elbow) coup m de coude (**in** dans) (b) (colloq) (jibe) **to take a** ∼ **at sb** lancer une pique (colloq) à qn (c) (in archaeology) fouilles fpl; **to go on a** ∼ aller faire des fouilles ②️ **digs** n pl (GB) chambre f (meublée) ③️ vtr (a) creuser ⟨*hole, tunnel, grave*⟩ (**in** dans) (b) bêcher ⟨*garden*⟩; fouiller ⟨*site*⟩ (c) extraire ⟨*coal*⟩ (**out of** de) ④️ vi ⟨*miner*⟩ creuser; ⟨*archaeologist*⟩ fouiller; ⟨*gardener*⟩ bêcher

■ **dig up** (a) déterrer ⟨*body, treasure, scandal*⟩; arracher ⟨*roots, weeds*⟩; excaver ⟨*road*⟩ (b) bêcher ⟨*garden*⟩

**digest** vtr digérer ⟨*food*⟩; assimiler ⟨*facts*⟩

**digestion** n digestion f

**digit** n (a) (number) chiffre m (b) (finger) doigt m; (toe) orteil m

**digital** adj ⟨*display, recording*⟩ numérique; ⟨*watch*⟩ à affichage numérique; ⟨*camera, TV*⟩ numérique

**dignified** adj ⟨*person*⟩ digne; ⟨*manner*⟩ empreint/-e de dignité

**dignity** n dignité f

**digress** vi faire une digression; **to** ∼ **from** s'écarter de

**dilapidated** adj délabré/-e

**dilate** ①️ vtr dilater ②️ vi se dilater

**dilemma** n dilemme m (**about** à propos de); **to be in a** ∼ être pris/-e dans un dilemme

**diligent** adj appliqué/-e

**dilute** vtr diluer (**with** avec)

**dim** ①️ adj (a) ⟨*room*⟩ sombre (b) ⟨*light*⟩ faible; **to grow** ∼ baisser (c) ⟨*outline*⟩ vague (d) ⟨*memory*⟩ vague (*before* n) (e) (colloq) (stupid) bouché/-e (colloq) ②️ vtr baisser ⟨*light, headlights*⟩; mettre [qch] en veilleuse ⟨*lamp*⟩

**dime** n (US) (pièce f de) dix cents mpl IDIOMS **they're a** ∼ **a dozen** (colloq) on en trouve à la pelle (colloq)

**dimension** n dimension f

**-dimensional** combining form **three**∼ à trois dimensions

**dime store** n (US) bazar m

**diminish** vtr, vi diminuer

**dimple** n fossette f

**din** n vacarme m

**dine** vi dîner

**diner** n (a) (person) dîneur/-euse m/f (b) (US) (restaurant) café-restaurant m

**dinghy** n (a) (*also* **sailing** ∼) dériveur m (b) (inflatable) canot m

**dingy** adj ⟨*colour*⟩ défraîchi/-e; ⟨*place*⟩ minable

**dining car** n wagon-restaurant m

**dining room** n (in house) salle f à manger; (in hotel) salle f de restaurant

**dinner** n (a) dîner m; **to go out to** ∼ dîner dehors; **to have** ∼ dîner (b) (banquet) dîner m (**for** en l'honneur de)

**dinner hour** n (GB Sch) heure f du déjeuner

**dinner jacket, DJ** n smoking m

**dinner party** n dîner m

**dinnertime** n heure f du dîner

**dinosaur** n dinosaure m

**dip** ①️ n (a) (in ground, road) creux m (b) (bathe) baignade f (c) (in prices, rate, sales) (mouvement m de) baisse f (**in** dans) (d) (Culin) sauce f ②️ vtr (a) tremper (**in, into** dans) (b) (GB) (Aut) baisser ⟨*headlights*⟩; ∼**ped headlights** codes mpl ③️ vi (a) ⟨*bird, plane*⟩ piquer (b) ⟨*land, road*⟩ être en pente

**(c) to ~ into** puiser dans ⟨savings⟩; parcourir ⟨novel⟩

**diploma** n diplôme m (**in** en)

**diplomacy** n diplomatie f

**diplomat** n diplomate mf

**diplomatic** adj diplomatique; **to be ~** avoir du tact

**dipstick** n jauge f de niveau d'huile

**direct** **1** adj (gen) direct/-e; ⟨person⟩ franc/franche

**2** adv directement; **to fly ~** prendre un vol direct

**3** vtr **(a)** (address, aim) adresser ⟨appeal, criticism⟩ (**at** à; **against** contre); cibler ⟨campaign⟩ (**at** sur); orienter ⟨effort, resource⟩ (**to, towards** vers)

**(b)** (control) diriger ⟨company, project⟩; régler ⟨traffic⟩

**(c)** diriger ⟨attack, light⟩ (**at** vers)

**(d)** réaliser ⟨film, programme⟩; mettre [qch] en scène ⟨play⟩; diriger ⟨actor, opera⟩

**(e)** (show route) **to ~ sb to sth** indiquer le chemin de qch à qn

**4** vi (in cinema, radio, TV) faire de la réalisation; (in theatre) faire de la mise en scène

**direct debit** n prélèvement m automatique

**direction** **1** n direction f; **in the right/wrong ~** dans la bonne/mauvaise direction; **to go in the opposite ~** aller en sens inverse; **from all ~s** de tous les côtés

**2 directions** n pl **(a)** (for route) indications fpl; **to ask for ~s** demander son chemin (**from** à)

**(b)** (for use) instructions fpl (**as to, about** sur); **~s for use** mode m d'emploi

**directly** adv **(a)** ⟨connect, challenge, go⟩ directement; ⟨point⟩ droit; ⟨above⟩ juste

**(b)** (at once) **~ after** aussitôt après; **~ before** juste avant

**(c)** (very soon) d'ici peu

**(d)** (frankly) ⟨speak⟩ franchement

**direct mail** n mailing m, publipostage m

**director** n **(a)** (of company) (sole) directeur/-trice m/f; (on board) administrateur/-trice m/f

**(b)** (of play, film) metteur m en scène; (of orchestra) chef m d'orchestre; (of choir) chef m des chœurs

**directory** n **(a)** (also **telephone ~**) annuaire m

**(b)** (for business use) répertoire m d'adresses; **street ~** répertoire m des rues

**(c)** (Comput) répertoire m

**directory assistance** n (US), **directory enquiries** n pl (GB) (service m des) renseignements mpl

**direct speech** n style m direct

**dirt** n **(a)** (on clothing, in room) saleté f; (on body, cooker) crasse f; (in carpet, engine, filter) saletés fpl

**(b)** (soil) terre f; (mud) boue f

**dirt track** n chemin m de terre battue

**dirty** **1** adj **(a)** ⟨face, clothing, street⟩ sale; ⟨work⟩ salissant/-e; **to get ~** se salir; **to get sth ~** salir qch

**(b)** ⟨needle⟩ qui a déjà servi; ⟨wound⟩ infecté/-e

**(c)** (colloq) ⟨book, joke⟩ cochon/-onne (colloq); ⟨mind⟩ mal tourné/-e

**(d)** (colloq) ⟨trick⟩ sale (**before** n)

**2** vtr salir

IDIOMS **to give sb a ~ look** (colloq) regarder qn d'un sale œil

**disability** n infirmité f; **mental/physical ~** handicap m mental/physique

**disable** vtr **(a)** ⟨accident⟩ rendre [qn] infirme

**(b)** immobiliser ⟨machine⟩

**(c)** (Comput) désactiver

**disabled** **1** n **the ~** les handicapés mpl

**2** adj handicapé/-e

**disabled access** n voie f d'accès pour handicapés

**disadvantage** n inconvénient m; **to be at a ~** être désavantagé/-e

**disadvantaged** adj défavorisé/-e

**disagree** vi **(a)** ne pas être d'accord (**with** avec; **on, about** sur); **we often ~** nous avons souvent des avis différents

**(b)** ⟨facts, accounts, result⟩ être en désaccord (**with** avec)

**(c) to ~ with sb** ⟨food⟩ ne pas réussir à qn

**disagreeable** adj désagréable

**disagreement** n **(a)** (difference of opinion) désaccord m (**about, over** sur)

**(b)** (argument) différend m (**about, over** sur)

**disallow** vtr **(a)** (Sport) refuser ⟨goal⟩

**(b)** (gen, Law) rejeter ⟨claim, decision⟩

**disappear** vi disparaître

**disappearance** n disparition f (**of** de)

**disappoint** vtr décevoir

**disappointed** adj déçu/-e (**about, with** sth par qch)

**disappointing** adj décevant/-e

**disappointment** n déception f; **to be a ~ to sb** décevoir qn

**disapproval** n désapprobation f (**of** de)

**disapprove** vi **to ~ of** désapprouver ⟨person, lifestyle⟩; être contre ⟨smoking⟩

**disapproving** adj désapprobateur/-trice

**disarm** vtr, vi désarmer

**disarmament** n désarmement m

**disaster** n catastrophe f; (long-term) désastre m

**disaster area** n région f sinistrée; (figurative) catastrophe f

**disaster fund** n fonds m de soutien

**disaster movie** n film m catastrophe

**disaster victim** n sinistré/-e m/f

**disastrous** adj désastreux/-euse

**disbelief** n incrédulité f

**disc, disk** (US) n **(a)** (gen, Mus) disque m

**(b) identity ~** plaque f d'identité; **tax ~** vignette f (automobile)

**discard** *vtr* **(a)** (get rid of) se débarrasser de ⟨*possessions*⟩; mettre [qch] au rebut ⟨*furniture*⟩
**(b)** (drop) abandonner ⟨*plan, policy*⟩; laisser tomber ⟨*person*⟩

**discerning** *adj* perspicace

**discharge** **1** *n* **(a)** (of patient) renvoi *m* au foyer
**(b)** (of gas, smoke) émission *f*; (of liquid) écoulement *m*; (of waste) déversement *m*
**(c)** (from eye, wound) sécrétions *fpl*
**2** *vtr* **(a)** renvoyer ⟨*patient*⟩; décharger ⟨*accused*⟩; **to be ~d from hospital** être autorisé/-e à quitter l'hôpital; **to be ~d from the army** être libéré/-e de l'armée
**(b)** renvoyer ⟨*employee*⟩
**(c)** émettre ⟨*gas*⟩; déverser ⟨*sewage*⟩
**(d)** (Med) **to ~ pus** suppurer

**discipline** **1** *n* discipline *f*
**2** *vtr* **(a)** (control) discipliner
**(b)** (punish) punir

**disciplined** *adj* discipliné/-e

**disclaim** *vtr* nier

**disclaimer** *n* démenti *m*

**disclose** *vtr* révéler ⟨*information*⟩

**disclosure** *n* révélation *f* (**of** de)

**disco** *n* discothèque *f*

**discomfort** *n* **(a)** (physical) sensation *f* pénible
**(b)** (embarrassment) sentiment *m* de gêne

**disconcerting** *adj* (worrying) troublant/-e; (unnerving) déconcertant/-e

**disconnect** *vtr* débrancher ⟨*pipe, fridge*⟩; couper ⟨*telephone*⟩; décrocher ⟨*carriage*⟩

**discontent** *n* mécontentement *m*

**discontented** *adj* mécontent/-e

**discontinue** *vtr* supprimer ⟨*service*⟩; arrêter ⟨*production*⟩; cesser ⟨*visits*⟩

**discount** **1** *n* remise *f* (**on** sur); **to give sb a ~** faire une remise à qn
**2** *vtr* écarter ⟨*idea, possibility*⟩; ne pas tenir compte de ⟨*advice, report*⟩

**discount store** *n* solderie *f*

**discourage** *vtr* décourager

**discover** *vtr* découvrir (**that** que)

**discovery** *n* découverte *f*

**discredit** *vtr* discréditer ⟨*person, organization*⟩; mettre en doute ⟨*report, theory*⟩

**discreet** *adj* discret/-ète

**discrepancy** *n* divergence *f*

**discretion** *n* discrétion *f*; **to use one's ~** agir à sa discrétion

**discriminate** *vi* **(a)** (act with bias) établir une discrimination (**against** envers; **in favour of** en faveur de)
**(b)** (distinguish) **to ~ between** faire une *or* la distinction entre

**discrimination** *n* discrimination *f*

**discus** *n* disque *m*

**discuss** *vtr* (talk about) discuter de; (in writing) examiner

**discussion** *n* discussion *f*; (in public) débat *m*

**disdainful** *adj* dédaigneux/-euse

**disease** *n* maladie *f*

**disembark** *vtr*, *vi* débarquer

**disenchanted** *adj* désabusé/-e

**disengage** *vtr* dégager (**from** de)

**disfigure** *vtr* défigurer

**disgrace** **1** *n* honte *f*; **to be in ~** (officially) être en disgrâce
**2** *vtr* déshonorer ⟨*team, family*⟩

**disgraceful** *adj* scandaleux/-euse

**disguise** **1** *n* déguisement *m*; **in ~** déguisé/-e
**2** *vtr* déguiser ⟨*person, voice*⟩; camoufler ⟨*blemish*⟩; cacher ⟨*emotion, fact*⟩

**disgust** **1** *n* (physical) dégoût *m*; (moral) écœurement *m* (**at** devant)
**2** *vtr* (physically) dégoûter; (morally) écœurer

**disgusting** *adj* (physically) répugnant/-e; (morally) écœurant/-e

**dish** *n* **(a)** plat *m*; **to do the ~es** faire la vaisselle
**(b)** (*also* **satellite ~**) antenne *f* parabolique
■ **dish out** distribuer ⟨*advice, compliments, money*⟩; servir ⟨*food*⟩

**dishcloth** *n* (for washing) lavette *f*; (for drying) torchon *m* (à vaisselle)

**dishevelled** *adj* ⟨*person*⟩ débraillé/-e; ⟨*hair*⟩ décoiffé/-e; ⟨*clothes*⟩ en désordre

**dishonest** *adj* malhonnête

**dishonesty** *n* (financial) malhonnêteté *f*; (moral) mauvaise foi *f*

**dishonour** (GB), **dishonor** (US) *n* déshonneur *m*

**dishtowel** *n* torchon *m*

**dishwasher** *n* (machine) lave-vaisselle *m inv*; (person) plongeur/-euse *m/f*

**disillusioned** *adj* désabusé/-e; **to be ~ with** perdre ses illusions sur

**disinfect** *vtr* désinfecter

**disinfectant** *n* désinfectant *m*

**disintegrate** *vi* se désagréger

**disinterested** *adj* impartial/-e

**disk** *n* **(a)** (Comput) disque *m*
**(b)** (US) = DISC

**disk drive (unit)** *n* unité *f* de disques

**dislike** **1** *n* aversion *f* (**for** pour); **to take a ~ to sb** prendre qn en aversion
**2** *vtr* ne pas aimer (**doing** faire)

**dislocate** *vtr* **to ~ one's shoulder** se démettre l'épaule

**dislodge** *vtr* déplacer ⟨*rock, tile, obstacle*⟩

**disloyal** *adj* déloyal/-e (**to** envers)

**dismal** *adj* **(a)** ⟨*place, sight*⟩ lugubre
**(b)** (colloq) ⟨*failure, attempt*⟩ lamentable

**dismantle** *vtr* **(a)** démonter ⟨*construction*⟩
**(b)** démanteler ⟨*organization*⟩

**dismay** *n* consternation *f* (**at** devant)

**dismiss** *vtr* **(a)** écarter ⟨*idea, suggestion*⟩; exclure ⟨*possibility*⟩ ···⟩

**(b)** chasser ⟨*thought, worry*⟩
**(c)** licencier ⟨*employee*⟩; démettre [qn] de ses fonctions ⟨*director, official*⟩
**(d)** (end interview with) congédier ⟨*person*⟩; (send out) ⟨*teacher*⟩ laisser sortir ⟨*class*⟩
**(e)** (Law) **the case was ∼ed** il y a eu non-lieu
**dismissal** *n* (of employee) licenciement *m*; (of manager, minister) destitution *f*
**dismissive** *adj* dédaigneux/-euse
**disobedient** *adj* désobéissant/-e
**disobey** ① *vtr* désobéir à ⟨*person*⟩; enfreindre ⟨*law*⟩
② *vi* ⟨*person*⟩ désobéir
**disorder** *n* **(a)** (lack of order) désordre *m*
**(b)** (disturbances) émeutes *fpl*
**(c)** (Med) (malfunction) troubles *mpl*; (disease) maladie *f*
**disorganized** *adj* désorganisé/-e
**disorientate** *vtr* désorienter
**disown** *vtr* renier ⟨*person*⟩; désavouer ⟨*document*⟩
**dispassionate** *adj* (impartial) objectif/-ive (about au sujet de)
**dispatch** ① *n* (report) dépêche *f*
② *vtr* envoyer ⟨*person*⟩ (to à); expédier ⟨*letter, parcel*⟩ (to à)
**dispel** *vtr* dissiper ⟨*doubt, fear, myth*⟩
**dispensary** *n* (GB) (in hospital) pharmacie *f*; (in chemist's) officine *f*
**dispense** *vtr* **(a)** ⟨*machine*⟩ distribuer ⟨*drinks, money*⟩
**(b)** ⟨*chemist*⟩ préparer ⟨*medicine, prescription*⟩
**(c)** (exempt) dispenser (**from sth** de qch; **from doing** de faire)
■ **dispense with (a)** se passer de ⟨*services, formalities*⟩
**(b)** abandonner ⟨*policy*⟩
**(c)** (make unnecessary) rendre inutile
**dispenser** *n* distributeur *m*
**disperse** ① *vtr* disperser ⟨*crowd, fumes*⟩
② *vi* **(a)** ⟨*crowd*⟩ se disperser
**(b)** ⟨*mist*⟩ se dissiper
**displaced person** *n* personne *f* déplacée
**display** ① *n* **(a)** (in shop) étalage *m*; (of furniture, vehicles) exposition *f*; **window ∼** vitrine *f*; **to be on ∼** être exposé/-e
**(b)** (demonstration) (of art, craft) démonstration *f*; (of dance, sport) exhibition *f*; **air ∼** fête *f* aéronautique
**(c)** (of emotion) démonstration *f*; (of strength) déploiement *m*; (of wealth) étalage *m*
**(d)** (Aut, Comput) écran *m*
② *vtr* **(a)** (show, set out) afficher ⟨*information, poster*⟩; exposer ⟨*object*⟩
**(b)** (reveal) faire preuve de ⟨*intelligence, interest, skill*⟩; révéler ⟨*emotion, vice, virtue*⟩
**(c)** (flaunt) faire étalage de ⟨*beauty, knowledge, wealth*⟩; exhiber ⟨*legs, chest*⟩
**displeased** *adj* mécontent/-e (**with, at** de)
**disposable** *adj* **(a)** (throwaway) jetable
**(b)** (available) disponible
**disposal** *n* **(a)** (of waste product) élimination *f*; **for ∼** à jeter

**(b)** (of company, property) vente *f*
**(c) to be at sb's ∼** être à la disposition de qn
**dispose** *v* ■ **dispose of (a)** se débarrasser de ⟨*body, rubbish*⟩; détruire ⟨*evidence*⟩; désarmer ⟨*bomb*⟩
**(b)** écouler ⟨*stock*⟩; vendre ⟨*car, shares*⟩
**disproportionate** *adj* disproportionné/-e (**to** par rapport à)
**disprove** *vtr* réfuter
**dispute** ① *n* **(a)** (quarrel) (between individuals) dispute *f*; (between groups) conflit *m* (**over, about** à propos de)
**(b)** (controversy) controverse *f* (**over, about** sur)
② *vtr* **(a)** contester ⟨*claim, figures*⟩
**(b)** se disputer ⟨*property, title*⟩
**disqualify** *vtr* **(a)** (gen) exclure; **to ∼ sb from doing** interdire à qn de faire
**(b)** (Sport) disqualifier
**(c)** (GB) (Aut) **to ∼ sb from driving** retirer le permis de conduire à qn
**disregard** ① *n* (for problem, person) indifférence *f* (**for sth** à qch; **for sb** envers qn); (for danger, life, law) mépris *m* (**for de**)
② *vtr* **(a)** ne pas tenir compte de ⟨*problem, evidence, remark*⟩; fermer les yeux sur ⟨*fault*⟩; mépriser ⟨*danger*⟩
**(b)** ne pas respecter ⟨*law, instruction*⟩
**disrepair** *n* délabrement *m*; **to fall into ∼** se délabrer
**disreputable** *adj* ⟨*person*⟩ peu recommandable; ⟨*place*⟩ mal famé/-e
**disrespect** *n* manque *m* de respect (**for** envers)
**disrespectful** *adj* ⟨*person*⟩ irrespectueux/-euse (**to, towards** envers)
**disrupt** *vtr* perturber ⟨*traffic, trade, meeting*⟩; bouleverser ⟨*lifestyle, schedule, routine*⟩; interrompre ⟨*power supply*⟩
**disruption** *n* (disorder) perturbations *fpl*; (of schedule) bouleversement *m*
**disruptive** *adj* perturbateur/-trice
**dissatisfaction** *n* mécontentement *m*
**dissatisfied** *adj* mécontent/-e (**with** de)
**dissect** *vtr* disséquer
**dissertation** *n* (GB Univ) mémoire *m* (**on** sur)
**dissident** *n, adj* dissident/-e (*m/f*)
**dissimilar** *adj* dissemblable; **∼ to** différent/-e de
**dissolve** ① *vtr* **(a)** ⟨*acid, water*⟩ dissoudre ⟨*solid, grease*⟩
**(b)** faire dissoudre ⟨*tablet, powder*⟩ (**in** dans)
**(c)** dissoudre ⟨*assembly, parliament, partnership*⟩
② *vi* **(a)** ⟨*tablet*⟩ se dissoudre (**in** dans; **into** en)
**(b)** ⟨*hope*⟩ s'évanouir; ⟨*outline, image*⟩ disparaître
**(c) to ∼ into tears** fondre en larmes
**dissuade** *vtr* dissuader (**from doing** de faire)
**distance** *n* distance *f* (**between** entre; **from**

de; **to ~ à**); **to keep one's ~** garder ses distances (**from** avec); **in the ~** au loin; **it's within walking ~** on peut y aller à pied

**distance learning** *n* enseignement *m* à distance

**distant** *adj* (a) (remote) éloigné/-e (b) (faint) ⟨*memory, prospect*⟩ lointain/-e (c) (cool) ⟨*person*⟩ distant/-e

**distaste** *n* dégoût *m*

**distinct** *adj* (gen) distinct/-e (**from** de); ⟨*resemblance, preference, progress*⟩ net/nette (*before n*); ⟨*advantage*⟩ indéniable

**distinction** *n* (a) (gen) distinction *f* (b) (Univ) mention *f* très bien

**distinctive** *adj* caractéristique (**of** de)

**distinguish** *vtr* distinguer (**from** de); **to be ~ed by** se caractériser par

**distinguished** *adj* (a) (elegant) distingué/-e (b) (famous) éminent/-e

**distinguishing** *adj* distinctif/-ive

**distort** *vtr* déformer

**distract** *vtr* distraire; **to ~ sb from doing** empêcher qn de faire

**distracting** *adj* gênant/-e

**distraction** *n* (a) (from concentration) distraction *f* (b) (diversion) diversion *f*

**distraught** *adj* éperdu/-e

**distress** ⎡1⎤ *n* (a) (emotional) désarroi *m*; **to cause sb ~** faire de la peine à qn (b) (physical) souffrance *f* (c) ⟨*ship*⟩ **in ~** en détresse ⎡2⎤ *vtr* faire de la peine à ⟨*person*⟩; (stronger) bouleverser ⟨*person*⟩ (**to do** de faire)

**distressed** *adj* (upset) peiné/-e (**at, by** par); (stronger) bouleversé/-e (**at, by** par)

**distressing** *adj* ⟨*case, event, idea*⟩ pénible; ⟨*news*⟩ navrant/-e; ⟨*sight*⟩ affligeant/-e

**distribute** *vtr* (a) (share out) distribuer ⟨*films, supplies, money*⟩ (**to** à; **among** entre) (b) (spread out) répartir ⟨*load, tax burden*⟩

**distribution** *n* distribution *f*

**distributor** *n* distributeur *m* (**for sth** de qch)

**district** *n* (in country) région *f*; (in city) quartier *m*; (administrative) district *m*

**district attorney** *n* (US) représentant *m* du ministère public

**distrust** *vtr* se méfier de

**disturb** *vtr* (a) (interrupt) déranger ⟨*person*⟩; troubler ⟨*silence, sleep*⟩ (b) (upset) troubler ⟨*person*⟩; (concern) inquiéter ⟨*person*⟩

**disturbance** *n* (a) (interruption, inconvenience) dérangement *m* (b) (riot) troubles *mpl*; (fight) altercation *f*

**disturbed** *adj* (a) ⟨*sleep*⟩ agité/-e (b) ⟨*child*⟩ perturbé/-e

**disturbing** *adj* ⟨*portrayal*⟩ troublant/-e; ⟨*book, film*⟩ perturbant/-e; ⟨*report, increase*⟩ inquiétant/-e

**disused** *adj* désaffecté/-e

**ditch** ⎡1⎤ *n* fossé *m* ⎡2⎤ *vtr* (colloq) laisser tomber ⟨*friend*⟩; abandonner ⟨*idea, vehicle*⟩; plaquer (colloq) ⟨*girlfriend, boyfriend*⟩

**dither** *vi* tergiverser (**about, over** sur)

**ditto** *adv* idem

**dive** ⎡1⎤ *n* (a) (by swimmer) plongeon *m* (b) (of plane, bird) piqué *m* ⎡2⎤ *vi* (a) ⟨*person*⟩ plonger (**off, from** de; **down to** jusqu'à) (b) (as hobby) faire de la plongée

**diver** *n* plongeur/-euse *m/f*; (deep-sea) scaphandrier *m*

**diverge** *vi* diverger; **to ~ from** s'écarter de

**diverse** *adj* (varied) divers/-e; (different) différent/-e

**diversify** *vi* se diversifier

**diversion** *n* (a) (distraction) diversion *f* (**from** à) (b) (of river, money) détournement *m* (c) (of traffic) déviation *f*

**diversity** *n* diversité *f*

**divert** *vtr* (a) détourner ⟨*water*⟩; dévier ⟨*traffic*⟩; dérouter ⟨*flight*⟩ (**to** sur); détourner ⟨*funds*⟩ (**to** au profit de) (b) (distract) détourner

**divide** ⎡1⎤ *vtr* (a) (*also* **~ up**) partager ⟨*food, money, time, work*⟩ (b) (separate) séparer (**from** de) (c) (split) diviser ⟨*friends, group*⟩ (d) (in mathematics) diviser (**by** par) ⎡2⎤ *vi* ⟨*road*⟩ bifurquer; ⟨*river, train*⟩ se séparer en deux; ⟨*group*⟩ (into two) se séparer en deux; ⟨*cell, organism*⟩ se diviser

**dividend** *n* dividende *m*

**dividing line** *n* ligne *f* de démarcation

**diving** *n* (from board) plongeon *m*; (under sea) plongée *f* sous-marine

**diving board** *n* plongeoir *m*

**diving suit** *n* scaphandre *m*

**division** *n* (gen) division *f*

**divisive** *adj* ⟨*policy*⟩ qui sème la discorde; **to be socially ~** créer des inégalités sociales

**divorce** ⎡1⎤ *n* divorce *m* ⎡2⎤ *vtr* **to ~ sb** divorcer de *or* d'avec qn; **they're ~d** ils ont divorcé; **she's ~d** elle est divorcée

**divorcee** *n* divorcé/-e *m/f*

**DIY** *n* (GB) (*abbr* = **do-it-yourself**) bricolage *m*

**dizzy** *adj* ⟨*height*⟩ vertigineux/-euse; **to make sb ~** donner le vertige à qn; **to feel ~** avoir la tête qui tourne

**DJ** *n* (*abbr* = **disc jockey**) DJ *mf*

**DNA** *n* (*abbr* = **deoxyribonucleic acid**) ADN *m*

**do** ⎡1⎤ *v aux* (a) (gen) **~ you like Mozart?** est-ce que tu aimes Mozart?, aimes-tu Mozart?; **I don't smoke** je ne fume pas; **don't shut the door** ne ferme pas la porte; **~ sit down** asseyez-vous; **I ~ like your dress** j'aime beaucoup ta robe; **he lives in London,** ⋯⟶

**doesn't he?** il habite à Londres, n'est-ce pas?; **Lola didn't phone, did she?** Lola n'a pas téléphoné par hasard? **don't ~ that!** ne fais pas ça!; **he said he'd tell her and he did** il a dit qu'il le lui dirait et il l'a fait; **so/neither does he** lui aussi/non plus

**(b)** (in short answers) **'I love peaches'—'so ~ I'** 'j'adore les pêches'—'moi aussi'; **'who wrote it?'—'I did'** 'qui l'a écrit?'—'moi'; **'shall I tell him?'—'no don't'** 'est-ce que je le lui dis?'—'non'; **'he knows the President'—'does he?'** 'il connaît le Président'—'vraiment?'; **'Tim didn't say that'** — **'yes he did'** 'Tim n'a pas dit ça' — 'si'

**2** vtr **(a)** (gen) faire; **to ~ the cooking/one's homework** faire la cuisine/ses devoirs; **to ~ sth again** refaire qch; **to ~ sb's hair** coiffer qn; **to ~ one's teeth** se brosser les dents; **what have you done to your hair?** qu'est-ce que vous avez fait à vos cheveux?; **what has he done with the newspaper?** qu'est-ce qu'il a fait du journal?; **to ~ 60** ⟨car, driver⟩ faire du 60 à l'heure

**(b)** (colloq) (cheat) **we've been done** on s'est fait avoir; **to ~ sb out of £5** refaire (colloq) qn de 5 livres sterling

**3** vi **(a)** (behave) **faire; ~ as you're told** (by me) fais ce que je te dis; (by others) fais ce qu'on te dit

**(b)** (serve purpose) faire l'affaire; **that box will ~** cette boîte fera l'affaire

**(c)** (be acceptable) **this really won't ~!** ⟨of situation, attitude⟩ ça ne peut pas continuer comme ça!; (of work) c'est franchement mauvais!

**(d)** (be enough) ⟨amount of money⟩ suffire

**(e)** (get on) ⟨person⟩ s'en sortir; ⟨business⟩ marcher

**(f)** (in health) **mother and baby are both ~ing well** la mère et l'enfant se portent bien; **the patient is ~ing well** le malade est en bonne voie

IDIOMS **how ~ you do** enchanté; **well done!** bravo!; **it doesn't ~ to be** ce n'est pas une bonne chose d'être; **it was all I could ~ not to laugh** je me suis retenu pour ne pas rire; **she does nothing but moan** elle ne fait que se plaindre

■ **do away with** se débarrasser de
■ **do up (a)** (fasten) nouer ⟨laces⟩; remonter ⟨zip⟩; **~ up your buttons** boutonne-toi
**(b)** (wrap) faire ⟨parcel⟩
**(c)** (renovate) restaurer ⟨house⟩
■ **do with (a)** **what's it (got) to ~ with you?** en quoi est-ce que ça te regarde?; **it has nothing to ~ with you** cela ne vous concerne pas
**(b)** (tolerate) supporter
**(c)** (need) **I could ~ with a holiday** j'aurais bien besoin de partir en vacances
**(d)** (finish) **it's all over and done with** c'est bien fini
■ **do without** se passer de ⟨person, advice⟩

**dock** **1** n **(a)** (in port) dock m; (for repairing ship) cale f
**(b)** (US) (wharf) appontement m
**(c)** (GB) (Law) banc m des accusés

**2** vi arriver au port
**dockworker** n docker m
**dockyard** n chantier m naval
**doctor** **1** n **(a)** (Med) médecin m, docteur m
**(b)** (Univ) docteur m
**2** vtr frelater ⟨food, wine⟩; falsifier ⟨figures⟩; altérer ⟨document⟩
**doctorate** n doctorat m
**docudrama** n docudrame m
**document** n document m
**documentary** n documentaire m (**about**, **on** sur)
**dodge** **1** n (GB) (colloq) (trick) combine f (colloq)
**2** vtr esquiver ⟨bullet, blow, question⟩
**dodgem (car)** n (GB) auto f tamponneuse
**dodgy** adj (colloq) (untrustworthy) louche (colloq); (risky) ⟨decision, plan⟩ risqué/-e; ⟨situation, moment⟩ délicat/-e
**dog** n **(a)** chien m; (female) chienne f
**(b)** (male fox, wolf) mâle m
IDIOMS **to go to the ~s** ⟨company, country⟩ aller à vau-l'eau
**dog collar** n **(a)** collier m de chien
**(b)** (clerical) col m romain
**dog-eared** adj écorné/-e
**dogged** adj ⟨attempt⟩ obstiné/-e; ⟨person, refusal⟩ tenace; ⟨resistance⟩ opiniâtre
**doghouse** n (US) niche f (à chien)
IDIOMS **to be in the ~** être tombé/-e en disgrâce
**dogmatic** adj dogmatique (**about** sur)
**dog paddle** n nage f à la manière d'un chien
**dogsbody** n (GB) (colloq) bonne f à tout faire
**doh** n (Mus) do m, ut m
**doing** n **this is her ~** c'est son ouvrage; **it takes some ~!** ce n'est pas facile du tout!
**dole** n (GB) (colloq) allocation f de chômage; **on the ~** au chômage
■ **dole out** (colloq) distribuer
**doll** n poupée f
**dollar** n dollar m
**dollar bill** n billet m d'un dollar
**dolphin** n dauphin m
**domain** n domaine m (**of** de)
**dome** n dôme m
**domestic** adj **(a)** ⟨market, flight⟩ intérieur/-e; ⟨crisis, issue⟩ de politique intérieure
**(b)** ⟨life, harmony⟩ familial/-e; ⟨dispute⟩ conjugal/-e; ⟨violence⟩ dans la famille
**domestic appliance** n appareil m électroménager
**domesticate** vtr domestiquer
**dominant** adj dominant/-e
**dominate** vtr, vi dominer
**domineering** adj autoritaire
**domino** n domino m; **to play ~es** jouer aux dominos

**donate** *vtr* faire don de (**to** à)

**donation** *n* don *m* (**of** de; **à** to)

**done** ⟨1⟩ *adj* ⟨*food*⟩ cuit/-e; **well** ∼ bien cuit/-e
⟨2⟩ *excl* ⟨*deal*⟩ marché conclu!
IDIOMS **it's not the** ∼ **thing** ça ne se fait pas

**donkey** *n* âne *m*

**donor** *n* (a) (of organ) donneur/-euse *m/f*
(b) (of money) donateur/-trice *m/f*

**donor card** *n* carte *f* de donneur d'organes

**doodle** *vi* gribouiller

**doom** *n* (of person) perte *f*; (of country) catastrophe *f*

**doomed** *adj* condamné/-e; **to be** ∼ **to failure** être voué/-e à l'échec

**door** *n* porte *f*; (in car, train) porte *f*, portière *f*; **behind closed** ∼**s** à huis clos

**doorbell** *n* sonnette *f*

**doorman** *n* portier *m*

**doormat** *n* paillasson *m*

**doorstep** *n* pas *m* de porte

**door-to-door** *adj* ⟨*canvassing*⟩ à domicile; ∼ **selling** porte à porte *m inv*

**doorway** *n* (a) (frame) embrasure *f*
(b) (entrance) porte *f*, entrée *f*

**dope** ⟨1⟩ *n* (colloq) (a) cannabis *m*
(b) (fool) imbécile *mf* (colloq)
⟨2⟩ *vtr* (Sport) doper ⟨*horse, athlete*⟩; (gen) droguer ⟨*person*⟩

**dope test** *n* (Sport) contrôle *m* antidopage

**dormant** *adj* (a) ⟨*emotion, talent*⟩ latent/-e
(b) ⟨*volcano*⟩ en repos

**dormitory** *n* (a) (GB) dortoir *m*
(b) (US Univ) résidence *f*, foyer *m*

**dormitory town** *n* ville *f* dortoir

**dormouse** *n* muscardin *m*

**dose** *n* dose *f* (**of** de); **a** ∼ **of flu** une bonne grippe

**dot** *n* (gen) point *m*; (on fabric) pois *m*
IDIOMS **at ten on the** ∼ à dix heures pile

**dot-com** ⟨1⟩ *n* (also ∼ **company**) société *f* Internet *or* virtuelle, société *f* dot-com
⟨2⟩ *adj* ⟨*shares*⟩ des sociétés Internet *or* virtuelles; ⟨*millionaire*⟩ du commerce électronique

**dote** *vi* **to** ∼ **on sb/sth** adorer qn/qch

**dotted line** *n* pointillé *m*

**double** ⟨1⟩ *n* (a) (drink) double *m*
(b) (of person) sosie *m*; (in film, play) doublure *f*
⟨2⟩ **doubles** *n pl* double *m*; **mixed** ∼**s** double mixte
⟨3⟩ *adj* double; **with a** ∼ **'n'** avec deux 'n'; **two** ∼ **four** (244) deux cent quarante-quatre
⟨4⟩ *adv* (a) ∼ **the amount** deux fois plus
(b) **to see** ∼ voir double
(c) ⟨*fold, bend*⟩ en deux
⟨5⟩ *vtr* doubler ⟨*amount, dose*⟩; multiplier [qch] par deux ⟨*number*⟩
⟨6⟩ *vi* (a) ⟨*sales, prices, salaries*⟩ doubler
(b) **to** ∼ **for sb** (actor) doubler qn
(c) **the sofa** ∼**s as a bed** le canapé fait aussi lit

IDIOMS **on** *or* **at the** ∼ au plus vite

■ **double back** rebrousser chemin

**double act** *n* duo *m*

**double-barrelled name** *n* (GB) ≈ nom *m* à particule

**double bass** *n* contrebasse *f*

**double bed** *n* lit *m* double, grand lit *m*

**double-breasted** *adj* ⟨*jacket*⟩ croisé/-e

**double-check** *vtr* vérifier [qch] à nouveau

**double chin** *n* double menton *m*

**double-click** *vi* double-cliquer

**double cream** *n* (GB) ≈ crème *f* fraîche

**double-cross** *vtr* (colloq) doubler, trahir ⟨*person*⟩

**double-decker** *n* (GB) (bus) autobus *m* à impériale *or* à deux étages

**double door** *n* porte *f* à deux battants

**double Dutch** *n* (colloq) baragouinage *m* (colloq)

**double glazing** *n* double vitrage *m*

**double-park** *vi* se garer en double file

**double room** *n* chambre *f* pour deux personnes

**double standard** *n* **to have** ∼**s** faire deux poids deux mesures

**double take** *n* **to do a** ∼ avoir une réaction à retardement

**double vision** *n* **to have** ∼ voir double

**double yellow line(s)** *n* (*pl*) (GB Aut) *marquage au sol interdisant le stationnement*

**doubt** ⟨1⟩ *n* doute *m*; **there is no** ∼ **(that)** il ne fait aucun doute que; **to have no** ∼ **(that)** être certain/-e que; **to be in** ∼ ⟨*person*⟩ être dans le doute; ⟨*outcome*⟩ être incertain/-e; **if** *or* **when in** ∼ dans le doute; **without (a)** ∼ sans aucun doute
⟨2⟩ *vtr* douter de ⟨*fact, ability, honesty, person*⟩; **I** ∼ **it!** j'en doute!; **I** ∼ **if he'll come** je doute qu'il vienne

**doubtful** *adj* (a) (unsure) incertain/-e
(b) ⟨*character, activity, taste*⟩ douteux/-euse

**dough** *n* (Culin) pâte *f*

**doughnut, donut** (US) *n* beignet *m*

**douse, dowse** *vtr* éteindre ⟨*fire*⟩; tremper ⟨*person*⟩; **to** ∼ **sth with petrol** arroser qch d'essence

**dove** *n* colombe *f*

**Dover** *pr n* Douvres

**dowdy** *adj* ⟨*person*⟩ mal fagoté/-e; ⟨*clothes*⟩ sans chic

**down**[1]

■ **Note** When used to indicate vague direction, *down* often has no explicit translation in French: *to go down to London* = aller à Londres; *down in Brighton* = à Brighton.
– For examples and further usages, see the entry below.

⟨1⟩ *adv* (a) **to go** *or* **come** ∼ descendre; **to fall** ∼ tomber; **to sit** ∼ **on the floor** s'asseoir par terre; **to pull** ∼ **a blind** baisser un store; ∼ **below** en bas; **the telephone lines are** ∼ ⋯▸

les lignes téléphoniques sont coupées; **face ∼** ⟨*fall*⟩ face contre terre; ⟨*lie*⟩ à plat ventre; (in water) le visage dans l'eau

**(b)** (lower) **profits are well ∼ on last year's** les bénéfices sont nettement inférieurs à ceux de l'année dernière; **to get one's weight ∼** maigrir; **I'm ∼ to my last cigarette** il ne me reste plus qu'une cigarette

**(c)** (Sport) **to be two sets ∼** ⟨*tennis player*⟩ perdre par deux sets

**(d)** (as deposit) **to pay £40 ∼** payer 40 livres sterling comptant

**2** *prep* **to go ∼ the street** descendre la rue; **to run ∼ the hill** descendre la colline en courant; **to go ∼ town** aller en ville; **they live ∼ the road** ils habitent un peu plus loin dans la rue

**3** *adj* **(a)** (colloq) **to feel ∼** être déprimé/-e

**(b)** ⟨*escalator*⟩ qui descend

**(c)** ⟨*computer*⟩ en panne

IDIOMS **it's ∼ to you to do it** c'est à toi de le faire; **∼ with tyrants!** à bas les tyrans!

**down²** *n* duvet *m*

**down-and-out** *n* clochard/-e *m/f*

**downbeat** *adj* **(a)** ⟨*pessimistic*⟩ pessimiste

**(b)** ⟨*laidback*⟩ décontracté/-e

**downfall** *n* chute *f*; **drink proved to be his ∼** c'est la boisson qui a causé sa perte

**downhearted** *adj* abattu/-e

**downhill** *adv* **to go ∼** ⟨*person, vehicle*⟩ descendre; **he's going ∼** ⟨*declining*⟩ il est sur le déclin

**downhill skiing** *n* ski *m* de piste

**download** *vtr* (Comput) télécharger

**downmarket** *adj* ⟨*products*⟩ bas de gamme *inv*; ⟨*area*⟩ populaire; ⟨*newspaper, programme*⟩ grand public *inv*

**down payment** *n* acompte *m*

**downplay** *vtr* minimiser l'importance de

**downpour** *n* averse *f*

**downright** **1** *adj* ⟨*insult*⟩ véritable (*before n*); ⟨*refusal*⟩ catégorique; ⟨*liar*⟩ fieffé/-e (*before n*)

**2** *adv* ⟨*stupid, rude*⟩ carrément

**downsize** *vi* réduire les effectifs

**Down's syndrome** *n* trisomie *f* 21

**downstairs** **1** *adj* ⟨*room*⟩ en bas; (on ground-floor) du rez-de-chaussée; **the ∼ flat** (GB) *or* **apartment** (US) l'appartement du rez-de-chaussée

**2** *adv* en bas; **to go** *or* **come ∼** descendre (l'escalier)

**downstream** *adj, adv* en aval (**of** de); **to go ∼** descendre le courant

**down-to-earth** *adj* pratique; **she's very ∼** (practical) elle a les pieds sur terre; (unpretentious) elle est très simple

**downtown** *adj* (US) ⟨*store, hotel*⟩ du centre ville

**downtrodden** *adj* tyrannisé/-e

**downturn** *n* (in economy, career) déclin *m* (**in** de); (in demand, profits) chute *f* (**in** de).

**down under** *adv* (colloq) en Australie

**downward** **1** *adj* ⟨*movement*⟩ vers le bas; **∼ trend** (Econ) tendance *f* à la baisse

**2** *adv* = DOWNWARDS

**downwards** *adv* (*also* **downward**) ⟨*look*⟩ vers le bas; **to slope ∼** descendre en pente (**to** vers)

**doze** *vi* somnoler

■ **doze off** (momentarily) s'assoupir; (to sleep) s'endormir

**dozen** *n* **(a)** (twelve) douzaine *f*; **a ∼ eggs** une douzaine d'œufs; **£1 a ∼** une livre sterling la douzaine

**(b)** (several) **∼s** des dizaines de ⟨*people, things, times*⟩

**drab** *adj* terne

**draft** **1** *n* **(a)** (of letter, speech) brouillon *m*; (of novel, play) ébauche *f*; (of contract, law) avant-projet *m*

**(b)** (on bank) traite *f* (**on** sur)

**(c)** (US) (conscription) service *m* militaire

**(d)** (US) = DRAUGHT

**2** *vtr* **(a)** faire le brouillon de ⟨*letter, speech*⟩; rédiger ⟨*contract, law*⟩

**(b)** (US) (conscript) incorporer (**into** dans)

**(c)** (GB) (transfer) détacher (**to** auprès de; **from** de)

■ **draft in** (GB) faire venir, amener ⟨*police, troops*⟩

**draft dodger** *n* (US Mil) insoumis *m*

**draftsman** (US) = DRAUGHTSMAN

**drag** **1** *n* **(a)** (colloq) **what a ∼!** quelle barbe! (colloq)

**(b)** ⟨*person*⟩ **in ∼** en travesti

**2** *adj* **(a)** ⟨*artist*⟩ de spectacle de travestis

**(b)** ⟨*racing*⟩ de dragsters

**3** *vtr* **(a)** (trail) traîner; (pull) tirer ⟨*boat, sledge*⟩; **to ∼ sth along the ground** traîner qch par terre; **to ∼ one's feet** traîner les pieds; (figurative) faire preuve de mauvaise volonté (**on** quant à); **don't ∼ my mother into this** ne mêle pas ma mère à ça

**(b)** draguer ⟨*river, lake*⟩

**(c)** (Comput) glisser

**4** *vi* **(a)** ⟨*hours, days*⟩ traîner; ⟨*story, plot*⟩ traîner en longueur

**(b)** (trail) **to ∼ in** ⟨*hem, belt*⟩ traîner dans ⟨*mud*⟩

**(c)** **to ∼ on** tirer une bouffée de ⟨*cigarette*⟩

■ **drag on** traîner en longueur

**drag and drop** *n* glisser-lâcher *m*

**drain** **1** *n* **(a)** (in street) canalisation *f*; (in building) canalisation *f* d'évacuation; (pipe) descente *f* d'eau; (ditch) fossé *m* d'écoulement

**(b)** (of people, skills, money) hémorragie *f*; **to be a ∼ on sb's resources** épuiser les ressources de qn

**2** *vtr* **(a)** drainer ⟨*land*⟩

**(b)** épuiser ⟨*resources*⟩

**(c)** vider ⟨*glass*⟩

**(d)** (Culin) égoutter ⟨*pasta, vegetables*⟩

**3** *vi* **(a)** ⟨*liquid*⟩ s'écouler (**out of, from** de; **into** dans)

**(b)** ⟨*dishes, food*⟩ s'égoutter

**drainage** *n* (of land) drainage *m*; (system) tout-à-l'égout *m inv*

**draining board** *n* égouttoir *m*

**drainpipe** *n* descente *f*

**drake** *n* canard *m* (mâle)

**drama** *n* (genre) théâtre *m*; (acting, directing) art *m* dramatique; (play, dramatic event) drame *m*; TV/radio ~ dramatique *f*; **to make a ~ out of sth** faire tout un drame de qch

**dramatic** *adj* ⟨art, effect, event⟩ dramatique; ⟨change, landscape⟩ spectaculaire; ⟨entrance⟩ théâtral/-e

**dramatist** *n* auteur *m* dramatique

**dramatize** *vtr* **(a)** (for stage) adapter [qch] à la scène; (for screen) adapter [qch] à l'écran; (for radio) adapter [qch] pour la radio **(b)** (make dramatic) donner un caractère dramatique à; (excessively) dramatiser

**drape** ① *n* (US) rideau *m* ② *vtr* draper (**in**, **with** de)

**drastic** *adj* ⟨policy, measure⟩ draconien/-ienne; ⟨reduction, remedy⟩ drastique; ⟨effect⟩ catastrophique; ⟨change⟩ radical/-e

**drastically** *adv* ⟨change, reduce⟩ radicalement; ⟨reduce, limit⟩ sévèrement

**draught** (GB), **draft** (US) *n* **(a)** (cold air) courant *m* d'air **(b)** **on ~** ⟨beer⟩ à la pression

**draughts** *n* (GB) jeu *m* de dames; **to play ~** jouer aux dames

**draughtsman** (GB), **draftsman** (US) *n* dessinateur/-trice *m/f*

**draughty** (GB), **drafty** (US) *adj* plein/-e de courants d'air

**draw** ① *n* **(a)** (in lottery) tirage *m* (au sort) **(b)** (Sport) match *m* nul; **it was a ~** (in race) ils sont arrivés ex aequo ② *vtr* **(a)** faire ⟨picture, plan⟩; dessiner ⟨person, object⟩; tracer ⟨line⟩ **(b)** (pull) ⟨animal, engine⟩ tirer **(c)** tirer ⟨conclusion⟩ (**from** de) **(d)** (attract) attirer ⟨crowd⟩ (**to** vers); susciter ⟨reaction⟩; **to ~ sb into** mêler qn à ⟨conversation⟩; entraîner qn dans ⟨argument, battle⟩ **(e)** retirer ⟨money⟩ (**from** de); tirer ⟨cheque⟩ (**on** sur); toucher ⟨wages, pension⟩ **(f)** (in lottery) tirer [qch] au sort ⟨ticket⟩ **(g)** sortir ⟨sword, knife⟩; **to ~ a gun on sb** sortir un pistolet et le braquer sur qn ③ *vi* **(a)** (make picture) dessiner **(b)** **to ~ ahead (of sb/sth)** (in race) gagner du terrain (sur qn/qch); (in contest, election) prendre de l'avance (sur qn/qch); **to ~ alongside** ⟨boat⟩ accoster; **to ~ near** ⟨time⟩ approcher; **to ~ level** se retrouver au même niveau **(c)** (in match) faire match nul IDIOMS **to ~ the line** fixer des limites; **to ~ the line at doing** se refuser à faire

■ **draw away** (move off) s'éloigner (**from** de); (move ahead) prendre de l'avance (**from** sur)

■ **draw in:** ¶ **~ in (a)** ⟨days, nights⟩ raccourcir **(b)** ⟨bus⟩ arriver; ⟨train⟩ entrer en gare ¶ **~ [sth] in** rentrer ⟨stomach, claws⟩

■ **draw out:** ¶ **~ out** ⟨train, bus⟩ partir; **the train drew out of the station** le train a quitté la gare ¶ **~ [sth] out (a)** (remove) tirer ⟨purse, knife⟩ (**of** de); retirer ⟨nail, cork⟩ (**of** de) **(b)** (withdraw) retirer ⟨money⟩ **(c)** (prolong) faire durer ¶ **~ [sb] out** faire sortir [qn] de sa coquille

■ **draw up (a)** établir ⟨contract⟩; dresser, établir ⟨list, report⟩ **(b)** approcher ⟨chair⟩ (**to** de)

**drawback** *n* inconvénient *m*

**drawer** *n* tiroir *m*

**drawing** *n* dessin *m*

**drawing board** *n* planche *f* à dessin

**drawing pin** *n* punaise *f*

**drawing room** *n* salon *m*

**drawl** *n* voix *f* traînante

**drawn** *adj* **(a)** **to look ~** avoir les traits tirés **(b)** ⟨game, match⟩ nul/nulle

**dread** *vtr* appréhender (**doing** de faire); (stronger) redouter (**doing** de faire)

**dreadful** *adj* épouvantable, affreux/-euse

**dreadfully** *adv* ⟨disappointed⟩ terriblement; ⟨suffer⟩ affreusement; ⟨behave⟩ abominablement; **I'm ~ sorry** je suis navré

**dream** ① *n* rêve *m* ② *adj* ⟨house, car, vacation⟩ de rêve ③ *vtr* rêver (**that** que) ④ *vi* rêver; **he dreamt about** *or* **of sth/doing** il a rêvé de qch/qu'il faisait; **I wouldn't ~ of selling the house** il ne me viendrait jamais à l'esprit de vendre la maison

■ **dream up** concevoir ⟨idea⟩; imaginer ⟨character, plot⟩

**dreamer** *n* **(a)** (inattentive person) rêveur/-euse *m/f* **(b)** (idealist) idéaliste *mf*

**dreary** *adj* ⟨weather, landscape, life⟩ morne; ⟨person⟩ ennuyeux/-euse

**dredge** *vtr* draguer ⟨river⟩

**dregs** *n pl* (of wine) lie *f*; (of coffee) marc *m*

**drench** *vtr* (in rain, sweat) tremper (**in** de)

**dress** ① *n* **(a)** (garment) robe *f* **(b)** (clothes) tenue *f*; **formal ~** tenue habillée ② *vtr* **(a)** habiller ⟨person⟩; **to get ~ed** s'habiller; **to be ~ed in** être vêtu/-e de **(b)** assaisonner ⟨salad⟩; préparer ⟨meat, fish⟩ **(c)** panser ⟨wound⟩

■ **dress up** (smartly) s'habiller; (in fancy dress) se déguiser (**as** en)

**dress circle** *n* premier balcon *m*

**dresser** *n* **(a)** **to be a stylish ~** s'habiller avec chic **(b)** (for dishes) buffet *m* **(c)** (US) (for clothes) commode-coiffeuse *f*

**dressing** *n* **(a)** (Med) pansement *m* **(b)** (sauce) assaisonnement *m* **(c)** (US) (stuffing) farce *f*

**dressing gown** *n* robe *f* de chambre

**dressing room** *n* loge *f*

**dressing table** *n* coiffeuse *f*

**dressmaker** *n* couturière *f*

**dress rehearsal** *n* (répétition *f*) générale *f*

**dress sense** *n* **to have** ~ s'habiller avec goût

**dribble** ⊡ *n* (of liquid) filet *m*; (of saliva) bave *f*
⊡ *vi* **(a)** ⟨*liquid*⟩ dégouliner (**on, onto** sur; **from** de); ⟨*person*⟩ baver
**(b)** (Sport) dribler

**dried** *adj* ⟨*fruit, herb*⟩ sec/sèche; ⟨*flower, vegetable*⟩ séché/-e; ⟨*milk, egg*⟩ en poudre

**drier** *n* séchoir *m*

**drift** ⊡ *n* **(a)** **the** ~ **of the current** le sens du courant
**(b)** (of snow) congère *f*; (of leaves) tas *m*
**(c)** (meaning) sens *m* (général)
⊡ *vi* **(a)** ⟨*boat*⟩ dériver; ⟨*balloon*⟩ voler à la dérive; ⟨*smoke, fog*⟩ flotter
⟨*snow*⟩ former des congères *fpl*; ⟨*leaves*⟩ s'amonceler
**(c)** **to** ~ **through life** errer sans but dans la vie
■ **drift apart** ⟨*friends*⟩ se perdre de vue; ⟨*lovers*⟩ se détacher progressivement l'un de l'autre

**driftwood** *n* bois *m* flotté

**drill** ⊡ *n* **(a)** (for wood, masonry) perceuse *f*; (for oil) trépan *m*; (for mining) foreuse *f*; (for teeth) roulette *f*
**(b)** (Mil) exercice *m*
**(c)** **fire** ~ exercice *m* d'évacuation en cas d'incendie
⊡ *vtr* **(a)** percer ⟨*hole, metal*⟩; passer la roulette à ⟨*tooth*⟩
**(b)** (Mil) entraîner ⟨*soldiers*⟩
⊡ *vi* **(a)** (in wood, masonry) percer un trou (**into** dans); **to** ~ **for sth** faire des forages pour trouver qch
**(b)** (Mil) ⟨*soldiers*⟩ faire de l'exercice

**drink** ⊡ *n* boisson *f*; **to have a** ~ boire quelque chose; (alcoholic) prendre un verre
⊡ *vtr* boire (**from** dans)
⊡ *vi* boire (**from** dans); **don't** ~ **and drive** ne conduisez pas si vous avez bu

**drinkable** *adj* (safe) potable; (nice) buvable

**drink-driving** *n* (GB) conduite *f* en état d'ivresse

**drinking water** *n* eau *f* potable

**drip** ⊡ *n* **(a)** (drop) goutte *f* (qui tombe)
**(b)** (GB) (Med) **to be on a** ~ être sous perfusion
⊡ *vi* **(a)** ⟨*liquid*⟩ tomber goutte à goutte; **to** ~ **from** *or* **off** dégouliner de
**(b)** ⟨*tap, branches*⟩ goutter; ⟨*washing*⟩ s'égoutter

**drive** ⊡ *n* **(a)** **to go for a** ~ aller faire un tour (en voiture); **it's a 40 km** ~ il y a 40 km de route
**(b)** (campaign) campagne *f* (**against** contre; **for, towards** pour; **to do** pour faire)
**(c)** (motivation) dynamisme *m*
**(d)** (Comput) entraînement *m* de disques
**(e)** (Aut) transmission *f*
**(f)** (*also* ~**way**) allée *f*

**(g)** (Sport) drive *m*
⊡ *vtr* **(a)** conduire ⟨*vehicle, passenger*⟩; piloter ⟨*racing car*⟩; **I** ~ **15 km every day** je fais 15 km en voiture chaque jour; **to** ~ **sth into** rentrer qch dans ⟨*garage, space*⟩
**(b)** (compel) pousser ⟨*person*⟩ (**to do** à faire)
**(c)** (power, propel) actionner ⟨*engine, pump*⟩
**(d) to** ~ **a nail through sth** enfoncer un clou dans qch
⊡ *vi* conduire; **to** ~ **along** rouler; **to** ~ **to work** aller au travail en voiture; **to** ~ **into** entrer dans ⟨*car park*⟩; rentrer dans ⟨*tree*⟩
■ **drive back (a)** repousser ⟨*people, animals*⟩
**(b)** ramener ⟨*passenger*⟩

**drive-by shooting** *n* attaque *f* criminelle (exécutée d'une voiture en marche)

**driver** *n* **(a)** conducteur/-trice *m/f*; ~**s** (motorists) automobilistes *mfpl*
**(b)** (of taxi) chauffeur *m*

**driver's license** *n* (US) permis *m* de conduire

**driving** ⊡ *n* conduite *f*
⊡ *adj* ⟨*rain*⟩ battant/-e; ⟨*wind, hail*⟩ cinglant/-e

**driving force** *n* (person) force *f* agissante (**behind** de); (money, ambition) moteur *m* (**behind** de)

**driving instructor** *n* moniteur/-trice *m/f* d'auto-école

**driving lesson** *n* leçon *f* de conduite

**driving licence** *n* (GB) permis *m* de conduire

**driving school** *n* auto-école *f*

**driving seat** *n* place *f* du conducteur
IDIOMS **to be in the** ~ être aux commandes

**driving test** *n* examen *m* du permis de conduire; **to take/pass one's** ~ passer/ réussir son permis (de conduire)

**drizzle** ⊡ *n* bruine *f*
⊡ *vi* bruiner

**drone** *n* **(a)** (of engine) ronronnement *m*; (of insects) bourdonnement *m*
**(b)** (Zool) faux bourdon *m*

**drool** *vi* baver; **to** ~ **over sb/sth** s'extasier sur qn/qch

**droop** *vi* ⟨*eyelids, head, shoulders*⟩ tomber; ⟨*plant*⟩ commencer à se faner

**drop** ⊡ *n* **(a)** (of liquid) goutte *f*
**(b)** (decrease) baisse *f* (**in** de); **a 5%** ~ **in sth** une baisse de 5% de qch
**(c)** (fall) **there's a** ~ **of 100 m** il y a un dénivelé de 100 m; **a steep** ~ **on either side** une pente abrupte de chaque côté; **a sheer** ~ un à-pic
**(d)** (delivery) (from aircraft) largage *m*
⊡ *vtr* **(a)** (by accident) laisser tomber; (on purpose) lâcher
**(b)** ⟨*aircraft*⟩ parachuter ⟨*person, supplies*⟩; larguer ⟨*bomb*⟩
**(c)** (*also* ~ **off**) déposer ⟨*person, object*⟩
**(d)** (lower) baisser ⟨*eyes, voice, level, price*⟩
**(e) to** ~ **a hint about sth** faire allusion à qch; **to** ~ **sb a line** envoyer un mot à qn

**(f)** laisser tomber ⟨*friend, school subject*⟩; renoncer à ⟨*habit, idea*⟩

**3** *vi* **(a)** (fall) ⟨*object*⟩ tomber; ⟨*person*⟩ (deliberately) se laisser tomber; (by accident) tomber; **the plane ∼ped to an altitude of 1,000 m** l'avion est descendu à une altitude de 1 000 m

**(b)** (decrease) baisser; **to ∼ (from sth) to sth** tomber (de qch) à qch

**IDIOMS a ∼ in the ocean** une goutte d'eau dans la mer

■ **drop in** passer; **to ∼ in on sb** passer voir qn

■ **drop off (a)** (fall off) tomber
**(b)** ∼ **off (to sleep)** s'endormir
**(c)** (decrease) diminuer

■ **drop out (a)** (fall out) tomber (of de)
**(b)** (from race) se désister; (from project) se retirer; (from school, university) abandonner ses études; (from society) se marginaliser

**drop-dead** *adv* (colloq) ∼ **gorgeous** super beau/belle (colloq)

**drop-down menu** *n* menu *m* déroulant

**dropout** *n* marginal/-e *m/f*

**droppings** *n pl* (of mouse, sheep) crottes *fpl*; (of horse) crottin *m*; (of bird) fiente *f*

**drop shot** *n* (Sport) amorti *m*

**drought** *n* sécheresse *f*

**drown** **1** *vtr* **(a)** noyer ⟨*person, animal*⟩
**(b)** (*also* ∼ **out**) couvrir ⟨*sound*⟩
**2** *vi* se noyer
**IDIOMS to ∼ one's sorrows** noyer son chagrin dans l'alcool

**drowning** *n* noyade *f*

**drowsy** *adj* à moitié endormi/-e; **to feel ∼** avoir envie de dormir

**drug** **1** *n* **(a)** (Med) médicament *m*; **to be on ∼s** prendre des médicaments
**(b)** (narcotic) drogue *f*; **to be on** *or* **to take ∼s** (gen) se droguer; ⟨*athlete*⟩ se doper
**2** *vtr* administrer des somnifères à ⟨*person*⟩

**drug abuse** *n* consommation *f* de stupéfiants

**drug addict** *n* toxicomane *mf*

**drug addiction** *n* toxicomanie *f*

**drugged** *adj* ⟨*person*⟩ drogué/-e; ⟨*drink*⟩ additionné/-e d'un narcotique

**drug habit** *n* accoutumance *f* à la drogue

**drug mule** *n* mule *f*

**drugs raid** *n* opération *f* antidrogue

**drugstore** *n* (US) drugstore *m*

**drug-taking** *n* usage *m* de stupéfiants; (in sport) dopage *m*.

**drug test** *n* (Sport) contrôle *m* antidopage

**drug user** *n* toxicomane *mf*

**drum** **1** *n* **(a)** (Mus) tambour *m*
**(b)** (barrel) bidon *m*; (larger) baril *m*
**2 drums** *n pl* batterie *f*; **to play ∼s** jouer de la batterie
**3** *vtr* **to ∼ one's fingers** tambouriner des doigts (on sur); **to ∼ sth into sb** enfoncer qch dans le crâne de qn (colloq)

■ **drum up** trouver ⟨*business*⟩; racoler ⟨*customers*⟩

**drummer** *n* (in army) tambour *m*; (jazz or pop) batteur *m*; (classical) percussionniste *mf*

**drumstick** *n* **(a)** (Mus) baguette *f* de tambour
**(b)** (of chicken, turkey) pilon *m*

**drunk** **1** *n* (*also* **drunkard**) ivrogne *m*
**2** *adj* ivre; **to get ∼** s'enivrer (**on** de)

**drunken** *adj* ⟨*person*⟩ ivre; ⟨*party*⟩ bien arrosé/-e; ⟨*sleep*⟩ éthylique; ⟨*state*⟩ d'ivresse

**dry** **1** *adj* **(a)** sec/sèche; **to keep sth ∼** tenir qch au sec; **on ∼ land** sur la terre ferme; **a ∼ day** un jour sans pluie
**(b)** ⟨*wit, person, remark*⟩ pince-sans-rire *inv*; ⟨*book*⟩ aride
**2** *vtr* faire sécher ⟨*clothes, washing*⟩; sécher ⟨*meat, produce*⟩; **to ∼ the dishes** essuyer la vaisselle; **to ∼ one's hands** se sécher les mains
**3** *vi* ⟨*clothes, washing*⟩ sécher

■ **dry out (a)** ⟨*cloth*⟩ sécher; ⟨*plant*⟩ se dessécher
**(b)** (colloq) ⟨*alcoholic*⟩ se faire désintoxiquer

■ **dry up:** ¶ ∼ **up (a)** ⟨*river, well*⟩ s'assécher
**(b)** (run out) se tarir
**(c)** (dry the dishes) essuyer la vaisselle
¶ ∼ **[sth] up** essuyer ⟨*dishes*⟩

**dry-clean** *vtr* **to have sth ∼ed** faire nettoyer qch (chez le teinturier)

**dry-cleaner's** *n* teinturerie *f*

**dryer** *n* séchoir *m*

**DTP** *n* (*abbr* = **desktop publishing**) PAO *f*

**dual** *adj* double

**dual carriageway** *n* (GB) route *f* à quatre voies

**dual nationality** *n* double nationalité *f*

**dub** *vtr* (into foreign language) doubler (**into** en); ∼**bed film** film doublé

**dubious** *adj* ⟨*reputation, answer*⟩ douteux/-euse; ⟨*claim*⟩ suspect/-e

**duchess** *n* duchesse *f*

**duck** **1** *n* canard *m*
**2** *vtr* **(a)** **to ∼ one's head** baisser vivement la tête
**(b)** (dodge) esquiver ⟨*blow*⟩
**(c)** se dérober de ⟨*responsibility*⟩
**3** *vi* baisser vivement la tête; ⟨*boxer*⟩ esquiver un coup; **to ∼ behind** se cacher derrière

**duckling** *n* caneton *m*

**duct** *n* **(a)** (for air, water) conduit *m*; (for wiring) canalisation *f*
**(b)** (Anat, Med) conduit *m*

**dud** *adj* (colloq) ⟨*banknote*⟩ faux/fausse (*before n*); ⟨*cheque*⟩ en bois (colloq); ⟨*book, movie*⟩ nul/nulle (colloq)

**due** **1** *n* dû *m*; **I must give her her ∼, she...** il faut lui rendre cette justice, elle...
**2** *adj* **(a)** ( payable) **to be/fall ∼** arriver/venir à échéance; **the rent is ∼ on the 6th** le loyer doit être payé le 6; **the balance ∼** le solde dû ⋯▸

(b) (owed) the respect ~ to him le respect auquel il a droit, le respect qu'on lui doit
(c) we are ~ (for) a wage increase soon nos salaires doivent bientôt être augmentés
(d) after ~ consideration après mûre réflexion; in ~ course (at the proper time) en temps voulu; (later) plus tard
(e) to be ~ to do devoir faire; to be ~ (in) ‹train, bus› être attendu/-e; ‹person› devoir arriver
**3** adv to face ~ north ‹building› être orienté/-e plein nord; to go ~ south aller droit vers le sud
**4** due to phr en raison de; to be ~ to ‹delay, cancellation› être dû/due à; ~ to unforeseen circumstances pour des raisons indépendantes de notre volonté

**dues** n pl (for membership) cotisation f; (for import, taxes) droits mpl

**duet** n duo m

**duffel bag** n sac m (de) marin

**duffel coat** n duffle-coat m

**duke** n duc m

**dull** **1** adj (a) ‹person, book› ennuyeux/-euse; ‹life, journey› monotone; ‹appearance› triste; ‹weather› maussade
(b) ‹eye, colour, complexion› terne
**2** vtr ternir ‹shine›; émousser ‹blade, pain›

**duly** adv (in proper fashion) dûment; (as expected, as arranged) comme prévu

**dumb** adj (a) muet/muette; to be struck ~ rester muet/muette (with de)
(b) (colloq) (stupid) ‹person› bête; ‹question, idea› idiot/-e

**dumb down** vtr abaisser le niveau intellectuel de ‹course, programme›

**dumbfounded** adj abasourdi/-e

**dummy** **1** n (a) (model) mannequin m
(b) (GB) (for baby) tétine f
**2** adj faux/fausse

**dummy run** n (trial) essai m

**dump** **1** n (a) (for rubbish) décharge f publique
(b) (Mil) arms ~ dépôt m d'armes
(c) (colloq) (town, village) trou m (colloq); (house) baraque f (colloq) minable
**2** vtr (a) jeter ‹refuse›; ensevelir ‹nuclear waste›; déverser ‹sewage›
(b) (colloq) plaquer (colloq) ‹boyfriend›; se débarrasser de ‹car›
IDIOMS to be down in the ~s (colloq) avoir le cafard (colloq)

**dumper (truck), dump truck** n tombereau m

**dunce** n cancre m (at, in en)

**dune** n dune f

**dung** n (for manure) fumier m

**dungarees** n pl (fashionwear) salopette f; (workwear) bleu m de travail

**Dunkirk** pr n Dunkerque

**duo** n duo m

**duplicate** **1** n (of document) double m (of de); (of painting, cassette) copie f
**2** adj (a) ‹cheque, receipt› en duplicata; a ~ key un double de clé
(b) (in two parts) ‹form, invoice› en deux exemplaires
**3** vtr (a) (copy) faire un double de ‹document›; copier ‹painting, cassette›
(b) (photocopy) photocopier

**durable** adj ‹material› résistant/-e; ‹equipment› solide; ‹friendship, tradition› durable

**duration** n durée f

**duress** n under ~ sous la contrainte

**during** prep pendant, au cours de

**dusk** n nuit f tombante, crépuscule m; at ~ à la nuit tombante

**dust** **1** n poussière f
**2** vtr épousseter ‹furniture›; saupoudrer ‹cake› (with de, avec)

**dustbin** n (GB) poubelle f

**dust cover** n (on book) jaquette f; (on furniture) housse f (de protection)

**duster** n chiffon m (à poussière)

**dustman** n (GB) éboueur m

**dustpan** n pelle f (à poussière)

**dusty** adj poussiéreux/-euse

**Dutch** **1** n (a) (people) the ~ les Néerlandais mpl
(b) (language) néerlandais m
**2** adj (gen) néerlandais/-e; ‹embassy› des Pays-Bas
IDIOMS to go ~ (colloq) payer chacun sa part; to go ~ with sb (colloq) faire fifty-fifty avec qn (colloq)

**duty** n (a) (obligation) devoir m (to envers); in the course of ~ (Mil) en service; (gen) dans l'exercice de ses fonctions
(b) (task) fonction f; to take up one's duties prendre ses fonctions
(c) (work) service m; to be on/off ~ (Mil, Med) être/ne pas être de service; (Sch) être/ne pas être de surveillance
(d) (tax) taxe f; customs duties droits mpl de douane

**duty-free** adj, adv hors taxe(s)

**duvet** n (GB) couette f

**duvet cover** n housse f de couette

**DVD** n (abbr = **digital video disc**) DVD m

**dwarf** n, adj nain/naine (m/f)

**dwell** v ■ dwell on (talk about) s'étendre sur; (think about) s'attarder sur

**dwindle** vi diminuer

**dye** **1** n teinture f
**2** vtr teindre; to ~ sth red teindre qch en rouge; to ~ one's hair se teindre les cheveux

**dying** adj ‹person, animal› mourant/-e; ‹art› en voie de disparition

**dyke** n (a) (on coast) digue f; (beside ditch) remblai m
(b) (GB) (ditch) fossé m

**dynamic** adj dynamique

**dynamite** n dynamite f

**dynamo** n (a) dynamo f

**(b)** (colloq) **he's a real** ~ il déborde d'énergie
**dysentery** n dysenterie f
**dysfunctional** adj dysfonctionnel/-elle

**dyslexia** n dyslexie f

**dyslexic** n, adj dyslexique (mf)

# Ee

**e, E** n **(a)** (letter) e, E m
**(b)** E (Mus) mi m
**(c)** E (drug) ecstasy m

**each** **1** det ⟨person, group, object⟩ chaque inv; ~ **morning** chaque matin, tous les matins; ~ **one** chacun/-e
**2** pron chacun/-e m/f; ~ **of you** chacun/-e de vous, chacun/-e d'entre vous; **oranges at 30p** ~ des oranges à 30 pence (la) pièce
**each other** pron

■ Note each other is very often translated by using a reflexive pronoun (nous, vous, se, s').

(also **one another**) **they know** ~ ils se connaissent; **to help** ~ s'entraider; **kept apart from** ~ séparés l'un de l'autre

**eager** adj ⟨person, acceptance⟩ enthousiaste; ⟨face⟩ où se lit l'enthousiasme; ⟨student⟩ plein d'enthousiasme; ~ **to do** (keen) désireux/-euse de faire; (impatient) pressé/-e de faire; ~ **for sth** avide de qch; **to be** ~ **to please** chercher à faire plaisir

**eagle** n aigle m

**ear** n **(a)** oreille f
**(b)** (of wheat, corn) épi m
**IDIOMS to play it by** ~ improviser

**earache** n **to have** ~ (GB) or **an** ~ avoir une otite

**eardrum** n tympan m

**earl** n comte m

**early** **1** adj **(a)** (one of the first) ⟨years, novels⟩ premier/-ière (before n); ~ **man** les premiers hommes
**(b)** ⟨delivery⟩ rapide; ⟨vegetable, fruit⟩ précoce; **to have an** ~ **lunch/night** déjeuner/ se coucher tôt; **in** ~ **childhood** dans la petite or première enfance; **at an** ~ **age** à un très jeune âge; **to be in one's** ~ **thirties** avoir entre 30 et 35 ans; **at the earliest** au plus tôt; **in the** ~ **spring** au début du printemps; **in the** ~ **afternoon** en début d'après-midi
**2** adv **(a)** tôt; **to get up** ~ se lever tôt or de bonne heure; **it's too** ~ il est trop tôt; **as I said earlier** comme je l'ai déjà dit
**(b)** (sooner than expected) en avance; **I'm a bit** ~ je suis un peu en avance

**early retirement** n retraite f anticipée

**earmark** vtr désigner ⟨person, money, site⟩

**earn** vtr **(a)** ⟨person⟩ gagner ⟨money⟩; ⟨investment⟩ rapporter ⟨interest⟩; **to** ~ **a** or **one's living** gagner sa vie

**(b) to** ~ **sb's respect** se faire respecter de qn

**earner** n salarié/-e m/f

**earnest** **1** n **in** ~ ⟨speak⟩ sérieusement; ⟨begin⟩ vraiment, pour de bon
**2** adj ⟨person⟩ sérieux/-ieuse; ⟨wish⟩ sincère

**earning power** n capacité f de gain

**earnings** n pl (of person) salaire m, revenu m (from de); (of company) gains mpl (from de); (from shares) (taux m de) rendement m

**earphones** n pl (over ears) casque m; (in ears) écouteurs mpl

**earring** n boucle f d'oreille

**earth** **1** n **(a)** terre f
**(b)** (colloq) **how/where/who on** ~...? comment/où/qui donc or diable (colloq)...?; **nothing on** ~ **would persuade me to come** je ne viendrais pour rien au monde
**2** vtr (GB) mettre [qch] à la terre

**earthenware** n faïence f

**earthquake** n tremblement m de terre

**earth tremor** n secousse f sismique

**earwig** n perce-oreille m

**ease** **1** n **(a)** (lack of difficulty) facilité f
**(b) to feel/to be at** ~ se sentir/être à l'aise; **to put sb's mind at** ~ rassurer qn (about à propos de)
**2** vtr **(a)** atténuer ⟨pain, tension, pressure⟩; réduire ⟨congestion⟩; diminuer ⟨burden⟩
**(b)** faciliter ⟨communication, transition⟩
**(c) to** ~ **sth into** introduire qch délicatement dans
**3** vi ⟨tension, pain, pressure⟩ s'atténuer; ⟨rain⟩ diminuer
■ **ease off** ⟨business⟩ ralentir; ⟨demand⟩ se réduire; ⟨traffic, rain⟩ diminuer; ⟨person⟩ relâcher son effort
■ **ease up** ⟨tense person, storm⟩ se calmer; ⟨authorities⟩ relâcher la discipline; **to** ~ **up on sb/on sth** être moins sévère envers qn/ pour qch

**easel** n chevalet m

**easily** adv facilement; **it's** ~ **the best** c'est de loin le meilleur; **she could** ~ **die** elle pourrait bien mourir

**east** **1** n **(a)** (compass direction) est m
**(b) the East** (Orient) l'Orient m; (part of country) l'Est m
**2** adj (gen) est inv; ⟨wind⟩ d'est

⸳⸳⸳⟩

**3** *adv* ⟨*move*⟩ vers l'est; ⟨*live, lie*⟩ à l'est (of de)

**Easter** **1** *n* Pâques *m*; **at ∼** à Pâques; **Happy ∼** Joyeuses Pâques
**2** *adj* ⟨*Sunday, egg*⟩ de Pâques

**eastern** *adj* (a) ⟨*coast*⟩ est *inv*; ⟨*town, accent*⟩ de l'est; **Eastern Europe** l'Europe de l'Est; **∼ France** l'est de la France
(b) (*also* **Eastern**) (oriental) oriental/-e

**East Timor** *pr n* Timor *m* oriental

**easy** **1** *adj* (a) ⟨*job, question, life, victim*⟩ facile; **it's ∼ to do** c'est facile à faire; **it's ∼ to make a mistake** il est facile de se tromper; **it isn't ∼ to do** ce n'est pas facile à faire; **it isn't ∼ to park** il n'est pas facile de se garer; **to make it** *or* **things easier** faciliter les choses (**for** pour)
(b) (relaxed) ⟨*smile, grace*⟩ décontracté/-e; ⟨*style*⟩ plein/-e d'aisance; **at an ∼ pace** d'un pas tranquille
(c) (colloq) **I'm ∼** ça m'est égal
**2** *adv* (a) **to take it** *or* **things ∼** ne pas s'en faire
(b) (colloq) **to go ∼ on** *or* **with** y aller doucement avec

**easygoing** *adj* ⟨*person*⟩ accommodant/-e; ⟨*manner, attitude*⟩ souple

**easy terms** *n pl* facilités *fpl* de paiement

**eat** **1** *vtr* manger ⟨*food*⟩; prendre ⟨*meal*⟩
**2** *vi* manger
■ **eat out** aller au restaurant

**eating disorder** *n* trouble *m* du comportement alimentaire

**eating habits** *n pl* habitudes *fpl* alimentaires

**eavesdrop** *vi* écouter aux portes

**ebb** **1** *n* reflux *m*
**2** *vi* ⟨*tide*⟩ descendre; ⟨*enthusiasm*⟩ décliner

**ebony** *n* (a) (wood) ébène *f*
(b) (colour) noir *m* d'ébène

**EC** *n* (*abbr* = **European Community**) CE *f*

**e-cash** *n* argent *m* électronique, argent *m* virtuel

**eccentric** *n, adj* excentrique (*mf*)

**ECG** *n* (*abbr* = **electrocardiogram**) ECG *m*

**echo** **1** *n* écho *m*
**2** *vtr* (a) répercuter ⟨*sound*⟩
(b) reprendre ⟨*ideas, opinions*⟩
**3** *vi* retentir, résonner

**eclipse** **1** *n* éclipse *f* (of de)
**2** *vtr* éclipser

**eco-friendly** *adj* qui ne nuit pas à l'environnement

**ecological** *adj* écologique

**ecologist** *n, adj* écologiste (*mf*)

**ecology** *n* écologie *f*

**e-commerce** *n* commerce *m* électronique

**economic** *adj* (gen) économique; (profitable) rentable

**economical** *adj* ⟨*person*⟩ économe; ⟨*machine, method*⟩ économique

**economics** *n* (science) économie *f*; (subject of study) sciences *fpl* économiques; (financial aspects) aspects *mpl* économiques (of de)

**economist** *n* économiste *mf*

**economize** *vtr, vi* économiser

**economy** *n* économie *f*

**economy class** *n* classe *f* économique

**economy drive** *n* campagne *f* de restriction

**eco-warrior** *n* éco-guerrier/-ière *m/f*

**ecstasy** *n* (a) extase *f*
(b) (drug) ecstasy *m*

**ecu, ECU** *n* (*abbr* = **European Currency Unit**) écu *m*, ÉCU *m*

**eczema** *n* eczéma *m*

**Eden** *pr n* Éden *m*, paradis *m* terrestre

**edge** **1** *n* (a) (outer limit) bord *m*; (of wood, clearing) lisière *f*; **the film had us on the ∼ of our seats** le film nous a tenus en haleine
(b) (of blade) tranchant *m*
(c) (of book, plank) tranche *f*
(d) **to be on ∼** ⟨*person*⟩ être énervé/-e
**2** *vi* **to ∼ forward** avancer doucement; **to ∼ towards** s'approcher à petits pas de

**edgeways, edgewise** *adv* ⟨*move*⟩ latéralement; ⟨*lay, put*⟩ sur le côté
IDIOMS **I can't get a word in ∼** je n'arrive pas à placer un mot

**edible** *adj* comestible

**Edinburgh** *pr n* Édimbourg

**edit** *vtr* (a) (in publishing) éditer
(b) (cut) couper ⟨*text, version*⟩
(c) monter ⟨*film, programme*⟩

**edition** *n* édition *f*

**editor** *n* (of newspaper) rédacteur/-trice *m/f* en chef (of de); (of book, manuscript) correcteur/-trice *m/f*; (of writer, works, anthology) éditeur/-trice *m/f*; (of film) monteur/-euse *m/f*

**editorial** **1** *n* éditorial *m* (on sur)
**2** *adj* (a) (in journalism) de la rédaction, rédactionnel/-elle
(b) (in publishing) éditorial/-e

**educate** *vtr* (a) ⟨*teacher*⟩ instruire; ⟨*parent*⟩ assurer l'instruction de; **to be ∼d in Paris** faire ses études à Paris
(b) informer ⟨*public*⟩ (**about, in** sur)

**educated** *adj* ⟨*person, classes*⟩ instruit/-e; ⟨*accent*⟩ élégant/-e

**education** *n* (a) éducation *f*, instruction *f*; **health ∼** hygiène *f*
(b) (formal schooling) études *fpl*; **to have had a university** *or* **college ∼** avoir fait des études supérieures
(c) (national system) enseignement *m*

**educational** *adj* (a) ⟨*establishment*⟩ d'enseignement
(b) ⟨*game, programme*⟩ éducatif/-ive; ⟨*talk*⟩ instructif/-ive

**EEC** *n* (*abbr* = **European Economic Community**) CEE *f*

**eel** *n* anguille *f*

**eerie** *adj* ⟨*silence, place*⟩ étrange et inquiétant/-e

**effect** ⟦1⟧ *n* **(a)** effet *m* (of de; on sur); **to take ~** ⟨*price increases*⟩ prendre effet; ⟨*pills, anaesthetic*⟩ commencer à agir; **to come into ~** ⟨*law, rate*⟩ entrer en vigueur; **she dresses like that for ~** elle s'habille comme ça pour faire de l'effet
**(b)** (repercussions) répercussions *fpl* (of de; on sur)
⟦2⟧ **effects** *n pl* effets *mpl*
⟦3⟧ *vtr* effectuer ⟨*repair, sale, change*⟩
⟦4⟧ **in effect** *phr* en fait, en réalité
**effective** *adj* efficace
**effectively** *adv* **(a)** (efficiently) efficacement
**(b)** (in effect) en fait, en réalité
**effeminate** *adj* efféminé/-e
**efficiency** *n* (of person, method, organization) efficacité *f* (**in doing** à faire); (of machine) rendement *m*
**efficient** *adj* **(a)** ⟨*person, management*⟩ efficace (**at doing** pour ce qui est de faire)
**(b)** ⟨*machine*⟩ économique
**effort** *n* effort *m*; **to make the ~** faire l'effort; **to spare no ~** ne pas ménager ses efforts; **to be worth the ~** en valoir la peine; **it is an ~ to do** il est pénible de faire
**EFL** *n* (*abbr* = **English as a Foreign Language**) anglais *m* langue étrangère
**eg** (*abbr* = **exempli gratia**) par ex
**egalitarian** *adj* égalitaire
**egg** *n* œuf *m*
■ **egg on** pousser ⟨*person*⟩
**eggcup** *n* coquetier *m*
**eggplant** *n* (US) aubergine *f*
**egg white** *n* blanc *m* d'œuf
**egg yolk** *n* jaune *m* d'œuf
**ego** *n* **(a)** amour-propre *m*; **it boosted his ~** ça lui a redonné confiance en lui-même
**(b)** (in psychology) moi *m*, ego *m*
**egoism** *n* égoïsme *m*
**egoist** *n* égoïste *mf*
**egotist** *n* égotiste *mf*
**Egypt** *pr n* Égypte *f*
**eiderdown** *n* édredon *m*
**eight** *n, pron, det* huit (*m*) *inv*
**eighteen** *n, pron, det* dix-huit (*m*) *inv*
**eighteenth** ⟦1⟧ *n* **(a)** (in order) dix-huitième *mf*
**(b)** (of month) dix-huit *m inv*
**(c)** (fraction) dix-huitième *m*
⟦2⟧ *adj, adv* dix-huitième
**eighth** ⟦1⟧ *n* **(a)** (in order) huitième *mf*
**(b)** (of month) huit *m inv*
**(c)** (fraction) huitième *m*
⟦2⟧ *adj, adv* huitième
**eighties** *n pl* **(a)** (era) **the ~** les années *fpl* quatre-vingt
**(b)** (age) **to be in one's ~** avoir entre quatre-vingts et quatre-vingt-dix ans
**eightieth** *n, adj, adv* quatre-vingtième (*mf*)
**eighty** *n, pron, det* quatre-vingts (*m*)
**eighty-one** *n, pron, det* quatre-vingt-un (*m*)

**Éire** *pr n* Éire *f*, République *f* d'Irlande
**either** ⟦1⟧ *pron, quantif* **(a)** (one or other) l'un/-e ou l'autre; **take ~ (of them)** prends l'un/-e ou l'autre; **I don't like ~ (of them)** je n'aime ni l'un/-e ni l'autre; **'which book do you want?'—'~'** 'quel livre veux-tu?'— 'n'importe'
**(b)** (both) **~ of the two is possible** les deux sont possibles
⟦2⟧ *det* **(a)** (one or other) n'importe lequel/ laquelle; **take ~ road** prenez n'importe laquelle des deux routes; **I can't see ~ child** je ne vois aucun des deux enfants
**(b)** (both) **in ~ case** dans un cas comme dans l'autre; **~ way, it will be difficult** de toute manière, ce sera difficile
⟦3⟧ *adv* non plus; **I can't do it ~** je ne peux pas le faire non plus
⟦4⟧ *conj* **(a)** (as alternatives) **~...or...** soit...soit..., (ou)...ou...
**(b)** (in the negative) **I wouldn't believe ~ Patrick or Emily** je ne croirais ni Patrick ni Emily
**eject** ⟦1⟧ *vtr* **(a)** ⟨*machine, system*⟩ rejeter ⟨*waste*⟩; ⟨*volcano*⟩ cracher ⟨*lava*⟩
**(b)** faire sortir ⟨*cassette*⟩
**(c)** expulser ⟨*troublemaker*⟩
⟦2⟧ *vi* ⟨*pilot*⟩ s'éjecter
**eject button** *n* touche *f* d'éjection
**eke** *v* ■ **eke out** faire durer ⟨*income, supplies*⟩ (**by** à force de; **by doing** en faisant); **to ~ out a living** essayer de joindre les deux bouts
**elaborate** ⟦1⟧ *adj* ⟨*excuse*⟩ compliqué/-e; ⟨*network, plan*⟩ complexe; ⟨*design*⟩ travaillé/-e; ⟨*painting, sculpture*⟩ ouvragé/-e
⟦2⟧ *vtr* élaborer ⟨*theory*⟩
⟦3⟧ *vi* entrer dans les détails; **to ~ on** s'étendre sur ⟨*proposal*⟩; développer ⟨*remark*⟩
**elapse** *vi* s'écouler
**elastic** *n, adj* élastique (*m*)
**elasticated** *adj* élastique
**elastic band** *n* élastique *m*
**elated** *adj* transporté/-e de joie
**elbow** *n* coude *m*
**elbow grease** *n* huile *f* de coude (colloq)
**elbowroom** *n* (room to move) espace *m* vital; (figurative) marge *f* de manœuvre
**elder** ⟦1⟧ *n* **(a)** (older person) aîné/-e *m/f*; (of tribe, group) ancien *m*
**(b)** (tree) sureau *m*
⟦2⟧ *adj* aîné/-e; **the ~ girl** l'aînée *f*, la fille aînée
**elderly** ⟦1⟧ *n* **the ~** les personnes *fpl* âgées
⟦2⟧ *adj* ⟨*person, population*⟩ âgé/-e
**eldest** ⟦1⟧ *n* aîné/-e *m/f*
⟦2⟧ *adj* aîné/-e; **the ~ child** l'aîné/-e
**elect** *vtr* **(a)** (by vote) élire (**from, from among** parmi)
**(b)** (choose) choisir (**to do** de faire)
**election** *n* élection *f*, scrutin *m*; **to win an ~** gagner aux élections

**election campaign** n campagne f électorale

**electoral** adj électoral/-e

**electorate** n électorat m, électeurs mpl

**electric** adj électrique

**electrical** adj électrique

**electric blanket** n couverture f chauffante

**electrician** n électricien/-ienne m/f

**electricity** n électricité f; **to turn off/on the ~** couper/rétablir le courant (électrique)

**electric shock** n décharge f électrique

**electrify** vtr (a) électrifier ⟨railway⟩ (b) électriser ⟨audience⟩

**electrocute** vtr électrocuter

**electronic** adj électronique

**electronic engineer** n électronicien/-ienne m/f

**electronic organizer** n ordinateur m de poche

**electronic publishing** n éditique f

**electronics** n électronique f

**electronic tagging** n marquage m électronique (des criminels)

**elegant** adj ⟨person, clothes, gesture⟩ élégant/-e; ⟨manners⟩ distingué/-e; ⟨restaurant⟩ chic

**element** n (a) élément m; **an ~ of luck** une part de chance (b) (in heater, kettle) résistance f

**elementary** adj (a) (basic) élémentaire (b) ⟨school⟩ primaire; ⟨teacher⟩ de primaire

**elephant** n éléphant m

**elevate** vtr élever (**to** au rang de)

**elevated** adj ⟨language, rank, style⟩ élevé/-e; ⟨railway, canal⟩ surélevé/-e

**elevator** n (a) (US) (lift) ascenseur m (b) (hoist) élévateur m

**eleven** n, pron, det onze (m) inv

**eleventh** ① n (a) (in order) onzième mf (b) (of month) onze m inv (c) (fraction) onzième m ② adj, adv onzième

**elf** n lutin m

**eligible** adj **to be ~ for** avoir droit à ⟨allowance, benefit, membership⟩; **to be ~ to do** être en droit de faire

**eliminate** vtr (gen) éliminer; écarter ⟨suspect⟩

**elimination** n élimination f; **by a process of ~** en procédant par élimination

**élite** ① n élite f ② adj ⟨group, minority⟩ élitaire; ⟨restaurant, club⟩ réservé/-e à l'élite; ⟨squad⟩ d'élite

**elm** n orme m

**elongated** adj allongé/-e

**elope** vi s'enfuir (**with** avec)

**eloquent** adj éloquent/-e

**else** ① adv d'autre; **somebody/nothing ~** quelqu'un/rien d'autre; **something ~** autre chose; **somewhere** or **someplace** (US) **~**

ailleurs; **how ~ can we do it?** comment le faire autrement?; **what ~ would you like?** qu'est-ce que tu voudrais d'autre? ② **or else** phr sinon

**elsewhere** adv ailleurs

**elusive** adj ⟨person, animal, happiness⟩ insaisissable; ⟨prize, victory⟩ hors d'atteinte

**emaciated** adj ⟨person, feature⟩ émacié/-e; ⟨limb, body⟩ décharné/-e; ⟨animal⟩ étique

**e-mail, email** ① n (medium) e-mail m, courrier m électronique; (item of mail) e-mail m, message m électronique ② vtr envoyer un e-mail à ⟨person⟩; envoyer [qch] par e-mail ⟨document⟩

**e-mail address** n adresse f électronique

**emancipate** vtr émanciper

**emancipation** n émancipation f

**embalm** vtr embaumer

**embankment** n (a) (for railway, road) remblai m (b) (by river) quai m, digue f

**embargo** n embargo m

**embark** vi (a) (on ship) s'embarquer (**for** pour) (b) **to ~ on** entreprendre ⟨journey⟩; se lancer dans ⟨career, process, project⟩

**embarkation** n embarquement m

**embarrass** vtr plonger [qn] dans l'embarras; **to be/to feel ~ed** être/se sentir gêné/-e

**embarrassing** adj embarrassant/-e

**embarrassment** n confusion f, gêne f (**about**, **at** devant); **to my ~** à ma grande confusion

**embassy** n ambassade f

**embers** n pl braises fpl

**embezzle** vtr détourner ⟨funds⟩ (**from** de)

**emblem** n emblème m

**embody** vtr incarner ⟨virtue, evil, ideal⟩

**embrace** ① n étreinte f ② vtr (a) (hug) étreindre (b) (include) comprendre ③ vi s'étreindre

**embroider** ① vtr (a) broder (**with** de) (b) embellir ⟨story, truth⟩ ② vi broder, faire de la broderie

**embroidery** n broderie f

**embryo** n embryon m

**emerald** n (a) (stone) émeraude f (b) (colour) émeraude m

**emerge** vi (a) ⟨person, animal⟩ sortir (**from** de) (b) ⟨problem, result⟩ se faire jour; ⟨pattern⟩ se dégager; ⟨truth⟩ apparaître

**emergency** ① n (gen) cas m d'urgence; (Med) urgence f; **in an ~, in case of ~** en cas d'urgence; **it's an ~** c'est urgent ② adj ⟨plan, repairs, call, stop⟩ d'urgence; ⟨brakes, vehicle⟩ de secours

**emergency exit** n sortie f de secours

**emergency landing** n atterrissage m d'urgence

**emergency services** n pl (police)

≈ police *f* secours; (ambulance) service *m* d'aide médicale d'urgence; (fire brigade) (sapeurs-)pompiers *mpl*

**emergency worker** *n* secouriste *mf*

**emigrant** *n* (about to leave) émigrant/-e *m/f*; (settled elsewhere) émigré/-e *m/f*

**emigrate** *vi* émigrer

**emission** *n* émission *f* (from provenant de)

**emit** *vtr* émettre

**emoticon** *n* (Comput) émoticône *f*, smiley *m* (colloq)

**emotion** *n* émotion *f*

**emotional** *adj* ⟨problem⟩ émotif/-ive; ⟨reaction⟩ émotionnel/-elle; ⟨tie, response⟩ affectif/-ive; ⟨speech⟩ passionné/-e; **to feel** ~ être ému/-e (**about** par); **she's rather** ~ elle est assez émotive

**emotionally** *adv* ⟨speak, react⟩ avec émotion; ~ **deprived** privé/-e d'affection; ~ **disturbed** caractériel/-ielle

**emotive** *adj* ⟨issue⟩ qui soulève les passions; ⟨word⟩ chargé/-e de connotations

**empathize** *vi* **to** ~ **with** s'identifier à ⟨person⟩

**emperor** *n* empereur *m*

**emphasis** *n* accent *m*; **to lay** *or* **put the** ~ **on sth** mettre l'accent sur qch

**emphasize** *vtr* mettre l'accent sur ⟨policy, need⟩; mettre [qch] en valeur ⟨eyes⟩

**emphatic** *adj* ⟨statement⟩ catégorique; ⟨voice, manner⟩ énergique; **to be** ~ **about** insister sur

**empire** *n* empire *m*

**employ** *vtr* (a) employer ⟨person, company⟩ (**as** en qualité de); **to be** ~**ed** avoir un emploi
(b) (use) utiliser ⟨machine, tool⟩; employer ⟨tactics, technique⟩; recourir à ⟨measures⟩

**employable** *adj* capable de faire un travail

**employee** *n* salarié/-e *m/f*

**employer** *n* employeur/-euse *m/f*

**employment** *n* travail *m*, emploi *m*

**employment agency** *n* bureau *m* de recrutement

**empower** *vtr* (legally) **to** ~ **sb to do** autoriser qn à faire; (politically) donner à qn le pouvoir de faire

**empress** *n* impératrice *f*

**empty** ⟦1⟧ *adj* (a) ⟨street⟩ désert/-e; ⟨desk⟩ libre; ⟨container⟩ vide; ⟨page⟩ vierge
(b) ⟨promise, threat⟩ en l'air; ⟨gesture⟩ vide de sens; ⟨life⟩ vide
⟦2⟧ *vtr, vi* = EMPTY OUT

■ **empty out**: ¶ ~ **out** ⟨building, container⟩ se vider; ⟨contents⟩ se répandre; ¶ ~ **[sth] out** vider ⟨container, drawer⟩; verser ⟨liquid⟩

**empty-handed** *adj* ⟨arrive, leave⟩ les mains vides; ⟨return⟩ bredouille *inv*

**emulate** *vtr* imiter

**emulsion** *n* émulsion *f*

**enable** *vtr* (a) **to** ~ **sb to do** permettre à qn de faire
(b) faciliter ⟨growth⟩; favoriser ⟨learning⟩

**enamel** *n* émail *m*

**enchant** *vtr* enchanter

**enchanting** *adj* enchanteur/-eresse

**encircle** *vtr* ⟨troops, police⟩ encercler; ⟨fence, wall⟩ entourer; ⟨belt, bracelet⟩ enserrer

**enclose** *vtr* (a) (gen) entourer (**with, by** de); (with fence, wall) clôturer (**with, by** avec)
(b) (in letter) joindre (**with, in** à); **please find** ~**d a cheque for £10** veuillez trouver ci-joint un chèque de dix livres sterling

**enclosure** *n* (a) (for animals) enclos *m*; (for racehorses) paddock *m*; (for officials) enceinte *f*
(b) (fence) clôture *f*

**encompass** *vtr* inclure, comprendre

**encore** ⟦1⟧ *n* bis *m*; **to play an** ~ jouer un bis
⟦2⟧ *excl* ~**!** bis!

**encounter** ⟦1⟧ *n* (gen) rencontre *f* (**with** avec); (Mil) affrontement *m*
⟦2⟧ *vtr* rencontrer ⟨opponent, resistance, problem⟩; essuyer ⟨setback⟩; croiser ⟨person⟩

**encourage** *vtr* (a) encourager (**to do** à faire)
(b) stimuler ⟨investment⟩; favoriser ⟨growth⟩

**encouragement** *n* encouragement *m*

**encouraging** *adj* encourageant/-e

**encroach** *vi* **to** ~ **on** ⟨person⟩ empiéter sur; ⟨sea, vegetation⟩ gagner du terrain sur ⟨land⟩

**encrypt** *vtr* crypter

**encyclop(a)edia** *n* encyclopédie *f*

**end** ⟦1⟧ *n* (a) (final part) fin *f*; **'The End'** 'Fin'; **to put an** ~ **to sth** mettre fin à qch; **to come to an** ~ se terminer; **in the** ~ **I went home** finalement je suis rentré chez moi; **for days on** ~ pendant des jours et des jours
(b) (extremity) bout *m*, extrémité *f*; **at the** ~ **of, on the** ~ **of** au bout de; **at the** ~ **of the garden** au fond du jardin; **the third from the** ~ le/la troisième avant la fin; **to stand sth on (its)** ~ mettre qch debout
(c) (aim) but *m*; **to this** ~ dans ce but; **a means to an** ~ un moyen d'arriver à ses fins
(d) (Sport) **to change** ~**s** changer de côté
⟦2⟧ *vtr* mettre fin à; **to** ~ **sth with** terminer qch par; **to** ~ **it all** en finir avec la vie
⟦3⟧ *vi* ⟨day, book⟩ se terminer (**in, with** par); ⟨contract, agreement⟩ expirer

■ **end up** finir par devenir ⟨president⟩; finir par être ⟨rich⟩; **to** ~ **up doing** finir par faire

**endanger** *vtr* mettre [qch] en danger ⟨health, life⟩; compromettre ⟨career, prospects⟩

**endangered species** *n* espèce *f* menacée

**endearing** *adj* ⟨person, habit⟩ attachant/-e; ⟨smile⟩ engageant/-e

**endeavour, endeavor** (US) ⟦1⟧ *n* tentative *f* (**to do** de faire)
⋯⟶

**2** *vtr* **to ~ to do** (do one's best) faire tout son possible pour faire; (find a means) trouver un moyen de faire

**ending** *n* fin *f*, dénouement *m*

**endive** *n* (GB) chicorée *f*; (US) endive *f*

**endless** *adj* ⟨patience, choice⟩ infini/-e; ⟨supply⟩ inépuisable; ⟨list, search, meeting⟩ interminable

**endorse** *vtr* donner son aval à ⟨policy⟩; appuyer ⟨decision⟩; approuver ⟨product⟩; endosser ⟨cheque⟩

**endow** *vtr* doter (**with** de)

**end result** *n* résultat *m* final

**endurance** *n* endurance *f*

**endure** **1** *vtr* endurer ⟨hardship⟩; supporter ⟨behaviour, person⟩; subir ⟨attack, defeat⟩
**2** *vi* durer

**enemy** **1** *n* ennemi/-e *m/f*
**2** *adj* ⟨forces, aircraft, territory⟩ ennemi/-e; ⟨agent⟩ de l'ennemi

**energetic** *adj* énergique

**energy** *n* énergie *f*

**energy policy** *n* politique *f* énergétique

**energy-saving** *adj* qui permet de faire des économies d'énergie

**enforce** *vtr* appliquer ⟨rule, policy⟩; faire respecter ⟨law, court order⟩

**engage** **1** *vtr* (a) **to be ~d in** se livrer à ⟨activity⟩; **to ~ sb in conversation** engager la conversation avec qn
(b) passer ⟨gear⟩; **to ~ the clutch** embrayer
**2** *vi* **to ~ in** se livrer à ⟨activity⟩; se lancer dans ⟨research⟩

**engaged** *adj* (a) **to be ~** être fiancé/-e (**to** à); **to get ~** se fiancer (**to** à)
(b) ⟨WC, phone⟩ occupé/-e

**engaged tone** *n* (GB) tonalité *f* 'occupé'

**engagement** *n* (a) (appointment) rendez-vous *m inv*
(b) (before marriage) fiançailles *fpl*

**engagement ring** *n* bague *f* de fiançailles

**engine** *n* (a) (gen) moteur *m*; (in ship) machines *fpl*
(b) locomotive *f*; **steam ~** locomotive à vapeur

**engine driver** *n* mécanicien *m*

**engineer** **1** *n* (graduate) ingénieur *m*; (in factory) mécanicien *m* monteur; (repairer) technicien *m*; (on ship) mécanicien *m*
**2** *vtr* (a) (plot) manigancer
(b) (build) construire

**engineering** *n* ingénierie *f*; **civil ~** génie *m* civil

**England** *pr n* Angleterre *f*

**English** **1** *n* (a) (people) **the ~** les Anglais
(b) (language) anglais *m*
**2** *adj* ⟨language, food⟩ anglais/-e; ⟨lesson, teacher⟩ d'anglais; ⟨ambassador, embassy⟩ d'Angleterre

**English Channel** *pr n* **the ~** la Manche

**Englishman** *n* Anglais *m*

**English-speaking** *adj* anglophone

**Englishwoman** *n* Anglaise *f*

**engrave** *vtr* graver

**engraving** *n* gravure *f*

**engrossed** *adj* **to be ~ in** être absorbé/-e par, être plongé/-e dans

**engulf** *vtr* engloutir

**enhance** *vtr* améliorer ⟨prospects, status⟩; mettre [qch] en valeur ⟨appearance, qualities⟩

**enigma** *n* énigme *f*

**enigmatic** *adj* énigmatique

**enjoy** **1** *vtr* (a) aimer (**doing** faire); **I didn't ~ the party** je ne me suis pas amusé à la soirée
(b) (have) jouir de ⟨good health, popularity⟩
**2** *v refl* **to ~ oneself** s'amuser

**enjoyable** *adj* agréable

**enjoyment** *n* plaisir *m*

**enlarge** **1** *vtr* agrandir
**2** *vi* (a) ⟨pupil, pores⟩ se dilater; ⟨tonsils⟩ enfler
(b) **to ~ on** s'étendre sur ⟨subject⟩; développer ⟨idea⟩

**enlighten** *vtr* éclairer (**on** sur)

**enlightening** *adj* instructif/-ive

**enlightenment** *n* (edification) instruction *f*; (clarification) éclaircissement *m*; **the (Age of) Enlightenment** le Siècle des lumières

**enlist** **1** *vtr* recruter; **to ~ sb's help** s'assurer l'aide de qn
**2** *vi* s'enrôler, s'engager

**enmity** *n* inimitié *f* (**towards** envers)

**enormity** *n* énormité *f*

**enormous** *adj* (gen) énorme; ⟨effort⟩ prodigieux/-ieuse

**enough**

■ Note When *enough* is used as a pronoun and if the sentence does not specify what it is enough of, the pronoun *en*, meaning of *it*/of *them*, must be added before the verb in French: *will there be enough?* = est-ce qu'il y en aura assez?

**1** *pron, quantif* assez; **have you had ~ to eat?** avez-vous assez mangé?; **more than ~** largement assez; **is that ~?** ça suffit?; **I've had ~ of him** j'en ai assez de lui
**2** *adv* assez; **curiously ~,...** aussi bizarre que cela puisse paraître...
**3** *det* assez de; **have you got ~ chairs?** avez-vous assez de chaises?

**enquire** **1** *vtr* demander
**2** *vi* se renseigner (**about** sur); **to ~ after sb** demander des nouvelles de qn

**enquiring** *adj* ⟨look, voice⟩ interrogateur/-trice; ⟨mind⟩ curieux/-ieuse

**enquiry** *n* demande *f* de renseignements; **to make enquiries** demander des renseignements (**about** sur); ▶ INQUIRY

**enrage** *vtr* rendre [qn] furieux/-ieuse

**enrich** *vtr* enrichir

**enrol, enroll** (US) ⟦1⟧ *vtr* (gen) inscrire; (Mil) enrôler
⟦2⟧ *vi* (gen) s'inscrire (**in, on** à); (Mil) s'engager (**in** dans)

**enrolment, enrollment** (US) *n* (gen) inscription *f* (**in, on** à); (Mil) enrôlement *m*

**ensuing** *adj* ‹*period*› qui suivit; ‹*event*› qui s'ensuivit

**en suite** *adj* attenant/-e

**ensure** *vtr* garantir; **to ∼ that...** s'assurer que...

**entail** *vtr* impliquer ‹*travel, work*›; entraîner ‹*expense*›; nécessiter ‹*effort*›

**enter** ⟦1⟧ *vtr* (a) entrer dans ‹*room, house, phase, period, profession, army*›; participer à ‹*race, competition*›; entrer à ‹*parliament*›; **to ∼ sb's mind** *or* **head** venir à l'idée *or* à l'esprit de qn
(b) engager ‹*horse*› (**for** dans); présenter ‹*poem, picture*› (**for** à)
(c) inscrire ‹*figure, fact*› (**in** dans); (in diary) noter ‹*appointment*› (**in** dans); (in computer) entrer ‹*data*›
⟦2⟧ *vi* (a) (come in) entrer
(b) **to ∼ for** s'inscrire à ‹*exam*›; s'inscrire pour ‹*race*›
■ **enter into** entrer en ‹*conversation*›; entamer ‹*negotiations*›; passer ‹*contract*›

**enterprise** *n* (a) (gen) entreprise *f*
(b) (initiative) esprit *m* d'initiative

**enterprising** *adj* ‹*person*› entreprenant/-e; ‹*plan*› audacieux/-ieuse

**entertain** ⟦1⟧ *vtr* (a) (keep amused) divertir; (make laugh) amuser; (keep occupied) distraire, occuper
(b) (play host to) recevoir ‹*guests*›
(c) entretenir ‹*idea*›; nourrir ‹*doubt, ambition, illusion*›
⟦2⟧ *vi* recevoir

**entertainer** *n* (comic) comique *mf*; (performer, raconteur) amuseur/-euse *m/f*

**entertaining** ⟦1⟧ *adj* divertissant/-e
⟦2⟧ *n* **they do a lot of ∼** ils reçoivent beaucoup

**entertainment** *n* (a) divertissement *m*, distractions *fpl*
(b) (event) spectacle *m*

**entertainment industry** *n* industrie *f* du spectacle

**enthusiasm** *n* enthousiasme *m* (**for** pour)

**enthusiast** *n* (for sport, DIY) passionné/-e *m/f*; (for music, composer) fervent/-e *m/f*

**enthusiastic** *adj* (gen) enthousiaste; ‹*discussion*› exalté/-e; ‹*worker, gardener*› passionné/-e

**entice** *vtr* (with offer, charms, prospects) attirer; (with food, money) appâter

**entire** *adj* entier/-ière; **the ∼ family** toute la famille, la famille entière

**entirely** *adv* ‹*destroy, escape*› entièrement; ‹*different, unnecessary*› complètement

**entirety** *n* ensemble *m*, totalité *f*

**entitle** *vtr* **to ∼ sb to sth** donner droit à qch à qn; **to be ∼d to sth** avoir droit à qch; **to be ∼d to do** avoir le droit de faire

**entitlement** *n* droit *m*

**entity** *n* entité *f*

**entrance** ⟦1⟧ *n* (gen) entrée *f*; **to gain ∼ to** être admis/-e à *or* dans ‹*club, university*›
⟦2⟧ *vtr* transporter, ravir

**entrance examination** *n* (GB) (Sch, Univ) examen *m* d'entrée; (for civil service) concours *m* d'entrée

**entrance fee** *n* droit *m* d'entrée

**entrance hall** *n* (in house) vestibule *m*; (in public building) hall *m*

**entrance requirements** *n pl* diplômes *mpl* requis

**entrant** *n* (in competition) participant/-e *m/f*; (in exam) candidat/-e *m/f*

**entreat** *vtr* implorer, supplier (**to do** de faire)

**entreaty** *n* prière *f*, supplication *f*

**entrepreneur** *n* entrepreneur/-euse *m/f*

**entrust** *vtr* confier; **to ∼ sb with sth, to ∼ sth to sb** confier qch à qn

**entry** *n* (a) (gen) entrée *f*; **to gain ∼ to** *or* **into** s'introduire dans ‹*building*›; accéder à ‹*computer file*›; **'no ∼'** (on door) 'défense d'entrer'; (in one way street) 'sens interdit'
(b) (in diary) note *f*; (in ledger) écriture *f*
(c) (for competition) œuvre *f* présentée à un concours

**entry form** *n* (for membership) fiche *f* d'inscription; (for competition) bulletin *m* de participation

**entry phone** *n* interphone *m*

**envelope** *n* enveloppe *f*

**envious** *adj* envieux/-ieuse; **to be ∼ of sb/sth** envier qn/qch

**environment** *n* (physical, cultural) environnement *m*; (social) milieu *m*

**environmental** *adj* ‹*conditions, changes*› du milieu; ‹*concern, issue*› lié/-e à l'environnement, écologique; ‹*protection, pollution*› de l'environnement; **∼ disaster** catastrophe *f* écologique

**environmental health** *n* hygiène *f* publique

**environmentally** *adv* **∼ safe, ∼ sound** qui ne nuit pas à l'environnement; **∼ friendly product** produit qui respecte l'environnement

**environmental studies** *n pl* (GB Sch) études *fpl* géographiques et biologiques de l'environnement

**envisage** *vtr* (anticipate) prévoir (**doing** de faire); (visualize) envisager (**doing** de faire)

**envoy** *n* envoyé/-e *m/f*

**envy** ⟦1⟧ *n* envie *f*; (long-term) jalousie *f*
⟦2⟧ *vtr* **to ∼ sb sth** envier qch à qn

**enzyme** *n* enzyme *f*

**epic** ⟦1⟧ *n* (gen) épopée *f*; (film) film *m* à grand spectacle; (novel) roman-fleuve *m*
⟦2⟧ *adj* épique

**epidemic** ① *n* épidémie *f*
  ② *adj* épidémique

**epidural** *n* péridurale *f*

**epilepsy** *n* épilepsie *f*

**epileptic** *n, adj* épileptique (*mf*)

**episode** *n* épisode *m*

**epitome** *n* épitomé *m*; **the ~ of kindness** la bonté incarnée

**epitomize** *vtr* personnifier, incarner

**epoch** *n* époque *f*

**equal** ① *n* égal/-e *m/f*
  ② *adj* (a) égal/-e (**to** à); **~ opportunities/rights** égalité *f* des chances/des droits
  (b) **to be ~ to** être à la hauteur de ⟨*task*⟩
  ③ *adv* ⟨*finish*⟩ à égalité
  ④ *vtr* égaler

**equality** *n* égalité *f*; **~ of opportunity** égalité des chances

**equalize** *vi* égaliser

**equally** *adv* ⟨*divide, share*⟩ en parts égales; **~ difficult** tout aussi difficile; **~, we might say that...** de même, on pourrait dire que...

**equate** *vtr* (identify) assimiler (**with, to** à); (compare) comparer (**with, to** à)

**equation** *n* équation *f*

**equator** *n* équateur *m*

**equilibrium** *n* équilibre *m*

**equip** *vtr* équiper (**for** pour; **with** de)

**equipment** *n* (gen) équipement *m*; (office, electrical, photographic) matériel *m*; **a piece** or **item of ~** un article

**equivalent** ① *n* équivalent *m*
  ② *adj* équivalent/-e

**era** *n* (in history, geology) ère *f*; (in politics, fashion) époque *f*

**eradicate** *vtr* éliminer ⟨*poverty, crime*⟩; éradiquer ⟨*disease*⟩

**erase** *vtr* effacer

**eraser** *n* (rubber) gomme *f*; (for blackboard) brosse *f* feutrée

**erect** ① *adj* ⟨*posture*⟩ droit/-e; ⟨*tail, ears*⟩ dressé/-e
  ② *vtr* ériger ⟨*building*⟩; monter ⟨*scaffolding, tent, screen*⟩

**erection** *n* (gen) érection *f*; (of building) construction *f*; (edifice) édifice *m*

**ermine** *n* hermine *f*

**erode** *vtr* éroder ⟨*rock, metal*⟩; saper ⟨*confidence*⟩

**erosion** *n* érosion *f*

**erotic** *adj* érotique

**err** *vi* (a) (make mistake) faire erreur
  (b) **to ~ on the side of caution** pécher par excès de prudence

**errand** *n* commission *f*, course *f*; **to run an ~ for sb** aller faire une commission pour qn

**erratic** *adj* ⟨*behaviour, person, driver*⟩ imprévisible; ⟨*moods*⟩ changeant/-e

**error** *n* (in spelling, grammar, typing) faute *f*; (in calculation, on computer) erreur *f*

**erupt** *vi* (a) ⟨*volcano*⟩ entrer en éruption
  (b) ⟨*violence*⟩ éclater

**eruption** *n* (of volcano) éruption *f*; (of violence, anger) explosion *f*

**escalate** *vi* ⟨*conflict, violence*⟩ s'intensifier; ⟨*prices*⟩ monter en flèche; ⟨*unemployment*⟩ augmenter rapidement

**escalator** *n* escalier *m* mécanique, escalator® *m*

**escapade** *n* frasque *f*

**escape** ① *n* fuite *f*, évasion *f* (**from** de; **to** vers); **to have a narrow** or **lucky ~** l'échapper belle
  ② *vtr* échapper à
  ③ *vi* (a) ⟨*person*⟩ s'enfuir, s'évader (**from** de); ⟨*animal*⟩ s'échapper (**from** de); (figurative) s'évader (**from** de); **to ~ with one's life** s'en sortir vivant
  (b) (leak) fuir

**escape clause** *n* clause *f* dérogatoire

**escape key** *n* touche *f* d'échappement

**escape route** *n* (in case of fire etc) plan *m* d'évacuation; (for fugitives) itinéraire *m* d'évasion

**escapism** *n* évasion *f* (du réel)

**escort** ① *n* (a) (for security) escorte *f*; **police ~** escorte de police
  (b) (companion) compagnon/compagne *m/f*
  (c) (in agency) hôtesse *f*; **~ agency** agence *f* d'hôtesses
  ② *vtr* (a) (for security) escorter; **to ~ sb in/out** faire entrer/sortir qn sous escorte
  (b) (to a function) accompagner; (home) raccompagner

**especially** *adv* (a) (above all) surtout, en particulier; **him ~** lui en particulier; **~ as it's so hot** d'autant plus qu'il fait si chaud
  (b) (on purpose) exprès, spécialement
  (c) (unusually) particulièrement

**espresso** *n* express *m inv*

**essay** *n* (a) (Sch) rédaction *f* (**on, about** sur); (extended) dissertation *f* (**on** sur)
  (b) (literary) essai *m* (**on** sur)

**essence** *n* essence *f*

**essential** ① *n* **a car is not an ~** une voiture n'est pas indispensable; **the ~s** l'essentiel *m*
  ② *adj* ⟨*role, feature, element*⟩ essentiel/-ielle; ⟨*ingredient, reading*⟩ indispensable; ⟨*difference*⟩ fondamental/-e; **it is ~ that we agree** il est indispensable que nous soyons d'accord

**essentially** *adv* essentiellement

**essential oil** *n* huile *f* essentielle

**establish** *vtr* (gen) établir; fonder ⟨*company*⟩

**establishment** *n* (a) (gen) établissement *m*
  (b) (shop, business) maison *f*
  (c) **the Establishment** l'ordre *m* établi

**estate** *n* (a) (stately home and park) domaine *m*, propriété *f*
  (b) = HOUSING ESTATE
  (c) (assets) biens *mpl*
  (d) (GB) (*also* **~ car**) break *m*

**estate agency** *n* (GB) agence *f* immobilière

**estate agent** *n* (GB) agent *m* immobilier

**esteem** *n* estime *f*

**estimate** 1 *n* (a) estimation *f* (b) (quote for client) devis *m* 2 *vtr* évaluer ⟨value, size, distance⟩; **to ~ that** estimer que 3 **estimated** *pp adj* ⟨cost, figure⟩ approximatif/-ive; **an ~d 300 people** environ 300 personnes

**Estonia** *pr n* Estonie *f*

**estranged** *adj* **~ from sb** séparé/-e de qn; **her ~ husband** son mari dont elle est séparée

**etc** *adv* (written abbr = **et cetera**) etc

**etching** *n* eau-forte *f*

**eternal** *adj* ⟨life⟩ éternel/-elle; ⟨chatter, optimist⟩ perpétuel/-elle

**ethical** *adj* ⟨problem, objection⟩ moral/-e; ⟨investment, theory⟩ éthique

**ethics** *n* (code) moralité *f*; **professional ~** déontologie *f*

**ethnic** *adj* ethnique

**ethnic cleansing** *n* purification *f* ethnique

**ethnic minority** *n* minorité *f* ethnique

**etiquette** *n* (a) (social) bienséance *f*, étiquette *f* (b) (professional, diplomatic) protocole *m*

**euphemism** *n* euphémisme *m*

**euphoria** *n* euphorie *f*

**euro** *n* euro *m*

**eurocheque** *n* Eurochèque *m*

**Eurocrat** *n* eurocrate *mf*

**Euro-MP** *n* député *m* européen

**Europe** *pr n* Europe *f*

**European** 1 *n* Européen/-éenne *m/f* 2 *adj* européen/-éenne

**European Commission** *n* Commission *f* européenne

**European Monetary System, EMS** *n* système *m* monétaire européen, SME *m*

**European Monetary Union, EMU** *n* Union *f* monétaire européenne

**European Union, EU** *n* Union *f* européenne, UE *f*

**eurosceptic** *n* eurosceptique *mf*

**euthanasia** *n* euthanasie *f*

**evacuate** *vtr* évacuer

**evacuee** *n* évacué/-e *m/f*

**evade** *vtr* esquiver ⟨blow⟩; éluder ⟨question, problem⟩

**evaluate** *vtr* évaluer

**evaluation** *n* évaluation *f*

**evaporate** *vi* ⟨liquid⟩ s'évaporer

**evaporated milk** *n* lait *m* condensé non sucré

**evasion** *n* (of responsibility) dérobade *f* (of à); **tax ~** évasion *f* fiscale

**evasive** *adj* ⟨answer⟩ évasif/-ive; ⟨look⟩ fuyant/-e

**eve** *n* veille *f*; **on the ~ of** à la veille de

**even**[1] 1 *adv* (a) (gen) même; **he didn't ~ try** il n'a même pas essayé; **don't tell anyone, not ~ Bob** ne dis rien à personne, pas même à Bob; **~ if/when** même si/quand (b) (with comparative) encore; **~ colder** encore plus froid 2 **even so** *phr* quand même 3 **even though** *phr* bien que (+ *subjunctive*)

**even**[2] *adj* ⟨surface, voice, temper⟩ égal/-e; ⟨teeth, hemline⟩ régulier/-ière; ⟨temperature⟩ constant/-e; ⟨number⟩ pair/-e; **to get ~ with sb** rendre à qn la monnaie de sa pièce

**evening** *n* soir *m*; (with emphasis on duration) soirée *f*; **in the ~** le soir; **all ~** toute la soirée; **every ~** tous les soirs

**evening class** *n* cours *m* du soir

**evening dress** *n* (formal clothes) tenue *f* de soirée

**event** *n* (a) (eventuality) événement *m* (b) (eventuality) cas *m*; **in the ~ of a fire** en cas d'incendie; **in any ~** de toute façon (c) (in athletics) épreuve *f*

**eventful** *adj* mouvementé/-e

**eventually** *adv* finalement; **to do sth ~** finir par faire qch

**ever** 1 *adv* (a) jamais; **no-one will ~ forget** personne n'oubliera jamais; **hardly ~** rarement, presque jamais; **has he ~ lived abroad?** est-ce qu'il a déjà vécu à l'étranger?; **do you ~ make mistakes?** est-ce qu'il t'arrive de te tromper?; **he's happier than he's ~ been** il n'a jamais été aussi heureux; **more beautiful than ~** plus beau/ belle que jamais (b) (always) toujours; **as cheerful as ~** toujours aussi gai; **the same as ~** toujours le même; **they lived happily ~ after** ils vécurent toujours heureux 2 **ever since** *phr* depuis; **~ since we arrived** depuis notre arrivée

**evergreen** *n* arbre *m* à feuilles persistantes

**everlasting** *adj* éternel/-elle

**every** 1 *det* (a) (each) chaque; **~ time** chaque fois; **~ house in the street** toutes les maisons de la rue; **I've read ~ one of her books** j'ai lu tous ses livres (b) (emphatic) **there is ~ chance that you'll have a place** il y a toutes les chances que tu aies une place; **to have ~ right to complain** avoir tous les droits de se plaindre (c) (indicating frequency) **~ day** tous les jours; **~ Thursday** tous les jeudis; **once ~ few days** tous les deux ou trois jours 2 **every other** *phr* **~ other day** tous les deux jours; **~ other Sunday** un dimanche sur deux

IDIOMS **~ now and then**, **~ so often** de temps en temps

**everybody** *pron* (also **everyone**) tout le monde

**everyday** *adj* ⟨*life*⟩ quotidien/-ienne; ⟨*clothes*⟩ de tous les jours; **in ~ use** d'usage courant

**everyone** = EVERYBODY

**everything** *pron* tout

**everywhere** *adv* partout

**evict** *vtr* expulser (**from** de)

**eviction** *n* expulsion *f*

**evidence** *n* (a) (proof) preuves *fpl* (**that** que; **of**, **for** de); (b) (testimony) témoignage *m* (**from** de); **to give ~** témoigner, déposer (**for sb** en faveur de qn; **against sb** contre qn); (c) (trace) trace *f* (**of** de)

**evident** *adj* manifeste

**evidently** *adv* (a) (apparently) apparemment (b) (patently) manifestement

**evil** ① *n* mal *m*
② *adj* ⟨*person, forces*⟩ malfaisant/-e; ⟨*act*⟩ diabolique; ⟨*spirit*⟩ maléfique; ⟨*smell*⟩ nauséabond/-e

**evolution** *n* évolution *f* (**from** à partir de)

**evolve** *vi* évoluer

**ewe** *n* brebis *f*

**ex-** *pref* ex-, ancien/-ienne (*before n*)

**exact** *adj* exact/-e; **to be (more) ~** plus précisément

**exactly** *adv* exactement

**exaggerate** *vtr*, *vi* exagérer

**exaggeration** *n* exagération *f*

**exam** *n* examen *m*

**examination** *n* examen *m* (**in** de); **French ~** examen *m* de français; **to take/pass an ~** passer/réussir un examen; **to have an ~** (Med) passer un examen médical

**examination paper** *n* sujets *mpl* d'examen

**examine** *vtr* examiner

**examiner** *n* examinateur/-trice *m/f*

**example** *n* exemple *m*; **for ~** par exemple; **to set a good ~** donner l'exemple; **to make an ~ of sb** punir qn pour l'exemple

**excavate** ① *vtr* fouiller ⟨*site*⟩; creuser ⟨*tunnel*⟩
② *vi* faire des fouilles

**exceed** *vtr* dépasser (**by** de)

**excel** *vi* exceller (**at**, **in** en; **at** *or* **in doing** à faire)

**excellent** *adj* excellent/-e

**except** ① *prep* sauf; **everybody ~ Lisa** tout le monde sauf Lisa, tout le monde à l'exception de *or* excepté Lisa; **who could have done it ~ him?** qui aurait pu le faire sinon lui?
② **except for** *phr* à part, à l'exception de

**exception** *n* (a) exception *f* (**for** pour); **with the ~ of** à l'exception de (b) **to take ~ to** prendre ⟨qch⟩ comme une insulte

**exceptional** *adj* exceptionnel/-elle

**excess** ① *n* excès *m* (**of** de)
② *adj* **~ weight** excès *m* de poids; **~ baggage** excédent *m* de bagages

**excessive** *adj* excessif/-ive

**exchange** ① *n* (a) échange *m*; **in ~** en échange (**for** de); **~ visit** voyage *m* d'échange (b) (in banking) change *m*; **the ~ rate** le taux de change (c) (*also* **telephone ~**) central *m* (téléphonique)
② *vtr* échanger (**for** contre; **with** avec)

**exchange control** *n* contrôle *m* des changes

**Exchange Rate Mechanism, ERM** *n* système *m* monétaire européen

**Exchequer** *pr n* (GB) **the ~** l'Échiquier *m*, le ministère des finances

**excite** *vtr* exciter

**excited** *adj* (gen) excité/-e; ⟨*voice, conversation*⟩ animé/-e

**excitement** *n* excitation *f*

**exciting** *adj* passionnant/-e

**exclaim** *vtr* s'exclamer

**exclamation mark, exclamation point** (US) *n* point *m* d'exclamation

**exclude** *vtr* exclure (**from** de)

**excluding** *prep* à l'exclusion de; **~ VAT** TVA non comprise

**exclusion zone** *n* zone *f* interdite

**exclusive** ① *n* (report) exclusivité *f*
② *adj* (a) ⟨*club*⟩ fermé/-e; ⟨*hotel*⟩ de luxe; ⟨*district*⟩ huppé/-e (b) ⟨*story, rights*⟩ exclusif/-ive; ⟨*interview*⟩ en exclusivité; **~ of meals** les repas non compris

**excruciating** *adj* ⟨*pain*⟩ atroce

**excursion** *n* (organized) excursion *f*

**excuse** ① *n* excuse *f* (**for sth** à qch; **for doing** pour faire; **to do** pour faire); **to make ~s** se trouver des excuses; **an ~ to leave early** un bon prétexte pour partir tôt; **there's no ~ for such behaviour** ce genre de conduite est inexcusable
② *vtr* (a) excuser ⟨*person*⟩ (**for doing** de faire, d'avoir fait); **~ me!** (apology) excusez-moi!, pardon!; (beginning an enquiry) excusez-moi; (pardon) pardon?
(b) (exempt) dispenser (**from sth** de qch; **from doing** de faire)

**ex-directory** *adj* sur la liste rouge

**execute** *vtr* exécuter

**execution** *n* exécution *f*

**executioner** *n* bourreau *m*

**executive** ① *n* (a) cadre *m*; **sales ~** cadre *m* commercial (b) (committee) exécutif *m*, comité *m* exécutif; **party ~** bureau *m* du parti
② *adj* (a) ⟨*post*⟩ de cadre (b) ⟨*power*⟩ exécutif/-ive

**exemplify** *vtr* illustrer, exemplifier

**exempt** ① *adj* exempt/-e (**from** de)
② *vtr* exempter (**from** de)

**exemption** *n* exemption *f*; (from exam) dispense *f*

**exercise** ① *n* exercice *m*

**2** *vtr* (a) exercer ‹body›; faire travailler ‹limb, muscles›
(b) faire preuve de ‹control, restraint›; exercer ‹power, right›
**3** *vi* faire de l'exercice

**exercise bike** *n* (at home) vélo *m* d'appartement; (in gym) vélo *m* d'entraînement

**exercise book** *n* cahier *m*

**exert** *vtr* exercer ‹pressure, influence› (on sur); **to ∼ oneself** se fatiguer

**exhale** *vi* ‹person› expirer

**exhaust** **1** *n* (a) (also ∼ **pipe**) pot *m* d'échappement
(b) (also ∼ **fumes**) gaz *mpl* d'échappement
**2** *vtr* épuiser; **∼ed** épuisé/-e

**exhaustion** *n* épuisement *m*

**exhibit** **1** *n* (a) œuvre *f* exposée
(b) (US) (exhibition) exposition *f*
**2** *vtr* exposer ‹work of art›; manifester ‹preference, sign›

**exhibition** *n* exposition *f*; **art ∼** exposition; **to make an ∼ of oneself** se donner en spectacle

**exhibition centre** (GB), **exhibition center** (US) *n* palais *m* des expositions

**exhilarating** *adj* ‹game› stimulant/-e; ‹experience› exaltant/-e; ‹speed› enivrant/-e

**exile** **1** *n* (a) (person) exilé/-e *m/f*
(b) (expulsion) exil *m* (from de); **in ∼** en exil
**2** *vtr* exiler (de from)

**exist** *vi* exister

**existence** *n* existence *f* (of de)

**existing** *adj* ‹laws, order› existant/-e; ‹policy, management› actuel/-elle

**exit** **1** *n* sortie *f*; **'no ∼'** 'interdit'
**2** *vi* sortir

**exodus** *n* exode *m*

**exotic** *adj* exotique

**expand** **1** *vtr* développer ‹business, network, range›; élargir ‹horizon, knowledge›; étendre ‹empire›; gonfler ‹lungs›
**2** *vi* ‹business, sector, town› se développer; ‹economy› être en expansion; ‹metal› se dilater

**expanse** *n* étendue *f*

**expansion** *n* développement *m* (in de; into dans); (of economy) expansion *f*; (of population) accroissement *m*

**expatriate** *n*, *adj* expatrié/-e (*m/f*)

**expect** **1** *vtr* (a) s'attendre à ‹event, victory, defeat, trouble›; **to ∼ the worst** s'attendre au pire; **to ∼ sb to do** s'attendre à ce que qn fasse; **I ∼ (that) I'll lose** je m'attends à perdre; **more than ∼ed** plus que prévu
(b) s'attendre à ‹sympathy, help› (from de la part de)
(c) attendre ‹baby, guest›
(d) (require) demander, attendre ‹hard work› (from de); **I ∼ you to be punctual** je vous demande d'être ponctuel
(e) (GB) (suppose) **I ∼ so** je pense que oui; **I ∼ he's tired** il doit être fatigué

**2** *vi* (a) **to ∼ to do** s'attendre à faire
(b) (require) **I ∼ to see you there** je compte bien vous y voir
(c) (be pregnant) **to be ∼ing** attendre un enfant

**expectant** *adj* (a) ‹look› plein d'attente
(b) ‹mother› futur/-e (before n)

**expectation** *n* (a) (prediction) prévision *f*; **against all ∼(s)** à l'encontre des prévisions générales
(b) (hope) aspiration *f*, attente *f*; **to live up to sb's ∼s** répondre à l'attente de qn

**expedient** *adj* (a) (appropriate) opportun/-e
(b) (advantageous) politique

**expedition** *n* expédition *f*; **to go on an ∼** partir en expédition

**expel** *vtr* (gen) expulser; renvoyer ‹pupil›

**expenditure** *n* dépense *f*

**expense** **1** *n* (a) (cost) frais *mpl*; (money spent) dépense *f*; **at one's own ∼** à ses propres frais; **to go to great ∼** dépenser beaucoup d'argent (**to do** pour faire); **to spare no ∼** ne pas regarder à la dépense
(b) **at the ∼ of** au détriment de ‹health, public, safety›; **at sb's ∼** ‹laugh, joke› aux dépens de qn
**2 expenses** *n pl* frais *mpl*

**expense account** *n* frais *mpl* de représentation

**expensive** *adj* (gen) cher/chère; ‹holiday, mistake› coûteux/-euse; ‹taste› de luxe

**experience** **1** *n* expérience *f*
**2** *vtr* connaître ‹loss, problem›; éprouver ‹emotion›

**experienced** *adj* (gen) expérimenté/-e; ‹eye› entraîné/-e

**experiment** **1** *n* expérience *f* (in en; on sur)
**2** *vi* expérimenter, faire des essais

**experimental** *adj* expérimental/-e

**experimentation** *n* expériences *fpl*

**expert** **1** *n* spécialiste *mf* (in en, de), expert *m* (in en)
**2** *adj* ‹opinion, advice› autorisé/-e; ‹witness› expert/-e; ‹eye› exercé/-e; **an ∼ cook** un cordon bleu

**expertise** *n* compétences *fpl*; (very specialized) expertise *f* (in dans le domaine de)

**expire** *vi* ‹deadline, offer› expirer; ‹period› arriver à terme; **my passport has ∼d** mon passeport est périmé

**expiry date** *n* (of credit card, permit) date *f* d'expiration

**explain** *vtr* expliquer (that que; to à)

**explanation** *n* explication *f* (of de; for à)

**explicit** *adj* explicite

**explode** **1** *vtr* (a) faire exploser ‹bomb›
(b) pulvériser ‹theory, rumour, myth›
**2** *vi* (gen) exploser; ‹boiler, building, ship› sauter

**exploit** **1** *n* exploit *m*
**2** *vtr* exploiter

**exploitation** *n* exploitation *f*

**explore** **1** *vtr* explorer ⋯⟶

**2** *vi* to go exploring partir en exploration

**explorer** *n* explorateur/-trice *m/f*

**explosion** *n* explosion *f*

**explosive** **1** *n* explosif *m*
**2** *adj* ⟨*device, force*⟩ explosif/-ive; ⟨*substance*⟩ explosible

**export** **1** *n* (process) exportation *f* (of de); (product) produit *m* d'exportation
**2** *vtr, vi* exporter

**exporter** *n* exportateur/-trice *m/f* (of de)

**expose** *vtr* (a) exposer (to à)
(b) (make public) révéler ⟨*identity*⟩; dénoncer ⟨*person, scandal*⟩
(c) to ~ oneself commettre un outrage à la pudeur

**exposure** *n* (a) (of secret, crime) révélation *f*
(b) (to light, sun, radiation) exposition *f* (to à)
(c) to die of ~ mourir de froid
(d) (*also* ~ **time**) temps *m* de pose
(e) (picture) pose *f*

**express** **1** *n* rapide *m*
**2** *adj* ⟨*letter, parcel*⟩ exprès; ⟨*delivery, train*⟩ rapide
**3** *adv* to send sth ~ envoyer qch en exprès
**4** *vtr* exprimer; to ~ oneself s'exprimer

**expression** *n* expression *f*

**expressive** *adj* expressif/-ive

**exquisite** *adj* exquis/-e

**extend** **1** *vtr* (a) agrandir ⟨*house*⟩; prolonger ⟨*runway*⟩; élargir ⟨*range*⟩; ~ed family famille *f* étendue
(b) prolonger ⟨*visit, visa*⟩
(c) étendre ⟨*arm, leg*⟩; tendre ⟨*hand*⟩
**2** *vi* s'étendre (as far as jusqu'à; from de)

**extension** *n* (a) (on cable, table) rallonge *f*; (to house) addition *f*
(b) (phone) poste *m* supplémentaire; ~ (number) (numéro *m* de) poste *m*
(c) (of deadline) délai *m* supplémentaire

**extension lead** *n* rallonge *f*

**extensive** *adj* (a) ⟨*network*⟩ vaste (before n); ⟨*list*⟩ long/longue (before n); ⟨*tests*⟩ approfondi/-e; ⟨*changes*⟩ important/-e
(b) ⟨*damage, loss*⟩ grave, considérable; ⟨*burns*⟩ grave

**extent** *n* (a) (of area, problem, power) étendue *f*; (of damage) ampleur *f*
(b) (degree) mesure *f*; to a certain/great ~ dans une certaine/large mesure

**exterior** **1** *n* extérieur *m* (of de)
**2** *adj* extérieur/-e (to à)

**exterminate** *vtr* éliminer ⟨*vermin*⟩; exterminer ⟨*people, race*⟩

**external** *adj* (gen) extérieur/-e (to à); ⟨*surface, injury, examiner*⟩ externe

**extinct** *adj* ⟨*species*⟩ disparu/-e; ⟨*volcano*⟩ éteint/-e; to become ~ ⟨*species, animal, plant*⟩ disparaître

**extinguish** *vtr* éteindre ⟨*fire, cigarette*⟩

**extinguisher** *n* extincteur *m*

**extra** **1** *n* (a) (feature) option *f*; the sunroof is an ~ le toit ouvrant est en option
(b) (actor) figurant/-e *m/f*

**2** *adj* supplémentaire; an ~ £1,000 1 000 livres sterling de plus
**3** *adv* ~ careful encore plus prudent (que d'habitude); you have to pay ~ il faut payer un supplément

**extra charge** *n* supplément *m*

**extract** **1** *n* extrait *m* (from de)
**2** *vtr* (a) extraire (from de)
(b) arracher ⟨*promise*⟩ (from à)

**extra-curricular** *adj* parascolaire

**extraordinary** *adj* extraordinaire

**extraterrestrial** *n, adj* extraterrestre (*mf*)

**extra time** *n* (in sport) prolongation *f*; to go into ~ jouer les prolongations

**extravagance** *n* (a) (trait) prodigalité *f*
(b) (luxury) luxe *m*

**extravagant** *adj* (a) ⟨*person*⟩ dépensier/-ière; ⟨*way of life*⟩ dispendieux/-ieuse; to be ~ with sth gaspiller qch
(b) (luxurious) luxueux/-euse

**extra virgin olive oil** *n* huile *f* d'olive extra vierge

**extreme** **1** *n* extrême *m*; to go to ~s pousser les choses à l'extrême
**2** *adj* (gen) extrême; ⟨*view, measure, reaction*⟩ extrémiste

**extremely** *adv* extrêmement

**extreme sports** *n pl* sports *mpl* extrêmes

**extremism** *n* extrémisme *m*

**extrovert** *n, adj* extraverti/-e (*m/f*)

**eye** **1** *n* (a) œil *m*; with blue ~s aux yeux bleus; in front of *or* before your (very) ~s sous vos yeux; to keep an ~ on sb/sth surveiller qn/qch; to have one's ~ on ⟨*watch*⟩ surveiller ⟨*person*⟩; (want) avoir envie de ⟨*house*⟩; viser ⟨*job*⟩; to catch sb's ~ attirer l'attention de qn; as far as the ~ can see à perte de vue; to have an ~ for avoir le sens de ⟨*detail*⟩
(b) (of needle) chas *m*
**2** *vtr* regarder
IDIOMS an ~ for an ~ œil pour œil; to make ~s at sb faire les yeux doux à qn; to see ~ to ~ with sb (about sth) partager le point de vue de qn (au sujet de qch)

**eyeball** *n* globe *m* oculaire

**eyebrow** *n* sourcil *m*

**eyebrow pencil** *n* crayon *m* à sourcils

**eye-catching** *adj* ⟨*design, poster*⟩ attrayant/-e; ⟨*advertisement, headline*⟩ accrocheur/-euse

**eyedrops** *n pl* gouttes *fpl* pour les yeux

**eyelash** *n* cil *m*

**eyelid** *n* paupière *f*

**eye liner** *n* eye-liner *m*

**eye shadow** *n* fard *m* à paupières

**eyesight** *n* vue *f*

**eye test** *n* examen *m* de la vue

**eyewitness** *n* témoin *m* oculaire

**e-zine** *n* magazine *m* électronique, e-zine *m*

# Ff

**f, F** *n* **(a)** (letter) f, F *m*
**(b)** F (Mus) fa *m*
**fable** *n* fable *f*
**fabric** *n* **(a)** (cloth) tissu *m*
**(b)** (of building) structure *f*; **the ~ of society** le tissu social
**fabricate** *vtr* **(a)** inventer [qch] de toutes pièces ⟨*story, evidence*⟩
**(b)** fabriquer ⟨*document*⟩
**fabric softener** *n* assouplissant *m*
**fabulous** *adj* **(a)** fabuleux/-euse
**(b)** (colloq) (wonderful) sensationnel/-elle (colloq)
**façade, facade** *n* façade *f* (**of** de)
**face** **1** *n* **(a)** (of person) visage *m*, figure *f*; (of animal) face *f*; **to slam the door/laugh in sb's ~** claquer la porte/rire au nez de qn; **to pull** *or* **make a ~** faire une grimace; (in disgust) faire la grimace
**(b) to lose ~** perdre la face; **to save ~** sauver la face
**(c)** (of clock, watch) cadran *m*; (of coin) côté *m*; (of planet) surface *f*; (of cliff, mountain) face *f*; (of playing card) face *f*; **~ up/down** à l'endroit/l'envers
**2** *vtr* **(a)** (look towards) ⟨*person*⟩ faire face à; ⟨*building, room*⟩ donner sur; **to ~ south** ⟨*person*⟩ regarder au sud; ⟨*building*⟩ être orienté/-e au sud
**(b)** se trouver face à ⟨*challenge, crisis*⟩; se trouver menacé/-e de ⟨*defeat, redundancy*⟩; affronter ⟨*rival, team*⟩; **to be ~d with** se trouver confronté/-e à ⟨*problem, decision*⟩
**(c)** (acknowledge) **~ the facts, you're finished!** regarde la réalité en face, tu es fini!; **let's ~ it, nobody's perfect** admettons-le, personne n'est parfait
**(d)** (tolerate prospect) **I can't ~ doing** je n'ai pas le courage de faire; **he couldn't ~ the thought of eating** l'idée de manger lui était insupportable
**(e)** revêtir ⟨*façade, wall*⟩ (**with** de)
**3 in the face of** *phr* **(a)** en dépit de ⟨*difficulties*⟩
**(b)** face à, devant ⟨*opposition, enemy, danger*⟩
**4 face to face** *adv* ⟨*be seated*⟩ face à face; **to come ~ to ~ with** se retrouver face à; **to talk to sb ~ to ~** parler à qn en personne
■ **face up to** faire face à ⟨*problem, responsibilities*⟩
**faceless** *adj* anonyme
**face-lift** *n* lifting *m*; **to have a ~** se faire faire un lifting; **to give [sth] a ~** rénover ⟨*building*⟩; réaménager ⟨*town centre*⟩
**facet** *n* facette *f*
**facetious** *adj* ⟨*remark*⟩ facétieux/-ieuse; ⟨*person*⟩ farceur/-euse

**face-to-face** **1** *adj* a **~ discussion, a ~ meeting** un face-à-face *inv*
**2 face to face** *adv* ⟨*be seated*⟩ face à face; **to come ~ with** se retrouver face à; **to meet sb ~** rencontrer qn en face-à-face
**face value** *n* (of coin) valeur *f* nominale; **to take [sth] at ~** prendre [qch] au pied de la lettre; **to take sb at ~** juger qn sur les apparences
**facilitate** *vtr* faciliter ⟨*progress, talks*⟩; favoriser ⟨*development*⟩
**facility** **1** *n* **(a)** (building) complexe *m*, installation *f*
**(b)** (ease) facilité *f*
**(c)** (feature) fonction *f*
**2 facilities** *n pl* (equipment) équipement *m*; (infrastructure) infrastructure *f*; **facilities for the disabled** installations *fpl* pour les handicapés; **parking facilities** parking *m*
**facsimile** *n* (gen) fac-similé *m*; (sculpture) reproduction *f*
**fact** *n* fait *m*; **~s and figures** les faits et les chiffres; **to know for a ~ that** savoir de source sûre que; **due to the ~ that** étant donné que; **as a matter of ~** en fait; **to be based on ~** être fondé-e sur des faits réels
**IDIOMS to know the ~s of life** savoir comment les enfants viennent au monde; **the (hard) ~s of life** les réalités de la vie
**fact-finding** *adj* ⟨*mission, tour*⟩ d'information
**faction** *n* (group) faction *f*
**factor** *n* facteur *m*; **common ~** point *m* commun; (in mathematics) facteur commun; **protection ~** indice *m* de protection
**factory** *n* usine *f*
**factory farming** *n* élevage *m* industriel
**factory shop** *n* magasin *m* d'usine
**factory worker** *n* ouvrier/-ière *m/f* (d'usine)
**fact sheet** *n* bulletin *m* d'informations
**factual** *adj* ⟨*evidence*⟩ factuel/-elle; ⟨*account, description*⟩ basé/-e sur les faits; **~ programme** reportage *m*
**faculty** *n* **(a)** (ability) faculté *f* (**for** de)
**(b)** (GB Univ) faculté *f*
**(c)** (US) (Univ, Sch) (staff) corps *m* enseignant
**fad** *n* **(a)** (craze) engouement *m* (**for** pour)
**(b)** (whim) (petite) manie *f*
**fade** **1** *vtr* décolorer
**2** *vi* ⟨*fabric*⟩ se décolorer, se défraîchir; ⟨*colour*⟩ passer; ⟨*lettering, smile, memory*⟩ s'effacer; ⟨*flowers*⟩ se faner; ⟨*image*⟩ s'estomper; ⟨*sound*⟩ s'affaiblir; ⟨*interest, excitement*⟩ s'évanouir; ⟨*hearing, light*⟩ baisser ····▷

■ **fade away** ⟨sound⟩ s'éteindre; ⟨sick
person⟩ dépérir
**faded** adj ⟨clothing⟩ décoloré/-e; ⟨jeans⟩
délavé/-e; ⟨photo⟩ jauni/-e; ⟨flower⟩ fané/-e
**faeces, feces** (US) n pl matières fpl
fécales
**fail** [1] n (in exam) échec m
  [2] vtr (a) échouer à ⟨exam, driving test⟩;
  échouer en ⟨subject⟩; coller (colloq)
  ⟨candidate, pupil⟩
  (b) (omit) to ~ to do manquer de faire; to ~
  to mention sth... omettre de signaler que...
  (c) (be unable) to ~ to do ne pas réussir à
  faire
  (d) ⟨person⟩ laisser tomber ⟨friend⟩;
  ⟨courage⟩ manquer à ⟨person⟩; ⟨memory⟩
  faire défaut à ⟨person⟩
  [3] vi (a) (not succeed) ne pas réussir; ⟨exam
  candidate, attempt, plan⟩ échouer; ⟨crop⟩ être
  mauvais/-e; if all else ~s en dernier recours
  (b) ⟨eyesight, hearing, light⟩ baisser; ⟨health⟩
  décliner
  (c) ⟨brakes⟩ lâcher; ⟨power⟩ être coupé/-e;
  ⟨heart⟩ lâcher
  [4] **without fail** phr ⟨arrive, do⟩ sans faute;
  ⟨happen⟩ à coup sûr
**failing** [1] n défaut m
  [2] prep ~ that, ~ this sinon
**failure** n (a) (lack of success) échec m (in à)
  (b) (person) raté/-e m/f (colloq); (venture or event)
  échec m
  (c) (of engine, machine) panne f
  (d) (Med) défaillance f
  (e) (omission) ~ to comply with the rules
  non-respect m de la réglementation; ~ to
  pay non-paiement m
**faint** [1] adj (a) ⟨smell, accent, breeze⟩
  léger/-ère; ⟨sound, voice, protest⟩ faible;
  ⟨markings⟩ à peine visible; ⟨recollection⟩
  vague; I haven't the ~est idea je n'en ai pas
  la moindre idée
  (b) to feel ~ se sentir mal, défaillir
  [2] vi s'évanouir (from sous l'effet de)
**fainthearted** n the ~ (cowardly) les
timorés mpl; (over-sensitive) les natures fpl
sensibles
**fair** [1] n (funfair, market) foire f; (for charity)
kermesse f; trade ~ foire commerciale
  [2] adj (a) (just) ⟨arrangement, person, trial,
  wage⟩ équitable (to pour); ⟨comment,
  decision, point⟩ juste; it's only ~ that she
  should be first ce n'est que justice qu'elle
  soit la première; it isn't ~ ce n'est pas juste
  (b) (quite good) assez bon/bonne
  (c) a ~ number of un bon nombre de; the
  house was a ~ size la maison était de bonne
  taille
  (d) ⟨weather⟩ beau/belle (before n); ⟨wind⟩
  favorable
  (e) ⟨hair⟩ blond/-e; ⟨complexion⟩ clair/-e
  (f) with her own ~ hands de ses blanches
  mains; the ~ sex le beau sexe
  [3] adv ⟨play⟩ franc jeu
  **IDIOMS to win ~ and square** remporter une
  victoire indiscutable
**fairground** n champ m de foire

**fair-haired** adj blond/-e
**fairly** adv (a) (quite, rather) assez; ⟨sure⟩
pratiquement
  (b) (justly) ⟨obtain, win⟩ honnêtement
**fair-minded** adj impartial/-e
**fairness** n (a) (of person) équité f; (of
judgment) impartialité f; in all ~ en toute
justice
  (b) (of complexion) blancheur f; (of hair)
  blondeur f
**fair play** n to have a sense of ~ jouer
franc jeu, être fair-play; to ensure ~ faire
respecter les règles du jeu
**fairy** n fée f
**fairy story, fairy tale** n conte m de fées
**faith** n (a) (confidence) confiance f; I have no
~ in her elle ne m'inspire pas confiance; in
good ~ en toute bonne foi
  (b) (belief) foi f (in en); the Muslim ~ la foi
  musulmane
**faithful** [1] n the ~ les fidèles mpl
  [2] adj fidèle (to à)
**faithfully** adv fidèlement; yours ~ (in letter)
veuillez agréer, Monsieur/Madame, mes/nos
salutations distinguées
**faith healer** n guérisseur m
**faith healing** n guérison f par la foi
**fake** [1] n (a) (jewel, work of art, note) faux m
  (b) (person) imposteur m
  [2] adj faux/fausse (before n)
  [3] vtr contrefaire ⟨signature, document⟩;
  falsifier ⟨results⟩; feindre ⟨emotion, illness⟩
  [4] vi faire semblant
**falcon** n faucon m
**Falklands** pr n pl (also **Falkland
Islands**) the ~ les îles fpl Malouines
**fall** [1] n (a) (gen) chute f (from de); (in
wrestling) tombé m
  (b) (decrease) baisse f (in de); (more drastic)
  chute f (in de)
  (c) (in pitch) descente f
  (d) (of government) chute f; (of monarchy)
  renversement m
  (e) (US) (autumn) automne m
  [2] **falls** n pl chutes fpl
  [3] vi (a) (gen) tomber (from, off, out of de;
  into dans); to ~ 10 metres tomber de 10
  mètres; to ~ down tomber dans ⟨hole,
  stairs⟩; to ~ on or to the floor or the ground
  tomber par terre; to ~ at sb's feet se jeter
  aux pieds de qn; to ~ from power tomber
  (b) ⟨quality, standard, level⟩ diminuer;
  ⟨temperature, price, production, number⟩
  baisser (by de); to ~ to/from descendre à/de
■ **fall apart (a)** ⟨bike, table⟩ être délabré/-e;
⟨shoes⟩ être usé/-e; ⟨car, house⟩ tomber en
ruine
  (b) ⟨country⟩ se désagréger; ⟨person⟩ craquer
  (colloq)
■ **fall back** reculer; (Mil) se replier
■ **fall back on** avoir recours à ⟨savings,
parents⟩
■ **fall behind** prendre du retard; to ~

behind with (GB) *or* in (US) prendre du retard
dans ⟨*work, project*⟩; être en retard pour
⟨*payments, rent*⟩

■ **fall down (a)** ⟨*person, poster*⟩ tomber;
⟨*tent, scaffolding*⟩ s'effondrer
**(b)** (GB) ⟨*argument, comparison*⟩ faiblir

■ **fall for**: ¶ ∼ **for** [sth] se laisser prendre à
⟨*trick, story*⟩; ¶ ∼ **for** [sb] tomber
amoureux/-euse de

■ **fall in (a)** ⟨*walls, roof*⟩ s'écrouler,
s'effondrer
**(b)** ⟨*soldiers*⟩ former les rangs

■ **fall off (a)** ⟨*person, hat, label*⟩ tomber
**(b)** ⟨*attendance, sales, output*⟩ diminuer;
⟨*quality*⟩ baisser; ⟨*support*⟩ retomber

■ **fall open** ⟨*book*⟩ tomber ouvert/-e; ⟨*robe*⟩
s'entrebâiller

■ **fall out (a)** tomber; his hair is ∼ing out il
perd ses cheveux
**(b)** (quarrel) se brouiller (**over** à propos de;
**with** avec)

■ **fall over**: ¶ ∼ **over** ⟨*person*⟩ tomber (par
terre); ⟨*object*⟩ se renverser; ¶ ∼ **over** [sth]
trébucher sur ⟨*object*⟩

■ **fall through** ⟨*plans, deal*⟩ échouer

**fallacy** *n* erreur *f*

**fallible** *adj* faillible

**fallout** *n* retombées *fpl*

**false** *adj* faux/fausse

**false alarm** *n* fausse alerte *f*

**false bottom** *n* (in bag, box) double fond
*m*

**falsely** *adv* **(a)** (wrongly) faussement;
(mistakenly) à tort
**(b)** ⟨*smile, laugh*⟩ avec affectation

**false pretences** *n pl* on *or* under ∼ en
utilisant un subterfuge; (by an action) par des
moyens frauduleux

**false start** *n* faux départ *m*

**false teeth** *n pl* dentier *m*

**falsify** *vtr* falsifier

**falsity** *n* fausseté *f*

**falter** *vi* **(a)** ⟨*person, courage*⟩ faiblir
**(b)** (when speaking) ⟨*person*⟩ bafouiller; ⟨*voice*⟩
trembloter
**(c)** (when walking) ⟨*person*⟩ chanceler;
⟨*footstep*⟩ hésiter

**faltering** *adj* ⟨*economy, demand*⟩ en déclin;
⟨*voice*⟩ hésitant/-e

**fame** *n* renommée *f* (as en tant que); ∼ and
fortune la gloire et la fortune

**familiar** *adj* familier/-ière (to à); her face
looked ∼ to me son visage m'était familier;
that name sounds ∼ ce nom me dit quelque
chose; it's a ∼ story c'est un scénario
connu; to be ∼ with sth connaître qch

**familiarity** *n* familiarité *f* (with avec)

**familiarize** ⒈ *vtr* to ∼ sb with
familiariser qn avec
⒉ *v refl* to ∼ oneself with se familiariser
avec ⟨*system, work*⟩; s'habituer à ⟨*person,
place*⟩

**family** *n* famille *f*; this must run in the ∼
ça doit être de famille

**family name** *n* nom *m* de famille

**family planning** *n* planning *m* familial

**family tree** *n* arbre *m* généalogique

**family unit** *n* cellule *f* familiale

**famine** *n* famine *f*

**famished** *adj* (colloq) I'm ∼ je meurs de
faim

**famous** *adj* (gen) célèbre (**for** pour);
⟨*school, university*⟩ réputé/-e (**for** pour)

**fan** ⒈ *n* **(a)** (of jazz) mordu/-e *m/f* (colloq); (of
star, actor) fan *mf* (colloq); (Sport) supporter *m*
**(b)** (for cooling) (mechanical) ventilateur *m*;
(hand-held) éventail *m*
⒉ *vtr* attiser ⟨*fire*⟩; to ∼ one's face
s'éventer le visage

■ **fan out**: ¶ ∼ **out** ⟨*police, troops*⟩ se
déployer (en éventail); ¶ ∼ [sth] **out** ouvrir
[qch] en éventail ⟨*cards, papers*⟩

**fanatic** *n* fanatique *mf*

**fanaticism** *n* fanatisme *m*

**fan belt** *n* courroie *f* de ventilateur

**fancy** ⒈ *n* **(a)** (liking) to take sb's ∼ ⟨*object*⟩
faire envie à qn; to take a ∼ to sb s'attacher
à qn; (sexually) (GB) s'enticher de qn
**(b)** (whim) caprice *m*; as the ∼ takes me
comme ça me prend
**(c)** (fantasy) imagination *f*; a flight of ∼ une
lubie
⒉ *adj* ⟨*equipment*⟩ sophistiqué/-e; ⟨*food,
hotel, restaurant*⟩ de luxe; ⟨*paper, box*⟩
fantaisie *inv*; ⟨*clothes*⟩ chic
⒊ *vtr* **(a)** (colloq) (want) avoir (bien) envie de
⟨*food, drink, object*⟩; what do you ∼ for
lunch? qu'est-ce qui te plairait pour le
déjeuner?
**(b)** (GB) (colloq) she fancies him elle s'est
entichée de lui
**(c)** ∼ seeing you here! (colloq) tiens donc, toi
ici!
**(d)** (Sport) voir [qn/qch] gagnant ⟨*athlete,
horse*⟩

**fancy dress** *n* (GB) déguisement *m*; in ∼
déguisé/-e

**fancy dress party** *n* bal *m* costumé

**fang** *n* (of dog, wolf) croc *m*; (of snake) crochet
*m* (à venin)

**fan mail** *n* lettres *fpl* envoyées par des
admirateurs

**fantasize** *vi* fantasmer (**about** sur); to ∼
**about** doing rêver de faire

**fantastic** *adj* **(a)** (colloq) (wonderful)
merveilleux/-euse, super *inv* (colloq)
**(b)** (unrealistic) ⟨*story*⟩ invraisemblable
**(c)** (colloq) (huge) ⟨*profit*⟩ fabuleux/-euse;
⟨*speed, increase*⟩ vertigineux/-euse
**(d)** (magical) fantastique

**fantasy** *n* **(a)** (dream) rêve *m*; (in psychology)
fantasme *m*
**(b)** (fiction) fantastique *m*

**fanzine** *n* magazine *m* des fans, fanzine *m*

**FAQ** *n* (*abbr* = **frequently asked
questions**) FAQ *f*, foire *f* aux questions

**far** ⒈ *adv* **(a)** (in space) loin; ∼ off, ∼ away
au loin; is it ∼ to York? est-ce que York est

loin d'ici?; **how** ∼ **is it to Leeds?** combien y
a-t-il (de kilomètres) jusqu'à Leeds?; **how** ∼
**is Glasgow from London?** Glasgow est à
quelle distance de Londres?; **as** ∼ **as** jusqu'à
**(b)** (in time) **as** ∼ **back as 1965** déjà en 1965;
**as** ∼ **back as he can remember** d'aussi loin
qu'il s'en souvienne; **the holidays are not** ∼
**off** c'est bientôt les vacances
**(c)** (very much) bien; ∼ **better** bien mieux; ∼
**too fast** bien trop vite
**(d) how** ∼ **have they got?** où en sont-ils?; **as**
∼ **as possible** autant que possible, dans la
mesure du possible; **as** ∼ **as we know** pour
autant que nous le sachions; **as** ∼ **as I am
concerned** quant à moi
**(e) to go too** ∼ aller trop loin; **to push sb
too** ∼ pousser qn à bout
**2** *adj* **(a) the** ∼ **north/south (of)** l'extrême
nord/sud (de); **the** ∼ **east/west (of)** tout à
fait à l'est/l'ouest (de)
**(b)** autre; **at the** ∼ **end of the room** à l'autre
bout de la pièce; **on the** ∼ **side of the wall** de
l'autre côté du mur
**(c)** (of party) **the** ∼ **right/left** l'extrême droite/
gauche
**3 by far** *phr* de loin
**4 far from** *phr* loin de; ∼ **from satisfied**
loin d'être satisfait/-e
**5 so far** *phr* **(a)** (up till now) jusqu'ici,
jusqu'à présent; **so** ∼**, so good** pour l'instant
tout va bien
**(b)** (up to a point) **you can only trust him so** ∼
tu ne peux pas lui faire entièrement
confiance
**IDIOMS not to be** ∼ **off** *or* **out** *or* **wrong** ne
pas être loin du compte; ∼ **and wide** partout;
**to be a** ∼ **cry from** être bien loin de; **she will
go** ∼ elle ira loin; **this wine won't go very** ∼
on ne va pas aller loin avec ce vin

**faraway** *adj* lointain/-e

**farce** *n* farce *f*

**farcical** *adj* ridicule

**fare** *n* (on bus, underground) prix *m* du ticket;
(on train, plane) prix du billet; **half/full** ∼
demi-/plein tarif *m*

**Far East** *pr n* Extrême-Orient *m*

**farewell** *n* adieu *m*

**far-fetched** *adj* tiré/-e par les cheveux
(colloq)

**farm** **1** *n* ferme *f*
**2** *vtr* cultiver, exploiter ⟨land⟩
■ **farm out**: ∼ **out [sth]** sous-traiter ⟨work⟩
(**to** à)

**farmer** *n* (gen) fermier *m*; (in official
terminology) agriculteur *m*; (arable) cultivateur
*m*; **pig** ∼ éleveur *m* de porcs

**farming** *n* (profession) agriculture *f*; (of land)
exploitation *f*; **sheep** ∼ élevage *m* de
moutons

**farmyard** *n* cour *f* de ferme

**far-off** *adj* lointain/-e

**far-reaching** *adj* ⟨effect⟩ considérable;
⟨change, reform⟩ radical/-e; ⟨plan, proposal⟩
d'une portée considérable

**far-sighted** *adj* **(a)** (prudent) ⟨person,
policy⟩ prévoyant/-e
**(b)** (US) ⟨person⟩ presbyte

**farther** *adj*, *adv* = FURTHER 1A,B 2B

**farthest** = FURTHEST

**fascinate** *vtr* (interest) passionner; (stronger)
fasciner

**fascinating** *adj* ⟨book, discussion⟩
passionnant/-e; ⟨person⟩ fascinant/-e

**fascination** *n* passion *f* (**with, for** pour)

**fascism** *n* fascisme *m*

**fascist** *n*, *adj* fasciste (*mf*)

**fashion** **1** *n* **(a)** mode *f* (**for** de); **in** ∼ à la
mode; **to go out of** ∼ se démoder, passer de
mode; **to be all the** ∼ faire fureur
**(b)** (manner) façon *f*, manière *f*; **after a** ∼ plus
ou moins bien
**2** *vtr* façonner ⟨clay, wood⟩ (**into** en);
fabriquer ⟨object⟩ (**out of, from** de)

**fashionable** *adj* ⟨clothes⟩ à la mode
(**among, with** parmi); ⟨resort, restaurant⟩ chic
(**among, with** parmi)

**fashion designer** *n* modéliste *mf*;
(world-famous) grand couturier *m*

**fashion house** *n* maison *f* de couture

**fashion model** *n* mannequin *m*

**fashion show** *n* présentation *f* de
collection

**fast** **1** *n* jeûne *m*
**2** *adj* **(a)** rapide; **to be a** ∼ **reader/runner**
lire/courir vite
**(b)** (ahead of time) **my watch is** ∼ ma montre
avance; **you're five minutes** ∼ ta montre
avance de cinq minutes
**3** *adv* **(a)** vite, rapidement; **how** ∼ **can you
run?** est-ce que tu cours vite?
**(b)** ⟨hold⟩ ferme; ⟨stuck⟩ bel et bien; ⟨shut⟩
bien; **to be** ∼ **asleep** dormir à poings fermés

**fasten** **1** *vtr* **(a)** fermer ⟨lid, case⟩; attacher
⟨belt, necklace⟩; boutonner ⟨coat⟩
**(b)** fixer ⟨notice, shelf⟩ (**to** à; **onto** sur);
attacher ⟨lead, rope⟩ (**to** à)
**2** *vi* ⟨box⟩ se fermer; ⟨necklace, skirt⟩
s'attacher

**fastener** *n* (gen) attache *f*; (hook) agrafe *f*;
(clasp) fermoir *m*

**fast food** *n* restauration *f* rapide

**fast food restaurant** *n* fast-food *m*,
restovite *m*

**fast-forward** **1** *n* avance *f* rapide
**2** *vtr* faire avancer rapidement ⟨tape⟩

**fast-growing** *adj* en pleine expansion

**fast lane** *n* voie *f* de dépassement

**fast track** **1** *n* promotion *f* accélérée
**2 fast-track** *vtr* former [qn] de façon
accélérée

**fat** **1** *n* **(a)** (in diet) matières *fpl* grasses;
**animal** ∼**s** graisses *fpl* animales
**(b)** (on meat) gras *m*
**(c)** (for cooking) matière *f* grasse
**(d)** (in body) graisse *f*
**2** *adj* **(a)** ⟨person, animal, body, bottom⟩
gros/grosse (*before n*); **to get** ∼ grossir

**(b)** ‹wallet› rebondi/-e; ‹envelope, file, magazine› épais/épaisse

**(c)** ‹profit, cheque› gros/grosse (before n)

**fatal** adj ‹accident, injury› mortel/-elle (**to** pour); ‹flaw, mistake› fatal/-e; ‹decision› funeste; ‹day, hour› fatidique

**fatalist** n fataliste mf

**fatality** n (person killed) mort m

**fatally** adv **(a)** ‹wounded› mortellement **(b)** ‹flawed› irrémédiablement

**fate** n sort m

**fateful** adj ‹decision› fatal/-e; ‹day› fatidique

**fat-free** adj sans matières grasses

**father** ⓵ n père m ⓶ vtr engendrer ‹child›

**Father Christmas** n (GB) le père Noël

**father-in-law** n beau-père m

**fatherly** adj paternel/-elle

**fathom** ⓵ n brasse f anglaise (= 1.83 m) ⓶ vtr (also ~ **out** (GB)) comprendre

**fatigue** n **(a)** (of person) épuisement m **(b)** metal ~ fatigue f du métal **(c)** (US) (Mil) corvée f

**fatten** vtr (also ~ **up**) engraisser ‹animal›; faire grossir ‹person›

**fattening** adj ‹food, drink› qui fait grossir

**fatty** adj ‹tissue, deposit› graisseux/-euse; ‹food, meat› gras/grasse

**fatuous** adj stupide

**faucet** n (US) robinet m

**fault** ⓵ n **(a)** (flaw) défaut m (**in** dans); he's always finding ~ il trouve toujours quelque chose à redire **(b)** (responsibility) faute f; **to be sb's ~** être (de) la faute de qn; **it's my own ~** c'est de ma faute **(c)** (in tennis) ~! faute! **(d)** (in earth) faille f ⓶ vtr prendre [qn/qch] en défaut; **it cannot be** ~**ed** c'est irréprochable

**faultless** adj ‹performance, manners› impeccable; ‹taste› irréprochable

**faulty** adj ‹wiring, machine› défectueux/-euse

**fauna** n faune f

**faux pas** n impair m

**favour** (GB), **favor** (US) ⓵ n **(a)** (kindness) service m; **to do sb a ~** rendre service à qn; **to return a** or **the ~** rendre la pareille **(b) to be in sb's ~** ‹situation› être avantageux/-euse pour qn; ‹financial rates, wind› être favorable à qn **(c) to win/lose ~ with sb** s'attirer/perdre les bonnes grâces de qn ⓶ vtr **(a)** (prefer) être pour ‹method, solution›; être partisan de ‹political party› **(b)** (benefit) ‹circumstances› favoriser ‹person›; ‹law› privilégier ‹person› ⓷ **in favour of** phr **(a)** (on the side of) en faveur de; **to be in ~ of sb/sth** être pour qn/qch

**(b)** (to the advantage of) **to work in sb's ~** avantager qn; **to decide in sb's ~** (Law) donner gain de cause à qn

**(c)** (out of preference for) ‹reject› au profit de

**favourable** (GB), **favorable** (US) adj ‹conditions, impression, reply› favorable (**to** à); ‹result, sign› bon/bonne (before n)

**favourably** (GB), **favorably** (US) adv ‹speak, write› en termes favorables; ‹look on› d'un œil favorable; **to compare ~ with sth** soutenir la comparaison avec qch

**favourite** (GB), **favorite** (US) ⓵ n (gen) préféré/-e m/f; (Sport) favori/-ite m/f ⓶ adj préféré/-e, favori/-ite

**favouritism** (GB), **favoritism** (US) n favoritisme m

**fawn** ⓵ n (Zool) faon m ⓶ vtr **to ~ on sb** flagorner qn

**fax** ⓵ n **(a)** (also ~ **message**) télécopie f, fax m **(b)** (also ~ **machine**) télécopieur m, fax m ⓶ vtr télécopier, faxer ‹document›; envoyer une télécopie or un fax à ‹person›

**fax number** n numéro m de télécopie or de fax

**faze** vtr (colloq) dérouter

**fear** ⓵ n **(a)** (fright) peur f **(b)** (apprehension) crainte f (**for** pour) **(c)** (possibility) **there's no ~ of him** or **his being late** il n'y a pas de danger qu'il soit en retard ⓶ vtr craindre; **to ~ the worst** craindre le pire, s'attendre au pire ⓷ vi **to ~ for sb/sth** craindre pour qn/qch

**fearless** adj sans peur, intrépide

**feasible** adj **(a)** ‹project› réalisable **(b)** ‹excuse, explanation› plausible

**feast** ⓵ n (meal) festin m; (religious) fête f ⓶ vi se régaler (**on** de)

**feat** n exploit m; **it was no mean ~** cela n'a pas été une mince affaire; **a ~ of engineering** une prouesse technologique

**feather** n plume f

**feature** ⓵ n **(a)** (distinctive characteristic) trait m, caractéristique f **(b)** (aspect) aspect m, côté m **(c)** (of face) trait m **(d)** (of car, computer, product) accessoire m **(e)** (report) (in paper) article m de fond (**on** sur); (on TV, radio) reportage m (**on** sur) ⓶ vtr ‹film, magazine› présenter ‹story, star›; ‹advert, poster› représenter ‹person› ⓷ vi **(a)** (figure) figurer **(b)** ‹performer› jouer (**in** dans)

**feature film** n long métrage m

**February** n février m

**federal** adj fédéral/-e

**federation** n fédération f

**fed up** adj (colloq) **to be ~** en avoir marre (colloq) (**of** de)

**fee** n **(a)** (for service) honoraires mpl; **school ~s** frais mpl de scolarité **(b)** (for admission) droit m d'entrée; (for membership) cotisation f

**feeble** adj (gen) faible; ⟨excuse⟩ peu convaincant/-e; ⟨joke, attempt⟩ médiocre

**feed** ⓵ n (for animals) ration f de nourriture; (for baby) (breast) tétée f; (bottle) biberon m
⓶ vtr **(a)** nourrir ⟨animal, plant, person⟩ (**on** de); donner à manger à ⟨pet⟩; ravitailler ⟨army⟩
**(b)** (supply) alimenter ⟨machine⟩; mettre des pièces dans ⟨meter⟩; faire passer ⟨ball⟩ (**to** à); **to ~ sth into** mettre or introduire qch dans

**feedback** n **(a)** (from people) remarques fpl (**on** sur; **from** de la part de)
**(b)** (on hi-fi) réaction f parasite

**feeding bottle** n biberon m

**feel** ⓵ n **(a)** (atmosphere) atmosphère f
**(b)** (sensation) sensation f
**(c) to get the ~ of** se faire à ⟨controls, system⟩; **to have a ~ for language** bien savoir manier la langue
⓶ vtr **(a)** éprouver ⟨affection, desire, pride⟩; ressentir ⟨hostility, obligation, effects⟩
**(b)** (believe) **to ~ (that)** estimer que
**(c)** sentir ⟨blow, draught, heat⟩; ressentir ⟨ache, stiffness, effects⟩
**(d)** (touch) tâter ⟨washing, cloth⟩; palper ⟨patient, shoulder, parcel⟩; **to ~ one's way** avancer à tâtons; (figurative) tâter le terrain
**(e)** avoir conscience de ⟨presence, tension⟩
⓷ vi **(a)** se sentir ⟨sad, happy, nervous, safe, ill, tired⟩; être ⟨sure, surprised⟩; avoir l'impression d'être ⟨trapped, betrayed⟩; **to ~ afraid/ashamed** avoir peur/honte; **to ~ hot/thirsty** avoir chaud/soif; **to ~ as if** or **as though** avoir l'impression que; **she isn't ~ing herself today** elle n'est pas dans son assiette aujourd'hui (colloq)
**(b)** (seem) être ⟨cold, smooth⟩; avoir l'air ⟨eerie⟩; **it ~s odd** ça fait drôle; **it ~s like (a) Sunday** on se croirait un dimanche
**(c)** (want) **to ~ like sth** avoir envie de qch; **I ~ like a drink** je prendrais bien un verre
**(d) to ~ (around** or **about) in** fouiller dans ⟨bag, pocket, drawer⟩; **to ~ along** tâtonner le long de ⟨edge, wall⟩
■ **feel for:** ¶ **~ (around) for [sth]** chercher [qch] à tâtons; ¶ **~ for [sb]** plaindre
■ **feel up to:** ¶ **~ up to (doing) sth** se sentir d'attaque (colloq) or assez bien pour (faire) qch

**feelgood** adj optimiste; **to play on the ~ factor** essayer de créer un sentiment de bien-être

**feeling** n **(a)** (emotion) sentiment m; **to hurt sb's ~s** blesser qn
**(b)** (opinion, belief) sentiment m; **~s are running high** les esprits s'échauffent
**(c)** (sensitivity) sensibilité f; **to speak with great ~** parler avec beaucoup de passion
**(d)** (impression) impression f; **I had a ~ you'd say that** je sentais que tu allais dire ça; **I've got a bad ~ about this** j'ai le pressentiment que cela va mal se passer
**(e)** (physical sensation) sensation f; **a dizzy ~** une sensation de vertige

**fee-paying** adj ⟨school⟩ payant/-e

**feign** vtr feindre ⟨innocence, surprise⟩; simuler ⟨illness, sleep⟩

**fell** ⓵ n montagne f
⓶ vtr abattre ⟨tree⟩; assommer ⟨person⟩
IDIOMS **in one ~ swoop** d'un seul coup

**fellow** ⓵ n **(a)** (colloq) (man) type m (colloq), homme m
**(b)** (of society, association) membre m (**of** de)
**(c)** (GB) (lecturer) membre m (du corps enseignant) d'un collège universitaire
**(d)** (US) (researcher) universitaire mf titulaire d'une bourse de recherche
⓶ adj **her ~ teachers** ses collègues professeurs; **a ~ Englishman** un compatriote anglais

**fellowship** n **(a)** (companionship) camaraderie f
**(b)** (association) association f

**felony** n crime m

**felt** n feutre m

**felt-tip (pen)** n feutre m

**female** ⓵ n **(a)** (Bot, Zool) femelle f
**(b)** (woman) femme f
⓶ adj **(a)** (Bot, Zool) femelle; **~ rabbit** lapine f
**(b)** ⟨population, role⟩ féminin/-e; ⟨voice⟩ de femme; **~ student** étudiante f
**(c)** ⟨plug, socket⟩ femelle

**feminine** ⓵ n féminin m
⓶ adj féminin/-e

**feminist** n, adj féministe (mf)

**fence** ⓵ n **(a)** clôture f
**(b)** (in showjumping) obstacle m; (in horseracing) haie f
⓶ vtr clôturer ⟨area, garden⟩
IDIOMS **to sit on the ~** ne pas prendre position

**fencing** n escrime f

**fend** vi **to ~ for oneself** se débrouiller (tout seul/toute seule)
■ **fend off** repousser ⟨attacker⟩; parer ⟨blow⟩; écarter ⟨question⟩

**fender** n **(a)** (for fire) garde-cendre m
**(b)** (US) (Aut) aile f

**fennel** n fenouil m

**fern** n fougère f

**ferocious** adj ⟨animal⟩ féroce; ⟨attack⟩ sauvage; ⟨heat⟩ accablant/-e

**ferret** n furet m
■ **ferret about** fureter, fouiller (**in** dans)

**ferry** ⓵ n (long-distance) ferry m; (over short distances) bac m
⓶ vtr transporter ⟨passenger, goods⟩

**fertile** adj ⟨land, imagination⟩ fertile; ⟨human, animal, egg⟩ fécond/-e

**fertility treatment** n traitement m contre la stérilité

**fertilize** vtr fertiliser ⟨land⟩; féconder ⟨animal, plant, egg⟩

**fertilizer** n engrais m

**fervent** adj ⟨admirer⟩ fervent/-e

**fester** vi ⟨wound, sore⟩ suppurer

**festival** n (gen) fête f; (arts event) festival m

**festivity** n réjouissance f

**fetch** *vtr* (a) aller chercher; ~! (to dog) rapporte!
(b) ⟨goods⟩ rapporter; **to ~ a good price** rapporter un bon prix; **these vases can ~ up to £600** le prix de ces vases peut atteindre 600 livres sterling

**fetching** *adj* ravissant/-e

**fête** *n* (church, village) kermesse *f* (paroissiale)

**fetus** (US) = FOETUS

**feud** ① *n* querelle *f*
② *vi* se quereller

**feudal** *adj* féodal/-e

**fever** *n* fièvre *f*; **to have a ~** avoir de la fièvre; **gold ~** la fièvre de l'or

**feverish** *adj* ⟨person, eyes⟩ fiévreux/-euse; ⟨dreams⟩ délirant/-e; ⟨excitement, activity⟩ fébrile

**fever pitch** *n* **to bring a crowd to ~** déchaîner une foule; **our excitement had reached ~** notre excitation était à son comble

**few**

■ **Note** When *a few* is used as a pronoun and if the sentence does not specify what it refers to, the pronoun *en* (= *of them*) must be added before the verb in French: *there were only a few* = il n'y en avait que quelques-uns/quelques-unes.

① *det* (a) (not many) peu de; **~ visitors/letters** peu de visiteurs/lettres
(b) (couple of) **every ~ days** tous les deux ou trois jours; **the first ~ weeks** les premières semaines
② *pron, quantif* peu; **~ of us succeeded** peu d'entre nous ont réussi
③ **a few** *det, quantif, pron* (a) (as determiner, quantifier) quelques; **a ~ people** quelques personnes; **quite a ~ people** pas mal (colloq) de gens, un bon nombre de personnes; **a ~ of the soldiers** quelques soldats; **a ~ of us** un certain nombre d'entre nous
(b) (as pronoun) quelques-uns/quelques-unes; **I would like a ~ more** j'en voudrais quelques-uns/quelques-unes de plus; **I only need a ~** il ne m'en faut que quelques-uns/quelques-unes
IDIOMS **they are ~ and far between** ils sont rarissimes

**fewer** ① *det* moins de; **~ and ~ pupils** de moins en moins d'élèves
② *pron* moins; **~ than 50 people** moins de 50 personnes; **no ~ than** pas moins de

**fewest** *det* le moins de

**fiancé** *n* fiancé *m*

**fiancée** *n* fiancée *f*

**fibre** (GB), **fiber** (US) *n* (a) (gen) fibre *f*
(b) (in diet) fibres *fpl*

**fibreglass** (GB), **fiberglass** (US) *n* fibres *fpl* de verre

**fibre optic** (GB), **fiber optic** (US) *adj* ⟨cable⟩ à fibres optiques; ⟨link⟩ par fibres optiques

**fickle** *adj* ⟨lover, friend⟩ inconstant/-e; ⟨fate, public opinion⟩ changeant/-e; ⟨weather⟩ capricieux/-ieuse

**fiction** *n* (a) (genre) le roman
(b) (invention) fiction *f*

**fictional** *adj* ⟨character, event⟩ imaginaire

**fictionalize** *vtr* romancer

**fictitious** *adj* (a) (false) ⟨name, address⟩ fictif/-ive
(b) (imaginary) imaginaire

**fiddle** ① *vtr* (colloq) falsifier ⟨tax return, figures⟩
② *vi* (a) (fidget) **to ~ with sth** tripoter qch
(b) (adjust) **to ~ with** tourner ⟨knobs, controls⟩

**fidelity** *n* fidélité *f* (of de; to à)

**fidget** *vi* ne pas tenir en place

**field** ① *n* (a) (gen) champ *m* (of de); (sports ground) terrain *m*; **football ~** terrain de football
(b) (of knowledge) domaine *m* (of de)
② *adj* (a) ⟨hospital⟩ de campagne
(b) ⟨test, study⟩ sur le terrain; ⟨work⟩ de terrain

**field day** *n* (a) (school trip) sortie *f* (éducative)
(b) (US) (sports day) journée *f* sportive
IDIOMS **to have a ~** (gen) s'amuser comme un fou/une folle; ⟨press, critics⟩ jubiler; (make money) ⟨shopkeepers⟩ faire d'excellentes affaires

**field trip** *n* (one day) sortie *f* éducative; (longer) voyage *m* d'études

**fieldwork** *n* travail *m* de terrain

**fierce** *adj* ⟨animal, expression, person⟩ féroce; ⟨battle, storm⟩ violent/-e; ⟨competition⟩ acharné/-e; ⟨flames, heat⟩ intense

**fiercely** *adv* ⟨oppose⟩ avec acharnement; ⟨fight⟩ sauvagement; ⟨shout⟩ violemment; ⟨burn⟩ avec intensité; ⟨competitive, critical⟩ extrêmement; ⟨determined, loyal⟩ farouchement

**fifteen** *n, pron, det* quinze (*m*) *inv*

**fifteenth** ① *n* (a) (in order) quinzième *mf*
(b) (of month) quinze *m inv*
(c) (fraction) quinzième *m*
② *adj, adv* quinzième

**fifth** ① *n* (a) (in order) cinquième *mf*
(b) (of month) cinq *m inv*
(c) (fraction) cinquième *m*
② *adj, adv* cinquième

**fifties** *n pl* (a) (era) **the ~** les années *fpl* cinquante
(b) (age) **to be in one's ~** avoir entre cinquante et soixante ans

**fiftieth** *n, adj, adv* cinquantième (*mf*)

**fifty** *n, pron, det* cinquante (*m*) *inv*

**fifty-fifty** ① *adj* **to have a ~ chance** avoir une chance sur deux (**of doing** de faire)
② *adv* **to share sth ~** partager qch moitié-moitié; **to go ~** faire moitié-moitié

**fig** *n* figue *f*

**fight** ① *n* (a) (gen) bagarre *f* (**between** ····⟩

entre; **over** pour); (Mil) bataille *f* (**between**
entre; **for** pour); (in boxing) combat *m*
(**between** entre)
**(b)** (struggle) lutte *f* (**against** contre; **for** pour;
**to do** pour faire)
**(c)** (argument) dispute *f* (**over** au sujet de; **with**
avec)
**2** *vtr* **(a)** se battre contre ⟨*person*⟩
**(b)** lutter contre ⟨*disease, opponent, emotion,
proposal*⟩; combattre ⟨*fire*⟩; mener
⟨*campaign, war*⟩ (**against** contre); **to ~ one's
way through** se frayer un passage dans
⟨*crowd*⟩
**3** *vi* **(a)** (gen, Mil) se battre
**(b)** (campaign) lutter
**(c)** (argue) se quereller (**over** à propos de)
■ **fight back**: ¶ **~ back** se défendre; ¶ **~
back** [sth] refréner ⟨*tears, fear, anger*⟩
■ **fight off**: ¶ **~ off** [sth], **~** [sth] **off** se
libérer de ⟨*attacker*⟩; repousser ⟨*attack*⟩; ¶ **~
off** [sth] lutter contre ⟨*illness*⟩; rejeter
⟨*criticism, proposal*⟩

**fighter** *n* **(a)** (Sport) boxeur *m*
**(b)** (determined person) lutteur/-euse *m/f*
**(c)** (also **~ plane**) avion *m* de chasse

**fighting** **1** *n* (gen) bagarre *f*, (Mil) combat *m*
**2** *adj* **(a)** ⟨*unit, force*⟩ de combat
**(b)** ⟨*talk*⟩ agressif/-ive

**fighting chance** *n* **to have a ~** avoir de
bonnes chances

**fighting fit** *adj* **to be ~** être en pleine
forme

**figment** *n* **a ~ of your imagination** un
produit de ton imagination

**figurative** *adj* figuré/-e

**figure** **1** *n* **(a)** chiffre *m*; **a four-~ number**
un nombre de quatre chiffres; **in double ~s**
à deux chiffres
**(b)** (person) personnage *m*; **well-known ~**
personnalité *f* célèbre; **father ~** image *f* du
père
**(c)** (body shape) ligne *f*; **to lose one's ~**
prendre de l'embonpoint
**(d)** (diagram, shape) figure *f*
**2** *vi* (appear) figurer (**in** dans)
■ **figure out** trouver ⟨*answer, reason*⟩; **to ~
out who/why** arriver à comprendre qui/
pourquoi

**figurehead** *n* (symbolic leader)
représentant/-e *m/f* nominal/-e; (of ship) figure
*f* de proue

**figure of speech** *n* figure *f* de
rhétorique

**figure skating** *n* patinage *m* artistique

**file** **1** *n* **(a)** (for papers) (gen) dossier *m*;
(cardboard) chemise *f*; (binder) classeur *m*
**(b)** (record) dossier *m* (**on** sur)
**(c)** (Comput) fichier *m*
**(d)** (tool) lime *f*
**(e)** **in single ~** en file indienne
**2** *vtr* **(a)** classer ⟨*invoice, letter, record*⟩
(**under** sous)
**(b)** déposer ⟨*application, complaint*⟩ (**with**
auprès de); **to ~ a lawsuit** (**against sb**)
intenter *or* faire un procès (à qn)

**(c)** limer ⟨*wood, metal*⟩; **to ~ one's nails** se
limer les ongles
**3** *vi* **they ~d into/out of the classroom** ils
sont entrés dans/sortis de la salle l'un après
l'autre

**file cabinet** (US), **filing cabinet** *n*
classeur *m* à tiroirs

**fill** **1** *vtr* **(a)** remplir ⟨*container, page*⟩ (**with**
de); garnir ⟨*cushion, pie, sandwich*⟩ (**with** de);
⟨*dentist*⟩ plomber ⟨*tooth, cavity*⟩
**(b)** ⟨*crowd, sound*⟩ remplir ⟨*room, street*⟩;
⟨*smoke, protesters*⟩ envahir ⟨*building, room*⟩;
occuper ⟨*time, day, hours*⟩; ⟨*emotion,
thought*⟩ remplir ⟨*mind, person*⟩
**(c)** boucher ⟨*crack, hole, void*⟩ (**with** avec)
**(d)** répondre à ⟨*need*⟩
**(e)** ⟨*company, university*⟩ pourvoir ⟨*post,
vacancy*⟩
**(f)** ⟨*applicant*⟩ occuper ⟨*post, vacancy*⟩
**(g)** ⟨*wind*⟩ gonfler ⟨*sail*⟩
**2** *vi* se remplir (**with** de)
■ **fill in**: **to ~ in for sb** remplacer qn; ¶ **~**
[sth] **in** remplir ⟨*form*⟩; donner ⟨*detail, name,
date*⟩; ¶ **~** [sb] **in** mettre [qn] au courant (**on**
de)
■ **fill out**: ¶ **~ out** ⟨*person*⟩ prendre du poids;
⟨*face*⟩ s'arrondir; ¶ **~** [sth] **out** remplir
⟨*form*⟩; faire ⟨*prescription*⟩
■ **fill up**: ¶ **~ up** ⟨*bath, theatre, bus*⟩ se
remplir (**with** de); ¶ **~** [sth] **up** remplir
⟨*kettle, box, room*⟩ (**with** de)

**filler** *n* **(a)** (for car body) mastic *m*; (for wall)
reboucheur *m*
**(b)** (TV show) bouche-trou *m*

**fillet** **1** *n* filet *m*; **~ steak** filet *m* de bœuf
**2** *vtr* enlever les arêtes de, fileter ⟨*fish*⟩

**filling** **1** *n* **(a)** (of sandwich, baked potato)
garniture *f*; (for peppers, meat) farce *f*
**(b)** (for tooth) plombage *m*
**2** *adj* ⟨*food, dish*⟩ bourratif/-ive (colloq)

**filling station** *n* station-service *f*

**film** **1** *n* **(a)** (movie) film *m*
**(b)** (for camera) pellicule *f*
**(c)** (layer) pellicule *f*
**2** *vtr* filmer
**3** *vi* tourner

**film fan** *n* cinéphile *mf*

**film festival** *n* festival *m* de cinéma

**film industry** *n* industrie *f*
cinématographique

**filming** *n* tournage *m*

**film set** *n* plateau *m* de tournage

**film star** *n* vedette *f* de cinéma

**film studio** *n* studio *m* de cinéma

**filter** **1** *n* filtre *m*
**2** *vtr* filtrer ⟨*liquid, gas*⟩; faire passer
⟨*coffee*⟩
**3** *vi* **to ~ into** ⟨*light, sound, water*⟩ pénétrer
dans ⟨*area*⟩

**filth** *n* **(a)** (dirt) crasse *f*
**(b)** (vulgarity) obscénités *fpl*; (swearing)
grossièretés *fpl*

**filthy** *adj* **(a)** (dirty) crasseux/-euse; (revolting)
répugnant/-e

**(b)** ⟨*language*⟩ ordurier/-ière; ⟨*mind*⟩ mal
tourné/-e
**(c)** (GB) ⟨*look*⟩ noir/-e
**fin** *n* (of fish, seal) nageoire *f*; (of shark) aileron
*m*
**final** [1] *n* (Sport) finale *f*
[2] *adj* **(a)** (last) dernier/-ière
**(b)** ⟨*decision*⟩ définitif/-ive; ⟨*result*⟩ final/-e
**finale** *n* finale *f*
**finalist** *n* finaliste *mf*
**finalize** *vtr* conclure ⟨*contract*⟩; arrêter
⟨*plan, details*⟩; faire la dernière mise au
point de ⟨*article*⟩; fixer ⟨*timetable, route*⟩
**finally** *adv* **(a)** (eventually) finalement, enfin
**(b)** (lastly) finalement, pour finir
**(c)** (definitively) définitivement
**finals** *n pl* (GB) (Univ) examens *mpl* de fin
d'études; (US) (Univ) examens *mpl* de fin de
semestre
**finance** [1] *n* **(a)** (gen) finance *f*
**(b)** (funds) fonds *mpl* (**for** pour; **from** auprès
de)
[2] *vtr* financer ⟨*project*⟩
**finance company** *n* société *f* de
financement
**finances** *n pl* situation *f* financière
**financial** *adj* financier/-ière
**financial year** *n* (GB) exercice *m*, année *f*
budgétaire
**find** [1] *n* **(a)** (gen) découverte *f*
**(b)** (good buy) trouvaille *f*
[2] *vtr* **(a)** trouver; **I can't ~ my keys** je ne
trouve pas mes clés; **I couldn't ~ the time** je
n'ai pas eu le temps
**(b)** (experience) éprouver ⟨*pleasure,
satisfaction*⟩ (**in** dans)
**(c)** (Law) **to ~ that** conclure que; **to ~ sb
guilty** déclarer qn coupable
■ **find out**: ¶ **~ out** se renseigner; **if he ever
~s out** si jamais il l'apprend; ¶ **~ [sth] out**
découvrir ⟨*fact, answer, name, cause, truth*⟩;
**~ out who/why/where** trouver qui/
pourquoi/où; ¶ **~ out about [sth]** **(a)** (learn by
chance) découvrir ⟨*plan, affair, breakage*⟩
**(b)** (research) faire des recherches sur
⟨*subject*⟩
**findings** *n pl* conclusions *fpl*
**fine** [1] *n* (gen) amende *f*; (for traffic offence)
contravention *f*
[2] *adj* **(a)** (very good) excellent/-e
**(b)** (satisfactory) bon/bonne (*before n*); **that's
~ très bien; '~, thanks'** 'très bien, merci'
**(c)** (nice) ⟨*weather, day*⟩ beau/belle (*before n*)
**(d)** (delicate) fin/-e
**(e)** (subtle) ⟨*adjustment, detail, distinction*⟩
subtil/-e
**(f)** (refined) ⟨*lady, clothes*⟩ beau/belle (*before
n*)
**(g)** (commendable) ⟨*person*⟩ merveilleux/-euse
[3] *adv* ⟨*get along, come along, do*⟩ très bien
[4] *vtr* (gen) condamner [qn] à une amende;
(for traffic offence) donner une contravention à
**fine art** *n* beaux-arts *mpl*
  IDIOMS **she's got cheating down to a ~** elle
est passée maître dans l'art de tricher

**fine-tune** *vtr* ajuster
**finger** [1] *n* doigt *m*
[2] *vtr* toucher ⟨*fruit, goods*⟩; tripoter (colloq)
⟨*necklace*⟩
  IDIOMS **to keep one's ~s crossed** croiser les
doigts (**for sb** pour qn)
**finger-nail** *n* ongle *m*
**fingerprint** *n* empreinte *f* digitale
**fingertip** *n* bout *m* du doigt
**finicky** *adj* ⟨*person*⟩ difficile (**about** pour);
⟨*job, task*⟩ minutieux/-ieuse
**finish** [1] *n* **(a)** (end) fin *f*
**(b)** (Sport) arrivée *f*
**(c)** (of wood, car) finition *f*; (of fabric, leather)
apprêt *m*
[2] *vtr* **(a)** finir, terminer ⟨*chapter, sentence,
task*⟩; terminer, achever ⟨*building, novel*⟩; **to
~ doing** finir de faire
**(b)** (leave) finir ⟨*work, school*⟩
**(c)** (consume) finir ⟨*cigarette, drink, meal*⟩
**(d)** ( put an end to) briser ⟨*career*⟩
[3] *vi* (gen) finir; ⟨*speaker*⟩ finir, se taire;
⟨*conference, programme, term*⟩ finir, se
terminer; ⟨*holidays*⟩ se terminer
■ **finish off** finir, terminer ⟨*letter, meal,
task*⟩
■ **finish up**: ¶ **~ up** finir; ¶ **~ [sth] up** finir
⟨*milk, paint, cake*⟩
**finishing line** (GB), **finish line** (US) *n*
ligne *f* d'arrivée
**finishing touch** *n* **to put the ~(es) to sth**
mettre la dernière main à qch
**finite** *adj* (gen) fini/-e; ⟨*resources*⟩ limité/-e
**Finland** *pr n* Finlande *f*
**Finn** *n* Finlandais/-e *m/f*
**Finnish** [1] *n* (language) finnois *m*
[2] *adj* **(a)** ⟨*culture, food, politics*⟩
finlandais/-e; ⟨*ambassador, embassy*⟩ de
Finlande
**(b)** ⟨*grammar*⟩ finnois/-e; ⟨*teacher, lesson*⟩ de
finnois
**fir** *n* (*also* **~ tree**) sapin *m*
**fire** [1] *n* **(a)** feu *m*; **to set ~ to sth** mettre le
feu à qch; **to be on ~** être en feu; **to catch ~**
prendre feu; **to sit by the ~** s'asseoir près
du feu *or* au coin du feu
**(b)** (blaze) incendie *m*; **to start a ~**
provoquer un incendie
**(c) to open ~ on sb** ouvrir le feu sur qn
[2] *excl* **(a)** (raising alarm) au feu!
**(b)** (Mil) feu!
[3] *vtr* **(a)** décharger ⟨*gun, weapon*⟩; tirer
⟨*shot*⟩; lancer ⟨*arrow, missile*⟩; **to ~
questions at sb** bombarder qn de questions
**(b)** (dismiss) renvoyer, virer (colloq) ⟨*person*⟩
[4] *vi* tirer (**at, on** sur)
**fire alarm** *n* alarme *f* incendie
**firearm** *n* arme *f* à feu
**firebomb** [1] *n* bombe *f* incendiaire
[2] *vtr* incendier ⟨*building*⟩
**fire brigade** *n* pompiers *mpl*
**fire engine** *n* voiture *f* de pompiers
**fire escape** *n* escalier *m* de secours
**fire exit** *n* sortie *f* de secours

**fire extinguisher** n extincteur m
**firefighter** n pompier m
**fireguard** n pare-étincelles m inv
**fireman** n pompier m
**fireplace** n cheminée f
**fireproof** adj ⟨door, clothing⟩ ignifugé/-e
**fire service** n (sapeurs-)pompiers mpl
**fire station** n caserne f de pompiers
**firewood** n bois m à brûler
**firework** n feu m d'artifice
**firing** n (of guns) tir m
**firing line** n to be in the ~ (Mil) être dans la ligne de tir; (under attack) faire l'objet de violentes critiques
**firing squad** n peloton m d'exécution
**firm** ⓵ n entreprise f, société f
   ⓶ adj (a) ⟨mattress, fruit, handshake⟩ ferme
   (b) ⟨basis, grasp⟩ solide
   (c) ⟨offer, intention, refusal⟩ ferme; ⟨evidence⟩ concret/-ète
   (d) ⟨person, leadership⟩ ferme (with sb avec qn)
   ⓷ adv to stand ~ tenir bon
**first** ⓵ n (a) (gen) premier/-ière m/f (to do à faire)
   (b) (of month) premier m inv; the ~ of May le premier mai
   (c) (GB) (Univ) (also ~-class honours degree) ≈ licence f avec mention très bien
   ⓶ adj premier/-ière (before n); the ~ three pages les trois premières pages; at ~ glance or sight à première vue; I'll ring ~ thing in the morning je vous appellerai en tout début de matinée
   ⓷ adv (a) ⟨arrive, leave⟩ le premier/la première; women and children ~ les femmes et les enfants d'abord; to come ~ ⟨contestant⟩ terminer premier/première (in à); ⟨career, family⟩ passer avant tout
   (b) (to begin with) d'abord; ~ of all tout d'abord
   (c) (for the first time) pour la première fois; I ~ met him in Paris je l'ai rencontré pour la première fois à Paris
   ⓸ at first phr au début
   IDIOMS ~ things ~ chaque chose en son temps
**first aid** n (a) (treatment) premiers soins mpl
   (b) (as skill) secourisme m
**first-aid kit** n trousse f de secours
**first class** adj (a) ⟨hotel, ticket⟩ de première (classe)
   (b) ⟨stamp, mail⟩ (au) tarif rapide
   (c) (GB) ⟨degree⟩ avec mention très bien
   (d) (excellent) excellent/-e
**first cousin** n (male) cousin m germain; (female) cousine f germaine
**first floor** n (GB) premier étage m; (US) rez-de-chaussée m
**first form** n (GB) (Sch) (classe f de) sixième f
**first grade** n (US Sch) cours m préparatoire
**firsthand** adj, adv de première main

**firstly** adv premièrement
**first name** n prénom m
**first night** n première f
**first-rate** adj excellent/-e
**first-time buyer** n personne f qui achète sa première maison
**fish** ⓵ n poisson m
   ⓶ vi pêcher; to ~ for trout pêcher la truite; to ~ for compliments rechercher les compliments
   ■ **fish out**: ~ out [sth] (a) (from bag, pocket) sortir
   (b) (from water) repêcher
**fish and chips** n poisson m frit avec des frites
**fish and chip shop** n (GB) friterie f
**fishbowl** n bocal m (à poissons)
**fisherman** n pêcheur m
**fishing** n pêche f; to go ~ aller à la pêche
**fishing boat** n bateau m de pêche
**fishing rod** n canne f à pêche
**fish market** n halle f aux poissons
**fishmonger** n (GB) poissonnier/-ière m/f; ~'s (shop) poissonnerie f
**fishnet** adj ⟨stockings⟩ à résille
**fish tank** n aquarium m
**fishy** adj (a) ⟨smell, taste⟩ de poisson
   (b) (colloq) (suspect) louche (colloq)
**fist** n poing m
**fit** ⓵ n (a) (Med) crise f, attaque f
   (b) (of anger, passion, panic) accès m; ~ of coughing quinte f de toux; to have sb in ~s (colloq) donner le fou rire à qn
   (c) (of garment) to be a good ~ être à la bonne taille; to be a tight ~ être juste
   ⓶ adj (a) ⟨person⟩ (in trim) en forme; (not ill) en bonne santé; to get ~ retrouver la forme
   (b) to be ~ for (worthy of) être digne de ⟨person, hero, king⟩; (capable of) être capable de faire ⟨job⟩; not ~ for human consumption impropre à la consommation; to see or think ~ to do juger bon de faire; to be in no ~ state to do ne pas être en état de faire
   ⓷ vtr (a) ⟨garment⟩ être à la taille de; ⟨shoe⟩ être à la pointure de; ⟨key⟩ aller dans ⟨lock⟩; aller dans ⟨envelope, space⟩
   (b) to ~ sth in or into trouver de la place pour qch dans ⟨room, house, car⟩
   (c) (install) mettre [qch] en place ⟨lock, door, kitchen, shower⟩
   (d) correspondre à ⟨description, requirements⟩
   ⓸ vi (a) ⟨garment⟩ être à ma/ta/sa taille, aller; ⟨shoes⟩ être à ma/ta/sa pointure, aller; ⟨key, lid, sheet⟩ aller
   (b) ⟨toys, books⟩ tenir (into dans); will the table ~ in that corner? y a-t-il de la place pour la table dans ce coin?
   (c) to ~ with correspondre à ⟨story, facts⟩
   IDIOMS in ~s and starts par à-coups
   ■ **fit in**: ¶ ~ in (a) ⟨key, object⟩ aller; will you all ~ in? (into car, room) est-ce qu'il y a de la place pour vous tous?
   (b) (figurative) ⟨person⟩ s'intégrer (with à); I'll

~ **in with your plans** j'accorderai mes projets avec les vôtres

¶ ~ **[sb/sth] in** caser ⟨objects⟩; caser ⟨game, meeting⟩; trouver le temps pour voir ⟨patient, colleague⟩

**fitness** n ( physical) forme f

**fitted** adj ⟨wardrobe⟩ encastré/-e; ⟨kitchen⟩ intégré/-e

**fitted carpet** n moquette f

**fitting** ⓵ n **(a)** ( part) installation f **(b)** (for clothes, hearing aid) essayage m ⓶ adj ⟨description⟩ adéquat/-e; ⟨memorial, testament⟩ qui convient

**fitting room** n salon m d'essayage

**five** n, pron, det cinq (m) inv

**five-a-side** n (also ~ **football**) football m à cinq ( joueurs)

**fix** ⓵ n **(a)** (difficulty) **to be in a ~** être dans le pétrin (colloq) **(b)** (colloq) (dose of drugs) shoot m (colloq) ⓶ vtr **(a)** fixer ⟨date, venue, price, limit⟩; déterminer ⟨position⟩ **(b)** arranger ⟨meeting, visit⟩; préparer ⟨drink, meal⟩; **to ~ one's hair** se donner un coup de peigne; **how are we ~ed for time/ money?** qu'est-ce qu'on a comme temps/ argent (colloq)? **(c)** (mend) réparer **(d)** fixer ⟨handle, shelf⟩ (**on** sur; **to** à) **(e)** fixer ⟨attention⟩ (**on** sur); tourner ⟨thoughts⟩ (**on** vers) **(f)** (colloq) truquer ⟨contest, election⟩ ⓷ **fixed** pp adj ⟨gaze, income, price⟩ fixe; ⟨expression⟩ figé/-e; ⟨menu⟩ à prix fixe ■ **fix up** organiser ⟨holiday, meeting⟩; décider de ⟨date⟩

**fixed-term contract** n contrat m à durée déterminée

**fixture** n **(a)** installation f; ~**s and fittings** équipements mpl **(b)** (Sport) rencontre f

**fizzle** v ■ **fizzle out** ⟨interest, romance⟩ s'éteindre; ⟨campaign, project⟩ faire fiasco; ⟨story⟩ se terminer en queue de poisson

**fizzy** adj gazeux/-euse

**flabby** adj ⟨skin, muscle⟩ flasque; ⟨person⟩ aux chairs flasques

**flag** ⓵ n drapeau m ⓶ vi ⟨interest⟩ faiblir; ⟨strength⟩ baisser; ⟨conversation⟩ languir; ⟨athlete⟩ flancher (colloq) ■ **flag down** faire signe de s'arrêter à ⟨person⟩; héler ⟨taxi⟩

**flagpole** n mât m

**flagrant** adj flagrant/-e

**flagstone** n dalle f

**flair** n **(a)** (talent) don; **to have a ~ for** être doué/-e pour ⟨languages⟩ **(b)** (style) classe f

**flake** ⓵ n (of snow) flocon m ⓶ vi (also ~ **off**) ⟨paint, varnish⟩ s'écailler; ⟨plaster, stone⟩ s'effriter; ⟨skin⟩ peler

**flamboyant** adj ⟨person⟩ haut/-e en couleur; ⟨lifestyle⟩ exubérant/-e; ⟨colour, clothes⟩ voyant/-e; ⟨gesture⟩ extravagant/-e

**flame** n flamme f; **in ~s** en flammes; **to go up in ~s** s'enflammer; **to burst into ~s** s'embraser

**flamer** n (Internet) auteur m d'un message injurieux

**flaming** ⓵ n (Internet) envoi m de messages injurieux ⓶ adj **(a)** ⟨vehicle, building⟩ en flammes **(b)** ⟨row⟩ violent/-e

**flamingo** n flamant m (rose)

**flammable** adj inflammable

**flan** n (savoury) quiche f, tarte f; (sweet) tarte f

**flank** ⓵ n flanc m ⓶ vtr **to be ~ed by** ⟨person⟩ être flanqué/-e par; ⟨place⟩ être bordé/-e par

**flannel** n **(a)** (wool) flanelle f; (cotton) pilou m **(b)** (GB) (also **face ~**) ≈ gant m de toilette

**flap** ⓵ n **(a)** (on pocket, envelope, tent) rabat m; (on table) abattant m **(b)** (of wings) battement m ⓶ vtr **the bird ~ped its wings** l'oiseau battait des ailes ⓷ vi ⟨wing⟩ battre; ⟨sail, flag⟩ claquer; ⟨clothes⟩ voleter

**flare** ⓵ n **(a)** (on runway) balise f lumineuse; (distress signal) fusée f (de détresse); (Mil) (on target) fusée f éclairante **(b)** (of match, lighter) lueur f ⓶ vi **(a)** ⟨firework, match⟩ jeter une brève lueur **(b)** ⟨skirt⟩ s'évaser; ⟨nostrils⟩ se dilater ■ **flare up (a)** ⟨fire⟩ s'embraser **(b)** ⟨violence⟩ éclater; ⟨person⟩ s'emporter **(c)** ⟨illness⟩ réapparaître; ⟨pain⟩ se réveiller

**flares** n pl pantalon m à pattes d'éléphant

**flash** ⓵ n **(a)** (of torch, headlights) lueur f soudaine; (of jewels, metal) éclat m; **a ~ of lightning** un éclair **(b)** **in** or **like a ~** en un clin d'œil **(c)** (on camera) flash m ⓶ vtr **(a)** **to ~ one's headlights (at)** faire un appel de phares (à) **(b)** lancer ⟨look, smile⟩ (**at** à) **(c)** (transmit) faire apparaître ⟨message⟩ **(d)** (colloq) (show) ⟨person⟩ montrer [qch] rapidement ⟨card, money⟩ **(e)** (also ~ **about**, ~ **around**) exhiber ⟨credit card⟩; étaler ⟨money⟩ ⓷ vi ⟨light⟩ clignoter; ⟨eyes⟩ lancer des éclairs; **to ~ on and off** clignoter ■ **flash by**, **flash past** ⟨person, bird⟩ passer comme un éclair; ⟨landscape⟩ défiler

**flashback** n **(a)** (in film) flash-back m (**to** à) **(b)** (memory) souvenir m

**flashing** adj ⟨light, sign⟩ clignotant/-e

**flash light** n lampe f de poche

**flashy** adj (colloq) ⟨car, dress, tie⟩ tape-à-l'œil inv; ⟨jewellery⟩ clinquant/-e

**flask** n thermos® f or m inv; (hip) ~ flasque f

**flat** ① n (a) (GB) appartement m;
**one-bedroom** ~ deux pièces m inv
(b) **the** ~ **of** le plat de ⟨hand, sword⟩
② adj (a) (gen) plat/-e; ⟨nose, face⟩ aplati/-e
(b) ⟨tyre, ball⟩ dégonflé/-e; **to have a** ~ **tyre**
avoir un pneu à plat
(c) ⟨refusal, denial⟩ catégorique
(d) ⟨fare, fee⟩ forfaitaire; ⟨charge, rate⟩ fixe
(e) ⟨beer⟩ éventé/-e
(f) (GB) ⟨car battery⟩ à plat; ⟨battery⟩ usé/-e
(g) (Mus) ⟨note⟩ bémol inv; ⟨voice, instrument⟩
faux/fausse
③ adv (a) ⟨lay, lie⟩ à plat; ~ **on one's back**
sur le dos
(b) **in 10 minutes** ~ en 10 minutes pile
(c) ⟨sing⟩ faux
**IDIOMS to fall** ~ ⟨joke⟩ tomber à plat; ⟨party⟩
tourner court; ⟨plan⟩ tomber à l'eau

**flatmate** n (GB) colocataire mf

**flat out** adv (colloq) ⟨drive⟩ à fond de train;
⟨work⟩ d'arrache-pied

**flat rate** ① n taux m fixe
② **flat-rate** adj ⟨fee, tax⟩ forfaitaire

**flatten** ① vtr (a) ⟨rain⟩ coucher ⟨crops,
grass⟩; abattre ⟨fence⟩; ⟨bombing⟩ raser
⟨building⟩
(b) (smooth out) aplanir ⟨surface⟩; aplatir
⟨metal⟩
(c) (crush) écraser ⟨fruit, object⟩
② v refl **to** ~ **oneself** s'aplatir (**against**
contre)

**flatter** vtr flatter (**on** sur)

**flattering** adj flatteur/-euse

**flattery** n flatterie f

**flaunt** vtr étaler ⟨wealth⟩; faire étalage de
⟨charms, knowledge⟩

**flavour** (GB), **flavor** (US) ① n goût m;
(subtler) saveur f; **full of** ~ savoureux/-euse
② vtr (gen) donner du goût à; (add specific
taste) parfumer (**with** à)

**flavouring** (GB), **flavoring** (US) n (for
sweet taste) parfum m; (for meat, fish)
assaisonnement m

**flaw** n défaut m

**flawed** adj défectueux/-euse

**flea** n puce f

**flea market** n marché m aux puces

**fleck** ① n (of colour, light) tache f; (of foam)
flocon m; (of blood, paint) petite tache f; (of dust)
particule f
② vtr ~**ed with** ⟨fabric⟩ moucheté/-e de
⟨colour⟩

**fledg(e)ling** n oisillon m

**flee** vtr, vi fuir

**fleece** n toison f; ~**-lined** fourré/-e

**fleet** n (a) (of ships) flotte f; (of small vessels)
flottille f
(b) (of vehicles) (on road) convoi m

**fleeting** adj ⟨memory, pleasure⟩ fugace;
⟨moment⟩ bref/brève (**before** n); ⟨glance⟩
rapide

**Flemish** ① n (a) **the** ~ les Flamands mpl
(b) (language) flamand m
② adj flamand/-e

**flesh** n chair f

**fleshy** adj charnu/-e

**flex** ① n (GB) fil m
② vtr faire jouer ⟨muscle⟩; fléchir ⟨limb⟩

**flexibility** n souplesse f, flexibilité f

**flexible** adj (a) ⟨arrangement, plan⟩
flexible
(b) ⟨person⟩ souple (**about** en ce qui
concerne)

**flexitime** n horaire m flexible or souple

**flick** ① n (with finger) chiquenaude f; (with
whip, cloth) petit coup m
② vtr (a) (with finger) donner une
chiquenaude à; (with tail, cloth) donner un petit
coup à; **he** ~**ed his ash on the floor** il a fait
tomber sa cendre par terre
(b) appuyer sur ⟨switch⟩

**flicker** vi ⟨fire, light⟩ vaciller, trembloter;
⟨image⟩ clignoter; ⟨eye, eyelid⟩ cligner
■ **flick through** feuilleter ⟨book⟩

**flick knife** n (GB) couteau m à cran d'arrêt

**flight** n (a) (gen) vol m (**to** vers; **from** de); **we**
**took the next** ~ (out) nous avons pris l'avion
suivant
(b) (escape) fuite f (**from** devant); **to take** ~
prendre la fuite
(c) **a** ~ **of steps** une volée de marches; **six**
~**s** (of stairs) six étages
(d) **a** ~ **of fancy** une invention

**flight attendant** n (male) steward m;
(female) hôtesse f de l'air

**flight bag** n bagage m à main

**flight path** n route f de vol

**flimsy** adj ⟨fabric⟩ léger/-ère; ⟨structure⟩
peu solide; ⟨excuse⟩ piètre (**before** n);
⟨evidence⟩ mince

**flinch** vi tressaillir; **without** ~**ing** sans
broncher; **to** ~ **from doing** hésiter à faire

**fling** ① n (a) (colloq) (spree) bon temps m
(b) (affair) aventure f
② vtr lancer
③ v refl **to** ~ **oneself** se jeter (**across** en
travers de; **over** par dessus)
■ **fling away**: ~ [sth] **away** jeter qch
■ **fling open**: ouvrir [qch] brusquement
⟨door⟩; ouvrir [qch] tout grand ⟨window⟩

**flint** n (a) (rock) silex m
(b) (in lighter) pierre f à briquet

**flip** ① n (somersault) tour m
② vtr (a) lancer ⟨coin⟩; faire sauter
⟨pancake⟩
(b) basculer ⟨switch⟩
■ **flip through** feuilleter ⟨book⟩

**flipchart** n tableau m de conférence,
paperboard m

**flip-flop** n (a) (sandal) tong f
(b) (US) (about-face) volte-face f inv

**flippant** adj ⟨remark, person⟩ désinvolte;
⟨tone, attitude⟩ cavalier/-ière

**flipper** n (a) (Zool) nageoire f
(b) (for swimmer) palme f

**flirt** ① n flirteur/-euse m/f
② vi flirter; **to** ~ **with** flirter avec ⟨person⟩;
jouer avec ⟨danger⟩; caresser ⟨idea⟩

**flirtatious** *adj* charmeur/-euse, dragueur/-euse (colloq derogatory)

**flit** *vi* **(a)** (*also* ~ **about**) ⟨*bird, moth*⟩ voleter; ⟨*person*⟩ aller d'un pas léger
**(b) a look of panic ~ted across his face** une expression de panique lui traversa le visage

**float** ⟨**1**⟩ *n* **(a)** (on net) flotteur *m*; (on line) bouchon *m*
**(b)** (GB) (swimmer's aid) planche *f*; (US) (life jacket) gilet *m* de sauvetage
**(c)** (carnival vehicle) char *m*
⟨**2**⟩ *vtr* **(a)** ⟨*person*⟩ faire flotter ⟨*boat, logs*⟩
**(b)** émettre ⟨*shares, loan*⟩; lancer [qch] en Bourse ⟨*company*⟩; laisser flotter ⟨*currency*⟩
⟨**3**⟩ *vi* **(a)** flotter; **to ~ on one's back** ⟨*swimmer*⟩ faire la planche; **the boat was ~ing out to sea** le bateau voguait vers le large; **to ~ up into the air** s'envoler
**(b)** ⟨*currency*⟩ flotter
■ **float off** ⟨*boat*⟩ dériver; ⟨*balloon*⟩ s'envoler

**floating** *adj* **(a)** ⟨*bridge*⟩ flottant/-e
**(b)** ⟨*population*⟩ instable

**floating voter** *n* électeur *m* indécis

**flock** ⟨**1**⟩ *n* **(a)** (of sheep, goats) troupeau *m*; (of birds) volée *f*
⟨**2**⟩ *vi* ⟨*animals, people*⟩ affluer (**around** autour de; **into** dans); **to ~ together** ⟨*people*⟩ s'assembler; ⟨*animals*⟩ se rassembler

**flog** *vtr* (beat) flageller

**flood** ⟨**1**⟩ *n* **(a)** inondation *f*
**(b) a ~ of** un flot de ⟨*people, memories*⟩; un déluge de ⟨*letters, complaints*⟩; **to be in ~s of tears** verser des torrents de larmes
⟨**2**⟩ *vtr* **(a)** inonder ⟨*area*⟩; faire déborder ⟨*river*⟩
**(b)** ⟨*light*⟩ inonder
**(c)** inonder ⟨*market*⟩ (**with** de)
**(d)** (Aut) noyer ⟨*engine*⟩
⟨**3**⟩ *vi* **(a)** ⟨*river*⟩ déborder
**(b) to ~ into sth** ⟨*light*⟩ inonder qch; ⟨*people*⟩ envahir qch; **to ~ over sb** ⟨*emotion*⟩ envahir qn

**floodgate** *n* vanne *f*

**floodlight** ⟨**1**⟩ *n* projecteur *m*; **under ~s** (Sport) en nocturne
⟨**2**⟩ *vtr* illuminer ⟨*building*⟩; éclairer ⟨*stage*⟩

**floor** ⟨**1**⟩ *n* **(a)** (of room) (wooden) plancher *m*, parquet *m*; (stone) sol *m*; (of car, lift) plancher *m*; **dance ~** piste *f* de danse; **on the ~** par terre
**(b)** (of stock exchange) parquet *m*; (of debating chamber) auditoire *m*; (of factory) atelier *m*
**(c)** (storey) étage *m*; **on the first ~** (GB) au premier étage; (US) au rez-de-chaussée
⟨**2**⟩ *vtr* **(a)** terrasser ⟨*attacker, boxer*⟩
**(b)** ⟨*question*⟩ décontenancer ⟨*candidate*⟩
**IDIOMS to wipe the ~ with sb** battre qn à plates coutures

**floorboard** *n* latte *f*, planche *f*

**floor cloth** *n* serpillière *f*

**floor show** *n* spectacle *m* ⟨*de cabaret*⟩

**flop** ⟨**1**⟩ *n* (colloq) (failure) fiasco *m* (colloq)
⟨**2**⟩ *vi* **(a) to ~ (down)** s'effondrer

**(b)** (colloq) ⟨*play, film*⟩ faire un four (colloq); ⟨*project, venture*⟩ être un fiasco (colloq)

**floppy** *adj* ⟨*ears*⟩ pendant/-e; ⟨*hat*⟩ à bords tombants

**floppy disk** *n* disquette *f*

**flora** *n* flore *f*

**floral** *adj* ⟨*design, fabric*⟩ à fleurs; ⟨*arrangement*⟩ floral/-e

**Florida** *pr n* Floride *f*

**florist** *n* (person) fleuriste *mf*; (shop) fleuriste *m*

**floss** *n* fil *m* dentaire

**flotsam** *n* ~ **and jetsam** épaves *fpl*

**flounce** ⟨**1**⟩ *n* (frill) volant *m*
⟨**2**⟩ *vi* **to ~ in/off** entrer/partir dans un mouvement d'indignation

**flounder** *vi* **(a)** ⟨*animal, person*⟩ se débattre (**in** dans)
**(b)** (falter) ⟨*speaker*⟩ bredouiller; ⟨*economy*⟩ stagner; ⟨*career, company*⟩ piétiner

**flour** *n* farine *f*

**flourish** ⟨**1**⟩ *n* **(a)** (gesture) geste *m* théâtral; **with a ~** ⟨*do*⟩ de façon théâtrale
**(b)** (in style) fioriture *f*
⟨**2**⟩ *vtr* brandir ⟨*ticket, document*⟩
⟨**3**⟩ *vi* prospérer

**flourishing** *adj* ⟨*garden, industry*⟩ florissant/-e; ⟨*business, town*⟩ prospère

**flout** *vtr* se moquer de ⟨*convention, rules*⟩

**flow** ⟨**1**⟩ *n* **(a)** (of liquid) écoulement *m*; (of blood, water) circulation *f*; (of refugees, words) flot *m*; (of information) circulation *f*; **in full ~** ⟨*speaker*⟩ en plein discours; **traffic ~** circulation *f*
**(b)** (of tide) flux *m*
⟨**2**⟩ *vi* **(a)** ⟨*liquid*⟩ couler (**into** dans); **the river ~s into the sea** le fleuve se jette dans la mer
**(b)** ⟨*conversation, words*⟩ couler; ⟨*wine, beer*⟩ couler à flots
**(c)** ⟨*blood, electricity*⟩ circuler (**through, round** dans)
**(d)** ⟨*hair, dress*⟩ flotter

**flowchart** *n* organigramme *m*

**flower** ⟨**1**⟩ *n* fleur *f*; **to be in ~** être en fleur
⟨**2**⟩ *vi* **(a)** ⟨*flower, tree*⟩ fleurir
**(b)** ⟨*love, person*⟩ s'épanouir

**flower arranging** *n* décoration *f* florale

**flower bed** *n* parterre *m* de fleurs

**flowering** ⟨**1**⟩ *n* floraison *f* (**of** de)
⟨**2**⟩ *adj* (producing blooms) à fleurs; (in bloom) en fleurs

**flower pot** *n* pot *m* de fleurs

**flower shop** *n* fleuriste *m*

**flowery** *adj* ⟨*design*⟩ à fleurs; ⟨*language, speech*⟩ fleuri/-e

**flu** *n* grippe *f*

**fluctuate** *vi* fluctuer (**between** entre)

**flue** *n* (of chimney) conduit *m*; (of stove, boiler) tuyau *m*

**fluency** *n* aisance *f*

**fluent** adj **(a)** her French is ∼ elle parle couramment français; **in** ∼ **English** dans un anglais parfait
**(b)** ⟨speech⟩ éloquent/-e; ⟨style⟩ coulant/-e

**fluently** adv couramment

**fluff** ① n (on clothes) peluche f; (on carpet) poussière f; (under furniture) mouton m, flocon m de poussière
② vtr **(a)** (also ∼ **up**) hérisser ⟨feathers⟩; faire bouffer ⟨hair⟩
**(b)** (colloq) rater ⟨cue, exam⟩

**fluffy** adj **(a)** ⟨toy⟩ en peluche; ⟨hair⟩ bouffant/-e
**(b)** (light) ⟨mixture⟩ léger/-ère; ⟨egg white, rice⟩ moelleux/-euse

**fluid** n, adj fluide (m)

**fluid ounce** n once f liquide ((GB) = 0.028 Tl; (US) = 0.030 l)

**fluke** n coup m de veine (colloq); **by a** ⟨sheer⟩ ∼ (tout à fait) par hasard

**fluorescent** adj fluorescent/-e

**fluoride** n fluorure m

**flurry** n **(a)** (gust) rafale f
**(b)** (bustle) agitation f soudaine; **a** ∼ **of activity** un tourbillon d'activité
**(c)** (of complaints, enquiries) vague f

**flush** ① n **(a)** (blush) rougeur f
**(b)** (surge) **a** ∼ **of** un élan de ⟨pleasure, pride⟩; un accès de ⟨anger, shame⟩
**(c)** (of toilet) chasse f d'eau
② vtr **to** ∼ **the toilet** tirer la chasse (d'eau); **to** ∼ **sth down the toilet** faire partir qch dans les toilettes
③ vi **(a)** (redden) rougir (**with** de)
**(b) the toilet doesn't** ∼ la chasse d'eau ne fonctionne pas
■ **flush out** débusquer ⟨sniper, spy⟩; **to** ∼ **sb/sth out of** faire sortir qn/qch de ⟨shelter⟩

**flushed** adj **(a)** ⟨cheeks⟩ rouge (**with** de); **to be** ∼ avoir les joues rouges
**(b)** ∼ **with** rayonnant/-e de ⟨pride⟩

**fluster** ① n agitation f
② vtr énerver; **to look** ∼**ed** avoir l'air énervé

**flute** n flûte f

**flutter** ① n (of wings, lashes) battement m
② vtr **(a) the bird** ∼**ed its wings** l'oiseau battait des ailes
**(b)** agiter ⟨fan, handkerchief⟩; **to** ∼ **one's eyelashes** battre des cils
③ vi **(a) the bird's wings** ∼**ed** l'oiseau battait des ailes
**(b)** ⟨flag⟩ flotter; ⟨clothes, curtains⟩ s'agiter; ⟨eyelids, lashes⟩ battre
**(c)** (also ∼ **down**) ⟨leaves⟩ tomber en voltigeant
**(d)** ⟨heart⟩ palpiter (**with** de); ⟨pulse⟩ battre faiblement

**flux** n **in** ⟨**a state of**⟩ ∼ dans un état de perpétuel changement

**fly** ① n mouche f
② **flies** n pl (of trousers) braguette f
③ vtr **(a)** piloter ⟨aircraft, balloon⟩; faire voler ⟨kite⟩

**(b)** (transport) emmener [qn] par avion ⟨person⟩
**(c)** ⟨bird, aircraft⟩ parcourir ⟨distance⟩
**(d)** ⟨ship⟩ arborer ⟨flag⟩
④ vi **(a)** ⟨bird, insect, aircraft, kite⟩ voler; **to** ∼ **over** or **across sth** survoler qch
**(b)** ⟨passenger⟩ voyager en avion, prendre l'avion; ⟨pilot⟩ piloter, voler; **to** ∼ **from Rome to Athens** aller de Rome à Athènes en avion
**(c)** ⟨sparks, insults⟩ voler; **to** ∼ **open** s'ouvrir brusquement; **to go** ∼**ing** (colloq) ⟨person⟩ faire un vol plané; ⟨object⟩ valdinguer (colloq); **to** ∼ **into a rage** se mettre en colère
**(d)** (also ∼ **past**, ∼ **by**) ⟨time, holidays⟩ passer très vite, filer (colloq)
**(e)** ⟨flag, scarf, hair⟩ flotter; **to** ∼ **in the wind** flotter au vent
■ **fly away** s'envoler

**fly-by-night** adj ⟨company⟩ douteux/-euse; ⟨person⟩ irresponsable

**fly-drive** adj avec formule avion plus voiture

**flying** ① n **to be afraid of** ∼ avoir peur de l'avion
② adj **(a)** ⟨insect, machine⟩ volant/-e; ⟨object, broken glass⟩ qui vole; **to take a** ∼ **leap** sauter avec élan
**(b)** ⟨visit⟩ éclair inv
IDIOMS **with** ∼ **colours** ⟨pass⟩ haut la main; **to get off to a** ∼ **start** prendre un très bon départ

**fly-on-the-wall** adj ⟨film⟩ pris/-e sur le vif

**flyover** n **(a)** (GB) pont m routier
**(b)** (US) (aerial display) défilé m aérien

**fly spray** n bombe f insecticide

**FM** n (abbr = **frequency modulation**) FM f

**foal** n poulain m

**foam** ① n **(a)** (on sea, from mouth) écume f; (on drinks) mousse f
**(b)** (chemical) mousse f
**(c)** (also ∼ **rubber**) mousse f
② vi **(a)** (also ∼ **up**) ⟨beer⟩ mousser; ⟨sea⟩ se couvrir d'écume; **to** ∼ **at the mouth** écumer; (figurative) écumer de rage
**(b)** ⟨horse⟩ suer

**foam bath** n bain m moussant

**fob** n (pocket) gousset m; (chain) chaîne f
■ **fob off** se débarrasser de ⟨enquirer, customer⟩; rejeter ⟨enquiry⟩

**focal point** n **(a)** (in optics) foyer m
**(b)** (of village, building) point m de convergence (**of** de; **for** pour)
**(c)** (main concern) point m central

**focus** ① n **(a)** (focal point) foyer m; **in** ∼ au point; **to go out of** ∼ ⟨device⟩ se dérégler; ⟨image⟩ devenir flou
**(b)** (device on lens) mise f au point
**(c)** (of attention, interest) centre m
**(d)** (emphasis) accent m
② vtr **(a)** concentrer ⟨ray⟩ (**on** sur); fixer ⟨eyes⟩ (**on** sur)

**(b)** mettre [qch] au point, régler ⟨lens, camera⟩

**3** vi to ~ **on** ⟨photographer⟩ cadrer sur; ⟨eyes, attention⟩ se fixer sur; ⟨report⟩ se concentrer sur

**4 focused** pp adj ⟨person⟩ déterminé/-e

**fodder** n fourrage m

**foe** n ennemi/-e m/f

**foetus, fetus** (US) n fœtus m

**fog** **1** n brouillard m

**2** vtr (also ~ **up**) ⟨steam⟩ embuer ⟨glass⟩; ⟨light⟩ voiler ⟨film⟩

**foggy** adj ⟨day, weather⟩ brumeux/-euse; it's ~ il y a du brouillard

**foghorn** n corne f de brume

**foible** n petite manie f

**foil** **1** n papier m d'aluminium; **silver ~** papier argenté

**2** vtr contrecarrer ⟨person⟩; déjouer ⟨attempt⟩

**foist** vtr to ~ sth on sb repasser qch à qn

**fold** **1** n **(a)** (in fabric, paper, skin) pli m

**(b)** (for sheep) parc m

**2** vtr **(a)** plier ⟨paper, shirt, chair⟩; replier ⟨wings⟩

**(b)** croiser ⟨arms⟩; joindre ⟨hands⟩

**3** vi **(a)** ⟨chair⟩ se plier

**(b)** (fail) ⟨play⟩ quitter l'affiche; ⟨company⟩ fermer

IDIOMS **to return to the ~** rentrer au bercail

■ **fold back** rabattre ⟨shutters, sheet, sleeve⟩

■ **fold in** incorporer ⟨sugar, flour⟩

■ **fold up** plier ⟨newspaper, chair⟩

**folder** n **(a)** (for papers) chemise f

**(b)** (for artwork) carton m

**folding** adj ⟨bed, table, chair⟩ pliant/-e; ⟨door⟩ en accordéon

**foliage** n feuillage m

**folk** **1** n (people) gens mpl

**2** adj **(a)** (traditional) ⟨tale, song⟩ folklorique

**(b)** (modern) ⟨music⟩ folk inv

**(c)** ⟨hero⟩ populaire

**folklore** n folklore m

**follow** **1** vtr (gen) suivre; poursuivre ⟨career⟩; ~**ed by** suivi/-e de

**2** vi **(a)** suivre; to ~ **in sb's footsteps** suivre les traces de qn; **there's ice cream to ~** ensuite il y a de la glace; **the results were as ~s** les résultats ont été les suivants

**(b)** (understand) suivre; **I don't ~** je ne suis pas

**(c)** it ~s that il s'ensuit que

■ **follow through** mener [qch] à terme ⟨project⟩; aller jusqu'au bout de ⟨idea⟩

■ **follow up** donner suite à ⟨letter, threat, offer⟩ (with par); suivre ⟨story, lead⟩

**follower** n **(a)** (of thinker, artist) disciple m; (of political leader) partisan/-e m/f

**(b)** (of team) supporter m

**following** **1** n (of religion, cult) adeptes mfpl; (of party, political figure) partisans/-anes mpl/fpl; (of soap opera, show) public m; (of sports team) supporters mpl

**2** adj suivant/-e

**3** prep suite à, à la suite de

**follow-up** **1** n **(a)** (film, record, single, programme) suite f (to à)

**(b)** (of patient, socialwork case) suivi m

**2** adj **(a)** (supplementary) ⟨work⟩ de suivi; ⟨check⟩ de contrôle; ⟨discussion, article⟩ complémentaire; ⟨letter⟩ de rappel

**(b)** (of patient, ex-inmate) ⟨visit⟩ de contrôle

**folly** n folie f

**fond** adj **(a)** ⟨embrace, farewell⟩ affectueux/-euse; ⟨eyes, smile⟩ tendre; ~ **memories de très bons souvenirs**

**(b)** ⟨wish, ambition⟩ cher/chère

**(c)** to be ~ **of sb** aimer beaucoup qn; **to be ~ of sth** aimer qch

**fondle** vtr caresser

**food** n nourriture f, alimentation f; **frozen ~** aliments surgelés; **Chinese ~** la cuisine chinoise; **that's ~ for thought** ça donne à réfléchir

**food aid** n aide f alimentaire

**foodie** n (colloq) amateur m de bonne bouffe (colloq)

**food poisoning** n intoxication f alimentaire

**food processor** n robot m ménager

**foodstuff** n denrée f alimentaire

**fool** **1** n **(a)** idiot/-e m/f (**to do** de faire); **you stupid ~!** (colloq) espèce d'idiot/-e!; **to make sb look a ~** faire passer qn pour un/-e idiot/-e; **to act the ~** faire l'imbécile

**(b)** (jester) fou m

**2** vtr tromper, duper

**foolhardy** adj téméraire

**foolish** adj **(a)** ⟨person⟩ bête (**to do** de faire)

**(b)** ⟨grin, expression⟩ stupide; **to feel ~** se sentir ridicule

**(c)** ⟨decision, question, remark⟩ idiot/-e

**foolproof** adj **(a)** ⟨method, plan⟩ infaillible

**(b)** ⟨machine⟩ d'utilisation très simple

**foot** **1** n **(a)** (of person) pied m; (of animal) patte f; (of sock, chair) pied m; **on ~** à pied; **from head to ~** de la tête aux pieds; **to put one's ~ down** faire acte d'autorité; (Aut) accélérer

**(b)** (measurement) pied m (= 0.3048 m)

**(c)** (of mountain) pied m (of de); **at the ~ of** au pied de ⟨bed⟩; à la fin de ⟨list, letter⟩; en bas de ⟨page, stairs⟩

**2** vtr to ~ **the bill** payer la facture (**for** de, pour)

IDIOMS **to be under sb's feet** être dans les jambes de qn; **rushed off one's feet** débordé/-e; **to put one's ~ in it** (colloq) faire une gaffe; **to stand on one's own two feet** se débrouiller tout seul/toute seule

**footage** n film m, pellicule f; **some ~ of** des images de

**foot and mouth (disease)** n fièvre f aphteuse

**football** n **(a)** (game) (GB) football m; (US) football m américain

**(b)** (ball) ballon m de football

**footballer** n (GB) joueur/-euse m/f de football

**foot brake** n (Aut) frein m (à pied)

**footbridge** n passerelle f

**foothold** n prise f (de pied); **to gain a ~** ⟨company⟩ prendre pied; ⟨ideology⟩ s'imposer

**footing** n (a) (basis) **on a firm ~** sur une base solide; **to be on an equal ~ with sb** être sur un pied d'égalité avec qn (b) (grip for feet) **to lose one's ~** perdre pied

**footlights** n pl rampe f

**footloose** adj libre comme l'air

**footnote** n note f de bas de page

**foot passenger** n passager m sans véhicule

**footpath** n (in countryside) sentier m; (in town) trottoir m

**footprint** n empreinte f (de pied)

**footstep** n pas m

**footstool** n repose-pied m

**footwear** n chaussures fpl

**for** prep (a) (gen) pour; **~ sb** pour qn; **he cooked dinner ~ us** il nous a préparé à manger; **what's it ~?** c'est pour quoi faire?, ça sert à quoi?; **to go ~ a swim** aller nager; **that's ~ us to decide** c'est à nous de décider; **she's the person ~ the job** elle est la personne qu'il faut pour le travail; **the reason ~ doing** la raison pour laquelle on fait; **if it weren't ~ her...** sans elle...; **'~ sale'** 'à vendre'; **it is impossible ~ me to stay** il m'est impossible de rester (b) ⟨work, play⟩ pour; ⟨MP⟩ de; **the minister ~ education** le ministre de l'éducation (c) (on behalf of) pour; **to be pleased ~ sb** être content/e pour qn; **say hello to him ~ me** dis-lui bonjour de ma part (d) (in time expressions) (with a completed action in the past) pendant; (with an incomplete action started in the past) depuis; (with a future time) pour; **I waited ~ two hours** j'ai attendu pendant deux heures; **I have/had been waiting for an hour** j'attends/j'attendais depuis une heure; **I'm going to Tokyo ~ five weeks** je vais à Tokyo pour cinq semaines; **the best show I've seen ~ years** le meilleur spectacle que j'aie vu depuis des années; **we've been together ~ two years** ça fait deux ans que nous sommes ensemble; **she's off to Paris ~ the weekend** elle va à Paris pour le week-end; **to stay ~ a year** rester un an; **to be away ~ a year** être absent/e pendant un an; **I was in Paris ~ two weeks** j'ai passé deux semaines à Paris; **the car won't be ready ~ another six weeks** la voiture ne sera pas prête avant six semaines; **it's time ~ bed** c'est l'heure d'aller au lit (e) (indicating distance) pendant; **to drive ~ miles** rouler pendant des kilomètres; **the last shop ~ 30 miles** le dernier magasin avant 50 kilomètres (f) (indicating cost, value) pour; **it was sold ~ £100** ça s'est vendu (pour) 100 livres sterling; **a cheque ~ £20** un chèque de 20 livres sterling

(g) (in favour of) **to be ~** être pour ⟨peace, divorce⟩; **the argument ~ recycling** l'argument en faveur du recyclage (h) **T ~ Tom** T comme Tom; **what's the French ~ 'boot'?** comment dit-on 'boot' en français? (i) **~ one thing... and ~ another...** premièrement... et deuxièmement...; **I, ~ one, agree with her** en tout cas moi, je suis d'accord avec elle

**forbid** vtr défendre, interdire; **to ~ sb to do** défendre or interdire à qn de faire; **to ~ sb sth** défendre or interdire qch à qn; **God ~!** Dieu m'en/l'en etc garde!

**forbidden** adj ⟨subject, fruit⟩ défendu/-e; ⟨place⟩ interdit/-e; **smoking is ~** il est interdit de fumer

**forbidding** adj ⟨building⟩ intimidant/-e; ⟨landscape⟩ inhospitalier/-ière; ⟨expression⟩ rébarbatif/-ive

**force** ① n force f; **by ~** par la force; **the police ~** la police; **a ~ 10 gale** un vent de force 10 ② **forces** n pl (also **armed ~s**) **the ~s** les forces fpl armées ③ vtr forcer (**to do** à faire) ④ **in force** phr (a) (in large numbers) en force (b) ⟨law, prices, ban⟩ en vigueur ■ **force on**: **~ [sth] on sb** imposer [qch] à qn, forcer qn à accepter [qch]

**forced** adj ⟨smile, landing⟩ forcé/-e; ⟨conversation⟩ peu naturel/-elle

**force-feed** vtr gaver ⟨animal, bird⟩; alimenter [qn] de force ⟨person⟩

**forceful** adj ⟨person, behaviour⟩ énergique; ⟨attack, speech⟩ vigoureux/-euse

**ford** ① n gué m ② vtr **to ~ a river** passer une rivière à gué

**fore** **n to the ~** en vue, en avant; **to come to the ~** ⟨person, issue⟩ s'imposer à l'attention; ⟨quality⟩ ressortir

**forearm** n avant-bras m inv

**foreboding** n pressentiment m

**forecast** ① n (a) (also **weather ~**) météo f, bulletin m météorologique (b) (outlook) (gen) pronostics mpl; (Econ) prévisions fpl ② vtr prévoir (**that** que)

**forecaster** n (a) (of weather) spécialiste mf de la météorologie (b) (economic) conjoncturiste mf

**forecourt** n (of shop) parking m; (of garage) aire f de stationnement; (of station) cour f de la gare

**forefinger** n index m

**forefront** n **at** or **in the ~ of** à la pointe de ⟨change, research, debate⟩; **au premier plan de** ⟨campaign, struggle⟩

**foregone** adj **it is a ~ conclusion** c'est couru d'avance

**foreground** n premier plan m

**forehand** n (Sport) coup m droit

**forehead** n front m

**foreign** adj (a) ⟨country, imports, policy⟩ étranger/-ère; ⟨market⟩ extérieur/-e; ⟨trade, travel⟩ à l'étranger
(b) (alien) ⟨concept⟩ étranger/-ère (**to** à)

**foreign affairs** n pl affaires fpl étrangères

**foreign body** n corps m étranger

**foreign correspondent** n correspondant/-e m/f à l'étranger

**foreigner** n étranger/-ère m/f

**foreign exchange** n devises fpl

**foreign exchange market** n marché m des changes

**foreign minister, foreign secretary** (GB) n ministre m des Affaires étrangères

**Foreign Office, FO** n (GB) ministère m des Affaires étrangères

**foreman** n (a) (supervisor) contremaître m
(b) (Law) président m (d'un jury)

**foremost** [1] adj premier/-ière (before n), plus grand
[2] adv **first and** ∼ avant tout

**forename** n prénom m

**forensic evidence** n résultats mpl des expertises médico-légales

**forensic science** n médecine f légale

**forensic scientist** n médecin m légiste

**forensic tests** n pl expertises fpl médico-légales

**forerunner** n (person) précurseur m; (institution, invention, model) ancêtre m

**foresee** vtr prévoir

**foreseeable** adj prévisible

**foreshadow** vtr annoncer

**foresight** n prévoyance f (**to do** de faire)

**foreskin** n prépuce m

**forest** n forêt f

**forester** n forestier/-ière m/f

**forest fire** n incendie m de forêt

**forestry** n (science) sylviculture f; (industry) exploitation f des forêts

**foretaste** n avant-goût m (**of** de)

**foretell** vtr prédire

**forever** adv pour toujours; **to go on** ∼ ⟨pain, noise, journey⟩ durer une éternité; **the desert seemed to go on** ∼ le désert semblait ne pas avoir de limites; **she is** ∼ **complaining** elle est toujours en train de se plaindre

**foreword** n avant-propos m inv

**forfeit** [1] n gage m
[2] vtr perdre ⟨right, liberty⟩

**forge** [1] n forge f
[2] vtr (a) forger ⟨metal⟩
(b) contrefaire ⟨banknotes, signature⟩; **a** ∼**d passport** un faux passeport
(c) forger ⟨alliance⟩; établir ⟨identity, link⟩
[3] vi **to** ∼ **ahead** accélérer; **to** ∼ **ahead with** aller de l'avant dans ⟨plan⟩

**forger** n (of documents) faussaire m; (of artefacts) contrefacteur/-trice m/f; (of money) faux-monnayeur m

**forgery** n contrefaçon f

**forget** [1] vtr oublier (**that** que; **to do** de faire)
[2] vi oublier
■ **forget about** oublier

**forgetful** adj distrait/-e

**forget-me-not** n myosotis m

**forgive** vtr pardonner à ⟨person⟩; pardonner ⟨act, remark⟩; **to** ∼ **sb sth** pardonner qch à qn; **to** ∼ **sb for doing** pardonner à qn d'avoir fait

**forgiveness** n pardon m

**forgo** vtr renoncer à

**fork** [1] n (a) (for eating) fourchette f
(b) (tool) fourche f
(c) (in river, on bicycle) fourche f; (in railway) embranchement m; (in road) bifurcation f
[2] vi (also ∼ **off**) bifurquer
■ **fork out** (colloq) casquer (colloq) (**for** pour)

**forked lightning** n éclair m ramifié

**forklift truck** n (GB) (also **forklift** (US)) chariot m élévateur à fourche

**forlorn** adj (a) (sad) ⟨appearance⟩ malheureux/-euse
(b) (desperate) ⟨attempt⟩ désespéré/-e

**form** [1] n (a) (gen) forme f; **in the** ∼ **of** sous forme de; **to be in good** ∼ être en bonne or pleine forme; **it is bad** ∼ **(to do)** cela ne se fait pas (de faire); **as a matter of** ∼ pour la forme
(b) (document) formulaire m; **blank** ∼ formulaire vierge
(c) (GB) (Sch) classe f; **in the first** ∼ ≈ en sixième
[2] vtr (a) former ⟨queue, circle, barrier⟩ (**from** avec); nouer ⟨friendship, relationship⟩; **to** ∼ **part of** faire partie de
(b) se faire ⟨impression, opinion⟩
(c) former ⟨personality, tastes, ideas, attitudes⟩
[3] vi se former

**formal** adj (a) (official) ⟨agreement, complaint, invitation⟩ officiel/-ielle
(b) (not casual) ⟨language⟩ soutenu/-e; ⟨occasion⟩ solennel/-elle; ⟨manner⟩ cérémonieux/-ieuse; ⟨clothing⟩ habillé/-e
(c) ⟨training⟩ professionnel/-elle; ⟨qualification⟩ reconnu/-e

**formal dress** n tenue f de soirée

**formality** n (a) (legal or social convention) formalité f
(b) (of occasion, manner) solennité f; (of language) caractère m soutenu

**formally** adv (a) (officially) officiellement
(b) (not casually) cérémonieusement

**format** [1] n format m
[2] vtr (Comput) formater

**formation** n formation f

**former** [1] n **the** ∼ (singular noun) celui-là/celle-là m/f; (plural noun) ceux-là/celles-là mpl/fpl
[2] adj (a) ⟨era, life⟩ antérieur/-e; ⟨size, state⟩ initial/-e, original/-e; **he's a shadow of his** ∼ **self** il n'est plus que l'ombre de lui-même ⋯⋯❯

**(b)** ⟨*leader, husband, champion*⟩
ancien/-ienne (*before n*)
**(c)** (first of two) premier/-ière (*before n*)
**formerly** *adv* autrefois
**formidable** *adj* **(a)** (intimidating) redoutable
**(b)** (awe-inspiring) impressionnant/-e
**formula** *n* **(a)** formule *f* (**for** de; **for doing**
pour faire)
**(b)** (baby milk) lait *m* en poudre
**fort** *n* fort *m*
**forte** *n* **to be sb's** ∼ être le fort de qn
**forth** *adv* **from this day** ∼ à partir
d'aujourd'hui; **from that day** ∼ à dater de ce
jour; ▶ BACK, SO
**forthcoming** *adj* **(a)** ⟨*event, book*⟩
prochain/-e (*before n*)
**(b) she wasn't very** ∼ **about it** elle était peu
disposée à en parler
**forthright** *adj* direct/-e
**forties** *n pl* **(a)** (era) **the** ∼ les années *fpl*
quarante
**(b)** (age) **to be in one's** ∼ avoir entre
quarante et cinquante ans
**fortieth** *n, adj, adv* quarantième (*mf*)
**fortified** *adj* ⟨*place*⟩ fortifié/-e; ∼ **wine** vin
*m* doux; ∼ **with vitamins** vitaminé/-e
**fortify** *vtr* fortifier
**fortnight** *n* (GB) quinze jours *mpl*; **the first**
∼ **in August** la première quinzaine d'août
**fortnightly** *adj* ⟨*meeting, visit*⟩ qui a lieu
toutes les deux semaines; ⟨*magazine*⟩
publié/-e toutes les deux semaines
**fortunate** *adj* heureux/-euse
**fortunately** *adv* heureusement
**fortune** *n* **(a)** fortune *f*; **to make a** ∼ faire
fortune
**(b) to have the good** ∼ **to do** avoir la chance
*or* le bonheur de faire
**(c) to tell sb's** ∼ dire la bonne aventure à qn
**fortune-teller** *n* diseur/-euse *m/f* de
bonne aventure
**forty** *n, pron, det* quarante (*m*) *inv*
**forward** ① *n* (Sport) avant *m*
② *adj* **(a)** (bold) effronté/-e
**(b)** (towards the front) ⟨*movement*⟩ en avant; **to**
**be too far** ∼ ⟨*seat*⟩ être trop en avant
**(c)** (advanced) avancé/-e; **he's no further** ∼ il
n'est pas plus avancé
③ *adv* (*also* **forwards**) **to step** ∼ faire un
pas en avant; **to fall** ∼ tomber en avant; **to**
**go** *or* **walk** ∼ avancer; **to move sth** ∼
avancer qch; **a way** ∼ une solution
④ *vtr* **(a)** expédier ⟨*goods*⟩; envoyer ⟨*parcel*⟩
**(b)** (send on) faire suivre, réexpédier ⟨*mail*⟩
**forwarding address** *n* nouvelle adresse
*f* (pour faire suivre le courrier)
**forward-looking** *adj* ⟨*company, person*⟩
tourné/-e vers l'avenir
**forward planning** *n* planification *f* à
long terme
**forwards** = FORWARD 3
**fossil** *n* fossile *m*
**fossil fuel** *n* combustible *m* fossile

**foster** ① *adj* ⟨*child, parent*⟩ adoptif/-ive
② *vtr* **(a)** (encourage) encourager ⟨*attitude*⟩;
promouvoir ⟨*activity*⟩
**(b)** prendre [qn] en placement ⟨*child*⟩
**foster family** *n* famille *f* de placement
**foster home** *n* foyer *m* de placement
**foul** ① *n* (Sport) faute *f* (**by** de; **on** sur)
② *adj* **(a)** ⟨*smell, air*⟩ fétide; ⟨*taste*⟩ infect/-e
**(b)** ⟨*weather, day*⟩ épouvantable; **to be in a** ∼
**mood** être d'une humeur massacrante
(colloq); **to have a** ∼ **temper** avoir un sale
caractère
**(c)** ⟨*language*⟩ ordurier/-ière
③ *adv* **to taste** ∼ avoir un goût infect
④ *vtr* **(a)** polluer ⟨*environment*⟩; souiller
⟨*pavement*⟩
**(b)** (Sport) commettre une faute contre
⟨*player*⟩
**foul-mouthed** *adj* grossier/-ière
**foul play** *n* acte *m* criminel; (in sport) jeu *m*
irrégulier
**foul-up** *n* (colloq) cafouillage *m* (colloq)
**found** *vtr* fonder (**on** sur)
**foundation** *n* **(a)** (founding) fondation *f*
**(b)** ∼**s** (of building) fondations *fpl*
**(c)** (*also* ∼ **cream**) fond *m* de teint
**foundation course** *n* (GB Univ) année *f*
de préparation à des études supérieures
**founder** *n* fondateur/-trice *m/f*
**foundry** *n* fonderie *f*
**fountain** *n* fontaine *f*
**fountain pen** *n* stylo *m* (à encre)
**four** *n, pron, det* quatre (*m*) *inv*
IDIOMS **on all** ∼**s** à quatre pattes
**four-by-four** *n* quatre-quatre *m inv*
**four-letter word** *n* mot *m* grossier
**four-star** ① *n* (GB) (*also* ∼ **petrol**)
super(carburant) *m*
② *adj* ⟨*hotel, restaurant*⟩ quatre étoiles
**fourteen** *n, pron, det* quatorze (*m*) *inv*
**fourteenth** ① *n* **(a)** (in order) quatorzième
*mf*
**(b)** (of month) quatorze *m inv*
**(c)** (fraction) quatorzième *m*
② *adj, adv* quatorzième
**fourth** ① *n* **(a)** (in order) quatrième *mf*
**(b)** (of month) quatre *m inv*
**(c)** (fraction) quatrième *m*
**(d)** (*also* ∼ **gear**) (Aut) quatrième *f*
② *adj, adv* quatrième
**four-wheel drive (vehicle)** *n*
quatre-quatre *m inv*
**fowl** *n* volaille *f*
**fox** *n* renard *m*
**foxhound** *n* fox-hound *m*
**fox hunting** *n* chasse *f* au renard
**fraction** *n* fraction *f* (**of** de)
**fracture** ① *n* fracture *f*
② *vtr* fracturer ⟨*bone, rock*⟩
③ *vi* ⟨*bone*⟩ se fracturer
**fragile** *adj* fragile
**fragment** *n* (of rock, manuscript) fragment *m*;
(of glass, china) morceau *m*

**fragrance** *n* parfum *m*

**fragrant** *adj* odorant/-e

**frail** *adj* ⟨person⟩ frêle; ⟨health, hope⟩ précaire

**frame** ⟨1⟩ *n* **(a)** (of building, boat, roof) charpente *f*; (of car) châssis *m*; (of bicycle, racquet) cadre *m*; (of bed) sommier *m*; (of tent) armature *f*
**(b)** (of picture, window) cadre *m*; (of door) encadrement *m*
**(c)** (body) corps *m*
⟨2⟩ **frames** *n pl* (of spectacles) monture *f*
⟨3⟩ *vtr* **(a)** encadrer ⟨picture, face⟩
**(b)** formuler ⟨question⟩

**frame of mind** *n* état *m* d'esprit; **to be in the right/wrong ~ for doing** être/ne pas être d'humeur à faire

**framework** *n* structure *f*; (figurative) cadre *m*

**franc** *n* franc *m*

**France** *pr n* France *f*

**franchise** *n* **(a)** (right to vote) droit *m* de vote
**(b)** (commercial) franchise *f*

**francophile** *n*, *adj* francophile (*mf*)

**frank** *adj* franc/franche

**Frankfurt** *pr n* Francfort

**frankly** *adv* franchement

**frantic** *adj* **(a)** ⟨activity⟩ frénétique
**(b)** ⟨effort, search⟩ désespéré/-e; **to be ~ with worry** être fou/folle d'inquiétude

**frantically** *adv* **(a)** (wildly) frénétiquement
**(b)** (desperately) désespérément

**fraternal** *adj* fraternel/-elle

**fraternity** *n* fraternité *f*

**fraud** *n* fraude *f*

**fraudulent** *adj* ⟨practice, use⟩ frauduleux/-euse; ⟨signature, cheque⟩ falsifié/-e; ⟨earnings⟩ illicite

**fraught** *adj* ⟨situation, atmosphere⟩ tendu/-e; ⟨person⟩ accablé/-e (**with** de); **to be ~ with** être lourd/-e de ⟨danger, difficulty⟩

**fray** *vi* ⟨material, rope⟩ s'effilocher

**frayed** *adj* ⟨nerves⟩ à bout; **tempers were ~** les gens s'énervaient

**frazzle** *n* (colloq) **to burn sth to a ~** calciner qch; **to be worn to a ~** être lessivé/-e (colloq)

**freak** ⟨1⟩ *n* **(a)** (strange person) original/-e *m/f*
**(b)** (at circus) phénomène *m*; **~ show** exhibition *f* de monstres
**(c)** (unusual occurrence) aberration *f*; **a ~ of nature** une bizarrerie de la nature
**(d)** (colloq) (enthusiast) mordu/-e *m/f* (colloq), fana *mf* (colloq)
⟨2⟩ *adj* ⟨accident, storm⟩ exceptionnel/-elle
■ **freak out** (get angry) piquer une crise (colloq); (go mad) flipper (colloq)

**freckle** *n* tache *f* de rousseur

**free** ⟨1⟩ *adj* **(a)** (gen) libre; **to be ~ to do** être libre de faire; **to set [sb/sth] ~** libérer ⟨person⟩; rendre la liberté à ⟨animal⟩
**(b)** (also **~ of charge**) gratuit/-e; **'admission ~'** 'entrée gratuite'

**(c) to be ~ with** être prodigue de ⟨advice⟩; **to be very ~ with money** dépenser sans compter
⟨2⟩ *adv* **(a)** ⟨run, roam⟩ librement, en toute liberté; **to go ~** ⟨hostage⟩ être libéré/-e; ⟨criminal⟩ circuler en toute liberté
**(b)** (without paying) gratuitement
⟨3⟩ *vtr* **(a)** (gen) libérer; (from wreckage) dégager
**(b)** débloquer ⟨money, resources⟩
⟨4⟩ **-free** *combining form* **smoke/sugar~** sans fumée/sucre; **interest-~** sans intérêt
⟨5⟩ **for free** *phr* gratuitement
IDIOMS **to have a ~ hand** avoir carte blanche (**in** pour); **to be a ~ agent** pouvoir agir à sa guise; **~ and easy** décontracté/-e

**freebee, freebie** *n* (colloq) (free gift) cadeau *m*; (newspaper) journal *m* gratuit; (trip) voyage *m* gratuit

**freedom** *n* liberté *f* (**to do** de faire); **~ of the press** liberté de la presse; **~ of information** libre accès *m* à l'information

**freedom fighter** *n* combattant *m* de la liberté

**freefall** *n* chute *f* libre

**Freefone®** *n* (also **Freephone®**) numéro *m* vert d'appel gratuit

**free-for-all** *n* mêlée *f* générale

**free gift** *n* cadeau *m*

**free kick** *n* coup *m* franc

**freelance** ⟨1⟩ *n* (also **freelancer**) free-lance *mf*
⟨2⟩ *adv* ⟨work⟩ en free-lance

**freely** *adv* (gen) librement; ⟨spend, give⟩ sans compter; ⟨admit⟩ volontiers

**free market** *n* (also **~ economy**) économie *f* de marché

**Freephone®** = FREEFONE ®

**freepost** *n* (GB) port *m* payé

**free-range** *adj* ⟨chicken⟩ élevé/-e en plein air; ⟨eggs⟩ de poules élevées en plein air

**free speech** *n* liberté *f* d'expression

**freestyle** *n* (in swimming) nage *f* libre; (in skiing) figures *fpl* libres; (in wrestling) lutte *f* libre

**free trade** *n* libre-échange *m*

**freeware** *n* freeware *m*, graticiel *m*

**freeway** *n* (US) autoroute *f*

**free will** *n* libre arbitre *m*; **of one's (own) ~** de plein gré

**freeze** ⟨1⟩ *n* **(a)** (in weather) gelées *fpl*
**(b)** (Econ) gel *m* (**on** de)
⟨2⟩ *vtr* **(a)** congeler ⟨food⟩; ⟨cold weather⟩ geler ⟨liquid, pipes⟩
**(b)** (Econ) bloquer, geler ⟨prices, wages, assets⟩
**(c)** (anaesthetize) insensibiliser ⟨gum, skin⟩
⟨3⟩ *vi* **(a)** ⟨water, pipes⟩ geler; ⟨food⟩ se congeler
**(b)** (feel cold) geler; **to be freezing to death** mourir de froid
**(c)** (not move) ⟨person, blood, smile⟩ se figer
⟨4⟩ *v impers* geler

**freeze-dried** *adj* lyophilisé/-e

**freeze frame** n arrêt m sur image

**freezer** n congélateur m

**freezer compartment** n freezer m

**freezing** 1 n zéro m; **below** ∼ en-dessous de zéro
2 adj **I'm** ∼ je suis gelé; **it's** ∼ **in here** on gèle ici

**freezing cold** adj ⟨room, wind⟩ glacial/-e; ⟨water⟩ glacé/-e

**freight** n (a) (goods) fret m, marchandises fpl
(b) (transport system) transport m
(c) (cost) (frais mpl de) port m

**freighter** n (a) (ship) cargo m
(b) (plane) avion-cargo m

**French** 1 n (a) (people) **the** ∼ les Français mpl
(b) (language) français m
2 adj ⟨culture, food, politics⟩ français/-e; ⟨teacher, lesson⟩ de français; ⟨ambassador, embassy⟩ de France

**French fries** n pl frites fpl

**Frenchman** n Français m

**French-speaking** adj francophone

**French toast** n pain m perdu

**French window** n porte-fenêtre f

**Frenchwoman** n Française f

**frenetic** adj ⟨activity⟩ frénétique; ⟨lifestyle⟩ trépidant/-e

**frenzied** adj ⟨activity⟩ frénétique; ⟨attempt⟩ désespéré/-e

**frenzy** n frénésie f, délire m

**frequency** n fréquence f (of de)

**frequent** adj (a) (common) ⟨expression⟩ courant/-e
(b) (happening often) fréquent/-e; **to make** ∼ **use of sth** se servir souvent or fréquemment de qch

**frequently** adv souvent, fréquemment

**fresco** n fresque f

**fresh** adj (a) frais/fraîche; **to smell** ∼ avoir une odeur fraîche; ∼ **orange juice** jus d'orange pressée; **while it is still** ∼ **in your mind** tant que tu l'as tout frais à l'esprit
(b) ⟨evidence, attempt⟩ nouveau/-elle (before n); ⟨linen⟩ propre; **to make a** ∼ **start** prendre un nouveau départ
(c) ⟨approach, outlook⟩ (tout) nouveau/ (toute) nouvelle (before n)
(d) **to feel** or **be** ∼ ⟨person⟩ être plein/-e d'entrain
(e) (colloq) (cheeky) impertinent/-e; **to be** ∼ **with sb** être un peu familier/-ière avec qn

**fresh air** n air m frais; **to get some** ∼ prendre l'air, s'oxygéner

**freshen** v ■ **freshen up** faire un brin de toilette

**freshly** adv fraîchement; ∼ **ironed/washed** qui vient d'être repassé/lavé

**fresh water** n eau f douce

**fret** vi (a) (be anxious) s'inquiéter (**over, about** pour, au sujet de)
(b) (cry) pleurer

**Freudian slip** n lapsus m

**friction** n (a) (rubbing) frottement m
(b) (conflict) conflits mpl (**between** entre); **to cause** ∼ être cause de friction

**Friday** n vendredi m

**fridge** n (GB) frigo m (colloq), réfrigérateur m

**fridge-freezer** n réfrigérateur-congélateur m

**friend** n ami/-e m/f (**of** de); **to make** ∼s se faire des amis; **to make** ∼s **with sb** devenir ami/-e m/f avec qn

**friendly** 1 adj ⟨person, attitude, argument, match⟩ amical/-e; ⟨animal⟩ affectueux/-euse; ⟨government, nation⟩ (after n); **to be** ∼ **with sb** être ami/-e m/f avec qn
2 **-friendly** combining form **environment-**∼ qui ne nuit pas à l'environnement; **user-**∼ d'utilisation facile, convivial/-e

**friendly fire** n (Mil) feu m allié

**friendship** n amitié f

**fright** n peur f; **to take** ∼ prendre peur, s'effrayer; **to give sb a** ∼ faire peur à qn, effrayer qn

**frighten** vtr faire peur à, effrayer

**frightened** adj **to be** ∼ avoir peur (**of** de; **to do** de faire)

**frightening** adj effrayant/-e

**frightful** adj (a) (inducing horror) abominable, épouvantable
(b) (colloq) (bad) ⟨prospect, mistake⟩ terrible; ⟨headache⟩ affreux/-euse

**frill** n (on dress) volant m; (on shirt) jabot m

**fringe** n (a) frange f; **on the** ∼**s of society** en marge de la société
(b) (in theatre) **the** ∼ théâtre m alternatif

**fringe benefits** n pl avantages mpl sociaux or en nature

**frisk** vtr fouiller ⟨person⟩

**fritter** n beignet m
■ **fritter away** gaspiller ⟨time, money⟩

**frivolous** adj frivole

**frizzy** adj ⟨hair⟩ crépu/-e

**frog** n grenouille f
IDIOMS **to have a** ∼ **in one's throat** avoir un chat dans la gorge

**frogman** n homme-grenouille m

**frogs' legs** n pl cuisses fpl de grenouille

**from** prep
■ Note from is often translated by de: from Rome = de Rome; from the sea = de la mer.
– Remember that de + le always becomes du (from the office = du bureau), and de + les always becomes des (from the United States = des États-Unis).
– For examples and particular usages, see the entry below.

(a) de; **where is he** ∼? d'où est-il?, d'où vient-il?; **she comes** ∼ **Oxford** elle vient d'Oxford; **paper** ∼ **Denmark** du papier provenant du Danemark; **a flight** ∼ **Nice** un vol en provenance de Nice; **a friend** ∼ **Chicago** un ami (qui vient) de Chicago; **a**

colleague ∼ Japan un collègue japonais; **a man ∼ the council** un homme qui travaille pour le conseil municipal; **a letter ∼ Tim** une lettre (de la part) de Tim; **who is it ∼?** c'est de la part de qui?; **alcohol can be made ∼ a wide range of products** on peut faire de l'alcool à partir de produits très variés; **10 km ∼ the sea** à 10 km de la mer; **15 years ∼ now** dans 15 ans, d'ici 15 ans
**(b)** ∼ ... **to...** de ... à...; **the journey ∼ A to B** le voyage de A à B; **the road ∼ A to B** la route qui va de A à B; **open ∼ 2 pm to 5 pm** ouvert de 14 à 17 heures; ∼ **June to August** du mois de juin au mois d'août; **to rise ∼ 10 to 17%** passer de 10 à 17%; ∼ **start to finish** du début à la fin; **everything ∼ paperclips to wigs** tout, des trombones aux perruques; ∼ **day to day** de jour en jour
**(c)** (starting from) à partir de; ∼ **today/May** à partir d'aujourd'hui/du mois de mai; **wine ∼ £5 a bottle** du vin à partir de 5 livres sterling la bouteille; ∼ **then on** dès lors; ∼ **the age of 8** depuis l'âge de 8 ans
**(d)** (based on) ∼ **a short story** d'après un conte; **to speak ∼ experience** parler d'expérience
**(e)** (among) **to choose** *or* **pick ∼** choisir parmi
**(f)** (in mathematics) **10 ∼ 27 leaves 17** 27 moins 10 égale 17
**(g)** (because of) **I know her ∼ work** je la connais car on travaille ensemble; ∼ **what I saw/he said** d'après ce que j'ai vu/ce qu'il a dit

**front** [1] *n* **(a)** (of house) façade *f*; (of shop) devanture *f*; (of cupboard, box, sweater, building) devant *m*; (of book) couverture *f*; (of card, coin, banknote) recto *m*; (of car, boat) avant *m*; (of fabric) endroit *m*; **to button at the ∼** se boutonner sur le devant; **on the ∼ of the envelope** au recto de l'enveloppe
**(b)** (of train, queue) tête *f*; (of auditorium) premier rang *m*; **at the ∼ of the line** en tête de la file; **to sit at the ∼ of the class** s'asseoir au premier rang de la classe; **I'll sit in the ∼** je vais m'asseoir devant; **at the ∼ of the coach** à l'avant du car
**(c)** (GB) (promenade) front *m* de mer, bord *m* de mer; **on the sea ∼** au bord de la mer
**(d)** (Mil) front *m*
**(e)** (in weather) front *m*
**(f)** (façade) façade *f*; **it's just a ∼** ce n'est qu'une façade
[2] *adj* ⟨entrance⟩ côté rue; ⟨garden, window⟩ de devant; ⟨bedroom⟩ qui donne sur la rue; ⟨wheel⟩ avant; ⟨seat⟩ (in cinema) au premier rang; (in vehicle) de devant; ⟨leg, paw, tooth⟩ de devant; ⟨before n⟩; ⟨view⟩ de face
[3] *vtr* **(a)** être à la tête de ⟨band⟩
**(b)** présenter ⟨TV show⟩
[4] *vi* **to ∼ onto** (GB) *or* **on** (US) donner sur
[5] **in front** *phr* ⟨walk⟩ devant; **the car in ∼** la voiture de devant; **the people in ∼** les gens qui sont devant; **to be in ∼** (in race) être en tête; **I'm 30 points in ∼** j'ai 30 points d'avance
[6] **in front of** *phr* devant

**front bench** *n* (GB Pol) (seats) rangs *mpl* du gouvernement
**front door** *n* porte *f* d'entrée
**frontier** *n* frontière *f*
**front line** *n* **(a)** (Mil) front *m*
**(b)** (exposed position) **to be in the ∼** être en première ligne
**front page** [1] *n* première page *f*
[2] **front-page** *adj* ⟨picture, story⟩ à la une (colloq); **the ∼ headlines** les gros titres, la manchette
**frost** *n* gel *m*
**frostbite** *n* gelures *fpl*
**frosted** *adj* ⟨nail varnish⟩ nacré/-e; ⟨glass⟩ dépoli/-e, opaque
**frosty** *adj* **(a)** ⟨morning⟩ glacial/-e; ⟨windscreen⟩ couvert/-e de givre; **it was a ∼ night** il gelait cette nuit-là
**(b)** (unfriendly) glacial/-e
**froth** *n* (on beer, champagne) mousse *f*; (on water) écume *f*; (around mouth) écume *f*
**frown** *vi* froncer les sourcils; **to ∼ at sb** regarder qn en fronçant les sourcils
■ **frown on, frown upon** désapprouver, critiquer
**frozen** *adj* **(a)** ⟨food⟩ congelé/-e
**(b)** ⟨lake, pipe, ground⟩ gelé/-e; **I'm ∼** je suis gelé; **to be ∼ stiff** être transi/-e de froid
**fruit** *n* fruit *m*; **a piece of ∼** un fruit
**fruit cake** *n* cake *m*
**fruition** *n* **to come to ∼** se réaliser; **to bring sth to ∼** réaliser qch
**fruit juice** *n* jus *m* de fruits
**fruit machine** *n* machine *f* à sous
**fruit salad** *n* salade *f* de fruits
**fruity** *adj* ⟨wine, fragrance⟩ fruité/-e
**frustrate** *vtr* frustrer ⟨person⟩; réduire [qch] à néant ⟨effort⟩; contrarier ⟨plan⟩; entraver ⟨attempt⟩
**frustrated** *adj* frustré/-e
**frustrating** *adj* **(a)** (irritating) énervant/-e
**(b)** (unsatisfactory) frustrant/-e
**frustration** *n* frustration *f* (at, with quant à)
**fry** [1] *vtr* faire frire
[2] **fried** *pp adj* **fried fish** poisson *m* frit; **fried food** friture *f*; **fried eggs** œufs *mpl* au plat; **fried potatoes** pommes *fpl* de terre sautées
**frying pan** *n* (GB) poêle *f* (à frire)
**fuel** [1] *n* (for heating) combustible *m*; (for car, plane) carburant *m*
[2] *vtr* **(a)** alimenter ⟨engine⟩
**(b)** ravitailler ⟨plane⟩
**(c)** aggraver ⟨tension⟩; attiser ⟨hatred⟩
**fuel tank** *n* (of car) réservoir *m*
**fugitive** *n* fugitif/-ive *m/f*, fuyard/-e *m/f*
**fulfil** (GB), **fulfill** (US) *vtr* **(a)** réaliser ⟨ambition⟩; répondre à ⟨desire, need⟩; **to feel ∼led** se sentir comblé/-e
**(b)** remplir ⟨duty, conditions, contract⟩
**fulfilment** (GB), **fulfillment** (US) *n* **(a)** (satisfaction) épanouissement *m*

**(b)** the ~ of la réalisation de ⟨ambition, need⟩

**full** ① adj **(a)** (gen) plein/-e ⟨of de⟩; ⟨hotel, flight, car park⟩ complet/-ète; ⟨theatre⟩ comble; **I'm ~ (up)** je n'en peux plus
**(b)** (busy) ⟨day, week⟩ chargé/-e, bien rempli/-e; **a very ~ life** une vie très remplie
**(c)** (complete) ⟨name, breakfast, story⟩ complet/-ète; ⟨price, control⟩ total/-e; ⟨responsibility⟩ entier/-ière; ⟨support⟩ inconditionnel/-elle
**(d)** ⟨member⟩ à part entière
**(e)** ⟨employment, bloom⟩ plein/-e (before n); **at ~ volume** à plein volume; **at ~ speed** à toute vitesse; **to get ~ marks** (GB) obtenir la note maximale
**(f)** (for emphasis) ⟨hour, kilo, month⟩ bon/ bonne (before n)
**(g)** (rounded) ⟨cheeks⟩ rond/-e; ⟨figure⟩ fort/-e; ⟨skirt, sleeve⟩ ample
② adv **to know ~ well that** savoir fort bien que; **with the heating up ~** avec le chauffage à fond
③ **in full** phr ⟨pay⟩ intégralement; **to write sth in ~** écrire qch en toutes lettres

**full blast** adv (colloq) **the TV was on (at) ~** la télé marchait à pleins tubes (colloq)
**full-blown** adj **(a)** ⟨disease⟩ déclaré/-e; ⟨epidemic⟩ extensif/-ive
**(b)** ⟨crisis, war⟩ à grande échelle
**full board** n (in hotel) pension f complète
**full-cream milk** n (GB) lait m entier
**full-length** adj ⟨coat, curtain⟩ long/longue; ⟨mirror⟩ en pied; **a ~ film** un long métrage
**full moon** n pleine lune f
**full name** n nom m et prénom m
**full price** adj, adv au prix fort
**full-scale** adj **(a)** ⟨drawing⟩ grandeur f nature
**(b)** ⟨investigation⟩ approfondi/-e
**(c)** ⟨alert⟩ général/-e; ⟨crisis⟩ généralisé/-e
**full-size(d)** adj grand format inv
**full stop** n (GB) point m
**full time** ① n (Sport) fin m du match
② **full-time** adj **(a)** (Sport) ⟨score⟩ final/-e
**(b)** ⟨job, student⟩ à plein temps
③ adv ⟨study, work⟩ à plein temps
**fully** adv **(a)** ⟨understand⟩ très bien; ⟨recover⟩ complètement; ⟨dressed⟩ entièrement; ⟨awake, developed⟩ complètement; **to be ~ qualified** avoir obtenu tous ses diplômes
**(b)** ⟨open⟩ à fond; **~ booked** complet/-ète
**fully-fledged** adj ⟨member⟩ à part entière; ⟨lawyer⟩ diplômé/-e
**fumble** vtr mal attraper ⟨ball⟩
∎ **fumble about** (in dark) tâtonner (**to do** pour faire); **to ~ about in** fouiller dans ⟨bag⟩
**fume** vi **(a)** ⟨chemical, mixture⟩ fumer
**(b)** (colloq) **to be fuming** être furibond/-e (colloq)
**fumes** n pl émanations fpl; **petrol ~** (GB), **gas ~** (US) vapeurs fpl d'essence
**fun** n plaisir m, amusement m; **to have ~**

s'amuser (**doing** en faisant; **with** avec); **windsurfing is ~** c'est amusant de faire de la planche à voile; **for ~** pour s'amuser; **she is great ~ to be with** on s'amuse beaucoup avec elle
IDIOMS **to make ~ of** or **poke ~ at sb/sth** se moquer de qn/qch

**function** ① n **(a)** (gen) fonction f
**(b)** (reception) réception f; (ceremony) cérémonie f (officielle)
② vi **(a)** (work properly) fonctionner
**(b)** **to ~ as** ⟨object⟩ faire fonction de, servir de; ⟨person⟩ jouer le rôle de
**functional** adj **(a)** (in working order) opérationnel/-elle
**(b)** ⟨furniture, design⟩ fonctionnel/-elle
**function key** n touche f de fonction
**fund** ① n fonds m; **relief ~** caisse f de secours; **disaster ~** collecte f en faveur des sinistrés
② **funds** n pl fonds mpl, capitaux mpl; **to be in ~s** avoir de l'argent
③ vtr financer ⟨company, project⟩
**fundamental** adj ⟨issue⟩ fondamental/-e; ⟨error, importance⟩ capital/-e; ⟨concern⟩ principal/-e
**fundamentalist** n, adj (gen) fondamentaliste (mf); (religious) intégriste (mf)
**funding** n financement m
**fund-raising** n collecte f de fonds
**funeral** n enterrement m, obsèques fpl (formal)
**funeral home** (US), **funeral parlour** n entreprise f de pompes funèbres
**fun fair** n fête f foraine
**fungus** n **(a)** (mushroom) champignon m
**(b)** (mould) moisissure f
**fun-loving** adj ⟨person⟩ qui aime s'amuser
**funnel** n **(a)** (for liquids) entonnoir m
**(b)** (on ship) cheminée f
**funny** adj (amusing) drôle, amusant/-e; (odd) bizarre; **to feel ~** (colloq) se sentir tout/-e chose (colloq)
**fur** ① n (of animal) poils mpl; (for garment) fourrure f
② adj ⟨collar, coat⟩ de fourrure
**furious** adj **(a)** furieux/-ieuse (**with, at** contre); **he's ~ about it** cela l'a rendu furieux
**(b)** ⟨debate, struggle⟩ acharné/-e; ⟨storm⟩ déchaîné/-e; **at a ~ rate** à un rythme effréné
**furnace** n (boiler) chaudière f; (in foundry) fourneau m; (for forging) four m
**furnish** vtr meubler ⟨room, apartment⟩
**furnishings** n pl ameublement m
**furniture** n mobilier m, meubles mpl; **a piece of ~** un meuble
**furry** adj ⟨toy⟩ en peluche; ⟨kitten⟩ au poil touffu
**further** ① adv **(a)** (gen) (also **farther**) plus loin (**than** que); **how much ~ is it?** c'est

encore loin?; ~ **back/forward** plus en arrière/en avant; ~ **away** *or* **off** plus loin; ~ **on** encore plus loin

**(b)** (in time) (*also* **farther**) ~ **back** than 1964 avant 1964; **we must look** ~ **ahead** nous devons regarder plus vers l'avenir

**(c) I haven't read** ~ **than page twenty** je n'ai pas lu au-delà de la page vingt; **prices fell (even)** ~ les prix ont baissé encore plus

**2** *adj* **(a)** (additional) **a** ~ **500 people** 500 personnes de plus; ~ **changes** d'autres changements; **without** ~ **delay** sans plus attendre

**(b)** (*also* **farther**) ⟨side, end⟩ autre

**3** *vtr* augmenter ⟨chances⟩; faire avancer ⟨career, plan⟩; servir ⟨cause⟩

**further education** *n* (GB Univ) ≈ enseignement *m* professionnel

**furthest** (*also* **farthest**) **1** *adj* le plus éloigné/la plus éloignée

**2** *adv* (*also* **the** ~) le plus loin

**furtive** *adj* ⟨glance, movement⟩ furtif/-ive; ⟨behaviour⟩ suspect/-e

**fury** *n* fureur *f*; **to be in a** ~ être en fureur

**fuse, fuze** (US) **1** *n* fusible *m*; **to blow a** ~ faire sauter un fusible; (get angry) piquer une crise (colloq)

**2** *vtr* **(a)** (GB) **to** ~ **the lights** faire sauter les plombs

**(b)** (join) fondre [qch] ensemble ⟨metals⟩

**fuse box** *n* boîte *f* à fusibles

**fuselage** *n* fuselage *m*

**fuse wire** *n* fusible *m*

**fuss** **1** *n* **(a)** (agitation) remue-ménage *m inv*; **to make a** ~ faire des histoires; **to make a** ~ **about sth** faire toute une histoire à propos de qch

**(b) to kick up a** ~ **about sth** (colloq) piquer une crise à propos de qch (colloq)

**(c)** (attention) **to make a** ~ **of** être aux petits soins avec *or* pour ⟨person⟩; caresser ⟨animal⟩

**2** *vi* **(a)** (worry) se faire du souci (**about** pour)

**(b)** (show attention) **to** ~ **over sb** (colloq) être aux petits soins avec *or* pour qn

**fussy** *adj* **to be** ~ **about one's food/about details** être maniaque sur la nourriture/sur les détails

**futile** *adj* **(a)** (vain) vain/-e
**(b)** (inane) futile

**future** **1** *n* **(a)** avenir *m*; **in the** ~ dans l'avenir; **in** ~ à l'avenir
**(b)** (*also* ~ **tense**) futur *m*
**2** *adj* ⟨generation, developments, investment, earnings⟩ futur/-e; ⟨prospects⟩ d'avenir; ⟨queen, king⟩ futur/-e (*before n*); **at some** ~ **date** à une date ultérieure

**fuze** (US) = FUSE

**fuzzy** *adj* **(a)** ⟨hair, beard⟩ crépu/-e
**(b)** ⟨image⟩ flou/-e; ⟨idea, mind⟩ confus/-e

**g**

# Gg

**g, G** *n* **(a)** (letter) g, G *m*
**(b) G** (Mus) sol *m*
**(c) g** (*written abbr* = **gram**) g

**gab**: *n* (colloq)
IDIOMS **to have the gift of the** ~ (colloq) avoir du bagou(t) (colloq)

**gadget** *n* gadget *m*

**gaffe** *n* bévue *f*

**gag** **1** *n* **(a)** (on mouth) bâillon *m*
**(b)** (colloq) (joke) blague *f* (colloq)
**2** *vtr* bâillonner ⟨person⟩
**3** *vi* avoir un haut-le-cœur

**gage** (US) = GAUGE

**gain** **1** *n* **(a)** (financial) gain *m*, profit *m*
**(b)** (increase) augmentation *f* (**in** de)
**(c)** (advantage) gain *m*; (advances) progrès *m* (**in** de)
**2** *vtr* **(a)** (gen) gagner; acquérir ⟨experience⟩ (**from** de); obtenir ⟨advantage⟩ (**from** grâce à); **we have nothing to** ~ nous n'avons rien à gagner
**(b) to** ~ **speed** prendre de la vitesse *or* de l'élan; **to** ~ **weight** prendre du poids

**3** *vi* **(a)** (increase) **to** ~ **in popularity** gagner en popularité; **to** ~ **in value** prendre de la valeur
**(b)** (profit) **she hasn't** ~**ed by it** cela ne lui a rien rapporté
■ **gain on** rattraper ⟨person, vehicle⟩

**galaxy** *n* galaxie *f*

**gale** *n* vent *m* violent

**gallery** *n* **(a)** (gen) galerie *f*
**(b)** (art) ~ musée *m* (d'art)
**(c)** (in theatre) dernier balcon *m*

**Gallic** *adj* (French) français/-e

**galling** *adj* vexant/-e

**gallon** *n* gallon *m* ((GB) = *4.546 l*; (US) = *3.785 l*)

**gallop** **1** *n* galop *m*
**2** *vi* galoper

**galore** *adv* ⟨prizes, bargains⟩ à profusion; ⟨drinks, sandwiches⟩ à volonté, à gogo (colloq)

**galvanize** *vtr* galvaniser ⟨group, community⟩; relancer ⟨campaign⟩; **to** ~ **sb into doing** pousser qn à faire

**gambit** *n* **(a)** tactique *f*                              ···⟩

**(b)** (in chess) gambit m

**gamble** ⟦1⟧ n pari m; **it's a ~** c'est risqué
  ⟦2⟧ vtr **(a)** jouer ⟨money⟩
  **(b)** (figurative) miser (**on** sur)
  ⟦3⟧ vi (at cards, on shares) jouer; (on horses)
  parier; (figurative) miser (**on** sur)

**gambler** n joueur/-euse m/f

**gambling** n jeu m (d'argent)

**game** ⟦1⟧ n **(a)** jeu m; **to play a ~** jouer à un
  jeu; **to have a ~ of** faire une partie de
  **(b)** (match) match m (**of** de); (in tennis) jeu m
  **(c)** (Culin) gibier m
  ⟦2⟧ **games** n pl **(a)** (GB) (Sch) sport m
  **(b)** (also **Games**) (sporting event) Jeux mpl
  IDIOMS **to give the ~ away** vendre la mèche

**gamekeeper** n garde-chasse m

**game plan** n stratégie f

**game reserve** n (for hunting) réserve f de
  chasse; (for protection) réserve f naturelle

**games console** n console f de jeux
  vidéo

**game show** n jeu m télévisé

**games room** n salle f de jeux

**games software** n logiciel m de jeux,
  ludiciel m

**gaming** n on-line **~** jeux mpl en ligne

**gaming zone** n (on Internet) salle f de jeux
  en ligne

**gammon** n jambon m

**gang** n **(a)** (of criminals) gang m; (of youths,
  friends) bande f
  **(b)** (of workmen, prisoners) équipe f
  ■ **gang up** se coaliser (**on, against** contre)

**gangland** n ≈ le Milieu

**gang leader** n chef m de bande

**gang-rape** n viol m collectif

**gangster** n gangster m

**gangway** n **(a)** (to ship) passerelle f
  **(b)** (GB) (in bus, cinema) allée f

**gap** n **(a)** (gen) trou m (**in** dans); (between
  planks, curtains) interstice m (**in** entre); (between
  cars) espace m (**in** entre); (in cloud) trouée f (**in**
  dans)
  **(b)** (of time) intervalle m; (in conversation)
  silence m
  **(c)** (discrepancy) écart m (**between** entre); **a
  15-year age ~** une différence d'âge de 15 ans
  **(d)** (in knowledge) lacune f (**in** dans)
  **(e)** (in market) créneau m

**gape** vi **(a)** (stare) rester bouche bée; **to ~ at
  sb/sth** regarder qn/qch bouche bée
  **(b) to ~ open** ⟨chasm⟩ s'ouvrir tout grand;
  ⟨wound⟩ être béant/-e; ⟨garment⟩ bâiller

**gaping** adj ⟨person⟩ bouche bée; ⟨wound,
  hole⟩ béant/-e

**gap year** n: année d'interruption des
  études entre le lycée et l'université

**garage** n garage m

**garbage** n **(a)** (US) (refuse) ordures fpl
  **(b)** (nonsense) âneries fpl, bêtises fpl

**garbage can** n (US) poubelle f

**garbage truck** n (US) camion m des
  éboueurs

**garbled** adj ⟨account, instructions⟩
  confus/-e

**garden** ⟦1⟧ n jardin m
  ⟦2⟧ vi jardiner, faire du jardinage

**garden centre** (GB), **garden center**
  (US) n jardinerie f

**gardener** n jardinier/-ière m/f

**gardening** n jardinage m

**gargle** vi se gargariser (**with** avec)

**garish** adj tape-à-l'œil inv

**garland** n guirlande f

**garlic** n ail m

**garment** n vêtement m

**garnish** ⟦1⟧ n garniture f
  ⟦2⟧ vtr garnir (**with** de)

**garter** n **(a)** (for stocking) jarretière f; (for
  socks) fixe-chaussette m
  **(b)** (US) (suspender) jarretelle f

**gas** ⟦1⟧ n **(a)** (fuel) gaz m
  **(b)** (anaesthetic) anesthésie f
  **(c)** (US) (petrol) essence f
  ⟦2⟧ vtr gazer

**gas chamber** n chambre f à gaz

**gas cooker** n cuisinière f à gaz

**gas fire** n (appareil m de) chauffage m à
  gaz

**gash** ⟦1⟧ n entaille f
  ⟦2⟧ vtr entailler

**gas mask** n masque m à gaz

**gasoline** n (US) essence f

**gas oven** n four m à gaz

**gasp** ⟦1⟧ n halètement m
  ⟦2⟧ vi **(a)** (for air) haleter
  **(b) to ~ (in amazement)** avoir le souffle
  coupé (par la surprise)

**gas pedal** n (US) accélérateur m

**gas station** n (US) station-service f

**gastro-enteritis** n gastro-entérite f

**gate** n (of field, level crossing) barrière f; (in
  town, prison, airport, garden) porte f; (of courtyard,
  palace) portail m; **at the ~** à l'entrée

**gatecrash** vtr (colloq) (without paying)
  resquiller (colloq) à; (without invitation) se pointer
  (colloq) sans invitation à

**gatecrasher** n (colloq) (at concert)
  resquilleur/-euse m/f; (at party) intrus/-e m/f

**gather** ⟦1⟧ n (in garment) fronce f
  ⟦2⟧ vtr **(a)** cueillir ⟨fruit, flowers⟩; ramasser
  ⟨fallen fruit, wood⟩; recueillir ⟨information⟩;
  rassembler ⟨courage, strength⟩; **to ~ speed**
  prendre de la vitesse
  **(b) to ~ that...** déduire que...; **I ~ (that) he
  was there** d'après ce que j'ai compris il était
  là
  **(c)** (in sewing) faire des fronces à
  ⟦3⟧ vi ⟨people, crowd⟩ se rassembler; ⟨family⟩
  se réunir; ⟨clouds⟩ s'amonceler

**gathering** n réunion f; **social/family ~**
  réunion entre amis/de famille

**gaudy** adj tape-à-l'œil inv

**gauge, gage** (US) ⟦1⟧ n **(a)** (of gun, screw)
  calibre m; (of metal, wire) épaisseur f
  **(b)** (of railway) écartement m (des voies)

g

**(c)** (measuring instrument) jauge $f$; **fuel** ∼ jauge d'essence

**2** *vtr* **(a)** mesurer ⟨*diameter*⟩; jauger ⟨*distance, quantity*⟩; calibrer ⟨*gun*⟩
**(b)** évaluer ⟨*mood, reaction*⟩

**gaunt** *adj* décharné/-e

**gauze** *n* (fabric) gaze $f$; (wire) grillage $m$

**gay** **1** *n* homosexuel/-elle $m/f$, gay $mf$
**2** *adj* **(a)** homosexuel/-elle
**(b)** (happy) gai/-e; ⟨*laughter*⟩ joyeux/-euse

**Gaza strip** *pr n* bande $f$ de Gaza

**gaze** **1** *n* regard $m$
**2** *vi* **to ∼ at** sb/sth regarder qn/qch; (in wonder) contempler qn/qch

**GCSE** *n* (*abbr* = **General Certificate of Secondary Education**) certificat $m$ d'études secondaires

**gear** *n* **(a)** (equipment) matériel $m$
**(b)** (clothes) fringues $fpl$ (colloq); **football ∼** tenue $f$ de football
**(c)** (Aut) vitesse $f$; **to be in third ∼** être en troisième; **to put a car in ∼** passer la vitesse; **you're not in ∼** tu es au point mort
■ **gear up** se préparer; **to be ∼ed up** être prêt/-e (**for** pour)

**gearbox** *n* boîte $f$ de vitesses

**gearstick** (GB), **gearshift** (US) *n* levier $m$ de vitesses

**gear wheel** *n* pignon $m$

**gel** **1** *n* gel $m$
**2** *vi* **(a)** (Culin) prendre
**(b)** (figurative) prendre forme

**gem** *n* (jewel) pierre $f$ précieuse

**Gemini** *n* Gémeaux $mpl$

**gender** *n* **(a)** (of word) genre $m$
**(b)** (of person, animal) sexe $m$

**gene** *n* gène $m$

**genealogy** *n* généalogie $f$

**gene library** *n* génothèque $f$

**gene pool** *n* patrimoine $m$ héréditaire

**general** **1** *n* général $m$
**2** *adj* général/-e
**3** **in general** *phr* (usually) en général; (overall) dans l'ensemble

**general election** *n* élections $fpl$ législatives.

**generalization** *n* généralisation $f$ (**about** sur)

**generalize** *vtr, vi* généraliser (**about** à propos de)

**general knowledge** *n* culture $f$ générale

**generally** *adv* **(a)** (usually) en général, généralement; **∼ speaking...** en règle générale...
**(b)** (overall) **the quality is ∼ good** dans l'ensemble la qualité est bonne
**(c)** ⟨*talk*⟩ d'une manière générale

**general practitioner, GP** *n* (médecin $m$) généraliste $mf$

**general public** *n* (grand) public $m$

**general-purpose** *adj* à usages multiples

**general strike** *n* grève $f$ générale

**generate** *vtr* produire ⟨*power, heat, income, waste*⟩; créer ⟨*employment*⟩; susciter ⟨*interest, tension, ideas*⟩; entraîner ⟨*profit, publicity*⟩

**generation** *n* **(a)** génération $f$; **the younger/older ∼** la jeune/l'ancienne génération
**(b)** (of electricity, data) production $f$

**generation gap** *n* fossé $m$ des générations

**generator** *n* (of electricity) générateur $m$; (in hospital, on farm) groupe $m$ électrogène

**generosity** *n* générosité $f$

**generous** *adj* (gen) généreux/-euse; ⟨*size*⟩ grand/-e (*before n*); ⟨*hem*⟩ bon/bonne (*before n*)

**gene therapy** *n* thérapie $f$ génique

**genetic** *adj* génétique

**genetically modified, GM** *adj* génétiquement modifié/-e

**genetic engineering** *n* génie $m$ génétique

**genetic fingerprinting** *n* empreintes $fpl$ génétiques

**genetics** *n* génétique $f$

**genetic testing** *n* tests $mpl$ de dépistage génétique

**Geneva** *pr n* Genève

**genial** *adj* cordial/-e

**genitals** *n pl* organes $mpl$ génitaux

**genius** *n* génie $m$

**genome** *n* génome $m$

**gentle** *adj* (gen) doux/douce; ⟨*hint, reminder*⟩ discret/-ète; ⟨*pressure, touch, breeze*⟩ léger/-ère; ⟨*exercise*⟩ modéré/-e

**gentleman** *n* **(a)** (man) monsieur $m$
**(b)** (well-bred) gentleman $m$

**gently** *adv* (gen) doucement; ⟨*treat, cleanse*⟩ avec douceur; ⟨*cook*⟩ à feu doux; ⟨*speak*⟩ gentiment; **to break the news ∼** annoncer la nouvelle avec ménagement

**gents** *n pl* (toilets) toilettes $fpl$; (on sign) 'Messieurs'

**genuine** *adj* ⟨*reason, motive*⟩ vrai/-e (*before n*); ⟨*work of art*⟩ authentique; ⟨*jewel, substance*⟩ véritable; ⟨*person, effort, interest*⟩ sincère; ⟨*buyer*⟩ sérieux/-ieuse

**genuinely** *adv* (really and truly) vraiment; (in reality) réellement

**geography** *n* géographie $f$

**geology** *n* géologie $f$

**geometry** *n* géométrie $f$

**gerbil** *n* gerbille $f$

**geriatric** *adj* ⟨*hospital, ward*⟩ gériatrique

**germ** *n* **(a)** (microbe) microbe $m$
**(b)** (seed) germe $m$

**German** **1** *n* **(a)** (person) Allemand/-e $m/f$
**(b)** (language) allemand $m$
**2** *adj* ⟨*custom, food*⟩ allemand/-e; ⟨*ambassador, embassy*⟩ d'Allemagne; ⟨*teacher, course*⟩ d'allemand

**German measles** *n* rubéole $f$

**Germany** *pr n* Allemagne $f$

**g**

**germinate** ① *vtr* faire germer
② *vi* germer

**germ warfare** *n* guerre *f* bactériologique

**gesticulate** *vi* gesticuler

**gesture** ① *n* geste *m* (of de)
② *vi* faire un geste; **to ~ at** or **towards sth** désigner qch d'un geste; **to ~ to sb** faire signe à qn

**get**

■ **Note** This much-used verb has no multi-purpose equivalent in French and therefore is very often translated by choosing a synonym: *to get lunch = to prepare lunch* = préparer le déjeuner.
– When *get* is used to express the idea that a job is done not by you but by somebody else (*to get a room painted*), *faire* is used in French followed by an infinitive (*faire repeindre une pièce*).
– When *get* has the meaning of *become* and is followed by an adjective (*to get rich*), *devenir* is sometimes useful but check the appropriate entry (RICH) as a single verb often suffices (*s'enrichir*).
– The phrasal verbs (*get around, get down, get on* etc.) are listed separately at the end of the entry GET.
– For examples and further uses of *get* see the entry below.

① *vtr* **(a)** (receive) recevoir ⟨*letter, grant*⟩; recevoir, percevoir ⟨*salary, pension*⟩; capter ⟨*channel*⟩
**(b)** (inherit) **to ~ sth from sb** hériter qch de qn ⟨*article, money*⟩; tenir qch de qn ⟨*trait*⟩
**(c)** (obtain) obtenir ⟨*permission, divorce*⟩; trouver ⟨*job*⟩
**(d)** (buy) acheter ⟨*item, newspaper*⟩ **(from** chez); avoir ⟨*ticket*⟩; **to ~ sb sth, to ~ sth for sb** (as gift) acheter qch à qn
**(e)** (acquire) se faire ⟨*reputation*⟩
**(f)** (achieve) obtenir ⟨*grade*⟩
**(g)** (fetch) chercher ⟨*person, help*⟩; **to ~ sb sth, to ~ sth for sb** aller chercher qch pour qn
**(h)** (move) **to ~ sb/sth downstairs** faire descendre qn/qch
**(i)** (help progress) **this is ~ting us nowhere** ça ne nous avance à rien; **where will that ~ you?** à quoi ça t'avancera?
**(j)** (deal with) **I'll ~ it** (of phone) je réponds; (of doorbell) j'y vais
**(k)** (prepare) préparer ⟨*breakfast, lunch*⟩
**(l)** (take hold of) attraper ⟨*person*⟩ **(by** par)
**(m)** (colloq) (oblige to give) **to ~ sth out of sb** faire sortir qch à qn ⟨*money*⟩; obtenir qch de qn ⟨*truth*⟩
**(n)** (contract) attraper ⟨*cold, disease*⟩; **he got measles from his sister** sa sœur lui a passé la rougeole
**(o)** (catch) prendre ⟨*bus, train*⟩
**(p)** (have) **to have got** avoir ⟨*object, money, friend*⟩; **I've got a headache** j'ai mal à la tête; **to ~ the idea that** se mettre dans la tête que
**(q)** **to ~ a surprise** être surpris/-e; **to ~ a shock** avoir un choc; **to ~ a bang on the head** recevoir un coup sur la tête

**(r)** (as punishment) prendre ⟨*five years*⟩; avoir ⟨*fine*⟩
**(s)** (understand, hear) comprendre
**(t)** (colloq) (annoy) **what ~s me is...** ce qui m'agace c'est que...
**(u)** **to ~ to like sb** finir par apprécier qn; **how did you ~ to hear of...?** comment avez-vous entendu parler de...?; **we got to know them last year** on a fait leur connaissance l'année dernière
**(v)** (have opportunity) **to ~ to do** avoir l'occasion de faire, pouvoir faire
**(w)** (must) **to have got to do** devoir faire ⟨*homework, chore*⟩; **it's got to be done** il faut le faire; **you've got to realize that...** il faut que tu te rendes compte que...
**(x)** (make) **to ~ sb to pay** faire payer qn; **to ~ sb to tell the truth** faire dire la vérité à qn
**(y)** (ask) **to ~ sb to wash the dishes** demander à qn de faire la vaisselle
**(z)** **to ~ the car repaired** faire réparer la voiture; **to ~ one's hair cut** se faire couper les cheveux; **to ~ the car going** faire démarrer la voiture; **to ~ one's socks wet** mouiller ses chaussettes; **to ~ one's finger trapped** se coincer le doigt; **to ~ a dress made** se faire faire une robe
② *vi* **(a)** (become) devenir ⟨*suspicious, old*⟩; **it's ~ting late** il se fait tard
**(b)** (forming passive) **to ~ killed** se faire tuer; **to ~ hurt** être blessé/-e
**(c)** (become involved in) **to ~ into** (colloq) se mettre à ⟨*hobby*⟩; commencer dans ⟨*profession*⟩; **to ~ into a fight** se battre
**(d)** (arrive) **to ~ there** arriver; **to ~ to the airport** arriver à l'aéroport; **how did you ~ here?** comment est-ce que tu es venu?; **where did you ~ to?** où est-ce que tu étais passé?
**(e)** (progress) **I'm ~ting nowhere with this essay** je n'avance pas dans cette dissertation; **now we're ~ting somewhere** il y a du progrès
**(f)** (put on) **to ~ into** mettre, enfiler ⟨*pyjamas*⟩

■ **get about (a)** (move) se déplacer
**(b)** (travel) voyager
■ **get across (a)** traverser ⟨*river, road*⟩
**(b)** faire passer ⟨*message*⟩ **(to** à)
■ **get ahead** (make progress) progresser
■ **get along (a) how are you ~ting along?** (in job, school) comment ça se passe?
**(b)** ⟨*people*⟩ bien s'entendre **(with** avec)
■ **get around:** ¶ **~ around** = GET ABOUT
**(b)** (manage to do) **she'll ~ around to visiting us eventually** elle va bien finir par venir nous voir; **I haven't got around to it yet** je n'ai pas encore eu le temps de m'en occuper; ¶ **~ around [sth]** contourner ⟨*problem, law*⟩
■ **get at** (colloq) **(a)** (reach) atteindre ⟨*object*⟩; découvrir ⟨*truth*⟩
**(b)** (criticize) être après ⟨*person*⟩
**(c)** (insinuate) **what are you ~ting at?** où est-ce que tu veux en venir?
■ **get away (a)** (leave) partir
**(b)** (escape) s'échapper

**(c)** to ∼ **away with a crime** échapper à la justice; **you won't** ∼ **away with it!** tu ne vas pas t'en tirer comme ça!

■ **get away from (a)** quitter ⟨place⟩; échapper à ⟨person⟩

**(b) there's no** ∼**ting away from it** on ne peut pas le nier

■ **get back**: ¶ ∼ **back (a)** (return) rentrer; (after short time) revenir

**(b)** (move backwards) reculer

¶ ∼ **back to [sth] (a)** (return to) rentrer à ⟨house, city⟩; revenir à ⟨office, point⟩; **when we** ∼ **back to London** à notre retour à Londres; **to** ∼ **back to sleep** se rendormir; **to** ∼ **back to normal** redevenir normal

**(b)** (return to earlier stage) revenir à ⟨main topic, former point⟩; ¶ ∼ **back to [sb]** revenir à; **I'll** ∼ **back to you** (on phone) je vous rappelle

¶ ∼ **[sth] back** (regain) récupérer ⟨lost object⟩; reprendre ⟨strength⟩; **she got her money back** elle a été remboursée

■ **get by (a)** (pass) passer

**(b)** (survive) s'en sortir (**on, with** avec)

■ **get down**

¶ ∼ **down (a)** (descend) descendre (**from, out of** de)

**(b)** (on floor) se coucher; (crouch) se baisser; **to** ∼ **down on one's knees** s'agenouiller

**(c)** to ∼ **down to** se mettre à ⟨work⟩; **to** ∼ **down to doing** se mettre à faire; ¶ ∼ **down [sth]** descendre ⟨slope⟩; ¶ ∼ **[sth] down** (from height) descendre

¶ ∼ **[sb] down** (colloq) (depress) déprimer

■ **get in**: ¶ ∼ **in (a)** (to building) entrer; (to vehicle) monter

**(b)** (return home) rentrer

**(c)** (arrive) arriver

**(d)** (penetrate) pénétrer

**(e)** ⟨party⟩ passer; ⟨candidate⟩ être élu/-e

**(f)** (Sch, Univ) ⟨applicant⟩ être admis/-e

¶ ∼ **[sth] in** (buy) acheter

■ **get into (a)** (enter) entrer dans ⟨building⟩; monter dans ⟨vehicle⟩

**(b)** (as member) devenir membre de; (as student) être admis/-e à

**(c)** (squeeze into) rentrer dans ⟨garment, size⟩

■ **get off**: ¶ ∼ **off (a)** (from bus) descendre (**at** à)

**(b)** (start on journey) partir

**(c)** (leave work) finir

**(d)** (colloq) (escape punishment) s'en tirer (**with** avec)

**(e) to** ∼ **off to a good start** prendre un bon départ; **to** ∼ **off to sleep** s'endormir

¶ ∼ **off [sth] (a)** descendre de ⟨wall, bus⟩

**(b)** s'écarter de ⟨subject⟩

¶ ∼ **[sth] off** (remove) enlever

■ **get on**: ¶ ∼ **on (a)** (climb aboard) monter

**(b)** (GB) (like each other) bien s'entendre

**(c)** (fare) **how did you** ∼ **on?** comment est-ce que ça s'est passé?; **how are you** ∼**ting on?** comment est-ce que tu t'en sors?

**(d)** (GB) (approach) **he's** ∼**ting on for 40** il approche des quarante ans; **it's** ∼**ting on for midnight** il est presque minuit

¶ ∼ **on [sth]** monter dans ⟨vehicle⟩

¶ ∼ **[sth] on** mettre ⟨garment, lid⟩; monter ⟨tyre⟩

■ **get on with**: ¶ **to** ∼ **on with one's work** continuer à travailler ¶ **to** ∼ **on with [sb]** (GB) s'entendre avec ⟨person⟩

■ **get out**: ¶ ∼ **out (a)** (exit) sortir (**through, by** par); ∼ **out!** va-t'en!

**(b)** (alight) descendre

**(c)** ⟨prisoner⟩ être libéré/-e

**(d)** ⟨news⟩ être révélé/-e

¶ ∼ **[sth] out (a)** (take out) sortir (**of** de)

**(b)** retirer ⟨cork⟩

**(c)** enlever ⟨stain⟩

**(d)** emprunter ⟨library book⟩

■ **get out of (a)** sortir de ⟨building⟩; descendre de ⟨vehicle⟩; être libéré/-e de ⟨prison⟩; quitter ⟨profession⟩

**(b) to** ∼ **out of doing** s'arranger pour ne pas faire; **I'll try to** ∼ **out of it** j'essaierai de me libérer

**(c)** perdre ⟨habit⟩

**(d) what do you** ∼ **out of your job?** qu'est-ce que ton travail t'apporte?; **what will you** ∼ **out of it?** qu'est-ce que vous en retirerez?

■ **get over (a)** traverser ⟨stream, bridge⟩; passer au-dessus de ⟨wall⟩

**(b)** se remettre de ⟨illness, shock⟩; **I can't** ∼ **over it** (amazed) je n'en reviens pas

**(c)** surmonter ⟨problem⟩; **to** ∼ **sth over with** en finir avec qch

■ **get round** (GB): ¶ ∼ **round** = GET AROUND; ¶ ∼ **round [sb]** (colloq) persuader [qn]

■ **get through**: ¶ ∼ **through (a)** (squeeze through) passer

**(b) to** ∼ **through to sb** (on phone) avoir qn au téléphone; (make oneself understood) se faire comprendre

**(c)** ⟨news, supplies⟩ arriver

**(d)** ⟨examinee⟩ réussir

¶ ∼ **through [sth] (a)** terminer ⟨book⟩; finir ⟨meal, task⟩; réussir à ⟨exam⟩

**(b)** (use) manger ⟨food⟩; dépenser ⟨money⟩

■ **get together**: ¶ ∼ **together** se réunir (**about, over** pour discuter de); ¶ ∼ **[sb/sth] together** réunir ⟨people⟩; former ⟨company⟩

■ **get up**: ¶ ∼ **up (a)** (from bed, chair) se lever (**from** de)

**(b)** (on ledge, wall) monter

**(c)** ⟨storm⟩ se préparer; ⟨wind⟩ se lever

**(d) what did you** ∼ **up to?** (enjoyment) qu'est-ce que tu as fait de beau?; (mischief) qu'est-ce que tu as fabriqué? (colloq)

¶ ∼ **up [sth] (a)** arriver en haut de ⟨hill, ladder⟩

**(b)** augmenter ⟨speed⟩

**get-together** n réunion f (entre amis)

**ghastly** adj horrible

**gherkin** n cornichon m

**ghetto** n ghetto m

**ghetto blaster** n (colloq) (gros) radiocassette m portable

**ghost** n fantôme m

**giant** **1** n géant m

**2** adj géant/-e

**gibberish** n charabia m

**giddy** adj (a) to feel ~ avoir la tête qui tourne
(b) ⟨height, speed⟩ vertigineux/-euse

**gift** n (a) (present) cadeau m (to à); **to give sb a ~** faire or offrir un cadeau à qn
(b) (donation) don m
(c) (talent) don m; **to have a ~ for doing** avoir le don de faire; **to have the ~ of the gab** avoir du bagou(t) (colloq)

**gifted** adj doué/-e

**gift shop** n magasin m de cadeaux

**gift token**, **gift voucher** n (GB) chèque-cadeau m

**gift wrap** n papier m cadeau

**gig** n (colloq) concert m de rock

**gigantic** adj gigantesque

**giggle** 1 n petit rire m; **to get the ~s** attraper le fou rire
2 vi rire

**gilt** 1 n dorure f
2 adj ⟨frame, paint⟩ doré/-e

**gimmick** n (scheme) truc m (colloq); (object) gadget m

**gin** n gin m; **~ and tonic** gin tonic m

**ginger** n (a) (Bot, Culin) gingembre m
(b) (colour) roux m

**ginger-haired** adj roux/rousse

**girl** n (a) (child) fille f; (teenager) jeune fille f; **baby ~** petite fille f, bébé m; **little ~** petite fille f, fillette f
(b) (daughter) fille f

**girlfriend** n (female friend) amie f; (sweetheart) (petite) amie f

**girl guide** (GB), **girl scout** (US) n éclaireuse f

**giro** n (GB) (system) système m de virement bancaire; (cheque) mandat m

**gist** n essentiel m (of de)

**give** 1 n élasticité f
2 vtr (gen) donner (to à); transmettre ⟨message⟩; transmettre, passer ⟨illness⟩ (to à); laisser ⟨seat⟩ (to à); accorder ⟨grant⟩ (to à); faire ⟨injection, massage⟩ (to à); faire ⟨speech⟩; **to ~ sb sth** donner qch à qn; (politely, as a gift) offrir qch à qn; **to ~ sb pleasure** faire plaisir à qn; **~ him my best (wishes)** transmets-lui mes amitiés; **she gave him a drink** elle lui a donné à boire; **to ~ sb enough room** laisser suffisamment de place à qn
3 vi ⟨mattress, sofa⟩ s'affaisser; ⟨shelf, floorboard⟩ fléchir; ⟨branch⟩ ployer
IDIOMS ~ or take an inch (or two) à quelques centimètres près; **to ~ and take** faire des concessions; **to ~ as good as one gets** rendre coup pour coup; **to ~ it all one's got** (colloq) (y) mettre le paquet
■ **give away**: ¶ ~ [sth] **away** (a) donner ⟨item, sample⟩
(b) révéler ⟨secret⟩
(c) laisser échapper ⟨match, goal, advantage⟩ (to au bénéfice de)

¶ ~ [sb] **away** (a) (betray) ⟨expression, fingerprints⟩ trahir; ⟨person⟩ dénoncer (to à); **to ~ oneself away** se trahir
(b) (in marriage) conduire [qn] à l'autel
■ **give back** rendre (to à)
■ **give in**: ¶ ~ **in** (a) (yield) céder (to à)
(b) (stop trying) abandonner; **I ~ in—tell me!** je donne ma langue au chat (colloq)—dis-le-moi!
¶ ~ [sth] **in** rendre ⟨work⟩; remettre ⟨ticket, key⟩
■ **give off** émettre ⟨signal, radiation, light⟩; dégager ⟨heat, fumes⟩
■ **give out**: ¶ ~ **out** ⟨strength⟩ s'épuiser; ⟨engine⟩ tomber en panne; ¶ ~ [sth] **out** (distribute) distribuer (to à)
■ **give up**: ¶ ~ **up** abandonner; **to ~ up on** laisser tomber ⟨diet, crossword, pupil, patient⟩; ne plus compter sur ⟨friend, partner⟩
¶ ~ **up** [sth] (a) renoncer à ⟨habit, title, claim⟩; sacrifier ⟨free time⟩; quitter ⟨job⟩; **to ~ up smoking/drinking** cesser de fumer/de boire
(b) abandonner ⟨search, hope, struggle⟩; renoncer à ⟨idea⟩
(c) céder ⟨seat, territory⟩
¶ ~ [sb] **up** (a) (hand over) livrer (to à); **to ~ oneself up** se livrer (to à)
(b) laisser tomber ⟨lover⟩
■ **give way** (a) (collapse) s'effondrer; ⟨fence, cable⟩ céder; **his legs gave way** ses jambes se sont dérobées sous lui
(b) (GB) (when driving) céder le passage (to à)
(c) (yield) céder; **to ~ way to** faire place à

**give-and-take** n concessions fpl mutuelles

**giveaway** n to be a ~ être révélateur/-trice

**given** 1 adj (a) ⟨point, level, number⟩ donné/-e; ⟨volume, length⟩ déterminé/-e; **at any ~ moment** à n'importe quel moment
(b) **to be ~ to sth/to doing** avoir tendance à qch/à faire; **I am not ~ to doing** je n'ai pas l'habitude de faire
2 prep (a) (in view of) ~ **(the fact) that** étant donné que
(b) (with) avec ⟨training, proper care⟩

**given name** n prénom m

**glad** adj content/-e, heureux/-euse (about de; that que; to do de faire); **he was only too ~ to help me** il ne demandait qu'à m'aider

**gladly** adv (willingly) volontiers; (with pleasure) avec plaisir

**glamorize** vtr peindre [qn/qch] sous de belles couleurs

**glamorous** adj ⟨person, image, look⟩ séduisant/-e; ⟨older person⟩ élégant/-e; ⟨dress⟩ splendide; ⟨occasion⟩ brillant/-e; ⟨job⟩ prestigieux/-ieuse

**glamour**, **glamor** (US) n (of person) séduction f; (of job) prestige m; (of travel, cars) fascination f

**glance** 1 n coup m d'œil
2 vi **to ~ at** jeter un coup d'œil à; **to ~ around the room** parcourir la pièce du regard

■ **glance off** ⟨*bullet, stone*⟩ ricocher sur *or* contre

**glancing** *adj* ⟨*blow, kick*⟩ oblique

**gland** *n* glande *f*; **to have swollen ~s** avoir des ganglions

**glandular fever** *n* mononucléose *f* infectieuse

**glare** ① *n* **(a)** (angry look) regard *m* furieux
**(b)** (from lights) lumière *f* éblouissante
② *vi* ⟨*person*⟩ lancer un regard furieux (**at** à)

**glaring** *adj* **(a)** ⟨*mistake, injustice*⟩ flagrant/-e
**(b)** ⟨*light*⟩ éblouissant/-e

**glass** ① *n* **(a)** verre *m*; **wine ~** verre à vin; **a ~ of wine** un verre de vin
**(b)** (mirror) miroir *m*
② *adj* ⟨*bottle, shelf*⟩ en verre; ⟨*door*⟩ vitré/-e
③ **glasses** *n pl* lunettes *fpl*

**glass ceiling** *n*: niveau professionnel que la discrimination empêche certains groupes sociaux de dépasser

**glassy-eyed** *adj* (from drink, illness) aux yeux vitreux; (hostile) au regard glacial

**glaze** ① *n* **(a)** (on pottery) vernis *m*
**(b)** (Culin) nappage *m*; (icing) glaçage *m*
② *vtr* **(a)** vernisser ⟨*pottery*⟩
**(b)** (Culin) glacer

**glazed** *adj* ⟨*door*⟩ vitré/-e; **to have a ~ look in one's eyes** avoir les yeux vitreux

**gleam** ① *n* (of light) lueur *f*; (of sunshine) rayon *m*; (of gold, polished surface) reflet *m*
② *vi* ⟨*light*⟩ luire; ⟨*knife, leather, surface*⟩ reluire; ⟨*eyes*⟩ briller

**gleaming** *adj* **(a)** ⟨*eyes, light*⟩ brillant/-e; ⟨*leather, surface*⟩ reluisant/-e
**(b)** (clean) étincelant/-e (de propreté)

**glide** *vi* ⟨*skater, boat*⟩ glisser (**on, over** sur); (in air) planer

**glider** *n* planeur *m*

**gliding** *n* vol *m* à voile

**glimpse** ① *n* **(a)** vision *f* fugitive (**of** de); **to catch a ~ of sth** entrevoir qch
**(b)** (insight) aperçu *m* (**of, at** de)
② *vtr* entrevoir

**glisten** *vi* ⟨*eyes, hair, surface*⟩ luire; ⟨*water*⟩ scintiller

**glitch** *n* (colloq) (gen) pépin *m* (colloq); (Comput) problème *m* technique

**glitter** ① *n* **(a)** (substance) paillettes *fpl*
**(b)** (sparkle) éclat *m*
② *vi* scintiller

**gloat** *vi* jubiler (**at, over** à l'idée de)

**global** *adj* **(a)** (world-wide) mondial/-e
**(b)** (comprehensive) global/-e

**global warming** *n* réchauffement *m* de la planète

**globe** *n* **(a)** **the ~** le globe
**(b)** (model) globe *m* terrestre

**gloom** *n* **(a)** (darkness) obscurité *f*
**(b)** (despondency) morosité *f* (**about, over** à propos de)

**gloomy** *adj* **(a)** (dark) sombre

**(b)** ⟨*expression, person, voice*⟩ lugubre; ⟨*weather*⟩ morose; ⟨*news, outlook*⟩ déprimant/-e

**glorify** *vtr* glorifier

**glorious** *adj* **(a)** ⟨*view, weather*⟩ magnifique; ⟨*holiday*⟩ merveilleux/-euse
**(b)** (illustrious) glorieux/-ieuse

**glory** ① *n* **(a)** (honour) gloire *f*
**(b)** (splendour) splendeur *f*
② *vi* **to ~ in** être très fier/fière de

**gloss** *n* **(a)** (shine) lustre *m*
**(b)** (paint) laque *f*
■ **gloss over** (pass rapidly over) glisser sur; (hide) dissimuler

**glossary** *n* glossaire *m*

**glossy** *adj* ⟨*hair, material*⟩ luisant/-e; ⟨*photograph*⟩ brillant/-e; ⟨*brochure*⟩ luxueux/-euse

**glossy magazine** *n* magazine *m* illustré (de luxe)

**glove** *n* gant *m*

**glove compartment** *n* boîte *f* à gants

**glow** ① *n* **(a)** (from fire) rougeoiement *m*; (of candle) lueur *f*
**(b)** (of complexion) éclat *m*
② *vi* **(a)** ⟨*metal, embers*⟩ rougeoyer; ⟨*lamp, cigarette*⟩ luire
**(b)** **to ~ with health** resplendir de santé; **to ~ with pride** rayonner de fierté

**glower** *vi* lancer des regards noirs (**at** à)

**glowing** *adj* **(a)** ⟨*ember*⟩ rougeoyant/-e; ⟨*face, cheeks*⟩ (from exercise) rouge; (from pleasure) radieux/-ieuse
**(b)** ⟨*account, terms*⟩ élogieux/-ieuse

**glue** ① *n* colle *f*
② *vtr* coller; **to ~ sth on** *or* **down** coller qch
③ **glued** (colloq) *pp adj* **to be ~d to the TV** être collé/-e devant la télé (colloq); **to be ~d to the spot** être cloué/-e sur place

**glue sniffer** *n* sniffeur/-euse *m/f* (colloq) de colle

**glue-sniffing** *n* inhalation *f* de colle

**glut** *n* surabondance *f*, excès *m*

**glutton** *n* glouton/-onne *m/f*

**glycerin(e)** *n* glycérine *f*

**GMT** *n* (*abbr* = **Greenwich Mean Time**) TU

**gnash** *vtr* **to ~ one's teeth** grincer des dents

**gnaw** ① *vtr* ronger ⟨*bone, wood*⟩
② *vi* **(a)** **to ~ at** *or* **on sth** ronger qch
**(b)** **to ~ at sb** ⟨*hunger, remorse, pain*⟩ tenailler qn

**GNP** *n* (*abbr* = **gross national product**) PNB *m*

**GNVQ** *n* (*abbr* = **General National Vocational Qualification**) ≈ baccalauréat *m* professionnel

**go**

■ **Note As an intransitive verb**
– go as a simple intransitive verb is translated

by *aller*: **where are you going?** = où vas-tu?; *Sasha went to London last week* = Sasha est allé à Londres la semaine dernière.

– Note that *aller* conjugates with *être* in compound tenses. For the conjugation of *aller*, see the French verb tables.

– The verb *go* produces a great many phrasal verbs (*go up, go down, go out, go back* etc). Many of these are translated by a single verb in French (*monter, descendre, sortir, retourner* etc). The phrasal verbs are listed separately at the end of the entry GO.

### As an auxiliary verb

– When *go* is used as an auxiliary to show intention, it is also translated by *aller*: *I'm going to buy a car* = je vais acheter une voiture; *I was going to talk to you about it* = j'allais t'en parler.

⎡1⎤ *vi* **(a)** aller (from **to**; **to** à, en); **to ~ to Paris/to California** aller à Paris/en Californie; **to ~ to town/to the country** aller en ville/à la campagne; **they went home** ils sont rentrés chez eux; **to ~ on holiday** partir en vacances; **to ~ for a drink** aller prendre un verre; **~ and ask her** va lui demander; **to ~ to school/work** aller à l'école/au travail; **to ~ to the doctor's** aller chez le médecin; **let's ~, let's get ~ing** allons-y
**(b)** (leave) partir; **I'm ~ing** je m'en vais
**(c)** (become) **to ~ red** rougir; **to ~ white** blanchir; **to ~ mad** devenir fou/folle
**(d)** **to ~ unnoticed** passer inaperçu/-e; **the question went unanswered** la question est restée sans réponse; **to ~ free** être libéré/-e
**(e)** (become impaired) **his memory is going** il perd la mémoire; **my voice is going** je n'ai plus de voix; **the battery is going** la pile est presque à plat
**(f)** (of time) passer, s'écouler
**(g)** (operate, function) ⟨*vehicle, machine, clock*⟩ marcher, fonctionner; **to get [sth] going** mettre [qch] en marche; **to keep going** ⟨*business*⟩ se maintenir; ⟨*machine*⟩ continuer à marcher; ⟨*person*⟩ continuer
**(h)** (belong, be placed) aller; **where do these plates ~?** où vont ces assiettes?; **it won't ~ into the box** ça ne rentre pas dans la boîte; **five into four won't ~** quatre n'est pas divisible par cinq
**(i)** (be about to) **to be going to do** aller faire; **it's going to snow** il va neiger
**(j)** (turn out) passer; **how did the party ~?** comment s'est passée la soirée?; **it went well/badly** ça s'est bien/mal passé
**(k)** (make sound, perform action or movement) (gen) faire; ⟨*bell, alarm*⟩ sonner; **she went like this with her fingers** elle a fait comme ça avec ses doigts
**(l)** (take one's turn) **you ~ next** c'est ton tour après, c'est à toi après; **you ~ first** après vous
**(m)** (match) **those two colours don't ~ together** ces deux couleurs ne vont pas ensemble
⎡2⎤ *vtr* faire ⟨*distance, number of miles*⟩
⎡3⎤ *n* (GB) (turn) tour *m*; (try) essai *m*; **whose ~ is it?** à qui le tour?; (in game) à qui de jouer?

⎡4⎤ **to go** *phr* **there are three days/pages to ~** il reste encore trois jours/pages
IDIOMS **to make a ~ of sth** réussir qch; **she's always on the ~** elle n'arrête jamais; **in one ~** d'un seul coup; **it goes without saying that** il va sans dire que; **as the saying goes** comme dit le proverbe; **anything goes** tout est permis
■ **go about** s'attaquer à ⟨*task*⟩; **to ~ about one's business** vaquer à ses occupations
■ **go ahead** ⟨*event*⟩ avoir lieu; **~ ahead!** vas-y!; **they are going ahead with the project** ils ont décidé de mettre le projet en route
■ **go along** aller; **to make sth up as one goes along** inventer qch au fur et à mesure
■ **go along with** être d'accord avec ⟨*person, view*⟩; accepter ⟨*plan*⟩
■ **go around (a)** se promener, circuler; **they ~ around everywhere together** ils vont partout ensemble
**(b)** ⟨*rumour*⟩ courir
■ **go away** partir; **~ away!** va-t-en!
■ **go back (a)** (return) retourner; (turn back) rebrousser chemin; **to ~ back to sleep** se rendormir; **to ~ back to work** se remettre au travail
**(b)** (date back) remonter (**to** à)
**(c)** (revert) revenir (**to** à)
■ **go back on** revenir sur ⟨*promise, decision*⟩
■ **go by**: ¶ **~ by** ⟨*person*⟩ passer; **as time goes by** avec le temps; ¶ **~ by** ⟨*sth*⟩ juger d'après ⟨*appearances*⟩, **to ~ by the rules** suivre le règlement
■ **go down**: ¶ **~ down (a)** (descend) (gen) descendre; ⟨*sun*⟩ se coucher; **to ~ down on one's knees** se mettre à genoux
**(b)** **to ~ down well/badly** être bien/mal reçu/-e
**(c)** ⟨*price, temperature, standard*⟩ baisser
**(d)** ⟨*swelling*⟩ désenfler; ⟨*tyre*⟩ se dégonfler
**(e)** (Comput) tomber en panne
¶ **~ down [sth]** descendre ⟨*hill*⟩
■ **go for**: ¶ **~ for [sb/sth] (a)** (colloq) (be keen on) aimer
**(b)** (apply to) **the same goes for him!** c'est valable pour lui aussi!
¶ **~ for [sb] (a)** (attack) attaquer
**(b)** **he has a lot going for him** il a beaucoup de choses pour lui
¶ **~ for [sth] (a)** essayer d'obtenir ⟨*honour, victory*⟩; **she's going for the world record** elle vise le record mondial; **~ for it!** (colloq) vas-y, fonce! (colloq)
**(b)** (choose) choisir, prendre
■ **go in (a)** (enter) entrer; (go back in) rentrer
**(b)** ⟨*troops*⟩ attaquer
**(c)** ⟨*sun*⟩ se cacher
■ **go in for (a)** (be keen on) aimer
**(b)** s'inscrire à ⟨*exam, competition*⟩
■ **go into (a)** (enter) entrer dans ⟨*building*⟩; se lancer dans ⟨*business, profession*⟩
**(b)** (examine) étudier ⟨*question*⟩
■ **go off**: ¶ **~ off (a)** ⟨*bomb*⟩ exploser
**(b)** ⟨*alarm clock*⟩ sonner; ⟨*fire alarm*⟩ se déclencher
**(c)** ⟨*person*⟩ partir, s'en aller

**(d)** (GB) ⟨*milk, cream*⟩ tourner; ⟨*meat*⟩ s'avarier; ⟨*butter*⟩ rancir; ⟨*performer, athlete*⟩ perdre sa forme
**(e)** ⟨*lights, heating*⟩ s'éteindre
**(f)** (happen, take place) **the concert went off very well** le concert s'est très bien passé
¶ ~ **off** [sb/sth] (GB) n'aimer plus
■ **go on**: ¶ ~ **on (a)** (happen) se passer; **how long has this been going on?** depuis combien de temps est-ce que ça dure?
**(b)** (continue on one's way) poursuivre son chemin
**(c)** (continue) continuer; **the list goes on and on** la liste est infinie
**(d)** (of time) (elapse) **as time went on, they...** avec le temps, ils...; **as the evening went on** au fur et à mesure que la soirée avançait
**(e) to ~ on about sth** ne pas arrêter de parler de qch
**(f)** (proceed) passer; **let's ~ on to the next item** passons au point suivant; **he went on to say that...** puis il a dit que...
**(g)** ⟨*heating, lights*⟩ s'allumer
**(h)** ⟨*actor*⟩ entrer en scène
¶ ~ **on** [sth] se fonder sur ⟨*evidence, information*⟩; **that's all we've got to ~ on** c'est tout ce que nous savons avec certitude
■ **go on at** s'en prendre à ⟨*person*⟩
■ **go out (a)** (leave, depart) sortir; **to ~ out for a drink** aller prendre un verre
**(b) to ~ out with sb** sortir avec qn
**(c)** ⟨*tide*⟩ descendre
**(d)** ⟨*fire, light*⟩ s'éteindre
■ **go over**
¶ ~ **over** (cross over) aller (**to** vers)
¶ ~ **over** [sth] (a) passer [qch] en revue ⟨*details, facts*⟩; vérifier ⟨*accounts, figures*⟩; relire ⟨*article*⟩
**(b)** (exceed) dépasser ⟨*limit, sum*⟩
■ **go round** (GB): ¶ ~ **round (a)** ⟨*wheel*⟩ tourner
**(b) to ~ round to see sb** aller voir qn
**(c)** ⟨*rumour*⟩ circuler
**(d)** (make detour) faire un détour
¶ ~ **round** [sth] faire le tour de ⟨*shops, house, museum*⟩
■ **go through**: ¶ ~ **through** ⟨*law*⟩ passer; ⟨*business deal*⟩ être conclu/-e
¶ ~ **through** [sth] (a) endurer, subir ⟨*experience*⟩; passer par ⟨*stage, phase*⟩; **she's gone through a lot** elle a beaucoup souffert
**(b)** (check) examiner
**(c)** (search) fouiller ⟨*belongings*⟩
**(d)** (perform) remplir ⟨*formalities*⟩
**(e)** (use up) dépenser ⟨*money*⟩; consommer ⟨*food, drink*⟩
■ **go through with** réaliser ⟨*plan*⟩; **I can't ~ through with it** je ne peux pas le faire
■ **go under** couler
■ **go up**: ¶ ~ **up (a)** (ascend) monter; **to ~ up to bed** monter se coucher
**(b)** ⟨*price, temperature*⟩ monter; ⟨*figures*⟩ augmenter; ⟨*curtain*⟩ se lever (**on** sur)
¶ ~ **up** [sth] monter, gravir ⟨*hill*⟩
■ **go without**: ¶ ~ **without** s'en passer
¶ ~ **without** [sth] se passer de

**go-ahead** *n* (colloq) **to give sb the ~** donner le feu vert à qn; **to get the ~** recevoir le feu vert
**goal** *n* but *m*
**goalkeeper** *n* gardien *m* de but
**goalpost** *n* poteau *m* de but
**goat** *n* chèvre *f*
**gobble** ⓵ *vtr* (also ~ **down**, ~ **up**) engloutir
⓶ *vi* ⟨*turkey*⟩ glouglouter
**gobbledygook** *n* (colloq) charabia *m* (colloq)
**go-between** *n* intermédiaire *mf*
**gobsmacked** *adj* (GB) (colloq) estomaqué/-e (colloq)
**god** *n* dieu *m*; **God** Dieu *m*
**godchild** *n* filleul/-e *m/f*
**goddaughter** *n* filleule *f*
**goddess** *n* déesse *f*
**godfather** *n* parrain *m*
**godmother** *n* marraine *f*
**godparent** *n* parrain/marraine *m/f*; **the ~s** le parrain et la marraine
**godsend** *n* aubaine *f*
**godson** *n* filleul *m*
**goggles** *n pl* lunettes *fpl*; (for swimming) lunettes *fpl* de plongée
**going** ⓵ *n* (a) (departure) départ *m*
**(b)** (progress) **that's good ~!** c'est rapide!; **it was slow ~** (on journey) ça a été long; (at work) ça n'avançait pas vite; **to be heavy ~** ⟨*book*⟩ être difficile à lire; ⟨*work, conversation*⟩ être laborieux/-ieuse
**(c)** when the ~ **gets tough** quand les choses vont mal; **she finds her new job hard ~** elle trouve que son nouveau travail est difficile; **they got out while the ~ was good** ils s'en sont tirés (colloq) avant qu'il ne soit trop tard
⓶ *adj* (a) ⟨*price*⟩ actuel/-elle, en cours; **the ~ rate** le tarif en vigueur
**(b) ~ concern** affaire *f* qui marche
**(c) it's the best model ~** c'est le meilleur modèle sur le marché
**goings-on** *n pl* (colloq) (events) événements *mpl*; (activities) activités *fpl*; (behaviour) conduite *f*
**go-kart** *n* kart *m*
**gold** ⓵ *n* or *m*
⓶ *adj* ⟨*jewellery, tooth*⟩ en or; ⟨*coin, ingot, ore, wire*⟩ d'or
IDIOMS **as good as ~** sage comme une image; **to be worth one's weight in ~** valoir son pesant d'or
**gold dust** *n* poudre *f* d'or; **to be like ~** être une denrée rare
**golden** *adj* (a) (made of gold) en or, d'or
**(b)** (gold coloured) doré/-e, d'or; ~ **hair** cheveux *mpl* blonds dorés
**(c)** ⟨*age, days*⟩ d'or; **a ~ opportunity** une occasion en or
**golden handshake** *n* prime *f* de départ
**golden rule** *n* règle *f* d'or
**goldfish** *n* poisson *m* rouge

**gold medal** n médaille f d'or
**gold mine** n mine f d'or
**gold-plated** adj plaqué/-e or
**gold rush** n ruée f vers l'or
**goldsmith** n orfèvre m
**golf** n golf m; **to play** ~ faire du golf
**golf club** n (place) club m de golf; (stick) crosse f de golf
**golf course** n (terrain m de) golf m
**golfer** n joueur/-euse m/f de golf, golfeur/-euse m/f
**gone** adj (a) (departed) parti/-e; (dead) disparu/-e
(b) (past) **it's** ~ **six o'clock** il est six heures passées
**gong** n gong m
**good** ① n (a) (virtue) bien m; ~ **and evil** le bien et le mal; **to be up to no** ~ (colloq) mijoter qch (colloq); **to come to no** ~ mal tourner
(b) (benefit) bien m; **it'll do you** ~ ça te fera du bien; **it didn't do my migraine any** ~ ça n'a pas arrangé ma migraine
(c) (use) **it's no** ~ **crying** ça ne sert à rien de pleurer; **what** ~ **would it do me?** à quoi cela me servirait-il?
② adj (a) (gen) bon/bonne (before n); **it's a** ~ **film** c'est un bon film; **it was a** ~ **party** c'était une soirée réussie; **the** ~ **weather** le beau temps; **she's a** ~ **swimmer** elle nage bien; **to be** ~ **at** être bon/bonne en ⟨Latin, physics⟩; être bon/bonne à ⟨badminton, chess⟩; **to be** ~ **with** savoir comment s'y prendre avec ⟨children, animals⟩; aimer ⟨figures⟩; **to have a** ~ **time** bien s'amuser; **it's** ~ **to see you again** je suis content de vous revoir; **I don't feel too** ~ je ne me sens pas très bien; **the** ~ **thing is that…** ce qui est bien c'est que…; **to taste** ~ avoir bon goût; **to smell** ~ sentir bon; **we had a** ~ **laugh** on a bien ri; **to wait/walk for a** ~ **hour** attendre/marcher une bonne heure
(b) (well-behaved) ⟨child, dog⟩ sage; **be** ~**!** sois sage!
(c) (high quality) ⟨hotel⟩ bon/bonne (before n); ⟨coat, china⟩ beau/belle (before n); ⟨degree⟩ avec mention
(d) (kind) ⟨person⟩ gentil/-ille; (virtuous) ⟨man, life⟩ vertueux/-euse; **to do sb a** ~ **turn** rendre service à qn; **would you be** ~ **enough to do** auriez-vous la gentillesse de faire
(e) (beneficial) **to be** ~ **for** faire du bien à ⟨person, plant⟩; être bon/bonne pour ⟨health, business, morale⟩
(f) (fortunate) **it's a** ~ **job** or **thing (that)** heureusement que; **it's a** ~ **job** or **thing too!** tant mieux!; ▶ BETTER, BEST
③ excl (expressing pleasure, satisfaction) c'est bien!; (with relief) tant mieux!; (to encourage, approve) très bien!
④ **as good as** phr quasiment; **to be as** ~ **as new** être comme neuf/neuve
⑤ **for good** phr pour toujours
IDIOMS ~ **for you!** bravo!; **it's too** ~ **to be true** c'est trop beau pour être vrai

**good afternoon** phr bonjour
**goodbye** phr au revoir
**good evening** phr bonsoir
**good-for-nothing** n bon/bonne m/f à rien
**good-humoured** (GB), **good-humored** (US) adj ⟨crowd, discussion⟩ détendu/-e; ⟨rivalry⟩ amical/-e; ⟨remark, smile⟩ plaisant/-e; **to be** ~ ⟨person⟩ avoir bon caractère
**good-looking** adj beau/belle (before n)
**good morning** phr bonjour
**good-natured** adj ⟨person⟩ agréable; ⟨animal⟩ placide
**goodness** ① n (a) (quality, virtue) bonté f
(b) (nourishment) **to be full of** ~ être plein/-e de bonnes choses
② excl (also ~ **gracious!**) mon Dieu!
IDIOMS **for** ~**! sake!** pour l'amour de Dieu!
**goodnight** phr bonne nuit
**goods** n pl articles mpl, marchandise f
**goods train** n (GB) train m de marchandises
**goodwill** n (a) (kindness) bonne volonté f
(b) (of business) clientèle f
**goose** n oie f
**gooseberry** n groseille f à maquereau
IDIOMS **to be a** or **play** ~ tenir la chandelle
**goose pimples** n pl chair f de poule
**gorge** ① n gorge f
② v refl **to** ~ **oneself** se gaver (on de)
**gorgeous** adj (a) (colloq) ⟨food, scenery⟩ formidable (colloq); ⟨kitten, baby⟩ adorable; ⟨weather, day, person⟩ splendide
(b) (sumptuous) somptueux/-euse
**gorilla** n gorille m
**gorse** n ajoncs mpl
**gory** adj sanglant/-e
**gosh** excl (colloq) ça alors! (colloq)
**go-slow** n (GB) grève f perlée
**gospel** n Évangile m
**gospel music** n gospel m
**gossip** ① n (a) (malicious) commérages mpl (about sur); (not malicious) nouvelles fpl (about sur)
(b) (person) commère f
② vi bavarder; (more maliciously) faire des commérages (about sur)
**gossip column** n échos mpl
**got: to have got** phr (a) **to have** ~ avoir
(b) **I've** ~ **to go** il faut que j'y aille
**gourd** n (a) (container) gourde f
(b) (fruit) calebasse f
**gout** n goutte f
**govern** ① vtr (a) gouverner ⟨country, state, city⟩; administrer ⟨colony, province⟩
(b) (control) régir ⟨use, conduct, treatment⟩
(c) (determine) déterminer ⟨decision⟩; régler ⟨flow, speed⟩
② vi ⟨parliament, president⟩ gouverner
**governess** n gouvernante f
**governing** adj ⟨party⟩ au pouvoir; ⟨class⟩ dirigeant/-e; **the** ~ **principle** l'idée directrice

**government** [1] n gouvernement m; (the state) l'État m; **in ~** au pouvoir
[2] adj ⟨minister, plan⟩ du gouvernement; ⟨department, majority, policy⟩ gouvernemental/-e; ⟨expenditure, borrowing⟩ de l'État; ⟨funds⟩ public/-ique

**governmental** adj gouvernemental/-e

**governor** n (of state, colony, bank) gouverneur m; (of prison) directeur m; (of school) membre m du conseil d'établissement

**gown** n (dress) robe f; (of judge, academic) toge f; (of surgeon) blouse f

**GP** n (abbr = **general practitioner**) (médecin m) généraliste mf

**grab** [1] vtr empoigner ⟨money, object⟩; saisir ⟨arm, person, opportunity⟩; **to ~ hold of** se saisir de
[2] vi **to ~ at** se jeter sur

**grace** n (a) (gen) grâce f; **sb's saving ~** ce qui sauve qn
(b) **to give sb two days' ~** accorder un délai de deux jours à qn
(c) (prayer) (before meal) bénédicité m; (after meal) grâces fpl
IDIOMS **to be full of airs and ~s** prendre des airs

**graceful** adj ⟨dancer, movement⟩ gracieux/-ieuse; ⟨person⟩ élégant/-e

**grade** [1] n (a) (quality) qualité f; **high-/low-~** de qualité supérieure/inférieure
(b) (mark) note f (**in** en)
(c) (rank) échelon m
(d) (US) (class) classe f
[2] vtr (by quality) classer (**according to** selon); (by size) calibrer (**according to** selon)

**grade school** n (US) école f primaire

**gradient** n pente f, inclinaison f

**gradual** adj (a) ⟨change, increase⟩ progressif/-ive
(b) ⟨slope⟩ doux/douce

**gradually** adv (slowly) peu à peu; (by degrees) progressivement

**graduate** [1] n diplômé/-e m/f
[2] vi (a) terminer ses études (**at** or **from** à); (US) (Sch) ≈ finir le lycée
(b) (progress) **to ~ (from sth) to** passer (de qch) à

**graduate training scheme** n programme m de formation professionnelle pour étudiants diplômés

**graduation** n (also **~ ceremony**) (cérémonie f de) remise f des diplômes

**graffiti** n graffiti mpl

**graffiti artist** n tagger m

**graft** [1] n greffe f; **skin ~** greffe de la peau
[2] vtr greffer (**onto** sur)

**grain** n (a) (of rice, wheat, sand, salt) grain m
(b) (crops) céréales fpl
(c) (figurative) (of truth, comfort) brin m
(d) (in wood, stone) veines fpl; (in leather, paper, fabric) grain m
IDIOMS **it goes against the ~** c'est contre tous mes/nos/leurs principes

**gram(me)** n gramme m

**grammar** n grammaire f

**grammar school** n (GB) ≈ lycée m (à recrutement sélectif)

**grammatical** adj (a) ⟨error⟩ de grammaire
(b) (correct) grammaticalement correct

**granary** n grenier m

**granary bread** n pain m aux céréales

**grand** adj ⟨building, ceremony⟩ grandiose; **on a ~ scale** à très grande échelle; **the Grand Canyon** le Grand Cañon m; **to play the ~ lady** jouer à la grande dame

**grandchild** n (girl) petite-fille f; (boy) petit-fils m; **his grandchildren** ses petits-enfants mpl

**granddaughter** n petite-fille f

**grandeur** n (of scenery) majesté f; (of building) caractère m grandiose

**grandfather** n grand-père m

**grandfather clock** n horloge f comtoise

**grandma** n (colloq) mémé f (colloq), mamy f (colloq), mamie f (colloq)

**grandmother** n grand-mère f

**grandpa** n (colloq) pépé m (colloq), papy m (colloq), papi m (colloq)

**grandparents** n pl grands-parents mpl

**grand piano** n piano m à queue

**grand slam** n grand chelem m

**grandson** n petit-fils m

**grandstand** n tribune f

**grand total** n total m

**granite** n granit(e) m

**granny** n (colloq) mémé f (colloq)

**grant** [1] n (gen) subvention f; (for study) bourse f
[2] vtr (a) accorder ⟨permission⟩; accéder à ⟨request⟩
(b) **to ~ sb [sth]** accorder [qch] à qn ⟨interview, leave, visa⟩; concéder [qch] à qn ⟨citizenship⟩
(c) **to ~ that** reconnaître que
IDIOMS **to take sth for ~ed** considérer qch comme allant de soi; **he takes his mother for ~ed** il croit que sa mère est à son service

**granulated** adj ⟨sugar⟩ cristallisé/-e

**granule** n (of sugar, salt) grain m; (of coffee) granulé m

**grape** n grain m de raisin; **a bunch of ~s** une grappe de raisin

**grapefruit** n pamplemousse m

**grapeseed oil** n huile f de pépins de raisin

**grapevine** n (in vineyard) pied m de vigne; (in greenhouse, garden) vigne f
IDIOMS **to hear sth on the ~** apprendre qch par le téléphone arabe

**graph** n graphique m

**graphic** adj (a) ⟨art, display, technique⟩ graphique
(b) ⟨account⟩ (pleasantly described) vivant/-e; (gory) cru/-e

**graphic design** n graphisme m

**g**

**graphic designer** n graphiste mf
**graphics** n pl (a) (on screen) visualisation f graphique
(b) **computer** ~ infographie f
(c) (in film, TV) images fpl; (in book) illustrations fpl
**graphics card** n carte f graphique
**graphics interface** n interface f graphique
**graph paper** n papier m millimétré
**grasp** [1] n (a) (hold, grip) prise f
(b) (understanding) maîtrise f
[2] vtr (a) empoigner ⟨rope, hand⟩; saisir ⟨opportunity⟩
(b) (comprehend) saisir, comprendre
[3] vi **to** ~ **at** tenter de saisir
**grasping** adj cupide
**grass** n herbe f; (lawn) pelouse f
IDIOMS **the** ~ **is greener (on the other side of the fence)** on croit toujours que c'est mieux ailleurs
**grass court** n court m en gazon
**grasshopper** n sauterelle f
**grassroots** [1] n pl **the** ~ le peuple
[2] adj ⟨movement⟩ populaire; ⟨support⟩ de base
**grate** [1] n grille f de foyer
[2] vtr râper ⟨carrot, cheese⟩
[3] vi (a) ⟨metal object⟩ grincer (**on** sur)
(b) (annoy) agacer; **that** ~**s** ça m'agace
**grateful** adj reconnaissant/-e (**to** à; **for** de)
**grater** n râpe f
**gratify** vtr faire plaisir à ⟨person⟩; satisfaire ⟨desire⟩; **to be gratified** être satisfait/-e
**grating** [1] n (bars) grille f
[2] adj ⟨noise⟩ grinçant/-e; ⟨voice⟩ désagréable
**gratitude** n reconnaissance f (**to**, **towards** envers; **for** de)
**gratuitous** adj gratuit/-e
**grave** [1] n tombe f
[2] adj (a) ⟨illness⟩ grave; ⟨risk⟩ sérieux/-ieuse grave; ⟨danger⟩ grand/-e (before n)
(b) (solemn) sérieux/-ieuse
**gravel** n (coarse) graviers mpl; (fine) gravillons mpl
**gravestone** n pierre f tombale
**graveyard** n cimetière m
**gravitate** vi **to** ~ **to(wards)** graviter vers
**gravity** n (a) pesanteur f; **centre of** ~ centre m de gravité
(b) (of situation) gravité f
**gravy** n sauce f (au jus de rôti)
**gravy boat** n saucière f
**gray** (US) = GREY
**graze** [1] n écorchure f
[2] vtr (a) **to** ~ **one's knee** s'écorcher le genou (**on**, **against** sur)
(b) (touch lightly) frôler
[3] vi ⟨sheep⟩ brouter; ⟨cow⟩ paître
**grease** [1] n graisse f
[2] vtr graisser
**greasy** adj ⟨hair, skin, food⟩ gras/grasse; ⟨overalls⟩ graisseux/-euse

**great** adj (a) (gen) grand/-e (before n); ⟨number, increase⟩ important/-e; ⟨heat⟩ fort/-e (before n); **a** ~ **deal (of)** beaucoup (de); **with** ~ **difficulty** avec beaucoup de mal
(b) (colloq) ⟨book, party, weather⟩ génial/-e (colloq), formidable (colloq); ⟨opportunity⟩ formidable (colloq); **to feel** ~ se sentir en pleine forme; ~! génial!
**great aunt** n grand-tante f
**great big** adj (très) grand/-e (before n), énorme
**Great Britain** pr n Grande-Bretagne f
**great grandchild** n (girl) arrière-petite-fille f; (garçon) arrière-petit-fils m
**great grandfather** n arrière-grand-père m
**great grandmother** n arrière-grand-mère f
**great-great grandchild** n (girl) arrière-arrière-petite-fille f; (boy) arrière-arrière-petit-fils m
**greatly** adv ⟨admire, regret⟩ beaucoup, énormément; ⟨surprised, distressed⟩ très, extrêmement; ⟨improved, changed⟩ considérablement
**greatness** n (of achievement) importance f; (of person) grandeur f
**great uncle** n grand-oncle m
**Greece** pr n Grèce f
**greed** n (a) (for money, power) avidité f (**for** de)
(b) (also **greediness**) (for food) gourmandise f
**greedy** adj (a) (for food) gourmand/-e; (stronger) goulu/-e; ⟨look⟩ avide; **a** ~ **pig** (colloq) un goinfre (colloq)
(b) (for money, power) avide (**for** de)
**Greek** [1] n (a) (person) Grec/Grecque m/f
(b) (language) grec m
[2] adj ⟨government, island⟩ grec/grecque; ⟨embassy⟩ de Grèce
IDIOMS **it's all** ~ **to me** c'est du chinois pour moi
**green** [1] n (a) (colour) vert m
(b) **village** ~ terrain m communal
(c) (in bowling) boulingrin m; (in golf) green m
(d) (person) écologiste mf; **the Greens** les Verts
[2] **greens** n pl (GB) légumes mpl verts
[3] adj (a) (in colour) vert/-e
(b) ⟨countryside⟩ verdoyant/-e
(c) (colloq) (naïve) naïf/naïve
(d) (inexperienced) novice
(e) ⟨policies, candidate, issues⟩ écologiste; ⟨product⟩ écologique
**green card** n (a) (driving insurance) carte f verte (internationale)
(b) (US) (residence and work permit) carte f de séjour
**greenery** n verdure f
**greenfield site** n terrain m vert
**greengrocer** n marchand m de fruits et légumes

**greenhouse** *n* serre *f*

**greenhouse effect** *n* effet *m* de serre

**Greenland** *pr n* Groenland *m*

**greet** *vtr* **(a)** (say hello to) saluer
**(b)** to be ~ed with *or* by provoquer ⟨*dismay, amusement*⟩

**greeting** ⟦1⟧ *n* salutation *f*
⟦2⟧ **greetings** *n pl* at Christmas ~s vœux *mpl* de Noël; **Season's** ~s meilleurs vœux

**greetings card** (GB), **greeting card** (US) *n* carte *f* de vœux

**grey** (GB), **gray** (US) ⟦1⟧ *n* gris *m*
⟦2⟧ *adj* **(a)** (in colour) gris/-e
**(b)** (grey-haired) to go *or* turn ~ grisonner
**(c)** (dull) ⟨*existence, day*⟩ morne; ⟨*person, town*⟩ terne

**grey area** *n* zone *f* floue

**grey-haired** *adj* aux cheveux gris

**greyhound** *n* lévrier *m*

**grid** *n* **(a)** grille *f*
**(b)** (GB) (network) réseau *m*

**gridlock** *n* embouteillage *m*, bouchon *m*

**grief** *n* chagrin *m*
IDIOMS to come to ~ ⟨*person*⟩ (have an accident) avoir un accident; (fail) échouer; ⟨*business*⟩ péricliter; **good** ~! mon Dieu!

**grief-stricken** *adj* accablé/-e de douleur

**grievance** *n* griefs *mpl* (**against** contre)

**grieve** *vi* to ~ **for** *or* **over** pleurer ⟨*person*⟩

**grievous bodily harm**, **GBH** *n* (Law) coups *mpl* et blessures *fpl*

**grill** ⟦1⟧ *n* gril *m*
⟦2⟧ *vtr* **(a)** faire griller ⟨*meat, fish*⟩
**(b)** (colloq) (interrogate) mettre [qn] sur la sellette (colloq)

**grille** *n* (gen) grille *f*; (on car) calandre *f*

**grim** *adj* **(a)** ⟨*news, town, future*⟩ sinistre; ⟨*sight, conditions*⟩ effroyable; ⟨*reality*⟩ dur/-e
**(b)** ⟨*struggle*⟩ acharné/-e; ⟨*resolve*⟩ terrible
**(c)** ⟨*face*⟩ grave

**grimace** ⟦1⟧ *n* grimace *f* (**of** de)
⟦2⟧ *vi* (involuntary) faire une grimace (**with, in** de); (pull a face) faire la grimace

**grime** *n* (of city) saleté *f*; (on object, person) crasse *f*

**grimy** *adj* ⟨*city*⟩ noir/-e; ⟨*hands, window*⟩ crasseux/-euse

**grin** ⟦1⟧ *n* sourire *m*
⟦2⟧ *vi* sourire (**at** à; **with** de)

**grind** ⟦1⟧ *n* (colloq) boulot *m* (colloq) *or* travail *m* monotone
⟦2⟧ *vtr* moudre ⟨*corn, coffee beans*⟩; écraser ⟨*grain*⟩; hacher ⟨*meat*⟩; to ~ **one's teeth** grincer des dents
⟦3⟧ *vi* ⟨*machine*⟩ grincer; to ~ **to a halt** ⟨*machine*⟩ s'arrêter; ⟨*vehicle*⟩ s'arrêter avec un grincement de freins; ⟨*factory, production*⟩ s'immobiliser

**grindstone** *n* meule *f* *or* pierre *f* à aiguiser
IDIOMS to keep *or* have one's nose to the ~ travailler sans relâche

**grip** ⟦1⟧ *n* **(a)** prise *f* (**on** sur)
**(b)** to lose one's ~ **on reality** perdre contact avec la réalité; to come to ~s **with sth** en venir aux prises avec qch; get a ~ **on yourself!** ressaisis-toi!
**(c)** (of tyre) adhérence *f*
⟦2⟧ *vtr* **(a)** (grab) agripper; (hold) serrer
**(b)** ⟨*tyres*⟩ adhérer à ⟨*road*⟩; ⟨*shoes*⟩ accrocher à ⟨*ground*⟩
**(c)** (captivate) captiver

**gripping** *adj* captivant/-e

**grisly** *adj* ⟨*story, sight*⟩ horrible; ⟨*remains*⟩ macabre

**gristle** *n* cartilage *m*

**grit** ⟦1⟧ *n* **(a)** (on lens) grains *mpl* de poussière; (sandy dirt) grains *mpl* de sable
**(b)** (GB) (for roads) sable *m*
⟦2⟧ *vtr* (GB) sabler ⟨*road*⟩
IDIOMS to ~ **one's teeth** serrer les dents

**grizzly** *n* (also ~ **bear**) grizzli *m*

**groan** ⟦1⟧ *n* (of pain, despair) gémissement *m*; (of disgust, protest) grognement *m*
⟦2⟧ *vi* (in pain) gémir; (in disgust, protest) grogner

**grocer** *n* (person) épicier/-ière *m/f*; ~'s (shop) épicerie *f*

**groceries** *n pl* provisions *fpl*

**grocery** *n* (also ~ **shop** (GB), ~ **store**) épicerie *f*

**groggy** *adj* groggy; to feel ~ avoir les jambes en coton (colloq)

**groin** *n* aine *f*

**groom** ⟦1⟧ *n* **(a)** (bridegroom) the ~ le jeune marié
**(b)** (for horse) palefrenier/-ière *m/f*
⟦2⟧ *vtr* **(a)** panser ⟨*horse*⟩
**(b)** to ~ **sb for** préparer qn à ⟨*exam, career*⟩

**groove** *n* (gen) rainure *f*; (on record) sillon *m*; (on screw) fente *f*

**grope** ⟦1⟧ *vtr* (colloq) (sexually) tripoter (colloq)
⟦2⟧ *vi* to ~ **for sth** chercher qch à tâtons

**gross** ⟦1⟧ *n* grosse *f*
⟦2⟧ *adj* **(a)** ⟨*income, profit*⟩ brut/-e
**(b)** ⟨*error, exaggeration*⟩ grossier/-ière; ⟨*abuse, inequality*⟩ choquant/-e; ⟨*injustice*⟩ flagrant/-e
**(c)** ⟨*behaviour*⟩ vulgaire; ⟨*language*⟩ cru/-e
**(d)** (colloq) (revolting) dégoûtant/-e
**(e)** (colloq) (obese) obèse
⟦3⟧ *vtr* ⟨*business, company*⟩ faire un bénéfice brut de

**grossly** *adv* ⟨*misleading, irresponsible*⟩ extrêmement; ⟨*underpaid*⟩ scandaleusement; ~ **overweight** obèse

**gross national product**, **GNP** *n* produit *m* national brut, PNB *m*

**grotesque** *n, adj* grotesque (*m*)

**grotto** *n* grotte *f*

**grotty** *adj* (colloq) minable (colloq); to feel ~ se sentir tout chose (colloq)

**ground** ⟦1⟧ *n* **(a)** (soil) sol *m*, terre *f*; on the ~ par terre; above ~ en surface; below ~ sous terre
**(b)** (area, territory) terrain *m*; a piece of ~ un terrain
**(c)** (sportsground) terrain *m* ····⫶

**2 grounds** *n pl* **(a)** (garden) parc *m* (of de) **(b)** (reasons) ~s for sth motifs *mpl* de qch; ~s for doing motifs pour faire; **on the ~s that** en raison du fait que
**3** *pp adj* ⟨*coffee, pepper*⟩ moulu/-e
**4** *vtr* **(a)** immobiliser ⟨*aircraft*⟩ **(b)** ⟨*ship*⟩ **to be ~ed** s'échouer
**IDIOMS to gain** ~ gagner du terrain (**on**, **over** sur); **to hold one's** ~ tenir bon; **to go to** ~ se terrer; **that suits me down to the** ~ ça me convient parfaitement

**ground floor** *n* rez-de-chaussée *m inv*; **on the** ~ au rez-de-chaussée

**grounding** *n* bases *fpl* (**in** en, de)

**groundnut oil** *n* huile *f* d'arachide

**ground rules** *n pl* grands principes *mpl*; **to change the** ~ modifier les règles du jeu

**groundsheet** *n* tapis *m* de sol

**ground troops** *n pl* troupes *fpl* terrestres

**groundwork** *n* travail *m* préparatoire (**for** à)

**group** **1** *n* groupe *m*; **in ~s** en groupes
**2** *vtr* grouper
**3** *vi* ~ **together** ⟨*people*⟩ se grouper

**group booking** *n* réservation *f* de groupe

**group therapy** *n* thérapie *f* de groupe

**group work** *n* travail *m* en groupes

**grouse** *n* tétras *m*

**grove** *n* bosquet *m*; **lemon** ~ verger *m* de citronniers

**grovel** *vi* ramper (**to, before** devant)

**grow** **1** *vtr* **(a)** cultiver ⟨*plant, crop*⟩ **(b)** laisser pousser ⟨*beard, nails*⟩; **to** ~ **5 cm** ⟨*person*⟩ grandir de 5 cm; ⟨*plant*⟩ pousser de 5 cm
**2** *vi* **(a)** ⟨*person*⟩ grandir (**by** de); ⟨*plant, hair*⟩ pousser (**by** de) **(b)** ⟨*population, tension*⟩ augmenter (**by** de); ⟨*company, economy*⟩ se développer; ⟨*opposition, support, problem*⟩ devenir plus important; ⟨*crisis*⟩ s'aggraver **(c)** devenir ⟨*hotter, stronger*⟩; **to** ~ **old** vieillir; **to** ~ **impatient** s'impatienter; **I grew to like him** j'ai appris à l'aimer
■ **grow apart** s'éloigner l'un de l'autre
■ **grow on: it** ~s **on you** on finit par l'aimer; **he's** ~ing **on me** je commence à le trouver plus sympathique
■ **grow out of (a) he's grown out of his suit** son costume est devenu trop petit pour lui **(b) he'll** ~ **out of it** (of habit) ça lui passera
■ **grow up** (gen) grandir; (become mature) devenir adulte; **when I** ~ **up** quand je serai grand

**grower** *n* (of fruit) producteur/-trice *m/f*; (of crops) cultivateur/-trice *m/f*

**growl** **1** *n* grondement *m*
**2** *vi* ⟨*dog*⟩ gronder

**grown-up** **1** *n* adulte *mf*, grande personne *f*
**2** *adj* adulte

**growth** *n* **(a)** (gen) croissance *f* (**in**, **of** de);

(of hair, nails) pousse *f*; (of economy) expansion *f* (**in**, **of** de); (in numbers, productivity) augmentation *f* (**in** de) **(b)** (tumour) grosseur *f*, tumeur *f*

**growth area** *n* secteur *m* en expansion

**growth industry** *n* industrie *f* en expansion

**growth rate** *n* taux *m* de croissance

**grubby** *adj* malpropre

**grudge** **1** *n* **to bear sb a** ~ en vouloir à qn
**2** *vtr* **to** ~ **sb their success** en vouloir à qn de sa réussite; **to** ~ **doing** rechigner à faire

**grudgingly** *adv* ⟨*admit*⟩ avec réticence

**gruelling**, **grueling** (US) *adj* exténuant/-e

**gruesome** *adj* horrible

**gruff** *adj* bourru/-e

**grumble** *vi* ⟨*person*⟩ ronchonner (**at sb** après qn; **to** auprès de); **to** ~ **about** se plaindre de

**grumpy** *adj* grincheux/-euse

**grunge** *n* (colloq) (dirt) crasse *f*; (style) grunge *m*

**grunt** **1** *n* grognement *m*
**2** *vi* grogner

**G-string** *n* (garment) string *m*

**guarantee** **1** *n* garantie *f*
**2** *vtr* garantir

**guard** **1** *n* **(a)** (for person) surveillant/-e *m/f*; (for place, object, at prison) gardien/-ienne *m/f*; (soldier) garde *m* **(b)** (military duty) garde *f*, surveillance *f*; **to be on** ~ être de garde **(c) to catch sb off** ~ prendre qn au dépourvu **(d)** (GB) (on train) chef *m* de train
**2** *vtr* **(a)** (protect) surveiller ⟨*place, object*⟩; protéger ⟨*person*⟩ **(b)** surveiller ⟨*hostage, prisoner*⟩ **(c)** garder ⟨*secret*⟩

**guard dog** *n* chien *m* de garde

**guarded** *adj* circonspect/-e (**about** à propos de)

**guardian** *n* **(a)** (gen) gardien/-ienne *m/f* (**of** de) **(b)** (of child) tuteur/-trice *m/f*

**guardian angel** *n* ange *m* gardien

**Guernsey** *pr n* Guernesey *f*

**guerrilla** *n* guérillero *m*

**guerrilla war** *n* guérilla *f*

**guess** **1** *n* supposition *f*, conjecture *f*; **at a** (rough) ~ **I would say that...** au hasard je dirais que...; **it's anybody's** ~! les paris sont ouverts!
**2** *vtr* **(a)** deviner; ~ **what!** tu sais quoi! (colloq) **(b)** (suppose) supposer
**3** *vi* deviner; **to keep sb** ~ing ne pas satisfaire la curiosité de qn

**guesswork** *n* conjecture *f*

**guest** *n* (in one's home) invité/-e *m/f*; (at hotel) client/-e *m/f*; **be my** ~! je vous en prie!

**guesthouse** *n* pension *f* de famille

**guest room** n chambre f d'amis

**guestworker** n travailleur immigré/ travailleuse immigrée m/f

**guidance** n conseils mpl (**from** de)

**guide** ⟨1⟩ n (a) (person, book) guide m (**to** de) (**b**) (idea) indication f; **as a rough** ∼ à titre d'indication
(**c**) (also **Girl Guide**) guide f
⟨2⟩ vtr guider (**to** vers)

**guide book** n guide m

**guide dog** n chien m d'aveugle

**guided tour** n visite f guidée

**guideline** n (rough guide) indication f; (in political context) directive f; (advice) conseils mpl

**guild** n (medieval) guilde f; (modern) association f

**guillotine** n (a) guillotine f
(**b**) (for paper) massicot m

**guilt** n culpabilité f

**guilty** adj coupable; **to feel** ∼ culpabiliser; **to feel** ∼ **about** se sentir coupable vis-à-vis de

**guinea-pig** n (a) (Zool) cochon m d'Inde
(**b**) (in experiment) cobaye m

**guitar** n guitare f

**guitarist** n guitariste mf

**gulch** n (US) ravin m

**gulf** n (a) golfe m; **the Gulf** la région f du Golfe
(**b**) (figurative) fossé m (**between** qui sépare)

**Gulf States** pr n pl **the** ∼ (in Middle East) les États mpl du Golfe

**Gulf War** pr n guerre f du Golfe

**gull** n mouette f

**gullible** adj crédule

**gully** n ravin m

**gulp** ⟨1⟩ n (of liquid) gorgée f; (of air) bouffée f, goulée f; (of food) bouchée f
⟨2⟩ vtr (also ∼ **down**) engloutir ⟨food, drink⟩
⟨3⟩ vi avoir la gorge serrée

**gum** n (a) (in mouth) gencive f
(**b**) (also **chewing** ∼) chewing-gum m
(**c**) (adhesive) colle f; (resin) gomme f

**gun** n (weapon) arme f à feu; (revolver) revolver m; (rifle) fusil m; (cannon) canon m; **to fire a** ∼ tirer
IDIOMS **to jump the** ∼ agir prématurément; **to stick to one's** ∼s (colloq) s'accrocher (colloq)

■ **gun down** abattre, descendre

**gunfire** n (from hand-held gun) coups mpl de feu; (from artillery) fusillade f

**gun laws** n pl législation f sur les armes à feu

**gun licence** n permis m de port d'armes

**gunman** n homme m armé

**gunpoint** n **to hold sb up at** ∼ tenir qn sous la menace d'une arme

**gunpowder** n poudre f

**gunshot** n coup m de feu

**gunshot wound** n blessure f par balle

**gurgle** ⟨1⟩ n (of water) gargouillement m; (of baby) gazouillis m
⟨2⟩ vi ⟨water⟩ gargouiller; ⟨baby⟩ gazouiller

**guru** n gourou m

**gush** vi jaillir

**gust** n rafale f

**gusto** n **with** ∼ avec enthousiasme

**gut** ⟨1⟩ n (colloq) bide m (colloq)
⟨2⟩ adj ⟨feeling, reaction⟩ viscéral/-e, instinctif/-ive
⟨3⟩ vtr ⟨fire⟩ ravager ⟨building⟩

**guts** n pl (colloq) (a) (of human) tripes fpl (colloq); (of animal) entrailles fpl
(**b**) (courage) cran m (colloq)

**gutsy** adj (colloq) (spirited) fougueux/-euse; (brave) courageux/-euse

**gutter** n (on roof) gouttière f; (in street) caniveau m

**gutter press** n presse f à sensation

**guy** n (colloq) type m (colloq); **a good/bad** ∼ (in films) un bon/méchant

**Guy Fawkes Day** n (GB) le 5 novembre (anniversaire de la Conspiration des Poudres)

**guzzle** vtr (colloq) engloutir

**gym** n (a) (abbr = **gymnasium**) salle f de gym (colloq), gymnase m
(**b**) (abbr = **gymnastics**) gym f (colloq)

**gymnasium** n gymnase m

**gymnast** n gymnaste mf

**gymnastics** n pl gymnastique f

**gym shoe** n tennis f

**gynaecologist** (GB), **gynecologist** (US) n gynécologue mf

**gypsy** n (gen) bohémien/-ienne m/f; (Central European) tzigane mf; (Spanish) gitan/-e m/f

# Hh

**h, H** *n* h, H *m*

**habit** *n* (a) habitude *f*; **to get into/out of the ~ of doing** prendre/perdre l'habitude de faire; **out of ~** par habitude
(b) (addiction) accoutumance *f*
(c) (of monk, nun) habit *m*

**habitable** *adj* habitable

**habitat** *n* habitat *m*

**habit-forming** *adj* **to be ~** créer une accoutumance

**habitual** *adj* ⟨behaviour, reaction⟩ habituel/-elle; ⟨drinker, smoker, liar⟩ invétéré/-e

**habitual offender** *n* récidiviste *mf*

**hack** [1] *n* (colloq) (writer) écrivaillon *m*; (journalist) journaliste *m/f* qui fait la rubrique des chiens écrasés
[2] *vtr* tailler dans ⟨bushes⟩ (with à coups de); **to ~ sb/sth to pieces** tailler qn/qch en pièces
[3] *vi* (a) **to ~ through sth** tailler dans qch
(b) (Comput) (colloq) pirater (colloq); **to ~ into** s'introduire dans ⟨system⟩

**hacker** *n* (computer) ~ pirate *m* informatique

**hacking** *n* (Comput) piratage *m* (colloq) informatique

**hackles** *n pl* (on dog) poils *mpl* du cou; **the dog's ~ began to rise** le chien se hérissait

**hackneyed** *adj* ⟨joke⟩ éculé/-e; ⟨subject⟩ rebattu/-e; **~ phrase** cliché *m*

**haddock** *n* églefin *m*

**haemophilia** (GB), **hemophilia** (US) *n* hémophilie *f*

**haemophiliac** (GB), **hemophiliac** (US) *n*, *adj* hémophile (*mf*)

**haemorrhage** (GB), **hemorrhage** (US) [1] *n* hémorragie *f*
[2] *vi* faire une hémorragie

**haemorrhoids** (GB), **hemorrhoids** (US) *n pl* hémorroïdes *fpl*

**haggard** *adj* ⟨appearance, person⟩ exténué/-e; ⟨face, expression⟩ défait/-e

**haggle** *vi* marchander; **to ~ over sth** discuter du prix de qch

**Hague** *pr n* **The ~** La Haye

**hail** [1] *n* grêle *f*
[2] *vtr* (a) héler ⟨person, taxi, ship⟩
(b) (praise) **to ~ sb as** acclamer qn comme; **to ~ sth as** saluer qch comme qch
[3] *v impers* grêler

**hailstone** *n* grêlon *m*

**hailstorm** *n* averse *f* de grêle

**hair** *n* (a) (on head) cheveux *mpl*; (on body)

poils *mpl*; (of animal) poil *m*; **to have one's ~ done** se faire coiffer; **long-~ed** ⟨person⟩ aux cheveux longs; ⟨animal⟩ à poil long
(b) (individually) (on head) cheveu *m*; (on body) poil *m*
IDIOMS **to split ~s** couper les cheveux en quatre

**hairband** *n* bandeau *m*

**hairbrush** *n* brosse *f* à cheveux

**haircut** *n* coupe *f* (de cheveux)

**hairdo** *n* (colloq) coiffure *f*

**hairdresser** *n* coiffeur/-euse *m/f*

**hairdrier** *n* (hand-held) sèche-cheveux *m inv*; (hood) casque *m*

**hair gel** *n* gel *m* coiffant

**hairgrip** *n* pince *f* à cheveux

**hairpin bend** *n* virage *m* en épingle à cheveux

**hair-raising** *adj* ⟨adventure, tale⟩ à vous faire dresser les cheveux sur la tête

**hair remover** *n* crème *f* dépilatoire

**hair-slide** *n* (GB) barrette *f*

**hairspray** *n* laque *f*

**hairstyle** *n* coiffure *f*

**hairy** *adj* poilu/-e

**halal** *adj* ⟨meat⟩ hallal *inv*

**half** [1] *n* (a) moitié *f*; **to cut sth in ~** couper qch en deux
(b) (fraction) demi *m*; **four and a ~** quatre et demi
(c) (GB) (colloq) (half pint) demi-pinte *f*
[2] *adj* **~ an hour** une demi-heure; **a ~-litre, ~ a litre** un demi-litre; **two and a ~ cups** deux tasses et demie
[3] *pron* (a) la moitié *f*; **~ of the students** la moitié des étudiants
(b) (in time) demi/-e *m/f*; **an hour and a ~** une heure et demie; **~ past two** (GB) deux heures et demie
[4] *adv* à moitié; **to ~ close sth** fermer qch à moitié; **it's ~ the price** c'est moitié moins cher; **I ~ expected it** je m'y attendais plus ou moins
IDIOMS **to go halves with sb** partager avec qn

**halfback** *n* (Sport) demi *m*

**half-board** *n* demi-pension *f*

**half-brother** *n* demi-frère *m*

**half day** *n* demi-journée *f*

**half fare** *n* demi-tarif *m*

**half-hearted** *adj* peu enthousiaste

**half-heartedly** *adv* sans conviction

**half hour** *n* demi-heure *f*; **on the ~** à la demie

**half-mast** *n* **at ~** en berne

**half-moon** *n* (a) demi-lune *f*

657

**(b)** (of fingernail) lunule *f*

**half price** *adv, adj* à moitié prix

**half-sister** *n* demi-sœur *f*

**half term** *n* (GB Sch) vacances *fpl* de la mi-trimestre

**half-time** *n* (Sport) mi-temps *f*; **at** ~ à la mi-temps

**halfway** *adv* **(a)** à mi-chemin (**between** entre; **to** de); ~ **up** *or* **down** à mi-hauteur de ⟨*stairs, tree*⟩; ~ **down the page** à mi-page **(b)** (in time) ~ **through** au milieu

**halfway house** *n* (rehabilitation centre) centre *m* de réadaptation

**hall** *n* **(a)** (in house) entrée *f*; (in hotel, airport) hall *m*; (for public events) (grande) salle *f* **(b)** (country house) manoir *m*

**hallelujah** *excl* alléluia!

**hallmark** [1] *n* **(a)** (GB) (on metal) poinçon *m* **(b)** (typical feature) caractéristique *f* [2] *vtr* poinçonner; **to be** ~**ed** porter un poinçon

**hall of residence** *n* résidence *f* universitaire

**Halloween** *n*: *la veille de la Toussaint*

**hallucinate** *vi* avoir des hallucinations

**hallucination** *n* hallucination *f*

**hallway** *n* entrée *f*

**halo** *n* **(a)** auréole *f* **(b)** (in astronomy) halo *m*

**halt** [1] *n* (stop) arrêt *m*; **to come to a** ~ ⟨*vehicle, troops*⟩ s'arrêter; ⟨*work*⟩ être interrompu/-e; **to call a** ~ **to sth** mettre fin à qch [2] *vtr* arrêter [3] *vi* s'arrêter

**halterneck** *n, adj* dos (*m inv*) nu

**halve** [1] *vtr* réduire [qch] de moitié ⟨*number, rate*⟩; couper [qch] en deux ⟨*carrot, cake*⟩ [2] *vi* ⟨*number, rate, time*⟩ diminuer de moitié

**ham** *n* jambon *m*

**hamburger** *n* **(a)** (burger) hamburger *m* **(b)** (US) (ground beef) pâté *m* de viande

**hammer** [1] *n* marteau *m* [2] *vtr* **(a)** marteler ⟨*metal, table*⟩; **to** ~ **sth into** enfoncer qch dans ⟨*wall, fence*⟩ **(b)** **to** ~ **sth into sb** faire entrer qch dans la tête de qn; **to** ~ **home a message** bien faire comprendre un message **(c)** (colloq) (defeat) battre [qn] à plates coutures [3] *vi* (pound) tambouriner (**on, at** contre)
■ **hammer out**: ~ **out** [sth], ~ [sth] **out** (negotiate) parvenir à [qch] après maintes discussions ⟨*agreement, policy, formula*⟩

**hamper** [1] *n* panier *m* à pique-nique [2] *vtr* entraver ⟨*movement, career, progress*⟩

**hamster** *n* hamster *m*

**hamstring** *n* tendon *m* du jarret

**hand** [1] *n* **(a)** main *f*; **he had a pencil in his** ~ il avait un crayon à la main; **to hold sb's** ~ tenir qn par la main; **to make sth by** ~

faire qch à la main; **the letter was delivered by** ~ la lettre a été remise en mains propres; **to give sb a (helping)** ~ donner un coup de main à qn; **to have sth to** ~ avoir qch sous la main; **to be on** ~ ⟨*person*⟩ être disponible; **to get out of** ~ devenir incontrôlable; **to take sb/sth in** ~ prendre qn/qch en main ⟨*situation, person*⟩ **(b)** (cards) jeu *m* **(c)** (worker) ouvrier/-ière *m/f*; (crew member) membre *m* de l'équipage **(d)** (on clock, dial) aiguille *f* **(e)** **on the one** ~..., **on the other** ~... d'une part..., d'autre part... [2] *vtr* **to** ~ **sth to sb** donner qch à qn [3] **hand in hand** *phr* ⟨*run, walk*⟩ la main dans la main; **to go** ~ **in** ~ aller de pair (**with** avec) [4] **out of hand** *phr* ⟨*reject*⟩ d'emblée
IDIOMS **to have one's** ~**s full** avoir assez à faire; **to try one's** ~ **at sth** s'essayer à; **to know sth like the back of one's** ~ connaître qch comme sa poche
■ **hand down** passer ⟨*object, clothes*⟩ (**to sb** à qn); transmettre ⟨*property*⟩
■ **hand in** remettre ⟨*form*⟩ (**to** à); rendre ⟨*homework, keys*⟩
■ **hand out** distribuer ⟨*food, leaflets*⟩
■ **hand over**: ¶ ~ **over to** [sb] passer l'antenne à ⟨*reporter*⟩; passer la main à ⟨*deputy, successor*⟩; ¶ ~ [sth] **over** rendre ⟨*weapon*⟩; céder ⟨*business*⟩; remettre ⟨*keys, money*⟩; ¶ ~ [sb] **over** livrer ⟨*prisoner*⟩

**handbag** *n* sac *m* à main

**hand baggage** *n* bagages *mpl* à main

**handball** *n* (Sport) handball *m*

**handbook** *n* manuel *m*; (technical) livret *m* technique

**handbrake** *n* frein *m* à main

**handcuffs** *n pl* menottes *fpl*

**handful** *n* **(a)** (fistful) poignée *f* **(b)** (of people) poignée *f*; (of buildings, objects) petit nombre *m* **(c)** (colloq) **to be a** ~ être épuisant/-e

**handgun** *n* arme *f* de poing

**hand-held** *adj* ⟨*camera*⟩ de reportage; ⟨*tool*⟩ à main; ⟨*device*⟩ portatif/-ive; ⟨*computer*⟩ de poche

**handicap** [1] *n* handicap *m* [2] *vtr* handicaper

**handicapped** *adj* ⟨*person*⟩ handicapé/-e; **mentally/physically** ~ **children** des enfants handicapés mentaux/physiques

**handicrafts** *n pl* (Sch) travaux *mpl* manuels

**handiwork** *n* ouvrage *m*

**handkerchief** *n* mouchoir *m*

**handle** [1] *n* (on door, drawer, bag) poignée *f*; (on bucket, cup, basket) anse *f*; (on frying pan) queue *f*; (on saucepan, cutlery, hammer, spade) manche *m*; (on wheelbarrow, pump) bras *m* [2] *vtr* **(a)** manipuler ⟨*explosives, food*⟩; manier ⟨*gun*⟩; '~ **with care**' 'fragile'

⋯⟶

**(b)** (manage) manier ⟨*horse*⟩; manœuvrer ⟨*car*⟩; **to know how to ~ children** savoir s'y prendre avec les enfants
**(c)** (deal with) faire face à ⟨*crisis*⟩; supporter ⟨*stress*⟩; ⟨*department, lawyer*⟩ s'occuper de ⟨*enquiries, case*⟩

**handlebars** *n pl* guidon *m*

**handling** *n* **(a)** (holding, touching) (of food, waste) manipulation *f*; (of tool, weapon) maniement *m*;
**(b)** (way of dealing) **her ~ of the theme** sa façon de traiter le thème; **their ~ of the economy** leur gestion de l'économie

**handling charge** *n* **(a)** (for goods) frais *mpl* de manutention
**(b)** (administrative) frais *mpl* administratifs

**hand luggage** *n* bagages *mpl* à main

**handmade** *adj* fait/-e à la main

**handout** *n* **(a)** (charitable) don *m*
**(b)** (leaflet) prospectus *m*

**handpick** *vtr* **(a)** cueillir [qch] à la main ⟨*grapes*⟩
**(b)** trier [qn] sur le volet ⟨*staff*⟩

**handshake** *n* poignée *f* de main

**handsome** *adj* beau/belle (*before n*)

**hands-on** *adj* ⟨*experience, manager*⟩ de terrain; ⟨*control*⟩ direct/-e; ⟨*approach*⟩ pragmatique

**handstand** *n* (Sport) équilibre *m*

**handwriting** *n* écriture *f*

**handwritten** *adj* manuscrit/-e

**handy** *adj* ⟨*book, skill*⟩ utile; ⟨*tool, pocket, size*⟩ pratique; ⟨*shop*⟩ bien situé/-e; **to keep/ have [sth] ~** garder/avoir [qch] sous la main ⟨*keys, passport*⟩

**handyman** *n* bricoleur *m*

**hang** ⟨**1**⟩ *n* **to get the ~ of sth** (colloq) piger qch (colloq)
⟨**2**⟩ *vtr* **(a)** (from hook, coat hanger) accrocher (**from** à; **by** par; **on** à); (from string, rope) suspendre (**from** à); (peg up) étendre ⟨*washing*⟩ (**on** sur)
**(b)** poser ⟨*wallpaper*⟩
**(c)** pendre ⟨*criminal, victim*⟩
⟨**3**⟩ *vi* **(a)** (on hook) être accroché/-e; (from height) être suspendu/-e; (on washing line) être étendu/-e
**(b)** ⟨*arm, leg*⟩ pendre
**(c)** ⟨*curtain, garment*⟩ tomber
**(d)** ⟨*person*⟩ être pendu/-e (**for** pour)
⟨**4**⟩ *v refl* **to ~ oneself** se pendre (**from** à)
■ **hang around** (colloq) **(a)** (*also* **~ about**) (wait) attendre; (aimlessly) traîner
**(b) to ~ around with sb** passer son temps avec qn
■ **hang back** (in fear) rester derrière; (figurative) être réticent/-e
■ **hang down** (gen) pendre; ⟨*hem*⟩ être défait/-e
■ **hang on**: ¶ **~ on (a)** (hold on) **to ~ on (to sth)** s'accrocher (à qch)
**(b)** (colloq) (wait) attendre
**(c)** (colloq) (survive) tenir (colloq); **~ on in there!** (colloq) tiens bon!
¶ **~ on [sth]** (depend on) dépendre de

■ **hang out**: ¶ **~ out (a)** (protrude) dépasser
**(b)** (colloq) (live) crécher (colloq)
**(c)** (colloq) (sit around) traîner (colloq)
¶ **~ [sth] out** étendre ⟨*washing*⟩; sortir ⟨*flag*⟩
■ **hang up**: ¶ **~ up** (on phone) raccrocher; **to ~ up on sb** raccrocher au nez de qn
¶ **~ [sth] up** (on hook) accrocher; (on hanger) suspendre; (on line) étendre

**hangar** *n* hangar *m*

**hanger-on** *n* (colloq) parasite *m*

**hang-glider** *n* deltaplane *m*

**hanging** *n* **(a)** (of person) pendaison *f*
**(b)** (curtain) rideau *m*; (on wall) tenture *f*

**hangover** *n* (from drink) gueule *f* de bois (colloq)

**hang-up** *n* (colloq) complexe *m*, problème *m*

**hanker** *vi* **to ~ after** *or* **for sth** rêver de qch

**hanky, hankie** (colloq) *n* mouchoir *m*

**haphazard** *adj* peu méthodique

**happen** *vi* **(a)** (occur) arriver, se passer, se produire; **what's ~ing?** qu'est-ce qui se passe?; **to ~ again** se reproduire; **whatever ~s** quoi qu'il arrive
**(b)** (occur by chance) **if you ~ to see her, say hello** si par hasard tu la vois, salue-la de ma part; **as it ~ed, the weather that day was bad** il s'est trouvé qu'il faisait mauvais ce jour-là

**happily** *adv* **(a)** (cheerfully) joyeusement; **a ~ married man** un mari heureux; **they all lived ~ ever after** ils vécurent heureux jusqu'à la fin de leurs jours
**(b)** (willingly) ⟨*admit*⟩ volontiers
**(c)** (luckily) heureusement

**happiness** *n* bonheur *m*

**happy** *adj* **(a)** heureux/-euse (**about** de; **that** que + *subjunctive*); **to be ~ with sth** être satisfait/-e de qch; **to keep a child ~** amuser un enfant; **to be ~ to do** être heureux/-euse de faire
**(b)** (in greetings) **Happy Birthday!** Bon anniversaire!; **Happy Christmas!** Joyeux Noël!; **Happy New Year!** Bonne année!

**happy ending** *n* heureux dénouement *m*

**happy medium** *n* juste milieu *m*

**harangue** *vtr* (about politics) haranguer; (moralize) sermonner

**harass** ⟨**1**⟩ *vtr* harceler
⟨**2**⟩ **harassed** *pp adj* excédé/-e

**harbour** (GB), **harbor** (US) ⟨**1**⟩ *n* port *m*
⟨**2**⟩ *vtr* nourrir ⟨*suspicion, illusion*⟩; receler ⟨*criminal*⟩

**hard** ⟨**1**⟩ *adj* **(a)** (firm) dur/-e; **to go ~** durcir
**(b)** (difficult) ⟨*problem, question, task*⟩ dur/-e, difficile; ⟨*choice, decision, life*⟩ difficile; **it's ~ to do** c'est dur *or* difficile à faire; **to find it ~ to do** avoir du mal à faire; **it was ~ work** ça a été dur *or* difficile; **to be a ~ worker** être travailleur/-euse
**(c)** (severe) ⟨*person, look, words*⟩ dur/-e, sévère; ⟨*blow*⟩ dur/-e, terrible; ⟨*winter*⟩ rude; **to be ~ on sb** ⟨*person*⟩ être dur/-e envers qn; **~ luck!** pas de chance!; **no ~ feelings!** sans rancune!
**(d)** ⟨*evidence, fact*⟩ solide

**(e)** ⟨*liquor*⟩ fort/-e; ⟨*drug*⟩ dur/-e
**(f)** ⟨*water*⟩ dur/-e, calcaire
**2** *adv* ⟨*push, hit, cry*⟩ fort; ⟨*work*⟩ dur;
⟨*study, think*⟩ sérieusement; ⟨*look, listen*⟩
attentivement; **to try ~** (mentally) faire
beaucoup d'efforts; (physically) essayer de
toutes ses forces

**hard and fast** *adj* ⟨*rule, distinction*⟩
absolu/-e

**hardback (book)** *n* livre *m* relié

**hardboard** *n* aggloméré *m*

**hard-boiled egg** *n* œuf *m* dur

**hard copy** *n* (Comput) tirage *m*

**hard core** **1** *n* (group, demonstrators) noyau
*m* dur
  **2 hard-core** *adj* **(a)** (established)
⟨*supporter, opponent, protest*⟩ irréductible
  **(b)** (extreme) ⟨*pornography, video*⟩ hard *inv*
(colloq)

**hard court** *n* court *m* en dur

**hard disk** *n* disque *m* dur

**hard-earned** *adj* ⟨*cash*⟩ durement
gagné/-e

**harden** **1** *vtr* **(a)** (faire) durcir ⟨*glue, wax*⟩
  **(b)** endurcir ⟨*person*⟩ **(to** à); durcir
⟨*attitude*⟩; **to ~ one's heart** s'endurcir (**to** à)
  **2** *vi* **(a)** ⟨*glue, wax, skin*⟩ durcir
  **(b)** ⟨*voice, stance*⟩ se durcir

**hardened** *adj* ⟨*criminal*⟩ endurci/-e;
⟨*drinker*⟩ invétéré/-e

**hard hat** *n* (helmet) casque *m*; (for riding)
bombe *f*

**hard-hearted** *adj* insensible

**hard-hitting** *adj* ⟨*speech, criticism*⟩
musclé/-e; ⟨*report*⟩ très critique

**hard labour** (GB), **hard labor** (US) *n*
travaux *mpl* forcés

**hardliner** *n* jusqu'au-boutiste *mf*; (political)
partisan/-e *m/f* de la ligne dure

**hardly** *adv* **(a)** (barely) ⟨*begin, know, see*⟩ à
peine; **~ had they set off when** à peine
étaient-ils partis que
  **(b)** (not really) **one can ~ expect that** on ne
peut guère s'attendre à ce que; **it's ~ likely**
c'est peu probable; **it's ~ surprising** ce n'est
guère étonnant; **I can ~ believe it!** j'ai peine
à le croire!
  **(c) ~ any/ever/anybody** presque pas/jamais/
personne; **he ~ ever writes** il n'écrit presque
jamais

**hard of hearing** *adj* **to be ~** entendre
mal

**hard-pressed, hard-pushed** *adj* en
difficulté; (for time) pressé/-e; **to be ~ to do**
avoir du mal à faire

**hardship** *n* **(a)** (difficulty) détresse *f*; (poverty)
privations *fpl*
  **(b)** (ordeal) épreuve *f*

**hard shoulder** *n* bande *f* d'arrêt
d'urgence

**hard up** *adj* (colloq) fauché/-e (colloq)

**hardware** *n* **(a)** (gen) articles *mpl* de
quincaillerie
  **(b)** (Comput) matériel *m* (informatique)

**(c)** (Mil) équipement *m*

**hardware shop, hardware store**
*n* quincaillerie *f*

**hard-working** *adj* travailleur/-euse

**hardy** *adj* ⟨*person*⟩ robuste; ⟨*plant*⟩
résistant/-e

**hare** *n* lièvre *m*

**haricot** *n* (GB) (**also ~ bean**) (dried)
haricot *m* blanc; (fresh) haricot *m* vert

**harm** **1** *n* mal *m*; **to do sb ~** faire du mal
à qn; **to do ~ to sth** endommager qch; **out
of ~'s way** en sûreté
  **2** *vtr* faire du mal à ⟨*person*⟩; endommager
⟨*crops, lungs*⟩; nuire à ⟨*population*⟩

**harmful** *adj* ⟨*chemical, ray*⟩ nocif/-ive;
⟨*behaviour, gossip*⟩ nuisible (**to** pour)

**harmless** *adj* **(a)** ⟨*chemical, virus*⟩
inoffensif/-ive (**to** pour); ⟨*growth*⟩ bénin/
bénigne
  **(b)** ⟨*person*⟩ inoffensif/-ive; ⟨*fun, joke*⟩
innocent/-e

**harmonica** *n* harmonica *m*

**harmonious** *adj* harmonieux/-ieuse

**harmonize** **1** *vtr* harmoniser
  **2** *vi* jouer en harmonie (**with** avec)

**harmony** *n* harmonie *f*

**harness** **1** *n* harnais *m*
  **2** *vtr* **(a)** harnacher ⟨*horse*⟩
  **(b)** (attach) atteler ⟨*animal*⟩ (**to** à)
  **(c)** exploiter ⟨*power, energy*⟩

**harp** *n* harpe *f*
■ **harp on** (colloq) rabâcher (colloq) toujours
la même chose sur ⟨*issue, event*⟩

**harpoon** *n* harpon *m*

**harrowing** *adj* ⟨*experience*⟩ atroce; ⟨*film,
image*⟩ déchirant/-e

**harsh** *adj* **(a)** ⟨*punishment, measures*⟩
sévère; ⟨*tone, regime, person*⟩ dur/-e;
⟨*conditions*⟩ difficile
  **(b)** ⟨*light, colour*⟩ cru/-e; ⟨*sound*⟩ rude,
dur/-e à l'oreille

**harshly** *adv* ⟨*treat, speak*⟩ durement;
⟨*punish*⟩ sévèrement

**harvest** **1** *n* (of wheat, fruit) récolte *f*; (of
grapes) vendange *f*
  **2** *vtr* moissonner ⟨*corn*⟩; récolter
⟨*vegetables*⟩; cueillir ⟨*fruit*⟩; vendanger
⟨*grapes*⟩

**has-been** *n* (colloq) homme fini/femme
finie *m/f*

**hassle** (colloq) **1** *n* complications *fpl*; **it
was a real ~** c'était enquiquinant (colloq)
  **2** *vtr* talonner (**about** à propos de)

**haste** *n* hâte *f*; **to act in ~** agir à la hâte

**hasten** **1** *vtr* accélérer ⟨*destruction*⟩;
précipiter ⟨*departure, death, decline*⟩
  **2** *vi* se hâter; **to ~ to do** s'empresser de
faire

**hasty** *adj* ⟨*talks, marriage, departure*⟩
précipité/-e; ⟨*meal*⟩ rapide; ⟨*note*⟩ écrit/-e à
la hâte; ⟨*decision*⟩ inconsidéré/-e;
⟨*conclusion*⟩ hâtif/-ive

**hat** *n* chapeau *m*

**hatch** [1] n (a) (on aircraft) panneau m
mobile; (in boat) écoutille f; (in car) portière f
(b) (also **serving ~**) passe-plats m inv
[2] vtr (a) faire éclore ‹eggs›
(b) tramer ‹plot, scheme›
[3] vi ‹chicks, fish eggs› éclore

**hatchback** n voiture f avec hayon

**hatchet** n hachette f

**hate** [1] n haine f
[2] vtr (a) (dislike) détester; (violently) haïr
(b) (not enjoy) avoir horreur de ‹sport, food›;
to ~ doing avoir horreur de faire
(c) (in apology) to ~ to do être désolé/-e de
faire

**hate mail** n lettres fpl d'injures

**hatred** n haine f (of de; for pour)

**hat trick** n triplé m

**haughty** adj ‹person› hautain/-e; ‹manner›
altier/-ière

**haul** [1] n (a) (taken by criminals) butin m
(b) (found by police, customs) saisie f; **arms ~**
saisie d'armes
(c) it's a long ~ la route est longue
(d) (of fish) pêche f
[2] vtr (drag) tirer

**haulage** n (a) (transport) transport m routier
(b) (cost) frais mpl de transport

**haunch** n hanche f

**haunt** [1] n lieu m de prédilection
[2] vtr hanter

**haunted** adj ‹house› hanté/-e; ‹face, look›
tourmenté/-e

**haunting** adj (gen) lancinant/-e; ‹memory›
obsédant/-e

**have** [1] vtr (a) (possess) avoir; she has (got)
a dog elle a un chien; I haven't (got) enough
time je n'ai pas assez de temps
(b) (with noun object) to ~ a wash se laver; to
~ a sandwich manger un sandwich; to ~ a
whisky boire un whisky; to ~ a cigarette
fumer une cigarette; to ~ breakfast prendre
le petit déjeuner; to ~ lunch déjeuner; I had
some more cake j'ai repris du gâteau
(c) (receive, get) recevoir ‹letter›; I've had no
news from him je n'ai pas eu de nouvelles de
lui; to let sb ~ sth donner qch à qn
(d) (hold) faire ‹party›; tenir ‹meeting›;
organiser ‹competition, exhibition›; avoir
‹conversation›
(e) (exert, exhibit) avoir ‹effect, influence›; avoir
‹courage, courtesy› (to do de faire)
(f) (spend) passer; to ~ a nice day passer une
journée agréable; to ~ a good time bien
s'amuser; to ~ a hard time traverser une
période difficile; to ~ a good holiday (GB) or
vacation (US) passer de bonnes vacances
(g) (also ~ got) to ~ sth to do avoir qch à
faire; I've got letters to write j'ai du courrier
à faire; I've got a lot of work to do j'ai
beaucoup de travail
(h) (suffer) avoir; to ~ (the) flu/a heart attack
avoir la grippe/une crise cardiaque; to ~
toothache avoir mal aux dents; he had his

car stolen il s'est fait voler sa voiture; she
has had her windows broken on lui a cassé
ses vitres
(i) to ~ the car fixed faire réparer la voiture;
to ~ the house painted faire peindre la
maison; to ~ one's hair cut se faire couper
les cheveux; to ~ an injection se faire faire
une piqûre
(j) (cause to become) she had them completely
baffled elle les a complètement déroutés; I
had it finished by 5 o'clock je l'avais fini
avant 5 heures
(k) (allow) tolérer; I won't ~ this kind of
behaviour! je ne tolérerai pas ce
comportement!
(l) (give birth to) ‹woman› avoir ‹child›;
‹animal› mettre bas, avoir ‹young›
[2] modal aux (must) I ~ to leave il faut que
je parte, je dois partir; something has (got)
to be done il faut faire quelque chose; you
don't ~ to leave so early tu n'as pas besoin
de or tu n'es pas obligé de partir si tôt
[3] v aux (a) avoir; (with movement and reflexive
verbs) être; she has lost her bag elle a perdu
son sac; she has already left elle est déjà
partie; he has hurt himself il s'est blessé;
having finished his breakfast, he went out
après avoir fini son petit déjeuner, il est
sorti
(b) (in tags, short answers) you've seen the film,
haven't you? tu as vu le film, n'est-ce pas?;
you haven't seen the film, ~ you? tu n'as pas
vu le film?; you haven't seen my bag, ~
you? tu n'as pas vu mon sac, par hasard?;
'~ you seen him?'—'yes, I ~' 'est-ce que tu
l'as vu?'—'oui'; 'you've never met him'—'yes
I ~!' 'tu ne l'as jamais rencontré'—'mais si!'
(c) (if) had I known, I wouldn't have bought it
si j'avais su, je ne l'aurais pas acheté
IDIOMS I've had it (up to here) with... colloq
j'en ai marre de... (colloq); to ~ it in for sb
(colloq) avoir qn dans le collimateur (colloq);
she doesn't ~ it in her to do elle est
incapable de faire; to ~ it out with sb
s'expliquer avec qn; the ~s and the ~-nots
les riches et les pauvres
■ **have on** (a) porter ‹coat, skirt›; he had
(got) nothing on il n'avait rien sur lui
(b) to ~ sth on (be busy) avoir qch de prévu
(c) to ~ sb on (colloq) faire marcher qn
(colloq)

**haven** n (a) (safe place) refuge m (for pour)
(b) (harbour) port m

**havoc** n dévastation f; to wreak ~
provoquer des dégâts; (figurative) tout mettre
sens dessus dessous

**Hawaii** pr n Hawaï m

**hawk** n faucon m

**hawthorn** n aubépine f

**hay** n foin m

**hay fever** n rhume m des foins

**haystack** n meule f de foin
IDIOMS it is/was like looking for a needle in a
~ autant chercher une aiguille dans une
botte de foin

**haywire** adj (colloq) **(a)** (faulty) to go ~
⟨plan⟩ dérailler; ⟨machinery⟩ se détraquer
**(b)** (crazy) détraqué/-e (colloq)

**hazard** [1] n risque m (to pour); **a health ~**
un risque pour la santé
[2] vtr hasarder ⟨opinion, guess⟩

**hazardous** adj dangereux/-euse

**haze** n (mist) brume f; (of smoke, dust) nuage
m

**hazel** [1] n noisetier m
[2] adj ⟨eyes⟩ (couleur de) noisette inv

**hazelnut** n noisette f

**hazy** adj ⟨weather, morning⟩
brumeux/-euse; ⟨sunshine⟩ voilé/-e; ⟨idea,
memory⟩ vague (before n)

**he** pron il; (emphatic) lui; ~'s seen us il nous
a vus; there ~ is le voilà; she lives in Oxford
but ~ doesn't elle habite Oxford mais lui
non; ~'s a genius c'est un génie; ~ and I lui
et moi

**head** [1] n **(a)** (gen) tête f; from ~ to foot or
toe de la tête aux pieds; to stand on one's ~
faire le poirier; £10 a ~ or per ~ 10 livres
sterling par personne
**(b)** (of family, church) chef m; (of organization)
responsable mf, directeur/-trice m/f; ~ of
State chef d'État
[2] **heads** n pl (of coin) face f; '~s or tails?'
'pile ou face?'
[3] adj **(a)** ⟨injury⟩ à la tête
**(b)** (chief) ⟨cashier, cook, gardener⟩ en chef
[4] vtr **(a)** être en tête de ⟨list, queue⟩; être à
la tête de ⟨firm, team⟩; mener ⟨expedition,
inquiry⟩
**(b)** ~ed writing paper papier m à lettres à
en-tête
**(c)** (steer) diriger ⟨vehicle⟩ (towards vers)
**(d)** (Sport) to ~ the ball faire une tête
[5] vi where was the train ~ed or ~ing? où
allait le train?; to ~ home rentrer; he's
~ing this way! il vient par ici!
IDIOMS to go to sb's ~ monter à la tête de
qn; to keep/lose one's ~ garder/perdre son
sang-froid; off the top of one's ~ ⟨say,
answer⟩ sans réfléchir
■ **head for (a)** se diriger vers ⟨place⟩
**(b)** courir à ⟨defeat⟩; courir vers ⟨trouble⟩

**headache** n mal m de tête; to have a ~
avoir mal à la tête

**headband** n bandeau m

**headbutt** vtr donner un coup de tête à

**head cold** n rhume m de cerveau

**headdress** n (of feathers) coiffure f; (of lace)
coiffe f

**header** n **(a)** (colloq) (dive) to take a ~
piquer une tête (colloq)
**(b)** (in sport) tête f

**headfirst** adv ⟨fall, plunge⟩ la tête la
première; ⟨rush into⟩ tête baissée

**head-hunt** vtr (seek to recruit) (chercher à)
recruter

**head-hunter** n chasseur m de têtes

**heading** n (of article, column) titre m; (of
subject area, topic) rubrique f; (on notepaper,
letter) en-tête m

**headlamp**, **headlight** n (of car) phare m

**headline** n (in paper) gros titre m; to hit the
~s faire la une (colloq); the front-page ~ la
manchette; the news ~s les grands titres
(de l'actualité)

**headlong** [1] adj a ~ dash une ruée
[2] adv ⟨fall⟩ la tête la première; ⟨run⟩ à
toute vitesse

**head office** n siège m social

**head-on** adj ⟨crash, collision⟩ de front

**headphones** n pl casque m

**headquarters** n pl (gen) siège m social;
(Mil) quartier m général

**head rest** n (gen) appui-tête m; (Aut)
repose-tête m inv

**head start** n to have a ~ avoir une
longueur d'avance (over sur)

**headstone** n pierre f tombale

**headstrong** adj ⟨person⟩ têtu/-e;
⟨attitude⟩ obstiné/-e

**head teacher** n directeur/-trice m/f

**headway** n to make ~ avancer, faire des
progrès

**heady** adj ⟨wine, mixture⟩ capiteux/-euse;
⟨perfume⟩ entêtant/-e; ⟨experience⟩ grisant/-e

**heal** [1] vtr guérir ⟨person, injury⟩
[2] vi ⟨wound, cut⟩ se cicatriser; the fracture
has ~ed l'os s'est ressoudé

**healer** n guérisseur/-euse m/f

**healing** [1] n guérison f
[2] adj ⟨power⟩ curatif/-ive; ⟨effect⟩ salutaire;
the ~ process le rétablissement

**health** n santé f; in good/bad ~ en bonne/
mauvaise santé; here's to your ~! à votre
santé!

**health club** n club m de remise en forme

**health farm** n: établissement pour cures
d'amaigrissement, de rajeunissement

**health food** n aliments mpl naturels,
aliments mpl diététiques

**healthily** adv sainement

**health insurance** n assurance f
maladie

**Health Service** n **(a)** (GB) (for public)
services mpl de santé
**(b)** (US) (Univ) infirmerie f

**healthy** adj ⟨person, dog⟩ en bonne santé;
⟨livestock, plant, lifestyle, diet⟩ sain/-e; ⟨air⟩
salutaire; ⟨appetite⟩ robuste; ⟨economy⟩
sain/-e; ⟨profit⟩ excellent/-e

**heap** [1] n **(a)** (pile) tas m
**(b)** (colloq) ~s of plein de
[2] vtr **(a)** (pile) entasser
**(b)** to ~ sth on sb couvrir qn de qch
⟨praise⟩; accabler qn de qch ⟨scorn⟩

**heaped** adj a ~ spoonful une bonne
cuillerée

**hear** [1] vtr **(a)** (gen) entendre; to make
oneself heard se faire entendre; (figurative)
faire entendre sa voix
**(b)** apprendre ⟨news, rumour⟩
**(c)** (listen to) écouter ⟨lecture, broadcast⟩;
⟨judge⟩ entendre ⟨case, evidence⟩

⋯⟩

[2] *vi* entendre; **to ~ about** entendre parler de
IDIOMS **~! ~!** bravo!
■ **hear from** avoir des nouvelles de ⟨person⟩
■ **hear of** entendre parler de; **I won't ~ of it!** il n'en est pas question!

**hearing** *n* (a) (sense) ouïe *f*, audition *f*; **his ~ is not very good** il n'a pas l'oreille très fine
(b) (before court) audience *f*

**hearing aid** *n* prothèse *f* auditive

**hearing-impaired** *adj* malentendant/-e

**hearsay** *n* ouï-dire *m inv*, on-dit *m inv*

**hearse** *n* corbillard *m*

**heart** *n* (a) (gen) cœur *m*; **by ~** ⟨learn, know⟩ par cœur; **to take sth to ~** prendre qch à cœur; **right in the ~ of London** en plein cœur de Londres; **the ~ of the matter** le fond du problème
(b) (in cards) ⟨**~(s)** cœur *m*
IDIOMS **to have one's ~ set on sth** vouloir qch à tout prix; **to take/lose ~** prendre/perdre courage

**heartache** *n* chagrin *m*

**heart attack** *n* crise *f* cardiaque, infarctus *m*

**heartbeat** *n* battement *m* de cœur

**heartbreaking** *adj* ⟨sight, story⟩ navrant/-e; ⟨cry, appeal⟩ déchirant/-e

**heartbroken** *adj* **to be ~** avoir le cœur brisé

**heart disease** *n* maladies *fpl* cardiaques

**heartening** *adj* encourageant/-e

**heart failure** *n* arrêt *m* du cœur

**heartfelt** *adj* sincère

**hearth** *n* foyer *m*; **~ rug** petit tapis *m*

**heartless** *adj* ⟨person⟩ sans cœur; ⟨attitude, treatment⟩ cruel/-elle

**heartthrob** *n* (colloq) idole *f*

**heart-to-heart** *n* **to have a ~ (with sb)** parler à cœur ouvert (avec qn)

**heart transplant** *n* greffe *f* du cœur

**hearty** *adj* ⟨welcome, greeting⟩ cordial/-e; ⟨person⟩ jovial/-e; ⟨laugh⟩ franc/franche; ⟨appetite⟩ solide; ⟨approval⟩ chaleureux/-euse

**heat** [1] *n* (a) chaleur *f*; **in this ~** par cette chaleur; **in the ~ of the moment** dans le feu de l'action
(b) (Sport) (round) épreuve *f* éliminatoire; (in athletics) série *f*
(c) (Zool) **to be on** *or* **in ~** être en chaleur
[2] *vtr* chauffer ⟨house, pool⟩; faire chauffer ⟨food, oven⟩
■ **heat up** faire chauffer ⟨food⟩; (reheat) faire réchauffer

**heated** *adj* (a) ⟨water, pool⟩ chauffé/-e
(b) ⟨debate, argument⟩ animé/-e

**heater** *n* appareil *m* de chauffage

**heathen** *n, adj* (irreligious) païen/-ïenne (*m/f*); (uncivilized) barbare (*mf*)

**heather** *n* bruyère *f*

**heating** *n* chauffage *m*

**heat stroke** *n* coup *m* de chaleur (*avec collapsus*)

**heatwave** *n* vague *f* de chaleur

**heave** [1] *vtr* (lift) hisser; (pull) traîner péniblement; (throw) lancer (at sur); **to ~ a sigh** pousser un soupir
[2] *vi* (a) ⟨sea, ground⟩ se soulever et s'abaisser
(b) (pull) tirer de toutes ses forces
(c) (retch) avoir un haut-le-cœur; (vomit) vomir

**heaven** *n* ciel *m*, paradis *m*; **thank ~(s)!** Dieu soit loué!; **good ~s!** grands dieux!

**heavenly** *adj* (a) ⟨choir, body⟩ céleste; ⟨peace⟩ divin/-e
(b) (colloq) (wonderful) divin/-e

**heavily** *adv* (a) ⟨lean, fall⟩ lourdement; ⟨sleep, sigh⟩ profondément; ⟨breathe⟩ (noisily) bruyamment; (with difficulty) péniblement; **~ underlined** souligné/-e d'un gros trait
(b) ⟨rain⟩ très fort; ⟨snow, invest, smoke, drink, rely⟩ beaucoup; ⟨bleed⟩ abondamment; ⟨taxed, armed⟩ fortement

**heavy** *adj* (gen) lourd/-e; ⟨shoes, frame⟩ gros/grosse (before n); ⟨line, features⟩ épais/épaisse; ⟨blow, fighting⟩ violent/-e; ⟨rain, frost, perfume, accent⟩ fort/-e; ⟨snow⟩ abondant/-e; ⟨traffic⟩ dense; ⟨gunfire⟩ nourri/-e; ⟨bleeding⟩ abondant/-e; ⟨sentence, fine⟩ sévère; ⟨cold⟩ gros/grosse (before n); **with a ~ heart** le cœur gros; **to be a ~ sleeper** avoir le sommeil lourd; **to be a ~ drinker** boire beaucoup

**heavy-handed** *adj* maladroit/-e

**heavy metal** *n* hard rock *m*

**heavyweight** *n* (a) (boxer) poids *m* lourd
(b) (figurative) (colloq) grosse légume *f* (colloq)

**Hebrew** [1] *n* (a) (person) Hébreu *m*
(b) (language) hébreu *m*
[2] *adj* ⟨language⟩ hébraïque; ⟨person⟩ hébreu/hébraïque

**heckle** [1] *vtr* interpeller
[2] *vi* chahuter

**hectic** *adj* ⟨activity⟩ intense; ⟨day, life, schedule⟩ mouvementé/-e

**hedge** [1] *n* haie *f*
[2] *vi* se dérober
IDIOMS **to ~ one's bets** se couvrir

**hedgehog** *n* hérisson *m*

**hedgerow** *n* haie *f*

**heed** [1] *n* **to take ~ of sb** tenir compte de ce que dit qn; **to take ~ of sth** tenir compte de qch
[2] *vtr* tenir compte de ⟨warning, advice⟩

**heel** *n* talon *m*
IDIOMS **to fall head over ~s in love with sb** tomber éperdument amoureux de qn; **to be hot on sb's ~s** talonner qn

**heel bar** *n* talon-minute *m*

**hefty** *adj* ⟨person⟩ costaud (colloq); ⟨object⟩ pesant/-e; ⟨blow⟩ puissant/-e; ⟨sum⟩ considérable

**heifer** *n* génisse *f*

**height** *n* (a) (of person) taille *f*; (of table, tower, tree) hauteur *f*

**(b)** (of plane) altitude *f*; **to be scared of** ∼s avoir le vertige

**(c)** (peak) **at the** ∼ **of the season** en pleine saison; **at the** ∼ **of** au plus fort de ⟨*storm, crisis*⟩; **the** ∼ **of** le comble de ⟨*luxury, stupidity, cheek*⟩; **to be the** ∼ **of fashion** être le dernier cri

**heighten** **1** *vtr* intensifier ⟨*emotion*⟩; augmenter ⟨*tension, suspense*⟩; accentuer ⟨*effect*⟩
**2** *vi* ⟨*tension*⟩ monter

**heir** *n* héritier/-ière *m/f* **(to** de)

**heiress** *n* héritière *f*

**heirloom** *n* héritage *m*; **a family** ∼ un objet de famille

**helicopter** *n* hélicoptère *m*

**hell** *n* **(a)** enfer *m*; **to make sb's life** ∼ rendre la vie infernale à qn
**(b)** (colloq) **a** ∼ **of a shock** un choc terrible; **a** ∼ **of a lot worse** nettement pire; **oh, what the** ∼**!** tant pis!; **why the** ∼**…?** pourquoi …, bon Dieu? (colloq); **what the** ∼ **is he doing?** qu'est-ce qu'il fait, bon Dieu? (colloq)
IDIOMS **for the** ∼ **of it** (colloq) par plaisir; **to raise** ∼ (colloq) faire une scène **(with sb** à qn)

**hello** *excl* **(a)** (greeting) bonjour!; (on the phone) allô!
**(b)** (in surprise) tiens!

**helm** *n* barre *f*; **at the** ∼ à la barre

**helmet** *n* casque *m*

**help** **1** *n* aide *f*; (in emergency) secours *m*; **with the** ∼ **of** à l'aide de ⟨*stick, knife*⟩; avec l'aide de ⟨*person*⟩; **it's/she's a (great)** ∼ ça/elle aide beaucoup; **to cry for** ∼ appeler au secours
**2** *excl* au secours!
**3** *vtr* **(a)** aider **(to do** à faire); (more urgently) secourir; **to** ∼ **each other** s'entraider; **to** ∼ **sb across** aider qn à traverser
**(b)** (serve) **to** ∼ **sb to** servir [qch] à qn ⟨*food, wine*⟩; **to** ∼ **oneself** se servir
**(c)** (prevent) **I couldn't** ∼ **laughing** je n'ai pas pu m'empêcher de rire; **it can't be** ∼ed! on n'y peut rien!; **he can't** ∼ **being stupid!** ce n'est pas de sa faute s'il est stupide!
**4** *vi* aider; **he never** ∼s **with the housework** il n'aide jamais à faire le ménage; **this map doesn't** ∼ **much** cette carte n'est pas d'un grand secours
■ **help out**: ¶ ∼ **out** aider, donner un coup de main (colloq); ¶ ∼ **[sb] out** aider, donner un coup de main à (colloq); (financially) dépanner (colloq)

**help desk** *n* service *m* d'assistance technique téléphonique

**helper** *n* aide *mf*, assistant/-e *m/f*; (for handicapped person) aide *f* sociale

**helpful** *adj* ⟨*person*⟩ serviable; ⟨*advice, suggestion*⟩ utile

**helping** *n* portion *f*

**helpless** *adj* **(a)** (powerless) ⟨*person*⟩ impuissant/-e; (because of infirmity, disability) impotent/-e
**(b)** (defenceless) ⟨*person*⟩ sans défense

**helpline** *n* service *m* d'assistance (téléphonique)

**hem** *n* ourlet *m*
■ **hem in** cerner ⟨*person*⟩

**hemisphere** *n* hémisphère *m*

**hemp** *n* chanvre *m*

**hen** *n* (chicken) poule *f*; (female bird) femelle *f*

**hence** *adv* **(a)** (for this reason) (before noun) d'où; (before adjective) donc
**(b)** (from now) d'ici

**henchman** *n* acolyte *m*

**henna** *n* henné *m*

**hen night** *n* soirée *f* passée entre femmes *(avant le mariage de l'une d'elles)*

**hen-pecked** *adj* ∼ **husband** mari *m* mené par le bout du nez

**hepatitis** *n* hépatite *f*

**her**

■ **Note** In French determiners agree in gender and number with the noun that follows. So *her*, when used as a determiner, is translated by *son* + masculine singular noun (son chien), or *sa* + feminine singular noun (sa maison) BUT by *son* + feminine noun beginning with a vowel or mute 'h' (son assiette) and by *ses* + plural noun (ses enfants).
– When *her* is stressed, *à elle* is added after the noun: HER *house* = sa maison à elle.

**1** *pron* **(a)** (direct object) la, l'; (indirect object) lui; **I saw** ∼ je l'ai vue; **he gave** ∼ **the book** il lui a donné le livre; **catch** ∼ atrappe-la!; **give it to** ∼ donne-le-lui
**(b)** (after preposition, to be) elle; **it's for** ∼ c'est pour elle; **it's** ∼ c'est elle
**2** *det* son/sa/ses

**herald** **1** *n* héraut *m*
**2** *vtr* (*also* ∼ **in**) annoncer

**heraldry** *n* héraldique *f*

**herb** *n* herbe *f*; **mixed** ∼s ≈ herbes de Provence

**herbal tea** *n* tisane *f*, infusion *f*

**herd** **1** *n* troupeau *m*
**2** *vtr* rassembler ⟨*animals*⟩; **to** ∼ **people into a room** conduire des gens dans une pièce
IDIOMS **to follow the** ∼ être un mouton de Panurge

**here** *adv*

■ **Note** When *here* is used to indicate the location of an object, a point etc close to the speaker, it is generally translated by *ici*: **come and sit here** = viens t'asseoir ici.
– When the location is not so clearly defined, *là* is the usual translation: **he's not here at the moment** = il n'est pas là pour l'instant.
– *voici* is used to translate *here is* and *here are* when the speaker is drawing attention to an object, a place, a person etc physically close to him or her.
– For examples and particular usages, see the entry below.

**(a)** ici; **near** ∼ près d'ici; **come over** ∼ ⋯⟩

venez par ici; **~ and there** par endroits; **~ they are/she comes!** les/la voici!; **~ are my keys** voici mes clés; **~ you are** tiens, tenez
**(b)** (indicating presence, arrival) **she's not ~ right now** elle n'est pas là pour le moment; **~ we are at last** nous voilà enfin; **we get off ~** c'est là qu'on descend; **now that summer's ~** maintenant que c'est l'été; **~'s our chance** voilà notre chance
IDIOMS **~'s to our success!** à notre succès!; **~'s to you!** à la tienne!

**hereabout** (US), **hereabouts** (GB) *adv* par ici

**hereafter** [1] *n* **the ~** l'au-delà *m*
[2] *adv* (Law) ci-après

**here and now** *n* **the ~** (present) le présent

**hereby** *adv* par la présente

**hereditary** *adj* héréditaire

**heredity** *n* hérédité *f*

**heresy** *n* hérésie *f*

**heritage** *n* patrimoine *m*

**hermit** *n* ermite *m*

**hernia** *n* hernie *f*

**hero** *n* héros *m*

**heroic** *adj* héroïque

**heroin** *n* héroïne *f*

**heroin addict** *n* héroïnomane *mf*

**heroine** *n* héroïne *f*

**heroism** *n* héroïsme *m*

**heron** *n* héron *m*

**hero-worship** [1] *n* culte *m* du héros, adulation *f*
[2] *vtr* aduler

**herring** *n* hareng *m*

**hers** *pron*

■ Note In French, possessive pronouns reflect the gender and number of the noun they are standing for; *hers* is translated by *le sien, la sienne, les siens, les siennes,* according to what is being referred to.

**my car is red but ~ is blue** ma voiture est rouge mais la sienne est bleue; **the green pen is ~** le stylo vert est à elle; **which house is ~?** laquelle est sa maison?; **I'm a friend of ~** c'est une amie à moi; **it's not ~** ce n'est pas à elle

**herself** *pron* **(a)** (reflexive) se, s'; **she's hurt ~** elle s'est blessée
**(b)** (after preposition) elle, elle-même; **for ~** pour elle, pour elle-même; **(all) by ~** toute seule
**(c)** (emphatic) elle-même; **she made it ~** elle l'a fait elle-même
**(d) she's not ~ today** elle n'est pas dans son assiette aujourd'hui

**hesitant** *adj* hésitant/-e; **to be ~ about doing** hésiter à faire

**hesitate** *vi* hésiter (**over** sur; **to do** à faire)

**hesitation** *n* hésitation *f*

**heterosexual** *n, adj* hétérosexuel/-elle (*m/f*)

**hexagon** *n* hexagone *m*

**hey** *excl* (colloq) (call for attention) hé!, eh!; (in protest) dis donc!

**heyday** *n* (gen) âge *m* d'or; (of person) beaux jours *mpl*

**HGV** *n* (GB) (*abbr* = **heavy goods vehicle**) PL *m*, poids *m* lourd

**hi** *excl* (colloq) salut! (colloq)

**hibernate** *vi* hiberner

**hiccup, hiccough** *n* **(a)** hoquet *m*; **to have (the) ~s** avoir le hoquet
**(b)** (setback) anicroche *f*

**hidden** *adj* caché/-e

**hide** [1] *n* (skin) peau *f*; (leather) cuir *m*
[2] *vtr* cacher ‹*object, person*› (**from** à); dissimuler ‹*feeling*› (**from** à)
[3] *vi* se cacher

**hide and seek** (GB), **hide-and-go-seek** (US) *n* cache-cache *m inv*

**hideaway** *n* retraite *f*

**hideous** *adj* ‹*person, monster, object*› hideux/-euse; ‹*noise*› affreux/-euse

**hiding** *n* **(a) to go into ~** se cacher; **to come out of ~** sortir de sa cachette
**(b)** (beating) correction *f*

**hiding place** *n* cachette *f*

**hierarchy** *n* hiérarchie *f*

**hieroglyph, hieroglyphic** *n* hiéroglyphe *m*

**hi-fi** *n* **(a)** (set of equipment) chaîne *f* hi-fi *inv*
**(b)** (*abbr* = **high fidelity**) hi-fi *f inv*

**high** [1] *n* **(a) to reach a new ~** atteindre son niveau le plus élevé
**(b)** (colloq) **to be on a ~** être en pleine euphorie
[2] *adj* **(a)** (gen) haut/-e; **how ~ is the cliff?** quelle est la hauteur de la falaise?; **it is 50 m ~** ça fait 50 m de haut
**(b)** ‹*number, price, volume*› élevé/-e; ‹*wind*› violent/-e; ‹*hope*› grand/-e (*before n*); **at ~ speed** à grande vitesse; **to have a ~ temperature** avoir de la fièvre; **~ in** riche en ‹*fat, iron*›
**(c)** ‹*quality, standard, rank*› supérieur/-e; **friends in ~ places** des amis haut placés
**(d)** ‹*ideal, principle*› noble
**(e)** ‹*pitch, voice*› aigu/aiguë; ‹*note*› haut/-e
**(f)** (colloq) (on drug) défoncé/-e (colloq); (happy) ivre de joie
[3] *adv* haut

**highbrow** *n, adj* intellectuel/-elle (*m/f*)

**high chair** *n* chaise *f* de bébé

**high-class** *adj* ‹*hotel, shop, car*› de luxe; ‹*goods*› de première qualité; ‹*area*› de grand standing

**high court** *n* cour *f* suprême

**high-definition TV, HDTV** *n* télévision *f* à haute définition

**higher education** *n* enseignement *m* supérieur

**high fashion** *n* haute couture *f*

**high-flier** *n* jeune loup *m*

**high-handed** *adj* despotique

**high heels** *n pl* hauts talons *mpl*

**high jump** *n* (Sport) saut *m* en hauteur

**Highlands** *pr n pl* Highlands *mpl*, Hautes-Terres *fpl* (d'Écosse)

**highlight** **1** *n* **(a)** (in hair) (natural) reflet *m*; (artificial) mèche *f*
**(b)** (of match, event) point *m* culminant; (of year, evening) point *m* fort
**2 highlights** *n pl* (on radio, TV) résumé *m*
**3** *vtr* **(a)** (with pen) surligner
**(b)** (emphasize) mettre l'accent sur

**highlighter** *n* (pen) surligneur *m*

**highly** *adv* ⟨*dangerous, intelligent*⟩ extrêmement; ~ **unlikely** fort peu probable; **to think ~ of sb** penser beaucoup de bien de qn

**highly-paid** *adj* très bien payé/-e

**highly-strung** *adj* très tendu/-e

**Highness** *n* His *or* Her (Royal) ~ Son Altesse *f*

**high-pitched** *adj* ⟨*voice, sound*⟩ aigu/ aiguë

**high point** *n* point *m* culminant

**high-powered** *adj* ⟨*car, engine*⟩ de grande puissance; ⟨*person*⟩ dynamique; ⟨*job*⟩ de haute responsabilité

**high-profile** *adj* ⟨*politician, group*⟩ bien en vue; ⟨*visit*⟩ qui fait beaucoup de bruit

**high-ranking** *adj* de haut rang

**high rise (building)** *n* tour *f* (d'habitation)

**high school** *n* (US Sch) ≈ lycée *m*; (GB Sch) établissement *m* secondaire

**high-speed** *adj* ⟨*train*⟩ à grande vitesse

**high street** (GB) *n* (*also* **High Street**) (in town) rue *f* principale; (in village) grand-rue *f*

**high-street shop** *n* boutique *f* appartenant à une chaîne

**high street spending** *n* dépenses *fpl* de consommation courante

**high-tech** *adj* ⟨*industry*⟩ de pointe; ⟨*equipment, car*⟩ ultramoderne

**high tide** *n* marée *f* haute

**highway** *n* (GB) route *f* nationale; (US) autoroute *f*

**Highway Code** *n* (GB) Code *m* de la Route

**hijack** *vtr* détourner ⟨*plane*⟩

**hijacker** *n* (of plane) pirate *m* (de l'air); (of bus, truck) pirate *m* (de la route)

**hijacking** *n* détournement *m*

**hike** **1** *n* randonnée *f*; **to go on a ~** faire une randonnée
**2** *vtr* (*also* **~ up**) augmenter ⟨*rate, price*⟩

**hiker** *n* randonneur/-euse *m/f*

**hiking** *n* randonnée *f*

**hilarious** *adj* désopilant/-e, hilarant/-e

**hill** *n* colline *f*; (hillside) coteau *m*; (incline) pente *f*, côte *f*

**hillside** *n* **on the ~** à flanc de coteau

**hilltop** *n* sommet *m* de colline

**hilly** *adj* vallonné/-e

**him** *pron* **(a)** (direct object) le, l'; (indirect object) lui; **I know ~** je le connais; **catch ~!** attrape-le!; **I gave ~ the book** je lui ai donné le livre; **phone ~!** téléphone-lui!
**(b)** (after preposition, to be) lui; **it's for ~** c'est pour lui; **it's ~** c'est lui

**Himalayas** *pr n pl* **the ~** (les montagnes *fpl* de) l'Himalaya *m*

**himself** *pron* **(a)** (reflexive) se, s'; **he's hurt ~** il s'est blessé
**(b)** (after preposition) lui, lui-même; **for ~** pour lui, pour lui-même; **(all) by ~** tout seul
**(c)** (emphatic) lui-même; **he made it ~** il l'a fait lui-même
**(d) he's not ~ today** il n'est pas dans son assiette aujourd'hui

**hinder** *vtr* entraver ⟨*development, career*⟩; freiner ⟨*progress, efforts*⟩

**hind legs** *n pl* pattes *fpl* de derrière

**hindrance** *n* entrave *f*; **to be a ~ to sb/ sth** gêner qn/qch

**hindsight** *n* **with (the benefit of) ~** avec le recul, rétrospectivement

**Hindu** **1** *n* Hindou/-e *m/f*
**2** *adj* hindou/-e

**hinge** **1** *n* charnière *f*; (lift-off) gond *m*
**2** *vi* **to ~ on** dépendre de

**hint** **1** *n* **(a)** (remark) allusion *f* (**about** à); **to drop ~s** faire des allusions
**(b)** (clue) indication *f*; (piece of advice) conseil *m*
**(c)** (of spice, accent) pointe *f*; (of colour) touche *f*; (of smile) ébauche *f*; (of irony) soupçon *m*
**2** *vtr* **to ~ that** laisser entendre que (**to** à)
**3** *vi* faire des allusions; **to ~ at** faire allusion à

**hip** **1** *n* hanche *f*
**2** *adj* (colloq) ⟨*person*⟩ branché/-e
**3** *excl* **~ hurrah!** hip hip hip hourra!

**hippie**, **hippy** *n, adj* hippie (*mf*)

**hippopotamus**, **hippo** *n* hippopotame *m*

**hire** **1** *n* location *f*; **for ~** ⟨*boat, skis*⟩ à louer; ⟨*taxi*⟩ libre
**2** *vtr* louer ⟨*equipment, vehicle*⟩; engager ⟨*person*⟩

**hire purchase**, **HP** *n* achat *m* à crédit; **on ~** à crédit

**his**

━ **Note** In French determiners agree in gender and number with the noun that follows. So *his*, when used as a determiner, is translated by *son* + masculine singular noun (son chien), by *sa* + feminine singular noun (sa maison) BUT by *son* + feminine noun beginning with a vowel or mute 'h' (son assiette) and by *ses* + plural noun (ses enfants).
− When *his* is stressed, *à lui* is added after the noun: HIS *house* = sa maison à lui.
− In French possessive pronouns reflect the gender and number of the noun they are standing for. When used as a possessive ⋯⋗

pronoun, *his* is translated by *le sien, la sienne, les siens* or *les siennes* according to what is being referred to.

**1** *det* son/sa/ses
**2** *pron* **all the drawings were good but ∼ was the best** tous les dessins étaient bons mais le sien était le meilleur; **the blue car is ∼** la voiture bleue est à lui; **it's not ∼** ce n'est pas à lui; **which house is ∼?** laquelle est sa maison?; **I'm a colleague of ∼** je suis un/-e de ses collègues

**hiss** **1** *n* sifflement *m*
**2** *vi* ⟨*person, steam, snake*⟩ siffler; ⟨*cat*⟩ cracher; ⟨*fat*⟩ grésiller

**historian** *n* historien/-ienne *m/f*

**historic(al)** *adj* historique

**history** *n* **(a)** histoire *f*; **to make ∼** entrer dans l'histoire
**(b)** (past experience) antécédents *mpl*; **to have a ∼ of violence** avoir un passé violent

**hit** **1** *n* **(a)** (blow, stroke) coup *m*
**(b)** (success) (play, film) succès *m*; (record) tube *m* (colloq); **to be a big ∼** avoir un succès fou
**(c)** (Comput) (visit to Website) hit *m* (colloq), visite *f* (à un site Web); (occurences in search) occurence *f*
**2** *vtr* **(a)** (strike) frapper ⟨*person, ball*⟩; **to ∼ one's head on sth** se cogner la tête contre qch
**(b)** atteindre ⟨*target, enemy*⟩
**(c)** (collide with) heurter ⟨*wall*⟩; ⟨*vehicle*⟩ renverser ⟨*person*⟩
**(d)** (affect adversely) affecter, toucher
**(e)** (reach) arriver à ⟨*motorway*⟩; rencontrer ⟨*traffic, bad weather*⟩; ⟨*figures, weight*⟩ atteindre ⟨*level*⟩
IDIOMS **to ∼ it off with sb** bien s'entendre avec qn
■ **hit back**: ¶ ∼ [sb] **back** rendre un coup à; ¶ ∼ [sth] **back** renvoyer ⟨*ball*⟩

**hit-and-run** *adj* ⟨*accident*⟩ où le chauffeur a pris la fuite

**hitch** **1** *n* problème *m*, pépin *m* (colloq)
**2** *vtr* **(a)** attacher ⟨*trailer*⟩ (**to** à)
**(b)** (colloq) **to ∼ a lift** faire du stop (colloq)
**3** *vi* (colloq) faire du stop (colloq)

**hitchhike** *vi* faire du stop (colloq); **to ∼ to Paris** aller à Paris en stop (colloq)

**hitchhiker** *n* auto-stoppeur/-euse *m/f*

**hitchhiking** *n* auto-stop *m*

**hit man** *n* tueur *m* à gages

**hit parade** *n* palmarès *m*, hit-parade *m*

**hit single** *n* tube *m* (colloq)

**HIV** *n* (abbr = **human immunodeficiency virus**) (virus *m*) VIH *m*; **∼ positive** séropositif/-ive; **∼ negative** séronégatif/-ive

**hive** *n* ruche *f*; **a ∼ of activity** une vraie ruche

**hoard** **1** *n* (of treasure) trésor *m*; (of provisions) provisions *fpl*; (of miser) magot *m* (colloq)
**2** *vtr* amasser ⟨*objects, money, food*⟩

**hoarding** *n* (GB) **(a)** (billboard) panneau *m* publicitaire
**(b)** (fence) palissade *f*

**hoarse** *adj* ⟨*voice*⟩ rauque; **to be ∼** être enroué/-e

**hoax** **1** *n* canular *m*
**2** *adj* ⟨*call, warning*⟩ bidon *inv* (colloq)

**hob** *n* (on cooker) table *f* de cuisson

**hobble** *vi* boitiller

**hobby** *n* passe-temps *m inv*

**hockey** *n* (GB) hockey *m*; (US) hockey *m* sur glace; **∼ stick** crosse *f* de hockey

**hoe** **1** *n* houe *f*, binette *f*
**2** *vtr* biner ⟨*ground*⟩; sarcler ⟨*flower beds*⟩

**hog** **1** *n* (US) (pig) porc *m*, verrat *m*
**2** *vtr* (colloq) monopoliser
IDIOMS **to go the whole ∼** (colloq) (be extravagant) faire les choses en grand; (go to extremes) aller jusqu'au bout

**hoist** *vtr* hisser ⟨*flag, sail, heavy object*⟩

**hold** **1** *n* **(a)** (grasp) prise *f*; **to get ∼ of** attraper ⟨*rope, handle*⟩
**(b)** **to get ∼ of** se procurer ⟨*book, ticket*⟩; découvrir ⟨*information*⟩
**(c)** **to get ∼ of sb** (contact) joindre qn; (find) trouver qn
**(d)** (control) emprise *f* (**on, over** sur); **to have a ∼ on** *or* **over sb** avoir de l'emprise sur qn; **to get a ∼ of oneself** se reprendre
**(e)** **to put a call on ∼** mettre un appel en attente
**(f)** (in plane) soute *f*; (on boat) cale *f*
**2** *vtr* **(a)** tenir; **to ∼ sth in one's hand** tenir qch à la main ⟨*brush, pencil*⟩; (enclosed) tenir qch dans la main ⟨*coin, sweet*⟩; **to ∼ sb (in one's arms)** serrer qn dans ses bras; **to ∼ sth in place** maintenir qch en place
**(b)** organiser ⟨*meeting, competition, reception*⟩; célébrer ⟨*church service*⟩; mener ⟨*inquiry*⟩; faire passer ⟨*interview*⟩
**(c)** (contain) ⟨*drawer, box, case*⟩ contenir ⟨*objects, possessions*⟩
**(d)** avoir ⟨*opinion, belief*⟩
**(e)** (keep against will) détenir ⟨*person*⟩; **to ∼ sb hostage** garder qn en otage
**(f)** détenir, avoir ⟨*power, record*⟩; être titulaire de ⟨*degree*⟩
**(g)** **to ∼ sb's attention** retenir l'attention de qn; **to ∼ sb responsible** tenir qn pour responsable
**(h)** (defend successfully) tenir ⟨*territory, city*⟩; conserver ⟨*title, seat*⟩; **to ∼ one's own** bien se défendre
**(i)** (on phone) **can you ∼ the line please?** ne quittez pas s'il vous plaît
**3** *vi* **(a)** ⟨*bridge, dam, rope*⟩ tenir
**(b)** ⟨*weather*⟩ se maintenir; ⟨*luck*⟩ durer
**(c)** (on phone) patienter
**(d)** **∼ still!** tiens-toi tranquille!
■ **hold against**: **to ∼ sth against sb** reprocher qch à qn
■ **hold back**: ¶ ∼ **back** se retenir (**from doing** de faire)
¶ ∼ [sb/sth] **back (a)** contenir ⟨*water, crowd, anger*⟩; retenir ⟨*tears, person*⟩
**(b)** entraver ⟨*development*⟩
■ **hold down (a)** tenir, maîtriser ⟨*person*⟩
**(b)** garder ⟨*job*⟩

■ **hold on (a)** (wait) attendre; '~ on...' (on phone) 'ne quittez pas...'
**(b)** (grip) s'accrocher; '~ on (tight)!' 'tiens-toi (bien)!'

■ **hold on to** s'agripper à ⟨branch, rope, person⟩; (to prevent from falling) retenir ⟨person⟩; serrer ⟨object, purse⟩

■ **hold out**: ¶ ~ out tenir bon; **to ~ out against** tenir bon devant ⟨threat, changes⟩ ¶ ~ [sth] out tendre ⟨hand⟩ (**to** à)

■ **hold to**: ~ **sb to** [sth] faire tenir [qch] à qn ⟨promise⟩

■ **hold up (a)** soutenir ⟨shelf⟩; tenir ⟨trousers⟩
**(b)** (raise) lever; **to ~ one's hand up** lever la main
**(c)** (delay) retarder ⟨person, flight⟩; ralentir ⟨production, traffic⟩
**(d)** (rob) attaquer

**holdall** n fourre-tout m, sac m

**holder** n (of passport, degree, post, account) titulaire mf; (of ticket, record) détenteur/-trice m/f; (of title) tenant/-e m/f

**hold-up** n **(a)** (delay) retard m; (on road) embouteillage m, bouchon m
**(b)** (robbery) hold-up m

**hole** n **(a)** (gen) trou m
**(b)** (GB) (in tooth) cavité f
**(c)** (of fox, rabbit) terrier m

**hole-in-the-wall** n (colloq) distributeur m automatique de billets de banque

**holiday** n **(a)** (GB) (vacation) vacances fpl; **to go on ~** partir en vacances
**(b)** (GB) (time off work) congé m
**(c)** (public, bank) jour m férié

**holiday home** n résidence f secondaire

**holiday job** n (in summer) job m (colloq) d'été

**holidaymaker** n (GB) vacancier/-ière m/f

**holiday resort** n lieu m de villégiature

**Holland** pr n Hollande f, Pays-Bas mpl

**hollow** ①  n creux m
②  adj ⟨object, cheeks⟩ creux/creuse; ⟨words⟩ faux/fausse, vain/-e; **a ~ laugh** un rire forcé; **to sound ~** sonner faux

**holly** n houx m

**holocaust** n holocauste m; **the Holocaust** l'Holocauste m

**hologram** n hologramme m

**holster** n étui m de revolver

**holy** adj (gen) saint/-e; ⟨water⟩ bénit/-e

**Holy Bible** n Sainte Bible f

**Holy Land** pr n Terre f Sainte

**Holy Spirit** n Saint-Esprit m

**homage** n hommage m; **to pay ~ to** rendre hommage à

**home** ① n **(a)** (house) maison f; (country) pays m natal; **broken ~** foyer désuni; **to leave ~** quitter la maison
**(b)** (institution) maison f; **to put sb in a ~** mettre qn dans un établissement spécialisé
**(c)** (Sport) **to play at ~** jouer à domicile
② adj **(a)** ⟨life⟩ de famille; ⟨comforts⟩ du foyer

**(b)** ⟨market, affairs⟩ intérieur/-e; ⟨news⟩ national/-e
**(c)** (Sport) ⟨match, win⟩ à domicile; ⟨team⟩ qui reçoit
③ adv **(a)** ⟨come, go⟩ (to house) à la maison, chez soi; (to country) dans son pays
**(b) to bring sth ~ to sb** faire comprendre or voir qch à qn; **to strike ~** toucher juste
④ **at home** phr **(a)** ⟨be, work, stay⟩ à la maison, chez soi
**(b)** (Sport) ⟨play⟩ à domicile
**(c)** (at ease) ⟨feel⟩ à l'aise (**with** avec); **make yourself at ~** fais comme chez toi

**home address** n adresse f personnelle

**home cooking** n bonne cuisine f familiale

**home economics** n (Sch) cours m d'économie domestique

**home help** n (GB) aide f familiale

**homeland** n pays m d'origine, patrie f

**homeless** n the ~ les sans-abri mpl

**homely** adj **(a)** (GB) (cosy, welcoming) accueillant/-e
**(b)** (GB) (unpretentious) simple
**(c)** (US) (plain) ⟨person⟩ sans attraits

**homemade** adj fait/-e maison, maison inv

**Home Office** n ministère m de l'Intérieur

**homeopathic** adj homéopathique

**home owner** n propriétaire mf

**home page** n page f d'accueil

**home rule** n gouvernement m autonome

**Home Secretary** n Ministre m de l'Intérieur

**home shopping** n téléachat m

**homesick** adj **to be ~** (for country) avoir le mal du pays

**home town** n ville f natale

**home video** n vidéo f d'amateur

**homeward** adv **to travel ~(s)** rentrer; **to be ~ bound** être sur le chemin de retour

**homework** n **(a)** (Sch) devoirs mpl
**(b)** (research) **to do some ~ on** faire quelques recherches au sujet de

**homeworker** n travailleur/-euse m/f à domicile

**homeworking** n travail m à domicile

**homicidal** adj homicide

**homicide** n **(a)** (murder) homicide m
**(b)** (person) meurtrier/-ière m/f

**homogenous** adj homogène

**homosexual** n, adj homosexuel/-elle (m/f)

**homosexuality** n homosexualité f

**honest** adj ⟨answer, account⟩ sincère; ⟨person⟩ (truthful, trustworthy) honnête; (frank) franc/franche; **to be ~ with sb** être franc/ franche avec qn; **to be ~, I don't care** à dire vrai, ça m'est égal

**honestly** adv **(a)** (truthfully) honnêtement
**(b)** (really) vraiment
**(c)** (sincerely) franchement

**honesty** n honnêteté f

**honey** n **(a)** (miel) miel m
**(b)** (colloq) (dear) chéri/-e m/f

**honeycomb** n (in hive) rayon m de miel; (for sale) gâteau m de miel

**honeymoon** n lune f de miel; **to go on** ~ partir en voyage de noces

**honeysuckle** n chèvrefeuille m

**Hong Kong** pr n Hongkong m

**honk** vtr **to** ~ **one's horn** donner un coup de klaxon®

**honor** (US) = HONOUR

**honorable** (US) = HONOURABLE

**honorary** adj honoraire

**honour** (GB), **honor** (US) ⓵ n **(a)** honneur m; **in** ~ **of** en l'honneur de
**(b)** (in titles) **Your Honour** Votre Honneur
⓶ vtr honorer ⟨person, cheque, contract⟩; tenir ⟨promise, commitment⟩

**honourable** (GB), **honorable** (US) adj (gen) honorable; ⟨person, intention⟩ honnête

**honours degree** n: licence réservée aux meilleurs étudiants

**hood** n **(a)** (of coat) capuchon m; (balaclava) cagoule f
**(b)** (on cooker) hotte f
**(c)** (GB) (on car, pram) capote f
**(d)** (US Aut) (bonnet) capot m
**(e)** (US) (colloq) (gangster) truand m

**hoof** n sabot m

**hook** ⓵ n **(a)** (on wall, for picture) crochet m
**(b)** (on fishing line) hameçon m
**(c)** (fastener) agrafe f; ~**s and eyes** agrafes fpl
**(d) to take the phone off the** ~ décrocher le téléphone
**(e)** (in boxing) crochet m; **left** ~ crochet du gauche
⓶ vtr accrocher (**on, onto** à)
IDIOMS **to get sb off the** ~ tirer qn d'affaire

**hooked** adj **(a)** ⟨nose, beak⟩ crochu/-e
**(b) to be** ~ **on** se camer (colloq) à ⟨drugs⟩; être mordu/-e (colloq) de ⟨films, computer games⟩

**hooligan** n vandale m, voyou m; **soccer** ~ hooligan m

**hoop** n (ring) cerceau m; (in croquet) arceau m

**hooray** excl hourra!

**hoot** ⓵ n (of owl) (h)ululement m; (of car) coup m de klaxon®
⓶ vtr **to** ~ **one's horn** donner un coup de klaxon®
⓷ vi ⟨owl⟩ (h)ululer; ⟨car⟩ klaxonner; ⟨person, crowd⟩ (derisively) huer; **to** ~ **with laughter** éclater de rire

**hoover** vtr (GB) **to** ~ **a room** passer l'aspirateur dans une pièce

**Hoover®** n (GB) aspirateur m

**hop** ⓵ n (of frog, rabbit, child) bond m; (of bird) sautillement m
⓶ **hops** n pl houblon m
⓷ vi ⟨person⟩ sauter; (on one leg) sauter à cloche-pied; ⟨bird⟩ sautiller; **to** ~ **into bed/off a bus** sauter dans son lit/d'un bus

**hope** ⓵ n espoir m (**of** de); **to raise sb's** ~**s**

faire naître l'espoir chez qn; **to give up** ~ abandonner tout espoir; **to have no** ~ **of sth** n'avoir aucune chance de qch
⓶ vtr espérer (**that** que); **to** ~ **to do** espérer faire; **I (do)** ~ **so/not** j'espère (bien) que oui/que non
⓷ vi espérer; **to** ~ **for a reward** espérer avoir une récompense; **let's** ~ **for the best** espérons que tout se passera bien

**hopeful** adj ⟨person, expression⟩ plein/-e d'espoir; ⟨attitude, mood⟩ optimiste; ⟨sign, situation⟩ encourageant/-e

**hopefully** adv **(a)** (with luck) avec un peu de chance
**(b)** (with hope) ⟨say⟩ avec optimisme

**hopeless** adj **(a)** ⟨attempt, case, struggle⟩ désespéré/-e; **it's** ~! inutile!
**(b)** (colloq) (incompetent) nul/nulle (colloq)

**hopelessness** n **(a)** (despair) désespoir m
**(b)** (futility) futilité f (**of doing** de faire)

**hopscotch** n marelle f

**horizon** n horizon m; **on the** ~ à l'horizon; (figurative) en vue

**horizontal** adj horizontal/-e

**hormone** n hormone f

**hormone replacement therapy, HRT** n hormonothérapie f substitutive

**horn** n **(a)** (of animal, snail) corne f
**(b)** (Mus) cor m
**(c)** (of car) klaxon® m; (of ship) sirène f

**hornet** n frelon m

**horoscope** n horoscope m

**horrendous** adj épouvantable

**horrible** adj **(a)** (unpleasant) ⟨place, clothes, smell⟩ affreux/-euse; ⟨weather, food, person⟩ épouvantable; **to be** ~ **to sb** être méchant/-e avec qn
**(b)** (shocking) ⟨death, crime⟩ horrible

**horrid** adj affreux/-euse

**horrific** adj atroce

**horrify** vtr horrifier

**horrifying** adj ⟨experience, sight⟩ horrifiant/-e; ⟨behaviour⟩ effroyable

**horror** n horreur f (**at** devant); **to have a** ~ **of sth/of doing** avoir horreur de qch/de faire

**horror film** n film m d'épouvante

**horror story** n histoire f d'épouvante

**horse** n cheval m
IDIOMS **from the** ~**'s mouth** de source sûre
■ **horse about, horse around** chahuter

**horseback** n **on** ~ à cheval

**horseback riding** n (US) équitation f

**horse chestnut** n (tree) marronnier m (d'Inde); (fruit) marron m (d'Inde)

**horsefly** n taon m

**horsepower** n puissance f (en chevaux)

**horse race** n course f de chevaux

**horseracing** n courses fpl de chevaux, courses fpl hippiques

**horseradish sauce** n sauce f au raifort

**horseriding** n équitation f

**horseshoe** n fer m à cheval

**horseshow** n concours m hippique

**horticulture** n horticulture f

**hose**, **hosepipe** (GB) n (gen) tuyau m; (for garden) tuyau m d'arrosage; (fire) ~ lance f à incendie

**hospice** n établissement m de soins palliatifs

**hospitable** adj hospitalier/-ière (**to** envers)

**hospital** n hôpital m; **to be taken to** ~ être hospitalisé/-e; **in** ~ à l'hôpital

**hospitality** n hospitalité f

**hospitalize** vtr hospitaliser

**host** 1 n (a) (gen) hôte m
(b) (on radio, TV) animateur/-trice m/f
(c) (multitude) foule f (**of** de)
2 vtr organiser ⟨party⟩; animer ⟨show⟩

**hostage** n otage m; **to hold sb** ~ garder qn en otage

**host country** n pays m hôte or d'accueil

**hostel** n (for workers, refugees) foyer m; (**youth**) ~ auberge f de jeunesse

**hostess** n hôtesse f

**hostile** adj hostile (**to** à)

**hostility** n hostilité f (**towards** à l'égard de)

**hot** adj (a) (gen) chaud/-e; **it's** ~ **here** il fait chaud ici; **to be** or **feel** ~ ⟨person⟩ avoir chaud; **to go** ~ **and cold** (with fever) être fiévreux/-euse; (with fear) avoir des sueurs froides
(b) (Culin) ⟨mustard, spice⟩ fort/-e; ⟨sauce, dish⟩ épicé/-e
(c) **to be** ~ **on sb's trail** être sur les talons de qn

**hot air balloon** n montgolfière f

**hotbed** n foyer m (**of** de)

**hot dog** n hot dog m

**hotel** n hôtel m

**hotelier**, **hotelkeeper** n (GB) hôtelier/-ière m/f

**hot-headed** adj ⟨person⟩ impétueux/-euse

**hotline** n (a) (for orders, tickets) ligne f ouverte, permanence f téléphonique
(b) (Mil, Pol) téléphone m rouge

**hotplate** n plaque f de cuisson

**hot seat** n
IDIOMS **to be in the** ~ être sur la sellette

**hotshot** n gros bonnet m (colloq)

**hot spot** n (colloq) (a) (trouble spot) point m chaud
(b) (sunny country) pays m chaud

**hot-tempered** adj colérique

**hot water bottle** n bouillotte f

**hound** 1 n chien m de chasse
2 vtr harceler, traquer ⟨person⟩
■ **hound out** chasser (**of** de)

**hour** n heure f; **£10 per** ~ 10 livres sterling (de) l'heure; **to be paid by the** ~ être payé/-e à l'heure; **60 km an hour** 60 km à l'heure; **in the early** ~s au petit matin

**hourly** 1 adj horaire
2 adv ⟨arrive, phone⟩ toutes les heures

**house** 1 n (a) (gen) maison f; **at my/his** ~ chez moi/lui; **to go to sb's** ~ aller chez qn; **on the** ~ aux frais de la maison
(b) (in theatre) (audience) assistance f; (auditorium) salle f; (performance) séance f
(c) (music) house music f
2 vtr loger ⟨person⟩; abriter ⟨collection⟩

**houseboat** n péniche f aménagée

**housebound** adj confiné/-e chez soi

**house call** n visite f à domicile

**household** 1 n maison f; (in survey) ménage m; **head of the** ~ chef m de famille
2 adj ⟨expenses⟩ du ménage; ⟨chore⟩ ménager/-ère

**household appliance** n appareil m électroménager

**householder** n (a) (occupier) occupant/-e m/f
(b) (owner) propriétaire mf

**household name** n **he's a** ~ il est célèbre

**house husband** n homme m au foyer

**housekeeper** n gouvernante f

**housekeeping** n (money) argent m du ménage

**House of Commons** n (GB) Chambre f des communes

**House of Lords** n (GB) Chambre f des lords, Chambre f haute

**House of Representatives** n (US) Chambre f des représentants

**houseplant** n plante f d'intérieur

**house-proud** adj fier/fière de son intérieur

**Houses of Parliament** n pl (GB) Parlement m Britannique

**house-to-house** adj ⟨search⟩ de maison en maison

**house-trained** adj (GB) propre

**house-warming (party)** n pendaison f de crémaillère

**housewife** n femme f au foyer; ménagère f

**housework** n travaux mpl ménagers; **to do the** ~ faire le ménage

**housing** n logements mpl

**housing estate** n (GB) cité f

**hover** vi ⟨eagle⟩ planer; ⟨helicopter⟩ faire du surplace; **to** ~ **around sb/sth** tourner autour de qn/qch

**hovercraft** n aéroglisseur m

**how** 1 adv (a) (gen) comment ~ **are you?** comment allez-vous?; ~**'s your brother?** comment va ton frère?; ~ **are things?** comment ça va?; ~ **do you do!** enchanté!; **to know** ~ **to do** savoir faire
(b) (in number, quantity questions) ~ **much is this?** combien ça coûte?; ~ **much do you weigh?** combien pèses-tu?; ~ **many people?** combien de personnes?; ~ **many times** combien de fois?; ~ **long will it take?** combien de temps cela va-t-il prendre?; ~ **tall are you?** combien mesures-tu?; ~ **far is** ····▷

it? c'est à quelle distance?; ~ old is she?
quel âge a-t-elle?; ~ soon can you get here?
dans combien de temps peux-tu être ici?
**(c)** (in exclamations) ~ wonderful/awful! c'est
fantastique/affreux!; ~ clever of you! comme
c'est intelligent de ta part!
2 (colloq) **how come** *phr* ~ come?
pourquoi?; ~ come you always get the best
place? comment ça se fait que tu aies
toujours la meilleure place?

**however** 1 *conj* (nevertheless) toutefois,
cependant
2 *adv* (no matter how) ~ hard I try, I can't j'ai
beau essayer, je n'y arrive pas; ~ difficult
the task is aussi difficile que soit la tâche; ~
small she may be si petite soit-elle; ~ much
it costs quel qu'en soit le prix; ~ long it
takes quel que soit le temps que ça prendra;
~ you like comme tu veux

**howl** 1 *n* hurlement *m*
2 *vi* hurler

**HQ** *n* (Mil) (*abbr* = **headquarters**) QG *m*

**HTML** *n* (*abbr* = **HyperText Markup
Language**) HTML *m*

**hub** *n* (of wheel) moyeu *m*; (figurative) centre *m*

**hubcap** *n* enjoliveur *m*

**huddle** *vi* to ~ around se presser autour de
⟨fire, radio⟩; to ~ together se serrer les uns
contre les autres

**hue** *n* **(a)** (colour) couleur *f*, teinte *f*
**(b)** ~ and cry tollé *m*

**huff** (colloq) 1 *n* in a ~ vexé/-e
2 *vi* souffler

**hug** 1 *n* étreinte *f*; to give sb a ~ serrer qn
dans ses bras
2 *vtr* **(a)** (embrace) serrer [qn] dans ses bras
**(b)** to ~ the coast/kerb serrer la côte/le
trottoir

**huge** *adj* ⟨object, garden, city, country⟩
immense; ⟨person, animal⟩ gigantesque;
⟨appetite, success⟩ énorme; ⟨debts, sum⟩ gros/
grosse (*before n*)

**hugely** *adv* **(a)** (emphatic) extrêmement
**(b)** ⟨increase, vary⟩ considérablement; ⟨enjoy⟩
énormément

**hull** *n* (of ship, plane) coque *f*; (of tank) carcasse
*f*

**hum** 1 *n* (of insect, traffic, voices)
bourdonnement *m*; (of machinery)
ronronnement *m*
2 *vi* ⟨person⟩ fredonner; ⟨insect, aircraft⟩
bourdonner; ⟨machine⟩ ronronner

**human** 1 *n* humain *m*
2 *adj* ⟨body, behaviour⟩ humain/-e;
⟨characteristic, rights⟩ de l'homme

**human being** *n* être *m* humain

**humane** *adj* ⟨person⟩ humain/-e; ⟨act⟩
d'humanité

**human interest story** *n* histoire *f*
vécue

**humanitarian** *adj* humanitaire

**humanity** *n* humanité *f*

**human nature** *n* nature *f* humaine

**human resources manager** *n*
responsable *mf* de la gestion des ressources
humaines

**humble** *adj* (gen) modeste; ⟨person⟩ humble

**humid** *adj* ⟨climate⟩ humide; ⟨weather⟩
lourd/-e

**humidity** *n* humidité *f*

**humiliate** *vtr* humilier

**humiliating** *adj* humiliant/-e

**humiliation** *n* humiliation *f*

**humorous** *adj* **(a)** ⟨story, book⟩
humoristique
**(b)** ⟨person, look⟩ plein/-e d'humour

**humour** (GB), **humor** (US) 1 *n* **(a)** (wit)
humour *m*; a good sense of ~ le sens de
l'humour
**(b)** (mood) humeur *f*; to be in good/bad ~
être de bonne/mauvaise humeur
2 *vtr* amadouer ⟨person⟩

**hump** *n* bosse *f*

**hunch** 1 *n* intuition *f*
2 *vtr* to ~ one's shoulders rentrer les
épaules

**hunched** *adj* ⟨back, figure⟩ voûté/-e;
⟨shoulders⟩ rentré/-e

**hundred** 1 *n* cent *m*; two ~ deux cents;
two ~ and one deux cent un; in nineteen ~
en mille neuf cents; in nineteen ~ and three
en mille neuf cent trois; ~s of times des
centaines de fois
2 *pron, det* cent; two ~ euros deux cents
euros; two ~ and five euros deux cent cinq
euros; about a ~ people une centaine de
personnes

**hundredth** *n, adj, adv* centième (*mf*)

**hundredweight** *n* (GB) = *50.80 kg*; (US) =
*45.36 kg*

**Hungarian** 1 *n* **(a)** (person) Hongrois/-e
*m/f*
**(b)** (language) hongrois *m*
2 *adj* hongrois/-e

**Hungary** *pr n* Hongrie *f*

**hunger** *n* faim *f*

**hunger strike** *n* grève *f* de la faim

**hung-over** *adj* (colloq) to be ~ avoir la
gueule de bois (colloq)

**hungry** *adj* to be ~ avoir faim; to make sb
~ donner faim à qn; ~ for assoiffé/-e de
⟨success, power⟩

**hunk** *n* **(a)** (of bread, cheese) gros morceau *m*
**(b)** (colloq) (man) beau mec *m* (colloq)

**hunt** 1 *n* **(a)** (for animals) chasse *f* (for à)
**(b)** (search) recherche *f* (for de)
2 *vtr* rechercher ⟨person⟩; chasser ⟨animal⟩
3 *vi* **(a)** (for prey) chasser
**(b)** (search) to ~ for sth chercher [qch]
partout ⟨object, person⟩

**hunter** *n* (person) chasseur/-euse *m/f*

**hunting** *n* chasse *f* (of à); to go ~ aller à la
chasse

**hunt saboteur** *n* opposant/-e *m/f* à la
chasse au renard

**hurdle** *n* **(a)** (Sport) haie *f*

(b) (obstacle) obstacle *m*

**hurl** *vtr* (a) (throw) lancer (**at** sur)
(b) (shout) **to ~ insults at sb** accabler qn d'injures

**hurrah**, **hurray** *n*, *excl* hourra (*m*)

**hurricane** *n* ouragan *m*

**hurry** ⓵ *n* hâte *f*, empressement *m*; **to be in a ~** être pressé/-e (**to do** de faire); **to leave in a ~** partir à la hâte
⓶ *vtr* terminer [qch] à la hâte ⟨*meal, task*⟩; bousculer ⟨*person*⟩
⓷ *vi* se dépêcher (**over doing** de faire); **to ~ out** sortir précipitamment
∎ **hurry up** se dépêcher; **~ up!** dépêche-toi!

**hurt** ⓵ *adj* (gen) blessé/-e; **to feel ~** être peiné/-e
⓶ *vtr* (a) (injure) **to ~ oneself** se blesser, se faire mal; **to ~ one's back** se blesser *or* se faire mal au dos
(b) (cause pain to) faire mal à; **you're ~ing my arm** vous me faites mal au bras
(c) (emotionally) blesser; (offend) froisser; **to ~ sb's feelings** blesser quelqu'un
⓷ *vi* (a) (be painful) faire mal; **my throat ~s** j'ai mal à la gorge
(b) (emotionally) blesser

**hurtful** *adj* blessant/-e

**hurtle** *vi* **to ~ down sth** dévaler qch; **to ~ along a road** foncer sur une route

**husband** *n* mari *m*; (on form) époux *m*

**hush** ⓵ *n* silence *m*
⓶ *excl* chut!
∎ **hush up**: ¶ **~ [sth] up** étouffer ⟨*affair*⟩
¶ **~ [sb] up** faire taire ⟨*person*⟩

**hush-hush** *adj* (colloq) très confidentiel/-ielle

**hustle** ⓵ *n* **~ (and bustle)** (lively) effervescence *f*; (tiring) agitation *f*
⓶ *vtr* pousser, bousculer ⟨*person*⟩

**hut** *n* (gen) cabane *f*; (dwelling) hutte *f*; (on beach) cabine *f* (de plage)

**hutch** *n* (for rabbits) clapier *m*

**hydrant** *n* (*also* **fire ~**) bouche *f* d'incendie

**hydraulic** *adj* hydraulique

**hydroelectricity** *n* hydroélectricité *f*

**hydrofoil** *n* (a) (craft) hydroptère *m*
(b) (foil) aile *f* portante

**hydrogen** *n* hydrogène *m*

**hyena** *n* hyène *f*

**hygiene** *n* hygiène *f*

**hygienic** *adj* hygiénique

**hymn** *n* cantique *m*

**hype** *n* (colloq) battage *m* publicitaire
∎ **hype up** faire du battage pour ⟨*film, star, book*⟩; gonfler ⟨*story*⟩

**hyper** *adj* (colloq) surexcité/-e

**hyperactive** *adj* hyperactif/-ive

**hyperlink** *n* lien *m* (hypertext)

**hypermarket** *n* (GB) hypermarché *m*

**hypertext** *n* hypertext *m*

**hyperventilate** *vi* être en hyperventilation

**hyphen** *n* trait *m* d'union

**hypnosis** *n* hypnose *f*

**hypnotherapy** *n* hypnothérapie *f*

**hypnotist** *n* hypnotiseur *m*

**hypnotize** *vtr* hypnotiser

**hypoallergenic** *adj* hypoallergénique

**hypocrisy** *n* hypocrisie *f*

**hypocrite** *n* hypocrite *mf*

**hypocritical** *adj* hypocrite

**hypodermic** *adj* hypodermique

**hypothermia** *n* hypothermie *f*

**hypothesis** *n* hypothèse *f*

**hysteria** *n* hystérie *f*

**hysterical** *adj* (a) ⟨*person, behaviour*⟩ hystérique
(b) (colloq) (funny) délirant/-e

**hysterics** *n* (a) (fit) crise *f* de nerfs; **to have ~** avoir une crise de nerfs
(b) (laughter) **to be in ~** rire aux larmes

# I i

**i, I¹** *n* i, I *m*

**I²** *pron* je, j'; **I am called Frances** je m'appelle Frances; **I closed the door** j'ai fermé la porte; **he's a student but I'm not** il est étudiant mais moi pas; **he and I went to the cinema** lui et moi sommes allés au cinéma

**ice** ⓵ *n* glace *f*; (on roads) verglas *m*; (in drink) glaçons *mpl*
⓶ *vtr* glacer ⟨*cake*⟩
⓷ **iced** *pp adj* ⟨*water*⟩ avec des glaçons; **~d tea** thé glacé
∎ **ice over** ⟨*windscreen, river*⟩ se couvrir de glace

**iceberg** *n* iceberg *m*

**icebox** *n* (a) (GB) (freezer compartment) freezer *m*
(b) (US) (fridge) réfrigérateur *m*

**ice-cold** *adj* glacé/-e

**ice cream** *n* glace *f*

**ice-cube** *n* glaçon *m*

**ice hockey** *n* hockey *m* sur glace

**Iceland** *pr n* Islande *f*

**Icelandic** ⓵ *n* (language) islandais *m*
⓶ *adj* ⟨*people, customs*⟩ islandais/-e

**ice rink** n patinoire f
**ice-skate** ⟦1⟧ n patin m à glace
⟦2⟧ vi faire du patin m à glace
**ice-skating** n patinage m sur glace
**icicle** n stalactite f (de glace)
**icing** n glaçage m
**icing sugar** n (GB) sucre m glace
**icon** n icône f
**iconize** vtr (Comput) iconiser
**icy** adj (a) ⟨road⟩ verglacé/-e
(b) ⟨wind⟩ glacial/-e; ⟨hands⟩ glacé/-e
(c) ⟨look, reception⟩ glacial/-e
**ID** n pièce f d'identité
**ID card** n carte f d'identité
**idea** n idée f (about, on sur); I have no ~ je
n'ai aucune idée; to have no ~ why/how ne
pas savoir pourquoi/comment; I've an ~ that
he might be lying j'ai dans l'idée qu'il ment
**ideal** ⟦1⟧ n idéal m
⟦2⟧ adj idéal/-e
**idealism** n idéalisme m
**idealist** n idéaliste mf
**idealistic** adj idéaliste
**idealize** vtr idéaliser
**ideally** adv (a) (preferably) ~, the tests
should be free l'idéal serait que les examens
soient gratuits; ~, we'd like to stay l'idéal
pour nous, ce serait de rester
(b) (perfectly) ~ situated idéalement situé/-e
**identical** adj identique (to, with à)
**identical twin** n vrai jumeau/vraie
jumelle m/f
**identification** n (a) identification f (with
à)
(b) (proof of identity) pièce f d'identité
**identify** ⟦1⟧ vtr identifier (as comme étant;
to à); (pick out) distinguer; to ~ sb/sth with
sb/sth identifier qn/qch à qn/qch
⟦2⟧ vi to ~ with s'identifier à
**identikit** n (also **Identikit**®)
portrait-robot m
**identity** n identité f
**identity bracelet** n gourmette f
**identity card** n carte f d'identité
**identity parade** n (GB) séance f
d'identification
**ideological** adj idéologique
**ideology** n idéologie f
**idiom** n (a) (phrase) idiome m
(b) (language) (of speakers) parler m; (of theatre,
sport) langue f; (of music) style m
**idiomatic** adj idiomatique
**idiosyncrasy** n particularité f
**idiosyncratic** adj particulier/-ière
**idiot** n idiot/-e m/f
**idiotic** adj bête
**idle** ⟦1⟧ adj (a) (lazy) ⟨person⟩ paresseux/-euse
(b) ⟨boast, threat⟩ vain/-e; ⟨curiosity⟩
oiseux/-euse; ⟨chatter⟩ inutile
(c) (without occupation) ⟨person⟩ oisif/-ive; ⟨day,
hour, moment⟩ de loisir
(d) ⟨dock, mine⟩ à l'arrêt; ⟨machine⟩ arrêté/-e

⟦2⟧ vi ⟨engine⟩ tourner au ralenti
■ **idle away** passer [qch] à ne rien faire
⟨day, time⟩
**idol** n idole f
**idolize** vtr adorer ⟨friend, parent⟩; idolâtrer
⟨star⟩
**idyllic** adj idyllique
**ie** (abbr = **that is**) c.-à-d
**if** ⟦1⟧ conj (a) si; ~ I won a lot of money, I
would travel si je gagnais beaucoup d'argent,
je voyagerais; ~ I had known, I would have
told you si j'avais su, je te l'aurais dit; ~ I
were you, I... (moi) à ta place, je...; ~ not
sinon; I wonder ~ they will come je me
demande s'ils vont venir; do you mind ~ I
smoke? cela vous dérange si je fume?; what
~ he died? et s'il mourait?
(b) (although) bien que; it's a good shop, ~ a
little expensive c'est un bon magasin, bien
qu'un peu cher
⟦2⟧ **if only** phr (a) (I wish) si seulement; ~
only I had known! si (seulement) j'avais su!
(b) ~ only because (of) ne serait-ce qu'à
cause de; ~ only for a moment ne serait-ce
que pour un instant
**iffy** adj (colloq) (dubious) suspect/-e
**igloo** n igloo m, iglou m
**ignite** ⟦1⟧ vtr faire exploser ⟨fuel⟩;
enflammer ⟨material⟩
⟦2⟧ vi ⟨petrol, gas⟩ s'enflammer; ⟨rubbish,
timber⟩ prendre feu
**ignition** n (a) (system) allumage m
(b) (also ~ **switch**) contact m
**ignition key** n clé f de contact
**ignorance** n ignorance f
**ignorant** adj (of a subject) ignorant/-e;
(uneducated) inculte; to be ~ about tout
ignorer de ⟨subject⟩; to be ~ of ignorer
⟨possibilities⟩
**ignore** vtr ignorer ⟨person⟩; ne pas relever
⟨mistake, remark⟩; ne pas tenir compte de
⟨feeling, fact⟩; ne pas suivre ⟨advice⟩; se
désintéresser complètement de ⟨problem⟩
**ill** ⟦1⟧ n mal m; to wish sb ~ souhaiter du
mal à qn
⟦2⟧ adj malade; I feel ~ je ne me sens pas
bien; to be taken ~, to fall ~ tomber malade
⟦3⟧ adv he is ~ suited to the post il n'est
guère fait pour ce poste; to speak ~ of sb
dire du mal de qn
**ill at ease** adj gêné/-e, mal à l'aise
**illegal** ⟦1⟧ n (US) immigrant/-e m/f
clandestin/-e
⟦2⟧ adj (gen) illégal/-e; ⟨parking⟩ illicite;
⟨immigrant⟩ clandestin/-e; (Sport)
irrégulier/-ière
**illegally** adv illégalement
**illegible** adj illisible
**illegitimate** adj illégitime
**ill-equipped** adj mal équipé/-e
**ill-fitting** adj ⟨garment, shoe⟩ qui va mal
**ill-health** n mauvaise santé f
**illicit** adj illicite
**ill-informed** adj mal informé/-e

**illiterate** n, adj analphabète (mf)

**illness** n maladie f

**illogical** adj illogique

**ill-treatment** n mauvais traitements mpl

**illuminate** vtr éclairer

**illuminated** adj ⟨sign⟩ lumineux/-euse

**illumination** n (lighting) éclairage m

**illuminations** n pl (GB) illuminations fpl

**illusion** n illusion f; **to have no ∼s** about sth ne pas se faire d'illusions sur qch; **to be** or **to labour under the ∼ that** s'imaginer que

**illustrate** vtr illustrer

**illustration** n illustration f

**illustrator** n illustrateur/-trice m/f

**ill will** n rancune f

**image** n (gen) image f; (of company, personality) image f de marque; **he is the (spitting) ∼ of you** c'est toi tout craché

**image-conscious** adj conscient/-e de son image de marque

**image maker** n professionnel/-elle m/f de l'image de marque

**image processing** n traitement m de l'image

**imagery** n images fpl

**imaginary** adj imaginaire

**imagination** n imagination f

**imaginative** adj ⟨person, performance⟩ plein d'imagination; ⟨mind⟩ imaginatif/-ive; ⟨solution, device⟩ ingénieux/-ieuse

**imagine** vtr (a) (visualize, picture) (s')imaginer; **to ∼ being rich/king** s'imaginer riche/roi; **you must have ∼d it** ce doit être un effet de ton imagination
(b) (suppose) supposer, imaginer (**that** que)

**imbalance** n déséquilibre m

**imbecile** n, adj imbécile (mf)

**imitate** vtr imiter

**imitation** ① n imitation f
② adj ⟨snow⟩ artificiel/-ielle; **∼ fur** imitation f fourrure; **∼ jewel** faux bijou m; **∼ leather** similicuir m

**imitator** n imitateur/-trice m/f

**immaculate** adj ⟨dress, manners⟩ impeccable; ⟨performance⟩ parfait/-e

**immaterial** adj (a) (unimportant) sans importance
(b) (intangible) immatériel/-ielle

**immature** adj (a) ⟨plant⟩ qui n'est pas arrivé à maturité
(b) (childish) immature; **don't be so ∼!** ne te conduis pas comme un enfant!

**immediate** adj (a) ⟨effect, reaction⟩ immédiat/-e; ⟨thought⟩ premier/-ière (before n)
(b) ⟨concern, goal⟩ premier/-ière (before n); ⟨problem, crisis⟩ urgent/-e
(c) ⟨vicinity⟩ immédiat/-e; **his ∼ family** ses proches; **in the ∼ future** dans l'avenir proche

**immediately** adv immédiatement; **∼ after/before** juste avant/après

**immense** adj immense

**immerse** vtr plonger (**in** dans)

**immersion course** n (GB) cours m avec immersion linguistique

**immigrant** n, adj (recent) immigrant/-e (m/f); (established) immigré/-e (m/f)

**immigration** n immigration f; **∼ laws** lois fpl sur l'immigration

**immigration control** n (system) contrôle m de l'immigration

**imminent** adj imminent/-e

**immobile** adj immobile

**immobilize** vtr paralyser ⟨traffic, organization⟩; immobiliser ⟨engine, patient, limb⟩

**immobilizer** n système m antidémarrage

**immoral** adj immoral/-e

**immorality** n immoralité f

**immortal** n, adj immortel/-elle (m/f)

**immortality** n immortalité f

**immortalize** vtr immortaliser

**immune** adj (a) (Med) ⟨person⟩ immunisé/-e (**to** contre); ⟨reaction, system⟩ immunitaire
(b) (oblivious) **∼ to** insensible à
(c) **to be ∼ from** être à l'abri de ⟨attack, arrest⟩; être exempté/-e de ⟨tax⟩

**immunity** n immunité f (**to, against** contre)

**immunize** vtr immuniser

**impact** n (a) (effect) impact m (**on** sur); **to make an ∼** faire de l'effet
(b) (of hammer, vehicle) choc m; (of bomb, bullet) impact m; **on ∼** au moment de l'impact

**impair** vtr affecter ⟨performance⟩; diminuer ⟨ability⟩; affaiblir ⟨hearing, vision⟩; détériorer ⟨health⟩

**impaired** adj ⟨hearing, vision⟩ affaibli/-e; **his speech is ∼** il a des problèmes d'élocution

**impart** vtr (a) transmettre ⟨knowledge, enthusiasm⟩ (**to** à); communiquer ⟨information⟩ (**to** à)
(b) donner ⟨atmosphere⟩

**impartial** adj ⟨advice, judge⟩ impartial/-e; ⟨account⟩ objectif/-ive

**impassable** adj ⟨obstacle⟩ infranchissable; ⟨road⟩ impraticable

**impassive** adj impassible

**impatience** n (a) (eagerness) impatience f (**to do** de faire)
(b) (irritation) agacement m (**with** à l'égard de; **at** devant)

**impatient** adj (a) (eager) ⟨person⟩ impatient/-e; ⟨gesture, tone⟩ d'impatience; **to be ∼ to do** être impatient/-e or avoir hâte de faire
(b) (irritable) agacé/-e (**at** par); **to be/get ∼ with sb** s'impatienter contre qn

**impeach** vtr mettre [qn] en accusation

**impeccable** adj ⟨behaviour⟩ irréprochable; ⟨appearance⟩ impeccable

**impede** vtr entraver

**impending** adj imminent/-e

**impenetrable** *adj* impénétrable
**imperative** ⓵ *n* impératif *m*
⓶ *adj* ⟨need⟩ urgent/-e; ⟨tone⟩
impérieux/-ieuse
**imperceptible** *adj* imperceptible
**imperfect** ⓵ *n* imparfait *m*
⓶ *adj* ⟨goods⟩ défectueux/-euse; ⟨logic,
knowledge⟩ imparfait/-e; **the ~ tense**
l'imparfait *m*
**imperial** *adj* (a) (gen) impérial/-e
(b) (GB) ⟨measure⟩ conforme aux normes
britanniques
**imperious** *adj* impérieux/-ieuse
**impersonal** *adj* impersonnel/-elle
**impersonate** *vtr* (imitate) imiter; ( pretend to
be) se faire passer pour ⟨police officer⟩
**impersonator** *n* imitateur/-trice *m/f*
**impertinent** *adj* impertinent/-e (**to**
envers)
**impervious** *adj* (to charm, suffering)
indifférent/-e (**to** à); (to demands) imperméable
(**to** à)
**impetuous** *adj* ⟨person⟩ impétueux/-euse;
⟨action⟩ impulsif/-ive
**impetus** *n* (a) impulsion *f* (**to** à)
(b) (momentum) élan *m*; **to gain/lose ~**
prendre/perdre de l'élan
**impinge** *vi* **to ~ on** (restrict) empiéter sur;
(affect) affecter
**implacable** *adj* implacable
**implant** ⓵ *n* implant *m*
⓶ *vtr* implanter (**in** dans)
**implausible** *adj* peu plausible
**implement** ⓵ *n* (gen) instrument *m*; (tool)
outil *m*; **farm ~s** outillage *m* agricole
⓶ *vtr* exécuter ⟨contract, decision, idea⟩;
mettre [qch] en application ⟨law⟩
**implementation** *n* (of contract, idea)
exécution *f*; (of law, policy) mise *f* en
application; (Comput) implémentation *f*
**implicate** *vtr* impliquer (**in** dans)
**implication** *n* (a) ( possible consequence)
implication *f*
(b) (suggestion) insinuation *f*
**implicit** *adj* (a) (implied) implicite (**in** dans)
(b) ⟨faith, trust⟩ absolu/-e
**imply** *vtr* (a) ⟨person⟩ (insinuate) insinuer
(**that** que); (make known) laisser entendre (**that**
que)
(b) (mean) ⟨argument⟩ impliquer; ⟨term,
word⟩ laisser supposer (**that** que)
**impolite** *adj* impoli/-e (**to** envers)
**import** ⓵ *n* importation *f*
⓶ *vtr* importer (**from** de; **to** en)
**importance** *n* importance *f*
**important** *adj* important/-e; **it is ~ that** il
est important que (+ *subjunctive*); **his
children are very ~ to him** ses enfants
comptent beaucoup pour lui
**importer** *n* importateur/-trice *m/f*
**impose** ⓵ *vtr* imposer ⟨embargo, rule⟩ (**on
sb** à qn; **on sth** sur qch); infliger ⟨sanction⟩

(**on** à); **to ~ a fine on sb** frapper qn d'une
amende; **to ~ a tax on tobacco** imposer le
tabac
⓶ *vi* s'imposer; **to ~ on sb's kindness**
abuser de la bonté de qn
**imposing** *adj* ⟨person⟩ imposant/-e; ⟨sight⟩
impressionnant/-e
**impossible** ⓵ *n* **the ~** l'impossible *m*
⓶ *adj* impossible; **to make it ~ for sb to do**
mettre qn dans l'impossibilité de faire
**impotent** *adj* impuissant/-e
**impound** *vtr* emmener [qch] à la fourrière
⟨vehicle⟩; confisquer ⟨goods⟩
**impractical** *adj* ⟨suggestion, idea⟩ peu
réaliste; **to be ~** ⟨person⟩ manquer d'esprit
pratique
**imprecise** *adj* imprécis/-e
**impress** ⓵ *vtr* (a) impressionner ⟨person⟩
(**with** par; **by doing** en faisant); **they were
~ed** ça leur a fait bonne impression
(b) **to ~ sth (up)on sb** faire bien
comprendre qch à qn
⓶ *vi* faire bonne impression
**impression** *n* (a) (gen) impression *f*; **to be
under** *or* **have the ~ that** avoir l'impression
que; **to make a good/bad ~** faire bonne/
mauvaise impression (**on** sur)
(b) (imitation) imitation *f*; **to do ~s** faire des
imitations
**impressionable** *adj* influençable
**impressive** *adj* (gen) impressionnant/-e;
⟨building, sight⟩ imposant/-e
**imprint** ⓵ *n* empreinte *f*
⓶ *vtr* (a) (fix) graver (**on** dans)
(b) ( print) imprimer (**on** sur)
**imprison** *vtr* emprisonner
**imprisonment** *n* emprisonnement *m*
**improbable** *adj* (unlikely to happen)
improbable; (unlikely to be true)
invraisemblable
**impromptu** *adj* impromptu/-e
**improper** *adj* (dishonest) irrégulier/-ière;
(indecent) indécent/-e; (incorrect) impropre,
abusif/-ive
**improve** ⓵ *vtr* (gen) améliorer; augmenter
⟨chances⟩; **to ~ one's mind** se cultiver
(l'esprit)
⓶ *vi* (a) s'améliorer
(b) **to ~ on** améliorer ⟨score⟩; renchérir sur
⟨offer⟩
**improvement** *n* (a) amélioration *f* (**in, of,
to** de); **the new edition is an ~ on the old one**
la nouvelle édition est bien meilleure que
l'ancienne
(b) (in house) aménagement *m*; **home ~s**
aménagements *mpl* du domicile
**improvise** ⓵ *vtr* improviser; **an ~d table**
une table de fortune
⓶ *vi* improviser
**impudent** *adj* insolent/-e, impudent/-e
**impulse** *n* impulsion *f*; **to have a sudden ~
to do** avoir une envie soudaine de faire; **on
(an) ~** sur un coup de tête
**impulse buy** *n* achat *m* d'impulsion

**impulsive** adj (spontaneous) spontané/-e; (rash) impulsif/-ive

**impure** adj impur/-e

**in** ① prep **(a)** (inside) dans; ~ **the box** dans la boîte; ~ **the newspaper** dans le journal; ~ **the school/town** dans l'école/la ville; ~ **school/town** à l'école/en ville; ~ **the country(side)** à la campagne; ~ **the photo** sur la photo; **chicken** ~ **a white wine sauce** du poulet à la sauce au vin blanc; ~ **Rome** à Rome; ~ **France/Spain** en France/Espagne; ~ **Canada/the United States** au Canada/aux États-Unis
**(b)** (showing occupation, activity) dans; ~ **insurance** dans les assurances; **to be** ~ **politics** faire de la politique; **to be** ~ **the team** faire partie de l'équipe
**(c)** (present in) chez; **it's rare** ~ **cats** c'est rare chez les chats; **he hasn't got it** ~ **him to succeed** il n'est pas fait pour réussir
**(d)** (showing manner, medium) en; ~ **Greek** en grec; ~ **B flat** en si bémol; ~ **a skirt** en jupe; **dressed** ~ **black** habillé/-e en noir; ~ **pencil/ink** au crayon/à l'encre; **to speak** ~ **a whisper** chuchoter; ~ **pairs** par deux; ~ **a circle** en cercle; ~ **the rain** sous la pluie
**(e)** (as regards) **rich** ~ **minerals** riche en minéraux; **deaf** ~ **one ear** sourd/-e d'une oreille; **10 cm** ~ **length** 10 cm de long
**(f)** (because of) dans; ~ **his hurry** dans sa précipitation; ~ **the confusion** dans la mêlée
**(g)** (with present participle) en; ~ **accepting** en acceptant; ~ **doing so** en faisant cela
**(h)** (with superlatives) de; **the tallest tower** ~ **the world** la plus grande tour du monde
**(i)** (in ratios) **a gradient of 1** ~ **4** une pente de 25%; **a tax of 20 pence** ~ **the pound** une taxe de 20 pence par livre sterling; **to have a one** ~ **five chance** avoir une chance sur cinq
**(j)** (with numbers) **she's** ~ **her twenties** elle a entre vingt et trente ans; **to cut sth** ~ **three** couper qch en trois; **the temperature was** ~ **the thirties** il faisait dans les trente degrés
**(k)** (during) ~ **May** en mai; ~ **1963** en 1963; ~ **summer** en été; ~ **the night** pendant la nuit; ~ **the morning(s)** le matin; **at four** ~ **the morning** à quatre heures du matin; ~ **the twenties** dans les années 20
**(l)** (within) ~ **ten minutes** en dix minutes; **I'll be back** ~ **half an hour** je serai de retour dans une demi-heure
**(m)** (for) depuis; **it hasn't rained** ~ **weeks** il n'a pas plu depuis des semaines
② adv **(a)** (to come) ~ entrer; **to run** ~ entrer en courant; **to ask** or **invite sb** ~ faire entrer qn
**(b)** (at home) **to be** ~ être là; **to stay** ~ rester à la maison
**(c)** (arrived) **the train is** ~ le train est en gare; **the ferry is** ~ le ferry est à quai
**(d) the tide is** ~ c'est marée haute
**(e)** (Sport) **the ball is** ~ la balle est bonne
**(f)** (in supply) **we don't have any** ~ nous n'en avons pas en stock; **to get some beer** ~ aller chercher de la bière

③ adj (colloq) **to be** ~, **to be the** ~ **thing** être à la mode
④ **in and out** phr **to come** ~ **and out** entrer et sortir; **to weave** ~ **and out of** se faufiler entre ⟨traffic, tables⟩
**IDIOMS he's** ~ **for a shock/surprise** il va avoir un choc/être surpris

**inability** n incapacité f (**to do** de faire)

**inaccessible** adj (out of reach) inaccessible; (hard to understand) peu accessible (**to** à)

**inaccuracy** n **(a)** (of report, estimate) inexactitude f
**(b)** (error) inexactitude f

**inaccurate** adj inexact/-e

**inactive** adj inactif/-ive

**inadequate** adj insuffisant/-e (**for** pour)

**inadvisable** adj inopportun/-e, à déconseiller

**inane** adj ⟨person, conversation⟩ idiot/-e; ⟨programme⟩ débile (colloq)

**inanimate** adj inanimé/-e

**inappropriate** adj **(a)** ⟨behaviour⟩ inconvenant/-e, peu convenable; ⟨remark⟩ inopportun/-e
**(b)** ⟨advice, word⟩ qui n'est pas approprié

**inarticulate** adj **(a) to be** ~ ne pas savoir s'exprimer
**(b)** ⟨mumble⟩ inarticulé/-e; ⟨speech⟩ inintelligible

**inasmuch: inasmuch as** phr (insofar as) dans la mesure où; (seeing as) vu que

**inattentive** adj ⟨pupil⟩ inattentif/-ive

**inaudible** adj inaudible

**inauguration** n (of exhibition) inauguration f; (of president) investiture f

**in-between** adj intermédiaire

**inbuilt** adj intrinsèque

**incapable** adj incapable (**of doing** de faire)

**incapacitate** vtr ⟨accident, illness⟩ immobiliser

**incendiary device** n engin m incendiaire

**incense** n encens m

**incensed** adj outré/-e (**at de; by** par)

**incentive** n **(a) to give sb the** ~ **to do** donner envie à qn de faire; **there is no** ~ **for people to save** rien n'incite les gens à faire des économies
**(b)** (also **cash** ~) prime f

**incentive scheme** n système m de primes d'encouragement

**incessant** adj incessant/-e

**incessantly** adv sans cesse

**incest** n inceste m

**incestuous** adj incestueux/-euse

**inch** n **(a)** pouce m (= 2.54 cm)
**(b)** ~ **by** ~ petit à petit; **to come within an** ~ **of winning** passer à deux doigts de la victoire

**incidence** n  the ∼ of la fréquence de ⟨thefts, deaths⟩; high/low ∼ of sth taux élevé/faible de qch

**incident** n incident m

**incidental** adj ⟨detail, remark⟩ secondaire

**incidentally** adv (by the way) à propos; (by chance) par la même occasion

**incident room** n bureau m des enquêteurs

**incinerate** vtr incinérer

**incite** vtr to ∼ violence inciter à la violence; to ∼ sb to do pousser or inciter qn à faire

**inclination** n inclination f

**incline** ⓵ vtr (a) incliner ⟨head⟩
(b) to be ∼d to do avoir tendance à faire; if you feel so ∼d si l'envie vous en prend
⓶ vi (a) (tend) to ∼ to or towards tendre vers
(b) ⟨road, tower⟩ s'incliner

**include** vtr inclure, comprendre; all the ministers, Blanc ∼d tous les ministres, Blanc inclu; breakfast is ∼d in the price le petit déjeuner est compris

**including** prep (y) compris; £50 ∼ VAT 50 livres sterling TVA comprise; ∼ service service compris; ∼ July y compris juillet; not ∼ July sans compter juillet

**inclusive** adj inclus/-e; ⟨price⟩ forfaitaire; all-∼ tout compris

**incoherent** adj incohérent/-e

**income** n revenus mpl, revenu m

**income bracket** n tranche f de revenu

**income tax** n impôt m sur le revenu

**incoming** adj ⟨call, mail⟩ qui vient de l'extérieur; ⟨government⟩ nouveau/-elle; ⟨tide⟩ montant/-e

**incomparable** adj sans pareil/-eille

**incompatible** adj incompatible

**incompetent** adj ⟨doctor, government⟩ incompétent/-e; ⟨work, performance⟩ mauvais/-e (before n)

**incomplete** adj (a) ⟨work, building⟩ inachevé/-e
(b) ⟨set⟩ incomplet/-ète

**incomprehensible** adj ⟨reason⟩ incompréhensible; ⟨speech⟩ inintelligible

**inconceivable** adj inconcevable

**inconclusive** adj ⟨meeting⟩ sans conclusion véritable; ⟨evidence⟩ peu concluant/-e

**incongruous** adj ⟨sight⟩ déconcertant/-e; ⟨appearance⟩ surprenant/-e

**inconsiderate** adj ⟨person⟩ peu attentif/-ive à autrui; ⟨remark⟩ maladroit/-e; to be ∼ towards sb manquer d'égards envers qn

**inconsistent** adj ⟨work⟩ inégal/-e; ⟨behaviour⟩ changeant/-e; ⟨argument⟩ incohérent/-e; ⟨attitude⟩ inconsistant/-e; to be ∼ with être en contradiction avec

**inconspicuous** adj ⟨person⟩ qui passe inaperçu/-e; ⟨place, clothing⟩ discret/-ète

**inconvenience** ⓵ n (a) (trouble) dérangement m; to put sb to great ∼ causer beaucoup de dérangement à qn
(b) (disadvantage) inconvénient m
⓶ vtr déranger

**inconvenient** adj ⟨location, arrangement⟩ incommode; ⟨time⟩ inopportun/-e

**incorporate** vtr (a) (make part of) incorporer (into dans)
(b) (contain) comporter
(c) Smith and Brown Incorporated Smith et Brown SA

**incorrect** adj incorrect/-e (to do de faire)

**incorrigible** adj incorrigible

**increase** ⓵ n (a) (in amount) augmentation f (in, of de); a 5% ∼ une augmentation de 5%
(b) (in degree) accroissement m; to be on the ∼ être en progression
⓶ vtr augmenter (by de; to jusqu'à)
⓷ vi augmenter (by de); to ∼ in value prendre de la valeur; to ∼ in size s'agrandir

**increased** adj ⟨demand, risk⟩ accru/-e

**increasing** adj ⟨number⟩ croissant/-e

**increasingly** adv de plus en plus

**incredible** adj incroyable

**incredulous** adj incrédule

**incriminating** adj ⟨statement, document⟩ compromettant/-e; ⟨evidence⟩ incriminant/-e

**incubator** n (for child) couveuse f; (for eggs, bacteria) incubateur m

**incur** vtr contracter ⟨debts⟩; subir ⟨loss⟩; encourir ⟨expense, risk, wrath⟩

**incurable** adj (a) ⟨disease⟩ incurable
(b) ⟨optimist, romantic⟩ incorrigible

**incursion** n (gen) intrusion f; (Mil) incursion f

**indebted** adj to be ∼ to sb (under an obligation) être redevable à qn; (grateful) être reconnaissant/-e à qn

**indecent** adj (a) (improper) indécent/-e
(b) (unreasonable) ⟨haste⟩ malséant/-e

**indecent assault** n attentat m à la pudeur

**indecent exposure** n outrage m public à la pudeur

**indecisive** adj (gen) indécis/-e (about quant à); ⟨battle, election⟩ peu concluant/-e

**indeed** adv (a) (certainly) en effet, effectivement; yes ∼! bien sûr que oui!; '∼ you can' 'bien sûr que oui'
(b) (in fact) en fait
(c) (for emphasis) vraiment; that was praise ∼ c'était vraiment un compliment; thank you very much ∼ merci mille fois

**indefinite** adj (a) (vague) vague
(b) ⟨period, delay⟩ illimité/-e; ⟨number⟩ indéterminé/-e
(c) the ∼ article l'article m indéfini

**indefinitely** adv ⟨continue, stay⟩ indéfiniment; ⟨postpone, ban⟩ pour une durée indéterminée

**indelible** adj ⟨ink, mark⟩ indélébile; ⟨impression⟩ ineffaçable

**independence** n indépendance f

**Independence Day** n (US) fête f de l'Indépendance

**independent** adj indépendant/-e (of de)

**in-depth** ⓵ adj ⟨analysis, study⟩ approfondi/-e; ⟨guide⟩ détaillé/-e
⓶ **in depth** adv ⟨examine, study⟩ en détail

**indescribable** adj ⟨chaos, noise⟩ indescriptible; ⟨pleasure, beauty⟩ inexprimable

**indestructible** adj indestructible

**index** n (a) (of book) index m inv
(b) (catalogue) catalogue m; **card ~** fichier m
(c) (Econ) indice m

**index card** n fiche f

**index finger** n index m inv

**index-linked** adj indexé/-e

**India** pr n Inde f

**Indian** ⓵ n (a) (from India) Indien/-ienne m/f
(b) (Native American) Indien/-ienne m/f d'Amérique
⓶ adj (a) (of India) indien/-ienne
(b) (Native American) indien/-ienne, amérindien/-ienne

**Indian Ocean** pr n the ~ l'océan m Indien

**Indian summer** n été m de la Saint Martin

**indicate** ⓵ vtr indiquer (that que; with de)
⓶ vi ⟨driver⟩ mettre son clignotant; ⟨cyclist⟩ faire signe

**indication** n indication f, indice m

**indicative** ⓵ n (in grammar) indicatif m
⓶ adj to be ~ of montrer

**indicator** n (a) (pointer) aiguille f
(b) (board) tableau m
(c) (on car) clignotant m

**indict** vtr inculper

**indictment** n (a) (Law) acte m d'accusation
(b) (criticism) mise f en accusation

**indie** adj (colloq) (Mus) indépendant/-e

**indifference** n indifférence f

**indifferent** adj (a) (uninterested) indifférent/-e (to, as to à)
(b) (mediocre) médiocre

**indigenous** adj indigène (to à)

**indigestion** n indigestion f; to have ~ avoir des brûlures d'estomac

**indignant** adj indigné/-e (at de; about, over par)

**indigo** n, adj indigo (m) inv

**indirect** adj indirect/-e

**indirectly** adv indirectement

**indirect speech** n discours m indirect

**indiscreet** adj indiscret/-ète

**indiscretion** n (lack of discretion) manque m de discrétion; (act) indiscrétion f

**indiscriminate** adj (a) (random) sans distinction
(b) ⟨person⟩ sans discernement

**indispensable** adj indispensable

**indisputable** adj ⟨champion⟩ indiscuté/-e; ⟨fact⟩ indiscutable

**indistinct** adj ⟨sound, markings⟩ indistinct/-e; ⟨memory⟩ confus/-e; ⟨photograph⟩ flou/-e

**individual** ⓵ n individu m
⓶ adj (a) ⟨effort, freedom, portion⟩ individuel/-elle; ⟨comfort, attitude⟩ personnel/-elle; ⟨tuition⟩ particulier/-ière
(b) (separate) **each ~ article** chaque article (individuellement)
(c) (idiosyncratic) particulier/-ière

**individuality** n individualité f

**individually** adv (personally, in person) individuellement; (one at a time) séparément

**indoctrinate** vtr endoctriner

**Indonesia** pr n Indonésie f

**indoor** adj ⟨pool, court⟩ couvert/-e; ⟨lavatory⟩ à l'intérieur; ⟨photography, shoes⟩ d'intérieur; ⟨sports facilities⟩ en salle

**indoors** adv à l'intérieur, dans la maison; **~ and outdoors** dedans et dehors; **to go ~** rentrer

**induce** vtr (a) (persuade) persuader (**to do** de faire); (stronger) inciter (**to** à; **to do** à faire)
(b) (bring about) provoquer

**induction course** n stage m d'introduction

**induction loop** n boucle f magnétique

**indulge** ⓵ vtr (a) céder à ⟨whim, desire⟩
(b) gâter ⟨child⟩; céder à ⟨adult⟩
⓶ vi to ~ in se livrer à ⟨speculation⟩; se complaire dans ⟨nostalgia⟩; se laisser tenter par ⟨food⟩
⓷ v refl to ~ oneself se faire plaisir

**indulgence** n (a) (tolerance) indulgence f (towards envers; for pour)
(b) ~ **in food** gourmandise f; it's my one ~ c'est mon péché mignon

**indulgent** adj indulgent/-e (to, towards pour, envers)

**industrial** adj (gen) industriel/-ielle; ⟨accident⟩ du travail

**industrial action** n (GB) (strike) grève f

**industrial estate** n zone f industrielle

**industrialize** vtr industrialiser

**industrial relations** n pl relations fpl entre les patrons et les ouvriers

**industrial waste** n déchets mpl industriels

**industrious** adj diligent/-e

**industry** n (a) industrie f; the oil ~ l'industrie du pétrole
(b) (diligence) zèle m (au travail)

**inedible** adj ⟨meal⟩ immangeable; ⟨plants⟩ non comestible

**ineffective** adj inefficace

**ineffectual** adj ⟨person⟩ incapable; ⟨policy⟩ inefficace; ⟨attempt⟩ infructueux/-euse

**inefficiency** n (lack of organization) manque ⋯⋗

*m* d'organisation; (incompetence) incompétence *f*; (of machine, method) inefficacité *f*

**inefficient** *adj* (disorganized) mal organisé/-e; (incompetent) incompétent/-e; (not effective) inefficace

**ineligible** *adj* to be ∼ (for job) ne pas remplir les conditions pour poser sa candidature (**for** à); (for election) être inéligible; (for pension, benefit) ne pas avoir droit (**for** à)

**inequality** *n* inégalité *f*

**inert** *adj* inerte

**inertia** *n* inertie *f*

**inevitable** *adj* inévitable (**that** que + *subjunctive*)

**inexcusable** *adj* inexcusable (**that** que + *subjunctive*)

**inexhaustible** *adj* inépuisable

**inexpensive** *adj* pas cher/chère

**inexperienced** *adj* inexpérimenté/-e

**inexplicable** *adj* inexplicable

**infallible** *adj* infaillible

**infamous** *adj* ⟨person⟩ tristement célèbre; ⟨crime⟩ infâme

**infancy** *n* (a) petite enfance *f*
(b) (figurative) débuts *mpl*; **in its** ∼ à ses débuts

**infant** *n* (baby) bébé *m*; (child) petit enfant *m*

**infantry** *n* infanterie *f*, fantassins *mpl*

**infant school** *n* ≈ école *f* maternelle

**infatuated** *adj* to be ∼ with être entiché/-e de

**infatuation** *n* engouement *m* (**with** pour)

**infect** *vtr* contaminer ⟨person, blood, food⟩; infecter ⟨wound⟩

**infection** *n* infection *f*

**infectious** *adj* (a) ⟨disease⟩ infectieux/-ieuse; ⟨person⟩ contagieux/-ieuse
(b) ⟨laughter⟩ communicatif/-ive

**infer** *vtr* déduire

**inferior** ⒈ *n* inférieur/-e *m/f*
⒉ *adj* (a) ⟨goods, work⟩ de qualité inférieure
(b) ⟨position⟩ inférieur/-e; **to make sb feel** ∼ donner un sentiment d'infériorité à qn

**inferiority** *n* infériorité *f* (**to** vis-à-vis de)

**inferiority complex** *n* complexe *m* d'infériorité

**inferno** *n* brasier *m*

**infertile** *adj* ⟨land⟩ infertile; ⟨person⟩ stérile

**infertility** *n* stérilité *f*

**infest** *vtr* infester (**with** de)

**infidelity** *n* infidélité *f*

**infighting** *n* conflits *mpl* internes

**infiltrate** *vtr* infiltrer ⟨organization, group⟩

**infinite** *adj* infini/-e

**infinitely** *adv* infiniment

**infinitive** *n* infinitif *m*; **in the** ∼ à l'infinitif

**infinity** *n* infini *m*

**infirmary** *n* (a) (hospital) hôpital *m*
(b) (in school, prison) infirmerie *f*

**inflamed** *adj* (Med) enflammé/-e

**inflammable** *adj* inflammable

**inflammation** *n* inflammation *f*

**inflatable** *adj* ⟨mattress, dinghy⟩ pneumatique; ⟨toy⟩ gonflable

**inflate** *vtr* gonfler ⟨tyre, dinghy⟩

**inflation** *n* inflation *f*

**inflexible** *adj* (a) ⟨person, attitude⟩ inflexible; ⟨system⟩ rigide
(b) ⟨material⟩ rigide

**inflict** *vtr* infliger ⟨pain, presence, defeat⟩ (**on** à); causer ⟨damage⟩ (**on** à)

**influence** ⒈ *n* influence *f*; **to be** *or* **have an** ∼ **on** avoir une influence sur; **to drive while under the** ∼ **of alcohol** conduire en état d'ébriété
⒉ *vtr* influencer ⟨person⟩ (**in** dans); influer sur ⟨decision, choice, result⟩; **to be** ∼**d by sb/ sth** se laisser influencer par qn/qch

**influential** *adj* influent/-e

**influenza** *n* grippe *f*

**influx** *n* afflux *m*

**info** *n* (colloq) renseignements *mpl*, tuyaux *mpl* (colloq)

**inform** ⒈ *vtr* informer, avertir (**of, about** de; **that** du fait que); **to keep sb** ∼**ed** tenir qn informé/-e *or* au courant (**of, as to** de)
⒉ *vi* **to** ∼ **on** *or* **against** dénoncer

**informal** *adj* (a) ⟨person⟩ sans façons; ⟨manner, style⟩ simple; ⟨language⟩ familier/-ière; ⟨clothes⟩ de tous les jours
(b) ⟨visit⟩ privé/-e; ⟨invitation⟩ verbal/-e; ⟨discussion, interview⟩ informel/-elle

**information** *n* (a) renseignements *mpl*, informations *fpl* (**on, about** sur); **a piece of** ∼ un renseignement, une information
(b) (US) (service *m* des) renseignements *mpl*

**information desk, information office** *n* bureau *m* des renseignements

**information pack** *n* documentation *f*

**information superhighway** *n* autoroutes *fpl* de l'information

**information technology, IT** *n* informatique *f*

**informative** *adj* instructif/-ive

**informer** *n* indicateur/-trice *m/f*

**infrared** *adj* infrarouge

**infrastructure** *n* infrastructure *f*

**infringe** ⒈ *vtr* enfreindre ⟨rule⟩; ne pas respecter ⟨rights⟩
⒉ *vi* **to** ∼ **on** *or* **upon** empiéter sur ⟨rights⟩

**infringement** *n* (of rule) infraction *f* (**of** à); (of rights) violation *f*

**infuriating** *adj* exaspérant/-e

**ingenious** *adj* ingénieux/-ieuse, astucieux/-ieuse

**ingenuity** *n* ingéniosité *f*

**ingenuous** *adj* ingénu/-e, candide

**ingot** *n* lingot *m*

**ingrained** *adj* ⟨dirt⟩ bien incrusté/-e; ⟨habit, hatred⟩ enraciné/-e

**ingratitude** *n* ingratitude *f*

**ingredient** *n* (Culin) ingrédient *m*; (figurative) élément *m* (**of** de)

**inhabit** *vtr* (a) habiter ⟨house, region, planet⟩
(b) vivre dans ⟨fantasy world⟩

**inhabitant** *n* habitant/-e *m/f*

**inhale** ① *vtr* aspirer, inhaler
② *vi* (breathe in) inspirer; (smoke) avaler la fumée

**inhaler** *n* inhalateur *m*

**inherent** *adj* inhérent/-e (to à)

**inherit** *vtr* hériter de ⟨money, property, title⟩; to ∼ sth from sb hériter qch de qn

**inheritance** *n* héritage *m*; to come into an ∼ faire un héritage

**inhibit** *vtr* inhiber ⟨person, reaction⟩; entraver ⟨activity, progress⟩

**inhibited** *adj* inhibé/-e, refoulé/-e

**inhibition** *n* inhibition *f*; to get rid of one's ∼s se libérer de ses inhibitions

**inhospitable** *adj* inhospitalier/-ière

**in-house** *adj* interne

**inhuman** *adj* inhumain/-e

**inhumanity** *n* inhumanité *f* (to envers)

**initial** ① *n* initiale *f*
② *adj* initial/-e; ∼ letter initiale *f*
③ *vtr* parapher, parafer

**initially** *adv* au départ

**initiate** ① *n* initié/-e *m/f*
② *vtr* (a) mettre en œuvre ⟨project, reform⟩; amorcer ⟨talks⟩; entamer, engager ⟨proceedings⟩
(b) (teach) to ∼ sb into initier qn à

**initiative** *n* initiative *f*; on one's own ∼ de son propre chef

**inject** *vtr* injecter ⟨vaccine⟩ (into dans); to ∼ sb (with sth) faire une injection *or* une piqûre (de qch) à qn

**injection** *n* (a) (Med) piqûre *f*
(b) (Tech) injection *f*

**injure** *vtr* (a) blesser ⟨person⟩; to ∼ one's hand se blesser la main
(b) nuire à, compromettre ⟨health, reputation⟩

**injured** ① *n* the ∼ les blessés *mpl*
② *adj* (a) (gen) blessé/-e
(b) (Law) the ∼ party la partie lésée

**injury** *n* blessure *f*; head injuries blessures à la tête

**injury time** *n* (Sport) arrêts *mpl* de jeu

**injustice** *n* injustice *f*

**ink** *n* encre *f*; in ∼ à l'encre

**inkjet printer** *n* imprimante *f* à jet d'encre

**inkling** *n* petite idée *f*; to have an ∼ that avoir idée que

**inland** ① *adj* intérieur/-e
② *adv* ⟨travel, lie⟩ à l'intérieur des terres

**Inland Revenue** *n* (GB) service *m* des impôts britannique

**in-laws** *n pl* (parents) beaux-parents *mpl*; (other relatives) belle-famille *f*, parents *mpl* par alliance

**inmate** *n* (of mental hospital) interné/-e *m/f*; (of prison) détenu/-e *m/f*

**inn** *n* (a) (hotel) auberge *f*
(b) (pub) pub *m*

**inner** *adj* intérieur/-e

**inner city** ① *n* the ∼ les quartiers *mpl* déshérités
② **inner-city** *n* ⟨problems⟩ des quartiers déshérités; ⟨area⟩ déshérité/-e

**innermost** *adj* sb's ∼ thoughts les pensées les plus intimes de qn

**innocence** *n* innocence *f*

**innocent** *n, adj* innocent/-e *(m/f)*

**innovation** *n* innovation *f*

**innovative** *adj* innovateur/-trice

**innovator** *n* innovateur/-trice *m/f*

**innuendo** *n* (veiled slights) insinuations *fpl*; (sexual references) allusions *fpl* grivoises

**inoculation** *n* vaccination *f*, inoculation *f*

**inoffensive** *adj* inoffensif/-ive

**in-patient** *n* malade *mf* hospitalisé/-e

**input** *n* (a) (of money) apport *m*; (of energy) alimentation *f* (of en)
(b) (contribution) contribution *f*
(c) (Comput) (data) données *fpl* d'entrée *or* à traiter

**inquest** *n* enquête *f* (on, into sur)

**inquire** = ENQUIRE

**inquiry** *n* enquête *f* (into sur); murder ∼ enquête criminelle; ▶ ENQUIRY

**inquisitive** *adj* curieux/-ieuse

**insane** *adj* (gen) fou/folle; (Law) aliéné/-e

**insanitary** *adj* insalubre, malsain/-e

**insanity** *n* (gen) folie *f*; (Law) aliénation *f* mentale

**insatiable** *adj* insatiable

**inscription** *n* inscription *f*

**insect** *n* insecte *m*; ∼ bite piqûre *f* d'insecte

**insecticide** *n, adj* insecticide *(m)*

**insect repellent** *n* insectifuge *m*, produit *m* anti-insecte

**insecure** *adj* (a) ⟨person⟩ qui manque d'assurance
(b) ⟨job⟩ précaire; ⟨investment⟩ risqué/-e

**insecurity** *n* (a) (psychological) manque *m* d'assurance
(b) (of position, situation) insécurité *f*

**insensitive** *adj* ⟨person⟩ (tactless) sans tact; (unfeeling) insensible (to à); ⟨remark⟩ indélicat/-e

**inseparable** *adj* inséparable (from de)

**insert** *vtr* insérer (in dans)

**inside** ① *n* intérieur *m*; to overtake on the ∼ (in Europe, US) doubler à droite; (in GB, Australia) doubler à gauche; people on the ∼ les gens qui sont dans la place
② *prep* (also (US) ∼ of) (a) à l'intérieur de; ∼ the box à l'intérieur de *or* dans la boîte; to be ∼ (the house) être à l'intérieur (de la maison)
(b) (under) ∼ (of) an hour en moins d'une heure
③ *adj* (a) ⟨cover, pocket⟩ intérieur/-e; ⟨toilet⟩ à l'intérieur ⋯⟶

**(b)** ⟨*information*⟩ de première main
**(c) the ~ lane** (of road) (in Europe, US) la voie de droite; (in GB, Australia) la voie de gauche; (of athletics track) le couloir intérieur
**4** *adv* (indoors) à l'intérieur; (in a container) à l'intérieur, dedans; **she's ~** elle est à l'intérieur; **to look ~** regarder à l'intérieur *or* dedans; **to go** *or* **come ~** entrer; **to bring sth ~** rentrer ⟨*chairs*⟩
**5 inside out** *phr* à l'envers; **to turn sth ~ out** retourner qch; **to know sb/sth ~ out** connaître qn/qch à fond
**insider dealing** *n* délit *m* d'initié
**insides** *n pl* (colloq) (of human) intestin *m*, estomac *m*, boyaux *mpl* (colloq)
**insight** *n* **(a)** (glimpse, understanding) aperçu *m*, idée *f* (into de)
**(b)** (intuition) perspicacité *f*, intuition *f*
**insignificant** *adj* ⟨*cost, difference*⟩ négligeable; ⟨*person, detail*⟩ insignifiant/-e
**insincere** *adj* peu sincère; **to be ~** manquer de sincérité
**insinuate** *vtr* insinuer (that que)
**insinuation** *n* insinuation *f*
**insipid** *adj* fade
**insist** **1** *vtr* **(a)** (demand) insister (that pour que)
**(b)** (maintain) affirmer (that que)
**2** *vi* insister; **to ~ on** exiger ⟨*punctuality, silence*⟩; **to ~ on doing** vouloir à tout prix faire, tenir à faire
**insistent** *adj* **to be ~** insister (about sur; that pour que + *subjunctive*)
**insofar: insofar as** *phr* **~ as** dans la mesure où
**insole** *n* semelle *f* (intérieure)
**insolent** *adj* insolent/-e
**insomnia** *n* insomnie *f*
**inspect** *vtr* examiner [qch] de près ⟨*document, product*⟩; contrôler, vérifier ⟨*accounts*⟩; inspecter ⟨*school, factory, pitch, wiring*⟩; contrôler ⟨*passport, ticket, baggage*⟩
**inspection** *n* (gen) inspection *f*; (of ticket, passport) contrôle *m*; **on closer ~** en y regardant de plus près
**inspector** *n* **(a)** (gen) inspecteur/-trice *m/f*
**(b)** (GB) **police ~** inspecteur *m* de police
**(c)** (GB) (on bus) contrôleur/-euse *m/f*
**inspiration** *n* inspiration *f* (for pour)
**inspire** *vtr* inspirer; **to be ~d by sth** s'inspirer de qch
**inspired** *adj* ⟨*person*⟩ inspiré/-e; ⟨*idea*⟩ lumineux/-euse; **an ~ guess** une heureuse inspiration
**inspiring** *adj* ⟨*person, speech*⟩ enthousiasmant/-e; ⟨*thought*⟩ exaltant/-e
**instal(l)** *vtr* **(a)** installer ⟨*equipment, software*⟩; poser ⟨*windows*⟩
**(b) to ~ sb in office** installer qn
**installation** *n* installation *f*
**instalment** (GB), **installment** (US) *n* versement *m* partiel; **in ~s** en plusieurs versements
**instance** *n* exemple *m*; **for ~** par exemple

**instant** **1** *n* instant *m*; **come here this ~!** viens ici tout de suite!
**2** *adj* **(a)** ⟨*access, effect, rapport, success*⟩ immédiat/-e; ⟨*solution*⟩ instantané/-e
**(b)** ⟨*coffee, soup*⟩ instantané/-e
**instant camera** *n* polaroïd® *m*
**instantly** *adv* immédiatement
**instead** **1** *adv* **we didn't go home—we went to the park ~** au lieu de rentrer nous sommes allés au parc; **let's take a taxi ~** prenons plutôt un taxi; **I was going to phone but wrote ~** j'allais téléphoner mais finalement j'ai écrit; **her son went ~** son fils y est allé à sa place
**2 instead of** *phr* **~ of sth/of doing** au lieu de qch/de faire; **use oil ~ of butter** utilisez de l'huile à la place du beurre; **~ of sb** à la place de qn
**instep** *n* cou-de-pied *m*
**instigate** *vtr* lancer ⟨*attack*⟩; engager ⟨*proceedings*⟩
**instil** (GB), **instill** (US) *vtr* inculquer ⟨*attitude*⟩ (in à); donner ⟨*confidence*⟩ (in à)
**instinct** *n* instinct *m* (for de)
**instinctive** *adj* instinctif/-ive
**institute** **1** *n* institut *m*
**2** *vtr* instituer
**institution** *n* **(a)** (gen) institution *f*; **financial ~** organisme *m* financier
**(b)** (home, hospital) établissement *m* spécialisé
**institutionalize** *vtr* **(a)** (place in care) placer [qn] dans un établissement spécialisé; (in mental hospital) interner
**(b)** (establish officially) institutionnaliser; **~d** ⟨*racism, violence*⟩ institutionnalisé/-e
**instruct** *vtr* **(a) to ~ sb to do** donner l'ordre à qn de faire; **to be ~ed to do** recevoir l'ordre de faire
**(b)** (teach) instruire; **to ~ sb in** enseigner [qch] à qn ⟨*subject*⟩
**instruction** *n* instruction *f*; **~s for use** mode *m* d'emploi
**instruction book** *n* livret *m* de l'utilisateur
**instructor** *n* **(a)** (in sports, driving) moniteur/-trice *m/f* (in de); (military) instructeur *m*
**(b)** (US) professeur *m*
**instrument** *n* instrument *m*; **to play an ~** jouer d'un instrument
**instrumental** **1** *n* instrumental *m*
**2** *adj* **(a) to be ~ in sth/in doing** contribuer à qch/à faire
**(b)** (Mus) instrumental/-e
**instrument panel** *n* tableau *m* de bord
**insufficient** *adj* **there are ~ copies** il n'y a pas assez d'exemplaires; **to be ~ for** être insuffisant/-e pour
**insulate** *vtr* isoler ⟨*roof, room, wire*⟩
**insulation** *n* isolation *f*
**insulin** *n* insuline *f*
**insult** **1** *n* insulte *f*
**2** *vtr* insulter

**insurance** n assurance f (**against** contre; **for** pour); **to take out ~ against sth** s'assurer contre qch

**insurance policy** n (police f d')assurance f

**insure** vtr assurer (**against** contre)

**intact** adj intact/-e

**intake** n (**a**) (consumption) consommation f
(**b**) (Sch, Univ) (admissions) admissions fpl
(**c**) **an ~ of breath** une inspiration f

**intangible** adj insaisissable

**integral** adj intégral/-e; ⟨part⟩ intégrant/-e; **~ to** intrinsèque à

**integrate** ① vtr (**a**) (incorporate, absorb) intégrer (**into** dans; **with** à)
(**b**) (combine) combiner ⟨systems⟩
② vi ⟨person⟩ s'intégrer (**with** à; **into** dans)

**integration** n intégration f (**with** à)

**integrity** n intégrité f

**intellect** n (**a**) (mental capacity) intelligence f
(**b**) (person) esprit m

**intellectual** n, adj intellectuel/-elle (m/f)

**intelligence** n (**a**) intelligence f (**to do de** faire)
(**b**) (gen, Mil) (information) renseignements mpl
(**c**) (Mil) (secret service) services mpl de renseignements

**intelligent** adj intelligent/-e

**intelligible** adj intelligible (**to** à)

**intend** vtr vouloir; **to ~ to do, to ~ doing** avoir l'intention de faire; **to be ~ed for** être destiné/-e à ⟨person⟩; être prévu/-e pour ⟨purpose⟩

**intense** adj (**a**) (gen) intense
(**b**) ⟨person⟩ sérieux/-ieuse

**intensify** ① vtr intensifier
② vi s'intensifier

**intensive** adj intensif/-ive

**intensive care** n **in ~** en réanimation

**intensive care unit** n service m de soins intensifs

**intent** adj ⟨person, expression⟩ absorbé/-e; **~ on doing** résolu/-e à faire
IDIOMS **to all ~s and purposes** quasiment, en fait

**intention** n intention f (**to do, of doing de** faire)

**intentional** adj intentionnel/-elle

**intentionally** adv intentionnellement, exprès

**interact** vi ⟨two factors, phenomena⟩ agir l'un sur l'autre; ⟨people⟩ communiquer; (Comput) dialoguer

**interactive** adj interactif/-ive

**intercept** vtr intercepter

**interchange** ① n (**a**) (road junction) échangeur m
(**b**) (exchange) échange m
② vtr échanger

**interchangeable** adj interchangeable

**intercom** n interphone® m

**intercourse** n rapports mpl (sexuels)

**interest** ① n (**a**) (gen) intérêt m (**in** pour);

**to hold sb's ~** retenir l'attention de qn; **it's in your** (own) **~(s) to do** il est dans ton intérêt de faire; **to have sb's best ~s at heart** vouloir le bien de qn
(**b**) (hobby) centre m d'intérêt
(**c**) (on loan, from investment) intérêts mpl (**on** de)
② vtr intéresser (**in** à)

**interested** adj ⟨expression, onlooker⟩ intéressé/-e; **to be ~ in** s'intéresser à ⟨subject, activity⟩; **I am ~ in doing** ça m'intéresse de faire

**interest-free** adj sans intérêt

**interesting** adj intéressant/-e

**interest rate** n taux m d'intérêt

**interface** ① n interface f
② vtr connecter, relier

**interfere** vi (**a**) **to ~ in** se mêler de ⟨affairs⟩; **she never ~s** elle ne se mêle jamais de ce qui ne la regarde pas
(**b**) (intervene) intervenir
(**c**) **to ~ with** ⟨person⟩ toucher, traficoter (colloq) ⟨machine⟩
(**d**) **to ~ with** ⟨activity⟩ empiéter sur ⟨family life⟩

**interference** n (on radio) parasites mpl

**interfering** adj ⟨person⟩ envahissant/-e

**interim** ① n **in the ~** entre-temps
② adj ⟨arrangement, government⟩ provisoire; ⟨post, employee⟩ intérimaire

**interior** ① n (**a**) intérieur m
(**b**) **Secretary/Department of the Interior** (US) ministre m/ministère m de l'Intérieur
② adj intérieur/-e

**interior decorator** n décorateur/-trice m/f

**interlink** vtr **to be ~ed** être lié/-e (**with** à)

**interlock** vi ⟨pipes⟩ s'emboîter; ⟨mechanisms⟩ s'enclencher; ⟨fingers⟩ s'entrelacer

**interlude** n (interval) intervalle m; (during play, concert) entracte m

**intermediary** n, adj intermédiaire (mf)

**intermediate** adj (**a**) (gen) intermédiaire
(**b**) (Sch) ⟨course⟩ de niveau moyen; ⟨level⟩ moyen/-enne

**intermission** n entracte m

**intern** ① n (US) (**a**) (Med) interne mf
(**b**) (gen) stagiaire mf
② vtr (Mil) interner

**internal** adj (**a**) (gen) interne
(**b**) (within country) intérieur/-e

**international** adj international/-e

**internationally** adv ⟨known, respected⟩ dans le monde entier

**internee** n interné/-e m/f

**Internet** n Internet m; **on the ~** sur Internet

**Internet access** n accès m Internet

**Internet kiosk** n borne f d'accès public à Internet

**Internet service provider**, **ISP** n fournisseur m d'accès Internet

**Internet user** n internaute mf
**interpret** [1] vtr interpréter (as comme)
[2] vi faire l'interprète
**interpreter** n interprète mf
**interrogate** vtr interroger
**interrogation** n interrogatoire m
**interrogative** n interrogatif m; in the ~ à la forme interrogative
**interrupt** vtr, vi interrompre
**interruption** n interruption f
**intersect** [1] vtr croiser
[2] vi ⟨roads⟩ se croiser; **to ~ with** croiser
**intersection** n intersection f
**interstate** n (US) (also ~ **highway**) autoroute f (inter-États)
**interval** n (a) intervalle m; **at regular ~s** à intervalles réguliers; **at four-hourly ~s** toutes les quatre heures; **at 100 metre ~s** à 100 mètres d'intervalle
(b) (GB) (in theatre) entracte m
**intervene** vi intervenir (**on behalf of** en faveur de)
**intervention** n intervention f (**on behalf of** en faveur de)
**interview** [1] n (a) (also **job ~**) entretien m
(b) (in newspaper) interview f
[2] vtr (a) faire passer un entretien à ⟨candidate⟩
(b) ⟨journalist⟩ interviewer ⟨celebrity⟩; ⟨police⟩ interroger ⟨suspect⟩
**interviewee** n (a) (for job) candidat/-e m/f
(b) (on TV, radio) personne f interviewée
**interviewer** n (a) (for job) personne f faisant passer l'entretien
(b) (on radio, TV, in press) intervieweur/-euse m/f
**interwar** adj **the ~ years** l'entre-deux-guerres m
**intestine** n intestin m
**intimacy** n intimité f
**intimate** adj (a) (gen) intime; **to be on ~ terms with sb** être intime avec qn
(b) ⟨knowledge⟩ approfondi/-e
**intimidate** vtr intimider
**intimidating** adj ⟨behaviour, person⟩ intimidant/-e; ⟨obstacle, sight, size⟩ impressionnant/-e; ⟨prospect⟩ redoutable
**into** prep (a) ⟨put, go, disappear⟩ dans ⟨place⟩; **to run ~ a wall** rentrer dans un mur; **to bang ~ sb/sth** heurter qn/qch; **to go ~ town/~ the office** aller en ville/au bureau; **to get ~ a car** monter dans une voiture; **to get ~ bed** se mettre au lit
(b) ⟨transform⟩ en; **to change dollars ~ euros** changer des dollars en euros; **to translate sth ~ French** traduire qch en français
(c) **to continue ~ the 18th century** continuer jusqu'au XVIIIᵉ siècle; **well ~ the afternoon** jusque tard dans l'après-midi
(d) (colloq) (keen on) **to be ~ sth** être fana de qch (colloq); **to be ~ drugs** se droguer

(e) (in division) **8 ~ 24 goes 3 times** or **is 3** 24 divisé par 8 égale 3
**intolerable** adj intolérable, insupportable
**intolerance** n intolérance f (**of, towards** vis-à-vis de; **to** à)
**intolerant** adj intolérant/-e (**of, towards** vis-à-vis de; **with** envers)
**intoxicated** adj ivre
**intoxicating** adj ⟨drink⟩ alcoolisé/-e; ⟨effect, substance⟩ toxique
**intranet** n intranet
**intransitive** adj intransitif/-ive
**intravenous** adj intraveineux/-euse
**intravenous drug user** n usager m de drogues par voie intraveineuse
**in-tray** n corbeille f arrivée
**intrepid** adj intrépide
**intricate** adj ⟨mechanism, pattern, plot⟩ compliqué/-e; ⟨problem⟩ complexe
**intrigue** [1] n intrigue f
[2] vtr intriguer; **she was ~d by his story** son histoire l'intriguait
**intriguing** adj ⟨person, smile⟩ fascinant/-e; ⟨story⟩ curieux/-ieuse, intéressant/-e
**introduce** vtr (a) présenter ⟨person⟩ (**as** comme; **to** à); **may I ~ my son?** je vous présente mon fils; **to ~ sb to** initier qn à ⟨painting, drugs⟩
(b) introduire ⟨law, reform, word, product, change⟩ (**in, into** dans)
(c) (on TV, radio) présenter ⟨programme⟩
**introduction** n (a) (of person) présentation f; **letter of ~** lettre de recommandation
(b) (of liquid, system, law) introduction f (**into** dans)
(c) (to speech, book) introduction f
**introductory** adj (a) ⟨speech, paragraph⟩ préliminaire; ⟨course⟩ d'initiation
(b) ⟨offer⟩ de lancement
**introvert** n introverti/-e m/f
**intrude** vi (a) **to ~ in** s'immiscer dans ⟨affairs, conversation⟩
(b) **to ~ (on sb's privacy)** être importun/-e
**intruder** n intrus/-e m/f
**intrusive** adj ⟨question, cameras⟩ indiscret/-ète; ⟨phone call, presence⟩ importun/-e
**intuition** n intuition f (**about** concernant)
**intuitive** adj intuitif/-ive
**inundate** vtr inonder ⟨land⟩; submerger ⟨organization, market⟩
**invade** vtr envahir
**invader** n envahisseur/-euse m/f
**invalid** [1] n (sick person) malade mf; (disabled person) infirme mf
[2] adj ⟨claim, passport⟩ pas valable; ⟨contract, marriage⟩ nul/nulle
**invaluable** adj ⟨assistance, experience⟩ inestimable; ⟨person, service⟩ précieux/-ieuse
**invasion** n invasion f; ~ **of (sb's) privacy** atteinte f à la vie privée (de qn)
**invent** vtr inventer
**invention** n invention f

**inventive** *adj* inventif/-ive

**inventor** *n* inventeur/-trice *m/f*

**inventory** *n* (a) inventaire *m*
(b) (US) stock *m*

**inverted commas** *n pl* (GB) guillemets *mpl*; **in** ~ entre guillemets

**invest** ⊞ *vtr* investir, placer ⟨*money*⟩; consacrer ⟨*time, energy*⟩ (**in** à)
⊡ *vi* (a) investir; **to** ~ **in shares** placer son argent en valeurs
(b) (buy) **to** ~ **in sth** s'acheter qch

**investigate** *vtr* (a) enquêter sur ⟨*crime, case*⟩; faire une enquête sur ⟨*person*⟩
(b) (study) examiner ⟨*possibility, report*⟩

**investigation** *n* (a) (inquiry) enquête *f* (**of, into** sur)
(b) (of accounts, reports) vérification *f*

**investment** *n* (financial) investissement *m*, placement *m*

**investment manager** *n* gérant/-e *m/f* de porte-feuille

**investor** *n* investisseur/-euse *m/f* (**in** dans); (in shares) actionnaire *mf*

**invigilate** *vtr* surveiller ⟨*examination*⟩

**invisible** *adj* invisible

**invisible ink** *n* encre *f* sympathique

**invitation** *n* invitation *f*

**invitation card** *n* carton *m* (d'invitation)

**invite** *vtr* inviter ⟨*person*⟩; **to** ~ **sb for a drink** inviter qn à prendre un verre; **to** ~ **sb in** inviter qn à entrer; **to** ~ **sb over** *or* **round (to one's house)** inviter qn chez soi

**inviting** *adj* ⟨*room*⟩ accueillant/-e; ⟨*meal*⟩ appétissant/-e; ⟨*prospect*⟩ alléchant/-e

**invoice** ⊞ *n* facture *f*
⊡ *vtr* envoyer une facture à ⟨*customer*⟩; **to** ~ **sb for sth** facturer qch à qn

**involve** *vtr* (a) (entail) impliquer, nécessiter ⟨*effort, travel*⟩; entraîner ⟨*problems*⟩
(b) (cause to participate) faire participer ⟨*person*⟩ (**in** à); **to be** ~**d in** participer à, être engagé/-e dans ⟨*business, project*⟩; être mêlé/-e à ⟨*scandal, robbery*⟩
(c) (affect) concerner, impliquer ⟨*person, animal, vehicle*⟩
(d) (engross) **to get** ~**d in** se laisser prendre par, se plonger dans ⟨*film, book, work*⟩
(e) **to get** ~**d with sb** avoir une liaison avec qn

**involved** *adj* (a) (complicated) ⟨*explanation*⟩ compliqué/-e
(b) ⟨*person, group*⟩ (implicated) impliqué/-e; (affected) concerné/-e
(c) (necessary) ⟨*effort*⟩ à fournir; **because of the expense** ~ à cause de la dépense que cela entraîne

**involvement** *n* (a) (in activity, task) participation *f* (**in** à); (in enterprise, politics) engagement *m* (**in** dans)
(b) (with group) liens *mpl*; (with person) relations *fpl*

**inward** ⊞ *adj* ⟨*satisfaction*⟩ personnel/-elle; ⟨*relief, calm*⟩ intérieur/-e

⊡ *adv* (*also* **inwards**) ⟨*open, move, grow*⟩ vers l'intérieur

**inward-looking** *adj* replié/-e sur soi-même

**inwards** = INWARD 2

**in-your-face** *adj* (colloq) agressif/-ive

**iodine** *n* (element) iode *m*; (antiseptic) teinture *f* d'iode

**IOU** *n* reconnaissance *f* de dette

**IQ** *n* (*abbr* = **intelligence quotient**) QI *m*

**Iran** *pr n* Iran *m*

**Iraq** *pr n* Iraq *m*

**irate** *adj* furieux/-ieuse (**about** au sujet de)

**Ireland** *pr n* Irlande *f*

**Irish** ⊞ *n* (a) (people) **the** ~ les Irlandais *mpl*
(b) (language) irlandais *m*
⊡ *adj* irlandais/-e

**Irishman** *n* Irlandais *m*

**Irish Republic** *pr n* République *f* d'Irlande

**Irish sea** *pr n* mer *f* d'Irlande

**Irishwoman** *n* Irlandaise *f*

**iron** ⊞ *n* (a) (metal) fer *m*; **scrap** ~ ferraille *f*
(b) (for clothes) fer *m* (à repasser)
⊡ *vtr* repasser ⟨*clothes*⟩

**ironic(al)** *adj* ironique

**ironing** *n* repassage *m*

**ironing board** *n* planche *f* à repasser

**ironmonger** *n* quincailler/-ière *m/f*; ~'s (shop) quincaillerie *f*

**irony** *n* ironie *f*

**irrational** *adj* ⟨*behaviour*⟩ irrationnel/-elle; ⟨*fear, hostility*⟩ sans fondement; **he's rather** ~ il n'est pas très raisonnable

**irregular** *adj* (a) irrégulier/-ière
(b) (US) ⟨*merchandise*⟩ de second choix

**irregularity** *n* irrégularité *f*

**irrelevant** *adj* (a) ⟨*remark*⟩ hors de propos; ⟨*fact*⟩ qui n'est pas pertinent; ⟨*question*⟩ sans rapport avec le sujet
(b) (unimportant) **the money's** ~ ce n'est pas l'argent qui compte

**irreligious** *adj* irréligieux/-ieuse

**irreparable** *adj* irréparable

**irreplaceable** *adj* irremplaçable

**irrepressible** *adj* ⟨*high spirits*⟩ irrépressible; ⟨*person*⟩ infatigable

**irresistible** *adj* irrésistible

**irrespective: irrespective of** *phr* sans tenir compte de ⟨*age, class*⟩; sans distinction de ⟨*race*⟩

**irresponsible** *adj* irresponsable

**irreversible** *adj* ⟨*process, decision*⟩ irréversible; ⟨*disease*⟩ incurable

**irritable** *adj* irritable

**irritable bowel syndrome** *n* colopathie *f* fonctionnelle

**irritate** *vtr* irriter

**irritating** adj irritant/-e

**Islam** n Islam m

**Islamic** adj islamique

**island** n (a) île f; (small) îlot m
(b) (also **traffic** ∼) refuge m

**islander** n insulaire mf, habitant/-e m/f
d'une île (or de l'île)

**Isle of Man** pr n île f de Man

**isolate** vtr isoler (**from** de)

**isolation** n isolement m

**Israel** pr n Israël (never with article)

**Israeli** ① n Israélien/-ienne m/f
② adj israélien/-ienne

**issue** ① n (a) problème m, question f; **to
make an** ∼ (**out**) **of** faire une histoire de; **at**
∼ en question
(b) (of stamps, shares) émission f; (of book)
publication f
(c) (journal, magazine) numéro m; **back** ∼
vieux numéro m
② vtr (a) (allocate) distribuer; **to** ∼ **sb with
sth** fournir qch à qn
(b) délivrer ⟨declaration⟩; émettre ⟨order,
warning⟩
(c) émettre ⟨stamps, shares⟩; publier ⟨book⟩

**it** pron (a) (subject pronoun) il, elle; **'where is
the chair?'** — **'it's in the kitchen'** 'où est la
chaise?' — 'elle est dans la cuisine'; **it's a
good film** c'est un bon film
(b) (object pronoun) le, la, l'; **I want** ∼ je le/la
veux
(c) (after a preposition) **about/from/of** ∼ en; **in/to**
∼ y; **I've heard about** ∼ j'en ai entendu
parler; **he went to** ∼ il y est allé
(d) (in questions) **who is** ∼? qui est-ce?, qui
c'est? (colloq); **where is** ∼? (of object) où est-il/
elle?; (of place) où est-ce?, où est-ce que c'est?,
c'est où? (colloq); **what is** ∼? (of object, noise)
qu'est-ce que c'est?, c'est quoi? (colloq); (what's
happening?) qu'est-ce qui se passe?; (what is the
matter?) qu'est-ce qu'il y a?
(e) (impersonal uses) **it's raining/snowing** il
pleut/neige; ∼ **is easy to learn English** il est
facile d'apprendre l'anglais; ∼ **doesn't matter**
ça ne fait rien; **it's time to eat** c'est l'heure
de manger; **it's me** c'est moi

**IT** n (abbr = **information technology**)
informatique f

**Italian** ① n (a) (person) Italien/-ienne m/f
(b) (language) italien m
② adj (gen) italien/-ienne; ⟨embassy⟩ d'Italie

**italics** n pl italique m; **in** ∼ en italique

**Italy** pr n Italie f

**itch** ① n démangeaison f
② vi avoir des démangeaisons; **my back is**
∼**ing** j'ai le dos qui me démange; **these
socks make me** ∼ ces chaussettes me
grattent

**itchy** adj (colloq) **I feel** ∼ **all over** ça me
gratte partout
IDIOMS **to have** ∼ **feet** (colloq) avoir la
bougeotte (colloq)

**item** n (a) article m; ∼**s of clothing**
vêtements mpl; **news** ∼ article m
(b) (on agenda) point m

**itemize** vtr détailler; ∼**d bill** facture f le
détaillée

**itinerary** n itinéraire m

**its** det son/sa/ses

■ **Note** In French determiners agree in number
and gender with the noun that follows. *its* is
translated by *son + masculine noun*: *its nose =
son nez*; by *sa + feminine noun*: *its tail = sa
queue*; BUT by *son + feminine noun beginning
with a vowel or mute 'h'*: *its ear = son oreille*;
and by *ses + plural noun*: *its ears = ses oreilles*.

**itself** pron (a) (reflexive) se, s'; **the cat hurt** ∼
le chat s'est fait mal
(b) (emphatic) lui-même/elle-même; **the house**
∼ **was pretty** la maison elle-même était jolie;
**he was kindness** ∼ c'était la bonté même or
personnifiée
(c) (after prepositions) **the heating comes on by**
∼ le chauffage se met en marche tout seul;
**learning French is not difficult in** ∼
l'apprentissage du français n'est pas difficile
en soi

**IVF** n (abbr= **in vitro fertilization**)
fécondation f in vitro

**ivory** n, adj ivoire (m)

**ivy** n lierre m

# Jj

**j, J** n j, J m

**jab** ① n (a) (GB) (vaccination) vaccin m;
(injection) piqûre f
(b) (in boxing) direct m
② vtr **to** ∼ **sth into sth** planter qch dans qch

**jabber** vi (chatter) jacasser; (in foreign language)
baragouiner

**jack** n (a) (for car) cric m
(b) (in cards) valet m (**of** de)

(c) (in bowls) cochonnet m
IDIOMS **to be a** ∼ **of all trades** être un/-e
touche-à-tout inv
■ **jack in** (GB) (colloq): ∼ **in** [sth], ∼ [sth] **in**
plaquer (colloq), laisser tomber ⟨job⟩

**jackal** n chacal m

**jackdaw** n choucas m

**jacket** n (a) (garment) veste f; (man's) veste f,
veston m

**(b)** (*also* **dust** ∼) jaquette *f*
**(c)** (US) (of record) pochette *f*
**jacket potato** *n* pomme *f* de terre en robe des champs (au four)
**jack-in-the-box** *n* diable *m* à ressort
**jackknife** *vi* ⟨*lorry*⟩ se mettre en portefeuille
**jackpot** *n* **to hit the** ∼ (win prize) gagner le gros lot; (have great success) faire un tabac (colloq)
**jade** *n* **(a)** (stone) jade *m*
**(b)** (*also* ∼ **green**) vert *m* jade
**jaded** *adj* **(a)** (exhausted) fatigué/-e
**(b)** (bored) ⟨*person, palate*⟩ blasé/-e
**jagged** *adj* ⟨*rock, cliff*⟩ déchiqueté/-e; ⟨*tooth, blade*⟩ ébréché/-e; ⟨*knife, saw*⟩ dentelé/-e
**jail** ⒈ *n* prison *f*
⒉ *vtr* mettre [qn] en prison
**jam** ⒈ *n* **(a)** confiture *f*; **apricot** ∼ confiture d'abricots
**(b)** (of traffic) embouteillage *m*
**(c)** (in machine, system) blocage *m*
**(d)** (colloq) (difficulty) pétrin *m* (colloq); **to be in a** ∼ être dans le pétrin (colloq)
**(e)** (*also* ∼ **session**) bœuf *m* (colloq), jam-session *f*
⒉ *vtr* **(a) to** ∼ **one's foot on the brake** freiner à bloc
**(b)** (wedge) coincer; **the key's** ∼**med** la clé s'est coincée
**(c)** (block) enrayer ⟨*mechanism*⟩; coincer ⟨*lock, door, system*⟩
**(d)** (*also* ∼ **up**) (crowd) encombrer; **cars** ∼**med (up) the roads** les routes étaient embouteillées
**(e)** (cause interference in) brouiller ⟨*frequency*⟩
⒊ *vi* **(a)** ⟨*mechanism*⟩ s'enrayer; ⟨*lock, door*⟩ se coincer
**(b)** (Mus) improviser
**Jamaica** *pr n* Jamaïque *f*
**jam-packed** *adj* bondé/-e; **to be** ∼ **with sth** être bourré/-e de qch
**jangle** ⒈ *n* (of bells, pots) tintement *m*; (of keys) cliquetis *m*
⒉ *vi* ⟨*bells*⟩ tinter; ⟨*bangles, keys*⟩ cliqueter
**janitor** *n* (US) gardien *m*
**January** *n* janvier *m*
**Japan** *pr n* Japon *m*
**Japanese** ⒈ *n* **(a)** (person) Japonais/-e *m/f*
**(b)** (language) japonais *m*
⒉ *adj* ⟨*culture, food, politics*⟩ japonais/-e; ⟨*teacher, lesson*⟩ de japonais; ⟨*ambassador, embassy*⟩ du Japon
**jar** ⒈ *n* **(a)** pot *m*; (large) bocal *m*; (earthenware) jarre *f*
**(b)** (jolt) secousse *f*, choc *m*
⒉ *vtr* **(a)** ébranler, secouer; **to** ∼ **one's shoulder** se cogner l'épaule
**(b)** (US) **to** ∼ **sb into action** pousser qn à agir
⒊ *vi* **(a)** ⟨*music, voice*⟩ rendre un son discordant; **to** ∼ **on sb's nerves** agacer qn
**(b)** (clash) ⟨*colours*⟩ jurer; ⟨*note*⟩ sonner faux

**jargon** *n* jargon *m*
**jasmine** *n* jasmin *m*
**jaundice** *n* jaunisse *f*
**jaundiced** *adj* (cynical) négatif/-ive
**javelin** *n* javelot *m*
**jaw** *n* mâchoire *f*
**jawbone** *n* mâchoire *f*
**jawline** *n* menton *m*
**jay** *n* geai *m*
**jazz** ⒈ *n* jazz *m*
⒉ *adj* ⟨*musician, singer*⟩ de jazz; ∼ **band** jazz-band *m*
**IDIOMS and all that** ∼ (colloq) et tout le bataclan (colloq)
■ **jazz up** (colloq) rajeunir ⟨*dress*⟩; égayer ⟨*room*⟩
**jazzy** *adj* **(a)** ⟨*colour*⟩ voyant/-e; ⟨*pattern, dress*⟩ bariolé/-e
**(b)** ⟨*music*⟩ jazzy *inv*
**jealous** *adj* jaloux/-ouse (of de); **to make sb** ∼ rendre qn jaloux
**jealousy** *n* jalousie *f*
**jeans** *n pl* jean *m*; **a pair of** ∼ un jean
**Jeep®** *n* jeep® *f*
**jeer** ⒈ *n* huée *f*
⒉ *vtr* huer
⒊ *vi* se moquer; **to** ∼ **at sb** ⟨*crowd*⟩ huer qn; ⟨*individual*⟩ railler qn
**jeering** *n* huées *fpl*
**jellied** *adj* en aspic; ∼ **eels** anguilles *fpl* en gelée
**Jell-o®** *n* (US) gelée *f* de fruits
**jelly** *n* **(a)** (savoury) gelée *f*; (sweet) gelée *f* de fruits
**(b)** (jam) gelée *f*
**jellyfish** *n* méduse *f*
**jeopardize** *vtr* compromettre ⟨*career, plans*⟩; mettre [qch] en péril ⟨*lives, troops*⟩
**jeopardy** *n* **in** ∼ en péril, menacé/-e
**jerk** ⒈ *n* **(a)** (jolt) (of vehicle) secousse *f*; (of muscle, limb) tressaillement *m*, (petit) mouvement *m* brusque; **with a** ∼ **of his head** d'un brusque mouvement de la tête
**(b)** (colloq) (idiot) abruti *m*
⒉ *vtr* tirer brusquement ⟨*object*⟩
⒊ *vi* ⟨*person, limb, muscle*⟩ tressaillir
**jerky** ⒈ *n* (US) (*also* **beef** ∼) bœuf *m* séché
⒉ *adj* ⟨*movement*⟩ saccadé/-e; ⟨*style, phrase*⟩ haché/-e
**jersey** *n* **(a)** (sweater) pull-over *m*
**(b)** (for sports) maillot *m*
**(c)** (fabric) jersey *m*
**Jersey** *pr n* Jersey *f*
**Jerusalem** *pr n* Jérusalem
**jest** ⒈ *n* plaisanterie *f*; **in** ∼ pour plaisanter
⒉ *vi* plaisanter
**jester** *n* bouffon *m*
**Jesuit** *n, adj* jésuite (*m*)
**Jesus** ⒈ *pr n* Jésus; ∼ **Christ** Jésus-Christ
⒉ *excl* (slang) ∼ **(Christ)!** nom de Dieu! (colloq)

**jet** [1] n (a) (also ~ **plane**) jet m, avion m à réaction
(b) (of water, flame) jet m
(c) (on hob) brûleur m; (of engine) gicleur m
(d) (stone) jais m
[2] vi to ~ **off to** s'envoler pour

**jet black** adj de jais inv

**jet engine** n moteur m à réaction, réacteur m

**jetfoil** n hydroglisseur m

**jetlag** n décalage m horaire

**jetlagged** adj to be ~ souffrir du décalage horaire

**jet setter** n to be a ~ faire partie du jet-set

**jet-skiing** n jet-ski m

**jettison** vtr (from ship) jeter [qch] par-dessus bord; (from plane) larguer

**jetty** n (of stone) jetée f; (of wood) appontement m

**Jew** n juif/juive m/f

**jewel** n (a) (gem) pierre f précieuse; (piece of jewellery) bijou m; (in watch) rubis m
(b) (person) perle f; (town, object) joyau m

**jeweller** (GB), **jeweler** (US) n (person) bijoutier/-ière m/f; ~'s (shop) bijouterie f

**jewellery** (GB), **jewelry** (US) n (gen) bijoux mpl; (in shop, workshop) bijouterie f; a piece of ~ un bijou

**Jewish** adj juif/juive

**jib** n (a) (sail) foc m
(b) (of crane) flèche f

**jibe** n moquerie f

**jiffy** n in a ~ en un clin d'œil

**Jiffy bag**® n enveloppe f matelassée

**jig** n gigue f

**jiggle** [1] vtr agiter
[2] vi (also ~ **about**, ~ **around**) gigoter; (impatiently) se trémousser

**jigsaw** n (a) (also ~ **puzzle**) puzzle m
(b) (saw) scie f sauteuse

**jilt** vtr abandonner, plaquer (colloq)

**jingle** [1] n (a) (of bells) tintement m; (of keys) cliquetis m
(b) (verse) ritournelle f; (for advert) refrain m publicitaire, sonal m
[2] vi (keys, coins) cliqueter

**jingoist** n, adj chauvin/-e (m/f)

**jinx** n (a) (curse) sort m; to put a ~ on jeter un sort à; there's a ~ on me j'ai la poisse (colloq)
(b) (unlucky person, object) it's a ~ ça porte la poisse

**jitters** n pl to have the ~ (person, stock market) être nerveux/-euse; (actor) avoir le trac

**job** [1] n (a) (employment) emploi m; (post) poste m; to get a ~ trouver un emploi; a teaching ~ un poste d'enseignant; what's her ~? qu'est-ce qu'elle fait (comme travail)?
(b) (role) fonction f; it's my ~ to do c'est à moi de faire

(c) (duty) travail m; she's only doing her ~ elle fait son travail
(d) (task) travail m; to find a ~ for sb to do trouver du travail pour qn
(e) (assignment) tâche f
(f) to make a good ~ of sth faire du bon travail avec qch
(g) (colloq) quite a ~ toute une affaire (colloq) (to do, doing de faire)
[2] adj (advert, offer) d'emploi; (pages) des emplois
IDIOMS that'll do the ~ ça fera l'affaire

**job centre** n (GB) bureau m des services nationaux de l'emploi

**job creation scheme** n (GB) plan m pour la création d'emplois

**job description** n description f de poste

**job-hunting** n chasse f à l'emploi

**jobless** n the ~ les sans-emplois mpl

**jobshare** n poste m partagé

**job sharing** n partage m de poste

**jockey** n jockey m

**jockey shorts** n pl (US) slip m (d'homme)

**jockstrap** n (colloq) suspensoir m

**jodhpurs** n pl jodhpurs mpl

**jog** [1] n (a) (with elbow) coup m de coude
(b) at a ~ au petit trot (colloq)
(c) (Sport) to go for a ~ aller faire un jogging
(d) (US) (in road) coude m
[2] vtr (with elbow) donner un coup de coude à; to ~ sb's memory rafraîchir la mémoire de qn
[3] vi to go ~ging faire du jogging

**jogger** n joggeur/-euse m/f

**jogging** n jogging m

**join** [1] n raccord m
[2] vtr (a) devenir membre de (organization, team); adhérer à (club); s'inscrire à (library); entrer dans (firm); s'engager dans (army); to ~ a union se syndiquer
(b) se mettre dans (queue)
(c) (meet up with) rejoindre (person); may I ~ you? (sit down) puis-je me joindre à vous?
(d) (connect) réunir, joindre (ends, pieces); assembler (parts); relier (points, towns) (to à)
(e) (road) rejoindre (motorway); (river) se jeter dans (sea)
[3] vi (a) (become member) (of party, club) adhérer; (of group, class) s'inscrire
(b) (pieces) se joindre; (wires) se raccorder; (roads) se rejoindre
■ **join in**: ¶ ~ in participer; ¶ ~ in [sth] participer à (talks, game); prendre part à (strike, demonstration, bidding); to ~ in the fun se joindre à la fête
■ **join up**
¶ ~ up (a) (enlist) s'engager
(b) (meet up) (people) se retrouver; (roads, tracks) se rejoindre
¶ ~ [sth] up relier (characters, dots)

**joiner** n menuisier/-ière m/f

**joint** [1] n (a) (Anat) articulation f; to be out of ~ (shoulder) être déboîté/-e

**(b)** (in carpentry) assemblage *m*; (in metalwork) joint *m*
**(c)** (of meat) rôti *m*
**(d)** (colloq) ( place) endroit *m*; (café) boui-boui *m* (colloq)
**(e)** (colloq) (cannabis) joint *m* (colloq)
**2** *adj* ⟨action⟩ collectif/-ive; ⟨programme, session⟩ mixte; ⟨measures, procedure⟩ commun/-e; ⟨winner⟩ ex aequo *inv*; ⟨talks⟩ multilatéral/-e

**joint account** *n* compte *m* joint
**joint effort** *n* collaboration *f*
**joint honours** *n pl* (GB Univ) licence *f* combinée
**jointly** *adv* conjointement; **to be ~ owned by** être la copropriété de
**joint owner** *n* copropriétaire *mf*
**joint venture** *n* **(a)** (Econ) coentreprise *f*
**(b)** (gen) projet *m* en commun
**joke** **1** *n* **(a)** plaisanterie *f*, blague *f* (colloq) (about sur); **to tell a ~** raconter une blague; **to play a ~ on sb** jouer un tour à qn; **it's no ~ doing** ce n'est pas facile de faire
**(b)** ( person) guignol *m*; (event, situation) farce *f*
**2** *vi* plaisanter, blaguer (colloq); **you must be joking!** tu veux rire!
**joker** *n* **(a)** ( prankster) farceur/-euse *m/f*
**(b)** (in cards) joker *m*
**jolly** **1** *adj* ⟨person⟩ enjoué/-e; ⟨tune⟩ joyeux/-euse
**2** *vtr* **to ~ sb along** amadouer qn
**jolt** **1** *n* **(a)** (jerk) secousse *f*
**(b)** (shock) choc *m*
**2** *vtr* secouer ⟨passenger⟩
**3** *vi* ⟨vehicle⟩ cahoter
**Jordan** *pr n* (country) Jordanie *f*
**jostle** *vi* se bousculer (**for** pour; **to do** pour faire)
**jot** *v* ■ **jot down** noter ⟨ideas, names⟩
**journal** *n* **(a)** (diary) journal *m*
**(b)** ( periodical) revue *f*; (newspaper) journal *m*
**journalism** *n* journalisme *m*
**journalist** *n* journaliste *mf*
**journey** *n* **(long)** voyage *m*; (short or habitual) trajet *m*; **bus ~** trajet en bus; **to go on a ~** partir en voyage
**jowl** *n* (jaw) mâchoire *f*; (fleshy fold) bajoue *f*
**joy** *n* **(a)** (delight) joie *f* (**at** devant)
**(b)** ( pleasure) plaisir *m*; **the ~ of doing** le plaisir de faire
**IDIOMS to be full of the ~s of spring** être en pleine forme
**joyrider** *n* jeune chauffard *m* en voiture volée
**joyriding** *n* rodéo *m* à la voiture volée
**joystick** *n* (in plane) manche *m* à balai; (for video game) manette *f*
**jubilant** *adj* ⟨person⟩ exultant/-e; ⟨crowd⟩ en liesse; ⟨expression, mood⟩ réjoui/-e
**jubilee** *n* jubilé *m*
**Judaism** *n* judaïsme *m*
**judge** **1** *n* **(a)** (in court) juge *m*

**(b)** (at competition) (gen) membre *m* du jury; (Sport) juge *m*
**(c) to be a good ~ of character** savoir juger les gens
**2** *vtr* **(a)** juger ⟨person⟩
**(b)** faire partie du jury de ⟨show, competition⟩
**(c)** estimer ⟨distance, age⟩; prévoir ⟨outcome, reaction⟩
**(d)** (consider) juger, estimer
**3** *vi* juger; **judging by** or **from...** à en juger d'après...
**judgment, judgement** *n* jugement *m*
**judicial** *adj* (gen) judiciaire; ⟨decision⟩ jurisprudentiel/-ielle
**judiciary** *n* **(a)** (system of courts) système *m* judiciaire
**(b)** ( judges) magistrature *f*
**judo** *n* judo *m*
**jug** *n* **(a)** (GB) (earthenware) pichet *m*; ( pot-bellied) cruche *f*; (glass) carafe *f*; (for cream, milk, water) pot *m*
**(b)** (US) (flagon) cruche *f*
**juggernaut** *n* (GB) poids *m* lourd
**juggle** *vi* jongler (**with** avec)
**juggler** *n* jongleur/-euse *m/f*
**jugular** *n, adj* jugulaire (*f*)
**juice** *n* **(a)** (from fruit, meat) jus *m*; **fruit ~** jus de fruit
**(b)** (sap) suc *m*
**(c) gastric ~s** sucs digestifs or gastriques
**juicy** *adj* **(a)** ⟨fruit⟩ juteux/-euse
**(b)** (colloq) ⟨story⟩ croustillant/-e
**jukebox** *n* juke-box *m*
**July** *n* juillet *m*
**jumble** *n* **(a)** (of papers, objects) tas *m*; (of ideas) fouillis *m*; (of words) fatras *m*
**(b)** (GB) (items for sale) bric-à-brac *m*, vieux objets *mpl*
■ **jumble up** mélanger ⟨letters, shapes⟩
**jumble sale** *n* (GB) vente *f* de charité
**jumbo** *n* (also ~ **jet**) gros-porteur *m*
**jump** **1** *n* **(a)** (leap) saut *m*, bond *m*; **parachute ~** saut en parachute
**(b)** (in horse race) obstacle *m*
**(c)** (in price, wages) bond *m* (**in** dans)
**2** *vtr* **(a)** sauter ⟨obstacle, ditch⟩
**(b) to ~ the lights** griller (colloq) le feu (rouge); **to ~ the queue** passer devant tout le monde
**(c) to ~ ship** ne pas rejoindre son bâtiment
**3** *vi* **(a)** (leap) sauter; **to ~ across** or **over sth** franchir qch d'un bond; **to ~ up and down** sautiller; (in anger) trépigner de colère
**(b)** (start in surprise) sursauter
**(c)** ⟨prices, rate⟩ monter en flèche
**(d) to ~ at** sauter sur ⟨opportunity⟩; accepter [qch] avec enthousiasme ⟨offer⟩
■ **jump back** ⟨person⟩ faire un bond en arrière; ⟨lever⟩ lâcher brusquement
■ **jump down** ⟨person⟩ sauter (**from** de)
■ **jump on:** ¶ **~ on** [sth] sauter dans ⟨bus, train⟩; sauter sur ⟨bicycle, horse⟩; ¶ **~ on** [sb] sauter sur qn ⋯⋗

■ **jump out** ⟨*person*⟩ sauter; **to ~ out of** sauter par ⟨*window*⟩; sauter de ⟨*bed, train*⟩
■ **jump up** ⟨*person*⟩ se lever d'un bond
**jumper** n **(a)** (GB) (sweater) pull m, pull-over m
**(b)** (US) (pinafore) robe f chasuble
**jump leads** n pl câbles mpl de démarrage
**jump-start** vtr faire démarrer [qch] avec des câbles ⟨*car*⟩
**jump suit** n combinaison f
**jumpy** adj (colloq) ⟨*person*⟩ nerveux/-euse; ⟨*market*⟩ instable
**junction** n **(a)** (of two roads) carrefour m; (on motorway) échangeur m
**(b)** (of railway lines) nœud m ferroviaire; (station) gare f de jonction
**June** n juin m
**jungle** n jungle f
**junior** ⚁ n **(a)** (younger person) cadet/-ette m/f
**(b)** (low-ranking worker) subalterne m/f
**(c)** (GB) (Sch) élève mf du primaire
**(d)** (US) (Univ) ≈ étudiant/-e m/f de premier cycle; (in high school) ≈ élève mf de première ⚁ adj **(a)** ⟨*colleague, rank, position*⟩ subalterne
**(b)** (Sport) ⟨*race, team*⟩ des cadets; ⟨*player*⟩ jeune
**(c)** (*also* **Junior**) Mortimer ~ Mortimer fils or junior
**junior high school** n (US) ≈ collège m
**junior minister** n secrétaire m d'État
**junior school** n (GB) école f (primaire)
**junk** n **(a)** (rubbish) camelote f (colloq)
**(b)** (second-hand) bric-à-brac m
**(c)** (boat) jonque f
**junk food** n nourriture f industrielle
**junkie** n (colloq) drogué/-e m/f
**junk mail** n prospectus mpl
**junk shop** n boutique f de bric-à-brac
**junkyard** n (for scrap) dépotoir m; (for old cars) cimetière f de voitures
**junta** n junte f
**Jupiter** pr n Jupiter f
**jurisdiction** n **(a)** (gen) compétence f (**over** sur)
**(b)** (Law) juridiction f (**over** sur)
**juror** n juré m
**jury** n jury m
**jury box** n banc m des jurés
**jury duty** (US), **jury service** (GB) n **to do ~** faire partie d'un jury
**just¹** ⚀ adv **(a) to have ~ done** venir (juste) de faire; **he had only ~ left** il venait tout juste de partir
**(b)** (immediately) juste; **~ before/after** juste avant/après
**(c)** (slightly) **~ over/under 20 kg** un peu plus/ moins de 20 kg
**(d)** (only, merely) juste; **~ for fun** juste pour rire; **~ two days ago** il y a juste deux jours; **he's ~ a child** ce n'est qu'un enfant

**(e)** (purposely) exprès; **he did it ~ to annoy us** il l'a fait exprès pour nous embêter
**(f)** (barely) tout juste; **~ on time** tout juste à l'heure; **he's ~ 20** il a tout juste 20 ans; **I (only) ~ caught the train** j'ai eu le train de justesse
**(g)** (simply) tout simplement; **~ tell the truth** dis la vérité, tout simplement; **she ~ won't listen** elle ne veut tout simplement pas écouter; **'~ a moment'** 'un instant'
**(h)** (exactly) exactement; **that's ~ what I want** c'est exactement ce que je veux; **it's ~ right** c'est parfait; **she looks ~ like her father** c'est son père tout craché (colloq); **it's ~ like him to forget** c'est bien de lui d'oublier
**(i)** (possibly) **it might** or **could ~ be true** il se peut que ce soit vrai
**(j)** (at this or that very moment) **to be ~ doing** être en train de faire; **to be ~ about to do** être sur le point de faire; **he was ~ leaving** il partait
**(k)** (positively, totally) vraiment; **that's ~ wonderful** c'est vraiment merveilleux
**(l)** (in requests) **if you could ~ hold this box** si vous pouviez tenir cette boîte
**(m)** (equally) **~ as big as...** (tout) aussi grand que...
**(n)** (with imperative) donc; **~ you dare!** essaie donc voir!; **~ imagine!** imagine donc!
⚁ **just about** phr presque; **~ about everything** à peu près tout; **I can ~ about see it** je peux tout juste le voir
⚂ **just as** phr **~ as he came** juste au moment où il est arrivé
⚃ **just now** phr en ce moment; **I saw him ~ now** je viens juste de le voir
**just²** adj ⟨*person, decision*⟩ juste; ⟨*demand*⟩ justifié/-e; ⟨*claim, criticism*⟩ légitime
**justice** n **(a)** (fairness) justice f; **the portrait doesn't do her ~** le portrait ne l'avantage pas
**(b)** (the law) justice f; **to bring sb to ~** traduire qn en justice
**Justice Department** n (US) ministère m de la justice
**Justice of the Peace** n juge m de paix
**justifiable** adj (that is justified) légitime; (that can be justified) justifiable
**justification** n raison f; **to have some ~ for doing** avoir des raisons de faire
**justified** adj justifié/-e; **to feel ~ in doing** se sentir en droit de faire
**justify** vtr justifier
**jut** vi (*also* **~ out**) ⟨*cliffs*⟩ avancer en saillie (**into** dans); ⟨*balcony*⟩ faire saillie (**over** sur)
**juvenile** n (gen) jeune mf; (Law) mineur/-e m/f
**juvenile delinquency** n délinquance f juvénile
**juvenile delinquent** n jeune délinquant/-e m/f
**juvenile offender** n délinquant/-e m/f mineur/-e
**juxtapose** vtr juxtaposer (**with** à)

# K k

**k**, **K** *n* k, K *m*

**kale** *n* (*also* **curly** ∼) chou *m* frisé

**kaleidoscope** *n* kaléidoscope *m*

**kangaroo** *n* kangourou *m*

**karaoke** *n* karaoké *m*

**karate** *n* karaté *m*

**Kashmir** *pr n* Cachemire *m*

**kayak**: *n* kayak *m*

**kebab** *n* (*also* **shish** ∼) chiche-kebab *m*

**kedgeree** *n* (GB) pilaf *m* de poisson

**keel** *n* quille *f*
■ **keel over** ⟨*boat*⟩ chavirer

**keen** *adj* (a) (eager) ⟨*artist, footballer, supporter*⟩ enthousiaste; ⟨*student*⟩ assidu/-e; **to be** ∼ **on** tenir à ⟨*plan, project*⟩; être chaud/-e pour (colloq) ⟨*idea*⟩; être passionné/-e de ⟨*activity*⟩; **to be** ∼ **on doing** *or* **to do** tenir à faire
(b) ⟨*appetite, interest*⟩ vif/vive; ⟨*eye, intelligence*⟩ vif/vive; ⟨*sight*⟩ perçant/-e; ⟨*hearing, sense of smell*⟩ fin/-e
(c) ⟨*competition*⟩ intense

**keep** ①  *n* (a) pension *f*; **to pay for one's** ∼ payer une pension
(b) (tower) donjon *m*
②  *vtr* (a) (retain) garder ⟨*receipt, money, letter, seat*⟩; **to** ∼ **sb/sth clean** garder qn/qch propre; **to** ∼ **sth warm** garder qch au chaud; **to** ∼ **sb warm** protéger qn du froid; **to** ∼ **sb waiting** faire attendre qn; **to** ∼ **sb talking** retenir qn; **to** ∼ **an engine running** laisser un moteur en marche
(b) (detain) retenir; **I won't** ∼ **you a minute** je n'en ai pas pour longtemps
(c) (tenir) ⟨*shop*⟩; élever ⟨*chickens*⟩
(d) (sustain) **to** ∼ **[sth] going** entretenir ⟨*conversation, fire*⟩; maintenir ⟨*tradition*⟩; **I'll make you a sandwich to** ∼ **you going** je te ferai un sandwich pour que tu tiennes le coup
(e) (store) mettre, ranger; **where do you** ∼ **your cups?** où rangez-vous vos tasses?
(f) (support) faire vivre, entretenir ⟨*family*⟩
(g) tenir ⟨*accounts, diary*⟩
(h) **to** ∼ **sth from sb** taire *or* cacher qch à qn; **to** ∼ **sth to oneself** garder qch pour soi
(i) (prevent) **to** ∼ **sb from doing** empêcher qn de faire
(j) tenir ⟨*promise*⟩; garder ⟨*secret*⟩; se rendre à ⟨*appointment*⟩
(k) (Mus) **to** ∼ **time** battre la mesure
③  *vi* (a) (continue) **to** ∼ **doing** continuer à *or* de faire, ne pas arrêter de faire; **to** ∼ **going** ⟨*person*⟩ continuer
(b) (remain) **to** ∼ **out of the rain** se protéger de la pluie; **to** ∼ **warm** se protéger du froid; **to** ∼ **calm** rester calme; **to** ∼ **silent** garder le silence

(c) ⟨*food*⟩ se conserver, se garder
(d) ⟨*news, business*⟩ attendre
(e) **'how are you** ∼**ing?'** 'comment allez-vous?'; **she's** ∼**ing well** elle va bien
④  *v refl* **to** ∼ **oneself to oneself** ne pas être sociable
⑤  **for keeps** *phr* pour de bon, pour toujours
■ **keep away**: ¶ ∼ **away** ne pas s'approcher (from de); ¶ ∼ **[sth/sb] away** empêcher [qch/qn] de s'approcher
■ **keep back**: ¶ ∼ **back** ne pas s'approcher (from de)
¶ ∼ **[sb/sth] back** (a) empêcher [qn] de s'approcher ⟨*crowd*⟩ (from de); ⟨*dam*⟩ retenir ⟨*water*⟩
(b) (retain) garder ⟨*money*⟩; conserver ⟨*food*⟩
■ **keep down** ¶ ∼ **[sth] down,** ∼ **down [sth]** limiter ⟨*number, speed, inflation*⟩; limiter l'augmentation de ⟨*prices, unemployment*⟩; ∼ **your voice down!** baisse la voix!
■ **keep off**: ¶ ∼ **off [sth]** (a) ne pas marcher sur ⟨*grass*⟩
(b) éviter ⟨*alcohol*⟩; s'abstenir de parler de ⟨*subject*⟩
¶ ∼ **[sth] off** éloigner ⟨*insects*⟩; **this plastic sheet will** ∼ **the rain off** cette housse en plastique protège de la pluie
■ **keep on**: ¶ ∼ **on doing** continuer à faire; **to** ∼ **on about** ne pas arrêter de parler de; **to** ∼ **on at sb** harceler qn (**to do** pour qu'il fasse); ¶ ∼ **[sb] on** garder
■ **keep out**: ¶ ∼ **out of [sth]** (a) ne pas entrer dans ⟨*house*⟩; **'**∼ **out!'** 'défense d'entrer'
(b) rester à l'abri de ⟨*sun, danger*⟩
(c) ne pas se mêler de ⟨*argument*⟩; **to** ∼ **out of sb's way** (not hinder) ne pas gêner qn; (avoid seeing) éviter qn
¶ ∼ **[sb/sth] out** ne pas laisser entrer ⟨*person, animal*⟩
■ **keep to** ne pas s'écarter de ⟨*road*⟩; respecter, s'en tenir à ⟨*facts*⟩; respecter ⟨*law, rules*⟩
■ **keep up**: ¶ ∼ **up** ⟨*car, runner, person*⟩ suivre; ¶ ∼ **[sth] up** (a) tenir ⟨*trousers*⟩
(b) continuer ⟨*attack, studies*⟩; entretenir ⟨*correspondence, friendship*⟩; maintenir ⟨*membership, tradition, pace*⟩; ¶ ∼ **[sb] up** ⟨*noise*⟩ empêcher [qn] de dormir
■ **keep up with** (a) aller aussi vite que ⟨*person*⟩; suivre ⟨*class*⟩; ⟨*wages*⟩ suivre ⟨*inflation*⟩; faire face à ⟨*demand*⟩
(b) suivre ⟨*fashion, developments*⟩

**keeper** *n* (curator) conservateur/-trice *m/f*; (guard) gardien/-ienne *m/f*

**keep fit** *n* gymnastique *f* d'entretien

**keeping** n (a) (custody) **in sb's ~** à la garde de qn; **to put sb/sth in sb's ~** confier qn/qch à qn
(b) (conformity) **in ~ with** conforme à ⟨law, tradition⟩; **to be in ~ with** correspondre à ⟨image, character⟩; s'harmoniser avec ⟨surroundings⟩

**keg** n (for liquid) fût m; (for gunpowder) baril m

**kennel** n (a) (GB) (for dog) niche f
(b) (establishment) chenil m

**Kenya** pr n Kenya m; **in ~** au Kenya

**kerb** n (GB) bord m du trottoir

**kernel** n (of nut, fruitstone) amande f

**kerosene, kerosine** n (a) (US) (paraffin) pétrole m (lampant)
(b) (fuel) kérosène m

**kestrel** n (faucon m) crécerelle f

**kettle** n bouilloire f; **to put the ~ on** mettre l'eau à chauffer

**kettledrum** n timbale f

**key** 1 n (a) clé f; **a front-door ~** une clé de maison; **a set** or **bunch of ~s** un jeu de clés; **under lock and ~** sous clé; **radiator ~** clavette f à radiateur
(b) (on computer, piano) touche f; (on oboe, flute) clé f
(c) (vital clue) clé f, secret m (**to** de)
(d) (on map) légende f; (to abbreviations, symbols) liste f; (for code) clé f
(e) (to test, riddle) solutions fpl; (Sch) corrigé m
(f) (Mus) ton m, tonalité f; **to sing in/off ~** chanter juste/faux
2 adj ⟨figure, role⟩ clé; ⟨point⟩ capital/-e
3 vtr (a) (also ~ **in**) saisir ⟨data⟩
(b) (adapt) adapter (**to** à)

**keyboard** n clavier m

**keyboards** n pl synthétiseur m

**keyed-up** adj (excited) excité/-e; (tense) tendu/-e

**keyhole** n trou m de serrure

**keyhole surgery** n chirurgie f endoscopique

**keynote speech** n discours m programme

**key-ring** n porte-clés m inv

**keyword** n mot m clé

**khaki** adj kaki inv

**kibbutz** n kibboutz m

**kick** 1 n (a) (of person, horse) coup m de pied; (of donkey, cow) coup m de sabot; (of swimmer) battement m de pieds; (of footballer) tir m
(b) (colloq) (thrill) **to get a ~ out of doing** prendre plaisir à faire
(c) (of firearm) recul m
2 vtr (once) ⟨person⟩ donner un coup de pied à ⟨person⟩; donner un coup de pied dans ⟨door, ball, tin can⟩; ⟨horse⟩ botter ⟨person⟩; ⟨donkey, cow⟩ donner un coup de sabot à ⟨person⟩; (repeatedly) ⟨person⟩ donner des coups de pied à ⟨person⟩; donner des coups de pieds dans ⟨object⟩; **to ~ sb on the leg**

⟨person, horse⟩ donner à qn un coup de pied à la jambe; ⟨donkey, cow⟩ donner à qn un coup de sabot dans la jambe
3 vi ⟨person⟩ (once) donner un coup de pied; (repeatedly) donner des coups de pied; ⟨swimmer⟩ faire des battements de pieds; ⟨cow⟩ ruer; ⟨horse⟩ botter
IDIOMS **to ~ the habit** (colloq) (of drug addiction) décrocher (colloq); (of smoking) arrêter de fumer; **I could have ~ed myself** je me serais donné des claques (colloq)
■ **kick around, kick about** donner des coups de pied dans, s'amuser avec ⟨ball⟩
■ **kick off** (a) (Sport) donner le coup d'envoi
(b) (colloq) (start) commencer
■ **kick out:** ¶ **~ out** ⟨animal⟩ ruer; ¶ **~ [sb] out** (colloq) virer (colloq)

**kick-off** n (Sport) coup m d'envoi

**kick-start** 1 n (also ~**-starter**) kick m
2 vtr (a) faire démarrer [qch] au pied ⟨motorbike⟩
(b) (colloq) relancer ⟨economy⟩

**kid** 1 n (a) (colloq) (child) enfant mf, gosse mf (colloq); (youth) gamin/-e m/f (colloq)
(b) (young goat) chevreau/-ette m/f
(c) (goatskin) chevreau m
2 vtr (colloq) charrier (colloq) (**about** à propos de)
3 vi (colloq) rigoler (colloq); **no ~ding!** sans blague! (colloq)
4 v refl (colloq) **to ~ oneself** se faire des illusions

**kidnap** vtr enlever

**kidnapper** n ravisseur/-euse m/f

**kidnapping** n enlèvement m

**kidney** n (a) (Anat) rein m
(b) (Culin) rognon m

**kidney bean** n haricot m rouge

**kidney machine** n rein m artificiel; **to be on a ~** être sous dialyse

**kill** 1 n mise f à mort
2 vtr (a) tuer ⟨person, animal⟩; **they ~ed each other** ils se sont entre-tués; **even if it ~s me!** (colloq) même si je dois y laisser ma peau! (colloq); **my feet are ~ing me** (colloq) j'ai mal aux pieds
(b) mettre fin à, étouffer ⟨rumour⟩; ⟨editor⟩ supprimer ⟨story⟩
(c) faire disparaître ⟨pain⟩; ôter ⟨appetite⟩
(d) (spend) **to ~ time** tuer le temps (**by doing** en faisant)
3 vi ⟨person, animal, drug⟩ tuer
4 v refl **to ~ oneself** se suicider

**killer** n (person) meurtrier m; (animal) tueur/-euse m/f; **heroin is a ~** l'héroïne tue

**killer whale** n épaulard m

**killing** n (of individual) meurtre m (**of** de); (of animal) mise f à mort (**of** de)

**killjoy** n rabat-joie mf inv

**kiln** n four m

**kilo** n kilo m

**kilobyte, KB** n kilo-octet m, Ko m

**kilogram(me)** n kilogramme m

**kilometre** (GB), **kilometer** (US) *n* kilomètre *m*

**kilowatt** *n* kilowatt *m*

**kind** ① *n* (a) (sort, type) sorte *f*, genre *m*, type *m*; this ~ of person ce genre de personne; all ~s of people toutes sortes de personnes; what ~ of dog is it? qu'est-ce que c'est comme chien?; what ~ of person is she? comment est-elle?, quel genre de personne est-ce?; this is one of a ~ il/elle est unique en son genre
(b) (in vague descriptions) a ~ of une sorte de; I heard a ~ of rattling noise j'ai entendu comme un cliquetis
(c) (classified type) espèce *f*, genre *m*; one's own ~ les gens de son espèce
② *adj* ⟨person, gesture, words⟩ gentil/-ille; ⟨act⟩ bon/bonne (before n); to be ~ to sb être gentil/-ille avec qn; to be ~ to animals bien traiter les animaux; that's very ~ of you c'est très gentil or aimable de votre part; would you be ~ enough to pass the salt? auriez-vous l'amabilité de me passer le sel?
③ **in kind** *phr* ⟨pay⟩ en nature
④ **kind of** *phr* (colloq) he's ~ of cute il est plutôt mignon; I ~ of like him en fait, je l'aime bien; 'is it interesting?'—'~ of' 'est-ce que c'est intéressant?'—'assez'

**kindergarten** *n* jardin *m* d'enfants

**kind-hearted** *adj* ⟨person⟩ de cœur

**kindle** *vtr* (a) allumer ⟨fire⟩
(b) attiser ⟨desire, passion⟩; susciter ⟨interest⟩

**kindly** ① *adj* ⟨person⟩ gentil/-ille; ⟨smile⟩ bienveillant/-e
② *adv* (a) (in a kind way) avec gentillesse; to speak ~ of sb dire du bien de qn
(b) (obligingly) gentiment; would you ~ do/ refrain from doing auriez-vous l'amabilité de faire/de ne pas faire
(c) (favourably) to take ~ to apprécier

**kindness** *n* gentillesse *f*, bonté *f*

**kindred spirit** *n* âme *f* sœur

**kinetics** *n* cinétique *f*

**king** *n* (a) (monarch) roi *m*; **King Charles** le roi Charles
(b) (in chess, cards) roi *m*; (in draughts, checkers) dame *f*

**kingdom** *n* (a) (country) royaume *m*
(b) (Bot, Zool) règne *m*; the animal ~ le règne animal

**kingfisher** *n* martin-pêcheur *m*

**king-size(d)** *adj* ⟨packet⟩ géant/-e; ⟨portion, garden⟩ énorme; ~ bed grand lit *m*; ~ cigarettes cigarettes *fpl* extra-longues

**kink** *n* (in rope, tube) nœud *m*; the hosepipe has a ~ in it le tuyau d'arrosage est tordu

**kiosk** *n* (a) (stand) kiosque *m*
(b) (GB) (phone box) cabine *f*

**kipper** *n* (GB) hareng *m* fumé et salé, kipper *m*

**kiss** ① *n* baiser *m*; to give sb a ~ embrasser qn, donner un baiser à qn
② *vtr* embrasser, donner un baiser à

⟨person⟩; to ~ sb on embrasser qn sur ⟨cheek, lips⟩; we ~ed each other nous nous sommes embrassés
③ *vi* s'embrasser

**kiss of life** *n* (GB) bouche-à-bouche *m inv*; to give sb the ~ faire le bouche-à-bouche à qn

**kit** *n* (a) (implements) trousse *f*
(b) (gear, clothes) affaires *fpl*; **football** ~ affaires de football
(c) (for assembly) kit *m*
(d) (Mil) paquetage *m*
■ **kit out** (GB) équiper (with de)

**kitbag** *n* (for sport) sac *m* de sport; (for travel) sac *m* de voyage; (Mil) sac *m* de soldat

**kitchen** *n* cuisine *f*

**kitchen foil** *n* papier *m* d'aluminium

**kitchen roll** *n* essuie-tout *m inv*

**kitchen sink** *n* évier *m*

**kitchen unit** *n* élément *m* de cuisine

**kite** *n* cerf-volant *m*; to fly a ~ faire voler un cerf-volant

**kitten** *n* chaton *m*

**kitty** *n* cagnotte *f*

**kiwi fruit** *n* kiwi *m*

**kleptomaniac** *n, adj* kleptomane (*mf*)

**knack** *n* (a) (dexterity) tour *m* de main (of doing pour faire); to get the ~ attraper le tour de main; to lose the ~ perdre la main
(b) (talent) don *m* (for doing de faire)

**knapsack** *n* sac *m* à dos

**knave** *n* (in cards) valet *m*

**knead** *vtr* pétrir ⟨dough⟩; masser ⟨flesh⟩

**knee** ① *n* genou *m*; on (one's) hands and ~s à quatre pattes
② *vtr* donner un coup de genou à ⟨person⟩
IDIOMS to go weak at the ~s avoir les jambes qui flageolent

**kneecap** *n* rotule *f*

**knee-deep** *adj* the water was ~ l'eau arrivait aux genoux

**kneel** *vi* (also ~ **down**) se mettre à genoux; (in prayer) s'agenouiller; to be ~ing être à genoux

**knee-length** *adj* ⟨skirt⟩ qui s'arrête au genou; ⟨boots⟩ haut/-e; ⟨socks⟩ long/longue

**knickers** *n pl* (GB) petite culotte *f*

**knick-knack** *n* bibelot *m*

**knife** ① *n* couteau *m*
② *vtr* donner un coup de couteau à; to be ~d recevoir un coup de couteau

**knife-edge** *n* to be (living) on a ~ ⟨person⟩ être au bord de l'abîme

**knife-point** *n* at ~ sous la menace d'un couteau

**knight** ① *n* (gen) chevalier *m*; (in chess) cavalier *m*
② *vtr* (GB) anoblir ⟨person⟩ (for pour)

**knighthood** *n* titre *m* de chevalier

**knit** ① *vtr* tricoter ⟨sweater, hat⟩; ~ted en tricot
② *vi* (a) tricoter
(b) ⟨broken bones⟩ se souder

**knitting** n tricot m

**knitwear** n tricots mpl

**knob** n (a) (of door) bouton m; (on bannister) boule f
(b) (control button) bouton m

**knobbly** (GB), **knobby** (US) adj ‹fingers› noueux/-euse; ‹knees› saillant/-e

**knock** ① n (a) (blow) coup m (on sur; with de); a ～ at the door un coup à la porte; ～! ～! toc! toc!
(b) (setback) coup m; to take a ～ en prendre un coup
② vtr (a) (strike) cogner ‹object›; to ～ one's head on sth se cogner la tête contre qch; to ～ sb unconscious assommer qn; to ～ sth off or out of sth faire tomber qch de qch
(b) (colloq) (criticize) dénigrer
③ vi (a) ‹branch, engine, object› cogner (on, against contre); ‹person› frapper (at, on à)
(b) (collide) to ～ into or against sth heurter qch

■ **knock down** (a) (deliberately) jeter [qn] à terre ‹person›; défoncer ‹door›; démolir ‹building›; (accidentally) renverser ‹person, object›; abattre ‹fence›
(b) ‹buyer› faire baisser ‹price›; ‹seller› baisser ‹price›

■ **knock off**: ¶ ～ off (colloq) arrêter de travailler
¶ ～ [sb/sth] off, ～ off [sb/sth] (a) (cause to fall) faire tomber ‹person, object›
(b) (colloq) (reduce) to ～ £10 off the price of sth réduire le prix de qch de 10 livres
(c) (colloq) ～ it off! ça suffit!

■ **knock out** (a) casser ‹tooth›
(b) (make unconscious) ‹person, blow› assommer; ‹drug› endormir; ‹boxer› mettre [qn] au tapis ‹opponent›
(c) (Sport) éliminer ‹opponent, team›

■ **knock over** renverser ‹person, object›

**knockdown** adj ‹price› sacrifié/-e

**knocker** n heurtoir m

**knocking** n (at door) coups mpl; (in engine) cognement m

**knock-kneed** adj cagneux/-euse

**knock-on effect** n implications fpl

**knock-out** ① n (in boxing) knock-out m
② adj (a) (Sport) ‹competition› avec tours éliminatoires
(b) (colloq) ‹pills› sédatif/-ive

**knot** ① n (a) nœud m; to tie a ～ faire un nœud; to tie sth in a ～ nouer qch
(b) (in wood) nœud m

(c) (group) petit groupe m (of de)
② vtr nouer (**together** ensemble)

**know** ① vtr (gen) savoir; (be acquainted or familiar with) connaître ‹place, person, way›; to ～ why/how savoir pourquoi/comment; to ～ how to do savoir faire; to ～ sb by sight connaître qn de vue; to get to ～ sb faire connaissance avec qn; he ～s all about it il est au courant; I knew it! j'en étais sûr!
② vi savoir; as you ～ comme vous le savez; to ～ about (have information) être au courant de ‹event›; (have skill) s'y connaître en ‹computing, engines›; to ～ of (from experience) connaître; (from information) avoir entendu parler de; to let sb ～ of or about tenir qn au courant de
IDIOMS to be in the ～ (colloq) être bien informé/-e

**know-all** n (GB) (colloq) je-sais-tout mf inv

**know-how** n (colloq) savoir-faire m inv

**knowing** adj ‹look, smile› entendu/-e

**knowledge** n (a) (awareness) connaissance f; to my ～ à ma connaissance; without sb's ～ à l'insu de qn
(b) (factual wisdom) connaissances fpl; (of specific field) connaissance f; technical ～ connaissances techniques

**knowledgeable** adj ‹person› savant/-e; to be ～ about s'y connaître en ‹subject›

**known** adj ‹authority, danger› reconnu/-e; ‹cure› connu/-e

**knuckle** n (a) (of person) jointure f, articulation f
(b) (Culin) (of lamb, mutton) manche m de gigot; (of pork, veal) jarret m

■ **knuckle down** (colloq) s'y mettre (sérieusement)

**knuckle-duster** n coup-de-poing m américain

**koala (bear)** n koala m

**Koran** n Coran m

**Korea** pr n Corée f

**kosher** adj (a) ‹food, restaurant› casher
(b) (colloq) (not illegal) it's ～ c'est réglo (colloq)

**Kosovan** ① n Kosovar/-e m/f
② adj kosovar/-e

**Kosovo** pr n Kosovo m

**Kurd** n Kurde mf

**Kurdish** adj kurde

**Kurdistan** pr n Kurdistan m

**Kuwait** pr n Koweït m

# Ll

**l, L** *n* l, L *m*

**lab** *n* labo *m* (colloq)

**lab coat** *n* blouse *f* blanche

**label** **1** *n* (a) (on clothing, jar) étiquette *f*
(b) (*also* **record** ∼) label *m*
(c) (Comput) label *m*
**2** *vtr* (a) étiqueter ⟨*clothing, jar*⟩
(b) classer, étiqueter (derogatory) ⟨*person*⟩ (as comme)

**labor** (US) = LABOUR

**laboratory** *n* laboratoire *m*

**laborer** (US) = LABOURER

**labor union** *n* (US) syndicat *m*

**labour** (GB), **labor** (US) **1** *n* (a) (work) travail *m*
(b) (*also* ∼ **force**) main-d'œuvre *f*
(c) (Med) accouchement *m*; **to be in** ∼ être en train d'accoucher
**2** *vi* travailler (dur) (at à; on sur; to do pour faire)
IDIOMS **to** ∼ **the point** insister lourdement

**Labour** **1** *n* (GB) parti *m* travailliste
**2** *adj* travailliste

**labourer** (GB), **laborer** (US) *n* ouvrier/-ière *m/f* du bâtiment

**Labour Party** *n* (GB) parti *m* travailliste

**labour-saving** *adj* ⟨*feature, system*⟩ qui facilite le travail; ∼ **device** appareil *m* ménager

**labyrinth** *n* labyrinthe *m*, dédale *m*

**lace** **1** *n* (a) (fabric) dentelle *f*
(b) (on shoe, boot, dress) lacet *m*; (on tent) cordon *m*
**2** *vtr* (a) lacer ⟨*shoes*⟩
(b) **to** ∼ **a drink with sth** mettre qch dans une boisson

**lace-up (shoe)** *n* chaussure *f* à lacet

**lack** **1** *n* manque *m* (of de); **through** ∼ **of** par manque de
**2** *vtr* manquer de
**3** *vi* **to be** ∼**ing** manquer; **to be** ∼**ing in** manquer de

**lacklustre** (GB), **lackluster** (US) *adj* terne

**lacquer** *n* (a) (for hair) laque *f*
(b) (varnish) laque *f*

**lacy** *adj* en *or* de dentelle

**lad** *n* (colloq) (boy) garçon *m*

**ladder** **1** *n* (a) (for climbing) échelle *f*
(b) (GB) (in stockings) échelle *f*, maille *f* filée
**2** *vtr, vi* filer

**laddish** *adj* (colloq) macho *inv* (colloq)

**ladle** *n* (Culin) louche *f*

**lady** **1** *n* (a) (woman) dame *f*; **ladies and gentlemen** mesdames et messieurs; **a little old** ∼ une petite vieille; **she's a real** ∼ elle est très distinguée
(b) (in titles) **Lady Churchill** Lady Churchill
**2** **ladies** *n pl* toilettes *fpl*; (on sign) 'Dames'

**ladybird** *n* coccinelle *f*

**ladylike** *adj* ⟨*behaviour*⟩ distingué/-e

**lag** **1** *n* (*also* **time** ∼) décalage *m*
**2** *vtr* calorifuger ⟨*pipe, tank*⟩; isoler ⟨*roof*⟩
■ **lag behind**: ¶ ∼ **behind** ⟨*person, prices*⟩ être à la traîne; ¶ ∼ **behind** [sb/sth] traîner derrière ⟨*person*⟩; être en retard sur ⟨*rival, product*⟩

**lager** *n* bière *f* blonde

**lager lout** *n* (GB) voyou *m* ⟨*qui se soûle à la bière*⟩

**lagoon** *n* lagune *f*

**laidback** *adj* (colloq) décontracté/-e

**laid up** *adj* **to be** ∼ être alité/-e

**lake** *n* lac *m*

**lamb** *n* agneau *m*; **leg of** ∼ gigot *m* d'agneau

**lamb's wool** *n* laine *f* d'agneau, lambswool *m*

**lame** *adj* boiteux/-euse

**lament** **1** *n* lamentation *f*
**2** *vtr* se lamenter sur ⟨*fate, misfortune*⟩

**lamentable** *adj* déplorable

**laminated** *adj* ⟨*plastic*⟩ stratifié/-e; ⟨*wood*⟩ contreplaqué/-e; ⟨*card*⟩ plastifié/-e

**lamp** *n* lampe *f*

**lamppost** *n* réverbère *m*

**lampshade** *n* abat-jour *m*

**lance** *vtr* percer ⟨*boil, abscess*⟩

**land** **1** *n* (a) (terrain, property) terrain *m*; (very large) terres *fpl*
(b) (farmland) terre *f*
(c) (country) pays *m*
(d) (not sea) terre *f*; **dry** ∼ terre ferme; **to reach** ∼ toucher terre; **by** ∼ par voie de terre
**2** *vtr* (a) ⟨*pilot*⟩ poser ⟨*aircraft*⟩; faire atterrir ⟨*space capsule*⟩
(b) prendre ⟨*fish*⟩
(c) (colloq) décrocher (colloq) ⟨*job, contract, prize*⟩
(d) (colloq) **to be** ∼**ed with sb/sth** se retrouver avec qn/qch sur les bras
**3** *vi* (a) ⟨*aircraft, passenger*⟩ atterrir
(b) ⟨*ship*⟩ accoster
(c) ⟨*person, animal, object*⟩ atterrir; ⟨*ball*⟩ toucher le sol; **most of the paint** ∼**ed on me** presque toute la peinture m'est tombée dessus

**landing** *n* (a) (at turn of stairs) palier *m*; (storey) étage *m*

**(b)** (from boat) (of people) débarquement m; (of cargo) déchargement m
**(c)** (by plane) atterrissage m (**on** sur)

**landing card** n carte f de débarquement

**landing gear** n train m d'atterrissage

**landing strip** n piste f d'atterrissage

**landlady** n (owner) propriétaire f; (live-in) logeuse f; (of pub) patronne f

**landlord** n (owner) propriétaire m; (live-in) logeur m; (of pub) patron m

**landmark** n (for bearings) point m de repère; (major step) étape f importante

**land mine** n mine f antipersonnel

**landowner** n propriétaire mf foncier/-ière

**landscape** n paysage m

**landscape gardener** n jardinier/-ière m/f paysagiste

**landslide** n **(a)** glissement m de terrain
**(b)** (also ∼ **victory**) victoire f écrasante

**lane** n **(a)** (in country) chemin m, petite route f; (in town) ruelle f
**(b)** (of road) voie f, file f; (air, sea) couloir m; (Sport) couloir m

**language** n **(a)** (system in general) langage m
**(b)** (of a particular nation) langue f; **the French** ∼ la langue française
**(c)** (of a particular group, style) langage m; **legal** ∼ langage juridique; **bad** or **foul** ∼ langage grossier
**(d)** (Comput) langage m

**language barrier** n obstacle m or barrière f de la langue

**language laboratory, language lab** n laboratoire m de langues

**languish** vi (remain neglected) ⟨person⟩ languir; ⟨object⟩ traîner

**lank** adj ⟨hair⟩ plat/-e

**lantern** n lanterne f

**lap** n **(a)** (of person) genoux mpl; **in one's** ∼ sur les genoux
**(b)** (Sport) (of track) tour m de piste; (of racecourse) tour m de circuit
IDIOMS **in the** ∼ **of luxury** dans le plus grand luxe
■ **lap up (a)** laper ⟨milk, water⟩
**(b)** boire [qch] comme du petit lait ⟨compliment, flattery⟩

**lap belt** n ceinture f ventrale

**lapel** n revers m

**lapse** **1** n **(a)** (slip) défaillance f; **a** ∼ **in concentration** un relâchement de l'attention
**(b)** (interval) intervalle m, laps m de temps
**2** vi **(a)** ⟨contract, membership⟩ expirer; ⟨insurance⟩ prendre fin
**(b)** **to** ∼ **into** se mettre à parler ⟨jargon, German⟩; tomber dans ⟨coma⟩; prendre ⟨bad habits⟩

**laptop** n (also ∼ **computer**) portable m

**lard** n saindoux m

**larder** n garde-manger m inv

**large** **1** adj **(a)** (gen) grand/-e (before n); ⟨appetite, piece, person, nose⟩ gros/grosse (before n); ⟨amount⟩ important/-e; ⟨crowd, family⟩ nombreux/-euse
**2** **at large** phr **(a)** ⟨prisoner, criminal⟩ en liberté
**(b)** ⟨society, population⟩ en général, dans son ensemble
IDIOMS **by and** ∼ en général

**large-scale** adj à grande échelle

**lark** n **(a)** (Zool) alouette f
**(b)** (colloq) (fun) **for a** ∼ pour rigoler (colloq)

**laryngitis** n laryngite f

**larynx** n larynx m

**lasagne** n lasagnes fpl

**laser** **1** n laser m
**2** adj ⟨beam, disc⟩ laser inv; ⟨printer⟩ à laser

**laser treatment** n thérapie f au laser

**lash** **1** n **(a)** (eyelash) cil m
**(b)** (whipstroke) coup m de fouet
**2** vtr fouetter ⟨person, animal⟩; ⟨rain⟩ cingler ⟨windows⟩
■ **lash out** ⟨person⟩ devenir violent/-e; **to** ∼ **out at sb** (physically) frapper qn; (verbally) invectiver qn

**last** **1** pron **the** ∼ le dernier/la dernière m/f (**to do** à faire); **the** ∼ **but one** l'avant-dernier/-ière; **the night before** ∼ (evening) avant-hier soir; (night) la nuit d'avant-hier; **the week before** ∼ il y a deux semaines
**2** adj dernier/-ière (before n); ∼ **week/year** la semaine/l'année dernière; ∼ **Christmas** à Noël l'an dernier; **over the** ∼ **ten years** durant ces dix dernières années; ∼ **night** (evening) hier soir; (night-time) la nuit dernière
**3** adv **(a) to come in** ∼ ⟨runner, racing car⟩ arriver en dernier; **the girls left** ∼ les filles sont parties les dernières; **to leave sth till** ∼ s'occuper de qch en dernier (lieu); ∼ **of all** en dernier lieu
**(b) she was** ∼ **here in 1976** la dernière fois qu'elle est venue ici, c'était en 1976
**4** vi **(a)** durer; **it's too good to** ∼! c'est trop beau pour que ça dure!; **he won't** ∼ **long here** il ne tiendra pas longtemps ici
**(b)** ⟨fabric⟩ faire de l'usage; ⟨perishables⟩ se conserver
**5** **at last** adv enfin

**last-ditch** adj ⟨attempt, stand⟩ désespéré/-e, ultime

**lasting** adj ⟨effect, impression⟩ durable; ⟨relationship⟩ sérieux/-ieuse

**lastly** adv enfin, finalement

**last-minute** adj de dernière minute

**last name** n nom m de famille

**last rites** n pl derniers sacrements mpl

**latch** n (fastening) loquet m; (spring lock) serrure f (de sûreté).
■ **latch on to** (colloq) s'accrocher à ⟨object, person⟩; exploiter ⟨idea⟩

**late** **1** adj **(a)** ⟨arrival⟩ tardif/-ive; **to be** ∼ **(for sth)** être en retard (pour qch); **to make**

sb ∼ retarder qn; **to be ∼ with the rent** payer son loyer avec du retard; **dinner will be a bit ∼** le dîner sera retardé
**(b)** ⟨*hour, supper, date*⟩ tardif/-ive; **to have a ∼ night** (aller) se coucher tard; **to be in one's ∼ fifties** approcher de la soixantaine; **in ∼ January** (à la) fin janvier; **in the ∼ 50s** à la fin des années 50
**(c)** (deceased) feu/-e (formal); **my ∼ wife** ma pauvre femme
**2** *adv* **(a)** ⟨*arrive, start, finish*⟩ en retard; **to be running ∼** ⟨*person*⟩ être en retard; ⟨*train, bus*⟩ avoir du retard; **to start three months ∼** commencer avec trois mois de retard
**(b)** ⟨*get up, open, close*⟩ tard; ⟨*marry*⟩ sur le tard; ∼ **last night/in the evening** tard hier soir/dans la soirée
**latecomer** *n* retardataire *mf*
**late developer** *n* **to be a ∼** ⟨*child*⟩ être lent/-e
**lately** *adv* ces derniers temps
**late-night** *adj* ⟨*film*⟩ dernier/-ière (*before n*); ⟨*session*⟩ en nocturne; **it's ∼ shopping on Thursdays** les magasins restent ouverts tard le jeudi
**later** **1** *adj* ⟨*date*⟩ ultérieur/-e; ⟨*model, novel*⟩ postérieur/-e
**2** *adv* plus tard; ∼ **on** plus tard; **six months ∼** six mois après; **to leave no ∼ than 6 am** partir au plus tard à 6 heures; **see you ∼!** à tout à l'heure!
**latest** **1** *adj* dernier/-ière (*before n*)
**2 at the latest** *phr* au plus tard
**latex** *n* latex *m*
**lathe** *n* tour *m*
**lather** *n* mousse *f*
**Latin** **1** *n* (language) latin *m*
**2** *adj* latin/-e
**Latin America** *pr n* Amérique *f* latine
**Latin American** *adj* latino-américain/-e
**latitude** *n* latitude *f*
**latter** *n* **the ∼** ce dernier/cette dernière *m/f*; ces derniers/ces dernières *mpl/fpl*
**Latvia** *pr n* Lettonie *f*
**laugh** **1** *n* rire *m*; **to like a good ∼** aimer bien rire; **to get a ∼** faire rire; **for a ∼** (colloq) pour rigoler (colloq)
**2** *vi* rire (about, over de); **to ∼ at sb/sth** rire de qn/qch; **the children ∼ed at the clown** le clown a fait rire les enfants; **he's afraid of being ∼ed at** il a peur qu'on se moque de lui
■ **laugh off** choisir de rire de ⟨*criticism, insult*⟩
**laughable** *adj* ridicule
**laughing stock** *n* risée *f*
**laughter** *n* rires *mpl*
**launch** **1** *n* **(a)** (for patrolling) vedette *f*; (for pleasure) bateau *m* de plaisance
**(b)** (of new boat, rocket) lancement *m*; (of lifeboat) mise *f* à l'eau; (of campaign, product) lancement *m*
**2** *vtr* **(a)** mettre ⟨qch⟩ à l'eau ⟨*dinghy, lifeboat*⟩; lancer ⟨*new ship, missile, rocket*⟩

**(b)** (start) lancer ⟨*campaign, career, product*⟩; ouvrir ⟨*investigation*⟩
**launch pad**, **launching pad** *n* aire *f* de lancement
**launder** *vtr* **(a)** laver ⟨*clothes*⟩
**(b)** blanchir ⟨*money*⟩
**launderette** (GB), **laundromat** (US) *n* laverie *f* automatique
**laundry** *n* **(a)** (place) (commercial) blanchisserie *f*; (in hotel, house) laverie *f*
**(b)** (linen) linge *m*; **to do the ∼** faire la lessive
**laurel** *n* laurier *m*
**lava** *n* lave *f*
**lavatory** *n* toilettes *fpl*
**lavender** *n* lavande *f*
**lavish** **1** *adj* ⟨*party, lifestyle*⟩ somptueux/-euse
**2** *vtr* prodiguer ⟨*money, affection*⟩ (on à)
**lavishly** *adv* ⟨*decorated*⟩ luxueusement; ⟨*spend*⟩ sans compter; ⟨*entertain*⟩ généreusement
**law** *n* **(a)** (gen) loi *f*; **to obey/break the ∼** respecter/enfreindre la loi; **to be against the ∼** être interdit/-e; **by ∼** conformément à la loi
**(b)** (Univ) droit *m*; **to study ∼** faire son droit
**law-abiding** *adj* respectueux/-euse des lois
**law and order** *n* ordre *m* public
**law court** *n* tribunal *m*
**law firm** *n* cabinet *m* d'avocats
**lawful** *adj* ⟨*owner, strike*⟩ légal/-e; ⟨*conduct*⟩ licite; ⟨*wife, husband*⟩ légitime
**lawless** *adj* ⟨*society*⟩ anarchique; ⟨*area, town*⟩ tombé/-e dans l'anarchie
**lawn** *n* pelouse *f*
**lawnmower** *n* tondeuse *f* (à gazon)
**law school** *n* faculté *f* de droit
**lawsuit** *n* procès *m*
**lawyer** *n* (who practises law) avocat/-e *m/f*; (expert in law) juriste *mf*
**lax** *adj* relâché/-e
**laxative** *n* laxatif *m*
**lay** **1** *adj* **(a)** (non-specialist) ∼ **person** profane *mf*
**(b)** ⟨*preacher, member*⟩ laïque
**2** *vtr* **(a)** (place) poser ⟨*object, card*⟩ (in dans; on sur); (spread out) étaler ⟨*rug, newspaper*⟩ (on sur); (arrange) disposer (on sur); **to ∼ the table (for)** mettre la table (pour)
**(b)** (prepare) préparer ⟨*plan, trail*⟩; poser ⟨*basis, foundation*⟩; tendre ⟨*trap*⟩
**(c)** (Zool) pondre ⟨*egg*⟩
**3** *vi* ⟨*bird*⟩ pondre
■ **lay down (a)** coucher ⟨*baby, patient*⟩; étaler ⟨*rug, cards*⟩; poser ⟨*book, implement*⟩; déposer ⟨*weapon*⟩
**(b) to ∼ down one's life for** sacrifier sa vie pour
**(c)** établir ⟨*rule*⟩; poser ⟨*condition*⟩
■ **lay off** (temporarily) mettre ⟨qn⟩ en chômage technique; (permanently) licencier ⋯✦

■ **lay on** prévoir ⟨*meal, transport*⟩; organiser ⟨*trip*⟩

■ **lay out (a)** disposer ⟨*goods, food*⟩; étaler ⟨*map, garment, fabric*⟩

**(b)** concevoir ⟨*building, article*⟩ présentation *f*; (of building) agencement *m*; (of town) plan *m*; (of garden) dessin *m*

**layabout** *n* (colloq) fainéant/-e *m/f* (colloq)

**lay-by** *n* (GB) aire *f* de repos

**layer** ⑴ *n* couche *f*
⑵ *vtr* **(a)** couper [qch] en dégradé ⟨*hair*⟩
**(b)** disposer [qch] en couches ⟨*cheese, potatoes*⟩

**layman** *n* profane *m*

**lay-off** *n* (permanent) licenciement *m*; (temporary) mise *f* en chômage technique

**layout** *n* (of page, book, computer screen) mise *f* en page; (of advert, article) présentation *f*; (of building) agencement *m*; (of town) plan *m*; (of garden) dessin *m*

**laze** *vi* (also ~ **about**, ~ **around**) paresser

**lazily** *adv* ⟨*move, wonder*⟩ nonchalamment; ⟨*lie, float*⟩ mollement; ⟨*flow, bob*⟩ doucement

**laziness** *n* paresse *f*

**lazy** *adj* ⟨*person*⟩ paresseux/-euse; ⟨*day, holiday*⟩ paisible; ⟨*movement, pace*⟩ lent/-e

**lead¹** ⑴ *n* **(a)** to be in the ~ être en tête; to go into the ~ passer en tête
**(b)** (initiative) to take the ~ prendre l'initiative; to follow sb's ~ suivre l'exemple de qn
**(c)** (clue) piste *f*
**(d)** (leading role) rôle *m* principal
**(e)** (wire) fil *m*
**(f)** (GB) (for dog) laisse *f*
⑵ *adj* ⟨*guitarist*⟩ premier/-ière (*before n*); ⟨*role, singer*⟩ principal/-e
⑶ *vtr* **(a)** (guide, escort) mener, conduire ⟨*person*⟩ (to sth à qch; to sb auprès de qn); to ~ sb away éloigner qn (from de)
**(b)** (bring) ⟨*path, sign*⟩ mener (to à)
**(c)** (cause) to ~ sb to do amener qn à faire
**(d)** mener ⟨*army, team, attack, strike*⟩; diriger ⟨*orchestra, research*⟩
**(e)** (conduct, have) mener ⟨*active life*⟩; to ~ a life of luxury vivre dans le luxe
⑷ *vi* **(a)** to ~ to ⟨*path*⟩ mener à; ⟨*door*⟩ s'ouvrir sur; ⟨*exit, trapdoor*⟩ donner accès à
**(b)** (result in) to ~ to entraîner ⟨*complication, discovery, accident*⟩
**(c)** ⟨*runner, car, company*⟩ être en tête; ⟨*team, side*⟩ mener; to ~ by 15 seconds avoir 15 secondes d'avance
**(d)** (in walk) aller devant; (in action, discussion) prendre l'initiative; (in dancing) conduire

■ **lead up to (a)** (precede) précéder ⟨*event*⟩
**(b)** (build up to) amener ⟨*topic*⟩

**lead²** *n* plomb *m*; (in pencil) mine *f*

**leaded petrol** (GB), **leaded gasoline** (US) *n* essence *f* au plomb

**leader** *n* **(a)** (of nation) chef *m* d'État, dirigeant/-e *m/f*; (of gang) chef *m*; (of party) leader *m*; (of trade union) secrétaire *mf*; (of strike, movement) meneur/-euse *m/f*

**(b)** (in competition) premier/-ière *m/f*; (horse) cheval *m* de tête; (in market, field) leader *m*

**leadership** *n* dirigeants *mpl*, direction *f*; under the ~ of sous la direction de

**leadership contest, leadership election** *n* (Pol) élection *f* à la direction du parti

**leadership qualities** *n pl* qualités *fpl* de leader

**lead-free** *adj* sans plomb

**leading** *adj* **(a)** ⟨*lawyer, politician*⟩ éminent/-e, important/-e; ⟨*company, bank*⟩ important/-e; ⟨*brand*⟩ dominant/-e
**(b)** ⟨*role*⟩ (main) majeur/-e; (in theatre) principal/-e
**(c)** (Sport) ⟨*driver, car*⟩ en tête de course; ⟨*team*⟩ en tête du classement

**leading edge** ⑴ *n* at the ~ of à la pointe de ⟨*technology*⟩
⑵ **leading-edge** *adj* ⟨*technology*⟩ de pointe

**lead story** *n* histoire *f* à la une (colloq)

**leaf** *n* **(a)** (of plant) feuille *f*
**(b)** (of book) page *f*
IDIOMS to turn over a new ~ tourner la page
■ **leaf through** feuilleter ⟨*papers, book*⟩

**leaflet** *n* (gen) dépliant *m*; (advertising) prospectus *m*

**league** *n* **(a)** (alliance) ligue *f*; to be in ~ with sb être de mèche avec qn (colloq)
**(b)** (GB) (Sport) (competition) championnat *m*; (association) ligue *f*
**(c)** they're not in the same ~ ils ne sont pas comparables

**league table** *n* classement *m*

**leak** ⑴ *n* fuite *f*
⑵ *vtr* divulguer ⟨*information, document*⟩
⑶ *vi* **(a)** ⟨*container, roof*⟩ fuir; ⟨*boat*⟩ faire eau
**(b)** ⟨*liquid, gas*⟩ s'échapper (from de)

**leaky** *adj* ⟨*container, pipe*⟩ qui fuit; ⟨*boat*⟩ qui prend l'eau

**lean** ⑴ *adj* **(a)** ⟨*body, face*⟩ mince; ⟨*meat*⟩ maigre
**(b)** ⟨*year, times*⟩ difficile
⑵ *vtr* appuyer (against contre)
⑶ *vi* ⟨*wall, building*⟩ pencher; to ~ against sth ⟨*bicycle, ladder*⟩ être appuyé/-e contre qch; ⟨*person*⟩ s'appuyer à qch; (with back) s'adosser à qch; to ~ out of the window se pencher par la fenêtre
■ **lean back** se pencher en arrière
■ **lean forward** se pencher en avant
■ **lean on:** ¶ ~ **on** [sth] s'appuyer sur ⟨*stick*⟩; s'accouder à ⟨*windowsill*⟩; ¶ ~ **on** [sb] (as support) s'appuyer sur ⟨*person*⟩; (depend on) compter sur ⟨*person*⟩; (pressurize) faire pression sur ⟨*person*⟩
■ **lean over:** ~ **over** [sth] se pencher par-dessus [qch]

**leap** ⑴ *n* **(a)** (jump) saut *m*, bond *m*
**(b)** (step in process) bond *m* (en avant)
**(c)** (in price) bond *m* (in dans)
⑵ *vi* **(a)** ⟨*person, animal*⟩ bondir, sauter; to

~ **to one's feet, to** ~ **up** se lever d'un bond; **to** ~ **across** *or* **over sth** franchir qch d'un bond
**(b)** ⟨*heart*⟩ bondir (**with** de)
**(c)** (*also* ~ **up**) ⟨*price, profit*⟩ grimper (**by** de)
■ **leap at**: ~ **at** [sth] sauter sur ⟨*chance, offer*⟩
■ **leap up (a)** (jump to one's feet) bondir sur ses pieds
**(b)** ⟨*price, rate*⟩ grimper

**leapfrog** *n* saute-mouton *m*

**leap year** *n* année *f* bissextile

**learn** ⒈ *vtr* (gen) apprendre; acquérir ⟨*skills*⟩ (**from** de); **to** ~ **(how) to do** apprendre à faire; **to** ~ **that** apprendre que
⒉ *vi* apprendre; **to** ~ **about sth** apprendre qch; **to** ~ **from one's mistakes** tirer la leçon de ses erreurs

**learned** *adj* ⟨*person, book*⟩ érudit/-e; ⟨*journal*⟩ spécialisé/-e; ⟨*society*⟩ savant/-e

**learner** *n* (beginner) débutant/-e *m/f*; **to be a fast/slow** ~ apprendre/ne pas apprendre vite

**learner driver** *n* élève *mf* d'auto-école

**learning** *n* **(a)** (knowledge) érudition *f*
**(b)** (process) apprentissage *m*

**learning difficulties** *n pl* (of schoolchildren) difficultés *fpl* scolaires; (of adults) difficultés *fpl* d'apprentissage

**lease** ⒈ *n* bail *m*
⒉ *vtr* louer [qch] à bail ⟨*house*⟩; louer ⟨*car*⟩

**leaseholder** *n* locataire *mf* à bail

**leash** *n* laisse *f*

**leasing** ⒈ *n* (by company) crédit-bail *m*; (by individual) location *f* avec option d'achat
⒉ *adj* ⟨*company, scheme*⟩ de leasing

**least** ⒈ *det* the ~ le moins de; (in negative constructions) le *or* la moindre; **they have the** ~ **money** ce sont eux qui ont le moins d'argent; **I haven't the** ~ **idea** je n'en ai pas la moindre idée
⒉ *pron* **the** ~ le moins; **we have the** ~ c'est nous qui en avons le moins; **it was the** ~ **I could do!** c'est la moindre des choses!
⒊ *adv* **(a)** (with adjective or noun) **the** ~ le/la moins; (with plural noun) les moins; **the** ~ **wealthy families** les familles les moins riches
**(b)** (with verbs) le moins *inv*; **I like that one (the)** ~ c'est celui-là que j'aime le moins; **nobody liked it,** ~ **of all John** personne ne l'aimait, John encore moins que les autres
⒋ **at least** *phr* (at the minimum) au moins; (qualifying statement) du moins; **she's at** ~ **40** elle a au moins 40 ans; **they could at** ~ **have phoned!** ils auraient au moins pu téléphoner!; **he's gone to bed—at** ~ **I think so** il est allé se coucher—du moins, je pense
⒌ **in the least** *phr* not in the ~ pas du tout
IDIOMS **last but not** ~, **last but by no means** ~ enfin et surtout

**leather** ⒈ *n* cuir *m*
⒉ *adj* ⟨*garment, object*⟩ de cuir, en cuir

**leave** ⒈ *n* congé *m*; **three days'** ~ trois jours de congé
⒉ *vtr* **(a)** (depart from) partir de ⟨*house, station etc*⟩; (more permanently) quitter ⟨*country, city etc*⟩; (go out of) sortir de ⟨*room, building*⟩; **he left home early** il est parti tôt de chez lui; **to** ~ **school** quitter l'école
**(b)** (forget) oublier ⟨*child, object*⟩
**(c)** quitter ⟨*partner*⟩
**(d)** laisser ⟨*instructions, tip*⟩ (**for** pour; **with** à); **to** ~ **sb sth** laisser qch à qn; **to** ~ **sb/sth in sb's care** confier qn/qch à qn
**(e)** laisser ⟨*food, drink, gap*⟩; **to** ~ **sth lying around** laisser traîner qch; **to** ~ **sth tidy** laisser qch en ordre
**(f)** **to** ~ **sth to sb** laisser [qch] à qn ⟨*job, task*⟩; **to** ~ **it (up) to sb to do** laisser à qn le soin de faire; **to** ~ **sb to it** laisser qn se débrouiller; ~ **it to** *or* **with me** je m'en occupe
**(g)** ⟨*oil, wine*⟩ faire ⟨*stain*⟩; ⟨*cup, plate*⟩ laisser ⟨*stain, mark*⟩
**(h)** (postpone) laisser ⟨*task, homework*⟩; ~ **it till tomorrow** laisse ça pour demain
**(i)** (bequeath) léguer (**to sb** à qn)
⒊ *vi* partir (**for** pour)
■ **leave behind (a)** (go faster than) distancer ⟨*person, competitor*⟩; **to be** *or* **get left behind** (physically) se faire distancer; (intellectually) ne pas suivre; (in business) ⟨*country, company*⟩ se laisser distancer
**(b)** ⟨*traveller*⟩ laisser [qch] derrière soi ⟨*town, country*⟩; quitter ⟨*family, husband*⟩; en finir avec ⟨*past*⟩
**(c)** (forget) oublier, laisser ⟨*object, child, animal*⟩
■ **leave out (a)** (accidentally) oublier ⟨*word, ingredient, person*⟩; (deliberately) omettre ⟨*name, fact*⟩; ne pas mettre ⟨*ingredient, object*⟩; tenir [qn] à l'écart ⟨*person*⟩; **to** ~ **sb out of** exclure qn de ⟨*group*⟩
**(b)** (outdoors) laisser [qch] dehors

**leaving** ⒈ *n* départ *m*
⒉ *adj* ⟨*party, present*⟩ d'adieu

**Lebanon** *pr n* **(the)** ~ (le) Liban *m*

**lecherous** *adj* lubrique

**lectern** *n* (in church) lutrin *m*; (for lecture notes) pupitre *m*

**lecture** ⒈ *n* conférence *f* (**on** sur); (GB) (Univ) cours *m* magistral (**on** sur)
⒉ *vtr* **(a)** (GB) (Univ) donner des cours à ⟨*class*⟩
**(b)** (scold) faire la leçon à ⟨*person*⟩
⒊ *vi* **(a)** (gen) donner une conférence (**on** sur)
**(b)** (GB) (Univ) **to** ~ **in sth** enseigner qch (à l'université)

**lecture notes** *n pl* notes *fpl* de cours

**lecturer** *n* **(a)** (speaker) conférencier/-ière *m/f*
**(b)** (GB) (Univ) enseignant/-e *m/f* (du supérieur)
**(c)** (US) (Univ) ≈ chargé *m* de cours

**lecture theatre** *n* amphithéâtre *m*

**ledge** *n* **(a)** (shelf) rebord *m*
**(b)** (on mountain) saillie *f* (rocheuse)

**ledger** n registre m de comptabilité, grand livre m

**leech** n sangsue f

**leek** n poireau m

**leer** vi to ~ at sb/sth lorgner qn/qch (colloq)

**leeway** n liberté f de manœuvre

**left** ⊡ n gauche f; on the ~ sur la gauche; (politically) à gauche
⊡ adj (a) ⟨eye, hand, shoe⟩ gauche
(b) (remaining) to be ~ rester; there are/we have five minutes ~ il reste/il nous reste cinq minutes; I've got one ~ il m'en reste un
⊡ adv ⟨go, look, turn⟩ à gauche

**left-hand** adj ⟨side⟩ de gauche

**left-hand drive** n voiture f avec la conduite à gauche

**left-handed** adj gaucher/-ère

**left-luggage (office)** n (GB) consigne f

**left-luggage lockers** n pl consigne f automatique

**leftovers** n pl restes mpl

**left wing** ⊡ n the ~ la gauche f
⊡ **left-wing** adj ⟨attitude⟩ de gauche; they are very ~ ils sont très à gauche

**leg** n (a) (of person, horse) jambe f; (of other animal) patte f
(b) (of furniture) pied m
(c) (Culin) (of lamb) gigot m; (of poultry, pork, frog) cuisse f
(d) (of trousers) jambe f
(e) (of journey, race) étape f
IDIOMS **to pull sb's** ~ faire marcher qn

**legacy** n (a) (Law) legs m
(b) (figurative) héritage m; (of war) séquelles fpl

**legal** adj (a) ⟨document, system⟩ juridique; ⟨costs⟩ de justice; **to take** ~ **advice** consulter un avocat
(b) ⟨heir, right, separation⟩ légal-e; ⟨owner, claim⟩ légitime

**legal action** n **to take** ~ **against sb** intenter un procès à qn

**legal aid** n aide f juridique

**legal holiday** n (US) jour m férié

**legalize** vtr légaliser

**legally** adv ⟨valid, void⟩ juridiquement; **this contract is** ~ **binding** ce contrat vous engage; ⟨act⟩ légalement

**legal proceedings** n pl poursuites fpl judiciaires

**legal tender** n monnaie f légale

**legend** n légende f (**of** de)

**legendary** adj légendaire

**leggings** n pl (for baby) collant m; (for woman) caleçon m

**legible** adj lisible

**legislation** n législation f

**legitimate** adj (a) (justifiable) ⟨action, question, request⟩ légitime; ⟨excuse⟩ valable
(b) (lawful) ⟨organization⟩ régulier/-ière; ⟨child, heir, owner⟩ légitime

**legitimize** vtr (legalize) légaliser; (justify) justifier

**leisure** ⊡ n loisirs mpl; **to do sth at (one's)** ~ prendre son temps pour faire qch
⊡ adj ⟨centre, facilities⟩ de loisirs

**leisure time** n loisirs mpl, temps m libre

**leisure wear** n vêtements mpl de sport

**lemon** n (fruit) citron m

**lemonade** n (fizzy) limonade f; (still) citronnade f; (US) (fresh) citron m pressé

**lemon juice** n jus m de citron; (GB) (drink) citron m pressé

**lemon tea** n thé m au citron

**lemon tree** n citronnier m

**lend** vtr (a) (loan) prêter ⟨object, money⟩; **to** ~ **sb sth, to** ~ **sth to sb** prêter qch à qn; **to** ~ **a hand** donner un coup de main
(b) (give) conférer ⟨quality, credibility⟩ (**to** à); prêter ⟨support⟩; **to** ~ **weight to sth** donner du poids à qch

**lender** n prêteur/-euse m/f

**lending** n prêt m

**length** ⊡ n (a) longueur f; **what** ~ **is the plank?** de quelle longueur est la planche?; **to be 50 cm in** ~ faire 50 cm de long
(b) (of book, film, list) longueur f; (of event, prison sentence) durée f; ~ **of time** temps m
(c) (of string, carpet, wood) morceau m; (of fabric) ≈ métrage m; (of pipe, track) tronçon m; **dress** ~ hauteur f de robe
(d) (Sport) longueur f
⊡ **at length** phr longuement
IDIOMS **to go to great** ~**s to do** se donner beaucoup de mal pour faire

**lengthen** ⊡ vtr rallonger ⟨garment⟩ (**by** de, par); prolonger ⟨shelf, road⟩ (**by** de, par); prolonger ⟨stay⟩
⊡ vi ⟨queue, list⟩ s'allonger; ⟨days⟩ rallonger

**lengthy** adj long/longue

**lenient** adj ⟨person⟩ indulgent/-e (**with** pour); ⟨punishment⟩ léger/-ère

**lens** n (in optical instruments) lentille f; (in spectacles) verre m; (in camera) objectif m; (contact) lentille f

**lens cap** n bouchon m d'objectif

**Lent** n carême m

**lentil** n lentille f

**Leo** pr n Lion m

**leopard** n léopard m

**leotard** n justaucorps m inv

**leper** n lépreux/-euse m/f

**leprosy** n lèpre f

**lesbian** n lesbienne f

**less** ⊡ det moins de; ~ **beer** moins de bière; **I have** ~ **money than him** j'ai moins d'argent que lui
⊡ pron moins; **I have** ~ **than you** j'en ai moins que toi; ~ **than 10** moins de dix; **in** ~ **than three hours** en moins de trois heures; **even** ~ encore moins
⊡ adv moins; **I read** ~ **these days** je lis moins à présent; **the more I see him, the** ~ **I like him** plus je le vois, moins je l'aime
⊡ prep moins; ~ **15% discount** moins 15% de remise; ~ **tax** avant impôts
⊡ **less and less** phr de moins en moins

**lessen** *vtr* diminuer ‹*influence, feelings*›; réduire ‹*cost*›; atténuer ‹*impact, pain*›

**lesser** ⟨1⟩ *adj* moindre; **to a ~ extent** à un moindre degré
⟨2⟩ *adv* moins; **~ known** moins connu

**lesson** *n* cours *m*, leçon *f*; **Spanish ~** cours d'espagnol; **driving ~** leçon de conduite; **I'm going to teach him a ~!** je vais lui donner une bonne leçon!

**let¹**

---

■ **Note** When *let* is used with another verb to make a suggestion (*let's do it at once*), the first person plural of the appropriate verb can generally be used to express this in French: *faisons-le tout de suite*. (Note that the verb alone translates *let us do* and no pronoun appears in French.)
– In the spoken language, however, French speakers will use the much more colloquial *on + present tense* or *si on + imperfect tense*:
– *let's go!* = allons-y *or* on y va!; *let's go to the cinema tonight* = si on allait au cinéma ce soir?
– These translations can also be used for suggestions in the negative:
– *let's not take* or *don't let's take the bus—let's walk* = on ne prend pas le bus, on y va à pied *or* ne prenons pas le bus, allons-y à pied.
– When *let* is used to mean *allow*, it is generally translated by the verb *laisser*. For more examples and particular usages, see the entry below.

---

*vtr* (a) (in suggestions, commands)
**~'s get out of here!** sortons d'ici!; **~'s not** *or* **don't ~'s** (GB) **talk about that!** n'en parlons pas!
(b) (allow) **to ~ sb do** laisser qn faire; **~ me explain** laisse-moi t'expliquer; **don't ~ it get you down** ne te laisse pas abattre; **she wanted to go but they wouldn't ~ her** elle voulait y aller mais ils ne l'ont pas laissée faire; **to ~ one's hair grow** se laisser pousser les cheveux
■ **let down**: ¶ **~ [sb] down (a)** (disappoint) laisser tomber [qn]; **to feel let down** être déçu/-e
(b) (embarrass) faire honte à [qn]
¶ **~ [sth] down (a)** (GB) dégonfler ‹*tyre*›
(b) rallonger ‹*garment*›
■ **let go**: ¶ **~ go** lâcher prise; **to ~ go of sb/sth** lâcher qn/qch
¶ **~ [sb] go (a)** relâcher ‹*prisoner*›
(b) lâcher ‹*person, arm*›
(c) licencier ‹*employee*›
(d) **to ~ oneself go** se laisser aller; ¶ **~ [sth] go** lâcher ‹*rope, bar*›
■ **let in**: ¶ **~ [sth] in** ‹*roof, window*› laisser passer ‹*rain*›; ‹*shoes*› prendre ‹*water*›; ‹*curtains*› laisser passer ‹*light*›
¶ **~ [sb] in (a)** (show in) faire entrer; (admit) laisser entrer
(b) **to ~ oneself in for** aller au devant de ‹*trouble*›
■ **let off**: ¶ **~ off [sth]** tirer ‹*fireworks*›; faire exploser ‹*bomb*›; faire partir ‹*gun*›
¶ **~ [sb] off (a)** (excuse) **to ~ sb off** dispenser qn de ‹*homework*›

(b) (leave unpunished) ne pas punir ‹*culprit*›
■ **let out**: ¶ **~ out** (US) ‹*school*› finir (at à); ¶ **~ out [sth] (a)** laisser échapper ‹*cry*›; **to ~ out a roar** beugler
(b) (GB) (reveal) révéler (**that** que); ¶ **~ [sth] out (a)** faire sortir ‹*animal*›; donner libre cours à ‹*anger*›
(b) élargir ‹*waistband*›
¶ **~ [sb] out** laisser sortir ‹*prisoner*› (of de); faire sortir ‹*pupils, employees*› (of de)
■ **let up** ‹*rain, wind*› se calmer; ‹*pressure*› s'arrêter; ‹*heat*› diminuer

**let²** *vtr* (*also* **~ out** (GB)) louer (**to** à); '**to ~**' 'à louer'

**letdown** *n* déception *f*

**lethal** *adj* ‹*substance, gas, dose*› mortel/-elle; ‹*weapon*› meurtrier/-ière

**lethargic** *adj* léthargique; (lazy) apathique; **to feel ~** se sentir engourdi/-e

**letter** *n* (a) lettre *f* (**to** pour; **from** de)
(b) (of alphabet) lettre *f*

**letter bomb** *n* lettre *f* piégée

**letter box** *n* boîte *f* à lettres

**letterhead** *n* en-tête *m*

**letters page** *n* courrier *m* des lecteurs

**lettuce** *n* salade *f*, laitue *f*

**letup** *n* accalmie *f*; (respite) pause *f*

**leuk(a)emia** *n* leucémie *f*

**level** ⟨1⟩ *n* (a) (gen) niveau *m*; **to be on the same ~ as sb** être du même niveau que qn; **at street ~** au niveau de la rue
(b) (of unemployment, illiteracy) taux *m*; (of spending) montant *m*; (of satisfaction, anxiety) degré *m*
(c) (in hierarchy) échelon *m*
⟨2⟩ *adj* (a) ‹*shelf, floor*› droit/-e; ‹*table*› horizontal/-e
(b) ‹*ground, surface, land*› plat/-e
(c) (Culin) ‹*teaspoonful*› ras/-e
(d) **to be ~** ‹*shoulders, windows*› être à la même hauteur; ‹*floor, building*› être au même niveau; **~ with the ground** au ras du sol
(e) **to remain ~** ‹*figures*› rester stable
⟨3⟩ *adv* **to draw ~** arriver à la même hauteur (**with** que)
⟨4⟩ *vtr* (a) (destroy) raser ‹*village*›
(b) lancer ‹*accusation*› (**at** contre); adresser ‹*criticism*› (**at** à); braquer ‹*gun*› (**at** sur)
(c) aplanir ‹*ground, surface*›
IDIOMS **to be ~-pegging** être à égalité; **to ~ with sb** être honnête avec qn
■ **level off** ‹*prices, curve*› se stabiliser

**level crossing** *n* passage *m* à niveau

**level-headed** *adj* sensé/-e

**lever** *n* (Aut, Tech) levier *m*; (small) manette *f*

**levy** ⟨1⟩ *n* taxe *f*, impôt *m*
⟨2⟩ *vtr* prélever ‹*tax, duty*›; imposer ‹*fine*›

**lewd** *adj* ‹*joke, gesture, remark*› obscène; ‹*person*› lubrique

**liability** ⟨1⟩ *n* (a) (Law) responsabilité *f*
(b) (drawback) handicap *m*
⟨2⟩ **liabilities** *n pl* passif *m*, dettes *fpl*

**liable** *adj* **(a)** (likely) **to be ~ to do** risquer de faire; **it's ~ to rain** il risque de pleuvoir, il se peut qu'il pleuve
**(b)** (legally subject) **to be ~ to** être passible de ⟨*fine*⟩; **to be ~ for tax** ⟨*person, company*⟩ être imposable; ⟨*goods*⟩ être soumis/-e à l'impôt
**liaise** *vi* travailler en liaison (**with** avec)
**liaison** *n* liaison *f*
**liar** *n* menteur/-euse *m/f*
**libel** 1 *n* diffamation *f*
2 *vtr* diffamer
**libellous** (GB), **libelous** (US) *adj* diffamatoire
**liberal** 1 *n* libéral/-e *m/f*
2 *adj* **(a)** (politically) libéral/-e
**(b)** ⟨*amount*⟩ généreux/-euse; ⟨*person*⟩ prodigue (**with** de)
**Liberal** *n* libéral/-e *m/f*
**Liberal Democrat** *n* (GB) libéral-démocrate *mf*
**liberalism** *n* libéralisme *m*
**liberalize** *vtr* libéraliser
**liberate** 1 *vtr* libérer (**from** de)
2 **liberated** *pp adj* ⟨*lifestyle, woman*⟩ libéré/-e
3 **liberating** *pres p adj* libérateur/-trice
**liberation** *n* libération *f* (**from** de); **women's ~** libération de la femme
**liberty** *n* liberté *f*
**Libra** *n* Balance *f*
**librarian** *n* bibliothécaire *mf*
**library** *n* bibliothèque *f*; **public ~** bibliothèque municipale; **mobile ~** (GB) bibliobus *m*
**lice** *n pl* poux *mpl*
**licence** (GB), **license** (US) *n* **(a)** (for trading) licence *f*
**(b)** (to drive, fish) permis *m*; (for TV) redevance *f*; **to lose one's** (driving) **~** se faire retirer son permis (de conduire)
**(c)** (freedom) licence *f*
**licence number** *n* (of car) numéro *m* minéralogique *or* d'immatriculation
**licence plate** *n* plaque *f* minéralogique *or* d'immatriculation
**license** 1 *n* (US) = LICENCE
2 *vtr* **(a)** (authorize) autoriser (**to do** à faire)
**(b)** faire immatriculer ⟨*vehicle*⟩
**licensed** *adj* **(a)** ⟨*restaurant*⟩ qui a une licence de débit de boissons
**(b)** ⟨*dealer, firm, taxi*⟩ agréé/-e; ⟨*pilot*⟩ breveté/-e; ⟨*vehicle*⟩ en règle
**licensing laws** *n pl* (GB) lois *fpl* réglementant la vente des boissons alcoolisées
**lick** 1 *n* **(a)** coup *m* de langue
**(b) a ~ of paint** un petit coup de peinture
2 *vtr* **(a)** lécher; **to ~ one's lips** se lécher les babines
**(b)** (colloq) écraser ⟨*team, opponent*⟩; **to get ~ed** se faire écraser
IDIOMS **to ~ one's wounds** panser ses blessures
**licorice** (US) = LIQUORICE

**lid** *n* **(a)** (cover) couvercle *m*
**(b)** (eyelid) paupière *f*
**lie** 1 *n* mensonge *m*; **to tell a ~** mentir
2 *vi* **(a)** (tell falsehood) mentir (**to sb** à qn; **about** à propos de); **he ~d about her** il a menti à son propos
**(b)** ⟨*person, animal*⟩ (action) s'allonger; (state) être allongé/-e; ⟨*objects*⟩ être couché/-e; **he was lying on the bed** il était allongé sur le lit; **to ~ on one's back** s'allonger sur le dos; **~ still** ne bougez pas; **here ~s John Brown** ci-gît John Brown
**(c)** (be situated) être; (remain) rester; **to ~ open** ⟨*book*⟩ être ouvert/-e; **that's where our future ~s** c'est là qu'est notre avenir; **to ~ before sb** ⟨*life, career*⟩ s'ouvrir devant qn; **what ~s ahead?** qu'est-ce qui nous attend?; **the house lay empty for years** la maison est restée vide pendant des années
**(d)** (can be found) résider; **their interests ~ elsewhere** leurs intérêts résident ailleurs; **to ~ in** ⟨*cause, secret, talent*⟩ résider dans; ⟨*popularity, strength, fault*⟩ venir de; **the responsibility ~s with them** ce sont eux qui sont responsables
IDIOMS **to ~ low** garder un profil bas; **to take it lying down** (colloq) se laisser faire
■ **lie around** traîner; **to leave sth lying around** laisser traîner qch
■ **lie down** (briefly) s'allonger; (for longer period) se coucher
**lie detector** *n* détecteur *m* de mensonge
**lie-in** *n* **to have a ~** faire la grasse matinée
**lieu** 1 **in lieu** *adv phr* **one week's holiday in ~** une semaine de vacances pour compenser
2 **in lieu of** *prep phr* à la place de
**life** *n* **(a)** (gen) vie *f*; **that's ~!** c'est la vie!; **the first time in my ~** la première fois de ma vie; **a job for ~** un emploi à vie; **a friend for ~** un ami pour la vie; **for the rest of one's ~** pour le restant de ses jours; **full of ~** plein/-e de vie; **to come to ~** ⟨*shy person*⟩ sortir de sa réserve; ⟨*fictional character*⟩ prendre vie; ⟨*party*⟩ s'animer
**(b)** (of machine, product) durée *f*
**(c)** (Law) **to serve ~** être emprisonné/-e à vie; **to sentence sb to ~** condamner qn à perpétuité
IDIOMS **to have the time of one's ~** s'amuser comme un fou/une folle
**lifebelt** *n* bouée *f* de sauvetage
**lifeboat** *n* canot *m* de sauvetage
**life drawing** *n* dessin *m* d'après modèle
**life-expectancy** *n* espérance *f* de vie; (of product) durée *f* probable
**lifeguard** *n* surveillant/-e *m/f* de baignade
**life imprisonment** *n* réclusion *f* à perpétuité
**life insurance** *n* assurance-vie *f*
**lifejacket** *n* gilet *m* de sauvetage
**lifeless** *adj* ⟨*body, object*⟩ inanimé/-e; ⟨*performance*⟩ peu vivant/-e; ⟨*voice*⟩ éteint/-e
**lifelike** *adj* très ressemblant/-e
**lifeline** *n* bouée *f* de sauvetage

**lifelong** *adj* ⟨*friendship, fear*⟩ de toute une vie; **to have had a ~ ambition to do** avoir toujours rêvé de faire

**lifesaving** *n* (gen) sauvetage *m*; (Med) secourisme *m*

**life sentence** *n* condamnation *f* à perpétuité

**life-size** *adj* grandeur nature *inv*

**life span** *n* durée *f* de vie

**life story** *n* vie *f*

**lifestyle** *n* style *m* de vie

**life-support machine** *n* **to be on a ~** être sous assistance respiratoire

**lifetime** *n* vie *f*; **in her ~** de son vivant; **the chance of a ~** une chance unique; **to seem like a ~** sembler une éternité

**lift** ① *n* (a) (GB) (elevator) ascenseur *m*; (for goods) monte-charge *m inv*
(b) (ride) **she asked me for a ~** elle m'a demandé de la conduire; **can I give you a ~?** je peux te déposer quelque part?
(c) (colloq) (boost) **to give sb a ~** remonter le moral à qn
② *vtr* (a) (pick up) soulever ⟨*object, person*⟩; **to ~ sth out of the box** sortir qch de la boîte
(b) (raise) lever ⟨*arm, head*⟩
(c) (remove) lever ⟨*ban, sanctions*⟩
(d) (boost) **to ~ sb's spirits** remonter le moral à qn
(e) (colloq) (steal) piquer (colloq) (**from** dans)
③ *vi* ⟨*bad mood, headache*⟩ disparaître; ⟨*fog*⟩ se dissiper

■ **lift off:** ¶ **~ off** ⟨*rocket*⟩ décoller; ⟨*top, cover*⟩ s'enlever; ¶ **~ [sth] off** enlever ⟨*cover, lid*⟩

■ **lift up** soulever ⟨*book, suitcase, lid*⟩; lever ⟨*head, veil, eyes*⟩; relever ⟨*jumper, coat*⟩

**lift-off** *n* lancement *m*

**ligament** *n* ligament *m*

**light** ① *n* (a) (brightness) lumière *f*; **against the ~** à contre-jour
(b) (in building, machine) lumière *f*; (in street) réverbère *m*; (on ship) feu *m*; (on dashboard) voyant *m* (lumineux)
(c) (Aut) (headlight) phare *m*; (rearlight) feu *m* arrière; (inside car) veilleuse *f*
(d) (flame) **to set ~ to** mettre le feu à; **have you got a ~?** tu as du feu?
(e) (aspect) jour *m*; **to see sth in a different ~** voir qch sous un jour différent
(f) **to come to** *or* **be brought to ~** être découvert/-e
② **lights** *n pl* (traffic) **~s** feu *m*, feux *mpl*; **the ~s are red** le feu est au rouge
③ *adj* (a) (bright) **to get** *or* **grow ~er** ⟨*sky*⟩ s'éclaircir; **while it's still ~** pendant qu'il fait encore jour
(b) ⟨*colour, wood, skin*⟩ clair/-e; **~ blue** bleu clair *inv*
(c) ⟨*material, wind, clothing, meal*⟩ léger/-ère; ⟨*rain*⟩ fin/-e; ⟨*drinker*⟩ modéré/-e; **to be a ~ sleeper** avoir le sommeil léger
(d) ⟨*knock, footsteps*⟩ léger/-ère
(e) ⟨*work*⟩ peu fatigant/-e; ⟨*exercise*⟩ léger/-ère

(f) ⟨*music*⟩ léger/-ère; **a bit of ~ relief** un peu de divertissement; **some ~ reading** quelque chose de facile à lire
④ *vtr* (a) allumer ⟨*oven, cigarette, fire*⟩; enflammer ⟨*paper*⟩; craquer ⟨*match*⟩
(b) ⟨*torch, lamp*⟩ éclairer

■ **light up** ⟨*lamp*⟩ s'allumer; ⟨*face*⟩ s'éclairer; ⟨*eyes*⟩ briller de joie

**light bulb** *n* ampoule *f*

**lighten** ① *vtr* éclaircir ⟨*colour, hair, skin*⟩; détendre ⟨*atmosphere*⟩
② *vi* ⟨*sky, hair*⟩ s'éclaircir; ⟨*atmosphere*⟩ se détendre

**light entertainment** *n* variétés *fpl*

**lighter** *n* (for smokers) briquet *m*; (for gas cooker) allume-gaz *m inv*

**lighter fuel** *n* (gas) gaz *m* à briquet; (liquid) essence *f* à briquet

**light-hearted** *adj* ⟨*person*⟩ enjoué/-e; ⟨*book*⟩ humoristique

**lighthouse** *n* phare *m*

**lighting** *n* éclairage *m*

**lightly** *adv* (a) ⟨*touch, kiss, season*⟩ légèrement
(b) ⟨*undertake, dismiss*⟩ à la légère
(c) **to get off ~** s'en tirer à bon compte

**lightning** ① *n* (in sky) éclairs *mpl*; (striking sth) foudre *f*; **a flash of ~** un éclair; **struck by ~** frappé/-e par la foudre
② *adj* ⟨*visit, raid*⟩ éclair *inv*

**light switch** *n* interrupteur *m*

**lightweight** *adj* ⟨*garment*⟩ léger/-ère; ⟨*champion*⟩ des poids légers

**light year** *n* année-lumière *f*

**like¹** ① *prep* (a) (gen) comme; **to be ~ sb/sth** être comme qn/qch; **to look ~** ressembler à; **big cities ~ London** les grandes villes comme Londres *or* telles que Londres; **you know what she's ~!** tu sais comment elle est!; **it was just ~ a fairytale!** on aurait dit un conte de fée!; **it looks ~ rain** on dirait qu'il va pleuvoir; **what's it ~?** c'est comment?; **what was the weather ~?** quel temps faisait-il?
(b) (typical of) **it's not ~ her to be late** ça ne lui ressemble pas *or* ce n'est pas son genre d'être en retard; **that's just ~ him!** c'est bien (de) lui!
② *conj* (a) (in the same way as) comme; **~ they used to** comme ils le faisaient autrefois
(b) (colloq) (as if) comme si; **he acts ~ he owns the place** il se conduit comme s'il était chez lui
③ *n* **fires, floods and the ~** les incendies, les inondations et autres catastrophes de ce genre; **she won't speak to the ~s of us!** (colloq) elle refuse de parler à des gens comme nous!

**like²** *vtr* (a) aimer bien ⟨*person*⟩; aimer (bien) ⟨*artist, food, music, style*⟩; **to ~ doing** *or* **to do** aimer (bien) faire; **to ~ A best** préférer A; **how do you ~ living in London?** ça te plaît de vivre à Londres?; **she doesn't ~ to be kept waiting** elle n'aime pas qu'on la fasse attendre    ⋯⊰

**(b)** (wish) vouloir, aimer; **I would ~ a ticket** je voudrais un billet; **I would ~ to do** je voudrais *or* j'aimerais faire; **would you ~ to come to dinner?** voudriez-vous venir dîner?; **we'd ~ her to come** nous voudrions *or* aimerions qu'elle vienne; **if you ~** si tu veux; **you can do what you ~** tu peux faire ce que tu veux

**likeable** *adj* ⟨person⟩ sympathique; ⟨novel, music⟩ agréable

**likelihood** *n* probabilité *f*, chances *fpl*; **in all ~** selon toute probabilité

**likely** *adj* **(a)** (probable) probable; ⟨explanation⟩ plausible; **prices are ~ to rise** les prix risquent d'augmenter; **it is** *or* **seems ~ that she'll come** il est probable qu'elle viendra; **it is hardly ~ that she'll come** il y a peu de chances qu'elle vienne; **a ~ story!** à d'autres! (colloq)
**(b)** (promising) ⟨candidate⟩ prometteur/-euse

**like-minded** *adj* du même avis

**liken** *vtr* comparer (**to** à)

**likeness** *n* **(a)** (similarity) ressemblance *f*; **family ~** air *m* de famille
**(b)** (picture) **to be a good ~** être ressemblant/-e

**likewise** *adv* (similarly) également, de même; (also) aussi, de même

**liking** *n* **to take a ~ to sb** se prendre d'affection pour qn; **to be to sb's ~** plaire à qn

**lilac** *n, adj* lilas (*m*) *inv*

**lily** *n* lys *m inv*

**lily of the valley** *n* muguet *m*

**limb** *n* **(a)** (arm, leg) membre *m*
**(b)** (of tree) branche *f* (maîtresse)

**limber** *v* ■ **limber up** s'échauffer

**limbo** *n* **(a)** (state) les limbes *mpl*; **to be in ~** être dans les limbes
**(b)** (dance) limbo *m*

**lime** *n* **(a)** (calcium) chaux *f*
**(b)** (fruit) citron *m* vert
**(c)** (*also* **~ tree**) tilleul *m*

**lime green** *n, adj* citron (*m*) vert *inv*

**lime juice** *n* jus *m* de citron vert

**limelight** *n* vedette *f*; **to be in the ~** tenir la vedette

**limestone** *n* calcaire *m*

**limit** **1** *n* limite *f*; **within ~s** dans une certaine limite; **to push sb to the ~** pousser qn à bout
**2** *vtr* limiter (**to** à)

**limitation** *n* **(a)** (restriction) restriction *f* (**on** à)
**(b)** (shortcoming) limite *f*; **to know one's (own) ~s** connaître ses propres limites

**limited** *adj* limité/-e

**limited company** *n* (GB) société *f* anonyme

**limousine** *n* limousine *f*

**limp** **1** *n* **to have a ~** boiter
**2** *adj* mou/molle
**3** *vi* boiter; **to ~ in/away** entrer/s'éloigner en boitant

**linchpin** *n* (essential element) **the ~ of** ⟨person⟩ le pilier de; ⟨principle⟩ la base de

**line** **1** *n* **(a)** (gen, Sport) ligne *f*; (shorter, thicker) trait *m*; (in drawing) trait *m*; **a straight ~** une ligne droite
**(b)** (of people, cars) file *f*; (of trees) rangée *f*; **to stand** *or* **wait in ~** faire la queue
**(c)** (on face) ride *f*
**(d)** (rope) corde *f*; (for fishing) ligne *f*; **to put the washing on the ~** étendre le linge
**(e)** (electric cable) ligne *f* (électrique)
**(f)** (phone connection) ligne *f*; **at the other end of the ~** au bout du fil; **the ~ went dead** la ligne a été coupée
**(g)** (rail route) ligne *f* (**between** entre); (rails) voie *f*
**(h)** (shipping company, airline) compagnie *f*
**(i)** (in genealogy) lignée *f*
**(j)** (in prose) ligne *f*; (in poetry) vers *m*; **to learn one's ~s** ⟨actor⟩ apprendre son texte
**(k)** **to fall into ~ with** s'aligner sur; **to bring sb into ~** ramener qn dans le rang; **to keep sb in ~** tenir qn en main
**(l)** (stance) **the official ~** la position officielle; **to take a firm ~ with sb** se montrer ferme avec qn
**(m)** (type of product) gamme *f*
**(n)** (Mil) **enemy ~s** lignes *fpl* ennemies
**2** *vtr* doubler ⟨garment⟩ (**with** avec); tapisser ⟨shelf⟩ (**with** de); border ⟨route⟩
**3 in line with** *phr* en accord avec ⟨policy, trend⟩; **to increase in ~ with** augmenter proportionnellement à
■ **line up**: ¶ **~ up** (side by side) se mettre en rang; (one behind the other) se mettre en file
¶ **~ [sth] up (a)** (align) aligner (**with** sur)
**(b)** (select) sélectionner ⟨team⟩

**lined** *adj* ⟨face⟩ ridé/-e; ⟨paper⟩ ligné/-e; ⟨curtains⟩ doublé/-e

**line manager** *n* responsable opérationnel/-elle *m/f*

**linen** *n* **(a)** (fabric) lin *m*
**(b)** (household) linge *m* de maison; (underwear) linge *m* de corps

**linen basket** *n* panier *m* à linge sale

**linen cupboard** (GB), **linen closet** (US) *n* armoire *f* à linge

**line of fire** *n* ligne *f* de tir

**line of work** *n* métier *m*

**liner** *n* paquebot *m* de grande ligne

**linesman** *n* (GB) (in tennis) juge *m* de ligne; (in football, hockey) juge *m* de touche

**line-up** *n* (Sport) équipe *f*; (personnel, pop group) groupe *m*

**linger** *vi* **(a)** ⟨person⟩ s'attarder; ⟨gaze⟩ s'attarder (**on** sur)
**(b)** ⟨memory, smell⟩ persister
**(c)** ⟨doubt, suspicion⟩ subsister

**lingerie** *n* lingerie *f*

**linguist** *n* linguiste *mf*

**linguistic** *adj* linguistique

**linguistics** *n* linguistique *f*

**lining** *n* doublure *f*

**link** **1** *n* **(a)** (in chain) maillon *m*
**(b)** (connection by rail, road) liaison *f*

**(c)** (between facts, events) rapport *m* **(between** entre); (between people) lien *m* **(with** avec)
**(d)** (tie) relation *f*, lien *m* **(with** avec; **between** entre)
**(e)** (in TV, radio, computing) liaison *f*
**2** *vtr* **(a)** ⟨*road, cable*⟩ relier ⟨*places, objects*⟩; **to ∼ A to B** *or* **A and B** relier A à B; **to ∼ arms** ⟨*people*⟩ se donner le bras
**(b) to ∼ sth to** *or* **with** lier qch à ⟨*inflation*⟩; établir un lien entre qch et ⟨*fact, crime, illness*⟩
**(c)** connecter ⟨*terminals*⟩
**(d)** (in TV, radio) établir une liaison entre ⟨*places*⟩ **(by** par);
**3 linked** *pp adj* ⟨*circles, symbols*⟩ entrelacé/-e; ⟨*issues, problems*⟩ lié/-e
■ **link up:** ¶ **∼ up** ⟨*firms*⟩ s'associer; **to ∼ up with** s'associer avec ⟨*college, firm*⟩; ¶ **∼ [sth] up** relier

**link road** *n* route *f* de raccordement
**link-up** *n* **(a)** (on TV, radio) liaison *f*
**(b)** (collaboration) association *f*
**lino** *n* lino *m*
**lint** *n* tissu *m* ouaté
**lion** *n* lion *m*
**lion cub** *n* lionceau *m*
**lioness** *n* lionne *f*
**lip** *n* **(a)** lèvre *f*
**(b)** (of jug) bec *m*
**liposuction** *n* liposuccion *f*
**lip-read** *vi* lire sur les lèvres de quelqu'un
**lipsalve** *n* baume *m* pour les lèvres
**lip service** *n* **to pay ∼ to feminism** se dire féministe pour la forme
**lipstick** *n* rouge *m* à lèvres
**liqueur** *n* liqueur *f*
**liquid** *n, adj* liquide (*m*)
**liquidate** *vtr* liquider
**liquidation** *n* liquidation *f*
**liquidizer** *n* (GB Culin) mixeur *m*
**liquor** *n* alcool *m*
**liquorice**, **licorice** (US) *n* **(a)** (plant) réglisse *f*
**(b)** (substance) réglisse *m*
**liquor store** *n* (US) magasin *m* de vins et spiritueux
**Lisbon** *pr n* Lisbonne
**lisp** *n* zézaiement *m*; **to have a ∼** zézayer
**list** **1** *n* liste *f* **(of** de)
**2** *vtr* **(a)** (gen) faire la liste de ⟨*objects, people*⟩; **to be ∼ed in a directory** être repris/-e dans un répertoire
**(b)** (Comput) lister
**3** *vi* ⟨*vessel*⟩ donner de la bande
**4 listed** *pp adj* (GB) ⟨*building*⟩ classé; ⟨*company*⟩ coté/-e en Bourse
**listen** *vi* écouter; **to ∼ to sb/sth** écouter qn/qch; **to ∼ to reason** écouter la voix de la raison; **to ∼ (out) for** guetter
■ **listen in** écouter (par indiscrétion)
**listener** *n* **(a) to be a good ∼** savoir écouter
**(b)** (to radio) auditeur/-trice *m/f*

**listeria** *n* (bacteria) listéria *f*; (illness) listériose *f*
**listing** **1** *n* **(a)** inscription *f* **(in** dans); **Stock Exchange ∼** liste *f* des sociétés cotées en Bourse
**(b)** (Comput) listing *m*
**2 listings** *n pl* pages *fpl* d'informations
**listless** *adj* ⟨*person*⟩ apathique
**list price** *n* prix *m* au catalogue
**literacy** *n* (in a population) taux *m* d'alphabétisation
**literal** *adj* **(a)** ⟨*meaning*⟩ littéral/-e
**(b)** ⟨*translation*⟩ mot à mot
**literally** *adv* ⟨*mean*⟩ littéralement; ⟨*translate*⟩ mot à mot; **to take sth ∼** prendre qch au pied de la lettre; (quite) **∼** bel et bien
**literary** *adj* littéraire
**literary criticism** *n* critique *f* littéraire
**literate** *adj* **(a)** (able to read and write) **to be ∼** savoir lire et écrire
**(b)** (cultured) ⟨*person*⟩ cultivé/-e
**literature** *n* **(a)** littérature *f*; **a work of ∼** une œuvre littéraire
**(b)** (pamphlets, brochures) documentation *f*
**lithe** *adj* leste
**Lithuania** *pr n* Lituanie *f*
**litigation** *n* litiges *mpl*
**litre**, **liter** (US) *n* litre *m*
**litter** **1** *n* **(a)** (rubbish) détritus *mpl*; (substantial) ordures *fpl*; (paper) papiers *mpl*
**(b)** (of young) portée *f*; **to have a ∼** mettre bas
**(c)** (for pet tray) litière *f*
**2** *vtr* **to be ∼ed with** ⟨*ground*⟩ être jonché/-e de
**litter bin** *n* poubelle *f*
**little**

■ **Note** When *a little* is used as a pronoun and if the sentence does not specify what it refers to, the pronoun *en* (= *of it*) must be added before the verb: *I have a little left* = il m'en reste un peu.

**1** *adj* **(a)** (small) petit/-e (*before n*)
**(b)** (not much) peu de; **∼ chance** peu de chances; **very ∼ damage** très peu de dégâts; **there's so ∼ time** il y a si peu de temps
**2** *pron* **a ∼** un peu; **I only ate a ∼** je n'en ai mangé qu'un peu; **he remembers very ∼** il ne se souvient pas bien; **there's ∼ I can do** je ne peux pas faire grand-chose; **to do as ∼ as possible** en faire le moins possible; **∼ or nothing** quasiment rien
**3** *adv* **(a)** (not much) peu; **I go there very ∼** j'y vais très peu; **the next results were ∼ better** les résultats suivants étaient à peine meilleurs; **∼ more than an hour ago** il y a à peine plus d'une heure
**(b)** (not at all) **∼ did they know that** ils étaient bien loin de se douter que
**4 a little (bit)** *phr* un peu; **a ∼ (bit) anxious** un peu inquiet/-iète; **a ∼ less/more** un peu moins/plus; **stay a ∼ longer** reste encore un peu      ···⫶

**5** **as little as** *phr* for as ∼ as 10 dollars a day pour seulement 10 dollars par jour; **as ∼ as £60** juste 60 livres sterling
IDIOMS ∼ **by** ∼ petit à petit

**little finger** *n* petit doigt *m*, auriculaire *m*
IDIOMS **to wrap** *or* **twist sb around one's** ∼ mener qn par le bout du nez

**live¹** *vi* (a) (gen) vivre; **as long as I** ∼… tant que je vivrai…; **to** ∼ **to regret sth** en venir à regretter qch; **long** ∼ **democracy!** vive la démocratie!; **to** ∼ **on** *or* **off** vivre de ⟨*fruit, charity*⟩; vivre sur ⟨*wage*⟩
(b) (dwell) ⟨*person*⟩ vivre, habiter (**with** avec); ⟨*animal*⟩ vivre; **they** ∼ **at number 7** ils habitent au numéro 7; **to** ∼ **in** vivre dans, habiter ⟨*house, apartment*⟩; **easy to** ∼ **with** facile à vivre
(c) (put up with) **to** ∼ **with** accepter ⟨*situation*⟩; supporter ⟨*decor*⟩
IDIOMS **to** ∼ **it up** (colloq) mener la grande vie
■ **live in** ⟨*maid*⟩ être logé/-e et nourri/-e
■ **live on** ⟨*reputation, tradition*⟩ se perpétuer
■ **live up to** ⟨*person*⟩ répondre à ⟨*expectations*⟩; être à la hauteur de ⟨*reputation*⟩

**live²** **1** *adj* (a) (alive) vivant/-e
(b) ⟨*broadcast*⟩ en direct; ⟨*performance*⟩ sur scène; ⟨*album*⟩ enregistré/-e en public; **before a** ∼ **audience** devant un public
(c) ⟨*cable*⟩ sous tension
**2** *adv* ⟨*appear, broadcast*⟩ en direct

**live-in** *adj* ⟨*maid, nanny*⟩ qui est logé/-e et nourri/-e; **to have a** ∼ **lover** vivre en concubinage

**livelihood** *n* gagne-pain *m*

**lively** *adj* (a) ⟨*person*⟩ plein/-e d'entrain; ⟨*place, atmosphere, conversation*⟩ animé/-e
(b) (fast) ⟨*pace*⟩ vif/vive; ⟨*music, dance*⟩ entraînant/-e

**liven** *v* ■ **liven up**: ¶ ∼ **up** s'animer; ¶ ∼ **[sth] up** animer ⟨*event*⟩

**liver** *n* foie *m*

**livery** *n* (a) (uniform) livrée *f*
(b) (boarding horses) **at** ∼ en pension

**livestock** *n* bétail *m*

**live wire** *n* boute-en-train *m inv*

**livid** *adj* (a) (furious) furieux/-ieuse
(b) (in colour) ⟨*face, scar*⟩ livide

**living** **1** *n* (a) vie *f*; **to work for a** ∼ travailler pour gagner sa vie; **what do you do for a** ∼**?** qu'est-ce que vous faites dans la vie?
(b) (lifestyle) vie *f*; **easy** ∼ une vie facile
**2** *adj* vivant/-e; **within** ∼ **memory** de mémoire d'homme

**living conditions** *n pl* conditions *fpl* de vie

**living expenses** *n pl* frais *mpl* de subsistance

**living room** *n* salle *f* de séjour, salon *m*

**living standards** *n pl* niveau *m* de vie

**living together** *n* cohabitation *f*

**living will** *n*: déclaration écrite (*de l'interessé*) refusant l'acharnement thérapeutique

**lizard** *n* lézard *m*

**llama** *n* lama *m*

**load** **1** *n* (a) (gen) charge *f*; (on vehicle, animal) chargement *m*; (on ship, plane) cargaison *f*; (figurative) fardeau *m*; **three (lorry-)∼s of sand** trois camions de sable
(b) (colloq) (a lot) **a (whole)** ∼ **of people** des tas (colloq) de gens; **that's a** ∼ **of nonsense** (colloq) c'est vraiment n'importe quoi (colloq)
**2** **loads** *n pl* (colloq) ∼**s of** (+ plural nouns) des tas (colloq) de; ∼**s of times** plein de *or* des tas (colloq) de fois; **we've got** ∼**s of time** nous avons tout notre temps; ∼**s of work** un travail fou (colloq)
**3** *vtr* (a) (gen) charger ⟨*vehicle, gun*⟩ (**with** de); mettre un film dans ⟨*camera*⟩
(b) (Comput) charger ⟨*program*⟩
(c) **to** ∼ **sb with** combler qn de ⟨*presents, honours*⟩

**loaded** *adj* (a) ⟨*tray, lorry, gun*⟩ chargé/-e (**with** de)
(b) (colloq) (rich) bourré/-e de fric (colloq)
(c) ⟨*question*⟩ tendancieux/-ieuse

**loaf** *n* pain *m*; **a** ∼ **of bread** un pain
■ **loaf about**, **loaf around** traînasser

**loafer** *n* (a) (shoe) mocassin *m*
(b) (idler) flemmard/-e *m/f* (colloq)

**loan** **1** *n* (when borrowing) emprunt *m*; (when lending) prêt *m*; **to be on** ∼ être prêté/-e (**to** à)
**2** *vtr* (also ∼ **out**) prêter (**to** à)

**loan shark** *n* (colloq) usurier/-ière *m/f*

**loath** *adj* **to be** ∼ **to do** répugner à faire

**loathe** *vtr* détester (**doing** faire)

**loathsome** *adj* répugnant/-e

**lobby** **1** *n* (a) (of hotel) hall *m*; (of theatre) lobby *m*
(b) (also ∼ **group**) lobby *m*
**2** *vi* faire pression (**for** pour obtenir)

**lobbying** *n* lobbying *m*

**lobe** *n* lobe *m*

**lobster** *n* homard *m*

**local** **1** *n* (a) **the** ∼**s** les gens *mpl* du coin
(b) (pub) pub *m* du coin
**2** *adj* (gen) local/-e; ⟨*library, shop*⟩ du quartier; ⟨*radio, news*⟩ régional/-e

**local anaesthetic** *n* anesthésique *m* local

**local authority** *n* (GB) autorités *fpl* locales

**local call** *n* communication *f* téléphonique locale

**local election** *n* élection *f* locale

**local government** *n* administration *f* locale

**locality** *n* (a) (neighbourhood) voisinage *m*
(b) (place) endroit *m*

**localized** *adj* localisé/-e

**locate** *vtr* (a) (find) retrouver ⟨*object*⟩; localiser ⟨*fault*⟩
(b) (position) situer ⟨*site*⟩

**location** *n* endroit *m*; **on ∼** ⟨*filmed*⟩ en extérieur

**lock** ⓵ *n* **(a)** (with key) serrure *f*; (with bolt) verrou *m*; **under ∼ and key** sous clé
**(b)** (of hair) mèche *f*
**(c)** (on canal) écluse *f*
**(d)** (Comput) verrouillage *m*
⓶ *vtr* fermer [qch] à clé
⓷ *vi* **(a)** ⟨*door, drawer*⟩ fermer à clé
**(b)** ⟨*steering wheel*⟩ se bloquer
■ **lock in** enfermer ⟨*person*⟩; **to ∼ oneself in** s'enfermer
■ **lock out**: **∼ sb out** enfermer qn dehors; **to ∼ oneself out** s'enfermer dehors
■ **lock together** ⟨*components, pieces*⟩ s'emboîter
■ **lock up**: ¶ **∼ up** fermer; ¶ **∼ [sth] up** fermer [qch] à clé ⟨*house*⟩; ¶ **∼ [sb] up** enfermer ⟨*hostage*⟩; mettre [qn] sous les verrous ⟨*killer*⟩

**locker** *n* casier *m*, vestiaire *m*

**locker room** *n* vestiaire *m*

**locket** *n* médaillon *m*

**locksmith** *n* serrurier *m*

**locomotive** *n* locomotive *f*

**locum** *n* (GB) remplaçant/-e *m/f*

**lodge** ⓵ *n* (small house) pavillon *m*; (for gatekeeper) loge *f* (du gardien)
⓶ *vtr* **to ∼ an appeal** faire appel; **to ∼ a complaint** porter plainte; **to ∼ a protest** protester
⓷ *vi* **(a)** ⟨*person*⟩ loger (**with** chez)
**(b)** ⟨*bullet*⟩ se loger; ⟨*small object*⟩ se coincer

**lodger** *n* (room only) locataire *mf*; (with meals) pensionnaire *mf*

**lodgings** *n pl* logement *m*

**loft** *n* **(a)** (attic) grenier *m*
**(b)** (US) (apartment) loft *m*

**loft conversion** *n* aménagement *m* de grenier

**log** ⓵ *n* **(a)** (of wood) rondin *m*; (for burning) bûche *f*
**(b)** (of ship) journal *m* de bord; (of plane) carnet *m* de vol
⓶ *vtr* **(a)** (record) noter
**(b)** ⟨*also* **∼ up**⟩ avoir à son actif ⟨*miles*⟩
IDIOMS **to sleep like a ∼** dormir comme une souche
■ **log in, log on** (Comput) ouvrir une session, se connecter
■ **log off, log out** (Comput) clore une session, se déconnecter

**log book** *n* (of car) ≈ carte *f* grise; (written record) registre *m*

**log cabin** *n* cabane *f* en rondins

**log fire** *n* feu *m* de bois

**loggerheads** *n pl* **to be at ∼** être en désaccord (**with** avec)

**logic** *n* logique *f*

**logical** *adj* logique

**logistics** *n* logistique *f*

**logo** *n* logo *m*

**log-off** *n* fin *f* de connexion

**log-on** *n* début *m* de connexion

**loin** *n* (Culin) (GB) ≈ côtes *fpl* premières; (US) ≈ filet *m*

**loiter** *vi* (idly) traîner; (pleasurably) flâner; (suspiciously) rôder

**loll** *vi* ⟨*person*⟩ se prélasser; ⟨*head*⟩ tomber; ⟨*tongue*⟩ pendre

**lollipop** *n* sucette *f*

**London** *pr n* Londres

**Londoner** *n* Londonien/-ienne *m/f*

**lone** *adj* solitaire

**loneliness** *n* (of person) solitude *f*; (of place) isolement *m*

**lonely** *adj* ⟨*person*⟩ seul/-e; ⟨*life*⟩ solitaire; ⟨*place*⟩ isolé/-e

**lonely hearts' column** *n* petites annonces *fpl* (de rencontre)

**loner** *n* solitaire *mf*

**lonesome** *adj* (US) solitaire

**long** ⓵ *adj* (gen) long/longue; ⟨*delay*⟩ important/-e; ⟨*grass*⟩ haut/-e; **to be 20 minutes ∼** durer 20 minutes; **to be 20 metres ∼** avoir *or* faire 20 mètres de long; **to get ∼er** ⟨*days, list, queue*⟩ s'allonger; ⟨*grass, hair*⟩ pousser; **she's been away a ∼ time** elle est restée longtemps absente; **it's been a ∼ time since...** ça fait longtemps que...; **to take a ∼ time** ⟨*person*⟩ être lent/-e; ⟨*task*⟩ prendre longtemps; **a ∼ way off** loin; **we've come a ∼ way** nous avons fait beaucoup de chemin
⓶ *adv* **(a)** (a long time) longtemps; **I won't be ∼** je n'en ai pas pour longtemps; **how ∼ will you be?** tu en as pour combien de temps?; **how ∼ did it take him?** il lui a fallu combien de temps?; **how ∼ is the interval?** combien de temps dure l'entracte?; **I haven't got ∼** je n'ai pas beaucoup de temps; **∼er than he thought** plus de temps qu'il ne le pensait; **before ∼** (in past) peu après; (in future) dans peu de temps; **not for ∼** pas longtemps; **∼ after** longtemps après; **not ∼ after** peu après; **∼ ago** il y a longtemps; **∼ before** bien avant; **he's no ∼er head** il n'est plus chef; **I can't stay any ∼er** je ne peux pas rester plus longtemps
**(b)** (for a long time) depuis longtemps; **those days are ∼ gone** ce temps-là n'est plus
⓷ *vi* **to ∼ for sth** avoir très envie de qch; **to do** rêver de faire
⓸ **as long as** *phr* (provided) du moment que (+ *indicative*), pourvu que (+ *subjunctive*)
IDIOMS **∼ time no see!** (colloq) ça fait une paye (colloq) qu'on ne s'est pas vus!; **so ∼!** (colloq) salut!

**long-awaited** *adj* longtemps attendu/-e

**long-distance** *adj* ⟨*runner*⟩ de fond; ⟨*telephone call*⟩ (within the country) interurbain/-e; (abroad) international/-e; **∼ lorry driver** (GB) routier *m*

**long-haired** *adj* ⟨*person*⟩ aux cheveux longs; ⟨*animal*⟩ à poil long

**longhand** *n* **in ∼** écrit/-e à la main

**long-haul** *adj* ⟨*flight, aircraft*⟩ long-courrier *inv*

**longing** *n* **(a)** grand désir *m* (**for** de; **to do** de faire)
**(b)** (nostalgia) nostalgie *f* (**for** de)

**longitude** *n* longitude *f*

**long jump** *n* (GB) saut *m* en longueur

**long-life** *adj* ⟨*milk*⟩ longue conservation *inv*; ⟨*battery*⟩ longue durée *inv*

**long-range** *adj* ⟨*missile*⟩ (à) longue portée; ⟨*forecast*⟩ à long terme

**long-sighted** *adj* presbyte

**long-standing** *adj* de longue date

**long term** ⟦1⟧ *n* **in the** ∼ à long terme ⟦2⟧ **long-term** *adj, adv* à long terme

**long-time** *adj* de longue date

**long-wave** *n* grandes ondes *fpl*

**long-winded** *adj* verbeux/-euse

**loo** *n* (GB) (colloq) vécés *mpl* (colloq), toilettes *fpl*

**look** ⟦1⟧ *n* **(a)** (glance) coup *m* d'œil; **to have** *or* **take a** ∼ **at sth** jeter un coup d'œil à *or* sur qch; **to have** *or* **take a good** ∼ **at** regarder [qch] de près; **to have a** ∼ **inside/ behind sth** regarder à l'intérieur de/derrière qch; **to have a** ∼ **round** faire un tour dans ⟨*park, town*⟩
**(b)** (search) **to have a (good)** ∼ (bien) chercher
**(c)** (expression) regard *m*; **a** ∼ **of sadness** un regard triste; **from the** ∼ **on his face...** à son expression...
**(d)** (appearance) (of person) air *m*; (of building, scenery) aspect *m*
⟦2⟧ **looks** *n pl* ∼**s aren't everything** il n'y a pas que la beauté qui compte; **he's losing his** ∼**s** il n'est pas aussi beau qu'autrefois
⟦3⟧ *vi* **(a)** regarder (**into** dans; **over** par-dessus); **to** ∼ **away** détourner le regard *or* les yeux; **to** ∼ **out of the window** regarder par la fenêtre
**(b)** (search) chercher, regarder
**(c)** (appear, seem) avoir l'air, paraître; **you** ∼ **cold** tu as l'air d'avoir froid; **he** ∼**s young for his age** il fait jeune pour son âge; **that makes you** ∼ **younger** ça te rajeunit; **the picture will** ∼ **good in the study** le tableau ira bien dans le bureau; **it doesn't** ∼ **right** ça ne va pas; **things are** ∼**ing good** les choses se présentent bien; **to** ∼ **like sb/sth** ressembler à qn/qch; **what does the house** ∼ **like?** comment est la maison?; **it** ∼**s like rain** on dirait qu'il va pleuvoir
⟦4⟧ *vtr* **(a)** (gaze, stare) regarder; **to** ∼ **sb in the eye** regarder qn dans les yeux
**(b)** (appear) **to** ∼ **one's age** faire son âge; **she's 40 but she doesn't** ∼ **it** elle a 40 ans mais elle ne les fait pas; **to** ∼ **one's best** être à son avantage
■ **look after** soigner ⟨*patient*⟩; garder ⟨*child*⟩; s'occuper de ⟨*customer, plant, finances, shop*⟩; surveiller ⟨*class, luggage*⟩; entretenir ⟨*car*⟩
■ **look around:** ¶ ∼ **around (a)** (glance) regarder autour de soi
**(b) to** ∼ **around for sb/sth** chercher qn/qch

**(c)** (in town) faire un tour
¶ ∼ **around [sth]** visiter ⟨*church, town*⟩
■ **look at (a)** regarder; (briefly) jeter un coup d'œil sur
**(b)** (examine) examiner ⟨*patient*⟩; jeter un coup d'œil à ⟨*car*⟩; étudier ⟨*problem, options*⟩
**(c)** (see, view) voir ⟨*life, situation*⟩; envisager ⟨*problem*⟩
■ **look back (a)** (turn around) se retourner (**at** pour regarder)
**(b) to** ∼ **back on** se tourner sur ⟨*past*⟩; repenser à ⟨*experience*⟩; ∼**ing back on it** rétrospectivement
■ **look down:** ¶ ∼ **down** (from a height) regarder en bas
¶ ∼ **down on** ⟨*sb/sth*⟩ **(a)** regarder [qch] d'en haut
**(b)** (condescendingly) mépriser
■ **look for** chercher ⟨*person, object*⟩
■ **look forward to** attendre [qch] avec impatience; **she's** ∼**ing forward to going on holiday** elle a hâte de partir en vacances; **I** ∼ **forward to hearing from you** (in letter) j'espère avoir bientôt de tes nouvelles; (formal) dans l'attente de votre réponse, je vous prie d'agréer mes sincères salutations
■ **look into** examiner ⟨*matter*⟩
■ **look on:** ¶ ∼ **on** (watch) regarder; (be present) assister à; ¶ ∼ **on** ⟨*sb/sth*⟩ considérer ⟨*person, event*⟩ (**as** comme; **with** avec)
■ **look out:** ¶ ∼ **out** (take care) faire attention (**for** à); (be wary) se méfier (**for** de); ∼ **out!** attention!; ¶ ∼ **out for** ⟨*sb/sth*⟩ guetter ⟨*person*⟩; être à l'affût de ⟨*bargain, new talent*⟩
■ **look round** ¶ (look behind) se retourner; (look about) regarder autour de soi; ¶ ∼ **round** ⟨*sth*⟩ visiter ⟨*town*⟩; **to** ∼ **round the shops** faire les magasins
■ **look through:** ¶ ∼ **through** ⟨*sth*⟩ **(a)** parcourir ⟨*report*⟩; feuilleter ⟨*magazine*⟩
**(b)** fouiller dans ⟨*belongings*⟩
¶ ∼ **through** ⟨*sb*⟩ faire semblant de ne pas voir
■ **look to (a)** (rely on) compter sur ⟨*qn/qch*⟩
**(b)** (turn to) se tourner vers ⟨*future, friends*⟩
■ **look up:** ¶ ∼ **up** (raise eyes) lever les yeux (**from** de); (raise head) lever la tête; **things are** ∼**ing up for us** les choses s'arrangent pour nous
¶ ∼ ⟨*sb/sth*⟩ **up (a)** chercher ⟨*phone number, price*⟩ (in dans)
**(b)** passer voir ⟨*acquaintance*⟩
¶ ∼ **up to** ⟨*sb*⟩ admirer ⟨*person*⟩

**look-alike** *n* sosie *m*

**look-in** *n* (GB) **to get a** ∼ avoir sa chance; **to give sb a** ∼ donner sa chance à qn

**look-out** *n* **(a) to be on the** ∼ **for** rechercher ⟨*stolen vehicle*⟩; être à l'affût de ⟨*bargain, new talent*⟩; guetter ⟨*visitor*⟩
**(b)** (place) poste *m* d'observation

**loom** ⟦1⟧ *n* métier *m* à tisser ⟦2⟧ *vi* **(a)** (also ∼ **up**) surgir (**out of** de; **over** au-dessus de)
**(b)** ⟨*war, crisis*⟩ menacer; ⟨*exam, interview*⟩ être imminent/-e; **to** ∼ **large** ⟨*issue*⟩ peser lourd

**loony** *adj* (colloq) farfelu/-e (colloq)

**loop** ⬛**1** *n* (gen, Comput) boucle *f*
⬛**2** *vtr* nouer
⬛**3** *vi* ⟨*road, path*⟩ faire une boucle

**loophole** *n* lacune *f*

**loose** *adj* **(a)** ⟨*knot, screw*⟩ desserré/-e;
⟨*handle, tooth*⟩ branlant/-e; ⟨*button*⟩ qui se
décroche; ⟨*thread*⟩ décousu/-e; **to hang ~**
⟨*hair*⟩ être dénoué/-e; **~ connection** faux
contact
**(b)** (free) **to break ~** ⟨*animal*⟩ s'échapper
(from de); **to cut sb ~** détacher qn; **to let ~**
libérer ⟨*animal, prisoner*⟩
**(c)** ⟨*page*⟩ détaché/-e; **~ change** petite
monnaie
**(d)** ⟨*jacket, trousers*⟩ ample; ⟨*collar*⟩ lâche
**(e)** ⟨*link, weave*⟩ lâche
**(f)** ⟨*translation, interpretation*⟩ assez libre;
⟨*wording*⟩ imprécis/-e; ⟨*connection,
guideline*⟩ vague; ⟨*style*⟩ relâché/-e
**(g)** ⟨*morals*⟩ dissolu/-e
IDIOMS **to be at a ~ end** (GB), **to be at ~
ends** (US) ne pas trop savoir quoi faire

**loosely** *adv* **(a)** ⟨*hold, wind, wrap*⟩ sans
serrer; **his clothes hung ~ on him** il flottait
dans ses vêtements
**(b)** ⟨*connected, organized*⟩ de façon souple
**(c)** ⟨*translate, describe*⟩ assez librement

**loosely knit** *adj* ⟨*group, structure*⟩ peu
uni/-e

**loosen** *vtr* desserrer ⟨*belt, strap, collar*⟩;
dégager ⟨*nail, post*⟩; relâcher ⟨*grip, rope,
control*⟩; dénouer ⟨*hair*⟩
■ **loosen up (a)** (sport) s'échauffer
**(b)** (relax) se détendre

**loot** ⬛**1** *n* butin *m*
⬛**2** *vtr* piller ⟨*shops*⟩

**looter** *n* pillard/-e *m/f*

**lopsided** *adj* ⟨*object, smile*⟩ de travers;
⟨*argument, view*⟩ irrationnel/-elle

**lord** *n* **(a)** ⟨*ruler*⟩ seigneur *m* (of de)
**(b)** ( peer) lord *m*; **the (House of) Lords** la
Chambre des Lords; **my Lord** (to noble)
Monsieur le comte/duc etc
IDIOMS **to ~ it over sb** (colloq) regarder qn
de haut

**Lord** *n* **(a)** (in prayers) Seigneur *m*
**(b)** (colloq) (in exclamations) **good ~!** grand
Dieu!

**Lord Mayor** *n* lord-maire *m*

**lordship** *n* (also **Lordship**) **your/his ~** (of
noble) Monsieur; (of judge) Monsieur le Juge

**lorry** *n* (GB) camion *m*

**lorry driver** *n* (GB) routier *m*, chauffeur
*m* de poids lourd

**lose** ⬛**1** *vtr* **(a)** (gen) perdre; **to ~ one's way**
se perdre; **to ~ interest in sth** se
désintéresser de qch
**(b)** ⟨*clock*⟩ retarder de ⟨*minutes, seconds*⟩
**(c)** (get rid of) semer (colloq) ⟨*pursuer*⟩
⬛**2** *vi* **(a)** (gen) perdre
**(b)** ⟨*clock*⟩ retarder
■ **lose out** être perdant/-e

**loser** *n* (gen, Sport) perdant/-e *m/f*

**loss** *n* perte *f* (of de); **to be at a ~** ( puzzled)
être perplexe; (helpless) être perdu/-e

**lost** *adj* **(a)** ⟨*person, animal*⟩ perdu/-e; **to get
~** ⟨*person, animal*⟩ se perdre; ⟨*object*⟩
s'égarer; **get ~!** (colloq) fiche le camp! (colloq)
**(b)** ⟨*opportunity*⟩ manqué/-e; ⟨*cause*⟩
perdu/-e; ⟨*civilization*⟩ disparu/-e; **to be ~
on sb** passer au-dessus de la tête de qn; **to
be ~ for words** être interloqué/-e; **to be ~ in**
être plongé/-e dans ⟨*book, thought*⟩

**lost and found** *n* objets *mpl* trouvés

**lost property** *n* (GB) objets *mpl* trouvés

**lot¹** ⬛**1** *pron* **(a)** (great deal) **a ~** beaucoup; **he
spent a ~** il a beaucoup dépensé, il a
dépensé beaucoup d'argent; **to mean a ~ to
sb** avoir beaucoup d'importance pour qn
**(b)** (colloq) **the ~** (le) tout
⬛**2** *quantif* **a ~ of money/time** beaucoup
d'argent/de temps; **I see a ~ of him** je le
vois beaucoup
⬛**3 lots** *quantif, pron* (colloq) **~s (and ~s) of**
des tas (colloq) de, beaucoup de; **~s of things**
des tas (colloq) de choses
⬛**4 a lot** *adv* beaucoup; **he's a ~ better/
worse** il va beaucoup mieux/plus mal; **this
happens quite a ~** cela arrive très souvent

**lot²** *n* **(a)** (destiny) sort *m*; (quality of life)
condition *f*
**(b)** (US) parcelle *f* (de terrain)
**(c)** (at auction) lot *m*
**(d) to draw ~s** tirer au sort
**(e)** (batch) fournée *f*

**lotion** *n* lotion *f*

**lottery** *n* loterie *f*

**loud** ⬛**1** *adj* **(a)** ⟨*music, voice*⟩ fort/-e; ⟨*noise,
scream*⟩ grand/-e (before n); ⟨*comment,
laugh*⟩ bruyant/-e; ⟨*applause*⟩ vif/vive
**(b)** ⟨*colour*⟩ criard/-e; ⟨*person, behaviour*⟩
exubérant/-e
⬛**2** *adv* fort; **out ~** à voix haute

**loudly** *adv* ⟨*knock, talk*⟩ bruyamment;
⟨*scream*⟩ fort; ⟨*protest*⟩ vivement

**loudspeaker** *n* (for announcements)
haut-parleur *m*; (for hi-fi) enceinte *f*

**lounge** *n* **(a)** (in house, hotel) salon *m*
**(b)** (in airport) **departure ~** salle *f*
d'embarquement
**(c)** (US) (also **cocktail ~**) bar *m*
■ **lounge about, lounge around**
paresser

**lousy** *adj* minable (colloq); **a ~ trick** un sale
tour

**lout** *n* malotru *m* (colloq)

**loutish** *adj* ⟨*person*⟩ grossier/-ière;
⟨*behaviour*⟩ de voyou

**louvred** (GB), **louvered** (US) *adj* ⟨*doors*⟩
à lamelles

**lovable** *adj* ⟨*person*⟩ sympathique; ⟨*child*⟩
adorable

**love** ⬛**1** *n* **(a)** amour *m*; **to be/fall in ~** être/
tomber amoureux/-euse (with de); **to make ~**
faire l'amour; **Andy sends his ~** Andy
t'embrasse; **with ~ from Bob**, **~ Bob**
affectueusement, Bob ····⫶

**(b)** (GB) (term of affection) mon chéri/ma chérie *m/f*
**(c)** (in tennis) zéro *m*
**2** *vtr* aimer; **to ~ each other** s'aimer; **to ~ doing** *or* **to do** aimer beaucoup faire; **'I'd ~ to!'** 'avec plaisir!'
IDIOMS **~ at first sight** le coup de foudre

**love affair** *n* liaison *f* (**with** avec; **between** entre)

**love-life** *n* vie *f* amoureuse

**lovely** *adj* **(a)** (beautiful) ⟨*colour, garden, woman*⟩ beau/belle (*before n*), joli/-e (*before n*); **to look ~** ⟨*child, dress*⟩ être ravissant/-e
**(b)** (pleasant) ⟨*letter, person*⟩ charmant/-e; ⟨*meal, smell*⟩ délicieux/-ieuse; ⟨*idea, surprise*⟩ bon/bonne (*before n*); ⟨*present, weather*⟩ magnifique

**lover** *n* **(a)** (male) amant *m*; (female) maîtresse *f*; **they are ~s** ils sont amants
**(b)** (person in love) amoureux/-euse *m/f*
**(c)** (enthusiast) amateur *m*; **jazz ~** amateur de jazz

**loving** *adj* (gen) tendre; ⟨*care*⟩ affectueux/-euse

**low** **1** *n* **(a)** (in weather) dépression *f*
**(b)** **to be at** *or* **have hit an all-time ~** être au plus bas
**2** *adj* **(a)** (gen) bas/basse; ⟨*speed*⟩ réduit/-e; ⟨*number, rate*⟩ faible (*before n*); ⟨*battery*⟩ presque à plat *inv*; **in a ~ voice** tout bas; **to be ~ on staff** manquer de personnel; **to be ~ in sugar** contenir peu de sucre
**(b)** ⟨*mark, quality*⟩ mauvais/-e (*before n*)
**(c)** (depressed) déprimé/-e
**(d)** ⟨*behaviour*⟩ ignoble
**3** *adv* **(a)** ⟨*aim*⟩ bas; ⟨*bend*⟩ très bas; ⟨*fly*⟩ à basse altitude
**(b)** (in importance) **it's very ~ (down) on the list** c'est tout à fait secondaire
**(c)** ⟨*speak, sing*⟩ bas; **to turn [sth] down ~** baisser ⟨*heating, light*⟩
**4** *vi* ⟨*cow*⟩ meugler

**low-alcohol** *adj* peu alcoolisé/-e

**lowbrow** *adj* ⟨*person*⟩ peu intellectuel/-elle

**low-budget** *adj* à petit budget

**low-calorie** *adj* ⟨*diet*⟩ hypocalorique; ⟨*food*⟩ à faible teneur en calories

**low-cost** *adj* économique, bon marché

**low-cut** *adj* décolleté/-e

**low-down** *adj* (colloq) tuyau *m* (colloq)

**lower** **1** *adj* inférieur/-e
**2** *vtr* **(a)** baisser ⟨*barrier, curtain, flag*⟩; abaisser ⟨*ceiling*⟩; **to ~ sb/sth** descendre qn/qch (**into** dans; **onto** sur)
**(b)** (reduce) baisser ⟨*prices, standards*⟩; réduire ⟨*pressure, temperature*⟩; abaisser ⟨*age limit*⟩; **to ~ one's voice** baisser la voix
**(c)** affaler ⟨*sail*⟩
**3** *v refl* **to ~ oneself (a)** s'abaisser
**(b)** **to ~ oneself into** s'asseoir précautionneusement dans ⟨*bath, armchair*⟩

**lower class** *n* **the ~(es)** la classe ouvrière

**lower sixth** *n* (GB Sch) ≈ classe *f* de première; **to be in the ~** ≈ être en première

**low-fat** *adj* ⟨*diet*⟩ sans matières grasses; ⟨*cheese*⟩ allégé/-e; ⟨*milk*⟩ écrémé/-e

**low-income** *adj* ⟨*family*⟩ à faible revenue; ⟨*bracket*⟩ des bas salaires

**low-key** *adj* ⟨*approach*⟩ discret/-ète; ⟨*meeting, talks*⟩ informel/-elle

**low-level** *adj* ⟨*bombing*⟩ à basse altitude; ⟨*talks*⟩ informel/-elle; ⟨*radiation*⟩ faible

**low-lying** *adj* à basse altitude

**low-paid** *adj* ⟨*job*⟩ faiblement rémunéré/-e; ⟨*worker*⟩ peu rémunéré/-e

**low-priced** *adj* à bas prix

**low-profile** *adj* discret/-ète

**low-quality** *adj* de qualité inférieure

**low-risk** *adj* à risque limité

**low season** *n* basse saison *f*

**low-tech** *adj* traditionnel/-elle

**low tide** *n* marée *f* basse

**loyal** *adj* ⟨*friend*⟩ loyal/-e (**to** envers); ⟨*customer*⟩ fidèle (**to** à)

**loyalty** *n* loyauté *f* (**to, towards** envers)

**loyalty card** *n* carte *f* de fidélité

**lozenge** *n* pastille *f*

**LP** *n* (disque *m*) 33 tours *m*

**L-plate** *n* (GB Aut) plaque *f* d'élève conducteur débutant accompagné

**Ltd** (GB) (*abbr* = **limited (liability)**) ≈ SARL

**lubricant** *n* lubrifiant *m*

**lucid** *adj* **(a)** (clear) clair/-e
**(b)** (sane) ⟨*person*⟩ lucide; ⟨*moment*⟩ de lucidité

**luck** *n* chance *f*; **good ~** chance *f*; **bad ~** malchance *f*; **to bring sb good/bad ~** porter bonheur/malheur à qn; **it's good ~** ça porte bonheur; **bad** *or* **hard ~!** pas de chance!; **good ~!** bonne chance!; **to be in/out of ~** avoir de la/ne pas avoir de chance

**luckily** *adv* heureusement (**for** pour)

**lucky** *adj* **(a)** (fortunate) **to be ~** avoir de la chance
**(b)** ⟨*charm, colour, number*⟩ porte-bonheur *inv*; **it's my ~ day!** c'est mon jour de chance!

**lucrative** *adj* lucratif/-ive

**ludicrous** *adj* grotesque

**luggage** *n* bagages *mpl*

**luggage rack** *n* porte-bagages *m inv*

**lukewarm** *adj* tiède

**lull** **1** *n* (in storm, fighting) accalmie *f*; (in conversation) pause *f*
**2** *vtr* **to ~ sb to sleep** endormir qn en le berçant; **to ~ sb into thinking that...** faire croire à qn que...; **to be ~ed into a false sense of security** se laisser aller à un sentiment de sécurité trompeur

**lullaby** *n* berceuse *f*

**lumber** **1** *n* (US) bois *m* de construction
**2** *vtr* (GB) (colloq) **to get** *or* **be ~ed with sb/sth** se retrouver avec qn/qch sur les bras
**3** *vi* (*also* **~ along**) avancer d'un pas lourd; ⟨*vehicle*⟩ avancer péniblement

**lumberjack** *n* bûcheron/-onne *m/f*

**luminous** *adj* lumineux/-euse
**lump** ☐1 *n* (a) (gen) morceau *m*; (of soil, clay) motte *f*; (in sauce) grumeau *m*
(b) (on body) (from knock) bosse *f* (on sur)
(c) (tumour) grosseur *f* (in, on à)
☐2 *vtr* to ~ X and Y together mettre X et Y dans le même panier (colloq)
IDIOMS to have a ~ in one's throat avoir la gorge serrée
**lump sum** *n* versement *m* unique
**lunar** *adj* ⟨landscape⟩ lunaire; ⟨eclipse⟩ de lune; ⟨landing⟩ sur la lune
**lunatic** *n* fou/folle *m/f*
**lunch** *n* déjeuner *m*; to have ~ déjeuner; to take sb out for ~ emmener qn déjeuner au restaurant; to close for ~ fermer le midi
**lunchbox** *n* boîte *f* à sandwichs
**lunchbreak** *n* pause-déjeuner *f*
**luncheon voucher**, **LV** *n* ticket-repas *m*, ticket-restaurant® *m*
**lunch hour** *n* heure *f* du déjeuner
**lunchtime** *n* heure *f* du déjeuner
**lung** *n* poumon *m*
**lunge** *vi* bondir (at vers; forward en avant)
**lurch** *vi* ⟨person, vehicle⟩ tanguer; to ~ forward ⟨car⟩ faire un bond en avant
IDIOMS to leave sb in the ~ abandonner qn
**lure** ☐1 *n* (a) (attraction) attrait *m* (of de)
(b) (in hunting) leurre *m*
☐2 *vtr* attirer (into dans; with avec); they ~d him out of his house ils ont réussi à le faire sortir de chez lui par la ruse

**lurid** *adj* (a) ⟨colour⟩ criard/-e
(b) ⟨detail, past⟩ épouvantable
**lurk** *vi* he was ~ing in the bushes il était tapi dans les buissons; to ~ in the garden rôder dans le jardin
**luscious** *adj* ⟨food⟩ succulent/-e; ⟨woman⟩ pulpeux/-euse
**lush** *adj* ⟨vegetation⟩ luxuriant/-e; ⟨hotel, surroundings⟩ luxueux/-euse
**lust** ☐1 *n* (a) désir *m*; (deadly sin) luxure *f*
(b) (for power, blood) soif *f* (for de)
☐2 *vi* to ~ for *or* after sb/sth convoiter qn/qch
**luvvy** *n* (colloq) acteur/-trice *m/f* prétentieux/-ieuse
**Luxembourg** *pr n* Luxembourg *m*
**luxurious** *adj* ⟨apartment, lifestyle⟩ de luxe (never after v); his apartment is ~ son appartement est luxueux
**luxury** ☐1 *n* luxe *m*
☐2 *adj* ⟨hotel, product, holiday⟩ de luxe
**lychee** *n* litchi *m*
**lying** *n* mensonges *mpl*
**lynch** *vtr* lyncher
**lynch mob** *n* lyncheurs *mpl*
**lyrical** *adj* lyrique; to wax ~ (about sth) disserter avec lyrisme (sur qch)
**lyrics** *n pl* paroles *fpl*
**lyric-writer** *n* parolier/-ière *m/f*

# M m

**m**, **M** *n* m, M *m*
**MA** *n* (abbr = **Master of Arts**) diplôme *m* supérieur de lettres
**macabre** *adj* macabre
**macaroni** *n* macaronis *mpl*
**mace** *n* (a) (spice) macis *m*
(b) (ceremonial staff) masse *f*
**Macedonia** *pr n* Macédoine *f*
**machete** *n* machette *f*
**machine** *n* machine *f*; sewing ~ machine à coudre; by ~ à la machine
**machine gun** *n* mitrailleuse *f*
**machine-readable** *adj* ⟨data⟩ directement exploitable; ⟨passport⟩ vérifiable par ordinateur
**machinery** *n* (a) (equipment) machines *fpl*; (working parts) mécanisme *m*, rouages *mpl*; a piece of ~ une machine
(b) (figurative) dispositifs *mpl*
**macho** *adj* macho (colloq)
**mackerel** *n* maquereau *m*

**mackintosh**, **macintosh** *n* imperméable *m*
**mad** *adj* (a) ⟨person⟩ fou/folle (with de); ⟨dog⟩ enragé/-e; ⟨idea, scheme⟩ insensé/-e; to go ~ devenir fou/folle; to drive sb ~ rendre qn fou
(b) (colloq) (angry) furieux/-ieuse; to be ~ at *or* with sb être très en colère contre qn; to go ~ se mettre dans une colère folle
(c) (colloq) (enthusiastic) ~ about *or* on fou/folle de (colloq) ⟨person, hobby⟩
(d) ⟨panic⟩ infernal/-e; the audience went ~ le public s'est déchaîné
IDIOMS to work like ~ travailler comme un fou/une folle
**madam** *n* madame *f*; Dear Madam (in letter) Madame
**mad cow disease** *n* maladie *f* de la vache folle
**maddening** *adj* ⟨person⟩ énervant/-e; ⟨delay, situation⟩ exaspérant/-e
**made** *adj* a ~ man un homme qui a réussi; ⋯⁖

**he's got it** ~ (colloq) (sure to succeed) sa réussite est assurée; (has succeeded) il n'a plus à s'en faire

**Madeira** *pr n* Madère

**made-to-measure** *adj* ⟨garment⟩ fait/-e sur mesure

**made-up** *adj* (a) (wearing make-up) maquillé/-e
(b) ⟨story⟩ fabriqué/-e

**madly** *adv* (a) (frantically) frénétiquement
(b) ⟨jealous⟩ follement; ~ **in love (with sb)** follement *or* éperdument amoureux/-euse (de qn)

**madman** *n* (colloq) fou *m* (colloq), malade *m* (colloq)

**madness** *n* folie *f*; **it is** ~ **to do** c'est de la folie de faire

**Mafia** *n* **the** ~ la Mafia

**magazine** *n* (a) revue *f*; (mainly photos) magazine *m*; **fashion** ~ magazine de mode; **women's** ~ journal *m* féminin
(b) (on radio, TV) magazine *m*
(c) (of gun, camera) magasin *m*

**maggot** *n* (in fruit) ver *m*; (for fishing) asticot *m*

**magic** ⊡ *n* magie *f*
⊡ *adj* magique

**magical** *adj* magique

**magic carpet** *n* tapis *m* volant

**magician** *n* (wizard) magicien *m*; (entertainer) illusionniste *m*

**magistrate** *n* magistrat *m*

**magistrate's court** *n* ≈ tribunal *m* de police

**magnanimous** *adj* magnanime

**magnate** *n* magnat *m*; **oil** ~ magnat du pétrole

**magnesium** *n* magnésium *m*

**magnet** *n* aimant *m*; (figurative) pôle *m* d'attraction (**for** pour)

**magnetic** *adj* (a) ⟨rod⟩ aimanté/-e; ⟨field, force, storm⟩ magnétique
(b) ⟨appeal⟩ irrésistible; **to have a** ~ **personality** avoir du charisme

**magnetism** *n* magnétisme *m*

**magnificent** *adj* magnifique

**magnify** *vtr* grossir

**magnifying glass** *n* loupe *f*

**magnitude** *n* ampleur *f* (**of** de)

**magnolia** *n* (a) ⟨also ~ **tree**⟩ magnolia *m*
(b) (colour) crème *f*

**magpie** *n* pie *f*

**mahogany** *n* acajou *m*

**maid** *n* (in house) bonne *f*; (in hotel) femme *f* de chambre

**maiden** ⊡ *n* jeune fille *f*
⊡ *adj* ⟨flight, voyage, speech⟩ inaugural/-e

**maiden name** *n* nom *m* de jeune fille

**mail** ⊡ *n* (a) (postal service) poste *f*; **by** ~ par la poste
(b) (letters) courrier *m*
(c) (e-mail) courrier *m* électronique
⊡ *vtr* envoyer, expédier ⟨letter, parcel⟩ (**to** à)

**mailbox** *n* (for posting) boîte *f* aux lettres; (for delivery) boîte *f* à lettres; (for e-mail) boîte *f* aux lettres électronique

**mailing** *n* (for advertising) publipostage *m*, mailing *m*

**mailing list** *n* fichier-clientèle *m*

**mailman** *n* (US) facteur *m*

**mail order** ⊡ *n* **to buy (by)** ~ acheter par correspondance
⊡ *adj* ⟨business, goods⟩ de vente *f* par correspondance

**maim** *vtr* estropier

**main** ⊡ *n* (a) (pipe) canalisation *f*
(b) **the** ~**s** (of electricity) secteur *m*; (of water, gas) le réseau de distribution; (of sewage) le réseau d'évacuation
⊡ *adj* principal/-e

**main course** *n* plat *m* principal

**mainframe** *n* ⟨also ~ **computer**⟩ ordinateur *m* central

**mainland** *n* territoire *m* continental; **on the** ~ sur le continent

**main line** ⊡ *n* grande ligne *f*
⊡ *adj* ⟨station⟩ de grande ligne
⊡ **mainline** *vi* (colloq) se piquer

**mainly** *adv* surtout, essentiellement

**main road** *n* (in country) route *f* principale; (in town) grande rue *f*

**mainstream** ⊡ *n* courant *m* dominant
⊡ *adj* (a) (conventional) traditionnel/-elle
(b) ~ **jazz** jazz mainstream

**maintain** *vtr* (a) (keep steady) maintenir
(b) subvenir aux besoins de ⟨family⟩; entretenir ⟨army, house, property⟩
(c) continuer à affirmer ⟨innocence⟩; **to** ~ **that** soutenir que

**maintenance** *n* (a) (upkeep) entretien *m* (**of** de)
(b) (GB) (Law) (alimony) pension *f* alimentaire

**maisonette** *n* duplex *m*

**maize** *n* maïs *m*

**majestic** *adj* majestueux/-euse

**majesty** *n* (a) (grandeur) majesté *f*
(b) **His/Her Majesty** sa Majesté

**major** ⊡ *n* (a) (Mil) commandant *m*
(b) (US) (Univ) matière *f* principale
(c) (Mus) ton *m* majeur
⊡ *adj* (a) ⟨event⟩ important/-e; ⟨role⟩ majeur/-e; ⟨significance⟩ capital/-e; **a** ~ **operation**, ~ **surgery** une grosse opération
(b) (main) principal/-e
(c) (Mus) majeur/-e; **in a** ~ **key** en majeur
⊡ *vi* (US) (Univ) **to** ~ **in** se spécialiser en

**Majorca** *pr n* Majorque *f*; **in** ~ à Majorque

**majority** *n* majorité *f* (**of** de); **to be in a** *or* **the** ~ être en majorité

**make** ⊡ *n* marque *f*
⊡ *vtr* (a) (gen) faire; **to** ~ **the bed** faire le lit; **to** ~ **a noise** faire du bruit; **to** ~ **a rule** établir une règle; **to** ~ **room/the time (for sth)** trouver de la place/du temps (pour qch); **to** ~ **friends/enemies** se faire des amis/des ennemis; **to** ~ **oneself understood** se faire comprendre; **it's made (out) of gold** c'est en

or; **made in France** fabriqué en France; **he was made treasurer** on l'a fait trésorier; **to ~ a habit/an issue of sth** faire de qch une habitude/une affaire; **it's been made into a film** on en a fait or tiré un film; **three and three ~ six** trois et trois font six
**(b)** (with adjective) **to ~ sb happy/ill** rendre qn heureux/malade; **to ~ sb hungry** donner faim à qn; **to ~ sth better/bigger/worse** améliorer/agrandir/aggraver qch
**(c)** (with infinitive) **to ~ sb cry** faire pleurer qn; **I made her smile** je l'ai fait sourire; **to ~ sb pay the bill** faire payer l'addition à qn; **to ~ sb wait** faire attendre qn; **they made me do it** ils m'ont obligé or forcé; **it ~s her voice sound funny** ça lui donne une drôle de voix
**(d)** (earn) gagner ⟨*salary*⟩; **to ~ a living** gagner sa vie; **to ~ a profit** réaliser des bénéfices; **to ~ a loss** subir des pertes
**(e)** (reach) arriver jusqu'à ⟨*place, position*⟩; atteindre ⟨*ranking, level*⟩; **we'll never ~ it** nous n'y arriverons jamais; **to ~ the front page** faire la une
**(f)** (estimate, say) **what time do you ~ it?** quelle heure as-tu?; **I ~ it five o'clock** il est cinq heures à ma montre; **let's ~ it five dollars** disons cinq dollars; **can we ~ it a bit later?** peut-on dire un peu plus tard?; **what do you ~ of it?** qu'en dis-tu?
**(g)** (cause success of) assurer la réussite de ⟨*holiday, meal*⟩; **it really made my day** ça m'a rendu heureux pour la journée
IDIOMS **to ~ it** (colloq) (in career, life) y arriver; (to party, meeting) réussir à venir; **I can't ~ it** je ne peux pas venir
■ **make do** faire avec; **to ~ do with** se contenter de qch
■ **make for (a)** (head for) se diriger vers
**(b)** (help create) permettre, assurer
■ **make good**: ¶ **~ good** réussir
¶ **~ good [sth] (a)** réparer ⟨*damage, omission*⟩; rattraper ⟨*lost time*⟩; combler ⟨*deficit*⟩
**(b)** tenir ⟨*promise*⟩
■ **make out**: ¶ **~ out** affirmer, prétendre (that que); ¶ **~ [sb/sth] out (a)** (see, distinguish) distinguer
**(b)** (claim) **to ~ sth out to be easy/difficult** prétendre que qch est facile/difficile
**(c)** (understand) comprendre (if si); **I can't ~ him out** je n'arrive pas à le comprendre
**(d)** (write out) faire, rédiger; **to ~ out a cheque to sb** faire un chèque à qn; **it is made out to X** il est à l'ordre de X
■ **make up**: ¶ **~ up (a)** (after quarrel) se réconcilier (with avec)
**(b) to ~ up for** rattraper ⟨*lost time, lost sleep*⟩; compenser ⟨*personal loss*⟩
¶ **~ [sth] up (a)** inventer ⟨*story, excuse*⟩
**(b)** (prepare) faire ⟨*parcel, garment, bed*⟩; préparer ⟨*prescription*⟩
**(c)** (constitute) faire; **to be made up of** être fait/-e or composé/-e de
**(d)** (compensate for) rattraper ⟨*loss, time*⟩; combler ⟨*deficit*⟩
**make-believe** n fantaisie f
**makeover** n transformation f

**maker** n (of clothes, food, appliance) fabricant m; (of cars, aircraft) constructeur m
**makeshift** adj improvisé/-e
**make-up** n (a) maquillage m; **to put on one's ~** se maquiller
**(b)** (character) caractère m
**make-up bag** n trousse f de maquillage
**make-up remover** n démaquillant m
**making** n (of film, programme) réalisation f; (of product) fabrication f; (of clothes) confection f; **his problems are of his own ~** ses ennuis sont de sa faute;
IDIOMS **to have all the ~s of** avoir tout pour faire
**maladjusted** adj inadapté/-e
**malaria** n paludisme m
**Malaysia** pr n Malaisie f
**male** ① n (a) (animal) mâle m
**(b)** (man) homme m
② adj (a) ⟨*plant, animal*⟩ mâle
**(b)** ⟨*population, role, trait*⟩ masculin/-e; ⟨*company*⟩ des hommes; **a ~ voice** une voix d'homme; **~ student** étudiant m
**(c)** ⟨*plug, socket*⟩ mâle
**male chauvinism** n machisme m
**male chauvinist** n phallocrate m
**male model** n mannequin m homme or masculin
**malevolent** adj malveillant/-e
**malformed** adj ⟨*limb, nose*⟩ difforme; ⟨*organ*⟩ malformé/-e
**malfunction** ① n (a) (poor operation) mauvais fonctionnement m
**(b)** (breakdown) défaillance f
② vi mal fonctionner
**malice** n méchanceté f (towards à)
**malicious** adj ⟨*comment, person*⟩ malveillant/-e; ⟨*act*⟩ méchant/-e; ⟨*lie*⟩ calomnieux/-ieuse
**malign** vtr calomnier
**malignant** adj (a) ⟨*look*⟩ malveillant/-e; ⟨*person*⟩ malfaisant/-e
**(b)** (Med) malin/-igne
**mall** n (a) (shopping arcade) (in town) galerie f marchande; (in suburbs) (US) centre m commercial
**(b)** (US) (street) rue f piétonne
**mallet** n maillet m
**malnutrition** n sous-alimentation f
**malpractice** n (a) (gen, Law) malversations fpl
**(b)** (US) (Med) erreur f médicale
**malt** n (a) (grain) malt m
**(b)** (whisky) whisky m pur malt
**(c)** (US) (malted milk) lait m malté
**Malta** pr n Malte f
**maltreat** vtr maltraiter
**mammal** n mammifère m
**mammoth** ① n mammouth m
② adj ⟨*task*⟩ gigantesque; ⟨*organization*⟩ géant/-e

m

**man** ☐ *n* **(a)** homme *m*; **an old** ~ un
vieillard; ~ **to** ~ d'homme à homme; ~ **and
wife** mari et femme
  **(b)** (mankind) l'humanité *f*
  **(c)** (in chess) pièce *f*; (in draughts) pion *m*
  ☐ *vtr* **(a)** tenir ‹*switchboard, desk*›
  **(b)** armer [qch] en hommes ‹*ship*›
  IDIOMS **every** ~ **for himself** chacun pour soi

**manage** ☐ *vtr* **(a) to** ~ **to do** réussir à
faire, se débrouiller (colloq) pour faire
  **(b)** diriger ‹*project, finances, organization*›;
gérer ‹*business, shop, hotel, estate*›; gérer
‹*money, time*›
  **(c)** (handle) savoir s'y prendre avec ‹*person,
animal*›; manier ‹*tool, boat*›
  ☐ *vi* se débrouiller

**manageable** *adj* ‹*size, car*› maniable;
‹*problem*› maîtrisable; ‹*person, animal*›
docile

**management** *n* **(a)** (system, field) gestion *f*;
**bad** ~ mauvaise gestion
  **(b)** (managers) direction *f*; **top** ~ la haute
direction; **the** ~ **team** l'équipe dirigeante

**management consultant** *n* conseiller
*m* en gestion

**management trainee** *n* apprenti
manager *m*

**manager** *n* (of firm, bank) directeur/-trice
*m/f*; (of shop) gérant/-e *m/f*; (of farm)
exploitant/-e *m/f*; (of project) responsable *mf*,
directeur/-trice *m/f*; (in show business)
directeur/-trice *m/f* artistique; (Sport)
manager *m*

**manageress** *n* (of firm, bank) directrice *f*;
(of shop, hotel) gérante *f*; (of project) responsable
*f*, directrice *f*; (in show business) directrice *f*
artistique

**managerial** *adj* ‹*experience*› en gestion;
‹*decision*› de la direction; ~ **staff** les cadres
*mpl*

**managing director**, **MD** *n*
directeur/-trice *m/f* général/-e

**mandarin** *n* **(a)** (fruit) mandarine *f*; (tree)
mandarinier *m*
  **(b)** (person) mandarin *m*

**mandate** *n* (authority) autorité *f*; (Pol)
mandat *m*

**mane** *n* crinière *f*

**manger** *n* mangeoire *f*

**mangle** *vtr* mutiler ‹*body*›; broyer ‹*vehicle*›

**mango** *n* (fruit) mangue *f*

**mangrove** *n* palétuvier *m*, manglier *m*

**mangy** *adj* ‹*dog*› galeux/-euse

**manhandle** *vtr* malmener, maltraiter

**manhole** *n* regard *m*

**manhood** *n* **(a)** âge *m* d'homme
  **(b)** (masculinity) masculinité *f*

**mania** *n* manie *f*

**maniac** *n* **(a)** (colloq) fou/folle *m/f*
  **(b)** (in psychology) maniaque *mf*

**manic** *adj* **(a)** (manic-depressive)
maniaco-dépressif/-ive; (obsessive)
obsessionnel/-elle
  **(b)** (figurative) ‹*activity, behaviour*› frénétique

**manicure** ☐ *n* manucure *f*
  ☐ *vtr* **to** ~ **one's nails** se faire les ongles

**manifest** ☐ *adj* manifeste, évident/-e
  ☐ *vtr* manifester

**manifesto** *n* manifeste *m*, programme *m*

**manipulate** *vtr* manipuler

**manipulative** *adj* manipulateur/-trice

**mankind** *n* humanité *f*

**manly** *adj* viril/-e

**man-made** *adj* ‹*fibre, fabric*› synthétique;
‹*lake*› artificiel/-ielle; ‹*tools*› fait/-e à la main

**manner** ☐ *n* **(a)** (way, method) manière *f*,
façon *f*; **in this** ~ de cette manière *or* façon;
**in a** ~ **of speaking** pour ainsi dire
  **(b)** (way of behaving) attitude *f*; **she has an
aggressive** ~ elle a une attitude agressive
  **(c)** (sort, kind) sorte *f*, genre *m* (**of** de)
  ☐ **manners** *n pl* **(a)** manières *fpl*; **to have
good/bad** ~**s** avoir de bonnes/mauvaises
manières; **it's bad** ~**s to do** il est mal élevé
de faire
  **(b)** (customs) mœurs *fpl*

**mannerism** *n* (habit) particularité *f*; (quirk)
manie *f*

**manoeuvre** (GB), **maneuver** (US) ☐ *n*
manœuvre *f*
  ☐ *vtr* **(a)** manœuvrer ‹*vehicle, object*›
  **(b)** (figurative) manœuvrer ‹*person*›; faire
dévier ‹*discussion*› (**to** vers)
  ☐ *vi* manœuvrer

**manor** *n* (also ~ **house**) manoir *m*

**manpower** *n* main-d'œuvre *f*

**mansion** *n* (in countryside) demeure *f*; (in
town) hôtel *m* particulier

**manslaughter** *n* homicide *m*
involontaire

**mantelpiece** *n* (manteau *m* de) cheminée
*f*

**manual** ☐ *n* manuel *m*
  ☐ *adj* ‹*labour, worker*› manuel/-elle;
‹*gearbox, typewriter*› mécanique

**manufacture** ☐ *n* (gen) fabrication *f*; (of
clothes) confection *f*; (of cars) construction *f*
  ☐ *vtr* (gen) fabriquer; construire ‹*cars*›

**manufacturer** *n* (gen) fabricant *m* (**of** de);
(of cars) constructeur *m*

**manure** *n* fumier *m*; **horse** ~ crottin *m* de
cheval

**manuscript** *n* manuscrit *m*

**many** ☐ *det* beaucoup de, un grand nombre
de; ~ **people** beaucoup de gens, un grand
nombre de personnes; ~ **times** de
nombreuses fois, bien des fois; **for** ~ **years**
pendant de nombreuses années; **how** ~
**people/times?** combien de personnes/fois?;
**too** ~ trop de; **I have as** ~ **books as you** (do)
j'ai autant de livres que toi; **so** ~ tant de
  ☐ *pron, quantif* beaucoup; **not** ~ pas
beaucoup; **too** ~ trop; **how** ~? combien?; **as**
~ **as you like** autant que tu veux; **I didn't
know there were so** ~ je ne savais pas qu'il
y en avait autant; ~ (**of them**) **were killed**
beaucoup d'entre eux ont été tués

**many-sided** *adj* à multiples facettes

**map** *n* carte *f* (**of** de); (of town, underground) plan *m* (**of** de); **street** ~ plan des rues
■ **map out** élaborer, mettre [qch] au point ⟨*plans, strategy*⟩; tracer ⟨*future*⟩

**maple** *n* érable *m*

**mar** *vtr* gâcher

**marathon** ① *n* marathon *m*
② *adj* (a) (Sport) ~ **runner** marathonien/-ienne *m/f*
(b) (massive) -marathon; **a** ~ **session** une séance-marathon

**marble** *n* (a) (stone) marbre *m*
(b) (Games) bille *f*; **to play** ~**s** jouer aux billes

**march** ① *n* marche *f*
② *vi* (a) (Mil) marcher au pas; **to** ~ (**for**) **40 km** faire une marche de 40 km; **forward** ~! en avant, marche!
(b) (in protest) manifester (**against** contre; **for** pour)
(c) **to** ~ **along** (walk briskly) marcher d'un pas vif; **to** ~ **in** (angrily) entrer l'air furieux; **she** ~**ed up to his desk** elle s'est dirigée droit sur son bureau

**March** *n* mars *m*

**marcher** *n* (in demonstration) manifestant/-e *m/f*; (in procession) marcheur/-euse *m/f*

**mare** *n* (horse) jument *f*; (donkey) ânesse *f*

**margarine** *n* margarine *f*

**margin** *n* marge *f*; **by a narrow** ~ de justesse, de peu

**marginal** *adj* marginal/-e

**marginalize** *vtr* marginaliser

**marigold** *n* souci *m*

**marijuana** *n* marijuana *f*

**marinade** *vtr* (*also* **marinate**) faire mariner

**marine** ① *n* (a) (soldier) fusilier *m* marin; **the Marines** les marines *mpl*
(b) (navy) **the merchant** ~ la marine marchande
② *adj* ⟨*mammal, biology*⟩ marin/-e; ⟨*explorer, life*⟩ sous-marin/-e; ⟨*insurance, law*⟩ maritime

**marital** *adj* conjugal/-e

**marital status** *n* situation *f* de famille

**marjoram** *n* marjolaine *f*

**mark** ① *n* (a) (gen) marque *f*; (stain) tache *f*
(b) **as a** ~ **of** en signe de ⟨*esteem, respect*⟩
(c) (Sch, Univ) note *f*
(d) **the high-tide** ~ le maximum de la marée haute; **at gas** ~ **7** à thermostat 7
(e) (Sport) **on your** ~**s!** à vos marques!
(f) (*also* **Deutschmark**) deutschmark *m*
② *vtr* (a) (gen) marquer; (stain) tacher
(b) ⟨*arrow, sign, label*⟩ indiquer ⟨*position, road*⟩
(c) (Sch, Univ) corriger; **to** ~ **sb absent** noter qn absent
(d) (Sport) marquer
③ *vi* (a) ⟨*teacher*⟩ faire des corrections
(b) (stain) se tacher
(c) (Sport) marquer

IDIOMS ~ **my words** crois-moi; **to** ~ **time** (Mil) marquer le pas; (figurative) (wait) attendre; (wait for right moment) attendre le bon moment

**marked** *adj* (a) ⟨*difference, increase, contrast*⟩ marqué/-e, net/nette (*before n*); ⟨*accent*⟩ prononcé/-e
(b) **he's a** ~ **man** on en veut à sa vie

**marker** *n* (a) (pen) marqueur *m*
(b) (tag) repère *m*

**market** ① *n* (a) (gen, Econ) marché *m*
(b) (stock market) Bourse *f*
② *vtr* (a) (sell) commercialiser, vendre
(b) (promote) lancer *or* mettre [qch] sur le marché

**market day** *n* jour *m* du marché

**market economy** *n* économie *f* de marché

**market forces** *n pl* forces *fpl* du marché

**market gardening** *n* culture *f* maraîchère

**marketing** *n* (a) (field) marketing *m*, mercatique *f*
(b) (department) service *m* de marketing

**marketing strategy** *n* stratégie *f* commerciale

**market leader** *n* (product) produit *m* vedette; (company) leader *m* du marché

**marketplace** *n* place *f* du marché

**market research** *n* étude *f* de marché

**market town** *n* bourg *m*

**market trader** *n* vendeur/-euse *m/f* sur un marché

**market value** *n* valeur *f* marchande

**markings** *n pl* (on animal) taches *fpl*; (on aircraft) marques *fpl*; **road** ~ signalisation *f* horizontale

**marksman** *n* tireur *m* d'élite

**marmalade** *n* confiture *f* *or* marmelade *f* d'oranges

**maroon** ① *n* bordeaux *m*
② *vtr* **to be** ~**ed on an island** être bloqué/-e sur une île; **the** ~**ed sailors** les naufragés

**marquee** *n* (a) (GB) (tent) grande tente *f*; (of circus) chapiteau *m*
(b) (US) (canopy) (grand) auvent *m*

**marriage** *n* mariage *m* (**to** avec)

**marriage certificate** *n* extrait *m* d'acte de mariage

**married** *adj* ⟨*person*⟩ marié/-e (**to** à); ⟨*life*⟩ conjugal/-e; ~ **couple** couple *m*

**marrow** *n* (a) (in bone) moelle *f*
(b) (GB) (vegetable) courge *f*; **baby** ~ (GB) courgette *f*

**marrowbone** *n* os *m* à moelle

**marry** ① *vtr* se marier avec, épouser ⟨*fiancé(e)*⟩; ⟨*priest*⟩ marier ⟨*couple*⟩; **to get married** se marier (**to** avec); **will you** ~ **me?** veux-tu m'épouser?
② *vi* se marier

**Mars** *pr n* Mars *f*

**marsh** *n* (*also* **marshland**) (terrain) marécage *m*; (region) marais *m*

**marshal** ① *n* (a) (Mil) maréchal *m* ⋯⋗

**(b)** (at rally, ceremony) membre *m* du service d'ordre

**(c)** (US) (in fire service) capitaine *m* des pompiers

②  *vtr* rassembler

**martial** *adj* ‹*art, law*› martial/-e; ‹*spirit*› guerrier/-ière

**martyr** ① *n* martyr/-e *m*/*f*

②  *vtr* martyriser

**martyrdom** *n* martyre *m*

**marvel** ① *n* merveille *f*

②  *vi* s'étonner (**at** de), être émerveillé/-e (**at** par)

**marvellous** (GB), **marvelous** (US) *adj* merveilleux/-euse; **that's ∼!** c'est formidable!

**marzipan** *n* pâte *f* d'amandes

**mascot** *n* mascotte *f*; **lucky ∼** porte-bonheur *m inv*

**masculine** *adj* masculin/-e

**masculinity** *n* masculinité *f*

**mash** ① *n* (for animals) pâtée *f*

②  *vtr* (*also* ∼ **up**) écraser

**mashed potatoes** *n pl* purée *f* de pommes de terre

**mask** ① *n* masque *m*; (for eyes only) loup *m*

②  *vtr* masquer

**masking tape** *n* ruban *m* adhésif

**masochist** *n, adj* masochiste *(mf)*

**mason** *n* **(a)** (in building) maçon *m*

**(b) Mason** (*also* **Free∼**) franc-maçon *m*

**masonry** *n* maçonnerie *f*

**masquerade** ① *n* bal *m* masqué; (figurative) mascarade *f*

②  *vi* **to ∼ as sb/sth** se faire passer pour qn/qch

**mass** ① *n* **(a)** masse *f* (**of** de); (of people) foule *f* (**of** de); (of details) quantité *f* (**of** de)

**(b)** (in church) messe *f*

②  **masses** *n pl* **(a) the ∼es** les masses *fpl*

**(b)** (GB) (colloq) **∼es of work** beaucoup *or* plein (colloq) de travail; **∼es of people** des tas (colloq) de gens

③  *adj* ‹*audience, movement, meeting, tourism*› de masse; ‹*exodus, protest, unemployment*› massif/-ive; **∼ hysteria** hystérie *f* collective

④  *vi* ‹*troops*› se regrouper; ‹*bees*› se masser; ‹*clouds*› s'amonceler

**massacre** ① *n* massacre *m*

②  *vtr* massacrer

**massage** ① *n* massage *m*

②  *vtr* masser

**mass grave** *n* charnier *m*

**massive** *adj* (gen) énorme; ‹*increase, cut*› massif/-ive

**mass-marketing** *n* commercialisation *f* massive

**mass media** *n* (mass) médias *mpl*

**mass murderer** *n* auteur *m* d'un massacre

**mass production** *n* fabrication *f* en série

**mast** *n* (on ship, for flags) mât *m*; (for aerial) pylône *m*

**master** ① *n* **(a)** (gen) maître *m*

**(b)** (Sch) (primary) maître *m*, instituteur *m*; (secondary) professeur *m*; (GB Univ) (of college) principal *m*

**(c)** (*also* ∼ **copy**) original *m*

②  *adj* ‹*chef, craftsman*› maître (*before n*); ‹*spy*› professionnel/-elle

③  *vtr* **(a)** maîtriser ‹*subject*›; posséder ‹*art, skill*›

**(b)** dominer ‹*feelings*›; surmonter ‹*phobia*›

**master key** *n* passe-partout *m inv*

**masterly** *adj* magistral/-e

**mastermind** ① *n* cerveau *m* (**of, behind** de)

②  *vtr* organiser ‹*robbery, event*›

**Master of Arts** *n* diplôme *m* supérieur de lettres

**master of ceremonies** *n* (in cabaret) animateur/-trice *m*/*f*; (at banquet) maître *m* des cérémonies

**Master of Science** *n* diplôme *m* supérieur en sciences

**masterpiece** *n* chef-d'œuvre *m*

**master plan** *n* plan *m* d'ensemble

**master's (degree)** *n* ≈ maîtrise (**in** de)

**mastery** *n* maîtrise *f* (**of** de)

**mat** ① *n* **(a)** (on floor) (petit) tapis *m*; (for wiping feet) paillasson *m*

**(b)** (on table) dessous-de-plat *m inv*; **place ∼** set *m* de table

②  *vi* ‹*hair*› s'emmêler; ‹*wool*› se feutrer; ‹*fibres*› s'enchevêtrer

**match** ① *n* **(a)** (Sport) match *m*

**(b)** (matchstick) allumette *f*

**(c)** **to be a ∼ for sb** être un adversaire à la mesure de qn; **to be no ∼ for sb** être trop faible pour qn

②  *vtr* **(a)** (gen) correspondre à; ‹*colour, bag*› être assorti/-e à; **to ∼ (up) the names to the photos** trouver les noms qui correspondent aux photos

**(b)** (equal) égaler ‹*record, achievement*›

③  *vi* ‹*colours, clothes, curtains*› être assortis/-ies; ‹*components*› aller ensemble; **with gloves to ∼** avec des gants assortis

**matchbox** *n* boîte *f* d'allumettes

**match point** *n* balle *f* de match

**matchstick** *n* allumette *f*

**mate** ① *n* **(a)** (GB) (colloq) (friend) copain *m* (colloq); (at work, school) camarade *mf*

**(b)** (Zool) (male) mâle *m*; (female) femelle *f*

**(c)** (assistant) aide *mf*

**(d)** (in navy) second *m*

②  *vtr* **(a)** accoupler ‹*animal*› (**with** à *or* avec)

**(b)** (in chess) faire mat

③  *vi* ‹*animal*› s'accoupler (**with** à, avec)

**material** ① *n* **(a)** (substance) (gen) matière *f*, substance *f*; (Tech) matériau *m*; **waste ∼** déchets *mpl*

**(b)** (fabric) tissu *m*, étoffe *f*

**(c)** (written matter) documentation *f*; **teaching ∼** matériel *m* pédagogique; **reading ∼** lecture *f*

**(d)** (potential) étoffe *f*; **she is star ~** elle a l'étoffe d'une vedette

**2 materials** *n pl* (equipment) matériel *m*; cleaning **~s** produits *mpl* d'entretien; building **~s** matériaux de construction **3** *adj* matériel/-ielle

**materialistic** *adj* matérialiste

**materialize** *vi* **(a)** ⟨*hope, offer, plan, threat*⟩ se concrétiser; ⟨*event, situation*⟩ se réaliser; ⟨*idea*⟩ prendre forme **(b)** (appear) ⟨*person, object*⟩ surgir; ⟨*spirit*⟩ se matérialiser

**maternal** *adj* maternel/-elle (**towards** avec)

**maternity** *n* maternité *f*

**maternity leave** *n* congé *m* de maternité

**maternity unit** *n* service *m* d'obstétrique

**maternity ward** *n* maternité *f*

**math** *n* (US) (colloq) math *fpl* (colloq)

**mathematical** *adj* mathématique

**mathematician** *n* mathématicien/-ienne *m/f*

**mathematics** *n* mathématiques *fpl*

**maths** *n* (GB) (colloq) maths *fpl* (colloq)

**matinée** *n* matinée *f*

**mating season** *n* saison *f* des amours

**matriculate** *vi* ⟨*student*⟩ s'inscrire

**matrimony** *n* mariage *m*

**matrix** *n* matrice *f*

**matron** *n* **(a)** (GB) (in hospital) infirmière *f* en chef; (in school) infirmière *f* **(b)** (of nursing home) directrice *f* **(c)** (US) (warder) gardienne *f*

**matt** (GB), **matte** (US) *adj* ⟨*paint*⟩ mat/-e; ⟨*photograph*⟩ sur papier mat

**matter** **1** *n* **(a)** (affair) affaire *f*; (requiring solution) problème *m*; (on agenda) point *m*; **it will be no easy ~** cela ne sera pas (une affaire) facile; **important ~s to discuss** des choses importantes à discuter; **private ~** affaire privée; **a ~ for the police** un problème qui relève de la police; **that's another ~** c'est une autre histoire; **the fact of the ~ is that** la vérité est que **(b)** (question) question *f*; **a ~ of** une question de ⟨*opinion, principle, taste*⟩; **a ~ of life and death** une question de vie ou de mort **(c)** (trouble) **is anything the ~?** y a-t-il un problème?; **what's the ~?** qu'est-ce qu'il y a?; **what's the ~ with Louise?** qu'est-ce qu'elle a, Louise?; **there's something the ~ with my car** ma voiture a un problème **(d)** (substance) matière *f*; **vegetable ~** matière végétale **(e)** printed **~** imprimés *mpl*; advertising **~** publicité *f*; reading **~** lecture *f*; subject **~** contenu *m* **(f)** (Med) (pus) pus *m* **2** *vi* être important/-e; **it doesn't ~** ça ne fait rien; **it doesn't ~ whether he comes or not** peu importe qu'il vienne ou pas **IDIOMS as a ~ of course** automatiquement;

**as a ~ of fact** en fait; **for that ~** d'ailleurs; **no ~ how late it is** peu importe l'heure; **no ~ what (happens)** quoi qu'il arrive; **and to make ~s worse** et pour ne rien arranger

**matter-of-fact** *adj* ⟨*voice, tone*⟩ détaché/-e; ⟨*person*⟩ terre à terre

**mattress** *n* matelas *m*

**mature** **1** *adj* **(a)** ⟨*plant, animal*⟩ adulte **(b)** ⟨*person*⟩ mûr/-e; ⟨*attitude, reader*⟩ adulte **(c)** ⟨*hard cheese*⟩ fort/-e; ⟨*soft cheese*⟩ affiné/-e; ⟨*whisky*⟩ vieux/vieille **2** *vi* **(a)** (physically) ⟨*person, animal*⟩ devenir adulte **(b)** (psychologically) ⟨*person*⟩ mûrir **(c)** ⟨*wine*⟩ vieillir; ⟨*cheese*⟩ s'affiner **(d)** ⟨*policy*⟩ arriver à échéance

**mature student** *n* personne *f* qui reprend des études (*après un temps au foyer ou dans la vie active*)

**maul** *vtr* ⟨*animal*⟩ lacérer

**mauve** *n, adj* mauve (*m*)

**maverick** *n, adj* nonconformiste (*mf*)

**maxim** *n* maxime *f*

**maximize** *vtr* maximiser ⟨*profit, sales*⟩; (Comput) agrandir

**maximum** **1** *n* maximum *m* **2** *adj* maximum (*inv*)

**maximum security prison** *n* prison *f* de haute surveillance

**may** *modal aux* **(a)** (expressing possibility) **it ~ rain** il pleuvra peut-être, il se peut qu'il pleuve; **she ~ not have seen him** elle ne l'a peut-être pas vu; **'are you going to accept?'—'I ~'** 'tu vas accepter'—'peut-être'; **he ~ not come** il risque de ne pas venir; **be that as it ~** quoi qu'il en soit; **come what ~** advienne que pourra **(b)** (expressing permission) **you ~ sit down** vous pouvez vous asseoir; **~ I come in?** puis-je entrer? **(c)** (wish) **~ he rest in peace** qu'il repose en paix

**May** *n* mai *m*

**maybe** *adv* peut-être; **~ they'll arrive early** peut-être qu'ils arriveront tôt

**mayday** *n* (distress signal) mayday *m*

**May Day** *n* premier mai *m*, fête *f* du travail

**mayhem** *n* (chaos) désordre *m*; (violence) grabuge *m* (colloq)

**mayor** *n* maire *m*

**mayoress** *n* (wife of mayor) femme *f* du maire; (lady mayor) mairesse *f*

**maze** *n* (puzzle, in gardens) labyrinthe *m*; (of streets, corridors) dédale *m*

**MBA** *n* (*abbr* = **Master of Business Administration**) ≈ maîtrise *f* de gestion

**MC** *n* (*abbr* = **Master of Ceremonies**) (in cabaret) animateur/-trice *m/f*; (at banquet) maître *m* des cérémonies

**me** *pron* **(a)** me, m'; **she knows ~** elle me connaît; **he loves ~** il m'aime ⋯❖

**(b)** (in imperatives, after prepositions and to be) moi; **give it to** ∼! donne-le-moi!; **it's for** ∼ c'est pour moi; **it's** ∼ c'est moi

**ME** n (abbr = **myalgic encephalomyelitis**) encéphalomyélite f myalgique

**meadow** n **(a)** (field) pré m
**(b)** (also ∼**land**) prés mpl, prairies fpl
**(c)** (also **water** ∼) prairie f inondable

**meagre** (GB), **meager** (US) adj maigre (before n)

**meal** n **(a)** (field) repas m; **to go out for a** ∼ aller (manger) au restaurant
**(b)** (from grain) farine f

**mean** 1 n moyenne f
2 adj **(a)** ⟨person⟩ avare, radin/-e (colloq); **he's** ∼ **with money** il est près de ses sous
**(b)** (unkind, vicious) méchant/-e (**to** avec); **a** ∼ **trick** un sale tour
**(c)** (average) ⟨weight, age⟩ moyen/-enne
**(d) that's no** ∼ **feat!** ce n'est pas un mince exploit!
3 vtr **(a)** ⟨word, phrase, symbol⟩ signifier, vouloir dire; ⟨sign⟩ vouloir dire; **the name** ∼**s nothing to me** ce nom ne me dit rien
**(b)** (intend) **to** ∼ **to do** avoir l'intention de faire; **to be meant for sb** être destiné/-e à qn; **I didn't** ∼ **to do it** je ne l'ai pas fait exprès; **she meant no offence** elle ne pensait pas à mal; **he doesn't** ∼ **you any harm** il ne te veut aucun mal; **to** ∼ **well** avoir de bonnes intentions; **he** ∼**s what he says** (he is sincere) il est sérieux; (he is menacing) il ne plaisante pas; **without** ∼**ing to** par inadvertance
**(c)** (entail) ⟨strike, law⟩ entraîner ⟨shortages, changes⟩
**(d)** (intend to say) vouloir dire; **what do you** ∼ **by that remark?** qu'est-ce que tu veux dire par là?; **I know what you** ∼ je comprends
**(e)** money ∼**s a lot to him** l'argent compte beaucoup pour lui; **your friendship** ∼**s a lot to me** ton amitié est très importante pour moi
**(f)** (be destined) **to be meant to do** être destiné/-e à faire; **it was meant to be** or **happen** cela devait arriver; **they were meant for each other** ils étaient faits l'un pour l'autre
**(g)** (be supposed to be) **he's meant to be/to be doing** il est censé être/faire

**meander** vi ⟨river, road⟩ serpenter

**meaning** n (of word, remark, action, life) sens m; (of symbol, film, dream) signification f

**meaningful** adj **(a)** (significant) ⟨word, statement, result⟩ significatif/-ive
**(b)** (profound) ⟨relationship, comment, lyrics⟩ sérieux/-ieuse; ⟨experience⟩ riche
**(c)** (eloquent) ⟨look, smile⟩ entendu/-e; ⟨gesture⟩ significatif/-ive

**meaningless** adj **(a)** ⟨word, phrase⟩ dépourvu/-e de sens
**(b)** (pointless) ⟨act, sacrifice⟩ futile, vain/-e; ⟨violence⟩ insensé/-e

**means** 1 n moyen m (**of doing** de faire); **a** ∼ **of** un moyen de ⟨communication, transport⟩; **by** ∼ **of** au moyen de; **yes, by all** ∼ oui, certainement; **it is by no** ∼ **certain** c'est loin d'être sûr
2 n pl moyens mpl, revenus mpl; **to live within one's** ∼ vivre selon ses moyens

**means test** n enquête f sur les ressources

**meantime** adv (in the) ∼ pendant ce temps; **for the** ∼ pour le moment

**meanwhile** adv **(a)** (during this time) pendant ce temps
**(b)** (until then) en attendant
**(c)** (since then) entre-temps

**measles** n rougeole f

**measure** 1 n **(a)** (gen) mesure f; **to take** ∼**s** prendre des mesures; **weights and** ∼**s** les poids et mesures mpl
**(b)** (measuring device) instrument m de mesure
2 vtr **(a)** mesurer; **to** ∼ **four by five metres** mesurer quatre mètres sur cinq
**(b)** (compare) **to** ∼ **sth against** comparer qch à
IDIOMS **for good** ∼ pour faire bonne mesure
■ **measure out** mesurer ⟨land, flour, liquid⟩; doser ⟨medicine⟩
■ **measure up** ⟨person⟩ avoir les qualités requises; **to** ∼ **up to** être à la hauteur de ⟨expectations⟩; soutenir la comparaison avec ⟨achievement⟩

**measurement** n **(a)** (of room, object) dimension f
**(b)** (of person) **to take sb's** ∼**s** prendre les mensurations de qn; **chest** ∼ tour m de poitrine; **leg** ∼ longueur f de jambe

**measuring jug** n verre m gradué

**meat** n viande f; **crab** ∼ chair f de crabe

**meat-eater** n (animal) carnivore m; (person) **they're not great** ∼**s** ils ne mangent pas beaucoup de viande

**meaty** adj **(a)** ⟨flavour, smell⟩ de viande
**(b)** ⟨article, book⟩ substantiel/-ielle
**(c)** ⟨person, hand⟩ épais/-aisse

**Mecca** pr n La Mecque

**mechanic** n mécanicien/-ienne m/f

**mechanical** adj mécanique

**mechanical engineering** n construction f mécanique

**mechanics** n pl **(a)** (field) mécanique f
**(b)** (workings) mécanisme m

**mechanism** n mécanisme m (**of** de)

**mechanization** n mécanisation f

**medal** n médaille f; **gold** ∼ médaille d'or

**medallion** n médaillon m

**medallist** (GB), **medalist** (US) n médaillé/-e m/f; **gold** ∼ médaillé/-e m/f d'or

**meddle** vi **to** ∼ **in** se mêler de ⟨affairs⟩; **to** ∼ **with** toucher à ⟨property⟩

**media** 1 n médias mpl
2 adj ⟨coverage, image, personality⟩ médiatique; ⟨power, reaction, report⟩ des médias

**median (strip)** n (US) terre-plein m central

**media studies** n pl communication f et journalisme m

**mediate** [1] *vtr* négocier ⟨*settlement, peace*⟩
[2] *vi* ⟨*person*⟩ arbitrer; **to ∼ in/between**
servir de médiateur dans/entre

**mediator** *n* médiateur/-trice *m/f*

**medical** [1] *n* (in school, army, for job) visite *f*
médicale; (private) examen *m* médical
[2] *adj* médical/-e

**medical insurance** *n*
assurance-maladie *f*

**medical student** *n* étudiant/-e *m/f* en
médecine

**medicated** *adj* (gen) médical/-e;
⟨*shampoo*⟩ traitant/-e

**medication** *n* médicaments *mpl*

**medicinal** *adj* ⟨*property, use*⟩
thérapeutique; ⟨*herb*⟩ médicinal/-e

**medicine** *n* (a) (field) médecine *f*
(b) (drug) médicament *m* (**for** pour)

**medicine cabinet, medicine
cupboard** *n* armoire *f* à pharmacie

**medicine man** *n* sorcier *m* guérisseur

**medieval** *adj* médiéval/-e

**mediocre** *adj* médiocre

**mediocrity** *n* (a) (state) médiocrité *f*
(b) (person) médiocre *mf*

**meditate** *vtr, vi* méditer

**Mediterranean** [1] *pr n* (a) **the ∼ (sea)**
la (mer) Méditerranée
(b) (region) **the ∼** les pays méditerranéens
[2] *adj* méditerranéen/-éenne

**medium** [1] *n* (a) (means) moyen *m*
(b) **to find** *or* **strike a happy ∼** trouver le
juste milieu
(c) (spiritualist) médium *m*
[2] *adj* moyen/-enne

**medium-dry** *adj* ⟨*drink*⟩ demi-sec

**medium-rare** *adj* ⟨*meat*⟩ à point

**medium-sized** *adj* de taille moyenne

**medley** *n* (a) (Mus) pot-pourri *m* (**of** de)
(b) (mixture) mélange *m*

**meek** *adj* docile

**meet** [1] *n* (a) (Sport) rencontre *f* (sportive);
**track ∼** (US) rencontre *f* d'athlétisme
(b) (GB) (in hunting) rendez-vous *m* de
chasseurs
[2] *vtr* (a) rencontrer ⟨*person, team, enemy*⟩
(b) (make acquaintance of) faire la
connaissance de ⟨*person*⟩; **have you met
each other?** vous vous connaissez?
(c) (await) attendre; (fetch) chercher; **she went
to ∼ them** elle est allée les attendre *or*
chercher; **to ∼ sb off** (GB) *or* **at** (US) **the
plane** attendre qn à l'aéroport
(d) répondre à, satisfaire à ⟨*criteria,
standards, needs*⟩; payer ⟨*bills, costs*⟩;
couvrir ⟨*debts*⟩; faire face à ⟨*obligations,
commitments*⟩; remplir ⟨*conditions*⟩
(e) se montrer à la hauteur de ⟨*challenge*⟩
[3] *vi* (a) ⟨*people, teams*⟩ se rencontrer;
⟨*committee, parliament*⟩ se réunir; **to ∼
again** ⟨*people*⟩ se revoir
(b) (by appointment) ⟨*people*⟩ se retrouver
(c) (make acquaintance) ⟨*people*⟩ se connaître

(d) ⟨*lips, roads*⟩ se rencontrer; **their eyes
met** leurs regards se croisèrent
**IDIOMS to make ends ∼** joindre les deux
bouts
■ **meet up** (colloq) se retrouver; **to ∼ up with**
(colloq) retrouver ⟨*friend*⟩
■ **meet with:** ¶ **∼ with** [sb] rencontrer
⟨*person, delegation*⟩; ¶ **∼ with** [sth]
rencontrer ⟨*opposition, success, suspicion*⟩;
être accueilli/-e avec ⟨*approval*⟩; subir
⟨*failure*⟩

**meeting** *n* (a) (official) réunion *f*; **in a ∼** en
réunion
(b) (informal) rencontre *f*
(c) (GB) (Sport) **athletics ∼** rencontre *f*
d'athlétisme; **race ∼** réunion *f* de courses

**meeting-place** *n* (lieu *m* de)
rendez-vous *m*

**meeting point** *n* point *m* de rencontre

**megabyte, MB** *n* mégaoctet *m*, Mo *m*

**megalomaniac** *n, adj* mégalomane (*mf*)

**megaphone** *n* porte-voix *m inv*

**megastore** *n* mégastore *m*

**melancholy** [1] *n* mélancolie *f*
[2] *adj* ⟨*person*⟩ mélancolique; ⟨*music,
occasion*⟩ triste

**mellow** [1] *adj* (a) ⟨*wine*⟩ moelleux/-euse;
⟨*flavour*⟩ suave; ⟨*tone*⟩ mélodieux/-ieuse
(b) ⟨*person*⟩ détendu/-e; ⟨*atmosphere*⟩
serein/-e
[2] *vtr* ⟨*experience*⟩ assagir ⟨*person*⟩
[3] *vi* ⟨*person, behaviour*⟩ s'assagir

**melodrama** *n* mélodrame *m*

**melodramatic** *adj* mélodramatique

**melody** *n* mélodie *f*

**melon** *n* melon *m*

**melt** [1] *vtr* (a) faire fondre ⟨*snow, plastic,
butter*⟩
(b) attendrir ⟨*heart*⟩
[2] *vi* (a) fondre; **to ∼ in your mouth** fondre
dans la bouche
(b) **to ∼ into** se fondre dans ⟨*crowd*⟩

**meltdown** *n* fusion *f* du cœur d'un
réacteur

**melting point** *n* point *m* de fusion

**member** *n* (a) membre *m*; **to be a ∼ of**
faire partie de ⟨*group*⟩; être membre de
⟨*club, committee*⟩; **∼ of staff** (gen) employé/-e
*m/f*; (Sch, Univ) enseignant/-e *m/f*; **∼ of the
public** (in street) passant/-e *m/f*; (in theatre,
cinema) spectateur/-trice *m/f*; **∼ state** état *m*
membre
(b) (*also* **Member**) (of parliament) député *m*
(c) (limb) membre *m*

**Member of Congress, MC** *n* (US)
membre *m* du Congrès

**Member of Parliament, MP** *n* (GB)
député *m* (**for** de)

**Member of the European
Parliament, MEP** *n* (GB) député *m* au
Parlement européen

**membership** *n* (a) (of club, organization)
adhésion *f* (**of** à)
(b) (fee) cotisation *f*

⋯⋫

**(c)** (members) membres *mpl*
**membrane** *n* membrane *f*
**memento** *n* souvenir *m* (of de)
**memo** *n* note *f* de service
**memoirs** *n pl* mémoires *mpl*
**memo pad** *n* bloc-notes *m*
**memorable** *adj* ⟨event⟩ mémorable; ⟨person, quality⟩ inoubliable
**memorial** **1** *n* mémorial *m* (to à)
**2** *adj* commémoratif/-ive
**memorize** *vtr* apprendre [qch] par cœur
**memory** *n* **(a)** mémoire *f*; from ∼ de mémoire; to have a good ∼ for faces être physionomiste; in (loving) ∼ of à la mémoire de
**(b)** (recollection) souvenir *m*; childhood memories souvenirs d'enfance
**menace** **1** *n* menace *f*
**2** *vtr* menacer (with de, avec)
**menacing** *adj* menaçant/-e
**mend** **1** *n* to be on the ∼ ⟨person⟩ être en voie de guérison; ⟨economy⟩ reprendre
**2** *vtr* réparer ⟨object, road⟩; (stitch) raccommoder; (darn) repriser; (add patch) rapiécer; that won't ∼ matters ça n'arrangera pas les choses
**3** *vi* ⟨injury⟩ guérir; ⟨person⟩ se rétablir
IDIOMS to ∼ one's ways s'amender
**menial** *adj* ⟨job⟩ subalterne; ⟨attitude⟩ servile; ∼ tasks basses besognes
**meningitis** *n* méningite *f*
**menopause** *n* ménopause *f*
**men's room** *n* (US) toilettes *fpl* pour hommes
**menstruation** *n* menstruation *f*
**menswear** *n* prêt-à-porter *m* pour hommes
**mental** *adj* (gen) mental/-e; ⟨ability, effort, energy⟩ intellectuel/-elle; ⟨hospital, institution⟩ psychiatrique
**mental block** *n* blocage *m* psychologique
**mentality** *n* mentalité *f*
**mentally** *adv* **(a)** ∼ handicapped handicapé/-e mental; the ∼ ill les malades mentaux
**(b)** ∼ exhausted surmené/-e intellectuellement
**mentholated** *adj* au menthol
**mention** **1** *n* mention *f* (of de); it got a ∼ on the radio on en a parlé à la radio
**2** *vtr* **(a)** faire mention de ⟨person, topic, fact⟩; please don't ∼ my name ne mentionnez pas mon nom; to ∼ sb/sth to sb parler de qn/qch à qn; not to ∼ sans parler de; without ∼ing any names sans nommer personne; don't ∼ it! je vous en prie!, je t'en prie!
**(b)** (acknowledge) citer ⟨name⟩
**menu** *n* menu *m*
**menu bar** *n* barre *f* de menu
**MEP** *n* (GB) (*abbr* = **Member of the European Parliament**) député *m* au Parlement européen

**mercenary** **1** *n* mercenaire *mf*
**2** *adj* ⟨person⟩ intéressé/-e
**merchandise** *n* marchandises *fpl*
**merchant** *n* (selling in bulk) négociant *m*; (selling small quantities) marchand *m*
**merchant bank** *n* (GB) banque *f* d'affaires
**merchant banker** *n* cadre *m* d'une banque d'affaires
**merchant navy** (GB), **merchant marine** (US) *n* marine *f* marchande
**merciful** *adj* **(a)** ⟨person⟩ clément/-e (to, towards envers); ⟨act⟩ charitable
**(b)** ⟨occurrence⟩ heureux/-euse; a ∼ release une délivrance
**merciless** *adj* ⟨ruler, criticism⟩ impitoyable (to, towards envers); ⟨heat⟩ implacable
**mercury** **1** *n* mercure *m*
**2** **Mercury** *pr n* Mercure *f*
**mercy** *n* clémence *f*; to have ∼ on sb avoir pitié de qn; to beg for ∼ demander grâce; at the ∼ of à la merci de
**mercy killing** *n* **(a)** euthanasie *f*
**(b)** (act) acte *m* d'euthanasie
**mere** *adj* **(a)** ⟨coincidence, nonsense⟩ pur/-e (before *n*); ⟨formality⟩ simple (before *n*); he's a ∼ child ce n'est qu'un enfant; the beach is a ∼ 2 km from here la plage n'est qu'à 2 km d'ici
**(b)** (very) ⟨idea⟩ simple (before *n*); the ∼ sight of her makes me nervous rien que de la voir, ça rend nerveux
**merely** *adv* simplement, seulement
**merge** **1** *vtr* **(a)** to ∼ sth with fusionner qch avec ⟨company, group⟩
**(b)** mélanger ⟨colours, designs⟩
**2** *vi* **(a)** (*also* ∼ **together**) ⟨companies, departments⟩ fusionner (with avec; ⟨roads, rivers⟩ se rejoindre
**(b)** ⟨colours, sounds⟩ se confondre
**merger** *n* fusion *f*
**meringue** *n* meringue *f*
**merit** **1** *n* mérite *m*
**2** *vtr* mériter
**mermaid** *n* sirène *f*
**merrily** *adv* **(a)** (happily) joyeusement
**(b)** (unconcernedly) avec insouciance
**merry** *adj* **(a)** (happy) joyeux/-euse, gai/-e; Merry Christmas! joyeux Noël!
**(b)** (colloq) (tipsy) éméché/-e
**merry-go-round** *n* manège *m*
**mesh** **1** *n* **(a)** (netting) (of string) filet *m*; (of metal) grillage *m*
**(b)** (net) mailles *fpl*
**2** *vi* (Tech) ⟨cogs⟩ s'engrener; to ∼ with s'emboîter dans
**mesmerize** **1** *vtr* hypnotiser
**2** **mesmerized** *pp adj* fasciné/-e, médusé/-e
**mess** **1** *n* **(a)** désordre *m*; what a ∼! quel désordre!, quelle pagaille! (colloq); to make a ∼ ⟨person⟩ mettre du désordre; this report is a ∼! ce rapport est fait n'importe comment!;

to make a ~ **on the carpet** salir la moquette;
to make a ~ **of the job** massacrer (colloq) le
travail
**(b)** (Mil) cantine *f*
2 *vi* (colloq) **(a) to ~ with** toucher à ‹*drugs*›
**(b) don't ~ with him** évite-le; **don't ~ with
me** ne me cherche pas
■ **mess about** (colloq), **mess around**
(colloq): ¶ ~ **around** faire l'imbécile; ¶ ~ **[sb]
around** (colloq) traiter qn par-dessus la jambe
(colloq), prendre qn pour un imbécile
■ **mess up** (colloq): ¶ ~ **up** (US) faire
l'imbécile
¶ ~ **[sth] up (a)** semer la pagaille dans
‹*papers*›; mettre du désordre dans ‹*kitchen*›
**(b)** (ruin) louper (colloq) ‹*exam*›; gâcher
‹*chances, life*›; ¶ ~ **[sb] up** ‹*drugs, alcohol*›
détruire; ‹*experience*› faire perdre les
pédales à qn (colloq)

**message** *n* message *m* **(about** au sujet de)
**message window** *n* (Comput) feuille *f* de
message
**messaging** *n* messagerie *f* électronique
**messenger** *n* messager/-ère *m/f*; (for hotel,
company) garçon *m* de courses, coursier/-ière
*m/f*
**messy** *adj* **(a)** ‹*house*› en désordre;
‹*appearance*› négligé/-e; ‹*handwriting*› peu
soigné/-e
**(b)** ‹*work, job*› salissant/-e; **he's a ~ eater** il
mange comme un cochon
**(c)** ‹*lawsuit*› compliqué/-e; **a ~ business**
une sale affaire
**metal** 1 *n* métal *m*
2 *adj* en métal
**metallic** *adj* ‹*substance*› métallique;
‹*paint, finish*› métallisé/-e; ‹*taste*› de métal
**metaphor** *n* métaphore *f*
**mete** *v* ■ **mete out** infliger ‹*punishment*›;
rendre ‹*justice*›
**meteor** *n* météore *m*
**meteorite** *n* météorite *f*
**meter** 1 *n* **(a)** compteur *m*; **gas ~**
compteur de gaz
**(b)** (also **parking ~**) parcmètre *m*
**(c)** (US) = METRE
2 *vtr* mesurer la consommation de
‹*electricity, gas*›
**method** *n* **(a)** (of teaching, contraception,
training) méthode *f* **(for doing** pour faire); (of
payment, treatment, production) mode *m* **(of** de)
**(b)** (orderliness) méthode *f*
**methodical** *adj* méthodique
**Methodist** *n, adj* méthodiste (*mf*)
**methylated spirit(s)** *n* alcool *m* à
brûler
**meticulous** *adj* méticuleux/-euse
**metre** (GB), **meter** (US) *n* mètre *m*
**metric** *adj* métrique
**metropolitan** *adj* **(a)** ‹*area, population*›
urbain/-e; ~ **New York** l'agglomération de
New York
**(b)** ~ **France** la France métropolitaine

**mettle** *n* courage *m*; **to be on one's ~** être
sur la sellette; **to put sb on his ~** amener qn
à montrer de quoi il est capable
**Mexico** *pr n* Mexique *m*
**miaow** 1 *n* miaou *m*
2 *vi* miauler
**microbe** *n* microbe *m*
**microchip** *n* puce *f*, circuit *m* intégré
**microcosm** *n* microcosme *m*
**microfilm** *n* microfilm *m*
**microlighting** *n* ULM *m*, ultra léger *m*
motorisé
**microphone** *n* microphone *m*
**microscope** *n* microscope *m*
**microwave** 1 *n* ~ **(oven)** four *m* à
micro-ondes
2 *vtr* passer [qch] au four à micro-ondes
**mid-** *pref* **in the ~20th century** au milieu du
vingtième siècle; ~**afternoon** milieu *m* de
l'après-midi; **(in)** ~**May** (à la) mi-mai; **he's in
his ~forties** il a environ quarante-cinq ans
**midair** 1 *adj* ‹*collision*› en plein vol
2 **in midair** *phr* (in mid-flight) en plein vol;
(in the air) en l'air
**midday** *n* midi *m*
**middle** 1 *n* **(a)** milieu *m*; **in the ~ of** au
milieu de; **in the ~ of May** à la mi-mai; **to be
in the ~ of doing** être en train de faire; **to
split [sth] down the ~** partager [qch] en
deux ‹*bill, work*›; diviser [qch] en deux
‹*group, opinion*›; **in the ~ of nowhere** en
pleine brousse (colloq)
**(b)** (waist) taille *f*
2 *adj* ‹*door, shelf*› du milieu; ‹*size,
difficulty*› moyen/-enne; **there must be a ~
way** il doit y avoir une solution
intermédiaire
**middle-aged** *adj* ‹*person*› d'âge mûr;
‹*outlook, view*› vieux jeu *inv*
**Middle Ages** *n pl* **the ~** le Moyen Âge
**middle class** 1 *n* classe *f* moyenne
2 **middle-class** *adj* ‹*person*› de la classe
moyenne; ‹*attitude, view*› bourgeois/-e
**Middle East** *pr n* Moyen-Orient *m*
**middle-eastern** *adj* du Moyen-Orient
**middleman** *n* intermédiaire *m*
**middle-size(d)** *adj* de taille moyenne
**middleweight** *n* poids *m* moyen
**middling** *adj* moyen/-enne; **fair to ~** pas
trop mal
**midfield** *n* milieu *m* du terrain
**midge** *n* moucheron *m*
**midget** *n* nain/-e *m/f*
**midnight** *n* minuit *m*
**midriff** *n* ventre *m*
**midst** *n* **in the ~ of** au beau milieu de; **in
the ~ of change/war** en plein changement/
pleine guerre; **in our ~** parmi nous
**midsummer** *n* milieu *m* de l'été
**Midsummer('s) Day** *n* la Saint-Jean
**midtown** *n* (US) centre-ville *m*
**midway** 1 *n* (US) attractions *fpl* foraines ⋯→

**2** *adj* ⟨*post, position*⟩ de mi-course; ⟨*stage, point*⟩ de mi-parcours

**3** *adv* ~ **between/along** à mi-chemin entre/ le long de; ~ **through** au milieu de

**midweek** **1** *adj* de milieu de semaine
**2** *adv* en milieu de semaine

**midwife** *n* sage-femme *f*; **male** ~ homme *m* sage-femme

**midwinter** *n* milieu *m* de l'hiver

**might¹** *modal aux* (a) (expressing possibility) peut-être; '**will you come?**'—'**I** ~' 'tu viendras?'—'peut-être'; **she** ~ **not have heard the news** elle n'a peut-être pas entendu la nouvelle; **I** ~ **lose my job** je risque de perdre mon travail
(b) (expressing annoyance) **you** ~ **have been killed!** tu aurais pu te faire tuer!; **I** ~ **have known!** j'aurais dû m'en douter!
(c) **I thought it** ~ **rain** j'ai pensé qu'il risquait de pleuvoir; **I thought you** ~ **say that** je m'attendais à ce que tu dises ça; **he said you** ~ **be hurt** il a dit que tu serais peut-être blessé
(d) ~ **I make a suggestion?** puis-je me permettre de faire une suggestion?; **it** ~ **be better to wait** ce serait peut-être mieux d'attendre

**might²** *n* (a) (power) puissance *f*
(b) (physical strength) force *f*; **with all his** ~ de toutes ses forces

**mighty** *adj* puissant/-e

**migrant** **1** *n* (person) migrant/-e *m/f*; (bird) oiseau *m* migrateur; (animal) animal *m* migrateur
**2** *adj* ⟨*labour*⟩ saisonnier/-ière; ⟨*bird, animal*⟩ migrateur/-trice

**migrate** *vi* (a) ⟨*person*⟩ émigrer
(b) ⟨*bird, animal*⟩ migrer

**mike** *n* (colloq) micro *m* (colloq)

**mild** *adj* (a) ⟨*surprise*⟩ léger/-ère; ⟨*interest, irritation*⟩ modéré/-e
(b) ⟨*weather, winter*⟩ doux/douce; ⟨*climate*⟩ tempéré/-e
(c) ⟨*beer, taste, tobacco*⟩ léger/-ère; ⟨*cheese*⟩ doux/douce; ⟨*curry*⟩ peu épicé/-e
(d) ⟨*soap, detergent*⟩ doux/douce
(e) ⟨*infection*⟩ bénin/-igne; ⟨*attack, sedative*⟩ léger/-ère
(f) ⟨*person, voice*⟩ doux/douce

**mildew** *n* moisissure *f*

**mile** *n* (a) mile *m* (= *1,609 m*); **it's 50** ~**s away** ≈ c'est à 80 kilomètres d'ici
(b) **to walk for** ~**s** marcher pendant des kilomètres; **it's** ~**s away!** c'est au bout du monde!; **to be** ~**s away** (daydreaming) être complètement ailleurs; ~**s from anywhere** loin de tout; **to stand out a** ~ sauter aux yeux

**mileage** *n* (a) nombre *m* de miles
(b) (done by car) kilométrage *m*
(c) (miles per gallon) consommation *f*

**milestone** *n* borne *f* (milliaire); (figurative) étape *f* importante

**militant** **1** *n* (activist) agitateur/-trice *m/f*
**2** *adj* militant/-e

**militarize** *vtr* militariser; ~**d zone** zone *f* militarisée

**military** **1** *n* **the** ~ (army) l'armée *f*; (soldiers) les militaires *mpl*
**2** *adj* militaire

**military service** *n* service *m* militaire

**militia** *n* milice *f*

**milk** **1** *n* lait *m*; **powdered** ~ lait en poudre; **full cream** ~ lait entier; **skimmed** ~ lait écrémé
**2** *vtr* (a) traire ⟨*cow*⟩
(b) (exploit) exploiter ⟨*situation, system*⟩; **to** ~ **sb dry** saigner qn à blanc

**milk chocolate** *n* chocolat *m* au lait

**milkman** *n* laitier *m*

**milkshake** *n* milkshake *m*

**milky** *adj* (a) ⟨*drink*⟩ au lait
(b) ⟨*skin, liquid, colour*⟩ laiteux/-euse

**Milky Way** *pr n* Voie *f* lactée

**mill** **1** *n* (a) moulin *m*; **water/pepper** ~ moulin à eau/à poivre
(b) (factory) fabrique *f*; **steel** ~ aciérie *f*
**2** *vtr* moudre ⟨*flour, pepper*⟩

**millenium bug** *n* bogue *m* de l'an 2000

**millennium** *n* millénaire *m*

**milligram(me)** *n* milligramme *m*

**millimetre** (GB), **millimeter** (US) *n* millimètre *m*

**million** **1** *n* million *m*; ~**s of** des millions de
**2** *adj* **a** ~ **people/pounds** un million de personnes/de livres

**millionaire** *n* millionnaire *mf*

**milometer** *n* (GB) ≈ compteur *m* kilométrique

**mime** **1** *n* mime *m*; ~ **show** pantomime *f*
**2** *vtr, vi* mimer

**mime artist** *n* mime *mf*

**mimic** **1** *n* imitateur/-trice *m/f*
**2** *vtr* imiter

**mince** **1** *n* (GB) viande *f* hachée; **beef** ~ bœuf *m* haché
**2** *vtr* hacher ⟨*meat*⟩

**mind** **1** *n* (a) esprit *m*; **peace of** ~ tranquillité d'esprit; **it's all in the** ~ c'est tout dans la tête (colloq); **to cross sb's** ~ venir à l'esprit de qn; **to have something on one's** ~ être préoccupé/-e; **to set sb's** ~ **at rest** rassurer qn; **nothing could be further from my** ~ loin de moi cette pensée; **to take sb's** ~ **off sth** distraire qn de qch; **my** ~**'s a blank** j'ai un trou de mémoire; **I can't get him out of my** ~ je n'arrive pas à l'oublier; **are you out of your** ~? (colloq) tu es fou/folle? (colloq)
(b) (brain) intelligence *f*; **with the** ~ **of a two-year-old** avec l'intelligence d'un enfant de deux ans
(c) (opinion) avis *m*; **to my** ~ à mon avis; **to make up one's** ~ **about/to do** se décider à propos de/à faire; **to change one's** ~ **about sth** changer d'avis sur qch; **to keep an open**

∼ **about sth** réserver son jugement sur qch;
**to know one's own** ∼ avoir des idées bien à
soi; **to speak one's** ∼ dire ce qu'on a à dire
②  *vtr* **(a)** surveiller ⟨*manners, language*⟩;
faire attention à ⟨*hazard*⟩
**(b) I don't** ∼ ça m'est égal, ça ne me
dérange pas; **I don't** ∼ **the cold** le froid ne
me dérange pas; **I don't** ∼ **cats, but I prefer
dogs** je n'ai rien contre les chats, mais je
préfère les chiens; **will they** ∼ **us being late?**
est-ce qu'ils seront fâchés si nous sommes
en retard?; **would you** ∼ **keeping my seat for
me?** est-ce que ça vous ennuierait de garder
ma place?; **I wouldn't** ∼ **a glass of wine** je
prendrais volontiers un verre de vin; **if you
don't** ∼ si cela ne vous fait rien; **never** ∼
(don't worry) ne t'en fais pas; (it doesn't matter)
peu importe; **he can't afford an apartment,
never** ∼ **a big house** il ne peut pas se
permettre un appartement encore moins
une grande maison
**(c)** s'occuper de ⟨*animal, children*⟩; tenir
⟨*shop*⟩
③  **in mind** *phr* I have something in ∼ for
this evening j'ai une idée pour ce soir; **to
bear sth in** ∼ (remember) ne pas oublier qch;
(take into account) prendre qch en compte
IDIOMS **to read sb's** ∼ lire dans les pensées
de qn; **to see sth in one's** ∼**'s eye** imaginer
qch; **to have a** ∼ **of one's own** savoir ce
qu'on veut

**mind-blowing** *adj* (colloq)
époustouflant/-e (colloq)

**mind-boggling** *adj* (colloq) stupéfiant/-e

**mindless** *adj* ⟨*person, programme*⟩ bête;
⟨*work*⟩ abrutissant/-e; ⟨*vandalism*⟩
gratuit/-e; ⟨*task*⟩ machinal/-e

**mine¹** *pron*

> ■ **Note** In French, possessive pronouns reflect
> the gender and number of the noun they are
> standing for. So *mine* is translated by *le mien, la
> mienne, les miens, les miennes,* according to
> what is being referred to.

**his car is red but** ∼ **is blue** sa voiture est
rouge mais la mienne est bleue; **which
(glass) is** ∼? lequel (de ces verres) est le
mien *or* est à moi?; **his children are older
than** ∼ ses enfants sont plus âgés que les
miens; **the blue car is** ∼ la voiture bleue est
à moi; **she's a friend of** ∼ c'est une amie à
moi; **it's not** ∼ ce n'est pas à moi

**mine²** ①  *n* mine *f*
②  *vtr* **(a)** extraire ⟨*gems, mineral*⟩; exploiter
⟨*area*⟩
**(b)** (Mil) miner ⟨*area*⟩

**minefield** *n* champ *m* de mines; (figurative)
terrain *m* miné

**miner** *n* mineur *m*

**mineral** ①  *n* (substance, class) minéral *m*;
(for extraction) minerai *m*
②  *adj* minéral/-e; ∼ **ore** minerai *m*

**mineral water** *n* eau *f* minérale

**mingle** *vi* **(a) to** ∼ **with** se mêler à ⟨*crowd,
guests*⟩

**(b)** ⟨*sounds*⟩ se confondre (with à); ⟨*smells,
feelings*⟩ se mêler (with à)

**miniature** ①  *n* miniature *f*
②  *adj* (gen) miniature; ⟨*dog, horse*⟩ nain/-e

**minicab** *n* (GB) taxi *m* (non agréé)

**minidisc** *n* minidisque *m*

**minimalist** *adj* minimaliste

**minimum** ①  *n* minimum *m* (of de)
②  *adj* minimum, minimal/-e

**mining** ①  *n* exploitation *f* minière
②  *adj* ⟨*industry, town*⟩ minier/-ière;
⟨*accident*⟩ de mine

**mini-skirt** *n* mini-jupe *f*

**minister** ①  *n* **(a)** (GB) ministre *m*; ∼ **of** *or*
**for Defence, Defence** ∼ ministre de la
Défense
**(b)** (clergyman) ministre *m* du culte
②  *vi* **to** ∼ **to** donner des soins à ⟨*person*⟩; **to**
∼ **to sb's needs** pourvoir aux besoins de qn

**minister of state** *n* (GB) ministre *m*
délégué

**ministry** *n* (GB) ministère *m*

**mink** *n* vison *m*

**minor** ①  *n* (Law) mineur/-e *m/f*
②  *adj* (gen, Mus) mineur/-e; ⟨*injury, burn*⟩
léger/-ère; ∼ **road** route secondaire

**minority** *n* minorité *f*; **to be in the** ∼ être
en minorité

**minstrel** *n* ménestrel *m*

**mint** ①  *n* **(a)** (herb) menthe *f*
**(b)** (sweet) bonbon *m* à la menthe
**(c)** (for coins) hôtel *m* des Monnaies
②  *adj* **in** ∼ **condition** à l'état neuf
③  *vtr* **(a)** frapper ⟨*coin*⟩
**(b)** forger ⟨*word, expression*⟩

**minuet** *n* menuet *m*

**minus** ①  *n* **(a)** (in mathematics) moins *m*
**(b)** (drawback) inconvénient *m*
②  *adj* ⟨*symbol, button*⟩ moins; ⟨*number,
quantity, value*⟩ négatif/-ive; ∼ **sign** signe
moins
③  *prep* **(a)** moins; **what is 20** ∼ **8?** combien
font 20 moins 8?; **it is** ∼ **15 (degrees)** il fait
moins 15 (degrés)
**(b)** (without) sans

**minuscule** *adj* minuscule

**minute¹** ①  *n* minute *f*; **five** ∼**s past ten**
dix heures cinq; **it's five** ∼**s' walk away** c'est
à cinq minutes à pied; **the** ∼ **I heard the
news** dès que j'ai appris la nouvelle; **any** ∼
**now** d'une minute à l'autre; **at the last** ∼ à
la dernière minute
②  **minutes** *n pl* compte-rendu *m*

**minute²** *adj* ⟨*particle*⟩ minuscule;
⟨*quantity*⟩ infime; ⟨*risk, variation*⟩ minime

**minute hand** *n* aiguille *f* des minutes

**miracle** *n* miracle *m*; **to work** *or* **perform**
∼**s** faire des miracles

**miraculous** *adj* **(a)** ⟨*escape, recovery*⟩
miraculeux/-euse
**(b)** ⟨*speed, strength*⟩ prodigieux/-ieuse

**mirror** ①  *n* **(a)** (gen) miroir *m*, glace *f*; (Aut)
rétroviseur *m*
**(b)** (figurative) reflet *m*                    ⋯⟶

**m**

**2** *vtr* refléter; **to be ~ed in** se refléter dans

**mirth** *n* (laughter) hilarité *f*; (joy) joie *f*

**misapprehension** *n* malentendu *m*, erreur *f*; **to be (labouring) under a ~** se tromper

**misappropriate** *vtr* détourner ⟨*funds*⟩

**misbehave** *vi* ⟨*child*⟩ se tenir mal; ⟨*adult*⟩ se conduire mal

**miscalculation** *n* erreur *f* de calcul; (figurative) mauvais calcul *m*

**miscarriage** *n* **(a)** (Med) fausse couche *f*; **to have a ~** faire une fausse couche **(b)** (Law) **a ~ of justice** une grave erreur judiciaire

**miscellaneous** *adj* divers/-e

**mischief** *n* espièglerie *f*; **to get into** *or* **make ~** faire des bêtises; **he's up to ~** il prépare quelque chose; **to be full of ~** être espiègle; **it keeps them out of ~** ça les occupe

**mischievous** *adj* ⟨*child, comedy, humour*⟩ espiègle; ⟨*smile, eyes*⟩ malicieux/-ieuse

**misconception** *n* idée *f* fausse

**misdemeanour, misdemeanor** (US) *n* délit *m*

**miser** *n* avare *mf*

**miserable** *adj* **(a)** ⟨*person, event, expression*⟩ malheureux/-euse; ⟨*thoughts*⟩ noir/-e; ⟨*weather*⟩ sale (before *n*); **to feel ~** avoir le cafard **(b)** ⟨*amount*⟩ misérable; ⟨*wage, life*⟩ de misère; ⟨*attempt, failure, performance*⟩ lamentable

**miserly** *adj* ⟨*person*⟩ avare; ⟨*amount*⟩ maigre

**misery** *n* **(a)** (unhappiness) souffrance *f*; (gloom) abattement *m*; **to make sb's life a ~** faire de la vie de qn un enfer **(b)** (misfortune) **the miseries of unemployment** le chômage et son cortège de misères **(c)** (GB) (colloq) (child) pleurnicheur/-euse *m/f*; (adult) rabat-joie *m inv*

**misfire** *vi* **(a)** ⟨*gun, rocket*⟩ faire long feu; ⟨*engine*⟩ avoir des ratés **(b)** ⟨*plan, joke*⟩ tomber à plat

**misfit** *n* marginal/-e *m/f*

**misfortune** *n* (unfortunate event) malheur *m*; (bad luck) malchance *f*

**misgiving** *n* crainte *f*; **to have ~s about sth** avoir des craintes quant à qch; **to have ~s about sb** avoir des doutes au sujet de qn

**misguided** *adj* ⟨*strategy, attempt*⟩ peu judicieux/-ieuse; ⟨*person*⟩ malavisé/-e

**mishandle** *vtr* **(a)** mal conduire ⟨*operation, meeting*⟩; mal s'y prendre avec ⟨*person*⟩ **(b)** (roughly) manier [qch] sans précaution ⟨*object*⟩; malmener ⟨*person, animal*⟩

**mishap** *n* incident *m*

**mishear** *vtr* mal entendre

**misinform** *vtr* mal renseigner

**misinterpret** *vtr* mal interpréter

**misinterpretation** *n* interprétation *f* erronée

**misjudge** *vtr* mal évaluer ⟨*speed, distance*⟩; mal calculer ⟨*shot*⟩; mal juger ⟨*person*⟩

**mislay** *vtr* égarer

**mislead** *vtr* (deliberately) tromper; (unintentionally) induire [qn] en erreur

**misleading** *adj* ⟨*impression, title, information*⟩ trompeur/-euse; ⟨*claim, statement, advertising*⟩ mensonger/-ère

**mismanage** *vtr* mal diriger ⟨*firm, project*⟩; mal gérer ⟨*finances*⟩

**misplace** *vtr* égarer

**misprint** *n* coquille *f*, faute *f* typographique

**mispronounce** *vtr* mal prononcer

**misread** *vtr* (read wrongly) mal lire; (misinterpret) mal interpréter ⟨*actions*⟩

**misrepresent** *vtr* présenter [qn] sous un faux jour ⟨*person*⟩; déformer ⟨*views, facts*⟩

**misrepresentation** *n* (of facts) déformation *f*

**miss** **1** *n* **(a)** (in game) coup *m* manqué *or* raté **(b)** **to give [sth] a ~** (colloq) ne pas aller à ⟨*film, lecture*⟩; se passer de ⟨*dish, drink, meal*⟩
**2** *vtr* **(a)** manquer ⟨*target*⟩ **(b)** rater ⟨*bus, plane, event, meeting*⟩; laisser passer ⟨*chance*⟩; **I ~ed the train by five minutes** j'ai raté le train de cinq minutes **(c)** ne pas saisir ⟨*joke, remark*⟩ **(d)** sauter ⟨*line, class*⟩; manquer ⟨*school*⟩ **(e)** (avoid) échapper à ⟨*death, injury*⟩; éviter ⟨*traffic, bad weather, rush hour*⟩; **he just ~ed being caught** il a failli être pris **(f)** **I ~ you** tu me manques; **he ~ed Paris** Paris lui manquait; **I'll ~ coming to the office** le bureau va me manquer
**3** *vi* **(a)** (Games, Sport, Mil) rater son coup; **~ed! raté! (b)** ⟨*engine*⟩ avoir des ratés
■ **miss out**: ¶ **~ out** être lésé/-e; ¶ **~ out on** [sth] laisser passer, louper (colloq); ¶ **~ [sb/ sth] out** sauter ⟨*line, verse*⟩; omettre ⟨*fact, point, person*⟩

**Miss** *n* Mademoiselle *f*; (written abbreviation) Mlle

**misshapen** *adj* ⟨*leg*⟩ difforme; ⟨*object*⟩ déformé/-e

**missile** *n* **(a)** (Mil) missile *m* **(b)** (rock, bottle) projectile *m*

**missing** *adj* **to be ~** manquer; **to go ~** ⟨*person, object*⟩ disparaître; **the ~ jewels/ child** les bijoux disparus/l'enfant disparu; **there are two books ~** il manque deux livres

**mission** *n* mission *f*

**missionary** *n* missionnaire *mf*

**mist** *n* brume *f*
■ **mist over, mist up** ⟨*lens, window*⟩ s'embuer

**mistake** **1** *n* (gen) erreur *f*; (in text, spelling, typing) faute *f*; **to make a ~** se tromper; **by ~** par erreur

**2** *vtr* **(a)** to ~ sth for sth else prendre qch pour qch d'autre; to ~ sb for sb else confondre qn avec qn d'autre
**(b)** mal interpréter ⟨*meaning*⟩

**mistaken** *adj* **(a)** to be ~ avoir tort; he was ~ in thinking it was over il avait tort de croire que c'était fini
**(b)** ⟨*enthusiasm, generosity*⟩ mal placé/-e

**mistletoe** *n* gui *m*

**mistranslation** *n* erreur *f* de traduction

**mistreat** *vtr* maltraiter

**mistress** *n* maîtresse *f*

**mistrust** **1** *n* méfiance *f* **(of** à l'égard de)
**2** *vtr* se méfier de

**misty** *adj* ⟨*conditions, morning*⟩ brumeux/-euse; ⟨*lens, window*⟩ embué/-e; ⟨*photo*⟩ flou/-e

**misunderstand** *vtr* mal comprendre; (completely) ne pas comprendre

**misunderstanding** *n* malentendu *m*

**misunderstood** *adj* to feel ~ se sentir incompris/-e

**misuse** **1** *n* (of equipment) mauvais usage *m*; (of word) usage *m* impropre; (of power, authority) abus *m*
**2** *vtr* faire mauvais usage de ⟨*equipment*⟩; mal employer ⟨*word, resources*⟩; abuser de ⟨*authority*⟩

**mitigate** *vtr* atténuer ⟨*effects, distress, sentence*⟩; réduire ⟨*risks*⟩; minimiser ⟨*loss*⟩

**mitre** (GB), **miter** (US) *n* mitre *f*

**mitten** *n* moufle *f*

**mix** **1** *n* **(a)** (gen) mélange *m*
**(b)** (Mus) mixage *m*, mix *m*
**2** *vtr* **(a)** (gen) mélanger (**with** avec; **and** à)
**(b)** préparer ⟨*drink*⟩; malaxer ⟨*cement, paste*⟩
**(c)** (Mus) mixer
**3** *vi* **(a)** (*also* ~ **together**) se mélanger (**with** avec, à)
**(b)** (socialize) être sociable; to ~ **with** fréquenter
■ **mix up (a)** (confuse) confondre; to get two things/people ~ed up confondre deux choses/personnes
**(b)** (jumble up) mélanger, mêler ⟨*papers, photos*⟩
**(c)** to get ~ed up in se trouver mêlé/-e à

**mixed** *adj* **(a)** ⟨*collection, programme, diet*⟩ varié/-e; ⟨*nuts, sweets*⟩ assorti/-e; ⟨*salad*⟩ composé/-e; ⟨*group, community*⟩ (socially, in age) mélangé/-e; (racially) d'origines diverses; of ~ **blood** de sang mêlé
**(b)** (for both sexes) mixte
**(c)** ⟨*reaction, feelings, reception*⟩ mitigé/-e

**mixed ability** *adj* (Sch) ⟨*class, teaching*⟩ sans groupes de niveau

**mixed race** *n* of ~ métis/-isse

**mixer** *n* **(a)** (Culin) batteur *m* électrique
**(b)** (drink) boisson *f* nonalcoolisée

**mixing** *n* (combining) mélange *m*; (Mus) mixage *m*

**mixture** *n* mélange *m* (**of** de)

**mix-up** *n* confusion *f* (**over** sur)

**moan** **1** *n* **(a)** (noise) gémissement *m*
**(b)** (colloq) (complaint) plainte *f* (**about** au sujet de)
**2** *vi* **(a)** (groan) gémir (**with** de)
**(b)** (colloq) (complain) râler (colloq) (**about** contre)

**moat** *n* douve *f*

**mob** **1** *n* foule *f* (**of** de)
**2** *vtr* assaillir ⟨*person*⟩; envahir ⟨*place*⟩

**mobile** **1** *n* mobile *m*
**2** *adj* **(a)** ⟨*object, population*⟩ mobile; ⟨*canteen*⟩ ambulant/-e
**(b)** to be ~ (able to walk) pouvoir marcher; (able to travel) pouvoir se déplacer

**mobile phone** *n* téléphone *m* portable, portable *m*

**mobilization** *n* mobilisation *f*

**mobilize** *vtr*, *vi* mobiliser

**mocha** *n* **(a)** (coffee) moka *m*
**(b)** (flavour) arôme *m* de café et de chocolat

**mock** **1** *n* (GB Sch) examen *m* blanc
**2** *adj* **(a)** ⟨*suede, ivory*⟩ faux/fausse (*before n*); ~ **leather** similicuir *m*
**(b)** (feigned) simulé/-e; in ~ **terror** en feignant la terreur
**3** *vtr* se moquer de ⟨*person, efforts, beliefs*⟩
**4** *vi* ⟨*person*⟩ se moquer

**mockery** *n* moquerie *f*

**mod con** *n* (GB) confort *m* (moderne)

**mode** *n* mode *m*

**model** **1** *n* **(a)** (of car, appliance, garment) modèle *m*
**(b)** ( person) (artist's) modèle *m*; (fashion) mannequin *m*
**(c)** (scale model) maquette *f*
**(d)** ( perfect example) modèle *m* (**of** de)
**2** *adj* **(a)** ⟨*railway, soldier, village*⟩ miniature; ⟨*aeroplane, boat, car*⟩ modèle réduit
**(b)** ⟨*husband, student, prison*⟩ modèle
**3** *vtr* **(a)** modeler ⟨*clay, wax*⟩
**(b)** ⟨*fashion model*⟩ présenter ⟨*garment*⟩
**4** *vi* **(a)** ⟨*artist's model*⟩ poser
**(b)** ⟨*fashion model*⟩ travailler comme mannequin

**modelling** (GB), **modeling** (US) *n* **(a)** (of clothes) to take up ~ devenir mannequin; have you done any ~? as-tu déjà travaillé comme mannequin?
**(b)** (Comput) modélisation *f*

**modem** *n* modem *m*

**moderate** **1** *adj* **(a)** (not extreme) modéré/-e (**in** dans)
**(b)** ⟨*success, income*⟩ moyen/-enne
**2** *vtr* modérer
**3** *vi* se modérer

**moderation** *n* modération *f* (**in** dans); in ~ avec modération

**modern** *adj* moderne; the ~ **world** le monde contemporain

**modernize** *vtr* moderniser

**modern languages** *n pl* langues *fpl* vivantes

**m**

**modest** *adj* (a) modeste (**about** au sujet de)
(b) ⟨*gift, aim*⟩ modeste; ⟨*sum, salary*⟩ modique

**modesty** *n* modestie *f*

**modify** *vtr* modifier

**modular** *adj* modulaire

**module** *n* module *m*

**mogul** *n* magnat *m*

**Mohammed, Mahomet** *pr n* Mahomet

**moist** *adj* ⟨*soil*⟩ humide; ⟨*cake*⟩ moelleux/-euse; ⟨*hands*⟩ moite; ⟨*skin*⟩ bien hydraté/-e

**moisten** *vtr* humecter

**moisture** *n* humidité *f*

**moisturizer** *n* (lotion) lait *m* hydratant; (cream) crème *f* hydratante

**molar** *n, adj* molaire (*f*)

**mold** (US) = MOULD

**mole** *n* (a) (Zool) taupe *f*
(b) (on skin) grain *m* de beauté

**molecule** *n* molécule *f*

**molest** *vtr* agresser [qn] sexuellement

**mollycoddle** *vtr* dorloter

**molt** (US) = MOULT

**molten** *adj* en fusion

**moment** *n* (a) (instant) instant *m*; **in a** ∼ dans un instant; **at any** ∼ à tout instant
(b) (point in time) moment *m*; **at the** ∼ en ce moment; **at the right** ∼ au bon moment

**momentarily** *adv* (a) (for an instant) momentanément
(b) (US) (very soon) dans un instant; (at any moment) d'un moment à l'autre

**momentary** *adj* passager/-ère

**momentous** *adj* capital/-e

**momentum** *n* (gen) élan *m*; (in physics) vitesse *f*

**monarch** *n* monarque *m*

**monarchy** *n* monarchie *f*

**monastery** *n* monastère *m*

**Monday** *n* lundi *m*

**monetary union** *n* union *f* monétaire

**money** *n* argent *m*; **to make** ∼ ⟨*person*⟩ gagner de l'argent; ⟨*business, project*⟩ rapporter de l'argent
IDIOMS **to get one's** ∼**'s worth, to get a good run for one's** ∼ en avoir pour son argent; **your** ∼ **or your life!** la bourse ou la vie!

**money belt** *n* ceinture *f* porte-monnaie

**moneybox** *n* tirelire *f*

**moneylender** *n* prêteur/-euse *m/f*

**moneymaker** *n* (product) article *m* qui rapporte beaucoup; (activity) activité *f* lucrative

**money order, MO** *n* mandat *m* postal

**mongrel** *n* (chien *m*) bâtard *m*

**monitor** ⓵ *n* (Comput, Med) moniteur *m*
⓶ *vtr* (a) surveiller ⟨*results, patient, breathing*⟩
(b) être à l'écoute de ⟨*broadcast*⟩

**monk** *n* moine *m*

**monkey** *n* (a) (Zool) singe *m*

(b) (colloq) (rascal) galopin *m* (colloq)

**monochrome** *adj* ⟨*film*⟩ en noir et blanc; ⟨*colour scheme*⟩ monochrome

**monogamous** *adj* monogame

**monogamy** *n* monogamie *f*

**monologue, monolog** (US) *n* monologue *m*

**monopolize** *vtr* (a) détenir le monopole de ⟨*market, supply*⟩
(b) (figurative) monopoliser

**monopoly** *n* monopole *m*

**monoski** *vi* faire du monoski

**monotonous** *adj* monotone

**monotony** *n* monotonie *f*

**monsoon** *n* mousson *f*

**monster** *n* monstre *m*

**monstrous** *adj* (a) (ugly) monstrueux/-euse; ⟨*building*⟩ hideux/-euse
(b) (huge) énorme

**month** *n* mois *m*; **in two** ∼**s, in two** ∼**s'** **time** dans deux mois; **every other** ∼ tous les deux mois; **in the** ∼ **of June** au mois de juin

**monthly** ⓵ *n* (journal) mensuel *m*
⓶ *adj* mensuel/-elle; ∼ **instalment** mensualité *f*
⓷ *adv* ⟨*pay, earn*⟩ au mois; ⟨*happen, visit, publish*⟩ tous les mois

**Montreal** *pr n* Montréal

**monument** *n* monument *m*

**moo** *vi* meugler

**mood** *n* (a) (humour) humeur *f*; **in a good/** **bad** ∼ de bonne/mauvaise humeur; **to be in** **the** ∼ **for doing** avoir envie de faire; **to be in** **no** ∼ **for doing** ne pas être d'humeur à faire
(b) (bad temper) saute *f* d'humeur; **to be in a** ∼ être de mauvaise humeur

**mood swing** *n* saute *f* d'humeur

**moody** *adj* (a) (unpredictable) d'humeur changeante, lunatique
(b) (sulky) de mauvaise humeur

**moon** *n* lune *f*
IDIOMS **to be over the** ∼ être aux anges; **once in a blue** ∼ tous les trente-six du mois (colloq); **the man in the** ∼ le visage de la Lune

**moonlight** ⓵ *n* clair *m* de lune
⓶ *vi* travailler au noir

**moonlit** *adj* éclairé/-e par la lune; **a** ∼ **night** une nuit de lune

**moor** ⓵ *n* lande *f*
⓶ *vtr* amarrer ⟨*boat*⟩
⓷ *vi* ⟨*boat*⟩ mouiller

**moorings** *n pl* amarres *fpl*

**moorland** *n* lande *f*

**moose** *n* (Canadian) orignal *m*; (European) élan *m*

**mop** ⓵ *n* (a) (of cotton) balai *m* à franges; (of sponge) balai *m* éponge
(b) ∼ **of hair** crinière *f* (colloq)
⓶ *vtr* (a) laver [qch] à grande eau ⟨*floor*⟩
(b) **to** ∼ **one's face/brow** s'éponger le visage/ le front
■ **mop up** éponger ⟨*milk, wine*⟩

**mope** *vi* se morfondre

■ **mope about**, **mope around** traîner
(comme une âme en peine)

**moped** *n* vélomoteur *m*

**moral** [1] *n* morale *f*
[2] **morals** *n pl* moralité *f*
[3] *adj* moral/-e

**morale** *n* moral *m*

**morality** *n* moralité *f*

**moral majority** *n* majorité *f*
bien-pensante

**morbid** *adj* morbide

**more** [1] *adv* (a) (comparative) plus (than
que); ~ **expensive** plus cher/chère; ~ **easily**
plus facilement
(b) (to a greater extent) plus, davantage; **you
must rest** ~ il faut que tu te reposes
davantage; **he is all the** ~ **angry because** il
est d'autant plus en colère que
(c) (longer) **I don't work there any** ~ je n'y
travaille plus
(d) (again) **once** ~ une fois de plus, encore
une fois
(e) (else) **nothing** ~ rien de plus; **something**
~ autre chose
[2] *det* plus de; **I have** ~ **money than him** j'ai
plus d'argent que lui; **some** ~ **books**
quelques livres de plus; **there's no** ~ **bread**
il n'y a plus de pain; **have some** ~ **beer!**
reprenez de la bière!
[3] *pron, quantif* (a) (larger amount or number)
plus; **it costs** ~ il/elle coûte plus cher (than
que); **he eats** ~ **than you** il mange plus que
toi
(b) (additional amount) davantage; (additional
number) plus; **I need** ~ **of them** il m'en faut
plus; **I need** ~ **of it** il m'en faut davantage
[4] **more and more** *phr* de plus en plus;
~ **and** ~ **work** de plus en plus de travail
[5] **more or less** *phr* plus ou moins
[6] **more than** *phr* (a) (greater amount or
number) plus de; ~ **than 20 people** plus de 20
personnes; ~ **than half** plus de la moitié; ~
**than enough** plus qu'assez
(b) (extremely) ~ **than generous** plus que
généreux

**moreover** *adv* de plus, qui plus est

**morning** [1] *n* matin *m*; (with emphasis on
duration) matinée *f*; **in the** ~ le matin; **on
Monday** ~s le lundi matin; (on) **Monday** ~
lundi matin; **later this** ~ plus tard dans la
matinée; **yesterday/tomorrow** ~ hier/demain
matin
[2] *excl* (good) ~! bonjour!

**morning-after pill** *n* pilule *f* du
lendemain

**Morocco** *pr n* Maroc *m*

**Morse (code)** *n* morse *m*; **in** ~ en morse

**morsel** *n* morceau *m*

**mortal** *n, adj* mortel/-elle (*m/f*)

**mortality** *n* mortalité *f*

**mortar** *n* mortier *m*

**mortgage** *n* emprunt-logement *m* (**on**
pour)

**mortgage rate** *n* taux *m* de
l'emprunt-logement

**mortuary** *n* morgue *f*

**mosaic** *n* mosaïque *f*

**Moscow** *pr n* Moscou

**Moslem** = MUSLIM

**mosque** *n* mosquée *f*

**mosquito** *n* moustique *m*

**mosquito repellent** *n* anti-moustique
*m*

**moss** *n* mousse *f*

**most**

■ **Note** When used to form the superlative of
adjectives, *most* is translated by *le plus* or *la
plus* depending on the gender of the noun and
by *les plus* with plural noun: *the most beautiful
woman in the room* = la plus belle femme de la
pièce; *the most expensive hotel in Paris* = l'hôtel
le plus cher de Paris; *the most difficult problems*
= les problèmes les plus difficiles. For examples
and further uses, see the entry below.

[1] *det* (a) (the majority of) la plupart de; ~
**people** la plupart des gens
(b) (in superlatives) le plus de; **she got the** ~
**votes** c'est elle qui a obtenu le plus de voix
[2] *pron* (a) (the greatest number) la plupart (**of**
de); (the largest part) la plus grande partie (**of**
de); ~ **of the time** la plupart du temps; ~ **of
us** la plupart d'entre nous; **for** ~ **of the day**
pendant la plus grande partie de la journée;
~ **of the bread** presque tout le pain
(b) (all) **the** ~ **you can expect is...** tout ce
que tu peux espérer c'est...
(c) (in superlatives) le plus; **John has got the** ~
c'est John qui en a le plus
[3] *adv* (a) (in superlatives) **the** ~ **beautiful
château in France** le plus beau château de
France; ~ **easily** le plus facilement
(b) (very) très, extrêmement; ~ **encouraging**
très *or* extrêmement encourageant; ~
**probably** très vraisemblablement
(c) (more than all the rest) le plus; **what
annoyed him** ~ (**of all**) **was** ce qui l'ennuyait
le plus c'était que
[4] **at (the) most** *phr* au maximum, au
plus
[5] **for the most part** *phr* (most of them)
pour la plupart; (most of the time) la plupart
du temps; (chiefly) surtout, essentiellement
[6] **most of all** *phr* par-dessus tout
**IDIOMS to make the** ~ **of** tirer le meilleur
parti de ⟨situation, resources, abilities⟩;
profiter de ⟨opportunity, good weather⟩

**mostly** *adv* (a) (chiefly) surtout,
essentiellement; (most of them) pour la
plupart
(b) (most of the time) la plupart du temps

**MOT** *n* (GB) (*also* ~ **test**) contrôle *m*
technique des véhicules

**moth** *n* papillon *m* de nuit; (in clothes) mite *f*

**mother** [1] *n* mère *f*
[2] *vtr* (coddle) dorloter

**motherboard** *n* carte *f* mère

**motherhood** *n* maternité *f*

**mother-in-law** *n* belle-mère *f*

**motherly** *adj* maternel/-elle

m

**mother-of-pearl** n nacre f
**Mother's Day** n fête f des Mères
**mother tongue** n langue f maternelle
**motion** [1] n (a) mouvement m; **to set [sth] in** ∼ mettre [qch] en marche ⟨machine⟩; mettre [qch] en route ⟨plan⟩; déclencher ⟨chain of events⟩
(b) (proposal) motion f
[2] vi **to** ∼ **to sb (to do)** faire signe à qn (de faire)
**motionless** adj immobile
**motivate** vtr motiver ⟨person⟩
**motivated** adj (a) ⟨person, pupil⟩ motivé/-e
(b) **politically/racially** ∼ ⟨act⟩ politique/raciste
**motivation** n motivation f
**motive** n (gen) motif m (**for, behind** de); (for crime) mobile m (**for** de)
**motley** adj ⟨crowd, gathering⟩ bigarré/-e; ⟨collection⟩ hétéroclite
**motor** [1] n moteur m
[2] adj (a) ⟨vehicle⟩ automobile; ⟨show⟩ de l'automobile
(b) ⟨mower⟩ à moteur
**motorbike** n moto f
**motorboat** n canot m automobile
**motorcycle** n motocyclette f
**motorcyclist** n motocycliste mf
**motor home** n auto-caravane f
**motorist** n automobiliste mf
**motor racing** n course f automobile
**motorway** n (GB) autoroute f
**mottled** adj ⟨skin, paper⟩ marbré/-e; ⟨hands⟩ tacheté/-e
**motto** n devise f
**mould** (GB), **mold** (US) [1] n (a) (Culin, figurative) moule m
(b) (fungi) moisissure f
[2] vtr modeler ⟨plastic, clay, shape⟩; façonner ⟨character, opinions⟩ (**into** pour en faire)
**mouldy** (GB), **moldy** (US) adj moisi/-e; **to go** ∼ moisir
**moult** (GB), **molt** (US) vi ⟨cat, dog⟩ perdre ses poils; ⟨bird⟩ muer
**mound** n (a) (hillock) tertre m
(b) (heap) monceau m (**of** de)
**mount** [1] vtr (a) monter sur ⟨platform, horse⟩
(b) monter ⟨jewel, picture, exhibit⟩
(c) organiser ⟨demonstration⟩
[2] vi (a) ⟨person, staircase⟩ monter (**to** jusqu'à)
(b) ⟨number, toll⟩ augmenter; ⟨concern⟩ grandir
(c) (on horse) se mettre en selle
**mountain** n montagne f
**mountain bike** n vélo m tout-terrain, VTT m
**mountaineer** n alpiniste mf
**mountaineering** n alpinisme m
**mountainous** adj montagneux/-euse

**mountain top** n cime f
**mourn** [1] vtr pleurer ⟨person, death⟩
[2] vi ⟨person⟩ porter le deuil; **to** ∼ **for sb/sth** pleurer qn/qch
**mourning** n deuil m
**mouse** n (Comput, Zool) souris f
**mousemat** n tapis m de souris
**mouse pointer** n pointeur m de la souris
**moustache, mustache** (US) n moustache f
**mouth** [1] n (a) (of human, horse) bouche f; (of other animal) gueule f
(b) (of cave, tunnel) entrée f; (of river) embouchure f; (of volcano) bouche f
[2] vtr articuler silencieusement
IDIOMS **by word of** ∼ de bouche à oreille
**mouthful** n (of food) bouchée f; (of liquid) gorgée f
**mouth organ** n harmonica m
**mouth-to-mouth resuscitation** n bouche-à-bouche m inv
**mouthwash** n eau f dentifrice
**mouth-watering** adj appétissant/-e
**move** [1] n (a) (movement) mouvement m; (gesture) geste m
(b) (of residence) déménagement m; (of company) transfert m
(c) (in game) coup m; **it's your** ∼ c'est ton tour
(d) (step, act) manœuvre f; **a good/bad** ∼ une bonne/mauvaise idée; **to make the first** ∼ faire le premier pas
[2] vtr (a) déplacer ⟨game piece, cursor, car, furniture⟩; transporter ⟨patient, army⟩; **to** ∼ **sth** (out of the way) enlever qch
(b) ⟨person⟩ bouger ⟨limb, head⟩; ⟨wind, mechanism⟩ faire bouger ⟨leaf, wheel⟩
(c) (relocate) muter ⟨staff⟩; transférer ⟨office⟩; **to** ∼ **house** déménager
(d) (affect) émouvoir; **to be deeply** ∼d être très ému/-e
[3] vi (a) (stir) bouger; ⟨lips⟩ remuer
(b) (travel) ⟨vehicle⟩ rouler; ⟨person⟩ avancer; ⟨procession, army⟩ être en marche; **to** ∼ **back** reculer; **to** ∼ **forward** s'avancer; **to** ∼ **away** s'éloigner
(c) (change home, location) déménager; **to** ∼ **to the countryside/to Japan** s'installer à la campagne/au Japon
(d) (change job) être muté/-e
(e) (act) agir
IDIOMS **to get a** ∼ **on** (colloq) se dépêcher
■ **move about, move around** ⟨person⟩ (fidget) remuer; (move home) déménager
■ **move along:** ¶ ∼ **along** (stop loitering) circuler; (proceed) avancer; (squeeze up) se pousser; ¶ ∼ **[sb/sth] along** faire circuler ⟨onlookers, crowd⟩
■ **move away** s'éloigner; (move house) déménager
■ **move in** (a) (to house) emménager; **to** ∼ **in with** s'installer avec ⟨friend, lover⟩
(b) (advance, attack) s'avancer (**on** sur)

■ **move on** ⟨*person, traveller*⟩ se mettre en route; ⟨*vehicle*⟩ repartir; **to ∼ on** to passer à ⟨*next item*⟩

■ **move out** (of house) déménager; **to ∼ out of** quitter

■ **move over** se pousser

■ **move up** (a) (make room) se pousser
**(b)** (be promoted) être promu/-e

**movement** *n* mouvement *m*; (of hand, arm) geste *m*

**movie** ⟦1⟧ *n* film *m*
⟦2⟧ **movies** *n pl* **the ∼s** le cinéma

**movie camera** *n* caméra *f*

**movie star** *n* vedette *f* de cinéma

**movie theater** *n* (US) cinéma *m*

**moving** *adj* (a) ⟨*vehicle*⟩ en marche; ⟨*parts, target*⟩ mobile; ⟨*staircase, walkway*⟩ roulant/-e
**(b)** ⟨*scene, speech*⟩ émouvant/-e

**mow** *vtr* tondre ⟨*grass, lawn*⟩

**mower** *n* tondeuse *f* à gazon

**MP** *n* (GB) (*abbr* = **Member of Parliament**) député *m* (for de)

**Mr** *n* M., Monsieur

**Mrs** *n* Mme, Madame

**Ms** *n* ≈ Mme

**MSc** *n* (*abbr* = **Master of Science**) diplôme *m* supérieur en sciences

**much** ⟦1⟧ *adv* beaucoup; **∼ more/less** beaucoup plus/moins; **∼ smaller** beaucoup plus petit; **I don't read ∼** je ne lis pas beaucoup; **we'd ∼ rather stay here** nous préférerions de beaucoup rester ici; **does it hurt ∼?** est-ce que ça fait très mal?; **we don't go out ∼** nous ne sortons pas beaucoup *or* souvent; **it's ∼ the same** c'est à peu près pareil (**as** que); **too ∼** trop; **very ∼** beaucoup; **thank you very ∼** merci beaucoup; **so ∼** tellement; **as ∼** autant (**as** que); **they hated each other as ∼ as ever** ils se détestaient toujours autant
⟦2⟧ *pron* beaucoup; **do you have ∼ left?** est-ce qu'il vous en reste beaucoup?; **we didn't eat ∼** nous n'avons pas mangé grand-chose; **I don't see ∼ of them now** je ne les vois pas beaucoup maintenant; **so ∼** tellement, tant; **we'd eaten so ∼ that** nous avions tellement mangé que; **too ∼** trop; **it costs too ∼** c'est trop cher; **twice as ∼** deux fois plus; **as ∼ as possible** autant que possible; **how ∼?** combien?; **it's not** *or* **nothing ∼** ce n'est pas grand-chose; **he's not ∼ to look at** il n'est pas très beau
⟦3⟧ *det* beaucoup de; **I haven't got ∼ time** je n'ai pas beaucoup de temps; **she didn't speak ∼ English** elle ne connaissait que quelques mots d'anglais; **too ∼ money** trop d'argent; **don't use so ∼ salt** ne mets pas tant de sel; **we paid twice as ∼** nous avons payé deux fois plus; **how ∼ time have we got left?** combien de temps nous reste-t-il?
⟦4⟧ **much as** *phr* bien que (+ *subjunctive*)
⟦5⟧ **so much as** *phr* without so **∼ as an apology** sans même s'excuser; **if you so ∼ as move** si tu fais le moindre mouvement

**muck** *n* saletés *fpl*; (mud) boue *f*

■ **muck about** (colloq), **muck around** (colloq): ¶ **∼ about** (fool about) faire l'imbécile; **to ∼ about with** traficoter (colloq) ⟨*appliance*⟩; toucher à ⟨*object*⟩; ¶ **∼ [sb] about** se ficher de (colloq) qn

■ **muck in** mettre la main à la pâte (colloq)

**mud** *n* boue *f*

**muddle** *n* (a) (mess) pagaille (colloq)
**(b)** (mix-up) malentendu *m* (**over** à propos de)
**(c)** to get into a **∼** ⟨*person*⟩ s'embrouiller

■ **muddle up**: ¶ **∼ [sth] up** (disorder) semer la pagaille (colloq) dans; ¶ **∼ [sb] up** embrouiller les idées de; ¶ **to get [sth] ∼d up** s'embrouiller dans ⟨*dates, names*⟩

**muddled** *adj* confus/-e

**muddy** *adj* ⟨*hand*⟩ couvert/-e de boue; ⟨*shoe, garment*⟩ crotté/-e; ⟨*road, water*⟩ boueux/-euse; ⟨*green, yellow*⟩ terne

**mudguard** *n* garde-boue *m inv*

**muffle** *vtr* assourdir ⟨*bell, drum*⟩

**mug** ⟦1⟧ *n* (a) grande tasse *f*
**(b)** (GB) (fool) poire *f* (colloq); **it's a ∼'s game** c'est un attrape-nigaud
⟦2⟧ *vtr* agresser; **to be ∼ged** se faire agresser

**mugger** *n* agresseur *m*

**mugging** *n* (attack) agression *f*; (crime) agressions *fpl*

**muggy** *adj* ⟨*room, day*⟩ étouffant/-e; ⟨*weather*⟩ lourd/-e

**Muhammad** *pr n* Mahomet

**mule** *n* mulet *m*, mule *f*
IDIOMS **as stubborn as a ∼** têtu/-e comme une mule

**mull** *v* ■ **mull over** retourner [qch] dans sa tête

**mulled wine** *n* vin *m* chaud

**multicultural** *adj* multiculturel/-elle

**multidisciplinary** *adj* pluridisciplinaire

**multi-ethnic** *adj* multi-ethnique

**multi-function** *adj* multifonctions *inv*

**multigym** *n* appareil *m* de musculation

**multilateral** *adj* multilatéral/-e

**multimedia** *n, adj* multimédia (*m*) *inv*

**multinational** *adj* multinational/-e

**multiple** *n, adj* multiple (*m*)

**multiple choice** *adj* à choix multiple

**multiple sclerosis**, **MS** *n* sclérose *f* en plaques

**multiplex** *n* (Cinema) complexe *m* multi-salles

**multiply** ⟦1⟧ *vtr* multiplier (**by** par)
⟦2⟧ *vi* se multiplier

**multipurpose** *adj* ⟨*tool, gadget*⟩ à usages multiples; ⟨*area, organization*⟩ polyvalent/-e

**multipurpose vehicle**, **MPV** *n* monospace *m*

**multi-racial** *adj* multiracial/-e

**multistorey** *adj* (GB) ⟨*car park*⟩ à niveaux multiples; ⟨*building*⟩ à étages

**multitrack** *adj* multipiste *inv*

**multitude** *n* multitude *f*

m

**mum, Mum** n (GB) (colloq) maman f
  IDIOMS **to keep** ∼ ne pas piper mot
**mumble** vtr, vi marmonner
**mumbo jumbo** n (colloq) charabia m
  (colloq)
**mummy** n (a) (colloq) (also **Mummy**)
  maman f
  (b) (embalmed body) momie f
**mumps** n oreillons mpl
**munch** vtr ⟨person⟩ mâcher; ⟨animal⟩
  mâchonner
**mundane** adj terre-à-terre, quelconque
**municipal** adj municipal/-e
**mural** n (wall painting) peinture f murale; (in
  cave) peinture f rupestre
**murder** [1] n meurtre m
  [2] vtr assassiner
  IDIOMS **to get away with** ∼ exercer ses
  talents en toute impunité
**murderer** n assassin m, meurtrier m
**murderess** n meurtrière f
**murderous** adj ⟨look⟩ assassin/-e; ⟨deeds,
  thoughts⟩ meurtrier/-ière
**murky** adj (a) ⟨light, water, colour⟩ glauque
  (b) ⟨past⟩ trouble
**murmur** [1] n murmure m (of de)
  [2] vtr, vi murmurer
**muscle** n muscle m
■ **muscle in** (colloq) s'imposer (on dans)
**muscle strain** n élongation f
**muscular** adj ⟨disease, tissue⟩ musculaire;
  ⟨person, body, limbs⟩ musclé/-e
**museum** n musée m
**mushroom** n (a) (Bot, Culin) champignon m
  (b) (colour) beige m rosé
**music** n musique f
**musical** [1] n comédie f musicale
  [2] adj (a) ⟨person⟩ musicien/-ienne
  (b) ⟨voice, laughter⟩ mélodieux/-ieuse; ⟨score⟩
  musical/-e
**musical instrument** n instrument m
  de musique
**musician** n musicien/-ienne m/f
**music video** n clip m (vidéo)
**musk** n musc m
**Muslim** (also **Moslem**) [1] n Musulman/-e
  m/f
  [2] adj musulman/-e
**mussel** n moule f
**must** [1] modal aux (a) (expressing obligation) I
  ∼ **go** je dois partir, il faut que je parte; **he** ∼
  **sit the exam in June** il faut qu'il passe
  l'examen au mois de juin; **you** ∼ **check your
  rear-view mirror first** il faut regarder dans le
  rétroviseur d'abord; **I** ∼ **say I was impressed**
  je dois dire que j'ai été impressionné; **we
  mustn't tell anyone** il ne faut en parler à
  personne, nous ne devons en parler à
  personne

  (b) (making deductions) **they** ∼ **really detest
  each other** ils doivent vraiment se détester;
  **it** ∼ **be pleasant living there** ça doit être
  agréable de vivre là-bas; **he** ∼ **have been
  surprised** il a dû être surpris
  [2] n **it's a** ∼ c'est indispensable; **this film is
  a** ∼ ce film est à voir or à ne pas rater; **a
  visit to the Louvre is a** ∼ une visite au
  Louvre s'impose
**mustache** (US) = MOUSTACHE
**mustard** n moutarde f
**muster** vtr (also ∼ **up**) rassembler
  ⟨troops⟩; rallier ⟨support⟩; trouver ⟨energy,
  enthusiasm⟩
  IDIOMS **to pass** ∼ être acceptable
**musty** adj **to smell** ∼ sentir le moisi or le
  renfermé
**mute** adj muet/-ette
**mutilate** vtr mutiler
**mutiny** n mutinerie f
**mutter** vtr, vi marmonner
**mutton** n mouton m
**mutual** adj (a) (reciprocal) réciproque; **the
  feeling is** ∼ c'est réciproque
  (b) ⟨friend, interests⟩ commun/-e; ⟨consent⟩
  mutuel/-elle; **by** ∼ **agreement** d'un commun
  accord
**mutual aid** n entraide f
**my**

■ **Note** In French, determiners agree in gender
and number with the noun that follows. So my is
translated by mon + masculine singular noun
(mon chien), ma + feminine singular noun (ma
maison) BUT by mon + feminine noun beginning
with a vowel or mute 'h' (mon assiette) and by
mes + plural noun (mes enfants).
– When my is stressed, à moi is added after the
noun: MY house = ma maison à moi.

  [1] det mon/ma/mes
  [2] excl ∼ ∼! ça alors!
**myself** pron (a) (reflexive) me, m'; **I've hurt**
  ∼ je me suis fait mal
  (b) (emphatic) moi-même; **I saw it** ∼ je l'ai vu
  moi-même; **(all) by** ∼ tout seul/toute seule
  (c) (after prepositions) moi, moi-même; **I feel
  proud of** ∼ je suis fier de moi
  (d) (expressions) **I'm not much of a dog-lover**
  ∼ personnellement je n'aime pas trop les
  chiens; **I'm not** ∼ **today** je ne suis pas dans
  mon assiette aujourd'hui
**mysterious** adj mystérieux/-ieuse
**mystery** n (a) mystère m
  (b) (book) roman m policier
**mystify** vtr laisser [qn] perplexe
**myth** n mythe m
**mythology** n mythologie f

# N n

**n, N** *n* n, N *m*

**naff** *adj* (GB) (colloq) ringard/-e (colloq)

**nag** *vtr* enquiquiner (colloq) (**about** au sujet de)

**nagging** *adj* (a) his ∼ wife sa mégère de femme
(b) ⟨*pain, doubt*⟩ tenace

**nail** [1] *n* (a) (on finger, toe) ongle *m*
(b) (Tech) clou *m*
[2] *vtr* clouer
■ **nail down**: ¶ ∼ [sth] down clouer; ¶ ∼ [sb] down coincer (colloq) ⟨*person*⟩

**nail-biting** *adj* ⟨*match, finish*⟩ palpitant/-e; ⟨*wait*⟩ angoissant/-e

**nailbrush** *n* brosse *f* à ongles

**nail file** *n* lime *f* à ongles

**nail varnish** *n* vernis *m* à ongles

**nail varnish remover** *n* dissolvant *m*

**naïve** *adj* naïf/naïve

**naked** *adj* nu/-e

**name** [1] *n* (a) (gen) nom *m*; (of book, film) titre *m*; **first** ∼ prénom *m*; **my** ∼ **is Louis** je m'appelle Louis
(b) (reputation) réputation *f*
(c) (insult) **to call sb** ∼**s** injurier qn
[2] *vtr* (a) (call) appeler ⟨*person, area*⟩; baptiser ⟨*boat*⟩; **they** ∼**d her after** (GB) *or* **for** (US) **her mother** ils l'ont appelée comme sa mère; **a boy** ∼**d Pascal** un garçon nommé Pascal
(b) (cite) citer; ∼ **three American States** citez trois États américains
(c) révéler ⟨*sources*⟩; révéler l'identité de ⟨*suspect*⟩; **to** ∼ ∼**s** donner des noms
(d) (state) indiquer ⟨*place, time*⟩; fixer ⟨*price, terms*⟩

**name-drop** *vi* citer des gens célèbres (*qu'on prétend connaître*)

**namely** *adv* à savoir

**namesake** *n* homonyme *m*

**nanny** *n* (GB) bonne *f* d'enfants

**nanny goat** *n* chèvre *f*

**nap** [1] *n* petit somme *m*; **afternoon** ∼ sieste *f*
[2] *vi* sommeiller

**nape** *n* nuque *f*; **the** ∼ **of the neck** la nuque

**napkin** *n* serviette *f* (de table)

**nappy** *n* (GB) couche *f* (de bébé)

**narcotic** [1] *n* (soporific) narcotique *m*; (illegal drug) stupéfiant *m*
[2] *adj* narcotique

**narked** *adj* (colloq) en rogne (colloq), en boule (colloq)

**narration** *n* récit *m*, narration *f*

**narrative** [1] *n* (account) récit *m*; (storytelling) narration *f*
[2] *adj* ⟨*prose, poem*⟩ narratif/-ive; ⟨*skill, talent*⟩ de conteur

**narrator** *n* narrateur/-trice *m/f*

**narrow** [1] *adj* (gen) étroit/-e; ⟨*views*⟩ étriqué/-e; ⟨*majority, margin*⟩ faible (*before n*); **to have a** ∼ **lead** avoir une légère avance; **to have a** ∼ **escape** l'échapper belle
[2] *vtr* (a) (limit) limiter (**to** à); **to** ∼ **the gap** réduire l'écart
(b) rétrécir ⟨*road, path, arteries*⟩; **to** ∼ **one's eyes** plisser les yeux
[3] *vi* (gen) se rétrécir; ⟨*gap, margin*⟩ se réduire (**to** à)
■ **narrow down** réduire ⟨*numbers, list, choice*⟩ (**to** à); limiter ⟨*investigation, research*⟩ (**to** à)

**narrowly** *adv* (barely) de justesse

**narrow-minded** *adj* borné/-e

**nasal** *adj* ⟨*vowel*⟩ nasal/-e; ⟨*accent, voice*⟩ nasillard/-e

**nasal spray** *n* nébuliseur *m* (*pour le nez*)

**nasty** *adj* (a) ⟨*person, expression, remark*⟩ méchant/-e; ⟨*experience, surprise, feeling, task*⟩ désagréable; ⟨*habit, smell, taste*⟩ mauvais/-e (*before n*); ⟨*trick*⟩ sale (*before n*); ⟨*cut, bruise*⟩ vilain/-e (*before n*); ⟨*accident*⟩ grave
(b) (ugly) affreux/-euse

**nation** *n* nation *f*; (people) peuple *m*

**national** [1] *n* ressortissant/-e *m/f*
[2] *adj* national/-e; **the** ∼ **press** (GB) les grands quotidiens *mpl*

**national anthem** *n* hymne *m* national

**National Curriculum** *n* (GB) programme *m* scolaire national

**National Front** *n* (GB) parti britannique d'extrême droite

**National Health Service, NHS** *n* (GB) services *mpl* de santé britanniques, ≈ Sécurité *f* Sociale

**National Insurance, NI** *n* (GB) securité *f* sociale britannique; ∼ **number** numéro *m* de sécurité sociale

**nationalism** *n* nationalisme *m*

**nationality** *n* nationalité *f*

**nationalize** *vtr* nationaliser ⟨*industry*⟩

**nationwide** [1] *adj* ⟨*appeal, coverage, strike*⟩ sur l'ensemble du territoire; ⟨*campaign*⟩ national/-e; ⟨*survey, poll*⟩ à l'échelle nationale
[2] *adv* dans tout le pays

**native** [1] *n* autochtone *mf*; **to be a** ∼ **of** être originaire de
[2] *adj* (a) ⟨*land*⟩ natal/-e; ⟨*tongue*⟩ maternel/-elle; ∼ **German speaker** personne *f* de langue maternelle allemande
(b) ⟨*flora, fauna, peoples*⟩ indigène

**n**

**Native American** n, adj
amérindien/-ienne (m/f)

**Nativity** n nativité f

**NATO** n (abbr = **North Atlantic Treaty Organization**) OTAN f

**natural** adj (a) (gen) naturel/-elle
(b) ⟨gift, talent⟩ inné/-e; ⟨artist, storyteller⟩ né/-e
(c) (unaffected) simple, naturel/-elle

**naturalize** vtr naturaliser ⟨person⟩; **to be ~d** se faire naturaliser

**naturally** adv (a) (obviously, of course) naturellement
(b) (by nature) de nature; **politeness comes ~ to him** il est d'un naturel poli
(c) ⟨behave, smile, speak⟩ avec naturel

**nature** n nature f; **let ~ take its course** laissez faire la nature; **it's not in her ~ to be aggressive** elle n'est pas agressive de nature; **it is in the ~ of things** il est dans l'ordre des choses

**nature conservancy** n protection f de la nature

**nature reserve** n réserve f naturelle

**nature trail** n sentier m écologique

**naughty** adj (a) (disobedient) vilain/-e
(b) (rude) ⟨joke, picture, story⟩ coquin/-e

**nausea** n nausée f

**nauseating** adj écœurant/-e

**nauseous** adj ⟨taste, smell⟩ écœurant/-e; **to feel ~** avoir la nausée

**nautical** adj nautique

**naval** adj ⟨battle, forces, base⟩ naval/-e; ⟨officer, recruit, uniform, affairs⟩ de la marine

**naval ring** n piercing m au nombril

**nave** n nef f

**navel** n nombril m

**navigate** 1 vtr (a) parcourir ⟨seas⟩
(b) piloter ⟨plane⟩; gouverner ⟨ship⟩
2 vi (in vessel, plane) naviguer; (in rally) faire le copilote; (on journey) tenir la carte

**navigation** n navigation f

**navigator** n (in vessel, plane) navigateur/-trice m/f; (in car) copilote mf

**navy** 1 n (a) (fleet) flotte f; (fighting force) marine f
(b) (also ~ **blue**) bleu m marine
2 adj (also ~ **blue**) bleu marine inv

**Nazi** n, adj nazi/-e (m/f)

**near** 1 adv (a) (close) près; **to live quite ~** habiter tout près; **to move ~er** s'approcher davantage (**to** de); **to bring sth ~er** approcher qch
(b) (nearly) **as ~ perfect as it could be** aussi proche de la perfection que possible; **nowhere ~ finished** loin d'être fini
2 prep (a) près de; ~ **here** près d'ici; ~ **the beginning of the article** presque au début de l'article; **he's no ~er (making) a decision** il n'est pas plus décidé
(b) (in time) ~**er the time** quand la date approchera; **it's getting ~ Christmas** Noël approche

3 adj proche; **in the ~ future** dans un avenir proche; **the ~est shops** les magasins les plus proches
4 vtr approcher de; **to ~ completion** toucher à sa fin
5 **near enough** phr à peu près
6 **near to** phr (a) (in space) près de; ~**er to** plus près de
(b) (on point of) au bord de ⟨tears, collapse⟩
(c) **to come ~ to doing** faillir faire

**nearby** 1 adj ⟨person⟩ qui se trouve/trouvait etc à proximité; ⟨town, village⟩ d'à côté
2 adv tout près; ⟨park, stand, wait⟩ à proximité

**nearly** adv presque; **I very ~ gave up** j'ai bien failli abandonner; **not ~ as talented as** loin d'être aussi doué que

**near miss** n **to have a ~** ⟨planes⟩ frôler la collision; ⟨cars⟩ faillir se percuter

**near-sighted** adj myope

**neat** 1 adj (a) ⟨person⟩ (in habits) ordonné/-e; (in appearance) soigné/-e; ⟨room, house, desk⟩ bien rangé/-e; ⟨garden, handwriting⟩ soigné/-e
(b) ⟨explanation, solution⟩ habile
(c) ⟨figure⟩ bien fait/-e; ⟨features⟩ régulier/-ière
(d) ⟨alcohol, spirits⟩ sans eau
2 adv ⟨drink whisky⟩ sec, sans eau

**neatly** adv (a) (tidily) ⟨dress, fold, arrange⟩ avec soin; ⟨write⟩ proprement
(b) (perfectly) ⟨illustrate, summarize⟩ parfaitement; ⟨link⟩ habilement

**necessarily** adv (definitely) forcément; (of necessity) nécessairement; **not ~** pas forcément

**necessary** adj (gen) nécessaire; ⟨qualification⟩ requis/-e; **if ~, as ~** si besoin est; **it is ~ for him to do** il faut qu'il fasse

**necessitate** vtr nécessiter

**necessity** n (a) (need) nécessité f; **from ~** par nécessité; **the ~ for** le besoin de
(b) (essential item) **to be an absolute ~** être indispensable

**neck** n (a) (of person) cou m; (of horse, donkey) encolure f
(b) (collar) col m; (neckline) encolure f
(c) (of bottle, vase, womb) col m
IDIOMS **to be ~ and ~** être à égalité; **to stick one's ~ out** (colloq) prendre des risques

**necklace** n collier m

**neckline** n encolure f

**necktie** n (US) cravate f

**nectar** n nectar m

**nectarine** n nectarine f, brugnon m

**need** 1 modal aux **you needn't finish it today** tu n'es pas obligé de le finir aujourd'hui; ~ **he reply?** est-ce qu'il faut qu'il réponde?, est-ce qu'il doit répondre?; **I needn't have hurried** ce n'était pas la peine de me dépêcher, ce n'était pas la peine que je me dépêche
2 vtr (a) (require) **to ~ sth/to do** avoir besoin de qch/de faire; **more money is ~ed**

nous avons besoin de plus d'argent; **everything you ∼ tout ce qu'il vous faut; everything you ∼ to know about computers** tout ce que vous devez savoir sur les ordinateurs
**(b)** (have to) **you'll ∼ to work hard** il va falloir que tu travailles dur; **he didn't ∼ to ask permission** il n'était pas obligé de demander la permission; **something ∼ed to be done** il fallait faire quelque chose
**3** *n* **(a)** (necessity) nécessité *f* **(for** de)**; I can't see the ∼ for it** je n'en vois pas la nécessité; **to feel the ∼ to do** éprouver le besoin de faire; **there's no ∼ to wait** inutile d'attendre; **there's no ∼ to worry** ce n'est pas la peine de s'inquiéter; **there's no ∼, I've done it** inutile, c'est fait; **if ∼ be** s'il le faut, si nécessaire
**(b)** (want, requirement) besoin *m* **(for** de)**; to be in ∼ of sth** avoir besoin de qch
**(c)** (poverty) **to be in ∼** être dans le besoin
**needle** **1** *n* aiguille *f*
**2** *vtr* harceler
**IDIOMS to have pins and ∼s** avoir des fourmis
**needless** *adj* ⟨anxiety, suffering⟩ inutile; ⟨intrusion, intervention⟩ inopportun/-e
**needlework** *n* couture *f*
**needy** *adj* ⟨person⟩ nécessiteux/-euse; ⟨sector, area⟩ sans ressources
**negate** *vtr* (cancel out) réduire [qch] à néant
**negative** **1** *n* **(a)** (of photo) négatif *m*
**(b)** (in grammar) négation *f*; **in the ∼** à la forme négative
**2** *adj* (gen) négatif/-ive; ⟨effect, influence⟩ néfaste
**neglect** **1** *n* **(a)** (of person) négligence *f*; (of building, garden) manque *m* d'entretien; (of health, appearance) manque *m* de soin
**(b)** (lack of interest) indifférence *f* **(of** à l'égard de)
**2** *vtr* **(a)** ne pas s'occuper de ⟨person, dog, plant⟩; ne pas entretenir ⟨garden, house⟩; négliger ⟨health, friend, work⟩
**(b)** (fail) **to ∼ to do** négliger de faire
**neglected** *adj* (gen) négligé/-e; ⟨garden, building⟩ mal entretenu/-e; **to feel ∼** se sentir délaissé/-e
**negligence** *n* négligence *f*
**negligent** *adj* ⟨person, procedure⟩ négligent/-e; ⟨air, manner⟩ nonchalant/-e
**negligible** *adj* négligeable
**negotiable** *adj* **(a)** ⟨rate, terms⟩ négociable
**(b)** ⟨road, pass⟩ praticable; ⟨obstacle⟩ franchissable
**negotiate** **1** *vtr* **(a)** (in business, diplomacy) négocier
**(b)** négocier ⟨bend⟩; franchir ⟨obstacle⟩
**2** *vi* négocier **(with** avec; **for** pour obtenir)
**3 negotiated** *pp adj* ⟨settlement, peace⟩ négocié/-e
**negotiation** *n* négociation *f*; **to be under ∼** être en cours de négociations
**negotiator** *n* négociateur/-trice *m/f*

**neigh** *vi* hennir
**neighbour** (GB)**, neighbor** (US) *n* voisin/-e *m/f*
**neighbourhood** (GB)**, neighborhood** (US) *n* **(a)** (district) quartier *m*
**(b)** (vicinity) **in the ∼** dans le voisinage
**neighbouring** (GB)**, neighboring** (US) *adj* voisin/-e
**neither** **1** *conj* **I have ∼ the time nor the money** je n'ai ni le temps ni l'argent; **∼ tea, nor milk** ni (le) thé, ni (le) lait; **'I can't sleep'—'∼ can I'** 'je n'arrive pas à dormir'— 'moi non plus'
**2** *det* aucun/-e des deux; **∼ book is suitable** aucun des deux livres ne convient; **∼ girl replied** aucune des deux filles n'a répondu
**3** *pron, quantif* ni l'un/-e ni l'autre *m/f*; **∼ of them came** ni l'un ni l'autre n'est venu
**neon** **1** *n* néon *m*
**2** *adj* ⟨light, sign⟩ au néon; ⟨atom⟩ de néon
**nephew** *n* neveu *m*
**Neptune** *pr n* (planet) Neptune *f*
**nerve** **1** *n* **(a)** (Anat) nerf *m*; (Bot) nervure *f*
**(b)** (courage) courage *m*; **to lose one's ∼** perdre son courage
**(c)** (colloq) (cheek) culot *m* (colloq)**; you've got a ∼!** tu as un sacré culot! (colloq)
**2 nerves** *n pl* (gen) nerfs *mpl*; (stage fright) trac *m* (colloq)**; to get on sb's ∼s** taper sur les nerfs de qn
**nerve-(w)racking** *adj* angoissant/-e
**nervous** *adj* **(a)** ⟨person⟩ (fearful) timide; (anxious) angoissé/-e; (highly strung) nerveux/-euse; ⟨smile, laugh, habit⟩ nerveux/-euse; **to be ∼ about doing** avoir peur de faire; **to feel ∼** (apprehensive) être angoissé/-e; (before performance) avoir le trac (colloq); (afraid) avoir peur; (ill at ease) se sentir mal à l'aise
**(b)** (Anat, Med) nerveux/-euse
**nervous breakdown** *n* dépression *f* nerveuse
**nervously** *adv* nerveusement
**nervous wreck** *n* (colloq) boule *f* de nerfs (colloq)
**nest** **1** *n* (of bird, animal) nid *m*
**(b)** **∼ of tables** tables *fpl* gigognes
**2** *vi* ⟨bird⟩ faire son nid
**nest egg** *n* magot *m* (colloq)
**nestle** *vi* **(a)** ⟨person, animal⟩ se blottir (**against** contre; **under** sous)
**(b)** ⟨village, house⟩ être niché/-e
**net** **1** *n* (gen) filet *m*; (in football) filets *mpl*
**2** *adj* (**also nett**) (gen) net/nette; ⟨loss⟩ sec/ sèche
**3** *vtr* **(a)** prendre [qch] au filet ⟨fish⟩
**(b)** (financially) ⟨person⟩ faire un bénéfice de; ⟨sale, export, deal⟩ rapporter
**Net** *n* Net *m*
**netball** *n*: sport d'équipe proche du basket joué par les femmes
**net curtain** *n* voilage *m*
**Netherlands** *pr n* **the ∼** les Pays-Bas *mpl*, la Hollande

**n**

**netiquette** *n* netiquette *f*

**netspeak** *n* jargon *m* Internet

**netting** *n* (of rope) filet *m*; (of metal, plastic) grillage *m*; (fabric) voile *m*

**nettle** *n* (also **stinging** ∼) ortie *f*

**network** ⒈ *n* réseau *m* (**of** de)
⒉ *vtr* (Comput) interconnecter
⒊ *vi* tisser un réseau de relations

**networking** *n* (a) (Comput) interconnexion *f*
(b) (establishing contacts) ∼ **is important** c'est important d'avoir des contacts

**network television** *n* (US) chaîne *f* nationale

**neurosis** *n* névrose *f*

**neurotic** *adj* névrosé/-e

**neuter** ⒈ *n* neutre *m*
⒉ *adj* neutre
⒊ *vtr* châtrer ‹*animal*›

**neutral** ⒈ *n* (Aut) **in/into** ∼ au point mort
⒉ *adj* neutre (**about** en ce qui concerne)

**neutrality** *n* neutralité *f*

**neutralize** *vtr* neutraliser

**never** *adv* (a) (not ever) **I** ∼ **go to London** je ne vais jamais à Londres; **she** ∼ **says anything** elle ne dit jamais rien; **it's now or** ∼ c'est le moment ou jamais; ∼ **again** plus jamais; ∼ **lie to me again!** ne me mens plus jamais!
(b) (emphatic negative) **he** ∼ **said a word** il n'a rien dit; **I** ∼ **knew that** je ne le savais pas; **he** ∼ **so much as apologized** il ne s'est même pas excusé

**never-ending** *adj* interminable

**nevertheless** *adv* (a) (all the same) quand même
(b) (nonetheless) pourtant, néanmoins

**new** *adj* nouveau/-elle (before n); (brand new) neuf/neuve; **I bought a** ∼ **computer** (to replace old one) j'ai acheté un nouvel ordinateur; (a brand new model) j'ai acheté un ordinateur neuf; **as good as** ∼ comme neuf; **to be** ∼ **to** ne pas être habitué/-e à ‹*job, way of life*›; **we're** ∼ **to the area** nous sommes nouveaux venus dans la région

**New Age** *adj* ‹*music, traveller*› New Age *inv*

**newborn** *adj* nouveau-né/-née

**newcomer** *n* (in place, job, club) nouveau venu/nouvelle venue *m/f*; (in sport, theatre, cinema) nouveau/-elle *m/f*

**newfound** *adj* tout nouveau/toute nouvelle

**new look** ⒈ *n* nouveau style *m*
⒉ **new-look** *adj* ‹*product*› nouvelle version *inv*; ‹*car, team*› nouveau/-elle (before n); ‹*edition, show*› remanié/-e

**newly** *adv* ‹*arrived, built, formed, qualified*› nouvellement; ‹*washed*› fraîchement

**newlyweds** *n pl* jeunes mariés *mpl*

**news** *n* (a) nouvelle(s) *f(pl)*; **a piece of** ∼ une nouvelle; (in newspaper) une information; **have you heard the** ∼**?** tu connais la nouvelle?
(b) (on radio, TV) **the** ∼ les informations *fpl*, le journal *m*

**news agency** *n* agence *f* de presse

**newsagent's** *n* (GB) magasin *m* de journaux

**news bulletin** (GB), **newscast** (US) *n* bulletin *m* d'information

**newscaster** *n* présentateur/-trice *m/f* des informations

**news conference** *n* conférence *f* de presse

**newsdealer** *n* (US) marchand *m* de journaux

**news editor** *n* rédacteur/-trice *m/f*

**newsgroup** *n* forum *m* de discussion

**news headlines** *n pl* (on TV) titres *mpl* de l'actualité

**news item** *n* sujet *m* d'actualité

**newsletter** *n* bulletin *m*

**newspaper** *n* journal *m*

**newsreader** *n* (GB) présentateur/-trice *m/f* des informations

**newsreel** *n* actualités *fpl*

**newsstand** *n* kiosque *m* à journaux

**New Year** *n* le nouvel an *m*; **to see in the** ∼ fêter la Saint-Sylvestre; **Happy** ∼**!** bonne année!

**New Year's day** (GB), **New Year's** (US) *n* le jour *m* de l'an

**New Year's Eve** *n* la Saint-Sylvestre

**New Zealand** *pr n* Nouvelle-Zélande *f*

**next**

■ Note When *next* is used as an adjective, it is generally translated by *prochain* when referring to something which is still to come or happen and by *suivant* when it generally means following: *I'll be 40 next year* = j'aurai 40 ans l'année prochaine; *the next year, he went to Spain* = l'année suivante il est allé en Espagne.
– For examples and further usages see the entry below.

⒈ *pron* **from one minute to the** ∼ d'un instant à l'autre; **the week after** ∼ dans deux semaines

⒉ *adj* (a) prochain/-e, suivant/-e; **get the** ∼ **train** prenez le prochain train; **he got on the** ∼ **train** il a pris le train suivant; **'**∼**!'** 'au suivant!'; **'you're** ∼**'** 'c'est à vous'; **the** ∼ **size (up)** la taille au-dessus; ∼ **Thursday** jeudi prochain; **he's due to arrive in the** ∼ **10 minutes** il devrait arriver d'ici 10 minutes; **this time** ∼ **week** dans une semaine; **the** ∼ **day** le lendemain
(b) ‹*room, street*› voisin/-e; ‹*building, house*› voisin/-e, d'à côté

⒊ *adv* (a) (afterwards) ensuite, après; **what happened** ∼**?** que s'est-il passé ensuite?
(b) (on a future occasion) **when I** ∼ **go there** la prochaine fois que j'irai
(c) (in order) **the** ∼ **tallest is Patrick** ensuite c'est Patrick qui est le plus grand

⒋ **next to** *phr* (a) (almost) presque; ∼ **to impossible** presque impossible; **to get sth for**

~ **to nothing** avoir qch pour quasiment rien; **in ~ to no time it was over** en un rien de temps c'était fini
**(b)** (beside, close to) à côté de; **two seats ~ to each other** deux sièges l'un à côté de l'autre; **to wear silk ~ to the skin** porter de la soie à même la peau

**next door** [1] *adj* (*also* **next-door**) d'à côté
[2] *adv* ⟨*live, move in*⟩ à côté

**next-door neighbour** *n* voisin/-e *m/f* (d'à côté)

**next of kin** *n* **to be sb's ~** être le parent le plus proche de qn

**nib** *n* plume *f*

**nibble** *vi* ⟨*animal*⟩ mordiller; ⟨*person*⟩ grignoter

**nice** *adj* **(a)** ⟨*drive, holiday, place*⟩ agréable; ⟨*house, picture, outfit, weather*⟩ beau/belle (*before n*); **did you have a ~ time?** tu t'es bien amusé?; ~ **to have met you** ravi d'avoir fait votre connaissance; **have a ~ day!** bonne journée!; **you look very ~** tu es très chic
**(b)** (tasty) bon/bonne (*before n*); **to taste ~** avoir bon goût
**(c)** ⟨*person*⟩ sympathique; **to be ~ to sb** être gentil/-ille avec qn
**(d)** ⟨*neighbourhood, school*⟩ comme il faut *inv*; **it is not ~ to tell lies** ce n'est pas bien de mentir
IDIOMS ~ **one!** (in admiration) bravo!; (ironic) il ne manquait plus que ça!

**nice-looking** *adj* beau/belle (*before n*)

**nicely** *adv* **(a)** (kindly) gentiment
**(b)** (attractively) agréablement
**(c)** (politely) poliment
**(d)** (satisfactorily) bien; **that'll do ~** cela fera l'affaire

**niche** *n* (recess) niche *f*; (figurative) place *f*; (in the market) créneau *m*

**niche market** *n* marché *m* spécialisé

**nick** [1] *n* encoche *f* (**in** dans)
[2] *vtr* **(a)** (cut) faire une entaille dans
**(b)** (GB) (colloq) (steal) piquer (colloq)
[3] (GB) (arrest) pincer (colloq)
IDIOMS **just in the ~ of time** juste à temps

**nickel** *n* **(a)** (US) pièce *f* de cinq cents
**(b)** (metal) nickel *m*

**nickname** [1] *n* surnom *m*
[2] *vtr* surnommer

**nicotine** *n* nicotine *f*

**nicotine patch** *n* patch *m* à la nicotine

**niece** *n* nièce *f*

**niggle** (colloq) [1] *n* (complaint) remarque *f*; **I've a ~ at the back of my mind** il y a quelque chose qui me travaille
[2] *vtr* (irritate) tracasser

**niggling** *adj* ⟨*doubt, worry*⟩ insidieux/-ieuse

**night** *n* nuit *f*; (before going to bed) soir *m*; **at ~** la nuit; **all ~ long** toute la nuit; **late at ~** tard le soir; **he arrived last ~** il est arrivé hier soir; **I slept badly last ~** j'ai mal dormi

cette nuit *or* la nuit dernière; **the ~ before last** avant-hier soir; **on Tuesday ~s** le mardi soir; **to get an early ~** se coucher tôt; **a ~ at the opera** une soirée à l'opéra

**nightclub** *n* boîte *f* de nuit

**nightclubbing** *n* **to go ~** aller en boîte (colloq)

**nightdress** *n* chemise *f* de nuit

**nightingale** *n* rossignol *m*

**nightlife** *n* vie *f* nocturne

**nightmare** *n* cauchemar *m*; **to have a ~** faire un cauchemar

**night school** *n* cours *mpl* du soir

**night shelter** *n* asile *m* de nuit

**night shift** *n* (period) **to be/work on the ~** être/travailler de nuit; (workers) équipe *f* de nuit

**nightshirt** *n* chemise *f* de nuit (d'homme)

**night spot** *n* (colloq) boîte *f* de nuit

**night-time** *n* nuit *f*; **at ~** la nuit

**night watchman** *n* veilleur *m* de nuit

**nil** *n* (gen) néant *m*; (Sport) zéro *m*

**Nile** *pr n* Nil *m*

**nimble** *adj* ⟨*person*⟩ agile; ⟨*fingers*⟩ habile

**nine** *n, pron, det* neuf (*m*) *inv*

**nineteen** *n, pron, det* dix-neuf (*m*) *inv*
IDIOMS **to talk ~ to the dozen** parler à n'en plus finir

**nineteenth** [1] *n* **(a)** (in order) dix-neuvième *mf*
**(b)** (of month) dix-neuf *m inv*
**(c)** (fraction) dix-neuvième *m*
[2] *adj, adv* dix-neuvième

**nineties** *n pl* **(a)** (era) **the ~** les années *fpl* quatre-vingt-dix
**(b)** (age) **to be in one's ~** avoir entre quatre-vingt-dix et cent ans

**ninetieth** *n, adj, adv* quatre-vingt-dixième (*mf*)

**nine-to-five** *adj* ⟨*job, routine*⟩ de bureau

**ninety** *n, pron, det* quatre-vingt-dix (*m*) *inv*

**ninth** [1] *n* **(a)** (in order) neuvième *mf*
**(b)** (of month) neuf *m inv*
**(c)** (fraction) neuvième *m*
[2] *adj, adv* neuvième

**nip** [1] *n* (pinch) pincement *m*; (bite) morsure *f*; **there's a ~ in the air** il fait frisquet (colloq)
[2] *vtr* (pinch) pincer; (bite) donner un petit coup de dent à; (playfully) mordiller
[3] *vi* (bite) mordre; (playfully) mordiller

**nipple** *n* mamelon *m*

**nippy** *adj* (colloq) **(a)** (cold) **it's a bit ~** il fait frisquet (colloq)
**(b)** (quick) ⟨*person*⟩ vif/vive; ⟨*car*⟩ rapide

**nit** *n* (egg) lente *f*; (larva) larve *f* de pou

**nit-pick** *vi* chercher la petite bête (colloq), pinailler (colloq)

**nitrogen** *n* azote *m*

**nitty-gritty** *n* (colloq) **to get down to the ~** passer aux choses sérieuses

**no** [1] *particle* non; ~ **thanks** non merci
[2] *det* **(a)** (none, not any) aucun/-e; **to have ~** ⋯✦

*n*

**money** ne pas avoir d'argent; **she has ~ talent** elle n'a aucun talent; **of ~ interest** sans intérêt
(b) (prohibiting) **~ smoking** défense de fumer; **~ parking** stationnement interdit; **~ talking!** silence!
(c) (for emphasis) **he's ~ expert** ce n'est certes pas un expert; **this is ~ time to cry** ce n'est pas le moment de pleurer
(d) (hardly any) **in ~ time** en un rien de temps
3 *adj* **it's ~ further/easier** ce n'est pas plus loin/facile; **I ~ longer work there** je n'y travaille plus; **~ later than Wednesday** pas plus tard que mercredi

**no., No.** (written abbr = **number**) nº

**nobility** *n* noblesse *f*

**noble** *n, adj* noble (*m*)

**nobody** 1 *pron* (also **no-one**) personne; **~ saw her** personne ne l'a vue; **there was ~ in the car** il n'y avait personne dans la voiture; **I heard ~** je n'ai entendu personne; **~ but me** personne sauf moi
2 *n* **to be a ~** être insignifiant/-e

**nocturnal** *adj* nocturne

**nod** 1 *n* **she gave him a ~** elle lui a fait un signe de (la) tête; (as greeting) elle l'a salué d'un signe de tête; (indicating assent) elle a fait oui de la tête
2 *vtr* **to ~ one's head** faire un signe de tête; (to indicate assent) hocher la tête
3 *vi* faire un signe de tête (**to** à); (in assent) faire oui de la tête

**no-go area** *n* quartier *m* chaud (*où la police etc ne s'aventure plus*)

**no-hoper** *n* (colloq) raté/-e *m/f* (colloq)

**noise** *n* bruit *m*; (shouting) tapage *m*; **to make a ~** faire du bruit

**noisy** *adj* ⟨person, place⟩ bruyant/-e; ⟨meeting, protest⟩ tumultueux/-euse

**nomad** *n* nomade *mf*

**nominal** *adj* (gen) nominal/-e; ⟨fee, sum⟩ minime; ⟨fine⟩ symbolique

**nominate** *vtr* (a) (propose) proposer; **to ~ sb for a prize** sélectionner qn pour un prix
(b) (appoint) nommer (**to sth** à qch); **to ~ sb (as) chairman** nommer qn président

**nomination** *n* (as candidate) proposition *f* de candidat; (for award) sélection *f*; (appointment) nomination *f* (**to** à)

**nominative** *n, adj* nominatif (*m*)

**nonaddictive** *adj* qui ne crée pas de dépendance

**nonalcoholic** *adj* non alcoolisé/-e

**nonbeliever** *n* non-croyant/-e *m/f*

**nonchalant** *adj* nonchalant/-e

**noncommittal** *adj* évasif/-ive

**noncompliance** *n* (with standards) non-conformité *f* (**with** à); (with orders) non-obéissance *f* (**with** à)

**nonconformist** *adj* non conformiste

**noncooperation** *n* refus *m* de coopération

**nondenominational** *adj* ⟨church⟩ œcuménique; ⟨school⟩ laïque

**nondescript** *adj* ⟨person, clothes⟩ insignifiant/-e; ⟨building⟩ quelconque

**none** *pron* (a) (not any) aucun/-e *m/f*; **~ of us/them** aucun de nous/d'entre eux; **~ of the wine was French** il n'y avait aucun vin français; **~ of the milk had been drunk** on n'avait pas touché au lait; **~ of the bread was fresh** tout le pain était rassis; **we have ~** nous n'en avons pas; **there's ~ left** il n'y en a plus; **~ of it was true** il n'y avait rien de vrai
(b) (nobody) personne; **~ but him** personne sauf lui

**nonentity** *n* (person) personne *f* insignifiante

**nonessentials** *n pl* (objects) accessoires *mpl*; (details) accessoire *m sg*

**nonetheless** *adv* pourtant, néanmoins

**nonexistent** *adj* inexistant/-e

**nonfiction** *n* œuvres *fpl* non fictionnelles

**no-nonsense** *adj* ⟨manner, attitude, policy⟩ direct/-e; ⟨person⟩ franc/franche

**nonplussed** *adj* perplexe

**non-profitmaking** *adj* ⟨organization⟩ à but non lucratif

**nonresident** *n* non-résident/-e *m/f*

**nonsense** *n* (foolishness) absurdités *fpl*; **to talk/write ~** dire/écrire n'importe quoi; **~!** balivernes! *fpl*; **I won't stand for this ~** j'en ai assez de ces bêtises

**nonsmoker** *n* non-fumeur/-euse *m/f*

**non-smoking** *adj* non fumeur *inv*

**nonstarter** *n* **to be a ~** ⟨plan, idea⟩ être voué/-e à l'échec

**nonstick** *adj* antiadhésif/-ive

**nonstop** 1 *adj* ⟨journey⟩ sans arrêt; ⟨train, flight⟩ direct/-e; ⟨noise⟩ incessant/-e
2 *adv* ⟨work, talk, drive, argue⟩ sans arrêt; ⟨fly⟩ sans escale

**non-taxable** *adj* non imposable

**noodles** *n pl* nouilles *fpl*

**nook** *n* coin *m*; **every ~ and cranny** tous les coins et recoins

**noon** *n* midi *m*; **at 12 ~** à midi

**no-one** = NOBODY 1

**noose** *n* (loop) nœud *m* coulant; (for hanging) corde *f*

**nor** *conj* **~ do I** moi non plus; **~ can he** lui non plus; **he was not a cruel man, ~ a mean one** il n'était ni cruel, ni méchant; **she hasn't written, ~ has she telephoned** elle n'a pas écrit, et elle n'a pas téléphoné non plus

**norm** *n* norme *f* (**for** pour; **to do** de faire)

**normal** 1 *n* normale *f*; **above/below ~** au-dessus/en dessous de la norme
2 *adj* (gen) normal/-e; ⟨place, time⟩ habituel/-elle

**normality** *n* normalité *f*

**normally** *adv* normalement

**Normandy** *pr n* Normandie *f*

**north** 1 *n* (a) (compass direction) nord *m*
(b) (part of world, country) **the North** le Nord

**2** *adj* (gen) nord *inv*; ⟨*wind*⟩ du nord; **in ∼ London** dans le nord de Londres

**3** *adv* ⟨*move*⟩ vers le nord; ⟨*lie, live*⟩ au nord (**of** de)

**North Africa** *pr n* Afrique *f* du Nord

**North America** *pr n* Amérique *f* du Nord

**northeast** **1** *n* nord-est *m*

**2** *adj* ⟨*coast, side*⟩ nord-est *inv*; ⟨*wind*⟩ de nord-est

**3** *adv* ⟨*move*⟩ vers le nord-est; ⟨*lie, live*⟩ au nord-est

**northern** *adj* ⟨*coast*⟩ nord *inv*; ⟨*town, accent*⟩ du nord; ⟨*hemisphere*⟩ Nord *inv*; **∼ England** le nord de l'Angleterre

**Northern Ireland** *pr n* Irlande *f* du Nord

**North Pole** *pr n* pôle *m* Nord

**North Sea** *pr n* **the ∼** la mer du Nord

**northwest** **1** *n* nord-ouest *m*

**2** *adj* ⟨*coast*⟩ nord-ouest *inv*; ⟨*wind*⟩ de nord-ouest

**3** *adv* ⟨*move*⟩ vers le nord-ouest; ⟨*lie, live*⟩ au nord-ouest

**Norway** *pr n* Norvège *f*

**Norwegian** **1** *n* (a) (person) Norvégien/-ienne *m/f*

(b) (language) norvégien *m*

**2** *adj* norvégien/-ienne

**nose** *n* nez *m*

IDIOMS **to look down one's ∼ at sb/sth** prendre qn/qch de haut; **to turn one's ∼ up at sth** faire le dégoûté/la dégoûtée devant qch; **to poke** *or* **stick one's ∼ into sth** (colloq) fourrer son nez dans qch (colloq)

■ **nose about, nose around** fouiner (**in** dans)

**nosebleed** *n* saignement *m* de nez

**nose-dive** *n* piqué *m*; **to go into a ∼** ⟨*plane*⟩ faire un piqué; (figurative) chuter

**nose ring** *n* piercing *m* au nez

**nostalgia** *n* nostalgie *f*

**nostalgic** *adj* nostalgique

**nostril** *n* (of person) narine *f*; (of horse) naseau *m*

**nosy** *adj* (colloq) fouineur/-euse (colloq)

**not** **1** *adv* (a) (with a verb) ne…pas; **she isn't at home** elle n'est pas chez elle; **we won't need a car** nous n'aurons pas besoin d'une voiture; **hasn't he seen it?** il ne l'a pas vu alors?; **I hope ∼** j'espère que non; **certainly ∼** sûrement pas; **∼ only** *or* **just** non seulement; **whether it rains or ∼** qu'il pleuve ou non; **why ∼?** pourquoi pas?; **∼ everyone likes it** ça ne plaît pas à tout le monde; **it's ∼ every day that** ce n'est pas tous les jours que; **∼ a sound was heard** on n'entendait pas un bruit; **∼ bad** pas mal

(b) (in question tags) **he likes fish doesn't he?** il aime le poisson, n'est-ce pas?

**2** **not at all** *phr* (in no way) pas du tout; (responding to thanks) de rien

**3** **not that** *phr* **∼ that I know of** pas

(autant) que je sache; **if she refuses, ∼ that she will…** si elle refuse, je ne dis pas qu'elle le fera…

**notable** *adj* ⟨*person*⟩ remarquable; ⟨*event, success, difference*⟩ notable

**notably** *adv* (in particular) notamment; (markedly) remarquablement

**notch** **1** *n* entaille *f*

**2** *vtr* encocher ⟨*stick*⟩

■ **notch up** (colloq) remporter ⟨*point, prize*⟩

**note** **1** *n* (a) (gen) note *f*; (short letter) mot *m*; **to take ∼ of** prendre note de

(b) (Mus) (sound, symbol) note *f*; (piano key) touche *f*

(c) (bank) **∼** billet *m*

**2** *vtr* noter

**3** **of note** *phr* ⟨*person*⟩ éminent/-e, réputé/-e; ⟨*development*⟩ digne d'intérêt

IDIOMS **to compare ∼s** échanger ses impressions (**with** avec)

■ **note down** noter

**notebook** *n* carnet *m*

**notebook pc** *n* ordinateur *m* portable

**noted** *adj* ⟨*intellectual, criminal*⟩ célèbre; **to be ∼ for** être réputé/-e pour

**notepad** *n* bloc-notes *m*

**notepaper** *n* papier *m* à lettres

**noteworthy** *adj* remarquable

**nothing**

---

■ Note When *nothing* is used alone as a reply to a question in English, it is translated by *rien*: *'what are you doing?'—'nothing'* = *'que fais-tu?'—'rien'.*

– *nothing* as a pronoun, when it is the subject of a verb, is translated by *rien ne* (+ verb or, in compound tenses, + auxiliary verb): *nothing changes* = *rien ne change*; *nothing has changed* = *rien n'a changé*.

– *nothing* as a pronoun, when it is the object of a verb, is translated by *ne…rien*; *ne* comes before the verb, and before the auxiliary in compound tenses, and *rien* comes after the verb or auxiliary: *I see nothing* = *je ne vois rien*; *I saw nothing* = *je n'ai rien vu*.

– When *ne rien* is used with an infinitive, the two words are not separated: *I prefer to say nothing* = *je préfère ne rien dire*.

– For more examples and particular usages, see the entry below.

---

**1** *pron* **I knew ∼ about it** je n'en savais rien; **we can do ∼ (about it)** nous n'y pouvons rien; **∼ much** pas grand-chose; **∼ else** rien d'autre; **I had ∼ to do with it!** je n'y étais pour rien!; **it's ∼ to do with us** ça ne nous regarde pas; **to stop at ∼** reculer devant rien (**to do** pour faire); **he means ∼ to me** il n'est rien pour moi; **the names meant ∼ to him** les noms ne lui disaient rien; **for ∼** (for free) gratuitement; (pointlessly) pour rien

**2** *adv* **it is ∼ like as difficult as** c'est loin d'être aussi difficile que; **she is** *or* **looks ∼ like her sister** elle ne ressemble pas du tout à sa sœur

**3** **nothing but** *phr* **he's ∼ but a coward**

ce n'est qu'un lâche; **they've done ~ but
moan** (colloq) ils n'ont fait que râler (colloq);
**it's caused me ~ but trouble** ça ne m'a valu
que des ennuis

**notice** [1] n **(a)** (written sign) pancarte f;
(advertisement) annonce f; (announcing birth,
marriage, death) avis m
**(b)** (attention) attention f; **to take ~** faire
attention (of à); **to take no ~ (of)** ne pas
faire attention (à)
**(c)** (notification) préavis m; **one month's ~** un
mois de préavis; **until further ~** jusqu'à
nouvel ordre; **at short ~** à la dernière
minute; **to give in one's ~** donner sa
démission
[2] vtr remarquer ⟨absence, mark⟩; **to get
oneself ~d** se faire remarquer

**noticeable** adj visible

**noticeboard** n panneau m d'affichage

**notification** n notification f; (in newspaper)
avis m; **to receive ~ that** être avisé/-e que

**notify** vtr notifier; **to ~ sb of** aviser qn de
⟨result, incident⟩; avertir qn de ⟨intention⟩;
informer qn de ⟨birth, death⟩

**notion** n **(a)** (idea) idée f
**(b)** (understanding) notion f

**notorious** adj ⟨criminal, organization⟩
notoire; ⟨district⟩ mal famé/-e; ⟨case⟩
tristement célèbre

**notoriously** adv notoirement; **they're ~
unreliable** il est bien connu qu'on ne peut
pas compter sur eux

**notwithstanding** [1] adv néanmoins
[2] prep (in spite of) en dépit de; (excepted)
exception faite de

**nought** n zéro m

**noun** n nom m, substantif m

**nourish** vtr nourrir (**with** avec; **on** de)

**nourishment** n nourriture f

**novel** [1] n roman m
[2] adj original/-e

**novelist** n romancier/-ière m/f

**novelty** n nouveauté f (**of doing** de faire)

**November** n novembre m

**novice** n débutant/-e m/f; (in religious order)
novice mf

**now** [1] conj **~ (that)** maintenant que
[2] adv **(a)** maintenant; **do it ~** fais-le
maintenant; **right ~** tout de suite; **any time
~** d'un moment à l'autre; (every) **~ and then**
or **again** de temps en temps
**(b)** (with preposition) **you should have phoned
him before ~** tu aurais dû lui téléphoner
avant; **before** or **until ~** jusqu'à présent; **he
should be finished by ~** il devrait avoir déjà
fini; **between ~ and next Friday** d'ici
vendredi prochain; **between ~ and then** d'ici
là; **from ~ on(wards)** dorénavant
**(c)** (in the past) **it was ~ 4 pm** il était alors 16
heures; **by ~ it was too late** à ce moment-là,
il était trop tard
**(d) ~ there's a man I can trust!** ah! voilà un

homme en qui on peut avoir confiance!;
**careful ~!** attention!; **~ then, let's get back
to work** bon, reprenons le travail

**nowadays** adv (these days) de nos jours;
(now) actuellement

**nowhere** [1] adv nulle part; **I've got ~ else
to go** je n'ai nulle part où aller; **there's ~ to
sit down** il n'y a pas d'endroit pour s'asseoir;
**all this talk is getting us ~** tout ce bavardage
ne nous avance à rien; **flattery will get you
~!** tu n'arriveras à rien en me flattant
[2] **nowhere near** phr loin de; **~ near
sufficient** loin d'être suffisant/-e

**noxious** adj nocif/-ive

**nozzle** n (of hose, pipe) ajutage m; (of hoover)
suceur m; (for icing) douille f

**nuance** n nuance f

**nuclear** adj nucléaire

**nuclear bomb** n bombe f atomique

**nuclear deterrent** n force f de
dissuasion nucléaire

**nuclear energy, nuclear power** n
énergie f nucléaire or atomique

**nuclear power station** n centrale f
nucléaire

**nuclear waste** n déchets mpl nucléaires

**nucleus** n noyau m

**nude** [1] n nu/-e m/f; **in the ~** nu/-e
[2] adj ⟨person⟩ nu/-e

**nudge** vtr (push) pousser du coude;
(accidentally) heurter; (brush against) frôler

**nudist** n, adj nudiste (mf)

**nugget** n pépite f

**nuisance** n (gen) embêtement m; (Law)
nuisance f; **what a ~!** que c'est agaçant!

**nuisance call** n appel m anonyme

**null** adj (Law) **~ and void** nul et non avenu

**nullify** vtr invalider, annuler

**numb** [1] adj **(a)** (from cold) engourdi/-e (**with**
par); (from anaesthetic) insensible; **to go ~**
s'engourdir
**(b)** (figurative) hébété/-e (**with** par)
[2] vtr ⟨cold⟩ engourdir; (Med) insensibiliser;
**to ~ the pain** endormir la douleur

**number** [1] n **(a)** (gen) nombre m; (written
figure) chiffre m; **a three-figure ~** un nombre
à trois chiffres; **a ~ of** un certain nombre de
**(b)** (of bus, house, page, telephone) numéro m; **a
wrong ~** un faux numéro
**(c)** (by performer) (act) numéro m; (song)
chanson f
[2] vtr **(a)** (allocate number to) numéroter
**(b)** (amount to, include) compter
IDIOMS **his days are ~ed** ses jours sont
comptés; **to look after ~ one** penser avant
tout à son propre intérêt

**numberplate** n (GB) plaque f
minéralogique or d'immatriculation

**numeracy** n aptitude f au calcul

**numeral** n chiffre m

**numerical** adj numérique

**numerous** adj nombreux/-euse

**nun** n religieuse f, bonne sœur f

**nurse** ① n (a) (Med) infirmier/-ière m/f;
male ∼ infirmier m
(b) = NURSEMAID
② vtr (a) soigner ⟨person, cold⟩
(b) allaiter ⟨baby⟩
(c) nourrir ⟨grievance, hope⟩

**nursemaid** n nurse f, bonne f d'enfants

**nursery** n (a) (also **day** ∼) crèche f; (in hotel, shop) garderie f
(b) (room) chambre f d'enfants
(c) (for plants) pépinière f

**nursery rhyme** n comptine f

**nursery school** n école f maternelle

**nursing** n profession f d'infirmier/-ière

**nursing home** n (a) (old people's) maison f de retraite; (convalescent) maison f de repos
(b) (GB) (maternity) clinique f obstétrique

**nurture** vtr (a) élever ⟨child⟩; soigner ⟨plant⟩
(b) nourrir ⟨hope, feeling, talent⟩

**nut** n (a) (walnut) noix f; (hazel) noisette f; (almond) amande f; (peanut) cacahuète f

(b) (Tech) écrou m

**nutcracker** n casse-noisettes m inv

**nutmeg** n noix f de muscade

**nutrition** n (process) nutrition f, alimentation f; (science) diététique f

**nutritional** adj ⟨value⟩ nutritif/-ive; ⟨composition, information⟩ nutritionnel/-elle

**nutritious** adj nourrissant/-e

**nutshell** n (a) coquille f de noix or noisette
(b) (figurative) **in a** ∼ en un mot

**nuzzle** vtr frotter son nez contre
■ **nuzzle up**: to ∼ up against or to sb se blottir contre qn

**NVQ** n (abbr = **National Vocational Qualification**) qualification f nationale professionnelle (obtenue par formation continue ou initiale)

**nylon** n nylon® m

**nymph** n nymphe f

# Oo

**o, O** n (a) (letter) o, O m
(b) **O** (spoken number) zéro

**oaf** n (clumsy) balourd/-e m/f; (loutish) mufle m

**oak** ① n chêne m
② adj de or en chêne

**OAP** n (GB) (abbr = **old age pensioner**) retraité/-e m/f

**oar** n rame f

**oasis** n (in desert) oasis f; (figurative) havre m

**oat** n ∼s avoine f
IDIOMS **to sow one's wild** ∼s jeter sa gourme

**oath** n (a) serment m; **under** ∼, **on** ∼ (GB) sous serment
(b) (swearword) juron m

**oatmeal** n (a) (cereal) farine f d'avoine
(b) (US) (porridge) bouillie f d'avoine

**obedience** n obéissance f (**to** à)

**obedient** adj obéissant/-e

**obese** adj obèse

**obesity** n obésité f

**obey** ① vtr obéir à ⟨person, instinct⟩; se conformer à ⟨instructions, law⟩
② vi ⟨person⟩ obéir

**obituary** n (also ∼ **notice**) nécrologie f

**object** ① n (a) (item) objet m
(b) (goal) but m (of de)
(c) (focus) **to be the** ∼ **of** être l'objet de
(d) (in grammar) complément m d'objet
② vtr objecter (**that** que)
③ vi soulever des objections; **to** ∼ **to**

protester contre ⟨attitude, comment⟩; **to** ∼ **to doing** se refuser à faire; **I** ∼ **to their behaviour** je trouve leur comportement inadmissible

**objection** n objection f (**to** à; **from** de la part de); **I've no** ∼(s) je n'y vois pas d'inconvénient

**objectionable** adj ⟨remark⟩ désobligeant/-e; ⟨behaviour, language⟩ choquant/-e; ⟨person⟩ insupportable

**objective** ① n objectif m
② adj objectif/-ive, impartial/-e

**objectively** adv objectivement

**obligation** n (a) (duty) devoir m (**towards, to** envers); **to be under (an)** ∼ **to do** être obligé/-e de faire
(b) (commitment) obligation f (**to** envers; **to do** de faire)
(c) (debt) dette f

**obligatory** adj obligatoire (**to do** de faire)

**oblige** vtr (a) (compel) obliger (**to do** à faire)
(b) (be helpful) rendre service à
(c) **to be** ∼**d to sb** être reconnaissant/-e à qn (**for** de)

**obliging** adj serviable

**obliterate** vtr effacer ⟨trace, word, memory⟩; anéantir ⟨landmark, city⟩

**oblivion** n oubli m

**oblivious** adj (unaware) inconscient/-e; **to be** ∼ **of** or **to** ne pas être conscient/-e de

**oblong** ① n rectangle m
② adj oblong/oblongue, rectangulaire

**obnoxious** *adj* odieux/-ieuse, exécrable

**obscene** *adj* obscène

**obscure** [1] *adj* obscur/-e; (indistinct) vague
[2] *vtr* obscurcir ⟨*truth*⟩; cacher ⟨*view*⟩; **to ~
the issue** embrouiller la question

**observant** *adj* observateur/-trice

**observation** *n* observation *f* (**of** de); **to
keep sb/sth under ~** surveiller qn/qch

**observe** *vtr* (a) (see, notice) observer (**that**
que)
(b) ⟨*doctor, police*⟩ surveiller
(c) (remark) faire observer (**that** que)
(d) observer ⟨*law, custom*⟩

**observer** *n* observateur/-trice *m/f* (**of** de)

**obsess** *vtr* obséder

**obsession** *n* obsession *f*

**obsessive** *adj* ⟨*person*⟩ maniaque;
⟨*neurosis*⟩ obsessionnel/-elle; ⟨*thought*⟩
obsédant/-e

**obsolescence** *n* (gen) désuétude *f*;
**built-in ~** obsolescence *f* planifiée

**obsolete** *adj* ⟨*technology*⟩ dépassé/-e;
⟨*custom, idea*⟩ démodé/-e; ⟨*word*⟩ désuet/-ète

**obstacle** *n* obstacle *m*; **to be an ~** faire
obstacle (**to** à)

**obstacle course** *n* (Mil) parcours *m* du
combattant; (figurative) course *f* d'obstacles

**obstacle race** *n* course *f* d'obstacles

**obstetrician** *n* obstétricien/-ienne *m/f*

**obstinate** *adj* ⟨*person*⟩ têtu/-e (**about** en ce
qui concerne); ⟨*behaviour, silence, effort*⟩
obstiné/-e; ⟨*resistance*⟩ acharné/-e

**obstruct** *vtr* cacher ⟨*view*⟩; bloquer ⟨*road*⟩;
gêner ⟨*traffic, person, progress*⟩; faire
obstruction à ⟨*player*⟩; entraver le cours de
⟨*justice*⟩

**obstruction** *n* (a) (to traffic, progress)
obstacle *m*; (in pipe) bouchon *m*
(b) (in sport) obstruction *f*

**obtain** *vtr* obtenir

**obtrusive** *adj* ⟨*noise*⟩ gênant/-e; ⟨*person,
behaviour*⟩ importun/-e

**obtuse** *adj* ⟨*person*⟩ obtus/-e; ⟨*remark*⟩
stupide

**obvious** [1] *n* **to state the ~** enfoncer les
portes ouvertes
[2] *adj* évident/-e (**to** pour)

**obviously** [1] *adv* manifestement; **she ~
needs help** il est évident qu'elle a besoin
d'aide; **he's ~ lying** il est clair qu'il ment
[2] *excl* bien sûr!, évidemment!

**occasion** *n* occasion *f*; **on one ~** une fois;
**to rise to the ~** se montrer à la hauteur des
circonstances; **on special ~s** dans les
grandes occasions

**occasional** *adj* ⟨*event*⟩ qui a lieu de temps
en temps; **the ~ letter** une lettre de temps en
temps

**occasionally** *adv* de temps à autre; **very
~** très rarement

**occult** *n* **the ~** les sciences *fpl* occultes

**occupant** *n* (a) (of building, bed) occupant/-e
*m/f*

(b) (of vehicle) passager/-ère *m/f*

**occupation** *n* (a) (Mil) occupation *f* (**de** of)
(b) (trade) métier *m*; (profession) profession *f*
(c) (activity) occupation *f*

**occupational** *adj* ⟨*accident*⟩ du travail;
⟨*risk*⟩ du métier; ⟨*safety*⟩ au travail

**occupational hazard** *n* **it's an ~** ça
fait partie des risques du métier

**occupier** *n* occupant/-e *m/f*

**occupy** *vtr* occuper; **to keep oneself
occupied** s'occuper (**by doing** en faisant)

**occur** *vi* (a) (happen) se produire
(b) (be present) se trouver
(c) **the idea ~red to me that...** l'idée m'est
venue à l'esprit que...; **it didn't ~ to me** ça
ne m'est pas venu à l'idée

**occurrence** *n* (a) (event) fait *m*; **to be a
rare ~** se produire rarement
(b) (instance) occurrence *f*
(c) (of disease, phenomenon) cas *m*

**ocean** *n* océan *m*

**o'clock** *adv* **at one ~** à une heure; **it's two
~** il est deux heures

**octagon** *n* octogone *m*

**octave** *n* octave *f*

**October** *n* octobre *m*

**octopus** *n* (a) (Zool) pieuvre *f*
(b) (Culin) poulpe *m*

**OD** *n, vi* (colloq) = OVERDOSE

**odd** [1] *adj* (a) (strange, unusual) ⟨*person,
object, occurrence*⟩ bizarre
(b) ⟨*socks, gloves*⟩ dépareillés
(c) (miscellaneous) **some ~ bits of cloth**
quelques bouts de tissu
(d) ⟨*number*⟩ impair/-e
(e) **to be the ~ one out** ⟨*person, animal,
plant*⟩ être l'exception *f*; ⟨*drawing, word*⟩
être l'intrus *m*; (when selecting team) ⟨*person*⟩
être sans partenaire
[2] **-odd** *combining form* **sixty-~ people/
years** une soixantaine de personnes/d'années

**oddity** *n* (odd thing) bizarrerie *f*; (person)
excentrique *mf*

**odd job** *n* (for money) petit boulot *m*; **~s** (in
house, garden) petits travaux *mpl*

**odd-job man** *n* homme *m* à tout faire

**odds** *n pl* (a) (in betting) cote *f* (**on** sur)
(b) (chance, likelihood) chances *fpl*; **the ~ are
against his winning** il y a peu de chances
qu'il gagne; **to win against the ~** gagner
contre toute attente
**IDIOMS at ~** (in dispute) être en conflit;
(inconsistent) en contradiction (**with** avec)

**odds and ends** *n pl* (GB) bricoles *fpl*
(colloq)

**odour** (GB), **odor** (US) *n* odeur *f*

**of** *prep*

■ **Note** In almost all its uses, the preposition *of* is
translated by *de*. For exceptions, see the entry
below.
– Remember that *de + le* always becomes *du*
and that *de + les* always becomes *des*.
– When *of it* or *of them* are used for something

already referred to, they are translated by *en*: *there's a lot of it* = il y en a beaucoup; *there are several of them* = il y en a plusieurs.

− Note, however, the following expressions used when referring to people: *there are six of them* = ils sont six; *there were several of them* = ils étaient plusieurs.

**(a)** (in most uses) de; **the leg ∼ the table** le pied de la table
**(b)** (made of) en; **a ring (made) ∼ gold** une bague en or
**(c) a friend ∼ mine** un ami à moi; **that's kind ∼ you** c'est très gentil de votre part *or* à vous; **some ∼ us/them** quelques-uns d'entre nous/d'entre eux

**off** [1] *adv* **(a)** (leaving) **to be ∼** partir, s'en aller; **it's time you were ∼** il est temps que tu partes; **I'm ∼** je m'en vais
**(b)** (at a distance) **to be 30 metres ∼** être à 30 mètres; **some way ∼** assez loin
**(c)** (ahead in time) **Easter is a month ∼** Pâques est dans un mois; **the exam is still several months ∼** l'examen n'aura pas lieu avant plusieurs mois
[2] *adj* **(a)** (free) **Tuesday's my day ∼** je ne travaille pas le mardi; **to have the morning ∼** avoir la matinée libre
**(b)** (turned off) **to be ∼** ⟨*water, gas*⟩ être coupé/-e; ⟨*tap*⟩ être fermé/-e; ⟨*light, TV*⟩ être éteint/-e
**(c)** (cancelled) ⟨*match, party*⟩ annulé/-e
**(d)** (removed) **the lid is ∼** il n'y a pas de couvercle; **with her make-up ∼** sans maquillage; **25% ∼** 25% de remise
**(e)** (colloq) (bad) **to be ∼** ⟨*food*⟩ être avarié/-e; ⟨*milk*⟩ avoir tourné/-e
[3] *prep* **(a)** (*also* **just ∼**) juste à côté de ⟨*kitchen*⟩; **∼ the west coast** au large de la côte ouest; **just ∼ the path** tout près du sentier
**(b) it is ∼ the point** là n'est pas la question
**(c)** (colloq) **to be ∼ one's food** ne pas avoir d'appétit
**IDIOMS to feel a bit ∼** (colloq) ne pas être dans son assiette (colloq); **to have an ∼ day** ne pas être dans un de ses bons jours

**off-centre** (GB), **off-center** (US) *adj* décentré/-e

**off-chance** *n* **just on the ∼** au cas où

**off-colour** *adj* (colloq) (unwell) patraque (colloq)

**offence** (GB), **offense** (US) *n* **(a)** (crime) délit *m*
**(b)** (insult) **to cause ∼ to sb** offenser qn; **to take ∼ (at)** s'offenser (de)
**(c)** (Mil) offensive *f*

**offend** [1] *vtr* offenser ⟨*person*⟩
[2] *vi* commettre une infraction (**against** à)

**offender** *n* **(a)** (Law) délinquant/-e *m/f*
**(b)** (culprit) coupable *mf*

**offensive** [1] *n* (Mil, Sport) offensive *f*
[2] *adj* ⟨*remark*⟩ injurieux/-ieuse (**to** pour); ⟨*behaviour*⟩ insultant/-e; ⟨*language*⟩ grossier/-ière

**offer** [1] *n* **(a)** offre *f* (**to do** de faire); **job ∼** offre d'emploi
**(b)** (of goods) **to be on special ∼** être en promotion
[2] *vtr* (gen) offrir; donner ⟨*advice, explanation, information*⟩; émettre ⟨*opinion*⟩; proposer ⟨*service*⟩; **to ∼ sb sth** offrir qch à qn; **to ∼ to do** se proposer pour faire
[3] *vi* se proposer

**offering** *n* (gift) cadeau *m*; (sacrifice) offrande *f*

**offhand** [1] *adj* désinvolte
[2] *adv* **∼, I don't know** comme ça au pied levé je ne sais pas

**office** *n* **(a)** (place) bureau *m*
**(b)** (position) fonction *f*, charge *f*; **public ∼** fonctions *fpl*; **to hold ∼** ⟨*president, mayor*⟩ être en fonction; ⟨*political party*⟩ être au pouvoir

**office block**, **office building** *n* (GB) immeuble *m* de bureaux

**officer** *n* **(a)** (in army, navy) officier *m*
**(b)** (*also* **police ∼**) policier *m*

**office worker** *n* employé/-e *m/f* de bureau

**official** [1] *n* fonctionnaire *mf*; (of party, union) officiel/-ielle *m/f*; (at town hall) employé/-e *m/f*
[2] *adj* officiel/-ielle

**offing** *n* **in the ∼** en perspective

**off-key** *adj* faux/fausse

**off-licence** *n* (GB) magasin *m* de vins et de spiritueux

**off-limits** *adj* interdit/-e

**off-line** *adj* (Comput) (not on the Internet) hors ligne; ⟨*processing*⟩ en différé

**off-load** *vtr* (get rid of) écouler ⟨*goods*⟩; **to ∼ the blame onto sb** rejeter la responsabilité sur qn

**off-message** *adj* (Pol) **to be ∼** être en désaccord avec la politique gouvernementale

**off-peak** *adj* ⟨*electricity*⟩ au tarif de nuit; ⟨*travel*⟩ en période creuse; ⟨*call*⟩ au tarif réduit

**off-putting** *adj* (GB) ⟨*manner*⟩ peu engageant/-e; **it was very ∼** c'était déroutant

**off-road** *vi* rouler en tout terrain

**off-road vehicle** *n* véhicule *m* tout terrain

**off-season** *adj* ⟨*cruise, holiday*⟩ hors saison

**offset** *vtr* compenser (**by** par); **to ∼ sth against sth** mettre qch et qch en balance

**offshore** *adj* ⟨*waters*⟩ du large; ⟨*fishing*⟩ au large; ⟨*oil rig*⟩ offshore *inv*

**offside** [1] *n* (GB) côté *m* conducteur
[2] *adj* **(a)** (GB) ⟨*lane*⟩ (in France) de gauche; (in UK) de droite
**(b)** (Sport) hors jeu *inv*

**offspring** *n* progéniture *f*

**offstage** *adj, adv* dans les coulisses

**off-the-cuff** *adj* ⟨*remark, speech*⟩ impromptu/-e

**off-the-peg** adj ⟨garment⟩ de prêt-à-porter

**off-the-shelf** adj ⟨goods⟩ disponible en magasin; ⟨software⟩ fixe

**off-the-wall** adj (colloq) loufoque (colloq)

**off-white** adj blanc cassé inv

**often** adv souvent; **as ~ as not, more ~ than not** le plus souvent; **how ~ do you meet?** vous vous voyez tous les combien?; **once too ~** une fois de trop; **every so ~** de temps en temps

**oh** excl oh!; **~ dear!** oh là là!; **~ (really)?** ah bon?

**oil** ① n (gen) huile f; (petroleum) pétrole m; **crude ~** pétrole brut; **engine ~** huile de moteur; **heating ~** fioul m
② vtr huiler

**oil change** n vidange f

**oilcloth** n toile f cirée

**oil field** n champ m pétrolifère

**oil painting** n peinture f à l'huile

**oil refinery** n raffinerie f de pétrole

**oil rig** n (offshore) plate-forme f pétrolière offshore; (on land) tour f de forage

**oilseed rape** n colza m

**oilskins** n pl (GB) ciré m

**oil slick** n marée f noire

**oil well** n puits m de pétrole

**oily** adj ⟨cloth, food, hair⟩ gras/grasse; ⟨dressing, substance⟩ huileux/-euse

**ointment** n pommade f

**okay, OK** (colloq) ① n to give sb/sth the **~** donner le feu vert à qn/qch
② adj it's **~** by me ça ne me dérange pas; is it **~** if...? est-ce que ça va si...?; he's **~** (nice) il est sympa (colloq); to feel **~** aller bien; I'm **~** ça va; 'how was the match?'—'**~**' 'comment as-tu trouvé le match?'—'pas mal'
③ adv ⟨cope, work out⟩ (assez) bien
④ particle (a) (giving agreement) d'accord
(b) (introducing topic) bien

**old** adj (a) ⟨person⟩ vieux/vieille (before n), âgé/-e; ⟨object, tradition, song⟩ vieux/vieille (before n); an **~** man un vieil homme, un vieillard; an **~** woman une vieille femme, une vieille; to get **~** vieillir; how **~** are you?** quel âge as-tu?; I'm ten years **~** j'ai dix ans; a six-year-**~** boy un garçon (âgé) de six ans; my **~**er brother mon frère aîné; I'm the **~**est c'est moi l'aîné/-e
(b) (former, previous) ⟨address, school, job, system⟩ ancien/-ienne (before n); in the **~** days autrefois

■ **Note** The irregular form vieil of the adjective vieux/vieille is used before masculine nouns beginning with a vowel or a mute 'h'.

**old age** n vieillesse f

**old-age pensioner, OAP** n (GB) retraité/-e m/f

**old-fashioned** adj ⟨person, ways⟩ vieux jeu inv; ⟨idea, attitude, garment, machine⟩ démodé/-e

**old people's home** n maison f de retraite

**old wives' tale** n conte m de bonne femme

**olive** ① n (a) (fruit) olive f
(b) (also **~ tree**) olivier m
② adj ⟨dress, eyes⟩ vert olive inv; ⟨complexion⟩ olivâtre

**olive green** n, adj vert (m) olive inv

**olive oil** n huile f d'olive

**Olympics** n pl (also **Olympic Games**) jeux mpl Olympiques

**ombudsman** n médiateur m

**omelette** n omelette f

**omen** n présage m

**ominous** adj ⟨cloud⟩ menaçant/-e; ⟨news⟩ inquiétant/-e; ⟨sign⟩ de mauvais augure

**omission** n omission f

**omit** vtr omettre (from de; to do de faire)

**omnipotent** adj omnipotent/-e

**omnipresent** adj omniprésent/-e

**on** ① prep (a) (position) sur ⟨table, coast, motorway⟩; **~ the beach** sur la plage; **~ top of the piano** sur le piano; **~ the floor** par terre; **there's a stain ~ it** il y a une tache dessus; **to live ~ Park Avenue** habiter Park Avenue; **a studio flat ~ Avenue Montaigne** un studio avenue Montaigne; **the paintings ~ the wall** les tableaux sur le mur; **I've got no small change ~ me** je n'ai pas de monnaie sur moi; **to have a smile ~ one's face** sourire; **to hang sth ~ a nail** accrocher qch à un clou; **~ a string** au bout d'une ficelle
(b) (about, on the subject of) sur; **~ Africa** sur l'Afrique
(c) to be **~** faire partie de ⟨team⟩; être membre de ⟨committee⟩
(d) (in expressions of time) **~ 22 February** le 22 février; **~ Friday** vendredi; **~ Saturdays** le samedi; **~ my birthday** le jour de mon anniversaire; **~ sunny days** quand il fait beau
(e) (immediately after) **~ his arrival** à son arrivée; **~ hearing the truth she...** quand elle a appris la vérité, elle...
(f) (taking) to be **~** steroids prendre des stéroïdes; to be **~** drugs se droguer
(g) (powered by) to run **~** batteries fonctionner sur piles; to run **~** electricity marcher à l'électricité
(h) (indicating a medium) **~** TV à la télé; **~** the news aux informations; **~** video en vidéo; **~** drums à la batterie
(i) (earning) to be **~** £20,000 a year gagner 20 000 livres sterling par an; to be **~** a low income avoir un bas salaire
(j) (paid for by) it's **~** me je t'invite
(k) (indicating transport) to travel **~** the bus voyager en bus; **~** the plane dans l'avion; to be **~** one's bike être à vélo; to leave **~** the first train prendre le premier train
② adj (a) while the meeting is **~** pendant la réunion; I've got a lot **~** je suis très occupé; the news is **~** in 10 minutes les informations sont dans 10 minutes; what's **~**? (on TV)

qu'est-ce qu'il y a à la télé?; (at the cinema, theatre) qu'est-ce qu'on joue?; **there's nothing** ~ il n'y a rien de bien
**(b) to be** ~ ⟨*TV, oven, light*⟩ être allumé/-e; ⟨*dishwasher, radio*⟩ marcher; ⟨*tap*⟩ être ouvert/-e; **the power is** ~ il y a du courant
**(c) to be** ~ ⟨*lid*⟩ être mis/-e
**3** *adv* **(a) to have nothing** ~ être nu/-e; **to have make-up** ~ être maquillé/-e; **with slippers** ~ en pantoufles
**(b) from that day** ~ à partir de ce jour-là; **20 years** ~ 20 ans plus tard; **to walk** ~ continuer à marcher; **to go to Paris then** ~ **to Marseilles** aller à Paris et de là à Marseille; **a little further** ~ un peu plus loin
**4** **on and off** *phr* de temps en temps
**5** **on and on** *phr* **to go** ~ **and** ~ ⟨*speaker*⟩ parler pendant des heures; ⟨*speech*⟩ durer des heures; **to go** ~ **and** ~ **about** ne pas arrêter de parler de
**IDIOMS it's just** *or* **simply not** ~ (GB) (out of the question) c'est hors de question; (not the done thing) ça ne se fait pas; (unacceptable) c'est inadmissible

**on-board** *adj* (in-car) embarqué/-e

**once** **1** *n* **just this** ~ pour cette fois; **for** ~ pour une fois
**2** *adv* **(a)** (one time) une fois; ~ **and for all** une (bonne) fois pour toutes; ~ **too often** une fois de trop; ~ **a day** une fois par jour
**(b)** (formerly) autrefois; ~ **upon a time there was a king** il était une fois un roi
**3** *conj* une fois que, dès que
**4** **at once** *phr* **(a)** (immediately) tout de suite; **all at** ~ tout d'un coup
**(b)** (simultaneously) à la fois

**once-over** *n* (colloq) **to give sth the** ~ jeter un rapide coup d'œil à qch; **to give sb the** ~ évaluer qn au premier coup d'œil

**oncoming** *adj* ⟨*car, vehicle*⟩ venant en sens inverse

**one** **1** *det* **(a)** (single) un/une; ~ **car** une voiture; ~ **dog** un chien; **to raise** ~ **hand** lever la main
**(b)** (unique, sole) seul/-e (*before n*); **my** ~ **vice** mon seul vice; **my** ~ **and only tie** ma seule et unique cravate; **the** ~ **and only Edith Piaf** l'incomparable Edith Piaf
**(c)** (same) même; **at** ~ **and the same time** en même temps
**2** *pron* **(a)** (indefinite) un/une *m/f*; **can you lend me** ~? tu peux m'en prêter un/une?; ~ **of them** ( person) l'un d'eux/l'une d'elles; (thing) l'un/l'une *m/f*
**(b)** (impersonal) (as subject) on; (as object) vous; ~ **never knows** on ne sait jamais
**(c)** (demonstrative) **the grey** ~ le gris/la grise; **this** ~ celui-ci/celle-ci; **which** ~? lequel/ laquelle?; **that's the** ~ c'est celui-là/celle-là; **he's/she's the** ~ **who** c'est lui/elle qui
**(e)** ~-**fifty** (in sterling) une livre cinquante
**3** *n* (number) un *m*; (referring to feminine) une *f*; ~ **o'clock** une heure; **in** ~**s and twos** par petits groupes
**4** **one by one** *phr* un par un/une par une
**IDIOMS to be** ~ **up on sb** (colloq) avoir un

avantage sur qn; **to go** ~ **better than sb** faire mieux que qn; **I for** ~ **think that** pour ma part je crois que

**one another** *pron* (*also* **each other**)

■ Note *one another* is very often translated by using a reflexive pronoun (*nous, vous, se, s'*).

**they love** ~ ils s'aiment; **to help** ~ s'entraider; **to worry about** ~ s'inquiéter l'un pour l'autre; **kept apart from** ~ séparés l'un de l'autre

**one-off** *adj* (GB) ⟨*experiment*⟩ unique; ⟨*event, payment*⟩ exceptionnel/-elle

**one-parent family** *n* famille *f* monoparentale

**one-piece** *adj* ~ **swimsuit** maillot *m* de bain une pièce

**one's** *det* son/sa/ses; ~ **books/friends** ses livres/amis; **to wash** ~ **hands** se laver les mains; **to do** ~ **best** faire de son mieux

**oneself** *pron* **(a)** (reflexive) se, s'; **to wash/ cut** ~ se laver/couper
**(b)** (for emphasis) soi-même
**(c)** (after prepositions) soi; **sure of** ~ sûr/-e de soi; **(all) by** ~ tout seul/toute seule

**one-sided** *adj* ⟨*account*⟩ partial/-e; ⟨*contest*⟩ inégal/-e; ⟨*deal*⟩ inéquitable

**one-time** *adj* ancien/-ienne (*before n*)

**one-to-one** *adj* ⟨*talk*⟩ en tête à tête; ~ **meeting** tête-à-tête *m inv*; ~ **tuition** cours *mpl* particuliers

**one-way** *adj* **(a)** ⟨*traffic*⟩ à sens unique; ~ **street** sens *m* unique
**(b)** ~ **ticket** aller *m* simple

**ongoing** *adj* ⟨*process*⟩ continu/-e; ⟨*battle, story*⟩ continuel/-elle

**onion** *n* oignon *m*

**on-line** *adj* (Comput) (on the Internet) en ligne; ⟨*mode*⟩ connecté/-e; ⟨*data processing*⟩ en direct

**onlooker** *n* spectateur/-trice *m/f*

**only** **1** *conj* mais, seulement; **I'd go** ~ **I'm too old** j'irais bien mais je suis trop vieux
**2** *adj* seul/-e; ~ **child** enfant unique
**3** *adv* **(a)** (exclusively) ~ **in Italy can one...** il n'y a qu'en Italie que l'on peut...; ~ **time will tell** seul l'avenir nous le dira; **'men** ~**'** 'réservé aux hommes'
**(b)** (in expressions of time) ~ **yesterday** pas plus tard qu'hier; **it seems like** ~ **yesterday** j'ai l'impression que c'était hier
**(c)** (merely) **you** ~ **had to ask** tu n'avais qu'à demander; **it's** ~ **fair** ce n'est que justice; **he** ~ **grazed his knees** il s'est juste égratigné les genoux; ~ **half the money** juste la moitié de l'argent
**4** **only just** *phr* **(a)** (very recently) **to have** ~ **just done** venir juste de faire
**(b)** (barely) ~ **just wide enough** juste assez large; ~ **just** (narrowly) de justesse
**5** **only too** *phr* ~ **too well** trop bien; ~ **too pleased** trop content/-e

**on-message** *adj* (Pol) **to be** ~ être en accord avec la politique gouvernementale

**o.n.o.** (GB) (*abbr* = **or nearest offer**) à débattre

**on-screen** *adj* sur l'écran

**onset** *n* début *m* (**of** de)

**onside** *adj, adv* en jeu

**on-site** *adj* sur place

**onslaught** *n* attaque *f* (**on** contre)

**on-target earnings, OTE** *n pl* '~ £40,000' 'salaire plus commission pouvant atteindre 40 000 livres sterling'

**on-the-job** *adj* ⟨*training*⟩ sur le lieu de travail

**on the spot** *adv* ⟨*decide*⟩ sur-le-champ; ⟨*killed*⟩ sur le coup; **to be** ~ être sur place

**onto** *prep* (*also* **on to**) sur
IDIOMS **to be** ~ **something** (colloq) être sur une piste

**onus** *n* obligation *f*; **the** ~ **is on sb to do** il incombe à qn de faire

**onward** ① *adj* ⟨*flight*⟩ correspondance *f* (**to** à destination de)
② *adv* = ONWARDS

**onwards** *adv* (*also* **onward**) **to carry** ~ continuer; **from now** ~ à partir d'aujourd'hui; **from that day** ~ à dater de ce jour

**ooze** ① *vtr* **the wound** ~**d blood** du sang suintait de la blessure
② *vi* **to** ~ **with** ⟨*person*⟩ rayonner de ⟨*charm, sexuality*⟩

**opal** *n* opale *f*

**opaque** *adj* opaque

**open** ① *n* **in the** ~ (outside) dehors, en plein air; **to bring sth out into the** ~ mettre qch au grand jour
② *adj* (a) (gen) ouvert/-e; **to be half** ~ ⟨*door*⟩ être entrouvert/-e; **the** ~ **air** le plein air; **in** ~ **country** en rase campagne; **on** ~ **ground** sur un terrain découvert; **the** ~ **road** la grand-route; **the** ~ **sea** la haute mer
(b) (not covered) ⟨*car, carriage*⟩ découvert/-e, décapoté/-e
(c) ~ **to** exposé/-e à ⟨*air, wind, elements*⟩; ~ **to attack** exposé/-e à l'attaque; **to lay oneself** ~ **to criticism** s'exposer (ouvertement) à la critique
(d) ⟨*access, competition*⟩ ouvert/-e à tous; ⟨*meeting*⟩ public/-ique
(e) (candid) ⟨*person*⟩ franc/franche (**about** à propos de)
(f) (blatant) ⟨*hostility, contempt*⟩ non dissimulé/-e
(g) **to leave the date** ~ laisser la date en suspens; **to keep an** ~ **mind** réserver son jugement
③ *vtr* (gen) ouvrir; entamer ⟨*discussions*⟩
④ *vi* (a) ⟨*door, flower, curtain*⟩ s'ouvrir; **to** ~ **onto sth** ⟨*door, window*⟩ donner sur qch
(b) ⟨*shop, bar*⟩ ouvrir; ⟨*meeting, play*⟩ commencer (**with** par)
(c) ⟨*film*⟩ sortir (sur les écrans)
■ **open up**: ¶ ~ **up** (a) ⟨*shop, branch*⟩ ouvrir
(b) ⟨*gap*⟩ se creuser
(c) (figurative) ⟨*person*⟩ se confier
¶ ~ **[sth] up** ouvrir

**open-air** *adj* ⟨*pool, stage*⟩ en plein air

**open day** *n* journée *f* portes ouvertes

**opener** *n* (for bottles) décapsuleur *m*; (for cans) ouvre-boîte *m*

**open-heart surgery** *n* (operation) opération *f* à cœur ouvert

**opening** ① *n* (a) (start) début *m*
(b) (of exhibition, shop) ouverture *f*; (of play, film) première *f*
(c) (gap) trouée *f*
(d) (opportunity) occasion *f* (**to do** de faire); (in market) débouché *m* (**for** pour); (for job) poste *m*
② *adj* ⟨*scene, move*⟩ premier/-ière (**before** *n*); ⟨*remarks*⟩ préliminaire; ⟨*ceremony*⟩ d'inauguration

**opening hours** *n pl* heures *fpl* d'ouverture

**open learning** *n*: formule d'enseignement à distance ou dans un centre ouvert à tous

**open market** *n* marché *m* libre

**open-minded** *adj* **to be** ~ avoir l'esprit ouvert

**open-necked** *adj* ⟨*shirt*⟩ à col ouvert

**open-plan** *adj* ⟨*office*⟩ paysagé/-e

**open ticket** *n* billet *m* ouvert

**Open University, OU** *n* (GB Univ) système d'enseignement universitaire par correspondance ouvert à tous

**opera** *n* opéra *m*

**opera glasses** *n* jumelles *fpl* de théâtre

**opera house** *n* opéra *m*

**operate** ① *vtr* (a) faire marcher ⟨*appliance, vehicle*⟩
(b) pratiquer ⟨*policy, system*⟩
(c) (manage) gérer
② *vi* (a) (do business) opérer
(b) (function) marcher
(c) (run) ⟨*service*⟩ fonctionner
(d) (Med) opérer; **to** ~ **on** opérer ⟨*person*⟩; **to** ~ **on sb's leg** opérer qn à la jambe

**operating instructions** *n pl* mode *m* d'emploi

**operating room** (US), **operating theatre** (GB) *n* salle *f* d'opération

**operating system** *n* système *m* d'exploitation

**operation** *n* (a) (gen, Med) opération *f*; **to have a heart** ~ se faire opérer du cœur
(b) **to be in** ~ ⟨*plan*⟩ être en vigueur; ⟨*machine*⟩ fonctionner; ⟨*oil rig, mine*⟩ être en exploitation

**operational** *adj* (a) (ready to operate) opérationnel/-elle
(b) ⟨*budget, costs*⟩ d'exploitation

**operative** ① *n* (worker) employé/-e *m/f*
② *adj* en vigueur

**operator** *n* (a) (on telephone) standardiste *mf*
(b) (of radio, computer) opérateur *m*
(c) **he's a smooth** ~ il sait s'y prendre

**opinion** *n* opinion *f* (**about** de), avis *m*

(**about, on** sur); **to have a high/low** ∼ **of sb/sth** avoir une bonne/mauvaise opinion de qn/qch; **in my** ∼ à mon avis

**opinionated** *adj* **to be** ∼ avoir des avis sur tout

**opinion poll** *n* sondage *m* d'opinion

**opponent** *n* (in contest) adversaire *mf*; (of regime) opposant/-e *m/f* (**of** à)

**opportune** *adj* ⟨*moment*⟩ opportun/-e

**opportunist** *n, adj* opportuniste ⟨*mf*⟩

**opportunity** *n* occasion *f* (**for** de); **to take the** ∼ **to do** profiter de l'occasion pour faire

**oppose** **1** *vtr* s'opposer à ⟨*plan, bill*⟩; **to be** ∼**d to sth/to doing** être contre qch/contre l'idée de faire

**2 opposing** *pres p adj* ⟨*party, team*⟩ adverse; ⟨*view, style*⟩ opposé/-e

**3 as opposed to** *phr* par opposition à

**opposite** **1** *n* contraire *m* (**to, of** de)

**2** *adj* (gen) opposé/-e; ⟨*building*⟩ d'en face; ⟨*page*⟩ ci-contre; ⟨*effect*⟩ inverse; **at** ∼ **ends of** aux deux bouts de ⟨*table, street*⟩

**3** *adv* en face; **directly** ∼ juste en face

**4** *prep* en face de ⟨*building, park, person*⟩

**opposite number** *n* (gen) homologue *m*; (Sport) adversaire *mf*

**opposition** *n* opposition *f* (**to** à); **the Opposition** (in politics) l'opposition *f*

**oppress** *vtr* opprimer ⟨*people, nation*⟩

**oppressive** *adj* (a) ⟨*law*⟩ oppressif/-ive; (b) ⟨*heat, atmosphere*⟩ oppressant/-e

**opt** *vi* **to** ∼ **for sth** opter pour qch; **to** ∼ **to do** choisir de faire

■ **opt out** décider de ne pas participer (**of** à)

**optical** *adj* optique

**optical illusion** *n* illusion *f* d'optique

**optician** *n* (selling glasses) opticien/-ienne *m/f*; (eye specialist) (GB) optométriste *mf*

**optimism** *n* optimisme *m*

**optimist** *n* optimiste *mf*

**optimistic** *adj* optimiste (**about** quant à)

**optimize** *vtr* optimiser

**optimum** *n, adj* optimum ⟨*m*⟩

**option** *n* option *f* (**to do** de faire); **to have the** ∼ **of doing** pouvoir choisir de faire; **I didn't have much** ∼ je n'avais guère le choix

**optional** *adj* facultatif/-ive; ∼ **extras** accessoires *mpl* en option

**or** *conj* (a) (gen) ou; **black** ∼ **white?** noir ou blanc?; **either here** ∼ **at Dave's** soit ici soit chez Dave; **whether he likes it** ∼ **not** que cela lui plaise ou non; **in a week** ∼ **so** dans huit jours environ; ∼ **should I say** ou bien devrais-je dire

(b) (linking alternatives in the negative) **I can't come today** ∼ **tomorrow** je ne peux venir ni aujourd'hui ni demain; **without food** ∼ **lodgings** sans nourriture ni abri

(c) (otherwise) sinon, autrement

**oral** **1** *n* oral *m*

**2** *adj* ⟨*examination, communication, contraceptive*⟩ oral/-e; ⟨*medicine*⟩ par voie orale

**orange** **1** *n* (a) (fruit) orange *f*

(b) (colour) orange *m*

**2** *adj* orange *inv*

**orange juice** *n* jus *m* d'orange

**orbit** **1** *n* orbite *f*

**2** *vtr* décrire une orbite autour de ⟨*sun, planet*⟩

**orchard** *n* verger *m*

**orchestra** *n* orchestre *m*

**orchestrate** *vtr* orchestrer

**orchid** *n* orchidée *f*

**ordain** *vtr* (a) (decree) décréter (**that** que)

(b) ordonner ⟨*priest*⟩

**ordeal** *n* épreuve *f*

**order** **1** *n* (a) (gen) ordre *m*; **in alphabetical** ∼ dans l'ordre alphabétique; **to restore** ∼ rétablir l'ordre

(b) (command) ordre *m* (**to do** de faire); **to be under** ∼**s to do** avoir (l')ordre de faire

(c) (in shop, restaurant) commande *f*

(d) (operational state) **in working** ∼ en état de marche; **to be out of** ∼ ⟨*phone line*⟩ être en dérangement; ⟨*lift, machine*⟩ être en panne

(e) (all right) **in** ∼ ⟨*documents*⟩ en règle; **that remark was way out of** ∼ cette remarque était tout à fait déplacée

(f) (also **religious** ∼) ordre *m*

**2** *vtr* (a) (command) ordonner; **to** ∼ **sb to do** ordonner à qn de faire

(b) commander ⟨*goods, meal*⟩; réserver ⟨*taxi*⟩ (**for** pour)

**3** *vi* ⟨*diner, customer*⟩ commander

**4 in order that** *phr* (with the same subject) afin de (+ *infinitive*), pour (+ *infinitive*); (when subject of verb changes) afin que (+ *subjunctive*), pour que (+ *subjunctive*)

**5 in order to** *phr* pour, afin de

■ **order about, order around: to** ∼ **people around** donner des ordres

**order form** *n* bon *m* or bulletin *m* de commande

**orderly** **1** *n* (medical) aide-soignant/-e *m/f*

**2** *adj* ⟨*queue*⟩ ordonné/-e; ⟨*pattern, row*⟩ régulier/-ière; ⟨*mind, system*⟩ méthodique; ⟨*crowd, demonstration*⟩ calme

**ordinary** **1** *n* **to be out of the** ∼ sortir de l'ordinaire

**2** *adj* (a) (normal) ⟨*family, life, person*⟩ ordinaire; ⟨*clothes*⟩ de tous les jours

(b) (average) ⟨*consumer, family*⟩ moyen/-enne

(c) (uninspiring) quelconque (derogatory)

**ore** *n* minerai *m*; **iron** ∼ minerai de fer

**organ** *n* (a) (gen) organe *m*

(b) (Mus) orgue *m*

**organ donor** *n* donneur/-euse *m/f* d'organes

**organic** *adj* ⟨*substance, development*⟩ organique; ⟨*produce, farming*⟩ biologique

**organism** *n* organisme *m*

**organization** *n* (a) (group) organisation *f*; (government) organisme *m*; (voluntary) association *f*

(b) (arrangement) organisation *f* (**of** de)

**organize** *vtr* organiser ⟨*event, time, life*⟩; ranger ⟨*books, papers*⟩

**organized crime** *n* grand banditisme *m*

**organizer** *n* (a) (person) organisateur/-trice *m/f*
(b) (*also* **personal ~**) (agenda *m*) organisateur *m*; **electronic ~ agenda** électronique

**organ transplant** *n* transplantation *f* d'organe

**orgy** *n* orgie *f*

**orient** **1** *n* **the Orient** l'Orient *m*
**2** *vtr* (*also* **orientate**) orienter (**towards** vers)

**oriental** *adj* (gen) oriental/-e; ⟨*appearance, eyes*⟩ d'Oriental; ⟨*carpet*⟩ d'Orient

**orienteering** *n* course *f* d'orientation

**origin** *n* origine *f*

**original** **1** *n* original *m*
**2** *adj* (a) (gen) original/-e
(b) (initial) ⟨*inhabitant, owner*⟩ premier/-ière (*before n*); ⟨*question, site*⟩ originel/-elle

**originality** *n* originalité *f*

**originally** *adv* (a) (initially) au départ
(b) (in the first place) à l'origine

**originate** *vi* ⟨*custom, style, tradition*⟩ voir le jour; ⟨*fire*⟩ se déclarer; **to ~ from** ⟨*goods*⟩ provenir de

**originator** *n* (a) (of idea, rumour) auteur *m*
(b) (of invention, system) créateur/-trice *m/f*

**ornament** *n* (a) (trinket) bibelot *m*
(b) (ornamentation) ornement *m*

**ornamental** *adj* ⟨*plant*⟩ ornemental/-e; ⟨*lake*⟩ d'agrément; ⟨*motif*⟩ décoratif/-ive

**ornate** *adj* richement orné/-e

**ornithology** *n* ornithologie *f*

**orphan** *n* orphelin/-e *m/f*

**orphanage** *n* orphelinat *m*

**orthodox** *adj* orthodoxe

**orthopaedic** (GB), **orthopedic** (US) *adj* orthopédique

**ostentatious** *adj* ostentatoire

**osteopath** *n* ostéopathe *mf*

**ostracize** *vtr* ostraciser

**ostrich** *n* autruche *f*

**other** **1** *adj* autre; **the ~ one** l'autre; **the ~ 25** les 25 autres; **~ people** les autres; **he was going the ~ way** il allait dans la direction opposée; **the ~ day** l'autre jour; **every ~ year** tous les deux ans; **every ~ Saturday** un samedi sur deux
**2** *pron* **the ~s** les autres; **~s** (as subject) d'autres; (as object) les autres; **one after the ~** l'un après l'autre; **someone or ~** quelqu'un; **some book or ~** un livre, je ne sais plus lequel; **somehow or ~** d'une manière ou d'une autre
**3** **other than** *phr* **~ than that** à part ça; **nobody knows ~ than you** tu es le seul à le savoir

**otherwise** **1** *adv* autrement; **no woman, married or ~** aucune femme, mariée ou non

**2** *conj* sinon; **it's quite safe, ~ I wouldn't do it** ce n'est pas dangereux du tout, sinon je ne le ferais pas

**otter** *n* loutre *f*

**ouch** *excl* aïe!

**ought** *modal aux* **I ~ to do/to have done** je devrais/j'aurais dû faire; **that ~ to fix it** ça devrait arranger les choses; **oughtn't we to ask?** ne croyez-vous pas que nous devrions demander?; **we ~ to say something** nous devrions dire quelque chose; **someone ~ to have accompanied her** quelqu'un aurait dû l'accompagner

**ounce** *n* once *f* (= *28.35 g*)

**our** *det* notre/nos

■ Note In French, determiners agree in gender and number with the noun that follows. So *our* is translated by *notre* + masculine or feminine singular noun (notre chien, notre maison) and *nos* + plural noun (nos enfants).
– When *our* is stressed, *à nous* is added after the noun: OUR house = notre maison à nous.

**ours** *pron*

■ Note In French, possessive pronouns reflect the number and gender of the noun they are standing for. Thus *ours* is translated by *le nôtre*, *la nôtre* or *les nôtres* according to what is being referred to.

**their children are older than ~** leurs enfants sont plus âgés que les nôtres; **which tickets are ~?** lesquels de ces billets sont les nôtres *or* à nous?; **a friend of ~** un ami à nous; **the blue car is ~** la voiture bleue est à nous; **it's not ~** ce n'est pas à nous

**ourselves** *pron* (a) (reflexive) nous; **we've hurt ~** nous nous sommes fait mal
(b) (emphatic) nous-mêmes; **we did it ~** nous l'avons fait nous-mêmes
(c) (after prepositions) **for ~** pour nous, pour nous-mêmes; **(all) by ~** tout seuls/toutes seules

**out**

■ Note When *out* is used as an adverb meaning *outside*, it often adds little to the sense of the phrase: *they're out in the garden = they're in the garden*. In such cases *out* will not usually be translated: *ils sont dans le jardin*.

**1** *vtr* révéler l'homosexualité de ⟨*person*⟩
**2** *adv* (a) (outside) dehors; **to stay ~ in the rain** rester (dehors) sous la pluie; **~ there** dehors
(b) **to go** *or* **walk ~** sortir; **I couldn't find my way ~** je ne trouvais pas la sortie; **when the tide is ~** à marée basse; **further ~** plus loin; **to invite sb ~ to dinner** inviter qn au restaurant
(c) (absent) **to be ~** être sorti/-e
(d) **to be ~** ⟨*book, exam results*⟩ être publié/-e
(e) **to be ~** ⟨*sun, moon, stars*⟩ briller
(f) **to be ~** ⟨*fire, light*⟩ être éteint/-e
(g) (Sport) **to be ~** ⟨*player*⟩ être éliminé/-e; **'~!'** (of ball) 'out!'

**(h)** (over) **before the week is** ~ avant la fin de la semaine
**(i)** (colloq) **to be** ~ **to do** être bien décidé/-e à faire; **he's just** ~ **for what he can get** c'est l'intérêt qui le guide
**3 out of** phr **(a)** **to go** or **walk** or **come** ~ **of** sortir de; **to jump** ~ **of the window** sauter par la fenêtre; **to take sth** ~ **of one's bag** prendre qch dans son sac
**(b)** (expressing ratio) sur; **two** ~ **of every three** deux sur trois
**(c)** hors de ⟨reach, sight⟩; en dehors de ⟨city⟩; à l'abri de ⟨sun⟩
**(d) to be (right)** ~ **of** ne plus avoir de ⟨item⟩
IDIOMS **to be** ~ **of it** (colloq) être dans les vapes (colloq)

**out-and-out** adj ⟨villain, liar⟩ fieffé/-e; ⟨supporter⟩ pur/-e et dur/-e; ⟨success, failure⟩ total/-e

**outback** n **the** ~ la brousse (australienne)

**outboard motor** n moteur m hors-bord

**outbreak** n (of war) début m; (of violence, spots) éruption f; (of disease) déclaration f

**outbuilding** n dépendance f

**outburst** n accès m

**outcast** n exclu/-e m/f

**outcome** n résultat m

**outcry** n tollé m (**about, against** contre)

**outdated** adj ⟨idea, practice, theory⟩ dépassé/-e; ⟨clothing⟩ démodé/-e

**outdo** vtr surpasser

**outdoor** adj ⟨life, activity, sport⟩ de plein air; ⟨restaurant⟩ en plein air

**outdoors** adv ⟨sit, work, play⟩ dehors; ⟨live⟩ en plein air; ⟨sleep⟩ à la belle étoile; **to go** ~ sortir

**outer** adj **(a)** (outside) extérieur/-e
**(b)** ⟨limit⟩ extrême

**outer space** n espace m (extra-atmosphérique)

**outfit** n tenue f

**outgoing** adj **(a)** (sociable) ouvert/-e et sociable
**(b)** ⟨government⟩ sortant/-e

**outgoings** n pl (GB) sorties fpl (de fonds)

**outgrow** vtr **(a)** (grow too big for) devenir trop grand pour
**(b)** (grow too old for) se lasser de [qch] avec le temps; **he'll** ~ **it** ça lui passera

**outlandish** adj bizarre

**outlast** vtr durer plus longtemps que

**outlaw** **1** n hors-la-loi m inv
**2** vtr déclarer illégal/-e ⟨practice, organization⟩

**outlay** n dépenses fpl (**on** en)

**outlet** n **(a)** (for gas, air, water) tuyau m de sortie
**(b)** retail ~ point m de vente
**(c)** (for emotion, talent) exutoire m
**(d)** (US) (socket) prise f de courant

**outline** **1** n **(a)** (silhouette) contour m
**(b)** (of plan, policy) grandes lignes fpl; (of essay) plan m

**2** vtr exposer brièvement ⟨aims, plan, reasons⟩

**outlive** vtr survivre à ⟨person⟩

**outlook** n **(a)** (attitude) vue f
**(b)** (prospects) perspectives fpl

**outlying** adj (away from city centre) excentré/-e; (remote) isolé/-e

**outnumber** vtr être plus nombreux/-euses que

**out-of-body experience** n **to have an** ~ faire une projection hors du corps

**out-of-date** adj ⟨ticket, passport⟩ périmé/-e; ⟨concept⟩ dépassé/-e

**outpatient** n malade mf externe; ~**s' department** service m de consultation

**outpost** n avant-poste m

**output** n (yield) rendement m; (of factory) production f

**outrage** **1** n **(a)** (anger) indignation f (**at** devant)
**(b)** (atrocity) atrocité f
**(c)** (scandal) scandale m
**2** vtr scandaliser ⟨public⟩

**outrageous** adj scandaleux/-euse; ⟨remark⟩ outrancier/-ière

**outright** **1** adj ⟨control, majority⟩ absolu/-e; ⟨ban⟩ catégorique; ⟨victory, winner⟩ incontesté/-e
**2** adv (gen) catégoriquement; ⟨killed⟩ sur le coup

**outset** n **at the** ~ au début; **from the** ~ dès le début

**outside** **1** n **(a)** extérieur m; **on the** ~ à l'extérieur
**(b)** (maximum) **at the** ~ au maximum
**2** adj extérieur/-e; ~ **lane** (in GB) voie f de droite; (in US, Europe) voie f de gauche; (on athletics track) couloir m extérieur; **an** ~ **chance** une faible chance
**3** adv dehors
**4** prep (also ~ **of**) **(a)** en dehors de ⟨city⟩; de l'autre côté de ⟨boundary⟩; à l'extérieur de ⟨building⟩
**(b)** (in front of) devant ⟨house, shop⟩

**outsider** n **(a)** (in community) étranger/-ère m/f
**(b)** (Sport) outsider m

**outsize** adj ⟨clothes⟩ grande taille

**outskirts** n pl périphérie f

**outsource** vtr sous-traiter

**outsourcing** n sous-traitance f

**outspoken** adj **to be** ~ parler sans détour

**outstanding** adj **(a)** (praiseworthy) remarquable
**(b)** (striking) frappant/-e
**(c)** ⟨bill⟩ impayé/-e; ⟨work⟩ inachevé/-e; ~ **debts** créances fpl à recouvrer

**outstay** vtr **to** ~ **one's welcome** s'éterniser

**outstretched** adj ⟨hand, arm⟩ tendu/-e; ⟨wings⟩ déployé/-e

**outstrip** vtr dépasser ⟨person⟩; excéder ⟨production, demand⟩

**o**

**outward** ① *adj* ⟨*appearance, sign*⟩
extérieur/-e; ⟨*calm*⟩ apparent/-e; ~ **journey**
aller *m*
② *adv* (*also* **outwards**) vers l'extérieur

**outwardly** *adv* (apparently) en apparence

**outwards** = OUTWARD 2

**outweigh** *vtr* l'emporter sur

**outwit** *vtr* être plus futé/-e que ⟨*person*⟩

**outworker** *n* travailleur/-euse *m/f* à
domicile

**oval** *n, adj* ovale (*m*)

**ovary** *n* ovaire *m*

**ovation** *n* ovation *f*; **to give sb a standing**
~ se lever pour ovationner qn

**oven** *n* four *m*

**oven glove** *n* manique *f*

**over**

■ Note *over* is often used with another
preposition in English (*to, in, on*) without altering
the meaning. In this case *over* is usually not
translated in French: *to be over in France* = être
en France; *to swim over to sb* = nager vers qn.

① *prep* (a) par-dessus; **he jumped** ~ **it** il a
sauté par-dessus; **to wear a sweater** ~ **one's
shirt** porter un pull par-dessus sa chemise; **a
bridge** ~ **the Thames** un pont sur la Tamise
(b) (across) **it's just** ~ **the road** c'est juste de
l'autre côté de la rue; ~ **here/there** par ici/
là; **come** ~ **here!** viens (par) ici!
(c) (above) au-dessus de; **they live** ~ **the shop**
ils habitent au-dessus de la boutique;
**children** ~ **six** les enfants de plus de six ans;
**temperatures** ~ **40°** des températures
supérieures à *or* au-dessus de 40°
(d) (in the course of) ~ **the weekend** pendant
le week-end; ~ **the last few days** au cours de
ces derniers jours; ~ **the years** avec le
temps; ~ **Christmas** à Noël
(e) **to be** ~ s'être remis/-e de ⟨*illness,
operation*⟩; **to be** ~ **the worst** avoir passé le
pire
(f) (by means of) ~ **the phone** par téléphone;
~ **the radio** à la radio
(g) (everywhere) **all** ~ **the house** partout dans
la maison
② *adj, adv* (a) (finished) **to be** ~ ⟨*term,
meeting*⟩ être terminé/-e; ⟨*war*⟩ être fini/-e
(b) (more) **children of six and** ~ les enfants
de plus de six ans
(c) **to invite** *or* **ask sb** ~ inviter qn; **we had
them** ~ **on Sunday** ils sont venus dimanche
(d) (on radio, TV) ~ **to you** à vous; **now** ~ **to
our Paris studios** nous passons l'antenne à
nos studios de Paris
(e) (showing repetition) **five times** ~ cinq fois de
suite; **to start all** ~ **again** recommencer à
zéro; **I had to do it** ~ (US) j'ai dû
recommencer; **I've told you** ~ **and** ~
(**again**)... je t'ai dit je ne sais combien de
fois...

**overact** *vi* en faire trop

**overall** ① *n* (GB) (coat-type) blouse *f*; (child's)
tablier *m*

② **overalls** *n pl* (GB) combinaison *f*; (US)
salopette *f*
③ *adj* ⟨*cost*⟩ global/-e; ⟨*improvement*⟩
général/-e; ⟨*effect*⟩ d'ensemble; ⟨*majority*⟩
absolu/-e
④ *adv* (a) (in total) en tout
(b) (in general) dans l'ensemble

**overawe** *vtr* intimider

**overbalance** *vi* ⟨*person*⟩ perdre
l'équilibre; ⟨*pile of objects*⟩ s'écrouler

**overboard** *adv* par-dessus bord, à l'eau

**overbook** *vtr, vi* surréserver

**overcast** *adj* ⟨*sky*⟩ couvert/-e

**overcharge** *vtr* faire payer trop cher à

**overcoat** *n* pardessus *m*

**overcome** ① *vtr* battre ⟨*opponent*⟩;
vaincre ⟨*enemy*⟩; surmonter ⟨*dislike, fear*⟩; **to
be** ~ **with despair** succomber au désespoir
② *vi* triompher

**overcook** *vtr* trop cuire

**overcrowded** *adj* ⟨*train, room*⟩ bondé/-e;
⟨*city*⟩ surpeuplé/-e; ⟨*class*⟩ surchargé/-e

**overcrowding** *n* (in city, institution)
surpeuplement *m*; (in transport)
surencombrement *m*; ~ **in classrooms** les
classes surchargées

**overdo** *vtr* **to** ~ **it** (when describing) exagérer;
(when performing) forcer la note (colloq); (when
working) en faire trop (colloq)

**overdose, OD** ① *n* (large dose) surdose *f*;
(lethal dose) dose *f* mortelle; (of medicine) dose *f*
drugs) overdose *f*; **to take an** ~ absorber une
dose excessive de médicaments
② *vi* (on medicine) prendre une dose mortelle
de médicaments; (on drugs) faire une overdose

**overdraft** *n* découvert *m*

**overdrawn** *adj* à découvert

**overdressed** *adj* trop habillé/-e

**overdrive** *n* **to go into** ~ ⟨*person*⟩ s'activer
intensivement

**overdue** *adj* ⟨*baby, work*⟩ en retard (by
de); ⟨*bill*⟩ impayé/-e; **this measure is long** ~
cette mesure aurait dû être prise il y a
longtemps

**overeat** *vi* manger à l'excès

**overestimate** *vtr* surestimer

**overexcited** *adj* surexcité/-e

**overflow** ① *vtr* ⟨*river*⟩ inonder ⟨*banks*⟩
② *vi* déborder (into dans; with de)

**overgrown** *adj* ⟨*garden*⟩ envahi/-e par la
végétation

**overhaul** ① *n* (of machine) révision *f*; (of
system) restructuration *f*
② *vtr* réviser ⟨*car, machine*⟩; restructurer
⟨*system*⟩

**overhead** ① *adj* ⟨*cable, railway*⟩
aérien/-ienne
② *adv* (a) (in sky) dans le ciel
(b) (above sb's head) au-dessus de ma/sa etc
tête

**overhead projector** *n* rétroprojecteur
*m*

**overheads** *n pl* frais *mpl* généraux

**overhear** *vtr* entendre par hasard

**overheat** *vi* ⟨*car, equipment*⟩ chauffer

**overindulge** *vi* faire des excès

**overjoyed** *adj* fou/folle de joie (**at** devant)

**overkill** *n* (excess publicity) matraquage *m*

**overland** ⟦1⟧ *adj* ⟨*route*⟩ terrestre; ⟨*journey*⟩ par route
⟦2⟧ *adv* par route

**overlap** *vi* se chevaucher

**overleaf** *adv* au verso

**overload** *vtr* surcharger (**with** de)

**overlook** *vtr* (a) ⟨*building, window*⟩ donner sur
(b) (miss) ne pas voir ⟨*detail, error*⟩; **to ~ the fact that** négliger le fait que
(c) (ignore) ignorer ⟨*effect, need*⟩

**overnight** ⟦1⟧ *adj* (a) ⟨*journey, train*⟩ de nuit; ⟨*stop*⟩ pour une nuit
(b) ⟨*success*⟩ immédiat/-e
⟦2⟧ *adv* (a) **to stay ~** passer la nuit
(b) ⟨*change, disappear, transform*⟩ du jour au lendemain

**overnight bag** *n* petit sac *m* de voyage

**overpopulated** *adj* surpeuplé/-e

**overpower** *vtr* (a) maîtriser ⟨*thief*⟩; vaincre ⟨*army*⟩
(b) ⟨*smell, smoke*⟩ accabler

**overpowering** *adj* ⟨*person*⟩ intimidant/-e; ⟨*desire, urge*⟩ irrésistible; ⟨*heat*⟩ accablant/-e; ⟨*smell*⟩ irrespirable

**overpriced** *adj* **it's ~** c'est trop cher pour ce que c'est

**overqualified** *adj* surqualifié/-e

**overrated** *adj* ⟨*person, work*⟩ surfait/-e

**overreact** *vi* réagir de façon excessive

**override** *vtr* l'emporter sur ⟨*consideration*⟩; passer outre à ⟨*decision*⟩

**overriding** *adj* ⟨*importance*⟩ primordial/-e; ⟨*priority*⟩ numéro un

**overrule** *vtr* **to be ~d** ⟨*decision*⟩ être annulé/-e

**overrun** *vtr* (a) (invade) envahir ⟨*country, site*⟩
(b) (exceed) dépasser ⟨*time, budget*⟩

**overseas** ⟦1⟧ *adj* (a) ⟨*student, investor*⟩ étranger/-ère
(b) ⟨*trade, market*⟩ extérieur/-e
⟦2⟧ *adv* à l'étranger

**overshadow** *vtr* éclipser ⟨*achievement*⟩

**oversight** *n* erreur *f*; **due to an ~** par inadvertance

**oversimplify** *vtr* simplifier [qch] à l'excès

**oversleep** *vi* se réveiller trop tard

**overspend** *vi* trop dépenser

**overstay** *vtr* **to ~ one's visa** dépasser la limite de validité de son visa

**overstep** *vtr* dépasser ⟨*bounds*⟩; **to ~ the mark** aller trop loin

**overt** *adj* évident/-e, manifeste

**overtake** *vtr*, *vi* dépasser

**over-the-top**, **OTT** *adj* (colloq) outrancier/-ière; **to go over the top** aller trop loin

**overthrow** *vtr* renverser ⟨*government, system*⟩

**overtime** ⟦1⟧ *n* heures *fpl* supplémentaires
⟦2⟧ *adv* **to work ~** ⟨*person*⟩ faire des heures supplémentaires

**overtone** *n* sous-entendu *m*, connotation *f*

**overture** *n* ouverture *f*

**overturn** ⟦1⟧ *vtr* (a) renverser ⟨*car, chair*⟩; faire chavirer ⟨*boat*⟩
(b) faire annuler ⟨*decision, sentence*⟩
⟦2⟧ *vi* ⟨*car, chair*⟩ se renverser; ⟨*boat*⟩ chavirer

**overweight** *adj* (a) ⟨*person*⟩ trop gros/grosse
(b) ⟨*suitcase*⟩ trop lourd/-e

**overwhelm** ⟦1⟧ *vtr* (a) ⟨*wave, avalanche*⟩ submerger; ⟨*enemy*⟩ écraser
(b) ⟨*shame, grief*⟩ accabler
⟦2⟧ **overwhelmed** *pp adj* (with letters, offers, kindness) submergé/-e (**with, by** de); (with shame, work) accablé/-e (**with, by** de); (by sight, experience) ébloui/-e (**by** par)

**overwhelming** *adj* ⟨*defeat, victory, majority*⟩ écrasant/-e; ⟨*desire*⟩ irrésistible; ⟨*heat, sorrow*⟩ accablant/-e; ⟨*support*⟩ massif/-ive

**overwork** *vi* se surmener

**overworked** *adj* surmené/-e

**owe** *vtr* devoir; **to ~ sth to sb** devoir qch à qn

**owing** ⟦1⟧ *adj* à payer, dû/-e
⟦2⟧ **owing to** *phr* en raison de

**owl** *n* hibou *m*; (with tufted ears) chouette *f*

**own** ⟦1⟧ *adj* propre; **her ~ car** sa propre voiture
⟦2⟧ *pron* **my ~** le mien, la mienne; **his/her ~** le sien, la sienne; **he has a room of his ~** il a sa propre chambre *or* une chambre à lui; **a house of our (very) ~** une maison (bien) à nous
⟦3⟧ *vtr* avoir ⟨*car, house, dog*⟩; **she ~s three shops** elle est propriétaire de trois magasins; **who ~s that house?** à qui est cette maison?
IDIOMS **to get one's ~ back** se venger (**on sb** de qn); **on one's ~** tout seul/toute seule
■ **own up** avouer

**owner** *n* propriétaire *mf*; **car ~** automobiliste *mf*; **home ~** propriétaire *mf*

**ownership** *n* propriété *f*; (of land) possession *f*

**ox** *n* bœuf *m*

**oxygen** *n* oxygène *m*

**oyster** *n* huître *f*

**ozone** *n* ozone *m*

**ozone layer** *n* couche *f* d'ozone

**O**

# Pp

**p, P** *n* p, P *m*

**PA** *n* (*abbr* = **personal assistant**) secrétaire *mf* de direction

**pace** ① *n* (step) pas *m*; (rate) rythme *m*; (speed) vitesse *f*; **at a fast/slow ~** vite/ lentement; **at walking ~** au pas
② *vi* **to ~ up and down** faire les cent pas; **to ~ up and down** arpenter ⟨*cage, room*⟩

**pacemaker** *n* (a) (Med) stimulateur *m* cardiaque
(b) (athlete) lièvre *m*

**Pacific** *pr n* **the ~** le Pacifique; **the ~ Ocean** l'océan Pacifique

**pacifist** *n*, *adj* pacifiste (*mf*)

**pacify** *vtr* apaiser ⟨*person*⟩; pacifier ⟨*country*⟩

**pack** ① *n* (a) (box) paquet *m*; (large box) boîte *f*; (bag) sachet *m*
(b) (group) bande *f*; (of hounds) meute *f*; **a ~ of lies** un tissu de mensonges
(c) (in rugby) pack *m*
(d) (of cards) jeu *m* de cartes
(e) (backpack) sac *m* à dos
② *vtr* (a) (in suitcase) mettre [qch] dans une valise ⟨*clothes*⟩; (in box, crate) emballer ⟨*ornaments, books*⟩
(b) emballer ⟨*box, crate*⟩; **to ~ one's suitcase** faire sa valise
(c) ⟨*crowd*⟩ remplir complètement ⟨*church, theatre*⟩
(d) tasser ⟨*snow, earth*⟩
③ *vi* (a) ⟨*person*⟩ faire ses valises
(b) **to ~ into** ⟨*crowd*⟩ s'entasser dans ⟨*place*⟩
■ **pack up**: ¶ **~ up** (a) ⟨*person*⟩ faire ses valises
(b) (colloq) (break down) ⟨*TV, machine*⟩ se détraquer (colloq); ⟨*car*⟩ tomber en panne
¶ **~** [sth] **up, ~ up** [sth] (in boxes, crates) emballer

**package** ① *n* (a) (parcel) paquet *m*, colis *m*
(b) (of proposals, measures, aid) ensemble *m* (**of** de)
(c) (Comput) progiciel *m*
② *vtr* conditionner, emballer

**package deal** *n* offre *f* globale

**package holiday** (GB), **package tour** *n* voyage *m* organisé

**packaging** *n* conditionnement *m*

**packed** *adj* comble; **~ with** plein/-e de

**packed lunch** *n* panier-repas *m*

**packet** *n* (gen) paquet *m*; (sachet) sachet *m*

**packing** *n* (a) (packaging) emballage *m*
(b) **to do one's ~** faire ses valises

**pact** *n* pacte *m*

**pad** ① *n* (a) (of paper) bloc *m*
(b) (for leg) jambière *f*
(c) (of paw) coussinet *m*; (of finger) pulpe *f*

(d) (*also* **launch ~**) rampe *f* de lancement
② *vtr* rembourrer ⟨*chair, shoulders, jacket*⟩ (**with** avec); capitonner ⟨*walls*⟩
③ *vi* **to ~ along/around** avancer/aller et venir à pas feutrés
■ **pad out** étoffer, délayer ⟨*essay, speech*⟩

**padded envelope** *n* enveloppe *f* matelassée

**padding** *n* (stuffing) rembourrage *m*

**paddle** ① *n* (a) (oar) pagaie *f*
(b) **to go for a ~** faire trempette *f*
② *vi* (a) (row) pagayer
(b) (wade) patauger
(c) ⟨*duck, swan*⟩ barboter

**paddling pool** *n* (public) pataugeoire *f*; (inflatable) piscine *f* gonflable

**padlock** ① *n* (on door) cadenas *m*; (for bicycle) antivol *m*
② *vtr* cadenasser ⟨*door, gate*⟩; mettre un antivol à ⟨*bicycle*⟩

**paediatrician** (GB), **pediatrician** (US) *n* pédiatre *mf*

**paedophile** (GB), **pedophile** (US) *n* pédophile *mf*

**pagan** *n*, *adj* païen/païenne (*m/f*)

**page** ① *n* (a) (in book) page *f*; **on ~ two** à la page deux
(b) (attendant) groom *m*; (US) coursier *m*
② *vtr* (on pager) rechercher; (over loudspeaker) faire appeler

**pageant** *n* (play) reconstitution *f* historique; (carnival) fête *f* à thème historique

**pageboy** *n* (at wedding) garçon *m* d'honneur

**pager** *n* récepteur *m* d'appel

**paid** *adj* ⟨*work, job*⟩ rémunéré/-e; ⟨*holiday*⟩ payé/-e; **~ assassin** tueur *m* à gages

**pain** ① *n* (a) douleur *f*; **to be in ~** souffrir; **period ~s** règles *fpl* douloureuses
(b) (colloq) (annoying person, thing) **he's/it's a ~** il est/c'est enquiquinant (colloq); **he's a ~ in the neck** (colloq) il est casse-pieds (colloq)
② **pains** *n pl* **to be at ~s to do** prendre grand soin de faire; **to take great ~s over** *or* **with sth** se donner beaucoup de mal pour qch

**painful** *adj* douloureux/-euse; ⟨*lesson, memory*⟩ pénible

**painkiller** *n* analgésique *m*

**painless** *adj* (a) (pain-free) indolore
(b) (trouble-free) sans peine

**painstaking** *adj* minutieux/-ieuse

**paint** ① *n* peinture *f*
② **paints** *n pl* couleurs *fpl*
③ *vtr* (a) (gen) peindre; peindre le portrait de ⟨*person*⟩; **to ~ one's nails** se vernir les ongles
(b) (depict) dépeindre

4 *vi* peindre

**paintbox** *n* boîte *f* de couleurs

**paintbrush** *n* pinceau *m*

**painter** *n* peintre *m*

**painting** *n* (a) (activity, art form) peinture *f*
(b) (work of art) tableau *m*; (unframed) toile *f*;
(of person) portrait *m*
(c) (decorating) peintures *fpl*

**pair** *n* (a) (gen) paire *f*; **to be one of a ∼**
faire partie d'une paire; **in ∼s** ⟨*work*⟩ en
groupes de deux; **a ∼ of scissors** une paire
de ciseaux; **a ∼ of trousers** un pantalon
(b) (couple) couple *m*
■ **pair off** (as a couple) se mettre ensemble;
(for temporary purposes) se mettre par deux
■ **pair up** ⟨*dancers, lovers*⟩ former un
couple; ⟨*competitors*⟩ faire équipe

**paisley** *n* tissu *m* à motifs cachemire

**pajamas** (US) = PYJAMAS

**Pakistan** *pr n* Pakistan *m*

**Pakistani** 1 *n* Pakistanais/-e *m/f*
2 *adj* pakistanais/-e

**palace** *n* palais *m*

**palatable** *adj* ⟨*food*⟩ savoureux/-euse;
⟨*solution, idea*⟩ acceptable

**palate** *n* palais *m*

**pale** 1 *adj* (gen) pâle; ⟨*light, dawn*⟩
blafard/-e; **to turn** *or* **go ∼** pâlir
2 *vi* pâlir; **to ∼ into insignificance** devenir
dérisoire

**Palestine** *pr n* Palestine *f*

**Palestinian** 1 *n* Palestinien/-ienne *m/f*
2 *adj* palestinien/-ienne

**palette** *n* palette *f*

**pallet** *n* (for loading) palette *f*

**pallid** *adj* ⟨*skin, light*⟩ blafard/-e

**palm** *n* (a) paume *f*; **in the ∼ of one's hand**
dans le creux de la main; **he read my ∼** il
m'a lu les lignes de la main
(b) (*also* ∼ **tree**) palmier *m*
(c) (*also* ∼ **leaf**) palme *f*
■ **palm off** (colloq): **to ∼ sth off** faire passer
qch (as pour); **to ∼ sth off on sb, to ∼ sb
off with sth** refiler (colloq) qch à qn

**Palm Sunday** *n* dimanche *m* des
Rameaux

**palmtop** *n* (*also* ∼ **computer**)
ordinateur *m* de poche

**palpable** *adj* ⟨*fear, tension*⟩ palpable; ⟨*lie,
error, nonsense*⟩ manifeste

**palpitate** *vi* palpiter (with de)

**paltry** *adj* ⟨*sum*⟩ dérisoire; ⟨*excuse*⟩ piètre
(before n)

**pamper** *vtr* choyer ⟨*person, pet*⟩

**pamphlet** *n* brochure *f*; (political) tract *m*

**pan** 1 *n* (saucepan) casserole *f*
2 *vtr* (a) (colloq) (criticize) éreinter
(b) (in photography) faire un panoramique de

**pancake** *n* crêpe *f*

**pancake day** *n* mardi *m* gras

**pandemonium** *n* tohu-bohu *m*

**pander** *vi* **to ∼ to** céder aux exigences de
⟨*person*⟩; flatter ⟨*whim*⟩

**pane** *n* vitre *f*, carreau *m*; **a ∼ of glass** une
vitre, un carreau

**panel** *n* (a) (of experts, judges) commission *f*;
(on discussion programme) invités *mpl*; (on quiz
show) jury *m*
(b) (section of wall) panneau *m*
(c) (of instruments, switches) tableau *m*

**pang** *n* (a) (emotional) serrement *m* de cœur;
**a ∼ of jealousy** une pointe de jalousie
(b) **∼s of hunger** crampes *fpl* d'estomac

**panhandler** *n* (US) (colloq) mendiant/-e *m/f*

**panic** 1 *n* panique *f*, affolement *m*
2 *vtr* affoler ⟨*person, animal*⟩; semer la
panique dans ⟨*crowd*⟩
3 *vi* s'affoler

**panic buying** *n* achats *mpl* par crainte
de la pénurie

**panic-stricken** *adj* pris/-e de panique

**panorama** *n* panorama *m*

**pansy** *n* pensée *f*

**pant** *vi* haleter

**panther** *n* (a) (leopard) panthère *f*
(b) (US) (puma) puma *m*

**pantomime** *n* (GB) spectacle *m* pour
enfants

**pantry** *n* garde-manger *m inv*

**pants** *n pl* (a) (US) (trousers) pantalon *m*
(b) (GB) (underwear) slip *m*

**panty hose** *n* (US) collant *m*

**panty-liner** *n* protège-slip *m*

**paper** 1 *n* (a) (for writing, drawing) papier *m*;
**a piece of ∼** (scrap) un bout de papier; (clean
sheet) une feuille (de papier); (for wrapping) un
morceau de papier; **writing/tissue ∼** papier
à lettres/de soie
(b) (*also* **wall∼**) papier *m* peint
(c) (newspaper) journal *m*
(d) article *m* (on sur); (lecture)
communication *f* (on sur)
(e) (exam) épreuve *f* (on de)
2 **papers** *n pl* (documents) papiers *mpl*
3 *adj* ⟨*bag, hat, handkerchief, napkin*⟩ en
papier; ⟨*plate, cup*⟩ en carton
4 *vtr* tapisser ⟨*room, wall*⟩

**paperback** *n* livre *m* de poche

**paperclip** *n* trombone *m*

**paper knife** *n* coupe-papier *m inv*

**paper round** *n* **he does a ∼** il livre des
journaux

**paper shop** *n* marchand *m* de journaux

**paper towel** *n* essuie-tout *m inv*

**paperweight** *n* presse-papier *m inv*

**paperwork** *n* (administration) travail *m*
administratif; (documentation) documents *mpl*

**par** *n* (a) **to be on a ∼ with** ⟨*performance*⟩
être comparable à; ⟨*person*⟩ être l'égal/-e de;
**to be up to ∼** être à la hauteur; **to be below**
*or* **under ∼** ⟨*performance*⟩ être en dessous de
la moyenne; ⟨*person*⟩ ne pas se sentir en
forme
(b) (in golf) par *m*

**parachute** 1 *n* parachute *m*
2 *vi* descendre en parachute

p

**parachute drop** n parachutage m
**parachute jump** n saut m en parachute
**parachuting** n parachutisme m
**parade** [1] n (a) (procession) parade f
(b) (Mil) défilé m
[2] vtr (display) faire étalage de
[3] vi défiler (**through** dans); **to ~ up and down** ⟨soldier, model⟩ défiler; ⟨child⟩ parader
**parade ground** n champ m de manœuvres
**paradise** n paradis m; **in ~** au paradis
**paradox** n paradoxe m
**paradoxical** adj paradoxal/-e
**paraffin** n (a) (GB) (fuel) pétrole m
(b) (also **~ wax**) paraffine f
**paragliding** n parapente m
**paragon** n modèle m (**of** de)
**paragraph** n paragraphe m
**parallel** [1] n (a) (gen) parallèle m
(b) (in mathematics) parallèle f
[2] adj (a) (gen) parallèle (**to, with** à)
(b) (similar) analogue (**to, with** à)
[3] adv **~ to, ~ with** parallèlement à
**paralyse** (GB), **paralyze** (US) vtr paralyser
**paralysis** n paralysie f
**paramedic** n auxiliaire mf médical/-e
**parameter** n paramètre m
**paramilitary** [1] n membre m d'une organisation paramilitaire
[2] adj paramilitaire
**paramount** adj **to be ~, to be of ~ importance** être d'une importance capitale
**paranoid** adj (Med) paranoïde; (gen) paranoïaque (**about** au sujet de)
**paraphernalia** n attirail m
**paraphrase** vtr paraphraser
**parascending** n parachutisme m ascensionnel
**parasite** n parasite m
**paratrooper** n parachutiste m
**parcel** n paquet m, colis m
IDIOMS **to be part and ~ of** faire partie intégrante de
■ **parcel up: ~ up** [sth], **~** [sth] **up** emballer
**parcel bomb** n colis m piégé
**parched** adj (a) (dry) desséché/-e
(b) (thirsty) **to be ~** mourir de soif
**parchment** n (document) parchemin m; (paper) papier-parchemin m
**pardon** [1] n (a) (gen) pardon m
(b) (Law) (also **free ~**) grâce f
[2] excl (what?) pardon?; (sorry!) pardon!
[3] vtr (a) (gen) pardonner; **~ me!** pardon!
(b) (Law) gracier ⟨criminal⟩
**parent** n parent m
**parental** adj des parents, parental/-e
**parent company** n maison f mère
**parenthood** n (fatherhood) paternité f; (motherhood) maternité f
**parenting** n éducation f des enfants

**parents' evening** n réunion f pour les parents d'élèves
**Paris** pr n Paris
**parish** n (a) paroisse f
(b) (GB) (administrative) commune f
**Parisian** [1] n Parisien/-ienne m/f
[2] adj parisien/-ienne
**park** [1] n (a) (public garden) jardin m public, parc m
(b) (estate) parc m
[2] vtr garer ⟨car⟩
[3] vi ⟨driver⟩ se garer
[4] **parked** pp adj en stationnement
**park-and-ride** n parking m relais
**parking** n stationnement m; **'No ~'** 'stationnement interdit'
**parking lot** n (US) parking m
**parking meter** n parcmètre m
**parking place, parking space** n place f
**parking ticket** n (fine) contravention f, PV m (colloq)
**parliament** n parlement m
**parliamentary** adj parlementaire
**parlour** (GB), **parlor** (US) n petit salon m
**parody** [1] n parodie f
[2] vtr parodier ⟨person, style⟩
**parole** n liberté f conditionnelle; **on ~** en liberté conditionnelle
**parrot** n perroquet m
**parry** vtr (a) (Sport) parer
(b) éluder ⟨question⟩
**parsley** n persil m
**parsnip** n panais m
**part** [1] n (a) (of whole) partie f; (of country) région f; **to be a ~ of** faire partie de; **that's the best/hardest ~** c'est ça le meilleur/le plus dur; **for the most ~** dans l'ensemble
(b) (Tech) (component) pièce f; **spare ~s** pièces détachées
(c) (of serial) épisode m
(d) (role) rôle m (**in** dans); **to take ~** participer (**in** à)
(e) (actor's role) rôle m (**of** de)
(f) (measure) mesure f
(g) (behalf) **on the ~ of** de la part de; **for my ~** pour ma part
(h) (US) (in hair) raie f
[2] adv en partie; **~ French, ~ Chinese** moitié français, moitié Chinois
[3] vtr séparer ⟨two people⟩; écarter ⟨legs⟩; entrouvrir ⟨lips, curtains⟩; **to ~ one's hair** se faire une raie
[4] vi (a) (split up) se séparer; **to ~ from sb** quitter qn
(b) ⟨crowd, clouds⟩ s'ouvrir
■ **part with** se séparer de ⟨object⟩; **to ~ with money** débourser
**part exchange** n (GB) reprise f; **to take sth in ~** reprendre qch
**partial** adj (a) (not complete) partiel/-ielle
(b) (biased) partial/-e
(c) (fond) **to be ~ to** avoir un faible pour

**partially sighted** n the ~ les malvoyants mpl

**participant** n participant/-e m/f (in à)

**participate** vi participer (in à)

**participation** n participation f (in à)

**participle** n participe m

**particle** n particule f

**particular** ①︎ adj (a) (gen) particulier/-ière; for no ~ reason sans raison particulière
(b) (fussy) méticuleux/-euse; to be ~ about être exigeant/-e sur ⟨cleanliness, punctuality⟩; prendre grand soin de ⟨appearance⟩; être difficile pour ⟨food⟩
②︎ in particular phr en particulier

**particularly** adv (a) (in particular) en particulier
(b) (especially) spécialement

**particulars** n pl (information) détails mpl; (name, address) coordonnées fpl

**parting** n (a) séparation f
(b) (GB) (in hair) raie f

**partisan** n (gen, Mil) partisan m

**partition** ①︎ n (a) (in room, house) cloison f
(b) (of country) partition f
②︎ vtr (a) cloisonner ⟨area, room⟩
(b) diviser ⟨country⟩

**partly** adv en partie

**partner** n (a) (professional) associé/-e m/f (in dans)
(b) (economic, political, sporting) partenaire m
(c) (married) époux/-se m/f; (unmarried) partenaire mf

**partnership** n association f; to go into ~ with s'associer à

**part of speech** n partie f du discours

**part-time** adj, adv à temps partiel

**party** n (a) (social event) fête f; (in evening) soirée f; (formal) réception f; to have a ~ faire une fête; **birthday** ~ (fête d')anniversaire m; **children's** ~ goûter m d'enfants
(b) (group) groupe m; (Mil) détachement m; **rescue** ~ équipe f de secouristes
(c) (in politics) parti m
(d) (Law) partie f

**party dress** n robe f de soirée; (for child) belle robe f

**party line** n (a) the ~ la ligne du parti
(b) (phone line) ligne f commune

**party political broadcast** n: émission dans laquelle un parti expose sa politique

**pass** ①︎ n (a) (permit) laissez-passer m inv; (for journalists) coupe-file m inv; **travel** ~ carte f d'abonnement
(b) (Sch, Univ) (in exam) moyenne f (in en); to get a ~ être reçu/-e
(c) (Sport) (in ball games) passe f; (in fencing) botte f
(d) (in mountains) col m
②︎ vtr (a) (gen) passer ⟨plate, ball, time⟩
(b) passer ⟨checkpoint, customs⟩; passer

devant ⟨building, area⟩; dépasser ⟨vehicle, level, expectation⟩; to ~ sb in the street croiser qn dans la rue
(c) ⟨person⟩ réussir ⟨test, exam⟩; ⟨car, machine⟩ passer [qch] (avec succès) ⟨test⟩
(d) adopter ⟨bill, motion⟩
(e) admettre ⟨candidate⟩
(f) prononcer ⟨sentence⟩
③︎ vi (gen) passer; (in exam) réussir
**IDIOMS** to make a ~ at sb faire du plat (colloq) à qn
■ **pass around**, **pass round** faire circuler ⟨document, photos⟩; faire passer ⟨food, plates⟩
■ **pass away** décéder
■ **pass by** ⟨procession⟩ défiler; ⟨person⟩ passer
■ **pass down** transmettre (from de; to à)
■ **pass off** faire passer ⟨person, incident⟩ (as pour)
■ **pass on** transmettre ⟨condolences, message⟩; passer ⟨clothes, cold⟩ (to à)
■ **pass out** (faint) perdre connaissance; (fall drunk) tomber ivre mort
■ **pass through** traverser

**passable** adj (a) ⟨standard, quality⟩ passable; ⟨knowledge, performance⟩ assez bon/bonne
(b) ⟨road⟩ praticable; ⟨river⟩ franchissable

**passage** n (a) (gen) passage
(b) (also ~**way**) (indoors) corridor m
(c) (journey) traversée f

**passenger** n (in car, plane, ship) passager/-ère m/f; (in train, bus, on underground) voyageur/-euse m/f

**passerby** n passant/-e m/f

**passing** adj (a) ⟨motorist, policeman⟩ qui passe/qui passait
(b) ⟨whim⟩ passager/-ère
(c) ⟨reference⟩ en passant inv
(d) ⟨resemblance⟩ vague (before n)

**passion** n passion f

**passionate** adj passionné/-e

**passive** ①︎ n the ~ le passif, la voix passive
②︎ adj passif/-ive

**passkey** n passe m

**pass mark** n moyenne f

**Passover** n Pâque f juive

**passport** n passeport m

**password** n mot m de passe

**past** ①︎ n passé m; in the ~ dans le passé
②︎ adj (a) (preceding) ⟨weeks, months⟩ dernier/-ière (before n); in the ~ two years dans les deux dernières années; during the ~ few days ces derniers jours
(b) (former) ⟨times, problems, experience⟩ passé/-e; ⟨president⟩ ancien/-ienne (before n); ⟨government⟩ précédent/-e; in times ~ autrefois, jadis
(c) summer is ~ l'été est fini; that's all ~ c'est du passé
③︎ prep (a) to walk or go ~ sb/sth passer devant qn/qch; to drive ~ sth passer devant qch (en voiture)

····⟶

**(b)** (in time) it's ∼ 6 il est 6 heures passées; **twenty** ∼ **two** deux heures vingt; **half** ∼ **two** deux heures et demie; **he is** ∼ **70** il a 70 ans passés
**(c)** (beyond) après; ∼ **the church** après l'église; **to be** ∼ **caring** ne plus s'en faire
[4] adv **to go** or **walk** ∼ passer
IDIOMS **to be** ∼ **it** (colloq) avoir passé l'âge; **to be** ∼ **its best** ⟨food⟩ être un peu avancé/-e; ⟨wine⟩ être un peu éventé/-e; **I wouldn't put it** ∼ **him (to do)** ça ne m'étonnerait pas de lui (qu'il fasse)

**pasta** n pâtes fpl (alimentaires)

**paste** [1] n **(a)** (glue) colle f
**(b)** (mixture) pâte f
**(c)** (Culin) (fish, meat) pâté m; (vegetable) purée f
[2] vtr (gen, Comput) coller (**onto** sur; **into** dans; **together** ensemble)

**pastel** [1] n pastel m
[2] adj ⟨colour, pink, shade⟩ pastel inv

**pasteurize** vtr pasteuriser

**pastime** n passe-temps m inv

**pastor** n pasteur m

**pastoral** n pastoral/-e; ⟨role, work⟩ de conseiller/-ère

**pastrami** n bœuf m fumé

**pastry** n **(a)** (mixture) pâte f
**(b)** (cake) pâtisserie f

**past tense** n passé m

**pasture** n pré m, pâturage m

**pat** [1] n **(a)** (gentle tap) petite tape f
**(b)** (of butter) noix f
[2] vtr tapoter ⟨hand⟩; caresser ⟨dog⟩
IDIOMS **to have sth off** (GB) or **down** ∼ connaître qch par cœur

**patch** [1] n **(a)** (in clothes) pièce f; (on tyre) rustine® f; (on eye) bandeau m
**(b)** (of snow, ice) plaque f; (of damp, rust, sunlight) tache f; (of fog) nappe f; (of blue sky) coin m
**(c)** (area of ground) zone f; (for planting) carré m; **a** ∼ **of grass** un coin d'herbe
**(d)** (GB) (colloq) (territory) territoire m
**(e)** (colloq) (period) période f
[2] vtr rapiécer ⟨hole, trousers⟩; réparer ⟨tyre⟩
■ **patch up**: ¶ ∼ **up** [sth], ∼ [sth] **up** soigner ⟨person⟩; rapiécer ⟨hole, trousers⟩; réparer ⟨ceiling, tyre⟩; (fig) rafistoler (colloq) ⟨marriage⟩; ¶ ∼ **up** [sth] résoudre ⟨differences⟩

**patchy** adj ⟨colour, essay, quality⟩ inégal/-e; ⟨knowledge⟩ incomplet/-ète; ∼ **cloud** nuages mpl épars

**paté** n pâté m; **salmon** ∼ terrine f de saumon

**patent** [1] n brevet m (**for**, **on** pour)
[2] adj (obvious) manifeste
[3] vtr faire breveter

**patent leather** n (cuir m) verni m

**paternal** adj paternel/-elle

**paternity** n paternité f

**paternity leave** n congé m de paternité

**path** n **(a)** (track) (also ∼**way**) chemin m; (narrower) sentier m; (in garden) allée f
**(b)** (course) (of projectile, vehicle, sun) trajectoire f; (of river) cours m; (of hurricane) itinéraire m
**(c)** (option) voie f

**pathetic** adj **(a)** (moving) pathétique
**(b)** (inadequate) misérable
**(c)** (colloq) (awful) lamentable

**pathological** adj ⟨fear, hatred⟩ pathologique; ⟨jealousy⟩ maladif/-ive

**pathology** n pathologie f

**patience** n **(a)** patience f (**with** avec)
**(b)** (card game) réussite f

**patient** [1] n patient/-e m/f
[2] adj patient (**with** avec)

**patiently** adv avec patience, patiemment

**patio** n **(a)** (terrace) terrasse f
**(b)** (courtyard) patio m

**patio doors** n pl porte-fenêtre f

**patriot** n patriote mf

**patriotic** adj ⟨mood, song⟩ patriotique; ⟨person⟩ patriote

**patriotism** n patriotisme m

**patrol** [1] n patrouille f
[2] vtr, vi patrouiller

**patrol boat**, **patrol vessel** n patrouilleur m

**patrol car** n voiture f de police

**patron** n **(a)** (of artist) mécène m; (of person) protecteur/-trice m/f; (of charity) bienfaiteur/-trice m/f
**(b)** (client) client/-e m/f (**of** de)

**patronage** n (support) patronage m; ∼ **of the arts** mécénat m

**patronize** vtr **(a)** traiter [qn] avec condescendance ⟨person⟩
**(b)** fréquenter ⟨restaurant, cinema⟩

**patronizing** adj condescendant/-e

**patron saint** n saint/-e m/f patron/-onne

**patter** [1] n **(a)** (of rain) crépitement m; ∼ **of footsteps** bruit m de pas rapides et légers
**(b)** (talk) baratin m
[2] vi ⟨child, mouse⟩ trottiner; ⟨rain⟩ crépiter

**pattern** n **(a)** (design) dessin m, motif m
**(b)** (of behaviour) mode m; **weather** ∼**s** tendances fpl climatiques
**(c)** (in dressmaking) patron m; (in knitting) modèle m
**(d)** (model, example) modèle m

**patterned** adj ⟨fabric⟩ à motifs

**paunch** n ventre m

**pauper** n indigent/-e m/f

**pause** [1] n **(a)** (silence) silence m
**(b)** (break) pause f
**(c)** (stoppage) interruption f
[2] vi **(a)** (stop speaking) marquer une pause
**(b)** (stop) s'arrêter; **to** ∼ **in** interrompre ⟨activity⟩; **to** ∼ **for thought** faire une pause pour réfléchir
**(c)** (hesitate) hésiter

**pave** vtr paver (**with** de); **to** ∼ **the way for sb/sth** ouvrir la voie à qn/qch

**pavement** n **(a)** (GB) (footpath) trottoir m
**(b)** (US) (roadway) chaussée f

**pavement café** n café m avec terrasse

**pavilion** *n* pavillon *m*
**paving slab**, **paving stone** *n* dalle *f*
**paw** ❘1❘ *n* patte *f*
  ❘2❘ *vtr* **to ~ the ground** ⟨*horse*⟩ piaffer; ⟨*bull*⟩ frapper le sol du sabot
**pawn** ❘1❘ *n* pion *m*
  ❘2❘ *vtr* mettre [qch] au mont-de-piété
**pawnbroker** *n* prêteur/-euse *m/f* sur gages
**pawnshop** *n* mont-de-piété *m*
**pay** ❘1❘ *n* salaire *m*
  ❘2❘ *vtr* **(a)** payer (**for** pour); **to ~ cash** payer comptant; **to ~ sth into** verser qch sur ⟨*account*⟩; **all expenses paid** tous frais payés
  **(b)** ⟨*account*⟩ rapporter ⟨*interest*⟩
  **(c)** (give) **to ~ attention to** faire attention à; **to ~ a tribute to sb** rendre hommage à qn; **to ~ sb a compliment** faire des compliments à qn; **to ~ sb a visit** rendre visite à qn
  **(d)** (benefit) **it would ~ him to do** il y gagnerait à faire; **it doesn't ~ to do** cela ne sert à rien de faire
  ❘3❘ *vi* **(a)** ⟨*person*⟩ payer; **to ~ for sth** payer qch; **you have to ~ to get in** l'entrée est payante; **to ~ one's own way** payer sa part; **the work doesn't ~ very well** le travail est mal payé
  **(b)** ⟨*business*⟩ rapporter; ⟨*activity*⟩ payer; **to ~ for itself** ⟨*business, purchase*⟩ s'amortir
  ■ **pay back** rembourser ⟨*person, money*⟩
  ■ **pay in** (GB) déposer ⟨*cheque, sum*⟩
  ■ **pay off**: ¶ ~ **off** être payant/-e
    ¶ ~ **[sb] off (a)** (dismiss) congédier ⟨*worker*⟩
    **(b)** (bribe) acheter le silence de ⟨*person*⟩; ¶ ~ **[sth] off** rembourser ⟨*debt*⟩
  ■ **pay up** (colloq) ~ **up** payer
**payable** *adj* **(a)** (gen) payable
  **(b)** **to make a cheque ~ to** faire un chèque à l'ordre de
**pay cheque** (GB), **pay check** (US) *n* chèque *m* de paie
**payday** *n* jour *m* de paie
**payee** *n* bénéficiaire *mf*
**payment** *n* (gen) paiement *m*; (in settlement) règlement *m*; (into account, of instalments) versement *m*; **monthly ~** mensualité *f*
**pay-packet** *n* enveloppe *f* de paie
**pay phone** *n* téléphone *m* public
**payslip** *n* bulletin *m* de salaire
**pay television** *n* télévision *f* à péage
**pc**, **PC** *n* (abbr = **personal computer**) ordinateur *m* (personnel), PC *m*
**PE** *n* (abbr = **physical education**) éducation *f* physique
**pea** *n* pois *m*
**peace** *n* paix *f*; **to keep the ~** (between countries, individuals) maintenir la paix; (in town) ⟨*police*⟩ maintenir l'ordre public; **I need a bit of ~ and quiet** j'ai besoin d'un peu de calme; **to find ~ of mind** trouver la paix
**peaceful** *adj* **(a)** (tranquil) paisible
  **(b)** (without conflict) pacifique
**peacefully** *adv* **(a)** ⟨*sleep*⟩ paisiblement
  **(b)** (without violence) pacifiquement

**peace-keeping forces** *n pl* forces *fpl* de maintien de la paix
**peacemaker** *n* (Pol) artisan *m* de la paix; (in family) conciliateur *m*
**peace process** *n* processus *m* de paix
**peace talks** *n pl* pourparlers *mpl* de paix
**peacetime** *n* temps *m* de paix
**peach** *n* pêche *f*
**peacock** *n* paon *m*
**peak** ❘1❘ *n* **(a)** (of mountain) pic *m* (**of** de)
  **(b)** (of cap) visière *f*
  **(c)** (of inflation, demand, price) maximum *m* (**in** dans; **of** de); (on a graph) sommet *m*
  **(d)** (of career, empire) apogée *m* (**of** de); (of fitness, form) meilleur *m* (**of** de); **in the ~ of condition** en excellente santé; **to be past its** *or* **one's ~** avoir fait son temps
  ❘2❘ *adj* ⟨*figure, level, price*⟩ maximum; ⟨*fitness*⟩ meilleur/-e
  ❘3❘ *vi* culminer (**at** à)
**peaked** *adj* **(a)** ⟨*cap, hat*⟩ à visière; ⟨*roof*⟩ pointu/-e
  **(b)** (US) pâlot/-otte
**peak period** *n* période *f* de pointe
**peak rate** *n* (for phone calls) tarif *m* rouge
**peak time** *n* (on TV) heures *fpl* de grande écoute; (for switchboard, traffic) heures *fpl* de pointe
**peaky** *adj* (colloq) pâlot/-otte
**peal** *n* (of bells) carillonnement *m*; (of thunder) grondement *m*; **~s of laughter** éclats *mpl* de rire
**peanut** *n* (nut) cacahuète *f*; (plant) arachide *f*
**peanut butter** *n* beurre *m* de cacahuètes
**pear** *n* poire *f*
**pearl** ❘1❘ *n* perle *f*
  ❘2❘ *adj* ⟨*necklace, brooch*⟩ de perles; ⟨*button*⟩ en nacre
**pear tree** *n* poirier *m*
**peasant** *n* paysan/-anne *m/f*
**peat** *n* tourbe *f*
**pebble** *n* caillou *m*; (on beach) galet *m*
**pecan** *n* noix *f* de pecan
**peck** ❘1❘ *n* **(a)** (from bird) coup *m* de bec
  **(b)** (colloq) **to give sb a ~** (on the cheek) faire une bise à qn
  ❘2❘ *vtr* ⟨*bird*⟩ picorer ⟨*food*⟩; donner un coup de bec à ⟨*person, animal*⟩
  ❘3❘ *vi* **(a)** ⟨*bird*⟩ **to ~ at** picorer ⟨*food*⟩
  **(b)** (colloq) **to ~ at one's food** ⟨*person*⟩ chipoter
**pecking order** *n* ordre *m* hiérarchique
**peckish** *adj* (colloq) **to be ~** avoir un petit creux (colloq)
**pectorals** *n pl* (also **pecs** (colloq)) pectoraux *mpl*
**peculiar** *adj* **(a)** (odd) bizarre
  **(b)** **to be ~ to** être particulier/-ière à *or* propre à
**peculiarity** *n* **(a)** (feature) particularité *f*
  **(b)** (strangeness) bizarrerie *f*
**pedal** ❘1❘ *n* pédale *f*

⋯⋯⁂

**2** *vi* pédaler
**pedal bin** *n* (GB) poubelle *f* à pédale
**pedal boat** *n* pédalo® *m*
**pedantic** *adj* pédant/-e
**peddle** *vtr* colporter ⟨*wares, ideas*⟩; **to ~ drugs** revendre de la drogue
**peddler** *n* (street vendor) colporteur *m*; **drug ~** trafiquant *m*
**pedestal** *n* socle *m*, piédestal *m*; **to put sb on a ~** mettre qn sur un piédestal
**pedestrian** **1** *n* piéton *m*
**2** *adj* ⟨*street, area*⟩ piétonnier/-ière, piéton/-onne
**pedestrian crossing** *n* passage *m* pour piétons, passage *m* clouté
**pedestrian precinct** *n* (GB) zone *f* piétonne
**pediatrician** (US) = PAEDIATRICIAN
**pedicure** *n* **to have a ~** se faire soigner les pieds
**pedigree** **1** *n* **(a)** (of animal) pedigree *m*; (of person) ascendance *f*
**(b)** (purebred animal) animal *m* avec pedigree
**2** *adj* ⟨*animal*⟩ de pure race
**pee** *n* (colloq) pipi *m* (colloq); **to have a ~** faire pipi (colloq)
**peek** *n* **to have a ~ at** jeter un coup d'œil furtif à
**peel** **1** *n* (gen) peau *f*; (of citrus fruit) écorce *f*; (of onion) pelure *f*; (peelings) épluchures *fpl*
**2** *vtr* éplucher ⟨*vegetable, fruit*⟩; décortiquer ⟨*prawn*⟩; écorcer ⟨*stick*⟩
**3** *vi* ⟨*skin*⟩ peler; ⟨*fruit, vegetable*⟩ s'éplucher
■ **peel off**: ¶ **~ off** ⟨*label*⟩ se détacher; ⟨*paint*⟩ s'écailler; ⟨*paper*⟩ se décoller; ¶ **~ [sth] off** enlever ⟨*clothing, label*⟩
**peeler** *n* économe *m*
**peelings** *n pl* épluchures *fpl*
**peep** **1** *n* **to have a ~ at sth** jeter un coup d'œil à qch; (furtively) regarder qch à la dérobée
**2** *vi* **(a)** jeter un coup d'œil (**over** par-dessus; **through** par); **to ~ at sb/sth** jeter un coup d'œil à qn/qch; (furtively) regarder qn/qch furtivement
**(b)** ⟨*chick*⟩ pépier
**peephole** *n* (in fence) trou *m*; (in door) judas *m*
**peer** **1** *n* **(a)** (equal) (in status) pair *m*; (in profession) collègue *m/f*
**(b)** (contemporary) (adult) personne *f* de la même génération; (child) enfant *mf* du même âge
**(c)** (GB) (*also* **~ of the realm**) pair *m*
**2** *vi* **to ~ at** scruter, regarder attentivement
**peerage** *n* (GB Pol) pairie *f*; **to be given a ~** être anobli/-e
**peer group** *n* **(a)** (of same status) pairs *mpl*
**(b)** (contemporaries) (adults) personnes *fpl* de la même génération; (children) enfants *mpl* du même âge
**peer group pressure** *n* pression *f* du groupe

**peg** *n* **(a)** (hook) patère *f*
**(b)** (GB) (*also* **clothes ~**) pince *f* à linge
**(c)** (of tent) piquet *m*
**(d)** (in carpentry) cheville *f*
**pejorative** *adj* péjoratif/-ive
**Peking** *pr n* Pékin
**pelican** *n* pélican *m*
**pellet** *n* **(a)** (of paper, wax, mud) boulette *f*
**(b)** (of shot) plomb *m*
**pelmet** *n* cantonnière *f*
**pelt** **1** *n* (fur) fourrure *f*; (hide) peau *f*
**2** *vtr* bombarder (**with sth** de qch)
**3** *vi* **(a)** (*also* **~ down**) ⟨*rain*⟩ tomber à verse
**(b)** (run) **to ~ along** courir à toutes jambes
**pelvis** *n* bassin *m*, pelvis *m*
**pen** *n* **(a)** (for writing) stylo *m*
**(b)** (for animals) parc *m*, enclos *m*
**penal** *n* ⟨*law, code, system*⟩ pénal/-e; ⟨*colony, institution*⟩ pénitentiaire
**penalize** *vtr* pénaliser
**penalty** *n* **(a)** (punishment) peine *f*, pénalité *f*; (fine) amende *f*
**(b)** (figurative) prix *m* (**for** de)
**(c)** (in soccer) penalty *m*; (in rugby) pénalité *f*
**pence** (GB) ▶ PENNY
**pencil** *n* crayon *m*; **in ~** au crayon
■ **pencil in**: **~ [sth] in**, **~ in [sth]** écrire [qch] au crayon; **let's ~ in the second of May** disons le deux mai pour l'instant
**pencil case** *n* trousse *f* (à crayons)
**pencil sharpener** *n* taille-crayon *m*
**pendant** *n* (on necklace) pendentif *m*
**pending** **1** *adj* **(a)** ⟨*case*⟩ en instance; ⟨*matter*⟩ en souffrance
**(b)** (imminent) imminent/-e
**2** *prep* en attendant
**pendulum** *n* pendule *m*, balancier *m*
**penetrate** *vtr* pénétrer; percer ⟨*cloud, silence, defences*⟩; traverser ⟨*wall*⟩; ⟨*spy*⟩ infiltrer ⟨*organization*⟩
**penetrating** *adj* ⟨*cold, eyes, question*⟩ pénétrant/-e; ⟨*sound, voice*⟩ perçant/-e
**pen friend** *n* correspondant/-e *m/f*
**penguin** *n* pingouin *m*, manchot *m*
**penicillin** *n* pénicilline *f*
**peninsula** *n* péninsule *f*
**penis** *n* pénis *m*
**penitent** *n, adj* pénitent/-e (*m/f*)
**penitentiary** *n* (US) prison *f*
**penknife** *n* canif *m*
**pennant** *n* **(a)** (flag) fanion *m*; (on boat) flamme *f*
**(b)** (US Sport) championnat *m*
**penniless** *adj* sans le sou, sans ressources
**penny** *n* **(a)** (GB) penny *m*; **a five pence** *or* **five p piece** une pièce de cinq pence; **a 25p stamp** un timbre-poste à 25 pence
**(b)** (US) cent *m*
IDIOMS **the ~ dropped** (colloq) ça a fait tilt (colloq); **not to have a ~ to one's name** être sans le sou

**pension** n (from state) pension f; (from employer) retraite f

**pensioner** n retraité/-e m/f

**pension scheme** n plan m de retraite

**pentagon** n (a) pentagone m
(b) the Pentagon (US) le Pentagone m

**Pentecost** n Pentecôte f

**penthouse** n appartement m de grand standing

**pent-up** adj ⟨energy, frustration⟩ contenu/-e; ⟨feelings⟩ réprimé/-e

**penultimate** adj avant-dernier/-ière

**people** ⟨1⟩ n (nation) peuple m
⟨2⟩ n pl (a) (in general) gens mpl; (specified or counted) personnes fpl; **old** ~ les personnes âgées; **they're nice** ~ ce sont des gens sympathiques; **there were a lot of** ~ il y avait beaucoup de monde; **other** ~'s **property** le bien des autres
(b) (of a town) habitants mpl; (of a country) peuple m
(c) (citizens) the ~ le peuple

■ Note gens is masculine plural and never countable. When counting people, you must use personnes rather than gens: three people = trois personnes.
– When used with gens, some adjectives such as vieux, bon, mauvais, petit, vilain placed before gens take the feminine form: les vieilles gens.

**people carrier** n monospace m

**pep** v ■ **pep up** remettre [qn] d'aplomb ⟨person⟩; animer ⟨party, team⟩

**pepper** n (a) (spice) poivre m
(b) (vegetable) poivron m

**peppercorn** n grain m de poivre

**pepper mill** n moulin m à poivre

**peppermint** n (a) (sweet) pastille f de menthe
(b) (plant) menthe f poivrée

**pepper pot, pepper shaker** n poivrier m

**pep talk** n (colloq) laïus m (colloq) d'encouragement

**per** prep par; ~ **annum** par an; ~ **head** par tête or personne; **80 km** ~ **hour** 80 km à l'heure; **£5** ~ **hour** 5 livres sterling (de) l'heure; **as** ~ **your instructions** conformément à vos instructions

**per capita** adj, adv par personne

**perceive** vtr percevoir

**per cent** n, adv pour cent (m)

**percentage** n pourcentage m

**perceptible** adj perceptible (to à)

**perception** n (a) (by senses) perception f
(b) (view) **my** ~ **of him** l'idée que je me fais de lui
(c) (insight) perspicacité f

**perceptive** adj ⟨person⟩ perspicace; ⟨analysis⟩ fin/-e; ⟨article⟩ intelligent/-e

**perch** ⟨1⟩ n (a) (gen) perchoir m
(b) (fish) perche f
⟨2⟩ vi se percher (on sur)

**percolator** n cafetière f à pression

**percussion** n (Mus) percussions fpl

**perennial** adj (a) perpétuel/-elle
(b) ⟨plant⟩ vivace

**perfect** ⟨1⟩ n parfait m; **in the** ~ au parfait
⟨2⟩ adj (gen) parfait/-e (for pour); ⟨moment, name, place, partner, solution⟩ idéal/-e (for pour); ⟨hostess⟩ exemplaire
⟨3⟩ vtr perfectionner

**perfection** n perfection f (of de)

**perfectionist** n, adj perfectionniste (mf)

**perfectly** adv (a) (totally) ⟨clear, happy⟩ tout à fait
(b) (very well) ⟨fit, illustrate⟩ parfaitement

**perforate** vtr perforer

**perform** ⟨1⟩ vtr (a) exécuter ⟨task⟩; accomplir ⟨duties⟩; procéder à ⟨operation⟩
(b) jouer ⟨play⟩; chanter ⟨song⟩; exécuter ⟨dance, trick⟩
(c) célébrer ⟨ceremony⟩
⟨2⟩ vi (a) ⟨actor, musician⟩ jouer
(b) **to** ~ **well/badly** ⟨team⟩ bien/mal jouer; ⟨interviewee⟩ faire bonne/mauvaise impression; ⟨exam candidate, company⟩ avoir de bons/de mauvais résultats

**performance** n (a) (rendition) interprétation f (of de)
(b) (concert, show, play) représentation f (of de); **to put on a** ~ **of Hamlet** donner une représentation d'Hamlet
(c) (of team, sportsman) performance f (in à)
(d) (of duties) exercice m (of de); (of task) exécution f (of de)
(e) (of car, engine) performances fpl

**performance artist** n artiste mf de performances

**performance indicators** n pl tableau m de bord

**performer** n artiste mf

**performing arts** n pl arts mpl scéniques

**perfume** ⟨1⟩ n parfum m
⟨2⟩ vtr parfumer

**perhaps** adv peut-être; ~ **she's forgotten** elle a peut-être oublié

**peril** n péril m, danger m

**perimeter** n périmètre m

**period** ⟨1⟩ n (a) (gen) période f; (era) époque f
(b) (US) (full stop) point m
(c) (menstruation) règles fpl
(d) (Sch) (lesson) cours m, leçon f; **to have a free** ~ ≈ avoir une heure de libre
⟨2⟩ adj (of a certain era) ⟨costume, furniture⟩ d'époque

**periodical** n, adj périodique (m)

**peripheral** adj ⟨vision, suburb⟩ périphérique; ⟨issue, investment⟩ annexe

**periphery** n périphérie f; **to remain on the** ~ rester à l'écart de ⟨event, movement⟩

**periscope** n périscope m

**perish** vi (a) (die) périr (from de)
(b) ⟨food⟩ se gâter; ⟨rubber⟩ se détériorer

**perishables** n pl denrées fpl périssables

**perjure** v refl to ~ oneself faire un faux témoignage

**perjury** n faux témoignage m

**perk** n (colloq) avantage m

■ **perk up** ⟨person⟩ se ragaillardir; ⟨business, life, plant⟩ reprendre

**perky** adj guilleret/-ette

**perm** n permanente f; to have a ~ se faire faire une permanente

**permanent** ⟨1⟩ n (US) permanente f
⟨2⟩ adj permanent/-e

**permanently** adv ⟨happy, tired⟩ en permanence; ⟨employed, disabled⟩ de façon permanente; ⟨close, emigrate, settle⟩ définitivement

**permeate** vtr (a) ⟨liquid, gas⟩ s'infiltrer dans; ⟨odour⟩ pénétrer dans
(b) ⟨ideas⟩ imprégner

**permissible** adj ⟨level, conduct⟩ admissible; ⟨error⟩ acceptable

**permission** n permission f; (official) autorisation f; to get ~ to do obtenir la permission or l'autorisation de faire

**permissive** adj permissif/-ive

**permit** ⟨1⟩ n (a) permis m; work ~ permis m de travail:
(b) (US Aut) permis m (de conduire)
⟨2⟩ vtr permettre; to ~ sb to do permettre à qn de faire; smoking is not ~ted il est interdit de fumer
⟨3⟩ vi permettre

**pernickety** adj (colloq) (a) (detail-conscious) pointilleux/-euse (about sur)
(b) (choosy) tatillon/-onne (about quant à)

**peroxide blonde** n blonde f décolorée

**perpendicular** adj perpendiculaire

**perpetrate** vtr perpétrer ⟨deed, fraud⟩; monter ⟨hoax⟩

**perpetrator** n auteur m (of de)

**perpetual** adj ⟨meetings, longing, turmoil⟩ perpétuel/-elle; ⟨darkness, stench⟩ permanent/-e

**perpetuate** vtr perpétuer

**perplexed** adj perplexe

**persecute** vtr persécuter

**persecution** n persécution f

**perseverance** n persévérance f

**persevere** vi persévérer (with, at dans)

**persist** vi persister (in dans; in doing à faire)

**persistence** n persévérance f

**persistent** adj (a) (persevering) persévérant/-e; (obstinate) obstiné/-e (in dans)
(b) ⟨rain, denial⟩ persistant/-e; ⟨enquiries, noise, pressure⟩ continuel/-elle; ⟨illness, fears, idea⟩ tenace

**persistent offender** n récidiviste mf

**person** n personne f; in ~ en personne; to have sth about one's ~ avoir qch sur soi

**personable** adj ⟨person⟩ qui présente bien

**personal** ⟨1⟩ n (US) petite annonce f personnelle
⟨2⟩ adj ⟨opinion, life, call, matter⟩

personnel/-elle; ⟨safety, choice, income, insurance⟩ individuel/-elle; ⟨service⟩ personnalisé/-e; to make a ~ appearance venir en personne (at à)

**personal ad** n petite annonce f personnelle

**personal column** n petites annonces fpl personnelles

**personality** n personnalité f

**personal loan** n emprunt m; (by bank etc) prêt m personnel

**personally** adv personnellement

**personal organizer** n ≈ agenda m

**personal property** n biens mpl personnels

**personal stereo** n baladeur m

**personify** vtr incarner ⟨ideal⟩

**personnel** n (a) (staff, troops) personnel m
(b) (department) service m du personnel

**perspective** n perspective f; to keep things in ~ garder un sens de la mesure; to put things into ~ relativiser les choses

**perspex®** n plexiglas® m

**perspiration** n (a) (sweat) sueur f
(b) (sweating) transpiration f

**perspire** vi transpirer

**persuade** vtr (a) (influence) persuader; to ~ sb to do persuader qn de faire
(b) (convince) convaincre (of de; that que)

**persuasion** n (a) (persuading) persuasion f
(b) (religion) confession f
(c) (political views) conviction f

**persuasive** adj ⟨person⟩ persuasif/-ive; ⟨argument, evidence⟩ convaincant/-e

**pert** adj ⟨person, manner⟩ espiègle; ⟨hat, nose⟩ coquin/-e

**pertinent** adj pertinent/-e

**perturb** vtr perturber

**perturbing** adj troublant/-e

**pervade** vtr imprégner

**perverse** adj (a) (twisted) ⟨person⟩ retors/-e; ⟨desire⟩ pervers/-e
(b) (contrary) ⟨refusal, attempt, attitude⟩ illogique; to take a ~ pleasure in doing prendre un malin plaisir à faire

**perversion** n (a) (deviation) perversion f
(b) (of facts, justice) travestissement m

**pervert** ⟨1⟩ n pervers/-e m/f
⟨2⟩ vtr (a) (corrupt) corrompre
(b) (misrepresent) travestir ⟨truth⟩; dénaturer ⟨meaning⟩; to ~ the course of justice entraver l'action de la justice

**perverted** adj (deviant) pervers/-e; (distorted) ⟨idea⟩ tordu/-e

**pessimism** n pessimisme m

**pessimist** n pessimiste mf

**pessimistic** adj pessimiste

**pest** n (a) (animal) animal m nuisible; (insect) insecte m nuisible
(b) (colloq) (person) enquiquineur/-euse m/f (colloq)

**pester** vtr harceler

**pesticide** n pesticide m

**pet** ⓵ n (a) (animal) animal m de compagnie
(b) (favourite) chouchou/chouchoute m/f
(colloq)
⓶ adj (a) (favourite) favori/-ite
(b) ~ **dog** chien
⓷ vtr caresser ⟨animal⟩
⓸ vi ⟨people⟩ échanger des caresses
**petal** n pétale m
**peter** v ■ **peter out** ⟨conversation⟩ tarir;
⟨supplies⟩ s'épuiser
**pet food** n aliments mpl pour chiens et
chats
**pet hate** (GB) n bête f noire
**petition** ⓵ n pétition f
⓶ vtr adresser une pétition à ⟨person, body⟩
⓷ vi **to** ~ **for divorce** demander le divorce
**pet name** n petit nom m
**pet project** n enfant m chéri ((figurative))
**petrified** adj pétrifié/-e
**petrol** (GB) n essence f; **to fill up with** ~
faire le plein (d'essence)
**petrol can** n bidon m à essence
**petroleum** n pétrole m
**petrol station** n (GB) station f d'essence
**pet shop** (GB), **pet store** (US) n
animalerie f
**petticoat** n (full slip) combinaison m; (half
slip) jupon m
**petty** adj ⟨person, squabble⟩ mesquin/-e;
⟨detail⟩ insignifiant/-e
**petty cash** n petite caisse f
**petty crime** n petite délinquance f
**petty officer** n ≈ maître m
**petty theft** n larcin m
**pew** n banc m (d'église)
**pewter** n étain m
**PGCE** n (abbr = **postgraduate
certificate in education**) diplôme m de
spécialisation dans l'enseignement
**pharmaceutical** adj pharmaceutique
**pharmacist** n pharmacien/-ienne m/f
**pharmacy** n pharmacie f
**phase** ⓵ n phase f; **it's just a** ~ (he's/
they're going through) ça lui/leur passera
⓶ vtr échelonner (**over** sur)
■ **phase in** introduire [qch]
progressivement
■ **phase out** supprimer [qch] peu à peu
**PhD** n (abbr = **Doctor of Philosophy**)
doctorat m
**pheasant** n faisan/-e m/f
**phenomenal** adj phénoménal/-e
**phenomenon** n phénomène m
**phew** excl (in relief) ouf!; (when too hot) pff!
**philanthropist** n philanthrope mf
**philistine** n béotien/-ienne m/f
**philosopher** n philosophe mf
**philosophic(al)** adj (a) ⟨knowledge,
question⟩ philosophique
(b) (calm, stoical) philosophe (**about** à propos
de)
**philosophy** n philosophie f

**phobia** n phobie f
**phone** ⓵ n téléphone m; **to be on the** ~ (be
talking) être au téléphone (**to sb** avec qn); (be
subscriber) avoir le téléphone
⓶ vtr (also ~ **up**) passer un coup de fil à
(colloq), téléphoner à, appeler
⓷ vi (also ~ **up**) téléphoner; **to** ~ **for a taxi**
appeler un taxi
**phone book** n annuaire m (téléphonique)
**phone booth, phone box** (GB) n
cabine f téléphonique
**phone call** n coup m de fil (colloq); (more
formal) communication f (téléphonique)
**phone card** n (GB) télécarte f
**phone-in** n émission f à ligne ouverte
**phone link** n liaison f téléphonique
**phone number** n numéro m de
téléphone
**phoney** (colloq) ⓵ n (a) (affected person)
poseur/-euse m/f
(b) (impostor) charlatan m
⓶ adj ⟨address, accent⟩ faux/fausse (before
n); ⟨company, excuse⟩ bidon inv (colloq);
⟨emotion⟩ simulé/-e
**phoney war** n the ~ la drôle de guerre
**phosphates** n pl phosphates mpl
**photo** = PHOTOGRAPH 1
**photo album** n album m de photos
**photo booth** n photomaton® m
**photo-call** n séance f de photos
**photocopier** n photocopieuse f
**photocopy** ⓵ n photocopie f
⓶ vtr photocopier
**photogenic** adj photogénique
**photograph** ⓵ n (also **photo**) photo f; **in
the** ~ sur la photo; **to take a** ~ **of sb/sth**
prendre qn/qch en photo
⓶ vtr photographier, prendre [qn/qch] en
photo
**photographer** n photographe mf
**photography** n photographie f
**photo opportunity** n séance f de photos
**photo session** n séance f de photos
**phrase** ⓵ n expression f
⓶ vtr formuler ⟨question, speech⟩
**phrasebook** n manuel m de conversation
**physical** ⓵ n (colloq) (check-up) bilan m de
santé
⓶ adj physique
**physical fitness** n forme f physique
**physically handicapped** adj **to be** ~
être handicapé/-e m/f physique
**physicist** n physicien/-ienne m/f
**physics** n physique f
**physiology** n physiologie f
**physiotherapy** n kinésithérapie f
**physique** n physique m
**pianist** n pianiste mf
**piano** n piano m
**pick** ⓵ n (a) (tool) pioche f, pic m; (of
climber) piolet m

···✦

**(b)** (choice) choix *m*; **to have one's ~ of** avoir le choix parmi; **take your ~** choisis
**(c) the ~ of the bunch** (singular) le meilleur/la meilleure du lot
**2** *vtr* **(a)** (choose) choisir ⟨from parmi⟩; (in sport) sélectionner ⟨player⟩ ⟨from parmi⟩; **to ~ a fight** chercher à se bagarrer (colloq) ⟨with avec⟩; (quarrel) chercher querelle ⟨with à⟩
**(b) to ~ one's way through** avancer avec précaution parmi ⟨rubble, litter⟩
**(c)** cueillir ⟨fruit, flowers⟩
**(d)** gratter ⟨spot, scab⟩; **to ~ sth from** *or* **off** enlever qch de; **to ~ one's teeth/nose** se curer les dents/le nez
**3** *vi* choisir

■ **pick at (a)** ⟨person⟩ manger [qch] du bout des dents ⟨food⟩; gratter ⟨spot, scab⟩
**(b)** ⟨bird⟩ picorer ⟨crumbs⟩

■ **pick on** harceler, s'en prendre à ⟨person⟩

■ **pick out (a)** (select) choisir; (single out) repérer
**(b)** distinguer ⟨landmark⟩; reconnaître ⟨person in photo⟩; repérer ⟨person in crowd⟩

■ **pick up**: ¶ **~ up** ⟨business⟩ reprendre; ⟨weather, health⟩ s'améliorer; ⟨ill person⟩ se rétablir
¶ **~ [sb/sth] up (a)** (lift up) ramasser ⟨object, litter, toys⟩; relever ⟨person⟩; **to ~ up the receiver** décrocher le téléphone; **to ~ oneself up** se relever
**(b)** prendre ⟨passenger, cargo⟩; passer prendre ⟨ticket, keys⟩; prendre, acheter ⟨milk, paper⟩; **could you ~ me up?** est-ce que tu peux venir me chercher?
**(c)** apprendre ⟨language⟩; prendre ⟨habit, accent⟩; développer ⟨skill⟩; **you'll soon ~ it up** tu t'y mettras vite
**(d)** trouver ⟨trail, scent⟩; ⟨radar⟩ détecter la présence de ⟨aircraft, person, object⟩; ⟨radio receiver⟩ capter ⟨signal⟩
**(e)** gagner ⟨point⟩; acquérir ⟨reputation⟩; **to ~ up speed** prendre de la vitesse
**(f)** (resume) reprendre ⟨conversation, career⟩
**(g)** ramasser ⟨partner, prostitute⟩

**pickaxe** (GB), **pickax** (US) *n* pioche *f*

**picket 1** *n* piquet *m* (de grève)
**2** *vtr* installer un piquet de grève aux portes de ⟨factory⟩

**picking 1** *n* (of crop) cueillette *f*
**2 pickings** *n pl* (rewards) gains *mpl*

**pickle 1** *n* **(a)** (preserves) conserves *fpl* au vinaigre
**(b)** (gherkin) cornichon *m*
**2** *vtr* (in vinegar) conserver [qch] dans du vinaigre
IDIOMS **to be in a ~** être dans le pétrin (colloq)

**pick-me-up** *n* remontant *m*

**pickpocket** *n* voleur *m* à la tire

**pickup truck** *n* (GB) pick-up *m inv*

**picnic** *n* pique-nique *m*; **to go for** *or* **on a ~** aller faire un pique-nique, pique-niquer

**picture 1** *n* **(a)** (painting) peinture *f*, tableau *m*; (drawing) dessin *m*; (in book) illustration *f*; (in mind) image *f*
**(b)** (description) description *f*

**(c)** (snapshot) photo *f*, photographie *f*
**(d) I get the ~** je vois; **to put sb in the ~** mettre qn au courant
**(e)** (film) film *m*
**(f)** (on TV screen) image *f*
**2** *vtr* s'imaginer

**picture card** *n* figure *f* ⟨carte⟩

**picture frame** *n* cadre *m*

**picture hook** *n* crochet *m* (à tableaux)

**picturesque** *adj* pittoresque

**pie** *n* tourte *f*; **meat ~** tourte à la viande

**piece** *n* **(a)** (gen) morceau *m*; (of string, ribbon) bout *m*; **a ~ of furniture** un meuble; **a ~ of luggage** une valise; **a ~ of advice** un conseil; **a ~ of information** un renseignement; **a ~ of luck** un coup de chance; **£20 a ~** 20 livres sterling pièce; **to fall to ~s** ⟨object⟩ tomber en morceaux; ⟨argument⟩ s'effondrer; **to go to ~s** (from shock) s'effondrer; (emotionally) craquer (colloq); (in interview) paniquer complètement
**(b)** (of jigsaw, machine, model) pièce *f*; **to take sth to ~s** démonter qch
**(c)** (article) article *m* ⟨on sur⟩
**(d)** (coin) **a 50p ~** une pièce de 50 pence
**(e)** (in chess) pièce *f*
IDIOMS **to give sb a ~ of one's mind** dire ses quatre vérités à qn

■ **piece together**: **~ [sth] together**, **~ together [sth]** reconstituer ⟨vase, letter⟩; assembler ⟨puzzle⟩; reconstituer ⟨facts⟩

**piecemeal 1** *adj* (random) fragmentaire; (at different times) irrégulier/-ière
**2** *adv* petit à petit

**pie chart** *n* diagramme *m* circulaire sectorisé, camembert *m* (colloq)

**pier** *n* (at seaside) jetée *f* (sur pilotis); (landing stage) embarcadère *f*

**pierce** *vtr* (make hole in) percer; (penetrate) transpercer

**piercing** *adj* ⟨scream, eyes⟩ perçant/-e; ⟨light⟩ intense; ⟨wind⟩ glacial/-e, pénétrant/-e

**pig** *n* **(a)** (animal) porc *m*, cochon *m*
**(b)** (colloq) ⟨person⟩ (greedy) goinfre *m* (colloq); (dirty) cochon/-onne *m/f* (colloq); (nasty) sale type *m* (colloq)

■ **pig out** (colloq) se goinfrer (colloq), s'empiffrer (colloq) ⟨on de⟩

**pigeon** *n* pigeon *m*

**pigeonhole** (GB) **1** *n* casier *m*
**2** *vtr* étiqueter, cataloguer

**pigeon-toed** *adj* **to be ~** marcher les pieds en dedans

**piggyback (ride)** *n* **to give sb a ~** porter qn sur son dos *or* sur ses épaules

**piggy bank** *n* tirelire *f*

**pigheaded** *adj* entêté/-e, obstiné/-e

**piglet** *n* porcelet *m*, petit cochon *m*

**pigment** *n* pigment *m*

**pigpen** (US) = PIGSTY

**pigskin** *n* peau *f* de porc

**pigsty, pigpen** (US) *n* porcherie *f*

**pigtail** *n* natte *f*

**pike** *n* (fish) brochet *m*

**pile** [1] *n* **(a)** (heap) tas *m* (**of** de); (stack) pile *f*
(**of** de); **in a ~** en tas *or* en pile
**(b)** (of fabric, carpet) poil *m*
**(c)** (colloq) **~s of** des tas (colloq) de ⟨*books,
letters*⟩; **~s of money** plein d'argent (colloq)
[2] **piles** *n pl* hémorroïdes *fpl*
[3] *vtr* entasser (**on** sur; **into** dans)
■ **pile up** ⟨*debts, problems, work*⟩
s'accumuler

**pileup** *n* carambolage *m*

**pilfer** [1] *vtr* dérober (**from** dans)
[2] *vi* commettre des larcins

**pilgrim** *n* pèlerin *m* (**to** de)

**pilgrimage** *n* pèlerinage *m*

**pill** *n* **(a)** (gen) comprimé *m*, cachet *m*
**(b)** (contraceptive) **the ~** la pilule

**pillage** *vtr, vi* piller

**pillar** *n* pilier *m*

**pillar box** *n* (GB) boîte *f* aux lettres

**pillion** [1] *n* (*also* **~ seat**) siège *m* de
passager
[2] *adv* **to ride ~** monter en croupe

**pillow** *n* oreiller *m*

**pillowcase** *n* taie *f* d'oreiller

**pilot** [1] *n* pilote *m*
[2] *adj* **(a)** ⟨*project, study*⟩ pilote; ⟨*series*⟩
expérimental/-e
**(b)** ⟨*error*⟩ de pilotage

**pilot light** *n* veilleuse *f*; (electric) voyant *m*
lumineux

**pilot scheme** *n* projet-pilote *m*

**pimp** *n* proxénète *m*

**pimple** *n* bouton *m*

**pimply** *adj* boutonneux/-euse

**pin** [1] *n* **(a)** (for cloth, paper) épingle *f*
**(b)** **three-~ plug** prise *f* à trois fiches
**(c)** (for wood, metal) goujon *m*
**(d)** (Med) broche *f*
**(e)** (brooch) barrette *f*
[2] *vtr* **(a)** épingler ⟨*dress, hem, curtain*⟩ (**to**
à)
**(b)** (trap) **to ~ sb** to coincer qn contre ⟨*wall,
floor*⟩
**(c)** (colloq) **to ~ sth on sb** mettre qch sur le
dos de qn ⟨*theft*⟩
■ **pin down**: ¶ **~** [sb] **down (a)** (physically)
immobiliser (**to** à)
**(b)** (figurative) coincer; **to ~ sb down to a
definite date** arriver à fixer une date ferme
avec qn
¶ **~** [sth] **down** identifier ⟨*concept, feeling*⟩
■ **pin up** accrocher ⟨*poster, notice*⟩ (**on** à)

**PIN (number)** *n* (*abbr* = **personal
identification number**) code *m*
confidentiel (pour carte bancaire)

**pinafore** *n* **(a)** (apron) tablier *m*
**(b)** (dress) robe-chasuble *f*

**pinball** *n* flipper *m*

**pincers** *n pl* tenailles *fpl*

**pinch** [1] *n* **(a)** (pincement *m*; **to give sb a ~**
pincer qn
**(b)** (of salt, spice) pincée *f*
[2] *vtr* **(a)** (on arm, leg) pincer
**(b)** ⟨*shoe*⟩ serrer

**(c)** (colloq) (steal) faucher (colloq) (**from** à)
[3] *vi* ⟨*shoe*⟩ serrer
**IDIOMS to feel the ~** avoir de la peine à
joindre les deux bouts

**pine** [1] *n* pin *m*
[2] *adj* ⟨*furniture*⟩ en pin
[3] *vi* ⟨*person*⟩ languir (**for** après); ⟨*animal*⟩
s'ennuyer (**for** de)

**pineapple** *n* ananas *m*

**pinecone** *n* pomme *f* de pin

**ping-pong**® *n* ping-pong® *m*

**pink** [1] *n* **(a)** (colour) rose *m*
**(b)** (flower) œillet *m* mignardise
[2] *adj* rose; **to go** *or* **turn ~** rosir; (blush)
rougir (**with** de)

**pinnacle** *n* **(a)** (on building) pinacle *m*
**(b)** (of rock) cime *f* (**of** de)
**(c)** (figurative) apogée *m* (**of** de)

**pinpoint** *vtr* indiquer ⟨*problem, causes,
location, site*⟩; déterminer ⟨*time*⟩

**pinstripe(d)** *adj* ⟨*fabric, suit*⟩ à fines
rayures

**pint** *n* pinte *f* ((GB) = *0.57 l*, (US) = *0.47 l*); **a
~ of milk** ≈ un demi-litre de lait; **a ~** (**of
beer**) un demi

**pinup** *n* (woman) pin-up *f* (colloq); (poster of
star) affiche *f* de vedette; (star) idole *f*

**pioneer** [1] *n* pionnier *m* (**of, in** de)
[2] *vtr* **to ~ the use of** être le premier/la
première à utiliser

**pious** *adj* pieux/pieuse

**pip** *n* **(a)** (seed) pépin *m*
**(b)** (on radio) top *m*
**IDIOMS to be ~ped at** *or* **to the post** se faire
souffler la victoire

**pipe** [1] *n* **(a)** (for gas, water) tuyau *m*;
(underground) conduite *f*
**(b)** (smoker's) pipe *f*
[2] **pipes** *n pl* (Mus) cornemuse *f*
[3] *vtr* **water is ~d across/to** l'eau est
acheminée par canalisation à travers/
jusqu'à
■ **pipe down** (colloq) faire moins de bruit
■ **pipe up** ⟨*voice*⟩ se faire entendre

**pipe-dream** *n* chimère *f*

**pipeline** *n* oléoduc *m*; **to be in the ~** être
prévu/-e

**piping hot** *adj* fumant/-e

**pique** *n* dépit *m*; **a fit of ~** un accès de
dépit

**pirate** [1] *n* pirate *m*
[2] *adj* ⟨*video, tape, radio*⟩ pirate (*after n*);
⟨*ship*⟩ de pirates
[3] *vtr* pirater ⟨*tape, video, software*⟩

**pirouette** *n* pirouette *f*

**Pisa** *pr n* Pise

**Pisces** *n* Poissons *mpl*

**pistol** *n* pistolet *m*

**piston** *n* piston *m*

**pit** [1] *n* **(a)** (in ground, in garage) fosse *f*; **gravel
~** carrière *f* de gravier
**(b)** (mine) mine *f*
**(c)** (in theatre) parterre *m*; **orchestra ~** fosse *f*
d'orchestre ···✦·

**(d)** (US) (in fruit) noyau *m*
**2** *vtr* to ~ sb against opposer qn à ⟨*opponent*⟩; to ~ one's wits against sb se mesurer à qn
**IDIOMS** it's the ~s! (colloq) c'est l'horreur!

**pit bull terrier** *n* pit bull *m*

**pitch** **1** *n* **(a)** (sportsground) terrain *m*; football ~ terrain de foot(ball)
**(b)** (of note, voice) hauteur *f*; (in music) ton *m*;
**(c)** (highest point) comble *m*
**(d)** (sales talk) boniment *m*
**(e)** (for street trader) emplacement *m*
**2** *vtr* **(a)** (throw) jeter (**into** dans); (Sport) lancer
**(b)** adapter ⟨*campaign, speech*⟩ (**at** à)
**(c)** ⟨*singer*⟩ trouver ⟨*note*⟩
**(d)** planter ⟨*tent*⟩; to ~ camp établir un camp
**3** *vi* **(a)** ⟨*boat*⟩ tanguer
**(b)** (US) (in baseball) lancer (la balle)
■ **pitch in** (colloq) (eat) attaquer (colloq); (help) donner un coup de main (colloq)

**pitch-black** *adj* tout/-e noir/-e

**pitcher** *n* **(a)** (jug) cruche *f*
**(b)** (US Sport) lanceur *m*

**pitchfork** *n* fourche *f*

**pitfall** *n* écueil *m* (of de)

**pith** *n* **(a)** (of fruit) peau *f* blanche
**(b)** (of plant) moelle *f*

**pitiful** *adj* ⟨*cry, sight*⟩ pitoyable; ⟨*state*⟩ lamentable; ⟨*amount*⟩ ridicule

**pitiless** *adj* impitoyable

**pittance** *n* to live on/earn a ~ vivre avec/gagner trois fois rien

**pity** **1** *n* **(a)** (compassion) pitié *f* (for pour); out of ~ par pitié; to take ~ on sb avoir pitié de qn
**(b)** (shame) dommage *m*; what a ~! quel dommage!
**2** *vtr* plaindre

**pivot** **1** *vtr* faire pivoter ⟨*lever*⟩; orienter ⟨*lamp*⟩
**2** *vi* **(a)** ⟨*lamp, device*⟩ pivoter (**on** sur)
**(b)** (figurative) ⟨*outcome, success*⟩ reposer (**on** sur)

**pixel** *n* pixel *m*

**pizza** *n* pizza *f*

**placard** *n* (at protest march) pancarte *f*; (on wall) affiche *f*

**place** **1** *n* **(a)** (location, position) endroit *m*; in ~s ⟨*hilly, damaged, worn*⟩ par endroits; ~ of birth/work lieu *m* de naissance/travail; ~ of residence domicile *m*; to be in the right ~ at the right time être là où il faut quand il le faut; to lose/find one's ~ (in book) perdre/retrouver sa page; (in paragraph, speech) perdre/retrouver le fil; all over the ~ (everywhere) partout
**(b)** (home) at Isabelle's ~ chez Isabelle; your ~ or mine? chez toi ou chez moi?
**(c)** (on bus, at table, in queue) place *f*
**(d)** (on team, with firm, on course) place *f* (on dans, **as** comme)
**(e)** (in competition, race) place *f*; to finish in first ~ terminer premier/-ière *or* à la première

place; in the first ~ (firstly, when listing) premièrement; (most importantly, most notably) tout d'abord, pour commencer
**(f)** (correct position) everything is in its ~ tout est bien à sa place; to hold sth in ~ maintenir qch en place; in ~ ⟨*law, system, scheme*⟩ en place; to put sb in his/her ~ remettre qn à sa place
**(g)** (personal level or position) it's not my ~ to do ce n'est pas à moi de faire; in his ~ à sa place
**(h)** (moment) moment *m*; in ~s ⟨*funny, boring, silly*⟩ par moments
**2** *vtr* **(a)** (gen) placer
**(b)** passer ⟨*order*⟩; to place a bet parier (**on** sur)
**(c)** (in competition, exam) classer
**(d)** (identify) situer ⟨*person*⟩; reconnaître ⟨*accent*⟩
**3** out of place *phr* déplacé/-e; to look out of ~ ⟨*building, person*⟩ détonner

**place mat** *n* set *m* de table

**placement** *n* (also **work** ~) stage *m*

**place-name** *n* nom *m* de lieu

**placid** *adj* placide

**plagiarize** *vtr, vi* plagier

**plague** **1** *n* **(a)** (bubonic) peste *f*
**(b)** (epidemic) épidémie *f*
**(c)** (of ants, locusts) invasion *f*
**(d)** (figurative) plaie *f*
**2** *vtr* **(a)** to be ~d by être en proie à ⟨*doubts, difficulties*⟩
**(b)** (harass) harceler

**plaice** *n* plie *f*, carrelet *m*

**plaid** *adj* écossais/-e

**plain** **1** *n* plaine *f*
**2** *adj* **(a)** (simple) simple
**(b)** (of one colour) uni/-e; ⟨*envelope*⟩ sans inscription; a ~ blue dress une robe toute bleue
**(c)** ⟨*woman*⟩ quelconque
**(d)** (obvious) évident/-e, clair/-e; it's ~ to see ça saute aux yeux
**(e)** ⟨*common sense*⟩ simple (before n); ⟨*ignorance*⟩ pur/-e et simple (after n)
**(f)** ⟨*yoghurt, rice*⟩ nature inv

**plain chocolate** *n* choclat *m* à croquer

**plain clothes** *adj* ⟨*policeman*⟩ en civil

**plainly** *adv* **(a)** (obviously) manifestement
**(b)** ⟨*see, remember*⟩ clairement
**(c)** ⟨*speak*⟩ franchement
**(d)** ⟨*dress, eat*⟩ simplement; ⟨*furnished*⟩ sobrement

**plait** *n* natte *f*

**plan** **1** *n* (gen) plan *m*; (definite aim) projet *m* (for de; to do pour faire); to go according to ~ se passer comme prévu
**2** *vtr* **(a)** (prepare, organize) planifier ⟨*future*⟩; organiser, préparer ⟨*timetable, meeting, expedition*⟩; organiser ⟨*day*⟩; faire un plan de ⟨*career*⟩; faire le plan de ⟨*essay, book*⟩; préméditer ⟨*crime*⟩
**(b)** (intend, propose) projeter ⟨*visit, trip*⟩; to ~ to do projeter de faire
**(c)** (design) concevoir

*p*

**3** *vi* prévoir; **to ~ for sth** prévoir qch; **to ~ on doing** compter faire
■ **plan ahead** (vaguely) faire des projets; (look, think ahead) prévoir

**plane** *n* **(a)** (aircraft) avion *m*
**(b)** (in geometry) plan *m*
**(c)** (tool) rabot *m*
**(d)** (*also* **~ tree**) platane *m*

**planet** *n* planète *f*

**plank** *n* planche *f*

**planner** *n* planificateur/-trice *m/f*; (in town planning) urbaniste *mf*

**planning** *n* **(a)** (of industry, economy, work) planification *f*; (of holiday, party) organisation *f*
**(b)** (in town) urbanisme *m*; (out of town) aménagement *m* du territoire

**planning permission** *n* permis *m* de construire

**plant** **1** *n* **(a)** (Bot) plante *f*
**(b)** (factory) usine *f*
**2** *vtr* **(a)** planter ‹seed, bulb, tree›
**(b)** placer ‹bomb, spy›; **to ~ drugs on sb** cacher de la drogue sur qn pour l'incriminer
**3** *v refl* **to ~ oneself between/in front of** se planter entre/devant

**plantation** *n* plantation *f*

**plaque** *n* **(a)** (on wall, monument) plaque *f*
**(b)** (on teeth) plaque *f* dentaire

**plaster** **1** *n* **(a)** (gen) plâtre *m*
**(b)** (GB) (*also* **sticking ~**) sparadrap *m*
**2** *vtr* **(a)** faire les plâtres de ‹house›
**(b)** (cover) couvrir (**with** de)

**plaster cast** *n* plâtre *m*

**plasterer** *n* plâtrier *m*

**plastic** **1** *n* plastique *m*; (credit cards) cartes *fpl* de crédit
**2** *adj* ‹bag, toys, container› en plastique

**plastic surgeon** *n* chirurgien *m* esthétique

**plastic surgery** *n* chirurgie *f* plastique

**plate** **1** **(a)** (dish) (for eating) assiette *f*; (for serving) plat *m*
**(b)** (sheet of metal) plaque *f*, tôle *f*
**(c)** (numberplate) plaque *f* minéralogique
**(d)** (illustration) planche *f*
**(e)** (in dentistry) dentier *m*
**(f)** (in earth's crust) plaque *f*
**2** **-plated** *combining form* **gold/silver-~d** plaqué/-e or/argent

**plate glass** *n* verre *m* à vitre

**platform** *n* **(a)** (for performance) estrade *f*; (at public meeting) tribune *f*
**(b)** (in scaffolding) plate-forme *f*
**(c)** (in politics) plate-forme *f* électorale
**(d)** (at station) quai *m*
**(e)** (Comput) plate-forme *f*

**platform shoes** *n pl* chaussures *fpl* à plateforme

**platinum** *n* platine *m*

**platinum blonde** *n* blonde *f* platine *or* platinée

**platonic** *adj* platonique

**platoon** *n* (of soldiers, police, firemen) section *f*; (in cavalry) peloton *m*

**platter** *n* (dish) plat *m*

**plausible** *adj* plausible, vraisemblable

**play** **1** *n* **(a)** (in theatre) pièce *f* (**about** sur)
**(b)** (recreation) jeu *m*
**(c)** (Sport) (game) partie *f*; **out of ~/in ~** ‹ball› hors jeu/en jeu
**(d)** (movement, interaction) jeu *m*; **to come into ~** entrer en jeu; **a ~ on words** un jeu de mots
**2** *vtr* **(a)** jouer à ‹game, cards›; jouer ‹card›; **to ~ hide and seek** jouer à cache-cache; **to ~ a joke on sb** jouer un tour à qn
**(b)** jouer de ‹instrument›; jouer ‹tune, symphony, chord›; jouer à ‹venue›
**(c)** (in theatre) interpréter, jouer ‹role›
**(d)** mettre ‹tape, video, CD›
**3** *vi* jouer
IDIOMS **to ~ for time** essayer de gagner du temps
■ **play along: to ~ along with sb** entrer dans le jeu de qn
■ **play down** minimiser ‹effects, disaster›
■ **play out: ~ out [sth]** vivre ‹fantasy›
■ **play up** (colloq) ‹computer, person› faire des siennes (colloq)

**play-acting** *n* comédie *f*, simagrées *fpl*

**playboy** *n* playboy *m*

**player** *n* (in sport, music) joueur/-euse *m/f*; (actor) comédien/-ienne *m/f*; **tennis ~** joueur/-euse *m/f* de tennis

**playful** *adj* ‹remark› taquin/-e; ‹child, kitten› joueur/-euse

**playground** *n* cour *f* de récréation

**playgroup** *n* ≈ halte-garderie *f*

**playhouse** *n* théâtre *m*

**playing card** *n* carte *f* à jouer

**playing field** *n* terrain *m* de sport

**play-off** *n* (GB) prolongation *f*; (US) match *m* crucial

**playroom** *n* salle *f* de jeux

**playschool** *n* ≈ halte-garderie *f*

**plaything** *n* jouet *m*

**playtime** *n* récréation *f*

**playwright** *n* auteur *m* dramatique

**plaza** *n* **(a)** (square) place *f*; **shopping ~** centre *m* commercial
**(b)** (US) péage *m*

**plc, PLC** *n* (GB) (*abbr* = **public limited company**) SA

**plea** *n* **(a)** (gen) appel *m* (**for** à); (for money, food) demande *f* (**for** de)
**(b)** (Law) **to enter a ~ of guilty/not guilty** plaider coupable/non coupable

**plead** **1** *vtr* plaider
**2** *vi* **(a)** **to ~ with sb** supplier qn
**(b)** (Law) plaider

**pleasant** *adj* agréable

**please** **1** *adv* s'il vous plaît; (informally) s'il te plaît; **'may I?'—'~ do'** 'je peux?'—'oui, je vous en prie' ····⟩

**p**

2 *vtr* faire plaisir à ⟨*person*⟩; **she is hard to**
~ elle est difficile (à contenter)
3 *vi* plaire; **do as you** ~ fais comme il te
plaira, fais comme tu veux

**pleased** *adj* content/-e (**that** que
+ *subjunctive*; **about, at** de; **with** de); **to look**
~ **with oneself** avoir l'air content de soi; **I**
**am** ~ **to announce that...** j'ai le plaisir
d'annoncer que...; ~ **to meet you** enchanté

**pleasing** *adj* ⟨*appearance, colour, voice*⟩
agréable; ⟨*manner, personality*⟩ avenant/-e;
⟨*effect, result*⟩ heureux/-euse

**pleasurable** *adj* agréable

**pleasure** *n* plaisir *m* (**of** de; **of doing** de
faire); **for** ~ par plaisir; **my** ~ (replying to
request for help) avec plaisir; (replying to thanks)
je vous en prie

**pleat** *n* pli *m*

**pleated** *adj* ⟨*skirt*⟩ plissé/-e; ⟨*trousers*⟩ à
plis (*after n*)

**pledge** 1 *n* (a) (promise) promesse *f*
(b) (money promised to charity) promesse *f* de
don
2 *vtr* promettre ⟨*allegiance, aid, support*⟩ (**to**
à); **to** ~ **one's word** donner sa parole

**plentiful** *adj* abondant/-e

**plenty** *quantif, pron* ~ **of** beaucoup de; ~
**to do** beaucoup à faire

**pliable** *adj* ⟨*twig, plastic*⟩ flexible; ⟨*person*⟩
malléable

**pliers** *n pl* pinces *fpl*; **a pair of** ~**s** des
pinces

**plight** *n* (a) (dilemma) situation *f* désespérée
(b) (suffering) détresse *f*

**plimsoll** *n* (GB) chaussure *f* de tennis

**plod** *v* ■ **plod along** ⟨*walk*⟩ avancer d'un
pas lent
■ **plod away** ⟨*work*⟩ travailler ferme, bosser
(colloq)

**plodder** *n* bûcheur/-euse *m/f* (colloq)

**plonk** (colloq) 1 *n* (wine) vin *m* ordinaire,
pinard *m* (slang)
2 *vtr* (*also* ~ **down**) planter ⟨*plate, bottle,*
*box*⟩ (**on** sur)

**plot** 1 *n* (a) (conspiracy) complot *m*
(b) (of novel, film, play) intrigue *f*
(c) ~ **of land** parcelle *f* de terre; **a vegetable**
~ un carré de légumes
(d) (building site) terrain *m* à bâtir
2 *vtr* (a) (plan) comploter ⟨*murder, attack,*
*return*⟩; fomenter ⟨*revolution*⟩
(b) (chart) relever [qch] sur une carte ⟨*course*⟩
(c) (on graph) tracer [qch] point par point
⟨*curve, graph*⟩
3 *vi* conspirer (**against** contre)

**plough** (GB), **plow** (US) 1 *n* charrue *f*
2 *vtr* (a) labourer ⟨*land, field*⟩; creuser
⟨*furrow*⟩
(b) (invest) **to** ~ **money into** investir
beaucoup d'argent dans ⟨*project, company*⟩
■ **plough back**: ~ [sth] **back**, ~ **back** [sth]
réinvestir ⟨*profits, money*⟩ (**into** dans)
■ **plough through** avancer péniblement
dans ⟨*mud, snow*⟩; ramer sur (colloq) ⟨*book*⟩

**ploy** *n* stratagème *m* (**to do** pour faire)

**pluck** 1 *n* courage *m*, cran *m* (colloq)
2 *vtr* (a) cueillir ⟨*flower, fruit*⟩
(b) plumer ⟨*chicken*⟩
(c) (in music) pincer ⟨*strings*⟩; pincer les
cordes de ⟨*guitar*⟩
(d) **to** ~ **one's eyebrows** s'épiler les sourcils
IDIOMS **to** ~ **up one's courage** prendre son
courage à deux mains

**plucky** *adj* courageux/-euse

**plug** 1 *n* (a) (on appliance) prise *f* (de
courant)
(b) (in bath, sink) bonde *f*
(c) (*also* **spark** ~) bougie *f*
(d) (in advertising) pub *f* (colloq), publicité *f* (**for**
pour)
2 *vtr* (a) boucher ⟨*hole*⟩ (**with** avec)
(b) (colloq) (promote) faire de la publicité pour
⟨*book, show, product*⟩
(c) **to** ~ **sth into** brancher qch à
■ **plug in**: ¶ ~ **in** se brancher; ¶ ~ [sth] **in**
brancher ⟨*appliance*⟩

**plug and play** *n* plug and play *m* (on
branche et ça marche)

**plughole** *n* (GB) bonde *f*

**plum** 1 *n* prune *f*
2 *adj* (a) (colour) prune *inv*
(b) (colloq) **to get a** ~ **job** décrocher un
boulot en or (colloq)

**plumb** 1 *adv* (a) (US) (colloq) ⟨*crazy*⟩
complètement
(b) (colloq) ~ **in the middle** en plein milieu
2 *vtr* sonder ⟨*depths*⟩; **to** ~ **the depths of**
toucher le fond de ⟨*despair, misery*⟩

**plumber** *n* plombier *m*

**plumbing** *n* plomberie *f*

**plummet** *vi* chuter, dégringoler (colloq)

**plump** *adj* ⟨*person, arm, leg*⟩ potelé/-e;
⟨*cheek, face*⟩ rond/-e, plein/-e

**plunge** 1 *vtr* plonger (**into** dans)
2 *vi* ⟨*road, cliff, waterfall*⟩ plonger; ⟨*bird,*
*plane*⟩ piquer; ⟨*person*⟩ (dive) plonger; (fall)
tomber (**from** de); ⟨*rate, value*⟩ chuter
IDIOMS **to take the** ~ se jeter à l'eau

**plunger** *n* ventouse *f*

**plural** 1 *n* pluriel *m*; **in the** ~ au pluriel
2 *adj* ⟨*noun, adjective*⟩ au pluriel; ⟨*form,*
*ending*⟩ du pluriel

**plus** 1 *n* avantage *m*
2 *adj* **the** ~ **side** le côté positif; **50** ~ plus
de 50; **the 65-**~ **age group** les personnes qui
ont 65 ans et plus
3 *prep* plus; **15** ~ **12** 15 plus 12
4 *conj* et; **bedroom** ~ **bathroom** chambre et
salle de bains

**plus-fours** *n pl* culotte *f* de golf

**plus sign** *n* signe *m* plus

**Pluto** *pr n* (planet) Pluton *f*

**plutonium** *n* plutonium *m*

**ply** 1 *vtr* (a) vendre ⟨*wares*⟩; **to** ~ **one's**
**trade** exercer son métier
(b) **to** ~ **sb with food/drink** ne cesser de
remplir l'assiette/le verre de qn

**2** *vi* ⟨*boat, bus*⟩ faire la navette (**between** entre)

**plywood** *n* contreplaqué *m*

**pm** *adv* (*abbr* = **post meridiem**) two ∼ deux heures de l'après-midi; **nine** ∼ neuf heures du soir

**pneumatic drill** *n* marteau *m* piqueur

**pneumonia** *n* pneumonie *f*

**poach** **1** *vtr* (a) chasser [qch] illégalement ⟨*game*⟩
(b) (Culin) faire pocher
**2** *vi* braconner

**poacher** *n* braconnier *m*

**PO Box** *n* boîte *f* postale

**pocket** **1** *n* (a) (in garment) poche *f*
(b) (in billiards) bourse *f*
**2** *adj* ⟨*diary, dictionary, edition*⟩ de poche
**3** *vtr* empocher

**pocketbook** *n* (US) (wallet) portefeuille *m*; (handbag) sac *m* à main

**pocketknife** *n* couteau *m* de poche

**pocket money** *n* argent *m* de poche

**podgy** *adj* (colloq) grassouillet/-ette

**podium** *n* (for speaker, conductor) estrade *f*; (for winner) podium *m*

**poem** *n* poème *m*

**poet** *n* poète *m*

**poetic** *adj* poétique

**poetry** *n* poésie *f*; **to write/read** ∼ écrire/lire des poèmes

**poignant** *adj* poignant/-e

**point** **1** *n* (a) (of knife, needle, pencil) pointe *f*
(b) (location, position on scale) point *m*; (less specific) endroit *m*
(c) (extent, degree) point *m*; **up to a** ∼ jusqu'à un certain point
(d) (moment) (precise) moment *m*; (stage) stade *m*; **to be on the** ∼ **of doing** être sur le point de faire; **at this** ∼ **in her career** à ce stade(-là) de sa carrière; **at some** ∼ **in the future** plus tard; **at one** ∼ à un moment donné
(e) (question, idea) point *m*; **to make the** ∼ **that** faire remarquer que; **you've made your** ∼ vous vous êtes exprimé; **to make a** ∼ **of doing** (as matter of pride) mettre un point d'honneur à faire; (do deliberately) faire exprès
(f) (central idea) point *m* essentiel; **to come straight to the** ∼ aller droit au fait; **to keep** *or* **stick to the** ∼ rester dans le sujet; **to miss the** ∼ ne pas comprendre; **that's beside the** ∼ là n'est pas la question; **to get the** ∼ comprendre; **that's not the** ∼ il ne s'agit pas de cela
(g) (purpose) objet *m*; **what's the** ∼ **of doing...?** à quoi bon faire...?; **there's no** ∼ **in doing** ça ne sert à rien de faire; **I don't see the** ∼ **of doing** je ne vois pas l'intérêt de faire
(h) (feature, characteristic) point *m*, côté *m*; **her strong** ∼ son point fort
(i) (in scoring) point *m*; **match** ∼ (in tennis) balle *f* de match
(j) (decimal point) virgule *f*

(k) (headland) pointe *f*
**2** *vtr* (a) (aim, direct) **to** ∼ **sth at sb** braquer qch sur qn ⟨*camera, gun*⟩; **to** ∼ **one's finger at sb** montrer qn du doigt
(b) (show) **to** ∼ **the way to** indiquer la direction de
(c) (in ballet, gym) **to** ∼ **one's toes** faire des pointes
**3** *vi* (a) (indicate) indiquer *or* montrer (du doigt); **to** ∼ **at sb/sth** montrer qn/qch du doigt
(b) ⟨*signpost, arrow, compass*⟩ indiquer; **to be** ∼**ing at sb** ⟨*gun, camera*⟩ être braqué/-e sur qn

■ **point out** montrer ⟨*place, person*⟩ (**to** à); faire remarquer ⟨*fact, discrepancy*⟩

**point-blank** *adv* (a) ⟨*shoot*⟩ à bout portant
(b) ⟨*refuse, deny*⟩ catégoriquement

**pointed** *adj* (a) ⟨*hat, stick, chin*⟩ pointu/-e
(b) ⟨*remark*⟩ qui vise quelqu'un

**pointer** *n* (a) (piece of information) indication *f*
(b) (on projector screen) flèche *f*
(c) (Comput) pointeur *m*

**pointless** *adj* ⟨*request, activity*⟩ absurde; **it's** ∼ **to do/for me to do** ça ne sert à rien de faire/que je fasse

**point of view** *n* point *m* de vue

**poise** *n* (a) (confidence) assurance *f*
(b) (physical elegance) aisance *f*

**poised** *adj* (a) (self-possessed) plein/-e d'assurance
(b) (elegant) plein/-e d'aisance
(c) (on the point of) **to be** ∼ **to do** être sur le point de faire

**poison** **1** *n* poison *m*
**2** *vtr* empoisonner ⟨*person, environment, relationship*⟩; ⟨*fumes*⟩ intoxiquer ⟨*person*⟩

**poisoning** *n* empoisonnement *m*

**poisonous** *adj* (a) ⟨*chemicals, gas*⟩ toxique; ⟨*mushroom, berry*⟩ vénéneux/-euse; ⟨*snake, insect, bite*⟩ venimeux/-euse
(b) ⟨*rumour, propaganda*⟩ pernicieux/-ieuse

**poke** *vtr* (a) (jab, prod) pousser [qn] du bout du doigt ⟨*person*⟩; donner un coup dans ⟨*pile, substance*⟩; tisonner ⟨*fire*⟩
(b) (push, put) **to** ∼ **sth into** enfoncer qch dans ⟨*hole, pot*⟩; **to** ∼ **one's head out of the window** passer la tête par la fenêtre

■ **poke around**, **poke about** farfouiller (**in** dans)

■ **poke out**: ¶ ∼ **out** ⟨*elbow, toe, blade*⟩ dépasser; ¶ ∼ **out [sth]**, ∼ **[sth] out** sortir ⟨*head, nose, tongue*⟩

**poker** *n* (a) (for fire) tisonnier *m*
(b) (cardgame) poker *m*
IDIOMS (as) **stiff as a** ∼ raide comme la justice

**poker-faced** *adj* ⟨*person*⟩ impassible

**Poland** *pr n* Pologne *f*

**polar** *adj* polaire

**pole** *n* (a) (stick) perche *f*; (for tent, flag) mât *m*; (for skiing) bâton *m*
(b) (of earth's axis) pôle *m*

**Pole** n Polonais/-e m/f
**pole star** n étoile f polaire
**pole vault** n saut m à la perche
**police** ① n (a) (police force) the ∼ la police
(b) (policemen) policiers mpl
② vtr maintenir l'ordre dans ⟨area⟩
**police constable**, **PC** n agent m de police
**Police Department**, **PD** n (US) services mpl de police (d'une ville)
**police force** n police f
**policeman** n agent m de police
**police officer** n policier m
**police station** n poste m de police; (larger) commissariat m
**policewoman** n femme f policier
**policing** n (a) (maintaining law and order) maintien m de l'ordre
(b) (of demonstration, match) organisation f du service d'ordre
(c) (of measures) contrôle m de l'application
**policy** n (a) (plan, rule) politique f (on sur)
(b) (in insurance) (cover) contrat m; (document) police f
**policyholder** n assuré/-e m/f
**policy unit** n comité m de conseillers politiques
**polio** n poliomyélite f
**polish** ① n (a) (for wood, floor) cire f; (for shoes) cirage m; (for brass, silver) pâte f à polir; (for car) lustre m
(b) (shiny surface) éclat m
(c) (of manner, performance) élégance f
② vtr (a) cirer ⟨shoes, furniture⟩; astiquer ⟨leather, car, glass, brass⟩; polir ⟨stone⟩
(b) (refine) soigner ⟨performance, image⟩; affiner ⟨style⟩
■ **polish off** (colloq) expédier (colloq) ⟨food, job⟩
**Polish** ① n (language) polonais m
② adj polonais/-e
**polished** adj (a) ⟨surface, wood⟩ poli/-e; ⟨floor, shoes⟩ ciré/-e
(b) ⟨manner⟩ raffiné/-e
(c) ⟨performance⟩ (bien) rodé/-e
**polite** adj poli/-e (to avec)
**politeness** n politesse f
**political** adj politique
**politically correct**, **PC** adj politiquement correct/-e
**political prisoner** n prisonnier/-ière m/f politique
**politician** n homme/femme m/f politique
**politicize** vtr politiser
**politics** n (a) (gen) politique f
(b) (subject) sciences fpl politiques
(c) (views) opinions fpl politiques
**poll** ① n (a) (vote casting) scrutin m, vote m; (election) élections fpl; to go to the ∼s se rendre aux urnes
(b) (survey) sondage m (on sur)
② vtr (a) obtenir ⟨votes⟩
(b) (canvass) interroger ⟨group⟩

**pollen** n pollen m
**polling booth** n isoloir m
**polling day** n jour m des élections
**polling station** n bureau m de vote
**poll tax** n (GB) ≈ impôts mpl locaux
**pollutant** n polluant m
**pollute** vtr polluer
**polluter** n pollueur/-euse m/f
**pollution** n pollution f
**polo** n polo m
**polo neck** n (GB) col m roulé
**poltergeist** n esprit m frappeur
**poly** ① n (GB) (colloq) abbr = POLYTECHNIC
② poly+ pref poly-
**polystyrene** n polystyrène m
**polytechnic** n (GB) (also **poly**) établissement m d'enseignement supérieur
**polythene** n (GB) polyéthylène m
**pomegranate** n grenade f
**pompom**, **pompon** n pompon m
**pompous** adj ⟨person⟩ plein/-e de suffisance; ⟨air, speech, style⟩ pompeux/-euse
**pond** n (large) étang m; (smaller) mare f; (in garden) bassin m
**ponder** vi réfléchir (on à); (more deeply) méditer (on sur)
**pontiff** n pontife m
**pontoon** n (a) (pier) ponton m
(b) (GB) (Games) vingt-et-un m
**pony** n poney m
**ponytail** n queue f de cheval
**poodle** n caniche m
**pool** ① n (a) (pond) étang m; (artificial) bassin m
(b) (also **swimming** ∼) piscine f
(c) (of water, light) flaque f; a ∼ of blood une mare de sang
(d) (kitty) cagnotte f; (in cards) mises fpl
(e) (of money, resources) pool m; (of ideas, experience) réservoir m
(f) (billiards) billard m américain
② **pools** n pl (GB) (also **football** ∼s) ≈ loto m sportif
③ vtr mettre [qch] en commun
**pool table** n table f de billard américain
**poor** adj (a) ⟨person, country⟩ pauvre (in en)
(b) ⟨quality, work, planning, weather, visibility⟩ mauvais/-e (before n); ⟨attendance⟩ faible
(c) (deserving pity) pauvre (before n); ∼ you! mon/ma pauvre!
(d) ⟨attempt, excuse⟩ piètre (before n)
**poorly** adv (a) ⟨live, dress, dressed⟩ pauvrement
(b) ⟨written, lit, paid⟩ mal
**pop** ① n (a) (sound) pan m; to go ∼ faire pan
(b) (colloq) (drink) soda m
(c) (music) musique f pop
② adj ⟨concert, group, music, song⟩ pop; ⟨record, singer⟩ de pop
③ vtr (a) faire éclater ⟨balloon, bubble⟩
(b) faire sauter ⟨cork⟩

**(c)** (colloq) (put) **to ~ sth in(to)** mettre qch
dans ‹*oven, cupboard, mouth*›
**4** *vi* **(a)** ‹*balloon*› éclater; ‹*cork, buttons*›
sauter
**(b)** ‹*ears*› se déboucher brusquement; **her
eyes were ~ping out of her head** les yeux
lui sortaient de la tête
**(c)** (GB) (colloq) (go) **to ~ into town/the bank**
faire un saut (colloq) en ville/à la banque
■ **pop in** (GB) (colloq) passer
■ **pop out** (GB) (colloq) sortir
■ **pop round, pop over** (GB) (colloq) passer
**pope** *n* pape *m*; **Pope Paul VI** le Pape Paul
VI
**poplar** *n* peuplier *m*
**poppy** *n* pavot *m*; **wild ~** coquelicot *m*
**pop sock** *n* mi-bas *m*
**popular** *adj* **(a)** ‹*actor, politician*›
populaire (**with, among** parmi); ‹*hobby,
sport*› répandu/-e (**with, among** chez); ‹*food,
dish*› prisé/-e (**with, among** par); ‹*product,
resort, colour, design*› en vogue (**with, among**
chez); **John is very ~** John a beaucoup
d'amis
**(b)** (of or for the people) ‹*music, movement,
press*› populaire; ‹*entertainment*› grand
public *inv*; ‹*science, history*› de vulgarisation
**popularity** *n* popularité *f* (**of** de; **with**
auprès de)
**popularize** *vtr* (make fashionable)
généraliser; (make accessible) vulgariser
**population** *n* population *f*
**pop-up menu** *n* menu *m* déroulant
**porcelain** *n* porcelaine *f*
**porch** *n* **(a)** (of house, church) porche *m*
**(b)** (US) (veranda) véranda *f*
**porcupine** *n* porc-épic *m*
**pore** *n* pore *m*
■ **pore over** être plongé/-e dans ‹*book*›;
étudier soigneusement ‹*map*›
**pork** *n* (viande *f* de) porc *m*
**pornographic** *adj* pornographique
**pornography** *n* pornographie *f*
**porpoise** *n* marsouin *m*
**porridge** *n* porridge *m* (*bouillie de flocons
d'avoine*)
**port** *n* **(a)** (harbour) port *m*; **in ~** au port; **~
of call** escale *f*; (figurative) arrêt *m*
**(b)** (drink) porto *m*
**(c)** (Comput) port *m*
**portable** *adj* portable
**porter** *n* **(a)** (in station, airport, hotel) porteur
*m*; (in hospital) brancardier *m*
**(b)** (GB) (doorman) (of hotel) portier *m*; (of
apartment block) gardien/-ienne *m/f*
**(c)** (US) (steward) employé *m* des wagons-lits
**portfolio** *n* **(a)** (case) porte-documents *m
inv*; (for drawings) carton *m* (à dessins)
**(b)** (sample) portfolio *m*
**(c)** (in politics, finance) portefeuille *m*
**porthole** *n* hublot *m*
**portion** *n* **(a)** (of house, machine, document,
country) partie *f* (**of** de)
**(b)** (share) (of money, blame) part *f* (**of** de)

**(c)** (at meal) portion *f*
**portrait** *n* portrait *m*
**portray** *vtr* **(a)** (depict) décrire ‹*place, era,
event*›; présenter ‹*person, situation*›
**(b)** ‹*actor*› interpréter ‹*character*›
**(c)** ‹*artist*› peindre ‹*person*›; ‹*picture, artist*›
représenter ‹*scene*›
**Portugal** *pr n* Portugal *m*
**Portuguese** **1** *n* **(a)** (person) Portugais/-e
*m/f*
**(b)** (language) portugais *m*
**2** *adj* portugais/-e
**pose** **1** *vtr* poser ‹*problem*› (**for** pour);
présenter ‹*challenge*› (**to** à); représenter
‹*threat, risk*› (**to** pour); soulever ‹*question*›
(**about** de)
**2** *vi* **(a)** ‹*artist's model*› poser; ‹*performer*›
prendre des poses
**(b) to ~ as** se faire passer pour
**(c)** (posture) frimer (colloq)
**poser** *n* (colloq) **(a)** (person) frimeur/-euse
*m/f* (colloq)
**(b)** (puzzle) colle *f* (colloq)
**posh** *adj* (colloq) ‹*person*› huppé/-e (colloq);
‹*house, area, clothes, car*› chic; ‹*voice*›
distingué/-e
**position** **1** *n* **(a)** (gen) position *f*; **to be in
~** (in place) être en place; (ready) être prêt/-e
**(b)** (situation, state) situation *f*; **to be in a ~ to
do** être en mesure de faire
**(c)** (Sport) poste *m*; **what ~ does he play?**
quel est son poste?
**(d)** (job) poste *m*
**2** *vtr* poster ‹*policemen, soldiers*›; disposer
‹*object*›
**positive** *adj* **(a)** (affirmative) ‹*answer,
reaction, result*› positif/-ive
**(b)** (optimistic) ‹*message, person, feeling, tone*›
positif/-ive
**(c)** (constructive) ‹*contribution, effect, progress*›
positif/-ive; ‹*advantage, good*› réel/réelle
(**before n**)
**(d)** (sure) ‹*identification, proof*› formel/-elle;
‹*fact*› indéniable; **to be ~** être sûr/-e (**about**
de; **that** que)
**(e)** (forceful) ‹*action*› catégorique
**(f)** (in mathematics, science) positif/-ive
**(g)** (extreme) ‹*pleasure*› pur/-e (**before n**);
‹*disgrace, outrage, genius*› véritable
(**before n**)
**positive discrimination** *n* mesures
*fpl* antidiscriminatoires
**possess** *vtr* **(a)** posséder ‹*property,
weapon, proof, charm*›; avoir ‹*power,
advantage*›; (illegally) détenir ‹*arms, drugs*›
**(b)** (take control of) ‹*anger, fury*› s'emparer de
‹*person*›; ‹*devil*› posséder ‹*person*›; **what
~ed you to do that?** qu'est-ce qui t'a pris de
faire ça?
**possession** **1** *n* **(a)** (gen) possession *f*
**(b)** (Law) (illegal) détention *f* (**of** de)
**2 possessions** *n pl* biens *mpl*
**possessive** **1** *n* (in grammar) possessif *m*
**2** *adj* possessif/-ive (**towards** à l'égard de;
**with** avec)

**possibility** n (a) (chance, prospect) possibilité f
(b) (eventuality) éventualité f

**possible** adj possible; **he did as much as** ~ il a fait tout son possible; **as far as** ~ dans la mesure du possible; **as quickly as** ~ le plus vite possible; **as soon as** ~ dès que possible

**possibly** adv (a) (maybe) peut-être
(b) (for emphasis) **how could they** ~ **understand?** comment donc pourraient-ils comprendre?; **we can't** ~ **afford it** nous n'en avons absolument pas les moyens

**post** ① n (a) (job) poste m (**as, of** de); **to hold a** ~ occuper un poste
(b) (GB) (postal system) poste f; (letters) courrier m; (delivery) distribution f; **by return of** ~ par retour du courrier; **it was lost in the** ~ cela s'est égaré dans le courrier
(c) (Mil) poste m
(d) (pole) poteau m
② **post-** pref post-; **in** ~**-1992 Europe** dans l'Europe d'après 1992
③ vtr (a) (GB) (send by post) poster, expédier [qch] (par la poste); (put in letterbox) mettre [qch] à la poste
(b) (stick up) afficher ⟨notice, poster⟩; annoncer ⟨details, results⟩
(c) (gen, Mil) (send abroad) affecter (**to** à)
(d) (station) poster ⟨guard, sentry⟩

**postage** n affranchissement m; **including** ~ **and packing** frais mpl d'expédition inclus; ~ **free** franc de port

**postal** adj ⟨charges, district⟩ postal/-e; ⟨application⟩ par la poste

**postal order, PO** n (GB) mandat m (**for** de)

**postbox** n (GB) boîte f aux lettres

**postcard** n carte f postale

**post code** n (GB) code m postal

**postdate** vtr postdater

**poster** n (for information) affiche f; (decorative) poster m

**posterity** n postérité f

**poster paint** n gouache f

**postgraduate** ① n ≈ étudiant/-e m/f de troisième cycle
② adj ≈ de troisième cycle

**posthumous** adj posthume

**postman** n facteur m

**postmark** n cachet m de la poste

**post-mortem** n autopsie f

**post-natal** adj post-natal/-e

**post office, PO** n poste f

**postpone** vtr reporter, remettre (**until** à; **for** de)

**postscript** n (in letter) post-scriptum m inv (**to** à); (to book) postface f (**to** à)

**posture** ① n (a) (pose) posture f; (figurative) (stance) position f
(b) (bearing) maintien m; **to have good/bad** ~ se tenir bien/mal
② vi poser, prendre des poses

**post-viral (fatigue) syndrome** n encéphalomyélite f myalgique

**postwar** adj d'après-guerre

**pot** ① n (a) (container) pot m
(b) (teapot) théière f; (coffee pot) cafetière f
(c) ~**s and pans** casseroles fpl
(d) (piece of pottery) poterie f
② vtr (a) mettre [qch] en pot ⟨jam⟩
(b) (in billiards) blouser ⟨ball⟩
(c) mettre [qch] en pot ⟨plant⟩
③ **potted** pp adj (a) ⟨plant⟩ en pot
(b) ⟨biography, history⟩ bref/brève (**before** n)
IDIOMS **to go to** ~ (colloq) ⟨person⟩ se laisser aller; ⟨situation⟩ aller à vau-l'eau; **to take** ~ **luck** (for meal) (GB) manger à la fortune du pot; (gen) prendre ce que l'on trouve

**potassium** n potassium m

**potato** n pomme f de terre

**potato chips** (US), **potato crisps** (GB) n pl chips fpl

**potato peeler** n épluche-légumes m inv

**pot belly** n bedaine f

**potent** adj (a) ⟨symbol, drug⟩ puissant/-e; ⟨drink⟩ fort/-e
(b) (sexually) viril/-e

**potential** ① n potentiel m (**as** en tant que; **for** de); **the** ~ **to do** les qualités fpl nécessaires pour faire; **to fulfil one's** ~ montrer de quoi on est capable
② adj ⟨buyer, danger, energy, market, victim⟩ potentiel/-ielle; ⟨champion, rival⟩ en puissance; ⟨investor⟩ éventuel/-elle

**pothole** n fondrière f, nid m de poule

**potholing** n (GB) spéléologie f

**pot plant** n plante f d'appartement

**potter** n potier m
■ **potter about, potter around** (GB) (do odd jobs) bricoler (colloq); (go about daily chores) suivre son petit train-train (colloq)

**pottery** n poterie f

**potting compost** n terreau m

**potty** (colloq) ① n pot m (d'enfant)
② adj (GB) ⟨person⟩ dingue (colloq); ⟨idea⟩ farfelu/-e (colloq); **to be** ~ **about** être toqué/-e de (colloq)

**pouch** n (a) (bag) petit sac m; (for tobacco) blague f (à tabac); (for ammunition) étui m (à munitions)
(b) (of marsupials) poche f ventrale

**poultry** n (birds) volailles fpl; (meat) volaille f

**pounce** vi bondir; **to** ~ **on** ⟨animal⟩ bondir sur ⟨prey, object⟩; ⟨person⟩ se jeter sur ⟨victim⟩

**pound** ① n (a) (weight measurement) livre f (= 453.6 g); **two** ~**s of apples** ≈ un kilo de pommes
(b) (unit of currency) livre f
(c) (for dogs, cars) fourrière f
② vtr (a) (Culin) piler ⟨spices, grain⟩; aplatir ⟨meat⟩
(b) ⟨waves⟩ battre ⟨shore⟩
(c) ⟨artillery⟩ pilonner ⟨city⟩
③ vi (a) **to** ~ **on** marteler ⟨door, wall⟩
(b) ⟨heart⟩ battre

**(c)** to ~ **up/down the stairs** monter/descendre l'escalier d'un pas lourd
**(d) my head is** ~**ing** j'ai l'impression que ma tête va éclater

**pour** **1** *vtr* **(a)** verser ⟨*liquid*⟩; couler ⟨*cement, metal, wax*⟩
**(b)** (*also* ~ **out**) servir ⟨*drink*⟩
**(c)** to ~ **money into** investir des sommes énormes dans
**2** *vi* **(a)** ⟨*liquid*⟩ couler (à flots); to ~ **into** ⟨*water, liquid*⟩ couler dans; ⟨*smoke, fumes*⟩ se répandre dans; ⟨*light*⟩ inonder ⟨*room*⟩; **tears** ~**ed down her face** les larmes ruisselaient sur son visage
**(b)** to ~ **into** ⟨*people*⟩ affluer dans; to ~ **out of** ⟨*people, cars*⟩ sortir en grand nombre de
**3** *v impers* **it's** ~**ing** (**with rain**) il pleut à verse
■ **pour away** vider
■ **pour in** ⟨*people*⟩ affluer; ⟨*letters, money*⟩ pleuvoir; ⟨*water*⟩ entrer à flots
■ **pour out:** ¶ ~ **out** ⟨*liquid, smoke, crowd*⟩ se déverser; ⟨*people*⟩ sortir en grand nombre ¶ ~ [**sth**] **out (a)** verser, servir ⟨*coffee, wine*⟩
**(b)** rejeter ⟨*fumes, sewage*⟩; to ~ **out one's troubles** *or* **heart to sb** s'épancher auprès de qn

**pout** *vi* faire la moue

**poverty** *n* pauvreté *f*; (more severe) misère *f*

**poverty line** *n* seuil *m* de pauvreté

**poverty-stricken** *adj* dans la misère

**POW** *n* (*abbr* = **prisoner of war**) prisonnier/-ière *m/f* de guerre

**powder** **1** *n* poudre *f*
**2** *vtr* to ~ **one's face** se poudrer le visage

**powdered** *adj* ⟨*egg, milk, coffee*⟩ en poudre

**powdery** *adj* ⟨*snow*⟩ poudreux/-euse; ⟨*stone*⟩ friable

**power** **1** *n* **(a)** (control) pouvoir *m*; **to be in/come to** ~ être/accéder au pouvoir; **to be in sb's** ~ être à la merci de qn
**(b)** (influence) influence *f* (**over** sur)
**(c)** (capability) pouvoir *m*; **to do everything in one's** ~ faire tout ce qui est en son pouvoir (**to do** pour faire)
**(d)** (*also* ~**s**) (authority) attributions *fpl*
**(e)** ( physical force) (of person, explosion) force *f*; (of storm) violence *f*
**(f)** (Tech) énergie *f*; (current) courant *m*; **to switch on the** ~ mettre le courant
**(g)** (of vehicle, plane) puissance *f*; **to be running at full/half** ~ fonctionner à plein/mi-régime
**(h)** (in mathematics) **6 to the** ~ **of 3** 6 puissance 3
**(i)** (country) puissance *f*
**2** *adj* ⟨*drill, cable*⟩ électrique; ⟨*brakes*⟩ assisté/-e
**3** *vtr* faire marcher ⟨*engine*⟩; propulser ⟨*plane, boat*⟩
IDIOMS **to do sb a** ~ **of good** faire à qn un bien fou; **the** ~**s that be** les autorités

**powerboat** *n* hors-bord *m inv*

**power cut** *n* coupure *f* de courant

**powerful** *adj* ⟨*person, engine, computer*⟩ puissant/-e; ⟨*smell, emotion, voice, government*⟩ fort/-e; ⟨*argument*⟩ solide

**powerless** *adj* impuissant/-e (**against** face à); **to be** ~ **to do** ne pas pouvoir faire

**power line** *n* ligne *f* à haute tension

**power of attorney** *n* procuration *f*

**power plant** (US), **power station** *n* centrale *f* (électrique)

**power sharing** *n* partage *m* du pouvoir

**power steering** *n* direction *f* assistée

**power user** *n* (Comput) utilisateur/-trice *mf* avancé/-e

**PR** *n* **(a)** (*abbr* = **public relations**) relations *fpl* publiques
**(b)** *abbr* = PROPORTIONAL REPRESENTATION

**practical** **1** *n* (exam) épreuve *f* pratique; (lesson) travaux *mpl* pratiques
**2** *adj* **(a)** (gen) pratique
**(b)** ⟨*plan*⟩ réalisable

**practicality** *n* **(a)** (of person) esprit *m* pratique; (of equipment) facilité *f* d'utilisation
**(b)** (of scheme, idea, project) aspect *m* pratique

**practical joke** *n* farce *f*

**practically** *adv* **(a)** (almost) pratiquement
**(b)** (in practical way) d'une manière pratique

**practice** **1** *n* **(a)** (exercises) exercices *mpl*; (experience) entraînement *m*; **to have had** ~ **in** *or* **at sth/in** *or* **at doing sth** avoir déjà fait qch; **to be out of** ~ être rouillé/-e (colloq)
**(b)** (for sport) entraînement *m*; (for music, drama) répétition *f*
**(c)** (procedure) pratique *f*, usage *m*; **it's standard** ~ **to do** il est d'usage de faire; **business** ~ usage en affaires
**(d)** (habit) habitude *f*
**(e)** (custom) coutume *f*
**(f)** (business of doctor, lawyer) cabinet *m*
**(g)** (not theory) pratique *f*; **in** ~ en pratique
**2** *adj* ⟨*game, match*⟩ d'essai; ⟨*flight*⟩ d'entraînement
**3** *vtr, vi* (US) = PRACTISE
IDIOMS ~ **makes perfect** c'est en forgeant qu'on devient forgeron (Proverb)

**practise** (GB), **practice** (US) **1** *vtr* **(a)** travailler ⟨*song, speech, French*⟩; s'exercer à ⟨*movement, shot*⟩; répéter ⟨*play*⟩; **to** ~ **the piano** travailler le piano; **to** ~ **doing** *or* **how to do** s'entraîner à faire
**(b)** (use) pratiquer ⟨*restraint, kindness*⟩; utiliser ⟨*method*⟩
**(c)** exercer ⟨*profession*⟩
**(d)** (observe) pratiquer ⟨*custom, religion*⟩
**2** *vi* **(a)** (at instrument) s'exercer; (for sports) s'entraîner; (for play, concert) répéter
**(b)** (work) exercer; **to** ~ **as** exercer la profession de ⟨*doctor, lawyer*⟩

**practising** (GB), **practicing** (US) *adj* ⟨*Christian, Muslim*⟩ pratiquant/-e; ⟨*doctor, lawyer*⟩ en exercice; ⟨*homosexual*⟩ actif/-ive

**pragmatic** *adj* pragmatique

**pragmatist** *n* pragmatiste *mf*

**prairie** *n* plaine *f* (herbeuse)

**praise** **1** *n* éloges *mpl*, louanges *fpl* ⋯❖

2 *vtr* (a) faire l'éloge de ⟨*person, book*⟩ (as en tant que)
(b) louer ⟨*God*⟩ (for pour)
**praiseworthy** *adj* digne d'éloges
**pram** *n* (GB) landau *m*
**prance** *vi* ⟨*horse*⟩ caracoler; ⟨*person*⟩ sautiller
**prank** *n* farce *f*
**prattle** *vi* bavarder; ⟨*children*⟩ babiller; to ∼ on about sth parler de qch à n'en plus finir
**prawn** *n* crevette *f* rose, bouquet *m*
**pray** *vi* prier (for pour)
**prayer** *n* prière *f*; to say one's ∼s faire sa prière
**preach** 1 *vtr* prêcher (to à)
2 *vi* prêcher (to à); (figurative) sermonner
IDIOMS to practise what one ∼es prêcher d'exemple
**preacher** *n* prédicateur *m*; (clergyman) pasteur *m*
**prearrange** *vtr* fixer [qch] à l'avance
**precarious** *adj* précaire
**precaution** *n* précaution *f* (against contre)
**precautionary** *adj* préventif/-ive
**precede** *vtr* précéder
**precedence** *n* (a) (in importance) priorité *f* (over sur)
(b) (in rank) préséance *f* (over sur)
**precedent** *n* précédent *m*; to set a ∼ créer un précédent
**preceding** *adj* précédent/-e
**precinct** *n* (a) (GB) (*also* **shopping** ∼) quartier *m* commerçant
(b) (GB) (*also* **pedestrian** ∼) zone *f* piétonne
(c) (US) (administrative district) circonscription *f*
**precious** *adj* (a) (valuable) précieux/-ieuse
(b) (held dear) ⟨*person*⟩ cher/chère (to à)
(c) (affected) précieux/-ieuse, affecté/-e
**precipice** *n* précipice *m*
**précis** *n* résumé *m*
**precise** *adj* (a) (exact) précis/-e
(b) ⟨*person, mind*⟩ méticuleux/-euse
**precisely** *adv* (a) (exactly) exactement, précisément; at ten o'clock ∼ à dix heures précises
(b) (accurately) ⟨*describe, record*⟩ avec précision
**precision** *n* précision *f*
**preclude** *vtr* exclure ⟨*possibility*⟩; empêcher ⟨*action*⟩
**precocious** *adj* précoce
**preconceived** *adj* préconçu/-e
**preconception** *n* opinion *f* préconçue
**precondition** *n* condition *f* requise
**precursor** *n* (person) précurseur *m*; (sign) signe *m* avant-coureur
**predate** *vtr* antidater ⟨*cheque*⟩; ⟨*discovery, building*⟩ être antérieur/-e à
**predator** *n* prédateur *m*
**predecessor** *n* prédécesseur *m*

**predetermine** *vtr* déterminer d'avance
**predicament** *n* situation *f* difficile
**predict** *vtr* prédire
**predictable** *adj* prévisible
**prediction** *n* prédiction *f* (that selon laquelle)
**predispose** *vtr* prédisposer
**predominant** *adj* prédominant/-e
**predominantly** *adv* principalement
**predominate** *vi* prédominer
**pre-eminent** *adj* éminent/-e
**pre-empt** *vtr* (a) anticiper ⟨*question, decision, move*⟩; devancer ⟨*person*⟩
(b) (thwart) contrecarrer ⟨*action, plan*⟩
**pre-emptive** *adj* préventif/-ive
**preen** *v refl* to ∼ oneself ⟨*bird*⟩ se lisser les plumes; ⟨*person*⟩ se pomponner
**prefab** *n* (bâtiment *m*) préfabriqué *m*
**preface** *n* (to book) préface *f*; (to speech) préambule *m*
**prefect** *n* (GB) (Sch) élève *m/f* chargé/-e de la surveillance
**prefer** *vtr* (a) (like better) préférer, aimer mieux; I ∼ painting to drawing je préfère la peinture au dessin; to ∼ it if aimer mieux que (+ *subjunctive*)
(b) (Law) to ∼ charges ⟨*police*⟩ déférer [qn] au parquet
**preferable** *adj* préférable (to à)
**preferably** *adv* de préférence
**preference** *n* préférence *f* (for pour)
**preferential** *adj* préférentiel/-ielle
**prefigure** *vtr* ⟨*event*⟩ préfigurer; ⟨*person*⟩ être le précurseur de
**prefix** *n* préfixe *m*
**pregnancy** *n* (gen) grossesse *f*; (Zool) gestation *f*
**pregnant** *adj* (gen) enceinte; (Zool) pleine; to get sb ∼ (colloq) faire un enfant à qn (colloq)
**preheat** *vtr* préchauffer ⟨*oven*⟩
**prehistoric** *adj* préhistorique
**prejudice** 1 *n* préjugé *m*; racial/political ∼ préjugés raciaux/en matière de politique
2 *vtr* (a) (bias) influencer; to ∼ sb against/in favour of prévenir qn contre/en faveur de
(b) porter préjudice à ⟨*claim, case*⟩; léser ⟨*person*⟩; compromettre ⟨*chances*⟩
**prejudiced** *adj* ⟨*person*⟩ plein/-e de préjugés; ⟨*account*⟩ partial/-e; ⟨*opinion*⟩ préconçu/-e
**preliminary** 1 *n* (a) (gen) as a ∼ to en prélude à
(b) (Sport) épreuve *f* éliminatoire
2 **preliminaries** *n pl* préliminaires *mpl* (to à)
3 *adj* préliminaire
**prelude** *n* prélude *m* (to à)
**premarital** *adj* avant le mariage
**premature** *adj* ⟨*baby, action*⟩ prématuré/-e; ⟨*ejaculation, menopause*⟩ précoce

**premeditate** *vtr* préméditer
**premier** [1] *n* premier ministre *m*
[2] *adj* premier/-ière (*before n*)
**première** [1] *n* première *f*
[2] *vtr* donner [qch] en première (*film, play*)
**premises** *n pl* locaux *mpl*; on the ~ sur place; off the ~ à l'extérieur; to leave the ~ quitter les lieux
**premium** *n* (a) (extra payment) supplément *m*
(b) (on stock exchange) prime *f* d'émission
(c) (in insurance) prime *f* (d'assurance)
(d) to be at a ~ valoir de l'or; to set a (high) ~ on sth mettre qch au (tout) premier plan
**premium bond** (GB) *n* obligation *f* à lots
**premonition** *n* prémonition *f*
**prenatal** *adj* prénatal/-e
**preoccupation** *n* préoccupation *f*
**preoccupied** *adj* préoccupé/-e
**preoccupy** *vtr* préoccuper
**prepaid** *adj* payé/-e d'avance; ~ envelope enveloppe *f* affranchie pour la réponse
**preparation** *n* préparation *f*; ~s préparatifs *mpl*; in ~ for sth en vue de qch
**preparatory** *adj* (*training, course, drawing*) préparatoire; (*meeting, report, investigations*) préliminaire
**preparatory school** *n* (a) (GB) école *f* primaire privée
(b) (US) lycée *m* privé
**prepare** [1] *vtr* préparer; to ~ to do se préparer à faire; to ~ sb for préparer qn à
[2] *vi* to ~ for se préparer à (*trip, talks, exam, war*); se préparer pour (*party, ceremony, game*); to ~ oneself se préparer
**prepared** *adj* (a) (willing) to be ~ to do être prêt/-e à faire
(b) (ready) to be ~ for être prêt/-e pour (*event*); to come ~ venir bien préparé/-e; to be ~ for the worst s'attendre au pire
**preposition** *n* préposition *f*
**preposterous** *adj* grotesque
**prerequisite** *n* (a) (gen) préalable *m* (of de; for à)
(b) (US) (Univ) unité *f* de valeur
**prerogative** *n* (official) prérogative *f*; (personal) droit *m*
**preschool** [1] *n* (US) école *f* maternelle
[2] *adj* préscolaire
**prescribe** *vtr* (a) (Med, figurative) prescrire (for sb à qn; for sth pour qch)
(b) imposer (*rule*)
**prescription** *n* ordonnance *f*; repeat ~ ordonnance renouvelable
**prescription charges** *n pl* frais *mpl* d'ordonnance
**presence** *n* présence *f*
**presence of mind** *n* présence *f* d'esprit
**present** [1] *n* (a) (gift) cadeau *m*; to give sb a ~ offrir un cadeau à qn
(b) the ~ le présent; for the ~ pour le moment, pour l'instant
(c) (*also* ~ **tense**) présent *m*

[2] *adj* (a) (attending) présent/-e; to be ~ at assister à
(b) (current) actuel/-elle; up to the ~ day jusqu'à ce jour
[3] *vtr* (a) (gen) présenter; offrir (*chance, opportunity*); to be ~ed with a choice se trouver face à un choix
(b) remettre (*prize, certificate*) (to à)
[4] *v refl* to ~ oneself se présenter; to ~ itself (*opportunity, thought*) se présenter
[5] **at present** *phr* (at this moment) en ce moment; (nowadays) actuellement
**presentable** *adj* présentable
**presentation** *n* (a) (gen) présentation *f*
(b) (talk) exposé *m*
(c) (of gift, award) remise *f* (of de)
(d) (portrayal) représentation *f*
**present-day** *adj* actuel/-elle
**presenter** *n* présentateur/-trice *m/f*
**presently** *adv* (currently) à présent; (soon, in future) bientôt
**present perfect** *n* passé *m* composé
**preservation** *n* (of building, wildlife, peace) préservation *f* (of de); (of food) conservation *f* (of de); (of life) protection *f* (of de)
**preservative** *n* (for food) agent *m* de conservation; (for wood) revêtement *m* (protecteur)
**preserve** [1] *n* (a) (Culin) (jam) confiture *f*; (pickle) conserve *f*
(b) (territory) chasse *f* gardée (of de)
[2] *vtr* (a) (save) préserver (*land, building, tradition*) (for pour); entretenir (*wood, leather, painting*)
(b) (maintain) préserver (*peace, standards, rights*); maintenir (*order*); garder (*humour, dignity, health*)
(c) conserver (*food*)
**preset** *vtr* régler (à l'avance) (*timer, cooker*); programmer (*video*)
**preside** *vi* présider; to ~ at sth présider qch; to ~ over présider (*conference, committee*)
**presidency** *n* présidence *f*
**president** *n* (a) président/-e *m/f*; to run for ~ être candidat/-e à la présidence
(b) (US) (managing director) président-directeur *m* général
**presidential** *adj* présidentiel/-ielle
**press** [1] *n* (a) the ~, the Press la presse *f*; to get a good/bad ~ avoir bonne/mauvaise presse
(b) (*also* **printing** ~) presse *f*
(c) (device for flattening) presse *f*
[2] *vtr* (a) (push) appuyer sur; to ~ sth in enfoncer qch; to ~ one's nose against sth coller son nez contre qch
(b) (squeeze) presser (*fruit, flower*); serrer (*arm, hand, person*)
(c) (iron) repasser (*clothes*)
(d) (urge) faire pression sur (*person*); mettre [qch] en avant (*issue*); to ~ sb to do presser qn de faire; to ~ a point insister
[3] *vi* (a) to ~ (down) appuyer

**p**

**(b)** ⟨crowd, person⟩ se presser (**forward** vers l'avant)
**4** v refl **to ~ oneself against** se plaquer contre ⟨wall⟩; se presser contre ⟨person⟩
■ **press for** faire pression pour obtenir ⟨change, release⟩; **to be ~ed for** ne pas avoir beaucoup de ⟨time, cash⟩
■ **press on** continuer; **to ~ on with** faire avancer ⟨reform, plan⟩

**press agency** n agence f de presse
**press conference** n conférence f de presse
**pressing** adj **(a)** (urgent) urgent/-e
**(b)** ⟨invitation⟩ pressant/-e
**press release** n communiqué m de presse
**press-stud** n (GB) (bouton-)pression m
**press-up** n pompe f (colloq)
**pressure** n **(a)** (gen) pression f; **to put ~ on sb** faire pression sur qn; **to do sth under ~** faire qch sous la contrainte
**(b)** (of traffic, tourists) flux m
**pressure cooker** n cocotte-minute® f
**pressure group** n groupe m de pression
**pressurize** vtr **(a)** pressuriser ⟨cabin, suit, gas⟩
**(b)** faire pression sur ⟨person⟩; **he was ~d into going** on a fait pression sur lui pour qu'il y aille
**prestige** n prestige m
**prestigious** adj prestigieux/-ieuse
**presumably** adv sans doute
**presume** vtr **(a)** (suppose) supposer, présumer
**(b)** (dare) **to ~ to do** se permettre de faire
**presumptuous** adj présomptueux/-euse, arrogant/-e
**presuppose** vtr présupposer ⟨that que⟩
**pre-tax** adj avant impôts inv
**pretence** (GB), **pretense** (US) n faux-semblant m; **to make a ~ of sth** feindre qch; **to make a ~ of doing** faire semblant de faire
**pretend** **1** vtr **to ~ that** faire comme si; **to ~ to do** faire semblant de faire
**2** vi faire semblant
**pretension** n prétention f
**pretentious** adj prétentieux/-ieuse
**preterite** n prétérit m
**pretext** n prétexte m
**pretty** **1** adj joli/-e; **it was not a ~ sight** ce n'était pas beau à voir
**2** adv (colloq) (very) vraiment; (fairly) assez; **~ good** pas mal du tout
**prevail** vi **(a)** (win) prévaloir (**against** contre)
**(b)** (be common) prédominer
■ **prevail upon** persuader ⟨person⟩
**prevailing** adj ⟨attitude, style⟩ qui prévaut; ⟨rate⟩ en vigueur; ⟨wind⟩ dominant/-e
**prevalent** adj **(a)** (widespread) répandu/-e
**(b)** (ruling) qui prévaut
**prevaricate** vi se dérober

**prevent** vtr prévenir ⟨fire, illness, violence⟩; éviter ⟨conflict, disaster, damage⟩; faire obstacle à ⟨marriage⟩; **to ~ sb from doing** empêcher qn de faire
**preventable** adj évitable
**prevention** n prévention f; **crime ~** lutte f contre la délinquance
**preventive** adj préventif/-ive
**preview** n (of film, play) avant-première f
**previous** adj précédent/-e; (further back in time) antérieur/-e
**previously** adv (before) auparavant, avant; (already) déjà
**prewar** adj d'avant-guerre inv
**prey** n proie f
■ **prey on (a)** (hunt) chasser
**(b)** (worry) **to ~ on sb's mind** préoccuper qn
**(c)** (exploit) exploiter ⟨fears, worries⟩
**price** **1** n **(a)** (cost) prix m; **to go up in ~** augmenter; **to pay a high ~ for sth** payer qch cher; **at any ~** à tout prix
**(b)** (value) valeur f; **to put a ~ on** évaluer ⟨object, antique⟩
**2** vtr fixer le prix de (**at** à)
**price cut** n baisse f du prix
**price freeze** n blocage m des prix
**priceless** adj **(a)** (extremely valuable) inestimable
**(b)** (colloq) (amusing) impayable (colloq)
**price list** n (in shop, catalogue) liste f des prix; (in bar, restaurant) tarif m
**price rise** n hausse f des prix
**price tag** n (label) étiquette f
**price war** n guerre f des prix
**prick** **1** n (of needle) piqûre f
**2** vtr piquer; **to ~ one's finger** se piquer le doigt
**3** vi piquer
■ **prick up: to ~ up one's ears** ⟨person⟩ dresser l'oreille; **the dog ~ed up its ears** le chien a dressé les oreilles
**prickle** **1** n (of hedgehog, plant) piquant m
**2** vi ⟨hairs⟩ se hérisser (**with** de)
**prickly** adj **(a)** ⟨bush, leaf⟩ épineux/-euse; ⟨animal⟩ armé/-e de piquants; ⟨thorn⟩ piquant/-e
**(b)** (itchy) qui gratte
**(c)** (colloq) (touchy) irritable (**about** à propos de)
**pride** **1** n **(a)** fierté f; **to take ~ in** être fier/fière de ⟨ability, achievement⟩; soigner ⟨appearance, work⟩; **to be sb's ~ and joy** être la (grande) fierté de qn
**(b)** (self-respect) amour-propre m; (excessive) orgueil m
**(c)** (of lions) troupe f
**2** v refl **to ~ oneself on sth/on doing** être fier/fière de qch/de faire
IDIOMS **to have ~ of place** occuper la place d'honneur
**priest** n prêtre m; **parish ~** curé m
**priesthood** n (calling) prêtrise f; **to enter the ~** entrer dans les ordres
**prig** n bégueule mf

**prim** *adj* (also ~ **and proper**) ‹*person, manner, appearance*› guindé/-e; ‹*expression*› pincé/-e; ‹*voice*› affecté/-e; ‹*clothing*› très convenable

**primarily** *adv* (chiefly) essentiellement; (originally) à l'origine

**primary** ⓵ *n* (US) (also ~ **election**) primaire *f*
⓶ *adj* (a) (main) principal/-e; ‹*sense, meaning, stage*› premier/-ière; **of ~ importance** de première importance
(b) (Sch) ‹*teaching, education*› primaire
(c) ‹*industry, products*› de base

**primary colour** (GB), **primary color** (US) *n* couleur *f* primaire

**primary school** *n* école *f* primaire

**primary (school) teacher** *n* (GB) instituteur/-trice *m/f*

**primate** *n* (a) (mammal) primate *m*
(b) (archbishop) primat *m* (of de)

**prime** ⓵ *n* **in one's ~** (professionally) à son apogée; (physically) dans la fleur de l'âge; **in its ~** à son apogée; **to be past its ~** avoir connu des jours meilleurs
⓶ *adj* (a) (chief) principal/-e; ‹*importance*› primordial/-e
(b) (good quality) ‹*site*› de premier ordre; ‹*meat, cuts*› de premier choix; **of ~ quality** de première qualité
(c) (classic) ‹*example*› excellent/-e (before n)
⓷ *vtr* (a) (brief) préparer; **to ~ sb about** mettre qn au courant de; **to ~ sb to say** souffler à qn de dire
(b) (Mil, Tech) amorcer

**prime minister**, **PM** *n* Premier ministre *m*

**prime mover** *n* (person) promoteur/-trice *m/f*

**prime number** *n* nombre *m* premier

**prime time** *n* heures *fpl* de grande écoute *m*

**primeval** *adj* primitif/-ive

**primitive** ⓵ *n* primitif *m*
⓶ *adj* primitif/-ive

**primrose** *n* primevère *f* (jaune)

**prince** *n* prince *m*

**princess** *n* princesse *f*

**principal** ⓵ *n* (of senior school) proviseur *m*; (of junior school, college) directeur/-trice *m/f*
⓶ *adj* principal/-e

**principle** *n* principe *m*; **in ~** en principe; **on ~** par principe

**print** ⓵ *n* (a) (typeface) caractères *mpl*; **the small** *or* **fine ~** les détails; **in ~** disponible en librairie; **out of ~** épuisé/-e
(b) (etching) estampe *f*; (engraving) gravure *f*
(c) (of photo) épreuve *f*
(d) (of finger, hand, foot) empreinte *f*; (of tyre) trace *f*
(e) (fabric) tissu *m* imprimé
⓶ *vtr* (a) imprimer ‹*book, banknote, pattern, design*›
(b) (publish) publier
(c) faire développer ‹*photos*›

(d) (write) écrire [qch] en script

■ **print off** tirer ‹*copies*›

■ **print out** imprimer

**printer** *n* (person, firm) imprimeur *m*; (machine) imprimante *f*

**printout** *n* sortie *f* sur imprimante; (perforated) listing *m*

**print-preview** *vtr* prévisualiser

**prior** ⓵ *adj* (a) (previous) préalable; ~ **notice** préavis *m*
(b) (more important) prioritaire
⓶ **prior to** *phr* avant

**priority** *n* priorité *f*

**priory** *n* prieuré *m*

**prise** *v* ■ **prise apart** séparer ‹*layers, people*›

■ **prise off** enlever [qch] en forçant ‹*lid*›

■ **prise open** ouvrir [qch] en forçant ‹*door*›

**prism** *n* prisme *m*

**prison** *n* prison *f*; **to put sb in ~** emprisonner qn

**prison camp** *n* camp *m* de prisonniers

**prisoner** *n* prisonnier/-ière *m/f*; (in jail) détenu/-e *m/f*

**prison officer** *n* surveillant/-e *m/f* de prison

**prison sentence** *n* peine *f* de prison

**pristine** *adj* immaculé/-e

**privacy** *n* (a) (private life) vie *f* privée; **to invade sb's ~** s'immiscer dans la vie privée de qn
(b) (solitude) intimité *f* (of de)

**private** ⓵ *n* simple soldat *m*
⓶ *adj* (a) ‹*property, vehicle, meeting, life*› privé/-e; ‹*letter, phone call*› personnel/-elle; ‹*sale*› de particulier à particulier; ‹*place*› tranquille; **room with ~ bath** chambre avec salle de bains particulière; **a ~ joke** une plaisanterie pour initiés
(b) ‹*sector, education, school, hospital*› privé/-e; ‹*accommodation, lesson*› particulier/-ière
⓷ **in private** *phr* en privé

**private eye** *n* (colloq) détective *m* privé

**privately** *adv* (a) (in private) en privé
(b) (not in public sector) dans le privé; ~-**owned** privé/-e

**privatization** *n* privatisation *f*

**privatize** *vtr* privatiser

**privilege** *n* privilège *m*

**privileged** *adj* ‹*minority, life*› privilégié/-e; ‹*information*› confidentiel/-ielle

**prize** ⓵ *n* (a) (award) prix *m*; (in lottery) lot *m*; **first ~** premier prix; (in lottery) gros lot
(b) (valued object) trésor *m*; (reward for effort) récompense *f*
⓶ *adj* (a) ‹*vegetable, bull*› primé/-e; ‹*pupil*› hors-pair *inv*
(b) ‹*possession*› précieux/-ieuse
(c) ‹*idiot, example*› parfait/-e (before n)

**prize draw** *n* (for charity) tombola *f*; (for advertising) tirage *m* au sort

**prize-giving** *n* remise *f* des prix

**prize money** n argent m du prix

**prizewinner** n (in lottery) gagnant/-e m/f; (of award) lauréat/-e m/f

**pro** [1] n (a) (colloq) (professional) pro mf (colloq)
(b) (advantage) **the ~s and cons** le pour et le contre; **the ~s and cons of sth** les avantages et les inconvénients de qch
[2] prep (colloq) (in favour of) pour

**proactive** adj ⟨approach, role⟩ dynamique

**probability** n (of desirable event) chances fpl; (of unwelcome event) risques mpl

**probable** adj probable

**probably** adv probablement

**probation** n (a) (for adult) sursis m avec mise à l'épreuve; (for juvenile) mise f en liberté surveillée
(b) (trial period) période f d'essai

**probationary** adj (trial) ⟨period, year⟩ d'essai; (training) ⟨period⟩ probatoire

**probation officer** n (for juveniles) délégué/-e m/f à la liberté surveillée; (for adults) agent m de probation

**probe** [1] n (a) (investigation) enquête f
(b) (instrument) sonde f
[2] vtr (Med, Tech) sonder (with avec)

**probing** adj ⟨look⟩ inquisiteur/-trice; ⟨question⟩ pénétrant/-e; ⟨examination⟩ très poussé/-e

**problem** [1] n problème m
[2] adj ⟨child⟩ difficile; ⟨family⟩ à problèmes

**problematic(al)** adj problématique

**problem page** n courrier m du cœur

**procedure** n procédure f

**proceed** vi (a) (set about) procéder; (continue) poursuivre; **to ~ with** poursuivre
(b) (be in progress) ⟨project, work⟩ avancer; ⟨interview, talks, trial⟩ se poursuivre
(c) ⟨person, road⟩ continuer; ⟨vehicle⟩ avancer

**proceedings** n pl (a) (meeting) réunion f; (ceremony) cérémonie f; (discussion) débats mpl
(b) (Law) poursuites fpl

**proceeds** n pl (of sale) produit m; (of event) recette f

**process** [1] n (a) (gen) processus m (of de); **to be in the ~ of doing** être en train de faire; **in the ~** en même temps
(b) (method) procédé m
[2] vtr (a) traiter ⟨applications, data⟩
(b) traiter ⟨raw materials, chemical, waste⟩
(c) développer ⟨film⟩
(d) (Culin) (mix) mixer; (chop) hacher

**processing** n traitement m; **the food ~ industry** l'industrie alimentaire

**procession** n (of demonstration, carnival) défilé m; (formal) cortège m; (religious) procession f

**processor** n (Comput) unité f centrale

**proclaim** vtr proclamer (that que)

**proclamation** n proclamation f

**procrastinate** vi atermoyer

**procure** vtr procurer; **to ~ sth for sb** procurer qch à qn; **to ~ sth for oneself** se procurer qch

**prod** [1] n (a) (poke) petit coup m
(b) (colloq) (reminder) **to give sb a ~** secouer (colloq) qn
[2] vtr (also ~ **at**) (with foot, instrument, stick) donner des petits coups à; (with finger) toucher

**prodigy** n prodige m

**produce** [1] n produits mpl
[2] vtr (a) (cause) produire ⟨result, effect⟩; provoquer ⟨reaction, change⟩
(b) ⟨region, farmer, company⟩ produire (from à partir de); ⟨worker, machine⟩ fabriquer
(c) (generate) produire ⟨heat, sound, energy⟩; rapporter ⟨profits⟩
(d) (present) produire ⟨passport, report⟩; fournir ⟨evidence, argument, example⟩; **to ~ sth from** sortir qch de ⟨pocket, bag⟩
(e) produire ⟨show, film⟩; (GB) mettre [qch] en scène ⟨play⟩
(f) (put together) préparer ⟨meal⟩; mettre au point ⟨timetable, package, solution⟩; éditer ⟨brochure, guide⟩

**producer** n (a) (of produce) producteur m; (of machinery, goods) fabricant m
(b) (of film) producteur/-trice m/f; (GB) (of play) metteur m en scène

**product** n produit m

**production** n (a) (of crop, foodstuffs, metal) production f (of de); (of machinery, furniture, cars) fabrication (of de)
(b) (output) production f
(c) (of film, opera) production f (of de); (of play) mise f en scène (of de)

**production line** n chaîne f de fabrication

**productive** adj ⟨factory, land, day⟩ productif/-ive; ⟨system, method, use⟩ efficace; ⟨discussion⟩ fructueux/-euse

**productivity** n productivité f

**profane** adj (a) (blasphemous) impie
(b) (secular) profane

**profession** n profession f

**professional** [1] n professionnel/-elle m/f
[2] adj professionnel/-elle

**professionalism** n (of person, organization) professionnalisme m; (of performance, work) (haute) qualité f

**professionally** adv (a) (expertly) ⟨designed⟩ par un professionnel
(b) (in work situation) dans un cadre professionnel
(c) ⟨play sport⟩ en professionnel/-elle; **he sings ~** il est chanteur professionnel
(d) (to a high standard) de manière professionnelle

**professor** n (a) (Univ) (chair holder) professeur m d'Université
(b) (US Univ) (teacher) professeur m

**proficiency** n (practical) compétence f (in, at en); (academic) niveau m (in en)

**proficient** adj compétent/-e

**profile** n (of face) profil m; (of body)

silhouette *f*; **in** ∼ de profil; **to have/maintain a high** ∼ occuper/rester sur le devant de la scène

**profiling** *n* (gen, Med) typage *m*

**profit** ①  *n* **(a)** bénéfice *m*, profit *m*; **gross/ net** ∼ bénéfice brut/net
**(b)** (figurative) profit *m*
② *vtr* profiter à ⟨*person, group*⟩
③ *vi* **to** ∼ **by** *or* **from sth** tirer profit de qch

**profitable** *adj* rentable; (figurative) fructueux/-euse

**profit margin** *n* marge *f* bénéficiaire

**profit sharing** *n* intéressement *m* des salariés aux bénéfices

**profound** *adj* profond/-e

**profuse** *adj* ⟨*praise, thanks*⟩ profus/-e; ⟨*bleeding*⟩ abondant/-e

**profusely** *adv* ⟨*sweat, bleed*⟩ abondamment; **to apologize** ∼ se confondre en excuses

**prognosis** *n* **(a)** (Med) pronostic *m* **(on, about** sur)
**(b)** (prediction) pronostics *mpl*

**program** ① *n* **(a)** (Comput) programme *m*
**(b)** (US) (on radio, TV) émission *f*
② *vtr, vi* programmer (**to do** pour faire)

**programme** (GB), **program** (US) ① *n*
**(a)** (broadcast) émission *f* (**about** sur)
**(b)** (schedule) programme *m*
**(c)** (for play, opera) programme *m*
② *vtr* programmer ⟨*machine*⟩ (**to do** pour faire)

**programmer** *n* programmeur/-euse *m/f*

**progress** ① *n* **(a)** (advances) progrès *m*; **to make** ∼ ⟨*person*⟩ faire des progrès
**(b)** (of person, inquiry) progression *f*; (of talks, disease, career) évolution *f*; **to be in** ∼ ⟨*discussions, exam*⟩ être en cours
② *vi* progresser

**progression** *n* **(a)** (evolution) évolution *f*
**(b)** (improvement) progression *f*
**(c)** (series) suite *f*

**progressive** *adj* **(a)** (gen) progressif/-ive
**(b)** (forward-looking) ⟨*person, policy*⟩ progressiste; ⟨*school*⟩ parallèle

**progress report** *n* (on construction work) rapport *m* sur l'état des travaux; (on project) rapport *m* sur l'état du projet; (on patient) bulletin *m* de santé

**prohibit** *vtr* interdire; **to** ∼ **sb from doing** interdire à qn de faire

**prohibition** *n* interdiction *f* (**on, against** de)

**prohibitive** *adj* prohibitif/-ive

**project** ① *n* **(a)** (scheme) projet *m* (**to do** pour faire)
**(b)** (Sch) dossier *m* (**on** sur); (Univ) mémoire *m* (**on** sur); **research** ∼ programme *m* de recherches
**(c)** (US) (state housing) (large) ≈ cité *f* HLM; (small) ≈ lotissement *m* HLM
② *vtr* **(a)** envoyer ⟨*missile*⟩; faire porter ⟨*voice*⟩
**(b)** projeter ⟨*guilt, anxiety*⟩ (**onto** sur)

**(c)** (estimate) prévoir
**(d)** projeter ⟨*image, slides*⟩

**projecting** *adj* saillant/-e

**projector** *n* projecteur *m*

**pro-life** *adj* contre l'avortement

**proliferate** *vi* proliférer

**prolific** *adj* (gen) prolifique; ⟨*decade*⟩ fécond/-e; ⟨*growth*⟩ rapide

**prologue** *n* prologue *m* (**to** de)

**prolong** *vtr* prolonger

**promenade** *n* (path) promenade *f*; (by sea) front *m* de mer

**prominent** *adj* **(a)** ⟨*figure, campaigner*⟩ très en vue; ⟨*artist*⟩ éminent/-e; **to play a** ∼ **part in sth** jouer un rôle de premier plan dans qch
**(b)** ⟨*place, feature*⟩ proéminent/-e; ⟨*ridge, cheekbone*⟩ saillant/-e; ⟨*eye*⟩ exorbité/-e

**promiscuity** *n* (sexual) vagabondage *m* sexuel

**promiscuous** *adj* ⟨*person*⟩ aux mœurs légères

**promise** ① *n* promesse *f*; **to break one's** ∼ manquer à sa promesse; **she shows great** ∼ elle promet beaucoup
② *vtr* promettre de faire; **to** ∼ **sb sth** promettre qch à qn
③ *vi* promettre; **do you** ∼? c'est promis?

**promising** *adj* ⟨*situation, result, future*⟩ prometteur/-euse; ⟨*artist, candidate*⟩ qui promet

**promote** *vtr* **(a)** (in rank) promouvoir (**to** à)
**(b)** (advertise) faire de la publicité pour; (market) promouvoir
**(c)** (encourage) promouvoir
**(d)** (GB) (in football) **to be** ∼**d from the fourth to the third division** passer de quatrième en troisième division

**promotion** *n* promotion *f*

**promotional video** *n* vidéo *f* publicitaire

**prompt** ① *adj* rapide; **to be** ∼ **to do** être prompt/-e à faire
② *vtr* **(a)** provoquer ⟨*reaction, decision*⟩; susciter ⟨*concern, comment*⟩; **to** ∼ **sb to do** inciter qn à faire
**(b)** (remind) souffler à ⟨*actor*⟩

**prompter** *n* **(a)** (in theatre) souffleur/-euse *m/f*
**(b)** (US) (teleprompter) téléprompteur *m*

**promptly** *adv* **(a)** (immediately) immédiatement
**(b)** (without delay) rapidement
**(c)** (punctually) à l'heure; ∼ **at six o'clock** à six heures précises

**prone** *adj* **(a) to be** ∼ **to** être sujet/-ette à ⟨*colds*⟩; être enclin/-e à ⟨*depression*⟩
**(b) to lie** ∼ être allongé/-e face contre terre

**pronoun** *n* pronom *m*

**pronounce** *vtr* prononcer
■ **pronounce on** se prononcer sur ⟨*case, matter*⟩

**pronounced** *adj* ⟨*accent, tendency*⟩ prononcé/-e; ⟨*change, increase*⟩ marqué/-e

**pronunciation** n prononciation f
**proof** n (a) (evidence) preuve f; ~ **of identity**
pièce f d'identité
(b) (in printing, photography) épreuve f
(c) (of alcohol) **to be 70%** ~ ≈ titrer 40°
d'alcool
**proof of purchase** n justificatif m
d'achat
**proofread** vtr corriger les épreuves de
**prop** ① n étai m
② **props** n pl accessoires mpl
③ vtr (a) (also ~ **up**) étayer
(b) **to** ~ **sb/sth against sth** appuyer qn/qch
contre qch
**propaganda** n propagande f
**propagate** vi se propager
**propel** vtr propulser
**propeller** n hélice f
**proper** adj (a) (right) ⟨term, spelling⟩
correct/-e; ⟨order, tool, response⟩ bon/bonne
(before n); ⟨clothing⟩ qu'il faut; **everything is
in the** ~ **place** tout est à sa place
(b) (adequate) ⟨recognition, facilities⟩
convenable; ⟨education, training⟩ bon/bonne
(before n); ⟨care⟩ requis/-e
(c) (respectable) ⟨person⟩ correct/-e;
⟨upbringing⟩ convenable
(d) (real, full) ⟨doctor, holiday, job⟩ vrai/-e
(before n)
(e) (actual) **in the village** ~ dans le village
même
**properly** adv (a) (correctly) correctement
(b) (fully) complètement; **I didn't have time to
thank you** ~ je n'ai pas eu le temps de vous
remercier
(c) (adequately) convenablement
**proper name, proper noun** n nom m
propre
**property** n (a) (belongings) propriété f, biens
mpl
(b) (real estate) biens mpl immobiliers
(c) (house) propriété f
(d) (characteristic) propriété f
**property developer** n promoteur m
immobilier
**property owner** n propriétaire mf
**prophecy** n prophétie f
**prophet** n prophète m
**proportion** ① n (a) (of group, population)
proportion f (of de); (of income, profit, work) part
f (of de)
(b) (ratio) proportion f
(c) (harmony) **out of/in** ~ hors de/en
proportion
(d) (perspective) **to get sth out of all** ~ faire
tout un drame de qch; **to be out of all** ~ être
tout à fait disproportionné/-e (**to** par rapport
à)
② **proportions** n pl dimensions fpl
**proportional** adj proportionnel/-elle
**proportional representation, PR** n
représentation f proportionnelle
**proposal** n (a) (suggestion) proposition f
(b) (of marriage) demande f en mariage

**propose** ① vtr proposer ⟨course of action,
solution⟩; présenter ⟨motion⟩
② vi faire sa demande en mariage (**to** à)
③ **proposed** pp adj ⟨action, reform⟩
envisagé/-e
**proposition** ① n (a) (suggestion)
proposition f
(b) (assertion) assertion f
② vtr faire une proposition à ⟨person⟩
**proprietor** n propriétaire mf (**of** de)
**propriety** n (a) (politeness) correction f
(b) (morality) décence f
**proscribe** vtr proscrire
**prose** n (a) prose f
(b) (GB) (translation) thème m
**prosecute** ① vtr poursuivre [qn] en
justice
② vi engager des poursuites
**prosecution** n (Law) (a) (accusation)
poursuites fpl (judiciaires)
(b) **the** ~ le/les plaignant/-s; (state, Crown) le
ministère public
**prosecutor** n (Law) procureur m
**prospect** ① n (a) (hope) espoir m, chance f
(b) (outlook) perspective f
② **prospects** n pl perspectives fpl
**prospective** adj ⟨buyer, candidate⟩
potentiel/-ielle; ⟨husband, wife⟩ futur/-e
(before n)
**prospectus** n brochure f
**prosper** vi prospérer
**prosperity** n prospérité f
**prosperous** adj prospère
**prostate** n (also ~ **gland**) prostate f
**prostitute** ① n prostituée f; **male** ~
prostitué m
② vtr prostituer ⟨person, talent⟩
**prostitution** n prostitution f
**prostrate** adj **to lie** ~ être allongé/-e de
tout son long; ~ **with grief** accablé/-e de
chagrin
**protagonist** n protagoniste mf
**protect** vtr (gen) protéger (**against** contre;
**from** de, contre); défendre ⟨consumer,
interests⟩ (**against** contre)
**protection** n protection f
**protection factor** n indice m de
protection
**protection racket** n racket m
**protective** adj protecteur/-trice
**protein** n protéine f
**protest** ① n (a) protestation f; **in** ~ en
signe de protestation
(b) (demonstration) manifestation f
② vtr (a) **to** ~ **that** protester que; **to** ~ **one's
innocence** protester de son innocence
(b) (US) (complain about) protester contre (**to**
auprès de)
③ vi (a) (complain) protester
(b) (demonstrate) manifester (**against** contre)
**Protestant** n, adj protestant/-e (m/f)
**protester** n manifestant/-e m/f
**protocol** n protocole m

**prototype** n prototype m (of de)

**protrude** vi (gen) dépasser; ⟨teeth⟩ avancer

**protruding** adj ⟨rock⟩ en saillie; ⟨eyes⟩ globuleux/-euse; ⟨ears⟩ décollé/-e; ⟨ribs⟩ saillant/-e; ⟨chin⟩ en avant

**proud** adj (a) fier/fière (of de); ⟨owner⟩ heureux/-euse (before n)
(b) ⟨day, moment⟩ grand/-e (before n)

**prove** [1] vtr prouver; (by demonstration) démontrer; **to ~ a point** montrer qu'on a raison
[2] vi **to ~ to be** s'avérer être
[3] v refl **to ~ oneself** faire ses preuves; **to ~ oneself (to be)** se révéler

**proverb** n proverbe m

**provide** vtr (a) (supply) fournir ⟨opportunity, evidence, jobs, meals⟩ (for à); apporter ⟨answer, support⟩ (for à); assurer ⟨service, access, training, shelter⟩ (for à)
(b) ⟨clause, law⟩ prévoir (that que)
■ **provide for** (a) envisager ⟨eventuality, expenses⟩
(b) subvenir aux besoins de ⟨family⟩; **to be well ~d for** être à l'abri du besoin

**provided, providing** conj (also ~ **that**) à condition que (+ subjunctive)

**province** n province f; **in the ~s** en province

**provincial** adj (a) ⟨newspaper, town⟩ de province; ⟨life⟩ provincial/-e
(b) (narrow) provincial/-e

**provision** [1] n (a) (of goods, equipment) fourniture f (of de; to à); (of service) prestation f; ~ **of food/supplies** approvisionnement m (to de)
(b) (for future) dispositions fpl
(c) (in agreement) clause f; (in bill, act) disposition f
[2] **provisions** n pl (supplies) provisions fpl

**provisional** adj provisoire

**provocative** adj (a) ⟨dress, remark⟩ provocant/-e
(b) ⟨book⟩ qui fait réfléchir

**provoke** vtr (a) (annoy) provoquer
(b) (cause) susciter ⟨anger, complaints⟩; provoquer ⟨laughter, reaction⟩

**prow** n proue f

**prowess** n (a) (skill) prouesses fpl
(b) (bravery) vaillance f

**prowl** [1] vtr **to ~ the streets** rôder dans les rues
[2] vi ⟨animal, person⟩ rôder

**proximity** n proximité f

**proxy** n (a) (person) mandataire mf
(b) **by ~** par procuration

**prudent** adj prudent/-e

**prudish** adj pudibond/-e, prude

**prune** [1] n (Culin) pruneau m
[2] vtr (cut back) tailler; (thin out) élaguer

**pry** vi **to ~ into** mettre son nez dans

**PS** n (abbr = **postscriptum**) PS m

**psalm** n psaume m

**pseudonym** n pseudonyme m

**psych** v ■ **psych up** (colloq): **to ~ oneself up** se préparer (psychologiquement) (for pour)

**psychiatric** adj psychiatrique

**psychiatrist** n psychiatre mf

**psychiatry** n psychiatrie f

**psychic** n médium m, voyant/-e m/f

**psychoanalysis** n psychanalyse f

**psychological** adj psychologique

**psychologist** n psychologue mf

**psychology** n psychologie f

**psychopath** n psychopathe mf

**psychotherapist** n psychothérapeute mf

**PTO** (abbr = **please turn over**) TSVP

**pub** n (GB) pub m

**puberty** n puberté f

**public** [1] n **the ~** le public
[2] adj (gen) public/-ique; ⟨library, amenity⟩ municipal/-e; ⟨duty, spirit⟩ civique; **to be in the ~ eye** occuper le devant de la scène
[3] **in public** phr en public

**public address (system)** n (système m de) sonorisation f

**public assistance** n (US) aide f sociale

**publication** n publication f

**public company** n société f anonyme par actions

**public convenience** n (GB) toilettes fpl

**public holiday** n (GB) jour m férié

**publicity** n publicité f; **to attract ~** attirer l'attention des médias

**publicity campaign** n (to sell product) campagne f publicitaire; (to raise social issue) campagne f de sensibilisation

**publicity stunt** n coup m publicitaire

**publicize** vtr (a) attirer l'attention du public sur ⟨issue, problem⟩
(b) rendre [qch] public ⟨information, facts⟩
(c) faire de la publicité pour ⟨show⟩

**publicly** adv publiquement

**public opinion** n opinion f publique

**public prosecutor** n procureur m général

**public relations, PR** n relations fpl publiques

**public school** n (GB) école f privée; (US) école f publique

**public sector** n secteur m public

**public transport** n transports mpl en commun

**publish** vtr publier ⟨book, letter, guide⟩; éditer ⟨newspaper, magazine⟩

**publisher** n (person) éditeur/-trice m/f; (also **publishing house**) maison f d'édition

**publishing** n édition f

**pudding** n (a) (GB) (dessert course) dessert m
(b) (cooked dish) pudding m ···⫶

**p**

**(c)** (GB) (sausage) **black/white** ~ boudin *m* noir/blanc

**puddle** *n* flaque *f*

**puff** ⟦1⟧ *n* (of air, smoke, steam) bouffée *f*; (of breath) souffle *m*
⟦2⟧ *vtr* tirer sur ⟨*pipe*⟩
⟦3⟧ *vi* **(a)** to ~ at tirer des bouffées de ⟨*cigarette, pipe*⟩
**(b)** (pant) souffler
■ **puff out (a)** gonfler ⟨*cheeks*⟩; ⟨*bird*⟩ hérisser ⟨*feathers*⟩
**(b)** to ~ out smoke lancer des bouffées de fumée
■ **puff up**: ¶ ~ up ⟨*feathers*⟩ se hérisser; ⟨*eye*⟩ devenir bouffi/-e; ⟨*rice*⟩ gonfler; ¶ ~ [sth] up hérisser ⟨*feathers, fur*⟩; ~ed up with pride rempli/-e d'orgueil

**puff pastry** *n* pâte *f* feuilletée

**puffy** *adj* bouffi/-e

**pull** ⟦1⟧ *n* **(a)** (tug) coup *m*; to give sth a ~ tirer sur qch
**(b)** (attraction) force *f*; (figurative) attrait *m* (of de)
**(c)** (colloq) (influence) influence *f* (over, with sur)
⟦2⟧ *vtr* **(a)** (gen) tirer; tirer sur ⟨*cord, rope*⟩; to ~ sb/sth through faire passer qn/qch par ⟨*hole, window*⟩; to ~ sth out of tirer qch de ⟨*pocket, drawer*⟩; to ~ sb out of retirer qn de ⟨*wreckage*⟩; sortir qn de ⟨*river*⟩
**(b)** (colloq) sortir ⟨*gun, knife*⟩; to ~ a gun on sb menacer qn avec un pistolet
**(c)** appuyer sur ⟨*trigger*⟩
**(d)** se faire une élongation à ⟨*muscle*⟩
**(e)** to ~ a face faire la grimace
⟦3⟧ *vi* tirer (at, on sur)
■ **pull apart (a)** (dismantle) démonter
**(b)** (destroy) ⟨*child*⟩ mettre en pièces; ⟨*animal*⟩ déchiqueter
■ **pull away**: ¶ ~ away ⟨*car*⟩ démarrer; ¶ ~ [sb/sth] away éloigner ⟨*person*⟩; retirer ⟨*hand*⟩; to ~ sb/sth away from écarter qn/qch de ⟨*window, wall*⟩
■ **pull back (a)** ⟨*troops*⟩ se retirer (from de)
**(b)** ⟨*car, person*⟩ reculer
■ **pull down** démolir ⟨*building*⟩; baisser ⟨*blind, trousers*⟩
■ **pull in** ⟨*car, bus, driver*⟩ s'arrêter
■ **pull off (a)** ôter ⟨*coat, sweater*⟩; enlever ⟨*shoes, lid, sticker*⟩
**(b)** conclure ⟨*deal*⟩; réaliser ⟨*feat*⟩
■ **pull out**: ¶ ~ out **(a)** ⟨*car, truck*⟩ déboîter; to ~ out of sth quitter qch ⟨*station, drive*⟩
**(b)** ⟨*troops, participants*⟩ se retirer (of de)
¶ ~ [sth] out **(a)** extraire ⟨*tooth*⟩; enlever ⟨*splinter*⟩; arracher ⟨*weeds*⟩
**(b)** (from pocket) sortir
■ **pull over**: ¶ ~ over ⟨*motorist, car*⟩ s'arrêter (sur le côté); ¶ ~ [sb/sth] over ⟨*police*⟩ forcer ⟨qn/qch⟩ à se ranger sur le côté
■ **pull through** ⟨*accident victim*⟩ s'en tirer
■ **pull together**: ¶ ~ together faire un effort; ¶ ~ oneself together se ressaisir
■ **pull up**: ¶ ~ up s'arrêter
¶ ~ up [sth], ~ [sth] up **(a)** (uproot) arracher

**(b)** lever ⟨*anchor*⟩; remonter ⟨*trousers, socks*⟩; prendre ⟨*chair*⟩
¶ ~ [sb] up **(a)** (lift) hisser
**(b)** (reprimand) réprimander
**(c)** arrêter ⟨*driver*⟩

**pull-down menu** *n* (Comput) menu *m* déroulant

**pulley** *n* poulie *f*

**pullover** *n* pull-over *m*

**pulp** ⟦1⟧ *n* (soft centre) pulpe *f*; (crushed mass) pâte *f*
⟦2⟧ *vtr* écraser ⟨*fruit, vegetable*⟩; réduire [qch] en pâte ⟨*wood, cloth*⟩; mettre [qch] au pilon ⟨*newspapers, books*⟩

**pulp fiction** *n* littérature *f* de gare

**pulpit** *n* chaire *f*

**pulse** *n* pouls *m*

**pulse rate** *n* pouls *m*

**pulverize** *vtr* pulvériser

**pump** ⟦1⟧ *n* **(a)** (for air) pompe *f*; bicycle ~ pompe à vélo
**(b)** (plimsoll) chaussure *f* de sport; (GB) (flat shoe) ballerine *f*; (US) (shoe with heel) chaussure *f* à talon
⟦2⟧ *vtr* **(a)** pomper ⟨*air, gas, water*⟩ (out of de)
**(b)** (colloq) (question) cuisiner (colloq) ⟨*person*⟩
**(c)** (Med) to ~ sb's stomach faire un lavage d'estomac à qn
⟦3⟧ *vi* ⟨*heart*⟩ battre violemment
■ **pump up** gonfler ⟨*tyre, air bed*⟩

**pumpkin** *n* citrouille *f*

**pun** *n* jeu *m* de mots, calembour *m*

**punch** ⟦1⟧ *n* **(a)** (blow) coup *m* de poing
**(b)** (of style, performance) énergie *f*
**(c)** (drink) punch *m*
⟦2⟧ *vtr* **(a)** donner un coup de poing à ⟨*person*⟩; to ~ sb in the face donner un coup de poing dans la figure de qn
**(b)** perforer ⟨*cards, tape*⟩; (manually) poinçonner ⟨*ticket*⟩

**Punch-and-Judy show** *n* ≈ (spectacle *m* de) guignol *m*

**punchbag** *n* (GB) sac *m* de sable

**punch line** *n* chute *f*

**punch-up** *n* (GB) (colloq) bagarre *f*

**punctual** *adj* ponctuel/-elle

**punctually** *adv* ⟨*start, arrive, leave*⟩ à l'heure

**punctuation** *n* ponctuation *f*

**punctuation mark** *n* signe *m* de ponctuation

**puncture** ⟦1⟧ *n* crevaison *f*; we had a ~ on the way on a crevé en chemin
⟦2⟧ *vtr* crever ⟨*tyre, balloon, air bed*⟩; to ~ a lung se perforer un poumon

**puncture (repair) kit** *n* boîte *f* de rustines®

**pundit** *n* expert/-e *m/f*

**pungent** *adj* ⟨*flavour*⟩ relevé/-e; ⟨*smell*⟩ fort/-e; ⟨*gas, smoke*⟩ âcre

**punish** *vtr* punir

**punishment** n punition f; (stronger) châtiment m

**punitive** adj punitif/-ive

**punk** ⓵ n (a) (music) punk m
(b) (punk rocker) punk mf
(c) (US) (colloq) voyou m
⓶ adj punk inv

**punnet** n (GB) barquette f

**punt** n (a) (boat) barque f (à fond plat)
(b) (Irish pound) livre f irlandaise

**puny** adj ⟨person, body⟩ chétif/-ive

**pup** n (a) (also **puppy**) chiot m
(b) (seal, otter) petit m

**pupil** n (a) (Sch) élève mf
(b) (in eye) pupille f

**puppet** n marionnette f

**purchase** ⓵ n achat m
⓶ vtr acheter

**purchasing power** n pouvoir m
d'achat

**pure** adj pur/-e

**puree** n purée f

**purely** adv purement

**purge** ⓵ n purge f
⓶ vtr purger ⟨party, system⟩ (of de); expier ⟨sin⟩

**purify** vtr (gen) purifier; épurer ⟨water, chemical⟩

**purist** n, adj puriste (mf)

**purity** n pureté f

**purple** ⓵ n violet m
⓶ adj (bluish) violet/-ette; (reddish) pourpre

**purpose** ⓵ n (a) (aim) but m; for the ~ of doing dans le but de faire
(b) (also **strength of** ~) résolution f
⓶ on ~ phr exprès

**purposely** adv exprès, intentionnellement

**purpose-made** adj fait/-e spécialement (for pour)

**purr** ⓵ n (of cat, engine) ronronnement m
⓶ vi ⟨cat, engine⟩ ronronner

**purse** n (for money) porte-monnaie m inv; (US) (handbag) sac m à main
IDIOMS to hold the ~-strings tenir les cordons de la bourse

**purser** n commissaire m de bord

**pursue** vtr (a) (chase) poursuivre
(b) poursuivre ⟨aim, ambition, studies⟩; mener ⟨policy⟩; se livrer à ⟨occupation, interest⟩; to ~ a career faire carrière (in dans)

**pursuer** n poursuivant/-e m/f

**pursuit** n (a) poursuite f; in ~ of à la poursuite de; in hot ~ à vos/ses etc trousses
(b) (hobby) passe-temps m inv; artistic ~s activités fpl artistiques

**push** ⓵ n poussée f; to give sb/sth a ~ pousser qn/qch
⓶ vtr (a) pousser ⟨person, car, pram⟩; appuyer sur ⟨button, switch⟩; to ~ sb/sth away repousser qn/qch; she ~ed him down

the stairs elle l'a poussé dans l'escalier; to ~ sb aside écarter qn; to ~ sb too far pousser qn à bout
(b) (colloq) (promote) promouvoir ⟨policy, theory⟩
(c) (colloq) (sell) vendre ⟨drugs⟩
⓷ vi pousser; to ~ past sb bousculer qn
IDIOMS at a ~ (GB) (colloq) s'il le faut; to ~ one's luck aller un peu trop loin
■ **push around** (colloq) (bully) bousculer ⟨person⟩
■ **push for** faire pression en faveur de ⟨reform⟩
■ **push in**: ¶ ~ in resquiller; ¶ ~ [sth] in enfoncer ⟨button, door, window⟩
■ **push over**: ¶ ~ over! pousse-toi!; ¶ ~ [sb/sth] over renverser ⟨person, table, car⟩
■ **push through** faire voter ⟨bill, legislation⟩; faire passer ⟨deal⟩

**push-button** adj ⟨telephone⟩ à touches

**pushchair** n (GB) poussette f

**pusher** n (colloq) (also **drug** ~) revendeur/-euse m/f de drogue

**push-start** vtr pousser ⟨qch⟩ pour le/la faire démarrer ⟨vehicle⟩

**push-up** n (Sport) pompe f (colloq)

**pushy** adj (colloq) (ambitious) arriviste; she's very ~ ⟨assertive⟩ elle s'impose

**put** vtr (a) (place) mettre ⟨object, person⟩ (in dans; on sur); to ~ sth through glisser qch dans ⟨letterbox⟩; to ~ sb through envoyer qn à ⟨university⟩; faire passer qn par ⟨ordeal⟩; faire passer [qch] à qn ⟨test⟩; to ~ one's hand to porter la main à ⟨mouth⟩
(b) (devote, invest) to ~ money/energy into sth investir de l'argent/son énergie dans qch; to ~ a lot into s'engager à fond pour ⟨work, project⟩; sacrifier beaucoup à ⟨marriage⟩
(c) to ~ money towards donner de l'argent pour ⟨gift⟩; ~ it towards some new clothes sers-t'en pour acheter des vêtements; to ~ tax on sth taxer qch
(d) (express) to ~ it bluntly pour parler franchement; let me ~ it another way laissez-moi m'exprimer différemment
IDIOMS I wouldn't ~ it past him! ça ne m'étonnerait pas de lui!
■ **put across** communiquer ⟨idea, case⟩
■ **put away** (a) (tidy away) ranger
(b) (save) mettre [qch] de côté
(c) (colloq) avaler ⟨food⟩; descendre (colloq) ⟨drink⟩
■ **put back** (a) (return) remettre; to ~ sth back where it belongs remettre qch à sa place
(b) remettre ⟨meeting⟩ (to à; until jusqu'à); repousser ⟨date⟩
(c) retarder ⟨clock, watch⟩
■ **put down**: ¶ ~ [sth] down (a) poser ⟨object⟩
(b) réprimer ⟨rebellion⟩
(c) (write down) mettre (par écrit)
(d) to ~ sth down to mettre qch sur le compte de; to ~ sth down to the fact that imputer qch au fait que

**(e)** (by injection) piquer ⟨*animal*⟩
**(f)** to ~ **down a deposit** verser des arrhes; **to ~ £50 down on sth** verser 50 livres sterling d'arrhes sur qch
¶ ~ **[sb] down (a)** déposer ⟨*passenger*⟩
**(b)** (colloq) (humiliate) rabaisser
■ **put forward (a)** (propose) avancer ⟨*theory, name*⟩; soumettre ⟨*plan*⟩; présenter la candidature de ⟨*person*⟩
**(b)** (in time) avancer ⟨*meeting, date, clock*⟩ (**by** de; **to** à)
■ **put in**: ¶ ~ **in (a)** ⟨*ship*⟩ faire escale (**at** à; **to** dans)
**(b)** to ~ **in for** postuler pour ⟨*job, promotion, rise*⟩; demander ⟨*transfer*⟩
¶ ~ **[sth] in (a)** installer ⟨*heating, units*⟩
**(b)** (make) faire ⟨*request, claim*⟩; **to ~ in an appearance** faire une apparition
**(c)** passer ⟨*time*⟩
**(d)** (insert) mettre
■ **put off**: ¶ ~ **[sth] off (a)** (delay, defer) remettre [qch] (à plus tard)
**(b)** (turn off) éteindre ⟨*light, radio*⟩
¶ ~ **[sb] off (a)** décommander ⟨*guest*⟩; dissuader ⟨*person*⟩; **to be easily put off** se décourager facilement
**(b)** (repel) ⟨*appearance, smell*⟩ dégoûter; ⟨*manner, person*⟩ déconcerter
■ **put on (a)** mettre ⟨*garment, make-up*⟩
**(b)** allumer ⟨*light, heating*⟩; mettre ⟨*record, music*⟩; **to ~ the kettle on** mettre de l'eau à chauffer
**(c)** prendre ⟨*weight, kilo*⟩
**(d)** (produce) monter ⟨*play, exhibition*⟩
**(e)** (adopt) prendre ⟨*accent, expression*⟩; **he's ~ting it on** il fait semblant
■ **put out (a)** (extend) tendre ⟨*hand*⟩; **to ~ out one's tongue** tirer la langue
**(b)** éteindre ⟨*fire, cigarette*⟩
**(c)** sortir ⟨*bin, garbage*⟩; faire sortir ⟨*cat*⟩
**(d)** diffuser ⟨*warning, statement*⟩
**(e)** mettre ⟨*food, towels*⟩

**(f)** (dislocate) se démettre ⟨*shoulder*⟩
**(g)** (inconvenience) déranger ⟨*person*⟩; (annoy) contrarier ⟨*person*⟩
■ **put through (a)** (implement) faire passer ⟨*bill, reform*⟩
**(b)** passer ⟨*caller*⟩ (**to** à)
■ **put together (a)** (assemble) assembler ⟨*pieces, parts*⟩; **to ~ sth back together** reconstituer qch
**(b)** (place together) mettre ensemble
**(c)** établir ⟨*list*⟩; faire ⟨*film, programme*⟩
**(d)** construire ⟨*argument*⟩
■ **put up**: ¶ ~ **up [sth]** opposer ⟨*resistance*⟩; **to ~ up a fight** combattre
¶ ~ **[sth] up (a)** hisser ⟨*flag, sail*⟩; relever ⟨*hair*⟩; **to ~ up one's hand** lever la main
**(b)** mettre ⟨*sign, plaque*⟩; afficher ⟨*list*⟩
**(c)** dresser ⟨*fence, tent*⟩
**(d)** augmenter ⟨*rent, prices, tax*⟩; faire monter ⟨*temperature*⟩
**(e)** (provide) fournir ⟨*money*⟩
¶ ~ **[sb] up (a)** (lodge) héberger
**(b)** to ~ **sb up to sth** pousser qn à qch
■ **put up with** supporter ⟨*person, situation*⟩

**put-down** *n* remarque *f* humiliante

**putty** *n* mastic *m*

**puzzle** ⟨1⟩ *n* **(a)** (mystery) mystère *m*
**(b)** (game) casse-tête *m inv*
⟨2⟩ *vtr* déconcerter

**puzzle book** *n* livre *m* de jeux

**puzzled** *adj* perplexe

**PVC** *n* (*abbr* = **polyvinyl chloride**) PVC *m*

**pygmy** *n* pygmée *mf*

**pyjamas** (GB), **pajamas** (US) *n pl* pyjama *m*; **a pair of ~** un pyjama

**pylon** *n* pylône *m*

**pyramid** *n* pyramide *f*

**python** *n* python *m*

# Qq

**q, Q** *n* q, Q *m*
**quack** ⟨1⟩ *n* **(a)** (of duck) coin-coin *m inv*
**(b)** (GB) (colloq) (doctor) toubib *m* (colloq)
**(c)** (impostor) charlatan *m*
⟨2⟩ *vi* cancaner
**quadrangle** *n* **(a)** (shape) quadrilatère *m*
**(b)** (courtyard) cour *f* carrée
**quadruple** ⟨1⟩ *n, adj* quadruple (*m*)
⟨2⟩ *vtr, vi* quadrupler
**quadruplet** *n* quadruplé/-e *m/f*
**quagmire** *n* bourbier *m*
**quail** ⟨1⟩ *n* caille *f*; **~'s egg** œuf *m* de caille
⟨2⟩ *vi* trembler
**quaint** *adj* **(a)** (pretty) pittoresque

**(b)** (old-world) au charme vieillot
**(c)** (odd) bizarre

**quake** *vi* trembler

**qualification** *n* **(a)** (diploma, degree) diplôme *m* (**in** en); (experience, skills) qualification *f*
**(b)** (restriction) restriction *f*; **without ~** sans réserves

**qualified** *adj* **(a)** (for job) (having diploma) diplômé/-e; (having experience, skills) qualifié/-e
**(b)** (competent) (having authority) qualifié/-e (**to do** pour faire); (having knowledge) compétent/-e (**to do** pour faire)
**(c)** (modified) nuancé/-e, mitigé/-e

**qualifier** n (contestant) qualifié/-e m/f; (match) éliminatoire f

**qualify** ① vtr (a) (modify) nuancer ⟨approval, opinion⟩; préciser ⟨statement, remark⟩
(b) (entitle) **to ~ sb to do** donner à qn le droit de faire
② vi (a) (get diploma, degree) obtenir son diplôme (**as** de, en)
(b) (be eligible) remplir les conditions (requises); **to ~ for** avoir droit à ⟨membership, legal aid⟩; **to ~ to do** avoir le droit de faire
(c) (Sport) se qualifier

**qualitative** adj qualitatif/-ive

**quality** ① n qualité f
② adj de qualité

**quality control** n contrôle m de qualité

**qualm** n scrupule m

**quandary** n embarras m; (serious) dilemme m

**quantifiable** adj facile à évaluer

**quantify** vtr quantifier

**quantitative** adj quantitatif/-ive

**quantity** n quantité f; **in ~** en grande quantité

**quantity surveyor** n métreur m

**quantum leap** n saut m quantique; (figurative) bond m prodigieux

**quarantine** ① n quarantaine f; **in ~** en quarantaine
② vtr mettre [qn/qch] en quarantaine

**quarrel** ① n dispute f (**between** entre; **over** au sujet de); **to have a ~** se disputer
② vi (a) (argue) se disputer
(b) (sever relations) se brouiller
(c) **to ~ with** contester ⟨claim, idea⟩; se plaindre de ⟨price, verdict⟩

**quarrelling** (GB), **quarreling** (US) n disputes fpl

**quarrelsome** adj ⟨person⟩ querelleur/-euse; ⟨remark⟩ agressif/-ive

**quarry** ① n (a) (in ground) carrière f
(b) (prey) proie f; (in hunting) gibier m
② vtr extraire ⟨stone⟩

**quarry tile** n carreau m de terre cuite

**quart** n (GB) = 1.136 l, (US) = 0.946 l

**quarter** ① n (a) (one fourth) quart m; **in ~ of an hour** dans un quart d'heure
(b) (three months) trimestre m
(c) (district) quartier m
② **quarters** n pl (Mil) quartiers mpl; (gen) logement m
③ pron (a) (25%) quart m; **only a ~ passed** seul le quart a réussi
(b) (in time phrases) **at (a) ~ to 11** (GB), **at a ~ of 11** (US) à onze heures moins le quart; **an hour and a ~** une heure et quart
④ adj **a ~ century** un quart de siècle
⑤ adv **a ~ full** au quart plein; **~ the price** quatre fois moins cher
⑥ vtr couper [qch] en quatre ⟨cake, apple⟩
⑦ **at close quarters** phr de près

**quarterfinal** n quart m de finale

**quarterly** ① adj trimestriel/-ielle
② adv tous les trois mois

**quartermaster** n (in army) intendant m; (in navy) maître m de timonerie

**quartet** n quatuor m; **jazz ~** quartette m

**quartz** n quartz m

**quash** vtr rejeter ⟨proposal⟩; réprimer ⟨rebellion⟩

**quasi(-)** pref quasi (+ adj), quasi- (+ n)

**quaver** ① n (a) (GB) (Mus) croche f
(b) (trembling) tremblement m (**in** dans)
② vi trembloter

**quay** n quai m; **on the ~** sur le quai

**quayside** n quai m

**queasiness** n nausée f

**queasy** adj **to be** or **feel ~** avoir mal au cœur

**Quebec** pr n Québec m; **in ~** (city) à Québec; (province) au Québec

**queen** n (a) (gen) reine f
(b) (in cards) dame f

**queen bee** n reine f des abeilles

**queen mother** n Reine mère f

**Queen's Counsel, QC** n (GB) (Law) avocat m éminent

**queer** adj (a) (strange) étrange, bizarre
(b) (suspicious) louche, suspect

**quell** vtr étouffer ⟨anger, anxiety, revolt⟩

**quench** vtr étancher ⟨thirst⟩; étouffer ⟨desire⟩

**querulous** adj grincheux/-euse

**query** ① n question f (**about** au sujet de); **a ~ from sb** une question venant de qn
② vtr mettre en doute; **to ~ whether** demander si

**quest** n quête f; **the ~ for sb/sth** la recherche de qn/qch

**question** ① n (a) (gen) question f (**about** sur); **to ask sb a ~** poser une question à qn; **it's a ~ of doing** il s'agit de faire; **that's another ~** c'est une autre affaire; **there was never any ~ of you paying** il n'a jamais été question que tu paies; **the person in ~** la personne en question; **it's out of the ~ for him to leave** il est hors de question qu'il parte
(b) (doubt) doute m; **to call sth into ~** mettre qch en doute; **it's open to ~** cela se discute
② vtr (a) (interrogate) questionner ⟨suspect, politician⟩
(b) (cast doubt upon) mettre en doute ⟨tactics, methods⟩

**questionable** adj (a) (debatable) discutable
(b) (dubious) douteux/-euse

**questioner** n interrogateur/-trice m/f

**questioning** n (of person) interrogation f; **to bring sb in for ~** amener qn pour interrogatoire

**question mark** n point m d'interrogation

**questionnaire** n questionnaire m (**on** sur)

**q**

**queue** 1 n (GB) (of people) queue f, file f
(d'attente); (of vehicles) file f; **to stand in a** ~
faire la queue; **to join the** ~ ⟨person⟩ se
mettre à la queue; ⟨car⟩ se mettre dans la
file; **to jump the** ~ (colloq) passer avant son
tour
2 vi (also ~ **up**) ⟨people⟩ faire la queue (**for**
pour); ⟨taxis⟩ attendre en ligne

**queue-jump** vi resquiller, passer avant
son tour

**quibble** vi chicaner (**about, over** sur)

**quick** 1 n **to bite one's nails to the** ~ se
ronger les ongles jusqu'au sang
2 adj (a) (speedy) ⟨pace, reply, profit, meal⟩
rapide; ⟨storm, shower⟩ bref/brève (before n);
**to have a** ~ **coffee** prendre un café en
vitesse; **to have a** ~ **wash** faire une toilette
rapide; **she's a** ~ **worker** elle travaille vite;
**the** ~**est way to do** le meilleur moyen de
faire; **to make a** ~ **recovery** se rétablir vite;
**be** ~ (**about it**)! dépêche-toi!
(b) (clever) ⟨child, student⟩ vif/vive d'esprit
(c) (prompt) ⟨reaction⟩ vif/vive; **to be a** ~
**learner** apprendre vite
3 adv ~! vite!; ~ **as a flash** avec la rapidité
de l'éclair
IDIOMS **to cut** or **sting sb to the** ~ piquer qn
au vif

**quicken** 1 vtr accélérer ⟨pace⟩; stimuler
⟨interest⟩
2 vi ⟨pace⟩ s'accélérer; ⟨anger⟩ s'intensifier

**quick-fire** adj rapide

**quicklime** n chaux f vive

**quickly** adv (rapidly) vite, rapidement;
(without delay) sans tarder; (come) ~! (viens)
vite!

**quick march** n (Mil) ≈ pas m cadencé

**quicksand** n sables mpl mouvants;
(figurative) bourbier m

**quicksilver** n mercure m

**quick-tempered** adj coléreux/-euse

**quick time** n (US) marche f rapide

**quid** n (GB) (colloq) livre f (sterling)

**quiet** 1 n (a) (silence) silence m
(b) (peace) tranquillité f
(c) (colloq) (secret) **on the** ~ discrètement
2 adj (a) (silent) ⟨church, person, room⟩
silencieux/-ieuse; **to keep** ~ garder le
silence; **to go** ~ se taire; **to keep sb** ~ faire
taire ⟨dog, child⟩; **be** ~ (stop talking) tais-toi;
(make no noise) ne fais pas de bruit
(b) (not noisy) ⟨voice⟩ bas/basse; ⟨engine⟩
silencieux/-ieuse; ⟨music⟩ doux/douce; **in a** ~
**voice** à voix basse; **to keep the children** ~
⟨activity⟩ tenir les enfants tranquilles
(c) (discreet) discret/-ète; **to have a** ~ **word**
**with sb** prendre qn à part pour lui parler
(d) (calm) ⟨village, holiday, night, life⟩
tranquille
(e) ⟨meal⟩ intime; ⟨wedding⟩ célébré/-e dans
l'intimité
(f) (secret) **to keep [sth]** ~ ne pas divulguer
⟨plans⟩; garder [qch] secret/-ète ⟨engagement⟩

**quieten** vtr (a) (calm) calmer ⟨person,
animal⟩

(b) (silence) faire taire ⟨critics, children⟩
■ **quieten down**: ¶ ~ **down** (a) (become
calm) ⟨person, activity⟩ se calmer
(b) (fall silent) se taire
¶ ~ [**sb/sth**] **down** (a) (calm) calmer
(b) (silence) faire taire

**quietly** adv (a) (not noisily) ⟨move⟩ sans
bruit; ⟨cough, speak⟩ doucement
(b) (silently) ⟨play, read, sit⟩ en silence
(c) (calmly) calmement

**quietness** n (a) (silence) silence m
(b) (of voice) faiblesse f
(c) (of place) tranquillité f

**quiff** n (GB) (on forehead) toupet m; (on top of
head) houppe f

**quill** n (a) (feather) penne f; (stem of feather)
tuyau m de plume
(b) (on porcupine) piquant m
(c) (also ~ **pen**) plume f d'oie

**quilt** 1 n (a) (GB) (duvet) couette f
(b) (bed cover) dessus m de lit
2 vtr matelasser

**quinine** n quinine f

**quintuplet** n quintuplé/-e m/f

**quip** 1 n trait m d'esprit
2 vi plaisanter

**quirk** n (of person) excentricité f; (of fate,
nature) caprice m

**quit** 1 vtr démissionner de ⟨job⟩; quitter
⟨place, person, profession⟩
2 vi (a) (give up) arrêter (**doing** de faire)
(b) (resign) démissionner

**quite** adv (a) (completely) ⟨new, ready,
understand⟩ tout à fait; ⟨alone, empty,
exhausted⟩ complètement; ⟨impossible⟩
totalement; ⟨extraordinary⟩ vraiment; **I** ~
**agree** je suis tout à fait d'accord; **you're** ~
**right** vous avez entièrement raison; **it's** ~ **all**
**right** c'est sans importance; **are you** ~ **sure?**
en êtes-vous certain?; ~ **clearly** (see) très
clairement
(b) (exactly) **not** ~ pas exactement; **I don't** ~
**know** je ne sais pas du tout
(c) (rather) ⟨big, easily, often⟩ assez; **it's** ~
**small** ce n'est pas très grand; **it's** ~ **warm**
**today** il fait bon aujourd'hui; **it's** ~ **likely**
**that** il est très probable que; **I** ~ **like Chinese**
**food** j'aime assez la cuisine chinoise; ~ **a**
**few** un bon nombre de ⟨people, examples⟩; ~
**a lot of money** pas mal d'argent; **I've thought**
**about it** ~ **a bit** j'y ai pas mal réfléchi
(d) (as intensifier) ~ **simply** tout simplement;
~ **a difference** une différence considérable;
**that will be** ~ **a change for you** ce sera un
grand changement pour toi; **she's** ~ **a**
**woman!** quelle femme!
(e) (expressing agreement) ~ (**so**) c'est sûr

**quits** adj (colloq) **to be** ~ être quitte (**with**
**sb** envers qn)

**quiver** 1 n (a) tremblement m
(b) (for arrows) carquois m
2 vi ⟨voice, lip, animal⟩ trembler (**with** de);
⟨leaves⟩ frémir; ⟨flame⟩ vaciller

**quiz** $\boxed{1}$ *n* **(a)** (game) jeu *m* de questions-réponses, quiz *m*; (written, in magazine) questionnaire *m* (**about** sur)
**(b)** (US Sch) interrogation *f*
$\boxed{2}$ *vtr* questionner (**about** au sujet de)
**quiz game**, **quiz show** *n* jeu *m* de questions-réponses
**quizzical** *adj* interrogateur/-trice
**quota** *n* **(a)** (prescribed number, amount) quota *m* (**of**, **for** de)
**(b)** (share) part *f* (**of** de); (officially allocated) quote-part *f*
**quotation** *n* **(a)** (quote) citation *f*
**(b)** (estimate) devis *m*
**quotation marks** *n pl* (also **quotes**) guillemets *mpl*; **in** ~ entre guillemets
**quote** $\boxed{1}$ *n* **(a)** (quotation) citation *f* (**from** de)

**(b)** (statement to journalist) déclaration *f*
**(c)** (estimate) devis *m*
$\boxed{2}$ **quotes** *n pl* = QUOTATION MARKS
$\boxed{3}$ *vtr* **(a)** citer ⟨*person, passage, proverb*⟩; rapporter ⟨*words*⟩; rappeler ⟨*reference number*⟩; **she was** ~**d as saying that...** elle aurait dit que...
**(b)** (state) indiquer ⟨*price, figure*⟩; **they** ~**d us £200** dans leur devis, ils ont demandé £200 sterling
**(c)** (on stock exchange) coter ⟨*share, price*⟩ (**at** à)
**(d)** (in betting) **to be** ~**d 6 to 1** être coté/-e entre 6 et 1
$\boxed{4}$ *vi* (from text, author) faire des citations; **to** ~ **from Keats** citer Keats

# Rr

**r, R** *n* r, R *m*
**rabbi** *n* rabbin *m*
**rabbit** *n* lapin *m*
**rabid** *adj* **(a)** (with rabies) enragé/-e
**(b)** (fanatical) fanatique
**rabies** *n* rage *f*
**race** $\boxed{1}$ *n* **(a)** (gen, Sport) course *f*; **to have a** ~ faire la course
**(b)** (ethnic group) race *f*
$\boxed{2}$ *vtr* faire la course avec ⟨*person, car, horse*⟩ (**to** jusqu'à)
$\boxed{3}$ *vi* **(a)** (gen, Sport) courir; **to** ~ **in/away** entrer/partir en courant
**(b)** (hurry) se dépêcher (**to do** de faire)
**(c)** ⟨*heart*⟩ battre précipitamment; ⟨*engine*⟩ s'emballer
**racehorse** *n* cheval *m* de course
**racer** *n* (bike) vélo *m* de course
**race relations** *n pl* relations *fpl* inter-raciales
**racetrack** *n* (for horses) champ *m* de courses; (for cars) circuit *m*; (for dogs, cycles) piste *f*
**racial** *adj* racial/-e
**racing** *n* courses *fpl*
**racing car** *n* voiture *f* de course
**racing cyclist** *n* coureur/-euse *m/f* cycliste
**racing driver** *n* coureur/-euse *m/f* automobile
**racism** *n* racisme *m*
**racist** *n, adj* raciste (*mf*)
**rack** $\boxed{1}$ *n* **(a)** (for plates) égouttoir *m*; (for clothes) portant *m*; (for bottles) casier *m*
**(b)** = ROOF RACK
**(c)** (torture) chevalet *m*

$\boxed{2}$ *vtr* ~**ed with** torturé/-e par ⟨*guilt*⟩
IDIOMS **to** ~ **one's brains** se creuser la cervelle (colloq)
**racket** *n* **(a)** (Sport) (also **racquet**) raquette *f*
**(b)** (colloq) (noise) vacarme *m*
**(c)** (swindle) escroquerie *f*
**racketeering** *n* racket *m*
**racquetball** *n* (US) ≈ squash *m*
**racy** *adj* **(a)** (lively) plein/-e de verve
**(b)** (risqué) osé/-e
**radar** *n* radar *m*
**radiant** *adj* radieux/-ieuse
**radiate** *vtr* **(a)** rayonner de ⟨*happiness*⟩; déborder de ⟨*confidence*⟩
**(b)** émettre ⟨*heat*⟩
**radiation** *n* (medical, nuclear) radiation *f*; (rays) radiations *fpl*
**radiation exposure** *n* irradiation *f*
**radiation sickness** *n* maladie *f* des rayons
**radiator** *n* radiateur *m*
**radical** *n, adj* radical/-e (*m/f*)
**radio** $\boxed{1}$ *n* radio *f*; **on the** ~ à la radio
$\boxed{2}$ *adj* ⟨*signal*⟩ radio *inv*; ⟨*programme*⟩ de radio
$\boxed{3}$ *vtr* **to** ~ **sth** (**to sb**) communiquer qch par radio (à qn)
$\boxed{4}$ *vi* **to** ~ **for help** appeler au secours par radio
**radioactive** *adj* radioactif/-ive
**radio alarm** *n* radio-réveil *m*
**radio announcer** *n* speaker/-erine *m/f*
**radio cassette (recorder)** *n* radiocassette *f*
**radiology** *n* radiologie *f*

**radio station** n (channel) station f de
radio; (installation) station f émettrice
**radiotherapy** n radiothérapie f
**radish** n radis m
**radius** n rayon m
**raffle** n tombola f
**raft** n radeau m
**rafter** n chevron m
**rag** n (a) (cloth) chiffon m
(b) (colloq) (newspaper) torchon m (colloq)
**rage** ⟦1⟧ n (a) rage f, colère f; **to fly into a ~**
entrer dans une colère noire
(b) (colloq) **to be (all) the ~** faire fureur
⟦2⟧ vi (a) ⟨storm, battle⟩ faire rage
(b) ⟨person⟩ tempêter (**at, against** contre)
**ragged** adj (a) ⟨garment⟩ en loques; ⟨cuff,
collar⟩ effiloché/-e; ⟨person⟩ dépenaillé/-e
(b) ⟨outline⟩ déchiqueté/-e
**raging** adj (a) ⟨passion, argument⟩
violent/-e; ⟨thirst, pain⟩ atroce; **a ~
toothache** une rage de dents
(b) ⟨blizzard, sea⟩ déchaîné/-e
**rags** n pl loques fpl; **in ~** en haillons
**raid** ⟦1⟧ n raid m (**on** sur); (on bank) hold-up
m (**on** de); (by police, customs) rafle f (**on** dans)
⟦2⟧ vtr ⟨military⟩ faire un raid sur; ⟨police⟩
faire une rafle dans; ⟨criminals⟩ attaquer
⟨bank⟩
**raider** n (a) (thief) pillard m
(b) (also **corporate ~**) raider m
**rail** n (a) (on balcony) balustrade f; (on tower)
garde-fou m; (handrail) rampe f
(b) (for curtains) tringle f
(c) (for train) rail m; **by ~** par chemin de fer
**railing** n (also **~s**) grille f
**railroad** n (US) (a) (network) chemin m de
fer
(b) (also **~ track**) voie f ferrée
**railroad car** n (US) wagon m
**railway** n (GB) (a) (network) chemin m de fer
(b) (also **~ line**) ligne f de chemin de fer
(c) (also **~ track**) voie f ferrée
**railway carriage** n (GB) wagon m
**railway station** n (GB) gare f
**rain** ⟦1⟧ n pluie f; **in the ~** sous la pluie
⟦2⟧ v impers pleuvoir; **it's ~ing (hard)** il pleut
(à verse)
**rainbow** n arc-en-ciel m
**raincoat** n imperméable m
**raindrop** n goutte f de pluie
**rainfall** n niveau m de précipitations
**rain forest** n forêt f tropicale
**rainy** adj ⟨afternoon, climate⟩
pluvieux/-ieuse
**rainy season** n saison f des pluies
**raise** ⟦1⟧ n (US) (pay rise) augmentation f
⟦2⟧ vtr (a) (lift) lever ⟨baton, barrier, curtain⟩;
hisser ⟨flag⟩; soulever ⟨lid⟩; renflouer
⟨sunken ship⟩; **to ~ one's hand/head** lever la
main/tête
(b) (increase) augmenter ⟨price, offer, salary⟩
(**from** de; **to** à); élever ⟨standard⟩; reculer
⟨age limit⟩; **to ~ one's voice** (to be heard)

parler plus fort; (in anger) hausser le ton; **to
~ the bidding** (in gambling) monter la mise; (at
auction) monter l'enchère
(c) (cause) faire naître ⟨fears⟩; soulever ⟨dust⟩
(d) (mention) soulever ⟨issue, objection⟩
(e) (bring up) élever ⟨child, family⟩
(f) (breed) élever ⟨livestock⟩
(g) (find) trouver ⟨capital⟩
(h) (collect) lever ⟨tax⟩; ⟨person⟩ collecter
⟨money⟩
(i) (end) lever ⟨ban⟩
(j) (give) **to ~ the alarm** donner l'alarme
**raised** adj ⟨platform, jetty⟩ surélevé/-e; **~
voices** des éclats de voix
**raisin** n raisin m sec
**rake** ⟦1⟧ n râteau m
⟦2⟧ vtr ratisser ⟨grass, leaves⟩
■ **rake up**: **~ up** [sth], **~** [sth] **up** ressusciter
⟨grievance⟩; remuer ⟨past⟩
**rally** ⟦1⟧ n (a) (meeting) rassemblement m
(b) (race) rallye m
(c) (in tennis) échange m
⟦2⟧ vtr rassembler ⟨support, troops⟩
⟦3⟧ vi (a) ⟨people⟩ se rallier (**to** à)
(b) (recover) ⟨patient⟩ se rétablir
**rallying call** n cri m de ralliement
**ram** ⟦1⟧ n bélier m
⟦2⟧ vtr (a) (crash into) rentrer dans, heurter
(b) (push) enfoncer
**RAM** n (Comput) (abbr = **random access
memory**) RAM f
**ramble** n randonnée f, balade f
■ **ramble on** discourir (**about** sur)
**rambler** n randonneur/-euse m/f
**rambling** adj (a) ⟨house⟩ plein/-e de coins
et de recoins
(b) ⟨talk, article⟩ décousu/-e
**ramification** n ramification f
**ramp** n rampe f; (GB) (to slow traffic)
ralentisseur m; (up to plane) passerelle f; (US)
(slip road) bretelle f
**rampage** n **to be** or **go on the ~** tout
saccager
**rampant** adj ⟨crime, disease⟩ endémique
**rampart** n rempart m
**ram raid** ⟦1⟧ n casse f à la voiture bélier
⟦2⟧ vtr dévaliser [qch] à l'aide d'une voiture
bélier
**ramshackle** adj délabré/-e
**ranch** n ranch m
**rancid** adj rance; **to go ~** rancir
**random** adj (fait/-e) au hasard
**range** ⟦1⟧ n (a) (of prices, products) gamme f;
(of activities) éventail m, choix m; (of radar,
weapon) portée f (**of** de)
(b) (US) (prairie) prairie f
(c) (of mountains) chaîne f
(d) (stove) (wood) fourneau m
(e) (also **shooting ~**) champ m de tir
⟦2⟧ vi (a) (vary) varier ⟨between entre⟩
(b) (cover) **to ~ over sth** couvrir qch
**ranger** n garde-forestier m

**rank** [1] n (a) (gen) rang m; (in military, police) grade m; **to break ∼s** ⟨soldiers⟩ rompre les rangs; **to close ∼s** serrer les rangs
(b) taxi ∼ station f de taxis
[2] adj (a) ⟨outsider, beginner⟩ complet/-ète
(b) ⟨odour⟩ fétide
[3] vtr classer (among parmi)
[4] vi se classer (among parmi)

**rank and file** n the ∼ la base f

**ranking** n classement m

**rankle** vi it still ∼s je ne l'ai pas encore digéré (colloq)

**ransack** vtr fouiller ⟨drawer⟩ (for pour trouver); mettre [qch] à sac ⟨house⟩

**ransom** n rançon f; **to hold sb to** (GB) or **for** (US) ∼ garder qn en otage

**rant** vi déclamer; **to ∼ and rave** tempêter

**rap** [1] n (a) (tap) coup m sec
(b) (music) rap m
[2] vtr frapper sur ⟨table, door⟩

**rape** [1] n (a) (attack) viol m
(b) (plant) colza m
[2] vtr violer

**rapid** adj rapide

**rapidly** adv rapidement

**rapids** n pl rapides mpl

**rapist** n violeur m

**rapper** n (Mus) rappeur/-euse m/f

**rapport** n bons rapports mpl

**rapture** n ravissement m; **to go into ∼s about sth** s'extasier sur qch

**rapturous** adj ⟨delight⟩ extasié/-e; ⟨applause⟩ frénétique

**rare** adj (a) (uncommon) rare
(b) ⟨steak⟩ saignant/-e

**rarely** adv rarement

**raring** adj to be ∼ to do être très impatient/-e de faire; **to be ∼ to go** piaffer d'impatience

**rarity** n (a) **to be a ∼** ⟨occurrence⟩ être rare; ⟨plant⟩ être une plante rare; ⟨collector's item⟩ être une pièce rare
(b) (rareness) rareté f

**rascal** n coquin/-e m/f

**rash** [1] n (a) (on skin) rougeurs fpl
(b) (figurative) vague f (of de)
[2] adj irréfléchi/-e

**rasher** n tranche f

**raspberry** n framboise f

**rasping** adj ⟨voice, sound⟩ râpeux/-euse

**rat** n rat m

**rate** [1] n (a) (speed) rythme m; **at this ∼** (figurative) à ce train-là
(b) (level) taux m; **the interest ∼** le taux d'intérêt
(c) (charge, fee) tarif m
(d) (in foreign exchange) cours m
[2] **rates** n pl (GB) impôts mpl locaux; **business ∼s** ≈ taxe f professionnelle
[3] vtr (a) (classify) **to ∼ sb as sth** considérer qn comme qch; **to ∼ sb among** classer qn parmi
(b) estimer ⟨honesty, friendship, person⟩

IDIOMS **at any ∼** en tout cas

**ratepayer** n (GB) contribuable mf

**rather** adv (a) plutôt (than que); **I ∼ like him** je le trouve plutôt sympathique; **it's ∼ like an apple** ça ressemble un peu à une pomme
(b) (preferably) **I would (much) ∼ do** je préférerais (de loin) faire (than que de faire); **I'd ∼ not** j'aimerais mieux pas

**ratify** vtr ratifier

**rating** n cote f

**ratings** n pl indice m d'écoute, audimat® m

**ratio** n proportion f, rapport m

**ration** [1] n ration f
[2] vtr rationner ⟨food⟩ (to à); limiter la ration de ⟨person⟩ (to à)

**rational** adj ⟨approach, argument⟩ rationnel/-elle; ⟨person⟩ sensé/-e

**rationale** n (a) (reasons) raisons fpl (for pour; for doing de faire)
(b) (logic) logique f (behind de)

**rationalize** vtr (a) (justify) justifier
(b) (GB) (streamline) rationaliser

**rationing** n rationnement m

**rat race** n foire f d'empoigne

**rat run** n: petite rue servant de raccourci

**rattle** [1] n (a) (of bottles, cutlery, chains) cliquetis m; (of window, engine) vibrations fpl
(b) (baby's) hochet m
[2] vtr ⟨wind⟩ faire vibrer ⟨window⟩; ⟨person⟩ s'acharner sur ⟨handle⟩
[3] vi ⟨bottles, cutlery, chains⟩ s'entrechoquer; ⟨window⟩ vibrer

**rattlesnake** n serpent m à sonnette, crotale m

**raucous** adj ⟨laugh⟩ éraillé/-e; ⟨person⟩ bruyant/-e

**raunchy** adj (colloq) ⟨performer, voice, song⟩ torride

**ravage** vtr ravager

**rave** [1] n (GB) (colloq) (party) bringue f (colloq) (branchée)
[2] adj (colloq) ⟨review⟩ dithyrambique
[3] vi (enthusiastically) parler avec enthousiasme (about de); (when fevered) délirer

**ravenous** adj ⟨animal⟩ vorace; **to be ∼** avoir une faim de loup

**ravine** n ravin m

**raving** adj (fanatical) enragé/-e; **a ∼ lunatic** un fou furieux/une folle furieuse

**ravioli** n ravioli mpl

**ravishing** adj ravissant/-e

**raw** adj (a) ⟨food⟩ cru/-e; ⟨rubber, sugar, data⟩ brut/-e; ⟨sewage⟩ non traité/-e
(b) (without skin) ⟨patch⟩ à vif
(c) (cold) ⟨weather⟩ froid/-e et humide
(d) (inexperienced) inexpérimenté/-e
IDIOMS **to get a ∼ deal** (colloq) être défavorisé/-e

**raw material** n matière f première

**ray** n rayon m; **a ∼ of** une lueur de ⟨hope⟩

r

**raze** *vtr* raser

**razor** *n* rasoir *m*

**razor blade** *n* lame *f* de rasoir

**re¹** *n* (Mus) ré *m*

**re²** *prep* (*abbr* = **with reference to**) (about) au sujet de; (in letterhead) 'objet'

**RE** *n* (Sch) (*abbr* = **Religious Education**) éducation *f* religieuse

**reach** ▢1 *n* portée *f*; **out of ~** hors de portée; **within (arm's) ~** à portée de (la) main; **within easy ~** ⟨*place*⟩ tout près
▢2 *vtr* (a) atteindre ⟨*place, person, object, switch*⟩; ⟨*sound, news, letter*⟩ parvenir à ⟨*person, place*⟩
(b) (come to) arriver à ⟨*decision, understanding*⟩; **to ~ a verdict** (Law) rendre un verdict
(c) toucher ⟨*audience, market*⟩
(d) (in height, length) arriver à ⟨*floor, ceiling*⟩
▢3 *vi* (a) **to ~ up/down** lever/baisser le bras; **to ~ out** tendre le bras
(b) (extend) **to ~ (up/down)** arriver jusqu'à

**reaches** *n pl* **the upper/lower ~** (of river) la partie supérieure/inférieure

**react** *vi* réagir (**to** à; **against** contre)

**reaction** *n* réaction *f*

**reactionary** *n*, *adj* réactionnaire (*mf*)

**reactor** *n* réacteur *m*

**read** ▢1 *vtr* (a) (gen) lire; **to ~ sb's mind** lire dans les pensées de qn
(b) (at university) faire des études de ⟨*history, French*⟩
(c) relever ⟨*meter*⟩
▢2 *vi* lire (**to sb** à qn)
■ **read out** lire [qch] à haute voix
■ **read up**: **to ~ up on sth/sb** étudier qch/qn à fond

**readable** *adj* (a) (legible) lisible
(b) (enjoyable) agréable à lire

**reader** *n* lecteur/-trice *m/f*

**readily** *adv* (a) (willingly) sans hésiter
(b) (easily) facilement

**reading** *n* (a) lecture *f*
(b) (on meter) relevé *m* (**on** de); (on instrument) indication *f* (**on** de)
(c) (interpretation) interprétation *f* (**of** de)

**reading glasses** *n pl* lunettes *fpl* (pour lire)

**reading list** *n* liste *f* d'ouvrages recommandés

**readjust** ▢1 *vtr* régler [qch] de nouveau
▢2 *vi* ⟨*person*⟩ se réadapter (**to** à)

**readvertise** *vtr* refaire paraître une annonce pour ⟨*post, item*⟩

**ready** *adj* (a) (prepared) prêt/-e (**for** pour; **to do** à faire); **to get ~** se préparer; **to get sth ~** préparer qch; **~, steady, go** à vos marques, prêts, partez!
(b) (willing) prêt/-e (**to do** à faire)

**ready-made** *adj* ⟨*clothes*⟩ de confection; ⟨*excuse*⟩ tout/-e fait/-e

**ready-to-wear** *adj* ⟨*garment*⟩ prêt-à-porter

**real** *adj* (a) (not imaginary) véritable, réel/réelle; **in ~ life** dans la réalité
(b) (genuine) ⟨*diamond, flower, leather*⟩ vrai/-e (*before n*), authentique
(c) (proper) ⟨*holiday, rest*⟩ véritable, vrai/-e (*before n*)
(d) (for emphasis) ⟨*charmer, pleasure*⟩ vrai/-e (*before n*)

**real estate** *n* (a) (property) biens *mpl* immobiliers
(b) (US) (profession) immobilier *m*

**realism** *n* réalisme *m*

**realist** *n*, *adj* réaliste (*mf*)

**realistic** *adj* réaliste

**reality** *n* réalité *f* (**of** de)

**realization** *n* prise *f* de conscience

**realize** *vtr* (a) se rendre compte de; **to ~ that** se rendre compte que; **to make sb ~ sth** faire comprendre qch à qn
(b) réaliser ⟨*idea, dream, goal*⟩; **to ~ one's potential** développer ses capacités

**reallocate** *vtr* réattribuer

**really** ▢1 *adv* (a) (gen) vraiment
(b) (in actual fact) en fait, réellement; **~?** (expressing disbelief) c'est vrai?
▢2 *excl* (*also* **well ~**) franchement!

**real time** *n* (Comput) temps *m* réel

**reap** *vtr* (a) moissonner ⟨*corn*⟩
(b) récolter ⟨*benefits*⟩

**reappear** *vi* reparaître

**reappearance** *n* réapparition *f*

**reapply** *vi* reposer sa candidature (**for** à)

**reappraise** *vtr* réexaminer ⟨*question*⟩; réévaluer ⟨*writer, work*⟩

**rear** ▢1 *n* (a) (of building, car, room) arrière *m*; (of procession, train) queue *f*
(b) (of person) derrière *m* (colloq)
▢2 *adj* (a) ⟨*door, garden*⟩ de derrière
(b) (of car) ⟨*light, seat, wheel*⟩ arrière *inv*
▢3 *vtr* élever ⟨*child, animals*⟩; cultiver ⟨*plants*⟩
▢4 *vi* (*also* **~ up**) ⟨*horse*⟩ se cabrer

**rearmament** *n* réarmement *m*

**rearrange** *vtr* réaménager ⟨*room*⟩; modifier ⟨*plans*⟩; changer ⟨*appointment*⟩

**rear-view mirror** *n* rétroviseur *m*

**reason** ▢1 *n* (a) (cause) raison *f* (**for, behind** de); **for no (good) ~** sans raison valable; **to have ~ to do** avoir des raisons de faire; **the ~ why...** la raison pour laquelle...; **I'll tell you the ~ why** je vais te *or* vous dire pourquoi; **to have every ~ to do** avoir tout lieu de faire; **with good ~** à juste titre
(b) (common sense) raison *f*; **to listen to** *or* **see ~** entendre raison; **it stands to ~ that** il va sans dire que; **within ~** dans la limite du raisonnable
▢2 *vi* **to ~ with sb** raisonner qn

**reasonable** *adj* (a) (sensible) raisonnable
(b) (moderately good) convenable

**reasonably** *adv* (a) (sensibly) raisonnablement
(b) (rather) assez

**reasoning** *n* raisonnement *m*

**reassert** *vtr* réaffirmer ⟨*authority, claim*⟩

**reassess** *vtr* réexaminer, reconsidérer

**reassurance** *n* (a) (comfort) réconfort *m* (b) (guarantee) garantie *f*

**reassure** *vtr* rassurer ⟨*person*⟩ (about sur)

**reassuring** *adj* rassurant/-e

**rebate** *n* remboursement *m*

**rebel** ① *n* rebelle *mf*
② *vi* se rebeller

**rebellion** *n* rébellion *f*, révolte *f*

**rebellious** *adj* rebelle, insoumis/-e

**rebuff** ① *n* rebuffade *f*
② *vtr* rabrouer ⟨*person*⟩; repousser ⟨*advances*⟩

**rebuild** *vtr* reconstruire

**rebuke** ① *n* réprimande *f*
② *vtr* réprimander (for pour)

**rebut** *vtr* réfuter

**recall** ① *n* (memory) mémoire *f*
② *vtr* (a) (remember) se souvenir de (b) (summon back) rappeler

**recapitulate** *vtr, vi* récapituler

**recapture** *vtr* recapturer ⟨*prisoner, animal*⟩; reprendre ⟨*town*⟩; recréer ⟨*period, atmosphere*⟩

**recede** *vi* (gen) s'éloigner; ⟨*hope, memory*⟩ s'estomper

**receding** *adj* ⟨*chin*⟩ fuyant/-e; he has a ∼ hairline son front se dégarnit

**receipt** ① *n* (a) (also ∼ desk) réception *m* (for pour); (from till) ticket *m* de caisse (b) (act of receiving) réception *f*
② **receipts** *n pl* (takings) recette *f* (from de)

**receive** ① *vtr* (a) (gen) recevoir; receler ⟨*stolen goods*⟩ (b) (greet) accueillir, recevoir ⟨*visitor, proposal, play*⟩ (with avec); to be well ∼d être bien reçu/-e
② **received** *pp adj* ⟨*ideas, opinions*⟩ reçu/-e

**receiver** *n* (a) (telephone) combiné *m* (b) (radio or TV) récepteur *m*

**receivership** *n* (GB) to go into ∼ être placé/-e sous administration judiciaire

**receiving** *n* (crime) recel *m*

**recent** *adj* ⟨*event, change, arrival, film*⟩ récent/-e; ⟨*acquaintance, development*⟩ nouveau/-elle (*before n*); in ∼ years au cours des dernières années

**recently** *adv* récemment; until ∼ jusqu'à ces derniers temps

**reception** *n* (a) (also ∼ desk) réception *f*
(b) (gathering) réception *f* (for sb en l'honneur de qn; for sth à l'occasion de qch) (c) (welcome) accueil *m* (for de) (d) (on radio, TV) réception *f* (on sur)

**receptionist** *n* réceptionniste *mf*

**receptive** *adj* réceptif/-ive (to à)

**recess** *n* (a) (in parliament) (holiday) vacances *fpl*
(b) (US) (break) (in school) récréation *f*; (during meeting) pause *f*

(c) (alcove) alcôve *f*, recoin *m*

**recession** *n* récession *f*

**recharge** *vtr* recharger

**rechargeable** *adj* rechargeable

**recipe** *n* recette *f* (for de)

**recipient** *n* (of letter) destinataire *mf*; (of benefits, aid, cheque) bénéficiaire *mf*; (of prize, award) lauréat/-e *m/f*

**reciprocal** *adj* réciproque

**reciprocate** ① *vtr* retourner ⟨*compliment*⟩; payer [qch] de retour ⟨*love*⟩; rendre ⟨*affection*⟩
② *vi* rendre la pareille

**recital** *n* récital *m*

**recite** *vtr, vi* réciter

**reckless** *adj* imprudent/-e

**recklessly** *adv* ⟨*act*⟩ avec imprudence; ⟨*promise, spend*⟩ de manière inconsciente

**reckon** *vtr* (a) (judge) considérer (that que) (b) (colloq) (think) to ∼ (that) croire que (c) (calculate) calculer ⟨*amount*⟩
■ **reckon on** (colloq): ¶ ∼ on [sb/sth] compter sur; ¶ ∼ on doing compter faire
■ **reckon with** compter avec

**reckoning** *n* (estimation) estimation *f*; (accurate calculation) calculs *mpl*

**reclaim** *vtr* (a) reconquérir ⟨*coastal land*⟩; assécher ⟨*marsh*⟩; défricher ⟨*forest*⟩; récupérer ⟨*glass, metal*⟩ (b) récupérer ⟨*deposit, money*⟩

**reclaimable** *adj* ⟨*waste product*⟩ récupérable

**recline** *vi* ⟨*person*⟩ s'allonger; ⟨*seat*⟩ s'incliner

**reclining** *adj* (a) ⟨*figure*⟩ allongé/-e (b) ⟨*seat*⟩ inclinable; ⟨*chair*⟩ réglable

**recluse** *n* reclus/-e *m/f*

**recognition** *n* reconnaissance *f*; in ∼ of en reconnaissance de

**recognizable** *adj* reconnaissable

**recognize** *vtr* reconnaître (by à)

**recoil** *vi* reculer (from devant)

**recollect** ① *vtr* se souvenir de, se rappeler
② *vi* se souvenir

**recollection** *n* souvenir *m*

**recommend** *vtr* (a) (commend) recommander (b) (advise) conseiller, recommander

**recommendation** *n* recommandation *f*; to give sb a ∼ recommander qn

**recommended reading** *n* livres *mpl* conseillés *or* recommandés

**recompense** *n* (a) (reward) récompense *f* (for de) (b) (compensation) dédommagement *m* (for pour)

**reconcile** *vtr* (a) réconcilier ⟨*people*⟩ (b) concilier ⟨*attitudes, views*⟩ (c) to become ∼d to sth se résigner à qch

**reconnaissance** *n* reconnaissance *f*

**reconnoitre** (GB), **reconnoiter** (US) ① *vtr* reconnaître      ···❖

② *vi* faire une reconnaissance

**reconsider** ① *vtr* réexaminer
② *vi* réfléchir

**reconstruct** *vtr* (a) (rebuild) reconstruire
⟨*building*⟩
(b) ⟨*police*⟩ faire une reconstitution de
⟨*crime*⟩

**reconstruction** *n* (a) (of building)
reconstruction *f*
(b) (of crime) reconstitution *f*

**record** ① *n* (a) (of events) compte-rendu *m*;
(of official proceedings) procès-verbal *m*; **to keep
a ~ of sth** noter qch; **to say sth off the ~**
dire qch en privé; **to set the ~ straight**
mettre les choses au clair
(b) (data) **~s** (historical, public) archives *fpl*;
(personal, administrative) dossier *m*
(c) (history) (of individual) passé *m*; (of organization,
group) réputation *f*
(d) (*also* **criminal ~**) casier *m* judiciaire
(e) (Mus) disque *m*
(f) (of athlete) record *m* (**for, in** de)
② *adj* (a) ⟨*company, label*⟩ de disques
(b) ⟨*sales, time*⟩ record (*after n*); **to be at a ~
high/low** être à son niveau le plus haut/bas
③ *vtr* (a) (note) noter ⟨*detail, idea, opinion*⟩
(b) (on disc, tape) enregistrer
(c) ⟨*instrument*⟩ enregistrer ⟨*temperature,
rainfall*⟩

**record book** *n* livre *m* des records

**recorded** *adj* (on tape) enregistré/-e;
(documented) ⟨*case, sighting*⟩ connu/-e

**recorded delivery** *n* (GB) **to send sth ~**
envoyer qch en recommandé

**recorder** *n* (Mus) flûte *f* à bec

**record-holder** *n* recordman/
recordwoman *m/f*

**recording** *n* enregistrement *m*

**record player** *n* tourne-disque *m*

**recourse** *n* recours *m* (**to** à)

**recover** ① *vtr* (a) retrouver, récupérer
⟨*money, vehicle*⟩; récupérer ⟨*territory*⟩; (from
water) repêcher, retrouver ⟨*body, wreck*⟩; **to ~
one's strength** reprendre des forces
(b) (recoup) réparer, compenser ⟨*losses*⟩
② *vi* (a) (from illness) se remettre (**from** de);
(from defeat) se ressaisir (**from** après)
(b) ⟨*economy*⟩ se redresser

**recovery** *n* (a) (getting better) rétablissement
*m*, guérison *f*
(b) (of economy, company, market) reprise *f*
(c) (getting back) (of vehicle) rapatriement *m*; (of
money) récupération *f*

**recovery vehicle** *n* camion *m* de
dépannage

**recreate** *vtr* recréer

**recreation** *n* (a) (leisure) loisirs *mpl*
(b) (playtime) récréation *f*

**recreational drug** *n*: drogue que l'on
prend de façon occasionnelle

**recreational vehicle, RV** *n*
camping-car *m*

**recrimination** *n* récrimination *f*

**recruit** ① *n* recrue *f*

② *vtr* recruter (**from** dans)

**recruiting officer** *n* officier *m* recruteur

**recruitment** *n* recrutement *m*

**rectangle** *n* rectangle *m*

**rectangular** *adj* rectangulaire

**rectify** *vtr* rectifier

**rector** *n* pasteur *m*

**recuperate** *vi* se rétablir (**from** de),
récupérer

**recur** *vi* ⟨*event, error*⟩ se reproduire;
⟨*illness*⟩ réapparaître; ⟨*theme*⟩ revenir

**recurrence** *n* (of illness) récurrence *f*; (of
symptom) réapparition *f*

**recurrent** *adj* récurrent/-e

**recycle** *vtr* recycler ⟨*paper, waste*⟩

**recycling** *n* recyclage *m*

**red** ① *n* (a) (colour) rouge *m*; **in ~** en rouge
(b) **to be in the ~** ⟨*person, account*⟩ être à
découvert; ⟨*company*⟩ être en déficit
② *adj* rouge (**with** de); ⟨*hair*⟩ roux/rousse; **to
go** *or* **turn ~** rougir
IDIOMS **to be caught ~-handed** être pris/-e la
main dans le sac (colloq)

**red alert** *n* alerte *f* rouge

**Red Cross** *n* Croix-Rouge *f*

**redcurrant** *n* groseille *f*

**redden** *vtr, vi* rougir

**redecorate** *vtr* repeindre et retapisser,
refaire

**redeem** *vtr* (a) retirer ⟨*pawned goods*⟩;
rembourser ⟨*debt*⟩
(b) racheter ⟨*sinner*⟩; **her one ~ing feature
is...** ce qui la rachète, c'est...

**redeploy** *vtr* redéployer ⟨*troops*⟩; réaffecter
⟨*staff*⟩

**redevelop** *vtr* réaménager ⟨*site, town*⟩

**red-faced** *adj* (embarrassed) penaud/-e

**redhead** *n* roux/rousse *m/f*

**red herring** *n* faux problème *m*

**red-hot** *adj* ⟨*metal, coal*⟩ chauffé/-e au
rouge

**redial** ① *vtr* refaire ⟨*number*⟩
② *vi* recomposer le numéro

**redial facility** *n* rappel *m* du dernier
numéro composé

**redirect** *vtr* canaliser ⟨*resources*⟩; dévier
⟨*traffic*⟩; réexpédier ⟨*mail*⟩

**rediscover** *vtr* redécouvrir

**red light area** *n* quartier *m* chaud

**redo** *vtr* refaire

**red pepper** *n* poivron *m* rouge

**redress** *vtr* **to ~ the balance** rétablir
l'équilibre

**red tape** *n* paperasserie *f*

**reduce** *vtr* (a) réduire ⟨*inflation, number,
pressure, sentence*⟩ (**by** de); baisser ⟨*prices,
temperature*⟩; **to ~ speed** ralentir; **to ~ sb to
tears** faire pleurer qn; **to be ~d to begging**
en être réduit/-e à la mendicité
(b) (in cooking) faire réduire ⟨*sauce, stock*⟩

**reduction** n **(a)** (in inflation, pressure, number) réduction f (**in** de); (of weight, size) diminution f (**in** de)
**(b)** (discount) réduction f, rabais m

**redundancy** n **(a)** (unemployment) chômage m
**(b)** (dismissal) licenciement m

**redundant** adj **(a)** (GB) (dismissed) licencié/-e; (out of work) au chômage; **to be made ~** être licencié/-e
**(b)** (not needed) superflu/-e

**reed** n **(a)** (plant) roseau m
**(b)** (Mus) anche f

**reef** n récif m, écueil m

**reek** vi **to ~ (of sth)** puer (qch)

**reel** 1 n bobine f; (for fishing) moulinet m
2 vi (sway) ⟨person⟩ tituber; **the blow sent him ~ing** le coup l'a projeté en arrière
■ **reel off** débiter ⟨list, names⟩

**re-elect** vtr réélire

**re-emerge** vi ⟨person, sun⟩ réapparaître; ⟨problem⟩ resurgir

**re-examine** vtr réexaminer

**refectory** n réfectoire m

**refer** 1 vtr renvoyer ⟨task, problem⟩ (**to** à); **to ~ sb to** ⟨person⟩ envoyer qn à ⟨department⟩
2 vi **(a)** (allude to) **to ~ to** parler de, faire allusion à ⟨person, topic, event⟩
**(b)** (relate, apply) **to ~ to** ⟨number, date, term⟩ se rapporter à
**(c)** (consult) **to ~ to** consulter ⟨notes, article⟩

**referee** 1 n **(a)** arbitre m
**(b)** (GB) (giving job reference) personne f pouvant fournir des références
2 vtr, vi arbitrer

**reference** 1 n **(a)** (allusion) référence f (**to** à), allusion f (**to** à)
**(b)** (consultation) **without ~ to sb/sth** sans consulter qn/qch; **for future ~** pour information
**(c)** (in book, letter) référence f
**(d)** (testimonial) références fpl
2 **with reference to** phr **with ~ to your letter** suite à votre lettre

**reference book** n ouvrage m de référence

**reference number** n numéro m de référence

**referendum** n référendum m

**referral** n (of matter, problem) renvoi m (**to** à)

**refill** 1 n (for ballpoint, lighter, perfume) recharge f
2 vtr recharger ⟨pen, lighter⟩; remplir [qch] à nouveau ⟨glass, bottle⟩

**refine** vtr **(a)** raffiner ⟨oil, sugar⟩
**(b)** (improve) peaufiner ⟨theory⟩

**refined** adj raffiné/-e

**refinement** n (elegance) raffinement m

**refinery** n raffinerie f

**reflect** 1 vtr **(a)** refléter ⟨image⟩; **to be ~ed in sth** se refléter dans qch
**(b)** renvoyer, réfléchir ⟨light, heat⟩
**(c)** (think) se dire

2 vi **(a)** (think) réfléchir (**on, upon** à)
**(b)** **to ~ well/badly on sb** faire honneur/du tort à qn

**reflection** n **(a)** (image) reflet m (**of** de), image f (**of** de)
**(b)** (thought) réflexion f; **on ~** à la réflexion

**reflector** n (on vehicle) catadioptre m

**reflex** 1 n réflexe m
2 adj réflexe; **a ~ action** un réflexe

**reflexive verb** n verbe m pronominal réfléchi

**reform** 1 n réforme f
2 vtr réformer

**reformation** n réforme f; **the Reformation** la Réforme

**refrain** 1 n refrain m
2 vi se retenir; **to ~ from doing** s'abstenir de faire

**refresh** vtr ⟨bath, drink⟩ rafraîchir; ⟨rest⟩ reposer; **to ~ sb's memory** rafraîchir la mémoire à qn

**refresher course** n cours m de recyclage

**refreshing** adj ⟨drink, shower⟩ rafraîchissant/-e; ⟨rest⟩ réparateur/-trice

**refreshments** n pl (drinks) rafraîchissements mpl; **light ~** repas m léger

**refrigerate** vtr frigorifier

**refrigerator** n réfrigérateur m, frigidaire® m

**refuel** vi se ravitailler en carburant

**refuge** n **(a)** (shelter, protection) refuge m (**from** contre); **to take ~ from** s'abriter de ⟨storm⟩
**(b)** (hostel) foyer m

**refugee** n réfugié/-e m/f

**refugee camp** n camp m de réfugiés

**refund** 1 n remboursement m
2 vtr rembourser

**refurbish** vtr rénover

**refusal** n refus m (**to do** de faire); (to application) réponse f négative

**refuse**[1] 1 vtr refuser (**to do** de faire)
2 vi refuser

**refuse**[2] n (GB) (household) ordures fpl; (industrial) déchets mpl; (garden) déchets mpl de jardinage

**refuse collector** n (GB) éboueur m

**refute** vtr réfuter

**regain** vtr retrouver ⟨health, strength, sight, composure⟩; reconquérir ⟨power, seat⟩; reprendre ⟨lead, control⟩; **to ~ consciousness** reprendre connaissance

**regal** adj royal/-e

**regale** vtr régaler (**with** de)

**regalia** n pl insignes mpl

**regard** 1 n **(a)** (consideration) égard m; **out of ~ for** par égard pour
**(b)** (esteem) estime f (**for** pour); **to hold sb/sth in high ~** avoir beaucoup d'estime pour qn/qch ⋯⋯

**(c) with** or **in ∼ to** en ce qui concerne; **in this ∼** à cet égard

**2** *vtr* considérer (**as** comme)

**regarding** *prep* concernant

**regardless** **1** *prep* **∼ of** sans tenir compte de

**2** *adv* malgré tout

**regards** *n pl* amitiés *fpl*; **give them my ∼** transmettez-leur mes amitiés

**regatta** *n* régate *f*

**regent** *n* régent/-e *m/f*

**reggae** *n* reggae *m*

**regime, régime** *n* régime *m*

**regiment** *n* régiment *m*

**region** *n* région *f*; (**somewhere**) **in the ∼ of £300** environ 300 livres sterling

**regional** *adj* régional/-e

**register** **1** *n* registre *m*; (at school) cahier *m* des absences

**2** *vtr* **(a)** déclarer ⟨*birth, death*⟩; faire immatriculer ⟨*vehicle*⟩; faire enregistrer ⟨*luggage, company*⟩; déposer ⟨*trademark, complaint*⟩

**(b)** ⟨*instrument*⟩ indiquer ⟨*speed, temperature*⟩; ⟨*person*⟩ exprimer ⟨*anger, disapproval*⟩

**(c)** envoyer [qch] en recommandé ⟨*letter*⟩

**3** *vi* (for course, school, to vote) s'inscrire; (at hotel) se présenter

**registered** *adj* **(a)** ⟨*voter*⟩ inscrit/-e; ⟨*vehicle, student*⟩ immatriculé/-e; ⟨*charity*⟩ ≈ agréé/-e

**(b)** ⟨*letter*⟩ recommandé/-e; **by ∼ post** en recommandé

**registered trademark** *n* marque *m* déposée

**registrar** *n* **(a)** (GB) (gen) officier *m* d'état civil; (medical) adjoint *m*

**(b)** (academic) responsable *mf* du bureau de la scolarité

**registration** *n* (of person) inscription *f*; (of trademark, patent) dépôt *m*; (of birth, death, marriage) déclaration *f*

**registration number** *n* numéro *m* d'immatriculation

**registry office** *n* (GB) bureau *m* de l'état civil; **to get married in a ∼** se marier civilement

**regress** *vi* régresser (**to** au stade de)

**regret** **1** *n* regret *m* (**about** à propos de); **to have no ∼s about doing** ne pas regretter d'avoir fait

**2** *vtr* regretter (**that** que + *subjunctive*); **to ∼ doing** regretter d'avoir fait; **I ∼ to inform you that** j'ai le regret de vous informer que

**regretfully** *adv* à regret

**regrettable** *adj* regrettable (**that** que + *subjunctive*)

**regular** **1** *n* **(a)** (client, visitor) habitué/-e *m/f*

**(b)** (US) (petrol) ordinaire *m*

**2** *adj* **(a)** (gen) régulier/-ière; **to take ∼ exercise** faire de l'exercice régulièrement

**(b)** (usual) ⟨*activity, customer, visitor*⟩ habituel/-elle; ⟨*viewer, listener*⟩ fidèle

**(c)** ⟨*army, soldier*⟩ de métier

**regularity** *n* régularité *f*

**regularly** *adv* régulièrement

**regulate** *vtr* **(a)** (gen, Econ) réguler

**(b)** (adjust) régler ⟨*mechanism*⟩

**regulation** **1** *n* **(a)** (gen) règlement *m*; (for safety, fire) consigne *f*; **under the (new) ∼s** selon la (nouvelle) réglementation; **against the ∼s** contraire au règlement or aux normes

**(b)** (controlling) réglementation *f*

**2** *adj* ⟨*width, length, uniform*⟩ réglementaire

**regurgitate** *vtr* régurgiter; (figurative) ressortir

**rehabilitate** *vtr* réinsérer ⟨*handicapped person, ex-prisoner*⟩; réhabiliter ⟨*addict, area*⟩

**rehabilitation centre** (GB), **rehabilitation center** (US) *n* (for the handicapped) centre *m* de rééducation; (for addicts etc) centre *m* de réinsertion

**rehearsal** *n* répétition *f* (**of** de)

**rehearse** **1** *vtr* répéter ⟨*scene*⟩; préparer ⟨*speech, excuse*⟩

**2** *vi* répéter (**for** pour)

**reheat** *vtr* réchauffer

**rehouse** *vtr* reloger

**reign** **1** *n* règne *m*

**2** *vi* régner (**over** sur)

**reimburse** *vtr* rembourser

**rein** *n* rêne *f*

**reincarnation** *n* réincarnation *f*

**reindeer** *n* renne *m*

**reinforce** *vtr* renforcer

**reinforced concrete** *n* béton *m* armé

**reinforcement** *n* (support) renfort *m*; **∼s** (Mil) renforts

**reinstate** *vtr* réintégrer ⟨*employee*⟩

**reiterate** *vtr* réitérer

**reject** **1** *n* marchandise *f* de deuxième choix

**2** *vtr* rejeter ⟨*advice, application, person, transplant*⟩; refuser ⟨*candidate, manuscript*⟩; démentir ⟨*claim, suggestion*⟩

**rejection** *n* (gen) rejet *m*; (of candidate, manuscript) refus *m*

**rejection letter** *n* lettre *f* de refus

**rejoice** *vi* se réjouir (**at, over** de)

**rejuvenate** *vtr* rajeunir

**rekindle** *vtr* ranimer

**relapse** **1** *n* rechute *f*

**2** *vi* (Med) rechuter; (gen) **to ∼ into** retomber dans

**relate** **1** *vtr* **(a)** (connect) faire le rapprochement entre

**(b)** raconter ⟨*story*⟩ (**to** à)

**2** *vi* **to ∼ to** (have connection) se rapporter à; (communicate) s'entendre avec

**related** *adj* **(a)** ⟨*person*⟩ apparenté/-e (**by, through** par; **to** à)

**(b)** (connected) ⟨*area, idea, incident*⟩ lié/-e (**to** à); **drug-∼** lié/-e à la drogue

**relation** ⟨1⟩ n (a) (relative) parent/-e m/f; my ~s ma famille
(b) (connection) rapport m
⟨2⟩ **relations** n pl (dealings) relations fpl (with avec)

**relationship** n (a) (between people) relations fpl; (with colleagues) rapports mpl
(b) (connection) rapport m (to, with avec)

**relative** ⟨1⟩ n parent/-e m/f; my ~s ma famille
⟨2⟩ adj (a) (gen) relatif/-ive
(b) (respective) respectif/-ive

**relatively** adv relativement; ~ speaking toutes proportions gardées

**relax** ⟨1⟩ vtr décontracter ⟨muscle⟩; assouplir ⟨restrictions, discipline⟩; détendre ⟨body⟩; relâcher ⟨efforts, grip, concentration⟩
⟨2⟩ vi (a) ⟨person⟩ se détendre
(b) ⟨grip⟩ se relâcher; ⟨jaw, muscle⟩ se décontracter

**relaxation** n (a) (of person) détente f
(b) (of restrictions, discipline) assouplissement m (in de)

**relaxed** adj détendu/-e, décontracté/-e

**relaxing** adj ⟨atmosphere, activity⟩ délassant/-e; ⟨vacation⟩ reposant/-e

**relay** ⟨1⟩ n (a) (of workers) équipe f (de relais)
(b) (also ~ **race**) course f de relais
⟨2⟩ vtr transmettre ⟨message⟩ (to à)

**release** ⟨1⟩ n (a) (liberation) libération f
(b) (relief) soulagement m
(c) (for press) communiqué m
(d) (of film) sortie f
(e) (film, video, record) (also **new ~**) nouveauté f
⟨2⟩ vtr (a) libérer ⟨prisoner⟩; dégager ⟨accident victim⟩; relâcher ⟨animal⟩; to ~ sb from dégager qn de ⟨promise⟩
(b) faire jouer ⟨catch, clasp⟩; déclencher ⟨shutter⟩; desserrer ⟨handbrake⟩; larguer ⟨bomb⟩
(c) (let go) lâcher ⟨object, arm, hand⟩
(d) faire sortir ⟨film, record⟩

**relegate** vtr (a) reléguer ⟨person, object⟩ (to à)
(b) (GB) (Sport) reléguer (to en)

**relegation** n relégation f

**relent** vi céder

**relentless** adj ⟨pressure⟩ implacable; ⟨noise, activity⟩ incessant/-e; ⟨attack⟩ acharné/-e

**relevant** adj (a) ⟨issue, facts, point⟩ pertinent/-e; ⟨information⟩ utile; to be ~ to avoir rapport à
(b) (appropriate) ⟨chapter⟩ correspondant/-e; ⟨period⟩ en question

**reliable** adj ⟨friend, witness⟩ digne de confiance, fiable; ⟨employee, firm⟩ sérieux/-ieuse; ⟨car, memory, account⟩ fiable; ⟨information, source⟩ sûr/-e

**reliant** adj to be ~ on être dépendant/-e de

**relic** n relique f

**relief** n (a) (from pain, distress) soulagement m
(b) (aid) aide f, secours m

(c) (in sculpture, geography) relief m

**relief agency** n organisation f humanitaire

**relief fund** n fonds m de secours

**relief supplies** n pl secours mpl

**relief work** n travail m humanitaire

**relief worker** n secouriste mf

**relieve** vtr (a) soulager ⟨pain, suffering, tension⟩; dissiper ⟨boredom⟩; remédier à ⟨poverty, famine⟩; to be ~d être soulagé/-e
(b) to ~ sb of débarrasser qn de ⟨coat, bag⟩; soulager qn de ⟨burden⟩
(c) (help) secourir ⟨troops, population⟩
(d) relever ⟨worker, sentry⟩

**religion** n religion f

**religious** adj (gen) religieux/-ieuse; ⟨person⟩ croyant/-e; ⟨war⟩ de religion

**relinquish** vtr renoncer à ⟨claim, right⟩ (to en faveur de); céder ⟨task, power⟩ (to à)

**relish** ⟨1⟩ n (a) with ~ ⟨eat, drink⟩ avec un plaisir évident
(b) (Culin) condiment m
⟨2⟩ vtr savourer ⟨food⟩; se réjouir de ⟨prospect⟩

**relocate** ⟨1⟩ vtr muter
⟨2⟩ vi ⟨company⟩ déménager; ⟨employee⟩ être muté/-e

**reluctance** n réticence f (to do à faire)

**reluctant** adj ⟨person⟩ peu enthousiaste; to be ~ to do être peu disposé/-e à faire

**reluctantly** adv à contrecœur

**rely** vi (a) (be dependent) to ~ on dépendre de ⟨person, aid, industry⟩; reposer sur ⟨method, technology, exports⟩
(b) (count) to ~ on sb/sth compter sur qn/qch (to do pour faire)

**remain** vi rester; to ~ silent garder le silence

**remainder** n reste m (of de)

**remains** n pl restes mpl

**remand** ⟨1⟩ n on ~ (in custody) en détention provisoire; (on bail) en liberté sous caution
⟨2⟩ vtr to be ~ed in custody être placé/-e en détention provisoire

**remand centre** n (GB) centre m de détention (provisoire)

**remark** ⟨1⟩ n remarque f
⟨2⟩ vtr (a) (comment) faire remarquer (that que; to à)
(b) (notice) remarquer (that que)

**remarkable** adj remarquable

**remarry** vi se remarier

**remedial** adj (Sch) ⟨class⟩ de rattrapage

**remedy** ⟨1⟩ n remède m (for à, contre)
⟨2⟩ vtr remédier à

**remember** ⟨1⟩ vtr (a) (recall) se souvenir de, se rappeler ⟨fact, name, place, event⟩; se souvenir de ⟨person⟩; to ~ doing se rappeler avoir fait, se souvenir d'avoir fait
(b) (not forget) to ~ to do penser à faire, ne pas oublier de faire
⟨2⟩ vi se souvenir

r

**remind** *vtr* rappeler; **to ~ sb of sb/sth** rappeler qn/qch à qn; **to ~ sb to do** rappeler à qn de faire

**reminder** *n* rappel *m* (**of** de; **that** du fait que)

**reminisce** *vi* évoquer ses souvenirs (**about** de)

**reminiscent** *adj* **to be ~ of sb/sth** faire penser à qn/qch

**remiss** *adj* négligent/-e

**remission** *n* (a) (of sentence, debt) remise *f* (b) (Med) rémission *f*

**remit** *n* attributions *fpl*

**remnant** *n* (gen) reste *m*; (of building, past) vestige *m*; (of fabric) coupon *m*

**remorse** *n* remords *m* (**for** de)

**remote** *adj* (a) ⟨*area, village*⟩ isolé/-e; ⟨*ancestor, country*⟩ éloigné/-e (b) (aloof) ⟨*person*⟩ distant/-e (c) (slight) ⟨*chance*⟩ vague, infime

**remote control** *n* télécommande *f*

**remote-controlled** *adj* télécommandé/-e

**remotely** *adv* ⟨*resemble*⟩ vaguement; **he's not ~ interested** ça ne l'intéresse pas du tout

**removal** *n* (a) (of furniture, parcel, rubbish) enlèvement *m*; (Med) ablation *f*; **stain ~** détachage *m* (b) (change of home) déménagement *m* (**from** de; **to** à)

**remove** *vtr* (a) (gen, Med) enlever (**from** de); enlever, ôter ⟨*clothes, shoes*⟩; supprimer ⟨*threat*⟩; chasser ⟨*doubt*⟩; **cousin once ~d** cousin au deuxième degré (b) **to ~ sb from office** démettre qn de ses fonctions

**remover** *n* déménageur *m*

**remuneration** *n* rémunération *f*

**Renaissance** *n* **the ~** la Renaissance

**render** *vtr* rendre

**rendezvous** ① *n* rendez-vous *m inv* ② *vi* **to ~ with sb** rejoindre qn

**renegade** *n* renégat/-e *m/f*

**renew** ① *vtr* (gen) renouveler; renouer ⟨*acquaintance*⟩; raviver ⟨*courage*⟩; faire prolonger ⟨*library book*⟩

**renewal** *n* (of contract, passport) renouvellement *m*; (of hostilities) reprise *f*; (of interest) regain *m*

**renewed** *adj* ⟨*interest, optimism*⟩ accru/-e; ⟨*attack, call*⟩ renouvelé/-e

**renounce** *vtr* (gen) renoncer à; renier ⟨*faith, friend*⟩

**renovate** *vtr* rénover ⟨*building*⟩

**renovation** *n* rénovation *f*; **~s** travaux *mpl* de rénovation

**renowned** *adj* célèbre (**for** pour)

**rent** ① *n* loyer *m*; **for ~** à louer ② *vtr* louer

**rental** *n* (of car, premises, equipment) location *f*; (of phone line) abonnement *m*

**rent boy** *n* jeune prostitué *m*

**reoffend** *vi* récidiver

**reopen** *vtr, vi* rouvrir

**reorganize** *vtr* réorganiser

**rep** *n* représentant/-e *m/f* (de commerce)

**repair** ① *n* réparation *f*; **to be (damaged) beyond ~** ne pas être réparable; **to be in good/bad ~** être en bon/mauvais état ② *vtr* réparer

**repairman** *n* réparateur *m*

**repatriate** *vtr* rapatrier

**repatriation** *n* rapatriement *m*

**repay** *vtr* rembourser ⟨*person, sum*⟩; rendre ⟨*hospitality, favour*⟩

**repayment** *n* remboursement *m* (**on** de)

**repeal** ① *n* abrogation *f* (**of** de) ② *vtr* abroger

**repeat** ① *n* (gen) répétition *f*; (on radio, TV) rediffusion *f*; (Mus) reprise *f* ② *vtr* (gen) répéter; (Sch) redoubler ⟨*year*⟩; rediffuser ⟨*programme*⟩

**repeated** *adj* ⟨*warnings, requests, attempts*⟩ répété/-e; ⟨*setbacks*⟩ successif/-ive

**repeatedly** *adv* plusieurs fois, à plusieurs reprises

**repel** *vtr* repousser

**repellent** *adj* repoussant/-e

**repent** *vi* se repentir

**repercussion** *n* répercussion *f*

**repertoire** *n* répertoire *m*

**repetition** *n* répétition *f*

**repetitive** *adj* répétitif/-ive

**repetitive strain injury, RSI** *n* microtraumatismes *mpl* répétés

**replace** *vtr* (a) (put back) remettre ⟨*lid, cork*⟩; remettre [qch] à sa place ⟨*book, ornament*⟩ (b) (provide replacement for) remplacer (**with** par)

**replacement** *n* (a) (person) remplaçant/-e *m/f* (**for** de) (b) (act) remplacement *m* (c) (spare part) pièce *f* de rechange

**replay** ① *n* (Sport) match *m* rejoué ② *vtr* rejouer

**replenish** *vtr* reconstituer ⟨*stocks*⟩

**replica** *n* réplique *f*, copie *f* (**of** de)

**reply** ① *n* réponse *f* ② *vtr, vi* répondre

**report** ① *n* (a) (written account) rapport *m* (**on** sur); (verbal account, minutes) compte-rendu *m*; (in media) communiqué *m*; (longer) reportage *m* (b) (GB) (Sch) (also **school ~**) bulletin *m* scolaire; (US) (Sch) (review) critique *f* ② *vtr* (a) signaler ⟨*fact, event, theft, accident*⟩; **to ~ sth to sb** transmettre qch à qn ⟨*result, decision, news*⟩ (b) (make complaint about) signaler ⟨*person*⟩; se plaindre de ⟨*noise*⟩ ③ *vi* (a) **to ~ on** faire un compte-rendu sur ⟨*talks, progress*⟩; ⟨*reporter*⟩ faire un reportage sur ⟨*events*⟩; ⟨*committee, group*⟩ faire son rapport sur (b) (present oneself) se présenter; **to ~ for duty** prendre son service

**(c) to ~ to** être sous les ordres (directs) de ⟨*manager, superior*⟩

**report card** *n* (US) bulletin *m* scolaire

**reporter** *n* journaliste *mf*, reporter *mf*

**repose** *n* repos *m*; **in ~** au repos

**repossess** *vtr* ⟨*bank*⟩ saisir ⟨*house*⟩; ⟨*creditor*⟩ reprendre possession de ⟨*property*⟩

**repossession** *n* saisie *f* immobilière

**reprehensible** *adj* répréhensible

**represent** *vtr* **(a)** (gen) représenter **(b)** (present) présenter ⟨*person, event*⟩ (**as** comme)

**representation** *n* **(a)** représentation *f* (**of** de; **by** par) **(b) to make ~s to sb** faire des démarches *fpl* auprès de qn

**representative** ⒈ *n* **(a)** représentant/-e *m/f* **(b)** (US) (politician) député *m* ⒉ *adj* représentatif/-ive (**of** de), typique (**of** de)

**repress** *vtr* réprimer ⟨*reaction, smile*⟩; refouler ⟨*feelings*⟩

**reprieve** ⒈ *n* **(a)** (Law) remise *f* de peine **(b)** (delay) sursis *m* **(c)** (respite) répit *m* ⒉ *vtr* accorder une remise de peine à ⟨*prisoner*⟩

**reprimand** ⒈ *n* réprimande *f* ⒉ *vtr* réprimander

**reprisal** *n* représailles *fpl*

**reproach** ⒈ *n* reproche *m*; **beyond ~** irréprochable ⒉ *vtr* reprocher à ⟨*person*⟩; **to ~ sb with** *or* **for sth** reprocher qch à qn

**reprocessing plant** *n* (*also* **nuclear ~**) usine *f* de retraitement (des déchets nucléaires)

**reproduce** ⒈ *vtr* reproduire ⒉ *vi* se reproduire

**reproduction** *n* reproduction *f*

**reproduction furniture** *n* meubles *mpl* de style

**reproductive** *adj* reproducteur/-trice

**reproof** *n* réprimande *f*

**reprove** *vtr* réprimander (**for doing** de faire)

**reptile** *n* reptile *m*

**republic** *n* république *f*

**republican** ⒈ *n* républicain/-e *m/f*; **Republican** (US) Républicain/-e *m/f* ⒉ *adj* (*also* **Republican**) républicain/-e

**repudiate** *vtr* rejeter

**repugnant** *adj* répugnant/-e

**repulse** *vtr* repousser

**repulsion** *n* répulsion *f*

**repulsive** *adj* repoussant/-e

**reputable** *adj* de bonne réputation

**reputation** *n* réputation *f* (**as** de)

**repute** *n* **of ~** réputé/-e

**reputed** *adj* (gen) réputé/-e; (Law) putatif/-ive; **he is ~ to be very rich** à ce que l'on dit il serait très riche

**request** ⒈ *n* **(a)** demande *f* (**for** de; **to** à), requête *f* (**for** de; **to** à); **on ~** sur demande **(b)** (on radio) dédicace *f* ⒉ *vtr* demander (**from** à); **to ~ sb to do** demander à qn de faire

**require** *vtr* **(a)** (need) avoir besoin de **(b)** (necessitate) ⟨*job, situation*⟩ exiger ⟨*funds, qualifications*⟩; **to be ~d to do** être tenu/-e de faire

**requirement** *n* **(a)** (need) besoin *m* **(b)** (condition) condition *f* **(c)** (obligation) obligation *f* (**to do** de faire) **(d)** (US) (Univ) matière *f* obligatoire

**requisite** *adj* exigé/-e, requis/-e

**requisition** *vtr* réquisitionner

**reschedule** *vtr* (change time) changer l'heure de; (change date) changer la date de

**rescue** ⒈ *n* **(a)** (aid) secours *m*; **to come/ go to sb's ~** venir/aller au secours de qn; **to come to the ~** venir à la rescousse **(b)** (operation) sauvetage *m* ⒉ *vtr* **(a)** (save) sauver **(b)** (aid) porter secours à **(c)** (release) libérer

**rescue worker** *n* secouriste *mf*

**research** ⒈ *n* recherche *f* (**into, on** sur) ⒉ *vtr* faire des recherches sur ⟨*topic*⟩; préparer ⟨*book, article*⟩

**research and development, R&D** *n* recherche-développement *f*, recherche *f* et développement *m*

**researcher** *n* chercheur/-euse *m/f*; (in TV) documentaliste *mf*

**resemblance** *n* ressemblance *f* (**between** entre; **to** avec)

**resemble** *vtr* ressembler à; **to ~ each other** se ressembler

**resent** *vtr* en vouloir à ⟨*person*⟩ (**for doing** d'avoir fait); ne pas aimer ⟨*tone*⟩

**resentful** *adj* plein/-e de ressentiment (**of sb** envers qn)

**resentment** *n* ressentiment *m*

**reservation** *n* **(a)** (doubt) réserve *f*; **without ~** sans réserve; **to have ~s about sth** avoir des doutes sur qch **(b)** (booking) réservation *f* **(c)** (US) (Indian) **~** réserve *f* (indienne)

**reservation desk** *n* bureau *m* des réservations

**reserve** ⒈ *n* **(a)** (stock) réserve *f*; **to keep sth in ~** tenir qch en réserve **(b)** (reticence) réserve *f* **(c)** (Mil) **the ~(s)** la réserve **(d)** (Sport) remplaçant/-e *m/f* **(e)** réserve *f*; **wildlife ~** réserve naturelle ⒉ *vtr* réserver

**reserved** *adj* réservé/-e

**reservoir** *n* réservoir *m*

**reset** *vtr* régler ⟨*machine*⟩; remettre [qch] à l'heure ⟨*clock*⟩

**reshuffle** *n* remaniement *m*

**reside** *vi* résider, habiter (**with** avec)

**residence** *n* résidence *f*

**residence permit** *n* permis *m* de séjour

**resident** ⓵ *n* (gen) résident/-e *m/f*; (of street) riverain/-e *m/f*; (of guest house) pensionnaire *mf*
⓶ *adj* ⟨*population*⟩ local/-e; ⟨*staff, tutor*⟩ à demeure

**residential** *adj* ⟨*area*⟩ résidentiel/-ielle; ⟨*staff*⟩ à demeure; ⟨*course*⟩ en internat; **to be in** ∼ **care** être pris en charge par une institution

**residue** *n* résidu *m* (**of** de)

**resign** ⓵ *vtr* démissionner de ⟨*post, job*⟩
⓶ *vi* démissionner (**as** du poste de; **from** de)
⓷ *v refl* **to** ∼ **oneself** se résigner (**to** à)

**resignation** *n* (a) (from post) démission *f* (**from** de; **as** du poste de)
(b) (patience) résignation *f*

**resigned** *adj* résigné/-e (**to** à)

**resilient** *adj* (morally) déterminé/-e; (physically) résistant/-e

**resin** *n* résine *f*

**resist** ⓵ *vtr* résister à
⓶ *vi* résister

**resistance** *n* résistance *f* (**to** à)

**Resistance** *n* **the** ∼ la Résistance

**resistance fighter** *n* résistant/-e *m/f*

**resistant** *adj* (a) heat-∼ résistant/-e à la chaleur; water-∼ imperméable
(b) (opposed) ∼ **to** réfractaire à

**resit** *vtr* (GB) repasser ⟨*exam, test*⟩

**reskill** *vtr* recycler

**resolute** *adj* ⟨*person*⟩ résolu/-e

**resolution** *n* résolution *f*; **to make a** ∼ **to do** prendre la résolution de faire

**resolve** ⓵ *n* détermination *f*
⓶ *vtr* (a) (gen) résoudre
(b) (decide) **to** ∼ **that** décider que; **to** ∼ **to do** résoudre de faire

**resonant** *adj* ⟨*voice*⟩ sonore

**resort** ⓵ *n* (a) recours *m*; **as a last** ∼ en dernier recours
(b) **seaside** ∼ station *f* balnéaire; **ski** ∼ station *f* de ski
⓶ *vi* **to** ∼ **to** recourir à

**resound** *vi* (a) ⟨*noise*⟩ retentir (**through** dans)
(b) ⟨*place*⟩ retentir (**with** de)

**resounding** *adj* ⟨*cheers*⟩ retentissant/-e; ⟨*success*⟩ éclatant/-e

**resource** *n* ressource *f*

**resource centre** (GB), **resource center** (US) *n* centre *m* de documentation

**resourceful** *adj* plein/-e de ressources, débrouillard/-e (colloq)

**respect** ⓵ *n* (a) (gen) respect *m*; **out of** ∼ par respect (**for** pour); **with (all due)** ∼ sauf votre respect; **with** ∼ **to** par rapport à
(b) (aspect) égard *m*; **in many** ∼**s** à bien des égards
⓶ **respects** *n pl* respects *mpl*; **to pay one's** ∼**s to sb** présenter ses respects à qn

⓷ *vtr* respecter

**respectable** *adj* (a) ⟨*person, family*⟩ respectable
(b) (adequate) ⟨*amount*⟩ respectable; ⟨*performance*⟩ honorable

**respectful** *adj* respectueux/-euse

**respective** *adj* respectif/-ive

**respiration** *n* respiration *f*

**respirator** *n* respirateur *m*

**respiratory** *adj* respiratoire

**respite** *n* répit *m* (**from** dans)

**respond** *vi* (a) (answer) répondre (**to** à; **with** par)
(b) (react) réagir (**to** à)

**response** *n* (a) (answer) réponse *f* (**to** à); **in** ∼ **to** en réponse à
(b) (reaction) réaction *f* (**to** à; **from** de)

**responsibility** *n* responsabilité *f* (**for** de); **to take** ∼ **for sth** prendre la responsabilité de qch

**responsible** *adj* (a) (to blame) responsable (**for** de)
(b) (in charge) ∼ **for doing** chargé/-e de faire
(c) (trustworthy) responsable
(d) ⟨*job*⟩ à responsabilités

**responsive** *adj* réceptif/-ive

**rest** ⓵ *n* (a) (remainder) **the** ∼ le reste (**of** de); **for the** ∼ **of my life** pour le restant de mes jours
(b) (other people) **the** ∼ **(of them)** les autres
(c) (repose) repos *m*; (break) pause *f*; **to have a** ∼ se reposer
⓶ *vtr* (a) (lean) **to** ∼ **sth on** appuyer qch sur
(b) reposer ⟨*legs*⟩; ne pas utiliser ⟨*injured limb*⟩
⓷ *vi* (a) se reposer; **to** ∼ **easy** être tranquille; **to let the matter** ∼ en rester là
(b) (be supported) **to** ∼ **on** reposer sur
(c) **to** ∼ **on** ⟨*decision*⟩ reposer sur ⟨*assumption*⟩
■ **rest with**: ∼ **with [sb/sth]** être entre les mains de

**restart** *vtr* (a) reprendre ⟨*talks*⟩
(b) remettre [qch] en marche ⟨*engine*⟩

**restaurant** *n* restaurant *m*

**restaurant car** *n* (GB) wagon-restaurant *m*

**restaurant owner** *n* restaurateur/-trice *m/f*

**restful** *adj* ⟨*holiday*⟩ reposant/-e; ⟨*place*⟩ paisible

**restless** *adj* ⟨*person*⟩ nerveux/-euse; ⟨*patient, sleep*⟩ agité/-e

**restock** *vtr* regarnir ⟨*shelf*⟩ (**with** en); réapprovisionner ⟨*shop*⟩ (**with** en)

**restoration** *n* restauration *f*

**restore** *vtr* (a) restituer ⟨*property*⟩ (**to** à)
(b) rétablir ⟨*health, peace, monarchy*⟩; rendre ⟨*faculty*⟩; **to** ∼ **sb to power** ramener qn au pouvoir
(c) (repair) restaurer

**restrain** ⓵ *vtr* retenir ⟨*person*⟩; contenir ⟨*crowd*⟩; maîtriser ⟨*animal*⟩
⓶ *v refl* **to** ∼ **oneself** se retenir

**restrained** adj ⟨manner⟩ calme; ⟨reaction⟩ modéré/-e; ⟨person⟩ posé/-e

**restraint** n **(a)** (moderation) modération f **(b)** (restriction) restriction f; **wage ~** contrôle m des salaires **(c)** (constraint) contrainte f

**restrict** vtr limiter ⟨activity, choice, growth⟩ (**to** à); restreindre ⟨freedom⟩; réserver ⟨access, membership⟩ (**to** à)

**restricted** adj ⟨growth, movement⟩ limité/-e; ⟨document⟩ confidentiel/-ielle; ⟨parking⟩ réglementé/-e

**restriction** n limitation f

**re-string** vtr changer les cordes de ⟨guitar⟩; recorder ⟨racket⟩; renfiler ⟨necklace⟩

**rest room** n (US) toilettes fpl

**result** ① n résultat m (**of** de); **as a ~ of** à la suite de; **as a ~** en conséquence ② vi résulter; **to ~ in** avoir pour résultat

**resume** vtr, vi reprendre

**résumé** n **(a)** (summary) résumé m **(b)** (US) (CV) curriculum vitae m inv

**resumption** n reprise f (**of** de)

**resurface** ① vtr refaire (la surface de) ⟨road⟩ ② vi ⟨submarine⟩ faire surface; ⟨person⟩ refaire surface

**resurrect** vtr ressusciter

**resurrection** n résurrection f; **the Resurrection** la Résurrection

**resuscitate** vtr (Med) réanimer

**resuscitation** n réanimation f

**retail** ① n vente f au détail ② adv au détail ③ vi **to ~ at** se vendre au détail à

**retailer** n détaillant m

**retail price** n prix m de détail

**retail sales** n pl ventes fpl au détail

**retail trade** n commerce m de détail

**retain** vtr garder ⟨control, identity⟩; conserver ⟨heat, title⟩; retenir ⟨water, fact⟩

**retaliate** vi réagir

**retaliation** n représailles fpl (**for** de)

**retarded** adj retardé/-e

**retch** vi avoir des haut-le-cœur

**rethink** n to have a ~ y repenser

**reticent** adj réticent/-e; **to be ~ about sth** être discret/-ète sur qch

**retina** n rétine f

**retinue** n escorte f

**retire** vi **(a)** (from work) prendre sa retraite **(b)** (withdraw) se retirer (**from** de)

**retired** adj retraité/-e

**retirement** n retraite f

**retirement age** n âge m de la retraite

**retirement home** n maison f de retraite

**retiring** adj (shy) réservé/-e

**retort** ① n riposte f ② vtr rétorquer (**that** que)

**retrace** vtr **to ~ one's steps** revenir sur ses pas

**retract** ① vtr rétracter ⟨statement, claws⟩; escamoter ⟨landing gear⟩ ② vi ⟨landing gear⟩ s'escamoter

**retrain** ① vtr recycler ⟨staff⟩ ② vi ⟨person⟩ se recycler

**retraining** n recyclage m

**retreat** ① n retraite f ② vi ⟨person⟩ se retirer (**into** dans; **from** de); ⟨army⟩ reculer; **to ~ into a dream world** se réfugier dans un monde imaginaire

**retrial** n nouveau procès m

**retrieve** vtr récupérer ⟨object⟩; redresser ⟨situation⟩; extraire ⟨data⟩

**retrograde** adj rétrograde

**retrospect**: **in retrospect** phr rétrospectivement

**retrospective** ① n (also **~ exhibition** or **~ show**) rétrospective f ② adj **(a)** (gen) rétrospectif/-ive **(b)** (Law) rétroactif/-ive

**return** ① n **(a)** (gen) retour m (**to** à; **from** de; **of** de); **by ~ of post** par retour du courrier **(b)** (on investment) rendement m (**on** de) ② vtr **(a)** (give back) rendre; (pay back) rembourser; **to ~ sb's call** rappeler qn **(b)** (bring back) rapporter (**to** à) **(c)** (put back) remettre **(d)** (send back) renvoyer; **'~ to sender'** 'retour à l'expéditeur' **(e)** (reciprocate) répondre à ⟨love⟩ **(f)** (Mil) riposter à ⟨fire⟩ **(g)** (Law) prononcer ⟨verdict⟩ **(h)** rapporter ⟨profit⟩ ③ vi **(a)** (come back) revenir (**from** de); retourner (**to** à); (get back from abroad) rentrer (**from** de); (get back home) rentrer chez soi **(b)** (resume) **to ~ to** reprendre ⟨activity⟩; **to ~ to power** revenir au pouvoir **(c)** (recur) ⟨symptom, doubt⟩ réapparaître ④ **in return** phr en échange (**for** de) IDIOMS **many happy ~s!** bon anniversaire!

**return fare** n prix m d'un billet aller-retour

**return flight** n vol m de retour

**return ticket** n billet m aller-retour

**return trip** n retour m

**reunification** n réunification f

**reunion** n réunion f

**reunite** vtr réunir ⟨family⟩; réunifier ⟨party⟩

**reuse** vtr réutiliser

**rev** vtr (colloq) monter le régime de ⟨engine⟩

**revalue** vtr réévaluer

**revamp** vtr rajeunir ⟨image⟩; réorganiser ⟨company⟩; retaper (colloq) ⟨building⟩

**reveal** vtr (gen) révéler; dévoiler ⟨truth, plan⟩; **to ~ sth to sb** révéler qch à qn

**revealing** adj **(a)** ⟨remark⟩ révélateur/-trice **(b)** ⟨blouse⟩ décolleté/-e

r

**revel** *vi* to ~ in sth/in doing se délecter de qch/à faire

**revelation** *n* révélation *f*

**revenge** ① *n* vengeance *f*; to get one's ~ se venger (for de; on sur)
② *v refl* to ~ oneself se venger

**revenue** *n* revenus *mpl*

**reverberate** *vi* résonner (with de; through dans, par); ⟨figurative⟩ se propager

**revere** *vtr* révérer

**reverence** *n* profond respect *m*

**Reverend** *n* (a) (Protestant) pasteur *m*
(b) (as title) the ~ Jones le révérend Jones; ~ Mother Révérende Mère

**reverent** *adj* ⟨hush⟩ religieux/-ieuse; ⟨expression⟩ de respect

**reverie** *n* rêverie *f*

**reversal** *n* (of policy, roles) renversement *m*; (of order, trend) inversion *f*; (of fortune) revers *m*

**reverse** ① *n* (a) (opposite) the ~ le contraire
(b) (back) the ~ (of coin) le revers; (of banknote) le verso; (of fabric) l'envers *m*
(c) (Aut) (also ~ gear) marche *f* arrière
② *adj* (a) ⟨effect⟩ contraire; in ~ order ⟨answer questions⟩ en commençant par le dernier/la dernière; ⟨list⟩ en commençant par la fin
(b) (Aut) ~ gear marche *f* arrière
③ *vtr* inverser ⟨trend, process⟩; renverser ⟨roles⟩; faire rouler [qch] en marche arrière ⟨car⟩; to ~ the charges appeler en PCV
④ *vi* ⟨driver⟩ faire marche arrière
⑤ in reverse *phr* en sens inverse

**reverse charge call** *n* appel *m* en PCV

**reversible** *adj* réversible

**revert** *vi* to ~ to reprendre ⟨habit, name⟩; redevenir ⟨wilderness⟩

**review** ① *n* (a) (reconsideration) révision *f* (of de); (report) rapport *m* (of sur)
(b) (of book, film) critique *f* (of de)
(c) (magazine) revue *f*
(d) (Mil) revue *f*
(e) (US) (Sch, Univ) révision *f*
② *vtr* (a) reconsidérer ⟨situation⟩; réviser ⟨attitude, policy⟩; passer [qch] en revue ⟨troops⟩
(b) faire la critique de ⟨book, film⟩
(c) (US) (Sch, Univ) réviser

**reviewer** *n* critique *m*

**revise** ① *vtr* (a) (alter) réviser, modifier ⟨estimate, figures⟩; to ~ one's opinion of sb/ sth réviser son jugement sur qn/qc
(b) (GB) (for exam) réviser ⟨subject⟩
(c) (correct) revoir, réviser ⟨text⟩
② *vi* (GB) ⟨student⟩ réviser

**revision** *n* révision *f*

**revitalize** *vtr* revitaliser

**revival** *n* (of economy) reprise *f*; (of interest) regain *m*; (of custom, language) renouveau *m*

**revive** ① *vtr* (a) ranimer ⟨person⟩
(b) raviver ⟨custom⟩; ranimer ⟨interest, hopes⟩; relancer ⟨movement, fashion⟩; revigorer ⟨economy⟩

② *vi* (a) ⟨person⟩ reprendre connaissance
(b) ⟨economy⟩ reprendre

**revoke** *vtr* révoquer ⟨will⟩; annuler ⟨decision⟩

**revolt** ① *n* révolte *f* (against contre)
② *vtr* dégoûter, révolter
③ *vi* se révolter (against contre)

**revolting** *adj* (a) (physically) répugnant/-e; (morally) révoltant/-e
(b) (colloq) ⟨food⟩ infect/-e; ⟨person⟩ affreux/-euse

**revolution** *n* (a) révolution *f* (in dans)
(b) (Aut, Tech) tour *m*

**revolutionary** *n, adj* révolutionnaire (*mf*)

**revolutionize** *vtr* révolutionner

**revolve** *vi* (a) (turn) tourner (around autour de)
(b) to ~ around (be focused on) être axé/-e sur

**revolving** *adj* ⟨chair⟩ pivotant/-e; ⟨stage⟩ tournant/-e; ~ door porte *f* à tambour

**revue** *n* revue *f*

**revulsion** *n* dégoût *m*

**reward** ① *n* récompense *f*; a £50 ~ 50 livres sterling de récompense
② *vtr* récompenser (for de, pour)

**rewarding** *adj* ⟨experience⟩ enrichissant/-e; ⟨job⟩ gratifiant/-e

**rewind** *vtr* rembobiner ⟨tape, film⟩

**rewind button** *n* bouton *m* de retour en arrière

**rewire** *vtr* refaire l'installation électrique de ⟨building⟩

**reword** *vtr* reformuler

**rework** *vtr* retravailler ⟨theme, metal⟩

**rewrite** *vtr* ré(é)crire ⟨story, history⟩

**rhapsody** *n* rhapsodie *f*

**rhetoric** *n* rhétorique *f*

**rhetorical** *adj* rhétorique

**rheumatism** *n* rhumatisme *m*

**Rhine** *pr n* Rhin *m*

**rhinoceros** *n* rhinocéros *m*

**rhubarb** *n* rhubarbe *f*

**rhyme** ① *n* (a) (gen) rime *f*
(b) (poem) vers *mpl*; (children's) comptine *f*
② *vi* rimer (with avec)

**rhythm** *n* rythme *m*

**rhythmic(al)** *adj* rythmique

**rib** *n* (a) (Anat, Culin) côte *f*
(b) (in umbrella) baleine *f*; (in plane, building) nervure *f*

**ribbon** *n* ruban *m*

**rib cage** *n* cage *f* thoracique

**rice** *n* riz *m*

**rich** ① *n* the ~ les riches *mpl*
② *adj* riche; to grow or get ~ s'enrichir; to make sb ~ enrichir qn

**riches** *n pl* richesses *fpl*

**richness** *n* richesse *f*

**rickety** *adj* branlant/-e

**rickshaw** *n* pousse-pousse *m inv*

**ricochet** *vi* ricocher (off sur)

**rid** ① *vtr* **to ~ sb/sth of** débarrasser qn/qch de

② *pp adj* **to get ~ of** se débarrasser de ⟨*old car, guests*⟩; éliminer ⟨*poverty*⟩

**riddance** *n*

IDIOMS **good ~ (to bad rubbish)!** bon débarras! (colloq)

**riddle** ① *n* **(a)** (puzzle) devinette *f*
**(b)** (mystery) énigme *f*

② *vtr* **to be ~d with** être criblé/-e de ⟨*bullets*⟩; être rongé/-e par ⟨*disease, guilt*⟩

**ride** ① *n* **(a)** (in vehicle, on bike) trajet *m* (in, on en, à); (for pleasure) tour *m*, promenade *f*; **to go for a ~** aller faire un tour; **to give sb a ~** (US) emmener qn (en voiture)
**(b)** (on horse) promenade *f* à cheval

② *vtr* **(a)** rouler à ⟨*bike*⟩; **to ~ a horse** monter à cheval; **can you ~ a bike?** sais-tu faire du vélo?
**(b)** (US) prendre ⟨*bus, subway*⟩; parcourir ⟨*range*⟩
**(c)** chevaucher ⟨*wave*⟩

③ *vi* (go horse-riding) faire du cheval; **to ~ in** *or* **on** prendre ⟨*bus*⟩

IDIOMS **to take sb for a ~** (colloq) rouler qn (colloq)

■ **ride out** surmonter ⟨*crisis*⟩; survivre à ⟨*recession*⟩; **to ~ out the storm** surmonter la crise

■ **ride up (a)** ⟨*rider*⟩ s'approcher (**to** de)
**(b)** ⟨*skirt*⟩ remonter

**rider** *n* **(a)** (on horse) cavalier/-ière *m/f*; (on motorbike) motocycliste *mf*; (on bike) cycliste *mf*
**(b)** (to document) annexe *f*

**ridge** *n* **(a)** (along mountain top) arête *f*, crête *f*
**(b)** (on rock, metal surface) strie *f*; (in ploughed land) crête *f*
**(c)** (on roof) faîte *m*, faîtage *m*

**ridicule** ① *n* ridicule *m*
② *vtr* tourner [qn/qch] en ridicule

**ridiculous** *adj* ridicule

**riding** *n* équitation *f*; **to go ~** faire de l'équitation

**riding school** *n* centre *m* équestre

**rife** *adj* **to be ~** être répandu/-e

**riffraff** *n* populace *f*

**rifle** ① *n* (firearm) fusil *m*
② *vtr* vider ⟨*wallet, safe*⟩
■ **rifle through** fouiller dans

**rift** *n* **(a)** (disagreement) désaccord *m*; (permanent) rupture *f*
**(b)** (in rock) fissure *f*; (in clouds) trouée *f*

**rig** ① *n* (for oil) (on land) tour *f* de forage; (offshore) plate-forme *f* pétrolière offshore
② *vtr* truquer ⟨*election, result*⟩
■ **rig up** installer ⟨*equipment*⟩; improviser ⟨*clothes line, shelter*⟩

**rigging** *n* **(a)** (on ship) gréement *m*
**(b)** (of election, competition, result) truquage *m*

**right** ① *n* **(a)** (side, direction) droite *f*; **on** *or* **to your ~** à votre droite
**(b)** (in politics) (*also* **Right**) **the ~** la droite
**(c)** (morally) bien *m*; **~ and wrong** le bien et le mal

**(d)** (just claim) droit *m*; **to have a ~ to sth** avoir droit à qch; **civil ~s** droits civils

② *adj* **(a)** (not left) droit/-e, de droite
**(b)** (morally, legally; fair) juste; **it is only ~ and proper** ce n'est que justice; **to do the ~ thing** faire ce qu'il faut
**(c)** (correct) ⟨*choice, direction, size, answer*⟩ bon/bonne (*before n*); ⟨*word*⟩ juste; ⟨*time*⟩ exact/-e; **to be ~** ⟨*person*⟩ avoir raison; ⟨*answer*⟩ être juste
**(d)** (suitable) qui convient; **the ~ person for the job** la personne qu'il faut pour le poste; **to be in the ~ place at the ~ time** être là où il faut au bon moment
**(e)** (in good order) **the engine isn't quite ~** le moteur ne fonctionne pas très bien; **I don't feel quite ~ these days** je ne me sens pas très bien ces jours-ci
**(f)** **to put** *or* **set ~** corriger ⟨*mistake*⟩; réparer ⟨*injustice*⟩; arranger ⟨*situation*⟩; réparer ⟨*machine*⟩
**(g)** ⟨*angle*⟩ droit/-e; **at ~ angles to** à angle droit avec, perpendiculaire à

③ *adv* **(a)** (not left) à droite; **to turn/look ~** tourner/regarder à droite
**(b)** (directly) droit, directement; **it's ~ in front of you** c'est droit *or* juste devant toi; **I'll be ~ back** je reviens tout de suite
**(c)** (exactly) **~ in the middle of the room** en plein milieu de la pièce; **~ now** (immediately) tout de suite; (US) (at this point in time) en ce moment
**(d)** (correctly) juste, comme il faut; **you're not doing it ~** tu ne fais pas ça comme il faut; **to guess ~** deviner juste
**(e)** (completely) tout; **go ~ back to the beginning** revenez tout au début; **~ at the bottom** tout au fond; **to turn the central heating ~ up** mettre le chauffage central à fond
**(f)** (very well) bon; **~, let's have a look** bon, voyons ça

④ *vtr* redresser

IDIOMS **by ~s** normalement, en principe

**right angle** *n* angle *m* droit

**right away** *adv* tout de suite

**righteous** *adj* vertueux/-euse

**rightful** *adj* légitime

**right-hand** *adj* du côté droit; **on the ~ side** sur la droite

**right-hand drive** *n* conduite *f* à droite

**right-handed** *adv* ⟨*person*⟩ droitier/-ière; ⟨*blow*⟩ du droit

**right-hand man** *n* bras *m* droit

**rightly** *adv* **(a)** (accurately) correctement
**(b)** (justifiably) à juste titre; **~ or wrongly** à tort ou à raison
**(c)** (with certainty) au juste; **I don't ~ know** je ne sais pas au juste

**right-of-centre** *adj* (Pol) centre-droite *inv*

**right of way** *n* **(a)** (Aut) priorité *f*
**(b)** (over land) droit *m* de passage; **'no ~'** 'entrée *f* interdite'

**right-on** adj (colloq) they're very ~ (colloq) ils s'appliquent à être idéologiquement corrects sur tout

**right-thinking** adj bien-pensant/-e

**right wing** [1] n the ~ la droite
[2] **right-wing** adj ⟨attitude⟩ de droite; they are very ~ ils sont très à droite

**rigid** adj ⟨rules, person, material⟩ rigide; ⟨controls, timetable⟩ strict/-e

**rigidly** adv ⟨oppose⟩ fermement; ⟨control⟩ rigoureusement; ⟨stick to, apply⟩ strictement

**rigorous** adj rigoureux/-euse

**rigour** (GB), **rigor** (US) n rigueur f

**rim** n bord m; (on wheel) jante f

**rind** n (a) (on cheese) croûte f; (on bacon) couenne f
(b) (on fruit) peau f

**ring** [1] n (a) anneau m; (with stone) bague f; a diamond ~ une bague de diamants; a wedding ~ une alliance
(b) (circle) cercle m; to have ~s under one's eyes avoir les yeux cernés
(c) (at door) coup m de sonnette; (of phone) sonnerie f
(d) (in circus) piste f; (in boxing) ring m
(e) (of smugglers, spies) réseau m
(f) (on cooker) (electric) plaque f; (gas) brûleur m
[2] vtr (a) sonner ⟨church bells⟩; to ~ the doorbell or bell sonner
(b) (GB) (also ~ **up**) appeler
[3] vi (a) ⟨bell, phone, person⟩ sonner; the doorbell rang on a sonné à la porte
(b) ⟨footsteps, laughter⟩ résonner; to ~ true sonner vrai
(c) (GB) (phone) téléphoner; to ~ for appeler ⟨taxi⟩
■ **ring off** (GB) raccrocher
■ **ring out** ⟨voice, cry⟩ retentir; ⟨bells⟩ sonner

**ring binder** n classeur m à anneaux

**ringing** n (a) (of bell, alarm) sonnerie f
(b) (in ears) bourdonnement m

**ringleader** n meneur/-euse m/f

**ringlet** n anglaise f

**ringroad** n (GB) périphérique m

**rinse** [1] n rinçage m
[2] vtr rincer; (wash) laver

**riot** [1] n (a) émeute f, révolte f; prison ~ mutinerie f
(b) a ~ of une profusion de ⟨colours⟩
[2] vi ⟨crowd, demonstrators⟩ se soulever; ⟨prisoners⟩ se mutiner
IDIOMS to run ~ ⟨crowd⟩ se déchaîner; ⟨imagination⟩ se débrider; ⟨plant⟩ proliférer

**rioter** n émeutier/-ière m/f; (in prison) mutin m

**riot gear** n tenue f antiémeutes

**rioting** n émeutes fpl, bagarres fpl

**riot police** n forces fpl antiémeutes

**rip** [1] vtr déchirer; to ~ sth out arracher qch
[2] vi ⟨fabric⟩ se déchirer
■ **rip off**: ¶ ~ off [sth], ~ [sth] off (a) arracher ⟨garment, roof⟩

(b) (colloq) (steal) rafler (colloq) ⟨idea, design⟩
¶ ~ [sb] off (colloq) arnaquer (slang)
■ **rip through**: ~ through [sth] ⟨bomb blast⟩ défoncer ⟨building⟩

**RIP** abbr qu'il/elle repose en paix

**ripe** adj ⟨fruit⟩ mûr/-e; ⟨cheese⟩ fait/-e

**ripen** [1] vtr mûrir ⟨fruit⟩; affiner ⟨cheese⟩
[2] vi ⟨fruit⟩ mûrir; ⟨cheese⟩ se faire

**rip-off** n (colloq) arnaque f (slang)

**ripple** [1] n ondulation f
[2] vi (a) ⟨water⟩ se rider; (making noise) clapoter
(b) ⟨hair, corn⟩ onduler; ⟨muscles⟩ saillir

**rise** [1] n (a) (increase) augmentation f (in de); (in prices, pressure) hausse f (in de); (in temperature) élévation f (in de)
(b) (of person) ascension f; (of empire) essor m
(c) (slope) montée f
[2] vi (a) ⟨water, tension⟩ monter; ⟨price, temperature⟩ augmenter; ⟨voice⟩ devenir plus fort/-e; ⟨hopes⟩ grandir
(b) (get up) ⟨person⟩ se lever; (after falling) relever; to ~ from the dead ressusciter; to ~ to the occasion se montrer à la hauteur
(c) ⟨road⟩ monter; ⟨cliff⟩ s'élever
(d) ⟨sun, moon⟩ se lever
(e) ⟨dough⟩ lever
IDIOMS to give ~ to donner lieu à ⟨rumours⟩; causer ⟨problem⟩

**rising** [1] n soulèvement m
[2] adj (gen) en hausse; ⟨tension⟩ grandissant/-e; ⟨sun, moon⟩ levant/-e

**risk** [1] n risque m; to run a ~ courir un risque; to take ~s prendre des risques; at ~ menacé/-e
[2] vtr risquer; to ~ doing courir le risque de faire

**risky** adj ⟨decision, undertaking⟩ risqué/-e; ⟨share, investment⟩ à risques

**risqué** adj osé/-e

**rite** n rite m

**ritual** [1] n rituel m, rites mpl
[2] adj rituel/-elle

**rival** [1] n (person) rival/-e m/f; (company) concurrent/-e m/f
[2] adj ⟨team, business⟩ rival/-e; ⟨claim⟩ opposé/-e
[3] vtr rivaliser avec (in de)

**rivalry** n rivalité f (between entre)

**river** n (flowing into sea) fleuve m; (tributary) rivière f

**riverbank** n berge f; along the ~ le long de la rivière

**riverside** [1] n berges fpl
[2] adj ⟨pub⟩ au bord de la rivière

**rivet** [1] n rivet m
[2] vtr (a) (Tech) riveter
(b) to be ~ed by être captivé/-e par; to be ~ed to the spot être cloué/-e sur place

**riveting** adj fascinant/-e

**Riviera** n the Italian ~ la Riviera; the French ~ la Côte d'Azur

**road** n (a) route f; the ~ to Leeds la route de Leeds

**(b)** (street) rue *f*
**(c)** (figurative) voie *f* (to de); **to be on the right**
**~** être sur la bonne voie
**roadblock** *n* barrage *m* routier
**road hump** *n* ralentisseur *m*
**road rage** *n* violence *f* au volant
**roadshow** *n* (play, show) spectacle *m* de
tournée; (publicity tour) tour *m* promotionnel
**roadside** *n* bord *m* de la route
**roadsign** *n* panneau *m* de signalisation
**road tax disc** *n* vignette *f*
**roadworks** *n pl* travaux *mpl* (routiers)
**roadworthy** *adj* en état de rouler
**roam** *vtr* parcourir ⟨countryside⟩; faire le
tour de ⟨shops⟩; traîner dans ⟨streets⟩
■ **roam around** ⟨person⟩ vadrouiller (colloq)
**roar** ⌐1⌐ *n* (of lion) rugissement *m*; (of person)
hurlement *m*; (of engine) vrombissement *m*;
(of traffic) grondement *m*; **a ~ of laughter** un
éclat de rire
⌐2⌐ *vi* ⟨lion⟩ rugir; ⟨person⟩ hurler; ⟨sea,
wind⟩ mugir; ⟨fire⟩ ronfler; ⟨engine⟩ vrombir
**roaring** *adj* (a) ⟨engine, traffic⟩
grondant/-e; **a ~ fire** une belle flambée
**(b)** ⟨success⟩ fou/folle
**roast** ⌐1⌐ *n* (Culin) rôti *m*; (US) barbecue *m*
⌐2⌐ *adj* ⟨meat, potatoes⟩ rôti/-e; **~ beef** rôti
de bœuf, rosbif *m*
⌐3⌐ *vtr* rôtir ⟨meat, potatoes⟩; (faire) griller
⟨chestnuts⟩; torréfier ⟨coffee beans⟩
**rob** *vtr* voler ⟨person⟩; dévaliser ⟨bank,
train⟩; **to ~ sb of sth** voler qch à qn;
(figurative) priver qn de qch
**robber** *n* voleur/-euse *m/f*
**robbery** *n* vol *m*
**robe** *n* robe *f*
**robin** *n* (also ~ **redbreast**) rouge-gorge
*m*
**robot** *n* robot *m*
**robust** *adj* robuste
**rock** ⌐1⌐ *n* (a) (substance) roche *f*; **solid ~**
roche dure
**(b)** (boulder) rocher *m*
**(c)** (also ~ **music**) rock *m*
⌐2⌐ *vtr* (a) balancer ⟨cradle⟩; bercer ⟨baby,
boat⟩
**(b)** ⟨tremor⟩ secouer ⟨town⟩; ⟨scandal⟩
ébranler ⟨government⟩
⌐3⌐ *vi* ⟨person⟩ se balancer; **to ~ back and
forth** se balancer d'avant en arrière
IDIOMS **on the ~s** ⟨drink⟩ avec des glaçons;
**to be on the ~s** ⟨marriage⟩ aller à vau-l'eau
**rock and roll** *n* (also **rock'n'roll**) rock
and roll *m*
**rock bottom** *n* **to hit ~** toucher le fond
**rock climber** *n* varappeur/-euse *m/f*
**rock climbing** *n* varappe *f*
**rockery** *n* (GB) rocaille *f*
**rocket** ⌐1⌐ *n* (a) (gen, Mil) fusée *f*
**(b)** (salad) roquette *f*
⌐2⌐ *vi* ⟨price, profit⟩ monter en flèche
**rock face** *n* paroi *f* rocheuse
**rockfall** *n* chute *f* de pierres

**rocking chair** *n* fauteuil *m* à bascule
**rocking horse** *n* cheval *m* à bascule
**rock star** *n* rock-star *f*
**rocky** *adj* (a) ⟨beach, path, road⟩
rocailleux/-euse; ⟨coast⟩ rocheux/-euse
**(b)** ⟨relationship, period⟩ difficile; ⟨business⟩
précaire
**Rocky Mountains** *pr n pl* (also
**Rockies**) **the ~** les montagnes *fpl*
Rocheuses
**rod** *n* (a) (gen, Tech) tige *f*; **curtain/stair ~**
tringle *f* à rideaux/de marche
**(b)** (for punishment) baguette *f*
**(c)** (for fishing) canne *f* à pêche
**rodent** *n* rongeur *m*
**roe** *n* œufs *mpl* (de poisson)
**roe deer** *n* (male) chevreuil *m*; (female)
chevrette *f*
**rogue** *n* (a) (rascal) coquin *m*
**(b)** (animal) solitaire *m*
**role** *n* rôle *m* (of de); **title ~** rôle-titre *m*
**role model** *n* modèle *m*
**role-play** *n* (Sch) jeu *m* de rôle; (for therapy)
psychodrame *m*
**roll** ⌐1⌐ *n* (a) (of paper, cloth) rouleau *m*; (of
banknotes) liasse *f*; (of flesh) bourrelet *m*; **a ~
of film** une pellicule
**(b)** (bread) petit pain *m*; **cheese ~** sandwich
*m* au fromage
**(c)** (of dice) lancer *m*
**(d)** (register) liste *f*; **to call the ~** faire l'appel
⌐2⌐ *vtr* (a) (gen) rouler; faire rouler ⟨dice⟩; **to
~ sth into a ball** faire une boulette de
⟨paper⟩; faire une boule de ⟨clay, dough⟩
**(b)** étirer ⟨dough⟩
⌐3⌐ *vi* (a) ⟨person, animal⟩ rouler (**onto** sur);
⟨car, plane⟩ faire un tonneau; ⟨ship⟩ tanguer
**(b)** ⟨thunder⟩ gronder; ⟨drum⟩ rouler
**(c)** ⟨camera, press⟩ tourner
■ **roll about** (GB), **roll around** ⟨animal,
person⟩ se rouler; ⟨marbles, tins⟩ rouler
■ **roll down** baisser ⟨blind, sleeve⟩
■ **roll over** se retourner
■ **roll up** enrouler ⟨rug, poster⟩; **to ~ up
one's sleeves** retrousser ses manches
**roller** *n* (a) (gen) rouleau *m*
**(b)** (curler) bigoudi *m*
**rollerblade** ⌐1⌐ *n* patin *m* en ligne
⌐2⌐ *vi* faire du patin en ligne
**roller blind** *n* store *m*
**roller coaster** *n* montagnes *fpl* russes
**roller-skate** *n* patin *m* à roulettes
**roller-skating** *n* patinage *m* à roulettes;
**to go ~** faire du patin à roulettes
**rolling pin** *n* rouleau *m* à pâtisserie
**rollneck** *n* col *m* roulé
**ROM** *n* (abbr = **read-only memory**)
ROM *f*, mémoire *f* morte
**Roman** ⌐1⌐ *n* Romain/-e *m/f*
⌐2⌐ *adj* romain/-e
**Roman Catholic** *n, adj* catholique (*mf*)
**romance** *n* (a) (of era, place) charme *m*; (of
travel) côté *m* romantique

**(b)** (love affair) histoire *f* d'amour; (love) amour *m*

**(c)** (novel) roman *m* d'amour; (film) film *m* d'amour

**Romania** *pr n* Roumanie *f*

**Romanian** ⓵ *n* **(a)** (person) Roumain/-e *m/f*

**(b)** (language) roumain *m*

⓶ *adj* roumain/-e

**romantic** ⓵ *n* romantique *mf*

⓶ *adj* **(a)** ‹setting, story, person› romantique

**(b)** ‹attachment› sentimental/-e

**(c)** ‹novel, film› d'amour

**romantic fiction** *n* (genre) romans *mpl* d'amour

**romanticize** *vtr* idéaliser

**Romany** *n* Tzigane *mf*, Romani *mf*

**romp** ⓵ *n* ébats *mpl*

⓶ *vi* s'ébattre

**rompers** *n pl* (*also* **romper suit**) barboteuse *f*

**roof** *n* **(a)** (on building) toit *m*

**(b)** (Anat) the ∼ of the mouth la voûte du palais

IDIOMS **to go through** *or* **hit the** ∼ (colloq) ‹person› sauter au plafond (colloq); ‹prices› battre tous les records

**roof rack** *n* galerie *f*

**rooftop** *n* toit *m*

**rook** *n* **(a)** (bird) (corbeau *m*) freux *m*

**(b)** (in chess) tour *f*

**room** ⓵ *n* **(a)** (bedroom) pièce *f*; (bedroom) chambre *f*; (for working) bureau *m*; (for meetings, teaching, operating) salle *f*

**(b)** (space) place *f*; **to make** ∼ faire de la place

⓶ *vi* (US) loger (**with** chez)

**roommate** *n* **(a)** (in same room) camarade *mf* de chambre

**(b)** (US) (flatmate) compagnon/compagne *m/f* d'appartement

**room service** *n* service *m* de chambre

**room temperature** *n* température *f* ambiante; **at** ∼ ‹wine› chambré/-e

**roomy** *adj* ‹car, house› spacieux/-ieuse; ‹garment› ample; ‹bag, cupboard› grand/-e (*before n*)

**roost** ⓵ *n* perchoir *m*

⓶ *vi* (in trees) percher (pour la nuit); (in attic) se nicher

IDIOMS **to rule the** ∼ faire la loi

**rooster** *n* coq *m*

**root** ⓵ *n* **(a)** racine *f*; **to take** ∼ ‹plant› prendre racine; ‹idea, value› s'établir; ‹industry› s'implanter

**(b)** (of problem) fond *m*; (of evil) origine *f*

⓶ *vtr* **to be** ∼**ed in** être ancré/-e dans; **deeply-**∼**ed** bien enraciné/-e; ∼**ed to the spot** figé/-e sur place

■ **root around**, **root about** fouiller (**in** dans)

■ **root out** traquer ‹corruption›; déloger ‹person›

**rootless** *adj* sans racines

**rope** ⓵ *n* (gen, Sport) corde *f*; (of pearls) rang *m*

⓶ *vtr* attacher ‹victim, animal› (**to** à); encorder ‹climber›

IDIOMS **to know the** ∼**s** connaître les ficelles (colloq)

■ **rope in** (colloq) : ∼ [sb] **in**, ∼ **in** [sb] (to help with task) embaucher (colloq)

**rope ladder** *n* échelle *f* de corde

**rosary** *n* (prayer) rosaire *m*; (beads) chapelet *m*

**rose** *n* rose *f*

**rosebud** *n* bouton *m* de rose

**rose bush** *n* rosier *m*

**rosemary** *n* romarin *m*

**rose-tinted** *adj*

IDIOMS **to see the world through** ∼ **spectacles** voir la vie en rose

**rosette** *n* (for winner) cocarde *f*

**roster** *n* (*also* **duty** ∼) tableau *m* de service

**rostrum** *n* estrade *f*

**rosy** *adj* ‹cheek, light› rose; **to paint a** ∼ **picture** peindre un tableau favorable

**rot** ⓵ *n* pourriture *f*

⓶ *vtr* pourrir

⓷ *vi* (*also* ∼ **away**) pourrir

**rota** *n* (GB) tableau *m* de service

**rotary** *adj* rotatif/-ive

**rotate** ⓵ *vtr* faire tourner ‹blade›

⓶ *vi* ‹blade, handle, wings› tourner

**rotation** *n* rotation *f*

**rote** *n* **by** ∼ par cœur

**rotten** *adj* **(a)** ‹produce› pourri/-e; ‹teeth› gâté/-e; ‹smell› de pourriture

**(b)** (corrupt) pourri/-e (colloq)

**(c)** (colloq) (bad) ‹weather› pourri/-e; ‹cook, driver› exécrable

**rouble** *n* rouble *m*

**rough** ⓵ *adj* **(a)** ‹material› rêche; ‹hand, skin, surface, rock› rugueux/-euse; ‹terrain› cahoteux/-euse

**(b)** ‹person, behaviour, sport› brutal/-e, violent/-e; ‹landing› brutal/-e; ‹area› dur/-e

**(c)** ‹description, map› sommaire; ‹figure, idea, estimate› approximatif/-ive

**(d)** (difficult) dur, difficile; **a** ∼ **time** une période difficile

**(e)** (crude) grossier/-ière

**(f)** (harsh) ‹voice, taste, wine› âpre

**(g)** (stormy) ‹sea, crossing› agité/-e

⓶ *adv* **to sleep** ∼ dormir à la dure

IDIOMS **to** ∼ **it** vivre à la dure

**roughage** *n* fibres *fpl*

**rough-and-ready** *adj* ‹person, manner› fruste; ‹conditions› rudimentaire; ‹method, system› sommaire

**roughen** *vtr* rendre [qch] rêche *or* rugueux

**roughly** *adv* **(a)** ‹calculate› grossièrement; ∼ **speaking** en gros; ∼ **10%** à peu près 10%

**(b)** ‹treat, hit› brutalement

**(c)** ‹make› grossièrement

**rough paper** *n* feuille *f* de brouillon

**roulette** n roulette f

**round** ⒈ adv (GB) **(a)** all ~ tout autour; **whisky all ~!** du whisky pour tout le monde!; **to go all the way** ~ faire tout le tour; **to go ~ and ~** tourner en rond **(b)** (to place, home) **to go ~ to sb's house** passer chez qn; **to ask sb ~** dire à qn de passer à la maison; **to invite sb ~ for lunch** inviter qn à déjeuner (chez soi) **(c)** **all year ~** toute l'année; **this time ~** cette fois-ci ⒉ prep (GB) **(a)** autour de ⟨table⟩; **to sit ~ the fire** s'asseoir au coin du feu **(b)** **to go ~ the corner** tourner au coin de la rue; **just ~ the corner** tout près; **to go ~ an obstacle** contourner un obstacle **(c)** **her sister took us ~ Oxford** sa sœur nous a fait visiter Oxford; **to go ~ the shops** faire les magasins ⒊ n **(a)** (of competition) manche f; (of golf, cards) partie f; (in boxing) round m; (in showjumping) parcours m; (in election) tour m; (of talks) série f; **a ~ of drinks** une tournée; **a ~ of ammunition** une cartouche; **a ~ of applause** une salve d'applaudissements; **a ~ of toast** un toast **(b)** **to do one's ~s** ⟨postman, milkman⟩ faire sa tournée; ⟨doctor⟩ visiter ses malades; ⟨guard⟩ faire sa ronde; **to go** or **do the ~s** ⟨rumour, flu⟩ circuler **(c)** (shape) rondelle f ⒋ adj **(a)** rond/-e; **in ~ figures, that's £100** si on arrondit, ça fait 100 livres sterling; **a ~ dozen** une douzaine exactement **(b)** **to have ~ shoulders** avoir le dos voûté; ⒌ vtr contourner ⟨headland⟩; **to ~ the corner** tourner au coin; **to ~ a bend** prendre un virage ⒍ **round about** phr **(a)** (approximately) à peu près, environ **(b)** (vicinity) **the people ~ about** les gens des environs
■ **round off (a)** finir ⟨meal, evening⟩ (**with** par); conclure ⟨speech⟩ **(b)** arrondir ⟨corner, figure⟩
■ **round on** (GB): ~ **on** [sb] attaquer violemment; **she ~ed on me** elle m'est tombée dessus (colloq)
■ **round up (a)** regrouper ⟨people⟩; rassembler ⟨livestock⟩ **(b)** arrondir [qch] au chiffre supérieur ⟨figure⟩

**roundabout** ⒈ n (GB) (in fairground) manège m; (in playground) tourniquet m; (for traffic) rond-point m ⒉ adj **to come by a ~ way** faire un détour; **by ~ means** par des moyens détournés; **a ~ way of saying** une façon détournée de dire

**rounders** n (GB) ≈ baseball m

**round-neck(ed) sweater** n pull-over m ras-de-cou inv

**round-the-clock** adj 24 heures sur 24

**round-the-world** adj autour du monde

**round trip** n aller-retour m

**roundup** n **(a)** (herding) rassemblement m (**of** de)

**(b)** (by police) rafle f

**rouse** vtr réveiller ⟨person⟩; susciter ⟨anger, interest⟩

**rousing** adj ⟨speech⟩ galvanisant/-e; ⟨music⟩ exaltant/-e

**rout** ⒈ n déroute f, défaite f ⒉ vtr (Mil) mettre en déroute; (figurative) battre à plates coutures

**route** ⒈ n chemin m, itinéraire m; (in shipping) route f; (in aviation) ligne f; (figurative) (to power) voie f (**to** de); **bus ~** ligne d'autobus ⒉ vtr expédier, acheminer ⟨goods⟩

**routine** ⒈ n **(a)** routine f **(b)** (act) numéro m ⒉ adj **(a)** ⟨enquiry, matter⟩ de routine **(b)** (uninspiring) routinier/-ière

**routinely** adv **(a)** ⟨check, review⟩ systématiquement **(b)** ⟨tortured, abused⟩ régulièrement

**row¹** ⒈ n **(a)** (of people, plants, stitches) rang m (**of** de); (of houses, seats, books) rangée f (**of** de) **(b)** (succession) **six times in a ~** six fois de suite; **the third week in a ~** la troisième semaine d'affilée ⒉ vtr **to ~ a boat up the river** remonter la rivière à la rame ⒊ vi (gen) ramer; (Sport) faire de l'aviron; **to ~ across** traverser [qch] à la rame ⟨lake⟩

**row²** ⒈ n **(a)** (quarrel) dispute f (**about** à propos de); (public) querelle f; **to have a ~ with** se disputer avec **(b)** (noise) tapage m ⒉ vi se disputer (**with** avec; **about, over** à propos de)

**rowboat** n (US) bateau m à rames

**rowdy** adj (noisy) tapageur/-euse; (in class) chahuteur/-euse

**rowing** n aviron m

**rowing boat** n (GB) bateau m à rames

**royal** adj royal/-e

**royal blue** n, adj bleu (m) roi inv

**Royal Highness** n **His ~** Son Altesse f royale; **Your ~** Votre Altesse f

**royalty** n **(a)** (persons) membres mpl d'une famille royale **(b)** (to author, composer) droits mpl d'auteur; (on patent) royalties fpl

**rub** ⒈ n **(a)** (massage) friction f **(b)** (polish) coup m de chiffon ⒉ vtr se frotter ⟨chin, eyes⟩; frotter ⟨stain, surface⟩; frictionner ⟨sb's back⟩; **to ~ sth into the skin** faire pénétrer qch dans la peau ⒊ vi frotter **IDIOMS to ~ sb up the wrong way** prendre qn à rebrousse-poil (colloq)
■ **rub out (a)** (erase) effacer
■ **rub in:** ~ [sth] **in,** ~ **in** [sth] faire pénétrer ⟨lotion⟩; **there's no need to ~ it in!** (colloq) inutile d'en rajouter! (colloq)

**rubber** ⒈ n **(a)** (substance) caoutchouc m **(b)** (GB) (eraser) gomme f ⒉ adj de or en caoutchouc

r

**rubber band** n élastique m

**rubber glove** n gant m en or de caoutchouc

**rubber plant** n caoutchouc m

**rubber stamp** n tampon m

**rubber tree** n hévéa m

**rubbish** ⌐1⌐ n (a) (refuse) déchets mpl; (domestic) ordures fpl; (on site) gravats mpl
(b) (inferior goods) camelote f (colloq); **this book is ∼!** (colloq) ce livre est nul! (colloq)
(c) (nonsense) bêtises fpl
⌐2⌐ vtr (GB) descendre [qn/qch] en flammes

**rubbish bin** n (GB) poubelle f

**rubbish dump** n (GB) décharge f (publique)

**rubbish heap** n tas m d'ordures

**rubble** n (after explosion) décombres mpl; (on site) gravats mpl

**ruby** ⌐1⌐ n (a) (gem) rubis m
(b) (also ∼ **red**) rouge m rubis
⌐2⌐ adj (a) ⟨liquid, lips⟩ vermeil/-eille; ∼ **wedding** noces fpl de vermeil
(b) ⟨bracelet, necklace⟩ de rubis

**rucksack** n sac m à dos

**rudder** n (on boat) gouvernail m; (on plane) gouverne f

**ruddy** adj ⟨cheeks⟩ coloré/-e

**rude** adj (a) (impolite) ⟨comment⟩ impoli/-e; ⟨person⟩ mal élevé/-e; **to be ∼ to sb** être impoli/-e envers qn
(b) (indecent) ⟨joke⟩ grossier/-ière; **a ∼ word** un gros mot

**rudimentary** adj rudimentaire

**rudiments** n pl rudiments mpl (**of** de)

**rueful** adj ⟨smile, thought⟩ triste

**ruff** n (of lace) fraise f; (of fur, feathers) collier m

**ruffle** ⌐1⌐ n (at sleeve) manchette f; (at neck) ruche f; (on shirt front) jabot m
⌐2⌐ vtr (a) ébouriffer ⟨hair, fur⟩; hérisser ⟨feathers⟩; rider ⟨water⟩
(b) (disconcert) énerver; (upset) froisser

**rug** n (a) tapis m; (by bed) descente f de lit
(b) (GB) (blanket) couverture f

**rugby** n rugby m

**rugby league** n rugby m à 13

**rugby union** n rugby m à 15

**rugged** adj (a) ⟨landscape⟩ accidenté/-e; ⟨coastline⟩ déchiqueté/-e
(b) ⟨man, features⟩ rude

**ruin** ⌐1⌐ n ruine f
⌐2⌐ vtr (a) ruiner ⟨economy, career⟩; **to ∼ one's eyesight** s'abîmer la vue
(b) gâcher ⟨holiday, meal⟩; abîmer ⟨clothes⟩
IDIOMS **to go to rack and ∼** se délabrer

**ruined** adj (a) (derelict) en ruines
(b) (spoilt) ⟨holiday, meal⟩ gâché/-e; ⟨clothes, furniture⟩ abîmé/-e; ⟨reputation⟩ ruiné/-e; (financially) ruiné/-e

**rule** ⌐1⌐ n (a) (of game, language) règle f; (of school, organization) règlement m; **against the**

∼**s** contraire aux règles or au règlement (**to do** de faire); ∼**s and regulations** réglementation f; **as a ∼** généralement
(b) (authority) domination f, gouvernement m
(c) (for measuring) règle f
⌐2⌐ vtr (a) ⟨ruler, law⟩ gouverner; ⟨monarch⟩ régner sur; ⟨party⟩ diriger; ⟨army⟩ commander
(b) ⟨factor⟩ dicter ⟨strategy⟩; **to be ∼d by** ⟨person⟩ être mené/-e par ⟨passions, spouse⟩
(c) (draw) faire, tirer ⟨line⟩
(d) ⟨court, umpire⟩ **to ∼ that** décréter que
⌐3⌐ vi (a) ⟨monarch, anarchy⟩ régner
(b) ⟨court, umpire⟩ statuer
■ **rule out** (a) exclure ⟨possibility, candidate⟩ (**of** de); **to ∼ out doing** exclure de faire
(b) interdire ⟨activity⟩

**ruler** n (a) (leader) dirigeant/-e m/f
(b) (measure) règle f

**ruling** ⌐1⌐ n décision f
⌐2⌐ adj (a) (in power) dirigeant/-e
(b) (dominant) dominant/-e

**rum** n rhum m

**rumble** ⌐1⌐ n (of thunder, artillery, trucks) grondement m; (of stomach) gargouillement m
⌐2⌐ vi ⟨thunder, artillery⟩ gronder; ⟨stomach⟩ gargouiller

**ruminate** vi (a) (think) **to ∼ on** or **about** ruminer sur
(b) (Zool) ruminer

**rummage** vi fouiller (**through** dans)

**rummy** n rami m

**rumour** (GB), **rumor** (US) n rumeur f, bruit m

**rumoured** (GB), **rumored** (US) adj **it is ∼ that** il paraît que, on dit que

**rump** n (a) (also ∼ **steak**) rumsteck m
(b) (of animal) croupe f

**rumple** vtr ébouriffer ⟨hair⟩; froisser ⟨clothes, sheets, papers⟩

**run** ⌐1⌐ n (a) course f; **a two-mile ∼** une course de deux miles; **to go for a ∼** aller courir; **to break into a ∼** se mettre à courir
(b) (flight) **on the ∼** en fuite; **to make a ∼ for it** fuir, s'enfuir
(c) (series) (of successes, failures) série f; (in printing) tirage m; **to have a ∼ of luck** être en veine
(d) (trip, route) trajet m
(e) (in cricket, baseball) point m
(f) (for rabbit, chickens) enclos m
(g) (in tights) échelle f
(h) (for skiing) piste f
(i) (in cards) suite f
⌐2⌐ vtr (a) courir ⟨distance, marathon⟩; **to ∼ a race** faire une course
(b) (drive) **to ∼ sb to the station** conduire qn à la gare
(c) (pass, move) **to ∼ one's hand over** passer la main sur; **to ∼ one's eye(s) over** parcourir rapidement
(d) (manage) diriger; **a well-/badly-run organization** une organisation bien/mal dirigée
(e) (operate) faire fonctionner ⟨machine⟩; faire

tourner ⟨*motor*⟩; exécuter ⟨*program*⟩; entretenir ⟨*car*⟩; **to ~ tests on** effectuer des tests sur
**(f)** (organize, offer) organiser ⟨*competition, course*⟩; mettre [qch] en place ⟨*bus service*⟩
**(g)** faire couler ⟨*bath*⟩; ouvrir ⟨*tap*⟩
**(h)** (enter) faire courir ⟨*horse*⟩; présenter ⟨*candidate*⟩
**3** *vi* **(a)** ⟨*person, animal*⟩ courir; **to ~ across/down** traverser/descendre qch en courant; **to ~ for the bus** courir pour attraper le bus; **to come ~ning** accourir **(towards** vers)
**(b)** (flee) fuir, s'enfuir; **to ~ for one's life** s'enfuir pour sauver sa peau (colloq)
**(c)** (colloq) (rush off) filer (colloq)
**(d)** (function) ⟨*machine*⟩ marcher; **to leave the engine ~ning** laisser tourner le moteur
**(e)** (continue, last) ⟨*contract, lease*⟩ être valide
**(f)** ⟨*play, musical*⟩ tenir l'affiche **(for** pendant)
**(g)** ( pass) **to ~ past/through** ⟨*road, frontier, path*⟩ passer/traverser; **to ~ (from) east to west** aller d'est en ouest
**(h)** (move) ⟨*sledge*⟩ glisser; ⟨*curtain*⟩ coulisser
**(i)** ⟨*bus, train*⟩ circuler
**(j)** (flow) couler; **tears ran down his face** les larmes coulaient sur son visage; **my nose is ~ning** j'ai le nez qui coule
**(k)** ⟨*dye, garment*⟩ déteindre; ⟨*make-up*⟩ couler
**(l)** (as candidate) se présenter; **to ~ for president** être candidat/-e à la présidence
**IDIOMS in the long ~** à long terme; **in the short ~** à brève échéance
■ **run about**, **run around** courir
■ **run away**: ¶ **~ away** s'enfuir; **to ~ away from home** ⟨*child*⟩ faire une fugue
¶ **~ away with** [sb/sth] **(a)** (flee) partir avec
**(b)** rafler (colloq) ⟨*prize, title*⟩
■ **run down**: ¶ **~ down** ⟨*battery*⟩ se décharger; ⟨*watch*⟩ retarder
¶ **~** [sb/sth] **down (a)** (in vehicle) renverser
**(b)** réduire ⟨*production, defences*⟩; user ⟨*battery*⟩
**(c)** (disparage) dénigrer
■ **run into (a)** heurter, rentrer dans (colloq) ⟨*car, wall*⟩
**(b)** (encounter) rencontrer ⟨*person, difficulty*⟩
**(c)** (amount to) s'élever à ⟨*hundreds, millions*⟩
■ **run off** partir en courant
■ **run out**: ¶ **~ out (a)** ⟨*supplies, oil*⟩ s'épuiser; **time is ~ning out** le temps manque
**(b)** ⟨*pen, machine*⟩ être vide
**(c)** ⟨*contract, passport*⟩ expirer
¶ **~ out of** ne plus avoir de ⟨*petrol, time, money, ideas*⟩; **to be ~ning out of** n'avoir presque plus de ⟨*petrol, time, money, ideas*⟩
■ **run over** (in vehicle) (injure) renverser; (kill) écraser
■ **run through** parcourir ⟨*list, article*⟩; répéter ⟨*scene, speech*⟩
■ **run up** accumuler ⟨*debt*⟩
■ **run up against** se heurter à ⟨*difficulty*⟩

**runaway** *adj* ⟨*teenager*⟩ fugueur/-euse; ⟨*slave*⟩ fugitif/-ive; ⟨*horse*⟩ emballé/-e
**rundown** *n* récapitulatif *m* **(on** de)
**run-down** *adj* **(a)** (exhausted) fatigué/-e, à plat (colloq)
**(b)** (shabby) décrépit/-e
**rung** *n* **(a)** (of ladder) barreau *m*
**(b)** (in hierarchy) échelon *m*
**run-in** *n* (colloq) prise *f* de bec (colloq)
**runner** *n* **(a)** (person, animal) coureur *m*
**(b)** (horse) partant/-e *m/f*
**(c)** (messenger) estafette *f*
**(d)** (for door, seat) glissière *f*; (for drawer) coulisseau *m*; (on sled) patin *m*
**(e)** (on stairs) chemin *m* d'escalier
**runner bean** *n* (GB) haricot *m* d'Espagne
**runner up** *n* second/-e *m/f* **(to** après)
**running** **1** *n* **(a)** (sport, exercise) course *f* à pied
**(b)** (management) direction *f* **(of** de)
**2** *adj* **(a)** ⟨*water*⟩ courant/-e; ⟨*tap*⟩ ouvert/-e
**(b) five days ~** cinq jours de suite
**IDIOMS to be in/out of the ~** être/ne plus être dans la course **(for** pour)
**running battle** *n* éternel conflit *m*
**running commentary** *n* commentaire *m* ininterrompu
**running total** *n* total *m* cumulé
**runny** *adj* ⟨*jam, sauce*⟩ liquide; ⟨*butter*⟩ fondu/-e; ⟨*omelette*⟩ baveux/-euse; **to have a ~ nose** avoir le nez qui coule
**run-of-the-mill** *adj* ordinaire, banal/-e
**runt** *n* **(a)** (of litter) le plus faible *m* de la portée
**(b)** (weakling) avorton *m*
**run-up** *n* **(a)** (for a jump) course *f* d'élan; **to take a ~** prendre son élan pour sauter
**(b)** (preceding period) **the ~ to** la dernière ligne droite avant
**runway** *n* piste *f* d'aviation
**rupee** *n* roupie *f*
**rupture** *n* rupture *f*
**rural** *adj* ⟨*country*⟩ rural/-e; ⟨*pastoral*⟩ champêtre
**ruse** *n* stratagème *m*
**rush** **1** *n* **(a)** (surge) ruée *f* **(to do** pour faire); **to make a ~ for sth** ⟨*crowd*⟩ se ruer vers qch; ⟨*individual*⟩ se précipiter vers qch
**(b)** (hurry) **to be in a ~** être pressé/-e **(to do** de faire); **to leave in a ~** partir en vitesse
**(c)** (of liquid, adrenalin) montée *f*; (of air) bouffée *f*
**(d)** ( plant) jonc *m*
**2** *vtr* **(a) to ~ sth** envoyer qch d'urgence à; **to be ~ed to the hospital** être emmené/-e d'urgence à l'hôpital
**(b)** expédier ⟨*task, speech*⟩
**(c)** (hurry) bousculer ⟨*person*⟩
**(d)** (charge at) sauter sur ⟨*person*⟩; prendre d'assaut ⟨*building*⟩
**3** *vi* ⟨*person*⟩ (hurry) se dépêcher **(to do** de faire); (rush forward) se précipiter **(to do** pour ···⟶

faire); **to ~ out of the room** se précipiter hors de la pièce; **to ~ down the stairs/past** descendre l'escalier/passer à toute vitesse
■ **rush into:** ¶ **to ~ into marriage/a purchase** se marier/acheter sans prendre le temps de réfléchir; ¶ **~ [sb] into doing** bousculer [qn] pour qu'il/elle fasse
■ **rush out:** ¶ **~ out** sortir en vitesse
■ **rush through:** ¶ **~ through** [sth] expédier ⟨*task*⟩; ¶ **~ [sth] through** adopter en vitesse ⟨*legislation*⟩; traiter en priorité ⟨*order, application*⟩

**rushed** *adj* ⟨*attempt, letter*⟩ expédié/-e
**rush hour** *n* heures *fpl* de pointe
**rusk** *n* biscuit *m* pour bébés
**russet** *adj* roussâtre
**Russia** *pr n* Russie *f*
**Russian** ⒈ *n* (a) (person) Russe *mf*
(b) (language) russe *m*
⒉ *adj* ⟨*culture, food, politics*⟩ russe; ⟨*teacher, lesson*⟩ de russe; ⟨*embassy*⟩ de Russie

**rust** ⒈ *n* rouille *f*
⒉ *vtr* rouiller ⟨*metal*⟩
⒊ *vi* ⟨*metal*⟩ se rouiller
**rustic** *adj* rustique
**rustle** ⒈ *n* (of paper, dry leaves) froissement *m*; (of leaves, silk) bruissement *m*
⒉ *vtr* froisser ⟨*papers*⟩
**rusty** *adj* rouillé/-e
**rut** *n* (a) (in ground) ornière *f*
(b) (routine) **be in a ~** être enlisé/-e dans la routine
(c) (Zool) **the ~** le rut
**ruthless** *adj* impitoyable (**in** dans)
**RV** *n* (US) (*abbr* = **recreational vehicle**) camping-car *m*, autocaravane *f*
**Rwanda** *pr n* Rwanda *m*
**rye** *n* (a) (cereal) seigle *m*
(b) (US) (*also* **~ whiskey**) whisky *m* à base de seigle
**rye bread** *n* pain *m* de seigle

# Ss

**s, S** *n* s, S *m*
**sabbath** *n* (*also* **Sabbath**) (Jewish) sabbat *m*; (Christian) jour *m* du seigneur
**sabbatical** *n* congé *m* sabbatique
**sabotage** ⒈ *n* sabotage *m*
⒉ *vtr* saboter
**saboteur** *n* saboteur/-euse *m/f*
**sabre, saber** (US) *n* sabre *m*
**sachet** *n* sachet *m*
**sack** ⒈ *n* (a) sac *m*
(b) **to get the ~** (colloq) se faire mettre à la porte (colloq)
⒉ *vtr* (a) (colloq) mettre [qn] à la porte (colloq) ⟨*employee*⟩
(b) mettre [qch] à sac ⟨*town*⟩
**sacrament** *n* sacrement *m*
**sacred** *adj* sacré/-e (**to** pour)
**sacrifice** ⒈ *n* sacrifice *m* (**to** à; **of** de)
⒉ *vtr* (a) (gen) sacrifier (**to** à)
(b) (to the gods) offrir [qch] en sacrifice (**to** à)
⒊ *v refl* **to ~ oneself** se sacrifier (**for** pour)
**sacrilege** *n* sacrilège *m*
**sacrosanct** *adj* sacro-saint/-e
**sad** *adj* triste (**that** que + *subjunctive*); **it makes me ~** cela me rend triste
**sadden** *vtr* attrister
**saddle** ⒈ *n* selle *f*
⒉ *vtr* (a) seller ⟨*horse*⟩
(b) **to ~ sb with** mettre [qch] sur les bras de qn ⟨*responsibility, task*⟩
**saddle bag** *n* sacoche *f*
**sadist** *n* sadique *mf*

**sadistic** *adj* sadique
**sadness** *n* tristesse *f*
**sae** *n abbr* = STAMPED ADDRESSED ENVELOPE
**safari** *n* safari *m*
**safari park** *n* parc *m* zoologique (*où les animaux vivent en semi-liberté*)
**safe** ⒈ *n* coffre-fort *m*
⒉ *adj* (a) (after ordeal, risk) ⟨*person*⟩ sain et sauf/saine et sauve; ⟨*object*⟩ intact/-e; **~ and sound** sain et sauf/saine et sauve
(b) (free from threat, harm) **to be ~** ⟨*person*⟩ être en sécurité; ⟨*document, valuables*⟩ être en lieu sûr; ⟨*company, job, reputation*⟩ ne pas être menacé/-e; **is the bike ~ here?** est-ce qu'on peut laisser le vélo ici sans risque?; **have a ~ journey!** bon voyage!
(c) (risk-free) ⟨*toy, level, method*⟩ sans danger; ⟨*place, vehicle*⟩ sûr/-e; ⟨*structure, building*⟩ solide; **it's not ~** c'est dangereux
(d) (prudent) ⟨*investment*⟩ sûr/-e; ⟨*choice*⟩ prudent/-e
(e) (reliable) **to be in ~ hands** être en bonnes mains
IDIOMS **better ~ than sorry!** mieux vaut prévenir que guérir!; **just to be on the ~ side** simplement par précaution
**safe bet** *n* **it's a ~** c'est quelque chose de sûr
**safe-conduct** *n* laissez-passer *m inv*
**safe-deposit box** *n* coffre *m* (à la banque)
**safeguard** ⒈ *n* garantie *f* (**for** pour; **against** contre)
⒉ *vtr* protéger (**against, from** contre)

**safe house** n refuge m
**safekeeping** n in sb's ~ à la garde de qn
**safely** adv (a) ⟨come back⟩ (of person) sans encombre; (of parcel, goods) sans dommage; (of plane) ⟨land, take off⟩ sans problème; **I arrived** ~ je suis bien arrivé
(b) **we can** ~ **assume that...** nous pouvons être certains que...
(c) ⟨locked, hidden⟩ bien
**safe sex** n rapports mpl sexuels sans risque
**safety** n sécurité f; **in** ~ en (toute) sécurité; **to reach** ~ parvenir en lieu sûr
**safety belt** n ceinture f de sécurité
**safety net** n filet m (de protection); (figurative) filet m de sécurité
**safety pin** n épingle f de sûreté
**sag** vi (a) ⟨beam, mattress⟩ s'affaisser; ⟨tent, rope⟩ ne pas être bien tendu-e
(b) ⟨breasts⟩ pendre; ⟨flesh⟩ être flasque
**saga** n saga f
**sage** n (a) (herb) sauge f
(b) (wise person) sage m
**Sagittarius** n Sagittaire m
**Sahara** pr n Sahara m; **the** ~ **desert** le désert du Sahara
**sail** ⃞1 n (a) (of boat) voile f; **to set sail** prendre la mer; **a ship in full** ~ un navire toutes voiles dehors
(b) (of windmill) aile f
⃞2 vtr (a) piloter ⟨ship, yacht⟩
(b) traverser [qch] en bateau ⟨ocean, channel⟩
⃞3 vi (a) ⟨person⟩ voyager en bateau; **to** ~ **around the world** faire le tour du monde en bateau
(b) ⟨ship⟩ **to** ~ **across** traverser ⟨ocean⟩; **the boat** ~**s at 10 am** le bateau part à 10 h
(c) (as hobby) **to go** ~**ing** faire de la voile
■ **sail through** gagner [qch] facilement ⟨match⟩; **to** ~ **through an exam** réussir un examen les doigts dans le nez (colloq)
**sailboard** n planche f à voile
**sailboarder** n véliplanchiste mf
**sailboat** n (US) bateau m à voiles
**sailing** n voile f
**sailing boat** n bateau m à voiles
**sailing ship** n voilier m
**sailor** n marin m
**saint** n saint/-e mf; **Saint Mark** saint Marc
**sake** n (a) **for the** ~ **of clarity** pour la clarté; **for the** ~ **of argument** à titre d'exemple; **to kill for the** ~ **of killing** tuer pour le plaisir de tuer; **for old times'** ~ en souvenir du bon vieux temps
(b) (benefit) **for the** ~ **of sb, for sb's** ~ par égard pour qn; **for God's/heaven's** ~! pour l'amour de Dieu/du ciel!
**salad** n salade f; **ham** ~ salade au jambon
**salad bar** n buffet m de crudités
**salad bowl** n saladier m
**salad dressing** n sauce f pour salade

**salami** n saucisson m sec
**salary** n salaire m
**sale** n (a) (gen) vente f (of de; to à); **for sale** à vendre; **on** ~ (GB) en vente
(b) (at cut prices) solde f; **the sales** les soldes; **in the** ~(s) (GB), **on** ~ (US) en solde
**sale price** n prix m soldé
**sales assistant** n (GB) vendeur/-euse mf
**sales executive** n cadre m commercial
**salesman** n (rep) représentant m; (in shop) vendeur m
**sales pitch** n baratin m (colloq) publicitaire
**sales rep, sales representative** n représentant/-e mf
**saleswoman** n (rep) représentante f; (in shop) vendeuse f
**saliva** n salive f
**salivate** vi saliver
**sallow** adj cireux/-euse
**salmon** n saumon m
**salmonella** n salmonelle f
**salon** n salon m
**saloon** n (a) (GB) (also ~ **car**) berline f
(b) (US) saloon m, bar m
(c) (on boat) salon m
**salt** ⃞1 n sel m
⃞2 vtr saler ⟨meat, fish, road, path⟩
**saltcellar** n salière f
**salty** adj ⟨water, food, flavour⟩ salé/-e
**salutary** adj salutaire
**salute** ⃞1 n salut m
⃞2 vtr, vi saluer
**salvage** ⃞1 n (a) (rescue) sauvetage m (of de)
(b) (goods rescued) biens mpl récupérés
⃞2 vtr (a) sauver ⟨cargo, materials, belongings⟩ (**from** de); effectuer le sauvetage de ⟨ship⟩
(b) sauver ⟨marriage, reputation, game⟩
(c) (for recycling) récupérer ⟨metal, paper⟩
**salvation** n salut m
**Salvation Army** n Armée f du Salut
**salve** ⃞1 n baume m
⃞2 vtr **to** ~ **one's conscience** soulager sa conscience
**Samaritan** n **the Good** ~ le bon Samaritain; **the** ~**s** les Samaritains mpl
**same** ⃞1 adj même (**as** que); **to be the** ~ être le/la même; **to look the** ~ être pareil/-eille; **to be the** ~ **as sth** être comme qch; **it amounts** or **comes to the** ~ **thing** cela revient au même; **it's all the** ~ **to me** ça m'est complètement égal; **if it's all the** ~ **to you** si ça ne te fait rien; **at the** ~ **time** en même temps; **to remain** or **stay the** ~ ne pas changer
⃞2 **the same** pron la même chose (**as** que); **I'll have the** ~ je prendrai la même chose; **to do the** ~ **as sb** faire comme qn; **the** ~ **to you!** (in greeting) à toi aussi, à toi de même!; (of insult) toi-même! (colloq)

**S**

3 **the same** adv ‹act, dress› de la même façon; **to feel the ~ as sb** penser comme qn IDIOMS **all the ~...**, **just the ~,...** tout de même,...; **thanks all the ~** merci quand même

**same-day** adj ‹service› effectué/-e dans la journée

**sample** 1 n (a) (of product, fabric) échantillon m
(b) (for analysis) prélèvement m
2 vtr (a) (taste) goûter (à) ‹food, wine›
(b) (test) essayer ‹products›; sonder ‹opinion, market›

**sanatorium** (GB), **sanitarium** (US) n sanatorium m

**sanctimonious** adj supérieur/-e

**sanction** 1 n sanction f; **to impose ~s** prendre des sanctions
2 vtr (permit) autoriser; (approve) sanctionner

**sanctity** n sainteté f

**sanctuary** n (a) (safe place) refuge m
(b) (holy place) sanctuaire m
(c) (for wildlife) réserve f; (for mistreated pets) refuge m

**sand** 1 n sable m
2 vtr (a) (also ~ **down**) poncer ‹floor›; frotter [qch] au papier de verre ‹woodwork›
(b) sabler ‹icy road›

**sandal** n sandale f

**sand castle** n château m de sable

**sand dune** n dune f

**sandpaper** 1 n papier m de verre
2 vtr poncer

**sandpit** n (quarry) sablière f; (for children) bac m à sable

**sandstone** n grès m

**sandwich** 1 n sandwich m; **cucumber ~** sandwich au concombre
2 vtr **to be ~ed between** ‹car, building, person› être pris/-e en sandwich entre

**sandwich bar** n sandwich bar m

**sandwich course** n (GB) cours m avec stage pratique

**sandy** adj (a) ‹beach› de sable; ‹path, soil› sablonneux/-euse
(b) ‹hair› blond roux inv; ‹colour› sable inv (after n)

**sane** adj (a) ‹person› sain/-e d'esprit
(b) ‹policy, judgment› sensé/-e

**sanitarium** (US) = SANATORIUM

**sanitary** adj (a) ‹engineer, installations› sanitaire
(b) (hygienic) hygiénique; (clean) propre

**sanitary towel** (GB), **sanitary napkin** (US) n serviette f hygiénique or périodique

**sanitation** n installations fpl sanitaires

**sanity** n équilibre m mental

**Santa (Claus)** pr n le père Noël

**sap** 1 n sève f
2 vtr saper ‹strength, courage, confidence›

**sapling** n jeune arbre m

**sapphire** n (a) (stone) saphir m
(b) (colour) bleu m saphir

**sarcasm** n sarcasme m

**sarcastic** adj sarcastique

**sardine** n sardine f

**Sardinia** pr n Sardaigne f

**sardonic** adj ‹laugh, look› sardonique; ‹person, remark› acerbe

**SAS** n (GB) (abbr = **Special Air Service**) commandos mpl britanniques aéroportés

**sash** n (round waist) large ceinture f; (ceremonial) écharpe f

**Satan** pr n Satan

**satanic** adj ‹rites› satanique; ‹pride, smile› démoniaque

**satchel** n cartable m (à bandoulière)

**satellite** n satellite m

**satellite dish** n antenne f parabolique

**satellite TV** n télévision f par satellite

**satin** 1 n satin m
2 adj ‹garment, shoe› de satin; **with a ~ finish** satiné/-e

**satire** n satire f (on sur)

**satiric(al)** adj satirique

**satirize** vtr faire la satire de

**satisfaction** n satisfaction f

**satisfactory** adj satisfaisant/-e

**satisfied** adj (a) (pleased) satisfait/-e (**with**, **about** de)
(b) (convinced) convaincu/-e (**by** par; **that** que)

**satisfy** vtr (a) satisfaire ‹person, need, desires, curiosity›; assouvir ‹hunger›
(b) (persuade) convaincre ‹person, public opinion› (**that** que)
(c) (meet) satisfaire à ‹demand, requirements, conditions›

**satisfying** adj (a) ‹meal› substantiel/-ielle
(b) ‹job› qui apporte de la satisfaction
(c) ‹result, progress› satisfaisant/-e

**saturate** vtr saturer (**with** de)

**saturated** adj (wet) ‹person, clothes› trempé/-e; ‹ground› détrempé/-e

**saturation point** n point m de saturation; **to reach ~** arriver à saturation

**Saturday** n samedi m; **he has a ~ job** il a un petit boulot (colloq) le samedi

**Saturn** pr n (planet) Saturne f

**sauce** n sauce f

**saucepan** n casserole f

**saucer** n soucoupe f

**Saudi Arabia** pr n Arabie f saoudite

**sauna** n sauna m

**saunter** vi (also ~ **along**) marcher d'un pas nonchalant; **to ~ off** s'éloigner d'un pas nonchalant

**sausage** n saucisse f

**sausage roll** n feuilleté m à la chair à saucisse

**savage** 1 n sauvage mf
2 adj (gen) féroce; ‹blow, beating› violent/-e; ‹attack› sauvage; ‹criticism› virulent/-e
3 vtr ‹dog› attaquer [qn/qch] sauvagement; ‹lion› déchiqueter

S

**save** [1] *n* (Sport) arrêt *m* de but
[2] *vtr* **(a)** (rescue) sauver (from de); **to ∼ sb's life** sauver la vie à qn
**(b)** (put by, keep) mettre [qch] de côté ⟨*money, food*⟩ (**to do** pour faire); garder ⟨*goods, documents*⟩ (**for** pour); sauvegarder ⟨*data, file*⟩; **to have money ∼d** avoir de l'argent de côté; **to ∼ sth for sb, to ∼ sb sth** garder qch pour qn
**(c)** (economize on) économiser ⟨*money*⟩ (**by doing** en faisant); gagner ⟨*time, space*⟩ (**by doing** en faisant); **to ∼ one's energy** ménager ses forces; **you'll ∼ money** vous ferez des économies; **to ∼ sb/sth (from) having to do** éviter à qn/qch de faire
**(d)** (Sport) arrêter
[3] *vi* **(a)** (put money by) = SAVE UP
**(b)** (economize) économiser, faire des économies; **to ∼ on** faire des économies de ⟨*energy, paper*⟩
■ **save up** faire des économies; **to ∼ up for** mettre de l'argent de côté pour s'acheter ⟨*car, house*⟩; mettre de l'argent de côté pour s'offrir ⟨*holiday*⟩

**saver** *n* épargnant/-e *m/f*

**saving grace** *n* bon côté *m*; **it's his ∼** c'est ce qui le sauve

**savings** *n pl* économies *fpl*

**savings account** *n* (GB) compte *m* d'épargne; (US) compte *m* rémunéré

**savings bank** *n* caisse *f* d'épargne

**saviour** (GB), **savior** (US) *n* sauveur *m*

**savour** (GB), **savor** (US) [1] *n* saveur *f*
[2] *vtr* savourer

**savoury** (GB), **savory** (US) *adj* (not sweet) salé/-e; (appetizing) appétissant/-e

**saw** [1] *n* scie *f*
[2] *vtr* scier; **to ∼ through/down/off** scier

**sawdust** *n* sciure *f* (de bois)

**sawn-off shotgun** *n* (GB) fusil *m* à canon scié

**saxophone** *n* saxophone *m*

**say** [1] *n* **to have one's ∼** dire ce qu'on a à dire (**on** sur); **to have a ∼/no ∼ in sth** avoir/ne pas avoir son mot à dire sur qch; **to have no ∼ in the matter** ne pas avoir voix au chapitre
[2] *vtr* **(a)** (gen) dire (**to** à); **'hello,' he said** 'bonjour,' dit-il; **to ∼ (that)** dire que; **they ∼ she's very rich, she is said to be very rich on** dit qu'elle est très riche; **to ∼ sth about sb/sth** dire qch au sujet de qn/qch; **to ∼ sth to oneself** se dire qch; **let's ∼ no more about it** n'en parlons plus; **it goes without ∼ing that** il va sans dire que; **that is to ∼** c'est-à-dire; **let's ∼ there are 20** mettons *or* supposons qu'il y en ait 20; **how high would you ∼ it is?** à ton avis, quelle en est la hauteur?; **I'd ∼ she was about 25** je lui donnerais environ 25 ans
**(b)** ⟨*sign, clock, dial, gauge*⟩ indiquer
[3] *vi* **stop when I ∼** arrête quand je te le dirai; **he wouldn't ∼** il n'a pas voulu le dire
IDIOMS **it ∼s a lot for sb/sth** c'est tout à l'honneur de qn/qch; **there's a lot to be said**

**for that method** cette méthode est très intéressante à bien des égards; **when all is said and done** tout compte fait, en fin de compte

**saying** *n* dicton *m*

**scab** *n* croûte *f*

**scaffolding** *n* échafaudage *m*

**scald** *vtr* ébouillanter

**scalding** *adj* brûlant/-e

**scale** [1] *n* **(a)** (gen) échelle *f*; **pay ∼, salary ∼** échelle des salaires; **on a ∼ of 1 to 10** sur une échelle allant de 1 à 10
**(b)** (extent) (of disaster, success, violence) étendue *f* (**of** de); (of defeat, recession, task) ampleur *f* (**of** de); (of activity, operation) envergure *f* (**of** de)
**(c)** (on ruler, gauge) graduation *f*
**(d)** (for weighing) balance *f*
**(e)** (Mus) gamme *f*
**(f)** (on fish, insect) écaille *f*
[2] **scales** *n pl* balance *f*
[3] *vtr* **(a)** escalader ⟨*wall, mountain*⟩
**(b)** écailler ⟨*fish*⟩
■ **scale down:** ∼ [sth] **down,** ∼ **down** [sth] réduire l'échelle de ⟨*drawing*⟩; réduire ⟨*activity*⟩

**scale drawing** *n* dessin *m* à l'échelle

**scale model** *n* maquette *f* à l'échelle

**scallop, scollop** *n* coquille *f* Saint-Jacques

**scalp** [1] *n* cuir *m* chevelu
[2] *vtr* scalper

**scam** *n* (colloq) escroquerie *f*

**scamper** *vi* **to ∼ about** *or* **around** ⟨*child, dog*⟩ gambader; ⟨*mouse*⟩ trottiner

**scan** [1] *n* (Med) (CAT) scanner *m*; (ultrasound) échographie *f*
[2] *vtr* **(a)** lire rapidement ⟨*page, newspaper*⟩
**(b)** (examine) scruter ⟨*face, horizon*⟩
**(c)** ⟨*beam of light, radar*⟩ balayer
**(d)** (Med) faire un scanner de ⟨*organ*⟩

**scandal** *n* scandale *m*

**scandalize** *vtr* scandaliser

**scandalous** *adj* scandaleux/-euse

**Scandinavia** *pr n* Scandinavie *f*

**scanner** *n* (Comput, Med) scanner *m*; (for bar codes) lecteur *m* optique

**scanty** *adj* ⟨*meal, supply*⟩ maigre (**before** *n*); ⟨*information*⟩ sommaire; ⟨*knowledge*⟩ rudimentaire; ⟨*swimsuit*⟩ minuscule

**scapegoat** *n* bouc *m* émissaire (**for** de)

**scar** [1] *n* cicatrice *f*; (on face from knife) balafre *f*
[2] *vtr* marquer; (on face with knife) balafrer; **to ∼ sb for life** laisser à qn une cicatrice permanente; (figurative) marquer qn pour la vie

**scarce** *adj* rare; **to become ∼** se faire rare

**scarcely** *adv* à peine; **∼ anybody believes it** presque personne ne le croit

**scare** [1] *n* **(a)** peur *f*; **to give sb a ∼** faire peur à qn
**(b)** (alert) alerte *f*; **bomb ∼** alerte à la bombe
[2] *vtr* faire peur à

····⫶·

■ **scare away**, **scare off** faire fuir
⟨animal, attacker⟩; (figurative) dissuader

**scarecrow** n épouvantail m

**scared** adj ⟨animal, person⟩ effrayé/-e;
⟨look⟩ apeuré/-e; **to be** or **feel ∼** avoir peur;
**to be ∼ stiff** (colloq) avoir une peur bleue
(colloq)

**scaremongering** n alarmisme m

**scarf** n (long) écharpe f; (square) foulard m

**scarlet** n, adj écarlate (f)

**scarlet fever** n scarlatine f

**scary** adj (colloq) qui fait peur

**scathing** adj ⟨remark, tone, wit⟩
cinglant/-e; ⟨criticism⟩ virulent/-e

**scatter** ⓵ vtr (a) (also ∼ **around**, ∼
**about**) répandre ⟨seeds, earth⟩; éparpiller
⟨books, papers, clothes⟩
(b) disperser ⟨crowd, herd⟩
⓶ vi ⟨people, animals, birds⟩ se disperser

**scatter-brained** adj ⟨person⟩ étourdi/-e;
⟨idea⟩ farfelu/-e (colloq)

**scattered** adj ⟨houses, trees, population,
clouds⟩ épars/-e; ⟨books, litter⟩ éparpillé/-e;
⟨support, resistance⟩ clairsemé/-e

**scatty** adj (colloq) (GB) étourdi/-e

**scavenge** vi **to ∼ for food** ⟨bird, animal⟩
chercher de la nourriture

**scavenger** n (a) (animal) charognard m
(b) (person) (for food) faiseur m de poubelles;
(for objects) récupérateur m

**scenario** n (gen) cas m de figure; (of film,
play) scénario m

**scene** n (a) (gen) scène f; **behind the ∼s**
dans les coulisses fpl; **you need a change of
∼** tu as besoin de changer de décor
(b) (of crime, accident) lieu m; **at** or **on the ∼**
sur les lieux
(c) (image, sight) image f
(d) (view) vue f

**scenery** n (a) (landscape) paysage m
(b) (in theatre) décors mpl

**scent** ⓵ n (a) (smell) odeur f
(b) (perfume) parfum m
(c) (of animal) fumet m; (in hunting) piste f
⓶ vtr (a) flairer ⟨prey, animal⟩
(b) pressentir ⟨danger, trouble⟩
(c) (perfume) parfumer ⟨air⟩

**sceptic** (GB), **skeptic** (US) n sceptique
m/f

**sceptical** (GB), **skeptical** (US) adj
sceptique

**scepticism** (GB), **skepticism** (US) n
scepticisme m

**schedule** ⓵ n (a) (of work, events)
programme m; (timetable) horaire m; **to be
ahead of/behind ∼** être en avance/en retard;
**to arrive on/ahead of ∼** ⟨bus, train, plane⟩
arriver à l'heure/en avance
(b) (list) liste f
⓶ vtr (plan) prévoir; (arrange) programmer

**scheduled flight** n vol m régulier

**scheme** ⓵ n (a) projet m, plan m (**to do**,
**for doing** pour faire); **pension ∼** régime m
de retraite

(b) (plot) combine f (**to do** pour faire)
⓶ vi comploter

**scheming** n machinations fpl

**schizophrenic** adj schizophrénique

**scholar** n érudit/-e m/f

**scholarship** n bourse f (**to** pour)

**school** ⓵ n (a) école f; **at ∼** à l'école
(b) (US) (university) université f
(c) (of fish) banc m
⓶ adj ⟨holiday, outing, trip, uniform, year⟩
scolaire

**schoolbag** n sac m de classe

**schoolboy** n (pupil) élève m; (primary)
écolier m; (secondary) collégien m

**schoolchild** n écolier/-ière m/f

**school fees** n pl frais mpl de scolarité

**schoolfriend** n camarade mf de classe

**schoolgirl** n (pupil) élève f; (primary)
écolière f; (secondary) collégienne f

**schooling** n scolarité f

**school-leaver** n (GB) jeune mf ayant fini
sa scolarité

**school leaving age** n âge m de fin de
scolarité

**school lunch** n repas m de la cantine
scolaire

**school report** (GB), **school report
card** (US) n bulletin m scolaire

**schoolteacher** n enseignant/-e m/f;
(primary) instituteur/-trice m/f; (secondary)
professeur m

**schoolwork** n travail m de classe

**science** ⓵ n science f; **to study ∼** étudier
les sciences
⓶ adj ⟨exam, subject⟩ scientifique; ⟨teacher,
textbook⟩ de sciences

**science fiction** n science-fiction f

**scientific** adj scientifique

**scientist** n scientifique mf

**scissors** n pl ciseaux mpl

**scoff** ⓵ vtr (GB) (colloq) (eat) engloutir
(colloq), bouffer (colloq)
⓶ vi se moquer (**at** de)

**scold** vtr gronder (**for doing** pour avoir fait)

**scoop** ⓵ n (a) (for measuring) mesure f
(b) (of ice cream) boule f
(c) (in journalism) exclusivité f
⓶ vtr (colloq) décrocher (colloq) ⟨prize, sum of
money, story⟩

**scooter** n (a) (child's) trottinette f
(b) (motorized) scooter m

**scope** n (a) (opportunity) possibilité f (**for** de)
(b) (of inquiry, report, book) portée f; (of plan)
envergure f
(c) (of person) compétences fpl

**scorch** ⓵ n (also ∼ **mark**) légère brûlure
f
⓶ vtr ⟨fire⟩ brûler; ⟨sun⟩ dessécher ⟨grass,
trees⟩; griller ⟨lawn⟩; ⟨iron⟩ roussir ⟨fabric⟩

**scorching** adj (colloq) (also ∼ **hot**) ⟨day⟩
torride; ⟨weather⟩ caniculaire

s

**score** [1] n (a) (Sport) score m; (in cards) marque f; **to keep (the) ~** marquer les points; (in cards) tenir la marque
(b) (in exam, test) note f, résultat m
(c) (Mus) (written music) partition f; (for film) musique f (de film)
(d) (twenty) **a ~** vingt m, une vingtaine f
(e) **on this** or **that ~** à ce sujet
[2] vtr (a) marquer ⟨goal, point⟩; remporter ⟨victory, success⟩; **to ~ 9 out of 10** avoir 9 sur 10
(b) (cut) entailler
[3] vi (gain point) marquer un point; (obtain goal) marquer un but
IDIOMS **to settle a ~** régler ses comptes

**scoreboard** n tableau m d'affichage

**scorn** [1] n mépris m (**for** pour)
[2] vtr (despise) mépriser; (reject) accueillir avec mépris ⟨claim, suggestion⟩

**scornful** adj méprisant/-e

**Scorpio** n Scorpion m

**Scot** n Écossais/-e m/f

**Scotch** [1] n (also ~ **whisky**) whisky m, scotch m
[2] adj écossais/-e

**Scotch tape**® n (US) scotch® m

**scot-free** adj **to get off ~** (unpunished) s'en tirer sans être inquiété/-e; (unharmed) s'en sortir indemne

**Scotland** pr n Écosse f

**Scottish** adj écossais/-e

**scour** vtr (a) (scrub) récurer
(b) (search) parcourir ⟨area, list⟩ (**for** à la recherche de)

**scourer** n tampon m à récurer

**scourge** n fléau m

**scout** n (a) (also **boy** ~) scout m
(b) (Mil) éclaireur m
(c) (also **talent** ~) découvreur/-euse m/f de nouveaux talents
■ **scout around** explorer; **to ~ around for sth** rechercher qch

**scowl** [1] n air m renfrogné
[2] vi prendre un air renfrogné

**scramble** [1] n (a) (rush) course f (**for** pour; **to do** pour faire)
(b) (climb) escalade f
[2] vtr brouiller ⟨signal⟩
[3] vi (a) **to ~ up** escalader; **to ~ down** dégringoler

**scrambled egg** n (also ~**s** pl) œufs mpl brouillés

**scrambling** n (sport) motocross m

**scrap** [1] n (a) (of paper, cloth) petit morceau m; (of news, information) fragment m
(b) (old iron) ferraille f
[2] **scraps** n pl (of food) restes mpl; (from butcher's) déchets mpl
[3] vtr (a) (colloq) abandonner ⟨idea, plan, system⟩
(b) détruire ⟨aircraft, equipment⟩

**scrapbook** n album m

**scrap dealer** n ferrailleur m

**scrape** [1] n **to get into a ~** (colloq) s'attirer des ennuis
[2] vtr (a) (clean) gratter ⟨vegetables, shoes⟩
(b) érafler ⟨car, paintwork, furniture⟩; **to ~ one's knees** s'écorcher les genoux
[3] vi **to ~ against sth** (rub) frotter contre qch; (scratch) érafler qch
■ **scrape by** (financially) s'en sortir à peine; (in situation) s'en tirer de justesse
■ **scrape in** (to university, class) entrer de justesse
■ **scrape out**: ¶ ~ **out [sth]**, ~ **[sth] out** nettoyer [qch] en grattant ⟨saucepan⟩
■ **scrape through**: ¶ ~ **through** s'en tirer de justesse; ¶ ~ **through [sth]** réussir de justesse à ⟨exam, test⟩

**scrap heap** n **to be thrown on the ~** être mis/-e au rebut

**scrap iron**, **scrap metal** n ferraille f

**scrap paper** n papier m brouillon

**scrap yard** n chantier m de ferraille, casse f

**scratch** [1] n (a) (on skin) égratignure f; (from a claw, fingernail) griffure f
(b) (on metal, furniture) éraflure f; (on record, glass) rayure f
(c) (sound) grattement m
(d) (colloq) **he/his work is not up to ~** il/son travail n'est pas à la hauteur
(e) **to start from ~** partir de zéro
[2] vtr (a) **to ~ one's initials on sth** graver ses initiales sur qch
(b) ⟨cat, person⟩ griffer ⟨person⟩; ⟨thorns, rose bush⟩ égratigner ⟨person⟩; érafler ⟨car, wood⟩; rayer ⟨record⟩; ⟨cat⟩ se faire les griffes sur ⟨furniture⟩; ⟨person⟩ **to ~ sb's eyes out** arracher les yeux à quelqu'un
(c) **to ~ sb's back** gratter le dos de qn
[3] vi se gratter

**scratch card** n jeu m de grattage

**scrawl** [1] n gribouillage m
[2] vtr, vi gribouiller

**scrawny** adj ⟨person, animal⟩ décharné/-e

**scream** [1] n (of person, animal) cri m (perçant); (stronger) hurlement m; (of brakes) grincement m; (of tyres) crissement m
[2] vtr crier
[3] vi crier; (stronger) hurler

**screech** [1] n (of person, animal) cri m strident; (of tyres) crissement m
[2] vi ⟨person, animal⟩ pousser un cri strident; ⟨tyres⟩ crisser

**screen** [1] n (a) (on TV, VDU, at cinema) écran m
(b) (furniture) paravent m
(c) (US) (in door) grille f
[2] vtr (a) (at cinema) projeter; (on TV) diffuser
(b) (conceal) cacher; (protect) protéger (**from** de)
(c) (test) examiner le cas de ⟨applicants, candidates⟩; contrôler ⟨baggage⟩; **to ~ sb for cancer** faire passer à qn des tests de dépistage du cancer

**screening** n (a) (showing) projection f; (on TV) diffusion f    ⋯⋗

**S**

**(b)** (of patients) examens *mpl* de dépistage
**(c)** (vetting) filtrage *m*
**screenplay** *n* scénario *m*
**screen saver** *n* économiseur *m* d'écran
**screenwriter** *n* scénariste *mf*
**screw** ⓵ *n* vis *f*
  ⓶ *vtr* visser (**into** dans; **onto** sur)
  ▪ **screw up (a)** froisser ⟨*piece of paper, material*⟩; **to ~ up one's eyes** plisser les yeux; **to ~ up one's face** faire la grimace
  **(b)** (colloq) faire foirer (colloq) ⟨*plan, task*⟩
**screwdriver** *n* **(a)** (tool) tournevis *m*
  **(b)** (cocktail) vodka-orange *f*
**scribble** *vtr, vi* griffonner, gribouiller
**scrimp** *vi* économiser; **to ~ and save** se priver de tout
**script** *n* **(a)** (for film, radio, TV) script *m*; (for play) texte *m*
  **(b)** (GB) (Sch, Univ) copie *f* (d'examen)
**scripture** *n* (*also* **Holy Scripture, Holy Scriptures**) (Christian) Écritures *fpl*; (other) textes *mpl* sacrés
**scriptwriter** *n* scénariste *mf*
**scroll** *n* rouleau *m*
  ▪ **scroll down:** ¶ **~ down** ⟨*person*⟩ faire défiler de haut en bas; ¶ **~ down [sth]** faire défiler [qch] de haut en bas ⟨*document*⟩
  ▪ **scroll up:** ¶ **~ up** ⟨*person*⟩ faire défiler de bas en haut; ¶**~ up [sth]** faire défiler [qch] de bas en haut ⟨*document*⟩
**scroll bar** *n* barre *f* de défilement
**scrounge** *vtr* (colloq) **to ~ sth off sb** piquer (colloq) qch à qn ⟨*cigarette*⟩; taper (colloq) qn de ⟨*money*⟩
**scrounger** *n* (colloq) parasite *m*
**scrub** ⓵ *n* **(a)** (clean) **to give sth a (good) ~** (bien) nettoyer qch
  **(b)** (Bot) broussailles *fpl*
  ⓶ *vtr* frotter ⟨*back, clothes*⟩; récurer ⟨*pan, floor*⟩; nettoyer ⟨*vegetable*⟩; **to ~ one's nails** se brosser les ongles
  ▪ **scrub up** ⟨*doctor*⟩ se stériliser les mains
**scrubbing brush, scrub brush** (US) *n* brosse *f* de ménage
**scruff** *n* **by the ~ of the neck** par la peau du cou
**scruffy** *adj* ⟨*clothes, person*⟩ dépenaillé/-e; ⟨*flat, town*⟩ délabré/-e
**scrum, scrummage** *n* (in rugby) mêlée *f*
**scrunchie** *n* chouchou *m*
**scruple** *n* scrupule *m* (**about** vis-à-vis de)
**scrupulous** *adj* scrupuleux/-euse
**scrutinize** *vtr* scruter ⟨*face, motives*⟩; examiner [qch] minutieusement ⟨*document, plan*⟩; vérifier ⟨*accounts, votes*⟩
**scrutiny** *n* examen *m*
**scuba diving** *n* plongée *f* sous-marine
**scuff** ⓵ *n* (*also* **~ mark**) (on floor, furniture) rayure *f*; (on leather) éraflure *f*
  ⓶ *vtr* érafler ⟨*shoes*⟩; rayer ⟨*floor, furniture*⟩
**scuffle** *n* bagarre *f*
**sculpt** *vtr, vi* sculpter
**sculptor** *n* sculpteur *m*

**sculpture** *n* sculpture *f*
**scum** *n* **(a)** (on pond) écume *f*
  **(b)** (on liquid) mousse *f*
  **(c) they're the ~ of the earth** c'est de la racaille
**scuttle** ⓵ *vtr* **(a)** saborder ⟨*ship*⟩
  **(b)** faire échouer ⟨*talks, project*⟩
  ⓶ *vi* **to ~ away** *or* **off** filer
**scythe** *n* faux *f inv*
**sea** ⓵ *n* mer *f*; **beside** *or* **by the ~** au bord de la mer; **the open ~** le large; **by ~** ⟨*travel*⟩ en bateau; ⟨*send*⟩ par bateau
  ⓶ *adj* ⟨*air, breeze*⟩ marin/-e; ⟨*bird, water*⟩ de mer; ⟨*crossing, voyage*⟩ par mer; ⟨*battle*⟩ naval/-e; ⟨*power*⟩ maritime
**seafood** *n* fruits *mpl* de mer
**seafront** *n* front *m* de mer
**seagull** *n* mouette *f*
**sea horse** *n* hippocampe *m*
**seal** ⓵ *n* **(a)** (Zool) phoque *m*
  **(b)** (stamp) sceau *m*
  **(c)** (on container) plomb *m*; (on package, letter) cachet *m*; (on door) scellés *mpl*
  ⓶ *vtr* **(a)** cacheter ⟨*document*⟩
  **(b)** fermer, cacheter ⟨*envelope*⟩
  **(c)** fermer [qch] hermétiquement ⟨*jar, tin*⟩; rendre [qch] étanche ⟨*window frame*⟩
  **(d)** sceller ⟨*alliance, friendship*⟩ (**with** par); **to ~ sb's fate** décider du sort de qn
  ▪ **seal off** isoler ⟨*ward*⟩; boucler ⟨*area, building*⟩; barrer ⟨*street*⟩
**sea lion** *n* lion *m* de mer
**seam** *n* (of garment) couture *f*
**seamless** *adj* ⟨*transition*⟩ sans heurts; ⟨*process, whole*⟩ continu/-e
**seaplane** *n* hydravion *m*
**search** ⓵ *n* **(a)** (for person, object) recherches *fpl* (**for sb/sth** pour retrouver qn/qch); **in ~ of** à la recherche de
  **(b)** (of place) fouille *f* (**of** de)
  **(c)** (Comput) recherche *f*
  ⓶ *vtr* **(a)** fouiller ⟨*area, building*⟩; fouiller dans ⟨*cupboard, drawer, memory*⟩
  **(b)** examiner (attentivement) ⟨*map, records*⟩
  ⓷ *vi* **(a)** chercher; **to ~ for** *or* **after sb/sth** chercher qn/qch; **to ~ through** fouiller dans ⟨*cupboard, bag*⟩; examiner ⟨*records, file*⟩
  **(b)** (Comput) **to ~ for** rechercher ⟨*data, file*⟩
  ▪ **search out:** **~ [sb/sth] out, ~ out [sb/sth]** découvrir
**search engine** *n* moteur *m* de recherche
**searching** *adj* ⟨*look, question*⟩ pénétrant/-e
**searchlight** *n* projecteur *m*
**search party** *n* équipe *f* de secours
**search warrant** *n* mandat *m* de perquisition
**sea salt** *n* sel *m* de mer
**seashell** *n* coquillage *m*
**seashore** *n* (part of coast) littoral *m*; (beach) plage *f*
**seasick** *adj* **to feel ~** avoir le mal de mer
**seaside** ⓵ *n* **the ~** le bord de la mer
  ⓶ *adj* ⟨*hotel*⟩ en bord de mer; ⟨*town*⟩ maritime; **~ resort** station *f* balnéaire

**season** [1] *n* saison *f*; **strawberries are in/ out of** ~ c'est/ce n'est pas la saison des fraises; **the holiday** ~ la période des vacances; **Season's greetings!** Joyeuses fêtes!
[2] *vtr* (with spices) relever; (with condiments) assaisonner

**seasonal** *adj* ⟨work, change⟩ saisonnier/-ière; ⟨fruit, produce⟩ de saison

**seasoned** *adj* ⟨soldier⟩ aguerri/-e; ⟨traveller⟩ grand/-e (before *n*); ⟨campaigner, performer⟩ expérimenté/-e; ⟨dish⟩ assaisonné/-e; **highly** ~ relevé/-e, épicé/-e

**seasoning** *n* assaisonnement *m*

**season ticket** *n* (for travel) carte *f* d'abonnement; (for theatre, matches) abonnement *m*

**seat** [1] *n* (a) (chair) siège *m*; (bench-type) banquette *f*
(b) (place) place *f*; **take** *or* **have a** ~ asseyez-vous; **to book a** ~ réserver une place
(c) (of trousers) fond *m*
[2] *vtr* (a) (place) ⟨person⟩
(b) **the car** ~**s five** c'est une voiture à cinq places; **the table** ~**s six** c'est une table de six couverts

**seatbelt** *n* ceinture *f* (de sécurité)

**-seater** *combining form* **a two-** ~ (plane) un avion *m* à deux places; (car) un coupé; (sofa) un (canapé) deux places

**seating** *n* places *fpl* assises; **I'll organize the** ~ je placerai les gens

**sea urchin** *n* oursin *m*

**sea view** *n* vue *f* sur la mer

**seaweed** *n* algue *f* marine

**seaworthy** *adj* en état de naviguer

**secateurs** *n pl* (GB) sécateur *m*

**secluded** *adj* retiré/-e

**seclusion** *n* isolement *m* (**from** à l'écart de)

**second** [1] *n* (a) (in order) deuxième *mf*, second/-e *m/f*
(b) (unit of time) seconde *f*; (instant) instant *m*
(c) (of month) deux *m inv*
(d) (Aut) (*also* ~ **gear**) deuxième *f*, seconde *f*
(e) (defective article) article *m* qui a un défaut
(f) (*also* ~**-class honours degree**) (GB) (Univ) ≈ licence *f* avec mention bien
[2] *adj* deuxième, second/-e; **to have a** ~ **helping** (**of sth**) reprendre (de qch); **to have a** ~ **chance to do sth** avoir une nouvelle chance de faire
[3] *adv* (a) (in second place) deuxième; **to come** *or* **finish** ~ arriver deuxième; **the** ~ **biggest building** le deuxième bâtiment de par sa grandeur
(b) (*also* **secondly**) deuxièmement
[4] *vtr* (in debate) appuyer ⟨proposal⟩
IDIOMS **to be** ~ **nature** être automatique; **to be** ~ **to none** être sans pareil; **on** ~ **thoughts** à la réflexion; **to have** ~ **thoughts** avoir quelques hésitations *or* doutes

**secondary** *adj* secondaire

**secondary school** *n* ≈ école *f* secondaire

**second class** [1] *adv* ⟨travel⟩ en deuxième classe; ⟨send⟩ au tarif lent
[2] **second-class** *adj*
(a) ⟨post, stamp⟩ au tarif lent
(b) ⟨carriage, ticket⟩ de deuxième classe
(c) (second-rate) de qualité inférieure

**second hand** [1] *n* (on watch, clock) trotteuse *f*
[2] **second-hand** *adj* ⟨clothes, car⟩ d'occasion; ⟨news, information⟩ de seconde main
[3] *adv* ⟨buy⟩ d'occasion; ⟨find out, hear⟩ indirectement

**secondly** *adv* deuxièmement

**second name** *n* (surname) nom *m* de famille; (second forename) deuxième prénom *m*

**second-rate** *adj* de second ordre

**seconds** *n pl* (colloq) rab *m* (colloq)

**secrecy** *n* secret *m*

**secret** [1] *n* secret *m*; **to tell sb a** ~ confier un secret à qn
[2] *adj* secret/-ète
[3] **in secret** *phr* en secret

**secretarial** *adj* ⟨skills, work⟩ de secrétaire; ⟨college⟩ de secrétariat

**secretary** *n* (a) (assistant) secrétaire *mf* (**to sb** de qn)
(b) **Foreign Secretary** (GB), **Secretary of State** (US) ministre *m* des Affaires étrangères

**secretive** *adj* ⟨person, organization⟩ secret/-ète; **to be** ~ **about sth** faire un mystère de qch

**secretly** *adv* secrètement

**secret weapon** *n* arme *f* secrète

**sect** *n* secte *f*

**section** *n* (a) (of train, aircraft, town, book) partie *f*; (of pipe, tunnel, road) tronçon *m*; (of object, kit) élément *m*; (of fruit) quartier *m*; (of population) tranche *f*
(b) (of company, department) service *m*; (of library, shop) rayon *m*
(c) (of act, bill, report) article *m*; (of newspaper) rubrique *f*

**sector** *n* secteur *m*

**secular** *adj* ⟨politics, society, education⟩ laïque; ⟨belief, music⟩ profane

**secure** [1] *adj* (a) ⟨job, marriage, income⟩ stable; ⟨basis, base⟩ solide
(b) ⟨hiding place⟩ sûr/-e
(c) ⟨padlock, knot⟩ solide; ⟨structure, ladder⟩ stable; ⟨rope⟩ bien attaché/-e; ⟨door, window⟩ bien fermé/-e
(d) **to feel** ~ se sentir en sécurité
[2] *vtr* (a) obtenir ⟨promise, release, right, victory⟩
(b) bien attacher ⟨rope⟩; bien fermer ⟨door, window⟩; stabiliser ⟨ladder⟩
(c) protéger ⟨house⟩; assurer ⟨position, future⟩
(d) garantir ⟨loan, debt⟩ (**against, on** sur)

**secure unit** *n* (in children's home) section ⋯⟶

*surveillée dans une maison de rééducation*; (in psychiatric hospital) quartier *m* de haute sécurité

**securities** *n pl* titres *mpl*

**security** [1] *n* (a) sécurité *f*; job ~ sécurité de l'emploi; national ~ sûreté *f* de l'État (b) (guarantee) garantie *f* (on sur) [2] *adj* ⟨camera, check, measures⟩ de sécurité; ⟨firm, staff⟩ de surveillance

**security guard** *n* garde *m* sécurité, vigile *m*

**security leak** *n* fuite *f* (d'information)

**sedate** [1] *adj* ⟨person⟩ posé/-e; ⟨lifestyle, pace⟩ tranquille [2] *vtr* mettre [qn] sous calmants ⟨patient⟩

**sedation** *n* sédation *f*; under ~ sous calmants

**sedative** *n* sédatif *m*, calmant *m*

**seduce** *vtr* séduire

**seductive** *adj* ⟨person⟩ séduisant/-e; ⟨smile⟩ aguicheur/-euse

**see** [1] *vtr* (a) voir; can you ~ him? est-ce que tu le vois?; I can't ~ him je ne le vois pas; to ~ the sights faire du tourisme; ~ you next week! à la semaine prochaine!; to ~ sb as considérer qn comme ⟨friend, hero⟩; it remains to be seen whether *or* if reste à voir si (b) (make sure) to ~ (to it) that veiller à ce que (+ *subjunctive*); ~ (to it) that the children are in bed by nine veillez à ce que les enfants soient couchés à neuf heures (c) (accompany) to ~ sb to the station accompagner qn à la gare; to ~ sb home raccompagner qn chez lui/elle [2] *vi* voir; I can't ~ je ne vois rien; I'll go and ~ je vais voir; we'll just have to wait and ~ il ne nous reste plus qu'à attendre; let's ~, let me ~ voyons (un peu) ■ **see off**: to ~ sb off dire au revoir à qn ■ **see out**: to ~ sb out raccompagner qn à la porte ■ **see through**: ¶ ~ through [sth] déceler ⟨deception, lie⟩; ¶ ~ through [sb] percer [qn] à jour; ¶ ~ [sth] through mener [qch] à bonne fin ■ **see to** s'occuper de ⟨arrangements⟩

**seed** *n* (a) (gen) graine *f*; (fruit pip) pépin *m*; (for sowing) semences *fpl*; to go to ~ ⟨plant⟩ monter en graine; ⟨person⟩ se ramollir; ⟨organization, country⟩ être en déclin (b) (Sport) tête *f* de série

**seedling** *n* plant *m*

**seedy** *adj* ⟨person⟩ louche; ⟨area, club⟩ mal famé/-e

**seek** *vtr* (a) chercher ⟨agreement, refuge, solution⟩; demander ⟨advice, help, permission⟩ (b) ⟨police, employer⟩ rechercher ⟨person⟩ ■ **seek out** aller chercher, dénicher

**seem** *vi* sembler; it ~s that il semble que (+ *subjunctive*); it ~s to me that il me semble que (+ *indicative*); he ~s happy/disappointed il a l'air heureux/déçu; it ~s odd (to me) ça (me) paraît bizarre; he ~s to be looking for someone on dirait qu'il cherche quelqu'un

**seep** *vi* suinter; to ~ away s'écouler; to ~ through sth ⟨water, gas⟩ s'infiltrer à travers qch; ⟨light⟩ filtrer à travers qch

**seesaw** [1] *n* tapecul *m* [2] *vi* ⟨price, rate⟩ osciller

**seethe** *vi* (a) to ~ with rage bouillir de colère; he was seething il était furibond (b) (teem) grouiller; the streets were seething with tourists les rues grouillaient de touristes

**see-through** *adj* transparent/-e

**segment** *n* segment *m*; (of orange) quartier *m*

**segregate** *vtr* (a) (separate) séparer (from de) (b) (isolate) isoler (from de)

**segregated** *adj* ⟨education, society⟩ ségrégationniste; ⟨area, school⟩ où la ségrégation raciale (*or* religieuse) est en vigueur

**segregation** *n* ségrégation *f* (from de)

**seize** *vtr* (a) saisir; to ~ hold of se saisir de ⟨person⟩; s'emparer de ⟨object⟩ (b) s'emparer de ⟨territory, prisoner, power⟩; prendre ⟨control⟩ ■ **seize up** ⟨engine⟩ se gripper; ⟨limb⟩ se bloquer

**seizure** *n* (a) (of territory, power) prise *f*; (of arms, drugs, property) saisie *f* (b) (Med) attaque *f*

**seldom** *adv* rarement

**select** [1] *adj* ⟨group⟩ privilégié/-e; ⟨hotel⟩ chic, sélect/-e; ⟨area⟩ chic, cossu/-e [2] *vtr* sélectionner (from, from among parmi)

**selection** *n* sélection *f*

**selective** *adj* ⟨memory, recruitment⟩ sélectif/-ive; ⟨admission, education⟩ basé/-e sur la sélection; ⟨account⟩ tendancieux/-ieuse

**self** *n* moi *m*; he's back to his old ~ again il est redevenu lui-même

**self-addressed envelope, SAE** *n* enveloppe *f* à mon/votre etc adresse

**self-adhesive** *adj* autocollant/-e

**self-assembly** *adj* en kit

**self-assured** *adj* plein/-e d'assurance

**self-catering** *adj* ⟨flat⟩ avec cuisine; ~ holiday vacances *fpl* en location

**self-centred** (GB), **self-centered** (US) *adj* égocentrique

**self-confessed** *adj* avoué/-e

**self-confidence** *n* assurance *f*

**self-confident** *adj* ⟨person⟩ sûr/-e de soi; ⟨attitude⟩ plein/-e d'assurance

**self-conscious** *adj* (a) (shy) timide; to be ~ about sth/about doing être gêné/-e par qch/de faire (b) ⟨style⟩ conscient/-e

**self-contained** *adj* ⟨flat⟩ indépendant/-e

**self-control** *n* sang-froid *m*

**self-defence** (GB), **self-defense** (US)
*n* (gen) autodéfense *f*; (Law) légitime défense *f*

**self-destructive** *adj*
autodestructeur/-trice

**self-determination** *n*
autodétermination *f*

**self-disciplined** *adj* autodiscipliné/-e

**self-effacing** *adj* effacé/-e

**self-employed** *adj* indépendant/-e; **to be**
~ travailler à son compte

**self-esteem** *n* amour-propre *m*

**self-evident** *adj* évident/-e

**self-explanatory** *adj* explicite

**self-expression** *n* expression *f* de soi/de
lui-même etc

**self-governing** *adj* autonome

**self-image** *n* image *f* de soi-même/de
lui-même etc

**self-important** *adj* suffisant/-e

**self-induced** *adj* auto-infligé/-e

**self-indulgent** *adj* complaisant/-e

**self-interested** *adj* intéressé/-e

**selfish** *adj* égoïste (**to do** de faire)

**selfishness** *n* égoïsme *m*

**selfless** *adj* ⟨*person*⟩ dévoué/-e; ⟨*devotion*⟩
désintéressé/-e

**self-pity** *n* apitoiement *m* sur soi-même

**self-portrait** *n* autoportrait *m*

**self-raising flour** (GB), **self-rising
flour** (US) *n* farine *f* à gâteau

**self-reliant** *adj* autosuffisant/-e

**self-respect** *n* respect *m* de soi

**self-respecting** *adj* ⟨*teacher, journalist,
comedian*⟩ qui se respecte

**self-righteous** *adj* satisfait/-e de
soi-même

**self-rule** *n* autonomie *f*

**self-sacrifice** *n* abnégation *f*

**self-satisfied** *adj* satisfait/-e de
soi-même

**self-service** ⓵ *n* libre-service *m*
⓶ *adj* ⟨*cafeteria*⟩ en libre-service

**self-sufficient** *adj* autosuffisant/-e

**self-taught** *adj* autodidacte

**sell** ⓵ *vtr* (a) vendre; **to** ~ **sth to sb, to** ~
**sb sth** vendre qch à qn; **to** ~ **sth for £5**
vendre qch 5 livres sterling
(b) (promote sale of) faire vendre
(c) faire accepter ⟨*idea, image, policy, party*⟩
⓶ *vi* (a) ⟨*person, shop, dealer*⟩ vendre (**to sb**
à qn)
(b) ⟨*goods, product, house, book*⟩ se vendre
■ **sell off:** ~ **[sth] off,** ~ **off [sth]** liquider;
(in sale) solder
■ **sell out** (a) ⟨*merchandise*⟩ se vendre;
**we've sold out of tickets** tous les billets ont
été vendus; **we've sold out** nous avons tout
vendu; **the play has sold out** la pièce affiche
complet
(b) (colloq) (betray one's principles) retourner sa
veste (colloq)

**sell-by date** *n* date *f* limite de vente

**seller's market** *n* marché *m* à la hausse

**selling** ⓵ *n* vente *f*
⓶ *adj* ⟨*price*⟩ de vente

**Sellotape**® ⓵ *n* scotch® *m*
⓶ **sellotape** *vtr* scotcher

**sellout** ⓵ *n* **the show was a** ~ le spectacle
affichait complet
⓶ *adj* ⟨*performance*⟩ à guichets fermés

**semen** *n* sperme *m*

**semester** *n* (US) semestre *m*

**semiautomatic** *n, adj* semi-automatique
(*m*)

**semibreve** *n* (GB) (Mus) ronde *f*

**semicircle** *n* demi-cercle *m*

**semicolon** *n* point-virgule *m*

**semiconscious** *adj* à peine conscient/-e

**semidarkness** *n* pénombre *f*, demi-jour
*m*

**semi-detached (house)** *n* maison *f*
jumelée

**semifinal** *n* demi-finale *f*

**semifinalist** *n* demi-finaliste *mf*

**seminar** *n* séminaire *m* (**on** sur)

**semi-skimmed** *adj* ⟨*milk*⟩
demi-écrémé/-e

**senate** *n* sénat *m*

**senator** *n* sénateur *m* (**for** de)

**send** *vtr* (a) envoyer; **to** ~ **sth to sb, to** ~
**sb sth** envoyer qch à qn; **to** ~ **sb home** (from
school, work) renvoyer qn chez lui/elle; **to** ~
**sb to prison** mettre qn en prison; ~ **her my
love!** embrasse-la de ma part; ~ **them my
regards** transmettez-leur mes amitiés
(b) **to** ~ **shivers down sb's spine** donner
froid dans le dos à qn; **to** ~ **sb to sleep**
endormir qn; **it sent him into fits of laughter**
ça l'a fait éclater de rire
IDIOMS **to** ~ **sb packing** (colloq) envoyer
balader qn (colloq)
■ **send away:** ¶ ~ **away for [sth]**
commander [qch] par correspondance; ¶ ~
**[sb/sth] away** faire partir; **to** ~ **an appliance
away to be mended** envoyer un appareil
chez le fabricant pour le faire réparer
■ **send for** appeler ⟨*doctor, plumber*⟩;
demander ⟨*reinforcements*⟩
■ **send in** envoyer ⟨*letter, form, troops*⟩;
faire entrer ⟨*visitor*⟩; **to** ~ **in one's
application** poser sa candidature
■ **send off:** ¶ ~ **off for [sth]** commander
[qch] par correspondance; ¶ ~ **[sth] off**
envoyer, expédier ⟨*letter*⟩; ¶ ~ **[sb] off** (Sport)
expulser
■ **send on** expédier [qch] à l'avance
⟨*baggage*⟩; faire suivre ⟨*letter, parcel*⟩
■ **send out** (a) émettre ⟨*light, heat*⟩
(b) faire sortir ⟨*pupil*⟩
■ **send up** (GB) (colloq) (parody) parodier

**sender** *n* expéditeur/-trice *m/f*

**send-off** *n* adieux *mpl*

**send-up** *n* (GB) (colloq) parodie *f*

**senile** *adj* sénile

**senile dementia** *n* démence *f* sénile

**senior** 1 n (a) (gen) aîné/-e m/f; **to be sb's**
~ être plus âgé/-e que qn
(b) (GB) (Sch) élève mf dans les grandes
classes; (US) (Sch) élève mf de terminale
2 adj (a) (older) ⟨person⟩ plus âgé/-e
(b) ⟨civil servant⟩ haut/-e (before n);
⟨partner⟩ principal/-e; ⟨officer, job, post⟩
supérieur/-e

**senior citizen** n personne f du troisième
âge

**senior high school** n (US Sch) ≈ lycée
m

**seniority** n (in years) âge m; (in rank) statut
m supérieur; (in years of service) ancienneté f

**senior management** n direction f

**senior school** n lycée m

**sensation** n sensation f; **to cause** or **create
a** ~ faire sensation

**sensational** adj sensationnel/-elle

**sensationalist** adj ⟨headline, story,
writer⟩ à sensation

**sensationalize** vtr faire un reportage à
sensation sur ⟨event, story⟩

**sense** 1 n (a) (faculty, ability) sens m; **a** ~ **of
humour/direction** le sens de l'humour/de
l'orientation; ~ **of hearing** ouïe f; ~ **of sight**
vue f; ~ **of smell** odorat m; ~ **of taste** goût
m; ~ **of touch** toucher m; **to lose all** ~ **of
time** perdre toute notion du temps
(b) (feeling) **a** ~ **of identity** un sentiment
d'identité; **a** ~ **of purpose** le sentiment
d'avoir un but
(c) (common) ~ bon sens m; **to have the** ~
**to do** avoir le bon sens de faire
(d) (meaning) sens m; (reason) **there's no** ~ **in
doing** cela ne sert à rien de faire; **to make** ~
**of sth** comprendre qch; **I can't make** ~ **of
this article** je ne comprends rien à cet
article; **to make** ~ ⟨sentence, film⟩ avoir un
sens
2 **senses** n pl **to come to one's senses**
revenir à la raison
3 vtr (a) deviner (that que); **to** ~ **danger**
sentir un danger
(b) ⟨machine⟩ détecter
**IDIOMS to see** ~ entendre raison; **to talk** ~
dire des choses sensées

**senseless** adj (a) ⟨violence⟩ gratuit/-e;
⟨discussion⟩ absurde; ⟨act, waste⟩ insensé/-e
(b) **to knock sb** ~ faire perdre connaissance
à qn

**sensible** adj ⟨person, attitude⟩ raisonnable;
⟨decision, solution⟩ judicieux/-ieuse;
⟨garment⟩ pratique; ⟨diet⟩ intelligent/-e

**sensitive** adj (a) (gen) sensible (**to** à)
(b) ⟨person⟩ (easily hurt) sensible, susceptible
(**to** à)
(c) ⟨situation⟩ délicat/-e; ⟨issue⟩ difficile;
⟨information⟩ confidentiel/-ielle

**sensitivity** n sensibilité f (**to** à)

**sensor** n détecteur m

**sensual** adj sensuel/-elle

**sentence** 1 n (a) (Law) peine f; **to serve a**
~ purger une peine
(b) (in grammar) phrase f

2 vtr condamner (**to** à; **to do** à faire; **for**
pour)

**sentiment** n (a) (feeling) sentiment m (**for**
pour; **towards** envers)
(b) (opinion) opinion f

**sentimental** adj sentimental/-e

**sentry** n sentinelle f

**separate** 1 adj (a) (independent, apart)
⟨piece, section⟩ à part; **she has a** ~ **room** elle
a une chambre à part; **the flat is** ~ **from the
rest of the house** l'appartement est
indépendant du reste de la maison; **keep the
knives** ~ rangez les couteaux séparément;
**keep the knives** ~ **from the forks** séparez les
couteaux des fourchettes
(b) (different) ⟨sections, problems⟩ différent/-e;
⟨organizations, agreements⟩ distinct/-e; **they
have** ~ **rooms** ils ont chacun leur chambre;
**they asked for** ~ **bills** (in restaurant) ils ont
demandé chacun leur addition
2 vtr (a) séparer (**from** de)
(b) (sort out) répartir ⟨people⟩; trier ⟨objects,
produce⟩
3 vi se séparer (**from** de)

**separately** adv séparément

**separates** n pl (garments) coordonnés mpl

**separation** n séparation f (**from** de)

**separatist** n, adj séparatiste (mf)

**September** n septembre m

**septic** adj infecté/-e; **to go** or **turn** ~
s'infecter

**septic tank** n fosse f septique

**sequel** n suite f (**to** à)

**sequence** n (a) (series) série f
(b) (order) ordre m; **in** ~ dans l'ordre
(c) (in film) séquence f

**Serbia** pr n Serbie f

**Serb, Serbian** 1 n Serbe mf
2 adj serbe

**serene** adj serein/-e

**sergeant** n (a) (GB) (Mil) sergent m
(b) (US) (Mil) caporal-chef m
(c) (in police) ≈ brigadier m

**serial** n feuilleton m; **TV** ~ feuilleton
télévisé

**serialize** vtr adapter [qch] en feuilleton

**serial killer** n tueur m en série

**serial number** n numéro m de série

**series** n série f; **a drama** ~ une série de
fiction

**serious** adj ⟨person, expression, discussion,
offer⟩ sérieux/-ieuse; ⟨accident, crime, crisis,
problem⟩ grave; ⟨literature, actor⟩ de qualité;
⟨attempt, concern⟩ réel/réelle; **to be** ~ **about
sth** prendre qch au sérieux; **to be** ~ **about
doing** avoir vraiment l'intention de faire

**seriously** adv (a) ⟨speak, think⟩
sérieusement; **to take sb/sth** ~ prendre
qn/qch au sérieux
(b) ⟨ill, injured⟩ gravement; ⟨underestimate⟩
vraiment

**seriousness** n (a) (of person, film, study)
sérieux m; (of tone, occasion, reply) gravité f; **in
all** ~ sérieusement

**(b)** (of illness, problem, situation) gravité *f*

**sermon** *n* sermon *m*

**serrated** *adj* dentelé/-e; **~ knife** couteau-scie *m*

**serum** *n* sérum *m*

**servant** *n* domestique *mf*

**serve** **1** *n* (Sport) service *m*

**2** *vtr* **(a)** servir ⟨*country, cause, public*⟩; travailler au service de ⟨*employer, family*⟩ **(b)** servir ⟨*customer, guest, meal, dish*⟩; **to ~ sb with sth** servir qch à qn **(c)** (provide facility) ⟨*power station, reservoir*⟩ alimenter; ⟨*public transport, library, hospital*⟩ desservir **(d)** (satisfy) servir ⟨*interests*⟩; satisfaire ⟨*needs*⟩ **(e) to ~ a purpose** être utile; **to ~ the or sb's purpose** faire l'affaire **(f)** purger ⟨*prison sentence*⟩ **(g)** (Law) délivrer ⟨*injunction*⟩ (**on sb** à qn); **to ~ a summons on sb** citer qn à comparaître **(h)** (Sport) servir

**3** *vi* **(a)** (in shop) servir; (at table) faire le service **(b) to ~ on** être membre de ⟨*committee, jury*⟩ **(c) to ~ as sth** servir de qch **(d)** (Mil) servir (**as** comme; **under** sous) **(e)** (Sport) servir (**for** pour); **Bruno to ~** au service, Bruno

IDIOMS **it ~s you right!** ça t'apprendra!

**server** *n* (Sport, Comput) serveur *m*

**service** **1** *n* **(a)** (gen) service *m*; (accident and) **emergency ~** service des urgences; **'out of ~'** (on machine) 'en panne' **(b)** (overhaul) révision *f* **(c)** (ceremony) office *m*; **Sunday ~** office du dimanche; **marriage ~** cérémonie *f* nuptiale

**2 services** *n pl* **(a)** (also **~ area**) aire *m* de services **(b)** (Mil) **the Services** les armées *f pl*

**3** *vtr* faire la révision de ⟨*vehicle*⟩; entretenir ⟨*machine, boiler*⟩; **to have one's car ~d** faire réviser sa voiture

**service centre** (GB), **service center** (US) *n* centre *m* de service après-vente

**service charge** *n* **(a)** (in restaurant) service *m*; **what is the ~?** le service est de combien? **(b)** (in banking) frais *mpl* de gestion de compte

**service engineer** *n* technicien *m* de maintenance

**serviceman** *n* militaire *m*

**service provider** *n* fournisseur *m* d'accès

**service station** *n* station-service *f*

**servicewoman** *n* femme *f* soldat

**serving** *n* portion *f*

**serving dish** *n* plat *m* (de service)

**serving spoon** *n* cuillère *f* de service

**session** *n* **(a)** (gen) séance *f* **(b)** (of parliament) session *f*

**(c)** (US) (Sch) (term) trimestre *m*; (period of lessons) cours *mpl*

**set** **1** *n* **(a)** (of keys, tools) jeu *m*; (of golf clubs, chairs) série *f*; (of cutlery) service *m*; (of rules, instructions, tests) série *f*; **a new ~ of clothes** des vêtements neufs; **they're sold in ~s of 10** ils sont vendus par lots de 10; **a ~ of fingerprints** des empreintes digitales; **a ~ of traffic lights** des feux *mpl* (de signalisation); **a chess ~** un jeu d'échecs; **a ~ of false teeth** un dentier **(b)** (Sport) (in tennis) set *m* **(c)** TV *or* **television ~** poste *m* de télévision **(d)** (scenery) (for play) décor *m*; (for film) plateau *m* **(e)** (GB) (Sch) groupe *m* **(f)** (hair-do) mise *f* en plis

**2** *adj* **(a)** ⟨*pattern, procedure, rule, task*⟩ bien déterminé/-e; ⟨*time, price*⟩ fixe; ⟨*menu*⟩ à prix fixe; **~ phrase** expression *f* consacrée; **to be ~ in one's ways** avoir ses habitudes **(b)** ⟨*expression, smile*⟩ figé/-e **(c)** (Sch, Univ) ⟨*text*⟩ au programme **(d)** (ready) prêt/-e (**for** pour; **to do** à faire) **(e) to be** (**dead**) **~ against sth/doing** être tout à fait contre qch/l'idée de faire; **to be ~ on doing** tenir absolument à faire **(f)** ⟨*jam, jelly, honey*⟩ épais/épaisse; ⟨*cement*⟩ dur/-e; ⟨*yoghurt*⟩ ferme

**3** *vtr* **(a)** (place) placer ⟨*object*⟩ (**on** sur); monter ⟨*gem*⟩ (**in** dans); **a house ~ among the trees** une maison située au milieu des arbres; **to ~ the record straight** mettre les choses au point; **his eyes are ~ very close together** ses yeux sont très rapprochés **(b)** mettre ⟨*table*⟩; tendre ⟨*trap*⟩ **(c)** fixer ⟨*date, deadline, price, target*⟩; lancer ⟨*fashion, trend*⟩; donner ⟨*tone*⟩; établir ⟨*precedent, record*⟩; **to ~ a good/bad example to sb** montrer le bon/mauvais exemple à qn; **to ~ one's sights on** viser **(d)** mettre ⟨qch⟩ à l'heure ⟨*clock*⟩; mettre ⟨*alarm clock, burglar alarm*⟩ **(e)** (start) **to ~ sth going** mettre qch en marche ⟨*machine*⟩; **to ~ sb laughing/thinking** faire rire/réfléchir qn **(f)** donner ⟨*homework, essay*⟩; **to ~ an exam** préparer les sujets d'examen **(g)** (in fiction, film) situer; **the film is ~ in Munich** le film se passe à Munich **(h) to ~ sth to music** mettre qch en musique **(i)** (Med) immobiliser ⟨*broken bone*⟩ **(j) to have one's hair ~** se faire faire une mise en plis

**4** *vi* **(a)** ⟨*sun*⟩ se coucher **(b)** ⟨*jam, concrete*⟩ prendre; ⟨*glue*⟩ sécher **(c)** (Med) ⟨*fracture*⟩ se ressouder

■ **set about** se mettre à ⟨*work*⟩; **to ~ about** (**the job** *or* **task of**) **doing** commencer à faire

■ **set apart** distinguer (**from** de)

■ **set aside** réserver ⟨*area, room, time*⟩ (**for** pour); mettre ⟨qch⟩ de côté ⟨*money, stock*⟩

■ **set back**: ¶ **~ back [sth]**, **~ [sth] back** (delay) retarder; ¶ **~ [sb] back** (colloq) coûter les yeux de la tête à ⟨colloq⟩

■ **set down**: ~ **down** [sth], ~ **[sth] down (a)**
(establish) fixer ⟨*conditions*⟩
**(b)** (record) enregistrer ⟨*fact*⟩
■ **set in** ⟨*infection*⟩ se déclarer; ⟨*depression*⟩
s'installer
■ **set off**: ¶ ~ **off** partir (for pour); **to** ~ **off**
**on a journey** partir en voyage
¶ ~ **[sth] off (a)** faire partir ⟨*firework*⟩; faire
exploser ⟨*bomb*⟩; déclencher ⟨*riot, panic,
alarm*⟩
**(b)** (enhance) mettre [qch] en valeur
⟨*garment*⟩
**(c) to** ~ **sth off against profits/debts** déduire
qch des bénéfices/des dettes; ¶ ~ **[sb] off**
faire pleurer ⟨*baby*⟩; **she laughed and that** ~
**me off** elle a ri et ça m'a fait rire à mon tour
■ **set on**: ¶ ~ **on** [sb] attaquer qn; ¶ ~ **[sth]
on** sb lâcher [qch] contre qn ⟨*dog*⟩
■ **set out**: ¶ ~ **out** se mettre en route (for
pour; **to do** pour faire); **to** ~ **out to do**
⟨*person*⟩ entreprendre de faire
¶ ~ **[sth] out (a)** disposer ⟨*goods, chairs,
food*⟩; préparer ⟨*board game*⟩
**(b)** présenter ⟨*ideas, proposals*⟩; formuler
⟨*objections, terms*⟩
■ **set up**: ¶ **to** ~ **up on one's own** s'établir à
son compte; **to** ~ **up in business** monter une
affaire
¶ ~ **[sth] up (a)** monter ⟨*stand, stall*⟩;
assembler ⟨*equipment, easel*⟩; ériger
⟨*roadblock*⟩; **to** ~ **up home** s'installer
**(b)** préparer ⟨*experiment*⟩; (Sport) préparer
⟨*goal, try*⟩
**(c)** créer ⟨*business, company*⟩; implanter
⟨*factory*⟩; former ⟨*support group, charity*⟩;
constituer ⟨*committee*⟩
**(d)** organiser ⟨*meeting*⟩; mettre [qch] en
place ⟨*procedures*⟩; ¶ ~ **[sb] up (a) she** ~ **her
son up (in business) as a gardener** elle a
aidé son fils à s'installer comme jardinier
**(b) that deal has** ~ **her up for life** grâce à ce
contrat elle n'aura plus à se soucier de rien
**(c)** (GB) (colloq) ⟨*police*⟩ tendre un piège à
⟨*criminal*⟩; ⟨*friend*⟩ monter un coup contre
⟨*person*⟩

**setback** *n* revers *m* (for pour)

**settee** *n* canapé *m*

**setting** *n* **(a)** (location) cadre *m*
**(b)** (in jewellery) monture *f*
**(c)** ( position on dial) position *f* (de réglage)

**setting-up** *n* (of scheme, business) création *f*;
(of factory) implantation *f*

**settle** ⟨**1**⟩ *vtr* **(a)** installer ⟨*person, animal*⟩
**(b)** calmer ⟨*stomach, nerves*⟩
**(c)** régler ⟨*matter, business, dispute*⟩; mettre
fin à ⟨*conflict, strike*⟩; régler, résoudre
⟨*problem*⟩; décider ⟨*match*⟩; **that's** ~**d** voilà
qui est réglé
**(d)** fixer ⟨*arrangements, price*⟩
**(e) to** ~ **one's affairs** mettre de l'ordre dans
ses affaires
**(f)** régler ⟨*bill, debt, claim*⟩
⟨**2**⟩ *vi* **(a)** ⟨*dust*⟩ se déposer; ⟨*bird, insect*⟩ se
poser
**(b)** (in new home) s'installer
**(c)** ⟨*contents, ground*⟩ se tasser

**(d)** ⟨*weather*⟩ se mettre au beau fixe
**(e)** (Law) régler; **to** ~ **out of court** parvenir à
un règlement à l'amiable
■ **settle down (a)** (get comfortable) s'installer
(on sur; in dans)
**(b)** (calm down) ⟨*person*⟩ se calmer
**(c)** (marry) se ranger
■ **settle for**: ~ **for sth** se contenter de qch
■ **settle in (a)** (move in) s'installer
**(b)** (become acclimatized) s'adapter
■ **settle up** (pay) payer

**settlement** *n* **(a)** (agreement) accord *m*
**(b)** (Law) règlement *m*
**(c)** (dwellings) village *m*; (colonial) territoire *m*

**set-top box** *n* décodeur *m*

**seven** *n, pron, det* sept (*m*) *inv*

**seventeen** *n, pron, det* dix-sept (*m*) *inv*

**seventeenth** ⟨**1**⟩ *n* **(a)** (in order)
dix-septième *mf*
**(b)** (of month) dix-sept *m inv*
**(c)** (fraction) dix-septième *m*
⟨**2**⟩ *adj, adv* dix-septième

**seventh** ⟨**1**⟩ *n* **(a)** (in order) septième *mf*
**(b)** (of month) sept *m inv*
**(c)** (fraction) septième *m*
⟨**2**⟩ *adj, adv* septième

**seventies** *n pl* **(a)** (era) **the** ~ les années
*fpl* soixante-dix
**(b)** (age) **to be in one's** ~ avoir plus de
soixante-dix ans

**seventieth** *n, adj, adv* soixante-dixième
(*mf*)

**seventy** *n, pron, det* soixante-dix (*m*) *inv*

**sever** *vtr* **(a)** sectionner ⟨*limb, artery*⟩;
couper ⟨*rope, branch*⟩
**(b)** rompre ⟨*link, relations*⟩; couper
⟨*communications*⟩

**several** ⟨**1**⟩ *quantif* ~ **of you/us** plusieurs
d'entre vous/d'entre nous
⟨**2**⟩ *det* plusieurs; ~ **books** plusieurs livres

**severe** *adj* **(a)** ⟨*problem, damage, shortage,
injury, depression, shock*⟩ grave; ⟨*weather,
cold, winter*⟩ rigoureux/-euse
**(b)** (harsh) sévère (with sb avec qn)
**(c)** ⟨*haircut, clothes*⟩ austère

**severely** *adv* ⟨*damage*⟩ sévèrement; ⟨*affect,
shock*⟩ durement; ⟨*disabled*⟩ gravement;
⟨*injured*⟩ grièvement; ⟨*beat*⟩ violemment

**severity** *n* (of problem, illness) gravité *f*; (of
punishment, treatment) sévérité *f*; (of climate)
rigueur *f*

**sew** ⟨**1**⟩ *vtr* coudre
⟨**2**⟩ *vi* coudre, faire de la couture
■ **sew up** recoudre ⟨*hole, tear*⟩; faire ⟨*seam*⟩;
(re)coudre ⟨*wound*⟩

**sewage** *n* eaux *fpl* usées

**sewer** *n* égout *m*

**sewing** *n* (activity) couture *f*; ( piece of work)
ouvrage *m*

**sewing machine** *n* machine *f* à coudre

**sex** ⟨**1**⟩ *n* **(a)** (gender) sexe *m*; **the opposite** ~
le sexe opposé
**(b)** (intercourse) (one act) rapport *m* sexuel;
(repeated) rapports *mpl* sexuels

**2** *adj* sexuel/-elle

**sex change** *n* to have a ∼ changer de sexe

**sex discrimination** *n* discrimination *f* sexuelle

**sex education** *n* éducation *f* sexuelle

**sexism** *n* sexisme *m*

**sexist** *n, adj* sexiste (*mf*)

**sex object** *n* objet *m* érotique

**sex offender** *n* délinquant/-e *m/f* sexuel/-elle

**sexual** *adj* sexuel/-elle

**sexual abuse** *n* violence *f* sexuelle

**sexual harassment** *n* harcèlement *m* sexuel

**sexuality** *n* sexualité *f*

**sexually transmitted disease, STD** *n* maladie *f* sexuellement transmissible, MST *f*

**sexy** *adj* (colloq) (*person, clothing*) sexy *inv* (colloq); (*book*) érotique

**shabby** *adj* (*person*) habillé/-e de façon miteuse; (*room, furnishings, clothing*) miteux/-euse; (*treatment*) mesquin/-e

**shack** *n* cabane *f*

**shade** **1** *n* (a) (shadow) ombre *f*; in the ∼ à l'ombre (of de)
(b) (of colour) ton *m*
(c) (*also* **lamp** ∼) abat-jour *m inv*
(d) (US) (*also* **window** ∼) store *m*
**2** *vtr* donner de l'ombre à; to ∼ one's eyes (with one's hand) s'abriter les yeux de la main
IDIOMS to put sb in the ∼ éclipser qn; to put sth in the ∼ surpasser *or* surclasser qch

**shadow** **1** *n* ombre *f*; to have ∼s under one's eyes avoir les yeux cernés
**2** *vtr* filer (*person*)

**shadow cabinet** *n* (GB) cabinet *m* fantôme

**shadowy** *adj* (dark) sombre; (indistinct) (*outline*) flou/-e; (*form*) indistinct/-e

**shady** *adj* (a) (*place*) ombragé/-e
(b) (*deal, businessman*) véreux/-euse

**shaft** *n* (a) (of tool) manche *m*; (of arrow) tige *f*; (in machine) axe *m*
(b) (passage, vent) puits *m*
(c) ∼ of light rai *m*; ∼ of lightning éclair *m*

**shaggy** *adj* (*hair, beard, eyebrows*) en broussailles; (*animal*) poilu/-e

**shake** **1** *n* (a) to give sb/sth a ∼ secouer qn/qch
(b) (*also* **milk-**∼) milk-shake *m*
**2** *vtr* (a) (gen) secouer; to ∼ one's head (in dismay) hocher la tête; (to say no) faire non de la tête; to ∼ hands with sb, to ∼ sb's hand serrer la main de qn, donner une poignée de main à qn
(b) ébranler (*confidence, faith, resolve*); (*event, disaster*) secouer (*person*)
**3** *vi* (a) trembler; to ∼ with trembler de (*fear, cold, emotion*); se tordre de (*laughter*)
(b) (shake hands) 'let's ∼ on it!' 'serrons-nous la main!'

■ **shake off** se débarrasser de (*cold, depression, habit, person*); se défaire de (*feeling*)

■ **shake up** (a) agiter (*bottle, mixture*)
(b) (*experience, news*) secouer (*person*)

**shaken** *adj* (shocked) choqué/-e

**shake-up** *n* réorganisation *f*; (Pol) remaniement *m*

**shaky** *adj* (a) (*chair, ladder*) branlant/-e; I feel a bit ∼ je me sens un peu flageolant
(b) (*relationship, position*) instable; (*evidence, argument*) peu solide; (*knowledge, memory*) peu sûr/-e; (*regime*) chancelant/-e; my French is a bit ∼ mon français est un peu hésitant

**shall** *modal aux* (a) (in future tense) I ∼ *or* I'll see you tomorrow je vous verrai demain; we ∼ not *or* shan't have a reply before Friday nous n'aurons pas de réponse avant vendredi
(b) (in suggestions) ∼ I set the table? est-ce que je mets la table?; ∼ we go to the cinema tonight? et si on allait au cinéma ce soir?; let's buy some peaches, ∼ we? et si on achetait des pêches?

**shallot** *n* (a) (GB) échalote *f*
(b) (US) cive *f*

**shallow** *adj* (*container, water, grave*) peu profond/-e; (*breathing, character, response*) superficiel/-ielle

**shallows** *n pl* bas-fonds *mpl*

**sham** **1** *n* (a) (person) imposteur *m*
(b) it's (all) a ∼ c'est de la comédie
**2** *adj* (*event*) prétendu/-e (*before n*); (*object, building, idea*) factice; (*activity, emotion*) feint/-e
**3** *vi* faire semblant

**shambles** *n* (colloq) pagaille *f* (colloq)

**shame** **1** *n* (a) (gen) honte *f*
(b) it's a (real) shame c'est (vraiment) dommage; it was a ∼ (that) she lost c'est dommage qu'elle ait perdu
**2** *vtr* (a) (embarrass) faire honte à
(b) (disgrace) déshonorer (**by doing** en faisant)

**shameful** *adj* honteux/-euse

**shameless** *adj* (*person*) éhonté/-e; (*attitude*) effronté/-e; (*negligence*) scandaleux/-euse

**shampoo** **1** *n* shampooing *m*
**2** *vtr* faire un shampooing à; to ∼ one's hair se faire un shampooing

**shamrock** *n* trèfle *m*

**shandy, shandygaff** (US) *n* panaché *m*

**shantytown** *n* bidonville *m*

**shape** **1** *n* forme *f*; a square ∼ une forme carrée; what ∼ is the room? quelle forme a la pièce?; to take ∼ prendre forme; to be in/out of ∼ (*person*) être/ne pas être en forme; to get in ∼ se mettre en forme; to knock sth into ∼ mettre qch au point (*project, idea, essay*)
**2** *vtr* (a) modeler (*clay*); sculpter (*wood*)
(b) (*person, event*) déterminer (*future, idea*); modeler (*character*)

**S**

■ **shape up** (a) (develop) ⟨person⟩ s'en sortir
(b) (meet expectations) être à la hauteur

**-shaped** *combining form* star-/V-∼ en forme d'étoile/de V

**shapeless** *adj* sans forme, informe

**shapely** *adj* ⟨woman⟩ bien fait/-e; ⟨ankle⟩ fin/-e; ⟨leg⟩ bien galbé/-e

**share** ① *n* (a) part *f* (of de); **to pay one's (fair)** ∼ payer sa part
(b) (in stock market) action *f*
② *vtr* partager (**with** avec); **we ∼ an interest in animals** nous aimons tous les deux les animaux
③ *vi* **to ∼ in** prendre part à

■ **share out** (amongst selves) partager ⟨food⟩; (amongst others) répartir ⟨food⟩ (**among, between** entre)

**shared** *adj* ⟨house, interest⟩ partagé/-e; ⟨facilities⟩ commun/-e

**shareholder** *n* actionnaire *mf*

**share option scheme** *n* plan *m* de participation par achat d'actions

**shareware** *n* shareware *m*, logiciel *m* contributif

**shark** *n* requin *m*

**sharp** ① *adj* (a) ⟨razor⟩ tranchant/-e; ⟨edge⟩ coupant/-e; ⟨blade, scissors, knife⟩ bien aiguisé/-e
(b) ⟨tooth, fingernail, end, needle⟩ pointu/-e; ⟨pencil⟩ bien taillé/-e; ⟨features⟩ anguleux/-euse
(c) ⟨angle⟩ aigu/aiguë; ⟨bend⟩ brusque; ⟨drop, incline⟩ fort/-e; ⟨fall, rise⟩ brusque, brutal/-e
(d) ⟨taste, smell⟩ âcre; ⟨fruit⟩ acide
(e) ⟨pain, cold⟩ vif/vive; ⟨cry⟩ aigu/aiguë; ⟨blow⟩ sévère; ⟨frost⟩ intense
(f) ⟨tongue⟩ acéré/-e; ⟨tone⟩ acerbe
(g) ⟨person, mind⟩ vif/vive; ⟨eyesight⟩ perçant/-e
(h) ⟨businessman⟩ malin/-igne; ∼ **operator** filou *m*
(i) ⟨image⟩ net/nette; ⟨contrast⟩ prononcé/-e
(j) (Mus) ⟨note⟩ dièse *inv*; (too high) aigu/aiguë
② *adv* (a) ⟨stop⟩ net; **to turn ∼ left** tourner brusquement vers la gauche
(b) (colloq) **at 9 o'clock ∼** à neuf heures pile (colloq)
(c) (Mus) ⟨sing, play⟩ trop haut

**sharpen** *vtr* aiguiser, affûter ⟨blade, scissors⟩; tailler ⟨pencil⟩

**sharpener** *n* taille-crayon *m*

**sharply** *adv* (a) ⟨turn, rise, fall⟩ brusquement, brutalement
(b) ⟨speak⟩ d'un ton brusque

**shatter** ① *vtr* fracasser ⟨window, glass⟩; rompre ⟨peace, silence⟩; briser ⟨hope⟩; démolir ⟨nerves⟩
② *vi* ⟨window, glass⟩ voler en éclats

**shattered** *adj* (a) ⟨dream⟩ brisé/-e; ⟨life, confidence⟩ anéanti/-e
(b) ⟨person⟩ (devastated) effondré/-e; (tired) (colloq) crevé/-e (colloq), épuisé/-e

**shave** ① *n* **to have a ∼** se raser

② *vtr* ⟨barber⟩ raser ⟨person⟩; **to ∼ one's beard off** se raser la barbe; **to ∼ one's legs** se raser les jambes
③ *vi* se raser
IDIOMS **that was a close ∼!** je l'ai/il l'a etc échappé belle!

**shaver** *n* (also **electric ∼**) rasoir *m* électrique

**shaving** ① *n* (a) (action) rasage *m*
(b) ∼**s** (of wood, metal) copeaux *mpl*
② *adj* ⟨cream, foam⟩ à raser

**shaving brush** *n* blaireau *m*

**shaving mirror** *n* petit miroir *m*

**shawl** *n* châle *m*

**she** *pron* elle; ∼**'s not at home** elle n'est pas chez elle; **here ∼ is** la voici; **there ∼ is** la voilà; ∼**'s a beautiful woman** c'est une belle femme

**sheaf** *n* (of corn, flowers) gerbe *f*; (of papers) liasse *f*

**shear** *vtr* tondre ⟨grass, sheep⟩

**shears** *n pl* (a) (for garden) cisaille *f*
(b) (for sheep) tondeuse *f*

**shed** ① *n* (in garden) remise *f*, abri *m*; (at factory site, port) hangar *m*
② *vtr* (a) verser ⟨tears⟩; perdre ⟨leaves, weight, antlers⟩; ⟨lorry⟩ déverser ⟨load⟩; verser ⟨blood⟩; **to ∼ skin** muer
(b) répandre ⟨light, happiness⟩

**sheep** *n* mouton *m*; (ewe) brebis *f*; **black ∼** brebis *f* galeuse

**sheep dog** *n* chien *m* de berger

**sheepish** *adj* penaud/-e

**sheepskin** *n* peau *f* de mouton

**sheer** *adj* (a) ⟨boredom, hypocrisy, stupidity⟩ pur/-e (*before n*)
(b) ⟨cliff⟩ à pic
(c) ⟨fabric⟩ léger/-ère, fin/-e; ⟨stockings⟩ extra-fin/-e

**sheet** *n* (a) (of paper, stamps) feuille *f*; (of metal, glass) plaque *f*
(b) (for bed) drap *m*; **dust ∼** housse *f*
(c) **fact ∼** bulletin *m* d'informations
(d) (of ice) couche *f*; (of flame) rideau *m*

**sheet lightning** *n* éclair *m* en nappe

**sheet metal** *n* tôle *f*

**sheik** *n* cheik *m*

**shelf** *n* (a) étagère *f*; (in oven) plaque *f*; (in shop, fridge) rayon *m*; (**a set of**) **shelves** une étagère
(b) (in rock, ice) corniche *f*

**shelf-life** *n* (of product) durée *f* de conservation; (of technology, pop music) durée *f* de vie

**shell** ① *n* (a) (of egg, nut, snail) coquille *f*; (of crab, tortoise, shrimp) carapace *f*; **sea ∼** coquillage *m*; **to come out of one's ∼** sortir de sa coquille
(b) (bomb) obus *m*; (cartridge) cartouche *f*
(c) (of building) carcasse *f*
② *vtr* (a) (Mil) pilonner ⟨town, installation⟩
(b) (Culin) écosser ⟨peas⟩; décortiquer ⟨prawn, nut⟩

**S**

■ **shell out** (colloq): ~ out [sth] débourser ⟨*sum*⟩ (**for** pour)

**shellfish** *n pl* (a) (Zool) crustacés *mpl*; (mussels, oysters) coquillages *mpl*
(b) (Culin) fruits *mpl* de mer

**shelter** [1] *n* (a) abri *m*; **to take ~ from** s'abriter de ⟨*weather*⟩
(b) (for homeless) refuge *m* (**for** pour); (for refugee) asile *m*
[2] *vtr* (a) (against weather) abriter (**from, against** de); (from truth) protéger (**from** de)
(b) donner refuge *or* asile à ⟨*refugee, criminal*⟩
[3] *vi* se mettre à l'abri; **to ~ from the storm** s'abriter de l'orage

**sheltered accommodation** *n* foyer-résidence *m*

**shelving** *n* (at home) étagères *fpl*; (in shop) rayons *mpl*

**shepherd** *n* berger *m*

**shepherd's pie** *n* hachis *m* Parmentier

**sheriff** *n* shérif *m*

**sherry** *n* xérès *m*, sherry *m*

**shield** [1] *n* (a) (Mil) bouclier *m*
(b) (on machine) écran *m* de protection; (around gun) pare-balles *m inv*
(c) (US) (policeman's badge) insigne *m*
[2] *vtr* protéger; **to ~ one's eyes** se protéger les yeux

**shift** [1] *n* (a) (change) changement *m* (**in** de), modification *f* (**in** de)
(b) (at work) période *f* de travail; (group of workers) équipe *f*; **to work an eight-hour ~** faire les trois-huit
[2] *vtr* (a) déplacer ⟨*furniture, vehicle*⟩; bouger, remuer ⟨*arm*⟩; changer ⟨*theatre scenery*⟩
(b) faire partir, enlever ⟨*stain, dirt*⟩
(c) rejeter ⟨*blame, responsibility*⟩ (**onto** sur); **to ~ attention away from a problem** détourner l'attention d'un problème
(d) (US Aut) **to ~ gear** changer de vitesse
[3] *vi* (*also* ~ **about**) ⟨*load*⟩ bouger; **to ~ from one foot to the other** se dandiner d'un pied sur l'autre

**shift key** *n* touche *f* de majuscule

**shiftless** *adj* paresseux/-euse, apathique

**shift work** *n* travail *m* posté

**shifty** *adj* louche, sournois/-e

**shimmer** *vi* (a) ⟨*jewels, water*⟩ scintiller; ⟨*silk*⟩ chatoyer
(b) (in heat) ⟨*landscape*⟩ vibrer

**shin, shinbone** *n* tibia *m*

**shine** [1] *n* lustre *m*
[2] *vtr* (a) braquer ⟨*headlights, spotlight, torch*⟩ (**on** sur)
(b) faire reluire ⟨*silver*⟩; cirer ⟨*shoes*⟩
[3] *vi* (a) ⟨*hair, light, sun*⟩ briller; ⟨*brass, floor*⟩ reluire; **the light is shining in my eyes** j'ai la lumière dans les yeux
(b) ⟨*eyes*⟩ briller (**with** de); ⟨*face*⟩ rayonner (**with** de)
(c) (excel) briller; **to ~ at** être brillant/-e en ⟨*science, languages*⟩

IDIOMS **to take a ~ to sb** (colloq) s'enticher de qn (colloq)

■ **shine through** ⟨*talent*⟩ éclater au grand jour

**shingle** [1] *n* (a) (on beach) galets *mpl*
(b) (on roof) bardeau *m*
[2] **shingles** *n pl* (Med) zona *m*

**shining** *adj* (a) ⟨*hair, metal, eyes*⟩ brillant/-e
(b) ⟨*face*⟩ radieux/-ieuse
(c) ⟨*example*⟩ parfait/-e (**before** *n*)

**shiny** *adj* (a) ⟨*metal, surface, hair*⟩ brillant/-e
(b) ⟨*shoes, wood*⟩ bien ciré/-e

**ship** [1] *n* navire *m*; (smaller) bateau *m*; **passenger ~** paquebot *m*
[2] *vtr* transporter [qch] par mer

**shipment** *n* cargaison *f*

**ship owner** *n* armateur *m*

**shipping** *n* navigation *f*, trafic *m* maritime

**shipping company** *n* compagnie *f* maritime

**shipwreck** [1] *n* (event) naufrage *m*; (ship) épave *f*
[2] *vtr* **to be ~ed** faire naufrage; **a ~ed sailor** un marin naufragé

**shipyard** *n* chantier *m* naval

**shirk** *vtr* esquiver ⟨*task, duty*⟩; fuir ⟨*responsibility*⟩

**shirt** *n* (man's) chemise *f*; (woman's) chemisier *m*; (for sport) maillot *m*

**shirt-sleeve** *n* manche *f* de chemise; **in one's ~s** en manches de chemise

**shirty** *adj* (GB) (colloq) **to get ~** prendre la mouche (colloq)

**shit** *excl* (slang) merde! (slang)

**shiver** [1] *n* frisson *m*; **to give sb the ~s** donner froid dans le dos à qn
[2] *vi* (with cold) grelotter (**with** de); (with fear) frémir (**with** de); (with disgust) frissonner (**with** de)

**shoal** *n* (of fish) banc *m*

**shock** [1] *n* (a) choc *m*; **to get** *or* **have a ~** avoir un choc; **to give sb a ~** faire un choc à qn; **to be in ~** être en état de choc
(b) (electrical) décharge *f*; **to get a ~** prendre une décharge
(c) (of collision) choc *m*; (of explosion) souffle *m*
(d) **a ~ of red hair** une tignasse rousse
[2] *vtr* (distress) consterner; (scandalize) choquer

**shock absorber** *n* amortisseur *m*

**shocking** *adj* ⟨*sight*⟩ consternant/-e; ⟨*news*⟩ choquant/-e

**shock wave** *n* remous *mpl*; **to send ~s through the stock market** provoquer des remous à la Bourse

**shoddy** *adj* ⟨*product*⟩ de mauvaise qualité; ⟨*work*⟩ mal fait/-e

**shoe** [1] *n* chaussure *f*; (for horse) fer *m*
[2] *vtr* ferrer ⟨*horse*⟩

**shoelace** *n* lacet *m* de chaussure

**shoe polish** *n* cirage *m*

**S**

**shoe shop** n magasin m de chaussures

**shoe size** n pointure f

**shoestring** n (US) lacet m de chaussure
**IDIOMS on a ~** (colloq) avec peu de moyens

**shoo** vtr (also ~ **away**) chasser

**shoot** ①  n (Bot) pousse f
② vtr (a) tirer ⟨bullet, arrow⟩ (at sur);
lancer ⟨missile⟩ (at sur)
(b) tirer sur ⟨person, animal⟩; (kill) abattre
⟨person, animal⟩; **she shot him in the leg** elle
lui a tiré dans la jambe; **to ~ sb dead**
abattre qn; **to ~ oneself** se tirer une balle
(c) **to ~ questions at sb** bombarder qn de
questions
(d) (film) tourner ⟨film, scene⟩; prendre [qch]
(en photo) ⟨subject⟩
(e) mettre ⟨bolt⟩
(f) **to ~ the rapids** franchir les rapides
(g) (US) jouer à ⟨pool⟩
③ vi (a) tirer (at sur)
(b) **to ~ forward** s'élancer à toute vitesse;
**the car shot past** la voiture est passée en
trombe
(c) (Sport) tirer, shooter
■ **shoot down** abattre, descendre (colloq)
⟨plane, pilot⟩
■ **shoot up:** ¶ ⟨flames, spray⟩ jaillir; ⟨prices,
profits⟩ monter en flèche; ¶ ~ **up [sth]**, ~
**[sth] up** (inject) (colloq) se shooter à (colloq)
⟨heroin⟩

**shooting** ①  n (a) (killing) meurtre m (par
arme à feu)
(b) (shots) coups mpl de feu, fusillade f
② adj ⟨pain⟩ lancinant/-e

**shooting range** n stand m de tir

**shooting star** n étoile f filante

**shoot-out** n (colloq) fusillade f

**shop** ①  n (a) magasin m; (small, fashionable)
boutique f; **to go to the ~s** aller faire les
courses
(b) (US) (in department store) rayon m
(c) (workshop) atelier m
② vi **to go ~ping** aller faire des courses;
(browse) aller faire les magasins
**IDIOMS to talk ~** parler boutique
■ **shop around** (compare prices) faire le tour
des magasins (**for** pour trouver); (compare
courses, services etc) bien chercher

**shopaholic** n (colloq) accro mf (colloq) du
shopping

**shop assistant** n (GB) vendeur/-euse m/f

**shopkeeper** n commerçant/-e m/f

**shoplifter** n voleur/-euse m/f à l'étalage

**shoplifting** n vol m à l'étalage

**shopping** n courses fpl

**shopping bag** n sac m à provisions

**shopping centre** (GB), **shopping
mall** (US) n centre m commercial

**shopping trolley** n caddie® m

**shop-soiled** adj ⟨garment⟩ sali/-e

**shop steward** n représentant/-e m/f
syndical/-e

**shop window** n vitrine f

**shore** n (of sea) côte f, rivage m; (of lake) rive
f; **on ~** à terre

**short** ①  n (a) (drink) alcool m fort
(b) (film) court métrage m
② **shorts** n pl short m; (underwear) caleçon
m
③ adj (a) ⟨stay, memory, period⟩ court/-e
(before n); ⟨course⟩ de courte durée;
⟨conversation, speech, chapter⟩ bref/brève
(before n); ⟨walk⟩ petit/-e (before n); **the days
are getting ~er** les jours diminuent or
raccourcissent
(b) ⟨hair, dress, distance, stick⟩ court/-e
(before n)
(c) ⟨person⟩ petit/-e (before n)
(d) **to be in ~ supply** être difficile à trouver;
**time is getting ~** le temps presse
(e) (lacking) **he is ~ of sth** il lui manque qch;
**to be ~ on** ⟨person⟩ manquer de ⟨talent,
tact⟩; **to run ~ of** manquer de ⟨clothes,
money, food⟩
(f) **Tom is ~ for Thomas** Tom est le
diminutif de Thomas
(g) (abrupt) **to be ~ with sb** être brusque avec
qn
(h) ⟨pastry⟩ brisé/-e
④ adv ⟨stop⟩ net; **to stop ~ of doing** se
retenir pour ne pas faire
⑤ **in short** phr bref
⑥ **short of** phr **~ of doing** à moins de
faire
**IDIOMS to sell oneself ~** se sous-estimer; **to
make ~ work of sth/sb** expédier qch/qn

**shortage** n pénurie f, manque m (**of** de)

**shortbread**, **shortcake** n sablé m

**short-change** vtr ne pas rendre toute sa
monnaie à

**short circuit** ①  n court-circuit m
② **short-circuit** vtr court-circuiter
③ **short-circuit** vi faire court-circuit

**shortcomings** n pl points mpl faibles

**shortcut** n raccourci m

**shorten** ①  vtr abréger ⟨visit, life⟩;
raccourcir ⟨garment, talk⟩; réduire ⟨time,
list⟩
② vi ⟨days⟩ diminuer

**shortfall** n (in budget, accounts) déficit m; (in
earnings, exports) manque m

**shorthand** n sténographie f, sténo f (colloq)

**shorthand-typist** n sténo-dactylo f

**shortlist** ①  n liste f des candidats
sélectionnés
② vtr sélectionner ⟨applicant⟩ (**for** pour)

**short-lived** adj **to be ~** ne pas durer
longtemps

**shortly** adv (a) ⟨return⟩ bientôt; ⟨be
published⟩ prochainement
(b) **~ after(wards)/before** peu (de temps)
après/avant
(c) (crossly) sèchement

**shortsighted** adj (a) myope
(b) (figurative) ⟨person⟩ peu clairvoyant/-e;
⟨policy, decision⟩ à courte vue

**short-sleeved** adj à manches courtes

**short-staffed** *adj* to be ∼ manquer de personnel

**short story** *n* nouvelle *f*

**short term** **1** *n* in the ∼ dans l'immédiat **2 short-term** *adj* à court terme

**shortwave** *n* ondes *fpl* courtes

**shot** **1** *n* **(a)** (from gun) coup *m* (de feu) **(b)** (Sport) (in tennis, golf, cricket) coup *m*; (in football) tir *m* **(c)** (snapshot) photo *f* **(of** de) **(d)** (in film-making) plan *m* **(of** de); **action** ∼ scène *f* d'action **(e)** (injection) piqûre *f* **(of** de) **(f) to have a** ∼ **at doing** essayer de faire **(g)** (person) **a good** ∼ un bon tireur **2** *adj* ⟨*silk*⟩ changeant/-e

**shotgun** *n* fusil *m*

**shot put** *n* (Sport) lancer *m* de poids

**should** *modal aux* **(a)** ∼ **I call the doctor?** est-ce que je devrais faire venir le médecin?; **why shouldn't I do it?** pourquoi est-ce que je ne le ferais pas?; **she** ∼ **learn to drive** elle devrait apprendre à conduire; **shouldn't you be at school?** tu ne devrais pas être à l'école? **(b) it shouldn't be difficult** ça ne devrait pas être difficile; **she** ∼ **have been here hours ago** elle aurait dû arriver il y a plusieurs heures déjà; **it shouldn't have cost so much** ça n'aurait pas dû coûter si cher **(c) I** ∼ **think she's about 40** à mon avis, elle doit avoir à peu près 40 ans; **I shouldn't be surprised** cela ne m'étonnerait pas **(d)** ∼ **you require any further information, please contact…** si vous souhaitez plus de renseignements, adressez-vous à… **(e) I** ∼ **think so!** je l'espère!; **I** ∼ **think not!** j'espère bien que non!; **how** ∼ **I know?** comment veux-tu que je le sache?; **flowers? you shouldn't have!** des fleurs? il ne fallait pas!

**shoulder** **1** *n* épaule *f* **2** *vtr* se charger de ⟨*burden, expense, task*⟩; endosser ⟨*responsibility*⟩ IDIOMS **to rub** ∼**s with sb** côtoyer qn

**shoulder blade** *n* omoplate *f*

**shoulder-length** *adj* ⟨*hair*⟩ mi-long/-ue

**shoulder pad** *n* épaulette *f*

**shout** **1** *n* cri *m* **(of** de) **2** *vtr* crier; (stronger) hurler **3** *vi* crier; **to** ∼ **at sb** crier après qn; **he was** ∼**ing to me** il me criait quelque chose ■ **shout out** pousser un cri

**shouting** *n* cris *mpl*

**shove** (colloq) **1** *n* **to give sb/sth a** ∼ pousser qn/qch **2** *vtr* **(a)** (push) pousser (**against** contre); **to** ∼ **sth into sth** fourrer qch dans qch **(b)** (jostle) bousculer ⟨*person*⟩ **3** *vi* pousser ■ **shove up** (colloq) se pousser

**shovel** **1** *n* pelle *f* **2** *vtr* enlever [qch] à la pelle ⟨*leaves, snow*⟩ **(off** de)

**show** **1** *n* **(a)** spectacle *m*; (in cinema) séance *f*; (on radio, TV) émission *f*; (of slides) projection *f* **(b)** (exhibition) exposition *f*; (of cars, boats) salon *m*; (of fashion) défilé *m*; **flower/dog** ∼ exposition florale/canine **(c)** (of feelings) semblant *m* **(of** de); (of strength) démonstration *f* **(of** de); (of wealth) étalage *m* **(of** de); **he made a** ∼ **of concern** il a affiché sa sollicitude; **to be just for** ∼ être de l'esbroufe (colloq) **2** *vtr* **(a)** montrer ⟨*person, object, photo, feelings*⟩; présenter ⟨*ticket*⟩ (**to** à); ⟨*TV channel, cinema*⟩ passer ⟨*film*⟩; ⟨*garment*⟩ laisser voir ⟨*underclothes, stain*⟩; indiquer ⟨*time, direction*⟩; **to** ∼ **sb sth** montrer qch à qn; **that carpet** ∼**s the dirt** cette moquette est salissante **(b)** (exhibit) présenter ⟨*animal*⟩; exposer ⟨*flower, vegetables*⟩ **(c)** (prove) démontrer ⟨*truth, guilt*⟩ **(d) to** ∼ **sb to their seat** placer qn; **to** ∼ **sb to their room** accompagner qn à sa chambre; **to** ∼ **sb to the door** reconduire qn **3** *vi* **(a)** ⟨*stain, label*⟩ se voir; ⟨*emotion*⟩ se voir; (in eyes) se lire **(b)** ⟨*film*⟩ passer IDIOMS **to have nothing to** ∼ **for sth** ne rien avoir tiré de qch ■ **show in**: ¶ ∼ [sb] **in** faire entrer ■ **show off**: ¶ ∼ **off** (colloq) faire le fier/la fière; ¶ ∼ [sb/sth] **off** faire admirer ⟨*skill*⟩; exhiber ⟨*baby, car*⟩ ■ **show out**: ¶ ∼ [sb] **out** accompagner [qn] à la porte ■ **show round**: ¶ ∼ [sb] **round** faire visiter ■ **show up**: ¶ ∼ **up** (colloq) (arrive) se montrer (colloq); ¶ ∼ [sth] **up** révéler ⟨*fault, mark*⟩; ¶ ∼ [sb] **up** faire honte à ⟨*person*⟩

**show business** *n* industrie *f* du spectacle

**showcase** *n* (for paintings, ideas) vitrine *f*; (for new artist etc) tremplin *m*

**showdown** *n* confrontation *f*

**shower** **1** *n* **(a)** douche *f*; **to have a** ∼ prendre une douche **(b)** (of rain) averse *f* **2** *vtr* **(a) to** ∼ **sb with sth** couvrir qn de ⟨*gifts, compliments, praise*⟩ **3** *vi* ⟨*person*⟩ prendre une douche

**show house** *n* maison-témoin *f*

**showjumping** *n* saut *m* d'obstacles

**show-off** *n* (colloq) m'as-tu-vu *mf inv* (colloq)

**show of hands** *n* vote *m* à mains levées

**showroom** *n* exposition *f*; **to look at cars in a** ∼ regarder les voitures exposées

**shrapnel** *n* éclats *mpl* d'obus

**shred** **1** *n* **(a)** (of paper, fabric) lambeau *m* **(b)** (of evidence, truth) parcelle *f* **2** *vtr* déchiqueter ⟨*paper*⟩; râper ⟨*vegetables*⟩

**shredder** *n* (for paper) déchiqueteuse *f*

**shrewd** *adj* ⟨*person*⟩ habile; ⟨*move, investment*⟩ astucieux/-ieuse

**S**

**shriek** ⟦1⟧ *n* (a) (of pain, fear) cri *m* perçant,
hurlement *m*; (of delight) cri *m*; **∼s of laughter**
éclats *mpl* de rire
  (b) (of bird) cri *m*
  ⟦2⟧ *vi* crier, hurler (**in, with** de)
**shrill** *adj* ⟨*voice, cry, laugh*⟩ perçant/-e;
⟨*whistle, tone*⟩ strident/-e
**shrimp** *n* crevette *f* grise
**shrine** *n* (a) (place) lieu *m* de pèlerinage
  (b) (building) chapelle *f*
  (c) (tomb) tombeau *m*
**shrink** ⟦1⟧ *vtr* faire rétrécir ⟨*fabric*⟩;
contracter ⟨*wood*⟩
  ⟦2⟧ *vi* (a) ⟨*fabric*⟩ rétrécir; ⟨*timber*⟩ se
contracter; ⟨*dough, meat*⟩ réduire; ⟨*sales*⟩
être en recul; ⟨*resources*⟩ s'amenuiser; ⟨*old
person, body*⟩ se tasser
  (b) **to ∼ from** se dérober devant ⟨*conflict,
responsibility*⟩; **to ∼ from doing** hésiter à
faire
**shrinking** *adj* ⟨*population, market*⟩ en
baisse; ⟨*audience*⟩ qui s'amenuise
**shrink-wrap** *vtr* emballer [qch] sous film
plastique
**shrivel** ⟦1⟧ *vtr* ⟨*sun, heat*⟩ flétrir ⟨*skin*⟩;
dessécher ⟨*plant, leaf*⟩
  ⟦2⟧ *vi* (*also* ∼ **up**) ⟨*fruit, vegetable*⟩ se
ratatiner; ⟨*skin*⟩ se flétrir; ⟨*plant, meat*⟩ se
dessécher
**shroud** ⟦1⟧ *n* linceul *m*
  ⟦2⟧ *vtr* envelopper (**in** dans)
**Shrove Tuesday** *n* mardi *m* gras
**shrub** *n* arbuste *m*
**shrubbery** *n* massif *m* d'arbustes
**shrug** ⟦1⟧ *n* haussement *m* d'épaules
  ⟦2⟧ *vtr* **to ∼ one's shoulders** hausser les
épaules
■ **shrug off** ignorer ⟨*problem, rumour*⟩
**shudder** ⟦1⟧ *n* (a) (of person) frisson *m* (of
de)
  (b) (of vehicle) secousse *f*
  ⟦2⟧ *vi* (a) ⟨*person*⟩ frissonner (**with** de)
  (b) ⟨*vehicle*⟩ **to ∼ to a halt** avoir quelques
soubresauts et s'arrêter
**shuffle** *vtr* (a) battre ⟨*cards*⟩
  (b) brasser ⟨*papers*⟩
  (c) **to ∼ one's feet** traîner les pieds
**shun** *vtr* fuir ⟨*people, publicity, temptation*⟩;
dédaigner ⟨*work*⟩
**shunt** ⟦1⟧ *vtr* aiguiller ⟨*wagon, engine*⟩ (**into**
sur)
  ⟦2⟧ *vi* ⟨*train*⟩ changer de voie
**shut** ⟦1⟧ *adj* fermé/-e; **her eyes were** ∼ elle
avait les yeux fermés; **to slam the door** ∼
claquer la porte (pour bien la fermer); **to
keep one's mouth** (colloq) ∼ se taire
  ⟦2⟧ *vtr* fermer
  ⟦3⟧ *vi* (a) ⟨*door, book, box, mouth*⟩ se fermer
  (b) ⟨*office, factory*⟩ fermer
■ **shut down**: ¶ ∼ **down** ⟨*business*⟩ fermer;
⟨*machinery*⟩ s'arrêter; ¶ ∼ [**sth**] **down** fermer
⟨*business*⟩; arrêter ⟨*machinery*⟩
■ **shut in**: ∼ [**sb/sth**] **in** enfermer
■ **shut off**: ∼ [**sth**] **off**, ∼ **off** [**sth**] couper
⟨*supply, motor*⟩

■ **shut out** (a) laisser [qn/qch] dehors
⟨*animal, person*⟩; éliminer ⟨*noise*⟩; **to be** ∼
**out** être à la porte
  (b) empêcher [qch] d'entrer ⟨*light*⟩
■ **shut up**: ¶ ∼ **up** (colloq) se taire (**about** au
sujet de)
  ¶ ∼ [**sb**] **up** (a) (colloq) (silence) faire taire
⟨*person*⟩
  (b) (confine) enfermer ⟨*person, animal*⟩ (**in**
dans)
  ¶ ∼ [**sth**] **up**, ∼ **up** [**sth**] fermer ⟨*house*⟩
**shutdown** *n* fermeture *f*
**shutter** *n* (a) (wooden, metal) volet *m*; (on
shop front) store *m*
  (b) (on camera) obturateur *m*
**shuttle** ⟦1⟧ *n* (a) navette *f*
  (b) (*also* ∼**cock**) volant *m*
  ⟦2⟧ *vtr* transporter ⟨*passengers*⟩
**shuttle service** *n* service *m* de navette
**shy** ⟦1⟧ *adj* ⟨*person*⟩ timide (**with, of** avec);
⟨*animal*⟩ farouche (**with, of** avec)
  ⟦2⟧ *vi* ⟨*horse*⟩ faire un écart (**at** devant)
■ **shy away** se tenir à l'écart (**from** de)
**Siberia** *pr n* Sibérie *f*
**sibling** *n* frère/sœur *m/f*
**Sicily** *pr n* Sicile *f*
**sick** *adj* (a) (ill) malade; **worried** ∼ malade
d'inquiétude
  (b) (nauseous) **to be** ∼ vomir; **to feel** ∼ avoir
mal au cœur
  (c) ⟨*joke, mind*⟩ malsain/-e
  (d) (disgusted) écœuré/-e, dégoûté/-e
  (e) (colloq) **to be** ∼ **of sb/sth** en avoir assez
*or* marre (colloq) de qn/qch
**sick bay** *n* infirmerie *f*
**sick building syndrome** *n* syndrome
*m* causé par un milieu de travail insalubre
**sicken** ⟦1⟧ *vtr* (disgust) écœurer
  ⟦2⟧ *vi* **to be** ∼**ing for sth** couver qch
**sickening** *adj* ⟨*sight*⟩ qui soulève le cœur;
⟨*smell, cruelty*⟩ écœurant/-e
**sick leave** *n* congé *m* de maladie
**sickly** *adj* (a) ⟨*person, plant*⟩ chétif/-ive
  (b) ⟨*smell, taste*⟩ écœurant/-e; ⟨*colour*⟩
fadasse; ∼ **sweet** douceâtre
**sickness** *n* (a) (illness) maladie *f*
  (b) (nausea) nausée *f*; **bouts of** ∼
vomissements *mpl*
**sick note** *n* (colloq) (for school) mot *m*
d'excuse; (for work) certificat *m* médical
**sickpay** *n* indemnité *f* de maladie
**sickroom** *n* infirmerie *f*
**side** ⟦1⟧ *n* (a) (gen) côté *m*; (of animal's body,
hill) flanc *m*; (of lake, road) bord *m*; **on one's/its**
∼ sur le côté; ∼ **by** ∼ côte à côte; **at** *or* **by
the** ∼ **of** au bord de ⟨*lake, road*⟩; à côté de
⟨*building*⟩
  (b) **to take** ∼**s** prendre position; **to change**
∼**s** changer de camp
  (c) (Sport) (team) équipe *f*
  ⟦2⟧ *adj* ⟨*door, window, entrance, view*⟩
latéral/-e
  ⟦3⟧ **on the side** *phr* **with salad on the** ∼

avec de la salade; **to work on the ∼** (in addition) travailler à côté; (illegally) travailler au noir

■ **side with** se mettre du côté de ⟨*person*⟩

**sideboard** *n* buffet *m*

**sideboards** (GB), **sideburns** *n pl* pattes *fpl*

**side effect** *n* (of drug) effet *m* secondaire; (of action) répercussion *f*

**side impact bars** *n pl* (Aut) renforts *mpl* latéraux

**sideline** *n* **(a)** as a ∼ comme à-côté **(b)** (Sport) ligne *f* de touche; **on the ∼s** sur la touche

**sidelong** *adj* ⟨*look*⟩ oblique

**side plate** *n* petite assiette *f*

**side saddle** *adv* en amazone

**side show** *n* attraction *f*

**sidestep** *vtr* éviter ⟨*opponent*⟩; éluder ⟨*issue*⟩

**side street** *n* petite rue *f*

**side stroke** *n* brasse *f* indienne

**sidetrack** *vtr* fourvoyer ⟨*person*⟩; **to get ∼ed** se fourvoyer

**sidewalk** *n* (US) trottoir *m*

**sideways** 1 *adj* ⟨*look, glance*⟩ de travers 2 *adv* ⟨*move*⟩ latéralement; ⟨*look at*⟩ de travers

**siding** *n* voie *f* de garage

**siege** *n* siège *m*; **to lay ∼ to sth** assiéger qch

**siesta** *n* sieste *f*; **to have a ∼** faire la sieste

**sieve** 1 *n* (for draining) passoire *f*; (for sifting) tamis *m* 2 *vtr* tamiser ⟨*flour*⟩

**sift** *vtr* **(a)** tamiser, passer [qch] au tamis ⟨*flour*⟩ **(b)** passer [qch] au crible ⟨*information*⟩

■ **sift through** trier ⟨*applications*⟩; fouiller (dans) ⟨*ashes*⟩

**sigh** 1 *n* soupir *m* 2 *vi* soupirer, pousser un soupir; **to ∼ with relief** pousser un soupir de soulagement

**sight** 1 *n* **(a)** vue *f*; **at first ∼** à première vue; **to catch ∼ of sb/sth** apercevoir qn/qch; **to lose ∼ of sb/sth** perdre qn/qch de vue; **I can't stand the ∼ of him!** je ne peux pas le voir (colloq) (en peinture)!; **to be in ∼** ⟨*land, border*⟩ être en vue; ⟨*peace, freedom*⟩ être proche; **to be out of ∼** être caché-e; **don't let her out of your ∼!** ne la quitte pas des yeux! **(b)** (scene) spectacle *m*; **it was not a pretty ∼!** ce n'était pas beau à voir! 2 **sights** *n pl* **(a)** attractions *fpl* touristiques (**of** de); **to see the ∼s** faire du tourisme **(b)** (on rifle, telescope) viseur *m* **(c)** **to set one's ∼s on sth** viser qch

**sightseeing** *n* tourisme *m*; **to go ∼** faire du tourisme

**sightseer** *n* touriste *mf*

**sign** 1 *n* **(a)** (gen) signe *m*; **the pound ∼** le symbole de la livre sterling

**(b)** (road sign) panneau *m* (**for** pour); (smaller) pancarte *f*; (outside shop) enseigne *f* 2 *vtr, vi* signer

■ **sign on (a)** (GB) (for benefit) pointer au chômage **(b)** (for course) s'inscrire (**for** à, dans)

■ **sign up (a)** (in forces) s'engager **(b)** (for course) s'inscrire (**for** à, dans)

**signal** 1 *n* signal *m* (**for** de) 2 *vtr* **to ∼** (**to sb**) **that** faire signe (à qn) que 3 *vi* **(a)** (gesture) faire des signes **(b)** (in car) mettre son clignotant

**signature** *n* signature *f*

**signature tune** *n* indicatif *m*

**significance** *n* **(a)** (importance) importance *f* **(b)** (meaning) signification *f*

**significant** *adj* ⟨*amount, impact*⟩ considérable; ⟨*event, role*⟩ important/-e; ⟨*name*⟩ significatif/-ive

**signify** *vtr* indiquer

**sign language** *n* code *m* or langage *m* gestuel

**signpost** *n* panneau *m* indicateur

**Sikh** *n, adj* sikh (*mf*)

**silence** 1 *n* silence *m*; **in ∼** en silence 2 *vtr* faire taire

**silencer** *n* silencieux *m*

**silent** *adj* **(a)** silencieux/-ieuse; **to be ∼** se taire **(b)** ⟨*disapproval, prayer*⟩ muet/muette **(c)** ⟨*film*⟩ muet/muette

**silhouette** *n* silhouette *f*

**silicon chip** *n* puce *f* électronique

**silk** *n* soie *f*

**silky** *adj* soyeux/-euse

**sill** *n* (of window) (interior) rebord *m*; (exterior) appui *m*

**silly** 1 *adj* ⟨*person*⟩ idiot/-e; ⟨*question, game*⟩ stupide; ⟨*behaviour, clothes*⟩ ridicule 2 *adv* **to drink oneself ∼** s'abrutir d'alcool; **to bore sb ∼** assommer qn

**silo** *n* silo *m*

**silt** *n* limon *m*, vase *f*

**silver** 1 *n* **(a)** (metal, colour) argent *m* **(b)** (silverware) argenterie *f* **(c)** (medal) médaille *f* d'argent 2 *adj* ⟨*ring, coin*⟩ en argent

**silver birch** *n* bouleau *m* argenté

**silver foil** *n* (GB) papier *m* d'aluminium

**silverware** *n* argenterie *f*

**similar** *adj* similaire, analogue; ∼ **to** analogue à, comparable à

**similarity** *n* ressemblance *f* (**to, with** avec)

**similarly** *adv* de la même façon

**simmer** *vi* **(a)** ⟨*soup*⟩ cuire à feu doux, mijoter; ⟨*water*⟩ frémir **(b)** ⟨*person*⟩ bouillonner (**with** de); ⟨*revolt, violence*⟩ couver

**simple** *adj* **(a)** (gen) simple; ⟨*dress, style*⟩ sobre    ⋯⋗

**S**

**(b)** (dimwitted) simplet/-ette (colloq), simple d'esprit

**simplicity** n simplicité f

**simplify** vtr simplifier

**simplistic** adj simpliste

**simply** adv **(a)** ⟨write, dress, live⟩ simplement, avec simplicité; **to put it ~...** en deux mots...
**(b)** (merely) simplement

**simulate** vtr (feign) simuler ⟨anger, illness⟩; affecter ⟨interest⟩; (reproduce) simuler

**simulator** n simulateur m

**simultaneous** adj simultané/-e

**sin** [1] n péché m, crime m
[2] vi pécher (**against** contre)

**since** [1] prep depuis; **I haven't seen him ~ then** je ne l'ai pas vu depuis; **I haven't been feeling well ~ Monday** je ne me sens pas bien depuis lundi; **I had been waiting ~ 9 o'clock** j'attendais depuis 9 heures
[2] conj **(a)** (from the time when) depuis que; **~ he's been away** depuis qu' il est absent; **ever ~ I married him** depuis que nous nous sommes mariés, depuis notre mariage; **I've known him ~ I was 12** je le connais depuis que j'ai 12 ans or depuis l'âge de 12 ans; **it's 10 years ~ we last met** cela fait 10 ans que nous ne nous sommes pas revus
**(b)** (because) comme; **~ you're so clever, do it yourself!** puisque tu es tellement malin, fais-le toi-même!
[3] adv **she has ~ qualified** depuis elle a obtenu son diplôme; **I haven't phoned her ~** je ne lui ai pas téléphoné depuis

**sincere** adj sincère

**sincerely** adv sincèrement; **Yours ~, Sincerely yours** (US) Veuillez agréer, Monsieur/Madame, l'expression de mes sentiments les meilleurs

**sincerity** n sincérité f

**sinew** n tendon m

**sing** [1] vtr chanter; **to ~ sb's praises** chanter les louanges de qn
[2] vi chanter

**Singapore** pr n Singapour f

**singe** vtr brûler [qch] légèrement ⟨hair, clothing⟩; (with iron) roussir ⟨clothes⟩

**singer** n chanteur/-euse m/f

**singing** n chant m

**single** [1] n **(a)** (also ~ **ticket**) aller m simple
**(b)** (also ~ **room**) chambre f pour une personne
**(c)** (record) 45 tours m
[2] adj **(a)** (sole) seul/-e (before n)
**(b)** (for one) ⟨sheet, bed, person⟩ pour une personne
**(c)** (unmarried) célibataire
**(d)** **every ~ day** tous les jours sans exception; **every ~ one of those people** chacune de ces personnes
■ **single out** choisir ⟨person⟩

**single cream** n ≈ crème f fraîche liquide

**single currency** n monnaie f unique

**single file** adv en file indienne

**single-handed(ly)** adv tout seul/toute seule

**single market** n marché m unique

**single-minded** adj tenace, résolu/-e

**single mother** n mère f qui élève ses enfants seule

**single-parent** adj ⟨family⟩ monoparental/-e

**singles** n pl (Sport) **the women's/men's ~** le simple dames/messieurs

**singles bar** n bar m de rencontres pour célibataires

**singles charts** n pl palmarès m des 45 tours

**single-sex** adj non mixte

**singlet** n (GB) **(a)** (Sport) maillot m
**(b)** (vest) maillot m de corps

**singular** [1] n singulier m
[2] adj singulier/-ière

**sinister** adj sinistre

**sink** [1] n (in kitchen) évier m; (in bathroom) lavabo m
[2] vtr **(a)** couler ⟨ship⟩
**(b)** forer ⟨oil well, shaft⟩; creuser ⟨foundations⟩; enfoncer ⟨post, pillar⟩ (**into** dans); **the dog sank its teeth into my arm** le chien a planté ses crocs dans mon bras
[3] vi **(a)** ⟨ship, object, person⟩ couler
**(b)** ⟨sun⟩ baisser; ⟨cake⟩ redescendre; **to ~ to the floor** s'effondrer; **to ~ into a chair** s'affaler dans un fauteuil; **to ~ into a deep sleep** sombrer dans un profond sommeil
**(c)** ⟨building, wall⟩ s'effondrer; **to ~ into** s'enfoncer dans ⟨mud⟩; sombrer dans ⟨anarchy, obscurity⟩
■ **sink in** ⟨news⟩ faire son chemin

**sinner** n pécheur/-eresse m/f

**sinus** n sinus m inv

**sip** [1] n petite gorgée f
[2] vtr boire [qch] à petites gorgées

**siphon** [1] n siphon m
[2] vtr (also ~ **off**) siphonner ⟨petrol, water⟩

**sir** n **(a)** Monsieur; **Dear Sir** Monsieur
**(b)** (GB) (in titles) **Sir James** Sir James

**siren** n sirène f

**sirloin** n aloyau m

**sister** n **(a)** (gen) sœur f
**(b)** (GB) (nurse) infirmière f chef

**sister-in-law** n belle-sœur f

**sit** [1] vtr (GB) se présenter à, passer ⟨exam⟩
[2] vi **(a)** s'asseoir (**at** à; **in** dans; **on** sur); **to be sitting** être assis/-e; **to ~ still** se tenir tranquille
**(b)** ⟨committee, court⟩ siéger
**(c)** **to ~ on** faire partie de ⟨committee, jury⟩
**(d)** ⟨hen⟩ **to ~ on** couver ⟨eggs⟩
■ **sit about, sit around** rester assis à ne rien faire
■ **sit down** s'asseoir (**at** à; **in** dans; **on** sur)
■ **sit in** ⟨observer⟩ assister (**on** à)
■ **sit up** se redresser; **to be ~ing up** être assis/-e; **~ up straight!** tiens-toi droit!

**sitcom** n (colloq) sitcom m

**site** n (a) (also **building** ∼) (before building) terrain m; (during building) chantier m
(b) (for tent) emplacement m; **caravan** ∼ (GB) terrain m de caravaning
(c) (archaeological) site m

**sitting** n (a) (session) séance f
(b) (in canteen) service m

**sitting room** n salon m

**sitting target** n cible f facile

**situate** vtr situer; **to be** ∼**d** être situé/-e, se trouver

**situation** n situation f

**sit-ups** n pl abdominaux mpl

**six** n, pron, det six (m) inv

**sixteen** n, pron, det seize (m) inv

**sixteenth** ◯1 n (a) (in order) seizième mf
(b) (of month) seize m inv
(c) (fraction) seizième m
◯2 adj, adv seizième

**sixth** ◯1 n (a) (in order) sixième mf
(b) (of month) six m inv
(c) (fraction) sixième m
◯2 adj, adv sixième

**sixth form** (GB) (Sch) n (lower) ≈ classes fpl de première; (upper) ≈ classes fpl de terminale

**sixth form college** n (GB) lycée m (n'ayant que des classes de première et terminale)

**sixth sense** n sixième sens m

**sixties** n pl (a) the ∼ les années fpl soixante
(b) to be in one's ∼ avoir entre soixante et soixante-dix ans

**sixtieth** n, adj, adv soixantième (mf)

**sixty** n, pron, det soixante (m) inv

**size** n (of person, paper, clothes) taille f; (of container, room, building, region) grandeur f; (of apple, egg, book, parcel) grosseur f; (of carpet, bed, machine) dimensions fpl; (of population, audience) importance f; (of class, company) effectif m; (of shoes, gloves) pointure f
IDIOMS to cut sb down to ∼ remettre qn à sa place, rabattre le caquet à qn (colloq)
■ **size up** se faire une opinion de ⟨person⟩; évaluer ⟨situation⟩; mesurer ⟨problem⟩

**sizeable** adj ⟨amount⟩ assez important/-e; ⟨house, field, town⟩ assez grand/-e

**sizzle** vi grésiller

**skate** ◯1 n (a) (ice) patin m à glace; (roller) patin m à roulettes
(b) (fish) raie f
◯2 vi patiner (**on**, **along** sur)

**skateboard** n skateboard m, planche f à roulettes

**skateboarder** n skateur/-euse m/f

**skater** n patineur/-euse m/f

**skating** n patinage m

**skating rink** n (ice) patinoire f; (roller-skating) piste f de patins à roulettes

**skeleton** n squelette m

**skeleton key** n passe-partout m inv

**skeptic** (US) = SCEPTIC

**skeptical** (US) = SCEPTICAL

**skepticism** (US) = SCEPTICISM

**sketch** ◯1 n (a) (drawing, draft) esquisse f; (hasty outline) croquis m; **rough** ∼ ébauche f
(b) (comic scene) sketch m
◯2 vtr faire une esquisse de; (hastily) faire un croquis de

**sketchbook** n carnet m à croquis

**sketchpad** n bloc m à dessin

**sketchy** adj ⟨information, details⟩ insuffisant/-e; ⟨memory⟩ vague

**skewer** ◯1 n (for kebab) brochette f; (for joint) broche f
◯2 vtr embrocher

**ski** ◯1 n ski m
◯2 vi faire du ski; **to** ∼ **down a slope** descendre une pente à skis

**ski boot** n chaussure f de ski

**skid** ◯1 n dérapage m
◯2 vi déraper (**on** sur)

**skier** n skieur/-ieuse m/f

**skiing** n ski m; **to go** ∼ faire du ski

**skiing holiday** n vacances fpl de neige

**ski jumping** n saut m à skis

**skilful** (GB), **skillful** (US) adj habile, adroit/-e

**ski lift** n remontée f mécanique

**skill** ◯1 n (a) (intellectual) habileté f, adresse f; (physical) dextérité f
(b) (special ability) (acquired) compétence f, capacités fpl; (practical) technique f
◯2 **skills** n pl (training) connaissances fpl

**skilled** adj (a) (trained) ⟨labour, work⟩ qualifié/-e
(b) (talented) consommé/-e

**skim** ◯1 vtr (a) (remove cream) écrémer; (remove scum) écumer
(b) ⟨plane, bird⟩ raser, frôler ⟨surface, treetops⟩
(c) to ∼ stones faire des ricochets avec des cailloux
◯2 vi to ∼ through parcourir ⟨book, article⟩; to ∼ over passer rapidement sur ⟨event, facts⟩

**skim(med) milk** n lait m écrémé

**skimp** vi to ∼ on lésiner sur

**skimpy** adj ⟨garment⟩ minuscule; ⟨portion, allowance, income⟩ maigre (before n)

**skin** ◯1 n peau f; (of onion) pelure f
◯2 vtr (a) écorcher ⟨animal⟩
(b) to ∼ one's knee s'écorcher le genou
IDIOMS to have a thick ∼ être insensible; to be or get soaked to the ∼ être trempé/-e jusqu'aux os (colloq); by the ∼ of one's teeth de justesse

**skin-deep** adj superficiel/-ielle

**skin diving** n plongée f sous-marine

**skinhead** n (GB) (youth) skin(head) m

**skinny** adj (colloq) maigre

**skint** adj (colloq) (GB) fauché/-e (colloq)

**skintight** adj moulant/-e

**skip** ◯1 n (a) (jump) petit bond m
(b) (GB) (container) benne f     ····∻

**S**

**2** *vtr* sauter ⟨*page, lunch, school*⟩
**3** *vi* **(a)** (once) bondir; (several times) sautiller **(b)** (with rope) sauter à la corde

**ski pants** *n* fuseau *m* (de ski)

**ski pass** *n* forfait-skieur *m*

**skipper** *n* (of ship) capitaine *m*; (of fishing boat) patron *m*; (of yacht) skipper *m*

**skipping rope** *n* corde *f* à sauter

**ski resort** *n* station *f* de ski

**skirt** **1** *n* jupe *f*
**2** *vtr* **(a)** contourner ⟨*wood, village, city*⟩ **(b)** esquiver ⟨*problem*⟩

**skirting board** *n* plinthe *f*

**ski slope** *n* piste *f*

**ski suit** *n* combinaison *f* de ski

**skittle** **1** *n* quille *f*
**2 skittles** *n pl* (jeu *m* de) quilles *fpl*

**skive** *vi* (GB) (colloq) (*also* ~ **off**) (shirk) tirer au flanc (colloq); (be absent) (from school) sécher l'école (colloq); (from work) ne pas aller au boulot (colloq)

**skulk** *vi* rôder; **to** ~ **out/off** sortir/s'éloigner furtivement

**skull** *n* crâne *m*

**skunk** *n* moufette *f*

**sky** *n* ciel *m*

**skydiving** *n* parachutisme *m* (en chute libre)

**sky-high** *adj* ⟨*prices, rates*⟩ exorbitant/-e

**skyjacker** *n* (colloq) pirate *m* de l'air

**skylight** *n* fenêtre *f* à tabatière

**skyline** *n* (in countryside) ligne *f* d'horizon; (in city) ligne *f* des toits

**skyscraper** *n* gratte-ciel *m inv*

**slab** *n* (of stone, wood, concrete) dalle *f*; (of meat, cheese, cake) pavé *m*; (of chocolate) tablette *f*

**slack** **1** *n* (in rope, cable) mou *m*
**2** *adj* **(a)** ⟨*worker*⟩ peu consciencieux/-ieuse; ⟨*work*⟩ peu soigné/-e **(b)** ⟨*period*⟩ creux/creuse (*after n*); ⟨*demand, sales*⟩ faible **(c)** ⟨*cable, rope, body*⟩ détendu/-e
**3** *vi* ⟨*worker*⟩ se relâcher dans son travail
■ **slack off** ⟨*business, trade*⟩ diminuer; ⟨*rain*⟩ se calmer

**slacken** **1** *vtr* **(a)** donner du mou à ⟨*rope*⟩; lâcher ⟨*reins*⟩ **(b)** réduire ⟨*pace*⟩
**2** *vi* **(a)** ⟨*rope*⟩ se relâcher **(b)** ⟨*activity, pace, speed, business*⟩ ralentir

**slalom** *n* slalom *m*

**slam** **1** *vtr* ⟨*person*⟩ claquer ⟨*door*⟩; ⟨*wind*⟩ faire claquer ⟨*door*⟩; **to** ~ **the door in sb's face** claquer la porte au nez de qn; **to** ~ **the ball into the net** renvoyer brutalement la balle dans le filet
**2** *vi* ⟨*door*⟩ claquer (**against** contre); **to** ~ **shut** se refermer en claquant

**slander** *n* (gen) calomnie *f* (**on** sur); (Law) diffamation *f* orale

**slang** *n* argot *m*

**slangy** *adj* (colloq) argotique

**slant** **1** *n* **(a)** (perspective) point *m* de vue (**on** sur) **(b)** (bias) tendance *f* **(c)** (slope) pente *f*
**2** *vi* ⟨*floor, ground*⟩ être en pente; ⟨*handwriting*⟩ pencher (**to** vers)

**slanting** *adj* ⟨*roof*⟩ en pente; ~ **eyes** yeux *mpl* bridés

**slap** **1** *n* tape *f* (**on** sur); (stronger) claque *f* (**on** sur); **a** ~ **in the face** une gifle
**2** *vtr* donner une tape à ⟨*person, animal*⟩; **to** ~ **sb in the face** gifler qn

**slap bang** *adv* (colloq) **he ran** ~ **into the wall** il s'est cogné en plein dans le mur en courant; ~ **in the middle (of)** au beau milieu (de)

**slapdash** *adj* (colloq) ⟨*person*⟩ brouillon/-onne (colloq); **in a** ~ **way** à la va-vite

**slash** **1** *n* **(a)** (wound) balafre *f* (**on** à) **(b)** (in fabric, seat, tyre) lacération *f*; (in painting) entaille *f*; (in skirt) fente *f* **(c)** (in printing) barre *f* oblique
**2** *vtr* **(a)** balafrer ⟨*cheek*⟩; faire une balafre à ⟨*person*⟩; couper ⟨*throat*⟩; ⟨*knife*⟩ entailler ⟨*face*⟩; **to** ~ **one's wrists** se tailler les veines **(b)** taillader ⟨*painting, fabric, tyres*⟩; trancher ⟨*cord*⟩ **(c)** (reduce) réduire [qch] (considérablement) ⟨*amount, spending*⟩; sacrifier ⟨*prices*⟩

**slat** *n* (of shutter, blind) lamelle *f*; (of bench, bed) lame *f*

**slate** **1** *n* ardoise *f*
**2** *vtr* **(a)** couvrir [qch] d'ardoises ⟨*roof*⟩ **(b)** (GB) (colloq) (criticize) taper sur (colloq) (**for** pour)
IDIOMS **to wipe the** ~ **clean** faire table rase

**slaughter** **1** *n* **(a)** (in butchery) abattage *m* **(b)** (massacre) massacre *m*, boucherie *f* (colloq)
**2** *vtr* **(a)** abattre ⟨*animal*⟩ **(b)** massacrer ⟨*people*⟩ **(c)** (colloq) (defeat) écraser

**slaughterhouse** *n* abattoir *m*

**Slav** **1** *n* Slave *mf*
**2** *adj* slave

**slave** **1** *n* esclave *mf*
**2** *vi* (*also* ~ **away**) travailler comme un forçat, trimer (colloq)

**slaver** *vi* ⟨*person, animal*⟩ baver

**slavery** *n* esclavage *m*

**slaw** (US) = COLESLAW

**slay** *vtr* faire périr ⟨*enemy*⟩; pourfendre ⟨*dragon*⟩

**sleaze** *n* (colloq) (pornography) pornographie *f*; (corruption) corruption *f*

**sleazy** *adj* (colloq) ⟨*club, area, character*⟩ louche; ⟨*story, aspect*⟩ scabreux/-euse; ⟨*café, hotel*⟩ borgne

**sled, sledge** (GB) **1** *n* luge *f*; (sleigh) traîneau *m*
**2** *vi* faire de la luge

**sledgehammer** *n* masse *f*

**sleek** *adj* **(a)** ⟨*hair*⟩ lisse et brillant/-e; ⟨*animal*⟩ au poil lisse et brillant

**(b)** ⟨shape⟩ élégant/-e; ⟨figure⟩ mince et harmonieux/-ieuse

**sleep** 1 n sommeil m; **to go to ~** s'endormir; **to go back to ~** se rendormir; **to send** or **put sb to ~** endormir qn; **to have a ~** dormir; **my leg has gone to ~** (colloq) j'ai la jambe engourdie; **to put an animal to ~** faire piquer un animal

2 vi dormir; **to ~ at a friend's house** coucher chez un ami

IDIOMS **to ~ like a log** or **top** dormir comme une souche or un loir

■ **sleep in** (stay in bed late) faire la grasse matinée; (oversleep) dormir trop tard

■ **sleep on: to ~ on a decision** attendre le lendemain pour prendre une décision

**sleeping bag** n sac m de couchage

**sleeping car** n voiture-lit f, wagon-lit m

**sleeping pill** n somnifère m

**sleepless** adj **to have a ~ night** passer une nuit blanche

**sleepover** n **she's having a ~** elle invite des amies à coucher chez elle

**sleepwalk** vi marcher en dormant, être somnambule

**sleepy** adj ⟨voice, village⟩ endormi/-e, somnolent/-e; **to feel** or **be ~** avoir envie de dormir, avoir sommeil; **to make sb ~** ⟨fresh air⟩ donner envie de dormir à qn; ⟨wine⟩ endormir qn, assoupir qn

**sleet** n neige f fondue

**sleeve** n (a) (of garment) manche f

**(b)** (of record) pochette f

**(c)** (Tech) (inner) chemise f; (outer) gaine f

IDIOMS **to have something up one's ~** avoir quelque chose en réserve

**sleeveless** adj sans manches

**sleigh** n traîneau m

**sleight of hand** n (a) (dexterity) dextérité f

**(b)** (trick) tour m de passe-passe

**slender** adj (a) ⟨person⟩ mince; ⟨waist⟩ fin/-e

**(b)** ⟨income, means⟩ modeste, maigre (before n)

**sleuth** n limier m, détective m

**slew** vi ⟨vehicle⟩ déraper; ⟨mast⟩ pivoter

**slice** 1 n (a) (of bread, meat) tranche f; (of cheese) morceau m; (of pie, tart) part m; (of lemon, cucumber, sausage) rondelle f

**(b)** (of profits) part f; (of territory, population) partie f

**(c)** (utensil) spatule f

2 vtr (a) couper [qch] (en tranches) ⟨loaf, roast⟩; couper [qch] en rondelles ⟨lemon, cucumber⟩

**(b)** fendre ⟨air⟩

**(c)** (Sport) slicer, couper ⟨ball⟩

3 vi **to ~ through** fendre ⟨water, air⟩; trancher ⟨timber, rope, meat⟩

**sliced bread** n pain m en tranches

**slice of life** n tranche f de vie

**slick** 1 n (also **oil ~**) (on water) nappe f de pétrole; (on shore) marée f noire

2 adj (a) ⟨production⟩ habile; ⟨operation⟩ mené/-e rondement

**(b)** (superficial) qui a un éclat plutôt superficiel

**(c)** ⟨person⟩ roublard/-e (colloq); ⟨answer⟩ astucieux/-ieuse; ⟨excuse⟩ facile

**(d)** (US) (slippery) ⟨road, surface⟩ glissant/-e; ⟨hair⟩ lissé/-e

**slide** 1 n (a) (in playground) toboggan m

**(b)** (photographic) diapositive f

**(c)** (microscope plate) lame f porte-objet

**(d)** (GB) (also **hair ~**) barrette f

**(e)** (decline) baisse f (**in** de)

2 vtr faire glisser

3 vi (a) ⟨car, person⟩ glisser, partir en glissade (**into** dans; **on** sur); **to ~ in and out** ⟨drawer⟩ coulisser

**(b)** ⟨prices, shares⟩ baisser

**slide projector** n projecteur m de diapositives

**slide rule** (GB), **slide ruler** (US) n règle f à calcul

**slide show** n (at exhibition) diaporama m; (at lecture, at home) séance f de projection

**sliding** adj ⟨door⟩ coulissant/-e; ⟨roof⟩ ouvrant/-e

**sliding scale** n échelle f mobile

**slight** 1 n affront m (**on** à; **from** de la part de)

2 adj (a) (gen) léger/-ère (before n); ⟨risk, danger⟩ faible (before n); ⟨pause, hesitation⟩ petit/-e (before n); **not to have the ~est difficulty** ne pas avoir la moindre difficulté

**(b)** (in build) mince

3 vtr (a) (offend) offenser; (stronger) humilier

**(b)** (US) (underestimate) sous-estimer

**slightly** adv ⟨fall, change⟩ légèrement; ⟨different, more, less⟩ un peu

**slim** 1 adj ⟨person, figure⟩ mince; ⟨ankle, leg⟩ fin/-e, mince; ⟨watch, calculator⟩ plat/-e

2 vi (GB) maigrir; **I'm ~ming** je fais un régime amaigrissant

**slime** n dépôt m gluant or visqueux; (of slug, snail) bave f

**sling** 1 n (a) (Med) écharpe f

**(b)** (for carrying baby) porte-bébé m; (for carrying load) élingue f

2 vtr lancer ⟨object, insult⟩ (**at** à)

**slip** 1 n (a) (error) erreur f; **~ of the tongue** lapsus m

**(b)** (receipt) reçu m; (for salary) bulletin m; **~ of paper** bout m de papier

**(c)** (stumble) faux pas m

**(d)** (petticoat) (full) combinaison f; (half) jupon m

2 vtr (a) (gen) glisser (**into** dans); **she ~ped the shirt over her head** (put on) elle a enfilé sa chemise; (take off) elle a retiré sa chemise

**(b)** ⟨dog⟩ se dégager de ⟨leash⟩; ⟨boat⟩ filer ⟨moorings⟩; **it had ~ped my mind (that)** j'avais complètement oublié (que); **to let ~ a remark** laisser échapper une remarque

**(c)** (Med) **to ~ a disc** se déplacer une vertèbre

⋯⟩

**3** *vi* (a) to ~ into passer ⟨dress, costume⟩; tomber dans ⟨coma⟩
(b) to ~ into/out of se glisser dans/hors de ⟨room, building⟩
(c) ⟨person, vehicle⟩ glisser (on sur; off de); ⟨knife, razor, pen⟩ glisser, déraper; to ~ through sb's fingers ⟨money, opportunity⟩ filer entre les doigts de qn
(d) (Aut) ⟨clutch⟩ patiner

**slipknot** *n* nœud *m* coulant
**slip-on (shoe)** *n* mocassin *m*
**slipped disc** *n* hernie *f* discale
**slipper** *n* pantoufle *f*
**slippery** *adj* glissant/-e
**slip road** *n* bretelle *f* d'accès
**slipshod** *adj* ⟨person⟩ négligent/-e; ⟨appearance, work⟩ négligé/-e, peu soigné/-e
**slip-up** *n* (colloq) bourde *f* (colloq)
**slit** **1** *n* fente *f* (in dans)
**2** *adj* ⟨eyes⟩ bridé/-e; ⟨skirt⟩ fendu/-e
**3** *vtr* (on purpose) faire une fente dans; (by accident) déchirer; to ~ sb's throat égorger qn; to ~ one's wrists s'ouvrir les veines
**slither** *vi* glisser
**sliver** *n* (of glass) éclat *m*; (of food) mince tranche *f*
**slob** *n* (colloq) (lazy) flemmard/-e *m/f* (colloq)
**slog** *vi* (colloq) (also ~ away) travailler dur, bosser (colloq)
**slogan** *n* slogan *m*
**slop** **1** *vtr* renverser ⟨liquid⟩
**2** *vi* (also ~ over) ⟨liquid⟩ déborder
**slope** **1** *n* pente *f*
**2** *vi* être en pente (towards vers); ⟨writing⟩ pencher (to vers)
**sloping** *adj* ⟨ground, roof⟩ en pente; ⟨ceiling⟩ incliné/-e; ⟨writing⟩ penché/-e
**sloppy** *adj* (a) (colloq) ⟨appearance⟩ débraillé/-e; ⟨work⟩ peu soigné/-e
(b) (colloq) (over-emotional) sentimental/-e
**slot** **1** *n* (a) (for coin, ticket) fente *f*; (for letters) ouverture *f*; (groove) rainure *f*
(b) (in timetable, schedule) créneau *m*
**2** *vtr* to ~ sth into a machine insérer qch dans une machine
**3** *vi* to ~ into sth ⟨coin, piece⟩ s'insérer dans qch; to ~ into place or position s'encastrer
■ **slot together** s'emboîter
**sloth** *n* (Zool) paresseux *m*
**slot machine** *n* (game) machine *f* à sous; (vending machine) distributeur *m* automatique
**slouch** *vi* être avachi/-e
**Slovakia** *pr n* Slovaquie *f*
**Slovenia** *pr n* Slovénie *f*
**slovenly** *adj* négligé/-e
**slow** **1** *adj* (a) (gen) lent/-e;
(b) ⟨business, market⟩ stagnant/-e
(c) (dull-witted) lent/-e (d'esprit)
(d) to be ~ ⟨clock, watch⟩ retarder; to be 10 minutes ~ retarder de 10 minutes
**2** *adv* lentement

**3** *vtr, vi* (also ~ down) ralentir
**slowly** *adv* lentement
**slow motion** *n* ralenti *m*; in ~ au ralenti
**slow-moving** *adj* lent/-e
**sludge** *n* (a) (also **sewage** ~) eaux *fpl* usées
(b) (mud) vase *f*
**slug** *n* limace *f*
**sluggish** *adj* (a) ⟨person, animal⟩ léthargique; ⟨circulation⟩ lent/-e
(b) ⟨market, trade⟩ qui stagne
**sluice** *n* (a) (also ~ **gate**) vanne *f*
(b) (also ~**way**) canal *m*
**slum** *n* (a) (area) quartier *m* pauvre
(b) (dwelling) taudis *m*
**slumber** **1** *n* sommeil *m*
**2** *vi* sommeiller
**slump** **1** *n* (in trade, prices) effondrement *m* (in de)
**2** *vi* (a) ⟨demand, trade, price⟩ chuter (from de; to à; by de); ⟨economy, market⟩ s'effondrer; ⟨popularity⟩ être en forte baisse
(b) ⟨person, body⟩ s'affaler (colloq)
**slur** **1** *n* (a) (in speech) marmonnement *m*
(b) (Mus) liaison *f*
(c) (aspersion) calomnie *f*
**2** *vi* avoir du mal à articuler
**3** **slurred** *pp adj* ⟨voice, speech⟩ inarticulé/-e
**slush** *n* neige *f* fondue
**slush fund** *n* caisse *f* noire
**sly** *adj* ⟨person, animal⟩ rusé/-e; ⟨remark, smile⟩ entendu/-e
IDIOMS on the ~ en douce (colloq), en cachette
**smack** **1** *n* claque *f*; (on face) gifle *f*
**2** *vtr* (on face) gifler ⟨person⟩; taper ⟨object⟩ (on sur; against contre); she ~ed him on the bottom elle lui a donné une tape sur les fesses
**3** *vi* to ~ of sentir
**small** **1** *n* the ~ of the back le creux du dos
**2** *adj* (a) (gen) petit/-e (before n); ⟨quantity, amount⟩ faible (before n)
(b) to feel ~ être dans ses petits souliers (colloq); to make sb feel or look ~ humilier qn
**3** *adv* ⟨write⟩ petit
**small ad** *n* (GB) petite annonce *f*
**small change** *n* petite monnaie *f*
**small talk** *n* banalités *fpl*; to make ~ faire la conversation
**smart** **1** *adj* (a) (elegant) ⟨person, clothes⟩ élégant/-e; ⟨restaurant, hotel, street⟩ chic
(b) (clever) malin/-e
(c) ⟨blow⟩ vif/vive; ⟨rebuke⟩ cinglant/-e; to walk at a ~ pace marcher à vive allure
(d) (Comput) intelligent/-e
**2** *vi* ⟨cut, cheeks⟩ brûler; his eyes were ~ing from the smoke la fumée lui brûlait les yeux
**smart bomb** *n* bombe *f* intelligente
**smart card** *n* carte *f* à puce

**smarten** *v* ■ **smarten up** embellir
⟨*room*⟩; **to ∼ oneself up** se faire beau

**smash** **1** *n* **(a)** (colloq) (*also* ∼**-up**)
(accident) collision *f*
**(b)** (colloq) (*also* ∼ **hit**) tube *m* (colloq)
**(c)** (in tennis) smash *m*
**(d)** (sound) fracas *m*
**2** *vtr* **(a)** briser ⟨*glass, door, car*⟩; (more
violently) fracasser
**(b)** démanteler ⟨*drugs ring, gang*⟩
**(c)** (Sport) **to ∼ the ball** faire un smash
**3** *vi* se briser, se fracasser

**smashing** *adj* (GB) (colloq) formidable
(colloq)

**smattering** *n* notions *fpl* (**of** de); **to have
a ∼ of Russian** avoir quelques
connaissances en russe

**smear** **1** *n* **(a)** (spot) tache *f*; (streak) traînée
*f*
**(b)** (defamation) propos *m* diffamatoire
**(c)** (Med) (*also* ∼ **test**) frottis *m*
**2** *vtr* **(a)** faire des taches sur ⟨*glass,
window*⟩; **her face was ∼ed with jam** elle
avait le visage barbouillé de confiture
**(b)** (spread) étaler ⟨*butter, paint*⟩; appliquer
⟨*lotion*⟩ (**on** sur)
**3** *vi* ⟨*ink, paint*⟩ s'étaler; ⟨*lipstick, make-up*⟩
couler

**smell** **1** *n* **(a)** odeur *f*
**(b)** (sense) odorat *m*
**2** *vtr* ⟨*person*⟩ sentir; ⟨*animal*⟩ renifler,
sentir; **I can ∼ burning** ça sent le brûlé
**3** *vi* sentir; **that ∼s nice/horrible** ça sent
bon/très mauvais; **to ∼ of sth** sentir qch

**smelling salts** *n pl* sels *mpl*

**smelly** *adj* malodorant/-e, qui sent
mauvais

**smile** **1** *n* sourire *m*
**2** *vi* sourire (**at sb** à qn)
■ **smile on**: ∼ **on** [sb/sth] ⟨*fortune, weather*⟩
sourire à; ⟨*person*⟩ être favorable à

**smiley** *n* (colloq) souriant *m*, smiley *m*
(colloq)

**smirk** **1** *n* (self-satisfied) petit sourire *m*
satisfait; (knowing) sourire *m* en coin
**2** *vi* (in a self-satisfied way) avoir un petit
sourire satisfait; (knowingly) avoir un sourire
en coin

**smithereens** *n pl* **in ∼** en mille
morceaux; **to smash sth to ∼** faire voler qch
en éclats

**smock** *n* blouse *f*, sarrau *m*

**smog** *n* smog *m*

**smoke** **1** *n* fumée *f*
**2** *vtr* fumer
**3** *vi* fumer

**smoke alarm** *n* détecteur *m* de fumée

**smoked** *adj* fumé/-e

**smoker** *n* fumeur/-euse *m/f*

**smoke screen** *n* (Mil) écran *m* de fumée;
(figurative) diversion *f*

**smoking** **1** *n* ∼ **and drinking** le tabac et
l'alcool; **to give up ∼** arrêter de fumer; 'no
∼' 'défense de fumer'

**2** *adj* ⟨*compartment, section*⟩ fumeurs (*after
n*)

**smoking-related** *adj* ⟨*disease*⟩
associé/-e au tabac

**smoky** *adj* ⟨*room*⟩ enfumé/-e; ⟨*cheese,
bacon*⟩ fumé/-e

**smooth** **1** *adj* **(a)** ⟨*stone, surface, skin,
fabric*⟩ lisse; ⟨*curve, breathing*⟩
régulier/-ière; ⟨*sauce*⟩ homogène; ⟨*crossing,
flight*⟩ sans heurts; ⟨*movement*⟩ aisé/-e
**(b)** ⟨*taste, wine, whisky*⟩ moelleux/-euse
**(c)** (suave) ⟨*person*⟩ mielleux/-euse;
⟨*manners, appearance*⟩ onctueux/-euse; **to be
a ∼ talker** être enjôleur/-euse
**2** *vtr* **(a)** (flatten out) lisser; (get creases out)
défroisser
**(b)** faciliter ⟨*transition, path*⟩
■ **smooth over**: ¶ ∼ **over** [sth] atténuer
⟨*differences*⟩; aplanir ⟨*difficulties, problems*⟩;
**to ∼ things over** arranger les choses

**smooth-running** *adj* ⟨*organization,
event*⟩ qui marche bien

**smother** *vtr* étouffer

**smoulder** (GB), **smolder** (US) *vi* **(a)**
⟨*cigarette, fire*⟩ se consumer
**(b)** ⟨*hatred, jealousy*⟩ couver; **to ∼ with** être
consumé/-e de

**smudge** **1** *n* trace *f*
**2** *vtr* étaler ⟨*make-up, print, ink, paint*⟩;
faire des traces sur ⟨*paper, paintwork*⟩
**3** *vi* ⟨*make-up, print, ink, paint*⟩ s'étaler

**smug** *adj* suffisant/-e

**smuggle** *vtr* faire du trafic de ⟨*arms,
drugs*⟩; faire passer [qch] en contrebande
⟨*watches, alcohol, cigarettes*⟩; **to ∼ sb/sth in**
faire entrer qn/qch clandestinement

**smuggler** *n* contrebandier/-ière *m/f*; **drug/
arms ∼** passeur/-euse *m/f* de drogue/
d'armes

**smuggling** *n* contrebande *f*; **drug/arms ∼**
trafic *m* de drogue/d'armes

**smutty** *adj* **(a)** (crude) grivois/-e
**(b)** (dirty) ⟨*face*⟩ noir/-e; ⟨*mark*⟩ noirâtre

**snack** **1** *n* **(a)** (small meal) repas *m* léger;
(instead of meal) casse-croûte *m inv*
**(b)** (crisps, peanuts) ∼**s** amuse-gueule *m inv*
**2** *vi* grignoter, manger légèrement

**snag** *n* **(a)** (hitch) inconvénient *m* (**in** de)
**(b)** (tear) accroc *m* (**in** à)

**snail** *n* escargot *m*

**snail mail** *n* (colloq) courrier *m* postal

**snake** *n* serpent *m*

**snap** **1** *n* **(a)** (of branch) craquement *m*; (of
fingers, elastic) claquement *m*
**(b)** (colloq) (photograph) photo *f*
**(c)** (game) ≈ bataille *f*
**2** *adj* ⟨*decision, judgment, vote*⟩ rapide
**3** *vtr* **(a)** faire claquer ⟨*fingers, jaws,
elastic*⟩
**(b)** (break) (faire) casser net
**(c)** (say crossly) dire [qch] hargneusement
**4** *vi* **(a)** (break) se casser
**(b)** (speak sharply) parler hargneusement
■ **snap at (a)** (speak sharply) parler
sèchement à

⋯⋗

**(b)** ⟨dog⟩ essayer de mordre

■ **snap up** sauter sur ⟨bargain⟩

**snappy** adj ⟨rhythm, reply⟩ rapide; ⟨advertisement⟩ accrocheur/-euse

**snapshot** n photo f

**snare** [1] n piège m

[2] vtr prendre [qn/qch] au piège

**snarl** vi ⟨animal⟩ gronder férocement; ⟨person⟩ grogner

**snarl-up** n (in traffic) embouteillage m; (in distribution network) blocage m

**snatch** [1] n **(a)** (of conversation) bribe f; (of tune) quelques notes fpl
**(b)** (theft) vol m
[2] vtr **(a)** (grab) attraper ⟨book, key⟩; **to ~ sth from sb** arracher qch à qn
**(b)** (colloq) (steal) voler ⟨handbag⟩ (from à)

**sneak** vi **to ~ in/out** entrer/sortir furtivement; **to ~ up on sb/sth** s'approcher sans bruit de qn/qch

**sneaker** n (US) basket f, (chaussure f de) tennis f

**sneaking** adj ⟨suspicion⟩ vague

**sneaky** adj sournois/-e

**sneer** [1] n sourire m méprisant
[2] vi sourire avec mépris

**sneeze** [1] n éternuement m
[2] vi éternuer

**snide** adj sournois/-e

**sniff** [1] n reniflement m
[2] vtr ⟨dog⟩ flairer; ⟨person⟩ sentir ⟨food⟩; inhaler ⟨glue, cocaine⟩
[3] vi renifler

**snigger** [1] n ricanement m
[2] vi ricaner

**snip** vtr découper (à petits coups de ciseaux) ⟨fabric, paper⟩; tailler ⟨hedge⟩

■ **snip off** couper

**sniper** n tireur m embusqué

**snippet** n (of conversation, information) bribes f; (of text, fabric, music) fragment m

**snivel** vi pleurnicher

**snob** n snob mf

**snobbery** n snobisme m

**snobbish** adj snob

**snooker** [1] n (game) snooker m
[2] vtr **(a)** (Sport, figurative) coincer ⟨player, person⟩
**(b)** (US) (deceive) avoir (colloq) ⟨person⟩

**snoop** (colloq) [1] n fouineur/-euse m/f
[2] vi fouiner, fureter

**snooze** (colloq) [1] n petit somme m
[2] vi sommeiller

**snore** [1] n ronflement m
[2] vi ronfler

**snorkel** n tuba m

**snorkelling** n plongée f avec tuba

**snort** [1] vi ⟨person, pig⟩ grogner; ⟨horse, bull⟩ s'ébrouer
[2] vtr sniffer ⟨drugs⟩

**snout** n museau m; (of pig) groin m

**snow** [1] n neige f
[2] v impers neiger; **it's ~ing** il neige

**snowball** [1] n boule f de neige
[2] vi faire boule de neige

**snowboard** [1] n surf m des neiges
[2] vi faire du surf des neiges

**snowdrift** n congère f

**snowdrop** n perce-neige m inv

**snowfall** n chute f de neige

**snowflake** n flocon m de neige

**snowman** n bonhomme m de neige

**snow mobile** n motoneige f

**snow plough** (GB), **snow plow** (US) n chasse-neige m inv

**snow shoe** n raquette f

**snub** [1] n rebuffade f
[2] vtr rembarrer

**snub-nosed** adj au nez retroussé

**snuff** n tabac m à priser

**snug** adj ⟨bed, room⟩ douillet/-ette; ⟨coat⟩ chaud/-e

**snuggle** vi se blottir

**so** [1] adv **(a)** (to such an extent) si, tellement; **~ happy/quickly** si or tellement heureux/vite; **~ much noise/many things** tant de bruit/de choses
**(b)** (in such a way) **~ arranged/worded that** organisé/rédigé d'une telle façon que; **and ~ on and ~ forth** et ainsi de suite; **~ be it!** soit!
**(c)** (thus) ainsi; (therefore) donc; **~ that's the reason** voilà donc pourquoi; **~ you're going are you?** alors tu y vas?
**(d)** (true) **is that ~?** c'est vrai?; **if (that's) ~** si c'est vrai
**(e)** (also) aussi; **~ is she** elle aussi, **~ do I** moi aussi
**(f)** (colloq) (thereabouts) environ; **20 or ~** environ 20
**(g)** (other uses) **I think/don't think ~** je crois/ne crois pas; **I'm afraid ~** j'ai bien peur que oui or si; **~ it would appear** c'est ce qu'il semble; **~ to speak** si je puis dire; **I told you ~** je te l'avais bien dit; **~ I see** je le vois bien; **who says ~?** qui dit ça?; **only more ~** mais encore plus; **he dived and as he did ~...** il a plongé et en le faisant...; **'it's broken'—'~ it is'** 'c'est cassé'—'je le vois bien!'; **~ (what)?** et alors?
[2] **so (that)** phr (in order that) pour que (+ subjunctive)
[3] **so as** phr pour; **~ as to attract attention** pour attirer l'attention
[4] **so much** phr tellement; **she worries ~ much** elle s'inquiète tellement; **she taught me ~ much** elle m'a tant appris; **thank you ~ much** merci beaucoup
**IDIOMS ~ much the better** tant mieux; **~ ~** comme ci comme ça

**soak** [1] vtr **(a)** ⟨rain⟩ tremper ⟨person, clothes⟩
**(b)** ⟨person⟩ faire tremper ⟨clothes, foods⟩
[2] vi **(a)** ⟨clothes, foods⟩ tremper
**(b)** ⟨liquid⟩ **to ~ into** être absorbé/-e par; **to ~ through** traverser

■ **soak up**: ¶ **~ [sth] up, ~ up [sth]**

absorber; ¶ ~ up [sth] s'imprégner de
⟨*atmosphere*⟩; **to ~ up the sun** faire le plein
(colloq) de soleil

**soaked** *adj* trempé/-e; **to be ~ through** *or*
~ **to the skin** être trempé/-e jusqu'aux os

**soaking** *adj* trempé/-e

**soap** *n* savon *m*; **a bar of ~** un savon

**soap opera** *n* feuilleton *m*

**soap powder** *n* lessive *f* (en poudre)

**soar** *vi* (a) ⟨*ball*⟩ filer; ⟨*bird, plane*⟩ prendre
son essor
(b) (glide) planer
(c) ⟨*price, temperature, costs*⟩ monter en
flèche; ⟨*hopes*⟩ grandir considérablement
(d) ⟨*tower, cliffs*⟩ se dresser

**soaring** *adj* ⟨*inflation, demand*⟩ en forte
progression; ⟨*prices, temperatures*⟩ en forte
hausse

**sob** ⓵ *n* sanglot *m*
⓶ *vi* sangloter

**sober** ⓵ *adj* (a) **I'm ~** (not drunk) je n'ai pas
bu d'alcool; (in protest) je ne suis pas ivre
(b) (no longer drunk) dessoûlé/-e
(c) (serious) ⟨*person*⟩ sérieux/-ieuse; ⟨*mood*⟩
grave
(d) ⟨*colour, suit*⟩ sobre
⓶ *vtr* ⟨*news, reprimand*⟩ calmer
■ **sober up** dessoûler

**sob story** *n* (colloq) mélo *m* (colloq)

**soccer** *n* football *m*

**sociable** *adj* ⟨*person*⟩ sociable; ⟨*evening*⟩
agréable

**social** *adj* (a) (gen) social/-e
(b) ⟨*call, visit*⟩ amical/-e

**social climber** *n* (still rising) arriviste *mf*;
(at his/her peak) parvenu/-e *mf*

**social club** *n* club *m*

**social gathering** *n* réunion *f* entre
amis

**socialism** *n* socialisme *m*

**socialist** *n, adj* (*also* **Socialist**)
socialiste (*mf*)

**socialite** *n* mondain/-e *m/f*

**socialize** *vi* rencontrer des gens; **to ~
with sb** fréquenter qn

**social life** *n* (of person) vie *f* sociale; (of
town) vie *f* culturelle

**social science** *n* science *f* sociale

**social security** *n* aide *f* sociale; **to be
on ~** recevoir l'aide sociale

**Social Services** *n pl* (GB) services *mpl*
sociaux

**social work** *n* travail *m* social

**social worker** *n* travailleur/-euse *m/f*
social/-e

**society** *n* (a) (gen) société *f*
(b) (club) société *f*; (for social contact)
association *f*
(c) (*also* **high ~**) haute société *f*

**sociologist** *n* sociologue *mf*

**sociology** *n* sociologie *f*

**sock** *n* chaussette *f*

**socket** *n* (a) (for plug) prise *f* (de courant);
(for bulb) douille *f*
(b) (of joint) cavité *f* articulaire; (of eye) orbite
*f*

**soda** *n* (a) (chemical) soude *f*
(b) (*also* **washing ~**) soude *f* ménagère
(c) (*also* **~ water**) eau *f* de seltz; **whisky
and ~** whisky *m* soda
(d) (*also* **~ pop**) (US) soda *m*

**sodden** *adj* ⟨*towel, clothing*⟩ trempé/-e;
⟨*ground*⟩ détrempé/-e

**sofa** *n* canapé *m*

**sofa bed** *n* canapé-lit *m*

**soft** *adj* (a) (gen) doux/douce; ⟨*ground*⟩
meuble; ⟨*bed, cushion*⟩ moelleux/-euse;
⟨*brush, hair*⟩ souple; ⟨*dough, butter*⟩ mou/
molle; ⟨*impact, touch*⟩ léger/-ère; ⟨*eyes,
heart*⟩ tendre; ⟨*fold*⟩ souple
(b) (lenient) ⟨*parent, teacher*⟩ (trop)
indulgent/-e

**soft cheese** *n* fromage *m* à pâte molle

**soft drink** *n* boisson *f* non alcoolisée

**soft drug** *n* drogue *f* douce

**soften** ⓵ *vtr* (a) adoucir ⟨*skin, water,
light, outline*⟩; ramollir ⟨*butter*⟩
(b) atténuer ⟨*blow, shock, pain*⟩
⓶ *vi* (a) ⟨*light, outline, music, colour*⟩
s'adoucir; ⟨*skin*⟩ devenir plus doux;
⟨*substance*⟩ se ramollir
(b) ⟨*person*⟩ s'assouplir (**towards sb** vis-à-vis
de qn)
■ **soften up**: ¶ ~ **up** amollir; ¶ ~ [sb] **up**
affaiblir ⟨*enemy, opponent*⟩; attendrir
⟨*customer*⟩

**softly** *adv* ⟨*speak, touch, blow*⟩ doucement;
⟨*fall*⟩ en douceur

**soft option** *n* **to take the ~** choisir la
facilité

**soft porn** *n* (colloq) soft *m* (colloq)

**soft spot** *n* (colloq) **to have a ~ for sb**
avoir un faible (colloq) pour qn

**soft-top** *n* décapotable *f*

**soft touch** *n* (colloq) poire *f* (colloq)

**soft toy** *n* peluche *f*

**software** *n* logiciel *m*

**software house** *n* fabricant *m* de
logiciels

**software package** *n* progiciel *m*

**software piracy** *n* piratage *m* de
logiciels

**soggy** *adj* ⟨*ground*⟩ détrempé/-e; ⟨*food*⟩
ramolli/-e

**soil** ⓵ *n* sol *m*, terre *f*
⓶ *vtr* salir

**soiled** *adj* (a) (dirty) sali/-e
(b) (*also* **shop-~**) vendu/-e avec défaut

**solace** ⓵ *n* (feeling of comfort) consolation *f*;
(source of comfort) réconfort *m*
⓶ *vtr* consoler (**for** de)

**solar** *adj* solaire

**solar eclipse** *n* éclipse *f* de soleil

**solar power** *n* énergie *f* solaire

**solder** *vtr, vi* souder (**onto, to** à)

**S**

**soldier** n soldat m
■ **soldier on** persévérer malgré tout

**sole** ① n (a) (fish) sole f
(b) (of foot) plante f; (of shoe, sock) semelle f
② adj (a) (single) seul/-e (before n), unique (before n)
(b) ⟨agent, right⟩ exclusif/-ive; ⟨trader⟩ indépendant

**solely** adv (wholly) entièrement; (exclusively) uniquement

**solemn** adj ⟨occasion, person, voice⟩ solennel/-elle; ⟨duty, warning⟩ formel/-elle

**solicit** ① vtr solliciter ⟨information, help, money, votes⟩; rechercher ⟨business, investment, orders⟩
② vi ⟨prostitute⟩ racoler

**soliciting** n racolage m

**solicitor** n (GB) (for documents, oaths) ≈ notaire m; (for court and police work) ≈ avocat/-e m/f

**solid** ① n solide m
② adj (a) (gen) solide; to go or become ～ se solidifier
(b) ⟨gold, marble⟩ massif/-ive; the gate was made of ～ steel le portail était tout en acier; cut through ～ rock taillé dans la roche
(c) ⟨crowd⟩ compact/-e; ⟨line⟩ continu/-e; five ～ days, five days ～ cinq jours entiers
(d) ⟨advice, worker⟩ sérieux/-ieuse; ⟨investment⟩ sûr/-e
③ adv ⟨freeze⟩ complètement; to be packed ～ ⟨hall⟩ être bondé/-e; the play is booked ～ la pièce affiche complet

**solidarity** n solidarité f

**solidify** ① vtr solidifier
② vi ⟨liquid⟩ se solidifier; ⟨honey, oil⟩ se figer

**solitary** adj (a) (unaccompanied) ⟨occupation, walker⟩ solitaire
(b) (lonely) ⟨person⟩ très seul/-e; ⟨farm, village⟩ isolé/-e
(c) (single) seul/-e

**solitary confinement** n isolement m cellulaire

**solo** ① n solo m
② adj, adv en solo

**soloist** n soliste mf

**solstice** n solstice m

**soluble** adj soluble

**solution** n solution f

**solve** vtr résoudre ⟨equation, problem⟩; élucider ⟨crime⟩; trouver la solution de ⟨mystery⟩; trouver la solution à ⟨clue, crossword⟩; trouver une solution à ⟨crisis, poverty, unemployment⟩

**solvent** ① n solvant m
② adj (in funds) solvable

**sombre** (GB), **somber** (US) adj sombre

**some**

■ Note When some is used to mean an unspecified amount of something, it is translated by du, de l' (before a vowel or mute 'h'), de la or des according to the gender and number of the noun that follows: I'd like some bread = je

voudrais du pain; have some water = prenez de l'eau; we've bought some beer = nous avons acheté de la bière; they've bought some peaches = ils ont acheté des pêches.
– But note that when a plural noun is preceded by an adjective in French, some is translated by de alone: some pretty dresses = de jolies robes.
– When some is used as a pronoun, it is translated by en which is placed before the verb in French: would you like some? = est-ce que vous en voulez?; I've got some = j'en ai.
– For further examples, see the entry below.

① det (a) (an unspecified amount or number) du/ de l'/de la/des; ～ old socks de vieilles chaussettes; ～ red socks des chaussettes rouges; I need ～ help j'ai besoin d'aide
(b) (certain) certain/-e (before n); ～ people say that certaines personnes disent que; to ～ extent dans une certaine mesure
(c) (a considerable amount or number) his suggestion was greeted with ～ hostility sa suggestion a été accueillie avec hostilité; it will take ～ doing ça ne va pas être facile à faire; we stayed there for ～ time nous sommes restés là assez longtemps
(d) (a little, a slight) the meeting did have ～ effect la réunion a eu un certain effet; you must have ～ idea where the house is tu dois avoir une idée de l'endroit où se trouve la maison
(e) (an unknown) he's doing ～ course il suit des cours; a car of ～ sort, ～ sort of car une voiture quelconque
② pron, quantif (a) (an unspecified amount or number) en; he took ～ of it/of them il en a pris un peu/quelques-uns; (do) have ～! servez-vous!
(b) (certain ones) certain/-e; ～ (of them) are blue certains sont bleus; ～ (of them) arrived early certains d'entre eux sont arrivés tôt
③ adv (a) (approximately) environ; ～ 20 people environ 20 personnes
(b) (US) (colloq) un peu

**somebody** pron (also **someone**) quelqu'un; ～ famous quelqu'un de célèbre

**somehow** adv (a) (also ～ or other) (of future action) d'une manière ou d'une autre; (of past action) je ne sais comment; we'll get there ～ on y arrivera d'une manière ou d'une autre; we managed it ～ nous avons réussi je ne sais comment
(b) (for some reason) ～ it doesn't seem very important en fait, ça ne semble pas très important

**someone** = SOMEBODY

**somersault** ① n (of gymnast) roulade f; (of child) galipette f; (accidental) culbute f
② vi ⟨gymnast⟩ faire une roulade; ⟨vehicle⟩ faire un tonneau

**something** ① pron quelque chose; ～ interesting quelque chose d'intéressant; ～ to do quelque chose à faire; there's ～ wrong il y a un problème; ～ or other quelque chose; in nineteen-sixty-～ en mille neuf cent soixante et quelques; **she's gone shopping or ~** elle est allée faire les courses ou quelque chose comme ça

**2 something of** *phr* **she is ~ of an expert on...** elle est assez experte en...; **it was ~ of a surprise** c'était assez étonnant

**sometime** *adv* **we'll have to do it ~** il va falloir qu'on le fasse un jour ou l'autre; **I'll tell you about it ~** je te raconterai ça un de ces jours; **I'll phone you ~ next week** je te téléphonerai dans le courant de la semaine prochaine

**sometimes** *adv* parfois, quelquefois

**somewhat** *adv* (with adjective) plutôt; (with verb, adverb) un peu

**somewhere** *adv* (some place) quelque part; **~ hot** un endroit chaud; **~ or other** je ne sais où; **~ between 50 and 100 people** entre 50 et 100 personnes

**son** *n* fils *m*

**sonata** *n* sonate *f*

**song** *n* chanson *f*; (of bird) chant *m*

**songwriter** *n* (of words) parolier/-ière *m/f*; (of words and music) auteur-compositeur *m* de chansons

**sonic** *adj* sonore

**sonic boom** *n* bang *m*

**son-in-law** *n* gendre *m*

**sonnet** *n* sonnet *m*

**soon** *adv* (a) (in a short time) bientôt; **see you ~!** à bientôt!
(b) (quickly) vite
(c) (early) tôt; **the ~er the better** le plus tôt sera le mieux; **as ~ as possible** dès que possible; **as ~ as you can** dès que tu pourras; **as ~ as he has finished** dès qu'il aura fini; **~er or later** tôt ou tard
(d) (not long) **~ afterwards** peu après; **no ~er had I finished than...** j'avais à peine fini que...

**soot** *n* suie *f*

**soothe** *vtr* calmer ⟨pain, nerves, person⟩; apaiser ⟨sunburn⟩

**soothing** *adj* ⟨music, voice⟩ apaisant/-e; ⟨cream, effect⟩ calmant/-e; ⟨words⟩ rassurant/-e

**sophisticated** *adj* (a) ⟨person⟩ (cultured) raffiné/-e; (affected) sophistiqué/-e; (elegant) chic; ⟨restaurant⟩ chic
(b) ⟨taste⟩ raffiné/-e; ⟨civilization⟩ évolué/-e
(c) ⟨equipment, technology⟩ sophistiqué/-e

**soporific** *adj* soporifique

**soprano** *n* (person) soprano *mf*; (voice, instrument) soprano *m*

**sorcerer** *n* sorcier *m*

**sordid** *adj* sordide

**sore** **1** *n* plaie *f*
**2** *adj* (a) ⟨eyes, gums⟩ irrité/-e; ⟨muscle, arm, foot⟩ endolori/-e; **to have a ~ throat** avoir mal à la gorge
(b) ⟨subject, point⟩ délicat/-e

**sorrow** *n* chagrin *m*

**sorrowful** *adj* ⟨look⟩ affligé/-e; ⟨voice⟩ triste

**sorry** **1** *adj* (a) désolé/-e; **I'm terribly ~** je suis vraiment désolé, je suis navré; **I'm ~ I'm late** je suis désolé d'être en retard; **to be ~ about sth** s'excuser de qch; **to say ~** s'excuser; **to be ~ to do** regretter de faire
(b) (pitying) **to be** *or* **feel ~ for sb** plaindre qn; **to feel ~ for oneself** s'apitoyer sur soi-même
(c) ⟨state, sight, business⟩ triste; ⟨person⟩ minable
**2** *excl* (a) (apologizing) pardon!, désolé!
(b) (pardon) **~?** pardon?

**sort** **1** *n* sorte *f*, genre *m*; **books, records— that ~ of thing** des livres, des disques, ce genre de choses; **I'm not that ~ of person** ce n'est pas mon genre; **some ~ of computer** une sorte d'ordinateur
**2** *vtr* classer ⟨data, files, stamps⟩; trier ⟨letters, apples, potatoes⟩; **to ~ books into piles** ranger des livres en piles
**3 of sorts, of a sort** *phr* **a duck of ~s** *or* **of a ~** une sorte de canard; **progress of ~s** un semblant de progrès
**4 sort of** *phr* (colloq) **~ of cute** plutôt mignon/-onne; **I ~ of understand** je comprends plus ou moins; **~ of blue-green** dans les bleu-vert; **it just ~ of happened** c'est arrivé comme ça
**IDIOMS to be** *or* **feel out of ~s** (ill) ne pas être dans son assiette; (grumpy) être de mauvais poil (colloq); **it takes all ~s (to make a world)** il faut de tout pour faire un monde
■ **sort out** (a) régler ⟨problem, matter⟩
(b) s'occuper de ⟨details, arrangements⟩; **I'll ~ it out** je m'en occuperai
(c) ranger ⟨cupboard, desk⟩; classer ⟨files, documents⟩; mettre de l'ordre dans ⟨finances, affairs⟩; clarifier ⟨ideas⟩
(d) trier ⟨photos, clothes⟩

**sort code** *n* code *m* d'agence

**SOS** *n* SOS *m*

**so-so** (colloq) **1** *adj* moyen/-enne
**2** *adv* comme ci comme ça (colloq)

**sought-after** *adj* ⟨person, skill⟩ demandé/-e, recherché/-e; ⟨job, brand, area⟩ prisé/-e

**soul** *n* (a) (gen) âme *f*
(b) (also **~ music**) soul *m*

**soul-destroying** *adj* abrutissant/-e

**soul mate** *n* âme *f* sœur

**soul-searching** *n* débat *m* intérieur

**sound** **1** *n* (a) (gen) son *m*; (noise) bruit *m* (of de); **to turn the ~ up/down** augmenter/baisser le volume; **the ~ of voices** un bruit de voix; **a grating** *or* **rasping ~** un grincement; **without a ~** sans bruit
(b) (figurative) **by the ~ of it, we're in for a rough crossing** d'après ce qu'on a dit, la traversée va être mauvaise
(c) (Med) sonde *f*
(d) (strait) détroit *m*
**2** *adj* (a) ⟨heart, constitution⟩ solide; ⟨health⟩ bon/bonne (before *n*); **to be of ~ mind** être sain/-e d'esprit ⋯⋯

**S**

**(b)** ⟨*basis, argument*⟩ solide; ⟨*judgment*⟩
sain/-e; ⟨*advice, investment*⟩ bon/bonne
(*before n*), sûr/-e
3 *vtr* faire retentir ⟨*siren, foghorn*⟩; **to ~
one's horn** klaxonner; **to ~ the alarm** sonner
l'alarme
4 *vi* **(a)** (seem) sembler; **it ~s as if he's
really in trouble** il semble qu'il ait vraiment
des ennuis; **it ~s like it might be dangerous**
ça a l'air dangereux; **to ~ boring** paraître
ennuyeux; **it ~s like a flute** on dirait une
flûte
**(b)** ⟨*alarm, buzzer, bugle*⟩ sonner
5 *adv* **to be ~ asleep** dormir à poings
fermés
■ **sound out** sonder, interroger ⟨*person*⟩

**sound barrier** *n* mur *m* du son

**sound bite** *n*: bref extrait d'une interview
enregistrée

**sound card** *n* (Comput) carte *f* son

**sound effect** *n* effet *m* sonore

**soundly** *adv* ⟨*sleep*⟩ à poings fermés;
⟨*defeat*⟩ à plates coutures

**soundproof** *adj* insonorisé/-e

**sound system** *n* (hi-fi) stéréo *f* (colloq); (for
disco etc) sono *f* (colloq)

**soundtrack** *n* (of film) bande *f* sonore; (on
record) bande *f* originale

**soup** *n* soupe *f*, potage *m*

**soup kitchen** *n* soupe *f* populaire

**soup plate** *n* assiette *f* creuse

**soupspoon** *n* cuillère *f* à soupe

**sour** 1 *adj* **(a)** aigre; **to go ~** ⟨*milk*⟩
tourner
**(b)** (bad-tempered) revêche
2 *vtr* gâter ⟨*relations, atmosphere*⟩

**source** *n* source *f*; **at ~** à la source; **~ of**
source *f* de ⟨*anxiety, resentment, satisfaction*⟩;
cause *f* de ⟨*problem, error, infection,
pollution*⟩

**sourdough** *n* (US) levain *m*

**south** 1 *n* **(a)** (compass direction) sud *m*
**(b)** (part of world, country) **the South** le Sud
2 *adj* (gen) sud *inv*; ⟨*wind*⟩ du sud; **in ~
London** dans le sud de Londres
3 *adv* ⟨*move*⟩ vers le sud; ⟨*lie, live*⟩ au sud
(of de)

**South Africa** *pr n* Afrique *f* du Sud

**South America** *pr n* Amérique *f* du Sud

**southeast** 1 *n* sud-est *m*
2 *adj* ⟨*coast, side*⟩ sud-est *inv*; ⟨*wind*⟩ de
sud-est
3 *adv* ⟨*move*⟩ vers le sud-est; ⟨*lie, live*⟩ au
sud-est

**southern** *adj* ⟨*coast*⟩ sud *inv*; ⟨*town,
accent*⟩ du sud; ⟨*hemisphere*⟩ Sud *inv*; **~
England** le sud de l'Angleterre

**South Pole** *pr n* pôle *m* Sud

**southwest** 1 *n* sud-ouest *m*
2 *adj* ⟨*coast*⟩ sud-ouest *inv*; ⟨*wind*⟩ de
sud-ouest
3 *adv* ⟨*move*⟩ vers le sud-ouest; ⟨*lie, live*⟩ au
sud-ouest

**souvenir** *n* souvenir *m*

**sovereign** 1 *n* **(a)** (monarch) souverain/-e
*m/f*
**(b)** (coin) souverain *m*
2 *adj* souverain/-e (*after n*)

**sovereignty** *n* souveraineté *f*

**Soviet Union** *pr n* Union *f* soviétique

**sow**[1] *n* truie *f*

**sow**[2] *vtr* **(a)** semer ⟨*seeds, corn*⟩
**(b)** ensemencer ⟨*field, garden*⟩ (**with** de)
**(c)** (figurative) semer

**soya** *n* soja *m*

**soya sauce, soy sauce** *n* sauce *f* soja

**spa** *n* **(a)** (town) station *f* thermale
**(b)** (US) (health club) club *m* de remise en
forme

**space** 1 *n* **(a)** (also **outer ~**) espace *m*
**(b)** (room) place *f*, espace *m*
**(c)** (gap) espace *m* (**between** entre); (on form)
case *f*
**(d)** (interval of time) intervalle *m*; **in the ~ of
five minutes** en l'espace de cinq minutes
**(e)** (area of land) espace *m*; **open ~s** espaces
libres
2 *adj* ⟨*programme, rocket*⟩ spatial/-e
3 *vtr* espacer
■ **space out** espacer ⟨*words, objects*⟩;
échelonner ⟨*payments*⟩

**space-bar** *n* barre *f* d'espacement

**spaced out** *adj* (colloq) **he's completely ~**
(colloq) il plane (colloq) complètement

**spaceship** *n* vaisseau *m* spatial

**space station** *n* station *f* orbitale

**spacesuit** *n* combinaison *f* spatiale

**spacing** *n* espacement *m*; (of payments)
échelonnement *m*; **in single/double ~** en
simple/double interligne

**spacious** *adj* spacieux/-ieuse

**spade** *n* **(a)** (implement) bêche *f*, pelle *f*
**(b)** (in cards) pique *m*

**spaghetti** *n* spaghetti *mpl inv*

**Spain** *pr n* Espagne *f*

**spamming** *n* (Internet) envoi *m* de
publicités à l'ensemble des connectés

**span** 1 *n* **(a)** (of time) durée *f*
**(b)** (of bridge) travée *f*; (wing)~ envergure *f*
2 *vtr* **(a)** ⟨*bridge, arch*⟩ enjamber
**(b)** (figurative) s'étendre sur

**Spaniard** *n* Espagnol/-e *m/f*

**spaniel** *n* épagneul *m*

**Spanish** 1 *n* **(a)** (people) **the ~** les
Espagnols *mpl*
**(b)** (language) espagnol *m*
2 *adj* (gen) espagnol/-e; ⟨*teacher, lesson*⟩
d'espagnol; ⟨*embassy*⟩ d'Espagne

**spank** *vtr* donner une fessée à

**spanner** *n* (GB) clé *f* (de serrage)

**spar** *vi* ⟨*boxers*⟩ échanger des coups

**spare** 1 *n* (part) pièce *f* de rechange; (wheel)
roue *f* de secours
2 *adj* **(a)** ⟨*cash*⟩ restant/-e; ⟨*seat*⟩ disponible;
⟨*copy*⟩ en plus; **I've got a ~ ticket** j'ai un
ticket en trop; **a ~ moment** un moment de
libre

S

**(b)** ⟨part⟩ de rechange; ⟨wheel⟩ de secours
**(c)** ⟨person, build⟩ élancé/-e
**3** vtr **(a) to have sth to** ∼ avoir qch de disponible; **to catch the train with five minutes to** ∼ prendre le train avec cinq minutes d'avance; **can you** ∼ **a minute?** as-tu un moment?
**(b)** (treat leniently) épargner; **to** ∼ **sb sth** épargner qch à qn
**(c)** (manage without) se passer de ⟨person⟩
IDIOMS **to** ∼ **no effort** faire tout son possible
**spare part** n pièce f de rechange
**spare room** n chambre f d'amis
**spare time** n loisirs mpl
**spare tyre** (GB), **spare tire** (US) n pneu m de rechange
**sparingly** adv ⟨use, add⟩ en petite quantité
**spark** **1** n étincelle f
**2** vtr (also ∼ **off**) provoquer ⟨reaction, panic⟩; être à l'origine de ⟨friendship, affair⟩
**sparkle** **1** n scintillement m; (in eye) éclair m
**2** vi ⟨flame, light⟩ étinceler; ⟨jewel, frost, metal, water⟩ scintiller; ⟨eyes⟩ briller; ⟨drink⟩ pétiller
**sparkler** n cierge m magique
**sparkling** adj **(a)** ⟨eyes⟩ brillant/-e
**(b)** ⟨wit⟩ plein/-e de brio
**(c)** ⟨drink⟩ pétillant/-e
**spark plug** n bougie f
**sparrow** n moineau m
**sparse** adj clairsemé/-e
**sparsely** adv peu; ∼ **wooded** peu boisé/-e; ∼ **populated** à faible population
**spasm** n (of pain) spasme m (**of** de); (of panic, rage) accès m (**of** de)
**spate** n **in full** ∼ (GB) ⟨river⟩ en pleine crue; ⟨person⟩ en plein discours
**(b) a** ∼ **of** une série de ⟨incidents⟩
**spatula** n spatule f
**speak** **1** vtr **(a)** parler ⟨language⟩; **can you** ∼ **English?** parlez-vous (l')anglais?
**(b)** dire ⟨truth⟩; prononcer ⟨word, name⟩; **to** ∼ **one's mind** dire ce qu'on pense
**2** vi parler (**to, with** à; **about, of** de); **who's** ∼**ing?** (on phone) qui est à l'appareil?; (**this is**) **Eileen** ∼**ing** c'est Eileen; **generally** ∼**ing** en règle générale; **roughly** ∼**ing** en gros; **strictly** ∼**ing** à proprement parler
■ **speak out** se prononcer
■ **speak up (a)** (louder) parler plus fort
**(b)** (dare to speak) intervenir
**speaker** n **(a)** (person talking) personne f qui parle; (public speaker) orateur/-trice m/f
**(b) a French** ∼ un/-e francophone; **a Russian** ∼ un/-e russophone
**(c)** (on stereo system) haut-parleur m
**-speaking** combining form **English-/ French-**∼ anglophone/francophone; **Welsh-**∼ ⟨person⟩ qui parle le gallois
**spear** n lance f
**spearhead** vtr mener ⟨campaign, revolt, reform⟩

**spearmint** n menthe f verte
**special** adj (gen) spécial/-e; ⟨case, reason, treatment⟩ particulier/-ière; ⟨friend⟩ très cher/chère
**special effect** n effet m spécial
**specialist** n spécialiste mf (**in** de)
**speciality** (GB), **specialty** (US) n spécialité f
**specialize** vi se spécialiser
**specially** adv **(a)** (specifically) spécialement; **I made it** ∼ **for you** je l'ai fait exprès pour toi
**(b)** (particularly) particulièrement; ⟨like, enjoy⟩ surtout
**special needs** n pl (Sch) difficultés fpl d'apprentissage scolaire
**special school** n établissement m médico-éducatif pour enfants handicapés
**species** n espèce f
**specific** adj précis/-e
**specifically** adv **(a)** (specially) spécialement
**(b)** (explicitly) explicitement
**(c)** (in particular) en particulier
**specify** **1** vtr stipuler; ⟨person⟩ préciser
**2 specified** pp adj ⟨amount, date, day⟩ spécifié/-e
**specimen** n (of rock, urine, handwriting) échantillon m; (of blood, tissue) prélèvement; (of species, plant) spécimen m
**speck** n (of dust, soot) grain m; (of dirt, mud, blood) petite tache f; (of light) point m
**spectacle** **1** n spectacle m
**2 spectacles** n pl lunettes fpl
**spectacular** adj spectaculaire
**spectator** n spectateur/-trice m/f
**spectre** (GB), **specter** (US) n spectre m
**spectrum** n **(a)** (of colours) spectre m
**(b)** (range) gamme f
**speculate** **1** vtr **to** ∼ **that** supposer que
**2** vi spéculer (**on** sur; **about** à propos de)
**speculation** n **(a)** (conjecture) spéculations fpl
**(b)** (financial) spéculation f (**in** sur)
**speech** n **(a)** discours m (**on** sur; **about** à propos de); **to give a** ∼ faire un discours
**(b)** (faculty) parole f
**(c)** (language) langage m
**speech day** n (GB) (Sch) (jour m de la) distribution f des prix
**speech impediment** n défaut m d'élocution
**speechless** adj muet/-ette (**with** de); **to be** ∼ **with** rester muet de; **I was** ∼ **at the news** la nouvelle m'a laissé sans voix
**speed** **1** n **(a)** vitesse f; (of response, reaction) rapidité f; **at top** ∼ à toute vitesse;
**(b)** (colloq) (drug) amphétamines fpl
**2** vtr hâter ⟨process, recovery⟩
**3** vi **(a) to** ∼ **along** ⟨driver, car⟩ rouler à toute allure; **to** ∼ **away** s'éloigner à toute allure
**(b)** (drive too fast) conduire trop vite                    ···❖

■ **speed up**: ¶ ~ up ⟨*walker*⟩ aller plus vite; ⟨*athlete, driver, car*⟩ accélérer; ⟨*worker*⟩ travailler plus vite; ¶ ~ [sth] up accélérer

**speedboat** *n* hors-bord *m*

**speed camera** *n* ≈ cinémomètre *m*

**speed hump** *n* ralentisseur *m*

**speeding** *n* excès *m* de vitesse

**speed limit** *n* limitation *f* de vitesse

**speedometer** *n* compteur *m* (de vitesse)

**spell** ① *n* (a) (period) moment *m*, période *f*; sunny ~ éclaircie *f*
(b) (magic words) formule *f* magique; to be under a ~ être envoûté/-e; to cast *or* put a ~ on sb jeter un sort à qn; to be under sb's ~ être sous le charme de qn
② *vtr* (a) écrire ⟨*word*⟩
(b) signifier ⟨*danger, disaster*⟩
③ *vi* he can't/can ~ il a une mauvaise/ bonne orthographe
■ **spell out** (a) épeler ⟨*word*⟩
(b) (explain) expliquer [qch] clairement

**spellbound** *adj* envoûté/-e (by par)

**spellcheck** *vtr* effectuer une correction orthographique sur ⟨*document*⟩

**spellchecker** *n* correcteur *m* orthographique.

**spelling** *n* orthographe *f*

**spend** ① *vtr* (a) dépenser ⟨*money, salary*⟩ (on en)
(b) passer ⟨*time*⟩ (doing à faire)
② *vi* dépenser

**spending cut** *n* réduction *f* des dépenses; (Pol) restriction *f* budgétaire

**spending power** *n* pouvoir *m* d'achat

**spending spree** *n* folie *f* (colloq) (de dépense); to go on a ~ faire des folies (colloq)

**spendthrift** *adj* ⟨*person*⟩ dépensier/-ière

**sperm** *n* sperme *m*

**sperm donor** *n* donneur *m* de sperme

**spew** *vtr* vomir

**sphere** *n* (a) (shape) sphère *f*
(b) (field) domaine *m* (of de); ~ of influence sphère *f* d'influence

**spherical** *adj* sphérique

**spice** *n* (Culin) épice *f*; (figurative) piment *m*

**spick-and-span** *adj* impeccable

**spicy** *adj* (a) ⟨*food*⟩ épicé/-e
(b) ⟨*detail*⟩ croustillant/-e

**spider** *n* araignée *f*

**spiderweb** *n* (US) toile *f* d'araignée

**spike** ① *n* pointe *f*
② *vtr* (colloq) corser ⟨*drink*⟩ (with de)

**spiky** *adj* ⟨*hair*⟩ en brosse *inv*; ⟨*branch*⟩ piquant/-e; ⟨*object*⟩ acéré/-e

**spill** ① *vtr* renverser ⟨*drink*⟩ (on, over sur)
② *vi* se répandre (onto sur; into dans)
■ **spill over** déborder; to ~ over into dégénérer en ⟨*looting, hostility*⟩

**spin** ① *n* (a) (of wheel) tour *m*; (of dancer, skater) pirouette *f*
(b) to go into a ~ ⟨*plane*⟩ descendre en vrille
(c) to go for a ~ (in car) aller faire un tour

② *vtr* (a) lancer ⟨*top*⟩; faire tourner ⟨*globe, wheel*⟩
(b) filer ⟨*wool, thread*⟩
(c) ⟨*spider*⟩ tisser ⟨*web*⟩
③ *vi* tourner; ⟨*weathercock, top*⟩ tournoyer; ⟨*dancer*⟩ pirouetter; my head is ~ning j'ai la tête qui tourne
■ **spin out** prolonger ⟨*visit*⟩; faire traîner [qch] en longueur ⟨*speech*⟩; faire durer ⟨*work, money*⟩
■ **spin round**: ¶ ~ round ⟨*person*⟩ se retourner rapidement; ⟨*dancer, skater*⟩ pirouetter; ⟨*car*⟩ faire un tête-à-queue; ¶ ~ [sb/sth] round faire tourner ⟨*wheel*⟩

**spinach** *n* (Culin) épinards *mpl*

**spinal cord** *n* moelle *f* épinière

**spindly** *adj* grêle

**spin doctor** *n* (Pol) consultant *m* en communication attaché à un parti politique

**spin-drier**, **spin dryer** *n* essoreuse *f*

**spine** *n* (a) (Anat) colonne *f* vertébrale
(b) (on hedgehog, cactus) piquant *m*
(c) (of book) dos *m*

**spineless** *adj* mou/molle

**spin-off** *n* (a) (incidental benefit) retombée *f* favorable
(b) (by-product) sous-produit *m*

**spinster** *n* célibataire *f*; (derogatory) vieille fille *f*

**spiral** ① *n* spirale *f*
② *adj* ⟨*structure*⟩ en spirale
③ *vi* ⟨*prices, costs*⟩ monter en flèche
④ **spiralling** (GB), **spiraling** (US) *pres p adj* qui monte en flèche

**spiral staircase** *n* escalier *m* en colimaçon

**spire** *n* flèche *f*

**spirit** ① *n* (a) (gen) esprit *m*
(b) (courage, determination) courage *m*
② **spirits** *n pl* (a) (alcohol) spiritueux *mpl*
(b) to be in good ~s être de bonne humeur; to be in high ~s être d'excellente humeur; to keep one's ~s up garder le moral

**spirited** *adj* ⟨*horse, debate, reply*⟩ fougueux/-euse; ⟨*attack, defence*⟩ vif/vive

**spirit level** *n* niveau *m* à bulle

**spiritual** ① *n* spiritual *m*
② *adj* spirituel/-elle

**spit** ① *n* (a) (saliva) salive *f*
(b) (Culin) broche *f*
② *vtr* ⟨*person*⟩ cracher; ⟨*pan*⟩ projeter ⟨*oil*⟩
③ *vi* ⟨*cat, person*⟩ cracher (at, on sur); ⟨*oil, sausage*⟩ grésiller; ⟨*logs, fire*⟩ crépiter
④ *v impers* it's ~ting (with rain) il bruine
IDIOMS to be the ~ting image of sb être le portrait tout craché de qn

**spite** ① *n* rancune *f*
② *vtr* faire du mal à; (less strong) embêter
③ **in spite of** *phr* malgré; in ~ of the fact that bien que

**spiteful** *adj* ⟨*person*⟩ rancunier/-ière; ⟨*remark*⟩ méchant/-e

**splash** ① *n* (a) (sound) plouf *m*

**splay ⋯⟶ sprain** ⋯⋯

**(b)** (of mud) tache *f*; (of water, oil) éclaboussure *f*; (of colour) touche *f*; (of tonic, soda) goutte *f*
2 *vtr* éclabousser; **to ~ water on to one's face** s'asperger le visage d'eau
3 *vi* faire des éclaboussures
∎ **splash out** (colloq) faire des folies; **to ~ out on sth** faire la folie de s'offrir qch

**splay** *vtr* écarter ⟨*feet, fingers*⟩

**spleen** *n* (Anat) rate *f*

**splendid** *adj* splendide; ⟨*idea, holiday, performance*⟩ merveilleux/-euse

**splendour** (GB), **splendor** (US) *n* splendeur *f*

**splice** *vtr* coller ⟨*tape, film*⟩; épisser ⟨*ends of rope*⟩

**splint** *n* (for injury) attelle *f*

**splinter** 1 *n* éclat *m*
2 *vi* ⟨*glass, windscreen*⟩ se briser; ⟨*wood*⟩ se fendre; ⟨*alliance*⟩ se scinder

**splinter group** *n* groupe *m* dissident

**split** 1 *n* **(a)** (in fabric) déchirure *f*; (in rock, wood) fissure *f*
**(b)** (in party, alliance) scission *f* (**in** de)
2 **splits** *n pl* **to do the ~s** faire le grand écart
3 *adj* ⟨*fabric*⟩ déchiré/-e; ⟨*seam*⟩ défait/-e; ⟨*log, lip*⟩ fendu/-e
4 *vtr* **(a)** fendre ⟨*log, rock*⟩ (**in, into** en); déchirer ⟨*garment*⟩
**(b)** diviser ⟨*party*⟩
**(c)** (share) partager (**between** entre)
5 *vi* **(a)** ⟨*wood, log, rock*⟩ se fendre (**in , into** en); ⟨*fabric, garment*⟩ se déchirer
**(b)** ⟨*party*⟩ se diviser
∎ **split up**: ¶ **~ up** ⟨*couple, band*⟩ se séparer; ¶ **~ [sth] up** diviser (**into** en)

**split second** *n* fraction *f* de seconde

**splutter** *vi* ⟨*person*⟩ bafouiller; ⟨*fire, fat*⟩ grésiller

**spoil** 1 *vtr* **(a)** (mar) gâcher ⟨*event, view, game*⟩; gâter ⟨*place, taste, effect*⟩; **to ~ sth for sb** gâcher qch à qn
**(b)** (ruin) abîmer ⟨*garment, crops*⟩
**(c)** (pamper) gâter ⟨*child, pet*⟩
2 *vi* ⟨*product, foodstuff*⟩ s'abîmer

**spoiled, spoilt** (GB) *adj* ⟨*child, dog*⟩ gâté/-e; **a ~ brat** (colloq) un gamin pourri (colloq)

**spoiler** *n* (Aut) becquet *m*

**spoils** *n pl* (of war) butin *m* (**of** de)

**spoilsport** *n* (colloq) **to be a ~** être un rabat-joie

**spoke** *n* rayon *m*

**spokesman** *n* porte-parole *m inv*

**spokeswoman** *n* porte-parole *m inv*

**sponge** 1 *n* **(a)** éponge *f*
**(b)** (*also* **~ cake**) génoise *f*
2 *vtr* éponger ⟨*material, stain, face*⟩
3 *vi* (colloq) **to ~ off** *or* **on** vivre sur le dos de ⟨*family, state*⟩

**sponge bag** *n* trousse *f* de toilette

**sponsor** 1 *n* **(a)** (advertiser, backer) sponsor *m*
**(b)** (patron) mécène *m*

2 *vtr* sponsoriser ⟨*event, team*⟩; financer ⟨*student*⟩; parrainer ⟨*child*⟩

**sponsorship** *n* sponsorat *m*

**spontaneous** *adj* spontané/-e

**spontaneously** *adv* spontanément

**spoof** *n* (colloq) (parody) parodie *f* (**on** de)

**spooky** *adj* (colloq) ⟨*house, atmosphere*⟩ sinistre; ⟨*story*⟩ qui fait froid dans le dos

**spool** *n* bobine *f*

**spoon** *n* cuillère *f*; (teaspoon) petite cuillère *f*

**spoonful** *n* cuillerée *f*, cuillère *f*

**sporadic** *adj* sporadique

**sport** *n* **(a)** sport *m*
**(b) he's a good ~** (good loser) il est beau joueur

**sporting** *adj* **(a)** ⟨*fixture, event*⟩ sportif/-ive
**(b)** (fair, generous) généreux/-euse; **to have a ~ chance of doing** avoir de bonnes chances de faire

**sports car** *n* voiture *f* de sport

**sports centre** (GB), **~s center** (US) *n* centre *m* sportif

**sports club** *n* club *m* sportif

**sports ground** *n* (large) stade *m*; (in school, club) terrain *m* de sports

**sports jacket** *n* (GB) veste *f* en tweed

**sportsman** *n* sportif *m*

**sports star** *n* vedette *f* sportive

**sportswear** *n* vêtements *mpl* de sport

**sportswoman** *n* sportive *f*

**sporty** *adj* (colloq) sportif/-ive

**spot** 1 *n* **(a)** (on animal) tache *f*; (on fabric) pois *m*; (on dice, domino) point *m*
**(b)** (stain) tache *f*
**(c)** (pimple) bouton *m*
**(d)** (place) endroit *m*; **on the ~** sur place; **to decide on the ~** décider sur-le-champ
**(e)** (colloq) (small amount) **a ~ of** un peu de
**(f)** (colloq) **to be in a (tight) ~** être dans une situation embêtante
2 *vtr* **(a)** apercevoir ⟨*person*⟩; repérer ⟨*difference, mistake*⟩
**(b)** (stain) tacher

**spot check** *n* contrôle *m* surprise

**spotless** *adj* impeccable

**spotlight** *n* **(a)** (light) projecteur *m*; (in home) spot *m*
**(b)** (focus of attention) **to be in** *or* **under the ~** ⟨*person*⟩ être sur la sellette; **the ~ is on Aids** le sida fait la une; **to turn** *or* **put the ~ on sb/sth** attirer l'attention sur qn/qch

**spotted** *adj* ⟨*fabric*⟩ à pois; ⟨*fur, dog*⟩ tacheté/-e

**spotty** *adj* (pimply) ⟨*skin*⟩ boutonneux/-euse; **he's very ~** il est plein de boutons; (patterned) à pois (**after** *n*)

**spouse** *n* époux/épouse *m/f*

**spout** 1 *n* (of kettle, teapot) bec *m* verseur
2 *vtr* **(a)** (spurt) faire jaillir ⟨*water*⟩
**(b)** (recite) débiter ⟨*poetry, statistics*⟩
3 *vi* ⟨*liquid*⟩ jaillir (**from, out of** de)

**sprain** 1 *n* entorse *f* ⋯⟶

**S**

**2** *vtr* to ~ one's ankle se faire une entorse à la cheville; (less severely) se fouler la cheville

**sprawl** **1** *n* (of suburbs, buildings) étendue *f*
**2** *vi* s'étaler

**spray** **1** *n* (a) (seawater) embruns *mpl*; (other) nuages *mpl* de (fines) gouttelettes
(b) (container) (for perfume) vaporisateur *m*; (can) bombe *f*; (for inhalant, throat, nose) pulvérisateur *m*
(c) (of flowers) (bunch) gerbe *f*; (single branch) rameau *m*
**2** *vtr* (a) vaporiser ⟨*liquid*⟩; asperger ⟨*person*⟩ (with de); to ~ sth onto sth (onto fire) projeter qch sur qch ⟨*foam, water*⟩; (onto surface, flowers) vaporiser qch sur qch ⟨*paint, water*⟩

**spray can** *n* bombe *f*, aérosol *m*

**spread** **1** *n* (a) (of disease, drugs) propagation *f*; (of news, information) diffusion *f*
(b) (Culin) pâte *f* à tartiner
**2** *vtr* (a) (unfold) étaler, étendre ⟨*cloth, newspaper, map*⟩ (on, over sur); ⟨*bird*⟩ déployer ⟨*wings*⟩
(b) étaler ⟨*butter, jam, glue*⟩ (on, over sur)
(c) (distribute) disperser ⟨*troops*⟩; répartir ⟨*workload, responsibility*⟩
(d) (also ~ out) étaler, échelonner ⟨*payments, meetings*⟩ (over sur)
(e) propager ⟨*disease, fire*⟩; semer ⟨*confusion, panic*⟩; faire circuler ⟨*rumour, story*⟩
**3** *vi* (a) ⟨*butter, jam, glue*⟩ s'étaler
(b) ⟨*forest, drought*⟩ s'étendre (over sur); ⟨*disease, fear, fire*⟩ se propager; ⟨*rumour, story*⟩ circuler; ⟨*stain, damp*⟩ s'étaler
■ **spread out**: ¶ ~ out ⟨*group*⟩ se disperser (over sur); ⟨*wings, tail*⟩ se déployer; ¶ ~ [sth] out étaler, étendre ⟨*cloth, map, rug*⟩ (on, over sur)

**spread-eagled** *adj* bras et jambes écartés

**spreadsheet** *n* tableur *m*

**spree** *n* to go on a ~ (drinking) faire la bringue (colloq); to go on a shopping ~ aller faire les folies dans les magasins

**sprig** *n* (of holly) petite branche *f*; (of parsley) brin *m*

**sprightly** *adj* alerte, gaillard

**spring** **1** *n* (a) (season) printemps *m*; in ~ au printemps
(b) (of wire) ressort *m*
(c) (leap) bond *m*
(d) (water source) source *f*
**2** *vtr* (a) déclencher ⟨*trap, lock*⟩
(b) to ~ a leak ⟨*tank, barrel*⟩ commencer à fuir
(c) to ~ [sth] on sb annoncer [qch] de but en blanc à qn ⟨*news, plan*⟩
**3** *vi* (a) (jump) bondir (onto sur)
(b) (originate) to ~ from venir de
■ **spring up** ⟨*new building*⟩ apparaître

**spring-clean** *vtr* nettoyer [qch] de fond en comble ⟨*house*⟩

**spring onion** *n* (GB) ciboule *f*

**springtime** *n* printemps *m*

**springy** *adj* ⟨*mattress, seat*⟩ élastique

**sprinkle** *vtr* to ~ sth with saupoudrer qch de ⟨*salt, sugar*⟩; parsemer qch de ⟨*herbs*⟩; to ~ sth with water humecter qch

**sprinkler** *n* (a) (for lawn) arroseur *m*
(b) (to extinguish fires) diffuseur *m*

**sprint** **1** *n* (race) sprint *m*, course *f* de vitesse
**2** *vi* (in athletics) sprinter; (to catch bus) courir (à toute vitesse)

**sprout** **1** *n* (also **Brussels** ~) chou *m* de Bruxelles
**2** *vi* ⟨*seed, shoot*⟩ germer; ⟨*grass, weeds*⟩ pousser

**spruce** **1** *n* (also ~ **tree**) épicéa *m*
**2** *adj* ⟨*person*⟩ soigné/-e; ⟨*house, garden*⟩ bien tenu/-e
■ **spruce up** astiquer ⟨*house*⟩; nettoyer ⟨*garden*⟩; to ~ oneself up se faire beau/belle

**spry** *adj* alerte, leste

**spun** *adj* ⟨*glass, gold, sugar*⟩ filé/-e

**spur** **1** *n* (a) (for horse) éperon *m*; (figurative) aiguillon *m*
(b) (of rock) contrefort *m*
**2** *vtr* (also ~ **on**) éperonner ⟨*horse*⟩; aiguillonner ⟨*person*⟩; to ~ sb to do inciter qn à faire
IDIOMS on the ~ of the moment sur une impulsion

**spurn** *vtr* refuser [qch] (avec mépris)

**spurt** **1** *n* (a) (gush) (of water, oil, blood) giclée *f*; (of flame) jaillissement *m*
(b) (of activity) regain *m*; (of energy) sursaut *m*; (in growth) poussée *f*; to put on a ~ ⟨*runner, cyclist*⟩ pousser une pointe de vitesse
**2** *vi* (also ~ **out**) jaillir (from, out of de)

**spy** **1** *n* espion/-ionne *m/f*
**2** *vtr* remarquer, discerner ⟨*figure, object*⟩
**3** *vi* to ~ on sb/sth espionner qn/qch

**spying** *n* espionnage *m*

**squabble** *vi* se disputer, se chamailler (colloq)

**squad** *n* (Mil) escouade *f*; (Sport) sélection *f*

**squad car** *n* voiture *f* de police

**squadron** *n* escadron *m*

**squalid** *adj* sordide

**squall** *n* (wind) bourrasque *f*, rafale *f* (of de); (at sea) grain *m*

**squalor** *n* (filth) saleté *f* repoussante; (wretchedness) misère *f* (noire)

**squander** *vtr* gaspiller

**square** **1** *n* (a) (shape) carré *m*
(b) (in town) place *f*
(c) (in game, crossword) case *f*; (of glass, linoleum) carreau *m*
(d) (colloq) (person) ringard/-e *m/f* (colloq)
**2** *adj* (a) (in shape) carré/-e; four ~ metres quatre mètres carrés
(b) (quits) to be ~ ⟨*people*⟩ être quitte
**3** *vtr* (a) to ~ one's shoulders redresser les épaules
(b) (settle) régler ⟨*account, debt*⟩
IDIOMS to go back to ~ one retourner à la case départ

S

■ **square up** (settle accounts) régler ses comptes

**square bracket** *n* crochet *m*; **in ∼s** entre crochets

**square root** *n* racine *f* carrée

**squash** **1** *n* **(a)** (sport) squash *m*
**(b)** (drink) sirop *m*
**(c)** (vegetable) courge *f*
**2** *vtr* écraser

■ **squash up** (colloq) se serrer (**against** contre)

**squat** **1** *adj* ⟨*person, structure, object*⟩ trapu/-e
**2** *vi* **(a)** (crouch) s'accroupir
**(b)** **to ∼ in** squatter ⟨*building*⟩

**squatter** *n* squatter *m*

**squawk** *vi* ⟨*hen*⟩ pousser des gloussements; ⟨*duck, parrot*⟩ pousser des cris rauques

**squeak** **1** *n* (of door, wheel, chalk) grincement *m*; (of mouse, soft toy) couinement *m*; (of furniture, shoes) craquement *m*
**2** *vi* ⟨*door, wheel, chalk*⟩ grincer; ⟨*mouse, soft toy*⟩ couiner; ⟨*shoes, furniture*⟩ craquer (**on** sur)

**squeaky** *adj* ⟨*voice*⟩ aigu/aiguë; ⟨*gate, hinge, wheel*⟩ grinçant/-e

**squeal** *vi* ⟨*person, animal*⟩ pousser des cris aigus

**squeamish** *adj* impressionnable, sensible

**squeeze** **1** *n* **(a)** (on credit, finances) resserrement *m* (**on** de)
**(b)** (colloq) (crush) **it will be a tight ∼** ce sera un peu juste
**2** *vtr* **(a)** presser ⟨*lemon, bottle, tube*⟩; serrer ⟨*arm, hand*⟩; appuyer sur ⟨*trigger*⟩; percer ⟨*spot*⟩; **to ∼ water out of** essorer, tordre ⟨*cloth*⟩
**(b)** (figurative) réussir à obtenir ⟨*money*⟩ (**out of** de); **to ∼ the truth out of sb** arracher la vérité à qn
**(c)** (fit) **to ∼ sth into sth** entasser qch dans qch

■ **squeeze in:** ¶ **∼ in** ⟨*person*⟩ se glisser; ¶ **∼ [sb] in** ⟨*doctor etc*⟩ faire passer [qn] entre deux rendez-vous

■ **squeeze past** ⟨*car, person*⟩ passer

**squelch** *vi* ⟨*water, mud*⟩ glouglouter; **to ∼ along** avancer en pataugeant

**squid** *n* calmar *m*, encornet *m*

**squiggle** *n* gribouillis *m*

**squint** **1** *n* strabisme *m*; **to have a ∼** loucher
**2** *vi* **(a)** (look) plisser les yeux
**(b)** (have eye condition) loucher

**squire** *n* ≈ châtelain *m*

**squirm** *vi* (wriggle) se tortiller; ⟨*person*⟩ (in pain) se tordre; (with embarrassment) être très mal à l'aise

**squirrel** *n* écureuil *m*

**squirt** **1** *vtr* faire gicler ⟨*liquid*⟩
**2** *vi* ⟨*liquid*⟩ jaillir (**from, out of** de)

**stab** **1** *n* **(a)** (act) coup *m* de couteau; **a ∼ in the back** (figurative) un coup en traître

**(b)** (of pain) élancement *m* (**of** de)
**2** *vtr* poignarder ⟨*person*⟩

**stabbing** *n* agression *f* au couteau

**stability** *n* stabilité *f*

**stabilize** **1** *vtr* stabiliser
**2** *vi* se stabiliser

**stable** **1** *n* écurie *f*; riding ∼s manège *m*
**2** *adj* **(a)** (steady) stable
**(b)** (psychologically) équilibré/-e

**stack** **1** *n* (pile) pile *f*; (of hay, straw) meule *f*
**2** *vtr* **(a)** (also ∼ **up**) (pile) empiler
**(b)** (fill) remplir ⟨*shelves*⟩
**(c)** mettre [qch] en attente ⟨*planes, calls*⟩

**stadium** *n* stade *m*

**staff** *n* (of company) personnel *m*; (of a school, college) personnel *m* enseignant

**staff meeting** *n* réunion *f* du personnel enseignant

**staff room** *n* salle *f* des professeurs

**stag** *n* cerf *m*

**stage** **1** *n* **(a)** (phase) (of illness, career, life) stade *m* (**of, in** de); (of project, process, plan) phase *f* (**of, in** de); (of journey, negotiations) étape *f* (**of, in** de)
**(b)** (raised platform) estrade *f*; (in theatre) scène *f*
**2** *vtr* **(a)** (organize) organiser ⟨*event, rebellion, strike*⟩
**(b)** (fake) simuler ⟨*quarrel, scene*⟩
**(c)** (in theatre) monter ⟨*play*⟩

**stagecoach** *n* diligence *f*

**stage fright** *n* trac *m*

**stage-manager** *n* régisseur/-euse *m/f*

**stagger** **1** *vtr* **(a)** (astonish) stupéfier, abasourdir
**(b)** échelonner ⟨*holidays, payments*⟩
**2** *vi* (from weakness) chanceler; (drunkenly) tituber

**staggering** *adj* ⟨*amount, increase*⟩ prodigieux/-ieuse; ⟨*news*⟩ renversant/-e; ⟨*achievement, contrast*⟩ stupéfiant/-e; ⟨*success*⟩ étourdissant/-e

**stagnant** *adj* stagnant/-e

**stagnate** *vi* stagner

**stag night**, **stag party** *n* soirée *f* pour enterrer une vie de garçon

**staid** *adj* guindé/-e

**stain** **1** *n* **(a)** (mark) tache *f*
**(b)** (dye) teinture *f*
**2** *vtr* **(a)** (soil) tacher ⟨*clothes, carpet, table*⟩
**(b)** teindre ⟨*wood*⟩

**stained glass** *n* verre *m* coloré

**stained glass window** *n* vitrail *m*

**stainless steel** *n* acier *m* inoxydable

**stain remover** *n* détachant *m*

**stair** **1** *n* (step) marche *f* (d'escalier)
**2 stairs** *n pl* **the ∼s** l'escalier; **to fall down the ∼s** tomber dans l'escalier

**staircase**, **stairway** *n* escalier *m*

**stake** **1** *n* **(a)** (amount risked) enjeu *m*; **to be at ∼** être en jeu
**(b)** (investment) participation *f* (**in** dans)
**(c)** (post) pieu *m*

····⊱

**S**

[2] *vtr* miser ⟨*money, property*⟩; risquer ⟨*reputation*⟩

■ **stake out**: ~ out [sth], ~ [sth] out surveiller ⟨*place*⟩

**stale** *adj* ⟨*bread, cake*⟩ rassis/-e; ⟨*beer*⟩ éventé/-e; ⟨*smell*⟩ de renfermé; ⟨*ideas*⟩ éculé/-e

**stalemate** *n* (a) (in chess) pat *m*
(b) (deadlock) impasse *f*

**stalk** [1] *n* (on plant, flower) tige *f*; (of leaf, apple) queue *f*; (of mushroom) pied *m*
[2] *vtr* ⟨*hunter, murderer*⟩ traquer ⟨*prey, victim*⟩; ⟨*animal*⟩ chasser ⟨*prey*⟩

**stall** [1] *n* (a) (at market, fair) stand *m*
(b) (in stable) stalle *f*
[2] **stalls** *n pl* (GB) orchestre *m*
[3] *vtr* caler ⟨*engine, car*⟩
[4] *vi* (a) ⟨*car*⟩ caler
(b) (play for time) temporiser

**stallholder** *n* marchand/-e *m/f*

**stallion** *n* étalon *m*

**stalwart** *adj* loyal/-e

**stamina** *n* résistance *f*, endurance *f*

**stammer** [1] *n* bégaiement *m*
[2] *vi* bégayer

**stamp** [1] *n* (a) (for envelope) timbre *m*
(b) (on passport, document) cachet *m*
(c) (marker) (rubber) tampon *m*; (metal) cachet *m*
[2] *vtr* (a) apposer [qch] au tampon ⟨*date, name*⟩ (on sur); tamponner ⟨*ticket, book*⟩; viser ⟨*document, passport*⟩
(b) to ~ one's foot (in anger) taper du pied
[3] *vi* ⟨*horse*⟩ piaffer; to ~ on écraser (du pied) ⟨*toy, foot*⟩; piétiner ⟨*soil, ground*⟩

**stamp-collecting** *n* philatélie *f*

**stamped addressed envelope, sae** *n* enveloppe *f* timbrée à votre/son etc adresse

**stampede** [1] *n* débandade *f*
[2] *vi* s'enfuir (pris d'affolement)

**stance** *n* position *f*

**stand** [1] *n* (a) (support, frame) support *m*; (for coats) portemanteau *m*
(b) (stall) (in market) éventaire *m*; (kiosk) kiosque *m*; (at exhibition, trade fair) stand *m*
(c) (in stadium) tribunes *fpl*
(d) (witness box) barre *f*
(e) (stance) to take a ~ on sth prendre position sur qch
(f) (to make) a last ~ (livrer) une dernière bataille
[2] *vtr* (a) (place) mettre ⟨*person, object*⟩ (against contre; in dans; on sur)
(b) (bear) supporter ⟨*cold, weight*⟩; tolérer ⟨*nonsense, bad behaviour*⟩; I can't ~ him je ne peux pas le supporter *or* le sentir; I can't ~ this town je déteste cette ville; I can't ~ doing je déteste faire
(c) (colloq) to ~ sb a drink payer un verre à qn
(d) to ~ trial passer en jugement
[3] *vi* (a) (also ~ up) se lever

(b) (be upright) ⟨*person*⟩ se tenir debout; ⟨*object*⟩ tenir debout; to remain ~ing rester debout
(c) ⟨*building, village*⟩ se trouver, être
(d) (step) to ~ on marcher sur ⟨*insect, foot*⟩
(e) (be) as things ~... étant donné l'état actuel des choses...; the total ~s at 300 le total est de 300; to ~ in sb's way (figurative) faire obstacle à qn
(f) (remain valid) ⟨*offer, agreement*⟩ rester valable
(g) (be a candidate) se présenter (as comme); to ~ for election se présenter aux élections

■ **stand back** ⟨*person, crowd*⟩ reculer (from de); (figurative) prendre du recul (from par rapport à)

■ **stand by**: ¶ ~ by ⟨*doctor, army*⟩ être prêt/-e à intervenir; ¶ ~ by [sb/sth] soutenir ⟨*person*⟩; s'en tenir à ⟨*principles, decision*⟩

■ **stand down** démissionner

■ **stand for** (a) (represent) représenter; ⟨*initials*⟩ vouloir dire
(b) (tolerate) tolérer

■ **stand in**: to ~ in for sb remplacer qn

■ **stand out** ⟨*person*⟩ sortir de l'ordinaire; ⟨*work, ability*⟩ être remarquable

■ **stand up**: ¶ ~ up (a) (rise) se lever
(b) (stay upright) se tenir debout
(c) ⟨*theory, story*⟩ tenir debout
(d) to ~ up to tenir tête à ⟨*person*⟩
(e) to ~ up for défendre ⟨*person, rights*⟩
¶ ~ [sth] up redresser ⟨*object*⟩
¶ ~ [sb] up (colloq) poser un lapin à (colloq)

**standard** [1] *n* (a) (level) niveau *m*; not to be up to ~ ne pas avoir le niveau requis
(b) (official specification) norme *f* (for de)
(c) (banner) étendard *m*
[2] *adj* ⟨*size, rate, pay*⟩ standard *inv*; ⟨*procedure*⟩ habituel/-elle; ⟨*image*⟩ traditionnel/-elle; it's ~ practice c'est l'usage

**Standard Assessment Task** *n* (GB) (Sch) test *m* d'aptitude scolaire (*par tranches d'âge*)

**standardize** *vtr* normaliser, standardiser

**standard lamp** *n* (GB) lampadaire *m*

**standard of living** *n* niveau *m* de vie

**standby** *n* (person) remplaçant/-e *m/f*; to be on ~ ⟨*army, emergency services*⟩ être prêt/-e à intervenir; (for airline ticket) être en stand-by

**stand-in** *n* remplaçant/-e *m/f*

**standing** [1] *n* (a) (reputation) réputation *f*, rang *m* (among parmi; with chez)
(b) (length of time) of long ~ de longue date
[2] *adj* (a) ⟨*army, committee, force*⟩ actif/-ive
(b) ⟨*invitation*⟩ permanent/-e

**standing charge** *n* frais *mpl* d'abonnement *m*

**standing order** *n* virement *m* automatique

**stand-off** *n* (US) impasse *f*

**standpoint** *n* point *m* de vue

**standstill** *n* to be at a ~ ⟨*traffic*⟩ être à l'arrêt; ⟨*factory, port*⟩ être au point mort;

⟨work⟩ être arrêté/e; ⟨talks⟩ être arrivé/-e à une impasse; **to come to a ∼** ⟨person, car⟩ s'arrêter

**stand-up** 1 n (also ∼ **comedy**) one man show m comique
2 adj ∼ **comedian** comique mf

**Stanley knife**® n cutter m

**staple** 1 n (a) (for paper) agrafe f
(b) (basic food) aliment m de base
2 adj ⟨product, food, diet⟩ de base
3 vtr agrafer (**to** à; **onto** sur)

**stapler** n agrafeuse f

**star** 1 n (a) (in sky) étoile f
(b) (celebrity) vedette f, star f
(c) (asterisk) astérisque m
(d) (ranking) **a three-∼ hotel** un hôtel (à) trois étoiles
2 vi ⟨actor⟩ jouer le rôle principal (**in** dans)
3 vtr ⟨film, play⟩ avoir [qn] pour vedette ⟨actor⟩

**starch** n (a) (carbohydrate) féculents mpl
(b) (for clothes) amidon m

**stardom** n célébrité f; **to rise to ∼** devenir une vedette

**stare** 1 n regard m fixe
2 vi **to ∼ at sb/sth** regarder fixement qn/qch

**starfish** n étoile f de mer

**stark** adj ⟨landscape⟩ désolé/-e; ⟨room, decor⟩ nu/-e; **in ∼ contrast to** en opposition totale avec
IDIOMS ∼ **naked** tout/-e nu/-e

**starry** adj ⟨night, sky⟩ étoilé/-e

**starry-eyed** adj ébloui/-e (**about** par)

**star sign** n signe m astrologique

**star-studded** adj avec de nombreuses vedettes

**start** 1 n (a) (beginning) début m
(b) (in sport) (advantage) avantage m; (in time, distance) avance f; (departure line) ligne f de départ
(c) (movement) **with a ∼** en sursaut
2 vtr (a) (begin) commencer; entamer ⟨bottle, packet⟩; **to ∼ doing** commencer à faire
(b) (cause, initiate) déclencher ⟨quarrel, war⟩; lancer ⟨fashion, rumour⟩
(c) faire démarrer ⟨car⟩; mettre [qch] en marche ⟨machine⟩
3 vi (a) (begin) commencer (**by doing** par faire); **to ∼ again** recommencer
(b) ⟨car, engine, machine⟩ démarrer
(c) (depart) partir
(d) (jump nervously) sursauter (**in** de)
4 **to start with** phr (a) (firstly) d'abord, premièrement
(b) (at first) au début
■ **start off**: ¶ ∼ **off (a)** (set off) ⟨train, bus⟩ démarrer; ⟨person⟩ partir
(b) (begin) ⟨person⟩ commencer; ⟨business, employee⟩ débuter (**as** comme; **in** dans)
¶ ∼ **[sth] off (a)** commencer ⟨visit, talk⟩ (**with** par)
(b) mettre [qch] en marche ⟨machine⟩
■ **start out** (on journey) partir

■ **start over** (US) recommencer (à zéro)
■ **start up**: ¶ ∼ **up** ⟨engine⟩ démarrer; ¶ ∼ **[sth] up** faire démarrer ⟨car⟩; ouvrir ⟨shop⟩; créer ⟨business⟩

**starter** n (a) (of race) starter m
(b) (on menu) hors-d'œuvre m inv
IDIOMS **for ∼s** (colloq) pour commencer

**startle** vtr (a) (take aback) surprendre
(b) (alarm) effrayer

**startling** adj saisissant/-e

**starvation** n famine f; **to die of ∼** mourir de faim

**starve** 1 vtr affamer; (figurative) priver (**of** de); **to ∼ oneself** se sous-alimenter
2 vi mourir de faim; **to be ∼d of** être en mal de ⟨company, conversation⟩

**starving** adj (hungry) **to be ∼** mourir de faim; (hunger-stricken) affamé/-e

**state** 1 n (a) état m; **he's not in a fit ∼ to drive** il n'est pas en état de conduire
(b) (government, nation) (also **State**) État m
2 **States** n pl **the States** les États-Unis mpl
3 adj (a) ⟨school, sector⟩ public/-ique; ⟨enterprise, pension⟩ d'État; ⟨subsidy⟩ de l'État
(b) ⟨occasion⟩ d'apparat; ⟨visit⟩ officiel/-ielle
4 vtr (a) (declare) exposer ⟨fact, opinion⟩; indiquer ⟨age, income⟩; **to ∼ that** ⟨person⟩ déclarer que
(b) (specify) spécifier ⟨amount, time, terms⟩; exprimer ⟨preference⟩
IDIOMS **to be in a ∼** être dans tous ses états

**State Department** n (US) ministère m des Affaires étrangères

**state-funded** adj subventionné/-e par l'État

**stateless** adj apatride

**stately** adj imposant/-e

**stately home** n (GB) château m

**statement** n (a) déclaration f; (official) communiqué m
(b) (also **bank ∼**) relevé m de compte

**state of the art** adj ⟨equipment⟩ ultramoderne; ⟨technology⟩ de pointe

**statesman** n homme m d'État

**static** 1 n (a) (also ∼ **electricity**) électricité f statique
(b) (interference) parasites mpl
2 adj (a) (stationary) ⟨image⟩ fixe; ⟨traffic⟩ bloqué/-e
(b) (stable) ⟨population, prices⟩ stationnaire

**station** 1 n (a) (also **railway ∼**) (GB)) gare f
(b) (radio, TV) station f
(c) (also **police ∼**) commissariat m; (small) poste m de police
2 vtr poster ⟨officer, guard⟩; stationner ⟨troops⟩

**stationary** adj immobile, à l'arrêt

**stationer** n (also ∼'s) papeterie f

**stationery** n fournitures fpl de bureau; (writing paper) papier m à lettres

**station wagon** n (US) break m

**S**

**statistic** n statistique f; ~s show that... d'après les statistiques...

**statistical** adj statistique

**statue** n statue f

**stature** n (a) (height) taille f
(b) (status) envergure f

**status** n (a) (position) position f
(b) (prestige) prestige m
(c) (legal, professional) statut m (as de);
financial ~ situation f financière

**status quo** n statu quo m

**status symbol** n signe m de prestige

**statute** n texte m de loi; by ~ par la loi

**statutory** adj légal/-e

**staunch** adj ⟨supporter, defence⟩ loyal/-e;
⟨Catholic, communist⟩ fervent/-e

**stave** n (Mus) portée f
■ **stave off** tromper ⟨hunger, fatigue⟩;
écarter ⟨threat⟩

**stay** ① n (a) (visit) séjour m
(b) ~ of execution sursis m
② vi (a) (remain) rester; to ~ for lunch rester
(à) déjeuner
(b) (have accommodation) loger; to ~ in a hotel/
with a friend loger à l'hôtel/chez un ami; to
~ overnight passer la nuit
(c) (visit) passer quelques jours (with chez)
■ **stay in** rester à la maison
■ **stay out**: to ~ out late/all night rentrer
tard/ne pas rentrer de la nuit; to ~ out of
trouble éviter les ennuis
■ **stay up** (a) (waiting for sb) veiller
(b) (as habit) se coucher tard
(c) (not fall down) tenir

**staying-power** n endurance f

**steadfast** adj tenace

**steadily** adv (a) (gradually) progressivement
(b) ⟨work, rain⟩ sans interruption

**steady** ① adj (a) (continual) ⟨stream,
increase⟩ constant/-e; ⟨rain⟩ incessant/-e;
⟨breathing, progress⟩ régulier/-ière
(b) (stable) stable; to hold [sth] ~ bien tenir
⟨ladder⟩
(c) ⟨voice, hand⟩ ferme; ⟨gaze⟩ calme
(d) (reliable) ⟨job⟩ stable; ⟨relationship⟩
durable
② vtr to ~ one's nerves se calmer les nerfs

**steak** n (of beef) steak m; (of fish) darne f

**steal** ① vtr voler (from sb à qn)
② vi (a) (thieve) voler
(b) (creep) to ~ into/out of a room entrer/
quitter une pièce subrepticement

**stealing** n vol m

**stealthy** adj ⟨step, glance⟩ furtif/-ive

**steam** ① n vapeur f
② vtr faire cuire [qch] à la vapeur
⟨vegetables⟩
③ vi fumer, dégager de la vapeur
IDIOMS to run out of ~ s'essouffler; to let off
~ décompresser
■ **steam up** ⟨window, glasses⟩ s'embuer

**steam engine** n locomotive f à vapeur

**steamer** n (boat) (bateau m à) vapeur m

**steamroller** n rouleau m compresseur

**steamy** adj (a) ⟨window⟩ embué/-e;
⟨climate⟩ chaud/-e et humide
(b) (colloq) (erotic) torride

**steel** ① n acier m
② v refl to ~ oneself s'armer de courage

**steelworks, steelyard** n installations
fpl sidérurgiques

**steep** ① adj (a) ⟨slope, stairs⟩ raide; ⟨street,
path⟩ escarpé/-e; ⟨roof⟩ en pente raide
(b) (sharp) ⟨rise, fall⟩ fort/-e (before n)
(c) (colloq) ⟨price⟩ exorbitant/-e
② vtr to ~ sth in faire tremper qch dans

**steeple** n (tower) clocher m; (spire) flèche f

**steer** ① n (animal) bouvillon m
② vtr (a) piloter ⟨ship, car⟩
(b) (guide) diriger ⟨person⟩
③ vi (in car) piloter; (in boat) gouverner
IDIOMS to ~ clear of sb/sth se tenir à l'écart
de qn/qch

**steering lock** n blocage m de direction

**steering wheel** n volant m

**stem** ① n (a) (of flower, leaf) tige f; (of fruit)
queue f
(b) (of glass) pied m
② vtr arrêter ⟨flow⟩; enrayer ⟨advance, tide⟩
③ vi to ~ from provenir de

**stencil** ① n pochoir m
② vtr décorer [qch] au pochoir ⟨fabric,
surface⟩

**stenography** n (US) sténographie f

**step** ① n (a) (pace) pas m
(b) (measure) mesure f; to take ~s prendre
des mesures
(c) (stage) étape f (in dans)
(d) (stair) marche f; ~s (small ladder) escabeau
m
② vi marcher (in dans; on sur); to ~ into
entrer dans ⟨lift⟩; monter dans ⟨dinghy⟩; to
~ off descendre de ⟨pavement⟩; to ~ over
enjamber ⟨fence⟩
IDIOMS one ~ at a time chaque chose en son
temps
■ **step back** (figurative) prendre du recul
(from par rapport à)
■ **step down** se retirer; (as electoral candidate)
se désister
■ **step in** intervenir (and do pour faire)
■ **step up** accroître ⟨production⟩; intensifier
⟨campaign⟩

**step aerobics** n step m

**stepbrother** n demi-frère m

**step-by-step** ① adj ⟨guide⟩ complet/-ète
② **step by step** adv ⟨explain⟩ étape par
étape

**stepchild** n beau-fils/belle-fille m/f

**stepdaughter** n belle-fille f

**stepfather** n beau-père m

**stepladder** n escabeau m

**stepmother** n belle-mère f

**stepping stone** n pierre f de gué;
(figurative) tremplin m

**stepsister** n demi-sœur f

**stepson** n beau-fils m

**stereo** n (a) (sound) stéréo f; in ~ en stéréo

**(b)** (*also* ~ **system**) chaîne *f* stéréo; **personal** ~ baladeur *m*

**stereotype** *n* stéréotype *m*

**sterile** *adj* stérile

**sterilize** *vtr* stériliser

**sterling** *n* livre *f* sterling *inv*

**stern** 1 *n* (of ship) poupe *f*
2 *adj* sévère

**steroid** *n* stéroïde *m*

**stew** 1 *n* ragoût *m*
2 *vtr* cuire (qch) en ragoût ⟨*meat*⟩; faire cuire ⟨*fruit*⟩; **~ed apples** compote *f* de pommes

**steward** *n* (on plane, ship) steward *m*; (of club) intendant/-e *m/f*; (at races) organisateur *m*

**stewardess** *n* (on plane) hôtesse *f* (de l'air)

**stick** 1 *n* **(a)** (of wood, chalk, dynamite) bâton *m*
**(b)** (*also* **walking** ~) canne *f*
**(c)** (in hockey) crosse *f*
2 *vtr* **(a) to ~ sth into sth** planter qch dans qch
**(b)** (colloq) (put) mettre
**(c)** (fix in place) coller ⟨*poster, stamp*⟩ (**on** sur; **to** à)
3 *vi* **(a) the thorn stuck in my finger** l'épine m'est restée dans le doigt
**(b)** ⟨*stamp, glue*⟩ coller; **to ~ to the pan** ⟨*sauce, rice*⟩ attacher (colloq)
**(c)** ⟨*drawer, door, lift*⟩ se coincer
**(d)** (remain) rester; **to ~ in sb's mind** rester gravé dans la mémoire de qn
■ **stick at**: ~ **at** [sth] persévérer dans ⟨*task*⟩
■ **stick out**: ¶ ~ **out** ⟨*nail, sharp object*⟩ dépasser (**of** de); **his ears ~ out** il a les oreilles décollées; ¶ ~ [sth] **out: to ~ out one's hand/foot** tendre la main/le pied; **to ~ one's tongue out** tirer la langue
■ **stick to (a)** (keep to) s'en tenir à ⟨*facts, point*⟩; maintenir ⟨*story, version*⟩
**(b)** (follow) suivre ⟨*river, road*⟩
■ **stick together (a)** ⟨*pages*⟩ se coller
**(b)** (colloq) (be loyal) être solidaires
**(c)** (colloq) (not separate) rester ensemble
■ **stick up** (project) se dresser; **to ~ up for sb** défendre qn

**sticker** *n* autocollant *m*

**sticking plaster** *n* pansement *m* adhésif, sparadrap *m*

**sticky** *n* **(a)** ⟨*floor, fingers*⟩ poisseux/-euse; ⟨*label*⟩ adhésif/-ive
**(b)** (sweaty) ⟨*hand, palm*⟩ moite

**sticky tape** *n* (colloq) Scotch® *m*, ruban *m* adhésif

**stiff** 1 *adj* **(a)** raide; (after sport, sleeping badly) courbaturé/-e; **~ neck** torticolis *m*; **to have ~ legs** (after sport) avoir des courbatures dans les jambes
**(b)** ⟨*lever, handle*⟩ dur/-e à manier
**(c)** ⟨*manner, style*⟩ compassé/-e
**(d)** (tough) ⟨*sentence*⟩ sévère; ⟨*exam, climb*⟩ difficile; ⟨*competition*⟩ rude
**(e)** (high) ⟨*charge, fine*⟩ élevé/-e

**(f)** a ~ **drink** un remontant
2 *adv* (colloq) **to bore sb ~** ennuyer qn à mourir; **to be scared ~** avoir une peur bleue

**stiffen** 1 *vtr* renforcer ⟨*card*⟩; empeser ⟨*fabric*⟩
2 *vi* **(a)** ⟨*person*⟩ se raidir
**(b)** ⟨*egg white*⟩ devenir ferme; ⟨*mixture*⟩ prendre de la consistance

**stifle** *vtr* étouffer

**stigma** *n* stigmate *m*

**stigmatize** *vtr* stigmatiser

**stile** *n* échalier *m*

**stiletto** *n* (*also* ~ **heel**) (shoe, heel) talon *m* aiguille

**still¹** *adv* **(a)** encore, toujours; **he's ~ as crazy as ever!** il est toujours aussi fou!; **they're ~ in town** ils sont encore en ville
**(b)** (referring to the future) encore; **I have four exams ~ to go** j'ai encore quatre examens à passer
**(c)** (nevertheless) quand même
**(d)** (with comparatives) encore; **better/worse ~** encore mieux/pire

**still²** 1 *n* **(a)** (for making alcohol) alambic *m*
**(b)** (photograph) photo *f* de plateau
2 *adj* **(a)** (motionless) ⟨*air, water*⟩ calme; ⟨*hand, person*⟩ immobile
**(b)** (peaceful) ⟨*countryside, streets*⟩ tranquille
**(c)** ⟨*drink*⟩ non gazeux/-euse
3 *adv* ⟨*lie, stay*⟩ immobile; **to sit ~** se tenir tranquille; **to stand ~** ne pas bouger

**still life** *n* nature *f* morte

**stilted** *adj* guindé/-e

**stimulant** *n* stimulant *m* (**to** de)

**stimulate** *vtr* stimuler

**stimulating** *adj* stimulant/-e

**stimulus** *n* **(a)** (physical) stimulus *m*
**(b)** (boost) impulsion *f*
**(c)** (incentive) stimulant *m*

**sting** 1 *n* **(a)** (part of insect) aiguillon *m*
**(b)** (result of being stung) piqûre *f*
2 *vtr* **(a)** ⟨*insect*⟩ piquer
**(b)** ⟨*wind*⟩ cingler
3 *vi* (gen) piquer; ⟨*cut*⟩ cuire

**stingy** *adj* radin/-e (colloq)

**stink** 1 *n* (mauvaise) odeur *f*
2 *vi* puer

**stint** 1 *n* **to do a three-year ~** travailler trois ans
2 *vi* **to ~ on** lésiner sur ⟨*drink, presents*⟩

**stipulate** *vtr* stipuler (**that** que)

**stir** 1 *n* **to cause (quite) a ~** faire sensation
2 *vtr* **(a)** remuer ⟨*liquid, sauce*⟩; mélanger ⟨*paint, powder*⟩; **to ~ sth into sth** incorporer qch à qch
**(b)** ⟨*breeze*⟩ agiter ⟨*leaves, papers*⟩
3 *vi* **(a)** ⟨*leaves, papers*⟩ trembler; ⟨*curtains*⟩ remuer
**(b)** (budge) bouger
■ **stir up** provoquer ⟨*trouble*⟩; attiser ⟨*hatred, unrest*⟩; exciter ⟨*crowd*⟩

**stir-fry** 1 *n* sauté *m* ⋯⋯

2 *vtr* faire sauter ⟨*beef, vegetable*⟩

**stirring** *adj* ⟨*story*⟩ passionnant/-e; ⟨*music, speech*⟩ enthousiasmant/-e

**stirrup** *n* étrier *m*

**stitch** 1 *n* (a) (in sewing, embroidery) point *m*; (in knitting, crochet) maille *f*
(b) (in wound) point *m* de suture
(c) (pain) point *m* de côté
2 *vtr* coudre (**to, onto** à); recoudre ⟨*wound*⟩

**stoat** *n* hermine *f*

**stock** 1 *n* (a) (supply) stock *m*; **we're out of ~** nous n'en avons plus
(b) (descent) souche *f*, origine *f*
(c) (Culin) bouillon *m*
(d) (livestock) bétail *m*
2 **stocks** *n pl* (a) (GB) (in finance) valeurs *fpl*, titres *mpl*; **~s and shares** valeurs *fpl* mobilières
(b) (US) actions *fpl*
(c) **the ~s** le pilori
3 *adj* ⟨*size*⟩ courant/-e; ⟨*answer*⟩ classique; ⟨*character*⟩ stéréotypé/-e
4 *vtr* (a) (sell) avoir, vendre
(b) remplir ⟨*fridge*⟩; garnir ⟨*shelves*⟩; approvisionner ⟨*shop*⟩
IDIOMS **to take ~** faire le point (**of** sur)
■ **stock up** s'approvisionner (**with, on** en)

**stockbroker** *n* agent *m* de change

**stock-cube** *n* bouillon-cube® *m*

**stock exchange** *n* **the ~** la Bourse

**Stockholm** *pr n* Stockholm

**stocking** *n* bas *m*

**stock market** *n* (a) (stock exchange) Bourse *f* (des valeurs)
(b) (prices, trading activity) marché *m* (des valeurs)

**stockpile** *vtr* stocker ⟨*weapons*⟩; faire des stocks de ⟨*food, goods*⟩

**stock room** *n* magasin *m*

**stock-still** *adv* **to stand ~** rester cloué/-e sur place

**stocktaking** *n* inventaire *m*

**stocky** *adj* trapu/-e

**stodgy** *adj* ⟨*food*⟩ bourratif/-ive

**stoical** *adj* stoïque

**stoke** *vtr* (*also* **~ up**) alimenter ⟨*fire, furnace*⟩

**stolid** *adj* ⟨*person, character*⟩ flegmatique

**stomach** 1 *n* estomac *m*; (belly) ventre *m*
2 *vtr* supporter ⟨*person, attitude*⟩

**stomach ache** *n* **to have** (a) **~** avoir mal au ventre

**stone** 1 *n* (a) pierre *f*; (pebble) caillou *m*
(b) (in fruit) noyau *m*
(c) (GB) (weight) = 6.35 kg
2 *vtr* dénoyauter ⟨*peach*⟩

**Stone Age** *n* âge *m* de pierre

**stone circle** *n* enceinte *f* de monolithes, cromlech *m*

**stone-cold** *adj* glacé/-e.

**stone mason** *n* tailleur *m* de pierre

**stonewall** *vi* faire de l'obstruction

**stone-washed** *adj* délavé/-e

**stony** *adj* (a) (rocky) pierreux/-euse
(b) ⟨*look, silence*⟩ glacial/-e

**stool** *n* tabouret *m*

**stoop** 1 *n* **to have a ~** avoir le dos voûté
2 *vi* être voûté/-e; (bend down) se baisser; **to ~ so low as to do** s'abaisser jusqu'à faire

**stop** 1 *n* (a) (gen) arrêt *m*; **to come to a ~** ⟨*vehicle, work, progress*⟩ s'arrêter; **to put a ~ to** mettre fin à
(b) (in telegram) stop *m*
2 *vtr* (a) (cease) arrêter; (temporarily) interrompre ⟨*activity*⟩; **to ~ doing** arrêter de faire
(b) (prevent) empêcher; **to ~ sb (from) doing** empêcher qn de faire
(c) supprimer ⟨*allowance*⟩; **to ~ a cheque** faire opposition à un chèque
(d) (plug) boucher ⟨*gap, hole, bottle*⟩
3 *vi* (a) s'arrêter
(b) (stay) rester; **to ~ for dinner** rester dîner; **I can't ~** je n'ai vraiment pas le temps
4 *v refl* **to ~ oneself** se retenir
■ **stop off** (on journey) faire un arrêt
■ **stop up**: **~** [*sth*] **up, ~ up** [*sth*] boucher ⟨*hole*⟩

**stopgap** *n* bouche-trou *m*

**stop-off** *n* (quick break) arrêt *m*; (longer) halte *f*

**stopover** *n* escale *f*

**stoppage** *n* (strike) arrêt *m* de travail

**stopper** *n* (for flask, jar) bouchon *m*

**stop sign** *n* (panneau *m* de) stop *m*

**stopwatch** *n* chronomètre *m*

**storage** 1 *n* (of food, fuel) stockage *m* (**of** de); **to be in ~** ⟨*furniture*⟩ être au garde-meuble
2 *adj* ⟨*space*⟩ de rangement

**storage heater** *n* radiateur *m* électrique à accumulation

**store** 1 *n* (a) (shop) magasin *m*; (smaller) boutique *f*
(b) (supply) provision *f*
(c) (place) (for food, fuel) réserve *f*; (for furniture) garde-meuble *m*
(d) **what does the future have in ~ for us?** qu'est-ce que l'avenir nous réserve?
2 *vtr* (a) conserver ⟨*food, information*⟩; ranger ⟨*furniture*⟩
(b) (Comput) mémoriser ⟨*data*⟩

**storekeeper** *n* (US) commerçant/-e *m/f*

**storeroom** *n* (in house, school, office) réserve *f*; (in factory, shop) magasin *m*

**storey** (GB), **story** (US) *n* étage *m*; **on the third ~** (GB) au troisième étage; (US) au quatrième étage

**stork** *n* cigogne *f*

**storm** 1 *n* tempête *f*; (thunderstorm) orage *m*
2 *vtr* prendre [qch] d'assaut ⟨*citadel, prison*⟩
3 *vi* **he ~ed off in a temper** il est parti furibond

**stormy** *adj* orageux/-euse; **~ scenes** éclats *mpl*

**story** *n* **(a)** (gen) histoire *f* **(about, of** de); **a
true ∼** une histoire vécue; **a ghost ∼** une
histoire de fantômes
**(b)** (in newspaper) article *m* (**on, about** sur)
**(c)** (rumour) rumeur *f* (**about** sur); **the ∼ goes
that** on raconte que
**(d)** (US) (floor) étage *m*
**storybook** *n* livre *m* de contes
**storyteller** *n* conteur/-euse *m/f*
**stout** *adj* **(a)** (fat) corpulent/-e
**(b)** (strong) ⟨*wall*⟩ épais/-aisse
**stove** *n* **(a)** (cooker) cuisinière *f*
**(b)** (heater) poêle *m*
**stow** *vtr* ranger ⟨*baggage*⟩
**stowaway** *n* passager/-ère *m/f*
clandestin/-e
**straddle** *vtr* enfourcher ⟨*horse, bike*⟩;
s'asseoir à califourchon sur ⟨*chair*⟩
**straggle** *vi* **(a)** ⟨*houses, villages*⟩ être
disséminé/-e le long de
**(b)** (dawdle) traîner
**straggler** *n* traînard/-e *m/f*
**straggly** *adj* ⟨*hair, beard*⟩ en désordre
**straight** **1** *adj* **(a)** ⟨*line, nose, road*⟩
droit/-e; ⟨*chair*⟩ raide; **in a ∼ line** en ligne
droite
**(b)** (level, upright) bien droit/-e; **the picture
isn't ∼** le tableau est de travers
**(c)** (tidy, in order) en ordre
**(d)** (clear) **to get sth ∼** comprendre qch; **to
set the record ∼** mettre les choses au clair
**(e)** (honest, direct) ⟨*person*⟩ honnête, droit/-e;
⟨*answer, question*⟩ clair/-e; **to be ∼ with sb**
jouer franc-jeu avec qn
**(f)** ⟨*choice*⟩ simple
**(g)** ⟨*spirits, drink*⟩ sec, sans eau
**(h)** ⟨*actor, role*⟩ sérieux/-ieuse
**2** *adv* **(a)** droit; **stand up ∼!** tenez-vous
droit!; **to go/keep ∼ ahead** aller/continuer
tout droit; **to look ∼ ahead** regarder droit
devant soi
**(b)** (without delay) directement; **to go ∼ back
to Paris** rentrer directement à Paris
**(c)** (frankly) tout net; **I'll tell you ∼** (colloq) je
vous le dirai tout net; **∼ out** carrément
**(d)** (neat) ⟨*drink*⟩ sec, sans eau
IDIOMS **to keep a ∼ face** garder son sérieux
**straightaway** *adv* tout de suite
**straighten** *vtr* tendre ⟨*arm, leg*⟩;
redresser ⟨*picture, teeth*⟩; ajuster ⟨*tie, hat*⟩;
défriser ⟨*hair*⟩
■ **straighten out: to ∼ things out** (resolve)
arranger les choses
■ **straighten up:** ¶ **∼ up** ⟨*person*⟩ se
redresser; ¶ **∼** [sth] **up** (tidy) ranger ⟨*objects,
room*⟩
**straightforward** *adj* ⟨*answer, person*⟩
franc/franche; ⟨*account*⟩ simple
**straight-laced** *adj* collet-monté *inv*
**strain** **1** *n* **(a)** (force) effort *m* (**on** sur)
**(b)** (pressure) (on person) stress *m*; (in relations)
tension *f*
**(c)** (of virus, bacteria) souche *f*
**2** *vtr* **(a) to ∼ one's eyes** (to see) plisser les
yeux; **to ∼ one's ears** tendre l'oreille

**(b)** (try) mettre [qch] à rude épreuve
⟨*patience*⟩
**(c)** (injure) **to ∼ a muscle** se froisser un
muscle; **to ∼ one's eyes** se fatiguer les
yeux; **to ∼ one's back** se faire un tour de
reins
**(d)** (sieve) passer ⟨*sauce*⟩; égoutter
⟨*vegetables, pasta, rice*⟩
**3** *vi* **to ∼ at** tirer sur ⟨*leash, rope*⟩
**strained** *adj* (tense) tendu/-e; (injured)
⟨*muscle*⟩ froissé/-e
**strainer** *n* passoire *f*
**strait** *n* détroit *m*
IDIOMS **to be in dire ∼s** être aux abois
**straitjacket** *n* camisole *f* de force
**strand** **1** *n* (gen) fil *m*; (of hair) mèche *f*
**2** *vtr* **to be ∼ed** être bloqué/-e; **to leave sb
∼ed** laisser qn en rade (colloq)
**strange** *adj* **(a)** (unfamiliar) inconnu/-e; **a ∼
man** un inconnu
**(b)** (odd) bizarre; **it is ∼ (that)** il est bizarre
que (+ *subjunctive*)
**strangely** *adv* ⟨*behave, react*⟩ d'une façon
étrange; ⟨*quiet, empty*⟩ étrangement; **∼
enough,...** chose étrange,...
**stranger** *n* (from elsewhere) étranger/-ère
*m/f*; (unknown person) inconnu/-e *m/f*
**strangle** *vtr* étrangler
**stranglehold** *n* (control) mainmise *f*
**strap** **1** *n* (on shoe) bride *f*; (on case, harness)
courroie *f*; (on watch) bracelet *m*; (on handbag)
bandoulière *f*; (on dress, bra) bretelle *f*
**2** *vtr* attacher (**to** à)
**strapless** *adj* sans bretelles
**strapped** *adj* (colloq) **to be ∼ for** être à
court de ⟨*cash, staff*⟩
**strapping** *adj* costaud/-e
**stratagem** *n* stratagème *m*
**strategic** *adj* stratégique
**strategy** *n* stratégie *f*
**straw** *n* paille *f*
IDIOMS **to clutch at ∼s** se raccrocher à
n'importe quoi; **the last ∼** la goutte qui fait
déborder le vase
**strawberry** **1** *n* fraise *f*; **strawberries and
cream** fraises à la crème
**2** *adj* ⟨*tart*⟩ aux fraises; ⟨*ice cream*⟩ à la
fraise; ⟨*jam*⟩ de fraises
**straw poll** *n* sondage *m* non-officiel
**stray** **1** *n* (dog) chien *m* errant; (cat) chat *m*
vagabond
**2** *adj* ⟨*dog*⟩ errant/-e; ⟨*cat*⟩ vagabond/-e;
⟨*bullet*⟩ perdu/-e; ⟨*tourist*⟩ isolé/-e
**3** *vi* **(a)** (wander) s'égarer; **to ∼ from the
road** s'écarter de la route
**(b)** ⟨*eyes, mind*⟩ errer
**streak** **1** *n* **(a)** (in character) côté *m*
**(b)** (period) **a winning/losing ∼** une bonne/
mauvaise passe
**(c)** (of paint) traînée *f*; **∼ of lightning** éclair *m*
**(d)** (in hair) mèche *f*
**2** *vtr* **(a)** strier ⟨*sea, sky*⟩
**(b) to get one's hair ∼ed** se faire faire des
mèches

**S**

**3** *vi* to ~ **past** passer comme une flèche
**streaky bacon** *n* (GB) bacon *m*
entrelardé
**stream** **1** *n* (a) (brook) ruisseau *m*
(b) **a** ~ **of** un flot de ⟨*traffic, questions*⟩; **a** ~
**of abuse** un torrent d'insultes
**2** *vi* (a) (flow) ruisseler; **sunlight was** ~**ing**
**into the room** le soleil entrait à flots dans la
pièce; **people** ~**ed out of the theatre** un flot
de gens sortait du théâtre
(b) ⟨*banners, hair*⟩ to ~ **in the wind** flotter
au vent
(c) ⟨*eyes, nose*⟩ couler
**streamer** *n* (of paper) banderole *f*
**streamline** *vtr* (a) (in design) caréner
(b) (make more efficient) rationaliser
⟨*distribution, production*⟩
(c) (cut) dégraisser ⟨*company*⟩
**streamlined** *adj* (a) ⟨*cooker, furniture*⟩
aux lignes modernes; ⟨*hull, body*⟩ caréné/-e
(b) ⟨*production, system*⟩ simplifié/-e
**street** *n* rue *f*; **in** *or* **on the** ~ dans la rue
**street cred** *n* (colloq) **to have** ~ être dans
le coup (colloq)
**streetlamp** *n* (old gas-lamp) réverbère *m*;
(modern) lampadaire *m*
**street market** *n* marché *m* en plein air
**street plan** *n* indicateur *m* des rues
**street value** *n* valeur *f* à la revente
**streetwise** *adj* (colloq) dégourdi/-e (colloq)
**strength** *n* (of wind, person, government, bond,
argument) force *f*; (of lens, magnet, voice, army)
puissance *f*; (of structure, equipment) solidité *f*;
(of material) résistance *f*; (of feeling) intensité *f*
**strengthen** *vtr* renforcer ⟨*building,
argument, love, position*⟩; consolider ⟨*bond,
links*⟩; affirmer ⟨*power, role*⟩; fortifier
⟨*muscles*⟩; raffermir ⟨*dollar*⟩
**strenuous** *adj* ⟨*exercise*⟩ énergique;
⟨*activity, job*⟩ ardu/-e
**stress** **1** *n* (a) (nervous) tension *f*, stress *m*;
**mental** ~ **tension nerveuse; to be under** ~
être stressé/-e
(b) (emphasis) accent *m* (**on** sur); **to lay** ~ **on**
insister sur ⟨*fact, problem*⟩
(c) (in physics) effort *m*
(d) (in pronouncing) accent *m*
**2** *vtr* mettre l'accent sur, insister sur; **to** ~
**the importance of sth** souligner l'importance
de qch; **to** ~ (**that**) souligner que
■ **stress out** (colloq) ¶ ~ [**sb**] **out** stresser [qn]
**stressed** *adj* (a) (also ~ **out**) stressé/-e
(b) ⟨*syllable*⟩ accentué/-e
**stressful** *adj* stressant/-e
**stretch** **1** *n* (a) (of road, track) tronçon *m*;
(of coastline, river) partie *f*
(b) (of water, countryside) étendue *f*
(c) (period) période *f*; **to work for 12 hours at**
**a** ~ travailler 12 heures d'affilée
**2** *adj* ⟨*cover, fabric, waist*⟩ extensible
**3** *vtr* (a) (extend) tendre ⟨*rope, net*⟩; étirer
⟨*arms, legs*⟩; **to** ~ **one's legs** (figurative) se
dégourdir les jambes
(b) étirer ⟨*elastic*⟩; élargir ⟨*shoe*⟩

(c) déformer ⟨*truth*⟩
(d) utiliser [qch] au maximum ⟨*budget,
resources*⟩
**4** *vi* (a) ⟨*person*⟩ s'étirer
(b) ⟨*road, track*⟩ s'étaler (**for, over** sur);
⟨*beach, moor*⟩ s'étendre (**for** sur)
(c) ⟨*elastic*⟩ s'étendre; ⟨*shoe*⟩ s'élargir
■ **stretch out**: ¶ ~ **out** s'étendre; ¶ ~ [**sth**]
**out** tendre ⟨*hand, foot*⟩ (**towards** vers);
étendre ⟨*arm, leg*⟩; étaler ⟨*nets, sheet*⟩
**stretcher** *n* brancard *m*
**strew** *vtr* éparpiller ⟨*litter, paper*⟩ (**on** sur);
~**n with** jonché/-e de
**stricken** *adj* (a) ⟨*face*⟩ affligé/-e; ⟨*area*⟩
sinistré/-e; ~ **by** frappé/-e de ⟨*illness*⟩; pris/-e
de ⟨*fear*⟩; accablé/-e de ⟨*guilt*⟩
(b) ⟨*plane, ship*⟩ en détresse
**strict** *adj* ⟨*person*⟩ strict/-e (**about** sur);
⟨*view*⟩ rigide; ⟨*silence*⟩ absolu/-e; ⟨*Methodist,
Catholic*⟩ de stricte observance; **in** ~
**confidence** à titre strictement confidentiel; **in**
~ **secrecy** dans le plus grand secret
**strictly** *adv* (a) ⟨*treat*⟩ avec sévérité
(b) ⟨*confidential, prohibited*⟩ strictement; ~
**speaking** à proprement parler
**stride** **1** *n* enjambée *f*
**2** *vi* **to** ~ **out/in** sortir/entrer à grands pas;
**to** ~ **across sth** enjamber qch
**IDIOMS to take sth in one's** ~ prendre qch
calmement
**strife** *n* conflits *mpl*
**strike** **1** *n* (a) grève *f*; **on** ~ en grève
(b) (attack) attaque *f*
**2** *vtr* (a) (hit) frapper ⟨*person, vessel*⟩;
heurter ⟨*rock, tree, pedestrian*⟩; **he struck his**
**head on the table** il s'est cogné la tête contre
la table; **to be struck by lightning** être
frappé/-e par la foudre
(b) (afflict) frapper ⟨*area, people*⟩
(c) ⟨*idea, thought*⟩ venir à l'esprit de
⟨*person*⟩; ⟨*resemblance*⟩ frapper; **to** ~ **sb as**
**odd** paraître étrange à qn
(d) (colloq) (find) tomber sur (colloq) ⟨*oil, gold*⟩
(e) (achieve) conclure ⟨*deal, bargain*⟩; **to** ~ **a**
**balance** trouver le juste milieu (**between**
entre)
(f) frotter ⟨*match*⟩
(g) ⟨*clock*⟩ sonner
**3** *vi* (a) (gen) frapper
(b) ⟨*workers*⟩ faire (la) grève
■ **strike down** terrasser ⟨*person*⟩
■ **strike off**: ¶ ~ **off**, ~ **off** [**sth**] (delete)
rayer; ¶ ~ [**sb**] **off** radier ⟨*doctor*⟩; ¶ ~ [**sb**/
**sth**] **off sth** rayer [qn/qch] de ⟨*list*⟩
■ **strike out**: ¶ ~ **out** (hit out) frapper; **to** ~
**out at** attaquer ⟨*adversary*⟩; s'en prendre à
⟨*critics*⟩; ¶ ~ [**sth**] **out** rayer
■ **strike up** ⟨*orchestra*⟩ commencer à jouer;
**to** ~ **up a conversation with** engager la
conversation avec; **to** ~ **up a friendship with**
se lier d'amitié avec
**strikebreaker** *n* briseur/-euse *m/f* de
grève
**strikebreaking** *n* retour *m* au travail
**strike force** *n* force *f* d'intervention

**striker** n (a) (person on strike) gréviste mf
(b) (in football) attaquant/-e m/f
**striking** adj ⟨person⟩ (good-looking) beau/
belle (before n); ⟨design, contrast⟩ frappant/-e
**string** [1] n (a) (twine) ficelle f; **a piece of ~**
un bout de ficelle
(b) (on bow, racket) corde f; (on puppet) fil m
(c) (series) **a ~ of** un défilé de ⟨visitors⟩; une
succession de ⟨successes, awards⟩
(d) (set) **~ of pearls** collier m de perles
[2] **strings** n pl (Mus) **the ~s** les cordes fpl
[3] vtr enfiler ⟨beads, pearls⟩ (**on** sur)
IDIOMS **to pull ~s** (colloq) faire jouer le
piston (colloq)
■ **string along** (GB) (colloq): ¶ **~ along**
suivre ¶ **~ [sb] along** mener qn en bateau
(colloq)
■ **string together** aligner ⟨words⟩
**string bean** n haricot m à écosser
**stringed instrument** n instrument m
à cordes
**stringent** adj rigoureux/-euse
**strip** [1] n bande f (**of** de)
[2] vtr (a) déshabiller ⟨person⟩; vider ⟨house,
room⟩; défaire ⟨bed⟩; **to ~ sb of** dépouiller
qn de ⟨belongings, rights⟩
(b) (remove paint from) décaper
(c) (dismantle) démonter
[3] vi se déshabiller
**strip cartoon** n bande f dessinée
**stripe** n (a) (on fabric, wallpaper) rayure f
(b) (on animal) (isolated) rayure f; (one of many)
zébrure f
**striped** adj rayé/-e
**strip lighting** n éclairage m au néon m
**stripper** n strip-teaseur/-euse m/f
**strive** vi s'efforcer (**to do** de faire)
**stroke** [1] n (a) (gen) coup m; **at a single ~**
d'un seul coup; **a ~ of luck** un coup de
chance; **a ~ of genius** un trait de génie
(b) (in swimming) mouvement m des bras;
(particular style) nage f
(c) (of pen) trait m; (of brush) touche f
(d) (Med) congestion f cérébrale
[2] vtr caresser
**stroll** [1] n promenade f, tour m
[2] vi se promener; (aimlessly) flâner
**stroller** n (US) (pushchair) poussette f
**strong** adj (a) (powerful) ⟨arm, person,
current, wind⟩ fort/-e; ⟨army, swimmer,
country⟩ puissant/-e
(b) ⟨heart, fabric, table⟩ solide; ⟨candidate,
argument⟩ de poids
(c) ⟨tea, medicine, glue⟩ fort/-e; ⟨coffee⟩
serré/-e
(d) ⟨smell, taste⟩ fort/-e
(e) ⟨desire, feeling⟩ profond/-e
(f) ⟨chance, possibility⟩ fort/-e (before n)
IDIOMS **to be still going ~** ⟨person⟩ se porter
toujours très bien; ⟨relationship⟩ aller
toujours bien; **it's not my ~ point** ce n'est
pas mon fort
**strongbox** n coffre-fort m
**stronghold** n forteresse f; (figurative) fief m

**strongly** adv (a) ⟨oppose, advise⟩
vivement; ⟨protest, deny⟩ énergiquement;
⟨suspect⟩ fortement; ⟨believe⟩ fermement; **I
feel ~ about this** c'est quelque chose qui me
tient à cœur
(b) (solidly) solidement
**strongroom** n chambre f forte
**strong-willed** adj obstiné/-e
**structural damage** n dégâts mpl
matériels
**structure** [1] n (a) (organization) structure f
(b) (building) construction f
[2] vtr structurer ⟨argument, essay, novel⟩;
organiser ⟨day, life⟩
**struggle** [1] n (gen) lutte f; (scuffle) rixe f
[2] vi (a) (put up a fight) se débattre (**to do**
pour faire); (tussle, scuffle) se battre
(b) (try hard) lutter (**to do** pour faire; **for**
pour)
**struggling** adj ⟨writer, artist⟩ qui essaie
de percer
**strum** vtr (carelessly) gratter ⟨guitar, tune⟩;
(gently) jouer doucement de ⟨guitar⟩
**strung out** adj (colloq) **to be ~ on** être
accro (colloq) à ⟨drug⟩; **to be ~ (from drugs)**
être en état de manque
**strut** [1] n montant m
[2] vi (also **~ about**, **~ around**) se
pavaner
**stub** [1] n (of pencil) bout m; (of cheque, ticket)
talon m; (of cigarette) mégot m
[2] vtr **to ~ one's toe** se cogner l'orteil
■ **stub out** écraser ⟨cigarette⟩
**stubble** n (a) (straw) chaume m
(b) (beard) barbe f de plusieurs jours
**stubborn** adj ⟨person, animal⟩ entêté/-e;
⟨behaviour⟩ obstiné/-e; ⟨refusal⟩ opiniâtre;
⟨stain⟩ rebelle
**stuck** adj (a) (jammed, trapped) coincé/-e; **to
get ~ in** rester coincé/-e dans ⟨lift⟩; s'enliser
dans ⟨mud⟩
(b) **to be ~ for an answer** ne pas savoir quoi
répondre
**stuck-up** adj (colloq) bêcheur/-euse (colloq)
**stud** n (a) (on jacket) clou m; (on door) clou m
à grosse tête; (on boot) crampon m
(b) (stallion) étalon m; (horse farm) haras m
(c) (earring) clou m d'oreille
**student** n étudiant/-e m/f
**student grant** n bourse f d'études
**student ID card** n carte f d'étudiant
**student nurse** n élève mf infirmier/-ière
**student teacher** n enseignant/-e m/f
stagiaire
**student union** n (building) maison f des
étudiants
**studio** n (gen) studio m; (of painter) atelier m
**studious** adj studieux/-ieuse
**study** [1] n (a) (work, research) étude f (**of, on**
de)
(b) (room) bureau m
[2] **studies** n pl études fpl; **computer
studies** informatique f; **social studies**
sciences fpl humaines ⋯⟶

**S**

**3** adj ⟨leave, group, visit⟩ d'étude; ~ **trip** voyage m d'études
**4** vtr étudier
**5** vi faire ses études

**study aid** n outil m pédagogique (destiné à l'élève)

**stuff** **1** n (things) choses fpl, trucs mpl (colloq); (personal belongings) affaires fpl; (rubbish, junk) bazar m (colloq); (substance) truc m (colloq)
**2** vtr (a) rembourrer ⟨cushion⟩ (**with** de); bourrer ⟨suitcase, room⟩ (**with** de)
(b) (shove) fourrer (colloq) (**in, into** dans)
(c) (Culin) farcir ⟨turkey, chicken⟩
(d) empailler ⟨dead animal, bird⟩

**stuffed** adj ⟨turkey, chicken⟩ farci/-e; ⟨toy animal⟩ en peluche; ⟨bird, fox⟩ empaillé/-e

**stuffing** n (a) (Culin) farce f
(b) (of furniture, pillow) rembourrage m

**stuffy** adj (a) (airless) étouffant/-e
(b) (staid) guindé/-e

**stumble** vi (a) (trip) trébucher (**against** contre; **on, over** sur)
(b) (in speech) hésiter
■ **stumble across** tomber par hasard sur ⟨rare find⟩

**stumbling block** n obstacle m

**stump** **1** n (of tree) souche f; (of candle, pencil, cigar) bout m; (of tooth) chicot m; (part of limb, tail) moignon m
**2** vtr (colloq) **to be ~ed by sth** être en peine d'expliquer qch; **I'm ~ed!** (in quiz) je sèche! (colloq); (nonplussed) aucune idée!
■ **stump up** (GB) (colloq) débourser (**for** pour)

**stun** vtr (a) (daze) assommer
(b) (amaze) stupéfier

**stunned** adj (dazed) assommé/-e
(b) (amazed) ⟨person⟩ stupéfait/-e; ⟨silence⟩ figé/-e

**stunning** adj (beautiful) sensationnel/-elle

**stunt** **1** n (a) (for attention) coup m organisé, truc m (colloq)
(b) (in film) cascade f
**2** vtr empêcher ⟨development⟩; nuire à ⟨plant growth⟩

**stunted** adj rabougri/-e

**stuntman** n cascadeur m

**stupefying** adj stupéfiant/-e

**stupendous** adj prodigieux/-ieuse

**stupid** adj bête, stupide; **I've done something ~** j'ai fait une bêtise

**stupidity** n bêtise f

**stupor** n stupeur f; **in a drunken ~** hébété/-e par l'alcool

**sturdy** adj robuste, solide

**stutter** vtr, vi bégayer

**St Valentine's Day** n la Saint-Valentin

**sty** n (a) (for pigs) porcherie f
(b) (also **stye**) orgelet m

**style** **1** n (a) (manner) style m
(b) (elegance) classe f; **to do things in ~** faire les choses en grand
(c) (design) (of car, clothing) modèle m; (of house) type m
(d) (fashion) mode f

**2** vtr couper ⟨hair⟩

**styling** **1** n (a) (design) conception f
(b) (in hairdressing) coupe f
**2** adj ⟨gel, mousse, product⟩ coiffant/-e

**stylish** adj ⟨car, coat, person⟩ élégant/-e; ⟨resort, restaurant⟩ chic

**stylist** n (a) (hairdresser) coiffeur/-euse m/f
(b) (designer) concepteur/-trice m/f

**stylistic** adj stylistique

**stylus** n pointe f de lecture

**suave** adj ⟨person⟩ mielleux/-euse

**subconscious** **1** n the ~ le subconscient
**2** adj inconscient/-e

**subcontinent** n sous-continent m

**subcontract** vtr sous-traiter (**out to** à)

**subcontractor** n sous-traitant m

**subdivide** vtr subdiviser

**subdue** vtr soumettre ⟨people, nation⟩

**subdued** adj ⟨person⟩ silencieux/-ieuse; ⟨excitement⟩ contenu/-e; ⟨lighting⟩ tamisé/-e

**subheading** n sous-titre m

**subject** **1** n (a) (topic) sujet m; **to change the ~** parler d'autre chose
(b) (at school, college) matière f; (for research, study) sujet m
(c) **to be the ~ of an inquiry** faire l'objet d'une enquête
(d) (citizen) sujet/-ette m/f
**2** adj (a) (liable) **to be ~ to** être sujet/-ette à ⟨flooding, fits⟩; être passible de ⟨tax⟩
(b) (dependent) **to be ~ to** dépendre de ⟨approval⟩; être soumis/-e à ⟨law⟩
**3** vtr **to ~ sb to sth** faire subir qch à qn

**subject heading** n sujet m

**subjective** adj subjectif/-ive

**subjugate** vtr subjuguer ⟨country, people⟩

**subjunctive** n subjonctif m

**sublet** vtr, vi sous-louer

**sublime** adj ⟨beauty, genius⟩ sublime; ⟨indifference⟩ suprême

**subliminal** adj subliminal/-e

**submachine gun** n mitraillette f

**submarine** n sous-marin m

**submerge** vtr ⟨sea, flood⟩ submerger; ⟨person⟩ immerger (**in** dans)

**submission** n soumission f (**to** à)

**submissive** adj ⟨person⟩ soumis/-e; ⟨behaviour⟩ docile

**submit** **1** vtr soumettre ⟨report, plan, script⟩ (**to** à); présenter ⟨bill, application⟩
**2** vi se soumettre; **to ~ to** subir ⟨indignity, injustice⟩; céder à ⟨will, demand⟩

**subnormal** adj ⟨person⟩ arriéré/-e

**subordinate** n, adj subalterne (mf)

**subpoena** vtr assigner [qn] à comparaître

**subscribe** vi (a) **to ~ to** partager ⟨view, values⟩
(b) **to ~ to** être abonné/-e à ⟨magazine⟩

**subscriber** n abonné/-e m/f (**to** de)

**subscription** n abonnement m (**to** à)

**s**

**subsequent** *adj* (in past) ultérieur/-e; (in future) à venir

**subsequently** *adv* par la suite

**subservient** *adj* servile (**to** envers)

**subside** *vi* (a) ⟨*storm, wind, noise*⟩ s'apaiser; ⟨*emotion*⟩ se calmer; ⟨*fever, excitement*⟩ retomber
(b) ⟨*building, land*⟩ s'affaisser

**subsidiary** ⟨1⟩ *n* (*also* ~ **company**) filiale *f*
⟨2⟩ *adj* secondaire (**to** par rapport à)

**subsidize** *vtr* subventionner

**subsidy** *n* subvention *f* (**to, for** à)

**subsist** *vi* subsister

**subsistence** *n* subsistance *f*

**subsistence level** *n* niveau *m* minimum pour vivre

**substance** *n* (a) (gen) substance *f*
(b) (of argument, talks) essentiel *m*; (of claim, accusation) fondement *m*

**substance abuse** *n* abus *m* de substances toxiques

**substandard** *adj* de qualité inférieure

**substantial** *adj* (a) (considerable) considérable; ⟨*sum, quantity*⟩ important/-e; ⟨*meal*⟩ substantiel/-ielle
(b) (solid) ⟨*proof, lock*⟩ solide

**substantiate** *vtr* justifier ⟨*allegation*⟩; appuyer [qch] par des preuves ⟨*statement*⟩

**substitute** ⟨1⟩ *n* (a) (person) remplaçant/-e *m/f*
(b) (product, substance) succédané *m*
⟨2⟩ *vtr* substituer (**for** à)

**subtitle** *n* sous-titre *m*

**subtitled** *adj* sous-titré/-e

**subtle** *adj* (gen) subtil/-e; ⟨*change*⟩ imperceptible; ⟨*hint*⟩ voilé/-e; ⟨*lighting*⟩ tamisé/-e

**subtlety** *n* subtilité *f*

**subtotal** *n* sous-total *m*

**subtract** *vtr* soustraire (**from** de)

**subtraction** *n* soustraction *f*

**suburb** ⟨1⟩ *n* banlieue *f*; **inner** ~ faubourg *m*
⟨2⟩ **suburbs** *n pl* **the** ~**s** la banlieue

**suburban** *adj* ⟨*street, shop, train*⟩ de banlieue; (US) ⟨*shopping mall*⟩ à l'extérieur de la ville

**suburbia** *n* banlieue *f*

**subversive** ⟨1⟩ *n* élément *m* subversif
⟨2⟩ *adj* subversif/-ive

**subway** *n* (a) (GB) (for pedestrians) passage *m* souterrain
(b) (US) (underground railway) métro *m*

**sub-zero** *adj* inférieur/-e à zéro

**succeed** ⟨1⟩ *vtr* succéder à ⟨*person*⟩
⟨2⟩ *vi* réussir; **to** ~ **in doing** réussir à faire

**succeeding** *adj* qui suit, suivant/-e

**success** *n* succès *m*, réussite *f*; **to be a** ~ ⟨*party*⟩ être réussi/-e; ⟨*film, person*⟩ avoir du succès

**successful** *adj* ⟨*attempt, operation*⟩ réussi/-e; ⟨*plan, campaign*⟩ couronné/-e de

succès; ⟨*film, book, writer*⟩ (profitable) à succès; (well regarded) apprécié/-e; ⟨*businessman*⟩ prospère; ⟨*career*⟩ brillant/-e; **to be** ~ réussir (**in doing** à faire)

**successfully** *adv* avec succès

**succession** *n* (a) (sequence) série *f* (**of** de); **in** ~ de suite; **in close** ~ coup sur coup
(b) (inheriting) succession *f* (**to** à)

**successive** *adj* successif/-ive; ⟨*day, week*⟩ consécutif/-ive

**successor** *n* successeur *m*

**success rate** *n* taux *m* de réussite

**success story** *n* réussite *f*

**succinct** *adj* succinct/-e

**succulent** *adj* succulent/-e

**succumb** *vi* succomber (**to** à)

**such** ⟨1⟩ *det* tel/telle; (similar) pareil/-eille; ~ **a situation** une telle situation; **in** ~ **a situation** dans une situation pareille; **some** ~ **remark** quelque chose comme ça; **there's no** ~ **thing** ça n'existe pas; **you'll do no** ~ **thing!** il n'en est pas question!; **in** ~ **a way that** d'une telle façon que; ~ **money as I have** le peu d'argent *or* tout l'argent que j'ai
⟨2⟩ *adv* (with adjectives) si, tellement; (with nouns) tel/telle; **in** ~ **a persuasive way** d'une façon si convaincante; ~ **a nice boy!** un garçon si gentil!; ~ **good quality** une telle qualité; **I hadn't seen** ~ **a good film for years** je n'avais pas vu un aussi bon film depuis des années; ~ **a lot of problems** tant de problèmes; **there were (ever** (colloq)) ~ **a lot of people** il y avait beaucoup de monde
⟨3⟩ **such as** *phr* comme, tel/telle que; **a house** ~ **as this** une maison comme celle-ci; **a person** ~ **as her** une personne comme elle; **have you** ~ **a thing as a screwdriver?** auriez-vous un tournevis par hasard?

**such and such** *det* tel/telle; **on** ~ **a topic** sur tel tel ou tel sujet

**suck** ⟨1⟩ *vtr* sucer ⟨*thumb, fruit, lollipop, pencil*⟩; (drink in) aspirer ⟨*liquid, air*⟩
⟨2⟩ *vi* **to** ~ **at** sucer; **to** ~ **on** tirer sur ⟨*pipe*⟩
■ **suck up:** ¶ ~ **up** (colloq) faire de la lèche (colloq); **to** ~ **up to sb** cirer les pompes à qn (colloq); ¶ ~ **[sth] up** pomper ⟨*liquid*⟩; aspirer ⟨*dirt*⟩

**sucker** *n* (a) (colloq) (dupe) bonne poire *f* (colloq)
(b) (on plant) surgeon *m*
(c) (pad) ventouse *f*

**suction** *n* succion *f*

**suction pad** *n* ventouse *f*

**sudden** *adj* (gen) soudain/-e; ⟨*movement*⟩ brusque; **all of a** ~ tout à coup

**sudden death play-off** *n*: penalties *pour départager deux équipes*

**suddenly** *adv* ⟨*die, grow pale*⟩ subitement; ⟨*happen*⟩ tout à coup

**suds** *n pl* (*also* **soap** ~) (foam) mousse *f* (de savon); (soapy water) eau *f* savonneuse

**sue** ⟨1⟩ *vtr* intenter un procès à; **to** ~ **sb for** ⋯⟩

S

**divorce** demander le divorce à qn; **to ~ sb for damages** réclamer à qn des dommages-intérêts
2 *vi* intenter un procès

**suede** 1 *n* daim *m*
2 *adj* ⟨*shoe, glove*⟩ en daim

**suffer** 1 *vtr* subir ⟨*loss, consequences, defeat*⟩; **to ~ a heart attack** avoir une crise cardiaque
2 *vi* (a) souffrir; **to ~ from** souffrir de ⟨*rheumatism, heat*⟩; avoir ⟨*headache, high blood pressure, cold*⟩; **to ~ from depression** être dépressif/-ive
(b) (do badly) ⟨*company, profits*⟩ souffrir; ⟨*health, quality, work*⟩ s'en ressentir

**sufferer** *n* victime *f*; **leukemia ~s** les leucémiques *mpl*

**suffering** 1 *n* souffrances *fpl* (of de)
2 *adj* souffrant/-e

**sufficient** *adj* suffisamment de, assez de; **to be ~** suffire

**sufficiently** *adv* suffisamment, assez

**suffocate** 1 *vtr* ⟨*smoke, fumes*⟩ asphyxier; ⟨*person, anger*⟩ étouffer
2 *vi* (a) (by smoke, fumes) être asphyxié/-e; (by pillow) être étouffé/-e
(b) (figurative) suffoquer

**suffocating** *adj* ⟨*smoke*⟩ asphyxiant/-e; ⟨*atmosphere, heat*⟩ étouffant/-e

**suffrage** *n* (right) droit *m* de vote; (system) suffrage *m*

**sugar** *n* sucre *m*; **brown ~** sucre *m* roux

**sugar beet** *n* betterave *f* à sucre

**sugar cane** *n* canne *f* à sucre

**sugar-free** *adj* sans sucre

**sugar lump** *n* morceau *m* de sucre

**suggest** *vtr* suggérer; **they ~ed that I (should) leave** ils m'ont suggéré de partir

**suggestion** *n* (a) (gen) suggestion *f*; **at sb's ~** sur le conseil de qn
(b) (hint) soupçon *m* (of de); (of smile) pointe *f*

**suggestive** *adj* suggestif/-ive

**suicidal** *adj* suicidaire

**suicide** *n* (action) suicide *m*; (person) suicidé/-e *m/f*; **to commit ~** se suicider

**suit** 1 *n* (a) (man's) costume *m*; (woman's) tailleur *m*; **a ~ of armour** une armure (complète)
(b) (lawsuit) procès *m*
(c) (in cards) couleur *f*
2 *vtr* (a) ⟨*colour, outfit*⟩ aller à ⟨*person*⟩
(b) ⟨*date, climate, arrangement*⟩ convenir à qn
3 *vi* convenir
4 *v refl* **to ~ oneself** faire comme on veut

**suitable** *adj* ⟨*accommodation, clothing, employment*⟩ adéquat/-e; ⟨*candidate*⟩ apte; ⟨*gift, gesture*⟩ approprié/-e; ⟨*moment*⟩ opportun/-e; **to be ~ for** convenir à ⟨*person*⟩; bien se prêter à ⟨*climate, activity, occasion*⟩

**suitably** *adv* convenablement

**suitcase** *n* valise *f*

**suite** *n* (a) (gen) suite *f*
(b) (furniture) mobilier *m*

**suited** *adj* **to be ~ to** ⟨*place, clothes*⟩ être commode pour; ⟨*game, style*⟩ convenir à; ⟨*person*⟩ être fait/-e pour

**sulk** *vi* bouder (**about, over** à cause de)

**sulky** *adj* boudeur/-euse; **to look ~** faire la tête

**sullen** *adj* ⟨*person, expression*⟩ renfrogné/-e; ⟨*day, sky, mood*⟩ maussade

**sulphur** (GB), **sulfur** (US) *n* soufre *m*

**sulphuric acid** *n* acide *m* sulfurique

**sultana** *n* (Culin) raisin *m* de Smyrne

**sultry** *adj* (a) ⟨*day*⟩ étouffant/-e; ⟨*weather*⟩ lourd/-e
(b) ⟨*look, smile*⟩ sensuel/-elle

**sum** *n* (a) (of money) somme *f*
(b) (calculation) calcul *m*
■ **sum up**: ¶ **~ up** récapituler; ¶ **~ up [sth]** résumer

**summarize** *vtr* résumer ⟨*book, problem*⟩; récapituler ⟨*argument, speech*⟩

**summary** *n* résumé *m*

**summer** 1 *n* été *m*; **in ~** en été
2 *adj* ⟨*evening, resort, clothes*⟩ d'été

**summer camp** *n* (US) colonie *f* de vacances

**summer holiday** (GB), **summer vacation** (US) *n* (gen) vacances *fpl* (d'été); (Sch, Univ) grandes vacances *fpl*

**summerhouse** *n* pavillon *m* (de jardin)

**summer school** *n* université *f* d'été

**summertime** *n* été *m*

**summit** *n* sommet *m*

**summon** *vtr* (a) (gen) faire venir
(b) (Law) citer
■ **summon up** rassembler ⟨*energy, strength*⟩ (to do pour faire)

**summons** 1 *n* (a) (Law) citation *f*
(b) (gen) injonction *f* (**from** de; **to** à)
2 *vtr* citer (**to** à; **to do** à faire; **for** pour)

**sumptuous** *adj* somptueux/-euse

**sum total** *n* (of money) montant *m* total; (of achievements) ensemble *m*

**sun** *n* soleil *m*; **in the ~** au soleil

**sunbathe** *vi* se faire bronzer

**sunbed** *n* (lounger) chaise *f* longue; (with sunlamp) lit *m* solaire

**sun block** *n* crème *f* écran total

**sunburn** *n* coup *m* de soleil

**sunburned**, **sunburnt** *adj* (burnt) brûlé/-e par le soleil; (tanned) (GB) bronzé/-e; **to get ~** attraper un coup de soleil

**Sunday** *n* dimanche *m*

**Sunday best** *n* (dressed) **in one's ~** endimanché/-e

**Sunday trading** *n* commerce *m* dominical

**sundial** *n* cadran *m* solaire

**sundress** *n* robe *f* bain de soleil

**sundries** *n pl* articles *mpl* divers

**sundry** *adj* divers/-e; **(to) all and ~** (à) tout le monde

**sunflower** *n* tournesol *m*

**sunglasses** *n pl* lunettes *fpl* de soleil

**sun hat** *n* chapeau *m* de soleil

**sunken** *adj* (a) ⟨*treasure, wreck*⟩ immergé/-e
(b) ⟨*cheek*⟩ creux/creuse; ⟨*eye*⟩ cave
(c) ⟨*bath*⟩ encastré/-e; ⟨*garden*⟩ en contrebas

**sunlamp** *n* lampe *f* à bronzer

**sunlight** *n* lumière *f* du soleil

**sunny** *adj* (a) ensoleillé/-e; **it's going to be** ∼ il va faire (du) soleil
(b) ⟨*child, temperament*⟩ enjoué/-e

**sunrise** *n* lever *m* du soleil

**sunroof** *n* toit *m* ouvrant

**sunset** *n* coucher *m* du soleil

**sunshade** *n* parasol *m*

**sunshield** *n* pare-soleil *m inv*

**sunshine** *n* soleil *m*

**sunstroke** *n* insolation *f*

**suntan** *n* bronzage *m*; **to get a** ∼ bronzer

**suntan lotion** *n* lotion *f* solaire

**suntanned** *adj* bronzé/-e

**suntan oil** *n* huile *f* solaire

**super** *adj, excl* (colloq) formidable

**superb** *adj* superbe

**supercilious** *adj* dédaigneux/-euse

**superficial** *adj* superficiel/-ielle

**superfluous** *adj* superflu/-e

**superimpose** *vtr* superposer (**on** à)

**superintendent** *n* (a) (supervisor) responsable *mf*
(b) (*also* **police** ∼) ≈ commissaire *m* de police
(c) (US) (for apartments) concierge *mf*
(d) (US) (*also* **school** ∼) inspecteur/-trice *m/f*

**superior** ⊡ *n* supérieur/-e *m/f*
⊡ *adj* (a) supérieur/-e (**to** à; **in** en); ⟨*product*⟩ de qualité supérieure
(b) (condescending) condescendant/-e

**superiority** *n* supériorité *f*

**superlative** ⊡ *n* superlatif *m*
⊡ *adj* ⟨*performance, service*⟩ superbe

**superman** *n* surhomme *m*

**supermarket** *n* supermarché *m*

**supermodel** *n* top model *m*

**supernatural** ⊡ *n* surnaturel *m*
⊡ *adj* surnaturel/-elle

**superpower** *n* superpuissance *f*

**supersede** *vtr* remplacer

**supersonic** *adj* supersonique

**superstar** *n* superstar *f*

**superstition** *n* superstition *f*

**superstitious** *adj* superstitieux/-ieuse

**superstore** *n* (large supermarket) hypermarché *m*; (specialist shop) grande surface *f*

**supervise** *vtr* superviser ⟨*activity, staff*⟩; surveiller ⟨*child, patient*⟩

**supervision** *n* (a) (of staff, work) supervision *f*
(b) (of child, patient) surveillance *f*

**supervisor** *n* (a) (for staff) responsable *m*
(b) (GB) (for thesis) directeur/-trice *m/f* de thèse
(c) (US Sch) directeur/-trice *m/f* d'études

**supper** *n* (evening meal) dîner *m*; (late snack) collation *f* (du soir); (after a show) souper *m*; **the Last Supper** la Cène *f*

**supple** *adj* souple

**supplement** ⊡ *n* (a) (fee) supplément *m*
(b) (to diet, income) complément *m* (**to** à)
(c) (in newspaper) supplément *m*
⊡ *vtr* compléter ⟨*diet, resources, training*⟩ (**with** de); augmenter ⟨*income, staff*⟩ (**with** de)

**supplementary** *adj* supplémentaire

**supplier** *n* fournisseur *m* (**of, to** de)

**supply** ⊡ *n* (a) (stock) réserves *fpl*; **in short** ∼ difficile à obtenir; **to get in a** ∼ **of sth** s'approvisionner en qch
(b) (source) (of fuel, gas, oxygen) alimentation *f*; (of food) approvisionnement *m*; (of equipment) fourniture *f*
⊡ **supplies** *n pl* (a) (equipment) réserves *fpl*; **food supplies** ravitaillement *m*
(b) (for office) fournitures *fpl*
⊡ *vtr* (provide) fournir (**to, for** à); approvisionner ⟨*factory, company*⟩ (**with** en); (with fuel, food) ravitailler ⟨*town, area*⟩ (**with** en)

**supply and demand** *n* l'offre *f* et la demande

**supply teacher** *n* (GB) suppléant/-e *m/f*

**support** ⊡ *n* (a) (moral, financial, political) soutien *m*, appui *m*; **to give sb/sth (one's)** ∼ apporter son soutien à qn/qch; **means of** ∼ (financial) moyens *mpl* de subsistance
(b) (physical, for weight) support *m*
(c) (person) soutien *m*; **to be a** ∼ **to sb** aider qn
⊡ *vtr* (a) (morally, financially) soutenir ⟨*person, cause, organization, currency*⟩; donner à ⟨*charity*⟩
(b) (physically) supporter ⟨*weight*⟩; soutenir ⟨*person*⟩
(c) confirmer ⟨*argument, theory*⟩
(d) (maintain) ⟨*breadwinner, farm*⟩ subvenir aux besoins de

**supporter** *n* (gen) partisan *m*; (Sport) supporter *m*; (of political party) sympathisant/-e *m/f*

**support group** *n* groupe *m* de soutien

**supporting** *adj* ∼ **actor/actress** second rôle masculin/féminin; **the** ∼ **cast** les seconds rôles *mpl*

**supportive** *adj* ⟨*person, organization*⟩ d'un grand secours; ⟨*role, network*⟩ de soutien

**suppose** *vtr* (a) (assume) supposer (**that** que); **I** ∼ **so/not** je suppose que oui/non
(b) (think) **to** ∼ (**that**) penser *or* croire que

**supposed** *adj* **to be** ∼ **to do/be** être censé/-e faire/être; **it's** ∼ **to be a good hotel** il paraît que c'est un bon hôtel

**supposing** *conj* ∼ (**that**) **he says no?** et s'il dit non?; ∼ **your income is X** supposons que ton revenu soit de X

**S**

**suppress** vtr supprimer ⟨evidence, information⟩; réprimer ⟨smile, urge, rebellion⟩; étouffer ⟨scandal, yawn⟩; dissimuler ⟨truth⟩

**supreme** adj suprême

**surcharge** n supplément m

**sure** ① adj (gen) sûr/-e (**about, of** de); **I'm not** ∼ **when he's coming** je ne sais pas trop quand il viendra; **we'll be there tomorrow for** ∼! on y sera demain sans faute!; **nobody knows for** ∼ personne ne (le) sait au juste; **to make** ∼ **that** (ascertain) s'assurer que; (ensure) faire en sorte que; **he's** ∼ **to fail** il va sûrement échouer; **to be** ∼ **of oneself** être sûr/-e de soi
② adv '∼!' (of course) 'bien sûr!'; ∼ **enough** effectivement

**sure-fire** adj (colloq) garanti/-e

**sure-footed** adj agile

**surely** adv sûrement, certainement

**surf** ① n (waves) vagues fpl (déferlantes); (foam) écume f
② vtr **to** ∼ **the Internet** naviguer or surfer sur Internet
③ vi (a) (Sport) faire du surf
(b) (Comput) naviguer or surfer sur Internet

**surface** ① n (a) surface f; **on the** ∼ (of liquid) à la surface; (of solid) sur la surface
(b) (of solid, cube) côté m
(c) (worktop) plan m de travail
② vi (a) ⟨person, object⟩ remonter à la surface; ⟨submarine⟩ faire surface
(b) ⟨problem⟩ se manifester

**surface area** n superficie f

**surfboard** n planche f de surf

**surfer** n (a) (on water) surfeur/-euse m/f
(b) (Comput) internaute mf

**surfing** n surf m

**surge** ① n (a) (of water, blood, energy) montée f (of de); (of anger, desire) accès m (of de)
(b) (in prices, unemployment) hausse f (in de); (in demand) accroissement m (in de)
② vi (a) ⟨water, waves⟩ déferler; ⟨blood, energy, emotion⟩ monter; **to** ∼ **forward** ⟨crowd⟩ s'élancer en avant
(b) ⟨prices, demand⟩ monter en flèche

**surgeon** n chirurgien m

**surgery** n (a) (operation) chirurgie f; **to have** ∼ se faire opérer
(b) (GB) (Med) (premises) cabinet m

**surgical** adj ⟨instrument⟩ chirurgical/-e; ⟨boot, stocking⟩ orthopédique

**surgical spirit** n alcool m (à 90 degrés)

**surly** adj revêche

**surname** n nom m de famille

**surpass** ① vtr surpasser (**in** en); dépasser ⟨expectations⟩
② v refl **to** ∼ **oneself** se surpasser

**surplus** ① n surplus m; (in business) excédent m
② adj (gen) en trop; (in business) excédentaire

**surprise** ① n surprise f; **to take sb by** ∼ (gen) prendre qn au dépourvu; (Mil) surprendre qn

② vtr (a) surprendre, étonner; **it** ∼**d them that no-one came** ils ont été surpris que personne ne vienne
(b) surprendre ⟨intruder⟩; attaquer [qch] par surprise ⟨garrison⟩

**surprised** adj étonné/-e; **I'm not** ∼ ça ne m'étonne pas

**surprising** adj étonnant/-e, surprenant/-e

**surprisingly** adv ⟨well, quickly⟩ étonnamment; ∼ **frank** d'une franchise étonnante

**surreal** adj surréaliste

**surrealist** n, adj surréaliste (mf)

**surrender** ① n (a) (of army) capitulation f (**to** devant); (of soldier, town) reddition f (**to** à)
(b) (of territory, rights) abandon m (**to** à); (of weapons, document) remise f (**to** à)
② vtr (a) livrer ⟨town⟩ (**to** à); céder ⟨weapons⟩ (**to** à)
(b) racheter ⟨insurance policy⟩; rendre ⟨passport⟩ (**to** à)
③ vi ⟨army, soldier⟩ se rendre (**to** à); ⟨country⟩ capituler (**to** devant)

**surrogate** ① n substitut m (**for** de)
② adj de substitution

**surrogate mother** n mère f porteuse

**surround** vtr (gen) entourer; ⟨police⟩ encercler ⟨building⟩; cerner ⟨person⟩

**surrounding** adj environnant/-e; **the** ∼ **area** les environs mpl

**surroundings** n pl cadre m; (of town) environs mpl; **natural** ∼ milieu m naturel

**surveillance** n surveillance f

**survey** ① n (a) (of trends, prices) enquête f (**of** sur); (by questioning people) sondage m; (study) étude f (**of** de)
(b) (GB) (of house) expertise f (**on** de)
(c) (of land) étude f topographique; (map) levé m topographique
② vtr (a) faire une étude de ⟨market, trends⟩
(b) (GB) faire une expertise de ⟨house⟩
(c) faire l'étude topographique de ⟨area⟩
(d) contempler ⟨scene, landscape⟩

**surveyor** n (a) (GB) (in housebuying) expert m (en immobilier)
(b) (for map-making) topographe mf

**survival** n (of person, animal) survie f (**of** de); (of custom, belief) survivance f (**of** de)

**survive** ① vtr (a) survivre à ⟨winter, heart attack⟩; réchapper de ⟨accident⟩; surmonter ⟨crisis⟩
(b) survivre à ⟨person⟩
② vi survivre; **to** ∼ **on sth** vivre de qch

**surviving** adj survivant/-e

**survivor** n (a) (of accident, attack) rescapé/-e m/f
(b) (Law) survivant/-e m/f

**susceptible** adj sensible (**to** à)

**suspect** ① n suspect/-e m/f
② adj suspect/-e
③ vtr (a) (believe) soupçonner ⟨murder, plot⟩; **to** ∼ **that** penser que
(b) (doubt) douter de ⟨truth, motives⟩
(c) (have under suspicion) soupçonner ⟨person⟩

**suspend** *vtr* **(a)** (gen) suspendre
**(b)** exclure [qn] temporairement ⟨*pupil*⟩
**(from** de)

**suspended sentence** *n* condamnation
*f* avec sursis

**suspender belt** *n* (GB) porte-jarretelles
*m inv*

**suspenders** *n pl* **(a)** (GB) (for stockings)
jarretelles *fpl*
**(b)** (US) (braces) bretelles *fpl*

**suspense** *n* (in film, novel) suspense *m*; **to
leave sb in** ∼ laisser qn dans l'expectative

**suspension** *n* **(a)** (gen, Aut) suspension *f*
**(b)** (of pupil) exclusion *f* temporaire

**suspicion** *n* méfiance *f* (**of** de); **to arouse**
∼ éveiller les soupçons; **to have** ∼**s about
sb/sth** avoir des doutes *mpl* sur qn/qch

**suspicious** *adj* **(a)** (wary) méfiant/-e; **to be**
∼ **of sth** se méfier de qch
**(b)** ⟨*person, object*⟩ suspect/-e; ⟨*behaviour,
activity*⟩ louche

**sustain** *vtr* **(a)** (maintain) maintenir
⟨*interest, success*⟩
**(b)** (Mus) soutenir ⟨*note*⟩
**(c)** (support) soutenir; ( physically) donner des
forces à; **to** ∼ **life** rendre la vie possible
**(d)** recevoir ⟨*injury, burn*⟩; éprouver ⟨*loss*⟩

**sustainable** *adj* ⟨*development, forestry*⟩
durable; ⟨*resource*⟩ renouvelable; ⟨*growth*⟩
viable

**sustenance** *n* nourriture *f*

**swab** *n* (Med) tampon *m*

**swagger** *vi* **(a)** (walk) se pavaner
**(b)** (boast) fanfaronner

**swallow** ⟦1⟧ *n* **(a)** (bird) hirondelle *f*
**(b)** (gulp) gorgée *f*
⟦2⟧ *vtr* **(a)** (eat) avaler
**(b)** ravaler ⟨*pride*⟩
**(c)** (colloq) (believe) avaler (colloq)
⟦3⟧ *vi* avaler; (nervously) avaler sa salive

**swamp** ⟦1⟧ *n* marais *m*, marécage *m*
⟦2⟧ *vtr* inonder

**swan** *n* cygne *m*

**swap** (colloq) ⟦1⟧ *n* échange *m*
⟦2⟧ *vtr* échanger; **to** ∼ **sth for sth** échanger
qch contre qch; **to** ∼ **places** changer de
place

**swarm** ⟦1⟧ *n* (of bees) essaim *m*; (of flies)
nuée *f*
⟦2⟧ *vi* ⟨*bees*⟩ essaimer; **to be** ∼**ing with**
grouiller de ⟨*people, maggots*⟩

**swarthy** *adj* basané/-e

**swastika** *n* croix *f* gammée, svastika *m*

**swat** *vtr* écraser ⟨*fly, wasp*⟩ (**with** avec)

**sway** ⟦1⟧ *n* **to hold** ∼ avoir une grande
influence; **to hold** ∼ **over** dominer
⟦2⟧ *vtr* **(a)** (influence) influencer
**(b)** (rock) osciller
⟦3⟧ *vi* ⟨*tree, bridge*⟩ osciller; ⟨*person*⟩
chanceler; (to music) se balancer

**swear** ⟦1⟧ *vtr* jurer (**to do** de faire); **to** ∼ **sb
to secrecy** faire jurer le secret à qn
⟦2⟧ *vi* **(a)** (curse) jurer

**(b)** (attest) **to** ∼ **to having done** jurer avoir
fait
∎ **swear by** (colloq) ∼ **by** [sth/sb] ne jurer
que par ⟨*remedy, expert*⟩
∎ **swear in**: ∼ **in** [sb], ∼ [sb] **in** faire prêter
serment à

**swearing** *n* jurons *mpl*

**swearword** *n* juron *m*, gros mot *m*

**sweat** ⟦1⟧ *n* sueur *f*; **to break out into a** ∼
se mettre à suer; **to be in a cold** ∼ **about sth**
avoir des sueurs froides à l'idée de qch
⟦2⟧ **sweats** *n pl* (US) survêtement *m*
⟦3⟧ *vi* ⟨*person, horse*⟩ transpirer, suer;
⟨*hands, feet, cheese*⟩ transpirer

**sweatband** *n* bandeau *m*

**sweater** *n* pull *m*

**sweat pants** *n pl* (US) pantalon *m* de
survêtement

**sweatshirt** *n* sweatshirt *m*

**sweatshop** *n* atelier *m* où on exploite le
personnel

**sweaty** *adj* ⟨*person*⟩ en sueur; ⟨*hand,
palm*⟩ moite

**swede** *n* (GB) rutabaga *m*

**Swede** *n* Suédois/-e *m/f*

**Sweden** *pr n* Suède *f*

**Swedish** ⟦1⟧ *n* (language) suédois *m*
⟦2⟧ *adj* suédois/-e

**sweep** ⟦1⟧ *n* **(a) to give sth a** ∼ donner un
coup de balai à qch
**(b)** (movement) **with a** ∼ **of his arm** d'un
grand geste du bras
**(c)** (of land, woods) étendue *f*
**(d)** (also **chimney** ∼) ramoneur *m*
⟦2⟧ *vtr* **(a)** balayer ⟨*floor, path*⟩; ramoner
⟨*chimney*⟩
**(b)** ( push) **to** ∼ **sth off the table** faire tomber
qch de la table (d'un grand geste de la
main); **to** ∼ **sb off his/her feet** (figurative) faire
perdre la tête à qn
**(c)** ⟨*beam, searchlight*⟩ balayer
⟦3⟧ *vi* **(a)** (clean) balayer
**(b) to** ∼ **in/out** (majestically) entrer/sortir
majestueusement
∎ **sweep aside** écarter ⟨*person, objection*⟩
∎ **sweep up** balayer

**sweeping** *adj* **(a)** ⟨*change, review*⟩
radical/-e
**(b)** ∼ **generalization** généralisation *f* à
l'emporte-pièce

**sweet** ⟦1⟧ *n* (GB) **(a)** (candy) bonbon *m*
**(b)** (dessert) dessert *m*
⟦2⟧ *adj* **(a)** (gen) doux/douce; ⟨*food, tea, taste*⟩
sucré/-e; **to have a** ∼ **tooth** aimer les
sucreries
**(b)** (kind) ⟨*person*⟩ gentil/-ille
**(c)** (cute) ⟨*baby, cottage*⟩ mignon/-onne
⟦3⟧ *adv* **to taste** ∼ avoir un goût sucré; **to
smell** ∼ sentir bon

**sweet-and-sour** *adj* aigre-doux/-douce

**sweetcorn** *n* maïs *m*

**sweeten** *vtr* **(a)** (Culin) sucrer (**with** avec)
**(b)** rendre [qch] plus tentant ⟨*offer*⟩
∎ **sweeten up** amadouer ⟨*person*⟩

**sweetener** n (a) (in food) édulcorant m
(b) (colloq) (bribe) incitation f; (illegal)
pot-de-vin m

**sweetheart** n (boyfriend) petit ami m;
(girlfriend) petite amie f

**sweetly** adv ⟨say, smile⟩ gentiment

**sweet potato** n patate f douce

**sweet-talk** vtr (colloq) baratiner (colloq)

**swell** ① n (of waves, sea) houle f
② vtr gonfler ⟨crowd, funds⟩; grossir ⟨river⟩
③ vi ⟨balloon, tyre, stomach⟩ se gonfler;
⟨wood⟩ gonfler; ⟨ankle, gland⟩ enfler; ⟨river⟩
grossir; ⟨crowd⟩ s'accroître

**swelling** n (on limb, skin) enflure f; (on head)
bosse f

**sweltering** adj (colloq) torride

**swerve** vi faire un écart; **to ~ off the road**
sortir de la route

**swift** ① n martinet m
② adj rapide, prompt/-e

**swill** n pâtée f (des porcs)

**swim** ① n baignade f; **to go for a ~** (in sea,
river) aller se baigner; (in pool) aller à la
piscine
② vtr nager ⟨distance, stroke⟩
③ vi (a) nager; **to ~ across sth** traverser
qch à la nage
(b) **to be ~ming in** baigner dans ⟨sauce, oil⟩
(c) ⟨scene, room⟩ tourner

**swimmer** n nageur/-euse m/f

**swimming** n natation f

**swimming costume** n (GB) maillot m
de bain

**swimming pool** n piscine f

**swimming trunks** n pl slip m de bain

**swimsuit** n maillot m de bain

**swindle** ① n escroquerie f
② vtr escroquer; **to ~ sb out of sth**
escroquer qch à qn

**swindler** n escroc m

**swing** ① n (a) (of pendulum, needle)
oscillation f; (of hips, body) balancement m
(b) (in public opinion) revirement m (in de); (in
prices, economy) fluctuation f (in de); (in mood)
saute f (in de)
(c) (in playground) balançoire f
② vtr (to and fro) balancer; **to ~ sb round and
round** faire tournoyer qn
③ vi (a) (to and fro) se balancer; ⟨pendulum⟩
osciller
(b) **to ~ open** s'ouvrir; **the car swung into
the drive** la voiture s'est engagée dans l'allée;
**to ~ around** ⟨person⟩ se retourner
(brusquement)
(c) (change) **to ~ from optimism to despair**
passer de l'optimisme au désespoir; **the party
swung towards the left** le parti a basculé
vers la gauche
**IDIOMS to get into the ~ of things** (colloq) se
mettre dans le bain (colloq); **to be in full ~**
battre son plein (colloq)

**swing door** (GB), **swinging door** (US)
n porte f battante

**swipe card** n carte f à piste magnétique

**swirl** vi tourbillonner

**Swiss** ① n Suisse mf
② adj suisse; ⟨embassy⟩ de Suisse

**switch** ① n (a) (change) changement m (in
de)
(b) (for light) interrupteur m; (on radio,
appliance) bouton m
② vtr (a) reporter ⟨attention⟩ (to sur); **to ~
flights** changer de vol
(b) intervertir ⟨objects, roles⟩; **I've ~ed the
furniture round** j'ai changé la disposition des
meubles
③ vi changer

■ **switch off** éteindre ⟨appliance, light,
engine⟩; couper ⟨supply⟩

■ **switch on** allumer ⟨appliance, light,
engine⟩

■ **switch over** (on TV) changer de chaîne

**switchboard** n standard m

**switchboard operator** n standardiste
mf

**switchover** n passage m (from de; to à)

**Switzerland** pr n Suisse f

**swivel** vtr faire pivoter ⟨chair, camera⟩;
tourner ⟨head, body⟩

■ **swivel round** pivoter

**swivel chair**, **swivel seat** n fauteuil
m tournant, chaise f tournante

**swollen** adj ⟨ankle, gland⟩ enflé/-e; ⟨eyes⟩
gonflé/-e; ⟨river⟩ en crue

**swoop** vi (a) ⟨bird, bat, plane⟩ plonger; **to
~ down** descendre en piqué; **to ~ down on**
fondre sur
(b) ⟨police, raider⟩ faire une descente

**sword** n épée f

**swordfish** n espadon m

**sworn** adj (a) ⟨statement⟩ fait/-e sous
serment
(b) ⟨enemy⟩ juré/-e; ⟨ally⟩ pour la vie

**swot** (colloq) ① n bûcheur/-euse m/f (colloq)
② vi bûcher (colloq)

**sycamore** n (also ~ **tree**) sycomore m

**syllable** n syllabe f

**syllabus** n programme m

**symbol** n symbole m (of, for de)

**symbolic** adj symbolique (of de)

**symbolism** n symbolisme m

**symbolize** vtr symboliser (by par)

**symmetric(al)** adj symétrique

**sympathetic** adj (compassionate)
compatissant/-e (to, towards envers);
(understanding) compréhensif/-ive; (kindly)
gentil/-ille; (well disposed) bien disposé/-e (to,
towards à l'égard de)

**sympathize** vi (a) témoigner de la
sympathie (with à); **I ~ with you in your grief**
je compatis à votre douleur
(b) (support) **to ~ with** souscrire à ⟨aims,
views⟩

**sympathizer** n sympathisant/-e m/f (of
de)

**sympathy** n (a) (compassion) compassion f
(b) (solidarity) solidarité f

**symphony** *n* symphonie *f*
**symphony orchestra** *n* orchestre *m* symphonique
**symptom** *n* symptôme *m*
**synagogue** *n* synagogue *f*
**synchronize** *vtr* synchroniser
**syndicate** *n* (gen) syndicat *m*; (of companies) consortium *m*
**syndrome** *n* syndrome *m*
**synonymous** *adj* synonyme (**with** de)
**synopsis** *n* (of play) synopsis *m*; (of book) résumé *m*
**syntax** *n* syntaxe *f*
**synthesis** *n* synthèse *f*
**synthesizer** *n* synthétiseur *m*
**synthetic** *adj* synthétique

**syringe** ⒈ *n* seringue *f*
  ⒉ *vtr* **to have one's ears ∼d** se faire déboucher les oreilles (avec une seringue)

**syrup** *n* sirop *m*

**system** *n* système *m* (**for doing, to do** pour faire); **road ∼** réseau *m* routier; **reproductive ∼** appareil *m* reproducteur; **to get sth out of one's ∼** oublier qch

**systematic** *adj* (a) (efficient) méthodique
  (b) (deliberate) systématique

**systematically** *adv* ⟨*work, list*⟩ méthodiquement; ⟨*arrange, destroy*⟩ systématiquement

**systems analyst** *n* analyste *mf* (de) systèmes

# Tt

**t, T** *n* t, T *m*
**tab** *n* (a) (loop) attache *f*
  (b) (on can) languette *f*
  (c) (label) étiquette *f*
  IDIOMS **to keep ∼s on sb** (colloq) tenir qn à l'œil (colloq)
**tabby (cat)** *n* chat/chatte *m/f* tigré/-e
**table** ⒈ *n* (a) table *f*; **to set the ∼** mettre le couvert
  (b) (list) table *f*, tableau *m*
  ⒉ *vtr* (a) (GB) (present) présenter
  (b) (US) (postpone) ajourner
**tablecloth** *n* nappe *f*
**table manners** *n pl* **to have good/bad ∼** savoir/ne pas savoir se tenir à table
**table mat** *n* (under plate) set *m* de table; (under serving-dish) dessous-de-plat *m inv*
**tablespoon** *n* (a) (object) cuillère *f* de service
  (b) (*also* **∼ful**) cuillerée *f* à soupe
**tablet** *n* comprimé *m* (**for** pour)
**table tennis** *n* tennis *m* de table, ping-pong® *m*
**tabloid** ⒈ *n* tabloïde *m*; **the ∼s** la presse populaire
  ⒉ *adj* ⟨*journalism, press*⟩ populaire
**taboo** *n, adj* tabou (*m*)
**tacit** *adj* tacite
**tack** ⒈ *n* (a) (nail) clou *m*
  (b) (US) (drawing pin) punaise *f*
  (c) (Naut) bordée *f*
  (d) (tactic) tactique *f*
  ⒉ *vtr* (a) (nail) **to ∼ sth to** clouer qch à
  (b) (in sewing) bâtir
  ⒊ *vi* ⟨*sailor*⟩ faire une bordée; ⟨*yacht*⟩ louvoyer

■ **tack on**: **∼ [sth] on, ∼ on [sth]** ajouter [qch] après coup ⟨*clause, ending, building*⟩ (**to** à)
**tackle** ⒈ *n* (a) (in soccer, hockey) tacle *m*; (in rugby, American football) plaquage *m*
  (b) (for fishing) articles *mpl* de pêche
  (c) (on ship) gréement *m*; (for lifting) palan *m*
  ⒉ *vtr* (a) s'attaquer à ⟨*task, problem*⟩
  (b) (confront) **to ∼ sb about** parler à qn de
  (c) (in soccer, hockey) tacler; (in rugby, American football) plaquer
**tacky** *adj* (a) (sticky) collant/-e
  (b) (colloq) (cheap) tocard/-e (colloq)
**tact** *n* tact *m*
**tactful** *adj* ⟨*person, letter*⟩ plein/-e de tact; ⟨*enquiry*⟩ discret/-ète
**tactical** *adj* tactique; **∼ voting** vote *m* utile
**tactics** *n pl* tactique *f*
**tactless** *adj* ⟨*person, question, suggestion*⟩ indélicat/-e; **to be ∼** ⟨*person, remark*⟩ manquer de tact
**tadpole** *n* têtard *m*
**tag** *n* (label) étiquette *f*; (on cat, dog) plaque *f*; (on file) onglet *m*
■ **tag along** suivre
**tail** *n* queue *f*
■ **tail off** (a) ⟨*figures, demand*⟩ diminuer
  (b) ⟨*voice*⟩ s'éteindre
**tailback** *n* bouchon *m*
**tailgate** *n* hayon *m*
**tail-off** *n* diminution *f*
**tailor** ⒈ *n* tailleur *m*
  ⒉ *vtr* **to ∼ sth to** adapter qch à ⟨*needs, person*⟩
**tailor-made** *adj* ⟨*garment*⟩ fait/-e sur mesure; (figurative) conçu/-e spécialement

**tails** n pl **(a)** (tailcoat) habit m
**(b)** (of coin) pile f; **heads or ∼?** pile ou face?

**tainted** adj ⟨food⟩ avarié/-e; ⟨water, air⟩ pollué/-e (**with** par); ⟨reputation⟩ entaché/-e

**take** **1** n (in film-making) prise f (de vues); (Mus) enregistrement m
**2** vtr **(a)** (gen) prendre; **he took the book off the shelf** il a pris le livre sur l'étagère; **she took a chocolate from the box** elle a pris un chocolat dans la boîte; **he took a pen out of his pocket** il a sorti un stylo de sa poche; **to ∼ an exam** passer un examen; **to ∼ a shower** prendre une douche; **to ∼ sb/sth seriously** prendre qn/qch au sérieux
**(b)** (carry with one) emporter, prendre ⟨object⟩; (carry to a place) emporter, porter ⟨object⟩; **to ∼ sb sth, to ∼ sth to sb** apporter qch à qn; **he took his umbrella with him** il a emporté son parapluie; **to ∼ a letter to the post office** porter une lettre à la poste; **to ∼ the car to the garage** emmener la voiture au garage; **to ∼ sth upstairs/downstairs** monter/descendre qch
**(c)** (accompany, lead) emmener ⟨person⟩; **to ∼ sb to** ⟨bus⟩ emmener qn à ⟨place⟩; ⟨road⟩ conduire or mener qn à ⟨place⟩; **I'll ∼ you to your room** je vais vous conduire à votre chambre; **he took her home** il l'a raccompagnée; **to ∼ a dog/a child for a walk** promener un chien/emmener un enfant faire une promenade
**(d)** (accept) ⟨person⟩ accepter ⟨job, bribe⟩; ⟨shop⟩ accepter ⟨credit card, cheque⟩; ⟨person⟩ supporter ⟨pain, criticism⟩; **she can't ∼ a joke** elle ne comprend pas la plaisanterie; **I can't ∼ any more!** je n'en peux plus!
**(e)** (require) demander, exiger ⟨patience, skill, courage⟩; **it ∼s patience to do** il faut de la patience pour faire; **it ∼s three hours to get there** il faut trois heures pour y aller; **it won't ∼ long** ça ne prendra pas longtemps; **it took her ten minutes to repair it** elle a mis dix minutes pour le réparer; **to have what it ∼s** avoir tout ce qu'il faut (**to do** pour faire)
**(f)** (assume) **I ∼ it that** je suppose que
**(g)** (hold) ⟨hall, bus⟩ pouvoir contenir ⟨50 people⟩; ⟨tank, container⟩ avoir une capacité de ⟨quantity⟩
**(h)** (wear) **what size do you ∼?** (in clothes) quelle taille faites-vous?; (in shoes) quelle pointure faites-vous?; **I ∼ a size 10** (in clothes) je m'habille en 36; **I ∼ a size 5** (in shoes) je chausse du 38
**(i)** (subtract) soustraire ⟨number, quantity⟩ (**from** de)
**3** vi ⟨drug⟩ faire effet; ⟨dye, plant⟩ prendre
**IDIOMS that's my last offer, ∼ it or leave it!** c'est ma dernière proposition, c'est à prendre ou à laisser!; **to ∼ a lot out of sb** fatiguer beaucoup qn
■ **take aback** interloquer; **to be ∼n aback** rester interloqué/-e
■ **take after** tenir de ⟨person⟩
■ **take apart** démonter ⟨car, machine⟩
■ **take away (a)** (carry away) emporter
**(b)** (remove) enlever ⟨object⟩; emmener ⟨person⟩

**(c)** (subtract) soustraire ⟨number⟩; **that doesn't ∼ anything away from his achievement** ça n'enlève rien à ce qu'il a accompli
■ **take back (a)** (to shop) rapporter ⟨goods⟩
**(b)** retirer ⟨statement, words⟩
**(c)** (accompany) ramener ⟨person⟩
**(d)** (accept again) reprendre
■ **take down (a)** enlever ⟨picture, curtains⟩; démonter ⟨tent, scaffolding⟩
**(b)** noter ⟨name, details⟩
■ **take hold** ⟨disease, epidemic⟩ s'installer; ⟨idea, ideology⟩ se répandre; **to ∼ hold of** prendre ⟨object, hand⟩
■ **take in (a)** (deceive) tromper; **I wasn't taken in by him** je ne me suis pas laissé prendre à son jeu
**(b)** recueillir ⟨refugee⟩; prendre ⟨lodger⟩
**(c)** (understand) saisir, comprendre ⟨situation⟩
**(d)** (observe) noter ⟨detail⟩
**(e)** (encompass) inclure
**(f)** (absorb) absorber ⟨nutrients, oxygen⟩
**(g)** ⟨boat⟩ prendre ⟨water⟩
**(h)** (in sewing) reprendre ⟨garment⟩
■ **take off: ¶ ∼ off (a)** ⟨plane⟩ décoller
**(b)** ⟨idea, fashion⟩ prendre
**¶ ∼ [sth] off (a) to ∼ £10 off (the price)** réduire le prix de 10 livres sterling
**(b) to ∼ two days off** prendre deux jours de congé
**¶ ∼ off [sth]** enlever ⟨clothing, shoes, lid⟩
**¶ ∼ [sb] off** (colloq) (imitate) imiter ⟨person⟩
■ **take on (a)** (employ) embaucher ⟨staff, worker⟩
**(b)** jouer contre ⟨team, player⟩; (fight) se battre contre ⟨person⟩
**(c)** (accept) prendre ⟨responsibilities, work⟩
■ **take out: ¶ ∼ [sth] out (a)** sortir ⟨object⟩ (**from, of** de); extraire ⟨tooth⟩; enlever ⟨appendix⟩; retirer ⟨money⟩
**(b) to ∼ [sth] out on sb** passer [qch] sur qn ⟨anger, frustration⟩; **to ∼ it out on sb** s'en prendre à qn
**¶ ∼ [sb] out** sortir avec ⟨person⟩; **to ∼ sb out to dinner** emmener qn dîner
■ **take over: ¶ ∼ over (a)** ⟨army, faction⟩ prendre le pouvoir
**(b)** (be successor) ⟨person⟩ prendre la suite; **to ∼ over from** remplacer ⟨predecessor⟩
**¶ ∼ over [sth]** prendre le contrôle de ⟨town, region⟩; reprendre ⟨business⟩
■ **take part** prendre part; **to ∼ part in** participer à
■ **take place** avoir lieu
■ **take to (a)** se prendre de sympathie pour ⟨person⟩
**(b)** (begin) **to ∼ to doing** se mettre à faire
**(c)** (go) se réfugier dans ⟨forest, hills⟩; **to ∼ to the streets** descendre dans la rue
■ **take up: ¶ to ∼ up with** s'attacher à ⟨person, group⟩
**¶ ∼ up [sth] (a)** (lift) enlever ⟨carpet, pavement⟩
**(b)** (start) se mettre à ⟨golf, guitar⟩; prendre ⟨job⟩; **to ∼ up one's duties** entrer dans ses fonctions
**(c)** (continue) reprendre ⟨story, cry, refrain⟩

**(d)** (accept) accepter ⟨*offer, invitation*⟩; relever ⟨*challenge*⟩
**(e) to ∼ sth up with sb** soulever [qch] avec qn ⟨*matter*⟩
**(f)** (occupy) prendre ⟨*space, time, energy*⟩
**(g)** prendre ⟨*position, stance*⟩
**(h)** (shorten) raccourcir ⟨*skirt, curtains*⟩
¶ **∼ sb up on (a)** reprendre qn sur ⟨*point, assertion*⟩
**(b) to ∼ sb up on an offer** accepter l'offre de qn

**take-away** *n* (GB) **(a)** (meal) repas *m* à emporter
**(b)** (restaurant) restaurant *m* qui fait des plats à emporter

**take-home pay** *n* salaire *m* net

**taken** *adj* **(a) to be ∼** ⟨*seat, room*⟩ être occupé/-e
**(b)** (impressed) **to be ∼ with** être emballé/-e ⟨*idea, person*⟩

**take-off** *n* **(a)** (by plane) décollage *m*
**(b)** (colloq) (imitation) imitation *f* (**of** de)

**take-out** *adj* (US) ⟨*food*⟩ à emporter

**takeover** *n* (of company) rachat *m*; (of political power) prise *f* de pouvoir

**takeover bid** *n* offre *f* publique d'achat, OPA *f*

**taker** *n* preneur/-euse *m/f*

**takings** *n pl* recette *f*

**talc, talcum (powder)** *n* talc *m*

**tale** *n* (story) histoire *f*; (fantasy story) conte *m*; (narrative, account) récit *m*

**talent** *n* talent *m*

**talent contest** *n* concours *m* de jeunes talents *or* d'amateurs

**talented** *adj* doué/-e, talentueux/-euse

**talisman** *n* talisman *m*

**talk** ⟨1⟩ *n* **(a)** (talking, gossip) propos *mpl*; **they are the ∼ of the town** on ne parle que d'eux
**(b)** (conversation) conversation *f*, discussion *f*
**(c)** (speech) exposé *m* (**about, on** sur); (more informal) causerie *f*
⟨2⟩ **talks** *n pl* négociations *fpl*; (political) pourparlers *mpl*; **peace ∼** pourparlers de paix
⟨3⟩ *vtr* parler; **to ∼ business** parler affaires; **to ∼ nonsense** raconter n'importe quoi; **to ∼ sb into/out of doing** persuader/dissuader qn de faire; **he ∼ed his way out of it** il s'en est tiré grâce à son bagout (colloq)
⟨4⟩ *vi* parler; (gossip) bavarder; **to ∼ to oneself** parler tout seul/toute seule

**talkative** *adj* bavard/-e

**talking** ⟨1⟩ *n* **I'll do the ∼** c'est moi qui parlerai; **'no ∼!'** 'silence!'
⟨2⟩ *adj* ⟨*bird, doll*⟩ qui parle

**talking book** *n* livre *m* enregistré (*à l'usage des non-voyants*)

**talking-to** *n* réprimande *f*

**talk show** *n* talk-show *m*

**tall** *adj* ⟨*person*⟩ grand/-e; ⟨*building, tree, chimney*⟩ haut/-e; **he's six feet ∼** ≈ il mesure un mètre quatre-vingts; **to grow ∼er** grandir

**tally** ⟨1⟩ *n* compte *m*
⟨2⟩ *vi* concorder

**tambourine** *n* tambourin *m*

**tame** ⟨1⟩ *adj* **(a)** ⟨*animal*⟩ apprivoisé/-e
**(b)** ⟨*story, party*⟩ sage; ⟨*reform*⟩ timide
⟨2⟩ *vtr* **(a)** apprivoiser ⟨*bird, wild animal*⟩; dompter ⟨*lion, tiger*⟩
**(b)** soumettre ⟨*person*⟩

**tamper** *vi* **to ∼ with** tripoter ⟨*machinery, lock*⟩; trafiquer ⟨*accounts, evidence*⟩

**tampon** *n* tampon *m*

**tan** ⟨1⟩ *n* **(a)** (*also* **sun∼**) bronzage *m*
**(b)** (colour) fauve *m*
⟨2⟩ *adj* fauve
⟨3⟩ *vtr* **(a)** bronzer ⟨*skin*⟩
**(b)** tanner ⟨*animal hide*⟩
⟨4⟩ *vi* ⟨*skin, person*⟩ bronzer

**tandem** *n* tandem *m*; **in ∼** en tandem

**tang** *n* (taste) goût *m* acidulé; (smell) odeur *f* piquante

**tangent** *n* tangente *f*; **to go off on a ∼** partir dans une digression

**tangerine** *n* tangerine *f*

**tangible** *adj* tangible

**tangle** ⟨1⟩ *n* (of hair, string, wires) enchevêtrement *m*; (of clothes, sheets) fouillis *m*
⟨2⟩ *vi* ⟨*hair, string, cable*⟩ s'emmêler
■ **tangle up**: ¶ **∼ up** s'embrouiller; ¶ **to get ∼d up** ⟨*hair, string, wires*⟩ s'emmêler

**tangy** *adj* acidulé/-e

**tank** *n* **(a)** (gen, Aut) réservoir *m*; (for oil) cuve *f*; (for water) citerne *f*; (for fish) aquarium *m*
**(b)** (Mil) char *m* (de combat)

**tankard** *n* chope *f*

**tanker** *n* **(a)** (ship) navire-citerne *m*; **oil ∼** pétrolier *m*
**(b)** (lorry) camion-citerne *m*

**tanned** *adj* (*also* **sun∼**) bronzé/-e

**Tannoy**® *n* (GB) **the ∼** le système de haut-parleurs

**tantalizing** *adj* ⟨*suggestion*⟩ tentant/-e; ⟨*possibility*⟩ séduisant/-e; ⟨*glimpse*⟩ excitant/-e

**tantamount** *adj* **to be ∼ to** équivaloir à, être équivalent/-e à

**tantrum** *n* crise *f* de colère; **to throw a ∼** piquer une crise (colloq)

**tap** ⟨1⟩ *n* **(a)** (for water, gas) robinet *m*
**(b)** (blow) petit coup *m*
⟨2⟩ *vtr* **(a)** (knock) taper (doucement); (repeatedly) tapoter
**(b)** mettre [qch] sur écoute ⟨*telephone*⟩
**(c)** inciser ⟨*rubber tree*⟩; exploiter ⟨*resources*⟩
■ **tap in: ∼ [sth] in, ∼ in [sth]** enfoncer ⟨*nail*⟩; taper ⟨*information, number*⟩

**tap dance** *n* (*also* **∼ dancing**) claquettes *fpl*

**tape** ⟨1⟩ *n* **(a)** bande *f* (magnétique); (cassette) cassette *f*; (video) cassette *f* vidéo; (recording) enregistrement *m*
**(b)** (*also* **adhesive ∼**) scotch® *m* ⋯⁖

t

**2** *vtr* **(a)** (record) enregistrer
**(b)** (stick) **to ~ sth to** coller qch à ⟨*surface, door*⟩

**tape deck** *n* platine *f* cassette

**tape measure** *n* mètre *m* ruban

**taper** *vi* ⟨*sleeve, trouser leg*⟩ se resserrer; ⟨*column, spire*⟩ s'effiler

**tape recorder** *n* magnétophone *m*

**tapestry** *n* tapisserie *f*

**tapeworm** *n* ver *m* solitaire, ténia *m*

**tap water** *n* eau *f* du robinet

**tar** *n* goudron *m*; (on roads) bitume *m*.

**target** **1** *n* **(a)** (in archery, shooting) cible *f*; (Mil) objectif *f*
**(b)** (butt) cible *f*; **to be the ~ of abuse** être insulté/-e
**(c)** (goal) objectif *m*
**2** *adj* ⟨*date, figure*⟩ prévu/-e; ⟨*audience, group*⟩ visé/-e, ciblé/-e
**3** *vtr* **(a)** diriger ⟨*weapon, missile*⟩; prendre [qch] pour cible ⟨*city, site*⟩
**(b)** (in marketing) viser ⟨*group, sector*⟩

**target language** *n* langue *f* cible

**tariff** *n* **(a)** (price list) tarif *m*
**(b)** (customs duty) droit *m* de douane

**tarmac** *n* **(a)** (*also* **Tarmac**®) macadam *m*
**(b)** (GB) (of airfield) piste *f*

**tarnish** **1** *vtr* ternir
**2** *vi* se ternir

**tarpaulin** *n* (material) toile *f* de bâche; (sheet) bâche *f*

**tarragon** *n* estragon *m*

**tart** *n* (small) tartelette *f*; (large) tarte *f*
■ **tart up** (GB) (colloq): ¶ **~ [sth] up, ~ up [sth]** retaper (colloq) ⟨*house, room*⟩; ¶ **~ oneself up** se pomponner (colloq)

**tartan** *adj* écossais/-e

**task** *n* tâche *f*; **a hard ~** une lourde tâche

**task bar** *n* barre *f* de tâches

**task force** *n* (Mil) corps *m* expéditionnaire; (committee) groupe *m* de travail

**taskmaster** *n* tyran *m*; **to be a hard ~** être très exigeant/-e

**tassel** *n* gland *m*

**taste** **1** *n* **(a)** (gen) goût *m*; **that's a matter of ~** ça dépend des goûts; **to be in bad ~** être de mauvais goût
**(b)** (brief experience) expérience *f*, (foretaste) avant-goût *m*
**2** *vtr* **(a)** (try) goûter ⟨*food, drink*⟩
**(b) I can ~ the brandy in this coffee** je sens le (goût du) cognac dans ce café
**(c)** (experience) goûter à ⟨*freedom, success*⟩
**3** *vi* **to ~ sweet** avoir un goût sucré; **to ~ horrible** avoir mauvais goût; **to ~ like sth** avoir le goût de qch; **to ~ of** avoir un goût de

**taste bud** *n* papille *f* gustative

**tasteful** *adj* de bon goût

**tasteless** *adj* **(a)** ⟨*remark, joke*⟩ de mauvais goût
**(b)** ⟨*food, drink*⟩ insipide

**tasty** *adj* ⟨*food*⟩ succulent/-e

**tatters** *n pl* **to be in ~** ⟨*clothing*⟩ être en lambeaux; ⟨*career, reputation*⟩ être en ruines

**tattoo** **1** *n* tatouage *m*
**2** *vtr* tatouer (**on** sur)

**tatty** *adj* (colloq) ⟨*carpet, garment*⟩ miteux/-euse; ⟨*book, shoes*⟩ en mauvais état

**taunt** *vtr* railler ⟨*person*⟩

**Taurus** *n* Taureau *m*

**taut** *adj* tendu/-e

**tauten** **1** *vtr* tendre
**2** *vi* se tendre

**tax** **1** *n* (on goods, services, property) taxe *f*; (on income, profits) impôt *m*
**2** *vtr* **(a)** imposer ⟨*earnings, person*⟩; taxer ⟨*luxury goods*⟩
**(b)** mettre [qch] à l'épreuve ⟨*patience*⟩

**taxation** *n* **(a)** (imposition of taxes) imposition *f*
**(b)** (revenue from taxes) impôts *mpl*

**tax bracket** *n* tranche *f* d'imposition du revenu

**tax collector** *n* percepteur *m*

**tax disc** *n* vignette *f* (automobile)

**tax evasion** *n* fraude *f* fiscale

**tax exile** *n*: *personne qui s'est expatriée pour raisons fiscales*

**tax-free** *adj* exempt/-e d'impôt

**tax haven** *n* paradis *m* fiscal

**taxi** *n* taxi *m*; **by ~** en taxi

**taxing** *adj* épuisant/-e

**taxi rank** (GB), **taxi stand** *n* station *f* de taxis

**tax office** *n* perception *f*

**taxpayer** *n* contribuable *mf*

**tax return** *n* **(a)** (form) feuille *f* d'impôts
**(b)** (declaration) déclaration *f* de revenus

**TB** *n* (*abbr* = **tuberculosis**) tuberculose *f*

**tea** *n* **(a)** (drink) thé *m*
**(b)** (GB) (afternoon meal) thé *m*; (for children) goûter *m*; (evening meal) dîner *m*

**tea bag** *n* sachet *m* de thé

**tea break** *n* (GB) pause-café *f*

**teach** **1** *vtr* enseigner à ⟨*children, adults*⟩; enseigner ⟨*subject*⟩; **to ~ sb** enseigner [qch] à qn ⟨*academic subject*⟩; apprendre [qch] à qn ⟨*practical skill*⟩; **to ~ school** (US) être instituteur/-trice; **to ~ sb a lesson** ⟨*person*⟩ donner une bonne leçon à qn; ⟨*experience*⟩ servir de leçon à qn
**2** *vi* enseigner

**teacher** *n* (in general) enseignant/-e *m/f*; (secondary) professeur *m*; (primary) instituteur/-trice *m/f*; (special needs) éducateur/-trice *m/f*

**teacher training** *n* formation *f* pédagogique

**teaching** **1** *n* enseignement *m*
**2** *adj* ⟨*post*⟩ d'enseignant; ⟨*method, qualification*⟩ pédagogique; ⟨*staff*⟩ enseignant/-e

**teaching hospital** *n* centre *m* hospitalo-universitaire, CHU *m*

**teacup** *n* tasse *f* à thé

**teak** *n* teck *m*

**team** *n* équipe *f*

**team member** *n* équipier/-ière *m/f*

**team spirit** *n* esprit *m* d'équipe

**teamwork** *n* collaboration *f*

**teapot** *n* théière *f*

**tear¹** ⓵ *n* (gen) accroc *m*; (Med) déchirure *f*
⓶ *vtr* déchirer ‹*garment, paper*›; **to ~ sth out of** arracher qch de ‹*book, notepad*›
⓷ *vi* (a) (rip) se déchirer
(b) (rush) **to ~ out/off** sortir/partir en trombe
■ **tear apart** (a) mettre [qch] en pièces ‹*prey*›; déchirer ‹*country*›
(b) (separate) séparer
(c) (colloq) (criticize) descendre [qn] en flammes
■ **tear off** (carefully) détacher; (violently) arracher
■ **tear open** ouvrir [qch] en le/la déchirant
■ **tear out** détacher ‹*coupon, cheque*›; arracher ‹*page*›
■ **tear up** déchirer ‹*letter, document*›

**tear²** *n* larme *f*; **to burst into ~s** fondre en larmes

**tearful** *adj* ‹*person, face*› en larmes; ‹*voice*› larmoyant/-e

**tear gas** *n* gaz *m* lacrymogène

**tease** *vtr* taquiner ‹*person*› (**about** à propos de); tourmenter ‹*animal*›

**teasing** *n* taquineries *fpl*

**teaspoon** *n* petite cuillère *f*, cuillère *f* à café

**teaspoonful** *n* cuillerée *f* à café

**teat** *n* (a) (of cow, goat, ewe) trayon *m*
(b) (GB) (on baby's bottle) tétine *f*

**teatime** *n* l'heure *f* du thé

**tea towel** *n* (GB) torchon *m* (à vaisselle)

**technical** *adj* technique

**technical college** *n* institut *m* d'enseignement technique

**technical drawing** *n* dessin *m* industriel

**technical hitch** *n* incident *m* technique

**technicality** *n* (a) (technical detail) détail *m* technique (**of** de)
(b) (minor detail) point *m* de détail
(c) (technical nature) technicité *f*

**technically** *adv* (a) (strictly speaking) théoriquement
(b) (technologically) techniquement

**technician** *n* technicien/-ienne *m/f*

**technique** *n* technique *f*

**techno** ⓵ *n* techno *f*
⓶ *adj* techno *inv*

**technological** *adj* technologique

**technology** *n* technologie *f*; **information ~** informatique *f*

**teddy** *n* (*also* **~ bear**) ours *m* en peluche

**tedious** *adj* ennuyeux/-euse

**teem** *vi* **to be ~ing with** grouiller de ‹*people*›

**teenage** *adj* ‹*son, daughter*› qui est adolescent/-e; ‹*singer, player*› jeune (*before n*); ‹*fashion*› des adolescents

**teenager** *n* jeune *mf*, adolescent/-e *m/f*

**teens** *n pl* adolescence *f*; **to be in one's ~** être adolescent/-e

**tee-shirt** *n* tee-shirt, T-shirt *m*

**teeter** *vi* vaciller

**teethe** *vi* faire ses dents

**teething troubles** *n pl* difficultés *fpl* initiales

**teetotal** *adj* **I'm ~** je ne bois jamais d'alcool

**teetotaller** (GB), **teetotaler** (US) *n* personne *f* qui ne boit jamais d'alcool

**TEFL** *n* (*abbr* = **Teaching of English as a Foreign Language**) enseignement *m* de l'anglais langue étrangère

**telecommunications** *n pl* télécommunications *fpl*

**telecommuting** *n* télétravail *m*

**teleconference** *n* téléconférence *f*

**telecottaging** *n* télétravail *m*

**telegram** *n* télégramme *m*

**telegraph** ⓵ *n* télégraphe *m*
⓶ *vtr* télégraphier

**telegraph pole** *n* poteau *m* télégraphique

**telemarketer** *n* téléprospecteur/-trice *m/f*

**telemarketing** *n* télémarketing *m*

**telepathy** *n* télépathie *f*

**telephone** ⓵ *n* téléphone *m*; **to be on the ~** (connected) avoir le téléphone; (talking) être au téléphone
⓶ *vtr* téléphoner à ‹*person*›; téléphoner ‹*instructions*›; **to ~ France** appeler la France
⓷ *vi* appeler, téléphoner

**telephone banking** *n* transactions *fpl* bancaires télématiques

**telephone booth, telephone box** (GB) *n* cabine *f* téléphonique

**telephone call** *n* appel *m* téléphonique

**telephone directory** *n* annuaire *m* (du téléphone)

**telephone number** *n* numéro *m* de téléphone

**telephone operator** *n* standardiste *mf*

**telephonist** *n* (GB) standardiste *mf*

**telephoto lens** *n* téléobjectif *m*

**telesales** *n* télévente *f*

**telescope** *n* télescope *m*

**teleshopping** *n* téléachat *m*

**teletext** *n* télétexte *m*

**televise** *vtr* téléviser

**television** *n* (a) (medium) télévision *f*; **on ~** à la télévision
(b) (set) téléviseur *m*

**television licence** *n* redevance *f* télévision

**television programme** *n* émission *f* de télévision

**television set** n téléviseur m, poste m de
télévision
**teleworking** n télétravail m
**telex** ⬚1 n télex m
⬚2 vtr télexer
**tell** ⬚1 vtr (a) (gen) dire; raconter ⟨joke,
story⟩; prédire ⟨future⟩; **to ~ sb about sth**
parler de qch à qn; **to ~ sb to do** dire à qn
de faire; **to ~ sb how to do/what to do**
expliquer à qn comment faire/ce qu'il faut
faire; **to ~ the time** ⟨clock⟩ indiquer or
marquer l'heure; ⟨person⟩ lire l'heure; **can
you ~ me the time please?** peux-tu me dire
l'heure (qu'il est), s'il te plaît?; **I was told
that** on m'a dit que; **I told you so!** je te
l'avais bien dit!
(b) (deduce) **you can ~ (that) he's lying** on
voit bien qu'il ment; **I can ~ (that) he's
disappointed** je sais qu'il est déçu
(c) (distinguish) distinguer; **can you ~ the
difference?** est-ce que vous voyez la
différence?; **how can you ~ them apart?**
comment peut-on les distinguer l'un de
l'autre?
⬚2 vi (a) (reveal secret) **don't ~!** ne le répète
pas!
(b) (know) savoir; **as far as I can ~** pour
autant que je sache; **how can you ~?**
comment le sais-tu?
(c) (show effect) **her age is beginning to ~** elle
commence à faire son âge
■ **tell off** réprimander ⟨person⟩
■ **tell on** (a) dénoncer ⟨person⟩ (**to** à)
(b) **the strain is beginning to ~ on him** on
commence à voir sur lui les effets de la
fatigue
**telling** adj ⟨remark, omission⟩
révélateur/-trice
**tell-tale** ⬚1 n rapporteur/-euse m/f
⬚2 adj ⟨sign⟩ révélateur/-trice
**telly** n (GB) (colloq) télé f (colloq)
**temp** (GB) (colloq) ⬚1 n intérimaire mf
⬚2 vi travailler comme intérimaire
**temper** ⬚1 n (a) (mood) humeur f; **to be in a
good/bad ~** être de bonne/mauvaise
humeur
(b) **to be in a ~** être en colère; **to lose one's
~** se mettre en colère (**with** contre)
(c) (nature) caractère m
⬚2 vtr (a) (moderate) tempérer
(b) tremper ⟨steel⟩
**temperament** n (a) (nature) tempérament
m
(b) (excitability) humeur f
**temperamental** adj (volatile)
capricieux/-ieuse
**temperate** adj ⟨climate, zone⟩ tempéré/-e;
⟨person, habit⟩ modéré/-e
**temperature** n température f; **to have a
~** avoir de la température or de la fièvre
**temper tantrum** n caprice m
**tempest** n tempête f
**tempestuous** adj turbulent/-e
**template** n gabarit m; (Comput) modèle m
**temple** n (a) (building) temple m

(b) (Anat) tempe f
**temporarily** adv (for a limited time)
temporairement; (provisionally) provisoirement
**temporary** adj ⟨job, contract⟩ temporaire;
⟨manager, secretary⟩ intérimaire;
⟨arrangement, accommodation⟩ provisoire
**tempt** vtr tenter; **to be ~ed to do** être
tenté/-e de faire
**temptation** n tentation f
**tempting** adj ⟨offer⟩ alléchant/-e; ⟨food,
smell⟩ appétissant/-e; ⟨idea⟩ tentant/-e
**ten** n, pron, det dix (m) inv
**tenacious** adj tenace
**tenancy** n location f
**tenant** n locataire mf
**tend** ⬚1 vtr soigner ⟨patient⟩; entretenir
⟨garden⟩; s'occuper de ⟨stall, store⟩
⬚2 vi **to ~ to do** avoir tendance à faire
**tendency** n tendance f (**to do** à faire)
**tender** ⬚1 n soumission
⬚2 adj (a) ⟨meat⟩ tendre
(b) ⟨kiss, love, smile⟩ tendre
(c) ⟨bruise, skin⟩ sensible
⬚3 présenter ⟨apology, fare⟩; donner
⟨resignation⟩
**tendon** n tendon m
**tendril** n vrille f
**tenement** n immeuble m ancien
**tenner** n (GB) (colloq) (note) billet m de dix
livres
**tennis** n tennis m
**tennis court** n court m de tennis, tennis
m inv
**tenor** n (Mus) ténor m
**tenpin bowling** (GB), **tenpins** (US) n
bowling m (à dix quilles)
**tense** ⬚1 n temps m; **the present ~** le
présent; **in the past ~** au passé
⬚2 adj ⟨person, atmosphere, conversation⟩
tendu/-e; ⟨moment⟩ de tension; **to make sb ~**
rendre qn nerveux
⬚3 vtr tendre ⟨muscle⟩; raidir ⟨body⟩
■ **tense up** ⟨person⟩ se crisper
**tension** n (a) (gen, Tech) tension f
(b) (suspense) suspense m
**tent** n tente f
**tentacle** n tentacule m
**tentative** adj ⟨smile, suggestion⟩ timide;
⟨conclusion, offer⟩ provisoire
**tenterhooks** n pl
IDIOMS **to be on ~** être sur des charbons
ardents; **to keep sb on ~** faire languir qn
**tenth** ⬚1 n (a) (in order) dixième mf
(b) (of month) dix m inv
(c) (fraction) dixième m
⬚2 adj, adv dixième
**tenuous** adj ⟨link⟩ ténu/-e; ⟨distinction,
theory⟩ mince
**tepid** adj tiède
**term** ⬚1 n (a) (period of time) (gen) période f,
terme m; (Sch, Univ) trimestre m; **autumn/
spring/summer ~** (Sch, Univ) premier/

deuxième/troisième trimestre **the president's first ~ of office** le premier mandat du président
**(b)** (word, phrase) terme *m*
**[2] terms** *n pl* **(a)** (conditions) termes *mpl*; (of financial arrangement) conditions *fpl* de paiement
**(b) to come to ~s with** assumer ⟨*identity, past, disability*⟩; accepter ⟨*death, defeat, failure*⟩; affronter ⟨*issue*⟩
**(c)** (relations) termes *mpl*; **to be on good ~s with** être en bons termes avec
**[3]** *vtr* appeler, nommer
**[4] in terms of** *phr* du point de vue de, sur le plan de
**terminal [1]** *n* **(a)** (at station) terminus *m*; (in airport) aérogare *f*; **ferry ~** gare *f* maritime
**(b)** (Comput) terminal *m*
**(c)** (for electricity) borne *f*
**[2]** *adj* ⟨*stage*⟩ terminal/-e; ⟨*illness*⟩ (incurable) incurable; (at final stage) en phase terminale
**terminate [1]** *vtr* mettre fin à ⟨*meeting, phase, relationship*⟩; résilier ⟨*contract*⟩; annuler ⟨*agreement*⟩; interrompre ⟨*pregnancy*⟩
**[2]** *vi* se terminer
**termination** *n* **(a)** (of contract) résiliation *f*; (of service) interruption *f*
**(b)** (Med) interruption *f* de grossesse
**terminology** *n* terminologie *f*
**terminus** *n* (GB) terminus *m*
**terrace [1]** *n* **(a)** (patio) terrasse *f*
**(b)** (row of houses) alignement *m* de maisons
**[2] terraces** *n pl* (GB) (in stadium) gradins *mpl*
**terrace(d) house** *n* maison *f* (située dans un alignement de maisons identiques et contiguës)
**terracotta** *n* **(a)** (earthenware) terre *f* cuite
**(b)** (colour) ocre brun *m*
**terrain** *n* terrain *m*
**terrible** *adj* **(a)** ⟨*pain, noise, sight*⟩ épouvantable; ⟨*accident, fight*⟩ terrible; ⟨*mistake*⟩ grave
**(b)** (colloq) ⟨*food, weather*⟩ affreux/-euse
**terribly** *adv* **(a)** (very) ⟨*pleased, obvious*⟩ très; ⟨*clever*⟩ extrêmement; **I'm ~ sorry** je suis navré
**(b)** (badly) ⟨*suffer*⟩ horriblement; ⟨*sing, drive*⟩ affreusement mal
**terrific** *adj* **(a)** (huge) ⟨*amount*⟩ énorme; ⟨*noise*⟩ épouvantable; ⟨*speed*⟩ fou/folle; ⟨*accident, shock*⟩ terrible
**(b)** (colloq) (wonderful) formidable
**terrifically** *adv* extrêmement
**terrified** *adj* terrifié/-e; **to be ~ of** avoir une peur folle de
**terrify** *vtr* terrifier
**terrifying** *adj* (frightening) terrifiant/-e; (alarming) effroyable
**territorial** *adj* territorial/-e
**territory** *n* territoire *m*; (figurative) domaine *m*
**terror [1]** *n* terreur *f*

**[2]** *adj* ⟨*tactic*⟩ d'intimidation; **a ~ campaign** une vague terroriste
**terrorism** *n* terrorisme *m*
**terrorist** *n* terroriste *mf*
**terrorize** *vtr* terroriser
**terry** *n* (*also* **~ towelling** (GB), **~ cloth** (US)) tissu *m* éponge
**terse** *adj* ⟨*style*⟩ succinct/-e; ⟨*person, statement*⟩ laconique
**tertiary** *adj* ⟨*sector*⟩ tertiaire; ⟨*education*⟩ supérieur/-e
**test [1]** *n* **(a)** (gen) test *m*; (Sch, Univ) (written) contrôle *m*; (oral) épreuve *f* orale; **to put sb/sth to the ~** mettre qn/qch à l'épreuve
**(b)** (of equipment, machine, new model) essai *m*
**(c)** (Med) (of blood, urine) analyse *f*; (of organ) examen *m*; (to detect virus, cancer) test *m* de dépistage; **to have a blood ~** se faire faire une analyse de sang
**(d)** (Aut) (*also* **driving ~**) examen *m* du permis de conduire
**[2]** *vtr* **(a)** (gen) évaluer ⟨*intelligence, efficiency*⟩; (Sch) (in classroom) interroger (**on** en); (at exam time) contrôler
**(b)** (new model, product) essayer; (Med) analyser ⟨*blood, sample*⟩; expérimenter ⟨*new drug*⟩; **to have one's eyes ~ed** se faire faire un examen des yeux
**(c)** mettre [qch] à l'épreuve ⟨*strength, patience*⟩
**testament** *n* **(a)** (proof) témoignage *m*; **to be a ~ to sth** témoigner de qch
**(b) the Old/the New Testament** l'Ancien/le Nouveau Testament
**test ban** *n* interdiction *f* d'essais nucléaires
**test case** *n* procès *m* qui fait jurisprudence
**test-drive** *vtr* faire un essai de route à, essayer
**testicle** *n* testicule *m*
**testify [1]** *vtr* témoigner (**that** que)
**[2]** *vi* témoigner; **to ~ to** témoigner de
**testimony** *n* témoignage *m*, déposition *f*
**testing** *n* (of drug, cosmetic) expérimentation *f*; (of blood, water etc) analyse *f*; (Sch) contrôles *mpl*
**test paper** *n* (Sch) interrogation *f* écrite
**test tube** *n* éprouvette *f*
**test-tube baby** *n* bébé-éprouvette *m*
**tetanus** *n* tétanos *m*
**tether** *vtr* attacher (**to** à)
**IDIOMS to be at the end of one's ~** être au bout du rouleau (colloq)
**text** *n* texte *m*
**textbook [1]** *n* manuel *m* (**about, on** sur) .
**[2]** *adj* ⟨*case*⟩ exemplaire; ⟨*example*⟩ parfait/-e
**textile** *n* textile *m*
**texture** *n* texture *f*
**Thames** *pr n* **the (river) ~** la Tamise

**than** ☐1 *prep* **(a)** (in comparisons) que; **he's
taller ~ me** il est plus grand que moi; **he has
more ~ me** il en a plus que moi
**(b)** (expressing quantity, degree, value) de; **more/
less ~ 100** plus/moins de 100; **more ~ half**
plus de la moitié; **temperatures lower ~ 30
degrees** des températures de moins de 30
degrés
☐2 *conj* **(a)** (in comparisons) que; **he's older ~ I
am** il est plus âgé que moi; **it took us longer
~ we expected** ça nous a pris plus de temps
que prévu
**(b)** (expressing preferences) **I'd sooner** *or* **rather
go to Rome ~ go to Venice** je préférerais
aller à Rome que d'aller à Venise, j'aimerais
mieux aller à Rome qu'à Venise
**(c)** (when) **hardly** *or* **no sooner had he left ~
the phone rang** à peine était-il parti que le
téléphone a sonné
**(d)** (US) **to be different ~ sth** être différent/-e
de qch

**thank** *vtr* remercier ‹*person*›; **~ God!** Dieu
merci!

**thankful** *adj* (grateful) reconnaissant/-e;
(relieved) soulagé/-e

**thankfully** *adv* **(a)** (luckily) heureusement
**(b)** (with relief) avec soulagement; (with gratitude)
avec gratitude

**thankless** *adj* ‹*task, person*› ingrat/-e

**thanks** ☐1 *n pl* remerciements *mpl*; **with ~**
avec mes/nos remerciements
☐2 *adv* (colloq) merci; **~ a lot** merci
beaucoup; **no ~** non merci
☐3 **thanks to** *phr* grâce à

**Thanksgiving (Day)** *n* (US) jour *m*
d'Action de Grâces

**thank you** ☐1 *n* (*also* **thank-you**,
**thankyou**) merci *m*; **to say ~ to sb** dire
merci à qn
☐2 *adj* ‹*letter, gift*› de remerciement
☐3 *adv* merci; **~ for coming** merci d'être
venu; **~ very much** merci beaucoup

**that**

■ Note **As a determiner**
– In French, determiners agree in gender and
number with the noun that follows; *that* is
translated by *ce* + masculine singular noun (*ce
monsieur*), by *cet* + masculine singular noun
beginning with a vowel or mute 'h' (*cet arbre, cet
homme*) and by *cette* + feminine singular noun
(*cette femme*). The plural form *those* is
translated by *ces*.
– Note, however, that the above translations are
also used for the English *this* (plural *these*). So
when it is necessary to insist on *that* as opposed
to others of the same sort *-là* is added to the
noun: *I prefer* THAT *version* = je préfère cette
version-là.
**As a pronoun** (*meaning that one*)
– In French, pronouns reflect the gender and
number of the noun they are standing for. So
*that* (meaning *that one*) is translated by *celui-là*
for a masculine noun, *celle-là* for a feminine

noun; *those* (meaning *those ones*) is translated
by *ceux-là* for a masculine plural noun and
*celles-là* for a feminine plural noun.

☐1 *det* /cet/cette/ces; **~ chair** cette chaise;
**those chairs** ces chaises; **at ~ moment** à ce
moment-là; **at ~ time** à cette époque-là; **you
can't do it ~ way** tu ne peux pas le faire
comme ça; **he went ~ way** il est allé par là;
**~ lazy son of yours** ton paresseux de fils
☐2 *dem pron* **(a)** (that one) celui-/celle-/ceux-/
celles-là
**(b)** (that thing, that person) **what's ~?** qu'est-ce
que c'est que ça?; **who's ~?** qui est-ce?; (on
phone) qui est à l'appareil?; **is ~ Françoise?**
c'est Françoise?; **who told you ~?** qui t'a dit
ça?; **~'s how he did it** c'est comme ça qu'il
l'a fait; **what did he mean by ~?** qu'est-ce
qu'il entendait par là?; **~'s the kitchen** ça,
c'est la cuisine
☐3 *rel pron* **(a)** (as subject) qui; (as object) que;
**the day ~ she arrived** le jour où elle est
arrivée
**(b)** (with a preposition) lequel, laquelle, lesquels,
lesquelles; **the chair ~ I was sitting on** la
chaise sur laquelle j'étais assis
**(c)** (with prepositions translated by *à*) auquel, à
laquelle, auxquels, auxquelles, **the girls ~ I
was talking to** les filles auxquelles je parlais
**(d)** (with prepositions translated by *de*) dont; **the
people ~ I've talked about** les personnes
dont j'ai parlé
☐4 *conj* que; **he said ~ he had finished** il a
dit qu'il avait fini
☐5 *adv* **it's about ~ thick** c'est à peu près
épais comme ça; **I can't do ~ much work in
one day** je ne peux pas faire autant de
travail dans une journée; **he can't swim ~
far** il ne peut pas nager aussi loin
IDIOMS **~ is (to say)...** c'est-à-dire...; **~'s it!**
(that's right) c'est ça!; (that's enough) ça suffit!; **I
don't want to see you again and ~'s ~!** je ne
veux pas te revoir point final!

**thatched cottage** *n* chaumière *f*

**thatched roof** *n* toit *m* de chaume

**thaw** ☐1 *n* dégel *m*
☐2 *vtr* faire fondre ‹*ice, snow*›; décongeler
‹*frozen food*›
☐3 *vi* **(a)** ‹*snow*› fondre; ‹*ground, frozen food*›
dégeler
**(b)** (figurative) se détendre

**the** *det* le/la/l'/les

■ Note In French, determiners agree in gender
and number with the noun that follows. So *the* is
translated by *le* or *l'* + masculine singular noun
(*le chien, l'ami*), by *la* or *l'* + feminine singular
noun (*la chaise, l'amie*) and by *les* + plural noun
(*les chaussures*).
– When *the* is used with a preposition that
translates by *de* in French *de* + *le* = masculine
singular noun = *du* (*du fromage*) and *de* + *les* +
plural noun = *des* (*des crayons*).
– When *the* is used with a preposition that
translates by *à* in French *à* + *le* + masculine
singular noun = *au* (*au cinéma*) and *à* + *les* +
plural noun = *aux* (*aux enfants*).

two chapters of ∼ **book** deux chapitres du livre; **I met them at** ∼ **supermarket** je les ai rencontrés au supermarché; ∼ **French** les Français; ∼ **wounded** les blessés; **she buys only** ∼ **best** elle n'achète que ce qu'il y a de mieux; ∼ **more I learn** ∼ **less I understand** plus j'apprends moins je comprends; ∼ **longer he waits** ∼ **harder it will be** plus il attendra plus ce sera difficile; ∼ **sooner** ∼ **better** le plus tôt sera le mieux; ∼ **fastest train** le train le plus rapide; ∼ **prettiest house in the village** la plus jolie maison du village; THE **book of the year** le meilleur livre de l'année; **do you mean** THE **Charlie Parker?** tu veux dire le célèbre Charlie Parker?; **Charles** ∼ **First** Charles 1$^{er}$ or Premier; ∼ **Smiths** les Smith

**theatre, theater** (US) n **(a)** théâtre m; **to go to the** ∼ aller au théâtre **(b)** (US) (cinema) cinéma m

**theatregoer** n amateur mf de théâtre

**theatrical** adj théâtral/-e; ⟨group⟩ de théâtre

**theft** n vol m (**of** de)

**their** det leur/leurs

■ **Note** In French, determiners agree in gender and number with the noun that follows. So *their* is translated by *leur* + masculine or feminine singular noun (*leur chien, leur maison*) and by *leurs* + plural noun (*leurs enfants*).
– When *their* is stressed, *à eux* is added after the noun: THEIR house = leur maison à eux.

**theirs** pron

■ **Note** In French, possessive pronouns reflect the gender and number of the noun they are standing for; *theirs* is translated by *le leur, la leur, les leurs*, according to what is being referred to.

**my car is red but** ∼ **is blue** ma voiture est rouge mais la leur est bleue; **my children are older than** ∼ mes enfants sont plus âgés que les leurs; **which house is** ∼**?** c'est laquelle leur maison?; **the money wasn't** ∼ **to give away** ils or elles n'avaient pas à donner cet argent

**them** pron **(a)** (direct object) les; **I've seen** ∼ je les ai vus; **catch** ∼**!** attrape-les!; **don't eat** ∼**!** ne les mange pas! **(b)** (indirect object) leur; **I gave it to** ∼ je le leur ai donné; **write to** ∼**!** écris-leur! **(c)** (with prepositions, with être) eux, elles; **with** ∼ avec eux/elles; **it's** ∼ c'est eux/elles **both of** ∼ tous/toutes les deux; **both of** ∼ **work in London** ils/elles travaillent à Londres tous/toutes les deux; **some of** ∼ quelques-uns d'entre eux/quelques-unes d'entre elles

**theme** n thème m

**theme park** n parc m d'attractions (à thème)

**theme song, theme tune** n (of film) musique f; (of radio, TV programme) indicatif m

**themselves** pron

■ **Note** When used as a reflexive pronoun, direct and indirect, *themselves* is translated by *se* (or *s'* before a vowel or mute 'h').
– When used for emphasis, the translation is *eux-mêmes* in the masculine and *elles-mêmes* in the feminine: *they did it themselves* = ils l'ont fait eux-mêmes or elles l'ont fait elles-mêmes.
– After a preposition, the translation is *eux* or *elles* or *eux-mêmes* or *elles-mêmes: they bought the painting for themselves* = (*masculine or mixed gender*) ils ont acheté le tableau pour eux or pour eux-mêmes; (*feminine gender*) elles ont acheté le tableau pour elles or pour elles-mêmes.

**(a)** (reflexive) se, s'; **they washed** ∼ ils se sont lavés
**(b)** (emphatic) eux-mêmes/elles-mêmes
**(c)** (after preposition) eux/elles, eux-mêmes/ elles-mêmes; **(all) by** ∼ tout seuls/toutes seules

**then** adv **(a)** (at that time) alors, à ce moment-là; (implying more distant past) en ce temps-là; **I was working in Oxford** ∼ je travaillais alors à Oxford; **since** ∼ depuis **(b)** (afterwards, next) puis, ensuite **(c)** (in that case, so) alors **(d)** (therefore) donc **(e)** (in addition, besides) puis, aussi

**thence** adv de là

**theology** n théologie f

**theorem** n théorème m

**theoretical** adj théorique

**theoretically** adv théoriquement; ∼ **speaking** en théorie

**theory** n théorie f; **in** ∼ en théorie

**therapeutic** adj thérapeutique

**therapist** n thérapeute mf

**therapy** n thérapie f

**there**

■ **Note** *there* is generally translated by *là* after prepositions (*near there* = près de là) and when emphasizing the location of an object/a point etc visible to the speaker: *put them there* = mettez-les là.
– *voilà* is used to draw attention to a visible place/object/person: *there's my watch* = voilà ma montre, whereas *il y a* is used for generalizations: *there's a village nearby* = il y a un village tout près.
– *there*, when unstressed with verbs such as *aller* and *être*, is translated by *y: we went there last year* = nous y sommes allés l'année dernière, but when more emphasis is made: *it was there that we went last year* = c'est là que nous sommes allés l'année dernière.
– For examples of the above and further uses, see the entry below.

**1** pron ∼ **is/are** il y a; ∼ **isn't any room** il n'y a pas de place; ∼ **are many reasons** il y a beaucoup de raisons; ∼ **are two** il y en a deux; ∼ **is some left** il en reste; ∼ **seems to be** il semble y avoir

**2** adv **(a)** là; **up to** ∼, **down to** ∼ jusque là; ⋯⟩

put it in ∼ mettez-le-là-dedans; **stand** ∼ mettez-vous là; **go over** ∼ va là-bas; **will she be** ∼ **now?** est-ce qu'elle y est maintenant? **(b)** (to person, activity) voilà; ∼ **you are** (seeing somebody arrive) vous voilà; (giving object) tenez, voilà; (that's done) et voilà; ∼**'s a bus coming** voilà un bus; **that paragraph** ∼ ce paragraphe **3** *excl* ∼∼! allez! allez!; ∼, **I told you!** voilà, je te l'avais bien dit!; ∼, **you've woken the baby!** c'est malin, tu as réveillé le bébé! **4 there again** *phr* (on the other hand) d'un autre côté

**thereabouts** (GB), **thereabout** (US) *adv* **(a)** (in the vicinity) par là **(b)** (roughly) **100 dollars or** ∼ 100 dollars environ

**thereby** *conj* ainsi

**therefore** *adv* donc, par conséquent

**thermal** *adj* thermique; ⟨*spring*⟩ thermal/-e; ⟨*garment*⟩ en thermolactyl®

**thermal imaging** *n* thermographie *f*

**thermometer** *n* thermomètre *m*

**Thermos**® *n* (*also* ∼ **flask**) bouteille *f* thermos®

**thermostat** *n* thermostat *m*

**thesaurus** *n* dictionnaire *m* analogique

**these** ▶ THIS

**thesis** *n* **(a)** (Univ) (doctoral) thèse *f*; (master's) mémoire *m* **(b)** (theory) thèse *f*

**they** *pron*

■ Note *they* is translated by *ils* (masculine) or *elles* (feminine). For a group of people or things of mixed gender, *ils* is always used. The emphatic form is *eux* (masculine) or *elles* (feminine).

∼ **have already gone** (masculine or mixed) ils sont déjà partis; (feminine) elles sont déjà parties; **here** ∼ **are!** les voici!; **there** ∼ **are!** les voilà!

**thick** **1** *adj* **(a)** (gen) épais/épaisse; ⟨*forest, vegetation, fog*⟩ dense, épais/épaisse; **to be 6 cm** ∼ faire 6 cm d'épaisseur **(b)** (colloq) (stupid) bête **2** *adv* **don't spread the butter on too** ∼ ne mets pas trop de beurre; **the snow lay** ∼ **on the ground** il y avait une épaisse couche de neige sur le sol IDIOMS **to be in the** ∼ **of** être au beau milieu de

**thicken** **1** *vtr* épaissir **2** *vi* s'épaissir; ⟨*voice*⟩ s'enrouer

**thicket** *n* fourré *m*

**thickly** *adv* ⟨*spread*⟩ en une couche épaisse; ⟨*cut*⟩ en morceaux épais

**thickness** *n* épaisseur *f*

**thickset** *adj* trapu/-e

**thick-skinned** *adj* insensible

**thief** *n* voleur/-euse *m/f*

**thieve** *vtr, vi* voler

**thigh** *n* cuisse *f*

**thimble** *n* dé *m* à coudre

**thin** **1** *adj* **(a)** ⟨*nose, lips, wall*⟩ mince; ⟨*line, stripe, wire, paper*⟩ fin/-e; ⟨*slice, layer*⟩ fin/-e, mince; ⟨*fabric, mist*⟩ léger/-ère **(b)** ⟨*mixture*⟩ liquide; ⟨*soup, sauce*⟩ clair/-e **(c)** ⟨*person, body*⟩ maigre; **to get** ∼ maigrir **(d) to wear** ∼ ⟨*joke, excuse*⟩ être usé/-e **2** *vtr* diluer ⟨*paint*⟩; allonger ⟨*sauce, soup*⟩ **3** *vi* (*also* ∼ **out**) ⟨*crowd*⟩ se disperser; ⟨*hair*⟩ se clairsemer

**thing** **1** *n* **(a)** (object) chose *f*, truc *m* (colloq); (action, task, event) chose *f*; **the best** ∼ **(to do) would be to go and see her** le mieux serait d'aller la voir; **I couldn't hear a** ∼ **(that) he said** je n'ai rien entendu de ce qu'il a dit; **the** ∼ **is, (that)...** ce qu'il y a, c'est que...; **the only** ∼ **is,...** la seule chose, c'est que... **(b)** (person, animal) **she's a pretty little** ∼ c'est une jolie petite fille; **you lucky** ∼**!** (colloq) veinard/-e! (colloq) **2 things** *n pl* **(a)** (personal belongings, equipment) affaires *fpl* **(b)** (situation, circumstances, matters) les choses *fpl*; **how are** ∼**s with you?** comment ça va?; **all** ∼**s considered** tout compte fait IDIOMS **for one** ∼**... (and) for another** ∼**...** premièrement... et deuxièmement...; **I must be seeing** ∼**s!** je dois avoir des visions!

**think** **1** *vtr* **(a)** (believe) croire, penser; **I** ∼ **so** je crois; **I don't** ∼ **so** je ne crois pas; **what do you** ∼ **it will cost?** combien ça va coûter à ton avis? **(b)** (imagine) croire, imaginer **(c)** (have opinion) **to** ∼ **a lot/not much of** penser/ne pas penser beaucoup de bien de; **what do you** ∼ **of him?** que penses-tu de lui? **2** *vi* **(a)** penser; (carefully) réfléchir; **to** ∼ **about** *or* **of sb/sth** penser à qn/qch; **I'll have to** ∼ **about it** il faudra que j'y réfléchisse; **to** ∼ **hard** bien réfléchir; **to be** ∼**ing of doing** envisager de faire; **to** ∼ **about doing** penser à faire **(b)** (consider) **to** ∼ **of sb as** considérer qn comme **(c)** (remember) **to** ∼ **of** se rappeler ■ **think again** (reflect more) se repencher sur la question; (change mind) changer d'avis ■ **think ahead** bien réfléchir (à l'avance) ■ **think back** se reporter en arrière (**to** à) ■ **think over**: ∼ **over** [sth], ∼ [sth] **over** réfléchir à ■ **think through** bien réfléchir à ⟨*proposal, action*⟩; faire le tour de ⟨*problem, question*⟩

**thinking** *n* (reflection) réflexion *f*; **current** ∼ **is that** la tendance actuelle de l'opinion est que; **to my way of** ∼ à mon avis

**think-tank** *n* groupe *m* de réflexion

**thinly** *adv* ⟨*slice*⟩ en tranches fines; ⟨*spread*⟩ en couche mince; ∼ **disguised** à peine déguisé/-e

**thinner** *n* diluant *m*

**third** **1** *n* **(a)** (in order) troisième *mf* **(b)** (of month) trois *m inv* **(c)** (fraction) tiers *m* **(d)** (*also* ∼**-class honours degree**) (GB Univ) ≈ licence *f* avec mention passable **(e)** (*also* ∼ **gear**) (Aut) troisième *f*

**2** *adj* troisième
**3** *adv* **(a)** ‹*come, finish*› troisième
**(b)** (*also* **thirdly**) troisièmement

**third-class** *adj* de troisième classe

**third degree** *n* (colloq) **to give sb the ~**
‹*parent, teacher*› soumettre qn à une
interrogation

**third party** *n* tiers *m*

**Third Way** *n* (GB Pol) troisième voie *f*

**Third World** *n* tiers-monde *m*

**thirst** *n* soif *f* (**for** de)

**thirsty** *adj* assoiffé/-e; **to be ~** avoir soif;
**to make sb ~** donner soif à qn

**thirteen** *n, pron, det* treize (*m*) *inv*

**thirteenth** **1** *n* **(a)** (in order) treizième *mf*
**(b)** (of month) treize *m inv*
**(c)** (fraction) treizième *m*
**2** *adj, adv* treizième

**thirties** *n pl* **(a)** (era) **the ~** les années *fpl*
trente
**(b)** (age) **to be in one's ~** avoir entre trente
et quarante ans

**thirtieth** **1** *n* **(a)** (in order) trentième *mf*
**(b)** (of month) trente *m inv*
**(c)** (fraction) trentième *m*
**2** *adj, adv* trentième

**thirty** *n, pron, det* trente (*m*) *inv*

**thirty-first** **1** *n* (of month) trente et un *m*
**2** *adj* trente et unième

**thirty something** *n*: jeune cadre de plus
de trente ans qui s'installe, fonde une famille,
etc

**this**

■ Note **As a determiner**
– In French, determiners agree in gender and
number with the noun that follows; *this* is
translated by *ce* + masculine singular noun (*ce
monsieur*) BUT by *cet* + masculine singular noun
beginning with a vowel or mute 'h' (*cet arbre,
cet homme*) and by *cette* + feminine singular
noun (*cette femme*). The plural form *these* is
translated by *ces* (*ces livres, ces histoires*).
– Note, however, that the above translations are
also used for the English *that* (plural *those*). So
when it is necessary to insist on *this* as opposed
to another or others of the same sort, the
adverbial tag *-ci* (*this one here*) is added to the
noun: *I prefer* THIS *version* = je préfère cette
version-ci.

**As a pronoun** (*meaning this one*)
– In French, pronouns reflect the gender and
number of the noun they are standing for. So
*this* (meaning *this one*) is translated by *celui-ci*
for a masculine noun, *celle-ci* for a feminine
noun; *those* (meaning *those ones*) is translated
by *ceux-ci* for a masculine plural noun, *celles-ci*
for a feminine plural noun: *of all the dresses this
is the prettiest one* = de toutes les robes celle-ci
est la plus jolie.
– For other uses of *this*, see the entry below.

**1** *det* **~ paper** ce papier; **~ lamp** cette
lampe; **do it ~ way not that way** fais-le
comme ça et pas comme ça
**2** *pron* **what's ~?** qu'est-ce que c'est?;

**who's ~?** qui est-ce?; (on telephone) qui est à
l'appareil?; **whose is ~?** à qui appartient
ceci?; **~ is the dining room** voici la salle à
manger; **~ is my sister Moira** (introduction)
voici ma sœur Moira; (on photo) c'est ma
sœur, Moira; **~ is not the right one** ce n'est
pas le bon; **who did ~?** qui a fait ça?; **~ is
what happens when** voilà ce qui se passe
quand
**3** *adv* **it's ~ big** c'est grand comme ça
IDIOMS **to talk about ~ and that** parler de
tout et de rien

**thistle** *n* chardon *m*

**thong** *n* **(a)** (on whip) lanière *f*
**(b)** (on shoe, garment) lacet *m*
**(c)** (underwear) string *m* ficelle

**thorn** *n* épine *f*

**thorough** *adj* **(a)** (detailed) ‹*analysis,
knowledge*› approfondi/-e; ‹*search, work*›
minutieux/-ieuse
**(b)** (meticulous) minutieux/-ieuse

**thoroughbred** **1** *n* pur-sang *m*
**2** *adj* de pure race

**thoroughfare** *n* rue *f*; **'no ~'** 'passage
interdit'

**thoroughly** *adv* **(a)** (meticulously) ‹*clean,
examine, read*› à fond; ‹*check, search*›
minutieusement
**(b)** (completely) ‹*clean, reliable, dangerous*›
tout à fait; ‹*agree*› parfaitement;
‹*recommend*› chaleureusement

**those** ▶ THAT

**though** **1** *conj* bien que (+ *subjunctive*); **a
foolish ~ courageous act** un acte stupide
quoique courageux
**2** *adv* quand même, pourtant; **it's very
expensive, ~** c'est très cher, pourtant

**thought** *n* **(a)** (idea) idée *f*, pensée *f*
**(b)** (reflection) pensée *f*; **deep in ~** plongé
dans ses pensées
**(c)** (consideration) considération *f*; **to give ~ to
sth** considérer qch

**thoughtful** *adj* **(a)** (reflective) pensif/-ive
**(b)** (considerate) ‹*person, gesture*›
prévenant/-e; ‹*letter*› gentil/-ille

**thoughtless** *adj* irréfléchi/-e

**thought-out** *adj* **well/badly ~** bien/mal
conçu/-e

**thought-provoking** *adj* qui fait
réfléchir

**thousand** *n, pron, det* mille *m inv*; **a ~
and two** mille deux; **about a ~** un millier;
**four ~ pounds** quatre mille livres sterling;
**~s of** des milliers de

**thousandth** *n, adj, adv* millième (*mf*)

**thrash** *vtr* **(a)** (whip) rouer [qn] de coups
**(b)** (Mil, Sport) (colloq) écraser
■ **thrash about, thrash around** se
débattre
■ **thrash out** venir à bout de ‹*problem*›;
réussir à élaborer ‹*plan*›

**thrashing** *n* raclée *f*

**thread** **1** *n* **(a)** (for sewing) fil *m*
**(b)** (of screw) filetage *m*

⋯⃕

**(c)** (of story, argument) fil *m*
2 *vtr* enfiler ⟨bead, needle⟩

**threadbare** *adj* usé/-e jusqu'à la corde

**threat** *n* menace *f* (**to** pour)

**threaten** 1 *vtr* menacer; **to ~ to do**
⟨person⟩ menacer de faire; ⟨event, thing⟩
risquer de faire; **to be ~ed with extinction**
risquer de disparaître
2 *vi* menacer

**three** *n, pron, det* trois (*m*) *inv*

**three-dimensional** *adj* en trois
dimensions

**threefold** 1 *adj* triple
2 *adv* triplement; **to increase ~** tripler

**three-piece suit** *n* (costume *m*)
trois-pièces *m inv*

**three-piece suite** *n* salon *m* trois
pièces

**three-quarters** *n* trois-quarts *mpl*; **~ of
an hour** trois-quarts d'heure

**thresh** *vtr* battre

**threshold** *n* seuil *m*

**thrift** *n* économie *f*

**thrifty** *adj* ⟨person⟩ économe (**in** dans)

**thrill** 1 *n* **(a)** (sensation) frisson *m*
**(b)** (pleasure) plaisir *m*
2 *vtr* transporter [qn] de joie
3 *vi* frissonner (**at, to** à)

**thrilled** *adj* ravi/-e; **~ed with** enchanté/-e
de

**thriller** *n* thriller *m*

**thrilling** *adj* ⟨adventure, match, story⟩
palpitant/-e; ⟨concert, moment, sensation⟩
exaltant/-e

**thrive** *vi* ⟨person⟩ se porter bien; ⟨plant⟩
pousser bien; ⟨business, community⟩
prospérer

**thriving** *adj* ⟨business, community⟩
florissant/-e; ⟨plant, animal⟩ en pleine santé

**throat** *n* gorge *f*; **to have a sore ~** avoir
mal à la gorge

**throb** *vi* **(a)** ⟨heart, pulse⟩ battre; **my head is
~bing** ça me lance dans la tête
**(b)** ⟨motor⟩ vibrer; ⟨music, building⟩
résonner

**throbbing** *adj* ⟨pain, ache, music⟩
lancinant/-e

**throne** *n* trône *m*

**throng** 1 *n* foule *f* (**of** de)
2 *vtr* envahir ⟨street, town⟩

**throttle** *n* (accelerator) accélérateur *m*

**through** 1 *prep* **(a)** (from one side to the
other) à travers; **the nail went right ~ the wall**
le clou a traversé le mur
**(b)** (via, by way of) **to go ~ the town centre**
passer par le centre-ville; **to look ~** regarder
avec ⟨telescope⟩; regarder par ⟨hole, window⟩;
**it was ~ her that I got this job** c'est par son
intermédiaire que j'ai eu ce travail
**(c)** (past) **to go ~** brûler ⟨red light⟩; **to get or
go ~** passer à travers ⟨barricade⟩; passer
⟨customs⟩; **she's been ~ a lot** elle en a vu
des vertes et des pas mures (colloq)

**(d)** (because of) **~ carelessness** par
négligence; **~ illness** pour cause de maladie
**(e)** (until the end of) **all or right ~ the day** toute
la journée
**(f)** (up to and including) jusqu'à; **from Friday ~
to Sunday** de vendredi jusqu'à dimanche
2 *adj* **(a)** ⟨train, ticket, route⟩ direct/-e;
⟨freight⟩ à forfait; **'no ~ road'** 'voie sans
issue'
**(b)** (successful) **to be ~ to the next round** être
sélectionné/-e pour le deuxième tour
**(c)** (colloq) (finished) fini/-e; **are you ~ with the
paper?** as-tu fini de lire le journal?
3 *adv* **the water went ~** l'eau est passée à
travers; **to let sb ~** laisser passer qn; **to read
sth right ~** lire qch jusqu'au bout
4 **through and through** *phr* **English ~
and ~** anglais jusqu'au bout des ongles

**throughout** 1 *prep* **(a)** (all over) **~ France**
dans toute la France; **~ the world** dans le
monde entier
**(b)** (for the duration of) tout au long de; **~ his
life** toute sa vie; **~ history** à travers
l'histoire
2 *adv* (in every part) partout; (the whole time)
tout le temps

**throughway** *n* (US) voie *f* rapide *or*
express

**throw** 1 *n* (in football) touche *f*; (of javelin)
lancer *m*; (in judo, wrestling) jeté *m*; (of dice)
coup *m*
2 *vtr* **(a)** (with careful aim) lancer; (downwards)
jeter; (with violence) projeter; **to ~ sth at sb**
lancer qch à qn; **to ~ a six** (in dice) faire un
six
**(b)** ⟨horse⟩ désarçonner ⟨rider⟩
**(c)** lancer ⟨punch⟩; jeter ⟨glance⟩; projeter
⟨light, shadow⟩ (**on** sur)
**(d)** (disconcert) désarçonner
**(e) to ~ a party** faire une fête (colloq)
**(f)** (in pottery) tourner
3 *vi* lancer

■ **throw away** jeter ⟨paper, old clothes⟩;
gâcher ⟨chance, life⟩
■ **throw back** rejeter ⟨fish⟩; relancer ⟨ball⟩
■ **throw in: ~ in** [sth], **[sth] in** (give free)
faire cadeau de; (add) ajouter
■ **throw out (a)** jeter ⟨rubbish⟩; expulser
⟨person⟩ (**of** de)
**(b)** rejeter ⟨application, decision⟩
■ **throw together:** ¶ **~** [sb] **together** réunir
⟨people⟩; ¶ **~** [sth] **together** improviser
■ **throw up:** ¶ **~ up** (colloq) vomir **~** [sth] **up**
**(a)** lever ⟨arms, hands⟩; lancer ⟨ball⟩
**(b)** (colloq) (abandon) laisser tomber ⟨job⟩

**throwaway** *adj* (discardable) jetable;
⟨society⟩ de consommation; ⟨remark⟩
désinvolte

**throwback** *n* survivance *f* (**to** de)

**thrush** *n* (Zool) grive *f*

**thrust** 1 *n* **(a)** (gen, Mil, Tech) poussée *f*;
**sword ~** coup *m* d'épée
**(b)** (of argument) portée *f*
2 *vtr* **to ~ sth towards** *or* **at sb** mettre
brusquement qch sous le nez de qn; **to ~ sth
into sth** enfoncer qch dans qch

**thud** ⟨1⟩ *n* bruit *m* sourd
⟨2⟩ *vi* faire un bruit sourd

**thug** *n* voyou *m*

**thumb** ⟨1⟩ *n* pouce *m*
⟨2⟩ *vtr* **(a)** (*also* ∼ **through**) feuilleter ⟨*book, magazine*⟩
**(b)** (colloq) **to** ∼ **a lift** faire du stop (colloq)
IDIOMS **to be under sb's** ∼ être sous la domination de qn

**thumbs down** *n* (colloq) **to give sb/sth the** ∼ rejeter qn/qch; **to get the** ∼ être rejeté/-e

**thumbs up** *n* (colloq) **to give sb/sth the** ∼ (approve) approuver qn/qch; **start the car when I give you the** ∼ démarre quand je te fais signe

**thumbtack** *n* punaise *f*

**thump** ⟨1⟩ *n* **(a)** (blow) (grand) coup *m*
**(b)** (sound) bruit *m* sourd
⟨2⟩ *vtr* taper sur; **he** ∼**ed me** il m'a tapé dessus
⟨3⟩ *vi* ⟨*heart*⟩ battre violemment; ⟨*music, rhythm*⟩ résonner

**thunder** ⟨1⟩ *n* **(a)** tonnerre *m*; **a peal of** ∼ un roulement de tonnerre
**(b)** (of hooves) fracas *m*; (of applause) tonnerre *m*
⟨2⟩ *v impers* tonner

**thunderbolt** *n* foudre *f*

**thunderclap** *n* coup *m* de tonnerre

**thunderstorm** *n* orage *m*

**thunderstruck** *adj* abasourdi/-e

**Thursday** *n* jeudi *m*

**thus** *adv* ainsi; ∼ **far** jusqu'à présent

**thwart** *vtr* contrarier ⟨*plan*⟩; contrecarrer les desseins de ⟨*person*⟩

**thyme** *n* thym *m*

**thyroid** *n* (*also* ∼ **gland**) thyroïde *f*

**tiara** *n* (woman's) diadème *m*; (Pope's) tiare *f*

**Tibet** *pr n* Tibet *m*

**tick** ⟨1⟩ *n* **(a)** (of clock) tic-tac *m*
**(b)** (mark) coche *f*
**(c)** (Zool) tique *f*
⟨2⟩ *vtr* cocher ⟨*box, name, answer*⟩
⟨3⟩ *vi* ⟨*bomb, clock, watch*⟩ faire tic-tac
■ **tick off** cocher ⟨*name, item*⟩

**ticket** *n* **(a)** (for plane, train, cinema, exhibition) billet *m* (**for** pour); (for bus, underground, cloakroom, left-luggage) ticket *m*; (for library) carte *f*; (label) étiquette *f*
**(b)** (Aut) (colloq) (for fine) PV *m* (colloq)
**(c)** (US) (of political party) liste *f* (électorale)

**ticket office** *n* (office) bureau *m* de vente (des billets); (booth) guichet *m*

**tickle** ⟨1⟩ *n* chatouillement *m*
⟨2⟩ *vtr* **(a)** ⟨*person, feather*⟩ chatouiller; ⟨*wool, garment*⟩ gratter
**(b)** (colloq) (gratify) chatouiller ⟨*palate, vanity*⟩
**(c)** (amuse) amuser
⟨3⟩ *vi* chatouiller

**tidal wave** *n* raz-de-marée *m inv*

**tide** *n* marée *f*; (figurative) (of emotion) vague *f*; (of events) cours *m*

**tidy** ⟨1⟩ *adj* **(a)** ⟨*house, room, desk*⟩ bien

rangé/-e; ⟨*garden, work, appearance*⟩ soigné/-e; ⟨*habits, person*⟩ ordonné/-e; ⟨*hair*⟩ bien coiffé/-e
**(b)** (colloq) ⟨*amount*⟩ beau/belle (*before n*)
⟨2⟩ *vtr, vi* = TIDY UP
■ **tidy up**: ¶ ∼ **up** faire du rangement; **to** ∼ **up after** ranger derrière ⟨*person*⟩; ¶ ∼ **up** [sth] ranger ⟨*house, room, objects*⟩; arranger ⟨*appearance, hair*⟩

**tie** ⟨1⟩ *n* **(a)** (piece of clothing) cravate *f*
**(b)** (bond) lien *m*
**(c)** (constraint) contrainte *f*
**(d)** (draw) match *m* nul
⟨2⟩ *vtr* **(a)** attacher ⟨*label, animal*⟩ (**to** à); ligoter ⟨*hands*⟩; ficeler ⟨*parcel*⟩ (**with** avec); nouer ⟨*scarf, cravate*⟩; attacher ⟨*laces*⟩; **to** ∼ **a knot in sth** faire un nœud à qch
**(b)** (link) associer (**to** à)
**(c) to be** ∼**d to** être rivé/-e à ⟨*job*⟩; être cloué/-e à (colloq) ⟨*house*⟩
⟨3⟩ *vi* **(a)** (fasten) s'attacher
**(b)** (draw) (in match) faire match nul; (in race) être ex aequo; (in vote) obtenir le même nombre de voix
■ **tie back** nouer [qch] derrière ⟨*hair*⟩
■ **tie down**: **she feels** ∼**d down** elle se sent coincée (colloq); **he doesn't want to be** ∼**d down** il ne veut pas perdre sa liberté; **to** ∼ **sb down to sth** (limit) imposer qch à qn
■ **tie in with** concorder avec ⟨*fact, event*⟩
■ **tie up (a)** ligoter ⟨*prisoner*⟩; ficeler ⟨*parcel*⟩; attacher ⟨*animal*⟩
**(b)** (freeze) immobiliser ⟨*capital*⟩
**(c) to be** ∼**d up** (busy) être pris/-e
**(d)** (finalize) conclure ⟨*deal*⟩; **to** ∼ **up the loose ends** régler les derniers détails

**tie break(er)** *n* (in tennis) tie-break *m*; (in quiz) question *f* subsidiaire

**tier** *n* (of cake, sandwich) étage *m*; (of system) niveau *m*; (of seating) gradin *m*

**tiff** *n* (petite) querelle *f*

**tiger** *n* tigre *m*

**tight** ⟨1⟩ *adj* **(a)** ⟨*grip*⟩ ferme; ⟨*knot*⟩ serré/-e; ⟨*rope, voice*⟩ tendu/-e
**(b)** (space) étroit/-e; ⟨*clothing*⟩ serré/-e; (closefitting) ⟨*jacket, shirt*⟩ ajusté/-e; **my shoes are too** ∼ mes chaussures me serrent
**(c)** (strict) ⟨*security, deadline*⟩ strict/-e; ⟨*budget, credit, schedule*⟩ serré/-e
⟨2⟩ *adv* ⟨*hold, grip*⟩ fermement; **hold** ∼**!** cramponne-toi!; **sit** ∼**!** ne bouge pas!

**tighten** ⟨1⟩ *vtr* serrer ⟨*lid, screw*⟩; resserrer ⟨*grip*⟩; renforcer ⟨*security, restrictions*⟩
⟨2⟩ *vi* ⟨*lips*⟩ se serrer; ⟨*muscle*⟩ se contracter

**tight-fisted** *adj* (colloq) radin/-e (colloq)

**tight-fitting** *adj* ajusté/-e

**tight-knit** *adj* uni/-e

**tightly** *adv* ⟨*grasp, hold*⟩ fermement; ⟨*embrace*⟩ bien fort; ⟨*fastened*⟩ bien

**tightrope** *n* corde *f* raide

**tightrope walker** *n* funambule *mf*

**tights** *n pl* (GB) collant *m*

**tile** ⟨1⟩ *n* (for roof) tuile *f*; (for floor, wall) carreau *m*

⋯⟶

**2** *vtr* poser des tuiles sur ⟨*roof*⟩; carreler ⟨*floor, wall*⟩

**till**[1] = UNTIL

**till**[2] *n* caisse *f*

**tiller** *n* barre *f*

**till receipt** *n* ticket *m* (de caisse)

**tilt** **1** *vtr* pencher ⟨*table, sunshade*⟩; incliner ⟨*head*⟩; rabattre ⟨*hat, cap*⟩
**2** *vi* (slant) pencher

**timber** *n* (for building) bois *m* (de construction); (trees) arbres *mpl*; (beam) poutre *f*

**time** **1** *n* (a) temps *m*; as ~ goes/went by avec le temps; **you've got plenty of** ~ tu as tout ton temps; **a long** ~ longtemps; **a long** ~ **ago** il y a longtemps; **in five days'** ~ dans cinq jours
(b) (hour of the day, night) heure *f*; **what** ~ **is it?, what's the** ~? quelle heure est-il?; **10 am French** ~ 10 heures, heure française; **this** ~ **last week** il y a exactement huit jours; **on** ~ à l'heure; **the train** ~**s** les horaires *mpl* des trains; **it's** ~ **for bed** c'est l'heure d'aller au lit; **it's** ~ **we started** il est temps de commencer; **about** ~ **too!** ce n'est pas trop tôt!; **in** ~ **for Christmas** à temps pour Noël
(c) (era, epoch) époque *f*; **at the** ~ à l'époque; **in former** ~**s** autrefois; **it's just like old** ~**s** c'est comme au bon vieux temps
(d) (moment) moment *m*; **at** ~**s** par moments; **at the right** ~ au bon moment; **this is no** ~ **for jokes** ce n'est pas le moment de plaisanter; **at all** ~**s** à tout moment; **any** ~ **now** d'un moment à l'autre; **by the** ~ **I finished the letter the post had gone** le temps de finir ma lettre et le courrier était parti; **some** ~ **next month** dans le courant du mois prochain; **for the** ~ **being** pour le moment
(e) (occasion) fois *f*; **nine** ~**s out of ten** neuf fois sur dix; **three** ~**s a month** trois fois par mois; **three at a** ~ trois à la fois; **from** ~ **to** ~ de temps en temps
(f) (experience) **to have a hard** ~ **doing** avoir du mal à faire; **he's having a hard** ~ il traverse une période difficile; **we had a good** ~ on s'est bien amusés
(g) (Mus) mesure *f*
(h) **ten** ~**s longer/stronger** dix fois plus long/plus fort; **eight** ~**s as much** huit fois autant
(i) (in mathematics) fois *f*
**2** *vtr* (a) (schedule) prévoir ⟨*holiday, visit, attack*⟩; fixer ⟨*appointment, meeting*⟩
(b) (judge) calculer ⟨*blow, shot*⟩
(c) chronométrer ⟨*athlete, cyclist*⟩
IDIOMS all in good ~ chaque chose en son temps; only ~ will tell l'avenir nous le dira; to have ~ on one's hands (for brief period) avoir du temps devant soi; (longer) avoir beaucoup de temps libre

**time bomb** *n* bombe *f* à retardement

**time-consuming** *adj* qui prend du temps

**time difference** *n* décalage *m* horaire

**time-frame** *n* (period envisaged) calendrier *m*; (period allocated) délai *m*

**timeless** *adj* éternel/-elle

**time-limit** *n* (a) (deadline) date *f* limite
(b) (maximum duration) durée *f* maximum

**timely** *adj* opportun/-e

**time off** *n* (leave) congé *m*; (free time) temps *m* libre

**timer** *n* (on light) minuterie *f*; (for cooking) minuteur *m*

**timeshare** *n* (house) maison *f* en multipropriété; (apartment) appartement *m* en multipropriété

**time-sheet** *n* feuille *f* de présence

**timespan** *n* durée *f*

**timetable** **1** *n* (Sch) emploi *m* du temps; (for plans, negotiations) calendrier *m*; (for buses, trains) horaire *m*
**2** *vtr* fixer l'heure de ⟨*class*⟩; fixer la date de ⟨*meeting*⟩

**time zone** *n* fuseau *m* horaire

**timid** *adj* timide; ⟨*animal*⟩ craintif/-ive

**timing** *n* (a) (gen) **the** ~ **of the announcement was unfortunate** le moment choisi pour la déclaration était inopportun
(b) (Aut) réglage *m* de l'allumage
(c) (Mus) sens *m* du rythme

**tin** *n* (a) (metal) étain *m*
(b) (GB) (can) boîte *f* (de conserve)
(c) (for biscuits, cake) boîte *f*; (for paint) pot *m*; (for baking) moule *m*; (for roasting) plat *m* (à rôtir)

**tin can** *n* boîte *f* en fer-blanc

**tin foil** *n* papier *m* (d')aluminium

**tinge** **1** *n* nuance *f*
**2** *vtr* teinter (with de)

**tingle** **1** *n* (physical) picotement *m*; (psychological) frisson *m*
**2** *vi* (physically) picoter; (psychologically) frissonner

**tinker** *vi* **to** ~ **with** bricoler ⟨*car*⟩; faire des retouches à ⟨*document*⟩

**tinkle** **1** *n* tintement *m*
**2** *vi* tinter

**tinned** *adj* ⟨*meat, fruit*⟩ en boîte, en conserve

**tinny** *adj* ⟨*sound*⟩ grêle; (badly made) de camelote (colloq)

**tin opener** *n* (GB) ouvre-boîtes *m inv*

**tinsel** *n* guirlandes *fpl*

**tint** *n* (trace) nuance *f*; (pale colour) teinte *f*; (hair colour) shampooing *m* colorant

**tinted** *adj* ⟨*glass, spectacles*⟩ fumé/-e; ⟨*hair*⟩ teint/-e

**tiny** *adj* tout/-e petit/-e

**tip** **1** *n* (a) (of stick, sword, pen, shoe, spire) pointe *f*; (of branch, leaf, shoot, tail, feather) extrémité *f*; (of finger, nose, tongue) bout *m*
(b) (gratuity) pourboire *m*
(c) (practical hint) truc *m* (colloq), conseil *m*; (in betting) tuyau *m* (colloq)
**2** *vtr* (a) (tilt) incliner; (pour) verser; (dump) déverser ⟨*waste, rubbish*⟩

**(b)** (predict) **to ~ sb/sth to win** prédire que qn/qch va gagner
**(c)** donner un pourboire à ⟨waiter, driver⟩
**3** vi (tilt) s'incliner
■ **tip off**: **~ off [sb]**, **~ [sb] off** avertir
■ **tip over** faire basculer ⟨chair⟩; renverser ⟨bucket, pile⟩
**tip-off** n dénonciation f
**tiptoe** **1** n **on ~** sur la pointe des pieds
**2** vi marcher sur la pointe des pieds
**tire** **1** n (US) pneu m
**2** vtr fatiguer
**3** vi **(a)** (get tired) se fatiguer
**(b)** (get bored) **to ~ of** se lasser de
■ **tire out** épuiser ⟨person⟩; **to be ~d out** être éreinté/-e
**tired** adj **(a)** (weary) ⟨person, face, legs⟩ fatigué/-e; ⟨voice⟩ las/lasse
**(b)** (bored) **to be ~ of sth/of doing** en avoir assez de qch/de faire; **to grow ~ of sth/of doing** se lasser de qch/de faire
**tiredness** n fatigue f
**tireless** adj ⟨person⟩ inlassable, infatigable; ⟨efforts⟩ constant/-e
**tiresome** adj ⟨person, habit⟩ agaçant/-e; ⟨problem, duty⟩ fastidieux/-ieuse
**tiring** adj fatigant/-e ⟨to do de faire⟩
**tissue** n **(a)** (handkerchief) mouchoir m en papier
**(b)** (also **~ paper**) papier m de soie
**(c)** (Anat, Bot) tissu m
**tit** n (Zool) mésange f
IDIOMS **~ for tat** un prêté pour un rendu
**titbit** n (GB) (of food) gâterie f; (of gossip) cancan m (colloq)
**title** **1** n titre m
**2 titles** n pl (in film) générique m
**3** vtr intituler ⟨book, play⟩
**title bar** n barre f de titre
**titleholder** n tenant/-e m/f du titre
**title role** n rôle m titre
**titter** **1** n ricanement m
**2** vi ricaner
**tizzy** n (colloq) **to be in a ~** être dans tous ses états
**to**
■ **Note** Remember that when to is translated by à then à + le = au and à + les = aux.
**1** infinitive particle **(a)** (expressing purpose) pour; **to do sth ~ impress one's friends** faire qch pour impressionner ses amis
**(b)** (linking consecutive acts) **he looked up ~ see...** en levant les yeux, il a vu...
**(c)** (after superlatives) à; **the youngest ~ do** le or la plus jeune à faire
**(d)** (avoiding repetition of verb) **'did you go?'—'no I promised not ~'** 'tu y es allé?'—'non j'avais promis de ne pas le faire'; **'are you staying? '—'I want ~ but...'** 'tu restes?'—'j'aimerais bien mais...'
**(e)** (following impersonal verb) **it is difficult ~ do** il est difficile de faire; **it's difficult ~**

understand c'est difficile à comprendre; **it's easy ~ read her writing** il est facile de lire son écriture
**2** prep **(a)** (in direction of) à ⟨shops, school⟩; (with purpose of visiting) chez ⟨doctor's⟩; (towards) vers; **she's gone ~ Mary's** elle est partie chez Mary; **~ Paris** à Paris; **~ Spain** en Espagne; **~ town** en ville; **the road ~ the village** la route qui mène au village; **turned ~ the wall** tourné vers le mur
**(b)** (up to) jusqu'à; **~ the end/this day** jusqu'à la fin/ce jour
**(c)** (in telling time) **ten (minutes) ~ three** trois heures moins dix; **it's five ~** il est moins cinq
**(d)** (introducing direct or indirect object) ⟨give, offer⟩ à; (to + personal pronoun) me/te/lui/ nous/vous/leur; **give the book ~ Sophie** donne le livre à Sophie; **be nice ~ your brother** sois gentil avec ton frère; **~ me it's just a minor problem** pour moi ce n'est qu'un problème mineur; **she gave it ~ them/ him** elle le leur/lui a donné
**(e)** (in toasts, dedications) à; **~ prosperity** à la prospérité; **~ our dear son** (on tombstone) à notre cher fils
**(f)** (in accordance with) **is it ~ your taste?** c'est à ton goût?; **to dance ~ the music** danser sur la musique
**(g)** (in relationships, comparisons) **to win by three goals ~ two** gagner par trois buts à deux; **next door ~ the school** à côté de l'école
**(h)** (showing accuracy) **three weeks ~ the day** trois semaines jour pour jour; **~ scale** à l'échelle
**(i)** (showing reason) **to invite sb ~ dinner** inviter qn à dîner; **~ this end** à cette fin
**(j)** (belonging to) de; **the key ~ the safe** la clé du coffre; **a room ~ myself** une chambre pour moi tout seul; **personal assistant ~ the director** assistant du directeur
**(k)** ⟨tied⟩ à; ⟨pinned⟩ à ⟨noticeboard⟩; sur ⟨lapel, dress⟩
**(l)** (showing reaction) à; **~ his surprise/dismay** à sa grande surprise/consternation
**toad** n crapaud m
**toadstool** n champignon m vénéneux
**to and fro** adv ⟨swing⟩ d'avant en arrière; **to go ~** ⟨person⟩ aller et venir
**toast** **1** n **(a)** (bread) toast m; **a slice of ~** un toast
**(b)** (drink) toast m; **to drink a ~** lever son verre
**2** vtr **(a)** faire griller ⟨bread⟩
**(b)** porter un toast à ⟨person, success⟩
**toaster** n grille-pain m inv
**tobacco** n tabac m
**toboggan** n luge f, toboggan m
**today** **1** n aujourd'hui m; **~ is Monday** (aujourd'hui) nous sommes lundi
**2** adv aujourd'hui; (nowadays) de nos jours; **~ week** dans une semaine aujourd'hui; **a week ago** il y a une semaine aujourd'hui; **later ~** plus tard dans la journée
**toddler** n très jeune enfant m

**toe** n (a) (Anat) orteil m; **big/little** ~ gros/petit orteil
(b) (of sock, shoe) bout m
IDIOMS **to** ~ **the line** marcher droit; **from top to** ~ de la tête aux pieds

**toehold** n (in climbing) prise f; **to get** or **gain a** ~ **in** s'introduire dans ⟨*market, organization*⟩

**toffee** n caramel m (au beurre)

**together** ⓵ adv (a) ensemble; **to get back** ~ **again** se remettre ensemble; **to be close** ~ être rapprochés/-es; **she's cleverer than all the rest of them put** ~ elle est plus intelligente que tous les autres réunis; **they belong** ~ (objects) ils vont ensemble; (people) ils sont faits l'un pour l'autre; **the talks brought the two sides closer** ~ les négociations ont rapproché les deux parties
(b) (at the same time) à la fois
⓶ **together with** phr (as well as) ainsi que; (in the company of) avec
IDIOMS **to get one's act** ~ s'organiser

**togetherness** n (in team, friendship) camaraderie f; (in family, couple) intimité f

**toil** ⓵ n labeur m
⓶ vi (a) (also **toil away**) (work) peiner
(b) (struggle) **to** ~ **up the hill** monter péniblement la côte

**toilet** n toilettes fpl; **public** ~(**s**) toilettes publiques

**toilet bag** n trousse f de toilette

**toilet paper**, **toilet tissue** n papier m hygiénique

**toiletries** n pl articles mpl de toilette

**toilet roll** n (roll) rouleau m de papier toilette; (tissue) papier m toilette

**token** ⓵ n (a) (for machine, phone) jeton m
(b) (voucher) bon m; **book/record** ~ chèque-cadeau m pour livre/pour disque
(c) témoignage m; **as a** ~ **of** en signe de
⓶ adj symbolique; **to make a** ~ **gesture** faire un geste pour la forme

**tolerable** adj (bearable) tolérable; (adequate) acceptable

**tolerance** n (gen, Med) tolérance f

**tolerant** adj tolérant/-e

**tolerate** vtr (permit) tolérer; (put up with) supporter

**toll** ⓵ n (a) death ~ nombre m de victimes (from de)
(b) (levy) (on road, bridge) péage m
(c) (of bell) son m; (for funeral) glas m
⓶ vtr, vi sonner

**toll call** n (US) communication f interurbaine

**tomato** ⓵ n tomate f
⓶ adj ⟨*puree*⟩ de tomate; ⟨*juice, salad*⟩ de tomates; ⟨*soup*⟩ à la tomate

**tomato sauce** n sauce f tomate

**tomb** n tombeau m

**tomboy** n garçon m manqué

**tombstone** n pierre f tombale

**tomcat** n matou m

**tomorrow** ⓵ n demain m; **I'll do it by** ~ je le ferai d'ici demain
⓶ adv demain; **see you** ~! à demain!; ~ **week** demain en huit; **a week ago** ~ il y aura une semaine demain

**tomorrow afternoon** n, adv demain après-midi

**tomorrow evening** n, adv demain soir

**tomorrow morning** n, adv demain matin

**ton** n (a) (in weight) (GB) (also **gross** ~ or **long** ~) tonne f britannique (= 1.016 kg); (US) (also **net** ~ or **short** ~) tonne f américaine (= 907 kg); **metric** ~ tonne f
(b) (colloq) (a lot) ~**s of** des tas de (colloq) ⟨*food, paper, bands*⟩

**tone** ⓵ n (a) (gen) ton m; **his** ~ **of voice** son ton; **to set the** ~ donner le ton à (**for** à)
(b) (Mus) timbre m; (on phone) tonalité f
(c) (of muscle) tonus m
⓶ vtr (also ~ **up**) tonifier ⟨*body, muscles*⟩
⓷ vi (also ~**in**) (blend) ⟨*colours*⟩ s'harmoniser
■ **tone down** atténuer ⟨*colours, criticism*⟩; adoucir le ton de ⟨*letter, statement*⟩

**tone-deaf** adj **to be** ~ ne pas avoir l'oreille musicale

**tongs** n pl (for coal) pincettes fpl; (in laboratory, for sugar) pince f

**tongue** n (a) (gen) langue f; **to stick one's** ~ **out at sb** tirer la langue à qn; **to lose one's** ~ (figurative) avaler sa langue
(b) (on shoe) languette f
IDIOMS **I have his name on the tip of my** ~ j'ai son nom sur le bout de la langue; **a slip of the** ~ un lapsus

**tongue-in-cheek** adj, adv au deuxième degré

**tongue stud** n piercing m de la langue

**tongue-tied** adj muet/-ette

**tongue-twister** n phrase f difficile à dire

**tonic** n (a) (also ~ **water**) eau f tonique; **a gin and** ~ un gin tonic
(b) (Med) remontant m

**tonight** ⓵ n ce soir
⓶ adv (this evening) ce soir; (after bedtime) cette nuit

**tonne** n tonne f

**tonsil** n amygdale f; **to have one's** ~**s out** se faire opérer des amygdales

**tonsillitis** n amygdalite f

**too** adv (a) (also) aussi; **have you been to India** ~? (like me) est-ce que toi aussi tu es allé en Inde?; (as well as other countries) est-ce que tu es allé en Inde aussi?
(b) (excessively) trop; ~ **big** trop grand/-e; ~ **many/** ~ **few people** trop de/trop peu de gens; **I ate** ~ **much** j'ai trop mangé; **you're** ~ **kind!** vous êtes trop aimable!; **I'm not** ~ **sure about that** je n'en suis pas si sûr

**tool** n outil m

**tool bar** n barre f d'outils

**toolbox** n boîte f à outils

**tool kit** n trousse f à outils

**tooth** *n* dent *f*

**toothache** *n* mal *m* de dents; **to have ~** (GB) *or* a **~** avoir mal aux dents

**toothbrush** *n* brosse *f* à dents

**toothpaste** *n* dentifrice *m*

**toothpick** *n* cure-dents *m inv*

**top** **1** *n* **(a)** (of page, ladder, stairs, wall) haut *m*; (of list) tête *f*; (of mountain, hill) sommet *m*; (of garden, field) (autre) bout *m*; (of vegetable) fane *f*; (of box, cake) dessus *m*; (surface) surface *f*; **at the ~ of** en haut de ⟨page, stairs, street, scale⟩; au sommet de ⟨hill⟩; en tête de ⟨list⟩; **at the ~ of the building** au dernier étage de l'immeuble; **at the ~ of the table** à la place d'honneur; **to be at the ~ of the agenda** être une priorité

**(b)** (highest position) **to aim for the ~** viser haut; **to get to** *or* **make it to the ~** réussir; **to be ~ of the class** être le premier/la première de la classe; **to be ~ of the bill** être la tête d'affiche

**(c)** (cap, lid) (of pen) capuchon *m*; (of bottle) bouchon *m*; (with serrated edge) capsule *f*; (of paint-tin, saucepan) couvercle *m*

**(d)** (item of clothing) haut *m*

**(e)** (toy) toupie *f*

**2** *adj* **(a)** (highest) ⟨step, storey⟩ dernier/-ière (before *n*); ⟨bunk⟩ de haut; ⟨button, shelf⟩ du haut; ⟨layer, lip⟩ supérieur/-e; ⟨speed⟩ maximum; ⟨concern, priority⟩ majeur/-e; **in the ~ left-hand corner** en haut à gauche; **to get ~ marks** (Sch) avoir dix sur dix *or* vingt sur vingt

**(b)** (furthest away) ⟨field, house⟩ du bout

**(c)** (leading) ⟨adviser, politician⟩ de haut niveau; ⟨job⟩ élevé/-e; ⟨wine, restaurant⟩ haut/-e de gamme

**3** *vtr* **(a)** être en tête de ⟨charts, polls⟩

**(b)** (exceed) dépasser ⟨sum, figure⟩

**(c)** (finish off) compléter (**with** par); (Culin) recouvrir ⟨cake⟩

**4** **on top of** *phr* **(a)** (on) sur ⟨cupboard, fridge, layer⟩

**(b)** (in addition to) en plus de ⟨salary, workload⟩

IDIOMS **on ~ of all this, to ~ it all** par-dessus le marché (colloq); **from ~ to bottom** de fond en comble; **to be over the ~, to be OTT** (colloq) ⟨behaviour, reaction⟩ être exagéré/-e; **to feel on ~ of the world** être aux anges; **to shout at the ~ of one's voice** crier à tue-tête

■ **top up** remplir (à nouveau) ⟨tank, glass⟩

**topaz** *n* topaze *f*

**top hat** *n* haut-de-forme *m*

**top-heavy** *adj* lourd/-e du haut

**topic** *n* (of conversation, conference) sujet *m*; (of essay, research) thème *m*

**topical** *adj* d'actualité

**topless** *adj* ⟨model⟩ aux seins nus

**top-level** *adj* ⟨talks, negotiations⟩ au plus haut niveau

**top management** *n* (haute) direction *f*

**top-of-the-range** *adj* haut de gamme *inv*

**topping** *n* (of jam, cream) nappage *m*

**topple** **1** *vtr* renverser

**2** *vi* (sway) ⟨vase, pile of books⟩ vaciller; (fall) (also **~ over**) ⟨vase, person⟩ basculer; ⟨pile of books⟩ s'effondrer

**top-ranking** *adj* important/-e

**top secret** *adj* ultrasecret/-ète

**topsy-turvy** *adj, adv* (colloq) sens dessus dessous

**torch** *n* **(a)** (GB) (flashlight) lampe *f* de poche

**(b)** (burning) flambeau *m*, torche *f*

**torment** **1** *n* supplice *m*

**2** *vtr* tourmenter

**tormentor** *n* persécuteur/-trice *m/f*

**torn** *adj* déchiré/-e

**tornado** *n* tornade *f*

**torpedo** *n* torpille *f*

**torrent** *n* torrent *m*; (figurative) flot *m*

**torrential** *adj* torrentiel/-ielle

**torrid** *adj* torride

**torso** *n* torse *m*

**tortoise** *n* tortue *f*

**tortoiseshell** *n* (shell) écaille *f*

**tortuous** *adj* tortueux/-euse

**torture** **1** *n* torture *f*; (figurative) supplice *m*

**2** *vtr* torturer; (figurative) tourmenter

**Tory** *n* (GB) Tory *mf*, conservateur/-trice *m/f*

**toss** **1** *n* **(a)** (throw) jet *m*; **a ~ of the head** un mouvement brusque de la tête

**(b)** **to decide sth on the ~ of a coin** décider qch à pile ou face

**2** *vtr* **(a)** (throw) lancer ⟨ball, stick, dice⟩; faire sauter ⟨pancake⟩; tourner ⟨salad⟩; **to ~ a coin** jouer à pile ou face

**(b)** ⟨animal⟩ secouer ⟨head, mane⟩; **to ~ one's head** ⟨person⟩ rejeter la tête en arrière

**(c)** ⟨horse⟩ désarçonner ⟨rider⟩

**(d)** ⟨wind⟩ agiter ⟨branches, leaves⟩

**3** *vi* **(a)** ⟨person⟩ se retourner; **I ~ed and turned all night** je me suis tourné et retourné toute la nuit

**(b)** (flip a coin) tirer à pile ou face; **to ~ for first turn** tirer le premier tour à pile ou face

■ **toss off** (colloq): **~** [sth] **off, ~ off** [sth] expédier

■ **toss out**: ¶ **~** [sth] **out, ~ out** [sth] jeter ⟨newspaper, empty bottles⟩; ¶ **~** [sb] **out** éjecter (**from** de)

**tot** *n* **(a)** (colloq) (toddler) tout/-e petit/-e enfant *m/f*

**(b)** (GB) (of whisky, rum) petite dose *f*

**total** **1** *n* total *m*; **in ~** au total

**2** *adj* **(a)** ⟨cost, amount, profit⟩ total/-e

**(b)** (complete) ⟨effect⟩ global/-e; ⟨disaster, eclipse⟩ total/-e; ⟨ignorance⟩ complet/-ète

**3** *vtr* **(a)** (add up) additionner ⟨figures⟩

**(b)** ⟨bill⟩ se monter à ⟨sum⟩

**totalitarian** *n, adj* totalitaire (*mf*)

**totally** *adv* ⟨blind, deaf⟩ complètement; ⟨unacceptable, convinced⟩ totalement; ⟨agree, change, new, different⟩ entièrement

**totem** *n* (pole) totem *m*; (symbol) symbole *m*

**totter** *vi* ⟨*person, regime, government*⟩
chanceler; ⟨*drunk person*⟩ tituber; ⟨*baby*⟩
trébucher; ⟨*pile of books, building*⟩ chanceler

**touch** [1] *n* **(a)** contact *m* (physique); **the ~
of her hand** le contact de sa main
**(b)** (sense) toucher *m*
**(c)** (style, skill) (of artist, writer) touche *f*; (of
musician) toucher *m*; **to lose one's ~** perdre la
main; **that's a clever ~!** ça, c'est génial!
**(d)** (little) **a ~** un petit peu
**(e)** (communication) **to get/stay in ~ with** se
mettre/rester en contact avec; **he's out of ~
with reality** il est déconnecté de la réalité
**(f)** (Sport) touche *f*
[2] *vtr* **(a)** toucher; (interfere with) toucher à; **to
~ sb on the shoulder** toucher l'épaule de qn;
**I never ~ alcohol** je ne prends jamais
d'alcool
**(b)** (affect) toucher; (adversely) affecter; (as
matter of concern) concerner; **we were most
~ed** nous avons été très touchés
[3] *vi* se toucher
IDIOMS **to be a soft ~** (colloq) être un pigeon
(colloq); **it's ~ and go whether he'll make it
through the night** il risque fort de ne pas
passer la nuit
■ **touch down (a)** ⟨*plane*⟩ atterrir
**(b)** (Sport) (in rugby) marquer un essai
■ **touch (up)on** effleurer ⟨*topic*⟩

**touchdown** *n* **(a)** (by plane) atterrissage *m*
**(b)** (Sport) essai *m*

**touched** *adj* **(a)** (emotionally) touché/-e
**(b)** (colloq) (mad) dérangé/-e (colloq)

**touching** *adj* touchant/-e

**touch line** *n* ligne *f* de touche

**touchpad** *n* tablette *f* tactile

**touch screen** *n* écran *m* tactile

**touch-tone** *adj* ⟨*telephone*⟩ à touches

**touch-type** *vi* taper au toucher

**touchy** *adj* susceptible (**about** sur la
question de)

**tough** [1] *adj* **(a)** ⟨*businessman*⟩ coriace;
⟨*criminal*⟩ endurci/-e; ⟨*policy, measure, law*⟩
sévère; ⟨*opposition, competition*⟩ rude; **a ~
guy** un dur (colloq)
**(b)** (difficult) difficile
**(c)** (robust) ⟨*person, animal*⟩ robuste; ⟨*plant,
material*⟩ résistant/-e
**(d)** ⟨*meat*⟩ coriace
**(e)** (rough) ⟨*area, school*⟩ dur/-e
[2] *excl* (colloq) tant pis pour toi!

**toughen** *vtr* **(a)** renforcer ⟨*leather, plastic*⟩;
tremper ⟨*glass, steel*⟩; durcir ⟨*skin*⟩
**(b)** (also **~ up**) endurcir ⟨*person*⟩; renforcer
⟨*law*⟩

**toupee** *n* postiche *m*

**tour** [1] *n* **(a)** (of country) circuit *m*; (of city)
tour *m*; (of building) visite *f*; (trip in bus)
excursion *f*
**(b)** (by team, band, theatre company) tournée *f*
[2] *vtr* **(a)** visiter ⟨*building, country, gallery*⟩
**(b)** ⟨*band, team*⟩ être en tournée en
⟨*country*⟩; ⟨*theatre production*⟩ tourner en
⟨*country*⟩
[3] *vi* ⟨*orchestra, play, team*⟩ être en tournée

**touring** *n* **(a)** (by tourist) tourisme *m*
**(b)** (by team, theatre company, band) tournée *f*

**tourism** *n* tourisme *m*

**tourist** *n* touriste *mf*

**tourist class** *n* (on flight) classe *f* touriste

**tourist (information) office** *n* (in
town) syndicat *m* d'initiative; (national
organization) office *m* du tourisme

**tourist trap** *n* piège *m* à touristes

**touristy** *adj* (colloq) envahi/-e par les
touristes

**tournament** *n* tournoi *m*

**tousle** *vtr* ébouriffer ⟨*hair*⟩

**tousled** *adj* ⟨*hair*⟩ ébouriffé/-e; ⟨*person,
appearance*⟩ débraillé/-e

**tout** *n* **(a)** (GB) (selling tickets) revendeur *m* de
billets au marché noir
**(b)** (soliciting custom) racoleur/-euse *m/f*
**(c)** (racing) vendeur *m* de tuyaux

**tow** [1] *n* (Aut) **to be on ~** être en remorque
[2] *vtr* remorquer, tracter ⟨*trailer, caravan*⟩
■ **tow away:** **~ away [sth], ~ [sth] away**
⟨*police*⟩ emmener [qch] à la fourrière;
⟨*recovery service*⟩ remorquer

**toward(s)** *prep*

■ **Note** When *towards* is used to talk about
direction or position, it is generally translated by
*vers:* she ran *toward(s)* him = elle a couru vers
lui.
– When *toward(s)* is used to mean *in relation to,*
it is translated by *envers:* his attitude *toward(s)*
his parents = son attitude envers ses parents.
For further examples, see the entry below.

**(a)** vers; **~ the east** vers l'est; **he was
standing with his back ~ me** il me tournait
le dos; **~ evening** vers le soir; **~ the end of**
vers la fin de ⟨*month, life*⟩
**(b)** envers; **to be friendly/hostile ~ sb** se
montrer cordial/hostile envers qn
**(c)** (as contribution) **the money will go ~ a new
car** l'argent servira à payer une nouvelle
voiture

**towel** *n* serviette *f* (de toilette)

**towelling** *n* (cloth) tissu *m* éponge

**tower** [1] *n* **(a)** (structure) tour *f*
**(b)** (Comput) boîtier *m* vertical, tour *f*
[2] *vi* **to ~ above** *or* **over** dominer
IDIOMS **to be a ~ of strength** être solide
comme un roc

**tower block** *n* (GB) tour *f* (d'habitation)

**towering** *adj* imposant/-e

**town** *n* ville *f*; **to go into ~** aller en ville
IDIOMS **to go to ~ on** ne pas lésiner sur
⟨*decor, catering*⟩; exploiter [qch] à fond
⟨*story, scandal*⟩; **he's the talk of the ~** on ne
parle que de lui

**town-and-country planning** *n*
aménagement *m* du territoire

**town centre** (GB), **town center** (US)
*n* centre-ville *m*

**town council** *n* (GB) conseil *m* municipal

**town hall** *n* mairie *f*

**town house** *n* petite maison *f* en centre ville; (mansion) hôtel *m* particulier

**town planning** *n* (GB) urbanisme *m*

**township** *n* commune *f*; (in South Africa) township *m*

**towpath** *n* chemin *m* de halage

**tow truck** *n* dépanneuse *f*

**toxic** *adj* toxique

**toxin** *n* toxine *f*

**toy** ① *n* jouet *m*
② *vi* to ~ with jouer avec ⟨object, feelings⟩; caresser ⟨idea⟩; **to ~ with one's food** chipoter

**toy boy** *n* (colloq) (GB) gigolo *m*

**toyshop** *n* magasin *m* de jouets

**trace** ① *n* trace *f*
② *vtr* (a) (locate) retrouver ⟨person, weapon, car⟩; dépister ⟨fault⟩; déterminer ⟨cause⟩; **the call was ~d to a London number** on a pu établir que le coup de téléphone venait d'un numéro à Londres
(b) (also ~ **back**) faire remonter ⟨origins, ancestry⟩ (**to** à)
(c) (draw) tracer; (copy) décalquer ⟨map, outline⟩

**tracing paper** *n* papier-calque *m*

**track** ① *n* (a) (print) (of animal, person, vehicle) traces *fpl*
(b) (course, trajectory) (of person) trace *f*; (of missile, aircraft, storm) trajectoire *f*; **to keep ~ of** ⟨person⟩ se tenir au courant de ⟨developments, events⟩; suivre le fil de ⟨conversation⟩; ⟨police⟩ suivre les mouvements de ⟨criminal⟩; **to lose ~ of** perdre de vue ⟨friend⟩; perdre la trace de ⟨document, aircraft, suspect⟩; perdre le fil de ⟨conversation⟩; **to lose ~ of (the) time** perdre la notion du temps
(c) (path, road) sentier *m*, chemin *m*; (Sport) piste *f*
(d) (railtrack) voie *f* ferrée; (US) (platform) quai *m*; **to leave the ~(s)** ⟨train⟩ dérailler
(e) (on record, tape, CD) morceau *m*
(f) (of tank, tractor) chenille *f*
(g) (US Sch) (stream) groupe *m* de niveau
② *vtr* suivre la trace de ⟨person, animal⟩; suivre la trajectoire de ⟨rocket, plane⟩
■ **track down** retrouver ⟨person, object⟩

**tracker ball** *n* boule *f* de commande

**tracker dog** *n* chien *m* policier

**track record** *n* **to have a good ~** avoir de bons antécédents

**track shoe** *n* chaussure *f* de course à pointes

**tracksuit** *n* survêtement *m*

**tract** *n* (a) (of land) étendue *f*
(b) (pamphlet) pamphlet *m*

**tractor** *n* tracteur *m*

**trade** ① *n* (a) (activity) commerce *m*; **to do a good ~** faire de bonnes affaires
(b) (sector of industry) industrie *f*
(c) (profession) (manual) métier *m*; (intellectual) profession *f*; **by ~** de métier
② *vtr* échanger (**for** contre)

③ *vi* faire du commerce
■ **trade in**: he ~d in his old car for a new one on lui a repris sa vieille voiture et il en a acheté une nouvelle

**trade fair** *n* salon *m*

**trade-in** *n* reprise *f* (d'un article usagé à l'achat d'un article neuf)

**trademark** *n* marque *f* déposée

**trade name** *n* nom *m* (de marque)

**trade-off** *n* compromis *m*

**trader** *n* (a) (shopkeeper, stallholder) commerçant/-e *m/f*
(b) (at stock exchange) opérateur/-trice *m/f* (en Bourse)

**tradesman's entrance** *n* entrée *f* de service

**Trades Union Congress, TUC** *n* (GB) Confédération *f* des syndicats (britanniques)

**trade union** *n* syndicat *m*

**trade union member** *n* syndiqué/-e *m/f*

**trading** *n* (a) (business) commerce *m*
(b) (at stock exchange) transactions *fpl* (boursières)

**trading estate** *n* zone *f* industrielle

**tradition** *n* tradition *f*

**traditional** *adj* traditionnel/-elle

**traditionalist** *n*, *adj* traditionaliste (*mf*)

**traffic** ① *n* (a) (on road) circulation *f*; (air, sea, rail) trafic *m*
(b) (in drugs, arms, slaves, goods) trafic *m* (**in** de)
② *vi* **to ~ in** faire du trafic de ⟨drugs, arms, stolen goods⟩

**traffic calming** *n* mesures *fpl* pour ralentir la circulation

**traffic jam** *n* embouteillage *m*

**trafficker** *n* trafiquant/-e *m/f* (**in** de)

**traffic lights** *n pl* feux *mpl* (de signalisation)

**traffic warden** *n* (GB) contractuel/-elle *m/f*

**tragedy** *n* tragédie *f*

**tragic** *adj* tragique

**trail** ① *n* (a) (path) chemin *m*, piste *f*
(b) (of blood, dust, slime) traînée *f*, trace *f*
(c) (trace) trace *f*, piste *f*
② *vtr* (a) (follow) ⟨animal, person⟩ suivre la piste de; ⟨car⟩ suivre
(b) (drag) traîner
③ *vi* (a) ⟨skirt, scarf⟩ traîner; ⟨plant⟩ pendre
(b) (shuffle) **to ~ in/out** entrer/sortir en traînant les pieds
(c) (lag) traîner; **our team were ~ing by 3 goals to 1** notre équipe avait un retard de 2 buts

**trail bike** *n* moto *f* tout terrain

**trail blazer** *n* pionnier/-ière *m/f*

**trailer** *n* (a) (vehicle, boat) remorque *f*
(b) (US) (caravan) caravane *f*
(c) (for film) bande-annonce *f*

**trailer park** n (US) terrain m de caravaning

**train** [1] n (a) (means of transport) train m; (underground) rame f; a ~ to Paris un train pour Paris; **to go to Paris by** ~ aller à Paris en train
(b) (succession) (of events) série f; my ~ of thought le fil de mes pensées
(c) (procession) (of animals, vehicles, people) file f; (of mourners) cortège m
(d) (of dress) traîne f
[2] vtr (a) former ⟨staff, worker, musician⟩; entraîner ⟨athlete, player⟩; dresser ⟨circus animal, dog⟩
(b) (aim) braquer ⟨gun, binoculars⟩ (on sur)
[3] vi (a) (for profession) être formé/-e, étudier; he's ~ing to be/he ~ed as a doctor il suit/il a reçu une formation de docteur
(b) (Sport) s'entraîner

**trained** adj ⟨staff⟩ qualifié/-e; ⟨professional⟩ diplômé/-e; ⟨voice, eye, ear⟩ exercé/-e; ⟨singer, actor⟩ professionnel/-elle; ⟨animal⟩ dressé/-e

**trainee** n stagiaire mf

**trainer** n (a) (of athlete, horse) entraîneur/-euse m/f; (of circus animal, dogs) dresseur/-euse m/f
(b) (GB) (shoe) (high) basket f; (low) tennis m

**training** n (a) (gen) formation f; (less specialized) apprentissage m
(b) (Mil, Sport) entraînement m

**training college** n (GB) école f professionnelle; (for teachers) centre m de formation pédagogique

**training course** n stage m de formation

**train spotter** n passionné/-e m/f de trains

**trait** n trait m

**traitor** n traître/traîtresse m/f (**to** à)

**tram** n (GB) tramway m

**tramp** n (rural) vagabond m; (urban) clochard/-e m/f

**trample** vtr piétiner

**trampoline** n trampoline m

**trance** n transe f; (figurative) état m second; **to go into a** ~ entrer en transe

**tranquil** adj tranquille

**tranquillizer, tranquilizer** (US) n tranquillisant m

**transaction** n transaction f

**transatlantic** adj ⟨crossing, flight⟩ transatlantique; ⟨accent⟩ d'outre-atlantique inv

**transcend** vtr (gen) transcender; (surpass) surpasser

**transcribe** vtr transcrire

**transcript** n (a) (copy) transcription f
(b) (US) (Sch) duplicata m de livret scolaire

**transfer** [1] n (a) (gen) transfert m; (of property, debt) cession f; (of funds) virement m; (of employee) mutation f
(b) (GB) (on skin, china, paper) décalcomanie f; (on T-shirt) transfert m
[2] vtr (a) transférer ⟨data, baggage⟩; virer ⟨money⟩; céder ⟨property, power⟩; reporter ⟨allegiance, support⟩; **I'm** ~ring you to reception je vous passe la réception
(b) (relocate) transférer ⟨office, prisoner, player⟩; muter ⟨employee⟩
[3] vi (a) ⟨player, passenger⟩ être transféré/-e; ⟨employee⟩ être muté/-e
(b) ⟨traveller⟩ changer d'avion

**transferable** adj (gen) transmissible; (in finance) négociable

**transfer passenger** n passager/-ère m/f en transit

**transferred charge call** n appel m en PCV

**transfixed** adj (fascinated) fasciné/-e; (horrified) paralysé/-e d'horreur

**transform** vtr transformer

**transformation** n transformation f

**transformer** n transformateur m

**transfusion** n transfusion f

**transgenic** adj transgénique

**transient** adj ⟨phase⟩ transitoire; ⟨emotion, beauty⟩ éphémère; ⟨population⟩ de passage

**transistor** n transistor m

**transit** n transit m; **in** ~ en transit

**transition** n transition f

**transitional** adj ⟨arrangement, measure⟩ transitoire; ⟨period⟩ de transition

**transitive** adj transitif/-ive

**translate** [1] vtr traduire
[2] vi (a) ⟨person⟩ traduire
(b) ⟨word, phrase, text⟩ se traduire

**translation** n traduction f; (school exercise) version f

**translator** n traducteur/-trice m/f

**transmission** n transmission f

**transmit** [1] vtr transmettre
[2] vi émettre

**transmitter** n (in radio, TV) émetteur m; (in telecommunications) capsule f microphonique

**transparency** n (slide) diapositive f; (for overhead projector) transparent m

**transparent** adj transparent/-e

**transplant** [1] n (operation) transplantation f; (organ, tissue transplanted) transplant m
[2] vtr transplanter

**transport** [1] n (also **transportation** (US)) transport m; **air/road** ~ transport aérien/par route; **to travel by public** ~ utiliser les transports en commun
[2] vtr transporter

**transportation** n transport m

**transpose** vtr transposer

**transsexual** n, adj transsexuel/-elle (m/f)

**transvestite** n travesti/-e m/f

**trap** [1] n (a) (snare) piège m
(b) (vehicle) cabriolet m
[2] vtr (a) (snare) prendre [qn/qch] au piège
(b) (catch) coincer ⟨person, finger⟩; retenir ⟨heat⟩

**trapdoor** n trappe f

**trash** n (a) (US) (refuse) (in streets) déchets mpl; (from household) ordures fpl

**(b)** (colloq) (low-grade goods) camelote *f* (colloq)
**(c)** (colloq) (nonsense) âneries *fpl*; **the film is
(absolute)** ∼ le film est (complètement) nul
(colloq)
**trashcan** *n* (US) poubelle *f*
**trashy** *adj* (colloq) ⟨*novel, film*⟩ nul/nulle
(colloq); ⟨*goods*⟩ de pacotille
**trauma** *n* traumatisme *m*
**traumatic** *adj* (psychologically)
traumatisant/-e; (Med) traumatique
**traumatize** *vtr* traumatiser
**travel** ⌐1⌐ *n* voyages *mpl*; **foreign** ∼ voyages
à l'étranger
⌐2⌐ *vtr* parcourir ⟨*country, road, distance*⟩
⌐3⌐ *vi* **(a)** (journey) voyager; **he** ∼**s widely** il
voyage beaucoup; **to** ∼ **abroad/to Brazil** aller
à l'étranger/au Brésil
**(b)** (move) ⟨*person, object, plane, boat*⟩ aller;
⟨*car, train*⟩ aller, rouler; ⟨*light, sound*⟩ se
propager; **to** ∼ **back in time** remonter le
temps
**(c) to** ∼ **well** ⟨*cheese, wine*⟩ supporter le
transport
**travel agency** *n* agence *f* de voyages
**travel agent** *n* agent *m* de voyages
**travel card** *n* carte *f* de transport
**travel insurance** *n* assurance *f* voyage
**traveller** (GB), **traveler** (US) *n* **(a)**
(voyager) voyageur/-euse *m/f*
**(b)** (GB) (gypsy) nomade *mf*
**traveller's cheque** (GB), **traveler's
check** (US) *n* chèque-voyage *m*
**travelling** (GB), **traveling** (US) ⌐1⌐ *n*
(touring) voyages *mpl*; (on single occasion)
voyage *m*; **to go** ∼ partir en voyage; **the job
involves** ∼ le poste exige des déplacements
⌐2⌐ *adj* **(a)** ⟨*actor, company, circus*⟩
itinérant/-e
**(b)** ⟨*companion, rug*⟩ de voyage; ⟨*conditions*⟩
(on road) de route
**(c)** ⟨*allowance, expenses*⟩ de déplacement
**travelling salesman** *n* voyageur *m* de
commerce
**travel-sick** *adj* **to be** *or* **get** ∼ souffrir du
mal des transports
**trawler** *n* chalutier *m*
**tray** *n* plateau *m*
**treacherous** *adj* traître/traîtresse
**treachery** *n* traîtrise *f*
**treacle** *n* (GB) (black) mélasse *f*; (golden
syrup) mélasse *f* raffinée
**tread** ⌐1⌐ *n* (of tyre) (pattern) sculptures *fpl*;
(outer surface) chape *f*
⌐2⌐ *vtr* fouler ⟨*street, path, area*⟩; **to** ∼ **water**
nager sur place
⌐3⌐ *vi* marcher; **to** ∼ **on** (walk) marcher sur;
(squash) piétiner; **to** ∼ **carefully** être
prudent/-e
**treason** *n* trahison *f*; **high** ∼ haute
trahison
**treasure** ⌐1⌐ *n* trésor *m*
⌐2⌐ *vtr* **(a)** (cherish) chérir ⟨*person, gift*⟩
**(b)** (prize) tenir beaucoup à ⟨*friendship*⟩

**treasurer** *n* **(a)** (on committee)
trésorier/-ière *m/f*
**(b)** (US) (in company) directeur *m* financier
**Treasury** *n* (*also* ∼ **Department**)
ministère *m* des finances
**treat** ⌐1⌐ *n* (pleasure) (petit) plaisir *m*; (food)
gâterie *f*; **I took them to the museum as a** ∼
je les ai emmenés au musée pour leur faire
plaisir; **it's my** ∼ (colloq) c'est moi qui paie
⌐2⌐ *vtr* **(a)** (gen, Med) traiter; **to** ∼ **sb well/
badly** bien traiter/maltraiter qn; **to** ∼ **sb/sth
with care** prendre soin de qn/qch; **they** ∼
**the house like a hotel** ils prennent la maison
pour un hôtel
**(b)** (pay for) **to** ∼ **sb to sth** payer *or* offrir
qch à qn; **to** ∼ **oneself to** s'offrir ⟨*holiday,
hairdo*⟩
**treatment** *n* traitement *m*
**treaty** *n* traité *m*
**treble** ⌐1⌐ *adj* triple
⌐2⌐ *vtr, vi* tripler
**tree** *n* arbre *m*; **an apple/a cherry** ∼ un
pommier/un cerisier
**tree stump** *n* souche *f*
**treetop** *n* cime *f* (d'un arbre)
**tree trunk** *n* tronc *m* d'arbre
**trek** ⌐1⌐ *n* (long journey) randonnée *f*; (laborious)
randonnée *f* pénible
⌐2⌐ *vi* **to** ∼ **across** traverser péniblement
⟨*desert*⟩
**trekking** *n* **to go** ∼ faire de la randonnée
pédestre
**tremble** *vi* trembler
**tremendous** *adj* ⟨*effort, improvement,
amount*⟩ énorme; ⟨*pleasure*⟩ immense;
⟨*storm, explosion*⟩ violent/-e; ⟨*success*⟩ fou/
folle (colloq)
**tremor** *n* **(a)** (in voice) tremblement *m*
**(b)** (in earthquake) secousse *f*
**trench** *n* tranchée *f*
**trench coat** *n* imperméable *m*,
trench-coat *m*
**trend** *n* **(a)** (tendency) tendance *f*
**(b)** (fashion) mode *f*; **to set a new** ∼ lancer
une nouvelle mode
**trendsetter** *n* innovateur/-trice *m/f*; **to be
a** ∼ lancer des modes
**trendy** *adj* (colloq) branché/-e (colloq)
**trespass** *vi* s'introduire illégalement; '**no**
∼**ing**' 'défense d'entrer'
**trespasser** *n* intrus/-e *m/f*
**trial** ⌐1⌐ *n* **(a)** (Law) procès *m*; **to go on** ∼, **to
stand** ∼ passer en jugement
**(b)** (test) (of machine, vehicle) essai *m*; (of drug,
new product) test *m*; **on** ∼ à l'essai; **by** ∼ **and
error** ⟨*learn*⟩ par l'expérience; ⟨*proceed*⟩ par
tâtonnements
**(c)** (Sport) épreuve *f*
**(d)** (trouble) épreuve *f*; (less strong) difficulté *f*
⌐2⌐ *adj* ⟨*period, separation*⟩ d'essai; **on a** ∼
**basis** à titre expérimental
**trial run** *n* essai *m*; **to take a car for a** ∼
essayer une voiture
**triangle** *n* triangle *m*

t

**tribe** *n* tribu *f*

**tribunal** *n* tribunal *m*

**tributary** *n* affluent *m*

**tribute** *n* hommage *m*; **to pay ~ to** rendre hommage à; **floral ~** (spray) gerbe *f*; (wreath) couronne *f*

**trick** **1** *n* **(a)** (to deceive) tour *m*, combine *f*; **to play a ~ on sb** jouer un tour à qn; **a ~ of the light** un effet de lumière
**(b)** (by magician, conjurer, dog) tour *m*; **to do a ~** faire un tour
**(c)** (knack, secret) astuce *f*
**(d)** (in cards) pli *m*; **to take** *or* **win a ~** faire un pli
**2** *adj* ⟨photo, shot⟩ truqué/-e
**3** *vtr* duper, rouler (colloq); **to ~ sb into doing sth** amener qn à faire qch par la ruse
IDIOMS **the ~s of the trade** les ficelles du métier; **that'll do the ~** ça fera l'affaire

**trickle** **1** *n* (of liquid) filet *m*; (of powder, sand) écoulement *m*; (of investment, orders) petite quantité *f*; (of people) petit nombre *m*
**2** *vi* **to ~ down** dégouliner le long de ⟨pane, wall⟩; **to ~ into** ⟨liquid⟩ s'écouler dans ⟨container⟩; ⟨people⟩ s'infiltrer dans ⟨country, organization⟩
■ **trickle away** ⟨water⟩ s'écouler lentement; ⟨people⟩ s'éloigner lentement

**trick question** *n* question *f* piège

**tricky** *adj* **(a)** ⟨decision, task⟩ difficile; ⟨problem⟩ épineux/-euse; ⟨situation⟩ délicat/-e
**(b)** (wily) malin/-igne

**tricycle** *n* (cycle) tricycle *m*

**trifle** **1** *n* **(a)** (GB) (Culin) ≈ diplomate *m*
**(b)** (triviality) bagatelle *f*
**2** *vi* **to ~ with** jouer avec ⟨feelings, affections⟩; **to ~ with sb** traiter qn à la légère

**trifling** *adj* ⟨sum, cost, detail⟩ insignifiant/-e

**trigger** *n* **(a)** (on gun) gâchette *f*
**(b)** (on machine) manette *f*
■ **trigger off** déclencher

**trilogy** *n* trilogie *f*

**trim** **1** *n* **(a)** (of hair) coupe *f* d'entretien
**(b)** (good condition) **to keep oneself in ~** se maintenir en bonne forme physique
**2** *adj* ⟨garden⟩ soigné/-e; ⟨boat, house⟩ bien tenu/-e; ⟨figure⟩ svelte; ⟨waist⟩ fin/-e
**3** *vtr* **(a)** (cut) couper ⟨hair, grass, material⟩; tailler ⟨beard, hedge⟩
**(b)** (reduce) réduire (by de)
**(c)** (Culin) dégraisser ⟨meat⟩
**(d)** (decorate) décorer ⟨tree, furniture⟩; border ⟨dress, handkerchief⟩

**trimming** *n* (on clothing) garniture *f*; **~s** (Culin) (with dish) accompagnements *mpl* traditionnels

**trinket** *n* babiole *f*

**trio** *n* trio *m* (of de)

**trip** **1** *n* **(a)** (journey) (abroad) voyage *m*; (excursion) excursion *f*; **business ~** voyage d'affaires
**(b)** (colloq) trip *m* (colloq)
**2** *vtr* (also **~ over, ~ up**) faire trébucher; (with foot) faire un croche-pied à

**3** *vi* **(a)** (also **~ over, ~ up**) (stumble) trébucher, faire un faux pas; **to ~ on** *or* **over** trébucher sur ⟨step, rock⟩; se prendre les pieds dans ⟨scarf, rope⟩
**(b)** (walk lightly) **to ~ along** ⟨child⟩ gambader; ⟨adult⟩ marcher d'un pas léger

**triple** *adj* triple

**triplet** *n* (child) triplé/-e *m/f*

**triplicate: in ~** *phr* en trois exemplaires

**tripod** *n* trépied *m*

**triumph** **1** *n* triomphe *m*
**2** *vi* triompher (**over** de)

**triumphant** *adj* ⟨person, team⟩ triomphant/-e; ⟨return, success⟩ triomphal/-e

**trivia** *n pl* futilités *fpl*

**trivial** *adj* ⟨matter, scale, film⟩ insignifiant/-e; ⟨error, offence⟩ léger/-ère (before n); ⟨conversation, argument, person⟩ futile

**trivialize** *vtr* banaliser; minimiser ⟨role⟩

**trolley** *n* **(a)** (GB) (for food, drinks, luggage, shopping) chariot *m*
**(b)** (US) tramway *m*

**trolley bus** *n* trolleybus *m*

**trolley car** *n* tramway *m*, tram *m*

**troop** *n* troupe *f*

**trooper** *n* **(a)** (Mil) homme *m* de troupe
**(b)** (US) (policeman) policier *m*

**trophy** *n* trophée *m*

**tropic** *n* tropique *m*; **in the ~s** sous les tropiques

**tropical** *adj* tropical/-e

**trot** **1** *n* trot *m*; **at a ~** au trot
**2** *vi* ⟨animal, rider⟩ trotter; ⟨person⟩ courir, trotter; ⟨child⟩ trottiner
IDIOMS **on the ~** (colloq) (one after the other) coup sur coup; (continuously) d'affilée
■ **trot out** (colloq): **~ out [sth]** débiter ⟨excuse, explanation⟩

**trouble** **1** *n* **(a)** (problems) problèmes *mpl*; (personal) ennuis *mpl*; (difficulties) difficultés *fpl*; **to be in** *or* **get into ~** ⟨person⟩ avoir des ennuis; ⟨company⟩ avoir des difficultés; **to get sb into ~** créer des ennuis à qn; **back ~** mal *m* de dos; **what's the ~?** qu'est-ce qui ne va pas?; **to have ~ doing** avoir du mal à faire; **to get sb out of ~** tirer qn d'affaire
**(b)** (effort, inconvenience) peine *f*; **it's not worth the ~** cela n'en vaut pas la peine; **to take the ~ to do, to go to the ~ of doing** se donner la peine de faire; **to save sb the ~ of doing** épargner à qn la peine de faire; **to go to a lot of ~** se donner beaucoup de mal
**2** **troubles** *n pl* soucis *mpl*; **money ~s** problèmes *mpl* d'argent
**3** *vtr* **(a)** (disturb, inconvenience) déranger ⟨person⟩; **may** *or* **could I ~ you to do?** puis-je vous demander de faire?
**(b)** (bother) **to be ~d by** être incommodé/-e par ⟨cough, pain⟩
**(c)** (worry) tracasser ⟨person⟩; **don't let that ~ you** ne te tracasse pas pour cela

**troubled** *adj* ⟨*person, expression*⟩
soucieux/-ieuse; ⟨*mind*⟩ inquiet/-iète; ⟨*sleep, times, area*⟩ agité/-e

**troublefree** *adj* sans problèmes

**troublemaker** *n* fauteur/-trice *m/f* de
troubles

**troubleshooter** *n* consultant/-e *m/f* en
gestion des entreprises

**troublesome** *adj* ⟨*person*⟩
ennuyeux/-euse; ⟨*problem*⟩ gênant/-e;
⟨*cough, pain*⟩ désagréable

**trouble spot** *n* point *m* chaud

**trough** *n* (a) (for drinking) abreuvoir *m*; (for
animal feed) auge *f*
(b) (between waves, hills, on graph) creux *m*
(c) (in weather) zone *f* dépressionnaire

**trousers** *n pl* pantalon *m*; **short ~** culotte
*f* courte

**trout** *n* truite *f*

**trowel** *n* (a) (for cement) truelle *f*
(b) (for gardening) déplantoir *m*

**truancy** *n* absentéisme *m*

**truant** *n* **to play ~** faire l'école
buissonnière

**truce** *n* trêve *f*

**truck** *n* (a) (lorry) camion *m*
(b) (rail wagon) wagon *m* de marchandises

**truck driver**, **trucker** (colloq) *n* routier
*m*

**trudge** *vi* marcher d'un pas lourd; **to ~
through the snow** marcher péniblement
dans la neige

**true** ⊞ *adj* (a) (based on fact, not a lie) ⟨*news,
fact, story*⟩ vrai/-e; (from real life) ⟨*story*⟩
vécu/-e
(b) (real, genuine) vrai/-e (*before n*); ⟨*identity,
age*⟩ véritable (*before n*); **to come ~** se
réaliser
(c) (heartfelt, sincere) ⟨*feeling, understanding*⟩
sincère; **~ love** le véritable amour
(d) (accurate) ⟨*copy*⟩ conforme; ⟨*assessment*⟩
correct, juste
(e) (faithful, loyal) fidèle; (**to** à)
(f) (Mus) ⟨*note, instrument*⟩ juste
⊠ *adv* ⟨*aim, fire*⟩ juste

**true-life** *adj* ⟨*adventure, story*⟩ vécu/-e

**truffle** *n* truffe *f*

**truly** *adv* (a) (gen) vraiment; **well and ~** bel
et bien
(b) (in letter) **yours ~** je vous prie d'agréer
l'expression de mes sentiments distingués
(formal)

**trump** *n* atout *m*
IDIOMS **to come up ~s** sauver la situation

**trumped-up** *adj* ⟨*charge*⟩ forgé/-e de
toutes pièces

**trumpet** *n* (a) (instrument, player) trompette *f*
(b) (elephant call) barrissement *m*
IDIOMS **to blow one's own ~** vanter ses
propres mérites

**trumpeter** *n* trompettiste *mf*

**truncheon** *n* matraque *f*

**trunk** *n* (a) (of tree, body) tronc *m*
(b) (of elephant) trompe *f*

(c) (for travel) malle *f*
(d) (US) (car boot) coffre *m*

**trunks** *n pl* slip *m* de bain

**truss** *n* (Med) bandage *m* herniaire
■ **truss up** brider, trousser ⟨*chicken*⟩;
ligoter ⟨*person*⟩

**trust** ⊞ *n* (a) (faith) confiance *f*; **to put one's
~ in** se fier à
(b) (Law) (arrangement) fidéicommis *m*;
(property involved) propriété *f* fiduciaire
⊠ *vtr* (a) (believe) se fier à ⟨*person,
judgment*⟩
(b) (rely on) faire confiance à
(c) (entrust) **to ~ sb with sth** confier qch à qn
③ *vi* **to ~ in** faire confiance à ⟨*person*⟩;
croire en ⟨*God, fortune*⟩; **to ~ to luck** se fier
au hasard
④ *v refl* **to ~ oneself to do** être sûr de
pouvoir faire

**trust company** *n* société *f* fiduciaire

**trusted** *adj* ⟨*friend*⟩ fidèle

**trusted third party**, **TTP** *n* tierce
partie *f* de confiance, TPC *f*

**trustee** *n* (a) (who administers property in trust)
fiduciaire *m*
(b) (of company) administrateur/-trice *m/f* (**of**
de)

**trust fund** *n* fonds *m* en fidéicommis

**trusting** *adj* ⟨*person*⟩ qui fait facilement
confiance aux gens

**trustworthy** *adj* ⟨*staff, firm*⟩
sérieux/-ieuse; ⟨*friend, lover*⟩ digne de
confiance

**truth** *n* (real facts) **the ~** la vérité; **there is
some ~ in it** il y a du vrai dans cela

**truthful** *adj* ⟨*person*⟩ honnête; ⟨*account,
version*⟩ vrai/-e

**try** ⊞ *n* (a) (attempt) essai *m*; **to have a ~**
essayer (**at doing** de faire)
(b) (Sport) essai *m*
⊠ *vtr* (a) (attempt) essayer de répondre à
⟨*exam question*⟩; **to ~ doing** or **to do** essayer
de faire; **to ~ hard to do** faire de gros efforts
pour faire; **to ~ one's best to do** faire tout
son possible pour faire
(b) (test out) essayer ⟨*tool, product, method,
activity*⟩; prendre [qn] à l'essai ⟨*person*⟩;
⟨*thief*⟩ essayer d'ouvrir ⟨*door, window*⟩;
tourner ⟨*door knob*⟩; **to ~ one's hand at sth**
s'essayer à qch
(c) (taste) goûter ⟨*food*⟩
(d) (consult) demander à ⟨*person*⟩; consulter
⟨*book*⟩; **~ the library** demandez à la
bibliothèque
(e) (subject to stress) **to ~ sb's patience**
pousser qn à bout
(f) (Law) juger ⟨*case, criminal*⟩
③ *vi* essayer; **to ~ again** (to perform task)
recommencer; (to see somebody) repasser; (to
phone) rappeler; **to ~ for** essayer d'obtenir
⟨*loan, university place*⟩; essayer de battre
⟨*world record*⟩; essayer d'avoir ⟨*baby*⟩; **keep
~ing!** essaie encore!
■ **try on** essayer ⟨*hat, dress*⟩
■ **try out**: **~ [sth] out**, **~ out [sth]** essayer

**trying** *adj* ⟨*person*⟩ pénible; ⟨*experience*⟩ éprouvant/-e

**T-shirt** *n* T-shirt *m*

**tub** *n* **(a)** (for flowers, water) bac *m*; (of ice cream, pâté) pot *m*
**(b)** (US) (bath) baignoire *f*

**tubby** *adj* (colloq) grassouillet/-ette (colloq)

**tube** *n* **(a)** (cylinder, container) tube *m*
**(b)** (GB) (colloq) **the** ~ le métro (londonien)
**(c)** (US) (colloq) (TV) télé *f* (colloq)
**(d)** (in TV set) tube *m* cathodique
**(e)** (in tyre) chambre *f* à air

**tuberculosis** *n* tuberculose *f*

**tuck** [1] *n* (in sewing) pli *m*
[2] *vtr* (put) glisser; **to** ~ **one's shirt into one's trousers** rentrer sa chemise dans son pantalon
■ **tuck away** (put away) ranger; (hide) cacher; **the house was** ~**ed away in the wood** la maison se cachait *or* était cachée dans le bois
■ **tuck in** rentrer ⟨*garment, shirt*⟩; border ⟨*bedclothes, person*⟩

**Tuesday** *n* mardi *m*

**tuft** *n* touffe *f*

**tug** [1] *n* **(a)** (pull) secousse *f*; **to give sth a** ~ tirer sur qch
**(b)** (*also* **tug boat**) remorqueur *m*
[2] *vtr* (pull) tirer
[3] *vi* **to** ~ **at** *or* **on** tirer sur ⟨*rope, hair*⟩

**tug-of-love** *n*: lutte *entre les parents pour la garde de l'enfant*

**tug-of-war** *n* (Sport) gagne-terrain *m*

**tuition** *n* cours *mpl*

**tuition fees** *n pl* frais *mpl* pédagogiques

**tulip** *n* tulipe *f*

**tumble** [1] *n* **(a)** (fall) chute *f*; **to take a** ~ ⟨*person*⟩ faire une chute
**(b)** (of clown, acrobat) culbute *f*
[2] *vi* **(a)** (fall) ⟨*person, object*⟩ tomber (**off, out of** de)
**(b)** ⟨*price, share, currency*⟩ chuter
**(c)** ⟨*clown, acrobat, child*⟩ faire des culbutes
■ **tumble down** ⟨*wall, building*⟩ s'écrouler

**tumble-drier, tumble-dryer** *n* sèche-linge *m inv*

**tumble-dry** *vtr* sécher (en machine)

**tumbler** *n* verre *m* droit

**tummy** *n* (colloq) ventre *m*

**tumour** (GB), **tumor** (US) *n* tumeur *f*

**tumult** *n* **(a)** (noise) tumulte *m*
**(b)** (disorder) agitation *f*

**tuna** *n* (*also* ~ **fish**) thon *m*

**tune** [1] *n* air *m*; **to be in/out of** ~ ⟨*instrument*⟩ être/ne pas être en accord; **to sing in/out of** ~ chanter juste/faux
[2] *vtr* accorder ⟨*musical instrument*⟩; régler ⟨*engine, radio, TV*⟩
■ **tune in**: ¶ ~ **in** mettre la radio; **to** ~ **in to** se mettre à l'écoute de ⟨*programme*⟩; régler sur ⟨*channel*⟩; ¶ ~ **[sth] in** régler (**to** sur)

**tunic** *n* (for gym) tunique *f*; (for nurse, schoolgirl) blouse *f*; (for soldier) vareuse *f*

**tuning fork** *n* diapason *m*

**tunnel** [1] *n* tunnel *m*
[2] *vtr, vi* creuser

**tunnel vision** *n* **to have** ~ (figurative) avoir des œillères

**turbine** *n* turbine *f*

**turbo** *n* (engine) turbo *m*; (car) turbo *f*

**turbocharged** *adj* turbo *inv*

**turbot** *n* turbot *m*

**turbulent** *adj* **(a)** ⟨*water*⟩ agité/-e
**(b)** ⟨*times, situation*⟩ agité/-e; ⟨*career, history*⟩ mouvementé/-e; ⟨*passions, character, faction*⟩ turbulent/-e

**tureen** *n* soupière *f*

**turf** [1] *n* (grass) gazon *m*; (peat) tourbe *f*
[2] *vtr* gazonner ⟨*lawn, pitch*⟩
■ **turf out**: ~ **out [sb/sth]**, ~ **[sb/sth] out** virer (colloq)

**Turk** *n* Turc/Turque *m/f*

**turkey** *n* **(a)** (bird) dinde *f*
**(b)** (US) (colloq) (flop) bide *m* (colloq); (bad film) navet *m* (colloq)

**Turkey** *pr n* Turquie *f*

**Turkish** [1] *n* (language) turc *m*
[2] *adj* turc/turque

**Turkish delight** *n* loukoum *m*

**turmoil** *n* désarroi *m*

**turn** [1] *n* **(a)** (in games, sequence) tour *m*; **whose** ~ **is it?** c'est à qui le tour?; **to be sb's** ~ **to do** être le tour de qn de faire; **to take** ~**s at sleeping, to take it in** ~**s to sleep** dormir à tour de rôle; **by** ~**s** tour à tour; **to speak out of** ~ commettre un impair
**(b)** (circular movement) tour *m*; **to give sth a** ~ tourner qch; **to do a** ~ ⟨*dancer*⟩ faire un tour
**(c)** (in vehicle) virage *m*; **to make** *or* **do a left/ right** ~ tourner à gauche/à droite
**(d)** (bend, side road) tournant *m*, virage *m*; **take the next right** ~, **take the next** ~ **on the right** prenez la prochaine (rue) à droite
**(e)** (change, development) tournure *f*; **to take a** ~ **for the better** ⟨*things, events, situation*⟩ prendre une meilleure tournure; **to take a** ~ **for the worse** ⟨*situation*⟩ se dégrader; ⟨*health*⟩ s'aggraver
**(f)** (GB) (colloq) (attack) crise *f*; **a dizzy** ~ un vertige; **it gave me quite a** ~, **it gave me a nasty** ~ ça m'a fait un coup (colloq)
**(g)** (act) numéro *m*
[2] *vtr* **(a)** (rotate) ⟨*person*⟩ tourner ⟨*wheel, handle*⟩; serrer ⟨*screw*⟩; ⟨*mechanism*⟩ faire tourner ⟨*cog, wheel*⟩
**(b)** (turn over, reverse) retourner ⟨*mattress, soil, steak, collar*⟩; tourner ⟨*page*⟩; **it** ~**s my stomach** ça me soulève le cœur
**(c)** (change direction of) tourner ⟨*chair, head, face, car*⟩
**(d)** (focus direction of) **to** ~ **[sth] on sb** braquer **[**qch**]** sur qn ⟨*gun, hose, torch*⟩
**(e)** (transform) **to** ~ **sth white/black** blanchir/ noircir qch; **to** ~ **sth opaque** rendre qch opaque; **to** ~ **sth into** transformer qch en ⟨*office, car park, desert*⟩; **to** ~ **a book into a**

**film** adapter un livre pour le cinéma; **to ~ sb into** ⟨*magician*⟩ changer qn en ⟨*frog*⟩; ⟨*experience*⟩ faire de qn ⟨*extrovert, maniac*⟩ **(f)** (deflect) détourner ⟨*person, conversation*⟩ **(towards** vers; **from** de) **(g)** (colloq) (pass the age of) **he has ~ed 50** il a 50 ans passés; **she has just ~ed 30** elle vient d'avoir 30 ans **(h)** (on lathe) tourner ⟨*wood, piece*⟩

**3** *vi* **(a)** (change direction) ⟨*person, car, plane, road*⟩ tourner; ⟨*ship*⟩ virer; **to ~ down** *or* **into** tourner dans ⟨*street, alley*⟩; **to ~ towards** tourner en direction de ⟨*village, mountains*⟩ **(b)** (reverse direction) ⟨*person, vehicle*⟩ faire demi-tour; ⟨*tide*⟩ changer; ⟨*luck*⟩ tourner **(c)** (revolve) ⟨*key, wheel, planet*⟩ tourner; ⟨*person*⟩ se tourner **(d)** (hinge) **to ~ on** ⟨*argument*⟩ tourner autour de ⟨*point, issue*⟩; ⟨*outcome*⟩ dépendre de ⟨*factor*⟩ **(e)** (spin round angrily) **to ~ on sb** ⟨*dog*⟩ attaquer qn; ⟨*person*⟩ se retourner contre qn **(f)** (resort to) **to ~ to** se tourner vers ⟨*person, religion*⟩; **to ~ to drink/drugs** se mettre à boire/se droguer; **I don't know where to ~** je ne sais plus où donner de la tête (colloq) **(g)** (change) **to ~ into** ⟨*person, tadpole*⟩ se transformer en ⟨*frog*⟩; ⟨*sofa*⟩ se transformer en ⟨*bed*⟩; ⟨*situation, evening*⟩ tourner à ⟨*farce, disaster*⟩; **to ~ to** ⟨*substance*⟩ se changer en ⟨*ice, gold*⟩; ⟨*fear, surprise*⟩ faire place à ⟨*horror, relief*⟩ **(h)** (become by transformation) devenir ⟨*pale, cloudy, green*⟩; **to ~ white/black/red** blanchir/noircir/rougir; **the weather is ~ing cold/warm** le temps se rafraîchit/se réchauffe **(i)** (go sour) ⟨*milk*⟩ tourner **(j)** ⟨*trees, leaves*⟩ jaunir

**4 in turn** *phr* ⟨*answer, speak*⟩ à tour de rôle; **she spoke to each of us in ~** elle nous a parlé chacun à notre tour **IDIOMS to do sb a good ~** rendre un service à qn

■ **turn against**: ¶ **~ against [sb/sth]** retourner contre; ¶ **~ [sb] against** retourner [qn] contre

■ **turn around (a)** (to face other way) ⟨*person*⟩ se retourner; ⟨*bus, vehicle*⟩ faire demi-tour **(b)** (revolve, rotate) ⟨*object, windmill, dancer*⟩ tourner ¶ **~ [sth] around** tourner [qch] dans l'autre sens ⟨*object*⟩

■ **turn aside** se détourner (**from** de)

■ **turn away**: ¶ **~ away** se détourner; ¶ **~ [sb] away** refuser ⟨*spectator, applicant*⟩; ne pas laisser entrer ⟨*salesman, caller*⟩

■ **turn back**: ¶ **~ back (a)** (on foot) rebrousser chemin; (in vehicle) faire demi-tour; **there's no ~ing back** il n'est pas question de revenir en arrière **(b)** (in book) revenir ¶ **~ [sth] back** reculer ⟨*dial, clock*⟩ ¶ **~ [sb] back** refouler ⟨*people, vehicles*⟩

■ **turn down (a)** (reduce) baisser ⟨*volume, radio, gas*⟩ **(b)** (fold over) rabattre ⟨*sheet, collar*⟩; retourner ⟨*corner of page*⟩ **(c)** (refuse) refuser ⟨*person, request*⟩; rejeter ⟨*offer, suggestion*⟩

■ **turn off**: ¶ **~ off (a)** ⟨*driver, walker*⟩ tourner **(b)** ⟨*motor, fan*⟩ s'arrêter ¶ **~ [sth] off (a)** éteindre ⟨*light, oven, TV, radio*⟩; fermer ⟨*tap*⟩; couper ⟨*water, gas, engine*⟩ **(b)** (leave) quitter ⟨*road*⟩ ¶ **~ [sb ] off** (colloq) rebuter

■ **turn on (a)** allumer ⟨*light, oven, TV, radio, gas*⟩; ouvrir ⟨*tap*⟩ **(b)** (colloq) exciter ⟨*person*⟩

■ **turn out**: ¶ **~ out (a)** (be eventually) **to ~ out well/badly** bien/mal se terminer; **it depends how things ~ out** cela dépend de la façon dont les choses vont tourner; **to ~ out to be wrong/easy** se révéler faux/facile; **it ~s out that they know each other already** il se trouve qu'ils se connaissent déjà **(b)** (come out) ⟨*crowd, people*⟩ venir ¶ **~ [sth] out (a)** (turn off) éteindre ⟨*light*⟩ **(b)** (empty) vider ⟨*pocket, bag*⟩; (Culin) démouler ⟨*mousse*⟩ **(c)** (produce) fabriquer ⟨*goods*⟩; former ⟨*scientists, graduates*⟩ ¶ **~ [sb] out** (evict) mettre [qn] à la porte

■ **turn over**: ¶ **~ over (a)** (roll over) ⟨*person, vehicle*⟩ se retourner **(b)** (turn page) tourner la page **(c)** ⟨*engine*⟩ se mettre en marche ¶ **~ [sb/sth] over (a)** (turn) tourner ⟨*page, paper*⟩; retourner ⟨*card, object, mattress, soil, patient*⟩ **(b)** (hand over) remettre ⟨*object, money, find, papers*⟩; livrer ⟨*person*⟩ (**to** à); remettre la succession de ⟨*company*⟩

■ **turn round** (GB) = TURN AROUND

■ **turn up**: ¶ **~ up (a)** (arrive, show up) arriver, se pointer (colloq); **don't worry—it will ~ up** ne t'inquiète pas—tu finiras par le retrouver **(b)** (present itself) ⟨*opportunity, job*⟩ se présenter **(c)** (point up) ⟨*corner, edge*⟩ être relevé/-e ¶ **~ [sth] up (a)** (increase, intensify) augmenter ⟨*heating, volume, gas*⟩; mettre [qch] plus fort ⟨*TV, radio, music*⟩ **(b)** (point up) relever ⟨*collar*⟩

**turnaround** *n* (in attitude) revirement *m*; (of fortune) revirement *m* (**in** de); (for the better) redressement *m* (**in** de)

**turning** *n* (GB) (in road) virage *m*

**turning point** *n* tournant *m* (**in, of** de)

**turnip** *n* navet *m*

**turnoff** *n* **(a)** (in road) embranchement *m* **(b)** (colloq) (person) **to be a real ~** être vraiment repoussant/-e

**turn of mind** *n* tournure *f* d'esprit

**turn of phrase** *n* (expression) expression *f*

**turnout** *n* (to vote, strike, demonstrate) taux *m* ⋯⃗

de participation; **there was a magnificent ~ for the parade** beaucoup de gens sont venus voir le défilé

**turnover** *n* **(a)** (of company) chiffre *m* d'affaires

**(b)** (of stock) rotation *f*; (of staff) taux *m* de renouvellement

**turnpike** *n* (tollgate) barrière *f* de péage; (US) (toll expressway) autoroute *f* à péage

**turnstile** *n* (gate) tourniquet *m*; (to count number of visitors) compteur *m* pour entrées

**turntable** *n* (on record player) platine *f*

**turnup** *n* (GB) (of trousers) revers *m*

**turpentine, turps** (colloq) *n* térébenthine *f*

**turret** *n* tourelle *f*

**turtle** *n* (GB) tortue *f* marine; (US) tortue *f*

**turtle dove** *n* tourterelle *f*

**turtleneck (sweater)** *n* pull-over *m* à col cheminée

**Tuscany** *pr n* Toscane *f*

**tusk** *n* défense *f*

**tussle** *n* empoignade *f* (**for** pour)

**tutor** *n* **(a)** (private teacher) professeur *m* particulier

**(b)** (GB Univ) chargé/-e *m/f* de travaux dirigés

**(c)** (US Univ) assistant/-e *m/f*

**tutorial** *n* (Univ) (group) classe *f* de travaux dirigés; (private) cours *m* privé

**tuxedo** *n* (US) smoking *m*

**TV** *n* (colloq) (*abbr* = **television**) télé *f* (colloq)

**TV dinner** *n* plateau *m* télé

**TV screen** *n* écran *m* télé

**twang** *n* (of string, wire) vibration *f*; (of tone) ton *m* nasillard

**tweak** *vtr* tordre ⟨*ear, nose*⟩; tirer ⟨*hair, moustache*⟩

**tweezers** *n pl* pincettes *fpl*; (for eyebrows) pince *f* à épiler

**twelfth** ① *n* **(a)** (in order) douzième *mf*

**(b)** (of month) douze *m inv*

**(c)** (fraction) douzième *m*

② *adj, adv* douzième

**twelve** *n, pron, det* douze (*m*) *inv*

**twenties** *n pl* **(a)** (era) **the ~** les années *fpl* vingt

**(b)** (age) **to be in one's ~** avoir entre vingt et trente ans

**twentieth** ① *n* **(a)** (in order) vingtième *mf*

**(b)** (of month) vingt *m*

**(c)** (fraction) vingtième *m*

② *adj, adv* vingtième

**twenty** *n, pron, det* vingt (*m*) *inv*

**twice** *adv* deux fois; **~ a day** *or* **daily** deux fois par jour; **she's ~ his age** elle a le double de son âge; **~ as much, ~ as many** deux fois plus

**twiddle** *vtr* tripoter; **to ~ one's thumbs** se tourner les pouces

**twig** *n* brindille *f*

**twilight** *n* crépuscule *m*

**twilight zone** *n* zone *f* d'ombre

**twin** ① *n* jumeau/-elle *m/f*

② *adj* **(a)** ⟨*brother, sister*⟩ jumeau/-elle

**(b)** ⟨*masts, propellers, beds*⟩ jumeaux/-elles (*after n*); ⟨*speakers*⟩ jumelés

③ *vtr* jumeler ⟨*town*⟩ (**with** avec)

**twine** *n* ficelle *f*

**twinge** *n* (of pain) élancement *m*; (of conscience, doubt) accès *m*; (of jealousy) pointe *f*

**twinkle** *vi* ⟨*light, star, jewel*⟩ scintiller; ⟨*eyes*⟩ pétiller

**twin town** *n* ville *f* jumelle

**twirl** ① *n* tournoiement *m*

② *vtr* faire tournoyer ⟨*baton, partner*⟩; entortiller ⟨*ribbon, vine*⟩

③ *vi* ⟨*dancer*⟩ tournoyer; **to ~ round** (turn round) se retourner brusquement

**twist** ① *n* **(a)** (in rope, cord, wool) tortillon *m*; (in road) zigzag *m*; (in river) coude *m*

**(b)** (in play, story) coup *m* de théâtre; (in events) rebondissement *m*

**(c)** (small amount) (of yarn, thread, hair) torsade *f*; **a ~ of lemon** une tranche de citron

② *vtr* **(a)** (turn) tourner ⟨*knob, handle*⟩; (open) dévisser ⟨*cap, lid*⟩; (close) visser ⟨*cap, lid*⟩; **he ~ed around in his chair** il s'est retourné dans son fauteuil

**(b)** (wind) enrouler; **to ~ threads together** torsader des fils

**(c)** (bend, distort) tordre ⟨*metal, rod, branch*⟩; déformer ⟨*words, facts, meaning*⟩; **his face was ~ed with pain** son visage était tordu de douleur

**(d)** (injure) **to ~ one's ankle/wrist** se tordre le bras/le poignet; **to ~ one's neck** attraper un torticolis

③ *vi* **(a)** ⟨*person*⟩ **to ~ round** (turn round) se retourner

**(b)** ⟨*rope, flex, coil*⟩ s'entortiller; **to ~ and turn** ⟨*road, path*⟩ serpenter

**twisted** *adj* ⟨*wire, metal*⟩ tordu/-e; ⟨*cord*⟩ entortillé/-e; ⟨*ankle, wrist*⟩ tordu/-e; ⟨*sense of humour*⟩ malsain/-e

**twit** *n* (colloq) idiot/-e *m/f*

**twitch** ① *n* **(a)** (tic) tic *m*

**(b)** (spasm) soubresaut *m*

② *vtr* tirer sur [qch] d'un coup sec ⟨*fabric, curtain*⟩

③ *vi* ⟨*person*⟩ avoir des tics; ⟨*mouth*⟩ trembler; ⟨*eye*⟩ cligner nerveusement; ⟨*limb, muscle*⟩ tressauter

**twitchy** *adj* agité/-e

**twitter** *vi* ⟨*bird*⟩ gazouiller

**two** *n, det, pron* deux (*m*) *inv*; **in ~s and threes** par deux ou trois, deux ou trois à la fois; **to break sth in ~** casser qch en deux

**IDIOMS to be in ~ minds about doing** hésiter à faire; **to put ~ and ~ together** faire le rapprochement

**two-faced** *adj* hypocrite, fourbe

**twofold** ① *adj* double

② *adv* doublement; **to increase ~** doubler

**two-piece** *n* (*also* **~ suit**) (woman's) tailleur *m*; (man's) costume *m* (deux-pièces)

**two-seater** *n* (car) voiture *f* à deux places; (plane) avion *m* à deux places

**two-tier** *adj* ‹society, health service› à deux vitesses

**two-time** *vtr* (colloq) être infidèle envers, tromper ‹partner›

**two-way** *adj* ‹street› à double sens; ‹traffic› dans les deux sens; ‹communication, exchange› bilatéral/-e

**two-way mirror** *n* glace *f* sans tain

**two-way radio** *n* émetteur-récepteur *m*

**tycoon** *n* magnat *m*

**type** ⓵ *n* (a) (variety, kind) type *m*, genre *m* (of de) (b) (in printing) caractères *mpl* ⓶ *vtr* taper (à la machine) ‹word, letter›; a ∼d letter une lettre dactylographiée ⓷ *vi* taper (à la machine)

**typecast** *vtr* cataloguer ‹person›

**typeface** *n* police *f* (de caractères)

**typewriter** *n* machine *f* à écrire

**typhoid** *n* typhoïde *f*

**typhoon** *n* typhon *m*

**typical** *adj* ‹case, example, day, village› typique; ‹generosity, compassion› caractéristique; **it's** ∼ **of him to be late** cela ne m'étonne pas de lui qu'il soit en retard

**typically** *adv* ‹react, behave› (of person) comme à mon/ton etc habitude; ∼ **English** ‹place, behaviour› typiquement anglais; **she's** ∼ **English** c'est l'Anglaise type

**typify** *vtr* ‹feature, behaviour› caractériser; ‹person, institution› être le type même de

**typing** *n* dactylo *f*

**typist** *n* dactylo *mf*

**typographic(al)** *adj* typographique

**typography** *n* typographie *f*

**tyrannize** *vtr* tyranniser

**tyranny** *n* tyrannie *f* (**over** sur)

**tyrant** *n* tyran *m*

**tyre** (GB), **tire** (US) *n* pneu *m*; **spare** ∼ (for car) pneu *m* de rechange; (fat) bourrelet *m*

**tyre pressure** *n* pression *f* des pneus

# U u

**u, U** *n* u, U *m*

**udder** *n* pis *m*

**UFO** *n* (*abbr* = **unidentified flying object**) ovni *m inv*

**ugly** *adj* (a) ‹person, building› laid/-e (b) ‹situation› dangereux/-euse

**UK** *pr n* (*abbr* = **United Kingdom**) Royaume-Uni *m*

**Ukraine** *pr n* the ∼ l'Ukraine *f*

**ulcer** *n* ulcère *m*

**ulterior** *adj* **without any** ∼ **motive** sans arrière-pensée

**ultimate** ⓵ *n* **the** ∼ **in** le nec plus ultra de ‹comfort, luxury› ⓶ *adj* ‹result, destination› final/-e; ‹sacrifice› ultime (*before n*)

**ultimately** *adv* en fin de compte, au bout du compte

**ultimatum** *n* ultimatum *m*

**ultramarine** *n, adj* outremer (*m*) *inv*

**ultrasound** *n* ultrasons *mpl*

**ultrasound scan** *n* échographie *f*

**ultraviolet** *adj* ultraviolet/-ette

**umbilical cord** *n* cordon *m* ombilical

**umbrella** *n* parapluie *m*

**umpire** *n* arbitre *m*

**UN** *n* (*abbr* = **United Nations**) the ∼ l'ONU *f*

**unable** *adj* **to be** ∼ **to do** (lacking means or opportunity) ne pas pouvoir faire; (lacking knowledge or skill) ne pas savoir faire; (incapable, not qualified) être incapable de faire

**unabridged** *adj* intégral/-e

**unacceptable** *adj* ‹proposal› inacceptable; ‹behaviour› inadmissible

**unaccompanied** *adj* (a) ‹child, baggage› non accompagné/-e; ‹man, woman› seul/-e (b) (Mus) sans accompagnement

**unaccounted** *adj* **to be** ∼ **for** (gen) être introuvable; **two of the crew are still** ∼ **for** deux membres de l'équipage sont toujours portés disparus

**unaccustomed** *adj* **to be** ∼ **to sth/to doing** ne pas avoir l'habitude de qch/de faire

**unaffected** *adj* (a) **to be** ∼ ne pas être affecté/-e (**by** par) (b) (natural) tout simple

**unafraid** *adj* ‹person› sans peur

**unaided** *adv* ‹stand, sit, walk› sans aide

**unambiguous** *adj* sans équivoque

**unanimous** *adj* unanime

**unanimously** *adv* ‹agree, condemn› unanimement; ‹vote› à l'unanimité

**unannounced** *adv* ‹arrive, call› sans prévenir

**unanswered** *adj* ‹letter, question› resté/-e sans réponse

**unappetizing** *adj* peu appétissant/-e

**unappreciative** *adj* ‹person, audience› ingrat/-e

**unapproachable** *adj* inaccessible

**unarmed** adj ⟨person⟩ non armé/-e; ⟨combat⟩ sans armes

**unashamedly** adv ouvertement

**unasked** adv ⟨come, attend⟩ sans être invité/-e; **to do sth** ~ faire qch spontanément

**unassuming** adj modeste

**unattached** adj (a) ⟨part, element⟩ détaché/-e
(b) (single) ⟨person⟩ célibataire

**unattainable** adj inaccessible

**unattractive** adj ⟨person⟩ peu attirant/-e; ⟨proposition⟩ peu intéressant/-e **(to** pour)

**unauthorized** adj fait/-e sans autorisation

**unavailable** adj **to be** ~ ⟨person⟩ ne pas être disponible

**unavoidable** adj inévitable

**unaware** adj (a) (not informed) **to be** ~ **that** ignorer que
(b) (not conscious) **to be** ~ **of sth** ne pas être conscient/-e de qch

**unawares** adv **to catch** or **take sb** ~ prendre qn au dépourvu

**unbearable** adj insupportable

**unbeatable** adj imbattable

**unbeknown** adv ~ **to sb** à l'insu de qn

**unbelievable** adj incroyable

**unbending** adj inflexible

**unbias(s)ed** adj impartial/-e

**unblock** vtr déboucher ⟨pipe, sink⟩

**unborn** adj ⟨child⟩ à naître; **her** ~ **child** l'enfant qu'elle porte/portait etc

**unbreakable** adj incassable

**unbroken** adj (a) ⟨sequence, silence, view⟩ ininterrompu/-e
(b) ⟨pottery⟩ intact/-e

**unbuckle** vtr déboucler ⟨belt⟩; défaire la boucle de ⟨shoe⟩

**unbutton** vtr déboutonner

**uncalled-for** adj ⟨remark⟩ déplacé/-e

**uncanny** adj ⟨resemblance⟩ étrange; ⟨accuracy⟩ étonnant/-e; ⟨silence⟩ troublant/-e

**uncaring** adj ⟨world⟩ indifférent/-e

**uncertain** ⟨1⟩ adj (a) (unsure) incertain/-e; **to be** ~ **about** ne pas être certain/-e de
(b) (changeable) ⟨temper⟩ instable; ⟨weather⟩ variable
⟨2⟩ **in no** ~ **terms** phr ⟨state⟩ en termes on ne peut plus clairs

**uncertainty** n incertitude f

**unchallenged** adj incontesté/-e; **to go** ~ ⟨statement, decision⟩ ne pas être récusé/-e

**unchanged** adj inchangé/-e

**uncharacteristic** adj ⟨generosity⟩ peu habituel/-elle; **it was** ~ **of him to...** ce n'est pas son genre de...

**uncharitable** adj peu charitable

**unchecked** adv de manière incontrôlée

**uncivilized** adj (a) (inhumane) ⟨treatment, conditions⟩ inhumain/-e
(b) (uncouth, rude) grossier/-ière

(c) (barbarous) ⟨people, nation⟩ non civilisé/-e

**uncle** n oncle m

**unclear** adj (a) ⟨motive, reason⟩ peu clair/-e; **it is** ~ **how/whether...** on ne sait pas très bien comment/si...
(b) ⟨instructions, voice⟩ pas clair/-e; ⟨answer⟩ peu clair/-e; ⟨handwriting⟩ difficile à lire

**uncomfortable** adj (a) ⟨shoes, garment, seat⟩ inconfortable; ⟨journey, heat⟩ pénible; **you look** ~ **in that chair** tu n'as pas l'air à l'aise dans ce fauteuil
(b) ⟨feeling, silence, situation⟩ pénible; **to make sb (feel)** ~ mettre qn mal à l'aise

**uncommon** adj rare

**uncommunicative** adj peu communicatif/-ive

**uncomplimentary** adj peu flatteur/-euse

**uncompromising** adj intransigeant/-e

**unconcerned** adj (uninterested) indifférent/-e (with à); (not caring) insouciant/-e; (untroubled) imperturbable

**unconditional** adj ⟨obedience, support, love⟩ inconditionnel/-elle; ⟨offer, surrender⟩ sans condition

**unconfirmed** adj non confirmé/-e

**unconnected** adj ⟨incidents, facts⟩ sans lien entre eux/elles; **to be** ~ **with** ⟨event, fact⟩ n'avoir aucun rapport avec; ⟨person⟩ n'avoir aucun lien avec

**unconscious** ⟨1⟩ n the ~ l'inconscient m
⟨2⟩ adj (a) (insensible) sans connaissance; **to knock sb** ~ assommer qn
(b) (unaware) **to be** ~ **of sth** ne pas être conscient/-e de qch
(c) ⟨bias, hostility⟩ inconscient/-e

**unconstitutional** adj inconstitutionnel/-elle

**uncontested** adj ⟨leader, fact⟩ incontesté/-e; ⟨seat⟩ non disputé/-e

**uncontrollable** adj ⟨emotion⟩ incontrôlable; ⟨tears⟩ qu'on ne peut retenir

**uncontrollably** adv ⟨laugh, sob⟩ sans pouvoir se contrôler

**unconventional** adj peu conventionnel/-elle

**unconvincing** adj peu convaincant/-e

**uncooked** adj non cuit/-e

**uncooperative** adj peu coopératif/-ive

**uncoordinated** adj ⟨efforts, service⟩ désordonné/-e; **to be** ~ ⟨person⟩ manquer de coordination

**uncouth** adj ⟨person⟩ grossier/-ière; ⟨accent⟩ peu raffiné/-e

**uncover** vtr dévoiler ⟨scandal⟩; découvrir ⟨evidence, body⟩

**uncritical** adj peu critique

**unctuous** adj onctueux/-euse, mielleux/-euse

**uncut** adj (a) ⟨film, version⟩ intégral/-e
(b) ⟨gem⟩ non taillé/-e

**undamaged** adj ⟨crops⟩ non endommagé/-e; ⟨building, reputation⟩ intact/-e

**undecided** adj ⟨person⟩ indécis/-e; ⟨outcome⟩ incertain/-e

**undemanding** adj ⟨task⟩ peu fatigant/-e; ⟨person⟩ peu exigeant/-e

**undemocratic** adj antidémocratique

**undemonstrative** adj peu démonstratif/-ive

**undeniable** adj indéniable

**under** ⟦1⟧ prep (a) sous; ∼ **the bed** sous le lit; ∼ **it** en dessous; **it's** ∼ **there** c'est là-dessous; ∼ **letter D** sous la lettre D
(b) (less than) ∼ **£10** moins de 10 livres sterling; **children** ∼ **five** les enfants de moins de cinq ans *or* au-dessous de cinq ans; **a number** ∼ **ten** un nombre inférieur à dix; **temperatures** ∼ **10°C** des températures inférieures à *or* au-dessous de 10°C
(c) (according to) ∼ **the law** selon la loi
(d) (subordinate to) sous; **I have 50 people** ∼ **me** j'ai 50 employés sous mes ordres
⟦2⟧ adv (a) ⟨crawl, sit, hide⟩ en dessous; **to go** ∼ ⟨diver, swimmer⟩ disparaître sous l'eau
(b) (less) moins; **£10 and** ∼ 10 livres sterling et moins; **children of six and** ∼ des enfants de six ans et au-dessous
(c) (anaesthetized) **to put sb** ∼ endormir qn

**underachieve** vi (Sch) ne pas obtenir les résultats dont on est capable

**underachiever** n (Sch) sous-performant/-e m/f

**underage** adj ∼ **drinking** la consommation d'alcool par les mineurs; **to be** ∼ être mineur/-e

**undercarriage** n train m d'atterrissage

**underclass** n classe f sous-prolétariat

**underclothes** n pl sous-vêtements mpl

**undercoat** n couche f de fond

**undercooked** adj pas assez cuit/-e; **the meat is** ∼ la viande n'est pas assez cuite

**undercover** adj ⟨activity, group⟩ clandestin/-e; ⟨agent⟩ secret/-ète

**undercurrent** n (in water) courant m profond; (in sea) courant m sous-marin; (figurative) courant m sous-jacent

**undercut** vtr concurrencer ⟨prices⟩

**underdeveloped** adj ⟨country⟩ sous-développé/-e; ⟨negative⟩ pas assez développé/-e

**underdog** n (in society) opprimé/-e m/f; (in game, contest) perdant/-e m/f

**underdone** adj ⟨food⟩ pas assez cuit/-e; ⟨steak⟩ (GB) saignant/-e

**underestimate** vtr sous-estimer

**underexpose** vtr sous-exposer

**underfed** adj sous-alimenté/-e

**underfoot** adv sous les pieds; **the ground was wet** ∼ le sol était humide

**underfunded** adj insuffisamment financé/-e

**undergo** vtr subir ⟨change, test, operation⟩; suivre ⟨treatment, training⟩; **to** ∼ **surgery** subir une intervention chirurgicale

**undergraduate** n étudiant/-e m/f

**underground** ⟦1⟧ n (a) (GB) (subway) métro m; **on the** ∼ dans le métro
(b) **the** ∼ (political) la clandestinité; (artistic) l'underground m
⟦2⟧ adj (a) (below ground) souterrain/-e
(b) (secret) clandestin/-e
(c) (artistic) underground inv
⟦3⟧ adv (a) (below ground) sous terre
(b) (secretly) **to go** ∼ passer dans la clandestinité

**underground train** n rame f (de métro)

**undergrowth** n sous-bois m

**underhand** adj (also **underhanded** (US)) ⟨person, method⟩ sournois/-e; ∼ **dealings** magouilles fpl (colloq)

**underline** vtr souligner

**underling** n subordonné/-e m/f

**underlying** adj ⟨problem⟩ sous-jacent/-e

**undermine** vtr saper ⟨foundations, authority, efforts⟩; ébranler ⟨confidence, position⟩

**underneath** ⟦1⟧ n dessous m
⟦2⟧ adv dessous, en dessous
⟦3⟧ prep sous, au-dessous de; **from** ∼ **a pile of books** de dessous une pile de livres

**undernourished** adj sous-alimenté/-e

**underpants** n pl slip m; **a pair of** ∼ un slip

**underpass** n (for traffic) voie f inférieure; (for pedestrians) passage m souterrain

**underpay** vtr sous-payer ⟨employee⟩

**underprivileged** adj défavorisé/-e

**underrate** vtr sous-estimer

**under-secretary** n (also ∼ **of state**) (GB) sous-secrétaire mf d'État

**undersell** ⟦1⟧ vtr vendre moins cher que ⟨competitor⟩
⟦2⟧ v refl **to** ∼ **oneself** se dévaloriser

**undershirt** n (US) maillot m de corps

**understaffed** adj **to be** ∼ manquer de personnel

**understand** ⟦1⟧ vtr (a) (gen) comprendre; **to make oneself understood** se faire comprendre
(b) (believe) **to** ∼ **that** croire que
⟦2⟧ vi comprendre (about à propos de)

**understandable** adj compréhensible; **it's** ∼ ça se comprend

**understandably** adv naturellement

**understanding** ⟦1⟧ n (a) (grasp of subject, issue) compréhension f
(b) (arrangement) entente f (about sur; between entre)
(c) (sympathy) compréhension f
(d) (powers of reason) entendement m
⟦2⟧ adj ⟨tone⟩ bienveillant/-e; ⟨person⟩ compréhensif/-ive

**understatement** n litote f

**understudy** n doublure f (to de)

**undertake** vtr (a) entreprendre ⟨search, study, trip⟩; se charger de ⟨mission, offensive⟩

⋯⋯⟩

u

**(b) to ~ to do** s'engager à faire

**undertaker** n (person) entrepreneur m de pompes funèbres; (company) entreprise f de pompes funèbres

**undertaking** n (a) (venture) entreprise f
**(b)** (promise) garantie f

**under-the-counter** adj (goods, trade) illicite; (payment) sous le manteau

**undertone** n (a) (low voice) voix f basse
**(b)** (hint) nuance f

**undervalue** vtr (a) (financially) sous-évaluer
**(b)** sous-estimer (person, quality)

**underwater** ① adj (cable, exploration) sous-marin/-e; (lighting) sous l'eau
② adv sous l'eau

**underway** adj to get ~ (vehicle) se mettre en route; (season) commencer

**underwear** n sous-vêtements mpl

**underweight** adj trop maigre

**underworld** n milieu m, pègre f

**undesirable** adj (aspect, habit, result) indésirable; (influence) néfaste; (friend) peu recommandable

**undetected** adv (break in, listen) sans être aperçu/-e; to go ~ (person) rester inaperçu/-e; (cancer) rester non décelé/-e; (crime) rester non découvert/-e

**undeterred** adj to be ~ by sb/sth ne pas se laisser démonter par qn/qch

**undeveloped** adj (person, organ, idea) non développé/-e; (land) inexploité/-e; (country) sous-développé/-e

**undignified** adj indigne

**undisciplined** adj indiscipliné/-e

**undiscovered** adj (secret) non révélé/-e; (land) inexploré/-e; (crime, document) non découvert/-e

**undiscriminating** adj sans discernement

**undisguised** adj non déguisé/-e

**undisputed** adj incontesté/-e

**undisturbed** adj (sleep) paisible, tranquille; to leave sb/sth ~ ne pas déranger qn/qch

**undivided** adj to give sb one's ~ attention accorder à qn toute son attention

**undo** vtr (a) défaire (button, lock); ouvrir (parcel)
**(b)** annuler (good, effort)

**undone** adj défait/-e; to come ~ (parcel, button) se défaire

**undoubtedly** adv indubitablement

**undress** ① vtr déshabiller
② vi se déshabiller

**undrinkable** adj (unpleasant) imbuvable; (dangerous) non potable

**undue** adj excessif/-ive

**unduly** adv (optimistic, surprised) excessivement; (neglect, worry) outre mesure

**unearthly** adj (light, landscape) surnaturel/-elle; (cry, silence) étrange; at an ~ hour à une heure indue

**uneasily** adv (a) (anxiously) avec inquiétude

**(b)** (uncomfortably) avec gêne

**uneasiness** n (worry) appréhension f (about au sujet de); (dissatisfaction) malaise m

**uneasy** adj (a) (person) inquiet/-iète (about, at au sujet de); (conscience) pas tranquille
**(b)** (compromise) difficile; (peace) boiteux/-euse; (silence) gêné/-e
**(c)** (sleep) agité/-e

**uneconomical** adj (wasteful) pas économique; (not profitable) pas rentable

**uneducated** adj (a) (person) sans instruction
**(b)** (person, speech) inculte; (accent, tastes) commun/-e

**unemotional** adj (person) impassible; (account, reunion) froid/-e

**unemployed** ① n the ~ les chômeurs mpl
② adj au chômage, sans emploi

**unemployment** n chômage m

**unemployment benefit** (GB), **unemployment compensation** (US) n allocations fpl de chômage

**unemployment rate** n taux m de chômage

**unenthusiastic** adj peu enthousiaste

**unenviable** adj peu enviable

**unequal** adj (amounts, contest, pay) inégal/-e

**unequivocal** adj (person, declaration) explicite; (answer, support) sans équivoque

**unethical** adj (gen) contraire à la morale; (Med) contraire à la déontologie

**uneven** adj (hem, teeth) irrégulier/-ière; (contest, surface) inégal/-e

**uneventful** adj (day, life, career) ordinaire; (journey, period) sans histoires

**unexciting** adj sans intérêt

**unexpected** adj (arrival, success) imprévu/-e; (ally, outcome) inattendu/-e; (death) inopiné/-e

**unexpectedly** adv (happen) à l'improviste; (large, small, fast) étonnamment

**unexplored** adj inexploré/-e

**unfailing** adj (support) fidèle; (optimism) à toute épreuve; (efforts) constant/-e

**unfair** adj injuste (to, on envers; to do de faire); (play, tactics) irrégulier/-ière; (trading) frauduleux/-euse

**unfair dismissal** n licenciement m abusif

**unfairness** n injustice f

**unfaithful** adj infidèle (to à)

**unfamiliar** adj (a) (face, name, place) inconnu/-e (to à); (concept, feeling, situation) inhabituel/-le (to à)
**(b)** to be ~ with sth ne pas connaître qch

**unfashionable** adj qui n'est pas à la mode

**unfasten** vtr défaire (clothing, button); ouvrir (bag)

u

**unfavourable** *adj* défavorable

**unfinished** *adj* ⟨work⟩ inachevé/-e; **to have ∼ business** avoir des choses à régler

**unfit** *adj* (a) (out of condition) qui n'est pas en forme
(b) ⟨housing⟩ inadéquat/-e; ⟨pitch, road⟩ impraticable (for à); **∼ for human consumption** impropre à la consommation humaine

**unflattering** *adj* peu flatteur/-euse

**unfold** ① *vtr* déplier ⟨paper, map, deck, chair⟩; déployer ⟨wings⟩; décroiser ⟨arms⟩
② *vi* (a) ⟨leaf⟩ se dérouler; ⟨mystery⟩ se dévoiler
(b) ⟨scene⟩ se dérouler; ⟨mystery⟩ se dévoiler

**unforeseeable** *adj* imprévisible

**unforeseen** *adj* imprévu/-e

**unforgettable** *adj* inoubliable

**unforgivable** *adj* impardonnable

**unforgiving** *adj* impitoyable

**unfortunate** *adj* (a) (pitiable) malheureux/-euse
(b) (regrettable) ⟨incident, choice⟩ malencontreux/-euse; ⟨remark⟩ fâcheux/-euse
(c) (unlucky) malchanceux/-euse

**unfortunately** *adv* malheureusement

**unfounded** *adj* sans fondement

**unfriendly** *adj* ⟨person, attitude, reception⟩ peu amical/-e; ⟨place⟩ inhospitalier/-ière

**unfulfilled** *adj* ⟨ambition⟩ non réalisé/-e; ⟨desire, need⟩ inassouvi/-e; **to feel ∼** se sentir insatisfait/-e

**unfurnished** *adj* non meublé/-e

**ungracious** *adj* désobligeant/-e (of de la part de)

**ungrammatical** *adj* incorrect/-e

**ungrateful** *adj* ingrat/-e (of de la part de; towards envers)

**unhappily** *adv* (a) (miserably) d'un air malheureux
(b) (unfortunately) malheureusement
(c) (inappropriately) malencontreusement

**unhappiness** *n* (a) (misery) tristesse *f*
(b) (dissatisfaction) mécontentement *m*

**unhappy** *adj* (a) ⟨person, childhood, situation⟩ malheureux/-euse; ⟨face, occasion⟩ triste
(b) (dissatisfied) mécontent/-e; **to be ∼ with sth** ne pas être satisfait/-e de qch
(c) (concerned) inquiet/-iète

**unharmed** *adj* ⟨person⟩ indemne; ⟨object⟩ intact/-e

**unhealthy** *adj* (a) ⟨person⟩ maladif/-ive; ⟨diet⟩ malsain/-e; ⟨conditions⟩ insalubre
(b) (unwholesome) malsain/-e

**unheard-of** *adj* (a) (shocking) inouï/-e
(b) ⟨price⟩ record; ⟨actor⟩ inconnu/-e

**unheeded** *adj* **to go ∼** ⟨warning, plea⟩ rester vain/-e

**unhelpful** *adj* ⟨employee⟩ peu serviable; ⟨attitude⟩ peu obligeant/-e

**unhindered** *adj* **∼ by** sans être entravé/-e par ⟨rules⟩; sans être encombré/-e par ⟨luggage⟩

**unhook** *vtr* dégrafer ⟨skirt⟩; décrocher ⟨picture⟩ (from de)

**unhurried** *adj* ⟨person⟩ posé/-e; ⟨pace, meal⟩ tranquille

**unhygienic** *adj* ⟨conditions⟩ insalubre; ⟨way, method⟩ peu hygiénique

**unidentified** *adj* non identifié/-e

**unification** *n* unification *f* (of de)

**uniform** ① *n* uniforme *m*
② *adj* identique; ⟨temperature⟩ constant/-e

**unify** *vtr* unifier

**unilateral** *adj* unilatéral/-e

**unimaginative** *adj* ⟨style⟩ sans originalité; **to be ∼** manquer d'imagination

**unimpeded** *adj* ⟨access, influx⟩ libre

**unimportant** *adj* sans importance

**unimpressed** *adj* **to be ∼ by** être peu impressionné/-e par ⟨person, performance⟩; n'être guère convaincu/-e par ⟨argument⟩

**uninhabitable** *adj* inhabitable

**uninhabited** *adj* inhabité/-e

**uninhibited** *adj* ⟨person⟩ sans complexes (about en ce qui concerne)

**uninitiated** *n* **the ∼** les profanes

**uninjured** *adj* indemne

**uninspired** *adj* ⟨approach⟩ terne; ⟨performance⟩ honnête; **to be ∼** ⟨person⟩ manquer d'inspiration; ⟨strategy⟩ manquer d'imagination

**unintelligible** *adj* incompréhensible

**unintended** *adj* ⟨slur, irony⟩ involontaire; ⟨consequence⟩ non voulu/-e

**unintentional** *adj* involontaire

**uninterested** *adj* indifférent/-e (in à)

**uninteresting** *adj* sans intérêt

**uninvited** *adj* ⟨attentions⟩ non sollicité/-e; ⟨remark⟩ gratuit/-e; **∼ guest** intrus/-e *m/f*

**uninviting** *adj* ⟨place⟩ rébarbatif/-ive; ⟨food⟩ peu appétissant/-e

**union** *n* (a) (also **trade ∼**) syndicat *m*
(b) (uniting) union *f*; (marriage) union *f*, mariage *m*

**Unionist** *n*, *adj* unioniste (*mf*)

**Union Jack** *n* drapeau *m* du Royaume-Uni

**unique** *adj* (a) (sole) unique; **to be ∼ to** être particulier/-ière à
(b) (remarkable) unique, exceptionnel/-elle

**unisex** *adj* unisexe

**unison** *n* **in ∼** à l'unisson

**unit** *n* (a) (gen) unité *f*
(b) (group) groupe *m*; (in army, police) unité *f*
(c) (department) (gen, Med) service *m*
(d) (piece of furniture) élément *m*

**unite** ① *vtr* unir (with à)
② *vi* s'unir (with à)

**united** *adj* ⟨group, front⟩ uni/-e (in dans); ⟨effort⟩ conjoint/-e

**United Kingdom** *pr n* Royaume-Uni *m*

u

**United Nations (Organization)** n
(Organisation f des) Nations fpl unies
**United States (of America)** pr n
États-Unis mpl (d'Amérique)
**unit trust** n ≈ société f d'investissement à
capital variable, SICAV f
**unity** n unité f
**universal** adj ⟨acclaim, reaction⟩
général/-e; ⟨education⟩ pour tous; ⟨principle,
truth⟩ universel/-elle
**universally** adv ⟨believed⟩ par tous,
universellement; ⟨known, loved⟩ de tous
**universe** n univers m
**university** n université f
**unjust** adj injuste (**to** envers)
**unjustified** adj injustifié/-e
**unkempt** adj ⟨appearance⟩ négligé/-e;
⟨hair⟩ ébouriffé/-e; ⟨beard⟩ peu soigné/-e
**unkind** adj ⟨person, thought, act⟩ pas très
gentil/-ille; ⟨remark⟩ désobligeant/-e; **to be ~
to sb** (by deed) ne pas être gentil avec qn;
(verbally) être méchant/-e avec qn
**unknown** ⓵ n (a) **the ~** l'inconnu m
(b) (person) inconnu/-e m/f
⓶ adj inconnu/-e
**unlace** vtr délacer
**unlawful** adj ⟨activity⟩ illégal/-e;
⟨detention⟩ arbitraire; **~ killing** meurtre m
**unlawfully** adv illégalement
**unleaded petrol** (GB), **unleaded
gasoline** (US) n essence f sans plomb
**unleavened** adj sans levain
**unless** conj à moins que (+ subjunctive), à
moins de (+ infinitive); **he won't come ~ you
invite him** il ne viendra pas à moins que tu
(ne) l'invites; **she can't take the job ~ she
finds a nanny** elle ne peut pas accepter le
poste à moins de trouver une nourrice
**unlike** prep (a) (in contrast to) contrairement
à, à la différence de; **~ me, he...**
contrairement à moi, il...
(b) (different from) différent/-e de
(c) (uncharacteristic of) **it's ~ her** (to be so
rude) ça ne lui ressemble pas (d'être aussi
impolie)
**unlikely** adj (a) (unexpected) improbable,
peu probable; **it is ~ that** il est peu probable
que (+ subjunctive)
(b) ⟨partner, choice, situation⟩ inattendu/-e
(c) ⟨story⟩ invraisemblable
**unlimited** adj illimité/-e; ⟨access⟩ libre
(before n)
**unlined** adj (a) ⟨garment, curtain⟩ sans
doublure
(b) ⟨paper⟩ non réglé
**unload** ⓵ vtr (a) décharger ⟨goods, vessel,
gun, camera⟩
(b) (get rid of) se décharger de ⟨feelings⟩
(on(to) sur); se débarrasser de ⟨goods⟩
⓶ vi ⟨truck, ship⟩ décharger
**unlock** vtr ouvrir ⟨door⟩; **to be ~ed** ne pas
être fermé/-e à clé
**unluckily** adv malheureusement (**for** pour)

**unlucky** adj (a) ⟨person⟩
malchanceux/-euse; ⟨event⟩
malencontreux/-euse; ⟨day⟩ de malchance
(b) ⟨number, colour⟩ néfaste, maléfique; **it's
~ to do** ça porte malheur de faire
**unmade** adj ⟨bed⟩ défait/-e
**unmanageable** adj ⟨child, dog⟩ difficile;
⟨system⟩ ingérable; ⟨hair⟩ rebelle
**unmarried** adj célibataire
**unmistakable** adj (a) (recognizable)
caractéristique (**of** de)
(b) (unambiguous) sans ambiguïté
(c) (marked) net/nette
**unmotivated** adj ⟨act⟩ gratuit/-e; ⟨person⟩
non motivé/-e
**unmoved** adj (unconcerned) indifférent/-e
(**by** à); (emotionally) insensible (**by** à)
**unnamed** adj (name not divulged) ⟨company,
source⟩ dont le nom n'a pas été divulgué;
(without name) **as yet ~** encore à la recherche
d'un nom
**unnatural** adj (a) (odd) anormal/-e; **it is ~
that** ce n'est pas normal que (+ subjunctive)
(b) ⟨style, laugh⟩ affecté/-e
(c) ⟨silence, colour⟩ insolite
**unnecessarily** adv inutilement
**unnecessary** adj (a) (not needed) inutile;
**it is ~ to do** il est inutile de faire; **it is ~ for
you to do** il est inutile que tu fasses
(b) (uncalled for) déplacé/-e
**unnerve** vtr déconcentancer, rendre [qn]
nerveux/-euse
**unnoticed** adj inaperçu/-e
**unobstructed** adj ⟨view, exit, road⟩
dégagé/-e
**unobtainable** adj ⟨supplies⟩ impossible à
se procurer; ⟨number⟩ impossible à obtenir
**unobtrusive** adj ⟨person⟩ effacé/-e; ⟨site,
object, noise⟩ discret/-ète
**unoccupied** adj ⟨house, shop⟩ inoccupé/-e;
⟨seat⟩ libre
**unofficial** adj ⟨figure⟩ officieux/-ieuse;
⟨candidate⟩ indépendant/-e; ⟨strike⟩ sauvage
**unorthodox** adj peu orthodoxe
**unpack** vtr défaire ⟨suitcase⟩; déballer
⟨belongings⟩
**unpaid** adj ⟨bill, tax⟩ impayé/-e; ⟨debt⟩ non
acquitté/-e; ⟨work⟩ non rémunéré/-e; **~ leave**
congé m sans solde
**unpalatable** adj (a) ⟨truth, statistic⟩
inconfortable; ⟨advice⟩ dur/-e à avaler
(b) ⟨food⟩ qui n'a pas bon goût
**unparalleled** adj (a) ⟨strength, luxury⟩
sans égal; ⟨success⟩ hors pair
(b) (unprecedented) sans précédent
**unpasteurized** adj ⟨milk⟩ cru/-e; ⟨cheese⟩
au lait cru
**unperturbed** adj imperturbable
**unplanned** adj ⟨stoppage, increase⟩
imprévu/-e; ⟨pregnancy, baby⟩ non prévu/-e
**unpleasant** adj désagréable
**unpleasantness** n (a) (of odour, experience,
remark) caractère m désagréable

**(b)** (bad feeling) dissensions *fpl* (**between** entre)

**unplug** *vtr* débrancher ⟨*appliance*⟩; déboucher ⟨*sink*⟩

**unpopular** *adj* impopulaire

**unprecedented** *adj* sans précédent

**unpredictable** *adj* ⟨*event*⟩ imprévisible; ⟨*weather*⟩ incertain/-e; **he's ~** on ne sait jamais à quoi s'attendre avec lui

**unpremeditated** *adj* non prémédité/-e

**unprepared** *adj* **(a)** ⟨*person*⟩ pas préparé/-e (**for** pour)
**(b)** ⟨*speech*⟩ improvisé/-e; ⟨*translation*⟩ non préparé/-e

**unprepossessing** *adj* peu avenant/-e

**unpretentious** *adj* sans prétention

**unproductive** *adj* improductif/-ive

**unprofessional** *adj* peu professionnel/-elle

**unprofitable** *adj* non rentable

**unprotected** *adj* ⟨*person, sex, area*⟩ sans protection (**from** contre)

**unprovoked** *adj* ⟨*attack, aggression*⟩ délibéré/-e

**unqualified** *adj* **(a)** ⟨*person*⟩ non qualifié/-e
**(b)** ⟨*support, respect*⟩ inconditionnel/-elle; ⟨*success*⟩ grand/-e (*before n*)

**unquestionable** *adj* incontestable

**unravel** ⟨1⟩ *vtr* défaire ⟨*knitting*⟩; démêler ⟨*thread, mystery*⟩
⟨2⟩ *vi* ⟨*knitting*⟩ se défaire; ⟨*mystery, thread*⟩ se démêler; ⟨*plot*⟩ se dénouer

**unreal** *adj* **(a)** (not real) irréel/-éelle
**(b)** (colloq) (unbelievable) incroyable

**unrealistic** *adj* irréaliste, peu réaliste

**unreasonable** *adj* **(a)** ⟨*behaviour, expectation*⟩ qui n'est pas raisonnable; **he's being very ~ about it** il n'est vraiment pas raisonnable
**(b)** ⟨*price, demand*⟩ excessif/-ive

**unrecognizable** *adj* méconnaissable

**unrelated** *adj* **(a)** (not connected) sans rapport (**to** avec)
**(b)** (as family) **to be ~** ne pas avoir de lien de parenté

**unrelenting** *adj* ⟨*heat, stare, person*⟩ implacable; ⟨*pursuit, zeal*⟩ acharné/-e

**unreliable** *adj* ⟨*evidence*⟩ douteux/-euse; ⟨*method, employee*⟩ peu sûr/-e; ⟨*equipment*⟩ peu fiable; **she's very ~** on ne peut pas compter sur elle

**unrepentant** *adj* impénitent/-e

**unrequited** *adj* ⟨*love*⟩ sans retour

**unresolved** *adj* irrésolu/-e

**unrest** *n* **(a)** (dissatisfaction) malaise *m*
**(b)** (agitation) troubles *mpl*

**unrestricted** *adj* ⟨*access*⟩ libre (*before n*); ⟨*power*⟩ illimité/-e

**unrewarding** *adj* (unfulfilling) peu gratifiant/-e; (thankless) ingrat/-e

**unripe** *adj* ⟨*fruit*⟩ pas mûr/-e

**unrivalled** *adj* sans égal

**unroll** *vtr* dérouler

**unruffled** *adj* **(a)** (calm) imperturbable
**(b)** ⟨*hair*⟩ lisse

**unruly** *adj* indiscipliné/-e

**unsafe** *adj* **(a)** ⟨*environment*⟩ malsain/-e; ⟨*drinking water*⟩ non potable; ⟨*goods, working conditions*⟩ dangereux/-euse
**(b)** (threatened) **to feel ~** ne pas se sentir en sécurité

**unsaid** *adj* **to leave sth ~** passer qch sous silence

**unsatisfactory** *adj* insatisfaisant/-e

**unsatisfied** *adj* ⟨*person*⟩ insatisfait/-e; ⟨*need*⟩ inassouvi/-e

**unsatisfying** *adj* peu satisfaisant/-e

**unsavoury** (GB), **unsavory** (US) *adj* ⟨*individual*⟩ louche, répugnant/-e

**unscathed** *adj* indemne

**unscheduled** *adj* ⟨*appearance, speech*⟩ surprise (*after n*); ⟨*flight*⟩ supplémentaire; ⟨*stop*⟩ qui n'a pas été prévu

**unscrew** *vtr* dévisser

**unscrupulous** *adj* ⟨*person*⟩ sans scrupules; ⟨*tactic*⟩ peu scrupuleux/-euse

**unseat** *vtr* désarçonner ⟨*rider*⟩

**unseen** *adv* ⟨*escape, slip away*⟩ sans être vu/-e

**unselfconscious** *adj* **(a)** (natural) naturel/-elle
**(b)** (uninhibited) sans complexes

**unselfish** *adj* ⟨*person*⟩ qui pense aux autres; ⟨*act*⟩ désintéressé/-e

**unsentimental** *adj* ⟨*account, film*⟩ qui ne donne pas dans la sensiblerie; ⟨*person*⟩ qui ne fait pas de sentiment

**unsettled** *adj* **(a)** ⟨*weather, climate*⟩ instable; ⟨*person*⟩ perturbé/-e
**(b)** ⟨*account*⟩ impayé/-e

**unsettling** *adj* ⟨*question, experience*⟩ troublant/-e; ⟨*work of art*⟩ dérangeant/-e

**unshaken** *adj* ⟨*person*⟩ imperturbable (**by** devant); ⟨*belief*⟩ inébranlable

**unshaven** *adj* pas rasé/-e

**unskilled** *adj* ⟨*worker, labour*⟩ non qualifié/-e; ⟨*job, work*⟩ qui n'exige pas de qualification professionnelle

**unsociable** *adj* peu sociable

**unsocial** *adj* **to work ~ hours** travailler en dehors des heures normales

**unsolicited** *adj* non sollicité/-e

**unsophisticated** *adj* ⟨*person*⟩ sans façons; ⟨*mind*⟩ simple; ⟨*analysis*⟩ simpliste

**unspeakable** *adj* **(a)** (dreadful) ⟨*pain, sorrow*⟩ inexprimable; ⟨*act*⟩ innommable
**(b)** (inexpressible) ⟨joy⟩ indescriptible

**unspoiled, unspoilt** *adj* ⟨*landscape, town*⟩ préservé/-e et intact

**unspoken** *adj* **(a)** (secret) inexprimé/-e
**(b)** (implicit) tacite

**unstable** *adj* instable

**unsteady** *adj* ⟨*steps, legs, voice*⟩ ⋯⟶

chancelant/-e; ⟨*ladder*⟩ instable; ⟨*hand*⟩
tremblant/-e; **to be ~ on one's feet** marcher
de façon mal assurée

**unstoppable** *adj* ⟨*force, momentum*⟩
irrésistible; ⟨*athlete, leader*⟩ imbattable

**unstuck** *adj* **to come ~** ⟨*stamp*⟩ se
décoller; ⟨*person*⟩ connaître un échec

**unsubstantiated** *adj* non corroboré/-e

**unsuccessful** *adj* **(a)** ⟨*attempt,
campaign*⟩ infructueux/-euse; ⟨*novel, film*⟩
sans succès; ⟨*effort, search*⟩ vain/-e; **to be ~**
⟨*attempt*⟩ échouer
**(b)** ⟨*candidate*⟩ (for job) malchanceux/-euse; (in
election) malheureux/-euse; ⟨*businessperson*⟩
malchanceux/-euse; ⟨*artist*⟩ inconnu/-e; **to be
~ in doing** ne pas réussir à faire

**unsuccessfully** *adv* ⟨*try*⟩ en vain;
⟨*challenge, bid*⟩ sans succès

**unsuitable** *adj* ⟨*location, clothing,
accommodation, time*⟩ inapproprié/-e;
⟨*moment*⟩ inopportun/-e; **to be ~** ne pas
convenir (**for sb** à qn); **to be ~ for a job** ne
pas convenir pour un travail

**unsupervised** *adj* ⟨*activity*⟩ non
encadré/-e; ⟨*child*⟩ laissé/-e sans surveillance

**unsure** *adj* peu sûr/-e (**of** de); **to be ~
about how/why/where** ne pas savoir très
bien comment/pourquoi/où; **to be ~ of
oneself** manquer de confiance en soi

**unsuspecting** *adj* ⟨*person*⟩ naïf/-ïve;
⟨*public*⟩ non averti/-e

**unsweetened** *adj* sans sucre, non
sucré/-e

**unsympathetic** *adj* **(a)** (uncaring) ⟨*person,
attitude, tone*⟩ peu compatissant/-e
**(b)** (unattractive) ⟨*person, character*⟩
antipathique

**untaxed** *adj* ⟨*goods*⟩ non taxé/-e; ⟨*car*⟩ sans
vignette

**untenable** *adj* ⟨*position*⟩ intenable; ⟨*claim,
argument*⟩ indéfendable

**unthinkable** *adj* impensable

**untidily** *adv* ⟨*scattered, strewn*⟩ en
désordre; **~ dressed** habillé/-e de façon
débraillée

**untidy** *adj* ⟨*person*⟩ (in habits) désordonné/-e;
(in appearance) peu soigné/-e; ⟨*habits, clothes*⟩
négligé/-e; ⟨*room*⟩ en désordre

**untie** *vtr* défaire, dénouer ⟨*knot, rope, laces*⟩;
défaire ⟨*parcel*⟩; délier ⟨*hands, hostage*⟩

**until** (*also* **till**)

───────────────────────────────
■ **Note** When used as a preposition in positive
sentences, *until* is translated by *jusqu'à*: *they're
staying until Monday* = ils restent jusqu'à lundi.
– Remember that *jusqu'à* + *le* becomes *jusqu'au*
and *jusqu'à* + *les* becomes *jusqu'aux*: *until the
right moment* = jusqu'au bon moment; *until the
exams* = jusqu'aux examens.
– In negative sentences, *not until* is translated
by *ne…pas avant*: *I can't see you until Friday* =
je ne peux pas vous voir avant vendredi.
– When used as a conjunction in positive
sentences, *until* is translated by *jusqu'à ce que* +
───────────────────────────────

*subjunctive*: *we'll stay here until Maya comes
back* = nous resterons ici jusqu'à ce que Maya
revienne.
– In negative sentences where the two verbs
have different subjects, *not until* is translated by
*ne…pas avant que* + *subjunctive*: *we won't leave
until Maya comes back* = nous ne partirons pas
avant que Maya revienne.
– In negative sentences where the two verbs
have the same subject, *not until* is translated by
*pas avant de* + *infinitive*: *we won't leave until
we've seen Claire* = nous ne partirons pas avant
d'avoir vu Claire.
– For more examples and particular usages, see
the entry below.
───────────────────────────────

**1** *prep* jusqu'à; (after negative verb) avant; **~
Tuesday** jusqu'à mardi; **~ the sixties**
jusqu'aux années soixante; **~ now** jusqu'à
présent; **~ then** jusqu'à ce moment-là,
jusque-là; (up) **~ 1901** jusqu'en *or* jusqu'à
1901; **valid** (up) **~ April 2006** valable jusqu'en
avril 2006; **to work from Monday ~ Saturday**
travailler du lundi au samedi
**2** *conj* jusqu'à ce que (+ *subjunctive*); (in
negative constructions) avant que (+ *subjunctive*),
avant de (+ *infinitive*); **we'll stay ~ a solution
is reached** nous resterons jusqu'à ce que
nous trouvions une solution; **let's watch TV
~ he's ready** regardons la télévision en
attendant qu'il soit prêt; **I'll wait ~ I get back**
j'attendrai d'être rentré (before doing pour
faire); **she waited ~ they were alone** elle a
attendu qu'ils soient seuls

**untimely** *adj* ⟨*arrival, announcement*⟩
inopportun/-e; ⟨*death*⟩ prématuré/-e

**untold** *adj* (not quantifiable); **~ millions** des
millions et des millions; **~ damage**
d'énormes dégâts; (endless) ⟨*misery, joy*⟩
indicible

**untrained** *adj* ⟨*worker*⟩ sans formation;
⟨*eye*⟩ inexercé/-e; **to be ~** n'avoir aucune
formation

**untranslatable** *adj* intraduisible (**into**
en)

**untroubled** *adj* ⟨*face, life*⟩ paisible; **to be
~** (by news) ne pas être troublé/-e (**by** par)

**untrue** *adj* faux/fausse

**untrustworthy** *adj* ⟨*information*⟩
douteux/-euse; ⟨*person*⟩ indigne de confiance

**unused¹** *adj* **to be ~ to sth/to doing** ne pas
être habitué/-e à qch/à faire

**unused²** *adj* ⟨*machine, building*⟩
inutilisé/-e; ⟨*stamp*⟩ neuf/neuve

**unusual** *adj* ⟨*colour, animal, flower*⟩ peu
commun/-e; ⟨*feature, occurrence, skill*⟩ peu
commun/-e, inhabituel/-elle; ⟨*dish, dress,
person*⟩ original/-e; **it is ~ to find/see** il est
rare de trouver/voir; **there's nothing ~
about it** cela n'a rien d'extraordinaire

**unusually** *adv* exceptionnellement

**unwanted** *adj* ⟨*goods, produce*⟩
superflu/-e; ⟨*pet*⟩ abandonné/-e; ⟨*visitor*⟩
indésirable; ⟨*child*⟩ non souhaité/-e; **to feel ~**
se sentir de trop

**unwarranted** *adj* injustifié/-e

**unwary** n the ~ les imprudents mpl

**unwelcome** adj ⟨visitor, interruption⟩ importun/-e; ⟨news⟩ fâcheux/-euse

**unwell** adj souffrant/-e; **he is feeling ~** il ne se sent pas très bien

**unwilling** adj ⟨attention, departure⟩ forcé/-e; **he is ~ to do it** il n'est pas disposé à le faire; (stronger) il ne veut pas le faire

**unwillingness** n réticence f **(to do à faire)**

**unwind** **1** vtr dérouler ⟨cable, bandage, scarf⟩
**2** vi **(a)** ⟨tape, cable, scarf⟩ se dérouler
**(b)** (relax) se relaxer

**unwise** adj ⟨choice, loan, decision⟩ peu judicieux/-ieuse; ⟨person⟩ imprudent/-e

**unwisely** adv imprudemment

**unwittingly** adv (innocently) innocemment; (without wanting to) involontairement

**unworthy** adj indigne **(of de)**

**unwrap** vtr déballer ⟨parcel⟩

**unwritten** adj ⟨rule, agreement⟩ tacite

**unzip** vtr **(a)** (open) défaire la fermeture à glissière de ⟨garment, bag⟩
**(b)** (Comput) dézipper, décompresser

**up** **1** adj **(a)** (out of bed) **she's ~** elle est levée; **we were ~ very late last night** nous nous sommes couchés très tard hier soir; **they were ~ all night** ils ont veillé toute la nuit; **I was still ~ at 2 am** j'étais toujours debout à 2 heures du matin
**(b)** (higher in amount, level) **sales are ~ (by 10%)** les ventes ont augmenté (de 10%); **numbers of students are ~** le nombre d'étudiants est en hausse
**(c)** (colloq) (wrong) **what's ~?** qu'est-ce qui se passe?; **what's ~ with him?** qu'est-ce qu'il a?
**(d)** (erected, affixed) **the notice is ~ on the board** l'annonce est affichée sur le panneau; **is the tent ~?** est-ce que la tente est déjà montée?; **he had his hand ~ for five minutes** il a gardé la main levée pendant cinq minutes
**(e)** (open) **the blinds were ~** les stores étaient levés; **when the lever is ~ the machine is off** si le levier est vers le haut la machine est arrêtée
**(f)** (finished) **'time's ~!'** 'c'est l'heure!'; **when the four days were ~** à la fin des quatre jours
**(g)** (facing upwards) **'this side ~'** 'haut'; **she was floating face ~** elle flottait sur le dos
**(h)** (pinned up) **her hair was ~** elle avait les cheveux relevés
**2** adv **(a)** **here/there** là-haut; **~ on the wardrobe** sur l'armoire; **~ in the tree/the clouds** dans l'arbre/les nuages; **~ in London** à Londres; **~ to/in Scotland** en Écosse; **~ North** au Nord; **four floors ~** quatre étages au-dessus; **on the second shelf ~** sur la deuxième étagère en partant du bas
**(b)** (ahead) d'avance; **to be four points ~ (on sb)** avoir quatre points d'avance (sur qn)

**(c)** (upwards) **T-shirts from £2 ~** des T-shirts à partir de deux livres
**3** prep **~ the tree** dans l'arbre; **the library is ~ the stairs** la bibliothèque se trouve en haut de l'escalier; **he ran ~ the stairs** il a monté l'escalier en courant; **he lives just ~ the road** il habite juste à côté; **to walk/drive ~ the road** remonter la rue; **he put it ~ his sleeve** il l'a mis dans sa manche
**4** **up above** phr au-dessus; **~ above sth** au-dessus de qch
**5** **up against** phr contre ⟨wall⟩; **to come ~ against** rencontrer ⟨opposition⟩
**6** **up and about** phr debout; **to be ~ and about again** être de nouveau sur pied
**7** **up and down** phr **(a)** (to and fro) **to walk ~ and down** aller et venir, faire les cent pas
**(b)** (throughout) **~ and down the country** dans tout le pays
**8** **up to** phr **(a)** (to particular level) jusqu'à; **~ to here/there** jusqu'ici/jusque là
**(b)** (as many as) jusqu'à, près de; **~ to 20 people/50 dollars** jusqu'à 20 personnes/50 dollars
**(c)** (until) jusqu'à; **~ to 1964** jusqu'en 1964; **~ to 10.30 pm** jusqu'à 22 h 30; **~ to now** jusqu'à maintenant
**(d)** **I'm not ~ to it** (not capable) je n'en suis pas capable; (not well enough) je n'en ai pas la force; (can't face it) je n'en ai pas le courage
**(e)** **it's ~ to him to do so** c'est à lui de faire; **it's ~ to you!** c'est à toi de décider!
**(f)** (doing) **what is he ~ to?** qu'est-ce qu'il fait?; **they're ~ to something** ils mijotent quelque chose (colloq)
IDIOMS **to be one ~ on sb** faire mieux que qn; **to be (well) ~ on** s'y connaître en ⟨art, history⟩; être au courant de ⟨news⟩; **the ~s and downs** les hauts et les bas **(of de)**

**up and coming** adj prometteur/-euse

**upbeat** adj optimiste

**upbringing** n éducation f

**update** vtr **(a)** (revise) mettre or remettre [qch] à jour ⟨database, information⟩; actualiser ⟨price, value⟩
**(b)** (modernize) moderniser
**(c)** (inform) mettre [qn] au courant **(on de)**

**upfront** adj (colloq) **(a)** (frank) franc/franche
**(b)** ⟨money⟩ payé/-e d'avance

**upgrade** **1** n (new version) nouvelle version f, mise f à jour; (in tourism) surclassement m
**2** vtr **(a)** (modernize) moderniser; (improve) améliorer
**(b)** (Comput) améliorer ⟨software, hardware⟩
**(c)** (raise) promouvoir ⟨person⟩; revaloriser ⟨job⟩

**upheaval** n **(a)** (disturbance) bouleversement m
**(b)** (instability) (political, emotional) bouleversements mpl; (physical) remue-ménage m inv

**uphill** **1** adj **(a)** ⟨road⟩ qui monte; **~ slope** côte f, montée f
**(b)** ⟨task⟩ difficile
**2** adv **to go/walk ~** monter

**u**

**uphold** *vtr* soutenir ‹*right*›; faire respecter ‹*law*›; confirmer ‹*decision*›

**upholstery** *n* (a) (covering) revêtement *m* (b) (stuffing) rembourrage *m*

**upkeep** *n* (a) (of property) entretien *m* (of de) (b) (cost) frais *mpl* d'entretien

**uplifting** *adj* tonique

**upload** *vtr* to ∼ sth to a server télécharger qch vers un serveur

**upmarket** *adj* ‹*car, hotel*› haut de gamme; ‹*area*› riche

**upon** *prep* (a) (on) sur (b) (linking two nouns) **thousands** ∼ **thousands of people** des milliers et des milliers de personnes

**upper** ⓵ *n* (of shoe) empeigne *f* ⓶ *adj* (a) ‹*shelf, cupboard*› du haut; ‹*floor, deck, lip*› supérieur/-e; ‹*teeth*› du haut (b) (in rank, scale) supérieur/-e (c) **the** ∼ **limit** la limite maximale (**on** de) IDIOMS **to have/get the** ∼ **hand** avoir/ prendre le dessus

**upper case** *adj* ∼ **letters** (lettres *fpl*) majuscules *fpl*

**upper class** *n* (*pl* ∼**es**) **the** ∼, **the** ∼**es** l'aristocratie *f* et la haute bourgeoisie

**uppermost** *adj* (a) (highest) ‹*branch*› le plus haut/la plus haute; (in rank) ‹*echelon*› le plus élevé/la plus élevée (b) **to be** ∼ **in sb's mind** être au premier plan des préoccupations de qn

**upper sixth** *n* (GB) (Sch) ≈ (classe *f*) terminale *f*

**upright** ⓵ *adj* (a) (physically) droit/-e; **to stay** ∼ ‹*person*› rester debout (b) (morally) droit/-e ⓶ *adv* **to stand** ∼ se tenir droit; **to sit** ∼ (action) se redresser

**uprising** *n* soulèvement *m* (**against** contre)

**uproar** *n* (noise) tumulte *m*; (protest) protestations *fpl*

**uproot** *vtr* déraciner

**upset** ⓵ *n* (a) (surprise, setback) revers *m* (b) (upheaval) bouleversement *m* (c) (distress) peine *f* (d) **to have a stomach** ∼ avoir l'estomac détraqué ⓶ *adj* **to be** *or* **feel** ∼ (distressed) être très affecté/-e; (annoyed) être contrarié/-e; **to get** ∼ (angry) se fâcher (**about** pour); (distressed) se tracasser (**about** pour) ⓷ *vtr* (a) (distress) ‹*sight, news*› bouleverser; ‹*person*› faire de la peine à (b) (annoy) contrarier (c) bouleverser ‹*plan*›; déjouer ‹*calculations*› (d) (destabilize) rompre ‹*balance*› (e) (Med) rendre [qn] malade ‹*person*›; perturber ‹*digestion*›

**upsetting** *adj* (distressing) navrant/-e; (annoying) contrariant/-e

**upside down** ⓵ *adj* à l'envers ⓶ *adv* à l'envers; **to turn the house** ∼ mettre la maison sens dessus dessous

**upstage** *vtr* éclipser

**upstairs** ⓵ *n* haut *m* ⓶ *adj* ‹*room*› du haut; **an** ∼ **bedroom** une chambre à l'étage ⓷ *adv* en haut; **to go** ∼ monter (l'escalier)

**upstart** *n, adj* arriviste (*mf*)

**upstream** *adv* ‹*travel*› vers l'amont; ∼ **from here** en amont d'ici

**uptake** *n* IDIOMS **to be quick/slow on the** ∼ (colloq) comprendre/ne pas comprendre vite

**uptight** *adj* (colloq) (a) (tense) tendu/-e (b) (inhibited) coincé/-e (colloq)

**up-to-date** *adj* (a) ‹*music, clothes*› à la mode; ‹*equipment*› moderne (b) ‹*records, timetable*› à jour; ‹*information*› récent/-e (c) (informed) ‹*person*› au courant (**with** de)

**up-to-the-minute** *adj* ‹*information*› dernier/-ière

**upward** ⓵ *adj* ‹*push, movement*› vers le haut; ‹*path, road*› qui monte; ‹*trend*› à la hausse ⓶ *adv* (also **upwards**) ‹*look, point*› vers le haut; **to go** *or* **move** ∼ monter; **from £10** ∼ à partir de 10 livres sterling

**upwardly mobile** *adj* en pleine ascension sociale

**upwards** = UPWARD 2

**uranium** *n* uranium *m*

**Uranus** *pr n* Uranus *f*

**urban** *adj* urbain/-e

**urban planning** *n* urbanisme *m*

**urban sprawl** *n* mitage *m*

**urchin** *n* gamin *m*

**Urdu** *n* urdu *m*

**urge** ⓵ *n* forte envie *f*, désir *m* (**to do** de faire) ⓶ *vtr* conseiller vivement, préconiser ‹*caution, restraint, resistance*›; **to** ∼ **sb to do** conseiller vivement à qn de faire; (stronger) pousser qn à faire

**urgency** *n* (of situation, appeal, request) urgence *f*; (of voice, tone) insistance *f*; **a matter of** ∼ une affaire urgente

**urgent** *adj* (a) (pressing) ‹*case, need*› urgent/-e, pressant/-e; ‹*message, demand*› urgent/-e; ‹*meeting, measures*› d'urgence (b) ‹*request, tone*› insistant/-e

**urgently** *adv* ‹*request*› d'urgence; ‹*plead*› instamment

**urinal** *n* (place) urinoir *m*; (fixture) urinal *m*

**urinate** *vi* uriner

**urine** *n* urine *f*

**URL** *n* (*abbr* = **Unified Resource Locator**) adresse *f* URL

**urn** *n* urne *f*

**us** *pron* nous; **she knows** ∼ elle nous connaît; **both of** ∼ tous/toutes les deux; **every single one of** ∼ chacun/-e d'entre nous; **some of** ∼ quelques-uns/-unes d'entre nous; **she's one of** ∼ elle est des nôtres

**US** *pr n* (*abbr* = **United States**) USA *mpl*

**USA** *pr n* (*abbr* = **United States of America**) USA *mpl*

**use** 1 *n* **(a)** (act of using) (of substance, object, machine) emploi *m*, utilisation *f* (of de); (of word, expression) emploi *m*, usage *m* (of de); **for the ~ of** à l'usage de ⟨*customer, staff*⟩; **for my own ~** pour mon usage personnel; **to make ~ of sth** utiliser qch; **to put sth to good ~** tirer parti de qch; **while the machine is in ~** lorsque la machine est en service *or* en fonctionnement; **to have the ~ of** avoir l'usage de ⟨*house, car, kitchen*⟩; avoir la jouissance de ⟨*garden*⟩; **to lose the ~ of one's legs** perdre l'usage de ses jambes **(b)** (way of using) (of resource, object, material) utilisation *f*; (of term) emploi *m*; **to have no further ~ for sb/sth** ne plus avoir besoin de qn/qch **(c)** (usefulness) **to be of ~** être utile (**to** à); **to be (of) no ~** ⟨*object*⟩ ne servir à rien; ⟨*person*⟩ n'être bon/bonne à rien; **what's the ~ of crying?** à quoi bon pleurer?; **it's no ~ (he won't listen)** c'est inutile (il n'écoutera pas)

2 *vtr* **(a)** se servir de, utiliser ⟨*object, car, room, money*⟩; employer ⟨*method, word*⟩; profiter de, saisir ⟨*opportunity*⟩; faire jouer ⟨*influence*⟩; avoir recours à ⟨*blackmail*⟩; utiliser ⟨*knowledge, talent*⟩; **to ~ sb/sth as** se servir de qn/qch comme; **to ~ sth to do** se servir de qch pour faire **(b)** (consume) consommer ⟨*fuel, food*⟩; utiliser ⟨*water, leftovers*⟩ **(c)** (exploit) se servir de ⟨*person*⟩

3 **used** *pp adj* ⟨*car*⟩ d'occasion; ⟨*envelope*⟩ qui a déjà servi

■ **use up** finir ⟨*food*⟩; dépenser ⟨*money*⟩; épuiser ⟨*supplies*⟩

**used**

■ **Note** To translate *used to do*, use the imperfect tense in French: *he used to live in York* = il habitait York.
– To emphasize a contrast between past and present, you can use *avant*: *I used to love sport* = avant, j'adorais le sport.

1 *modal aux* **I ~ to read a lot** je lisais beaucoup; **she ~ to smoke, didn't she?** elle fumait avant, non?; **she doesn't smoke now, but she ~ to** elle ne fume plus maintenant, mais elle fumait avant; **there ~ to be a pub here** il y avait un pub ici (dans le temps)

2 *adj* **to be ~ to sth** avoir l'habitude de qch, être habitué/-e à qch; **to get ~ to**

s'habituer à; **I'm not ~ to it** je n'ai pas l'habitude; **you'll get ~ to it** tu t'y habitueras

**useful** *adj* utile

**useless** *adj* **(a)** (not helpful) inutile **(b)** (not able to be used) inutilisable **(c)** (colloq) (incompetent) incapable, nul/nulle (colloq)

**user** *n* (of public service) usager *m*; (of product, machine) utilisateur/-trice *m/f*

**user-friendly** *adj* (Comput) convivial/-e; (gen) facile à utiliser

**user group** *n* groupe *m* d'utilisateurs

**usher** *vtr* conduire, escorter; **to ~ sb in/out** faire entrer/sortir qn

**usherette** *n* ouvreuse *f*

**USSR** *pr n* (*abbr* = **Union of Soviet Socialist Republics**) URSS *f*

**usual** *adj* (gen) habituel/-elle; ⟨*word, term*⟩ usuel/-elle; **it is ~ for sb to do** c'est normal pour qn de faire; **it is ~ to do** il est d'usage de faire; **as ~** comme d'habitude; **more/less than ~** plus/moins que d'habitude

**usually** *adv* d'habitude, normalement

**utensil** *n* ustensile *m*

**uterus** *n* utérus *m*

**utility** 1 *n* **(a)** (usefulness) utilité *f* **(b)** (*also* **public ~**) (service) service *m* public

2 **utilities** *n pl* (US) factures *fpl*

**utility company** *n* société *f* chargée d'assurer un service public

**utmost** 1 *n* **to do** *or* **try one's ~ to do** faire tout son possible pour faire; **to the ~ of one's abilities** au maximum de ses capacités

2 *adj* ⟨*caution, ease, secrecy*⟩ le plus grand/la plus grande (*before n*); ⟨*limit*⟩ extrême; **it is of the ~ importance that** il est extrêmement important que (+ *subjunctive*)

**Utopia** *n* utopie *f*

**utter** 1 *adj* ⟨*disaster, boredom, despair*⟩ total/-e; ⟨*honesty, sincerity*⟩ absolu/-e; ⟨*fool, stranger*⟩ parfait/-e (*before n*)

2 *vtr* prononcer ⟨*word, curse*⟩; pousser ⟨*cry*⟩; émettre ⟨*sound*⟩

**utterly** *adv* complètement; ⟨*condemn*⟩ avec vigueur

**U-turn** *n* demi-tour *m*; (figurative) volte-face *f inv*

**UV** *adj* (*abbr* = **ultraviolet**) ⟨*light, ray, radiation*⟩ ultraviolet/-ette

**u**

# Vv

**v**, **V** n (a) (letter) v, V m
(b) **v** (abbr = **versus**) contre

**vacancy** n (a) (room) 'vacancies' 'chambres
libres'; 'no vacancies' 'complet'
(b) (unfilled job) poste m à pourvoir, poste m
vacant

**vacant** adj (a) ⟨flat, room, seat⟩ libre,
disponible; ⟨office, land⟩ inoccupé/-e
(b) ⟨job, post⟩ vacant/-e, à pourvoir
(c) ⟨look, stare⟩ absent/-e; ⟨expression⟩ vide

**vacant possession** n jouissance f
immédiate

**vacate** vtr quitter ⟨house, premises, job⟩

**vacation** n vacances fpl; **on** ∼ en vacances

**vacationer** n (US) vacancier/-ière m/f

**vaccinate** vtr vacciner (**against** contre)

**vaccination** n vaccination f (**against**
contre)

**vaccine** n vaccin m (**against** contre)

**vacillate** vi hésiter

**vacuum** ①  n (a) (gen) vide m
(b) (also ∼ **cleaner**) aspirateur m
② vtr passer [qch] à l'aspirateur ⟨carpet⟩;
passer l'aspirateur dans ⟨room⟩

**vacuum pack** vtr emballer [qch] sous
vide

**vagrant** n, adj vagabond/-e (m/f)

**vague** adj (a) (gen) vague; **to be** ∼ **about**
rester vague sur or évasif/-ive au sujet de
⟨plans, past⟩
(b) (distracted) ⟨person, expression⟩ distrait/-e

**vaguely** adv (a) (gen) vaguement
(b) (distractedly) ⟨smile, gaze⟩ d'un air distrait
or vague

**vain** ① adj (a) (conceited) vaniteux/-euse,
vain/-e ⟨after n⟩
(b) (futile) ⟨attempt, promise, hope⟩ vain/-e
⟨before n⟩
② **in vain** phr en vain

**valentine card** n carte f de la
Saint-Valentin

**Valentine('s) Day** n la Saint-Valentin

**valet** n (a) (employee) valet m de chambre
(b) (US) (rack) valet m de nuit

**valet parking** n service m de voiturier

**valiant** adj ⟨soldier⟩ vaillant/-e; ⟨attempt⟩
courageux/-euse

**valid** adj (a) ⟨passport, licence⟩ valide;
⟨ticket, offer⟩ valable (**for** pour)
(b) ⟨argument, excuse⟩ valable; ⟨complaint⟩
fondé/-e; ⟨point, comment⟩ pertinent/-e

**validate** vtr (a) prouver le bien-fondé de
⟨claim, theory⟩
(b) valider ⟨document, passport⟩

**valley** n vallée f; (small) vallon m

**valour** (GB), **valor** (US) n bravoure f

**valuable** adj (a) ⟨object, asset⟩ de valeur;
**to be** ∼ avoir de la valeur; **a very** ∼ **ring** une
bague de grande valeur
(b) ⟨advice, information, lesson, member⟩
précieux/-ieuse

**valuables** n pl objets mpl de valeur

**valuation** n (of house, land, company)
évaluation f; (of antique, art) expertise f; **to
have a** ∼ **done on sth** faire évaluer qch

**value** ① n valeur f; novelty ∼ caractère
nouveau; **to be good** ∼ avoir un bon rapport
qualité-prix; **to get** ∼ **for money** en avoir
pour son argent
② vtr (a) évaluer ⟨house, asset, company⟩ (**at**
à); expertiser ⟨antique, jewel, painting⟩
(b) (appreciate) apprécier ⟨person, friendship,
opinion, help⟩; tenir à ⟨independence, life⟩

**value pack** n lot m économique

**valve** n (a) (in machine, engine) soupape f; (on
tyre, football) valve f
(b) (Anat) valvule f

**van** n (a) (small, for deliveries) fourgonnette f,
camionnette f; (larger, for removals) fourgon m
(b) (US) (camper) auto-caravane f,
camping-car m

**vandal** n vandale mf

**vandalism** n vandalisme m

**vandalize** vtr vandaliser

**van driver** n chauffeur m de camionnette

**vanguard** n avant-garde f; **in the** ∼ à
l'avant-garde

**vanilla** n vanille f

**vanish** vi disparaître (**from** de); **to** ∼ **into
thin air** se volatiliser

**vanity** n vanité f

**vantage point** n point m de vue, position
f élevée

**vaporizer** n vaporisateur m

**vapour** (GB), **vapor** (US) n vapeur f

**vapour trail** n traînée f de condensation,
traînée f d'avion

**variable** n, adj variable (f)

**variance** n **to be at** ∼ **with** ne pas
concorder avec ⟨evidence, facts⟩

**variant** n variante f (**of** de; **on** par rapport
à)

**variation** n (a) (change) variation f,
différence f (**in, of** de)
(b) (new version) variante f (**of** de); (in music)
variation f (**on** sur)

**varied** adj varié/-e

**variety** n (a) (diversity, range) variété f (**in, of**
de); **for a** ∼ **of reasons** pour diverses
raisons; **a** ∼ **of sizes/colours** un grand choix
de tailles/de coloris
(b) (type) type m; (of plant) variété f

**variety show** n spectacle de variétés
**various** adj (a) (different) différents/-es
(before n)
(b) (several) divers/-es
**varnish** ⓵ n vernis m
⓶ vtr vernir ⟨woodwork⟩; **to ~ one's nails**
se vernir les ongles
**vary** ⓵ vtr varier ⟨menu, programme⟩; faire
varier ⟨temperature⟩; changer de ⟨method,
pace, route⟩
⓶ vi varier (**with, according to** selon); **it
varies from one town to another** cela varie
d'une ville à l'autre
**varying** adj variable
**vase** n vase m; **flower ~** vase à fleurs
**vast** adj (a) ⟨amount, sum, improvement,
difference⟩ énorme; **the ~ majority** la très
grande majorité
(b) ⟨room, area, plain⟩ vaste (before n),
immense
**vat** n cuve f; **beer/wine ~** cuve à bière/vin
**VAT** n (GB) (abbr = **value-added tax**)
TVA f, taxe f à la valeur ajoutée
**Vatican** pr n Vatican m; **~ City** cité f du
Vatican
**vault** ⓵ n (a) (roof) voûte f
(b) (also **~s**) (of house, for wine) cave f; (of
bank) chambre f forte; (for safe-deposit boxes)
salle f des coffres
⓶ vtr sauter par-dessus ⟨fence, bar⟩
⓷ vi sauter (**over** par-dessus)
**VCR** n (abbr = **video cassette
recorder**) magnétoscope m
**VD** n (abbr = **venereal disease**) MST f
**VDU** n (abbr = **visual display unit**)
écran m de visualisation
**veal** n veau m
**veer** vi ⟨ship⟩ virer; (also **~ off**) ⟨person,
road⟩ tourner; **to ~ off course** dévier de sa
route
**vegan** n, adj végétalien/-ienne (m/f)
**veganism** n végétalisme m
**vegeburger**® ▶ VEGGIE BURGER
**vegetable** ⓵ n légume m
⓶ adj ⟨soup, patch⟩ de légumes; ⟨fat, oil⟩
végétal/-e; **~ garden** potager m
**vegetarian** n, adj végétarien/-ienne (m/f)
**vegetarianism** n végétarisme m
**vegetate** vi végéter
**vegetation** n végétation f
**veggie burger** n croquette f pour
végétariens
**vehement** adj véhément/-e
**vehicle** n véhicule m
**veil** ⓵ n (gen, figurative) voile m; (on hat)
voilette f
⓶ vtr ⟨mist, cloud⟩ voiler
**veiled** adj voilé/-e
**vein** n (blood vessel) veine f; (on insect wing,
leaf) nervure f; (in cheese) veinure f; (of ore)
veine f
**velocity** n vélocité f
**velour(s)** n velours m

**velvet** n velours m; **crushed ~** velours
frappé
**velvety** adj velouté/-e
**vending machine** n distributeur m
automatique
**vendor** n (a) (in street, kiosk) marchand/-e
m/f
(b) (as opposed to buyer) vendeur/-euse m/f
**veneer** n placage m; (figurative) vernis m
**venereal disease** n maladie f
vénérienne
**venetian blind** n store m vénitien
**Venezuela** pr n Venezuela m
**vengeance** n vengeance f; **with a ~** de
plus belle
**Venice** pr n Venise f
**venison** n (viande f de) chevreuil m
**venom** n venim m
**venomous** adj venimeux/-euse
**vent** ⓵ n (outlet for gas, pressure) bouche f,
conduit m; **air ~** bouche d'aération; **to give
~ to** décharger ⟨anger, feelings⟩
⓶ vtr décharger ⟨anger, frustration⟩ (**on**
sur)
**ventilate** vtr aérer ⟨room⟩
**ventilation** n (a) (gen) aération f,
ventilation f
(b) (of patient) ventilation f artificielle
**ventilator** n (for patient) respirateur m
artificiel
**ventriloquist** n ventriloque mf
**venture** ⓵ n (a) (undertaking) aventure f,
entreprise f; **a commercial ~** une entreprise
commerciale
(b) (experiment) essai m
⓶ vtr hasarder ⟨opinion, suggestion⟩; **to ~
to do** se risquer à faire
⓷ vi **to ~ into** s'aventurer dans ⟨place,
street, city⟩; **to ~ out(doors)** s'aventurer
dehors
**venture capital** n capital-risque m
**venue** n lieu m
**Venus** pr n Vénus f
**verb** n verbe m
**verbal** adj verbal/-e
**verbatim** ⓵ adj ⟨report, account⟩
textuel/-elle
⓶ adv ⟨describe, record⟩ mot pour mot
**verbose** adj verbeux/-euse
**verdict** n (a) (Law) verdict m; **a ~ of guilty/
not guilty** un verdict positif/négatif
(b) (figurative) (opinion) verdict m; **well, what's
the ~?** (colloq) eh bien, qu'est-ce que tu en
penses?
**verge** n (a) (GB) (by road) accotement m,
bas-côté m
(b) (brink) **on the ~ of** au bord de ⟨tears⟩; au
seuil de ⟨adolescence, death⟩; **on the ~ of
doing** sur le point de faire
■ **verge on** friser ⟨panic, stupidity,
contempt⟩
**verification** n vérification f
**verify** vtr vérifier

**V**

**vermicelli** *n* vermicelles *mpl*
**vermilion** *n, adj* vermillon (*m*) *inv*
**vermin** *n* (a) (rodents) animaux *mpl* nuisibles
(b) (lice, insects) vermine *f*
**verruca** *n* verrue *f* plantaire
**versatile** *adj* (a) ⟨person⟩ plein/-e de ressources, aux talents divers (*after n*); ⟨mind⟩ souple
(b) ⟨vehicle⟩ polyvalent/-e; ⟨equipment⟩ à usages multiples
**verse** *n* (a) (poems) poésie *f*
(b) (form) vers *mpl*; **in ~** en vers
(c) (part of poem) strophe *f*; (of song) couplet *m*
**version** *n* version *f* (**of** de)
**versus** *prep* contre
**vertebra** *n* vertèbre *f*
**vertebrate** *n* vertébré *m*
**vertical** *adj* vertical/-e; **a ~ drop** un à-pic
**vertigo** *n* vertige *m*; **to get ~** avoir le vertige
**verve** *n* brio *m*, verve *f*
**very** 1 *adj* (a) (actual) même (*after n*); **this ~ second** immédiatement
(b) (ideal) **the ~ person I need** exactement la personne qu'il me faut
(c) (ultimate) tout/-e; **from the ~ beginning** depuis le tout début; **at the ~ front** tout devant; **on the ~ edge** à l'extrême bord
(d) (mere) ⟨mention, thought, word⟩ seul/-e (*before n*); **the ~ idea!** quelle idée!
2 *adv* (a) (extremely) très; **I'm ~ sorry** je suis vraiment désolé; **~ well** très bien; **that's all ~ well but who's going to pay for it?** c'est bien beau, tout ça, mais qui va payer?; **~ much** beaucoup; **I didn't eat ~ much** je n'ai pas mangé grand-chose
(b) (absolutely) **the ~ best/worst thing** de loin la meilleure/pire chose; **at the ~ latest** au plus tard; **at the ~ least** tout au moins; **the ~ next day** le lendemain même; **a car of your ~ own** ta propre voiture
**vessel** *n* (a) (ship) vaisseau *m*
(b) (Anat) **blood ~** vaisseau *m* sanguin
(c) (container) vase *m*
**vest** *n* (a) (underwear) maillot *m* de corps
(b) (for sport, fashion) débardeur *m*
(c) (US) (waistcoat) gilet *m*
**vested interest** *n* **to have a ~** être personnellement intéressé/-e (**in** dans)
**vestige** *n* vestige *m*
**vet** 1 *n* (a) (*abbr* = **veterinary surgeon**) vétérinaire *mf*
(b) (US) (colloq) (Mil) ancien combattant *m*, vétéran *m*
2 *vtr* mener une enquête approfondie sur ⟨person⟩; passer [qch] en revue ⟨plan⟩; approuver ⟨publication⟩
**veteran** 1 *n* vétéran *m*
2 *adj* ⟨sportsman, politician⟩ chevronné/-e
**veterinarian** *n* (US) vétérinaire *mf*
**veterinary surgeon** *n* vétérinaire *mf*
**veterinary surgery** *n* clinique *f* vétérinaire

**veto** 1 *n* (a) (practice) veto *m*
(b) (right) droit *m* de veto (**over, on** sur)
2 *vtr* mettre *or* opposer son veto à
**vetting** *n* contrôle *m*
**vex** *vtr* (annoy) contrarier; (worry) tracasser
**vexed** *adj* (a) (annoyed) mécontent/-e (**with** de)
(b) ⟨question, issue⟩ épineux/-euse
**VHF** *n* (*abbr* = **very high frequency**) VHF
**via** *prep* (a) (by way of) (on ticket, timetable) via; (other contexts) en passant par; **we came ~ Paris** nous sommes venus en passant par Paris
(b) (by means of) par
**viability** *n* (of company) viabilité *f*; (of project, idea) validité *f*
**viable** *adj* ⟨company, government, farm⟩ viable; ⟨project, idea, plan⟩ réalisable, valable
**viaduct** *n* viaduc *m*
**vibrant** *adj* ⟨person, place, personality⟩ plein/-e de vie; ⟨colour⟩ éclatant/-e
**vibrate** *vi* vibrer (**with** de)
**vibration** *n* vibration *f*
**vicar** *n* pasteur *m*
**vicarage** *n* presbytère *m*
**vicarious** *adj* ⟨pleasure⟩ indirect/-e
**vice** *n* (a) vice *m*; (amusing weakness) faiblesse *f*
(b) (*also* = **vise** (US)) (tool) étau *m*
**vice-captain** *n* capitaine *m* en second
**vice-chancellor** *n* président/-e *m/f* d'Université
**vice-president** *n* vice-président/-e *m/f*
**vice squad** *n* brigade *f* des mœurs
**vicinity** *n* voisinage *m*; **in the (immediate) ~ of Oxford** à proximité (immédiate) d'Oxford
**vicious** *adj* ⟨animal⟩ malfaisant/-e; ⟨speech, attack⟩ brutal/-e; ⟨rumour, person, lie⟩ malveillant/-e
**vicious circle** *n* cercle *m* vicieux
**victim** *n* victime *f*
**victimization** *n* persécution *f*
**victimize** *vtr* persécuter
**victor** *n* vainqueur *m*
**Victorian** *adj* victorien/-ienne
**victorious** *adj* victorieux/-ieuse (**over** sur)
**victory** *n* victoire *f*
**video** 1 *n* (a) (*also* **~ recorder**) magnétoscope *m*
(b) (*also* **~ cassette**) cassette *f* vidéo; **on ~** en vidéo
(c) (*also* **~ film**) vidéo *f*
2 *adj* vidéo (*inv*)
3 *vtr* (a) (from TV) enregistrer [qch]
(b) (on camcorder) filmer [qch] en vidéo
**video camera** *n* caméra *f* vidéo
**video card** *n* (Comput) carte *f* vidéo
**video clip** *n* (from film) extrait *m*; (Mus) clip *m*

**videoconference** n vidéoconférence f
**videoconferencing** n vidéoconférence f
**videodisc** n vidéodisque m
**video game** n jeu m vidéo
**video jock** n (colloq) vidéo jockey mf
**video nasty** n vidéo f représentant des violences véritables
**videophone** n vidéophone m, visiophone m
**video shop** (GB), **video store** (US) n vidéoclub m
**videotape** n bande f vidéo
**vie** vi rivaliser (with avec; for pour; to do pour faire)
**Vienna** pr n Vienne
**view** **1** n (a) (gen) vue f; **in (full) ~ of sb** devant qn or sous les yeux de qn; **to disappear from ~** disparaître
(b) (personal opinion, attitude) avis m, opinion f; **point of ~** point m de vue; **in his ~** à son avis
**2** vtr (a) (consider) considérer; (envisage) envisager
(b) (look at) voir ⟨scene, building, collection, exhibition⟩; visiter ⟨house, castle⟩; regarder ⟨programme⟩
(c) (Comput) visualiser
**3** **in view of** phr (considering) vu, étant donné
**4** **with a view to** phr **with a ~ to doing** en vue de faire, afin de faire
**viewer** n (a) (of TV) téléspectateur/-trice m/f
(b) (of property) visiteur/-euse m/f
(c) (on camera) visionneuse f
**viewfinder** n viseur m
**viewing** **1** n (of exhibition, house) visite f; (of film) projection f; (of new range) présentation f
**2** adj ⟨habits, preferences⟩ des téléspectateurs; **~ figures** taux m d'écoute
**viewpoint** n (all contexts) point m de vue
**vigil** n (gen) veille f; (by sickbed) veillée f; (by demonstrators) manifestation f silencieuse
**vigilant** adj vigilant/-e
**vigilante** n membre m d'un groupe d'autodéfense
**vigorous** adj vigoureux/-euse
**vigour** (GB), **vigor** (US) n vigueur f
**vile** adj ⟨smell⟩ infect/-e; ⟨weather⟩ abominable; ⟨place, colour⟩ horrible; ⟨mood⟩ exécrable
**villa** n (in town) pavillon m; (in country, for holiday) villa f
**village** n village m
**village green** n terrain m communal
**village hall** n salle f des fêtes
**villager** n villageois/-e m/f
**villain** n (in book, film) méchant m; (child) coquin/-e m/f; (criminal) bandit m
**vindicate** vtr justifier
**vindictive** adj vindicatif/-ive
**vindictiveness** n esprit m de vengeance

**vine** n (a) (grapevine) vigne f
(b) (climbing plant) plante f grimpante
**vinegar** n vinaigre m
**vineyard** n vignoble m
**vintage** **1** n (wine) millésime m
**2** adj (a) ⟨wine, champagne⟩ millésimé/-e; ⟨port⟩ vieux/vieille
(b) ⟨comedy⟩ classique
**vintage car** n voiture f d'époque
**vinyl** **1** n vinyle m
**2** adj en vinyle; ⟨paint⟩ vinylique
**viola** n (violon m) alto m
**violate** vtr (a) violer ⟨law, agreement, rights⟩
(b) profaner ⟨sacred place⟩; troubler ⟨peace⟩
**violation** n violation f; **traffic ~** infraction f au code de la route
**violence** n violence f
**violent** adj (a) ⟨crime, behaviour, film, storm, emotion⟩ violent/-e
(b) ⟨contrast⟩ brutal/-e
(c) ⟨colour⟩ criard/-e
**violently** adv ⟨attack, react, shake⟩ violemment; ⟨brake, swerve⟩ brusquement
**violet** **1** n (a) (flower) violette f
(b) (colour) violet m
**2** adj violet/-ette
**violin** n violon m
**violinist** n violoniste mf
**VIP** (abbr = **very important person**)
**1** n personnalité f (en vue)
**2** adj ⟨area, lounge⟩ réservé/-e aux personnalités; **~ guest** hôte mf de marque; **to give sb (the) ~ treatment** recevoir qn en hôte de marque
**viper** n vipère f
**virgin** n, adj vierge (f)
**Virgo** n Vierge f
**virile** adj viril/-e
**virtual** adj (a) (gen) quasi-total/-e; **he was a ~ prisoner** il était pratiquement prisonnier
(b) (Comput) virtuel/-elle
**virtually** adv pratiquement, presque; **it's ~ impossible** c'est quasiment (colloq) impossible
**virtual reality** n réalité f virtuelle
**virtue** **1** n (a) (goodness) vertu f
(b) (advantage) avantage m
**2** **by virtue of** phr en raison de
**virtuoso** n virtuose mf (of de)
**virtuous** adj vertueux/-euse
**virus** n virus m
**virus checker** n logiciel m antivirus
**visa** n visa m; **tourist ~** visa de touriste
**vis-à-vis** prep (in relation to) par rapport à; (concerning) en ce qui concerne
**visibility** n visibilité f
**visible** adj (a) (able to be seen) visible; **clearly ~** bien visible
(b) (concrete) ⟨improvement, sign⟩ évident/-e
**visibly** adv ⟨moved, shocked⟩ manifestement

**V**

**vision** n (a) (idea, mental picture, hallucination) vision f
(b) (ability to see) vue f
(c) (foresight) sagacité f

**visionary** n, adj visionnaire (mf)

**visit** ⓵ n (gen) visite f; (stay) séjour m; a state ~ une visite officielle; **to pay a ~ to sb, to pay sb a ~** aller voir qn; (more formal) rendre visite à qn
⓶ vtr (a) **to ~ Paris** (see) visiter Paris; (stay) faire un séjour à Paris, aller passer quelques jours à Paris; **to ~ sb** (call) aller voir qn; (more formal) rendre visite à qn; (stay with) aller (passer quelques jours) chez qn
(b) (US) **to ~ with sb** aller voir qn

**visiting card** n (US) carte f de visite

**visiting hours** n pl heures fpl de visite

**visitor** n (a) (caller) invité/-e m/f
(b) (tourist) visiteur/-euse m/f

**visitor centre** n centre m d'accueil et d'information des visiteurs

**visitors' book** n (in exhibition) livre m d'or; (in hotel) registre m

**visor** n visière f

**vista** n panorama m; (figurative) perspective f

**visual** adj visuel/-elle

**visual aid** n support m visuel

**visual arts** n pl arts mpl plastiques

**visualize** vtr (a) (picture) s'imaginer
(b) (envisage) envisager

**visually impaired** n the ~ les malvoyants mpl

**vital** adj (a) (essential) (gen) primordial/-e; ⟨match, point, support, factor⟩ décisif/-ive; ⟨service, help⟩ indispensable; ⟨treatment, organ, force⟩ vital/-e; **of ~ importance** d'une importance capitale
(b) ⟨person⟩ plein/-e de vie

**vitality** n vitalité f

**vitally** adv ⟨important⟩ extrêmement; ⟨needed⟩ absolument

**vital statistics** n (of woman) mensurations fpl

**vitamin** n vitamine f

**viva** ⓵ n oral m
⓶ excl vive!

**vivacious** adj plein/-e de vivacité

**vivid** adj (a) (bright) ⟨colour, light⟩ vif/vive
(b) (graphic) ⟨imagination⟩ vif/vive; ⟨memory, picture⟩ (très) net/nette; ⟨dream, impression, description⟩ frappant/-e

**vividly** adv ⟨describe, illustrate⟩ de façon très vivante; ⟨remember, recall⟩ très bien

**vivisection** n vivisection f

**vixen** n (a) (fox) renarde f
(b) (woman) mégère f

**viz** adv (abbr = **videlicet**) à savoir

**V-neck** n (a) (neck) encolure f en V
(b) (sweater) pull m en V

**vocabulary** n vocabulaire m

**vocal** adj (a) (concerning speech) vocal/-e
(b) (vociferous) ⟨person⟩ qui se fait entendre

**vocalist** n chanteur/-euse m/f (dans un groupe pop)

**vocals** n pl chant m; **to do the backing ~** faire les chœurs

**vocation** n vocation f

**vocational** adj professionnel/-elle

**vocational course** n stage m de formation professionnelle

**vociferous** adj ⟨person, protest⟩ véhément/-e

**vogue** n vogue f (**for** de)

**voice** ⓵ n voix f; **in a loud ~** à haute voix; **in a low ~** à voix basse; **in a cross ~** d'une voix irritée; **to have lost one's ~** (when ill) être aphone; **at the top of one's ~** à tue-tête
⓶ vtr exprimer ⟨concern, grievance⟩

**voicemail** n messagerie f vocale

**voice-over** n voix-off f

**voice recognition** n reconnaissance f vocale

**void** ⓵ n vide m; **to fill the ~** combler le vide
⓶ adj (a) (Law) ⟨contract, agreement⟩ nul/ nulle; ⟨cheque⟩ annulé/-e
(b) (empty) vide; **~ of** dépourvu/-e de

**volatile** adj ⟨situation⟩ explosif/-ive; ⟨person⟩ lunatique; ⟨market, exchange rate⟩ instable

**volcano** n volcan m

**volley** ⓵ n (a) (in tennis) volée f
(b) (of gunfire) salve f (**of** de)
(c) (series) **a ~ of** un feu roulant de ⟨questions⟩; une bordée de ⟨insults, oaths⟩
⓶ vtr (in tennis) prendre [qch] de volée ⟨ball⟩
⓷ vi (in tennis) jouer à la volée

**volleyball** n volley(-ball) m

**volt** n volt m

**voltage** n tension f

**volume** n (a) (gen) volume m (**of** de); (of container) capacité f
(b) (book) volume m; (part of set) tome m

**volume control** n (bouton m de) réglage m du volume

**voluntarily** adv de plein gré, volontairement

**voluntary** adj (a) (gen) volontaire
(b) (unpaid) bénévole

**voluntary redundancy** n départ m volontaire

**volunteer** ⓵ n (a) (offering to do sth) volontaire mf
(b) (unpaid worker) bénévole mf
⓶ vtr (a) (offer) offrir; **to ~ to do** offrir de faire, se porter volontaire pour faire
(b) fournir [qch] spontanément ⟨information⟩
⓷ vi (a) se porter volontaire (**for** pour)
(b) (as soldier) s'engager comme volontaire

**voluptuous** adj voluptueux/-euse

**vomit** ⓵ n vomi m
⓶ vtr, vi vomir

**voodoo** n vaudou m

**voracious** adj vorace

**vortex** n tourbillon m

**V**

**vote** 1 *n* **(a)** (gen) vote *m*
**(b)** (franchise) **the ~** le droit de vote
2 *vtr* **(a)** (gen) voter; **to ~ sb into/out of office** élire/ne pas réélire qn
**(b)** (colloq) (propose) proposer
3 *vi* voter (**on** sur; **for sb** pour qn; **against** contre); **let's ~ on it** mettons-le aux voix; **to ~ to strike** voter la grève

**vote of confidence** *n* vote *m* de confiance (**in** en)

**vote of thanks** *n* discours *m* de remerciement

**voter** *n* électeur/-trice *m/f*

**voting** *n* scrutin *m*

**voting age** *n* majorité *f* électorale

**vouch** *v* ■ **vouch for (a)** (informally) répondre de ⟨*person*⟩; témoigner de ⟨*fact*⟩
**(b)** (officially) se porter garant de

**voucher** *n* bon *m*

**vow** 1 *n* (religious) vœu *m*; (of honour) serment *m*; **marriage** *or* **wedding ~s** promesses *fpl* du mariage
2 *vtr* faire vœu de ⟨*love, revenge, allegiance*⟩; **to ~ to do** jurer de faire

**vowel** *n* voyelle *f*

**voyage** *n* voyage *m*

**V-sign** *n* **(a)** (victory sign) V *m* de la victoire
**(b)** (GB) (offensive gesture) geste *m* obscène

**VSO** *n* (*abbr* = **Voluntary Service Overseas**) coopération *f* civile

**vulgar** *adj* **(a)** (tasteless) ⟨*furniture, clothes*⟩ de mauvais goût; ⟨*taste*⟩ douteux/-euse; ⟨*person*⟩ vulgaire
**(b)** (rude) grossier/-ière

**vulnerable** *adj* vulnérable (**to** à)

**vulture** *n* vautour *m*

# Ww

**w, W** *n* w, W *m*

**wad** *n* **(a)** (of banknotes, paper) liasse *f* (**of** de)
**(b)** (of cotton wool, padding) boule *f* (**of** de)

**waddle** *vi* ⟨*duck, person*⟩ se dandiner

**wade** *vi* **(a)** (in water) **to ~ into the water** entrer dans l'eau; **to ~ ashore** marcher dans l'eau jusqu'au rivage; **to ~ across** traverser à gué
**(b) he was wading through 'War and Peace'** il lisait 'Guerre et Paix', mais ça avançait lentement

**waders** *n pl* cuissardes *fpl*

**wafer** *n* (Culin) gaufrette *f*

**wafer-thin** *adj* ⟨*slice*⟩ ultrafin/-e

**waffle** 1 *n* **(a)** (Culin) gaufre *f*
**(b)** (colloq) (empty words) verbiage *m*
2 *vi* (colloq) (*also* **~ on**) (speaking) bavasser (colloq); (writing) faire du remplissage

**waft** *vi* **to ~ towards** flotter vers; **to ~ up** monter

**wag** 1 *vtr* remuer ⟨*tail*⟩
2 *vi* ⟨*tail*⟩ remuer, frétiller; **tongues will ~** ça va faire jaser

**wage** 1 *n* (*also* **~s** *pl*) salaire *m*
2 *vtr* mener ⟨*campaign*⟩; **to ~ (a) war against sb/sth** faire la guerre contre qn/qch

**wage earner** *n* **(a)** (person earning a wage) salarié/-e *m/f* (hebdomadaire)
**(b)** (breadwinner) soutien *m* de famille

**wage packet** *n* **(a)** (envelope) enveloppe *f* de paie
**(b)** (money) paie *f*

**wager** *n* pari *m*; **to make** *or* **lay a ~** parier, faire un pari

**wage slip** *n* feuille *f* de paie

**waggon** (GB), **wagon** *n* **(a)** (horse-drawn) chariot *m*
**(b)** (GB) (on rail) wagon *m* (de marchandises)
IDIOMS **to be on the ~** (colloq) être au régime sec

**wail** 1 *n* (of person) gémissement *m*; (of siren) hurlement *m*; (of musical instrument) son *m* plaintif
2 *vi* ⟨*person, wind*⟩ gémir; ⟨*siren*⟩ hurler; ⟨*music*⟩ pleurer

**waist** *n* taille *f*

**waistband** *n* ceinture *f*

**waistcoat** *n* (GB) gilet *m*

**waistline** *n* taille *f*

**waist measurement** *n* tour *m* de taille

**wait** 1 *n* attente *f*; **an hour's ~** une heure d'attente
2 *vtr* **(a)** attendre ⟨*one's turn*⟩
**(b)** (US) **to ~ table** servir à table
3 *vi* attendre; **to keep sb ~ing** faire attendre qn; **to ~ for sb/sth** attendre qn/qch; **to ~ for sb/sth to do** attendre que qn/qch fasse; **to ~ to do** attendre de faire; **I can't ~ to do** j'ai hâte de faire; (stronger) je meurs d'impatience de faire; **you'll have to ~ and see** attends et tu verras
IDIOMS **to lie in ~ for sb** guetter qn

■ **wait around, wait about** (GB) attendre

■ **wait behind** attendre un peu; **to ~ behind for sb** attendre qn

■ **wait on** servir ⟨*person*⟩; **to ~ on sb hand and foot** être aux petits soins pour qn

■ **wait up (a)** (stay awake) veiller; **to ~ up for sb** veiller jusqu'au retour de qn
**(b)** (US) **~ up!** attends!

W

**waiter** *n* serveur *m*; '~!' 'monsieur!'

**waiting game** *n* **to play a** ~ attendre son heure; (in politics) faire de l'attentisme

**waiting list** *n* liste *f* d'attente

**waiting room** *n* salle *f* d'attente

**waitress** *n* serveuse *f*; '~!' 'madame!','mademoiselle!'

**waive** *vtr* déroger à ‹rule›; renoncer à ‹claim, right›; supprimer ‹fee›

**wake** ① *vtr* réveiller; **to** ~ **sb from a dream** tirer qn d'un rêve
② *vi* se réveiller
■ **wake up**: ¶ ~ **up** se réveiller; ~ **up!** réveille-toi!; (to reality) ouvre les yeux!; ¶ ~ **[sb] up** réveiller

**wake-up call** *n* réveil *m* téléphoné

**Wales** *pr n* pays *m* de Galles

**walk** ① *n* (a) promenade *f*; (shorter) tour *m*; (hike) randonnée *f*; **it's about ten minutes'** ~ c'est à environ dix minutes à pied; **to go for a** ~ (aller) faire une promenade
(b) (gait) démarche *f*
(c) (pace) pas *m*
(d) (path) allée *f*
(e) (Sport) épreuve *f* de marche
② *vtr* (a) faire ‹qch› à pied ‹distance, path, road›
(b) conduire ‹horse›; promener ‹dog›; **to** ~ **sb home** raccompagner qn chez lui/elle
③ *vi* (in general) marcher; (for pleasure) se promener; (not run) aller au pas; (not ride or drive) aller à pied; **it's not very far, let's** ~ ce n'est pas très loin, allons-y à pied; **he** ~**ed up/down the road** il a remonté/descendu la rue (à pied)

───────────────────
■ **Note** à pied is often omitted with movement verbs if we already know that the person is on foot. If it is surprising or ambiguous, à pied should be included.
───────────────────

■ **walk around**: ¶ ~ **around** se promener; (aimlessly) traîner; ¶ ~ **around [sth]** (to and fro) faire un tour dans; (make circuit of) faire le tour de
■ **walk away** (a) s'éloigner (from de)
(b) (refuse to face) **to** ~ **away from** se désintéresser de ‹problem›
(c) (survive unscathed) sortir indemne (from de)
(d) (win easily) **to** ~ **away with** gagner ‹qch› haut la main ‹game, tournament›; remporter ‹qch› haut la main ‹election›; décrocher ‹prize, honour›
■ **walk back** revenir sur ses pas (to jusqu'à); **we** ~**ed back** (home) nous sommes rentrés à pied
■ **walk in** entrer; **I'd just** ~**ed in when** je venais à peine d'entrer quand
■ **walk into**: ~ **into [sth]** (a) (enter) entrer dans
(b) tomber dans ‹trap›; se fourrer dans ‹tricky situation›
(c) (bump into) rentrer dans ‹door, person›
■ **walk off**: ¶ ~ **off** (a) partir brusquement
(b) (colloq) **to** ~ **off with sth** (innocently) partir

avec qch; (as theft) filer (colloq) avec qch
¶ ~ **[sth] off** se promener pour faire passer ‹hangover, large meal›
■ **walk out** (a) sortir (of de)
(b) (desert) partir; **to** ~ **out on** laisser tomber (colloq) ‹lover›; rompre ‹contract, undertaking›
(c) (as protest) partir en signe de protestation; (on strike) se mettre en grève
■ **walk over**: ¶ ~ **over** s'approcher (to de)
¶ ~ **over [sb]** (colloq) (a) (defeat) battre [qn] à plates coutures
(b) (humiliate) marcher sur les pieds de
■ **walk round**: ¶ ~ **round** faire le tour; ¶ ~ **round [sth]** (round edge of) faire le tour de; (visit) visiter ‹town›
■ **walk through**: traverser ‹house, forest›; passer ‹door›; parcourir ‹streets›; marcher dans ‹snow, mud, grass›
■ **walk up**: **to** ~ **up to** s'approcher de

**walker** *n* (for pleasure) promeneur/-euse *m/f*; (for exercise) marcheur/-euse *m/f*

**walkie-talkie** *n* talkie-walkie *m*

**walking** *n* (for pleasure) promenades *fpl* à pied; (for exercise) marche *f* à pied

**walking boots** *n pl* chaussures *fpl* de marche

**walking distance** *n* **to be within** ~ être à quelques minutes de marche (**of** de)

**walking pace** *n* pas *m*; **at a** ~ au pas

**walking stick** *n* canne *f*

**walkman**® *n* walkman® *m*, baladeur *m*

**walkout** *n* (strike) grève *f* surprise

**walkover** *n* victoire *f* facile (**for** pour)

**walkway** *n* allée *f*

**wall** *n* (a) (construction) mur *m*
(b) (of cave, tunnel) paroi *f*
(c) (Anat) paroi *f*

**wall chart** *n* affiche *f*

**walled** *adj* ‹city› fortifié/-e; ‹garden› clos/-e

**wallet** *n* (for notes) portefeuille *m*; (for documents) porte-documents *m inv*

**wallflower** *n* giroflée *f* jaune
IDIOMS **to be a** ~ faire tapisserie

**wall light** *n* applique *f* murale

**wall-mounted** *adj* fixé/-e au mur

**wallow** *vi* **to** ~ **in** se vautrer dans ‹mud, luxury›; se complaire dans ‹self-pity, nostalgia›

**wallpaper** ① *n* (a) (for walls) papier *m* peint
(b) (Comput) fond *m* d'écran
② *vtr* tapisser ‹room›

**walnut** *n* (a) (nut) noix *f*
(b) (tree, wood) noyer *m*

**walrus** *n* morse *m*

**waltz** ① *n* valse *f*
② *vi* danser la valse (**with** avec)

**wand** *n* baguette *f*

**wander** ① *vtr* parcourir; **to** ~ **the streets** traîner dans la rue
② *vi* (a) (walk, stroll) se promener; **to** ~ **around town** se balader en ville

**(b)** (stray) errer; **to ∼ away** or **off** s'éloigner (**from** de)

**(c)** ⟨*eyes, hands*⟩ errer (**over** sur); ⟨*attention*⟩ se relâcher; **her mind is ∼ing** elle divague

■ **wander about, wander around** (stroll) se balader; (when lost) errer

**wane** *vi* ⟨*moon*⟩ décroître; ⟨*enthusiasm, popularity*⟩ diminuer

**wangle** (colloq) **⟨1⟩** *n* combine *f* (colloq)
**⟨2⟩** *vtr* soutirer ⟨*money, promise*⟩; se débrouiller pour avoir ⟨*leave*⟩; **to ∼ sth for sb** se débrouiller pour faire avoir qch à qn

**wannabe(e)** *n* (colloq): *personne qui rêve d'être célèbre*

**want** **⟨1⟩** *n* **(a)** (need) besoin *m*
**(b)** (lack) défaut *m*; **for ∼ of** à défaut or faute de; **it's not for ∼ of trying** ce n'est pas faute d'avoir essayé
**⟨2⟩** *vtr* **(a)** (desire) vouloir; **I ∼** (as general statement) je veux; (would like) je voudrais; (am seeking) je souhaite; **I don't ∼ to** je n'en ai pas envie; (flat refusal) je ne veux pas; **to ∼ to do** vouloir faire; **to ∼ sb to do** vouloir que qn fasse
**(b)** (colloq) (need) avoir besoin de
**(c)** (require presence of) demander; **if anyone ∼s me** si quelqu'un me demande; **you're ∼ed on the phone** on vous demande au téléphone; **to be ∼ed by the police** être recherché/-e par la police
**⟨3⟩** *vi* **to ∼ for** manquer de

**wanting** *adj* **to be ∼** faire défaut; **to be ∼ in** manquer de; **to be found ∼** s'avérer décevant/-e

**wanton** *adj* ⟨*cruelty, damage, waste*⟩ gratuit/-e; ⟨*disregard*⟩ délibéré/-e

**war** *n* guerre *f*; **in the ∼** à la guerre; **to wage ∼ on** faire la guerre contre; (figurative) mener une lutte contre

**ward** *n* **(a)** (in hospital) (unit) service *m*; (room) unité *f*; (separate building) pavillon *m*; **maternity ∼** service de maternité; **hospital ∼** salle *f* d'hôpital
**(b)** (electoral) circonscription *f* électorale
**(c)** (also **∼ of court**) (Law) pupille *m*

■ **ward off** chasser ⟨*evil, predator*⟩; faire taire ⟨*accusations, criticism*⟩; écarter ⟨*attack, threat*⟩; éviter ⟨*disaster*⟩

**warden** *n* (of institution, college) directeur/-trice *m/f*; (of park, estate) gardien/-ienne *m/f*

**warder** *n* (GB) gardien/-ienne *m/f*

**wardrobe** *n* **(a)** (furniture) armoire *f*
**(b)** (set of clothes) garde-robe *f*; (for theatre) costumes *mpl*

**warehouse** *n* entrepôt *m*

**wares** *n pl* marchandise *f*, marchandises *fpl*

**warfare** *n* guerre *f*

**war game** *n* jeu *m* de stratégie (militaire)

**warhead** *n* ogive *f*

**warlike** *adj* ⟨*people*⟩ guerrier/-ière; ⟨*mood, words*⟩ belliqueux/-euse

**warm** **⟨1⟩** *adj* **(a)** ⟨*place, food, temperature,*

*water, day, clothing*⟩ chaud/-e; **to be ∼** ⟨*person*⟩ avoir chaud; **it's ∼** il fait bon or chaud
**(b)** (affectionate) ⟨*person, atmosphere, welcome*⟩ chaleureux/-euse; ⟨*admiration, support*⟩ enthousiaste
**(c)** ⟨*colour*⟩ chaud/-e
**⟨2⟩** *vtr* chauffer ⟨*plate, food, water*⟩; réchauffer ⟨*implement, bed*⟩; **to ∼ oneself** se réchauffer; **to ∼ one's hands** se réchauffer les mains
**⟨3⟩** *vi* ⟨*food, liquid, object*⟩ chauffer

■ **warm to, warm towards** se prendre de sympathie pour ⟨*person*⟩; se faire à ⟨*idea*⟩; prendre goût à ⟨*task*⟩

■ **warm up**: ¶ **∼ up (a)** ⟨*person, room, house*⟩ se réchauffer; ⟨*food, liquid, engine*⟩ chauffer
**(b)** (become lively) s'animer
**(c)** ⟨*athlete*⟩ s'échauffer; ⟨*singer*⟩ s'échauffer la voix; ⟨*orchestra, musician*⟩ se préparer
¶ **∼ [sth] up** réchauffer ⟨*room, bed, person*⟩; faire réchauffer ⟨*food*⟩

**warm-hearted** *adj* chaleureux/-euse

**warmly** *adv* ⟨*smile, thank, recommend*⟩ chaleureusement; ⟨*speak, praise*⟩ avec enthousiasme

**warmth** *n* chaleur *f*

**warm-up** *n* échauffement *m*

**warn** **⟨1⟩** *vtr* avertir, prévenir; **to ∼ sb about** or **against sth** mettre qn en garde contre qch; **to ∼ sb to do** conseiller or dire à qn de faire; **to ∼ sb not to do** déconseiller à qn de faire
**⟨2⟩** *vi* **to ∼ of sth** annoncer qch

**warning** *n* avertissement *m*; (by an authority) avis *m*; (by light, siren) alerte *f*; **to give sb ∼** avertir qn (**of** de); **advance ∼** préavis *m*; **health ∼** mise en garde; **flood ∼** avis de crue

**warning light** *n* voyant *m* lumineux

**warning shot** *n* coup *m* de semonce

**warning sign** *n* (on road) panneau *m* d'avertissement; (of illness, stress) signe *m* annonciateur

**warning triangle** *n* (Aut) triangle *m* de présignalisation

**warp** **⟨1⟩** *vtr* **(a)** déformer ⟨*metal, wood, record*⟩
**(b)** pervertir ⟨*mind, personality*⟩
**⟨2⟩** *vi* se déformer

**warped** *adj* **(a)** ⟨*metal, wood, record*⟩ déformé/-e
**(b)** ⟨*mind, humour*⟩ tordu/-e; ⟨*personality, sexuality*⟩ perverti/-e; ⟨*account, view*⟩ faussé/-e

**warplane** *n* avion *m* militaire

**warrant** **⟨1⟩** *n* (Law) mandat *m*
**⟨2⟩** *vtr* justifier ⟨*action, measure*⟩

**warranty** *n* garantie *f*

**warren** *n* **(a)** (rabbits') garenne *f*
**(b)** (building, maze of streets) labyrinthe *m*

**warring** *adj* en conflit

**warrior** *n* guerrier/-ière *m/f*

**W**

**Warsaw** *pr n* Varsovie

**warship** *n* navire *m* de guerre

**wart** *n* verrue *f*

**wartime** *n* in ~ en temps de guerre

**war-torn** *adj* déchiré/-e par la guerre

**war veteran** *n* ancien combattant *m*

**wary** *adj* **(a)** (cautious) prudent/-e; **to be ~** montrer de la circonspection **(of** vis-à-vis de); **to be ~ of doing** hésiter à faire
**(b)** (distrustful) méfiant/-e; **to be ~** se méfier **(of** de)

**wash** ⚀ *n* **(a)** (clean) **to have a ~** se laver; **to give [sth] a ~** laver ⟨*window, floor*⟩; nettoyer ⟨*object*⟩; lessiver ⟨*paintwork, walls*⟩; **to give [sb] a ~** débarbouiller ⟨*child*⟩
**(b)** (laundry process) lavage *m*; **weekly ~** lessive *f* hebdomadaire; **in the ~** (about to be cleaned) au sale; (being cleaned) au lavage
**(c)** (from boat) remous *m*
⚁ *vtr* laver ⟨*person, clothes, floor*⟩; nettoyer ⟨*object, wound*⟩; lessiver ⟨*paintwork, surface*⟩; **to get ~ed** se laver; **to ~ one's hands/face** se laver les mains/le visage; **to ~ the dishes** faire la vaisselle
⚂ *vi* **(a)** ⟨*person*⟩ se laver, faire sa toilette; ⟨*animal*⟩ faire sa toilette
**(b)** (do laundry) faire la lessive
■ **wash away** emporter ⟨*structure, debris, person*⟩
■ **wash up:** ¶ ~ up **(a)** (GB) (do dishes) faire la vaisselle
**(b)** (US) (clean oneself) faire un brin de toilette (colloq)
¶ ~ [sth] up **(a)** (clean) laver ⟨*plate*⟩; nettoyer ⟨*pan*⟩
**(b)** ⟨*tide*⟩ rejeter ⟨*debris*⟩

**washable** *adj* lavable

**washbasin** *n* lavabo *m*

**washbowl** *n* (US) lavabo *m*

**washcloth** *n* (US) lavette *f*

**washed-out** *adj* **(a)** (faded) délavé/-e
**(b)** (tired) épuisé/-e, lessivé/-e (colloq)

**washed-up** *adj* (colloq) fichu/-e (colloq)

**washer** *n* (Tech) (as seal) joint *m*

**washer-dryer** *n* lave-linge/sèche-linge *m inv*

**washing** *n* (laundry) (to be cleaned) linge *m* sale; (when clean) linge *m*; **to do the ~** faire la lessive

**washing line** *n* corde *f* à linge

**washing machine** *n* machine *f* à laver

**washing powder** *n* (GB) lessive *f* (en poudre)

**washing-up** *n* (GB) vaisselle *f*

**washing-up liquid** *n* (GB) liquide *m* (à) vaisselle

**washout** *n* **(a)** (colloq) (project, system) fiasco *m*
**(b)** (colloq) (person) nullité *f* (colloq)
**(c)** (game, camp) fiasco *m* dû à la pluie

**washroom** *n* toilettes *fpl*

**wash-stand** *n* (US) lavabo *m*

**wasp** *n* guêpe *f*

**waspish** *adj* acerbe

**wastage** *n* **(a)** (of money, resources, talent) gaspillage *m*; (of heat, energy) déperdition *f*
**(b)** (*also* **natural ~**) élimination *f* naturelle

**waste** ⚀ *n* **(a)** (of food, money, energy) gaspillage *m* (**of** de); (of time) perte *f* (**of** de); **a ~ of effort** un effort inutile; **that car is such a ~ of money!** cette voiture, c'est vraiment de l'argent jeté par les fenêtres!; **to let sth go to ~** gaspiller qch
**(b)** (detritus) (*also* **wastes** (US)) déchets *mpl* (**from** de)
⚁ **wastes** *n pl* **(a)** (wilderness) étendues *fpl* sauvages
**(b)** (US) = WASTE 1B
⚂ *adj* **(a)** ⟨*heat, energy*⟩ gaspillé/-e; ⟨*water*⟩ usé/-e; **~ materials** déchets *mpl*
**(b)** ⟨*land*⟩ inculte
**(c)** **to lay ~ to** dévaster
⚃ *vtr* **(a)** (squander) gaspiller ⟨*food, resources, energy, money, talents*⟩; perdre ⟨*time, opportunity*⟩; user ⟨*strength*⟩
**(b)** (make thinner) décharner; (make weaker) atrophier

**wastebasket** *n* corbeille *f* à papier

**wastebin** *n* (GB) (for paper) corbeille *f* à papier; (for rubbish) poubelle *f*

**wasted** *adj* **(a)** ⟨*effort, life, vote*⟩ inutile; ⟨*energy, years*⟩ gaspillé/-e
**(b)** (fleshless) ⟨*body, limb*⟩ décharné/-e; (weak) ⟨*body, limb*⟩ atrophié/-e

**waste disposal** *n* traitement *m* des déchets

**waste disposal unit** *n* (GB) broyeur *m* d'ordures

**wasteful** *adj* ⟨*product, machine*⟩ qui consomme beaucoup; ⟨*method, process*⟩ peu économique; ⟨*person*⟩ gaspilleur/-euse

**wasteland** *n* (urban) terrain *m* vague; (rural) terre *f* à l'abandon

**wastepaper** *n* papier *m* or papiers *mpl* à jeter

**wastepaper basket**, **wastepaper bin** (GB) *n* corbeille *f* à papier

**waste pipe** *n* tuyau *m* de vidange

**wasting** *adj* ⟨*disease*⟩ débilitant/-e

**watch** ⚀ *n* **(a)** (timepiece) montre *f*
**(b)** (surveillance) surveillance *f* (**on** sur); **to keep ~** monter la garde; **to keep (a) ~ on sb/sth** surveiller qn/qch
⚁ *vtr* **(a)** (look at) regarder; (observe) observer
**(b)** (monitor) suivre ⟨*career, development*⟩; surveiller ⟨*situation*⟩
**(c)** (keep under surveillance) surveiller ⟨*person, movements*⟩
**(d)** (pay attention to) faire attention à ⟨*obstacle, dangerous object, money*⟩; surveiller ⟨*language, manners, weight*⟩; **to ~ one's step** (figurative) faire attention
**(e)** (look after) garder ⟨*person, property*⟩
⚂ *vi* regarder (**from** de)
■ **watch for** guetter ⟨*person, chance*⟩; surveiller l'apparition de ⟨*symptom*⟩
■ **watch out** (be careful) faire attention (**for** à); (keep watch) guetter; **~ out!** attention!

■ **watch over** veiller sur ⟨*person*⟩; veiller à ⟨*interests, rights, welfare*⟩

**watchable** *adj* qui se laisse regarder

**watchband** *n* (US) bracelet *m* de montre

**watchdog** *n* **(a)** (dog) chien *m* de garde
**(b)** (organization) organisme *m* de surveillance

**watchmaker** *n* horloger/-ère *m/f*

**watchman** *n* (guard) gardien *m*

**watch strap** *n* bracelet *m* de montre

**watchword** *n* slogan *m*

**water** ⊡ *n* eau *f*
⊡ *vtr* arroser ⟨*lawn, plant*⟩; irriguer ⟨*crop, field*⟩; abreuver ⟨*livestock*⟩
⊡ *vi* **the smell of cooking makes my mouth** ∼ l'odeur de cuisine me fait venir l'eau à la bouche; **the smoke made her eyes** ∼ la fumée l'a fait pleurer

■ **water down (a)** couper [qch] d'eau ⟨*beer, wine*⟩; diluer ⟨*syrup*⟩
**(b)** atténuer ⟨*effect, plans, policy*⟩; édulcorer ⟨*description, story*⟩

**water bed** *n* matelas *m* d'eau

**water bird** *n* oiseau *m* aquatique

**water birth** *n* accouchement *m* aquatique

**water bottle** *n* (for cyclist) bidon *m*

**water cannon** *n* canon *m* à eau

**watercolour** (GB), **watercolor** (US) *n* (paint) peinture *f* pour aquarelle; (painting) aquarelle *f*

**watercress** *n* cresson *m* (de fontaine)

**waterfall** *n* cascade *f*

**water filter** *n* filtre *m* à eau

**waterfront** *n* (on harbour) front *m* de mer; (by lakeside, riverside) bord *m* de l'eau

**water-heater** *n* chauffe-eau *m inv*

**watering can** *n* arrosoir *m*

**water jump** *n* rivière *f*

**water level** *n* niveau *m* d'eau

**water lily** *n* nénuphar *m*

**waterlogged** *adj* ⟨*ground, pitch*⟩ détrempé/-e

**water main** *n* canalisation *f* d'eau

**watermark** *n* (of sea) laisse *f*; (of river) ligne *f* des hautes eaux; (on paper) filigrane *m*

**watermelon** *n* pastèque *f*

**water power** *n* énergie *f* hydraulique

**waterproof** *adj* ⟨*coat*⟩ imperméable; ⟨*make-up*⟩ résistant/-e à l'eau

**waterproofs** *n pl* vêtements *mpl* imperméables

**water-resistant** *adj* qui résiste à l'eau

**water-ski** ⊡ *n* ski *m* nautique
⊡ *vi* faire du ski nautique

**water-skiing** *n* ski *m* nautique

**water slide** *n* toboggan *m* de piscine

**water sport** *n* sport *m* nautique

**water supply** *n* (in an area) approvisionnement *m* en eau; (to a building) alimentation *f* en eau

**watertight** *adj* **(a)** ⟨*container, seal*⟩ étanche

**(b)** ⟨*argument, case*⟩ incontestable; ⟨*alibi*⟩ irréfutable

**water tower** *n* château *m* d'eau

**water trough** *n* abreuvoir *m*

**waterway** *n* voie *f* navigable

**water wings** *n pl* bracelets *mpl* de natation

**watery** *adj* **(a)** ⟨*sauce, paint*⟩ trop liquide; ⟨*coffee*⟩ trop léger/-ère
**(b)** ⟨*colour, smile*⟩ pâle

**watt** *n* watt *m*

**wave** ⊡ *n* **(a)** (of hand) signe *m* (de la main)
**(b)** (of water) vague *f*; **to make** ∼**s** ⟨*wind*⟩ faire des vagues; (cause a stir) faire du bruit; (cause trouble) créer des histoires (colloq)
**(c)** (outbreak, surge) vague *f* (**of** de)
**(d)** (of light, radio) onde *f*
**(e)** (in hair) cran *m*
⊡ *vtr* **(a)** agiter ⟨*flag, ticket, banknote*⟩; brandir ⟨*umbrella, stick, gun*⟩
**(b) to** ∼ **goodbye to sb** faire au revoir de la main à qn
⊡ *vi* **(a)** (with hand) **to** ∼ **to** *or* **at sb** saluer qn de la main
**(b)** ⟨*branches*⟩ être agité/-e par le vent; ⟨*corn*⟩ ondoyer; ⟨*flag*⟩ flotter au vent

**wave band** *n* bande *f* de fréquence

**wavelength** *n* (on radio) longueur *f* d'onde
IDIOMS **to be on the same** ∼ **as sb** être sur la même longueur d'onde que qn

**waver** *vi* **(a)** (weaken) ⟨*person*⟩ vaciller; ⟨*courage, love*⟩ faiblir; ⟨*voice*⟩ trembler
**(b)** (hesitate) hésiter (**between** entre; **over** sur)

**wavy** *adj* ⟨*hair, line*⟩ ondulé/-e

**wax** ⊡ *n* (for candle, seal) cire *f*; (for skis) fart *m*; (in ear) cérumen *m*
⊡ *vtr* **(a)** cirer ⟨*floor*⟩; lustrer ⟨*car*⟩; farter ⟨*ski*⟩
**(b)** (depilate) épiler [qch] à la cire ⟨*legs*⟩
⊡ *vi* ⟨*moon*⟩ croître

**waxed jacket** *n* ciré *m*

**wax paper** *n* papier *m* paraffin

**waxwork** *n* personnage *m* en cire

**waxworks** *n* musée *m* de cire

**waxy** *adj* cireux/-euse

**way** ⊡ *n* **(a)** (route, road) chemin *m* (**from** de; **to** à); **the quickest** ∼ **to town** le chemin le plus court pour aller en ville; **to ask the** ∼ **to the station** demander le chemin pour aller à la gare; **there is no** ∼ **around the problem** il n'y a pas moyen de contourner le problème; **on the** ∼ **back from the meeting** en revenant de la réunion; **the** ∼ **in** l'entrée (**to** de); **the** ∼ **out** la sortie (**of** de); **a** ∼ **out of our difficulties** un moyen de nous sortir de nos difficultés; **the** ∼ **up** la montée; **on the** ∼ en route; **to be out of sb's** ∼ ⟨*place*⟩ ne pas être sur le chemin de qn; **don't go out of your** ∼ **to do** ne te donne pas de mal pour faire; **out of the** ∼ (isolated) isolé/-e; (unusual) extraordinaire; **by** ∼ **of** (via) en passant par; **to make one's** ∼ **towards** se diriger vers; **to** ····⊱

make one's ~ along avancer le long de; **to make one's own ~ there** y aller par ses propres moyens
**(b)** (direction) direction *f*, sens *m*; **which ~ did he go?** dans quelle direction est-il parti?; **he went that ~** il est parti par là; **come this ~** suivez-moi, venez par ici; **'this ~ up'** 'haut'; **to look the other ~** (to see) regarder de l'autre côté; (to avoid seeing unpleasant thing) détourner les yeux; (to ignore wrongdoing) fermer les yeux; **the other ~ up** dans l'autre sens; **the right ~ up** dans le bon sens; **the wrong ~ up** à l'envers; **to turn sth the other ~ around** retourner qch; **I didn't ask her, it was the other ~ around** ce n'est pas moi qui le lui ai demandé, c'est l'inverse; **the wrong/ right ~ around** dans le mauvais/bon sens
**(c)** (space in front, projected route) passage *m*; **to be in sb's ~** empêcher qn de passer; **to be in the ~** gêner le passage; **to get out of the ~** s'écarter (du chemin); **to get out of sb's ~** laisser passer qn; **to keep out of the ~** rester à l'écart; **to keep out of sb's ~** éviter qn; **to make ~** s'écarter; **to make ~ for sb/sth** faire place à qn/qch
**(d)** (distance) distance *f*; **it's a long ~** c'est loin (to jusqu'à); **to go all the ~ to China** aller jusqu'en Chine
**(e)** (manner) façon *f*, manière *f*; **do it this/that ~** fais-le comme ceci/cela; **to do another ~** faire autrement; **the French ~** à la française; **to write sth the right/wrong ~** écrire qch bien/mal; **try to see it my ~** mets-toi à ma place; **in his/her/its own ~** à sa façon; **to have a ~ with words** savoir manier les mots; **to have a ~ with children** savoir s'y prendre avec les enfants; **a ~ of doing** (method) une façon *or* manière de faire; (means) un moyen de faire; **I like the ~ he dresses** j'aime la façon dont il s'habille; **either ~, she's wrong** de toute façon, elle a tort; **one ~ or another** d'une façon ou d'une autre; **I don't care one ~ or the other** ça m'est égal; **you can't have it both ~s** on ne peut pas avoir le beurre et l'argent du beurre; **no ~!** (colloq) pas question! (colloq); **~ of life** mode de vie
**(f)** (respect, aspect) sens *m*; **in a ~ it's sad** en un sens c'est triste; **in a ~ that's true** dans une certaine mesure c'est vrai; **in many ~s** à bien des égards; **in some ~s** à certains égards; **in no ~, not in any ~** aucunement
**(g)** (custom, manner) coutume *f*, manière *f*; **that's the modern ~** c'est ce qui se fait de nos jours; **I know all her little ~s** je connais toutes ses petites habitudes; **that's just his ~** il est comme ça; **it's the ~ of the world** c'est la vie
**(h)** (will, desire) **to get one's ~, to have one's own ~** faire à son idée; **she likes (to have) her own ~** elle aime n'en faire qu'à sa tête; **if I had my ~** si cela ne tenait qu'à moi; **have it your (own) ~** comme tu voudras
2 *adv* **we went ~ over budget** le budget a été largement dépassé; **to be ~ out** (in guess, estimate) être loin du compte; **that's ~ out of order** je trouve ça un peu fort

3 **by the way** *phr* en passant; **by the ~,...** à propos,...; **what time is it, by the ~?** quelle heure est-il, au fait?

**waylay** *vtr* ⟨attacker⟩ attaquer; ⟨beggar, friend⟩ arrêter, harponner (colloq)

**waymark** *n* balise *f*

**way-out** *adj* (colloq) excentrique

**wayside** *n*
IDIOMS **to fall by the ~** (stray morally) quitter le droit chemin; (fail, not stay the course) abandonner en cours de route; (be cancelled, fall through) tomber à l'eau

**wayward** *adj* ⟨person, nature⟩ difficile; ⟨husband, wife⟩ volage

**we** *pron* nous

■ **Note** In standard French, *we* is translated by *nous* but in informal French, *on* is frequently used: *we're going to the cinema* = nous allons au cinéma *or more informally* on va au cinéma.
 – *on* is also used in correct French to refer to a large, vaguely defined group: *we shouldn't lie to our children* = on ne devrait pas mentir à ses enfants.

**~ saw her yesterday** nous l'avons vue hier; **~ left at six** nous sommes partis à six heures; (informal) on est partis (colloq) à six heures; **~ Scots like the sun** nous autres Écossais, nous aimons le soleil; **we didn't say that** nous, nous n'avons pas dit cela; (informal) nous, on n'a pas dit ça (colloq); **~ all make mistakes** tout le monde peut se tromper

**weak** *adj* **(a)** ⟨person, animal, muscle, limb⟩ faible; ⟨health, ankle, heart, nerves⟩ fragile; ⟨stomach⟩ délicat/-e; ⟨intellect⟩ médiocre; ⟨chin⟩ fuyant/-e; **to be ~ with** *or* **from hunger** être affaibli/-e par la faim; **to grow** *or* **become ~(er)** ⟨person⟩ s'affaiblir; ⟨pulse, heartbeat⟩ faiblir
**(b)** ⟨beam, support⟩ peu solide; ⟨structure⟩ fragile
**(c)** (lacking authority, strength) ⟨government, team, pupil, president⟩ faible; ⟨parent, teacher⟩ (not firm) qui manque de fermeté; (poor) piètre (before n); ⟨plot⟩ mince; ⟨actor, protest, excuse, argument⟩ peu convaincant/-e; **~ link** *or* **spot** point *m* faible
**(d)** (faint) ⟨light, current, concentration, sound⟩ faible; ⟨tea, coffee⟩ léger/-ère
**(e)** ⟨economy, dollar⟩ faible (**against** par rapport à)

**weaken** 1 *vtr* **(a)** (through illness, damage) affaiblir ⟨person, heart, structure⟩; diminuer ⟨resistance⟩; rendre [qch] moins solide ⟨joint, bank, wall⟩
**(b)** (undermine) nuire à l'autorité de ⟨government, president⟩; affaiblir ⟨team, company, authority, defence⟩; amoindrir ⟨argument, power⟩; nuire à ⟨morale⟩
**(c)** (dilute) diluer
2 *vi* **(a)** (physically) s'affaiblir
**(b)** ⟨government, resolve⟩ fléchir; ⟨support, alliance⟩ se relâcher
**(c)** (Econ) ⟨economy, currency⟩ être en baisse

**weakling** *n* (physically) gringalet *m*; (morally) mauviette *f*

**weakness** n (a) (weak point) point m faible
(b) (liking) faible m (for pour)
(c) (physical, moral) faiblesse f
(d) (lack of authority) faiblesse f; (of evidence, position) fragilité f
(e) (of light, current, sound) faiblesse f; (of tea, solution) légèreté f
(f) (of economy, currency) faiblesse f

**weak-willed** adj to be ∼ manquer de fermeté

**wealth** n (a) (possessions) fortune f
(b) (state) richesse f
(c) (large amount) a ∼ of une mine de ⟨information⟩; une profusion de ⟨detail⟩; énormément de ⟨experience, talent⟩

**wealthy** adj riche

**wean** vtr sevrer ⟨baby⟩; to ∼ sb away from or off sth détourner qn de qch

**weapon** n arme f

**weaponry** n matériel m de guerre

**wear** ⬚1 n (a) (clothing) children's/sports ∼ vêtements mpl pour enfants/de sport
(b) (use) for everyday ∼ de tous les jours; for summer ∼ pour l'été
(c) (damage) usure f (on de); ∼ and tear usure f; to be the worse for ∼ (drunk) être ivre; (tired) être épuisé/-e
⬚2 vtr (a) (be dressed in) porter; to ∼ blue s'habiller en bleu; to ∼ one's hair long/short avoir les cheveux longs/courts
(b) (put on, use) mettre; I haven't got a thing to ∼ je n'ai rien à me mettre; to ∼ make-up se maquiller
(c) (display) he wore a puzzled frown il fronçait les sourcils d'un air perplexe
(d) (damage by use) user; to ∼ a hole in trouer ⟨garment, sheet⟩
⬚3 vi ⟨carpet, shoes⟩ s'user; my patience is ∼ing thin je commence à être à bout de patience
■ **wear away** ⟨inscription⟩ s'effacer; ⟨tread, cliff, façade⟩ s'user
■ **wear down**: ¶ ∼ down s'user; to be worn down être usé/-e; ¶ ∼ [sth] down user ⟨steps⟩; saper ⟨resistance, resolve⟩; ¶ ∼ [sb] down épuiser
■ **wear off** (a) ⟨drug, effect⟩ se dissiper; ⟨sensation⟩ passer
(b) (come off) s'effacer
■ **wear out**: ¶ ∼ out s'user; ¶ ∼ [sth] out user; ¶ ∼ [sb] out épuiser
■ **wear through** ⟨elbow, trousers⟩ se trouer; ⟨sole, metal, fabric⟩ se percer

**weariness** n lassitude f

**wearing** adj (exhausting) fatigant/-e; (irritating) pénible

**weary** ⬚1 adj ⟨person, smile, sigh, voice⟩ las/lasse; ⟨eyes, limbs, mind⟩ fatigué/-e; to grow ∼ se lasser (of de; of doing de faire)
⬚2 vi se lasser (of de; of doing de faire)

**weasel** n (a) (Zool) belette f
(b) (sly person) sournois/-e m/f

**weather** ⬚1 n temps m; what's the ∼ like? quel temps fait-il?; the ∼ here is hot il fait

chaud ici; in hot/cold ∼ quand il fait chaud/froid; ∼ permitting si le temps le permet; in all ∼s par tous les temps
⬚2 vtr survivre à ⟨crisis, upheaval⟩; to ∼ the storm (figurative) surmonter la crise
IDIOMS to be under the ∼ ne pas se sentir bien

**weatherbeaten** adj ⟨face⟩ hâlé/-e; ⟨rocks, landscape⟩ battu/-e par les vents

**weathercock** n girouette f

**weather forecast** n bulletin m météorologique

**weather forecaster** n (on TV) présentateur/-trice m/f de la météo; (specialist) météorologue mf, météorologiste mf

**weatherproof** adj ⟨garment, shoe⟩ imperméable; ⟨shelter, door⟩ étanche

**weave** ⬚1 vtr (a) tisser ⟨rug, fabric⟩
(b) tresser ⟨cane, basket, wreath⟩
⬚2 vi to ∼ in and out se faufiler (of entre); to ∼ towards sth (drunk) s'approcher en titubant de qch

**weaving** n tissage m

**web** n (a) (also spider's ∼) toile f (d'araignée)
(b) (network) a ∼ of un réseau de ⟨ropes, lines⟩; a ∼ of lies un tissu de mensonges

**Web** n Web m, Toile f

**webbing** n (material) sangles fpl

**Web cam** n Webcam f

**web foot** n patte f palmée

**Webmaster** n Webmestre m, Webmaster m

**Web page** n page f Web

**Web server** n serveur m Web

**Website** n site m Web

**Web space** n espace m Web

**wed** n the newly ∼s les jeunes mariés mpl

**wedding** n mariage m; a church ∼ un mariage religieux

**wedding anniversary** n anniversaire m de mariage

**wedding day** n jour m des noces

**wedding dress, wedding gown** n robe f de mariée

**wedding reception** n repas m de mariage

**wedding ring** n alliance f

**wedge** ⬚1 n (a) (to insert in rock, wood) coin m; (to hold sth in position) cale f; (in rock climbing) piton m
(b) (of cake, pie, cheese) morceau m
⬚2 vtr (a) to ∼ sth in place caler qch; to ∼ a door open caler une porte pour la tenir ouverte
(b) (jam) to ∼ sth into enfoncer qch dans; to be ∼d between être coincé/-e entre
IDIOMS that's the thin end of the ∼ c'est le commencement de la fin

**Wednesday** n mercredi m

**wee** vi (GB) (colloq) faire pipi

**W**

**weed** [1] n mauvaise herbe f; (in water) herbes fpl aquatiques
[2] vtr, vi désherber
■ **weed out**: ¶ ~ [sb] out, ~ out [sb] (gen) éliminer; se débarrasser de ⟨employee⟩; ¶ ~ [sth] out, ~ out [sth] se débarrasser de ⟨stock, items⟩

**weedkiller** n désherbant m, herbicide m

**weedy** adj (colloq) ⟨person, build⟩ malingre; ⟨character, personality⟩ faible

**week** n semaine f; last/next ~ la semaine dernière/prochaine; this ~ cette semaine; the ~ before last il y a deux semaines; the ~ after next dans deux semaines; every other ~ tous les quinze jours; twice a ~ deux fois par semaine; ~ in ~ out toutes les semaines; a ~ today/on Monday (GB), today/Monday ~ aujourd'hui/lundi en huit; a ~ yesterday (GB), a ~ from yesterday (US) il y a eu huit jours or une semaine hier; in three ~s' time dans trois semaines; the working or work (US) ~ la semaine de travail

**weekday** n jour m de (la) semaine; on ~s en semaine

**weekend** n week-end m; at the ~ (GB), on the ~ (US) pendant le week-end; at ~s (GB), on ~s (US) le week-end

**weekend bag** n petit sac m de voyage

**weekend cottage** n résidence f secondaire

**weekly** [1] n (newspaper) journal m hebdomadaire; (magazine) (revue f) hebdomadaire m
[2] adj hebdomadaire; on a ~ basis à la semaine
[3] adv ⟨pay⟩ à la semaine; ⟨meet, visit⟩ une fois par semaine

**weep** vi (a) (cry) pleurer (over sur)
(b) (ooze) suinter

**weepy** adj ⟨mood, film⟩ larmoyant/-e; to feel ~ avoir envie de pleurer

**weigh** [1] vtr (a) (on scales) peser; to ~ 10 kilos peser 10 kilos; how much or what do you ~? combien pèses-tu?; to ~ oneself se peser
(b) (assess) évaluer ⟨arguments, advantages, options⟩; peser ⟨consequences, risks, words⟩
[2] vi to ~ on sb peser sur qn; to ~ on sb's mind préoccuper qn

■ **weigh down**: ¶ ~ down on [sb/sth] peser sur; ¶ ~ [sb/sth] down surcharger ⟨vehicle, boat⟩; faire plier ⟨branches⟩; ⟨responsibility, debt⟩ accabler; to be ~ed down with crouler sous le poids de ⟨luggage⟩; être accablé/-e de ⟨worry, guilt⟩

■ **weigh in** ⟨boxer, wrestler⟩ se faire peser; ⟨jockey⟩ aller au pesage

■ **weigh out** peser ⟨ingredients, quantity⟩

■ **weigh up** évaluer ⟨prospects, situation⟩; juger ⟨person⟩; mettre [qch] en balance ⟨options, benefits, risks⟩

**weighing machine** n (for people) balance f; (for luggage, freight) bascule f

**weight** [1] n poids m; to put on/lose ~ prendre/perdre du poids

[2] vtr lester ⟨net, arrow⟩
IDIOMS not to carry much ~ ne pas peser lourd (with pour); to be a ~ off one's mind être un grand soulagement; to pull one's ~ faire sa part de travail; to throw one's ~ about or around faire l'important/-e m/f

**weightlessness** n (in space) apesanteur f

**weight-lifter** n haltérophile m

**weight-lifting** n haltérophilie f

**weight problem** n problème m de poids

**weight training** n musculation f (en salle)

**weighty** adj (a) (serious) de grand poids
(b) (heavy) lourd/-e

**weir** n barrage m

**weird** adj (strange) bizarre; (eerie) mystérieux/-ieuse

**welcome** [1] n accueil m; to give sb a warm ~ faire un accueil chaleureux à qn
[2] adj (a) bienvenu/-e; to be ~ être le bienvenu/la bienvenue m/f; to make sb ~ (on arrival) réserver un bon accueil à qn
(b) 'thanks'—'you're ~' 'merci'—'de rien'
[3] excl (to respected guest) soyez le bienvenu/la bienvenue m/f chez nous!; (greeting friend) entre donc!; ~ back!, ~ home! je suis content que tu sois de retour!
[4] vtr accueillir ⟨person⟩; se réjouir de ⟨news, decision, change⟩; être heureux/-euse de recevoir ⟨contribution⟩; accueillir favorablement ⟨initiative, move⟩

**welcoming** adj ⟨atmosphere, person⟩ accueillant/-e; ⟨ceremony, committee⟩ d'accueil

**weld** vtr (also ~ **together**) souder; to ~ sth on or to souder qch à

**welfare** [1] n (a) (well-being) bien-être m inv; (interest) intérêt m
(b) (state assistance) assistance f sociale; (money) aide f sociale
[2] adj ⟨system⟩ de protection sociale; (US) ⟨meal⟩ gratuit/-e

**welfare benefit** n prestation f sociale

**welfare services** n pl services mpl sociaux

**welfare spending** n dépenses fpl sociales

**welfare state** n (as concept) État-providence m; (stressing state assistance) protection f sociale

**well**¹ [1] adj bien; to feel ~ se sentir bien; are you ~? vous allez bien?, tu vas bien?; she's not ~ enough to travel elle n'est pas en état de voyager; to get ~ se rétablir; that's all very ~, but tout ça c'est bien beau, mais; it would be just as ~ to check il vaudrait mieux vérifier; it would be as ~ for you not to get involved tu ferais mieux de ne pas t'en mêler; the flight was delayed, which was just as ~ le vol a été retardé, ce qui n'était pas plus mal
[2] adv bien; to do ~ at school être bon/bonne élève; mother and baby are both doing ~ la mère et l'enfant se portent bien; the operation went ~ l'opération s'est bien

passée; ~ **done!** bravo!; **you may** ~ **be right**
il se pourrait bien que tu aies raison; **we
may as** ~ **go home** on ferait aussi bien de
rentrer; **it was** ~ **worth waiting for** ça valait
vraiment la peine d'attendre; **to wish sb** ~
souhaiter beaucoup de chance à qn
**③** *excl* **(a)** (expressing astonishment) eh bien!;
(expressing indignation, disgust) ça alors!;
(expressing disappointment) tant pis!; (qualifying
statement) enfin; ~, **you may be right** après
tout, tu as peut-être raison; ~, **that's too
bad** c'est vraiment dommage; ~ **then, what's
the problem?** alors, quel est le problème?;
**very** ~ **then** très bien
**④** **as well** *phr* aussi
**⑤** **as well as** *phr* aussi bien que; **they
have a house in the country as** ~ **as an
apartment in Paris** ils ont à la fois une
maison à la campagne et un appartement à
Paris
IDIOMS **to be** ~ **in with sb** (colloq) être bien
avec qn (colloq); **to be** ~ **up in sth** s'y
connaître en qch; **to leave** ~ **alone** (GB) *or* ~
**enough alone** (US) ne pas s'en mêler

**well²** *n* (sunk in ground) puits *m*; (pool) source
*f*

**well-balanced** *adj* équilibré/-e

**well-behaved** *adj* ‹child› sage; ‹dog›
bien dressé/-e

**well-being** *n* bien-être *m inv*

**well-defined** *adj* ‹outline› net/nette; ‹role,
boundary› bien défini/-e

**well-disposed** *adj* **to be** ~ **towards** être
bien disposé/-e envers ‹person›; être
favorable à ‹regime, idea, policy›

**well done** *adj* ‹steak› bien cuit/-e; ‹task›
bien fait/-e

**well-educated** *adj* (having a good
education) instruit/-e; (cultured) cultivé/-e

**well-heeled** *adj* (colloq) riche

**well-informed** *adj* bien informé/-e
**(about** sur); **he's very** ~ il est très au
courant de l'actualité

**wellington (boot)** *n* (GB) botte *f* de
caoutchouc

**well-kept** *adj* ‹house, garden, village› bien
entretenu/-e

**well-known** *adj* ‹person, place› célèbre; **to
be** ~ **to sb** être connu/-e de qn; **it is** ~ **that,
it is a** ~ **fact that** il est bien connu que

**well-liked** *adj* très apprécié/-e

**well-made** *adj* bien fait/-e

**well-meaning** *adj* ‹person› bien
intentionné/-e; ‹advice› qui part d'une bonne
intention

**well-meant** *adj* **his offer was** ~ sa
proposition partait d'une bonne intention

**well-off** **①** *n* **the** ~ les gens *mpl* aisés; **the
less** ~ les plus défavorisés *mpl*
**②** *adj* (wealthy) aisé/-e; **to be** ~ **for** avoir
beaucoup de ‹space, provisions›

**well-read** *adj* cultivé/-e

**well-respected** *adj* très respecté/-e

**well-rounded** *adj* ‹education,
programme› complet/-ète; ‹individual› qui a
reçu une éducation complète

**well-thought-out** *adj* bien élaboré/-e

**well-timed** *adj* qui tombe/tombait à
point; **that was well timed!** (of entrance,
phonecall etc) c'est bien tombé!

**well-to-do** *adj* aisé/-e

**well-wisher** *n* personne *f* qui veut
témoigner sa sympathie

**well-worn** *adj* ‹carpet, garment› élimé/-e;
‹steps› usé/-e; ‹joke› rebattu/-e

**Welsh** **①** *n* **(a)** (people) **the** ~ les Gallois
*mpl*
**(b)** (language) gallois *m*
**②** *adj* gallois/-e

**welt** *n* (on skin) marque *f* (de coup)

**welterweight** *n* poids *m* welter

**west** **①** *n* **(a)** (compass direction) ouest *m*
**(b)** **the West** l'Occident *m*, l'Ouest *m*; (part of
country) l'Ouest *m*; (political entity) l'Occident *m*
**②** *adj* (gen) ouest *inv*; ‹wind› d'ouest
**③** *adv* ‹move› vers l'ouest; ‹lie, live› à
l'ouest (**of** de)

**West Bank** *pr n* Cisjordanie *f*.

**western** **①** *n* (film) western *m*
**②** *adj* **(a)** ‹coast› ouest *inv*; ‹town, accent›
de l'ouest; ~ **France** l'ouest de la France
**(b)** (Pol) occidental/-e

**westerner** *n* Occidental/-e *m/f*

**westernize** *vtr* occidentaliser; **to become**
~**d** s'occidentaliser

**west-facing** *adj* exposé/-e à l'ouest

**West Indian** **①** *n* Antillais/-e *m/f*
**②** *adj* antillais/-e

**West Indies** *pr n pl* Antilles *fpl*

**wet** **①** *adj* **(a)** (damp) ‹hair, clothes, grass,
surface› mouillé/-e; **to get** ~ se faire
mouiller; **to get one's feet** ~ se mouiller les
pieds; **to get the floor** ~ tremper le sol; ~
**through** trempé/-e
**(b)** (freshly applied) ‹cement, varnish› humide;
'~ **paint**' 'peinture fraîche'
**(c)** (rainy) ‹weather, day, night›
pluvieux/-ieuse; ‹season› des pluies; **when
it's** ~ quand il pleut
**(d)** (GB) ‹person› qui manque de caractère
**②** *vtr* **(a)** mouiller ‹floor, object, clothes›
**(b)** **to** ~ **one's pants/the bed** ‹adult›
mouiller sa culotte/le lit; ‹child› faire pipi
dans sa culotte/dans son lit

**wet blanket** *n* (colloq) rabat-joie *mf inv*

**wet-look** *adj* luisant/-e

**wet suit** *n* combinaison *f* de plongée

**whack** **①** *n* (blow) (grand) coup *m*
**②** *excl* paf!
**③** *vtr* **(a)** (hit) battre ‹person, animal›;
frapper ‹ball›
**(b)** (GB) (colloq) (defeat) piler (colloq)

**whacked** *adj* (colloq) (tired) vanné/-e (colloq)

**whacky** *adj* (colloq) ‹person› dingue (colloq);
‹sense of humour› farfelu/-e (colloq)

**whale** **①** *n* **(a)** (Zool) baleine *f*

⋯⋗

**(b)** (colloq) **to have a** ∼ **of a time** s'amuser comme un fou

**2** *vtr* (US) (colloq) (thrash) donner une raclée à (colloq)

**whaling** *n* pêche *f* à la baleine

**wharf** *n* quai *m*

**what**

■ Note **As a pronoun**

– When used in questions as an object pronoun *what* is translated by *qu'est-ce que* (*qu'est-ce qu'* in front of a vowel or mute 'h'): *what did you say?* qu'est-ce que tu as dit? Alternatively you can use *que* (*qu'* before a vowel or mute 'h'), but note that subject and verb are reversed and a hyphen is inserted before a pronoun: *what did you say?* qu'as-tu dit?

– As a subject pronoun in questions *what* is translated by *qu'est-ce qui: what is happening?* qu'est-ce qui se passe? Alternatively *que* can be used and the subject and verb are reversed and the subject becomes *il: what is happening?* que se passe-t-il?

– When *what* is used to introduce a clause it is translated by *ce que* (*ce qu'*) as the object of the verb: *I don't know what you want* je ne sais pas ce que tu veux. As the subject of the verb it is translated by *ce qui: what matters is that...* ce qui compte c'est que...

**1** *pron* **with** ∼? avec quoi?; **and** ∼ **else?** et quoi d'autre?; ∼ **for?** (why) pourquoi?; (about what) à propos de quoi? ∼'s **the matter?** qu'est-ce qu'il y a?; ∼'s **her telephone number?** quel est son numéro de téléphone?; ∼'s **that button for?** à quoi sert ce bouton?; ∼'s **it like?** comment c'est?; **do** ∼ **you want** fais ce que tu veux; **take** ∼ **you need** prends ce dont tu as besoin; ∼ **I need is** ce dont j'ai besoin c'est; **and** ∼'s **more** et en plus; **and** ∼'s **worse** et en plus; **he did** ∼? il a fait quoi?; **George** ∼? George comment?

**2** *det* quel/quelle/quels/quelles; **do you know** ∼ **train he took?** est-ce que tu sais quel train il a pris?; ∼ **a nice dress/car!** quelle belle robe/voiture!; ∼ **a strange thing to do!** quelle drôle d'idée!; ∼ **use is that?** à quoi ça sert?; ∼ **money he earns he spends** tout ce qu'il gagne, il le dépense; ∼ **few friends she had** les quelques amis qu'elle avait

**3 what about** *phr* **(a)** (to draw attention) ∼ **about the children?** et les enfants (alors)? **(b)** (to make suggestion) ∼ **about a meal out?** et si on dînait au restaurant?; ∼ **about Tuesday?** qu'est-ce que tu dirais de mardi?

**4 what if** *phr* et si; ∼ **if I bring the dessert?** et si j'apportais le dessert?

**5** *excl* quoi!, comment!

IDIOMS ∼ **with one thing and another** avec ceci et cela

**what-d'yer-call-it** *n* (colloq) machin *m* (colloq)

**whatever** **1** *pron* **(a)** (that which) (as subject) ce qui; (as object) ce que; **to do** ∼ **one can** faire ce qu'on peut
**(b)** (anything that) (as subject) tout ce qui; (as

object) tout ce que; **do** ∼ **you like** fais tout ce que tu veux; ∼ **you say** (as you like) tout ce qui vous plaira
**(c)** (no matter what) quoi que (+ *subjunctive*); ∼ **happens** quoi qu'il arrive; ∼ **she says, ignore it** quoi qu'elle dise n'en tiens pas compte; ∼ **it costs it doesn't matter** quel que soit le prix, ça n'a pas d'importance
**(d)** (what on earth) (as subject) qu'est-ce qui; (as object) qu'est-ce que; ∼'s **that?** qu'est-ce c'est que ça?

**2** *det* **(a)** (any) **they eat** ∼ **food they can get** ils mangent tout ce qu'ils trouvent à manger
**(b)** (no matter what) ∼ **their arguments** quels que soient leurs arguments; ∼ **the reason** quelle que soit la raison; **for** ∼ **reason** pour je ne sais quelle raison

**3** *adv* (*also* **whatsoever**) **to have no idea** ∼ ne pas avoir la moindre idée; **'any petrol?'—'none** ∼**'** 'il y a de l'essence?'—'pas du tout'

**what's-her-name** *n* (colloq) Machin *m* (colloq)

**what's-his-name** *n* (colloq) Machin *m* (colloq)

**wheat** *n* blé *m*

**wheat germ** *n* germe *m* de blé

**wheatmeal** *n* farine *f* complète

**wheedle** *vtr* **to** ∼ **sth out of sb** soutirer qch à qn par la cajolerie

**wheel** **1** *n* **(a)** (on vehicle) roue *f*; (on trolley, piece of furniture) roulette *f*
**(b)** (for steering) (in vehicle) volant *m*; (on boat) roue *f* (de gouvernail); **to be at** *or* **behind the** ∼ être au volant
**(c)** (in watch, mechanism, machine) rouage *m*
**(d)** (for pottery) tour *m*

**2** *vtr* pousser ⟨*bicycle, barrow*⟩; **they** ∼**ed me into the operating theatre** ils m'ont emmené dans la salle d'opération sur un chariot

**3** *vi* (*also* ∼ **round**) ⟨*person, regiment*⟩ faire demi-tour; ⟨*car, motorbike*⟩ braquer fortement; ⟨*ship*⟩ virer de bord

IDIOMS **to** ∼ **and deal** magouiller (colloq)

**wheelbarrow** *n* brouette *f*

**wheelchair** *n* fauteuil *m* roulant

**wheelclamp** *n* (Aut) sabot *m* de Denver

**wheeler dealer** *n* (colloq) magouilleur/-euse *m/f* (colloq)

**wheelie bin** *n* poubelle *f* à roulettes

**wheeze** *vi* avoir la respiration sifflante

**wheezy** *adj* ⟨*voice, cough*⟩ rauque; **to have a** ∼ **chest** avoir la respiration sifflante

**when**

■ Note *When* in questions is usually translated by *quand*.

– Note that there are three ways of asking questions using *quand*: *when did she leave?* = quand est-ce qu'elle est partie?, elle est partie quand?, quand est-elle partie?

– When talking about future time, *quand* will be used with the future tense of the verb: *tell him when you see him* = dis-lui quand tu le verras.

W

**1** *adv* **(a)** (in questions) quand; ~ **are we leaving?** quand est-ce qu'on part?; ~ **is the concert?** c'est quand le concert?; **I wonder ~ the film starts** je me demande à quelle heure commence le film; **say ~** dis-moi stop **(b)** (whenever) quand; **he's only happy ~ he's moaning** il n'est content que quand il rouspète; ~ **I eat ice cream, I feel ill** quand *or* chaque fois que je mange de la glace, j'ai mal au cœur

**2** *rel pron* où; **the week ~ it all happened** la semaine où tout cela s'est produit; **there are times ~ it's too stressful** il y a des moments où c'est trop stressant

**3** *conj* **(a)** (expressing time) quand; ~ **he was at school** quand il était à l'école, lorsqu'il était à l'école; ~ **I am 18** quand j'aurai 18 ans; ~ **he arrives, I'll let you know** quand il arrivera *or* dès qu'il arrivera, je te le dirai **(b)** (expressing contrast) alors que; **why buy their products ~ ours are cheaper?** pourquoi acheter leurs produits alors que les nôtres sont moins chers?

**4** *pron* quand; **until/since ~?** jusqu'à/depuis quand?; **1982, that's ~ I was born** 1982, c'est l'année où je suis né; **that's ~ I found out** c'est à ce moment-là que j'ai su

**whenever** *adv* **(a)** (no matter when) ~ **you want** quand tu veux; **I'll come ~ it is convenient** je viendrai quand cela vous arrangera **(b)** (every time that) chaque fois que; ~ **I see a black cat, I make a wish** chaque fois que je vois un chat noir, je fais un vœu

**where**

■ **Note** *where* in questions is usually translated by *où*: *where are the plates?* = où sont les assiettes?; *I don't know where the plates are* = je ne sais pas où sont les assiettes; *do you know where he is?* = est-ce que tu sais où il est?; *do you know where Paul is?* = est-ce que tu sais où est Paul?
— Note that *où + est-ce que* does not require a change in word order: *where did you see her?* = où est-ce que tu l'as vue?

**1** *adv* où; ~ **is my coat?** où est mon manteau?; ~ **do you work?** où est-ce que vous travaillez?; **ask him ~ he went** demande-lui où il est allé; **do you know ~ she's going?** est-ce tu sais où elle va?; **sit ~ you like** asseyez-vous où vous voulez; **it's cold ~ we live** il fait froid là où nous habitons; ~ **necessary** si nécessaire; ~ **possible** dans la mesure du possible **2** *pron* **from ~?** d'où?; **that's ~ I fell** c'est là que je suis tombé; **that is ~ he is mistaken** c'est là qu'il se trompe

**whereabouts** *n pl* **do you know his ~?** savez-vous où il est?

**whereas** *conj* **she likes dogs ~ I prefer cats** elle aime les chiens mais moi je préfère les chats; **he chose to stay quiet ~ I would have complained** il a choisi de ne rien dire alors que moi je me serais sûrement plaint

**whereby** *conj* **a system ~ all staff will** carry identification un système qui prévoit que tous les membres du personnel auront une carte

**wherever** *adv* **(a)** (in questions) ~ **has he got to?** où est-ce qu'il a bien pu passer? **(b)** (anywhere) ~ **she goes I'll go** où qu'elle aille, j'irai; ~ **you want** où tu veux; **we'll meet ~'s convenient for you** nous nous retrouverons là où ça t'arrange **(c)** (whenever) ~ **necessary** quand c'est nécessaire; ~ **possible** dans la mesure du possible

**whet** *vtr* **to ~ the appetite** stimuler l'appétit; **the books ~ted his appetite for travel** les livres lui donnèrent envie de voyager

**whether** *conj*

■ **Note** When *whether* is used to mean *if*, it is translated by *si*: *I wonder whether she got my letter* = je me demande si elle a reçu ma lettre.
— In *whether…or not* sentences, *whether* is translated by *que* and the verb that follows is in the subjunctive.

**(a)** (when outcome is uncertain) si; **I wasn't sure ~ to answer or not** je ne savais pas s'il fallait répondre; **can you check ~ it's cooked?** est-ce que tu peux vérifier si c'est cuit? **(b)** (no matter if) **you're coming ~ you like it or not!** tu viendras que cela te plaise ou non!; ~ **you have children or not, this book should interest you** que vous ayez des enfants ou non, ce livre devrait vous intéresser

**whew** *excl* (in relief) ouf!; (in hot weather) pff!; (in surprise) hein!

**which 1** *pron* **(a)** (in questions) lequel/laquelle/lesquels/lesquelles; **there are three peaches, ~ do you want?** il y a trois pêches, laquelle veux-tu?; **show her ~ you mean** montre-lui celui/celle etc dont tu parles; **I don't mind ~** ça m'est égal; **can you tell ~ is ~?** peux-tu les distinguer? **(b)** (relative pronoun) (as subject) qui; (as object) que; (with a preposition) lequel/laquelle/lesquels/lesquelles; (with a preposition translated by *de*) dont; **the book ~ is on the table** le livre qui est sur la table; **the book ~ I am reading** le livre que je lis; **the contract ~ he's spoken about** le contrat dont il a parlé; ~ **reminds me…** ce qui me fait penser que… **(c)** (with a superlative adjective) quel/quelle/quels/quelles; ~ **is the biggest?** (masculine objects) quel est le plus gros? **2** *det* quel/quelle/quels/quelles; ~ **books?** quels livres?; **she asked me ~ coach was leaving first** elle m'a demandé lequel des cars allait partir le premier; ~ **one of the children…?** lequel *or* laquelle des enfants…?; **you may wish to join, in ~ case…** vous voulez peut-être vous inscrire, auquel cas…

**whichever 1** *pron* **(a)** (the one that) (as subject) celui *m* qui, celle *f* qui; (as object) celui *m* que, celle *f* que; **'which restaurant?'—'~ is nearest'** 'quel

⋯✦

restaurant?'—'celui qui est le plus proche';
**come at 2 or 2.30, ~ suits you best** viens à
14 h ou 14 h 30, comme cela te convient le
mieux
**(b)** (no matter which one) (as subject) quel *m* que
soit celui qui, quelle *f* que soit celle qui; (as
object) quel *m* que soit celui que, quelle *f* que
soit celle que; **'do you want the big piece or
the small piece?'—'~'** 'est-ce que tu veux le
gros ou le petit morceau?'—'n'importe'
**2** *det* **(a)** (the one that) **let's go to ~ station is
nearest** allons à la gare la plus proche
**(b)** (no matter which) **I'll be happy ~ horse wins**
quel que soit le cheval qui gagne je serai
content

**whiff** *n* (of perfume, food) odeur *f*; (of smoke,
garlic) bouffée *f*

**while** **1** *conj* (*also* **whilst**) **(a)** (during the
time that) pendant que; **he made a sandwich ~
I phoned** il s'est fait un sandwich pendant
que je téléphonais; **~ in Spain, I visited
Madrid** pendant que j'étais en Espagne, j'ai
visité Madrid; **I fell asleep ~ watching TV** je
me suis endormi en regardant la télé; **close
the door ~ you're at it** ferme la porte
pendant que tu y es
**(b)** (although) bien que (+ *subjunctive*),
quoique (+ *subjunctive*)
**(c)** (whereas) alors que, tandis que; **she likes
dogs ~ I prefer cats** elle aime les chiens
mais moi je préfère les chats
**2** *n* **a ~ ago** il y a quelque temps; **a ~ later**
quelque temps plus tard; **for a good ~**
pendant longtemps; **a short ~ ago** il y a peu
de temps; **it will take a ~** cela va prendre un
certain temps; **after a (short) ~** au bout d'un
moment; **once in a ~** de temps en temps
■ **while away** tuer ⟨*time*⟩ **(doing, by doing**
en faisant)

**whilst** = WHILE 1

**whim** *n* caprice *m*; **on a ~** sur un coup de
tête

**whimper** **1** *n* gémissement *m* **(of** de)
**2** *vi* **(a)** ⟨*person, animal*⟩ gémir
**(b)** (whinge) ⟨*person*⟩ pleurnicher

**whimsical** *adj* ⟨*person*⟩ fantasque; ⟨*play,
tale, manner, idea*⟩ saugrenu/-e

**whine** *vi* (complain) se plaindre **(about** de);
(snivel) pleurnicher; ⟨*dog*⟩ gémir

**whinge** *vi* (colloq) râler

**whining** **1** *n* (complaints) jérémiades *fpl*; (of
dog) gémissements *mpl*
**2** *adj* ⟨*voice*⟩ geignard/-e; ⟨*child*⟩
pleurnicheur/-euse

**whinny** *vi* ⟨*horse*⟩ hennir doucement

**whip** **1** *n* **(a)** (for punishment) fouet *m*; (for
horse) cravache *f*
**(b)** (Culin) mousse *f*
**2** *vtr* **(a)** (beat) fouetter
**(b)** (Culin) fouetter ⟨*cream*⟩; battre [qch] en
neige ⟨*egg whites*⟩
**(c)** (colloq) **to ~ sth out** sortir qch
brusquement; (remove quickly) **he ~ped the
plates off the table** il a prestement retiré les
assiettes de la table; **I ~ped the key out of**

his hand je lui ai arraché la clé des mains;
**to ~ the crowd up into a frenzy** mettre la
foule en délire

**whiplash injury** *n* (Med) coup *m* du lapin

**whip-round** *n* (GB) (colloq) collecte *f*

**whirl** **1** *n* **(a)** (of activity, excitement) tourbillon
*m* **(of** de)
**(b)** (spiral motif) spirale *f*
**2** *vi* ⟨*dancer*⟩ tournoyer; ⟨*blade, propeller*⟩
tourner; ⟨*snowflakes, dust, thoughts*⟩
tourbillonner
IDIOMS **to give sth a ~** (colloq) essayer qch
■ **whirl round** ⟨*person*⟩ se retourner
brusquement; ⟨*blade, clock hand*⟩ tourner
brusquement

**whirlpool** *n* tourbillon *m*

**whirlpool bath** *n* bain *m* bouillonnant.

**whirlwind** *n* tourbillon *m*

**whirr** *vi* ⟨*motor*⟩ vrombir; ⟨*camera, fan*⟩
tourner; ⟨*insect*⟩ bourdonner; ⟨*wings*⟩ bruire

**whisk** **1** *n* (*also* **egg ~**) (manual) fouet *m*;
(electric) batteur *m*
**2** *vtr* **(a)** (Culin) battre
**(b)** (transport quickly) **he was ~ed off to meet
the president** on l'a emmené sur le champ
rencontrer le président; **she was ~ed off to
hospital** elle a été emmenée d'urgence à
l'hôpital

**whisker** **1** *n* (of animal) poil *m* de
moustache
**2 whiskers** *n pl* (of animal) moustaches *fpl*;
(of man) (beard) barbe *f*; (moustache) moustache
*f*

**whisper** **1** *n* chuchotement *m*; **to speak in
a ~ or in ~s** parler à voix basse
**2** *vtr* chuchoter **(to** à); **to ~ sth to sb**
chuchoter qch à qn; **'she's asleep', he ~ed**
'elle dort', dit-il en chuchotant
**3** *vi* chuchoter; **to ~ to sb** parler à voix
basse à qn

**whistle** **1** *n* **(a)** (object) sifflet *m*; **to blow
the or one's ~** donner un coup de sifflet
**(b)** (sound) (through mouth) sifflement *m*; (by
referee) coup *m* de sifflet; (of bird, train)
sifflement *m*
**2** *vtr* siffler; (casually) siffloter
**3** *vi* siffler; **to ~ at sb/sth** siffler qn/qch; **to
~ for** siffler ⟨*dog*⟩
IDIOMS **to blow the ~ on sb** dénoncer qn

**white** **1** *n* **(a)** (gen) blanc *m*
**(b)** (*also* **White**) (Caucasian) Blanc/Blanche
*m/f*
**(c)** (in chess, draughts) blancs *mpl*
**2** *adj* **(a)** blanc/blanche; **bright ~ teeth**
dents d'un blanc éclatant; **to go or turn ~**
devenir blanc, blanchir; **to paint sth ~**
peindre qch en blanc
**(b)** ⟨*race, child, skin*⟩ blanc/blanche; ⟨*area*⟩
habité/-e par des Blancs; ⟨*culture, prejudice*⟩
des Blancs; **a ~ man/woman** un Blanc/une
Blanche
**(c)** (pale) pâle **(with** de); **to go or turn ~** pâlir
(with de)

**whitebait** *n* (raw) blanchaille *f*; (fried) petite
friture *f*

**w**

**whiteboard** *n* tableau *m* blanc

**white coffee** *n* (at home) café *m* au lait; (in café) (café *m*) crème *m*

**white-collar** *adj* ⟨job, work⟩ d'employé de bureau; ⟨staff⟩ de bureau; **∼ worker** col *m* blanc, employé/-e *m/f* de bureau

**white elephant** *n* **(a)** (item, knicknack) bibelot *m*
**(b)** ( public project) réalisation *f* coûteuse et peu rentable

**white goods** *n pl* (appliances) gros électro-ménager *m*

**white horses** *n pl* (waves) moutons *mpl*

**White House** *n* the **∼** la Maison Blanche

**white-knuckle ride** *n* tour *m* de manège qui fait peur

**white lie** *n* pieux mensonge *m*

**whitener** *n* **(a)** (for clothes) agent *m* blanchissant
**(b)** (for shoes) produit *m* pour blanchir
**(c)** (for coffee, tea) succédané *m* de lait en poudre

**whiteness** *n* blancheur *f*

**white spirit** *n* white-spirit *m*

**whitewash** ☐1 *n* **(a)** (for walls) lait *m* de chaux
**(b)** (figurative) (cover-up) mise *f* en scène
☐2 *vtr* **(a)** blanchir [qch] à la chaux ⟨wall⟩
**(b)** (also **∼ over**) blanchir ⟨facts⟩

**white water** *n* eau *f* vive

**white water rafting** *n* rafting *m* en eau vive

**white wedding** *n* mariage *m* en blanc

**Whitsun** *n* (also **Whitsuntide**) Pentecôte *f*

**Whit Sunday** *n* Pentecôte *f*

**whittle** *vtr* tailler [qch] au couteau; **to ∼ sth away** *or* **down** réduire qch (**to** à)

**whizz** *vi* **to ∼ by** *or* **past** ⟨arrow, bullet⟩ passer en sifflant; ⟨car⟩ passer à toute allure; ⟨person⟩ passer rapidement

**whizz-kid** *n* (colloq) jeune prodige *m*

**who** *pron*

---

■ Note Note that there are three ways of asking questions using *qui* as the object of the verb: *who did he call?* = qui est-ce qu'il a appelé?, qui a-t-il appelé?, il a appelé qui?

---

**(a)** (in questions) (as subject) qui (est-ce qui); (as object) qui (est-ce que); (after prepositions) qui; **∼ knows the answer?** qui connaît la réponse?; **∼'s going to be there?** qui sera là?; **∼ did you invite?** qui est-ce que tu as invité?, qui as-tu invité?; **∼ was she with?** avec qui était-elle?; **∼ did you buy it for?** pour qui l'as-tu acheté?; **∼ did you get it from?** qui te l'a donné?
**(b)** (relative) (as subject) qui; (as object) que; (after prepositions) qui; **his friend, ∼ lives in Paris** son ami, qui habite Paris; **his friend ∼ he sees once a week** l'ami qu'il voit une fois par semaine

**(c)** (whoever) **bring ∼ you like** tu peux amener qui tu veux; **∼ do you think you are?** tu te prends pour qui?

**whodun(n)it** *n* polar *m* (colloq), roman *m* policier

**whoever** *pron* **(a)** (the one that) **∼ wins the election** celui ou celle qui gagnera les élections
**(b)** (anyone that) (as subject) quiconque; (as object) qui; **∼ saw the accident should contact us** quiconque a assisté à l'accident devrait nous contacter; **invite ∼ you like** invite qui tu veux
**(c)** (no matter who) **∼ you are** qui que vous soyez

**whole** ☐1 *n* **(a)** (total unit) tout *m*; **as a ∼** (not in separate parts) en entier; (overall) dans l'ensemble
**(b)** (all) **the ∼ of** tout/-e; **the ∼ of the weekend/August** tout le week-end/mois d'août; **the ∼ of London is talking about it** tout Londres en parle; **nearly the ∼ of Berlin was destroyed** Berlin a été presque entièrement détruit
☐2 *adj* **(a)** (entire) tout/-e, entier/-ière; (more emphatic) tout entier/-ière; **a ∼ hour** une heure entière; **a ∼ day** toute une journée; **for three ∼ weeks** pendant trois semaines entières; **his ∼ life** toute sa vie, sa vie entière; **the ∼ truth** toute la vérité; **the most beautiful city in the ∼ world** la plus belle ville du monde
**(b)** (emphatic use) **a ∼ new way of life** un mode de vie complètement différent; **that's the ∼ point of the exercise** c'est tout l'intérêt de l'exercice
**(c)** (intact) intact/-e
☐3 *adv* ⟨swallow, cook⟩ tout entier
☐4 **on the whole** *phr* dans l'ensemble

**wholefood** *n* (GB) produits *mpl* biologiques

**wholehearted** *adj* ⟨approval, support⟩ sans réserve; **to be in ∼ agreement with** être en accord total avec

**wholeheartedly** *adv* sans réserve

**wholemeal** *adj* (also **wholewheat**) complet/-ète

**whole milk** *n* lait *m* entier

**wholesale** ☐1 *adj* **(a)** ⟨business⟩ de gros
**(b)** (large-scale) ⟨destruction⟩ total/-e; ⟨acceptance, rejection⟩ en bloc; ⟨attack⟩ sur tous les fronts
☐2 *adv* **(a)** ⟨buy, sell⟩ en gros
**(b)** ⟨accept, reject⟩ en bloc

**wholesaler** *n* grossiste *mf*, marchand/-e *m/f* en gros

**wholesome** *adj* **(a)** (healthy) sain/-e
**(b)** (decent) ⟨person, appearance⟩ bien propre; ⟨entertainment⟩ innocent/-e

**wholewheat** = WHOLEMEAL

**wholly** *adv* entièrement, tout à fait

**whom** *pron* **(a)** (in questions) qui (est-ce que); (after prepositions) qui; **∼ did she meet?** qui ⋯❖

a-t-elle rencontré?, qui est-ce qu'elle a rencontré?; **to ∼ are you referring?** à qui est-ce que vous faites allusion?
**(b)** (relative) que; (after prepositions) qui; **the person to ∼/of ∼ I spoke** la personne à qui/ dont j'ai parlé

**whooping cough** n coqueluche f

**whopper** n (colloq) (large thing) monstre m

**whopping** adj (colloq) (also **∼ great**) monstre (colloq)

**whorl** n (of cream, chocolate) spirale f; (on fingerprint) volute f; (shell pattern) spire f; (of petals) verticille m

**whose** ⟨1⟩ pron **(a)** (in questions) à qui; **∼ is this?** à qui est ceci?
**(b)** (relative) dont; **the boy ∼ dog was killed** le garçon dont le chien a été tué; **the man ∼ daughter he was married to** l'homme dont il avait épousé la fille
⟨2⟩ det **∼ pen is that?** à qui est ce stylo?; **do you know ∼ car was stolen?** est-ce que tu sais à qui appartenait la voiture volée?; **∼ coat did you take?** tu as pris le manteau de qui?

### why

■ **Note** Note that there are three ways of asking questions using *why*:
– **why did you go?** = pourquoi est-ce que tu y es allé?, pourquoi y es-tu allé?, tu y es allé pourquoi?

⟨1⟩ adv **(a)** (in questions) pourquoi; **∼ do you ask?** pourquoi est-ce que tu me poses la question?, pourquoi tu me poses-tu la question?; **∼ bother?** pourquoi se tracasser?; **∼ the delay?** pourquoi ce retard?; **∼ not?** pourquoi pas?; **'tell them'—'∼ should I?'** 'dis-le-leur'—'et pourquoi (est-ce que je devrais le faire)?'
**(b)** (making suggestions) pourquoi; **∼ don't we go away for the weekend?** pourquoi ne pas partir quelque part pour le week-end?; **∼ don't I invite them for dinner?** et si je les invitais à manger?
⟨2⟩ conj pour ça; **that is ∼ they came** c'est pour ça qu'ils sont venus; **I need to know the reason ∼** j'ai besoin de savoir pourquoi

**wick** n mèche f

**wicked** adj **(a)** (evil) ⟨person⟩ méchant/-e; ⟨heart, deed⟩ cruel/-elle; ⟨plot⟩ pernicieux/-ieuse; ⟨intention⟩ mauvais/-e (before n)
**(b)** ⟨grin, humour⟩ malicieux/-ieuse; ⟨thoughts⟩ pervers/-e
**(c)** (vicious) ⟨wind⟩ méchant/-e; ⟨weapon⟩ redoutable; **to have a ∼ tongue** être mauvaise langue

**wicker** ⟨1⟩ n (also **wickerwork**) osier m
⟨2⟩ adj ⟨basket, furniture⟩ en osier

**wide** ⟨1⟩ adj **(a)** (broad) ⟨river, opening, mouth⟩ large; ⟨margin⟩ grand/-e; **how ∼ is your garden?** quelle est la largeur de votre jardin?; **it's 30 cm ∼** il fait 30 cm de large; **the river is 1 km across at its ∼st** le fleuve

fait or atteint 1 km à son point le plus large; **her eyes were ∼ with fear** ses yeux étaient agrandis par la peur
**(b)** (immense) ⟨ocean, desert, expanse⟩ vaste (before n)
**(c)** (extensive) ⟨variety, choice⟩ grand/-e (before n); **a ∼ range of opinions** une grande variété d'opinions; **a ∼ range of products** une vaste gamme de produits
**(d)** (Sport) ⟨ball, shot⟩ perdu/-e
⟨2⟩ adv **to open one's eyes ∼** ouvrir grand les yeux; **to open the door/window ∼** ouvrir la porte/la fenêtre en grand; **his eyes are (set) ∼ apart** il a les yeux très écartés; **his legs were ∼ apart** il avait les jambes écartées; **to be ∼ of the mark** ⟨ball, dart⟩ être à côté; ⟨guess⟩ être loin de la vérité

**wide-angle lens** n objectif m à grand angle

**wide awake** adj complètement éveillé/-e

**wide-eyed** adj **(a)** (with surprise, fear) **he was ∼** il ouvrait de grands yeux; **∼ with fear/ surprise** les yeux écarquillés de peur/ surprise; **she stared/listened ∼** elle regardait/écoutait les yeux écarquillés
**(b)** (naïve) ⟨person, innocence⟩ ingénu/-e

**widely** adv **(a)** (commonly) ⟨accepted, used⟩ largement; **this product is now ∼ available** on trouve maintenant ce produit partout
**(b)** ⟨spaced, planted⟩ à de grands intervalles; ⟨travel, differ, vary⟩ beaucoup

**widely-read** adj ⟨student⟩ qui a beaucoup lu; ⟨author⟩ très lu/-e

**widen** ⟨1⟩ vtr élargir ⟨road, gap⟩; étendre ⟨powers⟩; **this has ∼ed their lead in the opinion polls** ceci a renforcé leur position dominante dans les sondages
⟨2⟩ vi s'élargir

**widening** adj ⟨division⟩ de plus en plus grand/-e; ⟨gap⟩ qui s'élargit de plus en plus

**wide open** adj **(a)** ⟨door, window, eyes, mouth⟩ grand/-e ouvert/-e
**(b)** **the race is ∼** l'issue de la course est indécise

**wide-ranging** adj ⟨reforms⟩ de grande envergure; ⟨interests⟩ très variés

**wide screen** n grand écran m

**wide-screen TV** n téléviseur m à grand écran

**widespread** adj ⟨epidemic⟩ généralisé/-e; ⟨devastation⟩ étendu/-e; ⟨belief⟩ très répandu/-e

**widow** ⟨1⟩ n veuve f
⟨2⟩ vtr **to be ∼ed** devenir veuf/veuve m/f

**widower** n veuf m

**width** n **(a)** largeur f; **it is 30 metres in ∼** il fait or mesure 30 mètres de large
**(b)** (of fabric) lé m

**wield** vtr **(a)** brandir ⟨weapon, tool⟩
**(b)** exercer ⟨power⟩ (over sur)

**wife** n femme f; (more formally) épouse f; **the baker's/farmer's ∼** la boulangère/la fermière

**wig** n (whole head) perruque f; (partial) postiche m

**W**

**wiggle** (colloq) **1** *n* a ~ of the hips un roulement des hanches
**2** *vtr* faire bouger ⟨*tooth, wedged object*⟩; **to ~ one's hips** rouler les hanches; **to ~ one's fingers/toes** remuer les doigts/orteils
**3** *vi* ⟨*snake, worm*⟩ se tortiller

**wild** **1** *n* **in the ~** ⟨*conditions, life*⟩ en liberté; **to grow in the ~** pousser à l'état sauvage; **the call of the ~** l'appel de la nature
**2** *adj* **(a)** ⟨*animal, plant*⟩ sauvage; **the pony is still quite ~** le poney est encore assez farouche
**(b)** ⟨*landscape*⟩ sauvage
**(c)** ⟨*wind*⟩ violent/-e; ⟨*sea*⟩ agité/-e; **it was a ~ night** c'était une nuit de tempête
**(d)** ⟨*party, laughter, person*⟩ fou/folle; ⟨*imagination*⟩ délirant/-e; ⟨*applause*⟩ déchaîné/-e; **to go ~** se déchaîner
**(e)** (colloq) (furious) furieux/-ieuse; **he'll go** *or* **be ~!** ça va le mettre hors de lui!
**(f)** (colloq) (enthusiastic) **to be ~ about** être un/ une fana (colloq) de; **I'm not ~ about him/it** il/ça ne m'emballe (colloq) pas
**(g)** (outlandish) ⟨*idea, plan*⟩ fou/folle; ⟨*claim, promise, accusation*⟩ extravagant/-e; ⟨*story*⟩ farfelu/-e (colloq)
**3** *adv* ⟨*grow*⟩ à l'état sauvage; **the garden had run ~** le jardin était devenu une vraie jungle; **those children are allowed to run ~!** on permet à ces enfants de faire n'importe quoi!; **to let one's imagination run ~** laisser libre cours à son imagination

**wild boar** *n* sanglier *m*

**wilderness** *n* étendue *f* sauvage et désolée

**wild-eyed** *adj* au regard égaré

**wildfire** *n* **to spread like ~** se répandre comme une traînée de poudre

**wild flower** *n* fleur *f* des champs, fleur *f* sauvage

**wild-goose chase** *n* **it turned out to be a ~** ça n'a abouti à rien; **to lead sb on a ~** mettre qn sur une mauvaise piste

**wildlife** *n* (animals) faune *f*; (animals and plants) faune *f* et flore *f*

**wildlife park**, **wildlife reserve**, **wildlife sanctuary** *n* réserve *f* naturelle

**wildly** *adv* **(a)** ⟨*invest, spend, talk*⟩ de façon insensée; ⟨*fire, shoot*⟩ au hasard; **to hit out/ run ~** envoyer des coups/courir dans tous les sens
**(b)** ⟨*wave, gesture*⟩ de manière très agitée; ⟨*applaud*⟩ à tout rompre; **to fluctuate ~** subir des fluctuations violentes; **to beat ~** ⟨*heart*⟩ battre à tout rompre
**(c)** ⟨*enthusiastic, optimistic*⟩ extrêmement

**wilds** *n pl* **to live in the ~ of Arizona** habiter au fin fond de l'Arizona

**Wild West** *n* Far West *m*

**wilful** (GB), **willful** (US) *adj* **(a)** ⟨*person, behaviour*⟩ volontaire
**(b)** ⟨*damage, disobedience*⟩ délibéré/-e

**wilfully** (GB), **willfully** (US) *adv* **(a)** (in headstrong way) obstinément
**(b)** (deliberately) délibérément

**will¹** **1** *modal aux* **(a)** (expressing the future) **I'll see you tomorrow** je te verrai demain; **it won't rain** il ne pleuvra pas; **~ there be many people?** est-ce qu'il y aura beaucoup de monde?; **they'll come tomorrow** ils vont venir demain; **what ~ you do now?** qu'est-ce que tu vas faire maintenant?
**(b)** (expressing willingness or intention) **~ you help me?** est-ce que tu m'aideras?; **we won't stay too long** nous ne resterons pas trop longtemps; **he won't cooperate** il ne veut pas coopérer
**(c)** (in requests, commands) **~ you pass the salt please?** est-ce que tu peux me passer le sel s'il te plait; **~ you please be quiet!** est-ce que tu vas te taire?; **wait a minute, ~ you!** attends un peu!
**(d)** (in invitations) **~ you have some tea?** est-ce que vous voulez du thé?; **won't you join us for dinner?** est-ce que tu veux dîner avec nous?; **what ~ you have to drink?** qu'est-ce que tu prends?
**(e)** (in assumptions) **he'll be about 30 now** il doit avoir 30 ans maintenant; **you'll be tired, I expect** tu dois être fatigué je suppose
**(f)** (indicating sth predictable or customary) **they ~ ask for a deposit** ils demandent une caution; **these things ~ happen** ce sont des choses qui arrivent; **you ~ keep contradicting her!** il faut toujours que tu la contredises!
**(g)** (in short answers and tag questions) **you'll come again, won't you?** tu reviendras, n'est-ce pas?; **you won't forget, ~ you?** tu n'oublieras pas, n'est-ce pas?; **that'll be cheaper, won't it?** ça sera moins cher, non?; **'they won't be ready'—'yes, they ~'** 'ils ne seront pas prêts'—'(bien sûr que) si'; **'~ you call me?'—'yes, I ~'** 'est-ce que tu me téléphoneras?'—'bien sûr que oui'; **'she'll be furious'—'no, she won't!'** 'elle sera furieuse'—'bien sûr que non!'; **'I'll do it'—'no you won't!'** 'je le ferai'—'il n'en est pas question!'
**2** *vtr* **(a)** (urge mentally) **to ~ sb to do** supplier mentalement qn de faire; **to ~ sb to live** prier pour que qn vive
**(b)** (wish, desire) vouloir
**(c)** (Law) léguer ⟨*to* à⟩

**will²** **1** *n* **(a)** volonté *f* ⟨*to do* de faire⟩; **to have a ~ of one's own** n'en faire qu'à sa tête; **against my ~** contre mon gré; **to do with a ~** faire de bon cœur; **to lose the ~ to live** ne plus avoir envie de vivre
**(b)** (Law) testament *m*; **to leave sb sth in one's ~** léguer qch à qn
**2 at will** *phr* ⟨*select, take*⟩ à volonté; **they can wander about at ~** ils peuvent se promener comme ils veulent

**willing** *adj* **(a)** (prepared) **to be ~ to do** être prêt/-e à faire
**(b)** (eager) ⟨*pupil, helper*⟩ de bonne volonté; ⟨*slave*⟩ consentant/-e; ⟨*recruit, victim*⟩ volontaire; **to show ~** faire preuve de bonne volonté

W

**willingly** adv ⟨accept, help⟩ volontiers; ⟨work⟩ avec bonne volonté

**willingness** n (readiness) volonté f (**to do** de faire)

**willow** n (also ∼ **tree**) saule m

**will power** n volonté f (**to do** de faire)

**willy-nilly** adv (a) (regardless of choice) bon gré mal gré
(b) (haphazardly) au hasard

**wilt** vi (a) ⟨plant, flower⟩ se faner
(b) ⟨person⟩ (from heat, fatigue) se sentir faible; (at daunting prospect) perdre courage

**wimp** n (colloq) (ineffectual) lavette f (colloq); (fearful) poule f mouillée (colloq)

**win** ⌷1⌷ n victoire f (**over** sur)
⌷2⌷ vtr (a) gagner ⟨match, bet, battle, money⟩; remporter ⟨election⟩
(b) (acquire) obtenir ⟨delay, reprieve⟩; gagner ⟨friendship, heart⟩; s'attirer ⟨sympathy⟩; s'acquérir ⟨support⟩ (**of** de); **to** ∼ **sb's love/respect** se faire aimer/respecter de qn
⌷3⌷ vi gagner; **to** ∼ **against sb** l'emporter sur qn
■ **win back**: ¶ ∼ [sth] **back**, ∼ **back** [sth] récupérer ⟨support, votes⟩ (**from sb** sur qn); regagner ⟨affection, respect⟩; reprendre ⟨prize, territory⟩ (**from** à)
■ **win over**, **win round** convaincre ⟨person⟩

**wince** ⌷1⌷ n grimace f
⌷2⌷ vi grimacer, faire une grimace

**winch** ⌷1⌷ n treuil m
⌷2⌷ vtr **to** ∼ **sth down/up** descendre/hisser qch au treuil

**wind¹** ⌷1⌷ n (a) vent m; **the** ∼ **is blowing** il y a du vent; **which way is the** ∼ **blowing?** d'où vient le vent?
(b) (breath) **to knock the** ∼ **out of sb** couper le souffle à qn; **to get one's** ∼ reprendre souffle
(c) (flatulence) vents mpl; **to break** ∼ lâcher un vent
⌷2⌷ vtr (a) (make breathless) ⟨blow, punch⟩ couper la respiration à; ⟨climb⟩ essouffler
(b) faire faire son rot à ⟨baby⟩

**wind²** ⌷1⌷ vtr (a) (coil up) enrouler ⟨hair, rope, wire⟩ (**on, onto** sur; **round** autour de)
(b) (also ∼ **up**) remonter ⟨clock, toy⟩
(c) donner un tour de ⟨handle⟩
(d) **to** ∼ **its way** ⟨procession, road, river⟩ serpenter
⌷2⌷ vi ⟨road, river⟩ serpenter (**along** le long de); ⟨stairs⟩ tourner
■ **wind down**: ¶ ∼ **down** (a) ⟨organization⟩ réduire ses activités; ⟨activity, production⟩ toucher à sa fin; ⟨person⟩ se détendre
(b) ⟨clockwork⟩ être sur le point de s'arrêter
¶ ∼ [sth] **down** (a) baisser ⟨car window⟩
(b) mettre fin à ⟨activity, organization⟩
■ **wind up**: ¶ ∼ **up** (a) (finish) ⟨event⟩ se terminer (**with** par); ⟨speaker⟩ conclure
(b) (colloq) (end up) finir, se retrouver
¶ ∼ [sth] **up** (a) liquider ⟨business⟩; mettre fin à ⟨debate, meeting, project⟩

(b) remonter ⟨clock, car window⟩
¶ ∼ [sb] **up** (a) (tease) faire marcher ⟨person⟩
(b) (make tense) énerver

**wind chimes** n pl carillon m éolien

**wind energy** n énergie f éolienne

**windfall** n fruit m tombé par terre; (figurative) aubaine f

**windfall profit** n profit m inattendu

**winding** adj ⟨road, river⟩ sinueux/-euse; ⟨stairs⟩ en spirale

**wind instrument** n instrument m à vent

**windmill** n moulin m à vent

**window** n (a) (of house) fenêtre f; (of shop, public building) vitrine f; (of vehicle) (gen) vitre f; (of plane) hublot m; (stained glass) vitrail m; **to look out of** or **through the** ∼ regarder par la fenêtre
(b) (for service at bank or post office) guichet m

**window blind** n store m

**window box** n jardinière f

**window cleaner** n laveur/-euse m/f de carreaux

**window display** n vitrine f

**window ledge** n appui m de fenêtre

**windowpane** n carreau m

**window seat** n (a) (in room) banquette f
(b) (in plane, bus, train) place f côté vitre

**window-shopping** n **to go** ∼ faire du lèche-vitrines m inv (colloq)

**windowsill** n rebord m de fenêtre

**windpipe** n trachée-artère f

**windpower** n énergie f éolienne

**windscreen** (GB), **windshield** (US) n pare-brise m inv

**windscreen wiper** n (GB) essuie-glace m inv

**windshield** (US) = WINDSCREEN

**windsurf** vi faire de la planche à voile

**windsurfer** n (person) véliplanchiste mf; (board) planche f à voile

**windswept** adj venteux/-euse

**windy** adj ⟨place⟩ venteux/-euse; ⟨day⟩ de vent; **it was very** ∼ il faisait beaucoup de vent

**wine** n (a) (drink) vin m
(b) (colour) lie-de-vin m

**wine bar** n bar m à vin

**wine box** n ≈ cubitainer® m

**wine cellar** n cave f

**wine glass** n verre m à vin

**wine grower** n viticulteur/-trice m/f

**wine growing** ⌷1⌷ n viticulture f
⌷2⌷ adj ⟨region⟩ vinicole

**wine list** n carte f des vins

**wine rack** n casier m à bouteilles

**wine shop** n marchand m de vin

**wine tasting** n dégustation f de vins

**wine vinegar** n vinaigre m de vin

**wine waiter** n sommelier/-ière m/f

**wing** ⌷1⌷ n aile f

**2 wings** *n pl* (in theatre) **the ~s** les coulisses *fpl*; **to be waiting in the ~s** (figurative) attendre son heure

**winger** *n* (GB) (colloq) ailier *m*

**wing nut** *n* écrou *m* à oreilles

**wink** **1** *n* clin *m* d'œil; **we didn't get a ~ of sleep all night** nous n'avons pas fermé l'œil de la nuit

**2** *vi* cligner de l'œil; **to ~ at sb** faire un clin d'œil à qn

**winner** *n* **(a)** (victor) gagnant/-e *m/f*
**(b)** (success) **to be a ~** ⟨*film, book, song*⟩ avoir un gros succès

**winning** *adj* **(a)** (victorious) gagnant/-e
**(b)** ⟨*smile*⟩ engageant/-e; **to have ~ ways** avoir du charme

**winning post** *n* poteau *m* d'arrivée

**winnings** *n pl* gains *mpl*

**winning streak** *n* **to be on a ~** être dans une bonne période

**winter** **1** *n* hiver *m*; **in ~** en hiver
**2** *adj* ⟨*sports, clothes, weather*⟩ d'hiver
**3** *vi* passer l'hiver

**wintertime** *n* hiver *m*

**wipe** **1** *n* **(a)** **to give sth a ~** (clean, dust) donner un coup de chiffon à qch; (dry) essuyer qch
**(b)** (for face, baby) lingette *f*
**2** *vtr* essuyer ⟨*table, glass*⟩ (on sur; with avec); **to ~ one's hands/feet** s'essuyer les mains/les pieds; **to ~ one's nose** se moucher; **to ~ a baby's bottom** essuyer (les fesses d')un bébé; **to ~ the dishes** essuyer la vaisselle

■ **wipe away** essuyer ⟨*tears, sweat*⟩; faire partir ⟨*dirt, mark*⟩

■ **wipe out (a)** nettoyer ⟨*container, cupboard*⟩
**(b)** annuler ⟨*inflation*⟩; anéantir ⟨*species, enemy, population*⟩

■ **wipe up**: ¶ **~ up** essuyer la vaisselle; ¶ **~ [sth] up** essuyer

**wipe-clean** *adj* facile à nettoyer

**wire** **1** *n* **(a)** fil *m*; **electric/telephone ~** fil électrique/téléphonique
**(b)** (US) (telegram) télégramme *m*
**2** *vtr* **(a)** **to ~ a house** installer l'électricité dans une maison; **to ~ a plug/a lamp** connecter une prise/une lampe
**(b)** (telegraph) télégraphier à ⟨*person*⟩; télégraphier ⟨*money*⟩

**wiring** *n* (in house) installation *f* électrique; (in appliance) circuit *m* (électrique)

**wiry** *adj* **(a)** ⟨*person, body*⟩ mince et nerveux/-euse
**(b)** ⟨*hair*⟩ rêche

**wisdom** *n* sagesse *f*

**wisdom tooth** *n* dent *f* de sagesse

**wise** **1** *adj* ⟨*person, words, precaution, saying*⟩ sage; ⟨*choice, investment*⟩ judicieux/-ieuse; ⟨*smile, nod*⟩ avisé/-e; **a ~ man** un sage; **a ~ move** une décision judicieuse; **to be none the ~r** (understand no better) ne pas être plus avancé/-e; (not realize) ne s'apercevoir de rien

**2 -wise** *combining form* **(a)** (direction) dans le sens de; **length-~** dans le sens de la longueur
**(b)** (with regard to) pour ce qui est de; **work-~** pour ce qui est du travail

**wisecrack** *n* vanne *f* (colloq)

**wise guy** *n* (colloq) gros malin *m* (colloq)

**wisely** *adv* judicieusement

**wish** **1** *n* **(a)** (request) souhait *m* (for de); **to make a ~** faire un vœu; **her ~ came true** son souhait s'est réalisé
**(b)** (desire) désir *m* (for de; **to do** de faire); **to go against sb's ~es** aller contre la volonté de qn
**2 wishes** *n pl* vœux *mpl*; **good** *or* **best ~es** meilleurs vœux; (ending letter) bien amicalement; **best ~es on your birthday** meilleurs vœux pour votre anniversaire; **please give him my best ~es** je vous prie de lui faire toutes mes amitiés
**3** *vtr* **(a)** (expressing longing) **I ~ he were here/had been here** si seulement il était ici/ avait été ici; **he ~ed he had written** il regrettait de ne pas avoir écrit
**(b)** (express congratulations, greetings) souhaiter; **I ~ you good luck/a happy birthday** je vous souhaite bonne chance/un bon anniversaire; **I ~ him well** je souhaite que tout aille bien pour lui
**(c)** (want) souhaiter, désirer
**4** *vi* **(a)** (desire) vouloir; **just as you ~** comme vous voudrez
**(b)** (make a wish) faire un vœu

**wishful thinking** *n* **that's ~** c'est prendre ses désirs pour des réalités

**wishy-washy** *adj* (colloq) ⟨*colour*⟩ délavé/-e; ⟨*person*⟩ incolore et inodore (colloq)

**wisp** *n* (of hair) mèche *f*; (of straw) brin *m*; (of smoke, cloud) volute *f*

**wispy** *adj* ⟨*hair, beard*⟩ fin/-e; ⟨*cloud, smoke*⟩ léger/-ère

**wisteria** *n* glycine *f*

**wistful** *adj* (sad) mélancolique; (nostalgic) nostalgique

**wit** **1** *n* **(a)** (sense of humour) esprit *m*
**(b)** (witty person) personne *f* spirituelle
**2 to wit** *phr* à savoir

**witch** *n* sorcière *f*

**witchcraft** *n* sorcellerie *f*

**witch doctor** *n* shaman *m*

**witch-hunt** *n* chasse *f* aux sorcières

**with** *prep* **(a)** (gen) avec; **a meeting ~ sb** une réunion avec qn; **to hit sb ~ sth** frapper qn avec qch; **~ difficulty/pleasure** avec difficulté/plaisir; **to be patient ~ sb** être patient/-e avec qn; **delighted ~ sth** ravi/-e de qch; **to travel ~ sb** voyager avec qn; **to live ~ sb** (in one's own house) vivre avec qn; (in their house) vivre chez qn; **I'll be ~ you in a second** je suis à vous dans un instant; **take your umbrella ~ you** emporte ton parapluie; **bring the books back ~ you** rapporte les livres
**(b)** (in descriptions) à; avec; de; **a girl ~ black hair** une fille aux cheveux noirs; **the boy ~** ⋯⟶

the **broken leg** le garçon à la jambe cassée; **a boy ~ a broken leg** un garçon avec une jambe cassée; **a TV ~ remote control** une télévision avec télécommande; **furnished ~ antiques** meublé/-e avec des meubles anciens; **covered ~ mud** couvert/-e de boue; **to lie ~ one's eyes closed** être allongé/-e les yeux fermés; **to stand ~ one's arms folded** se tenir les bras croisés; **filled ~ sth** rempli/-e de qch
**(c)** (according to) **to increase ~ time** augmenter avec le temps; **to vary ~ the temperature** varier selon la température
**(d)** (owning, bringing) **passengers ~ tickets** les passagers munis de billets; **people ~ qualifications** les gens qualifiés; **somebody ~ your experience** quelqu'un qui a ton expérience; **have you got the report ~ you?** est-ce que tu as (amené) le rapport?
**(e)** (as regards) **how are things ~ you?** comment ça va?; **what's up ~ you?** qu'est-ce que tu as?; **what do you want ~ another car?** qu'est-ce que tu veux faire d'une deuxième voiture?
**(f)** (because of) **sick ~ worry** malade d'inquiétude; **he can see better ~ his glasses on** il voit mieux avec ses lunettes; **I can't do it ~ you watching** je ne peux pas le faire si tu me regardes
**(g)** (suffering from) **people ~ Aids/leukemia** les personnes atteintes du sida/de leucémie; **to be ill ~ flu** avoir la grippe
**(h)** (employed by, customer of) **a reporter ~ the Gazette** un journaliste de la Gazette; **he's ~ the UN** il travaille pour l'ONU; **I'm ~ Chemco** je travaille chez Chemco; **we're ~ the National Bank** nous sommes à la National Bank
**(i)** (in the same direction as) **to sail ~ the wind** naviguer dans le sens du vent; **to drift ~ the tide** dériver avec le courant

**withdraw** 1 *vtr* retirer ⟨*hand, money, application, permission, troops*⟩; renoncer à, retirer ⟨*claim*⟩; rétracter ⟨*accusation, statement*⟩
2 *vi* **(a)** (gen) se retirer (**from** de)
**(b)** (psychologically) se replier sur soi-même

**withdrawal** *n* **(a)** (of money, troops) retrait *m* (**of, from** de)
**(b)** (psychological reaction) repli *m* sur soi
**(c)** (of drug addict) état *m* de manque

**withdrawal symptoms** *n pl* symptômes *mpl* de manque; **to be suffering from ~** être en état de manque

**withdrawn** *adj* ⟨*person*⟩ renfermé/-e, replié/-e sur soi-même

**wither** 1 *vtr* flétrir
2 *vi* se flétrir

**withering** *adj* ⟨*look*⟩ plein/-e de mépris; ⟨*contempt, comment*⟩ cinglant/-e

**withhold** *vtr* différer ⟨*payment*⟩; retenir ⟨*tax, grant, rent*⟩; refuser ⟨*consent, permission*⟩; ne pas divulguer ⟨*information*⟩

**within** 1 *prep* **(a)** (inside) **~ the city walls**

dans l'enceinte de la ville; **~ the party** au sein du parti; **it's a play ~ a play** c'est une pièce dans la pièce
**(b)** (in expressions of time) **I'll do it ~ the hour** je le ferai en moins d'une heure; **15 burglaries ~ a month** 15 cambriolages en (moins d')un mois; **they died ~ a week of each other** ils sont morts à une semaine d'intervalle
**(c)** (not more than) **to be ~ several metres of sth** être à quelques mètres seulement de qch; **it's accurate to ~ a millimetre** c'est exact au millimètre près
**(d) to live ~ one's income** vivre selon ses moyens
2 *adv* à l'intérieur; **from ~** de l'intérieur

**without** 1 *prep* sans; **~ a key** sans clé; **~ any money** sans argent; **she left ~ it** elle est partie sans; **they left ~ me** ils sont partis sans moi; **~ looking** sans regarder; **it goes ~ saying** cela va de soi
2 *adv* à l'extérieur; **from ~** de l'extérieur

**withstand** *vtr* résister à

**witness** 1 *n* **(a)** (gen, Law) (person) témoin *m*; **she was a ~ to the accident** elle a été témoin de l'accident; **~ for the prosecution/ the defence** témoin à charge/à décharge
**(b)** (testimony) témoignage *m*; **to be** *or* **bear ~ to sth** témoigner de qch
2 *vtr* **(a)** (see) être témoin de, assister à ⟨*incident, attack*⟩
**(b)** servir de témoin lors de la signature de ⟨*will, treaty*⟩; être témoin à ⟨*marriage*⟩

**witness box** (GB), **witness stand** (US) *n* barre *f* des témoins

**wits** *n pl* (intelligence) intelligence *f*; (presence of mind) présence *f* d'esprit; **to collect** *or* **gather one's ~** rassembler ses esprits; **to frighten sb out of their ~** faire une peur épouvantable à qn; **to live by one's ~** vivre d'expédients; **a battle of ~** une joute verbale
IDIOMS **to be at one's ~ end** ne plus savoir quoi faire

**witticism** *n* bon mot *m*

**witty** *adj* spirituel/-elle

**wizard** *n* **(a)** (magician) magicien *m*
**(b)** (expert) **to be a ~ at chess/computing** être un as (colloq) aux échecs/en informatique

**wizened** *adj* ratatiné/-e

**wobble** *vi* ⟨*table, chair*⟩ branler; ⟨*pile of books, plates*⟩ osciller; ⟨*jelly*⟩ trembloter; ⟨*person*⟩ (on bicycle) osciller; (on ladder, tightrope) chanceler

**wobbly** *adj* ⟨*table, chair*⟩ bancal/-e; ⟨*tooth*⟩ branlant/-e

**woe** *n* malheur *m*; **a tale of ~** une histoire pathétique

**wolf** *n* loup *m*; **she-~** louve *f*
IDIOMS **to cry ~** crier au loup

**wolf-whistle** 1 *n* sifflement *m*
2 *vi* siffler

**woman** *n* femme *f*; **a ~ Prime Minister** une femme premier ministre; **he's always criticizing women drivers** il est toujours en train de critiquer les femmes au volant

**woman friend** n amie f

**womanizer** n coureur m (de jupons)

**womb** n (Anat) uterus m

**women's refuge** n foyer m pour femmes battues

**women's studies** n pl études fpl féministes

**wonder** ①n (a) (miracle) merveille f; **to do** or **work ~s** faire des merveilles (**for** pour; **with** avec); (**it's**) **no ~ that he's late** (ce n'est pas étonnant qu'il soit en retard
(b) (amazement) émerveillement m
②vtr (ask oneself) se demander; **I ~ how/ why/whether** je me demande comment/ pourquoi/si; (as polite request) **I ~ if you could help me?** pourriez-vous m'aider?; **it makes you ~** cela donne à penser; **it makes you ~ why** c'est à se demander pourquoi
③vi (a) (think) **to ~ about sth/about doing sth** penser à qch/à faire qch
(b) (be surprised) **to ~ at sth** s'étonner de qch; (admiringly) s'émerveiller de qch

**wonderful** adj ⟨book, film, meal, experience, holiday⟩ merveilleux/-euse; ⟨musician, teacher⟩ excellent/-e

**wonderfully** adv ⟨funny, exciting, clever⟩ très; ⟨work, cope, drive⟩ admirablement

**wonky** adj (colloq) (crooked) de traviole (colloq); (wobbly) ⟨furniture⟩ bancal/-e

**wont** adj **to be ~ to do** avoir coutume de faire; **as is his/their ~** comme à son/leur habitude

**woo** vtr courtiser

**wood** ①n bois m
②**woods** n pl bois mpl
③adj ⟨fire, smoke⟩ de bois; **~ floor** plancher m
IDIOMS **touch ~!** (GB), **knock on ~!** (US) touchons du bois!; **we are not out of the ~ yet** on n'est pas encore sorti de l'auberge

**wooden** adj (a) ⟨furniture, object, house⟩ en bois; ⟨leg, spoon⟩ de bois
(b) ⟨expression⟩ figé/-e

**woodland** n bois m

**woodpecker** n pic m

**wood pigeon** n pigeon m ramier

**woodwind** n pl bois mpl

**woodwork** n (a) (carpentry) menuiserie f
(b) (doors, windows) boiseries fpl

**woodworm** n ver m du bois

**wool** n laine f; **pure (new) ~** pure laine (vierge).
IDIOMS **to pull the ~ over sb's eyes** duper qn

**woollen** (GB), **woolen** (US) ①n (garment) lainage m
②adj ⟨garment⟩ de laine

**woolly** (GB), **wooly** (US) ①n (colloq) lainage m
②adj (a) ⟨garment⟩ de laine; ⟨animal coat, hair⟩ laineux/-euse; ⟨cloud⟩ cotonneux/-euse
(b) ⟨thinking⟩ flou/-e

**word** ①n (a) mot m; **to have the last ~** avoir le dernier mot; **I couldn't get a ~ in** je n'ai pas pu placer un mot; **in other ~s** en d'autres termes; **a ~ of warning** un avertissement; **a ~ of advice** un conseil; **too sad for ~s** trop triste; **I believed every ~ he said** je croyais tout ce qu'il me disait; **I mean every ~ of it** je pense ce que je dis; **a man of few ~s** un homme peu loquace; **not a ~ to anybody** pas un mot à qui que ce soit; **I don't believe a ~ of it** je n'en crois pas un mot
(b) (information) nouvelles fpl (**about** concernant); **there is no ~ of the missing climbers** on est sans nouvelles des alpinistes disparus; **~ got out that...** la nouvelle a transpiré que...; **to bring/send ~ that** annoncer/faire savoir que
(c) (promise, affirmation) parole f; **he gave me his ~** il m'a donné sa parole; **to keep/break one's ~** tenir/ne pas tenir parole; **to take sb's ~ for it** croire qn sur parole; **take my ~ for it!** crois-moi!
(d) (rumour) **~ has it that he's a millionaire** on dit qu'il est millionnaire; **~ got around that...** le bruit a couru que...
(e) (command) ordre m; **to give the ~ to do** donner l'ordre de faire
②**words** n pl (of play) texte m; (of song) paroles fpl
③vtr formuler ⟨reply, letter, statement⟩
IDIOMS **my ~!** (in surprise) ma parole!; **right from the ~ go** dès le départ; **to have a ~ with sb about sth** parler à qn à propos de qch; **to have ~s with sb** s'accrocher avec qn; **to put in a good ~ for sb** glisser un mot en faveur de qn

**word for word** adv ⟨copy, translate⟩ mot à mot; ⟨repeat⟩ mot pour mot

**wording** n formulation f

**wordlist** n liste f de mots

**word-of-mouth** ①adj verbal/-e
②**by word of mouth** phr verbalement

**word processing, WP** n traitement m de texte

**word processor** n machine f à traitement de texte

**work** ①n (a) (physical or mental activity) travail m (**on** sur); **it was hard ~ doing** ça a été dur de faire; **to be hard at ~** travailler dur; **it's thirsty ~** ça donne soif
(b) (occupation) travail m; **to be in ~** avoir du travail or un emploi; **place of ~** lieu m de travail; **to be off ~** (on vacation) être en congé; **to be off ~ with flu** être en arrêt de travail parce qu'on a la grippe; **to be out of ~** être au chômage
(c) (place of employment) **to go to ~** aller au travail
(d) (building, construction) travaux mpl (**on** sur)
(e) (essay, report) travail m; (artwork, novel, sculpture) œuvre f (**by** de); (study) ouvrage m (**by** de; **on** sur); (research) recherches fpl (**on** sur); **a ~ of reference** un ouvrage de référence; **a ~ of fiction** une œuvre de fiction; **the ~s of Racine** l'œuvre m de Racine; **this attack is the ~ of professionals** l'attaque est l'œuvre de professionnels ⋯▸

**2** **works** n pl (a) (factory) usine f
(b) (building work) travaux mpl
(c) (colloq) (everything) **the (full** or **whole) ∼s**
toute la panoplie (colloq)

**3** vtr (a) (drive) **to ∼ sb hard** surmener qn
(b) (labour) **to ∼ days/nights** travailler de
jour/de nuit; **to ∼ a 40 hour week** faire la
semaine de 40 heures; **he ∼ed his way
through college** il a travaillé pour payer ses
études
(c) (operate) se servir de ⟨computer, machine⟩
(d) (exploit commercially) exploiter ⟨mine, seam⟩
(e) (bring about) **to ∼ wonders** or **miracles**
faire des merveilles
(f) (use to one's advantage) **to ∼ the system**
exploiter le système
(g) (fashion) travailler ⟨clay, metal⟩
(h) (manoeuvre) **to ∼ sth into** introduire qch
dans ⟨slot, hole⟩; **to ∼ a lever up and down**
actionner un levier
(i) (exercise) faire travailler ⟨muscles⟩
(j) (move) **to ∼ one's way through** se frayer
un passage à travers ⟨crowd⟩; **to ∼ one's
way along** avancer le long de ⟨ledge,
windowsill⟩; **to ∼ one's hands free** se libérer
les mains; **it ∼ed its way loose, it ∼ed itself
loose** cela s'est desserré peu à peu

**4** vi (a) (do a job) travailler ⟨doing à faire⟩;
**to ∼ for a living** gagner sa vie
(b) (strive) **(against** contre; **for** pour; **to
do** pour faire); **to ∼ towards** aller vers
⟨solution⟩; s'acheminer vers ⟨compromise⟩;
négocier ⟨agreement⟩
(c) (function) fonctionner; **to ∼ on electricity**
marcher or fonctionner à l'électricité; **the
washing machine isn't ∼ing** la machine à
laver est en panne
(d) (act, operate) **it doesn't** or **things don't ∼
like that** ça ne marche pas comme ça; **to ∼ in
sb's favour** tourner à l'avantage de qn; **to ∼
against sb** jouer en la défaveur de qn
(e) (be successful) ⟨treatment⟩ avoir de l'effet;
⟨detergent, drug⟩ agir ⟨against contre; on
sur⟩; ⟨plan⟩ réussir; ⟨argument, theory⟩ tenir
debout; **flattery won't ∼ with me** la flatterie
ne marche pas avec moi
IDIOMS **to ∼ one's way up** gravir tous les
échelons; **to ∼ one's way up the company**
faire son chemin dans l'entreprise

■ **work in:** ∼ **in [sth]**, ∼ **[sth] in (a)** glisser
⟨joke⟩; mentionner ⟨fact, name⟩
(b) ((Culin)) incorporer

■ **work off (a)** (remove) retirer ⟨lid⟩
(b) (repay) travailler pour rembourser ⟨loan,
debt⟩
(c) (get rid of) se débarrasser de ⟨excess
weight⟩; dépenser ⟨excess energy⟩; passer
⟨anger, frustration⟩

■ **work on:** ¶ ∼ **on** continuer à travailler; ¶
∼ **on [sb]** travailler (colloq) ⟨person⟩; ¶ ∼ **on
[sth]** travailler à ⟨book, report⟩; travailler sur
⟨project⟩; s'occuper de ⟨case, problem⟩;
chercher ⟨cure, solution⟩; examiner ⟨idea,
theory⟩

■ **work out:** ¶ ∼ **out (a)** (exercise) s'entraîner
(b) (go according to plan) marcher

(c) (add up) **to ∼ out at (GB)** or **to (US)**
s'élever à
¶ ∼ **[sth] out (a)** (calculate) calculer ⟨amount⟩
(b) (solve) trouver ⟨answer, reason, culprit⟩;
résoudre ⟨problem⟩; comprendre ⟨clue⟩
(c) (devise) concevoir ⟨plan, scheme⟩; trouver
⟨route⟩
¶ ∼ **[sb] out** comprendre ⟨person⟩

■ **work up:** ¶ ∼ **up [sth]** développer
⟨interest⟩; accroître ⟨support⟩; **to ∼ up the
courage to do** trouver le courage de faire; **to
∼ up some enthusiasm for** s'enthousiasmer
pour; **to ∼ up an appetite** s'ouvrir l'appétit
¶ ∼ **up to [sth]** se préparer à ⟨confrontation,
announcement⟩
¶ ∼ **[sb] up (a)** (excite) exciter ⟨child, crowd⟩
(b) (annoy) **to get ∼ed up, to ∼ oneself up**
s'énerver

**workable** adj (a) ⟨idea, plan, suggestion⟩
réalisable; ⟨system⟩ pratique; ⟨arrangement,
compromise⟩ possible
(b) ⟨land, mine⟩ exploitable; ⟨cement⟩
maniable

**workaholic** n (colloq) bourreau m de
travail

**workbook** n (blank) cahier m; (with exercises)
livre m d'exercices

**worker** n (in manual job) ouvrier/-ière m/f; (in
white-collar job) employé/-e m/f

**work experience** n stage m

**workforce** n (in industry) main-d'œuvre f; (in
service sector) effectifs mpl

**working** adj (a) ⟨parent, woman⟩ qui
travaille; ⟨conditions, environment, methods⟩
de travail; ⟨population, life⟩ actif/-ive;
⟨breakfast, lunch, day⟩ de travail; **during ∼
hours** (in office) pendant les heures de bureau;
(in shop) pendant les heures d'ouverture
(b) (provisional) ⟨document⟩ de travail;
⟨definition, title⟩ provisoire
(c) (functional) ⟨model⟩ qui fonctionne; ⟨farm,
mine⟩ en exploitation; **in full ∼ order** en
parfait état de marche

**working class** **1** n classe f ouvrière; **the
∼es** les classes fpl laborieuses
**2** **working-class** adj ⟨area, background,
family, life⟩ ouvrier/-ière; ⟨culture, London⟩
prolétarien/-ienne; ⟨person⟩ de la classe
ouvrière

**workings** n pl rouages mpl

**workload** n charge f de travail

**workman** n ouvrier m

**workmanship** n **a carpenter famous for
sound ∼** un menuisier connu pour la qualité
de son travail; **furniture of the finest ∼** des
meubles d'une belle facture; **a piece of poor**
or **shoddy ∼** du travail mal fait or bâclé

**workmate** n collègue mf de travail

**work of art** n œuvre f d'art

**workout** n séance f de mise en forme

**workpack** n fiches fpl de travail

**work permit** n permis m de travail

**workplace** n lieu m de travail

**work-sharing** n partage m du travail

**worksheet** *n* (Sch) feuille *f* de questions

**workshop** *n* atelier *m*

**work station** *n* poste *m* de travail

**worktop** *n* plan *m* de travail

**work-to-rule** *n* grève *f* du zèle

**world** ⓵ *n* monde *m*; **throughout the** ∼ dans le monde entier; **to go round the** ∼ faire le tour du monde; **the biggest in the** ∼ le plus grand du monde; **more than anything in the** ∼ plus que tout au monde; **to go up in the** ∼ faire du chemin; **to go down in the** ∼ déchoir; **the Eastern/Western** ∼ les pays de l'Est/occidentaux; **the ancient** ∼ l'antiquité; **he lives in a** ∼ **of his own** il vit dans un monde à part

⓶ *adj* ⟨*events, market, leader, politics, rights, scale*⟩ mondial/-e; ⟨*record, tour, championship*⟩ du monde; ⟨*cruise*⟩ autour du monde

IDIOMS **to be on top of the** ∼ être aux anges; **to get the best of both** ∼**s** gagner sur les deux tableaux; **a man/woman of the** ∼ un homme/une femme d'expérience; **out of this** ∼ extraordinaire; **there's a** ∼ **of difference** il y a une différence énorme; **it did him the** *or* **a** ∼ **of good** ça lui a fait énormément de bien; **to think the** ∼ **of sb** penser le plus grand bien de qn; **what/ where/who in the** ∼? que/où/qui etc diable?; ∼**s apart** diamétralement opposé

**world-class** *adj* de niveau mondial

**World Cup** *n* Coupe *f* du Monde

**World Fair** *n* Exposition *f* universelle

**world-famous** *adj* mondialement connu/-e

**world leader** *n* (a) (politician) chef *m* d'État
(b) (athlete) meilleur/-e *m/f* du monde; (company) leader *m* mondial

**worldly** *adj* (a) (not spiritual) matériel/-ielle
(b) (experienced) ⟨*person*⟩ avisé/-e, qui a de l'expérience

**worldly-wise** *adj* avisé/-e, qui a de l'expérience

**world music** *n* musiques *fpl* du monde

**world power** *n* puissance *f* mondiale

**worldview** *n* vision *f* du monde

**world war** *n* guerre *f* mondiale; **the First/ Second World War** la Première/Seconde Guerre mondiale

**world-wide** ⓵ *adj* mondial/-e
⓶ *adv* dans le monde entier

**World Wide Web** *n* Toile *f* mondiale, Web *m*

**worm** *n* ver *m*

**worn** *adj* ⟨*carpet, clothing, shoe, tyre*⟩ usé/-e; ⟨*stone*⟩ abîmé/-e; ⟨*tread*⟩ lisse

**worn-out** *adj* (a) ⟨*carpet, brake*⟩ complètement usé/-e
(b) ⟨*person*⟩ épuisé/-e

**worried** *adj* ⟨*person, face*⟩ inquiet/-iète; **to be** ∼ **about sb/sth** se faire du souci *or* s'inquiéter pour qn/qch; **I'm** ∼ **(that) he might get lost** j'ai peur qu'il ne se perde

**worrier** *n* anxieux/-ieuse *m/f*

**worry** ⓵ *n* (a) (anxiety) soucis *mpl* (**about, over** à propos de)
(b) (problem) souci *m* (**about, over** au sujet de)
⓶ *vtr* (a) (concern) inquiéter; **I** ∼ **that he won't come** j'ai peur qu'il ne vienne pas; **it worried him that he couldn't find the keys** ça l'a inquiété de ne pas trouver les clés
(b) (bother) ennuyer; **would it** ∼ **you if I opened the window?** est-ce que ça vous ennuierait que j'ouvre la fenêtre?
(c) ⟨*dog*⟩ harceler ⟨*sheep*⟩
⓷ *vi* (be anxious) s'inquiéter; **to** ∼ **about** *or* **over sb/sth** s'inquiéter *or* se faire du souci pour qn/qch; **don't** ∼! ne t'inquiète pas!; **there's nothing to** ∼ **about** il n'y a pas lieu de s'inquiéter
⓸ *v refl* **to** ∼ **oneself** s'inquiéter, se faire de souci (**about sb** au sujet de qn; **about sth** à propos de qch); **to** ∼ **oneself sick over sth** se ronger les sangs (colloq) au sujet de qch
■ **worry at** ⟨*dog*⟩ mordiller, jouer avec ⟨*toy*⟩; ⟨*person*⟩ retourner [qch] dans tous les sens ⟨*problem*⟩

**worry beads** *n pl* chapelet *m* antistress

**worrying** *adj* inquiétant/-e

**worse** ⓵ *adj* pire (**than que**); **to get** ∼ ⟨*pressure, noise*⟩ augmenter; ⟨*conditions, weather*⟩ empirer; ⟨*illness, conflict*⟩ s'aggraver; **he's getting** ∼ (in health) il va plus mal; **the cough is getting** ∼ la toux empire; **to feel** ∼ (more ill) se sentir plus malade; (more unhappy) aller moins bien; **and what is** ∼ et le pire, c'est que; **and to make matters** ∼, **he lied** et pour ne rien arranger, il a menti
⓶ *n* **there is** ∼ **to come** ce n'est pas encore le pire; **to change for the** ∼ empirer
⓷ *adv* ⟨*play, sing*⟩ moins bien (**than que**); **to behave** ∼ se conduire plus mal; **she could do** ∼ **than follow his example** ce ne serait pas si mal si elle suivait son exemple

**worsen** ⓵ *vtr* aggraver ⟨*situation, problem*⟩
⓶ *vi* ⟨*condition, health, weather, situation*⟩ se détériorer; ⟨*problem, crisis, shortage, flooding*⟩ s'aggraver

**worsening** ⓵ *n* aggravation *f* (**of** de)
⓶ *adj* ⟨*situation*⟩ en voie de détérioration; ⟨*problem, shortage*⟩ en voie d'aggravation

**worse off** *adj* (a) (less wealthy) **to be** ∼ avoir moins d'argent (**than que**); **I'm £10 a week** ∼ j'ai dix livres de moins par semaine
(b) (in a worse situation) **to be** ∼ être dans une situation pire

**worship** ⓵ *n* (a) (religious devotion) culte *m*; **sun/ancestor** ∼ culte du soleil/des ancêtres; **place of** ∼ lieu *m* de culte
(b) (veneration) vénération *f*
⓶ **Worship** *pr n* (GB) **Your Worship** (to judge) Monsieur le juge; (to mayor) Monsieur le maire
⓷ *vtr* (a) (venerate) vénérer ⟨*God, Buddha*⟩; (give praise) rendre hommage à     ····⋗

**W**

**(b)** adorer, avoir un culte pour ⟨person⟩; avoir le culte de ⟨money, success⟩
[4] vi pratiquer sa religion

**worshipper** n fidèle mf

**worst** [1] n **(a)** (most difficult, unpleasant) **the ~** le/la pire m/f; **if the ~ came to the ~** (in serious circumstances) dans le pire des cas; (involving fatality) si le pire devait arriver
**(b)** (most negative trait) **to bring out the ~ in sb** mettre à jour ce qu'il y a de plus mauvais chez qn
**(c)** (of the lowest standard, quality) **the ~** le plus mauvais/la plus mauvaise m/f; **he's one of the ~** c'est un des plus mauvais; **to be the ~ at French** être le plus mauvais en français
[2] adj **(a)** (most unsatisfactory, unpleasant) pire, plus mauvais/-e; **the ~ book I've ever read** le plus mauvais livre que j'aie jamais lu; **the ~ thing about the film is...** ce qu'il y a de pire dans le film c'est...
**(b)** (most serious) plus grave; **one of the ~ recessions** une des crises les plus graves
[3] adv **the children suffer (the) ~** ce sont les enfants qui souffrent le plus; **they were (the) ~ hit by the strike** ce sont eux qui ont été les plus touchés par la grève; **~ of all,...** le pire de tout, c'est que...

**worth** [1] n **(a)** (quantity) **five pounds' ~ of sth** pour cinq livres de qch; **thousands of pounds' ~ of damage** des milliers de livres de dégâts; **a week's ~ of supplies** une semaine de provisions; **to get one's money's ~** en avoir pour son argent
**(b)** (value) valeur f; **of great ~** de grande valeur; **of no ~** sans valeur
[2] adj **(a)** (of financial value) **to be ~ sth** valoir qch; **how much is it ~?** combien cela vaut-il?; **the pound was ~ 10 francs then** à l'époque, la livre valait 10 francs
**(b)** (of abstract value) **to be ~ sth** valoir qch; **to be ~ it** (en) valoir la peine; **the book isn't ~ reading** le livre ne vaut pas la peine d'être lu; **that's ~ knowing** cela est bon à savoir; **those little pleasures that make life ~ living** ces petits plaisirs qui rendent la vie agréable
IDIOMS **for all one is ~** de toutes ses forces; **for what it's ~** pour ce que cela vaut; **to be ~ sb's while** valoir le coup

**worthless** adj sans valeur; **he's ~** c'est un bon à rien

**worthwhile** adj ⟨discussion, undertaking, visit⟩ qui en vaut la peine; ⟨career, project⟩ intéressant/-e; **to be ~ doing** valoir la peine de faire

**worthy** adj **(a)** (deserving) **to be ~ of sth** mériter qch, être digne de qch; **~ of note** digne d'intérêt; **to be ~ of doing** ⟨person⟩ être digne de faire
**(b)** (admirable) ⟨cause⟩ noble; ⟨citizen, friend⟩ digne

**would** modal aux **(a)** (expressing the conditional) **it ~ be nice if everyone were there, wouldn't it?** ce serait bien si tout le monde était là, n'est-ce pas?; **if he had more money, he'd buy a car** s'il avait plus d'argent il achèterait une voiture; **we ~ have missed**

the train if we had left later si nous étions partis plus tard, nous aurions raté le train; **we wouldn't have succeeded without him** nous n'aurions pas réussi sans lui
**(b)** (in indirect statements or questions) **we thought he'd forget** nous pensions qu'il oublierait; **did she say she ~ be coming?** est-ce qu'elle a dit qu'elle viendrait?; **I wish he ~ be quiet!** il ne pourrait pas se taire!
**(c)** (expressing willingness to act) **she wouldn't listen to me** elle ne voulait pas m'écouter; **he wouldn't do a thing to help us** il n'a rien voulu faire pour nous aider; **they asked me to leave but I wouldn't** ils m'ont demandé de partir mais j'ai refusé; **of course you ~ contradict him!** bien sûr il a fallu que tu le contredises!
**(d)** (in requests) **~ you give her the message?** est-ce que vous voulez bien lui transmettre le message?; **switch off the radio, ~ you?** éteins la radio, tu veux bien?; **~ you excuse me for a moment?** excusez-moi un instant
**(e)** (expressing one's wishes) **you like something to eat?** désirez-vous or voulez-vous manger quelque chose?; **I ~ like a beer** je voudrais une bière; **we ~ like to stay another night** nous aimerions rester une nuit de plus; **she'd have liked to stay here** elle aurait aimé rester ici; **I wouldn't mind another slice of cake** je prendrais bien un autre morceau de gâteau
**(f)** (offering advice) **if I were you, I wouldn't say anything** à ta place, je ne dirais rien; **it ~ be better to write** il vaudrait mieux écrire; **it ~ be a good idea to wait** ce serait une bonne idée d'attendre; **you ~ do well to check the timetable** tu ferais bien de vérifier l'horaire
**(g)** (in assumptions) **I ~ have been 12** je devais avoir 12 ans; **it ~ have been about midday** il devait être à peu près midi
**(h)** (used to) **she ~ talk for hours** elle parlait pendant des heures

**would-be** adj **(a)** (desirous of being) **~ emigrants/investors** personnes or ceux qui désirent émigrer/investir
**(b)** (so-called) **~ intellectuals** les soi-disant intellectuels
**(c)** (having intended to be) **the ~ thieves were arrested** les voleurs ont été arrêtés avant qu'ils aient pu passer à l'acte

**wound** [1] n **(a)** (injury) blessure f; (cut) plaie f; **bullet ~** blessure par balle; **knife ~** coup m de couteau; **a ~ to or in the head** une blessure à la tête
**(b)** (figurative) blessure f
[2] vtr blesser
IDIOMS **to lick one's ~s** panser ses blessures; **to rub salt into the ~** remuer le couteau dans la plaie

**wounded** [1] n **the ~** les blessés/blessées m/f
[2] adj blessé/-e; **~ in the arm** blessé au bras

**wrangle** [1] n querelle f
[2] vi se quereller (**over, about** sur, à propos de; **with** avec)

**wrap** [1] n (shawl) châle m; (stole) étole f

**2** *vtr* (in paper) emballer (**in** dans); (in blanket, garment) envelopper (**in** dans); **to be ~ped in** être emmitouflé/-e dans *‹blanket›*; être enveloppé/-e dans *‹newspaper›*; être enveloppé/-e de *‹mystery›*
IDIOMS **to keep sth/to be under ~s** garder qch/être secret/-ète
■ **wrap up**: ¶ **~ up** se couvrir; **~ up well** *or* **warm!** couvre-toi bien!
¶ **~ [sth] up (a)** faire *‹parcel›*; envelopper *‹gift, purchase›*; emballer *‹rubbish›*
**(b) to be ~ped up in** ne s'occuper que de *‹person, child›*; être absorbé/-e dans *‹activity, work›*; **they are completely ~ped up in each other** ils ne vivent que l'un pour l'autre
**(c)** dissimuler *‹meaning, facts, ideas›* (**in** derrière)
**wraparound** *adj ‹window, windscreen›* panoramique; *‹skirt›* portefeuille
**wraparound sunglasses** *n pl* lunettes *fpl* de soleil enveloppantes
**wrap-over** *adj ‹skirt›* portefeuille; *‹dress›* croisé/-e
**wrapper** *n* (of sweet) papier *m*
**wrapping** *n* emballage *m*
**wrapping paper** *n* (brown) papier *m* d'emballage; (decorative) papier *m* cadeau
**wreak** *vtr* assouvir *‹revenge›* (**on** sur); **to ~ havoc** *or* **damage** infliger des dégâts; **to ~ havoc** *or* **damage on sth** dévaster qch
**wreath** *n* couronne *f*; **to lay a ~** déposer une gerbe
**wreck** **1** *n* **(a)** (car, plane) (crashed) épave *f*; (burnt out) carcasse *f*
**(b)** (sunken ship) épave *f*
**(c)** ( person) épave *f*
**2** *vtr* **(a)** *‹explosion, fire, vandals›* dévaster *‹building, machinery›*; *‹person, driver, impact›* détruire *‹vehicle›*
**(b)** ruiner *‹career, chances, health, life, marriage›*; gâcher *‹holiday, weekend›*
**wreckage** *n* **(a)** (of plane, car, ship) épave *f*; (of building) décombres *mpl*
**(b)** (of hopes, plans) naufrage *m*
**wrecked** *adj* **(a)** *‹car, plane›* accidenté/-e; *‹ship›* naufragé/-e; *‹building›* démoli/-e
**(b)** *‹life, career, marriage›* ruiné/-e
**wren** *n* roitelet *m*
**wrench** **1** *n* **(a)** (tool) tourne-à-gauche *m* *inv*
**(b)** (emotional upheaval) déchirement *m*
**2** *vtr* tirer violemment sur *‹handle›*; **to ~ one's ankle/knee** se tordre la cheville/le genou; **to ~ sth from sb** arracher qch à qn; **to ~ sth away from sth** arracher qch de qch
**wrestle** **1** *vtr* **to ~ sb for sth** lutter contre qn pour qch; **to ~ sb to the ground** terrasser qn
**2** *vi* **(a)** (Sport) faire du catch
**(b)** (struggle) **to ~ with** se débattre avec *‹person, problem, homework, conscience›*; se battre avec *‹controls, zip, suitcase›*; lutter contre *‹temptation›*
**wrestler** *n* catcheur/-euse *m/f*
**wrestling** *n* catch *m*

**wretched** *adj ‹person›* infortuné/-e; *‹existence, appearance, conditions›* misérable; *‹weather›* affreux/-euse; *‹accommodation›* minable; *‹amount›* dérisoire
**wriggle** **1** *vtr* **to ~ one's toes/fingers** remuer les orteils/doigts; **to ~ one's way out of sth** se sortir de qch
**2** *vi ‹person›* s'agiter, gigoter; *‹snake, worm›* se tortiller; *‹fish›* frétiller; **to ~ out of** se défiler devant *‹duty, task›*
**wring** *vtr* **(a)** (also **~ out**) essorer *‹clothes, cloth›*
**(b)** (extract) arracher *‹confession, money›* (**from, out of** à)
**(c)** (twist) **to ~ sb's/sth's neck** tordre le cou à qn/qch; **to ~ one's hands** se tordre les mains; (figurative) se lamenter
**wrinkle** **1** *n* (on skin) ride *f*; (in fabric) pli *m*
**2** *vtr* **(a)** rider *‹skin›*; **to ~ one's nose** faire la grimace (**at** devant)
**(b)** froisser *‹fabric›*
**3** *vi ‹skin›* se rider; *‹fabric›* se froisser; *‹wallpaper›* gondoler
**wrist** *n* poignet *m*
**wristband** *n* (for tennis, on sleeve) poignet *m*
**wristwatch** *n* montre-bracelet *f*
**writ** *n* assignation *f* (**for** pour); **to issue** *or* **serve a ~ against sb, to serve sb with a ~** assigner qn en justice
**write** **1** *vtr* **(a)** écrire *‹letter, poem, novel›* (**to** à); composer *‹song, symphony›*; rédiger *‹business letter, article, report, prescription›*; faire *‹cheque›*; écrire *‹software, program›*; élaborer *‹legislation›*; **he wrote me a cheque for £100** il m'a fait un chèque de 100 livres sterling; **I wrote home** j'ai écrit à ma famille
**(b)** (US) écrire à *‹person›*
**2** *vi* écrire (**to sb** à qn)
■ **write back** répondre (**to** à)
■ **write down** noter *‹details, name›*; mettre [qch] par écrit *‹ideas, suggestions›*; consigner [qch] par écrit *‹information, findings›*
■ **write off**: ¶ **~ off** écrire une lettre (**to** à); **to ~ off for** écrire pour demander
¶ **~ [sb/sth] off (a)** (wreck) bousiller complètement (colloq) *‹car›*
**(b)** (in bookkeeping) passer [qch] aux pertes et profits *‹bad debt, loss›*; amortir *‹capital›*
**(c)** (end) annuler *‹debt, project, operation›*
■ **write out (a)** ( put down on paper) écrire
**(b)** (copy) copier
**write-off** *n* **(a)** (US) (in taxation) somme *f* déductible de la déclaration des revenus
**(b)** (wreck) épave *f*
**writer** *n* (author) (professional) écrivain *m*; (nonprofessional) auteur *m*
**writer's block** *n* l'angoisse *f* de la page blanche
**write-up** *n* **(a)** (review) critique *f*
**(b)** (account) rapport *m* (**of** sur)
**writhe** *vi* (also **~ about, ~ around**) se tortiller; **to ~ in agony** se tordre de douleur
**writing** *n* **(a)** (activity) **~ is her life** écrire, c'est sa vie

**W**

**(b)** (handwriting) écriture *f*; **his ∼ is poor/good** il écrit mal/bien
**(c)** (words and letters) écriture *f*; **to put sth in ∼** mettre qch par écrit
**(d)** (literature) littérature *f*

**writing pad** *n* bloc *m* de papier à lettres

**writing paper** *n* papier *m* à lettres

**writing table** *n* bureau *m*

**written** *adj* ⟨*reply, guarantee, proof*⟩ écrit/-e; **he failed the ∼ paper** il a échoué à l'écrit; **∼ evidence** *or* **proof** (Law) preuves *fpl* écrites; **the ∼ word** l'écriture

**wrong** ① *n* **(a)** (evil) mal *m*
**(b)** (injustice) tort *m*; **to right a ∼** réparer un tort
② *adj* **(a)** (incorrect) faux/fausse (*before n*); (ill-chosen) mauvais/-e (*before n*); **he took the ∼ key** il a pris la mauvaise clé; **it's the ∼ glue for the purpose** ce n'est pas la colle qu'il faut; **to go the ∼ way** se tromper de chemin; **I dialled the ∼ number** je me suis trompé de numéro, j'ai fait un faux *or* mauvais numéro; **you've got the ∼ number** vous faites erreur
**(b)** (reprehensible, unjust) **it is ∼ to cheat** c'est mal de tricher; **she hasn't done anything ∼** elle n'a rien fait de mal; **it was ∼ of me to do** je n'aurais pas dû faire; **it is ∼ that** c'est injuste que; **there's nothing ∼ with** *or* **in sth** il n'y a pas de mal à qch; **(so) what's ∼ with that?** où est le mal?
**(c)** (mistaken) **to be ∼** ⟨*person*⟩ avoir tort, se tromper; **to be ∼ about** se tromper sur; **she was ∼ about him** elle s'est trompée sur son compte; **to prove sb ∼** donner tort à qn

**(d)** (not as it should be) **there is something (badly) ∼** il y a quelque chose qui ne va pas (du tout); **there's something ∼ with this computer** il y a un problème avec cet ordinateur; **the wording is all ∼** la formulation ne va pas du tout; **what's ∼ with your arm?** qu'est-ce que tu as au bras?; **what's ∼ with you?** (to person suffering) qu'est-ce que tu as?; (to person behaving oddly) qu'est-ce qui t'arrive?; **your clock is ∼** votre pendule n'est pas à l'heure
③ *adv* **to get [sth] ∼** se tromper de ⟨*date, time, details*⟩; se tromper dans ⟨*calculations*⟩; **I think you've got it ∼** je pense que tu te trompes; **to go ∼** ⟨*person*⟩ se tromper; ⟨*machine*⟩ ne plus marcher
④ *vtr* faire du tort à ⟨*person, family*⟩
IDIOMS **to be in the ∼** être dans mon/ton etc tort; **to get on the ∼ side of sb** se faire mal voir de qn; **to go down the ∼ way** ⟨*food, drink*⟩ passer de travers

**wrongdoer** *n* malfaiteur *m*

**wrongfoot** *vtr* (Sport) prendre [qn] à contre-pied; (figurative) prendre [qn] au dépourvu

**wrongly** *adv* mal; **he concluded, ∼, that...** il a conclu, à tort, que...; **rightly or ∼** à tort ou à raison

**wrought** *adj* ⟨*silver, gold*⟩ travaillé/-e

**wrought iron** *n* fer *m* forgé

**wry** *adj* ⟨*smile, look, humour*⟩ narquois/-e; **to have a ∼ sense of humour** être pince-sans-rire

**x, X** *n* **(a)** (letter) x, X *m*
**(b)** (standing for number, name) **for x people** pour x personnes; **Ms X** Mme X; **X marks the spot** l'endroit est marqué d'une croix
**(c)** (kisses ending letter) grosses bises

**X-certificate** *adj* ⟨*film*⟩ interdit/-e aux moins de 18 ans

**xenophobia** *n* xénophobie *f*

**xerox**® *vtr* photocopier

**Xmas** *n* Noël *m*

**X-rated** *adj* ⟨*film, video*⟩ interdit/-e aux moins de 18 ans

**X-ray** ① *n* **(a)** (ray) rayon *m* X
**(b)** (photo) radiographie *f*, radio *f* (colloq); **to have an ∼** se faire radiographier; **to give sb an ∼** faire une radiographie à qn
② *vtr* radiographier

**X-ray unit** *n* service *m* de radiologie

# Yy

**y**, **Y** n y, Y m

**yacht** n yacht m

**yachting** n yachting m; **to go** ∼ faire du yachting

**yachtsman** n yachtman m

**yahoo** [1] n abruti/-e m (colloq)
[2] excl hourra!

**yak** n yack m

**Yale lock**® n serrure f de sûreté

**yam** n igname f

**yank** [1] n coup m sec; **to give sth a** ∼ tirer qch d'un coup sec
[2] vtr tirer ⟨person, rope⟩
■ **yank out** arracher

**Yank** n yankee mf

**Yankee** n yankee m

**yap** [1] n jappement m
[2] vi ⟨dog⟩ japper (at après)

**yapping** [1] n jappements mpl
[2] adj ⟨dog⟩ jappeur/-euse

**yard** n (a) yard m (= 0.9144 m)
(b) (of house, farm, prison, hospital) cour f
(c) (US) (garden) jardin m
(d) (for storage) dépôt m; (for construction) chantier m; **builder's** ∼ dépôt m de matériaux de construction

**yardarm** n bout m de vergue

**yardstick** n (figurative) critères mpl

**yarn** n (a) (fibre) fibre f textile; (wool) laine f
(b) (tale) histoire f; **to spin a** ∼ raconter des histoires

**yashmak** n voile m islamique

**yawn** [1] n bâillement m; **to give a** ∼ bâiller
[2] vi (a) ⟨person⟩ bâiller
(b) ⟨abyss, chasm⟩ béer

**yeah** particle (colloq) ouais (colloq), oui; **oh** ∼? vraiment?

**year** [1] n (a) (period of time) an m; (with emphasis on duration) année f; **in the** ∼ 1789/2000 en 1789/l'an 2000; **two** ∼**s ago** il y a deux ans; **all (the)** ∼ **round** toute l'année; **every** ∼ tous les ans; **over the** ∼**s** au cours des ans or des années; **the** ∼ **before last** il y a deux ans; **every** ∼ tous les ans; **they have been living in Paris for** ∼**s** ils habitent Paris depuis des années; **for the first time in** ∼**s** pour la première fois depuis des années; **it's a** ∼ **since I heard from him** je n'ai plus de ses nouvelles depuis un an; **they lived in Paris for** ∼**s** ils ont habité Paris pendant des années; **to earn £30,000 a** ∼ gagner 30 000 livres sterling par an
(b) (indicating age) **to be 19** ∼**s old** or **19** ∼**s of age** avoir 19 ans; **a two-**∼**-old child** un enfant de deux ans

(c) (pupil) **first/second-**∼ ≈ élève mf de sixième/cinquième
[2] **years** (colloq) n pl (a long time) **that would take** ∼**s!** ça prendrait une éternité!; **it's** ∼**s since we last met!** ça fait un siècle qu'on ne s'est pas vus!
IDIOMS **this job has put** ∼**s on me!** ce travail m'a vieilli de 10 ans!

**yearbook** n (a) (directory) annuaire m
(b) (US) album m de promotion

**yearlong** adj ⟨stay, course, absence⟩ d'un an, d'une année

**yearly** [1] adj ⟨visit, account, income⟩ annuel/-elle
[2] adv annuellement

**yearn** vi (a) **to** ∼ **for** désirer (avoir) ⟨child⟩; aspirer à ⟨freedom, unity⟩; attendre ⟨season, event⟩; **to** ∼ **to do** avoir très envie de faire
(b) (miss) **she** ∼**s for her son** son fils lui manque terriblement

**yearning** [1] n désir m ardent (**for** de; **to do** de faire)
[2] **yearnings** n pl aspirations fpl
[3] adj ⟨expression⟩ plein/-e de désir

**year out** n: année d'interruption des études entre le lycée et l'université.

**year tutor** n: professeur responsable de toutes les classes d'un même niveau

**yeast** n levure f

**yell** [1] n (shout) cri m; (of rage, pain) hurlement m
[2] vtr crier ⟨warning⟩; (louder) hurler ⟨insults⟩
[3] vi crier; **to** ∼ **at sb** crier après qn

**yelling** n cris mpl

**yellow** [1] n jaune m
[2] adj (a) (in colour) jaune; **to go** or **turn** ∼ jaunir
(b) (colloq) (cowardly) trouillard/-e (colloq)
[3] vi jaunir

**yellow-belly** n (colloq) trouillard/-e m/f (colloq)

**yellow card** n (Sport) carton m jaune

**yellowish** adj tirant sur le jaune; (unpleasantly) jaunâtre

**Yellow Pages**® n pl pages fpl jaunes

**yelp** [1] n glapissement m
[2] vi glapir

**Yemen** pr n Yémen m

**yen** n (a) (currency) yen m
(b) (colloq) (craving) **to have a** ∼ **for sth/to do** avoir grande envie de qch/de faire

**yeoman** n (also ∼ **farmer**) franc tenancier m

**yeoman of the guard** n (GB) membre m de la garde royale

y

**yep**, **yup** *particle* (colloq) (US) ouais (colloq), oui

**yes** *particle* oui; (in reply to negative question) si

■ Note *yes* is translated by *oui*, except when used in reply to a negative question in which case the translation is *si* or, more emphatically, *mais si*: *'did you see him?'*—*'yes (I did)'* = 'est-ce que tu l'as vu?'—'oui (je l'ai vu)'; *'you're not hungry, are you?'*—*'yes I am'* = 'tu n'as pas faim?'—'si (j'ai faim)'.
– Note that there are no direct equivalents in French for tag questions and short replies such as *yes I did, yes I am*.
– For some suggestions on how to translate these, see DO.

**yes-man** *n* (colloq) lèche-bottes *m inv*

**yesterday** ①*n* hier *m*; ∼'s newspaper le journal d'hier; ∼ was a sad day for all of us la journée d'hier a été triste pour nous tous; ∼ was the fifth of April hier nous étions le cinq avril; **the day before** ∼ avant-hier ②*adv* hier; **only** ∼ pas plus tard qu'hier; **all day** ∼ toute la journée d'hier

**yesterday afternoon** *n, adv* hier après-midi

**yesterday evening** *n, adv* hier soir

**yesterday morning** *n, adv* hier matin

**yesteryear** *n* temps *m* jadis; **the fashions of** ∼ la mode d'antan *or* du temps jadis

**yes-vote** *n* oui *m*

**yet** ①*conj* pourtant ②*adv* **(a)** (up till now, so far) encore; (in questions) déjà; (with superlatives) jusqu'ici; **it's not ready** ∼ ce n'est pas encore prêt; **has he arrived** ∼? est-il (déjà) arrivé?; **not** ∼ pas encore, pas pour l'instant; **it's the best** ∼ jusqu'ici, c'est le meilleur
**(b)** (*also* **just** ∼) tout de suite, encore; **don't start** ∼ ne commence pas tout de suite
**(c)** (still) encore; **they may** ∼ **come** ils pourraient encore arriver; **he'll finish it** ∼ il va le finir; **he won't come for hours** ∼ il ne viendra pas avant quelques heures
**(d)** (even, still) encore; ∼ **more cars** encore plus de voitures; ∼ **another attack** encore une autre attaque; ∼ **again** encore une fois

**yew** *n* (*also* ∼ **tree**) if *m*

**Y-fronts** *n pl* (GB) slip *m* ouvert

**YHA** *n* (GB) (*abbr* = **Youth Hostels Association**) association *f* des auberges de jeunesse

**yield** ①*n* rendement *m* ②*vtr* **(a)** (produce) produire
**(b)** (provide) donner, fournir ⟨*result, meaning*⟩; fournir ⟨*clue*⟩
**(c)** (surrender) céder (**to** à); **to** ∼ **ground** (figurative) céder du terrain
③*vi* **(a)** (to person, temptation, pressure, threats) céder (**to** à)
**(b)** (under weight, physical pressure) céder (**under** sous)
**(c)** (be superseded) **to** ∼ **to** ⟨*technology, phenomenon*⟩ céder le pas à
**(d)** (US) (driving) céder le passage

**yob**, **yobbo** *n* (GB) (colloq) loubard *m* (colloq), voyou *m*

**yodel** *vi* jodler, iodler

**yoga** *n* yoga *m*

**yoghurt** *n* yaourt *m*, yoghourt *m*

**yo-heave-ho** *excl* oh! hisse!

**yoke** ①*n* joug *m* ②*vtr* (*also* ∼ **up**) atteler

**yokel** *n* péquenaud/-e *m/f* (colloq), plouc *mf* (colloq)

**yolk** *n* jaune *m* (d'œuf)

**yonks** *n pl* (colloq) **I haven't seen him for** ∼ ça fait une éternité que je ne l'ai pas vu

**you** *pron*

■ Note In French *you* has two forms: *tu* and *vous*. The usual word to use to anyone you do not know very well is *vous*, also called the polite form: *can I help you?* est-ce que je peux vous aider? The more informal *tu* (plural *vous*) is used between groups of close friends and family members, within groups of children and young people and by adults when talking to children: *there's a biscuit for you* il y a un biscuit pour toi. If in doubt, use the *vous* form.

**(a)** (subject) tu, vous; (object) te, t', vous YOU **would never do that**
**(b)** (with preposition, for emphasis) toi, vous; (polite) vous, vous ne feriez jamais cela; (informal) toi, tu ne ferais jamais ça; ∼ **English** vous autres Anglais; ∼ **idiot!** (colloq) espèce d'imbécile! (colloq); ∼ **two can stay** vous deux, vous pouvez rester
**(c)** (as indefinite pronoun) (subject) on; (object, indirect object) vous, te; ∼ **never know!** on ne sait jamais!; **it makes** ∼ **sleepy** ça fait dormir

**you-know-what** *pron* (colloq) vous-savez-quoi, tu-sais-quoi

**you-know-who** *pron* (colloq) qui-vous-savez, qui-tu-sais

**young** ①*n* **(a)** (young people) **the** ∼ les jeunes *mpl*, la jeunesse *f*
**(b)** (animal's offspring) petits *mpl* ②*adj* (not very old) jeune; **to be** ∼ **at heart** avoir l'esprit jeune; **she is ten years** ∼**er than him** elle a dix ans de moins que lui; **I feel ten years** ∼**er** j'ai l'impression d'avoir rajeuni de dix ans; ∼ **lady** jeune femme *f*; ∼ **people** jeunes gens *mpl*; ∼ **person** jeune *m*; **the** ∼**er generation** la jeune génération; **her** ∼**er brother** son frère cadet; **I'm not as** ∼ **as I used to be** je n'ai plus 20 ans

**young blood** *n* sang *m* neuf

**youngish** *adj* assez jeune

**young-looking** *adj* **to be** ∼ faire (très) jeune

**young offender** *n* délinquant/-e *m/f*

**young professional** *n* jeune salarié/-e *m/f*

**youngster** *n* **(a)** (young person) jeune *m*
**(b)** (child) enfant *mf*

**your**

■ Note For a full note on the use of the *vous* and *tu* forms in French, see the entry YOU.

– In French, determiners agree in gender and number with the noun that follows: *your* + masculine singular noun = *ton, votre* (*your dog* ton/votre chien); *your* + feminine singular noun = *ta, votre* (*your house* ta/votre maison); *your* + plural noun = *tes, vos* (*your parents* tes/vos parents).

**(a)** *det* votre/vos; (more informally) ton/ta/tes
**(b)** (used impersonally) son, sa, ses; **you buy ∼ tickets at the door** on prend ses billets à l'entrée; **smoking is bad for ∼ health** le tabac est mauvais pour la santé
**(c)** (for emphasis) à vous, à toi; YOUR **house** votre maison à vous, ta maison à toi

**yours** *pron*

■ Note For a full note on the use of the *vous* and *tu* forms in French, see the note for the entry YOU.
– In French, possessive pronouns reflect the gender and number of the noun they are standing for. When *yours* is referring to only one person, it is translated by *le vôtre, la vôtre, les vôtres* or, more informally, *le tien, la tienne, les tiens, les tiennes*. When *yours* is referring to more than one person, it is translated by *le vôtre, la vôtre, les vôtres.*

**my car is red but ∼ is blue** ma voiture est rouge mais la vôtre *or* la tienne est bleue; **her children are older than ∼** ses enfants sont plus âgés que les vôtres *or* les tiens; **which house is ∼?** votre *or* ta maison c'est laquelle?; **he's a colleague of ∼** c'est un de vos *or* tes collègues; **it's not ∼** ce n'est pas à vous *or* à toi; **the money wasn't ∼ to give away** vous n'aviez pas à donner cet argent

**yourself** *pron*

■ Note For a full note on the use of the *vous* and *tu* forms in French, see the entry YOU.
– When used as a reflexive pronoun, direct and indirect, *yourself* is translated by *vous* or familiarly *te* (or *t'* before a vowel or mute 'h'): *you've hurt yourself* = vous vous êtes fait mal *or* tu t'es fait mal.
– In imperatives, the translation is *vous* or *toi*: *help yourself* = servez-vous *or* sers-toi. (Note the hyphens).
– When used for emphasis, the translation is *vous-même* or *toi-même*: *you yourself don't know* = vous ne savez pas vous-même *or* tu ne sais pas toi-même.

**(a)** (reflexive) vous, te, t'; **have you hurt ∼?** est-ce que tu t'es fait mal?
**(b)** (in imperatives) vous, toi
**(c)** (emphatic) vous-même, toi-même; **you ∼ said that…** vous avez dit vous-même que…, tu as dit toi-même que…
**(d)** (after prepositions) vous, vous-même, toi, toi-même
**(e)** (expressions) **(all) by ∼** tout seul/toute seule; **you're not ∼ today** tu n'as pas l'air dans ton assiette aujourd'hui

**yourselves** *pron*

■ Note
– When used as a reflexive pronoun, direct and indirect, *yourselves* is translated by *vous*: *help yourselves* = servez-vous.
– When used for emphasis, the translation is *vous-mêmes*: *do it yourselves* = faites-le vous-mêmes.

**(a)** (reflexive) vous
**(b)** (emphatic) vous-mêmes
**(c)** (after prepositions) vous, vous-mêmes; **all by ∼** tous seuls/toutes seules

**youth** *n* **(a)** (young man) jeune homme *m*; **a gang of ∼s** une bande de jeunes gens
**(b)** (period, state of being young) jeunesse *f*; **because of his ∼** à cause de son jeune âge
**(c)** (young people) jeunes *mpl*

**youth club** *n* centre *m* de jeunes

**youthful** *adj* **(a)** (young) jeune
**(b)** (typical of youth) **his ∼ looks** son air jeune

**youth hostel** *n* auberge *f* de jeunesse

**youth hostelling** *n* logement *m* en auberge de jeunesse

**youth work** *n* travail *m* social auprès des jeunes

**youth worker** *n* éducateur/-trice *m/f*

**yowl** *vi* ⟨*person, dog*⟩ hurler; ⟨*cat*⟩ miauler; ⟨*baby*⟩ brailler

**yoyo** *n* yo-yo *m*

**yuck** *excl* (GB) (colloq) berk (colloq)!

**yucky** *adj* (GB) (colloq) dégoûtant/-e

**Yugoslavia** *pr n* Yougoslavie *f*

**Yule log** *n* bûche *f* de Noël

**yummy** (colloq) **1** *adj* délicieux/-ieuse
**2** *excl* miam-miam (colloq)

**yuppie** *n* **1** jeune cadre *m* dynamique
**2** *adj* ⟨*image, style, fashion*⟩ de jeune cadre dynamique

**y**

# Zz

**z, Z** *n* z, Z *m*

**zany** *adj* loufoque (colloq)

**zap** (colloq) **[1]** *excl* paf!

**[2]** *vtr* **(a)** (destroy) détruire ⟨*town*⟩; tuer ⟨*person, animal*⟩

**(b)** (fire at) tirer sur ⟨*person*⟩

**(c)** (delete from computer screen) supprimer

**[3]** *vi* to ∼ **into town/a shop** faire un saut (colloq) en ville/dans un magasin; **to ∼ from channel to channel** zapper (colloq)

**zapper** *n* **(a)** (colloq) (TV remote control) télécommande *f*

**zeal** *n* **(a)** (fanaticism) zèle *m*; (religious) ferveur *f*

**(b)** (enthusiasm) ardeur *f*, zèle *m*

**zealot** *n* fanatique *mf*

**zebra** *n* zèbre *m*

**zebra crossing** *n* (GB) passage *m* (protégé) pour piétons

**zenith** *n* (figurative) apogée *m*

**zero** **[1]** *n* zéro *m*

**[2]** *adj* ⟨*altitude, growth, inflation, voltage*⟩ zéro *inv*; ⟨*confidence, interest, involvement, development*⟩ nul/nulle; **sub-∼ temperatures** des températures en dessous de zéro

■ **zero in**: **to ∼ in on** [sth] (Mil) viser ⟨*target*⟩; (figurative) cerner ⟨*problem*⟩; foncer droit sur ⟨*person*⟩; repérer ⟨*place*⟩

**zero hour** *n* heure *f* H

**zest** *n* (enthusiasm) entrain *m*; **his ∼ for life** sa joie de vivre

**zigzag** **[1]** *n* zigzag *m*

**[2]** *adj* ⟨*design, pattern*⟩ à zigzags; ⟨*route, road*⟩ en zigzag

**[3]** *vi* ⟨*person, vehicle, road*⟩ zigzaguer; ⟨*river, path*⟩ serpenter; **to ∼ up/down** monter/descendre en zigzag

**zilch** *n* (colloq) que dalle (slang)

**zimmer**® *n* déambulateur *m*

**zing** *n* (colloq) (energy) entrain *m*

**zip** **[1]** *n* **(a)** (*also* ∼ **fastener**, **zipper** (US)) fermeture *f* à glissière, fermeture *f* éclair®; **to do up/undo a ∼** tirer/défaire une fermeture à glissière

**(b)** (colloq) (energy) tonus *m*

**(c)** (US) (*also* ∼ **code**) code *m* postal

**[2]** *vtr* **(a)** (close) **to ∼ sth shut** fermer qch en tirant la fermeture à glissière

**(b)** (Comput) zipper, comprimer

**[3]** *vi* (colloq) **to ∼ along**, **to ∼ past** filer à toute allure; **to ∼ past sb/sth** dépasser qn/qch à toute allure

■ **zip through** (colloq): **to ∼ through a book** lire un livre en diagonale (colloq)

■ **zip up**: ¶ ∼ **up** ⟨*garment, bag*⟩ se fermer par une fermeture à glissière; ¶ ∼ [sth] **up** remonter la fermeture à glissière de qch

**zipper** (US) = ZIP 1A

**zip pocket** *n* poche *f* à fermeture à glissière

**zodiac** *n* zodiaque *m*

**zombie** *n* zombi(e) *m*; (figurative) abruti/-e *m/f* (colloq)

**zone** **[1]** *n* zone *f*

**[2]** *vtr* (divide) diviser [qch] en zones

**zonked** *adj* (colloq) (*also* **zonked out**) (tired) crevé/-e (colloq)

**zoo** *n* zoo *m*

**zoo keeper** *n* gardien/-ienne *m/f* de zoo

**zoologist** *n* zoologue *mf*, zoologiste *mf*

**zoology** *n* zoologie *f*

**zoom** **[1]** *n* (*also* ∼ **lens**) zoom *m*

**[2]** *vi* **(a)** (colloq) (move quickly) **to ∼ past** passer en trombe; **to ∼ around** passer à toute vitesse dans; **he's ∼ed off to Paris** il a foncé (colloq) à Paris

**(b)** (colloq) (rocket) ⟨*prices, profits*⟩ monter en flèche

**zucchini** *n* (US) courgette *f*

# Glossary of grammatical terms

**Abbreviation** A shortened form of a word or phrase made by leaving out some letters or by using only the initial letter of each word: etc., DNA

**Active** In the active form the subject of the verb performs the action: **she whistled = elle a sifflé**

**Adjective** A word describing a noun: **a** *red* **pencil = un crayon** *rouge*

**Adverb** A word that describes or changes the meaning of a verb, an adjective, or another adverb: **he drives** *fast* **= il conduit** *vite*; *fairly* **often = *assez* souvent**

**Article** The definite article, **the = le, la, l', les**, and indefinite article, **a/an = un, une**, are used in front of a noun

**Attributive** An adjective or noun is attributive when it is used directly before or directly after a noun: **the** *big* **dog = le** *grand* **chien;** *birthday* **card = carte d'anniversaire**

**Auxiliary verb** One of the verbs used to form the perfect, pluperfect, and future perfect tenses. In French the auxiliary verbs are **avoir** and **être: I have read the letter = j'*ai* lu la lettre; he had already gone = il *était* déjà parti**

**Cardinal number** A whole number representing a quantity: **one, two, three = un/une, deux, trois**

**Clause** A self-contained section of a sentence that contains a subject and a verb

**Collective noun** A noun that is singular in form but refers to a group of persons or things, e.g. **royalty, grain**

**Collocate** A word that regularly occurs with another; for example **book** is a typical collocate of the verb **to read**

**Comparative** The form of an adjective or adverb for comparing two or more nouns or pronouns, often using **more, less** or **as (plus, moins, aussi): smaller = plus petit; more frequently = plus fréquemment; as intelligent = aussi intelligent**

**Compound adjective** An adjective formed from two separate words : **tout-puissant = all-powerful; nord-américain = North American**

**Compound noun** A noun formed from two or more separate words: **porte-clés = keyring**

**Conditional tense** A tense of a verb that expresses what might happen if something else occurred: **I would invite them = je les inviterais**

**Conjugation** Variation of the form of a verb to show tense, person, etc.

**Conjunction** A word used to link clauses: **and = et, because = parce que**

**Consonant** All the letters other than a, e, i, o, u or y (y can be a vowel in French)

**Definite article**: the = **le, la, l', les**

**Demonstrative adjective** An adjective indicating the person or thing referred to: *this* **car = *cette* voiture;** *this* **pen = *ce* stylo**

**Demonstrative pronoun** A pronoun indicating the person or thing referred to: *this one* **is cheaper = *celui-ci* est moins cher**

**Determiner** A word used before a noun to make clear what is being referred to: **the = le, la, l', les; some = du/de l'/de la/des; my = mon/ma/mes**

**Direct object** the noun or pronoun directly affected by the verb: **she ate** *the apple* **= elle a mangé** *la pomme*

**Direct speech** A speaker's actual words or the use of these in writing

**Elliptical** Having a word or words omitted, especially where the sense can be guessed from the context

**Ending** Letters added to the stem of verbs, as well as to nouns and adjectives, according to tense, number, gender

**Exclamation** A sound, word, or remark expressing a strong feeling such as anger, fear, or joy: **ouch! = aïe!**

**Feminine** One of the two genders in French: **la femme = the woman; la carte = the card**

**Future tense** The tense of a verb that refers to something that will happen in the future: **I will go = j'irai**

**Gender** One of the two groups of nouns in French: masculine and feminine

**Imperative** A form of a verb that expresses a command: **hurry up! = dépêche-toi!**

**Imperfect tense** The tense of a verb that refers to an uncompleted or a habitual action in the past: **I went there every day = j'y allais tous les jours**

**Impersonal verb** A verb used in English only with 'it' and in French only with '**il**': **it is raining = il pleut**

**Indefinite article**: a/an = **un, une**

**Indefinite pronoun** A pronoun that does not identify a specific person or object: **one = on**; **something = quelque chose**

**Indicative form** The form of a verb used when making a statement of fact or asking questions of fact in various tenses: **we like animals = nous aimons les animaux**

**Indirect object** The noun or pronoun indirectly affected by the verb, at which the direct object is aimed: **she gave *him* the key = elle *lui* a donné la clé**

**Indirect speech** A report of what someone has said which does not reproduce the exact words

**Infinitive** The basic form of a verb: **to play = jouer**

**Inflect** To change the ending or form of a word to show its tense or its grammatical relation to other words: **donne** and **donnez** are inflected forms of the verb **donner**

**Interrogative pronoun** A pronoun that asks a question: **who? = qui?**

**Intransitive verb** A verb that does not have a direct object: **he died yesterday = il est mort hier**

**Invariable adjective** An adjective that has the same form in the plural as the singular, as French **ivoire, transmanche**

**Invariable noun** A noun that has the same form in the plural as the singular, as English **sheep, species**, French **aide-mémoire, rabais**

**Irregular verb** A verb that does not follow one of the set patterns and has its own individual forms, e.g. English **to be**, French **être**

**Masculine** One of the two genders in French: **le garçon = the boy; le livre = the book**

**Modal verb** A verb that is used with another verb to express permission, obligation, possibility, such as **might, should**. The French modal verbs are **devoir, pouvoir, savoir, vouloir, falloir**

**Negative** Expressing refusal or denial: **there aren't any = il n'y en a pas; he won't go = il ne veut pas partir**

**Noun** A word that names a person, thing, or concept such as **Peter, a child, a book, peace**

**Number** The state of being either singular or plural

**Object** The word or group of words which is immediately affected by the action indicated by the verb, as **livre** in **il a lu le livre**, or **voiture** in **elle lave la voiture**

**Ordinal number** A number that shows the position of a person or thing in a series: **the *third* time = la *troisième* fois, the *fourth* door on the left = la *quatrième* porte à gauche**

**Part of speech** A grammatical term for the function of a word; noun, verb, adjective, etc., are parts of speech

**Passive** In the passive form the subject of the verb experiences the action rather than performs it: **he was punished = il a été puni**

**Past participle** The part of a verb used to form past tenses: **she had *gone* = elle était *partie***

**Perfect tense** The tense of a verb that refers to an action that has taken place in a period of time that includes the present: **I have already eaten = j'ai déjà mangé; my bike has been stolen = on m'a volé mon vélo**

**Person** Any of the three groups of personal pronouns and forms taken by verbs. In the singular the **first person** (e.g. **I/je**) refers to the person speaking; **the second person** (e.g. **you/tu**) refers to the person spoken to; the **third person** (e.g. **he, she, it/il, elle**) refers to the person spoken about. The corresponding plural forms are **we/nous, you/vous, they/ils, elles**

**Personal pronoun** A pronoun that refers to a person or thing

**Phrasal verb** A verb in English combined with a preposition or an adverb to have a particular meaning: **run away = se sauver**. There are no phrasal verbs in French

**Phrase** A self-contained section of a sentence that does not contain a full verb

**Pluperfect tense** The tense of a verb that refers to something that happened before a particular point in the past: **when I arrived, he *had* already *left* = quand je suis arrivé, il *était* déjà *parti***

**Plural** Of nouns, etc., referring to more than one: **the children = les enfants**

**Possessive adjective** An adjective that shows possession, belonging to someone or something: **my = mon/ma/mes**

**Possessive pronoun** a pronoun that shows possession, belonging to someone or something: **mine = le mien/la mienne/les miens/les miennes**

**Postpositive** Placed after the word to which it relates, as **in stock** in the phrase **items in stock**

**Predicative** An adjective is predicative when it comes after a verb such as **be** or **become** in English, or after **être** or **devenir** in French: **she is beautiful = elle est belle**

**Prefix** A group of letters added to the beginning of a word to change its meaning, e.g. **anti-, ultra-, non-**

**Preposition** A word that stands in front of a noun or pronoun, usually indicating movement, position or time: *on* **the chair** = *sur* **la chaise**; *towards* **the car** = *vers* **la voiture**

**Present participle** The part of a verb in English that ends in –ing; the corresponding ending in French is **-ant**

**Present tense** The tense of a verb that refers to something happening now: **I make = je fais**

**Pronoun** A word that stands instead of a noun: **he = il, she = elle, mine = le mien/ la mienne/les miens/les miennes**

**Proper noun** A name of a person, place, institution etc. written with a capital letter at the start; **France, the Alps, Madeleine, l'Europe** are all proper nouns

**Reflexive pronoun** A pronoun that goes with a reflexive verb: in French **me, te, se, nous, vous, se**

**Reflexive verb** A verb whose object is the same as its subject. In French it is used with a reflexive pronoun and conjugated with **être**: **he washed himself = il s'est lavé**

**Regular verb** A verb that follows a set pattern in its different forms

**Relative pronoun** A pronoun that introduces a subordinate clause, relating to a person or thing mentioned in the main clause: **the book** *which* **I chose = le livre** *que* **j'ai choisi**

**Reported speech** Another name for Indirect speech

**Sentence** A sequence of words, with a subject and a verb, that can stand on their own to make a statement, ask a question, or give a command

**Singular** Of nouns, etc., referring to just one: **the tree = l'arbre**

**Stem** The part of a verb to which endings are added; **donn-** is the stem of **donner**

**Subject** In a clause or sentence, the noun or pronoun that causes the action of the verb: *he* **caught the ball** = *il* **a attrapé le ballon**

**Subjunctive** A verb form that is used to express doubt or uncertainty in English. It is more widely used in French, particularly after certain conjunctions and with verbs of wishing, fearing, ordering, forbidding followed by **que**: **I want you to be good = je veux que tu sois sage; you may be right = il est possible que tu aies raison**

**Subordinate clause** A clause which adds information to the main clause of a sentence, but cannot function as a sentence by itself, e.g. **when it rang in she answered the phone when it rang**

**Suffix** A group of letters joined to the end of a word to form another word, as **–able** in **workable**, or in French as **–eur** in **grandeur** or **–able** in **véritable**

**Superlative** The form of an adjective or adverb that makes it the 'most' or 'least': **the** *biggest* **house** = *la plus grande* **maison; the** *cheapest* **CD** = *le moins cher*

**Tense** The form of a verb that tells when the action takes place: present, future, imperfect, perfect, pluperfect are all tenses

**Transitive verb** A verb that is used with a direct object: **I wrote the letter = j'ai écrit la lettre**

**Verb** A word or group of words that describes an action: **the children are playing = les enfants jouent**

**Vowel** One of the following letters: **a, e, i, o, u** or **y** in French

# Summary of French grammar

Grammar provides a description of the rules by which a language functions. Many of these rules are complex and there are many exceptions to them. The following pages offer a summary of some of the most important features of French grammar.

## 1 Nouns and Gender

All French nouns are either masculine or feminine. The gender of nouns is shown by the definite and indefinite articles. Most nouns relating to male people are masculine and most relating to female people are feminine. Inanimate objects can be either gender and other nouns may be a particular gender for no clear reason, *une personne* = a person. A few have different genders according to their sense: *le mode* = method; *la mode* = fashion.

### 1.1 The definite article (= *the*)

|  | Singular | Plural |
|---|---|---|
| Masculine | le | les |
| Feminine | la | les |

- *le* and *la* are reduced to *l'* before:
  a singular noun starting with a vowel: *école* → *l'école*
  a singular noun starting with a silent *h*: *hôtel* → *l'hôtel*

- *les* is the plural in all cases: *les écoles, les hôtels*

- The preposition *à* + *le* become *au*: *au café* = at the café. Similarly *à* + *les* become *aux*

**Note:** Unlike in English, articles are rarely omitted, *les enfants aiment les bonbons* = children like sweets

### 1.2 The indefinite article (= *a* or *an*; plural = *some*)

|  | Singular | Plural |
|---|---|---|
| Masculine | un | des |
| Feminine | une | des |

- *un* and *une* also indicate the number 1 in counting: *un couteau* = one knife; *une pomme* = one apple

- *des* is the plural form for both masculine and feminine nouns: *des couteaux, des pommes*

But when specifying someone's occupation or profession, the article is dropped:

> *il est boucher* = he is a butcher    *ma sœur est avocat* = my sister is a lawyer

The article *le* is used to specify the day of the month:

> *aujourd'hui, c'est le six septembre* = today is the 6th of September
> *c'est le mardi deux juillet* = it's Tuesday 2 July

## 2 Nouns and Number

Nouns can be *singular* or *plural*, and this is referred to as *number*. This is an important consideration when choosing verb forms or adjectival agreements. Most nouns add an ending to form the plural.

### 2.1 Typical nouns:

Most nouns add -*s* in the plural:

> *chaise* → *chaises* (= chairs)     *chien* → *chiens* (= dogs)
> *voiture* → *voitures* (= cars)     *chat* → *chats* (= cats)

### 2.2 Nouns ending in -*au*, -*eu* or -*eau* usually add -*x* in the plural:

> *tuyau* → *tuyaux* (= pipes)     *jeu* → *jeux* (= games)
> *neveu* → *neveux* (= nephews)     *bureau* → *bureaux* (= desks)

### 2.3 Nouns ending in -*ail* usually add -*s*:

> *détail* → *détails* (= details)

But there are exceptions:

> *travail* → *travaux* (= works)

### 2.4 Nouns ending in -*al* usually change from -*al* to -*aux*:

> *rival* → *rivaux* (= rivals)     *cheval* → *chevaux* (= horses)

But there are exceptions:

> *bal* → *bals* (= dances)

### 2.5 Nouns ending in -*ou*:

These nouns usually add -*s* in the plural. But there are six common exceptions which add -*x*:

> *bijou* → *bijoux* (= jewels)     *genou* → *genoux* (= knees)
> *caillou* → *cailloux* (= pebbles)     *hibou* → *hiboux* (= owls)
> *chou* → *choux* (= cabbages)     *joujou* → *joujoux* (= toys)

### 2.6 Some nouns have unusual plurals and these have to be learnt individually:

> *ciel* → *cieux* (= skies)     *œil* → *yeux* (= eyes)

Note the plurals in the group: *monsieur* → *messieurs*; *madame* → *mesdames*; *mademoiselle* → *mesdemoiselles*: *mon-*, *ma-* in these words meant 'my' originally (as in 'my lord', 'my lady').

Surnames are not used in the plural in phrases such as: *les Dupont* = the Duponts; names of dynasties do however take *-s* in the plural: *les Bourbons* = the Bourbons.

### 2.7 Hyphenated nouns

The plurals of this group of nouns vary and depend on how the word is formed, ADJECTIVE + NOUN, VERB + NOUN, etc. In cases where there is an ADJECTIVE + NOUN, it is normal for both words in the compound to change:

> *beau-père* → *beaux-pères* (= fathers-in-law)
> *chou-fleur* → *choux-fleurs* (= cauliflowers)

If an element of a compound is neither a noun nor an adjective, it does not change in the plural.

> *le tire-bouchon* = corkscrew → *les tire-bouchons* (*tire* is part of the verb *tirer*)
> *un passe-partout* = skeleton key → *des passe-partout* (no noun: *passe* is a verb, *partout* is an adverb)

If in doubt it can be helpful to translate the compound word for word and find which element would logically become plural in English:

> *arc-en-ciel* (= rainbow) → *arcs-en-ciel* (= rainbows)
> (literally 'arc in the sky' → 'arcs in the sky')

### 2.8 Nouns which do not change in the plural

Nouns already ending in *-s*: *bois* → *bois* (= woods)
Nouns already ending in *-x*: *voix* → *voix* (= voices)
Nouns ending in *-z*: *nez* → *nez* (= noses)

## 3 *De* and expressions of quantity

*De* is used in many expressions of quantity. In many cases, it is translated in English by *some* or *any*.

Note how *de* is used with articles before nouns and how it may change:

> de + le → du     *le pain* → *du pain* = some bread
> de + la → de la     *la crème* → *de la crème* = some cream
> de + l' → de l'     *l'huile* → *de l'huile* = some oil
> de + les → des     *les oranges* → *des oranges* = some oranges

Note that after a negative the article is dropped and *de* alone is used:

> *j'ai du pain* = I have some bread
> *je n'ai pas de pain* = I don't have any bread
> *avez-vous de la crème* = do you have (some) cream?
> *nous n'avons pas de crème* = we do not have any cream

• • • • • • • • • • • • • • • • • • • • • • • • • • • • • • • • • •

If *de* comes before a vowel or a silent *h*, it is written *d'*:

  *achetez des oranges/de l'huile* = buy some oranges/oil
  *n'achetez pas d'oranges/d'huile* = don't buy any oranges/oil

There is more on Negatives in section 11, page 943.

If *de* comes before an adjective which qualifies a noun, it often remains *de* or *d'* rather than *des*:

  *de jolies fleurs* = some pretty flowers
  *d'énormes problèmes* = enormous problems
  *d'autres amis* = other friends

Expressions of quantity. The following always use *de* or *d'* before a vowel or silent 'h'.

  *un verre de vin* = a glass of wine
  *un kilo de haricots verts* = a kilo of French beans
  *deux kilos de pommes* = two kilos of apples
  *beaucoup de farine* = a lot of flour
  *beaucoup de cerises* = a lot of cherries
  *peu de mots* = few words
  *peu d'habitants* = not many inhabitants

But note the following:

  *encore du pain, s'il vous plaît* = some more bread, please

• • • • • • • • • • • • • • • • • • • • • • • • • • • • • • • • • •

## 4 Pronouns

### 4.1 Subject pronouns

Pronouns such as *I*, *we*, *they*, etc replace nouns as the subjects of sentences, and can refer to people or things. Subject pronouns determine the choice of endings for verbs, *je chante* = I sing, *tu chantes* = you sing, *nous chantons* = we sing, *vous chantez* = you (plural) sing.

| Singular | Plural |
| --- | --- |
| *je* = I | *nous* = we |
| *tu* = you | *vous* = you |
| *il* = he/it | *ils* = they [masculine or masculine + feminine] |
| *elle* = she/it | *elles* = they [feminine] |
| *on* = one* | |

- *tu* is used to speak to a child or someone who is well known
- *vous* is used in polite speech or to more than one person
- *ils* means 'they' referring to a male group, or a mixed male and female group

\**on* is used as a less specific subject pronoun to mean 'one', 'you', 'we', 'people', 'they'. It always takes the endings of the third person singular, see verb tables on p. 944.

  *on mange ici?* = shall we eat here?      *on n'aime pas refuser* = one doesn't like to refuse

. . . . . . . . . . . . . . . . . . . . . . . . . . . . . . . . . . . . . . . . . . . .

## 4.2 Object pronouns

### 4.2.a Direct object pronouns

Direct object pronouns in French, the equivalent of *it*, *her*, *him*, *us*, etc are used to replace noun objects. They can refer to people or things and can only be used with transitive verbs, marked *vtr* in this dictionary. Transitive verbs are those which affect or act on someone or something.

**frapper** *vtr* to hit: hit the ball; go on, hit it! = frappe la balle; allez, frappe-la!

| French | English | French | English |
|--------|---------|--------|---------|
| me/m' | me | nous | us |
| te/t' | you [*singular*] | vous | you [*plural*] |
| le/l' | him /it | les | them |
| la/l' | her/it | se/s' | themselves |
| se/s' | himself/herself/itself | | |

■ *m'/t'/l'/s'* are used if the word that follows begins with a vowel or a silent h:

*ils l'aiment* = they love her
*elle l'héberge gratuitement* = she puts him up for free

■ Object pronouns can affect the endings of past participles in compound tenses if the object is feminine or plural:

*elle a poli la table → elle l'a polie* (+e for feminine singular = she polished it)
*elle a poli les tables → elle les a polies* (+es for feminine plural = she polished them)

### 4.2.b Indirect object pronouns

Indirect object pronouns in French, the equivalent of *to it*, *to her*, *to him*, *to us*, etc are used to replace indirect noun objects. They can refer to people or things and are indirectly affected by the action of the verb.

*donnez-lui la balle!* = give the ball to him/to her
*il m'a montré la photo* = he showed me the photo
*donne-le-leur!* = give them that!/give that to them!

| French | English | French | English |
|--------|---------|--------|---------|
| me/m' | (to) me | nous | (to) us |
| te/t' | (to) you [*singular*] | vous | (to) you [*plural*] |
| lui | (to) him or it | leur | (to) them |
| lui | (to) her or it | | |

### 4.2.c Indirect object pronouns *y* and *en*

*y* is used in sentences with verbs which govern a preposition, e.g. *s'intéresser à, s'opposer à, penser à*

*il ne s'y intéresse pas* = he's not interested in it
*je m'y oppose* = I'm against it
*j'y pense* = I'm thinking about it

The indirect object pronoun referring to a quantity is: *en* = of it, of them, some

*j'en voudrais trois* = I'd like three (of them)
*offrez-leur-en* = offer them some

It is also used in sentences such as:

*nous en parlerons ce soir* = we'll talk about it this evening

## 4.3 Order of object pronouns in the sentence

Object pronouns come before most verb parts:

*elle leur rend les livres* = she is returning the books to them

Object pronouns come before an infinitive:

*elle va leur rendre les livres* = she is going to return the books to them

Object pronouns come before the first part of the compound tenses conjugated with *avoir* and *être*: see Verbs section 10.1.f

*elle leur a rendu les livres* = she returned the books to them

*il y est allé* = he went there

Object pronouns follow the imperative form of the verb and are linked to it by a hyphen:

*rends-leur les livres!* = give the books back to them!

Object pronouns return to normal order, object pronoun before verb, in imperative sentences if they are in the negative:

*ne les rendez pas!* = don't give them back!

### Order of Object Pronouns (see 4.2 for meanings):

When more than one object pronouns occur in the same sentence, they keep a fixed sequence as follows:

| | | | | |
|------|-----|------|---|----|
| me | le | lui | y | en |
| te | la | leur | | |
| se | les | | | |
| nous | | | | |
| vous | | | | |
| se | | | | |

- any combination of object pronouns will follow the above order:

  *nous le lui avons envoyé* = we sent it to her/him
  *ils le leur ont expliqué* = they explained it to them
  *elle leur en donne* = she gives them some
  *nous nous y opposons* = we're against it

- *me, te, nous, vous* can be both direct and indirect objects. They are also used with reflexive verbs [see Verbs section 10.1]

- *se* means: (to) himself, (to) herself, (to) oneself, (to) themselves, and is used with reflexive verbs

## 4.4 Emphatic or disjunctive pronouns

| | | | |
|------|-------|-------|------------------------------|
| *moi* | = me | *nous* | = us |
| *toi* | = you | *vous* | = you [plural or formal usage] |
| *lui* | = him | *eux* | = them |
| *elle* | = her | *elles* | = them [all female] |

The emphatic pronouns are used in the following situations:

- after prepositions:

  *avec moi* = with me    *sans elle* = without her
  *je pense à elle* = I'm thinking of her

- after *que* or *qu'* in comparative sentences [see Comparison section 8.1]:

  *plus petit que lui* = smaller than him    *plus grand que toi* = bigger than you

- to emphasize the subject:

  *lui, il n'aime pas le vin rouge mais elle, elle adore ça* =
  he doesn't like red wine but she loves it

- with *c'est, ce sont*

  *c'est moi!* = it's me!    *ce sont eux* = it's them

- with *même* meaning 'self' (myself, yourself, etc.):

  *toi-même* = yourself    *vous-mêmes* = yourselves

**Note:** -*s* is added to *même* in the plural

**Note:** *moi* and *toi* are used in imperatives when pronouns follow the verb:

  *donnez-le-moi!* = give it to me!    *mets-toi là!* = sit yourself there!

## 5 Adjectives

Adjectives are listed alphabetically according to the masculine form in this dictionary. In those cases where the feminine form is the same as the masculine, no further information is given. When the feminine is formed by adding an ending to the masculine, this is shown by the symbol ~ followed immediately by the ending: **lent, ~e** *adj* slow. If the change involves a spelling change to the masculine form, this is clearly shown: **langoureux, -euse** *adj*. Many determiners *ce, mon, tout* etc (= *this, my, all* etc) are adjectival and therefore must also agree with the nouns they qualify

### 5.1 Common adjectival endings:

Adjectives which add -*e* to form the feminine:

  *une jupe courte* = a short skirt

Adjectives which add -*s* to form the masculine plural:

  *des voyages intéressants* = interesting journeys

All adjectives follow this pattern in the plural unless the ending is -*x*, *curieux* → masculine plural *curieux*, or there is already a final -*s*, *bas* → masculine plural *bas*

Adjectives which add -*s* to the feminine to form the feminine plural

  *des histoires amusantes* = funny stories

. . . . . . . . . . . . . . . . . . . . . . . . . . . . . . . . .

## 5.2 Adjectives ending in -e

These are unchanged in the feminine: *aimable* → feminine *aimable*

-s is added in the normal way to form the plural for both masculine and feminine adjectives of this type: *aimable* → plural *aimables*

**Note:** If the adjective ends in -é, then the feminine form adds -e:

*aimé* → feminine *aimée*    plural: *aimés* → feminine *aimées*

## 5.3 Table of adjective endings and their typical feminine variants:

The following double the last letter and add an -e

| Typical ending | Adjective | Feminine | English |
|---|---|---|---|
| -as | *bas* | *basse* | low |
| -eil | *pareil* | *pareille* | similar |
| -el | *mortel* | *mortelle* | fatal |
| -en | *ancien* | *ancienne* | ancient |
| -et* | *muet* | *muette* | mute |
| -on | *bon* | *bonne* | good |
| -ul | *nul* | *nulle* | no good |

*Note that some adjectives ending in -et follow a different pattern: *inquiet* → *inquiète* = anxious

The following add a final -e and add an accent or change a consonant or consonant group

| Typical ending | Adjective | Feminine | English |
|---|---|---|---|
| -er | *premier* | *première* | first |
| -ef | *bref* | *brève* | brief |
| -if | *actif* | *active* | active |
| -eux | *fameux* | *fameuse* | infamous |
| -eur | *menteur* | *menteuse* | untruthful |
| -nc | *blanc* | *blanche* | white |
| -ic | *public* | *publique* | public |
| -gu | *aigu* | *aiguë* | acute |

The following are examples of irregular adjectives which show additional variations

*doux* → *douce* (= sweet)   *faux* → *fausse* (= false)
*favori* → *favorite* (= favourite)   *frais* → *fraîche* (= fresh)
*gentil* → *gentille* (= kind)   *jaloux* → *jalouse* (= jealous)
*malin* → *maligne* (= cunning)   *roux* → *rousse* (= red)
*sot* → *sotte* (= silly)

## 5.4 Position of adjectives

In French most adjectives follow the noun:

*un chocolat chaud* (= a hot chocolate)
*un homme grand* (= a tall man)
*un stylo noir* (= a black pen)

Some adjectives go before the noun. These are usually common adjectives:
*bon* = good, *gros* = big, *joli* = pretty, *nouveau* = new, *grand* = big, *petit* =
small

These may almost become part of the noun as a compound:

*un jeune homme* (= a young man)

They become part of a compound when they're joined to the noun by a
hyphen:

*les petits-enfants* (= the grandchildren)

Some adjectives radically change their meaning depending on whether
they precede or follow the noun, compare:

*la pauvre fille* (= the poor girl)  *la fille pauvre* (= the girl with little money)
*la mauvaise clé* (= the wrong key)  *un animal mauvais* (= a vicious animal)
*un grand homme* = a great man  *un homme grand* = a tall man

## 5.5 Adjectives which always precede the noun

The following classes of adjective always come before the nouns they
qualify:

Numbers, cardinal and ordinal:

*les trois filles* = the three girls  *la troisième fois* = the third time

Possessive and demonstrative adjectives:

*mon parapluie* = my umbrella  *cette église* = this church

Indefinite adjectives such as:

*chaque* = each, *tel* = such, *autre* = other
*chaque enfant* = each child  *une telle personne* = such a person

### beau, nouveau, vieux

These adjectives form a group because they have a variant spelling:

| Masculine | Masculine with vowel* | Plural | Feminine | Plural | English |
|---|---|---|---|---|---|
| beau | bel | beaux | belle | belles | beautiful |
| nouveau | nouvel | nouveaux | nouvelle | nouvelles | new |
| vieux | vieil | vieux | vieille | vieilles | old |

*une belle femme* (= a beautiful woman)
*de nouveaux livres* (= new books)
*de vieilles histoires* (= old stories)

*The variant spelling is used if the noun following is masculine
and begins with a vowel or a silent *h*:

*arbre* → *un bel arbre* (= a lovely tree)

# 6 Possession

## 6.1 Expressing possession

Possession is commonly expressed by *de*, meaning of.

> *le chien de Paul* (= literally: the dog of Paul) = Paul's dog
> *les vêtements de Sophie* (= literally: the clothes of Sophie) = Sophie's clothes

## 6.2 Possessive adjectives

The possessive adjectives are the equivalents of *my, your, his, her* etc.

POSSESSIVE ADJECTIVES

| Masculine | Feminine | Plural | English |
|-----------|----------|--------|---------|
| *mon* | *ma* | *mes* | my |
| *ton* | *ta* | *tes* | your |
| *son* | *sa* | *ses* | his/her/its/one's |
| *notre* | *notre* | *nos* | our |
| *votre* | *votre* | *vos* | your |
| *leur* | *leur* | *leurs* | their |

- The possessive adjective matches the gender and number of what is possessed NOT the possessor:

  *ma sœur* = my sister (the speaker may be male)     *sa femme* = his wife

- the feminine forms *ma, ta,* and *sa* end in vowels and are not used before a vowel. Instead the masculine form is used:

  *son élève* = his or her student     *son obligation* = her or his obligation

## 6.3 Possessive Pronouns

These are the equivalents of English *mine, yours, ours* etc. In French they reflect the gender and number of the what is possessed:

POSSESSIVE PRONOUNS

| Masculine | Feminine | Masculine Plural | Feminine Plural | English |
|-----------|----------|------------------|-----------------|---------|
| *le mien* | *la mienne* | *les miens* | *les miennes* | mine |
| *le tien* | *la tienne* | *les tiens* | *les tiennes* | yours |
| *le sien* | *la sienne* | *les siens* | *les siennes* | his/hers/its |
| *le nôtre* | *la nôtre* | *les nôtres* | *les nôtres* | ours |
| *le vôtre* | *la vôtre* | *les vôtres* | *les vôtres* | yours |
| *le leur* | *la leur* | *les leurs* | *les leurs* | theirs |

> *ce n'est pas sa veste, c'est la mienne* = it's not his jacket, it's mine (the speaker may be male)
> *ce ne sont pas ses chaussures, ce sont les miennes* = these are not his shoes, they're mine

# 7 Adverbs

Adverbs usually give additional information about a verb: i.e. they say 'how' (= in what way or manner), 'when', or 'where' something happens

Most French adverbs are formed from the feminine adjective by adding
*-ment*

> *heureux* → *heureuse* → *heureusement* (= happily, fortunately)
> *égal* → *égale* → *également* (= equally)

Exceptions include:

## 7.1 masculine adjectives ending in a vowel

The adverb is formed from the masculine adjective rather than the
feminine:

> *hardi* → *hardiment* (= robustly)     *résolu* → *résolument* (= resolutely)

## 7.2 adjectives ending in *-ant* or *-ent*

The *-nt* is dropped and the *-m-* is doubled:

> *constant* → *constamment* (= constantly)     *intelligent* → *intelligemment* (= intelligently)

Note however *lent* → *lentement* (= slowly). Some adverbs are irregular in
their formation:

> *bon* = good → *bien* = well          *bref* = brief → *brièvement* = briefly
> *gentil* = kind → *gentiment* = kindly     *mauvais* = bad → *mal* = badly

- - - - - - - - - - - - - - - - - - - - - - - - - - - - - - - - - - - - - - - - - - -

# 8 Comparison

## 8.1 Comparative of adjectives and adverbs

The comparative of adjectives and adverbs in English is usually expressed
by:

> 'more...'     *more interesting – adjective; more interestingly – adverb*
> 'as...'       *as easy – adjective; as easily – adverb*
> 'less...'     *less intelligent – adjective; less intelligently – adverb*

The comparative of adjectives and adverbs in French is expressed in most
cases by:

> 'plus...      *plus intéressant – adjective; plus facilement – adverb*
> aussi...'     *aussi grand – adjective (= as big); aussi facilement – adverb (= as easily)*
> 'moins...'    *moins intelligent – adjective (= less intelligent); moins facilement – adverb*
>               *(= less easily)*

Comparative adjectives and adverbs are followed by *que* (or *qu'* before a
vowel or silent *h*) to translate 'than' or 'as' in English.

> *plus intéressant que* = more interesting than
> *aussi facilement que* = as easily as
> *moins intelligent que* = less intelligent than

The comparative adjective reflects the gender and number of the noun
described:

> *il est plus grand que toi* = he is taller than you
> *cette rue est moins longue que celle-là* = this road is shorter than that one

SOME IRREGULAR:

| ADJECTIVE COMPARATIVES | | | ADVERB COMPARATIVES | | |
|---|---|---|---|---|---|
| **Adjective** | **Comparative** | **English** | **Adverb** | **Comparative** | **English** |
| *bon* = good | *meilleur* | better | *beaucoup* = much | plus | more |
| *mauvais* = bad | *pire* | worse | *bien* = well | *mieux* | better |
| | | | *mal* = badly | *pis* | worse |
| | | | *peu* = little | *moins* | less |

## 8.2 Superlative of adjectives and adverbs

The superlative of adjectives and adverbs in English is expressed by 'most…'

*most interesting – adjective, most interestingly – adverb*

The superlative adjective in French is expressed in most cases by:

'le/la/les plus + *adjective*'    le plus intéressant

The article is repeated reflecting the gender and number of the noun described:

*la ville la plus belle* = the most beautiful city

Note how *de* (or *du*) following the superlative in French is translated by *in* or *of* in English in sentences like:

*la ville la plus belle du monde* = the most beautiful city IN the world
*le meilleur épisode de la série* = the best episode OF the series

The superlative of adverbs in French closely resembles the adjective, but the article is always *le* (never: *la* or *les*): *le plus facilement* = the most easily

## 9 Time

Time phrases in French begin with *il est…* (= it is…) and the French equivalent of 'o'clock' is *heures*, except for 'one o'clock' *une heure*. The 24 hour clock is often used to distinguish between a.m. and p.m.

The number of hours is stated first and any minutes 'past' the hour are simply added to the end of the phrase:

*il est sept heures dix* = it's ten minutes past seven

'quarter past' is expressed by *et quart*:

*il est sept heures et quart* = it's quarter past seven *or* seven fifteen.

minutes 'to' the hour follow the word *moins* (= minus):

*il est quatre heures moins cinq* = it's five to four

'quarter to' is expressed by *moins le quart*:

*il est quatre heures moins le quart* = it's quarter to four

'half past' is expressed by *et demie*:

*il est trois heures et demie* = it's half past three

**Note:** *midi* (= midday) and *minuit* (= midnight) are masculine; therefore *et demie* changes to *et demi* with these two words:

> *il est midi/minuit et demi* = it's half past twelve (midday)/midnight

**Examples:**

> 1.00 = il est une heure
> 2.00 = il est deux heures
> 2.10 = il est deux heures dix
> 2.15 = il est deux heures et quart *or* il est deux heures quinze
> 2.30 = il est deux heures et demie *or* il est deux heures trente
> 2.35 = il est trois heures moins vingt-cinq *or* il est deux heures trente-cinq

## 10 Verbs

The infinitive is the basic form of the verb and the one you look up in the dictionary. Verbs are described as being *transitive* or *intransitive*. Transitive verbs, marked *vtr* in the dictionary, take an object. In *he kicks the ball*, 'kick' is the verb and 'the ball' is the object. Intransitive verbs, marked *vi*, function without objects; verbs like 'to die', 'to sleep', 'to live' are intransitive.

The tenses are the forms of the verb which convey the time at which something acts, happens, exists, etc. They are called the present tense, the future tense, the past tense etc. Verbs which follow the same pattern as others and make up a recognizable group are called regular verbs. Verbs which deviate from the general pattern or are unique in their verb forms are called irregular verbs. In the French-English section of the dictionary every French verb is cross-referenced to the verbs section by a number in square brackets, **déplacer** /deplase/ [12] ... This means that the relevant information will be found in table 12 of the section *French verbs* on page 950.

### 10.1 Verb patterns

In French there are three major groupings of regular verbs identified by their infinitive endings, -er, -ir, and -re. There are also many irregular verbs which don't follow the same patterns. Some verbs are reflexive which means that the object of the verb is the same as its subject.

> *je me lave* = I wash myself [see Pronouns section 4.3]

### 10.1.a Present tense

The present tense describes what is happening now (*it is raining*) or what regularly happens (*he plays football on Tuesdays*) or a current truth (*she loves chips*)

| parler 'to speak' | AN EXAMPLE OF AN -ER VERB |
|---|---|
| *je parle* = I speak | *nous parlons* = we speak |
| *tu parles* = you speak | *vous parlez* = you speak |
| *il parle* = he speaks | *ils parlent* = they speak (*masculine*) |
| *elle parle* = she speaks | *elles parlent* = they speak (*feminine*) |

■ the translation *I speak*, etc., may also be *I am speaking* and *I do speak*

| finir 'to finish' | AN EXAMPLE OF AN -IR VERB |
|---|---|
| *je finis* = I finish | *nous finissons* = we finish |
| *tu finis* = you finish | *vous finissez* = you finish |
| *il finit* = he finishes | *ils (masc) finissent* = they finish |
| *elle finit* = she finishes | *elles (fem) finissent* = they finish |

■ note the lengthened stem *-iss-* in the plural

| vendre 'to sell' | AN EXAMPLE OF AN -RE VERB |
|---|---|
| *je vends* = I sell | *nous vendons* = we sell |
| *tu vends* = you sell | *vous vendez* = you sell |
| *il vend* = he sells | *ils (masc) vendent* = they sell |
| *elle vend* = she sells | *elles (fem) vendent* = they sell |

■ note the dropped verb ending with *il* and *elle*

## 10.1.b Imperative

The imperative is the form of the verb for giving orders. Three parts of the present tense are used: *tu, nous, vous*

The *-s* is dropped from the *tu* part of the verb:

parle! (= talk!); parlons! (= let's talk!); parlez! (= talk!)

But there are exceptions [see Verb Tables]:

aie! (= have!); ayons! (= let's have!); ayez! (= have!)
sois! (= be!); soyons! (= let's be!); soyez! (= be!)
sache! (= know!); sachons! (= let's know!); sachez! (= know!)

## 10.1.c Imperfect tense

The imperfect tense describes what was happening in the past (*it was raining*) or what used to be a fact or a regular occurrence (*he used to like chocolate; he used to go to classes*)

il jouait au football tous les jeudis = he played football/used to play football every Tuesday

### Imperfect tense endings

| -ais | -ions |
|---|---|
| -ais | -iez |
| -ait | -aient |
| -ait | -aient |

These endings apply to all verbs and are added to the verb stem. The stem is taken from the *nous* form of the present tense, *nous finiss-ons* → *finiss-* → *je finissais*

The only irregular stem is *ét-* from *être*: *j'étais* (= I was), *tu étais* (= you were)… etc.

. . . . . . . . . . . . . . . . . . . . . . . . . . .

### 10.1.d Future tense

The future tense describes what will happen (*it will rain*) or what is expected to be a fact (*it will be easy*)

**Future tense endings**

| | |
|------|-------|
| -ai | -ons |
| -as | -ez |
| -a | -ont |
| -a | -ont |

These endings apply to all verbs and are added to the infinitive, which acts as the 'stem' for most verbs in the future tense:

*finir → je finirai* (= I shall finish)

But *-re* verbs drop the final *-e* of the infinitive:

*vendre → je vendrai* (= I shall sell)

The future may also be expressed by: the verb *aller* + Infinitive

*je vais finir…* (= I am going to finish…)

### Table of irregular future verb stems

| Infinitive | Future Stem | | Infinitive | Future Stem | |
|-----------|-------------|---|-----------|-------------|---|
| avoir | j'aurai | = I shall have | tenir | je tiendrai | = I shall hold |
| être | je serai | = I shall want | vouloir | je voudrai | = I shall be |
| faire | je ferai | = I shall make | pouvoir | je pourrai | = I shall be able |
| savoir | je saurai | = I shall know | recevoir | je recevrai | = I shall get |
| voir | je verrai | = I shall see | devoir | je devrai | = I shall have to |
| envoyer | j'enverrai | = I shall send | courir | je courrai | = I shall run |
| venir | je viendrai | = I shall come | mourir | je mourrai | = I shall die |

Compounds of the above verbs take the same the same stem as the basic verb:

*retenir* (= to hold back) *→ je retiendrai*     *défaire* (= to undo) *→ je déferai*

### 10.1.e Conditional tense

The conditional tense describes what would happen (*it would make him angry*) or what would be a fact (*it would be easy*). Conditionals are often preceded or followed by a phrase introduced by *si* (= if).

**Formation:** The conditional is made up of the Future Stem + Imperfect Endings. This applies to all verbs.

*il commencerait* (= he would begin)
*tu devrais* (= you ought to)
*il le ferait si tu le lui demandais* = he'd do it if you asked him

### 10.1.f Perfect tense

The perfect tense describes what has happened (*it has snowed*; *they have written*). In French it is also used for what happened and remained the case until a specific point in time (*ils y sont restés jusqu'à mardi* = they stayed there until Tuesday) or to state an action as part of a series, each action

• • • • • • • • • • • • • • • • • • • • • • • • • • • • • • • • • • • • • • • • • •

being complete in itself (*je me suis approché de la maison, j'ai sonné à la porte…* = I went up to the house, rang the doorbell…)

## Formation of the perfect tense:

Two common verbs are important in the formation of the perfect tense: *avoir* and *être*

| avoir = to have | | être = to be | |
|---|---|---|---|
| *j'ai* | *nous avons* | *je suis* | *nous sommes* |
| *tu as* | *vous avez* | *tu es* | *vous êtes* |
| *il a* | *ils ont* | *il est* | *ils sont* |
| *elle a* | *elles ont* | *elle est* | *elles sont* |

There are three elements in the perfect tense:

SUBJECT + *avoir/être* + PAST PARTICIPLE

The past participle of regular verbs is formed by removing the last syllable of the infinitive (*regarder, choisir, rendre*) and by replacing it with *-é, -i, -u* respectively:

-ER verbs:    *regarder → regardé → j'ai regardé* (= I have looked)
-IR verbs:    *choisir → choisi → tu as choisi* (= you have chosen)
-RE verbs:    *rendre → rendu → il a rendu* (= he has given back)

But some past participles are unique and have to be learnt by heart

## Table of common irregular past participles following the auxiliary verb *avoir*:

| Infinitive | Past Participle | | Infinitive | Past Participle | |
|---|---|---|---|---|---|
| avoir | *j'ai eu* | = I have had | croire | *j'ai cru* | = I have believed |
| être | *j'ai été* | = I have been | savoir | *j'ai su* | = I have known |
| faire | *j'ai fait* | = I have made | voir | *j'ai vu* | = I have seen |
| boire | *j'ai bu* | = I have drunk | pleuvoir | *il a plu* | = it has rained |
| pouvoir | *j'ai pu* | = I have been able | dire | *j'ai dit* | = I have said |
| devoir | *j'ai dû* | = I have had to | écrire | *j'ai écrit* | = I have written |
| lire | *j'ai lu* | = I have read | mettre | *j'ai mis* | = I have put |
| vouloir | *j'ai voulu* | = I have wanted | prendre | *j'ai pris* | = I have taken |

■ the past participle does not change its spelling after *avoir* unless there is a direct object preceding it: *j'ai vendu la table* (= I sold the table). No preceding direct object, no change to the past participle *vendu*. But in *tu l'as vendue* (= you've sold it), *l'* (referring to *la table*, feminine) makes *vendu* take the feminine ending *-e*.

Most verbs form their perfect tense with *avoir*. The exceptions are reflexive verbs and a small group of verbs of 'motion'. These take *être* and the past participle functions like an adjective qualifying the subject.

# Summary of French grammar

. . . . . . . . . . . . . . . . . . . . . . . . . . . . . . . . . . .

## 1 Reflexive verb: *se laver* = to get washed/to wash oneself

*je me suis lavé(e)* = I got washed
*tu t'es lavé(e)* = you got washed
*il s'est lavé* = he got washed
*elle s'est lavée* = she got washed

*nous nous sommes lavé(e)s* = we got washed
*vous vous êtes lavé(e)(s)* = you got washed
*ils se sont lavés* = they got washed
*elles se sont lavées* = they got washed

- The alternatives in brackets depend on gender (masculine or feminine) and number (singular or plural) of the subject: *je*, *tu*, *elle*, *nous*, etc

## 2 Verbs of motion which take *être*

| | | | | | |
|---|---|---|---|---|---|
| aller | *je suis allé(e)* | = I went | partir | *je suis parti(e)* | = I left |
| arriver | *je suis arrivé(e)* | = I arrived | rester | *je suis resté(e)* | = I stayed |
| descendre | *je suis descendu(e)* | = I went down | retourner | *je suis retourné(e)* | = I returned |
| entrer | *je suis entré(e)* | = I entered | revenir | *je suis revenu(e)* | = I came back |
| monter | *je suis monté(e)* | = I went up | sortir | *je suis sorti(e)* | = I went out |
| mourir | *je suis mort(e)* | = I died | tomber | *je suis tombé(e)* | = I fell |
| naître | *je suis né(e)* | = I was born | venir | *je suis venu(e)* | = I came |

- compounds of the above also take *être*: *devenir* (= to become) → *je suis devenu(e)*

### 10.1.g Pluperfect tense

The pluperfect tense describes what had happened (*it had snowed*; *they had written*) or what had been the case (*it had been easy*).

**Formation:** = Imperfect Tense of *avoir* or *être* + PAST PARTICIPLE

**Examples:**

*j'avais fini* = I had finished
*nous avions vendu l'appartement* = we had sold the flat
*elle s'était réveillée* = she had woken up
*nous étions partis* = we had left

- As with the perfect tense, past participles after *être* function like adjectives. They qualify the subject of the verb and reflect its gender and number.

### 10.1.h Future perfect tense

The future perfect tense describes what will have happened (*he will have arrived*) or what will have been the case (*it will not have been easy*)

**Formation:** = Future Tense of *avoir* or *être* + PAST PARTICIPLE

**Examples:**

*j'aurai fini* = I shall have finished
*nous aurons vendu la voiture* = we shall have sold the car
*nous serons descendus* = we shall have gone down

- As with the perfect tense, past participles after *être* function like adjectives. They qualify the subject of the verb and reflect its gender and number.

. . . . . . . . . . . . . . . . . . . . . . . . . . . . . . . . . . . . . . . . . . . . . .

## 11 Negatives

Negative is the idea expressed by words such as *no, never, nobody, nothing*, etc in English and *non, jamais, personne, rien*, etc in French. The negative of French verbs is formed by using *ne* before the verb, and *pas, jamais, plus*, etc after the verb according to the sense required.

ne … pas (= not)　　　　　　　ne … jamais (= never)
ne … personne (= nobody, no one)　ne … plus (= no longer)
ne … que (= only)　　　　　　ne … rien (= nothing)

In simple sentences *ne* is placed before the verb and *pas, jamais, plus* etc after it.

*je ne lis pas* = I am not reading

If there are pronouns before the verb, *ne* comes before them.

*je ne le lui donne jamais* = I never give it to him

If an auxiliary verb is used in a compound tense, it comes within *ne … pas, jamais, plus* etc.

*il n'a rien mangé* = he didn't eat anything

If an infinitive is used in the sentence, it comes after *ne … pas, jamais, plus* etc.

*il ne veut pas manger* = he doesn't want to eat

Neither … nor is expressed by *ni … ni*:

*ni Jean ni Luc ne voulaient venir* = neither Jean nor Luc wanted to come

If pronoun objects are used in the sentence they take the emphatic form.

*ni lui ni sa femme n'étaient là* = neither he nor his wife was there

If *personne* (= nobody) *or rien* (= nothing) is the subject it is followed only by *ne*:

*personne ne vous dérangera* = no one will disturb you
*rien n'est impossible* = nothing is impossible

Note also the following usage:

*qui a frappé? – personne* = who knocked? nobody
*qu'est-ce qui se passe? – rien* = what's going on? nothing

The use of the adjective *aucun/aucune* (= no) is very common; *aucun* is used with *ne* before the verb.

*il n'a aucun talent* = he has no talent
*elle n'avait aucune nouvelle de lui* = she hadn't heard from him

# French verbs

## Standard verb endings

|  |  | -er | -ir | -r, -re |
|---|---|---|---|---|
| **Indicative Present** | | | | |
| Singular | 1 | -e | -is | -s *or* -e |
|  | 2 | -es | -is | -s *or* -es |
|  | 3 | -e | -it | -t *or* -e |
| Plural | 1 | -ons | -(iss)ons | -ons |
|  | 2 | -ez | -(iss)ez | -ez |
|  | 3 | -ent | -(iss)ent | -ent |
| **Indicative Imperfect** | | | | |
| Singular | 1 | -ais | -(iss)ais | -ais |
|  | 2 | -ais | -(iss)ais | -ais |
|  | 3 | -ait | -(iss)ait | -ait |
| Plural | 1 | -ions | -(iss)ions | -ions |
|  | 2 | -iez | -(iss)iez | -iez |
|  | 3 | -aient | -(iss)aient | -aient |
| **Indicative Past historic** | | | | |
| Singular | 1 | -ai | -is | -s |
|  | 2 | -as | -is | -s |
|  | 3 | -a | -it | -t |
| Plural | 1 | -âmes | -îmes | -mes |
|  | 2 | -âtes | -îtes | -tes |
|  | 3 | -èrent | -irent | -rent |
| **Indicative Future** | | | | |
| Singular | 1 | -erai | -irai | -rai |
|  | 2 | -eras | -iras | -ras |
|  | 3 | -era | -ira | -ra |
| Plural | 1 | -erons | -irons | -rons |
|  | 2 | -erez | -irez | -rez |
|  | 3 | -eront | -iront | -ront |
| **Infinitive** | | | | |
| Present | | -er | -ir | -r *or* -re |

|  |  | -er | -ir | -r, -re |
|---|---|---|---|---|
| **Subjunctive Present** | | | | |
| Singular | 1 | -e | -(iss)e | -e |
|  | 2 | -es | -(iss)es | -es |
|  | 3 | -e | -(iss)e | -e |
| Plural | 1 | -ions | -(iss)ions | -ions |
|  | 2 | -iez | -(iss)iez | -iez |
|  | 3 | -ent | -(iss)ent | -ent |
| **Subjunctive Imperfect** | | | | |
| Singular | 1 | -asse | -isse | -sse |
|  | 2 | -asses | -isses | -sses |
|  | 3 | -ât | -ît | -ît *or* -ût |
| Plural | 1 | -assions | -issions | -ssions |
|  | 2 | -assiez | -issiez | -ssiez |
|  | 3 | -assent | -issent | -ssent |
| **Imperative Present** | | | | |
| Singular | 1 | | | |
|  | 2 | | | |
|  | 3 | -e | -is | -s |
| Plural | 1 | -ons | -(iss)ons | -ons |
|  | 2 | -ez | -(iss)ez | -ez |
| **Conditional Present** | | | | |
| Singular | 1 | -erais | -irais | -rais |
|  | 2 | -erais | -irais | -rais |
|  | 3 | -erait | -irait | -rait |
| Plural | 1 | -erions | -irions | -rions |
|  | 2 | -eriez | -iriez | -riez |
|  | 3 | -eraient | -iraient | -raient |
| **Participle** | | | | |
| Present | | -ant | -(iss)ant | -ant |
| Past | | -é | -i | -i *or* -u |

# 1 aimer

## Indicative

### Present

| | |
|---|---|
| j' | aime |
| tu | aimes |
| il | aime |
| nous | aimons |
| vous | aimez |
| ils | aiment |

### Imperfect

| | |
|---|---|
| j' | aimais |
| tu | aimais |
| il | aimait |
| nous | aimions |
| vous | aimiez |
| ils | aimaient |

### Past historic

| | |
|---|---|
| j' | aimai |
| tu | aimas |
| il | aima |
| nous | aimâmes |
| vous | aimâtes |
| ils | aimèrent |

### Future

| | |
|---|---|
| j' | aimerai |
| tu | aimeras |
| il | aimera |
| nous | aimerons |
| vous | aimerez |
| ils | aimeront |

### Perfect

| | | |
|---|---|---|
| j' | ai | aimé |
| tu | as | aimé |
| il | a | aimé |
| nous | avons | aimé |
| vous | avez | aimé |
| ils | ont | aimé |

### Pluperfect

| | | |
|---|---|---|
| j' | avais | aimé |
| tu | avais | aimé |
| il | avait | aimé |
| nous | avions | aimé |
| vous | aviez | aimé |
| ils | avaient | aimé |

## Imperative

### Present

| | |
|---|---|
| | aime |
| | aimons |
| | aimez |

### Past

| | |
|---|---|
| | aie | aimé |
| | ayons | aimé |
| | ayez | aimé |

## Subjunctive

### Present

| | |
|---|---|
| (que) j' | aime |
| (que) tu | aimes |
| (qu')il | aime |
| (que) nous | aimions |
| (que) vous | aimiez |
| (qu')ils | aiment |

### Perfect

| | | |
|---|---|---|
| (que) j' | aie | aimé |
| (que) tu | aies | aimé |
| (qu')il | ait | aimé |
| (que) nous | ayons | aimé |
| (que) vous | ayez | aimé |
| (qu')ils | aient | aimé |

### Pluperfect

| | | |
|---|---|---|
| (que) j' | eusse | aimé |
| (que) tu | eusses | aimé |
| (qu')il | eût | aimé |
| (que) nous | eussions | aimé |
| (que) vous | eussiez | aimé |
| (qu')ils | eussent | aimé |

## Conditional

### Present

| | |
|---|---|
| j' | aimerais |
| tu | aimerais |
| il | aimerait |
| nous | aimerions |
| vous | aimeriez |
| ils | aimeraient |

### Past I

| | | |
|---|---|---|
| j' | aurais | aimé |
| tu | aurais | aimé |
| il | aurait | aimé |
| nous | aurions | aimé |
| vous | auriez | aimé |
| ils | auraient | aimé |

## Participle

### Present aimant

### Past

| | |
|---|---|
| | aimé, -e |
| | ayant aimé |

## Infinitive

### Present aimer

### Past avoir aimé

# 2 plier

## Indicative

### Present

| | |
|---|---|
| je | plie |
| tu | plies |
| il | plie |
| nous | plions |
| vous | pliez |
| ils | plient |

### Imperfect

| | |
|---|---|
| je | pliais |
| tu | pliais |
| il | pliait |
| nous | pliions |
| vous | pliiez |
| ils | pliaient |

### Past historic

| | |
|---|---|
| je | pliai |
| tu | plias |
| il | plia |
| nous | pliâmes |
| vous | pliâtes |
| ils | plièrent |

### Future

| | |
|---|---|
| je | plierai |
| tu | plieras |
| il | pliera |
| nous | plierons |
| vous | plierez |
| ils | plieront |

### Perfect

| | | |
|---|---|---|
| j' | ai | plié |
| tu | as | plié |
| il | a | plié |
| nous | avons | plié |
| vous | avez | plié |
| ils | ont | plié |

### Pluperfect

| | | |
|---|---|---|
| j' | avais | plié |
| tu | avais | plié |
| il | avait | plié |
| nous | avions | plié |
| vous | aviez | plié |
| ils | avaient | plié |

## Imperative

### Present

| | |
|---|---|
| | plie |
| | plions |
| | pliez |

### Past

| | |
|---|---|
| | aie | plié |
| | ayons | plié |
| | ayez | plié |

## Subjunctive

### Present

| | |
|---|---|
| (que) je | plie |
| (que) tu | plies |
| (qu')il | plie |
| (que) nous | pliions |
| (que) vous | pliiez |
| (qu')ils | plient |

### Perfect

| | | |
|---|---|---|
| (que) j' | aie | plié |
| (que) tu | aies | plié |
| (qu')il | ait | plié |
| (que) nous | ayons | plié |
| (que) vous | ayez | plié |
| (qu')ils | aient | plié |

### Pluperfect

| | | |
|---|---|---|
| (que) j' | eusse | plié |
| (que) tu | eusses | plié |
| (qu')il | eût | plié |
| (que) nous | eussions | plié |
| (que) vous | eussiez | plié |
| (qu')ils | eussent | plié |

## Conditional

### Present

| | |
|---|---|
| je | plierais |
| tu | plierais |
| il | plierait |
| nous | plierions |
| vous | plieriez |
| ils | plieraient |

### Past I

| | | |
|---|---|---|
| j' | aurais | plié |
| tu | aurais | plié |
| il | aurait | plié |
| nous | aurions | plié |
| vous | auriez | plié |
| ils | auraient | plié |

## Participle

### Present pliant

### Past

| | |
|---|---|
| | plié, -e |
| | ayant plié |

## Infinitive

### Present plier

### Past avoir plié

## 3 finir

### Indicative

**Present**

| | |
|---|---|
| je | fin**is** |
| tu | fin**is** |
| il | fin**it** |
| nous | fin**issons** |
| vous | fin**issez** |
| ils | fin**issent** |

**Imperfect**

| | |
|---|---|
| je | fin**issais** |
| tu | fin**issais** |
| il | fin**issait** |
| nous | fin**issions** |
| vous | fin**issiez** |
| ils | fin**issaient** |

**Past historic**

| | |
|---|---|
| je | fin**is** |
| tu | fin**is** |
| il | fin**it** |
| nous | fin**îmes** |
| vous | fin**îtes** |
| ils | fin**irent** |

**Future**

| | |
|---|---|
| je | fin**irai** |
| tu | fin**iras** |
| il | fin**ira** |
| nous | fin**irons** |
| vous | fin**irez** |
| ils | fin**iront** |

**Perfect**

| | | |
|---|---|---|
| j' | ai | fin**i** |
| tu | as | fin**i** |
| il | a | fin**i** |
| nous | avons | fin**i** |
| vous | avez | fin**i** |
| ils | ont | fin**i** |

**Pluperfect**

| | | |
|---|---|---|
| j' | avais | fin**i** |
| tu | avais | fin**i** |
| il | avait | fin**i** |
| nous | avions | fin**i** |
| vous | aviez | fin**i** |
| ils | avaient | fin**i** |

### Imperative

**Present**

| | |
|---|---|
| | fin**is** |
| | fin**issons** |
| | fin**issez** |

**Past**

| | |
|---|---|
| aie | fin**i** |
| ayons | fin**i** |
| ayez | fin**i** |

### Subjunctive

**Present**

| | |
|---|---|
| (que) je | fin**isse** |
| (que) tu | fin**isses** |
| (qu')il | fin**isse** |
| (que) nous | fin**issions** |
| (que) vous | fin**issiez** |
| (qu')ils | fin**issent** |

**Perfect**

| | | |
|---|---|---|
| (que) j' | aie | fin**i** |
| (que) tu | aies | fin**i** |
| (qu')il | ait | fin**i** |
| (que) nous | ayons | fin**i** |
| (que) vous | ayez | fin**i** |
| (qu')ils | aient | fin**i** |

**Pluperfect**

| | | |
|---|---|---|
| (que) j' | eusse | fin**i** |
| (que) tu | eusses | fin**i** |
| (qu')il | eût | fin**i** |
| (que) nous | eussions | fin**i** |
| (que) vous | eussiez | fin**i** |
| (qu')ils | eussent | fin**i** |

### Conditional

**Present**

| | |
|---|---|
| je | fin**irais** |
| tu | fin**irais** |
| il | fin**irait** |
| nous | fin**irions** |
| vous | fin**iriez** |
| ils | fin**iraient** |

**Past I**

| | | |
|---|---|---|
| j' | aurais | fin**i** |
| tu | aurais | fin**i** |
| il | aurait | fin**i** |
| nous | aurions | fin**i** |
| vous | auriez | fin**i** |
| ils | auraient | fin**i** |

### Participle

**Present** fin**issant**

**Past** fin**i, -e**

ayant fin**i**

### Infinitive

**Present** fin**ir**

**Past** avoir fin**i**

## 4 offrir

### Indicative

**Present**

| | |
|---|---|
| j' | offre |
| tu | offr**es** |
| il | offre |
| nous | offr**ons** |
| vous | offr**ez** |
| ils | offr**ent** |

**Imperfect**

| | |
|---|---|
| j' | offr**ais** |
| tu | offr**ais** |
| il | offr**ait** |
| nous | offr**ions** |
| vous | offr**iez** |
| ils | offr**aient** |

**Past historic**

| | |
|---|---|
| j' | offr**is** |
| tu | offr**is** |
| il | offr**it** |
| nous | offr**îmes** |
| vous | offr**îtes** |
| ils | offr**irent** |

**Future**

| | |
|---|---|
| j' | offr**irai** |
| tu | offr**iras** |
| il | offr**ira** |
| nous | offr**irons** |
| vous | offr**irez** |
| ils | offr**iront** |

**Perfect**

| | | |
|---|---|---|
| j' | ai | offert |
| tu | as | offert |
| il | a | offert |
| nous | avons | offert |
| vous | avez | offert |
| ils | ont | offert |

**Pluperfect**

| | | |
|---|---|---|
| j' | avais | offert |
| tu | avais | offert |
| il | avait | offert |
| nous | avions | offert |
| vous | aviez | offert |
| ils | avaient | offert |

### Imperative

**Present**

| | |
|---|---|
| | offre |
| | offr**ons** |
| | offr**ez** |

**Past**

| | |
|---|---|
| aie | offert |
| ayons | offert |
| ayez | offert |

### Subjunctive

**Present**

| | |
|---|---|
| (que) j' | offre |
| (que) tu | offr**es** |
| (qu')il | offre |
| (que) nous | offr**ions** |
| (que) vous | offr**iez** |
| (qu')ils | offr**ent** |

**Perfect**

| | | |
|---|---|---|
| (que) j' | aie | offert |
| (que) tu | aies | offert |
| (qu')il | ait | offert |
| (que) nous | ayons | offert |
| (que) vous | ayez | offert |
| (qu')ils | aient | offert |

**Pluperfect**

| | | |
|---|---|---|
| (que) j' | eusse | offert |
| (que) tu | eusses | offert |
| (qu')il | eût | offert |
| (que) nous | eussions | offert |
| (que) vous | eussiez | offert |
| (qu')ils | eussent | offert |

### Conditional

**Present**

| | |
|---|---|
| j' | offr**irais** |
| tu | offr**irais** |
| il | offr**irait** |
| nous | offr**irions** |
| vous | offr**iriez** |
| ils | offr**iraient** |

**Past I**

| | | |
|---|---|---|
| j' | aurais | offert |
| tu | aurais | offert |
| il | aurait | offert |
| nous | aurions | offert |
| vous | auriez | offert |
| ils | auraient | offert |

### Participle

**Present** offrant

**Past** offert, -e

ayant offert

### Infinitive

**Present** offr**ir**

**Past** avoir offert

# 5 recevoir

## Indicative

**Present**

| | |
|---|---|
| je | reçois |
| tu | reçois |
| il | reçoit |
| nous | recevons |
| vous | recevez |
| ils | reçoivent |

**Imperfect**

| | |
|---|---|
| je | recevais |
| tu | recevais |
| il | recevait |
| nous | recevions |
| vous | receviez |
| ils | recevaient |

**Past historic**

| | |
|---|---|
| je | reçus |
| tu | reçus |
| il | reçut |
| nous | reçûmes |
| vous | reçûtes |
| ils | reçurent |

**Future**

| | |
|---|---|
| je | recevrai |
| tu | recevras |
| il | recevra |
| nous | recevrons |
| vous | recevrez |
| ils | recevront |

**Perfect**

| | | |
|---|---|---|
| j' | ai | reçu |
| tu | as | reçu |
| il | a | reçu |
| nous | avons | reçu |
| vous | avez | reçu |
| ils | ont | reçu |

**Pluperfect**

| | | |
|---|---|---|
| j' | avais | reçu |
| tu | avais | reçu |
| il | avait | reçu |
| nous | avions | reçu |
| vous | aviez | reçu |
| ils | avaient | reçu |

## Imperative

**Present**

| | |
|---|---|
| | reçois |
| | recevons |
| | recevez |

**Past**

| | |
|---|---|
| | aie reçu |
| | ayons reçu |
| | ayez reçu |

## Subjunctive

**Present**

| | |
|---|---|
| (que) je | reçoive |
| (que) tu | reçoives |
| (qu')il | reçoive |
| (que) nous | recevions |
| (que) vous | receviez |
| (qu')ils | reçoivent |

**Perfect**

| | | |
|---|---|---|
| (que) j' | aie | reçu |
| (que) tu | aies | reçu |
| (qu')il | ait | reçu |
| (que) nous | ayons | reçu |
| (que) vous | ayez | reçu |
| (qu')ils | aient | reçu |

**Pluperfect**

| | | |
|---|---|---|
| (que) j' | eusse | reçu |
| (que) tu | eusses | reçu |
| (qu')il | eût | reçu |
| (que) nous | eussions reçu |
| (que) vous | eussiez reçu |
| (qu')ils | eussent reçu |

## Conditional

**Present**

| | |
|---|---|
| je | recevrais |
| tu | recevrais |
| il | recevrait |
| nous | recevrions |
| vous | receviez |
| ils | recevraient |

**Past I**

| | | |
|---|---|---|
| j' | aurais | reçu |
| tu | aurais | reçu |
| il | aurait | reçu |
| nous | aurions | reçu |
| vous | auriez | reçu |
| ils | auraient reçu |

## Participle

| | |
|---|---|
| **Present** | recevant |
| **Past** | reçu, -e |
| | ayant reçu |

## Infinitive

| | |
|---|---|
| **Present** | recevoir |
| **Past** | avoir reçu |

# 6 rendre

## Indicative

**Present**

| | |
|---|---|
| je | rends |
| tu | rends |
| il | rend |
| nous | rendons |
| vous | rendez |
| ils | rendent |

**Imperfect**

| | |
|---|---|
| je | rendais |
| tu | rendais |
| il | rendait |
| nous | rendions |
| vous | rendiez |
| ils | rendaient |

**Past historic**

| | |
|---|---|
| je | rendis |
| tu | rendis |
| il | rendit |
| nous | rendîmes |
| vous | rendîtes |
| ils | rendirent |

**Future**

| | |
|---|---|
| je | rendrai |
| tu | rendras |
| il | rendra |
| nous | rendrons |
| vous | rendrez |
| ils | rendront |

**Perfect**

| | | |
|---|---|---|
| j' | ai | rendu |
| tu | as | rendu |
| il | a | rendu |
| nous | avons | rendu |
| vous | avez | rendu |
| ils | ont | rendu |

**Pluperfect**

| | | |
|---|---|---|
| j' | avais | rendu |
| tu | avais | rendu |
| il | avait | rendu |
| nous | avions | rendu |
| vous | aviez | rendu |
| ils | avaient | rendu |

## Imperative

**Present**

| | |
|---|---|
| | rends |
| | rendons |
| | rendez |

**Past**

| | |
|---|---|
| | aie rendu |
| | ayons rendu |
| | ayez rendu |

## Subjunctive

**Present**

| | |
|---|---|
| (que) je | rende |
| (que) tu | rendes |
| (qu')il | rende |
| (que) nous | rendions |
| (que) vous | rendiez |
| (qu')ils | rendent |

**Perfect**

| | | |
|---|---|---|
| (que) j' | aie | rendu |
| (que) tu | aies | rendu |
| (qu')il | ait | rendu |
| (que) nous | ayons | rendu |
| (que) vous | ayez | rendu |
| (qu')ils | aient | rendu |

**Pluperfect**

| | | |
|---|---|---|
| (que) j' | eusse | rendu |
| (que) tu | eusses | rendu |
| (qu')il | eût | rendu |
| (que) nous | eussions rendu |
| (que) vous | eussiez rendu |
| (qu')ils | eussent rendu |

## Conditional

**Present**

| | |
|---|---|
| je | rendrais |
| tu | rendrais |
| il | rendrait |
| nous | rendrions |
| vous | rendriez |
| ils | rendraient |

**Past I**

| | | |
|---|---|---|
| j' | aurais | rendu |
| tu | aurais | rendu |
| il | aurait | rendu |
| nous | aurions | rendu |
| vous | auriez | rendu |
| ils | auraient rendu |

## Participle

| | |
|---|---|
| **Present** | rendant |
| **Past** | rendu, -e |
| | ayant rendu |

## Infinitive

| | |
|---|---|
| **Present** | rendre |
| **Past** | avoir rendu |

## 7 être

### Indicative

**Present**

| | |
|---|---|
| je | suis |
| tu | es |
| il | est |
| nous | sommes |
| vous | êtes |
| ils | sont |

**Imperfect**

| | |
|---|---|
| j' | étais |
| tu | étais |
| il | était |
| nous | étions |
| vous | étiez |
| ils | étaient |

**Past historic**

| | |
|---|---|
| je | fus |
| tu | fus |
| il | fut |
| nous | fûmes |
| vous | fûtes |
| ils | furent |

**Future**

| | |
|---|---|
| je | serai |
| tu | seras |
| il | sera |
| nous | serons |
| vous | serez |
| ils | seront |

**Perfect**

| | | |
|---|---|---|
| j' | ai | été |
| tu | as | été |
| il | a | été |
| nous | avons | été |
| vous | avez | été |
| ils | ont | été |

**Pluperfect**

| | | |
|---|---|---|
| j' | avais | été |
| tu | avais | été |
| il | avait | été |
| nous | avions | été |
| vous | aviez | été |
| ils | avaient | été |

### Imperative

**Present**

| | |
|---|---|
| | sois |
| | soyons |
| | soyez |

**Past**

| | |
|---|---|
| aie | été |
| ayons | été |
| ayez | été |

### Subjunctive

**Present**

| | |
|---|---|
| (que) je | sois |
| (que) tu | sois |
| (qu')il | soit |
| (que) nous | soyons |
| (que) vous | soyez |
| (qu')ils | soient |

**Perfect**

| | | |
|---|---|---|
| (que) j' | aie | été |
| (que) tu | aies | été |
| (qu')il | ait | été |
| (que) nous | ayons | été |
| (que) vous | ayez | été |
| (qu')ils | aient | été |

**Pluperfect**

| | | |
|---|---|---|
| (que) j' | eusse | été |
| (que) tu | eusses | été |
| (qu')il | eût | été |
| (que) nous | eussions | été |
| (que) vous | eussiez | été |
| (qu')ils | eussent | été |

### Conditional

**Present**

| | |
|---|---|
| je | serais |
| tu | serais |
| il | serait |
| nous | serions |
| vous | seriez |
| ils | seraient |

**Past I**

| | | |
|---|---|---|
| j' | aurais | été |
| tu | aurais | été |
| il | aurait | été |
| nous | aurions | été |
| vous | auriez | été |
| ils | auraient | été |

### Participle

**Present** étant

**Past** été (invariable)
ayant été

### Infinitive

**Present** être

**Past** avoir été

## 8 avoir

### Indicative

**Present**

| | |
|---|---|
| j' | ai |
| tu | as |
| il | a |
| nous | avons |
| vous | avez |
| ils | ont |

**Imperfect**

| | |
|---|---|
| j' | avais |
| tu | avais |
| il | avait |
| nous | avions |
| vous | aviez |
| ils | avaient |

**Past historic**

| | |
|---|---|
| j' | eus |
| tu | eus |
| il | eut |
| nous | eûmes |
| vous | eûtes |
| ils | eurent |

**Future**

| | |
|---|---|
| j' | aurai |
| tu | auras |
| il | aura |
| nous | aurons |
| vous | aurez |
| ils | auront |

**Perfect**

| | | |
|---|---|---|
| j' | ai | eu |
| tu | as | eu |
| il | a | eu |
| nous | avons | eu |
| vous | avez | eu |
| ils | ont | eu |

**Pluperfect**

| | | |
|---|---|---|
| j' | avais | eu |
| tu | avais | eu |
| il | avait | eu |
| nous | avions | eu |
| vous | aviez | eu |
| ils | avaient | eu |

### Imperative

**Present**

| | |
|---|---|
| | aie |
| | ayons |
| | ayez |

**Past**

| | |
|---|---|
| aie | eu |
| ayons | eu |
| ayez | eu |

### Subjunctive

**Present**

| | |
|---|---|
| (que) j' | aie |
| (que) tu | aie |
| (qu')il | ait |
| (que) nous | ayons |
| (que) vous | ayez |
| (qu')ils | aient |

**Perfect**

| | | |
|---|---|---|
| (que) j' | aie | eu |
| (que) tu | aies | eu |
| (qu')il | ait | eu |
| (que) nous | ayons | eu |
| (que) vous | ayez | eu |
| (qu')ils | aient | eu |

**Pluperfect**

| | | |
|---|---|---|
| (que) j' | eusse | eu |
| (que) tu | eusses | eu |
| (qu')il | eût | eu |
| (que) nous | eussions | eu |
| (que) vous | eussiez | eu |
| (qu')ils | eussent | eu |

### Conditional

**Present**

| | |
|---|---|
| j' | aurais |
| tu | aurais |
| il | aurait |
| nous | aurions |
| vous | auriez |
| ils | auraient |

**Past I**

| | | |
|---|---|---|
| j' | aurais | eu |
| tu | aurais | eu |
| il | aurait | eu |
| nous | aurions | eu |
| vous | auriez | eu |
| ils | auraient | eu |

### Participle

**Present** ayant

**Past** eu, -e
ayant eu

### Infinitive

**Present** avoir

**Past** avoir eu

# 9 aller

## Indicative

**Present**

| je | vais |
|----|------|
| tu | vas |
| il | va |
| nous | allons |
| vous | allez |
| ils | vont |

**Imperfect**

| j' | allais |
|----|--------|
| tu | allais |
| il | allait |
| nous | allions |
| vous | alliez |
| ils | allaient |

**Past historic**

| j' | allai |
|----|-------|
| tu | allas |
| il | alla |
| nous | allâmes |
| vous | allâtes |
| ils | allèrent |

**Future**

| j' | irai |
|----|------|
| tu | iras |
| il | ira |
| nous | irons |
| vous | irez |
| ils | iront |

**Perfect**

| je | suis | allé |
|----|------|------|
| tu | es | allé |
| il | est | allé |
| nous | sommes | allés |
| vous | êtes | allés |
| ils | sont | allés |

**Pluperfect**

| j' | étais | allé |
|----|-------|------|
| tu | étais | allé |
| il | était | allé |
| nous | étions | allés |
| vous | étiez | allés |
| ils | étaient | allés |

## Imperative

**Present**

| | va |
|--|-----|
| | allons |
| | allez |

**Past**

| | sois | allé |
|--|------|------|
| | soyons | allés |
| | soyez | allés |

## Subjunctive

**Present**

| (que) j' | aille |
|----------|-------|
| (que) tu | ailles |
| (qu')il | aille |
| (que) nous | allions |
| (que) vous | alliez |
| (qu')ils | aillent |

**Perfect**

| (que) je | sois | allé |
|----------|------|------|
| (que) tu | sois | allé |
| (qu')il | soit | allé |
| (que) nous | soyons | allés |
| (que) vous | soyez | allés |
| (qu')ils | soient | allés |

**Pluperfect**

| (que) je | fusse | allé |
|----------|-------|------|
| (que) tu | fusses | allé |
| (qu')il | fût | allé |
| (que) nous | fussions | allés |
| (que) vous | fussiez | allés |
| (qu')ils | fussent | allés |

## Conditional

**Present**

| j' | irais |
|----|-------|
| tu | irais |
| il | irait |
| nous | irions |
| vous | iriez |
| ils | iraient |

**Past I**

| je | serais | allé |
|----|--------|------|
| tu | serais | allé |
| il | serait | allé |
| nous | serions | allés |
| vous | seriez | allés |
| ils | seraient | allés |

## Participle

**Present** allant

**Past** allé, -e
étant allé

## Infinitive

**Present** aller

**Past** être allé

# 10 faire

## Indicative

**Present**

| je | fais |
|----|------|
| tu | fais |
| il | fait |
| nous | faisons |
| vous | faites |
| ils | font |

**Imperfect**

| je | faisais |
|----|---------|
| tu | faisais |
| il | faisait |
| nous | faisions |
| vous | faisiez |
| ils | faisaient |

**Past historic**

| je | fis |
|----|-----|
| tu | fis |
| il | fit |
| nous | fîmes |
| vous | fîtes |
| ils | firent |

**Future**

| je | ferai |
|----|-------|
| tu | feras |
| il | fera |
| nous | ferons |
| vous | ferez |
| ils | feront |

**Perfect**

| j' | ai | fait |
|----|-----|------|
| tu | as | fait |
| il | a | fait |
| nous | avons | fait |
| vous | avez | fait |
| ils | ont | fait |

**Pluperfect**

| j' | avais | fait |
|----|-------|------|
| tu | avais | fait |
| il | avait | fait |
| nous | avions | fait |
| vous | aviez | fait |
| ils | avaient | fait |

## Imperative

**Present**

| | fais |
|--|------|
| | faisons |
| | faites |

**Past**

| | aie | fait |
|--|-----|------|
| | ayons | fait |
| | ayez | fait |

## Subjunctive

**Present**

| (que) je | fasse |
|----------|-------|
| (que) tu | fasses |
| (qu')il | fasse |
| (que) nous | fassions |
| (que) vous | fassiez |
| (qu')ils | fassent |

**Perfect**

| (que) j' | aie | fait |
|----------|-----|------|
| (que) tu | aies | fait |
| (qu')il | ait | fait |
| (que) nous | ayons | fait |
| (que) vous | ayez | fait |
| (qu')ils | aient | fait |

**Pluperfect**

| (que) j' | eusse | fait |
|----------|-------|------|
| (que) tu | eusses | fait |
| (qu')il | eût | fait |
| (que) nous | eussions | fait |
| (que) vous | eussiez | fait |
| (qu')ils | eussent | fait |

## Conditional

**Present**

| je | ferais |
|----|--------|
| tu | ferais |
| il | ferait |
| nous | ferions |
| vous | feriez |
| ils | feraient |

**Past I**

| j' | aurais | fait |
|----|--------|------|
| tu | aurais | fait |
| il | aurait | fait |
| nous | aurions | fait |
| vous | auriez | fait |
| ils | auraient | fait |

## Participle

**Present** faisant

**Past** fait, -e
ayant fait

## Infinitive

**Present** faire

**Past** avoir fait

# French verbs

| Infinitive | Rules | Indicative Present | Imperfect | Past Historic | Future |
|---|---|---|---|---|---|
| **11 créer** | *always* é | je crée, -es, -e, -ent<br>nous créons, -ez | je créais ... | je créai ... | je créerai ... |
| **12 placer** | c | je place, -es, -e, -ez, -ent | nous placions, -iez | ils placèrent | je placerai ... |
| | ç *before* a *and* o | nous plaçons | je plaçais, -ais, -ait, -aient | je plaçai, -as, -a, -âmes, -âtes | |
| **13 manger** | g | je mange, -es, -e, -ez, -ent | nous mangions, -iez | ils mangèrent | je mangerai ... |
| | ge *before* a *and* o | nous mangeons | je mangeais, -eais, -eait, -eaient | je mangeai, -as, -a, -âmes, -âtes | |
| **14 céder** | è *before silent final syllable* | je cède, -es, -e, -ent | | | |
| | é | nous cédons, -ez | je cédais ... | je cédai ... | je céderai ... |
| **15 assiéger** | è *before silent final syllable* | j'assiège, -es, -e, -ent | | | |
| | ge *before* a *and* o | nous assiégeons | j'assiégeais, -eais, -eait, -eaient | j'assiégeai | |
| | é *before silent syllable* | | | | j'assiégerai ... |
| **16 lever** | è *before silent syllable* | je lève, -es, -e, -ent | | | je lèverai ... |
| | e | nous levons, -ez | je levais ... | je levai ... | |
| **17 geler** | è *before silent syllable* | je gèle, -es, -e, -ent | | | je gèlerai ... |
| | e | nous gelons, -ez | je gelais ... | je gelai ... | |
| **18 acheter** | è *before silent syllable* | j'achète, -es, -e, -ent | | | j'achèterai ... |
| | e | nous achetons, -ez | j'achetais ... | j'achetai ... | |
| **19 appeler** | ll *before mute* e | j'appelle, -es, -e, -ent | | | j'appellerai ... |
| | l | nous appelons, -ez | j'appelais ... | j'appelai ... | |
| **20 jeter** | tt *before mute* e | je jette, -es, -e, -ent | | | je jetterai ... |
| | t | nous jetons, -ez | je jetais ... | je jetai ... | |
| **21 payer** | i *before mute* e | je paie, -es, -e, -ent | | | je paierai ... |
| | *or* y | je paye, -es, -e, -ent<br>nous payons, -ez | je payais ... | je payai ... | je payerai ... |

| Conditional Present | Subjunctive Present | Imperative | Participle Present | Past | |
|---|---|---|---|---|---|
| je créerais … | que je crée … | crée | créant | créé, -e | 11 |
| | | créons, -ez | | | |
| je placerais … | que je place … | place, -ez | | placé, -e | 12 |
| | | plaçons | plaçant | | |
| je mangerais … | que je mange … | mange, -ez | | mangé, -e | 13 |
| | | mangeons | mangeant | | |
| | que je cède, -es, -e, -ent | cède | | | 14 |
| je céderais … | que nous cédions, -iez | cédons, -ez | cédant | cédé, -e | |
| | que j'assiège … | assiège | | | 15 |
| j'assiégerais … | que nous assiégions , -iez | assiégeons | assiégeant | assiégé, -e | |
| je lèverais … | que je lève, -es, -e, -ent | lève | | | 16 |
| | que nous levions, -iez | levons, -ez | levant | levé, -e | |
| je gèlerais … | que je gèle, -es, -e, -ent | gèle | | | 17 |
| | que nous gelions, -iez | gelons, -ez | gelant | gelé, -e | |
| j'achèterais … | que j'achète, -es, -e, -ent | achète | | | 18 |
| | que nous achetions, -iez | achetons, -ez | achetant | acheté, -e | |
| j'appellerais … | que j'appelle, -es, -e, -ent | appelle | | | 19 |
| | que nous appelions, -iez | appelons, -ez | appelant | appelé, -e | |
| je jetterais … | que je jette, -es, -e, -ent | jette | | | 20 |
| | que nous jetions, -iez | jetons, -ez | jetant | jeté, -e | |
| je paierais … | que je paie, -es, -e, -ent | paie | | | 21 |
| je payerais … | que je paye, -es, -e, -ent | paye | | | |
| | que nous payions, -iez | payons, -ez | payant | payé, -e | |

# French verbs

| Infinitive | Rules | Indicative Present | Imperfect | Past Historic | Future |
|---|---|---|---|---|---|
| **22 essuyer** | i *before mute* e | j'essuie, -es, -e, -ent | | | j'essuierai ... |
| | y | nous essuyons, -ez | j'essuyais ... | j'essuyai ... | |
| **23 employer** | i *before mute* e | j'emploie, -es, -e, -ent | | | j'emploierai ... |
| | y | nous employons, -ez | j'employais ... | j'employai ... | |
| **24 envoyer** | i *before mute* e | j'envoie, -es, -e, -ent | | | |
| | y | nous envoyons, -ez | j'envoyais ... | j'envoyai ... | |
| | err | | | | j'enverrai ... |
| **25 haïr** | i | je hais, -s, -t | | | |
| | ï | nous haïssons, -ez, -ent | je haïssais ... | je haïs ... (haïmes, haïtes) | je haïrai ... |
| **26 courir** | | je cours ... | je courais ... | je courus ... | je courrai ... |
| **27 cueillir** | | je cueille, -es, -e, nous cueillons ... | je cueillais ... | je cueillis ... | je cueillerai ... |
| **28 assaillir** | | j'assaille, -es, -e, nous assaillons, -ez, -ent | j'assaillais ... | j'assaillis ... | j'assaillirai ... |
| **29 fuir** | i *before consonants and* e | je fuis, -s, -t, -ent | | je fuis ... | je fuirai ... |
| | y *before* a, ez, i, o | nous fuyons, -ez | je fuyais ... | | |
| **30 partir** | *without* t | je pars ... | | | |
| | *with* t | il part ... | je partais ... | je partis ... | je partirai ... |
| **31 bouillir** | ou | je bous, s, t | | | |
| | ouill | nous bouillons ... | je bouillais ... | je bouillis ... | je bouillirai ... |
| **32 couvrir** | | je couvre, -es, -e, nous couvrons ... | je couvrais ... | je couvris ... | je couvrirai ... |
| **33 vêtir** | | je vêts ... | je vêtais ... | je vêtis ... | je vêtirai ... |
| **34 mourir** | eur | je meurs, -s, -t, -ent | | | |
| | our | nous mourons, -ez | je mourais ... | je mourus ... | je mourrai ... |
| **35 acquérir** | quier | j'acquiers, -s, -t, -ièrent | | | |
| | quér | nous acquérons -ez | j'acquérais ... | | j'acquerrai ... |
| | qu | | | j'acquis ... | |

| Conditional Present | Subjunctive Present | Imperative | Participle Present | Past | |
|---|---|---|---|---|---|
| j'essuierais ... | que j'essuie, -es, -e, -ent | essuie | | | 22 |
| | que nous essuyions, -iez | essuyons, -ez | essuyant | essuyé, e | |
| j'emploierais ... | que j'emploie, -es, -e, -ent | emploie | | | 23 |
| | que nous employions, -iez | employons, -ez | employant | employé, -e | |
| | que j'envoie, -es, -e, -ent | envoie | | | 24 |
| | que nous envoyions, -iez | envoyons, -ez | envoyant | envoyé, -e | |
| j'enverrais ... | | | | | |
| | | hais | | | 25 |
| je haïrais ... | que je haïsse, qu'il haïsse | haïssons, haïssez | haïssant | haï, -e | |
| je courrais ... | que je coure ... | cours, courons, -ez | courant | couru, -e | 26 |
| je cueillerais ... | que je cueille ... | cueille cueillons, -ez | cueillant | cueilli, -e | 27 |
| | | assaille | | | 28 |
| j'assaillirais ... | que j'assaille ... | assaillons, -ez | assaillant | assailli, -e | |
| je fuirais ... | que je fuie, -es, -e, -ent | fuis | | fui, -e | 29 |
| | que nous fuyions, -iez | fuyons, -ez | fuyant | | |
| | | pars | | | 30 |
| je partirais ... | que je parte ... | partons, -ez | partant | parti, -e | |
| | | bous | | | 31 |
| je bouillirais ... | que je bouille ... | bouillons, -ez | bouillant | bouilli, -e | |
| je couvrirais ... | que je couvre, -es, -e, -ent | couvre | | | 32 |
| | que nous couvrions ... | couvrons, -ez | couvrant | couvert, -e | |
| je vêtirais ... | que je vête ... | vêts vêtons, vêtez | vêtant | vêtu, -e | 33 |
| | que je meure ... | meurs | | mort, -e | 34 |
| je mourrais ... | | mourons, -ez | mourant | | |
| | que j'acquière, -es, -e, -ent | acquiers | | | 35 |
| j'acquerrais ... | que nous acquérions, -iez | acquérons, -ez | acquérant | | |
| | | | | acquis, -e | |

# French verbs

| Infinitive | Rules | Indicative Present | Imperfect | Past Historic | Future |
|---|---|---|---|---|---|
| **36 venir** | i | je viens, -s, -t, -nent | | je vins … ils vinrent | je viendrai … |
| | e | nous venons, -ez | je venais … | | |
| **37 gésir** | Defective | je gis, tu gis, il gît, nous gisons, -ez, -ent | je gisais … | | |
| **38 ouïr** | Archaic | j'ois … nous oyons … | j'oyais … | j'ouïs … | j'ouïrai … |
| **39 pleuvoir** | | il pleut ils pleuvent | il pleuvait ils pleuvaient | il plut ils plurent | il pleuvra ils pleuvront |
| **40 pourvoir** | i | je pourvois, -s, -t, -ent | | | je pourvoirai … |
| | y | nous pourvoyons, -ez | je pourvoyais … | | |
| | u | | | je pourvus … | |
| **41 asseoir** | ie | j'assieds, -ds, -d | | | j'assiérai … |
| | ey | nous asseyons, -ez, -ent | j'asseyais … | | |
| | i | | | j'assis … | |
| **asseoir** (oi/oy replace ie/ey) | oi | j'assois, -s, -t, -ent | | | j'assoirai … |
| | oy | nous assoyons, -ez | j'assoyais … | | |
| **42 prévoir** | oi | je prévois, -s, -t, -ent | | | je prévoirai … |
| | oy | nous prévoyons, -ez | je prévoyais … | | |
| | i/u | | | je prévis … | |
| **43 mouvoir** | eu | je meus, -s, -t, -vent | | | |
| | ou | nous mouvons, -ez | je mouvais … | | je mouvrai … |
| | u | | | je mus, -s, -t, -(û)mes, -(û)tes, -rent | |
| **44 devoir** | û in the past participle masc. sing. | je dois, -s, -t -vent | | je dus … | |
| | | nous devons, -ez | je devais … | | je devrai … |
| **45 valoir** | au, aille | je vaux, -x, -t | | | je vaudrai … |
| | al | nous valons, -ez, -ent | je valais … | je valus … | |
| **prévaloir** | | | | | |

| Conditional Present | Subjunctive Present | Imperative | Participle Present | Past | |
|---|---|---|---|---|---|
| je viendrais … | que je vienne, -es, -e, -ent | viens | | | 36 |
| | que nous venions, -iez | venons, -ez | venant | venu, -e | |
| | | | gisant | | 37 |
| j'ouïrais … | que j'oie … | ois | | ouï, -e | 38 |
| | que nous oyions … | oyons, -ez | oyant | | |
| il pleuvrait ils pleuvraient | qu'il pleuve qu'ils pleuvent | | pleuvant | plu | 39 |
| je pourvoirais … | que je pourvoie, -es, -e, -ent | pourvois | | | 40 |
| | que nous pourvoyions, -iez | pourvoyons, -ez | pourvoyant | | |
| | | | | pourvu, -e | |
| j'assiérais … | | assieds | | | 41 |
| | que j' asseye … | asseyons, -ez | asséyant | | |
| | que nous asseyions … | | | assis, -e | |
| j'assoirais … | que j'assoie, -es, -e, -ent | assois | | | |
| | que nous assoyions, -iez | assoyons, -ez | assoyant | | |
| je prévoirais … | que je prévoie, -es, -e, -ent | prévois | | | 42 |
| | que ns prévoyions, -iez | prévoyons, -ez | prévoyant | | |
| | | | | prévu, -e | |
| | que je meuve, -es, -e, -ent | meus | | | 43 |
| je mouvrais … | que nous mouvions, -iez | mouvons, -ez | mouvant | | |
| | | | | mû, mue | |
| | que je doive, -es, -e, -ent | dois | | dû, due | 44 |
| je devrais … | que nous devions, -iez | devons, -ez | devant | | |
| je vaudrais … | que je vaille, -es, -e, -ent | vaux | | | 45 |
| | que nous valions, -iez | valons, -ez | valant | valu, -e | |
| | que je prévale, -es, -e | | | | |

| Infinitive | Rules | Indicative | | | |
|---|---|---|---|---|---|
| | | Present | Imperfect | Past Historic | Future |
| **46 voir** | oi | je vois, -s, -t, -ent | | | |
| | oy | nous voyons, -ez | je voyais ... | | |
| | i/e/u | | | je vis ... | je verrai ... |
| **47 savoir** | 5 forms | je sais, -s, -t, | | je sus ... | je saurai ... |
| | | nous savons, -ez, -ent | je savais ... | | |
| **48 vouloir** | veu/veuil | je veux, -x, -t, veulent | | | |
| | voul/voudr | nous voulons, -ez | je voulais ... | je voulus ... | je voudrai ... |
| **49 pouvoir** | eu/u(i) | je peux, -x, -t, peuvent | | je pus ... | |
| | ouv/our | nous pouvons, -ez | je pouvais ... | | je pourrai ... |
| **50 falloir** | *Impersonal* | il faut | il fallait | il fallut | il faudra |
| **51 déchoir** | choir *and* échoir *are defective* | je déchois, -s, -t, -ent | | | |
| | | nous déchoyons, -ez | je déchoyais ... | je déchus ... | je décherrai ... |
| **52 prendre** | prend | je prends, -ds, -d | | | je prendrai ... |
| | pren | nous prenons, -ez ils prennent | je prenais ... | | |
| | pri(s) | | | je pris ... | |
| **53 rompre** | | je romps, -ps, -pt nous rompons ... | je rompais ... | je rompis ... | je romprai ... |
| **54 craindre** | ain/aind | je crains, -s, -t | | | je craindrai ... |
| | aign | nous craignons, -ez, -ent | je craignais ... | je craignis ... | |
| **55 peindre** | ein | je peins, -s, -t | | | je peindrai ... |
| | eign | nous peignons, -ez, -ent | je peignais ... | je peignis ... | |
| **56 joindre** | oin/oind | je joins, -s, -t | | | je joindrai ... |
| | oign | nous joignons, -ez, -ent | je joignais ... | je joignis ... | |
| **57 vaincre** | ainc | je vaincs, -cs, -c | | | je vaincrai ... |
| | ainqu | nous vainquons, -ez, -ent | je vainquais ... | je vainquis ... | |
| **58 traire** | i | je trais, -s, -t, -ent | | (obsolete) | je trairai ... |
| | y | nous trayons, -ez | je trayais ... | | |

| Conditional Present | Subjunctive Present | Imperative | Participle Present | Past | |
|---|---|---|---|---|---|
| | que je voie, -es, -e, -ent | vois | | | **46** |
| | que nous voyions, -iez | voyons, -ez | voyant | | |
| je verrais ... | | | | vu, -e | |
| je saurais ... | que je sache ... | sache, -ons, -ez | sachant | su, -e | **47** |
| | que je veuille, -es, -e, -ent | veux (veuille) | | | **48** |
| je voudrais ... | que nous voulions, -iez | voulons, -ez (veuillez) | voulant | voulu, -e | |
| | que je puisse ... | (obsolete) | | pu | **49** |
| je pourrais ... | | | pouvant | | |
| il faudrait | qu'il faille | (no form) | (obsolete) | fallu | **50** |
| | que je déchoie, -es, -e, -ent | déchois | (no form but échéant) | | **51** |
| je décherrais ... | que nous déchoyions, -iez | déchoyons, -ez | | déchu, -e | |
| je prendrais ... | | prends | | | **52** |
| | que je prenne ... | prenons, -ez | prenant | | |
| | | | | pris, -e | |
| je romprais ... | que je rompe ... | romps -pons, -pez | rompant | rompu, -e | **53** |
| je craindrais ... | | crains | | craint, -e | **54** |
| | que je craigne ... | craignons, -ez | craignant | | |
| je peindrais ... | | peins | | peint, -e | **55** |
| | que je peigne ... | peignons, -ez | peignant | | |
| je joindrais ... | | joins | | joint, -e | **56** |
| | que je joigne ... | joignons, -ez | joignant | | |
| je vaincrais ... | | vaincs | | vaincu, -e | **57** |
| | que je vainque ... | vainquons, -ez | vainquant | | |
| je trairais ... | que je traie, -es, -e, -ent | trais | | trait, -e | **58** |
| | que nous trayions, | trayons, -ez | trayant | | |

# French verbs

| Infinitive | Rules | Indicative | | | |
|---|---|---|---|---|---|
| | | Present | Imperfect | Past Historic | Future |
| 59 plaire | ai | je plais,<br>tu plais, il plaît<br>(but il tait)<br>nous plaisons … | je plaisais … | | je plairai … |
| | u | | | je plus … | |
| 60 mettre | met | je mets,<br>nous mettons | je mettais … | | je mettrai … |
| | mis | | | je mis … | |
| 61 battre | t | je bats, -ts, -t | | | |
| | tt | nous battons … | je battais … | je battis … | je battrai … |
| 62 suivre | ui | je suis, -s, -t | | | |
| | uiv | nous suivons … | je suivais … | je suivis … | je suivrai … |
| 63 vivre | vi/viv | je vis, -s, -t,<br>nous vivons … | je vivais … | | je vivrai … |
| | véc | | | je vécus … | |
| 64 suffire | | je suffis, -s, -t,<br>nous suffisons … | je suffisais … | je suffis … | je suffirai … |
| 65 médire | | je médis, -s, -t,<br>nous médisons,<br>vous médisez<br>(but vous dites,<br>redites) | je médisais … | je médis … | je médirai … |
| 66 lire | i | je lis, -s, -t | | | je lirai … |
| | is | nous lisons,<br>-ez, -ent | je lisais … | | |
| | u | | | je lus … | |
| 67 écrire | i | j'écris, -s, -t | | | j'écrirai … |
| | iv | nous écrivons,<br>-ez, -ent | j'écrivais … | j'écrivis … | |
| 68 rire | | je ris, -s, -t,<br>nous rions … | je riais …<br>nous riions,<br>-iez | je ris …<br>nous rîmes … | je rirai … |
| 69 conduire | | je conduis … | je conduisais … | je conduisis… | je conduirai … |
| 70 boire | oi | je bois, -s, -t,<br>-vent | | | je boirai … |
| | u(v) | nous buvons, -ez | je buvais … | je bus … | |
| 71 croire | oi | je crois, -s, -t,<br>ils croient | | | je croirai … |
| | oy | nous croyons, -ez | je croyais … | | |
| | u | | | je crus … | |

| Conditional Present | Subjunctive Present | Imperative | Participle Present | Past | |
|---|---|---|---|---|---|
| je plairais ... | que je plaise ... | plais<br>plaisons, -ez | plaisant | | 59 |
| | | | | plu | |
| je mettrais ... | que je mette ... | mets<br>mettons, -ez | mettant | | 60 |
| | | | | mis, -e | |
| je battrais ... | que je batte ... | bats<br>battons, -ez | battant | battu, -e | 61 |
| je suivrais ... | que je suive ... | suis<br>suivons, -ez | suivant | suivi, -e | 62 |
| je vivrais ... | que je vive ... | vis<br>vivons, -ez | vivant | | 63 |
| | | | | vécu, -e | |
| je suffirais ... | que je suffise ... | suffis<br>suffisons, -ez | suffisant | suffi<br>(but confit,<br>déconfit, frit,<br>circoncis) | 64 |
| je médirais ... | que je médise ...<br>que nous médisions,<br>-iez | médis<br>médisons<br>médisez<br>(but dites,<br>redites) | médisant | médit | 65 |
| je lirais ... | que je lise ... | lis<br>lisons, -ez | lisant | | 66 |
| | | | | lu, -e | |
| j'écrirais ... | que j'écrive ... | écris<br>écrivons, -ez | écrivant | écrit, -e | 67 |
| je rirais ... | que je rie ...<br>que nous riions, -iez | ris, rions,<br>riez | riant | ri | 68 |
| je conduirais ... | que je conduise ... | conduis<br>conduisons, -ez | conduisant | conduit, -e<br>(but lui, nui) | 69 |
| je boirais ... | que je boive, -es, -e,<br>-ent<br>que nous buvions,<br>-iez | bois<br>buvons, -ez | buvant | bu, -e | 70 |
| je croirais ... | que je croie ... | crois<br>croyons, -ez | croyant | cru, -e | 71 |

# French verbs

| Infinitive | Rules | Indicative | | | |
|---|---|---|---|---|---|
| | | Present | Imperfect | Past Historic | Future |
| 72 croître | oî | je croîs, -s, -t | | | je croîtrai … |
| | oiss | nous croissons, -ez, -ent | je croissais … | | |
| | û | | | je crûs … | |
| 73 connaître | | je connais, -s, -ssons, -ssez, -ssent | je connaissais … | je connus … | |
| | î before t | il connaît | | | je connaîtrai … |
| 74 naître | î before t | je nais, nais, naît | | | je naîtrai … |
| | naisse | nous naissons, -ez, -ent | je naissais … | | |
| | naqu | | | je naquis … | |
| 75 résoudre | ou | je résous, -s, -t | | (absoudre and dissoudre have no past historic) | je résoudrai … |
| | ol/olv | nous résolvons, -ez, -ent | je résolvais … | | |
| | olu | | | je résolus … | |
| 76 coudre | oud | je couds, -ds, -d | | | je coudrai … |
| | ous | nous cousons, -ez, -ent | je cousais … | je cousis … | |
| 77 moudre | moud | je mouds, -ds, -d | | | je moudrai … |
| | moul | nous moulons, -ez, -ent | je moulais … | je moulus … | |
| 78 conclure | | je conclus, -s, -t, nous concluons, -ez, -ent | je concluais … | je conclus … | je conclurai … |
| 79 clore | Defective | je clos, -os, -ôt ils closent | (obsolete) | (obsolete) | je clorai … |
| 80 maudire | | je maudis, -s, -t nous maudissons, -ez, -ent | je maudissais … | je maudis … | je maudirai … |

| Conditional Present | Subjunctive Present | Imperative | Participle Present | Past | |
|---|---|---|---|---|---|
| je croîtrais... | | croîs | | | 72 |
| | que je croisse ... | croissons, -ez | croissant | | |
| | | | | crû, crue (but accru, -e) | |
| | que je connaisse ... | connais, -ssons, -ssez | connaissant | connu, -e | 73 |
| je connaîtrais ... | | | | | |
| | | nais | | né, -e | 74 |
| je naîtrais ... | | | | | |
| | que je naisse ... | naissons, -ez | naissant | | |
| je résoudrais ... | | résous | | (absous, -oute; dissous, -oute) | 75 |
| | que je résolve ... | résolvons, -ez | résolvant | | |
| | | | | résolu, -e | |
| je coudrais ... | | couds | | | 76 |
| | que je couse ... | cousons, -ez | cousant | cousu, -e | |
| je moudrais ... | | mouds | | | 77 |
| | que je moule ... | moulons, -ez | moulant | moulu, -e | |
| je conclurais ... | que je conclue ... | conclus concluons, -ez | concluant | conclu, -e (but inclus, -e) | 78 |
| je clorais ... | que je close ... | clos | closant | clos, -e | 79 |
| je maudirais ... | que je maudisse qu'il maudisse | maudis -ssons, -ssez | maudissant | maudit, -e | 80 |

# Numbers

## Cardinal numbers

| | | | |
|---|---|---|---|
| 0 zéro* | 16 seize | 90 quatre-vingt-dix | 1 200 mille** deux cents |
| 1 un† | 17 dix-sept | 91 quatre-vingt-onze | 2 000 deux mille†† |
| 2 deux | 18 dix-huit | 92 quatre-vingt-douze | 10 000 dix mille |
| 3 trois | 19 dix-neuf | 99 quatre-vingt-dix-neuf | 100 000 cent mille |
| 4 quatre | 20 vingt | 101 cent un† | 102 000 cent deux mille |
| 5 cinq | 21 vingt et un | 102 cent deux | 1 000 000 un million‡‡ |
| 6 six | 22 vingt-deux | 110 cent dix | 1 264 932 un million |
| 7 sept | 30 trente | 187 cent quatre-vingt- | deux cent soixante- |
| 8 huit | 40 quarante | sept | quatre mille neuf cent |
| 9 neuf | 50 cinquante | 200 deux cents | trente-deux |
| 10 dix | 60 soixante | 250 deux cent◊ | 1 000 000 000 un |
| 11 onze | 70 soixante-dix | cinquante | milliard‡‡ |
| 12 douze | 71 soixante et onze | 1 000 mille∞ | 1 000 000 000 000 un |
| 13 treize | 80 quatre-vingts§ | 1 001 mille un† | billion‡‡ |
| 14 quatorze | 81 quatre-vingt-un¶ | 1 002 mille deux | |
| 15 quinze | 82 quatre-vingt-deux | 1 020 mille vingt | |

\* In English *0* may be called *nought*, *zero* or even *nothing*; French is always *zéro:* **a nought = un zéro.**

† **one** is **une** in French when it agrees with a feminine noun, so *un crayon* but *une table*, *une des tables*, *vingt et une tables*, etc.

§ Note that when *80* is used as a page number it has no *s:* **page eighty = page quatre-vingt.**

¶ **vingt** has no *s* when it is in the middle of a number. The only exception to this rule is when *quatre-vingts* is followed by *millions*, *milliards* or *billions*, eg **quatre-vingts millions, quatre-vingts billions** etc.

◊ **cent** does not take an *s* when it is in the middle of a number. The only exception to this rule is when it is followed by *millions*, *milliards* or *billions*, eg **trois cents millions, six cents billions** etc. It has a normal plural when it modifies other nouns: **200 inhabitants = deux cents habitants.**

∞ Where English would have a comma, French has simply a space. A full stop (period) can be used, e.g. **1.000.** As in English, there is no separation in dates between thousands and hundreds: **in 2004 = en 2004.**

\*\* In dates, the spelling **mil** is preferred to **mille**, i.e. **en 1200 = en mil deux cents.** However, when the year is a round number of thousands, the spelling is always **mille**, so **en l'an mille, en l'an deux mille** etc.

†† **mille** is invariable; it never takes an *s.*

‡‡ The French words **million, milliard** and **billion** are nouns, and when written out in full they take **de** before another noun, eg **a million inhabitants = un million d'habitants.** However, when written in figures, **1,000,000 inhabitants = 1 000 000 habitants,** but is still spoken as *un million d'habitants.* When **million** etc. is part of a complex number, **de** is not used before the nouns, eg **6,000,210 people = six millions deux cent dix personnes.**

## Ordinal numbers§

| | | | | | | |
|---|---|---|---|---|---|---|
| 1st | 1er‡ | premier (fem. première) | 30th | 30e | trentième |
| 2nd | 2e | second (fem. seconde) or deuxième | 31st | 31e | trente et unième |
| | | | 40th | 40e | quarantième |
| 3rd | 3e | troisième | 50th | 50e | cinquantième |
| 4th | 4e | quatrième | 60th | 60e | soixantième |
| 5th | 5e | cinquième | 70th | 70e | soixante-dixième |
| 6th | 6e | sixième | 71st | 71e | soixante et onzième |
| 7th | 7e | septième | 72nd | 72e | soixante-douzième |
| 8th | 8e | huitième | 73rd | 73e | soixante-treizième |
| 9th | 9e | neuvième | 74th | 74e | soixante-quartorzième |
| 10th | 10e | dixième | 75th | 75e | soixante-quinzième |
| 11th | 11e | onzième | 79th | 79e | soixante-dix-neuvième |
| 12th | 12e | douzième | 80th | 80e | quatre-vingtième |
| 13th | 13e | treizième | 81st | 81e | quatre-vingt-unième |
| 14th | 14e | quatorzième | 90th | 90e | quatre-vingt-dixième |
| 15th | 15e | quinzième | 91st | 91e | quatre-vingt-onzième |
| 16th | 16e | seizième | 99th | 99e | quatre-vingt-dix-neuvième |
| 17th | 17e | dix-septième | 100th | 100e | centième |
| 18th | 18e | dix-huitième | 101st | 101e | cent et unième |
| 19th | 19e | dix-neuvième | 102nd | 102e | cent-deuxième |
| 20th | 20e | vingtième | 200th | 200e | deux centième |
| 21st | 21e | vingt et unième | 1,000th | 1 000e | millième |
| 22nd | 22e | vingt-deuxième | 2,000th | 2 000e | deux millième |
| 23rd | 23e | vingt-troisième | 1,000,000th | 1 000 000e | millionième |
| 24th | 24e | vingt-quatrième | | | |
| 25th | 25e | vingt-cinquième | | | |

Like English, French makes nouns by adding the definite article:

the first . . . . . . . . . . = le premier (or la première, or les premiers *m pl* or les premières *f pl*)

the second . . . . . . . = le second (or la seconde etc)

the first three . . . . . = les trois premiers *or* les trois premières

Note the French word order in:

*the third richest* = le troisième
*country in the* pays le plus
*world* riche du monde

§ All the ordinal numbers in French behave like ordinary adjectives and take normal plural endings where appropriate.

‡ This is the masculine form; the feminine is **1re** and the plural **1ers** (m) or **1res** (f). All the other abbreviations of ordinal numbers are invariable.

## Use of en

Note the use of **en** in the following examples:

*there are six* . . . . . . . . . . . = il y en a six
*I've got a hundred* . . . . . . . = j'en ai cent

**en** must be used when the thing you are talking about is not expressed (the French says literally *there of them are six, I of them have a hundred* etc.). However, **en** is not needed when the object is specified:

*there are six apples* . . . = il y a six pommes

## Decimals in French

Note that French uses a comma where English has a decimal point.

| written as | spoken as |
|---|---|
| 0,25 . . . . . . . . . . . | zéro virgule vingt-cinq |
| 0,05 . . . . . . . . . . . | zéro virgule zéro cinq |
| 3,45 . . . . . . . . . . . | trois virgule quarante-cinq |
| 8,195 . . . . . . . . . . | huit virgule cent quatre-vingt-quinze |

## Approximate numbers

When you want to say 'about ...' , remember the French ending *-aine*:

| | |
|---|---|
| *about ten* ............ | = une dizaine |
| *about ten books* ...... | = une dizaine de livres |
| *about fifteen* ......... | = une quinzaine |
| *about fifteen people* ... | = une quinzaine de personnes |

Similarly *une trentaine, une quarantaine, une cinquantaine, une soixantaine* and *une centaine* (and *une douzaine* means *a dozen*). For other numbers, use **environ** (*about*):

| | |
|---|---|
| *about thirty-five* ...... | = environ trente-cinq |
| *hundreds of books* ... | = des centaines de livres |
| *thousands of books* ... | = des milliers de livres |
| *I've got thousands* .... | = j'en ai des milliers |

## Percentages in French

| *written as* | *spoken as* |
|---|---|
| 25% | ...........vingt-cinq pour cent |
| 50% | ...........cinquante pour cent |
| 100% | ...........cent pour cent |
| 200% | ...........deux cents pour cent |
| 365% | ...........trois cent soixante-cinq pour cent |
| 4,25% | .........quatre virgule vingt-cinq pour cent |

## Fractions in French

| *in figures* | *in words* |
|---|---|
| $1/2$ ............ | un demi* |
| $1/3$ ............ | un tiers |
| $1/4$ ............ | un quart |
| $1/5$ ............ | un cinquième |
| $1/6$ ............ | un sixième |
| $1/7$ ............ | un septième |
| $1/8$ ............ | un huitième |
| $1/9$ ............ | un neuvième |
| $1/10$............ | un dixième |
| $1/11$............ | un onzième |
| $1/12$............ | un douzième (*etc*) |

\* Note that **half**, when not a fraction, is translated by the noun **moitié** or the adjective **demi**; see the dictionary entry.

## Phrases

| | |
|---|---|
| *numbers up to ten* ....| = les nombres jusqu'à dix |
| *to count up to ten* ....| = compter jusqu'à dix |
| *almost ten* ..........| = presque dix |
| *less than ten* ........| = moins de dix |
| *more than ten* .......| = plus de dix |
| *all ten of them* ......| = tous les dix |
| *all ten boys* .........| = les dix garçons |
| *my last ten pounds* ...| = mes dix dernières livres |
| *the next twelve weeks* ..| = les douze prochaines semaines |
| *the other two* ........| = les deux autres |
| *the last four* .........| = les quatre derniers |

## Calculations in French

| | |
|---|---|
| $10 + 3 = 13$ ....... | dix et trois font *or* égalent treize |
| $10 - 3 = 7$ ....... | trois ôté de dix il reste sept *or* dix moins trois égale sept |
| $10 \times 3 = 30$ ...... | dix fois trois égalent trente |
| $30 : 3 = 10$ ...... | trente divisé par trois |
| $(30 \div 3 = 10)$ | égale dix |
| $5^2$ | .........cinq au carré |
| $5^3$ | .........cinq puissance trois |
| $\sqrt{12}$ | .........racine carrée de douze |

| *in figures* | *in words* |
|---|---|
| $2/3$ ............ | deux tiers† |
| $2/5$ ............ | deux cinquièmes |
| $3/4$ ............ | trois quarts |
| $3/10$............ | trois dixièmes |
| $1\,1/2$ ............ | un et demi |
| $1\,1/3$ ............ | un (et) un tiers |
| $1\,1/4$ ............ | un et quart |
| $1\,1/5$ ............ | un (et) un cinquième |
| $5\,2/3$ ............ | cinq (et) deux tiers |
| $5\,3/4$ ............ | cinq (et) trois quarts |

† Note the use of **les** and **d'entre** when these fractions are used about a group of people or things: **two-thirds of them** = **les deux tiers d'entre eux**.

# Also available from Oxford University Press

## Oxford-Hachette French Dictionary

■ Over 900,000 words, phrases, and translations

0-19-860363-0

## Concise Oxford-Hachette French Dictionary

■ Over 445,000 words, phrases, and translations

0-19-860242-1
0-19-860465-3
(Book and CD-ROM)

## Oxford Business French Dictionary

■ 50,000 words and phrases

0-19-860483-1

## Oxford Colour French Dictionary Plus

■ Over 100,000 words, phrases, and translations

0-19-864560-0
0-19-864564-3
(US edition)

## Oxford French Minidictionary

■ Over 100,000 words, phrases, and translations

0-19-860467-X

## Oxford Take off in French

■ Language learning course with almost 5 hours of audio

0-19-860298-7
(Book + 4 CDs)
0-19-860274-X
(Book + 4 cassettes)

## Quick Take off in French

■ Language learning course with almost 3 hours of audio

0-19-860663-X
(Book +2 CDs)
0-19-860662-1
(Book + 2 cassettes)

OXFORD
UNIVERSITY PRESS